CORPORATIONS OTHER BUSINESS ORGANIZATIONS

STATUTES, RULES, MATERIALS, AND FORMS

2019 Edition

Selected and Edited by

JAMES D. COX

Brainerd Currie Professor of Law
Duke University

MELVIN A. EISENBERG

Jesse H. Choper Professor of Law, Emeritus
University of California at Berkeley

FOUNDATION PRESS

© 1988–2004 FOUNDATION PRESS
© 2005–2012 THOMSON REUTERS/FOUNDATION PRESS
© 2013 LEG, Inc. d/b/a West Academic Publishing
© 2014–2018 LEG, Inc. d/b/a West Academic
© 2019 LEG, Inc. d/b/a West Academic
    444 Cedar Street, Suite 700
    St. Paul, MN 55101
    1-877-888-1330

Printed in the United States of America

ISBN: 978-1-64242-931-2

PREFACE

This Supplement is designed to provide students with the essential statutory provisions, rules, materials, and forms needed in courses in Corporations and Other Business Organizations, and to give students a hand's-on grasp of the tools with which the profession works in these areas.

This Supplement includes state and federal statutes and rules; extensive excerpts from the Second and Third Restatements of Agency; the virtually complete text of the ALI's Principles of Corporate Governance, together with selected Comments; selected forms; and other materials.

In general, the federal materials have been edited much more heavily than the other materials, because much of the federal material is more relevant to courses in Securities Regulation than to courses in Corporations and Business Associations. The aim of the editing of the federal materials has been to preserve the substance and the flow of the material, but to winnow out details that are unnecessary for the study of corporation law.

The following conventions have been used in the preparation of this Supplement:

(1) Omissions within a statutory section, rule, form, official comment, instruction, note, or other material are indicated by ellipses (. . .). The omission of an entire statutory section, rule, form, official comment, instruction, or note is not so indicated. However, in the case of the Delaware statute, the Model Business Corporation Act, the Uniform Partnership Act, the Revised Uniform Partnership Act, the Revised Uniform Limited Partnership Act, the Securities Act, the Securities Exchange Act, the Delaware Limited Liability Company Act, and the Uniform Limited Liability Company Act, the omission of an entire section is indicated in the Table of Contents by an asterisk following the title of the omitted section.

(2) Editorial insertions in the text are indicated by brackets. In some cases, an official text itself includes bracketed material, but the context usually makes clear whether bracketed material consists of editorial insertions or original text.

(3) Sections of the securities acts have been numbered serially, beginning with Section 1, rather than with the number-and-letter combinations used in the United States Code. Rules and forms under those acts have been numbered without the prefatory Part numbers that appear in the Code of Federal Regulations.

(4) This supplement does not include temporary SEC rules.

We thank the authors, publishers and copyrightholders who permitted us to reprint all or portions of the following works, including:

American Bar Association, Section of Business Law, Committee on Corporate Laws, Model Business Corporation Act.

American Law Institute, Restatement (Second) of Agency, Restatement (Third) of Agency, and Principles of Corporate Governance: Analysis and Recommendations.

R.F. Balotti and J. Finkelstein, The Delaware Law of Corporations and Business Organizations (3d ed. 1998).

National Conference of Commissioners on Uniform State Laws, Uniform Limited Liability Company Act (1995), Uniform Partnership Act, Revised Uniform Limited Partnership Act (1995), and Revised Uniform Limited Partnership Act.

JAMES D. COX
MELVIN A. EISENBERG

May 2019

TABLE OF CONTENTS

PREFACE..III

Restatement (Third) of Agency (2006) (Selected Provisions)...1

Uniform Partnership Act...47

Revised Uniform Partnership Act (1997) 61

Form of Partnership Agreement 135

Uniform Limited Partnership Act (2001) 149

Delaware Limited Liability Company Act 223

Delaware Statutory Public Benefit Liability Companies 271

Uniform Limited Liability Company Act (2006) 275

Limited Liability Company Agreement—Short-Form 435

Delaware General Corporation Law 441

Model Business Corporation Act...543

California Corporations Code (Selected Provisions) 753

Connecticut General Statutes Ann. § 33–756 825

Ind. Code Ann. Title 23..827

Maryland Ann. Code Corporations and Associations, Title 4 833

Mich. Comp. Laws § 450.1489...841

Minnesota Stats. Ann. § 302A.751 843

Nev. Rev. Stat. § 78.138..845

New York Business Corporation Law (Selected Provisions) 847

North Dakota Publicly Traded Corporations Act 901

Pennsylvania Consol. Stats. Ann. Title 15 (Excerpts) 913

Virginia Corporations Code §§ 13.1–690, 13.1–692.1 929

Uniform Commercial Code § 8–204 931

Federal Rules of Civil Procedure, Rules 11, 23, 23.1..933

v

Uniform Fraudulent Transfer Act (Selected Provisions)..939

Bankruptcy Code 11 U.S.C.A. §§ 101(32), 548(a) 943

New York Stock Exchange Listed Company Manual (Excerpts) 945

New York Stock Exchange Rules and Constitution—Operation of Member
    Organizations 967

ABA Model Rules of Professional Conduct, Rules 1.6, 1.7, 1.13...............................969

American Law Institute Principles of Corporate Governance: Analysis and
    Recommendations (1994) 975

Corporate Forms 1023

    Simple Form of Certificate of Incorporation 1025

    Form of By-Laws...1027

    Form of Minutes of Organization Meeting..1033

    Selected ISS United States Proxy Voting Guidelines....................................1037

    Form of Stock Certificate 1057

    Form of Proxy Statement and Form of Proxy..1059

    Richards, Layton & Finger, P.A. Forum Selection Bylaw 1111

    Agreement Between Activist Investor and Public Company 1113

    Wachtell, Lipton, Rosen & Katz, Share Purchase Rights Plan 1125

    Form of Chubb's Directors and Officers Liability Policy...............................1155

Securities Act of 1933 1173

Rules and Forms Under the Securities Act of 1933 (Selected Provisions)...................1213

Regulation Crowdfunding—General Rules and Regulations (Selected
    Provisions) 1291

Regulation S–X—Form and Content of and Requirements for Financial
    Statements...1303

Regulation S–T—General Rules and Regulations for Electronic Filings....................1317

Regulation S–K—Standard Instructions for Filing Forms Under Securities Act
    of 1933 [and] Securities Exchange Act of 1934 (Selected Provisions) 1319

Regulation M–A...1369

Securities Exchange Act of 1934 1381

Rules and Forms Under the Securities Exchange Act of 1934 (Selected
    Provisions) 1445

Jobs Act Provisions Not Amending Other Federal Statutes 1583

Regulation FD 1585

Securities and Exchange Commission Release No. 33–7881 (2000) 1589

Example of SEC No-Action Letter: Selected Items from Johnson & Johnson
    Arbitration Bylaw Proposal 1599

Division of Corporation Finance, Securities and Exchange Commission 1619

Division of Corporation Finance, Securities and Exchange Commission:
    Staff Legal Bulletin No. 14C 1625

Division of Corporation Finance, Securities and Exchange Commission:
    Staff Legal Bulletin No. 14H 1629

Division of Corporation Finance, Securities and Exchange Commission:
    Staff Legal Bulletin No. 14J (CF) 1633

Proxy Voting: Disclosure of Proxy Voting Policies and Proxy Voting Records by
    Mutual Funds and Other Registered Management Investment Companies 1639

Voting Activities by Investment Advisers 1641

Regulation AC (Analyst Certification) 1643

Sarbanes-Oxley Act 1647

Federal Mail Fraud Act 1677

U.S.C. § 1658 1679

Racketeer Influence and Corrupt Organizations (RICO) 1681

Hart-Scott-Rodino Antitrust Improvements Act 1683

Regulations Under the Hart-Scott-Rodino Antitrust Improvements Act 1687

CORPORATIONS AND OTHER BUSINESS ORGANIZATIONS

STATUTES, RULES, MATERIALS, AND FORMS

2019 Edition

RESTATEMENT (THIRD) OF AGENCY (2006) (SELECTED PROVISIONS)

TABLE OF CONTENTS

Chapter 1

INTRODUCTORY MATTERS

TOPIC 1.   DEFINITIONS AND TERMINOLOGY

Sec.		Page
1.01	Agency Defined	4
1.02	Parties' Labeling and Popular Usage Not Controlling	4
1.03	Manifestation	4
1.04	Terminology	4

Chapter 2

PRINCIPLES OF ATTRIBUTION

TOPIC 1.   ACTUAL AUTHORITY

2.01	Actual Authority	5
2.02	Scope of Actual Authority	7

TOPIC 2.   APPARENT AUTHORITY

2.03	Apparent Authority	13

TOPIC 3.   RESPONDEAT SUPERIOR

2.04	Respondeat Superior	14
2.05	Estoppel to Deny Existence of Agency Relationship	14
2.06	Liability of Undisclosed Principal	14
2.07	Restitution of Benefit	14

Chapter 3

CREATION AND TERMINATION OF AUTHORITY AND AGENCY RELATIONSHIPS

TOPIC 1.   CREATING AND EVIDENCING ACTUAL AUTHORITY

3.01	Creation of Actual Authority	14
3.02	Formal Requirements	14

TOPIC 2.   CREATING APPARENT AUTHORITY

3.03	Creation of Apparent Authority	15

TOPIC 4.   TERMINATION OF AGENT'S POWER

TITLE A. TERMINATION OF ACTUAL AUTHORITY

3.10	Manifestation Terminating Actual Authority	15

TITLE B. TERMINATION OF APPARENT AUTHORITY

3.11   Termination of Apparent Authority.. 15

TITLE C. IRREVOCABLE POWERS

3.12   Power Given as Security; Irrevocable Proxy 15
3.13   Termination of Power Given as Security or Irrevocable Proxy 19

TOPIC 5.   AGENTS WITH MULTIPLE PRINCIPALS

3.14   Agents with Multiple Principals 20
3.15   Subagency 20
3.16   Agent for Coprincipals 21

Chapter 4

RATIFICATION

4.01   Ratification Defined.. 21
4.02   Effect of Ratification 21
4.03   Acts That May Be Ratified 21
4.04   Capacity to Ratify 21
4.05   Timing of Ratification 24
4.06   Knowledge Requisite to Ratification 24
4.07   No Partial Ratification 24
4.08   Estoppel to Deny Ratification 24

Chapter 5

NOTIFICATIONS AND NOTICE

5.01   Notifications and Notice—In General 24
5.02   Notification Given by or to an Agent 24
5.03   Imputation of Notice of Fact to Principal 25
5.04   An Agent Who Acts Adversely to a Principal 25

Chapter 6

CONTRACTS AND OTHER TRANSACTIONS
WITH THIRD PARTIES

TOPIC 1.   PARTIES TO CONTRACTS

6.01   Agent for Disclosed Principal... 25
6.02   Agent for Unidentified Principal 26
6.03   Agent for Undisclosed Principal 27
6.04   Principal Does Not Exist or Lacks Capacity 28

TOPIC 2.   RIGHTS, LIABILITIES, AND DEFENSES

TITLE A. IN GENERAL

6.05   Contract That Is Unauthorized in Part or That Combines Orders of Several
        Principals 29
6.06   Setoff 30

TITLE B. SUBSEQUENT DEALINGS BETWEEN THIRD PARTY
AND PRINCIPAL OR AGENT

6.07   Settlement with Agent by Principal or Third Party 30
6.08   Other Subsequent Dealings Between Third Party and Agent 31
6.09   Effect of Judgment Against Agent or Principal 31

TITLE C. AGENT'S WARRANTIES AND REPRESENTATIONS

6.10   Agent's Implied Warranty of Authority 31
6.11   Agent's Representations 32

Chapter 7

TORTS—LIABILITY OF AGENT AND PRINCIPAL

TOPIC 1.   AGENT'S LIABILITY

7.01   Agent's Liability to Third Party 33
7.02   Duty to Principal; Duty to Third Party 33

TOPIC 2.   PRINCIPAL'S LIABILITY

7.03   Principal's Liability—In General 33
7.04   Agent Acts with Actual Authority 33
7.05   Principal's Negligence in Conducting Activity Through Agent; Principal's Special
        Relationship with Another Person 34
7.06   Failure in Performance of Principal's Duty of Protection 34
7.07   Employee Acting Within Scope of Employment 35
7.08   Agent Acts with Apparent Authority 37

Chapter 8

DUTIES OF AGENT AND PRINCIPAL TO EACH OTHER

TOPIC 1.   AGENT'S DUTIES TO PRINCIPAL

TITLE A. GENERAL FIDUCIARY PRINCIPLE

8.01   General Fiduciary Principle 38

TITLE B. DUTIES OF LOYALTY

8.02   Material Benefit Arising Out of Position 39
8.03   Acting as or on Behalf of an Adverse Party 40
8.04   Competition 41
8.05   Use of Principal's Property; Use of Confidential Information 41
8.06   Principal's Consent 42

TITLE C. DUTIES OF PERFORMANCE

8.07   Duty Created by Contract 43
8.08   Duties of Care, Competence, and Diligence 43
8.09   Duty to Act Only Within Scope of Actual Authority and to Comply with Principal's
        Lawful Instructions 44
8.10   Duty of Good Conduct 44
8.11   Duty to Provide Information 44
8.12   Duties Regarding Principal's Property—Segregation, Record-Keeping, and
        Accounting 45

TOPIC 2.   PRINCIPAL'S DUTIES TO AGENT

8.13   Duty Created by Contract 45
8.14   Duty to Indemnify 45
8.15   Principal's Duty to Deal Fairly and in Good Faith 46

CHAPTER 1

INTRODUCTORY MATTERS

TOPIC 1.   DEFINITIONS AND TERMINOLOGY

§ 1.01   Agency Defined

[handwritten: relationship terminates when A breaches f. duciary duty]

Agency is the fiduciary relationship that arises when one person (a "principal") manifests assent to another person (an "agent") that the agent shall act on the principal's behalf and subject to the principal's control, and the agent manifests assent or otherwise consents so to act.

§ 1.02   Parties' Labeling and Popular Usage Not Controlling

An agency relationship arises only when the elements stated in § 1.01 are present. Whether a relationship is characterized as agency in an agreement between parties or in the context of industry or popular usage is not controlling.

§ 1.03   Manifestation

A person manifests assent or intention through written or spoken words or other conduct.

§ 1.04   Terminology

(1) Coagents. Coagents have agency relationships with the same principal. A coagent may be appointed by the principal or by another agent actually or apparently authorized by the principal to do so.

(2) *Disclosed, undisclosed, and unidentified principals.*

(a) *Disclosed principal.* A principal is disclosed if, when an agent and a third party interact, the third party has notice that the agent is acting for a principal and has notice of the principal's identity.

(b) *Undisclosed principal.* A principal is undisclosed if, when an agent and a third party interact, the third party has no notice that the agent is acting for a principal.

(c) *Unidentified principal.* A principal is unidentified if, when an agent and a third party interact, the third party has notice that the agent is acting for a principal but does not have notice of the principal's identity.

(3) *Gratuitous agent.* A gratuitous agent acts without a right to compensation.

(4) *Notice.* A person has notice of a fact if the person knows the fact, has reason to know the fact, has received an effective notification of the fact, or should know the fact to fulfill a duty owed to another person. Notice of a fact that an agent knows or has reason to know is imputed to the principal as stated in §§ 5.03 and 5.04. A notification given to or by an agent is effective as notice to or by the principal as stated in § 5.02.

(5) *Person.* A person is (a) an individual; (b) an organization or association that has legal capacity to possess rights and incur obligations; (c) a government, political subdivision, or instrumentality or entity created by government; or (d) any other entity that has legal capacity to possess rights and incur obligations.

(6) *Power given as security.* A power given as security is a power to affect the legal relations of its creator that is created in the form of a manifestation of actual authority and held for the benefit of the holder or a third person. It is given to protect a legal or equitable title or to secure the performance of a duty apart from any duties owed the holder of the power by its creator that are incident to a relationship of agency under § 1.01.

(7) *Power of attorney.* A power of attorney is an instrument that states an agent's authority.

(8) *Subagent.* A subagent is a person appointed by an agent to perform functions that the agent has consented to perform on behalf of the agent's principal and for whose conduct the appointing agent is responsible to the principal. The relationship between an appointing agent and a subagent is one of agency, created as stated in § 1.01.

(9) *Superior and subordinate coagents.* A superior coagent has the right, conferred by the principal, to direct a subordinate coagent.

(10) *Trustee and agent-trustee.* A trustee is a holder of property who is subject to fiduciary duties to deal with the property for the benefit of charity or for one or more persons, at least one of whom is not the sole trustee. An agent-trustee is a trustee subject to the control of the settlor or of one or more beneficiaries.

CHAPTER 2

PRINCIPLES OF ATTRIBUTION

TOPIC 1.   ACTUAL AUTHORITY

§ 2.01   Actual Authority

An agent acts with actual authority when, at the time of taking action that has legal consequences for the principal, the agent reasonably believes, in accordance with the principal's manifestations to the agent, that the principal wishes the agent so to act.

Comment:

a.   Scope and cross-references. Section 1.03 defines manifestation. Section 2.02 covers the scope of actual authority, including criteria with which to assess the reasonableness of the agent's belief. Sections 3.01 and 3.02 state the means by which a principal creates actual authority, including circumstances in which a writing is required.

b.   Terminology. As defined in this section, "actual authority" is a synonym for "true authority," a term used in some opinions. The definition in this section does not attempt to classify different types of actual authority on the basis of the degree of detail in the principal's manifestation, which may consist of written or spoken words or other conduct. See § 1.03. As commonly used, the term "express authority" often means actual authority that a principal has stated in very specific or detailed language.

The term "implied authority" has more than one meaning. "Implied authority" is often used to mean actual authority either (1) to do what is necessary, usual, and proper to accomplish or perform an agent's express responsibilities or (2) to act in a manner in which an agent believes the principal wishes the agent to act based on the agent's reasonable interpretation of the principal's manifestation in light of the principal's objectives and other facts known to the agent. These meanings are not mutually exclusive. Both fall within the definition of actual authority. Section 2.02, which delineates the scope of actual authority, subsumes the practical consequences of implied authority.

The term "inherent agency power," used in the Restatement Second of Agency and defined therein by § 8 A, is not used in this Restatement. Inherent agency power is defined as "a term used . . . to indicate the power of an agent which is derived not from authority, apparent authority or estoppel, but solely from the agency relation and exists for the protection of persons harmed by or dealing with a servant or other agent." Other doctrines stated in this Restatement encompass the justifications underpinning § 8 A, including the importance of interpretation by the agent in the agent's relationship with the principal, as well as the doctrines of apparent authority, estoppel, and restitution.

c.   Rationale. Actual authority is a consequence of a principal's expressive conduct toward the agent, through which the principal manifests assent to be affected by the agent's action, and the agent's reasonable understanding of the principal's manifestation. An agent's actions establish the agent's consent to act on the principal's behalf, as does any separate manifestation of assent by the agent. When an agent acts with actual authority, the agent's power to affect the principal's legal relations with third parties is coextensive with the agent's right to do so, which actual authority creates. In contrast, although an agent who acts with only apparent authority also affects the principal's legal relations, the agent lacks the right to do so, and the agent's act is not rightful as toward the principal. Actual authority often overlaps with the presence of apparent authority. . . .

The focal point for determining whether an agent acted with actual authority is the agent's reasonable understanding at the time the agent takes action. Although it is commonly said that a principal grants or confers actual authority, the principal's initial manifestation to the agent may often be modified or supplemented by subsequent manifestations from the principal and by other developments that the agent should reasonably consider in determining what the principal wishes to be done. A principal's manifestations may reach the agent directly or indirectly. Often a principal's manifestation will state that the agent should refrain from acting in a particular way. In that situation, the agent's failure to act conforms to the principal's expressed wishes.

Illustration:

    1.   P gives A a power of attorney authorizing A to sell a piece of property owned by P. P subsequently says to A, "Don't sell the property. Lease it instead." After P's statement, A has actual authority only to lease.

The presence of actual authority requires that an agent's belief be reasonable at the time the agent acts. It is also necessary that the agent in fact believes that the principal desires the action taken by the agent.

Illustrations:

    2.   Same facts as Illustration 1, except that A overhears P say to a third party that P no longer wishes to sell the property and wishes A to lease it. A has actual authority only to lease because A knows P does not wish the property to be sold.

    3.   Same facts as Illustration 1, except that, after telling A to lease the property instead of selling it, P tells F that P regrets making this statement and wishes that the property be sold. A is unaware of P's statement to F. A sells the property to T, showing T the power of attorney. T is unaware of P's oral statements to A and F. A did not have actual authority to sell the property. A acted with apparent authority as defined in § 2.03.

Unless a principal's manifestation expressly states that the authority is irrevocable and constitutes a power given as security or an irrevocable proxy as defined in § 3.12, the principal has power to revoke actual authority even when the principal has contracted not to do so. If a principal's revocation of actual authority breaches a contract with the agent, the agent's authority terminates but the principal is subject to liability to the agent for breach of contract.

Illustration:

    4.   Same facts as Illustration 1, except that the power of attorney states that A's authority to sell shall be irrevocable by P for six months, in exchange for A's promise to use best efforts to sell the property. At the end of three months, P tells A that P revokes A's authority. A's authority is terminated, but P is subject to liability for breach of contract.

A principal's manifestation to an agent often consists of an intentional act. However, a principal may also convey actual authority to the agent through unintended conduct that the agent reasonably believes to constitute an expression of the principal's intentions.

Illustrations:

    5.   P drafts and executes a power of attorney authorizing A to sell a piece of property. Following a change of mind, P drafts and executes a second power authorizing A only to lease the property. P inadvertently sends the first power to A and does not otherwise communicate with A regarding the nature of A's authority. A has actual authority to sell the property.

    6.   Same facts as Illustration 5, except that after A receives the power of attorney from P, P sends A a letter asking for a status report on A's efforts to lease the property. The letter also states that P is glad the property will not be sold. After receiving P's letter, A lacks actual

authority to sell the property because it is not reasonable for A to believe that P wishes A to sell it. . . .

§ 2.02   Scope of Actual Authority

(1) An agent has actual authority to take action designated or implied in the principal's manifestations to the agent and acts necessary or incidental to achieving the principal's objectives, as the agent reasonably understands the principal's manifestations and objectives when the agent determines how to act.

(2) An agent's interpretation of the principal's manifestations is reasonable if it reflects any meaning known by the agent to be ascribed by the principal and, in the absence of any meaning known to the agent, as a reasonable person in the agent's position would interpret the manifestations in light of the context, including circumstances of which the agent has notice and the agent's fiduciary duty to the principal.

(3) An agent's understanding of the principal's objectives is reasonable if it accords with the principal's manifestations and the inferences that a reasonable person in the agent's position would draw from the circumstances creating the agency.

Comment . . .

e. Agent's reasonable understanding of principal's manifestation. An agent does not have actual authority to do an act if the agent does not reasonably believe that the principal has consented to its commission. Whether an agent's belief is reasonable is determined from the viewpoint of a reasonable person in the agent's situation under all of the circumstances of which the agent has notice. Lack of actual authority is established by showing either that the agent did not believe, or could not reasonably have believed, that the principal's grant of actual authority encompassed the act in question. This standard requires that the agent's belief be reasonable, an objective standard, and that the agent actually hold the belief, a subjective standard.

Illustration:

4.   P, a photographer, employs A as a business manager. P authorizes A to endorse and deposit checks P receives from publishers of photographs taken by P. Based on P's statements to A, A believes A's authority is limited to endorsing and depositing checks and does not include entering into agreements that bind P in other respects. A endorses and deposits a check from T, a magazine publisher, made payable to P. Printed on the back of the check is a legend: "Endorsement constitutes a release of all claims." It is beyond the scope of A's actual authority to release claims that P has against T.

The context in which principal and agent interact, including the nature of the principal's business or the principal's personal situation, frames the reasonableness of an agent's understanding of the principal's objectives. An agent's actual authority encompasses acts necessary to accomplish the end the principal has directed that the agent achieve. In exigent circumstances not known to the principal, the agent may reasonably believe that the principal would wish the agent to act beyond the specifics detailed by the principal.

Illustrations:

5.   P Corporation employs A as the Facilities Manager at an amusement park owned by P Corporation. A reports to B, P Corporation's Vice President for Leisure Activities. B directs A to arrange for the reseeding of the badly deteriorated lawn adjacent to the park's entrance. B also directs A to complete the reseeding by the end of the week. A purchases grass seed and directs groundskeepers to schedule time for reseeding. A then learns that the park location is in the path of a forecasted hurricane. A has actual authority to postpone the reseeding.

6.   Same facts as Illustration 5, except weather conditions do not interrupt the reseeding. A knows that the lawn could be reseeded either at much higher cost to achieve turf conditions suitable for a golf course, or at lower cost to achieve conditions that are visually attractive but not suitable for use as a golf course. Absent other manifestations from B, or other knowledge of P Corporation's practices, A lacks actual authority to reseed to achieve the golf-course standard. In light of the use P Corporation will make of the lawn, it is not reasonable for A to believe that P Corporation's objectives require that the lawn be usable as a golf course.

Factors relevant to the reasonableness of an agent's understanding of the principal's manifestation include the fiduciary character of the agent's relationship with the principal and the agent's inability to react to the principal's unexpressed interests or wishes. An agent's fiduciary position obliges the agent to act loyally to serve the principal's interests and objectives that the agent knows or should know. See § 8.01. The relevant interests and objectives are those with respect to the agency and do not encompass other objectives or interests that a principal may have. A principal's situation, if known to the agent at the time the agent acts, may affect the agent's authority to do a particular act. Additionally, the principal may revoke or limit authority subsequent to granting it. An agent's understanding at the time the agent acts is controlling. If an agent knows that the principal's reason for previously authorizing the agent to do an act is no longer operative, the agent does not have actual authority to do the act. An agent's actual authority is not affected by changes in the principal's situation that are not known to the agent. . . .

Illustrations:

7.   The directors of P Corporation approve a plan to upgrade a plant that is suitable for the manufacture of one product line. P Corporation's Executive Vice President tells M, the plant manager, to contract with an engineering firm for a redesign of the production process that must precede the upgrade work. After adopting the resolution, the directors abandon the upgrade plan and so notify the Executive Vice President. No one tells M, who on behalf of P Corporation enters into a contract with T, an engineering firm, to do the redesign. P Corporation is bound by the contract. M had actual authority to make the contract.

8.   Same facts as Illustration 7, except that M reads in the newspaper that P Corporation's directors have discontinued the sole product line manufactured in the plant. M no longer has actual authority to make the contract with T. M may have apparent authority as defined in § 2.03 if T reasonably believes M has authority to make the contract. T's belief will not be reasonable if T is also aware that the product line has been discontinued.

9.   Same facts as Illustration 7, except that the upgrade plan depends on using a particular building technology. M is aware of this fact. After the directors adopt the resolution and M is directed to contract for the redesign work, M learns that regulatory restrictions will prevent P Corporation from using the particular technology on which the plan depends. M no longer has actual authority to make the contract with T. M may have apparent authority as defined in § 2.03 if T reasonably believes that M has authority to make the contract.

10.   Same facts as Illustration 7, except that P Corporation's Chief Financial Officer tells M that the upgrade plans have been abandoned. M no longer has actual authority even though M does not report to the Chief Financial Officer.

The nature of actual authority means that the relevant inquiry always focuses on the time the agent acts. In Illustrations 8, 9, and 10, the temporal focus, which is the time the agent acts, is not the time of the principal's initial manifestation to the agent. An alternative formulation, which would reach the same outcomes on these Illustrations, is to say that M had actual authority but that subsequent developments terminated it. This formulation unnecessarily adds two elements, the initial presence of authority and its subsequent termination, to the determinative inquiry, which is the reasonableness of M's belief at the time of determining the action to take. . . .

An agent's understanding of the principal's interests and objectives is an element of the agent's reasonable interpretation of the principal's conduct. If a literal interpretation of a principal's communication to the agent would authorize an act inconsistent with the principal's interests or objectives known to the agent, it is open to question whether the agent's literal interpretation is reasonable.

Illustration:

11.   P, a toy designer, employs A as an agent to present P's designs to toy manufacturers. P says to A, "Before you show the design, sign whatever forms the manufacturer requires." A knows that P's practice is to retain all copyright and other intellectual-property interests in P's designs. It may not be reasonable for A to interpret P's instruction to authorize A to sign a form that assigns or releases all of P's interests in the design to T, a toy manufacturer. If T, an

important presence in the industry, always demands that such a release be executed, when feasible A should contact P for further instructions. When not feasible, it is a question of fact whether A acted reasonably in signing the form presented by T. A has apparent authority as defined in § 2.03 only if based on P's conduct it is reasonable for T to believe that A has authority to sign the form.

Interactions between principal and agent do not occur in a vacuum. Prior dealings between them are relevant to the reasonableness of the agent's understanding of the principal's manifestation. If a principal and an agent share an idiosyncratic understanding of what is meant by the principal's manifestation, that understanding controls the scope of the agent's actual authority, not the understanding that a reasonable person would have. Unlike a party dealing at arm's length with another, the focus for an agent is interpreting the principal's manifestations so as to further the principal's objectives.

Illustrations:

12. P, who owns a number of residential rental properties, retains A to manage them. P directs A, "Install smoke detectors in each room." Based on A's prior dealings with P, A knows that by "each room," P means "each room in which the housing code requires a smoke detector." A also knows that P views compliance with the housing code as a business necessity. A's actual authority to install smoke detectors is limited to rooms in which the housing code requires their installation.

13. Same facts as Illustration 12, except that after P's directive to A, the housing code is amended to require the installation of smoke detectors in hallways as well as rooms. A has actual authority to install smoke detectors in hallways as well as rooms.

In determining whether an agent's action reflected a reasonable understanding of the principal's manifestations of consent, it is relevant whether the principal knew of prior similar actions by the agent and acquiesced in them.

Illustration:

14. Same facts as Illustration 12, except that P knows that, given the same directive in the past, A has installed smoke detectors in all rooms. P has not objected or complained. A has actual authority to install smoke detectors in all rooms.

The context in which principal and agent interact will often include customs and usages that are particular to a type of business or a geographic locale. A person carrying on business has reason to know of such customs and usages and thus has notice of them as defined in § 1.04(4). If an agent has notice that the principal does not know of a custom or usage, the agent is not authorized to act in accordance with it if doing so would result in a transaction different from that which the agent has notice is desired by the principal.

If a principal states the agent's authority in terms that contemplate that the agent will use substantial discretion to determine the particulars, it is ordinarily reasonable for the agent to believe that following usage and custom will be acceptable to the principal. In contrast, if a principal's express statement of authority is highly detailed, it is not reasonable for the agent to believe the principal intended that the agent should follow a custom or usage that is at odds with the terms of the principal's express authorization. When a practice is common in a particular industry, it will be difficult for the principal credibly to claim no notice of it. Cases addressing the relevance of usage and custom reflect some division whether it is necessary to show that the principal had notice of the existence of the customs, usages, or practices at issue. This issue should be treated as an aspect of a broader inquiry into the reasonableness of the agent's belief that the agent had authority.

f. Interpretation by agent. In order to determine with specificity what a principal would wish the agent to do, the agent must interpret the language the principal uses or assess the principal's conduct or the situation in which the principal has placed the agent. An agent's position requires such interpretation regardless of the circumstances under which the principal created actual authority. Thus, interpretation by the agent is necessary whether the agent has received explicit instructions from the principal, has received a general directive, or has been appointed to a position in an organization with delegated powers. The benchmark for interpretation reflects the agent's fiduciary position. If the principal gives imperative instructions using clear and precise language and the instructions do not demand illegal conduct and do not appear to have been issued in error, the agent should follow the instructions even if they conflict with industry usage or custom. A reasonable agent would understand the principal's choice of precise language, imperatively stated, as an accurate reflection of the principal's wishes. An industry custom or practice contrary to the principal's definite instructions does not excuse the agent's violation of the principal's instructions.

A principal's ability to communicate with the agent is a basic component of the principal's exercise of the right of control. In particular, a principal has the opportunity to state instructions to the agent with clarity and specificity. Moreover, much that underlies the occurrence of the risk that the agent will depart from instructions is within the principal's control. The principal's instructions may be insufficiently clear in their import to enable the agent to discern what acts the principal wishes the agent to do or to refrain from doing. The principal's instructions, albeit clear as far as they go, may be incomplete in some significant respect, or the instructions may reasonably be understood by the agent to authorize the agent to exercise discretion. Moreover, an agent may depart from instructions because the agent interprets the instructions from a perspective that differs in significant respects from the perspective from which the principal would interpret the identical language. Although not all factors that underlie such differences in perspective are always within the principal's control, in significant respects the principal makes decisions that shape the viewpoint from which the agent interprets instructions.

Occasionally, it may be open to doubt what a principal's instructions mean, even when they are interpreted literally. As a result, the agent may interpret them differently from the interpretation the principal would have preferred. The agent's fiduciary duty to the principal obliges the agent to interpret the principal's manifestations so as to infer, in a reasonable manner, what the principal desires to be done in light of facts of which the agent has notice at the time of acting. Within this basic framework, however, it is not surprising that more than one reasonable interpretation of instructions might be possible. Not all agents are equally gifted in their capacity for reasonable interpretation, especially when the instructions themselves are not specific or when the principal has not furnished the agent with a separate instruction that specifies how to resolve doubtful cases.

A principal may take steps that, by reducing ambiguity or other lack of clarity, reduce the risk that the agent's actions will deviate from the principal's wishes, interests, or objectives. Giving an agent a formal written set of instructions reduces the agent's discretion and potential to err in determining what actions to take. A principal may also reduce the risk of deviation by monitoring the agent, for example by requiring prompt checks on the agent's actions by a superior coagent or an external auditor. How an organizational principal structures itself, including titles given to individuals and habitual patterns of interaction among them, may also reduce the risk of deviation by orienting individuals to defined roles and organizationally specified constraints on action.

An organizational principal, like any principal, is at risk of misunderstanding and misinterpretation. Detailed instructions may be so complex that lapses occur because an agent's attentiveness slips. Prolix instructions may cause some agents to decide that certain instructions may be ignored as trivial or as unwittingly imposed obstacles to achieving what the agent perceives to be the principal's overriding objective. An agent is not privileged to disregard instructions unless the agent reasonably believes that the principal wishes the agent to do so. If third parties with whom the agent interacts reasonably believe the agent to be authorized, the doctrine of apparent authority, defined in § 2.03, may apply to protect the third party. It does not protect an agent who departs from instructions. See § 8.09(2) on an agent's duty to comply with all lawful instructions received from the principal.

Interactions among coagents within an organization often involve superior agents giving instructions to junior or subordinate agents. See § 1.04(9). A subordinate agent may realize correctly that the superior agent is not the principal. Whether correctly or mistakenly, the subordinate agent may believe that the principal's interests would best be served by disregarding the superior agent's instructions. Each separate occasion for the communication and interpretation of instruction downward within a sequential chain of agents enhances the likelihood of miscommunication, misunderstanding, and departure from instructions.

A principal may believe when initially giving instructions to the agent that the principal's best interests will be served by investing the agent with a large measure of discretion, a decision later regretted by the principal when reviewing the agent's actual use of discretion. Regardless of any later regret, the principal is bound by the agent's acts so long as the agent's interpretation was reasonable.

Illustrations:

15. A is the manager of a retail clothing store owned by P, who owns several such stores. P authorizes store managers to buy, from vendors specified by P, inventory of items specified by P for their stores up to limits specified in dollar amount. P identifies "men's dress shirts" as an inventory type that A has authority to buy. A knows that by "dress shirts" P means "shirts suitable for wearing with a tuxedo." A does not have actual authority to buy dress shirts not suitable for tuxedo wear.

16. Same facts as Illustration 15, except that P ascribes no unusual meaning to "men's dress shirts" that is known to A. P provides A with no directions as to the color assortment of shirts. At the time A places the order, a particular color is fashionable and A orders many shirts in that color, believing that the fashion will continue. The shirts fail to sell. A had actual authority to buy the shirts.

17. Same facts as Illustration 16, except that A believes P has set the dollar limit at an unnecessarily low level. A also believes that the limit will result in an inadequate range of selections for P's customers. A purchases men's dress shirts in a quantity that exceeds the dollar limit set by P. A does not have actual authority to exceed P's limit.

18. Same facts as Illustration 17, except that A purchases shirts in a quantity exceeding the limit set by P because A does not notice the limit, failing carefully to read the written statement that A received from P. A lacks actual authority to buy beyond the limit.

19. P Corporation, a financial firm, employs A as a trader in financial instruments on P Corporation's own account. P Corporation imposes no express limits on the type of financial instrument in which A may take trading positions. Additionally, P Corporation awards bonuses to A based on the overall profitability of the portfolio that A manages. A commits P Corporation to a series of risky and unusual investments that result in a substantial loss sustained by the portfolio as a whole. A had actual authority to make the risky and unusual investments. P Corporation imposed no explicit limits on A, and P Corporation's prior treatment of A's investment decisions would not give A a basis for inferring a limit.

An agent who knowingly contravenes or exceeds the principal's instructions may believe that to do so best serves the principal's interests. The agent may believe that circumstances have changed since the initial instructions and that, were the principal to reconsider the matter, different instructions would be given. Unless it is reasonable for the agent to believe that the principal wishes the agent to construe the instructions in light of changed circumstances, the agent lacks actual authority to violate instructions.

Illustrations:

20. P retains A, directing A to buy Blackacre but to offer no more than $250,000. A then learns that Blackacre has increased substantially in value and, if purchased for $300,000, would represent a bargain. As A knows, it is financially feasible for P to pay $300,000 for Blackacre. A does not have actual authority to offer more than $250,000 for Blackacre.

21. Same facts as Illustration 20, except that Blackacre is to be sold at an auction in which the successful bidder will be required to deposit a check in an amount equal to 10 percent of the bid. P gives A a blank check to use in making the deposit. A does not have actual authority to bid more than $250,000 for Blackacre.

22. Same facts as Illustration 20, except that P owns and operates a golf course on land that almost entirely surrounds Blackacre. A has notice of P's long-term business plan to enhance the aesthetic and athletic qualities of the course and thereby make it more profitable. At the auction of Blackacre, A learns for the first time that there will be one other bidder, B. A also learns that B's plan for using Blackacre is to construct a cement factory on it. A is unable to

contact P to relay this information and receive further instructions. A succeeds in purchasing Blackacre for P by bidding $260,000. A acted with actual authority. . . .

It is often feasible for an agent to contact the principal to inquire what the principal now wishes to be done. In an era of rapid electronic communication, it is often cheap and easy for an agent to inquire before proceeding. The agent's inquiry gives the principal the opportunity to clarify or supplement the prior instructions. However, an agent may believe that it is infeasible to contact the principal for clarification or that the advantage promised by the transaction will be lost if the agent does not conclude it promptly. Unless the agent has a basis reasonably to believe that the principal does not wish to resolve the question, the agent should attempt to contact the principal prior to exercising discretion to disregard prior instructions. If the principal does not respond to the agent's inquiry and viewed objectively the action then taken by the agent reasonably serves the principal's interests as the agent could best discern them, the agent acted with actual authority.

A principal's instructions may not address prior occasions on which the agent has contravened instructions. On prior occasions the principal may have affirmatively approved of the agent's unauthorized act or silently acquiesced in it by failing to voice affirmative disapproval. The history is likely to influence the agent's subsequent interpretation of instructions. If the principal's subsequent instructions do not address the history, the agent may well infer from the principal's silence that the principal will not demand compliance with the instructions to any degree greater than the principal has done in the past. It is a question of fact whether the agent is reasonable in drawing such an inference. It will probably not be reasonable if the principal has recently renewed the instructions or newly emphasized the importance of complying with them.

An agent may believe, whether correctly or erroneously, that the agent knows the principal's best interests better than the principal does. What appears to be hubris on the agent's part may be present when the agent in fact has greater expertise or knowledge than does the principal as to matters within the scope of the agency relationship. Agents are often said to depart from their instructions due to an "excess of zeal." One explanation for this phenomenon is the agent's belief in a superior understanding of the principal's best interests. Additionally, agents sometimes exhibit an "excess of zeal" because they have information about the principal's situation that differs from the principal's own information and beliefs based upon it. Matters that seem urgent or imperative to the agent may seem less so to the principal, whose knowledge will often be broader in scope and whose time horizon will often extend farther into the future than will the agent's.

The incentive structure embedded in an agent's relationship with the principal may aggravate differences in perspective. Lapses from instructions may well follow if the agent's compensation depends on the volume of transactions concluded by the agent or on their dollar value, or if the agent fears the principal will terminate the agency relationship if the agent does not achieve success. Regardless of the explanation for the lapse, the agent does not have actual authority to disregard instructions unless it is reasonable for the agent to believe that the principal wishes the agent to do so.

Illustrations:

23. VP, the vice president of P Corporation in charge of P Corporation's information technology, enters into negotiations with T Corporation to buy a new computer system. Before VP begins negotiations with T Corporation, the board of directors of P Corporation authorizes the expenditure of up to $5 million on a new computer system. The CEO of P Corporation then directs VP not to buy a computer system from T Corporation because the CEO has been told by other CEOs that T Corporation's products demand a high level of user sophistication. Believing that the CEO has underestimated the computer skills of P Corporation's work force, VP enters into a contract with T Corporation to buy a computer system for $4 million. VP did not have actual authority to enter into a transaction specifically forbidden by the CEO.

24. Same facts as Illustration 23, except that VP, additionally, has good reason to believe that the computer system is a bargain at the $4 million price. VP does not have actual authority to contract to buy it.

g. *Explicit instructions.* A principal may direct an agent to do or refrain from doing a specific act. The agent's fiduciary duty to the principal obliges the agent to interpret the principal's instructions so as to infer, in a reasonable manner, what the principal would wish the agent to do in light of the facts of which the agent has notice at the time of acting.

Although an agent's task of interpretation is often straightforward when given specific instructions, the principal's language does not interpret itself. Circumstances may require the agent to exercise discretion in ascertaining the principal's wishes. Suppose the principal (P), the owner of a menagerie, makes a statement that P believes directs the general manager of the menagerie (A) to buy no more horses. If A enters into an agreement to buy another horse for the menagerie, A did not act with actual authority unless A reasonably believed that P wished the purchase to be made.

Consider the variety of explanations for A's purchase of the horse on P's account despite what appears to be P's direction to the contrary. First, P's statement might not have expressed P's wishes clearly. Perhaps P said, "I'm not into horses anymore," which is not a categorical statement of an instruction to A. If A sought clarification from P, P might have responded, "What I meant was, buy no more horses." A's purchase of the additional horse would be unauthorized. A might, however, reasonably believe that no clarification was necessary. Perhaps A believed that P meant to discontinue P's private use of horses, separate from the menagerie business. A's belief is not reasonable, though, in the absence of some reason to ascribe that interpretation to P's statement. A might fail to seek clarification from P if logistics make it difficult or impossible to do so or if P seems too rushed or distracted to explain further. It is a question of fact whether A's failure to seek clarification is reasonable under the circumstances.

Suppose P said to A originally (or in response to A's request for clarification): "Buy no more horses." This instruction, clear on its face, might nonetheless leave A in doubt in some circumstances. P's language does not itself define the word "horse" and does not eliminate A's need to interpret P's language to determine whether P intends to prohibit A's purchase of a pony or a zebra or toy horses for sale in the menagerie's gift shop. A's interpretation will not be reasonable unless it takes into account A's prior experience with P which is likely to reveal how P uses language when referring to the menagerie.

Moreover, A might wonder how absolutely or unconditionally to interpret P's instruction. Would it contravene the instruction to buy an additional horse after the death of one of the horses on display in the menagerie? Should A understand P to mean that the value of an additional horse, relative to the sale price, is totally irrelevant? Must A pass on the opportunity to buy an especially valuable horse at a very low price? A may believe that P's best interests would be served by ignoring the literal interpretation of P's instruction. Unless A has reason to believe that P wishes A to do so, however, it is not reasonable for A to disregard the instruction rather than contacting P, if feasible, for further clarification.

A might decide to contravene P's instruction if A believes it to be a mistake from the standpoint of the business interest of the menagerie itself. Although A's departure from P's instructions may well be understandable, it is not consistent with A's duty of loyalty, which is owed to P and not to the menagerie itself. A lacks authority to depart from P's instructions to serve A's perception of what is required to further the interests of the menagerie.

Regardless of the breadth or narrowness with which a principal has conveyed authority to the agent, an agent's actual authority extends only to acts that the agent reasonably believes the principal has authorized or wishes the agent to perform. The fiduciary character of the agency relationship shapes the agent's permissible interpretation of authority, disallowing an interpretation that is inconsistent with interests of the principal that the agent knows or should know. . . .

TOPIC 2. APPARENT AUTHORITY

§ 2.03 Apparent Authority

Apparent authority is the power held by an agent or other actor to affect a principal's legal relations with third parties when a third party reasonably believes the actor has authority to act on behalf of the principal and that belief is traceable to the principal's manifestations.

TOPIC 3.   RESPONDEAT SUPERIOR

§ 2.04   Respondeat Superior

An employer is subject to liability for torts committed by employees while acting within the scope of their employment. → if employer is vicariously liable, both liable joint and severally

§ 2.05   Estoppel to Deny Existence of Agency Relationship

A person who has not made a manifestation that an actor has authority as an agent and who is not otherwise liable as a party to a transaction purportedly done by the actor on that person's account is subject to liability to a third party who justifiably is induced to make a detrimental change in position because the transaction is believed to be on the person's account, if

(1) the person intentionally or carelessly caused such belief, or

(2) having notice of such belief and that it might induce others to change their positions, the person did not take reasonable steps to notify them of the facts.

§ 2.06   Liability of Undisclosed Principal

(1) An undisclosed principal is subject to liability to a third party who is justifiably induced to make a detrimental change in position by an agent acting on the principal's behalf and without actual authority if the principal, having notice of the agent's conduct and that it might induce others to change their positions, did not take reasonable steps to notify them of the facts.

(2) An undisclosed principal may not rely on instructions given an agent that qualify or reduce the agent's authority to less than the authority a third party would reasonably believe the agent to have under the same circumstances if the principal had been disclosed.

§ 2.07   Restitution of Benefit

If a principal is unjustly enriched at the expense of another person by the action of an agent or a person who appears to be an agent, the principal is subject to a claim for restitution by that person.

CHAPTER 3

CREATION AND TERMINATION OF AUTHORITY AND AGENCY RELATIONSHIPS

TOPIC 1.   CREATING AND EVIDENCING ACTUAL AUTHORITY

§ 3.01   Creation of Actual Authority

Actual authority, as defined in § 2.01, is created by a principal's manifestation to an agent that, as reasonably understood by the agent, expresses the principal's assent that the agent take action on the principal's behalf.

§ 3.02   Formal Requirements

If the law requires a writing or record signed by the principal to evidence an agent's authority to bind a principal to a contract or other transaction, the principal is not bound in the absence of such a writing or record. A principal may be estopped to assert the lack of such a writing or record when a third party has been induced to make a detrimental change in position by the reasonable belief that an agent has authority to bind the principal that is traceable to a manifestation made by the principal.

TOPIC 2. CREATING APPARENT AUTHORITY

§ 3.03 Creation of Apparent Authority

Apparent authority, as defined in § 2.03, is created by a person's manifestation that another has authority to act with legal consequences for the person who makes the manifestation, when a third party reasonably believes the actor to be authorized and the belief is traceable to the manifestation. . . .

TOPIC 4. TERMINATION OF AGENT'S POWER

TITLE A. TERMINATION OF ACTUAL AUTHORITY

§ 3.10 Manifestation Terminating Actual Authority

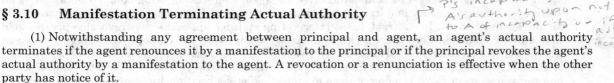

[handwritten margin note: P's incapacity terminates A's authority upon notice to A of incapacity or if adjudged incompetent]

(1) Notwithstanding any agreement between principal and agent, an agent's actual authority terminates if the agent renounces it by a manifestation to the principal or if the principal revokes the agent's actual authority by a manifestation to the agent. A revocation or a renunciation is effective when the other party has notice of it.

(2) A principal's manifestation of revocation is, unless otherwise agreed, ineffective to terminate a power given as security or to terminate a proxy to vote securities or other membership or ownership interests that is made irrevocable in compliance with applicable legislation. See §§ 3.12–3.13.

TITLE B. TERMINATION OF APPARENT AUTHORITY

§ 3.11 Termination of Apparent Authority

(1) The termination of actual authority does not by itself end any apparent authority held by an agent.

(2) Apparent authority ends when it is no longer reasonable for the third party with whom an agent deals to believe that the agent continues to act with actual authority.

TITLE C. IRREVOCABLE POWERS

§ 3.12 Power Given as Security; Irrevocable Proxy

(1) A power given as security is a power to affect the legal relations of its creator that is created in the form of a manifestation of actual authority and held for the benefit of the holder or a third person. This power is given to protect a legal or equitable title or to secure the performance of a duty apart from any duties owed the holder of the power by its creator that are incident to a relationship of agency under § 1.01. It is given upon the creation of the duty or title or for consideration. It is distinct from actual authority that the holder may exercise if the holder is an agent of the creator of the power.

(2) A power to exercise voting rights associated with securities or a membership interest may be conferred on a proxy through a manifestation of actual authority. The power may be given as security under (1) and may be made irrevocable in compliance with applicable legislation.

Comment . . .

b. Distinguished from agency and actual authority. A power given as security creates neither a relationship of agency as defined in § 1.01 nor actual authority as defined in § 2.01, although the power enables its holder to affect the legal relations of the creator of the power. The power arises from a manifestation of assent by its creator that the holder of the power may properly create liability against the creator, or dispose of property or other interests of the creator, or perfect or otherwise protect a title already held by the holder of the power or the person for whose benefit the holder is to act. If the power is given as security for the performance of a duty, it must be supported by consideration, but consideration is not necessary if the power is given to facilitate transfers of title to the power holder.

The rights created by a power given as security, or by an irrevocable proxy, entitle the holder to take specific actions. If the creator of a validly created power given as security purports to revoke the holder's authority contrary to the agreement pursuant to which the creator granted the power, specific enforcement of the holder's rights is an appropriate remedy, subject to the court's discretion in granting an equitable remedy. Likewise, specific enforcement may be warranted to protect the rights of the holder of a validly created irrevocable proxy. In both cases, it will often be difficult or impossible for the holder to prove quantifiable damages or to obtain a substitute performance. See Restatement Second, Contracts § 360, Comments *b* and *c*.

A power given as security does not create a relationship of agency as defined in § 1.01 because it is neither given for, nor exercised for, the benefit of the person who creates it. The holder is not subject to the creator's control and the holder does not owe fiduciary duties to the creator. An agent's right to act, created by actual authority, does not constitute a power given as security although the agent has an interest in earning a commission by performing services and the principal has contracted with the agent not to revoke the agent's actual authority. An agent's interest in being paid a commission is an ordinary incident of agency and its presence does not convert the agent's authority into a power held for the agent's benefit. In contrast, cases interpreting statutes applicable to irrevocable proxies hold that a proxy holder's interest in an employment agreement with the corporation suffices to support irrevocability. See Comment *d*. However, if a power holder has a distinct interest in the subject matter of an agency relationship, separate from acting as an agent, a power given to protect that interest is a power given as security, as is a power given to protect a distinct relationship, separate from the agency relationship, between the agent and the principal. A power may be granted irrevocably for the benefit of its creator as well as the holder.

A power given as security may also be created and held for the benefit of a third party, other than the holder of the power. The creator of the power and the holder have the ability to create an enforceable right in a third party to benefit from the power, just as two parties to a contract have the ability to create a right in a third-party beneficiary. See Restatement Second, Contracts § 304, Comment *b*.

Illustrations:

1. P owns Blackacre, which is situated next to Whiteacre, on which P operates a restaurant. To finance renovations and expansions, P borrows money from A. A written agreement between P and A provides that A shall irrevocably have P's authority to transfer ownership of Blackacre to A in the event P defaults on the loan. A has a power given as security.

2. Same facts as Illustration 1, except that A is a corporation and the agreement with P provides that M, an officer of A, shall have P's authorization to transfer ownership of Blackacre. M has a power given as security. The power was given by P for the benefit of A.

3. P owns a resort hotel. P engages A to manage the hotel for a term of 10 years, in an agreement that expressly provides that P may not revoke A's authority except pursuant to mutual agreement. The agreement states that P's promise not to revoke A's authority constitutes security to A for A's interest in receiving the management fee specified in the agreement, which is three percent of gross revenues for the first five years, and five percent for the second five years. A does not have a power given as security. If P revokes A's authority, A will not have a specifically enforceable right to continue to manage the hotel. A may claim that P's revocation is a breach of contract and seek money damages from P.

4. P develops a mechanical invention and engages A to patent the invention and arrange for its commercial manufacture. P authorizes A to file patent documents on P's behalf and to enter into contracts with suitable manufacturers. P agrees to pay A's expenses and agrees to pay A half of P's profits. Even if A's authority is stated to be irrevocable, A does not hold a power given as security.

5. Same facts as Illustration 4, except that P grants A a one-half ownership interest in the invention and P's rights in it, and A agrees to cover the expenses of A's efforts. It may be found that A has a power given as security. A will exercise the power for A's benefit as well as P's.

6. Same facts as Illustration 5, except that P, at A's request, grants the one-half ownership interest to C, to whom A is indebted. It may be found that A has a power given as security, to be exercised for the benefit of C.

 c. *Power coupled with an interest.* Some jurisdictions follow a test narrower than that stated in this section, under which it is necessary that a power holder possess a proprietary interest in the "subject matter of the agency itself." This test also requires that the power and the proprietary interest be united in the same person. The narrower test has a distinguished lineage, beginning with Chief Justice Marshall's opinion in *Hunt v. Rousmanier's Administrators*, 21 U.S. (8 Wheat.) 174 (1823). Rousmanier had given Hunt a power of attorney to sell a brig and a schooner owned by Rousmanier, to be exercisable if Rousmanier defaulted in repaying loans he owed to Hunt. After Rousmanier died insolvent, following his default on the loans, the court held that the power was not enforceable. The court held that the power created only a revocable agency, which perished with Rousmanier's death, as opposed to "a power coupled with an interest" that survives its creator's death and may be exercised after it. 21 U.S. at 203. To create such a power, the holder must be vested with an interest or estate that accompanies the power. The focus of the court's opinion is the demise of Rousmanier's legal personality with his death, not the commercial function of the power, which the parties intended as a substitute for a mortgage on the ships that might not have been enforceable.

 The difference between the test for irrevocability derived from *Hunt*, and that stated in this section, has practical consequences in two situations. First, under the "power coupled with an interest" approach, the power P granted to A in Illustration 1 is revocable because it does not accompany any proprietary interest of A in Blackacre itself. More generally, if a power must be coupled with a property interest to be made irrevocable, granting a power of sale as to property owned by the debtor, in which a creditor has no proprietary interest, will not effectively protect the creditor's interests. Unsurprisingly, the law applicable to loan transactions has itself evolved to overcome this obstacle. For example, a mortgage lender by statute has the right in every jurisdiction to cause the sale of the mortgaged property through judicial foreclosure. Additionally, in about 60 percent of the states, statutes authorize a mortgagee to sell pursuant to a power of sale, created by the mortgagor by conveying the property to a trustee who holds the property and the power to sell it as a fiduciary for the benefit of the mortgagee-beneficiary. The trustee exercises the power of sale. Separately, in secured financing under U.C.C. Article 9, it is irrelevant whether a lender obtains title to the collateral. A secured lender's rights concerning collateral, including the right to dispose of it after the borrower's default, are specified and regulated by the Code.

 Second, the test derived from *Hunt* requires that the same person hold both the interest and the power. As a consequence, it does not recognize the irrevocability of a power created in one person when the creator transfers the requisite proprietary interest to another person, even if the holder and the transferor are closely related, such as affiliated corporations in the same group. Illustration 6 presents such a situation. The rule stated in this section permits an irrevocable power to be held for the benefit of a third party, which implies that the power holder and the interest-holder may be distinct persons.

 Distinguished lineage aside, the quest for an interest to which a power has been coupled is not a useful exercise when it is clear that the power has been created for the benefit of a person other than the creator, as in *Hunt* itself. It is unnecessary to impose further limits on the creator's range of choices.

 d. *Irrevocable proxies.* A right to vote associated with securities may be delegated by the owner to an agent. Likewise, many organizational statutes contemplate that members of not-for-profit corporations may delegate voting rights to agents, as may members of limited-liability companies (LLCs). In such statutes, the treatment of voting by proxy is less fully developed than in business-corporation statutes.

 Designating a proxy to vote creates a relationship of agency as defined in § 1.01 unless the proxy is irrevocable. Thus, the principal may revoke a proxy holder's actual authority. The principal lacks power to revoke the proxy holder's authority to vote when such authority is expressly made irrevocable and the holder receives the proxy as a power given as security as defined in § 3.12(1), or the proxy is supported by an interest that suffices to make it irrevocable under the applicable organizational statute. Revocation requires a manifestation from the principal, which may be made by conduct from which dissent to the proxy holder's authority may be inferred. See Comment *c*. The death of the proxy holder revokes a proxy that has expressly been made irrevocable only when the proxy was given to support an interest that terminates with the holder's death. See § 3.13.

An irrevocable proxy separates voting power from stock ownership; even when the proxy holder owns stock, the ability to vote stock owned by another augments the proxy holder's voting power. An irrevocable proxy thereby distorts the allocation of voting power to or among a corporation's residual economic claimants, who own its stock. The proxy holder's interests may not always be aligned with those of stockholders. For example, if the holder owns no stock but has an interest in employment by the corporation or an interest in commercial transactions with it, the proxy holder's interests may diverge from the stockholders' interests.

This potential for divergence in interests explains why, in many cases, courts refused to enforce irrevocable proxies. Courts enforced irrevocable proxies only when the holder had a proprietary interest in the shares themselves, as would a pledgee who has lent money on the security of the shares to their owner. Even when coupled with such an interest, an irrevocable proxy always operates with regard to two subjects: first, the shares; and, as a secondary subject, the corporation. The holder's vote affects the interests, but not the legal relations, of all of the corporation's shareholders. The spillover effect from the principal to the corporation and its other shareholders may also explain why irrevocable proxies attracted skepticism. An irrevocable proxy affects the interests of all shareholders because, if the holder has majority control, the holder ordinarily has power to choose the corporation's directors and holds veto power over fundamental transactions that require a shareholder vote.

Judicial skepticism lessened in some jurisdictions. Irrevocability was a practical necessity to combinations among shareholders because it enabled the coalescence of voting power in a predictable and enforceable manner. Only specific enforcement of the proxy by its terms, and not money damages, can provide control over voting. In response, some courts recast the terms of analysis to examine the grantor's motive or objective in granting the proxy. Such cases focus on whether the grantor had the pursuit of purely personal gain as an objective, as opposed to the good of all shareholders. This test has proven difficult to state or apply with precision. Business-corporation statutes also evolved to permit stockholders to form voting trusts, or to enter into specifically enforceable voting agreements, both devices that separate control over voting from stock ownership.

Most business-corporation statutes now address the question of irrevocability, albeit against the background sketched above. The statutes, and recent cases interpreting them, broaden the circumstances in which a proxy may be made irrevocable well beyond those applicable more generally to powers given as security, defined in § 3.12(1). Most business-corporation statutes provide that a proxy shall be irrevocable if it expressly so states and if the proxy is "coupled with an interest." The statutes vary in the extent to which they specify what shall suffice as an interest and in whether the statute makes the specification exclusive. Many statutes specify a nonexclusive list of relationships that suffice as an interest. The typical statement is that the appointment of a proxy is coupled with an interest when the appointee is a pledgee, a person who has purchased or agreed to purchase the shares, a creditor who extended credit to the corporation under terms requiring the appointment, an employee whose employment contract with the corporation requires the appointment, or a party to a voting agreement created pursuant to the statute. In some statutes, including those of New York and California, the list of specified interests is exclusive. Several statutes, including those of Delaware and Massachusetts, use broader language without specifying particular interests. Under the Delaware statute, "[a] duly executed proxy shall be irrevocable if it states that it is irrevocable and if, and only as long as, it is coupled with an interest sufficient in law to support an irrevocable power. A proxy may be made irrevocable regardless of whether the interest with which it is coupled is an interest in the stock itself or an interest in the corporation generally." Del. Code Ann., tit. 8, § 212(e) (2005).

Recent Delaware authority holds that an interest in employment constitutes "an interest in the corporation generally." This possibility is present as well under statutes that define interest to include an employment contract that requires the irrevocable proxy. So treating an interest in employment is at odds with the cases defining the more general doctrine of power given as security, stated in § 3.12(1). An agent's interest in receiving commissions or other compensation is insufficient to support such a power because it is an ordinary incident of the agency itself.

Competing policies apply to the treatment of interests in employment. The policy factors are especially pertinent when the relevant organizational statute authorizes voting by proxy but does not specify when a proxy may be made irrevocable. For example, some LLC statutes, like some not-for-profit corporation statutes, authorize voting by proxy but are silent on irrevocability. A proxy holder's self-interest in employment could lead to the election of directors, or to votes on fundamental transactions, that disserve the interests of most shareholders or members. This risk, however, may not warrant a stricter rule or at least not a categorically stricter rule. The risk will not materialize unless the holder's vote controls the voting outcome. Even when a proxy holder has effective control, other legal doctrines regulate how that control may be used. For example, corporate law regulates the use of voting control through doctrines specifically applicable to shareholders who use control to benefit themselves at the expense of other shareholders. See Principles of Corporate Governance: Analysis and Recommendations §§ 5.10–5.14. Moreover, a corporation's directors, regardless of how or by whom elected, owe fiduciary duties to the entire corporation, which encompasses the interests of its noncontrolling shareholders. See id. §§ 5.02–5.09. The terms of the employment contract between a proxy holder and the organization may also mitigate the risk, for example by tying the holder's compensation to performance-related criteria, and thereby aligning the holder's economic interests more closely to those of stockholders or members.

In general, irrevocable proxies to vote sufficient shares to constitute control are much more likely in closely held corporations or other business organizations than in publicly held corporations. In closely held enterprises, it is also more likely that most members will assent to, or at least be aware of, the circumstances that led to the proxy holder's irrevocable appointment.

§ 3.13 Termination of Power Given as Security or Irrevocable Proxy

(1) A power given as security or an irrevocable proxy is terminated by an event that

(a) discharges the obligation secured by the power or terminates the interest secured or supported by the proxy, or

(b) makes its execution illegal or impossible, or

(c) constitutes an effective surrender of the power or proxy by the person for whose benefit it was created or conferred.

(2) Unless otherwise agreed, neither a power given as security nor a proxy made irrevocable as provided in § 3.12(2) is terminated by:

(a) a manifestation revoking the power or proxy made by the person who created it; or

(b) surrender of the power or proxy by its holder if it is held for the benefit of another person, unless that person consents; or

(c) loss of capacity by the creator or the holder of the power or proxy; or

(d) death of the holder of the power or proxy, unless the holder's death terminates the interest secured or supported by the power or proxy; or

(e) death of the creator of the power or proxy, if the power or proxy is given as security for the performance of a duty that does not terminate with the death of its creator.

Comment . . .

b. Distinguished from revocation and renunciation of actual authority. Powers given as security and irrevocable proxies do not create relationships of agency as defined in § 1.01 and, despite their form, do not create actual authority under §§ 2.01 and 3.01. The power or proxy is held for the benefit of the holder or a third party and not solely for the benefit of its creator. A power given as security is not terminated by a manifestation of revocation by the creator of the power unless the parties have so agreed. A proxy made irrevocable in compliance with applicable legislation is not terminated by a manifestation of revocation from the owner of the securities or interest. In contrast, a manifestation of revocation by a principal terminates an agent's actual authority, notwithstanding any prior contrary agreement between principal and agent. See § 3.10.

Three basic concepts explain when powers given as security and irrevocable proxies will always terminate. Additionally, if the creator and holder of the power so agree, the power or proxy may be made subject to additional circumstances that result in termination. First, a power given as security or an irrevocable proxy is by definition tied to or supported by an interest or obligation that differentiates the power or proxy from a relationship of agency. Duration of the power or proxy is thus coterminous with such interest or obligation, with the consequence that terminating the interest or obligation terminates the power or proxy as well. For example, if the creator grants the power as security to a creditor, discharging the creator's obligation to the creditor terminates the power. If the creator grants the power to protect an ownership interest of the holder, the power terminates when the holder no longer has the ownership interest.

Second, a power given as security or an irrevocable proxy terminates when the power cannot be executed, either practically or legally, or when it is no longer possible for the proxy holder to vote because the grantor of the proxy no longer owns the securities or membership interest. For example, if the power is a power to sell property, the creator's sale of the same property to a bona fide purchaser who lacks notice of the power terminates the holder's power of sale.

Third, a power given as security or an irrevocable proxy terminates with the consent of the person for whose benefit it was created, manifested by surrendering the power or proxy. If the power was created for the benefit of a person other than the holder, the holder's surrender or renunciation does not terminate the power without the beneficiary's consent. This limit on surrender is analogous to the doctrine protecting the right of a third-party beneficiary to performance of a promise when the promisor and promisee have agreed that the third-party beneficiary shall hold a right to performance that may not be varied without the beneficiary's consent. See Restatement Second, Contracts § 311(1) and Comment *a*.

Under statutes in many states, the interests that may support an irrevocable proxy are broader than those requisite for a power granted as security. These interests include those created by an employment agreement with the corporation that requires the proxy, as well as by a voting agreement among shareholders. See § 3.12, Comment *d*. Some statutes formulate the requisite interest in nonspecific terms, such as "an interest in the corporation generally." See Del. Code Ann. tit. 8, § 212(e) (2005). The power irrevocably conferred by the proxy terminates when the holder's interest ends. . . .

TOPIC 5.   AGENTS WITH MULTIPLE PRINCIPALS

§ 3.14   Agents with Multiple Principals

An agent acting in the same transaction or matter on behalf of more than one principal may be one or both of the following:

    (a) a subagent, as stated in § 3.15; or

    (b) an agent for coprincipals, as stated in § 3.16.

§ 3.15   Subagency

(1) A subagent is a person appointed by an agent to perform functions that the agent has consented to perform on behalf of the agent's principal and for whose conduct the appointing agent is responsible to the principal. The relationships between a subagent and the appointing agent and between the subagent and the appointing agent's principal are relationships of agency as stated in § 1.01.

(2) An agent may appoint a subagent only if the agent has actual or apparent authority to do so.

Comment . . .

    b.   Subagency contrasted with coagency. Agency creates a personal relationship between principal and agent; an agent's delegation of power to another person to act on behalf of the principal is inconsistent with the undertaking made when a person consents to act as agent on behalf of a principal. However, a principal may empower an agent to appoint another agent to act on the principal's behalf. The second agent may be a subagent or a coagent. . . .

An agent who appoints a subagent delegates to the subagent power to act on behalf of the principal that the principal has conferred on the agent. A subagent acts subject to the control of the appointing agent, and the principal's legal position is affected by action taken by the subagent as if the action had been taken by the appointing agent. Thus, a subagent has two principals, the appointing

20

agent and that agent's principal. Although an appointing agent has the right and duty to control a subagent, the interests and instructions of the appointing agent's principal are paramount. . . .

§ 3.16 Agent for Coprincipals

Two or more persons may as coprincipals appoint an agent to act for them in the same transaction or matter.

CHAPTER 4

RATIFICATION

§ 4.01 Ratification Defined

(1) Ratification is the affirmance of a prior act done by another, whereby the act is given effect as if done by an agent acting with actual authority.

(2) A person ratifies an act by

(a) manifesting assent that the act shall affect the person's legal relations, or

(b) conduct that justifies a reasonable assumption that the person so consents.

(3) Ratification does not occur unless

(a) the act is ratifiable as stated in § 4.03,

(b) the person ratifying has capacity as stated in § 4.04,

(c) the ratification is timely as stated in § 4.05, and

(d) the ratification encompasses the act in its entirety as stated in § 4.07.

§ 4.02 Effect of Ratification

(1) Subject to the exceptions stated in subsection (2), ratification retroactively creates the effects of actual authority.

(2) Ratification is not effective:

(a) in favor of a person who causes it by misrepresentation or other conduct that would make a contract voidable;

(b) in favor of an agent against a principal when the principal ratifies to avoid a loss; or

(c) to diminish the rights or other interests of persons, not parties to the transaction, that were acquired in the subject matter prior to the ratification.

§ 4.03 Acts That May Be Ratified

A person may ratify an act if the actor acted or purported to act as an agent on the person's behalf.

§ 4.04 Capacity to Ratify

(1) A person may ratify an act if

(a) the person existed at the time of the act, and

(b) the person had capacity as defined in § 3.04 at the time of ratifying the act.

(2) At a later time, a principal may avoid a ratification made earlier when the principal lacked capacity as defined in § 3.04.

Comment . . .

   b.   Capacity to be a principal. . . .

   Earlier statements of ratification doctrine were more stringent on this score, requiring that the principal have had capacity at the time of the original act as well as at the time of ratification. See Restatement Second, Agency § 84(1). . . .

   c.   Nonexistent principals, including corporations yet to be formed. Under the rule stated in subsection (1)(a), a person not in existence at the time of an act or transaction may not subsequently ratify it. Instead, a person may elect to become bound under such circumstances by adopting what was done prior to the person's existence. Adoption operates analogously to ratification because it requires assent or affirmance on the part of the ratifier. Unlike ratification, adoption does not have a relation-back effect. Additionally, an adoption, unlike a novation, does not itself release obligors from liabilities created by the original transaction.

Illustration:

   1.   A, acting on behalf of P Corporation, which is not yet incorporated, enters into an oral employment contract for a term of 18 months with B. Once formed, P Corporation adopts the contract 13 months after A made the contract with B. The applicable Statute of Frauds requires that contracts not to be performed within one year of their making, including contracts of employment, be evidenced by a writing signed by the party to be charged. B's contract is enforceable notwithstanding the Statute of Frauds because P Corporation's adoption does not relate back to the time of the original contract.

   This limit on ratification has a long lineage in disputes involving transactions made by promoters on behalf of corporations that have not yet been formed. Comparable questions may arise concerning promoters' transactions on behalf of not-yet-formed limited partnerships and limited-liability companies. A corporation should not be bound by the terms of a contract made prior to its existence until its own mechanisms of governance are in place and able to assess the merits of the transaction. A promoter's interests are often not identical to the interests of those who own equity in a corporation once it is formed.

   If a promoter enters into a contract with a third party on behalf of a corporation that has not yet commenced legal existence, the corporation itself cannot be a party to the contract prior to its existence. This is so whether the contract purports to be made on behalf of a corporation characterized as one yet to be formed or characterizes the corporation as one presently in existence. If the contract is to bind the third party prior to the existence of the corporation, unless the relationship is structured as an option that may be exercised by the corporation when formed, either the promoter or someone else must be liable on the contract. The parties' intention must often be determined on the basis of inferences to be drawn from the circumstances, which include whether the promoter and the other party are aware that the corporation does not yet exist. A third party may agree in a contract made by a promoter to release the promoter's liability when and if the corporation adopts the contract. In the absence of an express agreement by the third party to release the promoter, some cases permit the promoter to establish that the parties intended that the promoter would not be personally liable. A corporation may adopt a contract made by a promoter by accepting its benefits with knowledge of its terms.

   This doctrine has the potential to carry harsh consequences for promoters when a third party does not agree to release a promoter's individual liability when and if the corporation adopts the contract. The third party may determine that the corporation's ability to perform under the contract looks risky and decline to release the promoter or, regardless of its assessment of prospects of the corporation's performance, the third party may prefer to have more rather than fewer obligors on the contract. When a third party knows at the time of contracting with a promoter that the corporation has not yet been formed, the promoter's conduct has not deceived the third party. Moreover, even if the corporation agrees to indemnify the promoter against loss stemming from the promoter's individual liability, the indemnity will not protect the promoter if the corporation is insolvent and cannot pay when the promoter seeks to be indemnified.

Viewed in a broader perspective, the risk of individual liability may be beneficial because it encourages promoters to complete the formal requisites for incorporation sooner rather than later. The process requisite to incorporation under contemporary corporation statutes is not cumbersome. Moreover, duly completing the process of forming a corporation creates a publicly accessible document, filed with the state, that furnishes useful albeit minimal information, including the corporation's name and the name and address of the agent it has designated to receive service of process. Such a formal record provides a source of information that enables the state to enforce applicable law, as well as enabling private parties to pursue legal process.

Provisions in corporation statutes reflect different judgments about how contractual risk should be allocated as between promoter and third party when a contract purports to be made on behalf of a not-yet-formed corporation as if it had present existence. Several states have adopted verbatim the language of § 2.04 of the Model Business Corporation Act, which provides that "[a]ll persons purporting to act as or on behalf of a corporation, knowing there was no incorporation under this act, are jointly and severally liable for all liabilities created while so acting." In a few states, a promoter must have "actual knowledge" that there was no incorporation, while in several other states, the promoter is liable whether or not the promoter knows that the corporation has not yet been incorporated. A few states excuse a promoter from liability when the promoter believes in good faith that incorporation has occurred or do not permit a person "who also knew that there was no incorporation" to hold the promoter liable.

A court may determine that a third party should be estopped from seeking a promoter's personal liability. For example, if a promoter is reluctant to enter into a contract personally but a third party persuades the promoter to contract in the name of a nonexistent corporation, the third party has induced the promoter to take action the promoter would likely not have taken otherwise.

REPORTER'S NOTES . . .

c.   *Nonexistent principals, including corporations yet to be formed.* Illustration 1 is based on McArthur v. Times Printing Co., 51 N.W. 216, 217 (1892).

For the proposition that a corporation may adopt preincorporation transactions, see Illinois Controls, Inc. v. Langham, 639 N.E.2d 771, 780 (Ohio 1994). See also Madeja v. Olympic Packer, LLC, 155 F. Supp. 2d 1183, 1204 (D. Hawaii 2001), aff'd, 310 F.3d 628 (9th Cir. 2002) (holding that charter agreement was not void because made prior to incorporation of company that chartered vessel; either corporation or individual who signed charter on its behalf as president would be required to perform terms of charter).

Cases holding that a corporation once formed may "adopt" but not ratify promoters' contracts include Commissioners of Lewes v. Breakwater Fisheries Co., 117 A. 823 (Del. Ch. 1922); Davis & Rankin Bldg. & Mfg. Co. v. Hillsboro Creamery Co., 37 N.E. 549 (Ind. App. 1894); McCrillis v. A & W Enters., Inc., 155 S.E.2d 281 (N.C. 1967). The sole authority to the contrary appears to be Stanton v. New York & E.Ry. Co., 22 A. 300 (Conn. 1890).

Some opinions use the terms "ratification" and "adoption" interchangeably when no operative consequences follow. See Yost v. Early, 589 A.2d 1291, 1300 (Md. App. 1991); Eden Temp. Servs., Inc. v. House of Excellence, Inc., 704 N.Y.S.2d 239, 240 (App. Div. 2000); Coastal Shutters & Insulation, Inc. v. Derr, 809 S.W.2d 916, 920 (Tex. App. 1991).

Cases holding that a promoter retains individual liability despite the corporation's adoption of the contract include Allen Steel Supply Co. v. Bradley, 402 P.2d 394 (Idaho 1965); Jacobson v. Stern, 605 P.2d 198 (Nev. 1980). This gives the third party "double security." See Carle v. Corhan, 103 S.E. 699, 702 (Va. 1920); Eddie Flores, The Case for Eliminating Promoter Liability on Preincorporation Agreements, 32 Ariz. L. Rev. 405, 407 (1990).

Cases looking to the parties' intention to determine whether a promoter is personally liable include Quaker Hill, Inc. v. Parr, 364 P.2d 1056 (Colo. 1961) (no intention to hold promoters personally liable when contract signed in name of corporation and other party knew corporation not in existence); Tin Cup Pass Ltd. P'ship v. Daniels, 553 N.E.2d 82 (Ill. App. Ct. 1990) (holding promoters not liable when lease signed in name of corporation that both parties knew had not been formed); Company Stores Dev. Corp. v. Pottery Warehouse, Inc., 733 S.W.2d 886, 887 (Tenn. Ct. App. 1987) (holding promoter not liable on lease when lessor agreed to look only to named lessee as " 'a corporation to be formed' "). . . .

§ 4.05   Timing of Ratification

A ratification of a transaction is not effective unless it precedes the occurrence of circumstances that would cause the ratification to have adverse and inequitable effects on the rights of third parties. These circumstances include:

    (1) any manifestation of intention to withdraw from the transaction made by the third party;

    (2) any material change in circumstances that would make it inequitable to bind the third party, unless the third party chooses to be bound; and

    (3) a specific time that determines whether a third party is deprived of a right or subjected to a liability.

§ 4.06   Knowledge Requisite to Ratification

A person is not bound by a ratification made without knowledge of material facts involved in the original act when the person was unaware of such lack of knowledge.

§ 4.07   No Partial Ratification

A ratification is not effective unless it encompasses the entirety of an act, contract, or other single transaction.

§ 4.08   Estoppel to Deny Ratification

If a person makes a manifestation that the person has ratified another's act and the manifestation, as reasonably understood by a third party, induces the third party to make a detrimental change in position, the person may be estopped to deny the ratification.

CHAPTER 5

NOTIFICATIONS AND NOTICE

§ 5.01   Notifications and Notice—In General

    (1) A notification is a manifestation that is made in the form required by agreement among parties or by applicable law, or in a reasonable manner in the absence of an agreement or an applicable law, with the intention of affecting the legal rights and duties of the notifier in relation to rights and duties of persons to whom the notification is given.

    (2) A notification given to or by an agent is effective as notification to or by the principal as stated in § 5.02.

    (3) A person has notice of a fact if the person knows the fact, has reason to know the fact, has received an effective notification of the fact, or should know the fact to fulfill a duty owed to another person.

    (4) Notice of a fact that an agent knows or has reason to know is imputed to the principal as stated in §§ 5.03 and 5.04.

§ 5.02   Notification Given by or to an Agent

    (1) A notification given to an agent is effective as notice to the principal if the agent has actual or apparent authority to receive the notification, unless the person who gives the notification knows or has reason to know that the agent is acting adversely to the principal as stated in § 5.04.

    (2) A notification given by an agent is effective as notification given by the principal if the agent has actual or apparent authority to give the notification, unless the person who receives the notification knows or has reason to know that the agent is acting adversely to the principal as stated in § 5.04.

§ 5.03 Imputation of Notice of Fact to Principal

For purposes of determining a principal's legal relations with a third party, notice of a fact that an agent knows or has reason to know is imputed to the principal if knowledge of the fact is material to the agent's duties to the principal, unless the agent

(a) acts adversely to the principal as stated in § 5.04, or

(b) is subject to a duty to another not to disclose the fact to the principal.

§ 5.04 An Agent Who Acts Adversely to a Principal

For purposes of determining a principal's legal relations with a third party, notice of a fact that an agent knows or has reason to know is not imputed to the principal if the agent acts adversely to the principal in a transaction or matter, intending to act solely for the agent's own purposes or those of another person. Nevertheless, notice is imputed

(a) when necessary to protect the rights of a third party who dealt with the principal in good faith; or

(b) when the principal has ratified or knowingly retained a benefit from the agent's action.

A third party who deals with a principal through an agent, knowing or having reason to know that the agent acts adversely to the principal, does not deal in good faith for this purpose.

CHAPTER 6

CONTRACTS AND OTHER TRANSACTIONS WITH THIRD PARTIES

TOPIC 1.   PARTIES TO CONTRACTS

§ 6.01 Agent for Disclosed Principal

When an agent acting with actual or apparent authority makes a contract on behalf of a disclosed principal,

(1) the principal and the third party are parties to the contract; and

(2) the agent is not a party to the contract unless the agent and third party agree otherwise.

Comment . . .

b. Bases and consequences of contractual liability when agent acts on behalf of disclosed principal. An agent acts on behalf of a disclosed principal when the third party with whom the agent deals has notice that the agent acts for a principal and also has notice of the principal's identity. See § 1.04(2)(a). An agent has power to make contracts on behalf of the agent's principal when the agent acts with actual or apparent authority. . . .

Illustration:

1.   P, a wine merchant, engages A to dispose of portions of P's inventory. P directs A to sell all of P's inventory of French wines to T, another wine merchant. A makes an offer to T on P's behalf. T replies: "I do not believe that you have authority to sell all of P's French wine, but I will chance it and accept the offer." There is a contract between P and T. A had actual authority to bind P, although T doubts whether this is so. . . .

An agent who enters into a contract on behalf of a disclosed principal does not become a party to the contract and is not subject to liability as a guarantor of the principal's performance unless the agent and the third party so agree. Thus, in the absence of such agreement, an agent for a disclosed principal who enters into a contract on the principal's behalf is not subject to liability if the principal fails to perform obligations created by the contract. As a consequence, the agent is not a necessary party to breach-of-contract litigation between a disclosed principal and the third party to a contract made by the agent on the principal's behalf.

Through ratification, a person may become a party to a contract purportedly made on that person's behalf by another who acted without actual or apparent authority. See Chapter 4.

[The] parties to a contract, a principal and third party, have the same rights, liabilities, and defenses against each other as if the principal had made the contract directly, subject to §§ 6.05–6.09. A disclosed principal may assert against the third party all defenses that arise out of the contract itself and all defenses that are personal to the principal. The principal may not assert defenses that would have been personal to the agent had the agent been a party to the contract. . . .

    c.   *Contract made on behalf of a disclosed principal.* If an agent makes a contract in the name of a principal or a description in the contract is sufficient to identify the principal, the principal is a disclosed principal and is a party to the contract. When a disclosed principal is a corporation or other organization with separate legal personality, the corporation becomes a party to contracts made on its behalf by its agents. Corporate or other organizational agents, like agents for other disclosed principals, are not parties to a corporate contract unless the agent and the third party so agree. . . .

Illustration:

    4.   P, a farmer, incorporates the farm business under the name "P Farms Corp." P operates the business of P Farms Corp. as its chief executive officer. On behalf of and in the name of P Farms Corp., P purchases supplies on credit from T. P is not a party to, and is not subject to liability on, contracts between P Farms Corp. and T. . . .

§ 6.02   Agent for Unidentified Principal

When an agent acting with actual or apparent authority makes a contract on behalf of an unidentified principal,

    (1) the principal and the third party are parties to the contract; and

    (2) the agent is a party to the contract unless the agent and the third party agree otherwise.

Comment . . .

    b.   *Bases of contractual liability when agent acts on behalf of unidentified principal.* An agent acts on behalf of an unidentified principal when the third party with whom the agent deals has notice that the agent acts on behalf of a principal but does not have notice of the principal's identity. See § 1.04(2)(c). Many cases, like Restatement Second, Agency § 4(2), refer to such a principal as a "partially disclosed principal." This Restatement instead uses the term "unidentified principal." . . .

An agent has power to make contracts on behalf of an unidentified principal when the agent acts with actual or apparent authority, just as an agent acting with actual or apparent authority has power to make contracts on behalf of a disclosed principal. See § 6.01(1). If an agent purports to act on behalf of an unidentified principal but lacks actual or apparent authority to bind the principal, the agent is subject to liability on the agent's implied warranty of authority. . . .

Unless the third party and the agent agree otherwise, an agent who makes a contract on behalf of a disclosed principal does not become a party to the contract. See § 6.01(2). In contrast, as stated in subsection (2) of this section, an agent who makes a contract on behalf of an unidentified principal becomes a party to the contract unless the third party and the agent agree otherwise. When a third party has notice that an agent deals on behalf of a principal but does not have notice of the principal's identity, it is not likely that the third party will rely solely on the principal's solvency or ability to perform obligations arising from the contract. Without notice of a principal's identity, a third party will be unable to assess the principal's reputation, assets, and other indicia of creditworthiness and ability to perform duties under the contract. If an agent provides reassurances about the principal's soundness only generally or describes the principal, the third party will be unable to verify such claims without notice of the principal's identity. . . .

Illustrations:

1.   P, who deals in antiques, retains A to purchase antiques on P's behalf. P directs A not to disclose P's identity to persons with whom A deals. A complies. A contracts to buy an antique clock owned by T, telling T that A is purchasing the clock on behalf of A's principal. P is A's unidentified principal. P and T are parties to the contract for the sale of the clock. A is also a party to the contract unless A and T agree otherwise.

2.   Same facts as Illustration 1, except that, prior to contracting to sell the clock, T learns from a friend that A represents P. As to T, P is A's disclosed principal. T knew P's identity when making the contract with A. P and T are parties to the contract for the sale of the clock. A is not a party unless A and T agree otherwise. See § 6.01(2). . . .

e.   Agent's position as party to contract. In an action by a third party against an agent who has made a contract on behalf of an unidentified principal, the agent may assert all defenses that arise from the transaction itself and defenses available to the agent personally.

§ 6.03   Agent for Undisclosed Principal

When an agent acting with actual authority makes a contract on behalf of an undisclosed principal,

(1) unless excluded by the contract, the principal is a party to the contract;

(2) the agent and the third party are parties to the contract; and

(3) the principal, if a party to the contract, and the third party have the same rights, liabilities, and defenses against each other as if the principal made the contract personally, subject to §§ 6.05–6.09.

Comment . . .

b.   Rationales for contractual liability. . . .

. . . [W]ell-settled doctrine treats an undisclosed principal as a party to a contract that an agent makes on behalf of the principal, unless the contract excludes the principal as a party. . . .

Illustration:

1.   A, the sole proprietor of a construction business, deals over several years with T, who is in the building-supplies business. A maintains an account with T that requires A to pay for supplies 30 days following delivery. Without notice to T, A incorporates A's business as "A Construction Corp." and transfers to A Construction Corp. ownership of all assets used by A in operating the business. A continues to run the business as before and continues to purchase supplies on credit from T. Both A and A Construction Corp. are subject to liability for payment owed to T for supplies delivered by T to A's business after A incorporates it. A acted as the agent of A Construction Corp., A's undisclosed principal.

An agent who makes a contract on behalf of an undisclosed principal also becomes a party to the contract. The basis for treating the agent as a party to the contract is the expectation of the third party. The agent has dealt with the third party as if the agent were the sole party whose legal relations would be affected as a consequence of making the contract. . . .

d.   Circumstances that affect rights or liabilities of undisclosed principal; contract excluding undisclosed principal as party. . . .

The nature of the performance that a contract requires determines whether performance by an undisclosed principal will be effective as performance under the contract and whether an undisclosed principal can require that the third party render performance to the principal. Performance by an undisclosed principal is not effective as performance under a contract if the third party has a substantial interest in receiving performance from the agent who made the contract. This limit corresponds to the limit on delegability of performance of a duty as stated in Restatement Second, Contracts § 318(2).

Illustrations:

6.   T enters into a contract with A in which A promises to manage T's investment portfolio. A does not disclose that A makes the contract on behalf of P. P offers to manage T's portfolio. T is free to accept or reject P's offer of performance. P's offer does not constitute an offer of performance of the contract made by A. T has a substantial interest in receiving investment-management services from A.

7.   T enters into a contract to purchase a quantity of coal of a specified kind from A. A does not disclose that A makes the contract on behalf of P. P tenders coal to T of the specified kind and quantity. P's tender has the effect of a tender by A because T has no substantial interest in receiving the coal from A.

The nature of the performance that a contract requires from a third party determines whether an undisclosed principal is entitled to receive that performance. An undisclosed principal may not require that a third party render performance to the principal if rendering performance to the principal would materially change the nature of the third party's duty, materially increase the burden or risk imposed on the third party, or materially impair the third party's chance of receiving return performance. These limits correspond to the limits imposed on assignment of a contractual right. See Restatement Second, Contracts § 317(2).

Illustrations:

8.   T agrees to work as a nanny for A. P, A's undisclosed principal, cannot require T to work as a nanny for P. The contract between T and A requires that T render personal services in an ongoing close association. Requiring T to render the services to P would materially change the nature of T's duties.

9.   T agrees to sell Blackacre in exchange for cash to A, who acts on behalf of P, A's undisclosed principal. P may require performance from T. The contract made by A requires only the payment of money in exchange for Blackacre.

e.   Position of agent as party to contract. As a party to a contract made on behalf of an undisclosed principal, an agent may sue the third party in the agent's own name. The agent is subject to liability on the contract. If sued on the contract, the agent may assert all defenses arising from the transaction and defenses personal to the agent.

Illustration:

10.   P owns a farm which A manages. A makes a contract to sell a quantity of potatoes from P's farm to T, expressly warranting that they are seed potatoes. T does not have notice that A acts on behalf of P. After T takes delivery of the potatoes, pays for them, and resells them, T discovers that they are not seed potatoes. A and P are subject to liability to T for breach of warranty. . . .

§ 6.04   Principal Does Not Exist or Lacks Capacity

Unless the third party agrees otherwise, a person who makes a contract with a third party purportedly as an agent on behalf of a principal becomes a party to the contract if the purported agent knows or has reason to know that the purported principal does not exist or lacks capacity to be a party to a contract.

Comment . . .

c.   Contracts made on behalf of entities yet to be formed. The rule stated in this section is applicable when a person purports to make a contract with a third party on behalf of an entity that does not exist. If that person and the third party manifest assent that the contract shall bind the third party, the person who purports to act on behalf of the entity is personally liable on the contract.

Illustration:

2.   A is the president and sole shareholder of "Marketing Designs, Inc." Wishing to do business as a wholesaler of seafood, A makes a contract to purchase salmon from T, a fish importer. A expressly makes the contract on behalf of "Boston International Seafood Exchange,

Inc.," believing that the name more closely identifies A with the seafood industry. A knows that Boston International Seafood Exchange, Inc., does not exist. Payment for the salmon is not made as required by the contract. A is subject to liability on the contract with T. As A knew, the corporation on whose behalf A purportedly made the contract did not exist.

The classic instance of this situation arises when a person enters into a contract purportedly on behalf of an entity that has not yet been formed, such as a business or a not-for-profit corporation or a limited-liability company. Promoters of entities yet-to-be-formed may find it attractive and even imperative to obtain binding commitments from third parties before the formal process of organization has been completed. The statute applicable to forming the particular type of entity may address the circumstances under which a promoter will be subject to individual liability on a contract made on behalf of a not-yet-formed entity. When an entity comes into existence, it may adopt the contract made by the promoter. See §4.04, Comment *c*. An entity's adoption of a contract made by a promoter does not by itself release the promoter from any individual liability that the promoter may have on the contract. See id.

If a promoter enters into a contract with a third party on behalf of an entity that has not yet commenced legal existence, the entity itself cannot be a party to the contract prior to its existence. This is so whether the contract purports to be made on behalf of an entity characterized as one yet to be formed or characterizes the entity as one presently in existence. If the contract is to bind the third party prior to the entity's existence, unless the relationship is structured as an option that may be exercised by the entity when formed, either the promoter or someone else must be liable on the contract. The parties' intention must often be determined on the basis of inferences to be drawn from the circumstances, which include whether the promoter and the other party are aware that the entity does not yet exist. A third party may agree in a contract made by a promoter to release the promoter's liability when and if the entity adopts the contract. In the absence of an express agreement by the third party to release the promoter, some cases permit the promoter to establish that the parties intended that the promoter would not be personally liable. An entity may adopt a contract made by a promoter by accepting its benefits with knowledge of its terms. For further discussion, see §4.04, Comment *c*.

Similar questions arise when a person purports to take action on behalf of an entity when its powers have been suspended or forfeited, or when the entity has been dissolved. The organizational statute applicable to the entity may specify the circumstances under which such action will result in individual liability to third parties. . . .

TOPIC 2.   RIGHTS, LIABILITIES, AND DEFENSES

TITLE A. IN GENERAL

§6.05   Contract That Is Unauthorized in Part or That Combines Orders of Several Principals

(1) If an agent makes a contract with a third party that differs from the contract that the agent had actual or apparent authority to make only in an amount or by the inclusion or exclusion of a separable part, the principal is subject to liability to the third party to the extent of the contract that the agent had actual or apparent authority to make if

(a) the third party seasonably makes a manifestation to the principal of willingness to be bound; and

(b) the principal has not changed position in reasonable reliance on the belief that no contract bound the principal and the third party.

(2) Two or more principals may authorize the same agent to make separate contracts for them. If the agent makes a single contract with a third party on the principals' behalves that combines the principals' separate orders or interests and calls for a single performance by the third party,

(a) if the agent purports to make the combined contract on behalf of disclosed principals, the agent is subject to liability to the third party for breach of the agent's warranty of authority as stated in §6.10, unless the separate principals are bound by the combined contract;

(b) if the principals are unidentified or undisclosed, the third party and the agent are the only parties to the combined contract; and

(c) unless the agent acted with actual or apparent authority to bind each of the principals to the combined contract,

(i) subject to (1), none of the separate principals is subject to liability on the combined contract; and

(ii) the third party is not subject to liability on the combined contract to any of the separate principals.

§ 6.06   Setoff

(1) When an agent makes a contract on behalf of a disclosed or unidentified principal, unless the principal and the third party agree otherwise,

(a) the third party may not set off any amount that the agent independently owes the third party against an amount the third party owes the principal under the contract; and

(b) the principal may not set off any amount that the third party independently owes the agent against an amount the principal owes the third party under the contract.

(2) When an agent makes a contract on behalf of an undisclosed principal,

(a) the third party may set off

(i) any amount that the agent independently owed the third party at the time the agent made the contract and

(ii) any amount that the agent thereafter independently comes to owe the third party until the third party has notice that the agent acts on behalf of a principal against an amount the third party owes the principal under the contract;

(b) after the third party has notice that the agent acts on behalf of a principal, the third party may not set off any amount that the agent thereafter independently comes to owe the third party against an amount the third party owes the principal under the contract unless the principal consents; and

(c) the principal may not set off any amount that the third party independently owes the agent against an amount that the principal owes the third party under the contract, unless the principal and the third party agree otherwise.

(3) Unless otherwise agreed, an agent who is a party to a contract may not set off any amount that the principal independently owes the agent against an amount that the agent owes the third party under the contract. However, with the principal's consent, the agent may set off any amount that the principal could set off against an amount that the principal owes the third party under the contract.

TITLE B. SUBSEQUENT DEALINGS BETWEEN THIRD PARTY AND PRINCIPAL OR AGENT

§ 6.07   Settlement with Agent by Principal or Third Party

(1) A principal's payment to or settlement of accounts with an agent discharges the principal's liability to a third party with whom the agent has made a contract on the principal's behalf only when the principal acts in reasonable reliance on a manifestation by the third party, not induced by misrepresentation by the agent, that the agent has settled the account with the third party.

(2) A third party's payment to or settlement of accounts with an agent discharges the third party's liability to the principal if the agent acts with actual or apparent authority in accepting the payment or settlement.

(3) When an agent has made a contract on behalf of an undisclosed principal,

(a) until the third party has notice of the principal's existence, the third party's payment to or settlement of accounts with the agent discharges the third party's liability to the principal;

(b) after the third party has notice of the principal's existence, the third party's payment to or settlement of accounts with the agent discharges the third party's liability to the principal if the agent acts with actual or apparent authority in accepting the payment or settlement; and

(c) after receiving notice of the principal's existence, the third party may demand reasonable proof of the principal's identity and relationship to the agent. Until such proof is received, the third party's payment to or settlement of accounts in good faith with the agent discharges the third party's liability to the principal.

§ 6.08 Other Subsequent Dealings Between Third Party and Agent

(1) When an agent has made a contract with a third party on behalf of a disclosed or unidentified principal, subsequent dealings between the agent and the third party may increase or diminish the principal's rights or liabilities to the third party if the agent acts with actual or apparent authority or the principal ratifies the agent's action.

(2) When an agent has made a contract with a third party on behalf of an undisclosed principal,

(a) until the third party has notice of the principal's existence, subsequent dealings between the third party and the agent may increase or diminish the rights or liabilities of the principal to the third party if the agent acts with actual authority, or the principal ratifies the agent's action; and

(b) after the third party has notice of the principal's existence, subsequent dealings between the third party and the agent may increase or diminish the principal's rights or liabilities to the third party if the agent acts with actual or apparent authority or the principal ratifies the agent's action.

§ 6.09 Effect of Judgment Against Agent or Principal

When an agent has made a contract with a third party on behalf of a principal, unless the contract provides otherwise,

(1) the liability, if any, of the principal or the agent to the third party is not discharged if the third party obtains a judgment against the other; and

(2) the liability, if any, of the principal or the agent to the third party is discharged to the extent a judgment against the other is satisfied.

TITLE C. AGENT'S WARRANTIES AND REPRESENTATIONS

§ 6.10 Agent's Implied Warranty of Authority

A person who purports to make a contract, representation, or conveyance to or with a third party on behalf of another person, lacking power to bind that person, gives an implied warranty of authority to the third party and is subject to liability to the third party for damages for loss caused by breach of that warranty, including loss of the benefit expected from performance by the principal, unless

(1) the principal or purported principal ratifies the act as stated in § 4.01; or

(2) the person who purports to make the contract, representation, or conveyance gives notice to the third party that no warranty of authority is given; or

(3) the third party knows that the person who purports to make the contract, representation, or conveyance acts without actual authority.

Comment . . .

b. Agent's implied warranty of authority—in general. . . .

The measure of recovery for breach of an implied warranty of authority should reflect the fact that the third party may have been deprived of a benefit that the third party would have realized, had the principal been bound as the agent purported to have authority to do. Thus, if an agent purports to bind a principal to a contract, the third party's measure of recovery should compensate the third party for loss suffered and should include the benefit of the bargain to the third party, had the principal been bound by the contract. Some courts, in contrast, limit the third party's recovery to the damage or loss the third party suffered and exclude the third party's expected gain from the contract. Some cases explicitly characterize the third party's claim for breach of warranty as equivalent to a tort claim based on a misrepresentation.

The better rule recognizes that the function of the agent's implied warranty is to safeguard the third party's expectation that the agent in fact has power to bind the principal to the legal consequences of the agent's actions. Although the agent's implied warranty of authority is grounded in an implied representation made by the agent, the representation is that the agent's actions will bind the principal whom the agent purports to represent. When an agent purports to bind a principal to a contract but lacks power to do so, the third party has been deprived of the anticipated benefit of a bargain. The third party's recovery against the agent should include the value of this anticipated benefit. As noted above, an agent's implied representation may, separately, subject the agent to tort liability. . . .

§ 6.11   Agent's Representations

(1) When an agent for a disclosed or unidentified principal makes a false representation about the agent's authority to a third party, the principal is not subject to liability unless the agent acted with actual or apparent authority in making the representation and the third party does not have notice that the agent's representation is false.

(2) A representation by an agent made incident to a contract or conveyance is attributed to a disclosed or unidentified principal as if the principal made the representation directly when the agent had actual or apparent authority to make the contract or conveyance unless the third party knew or had reason to know that the representation was untrue or that the agent acted without actual authority in making it.

(3) A representation by an agent made incident to a contract or conveyance is attributed to an undisclosed principal as if the principal made the representation directly when

    (a) the agent acted with actual authority in making the representation, or

    (b) the agent acted without actual authority in making the representation but had actual authority to make true representations about the same matter.

The agent's representation is not attributed to the principal when the third party knew or had reason to know it was untrue.

(4) When an agent who makes a contract or conveyance on behalf of an undisclosed principal falsely represents to the third party that the agent does not act on behalf of a principal, the third party may avoid the contract or conveyance if the principal or agent had notice that the third party would not have dealt with the principal.

Comment . . .

    b.   Agent's representation concerning agent's own authority. An agent's own statements about the nature or extent of the agent's authority to act on behalf of the principal do not create apparent authority by themselves. An agent acts with apparent authority only when a third party's belief that the agent acts with authority is reasonable and is traceable to a manifestation made by the principal. . . .

Illustrations:

    1.   P, who owns a tree nursery, tells T, who owns a garden center, that A is authorized to sell P's trees only at prices set by P and communicated by P to T. A tells T that A now has P's authority to set the prices for P's trees. A's statement to T does not by itself create apparent authority to bind P to sell trees to T at prices set by A. . . .

CHAPTER 7

TORTS—LIABILITY OF AGENT AND PRINCIPAL

TOPIC 1.   AGENT'S LIABILITY

§ 7.01   Agent's Liability to Third Party

An agent is subject to liability to a third party harmed by the agent's tortious conduct. Unless an applicable statute provides otherwise, an actor remains subject to liability although the actor acts as an agent or an employee, with actual or apparent authority, or within the scope of employment.

§ 7.02   Duty to Principal; Duty to Third Party

An agent's breach of a duty owed to the principal is not an independent basis for an agent's tort liability to a third party. An agent is subject to tort liability to a third party harmed by the agent's conduct only when the agent's conduct breaches a duty that the agent owes to the third party.

TOPIC 2.   PRINCIPAL'S LIABILITY

§ 7.03   Principal's Liability—In General

(1) A principal is subject to direct liability to a third party harmed by an agent's conduct when

     (a) as stated in § 7.04, the agent acts with actual authority or the principal ratifies the agent's conduct and

         (i) the agent's conduct is tortious, or

         (ii) the agent's conduct, if that of the principal, would subject the principal to tort liability;
or

     (b) as stated in § 7.05, the principal is negligent in selecting, supervising, or otherwise controlling the agent; or

     (c) as stated in § 7.06, the principal delegates performance of a duty to use care to protect other persons or their property to an agent who fails to perform the duty.

(2) A principal is subject to vicarious liability to a third party harmed by an agent's conduct when → *if vicarious liability then both jointly severally liable*

     (a) as stated in § 7.07, the agent is an employee who commits a tort while acting within the scope of employment; or → *doesn't apply to Ind. K (exception – if inherently dangerous activities, knowing/negligent choosing of I-d. K, nondelegable duties)*

     (b) as stated in § 7.08, the agent commits a tort when acting with apparent authority in dealing with a third party on or purportedly on behalf of the principal.

§ 7.04   Agent Acts with Actual Authority

A principal is subject to liability to a third party harmed by an agent's conduct when the agent's conduct is within the scope of the agent's actual authority or ratified by the principal; and

(1) the agent's conduct is tortious, or

(2) the agent's conduct, if that of the principal, would subject the principal to tort liability.

Comment . . .

     b.   *In general.* When an agent acts with actual authority, the agent reasonably believes, in accordance with manifestations of the principal, that the principal wishes the agent so to act. . . .

Illustrations:

     1.   P, who publishes a newspaper, engages D to deliver copies of the newspaper to a neighboring community. P directs D to deliver the newspapers in the midst of an ice storm when both P and D know that driving conditions are hazardous, that the vehicle D will use is not

equipped for such conditions, and that D lacks experience in driving under such conditions. In the course of making deliveries, D skids on an icy road, injuring T. P is subject to liability to T. P's instruction to D directed D to act in a negligent manner. D is also subject to liability to T. See § 7.01. . . .

    c.   When actor is not personally subject to liability. A person may be subject to tort liability because of an actor's conduct although the actor is not subject to liability. For example, a person who directs conduct may have notice of facts that the actor lacks.

Illustration:

    5.   P, in the produce business, directs A to make a delivery to a customer using a particular truck. P knows that the truck's brakes do not work properly. A does not know this and has no reason or duty to know it. T, a pedestrian, is injured when the truck's brakes fail while A is driving the truck to make the delivery and attempts to stop at a stop sign. P is subject to liability to T. A is not subject to liability to T. . . .

§ 7.05   Principal's Negligence in Conducting Activity Through Agent; Principal's Special Relationship with Another Person

(1) A principal who conducts an activity through an agent is subject to liability for harm to a third party caused by the agent's conduct if the harm was caused by the principal's negligence in selecting, training, retaining, supervising, or otherwise controlling the agent.

(2) When a principal has a special relationship with another person, the principal owes that person a duty of reasonable care with regard to risks arising out of the relationship, including the risk that agents of the principal will harm the person with whom the principal has such a special relationship.

Comment . . .

    b. In general; relationship to other bases for liability. . . .

A foreseeable risk of harm may be created when one person conducts an activity through another person. For example, the actor chosen for a task may lack competence to perform it without endangering others. A task may require using an instrumentality that is dangerous to others unless the user has appropriate skill or supervision. Some tasks require performance in settings that pose a foreseeable risk of criminal or other intentional misconduct against third parties or their property unless the actor is chosen with due care in reference to that risk.

Illustrations:

    1.   P, who owns an apartment building, employs A as its on-site manager. P knows that A is impatient and has a violent temper. T, one of P's tenants, complains to A about the lack of heat in T's apartment. Enraged, A assaults T. P is subject to liability to T. P hired A knowing that A's temperament was not suited to the foreseeable demands of on-site residential management. P's liability to T under this section is independent of whether P is subject to liability to T under § 7.07 on the basis that A's conduct was within the scope of A's employment by P. . . .

    3.   P, who owns a furniture store, employs A to deliver furniture to retail customers. A's duties include entering customers' homes to situate items they have purchased. Having entered T's home to deliver a sofa, A assaults T. Prior to employing A, P conducted no check of A's background. Had P done so, P would have discovered criminal convictions for assault. Had P known of A's criminal history, P would not have employed A to make deliveries. P is subject to liability to T. . . .

§ 7.06   Failure in Performance of Principal's Duty of Protection

A principal required by contract or otherwise by law to protect another cannot avoid liability by delegating performance of the duty, whether or not the delegate is an agent.

§ 7.07 Employee Acting Within Scope of Employment

(1) An employer is subject to vicarious liability for a tort committed by its employee acting within the scope of employment.

(2) An employee acts within the scope of employment when performing work assigned by the employer or engaging in a course of conduct subject to the employer's control. An employee's act is not within the scope of employment when it occurs within an independent course of conduct not intended by the employee to serve any purpose of the employer.

(3) For purposes of this section,

(a) an employee is an agent whose principal controls or has the right to control the manner and means of the agent's performance of work, and

(b) the fact that work is performed gratuitously does not relieve a principal of liability.

Comment . . .

b. When tortious conduct is within the scope of employment—in general. An employee's conduct, although tortious, may be within the scope of employment as defined in subsection (2). If an employee commits a tort while performing work assigned by the employer or while acting within a course of conduct subject to the employer's control, the employee's conduct is within the scope of employment unless the employee was engaged in an independent course of conduct not intended to further any purpose of the employer. The formulation in subsection (2) reflects the definition of scope of employment applied in most cases and in most jurisdictions. . . .

[R]espondeat superior subjects an employer to vicarious liability for employee torts committed within the scope of employment, distinct from whether the employer is subject to direct liability. An employer's ability to exercise control over its employees' work-related conduct enables the employer to take measures to reduce the incidence of tortious conduct. It may be difficult, after the fact of an employee's tortious conduct, to identify an instance of negligence on the part of the employer. This may be so even when, before the fact of the employee's tortious conduct, steps were available to the employer that, if taken, would have prevented the tort. In contrast, when an employee's tortious conduct is outside the range of activity that an employer may control, subjecting the employer to liability would not provide incentives for the employer to take measures to reduce the incidence of such tortious conduct. Moreover, for an employer to insure against a risk of liability, whether from third-party sources or its own assets, the risk must be at least to some degree ascertainable and quantifiable.

In assessing the scope of employment limitation on respondeat superior, it is helpful to recognize that the range of tortious conduct by employees to which the doctrine is relevant is not all-encompassing. Respondeat superior is not the sole basis for liability when an employer itself is at fault, see §§ 7.04, 7.05, and 7.06, nor is it the sole basis for vicarious liability when an employee's apparent authority enables the employee to commit a tort, see § 7.08. . . .

Under subsection (2), an employee's tortious conduct is outside the scope of employment when the employee is engaged in an independent course of conduct not intended to further any purpose of the employer. An independent course of conduct represents a departure from, not an escalation of, conduct involved in performing assigned work or other conduct that an employer permits or controls. When an employee commits a tort with the sole intention of furthering the employee's own purposes, and not any purpose of the employer, it is neither fair nor true-to-life to characterize the employee's action as that of a representative of the employer. The employee's intention severs the basis for treating the employee's act as that of the employer in the employee's interaction with the third party. . . .

c. Conduct in the performance of work and scope of employment. An employee's conduct is within the scope of employment when it constitutes performance of work assigned to the employee by the employer. The fact that the employee performs the work carelessly does not take the employee's conduct outside the scope of employment, nor does the fact that the employee otherwise makes a mistake in performing the work. Likewise, conduct is not outside the scope of employment merely because an employee disregards the employer's instructions.

Illustrations:

    1.   P, who writes bail bonds, employs A as a bond "runner." A's assigned work is to locate persons for whom P has written bonds who jump bail and return them to custody. P directs A to search for J. A mistakenly identifies T as J, breaks down the door of T's home, and holds T at gunpoint. Under applicable law, A's conduct toward T is tortious. P is subject to liability to T. A's actions constituted performance of work P assigned to A.

    2.   Same facts as Illustration 1, except that P instructs its runners to contact P's office prior to attempting a forcible entry into a residence. A neglects to do this before breaking down the door of T's home. Same result.

In Illustration 2, A's conduct is within the scope of employment, despite A's disregard for P's instruction, because A is engaged in doing work assigned by P. Likewise, had A contravened an instruction not to exceed the speed limit while pursuing a bail jumper and caused an accident that injured another driver or a pedestrian, A would have been acting within the scope of employment. Thus, the fact that an employee's action violates a generally applicable law, such as a speeding limit, does not by itself place the employee's conduct outside the scope of employment. These results are not surprising. An employee may believe that the employer wishes the employee to disregard an inconvenient constraint when the employee fears that compliance would jeopardize completing the employee's assigned mission at all or completing it on or ahead of schedule. Although the employee's belief may be mistaken, it is compatible with acting in an assigned role to do an assigned task. However, the character, extreme nature, or other circumstances accompanying an employee's actions may demonstrate that the employee's course of conduct is independent of performing work assigned by the employer and intended solely to further the employee's own purposes. . . .

    e.   *Peregrinations.* In general, travel required to perform work, such as travel from an employer's office to a job site or from one job site to another, is within the scope of an employee's employment while traveling to and from work is not. However, an employer may place an employee's travel to and from work within the scope of employment by providing the employee with a vehicle and asserting control over how the employee uses the vehicle so that the employee may more readily respond to the needs of the employer's enterprise. An employee's travel to and from work may also be within the scope of employment if the employee does more than simply travel to and from work, for example by stopping for the employer's benefit to accomplish a task assigned by the employer.

An employee's travel during the work day that is not within the scope of employment has long been termed a "frolic" of the employee's own. De minimis departures from assigned routes are not "frolics." A "frolic" may also consist of activity on an employer's premises and within working hours. . . . The conventional meaning of the term "detour" is a deviation from travel on an assigned route that is still within the scope of employment.

Illustrations:

    12.   P, who owns a tree-maintenance service, employs A as foreman for a crew that provides tree-trimming services for utility companies and owners of commercial and residential property. P furnishes A with a pickup truck and authorizes A to use the truck to commute between A's residence and the day's job site. P also directs A to use the truck to make sales calls to prospective customers. En route from home to a utility job site, A stops to visit C, a prospective residential customer. As A turns to pull into C's driveway, A injures T, a pedestrian whom A negligently failed to notice. P is subject to liability to T. Visiting C was part of A's assigned work for P.

    13.   Same facts as Illustration 12, except that en route to visit C, A departs slightly from the most direct route to visit A's favorite take-out restaurant. A's departure is within the scope of employment.

    14.   P, who owns a nursery, employs A. A's assigned duties include caring for the nursery's lawn and keeping the nursery's lawn mower filled with gas. En route to the nursery from home, A stops at a drugstore to pick up medicine for A's spouse, then stops at a gas station across the street to buy a can of gas for the nursery's lawn mower. A next returns home to drop off the medicine, then stops at another gas station to buy gas for A's truck. Leaving this second gas station, A drives negligently and collides with T. P is subject to liability to T. A was transporting

36

gas to fill the nursery's lawnmower, necessary for A to perform A's assigned work. A's stop for gas was an incidental deviation from A's performance of assigned work. . . .

f. Definition of employee. For purposes of respondeat superior, an agent is an employee only when the principal controls or has the right to control the manner and means through which the agent performs work. The definition has the consequence of distinguishing between employees and agents who are not employees because they retain the right to control how they perform their work. If a person has no right to control an actor and exercises no control over the actor, the actor is not an agent. . . .

Numerous factual indicia are relevant to whether an agent is an employee. These include: the extent of control that the agent and the principal have agreed the principal may exercise over details of the work; whether the agent is engaged in a distinct occupation or business; whether the type of work done by the agent is customarily done under a principal's direction or without supervision; the skill required in the agent's occupation; whether the agent or the principal supplies the tools and other instrumentalities required for the work and the place in which to perform it; the length of time during which the agent is engaged by a principal; whether the agent is paid by the job or by the time worked; whether the agent's work is part of the principal's regular business; whether the principal and the agent believe that they are creating an employment relationship; and whether the principal is or is not in business. Also relevant is the extent of control that the principal has exercised in practice over the details of the agent's work.

In some employment relationships, an employer's right of control may be attenuated. For example, senior corporate officers, like captains of ships, may exercise great discretion in operating the enterprises entrusted to them, just as skilled professionals exercise discretion in performing their work. Nonetheless, all employers retain a right of control, however infrequently exercised. . . .

§ 7.08 Agent Acts with Apparent Authority

A principal is subject to vicarious liability for a tort committed by an agent in dealing or communicating with a third party on or purportedly on behalf of the principal when actions taken by the agent with apparent authority constitute the tort or enable the agent to conceal its commission.

Comment:

a. Scope and cross-references. The rule stated in this section applies to (1) agents, whether or not they are employees as defined in § 7.07(3); and (2) agents who are employees as defined in § 7.07(3) whose tortious conduct is not within the scope of employment under § 7.07(2). The torts to which this section applies are those in which an agent appears to deal or communicate on behalf of a principal and the agent's appearance of authority enables the agent to commit a tort or conceal its commission. Such torts include fraudulent and negligent misrepresentations, defamation, tortious institution of legal proceedings, and conversion of property obtained by an agent purportedly at the principal's direction. . . .

Illustrations:

1. P Numismatics Company urges its customers to seek investment advice from its retail salespeople, including A. T, who wishes to invest in gold coins, seeks A's advice at an office of P Numismatics Company. A encourages T to purchase a particular set of gold coins, falsely representing material facts relevant to their value. T, reasonably relying on A's representations, purchases the set of coins. P is subject to liability to T. A is also subject to liability to T. See § 7.01.

2. Same facts as Illustration 1, except that A persuades T to pay cash for the coins and to leave the coins with A so that they may be safely stored by P Numismatics Company. A then absconds with both the coins and the cash paid by T. Same results. . . .

CHAPTER 8

DUTIES OF AGENT AND PRINCIPAL TO EACH OTHER

TOPIC 1.   AGENT'S DUTIES TO PRINCIPAL
TITLE A. GENERAL FIDUCIARY PRINCIPLE

§ 8.01   General Fiduciary Principle

An agent has a fiduciary duty to act loyally for the principal's benefit in all matters connected with the agency relationship.

Comment . . .

d(1). Remedies for breach of fiduciary duty—in general. An agent's breach of fiduciary duty may create several distinct bases on which the principal may recover monetary relief or receive another remedy. Under appropriate circumstances, an agent's breach or threatened breach of fiduciary duty is a basis on which the principal may receive specific nonmonetary relief through an injunction. An agent's breach of fiduciary obligation may also furnish a basis on which the principal may avoid or rescind a contract entered into with the agent or a third party.

An agent's breach also creates distinct bases on which the principal may recover monetary relief. An agent's breach subjects the agent to liability for loss that the breach causes the principal. See Restatement Second, Torts § 874. A breach of fiduciary duty may also subject the agent to liability for punitive damages when the circumstances satisfy generally applicable standards for their imposition. For general standards applicable to awards of punitive damages, see Restatement Second, Torts § 908(2). In these respects, the consequences of a breach of fiduciary duty do not differ from those of other torts that an agent may commit against a principal.

The law of restitution and unjust enrichment also creates a basis for an agent's liability to a principal when the agent breaches a fiduciary duty, even though the principal cannot establish that the agent's breach caused loss to the principal. If through the breach the agent has realized a material benefit, the agent has a duty to account to the principal for the benefit, its value, or its proceeds. The agent is subject to liability to deliver the benefit, its proceeds, or its value to the principal. . . . An agent must also account to the principal for the value of the agent's use of property of the principal when the use violates the agent's duty to the principal, although the principal cannot establish that the use was harmful. . . . If an agent's breach of duty is in connection with a transaction as or on behalf of an adverse party, an alternate remedy that may be available to the principal is avoiding the transaction. . . .

(2).   Remedies for breach of fiduciary duty—forfeiture of commissions and other compensation. An agent's breach of fiduciary duty is a basis on which the agent may be required to forfeit commissions and other compensation paid or payable to the agent during the period of the agent's disloyalty. The availability of forfeiture is not limited to its use as a defense to an agent's claim for compensation.

Forfeiture may be the only available remedy when it is difficult to prove that harm to a principal resulted from the agent's breach or when the agent realizes no profit through the breach. In many cases, forfeiture enables a remedy to be determined at a much lower cost to litigants. Forfeiture may also have a valuable deterrent effect because its availability signals agents that some adverse consequence will follow a breach of fiduciary duty.

Although forfeiture is generally available as a remedy for breach of fiduciary duty, cases are divided on how absolute a measure to apply. Some cases require forfeiture of all compensation paid or payable over the period of disloyalty, while others permit apportionment over a series of tasks or specified items of work when only some are tainted by the agent's disloyal conduct. The better rule permits the court to consider the specifics of the agent's work and the nature of the agent's breach of duty and to evaluate whether the agent's breach of fiduciary duty tainted all of the agent's work or was confined to discrete transactions for which the agent was entitled to apportioned compensation. . . .

Illustration:

9. P Bank employs A, an advisor and facilitator, and assigns A to work on a series of transactions. P Bank agrees to compensate A by paying A an annual salary plus an amount to be determined by P Bank on the basis of P Bank's annual profitability. Without P Bank's knowledge or consent, during A's last year and a half working for P Bank, A accepts for A's personal account investment opportunities from three clients with whom A worked on transactions on P Bank's account. A also does work on a fourth transaction in which A accepts no such opportunity for A's own account. All of A's compensation for the year and a half may be forfeited to P Bank. A's agreement with P Bank did not allocate A's compensation on a transaction-specific basis. A is also subject to liability to P Bank for profits made by A, or property that A obtained, through A's receipt of material benefits from third parties. See § 8.02.

Some cases permit an agent to establish that the agent's work on balance was of benefit to the principal or require the principal to establish that on balance it was damaged by the agent's breach. The better rule does not condition the availability of forfeiture as a remedy on whether a principal can establish damage. The requirement that a principal establish damage is inconsistent with a basic premise of remedies available for breach of fiduciary duty, which is that a principal need not establish harm resulting from an agent's breach to require the agent to account. See Comments *b* and *d(1)*. The requirement may also tempt an agent to undertake conduct that breaches the agent's fiduciary duty in the hope that no harm will befall the principal or that, if it does, the principal will be unable to establish it or unable or unwilling to expend the necessary resources required to litigate the question.

Likewise, the better rule does not allow an agent to offset amounts otherwise forfeitable to the principal by showing benefits gained by the principal through the agent's work. The benefits generated by a disloyal agent may be difficult to quantify, especially when incentives created by the agent's disloyalty reshape how the agent performs assigned work.

TITLE B. DUTIES OF LOYALTY

§ 8.02 Material Benefit Arising Out of Position

An agent has a duty not to acquire a material benefit from a third party in connection with transactions conducted or other actions taken on behalf of the principal or otherwise through the agent's use of the agent's position.

Comment . . .

b. Rationale. This rule stems from the ordinary expectation that a person who acts as an agent does so to further the interests of the principal and that it is the principal who should benefit from turns of good fortune that may occur in connection with transactions that the agent undertakes on the principal's behalf. This expectation may stem from the fact when an agent acts with actual or apparent authority, the principal risks being bound by transactions that may turn out to be disadvantageous to the principal in some respect.

An additional rationale for this rule stems from risks to a principal's interests that may arise when an agent pursues material benefits from third parties in connection with actions taken on behalf of the principal. For example, an agent's interest in acquiring a benefit from a third party may supersede the agent's commitment to obtain terms from the third party that are best from the standpoint of the principal. Although the agent may believe that no harm will befall the principal, the agent is not in a position disinterestedly to assess whether harm may occur or whether the principal's interests would be better served if the agent did not pursue or acquire the benefit from the third party. Only the principal can assess the potential impact on the principal's interests of an agent's anticipated receipt of a material benefit to be furnished by a third party. By providing a material benefit to a person known to act as an agent, a third party may become subject to liability to the principal. A third party who provides substantial assistance or encouragement to an agent in breaching the agent's duty to the principal is also subject to liability to the principal. . . .

Illustration:

    1.   P, who owns a racehorse, Grace, engages A, a jockey, to ride Grace in an upcoming race. P agrees to pay A a fee of $500. T, who has made a large bet that Grace will win the race, promises to pay A $5000 if Grace wins the race. T asks A not to tell P about T's promise. Neither A nor T tells P about T's promise. Grace, ridden by A, wins the race. T pays A $5000. A and T are subject to liability to P. A's receipt of $5000 from T breached A's duty to P. T knowingly provided substantial assistance and encouragement to A in A's breach of duty to P. For discussion of remedies available to P, see Comment *e*. . . .

The purpose of this rule is prophylactic. To establish that the agent is subject to liability, it is not necessary that the principal show that the agent's acquisition of a material benefit harmed the principal. The benefit realized by the agent can often be calculated more readily than any harm suffered by the principal. However, when the principal can establish that the agent's conduct resulted in harm to the principal, the principal may recover compensatory damages from the agent.

Moreover, an agent's acquisition of a material benefit may breach this rule even though the agent's ability to acquire the benefit depends on achieving an outcome that may appear consistent with the principal's interests. In Illustration 1, P presumably wishes that Grace will win the race, as do T and A. However, T's promise to pay A if Grace wins the race undermines P's ability to exercise control over A and may thwart P's objectives as P understands them. T's promise may induce A to spur Grace on to assure that Grace wins the race and A receives an additional $5000. However, P, unbeknownst to A, may plan to enter Grace in another race that P views as more important and thus may wish that Grace's energies not be overtaxed. Thus, the point of the rule is to focus the agent's efforts on furthering the principal's interests as the agent reasonably understands them, taking into account manifestations made by the principal. Permitting an agent's focus to encompass additional incentives offered by a third party is inconsistent with the singleness of focus due the principal. . . .

Illustrations:

    3.   P, who owns a used-car lot, employs A as its general manager. A's duties include contracting with suppliers of used cars to replenish P's inventory. One supplier, T, pays A $500 for each car that A purchases for sale on P's lot. A is subject to liability to P. The payments A received from T are material benefits that A acquired in connection with transactions A conducted on P's behalf.

    4.   Same facts as Illustration 3, except that T does not pay A for cars that A purchases on behalf of P. Instead, T gives A a three-year-old BMW, stating, "This is a gift from me to you in gratitude for our good relationship." Same result. A is subject to liability to P. . . .

    e.   *Remedies.* When an agent breaches the duty stated in this section, the principal may recover monetary relief from the agent and, in appropriate circumstances, from any third party who participated in the agent's breach. A principal may avoid a contract entered into by the agent with a third party who participated in the agent's breach of duty. The principal may recover any material benefit received by the agent through the agent's breach, the value of the benefit, or proceeds of the benefit retained by the agent. The principal may also recover damages for any harm caused by the agent's breach. If an agent's breach of duty involves a wrongful disposal of assets of the principal, the principal cannot recover both the value of the asset and what the agent received in exchange. If a principal recovers damages from a third party as a consequence of an agent's breach of fiduciary duty, the principal remains entitled to recover from the agent any benefit that the agent improperly received from the transaction. . . .

§ 8.03   Acting as or on Behalf of an Adverse Party

An agent has a duty not to deal with the principal as or on behalf of an adverse party in a transaction connected with the agency relationship.

Comment . . .

 b. *Rationale.* As a fiduciary, an agent has a duty to the principal to act loyally in the principal's interest in all matters in connection with the agency relationship. See § 8.01. The rule stated in this section is a specific application of this general principle. . . .

 A principal may consent to conduct by an agent that would otherwise constitute a breach of the agent's duty. . . .

Illustrations:

 1. P Corporation, which sells fabric-forming systems used for purposes such as lining ditches, uses polypropylene fabric as a principal component in constructing systems. P Corporation hires A to make sales and perform marketing functions. A's duties do not involve negotiating the terms of P Corporation's purchase of polypropylene fabric. Unbeknownst to P Corporation, A owns one-half of the equity of T Corporation, the principal supplier of polypropylene to P Corporation. A has breached A's duty to P Corporation. A's ownership interest in T Corporation makes A an adverse party in P Corporation's dealings with T Corporation.

 2. Same facts as Illustration 1, except that A tells C, P Corporation's President, that A owns an interest in T Corporation. P Corporation, through C, has knowledge that in dealing with T Corporation, it deals with A as an adverse party.

 A principal's knowledge that an agent deals as or on behalf of an adverse party does not relieve the agent of duties to the principal in connection with that transaction. Under the rule stated in § 8.06, the agent has a duty to deal fairly with the principal and to disclose to the principal all facts of which the agent has notice that are reasonably relevant to the principal's exercise of judgment, unless the principal has manifested that the principal already knows them or does not wish to know them. Thus, a principal's knowledge that its agent acts as or on behalf of an adverse party does not convert the relationship between principal and agent into an arm's-length relationship. Moreover, as stated in § 8.11, an agent has a duty to use reasonable effort to furnish information to the principal although the agent does not deal as or on behalf of an adverse party.

Illustration:

 3. Same facts as Illustration 2, except that A knows that T Corporation is well along in the process of developing a new line of polypropylene fabric that could be superior for P Corporation's purposes. A has a duty to disclose this fact to P Corporation. That a superior product is in the offing is a fact that a user of the current product would reasonably take into account in determining how much of the current product to purchase. . . .

§ 8.04 Competition

 Throughout the duration of an agency relationship, an agent has a duty to refrain from competing with the principal and from taking action on behalf of or otherwise assisting the principal's competitors. During that time, an agent may take action, not otherwise wrongful, to prepare for competition following termination of the agency relationship.

§ 8.05 Use of Principal's Property; Use of Confidential Information

 An agent has a duty

 (1) not to use property of the principal for the agent's own purposes or those of a third party; and

 (2) not to use or communicate confidential information of the principal for the agent's own purposes or those of a third party.

Comment . . .

 b. *Use of principal's property.* An agent who has possession of property of the principal has a duty to use it only on the principal's behalf, unless the principal consents to such use. See § 8.06. This rule is a specific application of an agent's basic fiduciary duty stated in § 8.01. . . . The rule is also a corollary of a principal's right, as an owner of property, to exclude usage by others. An agent is subject to this duty whether or not the agent uses property of the principal to compete with the principal or causes harm to the principal through the use. An agent may breach this duty even when the agent's use is beneficial in some sense to the property or to the principal. An agent is subject to liability to the principal for any profit made by the agent while using the principal's property when the use facilitates making the profit, or otherwise for the value of the use.

Illustrations:

> 1.   P, who owns a stable of horses, employs A to take care of them. While P is absent for a month, and without P's consent, A rents the horses to persons who ride them. Although being ridden is beneficial to the horses, A is subject to liability to P for the amount A receives for the rentals.

> 2.   Same facts as Illustration 1, except that A permits A's friends to ride P's horses for free during P's absence. A is subject to liability to P for the value of the use made of the horses. . . .

§ 8.06   Principal's Consent

(1) Conduct by an agent that would otherwise constitute a breach of duty as stated in §§ 8.01, 8.02, 8.03, 8.04, and 8.05 does not constitute a breach of duty if the principal consents to the conduct, provided that

(a) in obtaining the principal's consent, the agent

(i) acts in good faith,

(ii) discloses all material facts that the agent knows, has reason to know, or should know would reasonably affect the principal's judgment unless the principal has manifested that such facts are already known by the principal or that the principal does not wish to know them, and

(iii) otherwise deals fairly with the principal; and

(b) the principal's consent concerns either a specific act or transaction, or acts or transactions of a specified type that could reasonably be expected to occur in the ordinary course of the agency relationship.

(2) An agent who acts for more than one principal in a transaction between or among them has a duty

(a) to deal in good faith with each principal,

(b) to disclose to each principal

(i) the fact that the agent acts for the other principal or principals, and

(ii) all other facts that the agent knows, has reason to know, or should know would reasonably affect the principal's judgment unless the principal has manifested that such facts are already known by the principal or that the principal does not wish to know them, and

(c) otherwise to deal fairly with each principal.

Comment . . .

b.   In general. This section defines the circumstances under which conduct of a principal is effective as consent to conduct by an agent that would otherwise constitute a breach of the agent's duties of loyalty.

Common-law agency does not accord effect to all manifestations of assent by a principal that purport to eliminate or otherwise affect the fiduciary duties owed by an agent. This is so for two distinct reasons: (1) the law, and not the parties, determines whether a particular relationship is one of agency as defined in § 1.01; and (2) the law imposes restrictions on the efficacy of a principal's manifestations of assent in the interest of safeguarding the principal's intention in creating a relationship of common-law agency. . . .

Moreover, although a person may empower another to take action without regard to the interests of the person who grants the power, the law applicable to relationships of agency as defined in § 1.01 imposes mandatory limits on the circumstances under which an agent may be empowered to take disloyal action. These limits serve protective and cautionary purposes. Thus, an agreement that contains general or broad language purporting to release an agent in advance from the agent's general fiduciary obligation to the principal is not likely to be enforceable. This is because a broadly sweeping release of an agent's fiduciary duty may not reflect an adequately informed judgment on the part of the principal; if effective, the release would expose the principal to the risk that the agent will exploit the agent's position in ways not foreseeable by the principal at the time the principal agreed to the release.

In contrast, when a principal consents to specific transactions or to specified types of conduct by the agent, the principal has a focused opportunity to assess risks that are more readily identifiable. Likewise, when a principal consents after-the-fact to action taken by an agent that would otherwise breach the agent's fiduciary duty to the principal, the principal has the opportunity to assess what the agent has done with a degree of specificity not available before the agent takes action. . . .

An agent bears the burden of establishing that the requirements stated in this section have been fulfilled. . . .

TITLE C. DUTIES OF PERFORMANCE

§ 8.07 Duty Created by Contract

An agent has a duty to act in accordance with the express and implied terms of any contract between the agent and the principal.

§ 8.08 Duties of Care, Competence, and Diligence

Subject to any agreement with the principal, an agent has a duty to the principal to act with the care, competence, and diligence normally exercised by agents in similar circumstances. Special skills or knowledge possessed by an agent are circumstances to be taken into account in determining whether the agent acted with due care and diligence. If an agent claims to possess special skills or knowledge, the agent has a duty to the principal to act with the care, competence, and diligence normally exercised by agents with such skills or knowledge.

Comment . . .

c.   Duty of competence. The specific skills that an agent must possess to be competent depend on the nature of the service that the agent undertakes to provide and the circumstances under which it will be provided, such as the magnitude and complexity of transactions that the agent will conduct on the principal's account. For example, an agent may be competent to lease apartments in a residential building but lack the competence required to negotiate a complex lease of commercial space.

If an agent undertakes to perform services as a practitioner of a trade or profession, the agent "is required to exercise the skill and knowledge normally possessed by members of that profession or trade in good standing in similar communities" unless the agent represents that the agent possesses greater or lesser skill. Restatement Second, Torts § 299A. An agent may reasonably be expected to know at least the basic rules and practices under which the agent's industry or profession operates. . . .

An agent's level of skill or knowledge may exceed the norm for similarly situated agents. Alternatively, an agent may falsely represent that this is so. An agent's performance should be evaluated consistently with the agent's claimed level of skill or knowledge unless the agent establishes that the principal knew the agent's claim to be false. The agent's professed level of skill or knowledge becomes the standard against which the agent's performance should be assessed. For a comparable rule applicable to trustees, see Restatement Third, Trusts § 77(3) (Tentative Draft No. 4, 2005). When an agent does not claim to possess special skills or knowledge but in fact has a level of skill or knowledge that exceeds the norm, the trier of fact may consider the agent's actual knowledge and skills in determining whether the agent acted with due care under the circumstances. See Restatement Third, Torts: Liability for Physical Harm § 12, Comment *a* (Proposed Final Draft No. 1, 2005). An actor's actual state of knowledge will always be relevant to determining whether the actor behaved with due care, regardless of the source of that knowledge. Id., Comment *a*. An actor's knowledge and skills are combined to a degree that makes it difficult to disaggregate them. Id. . . .

d.   Duty of diligence. An agent's duty of diligence requires the agent to bring the agent's competence to bear on matters undertaken on behalf of the principal. Ordinarily, the scope of an agent's duty to be diligent is limited by the scope of the services the agent undertakes to perform for the principal. The scope of an agent's duty may be expanded by contract or by the existence of a special relationship of trust and confidence between agent and principal. For example, a securities broker's duty of diligence to a client who directs trading in the client's own account (a "nondiscretionary" account) is limited to executing the client's orders to purchase and sell securities in the account and does not extend to advising the client or issuing risk warnings on an ongoing basis. In contrast, a securities broker's duty may include the provision of advice and warnings when the broker's relationship with the client is one in which the client's trust and confidence are invited by the broker and given by the client.

Although an agent has a duty of diligence, that duty is to make reasonable efforts to achieve a result and not a duty to achieve the result regardless of the effort, risk, and cost involved. If an agent makes a reasonable effort, the agent is not subject to liability to the principal if the effort fails to accomplish the end desired by the principal. . . .

§ 8.09   Duty to Act Only Within Scope of Actual Authority and to Comply with Principal's Lawful Instructions

(1) An agent has a duty to take action only within the scope of the agent's actual authority.

(2) An agent has a duty to comply with all lawful instructions received from the principal and persons designated by the principal concerning the agent's actions on behalf of the principal.

Comment . . .

b.   Duty to act only within scope of actual authority. . . .

If an agent takes action beyond the scope of the agent's actual authority, the agent is subject to liability to the principal for loss caused the principal. The principal's loss may stem from actions taken by the agent with apparent authority, on the basis of which the principal became subject to liability to third parties. . . .

§ 8.10   Duty of Good Conduct

An agent has a duty, within the scope of the agency relationship, to act reasonably and to refrain from conduct that is likely to damage the principal's enterprise.

§ 8.11   Duty to Provide Information

An agent has a duty to use reasonable effort to provide the principal with facts that the agent knows, has reason to know, or should know when

(1) subject to any manifestation by the principal, the agent knows or has reason to know that the principal would wish to have the facts or the facts are material to the agent's duties to the principal; and

(2) the facts can be provided to the principal without violating a superior duty owed by the agent to another person.

Comment . . .

b.   In general. A principal's agents link the principal to the external world for purposes of acquiring information as well as for purposes of taking action. . . . An agent owes the principal a duty to provide information to the principal that the agent knows or has reason to know the principal would wish to have. An agent also owes the principal a duty, subject to any manifestation by the principal, to provide information to the principal that is material to the agent's duties to the principal. . . .

Illustrations:

1.   A represents P Insurance Co. and solicits applications for insurance policies to be issued by it. A submits an application for life insurance completed by T to P Insurance Co. After submitting the application but before P Insurance Co. issues a policy to T, A learns that T's health

has deteriorated substantially. As A knows, this is information that P Insurance Co. would desire to have in determining whether to issue a policy of life insurance to T. A has a duty to use reasonable effort to provide this information to P Insurance Co. . . .

3. P, who owns a house, retains A as a rental agent. A learns that T, the tenant who occupies the house, has vacated it and that the water pipes in the house have frozen and then thawed, causing damage to the house's flooring. As A knows, P would desire to have this information to determine what steps to take. A has a duty to use reasonable effort to provide this information to P.

4. P, who owns Blackacre, lists it for sale with A. T makes an offer to buy Blackacre for $100,000. Before T's offer is accepted, A learns that S is willing to pay $120,000 for Blackacre. As A knows, P would desire to have this information. A has a duty to use reasonable effort to provide the information to P. . . .

11. P opens an account with A for the purpose of trading in a complex and unusual type of overseas commodities option contract. A provides P with a document stating that each option contract has three components: (1) a premium for the option; (2) a commission; and (3) a foreign service fee of 20 percent of the premium. A does not tell P that the "foreign service fee" does not represent any additional expense that A must incur to execute a transaction but, instead, is an additional commission to be retained by A. Few investors at the time understand the complexities of such transactions and P could not know what expenses a broker like A would incur in executing them. A has a duty to P to inform P that the "foreign service fee" represents monies that A will retain. P is uniquely dependent on A for this information, which was material to P's decision whether engaging in such transactions could be to P's advantage. . . .

§ 8.12 Duties Regarding Principal's Property—Segregation, Record-Keeping, and Accounting

An agent has a duty, subject to any agreement with the principal,

(1) not to deal with the principal's property so that it appears to be the agent's property;

(2) not to mingle the principal's property with anyone else's; and

(3) to keep and render accounts to the principal of money or other property received or paid out on the principal's account.

TOPIC 2. PRINCIPAL'S DUTIES TO AGENT

§ 8.13 Duty Created by Contract

A principal has a duty to act in accordance with the express and implied terms of any contract between the principal and the agent.

§ 8.14 Duty to Indemnify

A principal has a duty to indemnify an agent

(1) in accordance with the terms of any contract between them; and

(2) unless otherwise agreed,

(a) when the agent makes a payment

(i) within the scope of the agent's actual authority, or

(ii) that is beneficial to the principal, unless the agent acts officiously in making the payment; or

(b) when the agent suffers a loss that fairly should be borne by the principal in light of their relationship.

Comment . . .

    b.   Agent's right to indemnification—in general. In general, a principal's obligation to indemnify an agent arises when the agent makes a payment or incurs an expense or other loss while acting on behalf of the principal. An agent's actions on behalf of a principal may result in pecuniary loss for the agent. For example, an agent may be required to make payments to third parties to carry out the agent's work for the principal. Actions taken by an agent may also result in litigation against the agent brought by third parties with whom the agent has interacted on the principal's behalf. A contract between a principal and an agent may anticipate the possibility that the agent will incur pecuniary losses, specify when and to what extent the principal has a duty to indemnify the agent, and prescribe procedures to be followed by the agent in claiming rights to indemnity under the contract.

    In the absence of such a contract, a principal has duties to indemnify the agent as stated in subsection (2). If an agent acts with actual authority in making a payment to a third party, the principal has a duty to indemnify the agent unless otherwise agreed.

Illustration:

    1.   P retains A, an import broker, to handle importation of a large quantity of herbicide. A learns that the amount of duty payable on the herbicide will exceed a prior estimate given by the customs service because the herbicide contains various chemicals not listed on its label. Fearing forfeiture of the security bond A has posted for the duty, A pays the additional amount under protest and seeks indemnity from P. P has a duty to indemnify A. A acted with actual authority in making the payment. . . .

    d.   Rights to indemnification in connection with litigation. In the absence of an express contractual provision that requires the principal to indemnify an agent in connection with litigation against the agent, a principal has a duty to indemnify the agent against expenses and other losses incurred by the agent in defending against actions brought by third parties if the agent acted with actual authority in taking the action challenged by the third party's suit. . . .

§ 8.15   Principal's Duty to Deal Fairly and in Good Faith

    A principal has a duty to deal with the agent fairly and in good faith, including a duty to provide the agent with information about risks of physical harm or pecuniary loss that the principal knows, has reason to know, or should know are present in the agent's work but unknown to the agent.

Comment . . .

    b.   Duty to deal with agent fairly and in good faith. A principal has a duty to deal fairly and in good faith with an agent. This duty does not supersede the principal's power to terminate the agent's authority as stated in § 3.10(1). This general duty encompasses more specific duties. The general duty obliges the principal to refrain from engaging in conduct that will foreseeably result in loss for the agent when the agent's own conduct is without fault.

Illustration:

    1.   P Corporation, wishing to do business in Taiwan, engages A as its general manager in Taiwan. P Corporation designates A as its "responsible person" or legal representative in Taiwan, which requires such a designation to conduct business in the country. As P Corporation's designated "responsible person," A affixes A's "chop" or signature-equivalent, to tax returns that P Corporation prepares and files in Taiwan. Having decided to cease doing business in Taiwan, P Corporation terminates A's engagement but does not remove its designation of A as its "responsible person," although A requests several times that P Corporation do so and tells P Corporation that A is concerned that A may be subject to liability in the event of tax-related disputes between P Corporation and Taiwan. Taiwan assesses a tax liability against P Corporation that P Corporation contests and then, following an adverse final determination, does not pay. Taiwanese authorities notify A that A is forbidden to leave the country until its tax dispute with P Corporation is resolved. P Corporation has breached its duty of good faith. P Corporation is subject to liability for loss suffered by A, including attorney's fees incurred by A to resolve A's predicament. . . .

UNIFORM PARTNERSHIP ACT

TABLE OF CONTENTS

(looks from perspective of individuals/partners aggregate)

PART I.   PRELIMINARY PROVISIONS

Sec.		Page
1.	Name of Act	48
2.	Definition of Terms	48
3.	Interpretation of Knowledge and Notice	48
4.	Rules of Construction	48
5.	Rules for Cases Not Provided for in This Act	49

PART II.   NATURE OF PARTNERSHIP

6.	Partnership Defined	49
7.	Rules for Determining the Existence of a Partnership	49
8.	Partnership Property	49

PART III.   RELATIONS OF PARTNERS TO PERSONS DEALING WITH THE PARTNERSHIP

9.	Partner Agent of Partnership as to Partnership Business	50
10.	Conveyance of Real Property of the Partnership	50
11.	Partnership Bound by Admission of Partner	51
12.	Partnership Charged With Knowledge of or Notice to Partner	51
13.	Partnership Bound by Partner's Wrongful Act	51
14.	Partnership Bound by Partner's Breach of Trust	51
15.	Nature of Partner's Liability	51
16.	Partner by Estoppel	51
17.	Liability of Incoming Partner	52

PART IV.   RELATIONS OF PARTNERS TO ONE ANOTHER

18.	Rules Determining Rights and Duties of Partners	52
19.	Partnership Books	52
20.	Duty of Partners to Render Information	52
21.	Partner Accountable as a Fiduciary	52
22.	Right to an Account	53
23.	Continuation of Partnership Beyond Fixed Term	53

PART V.   PROPERTY RIGHTS OF A PARTNER

24.	Extent of Property Rights of a Partner	53
25.	Nature of a Partner's Right in Specific Partnership Property	53
26.	Nature of Partner's Interest in the Partnership	53
27.	Assignment of Partner's Interest	54
28.	Partner's Interest Subject to Charging Order	54

PART VI.   DISSOLUTION AND WINDING UP

29.	Dissolution Defined	54
30.	Partnership Not Terminated by Dissolution	54
31.	Causes of Dissolution	54
32.	Dissolution by Decree of Court	55
33.	General Effect of Dissolution on Authority of Partner	55
34.	Right of Partner to Contribution From Co-partners After Dissolution	56

35.   Power of Partner to Bind Partnership to Third Persons After Dissolution 56
36.   Effect of Dissolution on Partner's Existing Liability 57
37.   Right to Wind Up.. 57
38.   Rights of Partners to Application of Partnership Property 57
39.   Rights Where Partnership Is Dissolved for Fraud or Misrepresentation 58
40.   Rules for Distribution... 58
41.   Liability of Persons Continuing the Business in Certain Cases 59
42.   Rights of Retiring or Estate of Deceased Partner When the Business Is Continued.................. 59
43.   Accrual of Actions 60

PART VII. MISCELLANEOUS PROVISIONS*

44.   When Act Takes Effect.*
45.   Legislation Repealed.*

PART I

PRELIMINARY PROVISIONS

§ 1.   Name of Act

This act may be cited as Uniform Partnership Act.

§ 2.   Definition of Terms

In this act, "Court" includes every court and judge having jurisdiction in the case.

"Business" includes every trade, occupation, or profession.

"Person" includes individuals, partnerships, corporations, and other associations.

"Bankrupt" includes bankrupt under the Federal Bankruptcy Act or insolvent under any state insolvent act.

"Conveyance" includes every assignment, lease, mortgage, or encumbrance.

"Real property" includes land and any interest or estate in land.

§ 3.   Interpretation of Knowledge and Notice

(1) A person has "knowledge" of a fact within the meaning of this act not only when he has actual knowledge thereof, but also when he has knowledge of such other facts as in the circumstances shows bad faith.

(2) A person has "notice" of a fact within the meaning of this act when the person who claims the benefit of the notice:

(a) States the fact to such person, or

(b) Delivers through the mail, or by other means of communication, a written statement of the fact to such person or to a proper person at his place of business or residence.

§ 4.   Rules of Construction

(1) The rule that statutes in derogation of the common law are to be strictly construed shall have no application to this act.

(2) The law of estoppel shall apply under this act.

---

*   Omitted.

(3) The law of agency shall apply under this act.

(4) This act shall be so interpreted and construed as to effect its general purpose to make uniform the law of those states which enact it.

(5) This act shall not be construed so as to impair the obligations of any contract existing when the act goes into effect, nor to affect any action or proceedings begun or right accrued before this act takes effect.

§ 5.　Rules for Cases Not Provided for in This Act

In any case not provided for in this act the rules of law and equity, including the law merchant, shall govern.

PART II

NATURE OF PARTNERSHIP

§ 6.　Partnership Defined

↦ need at least two persons

(1) A partnership is an association of two or more persons to carry on as co-owners a business for profit.

(2) But any association formed under any other statute of this state, or any statute adopted by authority, other than the authority of this state, is not a partnership under this act, unless such association would have been a partnership in this state prior to the adoption of this act; but this act shall apply to limited partnerships except in so far as the statutes relating to such partnerships are inconsistent herewith.

§ 7.　Rules for Determining the Existence of a Partnership

In determining whether a partnership exists, these rules shall apply:

(1) Except as provided by section 16 persons who are not partners as to each other are not partners as to third persons.

(2) Joint tenancy, tenancy in common, tenancy by the entireties, joint property, common property, or part ownership does not of itself establish a partnership, whether such co-owners do or do not share any profits made by the use of the property.

(3) The sharing of gross returns does not of itself establish a partnership, whether or not the persons sharing them have a joint or common right or interest in any property from which the returns are derived.

(4) The receipt by a person of a share of the profits of a business is prima facie evidence that he is a partner in the business, but no such inference shall be drawn if such profits were received in payment:

(a) As a debt by installments or otherwise,

(b) As wages of an employee or rent to a landlord,

(c) As an annuity to a widow or representative of a deceased partner,

(d) As interest on a loan, though the amount of payment vary with the profits of the business,

(e) As the consideration for the sale of a good-will of a business or other property by installments or otherwise.

§ 8.　Partnership Property

(1) All property originally brought into the partnership stock or subsequently acquired by purchase or otherwise, on account of the partnership, is partnership property.

(2) Unless the contrary intention appears, property acquired with partnership funds is partnership property.

(3) Any estate in real property may be acquired in the partnership name. Title so acquired can be conveyed only in the partnership name.

(4) A conveyance to a partnership in the partnership name, though without words of inheritance, passes the entire estate of the grantor unless a contrary intent appears.

PART III

RELATIONS OF PARTNERS TO PERSONS DEALING WITH THE PARTNERSHIP

§ 9.   Partner Agent of Partnership as to Partnership Business

(1) Every partner is an agent of the partnership for the purpose of its business, and the act of every partner, including the execution in the partnership name of any instrument, for apparently carrying on in the usual way the business of the partnership of which he is a member binds the partnership, unless the partner so acting has in fact no authority to act for the partnership in the particular matter, and the person with whom he is dealing has knowledge of the fact that he has no such authority.

(2) An act of a partner which is not apparently for the carrying on of the business of the partnership in the usual way does not bind the partnership unless authorized by the other partners.

(3) Unless authorized by the other partners or unless they have abandoned the business, one or more but less than all the partners have no authority to:

(a) Assign the partnership property in trust for creditors or on the assignee's promise to pay the debts of the partnership,

(b) Dispose of the good-will of the business,

(c) Do any other act which would make it impossible to carry on the ordinary business of a partnership,

(d) Confess a judgment,

(e) Submit a partnership claim or liability to arbitration or reference.

(4) No act of a partner in contravention of a restriction on authority shall bind the partnership to persons having knowledge of the restriction.

§ 10.   Conveyance of Real Property of the Partnership

(1) Where title to real property is in the partnership name, any partner may convey title to such property by a conveyance executed in the partnership name; but the partnership may recover such property unless the partner's act binds the partnership under the provisions of paragraph (1) of section 9, or unless such property has been conveyed by the grantee or a person claiming through such grantee to a holder for value without knowledge that the partner, in making the conveyance, has exceeded his authority.

(2) Where title to real property is in the name of the partnership, a conveyance executed by a partner, in his own name, passes the equitable interest of the partnership, provided the act is one within the authority of the partner under the provisions of paragraph (1) of section 9.

(3) Where title to real property is in the name of one or more but not all the partners, and the record does not disclose the right of the partnership, the partners in whose name the title stands may convey title to such property, but the partnership may recover such property if the partners' act does not bind the partnership under the provisions of paragraph (1) of section 9, unless the purchaser or his assignee, is a holder for value, without knowledge.

(4) Where the title to real property is in the name of one or more or all the partners, or in a third person in trust for the partnership, a conveyance executed by a partner in the partnership name, or in his own name, passes the equitable interest of the partnership, provided the act is one within the authority of the partner under the provisions of paragraph (1) of section 9.

(5) Where the title to real property is in the names of all the partners a conveyance executed by all the partners passes all their rights in such property.

§ 11. Partnership Bound by Admission of Partner

An admission or representation made by any partner concerning partnership affairs within the scope of his authority as conferred by this act is evidence against the partnership.

§ 12. Partnership Charged With Knowledge of or Notice to Partner

Notice to any partner of any matter relating to partnership affairs, and the knowledge of the partner acting in the particular matter, acquired while a partner or then present to his mind, and the knowledge of any other partner who reasonably could and should have communicated it to the acting partner, operate as notice to or knowledge of the partnership, except in the case of a fraud on the partnership committed by or with the consent of that partner.

§ 13. Partnership Bound by Partner's Wrongful Act

Where, by any wrongful act or omission of any partner acting in the ordinary course of the business of the partnership or with the authority of his co-partners, loss or injury is caused to any person, not being a partner in the partnership, or any penalty is incurred, the partnership is liable therefor to the same extent as the partner so acting or omitting to act.

§ 14. Partnership Bound by Partner's Breach of Trust

The partnership is bound to make good the loss: → like theft (a tort)

(a) Where one partner acting within the scope of his apparent authority receives money or property of a third person and misapplies it; and

(b) Where the partnership in the course of its business receives money or property of a third person and the money or property so received is misapplied by any partner while it is in the custody of the partnership.

§ 15. Nature of Partner's Liability

All partners are liable

→ for all torts-based liabilities

(a) Jointly and severally for everything chargeable to the partnership under sections 13 and 14.

(b) Jointly for all other debts and obligations of the partnership; but any partner may enter.

§ 16. Partner by Estoppel

(1) When a person, by words spoken or written or by conduct, represents himself, or consents to another representing him to any one, as a partner in an existing partnership or with one or more persons not actual partners, he is liable to any such person to whom such representation has been made, who has, on the faith of such representation, given credit to the actual or apparent partnership, and if he has made such representation or consented to its being made in a public manner he is liable to such person, whether the representation has or has not been made or communicated to such person so giving credit by or with the knowledge of the apparent partner making the representation or consenting to its being made.

(a) When a partnership liability results, he is liable as though he were an actual member of the partnership.

(b) When no partnership liability results, he is liable jointly with the other persons, if any, so consenting to the contract or representation as to incur liability, otherwise separately.

(2) When a person has been thus represented to be a partner in an existing partnership, or with one or more persons not actual partners, he is an agent of the persons consenting to such representation to bind them to the same extent and in the same manner as though he were a partner in fact, with respect to persons who rely upon the representation. Where all the members of the existing partnership consent to the representation, a partnership act or obligation results; but in all other cases it is the joint act or obligation of the person acting and the persons consenting to the representation.

§ 17. Liability of Incoming Partner

A person admitted as a partner into an existing partnership is liable for all the obligations of the partnership arising before his admission as though he had been a partner when such obligations were incurred, except that this liability shall be satisfied only out of partnership property.

PART IV

RELATIONS OF PARTNERS TO ONE ANOTHER

§ 18. Rules Determining Rights and Duties of Partners

The rights and duties of the partners in relation to the partnership shall be determined, subject to any agreement between them, by the following rules:

(a) Each partner shall be repaid his contributions, whether by way of capital or advances to the partnership property and share equally in the profits and surplus remaining after all liabilities, including those to partners, are satisfied; and must contribute towards the losses, whether of capital or otherwise, sustained by the partnership according to his share in the profits. → §401(a) RUPA pg 86

(b) The partnership must indemnify every partner in respect of payments made and personal liabilities reasonably incurred by him in the ordinary and proper conduct of its business, or for the preservation of its business or property.

(c) A partner, who in aid of the partnership makes any payment or advance beyond the amount of capital which he agreed to contribute, shall be paid interest from the date of the payment or advance.

(d) A partner shall receive interest on the capital contributed by him only from the date when repayment should be made.

(e) All partners have equal rights in the management and conduct of the partnership business.

(f) No partner is entitled to remuneration for acting in the partnership business, except that a surviving partner is entitled to reasonable compensation for his services in winding up the partnership affairs.

(g) No person can become a member of a partnership without the consent of all the partners.

(h) Any difference arising as to ordinary matters connected with the partnership business may be decided by a majority of the partners; but no act in contravention of any agreement between the partners may be done rightfully without the consent of all the partners.

§ 19. Partnership Books

The partnership books shall be kept, subject to any agreement between the partners, at the principal place of business of the partnership, and every partner shall at all times have access to and may inspect and copy any of them.

§ 20. Duty of Partners to Render Information

Partners shall render on demand true and full information of all things affecting the partnership to any partner or the legal representative of any deceased partner or partner under legal disability.

§ 21. Partner Accountable as a Fiduciary

(1) Every partner must account to the partnership for any benefit, and hold as trustee for it any profits derived by him without the consent of the other partners from any transaction connected with the formation, conduct, or liquidation of the partnership or from any use by him of its property.

(2) This section applies also to the representatives of a deceased partner engaged in the liquidation of the affairs of the partnership as the personal representatives of the last surviving partner.

§ 22. Right to an Account

Any partner shall have the right to a formal account as to partnership affairs:

(a) If he is wrongfully excluded from the partnership business or possession of its property by his co-partners,

(b) If the right exists under the terms of any agreement,

(c) As provided by section 21,

(d) Whenever other circumstances render it just and reasonable.

§ 23. Continuation of Partnership Beyond Fixed Term

(1) When a partnership for a fixed term or particular undertaking is continued after the termination of such term or particular undertaking without any express agreement, the rights and duties of the partners remain the same as they were at such termination, so far as is consistent with a partnership at will.

(2) A continuation of the business by the partners or such of them as habitually acted therein during the term, without any settlement or liquidation of the partnership affairs, is prima facie evidence of a continuation of the partnership.

PART V

PROPERTY RIGHTS OF A PARTNER

§ 24. Extent of Property Rights of a Partner

The property rights of a partner are (1) his rights in specific partnership property, (2) his interest in the partnership, and (3) his right to participate in the management.

§ 25. Nature of a Partner's Right in Specific Partnership Property

(1) A partner is co-owner with his partners of specific partnership property holding as a tenant in partnership.

(2) The incidents of this tenancy are such that:

(a) A partner, subject to the provisions of this act and to any agreement between the partners, has an equal right with his partners to possess specific partnership property for partnership purposes; but he has no right to possess such property for any other purpose without the consent of his partners.

(b) A partner's right in specific partnership property is not assignable except in connection with the assignment of rights of all the partners in the same property.

(c) A partner's right in specific partnership property is not subject to attachment or execution, except on a claim against the partnership. When partnership property is attached for a partnership debt the partners, or any of them, or the representatives of a deceased partner, cannot claim any right under the homestead or exemption laws.

(d) On the death of a partner his right in specific partnership property vests in the surviving partner or partners, except where the deceased was the last surviving partner, when his right in such property vests in his legal representative. Such surviving partner or partners, or the legal representative of the last surviving partner, has no right to possess the partnership property for any but a partnership purpose.

(e) A partner's right in specific partnership property is not subject to dower, curtesy, or allowances to widows, heirs, or next of kin.

§ 26. Nature of Partner's Interest in the Partnership

A partner's interest in the partnership is his share of the profits and surplus, and the same is personal property.

§ 27.   Assignment of Partner's Interest

(1) A conveyance by a partner of his interest in the partnership does not of itself dissolve the partnership, nor, as against the other partners in the absence of agreement, entitle the assignee, during the continuance of the partnership, to interfere in the management or administration of the partnership business or affairs, or to require any information or account of partnership transactions, or to inspect the partnership books; but it merely entitles the assignee to receive in accordance with his contract the profits to which the assigning partner would otherwise be entitled.

(2) In case of a dissolution of the partnership, the assignee is entitled to receive his assignor's interest and may require an account from the date only of the last account agreed to by all the partners.

§ 28.   Partner's Interest Subject to Charging Order

(1) On due application to a competent court by any judgment creditor of a partner, the court which entered the judgment, order, or decree, or any other court, may charge the interest of the debtor partner with payment of the unsatisfied amount of such judgment debt with interest thereon; and may then or later appoint a receiver of his share of the profits, and of any other money due or to fall due to him in respect of the partnership, and make all other orders, directions, accounts and inquiries which the debtor partner might have made, or which the circumstances of the case may require.

(2) The interest charged may be redeemed at any time before foreclosure, or in case of a sale being directed by the court may be purchased without thereby causing a dissolution:

(a) With separate property, by any one or more of the partners, or

(b) With partnership property, by any one or more of the partners with the consent of all the partners whose interests are not so charged or sold.

(3) Nothing in this act shall be held to deprive a partner of his right, if any, under the exemption laws, as regards his interest in the partnership.

PART VI

DISSOLUTION AND WINDING UP

§ 29.   Dissolution Defined

The dissolution of a partnership is the change in the relation of the partners caused by any partner ceasing to be associated in the carrying on as distinguished from the winding up of the business.

Official Comment

. . . In this act dissolution designates the point in time when the partners cease to carry on the business together; termination is the point in time when all the partnership affairs are wound up; winding up, the process of settling partnership affairs after dissolution.

§ 30.   Partnership Not Terminated by Dissolution

On dissolution the partnership is not terminated, but continues until the winding up of partnership affairs is completed.

§ 31.   Causes of Dissolution

Dissolution is caused:

(1) Without violation of the agreement between the partners,

(a) By the termination of the definite term or particular undertaking specified in the agreement,

(b) By the express will of any partner when no definite term or particular undertaking is specified,

(c) By the express will of all the partners who have not assigned their interests or suffered them to be charged for their separate debts, either before or after the termination of any specified term or particular undertaking,

(d) By the expulsion of any partner from the business bona fide in accordance with such a power conferred by the agreement between the partners;

(2) In contravention of the agreement between the partners, where the circumstances do not permit a dissolution under any other provision of this section, by the express will of any partner at any time;

(3) By any event which makes it unlawful for the business of the partnership to be carried on or for the members to carry it on in partnership;

(4) By the death of any partner;

(5) By the bankruptcy of any partner or the partnership;

(6) By decree of court under section 32.

Official Comment

Paragraph (2) will settle a matter on which at present considerable confusion and uncertainty exists. The paragraph as drawn allows a partner to dissolve a partnership in contravention of the agreement between the partners. . . .

The relation of partners is one of agency. The agency is such a personal one that equity cannot enforce it even where the agreement provides that the partnership shall continue for a definite time. The power of any partner to terminate the relation, even though in doing so he breaks a contract, should, it is submitted, be recognized.

The rights of the parties upon a dissolution in contravention of the agreement are safeguarded by section 38(2), infra.

§ 32. Dissolution by Decree of Court

(1) On application by or for a partner the court shall decree a dissolution whenever:

(a) A partner has been declared a lunatic in any judicial proceeding or is shown to be of unsound mind,

(b) A partner becomes in any other way incapable of performing his part of the partnership contract,

(c) A partner has been guilty of such conduct as tends to affect prejudicially the carrying on of the business,

(d) A partner wilfully or persistently commits a breach of the partnership agreement, or otherwise so conducts himself in matters relating to the partnership business that it is not reasonably practicable to carry on the business in partnership with him,

(e) The business of the partnership can only be carried on at a loss,

(f) Other circumstances render a dissolution equitable.

(2) On the application of the purchaser of a partner's interest under sections 28 or 29:[1]

(a) After the termination of the specified term or particular undertaking,

(b) At any time if the partnership was a partnership at will when the interest was assigned or when the charging order was issued.

§ 33. General Effect of Dissolution on Authority of Partner

Except so far as may be necessary to wind up partnership affairs or to complete transactions begun but not then finished, dissolution terminates all authority of any partner to act for the partnership,

(1) With respect to the partners,

---

[1] So in original. Probably should read "sections 27 or 28."

(a) When the dissolution is not by the act, bankruptcy or death of a partner; or

(b) When the dissolution is by such act, bankruptcy or death of a partner, in cases where section 34 so requires.

(2) With respect to persons not partners, as declared in section 35.

§ 34. Right of Partner to Contribution From Co-partners After Dissolution

Where the dissolution is caused by the act, death or bankruptcy of a partner, each partner is liable to his co-partners for his share of any liability created by any partner acting for the partnership as if the partnership had not been dissolved unless

(a) The dissolution being by act of any partner, the partner acting for the partnership had knowledge of the dissolution, or

(b) The dissolution being by the death or bankruptcy of a partner, the partner acting for the partnership had knowledge or notice of the death or bankruptcy.

§ 35. Power of Partner to Bind Partnership to Third Persons After Dissolution

(1) After dissolution a partner can bind the partnership except as provided in Paragraph (3)

(a) By any act appropriate for winding up partnership affairs or completing transactions unfinished at dissolution;

(b) By any transaction which would bind the partnership if dissolution had not taken place, provided the other party to the transaction

(I) Had extended credit to the partnership prior to dissolution and had no knowledge or notice of the dissolution; or

(II) Though he had not so extended credit, had nevertheless known of the partnership prior to dissolution, and, having no knowledge or notice of dissolution, the fact of dissolution had not been advertised in a newspaper of general circulation in the place (or in each place if more than one) at which the partnership business was regularly carried on.

(2) The liability of a partner under Paragraph (1b) shall be satisfied out of partnership assets alone when such partner had been prior to dissolution

(a) Unknown as a partner to the person with whom the contract is made; and

(b) So far unknown and inactive in partnership affairs that the business reputation of the partnership could not be said to have been in any degree due to his connection with it.

(3) The partnership is in no case bound by any act of a partner after dissolution

(a) Where the partnership is dissolved because it is unlawful to carry on the business, unless the act is appropriate for winding up partnership affairs; or

(b) Where the partner has become bankrupt; or

(c) Where the partner has no authority to wind up partnership affairs; except by a transaction with one who

(I) Had extended credit to the partnership prior to dissolution and had no knowledge or notice of his want of authority; or

(II) Had not extended credit to the partnership prior to dissolution, and, having no knowledge or notice of his want of authority, the fact of his want of authority has not been advertised in the manner provided for advertising the fact of dissolution in Paragraph (1bII).

(4) Nothing in this section shall affect the liability under Section 16 of any person who after dissolution represents himself or consents to another representing him as a partner in a partnership engaged in carrying on business.

§ 36. Effect of Dissolution on Partner's Existing Liability

(1) The dissolution of the partnership does not of itself discharge the existing liability of any partner.

(2) A partner is discharged from any existing liability upon dissolution of the partnership by an agreement to that effect between himself, the partnership creditor and the person or partnership continuing the business; and such agreement may be inferred from the course of dealing between the creditor having knowledge of the dissolution and the person or partnership continuing the business.

(3) Where a person agrees to assume the existing obligations of a dissolved partnership, the partners whose obligations have been assumed shall be discharged from any liability to any creditor of the partnership who, knowing of the agreement, consents to a material alteration in the nature or time of payment of such obligations.

(4) The individual property of a deceased partner shall be liable for all obligations of the partnership incurred while he was a partner but subject to the prior payment of his separate debts.

§ 37. Right to Wind Up

Unless otherwise agreed the partners who have not wrongfully dissolved the partnership or the legal representative of the last surviving partner, not bankrupt, has the right to wind up the partnership affairs; provided, however, that any partner, his legal representative or his assignee, upon cause shown, may obtain winding up by the court. → same people have standing for supervision of winding up

§ 38. Rights of Partners to Application of Partnership Property

(1) When dissolution is caused in any way, except in contravention of the partnership agreement, each partner, as against his co-partners and all persons claiming through them in respect of their interests in the partnership, unless otherwise agreed, may have the partnership property applied to discharge its liabilities, and the surplus applied to pay in cash the net amount owing to the respective partners. But if dissolution is caused by expulsion of a partner, bona fide under the partnership agreement and if the expelled partner is discharged from all partnership liabilities, either by payment or agreement under section 36(2), he shall receive in cash only the net amount due him from the partnership.

(2) When dissolution is caused in contravention of the partnership agreement the rights of the partners shall be as follows:

(a) Each partner who has not caused dissolution wrongfully shall have,

(I) All the rights specified in paragraph (1) of this section, and

(II) The right, as against each partner who has caused the dissolution wrongfully, to damages for breach of the agreement.

(b) The partners who have not caused the dissolution wrongfully, if they all desire to continue the business in the same name, either by themselves or jointly with others, may do so, during the agreed term for the partnership and for that purpose may possess the partnership property, provided they secure the payment by bond approved by the court, or pay to any partner who has caused the dissolution wrongfully, the value of his interest in the partnership at the dissolution, less any damages recoverable under clause (2aII) of this section, and in like manner indemnify him against all present or future partnership liabilities.

(c) A partner who has caused the dissolution wrongfully shall have:

I.   If the business is not continued under the provisions of paragraph (2b) all the rights of a partner under paragraph (1), subject to clause (2aII), of this section,

II.   If the business is continued under paragraph (2b) of this section the right as against his co-partners and all claiming through them in respect of their interests in the partnership, to have the value of his interest in the partnership, less any damages caused to his co-partners by the dissolution, ascertained and paid to him in cash, or the payment secured by bond approved by the court, and to be released from all existing liabilities of the partnership; but in ascertaining the value of the partner's interest the value of the good-will of the business shall not be considered.

Official Comment

The right given to each partner, where no agreement to the contrary has been made, to have his share of the surplus paid to him in cash makes certain an existing uncertainty. At present it is not certain whether a partner may or may not insist on a physical partition of the property remaining after third persons have been paid.

§ 39. Rights Where Partnership Is Dissolved for Fraud or Misrepresentation

Where a partnership contract is rescinded on the ground of the fraud or misrepresentation of one of the parties thereto, the party entitled to rescind is, without prejudice to any other right, entitled,

(a) To a lien on, or a right of retention of, the surplus of the partnership property after satisfying the partnership liabilities to third persons for any sum of money paid by him for the purchase of an interest in the partnership and for any capital or advances contributed by him; and

(b) To stand, after all liabilities to third persons have been satisfied, in the place of the creditors of the partnership for any payments made by him in respect of the partnership liabilities; and

(c) To be indemnified by the person guilty of the fraud or making the representation against all debts and liabilities of the partnership.

§ 40. Rules for Distribution

In settling accounts between the partners after dissolution, the following rules shall be observed, subject to any agreement to the contrary:

(a) The assets of the partnership are:

I.   The partnership property,

II.   The contributions of the partners necessary for the payment of all the liabilities specified in clause (b) of this paragraph.

(b) The liabilities of the partnership shall rank in order of payment, as follows:

I.   Those owing to creditors other than partners,

II.   Those owing to partners other than for capital and profits,

III.   Those owing to partners in respect of capital,

IV.   Those owing to partners in respect of profits.

(c) The assets shall be applied in order of their declaration in clause (a) of this paragraph to the satisfaction of the liabilities.

(d) The partners shall contribute, as provided by section 18(a) the amount necessary to satisfy the liabilities; but if any, but not all, of the partners are insolvent, or, not being subject to process, refuse to contribute, the other partners shall contribute their share of the liabilities, and, in the relative proportions in which they share the profits, the additional amount necessary to pay the liabilities.

(e) An assignee for the benefit of creditors or any person appointed by the court shall have the right to enforce the contributions specified in clause (d) of this paragraph.

(f) Any partner or his legal representative shall have the right to enforce the contributions specified in clause (d) of this paragraph, to the extent of the amount which he has paid in excess of his share of the liability.

(g) The individual property of a deceased partner shall be liable for the contributions specified in clause (d) of this paragraph.

(h) When partnership property and the individual properties of the partners are in possession of a court for distribution, partnership creditors shall have priority on partnership property and separate creditors on individual property, saving the rights of lien or secured creditors as heretofore.

58

(i) Where a partner has become bankrupt or his estate is insolvent the claims against his separate property shall rank in the following order:

I.   Those owing to separate creditors,

II.   Those owing to partnership creditors,

III.   Those owing to partners by way of contribution.

§ 41.   Liability of Persons Continuing the Business in Certain Cases

(1) When any new partner is admitted into an existing partnership, or when any partner retires and assigns (or the representative of the deceased partner assigns) his rights in partnership property to two or more of the partners, or to one or more of the partners and one or more third persons, if the business is continued without liquidation of the partnership affairs, creditors of the first or dissolved partnership are also creditors of the partnership so continuing the business.

(2) When all but one partner retire and assign (or the representative of a deceased partner assigns) their rights in partnership property to the remaining partner, who continues the business without liquidation of partnership affairs, either alone or with others, creditors of the dissolved partnership are also creditors of the person or partnership so continuing the business.

(3) When any partner retires or dies and the business of the dissolved partnership is continued as set forth in paragraphs (1) and (2) of this section, with the consent of the retired partners or the representative of the deceased partner, but without any assignment of his right in partnership property, rights of creditors of the dissolved partnership and of the creditors of the person or partnership continuing the business shall be as if such assignment had been made.

(4) When all the partners or their representatives assign their rights in partnership property to one or more third persons who promise to pay the debts and who continue the business of the dissolved partnership, creditors of the dissolved partnership are also creditors of the person or partnership continuing the business.

(5) When any partner wrongfully causes a dissolution and the remaining partners continue the business under the provisions of section 38(2b), either alone or with others, and without liquidation of the partnership affairs, creditors of the dissolved partnership are also creditors of the person or partnership continuing the business.

(6) When a partner is expelled and the remaining partners continue the business either alone or with others, without liquidation of the partnership affairs, creditors of the dissolved partnership are also creditors of the person or partnership continuing the business.

(7) The liability of a third person becoming a partner in the partnership continuing the business, under this section, to the creditors of the dissolved partnership shall be satisfied out of partnership property only.

(8) When the business of a partnership after dissolution is continued under any conditions set forth in this section the creditors of the dissolved partnership, as against the separate creditors of the retiring or deceased partner or the representative of the deceased partner, have a prior right to any claim of the retired partner or the representative of the deceased partner against the person or partnership continuing the business, on account of the retired or deceased partner's interest in the dissolved partnership or on account of any consideration promised for such interest or for his right in partnership property.

(9) Nothing in this section shall be held to modify any right of creditors to set aside any assignment on the ground of fraud.

(10) The use by the person or partnership continuing the business of the partnership name, or the name of a deceased partner as part thereof, shall not of itself make the individual property of the deceased partner liable for any debts contracted by such person or partnership.

§ 42.   Rights of Retiring or Estate of Deceased Partner When the Business Is Continued

When any partner retires or dies, and the business is continued under any of the conditions set forth in section 41(1, 2, 3, 5, 6), or section 38(2b) without any settlement of accounts as between him or his estate and the person or partnership continuing the business, unless otherwise agreed, he or his legal representative as against such persons or partnership may have the value of his interest at the date of dissolution ascertained, and shall receive as an ordinary creditor an amount equal to the value of his interest in the dissolved partnership with interest, or, at his option or at the option of his legal representative, in lieu of interest, the profits attributable to the use of his right in the property of the dissolved partnership; provided that the creditors of the dissolved partnership as against the separate creditors, or the representative of the retired or deceased partner, shall have priority on any claim arising under this section, as provided by section 41(8) of this act.

§ 43.   Accrual of Actions

The right to an account of his interest shall accrue to any partner, or his legal representative, as against the winding up partners or the surviving partners or the person or partnership continuing the business, at the date of dissolution, in the absence of any agreement to the contrary.

Default Rules

REVISED UNIFORM PARTNERSHIP ACT (1997)

(Last Amended 2013)

(looks from perspective of an entity! partnership)

TABLE OF CONTENTS

[ARTICLE] 1
GENERAL PROVISIONS

Sec.		Page
101.	Short Title.	65
102.	Definitions.	65
103.	Knowledge; Notice.	69
104.	Governing Law.	70
105.	Partnership Agreement; Scope, Function, and Limitations.	70
106.	Partnership Agreement; Effect on Partnership and Person Becoming Partner; Preformation Agreement.	74
107.	Partnership Agreement; Effect on Third Parties and Relationship to Records Effective on Behalf of Partnership.	75
118.	Reservation of Power to Amend or Repeal.	75
119.	Supplemental Principles of Law.	76

[ARTICLE] 2
NATURE OF PARTNERSHIP

201.	Partnership As Entity.	76
202.	Formation of Partnership.	76
203.	Partnership Property.	78
204.	When Property Is Partnership Property.	78

[ARTICLE] 3
RELATIONS OF PARTNERS TO PERSONS
DEALING WITH PARTNERSHIP

301.	Partner Agent of Partnership.	79
302.	Transfer of Partnership Property.	80
303.	Statement of Partnership Authority.	81
304.	Statement of Denial.	82
305.	Partnership Liable for Partner's Actionable Conduct.	83
306.	Partner's Liability.	83 → shield
307.	Actions by and Against Partnership and Partners.	85
308.	Liability of Purported Partner.	85

[ARTICLE] 4
RELATIONS OF PARTNERS TO EACH
OTHER AND TO PARTNERSHIP

401.	Partner's Rights and Duties.	86
402.	Becoming Partner.	88
403.	Form of Contribution.	89
404.	Liability for Contribution.	89
405.	Sharing of and Right to Distributions Before Dissolution.	89
406.	Limitations on Distributions by Limited Liability Partnership.	89
407.	Liability for Improper Distributions by Limited Liability Partnership.	91
408.	Rights to Information of Partners and Persons Dissociated as Partner.	91
409.	Standards of Conduct for Partners.	93
410.	Actions by Partnership and Partners.	96

411.   Continuation of Partnership Beyond Definite Term or Particular Undertaking. 96

[ARTICLE] 5
TRANSFERABLE INTERESTS AND RIGHTS
OF TRANSFEREES AND CREDITORS

501.   Partner Not Co-Owner of Partnership Property. 97
502.   Nature of Transferable Interest. 97
503.   Transfer of Transferable Interest. 97
504.   Charging Order. 98
505.   Power of Legal Representative of Deceased Partner. 99

[ARTICLE] 6
DISSOCIATION

601.   Events Causing Dissociation. 99
602.   Power to Dissociate as Partner; Wrongful Dissociation. 101
603.   Effect of Dissociation. 102

[ARTICLE] 7
PERSON'S DISSOCIATION AS A PARTNER
WHEN BUSINESS NOT WOUND UP

701.   Purchase of Interest of Person Dissociated as Partner. 103
702.   Power to Bind and Liability of Person Dissociated as Partner. 104
703.   Liability of Person Dissociated as Partner to Other Persons. 105
704.   Statement of Dissociation. 106
705.   Continued Use of Partnership Name. 106

[ARTICLE] 8
DISSOLUTION AND WINDING UP

801.   Events Causing Dissolution. 106
802.   Winding Up. 109
803.   Rescinding Dissolution. 109
804.   Power to Bind Partnership After Dissolution. 110
805.   Liability After Dissolution of Partner and Person Dissociated as Partner. 110
806.   Disposition of Assets in Winding Up; When Contributions Required. 111
807.   Known Claims Against Dissolved Limited Liability Partnership. 112
808.   Other Claims Against Dissolved Limited Liability Partnership. 113
809.   Court Proceedings. 114
810.   Liability of Partner and Person Dissociated as Partner When Claim Against Partnership Barred. 114

[ARTICLE] 9
LIMITED LIABILITY PARTNERSHIP

901.   Statement of Qualification. 114
902.   Permitted Names. 116
908.   Registered Agent. 116
912.   Service of Process, Notice, or Demand. 117
913.   [Annual] [Biennial] Report for [Secretary of State]. 117

[ARTICLE] 10
FOREIGN LIMITED LIABILITY PARTNERSHIP

1001.   Governing Law. 118
1002.   Registration to Do Business in This State. 118

[ARTICLE] 11
MERGER, INTEREST EXCHANGE, CONVERSION, AND DOMESTICATION

[PART] 1
GENERAL PROVISIONS

1101. Definitions...119
1102. Relationship of [Article] to Other Laws...................................123
1103. Required Notice or Approval..123
1104. Nonexclusivity...124
1106. Appraisal Rights...124

[PART] 2
MERGER

1121. Merger Authorized...124
1122. Plan of Merger..125
1123. Approval of Merger...125
1126. Effect of Merger..126

[PART] 3
INTEREST EXCHANGE

1131. Interest Exchange Authorized..127
1132. Plan of Interest Exchange..128
1133. Approval of Interest Exchange...128
1136. Effect of Interest Exchange..129

[PART] 4
CONVERSION

1141. Conversion Authorized...130
1142. Plan of Conversion..130
1143. Approval of Conversion..130
1146. Effect of Conversion...131

[PART] 5
DOMESTICATION

1151. Domestication Authorized..132
1152. Plan of Domestication..133
1153. Approval of Domestication...133
1156. Effect of Domestication...133

PREFATORY NOTE TO 2011 AND 2013 HARMONIZATION AMENDMENTS

From 2009 to 2013, the Uniform Law Conference undertook an intensive effort to harmonize, to the extent possible, all uniform acts pertaining to unincorporated organizations. As part of that effort, the Uniform Partnership Act (1997) underwent four types of changes: substantive; major improvements in language; minor revisions in language for the sake of harmonization; and relocation within this particular "spoke" of provisions that are part of the "HUB" in the new Uniform Business Organizations Code ("UBOC").

Substantive Changes

The most significant substantive changes are:

- simplifying the section on "knowledge" and "notice," Section 103;

- centralizing constructive notice provisions, Section 103(d);

- revising and expanding provisions pertaining to the partnership agreement, Sections 105–107;

- updating various filing provisions pertaining to limited liability partnerships, Sections 108–118;

- providing that, in the context of a claim to "pierce the veil" of a limited liability partnership, "[t]he failure of [the] limited liability partnership to observe formalities relating to the exercise of its powers or management of its business is not a ground for imposing liability on a partner for a debt, obligation, or other liability of the partnership," Section 306(d);

- providing rules on unlawful distributions, Sections 406–407;

- "uncabining" (*i.e.*, making non-exhaustive) the codification of fiduciary duties, Section 409 (a)–(b);

- making clear that the act's obligation of good faith and fair dealing is the common law obligation of contract law, Section 409(d);

- adding as an event causing dissolution "the passage of 90 consecutive days during which the partnership does not have at least two partners," Section 801(6); and

- adding the comprehensive provisions of the Model Entity Transactions Act, Article 11.

Substantial Improvements to Language

The most significant improvements in language appear in Section 105 (formerly Section 103), the first of three sections addressing the partnership agreement. The structure of Section 105 is far less complicated than the structure of former Section 103.

Harmonization-Based Language Changes

Minor changes in language for the sake of harmonization appear throughout the act.

Relocation and Renumbering of HUB-Based Provisions

The Harmonization Project included both the harmonization of various stand-alone acts and the compilation of UBOC, which comprises a "HUB" (somewhat analogous to Article 1 of the Uniform Commercial Code) and various spokes. Each spoke pertains to a different type of organization (*e.g.*, general partnership, limited partnership, limited liability company, statutory trust entity). Naturally, spokes in the Code do not repeat the provisions from the HUB. In contrast, each stand-alone act includes provisions that appear in the HUB in the Code.

So that the section numbers of this "spoke" correspond with the spoke provisions in the Code, HUB-based provisions of this Act have been renumbered to appear at the end of articles. *See, e.g.*, Sections 112–121. . . .

[ARTICLE] 1

GENERAL PROVISIONS

Sec.
101. Short Title.
102. Definitions.
103. Knowledge; Notice.
104. Governing Law.
105. Partnership Agreement; Scope, Function, and Limitations.
106. Partnership Agreement; Effect on Partnership and Person Becoming Partner; Preformation Agreement.
107. Partnership Agreement; Effect on Third Parties and Relationship to Records Effective on Behalf of Partnership.
118. Reservation of Power to Amend or Repeal.
119. Supplemental Principles of Law.

§ 101. SHORT TITLE.

This [act] may be cited as the Uniform Partnership Act.

§ 102. DEFINITIONS.

In this [act]:

(1) "Business" includes every trade, occupation, and profession.

(2) "Contribution", except in the phrase "right of contribution", means property or a benefit described in Section 403 which is provided by a person to a partnership to become a partner or in the person's capacity as a partner.

(3) "Debtor in bankruptcy" means a person that is the subject of:

(A) an order for relief under Title 11 of the United States Code or a comparable order under a successor statute of general application; or

(B) a comparable order under federal, state, or foreign law governing insolvency.

(4) "Distribution" means a transfer of money or other property from a partnership to a person on account of a transferable interest or in a person's capacity as a partner. The term:

(A) includes:

(i) a redemption or other purchase by a partnership of a transferable interest; and

(ii) a transfer to a partner in return for the partner's relinquishment of any right to participate as a partner in the management or conduct of the partnership's business or have access to records or other information concerning the partnership's business; and

(B) does not include amounts constituting reasonable compensation for present or past service or payments made in the ordinary course of business under a bona fide retirement plan or other bona fide benefits program.

(5) "Foreign limited liability partnership" means a foreign partnership whose partners have limited liability for the debts, obligations, or other liabilities of the foreign partnership under a provision similar to Section 306(c).

(6) "Foreign partnership" means an unincorporated entity formed under the law of a jurisdiction other than this state which would be a partnership if formed under the law of this state. The term includes a foreign limited liability partnership.

(7) "Jurisdiction", used to refer to a political entity, means the United States, a state, a foreign country, or a political subdivision of a foreign country.

(8) "Jurisdiction of formation" means the jurisdiction whose law governs the internal affairs of an entity.

(9) "Limited liability partnership", except in the phrase "foreign limited liability partnership" and in [Article] 11, means a partnership that has filed a statement of qualification under Section 901 and does not have a similar statement in effect in any other jurisdiction.

(10) "Partner" means a person that:

(A) has become a partner in a partnership under Section 402 or was a partner in a partnership when the partnership became subject to this [act] under Section 110; and

(B) has not dissociated as a partner under Section 601.

(11) "Partnership", except in [Article] 11, means an association of two or more persons to carry on as co-owners a business for profit formed under this [act] or that becomes subject to this [act] under [Article] 11 or Section 110. The term includes a limited liability partnership.

(12) "Partnership agreement" means the agreement, whether or not referred to as a partnership agreement and whether oral, implied, in a record, or in any combination thereof, of all the partners of

a partnership concerning the matters described in Section 105(a). The term includes the agreement as amended or restated.

(13) "Partnership at will" means a partnership in which the partners have not agreed to remain partners until the expiration of a definite term or the completion of a particular undertaking.

(14) "Person" means an individual, business corporation, nonprofit corporation, partnership, limited partnership, limited liability company, [general cooperative association,] limited cooperative association, unincorporated nonprofit association, statutory trust, business trust, common-law business trust, estate, trust, association, joint venture, public corporation, government or governmental subdivision, agency, or instrumentality, or any other legal or commercial entity.

(15) "Principal office" means the principal executive office of a partnership or a foreign limited liability partnership, whether or not the office is located in this state.

(16) "Property" means all property, whether real, personal, or mixed or tangible or intangible, or any right or interest therein.

(17) "Record", used as a noun, means information that is inscribed on a tangible medium or that is stored in an electronic or other medium and is retrievable in perceivable form.

(18) "Registered agent" means an agent of a limited liability partnership or foreign limited liability partnership which is authorized to receive service of any process, notice, or demand required or permitted by law to be served on the partnership.

(19) "Registered foreign limited liability partnership" means a foreign limited liability partnership that is registered to do business in this state pursuant to a statement of registration filed by the [Secretary of State].

(20) "Sign" means, with present intent to authenticate or adopt a record:

    (A)   to execute or adopt a tangible symbol; or

    (B)   to attach to or logically associate with the record an electronic symbol, sound, or process.

(21) "State" means a state of the United States, the District of Columbia, Puerto Rico, the United States Virgin Islands, or any territory or insular possession subject to the jurisdiction of the United States.

(22) "Transfer" includes:

    (A)   an assignment;

    (B)   a conveyance;

    (C)   a sale;

    (D)   a lease;

    (E)   an encumbrance, including a mortgage or security interest;

    (F)   a gift; and

    (G)   a transfer by operation of law.

(23) "Transferable interest" means the right, as initially owned by a person in the person's capacity as a partner, to receive distributions from a partnership, whether or not the person remains a partner or continues to own any part of the right. The term applies to any fraction of the interest, by whomever owned.

(24) "Transferee" means a person to which all or part of a transferable interest has been transferred, whether or not the transferor is a partner.

Comment

UPA (1997) section 101 defined fourteen terms. This section defines twenty-four terms. The increase is generally due to harmonization and more particularly to changes made to bring the LLP provisions pertaining to limited liability and filings into line with the corresponding provisions of . . . [the other uniform acts].

"Foreign limited liability partnership" and "Foreign partnership" [(5) and (6)]—These definitions intend a flexible, comparative approach. Under Paragraph 6, if a particular type of foreign entity has key legal characteristics that approximate the essential legal characteristics of a domestic general partnership, that particular type of foreign entity is a foreign partnership under this act. Likewise, under Paragraph 5, if a foreign partnership has a liability shield similar to the shield provided under this act for a domestic LLP, the foreign partnership is a foreign limited liability partnership. . . .

"Limited liability partnership" [(9)]—Under this act (and most, if not all, LLP statutes), a general partnership obtains its LLP status from only one jurisdiction. The resulting LLP is "domestic" with regard to that jurisdiction and "foreign" with regard to all others. . . .

"Partner" [(10)]—Under Section 202(a), any "person" can be a partner. Paragraph 14 of this section defines "person" very broadly to include individuals and "any . . . legal or commercial entity." At common law, "[t]he general rule . . . [was] that every person of sound mind, *sui juris*, and not otherwise restrained by law, may enter into a contract of partnership." JOSEPH STORY, COMMENTARIES ON THE LAW ON PARTNERSHIP § 7, at 10 (2d ed. 1850). The phrase "sound mind" and the term *"sui juris"* suggest that at common law a partner was necessarily an individual. *See* BLACK'S LAW DICTIONARY (9th ed. 2009) (defining *sui juris* as one "[o]f full age and capacity"). UPA (1914) § 2 defined "person" to include "partnerships, corporations, and other associations." *See, e.g., Williams v. Mammoth of Alaska, Inc.,* 890 P.2d 581, 584 n.8 (Alaska 1995*)* (stating that under UPA (1914) "[a] partner need not be a natural person").

After a person has been dissociated as a partner under Section 602, the term "partner" continues to apply to the person's conduct while a partner. *See* Section 603(b).

"Partnership" [(11)]—This definition, combined with Section 202(a), makes clear that a general partnership is a *business* organization. This definition makes no reference to a partnership having partners upon formation, but Section 202(a) does.

"Partnership agreement" [(12)]—This definition must be read in conjunction with Sections 105 through 107, which further describe the partnership agreement. In particular, although this definition refers to "the agreement . . . of all the partners," the partnership itself is bound by and may enforce the agreement. Section 106(a).

A partnership agreement is a contract, and therefore all statutory language pertaining to the partnership agreement must be understood in the context of the law of contracts.

The definition in Paragraph 12 is very broad and recognizes a wide scope of authority for the partnership agreement: "the matters described in Section 105(a)." Those matters include not only all relations *inter se* the partners and the partnership but also "the business of the partnership and the conduct of that business." Section 105(a)(2). Moreover, the definition puts no limits on the form of the partnership agreement. To the contrary, the definition contains the phrase "whether oral, implied, in a record, or in any combination thereof."

Unless the partnership agreement itself provides otherwise:

- A partnership agreement may comprise a number of separate documents (or records), however denominated; and

- Subject to Section 106(b) (deeming new partners to assent to the then-existing partnership agreement), a document, record, understanding, etc. can be part of the partnership agreement only with the assent of all persons then partners.

An agreement among less than all partners might well be enforceable among those partners as parties, but would not be part of the partnership agreement. However, under Section 105(a)(3), an amendment to a partnership agreement can be made with less than unanimous consent if the partnership agreement itself so provides.

An agreement to form a partnership is not itself a partnership agreement. The term "partnership agreement" presupposes "partners," and a person cannot be a partner in a partnership before the partnership exists. However, as soon as a partnership comes into existence, it perforce has a partnership agreement. For example, suppose: (i) two persons orally and informally agree to join their activities in a manner that satisfies Section 202 (formation of partnership); (ii) the partnership is thus formed; and (iii) without further ado or agreement, the persons become the partnership's initial partners. A partnership agreement exists. In the words of Paragraph 12 "all the partners" have agreed who the partners are and that, as "all the partners," they will conduct a business. That agreement—no matter how informal or rudimentary—is an agreement "concerning the matters described in Section 105(a)." To the extent the agreement does not provide the *inter se* "rules of the game," the "default rules" of this act "fill in the gaps." Section 105(b).

This act states no rule as to whether the statute of frauds applies to partnership agreements. Case law suggests that the answer is yes:

Partnership agreements, like other contracts, are subject to the Statute of Frauds. A contract of partnership for a term exceeding one year is within the Statute of Frauds and is void unless it is in writing [and signed by the party to be bound]; however, a contract establishing a partnership terminable at the will of any partner is generally held to be capable of performance by its terms within one year of its making and, therefore, to be outside the Statute of Frauds.

Abbott v. Hurst, 643 So. 2d 589, 592 (Ala. 1994) (citations omitted).

Likewise, the land provision of the statute of frauds:

applies to an oral contract to transfer or convey partnership real property, and the interest of the other partners therein, to one partner as an individual, as well as to a parol contract by one of the parties to convey certain land owned by him individually to the partnership, or to another partner, or to put it into the partnership stock.

Froiseth v. Nowlin, 287 P. 55, 56 (Wash. 1930) (quoting 27 C.J.S. § 220). . . .

In contrast, the land provision does not apply to a partner's interest in a partnership, no matter how much the partnership owns or deals in real property. Interests in a partnership are personal property and reflect no direct interest in the entity's assets. *See* Sections 102(23), 501. Thus, the real property issues pertaining to a partnership ownership of land do not "flow through" to the partners and partnership interests. . . .

"Partnership at will" [(13)]—This paragraph defines "partnership at will" in the negative (*i.e.*, by stating what the defined term is not). A partnership is "at will" if the partners' agreement does not obligate them to remain in the partnership until the passage of a specified time (a term) or the completion of a specified task, job, project, etc. (an undertaking).

"Partnership at will" is thus the default mode under this act; that is, a partnership is "at will" unless the partners have agreed otherwise. Absent such agreement, a partner may rightfully leave the partnership at any time (dissociate), Sections 601(1), 602(b)(2), and rightfully cause or seek the winding up of the partnership and its business (dissolution), Section 801(1). . . .

This act does not directly define "partnership for a term" and "partnership for an undertaking," but their respective meanings are clear from this paragraph's wording and the case law. . . .

"Principal office" [(15)]—. . . UPA (1997) referred to a partnership's "chief executive office," *e.g.*, UPA (1997) § 106(a), but did not define the term. *Id.*, cmt. The Harmonization Project substituted "principal office," as a more traditional and better-understood term in business entity statutes. In most cases, a partnership's principal office will be the same as the partnership's chief executive office (however defined). . . .

"Transferable interest" [(23)]—Absent a contrary provision in the partnership agreement or the consent of the partners, a "transferable interest" is the only interest in a partnership which can be transferred to a non-partner. . . .

UPA (1997) took a different approach, defining the entirety of a partner's rights directly and identifying the economic aspect through a limit on transferability. *See* UPA (1997) §§ 101(9) (defining "[p]artnership interest" or "partner's interest in the partnership" as "all of a partner's interests in the partnership, including the partner's transferable interest and all management and other rights"), 502 (stating that "the only transferable interest of a partner in the partnership is the partner's share of the profits and losses of the partnership and the partner's right to receive distributions").

This act defines "[t]ransferable interest" as an interest "initially owned by a person in the person's capacity as a partner," because this act does not contemplate a partnership directly creating interests that comprise only economic rights. *See* Sections 402 (addressing how a person becomes a partner), 503 (addressing how a person becomes a transferee).

§ 103.   KNOWLEDGE; NOTICE.

(a)   A person knows a fact if the person:

(1)   has actual knowledge of it; or

(2)   is deemed to know it under subsection (d)(1) or law other than this [act].

(b)   A person has notice of a fact if the person:

(1)   has reason to know the fact from all the facts known to the person at the time in question; or

(2)   is deemed to have notice of the fact under subsection (d)(2).

(c)   Subject to Section 117(f), a person notifies another person of a fact by taking steps reasonably required to inform the other person in ordinary course, whether or not those steps cause the other person to know the fact.

(d)   A person not a partner is deemed:

(1)   to know of a limitation on authority to transfer real property as provided in Section 303(g); and

(2)   to have notice of:

(A)   a person's dissociation as a partner 90 days after a statement of dissociation under Section 704 becomes effective; and

(B)   a partnership's:

(i)   dissolution 90 days after a statement of dissolution under Section 802 becomes effective;

(ii)   termination 90 days after a statement of termination under Section 802 becomes effective; and

(iii)   participation in a merger, interest exchange, conversion, or domestication, 90 days after articles of merger, interest exchange, conversion, or domestication under [Article] 11 become effective.

(e)   A partner's knowledge or notice of a fact relating to the partnership is effective immediately as knowledge of or notice to the partnership, except in the case of a fraud on the partnership committed by or with the consent of that partner.

Comment

The Harmonization Project made two important changes to this section. First, unlike UPA (1997), this act contains no generally applicable provisions determining when an organization other than a partnership is charged with knowledge or notice, because those imputation rules: (i) comprise core topics within the law of agency; (ii) are very complicated; (iii) should not have any different content under this act than in other circumstances; and (iv) are the subject of considerable attention in the Restatement (Third) of Agency (2006). However, Subsection (e) does provide a rule for attributing to a partnership knowledge or notice possessed by a partner.

Second, this act does not define "notice" to include "knowledge." Although conceptualizing the latter as giving the former makes logical sense and has a long pedigree, that conceptualization is counter-intuitive for the uninitiated. In ordinary usage, notice has a meaning separate from knowledge. This act follows ordinary usage and therefore contains some references to "knowledge or notice.". . .

Subsection (d)—Following the pioneering approach of UPA (1997), this subsection provides constructive notice of facts stated in specified filed public records. . . .

UPA (1997) used an oblique and decentralized approach to constructive notice . . . [by scattering its treatment of constructive notice among several provisions]. As revised by the Harmonization Project, this subsection provides directly for constructive notice and centralizes all of this act's constructive notice provisions except for those pertaining to statements of authority under Section 303.

Subsection (e)—This subsection states the rule for imputing a partner's knowledge or notice to the partnership. The rule was part of the common law. *Peoples' Bank of Baltimore v. Keech*, 26 Md. 521, 533 (Md. 1867) (holding that "the firm is bound by notice to one of the co-partners; because each represents the firm and is general agent of all"). . . .

§ 104.   GOVERNING LAW.

The internal affairs of a partnership and the liability of a partner as a partner for a debt, obligation, or other liability of the partnership are governed by:

(1)   in the case of a limited liability partnership, the law of this state; and

(2)   in the case of a partnership that is not a limited liability partnership, the law of the jurisdiction in which the partnership has its principal office.

Comment

. . .

Like any other legal concept, "internal affairs" may be indeterminate at its edges. However, the concept certainly includes interpretation and enforcement of the partnership agreement, relations among the partners as partners, and relations between the partnership and a partner as a partner. . . .

"Internal affairs" do not encompass the power *vel non* of a person to bind a partnership. RESTATEMENT (SECOND) OF CONFLICT OF LAWS §§ 292(2) (1971) ("The principal will be held bound by the agent's action if he would so be bound under the local law of the state where the agent dealt with the third person, provided at least that the principal had authorized the agent to act on his behalf in that state or had led the third person reasonably to believe that the agent had such authority."), 295(1) ("Whether a partnership is bound by action taken on its behalf by an agent in dealing with a third person is determined by the local law of the state selected by application of the rule of § 292."); RESTATEMENT (FIRST) OF CONFLICT OF LAWS § 345, cmt. c (1934) (Law Governing Effect of Act of Agent or Partner) ("If . . . the principal or partner sends the agent or other partner into a state to act on his behalf, he assumes the risk of liability not only for authorized but for unauthorized conduct of the agent or partner in accordance with the law of that state."); *see also Farm & Ranch Services, Ltd. v. LT Farm & Ranch, L.L.C.*, 779 F. Supp. 2d 949, 960 (S.D. Iowa 2011).

"Internal affairs" and the "liability of a partner as a partner" are mentioned separately, because it can be argued that the liability of partners to third parties is not an internal affair. *See, e.g.*, RESTATEMENT (SECOND) OF CONFLICT OF LAWS § 307 (1971) (treating shareholders' liability separately from the internal affairs doctrine). A few cases subsume owner/manager liability into internal affairs. . . .

§ 105.   PARTNERSHIP AGREEMENT; SCOPE, FUNCTION, AND LIMITATIONS.

(a)   Except as otherwise provided in subsections (c) and (d), the partnership agreement governs:

(1)   relations among the partners as partners and between the partners and the partnership;

(2)   the business of the partnership and the conduct of that business; and

(3)   the means and conditions for amending the partnership agreement.

(b)   To the extent the partnership agreement does not provide for a matter described in subsection (a), this [act] governs the matter.

(c)   A partnership agreement may not:

(1)   vary the law applicable under Section 104(1);

(2)   vary the provisions of Section 110;

(3)   vary the provisions of Section 307;

(4)   unreasonably restrict the duties and rights under Section 408, but the partnership agreement may impose reasonable restrictions on the availability and use of information obtained under that section and may define appropriate remedies, including liquidated damages, for a breach of any reasonable restriction on use;

(5)   alter or eliminate the duty of loyalty or the duty of care, except as otherwise provided in subsection (d);

(6)   eliminate the contractual obligation of good faith and fair dealing under Section 409(d), but the partnership agreement may prescribe the standards, if not manifestly unreasonable, by which the performance of the obligation is to be measured;

(7)   unreasonably restrict the right of a person to maintain an action under Section 410(b);

(8)   relieve or exonerate a person from liability for conduct involving bad faith, willful or intentional misconduct, or knowing violation of law;

(9)   vary the power of a person to dissociate as a partner under Section 602(a), except to require that the notice under Section 601(1) be in a record;

(10) vary the grounds for expulsion specified in Section 601(5);

(11) vary the causes of dissolution specified in Section 801(4) or (5);

(12) vary the requirement to wind up the partnership's business as specified in Section 802(a), (b)(1), and (d);

(13) vary the right of a partner under Section 901(f) to vote on or consent to a cancellation of a statement of qualification;

(14) vary the right of a partner to approve a merger, interest exchange, conversion, or domestication under Section 1123(a)(2), 1133(a)(2), 1143(a)(2), or 1153(a)(2);

(15) vary the required contents of a plan of merger under Section 1122(a), plan of interest exchange under Section 1132(a), plan of conversion under Section 1142(a), or plan of domestication under Section 1152(a);

(16) vary any requirement, procedure, or other provision of this [act] pertaining to:

(A)   registered agents; or

(B)   the [Secretary of State], including provisions pertaining to records authorized or required to be delivered to the [Secretary of State] for filing under this [act]; or

(17) except as otherwise provided in Sections 106 and 107(b), restrict the rights under this [act] of a person other than a partner.

(d)   Subject to subsection (c)(8), without limiting other terms that may be included in a partnership agreement, the following rules apply:

(1)   The partnership agreement may:

(A)   specify the method by which a specific act or transaction that would otherwise violate the duty of loyalty may be authorized or ratified by one or more disinterested and independent persons after full disclosure of all material facts; and

(B)   alter the prohibition in Section 406(a)(2) so that the prohibition requires only that the partnership's total assets not be less than the sum of its total liabilities.

(2)   To the extent the partnership agreement expressly relieves a partner of a responsibility that the partner would otherwise have under this [act] and imposes the responsibility on one or more other partners, the agreement also may eliminate or limit any fiduciary duty of the partner relieved of the responsibility which would have pertained to the responsibility.

(3)   If not manifestly unreasonable, the partnership agreement may:

(A)   alter or eliminate the aspects of the duty of loyalty stated in Section 409(b);

(B)   identify specific types or categories of activities that do not violate the duty of loyalty;

(C)   alter the duty of care, but may not authorize conduct involving bad faith, willful or intentional misconduct, or knowing violation of law; and

(D)   alter or eliminate any other fiduciary duty.

(e)   The court shall decide as a matter of law whether a term of a partnership agreement is manifestly unreasonable under subsection (c)(6) or (d)(3). The court:

    (1)   shall make its determination as of the time the challenged term became part of the partnership agreement and by considering only circumstances existing at that time; and

    (2)   may invalidate the term only if, in light of the purposes and business of the partnership, it is readily apparent that:

        (A)   the objective of the term is unreasonable; or

        (B)   the term is an unreasonable means to achieve the term's objective.

Comment

The Harmonization Project re-wrote this section, for the most part conforming this section to the corresponding section of ULLCA (2006).

Principal Provisions of the Act Concerning the Partnership Agreement

The partnership agreement is pivotal to a partnership, and Sections 105 through 107 are pivotal to this act. They must be read together, along with Section 102(12) (defining the partnership agreement).

This section performs five essential functions. Subsection (a) establishes the primacy of the partnership agreement in establishing *inter se* relations among the partners and partnership. Subsection (b) recognizes this act as comprising mostly default rules (*i.e.*, gap fillers for issues as to which the partnership agreement provides no rule). Subsection (c) lists the few mandatory provisions of the act. Subsection (d) lists some provisions frequently found in partnership agreements, authorizing some unconditionally and others so long as "not manifestly unreasonable." Subsection (e) delineates in detail both the meaning of "not manifestly unreasonable" and the information relevant to determining a claim that a provision of a partnership agreement is manifestly unreasonable.

Section 106 details the effect of a partnership agreement on the partnership and on persons becoming partners. Section 107 concerns the effect of a partnership agreement on third parties.

Role and Inevitability of Partnership Agreement

. . .

The partnership agreement is the exclusive consensual process for modifying this act's various default rules pertaining to relationships *inter se* the partners and between the partners and the partnership. . . .

The Partnership Agreement and the Fiduciary and Other Duties of Those Who Manage

One of the most complex questions in the law of unincorporated business organizations is the extent to which an agreement among the organization's owners can affect the fiduciary and other duties of those who have ultimate power to manage the organization—in a general partnership, the partners themselves. As explained in detail in the comment to Subsection (d)(3), this act rejects the notion that a contract can completely transform an inherently fiduciary relationship into a merely arm's length association. Within that limitation, however, this section provides substantial power to the partnership agreement to reshape, limit, and eliminate fiduciary and other managerial duties.

Subsection (a) recognizes that the partnership agreement is the map to the parties' deal and that any claim by a partner of managerial misconduct must be assessed first under the relevant terms of the partnership agreement. Subsection (d) specifically validates arrangements commonly used to reshape managerial duties and limit the consequences of breaching those duties. Subsection (c) contains relevant limitations, but those limitations: (i) must be read together with Subsection (d); and (ii) do not preclude the partnership agreement fundamentally redesigning the duties applicable to the partners. For the act's design of those duties, see Sections 408 and 409.

Subsection (a)—This section describes the very broad scope of a partnership's partnership agreement, which includes all matters constituting "internal affairs." . . .

Subsection (a)(3)—Under this provision, the partnership agreement can control both the quantum of consent required (*e.g.*, majority of partners) and the means by which the consent is manifested (*e.g.*, prohibiting modifications except when consented to in writing). . . .

If the partnership agreement does not address the issue, Section 401(k) applies . . .

Subsection (c)—This subsection lists provisions of this act whose respective effects cannot be varied or may be varied subject to a stated limitation. . . .

Subsection (c)(3)—Under this act, a partnership is emphatically an entity, and the partners lack the power to alter that characteristic. . . .

Subsection (c)(5)—This limitation is less powerful than might first appear, because Subsection (d) specifically authorizes substantial alterations to the duties of loyalty and care, including restricting and substantially eliminating those duties.

Subsection (c)(6)—Section 409(d) refers to the "contractual obligation of good faith and fair dealing," which contract law implies in every contract. The partnership agreement cannot eliminate this obligation, neither in whole (*i.e.*, generally) nor in part (*i.e.*, as applicable to specified situations).

However, a partnership agreement may "prescribe the standards . . . by which the performance of [that] obligation is to be measured."

EXAMPLE: A partnership agreement designates a managing partner, provides that partner almost total control of the partnership's operations, and grants the partner the discretion to cause the partnership to enter into contracts with affiliates of the partner (so-called "Conflict Transactions"). The agreement further provides: "When causing the Company to enter into a Conflict Transaction, the Managing Partner complies with Section 409(d) of [this act] if a disinterested person, knowledgeable in the subject matter, states in writing that the terms and conditions of the Conflict Transaction are equivalent to the terms and conditions that would be agreed to by persons at arm's length in comparable circumstances." This provision "prescribes[s] the standards by which the performance of the [Section 409(d)] obligation is to be measured.". . .

Subsection (c)(7)—Section 410(b) delineates a partner's rights to "maintain an action against the partnership or another partner." It would be unreasonable to frustrate these rights but not unreasonable to channel their exercise. For example, the partnership agreement might select a forum, require pre-suit mediation, provide for arbitration, or require a pre-suit demand on a management committee before a partner files suit against the partnership. Similarly, it is not unreasonable to provide for liquidated damages consonant with the law of contracts. In contrast, it would be unreasonable for a partnership agreement to both: (i) require a partner intending to sue the partnership to make demand on a management committee before filing suit against the partnership regardless of futility; and (ii) bar taking the claim to court no matter how long the management committee ponders the demand.

Subsection (c)(8)—These restrictions are ubiquitous in the law of business entities and, in conjunction with other provisions of this section, control the otherwise very broad power of a partnership agreement to affect fiduciary and other duties. The restrictions are central to the raft of exculpatory provisions that sprung up in corporate statutes in response to *Smith v. Van Gorkum*, 488 A.2d 858 (Del. 1985). . . .

Subsection (c)(9)—As a result of this restriction, a partner always has the power to dissociate; the partnership agreement can only negate the right. This approach is consistent with the notions that: (i) a partnership is a voluntary association, *see, e.g., Gangl v. Gangl*, 281 N.W.2d 574, 580 (N.D. 1979) (stating that "[t]he term [association] connotes not only a group of two or more persons but also voluntariness"); (ii) the partnership relationship is essentially contractual, *see, e.g., Wallner v. Schmitz*, 239 Minn. 93, 95, 57 N.W.2d 821, 823 (1953) (stating that "[a] partnership is a contractual relationship as between the parties"); and (iii) only in exceptional circumstances does a party to a contract lack the power to breach, and courts will not enjoin a person to remain in an ongoing contractual relationship that involves trust and confidence. E. ALLAN FARNSWORTH, CONTRACTS § 12.7, at 781 (3d ed.1999) ("A court will not grant specific performance of a contract to provide a service that is personal in nature. This refusal . . . is based [in part] of the undesirability of compelling the continuance of personal relations after disputes have arisen and confidence and loyalty have been shaken and the undesirability, in some instances, of imposing what might seem like involuntary servitude."). . . .

Subsection (c)(11)—The partnership agreement may not change the stated grounds for dissolution but may determine the forum in which a claim for dissolution under Section 801(4) or (5) is determined. For example, arbitration and forum selection clauses are commonplace in business relationships in general and in partnership agreements in particular. . . .

Subsection (c)(17)—This limitation pertains only to "the rights under this [act] of" third parties" other than partners. Moreover, the limitation is subject to two major exceptions: Section 106 (pertaining to the partnership agreement's relationship to the partnership itself and to persons becoming partners) and Section 107(b) (pertaining to the partnership agreement's power over the rights of transferees).

Subsection (d)—The partnership agreement has plenipotentiary power over the matters described in Subsection (a), except as specifically limited by Subsections (c) and (d)(3). However, for the convenience of practitioners and the courts, Paragraphs 1 and 2 list various terms often found in partnership agreements. No negative inference should be drawn about terms not listed; the listing is provided "without limiting other terms that may be included in a partnership agreement."

Paragraph 3 lists arrangements subject to the "not manifestly unreasonable" standard. Subsection (e) delineates that standard. The same standard applies to terms of a partnership agreement which seek to "prescribe the standards . . . by which the performance of the [contractual] obligation [of good faith and fair dealing under Section 409(d)] is to be measured." Subsection (c)(6).

Section (d)(3)—This act rejects the ultra-contractarian notion that fiduciary duty within a business organization is merely a set of default rules and seeks instead to balance the virtues of "freedom of contract" against the dangers that inescapably exist when some persons have power over the interests of others.

Nonetheless, a properly drafted partnership agreement may substantially alter and even eliminate fiduciary duties. Two important limitations exist. First, arrangements subject to this subsection may not be "manifestly unreasonable." *See* Subsection (e) (delineating this standard).

Second, the partnership agreement may not transform the relationship *inter se* partners and the partnership into an entirely arm's length arrangement. For example, displacement of fiduciary duties is effective only to the extent that the displacement is stated clearly and with particularity. This rule is fundamental in the jurisprudence of fiduciary duty. . . .

Although Subsection (d)(3) does not expressly address contracts between a partnership and a partner, the stated constraints must also apply to such contracts. . . .

Subsection (e)—The "not manifestly unreasonable" concept became part of uniform business entity statutes when UPA (1997) imported the concept from the Uniform Commercial Code. . . .

Subsection (e) is fundamental to this act, because: (i) this act generally defers to the agreement among the partners; and (ii) Subsection (e) safeguards the partnership agreement in at least four ways:

- Determining manifest unreasonableness *inter se* owners of an organization is a different task than doing so in a commercial context, where concepts like "usages of trade" are available to inform the analysis. Each business organization must be understood in its own terms and context.

- If loosely applied, the concept of "manifestly unreasonable" would permit a court to rewrite the partners' agreement, which would destroy the balance this act seeks to establish between freedom of contract and fiduciary duty.

- Case law has not adequately delineated the concept. . . .

- In the context of statutes permitting stock transfer restrictions unless "manifestly unreasonable," courts have often ignored the word "manifestly." . . .

§ 106. PARTNERSHIP AGREEMENT; EFFECT ON PARTNERSHIP AND PERSON BECOMING PARTNER; PREFORMATION AGREEMENT.

(a)   A partnership is bound by and may enforce the partnership agreement, whether or not the partnership has itself manifested assent to the agreement.

(b)   A person that becomes a partner is deemed to assent to the partnership agreement.

(c)   Two or more persons intending to become the initial partners of a partnership may make an agreement providing that upon the formation of the partnership the agreement will become the partnership agreement.

Comment

Subsection (a)—This subsection resolves twin questions that have troubled some courts—namely, whether an unincorporated entity that has not signed its foundational agreement nonetheless is bound by and may enforce the agreement. . . .

This subsection answers the twin questions, categorically and in the affirmative. . . .

§ 107. PARTNERSHIP AGREEMENT; EFFECT ON THIRD PARTIES AND RELATIONSHIP TO RECORDS EFFECTIVE ON BEHALF OF PARTNERSHIP.

(a)   A partnership agreement may specify that its amendment requires the approval of a person that is not a party to the agreement or the satisfaction of a condition. An amendment is ineffective if its adoption does not include the required approval or satisfy the specified condition.

(b)   The obligations of a partnership and its partners to a person in the person's capacity as a transferee or person dissociated as a partner are governed by the partnership agreement. Subject only to a court order issued under Section 504(b)(2) to effectuate a charging order, an amendment to the partnership agreement made after a person becomes a transferee or is dissociated as a partner:

(1)   is effective with regard to any debt, obligation, or other liability of the partnership or its partners to the person in the person's capacity as a transferee or person dissociated as a partner; and

(2)   is not effective to the extent the amendment:

(A)   imposes a new debt, obligation, or other liability on the transferee or person dissociated as a partner; or

(B)   prejudices the rights under Section 701 of a person that dissociated as a partner before the amendment was made.

(c)   If a record delivered by a partnership to the [Secretary of State] for filing becomes effective and contains a provision that would be ineffective under Section 105(c) or (d)(3) if contained in the partnership agreement, the provision is ineffective in the record.

(d)   Subject to subsection (c), if a record delivered by a partnership to the [Secretary of State] for filing becomes effective and conflicts with a provision of the partnership agreement:

(1)   the agreement prevails as to partners, persons dissociated as partners, and transferees; and

(2)   the record prevails as to other persons to the extent they reasonably rely on the record.

Comment

. . .

Subsection (b)—The law of unincorporated business organizations is only beginning to grapple in a modern way with the tension between the rights of an organization's owners to carry on their activities as they see fit (or have agreed) and the rights of transferees of the organization's economic interests. If, as is often the situation, the partnership agreement overrides Section 701 (Purchase of Interest of Person Dissociated as Partner), such transferees can include the heirs of the partnership's founders as well as former partners who, by agreement, are "locked in" as transferees of their own interests. . . .

This subsection . . . expressly subject[s]. . . transferees (including a person dissociated as a partner) to partnership agreement amendments made after the transfer or dissociation, except amendments that increase obligations on transferees. For example, an amendment might extend the duration of a partnership but may not institute a new capital call obligation on transferees.

The issue of whether, in extreme and sufficiently harsh circumstances, transferees might be able to claim some type of duty or obligation to protect against expropriation awaits development in the case law. An unreported LLC case suggests the answer might be yes, but the decision rests primarily on the wording of the LLC's operating agreement. In *Kohannim v. Katoli*, 08-11-00155-CV, 2013 WL 3943078, at *10–11 (Tex. App. July 24, 2013). . . .

For the very limited statutory rights of transferees, see Section 503.

§ 118.   RESERVATION OF POWER TO AMEND OR REPEAL.

The [legislature of this state] has power to amend or repeal all or part of this [act] at any time, and all limited liability partnerships and foreign limited liability partnerships subject to this [act] are governed by the amendment or repeal.

Comment

Provisions similar to this section have their genesis in *Trustees of Dartmouth College v. Woodward*, 17 U.S. (4 Wheat) 518 (1819), which held that the United States Constitution prohibited the application of newly enacted statutes to existing corporations while suggesting the efficacy of a reservation of power similar to this section. . . .

§ 119.   SUPPLEMENTAL PRINCIPLES OF LAW.

Unless displaced by particular provisions of this [act], the principles of law and equity supplement this [act].

[ARTICLE] 2

NATURE OF PARTNERSHIP

Sec.
201.   Partnership As Entity.
202.   Formation of Partnership.
203.   Partnership Property.
204.   When Property Is Partnership Property.

§ 201.   PARTNERSHIP AS ENTITY.

(a)   A partnership is an entity distinct from its partners.

(b)   A partnership is the same entity regardless of whether the partnership has a statement of qualification in effect under Section 901.

Comment

Subsection (a)—The law of general partnerships long struggled with the question of whether a partnership is merely an aggregate of its partners or an entity distinct from its partners. . . .

According to the comment to this section, UPA (1997) "embrace[d] the entity theory of the partnership," characterized "the entity theory as the dominant model" for the act, and highlighted a key problem arising from the aggregate aspect of UPA (1914)—namely, "the necessity of a deed to convey title from the 'old' partnership to the 'new' partnership every time there is a change of cast among the partners." . . .

The Harmonization process made no changes to this aspect of UPA (1997). . . .

§ 202.   FORMATION OF PARTNERSHIP.

(a)   Except as otherwise provided in subsection (b), the association of two or more persons to carry on as co-owners a business for profit forms a partnership, whether or not the persons intend to form a partnership.

(b)   An association formed under a statute other than this [act], a predecessor statute, or a comparable statute of another jurisdiction is not a partnership under this [act].

(c)   In determining whether a partnership is formed, the following rules apply:

(1)   Joint tenancy, tenancy in common, tenancy by the entireties, joint property, common property, or part ownership does not by itself establish a partnership, even if the co-owners share profits made by the use of the property.

(2)   The sharing of gross returns does not by itself establish a partnership, even if the persons sharing them have a joint or common right or interest in property from which the returns are derived.

(3)   A person who receives a share of the profits of a business is presumed to be a partner in the business, unless the profits were received in payment:

(A)   of a debt by installments or otherwise;

[handwritten: ↓ rebuttable by list following]

*[handwritten bottom left: *no formal agreement required, intent may be implied from their conduct]*

*[handwritten bottom right: *writing generally not required (should if partnership over a year)]*

(B)   for services as an independent contractor or of wages or other compensation to an employee;

(C)   of rent;

(D)   of an annuity or other retirement or health benefit to a deceased or retired partner or a beneficiary, representative, or designee of a deceased or retired partner;

(E)   of interest or other charge on a loan, even if the amount of payment varies with the profits of the business, including a direct or indirect present or future ownership of the collateral, or rights to income, proceeds, or increase in value derived from the collateral; or

(F)   for the sale of the goodwill of a business or other property by installments or otherwise.

Comment

UPA (1997) § 202 combined UPA (1914) §§ 6 and 7, recasting the "definition" of a partnership in UPA (1914) § 6(1) "as an operative rule of law—*i.e.*, "[a] partnership is an association of two or more persons. . . ." became "the association of two or more persons. . . forms." The change was stylistic and made no substantive change in the law. The Harmonization Project made no substantive change to this section. . . .

The addition of the phrase, "whether or not the persons intend to form a partnership," merely codifies the universal judicial construction of UPA (1914) § 6(1) that a partnership is created by the association of persons whose intent is to carry on as co-owners a business for profit, regardless of their subjective intention to be "partners." Indeed, they may inadvertently create a partnership despite their expressed subjective intention not to do so. The language of Section 202 alerts readers to this possibility.

Subsection (a)—Consistent with the common law and UPA (1914), under this act "co-ownership" is a key concept. Ownership involves the power of ultimate control (albeit a power that can be substantially diminished by agreement) and a right to share in the profits of the co-owned business. To state that partners are co-owners of a business is to state that: (i) they share in the profits (if any) of the enterprise; and (ii) *ab initio* at least, they collectively have the power of ultimate control. Consequently:

- mere passive co-ownership of property, as distinguished from using the property to carry on a business, does not establish a partnership, Subsection (c)(1); and

- merely sharing gross revenues is likewise insufficient, Subsection (c)(2).

UPA (1997) added, "whether or not the persons intend to form a partnership" to the UPA (1914) formulation, thereby codifying a rule uniformly applied by courts: Subjective intent to create the legal relationship of "partnership" is irrelevant. What matters is the intent *vel non* to establish the business relationship that the law labels a "partnership." Thus, a disclaimer of partnership status is ineffective to the extent the parties' intended arrangements meet the criteria stated in this subsection.

Subsection (b)—This subsection continues the UPA (1914) concept that the general partnership is the residual form of business association. Accordingly, partnership-like organizations formed under specially applicable statutes are not within this act. . . .

An arrangement labeled a "joint venture" is a partnership if the arrangement meets the criteria stated in Subsection (a). . . .

A limited partnership is not a partnership under this act; a limited partnership is "formed under a statute other than this [act]" (*i.e.*, ULPA (2001) (Last Amended 2013) § 201). . . .

Subsection (c)—UPA (1997) derived this subsection from UPA (1914) § 7 and with one exception, made no substantive change to the law. The substantive change pertains to the sharing of profits, which UPA (1997) recast as creating a rebuttable presumption of partnership rather merely constituting *prima facie* evidence. "*Prima facie*" means that the party with the burden of proof has adduced sufficient evidence to carry that burden, subject to the finder of fact's view of any contrary evidence. The burden of persuasion is unchanged. In contrast, "rebuttable presumption" switches the burden of persuasion.

Subsection (c)(3)—The protected categories listed in this paragraph apply regardless of whether the profit share is a single, unvarying percentage or a ratio that varies; for example, after reaching a dollar floor or different levels of profits. Like UPA (1914), this act makes no attempt to answer in every case whether a partnership is formed. Whether a relationship is more properly characterized as that of borrower and lender, employer and employee, or landlord and tenant is left to the trier of fact. As under UPA (1914), a person may function in both partner and non-partner capacities.

Subsection (c)(3)(E)—UPA (1997) added this protected category, excepting from the rebuttable presumption a share of the profits received in payment of interest or other charges on a loan, "including a direct or indirect present or future ownership in the collateral, or rights to income, proceeds, or increase in value derived from the collateral." . . .

§ 203. PARTNERSHIP PROPERTY.

Property acquired by a partnership is property of the partnership and not of the partners individually.

§ 204. WHEN PROPERTY IS PARTNERSHIP PROPERTY.

(a) Property is partnership property if acquired in the name of:

(1) the partnership; or

(2) one or more partners with an indication in the instrument transferring title to the property of the person's capacity as a partner or of the existence of a partnership but without an indication of the name of the partnership.

(b) Property is acquired in the name of the partnership by a transfer to:

(1) the partnership in its name; or

(2) one or more partners in their capacity as partners in the partnership, if the name of the partnership is indicated in the instrument transferring title to the property.

(c) Property is presumed to be partnership property if purchased with partnership assets, even if not acquired in the name of the partnership or of one or more partners with an indication in the instrument transferring title to the property of the person's capacity as a partner or of the existence of a partnership.

(d) Property acquired in the name of one or more of the partners, without an indication in the instrument transferring title to the property of the person's capacity as a partner or of the existence of a partnership and without use of partnership assets, is presumed to be separate property, even if used for partnership purposes. → separate property

Comment

Section 204 states the rules *inter se the partners and partnership* for determining when property is acquired by the partnership and so becomes partnership property. These rules apply to "all property, whether real, personal, or mixed or tangible or intangible, or any right or interest therein." Section 102(16) (defining "property").

These rules provide three separate approaches—according to:

- the name or names used in acquiring the property;

- when a partner's name appears as a transferee, the capacity in which the partner is acting; and

- for property acquired by purchase, whether the partnership provided the consideration for the property.

These approaches are complementary, not mutually exclusive. . . .

Subsections (c) and (d)—At least *inter se* the partners and partnership, it is the intention of the partners that controls whether property belongs to the partnership or to one or more of the partners in their individual capacities. These subsections each contain a rebuttable presumption as to the partners' intent. . . .

[ARTICLE] 3

RELATIONS OF PARTNERS TO PERSONS DEALING WITH PARTNERSHIP

Sec.
301. Partner Agent of Partnership.
302. Transfer of Partnership Property.
303. Statement of Partnership Authority.
304. Statement of Denial.
305. Partnership Liable for Partner's Actionable Conduct.
306. Partner's Liability.
307. Actions by and Against Partnership and Partners.
308. Liability of Purported Partner.

§ 301. PARTNER AGENT OF PARTNERSHIP.

Subject to the effect of a statement of partnership authority under Section 303, the following rules apply:

(1) Each partner is an agent of the partnership for the purpose of its business. An act of a partner, including the signing of an instrument in the partnership name, for apparently carrying on in the ordinary course the partnership business or business of the kind carried on by the partnership binds the partnership, unless the partner did not have authority to act for the partnership in the particular matter and the person with which the partner was dealing knew or had notice that the partner lacked authority.

(2) An act of a partner which is not apparently for carrying on in the ordinary course the partnership's business or business of the kind carried on by the partnership binds the partnership only if the act was actually authorized by all the other partners.

Comment

. . .

This section's principal purpose is to delineate a partner's statutory apparent authority. The partnership agreement and Section 401 govern the rights of the partners among themselves, including the right to restrict a partner's actual authority.

Section 301(1)—This paragraph retains the basic principles reflected in UPA (1914) § 9(1) and in effect characterizes a partner as a general managerial agent. Such agents have both actual and apparent authority, and this section delineates the apparent authority. . . .

The agency law origins of statutory apparent authority has informed courts' application of UPA (1914) § 9(1), and that case law is equally applicable under this act. . . .

[P]er the law of apparent authority, a partner can bind a partnership under this section even if the partner intends to take and does take the resulting benefits for the partner's own benefit. *See Wolfe v. Harms*, 413 S.W.2d 204, 216 (Mo. 1967) (stating that partnership is liable for partner's acts "even if the predominant motive of the partner was to benefit himself or third persons"). . . .

UPA (1997) § 301(1) effected three changes from UPA (1914) § 9(1). First, Section 301(1) clarified that a partner's apparent authority includes acts for carrying on in the ordinary course "business of the kind carried on by the partnership," not just the business of the particular partnership in question. . . .

The Harmonization Project preserved this UPA (1997) change, the significance of which depends on how broadly courts construe "business of the kind carried on by the partnership." For example, does a partnership that acts as a grain broker (never taking a position in grain) do business "of the kind carried on" by a partnership that buys grain for resale?

Second, UPA (1997) used "carrying on in the ordinary course" in lieu of the UPA (1914) phrase "in the usual way." . . .

The change in language had the benefit of aligning Section 301(1) with Section 305 (establishing attribution rules for a partner's wrongful conduct and referring to "ordinary course of business of the partnership" and "the ordinary course of the partnership's business"). The Harmonization Project also preserved this UPA (1997) change. . . .

UPA (1997)'s third change . . . concerned the allocation of risk of a partner's lack of authority. Under UPA (1914) § 9(1) and (4), a restriction on a partner's authority binds only a person with knowledge of the restriction. In contrast, UPA (1997) § 301(1) provides that a person who has received a notification of a restriction is also bound. Thus, UPA (1997) shifted the risk of lack of authority somewhat away from the partnership and somewhat toward third parties dealing with partners.

The Harmonization Project shifted the risk a bit further, binding third parties who know or *have reason to know* of a restriction. Section 301(1). (However, it is arguable that the Harmonization Project merely made explicit a rule implicit in the case law. As noted above, the case law requires a third party to show a *reasonable* belief in the partner's authority. A third party who has reason to know of a partner's lack of authority will be hard pressed to make that showing.)

Statements of partnership authority, Section 303, affect the application of this paragraph only in two ways. First, under Section 303(e) all persons (other than partners) are deemed to know of a limitation on the authority of a partner to transfer real property contained in a statement recorded in the appropriate land records. Second, a person (other than a partner) with actual knowledge of a grant or limitation of a partner's authority may rely on that knowledge. . . .

§ 302. TRANSFER OF PARTNERSHIP PROPERTY.

(a)   Partnership property may be transferred as follows:

(1)   Subject to the effect of a statement of partnership authority under Section 303, partnership property held in the name of the partnership may be transferred by an instrument of transfer signed by a partner in the partnership name.

(2)   Partnership property held in the name of one or more partners with an indication in the instrument transferring the property to them of their capacity as partners or of the existence of a partnership, but without an indication of the name of the partnership, may be transferred by an instrument of transfer signed by the persons in whose name the property is held.

(3)   Partnership property held in the name of one or more persons other than the partnership, without an indication in the instrument transferring the property to them of their capacity as partners or of the existence of a partnership, may be transferred by an instrument of transfer signed by the persons in whose name the property is held.

(b)   A partnership may recover partnership property from a transferee only if it proves that signing of the instrument of initial transfer did not bind the partnership under Section 301 and:

(1)   as to a subsequent transferee who gave value for property transferred under subsection (a)(1) and (2), proves that the subsequent transferee knew or had been notified that the person who signed the instrument of initial transfer lacked authority to bind the partnership; or

(2)   as to a transferee who gave value for property transferred under subsection (a)(3), proves that the transferee knew or had been notified that the property was partnership property and that the person who signed the instrument of initial transfer lacked authority to bind the partnership.

(c)   A partnership may not recover partnership property from a subsequent transferee if the partnership would not have been entitled to recover the property, under subsection (b), from any earlier transferee of the property.

(d)   If a person holds all the partners' interests in the partnership, all the partnership property vests in that person. The person may sign a record in the name of the partnership to evidence vesting of the property in that person and may file or record the record.

§ 303. STATEMENT OF PARTNERSHIP AUTHORITY.

(a) A partnership may deliver to the [Secretary of State] for filing a statement of partnership authority. The statement:

(1) must include the name of the partnership and:

(A) if the partnership is not a limited liability partnership, the street and mailing addresses of its principal office; or

(B) if the partnership is a limited liability partnership, the name and street and mailing addresses of its registered agent;

(2) with respect to any position that exists in or with respect to the partnership, may state the authority, or limitations on the authority, of all persons holding the position to:

(A) sign an instrument transferring real property held in the name of the partnership; or

(B) enter into other transactions on behalf of, or otherwise act for or bind, the partnership; and

(3) may state the authority, or limitations on the authority, of a specific person to:

(A) sign an instrument transferring real property held in the name of the partnership; or

(B) enter into other transactions on behalf of, or otherwise act for or bind, the partnership.

(b) To amend or cancel a statement of authority filed by the [Secretary of State], a partnership must deliver to the [Secretary of State] for filing an amendment or cancellation stating:

(1) the name of the partnership;

(2) if the partnership is not a limited liability partnership, the street and mailing addresses of the partnership's principal office;

(3) if the partnership is a limited liability partnership, the name and street and mailing addresses of its registered agent;

(4) the date the statement being affected became effective; and

(5) the contents of the amendment or a declaration that the statement is canceled.

(c) A statement of authority affects only the power of a person to bind a partnership to persons that are not partners.

(d) Subject to subsection (c) and Section 103(d)(1), and except as otherwise provided in subsections (f), (g), and (h), a limitation on the authority of a person or a position contained in an effective statement of authority is not by itself evidence of any person's knowledge or notice of the limitation.

(e) Subject to subsection (c), a grant of authority not pertaining to transfers of real property and contained in an effective statement of authority is conclusive in favor of a person that gives value in reliance on the grant, except to the extent that if the person gives value:

(1) the person has knowledge to the contrary;

(2) the statement has been canceled or restrictively amended under subsection (b); or

(3) a limitation on the grant is contained in another statement of authority that became effective after the statement containing the grant became effective.

(f) Subject to subsection (c), an effective statement of authority that grants authority to transfer real property held in the name of the partnership, a certified copy of which statement is recorded in the office for recording transfers of the real property, is conclusive in favor of a person that gives value in reliance on the grant without knowledge to the contrary, except to the extent that when the person gives value:

(1) the statement has been canceled or restrictively amended under subsection (b), and a certified copy of the cancellation or restrictive amendment has been recorded in the office for recording transfers of the real property; or

(2)   a limitation on the grant is contained in another statement of authority that became effective after the statement containing the grant became effective, and a certified copy of the later-effective statement is recorded in the office for recording transfers of the real property.

(g)   Subject to subsection (c), if a certified copy of an effective statement containing a limitation on the authority to transfer real property held in the name of a partnership is recorded in the office for recording transfers of that real property, all persons are deemed to know of the limitation.

(h)   Subject to subsection (i), an effective statement of dissolution is a cancellation of any filed statement of authority for the purposes of subsection (f) and is a limitation on authority for purposes of subsection (g).

(i)   After a statement of dissolution becomes effective, a partnership may deliver to the [Secretary of State] for filing and, if appropriate, may record a statement of authority that is designated as a post-dissolution statement of authority. The statement operates as provided in subsections (f) and (g).

(j)   Unless canceled earlier, an effective statement of authority is canceled by operation of law five years after the date on which the statement, or its most recent amendment, becomes effective. The cancellation is effective without recording under subsection (f) or (g).

(k)   An effective statement of denial operates as a restrictive amendment under this section and may be recorded by certified copy for purposes of subsection (f)(1).

Comment

UPA (1997) § 303 pioneered this concept, which was refined in ULLCA (2006) and further refined in the Harmonization Project. This section is conceptually divided into two realms: (i) statements pertaining to the power to transfer interests in the partnership real property; and (ii) statements pertaining to other matters. In the latter realm, statements are filed only in the records of the filing office and operate only to the extent the statements are actually known and relied on by a third party. Section 303(d), (e).

As to interests in real property, in contrast, this section: (i) requires double filing—with the filing office and in the appropriate land records; and (ii) provides for constructive knowledge of statements limiting authority. Thus, a properly filed and recorded statement can protect the partnership, Section 303(g), and, in order for a statement pertaining to real property to be a sword in the hands of a third party, the statement must have been both filed and properly recorded, Section 303(f). Experience suggests that statements of authority will most often be used in connection with transactions in real estate.

By its terms, this section applies only to domestic general partnerships. . . .

Subsections (f)–(h)—These subsections: (i) pertain to transactions in real property; (ii) provide a mechanism by which authority to transfer a partnership's real property can be made to appear in the real estate records; and (iii) thus address the principal concerns (raised by real estate lawyers) that led the drafters of UPA (1997) to provide for statements of authority.

Subsection (f)—This subsection provides a sword for a vendee of real property. If the vendee has "give[n] value in reliance on the grant without knowledge to the contrary," the statement of authority protects the vendee against claims that contradict the grant. . . .

Subsection (g)—This subsection provides a shield for the partnership as alleged vendor. If a vendee's claim contradicts the stated limitation, constructive notice knowledge ("deemed to know") defeats the claim even if the vendee gave value and lacked actual knowledge. . . .

Subsection (k)—Presumably, when real property is involved, a person who obtains the filing of a statement of denial under Section 304 will cause a certified copy of the statement to be "recorded by certified copy for purposes of subsection (f)(1)" [undercutting constructive notice as to authority to transfer real property]. However, nothing in this subsection prevents the partnership from causing a certified copy to appear in the land records; due the section's use of the passive voice ("may be recorded"), the act does not delimit who has the authority to act under this subsection.

§ 304.   STATEMENT OF DENIAL.

A person named in a filed statement of authority granting that person authority may deliver to the [Secretary of State] for filing a statement of denial that:

(1)   provides the name of the partnership and the caption of the statement of authority to which the statement of denial pertains; and

(2)   denies the grant of authority.

§ 305.   PARTNERSHIP LIABLE FOR PARTNER'S ACTIONABLE CONDUCT.

(a)   A partnership is liable for loss or injury caused to a person, or for a penalty incurred, as a result of a wrongful act or omission, or other actionable conduct, of a partner acting in the ordinary course of business of the partnership or with the actual or apparent authority of the partnership.

(b)   If, in the course of the partnership's business or while acting with actual or apparent authority of the partnership, a partner receives or causes the partnership to receive money or property of a person not a partner, and the money or property is misapplied by a partner, the partnership is liable for the loss.

Comment

Subsection (a)—. . .

To successfully invoke this provision, a plaintiff must show; (i) "a wrongful act or omission or other actionable conduct" by a partner; (ii) that caused "loss or injury"; and (iii) that at the relevant moment, the partner was acting with actual authority, apparent authority (if relevant), or within "the ordinary course of business of the partnership."

Extrapolating from agency law, apparent authority is relevant only when the appearance of authority augments the impact of the wrongful act. . . .

An act or omission may be "in the ordinary course of business of the partnership" even though the act is wrongful. Any other interpretation would vitiate the "ordinary course" element. "The proper question . . . is not whether the specific wrongful act is 'ordinary course' . . ., but rather whether that type of act, if done rightfully, would be." DANIEL S. KLEINBERGER, AGENCY, PARTNERSHIP AND LLCS: EXAMPLES AND EXPLANATIONS § 10.5.1, at 350 (4th ed. 2012). . . .

Subsection (b)—. . . It is not necessary that the partner "receiv[ing] or caus[ing] the partnership to receive money or property" do so wrongfully. Culpability is necessary at the second phase—*i.e.* when "the money or property is misapplied by a partner."

§ 306.   PARTNER'S LIABILITY.

[handwritten: → use agency law if not under RUPA and its a general partnership]

(a)   Except as otherwise provided in subsections (b) and (c), all partners are liable jointly and severally for all debts, obligations, and other liabilities of the partnership unless otherwise agreed by the claimant or provided by law.

(b)   A person that becomes a partner is not personally liable for a debt, obligation, or other liability of the partnership incurred before the person became a partner.

(c)   A debt, obligation, or other liability of a partnership incurred while the partnership is a limited liability partnership is solely the debt, obligation, or other liability of the limited liability partnership. A partner is not personally liable, directly or indirectly, by way of contribution or otherwise, for a debt, obligation, or other liability of the limited liability partnership solely by reason of being or acting as a partner. This subsection applies:

(1)   despite anything inconsistent in the partnership agreement that existed immediately before the vote or consent required to become a limited liability partnership under Section 901(b); and

(2)   regardless of the dissolution of the limited liability partnership.

(d)   The failure of a limited liability partnership to observe formalities relating to the exercise of its powers or management of its business is not a ground for imposing liability on a partner for a debt, obligation, or other liability of the partnership.

(e)   The cancellation or administrative revocation of a limited liability partnership's statement of qualification does not affect the limitation in this section on the liability of a partner for a debt, obligation, or other liability of the partnership incurred while the statement was in effect.

Comment

. . .

Subsection (c)—This subsection provides a corporate/LLC-like liability shield for partners, protecting them from (and only from) the debts, obligations and liabilities of the partnership—*i.e.*, against a partner's alleged vicarious liability for the obligations of the entity.

Full Liability Shield

This act provides a full liability shield—*i.e.*, the shield applies regardless of the law giving rise to a claim against an LLP. A few jurisdictions provide only a partial shield. *See, e.g.*, 15 PA. CONS. STAT. ANN. § 8204 (West 2013) (providing the partners of an LLP a shield for claims against the partnership "whether sounding in contract or tort or otherwise," but only the claims that "arise from any negligent or wrongful acts or misconduct committed by another partner or other representative of the partnership"). The resulting partial shield does not protect partners against liability for the partnership's ordinary commercial debts, such as liability for lease payments.

Shield Applicable Regardless of the Identity of the Plaintiff

What makes the shield relevant is the nature of the claim. If the complaint seeks to hold a partner vicariously liability for the LLP's obligations, the shield applies. If not, not. Thus, there is no distinction among a claim arising from an LLP's debt to a commercial creditor, a partner's claim that the LLP has failed to return a contribution as required by the partnership agreement, and a claim by a former partner that the LLP has failed to follow through on a buy-out agreement. . . .

Shield Inapposite for Claims Arising from a Partner's Own Conduct

Because the partner liability at issue is solely vicarious, the LLP shield is irrelevant to claims seeking to hold a partner directly liable on account of the partner's own conduct. . . .

Subsection (c) pertains only to claims based on the LLP's liability and is irrelevant to claims by a limited liability partnership or a partner against another partner and *vice versa*. *See* Sections 307 (pertaining to actions by partners), 409 (pertaining to management duties). . . .

Subsection (c)(2)—*The Shield and Dissolution*. The rule stated here is inherent in the nature of partnership dissolution. "[D]issolution does not end a partnership's existence but rather changes the purpose of that existence." Section 801, cmt. . . .

This subsection makes this point expressly. . .

The Shield and Termination. This subsection does not expressly provide that, when a limited liability partnership's existence terminates, the LLP shield remains in place as to any debt, obligation, or other liability of the partnership incurred before the termination. However, the point follows ineluctably from Subsection 306(b). . . .

Subsection (d)—This subsection was added during the Harmonization Project and pertains to the equitable doctrine of "piercing the veil"—*i.e.*, conflating an entity and its owners to hold one liable for the obligations of the other. The doctrine of "piercing the corporate veil" is well established, and courts should apply the doctrine to limited liability partnerships for the same reasons that courts have regularly (and sometimes almost reflexively) applied the doctrine to limited liability companies. . . .

However, as with LLC piercing, LLP piercing involves one important distinction from the corporate realm. While under corporate law "disregard of corporate formalities" is a key piercing factor, that factor is inapposite in the law of unincorporated organizations. Corporate formalities reflect statutory mandates. LLP formalities derive for the most part from the agreement among the partners. From a policy perspective, disregarding formalities adopted by agreement differs substantially from disregarding formalities imposed by law. . . .

In contrast, this subsection is inapposite to another key piercing factor—disregard of the separateness between entity and owner. . . .

EXAMPLE: A partner in a limited liability partnership uses a car titled in the partnership's name for personal purposes and writes checks on the partnership's account to pay for personal expenses. These facts are relevant to a piercing claim; they pertain to economic separateness, not Subsection (b) formalities.

. . .

§ 307. ACTIONS BY AND AGAINST PARTNERSHIP AND PARTNERS.

(a)   A partnership may sue and be sued in the name of the partnership.

(b)   To the extent not inconsistent with Section 306, a partner may be joined in an action against the partnership or named in a separate action.

(c)   A judgment against a partnership is not by itself a judgment against a partner. A judgment against a partnership may not be satisfied from a partner's assets unless there is also a judgment against the partner.

(d)   A judgment creditor of a partner may not levy execution against the assets of the partner to satisfy a judgment based on a claim against the partnership unless the partner is personally liable for the claim under Section 306 and:

(1)   a judgment based on the same claim has been obtained against the partnership and a writ of execution on the judgment has been returned unsatisfied in whole or in part;

(2)   the partnership is a debtor in bankruptcy;

(3)   the partner has agreed that the creditor need not exhaust partnership assets;

(4)   a court grants permission to the judgment creditor to levy execution against the assets of a partner based on a finding that partnership assets subject to execution are clearly insufficient to satisfy the judgment, that exhaustion of partnership assets is excessively burdensome, or that the grant of permission is an appropriate exercise of the court's equitable powers; or

(5)   liability is imposed on the partner by law or contract independent of the existence of the partnership.

(e)   This section applies to any debt, liability, or other obligation of a partnership which results from a representation by a partner or purported partner under Section 308.

Comment

Section 307 reflects the entity construct. . . .

Subsection (b)—. . .

The reference to "not inconsistent with Section 306" is the procedural analog to the substantive protections of Section 306(b) (incoming partner not liable for pre-existing partnership obligations) and (c) (partners not liable for partnership obligations incurred by an LLP). When a partner has personally guaranteed a partnership obligation, naming that partner in a suit against the partnership is "not inconsistent with Section 306." . . .

Subsection (c)—Reflecting the entity construct, . . . this subsection provides that a judgment against the partnership: (i) is not, standing alone, a judgment against the partners; and (ii) cannot be satisfied from a partner's personal assets absent a judgment against the partner.

As did UPA (1914) and UPA (1997), this act leaves to the law of judgments to determine the collateral effects to be accorded a prior judgment for or against the partnership in a subsequent action against a partner individually. . . .

This subsection and Subsection (d) combine to create a trap for the unwary. For statute of limitations purposes, a creditor's claim against the partners accrues simultaneously with the claim against the partnership. If a creditor chooses not to sue the partners in its suit against the partnership, the statute of limitations may run before the creditor commences suit against the partners. . . .

§ 308.   LIABILITY OF PURPORTED PARTNER.

(a)   If a person, by words or conduct, purports to be a partner, or consents to being represented by another as a partner, in a partnership or with one or more persons not partners, the purported partner is liable to a person to whom the representation is made, if that person, relying on the representation, enters into a transaction with the actual or purported partnership. If the representation, either by the purported partner or by a person with the purported partner's consent, is made in a public manner, the purported partner is liable to a person who relies upon the purported partnership even if the purported partner is not aware of being held out as a partner to the claimant. If partnership liability results, the purported partner is liable with respect to that liability as if the purported partner were a partner. If no partnership liability results, the purported partner is liable with respect to that liability jointly and severally with any other person consenting to the representation.

(b) If a person is thus represented to be a partner in an existing partnership, or with one or more persons not partners, the purported partner is an agent of persons consenting to the representation to bind them to the same extent and in the same manner as if the purported partner were a partner with respect to persons who enter into transactions in reliance upon the representation. If all the partners of the existing partnership consent to the representation, a partnership act or obligation results. If fewer than all the partners of the existing partnership consent to the representation, the person acting and the partners consenting to the representation are jointly and severally liable.

(c) A person is not liable as a partner merely because the person is named by another as a partner in a statement of partnership authority.

(d) A person does not continue to be liable as a partner merely because of a failure to file a statement of dissociation or to amend a statement of partnership authority to indicate the person's dissociation as a partner.

(e) Except as otherwise provided in subsections (a) and (b), persons who are not partners as to each other are not liable as partners to other persons.

[ARTICLE] 4

RELATIONS OF PARTNERS TO EACH OTHER AND TO PARTNERSHIP

Sec.
401.　Partner's Rights and Duties.
402.　Becoming Partner.
403.　Form of Contribution.
404.　Liability for Contribution.
405.　Sharing of and Right to Distributions Before Dissolution.
406.　Limitations on Distributions by Limited Liability Partnership.
407.　Liability for Improper Distributions by Limited Liability Partnership.
408.　Rights to Information of Partners and Persons Dissociated as Partner.
409.　Standards of Conduct for Partners.
410.　Actions by Partnership and Partners.
411.　Continuation of Partnership Beyond Definite Term or Particular Undertaking.

§ 401. PARTNER'S RIGHTS AND DUTIES.

(a) Each partner is entitled to an equal share of the partnership distributions and, except in the case of a limited liability partnership, is chargeable with a share of the partnership losses in proportion to the partner's share of the distributions.

(b) A partnership shall reimburse a partner for any payment made by the partner in the course of the partner's activities on behalf of the partnership, if the partner complied with this section and Section 409 in making the payment.

(c) A partnership shall indemnify and hold harmless a person with respect to any claim or demand against the person and any debt, obligation, or other liability incurred by the person by reason of the person's former or present capacity as a partner, if the claim, demand, debt, obligation, or other liability does not arise from the person's breach of this section or Section 407 or 409.

(d) In the ordinary course of its business, a partnership may advance reasonable expenses, including attorney's fees and costs, incurred by a person in connection with a claim or demand against the person by reason of the person's former or present capacity as a partner, if the person promises to repay the partnership if the person ultimately is determined not to be entitled to be indemnified under subsection (c).

(e)   A partnership may purchase and maintain insurance on behalf of a partner against liability asserted against or incurred by the partner in that capacity or arising from that status even if, under Section 105(c)(7), the partnership agreement could not eliminate or limit the person's liability to the partnership for the conduct giving rise to the liability.

(f)   A partnership shall reimburse a partner for an advance to the partnership beyond the amount of capital the partner agreed to contribute.

(g)   A payment or advance made by a partner which gives rise to a partnership obligation under subsection (b) or (f) constitutes a loan to the partnership which accrues interest from the date of the payment or advance.

(h)   Each partner has equal rights in the management and conduct of the partnership's business.

(i)   A partner may use or possess partnership property only on behalf of the partnership.

(j)   A partner is not entitled to remuneration for services performed for the partnership, except for reasonable compensation for services rendered in winding up the business of the partnership.

(k)   A difference arising as to a matter in the ordinary course of business of a partnership may be decided by a majority of the partners. An act outside the ordinary course of business of a partnership and an amendment to the partnership agreement may be undertaken only with the affirmative vote or consent of all the partners.

Comment

For the most part, Section 401 merely restates the rules of UPA (1914) § 18, thereby establishing many of the default rules that govern the relations among partners. All of these rules are, however, subject to contrary agreement of the partners. . . . as provided in Sections 105 through 107.

UPA (1997) § 401(a) experimented with providing a default configuration for capital accounts. For the reasons stated in Section 405, comment, the Harmonization Project ended the experiment and eliminated the configuration.

Subsection (a)—. . . [T]he Harmonization Project substituted "distribution" for "profits." Distributions are shared equally and losses are shared in proportion to each partner's share of distributions. Thus, under this default rule, partners share distributions per capita and not in proportion to capital contribution (per capital).

If partners agree to share distributions other than equally, losses will be shared in the same proportion as distributions, absent agreement to do otherwise. This rule, carried over from UPA (1914) rests on the assumption that partners would likely agree to share losses on the same basis as distributions, but may fail to say so. . . .

It may seem unfair that the contributor of services, who contributes little or no capital, should be obligated to contribute toward the capital loss of the large contributor who contributed no services. In entering a partnership with such a capital structure, the partners should foresee that application of the default rule might bring about unusual results and take advantage of their power to vary by agreement the allocation of capital losses.

Subsections (b) and (c)—A partnership's obligation, if any, to reimburse or indemnify others (*e.g.*, employees, other agents, and independent contractors) is a question for other law, including the law of agency, contract, and restitution. . . .

Subsection (b)— . . .

The reimbursement obligation stated here is a default rule and roughly parallels a rule of agency law. Restatement (Third) of Agency § 8.14(2) (2006) (stating that "[a] principal has a duty to indemnify an agent . . . when the agent makes a payment (i) within the scope of the agent's actual authority, or (ii) that is beneficial to the principal, unless the agent acts officiously in making the payment"). . . .

Subsection (h)—This subsection was UPA (1997) § 401(f) and is based on UPA (1914) § 18(e). UPA (1997) § 401, comment 7, suggests that UPA (1914) § 18(e) case law continues to be relevant and notes that Section 18(e) "has been interpreted broadly to mean that, absent contrary agreement, each partner has a continuing right to participate in the management of the partnership and to be informed about the partnership business, even if, per the partnership agreement, the partner's assent to partnership business decisions is not required." . . .

The actual authority of a partner is a question of agency law and depends fundamentally on the contents of the partnership agreement. If, however, the partnership agreement is silent on the issue, this subsection helps delineate that actual authority. Acting individually, a partner:

- has no actual authority to commit the partnership to any matter for which this act requires the affirmative vote or consent of all partners;

- has the actual authority to commit the partnership to usual and customary matters, unless the partner has reason to know that: (i) other partners might disagree; or (ii) for some other reason consultation with fellow partners is appropriate; and

- has no actual authority to take unusual or non-customary actions that will have a substantial effect on the partnership. . . .

Finally, the authority granted by this subsection includes the authority to delegate. Delegation does not relieve the delegating partner or partners of their duties under Section 409. However, the fact of delegation is a fact relevant to any breach of duty analysis.

EXAMPLE: A partner personally handles all important paperwork for a partnership. The partner neglects to renew the fire insurance coverage on a building owned by the partnership, despite having received and read a warning notice from the insurance company. The building subsequently burns to the ground and is a total loss. The partner might be liable for breach of the duty of care under Section 409(c) (gross negligence).

EXAMPLE: A partner delegates responsibility for insurance renewals to the partnership's office manager, and that manager neglects to renew the fire insurance coverage on the building. Even assuming that the office manager has been grossly negligent, the partner is not necessarily liable under Section 409(c). The office manager's gross negligence is not automatically attributed to the partner. Under Section 409(c), the question is whether the partner was grossly negligent (or worse) in selecting the office manager, delegating insurance renewal matters to the office manager, and supervising the general manager after the delegation. . . .

§ 402.   BECOMING PARTNER.

(a)   Upon formation of a partnership, a person becomes a partner under Section 202(a).

(b)   After formation of a partnership, a person becomes a partner:

   (1)   as provided in the partnership agreement;

   (2)   as a result of a transaction effective under [Article] 11; or

   (3)   with the affirmative vote or consent of all the partners. *(need unanimous)*

(c)   A person may become a partner without:

   (1)   acquiring a transferable interest; or

   (2)   making or being obligated to make a contribution to the partnership.

Comment

This section was adopted in the 2011 and 2013 Harmonization amendments and changes UPA (1997) both in style and substance. . . .

Subsection (b)(3)—A partnership being a creature of contract, consent is determined on an objective basis (*i.e.*, contract law's "reasonable person" standard). Depending on the terms of the partnership agreement, the partners' manifestation of consent might involve detailed formalities, entirely informal activities, or anything in between. Moreover, the partnership agreement might reduce the quantum of consent necessary or shift the consent right to the management committee or managing partners.

A partnership being a voluntary association, a person cannot become a partner without manifesting consent to do so. That consent also is judged objectively.

Under Section 106(b), "[a] person that becomes a partner is deemed to assent to the partnership agreement," and the agreement binds the partner regardless of whether the partner has actually indicated assent in any way.

Subsection (c)(1)—To accommodate business practices, this provision permits so-called "non-economic partners."

§ 403.   FORM OF CONTRIBUTION.

A contribution may consist of property transferred to, services performed for, or another benefit provided to the partnership or an agreement to transfer property to, perform services for, or provide another benefit to the partnership.

Comment

This section is derived from ULLCA (2006) § 402, was adopted as part of the 2011 and 2013 Harmonization amendments, is intentionally quite broad, and encompasses past, present, and promised benefits. . . .

This act does not contain a statute of frauds specifically applicable to promised contributions. Generally applicable statutes of fraud might apply, however. For example, a promise to contribute land to a partnership would be subject to the statute of frauds pertaining to land transfers. Likewise, a promise that by its terms requires performance that extends beyond one year from the making of the contract would be subject to the one-year provision of the statute of frauds. . . .

§ 404.   LIABILITY FOR CONTRIBUTION.

(a)   A person's obligation to make a contribution to a partnership is not excused by the person's death, disability, termination, or other inability to perform personally.

(b)   If a person does not fulfill an obligation to make a contribution other than money, the person is obligated at the option of the partnership to contribute money equal to the value of the part of the contribution which has not been made.

(c)   The obligation of a person to make a contribution may be compromised only by the affirmative vote or consent of all the partners. If a creditor of a limited liability partnership extends credit or otherwise acts in reliance on an obligation described in subsection (a) without knowledge or notice of a compromise under this subsection, the creditor may enforce the obligation.

§ 405.   SHARING OF AND RIGHT TO DISTRIBUTIONS BEFORE DISSOLUTION.

(a)   Any distribution made by a partnership before its dissolution and winding up must be in equal shares among partners, except to the extent necessary to comply with a transfer effective under Section 503 or charging order in effect under Section 504.

(b)   Subject to Section 701, a person has a right to a distribution before the dissolution and winding up of a partnership only if the partnership decides to make an interim distribution.

(c)   A person does not have a right to demand or receive a distribution from a partnership in any form other than money. Except as otherwise provided in Section 806, a partnership may distribute an asset in kind only if each part of the asset is fungible with each other part and each person receives a percentage of the asset equal in value to the person's share of distributions.

(d)   If a partner or transferee becomes entitled to receive a distribution, the partner or transferee has the status of, and is entitled to all remedies available to, a creditor of the partnership with respect to the distribution. However, the partnership's obligation to make a distribution is subject to offset for any amount owed to the partnership by the partner or a person dissociated as partner on whose account the distribution is made.

§ 406.   LIMITATIONS ON DISTRIBUTIONS BY LIMITED LIABILITY PARTNERSHIP.

(a)   A limited liability partnership may not make a distribution, including a distribution under Section 806, if after the distribution:

(1)   the partnership would not be able to pay its debts as they become due in the ordinary course of the partnership's business; or

(2)   the partnership's total assets would be less than the sum of its total liabilities plus the amount that would be needed, if the partnership were to be dissolved and wound up at the time of the distribution, to satisfy the preferential rights upon dissolution and winding up of partners and transferees whose preferential rights are superior to the rights of persons receiving the distribution.

(b)   A limited liability partnership may base a determination that a distribution is not prohibited under subsection (a) on:

(1)   financial statements prepared on the basis of accounting practices and principles that are reasonable in the circumstances; or

(2)   a fair valuation or other method that is reasonable under the circumstances.

(c)   Except as otherwise provided in subsection (e), the effect of a distribution under subsection (a) is measured:

(1)   in the case of a distribution as defined in Section 102(4)(A), as of the earlier of:

(A)   the date money or other property is transferred or debt is incurred by the limited liability partnership; or

(B)   the date the person entitled to the distribution ceases to own the interest or rights being acquired by the partnership in return for the distribution;

(2)   in the case of any other distribution of indebtedness, as of the date the indebtedness is distributed; and

(3)   in all other cases, as of the date:

(A)   the distribution is authorized, if the payment occurs not later than 120 days after that date; or

(B)   the payment is made, if the payment occurs more than 120 days after the distribution is authorized.

(d)   A limited liability partnership's indebtedness to a partner or transferee incurred by reason of a distribution made in accordance with this section is at parity with the partnership's indebtedness to its general, unsecured creditors, except to the extent subordinated by agreement.

(e)   A limited liability partnership's indebtedness, including indebtedness issued as a distribution, is not a liability for purposes of subsection (a) if the terms of the indebtedness provide that payment of principal and interest is made only if and to the extent that a payment of a distribution could then be made under this section. If the indebtedness is issued as a distribution, each payment of principal or interest is treated as a distribution, the effect of which is measured on the date the payment is made.

(f)   In measuring the effect of a distribution under Section 806, the liabilities of a dissolved limited liability partnership do not include any claim that has been disposed of under Section 807, 808, or 809.

Comment

Both this section and Section 407 were derived essentially from the Model Business Corporation Act section 6.40, and were added during the Harmonization Project. Both sections are necessary and appropriate because a limited liability partnership provides the partners a corporate-like liability shield. With the exception noted in the comment to Subsection (a)(2), the provisions of this section are non-waivable. Section 105(c)(17). . . .

Subsection (a)(2)—The reference to "preferential rights upon dissolution and winding up" is a default rule, because removing this protection for preferred partners or transferees is an *inter se* matter. *See* Section 105(d)(1)(B). The rest of the section is not subject to change in the partnership agreement. Section 105(c)(17). . . .

Subsection (c)—This subsection provides three alternative rules for determining the point(s) in time of as which to apply the solvency tests stated in Subsection (a). The timing depends on which of three categories encompasses a distribution: (i) a distribution in the nature of a redemption (regardless of whether the distribution includes a distribution of indebtedness); (ii) any distribution of indebtedness other than a distribution in the nature of a redemption; and (iii) any distribution that involves neither a redemption nor a distribution of indebtedness. A requirement for additional solvency testing pertaining to distributions of indebtedness appears in Subsection (e). . . .

Subsection (e)—This subsection contains two rules pertaining to indebtedness issued as part of a distribution and the Subsection (a) solvency tests. The first sentence states the sensible rule that indebtedness that is essentially subordinated to the solvency requirement (*i.e.*, not payable if making payment would transgress that requirement) is not counted in determining liabilities for purposes of the solvency tests. The second sentence applies the solvency tests to each payment of principal and interest on any indebtedness issued as a distribution, in addition to any previous testing required by Subsection (c)(1)(A) or (c)(2).

EXAMPLE: A limited liability partnership and one of its partners agree that the LLP will buy out the person's entire ownership interest in the LLP in return for a promissory note from the LLP, payable in installments. Under the redemption agreement: (i) on January 15 the person surrenders all its interests and rights and dissociates as a partner; and (ii) the LLP signs and delivers the note to the person on February 15. Under the note, payment of interest is due monthly beginning March 15, with a balloon payment of the principal due December 30.

Under Subsection (c)(1)(B), the solvency tests are applied as of January 15. Under Subsection (e), the solvency tests are again applied on the March 15, April 15, etc., and again on December 30. . . .

§ 407. LIABILITY FOR IMPROPER DISTRIBUTIONS BY LIMITED LIABILITY PARTNERSHIP. *refers to §6.4 of MBCA*

(a) Except as otherwise provided in subsection (b), if a partner of a limited liability partnership consents to a distribution made in violation of Section 406 and in consenting to the distribution fails to comply with Section 409, the partner is personally liable to the partnership for the amount of the distribution which exceeds the amount that could have been distributed without the violation of Section 406.

(b) To the extent the partnership agreement of a limited liability partnership expressly relieves a partner of the authority and responsibility to consent to distributions and imposes that authority and responsibility on one or more other partners, the liability stated in subsection (a) applies to the other partners and not to the partner that the partnership agreement relieves of the authority and responsibility.

(c) A person that receives a distribution knowing that the distribution violated Section 406 is personally liable to the limited liability partnership but only to the extent that the distribution received by the person exceeded the amount that could have been properly paid under Section 406.

(d) A person against which an action is commenced because the person is liable under subsection (a) may:

(1) implead any other person that is liable under subsection (a) and seek to enforce a right of contribution from the person; and

(2) implead any person that received a distribution in violation of subsection (c) and seek to enforce a right of contribution from the person in the amount the person received in violation of subsection (c).

(e) An action under this section is barred unless commenced not later than two years after the distribution.

§ 408. RIGHTS TO INFORMATION OF PARTNERS AND PERSONS DISSOCIATED AS PARTNER.

(a) A partnership shall keep its books and records, if any, at its principal office.

(b) On reasonable notice, a partner may inspect and copy during regular business hours, at a reasonable location specified by the partnership, any record maintained by the partnership regarding the partnership's business, financial condition, and other circumstances, to the extent the information is material to the partner's rights and duties under the partnership agreement or this [act].

(c) The partnership shall furnish to each partner:

(1) without demand, any information concerning the partnership's business, financial condition, and other circumstances which the partnership knows and is material to the proper exercise of the

partner's rights and duties under the partnership agreement or this [act], except to the extent the partnership can establish that it reasonably believes the partner already knows the information; and

(2)   on demand, any other information concerning the partnership's business, financial condition, and other circumstances, except to the extent the demand or the information demanded is unreasonable or otherwise improper under the circumstances.

(d)   The duty to furnish information under subsection (c) also applies to each partner to the extent the partner knows any of the information described in subsection (c).

(e)   Subject to subsection (j), on 10 days' demand made in a record received by a partnership, a person dissociated as a partner may have access to information to which the person was entitled while a partner if:

(1)   the information pertains to the period during which the person was a partner;

(2)   the person seeks the information in good faith; and

(3)   the person satisfies the requirements imposed on a partner by subsection (b).

(f)   Not later than 10 days after receiving a demand under subsection (e), the partnership in a record shall inform the person that made the demand of:

(1)   the information that the partnership will provide in response to the demand and when and where the partnership will provide the information; and

(2)   the partnership's reasons for declining, if the partnership declines to provide any demanded information.

(g)   A partnership may charge a person that makes a demand under this section the reasonable costs of copying, limited to the costs of labor and material.

(h)   A partner or person dissociated as a partner may exercise the rights under this section through an agent or, in the case of an individual under legal disability, a legal representative. Any restriction or condition imposed by the partnership agreement or under subsection (j) applies both to the agent or legal representative and to the partner or person dissociated as a partner.

(i)   Subject to Section 505, the rights under this section do not extend to a person as transferee.

(j)   In addition to any restriction or condition stated in its partnership agreement, a partnership, as a matter within the ordinary course of its business, may impose reasonable restrictions and conditions on access to and use of information to be furnished under this section, including designating information confidential and imposing nondisclosure and safeguarding obligations on the recipient. In a dispute concerning the reasonableness of a restriction under this subsection, the partnership has the burden of proving reasonableness.

Comment

. . . The rules stated here might be termed "quasi-default rules"—subject to some change by the partnership agreement. *See* Section 105(c)(4) (prohibiting unreasonable restrictions on the information rights stated in this section).

Although the rights and duties stated in this section are extensive, they are not necessarily all-inclusive. This act's statement of fiduciary duties is not exhaustive, *see* . . . *Bakerman v. Sidney Frank Importing Co., Inc.*, No. Civ.A. 1844-N, 2006 WL 3927242, at *14 (Del. Ch. Oct. 16, 2006) (holding that an LLC manager owed "certain duties to members of the LLC" and stating that "[w]hen fiduciaries communicate with their beneficiaries in the context of asking the beneficiary to make a discretionary decision—such as whether to consent to a sale of substantially all the assets of an LLC—the fiduciary has a duty to disclose all material facts bearing on the decision at issue"). . . .

Subsection (a)—A general partnership is often a very informal organization. Accordingly, this subsection states a default-required location for any books and records a partnership may have but does not require that books and records be kept. Other law may so require, however—particularly tax law. This subsection applies to any books and records kept to satisfy other law.

Subsection (b)—This subsection states the rule pertaining to information memorialized in "any record maintained by the partnership." For the meaning of "material" as applied to information, see Section 409(f), comment.

Subsections (c) and (d)—In appropriate circumstances, violation of either or both of these provisions might cause a court to enjoin or even rescind action taken by the partnership, especially when the violation has interfered with an approval or veto mechanism involving partner consent. *E.g., Blue Chip Emerald L.L.C. v. Allied Partners Inc.*, 299 A.D.2d 278, 279–80 (N.Y. App. Div. 2002) (invoking partnership law precedent as reflecting a duty of full disclosure and holding that "[a]bsent such full disclosure, the transaction is voidable").

Subsection (c)—This subsection imposes a duty on the partnership, not the partners. However, a partner could be liable in damages if the partner were to: (i) breach a duty under Section 409 or the partnership agreement; and (ii) in doing so cause or suffer the partnership to breach the duty stated in this paragraph.

Subsection (c)(1)—This provision imposes an affirmative duty to volunteer information. . . . [However,] the obligation is limited to information that is both material and known by the partnership. "Knowledge" is viewed subjectively (*i.e.*, actual knowledge). Section 103(a)(1). Materiality is viewed objectively. Thus, the duty applies to known, material information, even if the partnership does not know that the information is material.

A partnership will "know" what its partners know. Under Section 103(e), "[a] partner's knowledge . . . of a fact relating to the partnership is effective immediately as knowledge of or notice to the partnership." . . .

Subsection (d)—. . .

Because this subsection imposes duties directly on partner, the duties are in the nature of a contractual obligation, and breach is a matter of strict liability. For example, it is no defense for a partner under this section to assert that, although the partner failed to furnish required information, the failure did not amount to gross negligence under Section 409(c). . . .

Subsection (e)(2)—A duty of good faith is needed here, because a person claiming access under this subsection is no longer a partner and is no longer subject to a partner's obligation of good faith and fair dealing under Section 409(d). . . .

Subsection (j)—This subsection provides fallback protection for gaps in the partnership agreement. For example, the partners may protect trade secrets from disclosure and prohibit various misuses of confidential information even if the partnership agreement omits to do so. . . .

§ 409.   STANDARDS OF CONDUCT FOR PARTNERS.

(a)   A partner owes to the partnership and the other partners the duties of loyalty and care stated in subsections (b) and (c).

(b)   The fiduciary duty of loyalty of a partner includes the duties:

(1)   to account to the partnership and hold as trustee for it any property, profit, or benefit derived by the partner:

(A)   in the conduct or winding up of the partnership's business;

(B)   from a use by the partner of the partnership's property; or

(C)   from the appropriation of a partnership opportunity;   → Meinhard case (look @ comment)

(2)   to refrain from dealing with the partnership in the conduct or winding up of the partnership business as or on behalf of a person having an interest adverse to the partnership; and

(3)   to refrain from competing with the partnership in the conduct of the partnership's business before the dissolution of the partnership.

(c)   The duty of care of a partner in the conduct or winding up of the partnership business is to refrain from engaging in grossly negligent or reckless conduct, willful or intentional misconduct, or a knowing violation of law.

(d)   A partner shall discharge the duties and obligations under this [act] or under the partnership agreement and exercise any rights consistently with the contractual obligation of good faith and fair dealing.

(e)   A partner does not violate a duty or obligation under this [act] or under the partnership agreement solely because the partner's conduct furthers the partner's own interest.

(f)   All the partners may authorize or ratify, after full disclosure of all material facts, a specific act or transaction by a partner that otherwise would violate the duty of loyalty.

(g)   It is a defense to a claim under subsection (b)(2) and any comparable claim in equity or at common law that the transaction was fair to the partnership.

(h)   If, as permitted by subsection (f) or the partnership agreement, a partner enters into a transaction with the partnership which otherwise would be prohibited by subsection (b)(2), the partner's rights and obligations arising from the transaction are the same as those of a person that is not a partner.

Comment

This section originated as UPA (1997) § 404. The 2011 and 2013 Harmonization amendments made one major substantive change; they "un-cabined" fiduciary duty. UPA (1997) § 404 had deviated substantially from UPA (1914) by purporting to codify all fiduciary duties owed by partners. This approach had a number of problems. Most notably, the exhaustive list of fiduciary duties left no room for the fiduciary duty owed by partners to each other. . . .

"Un-cabining" harmonized this act to ULLCA (2006), and this section states some of the core aspects of the fiduciary duty of loyalty, provides a duty of care, and incorporates the contractual obligation of good faith and fair dealing. The duties stated in this section are subject to the partnership agreement, but Sections 105(c) and (d) contain important limitations on the power of the partnership agreement to affect fiduciary and other duties and the obligation of good faith and fair dealing. . . .

Subsection (a)—This subsection recognizes two core managerial duties but, unlike UPA (1997), does not purport to be exhaustive. . . .

Subsection (b)—This subsection states three core aspects of the fiduciary duty of loyalty. . . .

This subsection applies beginning with "the partnership's business," which by definition cannot exist before the partnership does; thus the stated duties do not apply to pre-formation activities. . . .

Subsection (b)(1)—The phrase "hold as trustee" . . . reflects the availability of disgorgement remedies, such as a constructive trust. . . .

Subsection (b)(1)(A)—This provision is consistent with a basic principle of agency law—namely, that an agent may not benefit at all from the performance of the agency unless the principal consents. . . .

Subsection (b)(1)(C)—This act does not specify what constitutes "a partnership opportunity," but ample case law exists. . . .

Subsection (b)(2)—In this context, the phrase "adverse interest" is a term of art, meaning "to be on the other side of the table" in some dealing with the partnership. Absent informed consent by the partnership, this duty is breached by the mere existence of the conflict of interest and the partnership need not prove that the outcome of the dealing was adverse to the partnership. *But see* Subsection (g) (permitting the defense of fairness).This duty continues through winding up.

Subsection (c)—This act no longer refers to the duty of care as a fiduciary duty, because: (i) the duty of care applies in many non-fiduciary situations; and (ii) breach of the duty of care is remediable in damages while breach of a fiduciary duty gives rise also to equitable remedies, including disgorgement, constructive trust, and rescission. . . .

However, the label change is merely semantics; no change in the law is intended. . . .

Subsection (d)—This subsection refers to the "*contractual* obligation of good faith and fair dealing" (emphasis added) and thereby invokes the implied obligation that exists in every contract. *See* RESTATEMENT (SECOND) CONTRACTS § 205 (1981) ("Every contract imposes upon each party a duty of good faith and fair dealing in its performance and its enforcement."). The adjective ("contractual") should help avoid decisions like *Phelps v. Frampton*, 170 P.3d 474, 483 (Mont. 2007) (holding that Montana's version of UPA (1997) creates a statutory obligation of good faith and fair dealing separate from the implied contractual covenant).

At first glance, it may seem strange to apply a contractual obligation to statutory duties and rights—*i.e.*, duties and rights "under this [act]." However, for the most part those duties and rights apply to relationships *inter se* the partners and the partnership and function only to the extent not displaced by the partnership agreement. Those statutory default rules are thus intended to function like a contract; applying the contractual notion of good faith and fair dealing therefore makes sense.

The contractual obligation of "good faith" has nothing to do with the corporate concept of good faith that for years bedeviled courts and attorneys trying to understand: . . . . In that context, good faith is an aspect of the duty of loyalty. . . .

Likewise, the contractual obligation of good faith and fair dealing has nothing to do with the "utmost good faith" sometimes used to describe the fiduciary duties that owners of closely held businesses owe each other. . . .

To the contrary, the contractual obligation of good faith and fair dealing is not a fiduciary duty, does not command altruism or self-abnegation, and does not prevent a partner from acting in the partner's own self-interest:

"Fair dealing" is not akin to the fair process component of entire fairness, *i.e.*, whether the fiduciary acted fairly when engaging in the challenged transaction as measured by duties of loyalty and care. . . . It is rather a commitment to deal "fairly" in the sense of consistently with the terms of the parties' agreement and its purpose. Likewise "good faith" does not envision loyalty to the contractual counterparty, but rather faithfulness to the scope, purpose, and terms of the parties' contract. Both necessarily turn on the contract itself and what the parties would have agreed upon had the issue arisen when they were bargaining originally.

Gerber v. Enter. Prods. Holdings, L.L.C., 67 A.3d 400, 418–19 (Del. 2013). . . .

Courts should not use the contractual obligation to change *ex post facto* the parties' or this act's allocation of risk and power. To the contrary, the obligation should be used only to protect agreed-upon arrangements from conduct that is manifestly beyond what a reasonable person could have contemplated when the arrangements were made.

The partnership agreement or this act may grant discretion to a partner, and the contractual obligation of good faith and fair dealing is especially salient when discretion is at issue. However, a partner may properly exercise discretion even though another partner suffers as a consequence. Conduct does not violate the obligation of good faith and fair dealing merely because that conduct substantially prejudices a party. Indeed, parties allocate risk precisely because prejudice may occur.

The exercise of discretion constitutes a breach of the obligation of good faith and fair dealing only when the party claiming breach shows that the conduct has no honestly held purpose that legitimately comports with the parties' agreed-upon arrangements:

An implied covenant claim . . . looks to the past. It is not a free-floating duty unattached to the underlying legal documents. It does not ask what duty the law should impose on the parties given their relationship at the time of the wrong, but *rather what the parties would have agreed to themselves had they considered the issue in their original bargaining positions at the time of contracting.*

Gerber v. Enter. Prods. Holdings, L.L.C., 67 A.3d 400, 418 (Del. 2013). . . .

In sum, the purpose of the contractual obligation of good faith and fair dealing is to protect the arrangement the partners have chosen for themselves, not to restructure that arrangement under the guise of safeguarding it. . . .

Subsection (e)—A partner in a general partnership has at least two different roles: (i) as a party to the partnership agreement, with rights and obligations under that agreement; and (ii) as co-manager of the enterprise. This provision pertains to the first role. A partner's exercise of rights under the partnership agreement is subject to the obligation of good faith and fair dealing, Subsection (d), but a partner does not breach that contractual obligation "solely because the partner's conduct furthers the partner's own interest." In contrast, this provision is ineffective with regard to a partner's duties as co-manager. For example, a partner's liability under Section 409(b)(3) (prohibiting competition) is not "solely because the partner's conduct furthers the partner's own interest." Rather, the liability results from the breach of a specific obligation—*i.e.*, the codified aspect of the duty of loyalty that prohibits competition. . . .

Subsection (g)—This subsection codifies judge-made law applicable to all business entities. *See, e.g., Kahn v. Lynch Commc'n Sys., Inc.*, 638 A.2d 1110, 1116 (Del. 1994) (discussing "entire fairness" in the context of a corporation's merger with an affiliate). . . .

Subsection (h)—This subsection is the modern, reformulated version of a language that sought to overturn the now-defunct notion that debts to partners were categorically inferior to debts to non-partner creditors. . . . The reformulation makes clear that this provision has nothing to do with the fiduciary duty pertaining to conflict of interests. . . .

This subsection states a default rule. The partnership agreement may provide that debt to a partner (or partners generally) is subordinate to other partnership obligations. The agreement that creates the debt may do likewise.

§ 410.   ACTIONS BY PARTNERSHIP AND PARTNERS.

(a)   A partnership may maintain an action against a partner for a breach of the partnership agreement, or for the violation of a duty to the partnership, causing harm to the partnership.

(b)   A partner may maintain an action against the partnership or another partner, with or without an accounting as to partnership business, to enforce the partner's rights and protect the partner's interests, including rights and interests under the partnership agreement or this [act] or arising independently of the partnership relationship.

(c)   A right to an accounting on dissolution and winding up does not revive a claim barred by law.

Comment

In UPA (1997) this section was Section 405. The Harmonization Project did not change the section other than to renumber it. . . .

This subsection authorizes a partner to bring claims "to enforce the partner's rights and protect the partner's interests"—*i.e.*, direct claims. The statutory language does not contemplate derivative claims; thus, this act neither authorizes nor precludes such claims. . . .

The case law does generally recognize the direct/derivative distinction in the context of general partnerships, and some cases permit a partner to sue derivatively. . . .

Despite the conflict and confusion in the cases, one proposition does appears reasonably certain: A minority partner in a general partnership must have some right to sue "where the controlling partners, for improper, ulterior motives and not because of what they in good faith believe to be the best interests of the partnership, decline to sue on a valid, valuable *partnership cause of action* which it is advantageous to the partnership to pursue." . . . [*Cates v. International Tel. & Tel. Corp.*, 756 F.2d 1161, 1179 (5th Cir.1985)].

Subsection (c)—. . . This subsection inevitably implies that other law governs the accrual of a claim under Subsection (b) as well as the statute of limitations applicable to those claims. As a result, partners must take care not to "to sit on their claims" waiting for the partnership to dissolve. . . .

§ 411.   CONTINUATION OF PARTNERSHIP BEYOND DEFINITE TERM OR PARTICULAR UNDERTAKING.

(a)   If a partnership for a definite term or particular undertaking is continued, without an express agreement, after the expiration of the term or completion of the undertaking, the rights and duties of the partners remain the same as they were at the expiration or completion, so far as is consistent with a partnership at will.

(b)   If the partners, or those of them who habitually acted in the business during the term or undertaking, continue the business without any settlement or liquidation of the partnership, they are presumed to have agreed that the partnership will continue.

[ARTICLE] 5

TRANSFERABLE INTERESTS AND RIGHTS OF TRANSFEREES AND CREDITORS

Sec.
501. Partner Not Co-Owner of Partnership Property.
502. Nature of Transferable Interest.
503. Transfer of Transferable Interest.
504. Charging Order.
505. Power of Legal Representative of Deceased Partner.

§ 501. PARTNER NOT CO-OWNER OF PARTNERSHIP PROPERTY.

A partner is not a co-owner of partnership property and has no interest in partnership property which can be transferred, either voluntarily or involuntarily.

§ 502. NATURE OF TRANSFERABLE INTEREST.

A transferable interest is personal property.

§ 503. TRANSFER OF TRANSFERABLE INTEREST.

(a) A transfer, in whole or in part, of a transferable interest:

(1) is permissible;

(2) does not by itself cause a person's dissociation as a partner or a dissolution and winding up of the partnership business; and

(3) subject to Section 505, does not entitle the transferee to:

(A) participate in the management or conduct of the partnership's business; or

(B) except as otherwise provided in subsection (c), have access to records or other information concerning the partnership's business.

(b) A transferee has the right to:

(1) receive, in accordance with the transfer, distributions to which the transferor would otherwise be entitled; and

(2) seek under Section 801(5) a judicial determination that it is equitable to wind up the partnership business.

(c) In a dissolution and winding up of a partnership, a transferee is entitled to an account of the partnership's transactions only from the date of dissolution.

(d) A partnership need not give effect to a transferee's rights under this section until the partnership knows or has notice of the transfer.

(e) A transfer of a transferable interest in violation of a restriction on transfer contained in the partnership agreement is ineffective if the intended transferee has knowledge or notice of the restriction at the time of transfer.

(f) Except as otherwise provided in Section 601(4)(B), if a partner transfers a transferable interest, the transferor retains the rights of a partner other than the transferable interest transferred and retains all the duties and obligations of a partner.

(g) If a partner transfers a transferable interest to a person that becomes a partner with respect to the transferred interest, the transferee is liable for the partner's obligations under Sections 404 and 407 known to the transferee when the transferee becomes a partner.

Comment

One of the most fundamental characteristics of partnership law is its fidelity to the "pick your partner" principle. . . . This section is the core of the act's provisions reflecting and protecting that principle. A partner's rights in a partnership are bifurcated into economic rights (the transferable interest) and governance rights (including management rights, consent rights, rights to information, rights to seek judicial intervention). Unless the partnership agreement otherwise provides, a partner acting without the consent of all other partners lacks both the power and the right to: (i) bestow partnership on a non-partner, Section 402(b)(3); or (ii) transfer to a non-partner anything other than some or all of the partner's transferable interest, Section 503(a)(3). The rights of a mere transferee are quite limited (*i.e.,* to receive distributions), Section 503(b), and, if the partnership dissolves and winds up, to receive specified information pertaining to the partnership from the date of dissolution, Section 503(c).

This section applies regardless of whether the transferor is a partner, a transferee of a partner, a transferee of a transferee, etc. . . .

This section does not directly consider whether a partner may transfer governance rights to another partner without obtaining consent from all the other partners. As noted in Section 502, comment, the question is moot under this act's default rule for allocating governance rights.

However, the question can be pivotal when the partnership agreement displaces the default rule on governance rights but does not determine whether transfer restrictions (whether contractual, statutory, or both) apply to transfers of governance rights from one partner to another. Case law is scant and pertains to limited liability companies. Nonetheless, the cases suggest that this act does not protect partners from control shifts that result from transfers among partners. . . . *Blythe v. Bell*, No. 11 CVS 933, 2012 WL 7807800, at ¶ 6 (N.C. Dist. Dec. 10, 2012) (holding in a case of "first impression in North Carolina" that "in the absence of articles of incorporation or an operating agreement to the contrary . . . the assignment of control [*i.e.,* governance] interests between members is effective without unanimous member consent"); *Achaian, Inc. v. Leemon Family LLC*, 25 A.3d 800, 810 (Del. Ch. 2011) (Strine, Ch.). . . [(same)]. . . .

Subsection (f)—Under this subsection, a partner remains a partner (with all attendant rights and obligations) even after permanently transferring the entirety of the transferable interest, unless: (i) the other partners opt for expulsion under Section 601(4)(B); or (ii) as otherwise provided in the partnership agreement.

§ 504.   CHARGING ORDER.

(a)   On application by a judgment creditor of a partner or transferee, a court may enter a charging order against the transferable interest of the judgment debtor for the unsatisfied amount of the judgment. A charging order constitutes a lien on a judgment debtor's transferable interest and requires the partnership to pay over to the person to which the charging order was issued any distribution that otherwise would be paid to the judgment debtor.

(b)   To the extent necessary to effectuate the collection of distributions pursuant to a charging order in effect under subsection (a), the court may:

(1)   appoint a receiver of the distributions subject to the charging order, with the power to make all inquiries the judgment debtor might have made; and

(2)   make all other orders necessary to give effect to the charging order.

(c)   Upon a showing that distributions under a charging order will not pay the judgment debt within a reasonable time, the court may foreclose the lien and order the sale of the transferable interest. The purchaser at the foreclosure sale obtains only the transferable interest, does not thereby become a partner, and is subject to Section 503.

(d)   At any time before foreclosure under subsection (c), the partner or transferee whose transferable interest is subject to a charging order under subsection (a) may extinguish the charging order by satisfying the judgment and filing a certified copy of the satisfaction with the court that issued the charging order.

(e)   At any time before foreclosure under subsection (c), a partnership or one or more partners whose transferable interests are not subject to the charging order may pay to the judgment creditor the full amount due under the judgment and thereby succeed to the rights of the judgment creditor, including the charging order.

(f)   This [act] does not deprive any partner or transferee of the benefit of any exemption law applicable to the transferable interest of the partner or transferee.

(g)   This section provides the exclusive remedy by which a person seeking in the capacity of a judgment creditor to enforce a judgment against a partner or transferee may satisfy the judgment from the judgment debtor's transferable interest.

§ 505.   POWER OF LEGAL REPRESENTATIVE OF DECEASED PARTNER.

If a partner dies, the deceased partner's legal representative may exercise:

(1)   the rights of a transferee provided in Section 503(c); and

(2)   for purposes of settling the estate, the rights the deceased partner had under Section 408.

[ARTICLE] 6

DISSOCIATION

Sec.
601.   Events Causing Dissociation.
602.   Power to Dissociate as Partner; Wrongful Dissociation.
603.   Effect of Dissociation.

§ 601.   EVENTS CAUSING DISSOCIATION.

A person is dissociated as a partner when:

(1)   the partnership knows or has notice of the person's express will to withdraw as a partner, but, if the person has specified a withdrawal date later than the date the partnership knew or had notice, on that later date;

(2)   an event stated in the partnership agreement as causing the person's dissociation occurs;

(3)   the person is expelled as a partner pursuant to the partnership agreement;

(4)   the person is expelled as a partner by the affirmative vote or consent of all the other partners if:

(A)   it is unlawful to carry on the partnership business with the person as a partner;

(B)   there has been a transfer of all of the person's transferable interest in the partnership, other than:

(i)   a transfer for security purposes; or

(ii)   a charging order in effect under Section 504 which has not been foreclosed;

(C)   the person is an entity and:

(i)   the partnership notifies the person that it will be expelled as a partner because the person has filed a statement of dissolution or the equivalent, the person has been administratively dissolved, the person's charter or the equivalent has been revoked, or the person's right to conduct business has been suspended by the person's jurisdiction of formation; and

(ii)   not later than 90 days after the notification, the statement of dissolution or the equivalent has not been withdrawn, rescinded, or revoked, or the person's charter or the equivalent or right to conduct business has not been reinstated; or

(D)   the person is an unincorporated entity that has been dissolved and whose activities and affairs are being wound up;

(5)   on application by the partnership or another partner, the person is expelled as a partner by judicial order because the person:

(A) has engaged or is engaging in wrongful conduct that has affected adversely and materially, or will affect adversely and materially, the partnership's business;

(B) has committed willfully or persistently, or is committing willfully or persistently, a material breach of the partnership agreement or a duty or obligation under Section 409; or

(C) has engaged or is engaging in conduct relating to the partnership's business which makes it not reasonably practicable to carry on the business with the person as a partner;

(6)   the person:

(A) becomes a debtor in bankruptcy;

(B) signs an assignment for the benefit of creditors; or

(C) seeks, consents to, or acquiesces in the appointment of a trustee, receiver, or liquidator of the person or of all or substantially all the person's property;

(7)   in the case of an individual:

(A) the individual dies;

(B) a guardian or general conservator for the individual is appointed; or

(C) a court orders that the individual has otherwise become incapable of performing the individual's duties as a partner under this [act] or the partnership agreement;

(8)   in the case of a person that is a testamentary or inter vivos trust or is acting as a partner by virtue of being a trustee of such a trust, the trust's entire transferable interest in the partnership is distributed;

(9)   in the case of a person that is an estate or is acting as a partner by virtue of being a personal representative of an estate, the estate's entire transferable interest in the partnership is distributed;

(10) in the case of a person that is not an individual, the existence of the person terminates;

(11) the partnership participates in a merger under [Article] 11 and:

(A) the partnership is not the surviving entity; or

(B) otherwise as a result of the merger, the person ceases to be a partner;

(12) the partnership participates in an interest exchange under [Article] 11 and, as a result of the interest exchange, the person ceases to be a partner;

(13) the partnership participates in a conversion under [Article] 11;

(14) the partnership participates in a domestication under [Article] 11 and, as a result of the domestication, the person ceases to be a partner; or

(15) the partnership dissolves and completes winding up.

Comment

This section mostly states default rules, which the partnership agreement may vary. . . .

Paragraph (1)—Partnership agreements often require notice of dissociation to be in writing and to specify the effective date of the dissociation. The partnership cannot eliminate the power of a partner to dissociate by express will, Section 110(c)(9), but can eliminate the right and thereby make the dissociation wrongful.

Paragraph (3)—General partnership agreements often provide for "no cause" expulsion, and courts differ somewhat in how they approach such provisions. . . .

Paragraph (5)—. . .

For an analysis that helps distinguish Paragraph (5)(C) from Paragraphs (5)(A) and (B), *see All Saints University of Medicine Aruba v. Chilana*, A-2628-09T1, 2012 WL 6652510, at *15 (N.J. Super. Ct. App. Div. Dec. 24, 2012) (interpreting predecessor law and noting that the "not reasonably practicable standard" does not require a showing of wrongful conduct). . . .

Where grounds exist for both dissociation and dissolution, a court has the discretion to choose between the alternatives. *Robertson v. Jacobs Cattle Co.*, 830 N.W.2d 191, 201–02 (Neb. 2013). "[T]here is no textual basis for imposing a higher burden of proof for dissociation than dissolution." *Brennan v. Brennan Assocs.*, 977 A.2d 107, 121 (Conn. 2009).

The partnership agreement cannot vary the stated grounds for expulsion, Section 105(c)(10), but can choose an alternate forum—*e.g.*, arbitration. *Compare* Section 801(a)(4) (containing analogous grounds for dissolution by court order), *with* Section 105(c)(11) (making the Section 701(a)(4) grounds non-waivable). . . .

§ 602.   POWER TO DISSOCIATE AS PARTNER; WRONGFUL DISSOCIATION.

(a)   A person has the power to dissociate as a partner at any time, rightfully or wrongfully, by withdrawing as a partner by express will under Section 601(1).

(b)   A person's dissociation as a partner is wrongful only if the dissociation:

(1)   is in breach of an express provision of the partnership agreement; or

(2)   in the case of a partnership for a definite term or particular undertaking, occurs before the expiration of the term or the completion of the undertaking and:

(A)   the person withdraws as a partner by express will, unless the withdrawal follows not later than 90 days after another person's dissociation by death or otherwise under Section 601(6) through (10) or wrongful dissociation under this subsection;

(B)   the person is expelled as a partner by judicial order under Section 601(5);

(C)   the person is dissociated under Section 601(6); or

(D)   in the case of a person that is not a trust other than a business trust, an estate, or an individual, the person is expelled or otherwise dissociated because it willfully dissolved or terminated.

(c)   A person that wrongfully dissociates as a partner is liable to the partnership and to the other partners for damages caused by the dissociation. The liability is in addition to any debt, obligation, or other liability of the partner to the partnership or the other partners.

Comment

Subsection (a)—A general partnership is a voluntary association, *see* Section 105(c)(9), and voluntary. . . .

The phrase "rightfully or wrongfully" reflects the distinction between a partner's *power* to withdraw in contravention of the partnership agreement and a partner's *right* to do so. Thus, although a partner cannot be enjoined from exercising the power to dissociate, the dissociation may be wrongful under Subsection (b).

Subsection (b)—This subsection list exhaustively ("only if") the dissociations that are "wrongful." The label has three consequences:

- under Subsection (c) liability for resulting damages, which, under Section 701(c), may be offset against the amount of the buyout price due to the partner under Section 701(a);

- under Section 701(h) postponement of payment of the buyout price until the term expires or the undertaking is completed; and

- under Section 804, exclusion from the winding up process, if the dissociation results in dissolution of the partnership.

This subsection states a default rule. The partnership agreement can expand the list (*e.g.*, by making wrongful a dissociation that beaches the implied contractual covenant of good faith and fair dealing). In theory, the partnership agreement can provide for liquidated damages (subject to the requirements of contract law) and, in theory, can also shrink or even eliminate the list of wrongful dissociations. . . .

Subsection (c)—A partner who prematurely dissociates from a partnership for an agreed term or undertaking risks liability for any resulting damages. For example, the partnership might incur substantial expenses in replacing the general partner's expertise, reputation, or creditworthiness.

In effect, this subsection equates wrongful dissociation with breach of contract. Accordingly, courts should look to contract law to determine what consequential damages are recoverable. . . .

§ 603. EFFECT OF DISSOCIATION.

(a)   If a person's dissociation results in a dissolution and winding up of the partnership business, [Article] 8 applies; otherwise, [Article] 7 applies.

(b)   If a person is dissociated as a partner:

(1)   the person's right to participate in the management and conduct of the partnership's business terminates, except as otherwise provided in Section 802(c); and

(2)   the person's duties and obligations under Section 409 end with regard to matters arising and events occurring after the person's dissociation, except to the extent the partner participates in winding up the partnership's business pursuant to Section 802.

(c)   A person's dissociation does not of itself discharge the person from any debt, obligation, or other liability to the partnership or the other partners which the person incurred while a partner.

Comment

Subsection (a)—This subsection is a "switching" provision, invoking either Article 7 or 8 depending on whether a person's dissociation as a partner results in dissolution. . . .

Subsection (b)—This section originated as UPA (1997) § 603(b) and deals with some of the internal effects of a person's dissociation as a partner.

Subsection (b)(1)—A person's dissociation as a partner ends immediately the person's right to participate in the management of the business, unless the dissociation results in dissolution of the partnership. *See* Section 802(c) ("A person whose dissociation as a partner resulted in dissolution may participate in winding up as if still a partner, unless the dissociation was wrongful.").

Subsection (b)(2)—Unless a person's dissociation as a partner results in dissolution and the person participates in winding up, Section 802(c), this provision establishes a dividing line, separating out "matters arising and events occurring after the person's dissociation." If the partnership has continuing projects with clients, ongoing relationships with clients, or both, the dividing line requires special attention with regard to non-competition and partnership opportunities duties. *See* Section 409(b)(1), (3). . . .

This provision does not determine the effect of a person's dissociation as a partner on the person's future obligations or rights under the partnership agreement. Some contractual obligations typically extend beyond dissociation—*e.g.*, non-competition agreements, buyout arrangements. To the extent provisions of the partnership agreement continue to apply, the common law obligation of good faith continues to apply as well. *See* the comment to Section 409(d) (explaining that the subsection "invokes the implied obligation that exists in every contract" as a matter of common law).

Subsection (c)—A partner's obligation to safeguard trade secrets and other confidential or proprietary information is incurred when the partner learns or otherwise obtains the information. This subsection preserves the obligation post-dissociation.

[ARTICLE] 7

PERSON'S DISSOCIATION AS A PARTNER WHEN BUSINESS NOT WOUND UP

Sec.
701.   Purchase of Interest of Person Dissociated as Partner.
702.   Power to Bind and Liability of Person Dissociated as Partner.
703.   Liability of Person Dissociated as Partner to Other Persons.
704.   Statement of Dissociation.
705.   Continued Use of Partnership Name.

§ 701. PURCHASE OF INTEREST OF PERSON DISSOCIATED AS PARTNER.

(a)   If a person is dissociated as a partner without the dissociation resulting in a dissolution and winding up of the partnership business under Section 801, the partnership shall cause the person's interest in the partnership to be purchased for a buyout price determined pursuant to subsection (b).

(b)   The buyout price of the interest of a person dissociated as a partner is the amount that would have been distributable to the person under Section 806(b) if, on the date of dissociation, the assets of the partnership were sold and the partnership were wound up, with the sale price equal to the greater of:

(1)   the liquidation value; or

(2)   the value based on a sale of the entire business as a going concern without the person.

(c)   Interest accrues on the buyout price from the date of dissociation to the date of payment, but damages for wrongful dissociation under Section 602(b), and all other amounts owing, whether or not presently due, from the person dissociated as a partner to the partnership, must be offset against the buyout price.

(d)   A partnership shall defend, indemnify, and hold harmless a person dissociated as a partner whose interest is being purchased against all partnership liabilities, whether incurred before or after the dissociation, except liabilities incurred by an act of the person under Section 702.

(e)   If no agreement for the purchase of the interest of a person dissociated as a partner is reached not later than 120 days after a written demand for payment, the partnership shall pay, or cause to be paid, in money to the person the amount the partnership estimates to be the buyout price and accrued interest, reduced by any offsets and accrued interest under subsection (c).

(f)   If a deferred payment is authorized under subsection (h), the partnership may tender a written offer to pay the amount it estimates to be the buyout price and accrued interest, reduced by any offsets under subsection (c), stating the time of payment, the amount and type of security for payment, and the other terms and conditions of the obligation.

(g)   The payment or tender required by subsection (e) or (f) must be accompanied by the following:

(1)   a statement of partnership assets and liabilities as of the date of dissociation;

(2)   the latest available partnership balance sheet and income statement, if any;

(3)   an explanation of how the estimated amount of the payment was calculated; and

(4)   written notice that the payment is in full satisfaction of the obligation to purchase unless, not later than 120 days after the written notice, the person dissociated as a partner commences an action to determine the buyout price, any offsets under subsection (c), or other terms of the obligation to purchase.

(h)   A person that wrongfully dissociates as a partner before the expiration of a definite term or the completion of a particular undertaking is not entitled to payment of any part of the buyout price until the expiration of the term or completion of the undertaking, unless the person establishes to the satisfaction of the court that earlier payment will not cause undue hardship to the business of the partnership. A deferred payment must be adequately secured and bear interest.

(i)   A person dissociated as a partner may maintain an action against the partnership, pursuant to Section 410(b)(2), to determine the buyout price of that person's interest, any offsets under subsection (c), or other terms of the obligation to purchase. The action must be commenced not later than 120 days after the partnership has tendered payment or an offer to pay or within one year after written demand for payment if no payment or offer to pay is tendered. The court shall determine the buyout price of the person's interest, any offset due under subsection (c), and accrued interest, and enter judgment for any additional payment or refund. If deferred payment is authorized under subsection (h), the court shall also determine the security for payment and other terms of the obligation to purchase. The court may assess reasonable attorney's fees and the fees and expenses of appraisers or other experts for a party to the action, in amounts the court finds equitable, against a party that the court finds acted arbitrarily, vexatiously, or not in good faith. The finding may be based on the partnership's failure to tender payment or an offer to pay or to comply with subsection (g).

Comment

Article 7 originated in UPA (1997) and provides for the buyout of the interest of a person dissociated as a partner if the dissociation does not result in a dissolution and winding up of the partnership's business under Article 8. *See* Section 603(a). If there is no dissolution, the remaining partners have a right to continue the business and the person dissociated as a partner has a right to be bought out. . . .

The rules in this section are merely default rules. The partners may, in the partnership agreement, fix the method or formula for determining the buyout price and all of the other terms and conditions of the buyout right. Indeed, the very right to a buyout itself may be modified, although a provision providing for a complete forfeiture would probably not be enforceable. *See* Section 119 (Supplemental Principles of Law).

Subsection (a)—This subsection provides that, if a person's dissociation as a partner does not result in a windup of the business, the partnership shall cause the interest of the dissociating partner to be purchased for a buyout price determined pursuant to Subsection (b). The buyout is mandatory, unless the partnership provides otherwise. The "cause to be purchased" language is intended to accommodate a purchase by the partnership, one or more of the remaining partners, or a third party.

Subsection (b)—This subsection provides how the "buyout price" is to be determined. The terms "fair market value" or "fair value" were not used because they are often considered terms of art having a special meaning depending on the context, such as in tax or corporate law. "Buyout price" was a new term in UPA (1997). Under Subsection (b), the buyout price is the amount that would have been distributable to the dissociating partner under Section 807(b) if, on the date of dissociation, the assets of the partnership were sold at a price equal to the greater of liquidation value or going concern value without the departing partner. Liquidation value is not intended to mean distress sale value. Under general principles of valuation, the hypothetical selling price in either case should be the price that a willing and informed buyer would pay a willing and informed seller, with neither being under any compulsion to deal. The notion of a minority discount in determining the buyout price is negated by valuing the business as a going concern. Other discounts, such as for a lack of marketability or the loss of a key partner, may be appropriate, however. . . .

Since the buyout price is based on the value of the business at the time of dissociation, the partnership must pay interest on the amount due from the date of dissociation until payment to compensate the dissociating partner for the use of his interest in the firm. . . .

Under this section, unless the partnership's goodwill is damaged by the wrongful dissociation, the value of the wrongfully dissociating partner's interest will include any goodwill value of the partnership. If the firm's goodwill is damaged, the amount of the damages suffered by the partnership and the remaining partners will be offset against the buyout price.

Subsection (c)—This subsection provides that the partnership may offset against the buyout price all amounts owing by the person dissociated as a partner to the partnership, whether or not presently due, including any damages for wrongful dissociation under Section 602(c). This rule has the effect of accelerating payment of amounts not yet due from the former partner to the partnership, including a long-term loan by the partnership to the former partner. . . .

Subsection (f)—Under this subsection, when deferred payment is authorized in the case of a wrongfully dissociating partner, a written offer stating the amount the partnership estimates to be the purchase price should be tendered within the 120-day period, even though actual payment of the amount may be deferred, possibly for many years. *See* the comment to Subsection (h). The dissociated partner is entitled to know at the time of dissociation what amount the remaining partners think is due, including the estimated amount of any damages allegedly caused by the partner's wrongful dissociation that may be offset against the buyout price. . . .

Subsection (i)—This subsection provides that a person dissociated as a partner may maintain an action against the partnership to determine the buyout price, any offsets, or other terms of the purchase obligation. . . .

§ 702. POWER TO BIND AND LIABILITY OF PERSON DISSOCIATED AS PARTNER.

(a)   After a person is dissociated as a partner without the dissociation resulting in a dissolution and winding up of the partnership business and before the partnership is merged out of existence, converted, or domesticated under [Article] 11, or dissolved, the partnership is bound by an act of the person only if:

(1)   the act would have bound the partnership under Section 301 before dissociation; and

(2)   at the time the other party enters into the transaction:

    (A)   less than two years has passed since the dissociation; and

    (B)   the other party does not know or have notice of the dissociation and reasonably believes that the person is a partner.

    (b)   If a partnership is bound under subsection (a), the person dissociated as a partner which caused the partnership to be bound is liable:

    (1)   to the partnership for any damage caused to the partnership arising from the obligation incurred under subsection (a); and

    (2)   if a partner or another person dissociated as a partner is liable for the obligation, to the partner or other person for any damage caused to the partner or other person arising from the liability.

Comment

A person's dissociation as a partner ends immediately the person's actual authority to act for the partnership, unless the dissociation results in a dissolution and winding up of the business of the partnership. *See* Section 603(b)(1). However, the person's apparent authority may linger.

This section does not affect a person's power to bind a partnership in another capacity—*e.g.*, as an employee with actual authority.

Subsection (a)—This subsection codifies and constrains the lingering apparent authority of a person dissociated as a partner. The constraint is in the phrase "only if."

The provision applies until the partnership dissolves or under Article 11 ceases to be governed by this act. Once a partnership dissolves, Section 804 applies.

With respect to authority of a person dissociated as a partner to transfer partnership real property, Section 303(e) provides that third parties are deemed to have knowledge of a limitation on the person's authority to transfer real property held in the partnership name upon the proper recording of a statement containing such a limitation. Section 704(b) provides that a statement of dissociation operates as a limitation on the person's authority for the purposes of Section 303(e). Thus, a properly recorded statement of dissociation provides, immediately upon recording, constructive knowledge of the lack of authority of a person dissociated as a partner to transfer real property held in the partnership name. . . .

§ 703.   LIABILITY OF PERSON DISSOCIATED AS PARTNER TO OTHER PERSONS.

    (a)   Except as otherwise provided in subsection (b), a person dissociated as a partner is not liable for a partnership obligation incurred after dissociation.

    (b)   A person that is dissociated as a partner is liable on a transaction entered into by the partnership after the dissociation only if:

    (1)   a partner would be liable on the transaction; and

    (2)   at the time the other party enters into the transaction:

    (A)   less than two years has passed since the dissociation; and

    (B)   the other party does not have knowledge or notice of the dissociation and reasonably believes that the person is a partner.

    (c)   By agreement with a creditor of a partnership and the partnership, a person dissociated as a partner may be released from liability for a debt, obligation, or other liability of the partnership.

    (d)   A person dissociated as a partner is released from liability for a debt, obligation, or other liability of the partnership if the partnership's creditor, with knowledge or notice of the person's dissociation but without the person's consent, agrees to a material alteration in the nature or time of payment of the debt, obligation, or other liability.

§ 704.   STATEMENT OF DISSOCIATION.

(a)   A person dissociated as a partner or the partnership may deliver to the [Secretary of State] for filing a statement of dissociation stating the name of the partnership and that the person has dissociated from the partnership.

(b)   A statement of dissociation is a limitation on the authority of a person dissociated as a partner for the purposes of Section 303.

§ 705.   CONTINUED USE OF PARTNERSHIP NAME.

Continued use of a partnership name, or the name of a person dissociated as a partner as part of the partnership name, by partners continuing the business does not of itself make the person dissociated as a partner liable for an obligation of the partners or the partnership continuing the business.

[ARTICLE] 8

DISSOLUTION AND WINDING UP

Sec.

801.   Events Causing Dissolution.
802.   Winding Up.
803.   Rescinding Dissolution.
804.   Power to Bind Partnership After Dissolution.
805.   Liability After Dissolution of Partner and Person Dissociated as Partner.
806.   Disposition of Assets in Winding Up; When Contributions Required.
807.   Known Claims Against Dissolved Limited Liability Partnership.
808.   Other Claims Against Dissolved Limited Liability Partnership.
809.   Court Proceedings.
810.   Liability of Partner and Person Dissociated as Partner When Claim Against Partnership Barred.

§ 801.   EVENTS CAUSING DISSOLUTION.

A partnership is dissolved, and its business must be wound up, upon the occurrence of any of the following:

(1)   in a partnership at will, the partnership knows or has notice of a person's express will to withdraw as a partner, other than a partner that has dissociated under Section 601(2) through (10), but, if the person has specified a withdrawal date later than the date the partnership knew or had notice, on the later date;

(2)   in a partnership for a definite term or particular undertaking:

(A)   within 90 days after a person's dissociation by death or otherwise under Section 601(6) through (10) or wrongful dissociation under Section 602(b), the affirmative vote or consent of at least half of the remaining partners to wind up the partnership business, for which purpose a person's rightful dissociation pursuant to Section 602(b)(2)(A) constitutes that partner's consent to wind up the partnership business;

(B)   the affirmative vote or consent of all the partners to wind up the partnership business; or

(C)   the expiration of the term or the completion of the undertaking;

(3)   an event or circumstance that the partnership agreement states causes dissolution;

(4)   on application by a partner, the entry by [the appropriate court] of an order dissolving the partnership on the grounds that:

(A)   the conduct of all or substantially all the partnership's business is unlawful;

(B)   the economic purpose of the partnership is likely to be unreasonably frustrated;

(C)   another partner has engaged in conduct relating to the partnership business which makes it not reasonably practicable to carry on the business in partnership with that partner; or

(D)   it is otherwise not reasonably practicable to carry on the partnership business in conformity with the partnership agreement;

(5)   on application by a transferee, the entry by [the appropriate court] of an order dissolving the partnership on the ground that it is equitable to wind up the partnership business:

(A)   after the expiration of the term or completion of the undertaking, if the partnership was for a definite term or particular undertaking at the time of the transfer or entry of the charging order that gave rise to the transfer; or

(B)   at any time, if the partnership was a partnership at will at the time of the transfer or entry of the charging order that gave rise to the transfer; or

(6)   the passage of 90 consecutive days during which the partnership does not have at least two partners.

Comment

"Dissolution" has been a term of art in the law of unincorporated business organizations . . . Dissolution does not end a partnership's existence but rather changes the purpose of that existence: "A dissolved partnership shall wind up its business and. . . the partnership continues after dissolution only for the purpose of winding up." Section 802(a). The partnership may, but need not, file a statement of dissolution. Section 802(b)(2)(A). The partnership terminates when winding up is complete. The partnership may, but need not, file a statement of termination. Section 802(b)(2)(F).

UPA (1914) took a strictly aggregate approach to dissolution; under UPA (1914) § 29, the departure of any partner under any circumstances inevitably caused the partnership to dissolve. . . .

UPA (1997) fundamentally changed this . . ., making the partnership entity much more durable than the UPA (1914) aggregate. For example, expelling a partner does not cause the partnership to dissolve, even if the partnership is at-will. Section 801(1). More generally, the grounds for dissolution stated in Section 801 are exhaustive, unless the partnership agreement states otherwise.

Given this act's built-in transfer restrictions, Section 503, increasing the partnership's durability necessarily decreases each partner's exit rights. . . . Eliminating that power creates a risk of "lock-in."

UPA (1997) addressed the lock-in issue through UPA (1997) § 701. When a person dissociates as a partner, whether rightfully or wrongfully, the partnership is obligated to buy out the person's interest. Note, however, that Section 701, like UPA (1997) § 701, is a default rule.

Except for Paragraphs 4 and 5, this section comprises default rules. Paragraphs 4 and 5 are mandatory only with regard to the stated grounds for dissolution. . . .

The Harmonization Project added Paragraph 6 but otherwise made no significant changes to this section. . . .

Paragraph (2)(A)—This provision: (i) originated in UPA (1997); (ii) helps make the partnership entity more durable; (iii) protects the remaining partners where the dissociating partner is crucial to the successful continuation of the business; and (iv) reverses the approach of UPA (1914). . . .

A person's dissociation as a partner by death or otherwise under Section 601(6) to (10) or wrongful dissociation under Section 602(b), makes a term partnership *susceptible* to dissolution. If within ninety days after the dissociation at least half of the remaining partners express their will to dissolve the partnership, the partnership dissolves. Section 601(6) to (10) pertain, respectively, to a partner's bankruptcy or similar financial impairment (6); a partner's death or incapacity (7); the distribution by a trust-partner of its entire transferable interest (8); the distribution by an estate-partner of its entire transferable interest; and the termination of an entity-partner (10).

During the same ninety-day window, Section 602(b)(2)(A) permits each remaining partner to withdraw rightfully by express will. A partner does not express a desire to withdraw solely by reason of voting for or consenting to the winding up of the partnership business. However, the converse is true: "[A] person's rightful dissociation pursuant to Section 602(b)(2)(A) constitutes the expression of that partner's consent to wind up the partnership business." Section 801(2)(A).

EXAMPLE: A term partnership has seven partners, and one of the partners dissociates by dying before the end of the term. Section 601(7). The partnership will dissolve if within ninety days after the dissociation three of the remaining five partners affirmatively vote or consent to dissolution.

EXAMPLE: Same facts, except the partner dissociates in breach of the partnership agreement. Same result.

EXAMPLE: Same facts, except that the partner is "a person that . . . is acting as a partner by virtue of being a trustee of . . . a trust, [and] the trust's entire transferable interest in the partnership [has been] distributed. Section 601(8). Same result.

. . .

Paragraph (2)(C)—. . . This provision must be read in conjunction with Section 411. Under Section 411(a), if the partners continue the business after the expiration of the term or the completion of the undertaking, the partnership will be treated as a partnership at will. Moreover, if the partners continue the business without any settlement or liquidation of the partnership, under Section 411(b) they are presumed to have agreed that the partnership will continue, despite the lack of a formal agreement.

Paragraph (3)—The partners can avoid the effects of this paragraph either by amending the partnership agreement before dissolution occurs or using Section 803 to rescind dissolution. . . .

Paragraph (4)—The partnership agreement cannot vary the stated grounds for dissolution.

Paragraph (4)(A)—The "all or substantially all" proviso is intended to avoid dissolution for insubstantial or innocent regulatory violations.

Paragraph (4)(B)–(D)—The Virginia Supreme Court has referred to "these statutory bases for judicial dissolution as the economic purpose test, the partner conduct test, and the business operations test, respectively." *Russell Realty Assocs. v. Russell*, 724 S.E.2d 690, 693 (Va. 2012). . . . These tests somewhat overlap and are often pled together. *E.g.*, *Wood v. Apodaca*, 375 F. Supp. 2d 942, 948 (N.D. Cal. 2005).

Some courts have held that, if the trial court finds grounds for dissolution under one or more of these provisions, that court has no power to order a lesser remedy, such as a buyout. . . .

Paragraph (4)(B)—"[P]oor financial performance" is neither sufficient nor necessary to satisfy this provision. *Russell Realty Assocs. v. Russell*, 724 S.E.2d 690, 694 (Va. 2012). . . . That provision might result in a dissolution contrary to the partners' expectations in a start-up or tax shelter situation, in which case 'book' or 'tax' losses do not signify business failure.").

As for the second point (not always necessary), see *Russell Realty Assocs. v. Russell*, 724 S.E.2d 690, 694–55 (Va. 2012) (noting that the partnership's purpose was "to acquire, hold, invest in, and lease and sell investment properties"; stating with regard to the Virginia analog to Paragraph 4(B) that "[t]he partners' expectations for realizing these purposes included not only expectations of economic success, but also the ability to undertake these activities in an efficient and productive manner to maximize return to the partnership"; and listing numerous ways in which the relationship between the partners frustrated the economic purpose of the partnership).

Paragraph (4)(C)—A partner can trigger this provision without necessarily breaching the partnership agreement. *E.g.*, *Robertson v. Jacobs Cattle Co.*, 830 N.W.2d 191, 202 (Neb. 2013) (stating that "the somewhat autocratic manner in which Ardith conducted the affairs of the partnership in recent years, even if not in violation of the partnership agreement, would constitute grounds for dissolution under [the UPA (1997) version of] this provision").

Paragraph (4)(D)—The specific terms of the partnership agreement are the frame of reference for applying this provision. *Sriram v. Preferred Income Fund III Ltd. P'ship*, 22 F.3d 498, 502 (2d Cir. 1994) ("The issue is not whether the partnerships can effectively carry out the general purpose of the Agreements after considerable modification of their terms. Rather, the query . . . is whether the purpose of the Agreements can be carried out 'in conformity with the partnership agreement,' that is, in conformity with the terms and conditions of the Agreements to which the limited partners ascribed and on which they relied when choosing to part with their capital."). . . .

Paragraph (5)—This paragraph gives a transferee rights comparable to a partner who seeks dissolution because the other partners are continuing the business in derogation of the partner's rights to obtain dissolution. . . .

Paragraph (6)—The Harmonization Project added this provision, which is consistent with Section 202(a) (stating that "the association of two or more persons to carry on as co-owners a business for profit forms a partnership"). . . . *See* the comment to Section 302(d); *Pemstein v. Pemstein*, G030217, 2004 WL 1260034 (Cal. Ct. App. June 9, 2004) (" 'Can one person carry on a partnership?' In short, the answer is no. . . . Just as it takes two to form a marriage, it takes a minimum of two to run a viable partnership. . . .")

§ 802. WINDING UP.

(a)   A dissolved partnership shall wind up its business and, except as otherwise provided in Section 803, the partnership continues after dissolution only for the purpose of winding up.

(b)   In winding up its business, the partnership:

(1)   shall discharge the partnership's debts, obligations, and other liabilities, settle and close the partnership's business, and marshal and distribute the assets of the partnership; and

(2)   may:

(A)   deliver to the [Secretary of State] for filing a statement of dissolution stating the name of the partnership and that the partnership is dissolved;

(B)   preserve the partnership business and property as a going concern for a reasonable time;

(C)   prosecute and defend actions and proceedings, whether civil, criminal, or administrative;

(D)   transfer the partnership's property;

(E)   settle disputes by mediation or arbitration;

(F)   deliver to the [Secretary of State] for filing a statement of termination stating the name of the partnership and that the partnership is terminated; and

(G)   perform other acts necessary or appropriate to the winding up.

(c)   A person whose dissociation as a partner resulted in dissolution may participate in winding up as if still a partner, unless the dissociation was wrongful.

(d)   If a dissolved partnership does not have a partner and no person has the right to participate in winding up under subsection (c), the personal or legal representative of the last person to have been a partner may wind up the partnership's business. If the representative does not exercise that right, a person to wind up the partnership's business may be appointed by the affirmative vote or consent of transferees owning a majority of the rights to receive distributions at the time the consent is to be effective. A person appointed under this subsection has the powers of a partner under Section 804 but is not liable for the debts, obligations, and other liabilities of the partnership solely by reason of having or exercising those powers or otherwise acting to wind up the partnership's business.

(e)   On the application of any partner or person entitled under subsection (c) to participate in winding up, the [appropriate court] may order judicial supervision of the winding up of a dissolved partnership, including the appointment of a person to wind up the partnership's business, if:

(1)   the partnership does not have a partner and within a reasonable time following the dissolution no person has been appointed under subsection (d); or

(2)   the applicant establishes other good cause.

§ 803. RESCINDING DISSOLUTION.

(a)   A partnership may rescind its dissolution, unless a statement of termination applicable to the partnership has become effective or [the appropriate court] has entered an order under Section 801(4) or (5) dissolving the partnership.

(b)   Rescinding dissolution under this section requires:

(1)   the affirmative vote or consent of each partner; and

(2) if the partnership has delivered to the [Secretary of State] for filing a statement of dissolution and:

(A) the statement has not become effective, delivery to the [Secretary of State] for filing of a statement of withdrawal under Section 115 applicable to the statement of dissolution; or

(B) the statement of dissolution has become effective, delivery to the [Secretary of State] for filing of a statement of rescission stating the name of the partnership and that dissolution has been rescinded under this section.

(c) If a partnership rescinds its dissolution:

(1) the partnership resumes carrying on its business as if dissolution had never occurred;

(2) subject to paragraph (3), any liability incurred by the partnership after the dissolution and before the rescission has become effective is determined as if dissolution had never occurred; and

(3) the rights of a third party arising out of conduct in reliance on the dissolution before the third party knew or had notice of the rescission may not be adversely affected.

Comment

The Harmonization Project added this section, replacing UPA (1997) § 802(b) (permitting the partners to "waive the right to have the partnership's business wound up and the partnership terminated" after which "the partnership resumes carrying on its business as if dissolution had never occurred")....

§ 804. POWER TO BIND PARTNERSHIP AFTER DISSOLUTION.

(a) A partnership is bound by a partner's act after dissolution which:

(1) is appropriate for winding up the partnership business; or

(2) would have bound the partnership under Section 301 before dissolution if, at the time the other party enters into the transaction, the other party does not know or have notice of the dissolution.

(b) A person dissociated as a partner binds a partnership through an act occurring after dissolution if:

(1) at the time the other party enters into the transaction:

(A) less than two years has passed since the dissociation; and

(B) the other party does not know or have notice of the dissociation and reasonably believes that the person is a partner; and

(2) the act:

(A) is appropriate for winding up the partnership's business; or

(B) would have bound the partnership under Section 301 before dissolution and at the time the other party enters into the transaction the other party does not know or have notice of the dissolution.

§ 805. LIABILITY AFTER DISSOLUTION OF PARTNER AND PERSON DISSOCIATED AS PARTNER.

(a) If a partner having knowledge of the dissolution causes a partnership to incur an obligation under Section 804(a) by an act that is not appropriate for winding up the partnership business, the partner is liable:

(1) to the partnership for any damage caused to the partnership arising from the obligation; and

(2) if another partner or person dissociated as a partner is liable for the obligation, to that other partner or person for any damage caused to that other partner or person arising from the liability.

(b)   Except as otherwise provided in subsection (c), if a person dissociated as a partner causes a partnership to incur an obligation under Section 804(b), the person is liable:

(1)   to the partnership for any damage caused to the partnership arising from the obligation; and

(2)   if a partner or another person dissociated as a partner is liable for the obligation, to the partner or other person for any damage caused to the partner or other person arising from the obligation.

(c)   A person dissociated as a partner is not liable under subsection (b) if:

(1)   Section 802(c) permits the person to participate in winding up; and

(2)   the act that causes the partnership to be bound under Section 804(b) is appropriate for winding up the partnership's business.

§ 806.   DISPOSITION OF ASSETS IN WINDING UP; WHEN CONTRIBUTIONS REQUIRED.

(a)   In winding up its business, a partnership shall apply its assets, including the contributions required by this section, to discharge the partnership's obligations to creditors, including partners that are creditors.

(b)   After a partnership complies with subsection (a), any surplus must be distributed in the following order, subject to any charging order in effect under Section 504:

(1)   to each person owning a transferable interest that reflects contributions made and not previously returned, an amount equal to the value of the unreturned contributions; and

(2)   among persons owning transferable interests in proportion to their respective rights to share in distributions immediately before the dissolution of the partnership.

(c)   If a partnership's assets are insufficient to satisfy all its obligations under subsection (a), with respect to each unsatisfied obligation incurred when the partnership was not a limited liability partnership, the following rules apply:

(1)   Each person that was a partner when the obligation was incurred and that has not been released from the obligation under Section 703(c) and (d) shall contribute to the partnership for the purpose of enabling the partnership to satisfy the obligation. The contribution due from each of those persons is in proportion to the right to receive distributions in the capacity of a partner in effect for each of those persons when the obligation was incurred.

(2)   If a person does not contribute the full amount required under paragraph (1) with respect to an unsatisfied obligation of the partnership, the other persons required to contribute by paragraph (1) on account of the obligation shall contribute the additional amount necessary to discharge the obligation. The additional contribution due from each of those other persons is in proportion to the right to receive distributions in the capacity of a partner in effect for each of those other persons when the obligation was incurred.

(3)   If a person does not make the additional contribution required by paragraph (2), further additional contributions are determined and due in the same manner as provided in that paragraph.

(d)   A person that makes an additional contribution under subsection (c)(2) or (3) may recover from any person whose failure to contribute under subsection (c)(1) or (2) necessitated the additional contribution. A person may not recover under this subsection more than the amount additionally contributed. A person's liability under this subsection may not exceed the amount the person failed to contribute.

(e)   If a partnership does not have sufficient surplus to comply with subsection (b)(1), any surplus must be distributed among the owners of transferable interests in proportion to the value of the respective unreturned contributions.

(f)   All distributions made under subsections (b) and (c) must be paid in money.

Comment

Subsection (a)—This subsection is non-waivable as to creditors who are not partners. . . . However, if a creditor is willing, a dissolved partnership may certainly make agreements with the creditor specifying the terms under which the partnership will "discharge its obligations" to the creditor. . . .

Subsection (b)—For the most part, this subsection states default rules. For example, partnership agreements often provide for different distribution rights upon liquidation than during operations. . . .

Subsection (c)—This section applies obligation by obligation, because a person—*qua* partner or person dissociated as a partner—is required to contribute to the partnership to satisfy a partnership obligation only if, when the obligation was incurred: (i) the person was a partner; and (ii) the partnership was not an LLP. *See* Section 306(b), (c). . . .

Subsection (c)(2) and (3)—These provisions are analogous to buy-sell provisions that: (i) provide that an owner's effort to sell the ownership interest triggers an option to purchase allocated among all the other owners; (ii) make the option conditional on the entire interest being purchased; and (iii) provide for successive allocations to take up any previous allocations that were not unexercised.

Subsection (e)—If a partnership has been a limited liability partnership throughout the partnership's existence, this subsection is consistent with this act's approach to loss sharing. If a partnership has been a limited liability partnership during only part of the partnership's existence, the issue of loss sharing upon dissolution: (i) can be exceedingly complicated, varying radically depending on the circumstances; (ii) is therefore not amenable to a statutory "gap filler"; and (iii) thus should always be addressed in the partnership agreement.

However, in case the partnership agreement does not address the issue, this act must provide a default rule. . . . This subsection applies to fill the gap. This approach has the virtues of simplicity and certainty but in no way resembles what "typical" partners might agree if they were to consider the matter *ab initio*, especially if the partnership was never an LLP. *Cf.* Robert W. Hillman, *Private Ordering Within Partnerships*, 41 U. MIAMI L. REV. 425, 448 (1987) ("[T]he various norms established by the Act, applicable in the absence of agreements to the contrary, represent the supposed understandings partners most likely reach if they choose to bargain on the various issues.").

§ 807. KNOWN CLAIMS AGAINST DISSOLVED LIMITED LIABILITY PARTNERSHIP.

(a)   Except as otherwise provided in subsection (d), a dissolved limited liability partnership may give notice of a known claim under subsection (b), which has the effect provided in subsection (c).

(b)   A dissolved limited liability partnership may in a record notify its known claimants of the dissolution. The notice must:

(1)   specify the information required to be included in a claim;

(2)   state that a claim must be in writing and provide a mailing address to which the claim is to be sent;

(3)   state the deadline for receipt of a claim, which may not be less than 120 days after the date the notice is received by the claimant;

(4)   state that the claim will be barred if not received by the deadline; and

(5)   unless the partnership has been throughout its existence a limited liability partnership, state that the barring of a claim against the partnership will also bar any corresponding claim against any partner or person dissociated as a partner which is based on Section 306.

(c)   A claim against a dissolved limited liability partnership is barred if the requirements of subsection (b) are met and:

(1)   the claim is not received by the specified deadline; or

(2)   if the claim is timely received but rejected by the limited liability partnership:

(A)   the partnership causes the claimant to receive a notice in a record stating that the claim is rejected and will be barred unless the claimant commences an action against the partnership to enforce the claim not later than 90 days after the claimant receives the notice; and

(B)   the claimant does not commence the required action not later than 90 days after the claimant receives the notice.

(d)   This section does not apply to a claim based on an event occurring after the date of dissolution or a liability that on that date is contingent.

Comment

Source—Added during the Harmonization Project, this section is derived almost verbatim from Model Business Corporation Act section 14.06. . . .

§ 808. OTHER CLAIMS AGAINST DISSOLVED LIMITED LIABILITY PARTNERSHIP.

(a)   A dissolved limited liability partnership may publish notice of its dissolution and request persons having claims against the partnership to present them in accordance with the notice.

(b)   A notice under subsection (a) must:

(1)   be published at least once in a newspaper of general circulation in the [county] in this state in which the dissolved limited liability partnership's principal office is located or, if the principal office is not located in this state, in the [county] in which the office of the partnership's registered agent is or was last located;

(2)   describe the information required to be contained in a claim, state that the claim must be in writing, and provide a mailing address to which the claim is to be sent;

(3)   state that a claim against the partnership is barred unless an action to enforce the claim is commenced not later than three years after publication of the notice; and

(4)   unless the partnership has been throughout its existence a limited liability partnership, state that the barring of a claim against the partnership will also bar any corresponding claim against any partner or person dissociated as a partner which is based on Section 306.

(c)   If a dissolved limited liability partnership publishes a notice in accordance with subsection (b), the claim of each of the following claimants is barred unless the claimant commences an action to enforce the claim against the partnership not later than three years after the publication date of the notice:

(1)   a claimant that did not receive notice in a record under Section 807;

(2)   a claimant whose claim was timely sent to the partnership but not acted on; and

(3)   a claimant whose claim is contingent at, or based on an event occurring after, the date of dissolution.

(d)   A claim not barred under this section or Section 807 may be enforced:

(1)   against a dissolved limited liability partnership, to the extent of its undistributed assets;

(2)   except as otherwise provided in Section 809, if assets of the partnership have been distributed after dissolution, against a partner or transferee to the extent of that person's proportionate share of the claim or of the partnership's assets distributed to the partner or transferee after dissolution, whichever is less, but a person's total liability for all claims under this paragraph may not exceed the total amount of assets distributed to the person after dissolution; and

(3)   against any person liable on the claim under Sections 306, 703, and 805.

Comment

Source—Added during the Harmonization Project, this section is derived almost verbatim from Model Business Corporation Act section 14.07. . . .

§ 809.　COURT PROCEEDINGS.

(a)　A dissolved limited liability partnership that has published a notice under Section 808 may file an application with [the appropriate court] in the [county] where the partnership's principal office is located or, if the principal office is not located in this state, where the office of its registered agent is or was last located, for a determination of the amount and form of security to be provided for payment of claims that are reasonably expected to arise after the date of dissolution based on facts known to the partnership and:

　　(1)　at the time of the application:

　　　　(A)　are contingent; or

　　　　(B)　have not been made known to the partnership; or

　　(2)　are based on an event occurring after the date of dissolution.

(b)　Security is not required for any claim that is or is reasonably anticipated to be barred under Section 807.

(c)　Not later than 10 days after the filing of an application under subsection (a), the dissolved limited liability partnership shall give notice of the proceeding to each claimant holding a contingent claim known to the partnership.

(d)　In any proceeding under this section, the court may appoint a guardian ad litem to represent all claimants whose identities are unknown. The reasonable fees and expenses of the guardian, including all reasonable expert witness fees, must be paid by the dissolved limited liability partnership.

(e)　A dissolved limited liability partnership that provides security in the amount and form ordered by the court under subsection (a) satisfies the partnership's obligations with respect to claims that are contingent, have not been made known to the partnership, or are based on an event occurring after the date of dissolution, and such claims may not be enforced against a partner or transferee on account of assets received in liquidation.

Comment

Source—Added during the Harmonization Project, this section is derived almost verbatim from Model Business Corporation Act section 14.08.

§ 810.　LIABILITY OF PARTNER AND PERSON DISSOCIATED AS PARTNER WHEN CLAIM AGAINST PARTNERSHIP BARRED.

If a claim against a dissolved partnership is barred under Section 807, 808, or 809, any corresponding claim under Section 306, 703, or 805 is also barred.

[ARTICLE] 9

LIMITED LIABILITY PARTNERSHIP

Sec.
901.　　　Statement of Qualification.
902.　　　Permitted Names.
908.　　　Registered Agent.
912.　　　Service of Process, Notice, or Demand.
913.　　　[Annual] [Biennial] Report for [Secretary of State].

§ 901.　STATEMENT OF QUALIFICATION.

(a)　A partnership may become a limited liability partnership pursuant to this section.

(b)　The terms and conditions on which a partnership becomes a limited liability partnership must be approved by the affirmative vote or consent necessary to amend the partnership agreement except, in the case of a partnership agreement that expressly addresses obligations to contribute to the partnership, the affirmative vote or consent necessary to amend those provisions.

(c)   After the approval required by subsection (b), a partnership may become a limited liability partnership by delivering to the [Secretary of State] for filing a statement of qualification. The statement must contain:

(1)   the name of the partnership which must comply with Section 902;

(2)   the street and mailing addresses of the partnership's principal office and, if different, the street address of an office in this state, if any;

(3)   the name and street and mailing addresses in this state of the partnership's registered agent; and

(4)   a statement that the partnership elects to become a limited liability partnership.

(d)   A partnership's status as a limited liability partnership remains effective, regardless of changes in the partnership, until it is canceled pursuant to subsection (f) or administratively revoked pursuant to Section 903.

(e)   The status of a partnership as a limited liability partnership and the protection against liability of its partners for the debts, obligations, or other liabilities of the partnership while it is a limited liability partnership is not affected by errors or later changes in the information required to be contained in the statement of qualification.

(f)   A limited liability partnership may amend or cancel its statement of qualification by delivering to the [Secretary of State] for filing a statement of amendment or cancellation. The statement must be approved by the affirmative vote or consent of all the partners and state the name of the limited liability partnership and in the case of:

(1)   an amendment, state the text of the amendment; and

(2)   a cancellation, state that the statement of qualification is canceled.

Comment

Subsection (a)—Every partnership governed by this act may become a limited liability partnership, and the necessary formalities are straightforward: approval of the decision by the partners and delivering to the filing office for filing a simple statement of qualification. A partnership becomes a limited liability partnership when the filing office files the statement of qualification and the statement takes effect. For the consequences of LLP status, see Section 306(c), comment.

Subsection (b)—In the default mode, becoming a limited liability partnership requires the agreement of all partners. . . .

Subsection (c)—Although a statement of qualification does not create a new entity, Section 201(b), the requirements stated here are comparable to the requirements for a certificate of formation for a limited liability company, ULLCA (2006) (Last Amended 2013), and a certificate of limited partnership, ULPA (2001) (Last Amended 2013). The liability shield—a privilege granted by state—justifies requiring an LLP to meet these requirements.

Subsection (d)—Under some early LLP statutes, an LLP's failure to file an annual renewal ended LLP status and terminated the shield. This subsection eschews that draconian result. However, an LLP's failure to file an annual/biennial report, Section 913, is grounds for administrative revocation. *See* Section 903(d). . . .

Subsection (f)—The unanimity requirement for amending a statement of qualification is a default rule. The unanimity requirement for cancelling a statement of qualification is mandatory. Section 105(c)(13). The difference reflects the very different consequences of amendment and cancellation. Subsection (b) requires very little information in a statement of qualification and does not contemplate additional information. . . . Therefore, an amendment can do no substantial harm to any partner's interest. In contrast, cancelling a statement of qualification makes every partner vicariously liable for all partnership obligations. . . .

§ 902.   PERMITTED NAMES.

(a)   The name of a partnership that is not a limited liability partnership may not contain the phrase "Registered Limited Liability Partnership" or "Limited Liability Partnership" or the abbreviation "R.L.L.P.", "L.L.P.", "RLLP", or "LLP".

(b)   The name of a limited liability partnership must contain the phrase "Registered Limited Liability Partnership" or "Limited Liability Partnership" or the abbreviation "R.L.L.P.", "L.L.P.", "RLLP", or "LLP".

(c)   Except as otherwise provided in subsection (f), the name of a limited liability partnership, and the name under which a foreign limited liability partnership may register to do business in this state, must be distinguishable on the records of the [Secretary of State] from any:

(1)   name of an existing person whose formation required the filing of a record by the [Secretary of State] and which is not at the time administratively dissolved;

(2)   name of a limited liability partnership whose statement of qualification is in effect;

(3)   name under which a person that is registered to do business in this state by the filing of a record by the [Secretary of State];

(4)   name that is reserved under Section 903 or other law of this state providing for the reservation of a name by a filing of a record by the [Secretary of State];

(5)   name that is registered under Section 904 or other law of this state providing for the registration of a name by a filing of a record by the [Secretary of State]; and

(6)   a name registered under [this state's assumed or fictitious name statute].

(d)   If a person consents in a record to the use of its name and submits an undertaking in a form satisfactory to the [Secretary of State] to change its name to a name that is distinguishable on the records of the [Secretary of State] from any name in any category of names in subsection (c), the name of the consenting person may be used by the person to which the consent was given.

(e)   Except as otherwise provided in subsection (f), in determining whether a name is the same as or not distinguishable on the records of the [Secretary of State] from the name of another person, words, phrases, or abbreviations indicating a type of entity, such as "corporation", "corp.", "incorporated", "Inc.", "professional corporation", "PC", "P.C.", "professional association", "PA", "P.A.", "Limited", "Ltd.", "limited partnership", "LP", "L.P.", "limited liability partnership", "LLP", "L.L.P.", "registered limited liability partnership", "RLLP", "R.L.L.P.", "limited liability limited partnership", "LLLP", "L.L.L.P.", "registered limited liability limited partnership", "RLLLP", "R.L.L.L.P.", "limited liability company", "LLC", or "L.L.C.", "limited cooperative association", "limited cooperative", "LCA", or "L.C.A." may not be taken into account.

(f)   A person may consent in a record to the use of a name that is not distinguishable on the records of the [Secretary of State] from its name except for the addition of a word, phrase, or abbreviation indicating the type of person as provided in subsection (e). In such a case, the person need not change its name pursuant to subsection (d).

(g)   The name of a limited liability partnership or foreign limited liability partnership may not contain the words [insert prohibited words or words that may be used only with approval by an appropriate state agency].

(h)   A limited liability partnership or foreign limited liability partnership may use a name that is not distinguishable from a name described in subsection (c)(1) through (6) if the partnership delivers to the [Secretary of State] a certified copy of a final judgment of a court of competent jurisdiction establishing the right of the partnership to use the name in this state.

§ 908.   REGISTERED AGENT.

(a)   Each limited liability partnership and each registered foreign limited liability partnership shall designate and maintain a registered agent in this state. The designation of a registered agent is an affirmation of fact by the partnership or foreign partnership that the agent has consented to serve.

(b)   A registered agent for a limited liability partnership or registered foreign limited liability partnership must have a place of business in this state.

(c)   The only duties under this [act] of a registered agent that has complied with this [act] are:

(1)   to forward to the limited liability partnership or registered foreign limited liability partnership at the address most recently supplied to the agent by the partnership or foreign partnership any process, notice, or demand pertaining to the partnership or foreign partnership which is served on or received by the agent;

(2)   if the registered agent resigns, to provide the notice required by Section 907(c) to the partnership or foreign partnership at the address most recently supplied to the agent by the partnership or foreign partnership; and

(3)   to keep current the information with respect to the agent in the statement of qualification or foreign registration statement.

§ 912.   SERVICE OF PROCESS, NOTICE, OR DEMAND.

(a)   A limited liability partnership or registered foreign limited liability partnership may be served with any process, notice, or demand required or permitted by law by serving its registered agent.

(b)   If a limited liability partnership or registered foreign limited liability partnership ceases to have a registered agent, or if its registered agent cannot with reasonable diligence be served, the partnership or foreign partnership may be served by registered or certified mail, return receipt requested, or by similar commercial delivery service, addressed to the partnership or foreign partnership at its principal office. The address of the principal office must be as shown in the partnership's or foreign partnership's most recent [annual] [biennial] report filed by the [Secretary of State]. Service is effected under this subsection on the earliest of:

(1)   the date the partnership or foreign partnership receives the mail or delivery by the commercial delivery service;

(2)   the date shown on the return receipt, if signed by the partnership or foreign partnership; or

(3)   five days after its deposit with the United States Postal Service, or with the commercial delivery service, if correctly addressed and with sufficient postage or payment.

(c)   If process, notice, or demand cannot be served on a limited liability partnership or registered foreign limited liability partnership pursuant to subsection (a) or (b), service may be made by handing a copy to the individual in charge of any regular place of business of the partnership or foreign partnership if the individual served is not a plaintiff in the action.

(d)   Service of process, notice, or demand on a registered agent must be in a written record.

(e)   Service of process, notice, or demand may be made by other means under law other than this [act].

§ 913.   [ANNUAL] [BIENNIAL] REPORT FOR [SECRETARY OF STATE].

(a)   A limited liability partnership or registered foreign limited liability partnership shall deliver to the [Secretary of State] for filing [an annual] [a biennial] report that states:

(1)   the name of the partnership or registered foreign partnership;

(2)   the name and street and mailing addresses of its registered agent in this state;

(3)   the street and mailing addresses of its principal office;

(4)   the name of at least one partner; and

(5)   in the case of a foreign partnership, its jurisdiction of formation and any alternate name adopted under Section 1006.

(b)   Information in the [annual] [biennial] report must be current as of the date the report is signed by the limited liability partnership or registered foreign limited liability partnership.

(c)   The first [annual] [biennial] report must be delivered to the [Secretary of State] for filing after [January 1] and before [April 1] of the year following the calendar year in which the limited liability partnership's statement of qualification became effective or the registered foreign limited liability partnership registered to do business in this state. Subsequent [annual] [biennial] reports must be delivered to the [Secretary of State] for filing after [January 1] and before [April 1] of each [second] calendar year thereafter.

(d)   If [an annual] [a biennial] report does not contain the information required by this section, the [Secretary of State] promptly shall notify the reporting limited liability partnership or registered foreign limited liability partnership in a record and return the report for correction.

(e)   If [an annual] [a biennial] report contains the name or address of a registered agent which differs from the information shown in the records of the [Secretary of State] immediately before the report becomes effective, the differing information is considered a statement of change under Section 909.

[ARTICLE] 10

FOREIGN LIMITED LIABILITY PARTNERSHIP

Sec.
1001.   Governing Law.
1002.   Registration to Do Business in This State.

§ 1001.   GOVERNING LAW.

(a)   The law of the jurisdiction of formation of a foreign limited liability partnership governs:

(1)   the internal affairs of the partnership; and

(2)   the liability of a partner as partner for a debt, obligation, or other liability of the foreign partnership.

(b)   A foreign limited liability partnership is not precluded from registering to do business in this state because of any difference between the law of its jurisdiction of formation and the law of this state.

(c)   Registration of a foreign limited liability partnership to do business in this state does not authorize the foreign partnership to engage in any business or exercise any power that a limited liability partnership may not engage in or exercise in this state.

§ 1002.   REGISTRATION TO DO BUSINESS IN THIS STATE.

(a)   A foreign limited liability partnership may not do business in this state until it registers with the [Secretary of State] under this [article].

(b)   A foreign limited liability partnership doing business in this state may not maintain an action or proceeding in this state unless it has registered to do business in this state.

(c)   The failure of a foreign limited liability partnership to register to do business in this state does not impair the validity of a contract or act of the foreign partnership or preclude it from defending an action or proceeding in this state.

(d)   A limitation on the liability of a partner of a foreign limited liability partnership is not waived solely because the foreign partnership does business in this state without registering to do business in this state.

(e)   Section 1001(a) and (b) applies even if a foreign limited liability partnership fails to register under this [article].

[ARTICLE] 11

MERGER, INTEREST EXCHANGE, CONVERSION, AND DOMESTICATION

Introductory Comment

This article deals comprehensively with both same-type and cross-type mergers and interest exchanges and with conversions and domestications. For this article to apply, at least one participant organization must be a domestic general partnership (regardless of whether the partnership is an LLP). For a foreign organization to be involved, its organic law must permit the organization's participation. . . .

[PART] 1

GENERAL PROVISIONS

Sec.
1101. Definitions.
1102. Relationship of [Article] to Other Laws.
1103. Required Notice or Approval.
1104. Nonexclusivity.
1106. Appraisal Rights.

§ 1101. DEFINITIONS.

In this [article]:

(1) "Acquired entity" means the entity, all of one or more classes or series of interests of which are acquired in an interest exchange.

(2) "Acquiring entity" means the entity that acquires all of one or more classes or series of interests of the acquired entity in an interest exchange.

(3) "Conversion" means a transaction authorized by [Part] 4.

(4) "Converted entity" means the converting entity as it continues in existence after a conversion.

(5) "Converting entity" means the domestic entity that approves a plan of conversion pursuant to Section 1143 or the foreign entity that approves a conversion pursuant to the law of its jurisdiction of formation.

(6) "Distributional interest" means the right under an unincorporated entity's organic law and organic rules to receive distributions from the entity.

(7) "Domestic", with respect to an entity, means governed as to its internal affairs by the law of this state.

(8) "Domesticated limited liability partnership" means a domesticating limited liability partnership as it continues in existence after a domestication.

(9) "Domesticating limited liability partnership" means the domestic limited liability partnership that approves a plan of domestication pursuant to Section 1153 or the foreign limited liability partnership that approves a domestication pursuant to the law of its jurisdiction of formation.

(10) "Domestication" means a transaction authorized by [Part] 5.

(11) "Entity":

(A) means:

(i) a business corporation;

(ii) a nonprofit corporation;

  (iii) a general partnership, including a limited liability partnership;

  (iv) a limited partnership, including a limited liability limited partnership;

  (v) a limited liability company;

  [(vi) a general cooperative association;]

  (vii) a limited cooperative association;

  (viii) an unincorporated nonprofit association;

  (ix) a statutory trust, business trust, or common-law business trust; or

  (x) any other person that has:

    (I) a legal existence separate from any interest holder of that person; or

    (II) the power to acquire an interest in real property in its own name; and

 (B) does not include:

  (i) an individual;

  (ii) a trust with a predominantly donative purpose or a charitable trust;

  (iii) an association or relationship that is not an entity listed in subparagraph (A) and is not a partnership under the rules stated in [Section 202(c) of the Uniform Partnership Act (1997) (Last Amended 2013)] [Section 7 of the Uniform Partnership Act (1914)] or a similar provision of the law of another jurisdiction;

  (iv) a decedent's estate; or

  (v) a government or a governmental subdivision, agency, or instrumentality.

 (12) "Filing entity" means an entity whose formation requires the filing of a public organic record. The term does not include a limited liability partnership.

 (13) "Foreign", with respect to an entity, means an entity governed as to its internal affairs by the law of a jurisdiction other than this state.

 (14) "Governance interest" means a right under the organic law or organic rules of an unincorporated entity, other than as a governor, agent, assignee, or proxy, to:

 (A) receive or demand access to information concerning, or the books and records of, the entity;

 (B) vote for or consent to the election of the governors of the entity; or

 (C) receive notice of or vote on or consent to an issue involving the internal affairs of the entity.

 (15) "Governor" means:

 (A) a director of a business corporation;

 (B) a director or trustee of a nonprofit corporation;

 (C) a general partner of a general partnership;

 (D) a general partner of a limited partnership;

 (E) a manager of a manager-managed limited liability company;

 (F) a member of a member-managed limited liability company;

 [(G) a director of a general cooperative association;]

 (H) a director of a limited cooperative association;

 (I) a manager of an unincorporated nonprofit association;

 (J) a trustee of a statutory trust, business trust, or common-law business trust; or

(K)   any other person under whose authority the powers of an entity are exercised and under whose direction the activities and affairs of the entity are managed pursuant to the organic law and organic rules of the entity.

(16) "Interest" means:

(A)   a share in a business corporation;

(B)   a membership in a nonprofit corporation;

(C)   a partnership interest in a general partnership;

(D)   a partnership interest in a limited partnership;

(E)   a membership interest in a limited liability company;

[(F) a share in a general cooperative association;]

(G)   a member's interest in a limited cooperative association;

(H)   a membership in an unincorporated nonprofit association;

(I)   a beneficial interest in a statutory trust, business trust, or common-law business trust; or

(J)   a governance interest or distributional interest in any other type of unincorporated entity.

(17) "Interest Exchange" means a transaction authorized by [Part] 3.

(18) "Interest holder" means:

(A)   a shareholder of a business corporation;

(B)   a member of a nonprofit corporation;

(C)   a general partner of a general partnership;

(D)   a general partner of a limited partnership;

(E)   a limited partner of a limited partnership;

(F)   a member of a limited liability company;

[(G) a shareholder of a general cooperative association;]

(H)   a member of a limited cooperative association;

(I)   a member of an unincorporated nonprofit association;

(J)   a beneficiary or beneficial owner of a statutory trust, business trust, or common-law business trust; or

(K)   any other direct holder of an interest.

(19) "Interest holder liability" means:

(A)   personal liability for a liability of an entity which is imposed on a person:

(i)   solely by reason of the status of the person as an interest holder; or

(ii)   by the organic rules of the entity which make one or more specified interest holders or categories of interest holders liable in their capacity as interest holders for all or specified liabilities of the entity; or

(B)   an obligation of an interest holder under the organic rules of an entity to contribute to the entity.

(20) "Merger" means a transaction authorized by [Part] 2.

(21) "Merging entity" means an entity that is a party to a merger and exists immediately before the merger becomes effective.

(22) "Organic law" means the law of an entity's jurisdiction of formation governing the internal affairs of the entity.

(23) "Organic rules" means the public organic record and private organic rules of an entity.

(24) "Plan" means a plan of merger, plan of interest exchange, plan of conversion, or plan of domestication.

(25) "Plan of conversion" means a plan under Section 1142.

(26) "Plan of domestication" means a plan under Section 1152.

(27) "Plan of interest exchange" means a plan under Section 1132.

(28) "Plan of merger" means a plan under Section 1122.

(29) "Private organic rules" means the rules, whether or not in a record, that govern the internal affairs of an entity, are binding on all its interest holders, and are not part of its public organic record, if any. The term includes:

(A)   the bylaws of a business corporation;

(B)   the bylaws of a nonprofit corporation;

(C)   the partnership agreement of a general partnership;

(D)   the partnership agreement of a limited partnership;

(E)   the operating agreement of a limited liability company;

[(F)   the bylaws of a general cooperative association;]

(G)   the bylaws of a limited cooperative association;

(H)   the governing principles of an unincorporated nonprofit association; and

(I)   the trust instrument of a statutory trust or similar rules of a business trust or common-law business trust.

(30) "Protected agreement" means:

(A)   a record evidencing indebtedness and any related agreement in effect on [the effective date of this [act]];

(B)   an agreement that is binding on an entity on [the effective date of this [act]];

(C)   the organic rules of an entity in effect on [the effective date of this [act]]; or

(D)   an agreement that is binding on any of the governors or interest holders of an entity on [the effective date of this [act]].

(31) "Public organic record" means the record the filing of which by the [Secretary of State] is required to form an entity and any amendment to or restatement of that record. The term includes:

(A)   the articles of incorporation of a business corporation;

(B)   the articles of incorporation of a nonprofit corporation;

(C)   the certificate of limited partnership of a limited partnership;

(D)   the certificate of organization of a limited liability company;

[(E)   the articles of incorporation of a general cooperative association;]

(F)   the articles of organization of a limited cooperative association; and

(G)   the certificate of trust of a statutory trust or similar record of a business trust.

(32) "Registered foreign entity" means a foreign entity that is registered to do business in this state pursuant to a record filed by the [Secretary of State].

(33) "Statement of conversion" means a statement under Section 1145.

(34) "Statement of domestication" means a statement under Section 1155.

(35) "Statement of interest exchange" means a statement under Section 1135.

(36) "Statement of merger" means a statement under Section 1125.

(37) "Surviving entity" means the entity that continues in existence after or is created by a merger.

(38) "Type of entity" means a generic form of entity:

　　(A)　recognized at common law; or

　　(B)　formed under an organic law, whether or not some entities formed under that organic law are subject to provisions of that law that create different categories of the form of entity.

§ 1102.　RELATIONSHIP OF [ARTICLE] TO OTHER LAWS.

(a)　This [article] does not authorize an act prohibited by, and does not affect the application or requirements of, law other than this [article].

(b)　A transaction effected under this [act] may not create or impair a right, duty, or obligation of a person under the statutory law of this state relating to a change in control, takeover, business combination, control-share acquisition, or similar transaction involving a domestic merging, acquired, converting, or domesticating business corporation unless:

　　(1)　if the corporation does not survive the transaction, the transaction satisfies any requirements of the law; or

　　(2)　if the corporation survives the transaction, the approval of the plan is by a vote of the shareholders or directors which would be sufficient to create or impair the right, duty, or obligation directly under the law.

Comment

This section preserves existing regulatory law in an adopting state in general terms. . . .

Laws other than this act that will apply to transactions under the act include, for example, uniform fraudulent transfer and fraudulent conveyance acts, state insolvency statutes, federal bankruptcy law, and Articles 8 and 9 of the Uniform Commercial Code.

Subsection (b)—Many states have enacted "antitakeover" statutes intended to make it more difficult to acquire control of a publicly traded corporation. . . .

This subsection protects the application of antitakeover statutes from being affected by a transaction under this act by requiring that the transaction be approved in a manner that would be sufficient to approve changing the application of the antitakeover statute. . . .

§ 1103.　REQUIRED NOTICE OR APPROVAL.

(a)　A domestic or foreign entity that is required to give notice to, or obtain the approval of, a governmental agency or officer of this state to be a party to a merger must give the notice or obtain the approval to be a party to an interest exchange, conversion, or domestication.

(b)　Property held for a charitable purpose under the law of this state by a domestic or foreign entity immediately before a transaction under this [article] becomes effective may not, as a result of the transaction, be diverted from the objects for which it was donated, granted, devised, or otherwise transferred unless, to the extent required by or pursuant to the law of this state concerning cy pres or other law dealing with nondiversion of charitable assets, the entity obtains an appropriate order of [the appropriate court] [the Attorney General] specifying the disposition of the property.

(c)　A bequest, devise, gift, grant, or promise contained in a will or other instrument of donation, subscription, or conveyance which is made to a merging entity that is not the surviving entity and which takes effect or remains payable after the merger inures to the surviving entity.

(d)   A trust obligation that would govern property if transferred to a nonsurviving entity applies to property that is transferred to the surviving entity under this section.

§ 1104.   NONEXCLUSIVITY.

The fact that a transaction under this [article] produces a certain result does not preclude the same result from being accomplished in any other manner permitted by law other than this [article].

Comment

This section allows a transaction that has the same end result as one of the transactions governed by this act, but that is accomplished in a manner not within the scope of this act, to be exempt from this act. For example, a sale of assets and transfer of liabilities by two entities to a third entity followed by the liquidation of the two transferring entities can be accomplished pursuant to statutory provisions pertaining to sale of assets rather than under Part 2 of this article, even though the end result of the transaction is essentially the same as if the two entities had merged into a third entity.

§ 1106.   APPRAISAL RIGHTS.

An interest holder of a domestic merging, acquired, converting, or domesticating partnership is entitled to contractual appraisal rights in connection with a transaction under this [article] to the extent provided in:

(1)   the partnership's organic rules; or

(2)   the plan.

Comment

In corporate law, appraisal rights developed when corporate statutes were amended to permit mergers with less than unanimous consent of the shareholders. This article provides no appraisal rights, because as a default rule transactions under this article require the consent or affirmative vote of all the partners. Where the partnership agreement changes this default rule, parties may wish to consider contractual appraisal rights. . . .

[PART] 2

MERGER

Sec.

1121.   Merger Authorized.
1122.   Plan of Merger.
1123.   Approval of Merger.
1126.   Effect of Merger.

§ 1121.   MERGER AUTHORIZED.

(a)   By complying with this [part]:

(1)   one or more domestic partnerships may merge with one or more domestic or foreign entities into a domestic or foreign surviving entity; and

(2)   two or more foreign entities may merge into a domestic partnership.

(b)   By complying with the provisions of this [part] applicable to foreign entities, a foreign entity may be a party to a merger under this [part] or may be the surviving entity in such a merger if the merger is authorized by the law of the foreign entity's jurisdiction of formation.

Comment

The merger transaction authorized by this act involves the combination of one or more domestic general partnerships with or into one or more other domestic or foreign entities. It also contemplates the consolidation of two or more foreign entities into a single domestic general partnership. Upon the effective date of the merger, all the assets and liabilities of the constituent entities vest in the surviving entity as a matter of law. As such, mergers require the existence of at least two separate entities before the transaction and only one entity may survive the merger. If independent existence of the constituent entities is desired following the conclusion of the transaction, a restructuring transaction other than a merger must be used to accomplish the transfer of assets and liabilities. . . .

§ 1122. PLAN OF MERGER.

(a) A domestic partnership may become a party to a merger under this [part] by approving a plan of merger. The plan must be in a record and contain:

(1) as to each merging entity, its name, jurisdiction of formation, and type of entity;

(2) if the surviving entity is to be created in the merger, a statement to that effect and the entity's name, jurisdiction of formation, and type of entity;

(3) the manner of converting the interests in each party to the merger into interests, securities, obligations, money, other property, rights to acquire interests or securities, or any combination of the foregoing;

(4) if the surviving entity exists before the merger, any proposed amendments to:

(A) its public organic record, if any; or

(B) its private organic rules that are, or are proposed to be, in a record;

(5) if the surviving entity is to be created in the merger:

(A) its proposed public organic record, if any; and

(B) the full text of its private organic rules that are proposed to be in a record;

(6) the other terms and conditions of the merger; and

(7) any other provision required by the law of a merging entity's jurisdiction of formation or the organic rules of a merging entity.

(b) In addition to the requirements of subsection (a), a plan of merger may contain any other provision not prohibited by law.

§ 1123. APPROVAL OF MERGER.

(a) A plan of merger is not effective unless it has been approved:

(1) by a domestic merging partnership, by all the partners of the partnership entitled to vote on or consent to any matter; and

(2) in a record, by each partner of a domestic merging partnership which will have interest holder liability for debts, obligations, and other liabilities that are incurred after the merger becomes effective, unless:

(A) the partnership agreement of the partnership provides in a record for the approval of a merger in which some or all of its partners become subject to interest holder liability by the affirmative vote or consent of fewer than all the partners; and

(B) the partner consented in a record to or voted for that provision of the partnership agreement or became a partner after the adoption of that provision.

(b) A merger involving a domestic merging entity that is not a partnership is not effective unless the merger is approved by that entity in accordance with its organic law.

(c) A merger involving a foreign merging entity is not effective unless the merger is approved by the foreign entity in accordance with the law of the foreign entity's jurisdiction of formation.

Comment

Subsection (a)—In the uniform acts pertaining to unincorporated business organizations, unanimity is the default rule for approving a merger. The partnership agreement certainly can change this rule, but care should be taken in doing so. For example, a merger can revise the partnership agreement. Section 1122(a)(4). Thus, if a merger requires less-than-unanimous consent, the partnership agreement is subject to amendment by the same quantum of consent. "Exit rights" also require consideration. This act does not provide appraisal rights, because those rights are inapposite when unanimous consent is required. *See* the comment to Section 1106. . . .

Subsection (c)—Where a foreign entity is a party to a merger under this act, this subsection defers to the laws of the foreign jurisdiction for the requirements for approval of the merger by the foreign entity. Those laws will include the organic law of the foreign entity and other applicable laws. The laws of the foreign jurisdiction will also control the application of any special approval requirements found in the organic rules of the foreign entity.

§ 1126. EFFECT OF MERGER.

(a)   When a merger becomes effective:

(1)   the surviving entity continues or comes into existence;

(2)   each merging entity that is not the surviving entity ceases to exist;

(3)   all property of each merging entity vests in the surviving entity without transfer, reversion, or impairment;

(4)   all debts, obligations, and other liabilities of each merging entity are debts, obligations, and other liabilities of the surviving entity;

(5)   except as otherwise provided by law or the plan of merger, all the rights, privileges, immunities, powers, and purposes of each merging entity vest in the surviving entity;

(6)   if the surviving entity exists before the merger:

(A)   all its property continues to be vested in it without transfer, reversion, or impairment;

(B)   it remains subject to all its debts, obligations, and other liabilities; and

(C)   all its rights, privileges, immunities, powers, and purposes continue to be vested in it;

(7)   the name of the surviving entity may be substituted for the name of any merging entity that is a party to any pending action or proceeding;

(8)   if the surviving entity exists before the merger:

(A)   its public organic record, if any, is amended as provided in the statement of merger; and

(B)   its private organic rules that are to be in a record, if any, are amended to the extent provided in the plan of merger;

(9)   if the surviving entity is created by the merger, its private organic rules become effective and:

(A)   if it is a filing entity, its public organic record becomes effective; and

(B)   if it is a limited liability partnership, its statement of qualification becomes effective; and

(10) the interests in each merging entity which are to be converted in the merger are converted, and the interest holders of those interests are entitled only to the rights provided to them under the plan of merger and to any appraisal rights they have under Section 1106 and the merging entity's organic law.

(b)   Except as otherwise provided in the organic law or organic rules of a merging entity, the merger does not give rise to any rights that an interest holder, governor, or third party would have upon a dissolution, liquidation, or winding up of the merging entity.

(c)   When a merger becomes effective, a person that did not have interest holder liability with respect to any of the merging entities and becomes subject to interest holder liability with respect to a domestic entity as a result of the merger has interest holder liability only to the extent provided by the organic law of that entity and only for those debts, obligations, and other liabilities that are incurred after the merger becomes effective.

(d)   When a merger becomes effective, the interest holder liability of a person that ceases to hold an interest in a domestic merging partnership with respect to which the person had interest holder liability is subject to the following rules:

(1)   The merger does not discharge any interest holder liability under this [act] to the extent the interest holder liability was incurred before the merger became effective.

(2)   The person does not have interest holder liability under this [act] for any debt, obligation, or other liability that is incurred after the merger becomes effective.

(3)   This [act] continues to apply to the release, collection, or discharge of any interest holder liability preserved under paragraph (1) as if the merger had not occurred and the surviving entity were the domestic merging entity.

(4)   The person has whatever rights of contribution from any other person as are provided by this [act], law other than this [act], or the partnership agreement of the domestic merging partnership with respect to any interest holder liability preserved under paragraph (1) as if the merger had not occurred.

(e)   When a merger has become effective, a foreign entity that is the surviving entity may be served with process in this state for the collection and enforcement of any debts, obligations, or other liabilities of a domestic merging partnership as provided in Section 119.

(f)   When a merger has become effective, the registration to do business in this state of any foreign merging entity that is not the surviving entity is canceled.

[PART] 3

INTEREST EXCHANGE

Sec.

1131.   Interest Exchange Authorized.
1132.   Plan of Interest Exchange.
1133.   Approval of Interest Exchange.
1136.   Effect of Interest Exchange.

§ 1131.   INTEREST EXCHANGE AUTHORIZED.

(a)   By complying with this [part]:

(1)   a domestic partnership may acquire all of one or more classes or series of interests of another domestic entity or a foreign entity in exchange for interests, securities, obligations, money, other property, rights to acquire interests or securities, or any combination of the foregoing; or

(2)   all of one or more classes or series of interests of a domestic partnership may be acquired by another domestic entity or a foreign entity in exchange for interests, securities, obligations, money, other property, rights to acquire interests or securities, or any combination of the foregoing.

(b)   By complying with the provisions of this [part] applicable to foreign entities, a foreign entity may be the acquiring or acquired entity in an interest exchange under this [part] if the interest exchange is authorized by the law of the foreign entity's jurisdiction of formation.

(c)   If a protected agreement contains a provision that applies to a merger of a domestic partnership but does not refer to an interest exchange, the provision applies to an interest exchange in which the domestic partnership is the acquired entity as if the interest exchange were a merger until the provision is amended after [the effective date of this [act]].

Comment

An interest exchange is the same type of transaction as the share exchange provided for in section 11.03 of the Model Business Corporation Act. The effect of an interest exchange is that: (i) the separate existence of the acquired entity is not affected; and (ii) the acquiring entity acquires all of the interests of one or more classes of the acquired entity. An interest exchange also allows an indirect acquisition through the use of consideration in the exchange that is not provided by the acquiring entity (*e.g.*, consideration from another or related entity).

Neither share exchanges nor interest exchanges are universally recognized in either corporation or unincorporated entity laws. The effect of an interest exchange can be achieved through a triangular merger in which the acquiring entity forms a new subsidiary and the acquired entity is then merged into the new subsidiary. Part 3 allows the interest exchange to be accomplished directly in a single step, rather than indirectly through the triangular merger route. . . .

§ 1132.　PLAN OF INTEREST EXCHANGE.

(a)　A domestic partnership may be the acquired entity in an interest exchange under this [part] by approving a plan of interest exchange. The plan must be in a record and contain:

(1)　the name of the acquired entity;

(2)　the name, jurisdiction of formation, and type of entity of the acquiring entity;

(3)　the manner of converting the interests in the acquired entity into interests, securities, obligations, money, other property, rights to acquire interests or securities, or any combination of the foregoing;

(4)　any proposed amendments to the partnership agreement that are, or are proposed to be, in a record of the acquired entity;

(5)　the other terms and conditions of the interest exchange; and

(6)　any other provision required by the law of this state or the partnership agreement of the acquired entity.

(b)　In addition to the requirements of subsection (a), a plan of interest exchange may contain any other provision not prohibited by law.

§ 1133.　APPROVAL OF INTEREST EXCHANGE.

(a)　A plan of interest exchange is not effective unless it has been approved:

(1)　by all the partners of a domestic acquired partnership entitled to vote on or consent to any matter; and

(2)　in a record, by each partner of the domestic acquired partnership that will have interest holder liability for debts, obligations, and other liabilities that are incurred after the interest exchange becomes effective, unless:

(A)　the partnership agreement of the partnership provides in a record for the approval of an interest exchange or a merger in which some or all its partners become subject to interest holder liability by the affirmative vote or consent of fewer than all the partners; and

(B)　the partner consented in a record to or voted for that provision of the partnership agreement or became a partner after the adoption of that provision.

(b)　An interest exchange involving a domestic acquired entity that is not a partnership is not effective unless it is approved by the domestic entity in accordance with its organic law.

(c)　An interest exchange involving a foreign acquired entity is not effective unless it is approved by the foreign entity in accordance with the law of the foreign entity's jurisdiction of formation.

(d)　Except as otherwise provided in its organic law or organic rules, the interest holders of the acquiring entity are not required to approve the interest exchange.

§ 1136. EFFECT OF INTEREST EXCHANGE.

(a)   When an interest exchange in which the acquired entity is a domestic partnership becomes effective:

(1)   the interests in the acquired partnership which are the subject of the interest exchange are converted, and the partners holding those interests are entitled only to the rights provided to them under the plan of interest exchange and to any appraisal rights they have under Section 1106;

(2)   the acquiring entity becomes the interest holder of the interests in the acquired partnership stated in the plan of interest exchange to be acquired by the acquiring entity; and

(3)   the provisions of the partnership agreement of the acquired partnership that are to be in a record, if any, are amended to the extent provided in the plan of interest exchange.

(b)   Except as otherwise provided in the partnership agreement of a domestic acquired partnership, the interest exchange does not give rise to any rights that a partner or third party would have upon a dissolution, liquidation, or winding up of the acquired partnership.

(c)   When an interest exchange becomes effective, a person that did not have interest holder liability with respect to a domestic acquired partnership and becomes subject to interest holder liability with respect to a domestic entity as a result of the interest exchange has interest holder liability only to the extent provided by the organic law of the entity and only for those debts, obligations, and other liabilities that are incurred after the interest exchange becomes effective.

(d)   When an interest exchange becomes effective, the interest holder liability of a person that ceases to hold an interest in a domestic acquired partnership with respect to which the person had interest holder liability is subject to the following rules:

(1)   The interest exchange does not discharge any interest holder liability under this [act] to the extent the interest holder liability was incurred before the interest exchange became effective.

(2)   The person does not have interest holder liability under this [act] for any debt, obligation, or other liability that is incurred after the interest exchange becomes effective.

(3)   This [act] continues to apply to the release, collection, or discharge of any interest holder liability preserved under paragraph (1) as if the interest exchange had not occurred.

(4)   The person has whatever rights of contribution from any other person as are provided by this [act], law other than this [act], or the partnership agreement of the domestic acquired partnership with respect to any interest holder liability preserved under paragraph (1) as if the interest exchange had not occurred.

Comment

. . .

When an interest exchange becomes effective: (i) the interests of the acquired domestic general partnership are exchanged, converted, or canceled as provided in the plan; (ii) the only rights of the former partners and transferees of the acquired partnership whose interests are affected by the interest exchange are those rights related to the exchange, conversion, or cancellation; (iii) the acquiring entity becomes the owner of the acquired partnership's interests as provided in the plan; and (iv) the provisions of the partnership agreement of the acquired partnership that are to be in a record, if any, are amended to the extent provided in the plan of interest exchange. . . .

[PART] 4

CONVERSION

Sec.

1141.   Conversion Authorized.
1142.   Plan of Conversion.

129

1143.   Approval of Conversion.
1146.   Effect of Conversion.

§ 1141.   CONVERSION AUTHORIZED.

(a)   By complying with this [part], a domestic partnership may become:

(1)   a domestic entity that is a different type of entity; or

(2)   a foreign entity that is a different type of entity, if the conversion is authorized by the law of the foreign entity's jurisdiction of formation.

(b)   By complying with the provisions of this [part] applicable to foreign entities, a foreign entity that is not a foreign partnership may become a domestic partnership if the conversion is authorized by the law of the foreign entity's jurisdiction of formation.

(c)   If a protected agreement contains a provision that applies to a merger of a domestic partnership but does not refer to a conversion, the provision applies to a conversion of the partnership as if the conversion were a merger until the provision is amended after [the effective date of this [act]].

Comment

This part of Article 11 permits an entity to change to a different type of entity. A transaction in which an entity changes its jurisdiction of organization but does not change its type is a domestication and is the subject of Part 5. . . .

§ 1142.   PLAN OF CONVERSION.

(a)   A domestic partnership may convert to a different type of entity under this [part] by approving a plan of conversion. The plan must be in a record and contain:

(1)   the name of the converting partnership;

(2)   the name, jurisdiction of formation, and type of entity of the converted entity;

(3)   the manner of converting the interests in the converting partnership into interests, securities, obligations, money, other property, rights to acquire interests or securities, or any combination of the foregoing;

(4)   the proposed public organic record of the converted entity if it will be a filing entity;

(5)   the full text of the private organic rules of the converted entity which are proposed to be in a record;

(6)   the other terms and conditions of the conversion; and

(7)   any other provision required by the law of this state or the partnership agreement of the converting partnership.

(b)   In addition to the requirements of subsection (a), a plan of conversion may contain any other provision not prohibited by law.

§ 1143.   APPROVAL OF CONVERSION.

(a)   A plan of conversion is not effective unless it has been approved:

(1)   by a domestic converting partnership, by all the partners of the partnership entitled to vote on or consent to any matter; and

(2)   in a record, by each partner of a domestic converting partnership which will have interest holder liability for debts, obligations, and other liabilities that are incurred after the conversion becomes effective, unless:

(A)   the partnership agreement of the partnership provides in a record for the approval of a conversion or a merger in which some or all of its partners become subject to interest holder liability by the affirmative vote or consent of fewer than all the partners; and

(B)   the partner voted for or consented in a record to that provision of the partnership agreement or became a partner after the adoption of that provision.

(b)   A conversion involving a domestic converting entity that is not a partnership is not effective unless it is approved by the domestic converting entity in accordance with its organic law.

(c)   A conversion of a foreign converting entity is not effective unless it is approved by the foreign entity in accordance with the law of the foreign entity's jurisdiction of formation.

§ 1146.   EFFECT OF CONVERSION.

(a)   When a conversion becomes effective:

(1)   the converted entity is:

(A)   organized under and subject to the organic law of the converted entity; and

(B)   the same entity without interruption as the converting entity;

(2)   all property of the converting entity continues to be vested in the converted entity without transfer, reversion, or impairment;

(3)   all debts, obligations, and other liabilities of the converting entity continue as debts, obligations, and other liabilities of the converted entity;

(4)   except as otherwise provided by law or the plan of conversion, all the rights, privileges, immunities, powers, and purposes of the converting entity remain in the converted entity;

(5)   the name of the converted entity may be substituted for the name of the converting entity in any pending action or proceeding;

(6)   if the converted entity is a limited liability partnership, its statement of qualification becomes effective;

(7)   the provisions of the partnership agreement of the converted entity which are to be in a record, if any, approved as part of the plan of conversion become effective; and

(8)   the interests in the converting entity are converted, and the interest holders of the converting entity are entitled only to the rights provided to them under the plan of conversion and to any appraisal rights they have under Section 1106.

(b)   Except as otherwise provided in the partnership agreement of a domestic converting partnership, the conversion does not give rise to any rights that a partner or third party would have upon a dissolution, liquidation, or winding up of the converting entity.

(c)   When a conversion becomes effective, a person that did not have interest holder liability with respect to the converting entity and becomes subject to interest holder liability with respect to a domestic entity as a result of the conversion has interest holder liability only to the extent provided by the organic law of the entity and only for those debts, obligations, and other liabilities that are incurred after the conversion becomes effective.

(d)   When a conversion becomes effective, the interest holder liability of a person that ceases to hold an interest in a domestic converting partnership with respect to which the person had interest holder liability is subject to the following rules:

(1)   The conversion does not discharge any interest holder liability under this [act] to the extent the interest holder liability was incurred before the conversion became effective.

(2)   The person does not have interest holder liability under this [act] for any debt, obligation, or other liability that is incurred after the conversion becomes effective.

(3)   This [act] continues to apply to the release, collection, or discharge of any interest holder liability preserved under paragraph (1) as if the conversion had not occurred.

(4)   The person has whatever rights of contribution from any other person as are provided by this [act], law other than this [act], or the organic rules of the converting entity with respect to any interest holder liability preserved under paragraph (1) as if the conversion had not occurred.

(e)   When a conversion has become effective, a foreign entity that is the converted entity may be served with process in this state for the collection and enforcement of any of its debts, obligations, and other liabilities as provided in Section 119.

(f)   If the converting entity is a registered foreign entity, its registration to do business in this state is canceled when the conversion becomes effective.

(g)   A conversion does not require the entity to wind up its affairs and does not constitute or cause the dissolution of the entity.

Comment

. . .

When a conversion becomes effective, the internal affairs of the converting entity are no longer governed by its former organic law but instead by the organic law of the converted entity. As a result, filings that may have been made under the organic law of the converting entity, such as the following, will no longer be effective: a statement of qualification as a limited liability partnership under UPA (1997) (Last Amended 2013) § 901, a statement of partnership authority under Section 303 of that act, a statement of authority under Section of the ULLCA (2006) (Last Amended 2013) § 302, or under Uniform Unincorporated Nonprofit Association Act (2008) (Last Amended 2013) § 7. . . .

[PART] 5

DOMESTICATION

Sec.

1151.   Domestication Authorized.
1152.   Plan of Domestication.
1153.   Approval of Domestication.
1156.   Effect of Domestication.

§ 1151.   DOMESTICATION AUTHORIZED.

(a)   By complying with this [part], a domestic limited liability partnership may become a foreign limited liability partnership if the domestication is authorized by the law of the foreign jurisdiction.

(b)   By complying with the provisions of this [part] applicable to foreign limited liability partnerships, a foreign limited liability partnership may become a domestic limited liability partnership if the domestication is authorized by the law of the foreign limited liability partnership's jurisdiction of formation.

(c)   If a protected agreement contains a provision that applies to a merger of a domestic limited liability partnership but does not refer to a domestication, the provision applies to a domestication of the limited liability partnership as if the domestication were a merger until the provision is amended after [the effective date of this [act]].

Comment

A domestication authorized by Part 5 of Article 11 differs from a conversion in that a domestication requires that the domesticating entity be the same type of entity as the domesticated entity. In a conversion, by contrast, the converting entity changes its type.

As with a conversion, all rights and privileges, debts, obligations and other liabilities, and actions or proceedings of a domesticating entity remain vested in the domesticated entity. A domestication is not a sale, transfer, assignment, or conveyance and does not give rise to a claim of reverter or impairment of title. . . .

§ 1152. PLAN OF DOMESTICATION.

(a)   A domestic limited liability partnership may become a foreign limited liability partnership in a domestication by approving a plan of domestication. The plan must be in a record and contain:

(1)   the name of the domesticating limited liability partnership;

(2)   the name and jurisdiction of formation of the domesticated limited liability partnership;

(3)   the manner of converting the interests in the domesticating limited liability partnership into interests, securities, obligations, money, other property, rights to acquire interests or securities, or any combination of the foregoing;

(4)   the proposed statement of qualification of the domesticated limited liability partnership;

(5)   the full text of the provisions of the partnership agreement of the domesticated limited liability partnership that are proposed to be in a record;

(6)   the other terms and conditions of the domestication; and

(7)   any other provision required by the law of this state or the partnership agreement of the domesticating limited liability partnership.

(b)   In addition to the requirements of subsection (a), a plan of domestication may contain any other provision not prohibited by law.

§ 1153. APPROVAL OF DOMESTICATION.

(a)   A plan of domestication of a domestic domesticating limited liability partnership is not effective unless it has been approved:

(1)   by all the partners entitled to vote on or consent to any matter; and

(2)   in a record, by each partner that will have interest holder liability for debts, obligations, and other liabilities that are incurred after the domestication becomes effective, unless:

(A)   the partnership agreement of the domesticating partnership in a record provides for the approval of a domestication or merger in which some or all of its partners become subject to interest holder liability by the affirmative vote or consent of fewer than all the partners; and

(B)   the partner voted for or consented in a record to that provision of the partnership agreement or became a partner after the adoption of that provision.

(b)   A domestication of a foreign domesticating limited liability partnership is not effective unless it is approved in accordance with the law of the foreign limited liability partnership's jurisdiction of formation.

§ 1156. EFFECT OF DOMESTICATION.

(a)   When a domestication becomes effective:

(1)   the domesticated entity is:

(A)   organized under and subject to the organic law of the domesticated entity; and

(B)   the same entity without interruption as the domesticating entity;

(2)   all property of the domesticating entity continues to be vested in the domesticated entity without transfer, reversion, or impairment;

(3)   all debts, obligations, and other liabilities of the domesticating entity continue as debts, obligations, and other liabilities of the domesticated entity;

(4)   except as otherwise provided by law or the plan of domestication, all the rights, privileges, immunities, powers, and purposes of the domesticating entity remain in the domesticated entity;

(5)   the name of the domesticated entity may be substituted for the name of the domesticating entity in any pending action or proceeding;

(6)   the statement of qualification of the domesticated entity becomes effective;

(7)   the provisions of the partnership agreement of the domesticated entity that are to be in a record, if any, approved as part of the plan of domestication become effective; and

(8)   the interests in the domesticating entity are converted to the extent and as approved in connection with the domestication, and the partners of the domesticating entity are entitled only to the rights provided to them under the plan of domestication and to any appraisal rights they have under Section 1106.

(b)   Except as otherwise provided in the organic law or partnership agreement of the domesticating limited liability partnership, the domestication does not give rise to any rights that a partner or third party would otherwise have upon a dissolution, liquidation, or winding up of the domesticating partnership.

(c)   When a domestication becomes effective, a person that did not have interest holder liability with respect to the domesticating limited liability partnership and becomes subject to interest holder liability with respect to a domestic limited liability partnership as a result of the domestication has interest holder liability only to the extent provided by this [act] and only for those debts, obligations, and other liabilities that are incurred after the domestication becomes effective.

(d)   When a domestication becomes effective, the interest holder liability of a person that ceases to hold an interest in a domestic domesticating limited liability partnership with respect to which the person had interest holder liability is subject to the following rules:

(1)   The domestication does not discharge any interest holder liability under this [act] to the extent the interest holder liability was incurred before the domestication became effective.

(2)   A person does not have interest holder liability under this [act] for any debt, obligation, or other liability that is incurred after the domestication becomes effective.

(3)   This [act] continues to apply to the release, collection, or discharge of any interest holder liability preserved under paragraph (1) as if the domestication had not occurred.

(4)   A person has whatever rights of contribution from any other person as are provided by this [act], law other than this [act], or the partnership agreement of the domestic domesticating limited liability partnership with respect to any interest holder liability preserved under paragraph (1) as if the domestication had not occurred.

(e)   When a domestication becomes effective, a foreign limited liability partnership that is the domesticated partnership may be served with process in this state for the collection and enforcement of any of its debts, obligations, and other liabilities as provided in Section 119.

(f)   If the domesticating limited liability partnership is a registered foreign entity, the registration of the partnership is canceled when the domestication becomes effective.

(g)   A domestication does not require a domestic domesticating limited liability partnership to wind up its business and does not constitute or cause the dissolution of the partnership.

FORM OF PARTNERSHIP AGREEMENT

by

JACK S. JOHAL, ERIK S. SCHIMMELBUSCH & HILTON S. WILLIAMS

The following Annotated Form of Partnership Agreement was drafted by Jack S. Johal, Erik S. Schimmelbusch, and Hilton S. Williams. The form was originally published in the State Bar of California's Business Law News, Summer 1997, at p. 15.

The Form was prepared with California partnerships in mind, but since the California statute is based on RUPA (although it differs from RUPA in certain respects), the Form would by and large be an appropriate starting-point for drafting a partnership agreement under most or all versions of RUPA. As originally published, the form made cross-references to the California statute. For ease of use in this Supplement, the editor of the Supplement has inserted, in place of the California cross-references, cross-references to RUPA.

General Partnership Agreement for

_____,

a California General Partnership

This Agreement of General Partnership (**"Agreement"**), dated for reference purposes only _____, 19__ (**"Effective Date"**), is entered into by and between the parties listed on the signature pages of this Agreement (collectively referred to as **"Partners"** and individually as **"Partner"**).

AGREEMENT

1. FORMATION AND ORGANIZATION.

1.1 _Formation_. The Partners hereby form a general partnership ("Partnership") pursuant to the laws of the State of California, which Partnership shall be governed by and in accordance with the Uniform Partnership Act of 1994, ("Partnership Act").

1.2 _Name_. The Partnership's name shall be "_____" and the Partnership's business shall continue to be conducted under said name.

1.3 _Principal Place of Business_. The Partnership's principal place of business shall be located at (i) _____, or (ii) such other place or places in California as a majority interest of the Partners may select from time to time upon written notice thereof to the other Partners.

1.4 _Business_. The Partnership's business shall be to _____

The Partnership shall have the power to do all acts and things in furtherance of and incidental to the foregoing business.

1.5 _Filings_.

1.5.1 _Fictitious Business Name_. As soon after the Effective Date as is reasonably practicable, the Partners shall execute, file, and publish an appropriate fictitious business name statement for the Partnership in accordance with the California Business and Professions Code.

1.5.2 _Statement of Partnership Authority_. As soon after the Effective Date as is reasonably practicable, the Partners shall (i) sign, acknowledge and verify a statement of partnership authority pursuant to RUPA § 303, (ii) file such statement in the Secretary of State's office, and (iii) cause said statement to be recorded in each county in California in which the Partnership owns or contemplates owning real property or any interest in real property. Promptly following any change in the Partners of the Partnership, the Partners shall amend such statement, file such statement with the Secretary of State's office and cause said amended statement to be recorded in each county in California in which the Partnership owns or contemplates owning real property or any interest in real property.[3]

    1.5.3 <u>Percentage Interests</u>. As used in this Agreement, a Partner's **"Percentage Interest"** shall mean the percentage set forth below opposite such Partner's name:

        _____ ____%

        _____ ____%

    As used in this Agreement, **"Percentage Interests"** shall mean the aggregate of all such percentages, unless the context requires otherwise. **"Majority Interest"** shall mean those Partners who hold a majority of the Percentage Interests which all Partners hold.

    1.6 <u>Term</u>. The Partnership shall commence upon the Effective Date and shall continue for a period of forty (40) years thereafter, unless sooner terminated in accordance with Section 10 below.

2. CAPITAL CONTRIBUTIONS.

    2.1 <u>Initial Capital</u>.

    2.1.1 <u>Partner #1</u>. Upon the formation of the Partnership, Partner #1 shall contribute cash in the amount of One Hundred Thousand Dollars ($100,000) to the Partnership. Partner #1 shall receive a corresponding credit to its Capital Account.

    2.1.2 <u>Partner #2</u>. Upon the formation of the Partnership, Partner #2 shall contribute to the Partnership all of its right, title, and interest in and to that certain real property described on the attached Exhibit "___." The Partners agree that such property has a net fair market value of One Hundred Thousand Dollars ($100,000). Partner #2 shall receive a credit to its Capital Account equal to such net fair market value.

    2.1.3 <u>Partner #3</u>. Upon the formation of the Partnership, Partner #3 shall contribute to the Partnership all of his or her right to acquire that certain real property described on the attached Exhibit "___" pursuant to that certain Purchase Agreement, dated April 1, 1995, by and between Partner #3 and John Doe. The Partners agree that such right has a net fair market value of One Hundred Thousand Dollars ($100,000). Partner #3 shall receive a credit to his or her Capital Account equal to such value.

    2.1.4 As used in this agreement, **"Capital Contribution"** shall mean any cash or its equivalent in property, both real and personal, contributed to the capital of the Partnership.

    2.2 <u>Additional Capital</u>. No Partner shall be required to make any additional Capital Contributions. To the extent *[unanimously or by Majority Interest]* approved by the Partners, from time to time, the Partners may be permitted to make additional Capital Contributions if and to the extent they so desire, and if the Partners determine that such additional Capital Contributions are necessary or appropriate for the conduct of the Partnership's business *[including, without limitation, expansion or diversification]*. In that event, the Partners shall have the opportunity, but not the obligation, to participate in such Capital Contributions on a pro rata basis in accordance with their Percentage Interests. Each Partner shall receive a credit to its Capital Account in the amount of any additional capital which it contributes to the Partnership. Immediately following such Capital Contributions, the Percentage Interests shall be adjusted by the Partners to reflect the new relative proportions of the Capital Accounts of the Partners.

    2.3 <u>Capital Accounts</u>. The Partnership shall establish and maintain an individual capital account (**"Capital Account"**) for each Partner in accordance with [Internal Revenue Code Treasury] Regulations Section 1.704–1(b)(2)(iv).[4] If a Partner transfers all or part of its Partnership Interest in accordance with

---

    [3] *Comment:* Pursuant to RUPA § 303(a), a partnership may file a Statement of Partnership Authority with the Secretary of State. The Statement may specify the authority, or limitations on authority, of some or all of the partners to enter into transactions on behalf of the partnership. A filed Statement of Partnership Authority binds the partnership in favor of third parties who lack knowledge contrary to the statements in the document as to personal property transactions, and as to real property transactions if the Statement is recorded in the office for recording transfers of that property.

    [4] *Comment:* For tax purposes, allocations of income, gain, loss, deduction and credit must be made in accordance with the partners' respective interests in the partnership. I.R.C. § 704. Allocations which have substantial economic effect are deemed to be in accordance with the partners' respective interests for these purposes. Allocations will have economic

this Agreement, such Partner's Capital Account attributable to the transferred Partnership Interest shall carry over to the new owner of such Partnership Interest pursuant to Regulations Section 1.704–1(b)(2)(iv)(1).

2.4 <u>No Interest</u>. No Partner shall be entitled to interest on the unreturned portion of his capital contributions.

2.5 <u>Withdrawal of Partner or Capital</u>. No Partner may withdraw as a partner of, or withdraw capital from, the Partnership without the consent of a Majority Interest of the Partners.[5]

2.6 <u>Return of Capital</u>. No Partner guarantees the return of another Partner's capital contributions.

3. DISTRIBUTIONS.

3.1 <u>Cash Available for Distribution</u>. As used in this Agreement, the term **"Cash Available for Distribution"** shall mean the amount of cash which *[all or a Majority Interest]* of the Partners deem available for distribution to the Partners, taking into account, among other factors, (i) all Partnership obligations then due and payable (including any compensation payable to the Partners in accordance with Section 5.6 below), (ii) anticipated Partnership expenditures, and (iii) those amounts which the Partners deem reasonably necessary, in [their] sole discretion, to place into reserves to satisfy customary and usual costs and claims with respect to the Partnership's business.

3.2 <u>Manner of Distribution</u>. The Partnership shall distribute Cash Available For Distribution to the Partners in the following order of priority:

(a) First, to the Partners, pro rata, in accordance with the amount of capital which the Partners have contributed to the Partnership, until each Partner has received distributions under this subsection (a) which, in the aggregate, equal one hundred percent (100%) of the capital which such Partner has contributed to the Partnership; and

(b) Thereafter, to the Partners, pro rata, in accordance with their respective Percentage Interests.

3.3 <u>Time of Distribution</u>. The Partnership shall distribute Cash Available For Distribution to the Partners pursuant to Section 3.2 above in such amounts and at such times as *[all or a Majority Interest]* of the Partners shall determine.

3.4 <u>Withholding</u>. The Partnership shall withhold and pay all [state] withholding taxes in accordance with the provisions [of state law].

4. PROFITS AND LOSSES.

4.1 <u>Determination of Profits and Losses</u>. Partnership profits and losses shall be determined in accordance with Internal Revenue Code Sections 703 and 704, as amended **("Code")**, and the Treasury Regulations promulgated thereunder.

4.2 <u>Allocation of Profits and Losses</u>. *[RUPA § 401(b)]*

4.2.1 <u>Losses</u>. Subject to Section 4.3 below, Partnership losses shall be allocated to the Partners in the following order of priority:

(a) First, to the Partners in the amount of any profits previously allocated to them pursuant to Section 4.2.2(b) below (to the extent such profits have not been offset by prior loss allocations under this subsection (a));

---

effect if the partnership agreement incorporates the "safe harbor" provisions, set forth in Treasury Regulations Section 1.704–1(b)(2). Pursuant to such "safe harbor" provisions, (i) capital accounts must be maintained in accordance with Treasury Regulations Section 1.704–1(b)(2)(iv), (ii) liquidating distributions must be made in accordance with positive capital account balances, and (iii) each partner must be obligated to restore any deficit balance in its capital account upon liquidation of its interest in the partnership. In lieu of a deficit restoration requirement, the partnership agreement can include "qualified income offset" and corresponding "loss limitation" provisions drafted to comply with treasury Regulations Section 1.704–1(b)(2)(ii)(d). In order to ensure that allocations will be respected for tax purposes, the partnership agreement should contain a provision which requires capital accounts to be maintained in accordance with Treasury Regulations Section 1.704–1(b)(2)(iv), as well as provisions which satisfy the remaining "safe harbor" requirements.

[5] *See* Section 9 of the Agreement concerning dissociation.

(b) Second, to the Partners, pro rata, in proportion to their positive Capital Account balances, until no Partner has a positive Capital Account balance; and

(c) Thereafter, to the Partners, pro rata, in accordance with their respective Percentage Interests.

4.2.2   <u>Profits</u>. Subject to Section 4.3 below, Partnership profits shall be allocated to the Partners in the following order of priority:

(a) First, to the Partners in the amount of any losses previously allocated to them pursuant to Sections 4.2.1(b) and 4.2.1(c) above (to the extent such losses have not been offset by prior profit allocations under this subsection (a)); and

(b) Thereafter, to the Partners, pro rata, in accordance with their respective Percentage Interests.

4.3   <u>Special Allocations</u>.

4.3.1   <u>Minimum Gain Chargeback</u>. If there is a net decrease in "Partnership Minimum Gain" (as defined in Treasury Regulations Section 1.704–2(d)) during any fiscal year of the Partnership, each Partner shall be specially allocated items of Partnership income and gain for such fiscal year (and, if necessary, in subsequent fiscal years) in an amount equal to the portion of such Partner's share of the net decrease in Partnership Minimum Gain that is allocable to the disposition of any Partnership property which is subject to a "Nonrecourse Liability" (as defined in Treasury Regulations Section 1.752–1(a)(2)), which share of such net decrease shall be determined in accordance with Treasury Regulations Section 1.704–2(g)(2). Allocations pursuant to this Section 4.3.1 shall be made in proportion to the respective amounts required to be allocated to each Partner under this Section 4.3.1. The items to be so allocated shall be determined in accordance with Treasury Regulations Section 1.704–2(f). This Section 4.3.1 is intended to comply and shall be interpreted consistently with the minimum gain chargeback requirement contained in Treasury Regulations Section 1.704–2(f).

4.3.2   <u>Chargeback of Minimum Gain Attributable To Partner Nonrecourse Debt</u>. If there is a net decrease in Partnership Minimum Gain attributable to a "Partner Nonrecourse Debt" (as defined in Treasury Regulations Section 1.704–2(b)(4)) during any Partnership fiscal year, each Partner who has a share of the Partnership Minimum Gain attributable to such Partner Nonrecourse Debt (determined in accordance with Treasury Regulations Section 1.704–2(i)(5)) shall be specially allocated items of Partnership income and gain for such fiscal year (and, if necessary, in subsequent fiscal years) in an amount equal to that portion of such Partner's share of the net decrease in Partnership Minimum Gain attributable to such Partner Nonrecourse Debt that is allocable to the disposition of Partnership property subject to such Partner Nonrecourse Debt (which share of such net decrease shall be determined in accordance with Treasury Regulations Section 1.704–2(i)(5)). Allocations pursuant to this Section 4.3.2 shall be made in proportion to the respective amounts required to be allocated to each Partner under this Section 4.3.2. The items to be so allocated shall be determined in accordance with Treasury Regulations Section 1.704–2(i)(4). This Section 4.3.2 is intended to comply and shall be interpreted consistently with the minimum gain chargeback requirement contained in Treasury Regulations Section 1.704–2(i)(4).

4.3.3   <u>Nonrecourse Deductions</u>. Any nonrecourse deductions (as defined in Treasury Regulations Section 1.704–2(b)(1)) for any fiscal year or other period shall be specially allocated to the Partners, pro rata, in accordance with their respective Percentage Interests.

4.3.4   <u>Partner Nonrecourse Deductions</u>. Any items of Partnership loss, deduction, or [Internal Revenue] Code Section 705(a)(2)(B) expenditures attributable to a Partner Nonrecourse Debt for any fiscal year or other period shall be specially allocated to the Partner who bears the economic risk of loss with respect to the Partner Nonrecourse Debt to which such items of Partnership loss, deduction, or Code Section 705(a)(2)(B) expenditures are attributable in accordance with Treasury Regulations Section 1.704–2(i).

4.4   <u>Code Section 704(c) Allocations</u>. Notwithstanding Sections 4.2 and 4.3 above, in accordance with Code Section 704(c) and the Treasury Regulations promulgated thereunder, income, gain, loss, and deduction with respect to any Partnership property contributed to the capital of the Partnership shall be allocated between the Partners so as to take account of any variation between the adjusted basis of such property to the Partnership for federal income tax purposes and its fair market value on the date of contribution. Allocations pursuant to this Section 4.4 are solely for purposes of federal, state, and local taxes. As such, they shall not affect or in any way be taken into account in computing a Partner's Capital Account or share of profits, losses, or other items of distributions pursuant to this Agreement.

5. MANAGEMENT AND AUTHORITY.

5.1 <u>Participation by Partners</u>. Except as expressly provided otherwise in this Agreement, (i) each Partner shall participate in the control, management and direction of the Partnership's business, and (ii) all Partnership matters shall be decided by a Majority Interest of the Partners. *[RUPA § 401(f)]*[6]

5.2 <u>Fiduciary Duties</u>. Each Partner owes to the Partnership the duty of loyalty and the duty of care. Accordingly, each Partner shall (i) account to the Partnership for any property, profit, or benefit obtained by such Partner in the conduct of the Partnership's business, and (ii) refrain from dealing with the Partnership as or on behalf of a party having an adverse interest to that of the Partnership.[7]

5.3 <u>Rights and Responsibilities</u>. The Partners shall be responsible for the day-to-day management and operation of the Partnership's business. In addition, all things to be done by the Partnership shall be, except as expressly provided otherwise in this Agreement, decided by a Majority Interest of the Partners including the following *[RUPA § 401(j)]*:

(a) Execute all contracts, notes, deeds of trust, grant deeds, agreements for sale, escrow instructions, releases, easements, and other documents and instruments in connection with the Partnership's business;

(b) [Sell,] lease, exchange or otherwise dispose of all or any part of the Partnership's property;

(c) Exercise the Partnership's rights and fulfill the Partnership's obligations with respect to any partnership in which the Partnership is a partner, whether such rights and obligations are conferred by law or set forth in the governing instrument for such other partnership;

(d) Employ or discharge, at the Partnership's expense, . . . agents, employees, independent contractors, attorneys, and/or accountants;

(e) Operate and maintain Partnership property;

(f) Obtain insurance necessary for the proper protection of the Partnership and the Partners; and

(g) Adjust any and all claims against the Partnership.

---

[6] *Comment:* Under RUPA, in the absence of a contrary agreement, each partner has equal rights in the management and conduct of the partnership business, and may possess partnership property only on behalf of the partnership. A majority of the partners may resolve a difference arising as to a matter in the ordinary course of business of the partnership; however, an act outside the ordinary course of business and/or an amendment to the partnership agreement requires the consent of all of the partners. *See* Section 5.4 below, providing for decisions to be made by unanimous vote of the partners with respect to matters in the ordinary course of the partnership's business.

[7] *Comment:* RUPA sets forth specific duties owed by a partner to the partnership and the other partners. The two principal duties that a partner owes to the partnership and the other partners are (i) the duty of loyalty, and (ii) the duty of care. The duty of loyalty includes (i) the duty to account to the partnership for any property, profit, or benefit obtained by the partner in the conduct of the partnership business or from the use of partnership property or information including the appropriation of a partnership opportunity; (ii) the duty to refrain from dealing with the partnership in the conduct or winding up of the partnership business as or on behalf of a party having an interest adverse to the partnership; and (iii) the duty to refrain from competing with the partnership in the conduct of the partnership business before the partnership's dissolution. A partner's duty of care to the partnership and the other partners is limited to refraining from engaging in grossly negligent or reckless conduct, intentional misconduct, or a knowing violation of law. Certain provisions of RUPA regarding fiduciary duties may not be varied by the partnership agreement. The partnership agreement may not eliminate the duty of loyalty. If not manifestly unreasonable, however, the partnership agreement may (i) identify specific types or categories of activities that do not violate the duty of loyalty; or (ii) provide that a specified percentage of the partners may authorize or ratify, after full disclosure of all material facts, a specific act or transaction that would otherwise violate the duty of loyalty. In addition, the partnership agreement may not unreasonably reduce the duty of care or eliminate the obligation of good faith and fair dealing. The partnership agreement may, however, prescribe the standards by which the performance of the obligation is to be measured, provided that such standards are not manifestly unreasonable.

5.4   <u>Unanimous Consent Required</u>. Notwithstanding Section 5.3 above, none of the following shall be effected without the unanimous prior written consent of all Partners *[RUPA § 401(j)]*

(a) Admit an additional Partner to the Partnership;

(b) Borrow money on behalf of the Partnership in excess of _____;

(c) Prepay (in whole or in part), refinance, increase, modify, or extend any Partnership obligation;

(d) Pledge, hypothecate or otherwise encumber all or any part of the Partnership's assets;

(e) Dissolve the Partnership;

(f) Assign the Partnership's property in trust for creditors or on the assignee's promise to pay the Partnership's debts;

(g) Confess a judgment;

(h) Do any act which would make it impossible for the Partners to carry on the ordinary business of the Partnership;

(i) Submit a Partnership claim or liability to arbitration or reference. . . .

(j) Authorize the merger *[RUPA §§ 905–907]*[8] with, or conversion *[RUPA §§ 901–904]*[9] into, a foreign or domestic other business entity[; or]

(k) Do any act in contravention of this Agreement.

---

[8]   *Comment:* RUPA provides for the merger of one or more partnerships into one partnership or any other number of business entities provided that the entities that are parties to the merger are permitted under the laws of their respective states of organization to effect the merger. Each party must approve an Agreement containing (i) terms and conditions of the merger; (ii) name and place of organization of the surviving entity; (iii) the manner of converting interests; (iv) any other details or provisions as are required by the laws under which constituent entities are organized; and (v) any other desired provisions.

A Statement of Merger may be filed pursuant to RUPA § 915 to evidence a merger in which (i) only partnerships are involved; and (ii) a domestic partnership is a party and no other party is a domestic entity. Although it is optional, a Statement of Merger should be filed whenever a constituent partnership owns real property and recorded in each county in which real property is owned.

Upon a merger, the separate existence of the non-surviving entities ceases, and the surviving entity succeeds to all rights and property of the non-surviving entities without further act or deed and is subject to the obligations of the disappearing entities.

[9]   *Comment:* RUPA provides that a partnership may be converted into a domestic limited partnership, limited liability company, or a foreign other business entity if each of the partners would, pursuant to the proposed conversion, receive a percentage interest in the profits and capital of the converted business entity equal to the partner's percentage interest in profits and capital of the converting partnership as of the effective time of the conversion. The conversion may be effected only if (i) the law under which the new entity will exist expressly permits the formation of such new entity pursuant to a conversion; and (ii) the partnership complies with all of the requirements of such other law that applies to the conversion of such other business entity.

The partnership must approve a plan of conversion that states (i) the terms and conditions of the conversion; (ii) the place of the organization of the converted entity and of the converting partnership; (iii) the name of the converted entity after conversion, if different from that of the converting partnership; (iv) the manner of converting the partnership interests of each of the partners into securities of or interests in the converted entity; (v) the provisions of the governing document for the converted entity to which the holders of interest in the converted entity are to be bound; (vi) any other details or provisions required by law under which the converted entity is organized; and (vii) any other details or provisions desired by the parties.

An entity that converts into another entity is for all purposes considered the same entity that existed prior to the conversion. When a conversion takes effect, all of the following apply: (i) all rights and property of the converting entity remain vested in the converted entity; (ii) all debts, liabilities and obligations of the converting entity continue as debts, liabilities and obligations of the converted entity; (iii) all rights of creditors and liens upon the property of the converting entity are preserved and remain enforceable against the converted entity; and (iv) any action or proceeding pending by or against the converting entity may be continued against the converted entity as if the conversion had never occurred.

The personal liability of a partner of a converting partnership is unchanged regarding all obligations for which the partner was personally liable prior to the conversion. Similarly, a partner of a partnership that converted from another business entity is liable for any obligations of the converting other business entity for which the partner was personally liable prior to the conversion. . . .

5.5   Time and Opportunities. The Partners shall devote to the Partnership such time as is reasonably necessary to carry out their respective obligations under this Agreement. During the term of this Partnership, each Partner may engage in any business activity for his own profit or advantage without the other Partners' consent, provided such other activity is not in competition with the Partnership's business. *[RUPA § 404(b)(3)]*

5.6   Expenses. Each Partner shall be entitled to reimbursement from the Partnership for those out-of-pocket expenses which such Partner reasonably incurs in the proper conduct of the Partnership's business. Each Partner shall itemize all such expenses in reasonable detail.

5.7   Compensation.

5.7.1   In General. Except as expressly provided otherwise in this Section, no Partner shall be entitled to receive compensation for services rendered to the Partnership, unless such compensation is approved in writing by *[all or a Majority Interest]* of the Partners. *[RUPA § 401(h)]*

5.7.2   Contracts With Partners and Affiliates. The Partnership may enter into contracts with a Partner or an affiliate of a Partner for the performance of services upon such terms and conditions as the Partners deem to be in the Partnership's best interests; provided, however, such contracts must provide for commercially reasonable fees, compensation, and/or other monetary payments.[10]

5.7.3   Tax Treatment. Any compensation which the Partnership pays to a Partner in accordance with this Section shall be treated as a payment made to one who is not a partner under Code Section 707(a) or 707(c).

5.8   Indemnification. The Partnership shall bear the cost of all expenditures and liabilities which the Partners incur in the proper conduct of the Partnership's business. The Partnership, to the extent of its assets, shall indemnify, defend and hold harmless a Partner from and against any and all liabilities of every kind, arising in any manner out of or in connection with the operation of the Partnership's business, except as to those matters arising by reason of such Partner's fraud, gross negligence, willful misconduct, or breach of fiduciary duty.

6.   ACCOUNTING AND BANKING.

6.1   Fiscal Year. The fiscal year of the Partnership shall be the calendar year.

6.2   Accounting Method. The Partnership's books shall be kept on the method of accounting which the Partners select, provided the Partnership is entitled under the Code to use such method of accounting. The Partnership shall prepare, or cause to be prepared, financial statements for financial reporting purposes on such method of accounting in accordance with those accounting principles used to prepare the Partnership's federal income tax returns, consistently applied.

6.3   Books and Records. The Partners shall keep, or cause to be kept, (i) accurate records of all transactions entered into with respect to the Partnership's business, and (ii) accurate books and accounts with respect to the Partnership's management and operation. The Partners shall (i) maintain the Partnership's books of account and other records at the Partnership's principal place of business, and (ii) make such documents available at ordinary business hours for inspection and copying by each Partner or its designated representative. Any copies which a Partner makes of the documents specified herein shall be at such Partner's expense. *[RUPA § 403]*

6.4   Bank Accounts. The Partners shall open and thereafter maintain a separate bank account(s) in the Partnership's name, in which all Partnership funds shall be deposited. All withdrawals from the Partnership's bank account(s) shall be made only by checks requiring the signature of such person or persons as *[all or a Majority Interest]* of the Partners shall designate.

---

[10]   *Comment:* Partners should be advised that notwithstanding the foregoing provision, they must ensure that if they or their affiliates enter into contracts with the Partnership, that they do not violate the duties of loyalty and care discussed above with respect to Section 5.2.

6.5   Tax Matters.

6.5.1   Tax Returns. The Partners shall prepare and file, or cause to be prepared and filed, at the Partnership's expense, all federal and state tax returns on behalf of the Partnership in a timely manner.

6.5.2   Tax Elections. The Partners may cause the Partnership to make any tax elections available to the Partnership under the Code or any state revenue or taxation law.

7.   TRANSFERS OF PARTNERSHIP INTERESTS.

7.1   General Prohibition. No Partner may sell, assign, pledge, hypothecate, or otherwise transfer or encumber all or any part of its interest in the Partnership without the other Partners' prior written consent, which consent may be withheld for any reason or for no reason at all. Any attempted sale, assignment, pledge, hypothecation, or other transfer or encumbrance of a Partner's interest in the Partnership in violation of this Section 7.1 shall be invalid. As such, it shall neither (i) relieve the transferor Partner of any of its obligations under this Agreement, nor (ii) entitle the transferee to any rights as a partner of the Partnership, as such rights are set forth in this Agreement and/or conferred by law.

7.2   Permitted Transfers. A Partner *[without the other Partners' consent]* may, transfer all or any part of his interest in the Partnership in trust for the benefit of himself, his spouse, his children, or grandchildren, or any combination thereof, provided (i) such Partner is a trustee or co-trustee of such trust, and (ii) such Partner, as trustee or co-trustee, agrees in writing to abide by the terms and conditions of this Agreement.

7.3   Transferee As Partner. Any transferee which acquires an interest in the Partnership in accordance with Sections 7.1 or 7.2 above shall satisfy each of the following conditions:

(a) The transferee must execute a written agreement whereby such transferee agrees to be bound by all of the terms, conditions, restrictions, and limitations set forth in this Agreement;

(b) The spouse of such transferee, if any, must consent in writing to be bound by all of the terms, conditions, restrictions, and limitations set forth in this Agreement; and

(c) The transferee must reimburse the Partnership for all reasonable legal and accounting fees and other costs which the Partnership must pay as a result of the transaction.

7.4   Status of Transferee. Upon the satisfaction of those conditions set forth in Section 7.3 above, the transferee shall succeed to the Partnership interest of the transferor Partner in the same capacity as the transferor Partner held in the Partnership. Accordingly, the transferee shall acquire all rights and obligations with respect to title, management, capital, allocations, and distributions which the transferor Partner held in the Partnership, as such rights and obligations are set forth in this Agreement and/or conferred by law. If any of the conditions set forth in Section 7.3 above are not satisfied or waived in writing by the Partners, then (i) the transferor Partner shall not be relieved of any of its obligations as a Partner of the Partnership (as such obligations are set forth in this Agreement and/or conferred by law), and (ii) the transferee shall not be entitled to any rights of a Partner under this Agreement, other than the right to receive as much of the transferor Partner's share of Partnership profits, losses and distributions to which the transferor Partner otherwise would be entitled under this Agreement.[11] *[RUPA § 503]*

7.5   Transfers By Operation of Law. Any party who acquires any interest in the Partnership by operation of law, including by death or court decree, shall not be entitled to vote or otherwise participate in the Partnership's business.

---

[11]   *Comment:* RUPA § 502 provides that a partner's only "transferable interest" in the partnership under RUPA is the partner's share of the profits, losses, and distributions. The interest is characterized as personal property. Although a partner may transfer his or her interest in the partnership, RUPA § 503(a) provides that such transfer does not (i) by itself cause the partner's dissociation or a dissolution of the partnership; or (ii) entitle the transferee to participate in the management or conduct of the partnership business; or (iii) entitle the transferee to access to partnership information or inspect or copy the partnership books or records. Despite these limitations, a transferee has a right to (i) receive distributions to which the transferor would otherwise be entitled; (ii) receive a net amount otherwise distributable to the transferor upon the dissolution and winding up of the partnership's business; and (iii) seek a judicial determination that it is equitable to wind up the partnership business.

8. ADDITIONAL PARTNERS.

8.1 <u>Admission</u>. A person or entity may be admitted as an additional Partner in the Partnership only with the written consent of all Partners, which consent may be withheld for any reason or for no reason at all. *[RUPA § 401(i)]*

8.2 <u>Amendment</u>. Upon the admission of an additional Partner pursuant to Section 8.1 above, each Partner (including the additional Partner) shall execute an amendment to this Agreement (i) evidencing the additional Partner's consent to be bound by all of the provisions contained in this Agreement, and (ii) reflecting the Partners' new Percentage Interests.

9. DISSOCIATION OF A PARTNER.

A Partner shall cease to be a Partner, and shall be deemed "dissociated" within the meaning of [RUPA §§ 601–603], upon the occurrence of any of the events described in Section 9.1 below.

9.1 <u>Events of Dissociation</u>. The following events shall result in a Partner's dissociation from the Partnership *[RUPA § 601]*:

(a) Such Partner's expulsion pursuant to the unanimous vote of the other Partners;

(b) Such Partner's expulsion pursuant to an order of a court of competent jurisdiction;

(c) Such Partner becomes a debtor in bankruptcy;

(d) In the case of a Partner who is an individual, such Partner's death or incapacity;

(e) In the case of a Partner that is a trust or an estate, the distribution of the trust's or estate's entire transferable interest in the Partnership; or

(f) The termination of a Partner who is not an individual, partnership, corporation, trust, or estate.[12]

9.2 <u>Wrongful Dissociation</u>.

9.2.1 <u>Events Causing Wrongful Dissociation</u>. A Partner's dissociation shall be deemed wrongful if such dissociation (i) resulted from an event described in paragraphs (b), (c), (e) or (f) of Section 9.1 above, or (ii) resulted from an event not described in Section 9.1 above.[13] *[RUPA § 602]*

9.2.2 <u>Liability of Wrongfully Dissociated Partner</u>. A Partner who wrongfully dissociates is liable to the Partnership and to the other Partners for any damages caused by such wrongful dissociation, and such liability is in addition to any other obligation owed by the Partner to the Partnership.[14] *[RUPA § 602(c)]*

---

[12] *Comment:* Under the UPA, the death or withdrawal of a partner automatically triggered a dissolution of the partnership. Accordingly, the termination of a partner's relationship with the partnership was discussed only in the context of dissolution. In contrast, RUPA treats the dissolution of a partnership and the withdrawal of a partner as two separate concepts. The withdrawal of a partner from a partnership is referred to as "dissociation" in RUPA. RUPA § 601 lists events, which include those described above, which result in a partner's dissociation. In addition, the partnership agreement may identify other events causing a partner's dissociation.

[13] *Comment:* A partner has the power to dissociate at any time by express will, irrespective of whether such dissociation is rightful or wrongful. A partner's dissociation is wrongful if it is in breach of an express provision of the partnership agreement. Dissociation is also wrongful if, in the case of a partnership for a definite term or particular undertaking, (i) the partner withdraws by express will (except as specified under limited circumstances); (ii) the partner is expelled by judicial determination; (iii) the partner is dissociated by becoming a debtor in bankruptcy; or (iv) in the case of a partner who is not an individual, trust other than a business trust, or estate, the partner is expelled or dissociated because it willfully dissolved or terminated. A partner who wrongfully dissociates is liable to the partnership and to the other partners for any damages caused by such wrongful dissociation, and such liability is in addition to any other obligation owed by the partner to the partnership. Accordingly, the partnership agreement may specify additional consequences of a partner's wrongful dissociation.

[14] *Comment:* The language contained in Section 9.2.2 mirrors the language of RUPA § 602(c). Under RUPA, a partner's liability for wrongfully dissociating, as described above, is in addition to any other obligation owed by the partner to the partnership. Accordingly, a wrongfully dissociating partner will be held liable for any other breach of the partnership agreement and the partnership agreement may specify additional consequences of a partner's wrongful dissociation.

9.3 <u>Liability of Dissociated Partner</u>. A dissociated Partner is liable to the Partnership for any obligation incurred prior to that Partner's dissociation. A dissociated Partner may be liable for a transaction entered into by the Partnership within two years after the Partner's dissociation, provided the requirements set forth in RUPA § 703(b) are satisfied.[15] *[RUPA § 702]*

10. DISSOLUTION AND TERMINATION OF PARTNERSHIP.

10.1 <u>Events of Dissolution</u>.[16] The Partnership shall dissolve upon the occurrence of any of the following events:

(a) The expiration of the Partnership's term, as set forth in Section 1.6 above;[17] *[RUPA § 801(2)(iii)]*

(b) The Partners' unanimous written consent to dissolve the Partnership;[18] *[RUPA § 801(2)(ii)]*

(c) The sale, transfer or other disposition of all or substantially all of the Partnership's assets;

(d) The occurrence of any event which makes it unlawful for the Partners to carry on the Partnership's business; *[RUPA § 801(4)]* or

(e) Whenever a court of competent jurisdiction so properly decrees.[19] *[RUPA § 801(5)]*

10.2 <u>Winding-Up</u>. Upon the Partnership's dissolution, the Partnership's business shall be wound up within a reasonable period of time, its assets liquidated, a final accounting made, and the Partnership's

---

[15] *Comment:* Under RUPA, a partner is not discharged from liability for a partnership obligation incurred before dissociation merely because he or she has dissociated from the partnership. Generally, a dissociated partner is not liable for partnership obligations incurred after dissociation. A dissociated partner may, however, be liable to a third party for transactions entered into by the partnership within two years after the partner's dissociation, if (i) the other party reasonably believed that the dissociated partner was then a partner; (ii) the other party did not have notice of the partner's dissociation; and (iii) the other party is not deemed to have had knowledge or notice by reason of the filing of a Statement of Partnership Authority or Statement of Dissociation. A dissociated partner may be released from liability for a partnership obligation by agreement with the partnership creditor and the partners continuing the partnership business. In addition, a dissociated partner is released from liability for a partnership obligation if a partnership creditor, with notice of the partner's dissociation but without the partner's consent, agrees to a material alteration in the form of nature or time of payment of a partnership obligation.

[16] *Comment:* In a partnership at will, RUPA provides that the partnership will dissolve by the express will of at least half of the partners, including partners, other than wrongfully dissociating partners, who have dissociated within the preceding 90 days and for which purpose such dissociation constitutes an expression of that partner's will to dissolve and wind up the partnership business.

Regardless of whether a partnership is at will or for a definite term or undertaking, RUPA provides that the partnership will be dissolved and must be wound up upon the occurrence of (i) an event agreed to in the partnership agreement; (ii) an event that makes it unlawful for all or substantially all of the business of the partnership to be continued, unless such illegality is cured within 90 days after notice to the partnership of such event; or (iii) on application by a partner, a judicial determination that any of the following provisions of RUPA § 801 apply: (1) the partnership's economic purpose is likely to be frustrated; (2) another partner has engaged in conduct relating to the partnership business that makes it not reasonably practicable to carry on the business in partnership with that partner, or (3) it is not otherwise reasonably practical to conduct the partnership business in conformity with the partnership agreement.

[17] *Comment:* In a partnership for a definite term, dissolution is triggered by (i) the expiration of 90 days after a partner's dissociation by several specified events, including, without limitation, a partner's death, bankruptcy, or wrongful dissociation, unless before that time a majority in interest of the partners (including partners who have rightfully dissociated) agree to continue the partnership; (ii) the expiration of the term.

[18] *Comment:* Where the partnership is for a definite term, RUPA § 801(2)(ii) requires the express will of all of the partners to wind up the partnership business.

[19] *Comment:* To obtain a judicial decree that a partnership should be dissolved, a partner must make application for such decree, and the court must determine that one of the requirements contained in RUPA § 801 is fulfilled (See, footnote 13). In addition, a partnership is dissolved if, on application by a transferee of a partner's interest, a judicial determination is made that it is equitable to wind up the partnership business after the expiration of the term or completion of the undertaking, provided that the partnership was for a definite term or specific undertaking at the time of the transfer or entry of the charging order that gave rise to the transfer.

books closed. The Partners shall liquidate the Partnership's real property in an orderly fashion over a reasonable period of time pursuant to established real estate practices.[20] *[RUPA §§ 801–807]*

10.3 <u>Manner of Distribution</u>. Those proceeds which the Partnership derives from the liquidation of its assets shall be applied and distributed in the following order of priority:

(a) First, to the payment of expenses of liquidation and Partnership debts owing to creditors other than Partners;

(b) Second, to the payment of any Partnership debts owing to Partners; and

(c) Thereafter, to the Partners in accordance with their positive Capital Account balances, after taking into account income and loss allocations for the Partnership taxable year during which liquidation occurs. These liquidating distributions shall be made by the end of the Partnership taxable year in which the Partnership is liquidated, or, if later, within ninety (90) days after the date of such liquidation.

10.4 <u>Deficit Restoration Requirement</u>. If, upon liquidation, any Partner has a deficit balance in his Capital Account, after taking into account all Capital Account adjustments for the Partnership taxable year during which liquidation occurs, such Partner shall contribute cash to the capital of the Partnership in the amount necessary to eliminate such deficit balance by the end of the Partnership taxable year during which liquidation occurs or, if later, within ninety (90) days after the date of such liquidation. *[RUPA § 807(b)]*

10.5 <u>Termination</u>. Immediately after the application and distribution of liquidation proceeds in accordance with Section 10.3 above, the Partnership shall terminate.[21]

11. MISCELLANEOUS.

11.1 <u>Amendment</u>. This Agreement is subject to amendment only with the written consent of those Partners whose consent is required under this Agreement to accomplish the action reflected in such amendment.

11.2 <u>Binding Effect</u>. Subject to the restrictions set forth herein, this Agreement shall be binding upon the Partners and their respective successors, assigns, representatives, and beneficiaries.

11.3 <u>Captions and Headings.</u> Captions and headings used in this Agreement are for convenience purposes only. As such, they shall not control, affect, modify, amend or change the meaning and/or construction of any term or provision contained in this Agreement.

---

[20] *Comment:* Any partner who has not dissociated may participate in winding up the partnership's business. Upon application by any partner, however, a court may order judicial supervision of the winding up. The person winding up the partnership's business may do the following:

(i) preserve the partnership business or property as a going concern for a reasonable time; (ii) prosecute and defend actions and proceedings, whether civil, criminal, or administrative; (iii) settle and close the partnership's business; (iv) dispose of and transfer the partnership's property; (v) discharge the partnership's liabilities; (vi) distribute the partnership's assets; (vii) settle disputes by mediation or arbitration; and (viii) perform other necessary acts.

Under limited circumstances, a partnership may be bound by acts that occur during the winding up process. A partnership is bound by a partner's act after dissolution that is (i) appropriate for winding up the partnership's business; or (ii) would have bound the partnership before dissolution, if the other party to the transaction did not have notice of the dissolution.

RUPA provides that a partner who has not wrongfully dissociated may file a statement of dissolution stating, (i) the name of the partnership as filed with the Secretary of State; (ii) any identification number issued by the Secretary of State; and (iii) that the partnership has dissolved and is winding up its business. A Statement of Dissolution cancels a filed Statement of Partnership Authority, and is a limitation on authority for purposes of RUPA § 303(e). A third party is deemed to have notice of the dissolution and limitation of a partner's authority as a result of the Statement of Dissolution 90 days after it is filed.

After filing a Statement of Dissolution, a dissolved partnership may file and, if appropriate, record a Statement of Partnership Authority that will be valid with respect to any transaction, whether or not the transaction is appropriate for winding up the partnership's business.

[21] *Comment:* RUPA provides that a partnership continues after dissolution only for the purpose of winding up its business. The partnership is terminated when the winding [up is completed].

11.4 <u>Counterparts and Facsimiles</u>. The Partners may execute this Agreement simultaneously, in any number of counterparts, or on facsimile copies, each of which shall be deemed an original, but all of which together shall constitute one and the same Agreement.

11.5 <u>Entire Agreement</u>. This Agreement contains the Partners' entire agreement and supersedes any prior oral or written agreements among them with respect to the subject matter contained herein. There are no representations, agreements, arrangements, or understandings (oral or written) among the Partners relating to the subject matter of this Agreement which are not fully expressed herein.

11.6 <u>Further Documents</u>. Each party agrees to execute, with acknowledgment and affidavit if required, any and all documents in writing which may be required under this Agreement.

11.7 <u>Governing Law</u>. This Agreement, together with the Partners' respective rights and obligations hereunder, shall be governed by and construed in accordance with the laws of the State of California.

11.8 <u>Notices</u>. Any notice required or permitted hereunder shall be given in writing and shall be deemed effectively given upon (i) personal delivery, (ii) twenty-four (24) hours after deposit with Federal Express or a comparable express courier, addressed to a party at the address set forth below his signature hereto, or (iii) forty-eight (48) hours after deposit in the United States mail, by certified mail, return receipt requested, postage prepaid, addressed to a Partner at the address set forth below his signature hereto. A Partner may designate another address for notice purposes upon written notice thereof to the Partnership.

11.9 <u>Partition—No Right</u>. No Partner shall have any right to seek or demand (i) partition of all or any part of the Partnership's assets, or (ii) any specific Partnership assets upon the liquidation of the Partnership.

11.10 <u>Prevailing Party's Fees</u>. If any party commences an action against another party to interpret or enforce any of the terms of this Agreement, or because of the other party's breach of any provision set forth in this Agreement, the losing party shall pay to the prevailing party reasonable attorneys' fees, costs and expenses, court costs and other costs of action incurred in connection with the prosecution or defense of such action, whether or not the action is prosecuted to a final judgment. For purposes of this Agreement, the terms "attorneys' fees" or "attorneys' fees and costs" shall mean the fees and expenses of counsel to the parties hereto, which may include, without limitation, printing, photostating, duplicating and other expenses, air freight charges, and fees billed for law clerks, paralegals, librarians and others not admitted to the bar but performing services under the supervision of an attorney. The terms "attorneys' fees" or "attorneys' fees and costs" shall also include, without limitation, all such fees and expenses incurred with respect to appeals, arbitrations and bankruptcy proceedings, and whether or not any action or proceeding is brought with respect to the matter for which said fees and expenses were incurred. The term "attorney" shall have the same meaning as the term "counsel."

11.11 <u>Pronouns and Gender</u>. Any pronouns or references used in this Agreement shall be deemed to include the masculine, feminine, or neuter gender, as appropriate. Any expression in the singular or plural shall, if appropriate in the context, include both the singular and the plural.

11.12 <u>Recitals and Exhibits</u>. All recitals set forth in this Agreement and all exhibits referenced in this Agreement are incorporated into this Agreement by this reference.

11.13 <u>Severability</u>. If a court of competent jurisdiction finds any provision in this Agreement to be invalid, such invalidity shall not affect the remainder of the Agreement. In such event, the invalid provision shall be deemed severed therefrom and the remainder of the Agreement shall remain enforceable in accordance with its terms and of full force and effect.

11.14 <u>Third Parties—No Interest</u>. Nothing in this Agreement (whether express or implied) is intended to or shall (i) confer any rights or remedies under or by reason of this Agreement on any persons other than the parties hereto and their respective successors and assigns, (ii) relieve or discharge the obligation or liability of any third person to any party hereto, or (iii) give any third person any right of subrogation or action against any party to this Agreement.

11.15 <u>Waiver</u>. A party's waiver of any breach of any provision contained in this Agreement shall not constitute a continuing waiver or a waiver of any subsequent breach of such provision or any other provision contained in this Agreement.

11.16 <u>Time of Essence</u>. Time is of the essence of this Agreement and all terms, covenants, conditions and provisions set forth in this Agreement.

12. EXECUTION.

IN WITNESS WHEREOF, the Partners have executed this Agreement effective as of the Effective Date as set forth in the Agreement.

Date: _____

_____

Signature

_____

Typed Name

_____

Residence Address

Date: _____

_____

Signature

_____

Typed Name

_____

Residence Address

13. CONSENT OF SPOUSES.

We certify that:

(1) We are the spouses of the persons who signed the foregoing Partnership Agreement and who constitute the members of the Partnership described in that Agreement.

(2) We have read and approve the provisions of that Partnership Agreement, including but not limited to those relating to the purchase, sale, or other disposition of the interest of a deceased, retiring, withdrawing, or terminating partner.

(3) We agree to be bound by and accept those provisions of that Partnership Agreement in lieu of all other interests we, or any of us, may have in that Partnership, whether the interest be community property or otherwise.

(4) Our spouses shall have the full power of management of their interests in the Partnership, including any portion of those interests that are our community property, and they have the full right, without our further approval, to exercise their voting rights as partners in the Partnership, to execute any amendments to the Partnership Agreement, and to sell, transfer, encumber, and deal in any manner with those Partnership interests, including any portion of those interests that are our community property.

Executed on Date: _____, at: _____, California.

_____

Signature

FORM OF PARTNERSHIP AGREEMENT

_____

Typed Name

_____

Signature

_____

Typed Name

UNIFORM LIMITED PARTNERSHIP ACT (2001)

(Last Amended 2013)

TABLE OF CONTENTS

[ARTICLE] 1
GENERAL PROVISIONS

Sec.		Page
101.	Short Title.	160
102.	Definitions.	160
103.	Knowledge; Notice.	163
104.	Governing Law.	164
105.	Partnership Agreement; Scope, Function, and Limitations.	164
106.	Partnership Agreement; Effect on Limited Partnership and Person Becoming Partner; Preformation Agreement.	167
107.	Partnership Agreement; Effect on Third Parties and Relationship to Records Effective on Behalf of Limited Partnership.	167
108.	Required Information.	168
109.	Dual Capacity.	168
110.	Nature, Purpose, and Duration of Limited Partnership.	169
111.	Powers.	169
113.	Supplemental Principles of Law.	169
114.	Permitted Names.	169
117.	Registered Agent.	170
118.	Change of Registered Agent or Address for Registered Agent by Limited Partnership.	170
123.	Reservation of Power to Amend or Repeal.	171

[ARTICLE] 2
FORMATION; CERTIFICATE OF LIMITED
PARTNERSHIP AND OTHER FILINGS

201.	Formation of Limited Partnership; Certificate of Limited Partnership.	171
202.	Amendment or Restatement of Certificate of Limited Partnership.	172
212.	[Annual] [Biennial] Report for [Secretary of State].	172

[ARTICLE] 3
LIMITED PARTNERS

301.	Becoming Limited Partner.	173
302.	No Agency Power of Limited Partner as Limited Partner.	173
303.	No Liability as Limited Partner for Limited Partnership Obligations.	174
304.	Rights to Information of Limited Partner and Person Dissociated as Limited Partner.	175
305.	Limited Duties of Limited Partners.	177
306.	Person Erroneously Believing Self to Be Limited Partner.	177

[ARTICLE] 4
GENERAL PARTNERS

401.	Becoming General Partner.	178
402.	General Partner Agent of Limited Partnership.	178
403.	Limited Partnership Liable for General Partner's Actionable Conduct.	178
404.	General Partner's Liability.	179
405.	Actions by and Against Partnership and Partners.	179
406.	Management Rights of General Partner.	180

407. Rights to Information of General Partner and Person Dissociated as General Partner............181
408. Reimbursement; Indemnification; Advancement; and Insurance.................................182
409. Standards of Conduct for General Partners...182

[ARTICLE] 5
CONTRIBUTIONS AND DISTRIBUTIONS

501. Form of Contribution...184
502. Liability for Contribution..185
503. Sharing of and Right to Distributions Before Dissolution....................................185
504. Limitations on Distributions..185
505. Liability for Improper Distributions..186

[ARTICLE] 6
DISSOCIATION

601. Dissociation as Limited Partner...187
602. Effect of Dissociation as Limited Partner...189
603. Dissociation as General Partner...189
604. Power to Dissociate as General Partner; Wrongful Dissociation...............................190
605. Effect of Dissociation as General Partner...191
606. Power to Bind and Liability of Person Dissociated as General Partner.........................192
607. Liability of Person Dissociated as General Partner to Other Persons..........................192

[ARTICLE] 7
TRANSFERABLE INTERESTS AND RIGHTS
OF TRANSFEREES AND CREDITORS

701. Nature of Transferable Interest...193
702. Transfer of Transferable Interest...193
703. Charging Order...195
704. Power of Legal Representative of Deceased Partner...195

[ARTICLE] 8
DISSOLUTION AND WINDING UP

801. Events Causing Dissolution..196
802. Winding Up...197
804. Power to Bind Partnership After Dissolution...198
805. Liability After Dissolution of General Partner and Person Dissociated as General Partner....199
806. Known Claims Against Dissolved Limited Partnership..199
807. Other Claims Against Dissolved Limited Partnership..200
808. Court Proceedings..200
809. Liability of General Partner and Person Dissociated as General Partner When Claim
     Against Limited Partnership Barred...201
810. Disposition of Assets in Winding Up; When Contributions Required............................201

[ARTICLE] 9
ACTIONS BY PARTNERS

901. Direct Action by Partner..202
902. Derivative Action..202
903. Proper Plaintiff...203
904. Pleading..203
905. Special Litigation Committee...203
906. Proceeds and Expenses..204

[ARTICLE] 10
FOREIGN LIMITED PARTNERSHIPS

1001.   Governing Law..204

[ARTICLE] 11
MERGER, INTEREST EXCHANGE, CONVERSION, AND DOMESTICATION

[PART] 1
GENERAL PROVISIONS

1101.   Definitions...204
1102.   Relationship of [Article] to Other Laws...........................208
1103.   Required Notice or Approval..209
1104.   Nonexclusivity..209
1106.   Appraisal Rights...209

[PART] 2
MERGER

1121.   Merger Authorized..210
1122.   Plan of Merger..210
1123.   Approval of Merger..211
1126.   Effect of Merger..211

[PART] 3
INTEREST EXCHANGE

1131.   Interest Exchange Authorized...213
1132.   Plan of Interest Exchange...213
1133.   Approval of Interest Exchange..214
1134.   Amendment or Abandonment of Plan of Interest Exchange.........214
1136.   Effect of Interest Exchange...215

[PART] 4
CONVERSION

1141.   Conversion Authorized...216
1142.   Plan of Conversion...216
1143.   Approval of Conversion..216
1146.   Effect of Conversion...217

[PART] 5
DOMESTICATION

1151.   Domestication Authorized..218
1152.   Plan of Domestication..219
1153.   Approval of Domestication...219
1154.   Amendment or Abandonment of Plan of Domestication..............219
1156.   Effect of Domestication..220

[ARTICLE] 12
MISCELLANEOUS PROVISIONS

1201.   Uniformity of Application and Construction.*

---

*   Omitted.

1202. Relation to Electronic Signatures in Global and National Commerce Act.*
1203. Savings Clause.*
[1204. Severability Clause.]*
1205. Repeals.*
1206. Effective Date.*

2001 PREFATORY NOTE

The Act's Overall Approach

The new Limited Partnership Act is a "stand alone" act, "de-linked" from both the original general partnership act ("UPA") and the Revised Uniform Partnership Act ("RUPA"). To be able to stand alone, the Limited Partnership incorporates many provisions from RUPA and some from the Uniform Limited Liability Company Act ("ULLCA"). As a result, the new Act is far longer and more complex than its immediate predecessor, the Revised Uniform Limited Partnership Act ("RULPA").

The new Act has been drafted for a world in which limited liability partnerships and limited liability companies can meet many of the needs formerly met by limited partnerships. This Act therefore targets two types of enterprises that seem largely beyond the scope of LLPs and LLCs: (i) sophisticated, manager-entrenched commercial deals whose participants commit for the long term, and (ii) estate planning arrangements (family limited partnerships). This Act accordingly assumes that, more often than not, people utilizing it will want:

- strong centralized management, strongly entrenched, and

- passive investors with little control over or right to exit the entity

The Act's rules, and particularly its default rules, have been designed to reflect these assumptions.

The Decision to "De-Link" and Create a Stand Alone Act

Unlike this Act, RULPA is not a stand alone statute. RULPA was drafted to rest on and link to the UPA. RULPA Section 1105 states that "In any case not provided for in this [Act] the provisions of the Uniform Partnership Act govern." UPA Section 6(2) in turn provides that "this Act shall apply to limited partnerships except in so far as the statutes relating to such partnerships are inconsistent herewith." More particularly, RULPA Section 403 defines the rights, powers, restrictions and liabilities of a "general partner of a limited partnership" by equating them to the rights, powers, restrictions and liabilities of "a partner in a partnership without limited partners."

This arrangement has not been completely satisfactory, because the consequences of linkage are not always clear. *See, e.g., Frye v. Manacare Ltd.*, 431 So.2d 181, 183–84 (Fla. Dist. Ct. App. 1983) (applying UPA Section 42 in favor of a limited partner), *Porter v. Barnhouse*, 354 N.W.2d 227, 232–33 (Iowa 1984) (declining to apply UPA Section 42 in favor of a limited partner) and *Baltzell-Wolfe Agencies, Inc. v. Car Wash Investments No. 1, Ltd.*, 389 N.E.2d 517, 518–20 (Ohio App. 1978) (holding that neither the specific provisions of the general partnership statute nor those of the limited partnership statute determined the liability of a person who had withdrawn as general partner of a limited partnership). Moreover, in some instances the "not inconsistent" rules of the UPA can be inappropriate for the fundamentally different relations involved in a limited partnership.

In any event, the promulgation of RUPA unsettled matters. RUPA differs substantially from the UPA, and the drafters of RUPA expressly declined to decide whether RUPA provides a suitable base and link for the limited partnership statute. According to RUPA's Prefatory Note:

Partnership law no longer governs limited partnerships pursuant to the provisions of RUPA itself. First, limited partnerships are not "partnerships" within the RUPA definition. Second, UPA Section 6(2), which provides that the UPA governs limited partnerships in cases not provided for in the Uniform Limited Partnership Act (1976) (1985) ("RULPA") has been deleted. No substantive change in result is intended,

---

* Omitted.

however. Section 1105 of RULPA already provides that the UPA governs in any case not provided for in RULPA, and thus the express linkage in RUPA is unnecessary. Structurally, it is more appropriately left to RULPA to determine the applicability of RUPA to limited partnerships. It is contemplated that the Conference will review the linkage question carefully, although no changes in RULPA may be necessary despite the many changes in RUPA.

The linkage question was the first major issue considered and decided by this Act's Drafting Committee. Since the Conference has recommended the repeal of the UPA, it made no sense to recommend retaining the UPA as the base and link for a revised or new limited partnership act. The Drafting Committee therefore had to choose between recommending linkage to the new general partnership act (*i.e.*, RUPA) or recommending de-linking and a stand alone act.

The Committee saw several substantial advantages to de-linking. A stand alone statute would:

- be more convenient, providing a single, self-contained source of statutory authority for issues pertaining to limited partnerships;

- eliminate confusion as to which issues were solely subject to the limited partnership act and which required reference (*i.e.*, linkage) to the general partnership act; and

- rationalize future case law, by ending the automatic link between the cases concerning partners in a general partnership and issues pertaining to general partners in a limited partnership.

Thus, a stand alone act seemed likely to promote efficiency, clarity, and coherence in the law of limited partnerships.

In contrast, recommending linkage would have required the Drafting Committee to (1) consider each provision of RUPA and determine whether the provision addressed a matter provided for in RULPA; (2) for each RUPA provision which addressed a matter not provided for in RULPA, determine whether the provision stated an appropriate rule for limited partnerships; and (3) for each matter addressed both by RUPA and RULPA, determine whether RUPA or RULPA stated the better rule for limited partnerships.

That approach was unsatisfactory for at least two reasons. No matter how exhaustive the Drafting Committee's analysis might be, the Committee could not guarantee that courts and practitioners would reach the same conclusions. Therefore, in at least some situations linkage would have produced ambiguity. In addition, the Drafting Committee could not guarantee that all currently appropriate links would remain appropriate as courts begin to apply and interpret RUPA. Even if the Committee recommended linkage, RUPA was destined to be interpreted primarily in the context of general partnerships. Those interpretations might not make sense for limited partnership law, because the modern limited partnership involves fundamentally different relations than those involved in "the small, often informal, partnership" that is "[t]he primary focus of RUPA." RUPA, Prefatory Note.

The Drafting Committee therefore decided to draft and recommend a stand alone act.

Availability of LLLP Status

Following the example of a growing number of States, this Act provides for limited liability limited partnerships. In a limited liability limited partnership ("LLLP"), no partner—whether general or limited—is liable on account of partner status for the limited partnership's obligations. Both general and limited partners benefit from a full, status-based liability shield that is equivalent to the shield enjoyed by corporate shareholders, LLC members, and partners in an LLP.

This Act is designed to serve preexisting limited partnerships as well as limited partnerships formed after the Act's enactment. Most of those preexisting limited partnership will not be LLLPs, and accordingly the Act does not prefer or presume LLLP status. Instead, the Act makes LLLP status available through a simple statement in the certificate of limited partnership. *See* Sections 102(9), 201(a)(4) and 404(c).

Liability Shield for Limited Partners

RULPA provides only a restricted liability shield for limited partners. The shield is at risk for any limited partner who "participates in the control of the business." RULPA Section 303(a). Although this "control rule" is subject to a lengthy list of safe harbors, RULPA Section 303(b), in a world with LLPs, LLCs and, most importantly, LLLPs, the rule is an anachronism. This Act therefore eliminates the control rule and provides a full, status-based shield against limited partner liability for entity obligations. The shield applies whether or not the limited partnership is an LLLP. *See* Section 303.

Transition Issues

Following RUPA's example, this Act provides (i) an effective date, after which all newly formed limited partnerships are subject to this Act; (ii) an optional period, during which limited partnerships formed under a predecessor statute may elect to become subject to this Act; and (iii) a mandatory date, on which all preexisting limited partnerships become subject to this Act by operation of law.

A few provisions of this Act differ so substantially from prior law that they should not apply automatically to a preexisting limited partnership. Section 1206(c) lists these provisions and states that each remains inapplicable to a preexisting limited partnership, unless the limited partnership elects for the provision to apply.

Comparison of RULPA and this Act

The following table compares some of the major characteristics of RULPA and this Act. In most instances, the rules involved are "default" rules—*i.e.*, subject to change by the partnership agreement.

Characteristic	RULPA	This Act
relationship to general partnership act	linked, Sections 1105, 403; UPA Section 6(2)	de-linked (but many RUPA provisions incorporated)
permitted purposes	subject to any specified exceptions, "any business that a partnership without limited partners may carry on," Section 106	any lawful purpose, Section 104(b)
constructive notice via publicly filed documents	only that limited partnership exists and that designated general partners are general partners, Section 208	RULPA constructive notice provisions carried forward, Section 103(c), plus constructive notice, 90 days after appropriate filing, of: general partner dissociation and of limited partnership dissolution, termination, merger and conversion, Section 103(d)
duration	specified in certificate of limited partnership, Section 201(a)(4)	perpetual, Section 104(c); subject to change in partnership agreement
use of limited partner name in entity name	prohibited, except in unusual circumstances, Section 102(2)	permitted, Section108(a)
annual report	none	required, Section 210
limited partner liability for entity debts	none unless limited partner "participates in the control of the business" and person "transact[s] business with the limited partnership reasonably believing . . . that the limited partner is a general partner," Section 303(a); safe harbor lists many activities that do not constitute participating in the	none, regardless of whether the limited partnership is an LLLP, "even if the limited partner participates in the management and control of the limited partnership," Section 303

Characteristic	RULPA	This Act
	control of the business, Section 303(b)	
limited partner duties	none specified	no fiduciary duties "solely by reason of being a limited partner," Section 305(a); each limited partner is obliged to "discharge duties . . . and exercise rights consistently with the obligation of good faith and fair dealing," Section 305(b)
partner access to information—required records/information	all partners have right of access; no requirement of good cause; Act does not state whether partnership agreement may limit access; Sections 105(b) and 305(1)	list of required information expanded slightly; Act expressly states that partner does not have to show good cause; Sections 304(a), 407(a); however, the partnership agreement may set reasonable restrictions on access to and use of required information, Section 110(b)(4), and limited partnership may impose reasonable restrictions on the use of information, Sections 304(g) and 407(f)
partner access to information—other information	limited partners have the right to obtain other relevant information "upon reasonable demand," Section 305(2); general partner rights linked to general partnership act, Section 403	for limited partners, RULPA approach essentially carried forward, with procedures and standards for making a reasonable demand stated in greater detail, plus requirement that limited partnership supply known material information when limited partner consent sought, Section 304; general partner access rights made explicit, following ULLCA and RUPA, including obligation of limited partnership and general partners to volunteer certain information, Section 407; access rights provided for former partners, Sections 304 and 407
general partner liability for entity debts	complete, automatic and formally inescapable, Section 403(b) (n.b.—in practice, most modern limited partnerships have used a general partner that has its own liability shield; e.g., a	LLLP status available via a simple statement in the certificate of limited partnership, Sections 102(9), 201(a)(4); LLLP status provides a full liability shield to all general partners, Section

Characteristic	RULPA	This Act
	corporation or limited liability company)	404(c); if the limited partnership is not an LLLP, general partners are liable just as under RULPA, Section 404(a)
general partner duties	linked to duties of partners in a general partnership, Section 403	RUPA general partner duties imported, Section 408; general partner's non-compete duty continues during winding up, Section 408(b)(3)
allocation of profits, losses and distributions	provides separately for sharing of profits and losses, Section 503, and for sharing of distributions, Section 504; allocates each according to contributions made and not returned	eliminates as unnecessary the allocation rule for profits and losses; allocates distributions according to contributions made, Section 503 (n.b.—in the default mode, the Act's formulation produces the same result as RULPA formulation)
partner liability for distributions	recapture liability if distribution involved "the return of . . . contribution"; one year recapture liability if distribution rightful, Section 608(a); six year recapture liability if wrongful, Section 608(b)	following ULLCA Sections 406 and 407, the Act adopts the RMBCA approach to improper distributions, Sections 508 and 509
limited partner voluntary dissociation	theoretically, limited partner may withdraw on six months notice unless partnership agreement specifies a term for the limited partnership or withdrawal events for limited partner, Section 603; practically, virtually every partnership agreement specifies a term, thereby eliminating the right to withdraw (n.b.—due to estate planning concerns, several States have amended RULPA to prohibit limited partner withdrawal unless otherwise provided in the partnership agreement)	no "right to dissociate as a limited partner before the termination of the limited partnership," Section 601(a); power to dissociate expressly recognized, Section 601(b)(1), but can be eliminated by the partnership agreement
limited partner involuntary dissociation	not addressed	lengthy list of causes, Section 601(b), taken with some modification from RUPA
limited partner dissociation—payout	"fair value . . . based upon [the partner's] right to share in distributions," Section 604	no payout; person becomes transferee of its own transferable interest, Section 602(3)

Characteristic	RULPA	This Act
general partner voluntary dissociation	right exists unless otherwise provided in partnership agreement, Section 602; power exists regardless of partnership agreement, Section 602	RULPA rule carried forward, although phrased differently, Section 604(a); dissociation before termination of the limited partnership is defined as wrongful, Section 604(b)(2)
general partner involuntary dissociation	Section 402 lists causes	following RUPA, Section 603 expands the list of causes, including expulsion by court order, Section 603(5)
general partner dissociation—payout	"fair value . . . based upon [the partner's] right to share in distributions," Section 604, subject to offset for damages caused by wrongful withdrawal, Section 602	no payout; person becomes transferee of its own transferable interest, Section 605(5)
transfer of partner interest—nomenclature	"Assignment of Partnership Interest," Section 702	"Transfer of Partner's Transferable Interest," Section 702
transfer of partner interest—substance	economic rights fully transferable, but management rights and partner status are not transferable, Section 702	same rule, but Sections 701 and 702 follow RUPA's more detailed and less oblique formulation
rights of creditor of partner	limited to charging order, Section 703	essentially the same rule, but, following RUPA and ULLCA, the Act has a more elaborate provision that expressly extends to creditors of transferees, Section 703
dissolution by partner consent	requires unanimous written consent, Section 801(3)	requires consent of "all general partners and of limited partners owning a majority of the rights to receive distributions as limited partners at the time the consent is to be effective," Section 801(2)
dissolution following dissociation of a general partner	occurs automatically unless all partners agree to continue the business and, if there is no remaining general partner, to appoint a replacement general partner, Section 801(4)	if at least one general partner remains, no dissolution unless "within 90 days after the dissociation . . . partners owning a majority of the rights to receive distributions as partners" consent to dissolve the limited partnership; Section 801(3)(A); if no general partner remains, dissolution occurs upon the passage of 90 days after the dissociation, unless before that deadline limited partners owning a

Characteristic	RULPA	This Act
		majority of the rights to receive distributions owned by limited partners consent to continue the business and admit at least one new general partner and a new general partner is admitted, Section 801(3)(B)
filings related to entity termination	certificate of limited partnership to be cancelled when limited partnership dissolves and begins winding up, Section 203	limited partnership may amend certificate to indicate dissolution, Section 803(b)(1), and may file statement of termination indicating that winding up has been completed and the limited partnership is terminated, Section 203
procedures for barring claims against dissolved limited partnership	none	following ULLCA Sections 807 and 808, the Act adopts the RMBCA approach providing for giving notice and barring claims, Sections 806 and 807
conversions and mergers	no provision	Article 11 permits conversions to and from and mergers with any "organization," defined as "a general partnership, including a limited liability partnership; limited partnership, including a limited liability limited partnership; limited liability company; business trust; corporation; or any other entity having a governing statute . . . [including] domestic and foreign entities regardless of whether organized for profit." Section1101(8)
writing requirements	some provisions pertain only to written understandings; *see, e.g.*, Sections 401 (partnership agreement may "provide in writing for the admission of additional general partners"; such admission also permitted "with the written consent of all partners"), 502(a) (limited partner's promise to contribute "is not enforceable unless set out in a writing signed by the limited partner"), 801(2) and (3) (dissolution occurs "upon the happening of events specified in writing in the	removes virtually all writing requirements; but does require that certain information be maintained in record form, Section 111

Characteristic	RULPA	This Act
	partnership agreement" and upon "written consent of all partners"), 801(4) (dissolution avoided following withdrawal of a general partner if "all partners agree in writing")	

PREFATORY NOTE TO 2011 AND 2013 HARMONIZATION AMENDMENTS

From 2009 to 2011, the Uniform Law Conference undertook an intensive effort to harmonize, to the extent possible, all uniform acts pertaining to unincorporated organizations. As part of that effort, the Uniform Limited Partnership Act ("ULPA") underwent four types of changes: substantive, major improvements in language, minor revisions in language for the sake of harmonization; and relocation within this particular "spoke" of provisions that are part of the "HUB" in the new Uniform Business Organizations Code ("UBOC").

Substantive Changes

The most significant substantive changes is the "un-cabining" fiduciary duty; *i.e.*, ceasing to characterize the Act's codification of fiduciary duty as exhaustive, Section 409.

Other substantive changes include: (i) providing a narrow exception to the rule that the amendments to the partnership agreement control the rights of persons previously dissociated as partners and of persons that had previously become transferees, Section 107(b)(2); (ii) eliminating the requirement that a domestic limited partnership designate and maintain an in-state office, Section 201; (iii) requiring that the annual report list the name of at least one general partner, Section 212(a)(4); and (iv) expressly authorizing a limited partnership to provide advancements to a person entitled to indemnification, Section 408(c).

Substantial Improvements to Language

The most significant improvements in language appear in Section 105 (formerly Section 110), the first of three sections addressing the partnership agreement. The structure of Section 105 is far less complicated than the structure of former Section 110.

Harmonization-Based Language Changes

Minor changes in language for the sake of harmonization appear throughout the act. For example, Section 202(b) is revised as follows:

(b) ~~In order to~~ To amend its certificate of limited partnership, a limited partnership must deliver to the [Secretary of State] for filing an amendment ~~or, pursuant to [Article] 11, articles of merger~~ stating:

(1) the name of the ~~limited~~ partnership;

(2) the date of filing of its initial certificate of limited partnership; and

(3) ~~the changes~~ the amendment ~~makes to the certificate as most recently amended or restated.~~

Relocation and Renumbering of HUB-Based Provisions

The harmonization process included both the harmonization of various stand-alone acts and UBOC, which comprises a "HUB" (somewhat analogous to Article 1 of the Uniform Commercial Code) and various spokes. Each spoke pertains to a different type of organization (*e.g.*, limited partnership, statutory entity trust). Naturally, spokes in the Code do not repeat the provisions from the HUB. In contrast, each stand-alone act includes provisions that appear in the HUB in the Code.

So that the section numbers this "spoke" correspond with the spoke provisions in the Code, "HUB"-based provisions of this Act have been renumbered to appear at the end of articles. *See, e.g.*, Sections 112 through 122. . . .

[ARTICLE] 1

GENERAL PROVISIONS

§ 101.　SHORT TITLE.

This [act] may be cited as the Uniform Limited Partnership Act.

§ 102.　DEFINITIONS.

In this [act]:

　　(1)　"Certificate of limited partnership" means the certificate required by Section 201. The term includes the certificate as amended or restated.

　　(2)　"Contribution", except in the phrase "right of contribution", means property or a benefit described in Section 501 which is provided by a person to a limited partnership to become a partner or in the person's capacity as a partner.

　　(3)　"Debtor in bankruptcy" means a person that is the subject of:

　　　　(A)　an order for relief under Title 11 of the United States Code or a comparable order under a successor statute of general application; or

　　　　(B)　a comparable order under federal, state, or foreign law governing insolvency.

　　(4)　"Distribution" means a transfer of money or other property from a limited partnership to a person on account of a transferable interest or in the person's capacity as a partner. The term:

　　　　(A)　includes:

　　　　　　(i)　a redemption or other purchase by a limited partnership of a transferable interest; and

　　　　　　(ii)　a transfer to a partner in return for the partner's relinquishment of any right to participate as a partner in the management or conduct of the partnership's activities and affairs or to have access to records or other information concerning the partnership's activities and affairs; and

　　　　(B)　does not include amounts constituting reasonable compensation for present or past service or payments made in the ordinary course of business under a bona fide retirement plan or other bona fide benefits program.

　　(5)　"Foreign limited liability limited partnership" means a foreign limited partnership whose general partners have limited liability for the debts, obligations, or other liabilities of the foreign partnership under a provision similar to Section 404(c).

　　(6)　"Foreign limited partnership" means an unincorporated entity formed under the law of a jurisdiction other than this state which would be a limited partnership if formed under the law of this state. The term includes a foreign limited liability limited partnership.

　　(7)　"General partner" means a person that:

　　　　(A)　has become a general partner under Section 401 or was a general partner in a partnership when the partnership became subject to this [act] under Section 112; and

　　　　(B)　has not dissociated as a general partner under Section 603.

(8) "Jurisdiction", used to refer to a political entity, means the United States, a state, a foreign country, or a political subdivision of a foreign country.

(9) "Jurisdiction of formation" means the jurisdiction whose law governs the internal affairs of an entity.

(10) "Limited liability limited partnership", except in the phrase "foreign limited liability limited partnership" and in [Article] 11, means a limited partnership whose certificate of limited partnership states that the partnership is a limited liability limited partnership.

(11) "Limited partner" means a person that:

    (A) has become a limited partner under Section 301 or was a limited partner in a limited partnership when the partnership became subject to this [act] under Section 112; and

    (B) has not dissociated under Section 601.

(12) "Limited partnership", except in the phrase "foreign limited partnership" and in [Article] 11, means an entity formed under this [act] or which becomes subject to this [act] under [Article] 11 or Section 112. The term includes a limited liability limited partnership.

(13) "Partner" means a limited partner or general partner.

(14) "Partnership agreement" means the agreement, whether or not referred to as a partnership agreement and whether oral, implied, in a record, or in any combination thereof, of all the partners of a limited partnership concerning the matters described in Section 105(a). The term includes the agreement as amended or restated.

(15) "Person" means an individual, business corporation, nonprofit corporation, partnership, limited partnership, limited liability company, [general cooperative association,] limited cooperative association, unincorporated nonprofit association, statutory trust, business trust, common-law business trust, estate, trust, association, joint venture, public corporation, government or governmental subdivision, agency, or instrumentality, or any other legal or commercial entity.

(16) "Principal office" means the principal executive office of a limited partnership or foreign limited partnership, whether or not the office is located in this state.

(17) "Property" means all property, whether real, personal, or mixed or tangible or intangible, or any right or interest therein.

(18) "Record", used as a noun, means information that is inscribed on a tangible medium or that is stored in an electronic or other medium and is retrievable in perceivable form.

(19) "Registered agent" means an agent of a limited partnership or foreign limited partnership which is authorized to receive service of any process, notice, or demand required or permitted by law to be served on the partnership.

(20) "Registered foreign limited partnership" means a foreign limited partnership that is registered to do business in this state pursuant to a statement of registration filed by the [Secretary of State].

(21) "Required information" means the information that a limited partnership is required to maintain under Section 108.

(22) "Sign" means, with present intent to authenticate or adopt a record:

    (A) to execute or adopt a tangible symbol; or

    (B) to attach to or logically associate with the record an electronic symbol, sound, or process.

(23) "State" means a state of the United States, the District of Columbia, Puerto Rico, the United States Virgin Islands, or any territory or insular possession subject to the jurisdiction of the United States.

(24) "Transfer" includes:

    (A)   an assignment;

    (B)   a conveyance;

    (C)   a sale;

    (D)   a lease;

    (E)   an encumbrance, including a mortgage or security interest;

    (F)   a gift; and

    (G)   a transfer by operation of law.

    (25) "Transferable interest" means the right, as initially owned by a person in the person's capacity as a partner, to receive distributions from a limited partnership, whether or not the person remains a partner or continues to own any part of the right. The term applies to any fraction of the interest, by whomever owned.

    (26) "Transferee" means a person to which all or part of a transferable interest has been transferred, whether or not the transferor is a partner. The term includes a person that owns a transferable interest under Section 602(a)(3) or 605(a)(4).

Comment

    This section contains definitions for terms used throughout the act, while Section 1011 contains definitions specific to Article 11's provisions on mergers, conversions, interest exchanges, and domestications. . . .

    "Limited liability limited partnership" [(10)]—Typically, a general partnership becomes a limited liability partnership when the filing office files a statement of qualification submitted by the partnership. In contrast, LLLP status results from a statement in a limited partnership's certificate of limited partnership. Section 201(b)(5) requires a limited partnership's certificate of limited partnership to state "whether the limited partnership is a limited liability limited partnership."

    The definition makes an exception for Article 11, because in that article the phrase "limited liability limited partnership" encompasses both domestic and foreign LLLPs. . . .

    "Partnership agreement" [(14)]—This definition must be read in conjunction with Sections 105 through 107, which further describe the partnership agreement. In particular, although this definition refers to "the agreement . . . of all the partners," the limited partnership itself is bound by and may enforce the agreement. Section 106(a).

    A partnership agreement is a contract, and therefore all statutory language pertaining to the partnership agreement must be understood in the context of the law of contracts.

    The definition in Paragraph 14 is very broad and recognizes a wide scope of authority for the partnership agreement . . .

    This act states no rule as to whether the statute of frauds applies to partnership agreements. Case law suggests that the answer is yes:

> Partnership agreements, like other contracts, are subject to the Statute of Frauds. A contract of partnership for a term exceeding one year is within the Statute of Frauds and is void unless it is in writing [and signed by the party to be bound]; however, a contract establishing a partnership terminable at the will of any partner is generally held to be capable of performance by its terms within one year of its making and, therefore, to be outside the Statute of Frauds.

Abbott v. Hurst, 643 So.2d 589, 592 (Ala. 1994) (citations omitted). . .

    "Transfer" [(24)]—The term "transfer" is broadly defined to include all types of conveyances of interests in property. The reference to "transfer by operation of law" is significant in connection with Section 702 (Transfer of Transferable Interest). That section severely restricts a transferee's rights (absent the consent of the partners), and this definition makes those restrictions applicable, for example, to transfers ordered by a family court as part of a divorce proceeding and transfers resulting from the death of a partner. The restrictions also apply to transfers in the context of a partner's bankruptcy, except to the extent that bankruptcy law supersedes this act.

"Transferable interest" [(25)] . . .

This act defines "[t]ransferable interest" as an interest "initially owned by a person in the person's capacity as a partner," because this act does not contemplate a limited partnership directly creating interests that comprise only economic rights. *See* Sections 301 and 401 (addressing how a person becomes a limited and general partner) and 702 (addressing how a person becomes a transferee).

"Transferee" [(26)]—This definition should be read in light of Sections 602(a)(3) and 605(a)(4), which subject to limited exceptions provide that "any transferable interest owned by [a general or limited partner] in the person's capacity as a [general or limited] partner immediately before dissociation is owned by the person solely as a transferee."

§ 103. KNOWLEDGE; NOTICE.

(a)   A person knows a fact if the person:

    (1)   has actual knowledge of it; or

    (2)   is deemed to know it under law other than this [act].

(b)   A person has notice of a fact if the person:

    (1)   has reason to know the fact from all the facts known to the person at the time in question; or

    (2)   is deemed to have notice of the fact under subsection (c) or (d).

(c)   A certificate of limited partnership on file in the office of the [Secretary of State] is notice that the partnership is a limited partnership and the persons designated in the certificate as general partners are general partners. Except as otherwise provided in subsection (d), the certificate is not notice of any other fact.

(d)   A person not a partner is deemed to have notice of:

    (1)   a person's dissociation as a general partner 90 days after an amendment to the certificate of limited partnership which states that the other person has dissociated becomes effective or 90 days after a statement of dissociation pertaining to the other person becomes effective, whichever occurs first;

    (2)   a limited partnership's:

        (A)   dissolution 90 days after an amendment to the certificate of limited partnership stating that the limited partnership is dissolved becomes effective;

        (B)   termination 90 days after a statement of termination under Section 802(b)(2)(F) becomes effective; and

        (C)   participation in a merger, interest exchange, conversion, or domestication, 90 days after articles of merger, interest exchange, conversion, or domestication under [Article] 11 become effective.

(e)   Subject to Section 210(f), a person notifies another person of a fact by taking steps reasonably required to inform the other person in ordinary course, whether or not those steps cause the other person to know the fact.

(f)   A general partner's knowledge or notice of a fact relating to the limited partnership is effective immediately as knowledge of or notice to the partnership, except in the case of a fraud on the partnership committed by or with the consent of the general partner. A limited partner's knowledge or notice of a fact relating to the partnership is not effective as knowledge of or notice to the partnership.

Comment

Three aspects of this section warrant particular note. First, this section is substantially slimmer than the corresponding provisions of previous uniform acts pertaining to business organizations. . . .

Second, the section contains no generally applicable provisions determining when an organization is charged with knowledge or notice, because those imputation rules: (i) comprise core topics within the law of agency; (ii) are very complicated; (iii) should not have any different content under this act than in other circumstances; and (iv) are the subject of considerable attention in the RESTATEMENT (THIRD) OF AGENCY (2006).

Third, this act does not define "notice" to include "knowledge." Although conceptualizing the latter as giving the former makes logical sense and has a long pedigree, that conceptualization is counter-intuitive for the uninitiated. In ordinary usage, notice has a meaning separate from knowledge. This act follows ordinary usage and therefore contains some references to "knowledge or notice." . . .

§ 104. GOVERNING LAW.

The law of this state governs:

(1)　the internal affairs of a limited partnership; and

(2)　the liability of a partner as partner for a debt, obligation, or other liability of a limited partnership.

§ 105. PARTNERSHIP AGREEMENT; SCOPE, FUNCTION, AND LIMITATIONS.

(a)　Except as otherwise provided in subsections (c) and (d), the partnership agreement governs:

(1)　relations among the partners as partners and between the partners and the limited partnership;

(2)　the activities and affairs of the partnership and the conduct of those activities and affairs; and

(3)　the means and conditions for amending the partnership agreement.

(b)　To the extent the partnership agreement does not provide for a matter described in subsection (a), this [act] governs the matter.

(c)　A partnership agreement may not:

(1)　vary the law applicable under Section 104;

(2)　vary a limited partnership's capacity under Section 111 to sue and be sued in its own name;

(3)　vary any requirement, procedure, or other provision of this [act] pertaining to:

(A)　registered agents; or

(B)　the [Secretary of State], including provisions pertaining to records authorized or required to be delivered to the [Secretary of State] for filing under this [act];

(4)　vary the provisions of Section 204;

(5)　vary the right of a general partner under Section 406(b)(2) to vote on or consent to an amendment to the certificate of limited partnership which deletes a statement that the limited partnership is a limited liability limited partnership;

(6)　alter or eliminate the duty of loyalty or the duty of care except as otherwise provided in subsection (d);

(7)　eliminate the contractual obligation of good faith and fair dealing under Sections 305(a) and 409(d), but the partnership agreement may prescribe the standards, if not manifestly unreasonable, by which the performance of the obligation is to be measured;

(8)　relieve or exonerate a person from liability for conduct involving bad faith, willful or intentional misconduct, or knowing violation of law;

(9)　vary the information required under Section 108 or unreasonably restrict the duties and rights under Section 304 or 407, but the partnership agreement may impose reasonable restrictions on the availability and use of information obtained under those sections and may define appropriate remedies, including liquidated damages, for a breach of any reasonable restriction on use;

(10)　vary the grounds for expulsion specified in Section 603(5)(B);

(11) vary the power of a person to dissociate as a general partner under Section 604(a), except to require that the notice under Section 603(1) be in a record;

(12) vary the causes of dissolution specified in Section 801(a)(6);

(13) vary the requirement to wind up the partnership's activities and affairs as specified in Section 802(a), (b)(1), and (d);

(14) unreasonably restrict the right of a partner to maintain an action under [Article] 9;

(15) vary the provisions of Section 905, but the partnership agreement may provide that the partnership may not have a special litigation committee;

(16) vary the right of a partner to approve a merger, interest exchange, conversion, or domestication under Section 1123(a)(2), 1133(a)(2), 1143(a)(2), or 1153(a)(2);

(17) vary the required contents of a plan of merger under Section 1122(a), plan of interest exchange under Section 1132(a), plan of conversion under Section 1142(a), or plan of domestication under Section 1152(a); or

(18) except as otherwise provided in Sections 106 and 107(b), restrict the rights under this [act] of a person other than a partner.

(d) Subject to subsection (c)(8), without limiting other terms that may be included in a partnership agreement, the following rules apply:

(1) The partnership agreement may:

(A) specify the method by which a specific act or transaction that would otherwise violate the duty of loyalty may be authorized or ratified by one or more disinterested and independent persons after full disclosure of all material facts; and

(B) alter the prohibition in Section 504(a)(2) so that the prohibition requires only that the partnership's total assets not be less than the sum of its total liabilities.

(2) If not manifestly unreasonable, the partnership agreement may:

(A) alter or eliminate the aspects of the duty of loyalty stated in Section 409(b);

(B) identify specific types or categories of activities that do not violate the duty of loyalty;

(C) alter the duty of care, but may not authorize conduct involving bad faith, willful or intentional misconduct, or knowing violation of law; and

(D) alter or eliminate any other fiduciary duty.

(e) The court shall decide as a matter of law whether a term of a partnership agreement is manifestly unreasonable under subsection (c)(7) or (d)(2). The court:

(1) shall make its determination as of the time the challenged term became part of the partnership agreement and by considering only circumstances existing at that time; and

(2) may invalidate the term only if, in light of the purposes, activities, and affairs of the limited partnership, it is readily apparent that:

(A) the objective of the term is unreasonable; or

(B) the term is an unreasonable means to achieve its objective.

Comment

The Harmonization Project rewrote this section to conform, for the most part, to the corresponding section of ULLCA (2006) (Last Amended).

Principal Provisions of the Act Concerning the Partnership Agreement

The partnership agreement is pivotal to a limited partnership, and Sections 105 through 107 are pivotal to this act. They must be read together, along with Section 102(14) (defining the partnership agreement).

This Section performs five essential functions. Subsection (a) establishes the primacy of the partnership agreement in establishing relations *inter se* the limited partnership and its partners. Subsection (b) recognizes this act as comprising mostly default rules—*i.e.*, gap fillers for issues as to which the partnership agreement provides no rule. Subsection (c) lists the few mandatory provisions of the act. Subsection (d) lists some provisions frequently found in partnership agreements, authorizing some provisions unconditionally and other provisions so long as "not manifestly unreasonable." Subsection (e) delineates in detail both the meaning of "not manifestly unreasonable" and the information relevant to a determining a claim that a provision of a partnership agreement is manifestly unreasonable.

Section 106 details the effect of a partnership agreement on the limited partnership and on persons becoming partners. Section 107 concerns the effect of a partnership agreement on third parties. . . .

The Partnership Agreement and the Fiduciary and Other Duties of the General Partner

One of the most complex questions in the law of unincorporated business organizations is the extent to which an agreement among the organization's owners can affect the fiduciary and other duties of those who manage the organization—in the case of a limited partnership, the general partner (or partners). As explained in detail in the comment to Subsection (d)(3), this act rejects the notion that a contract can completely transform an inherently fiduciary relationship into a merely arm's length association. Within that limitation, however, this section provides substantial power to the partnership agreement to reshape, limit, and eliminate fiduciary and other managerial duties. . . .

Subsection (a) recognizes that the partnership agreement is the map to the parties' deal and that any claim by a partner of managerial misconduct must be assessed first under the relevant terms of the partnership agreement. Subsection (d) specifically validates arrangements commonly used to reshape managerial duties and limit the consequences of breaching those duties. Subsection (c) contains relevant limitations, but those limitations: (i) must be read together with Subsection (d); and (ii) do not preclude the partnership agreement fundamentally redesigning the duties applicable to the general partners. . . .

Subsection (a)(1)—This paragraph encompasses all the rights and duties of each partner, including rights and duties pertaining to transactions under Article 11.

Subsection (a)(3)—Under this provision, the partnership agreement can control both the quantum of consent required (*e.g.*, majority of partners) and the means by which the consent is manifested (*e.g.*, prohibiting modifications except when consented to in writing). *See also* Section 107(a), cmt.

If the partnership agreement does not address the issue, this act provides the rule. Section 407(b)(4)(C) (requiring the affirmative vote or consent of all the partners) and 407(c)(3)(C) (same). Under Section 111 (supplemental principles of law), the parol evidence rule will apply to a written partnership agreement when appropriate under contract law.

Subsection (b)—To the extent the partnership agreement does not determine an *inter se* matter, this act determines the matter. The partnership agreement may vary any provision of this act pertaining to *inter se* matters, except as provided in Subsections (c) and (d). . . .

Subsection (c)(7)—Sections 305(a) and 409(d) refer to the "contractual obligation of good faith and fair dealing," which . . .T]he partnership agreement cannot eliminate . . . in whole (*i.e.*, generally) nor in part (*i.e.*, as applicable to specified situations).

However, a partnership agreement may "prescribe the standards . . . by which the performance of the obligation is to be measured."

EXAMPLE: The partnership agreement of a limited partnership gives the general partner the discretion to cause the limited partnership to enter into contracts with affiliates of the general partner (so-called "Conflict Transactions"). The agreement further provides: "When causing the Limited Partnership to enter into a Conflict Transaction, the general partner complies with Section 409(d) of [this act] if a disinterested person, knowledgeable in the subject matter, states in writing that the terms and conditions of the Transaction are equivalent to the terms and conditions that would be agreed to by persons at arm's length in comparable circumstances." This provision "prescribe[s] the standards by which the performance of the [Section 409(d)] obligation is to be measured." . . .

Subsection (c)(12)—The partnership agreement may not change the stated grounds for judicial dissolution . . .

The approach of this paragraph differs from the law of Delaware. *See Huatuco v. Satellite Healthcare*, CV 8465-VCG, 2013 WL 6460898 at *1 and n.2 (Del. Ch. Dec. 9, 2013) (stating that "the right to judicial dissolution is a default right which the parties may eschew by contract" but reserving the question of "[w]hether the parties may, by contract, divest this Court of its authority to order a dissolution in all circumstances, even where it appears manifest that equity so requires—leaving, for instance, irreconcilable members locked away together forever like some alternative entity version of Sartre's *Huis Clos*"). . . .

Section (d)(2)—This act rejects the ultra-contractarian notion that fiduciary duty within a business organization is merely a set of default rules and seeks instead to balance the virtues of "freedom of contract" against the dangers that inescapably exist when some have power over the interests of others.

Nonetheless, a properly drafted partnership agreement may substantially alter and even eliminate fiduciary duties. Two important limitations exist. First, arrangements subject to this subsection may not be "manifestly unreasonable." *See* Subsection (e) (delineating this standard).

Second, the partnership agreement may not transform the relationship *inter se* the general partners to the limited partnership and limited partners into an entirely arm's length arrangement. For example, displacement of fiduciary duties is effective only to the extent that the displacement is stated clearly and with particularity. This rule is fundamental in the jurisprudence of fiduciary duty. *See, e.g., Paige Capital Mgmt., LLC v. Lerner Master Fund, LLC*, Civ. A. No. 5502-CS, 2011 WL 3505355 at *31 (Del. Ch. Aug. 8 2011) (stating that, even under a statute that "permits the waiver of fiduciary duties . . . such waivers must be set forth clearly"); *Kelly v. Blum*, Civ. A. No. 4516-VCP, 2010 WL 629850, at *10 n.70 (Del. Ch. Feb. 24, 2010) ("Having been granted great contractual freedom by the LLC Act, drafters of or parties to an LLC agreement should be expected to provide . . . clear and unambiguous provisions when they desire to expand, restrict or eliminate the operation of traditional fiduciary duties"). It would therefore be manifestly unreasonable for a partnership agreement to negate this rule. . . .

Subsection (d)(2)(A)—Subject to the "not manifestly unreasonable" standard, this paragraph empowers the partnership agreement to eliminate *all* aspects of the duty of loyalty listed in Section 409(b). The obligation of good faith and fair dealing, Section 409(d), would remain. . . .

§ 106. PARTNERSHIP AGREEMENT; EFFECT ON LIMITED PARTNERSHIP AND PERSON BECOMING PARTNER; PREFORMATION AGREEMENT.

(a)   A limited partnership is bound by and may enforce the partnership agreement, whether or not the partnership has itself manifested assent to the agreement.

(b)   A person that becomes a partner is deemed to assent to the partnership agreement.

(c)   Two or more persons intending to become the initial partners of a limited partnership may make an agreement providing that upon the formation of the partnership the agreement will become the partnership agreement.

Comment

Subsection (a)—This subsection resolves twin questions that have troubled some courts—namely, whether an unincorporated entity that has not signed its foundational agreement nonetheless is bound by and may enforce the agreement. . . .

This subsection answers the twin questions, categorically and in the affirmative. . . .

§ 107. PARTNERSHIP AGREEMENT; EFFECT ON THIRD PARTIES AND RELATIONSHIP TO RECORDS EFFECTIVE ON BEHALF OF LIMITED PARTNERSHIP.

(a)   A partnership agreement may specify that its amendment requires the approval of a person that is not a party to the agreement or the satisfaction of a condition. An amendment is ineffective if its adoption does not include the required approval or satisfy the specified condition.

(b)   The obligations of a limited partnership and its partners to a person in the person's capacity as a transferee or person dissociated as a partner are governed by the partnership agreement. Subject only to a court order issued under Section 703(b)(2) to effectuate a charging order, an amendment to the partnership agreement made after a person becomes a transferee or is dissociated as a partner:

(1)   is effective with regard to any debt, obligation, or other liability of the partnership or its partners to the person in the person's capacity as a transferee or person dissociated as a partner; and

(2)   is not effective to the extent the amendment imposes a new debt, obligation, or other liability on the transferee or person dissociated as a partner.

(c)   If a record delivered by a limited partnership to the [Secretary of State] for filing becomes effective and contains a provision that would be ineffective under Section 105(c) or (d)(2) if contained in the partnership agreement, the provision is ineffective in the record.

(d)   Subject to subsection (c), if a record delivered by a limited partnership to the [Secretary of State] for filing becomes effective and conflicts with a provision of the partnership agreement:

(1)   the agreement prevails as to partners, persons dissociated as partners, and transferees; and

(2)   the record prevails as to other persons to the extent they reasonably rely on the record.

§ 108.   REQUIRED INFORMATION.

A limited partnership shall maintain at its principal office the following information:

(1)   a current list showing the full name and last known street and mailing address of each partner, separately identifying the general partners, in alphabetical order, and the limited partners, in alphabetical order;

(2)   a copy of the initial certificate of limited partnership and all amendments to and restatements of the certificate, together with signed copies of any powers of attorney under which any certificate, amendment, or restatement has been signed;

(3)   a copy of any filed articles of merger, interest exchange, conversion, or domestication;

(4)   a copy of the partnership's federal, state, and local income tax returns and reports, if any, for the three most recent years;

(5)   a copy of any partnership agreement made in a record and any amendment made in a record to any partnership agreement;

(6)   a copy of any financial statement of the partnership for the three most recent years;

(7)   a copy of the three most recent [annual] [biennial] reports delivered by the partnership to the [Secretary of State] pursuant to Section 212;

(8)   a copy of any record made by the partnership during the past three years of any consent given by or vote taken of any partner pursuant to this [act] or the partnership agreement; and

(9)   unless contained in a partnership agreement made in a record, a record stating:

(A)   a description and statement of the agreed value of contributions other than money made and agreed to be made by each partner;

(B)   the times at which, or events on the happening of which, any additional contributions agreed to be made by each partner are to be made;

(C)   for any person that is both a general partner and a limited partner, a specification of what transferable interest the person owns in each capacity; and

(D)   any events upon the happening of which the partnership is to be dissolved and its activities and affairs wound up.

§ 109.   DUAL CAPACITY.

A person may be both a general partner and a limited partner. A person that is both a general and limited partner has the rights, powers, duties, and obligations provided by this [act] and the partnership agreement in each of those capacities. When the person acts as a general partner, the person is subject to the obligations, duties, and restrictions under this [act] and the partnership agreement for general partners.

When the person acts as a limited partner, the person is subject to the obligations, duties, and restrictions under this [act] and the partnership agreement for limited partners.

§ 110. NATURE, PURPOSE, AND DURATION OF LIMITED PARTNERSHIP.

(a)   A limited partnership is an entity distinct from its partners. A limited partnership is the same entity regardless of whether its certificate states that the limited partnership is a limited liability limited partnership.

(b)   A limited partnership may have any lawful purpose, regardless of whether for profit.

(c)   A limited partnership has perpetual duration.

§ 111. POWERS.

A limited partnership has the capacity to sue and be sued in the name of the partnership and the power to do all things necessary or convenient to carry on the partnership's activities and affairs.

Comment

Continuing the approach initiated in ULPA (2001) § 105, this act omits as unnecessary any detailed list of specific powers. . . .

§ 113. SUPPLEMENTAL PRINCIPLES OF LAW.

Unless displaced by particular provisions of this [act], the principles of law and equity supplement this [act].

§ 114. PERMITTED NAMES.

(a)   The name of a limited partnership may contain the name of any partner.

(b)   The name of a limited partnership that is not a limited liability limited partnership must contain the phrase "limited partnership" or the abbreviation "LP" or "L.P." and may not contain the phrase "limited liability limited partnership" or the abbreviation "LLLP" or "L.L.L.P.".

(c)   The name of a limited liability limited partnership must contain the phrase "limited liability limited partnership" or the abbreviation "LLLP" or "L.L.L.P." and must not contain the abbreviation "LP" or "L.P.".

(d)   Except as otherwise provided in subsection (g), the name of a limited partnership, and the name under which a foreign limited partnership may register to do business in this state, must be distinguishable on the records of the [Secretary of State] from any:

(1)   name of an existing person whose formation required the filing of a record by the [Secretary of State] and which is not at the time administratively dissolved;

(2)   name of a limited liability partnership whose statement of qualification is in effect;

(3)   name under which a person is registered to do business in this state by the filing of a record by the [Secretary of State];

(4)   name reserved under Section 115 or other law of this state providing for the reservation of a name by the filing of a record by the [Secretary of State];

(5)   name registered under Section 116 or other law of this state providing for the registration of a name by the filing of a record by the [Secretary of State]; and

(6)   name registered under [this state's assumed or fictitious name statute].

(e)   If a person consents in a record to the use of its name and submits an undertaking in a form satisfactory to the [Secretary of State] to change its name to a name that is distinguishable on the records of the [Secretary of State] from any name in any category of names in subsection (d), the name of the consenting person may be used by the person to which the consent was given.

(f)   Except as otherwise provided in subsection (g), in determining whether a name is the same as or not distinguishable on the records of the [Secretary of State] from the name of another person, words, phrases, or abbreviations indicating the type of person, such as "corporation", "corp.", "incorporated", "Inc.", "professional corporation", "PC", "P.C.", "professional association", "PA", "P.A.", "Limited", "Ltd.", "limited partnership", "LP", "L.P.", "limited liability partnership", "LLP", "L.L.P.", "registered limited liability partnership", "RLLP", "R.L.L.P.", "limited liability limited partnership", "LLLP", "L.L.L.P.", "registered limited liability limited partnership", "RLLLP", "R.L.L.L.P.", "limited liability company", "LLC", "L.L.C.", "limited cooperative association", "limited cooperative", "LCA", or "L.C.A." may not be taken into account.

(g)   A person may consent in a record to the use of a name that is not distinguishable on the records of the [Secretary of State] from its name except for the addition of a word, phrase, or abbreviation indicating the type of person as provided in subsection (f). In such a case, the person need not change its name pursuant to subsection (e).

(h)   The name of a limited partnership or foreign limited partnership may not contain the words [insert prohibited words or words that may be used only with approval by an appropriate state agency].

(i)   A limited partnership or foreign limited partnership may use a name that is not distinguishable from a name described in subsection (d)(1) through (6) if the partnership delivers to the [Secretary of State] a certified copy of a final judgment of a court of competent jurisdiction establishing the right of the partnership to use the name in this state.

§ 117.   REGISTERED AGENT.

(a)   Each limited partnership and each registered foreign limited partnership shall designate and maintain a registered agent in this state. The designation of a registered agent is an affirmation of fact by the limited partnership or registered foreign limited partnership that the agent has consented to serve.

(b)   A registered agent for a limited partnership or registered foreign limited partnership must have a place of business in this state.

(c)   The only duties under this [act] of a registered agent that has complied with this [act] are:

(1)   to forward to the limited partnership or registered foreign limited partnership at the address most recently supplied to the agent by the partnership or foreign partnership any process, notice, or demand pertaining to the partnership or foreign partnership which is served on or received by the agent;

(2)   if the registered agent resigns, to provide the notice required by Section 119(c) to the partnership or foreign partnership at the address most recently supplied to the agent by the partnership or foreign partnership; and

(3)   to keep current the information with respect to the agent in the certificate of limited partnership.

§ 118.   CHANGE OF REGISTERED AGENT OR ADDRESS FOR REGISTERED AGENT BY LIMITED PARTNERSHIP.

(a)   A limited partnership or registered foreign limited partnership may change its registered agent or the address of its registered agent by delivering to the [Secretary of State] for filing a statement of change that states:

(1)   the name of the partnership or foreign partnership; and

(2)   the information that is to be in effect as a result of the filing of the statement of change.

(b)   The general or limited partners of a limited partnership need not approve the [delivery to the Secretary of State] for filing of:

(1)   a statement of change under this section; or

(2)   a similar filing changing the registered agent or registered office, if any, of the partnership in any other jurisdiction.

(c)   A statement of change under this section designating a new registered agent is an affirmation of fact by the limited partnership or registered foreign limited partnership that the agent has consented to serve.

(d)   As an alternative to using the procedure in this section, a limited partnership may amend its certificate of limited partnership.

§ 123.   RESERVATION OF POWER TO AMEND OR REPEAL.

The [legislature of this state] has power to amend or repeal all or part of this [act] at any time, and all limited partnerships and foreign limited partnerships subject to this [act] are governed by the amendment or repeal.

[ARTICLE] 2

FORMATION; CERTIFICATE OF LIMITED PARTNERSHIP AND OTHER FILINGS

§ 201.   FORMATION OF LIMITED PARTNERSHIP; CERTIFICATE OF LIMITED PARTNERSHIP.

(a)   To form a limited partnership, a person must deliver a certificate of limited partnership to the [Secretary of State] for filing.

(b)   A certificate of limited partnership must state:

(1)   the name of the limited partnership, which must comply with Section 114;

(2)   the street and mailing addresses of the partnership's principal office;

(3)   the name and street and mailing addresses in this state of the partnership's registered agent;

(4)   the name and street and mailing addresses of each general partner; and

(5)   whether the limited partnership is a limited liability limited partnership.

(c)   A certificate of limited partnership may contain statements as to matters other than those required by subsection (b), but may not vary or otherwise affect the provisions specified in Section 105(c) and (d) in a manner inconsistent with that section.

(d)   A limited partnership is formed when:

(1)   the certificate of limited partnership becomes effective;

(2)   at least two persons have become partners;

(3)   at least one person has become a general partner; and

(4)   at least one person has become a limited partner.

Comment

For a limited partnership to be formed (*i.e.*, to come into existence), four conditions must be met: (i) a certificate of limited partnership must become effective; (ii) at least two persons must become a partners; (iii) at least one person must become a general partner; and (iv) at least one person must become a limited partner. . . .

Section (b)(5)—This act permits a limited partnership to be a limited liability limited partnership ("LLLP"), and this provision requires the certificate of limited partnership to state whether the limited partnership is an LLLP. The requirement is intended to force the organizers of a limited partnership to decide whether the limited partnership is to be an LLLP.

Subject to Sections 406(b)(2) and 105(c)(5), a limited partnership may amend its certificate of limited partnership to add or delete a statement that the limited partnership is a limited liability limited partnership. An amendment deleting such a statement must be accompanied by an amendment stating that the limited partnership is *not* a limited liability limited partnership. Section 201(b)(5) does not permit a certificate of limited partnership to be silent on this point, except for pre-existing partnerships that become subject to this act under Section 112. *See* Section 112(c)(2). . . .

§ 202. AMENDMENT OR RESTATEMENT OF CERTIFICATE OF LIMITED PARTNERSHIP.

(a) A certificate of limited partnership may be amended or restated at any time.

(b) To amend its certificate of limited partnership, a limited partnership must deliver to the [Secretary of State] for filing an amendment stating:

    (1) the name of the partnership;

    (2) the date of filing of its initial certificate; and

    (3) the text of the amendment.

(c) To restate its certificate of limited partnership, a limited partnership must deliver to the [Secretary of State] for filing a restatement, designated as such in its heading.

(d) A limited partnership shall promptly deliver to the [Secretary of State] for filing an amendment to a certificate of limited partnership to reflect:

    (1) the admission of a new general partner;

    (2) the dissociation of a person as a general partner; or

    (3) the appointment of a person to wind up the limited partnership's activities and affairs under Section 802(c) or (d).

(e) If a general partner knows that any information in a filed certificate of limited partnership was inaccurate when the certificate was filed or has become inaccurate due to changed circumstances, the general partner shall promptly:

    (1) cause the certificate to be amended; or

    (2) if appropriate, deliver to the [Secretary of State] for filing a statement of change under Section 118 or a statement of correction under Section 209.

§ 212. [ANNUAL] [BIENNIAL] REPORT FOR [SECRETARY OF STATE].

(a) A limited partnership or registered foreign limited partnership shall deliver to the [Secretary of State] for filing [an annual] [a biennial] report that states:

    (1) the name of the partnership or foreign partnership;

    (2) the name and street and mailing addresses of its registered agent in this state;

    (3) the street and mailing addresses of its principal office;

    (4) the name of at least one general partner; and

    (5) in the case of a foreign partnership, its jurisdiction of formation and any alternate name adopted under Section 1006(a).

(b) Information in the [annual] [biennial] report must be current as of the date the report is signed by the limited partnership or registered foreign limited partnership.

(c) The first [annual] [biennial] report must be delivered to the [Secretary of State] for filing after [January 1] and before [April 1] of the year following the calendar year in which the limited partnership's certificate of limited partnership became effective or the registered foreign limited partnership registered to do business in this state. Subsequent [annual] [biennial] reports must be delivered to the [Secretary of State] for filing after [January 1] and before [April 1] of each [second] calendar year thereafter.

(d)   If [an annual] [a biennial] report does not contain the information required by this section, the [Secretary of State] promptly shall notify the reporting limited partnership or registered foreign limited partnership in a record and return the report for correction.

(e)   If [an annual] [a biennial] report contains the name or address of a registered agent which differs from the information shown in the records of the [Secretary of State] immediately before the report becomes effective, the differing information is considered a statement of change under Section 118.

[ARTICLE] 3

LIMITED PARTNERS

§ 301.   BECOMING LIMITED PARTNER.

(a)   Upon formation of a limited partnership, a person becomes a limited partner as agreed among the persons that are to be the initial partners.

(b)   After formation, a person becomes a limited partner:

(1)   as provided in the partnership agreement;

(2)   as the result of a transaction effective under [Article] 11;

(3)   with the affirmative vote or consent of all the partners; or

(4)   as provided in Section 801(a)(4) or (a)(5).

(c)   A person may become a limited partner without:

(1)   acquiring a transferable interest; or

(2)   making or being obligated to make a contribution to the limited partnership.

§ 302.   NO AGENCY POWER OF LIMITED PARTNER AS LIMITED PARTNER.

(a)   A limited partner is not an agent of a limited partnership solely by reason of being a limited partner.

(b)   A person's status as a limited partner does not prevent or restrict law other than this [act] from imposing liability on a limited partnership because of the person's conduct.

Comment

Subsection (a)—In this respect a limited partner is analogous to a shareholder in a corporation; in each case, status as owner provides neither the right to manage nor a reasonable appearance of that right. The phrase "solely by reason of being a limited partner" conforms to Subsection (b).

Subsection (b)—The phrase "as a limited partner" indicates that: (i) this section does not disable a general partner that also owns a limited partner interest; (ii) the partnership agreement may as a matter of contract allocate managerial rights to one or more limited partners; and (iii) a separate agreement can empower and entitle a person that is a limited partner to act for the limited partnership in another capacity, *e.g.*, as an agent. *See* Section 305(a), cmt.

The fact that a limited partner *qua* limited partner has no power to bind the limited partnership means that, subject to Section 109 (Dual Capacity), information possessed by a limited partner is not attributed to the limited partnership. *See* Section 103(f).

This act specifies various circumstances in which limited partners have consent rights, including:

- admission of a limited partner, Section 301(b)(3)

- admission of a general partner, Section 401(b)(3)

- amendment of the partnership agreement, Section 406(b)(1)

- the decision to amend the certificate of limited partnership so as to obtain or relinquish LLLP status, Section 406(b)(2)

- the disposition of all or substantially all of the limited partnership's property, outside the usual and regular course of its activities and affairs, Section 406(b)(3)

- the compromise of a partner's obligation to make a contribution or return an improper distribution, Section 502(c)

- expulsion of a limited partner by consent of the other partners, Section 601(b)(4)

- expulsion of a general partner by consent of the other partners, Section 603(4)

- causing dissolution by consent, Section 801(a)(2)

- causing dissolution by consent following the dissociation of a general partner, when at least one general partner remains, Section 801(a)(3)(A)

- avoiding dissolution and appointing a successor general partner, following the dissociation of the sole general partner, Section 801(a)(3)(B)(i)

- appointing a person to wind up the limited partnership when there is no general partner, Section 802(c)

- rescinding dissolution, Section 803(b)(1)

- approving, amending or abandoning a plan of:

   o   merger, Sections 1123–24;

   o   interest exchange, Sections 1133–34;

   o   conversion, Sections 1143–44; and

   o   domestication, Sections 1153–54.

§ 303.   NO LIABILITY AS LIMITED PARTNER FOR LIMITED PARTNERSHIP OBLIGATIONS.

(a)   A debt, obligation, or other liability of a limited partnership is not the debt, obligation, or other liability of a limited partner. A limited partner is not personally liable, directly or indirectly, by way of contribution or otherwise, for a debt, obligation, or other liability of the partnership solely by reason of being or acting as a limited partner, even if the limited partner participates in the management and control of the limited partnership. This subsection applies regardless of the dissolution of the partnership.

(b)   The failure of a limited partnership to observe formalities relating to the exercise of its powers or management of its activities and affairs is not a ground for imposing liability on a limited partner for a debt, obligation, or other liability of the partnership.

Comment

Elimination of the "Control Rule"

ULPA (2001) eliminated the so-called "control rule," which had impaired the liability protection accorded limited partners and had become an anachronism in a world with LLPs, LLCs and, most importantly, LLLPs.

The "control rule" first appeared in a uniform act in 1916, although the concept is much older. Section 7 of the original Uniform Limited Partnership Act provided that "a limited partner shall not become liable as a general partner [*i.e.*, for the obligations of the limited partnership] unless . . . he takes part in the control of the business."

ULPA (1976) "carrie[d] over the basic test from former Section 7," but recognized "the difficulty of determining when the control line has been overstepped." ULPA (1976) § 303, cmt. Accordingly, ULPA (1976) tried to buttress the limited partner's shield by: (i) providing a safe harbor for a lengthy list of activities deemed not to constitute participating in control, Section 303(b); and (ii) limiting a limited partner's "control rule" liability "only to persons who transact business with the limited partnership with actual knowledge of [the limited partner's] participation in control," Section 303(a). However, these protections were complicated by a countervailing rule which made a limited partner generally liable for the limited partnership's obligations "if the limited partner's participation in the control of the business is . . . substantially the same as the exercise of the powers of a general partner." Section 303(a).

The 1985 amendments to ULPA (1976) further buttressed the limited partner's shield, removing the "substantially the same" rule, expanding the list of safe harbor activities and limiting "control rule" liability "only to persons who transact business with the limited partnership reasonably believing, based upon the limited partner's conduct, that the limited partner is a general partner." ULPA (1976/1985) § 303(a).

ULPA (2001) took the logical next step, bringing limited partners into parity with corporate shareholders, LLC members, and LLP partners.

Subsection (a)—This subsection provides a corporate-like liability shield for limited partners, protecting them against the debts, obligations and other liabilities of the limited partnership—*i.e.*, against vicarious liability for the obligations of the entity. Because a dissolved limited partnership is nonetheless an entity formed under this act, dissolution has no effect on the liability shield. . . .

§ 304. RIGHTS TO INFORMATION OF LIMITED PARTNER AND PERSON DISSOCIATED AS LIMITED PARTNER.

(a)   On 10 days' demand, made in a record received by the limited partnership, a limited partner may inspect and copy required information during regular business hours in the limited partnership's principal office. The limited partner need not have any particular purpose for seeking the information.

(b)   During regular business hours and at a reasonable location specified by the limited partnership, a limited partner may inspect and copy information regarding the activities, affairs, financial condition, and other circumstances of the limited partnership as is just and reasonable if:

(1)   the limited partner seeks the information for a purpose reasonably related to the partner's interest as a limited partner;

(2)   the limited partner makes a demand in a record received by the limited partnership, describing with reasonable particularity the information sought and the purpose for seeking the information; and

(3)   the information sought is directly connected to the limited partner's purpose.

(c)   Not later than 10 days after receiving a demand pursuant to subsection (b), the limited partnership shall inform in a record the limited partner that made the demand of:

(1)   what information the partnership will provide in response to the demand and when and where the partnership will provide the information; and

(2)   the partnership's reasons for declining, if the partnership declines to provide any demanded information.

(d)   Whenever this [act] or a partnership agreement provides for a limited partner to vote on or give or withhold consent to a matter, before the vote is cast or consent is given or withheld, the limited partnership shall, without demand, provide the limited partner with all information that is known to the partnership and is material to the limited partner's decision.

(e)   Subject to subsection (j), on 10 days' demand made in a record received by a limited partnership, a person dissociated as a limited partner may have access to information to which the person was entitled while a limited partner if:

(1)   the information pertains to the period during which the person was a limited partner;

(2)   the person seeks the information in good faith; and

(3)   the person satisfies the requirements imposed on a limited partner by subsection (b).

(f)   A limited partnership shall respond to a demand made pursuant to subsection (e) in the manner provided in subsection (c).

(g)   A limited partnership may charge a person that makes a demand under this section reasonable costs of copying, limited to the costs of labor and material.

(h)   A limited partner or person dissociated as a limited partner may exercise the rights under this section through an agent or, in the case of an individual under legal disability, a legal representative. Any restriction or condition imposed by the partnership agreement or under subsection (j) applies both to the agent or legal representative and to the limited partner or person dissociated as a limited partner.

(i)   Subject to Section 704, the rights under this section do not extend to a person as transferee.

(j)   In addition to any restriction or condition stated in its partnership agreement, a limited partnership, as a matter within the ordinary course of its activities and affairs, may impose reasonable restrictions and conditions on access to and use of information to be furnished under this section, including designating information confidential and imposing nondisclosure and safeguarding obligations on the recipient. In a dispute concerning the reasonableness of a restriction under this subsection, the partnership has the burden of proving reasonableness.

Comment

This section balances two countervailing concerns relating to information: the need of limited partners and former limited partners for access versus the limited partnership's need to protect confidential business data and other intellectual property. The balance must be understood in the context of fiduciary duties. The general partners are obliged through their duties of care and loyalty to protect information whose confidentiality is important to the limited partnership or otherwise inappropriate for dissemination. *See* Section 409 (general standards of general partner conduct). A limited partner, in contrast, "does not have any [fiduciary] duty to the limited partnership or to any other partner solely by reason of acting as a limited partner." Section 305(b).

Like predecessor law, this act divides limited partner access rights into two categories: required information and other information. However, this act builds on predecessor law by:

- expanding slightly the category of required information and stating explicitly that a limited partner may have access to that information without having to show cause;

- specifying a procedure for limited partners to follow when demanding access to other information;

- specifying how a limited partnership must respond to such a demand and setting a time limit for the response;

- retaining predecessor law's "just and reasonable" standard for determining a limited partner's right to other information, while recognizing that, to be "just and reasonable," a limited partner's demand for other information must meet minimum standards of relatedness and particularity;

- expressly requiring the limited partnership to volunteer known, material information when seeking or obtaining consent from limited partners;

- codifying (while limiting) the power of the partnership agreement to vary limited partner access rights;

- permitting the limited partnership to establish other reasonable limits on access; and

- providing access rights for former limited partners.

Although the rights and duties stated in this section are extensive, they are not necessarily all-inclusive. This act's statement of fiduciary duties is not exhaustive. *See* Section 409(a), cmt., and some cases characterize owners' information rights as reflecting a fiduciary duty of those with management power. . . . Also, the rights stated in this section are in addition to whatever discovery rights a party has in a civil suit.

In contrast, the rights of transferees are limited to those stated in this section and Subsection 702(c); general partners do not owe fiduciary duties to transferees.

The rights stated in this section are personal to limited partners and transferees, and are enforceable through a direct action. *See* Section 901(b), cmt.

Subsection (a)—The phrase "required information" is a defined term. *See* Sections 102(21) and 108. This subsection's broad right of access is subject not only to reasonable limitations in the partnership agreement, Section 105(c)(9), but also to the power of the limited partnership to impose reasonable limitations on use, Subsection (j). Unless the partnership agreement provides otherwise, general partners have the authority to use that power. *See* Section 406(a).

Subsection (b)—. . . This subsection does not itself impose a requirement of good faith because Section 305(a) contains a generally applicable obligation of good faith and fair dealing for limited partners. *But see* Subsection (e)(2) (establishing a duty of good faith applicable to a former limited partner).

Subsection (d)—The duty stated in this subsection is at the core of the duties owed by a limited partnership and its general partners to the limited partners, and imposes an affirmative duty to volunteer information. The obligation is limited to information which is both material and known by the limited partnership.

"Knowledge" is viewed subjectively—*i.e.*, actual knowledge. Section 103(a)(1). A limited partnership will "know" what its general partners know. Under Section 103(f), "[a] general partner's knowledge . . . of a fact relating to the limited partnership is effective immediately as knowledge of or notice to the partnership." As to others acting or reasonably appearing to act on behalf of the limited partnership, common law agency rules will apply. RESTATEMENT (THIRD) OF AGENCY § 5.03 (2006) (Imputation of Notice of Fact to Principal).

In contrast, materiality is viewed objectively. Thus, this subsection applies to known, material information, even if the limited partnership does not know that the information is material. . . .

§ 305. LIMITED DUTIES OF LIMITED PARTNERS.

(a)　A limited partner shall discharge any duties to the partnership and the other partners under the partnership agreement and exercise any rights under this [act] or the partnership agreement consistently with the contractual obligation of good faith and fair dealing.

(b)　Except as otherwise provided in subsection (a), a limited partner does not have any duty to the limited partnership or to any other partner solely by reason of acting as a limited partner.

(c)　If a limited partner enters into a transaction with a limited partnership, the limited partner's rights and obligations arising from the transaction are the same as those of a person that is not a partner.

Comment

[handwritten: → no fiduciary duty typically as a limited partner]

Subsection (a)—Fiduciary duty typically attaches to a person whose status or role creates significant power for that person over the interests of another person. Under this act, limited partners have very limited power of any sort in the regular activities of the limited partnership and no power whatsoever justifying the imposition of fiduciary duties either to the limited partnership or fellow partners. . . .

It is possible for a partnership agreement to allocate significant managerial authority and power to a limited partner, but in that case the power exists not as a matter of status or role but rather as a matter of contract. *E.g.*, *DV Realty Advisors LLC v. Policemen's Annuity & Ben. Fund of Chicago*, 75 A.3d 101, 111 (Del. 2013) (pertaining to a limited partnership agreement that allowed the limited partners to remove the general partner). The proper limit on such contract-based power is the contract itself (including the implied obligation of good faith and fair dealing), not fiduciary duty, unless the partnership agreement itself: (i) expressly imposes a fiduciary duty; or (ii) creates a role for a limited partner which, as a matter of other law, gives rise to a fiduciary duty. For example, if the partnership agreement makes a limited partner an agent for the limited partnership as to particular matters, the law of agency will impose fiduciary duties on the limited partner with respect to the limited partner's role as agent.

This subsection refers to the "contractual obligation of good faith and fair dealing" to emphasize that the obligation is not an invitation to re-write agreements among the partners. At first glance, it may seem strange to apply a contractual obligation to statutory duties and rights—*i.e.*, duties and rights "under this [act]." However, for the most part those duties and rights apply to relationships *inter se* the partners and the limited partnership and function only to the extent not displaced by the partnership agreement. Those statutory default rules are thus intended to function like a contract; applying the contractual notion of good faith and fair dealing therefore makes sense. . . .

§ 306. PERSON ERRONEOUSLY BELIEVING SELF TO BE LIMITED PARTNER.

(a)　Except as otherwise provided in subsection (b), a person that makes an investment in a business enterprise and erroneously but in good faith believes that the person has become a limited partner in the enterprise is not liable for the enterprise's obligations by reason of making the investment, receiving distributions from the enterprise, or exercising any rights of or appropriate to a limited partner, if, on ascertaining the mistake, the person:

(1)   causes an appropriate certificate of limited partnership, amendment, or statement of correction to be signed and delivered to the [Secretary of State] for filing; or

(2)   withdraws from future participation as an owner in the enterprise by signing and delivering to the [Secretary of State] for filing a statement of negation under this section.

(b)   A person that makes an investment described in subsection (a) is liable to the same extent as a general partner to any third party that enters into a transaction with the enterprise, believing in good faith that the person is a general partner, before the [Secretary of State] files a statement of negation, certificate of limited partnership, amendment, or statement of correction to show that the person is not a general partner.

(c)   If a person makes a diligent effort in good faith to comply with subsection (a)(1) and is unable to cause the appropriate certificate of limited partnership, amendment, or statement of correction to be signed and delivered to the [Secretary of State] for filing, the person has the right to withdraw from the enterprise pursuant to subsection (a)(2) even if the withdrawal would otherwise breach an agreement with others that are or have agreed to become co-owners of the enterprise.

[ARTICLE] 4
GENERAL PARTNERS

§ 401.   BECOMING GENERAL PARTNER.

[handwritten: → default rule: general partner bind the limited partnership if done in the ordinary course of biz]

(a)   Upon formation of a limited partnership, a person becomes a general partner as agreed among the persons that are to be the initial partners.

(b)   After formation of a limited partnership, a person becomes a general partner:

(1)   as provided in the partnership agreement;

(2)   as the result of a transaction effective under [Article] 11;

(3)   with the affirmative vote or consent of all the partners; or

(4)   as provided in Section 801(a)(3)(B).

(c)   A person may become a general partner without:

(1)   acquiring a transferable interest; or

(2)   making or being obligated to make a contribution to the partnership.

§ 402.   GENERAL PARTNER AGENT OF LIMITED PARTNERSHIP.

(a)   Each general partner is an agent of the limited partnership for the purposes of its activities and affairs. An act of a general partner, including the signing of a record in the partnership's name, for apparently carrying on in the ordinary course the partnership's activities and affairs or activities and affairs of the kind carried on by the partnership binds the partnership, unless the general partner did not have authority to act for the partnership in the particular matter and the person with which the general partner was dealing knew or had notice that the general partner lacked authority.

(b)   An act of a general partner which is not apparently for carrying on in the ordinary course the limited partnership's activities and affairs or activities and affairs of the kind carried on by the partnership binds the partnership only if the act was actually authorized by all the other partners.

§ 403.   LIMITED PARTNERSHIP LIABLE FOR GENERAL PARTNER'S ACTIONABLE CONDUCT.

(a)   A limited partnership is liable for loss or injury caused to a person, or for a penalty incurred, as a result of a wrongful act or omission, or other actionable conduct, of a general partner acting in the ordinary course of activities and affairs of the partnership or with the actual or apparent authority of the partnership.

(b)   If, in the course of a limited partnership's activities and affairs or while acting with actual or apparent authority of the partnership, a general partner receives or causes the partnership to receive money or property of a person not a partner, and the money or property is misapplied by a general partner, the partnership is liable for the loss.

§ 404.   GENERAL PARTNER'S LIABILITY.

(a)   Except as otherwise provided in subsections (b) and (c), all general partners are liable jointly and severally for all debts, obligations, and other liabilities of the limited partnership unless otherwise agreed by the claimant or provided by law.

(b)   A person that becomes a general partner is not personally liable for a debt, obligation, or other liability of the limited partnership incurred before the person became a general partner.

(c)   A debt, obligation, or other liability of a limited partnership incurred while the partnership is a limited liability limited partnership is solely the debt, obligation, or other liability of the limited liability limited partnership. A general partner is not personally liable, directly or indirectly, by way of contribution or otherwise, for a debt, obligation, or other liability of the limited liability limited partnership solely by reason of being or acting as a general partner. This subsection applies:

(1)   despite anything inconsistent in the partnership agreement that existed immediately before the vote or consent required to become a limited liability limited partnership under Section 406(b)(2); and

(2)   regardless of the dissolution of the partnership.

(d)   The failure of a limited liability limited partnership to observe formalities relating to the exercise of its powers or management of its activities and affairs is not a ground for imposing liability on a general partner for a debt, obligation, or other liability of the partnership.

(e)   An amendment of a certificate of limited partnership which deletes a statement that the limited partnership is a limited liability limited partnership does not affect the limitation in this section on the liability of a general partner for a debt, obligation, or other liability of the limited partnership incurred before the amendment became effective.

§ 405.   ACTIONS BY AND AGAINST PARTNERSHIP AND PARTNERS.

(a)   To the extent not inconsistent with Section 404, a general partner may be joined in an action against the limited partnership or named in a separate action.

(b)   A judgment against a limited partnership is not by itself a judgment against a general partner. A judgment against a partnership may not be satisfied from a general partner's assets unless there is also a judgment against the general partner.

(c)   A judgment creditor of a general partner may not levy execution against the assets of the general partner to satisfy a judgment based on a claim against the limited partnership, unless the partner is personally liable for the claim under Section 404 and:

(1)   a judgment based on the same claim has been obtained against the limited partnership and a writ of execution on the judgment has been returned unsatisfied in whole or in part;

(2)   the partnership is a debtor in bankruptcy;

(3)   the general partner has agreed that the creditor need not exhaust partnership assets;

(4)   a court grants permission to the judgment creditor to levy execution against the assets of a general partner based on a finding that partnership assets subject to execution are clearly insufficient to satisfy the judgment, that exhaustion of assets is excessively burdensome, or that the grant of permission is an appropriate exercise of the court's equitable powers; or

(5)   liability is imposed on the general partner by law or contract independent of the existence of the partnership.

§ 406.   MANAGEMENT RIGHTS OF GENERAL PARTNER.

(a)   Each general partner has equal rights in the management and conduct of the limited partnership's activities and affairs. Except as otherwise provided in this [act], any matter relating to the activities and affairs of the partnership is decided exclusively by the general partner or, if there is more than one general partner, by a majority of the general partners.

(b)   The affirmative vote or consent of all the partners is required to:

(1)   amend the partnership agreement;

(2)   amend the certificate of limited partnership to add or delete a statement that the limited partnership is a limited liability limited partnership; and

(3)   sell, lease, exchange, or otherwise dispose of all, or substantially all, of the limited partnership's property, with or without the good will, other than in the usual and regular course of the limited partnership's activities and affairs.

(c)   A limited partnership shall reimburse a general partner for an advance to the partnership beyond the amount of capital the general partner agreed to contribute.

(d)   A payment or advance made by a general partner which gives rise to a limited partnership obligation under subsection (c) or Section 408(a) constitutes a loan to the limited partnership which accrues interest from the date of the payment or advance.

(e)   A general partner is not entitled to remuneration for services performed for the limited partnership.

Comment

Subsection (a)—As explained in the Prefatory Note to ULPA (2001), this act assumes that, more often than not, people utilizing the act will want: (i) strong centralized management, strongly entrenched; and (ii) passive investors with little control over the entity. Section 302 essentially excludes limited partners from the ordinary management of a limited partnership's activities and affairs, unless the partnership agreement provides otherwise.

This subsection states affirmatively the general partners' commanding role. Only the partnership agreement and the express provisions of this act can limit that role.

The authority granted by this subsection includes the authority to delegate. Delegation does not relieve the delegating general partner or partners of their duties under Section 409. However, the fact of delegation is a fact relevant to any breach of duty analysis.

EXAMPLE: A sole general partner personally handles all important paperwork for a limited partnership. The general partner neglects to renew the fire insurance coverage on a building owned by the limited partnership, despite having received and read a warning notice from the insurance company. The building subsequently burns to the ground and is a total loss. The general partner might be liable for breach of the duty of care under Section 409(c) (gross negligence).

EXAMPLE: A sole general partner delegates responsibility for insurance renewals to the limited partnership's office manager, and that manager neglects to renew the fire insurance coverage on the building. Even assuming that the office manager has been grossly negligent, the general partner is not necessarily liable under Section 409(c). The office manager's gross negligence is not automatically attributed to the general partner. Under Section 409(c), the question is whether the general partner was grossly negligent (or worse) in selecting the office manager, delegating insurance renewal matters to the office manager, and supervising the office manager after the delegation. . . .

For limited partnerships that have more than one general partner, this act provides that in most circumstances a "matter relating to the activities and affairs of the partnership is decided . . . by a majority of the general partners." However, unlike corporate statutes, this act does not provide a rule for the quantum of participation necessary to constitute "a majority." *Cf., e.g.*, MINN. STAT. § 302A.237 (2014) (providing rules for determining the votes need to constitute "an act of the board"). If a limited partnership has more than one general partner, the partnership agreement should consider what "a majority" means in the event a general partner position is vacant. . . .

Subsection (b)—Other provisions of this act also contain default rules providing for unanimous consent. *E.g.*, Sections 301(b)(3) (for a person to become a limited partner after formation of the limited partnership), 401(b)(3) (same as to becoming a general partner), and 502(3) (for compromising a person's obligation to make a contribution). In addition, the transactions authorized under Article 11 each have a default unanimous consent requirement.

Subsections (a) and (b)—These subsections have important implications for a partner's actual authority to act on behalf of the partnership. The actual authority of a general partner is a question of agency law, *see* RESTATEMENT (THIRD) OF AGENCY § 3.01 (2006) (Creation of Actual Authority), and depends fundamentally on the contents of the partnership agreement. If, however, the partnership agreement is silent on the issue, this subsection helps delineate that actual authority. . . .

§ 407. RIGHTS TO INFORMATION OF GENERAL PARTNER AND PERSON DISSOCIATED AS GENERAL PARTNER.

(a)   A general partner may inspect and copy required information during regular business hours in the limited partnership's principal office, without having any particular purpose for seeking the information.

(b)   On reasonable notice, a general partner may inspect and copy during regular business hours, at a reasonable location specified by the limited partnership, any record maintained by the partnership regarding the partnership's activities, affairs, financial condition, and other circumstances, to the extent the information is material to the general partner's rights and duties under the partnership agreement or this [act].

(c)   A limited partnership shall furnish to each general partner:

(1)   without demand, any information concerning the partnership's activities, affairs, financial condition, and other circumstances which the partnership knows and is material to the proper exercise of the general partner's rights and duties under the partnership agreement or this [act], except to the extent the partnership can establish that it reasonably believes the general partner already knows the information; and

(2)   on demand, any other information concerning the partnership's activities, affairs, financial condition, and other circumstances, except to the extent the demand or the information demanded is unreasonable or otherwise improper under the circumstances.

(d)   The duty to furnish information under subsection (c) also applies to each general partner to the extent the general partner knows any of the information described in subsection (b).

(e)   Subject to subsection (j), on 10 days' demand made in a record received by a limited partnership, a person dissociated as a general partner may have access to the information and records described in subsections (a) and (b) at the locations specified in those subsections if:

(1)   the information or record pertains to the period during which the person was a general partner;

(2)   the person seeks the information or record in good faith; and

(3)   the person satisfies the requirements imposed on a limited partner by Section 304(b).

(f)   A limited partnership shall respond to a demand made pursuant to subsection (e) in the manner provided in Section 304(c).

(g)   A limited partnership may charge a person that makes a demand under this section the reasonable costs of copying, limited to the costs of labor and material.

(h)   A general partner or person dissociated as a general partner may exercise the rights under this section through an agent or, in the case of an individual under legal disability, a legal representative. Any restriction or condition imposed by the partnership agreement or under subsection (j) applies both to the agent or legal representative and to the general partner or person dissociated as a general partner.

(i)   The rights under this section do not extend to a person as transferee, but if:

(1)   a general partner dies, Section 704 applies; and

(2) an individual dissociates as a general partner under Section 603(6)(B) or (C), the legal representative of the individual may exercise the rights under subsection (c) of a person dissociated as a general partner.

(j) In addition to any restriction or condition stated in its partnership agreement, a limited partnership, as a matter within the ordinary course of its activities and affairs, may impose reasonable restrictions and conditions on access to and use of information to be furnished under this section, including designating information confidential and imposing nondisclosure and safeguarding obligations on the recipient. In a dispute concerning the reasonableness of a restriction under this subsection, the partnership has the burden of proving reasonableness.

Comment

Subsection (a)—The phrase "required information" is a defined term. *See* Sections 102(21) and 108. This subsection's broad right of access is subject both to reasonable limitations in the partnership agreement, Section 105(c)(9), and also the power of the limited partnership to impose reasonable limitations on use, Subsection (j). However, limiting a general partner's access to this information or any other information would be quite unusual. . . .

§ 408. REIMBURSEMENT; INDEMNIFICATION; ADVANCEMENT; AND INSURANCE.

(a) A limited partnership shall reimburse a general partner for any payment made by the general partner in the course of the general partner's activities on behalf of the partnership, if the general partner complied with Sections 406, 409, and 504 in making the payment.

(b) A limited partnership shall indemnify and hold harmless a person with respect to any claim or demand against the person and any debt, obligation, or other liability incurred by the person by reason of the person's former or present capacity as a general partner, if the claim, demand, debt, obligation, or other liability does not arise from the person's breach of Section 406, 409, or 504.

(c) In the ordinary course of its activities and affairs, a limited partnership may advance reasonable expenses, including attorney's fees and costs, incurred by a person in connection with a claim or demand against the person by reason of the person's former or present capacity as a general partner, if the person promises to repay the partnership if the person ultimately is determined not to be entitled to be indemnified under subsection (b).

(d) A limited partnership may purchase and maintain insurance on behalf of a general partner against liability asserted against or incurred by the general partner in that capacity or arising from that status even if, under Section 105(c)(8), the partnership agreement could not eliminate or limit the person's liability to the partnership for the conduct giving rise to the liability.

Comment

Subsections (a) and (b)—These subsections apply only to general partners. A limited partnership's obligation, if any, to reimburse or indemnify others (*e.g.,* employees, independent contractors, other agents) is a question for other law, including the law of agency, contract and restitution. The fact a person has dissociated as a partner does not affect any obligations incurred by the partnership under these subsections for conduct occurring before the dissociation. . . .

§ 409. STANDARDS OF CONDUCT FOR GENERAL PARTNERS.

(a) A general partner owes to the limited partnership and, subject to Section 901, the other partners the duties of loyalty and care stated in subsections (b) and (c).

(b) The fiduciary duty of loyalty of a general partner includes the duties:

(1) to account to the limited partnership and hold as trustee for it any property, profit, or benefit derived by the general partner:

(A) in the conduct or winding up of the partnership's activities and affairs;

(B) from a use by the general partner of the partnership's property; or

(C)   from the appropriation of a partnership opportunity;

(2)   to refrain from dealing with the partnership in the conduct or winding up of the partnership's activities and affairs as or on behalf of a person having an interest adverse to the partnership; and

(3)   to refrain from competing with the partnership in the conduct or winding up of the partnership's activities and affairs.

(c)   The duty of care of a general partner in the conduct or winding up of the limited partnership's activities and affairs is to refrain from engaging in grossly negligent or reckless conduct, willful or intentional misconduct, or knowing violation of law.

(d)   A general partner shall discharge the duties and obligations under this [act] or under the partnership agreement and exercise any rights consistently with the contractual obligation of good faith and fair dealing.

(e)   A general partner does not violate a duty or obligation under this [act] or under the partnership agreement solely because the general partner's conduct furthers the general partner's own interest.

(f)   All the partners of a limited partnership may authorize or ratify, after full disclosure of all material facts, a specific act or transaction by a general partner that otherwise would violate the duty of loyalty.

(g)   It is a defense to a claim under subsection (b)(2) and any comparable claim in equity or at common law that the transaction was fair to the limited partnership.

(h)   If, as permitted by subsection (f) or the partnership agreement, a general partner enters into a transaction with the limited partnership which otherwise would be prohibited by subsection (b)(2), the general partner's rights and obligations arising from the transaction are the same as those of a person that is not a general partner.

Comment

. . .

The 2011 and 2013 Harmonization amendments "un-cabined" fiduciary duty in both partnership acts, thereby harmonizing them to ULLCA (2006). As harmonized, this section states some of the core aspects of the fiduciary duty of loyalty, provides a duty of care, and incorporates the contractual obligation of good faith and fair dealing. The duties stated in this section are subject to the limited partnership agreement, but Section 105(c) and (d) contain important limitations on the power of the partnership agreement to affect fiduciary and other duties and the obligation of good faith and fair dealing. . . .

Subsection (a)—This subsection recognizes two core managerial duties but, unlike UPA (1997) and ULPA (2001), does not purport to be exhaustive. For example, many cases characterize a manager's duty to disclose as a fiduciary duty. *E.g., Lonergan v. EPE Holdings, LLC,* 5 A.3d 1008, 1023 (Del. Ch. 2010) (stating that "in the limited partnership context, absent contractual modification, a general partner owes fiduciary duties that include a duty of full disclosure") (quotation marks and citation omitted); *Exxon Corp. v. Burglin*, 4 F.3d 1294, 1298 (5th Cir. 1993) ("Under Alaska law, a general partner stands in a fiduciary relationship with the limited partnership and thereby owes 'a fiduciary duty . . . to disclose information concerning partnership affairs.'") (quoting *Parker v. Northern Mixing Co.*, 756 P.2d 881, 894 (Alaska 1988)). . . .

Subsection (c)—This act no longer refers to the duty of care as a fiduciary duty, because: (i) the duty of care applies in many non-fiduciary situations; and (ii) breach of the duty of care is remediable only in damages while breach of a fiduciary duty gives rise also to equitable remedies, including disgorgement, constructive trust, and rescission.

The change in label is consistent with the RESTATEMENT (THIRD) OF AGENCY § 8.02 (2006), which refers to the agent's "fiduciary duty" to act loyally, but eschews the word "fiduciary" when stating the agent's duties of "care, competence, and diligence." *Id.* § 8.08. However, the label change is merely semantics; no change is the law is intended. . . .

Subsection (d)—This subsection refers to the "*contractual* obligation of good faith and fair dealing" (emphasis added) and thereby invokes the implied obligation that exists in every contract. . . .

[T]he contractual obligation of good faith and fair dealing is not a fiduciary duty, does not command altruism or self-abnegation, and does not prevent a general partner from acting in the general partner's own self-interest:

"Fair dealing" is not akin to the fair process component of entire fairness, *i.e.*, whether the fiduciary acted fairly when engaging in the challenged transaction as measured by duties of loyalty and care . . . It is rather a commitment to deal "fairly" in the sense of consistently with the terms of the parties' agreement and its purpose. Likewise "good faith" does not envision loyalty to the contractual counterparty, but rather faithfulness to the scope, purpose, and terms of the parties' contract. Both necessarily turn on the contract itself and what the parties would have agreed upon had the issue arisen when they were bargaining originally.

Gerber v. Enter. Products Holdings, LLC, 67 A.3d 400, 418–19 (Del. 2013). . . .

Courts should not use the contractual obligation to change *ex post facto* the parties' or this act's allocation of risk and power. To the contrary, the obligation should be used only to protect agreed-upon arrangements from conduct that is manifestly beyond what a reasonable person could have contemplated when the arrangements were made.

The partnership agreement or this act may grant discretion to a general partner, and the contractual obligation of good faith and fair dealing is especially salient when discretion is at issue. However, a general partner may properly exercise discretion even though another partner (whether general or limited) suffers as a consequence. Conduct does not violate the obligation of good faith and fair dealing merely because that conduct substantially prejudices a party. Indeed, parties allocate risk precisely because prejudice may occur.

The exercise of discretion constitutes a breach of the obligation of good faith and fair dealing only when the party claiming breach shows that the conduct has no honestly-held purpose that legitimately comports with the parties' agreed-upon arrangements:

An implied covenant claim . . . looks to the past. It is not a free-floating duty unattached to the underlying legal documents. It does not ask what duty the law should impose on the parties given their relationship at the time of the wrong, but *rather what the parties would have agreed to themselves had they considered the issue in their original bargaining positions at the time of contracting.*

Gerber v. Enter. Prods. Holdings, LLC, 67 A.3d 400, 418 (Del. 2013). . . .

In sum, the purpose of the contractual obligation of good faith and fair dealing is to protect the arrangement the partners have chosen for themselves, not to restructure that arrangement under the guise of safeguarding it. . . .

Subsection (h)—This subsection is the modern, reformulated version of a language that sought to overturn the now-defunct notion that debts to partners were categorically inferior to debts to non-partner creditors. *See, e.g.,* ULPA (2001) § 112 ("A partner may lend money to and transact other business with the limited partnership and has the same rights and obligations with respect to the loan or other transaction as a person that is not a partner."). The reformulation makes clear that this provision has nothing to do with the fiduciary duty pertaining to conflict of interests. *See BT-I v. Equitable Life Assurance Soc'y of the United States*, 75 Cal. App. 4th 1406, 1415, 89 Cal. Rptr. 2d 811 (1999) (examining the prior formulation, explaining its history and stating "[w]e cannot discern anything in the purpose of [the prior formulation] that suggests an intent to affect a general partner's fiduciary duty to limited partners").

This subsection states a default rule. The partnership agreement may provide that debt to a general partner (or general partners generally) is subordinate to other partnership obligations. The agreement that creates the debt may do likewise.

[ARTICLE] 5

CONTRIBUTIONS AND DISTRIBUTIONS

§ 501.　　FORM OF CONTRIBUTION.

A contribution may consist of property transferred to, services performed for, or another benefit provided to the limited partnership or an agreement to transfer property to, perform services for, or provide another benefit to the partnership.

§ 502. LIABILITY FOR CONTRIBUTION.

(a)   A person's obligation to make a contribution to a limited partnership is not excused by the person's death, disability, termination, or other inability to perform personally.

(b)   If a person does not fulfill an obligation to make a contribution other than money, the person is obligated at the option of the limited partnership to contribute money equal to the value, as stated in the required information, of the part of the contribution which has not been made.

(c)   The obligation of a person to make a contribution may be compromised only by the affirmative vote or consent of all the partners. If a creditor of a limited partnership extends credit or otherwise acts in reliance on an obligation described in subsection (a) without knowledge or notice of a compromise under this subsection, the creditor may enforce the obligation.

§ 503. SHARING OF AND RIGHT TO DISTRIBUTIONS BEFORE DISSOLUTION.

(a)   Any distribution made by a limited partnership before its dissolution and winding up must be shared among the partners on the basis of the value, as stated in the required information when the limited partnership decides to make the distribution, of the contributions the limited partnership has received from each partner, except to the extent necessary to comply with a transfer effective under Section 702 or charging order in effect under Section 703.

(b)   A person has a right to a distribution before the dissolution and winding up of a limited partnership only if the partnership decides to make an interim distribution. A person's dissociation does not entitle the person to a distribution.

(c)   A person does not have a right to demand or receive a distribution from a limited partnership in any form other than money. Except as otherwise provided in Section 810(f), a partnership may distribute an asset in kind only if each part of the asset is fungible with each other part and each person receives a percentage of the asset equal in value to the person's share of distributions.

(d)   If a partner or transferee becomes entitled to receive a distribution, the partner or transferee has the status of, and is entitled to all remedies available to, a creditor of the limited partnership with respect to the distribution. However, the partnership's obligation to make a distribution is subject to offset for any amount owed to the partnership by the partner or a person dissociated as a partner on whose account the distribution is made.

§ 504. LIMITATIONS ON DISTRIBUTIONS. *refers to § 6.4 MBCA*

(a)   A limited partnership may not make a distribution, including a distribution under Section 810, if after the distribution:

(1)   the partnership would not be able to pay its debts as they become due in the ordinary course of the partnership's activities and affairs; or

(2)   the partnership's total assets would be less than the sum of its total liabilities plus the amount that would be needed, if the partnership were to be dissolved and wound up at the time of the distribution, to satisfy the preferential rights upon dissolution and winding up of partners and transferees whose preferential rights are superior to the rights of persons receiving the distribution.

(b)   A limited partnership may base a determination that a distribution is not prohibited under subsection (a) on:

(1)   financial statements prepared on the basis of accounting practices and principles that are reasonable in the circumstances; or

(2)   a fair valuation or other method that is reasonable under the circumstances.

(c)   Except as otherwise provided in subsection (e), the effect of a distribution under subsection (a) is measured:

(1)   in the case of a distribution as defined in Section 102(4)(A), as of the earlier of:

(A)   the date money or other property is transferred or debt is incurred by the limited partnership; or

(B)   the date the person entitled to the distribution ceases to own the interest or right being acquired by the partnership in return for the distribution;

(2)   in the case of any other distribution of indebtedness, as of the date the indebtedness is distributed; and

(3)   in all other cases, as of the date:

(A)   the distribution is authorized, if the payment occurs not later than 120 days after that date; or

(B)   the payment is made, if the payment occurs more than 120 days after the distribution is authorized.

(d)   A limited partnership's indebtedness to a partner or transferee incurred by reason of a distribution made in accordance with this section is at parity with the partnership's indebtedness to its general, unsecured creditors, except to the extent subordinated by agreement.

(e)   A limited partnership's indebtedness, including indebtedness issued as a distribution, is not a liability for purposes of subsection (a) if the terms of the indebtedness provide that payment of principal and interest is made only if and to the extent that payment of a distribution could then be made under this section. If the indebtedness is issued as a distribution, each payment of principal or interest is treated as a distribution, the effect of which is measured on the date the payment is made.

(f)   In measuring the effect of a distribution under Section 810, the liabilities of a dissolved limited partnership do not include any claim that has been disposed of under Section 806, 807, or 808.

Comment

Both this section and Section 505 were derived essentially from the Model Business Corporation Act section 6.40. Both sections are necessary and appropriate because a limited partnership provides its limited partners a corporate-like liability shield and a limited liability limited partnership provides the shield to general partners as well. With the exception noted in the comment to Subsection (a)(2), the provisions of this section are non-waivable. Section 105(c)(18)....

§ 505.   LIABILITY FOR IMPROPER DISTRIBUTIONS.

(a)   If a general partner consents to a distribution made in violation of Section 504 and in consenting to the distribution fails to comply with Section 409, the general partner is personally liable to the limited partnership for the amount of the distribution which exceeds the amount that could have been distributed without the violation of Section 504.

(b)   A person that receives a distribution knowing that the distribution violated Section 504 is personally liable to the limited partnership but only to the extent that the distribution received by the person exceeded the amount that could have been properly paid under Section 504.

(c)   A general partner against which an action is commenced because the general partner is liable under subsection (a) may:

(1)   implead any other person that is liable under subsection (a) and seek to enforce a right of contribution from the person; and

(2)   implead any person that received a distribution in violation of subsection (b) and seek to enforce a right of contribution from the person in the amount the person received in violation of subsection (b).

(d)   An action under this section is barred unless commenced not later than two years after the distribution.

Comment

. . .

This section contemplates two categories of liability: liability of those who have authorized improper distributions, Subsection (a), and the liability of those who have received improper distributions, Subsection (c). Liability that has accrued under this section is not affected by a person subsequently ceasing to be a partner or transferee.

The liability is to the entity, not to the creditors of an insolvent entity. . . .

This section does not preclude or interfere with claims for fraudulent transfer. *See* Subsection (d), cmt.

Subsection (a)—The liability is not strict liability but rather attaches only to the extent a decision maker has failed to comply with the duties stated in Section 409. . . .

[ARTICLE] 6

DISSOCIATION

§ 601.   DISSOCIATION AS LIMITED PARTNER.

(a)   A person does not have a right to dissociate as a limited partner before the completion of the winding up of the limited partnership.

(b)   A person is dissociated as a limited partner when:

(1)   the limited partnership knows or has notice of the person's express will to withdraw as a limited partner, but, if the person has specified a withdrawal date later than the date the partnership knew or had notice, on that later date;

(2)   an event stated in the partnership agreement as causing the person's dissociation as a limited partner occurs;

(3)   the person is expelled as a limited partner pursuant to the partnership agreement;

(4)   the person is expelled as a limited partner by the affirmative vote or consent of all the other partners if:

(A)   it is unlawful to carry on the limited partnership's activities and affairs with the person as a limited partner;

(B)   there has been a transfer of all the person's transferable interest in the partnership, other than:

(i)   a transfer for security purposes; or

(ii)   a charging order in effect under Section 703 which has not been foreclosed;

(C)   the person is an entity and:

(i)   the partnership notifies the person that it will be expelled as a limited partner because the person has filed a statement of dissolution or the equivalent, the person has been administratively dissolved, the person's charter or the equivalent has been revoked, or the person's right to conduct business has been suspended by the person's jurisdiction of formation; and

(ii)   not later than 90 days after the notification, the statement of dissolution or the equivalent has not been withdrawn, rescinded, or revoked, the person has not been reinstated, or the person's charter or the equivalent or right to conduct business has not been reinstated; or

(D)   the person is an unincorporated entity that has been dissolved and whose activities and affairs are being would up;

(5) on application by the limited partnership or a partner in a direct action under Section 901, the person is expelled as a limited partner by judicial order because the person:

(A) has engaged or is engaging in wrongful conduct that has affected adversely and materially, or will affect adversely and materially, the partnership's activities and affairs;

(B) has committed willfully or persistently, or is committing willfully and persistently, a material breach of the partnership agreement or the contractual obligation of good faith and fair dealing under Section 305(a); or

(C) has engaged or is engaging in conduct relating to the partnership's activities and affairs which makes it not reasonably practicable to carry on the activities and affairs with the person as a limited partner;

(6) in the case of an individual, the individual dies;

(7) in the case of a person that is a testamentary or inter vivos trust or is acting as a limited partner by virtue of being a trustee of such a trust, the trust's entire transferable interest in the limited partnership is distributed;

(8) in the case of a person that is an estate or is acting as a limited partner by virtue of being a personal representative of an estate, the estate's entire transferable interest in the limited partnership is distributed;

(9) in the case of a person that is not an individual, the existence of the person terminates;

(10) the limited partnership participates in a merger under [Article] 11 and:

(A) the partnership is not the surviving entity; or

(B) otherwise as a result of the merger, the person ceases to be a limited partner;

(11) the limited partnership participates in an interest exchange under [Article] 11 and, as a result of the interest exchange, the person ceases to be a limited partner;

(12) the limited partnership participates in a conversion under [Article] 11;

(13) the limited partnership participates in a domestication under [Article] 11 and, as a result of the domestication, the person ceases to be a limited partner; or

(14) the limited partnership dissolves and completes winding up.

Comment

Subsection (b)(5)—...

Although the partnership agreement can revise or eliminate the possibility of judicial expulsion, doing so requires careful planning. *Cf. Huatuco v. Satellite Healthcare*, CV 8465-VCG, 2013 WL 6460898, at *1, n.2 (Del. Ch. Dec. 9, 2013) (stating that "the right to judicial dissolution is a default right which the parties may eschew by contract" while reserving the question of "[w]hether the parties may, by contract, divest this Court of its authority to order a dissolution in all circumstances, even where it appears manifest that equity so requires—leaving, for instance, irreconcilable members locked away together forever like some alternative entity version of Sartre's Huis Clos").

For examples of conduct warranting an expulsion order in various contexts, see *All Saints Univ. of Med. Aruba v. Chilana*, A-2628-09T1, 2012 WL 6652510 (N.J. Super. Ct. App. Div. Dec. 24, 2012) (discussing a pattern of conduct); *Sherwood Park Bus. Ctr., L.L.C. v. Taggart*, 323 P.3d 551, 561 (Or. Ct. App. 2014) (upholding expulsion of a member who "had stolen a large amount of money from [the limited liability company], had intentionally failed to provide financial information, and had made himself unavailable to carry on the business"); *CCD, L.C. v. Millsap*, 116 P.3d 366, 373 (Utah 2005) (holding that a member's "misappropriat[ion of] trust account funds totaling at least $11,540.06 for his personal use" warranted expulsion, where the member's "misconduct continued the pattern of behavior that [had previously] resulted in losses to the company of $625,000[, where the new misconduct] . . . took place after [the member's] prior wrongdoing had been discovered and after [the limited liability company] had assented to permit [the member] to atone for his misdeeds by fulfilling the terms of the amended operating agreement"). . . .

§ 602. EFFECT OF DISSOCIATION AS LIMITED PARTNER.

(a)   If a person is dissociated as a limited partner:

(1)   subject to Section 704, the person does not have further rights as a limited partner;

(2)   the person's contractual obligation of good faith and fair dealing as a limited partner under Section 305(a) ends with regard to matters arising and events occurring after the person's dissociation; and

(3)   subject to Section 704 and [Article] 11, any transferable interest owned by the person in the person's capacity as a limited partner immediately before dissociation is owned by the person solely as a transferee.

(b)   A person's dissociation as a limited partner does not of itself discharge the person from any debt, obligation, or other liability to the limited partnership or the other partners which the person incurred while a limited partner.

§ 603. DISSOCIATION AS GENERAL PARTNER.

A person is dissociated as a general partner when:

(1)   the limited partnership knows or has notice of the person's express will to withdraw as a general partner, but, if the person has specified a withdrawal date later than the date the partnership knew or had notice, on that later date;

(2)   an event stated in the partnership agreement as causing the person's dissociation as a general partner occurs;

(3)   the person is expelled as a general partner pursuant to the partnership agreement;

(4)   the person is expelled as a general partner by the affirmative vote or consent of all the other partners if:

(A)   it is unlawful to carry on the limited partnership's activities and affairs with the person as a general partner;

(B)   there has been a transfer of all the person's transferable interest in the partnership, other than:

(i)   a transfer for security purposes; or

(ii)   a charging order in effect under Section 703 which has not been foreclosed;

(C)   the person is an entity and:

(i)   the partnership notifies the person that it will be expelled as a general partner because the person has filed a statement of dissolution or the equivalent, the person has been administratively dissolved, the person's charter or the equivalent has been revoked, or the person's right to conduct business has been suspended by the person's jurisdiction of formation; and

(ii)   not later than 90 days after the notification, the statement of dissolution or the equivalent has not been withdrawn, rescinded, or revoked, the person has not been reinstated, or the person's charter or the equivalent or right to conduct business has not been reinstated; or

(D)   the person is an unincorporated entity that has been dissolved and whose activities and affairs are being would up;

(5)   on application by the limited partnership or a partner in a direct action under Section 901, the person is expelled as a general partner by judicial order because the person:

(A)   has engaged or is engaging in wrongful conduct that has affected adversely and materially, or will affect adversely and materially, the partnership's activities and affairs;

(B)   has committed willfully or persistently, or is committing willfully or persistently, a material breach of the partnership agreement or a duty or obligation under Section 409; or

(C)   has engaged or is engaging in conduct relating to the partnership's activities and affairs which makes it not reasonably practicable to carry on the activities and affairs of the limited partnership with the person as a general partner;

(6)   in the case of an individual:

(A)   the individual dies;

(B)   a guardian or general conservator for the individual is appointed; or

(C)   a court orders that the individual has otherwise become incapable of performing the individual's duties as a general partner under this [act] or the partnership agreement;

(7)   the person:

(A)   becomes a debtor in bankruptcy;

(B)   executes an assignment for the benefit of creditors; or

(C)   seeks, consents to, or acquiesces in the appointment of a trustee, receiver, or liquidator of the person or of all or substantially all the person's property;

(8)   in the case of a person that is a testamentary or inter vivos trust or is acting as a general partner by virtue of being a trustee of such a trust, the trust's entire transferable interest in the limited partnership is distributed;

(9)   in the case of a person that is an estate or is acting as a general partner by virtue of being a personal representative of an estate, the estate's entire transferable interest in the limited partnership is distributed;

(10) in the case of a person that is not an individual, the existence of the person terminates;

(11) the limited partnership participates in a merger under [Article] 11 and:

(A)   the partnership is not the surviving entity; or

(B)   otherwise as a result of the merger, the person ceases to be a general partner;

(12) the limited partnership participates in an interest exchange under [Article] 11 and, as a result of the interest exchange, the person ceases to be a general partner;

(13) the limited partnership participates in a conversion under [Article] 11;

(14) the limited partnership participates in a domestication under [Article] 11 and, as a result of the domestication, the person ceases to be a general partner; or

(15) the limited partnership dissolves and completes winding up.

§ 604.   POWER   TO   DISSOCIATE   AS   GENERAL   PARTNER;   WRONGFUL DISSOCIATION.

(a)   A person has the power to dissociate as a general partner at any time, rightfully or wrongfully, by withdrawing as a general partner by express will under Section 603(1).

(b)   A person's dissociation as a general partner is wrongful only if the dissociation:

(1)   is in breach of an express provision of the partnership agreement; or

(2)   occurs before the completion of the winding up of the limited partnership, and:

(A)   the person withdraws as a general partner by express will;

(B)   the person is expelled as a general partner by judicial order under Section 603(5);

(C)   the person is dissociated as a general partner under Section 603(7); or

(D)   in the case of a person that is not a trust other than a business trust, an estate, or an individual, the person is expelled or otherwise dissociated as a general partner because it willfully dissolved or terminated.

(c)   A person that wrongfully dissociates as a general partner is liable to the limited partnership and, subject to Section 901, to the other partners for damages caused by the dissociation. The liability is in addition to any debt, obligation, or other liability of the general partner to the partnership or the other partners.

Comment

Subsection (a)—The limited partnership agreement may not eliminate this power. *See* Section 105(c)(11). In this respect, a general partner in a limited partnership is analogous to a general partner in general partnership. *See* UPA (1997) (Last Amended 2013) § 105(c)(9).

Subsection (b)—This subsection list exhaustively ("only if") the dissociations that are "wrongful," but the list is a default rule. The limited partnership agreement can expand the list; *e.g.,* by making wrongful a dissociation that beaches the implied contractual covenant of good faith and fair dealing. In theory, the partnership agreement can provide for liquidated damages (subject to the requirements of contract law) and, in theory, can also contract or even eliminate the list of wrongful dissociations. . . .

Subsection (c)—A person who prematurely dissociates as a general partner risks liability for any resulting damages. For example, the limited partnership might incur substantial expenses in replacing the general partner's expertise, reputation, or creditworthiness.

In effect, this subsection equates wrongful dissociation with breach of contract. Accordingly, courts should look to contract law to determine what consequential damages are recoverable. . . .

§ 605.   EFFECT OF DISSOCIATION AS GENERAL PARTNER.

(a)   If a person is dissociated as a general partner:

(1)   the person's right to participate as a general partner in the management and conduct of the limited partnership's activities and affairs terminates;

(2)   the person's duties and obligations as a general partner under Section 409 end with regard to matters arising and events occurring after the person's dissociation;

(3)   the person may sign and deliver to the [Secretary of State] for filing a statement of dissociation pertaining to the person and, at the request of the limited partnership, shall sign an amendment to the certificate of limited partnership which states that the person has dissociated as a general partner; and

(4)   subject to Section 704 and [Article] 11, any transferable interest owned by the person in the person's capacity as a general partner immediately before dissociation is owned by the person solely as a transferee.

(b)   A person's dissociation as a general partner does not of itself discharge the person from any debt, obligation, or other liability to the limited partnership or the other partners which the person incurred while a general partner.

Comment

Subsection (a)(1)—Once a person dissociates as a general partner, the person loses all management rights as a general partner regardless of what happens to the limited partnership. . . .

Subsection (a)(2)—This provision establishes a dividing line, separating out "matters arising and events occurring after the person's dissociation." If the limited partnership has continuing projects with clients, ongoing relationships with clients, or both, the dividing line requires special attention with regard to non-competition and partnership opportunities duties. *See* Section 409(b)(1) and (3). . . .

This provision does not determine the effect of a person's dissociation as a general partner on the person's future obligations or rights under the partnership agreement. Some contractual obligations typically extend beyond dissociation—*e.g.*, non-competition provisions, buyout arrangements. To the extent provisions of the partnership agreement continue to apply, the common law obligation of good faith continues to apply as well. . . .

    Subsection (b)—A general partner's obligation to safeguard trade secrets and other confidential or proprietary information is incurred when the partner learns or otherwise obtains the information. This subsection preserves the obligation post-dissociation.

§ 606. POWER TO BIND AND LIABILITY OF PERSON DISSOCIATED AS GENERAL PARTNER.

    (a)   After a person is dissociated as a general partner and before the limited partnership is merged out of existence, converted, or domesticated under [Article] 11, or dissolved, the partnership is bound by an act of the person only if:

        (1)   the act would have bound the partnership under Section 402 before the dissociation; and

        (2)   at the time the other party enters into the transaction:

            (A)   less than two years has passed since the dissociation; and

            (B)   the other party does not know or have notice of the dissociation and reasonably believes that the person is a general partner.

    (b)   If a limited partnership is bound under subsection (a), the person dissociated as a general partner which caused the partnership to be bound is liable:

        (1)   to the partnership for any damage caused to the partnership arising from the obligation incurred under subsection (a); and

        (2)   if a general partner or another person dissociated as a general partner is liable for the obligation, to the general partner or other person for any damage caused to the general partner or other person arising from the liability.

Comment

    A person's dissociation as a general partner ends immediately the person's actual authority to act for the partnership. *See* Section 605(a)(1). However, the person's apparent authority may linger. . . .

§ 607. LIABILITY OF PERSON DISSOCIATED AS GENERAL PARTNER TO OTHER PERSONS.

    (a)   A person's dissociation as a general partner does not of itself discharge the person's liability as a general partner for a debt, obligation, or other liability of the limited partnership incurred before dissociation. Except as otherwise provided in subsections (b) and (c), the person is not liable for a partnership obligation incurred after dissociation.

    (b)   A person whose dissociation as a general partner results in a dissolution and winding up of the limited partnership's activities and affairs is liable on an obligation incurred by the partnership under Section 805 to the same extent as a general partner under Section 404.

    (c)   A person that is dissociated as a general partner without the dissociation resulting in a dissolution and winding up of the limited partnership's activities and affairs is liable on a transaction entered into by the partnership after the dissociation only if:

        (1)   a general partner would be liable on the transaction; and

        (2)   at the time the other party enters into the transaction:

            (A)   less than two years has passed since the dissociation; and

            (B)   the other party does not have knowledge or notice of the dissociation and reasonably believes that the person is a general partner.

    (d)   By agreement with a creditor of a limited partnership and the partnership, a person dissociated as a general partner may be released from liability for a debt, obligation, or other liability of the partnership.

192

(e)   A person dissociated as a general partner is released from liability for a debt, obligation, or other liability of the limited partnership if the partnership's creditor, with knowledge or notice of the person's dissociation as a general partner but without the person's consent, agrees to a material alteration in the nature or time of payment of the debt, obligation, or other liability.

Comment

. . .

Subsection (a)—A person's dissociation as a general partner does not categorically preclude the person being liable as a general partner for subsequently incurred obligations of the limited partnership. If the dissociation results in dissolution, Subsection (b) applies and the person will be liable as a general partner on any partnership obligation incurred under Section 805. If the dissociation does not result in dissolution, Subsection (c) applies. . . .

[ARTICLE] 7

TRANSFERABLE INTERESTS AND RIGHTS OF TRANSFEREES AND CREDITORS

§ 701.   NATURE OF TRANSFERABLE INTEREST.

A transferable interest is personal property.

Comment

For the definition of transferable interest, see Section 102(25). Absent a contrary provision in the partnership agreement or the consent of the partners, a "transferable interest" is the only interest in a limited partnership that can be transferred to a person not already a partner. *See* Section 702. As to whether a partner may transfer governance rights to a fellow partner, the question is moot absent a provision in the partnership agreement changing the default rule. *See* Section 406(a) (allocating general partner governance rights *per capita*) and 406(b) (requiring unanimous agreement of all partners to take specified action). In the default mode, a general partner's transfer of governance rights to another general partner: (i) does not increase the transferee's governance rights; (ii) eliminates the transferor's governance rights; and (iii) thereby changes the denominator but not the numerator in calculating governance rights

EXAMPLE: LCN Company is a limited partnership with three general partners, Laura, Charles, and Nora. The partnership agreement does not displace this act's default rule on the allocation of governance rights among general partners. Thus, each general partner has 1/3 of those rights. Laura transfers her entire ownership interest to Charles. The transfer does not increase Charles's governance rights but does eliminate Laura's. After the transfer, Laura has no governance rights (regardless of whether Charles and Nora agree to expel Laura under Section 603(4)(B)). As a result, Charles and Nora each have 1/2 of the governance rights. . . .

§ 702.   TRANSFER OF TRANSFERABLE INTEREST.

(a)   A transfer, in whole or in part, of a transferable interest:

(1)   is permissible;

(2)   does not by itself cause a person's dissociation as a partner or a dissolution and winding up of the limited partnership's activities and affairs; and

(3)   subject to Section 704, does not entitle the transferee to:

(A)   participate in the management or conduct of the partnership's activities and affairs; or

(B)   except as otherwise provided in subsection (c), have access to required information, records, or other information concerning the partnership's activities and affairs.

(b)   A transferee has the right to receive, in accordance with the transfer, distributions to which the transferor would otherwise be entitled.

(c)   In a dissolution and winding up of a limited partnership, a transferee is entitled to an account of the partnership's transactions only from the date of dissolution.

(d)   A transferable interest may be evidenced by a certificate of the interest issued by a limited partnership in a record, and, subject to this section, the interest represented by the certificate may be transferred by a transfer of the certificate.

(e)   A limited partnership need not give effect to a transferee's rights under this section until the partnership knows or has notice of the transfer.

(f)   A transfer of a transferable interest in violation of a restriction on transfer contained in the partnership agreement is ineffective if the intended transferee has knowledge or notice of the restriction at the time of transfer.

(g)   Except as otherwise provided in Sections 601(b)(4)(B) and 603(4)(B), if a general or limited partner transfers a transferable interest, the transferor retains the rights of a general or limited partner other than the transferable interest transferred and retains all the duties and obligations of a general or limited partner.

(h)   If a general or limited partner transfers a transferable interest to a person that becomes a general or limited partner with respect to the transferred interest, the transferee is liable for the transferor's obligations under Sections 502 and 505 known to the transferee when the transferee becomes a partner.

Comment

One of the most fundamental characteristics of limited partnership law is its fidelity to the "pick your partner" principle. . . .

This section is the core of the act's provisions reflecting and protecting that principle. The provisions of this section apply regardless of whether the interest pertains to a general partner or a limited partner. A partner's rights in a limited partnership are bifurcated into economic rights (the transferable interest) and governance rights (including management rights, consent rights, rights to information, rights to seek judicial intervention). Unless the partnership agreement otherwise provides, a partner acting without the consent of all other partners lacks both the power and the right to: (i) bestow partnership on a non-partner, Sections 301(b)(3), 401(b)(3); or (ii) transfer to a non-partner anything other than some or all of the partner's transferable interest, Section 702(a)(3). The rights of a mere transferee are quite limited—*i.e.*, to receive distributions), Section 702(b), and, if the limited partnership dissolves and winds up, to receive specified information pertaining to the limited partnership from the date of dissolution. Section 702(c). . . .

This section does not directly consider whether a partner may transfer governance rights to another partner without obtaining consent from all the other partners. As noted above, Section 701, cmt., the question is moot under this act's default rule for allocating governance rights.

However, the question can be pivotal when the partnership agreement displaces the default rule on governance rights but does not determine whether transfer restrictions (whether contractual, statutory, or both) apply to transfers of governance rights from one partner to another. Case law is scant and pertains to LLCs. Nonetheless, the case law suggests that this act does not protect partners from control shifts that result from transfers among partners (as distinguished from transfers to non-partners who seek thereby to become partners).). *Blythe v. Bell*, No. 11 CVS 933. 2012 WL 7807800, at ¶ 6 (N.C. Dist. Dec. 10, 2012) (holding in a case of "first impression in North Carolina" that "in the absence of articles of incorporation or an operating agreement to the contrary . . . the assignment of control [(*i.e.*, governance)] interests between members is effective without unanimous member consent"); *Achaian, Inc. v. Leemon Family L.L.C.*, 25 A.3d 800, 810 (Del. Ch. 2011) (Strine, Ch.) (holding that the terms of the LLC agreement did not preclude one member of a three-member LLC from transferring the member's entire interest (including governance rights) to a second member without first having the consent of the third member; stating that the third member's "argument relies on a very thinly sliced version of [the 'pick-your-partner principle, the strained version being] . . . that once one chooses his initial co-members, one continues to hold a veto over how much additional voting power they may acquire'; explaining that '[t]he problem for [the third member] is that nothing in the LLC Agreement supports [that member's] reading of it that would require an already admitted Member, like [the acquirer (*i.e.*, the second member)], to be become once, twice (or even three times) a Member each and every time that Member acquires an additional block of Interests' "). . . .

Subsection (a)—The definition of "transfer," Section 102(24), and this subsection's reference to "in whole or in part" combine to mean that this section encompasses not only unconditional, permanent, and complete transfers but also temporary, contingent, and partial ones. Thus, for example, a charging order under Section 703 effects a transfer of part of the judgment debtor's transferable interest, as does the pledge of a transferable interest as collateral for a loan and the gift of a life-interest in a partner's rights to distribution.

Subsection (a)(2)—The phrase "by itself" contemplates Sections 601(b)(4)(B) and 603(4)(B); each create a risk of dissociation via expulsion when a partner transfers all of the partner's transferable interest.

Subsection (a)(3)—Mere transferees have no right to participate in management or otherwise intrude as the partners carry on the affairs of the limited partnership and their activities as partners.

Because Section 102(24) defines "transfer" to include "a transfer by operation of law," this section affects the power of other law to effect transfers of a partner's ownership interest. For example, a divorce court lacks the power to award a partner's spouse anything beyond the partner's transferable interest. Nor does the partner have the power to enter into a property settlement purporting to effect any greater transfer. . . .

§ 703. CHARGING ORDER.

(a)   On application by a judgment creditor of a partner or transferee, a court may enter a charging order against the transferable interest of the judgment debtor for the unsatisfied amount of the judgment. A charging order constitutes a lien on a judgment debtor's transferable interest and requires the limited partnership to pay over to the person to which the charging order was issued any distribution that otherwise would be paid to the judgment debtor.

(b)   To the extent necessary to effectuate the collection of distributions pursuant to a charging order in effect under subsection (a), the court may:

(1)   appoint a receiver of the distributions subject to the charging order, with the power to make all inquiries the judgment debtor might have made; and

(2)   make all other orders necessary to give effect to the charging order.

(c)   Upon a showing that distributions under a charging order will not pay the judgment debt within a reasonable time, the court may foreclose the lien and order the sale of the transferable interest. The purchaser at the foreclosure sale obtains only the transferable interest, does not thereby become a partner, and is subject to Section 702.

(d)   At any time before foreclosure under subsection (c), the partner or transferee whose transferable interest is subject to a charging order under subsection (a) may extinguish the charging order by satisfying the judgment and filing a certified copy of the satisfaction with the court that issued the charging order.

(e)   At any time before foreclosure under subsection (c), a limited partnership or one or more partners whose transferable interests are not subject to the charging order may pay to the judgment creditor the full amount due under the judgment and thereby succeed to the rights of the judgment creditor, including the charging order.

(f)   This [act] does not deprive any partner or transferee of the benefit of any exemption law applicable to the transferable interest of the partner or transferee.

(g)   This section provides the exclusive remedy by which a person seeking in the capacity of a judgment creditor to enforce a judgment against a partner or transferee may satisfy the judgment from the judgment debtor's transferable interest.

§ 704.   POWER OF LEGAL REPRESENTATIVE OF DECEASED PARTNER.

If a partner dies, the deceased partner's legal representative may exercise:

(1)   the rights of a transferee provided in Section 702(c); and

(2)   for the purposes of settling the estate, the rights of a current limited partner under Section 304.

[ARTICLE] 8

DISSOLUTION AND WINDING UP

§ 801.   EVENTS CAUSING DISSOLUTION.

(a)   A limited partnership is dissolved, and its activities and affairs must be wound up, upon the occurrence of any of the following:

(1)   an event or circumstance that the partnership agreement states causes dissolution;

(2)   the affirmative vote or consent of all general partners and of limited partners owning a majority of the rights to receive distributions as limited partners at the time the vote or consent is to be effective;

(3)   after the dissociation of a person as a general partner:

(A)   if the partnership has at least one remaining general partner, the affirmative vote or consent to dissolve the partnership not later than 90 days after the dissociation by partners owning a majority of the rights to receive distributions as partners at the time the vote or consent is to be effective; or

(B)   if the partnership does not have a remaining general partner, the passage of 90 days after the dissociation, unless before the end of the period:

(i)   consent to continue the activities and affairs of the partnership and admit at least one general partner is given by limited partners owning a majority of the rights to receive distributions as limited partners at the time the consent is to be effective; and

(ii)   at least one person is admitted as a general partner in accordance with the consent;

(4)   the passage of 90 consecutive days after the dissociation of the partnership's last limited partner, unless before the end of the period the partnership admits at least one limited partner;

(5)   the passage of 90 consecutive days during which the partnership has only one partner, unless before the end of the period:

(A)   the partnership admits at least one person as a partner;

(B)   if the previously sole remaining partner is only a general partner, the partnership admits the person as a limited partner; and

(C)   if the previously sole remaining partner is only a limited partner, the partnership admits a person as a general partner;

(6)   on application by a partner, the entry by [the appropriate court] of an order dissolving the partnership on the grounds that:

(A)   the conduct of all or substantially all the partnership's activities and affairs is unlawful; or

(B)   it is not reasonably practicable to carry on the partnership's activities and affairs in conformity with the certificate of limited partnership and partnership agreement; or

(7)   the signing and filing of a statement of administrative dissolution by the [Secretary of State] under Section 811.

(b)   If an event occurs that imposes a deadline on a limited partnership under subsection (a) and before the partnership has met the requirements of the deadline, another event occurs that imposes a different deadline on the partnership under subsection (a):

(1)   the occurrence of the second event does not affect the deadline caused by the first event; and

(2)   the partnership's meeting of the requirements of the first deadline does not extend the second deadline.

Comment

. . .

Except for Paragraphs (a)(6) and (7), this section comprises default rules. Paragraph 7 is fully mandatory, Section 105(c)(3)(B); Paragraph 6 is mandatory only with regard to the stated grounds for dissolution. *See* Section 105(c)(12), cmt. Moreover, a partnership agreement can provide additional causes of dissolution. *See* Subsection (a)(1). Variations to the statutory causes of dissolution are commonplace. . . .

Subsection (a)(2)—Although most actions involving limited partner consent require unanimous consent (*e.g.*, Section 406(b)), this provision requires only the specified majority consent. Rights to receive distributions owned by a person that is both a general and a limited partner figure into the limited partner determination only to the extent those rights are owned in the person's capacity as a limited partner. *See* Section 108(9)(C).

Example: XYZ is a limited partnership with three general partners, each of whom is also a limited partner, and five other limited partners. Rights to receive distributions are allocated as follows:

Partner #1 as general partner—3%

Partner #2 as general partner—2%

Partner #3 as general partner—1%

Partner #1 as limited partner—7%

Partner #2 as limited partner—3%

Partner #3 as limited partner—4%

Partner #4 as limited partner—5%

Partner #5 as limited partner—5%

Partner #6 as limited partner—5%

Partner #7 as limited partner—5%

Partner #8 as limited partner—5%

Several non-partner transferees, in the aggregate—55%

Distribution rights owned by persons as limited partners amount to 39% of total distribution rights. A majority is therefore anything greater than 19.5%. If only Partners 1, 2, 3, and 4 consent to dissolve, the limited partnership is not dissolved. Together these partners own as limited partners 19% of the distribution rights owned by persons as limited partners—just short of the necessary majority. For purposes of this calculation, distribution rights owned by non-partner transferees are irrelevant. So, too, are distribution rights owned by persons as general partners. (However, dissolution under this provision requires "the consent of all general partners.") . . .

Subsection (a)(3)(A)—Unlike Subsection (a)(2), this provision makes no distinction between distribution rights owned by persons as general partners and distribution rights owned by persons as limited partners. Distribution rights owned by non-partner transferees are irrelevant. . . .

§ 802. WINDING UP.

(a)   A dissolved limited partnership shall wind up its activities and affairs and, except as otherwise provided in Section 803, the partnership continues after dissolution only for the purpose of winding up.

(b)   In winding up its activities and affairs, the limited partnership:

(1)   shall discharge the partnership's debts, obligations, and other liabilities, settle and close the partnership's activities and affairs, and marshal and distribute the assets of the partnership; and

(2)   may:

(A)   amend its certificate of limited partnership to state that the partnership is dissolved;

(B)   preserve the partnership activities, affairs, and property as a going concern for a reasonable time;

(C)   prosecute and defend actions and proceedings, whether civil, criminal, or administrative;

(D)   transfer the partnership's property;

(E)   settle disputes by mediation or arbitration;

(F)   deliver to the [Secretary of State] for filing a statement of termination stating the name of the partnership and that the partnership is terminated; and

(G)   perform other acts necessary or appropriate to the winding up.

(c)   If a dissolved limited partnership does not have a general partner, a person to wind up the dissolved partnership's activities and affairs may be appointed by the affirmative vote or consent of limited partners owning a majority of the rights to receive distributions as limited partners at the time the vote or consent is to be effective. A person appointed under this subsection:

(1)   has the powers of a general partner under Section 804 but is not liable for the debts, obligations, and other liabilities of the partnership solely by reason of having or exercising those powers or otherwise acting to wind up the dissolved partnership's activities and affairs; and

(2)   shall deliver promptly to the [Secretary of State] for filing an amendment to the partnership's certificate of limited partnership stating:

(A)   that the partnership does not have a general partner;

(B)   the name and street and mailing addresses of the person; and

(C)   that the person has been appointed pursuant to this subsection to wind up the partnership.

(d)   On the application of a partner, the [appropriate court] may order judicial supervision of the winding up of a dissolved limited partnership, including the appointment of a person to wind up the partnership's activities and affairs, if:

(1)   the partnership does not have a general partner and within a reasonable time following the dissolution no person has been appointed pursuant to subsection (c); or

(2)   the applicant establishes other good cause.

§ 804.   POWER TO BIND PARTNERSHIP AFTER DISSOLUTION.

(a)   A limited partnership is bound by a general partner's act after dissolution which:

(1)   is appropriate for winding up the partnership's activities and affairs; or

(2)   would have bound the partnership under Section 402 before dissolution if, at the time the other party enters into the transaction, the other party does not know or have notice of the dissolution.

(b)   A person dissociated as a general partner binds a limited partnership through an act occurring after dissolution if:

(1)   at the time the other party enters into the transaction:

(A)   less than two years has passed since the dissociation; and

(B)   the other party does not know or have notice of the dissociation and reasonably believes that the person is a general partner; and

(2)   the act:

(A)   is appropriate for winding up the partnership's activities and affairs; or

(B)   would have bound the partnership under Section 402 before dissolution and at the time the other party enters into the transaction the other party does not know or have notice of the dissolution.

§ 805. LIABILITY AFTER DISSOLUTION OF GENERAL PARTNER AND PERSON DISSOCIATED AS GENERAL PARTNER.

(a) If a general partner having knowledge of the dissolution causes a limited partnership to incur an obligation under Section 804(a) by an act that is not appropriate for winding up the partnership's activities and affairs, the general partner is liable:

(1) to the partnership for any damage caused to the partnership arising from the obligation; and

(2) if another general partner or a person dissociated as a general partner is liable for the obligation, to that other general partner or person for any damage caused to that other general partner or person arising from the liability.

(b) If a person dissociated as a general partner causes a limited partnership to incur an obligation under Section 804(b), the person is liable:

(1) to the partnership for any damage caused to the partnership arising from the obligation; and

(2) if a general partner or another person dissociated as a general partner is liable for the obligation, to the general partner or other person for any damage caused to the general partner or other person arising from the obligation.

§ 806. KNOWN CLAIMS AGAINST DISSOLVED LIMITED PARTNERSHIP.

(a) Except as otherwise provided in subsection (d), a dissolved limited partnership may give notice of a known claim under subsection (b), which has the effect provided in subsection (c).

(b) A dissolved limited partnership may in a record notify its known claimants of the dissolution. The notice must:

(1) specify the information required to be included in a claim;

(2) state that a claim must be in writing and provide a mailing address to which the claim is to be sent;

(3) state the deadline for receipt of a claim, which may not be less than 120 days after the date the notice is received by the claimant;

(4) state that the claim will be barred if not received by the deadline; and

(5) unless the partnership has been throughout its existence a limited liability limited partnership, state that the barring of a claim against the partnership will also bar any corresponding claim against any general partner or person dissociated as a general partner which is based on Section 404.

(c) A claim against a dissolved limited partnership is barred if the requirements of subsection (b) are met and:

(1) the claim is not received by the specified deadline; or

(2) if the claim is timely received but rejected by the partnership:

(A) the partnership causes the claimant to receive a notice in a record stating that the claim is rejected and will be barred unless the claimant commences an action against the partnership to enforce the claim not later than 90 days after the claimant receives the notice; and

(B) the claimant does not commence the required action not later than 90 days after the claimant receives the notice.

(d) This section does not apply to a claim based on an event occurring after the date of dissolution or a liability that on that date is contingent.

§ 807.   OTHER CLAIMS AGAINST DISSOLVED LIMITED PARTNERSHIP.

(a)   A dissolved limited partnership may publish notice of its dissolution and request persons having claims against the partnership to present them in accordance with the notice.

(b)   A notice under subsection (a) must:

(1)   be published at least once in a newspaper of general circulation in the [county] in this state in which the dissolved limited partnership's principal office is located or, if the principal office is not located in this state, in the [county] in which the office of the partnership's registered agent is or was last located;

(2)   describe the information required to be contained in a claim, state that the claim must be in writing, and provide a mailing address to which the claim is to be sent;

(3)   state that a claim against the partnership is barred unless an action to enforce the claim is commenced not later than three years after publication of the notice; and

(4)   unless the partnership has been throughout its existence a limited liability limited partnership, state that the barring of a claim against the partnership will also bar any corresponding claim against any general partner or person dissociated as a general partner which is based on Section 404.

(c)   If a dissolved limited partnership publishes a notice in accordance with subsection (b), the claim of each of the following claimants is barred unless the claimant commences an action to enforce the claim against the partnership not later than three years after the publication date of the notice:

(1)   a claimant that did not receive notice in a record under Section 806;

(2)   a claimant whose claim was timely sent to the partnership but not acted on; and

(3)   a claimant whose claim is contingent at, or based on an event occurring after, the date of dissolution.

(d)   A claim not barred under this section or Section 806 may be enforced:

(1)   against the dissolved limited partnership, to the extent of its undistributed assets;

(2)   except as otherwise provided in Section 808, if assets of the partnership have been distributed after dissolution, against a partner or transferee to the extent of that person's proportionate share of the claim or of the partnership's assets distributed to the partner or transferee after dissolution, whichever is less, but a person's total liability for all claims under this paragraph may not exceed the total amount of assets distributed to the person after dissolution; and

(3)   against any person liable on the claim under Sections 404 and 607.

§ 808.   COURT PROCEEDINGS.

(a)   A dissolved limited partnership that has published a notice under Section 807 may file an application with [the appropriate court] in the [county] where the partnership's principal office is located or, if the principal office is not located in this state, where the office of its registered agent is or was last located, for a determination of the amount and form of security to be provided for payment of claims that are contingent, have not been made known to the partnership, or are based on an event occurring after the date of dissolution but which, based on the facts known to the partnership, are reasonably expected to arise after the date of dissolution. Security is not required for any claim that is or is reasonably anticipated to be barred under Section 807.

(b)   Not later than 10 days after the filing of an application under subsection (a), the dissolved limited partnership shall give notice of the proceeding to each claimant holding a contingent claim known to the partnership.

(c)   In a proceeding brought under this section, the court may appoint a guardian ad litem to represent all claimants whose identities are unknown. The reasonable fees and expenses of the guardian, including all reasonable expert witness fees, must be paid by the dissolved limited partnership.

(d)   A dissolved limited partnership that provides security in the amount and form ordered by the court under subsection (a) satisfies the partnership's obligations with respect to claims that are contingent, have not been made known to the partnership, or are based on an event occurring after the date of dissolution, and such claims may not be enforced against a partner or transferee on account of assets received in liquidation.

§ 809.   LIABILITY OF GENERAL PARTNER AND PERSON DISSOCIATED AS GENERAL PARTNER WHEN CLAIM AGAINST LIMITED PARTNERSHIP BARRED.

If a claim against a dissolved limited partnership is barred under Section 806, 807, or 808, any corresponding claim under Section 404 or 607 is also barred.

§ 810.   DISPOSITION OF ASSETS IN WINDING UP; WHEN CONTRIBUTIONS REQUIRED.

(a)   In winding up its activities and affairs, a limited partnership shall apply its assets, including the contributions required by this section, to discharge the partnership's obligations to creditors, including partners that are creditors.

(b)   After a limited partnership complies with subsection (a), any surplus must be distributed in the following order, subject to any charging order in effect under Section 703:

(1)   to each person owning a transferable interest that reflects contributions made and not previously returned, an amount equal to the value of the unreturned contributions; and

(2)   among persons owning transferable interests in proportion to their respective rights to share in distributions immediately before the dissolution of the partnership.

(c)   If a limited partnership's assets are insufficient to satisfy all of its obligations under subsection (a), with respect to each unsatisfied obligation incurred when the partnership was not a limited liability limited partnership, the following rules apply:

(1)   Each person that was a general partner when the obligation was incurred and that has not been released from the obligation under Section 607 shall contribute to the partnership for the purpose of enabling the partnership to satisfy the obligation. The contribution due from each of those persons is in proportion to the right to receive distributions in the capacity of a general partner in effect for each of those persons when the obligation was incurred.

(2)   If a person does not contribute the full amount required under paragraph (1) with respect to an unsatisfied obligation of the partnership, the other persons required to contribute by paragraph (1) on account of the obligation shall contribute the additional amount necessary to discharge the obligation. The additional contribution due from each of those other persons is in proportion to the right to receive distributions in the capacity of a general partner in effect for each of those other persons when the obligation was incurred.

(3)   If a person does not make the additional contribution required by paragraph (2), further additional contributions are determined and due in the same manner as provided in that paragraph.

(d)   A person that makes an additional contribution under subsection (c)(2) or (3) may recover from any person whose failure to contribute under subsection (c)(1) or (2) necessitated the additional contribution. A person may not recover under this subsection more than the amount additionally contributed. A person's liability under this subsection may not exceed the amount the person failed to contribute.

(e)   All distributions made under subsections (b) and (c) must be paid in money.

Comment

In some circumstances, this act requires a partner to make payments to the limited partnership. *See, e.g.,* Sections 502(b), 505(a), 505(b), 810(c). In other circumstances, this act requires a partner to make payments to other partners. *See, e.g.,* Sections 505(c), 810(d). In no circumstances does this act require a partner to make a payment for the purpose of equalizing or otherwise reallocating capital losses incurred by partners.

EXAMPLE: XYZ Limited Partnership ("XYZ") has one general partner and four limited partners. As indicated by its name, XYZ is not a limited liability limited partnership. According to XYZ's required information, the value of each partner's contributions to XYZ are:

General partner—$5,000

Limited partner #1—$10,000

Limited partner #2—$15,000

Limited partner #3—$20,000

Limited partner #4—$25,000

XYZ is unsuccessful and eventually dissolves without ever having made a distribution to its partners. XYZ lacks any assets with which to return to the partners the value of their respective contributions. No partner is obliged to make any payment either to the limited partnership or to fellow partners to adjust these capital losses. These losses are not part of "the limited partnership's obligations to creditors." Section 810(a).

EXAMPLE: Same facts, except that Limited Partner #4 loaned $25,000 to XYZ, and XYZ lacks the assets to repay the loan. The general partner must contribute to the limited partnership whatever funds are necessary to enable XYZ to satisfy the obligation owned to Limited Partner #4 on account of the loan. Section 810(a) and (c).

[ARTICLE] 9

ACTIONS BY PARTNERS

§ 901. DIRECT ACTION BY PARTNER.

(a) Subject to subsection (b), a partner may maintain a direct action against another partner or the limited partnership, with or without an accounting as to the partnership's activities and affairs, to enforce the partner's rights and otherwise protect the partner's interests, including rights and interests under the partnership agreement or this [act] or arising independently of the partnership relationship.

(b) A partner maintaining a direct action under this section must plead and prove an actual or threatened injury that is not solely the result of an injury suffered or threatened to be suffered by the limited partnership.

(c) A right to an accounting on a dissolution and winding up does not revive a claim barred by law.

Comment

Subsection (b)—. . .

Although in ordinary contractual situations it is axiomatic that each party to a contract has standing to sue for breach of that contract, within a limited partnership different circumstances typically exist. A partner does not have a direct claim against a general partner merely because the general partner has breached the partnership agreement. Likewise a general partner's violation of this act does not automatically create a direct claim for every other partner. To have standing in his, her, or its own right, a partner plaintiff must be able to show a harm that occurs independently of the harm caused or threatened to be caused to the limited partnership. . . .

The reference to "threatened injury" is to encompass potential claims for preventative relief, such as a temporary restraining order or preliminary injunction. . . .

This section's standing rule is subject to reasonable alterations by the partnership agreement. *See* Section 105(c)(14), cmt.

§ 902. DERIVATIVE ACTION.

A partner may maintain a derivative action to enforce a right of a limited partnership if:

(1) the partner first makes a demand on the general partners, requesting that they cause the partnership to bring an action to enforce the right, and the general partners do not bring the action within a reasonable time; or

(2)   a demand under paragraph (1) would be futile.

§ 903.   PROPER PLAINTIFF.

A derivative action to enforce a right of a limited partnership may be maintained only by a person that is a partner at the time the action is commenced and:

(1)   was a partner when the conduct giving rise to the action occurred; or

(2)   whose status as a partner devolved on the person by operation of law or pursuant to the terms of the partnership agreement from a person that was a partner at the time of the conduct.

§ 904.   PLEADING.

In a derivative action, the complaint must state with particularity:

(1)   the date and content of plaintiff's demand and the response to the demand by the general partner; or

(2)   why demand should be excused as futile.

§ 905.   SPECIAL LITIGATION COMMITTEE.

(a)   If a limited partnership is named as or made a party in a derivative proceeding, the partnership may appoint a special litigation committee to investigate the claims asserted in the proceeding and determine whether pursuing the action is in the best interests of the partnership. If the partnership appoints a special litigation committee, on motion by the committee made in the name of the partnership, except for good cause shown, the court shall stay discovery for the time reasonably necessary to permit the committee to make its investigation. This subsection does not prevent the court from:

(1)   enforcing a person's right to information under Section 304 or 407; or

(2)   granting extraordinary relief in the form of a temporary restraining order or preliminary injunction.

(b)   A special litigation committee must be composed of one or more disinterested and independent individuals, who may be partners.

(c)   A special litigation committee may be appointed:

(1)   by a majority of the general partners not named as parties in the proceeding; or

(2)   if all general partners are named as parties in the proceeding, by a majority of the general partners named as defendants.

(d)   After appropriate investigation, a special litigation committee may determine that it is in the best interests of the limited partnership that the proceeding:

(1)   continue under the control of the plaintiff;

(2)   continue under the control of the committee;

(3)   be settled on terms approved by the committee; or

(4)   be dismissed.

(e)   After making a determination under subsection (d), a special litigation committee shall file with the court a statement of its determination and its report supporting its determination and shall serve each party with a copy of the determination and report. The court shall determine whether the members of the committee were disinterested and independent and whether the committee conducted its investigation and made its recommendation in good faith, independently, and with reasonable care, with the committee having the burden of proof. If the court finds that the members of the committee were disinterested and independent and that the committee acted in good faith, independently, and with reasonable care, the court shall enforce the determination of the committee. Otherwise, the court shall dissolve the stay of discovery entered under subsection (a) and allow the action to continue under the control of the plaintiff.

Comment

Although special litigation committees are best known in the corporate field, they are no more inherently corporate than derivative litigation or the notion that an organization is a person distinct from its owners. An "SLC" can serve as an ADR mechanism, help protect an agreed upon arrangement from strike suits, protect the interests of partners who are neither plaintiffs nor defendants (if any), and bring the benefits of a specially tailored business judgment to any judicial decision.

This section's approach corresponds to established law in most jurisdictions, modified to fit the typical governance structures of a limited partnership. Use of an SLC is optional. . . .

§ 906.   PROCEEDS AND EXPENSES.

(a)   Except as otherwise provided in subsection (b):

(1)   any proceeds or other benefits of a derivative action, whether by judgment, compromise, or settlement, belong to the limited partnership and not to the plaintiff; and

(2)   if the plaintiff receives any proceeds, the plaintiff shall remit them immediately to the partnership.

(b)   If a derivative action is successful in whole or in part, the court may award the plaintiff reasonable expenses, including reasonable attorney's fees and costs, from the recovery of the limited partnership.

(c)   A derivative action on behalf of a limited partnership may not be voluntarily dismissed or settled without the court's approval.

[ARTICLE] 10

FOREIGN LIMITED PARTNERSHIPS

§ 1001.   GOVERNING LAW.

(a)   The law of the jurisdiction of formation of a foreign limited partnership governs:

(1)   the internal affairs of the partnership;

(2)   the liability of a partner as partner for a debt, obligation, or other liability of the partnership; and

(3)   the liability of a series of the partnership.

(b)   A foreign limited partnership is not precluded from registering to do business in this state because of any difference between the law of its jurisdiction of formation and the law of this state.

(c)   Registration of a foreign limited partnership to do business in this state does not authorize the foreign partnership to engage in any activities and affairs or exercise any power that a limited partnership may not engage in or exercise in this state.

[ARTICLE] 11

MERGER, INTEREST EXCHANGE, CONVERSION, AND DOMESTICATION

[PART] 1

GENERAL PROVISIONS

§ 1101.   DEFINITIONS.

In this [article]:

(1) "Acquired entity" means the entity, all of one or more classes or series of interests of which are acquired in an interest exchange.

(2) "Acquiring entity" means the entity that acquires all of one or more classes or series of interests of the acquired entity in an interest exchange.

(3) "Conversion" means a transaction authorized by [Part] 4.

(4) "Converted entity" means the converting entity as it continues in existence after a conversion.

(5) "Converting entity" means the domestic entity that approves a plan of conversion pursuant to Section 1143 or the foreign entity that approves a conversion pursuant to the law of its jurisdiction of formation.

(6) "Distributional interest" means the right under an unincorporated entity's organic law and organic rules to receive distributions from the entity.

(7) "Domestic", with respect to an entity, means governed as to its internal affairs by the law of this state.

(8) "Domesticated limited partnership" means the domesticating limited partnership as it continues in existence after a domestication.

(9) "Domesticating limited partnership" means the domestic limited partnership that approves a plan of domestication pursuant to Section 1153 or the foreign limited partnership that approves a domestication pursuant to the law of its jurisdiction of formation.

(10) "Domestication" means a transaction authorized by [Part] 5.

(11) "Entity":

(A) means:

(i) a business corporation;

(ii) a nonprofit corporation;

(iii) a general partnership, including a limited liability partnership;

(iv) a limited partnership, including a limited liability limited partnership;

(v) a limited liability company;

[(vi) a general cooperative association;]

(vii) a limited cooperative association;

(viii) an unincorporated nonprofit association;

(ix) a statutory trust, business trust, or common-law business trust; or

(x) any other person that has:

(I) a legal existence separate from any interest holder of that person; or

(II) the power to acquire an interest in real property in its own name; and

(B) does not include:

(i) an individual;

(ii) a trust with a predominantly donative purpose or a charitable trust;

(iii) an association or relationship that is not an entity listed in subparagraph A and is not a partnership under the rules stated in [Section 202(c) of the Uniform Partnership Act (1997) (Lasted Amended 2013)] [Section 7 of the Uniform Partnership Act (1914)] or a similar provision of the law of another jurisdiction;

(iv) a decedent's estate; or

(v)   a government or a governmental subdivision, agency, or instrumentality.

(12) "Filing entity" means an entity whose formation requires the filing of a public organic record. The term does not include a limited liability partnership.

(13) "Foreign", with respect to an entity, means an entity governed as to its internal affairs by the law of a jurisdiction other than this state.

(14) "Governance interest" means a right under the organic law or organic rules of an unincorporated entity, other than as a governor, agent, assignee, or proxy, to:

(A)   receive or demand access to information concerning, or the books and records of, the entity;

(B)   vote for or consent to the election of the governors of the entity; or

(C)   receive notice of or vote on or consent to an issue involving the internal affairs of the entity.

(15) "Governor" means:

(A)   a director of a business corporation;

(B)   a director or trustee of a nonprofit corporation;

(C)   a general partner of a general partnership;

(D)   a general partner of a limited partnership;

(E)   a manager of a manager-managed limited liability company;

(F)   a member of a member-managed limited liability company;

[(G) a director of a general cooperative association;]

(H)   a director of a limited cooperative association;

(I)   a manager of an unincorporated nonprofit association;

(J)   a trustee of a statutory trust, business trust, or common-law business trust; or

(K)   any other person under whose authority the powers of an entity are exercised and under whose direction the activities and affairs of the entity are managed pursuant to the organic law and organic rules of the entity.

(16) "Interest" means:

(A)   a share in a business corporation;

(B)   a membership in a nonprofit corporation;

(C)   a partnership interest in a general partnership;

(D)   a partnership interest in a limited partnership;

(E)   a membership interest in a limited liability company;

[(F) a share in a general cooperative association;]

(G)   a member's interest in a limited cooperative association;

(H)   a membership in an unincorporated nonprofit association;

(I)   a beneficial interest in a statutory trust, business trust, or common-law business trust; or

(J)   a governance interest or distributional interest in any other type of unincorporated entity.

(17) "Interest exchange" means a transaction authorized by [Part] 3.

(18) "Interest holder" means:

    (A)   a shareholder of a business corporation;

    (B)   a member of a nonprofit corporation;

    (C)   a general partner of a general partnership;

    (D)   a general partner of a limited partnership;

    (E)   a limited partner of a limited partnership;

    (F)   a member of a limited liability company;

    [(G) a shareholder of a general cooperative association;]

    (H)   a member of a limited cooperative association;

    (I)   a member of an unincorporated nonprofit association;

    (J)   a beneficiary or beneficial owner of a statutory trust, business trust, or common-law business trust; or

    (K)   any other direct holder of an interest.

(19) "Interest holder liability" means:

    (A)   personal liability for a liability of an entity which is imposed on a person:

       (i)   solely by reason of the status of the person as an interest holder; or

       (ii) by the organic rules of the entity which make one or more specified interest holders or categories of interest holders liable in their capacity as interest holders for all or specified liabilities of the entity; or

    (B)   an obligation of an interest holder under the organic rules of an entity to contribute to the entity.

(20) "Merger" means a transaction authorized by [Part] 2.

(21) "Merging entity" means an entity that is a party to a merger and exists immediately before the merger becomes effective.

(22) "Organic law" means the law of an entity's jurisdiction of formation governing the internal affairs of the entity.

(23) "Organic rules" means the public organic record and private organic rules of an entity.

(24) "Plan" means a plan of merger, plan of interest exchange, plan of conversion, or plan of domestication.

(25) "Plan of conversion" means a plan under Section 1142.

(26) "Plan of domestication" means a plan under Section 1152.

(27) "Plan of interest exchange" means a plan under Section 1132.

(28) "Plan of merger" means a plan under Section 1122.

(29) "Private organic rules" means the rules, whether or not in a record, that govern the internal affairs of an entity, are binding on all its interest holders, and are not part of its public organic record, if any. The term includes:

    (A)   the bylaws of a business corporation;

    (B)   the bylaws of a nonprofit corporation;

    (C)   the partnership agreement of a general partnership;

    (D)   the partnership agreement of a limited partnership;

    (E)   the operating agreement of a limited liability company;

    [(F)   the bylaws of a general cooperative association;]

(G)   the bylaws of a limited cooperative association;

(H)   the governing principles of an unincorporated nonprofit association; and

(I)   the trust instrument of a statutory trust or similar rules of a business trust or a common-law business trust.

(30)   "Protected agreement" means:

(A)   a record evidencing indebtedness and any related agreement in effect on [the effective date of this [act]];

(B)   an agreement that is binding on an entity on [the effective date of this [act]];

(C)   the organic rules of an entity in effect on [the effective date of this [act]]; or

(D)   an agreement that is binding on any of the governors or interest holders of an entity on [the effective date of this [act]].

(31)   "Public organic record" means the record the filing of which by the [Secretary of State] is required to form an entity and any amendment to or restatement of that record. The term includes:

(A)   the articles of incorporation of a business corporation;

(B)   the articles of incorporation of a nonprofit corporation;

(C)   the certificate of limited partnership of a limited partnership;

(D)   the certificate of organization of a limited liability company;

[(E)   the articles of incorporation of a general cooperative association;]

(F)   the articles of organization of a limited cooperative association; and

(G)   the certificate of trust of a statutory trust or similar record of a business trust.

(32)   "Registered foreign entity" means a foreign entity that is registered to do business in this state pursuant to a record filed by the [Secretary of State].

(33)   "Statement of conversion" means a statement under Section 1145.

(34)   "Statement of domestication" means a statement under Section 1155.

(35)   "Statement of interest exchange" means a statement under Section 1135.

(36)   "Statement of merger" means a statement under Section 1125.

(37)   "Surviving entity" means the entity that continues in existence after or is created by a merger.

(38)   "Type of entity" means a generic form of entity:

(A)   recognized at common law; or

(B)   formed under an organic law, whether or not some entities formed under that organic law are subject to provisions of that law that create different categories of the form of entity.

§ 1102.   RELATIONSHIP OF [ARTICLE] TO OTHER LAWS.

(a)   This [article] does not authorize an act prohibited by, and does not affect the application or requirements of, law other than this [article].

(b)   A transaction effected under this [article] may not create or impair a right, duty, or obligation of a person under the statutory law of this state relating to a change in control, takeover, business combination, control-share acquisition, or similar transaction involving a domestic merging, acquired, converting, or domesticating business corporation unless:

(1)   if the corporation does not survive the transaction, the transaction satisfies any requirements of the law; or

(2)   if the corporation survives the transaction, the approval of the plan is by a vote of the shareholders or directors which would be sufficient to create or impair the right, duty, or obligation directly under the law.

Comment

This section preserves existing regulatory law in an adopting state in general terms. . . .

Laws other than this act that will apply to transactions under the act include, for example, uniform fraudulent transfer and fraudulent conveyance acts, state insolvency statutes, federal bankruptcy law, and Articles 8 and 9 of the Uniform Commercial Code.

Subsection (b)—Many states have enacted "antitakeover" statutes intended to make it more difficult to acquire control of a publicly traded corporation. . . .

This subsection protects the application of antitakeover statutes from being affected by a transaction under this act by requiring that the transaction be approved in a manner that would be sufficient to approve changing the application of the antitakeover statute. . . .

§ 1103.   REQUIRED NOTICE OR APPROVAL.

(a)   A domestic or foreign entity that is required to give notice to, or obtain the approval of, a governmental agency or officer of this state to be a party to a merger must give the notice or obtain the approval to be a party to an interest exchange, conversion, or domestication.

(b)   Property held for a charitable purpose under the law of this state by a domestic or foreign entity immediately before a transaction under this [article] becomes effective may not, as a result of the transaction, be diverted from the objects for which it was donated, granted, devised, or otherwise transferred unless, to the extent required by or pursuant to the law of this state concerning cy pres or other law dealing with nondiversion of charitable assets, the entity obtains an appropriate order of [the appropriate court] [the Attorney General] specifying the disposition of the property.

(c)   A bequest, devise, gift, grant, or promise contained in a will or other instrument of donation, subscription, or conveyance which is made to a merging entity that is not the surviving entity and which takes effect or remains payable after the merger inures to the surviving entity.

(d)   A trust obligation that would govern property if transferred to a nonsurviving entity applies to property that is transferred to the surviving entity under this section.

§ 1104.   NONEXCLUSIVITY.

The fact that a transaction under this [article] produces a certain result does not preclude the same result from being accomplished in any other manner permitted by law other than this [article].

Comment

This section allows a transaction that has the same end result as one of the transactions governed by this act, but that is accomplished in a manner not within the scope of this act, to be exempt from this act. For example, a sale of assets and transfer of liabilities by two entities to a third entity followed by the liquidation of the two transferring entities can be accomplished pursuant to statutory provisions pertaining to sale of assets rather than under Part 2 of this article, even though the end result of the transaction is essentially the same as if the two entities had merged into a third entity.

§ 1106.   APPRAISAL RIGHTS.

An interest holder of a domestic merging, acquired, converting, or domesticating limited partnership is entitled to contractual appraisal rights in connection with a transaction under this [article] to the extent provided in:

(1)   the partnership agreement; or

(2)   the plan.

Comment

In corporate law, appraisal rights developed when corporate statutes were amended to permit mergers with less than unanimous consent of the shareholders. This article provides no appraisal rights, because, as a default rule, transactions under this article require the consent or affirmative vote of all the partners. Where the limited partnership agreement changes this default rule, parties may wish to consider contractual appraisal rights. . . .

[PART] 2

MERGER

§ 1121. MERGER AUTHORIZED.

(a)   By complying with this [part]:

(1)   one or more domestic limited partnerships may merge with one or more domestic or foreign entities into a domestic or foreign surviving entity; and

(2)   two or more foreign entities may merge into a domestic limited partnership.

(b)   By complying with the provisions of this [part] applicable to foreign entities, a foreign entity may be a party to a merger under this [part] or may be the surviving entity in such a merger if the merger is authorized by the law of the foreign entity's jurisdiction of formation.

Comment

The merger transaction authorized by this act involves the combination of one or more domestic limited partnerships with or into one or more other domestic or foreign entities. It also contemplates the consolidation of two or more foreign entities into a single domestic limited partnership. Upon the effective date of the merger, all the assets and liabilities of the constituent entities vest in the surviving entity as a matter of law. As such, mergers require the existence of at least two separate entities before the transaction and only one entity may survive the merger. If independent existence of the constituent entities is desired following the conclusion of the transaction, a restructuring transaction other than a merger must be used to accomplish the transfer of assets and liabilities. . . .

§ 1122. PLAN OF MERGER.

(a)   A domestic limited partnership may become a party to a merger under this [part] by approving a plan of merger. The plan must be in a record and contain:

(1)   as to each merging entity, its name, jurisdiction of formation, and type of entity;

(2)   if the surviving entity is to be created in the merger, a statement to that effect and the entity's name, jurisdiction of formation, and type of entity;

(3)   the manner of converting the interests in each party to the merger into interests, securities, obligations, money, other property, rights to acquire interests or securities, or any combination of the foregoing;

(4)   if the surviving entity exists before the merger, any proposed amendments to:

(A)   its public organic record, if any; and

(B)   its private organic rules that are, or are proposed to be, in a record;

(5)   if the surviving entity is to be created in the merger:

(A)   its proposed public organic record, if any; and

(B)   the full text of its private organic rules that are proposed to be in a record;

(6)   the other terms and conditions of the merger; and

(7)   any other provision required by the law of a merging entity's jurisdiction of formation or the organic rules of a merging entity.

(b) In addition to the requirements of subsection (a), a plan of merger may contain any other provision not prohibited by law.

§ 1123. APPROVAL OF MERGER.

(a) A plan of merger is not effective unless it has been approved:

(1) by a domestic merging limited partnership, by all the partners of the partnership entitled to vote on or consent to any matter; and

(2) in a record, by each partner of a domestic merging limited partnership which will have interest holder liability for debts, obligations, and other liabilities that are incurred after the merger becomes effective, unless:

(A) the partnership agreement of the partnership provides in a record for the approval of a merger in which some or all of its partners become subject to interest holder liability by the affirmative vote or consent of fewer than all the partners; and

(B) the partner consented in a record to or voted for that provision of the partnership agreement or became a partner after the adoption of that provision.

(b) A merger involving a domestic merging entity that is not a limited partnership is not effective unless the merger is approved by that entity in accordance with its organic law.

(c) A merger involving a foreign merging entity is not effective unless the merger is approved by the foreign entity in accordance with the law of the foreign entity's jurisdiction of formation.

Comment

Subsection (a)—In the uniform acts pertaining to unincorporated business organizations, unanimity is the default rule for approving a merger. The limited partnership agreement certainly can change this rule, but care should be taken in doing so. For example, a merger can revise the partnership agreement. Section 1122(a)(4). Thus, if a merger requires less-than-unanimous consent, the partnership agreement is subject to amendment by the same quantum of consent. "Exit rights" also require consideration. . . .

Subsection (c)—Where a foreign entity is a party to a merger under this act, this subsection defers to the laws of the foreign jurisdiction for the requirements for approval of the merger by the foreign entity. Those laws will include the organic law of the foreign entity and other applicable laws. The laws of the foreign jurisdiction will also control the application of any special approval requirements found in the organic rules of the foreign entity.

§ 1126. EFFECT OF MERGER.

(a) When a merger becomes effective:

(1) the surviving entity continues or comes into existence;

(2) each merging entity that is not the surviving entity ceases to exist;

(3) all property of each merging entity vests in the surviving entity without transfer, reversion, or impairment;

(4) all debts, obligations, and other liabilities of each merging entity are debts, obligations, and other liabilities of the surviving entity;

(5) except as otherwise provided by law or the plan of merger, all the rights, privileges, immunities, powers, and purposes of each merging entity vest in the surviving entity;

(6) if the surviving entity exists before the merger:

(A) all its property continues to be vested in it without transfer, reversion, or impairment;

(B) it remains subject to all its debts, obligations, and other liabilities; and

(C) all its rights, privileges, immunities, powers, and purposes continue to be vested in it;

(7)   the name of the surviving entity may be substituted for the name of any merging entity that is a party to any pending action or proceeding;

(8)   if the surviving entity exists before the merger:

   (A)   its public organic record, if any, is amended to the extent provided in the statement of merger; and

   (B)   its private organic rules that are to be in a record, if any, are amended to the extent provided in the plan of merger;

(9)   if the surviving entity is created by the merger, its private organic rules become effective and:

   (A)   if it is a filing entity, its public organic record becomes effective; and

   (B)   if it is a limited liability partnership, its statement of qualification becomes effective; and

(10)   the interests in each merging entity which are to be converted in the merger are converted, and the interest holders of those interests are entitled only to the rights provided to them under the plan of merger and to any appraisal rights they have under Section 1106 and the merging entity's organic law.

(b)   Except as otherwise provided in the organic law or organic rules of a merging entity, the merger does not give rise to any rights that an interest holder, governor, or third party would have upon a dissolution, liquidation, or winding up of the merging entity.

(c)   When a merger becomes effective, a person that did not have interest holder liability with respect to any of the merging entities and becomes subject to interest holder liability with respect to a domestic entity as a result of the merger has interest holder liability only to the extent provided by the organic law of that entity and only for those debts, obligations, and other liabilities that are incurred after the merger becomes effective.

(d)   When a merger becomes effective, the interest holder liability of a person that ceases to hold an interest in a domestic merging limited partnership with respect to which the person had interest holder liability is subject to the following rules:

(1)   The merger does not discharge any interest holder liability under this [act] to the extent the interest holder liability was incurred before the merger became effective.

(2)   The person does not have interest holder liability under this [act] for any debt, obligation, or other liability that is incurred after the merger becomes effective.

(3)   This [act] continues to apply to the release, collection, or discharge of any interest holder liability preserved under paragraph (1) as if the merger had not occurred.

(4)   The person has whatever rights of contribution from any other person as are provided by this [act], law other than this [act], or the partnership agreement of the domestic merging limited partnership with respect to any interest holder liability preserved under paragraph (1) as if the merger had not occurred.

(e)   When a merger becomes effective, a foreign entity that is the surviving entity may be served with process in this state for the collection and enforcement of any debts, obligations, or other liabilities of a domestic merging limited partnership as provided in Section 121.

(f)   When a merger becomes effective, the registration to do business in this state of any foreign merging entity that is not the surviving entity is canceled.

[PART] 3

INTEREST EXCHANGE

§ 1131. INTEREST EXCHANGE AUTHORIZED.

(a) By complying with this [part]:

(1) a domestic limited partnership may acquire all of one or more classes or series of interests of another domestic entity or a foreign entity in exchange for interests, securities, obligations, money, other property, rights to acquire interests or securities, or any combination of the foregoing; or

(2) all of one or more classes or series of interests of a domestic limited partnership may be acquired by another domestic entity or a foreign entity in exchange for interests, securities, obligations, money, other property, rights to acquire interests or securities, or any combination of the foregoing.

(b) By complying with the provisions of this [part] applicable to foreign entities, a foreign entity may be the acquiring or acquired entity in an interest exchange under this [part] if the interest exchange is authorized by the law of the foreign entity's jurisdiction of formation.

(c) If a protected agreement contains a provision that applies to a merger of a domestic limited partnership but does not refer to an interest exchange, the provision applies to an interest exchange in which the domestic limited partnership is the acquired entity as if the interest exchange were a merger until the provision is amended after [the effective date of this [act]].

Comment

An interest exchange is the same type of transaction as the share exchange provided for in section 11.03 of the Model Business Corporation Act. The effect of an interest exchange is that: (i) the separate existence of the acquired entity is not affected; and (ii) the acquiring entity acquires all of the interests of one or more classes of the acquired entity. An interest exchange also allows an indirect acquisition through the use of consideration in the exchange that is not provided by the acquiring entity (*e.g.*, consideration from another or related entity).

Neither share exchanges nor interest exchanges are universally recognized in either corporation or unincorporated entity laws. The effect of an interest exchange can be achieved through a triangular merger in which the acquiring entity forms a new subsidiary and the acquired entity is then merged into the new subsidiary. Part 3 allows the interest exchange to be accomplished directly in a single step, rather than indirectly through the triangular merger route. . . .

§ 1132. PLAN OF INTEREST EXCHANGE.

(a) A domestic limited partnership may be the acquired entity in an interest exchange under this [part] by approving a plan of interest exchange. The plan must be in a record and contain:

(1) the name of the acquired entity;

(2) the name, jurisdiction of formation, and type of entity of the acquiring entity;

(3) the manner of converting the interests in the acquired entity into interests, securities, obligations, money, other property, rights to acquire interests or securities, or any combination of the foregoing;

(4) any proposed amendments to:

(A) the certificate of limited partnership of the acquired entity; and

(B) the partnership agreement of the acquired entity that are, or are proposed to be, in a record;

(5) the other terms and conditions of the interest exchange; and

(6) any other provision required by the law of this state or the partnership agreement of the acquired entity.

(b)   In addition to the requirements of subsection (a), a plan of interest exchange may contain any other provision not prohibited by law.

§ 1133.   APPROVAL OF INTEREST EXCHANGE.

(a)   A plan of interest exchange is not effective unless it has been approved:

(1)   by all the partners of a domestic acquired limited partnership entitled to vote on or consent to any matter; and

(2)   in a record, by each partner of the domestic acquired limited partnership that will have interest holder liability for debts, obligations, and other liabilities that are incurred after the interest exchange becomes effective, unless:

(A)   the partnership agreement of the partnership provides in a record for the approval of an interest exchange or a merger in which some or all its partners become subject to interest holder liability by the affirmative vote or consent of fewer than all of the partners; and

(B)   the partner consented in a record to or voted for that provision of the partnership agreement or became a partner after the adoption of that provision.

(b)   An interest exchange involving a domestic acquired entity that is not a limited partnership is not effective unless it is approved by the domestic entity in accordance with its organic law.

(c)   An interest exchange involving a foreign acquired entity is not effective unless it is approved by the foreign entity in accordance with the law of the foreign entity's jurisdiction of formation.

(d)   Except as otherwise provided in its organic law or organic rules, the interest holders of the acquiring entity are not required to approve the interest exchange.

Section 1123(a)(2), comment.

§ 1134.   AMENDMENT OR ABANDONMENT OF PLAN OF INTEREST EXCHANGE.

(a)   A plan of interest exchange may be amended only with the consent of each party to the plan, except as otherwise provided in the plan.

(b)   A domestic acquired limited partnership may approve an amendment of a plan of interest exchange:

(1)   in the same manner as the plan was approved, if the plan does not provide for the manner in which it may be amended; or

(2)   by its partners in the manner provided in the plan, but a partner that was entitled to vote on or consent to approval of the interest exchange is entitled to vote on or consent to any amendment of the plan that will change:

(A)   the amount or kind of interests, securities, obligations, money, other property, rights to acquire interests or securities, or any combination of the foregoing, to be received by any of the partners of the acquired partnership under the plan;

(B)   the certificate of limited partnership or partnership agreement of the acquired partnership that will be in effect immediately after the interest exchange becomes effective, except for changes that do not require approval of the partners of the acquired partnership under this [act] or the partnership agreement; or

(C)   any other terms or conditions of the plan, if the change would adversely affect the partner in any material respect.

(c)   After a plan of interest exchange has been approved and before a statement of interest exchange becomes effective, the plan may be abandoned as provided in the plan. Unless prohibited by the plan, a domestic acquired limited partnership may abandon the plan in the same manner as the plan was approved.

(d)   If a plan of interest exchange is abandoned after a statement of interest exchange has been delivered to the [Secretary of State] for filing and before the statement becomes effective, a statement of abandonment, signed by the acquired limited partnership, must be delivered to the [Secretary of State] for filing before the statement of interest exchange becomes effective. The statement of abandonment takes effect on filing, and the interest exchange is abandoned and does not become effective. The statement of abandonment must contain:

    (1)   the name of the acquired partnership;

    (2)   the date on which the statement of interest exchange was filed by the [Secretary of State]; and

    (3)   a statement that the interest exchange has been abandoned in accordance with this section.

§ 1136. EFFECT OF INTEREST EXCHANGE.

(a)   When an interest exchange in which the acquired entity is a domestic limited partnership becomes effective:

    (1)   the interests in the acquired partnership which are the subject of the interest exchange are converted, and the partners holding those interests are entitled only to the rights provided to them under the plan of interest exchange and to any appraisal rights they have under Section 1106;

    (2)   the acquiring entity becomes the interest holder of the interests in the acquired partnership stated in the plan of interest exchange to be acquired by the acquiring entity;

    (3)   the certificate of limited partnership of the acquired partnership is amended to the extent provided in the statement of interest exchange; and

    (4)   the provisions of the partnership agreement of the acquired partnership that are to be in a record, if any, are amended to the extent provided in the plan of interest exchange.

(b)   Except as otherwise provided in the certificate of limited partnership or partnership agreement of a domestic acquired limited partnership, the interest exchange does not give rise to any rights that a partner or third party would have upon a dissolution, liquidation, or winding up of the acquired partnership.

(c)   When an interest exchange becomes effective, a person that did not have interest holder liability with respect to a domestic acquired limited partnership and becomes subject to interest holder liability with respect to a domestic entity as a result of the interest exchange has interest holder liability only to the extent provided by the organic law of the entity and only for those debts, obligations, and other liabilities that are incurred after the interest exchange becomes effective.

(d)   When an interest exchange becomes effective, the interest holder liability of a person that ceases to hold an interest in a domestic acquired limited partnership with respect to which the person had interest holder liability is subject to the following rules:

    (1)   The interest exchange does not discharge any interest holder liability under this [act] to the extent the interest holder liability was incurred before the interest exchange became effective.

    (2)   The person does not have interest holder liability under this [act] for any debt, obligation, or other liability that is incurred after the interest exchange becomes effective.

    (3)   This [act] continues to apply to the release, collection, or discharge of any interest holder liability preserved under paragraph (1) as if the interest exchange had not occurred.

    (4)   The person has whatever rights of contribution from any other person as are provided by this [act], law other than this [act], or the partnership agreement of the domestic acquired partnership with respect to any interest holder liability preserved under paragraph (1) as if the interest exchange had not occurred.

Comment

. . .

When an interest exchange becomes effective: (i) the interests of the acquired domestic limited partnership are exchanged, converted, or canceled as provided in the plan; (ii) the only rights of the former partners and transferees of the acquired limited partnership whose interests are affected by the interest exchange are those rights related to the exchange, conversion, or cancellation; (iii) the acquiring entity becomes the owner of the acquired limited partnership's interests as provided in the plan; (iv) the certificate of limited partnership of the acquired limited partnership is amended as provided in the statement of interest exchange, thus obviating the need for repetitive filings (*i.e.*, a filing as to the entity interest exchange and another filing to reflect amendments to certificate); and (v) the provisions of the partnership agreement of the acquired limited partnership that are to be in a record, if any, are amended to the extent provided in the plan of interest exchange. . . .

[PART] 4

CONVERSION

§ 1141. CONVERSION AUTHORIZED.

(a)   By complying with this [part], a domestic limited partnership may become:

(1)   a domestic entity that is a different type of entity; or

(2)   a foreign entity that is a different type of entity, if the conversion is authorized by the law of the foreign entity's jurisdiction of formation.

(b)   By complying with the provisions of this [part] applicable to foreign entities, a foreign entity that is not a foreign limited partnership may become a domestic limited partnership if the conversion is authorized by the law of the foreign entity's jurisdiction of formation.

(c)   If a protected agreement contains a provision that applies to a merger of a domestic limited partnership but does not refer to a conversion, the provision applies to a conversion of the partnership as if the conversion were a merger until the provision is amended after [the effective date of this [act]].

Comment

This part of Article 11 permits an entity to change to a different type of entity. A transaction in which an entity changes its jurisdiction of organization but does not change its type is a domestication and is the subject of Part 5. . . .

§ 1142. PLAN OF CONVERSION.

(a)   A domestic limited partnership may convert to a different type of entity under this [part] by approving a plan of conversion. The plan must be in a record and contain:

(1)   the name of the converting limited partnership;

(2)   the name, jurisdiction of formation, and type of entity of the converted entity;

(3)   the manner of converting the interests in the converting limited partnership into interests, securities, obligations, money, other property, rights to acquire interests or securities, or any combination of the foregoing;

(4)   the proposed public organic record of the converted entity if it will be a filing entity;

(5)   the full text of the private organic rules of the converted entity which are proposed to be in a record;

(6)   the other terms and conditions of the conversion; and

(7)   any other provision required by the law of this state or the partnership agreement of the converting limited partnership.

(b)   In addition to the requirements of subsection (a), a plan of conversion may contain any other provision not prohibited by law.

§ 1143. APPROVAL OF CONVERSION.

(a)   A plan of conversion is not effective unless it has been approved:

(1)   by a domestic converting limited partnership, by all the partners of the limited partnership entitled to vote on or consent to any matter; and

(2)   in a record, by each partner of a domestic converting limited partnership which will have interest holder liability for debts, obligations, and other liabilities that are incurred after the conversion becomes effective, unless:

(A)   the partnership agreement of the partnership provides in a record for the approval of a conversion or a merger in which some or all of its partners become subject to interest holder liability by the affirmative vote or consent of fewer than all the partners; and

(B)   the partner voted for or consented in a record to that provision of the partnership agreement or became a partner after the adoption of that provision.

(b)   A conversion involving a domestic converting entity that is not a limited partnership is not effective unless it is approved by the domestic converting entity in accordance with its organic law.

(c)   A conversion of a foreign converting entity is not effective unless it is approved by the foreign entity in accordance with the law of the foreign entity's jurisdiction of formation.

§ 1146.   EFFECT OF CONVERSION.

(a)   When a conversion becomes effective:

(1)   the converted entity is:

(A)   organized under and subject to the organic law of the converted entity; and

(B)   the same entity without interruption as the converting entity;

(2)   all property of the converting entity continues to be vested in the converted entity without transfer, reversion, or impairment;

(3)   all debts, obligations, and other liabilities of the converting entity continue as debts, obligations, and other liabilities of the converted entity;

(4)   except as otherwise provided by law or the plan of conversion, all the rights, privileges, immunities, powers, and purposes of the converting entity remain in the converted entity;

(5)   the name of the converted entity may be substituted for the name of the converting entity in any pending action or proceeding;

(6)   the certificate of limited partnership of the converted entity becomes effective;

(7)   the provisions of the partnership agreement of the converted entity which are to be in a record, if any, approved as part of the plan of conversion become effective; and

(8)   the interests in the converting entity are converted, and the interest holders of the converting entity are entitled only to the rights provided to them under the plan of conversion and to any appraisal rights they have under Section 1106.

(b)   Except as otherwise provided in the partnership agreement of a domestic converting limited partnership, the conversion does not give rise to any rights that a partner or third party would have upon a dissolution, liquidation, or winding up of the converting entity.

(c)   When a conversion becomes effective, a person that did not have interest holder liability with respect to the converting entity and becomes subject to interest holder liability with respect to a domestic entity as a result of the conversion has interest holder liability only to the extent provided by the organic law of the entity and only for those debts, obligations, and other liabilities that are incurred after the conversion becomes effective.

(d)   When a conversion becomes effective, the interest holder liability of a person that ceases to hold an interest in a domestic converting limited partnership with respect to which the person had interest holder liability is subject to the following rules:

(1)　The conversion does not discharge any interest holder liability under this [act] to the extent the interest holder liability was incurred before the conversion became effective.

(2)　The person does not have interest holder liability under this [act] for any debt, obligation, or other liability that is incurred after the conversion becomes effective.

(3)　This [act] continues to apply to the release, collection, or discharge of any interest holder liability preserved under paragraph (1) as if the conversion had not occurred.

(4)　The person has whatever rights of contribution from any other person as are provided by this [act], law other than this [act], or the organic rules of the converting entity with respect to any interest holder liability preserved under paragraph (1) as if the conversion had not occurred.

(e)　When a conversion becomes effective, a foreign entity that is the converted entity may be served with process in this state for the collection and enforcement of any of its debts, obligations, and other liabilities as provided in Section 121.

(f)　If the converting entity is a registered foreign entity, its registration to do business in this state is canceled when the conversion becomes effective.

(g)　A conversion does not require the entity to wind up its affairs and does not constitute or cause the dissolution of the entity.

Comment

When a conversion becomes effective, the internal affairs of the converting entity are no longer governed by its former organic law but instead by the organic law of the converted entity. As a result, filings that may have been made under the organic law of the converting entity, such as the following, will no longer be effective: a statement of qualification as a limited liability partnership under UPA (1997) (Last Amended 2013) § 901, a statement of partnership authority under section 303 of that act, a statement of authority under Section of the ULLCA (2006) (Last Amended 2013) § 302, or under Uniform Unincorporated Nonprofit Association Act (2008) (Last Amended 2013) § 7. . . .

[PART] 5

DOMESTICATION

§ 1151.　DOMESTICATION AUTHORIZED.

(a)　By complying with this [part], a domestic limited partnership may become a foreign limited partnership if the domestication is authorized by the law of the foreign jurisdiction.

(b)　By complying with the provisions of this [part] applicable to foreign limited partnerships, a foreign limited partnership may become a domestic limited partnership if the domestication is authorized by the law of the foreign limited partnership's jurisdiction of formation.

(c)　If a protected agreement contains a provision that applies to a merger of a domestic limited partnership but does not refer to a domestication, the provision applies to a domestication of the limited partnership as if the domestication were a merger until the provision is amended after [the effective date of this [act]].

Comment

A domestication authorized by Part 5 of Article 11 differs from a conversion in that a domestication requires that the domesticating entity be the same type of entity as the domesticated entity. In a conversion, by contrast, the converting entity changes its type.

As with a conversion, all rights and privileges, debts, obligations and other liabilities, and actions or proceedings of a domesticating entity vest unimpaired in the domesticated entity. A domestication is not a sale, transfer, assignment, or conveyance and does not give rise to a claim of reverter or impairment of title. . . .

§ 1152. PLAN OF DOMESTICATION.

(a)   A domestic limited partnership may become a foreign limited partnership in a domestication by approving a plan of domestication. The plan must be in a record and contain:

(1)   the name of the domesticating limited partnership;

(2)   the name and jurisdiction of formation of the domesticated limited partnership;

(3)   the manner of converting the interests in the domesticating limited partnership into interests, securities, obligations, money, other property, rights to acquire interests or securities, or any combination of the foregoing;

(4)   the proposed certificate of limited partnership of the domesticated limited partnership;

(5)   the full text of the provisions of the partnership agreement of the domesticated limited partnership, that are proposed to be in a record;

(6)   the other terms and conditions of the domestication; and

(7)   any other provision required by the law of this state or the partnership agreement of the domesticating limited partnership.

(b)   In addition to the requirements of subsection (a), a plan of domestication may contain any other provision not prohibited by law.

§ 1153. APPROVAL OF DOMESTICATION.

(a)   A plan of domestication of a domestic domesticating limited partnership is not effective unless it has been approved:

(1)   by all the partners entitled to vote on or consent to any matter; and

(2)   in a record, by each partner that will have interest holder liability for debts, obligations, and other liabilities that are incurred after the domestication becomes effective, unless:

(A)   the partnership agreement of the domesticating partnership in a record provides for the approval of a domestication or merger in which some or all of its partners become subject to interest holder liability by the affirmative vote or consent of fewer than all the partners; and

(B)   the partner voted for or consented in a record to that provision of the partnership agreement or became a partner after the adoption of that provision.

(b)   A domestication of a foreign domesticating limited partnership is not effective unless it is approved in accordance with the law of the foreign limited partnership's jurisdiction of formation.

§ 1154. AMENDMENT OR ABANDONMENT OF PLAN OF DOMESTICATION.

(a)   A plan of domestication of a domestic domesticating limited partnership may be amended:

(1)   in the same manner as the plan was approved, if the plan does not provide for the manner in which it may be amended; or

(2)   by its partners in the manner provided in the plan, but a partner that was entitled to vote on or consent to approval of the domestication is entitled to vote on or consent to any amendment of the plan that will change:

(A)   the amount or kind of interests, securities, obligations, money, other property, rights to acquire interests or securities, or any combination of the foregoing, to be received by any of the partners of the domesticating limited partnership under the plan;

(B)   the certificate of limited partnership or partnership agreement of the domesticated limited partnership that will be in effect immediately after the domestication becomes effective, except for changes that do not require approval of the partners of the domesticated limited partnership under its organic law or partnership agreement; or

(C) any other terms or conditions of the plan, if the change would adversely affect the partner in any material respect.

(b) After a plan of domestication has been approved by a domestic domesticating limited partnership and before a statement of domestication becomes effective, the plan may be abandoned as provided in the plan. Unless prohibited by the plan, a domestic domesticating limited partnership may abandon the plan in the same manner as the plan was approved.

(c) If a plan of domestication is abandoned after a statement of domestication has been delivered to the [Secretary of State] for filing and before the statement becomes effective, a statement of abandonment, signed by the domesticating limited partnership, must be delivered to the [Secretary of State] for filing before the statement of domestication becomes effective. The statement of abandonment takes effect on filing, and the domestication is abandoned and does

§ 1156. EFFECT OF DOMESTICATION.

(a) When a domestication becomes effective:

(1) the domesticated entity is:

(A) organized under and subject to the organic law of the domesticated entity; and

(B) the same entity without interruption as the domesticating entity;

(2) all property of the domesticating entity continues to be vested in the domesticated entity without transfer, reversion, or impairment;

(3) all debts, obligations, and other liabilities of the domesticating entity continue as debts, obligations, and other liabilities of the domesticated entity;

(4) except as otherwise provided by law or the plan of domestication, all the rights, privileges, immunities, powers, and purposes of the domesticating entity remain in the domesticated entity;

(5) the name of the domesticated entity may be substituted for the name of the domesticating entity in any pending action or proceeding;

(6) the certificate of limited partnership of the domesticated entity becomes effective;

(7) the provisions of the partnership agreement of the domesticated entity that are to be in a record, if any, approved as part of the plan of domestication become effective; and

(8) the interests in the domesticating entity are converted to the extent and as approved in connection with the domestication, and the partners of the domesticating entity are entitled only to the rights provided to them under the plan of domestication and to any appraisal rights they have under Section 1106.

(b) Except as otherwise provided in the organic law or partnership agreement of the domesticating limited partnership, the domestication does not give rise to any rights that an partner or third party would have upon a dissolution, liquidation, or winding up of the domesticating partnership.

(c) When a domestication becomes effective, a person that did not have interest holder liability with respect to the domesticating limited partnership and becomes subject to interest holder liability with respect to a domestic limited partnership as a result of the domestication has interest holder liability only to the extent provided by this [act] and only for those debts, obligations, and other liabilities that are incurred after the domestication becomes effective.

(d) When a domestication becomes effective, the interest holder liability of a person that ceases to hold an interest in a domestic domesticating limited partnership with respect to which the person had interest holder liability is subject to the following rules:

(1) The domestication does not discharge any interest holder liability under this [act] to the extent the interest holder liability was incurred before the domestication became effective.

(2) A person does not have interest holder liability under this [act] for any debt, obligation, or other liability that is incurred after the domestication becomes effective.

(3) This [act] continues to apply to the release, collection, or discharge of any interest holder liability preserved under paragraph (1) as if the domestication had not occurred.

(4) A person has whatever rights of contribution from any other person as are provided by this [act], law other than this [act], or the partnership agreement of the domestic domesticating limited partnership with respect to any interest holder liability preserved under paragraph (1) as if the domestication had not occurred.

(e) When a domestication becomes effective, a foreign limited partnership that is the domesticated partnership may be served with process in this state for the collection and enforcement of any of its debts, obligations, and other liabilities as provided in Section 121.

(f) If the domesticating limited partnership is a registered foreign entity, the registration of the partnership is canceled when the domestication becomes effective.

(g) A domestication does not require a domestic domesticating limited partnership to wind up its affairs and does not constitute or cause the dissolution of the partnership.

DELAWARE LIMITED LIABILITY COMPANY ACT

TABLE OF CONTENTS

DEL. CODE ANN. TITLE 6, CHAPTER 18

SUBCHAPTER I. GENERAL PROVISIONS

Sec.		Page
18–101.	Definitions	225
18–102.	Name Set Forth in Certificate	227
18–103.	Reservation of Name*	
18–104.	Registered Office; Registered Agent	227
18–105.	Service of Process on Domestic Limited Liability Companies	227
18–106.	Nature of Business Permitted; Powers	228
18–107.	Business Transactions of Member or Manager With the Limited Liability Company	229
18–108.	Indemnification	229
18–109.	Service of Process on Managers and Liquidating Trustees	229
18–110.	Contested Matters Relating to Managers; Contested Votes	230
18–111.	Interpretation and Enforcement of Limited Liability Company Agreement	231
18–112.	Judicial Cancellation of Certificate of Formation; Proceedings	231

SUBCHAPTER II. FORMATION; CERTIFICATE OF FORMATION

18–201.	Certificate of Formation	231
18–202.	Amendment to Certificate of Formation	232
18–203.	Cancellation of Certificate	232
18–204.	Execution	232
18–205.	Execution, Amendment or Cancellation by Judicial Order	233
18–206.	Filing	233
18–207.	Notice	233
18–208.	Restated Certificate*	
18–209.	Merger and Consolidation	234
18–210.	Contractual Appraisal Rights	237
18–211.	Certificate of Correction	237
18–212.	Domestication of Non-United States Entities	237
18–213.	Transfer or Continuance of Domestic Limited Liability Companies	239
18–214.	Conversion of Certain Entities to a Limited Liability Company	242
18–215.	Series of Members, Managers, Limited Liability Company Interests or Assets	243
18–216.	Approval of Conversion of a Limited Liability Company	247
18–217.	Division of a Limited Liability Company	249
18–218.	Registered Series of Members, Managers, Limited Liability Company Interests or Assets	250
18–219.	Approval of Conversion of a Protected Series of a Domestic Limited Liability Company to a Registered Series of Such Domestic Limited Liability Company	252
18–220.	Approval of Conversion of a Registered Series of a Domestic Limited Liability Company to a Protected Series of Such Domestic Limited Liability Company	252
18–221.	Merger and Consolidation of Registered Series	253

SUBCHAPTER III. MEMBERS

18–301.	Admission of Members	253
18–302.	Classes and Voting	254
18–303.	Liability to Third Parties	255
18–304.	Events of Bankruptcy	255

---

*   Omitted.

18–305. Access to and Confidentiality of Information; Records 256
18–306. Remedies for Breach of Limited Liability Company Agreement by Member.................... 257

SUBCHAPTER IV.   MANAGERS

18–401. Admission of Managers.. 257
18–402. Management of Limited Liability Company... 258
18–403. Contributions by a Manager... 258
18–404. Classes and Voting.. 258
18–405. Remedies for Breach of Limited Liability Company Agreement by Manager 259
18–406. Reliance on Reports and Information by Member or Manager.......................... 259
18–407. Delegation of Rights and Powers to Manage 259

SUBCHAPTER V.   FINANCE

18–501. Form of Contribution 260
18–502. Liability for Contribution 260
18–503. Allocation of Profits and Losses... 260
18–504. Allocation of Distributions.. 260
18–505. Defense of Usury Not Available*

SUBCHAPTER VI.   DISTRIBUTIONS AND RESIGNATION

18–601. Interim Distributions.. 261
18–602. Resignation of Manager 261
18–603. Resignation of Member 261
18–604. Distribution Upon Resignation 261
18–605. Distribution in Kind... 261
18–606. Right to Distribution.. 261
18–607. Limitations on Distribution.. 262

SUBCHAPTER VII.   ASSIGNMENT OF LIMITED LIABILITY COMPANY INTERESTS

18–701. Nature of Limited Liability Company Interest.. 262
18–702. Assignment of Limited Liability Company Interest...................................... 262
18–703. Member's Limited Liability Company Interest Subject to Charging Order........... 263
18–704. Right of Assignee to Become Member.. 263
18–705. Powers of Estate of Deceased or Incompetent Member 264

SUBCHAPTER VIII.   DISSOLUTION

18–801. Dissolution... 264
18–802. Judicial Dissolution 265
18–803. Winding Up 265
18–804. Distribution of Assets 265
18–805. Trustees or Receivers for Limited Liability Companies; Appointment; Powers; Duties*
18–806. Revocation of Dissolution.. 266

SUBCHAPTER IX.   FOREIGN LIMITED LIABILITY COMPANIES

18–901. Law Governing.. 267
18–902. Registration Required; Application... 267
18–903. Issuance of Registration*
18–904. Name; Registered Office; Registered Agent*

_____

* Omitted.

18–905.   Amendments to Application*
18–906.   Cancellation of Registration*
18–907.   Doing Business Without Registration*
18–908.   Foreign Limited Liability Companies Doing Business Without Having Qualified;
            Injunctions*
18–909.   Execution; Liability*
18–910.   Service of Process on Registered Foreign Limited Liability Companies*
18–911.   Service of Process on Unregistered Foreign Limited Liability Companies*
18–912.   Activities Not Constituting Doing Business 267

SUBCHAPTER X.   DERIVATIVE ACTIONS

18–1001.   Right to Bring Action 268
18–1002.   Proper Plaintiff 268
18–1003.   Complaint 268
18–1004.   Expenses 268

SUBCHAPTER XI.   MISCELLANEOUS

18–1101.   Construction and Application of Chapter and Limited Liability Company
            Agreement 268
18–1102.   Short Title 269
18–1103.   Severability*
18–1104.   Cases Not Provided for in This Chapter 269
18–1105.   Fees*
18–1106.   Reserved Power of State of Delaware to Alter or Repeal Chapter 269
18–1107.   Taxation of Limited Liability Companies 269
18–1108.   Cancellation of Certificate of Formation for Failure to Pay Taxes*
18–1109.   Revival of Domestic Limited Liability Company*

SUBCHAPTER I. GENERAL PROVISIONS

§ 18–101.   Definitions

As used in this chapter unless the context otherwise requires:

(1) "Bankruptcy" means an event that causes a person to cease to be a member as provided in § 18–304 of this title.

(2) "Certificate of formation" means the certificate referred to in § 18–201 of this title, and the certificate as amended.

(3) "Contribution" means any cash, property, services rendered or a promissory note or other obligation to contribute cash or property or to perform services, which a person contributes to a limited liability company in his capacity as a member.

(4) "Foreign limited liability company" means a limited liability company formed under the laws of any state or under the laws of any foreign country or other foreign jurisdiction and denominated as such under the laws of such state or foreign country or other foreign jurisdiction.

(5) "Knowledge" means a person's actual knowledge of a fact, rather than the person's constructive knowledge of the fact.

(6) "Limited liability company" and "domestic limited liability company" means a limited liability company formed under the laws of the State of Delaware and having 1 or more members.

---

*   Omitted.

225

(7) "Limited liability company agreement" means any agreement (whether referred to as a limited liability company agreement, an operating agreement, or otherwise), written, oral or implied, of the member or members as to the affairs of a limited liability company and the conduct of its business. A member or manager of a limited liability company or an assignee of a limited liability company interest is bound by the limited liability company agreement whether or not the member or manager or assignee executes the limited liability company agreement. A limited liability company is not required to execute its limited liability company agreement. A limited liability company is bound by its limited liability company agreement whether or not the limited liability company executes the limited liability company agreement. A limited liability company agreement of a limited liability company having only one member shall not be unenforceable by reason of there being only one person who is a party to the limited liability company agreement. A limited liability company agreement is not subject to any statute of frauds. . . . A limited liability company agreement may provide rights to any person, including a person who is not a party to the limited liability company agreement, to the extent set forth therein. A written limited liability company agreement or another written agreement or writing:

　　a.　　May provide that a person shall be admitted as a member of a limited liability company, or shall become an assignee of a limited liability company interest or other rights or powers of a member to the extent assigned:

　　　　1.　　If such person (or a representative authorized by such person orally, in writing or by other action such as payment for a limited liability company interest) executes the limited liability company agreement or any other writing evidencing the intent of such person to become a member or assignee; or

　　　　2.　　Without such execution, if such person (or a representative authorized by such person orally, in writing or by other action such as payment for a limited liability company interest) complies with the conditions for becoming a member or assignee as set forth in the limited liability company agreement or any other writing; and

　　b.　　Shall not be unenforceable by reason of its not having been signed by a person being admitted as a member or becoming an assignee as provided in subparagraph a. of this paragraph, or by reason of its having been signed by a representative as provided in this chapter.

(8) "Limited liability company interest" means a member's share of the profits and losses of a limited liability company and a member's right to receive distributions of the limited liability company's assets.

(9) "Liquidating trustee" means a person carrying out the winding up of a limited liability company.

(10) "Manager" means a person who is named as a manager of a limited liability company in, or designated as a manager of a limited liability company pursuant to, a limited liability company agreement or similar instrument under which the limited liability company is formed.

(11) "Member" means a person who is admitted to a limited liability company as a member as provided in § 18–301 of this title or, in the case of a foreign limited liability company, in accordance with the laws of the state or foreign country or other foreign jurisdiction under which the foreign limited liability company is formed.

(12) "Person" means a natural person, partnership (whether general or limited), limited liability company, trust (including a common law trust, business trust, statutory trust, voting trust or any other form of trust), estate, association (including any group, organization, co-tenancy, plan, board, council or committee), corporation, government (including a country, state, county or any other governmental subdivision, agency or instrumentality), custodian, nominee or any other individual or entity (or series thereof) in its own or any representative capacity, in each case, whether domestic or foreign.

(13) "Personal representative" means, as to a natural person, the executor, administrator, guardian, conservator or other legal representative thereof and, as to a person other than a natural person, the legal representative or successor thereof.

(14) "Protected series" means a designated series of members, limited liability company interests or assets that is established in accordance with § 18–215(b) of this title.

(15) "Registered series" means a designated series of members, managers, limited liability company interests or assets that is formed in accordance with § 18–218 of this title.

(16) "Series" means a designated series of members, limited liability company interests or assets that is a protected series or a registered series, or that is neither a protected series nor a registered series.

(17) "State" means the District of Columbia or the Commonwealth of Puerto Rico or any state, territory, possession or other jurisdiction of the United States other than the State of Delaware.

§ 18–102. Name Set Forth in Certificate

The name of each limited liability company as set forth in its certificate of formation:

(1) Shall contain the words "Limited Liability Company" or the abbreviation "L.L.C." or the designation LLC;

(2) May contain the name of a member or manager;

(3) Must be such as to distinguish it upon the records in the office of the Secretary of State from the name on such records of any corporation, partnership, limited partnership, statutory trust or limited liability company or registered series reserved, registered, formed or organized under the laws of the State of Delaware or qualified to do business or registered as a foreign corporation, foreign limited partnership, foreign statutory trust, foreign partnership or foreign limited liability company in the State of Delaware; provided however, that a limited liability company may register under any name which is not such as to distinguish it upon the records in the office of the Secretary of State from the name on such records of any domestic or foreign corporation, partnership, limited partnership, statutory trust, registered series or foreign limited liability company reserved, registered, formed or organized under the laws of the State of Delaware with the written consent of the other corporation, partnership, limited partnership, statutory trust, registered series or foreign limited liability company, which written consent shall be filed with the Secretary of State; . . . and

(4) May contain the following words: "Company," "Association," "Club," "Foundation," "Fund," "Institute," "Society," "Union," "Syndicate," "Limited," "Public Benefit" or "Trust" (or abbreviations of like import). . . .

§ 18–104. Registered Office; Registered Agent

(a) Each limited liability company shall have and maintain in the State of Delaware:

(1) A registered office, which may but need not be a place of its business in the State of Delaware; and

(2) A registered agent for service of process on the limited liability company, having a business office identical with such registered office, which agent may be any of

    a.   the limited liability company itself,

    b.   an individual resident in the State of Delaware,

    c.   a domestic limited liability company (other than the limited liability company itself), a domestic corporation, a domestic partnership (whether general (including a limited liability partnership) or limited (including a limited liability limited partnership)), or a domestic statutory trust, or

    d.   a foreign corporation, a foreign partnership (whether general (including a limited liability partnership) or limited (including a limited liability limited partnership)), a foreign limited liability company, or a foreign statutory trust. . . .

§ 18–105. Service of Process on Domestic Limited Liability Companies

(a) Service of legal process upon any domestic limited liability company or any protected series or registered series thereof shall be made by delivering a copy personally to any manager of the limited liability company in the State of Delaware or the registered agent of the limited liability company in the State of Delaware, or by leaving it at the dwelling house or usual place of abode in the State of Delaware of any such manager or registered agent (if the registered agent be an individual), or at the registered office or other place of business of the limited liability company in the State of Delaware. If service of legal process is made upon the registered agent of the limited liability company in the State of Delaware on behalf of any such protected series or registered series, such process shall include the name of the limited liability company and the name of such protected series or registered series. If the registered agent be a corporation, service of process upon it as such may be made by serving, in the State of Delaware, a copy thereof on the president, vice-president, secretary, assistant secretary or any director of the corporate registered agent. Service by copy left at the dwelling house or usual place of abode of a manager or registered agent, or at the registered office or other place of business of the limited liability company in the State of Delaware, to be effective, must be delivered thereat at least 6 days before the return date of the process, and in the presence of an adult person, and the officer serving the process shall distinctly state the manner of service in his return thereto. Process returnable forthwith must be delivered personally to the manager or registered agent.

(b) In case the officer whose duty it is to serve legal process cannot by due diligence serve the process in any manner provided for by subsection (a) of this section, it shall be lawful to serve the process against the limited liability company or any protected series or registered series thereof upon the Secretary of State, and such service shall be as effectual for all intents and purposes as if made in any of the ways provided for in subsection (a) of this section. If service of legal process is made upon the Secretary of State on behalf of any such protected series or registered series, such process shall include the name of the limited liability company and the name of such protected series or registered series. Process may be served upon the Secretary of State under this subsection by means of electronic transmission but only as prescribed by the Secretary of State. The Secretary of State is authorized to issue such rules and regulations with respect to such service as the Secretary of State deems necessary or appropriate. In the event that service is effected through the Secretary of State in accordance with this subsection, the Secretary of State shall forthwith notify the limited liability company by letter, directed to the limited liability company at its address as it appears on the records relating to such limited liability company on file with the Secretary of State or, if no such address appears, at its last registered office. Such letter shall be sent by a mail or courier service that includes a record of mailing or deposit with the courier and a record of delivery evidenced by the signature of the recipient. Such letter shall enclose a copy of the process and any other papers served on the Secretary of State pursuant to this subsection. It shall be the duty of the plaintiff in the event of such service to serve process and any other papers in duplicate, to notify the Secretary of State that service is being effected pursuant to this subsection, and to pay the Secretary of State the sum of $50 for the use of the State of Delaware, which sum shall be taxed as part of the costs in the proceeding if the plaintiff shall prevail therein. The Secretary of State shall maintain an alphabetical record of any such service setting forth the name of the plaintiff and defendant, the title, docket number and nature of the proceeding in which process has been served upon the Secretary, the fact that service has been effected pursuant to this subsection, the return date thereof, and the day and hour when the service was made. The Secretary of State shall not be required to retain such information for a period longer than 5 years from the Secretary's receipt of the service of process.

§ 18–106.   Nature of Business Permitted; Powers

(a) A limited liability company may carry on any lawful business, purpose or activity, whether or not for profit, with the exception of the business of banking as defined in § 126 of Title 8.

(b) A limited liability company shall possess and may exercise all the powers and privileges granted by this chapter or by any other law or by its limited liability company agreement, together with any powers incidental thereto, including such powers and privileges as are necessary or convenient to the conduct, promotion or attainment of the business, purposes or activities of the limited liability company.

(c) Notwithstanding any provision of this chapter to the contrary, without limiting the general powers enumerated in subsection (b) above, a limited liability company shall, subject to such standards and restrictions, if any, as are set forth in its limited liability company agreement, have the power and authority to make contracts of guaranty and suretyship, and enter into interest rate, basis, currency, hedge or other swap agreements, or cap, floor, put, call, option, exchange or collar agreements, derivative agreements or other agreements similar to any of the foregoing.

(d) Unless otherwise provided in a limited liability company agreement, a limited liability company has the power and authority to grant, hold or exercise a power of attorney, including an irrevocable power of attorney.

§ 18–107. Business Transactions of Member or Manager With the Limited Liability Company

Except as provided in a limited liability company agreement, a member or manager may lend money to, borrow money from, act as a surety, guarantor or endorser for, guarantee or assume 1 or more obligations of, provide collateral for, and transact other business with, a limited liability company and, subject to other applicable law, has the same rights and obligations with respect to any such matter as a person who is not a member or manager.

§ 18–108. Indemnification

Subject to such standards and restrictions, if any, as are set forth in its limited liability company agreement, a limited liability company may, and shall have the power to, indemnify and hold harmless any member or manager or other person from and against any and all claims and demands whatsoever.

§ 18–109. Service of Process on Managers and Liquidating Trustees

(a) A manager or a liquidating trustee of a limited liability company may be served with process in the manner prescribed in this section in all civil actions or proceedings brought in the State of Delaware involving or relating to the business of the limited liability company or a violation by the manager or the liquidating trustee of a duty to the limited liability company, or any member of the limited liability company, whether or not the manager or the liquidating trustee is a manager or a liquidating trustee at the time suit is commenced. A manager's or a liquidating trustee's serving as such constitutes such person's consent to the appointment of the registered agent of the limited liability company (or, if there is none, the Secretary of State) as such person's agent upon whom service of process may be made as provided in this section. Such service as a manager or a liquidating trustee shall signify the consent of such manager or liquidating trustee that any process when so served shall be of the same legal force and validity as if served upon such manager or liquidating trustee within the State of Delaware and such appointment of the registered agent (or, if there is none, the Secretary of State) shall be irrevocable. As used in this subsection (a) and in subsection (b), (c), and (d) of this § 18–109, the term "manager" refers (i) to a person who is a manager as defined in § 18–101(10) of this chapter and (ii) to a person, whether or not a member of a limited liability company, who, although not a manager as defined in § 18–101(10) of this chapter, participates materially in the management of the limited liability company, provided, however, that the power to elect or otherwise select or to participate in the election or selection of a person to be a manager as defined in § 18–101(10) of this chapter shall not, by itself, constitute participation in the management of the limited liability company.

(b) Service of process shall be effected by serving the registered agent (or, if there is none, the Secretary of State) with 1 copy of such process in the manner provided by law for service of writs of summons. In the event service is made under this subsection upon the Secretary of State, the plaintiff shall pay to the Secretary of State the sum of $50 for the use of the State of Delaware, which sum shall be taxed as part of the costs of the proceeding if the plaintiff shall prevail therein. In addition, the Prothonotary or the Register in Chancery of the court in which the civil action or proceeding is pending shall, within 7 days of such service, deposit in the United States mails, by registered mail, postage prepaid, true and attested copies of the process, together with a statement that service is being made pursuant to this section, addressed to such manager or liquidating trustee at the registered office of the limited liability company and at his address last known to the party desiring to make such service.

(c) In any action in which any such manager or liquidating trustee has been served with process as hereinabove provided, the time in which a defendant shall be required to appear and file a responsive pleading shall be computed from the date of mailing by the Prothonotary or the Register in Chancery as provided in subsection (b) of this section; however, the court in which such action has been commenced may order such continuance or continuances as may be necessary to afford such manager or liquidating trustee reasonable opportunity to defend the action.

(d) In a written limited liability company agreement or other writing, a manager or member may consent to be subject to the nonexclusive jurisdiction of the courts of, or arbitration in, a specified jurisdiction, or the exclusive jurisdiction of the courts of the State of Delaware, or the exclusivity of arbitration in a specified jurisdiction or the State of Delaware, and to be served with legal process in the manner prescribed in such limited liability company agreement or other writing. Except by agreeing to arbitrate any arbitrable matter in a specified jurisdiction or in the State of Delaware, a member who is not a manager may not waive its right to maintain a legal action or proceeding in the courts of the State of Delaware with respect to matters relating to the organization or internal affairs of a limited liability company.

(e) Nothing herein contained limits or affects the right to serve process in any other manner now or hereafter provided by law. This section is an extension of and not a limitation upon the right otherwise existing of service of legal process upon nonresidents.

(f) The Court of Chancery and the Superior Court may make all necessary rules respecting the form of process, the manner of issuance and return thereof and such other rules which may be necessary to implement this section and are not inconsistent with this section.

§ 18–110.　　Contested Matters Relating to Managers; Contested Votes

(a) Upon application of any member or manager, the Court of Chancery may hear and determine the validity of any admission, election, appointment, removal or resignation of a manager of a limited liability company, and the right of any person to become or continue to be a manager of a limited liability company, and, in case the right to serve as a manager is claimed by more than 1 person, may determine the person or persons entitled to serve as managers; and to that end make such order or decree in any such case as may be just and proper, with power to enforce the production of any books, papers and records of the limited liability company relating to the issue. In any such application the limited liability company shall be named as a party and service of copies of the application upon the registered agent of the limited liability company shall be deemed to be service upon the limited liability company and upon the person or persons whose right to serve as a manager is contested and upon the person or persons, if any, claiming to be a manager or claiming the right to be a manager; and the registered agent shall forward immediately a copy of the application to the limited liability company and to the person or persons whose right to serve as a manager is contested and to the person or persons, if any, claiming to be a manager or the right to be a manager, in a postpaid, sealed, registered letter addressed to such limited liability company and such person or persons at their post-office addresses last known to the registered agent or furnished to the registered agent by the applicant member or manager. The Court may make such order respecting further or other notice of such application as it deems proper under [the] circumstances.

(b) Upon application of any member or manager, the Court of Chancery may hear and determine the result of any vote of members or managers upon matters as to which the members or managers of the limited liability company, or any class or group of members or managers, have the right to vote pursuant to the limited liability company agreement or other agreement or this chapter (other than the admission, election, appointment, removal or resignation of managers). In any such application, the limited liability company shall be named as a party and service of the application upon the registered agent of the limited liability company shall be deemed to be service upon the limited liability company, and no other party need be joined in order for the Court to adjudicate the result of the vote. The Court may make such order respecting further or other notice of such application as it deems proper under [the] circumstances.

(c) As used in this section, the term "manager" refers (i) to a person who is a manager as defined in § 18–101(10) of this Title, and (ii) to a person, whether or not a member of a limited liability company, who although not a manager as defined in 18–101(10) of this Title, participates materially in the management of the limited liability company; provided however, that the power to elect or otherwise select or to participate in the election or selection of a person to be a manager as defined in 18–101(10) of this Title shall not, by itself, constitute participation in the management of the limited liability company.

(d) Nothing herein contained limits or affects the right to serve process in any other manner now or hereafter provided by law. This section is an extension of and not a limitation upon the right otherwise existing of service of legal process upon nonresidents.

§ 18–111.   Interpretation and Enforcement of Limited Liability Company Agreement

Any action to interpret, apply or enforce the provisions of a limited liability company agreement, or the duties, obligations or liabilities of a limited liability company to the members or managers of the limited liability company, or the duties, obligations or liabilities among members or managers and of members or managers to the limited liability company, or the rights or powers of, or restrictions on, the limited liability company, members or managers, or any provision of this chapter, or any other instrument, document, agreement or certificate contemplated by any provision of this chapter, may be brought in the Court of Chancery. As used in this section, the term "manager" refers (i) to a person who is a manager as defined in § 18–101(10) of this Title, and (ii) to a person, whether or not a member of a limited liability company, who, although not a manager as defined in § 18–101(10) of this Title, participates materially in the management of the limited liability company; provided however, that the power to elect or otherwise select or to participate in the election or selection of a person to be a manager as defined in § 18–101(10) of this Title shall not, by itself, constitute participation in the management of the limited liability company.

§ 18–112.   Judicial Cancellation of Certificate of Formation; Proceedings

(a) Upon motion by the Attorney General, the Court of Chancery shall have jurisdiction to cancel the certificate of any domestic limited liability company for abuse or misuse of its limited liability company powers, privileges or existence. The Attorney General shall proceed for this purpose in the Court of Chancery.

(b) The Court of Chancery shall have power, by appointment of trustees, receivers, or otherwise, to administer and wind up the affairs of any domestic limited liability company whose certificate of formation shall be canceled by the Court of Chancery under this section, and to make such orders and decrees with respect thereto as shall be just and equitable respecting its affairs and assets and the rights of its members and creditors.

SUBCHAPTER II. FORMATION; CERTIFICATE OF FORMATION

§ 18–201.   Certificate of Formation

(a) In order to form a limited liability company, 1 or more authorized persons must execute a certificate of formation. The certificate of formation shall be filed in the office of the Secretary of State and set forth:

(1) The name of the limited liability company;

(2) The address of the registered office and the name and address of the registered agent for service of process required to be maintained by § 18–104 of this title; and

(3) Any other matters the members determine to include therein.

(b) A limited liability company is formed at the time of the filing of the initial certificate of formation in the office of the Secretary of State or at any later date or time specified in the certificate of formation if, in either case, there has been substantial compliance with the requirements of this section. A limited liability company formed under this chapter shall be a separate legal entity, the existence of which as a separate legal entity shall continue until cancellation of the limited liability company's certificate of formation.

(c) The filing of the certificate of formation in the office of the Secretary of State shall make it unnecessary to file any other documents under Chapter 31 of this title.

(d) A limited liability company agreement shall be entered into or otherwise existing either before, after or at the time of the filing of a certificate of formation and, whether entered into or otherwise existing before, after or at the time of such filing, may be made effective as of the effective time of such filing or at such other time or date as provided in or reflected by the limited liability company agreement.

§ 18–202.   Amendment to Certificate of Formation

(a) A certificate of formation is amended by filing a certificate of amendment thereto in the office of the Secretary of State. The certificate of amendment shall set forth:

(1) The name of the limited liability company; and

(2) The amendment to the certificate of formation.

(b) A manager or, if there is no manager, then any member who becomes aware that any statement in a certificate of formation was false when made, or that any matter described has changed making the certificate of formation false in any material respect, shall promptly amend the certificate of formation.

(c) A certificate of formation may be amended at any time for any other proper purpose.

(d) Unless otherwise provided in this chapter or unless a later effective date or time (which shall be a date or time certain) is provided for in the certificate of amendment, a certificate of amendment shall be effective at the time of its filing with the Secretary of State.

§ 18–203.   Cancellation of Certificate

(a) A certificate of formation shall be cancelled upon the dissolution and the completion of winding up of a limited liability company, or as provided in § 18–104(d), § 18–104(i)(4), § 18–112 or § 18–1108 [cancellation of certificate of formation for failure to pay taxes] of this chapter, or upon the filing of a certificate of merger or consolidation or a certificate of ownership and merger if the limited liability company is not the surviving or resulting entity in a merger or consolidation, or upon the future effective date or time of a certificate of merger or consolidation or a certificate of ownership and merger if the limited liability company is not the surviving or resulting entity in a merger or consolidation, or upon the filing of a certificate of transfer or upon the future effective date or time of a certificate of transfer, or upon the filing of a certificate of conversion to non-Delaware entity or upon the filing of a certificate of division if the limited liability company is a dividing company that is not a surviving company or upon the future effective date or time of a certificate of division if the limited liability company is a dividing company that is not a surviving company. A certificate of cancellation shall be filed in the office of the Secretary of State to accomplish the cancellation of a certificate of formation upon the dissolution and the completion of winding up of a limited liability company and shall set forth:

(1) The name of the limited liability company;

(2) The date of filing of its certificate of formation;

(3) If the limited liability company has formed one or more registered series whose certificate of registered series has not been canceled prior to the filing of the certificate of cancellation, the name of each such registered series;

(4) The future effective date or time (which shall be a date or time certain) of cancellation if it is not to be effective upon the filing of the certificate; and

(5) Any other information the person filing the certificate of cancellation determines. . . .

(c) The Secretary of State shall not issue a certificate of good standing with respect to a limited liability company (or any registered series thereof) if its certificate of formation is cancelled.

§ 18–204.   Execution

(a) Each certificate required by this subchapter to be filed in the office of the Secretary of State shall be executed by 1 or more authorized persons or, in the case of a certificate of conversion to limited liability company or certificate of limited liability company domestication, by any person authorized to execute such certificate on behalf of the other entity or non-United States entity, respectively, except that a certificate of merger or consolidation filed by a surviving or resulting other business entity shall be executed by any person authorized to execute such certificate on behalf of such other business entity.

(b) Unless otherwise provided in a limited liability company agreement, any person may sign any certificate or amendment thereof or enter into a limited liability company agreement or amendment thereof by an agent, including an attorney-in-fact. An authorization, including a power of attorney, to sign any certificate or amendment thereof or to enter into a limited liability company agreement or amendment thereof need not be in writing, need not be sworn to, verified or acknowledged, and need not be filed in the office of the Secretary of State, but if in writing, must be retained by the limited liability company.

(c) For all purposes of the laws of the State of Delaware, unless otherwise provided in a limited liability company agreement, a power of attorney or proxy with respect to a limited liability company granted to any person shall be irrevocable if it states that it is irrevocable and it is coupled with an interest sufficient in law to support an irrevocable power. Such irrevocable power of attorney, unless otherwise provided therein, shall not be affected by subsequent death, disability, incapacity, dissolution, termination of existence or bankruptcy of, or any other event concerning, the principal. A power of attorney with respect to matters relating to the organization, internal affairs or termination of a limited liability company or granted by a person as a member or an assignee of a limited liability company interest or by a person seeking to become a member or an assignee of a limited liability company interest and, in either case, granted to the limited liability company, a manager or member thereof, or any of their respective officers, directors, managers, members, partners, trustees, employees or agents shall be deemed coupled with an interest sufficient in law to support an irrevocable power or proxy. The provisions of this subsection shall not be construed to limit the enforceability of a power of attorney or proxy that is part of a limited liability company agreement.

(d) The execution of a certificate by a person who is authorized by this Chapter to execute such certificate constitutes an oath or affirmation, under the penalties of perjury in the third degree, that, to the best of such person's knowledge and belief, the facts stated therein are true.

§ 18–205.   Execution, Amendment or Cancellation by Judicial Order

(a) If a person required to execute a certificate required by this subchapter fails or refuses to do so, any other person who is adversely affected by the failure or refusal may petition the Court of Chancery to direct the execution of the certificate. If the Court finds that the execution of the certificate is proper and that any person so designated has failed or refused to execute the certificate, it shall order the Secretary of State to record an appropriate certificate.

(b) If a person required to execute a limited liability company agreement or amendment thereof fails or refuses to do so, any other person who is adversely affected by the failure or refusal may petition the Court of Chancery to direct the execution of the limited liability company agreement or amendment thereof. If the Court finds that the limited liability company agreement or amendment thereof should be executed and that any person required to execute the limited liability company agreement or amendment thereof has failed or refused to do so, it shall enter an order granting appropriate relief.

§ 18–206.   Filing

(a) The signed copy of any certificate authorized to be filed under this chapter shall be delivered to the Secretary of State. A person who executes a certificate as an agent or fiduciary need not exhibit evidence of his authority as a prerequisite to filing. Any signature on any certificate authorized to be filed with the Secretary of State under any provision of this chapter may be a facsimile, a conformed signature or an electronically transmitted signature. Upon delivery of any certificate, the Secretary of State shall record the date and time of its delivery. . . .

§ 18–207.   Notice

The fact that a certificate of formation is on file in the office of the Secretary of State is notice that the entity formed in connection with the filing of the certificate of formation is a limited liability company formed under the laws of the State of Delaware and is notice of all other facts set forth therein which are required to be set forth in a certificate of formation by § 18–201(a)(1) and (2) or § 18–1202 of this title and which are permitted to be set forth in a certificate of formation by § 18–215(b) or § 18–218(b) of this title. The fact that a certificate of registered series is on file in the office of the Secretary of State is notice that the registered series named in such certificate of registered series has been formed pursuant to § 18–218 of this title and is notice of all other facts set forth therein which are required to be set forth in a certificate of registered series by § 18–218(d) of this title.

§ 18–209.   Merger and Consolidation

(a) As used in this section and in §§ 18–204, 18–217, 18–219, 18–220 and 18–221 of this title, "other business entity" means a corporation, a statutory trust, a business trust, an association, a real estate investment trust, a common-law trust, or any other unincorporated business or entity, including a partnership (whether general (including a limited liability partnership) or limited (including a limited liability partnership)), and a foreign limited liability company, but excluding a domestic limited liability company. As used in this section and in §§ 18–210 and 18–301 of this title, "plan of merger" means a writing approved by a domestic limited liability company, in the form of resolutions or otherwise, that states the terms and conditions of a merger under subsection (i) of this section.

(b) Pursuant to an agreement of merger or consolidation, 1 or more domestic limited liability companies may merge or consolidate with or into 1 or more domestic limited liability companies or 1 or more other business entities formed or organized under the laws of the State of Delaware or any other state or the United States or any foreign country or other foreign jurisdiction, or any combination thereof, with such domestic limited liability company or other business entity as the agreement shall provide being the surviving or resulting domestic limited liability company or other business entity. Unless otherwise provided in the limited liability company agreement, an agreement of merger or consolidation or a plan of merger shall be approved by each domestic limited liability company which is to merge or consolidate by members who own more than 50 percent of the then current percentage or other interest in the profits of the domestic limited liability company owned by all of the members. In connection with a merger or consolidation hereunder, rights or securities of, or interests in, a domestic limited liability company or other business entity which is a constituent party to the merger or consolidation may be exchanged for or converted into cash, property, rights or securities of, or interests in, the surviving or resulting domestic limited liability company or other business entity or, in addition to or in lieu thereof, may be exchanged for or converted into cash, property, rights or securities of, or interests in, a domestic limited liability company or other business entity which is not the surviving or resulting limited liability company or other business entity in the merger or consolidation, may remain outstanding or may be cancelled. Notwithstanding prior approval, an agreement of merger or consolidation or a plan of merger may be terminated or amended pursuant to a provision for such termination or amendment contained in the agreement of merger or consolidation or plan of merger. Unless otherwise provided in a limited liability company agreement, a limited liability company, whose original certificate of formation was filed with the Secretary of State and effective on or prior to July 15, 2015, shall continue to be governed by the second sentence of this subsection as in effect on July 15, 2015.

(c) Except in the case of a merger under subsection (i) of this section, if a domestic limited liability company is merging or consolidating under this section, the domestic limited liability company or other business entity surviving or resulting in or from the merger or consolidation shall file a certificate of merger or consolidation executed by one or more persons on behalf of the domestic limited liability company when it is the surviving or resulting entity in the office of the Secretary of State. The certificate of merger or consolidation shall state:

(1) The name and jurisdiction of formation or organization and type of entity of each of the domestic limited liability companies and other business entities which is to merge or consolidate;

(2) That an agreement of merger or consolidation has been approved and executed by each of the domestic limited liability companies and other business entities which is to merge or consolidate;

(3) The name of the surviving or resulting domestic limited liability company or other business entity;

(4) In the case of a merger in which a domestic limited liability company is the surviving entity, such amendments, if any, to the certificate of formation of the surviving domestic limited liability company to change its name, registered office or registered agent as are desired to be effected by the merger;

(5) The future effective date or time (which shall be a date or time certain) of the merger or consolidation if it is not to be effective upon the filing of the certificate of merger or consolidation;

(6) That the agreement of merger or consolidation is on file at a place of business of the surviving or resulting domestic limited liability company or other business entity, and shall state the address thereof;

(7) That a copy of the agreement of merger or consolidation will be furnished by the surviving or resulting domestic limited liability company or other business entity, on request and without cost, to any member of any domestic limited liability company or any person holding an interest in any other business entity which is to merge or consolidate; and

(8) If the surviving or resulting entity is not a domestic limited liability company, or a corporation, partnership (whether general (including a limited liability partnership) or limited (including a limited liability limited partnership)) or statutory trust organized under the laws of the State of Delaware, a statement that such surviving or resulting other business entity agrees that it may be served with process in the State of Delaware in any action, suit or proceeding for the enforcement of any obligation of any domestic limited liability company which is to merge or consolidate, irrevocably appointing the Secretary of State as its agent to accept service of process in any such action, suit or proceeding and specifying the address to which a copy of such process shall be mailed to it by the Secretary of State. Process may be served upon the Secretary of State under this subsection by means of electronic transmission but only as prescribed by the Secretary of State. The Secretary of State is authorized to issue such rules and regulations with respect to such service as the Secretary of State deems necessary or appropriate. In the event of service hereunder upon the Secretary of State, the procedures set forth in § 18–911(c) of this title shall be applicable, except that the plaintiff in any such action, suit or proceeding shall furnish the Secretary of State with the address specified in the certificate of merger or consolidation provided for in this section and any other address which the plaintiff may elect to furnish, together with copies of such process as required by the Secretary of State, and the Secretary of State shall notify such surviving or resulting other business entity at all such addresses furnished by the plaintiff in accordance with the procedures set forth in § 18–911(c) of this title.

(d) Unless a future effective date or time is provided in a certificate of merger or consolidation, or in the case of a merger under subsection (i) of this section a certificate of ownership and merger, in which event a merger or consolidation shall be effective at any such future effective date or time, a merger or consolidation shall be effective upon the filing in the office of the Secretary of State of a certificate of merger or consolidation or a certificate of ownership and merger.

(e) A certificate of merger or consolidation or a certificate of ownership and merger shall act as a certificate of cancellation for a domestic limited liability company which is not the surviving or resulting entity in the merger or consolidation. A certificate of merger that sets forth any amendment in accordance with Subsection (c)(4) of this Section shall be deemed to be an amendment to the certificate of formation of the limited liability company, and the limited liability company shall not be required to take any further action to amend its certificate of formation under § 18–202 of this Title with respect to such amendments set forth in the certificate of merger. Whenever this section requires the filing of a certificate of merger or consolidation, such requirement shall be deemed satisfied by the filing of an agreement of merger or consolidation containing the information required by this section to be set forth in the certificate of merger or consolidation.

(f) An agreement of merger or consolidation or a plan of merger approved in accordance with subsection (b) of this section may:

(1) Effect any amendment to the limited liability company agreement; or

(2) Effect the adoption of a new limited liability company agreement . . . for a limited liability company if it is the surviving or resulting limited liability company in the merger or consolidation.

Any amendment to a limited liability company agreement or adoption of a new limited liability company agreement made pursuant to the foregoing sentence shall be effective at the effective time or date of the merger or consolidation and shall be effective notwithstanding any provision of the limited liability company agreement relating to amendment or adoption of a new limited liability company agreement, other than a provision that by its terms applies to an amendment to the limited liability company agreement or the adoption of a new limited liability company agreement, in either case, in connection with a merger or consolidation. The provisions of this subsection shall not be construed to limit the accomplishment of a merger or of any of the matters referred to herein by any other means provided for in a limited liability company agreement or other agreement or as otherwise permitted by law, including that the limited liability company agreement of any constituent limited liability company to the merger or consolidation (including a limited liability company formed for the purpose of consummating a merger or consolidation) shall be the limited liability company agreement of the surviving or resulting limited liability company.

(g) When any merger or consolidation shall have become effective under this section, for all purposes of the laws of the State of Delaware, all of the rights, privileges and powers of each of the domestic limited liability companies and other business entities that have merged or consolidated, and all property, real, personal and mixed, and all debts due to any of said domestic limited liability companies and other business entities, as well as all other things and causes of action belonging to each of such domestic limited liability companies and other business entities, shall be vested in the surviving or resulting domestic limited liability company or other business entity, and shall thereafter be the property of the surviving or resulting domestic limited liability company or other business entity as they were of each of the domestic limited liability companies and other business entities that have merged or consolidated, and the title to any real property vested by deed or otherwise, under the laws of the State of Delaware, in any of such domestic limited liability companies and other business entities, shall not revert or be in any way impaired by reason of this chapter; but all rights of creditors and all liens upon any property of any of said domestic limited liability companies and other business entities shall be preserved unimpaired, and all debts, liabilities and duties of each of the said domestic limited liability companies and other business entities that have merged or consolidated shall thenceforth attach to the surviving or resulting domestic limited liability company or other business entity, and may be enforced against it to the same extent as if said debts, liabilities and duties had been incurred or contracted by it. Unless otherwise agreed, a merger or consolidation of a domestic limited liability company, including a domestic limited liability company which is not the surviving or resulting entity in the merger or consolidation, shall not require such domestic limited liability company to wind up its affairs under § 18–803 of this title or pay its liabilities and distribute its assets under § 18–804 of this title and the merger or consolidation shall not constitute a dissolution of such limited liability company.

(h) A limited liability company agreement may provide that a domestic limited liability company shall not have the power to merge or consolidate as set forth in this section.

(i) In any case in which (x) at least 90% of the outstanding shares of each class of the stock of a corporation or corporations (other than a corporation which has in its certificate of incorporation the provision required by § 251(g)(7)(i) of Title 8), of which class there are outstanding shares that, absent § 267(a) of Title 8, would be entitled to vote on such merger, is owned by a domestic limited liability company, (y) 1 or more of such corporations is a corporation of the State of Delaware, and (z) any corporation that is not a corporation of the State of Delaware is a corporation of any other state or the District of Columbia or another jurisdiction, the laws of which do not forbid such merger, the domestic limited liability company having such stock ownership may either merge the corporation or corporations into itself and assume all of its or their obligations, or merge itself, or itself and 1 or more of such corporations, into 1 of the other corporations, pursuant to a plan of merger. If a domestic limited liability company is causing a merger under this subsection, the domestic limited liability company shall file a certificate of ownership and merger executed by 1 or more authorized persons on behalf of the domestic limited liability company in the office of the Secretary of State. The certificate of ownership and merger shall certify that such merger was authorized in accordance with the domestic limited liability company's limited liability company agreement and this chapter, and if the domestic limited liability company shall not own all the outstanding stock of all the corporations that are parties to the merger, shall state the terms and conditions of the merger, including the securities, cash, property, or rights to be issued, paid, delivered or granted by the surviving domestic limited liability company or corporation upon surrender of each share of the corporation or corporations not owned by the domestic limited liability company, or the cancellation of some or all of such shares. If a corporation surviving a merger under this subsection is not a corporation organized under the laws of the State of Delaware, then the terms and conditions of the merger shall obligate such corporation to agree that it may be served with process in the State of Delaware in any proceeding for enforcement of any obligation of the domestic limited liability company or any obligation of any constituent corporation of the State of Delaware, as well as for enforcement of any obligation of the surviving corporation, including any suit or other proceeding to enforce the right of any stockholders as determined in appraisal proceedings pursuant to § 262 of Title 8, and to irrevocably appoint the Secretary of State as its agent to accept service of process in any such suit or other proceedings, and to specify the address to which a copy of such process shall be mailed by the Secretary of State. Process may be served upon the Secretary of State under this subsection by means of electronic transmission but only as prescribed by the Secretary of State. The Secretary of State is authorized to issue such rules and regulations with respect to such service as the Secretary of State deems necessary or appropriate. In the event of such service upon the Secretary of State in accordance with this subsection, the Secretary of State shall forthwith notify such surviving corporation thereof by letter, directed to such surviving corporation at its address so specified, unless such surviving corporation shall have designated in writing to the Secretary of State a different address for such purpose, in which case it shall be mailed to the last address so designated. Such letter shall be sent by a mail or courier service that includes a record of mailing or deposit with the courier and a record of delivery evidenced by the signature of the recipient. Such letter shall enclose a copy of the process and any other papers served on the Secretary of State pursuant to this subsection. It shall be the duty of the plaintiff in the event of such service to serve process and any other papers in duplicate, to notify the Secretary of State that service is being effected pursuant to this subsection and to pay the Secretary of State the sum of $50 for the use of the State of Delaware, which sum shall be taxed as part of the costs in the proceeding, if the plaintiff shall prevail therein. The Secretary of State shall maintain an alphabetical record of any such service setting forth the name of the plaintiff and the defendant, the title, docket number and nature of the proceeding in which process has been served, the fact that service has been effected pursuant to this subsection, the return date thereof, and the day and hour service was made. The Secretary of State shall not be required to retain such information longer than 5 years from receipt of the service of process.

§ 18–210. Contractual Appraisal Rights

A limited liability company agreement or an agreement of merger or consolidation or a plan of merger may provide that contractual appraisal rights with respect to a limited liability company shall be available for any class or group or series of members or limited liability company interests in connection with any amendment of a limited liability company agreement, any merger or consolidation in which the limited liability company is a constituent party to the merger or consolidation, any conversion of the limited liability company to another business form, any transfer to or domestication or continuance in any jurisdiction by the limited liability company, or the sale of all or substantially all of the limited liability company's assets. The Court of Chancery shall have jurisdiction to hear and determine any matter relating to any such appraisal rights.

§ 18–211. Certificate of Correction

(a) Whenever any certificate authorized to be filed with the office of the Secretary of State under any provision of this chapter has been so filed and is an inaccurate record of the action therein referred to, or was defectively or erroneously executed, such certificate may be corrected by filing with the office of the Secretary of State a certificate of correction of such certificate. The certificate of correction shall specify the inaccuracy or defect to be corrected, shall set forth the portion of the certificate in corrected form and shall be executed and filed as required by this chapter. The certificate of correction shall be effective as of the date the original certificate was filed, except as to those persons who are substantially and adversely affected by the correction, and as to those persons the certificate of correction shall be effective from the filing date. . . .

§ 18–212. Domestication of Non-United States Entities

(a) As used in this section and in § 18–204, "non-United States entity" means a foreign limited liability company (other than one formed under the laws of a state) or a corporation, a statutory trust, a business trust, an association, a real estate investment trust, a common-law trust or any other unincorporated business or entity, including a partnership (whether general (including a limited liability partnership) or limited (including a limited liability limited partnership)) formed, incorporated, created or that otherwise came into being under the laws of any foreign country or other foreign jurisdiction (other than any state).

(b) Any non-United States entity may become domesticated as a limited liability company in the State of Delaware by complying with subsection (g) of this section and filing in the office of the Secretary of State in accordance with § 18–206 of this title:

(1) A certificate of limited liability company domestication that has been executed in accordance with § 18–204 of this title; and

(2) A certificate of formation that complies with § 18–201 of this title and has been executed by 1 or more authorized persons in accordance with § 18–204 of this title. . . .

(c) The certificate of limited liability company domestication shall state:

(1) The date on which and jurisdiction where the non-United States entity was first formed, incorporated, created or otherwise came into being;

(2) The name of the non-United States entity immediately prior to the filing of the certificate of limited liability company domestication;

(3) The name of the limited liability company as set forth in the certificate of formation filed in accordance with subsection (b) of this section;

(4) The future effective date or time (which shall be a date or time certain) of the domestication as a limited liability company if it is not to be effective upon the filing of the certificate of limited liability company domestication and the certificate of formation;

(5) The jurisdiction that constituted the seat, siege social, or principal place of business or central administration of the non-United States entity, or any other equivalent thereto under applicable law, immediately prior to the filing of the certificate of limited liability company domestication; and

(6) That the domestication has been approved in the manner provided for by the document, instrument, agreement or other writing, as the case may be, governing the internal affairs of the non-United States entity and the conduct of its business or by applicable non-Delaware law, as appropriate.

(d) Upon the filing in the office of the Secretary of State of the certificate of limited liability company domestication and the certificate of formation or upon the future effective date or time of the certificate of limited liability company domestication and the certificate of formation, the non-United States entity shall be domesticated as a limited liability company in the State of Delaware and the limited liability company shall thereafter be subject to all of the provisions of this chapter, except that notwithstanding § 18–201 of this title, the existence of the limited liability company shall be deemed to have commenced on the date the non-United States entity commenced its existence in the jurisdiction in which the non-United States entity was first formed, incorporated, created or otherwise came into being.

(e) The domestication of any non-United States entity as a limited liability company in the State of Delaware shall not be deemed to affect any obligations or liabilities of the non-United States entity incurred prior to its domestication as a limited liability company in the State of Delaware, or the personal liability of any person therefor.

(f) The filing of a certificate of limited liability company domestication shall not affect the choice of law applicable to the non-United States entity, except that from the effective date or time of the domestication, the law of the State of Delaware, including the provisions of this chapter, shall apply to the non-United States entity to the same extent as if the non-United States entity had been formed as a limited liability company on that date.

(g) Prior to the filing of a certificate of limited liability company domestication with the Office of the Secretary of State, the domestication shall be approved in the manner provided for by the document, instrument, agreement or other writing, as the case may be, governing the internal affairs of the non-United States entity and the conduct of its business or by applicable non-Delaware law, as appropriate, and a limited liability company agreement shall be approved by the same authorization required to approve the domestication.

(h) When any domestication shall have become effective under this section, for all purposes of the laws of the State of Delaware, all of the rights, privileges and powers of the non-United States entity that has been domesticated, and all property, real, personal and mixed, and all debts due to such non-United States entity, as well as all other things and causes of action belonging to such non-United States entity, shall remain vested in the domestic limited liability company to which such non-United States entity has been domesticated (and also in the non-United States entity, if and for so long as the non-United States entity continues its existence in the foreign jurisdiction in which it was existing immediately prior to the domestication) and shall be the property of such domestic limited liability company (and also in the non-United States entity, if and for so long as the non-United States entity continues its existence in the foreign jurisdiction in which it was existing immediately prior to the domestication), and the title to any real property vested by deed or otherwise in such non-United States entity shall not revert or be in any way impaired by reason of this chapter; but all rights of creditors and all liens upon any property of such non-United States entity shall be preserved unimpaired, and all debts, liabilities and duties of the non-United States entity that has been domesticated shall remain attached to the domestic limited liability company to which such non-United States entity has been domesticated (and also to the non-United States entity, if and for so long as the non-United States entity continues its existence in the foreign jurisdiction in which it was existing immediately prior to the domestication), and may be enforced against it to the same extent as if said debts, liabilities and duties had originally been incurred or contracted by it in its capacity as a domestic limited liability company. The rights, privileges, powers and interests in property of the non-United States entity, as well as the debts, liabilities and duties of the non-United States entity, shall not be deemed, as a consequence of the domestication, to have been transferred to the domestic limited liability company to which such non-United States entity has domesticated for any purpose of the laws of the State of Delaware.

(i) When a non-United States entity has become domesticated as a limited liability company pursuant to this section, for all purposes of the laws of the State of Delaware, the limited liability company shall be deemed to be the same entity as the domesticating non-United States entity and the domestication shall constitute a continuation of the existence of the domesticating non-United States entity in the form of a domestic limited liability company. Unless otherwise agreed, for all purposes of the laws of the State of Delaware, the domesticating non-United States entity shall not be required to wind up its affairs or pay its liabilities and distribute its assets, and the domestication shall not be deemed to constitute a dissolution of such non-United States entity. If, following domestication, a non-United States entity that has become domesticated as a limited liability company continues its existence in the foreign country or other foreign jurisdiction in which it was existing immediately prior to domestication, the limited liability company and such non-United States entity shall, for all purposes of the laws of the State of Delaware, constitute a single entity formed, incorporated, created or otherwise having come into being, as applicable, and existing under the laws of the State of Delaware and the laws of such foreign country or other foreign jurisdiction.

(j) In connection with a domestication hereunder, rights or securities of, or interests in, the non-United States entity that is to be domesticated as a domestic limited liability company may be exchanged for or converted into cash, property, rights or securities of, or interests in, such domestic limited liability company or, in addition to or in lieu thereof, may be exchanged for or converted into cash, property, rights or securities of, or interests in, another domestic liability company or entity, may remain outstanding or may be cancelled.

§ 18–213. Transfer or Continuance of Domestic Limited Liability Companies

(a) Upon compliance with the provisions of this section, any limited liability company may transfer to or domesticate or continue in any jurisdiction, other than any state, and, in connection therewith, may elect to continue its existence as a limited liability company in the State of Delaware.

(b) If the limited liability company agreement specifies the manner of authorizing a transfer or domestication or continuance described in subsection (a) of this section, the transfer or domestication or continuance shall be authorized as specified in the limited liability company agreement. If the limited liability company agreement does not specify the manner of authorizing a transfer or domestication or continuance described in subsection (a) of this section and does not prohibit such a transfer or domestication or continuance, the transfer or domestication or continuance shall be authorized in the same manner as is specified in the limited liability company agreement for authorizing a merger or consolidation that involves the limited liability company as a constituent party to the merger or consolidation. If the limited liability company agreement does not specify the manner of authorizing a transfer or domestication or continuance described in subsection (a) of this section or a merger or consolidation that involves the limited liability company as a constituent party and does not prohibit such a transfer or domestication or continuance, the transfer or domestication or continuance shall be authorized by the approval by the members who own more than 50% of the then current percentage or other interest in the profits of the domestic limited liability company owned by all of the members. If a transfer or domestication or continuance described in subsection (a) of this section shall be authorized as provided in this subsection (b), a certificate of transfer if the limited liability company's existence as a limited liability company of the State of Delaware is to cease, or a certificate of transfer and domestic continuance if the limited liability company's existence as a limited liability company in the State of Delaware is to continue, executed in accordance with § 18–204 of this title, shall be filed in the Office of the Secretary of State in accordance with § 18–206 of this title. The certificate of transfer or the certificate of transfer and domestic continuance shall state:

(1) The name of the limited liability company and, if it has been changed, the name under which its certificate of formation was originally filed;

(2) The date of the filing of its original certificate of formation with the Secretary of State;

(3) The jurisdiction to which the limited liability company shall be transferred or in which it shall be domesticated or continued and the name of the entity or business form formed, incorporated, created or that otherwise comes into being as a consequence of the transfer of the limited liability company to, or its domestication or continuance in, such foreign jurisdiction;

(4) The future effective date or time (which shall be a date or time certain) of the transfer to or domestication or continuance in the jurisdiction specified in subsection (b)(3) of this section if it is not to be effective upon the filing of the certificate of transfer or the certificate of transfer and domestic continuance;

(5) That the transfer or domestication or continuance of the limited liability company has been approved in accordance with the provisions of this section;

(6) In the case of a certificate of transfer, (i) that the existence of the limited liability company as a limited liability company of the State of Delaware shall cease when the certificate of transfer becomes effective, and (ii) the agreement of the limited liability company that it may be served with process in the State of Delaware in any action, suit or proceeding for enforcement of any obligation of the limited liability company arising while it was a limited liability company of the State of Delaware, and that it irrevocably appoints the Secretary of State as its agent to accept service of process in any such action, suit or proceeding;

(7) The address (which may not be that of the limited liability company's registered agent without the written consent of the limited liability company's registered agent, such consent to be filed with the certificate of transfer) to which a copy of the process referred to in subsection (b)(6) of this section shall be mailed to it by the Secretary of State. Process may be served upon the Secretary of State under subsection (b)(6) of this section by means of electronic transmission but only as prescribed by the Secretary of State. The Secretary of State is authorized to issue such rules and regulations with respect to such service as the Secretary of State deems necessary or appropriate. In the event of service hereunder upon the Secretary of State, the procedures set forth in § 18–911(c) of this title shall be applicable, except that the plaintiff in any such action, suit or proceeding shall furnish the Secretary of State with the address specified in this subsection and any other address that the plaintiff may elect to furnish, together with copies of such process as required by the Secretary of State, and the Secretary of State shall notify the limited liability company that has transferred or domesticated or continued out of the State of Delaware at all such addresses furnished by the plaintiff in accordance with the procedures set forth in § 18–911(c) of this title; and

(8) In the case of a certificate of transfer and domestic continuance, that the limited liability company will continue to exist as a limited liability company of the State of Delaware after the certificate of transfer and domestic continuance becomes effective.

Unless otherwise provided in a limited liability company agreement, a limited liability company whose original certificate of formation was filed with the Secretary of State and effective on or prior to July 31, 2015, shall continue to be governed by the third sentence of this subsection as in effect on July 31, 2015.

(c) Upon the filing in the Office of the Secretary of State of the certificate of transfer or upon the future effective date or time of the certificate of transfer and payment to the Secretary of State of all fees prescribed in this chapter, the Secretary of State shall certify that the limited liability company has filed all documents and paid all fees required by this chapter, and thereupon the limited liability company shall cease to exist as a limited liability company of the State of Delaware. Such certificate of the Secretary of State shall be *prima facie* evidence of the transfer or domestication or continuance by such limited liability company out of the State of Delaware.

(d) The transfer or domestication or continuance of a limited liability company out of the State of Delaware in accordance with this section and the resulting cessation of its existence as a limited liability company of the State of Delaware pursuant to a certificate of transfer shall not be deemed to affect any obligations or liabilities of the limited liability company incurred prior to such transfer or domestication or continuance or the personal liability of any person incurred prior to such transfer or domestication or continuance, nor shall it be deemed to affect the choice of law applicable to the limited liability company with respect to matters arising prior to such transfer or domestication or continuance. Unless otherwise agreed, the transfer or domestication or continuance of a limited liability company out of the State of Delaware in accordance with this section shall not require such limited liability company to wind up its affairs under § 18–803 of this title or pay its liabilities and distribute its assets under § 18–804 of this title and shall not be deemed to constitute a dissolution of such limited liability company.

(e) If a limited liability company files a certificate of transfer and domestic continuance, after the time the certificate of transfer and domestic continuance becomes effective, the limited liability company shall continue to exist as a limited liability company of the State of Delaware, and the laws of the State of Delaware, including the provisions of this chapter, shall apply to the limited liability company, to the same extent as prior to such time. So long as a limited liability company continues to exist as a limited liability company of the State of Delaware following the filing of a certificate of transfer and domestic continuance, the continuing domestic limited liability company and the entity or business form formed, incorporated, created or that otherwise came into being as a consequence of the transfer of the limited liability company to, or its domestication or continuance in, a foreign country or other foreign jurisdiction shall, for all purposes of the laws of the State of Delaware, constitute a single entity formed, incorporated, created or otherwise having come into being, as applicable, and existing under the laws of the State of Delaware and the laws of such foreign country or other foreign jurisdiction.

(f) In connection with a transfer or domestication or continuance of a domestic limited liability company to or in another jurisdiction pursuant to subsection (a) of this section, rights or securities of, or interests in, such limited liability company may be exchanged for or converted into cash, property, rights or securities of, or interests in, the entity or business form in which the limited liability company will exist in such other jurisdiction as a consequence of the transfer or domestication or continuance or, in addition to or in lieu thereof, may be exchanged for or converted into cash, property, rights or securities of, or interests in, another entity or business form, may remain outstanding or may be cancelled.

(g) When a limited liability company has transferred or domesticated or continued out of the State of Delaware pursuant to this section, the transferred or domesticated or continued entity or business form shall, for all purposes of the laws of the State of Delaware, be deemed to be the same entity as the limited liability company and shall constitute a continuance of the existence of such limited liability company in the form of the transferred or domesticated or continued entity or business form. When any transfer or domestication or continuance of a limited liability company out of the State of Delaware shall have become effective under this section, for all purposes of the laws of the State of Delaware, all of the rights, privileges and powers of the limited liability company that has transferred or domesticated or continued, and all property, real, personal and mixed, and all debts due to such limited liability company, as well as all other things and causes of action belonging to such limited liability company, shall remain vested in the transferred or domesticated or continued entity or business form (and also in the limited liability company that has transferred, domesticated or continued, if and for so long as such limited liability company continues its existence as a domestic limited liability company) and shall be the property of such transferred or domesticated or continued entity or business form (and also of the limited liability company that has transferred, domesticated or continued, if and for so long as such limited liability company continues its existence as a domestic limited liability company), and the title to any real property vested by deed or otherwise in such limited liability company shall not revert or be in any way impaired by reason of this chapter; but all rights of creditors and all liens upon any property of such limited liability company shall be preserved unimpaired, and all debts, liabilities and duties of the limited liability company that has transferred or domesticated or continued shall remain attached to the transferred or domesticated or continued entity or business form (and also to the limited liability company that has transferred, domesticated or continued, if and for so long as such limited liability company continues its existence as a domestic limited liability company), and may be enforced against it to the same extent as if said debts, liabilities and duties had originally been incurred or contracted by it in its capacity as the transferred or domesticated or continued entity or business form. The rights, privileges, powers and interests in property of the limited liability company that has transferred or domesticated or continued, as well as the debts, liabilities and duties of such limited liability company, shall not be deemed, as a consequence of the transfer or domestication or continuation out of the State of Delaware, to have been transferred to the transferred or domesticated or continued entity or business form for any purpose of the laws of the State of Delaware.

(h) A limited liability company agreement may provide that a domestic limited liability company shall not have the power to transfer, domesticate or continue as set forth in this section.

§ 18–214.   Conversion of Certain Entities to a Limited Liability Company

(a) As used in this section and in § 18–204, the term "other entity" means a corporation, a statutory trust, a business trust, an association, a real estate investment trust, a common-law trust or any other unincorporated business or entity, including a partnership (whether general (including a limited liability partnership) or limited (including a limited liability limited partnership)) or a foreign limited liability company.

(b) Any other entity may convert to a domestic limited liability company by complying with subsection (h) of this section and filing in the office of the Secretary of State in accordance with § 18–206 of this title:

(1) A certificate of conversion to limited liability company that has been executed in accordance with § 18–204 of this title; and

(2) A certificate of formation that complies with § 18–201 of this title and has been executed by 1 or more authorized persons in accordance with § 18–204 of this title. . . .

(c) The certificate of conversion to limited liability company shall state:

(1) The date on which and jurisdiction where the other entity was first created, incorporated, formed or otherwise came into being and, if it has changed, its jurisdiction immediately prior to its conversion to a domestic limited liability company;

(2) The name and type of entity of the other entity immediately prior to the filing of the certificate of conversion to limited liability company;

(3) The name of the limited liability company as set forth in its certificate of formation filed in accordance with subsection (b) of this section; and

(4) The future effective date or time (which shall be a date or time certain) of the conversion to a limited liability company if it is not to be effective upon the filing of the certificate of conversion to limited liability company and the certificate of formation.

(d) Upon the filing in the office of the Secretary of State of the certificate of conversion to limited liability company and the certificate of formation or upon the future effective date or time of the certificate of conversion to limited liability company and the certificate of formation, the other entity shall be converted into a domestic limited liability company and the limited liability company shall thereafter be subject to all of the provisions of this chapter, except that notwithstanding § 18–201 of this title, the existence of the limited liability company shall be deemed to have commenced on the date the other entity commenced its existence in the jurisdiction in which the other entity was first created, formed, incorporated or otherwise came into being.

(e) The conversion of any other entity into a domestic limited liability company shall not be deemed to affect any obligations or liabilities of the other entity incurred prior to its conversion to a domestic limited liability company or the personal liability of any person incurred prior to such conversion.

(f) When any conversion shall have become effective under this section, for all purposes of the laws of the State of Delaware, all of the rights, privileges and powers of the other entity that has converted, and all property, real, personal and mixed, and all debts due to such other entity, as well as all other things and causes of action belonging to such other entity, shall remain vested in the domestic limited liability company to which such other entity has converted and shall be the property of such domestic limited liability company, and the title to any real property vested by deed or otherwise in such other entity shall not revert or be in any way impaired by reason of this chapter; but all rights of creditors and all liens upon any property of such other entity shall be preserved unimpaired, and all debts, liabilities and duties of the other entity that has converted shall remain attached to the domestic limited liability company to which such other entity has converted, and may be enforced against it to the same extent as if said debts, liabilities and duties had originally been incurred or contracted by it in its capacity as a domestic limited liability company. The rights, privileges, powers and interests in property of the other entity, as well as the debts, liabilities and duties of the other entity, shall not be deemed, as a consequence of the conversion, to have been transferred to the domestic limited liability company to which such other entity has converted for any purpose of the laws of the State of Delaware.

(g) Unless otherwise agreed, for all purposes of the laws of the State of Delaware, the converting other entity shall not be required to wind up its affairs or pay its liabilities and distribute its assets, and the conversion shall not be deemed to constitute a dissolution of such other entity. When an other entity has been converted to a limited liability company pursuant to this section, for all purposes of the laws of the State of Delaware, the limited liability company shall be deemed to be the same entity as the converting other entity and the conversion shall constitute a continuation of the existence of the converting other entity in the form of a domestic limited liability company.

(h) Prior to filing a certificate of conversion to limited liability company with the office of the Secretary of State, the conversion shall be approved in the manner provided for by the document, instrument, agreement or other writing, as the case may be, governing the internal affairs of the other entity and the conduct of its business or by applicable law, as appropriate and a limited liability company agreement shall be approved by the same authorization required to approve the conversion.

(i) In connection with a conversion hereunder, rights or securities of, or interests in, the other entity which is to be converted to a domestic limited liability company may be exchanged for or converted into cash, property, rights or securities or, or interests in, such domestic limited liability company or, in addition to or in lieu thereof, may be exchanged for or converted into cash, property, rights or securities or, or interests in, another domestic limited liability company or other entity, may remain outstanding or may be cancelled.

(j) The provisions of this section shall not be construed to limit the accomplishment of a change in the law governing, or the domicile of, an other entity to the State of Delaware by any other means provided for in a limited liability company agreement or other agreement or as otherwise permitted by law, including by the amendment of a limited liability company agreement or other agreement.

§ 18–215. Series of Members, Managers, Limited Liability Company Interests or Assets

(a) A limited liability company agreement may establish or provide for the establishment of 1 or more designated series of members, managers, limited liability company interests or assets. Any such series may have separate rights, powers or duties with respect to specified property or obligations of the limited liability company or profits and losses associated with specified property or obligations, and any such series may have a separate business purpose or investment objective. No provision of subsection (b) of this section or § 18–218 of this title shall be construed to limit the application of the principle of freedom of contract to a series that is not a protected series or a registered series. Other than pursuant to §§ 18–219, 18–220 and 18–221, a series may not merge, convert or consolidate pursuant to any section of this title or any other statute of this State.

(b) A series established in accordance with the following sentence is a protected series. Notwithstanding anything to the contrary set forth in this chapter or under other applicable law, in the event that a limited liability company agreement establishes or provides for the establishment of 1 or more series, and to the extent the records maintained for any such series account for the assets associated with such series separately from the other assets of the limited liability company, or any other series thereof, and if the limited liability company agreement so provides, and if notice of the limitation on liabilities of a series as referenced in this subsection is set forth in the certificate of formation of the limited liability company, then the debts, liabilities, obligations and expenses incurred, contracted for or otherwise existing with respect to such series shall be enforceable against the assets of such series only, and not against the assets of the limited liability company generally or any other series thereof, and, unless otherwise provided in the limited liability company agreement, none of the debts, liabilities, obligations and expenses incurred, contracted for or otherwise existing with respect to the limited liability company generally or any other series thereof shall be enforceable against the assets of such series. Neither the preceding sentence nor any provision pursuant thereto in a limited liability company agreement or certificate of formation shall (i) restrict a protected series or limited liability company on behalf of a protected series from agreeing in the limited liability company agreement or otherwise that any or all of the debts, liabilities, obligations and expenses incurred, contracted for or otherwise existing with respect to the limited liability company generally or any other series thereof shall be enforceable against the assets of such protected series or (ii) restrict a limited liability company from agreeing in the limited liability company agreement or otherwise that any or all of the debts, liabilities, obligations and expenses incurred, contracted for or otherwise existing with respect to a protected series shall be enforceable against the assets of the limited liability company generally. Assets associated with a protected series may be held directly or indirectly, including in the name of such series, in the name of the limited liability company, through a nominee or otherwise. Records maintained for a protected series that reasonably identify its assets, including by specific listing, category, type, quantity, computational or allocational formula or procedure (including a percentage or share of any asset or assets) or by any other method where the identity of such assets is objectively determinable, will be deemed to account for the assets associated with such series separately from the other assets of the limited liability company, or any other series thereof. Notice in a certificate of formation of the limitation on liabilities of a protected series as referenced in this subsection shall be sufficient for all purposes of this subsection whether or not the limited liability company has established any protected series when such notice is included in the certificate of formation, and there shall be no requirement that any specific protected series of the limited liability company be referenced in such notice. The fact that a certificate of formation that contains the foregoing notice of the limitation on liabilities of a protected series is on file in the office of the Secretary of State shall constitute notice of such limitation on liabilities of a protected series. As used in this chapter, a reference to assets of a protected series includes assets associated with such series, a reference to assets associated with a protected series includes assets of such series, a reference to members or managers of a protected series includes members or managers associated with such series, and a reference to members or managers associated with a protected series includes members or managers of such series. The following shall apply to a protected series:

(1) A protected series may carry on any lawful business, purpose or activity, whether or not for profit, with the exception of the business of banking as defined in § 126 of Title 8. Unless otherwise provided in a limited liability company agreement, a protected series shall have the power and capacity to, in its own name, contract, hold title to assets (including real, personal and intangible property), grant liens and security interests, and sue and be sued.

(2) Except as otherwise provided by this chapter, no member or manager of a protected series shall be obligated personally for any debt, obligation or liability of such series, whether arising in contract, tort or otherwise, solely by reason of being a member or acting as a manager of such series. Notwithstanding the preceding sentence, under a limited liability company agreement or under another agreement, a member or manager may agree to be obligated personally for any or all of the debts, obligations and liabilities of one or more protected series.

(3) A limited liability company agreement may provide for classes or groups of members or managers associated with a protected series having such relative rights, powers and duties as the limited liability company agreement may provide, and may make provision for the future creation in the manner provided in the limited liability company agreement of additional classes or groups of members or managers associated with such series having such relative rights, powers and duties as may from time to time be established, including rights, powers and duties senior to existing classes and groups of members or managers associated with such series. A limited liability company agreement may provide for the taking of an action, including the amendment of the limited liability company agreement, without the vote or approval of any member or manager or class or group of members or managers, including an action to create under the provisions of the limited liability company agreement a class or group of a protected series of limited liability company interests that was not previously outstanding. A limited liability company agreement may provide that any member or class or group of members associated with a protected series shall have no voting rights.

(4) A limited liability company agreement may grant to all or certain identified members or managers or a specified class or group of the members or managers associated with a protected series the right to vote separately or with all or any class or group of the members or managers associated with such series, on any matter. Voting by members or managers associated with a protected series may be on a per capita, number, financial interest, class, group or any other basis.

(5) Unless otherwise provided in a limited liability company agreement, the management of a protected series shall be vested in the members associated with such series in proportion to the then current percentage or other interest of members in the profits of such series owned by all of the members associated with such series, the decision of members owning more than 50 percent of the said percentage or other interest in the profits controlling; provided, however, that if a limited liability company agreement provides for the management of a protected series, in whole or in part, by a manager, the management of such series, to the extent so provided, shall be vested in the manager who shall be chosen in the manner provided in the limited liability company agreement. The manager of a protected series shall also hold the offices and have the responsibilities accorded to the manager as set forth in a limited liability company agreement. A protected series may have more than 1 manager. Subject to § 18–602 of this title, a manager shall cease to be a manager with respect to a protected series as provided in a limited liability company agreement. Except as otherwise provided in a limited liability company agreement, any event under this chapter or in a limited liability company agreement that causes a manager to cease to be a manager with respect to a protected series shall not, in itself, cause such manager to cease to be a manager of the limited liability company or with respect to any other series thereof.

(6) Notwithstanding § 18–606 of this title, but subject to subsections (b)(7) and (b)(10) of this section, and unless otherwise provided in a limited liability company agreement, at the time a member of a protected series becomes entitled to receive a distribution with respect to such series, the member has the status of, and is entitled to all remedies available to, a creditor of such series, with respect to the distribution. A limited liability company agreement may provide for the establishment of a record date with respect to allocations and distributions with respect to a protected series.

(7) Notwithstanding § 18–607(a) of this title, a limited liability company may make a distribution with respect to a protected series. A limited liability company shall not make a distribution with respect to a protected series to a member to the extent that at the time of the distribution, after giving effect to the distribution, all liabilities of such series, other than liabilities to members on account of their limited liability company interests with respect to such series and liabilities for which the recourse of creditors is limited to specified property of such series, exceed the fair value of the assets associated with such series, except that the fair value of property of such series that is subject to a liability for which the recourse of creditors is limited shall be included in the assets associated with such series only to the extent that the fair value of that property exceeds that liability. For purposes of the immediate preceding sentence, the term "distribution" shall not include amounts constituting reasonable compensation for present or past services or reasonable payments made in the ordinary course of business pursuant to a bona fide retirement plan or other benefits program. A member who receives a distribution in violation of this subsection, and who knew at the time of the distribution that the distribution violated this subsection, shall be liable to the protected series for the amount of the distribution. A member who receives a distribution in violation of this subsection, and who did not know at the time of the distribution that the distribution violated this subsection, shall not be liable for the amount of the distribution. Subject to § 18–607(c) of this title, which shall apply to any distribution made with respect to a protected series under this subsection, this subsection shall not affect any obligation or liability of a member under an agreement or other applicable law for the amount of a distribution.

(8) Unless otherwise provided in the limited liability company agreement, a member shall cease to be associated with a protected series and to have the power to exercise any rights or powers of a member with respect to such series upon the assignment of all of the member's limited liability company interest with respect to such series. Except as otherwise provided in a limited liability company agreement, any event under this chapter or a limited liability company agreement that causes a member to cease to be associated with a protected series shall not, in itself, cause such member to cease to be associated with any other series or terminate the continued membership of a member in

the limited liability company or cause the termination of the protected series, regardless of whether such member was the last remaining member associated with such series.

(9) Subject to § 18–801 of this title, except to the extent otherwise provided in the limited liability company agreement, a protected series may be terminated and its affairs wound up without causing the dissolution of the limited liability company. The termination of a protected series shall not affect the limitation on liabilities of such series provided by this subsection (b). A protected series is terminated and its affairs shall be wound up upon the dissolution of the limited liability company under § 18–801 of this title or otherwise upon the first to occur of the following:

   a. At the time specified in the limited liability company agreement;

   b. Upon the happening of events specified in the limited liability company agreement;

   c. Unless otherwise provided in the limited liability company agreement, upon the affirmative vote or written consent of the members associated with such series who own more than two-thirds of the then-current percentage or other interest in the profits of the series of the limited liability company owned by all of the members associated with such series; or

   d. The termination of such series under subsection (b)(11) of this section.

Unless otherwise provided in a limited liability company agreement, a limited liability company whose original certificate of formation was filed with the Secretary of State and effective on or prior to July 15, 2015, shall continue to be governed by paragraph (3) of this subsection as in effect on July 15, 2015 (except that "affirmative" and "written" shall be deleted from such paragraph (k)(30).

(10) Notwithstanding § 18–803(a) of this title, unless otherwise provided in the limited liability company agreement, a manager associated with a protected series who has not wrongfully terminated such series or, if none, the members associated with such series, in either case, by members who own more than 50 percent of the then current percentage or other interest in the profits of such series owned by all of the members associated with such series, may wind up the affairs of such series; but the Court of Chancery, upon cause shown, may wind up the affairs of a protected series upon application of any member or manager associated with such protected series, or the member's personal representative or assignee, and in connection therewith, may appoint a liquidating trustee. The persons winding up the affairs of a protected series may, in the name of the limited liability company and for and on behalf of the limited liability company and such series, take all actions with respect to such protected series as are permitted under § 18–803(b) of this title, which section shall apply to the winding up and distribution of assets of a series. The persons winding up the affairs of a protected series shall provide for the claims and obligations of such protected series as provided in § 18–804(b) of this title and distribute the assets of such series as provided in § 18–804 of this title, which section shall apply to the winding up and distribution of assets of a protected series. Actions taken in accordance with this subsection shall not affect the liability of members and shall not impose liability on a liquidating trustee. Unless otherwise provided in a limited liability company agreement, a limited liability company whose original certificate of formation was filed with the Secretary of State and effective on or prior to July 31, 2015, shall continue to be governed by the first sentence of this subsection as in effect on July 31, 2015.

(11) On application by or for a member or manager associated with a protected series, the Court of Chancery may decree termination of such series whenever it is not reasonably practicable to carry on the business of such series in conformity with a limited liability company agreement.

(12) For all purposes of the laws of the State of Delaware, a protected series is an association, regardless of the number of members or managers, if any, of such series.

(c) If a foreign limited liability company that is registering to do business in the State of Delaware in accordance with § 18–902 of this title is governed by a limited liability company agreement that establishes or provides for the establishment of designated series of members, managers, limited liability company interests or assets having separate rights, powers or duties with respect to specified property or obligations of the foreign limited liability company or profits and losses associated with specified property or obligations, that fact shall be so stated on the application for registration as a foreign limited liability company. In addition, the foreign limited liability company shall state on such application whether the debts, liabilities and obligations incurred, contracted for or otherwise existing with respect to a particular series, if any, shall be enforceable against the assets of such series only, and not against the assets of the foreign limited liability company generally or any other series thereof, and, whether any of the debts, liabilities, obligations and expenses incurred, contracted for or otherwise existing with respect to the foreign limited liability company generally or any other series thereof shall be enforceable against the assets of such series. Unless otherwise provided in a limited liability company agreement, a limited liability company whose original certificate of formation was filed with the Secretary of State and effective on or prior to July 15, 2015, shall continue to be governed by the third sentence of this subsection as in effect on July 15, 2015.

§ 18–216.   Approval of Conversion of a Limited Liability Company

(a) Upon compliance with this section, a domestic limited liability company may convert to a corporation, a statutory trust, a business trust, an association, a real estate investment trust, a common-law trust or any other unincorporated business or entity, including a partnership (whether general (including a limited liability partnership) or limited (including a limited liability limited partnership)) or a foreign limited liability company.

(b) If the limited liability company agreement specifies the manner of authorizing a conversion of the limited liability company, the conversion shall be authorized as specified in the limited liability company agreement. If the limited liability company agreement does not specify the manner of authorizing a conversion of the limited liability company and does not prohibit a conversion of the limited liability company, the conversion shall be authorized in the same manner as is specified in the limited liability company agreement for authorizing a merger or consolidation that involves the limited liability company as a constituent party to the merger or consolidation. If the limited liability company agreement does not specify the manner of authorizing a conversion of the limited liability company or a merger or consolidation that involves the limited liability company as a constituent party and does not prohibit a conversion of the limited liability company, the conversion shall be authorized by the approval by members who own more than 50 percent of the then current percentage or other interest in the profits of the domestic limited liability company owned by all of the members.

(c) Unless otherwise agreed, the conversion of a domestic limited liability company to another entity or business form pursuant to this section shall not require such limited liability company to wind up its affairs under § 18–803 of this title or pay its liabilities and distribute its assets under § 18–804 of this title, and the conversion shall not constitute a dissolution of such limited liability company. When a limited liability company has converted to another entity or business form pursuant to this section, for all purposes of the laws of the State of Delaware, the other entity or business form shall be deemed to be the same entity as the converting limited liability company and the conversion shall constitute a continuation of the existence of the limited liability company in the form of such other entity or business form.

(d) In connection with a conversion of a domestic limited liability company to another entity or business form pursuant to this section, rights or securities of or interests in the domestic limited liability company which is to be converted may be exchanged for or converted into cash, property, rights or securities of or interests in the entity or business form into which the domestic limited liability company is being converted or, in addition to or in lieu thereof, may be exchanged for or converted into cash, property, rights or securities of or interests in another entity or business form, may remain outstanding or may be cancelled.

(e) If a limited liability company shall convert in accordance with this section to another entity or business form organized, formed or created under the laws of a jurisdiction other than the State of Delaware, a certificate of conversion to non-Delaware entity executed in accordance with § 18–204 of this title, shall be filed in the office of the Secretary of State in accordance with § 18–206 of this title. The certificate of conversion to non-Delaware entity shall state:

(1) The name of the limited liability company and, if it has been changed, the name under which its certificate of formation was originally filed;

(2) The date of filing of its original certificate of formation with the Secretary of State;

(3) The jurisdiction in which the entity or business form, to which the limited liability company shall be converted, is organized, formed or created, and the name of such entity or business form;

(4) The future effective date or time (which shall be a date or time certain) of the conversion if it is not to be effective upon the filing of the certificate of conversion to non-Delaware entity;

(5) That the conversion has been approved in accordance with this section;

(6) The agreement of the limited liability company that it may be served with process in the State of Delaware in any action, suit or proceeding for enforcement of any obligation of the limited liability company arising while it was a limited liability company of the State of Delaware, and that it irrevocably appoints the Secretary of State as its agent to accept service of process in any such action, suit or proceeding;

(7) The address to which a copy of the process referred to in paragraph (6) of this subsection shall be mailed to it by the Secretary of State. Process may be served upon the Secretary of State under paragraph (6) of this subsection by means of electronic transmission but only as prescribed by the Secretary of State. The Secretary of State is authorized to issue such rules and regulations with respect to such service as the Secretary of State deems necessary or appropriate. In the event of service hereunder upon the Secretary of State, the procedures set forth in § 18–911(c) of this title shall be applicable, except that the plaintiff in any such action, suit or proceeding shall furnish the Secretary of State with the address specified in this subdivision and any other address that the plaintiff may elect to furnish, together with copies of such process as required by the Secretary of State, and the Secretary of State shall notify the limited liability company that has converted out of the State of Delaware at all such addresses furnished by the plaintiff in accordance with the procedures set forth in § 18–911(c) of this title.

(f) Upon the filing in the office of the Secretary of State of the certificate of conversion to non-Delaware entity or upon the future effective date or time of the certificate of conversion to [a] non-Delaware entity and payment to the Secretary of State of all fees prescribed in this chapter, the Secretary of State shall certify that the limited liability company has filed all documents and paid all fees required by this chapter, and thereupon the limited liability company shall cease to exist as a limited liability company of the State of Delaware. Such certificate of the Secretary of State shall be prima facie evidence of the conversion by such limited liability company out of the State of Delaware.

(g) The conversion of a limited liability company out of the State of Delaware in accordance with this section and the resulting cessation of its existence as a limited liability company of the State of Delaware pursuant to a certificate of conversion to non-Delaware entity shall not be deemed to affect any obligations or liabilities of the limited liability company incurred prior to such conversion or the personal liability of any person incurred prior to such conversion, nor shall it be deemed to affect the choice of law applicable to the limited liability company with respect to matters arising prior to such conversion.

(h) When any conversion shall have become effective under this Section for all purposes of the laws of the State of Delaware, all of the rights, privileges and powers of the limited liability company that has converted, and all property, real, personal and mixed, and all debts due to such limited liability company, as well as all other things and causes of action belonging to such limited liability company, shall remain vested in the other entity or business form to which such limited liability company has converted and shall be the property of such other entity or business form, and the title to any real property vested deed or otherwise in such limited liability company shall not revert or be in any way impaired by reason of this Chapter; but all rights of creditors and all liens upon any property of such limited liability company shall be preserved unimpaired, and all debts, liabilities and duties of the limited liability company that has converted shall remain attached to the other entity or business form to which such limited liability company has converted, and may be enforced against it to the same extent as if said debts, liabilities and duties had originally been incurred or contracted by it in its capacity as such other entity or business form. The rights, privileges, powers and interests in property of the limited liability company that has converted, as well as the debts, liabilities and duties of such limited liability company, shall not be deemed, as a consequence of the conversion, to have been transferred to the other entity or business form to which such limited liability company has converted for any purpose of the laws of the State of Delaware.

(i) A limited liability company agreement may provide that a domestic limited liability company shall not have the power to convert as set forth in this section.

§ 18–217.   Division of a Limited Liability Company

(a) As used in this section and §§ 18–203 and 18–1203:

(1) "Dividing company" means the domestic limited liability company that is effecting a division in the manner provided in this section.

(2) "Division" means the division of a dividing company into two or more domestic limited liability companies in accordance with this section.

(3) "Division company" means a surviving company, if any, and each resulting company.

(4) "Division contact" means, in connection with any division, a natural person who is a Delaware resident, any division company in such division or any other domestic limited liability company or other business entity as defined in § 18–209 of this title formed or organized under the laws of the State of Delaware, which division contact shall maintain a copy of the plan of division for a period of six (6) years from the effective date of the division and shall comply with subsection (g)(3) of this section.

(5) "Organizational documents" means the certificate of formation and limited liability company agreement of a domestic limited liability company.

(6) "Resulting company" means a domestic limited liability company formed as a consequence of a division.

(7) "Surviving company" means a dividing company that survives the division.

(b) Pursuant to a plan of division, any domestic limited liability company may, in the manner provided in this section, be divided into two or more domestic limited liability companies. The division of a domestic limited liability company in accordance with this section and, if applicable, the resulting cessation of the existence of the dividing company pursuant to a certificate of division shall not be deemed to affect the personal liability of any person incurred prior to such division with respect to matters arising prior to such division, nor shall it be deemed to affect the validity or enforceability of any obligations or liabilities of the dividing company incurred prior to such division; provided, that such obligations and liabilities shall be allocated to and vested in, and valid and enforceable obligations of, such division company or companies to which such obligations and liabilities have been allocated pursuant to the plan of division, as provided in subsection (*l*) of this section. Each resulting company in a division shall be formed in compliance with the requirements of this chapter and subsection (i) of this section.

(c) If the limited liability company agreement of the dividing company specifies the manner of adopting a plan of division, the plan of division shall be adopted as specified in the limited liability company agreement. If the limited liability company agreement of the dividing company does not specify the manner of adopting a plan of division and does not prohibit a division of the limited liability company, the plan of division shall be adopted in the same manner as is specified in the limited liability company agreement for authorizing a merger or consolidation that involves the limited liability company as a constituent party to the merger or consolidation. If the limited liability company agreement of the dividing company does not specify the manner of adopting a plan of division or authorizing a merger or consolidation that involves the limited liability company as a constituent party and does not prohibit a division of the limited liability company, the adoption of a plan of division shall be authorized by the approval by members who own more than 50 percent of the then current percentage or other interest in the profits of the dividing company owned by all of the members. Notwithstanding prior approval, a plan of division may be terminated or amended pursuant to a provision for such termination or amendment contained in the plan of division.

(d) Unless otherwise provided in a plan of division, the division of a domestic limited liability company pursuant to this section shall not require such limited liability company to wind up its affairs under § 18–803 of this title or pay its liabilities and distribute its assets under § 18–804 of this title, and the division shall not constitute a dissolution of such limited liability company.

(e) In connection with a division under this section, rights or securities of, or interests in, the dividing company may be exchanged for or converted into cash, property, rights or securities of, or interests in, the surviving company or any resulting company or, in addition to or in lieu thereof, may be exchanged for or converted into cash, property, rights or securities of, or interests in, a domestic limited liability company or any other business entity which is not a division company or may be canceled or remain outstanding (if the dividing company is a surviving company). . . .

§ 18–218. Registered Series of Members, Managers, Limited Liability Company Interests or Assets

(a) If a limited liability company agreement provides for the establishment or formation of 1 or more series, then a registered series may be formed by complying with this § 18–218. A limited liability company agreement does not need to use the term registered when referencing series or refer to this § 18–218, and a reference in a limited liability company agreement for a registered series, including a registered series resulting from the conversion of a protected series to a registered series, may continue to refer to § 18–215 of this title, which reference shall be deemed a reference to this § 18–218 with respect to such registered series. A registered series is formed by the filing of a certificate of registered series in the office of the Secretary of State.

(b) Notice of the limitation on liabilities of a registered series as referenced in § 18–218(c) shall be set forth in the certificate of formation of the limited liability company. Notice in a certificate of formation of the limitation on liabilities of a registered series as referenced in § 18–218(c) shall be sufficient for all purposes of this subsection whether or not the limited liability company has formed any registered series when such notice is included in the certificate of formation, and there shall be no requirement that (i) any specific registered series of the limited liability company be referenced in such notice, (ii) such notice use the term registered when referencing series or include a reference to this § 18–218, or (iii) the certificate of formation be amended if it includes a reference to § 18–215 of this title. Any reference to § 18–215 of this title in a certificate of formation of a limited liability company that has one or more registered series shall be deemed a reference to this § 18–218 with respect to such registered series. The fact that a certificate of formation that contains the foregoing notice of the limitation on liabilities of a series is on file in the office of the Secretary of State shall constitute notice of such limitation on liabilities of a registered series.

(c) Notwithstanding anything to the contrary set forth in this chapter or under other applicable law, to the extent the records maintained for a registered series account for the assets associated with such series separately from the other assets of the limited liability company, or any other series thereof, then the debts, liabilities, obligations and expenses incurred, contracted for or otherwise existing with respect to such series shall be enforceable against the assets of such series only, and not against the assets of the limited liability company generally or any other series thereof, and, unless otherwise provided in the limited liability company agreement, none of the debts, liabilities, obligations and expenses incurred, contracted for or otherwise existing with respect to the limited liability company generally or any other series thereof shall be enforceable against the assets of such series. Neither the preceding sentences nor any provision pursuant thereto in a limited liability company agreement, certificate of formation or certificate of registered series shall (i) restrict a registered series or limited liability company on behalf of a registered series from agreeing in the limited liability company agreement or otherwise that any or all of the debts, liabilities, obligations and expenses incurred, contracted for or otherwise existing with respect to the limited liability company generally or any other series thereof shall be enforceable against the assets of such registered series or (ii) restrict a limited liability company from agreeing in the limited liability company agreement or otherwise that any or all of the debts, liabilities, obligations and expenses incurred, contracted for or otherwise existing with respect to a registered series shall be enforceable against the assets of the limited liability company generally. Assets associated with a registered series may be held directly or indirectly, including in the name of such series, in the name of the limited liability company, through a nominee or otherwise. Records maintained for a registered series that reasonably identify its assets, including by specific listing, category, type, quantity, computational or allocational formula or procedure (including a percentage or share of any asset or assets) or by any other method where the identity of such assets is objectively determinable, will be deemed to account for the assets associated with such series separately from the other assets of the limited liability company, or any other series thereof. As used in this chapter, a reference to assets of a registered series includes assets associated with such series, a reference to assets associated with a registered series includes assets of such series, a reference to members or managers of a registered series includes members or managers associated with such series, and a reference to members or managers associated with a registered series includes members or managers of such series. The following shall apply to a registered series:

(1) A registered series may carry on any lawful business, purpose or activity, whether or not for profit. . . .

(2) Except as otherwise provided by this chapter, no member or manager of a registered series shall be obligated personally for any debt, obligation or liability of such series, whether arising in contract, tort or otherwise, solely by reason of being a member or acting as manager of such series. . . .

(3) A limited liability company agreement may provide for classes or groups of members or managers associated with a registered series having such relative rights, powers and duties as the limited liability company agreement may provide, and may make provision for the future creation in the manner provided in the limited liability company agreement of additional classes or groups of members or managers associated with such series having such relative rights, powers and duties as may from time to time be established, including rights, powers and duties senior to existing classes and groups of members or managers associated with such series. A limited liability company agreement may provide for the taking of an action, including the amendment of the limited liability company agreement, without the vote or approval of any member or manager or class or group of members or managers, including an action to create under the provisions of the limited liability company agreement a class or group of a registered series of limited liability company interests that was not previously outstanding. A limited liability company agreement may provide that any member or class or group of members associated with a registered series shall have no voting rights.

(4) A limited liability company agreement may grant to all or certain identified members or managers or a specified class or group of the members or managers associated with a registered series the right to vote separately or with all or any class or group of the members or managers associated with such series, on any matter. Voting by members or managers associated with a registered series may be on a per capita, number, financial interest, class, group or any other basis.

(5) Unless otherwise provided in a limited liability company agreement, the management of a registered series shall be vested in the members associated with such series in proportion to the then current percentage or other interest of members in the profits of such series owned by all of the members associated with such series, the decision of members owning more than 50 percent of the said percentage or other interest in the profits controlling; provided, however, that if a limited liability company agreement provides for the management of a registered series, in whole or in part, by a manager, the management of such series, to the extent so provided, shall be vested in the manager who shall be chosen in the manner provided in the limited liability company agreement. . . .

(7) . . . A limited liability company shall not make a distribution with respect to a registered series to a member to the extent that at the time of the distribution, after giving effect to the distribution, all liabilities of such series, other than liabilities to members on account of their limited liability company interests with respect to such series and liabilities for which the recourse of creditors is limited to specified property of such series, exceed the fair value of the assets associated with such series, except that the fair value of property of such series that is subject to a liability for which the recourse of creditors is limited shall be included in the assets associated with such series only to the extent that the fair value of that property exceeds that liability. . . .

(8) Unless otherwise provided in the limited liability company agreement, a member shall cease to be associated with a registered series and to have the power to exercise any rights or powers of a member with respect to such series upon the assignment of all of the member's limited liability company interest with respect to such series. . . .

(9) . . . A registered series is dissolved and its affairs shall be wound up upon the dissolution of the limited liability company under § 18–801 of this title or otherwise upon the first to occur of the following:

a. At the time specified in the limited liability company agreement;

b. Upon the happening of events specified in the limited liability company agreement;

c. Unless otherwise provided in the limited liability company agreement, upon the vote or consent of members associated with such series who own more than 2/3 of the then-current percentage or other interest in the profits of such series of the limited liability company owned by all of the members associated with such series; or

d. The dissolution of such series under subsection (b)(11) of this section.

(10) Notwithstanding § 18–803(a) of this title, unless otherwise provided in the limited liability company agreement, a manager associated with a registered series who has not wrongfully dissolved such series or, if none, the members associated with such series or a person approved by the members associated with such series, in either case, by members who own more than 50 percent of the then current percentage or other interest in the profits of such series owned by all of the members associated with such series, may wind up the affairs of such series; but the Court of Chancery, upon cause shown, may wind up the affairs of a registered series upon application of any member or manager associated with such series, or the member's personal representative or assignee, and in connection therewith, may appoint a liquidating trustee. The persons winding up the affairs of a registered series may, in the name of the limited liability company and for and on behalf of the limited liability company and such series, take all actions with respect to such series as are permitted under § 18–803(b) of this title. The persons winding up the affairs of a registered series shall provide for the claims and obligations of such series and distribute the assets of such series as provided in § 18–804 of this title, which section shall apply to the winding up and distribution of assets of a registered series. Actions taken in accordance with this subsection shall not affect the liability of members and shall not impose liability on a liquidating trustee.

(11) On application by or for a member or manager associated with a registered series, the Court of Chancery may decree dissolution of such series whenever it is not reasonably practicable to carry on the business of such series in conformity with a limited liability company agreement.

(12) For all purposes of the laws of the State of Delaware, a registered series is an association, regardless of the number of members or managers, if any, of such series.

(d) In order to form a registered series of a limited liability company, a certificate of registered series must be filed in accordance with this § 18–218(d). . . .

§ 18–219. Approval of Conversion of a Protected Series of a Domestic Limited Liability Company to a Registered Series of Such Domestic Limited Liability Company

(a) A protected series of a domestic limited liability company may convert to a registered series of such domestic limited liability company by complying with this section and filing in the office of the Secretary of State in accordance with § 18–206 of this title. . . .

§ 18–220. Approval of Conversion of a Registered Series of a Domestic Limited Liability Company to a Protected Series of Such Domestic Limited Liability Company

(a) Upon compliance with this section, a registered series of a domestic limited liability company may convert to a protected series of such domestic limited liability company. An existing registered series may not become a protected series other than pursuant to this § 18–220.

(b) If the limited liability company agreement specifies the manner of authorizing a conversion of a registered series of such limited liability company to a protected series of such limited liability company, the conversion of a registered series to a protected series shall be authorized as specified in the limited liability company agreement. If the limited liability company agreement does not specify the manner of authorizing a conversion of a registered series of such limited liability company to a protected series of such limited liability company and does not prohibit a conversion of a registered series to a protected series, the conversion shall be authorized by members of such registered series who own more than 50 percent of the then current percentage or other interest in the profits of such registered series owned by all of the members of such registered series.

(c) Unless otherwise agreed, the conversion of a registered series of a limited liability company to a protected series of such limited liability company pursuant to this section shall not require such limited liability company or such registered series of such limited liability company to wind up its affairs under § 18–803 or § 18–218 of this title or pay its liabilities and distribute its assets under § 18–804 or § 18–218 of this title, and the conversion of a registered series of a limited liability company to a protected series of such limited liability company shall not constitute a dissolution of such limited liability company or of such registered series. . . .

§ 18–221. Merger and Consolidation of Registered Series

(a) Pursuant to an agreement of merger or consolidation, 1 or more registered series may merge or consolidate with or into 1 or more other registered series of the same limited liability company with such registered series as the agreement shall provide being the surviving or resulting registered series. Unless otherwise provided in the limited liability company agreement, an agreement of merger or consolidation shall be approved by each registered series which is to merge or consolidate by members of such registered series who own more than 50 percent of the then current percentage or other interest in the profits of such registered series owned by all of the members of such registered series. In connection with a merger or consolidation hereunder, rights or securities of, or interests in, a registered series which is a constituent party to the merger or consolidation may be exchanged for or converted into cash, property, rights or securities of, or interests in, the surviving or resulting registered series or, in addition to or in lieu thereof, may be exchanged for or converted into cash, property, rights or securities of, or interests in, a domestic limited liability company or other business entity which is not the surviving or resulting registered series in the merger or consolidation, may remain outstanding or may be canceled. Notwithstanding prior approval, an agreement of merger or consolidation may be terminated or amended pursuant to a provision for such termination or amendment contained in the agreement of merger or consolidation. . . .

SUBCHAPTER III. MEMBERS

§ 18–301. Admission of Members

(a) In connection with the formation of a limited liability company, a person is admitted as a member of the limited liability company upon the later to occur of:

(1) The formation of the limited liability company; or

(2) The time provided in and upon compliance with the limited liability company agreement or, if the limited liability company agreement does not so provide, when the person's admission is reflected in the records of the limited liability company.

(b) After the formation of a limited liability company, a person is admitted as a member of the limited liability company:

(1) In the case of a person who is not an assignee of a limited liability company interest, including a person acquiring a limited liability company interest directly from the limited liability company and a person to be admitted as a member of the limited liability company without acquiring a limited liability company interest in the limited liability company, at the time provided in and upon compliance with the limited liability company agreement or, if the limited liability company agreement does not so provide, upon the consent of all members and when the person's admission is reflected in the records of the limited liability company;

(2) In the case of an assignee of a limited liability company interest, as provided in § 18–704(a) of this title and at the time provided in and upon compliance with the limited liability company agreement or, if the limited liability company agreement does not so provide, when any such person's permitted admission is reflected in the records of the limited liability company; or

(3) In the case of a person being admitted as a member of a surviving or resulting limited liability company pursuant to a merger or consolidation approved in accordance with § 18–209(b) of this title, as provided in the limited liability company agreement of the surviving or resulting limited liability company or in the agreement of merger or consolidation or plan of merger, and in the event of any inconsistency, the terms of the agreement of merger or consolidation or plan of merger shall control; and in the case of a person being admitted as a member of a limited liability company pursuant to a merger or consolidation in which such limited liability company is not the surviving or resulting limited

liability company in the merger or consolidation, as provided in the limited liability company agreement of such limited liability company.

(c) In connection with the domestication of a non-United States entity (as defined in § 18–212 of this title) as a limited liability company in the State of Delaware in accordance with § 18–212 of this title or the conversion of an other entity (as defined in § 18–214 of this title) to a domestic limited liability company in accordance with § 18–214 of this title, a person is admitted as a member of the limited liability company as provided in the limited liability company agreement.

(d) A person may be admitted to a limited liability company as a member of the limited liability company and may receive a limited liability company interest in the limited liability company without making a contribution or being obligated to make a contribution to the limited liability company. Unless otherwise provided in a limited liability company agreement, a person may be admitted to a limited liability company as a member of the limited liability company without acquiring a limited liability company interest in the limited liability company. Unless otherwise provided in a limited liability company agreement, a person may be admitted as the sole member of a limited liability company without making a contribution or being obligated to make a contribution to the limited liability company or without acquiring a limited liability company interest in the limited liability company.

(e) Unless otherwise provided in a limited liability company agreement or another agreement, a member shall have no preemptive right to subscribe to any additional issue of limited liability company interests or another interest in a limited liability company.

§ 18–302.   Classes and Voting

(a) A limited liability company agreement may provide for classes or groups of members having such relative rights, powers and duties as the limited liability company agreement may provide, and may make provision for the future creation in the manner provided in the limited liability company agreement of additional classes or groups of members having such relative rights, powers and duties as may from time to time be established, including rights, powers and duties senior to existing classes and groups of members. A limited liability company agreement may provide for the taking of an action, including the amendment of the limited liability company agreement, without the vote or approval of any member or class or group of members, including an action to create under the provisions of the limited liability company agreement a class or group of limited liability company interests that was not previously outstanding. A limited liability company agreement may provide that any member or class or group of members shall have no voting rights.

(b) A limited liability company agreement may grant to all or certain identified members or a specified class or group of the members the right to vote separately or with all or any class or group of the members or managers, on any matter. Voting by members may be on a per capita, number, financial interest, class, group or any other basis.

(c) A limited liability company agreement may set forth provisions relating to notice of the time, place or purpose of any meeting at which any matter is to be voted on by any members, waiver of any such notice, action by consent without a meeting, the establishment of a record date, quorum requirements, voting in person or by proxy, or any other matter with respect to the exercise of any such right to vote.

(d) Unless otherwise provided in a limited liability company agreement, meetings of members may be held by means of conference telephone or other communications equipment by means of which all persons participating in the meeting can hear each other, and participation in a meeting pursuant to this subsection shall constitute presence in person at the meeting. Unless otherwise provided in a limited liability company agreement, on any matter that is to be voted on, consented to or approved by members, the members may take such action without a meeting, without prior notice and without a vote if consented to or approved, in writing, by electronic transmission or by any other means permitted by law, by members having not less than the minimum number of votes that would be necessary to authorize or take such action at a meeting at which all members entitled to vote thereon were present and voted. Unless otherwise provided in a limited liability company agreement, if a person (whether or not then a member) consenting as a member to any matter provides that such consent will be effective at a future time (including a time determined upon the happening of an event), then such person shall be deemed to have consented as a member at such future time so long as such person is then a member. Unless otherwise provided in a limited liability company agreement, on any matter that is to be voted on by members, the members may vote in person or by proxy, and such proxy may be granted in writing, by means of electronic transmission or as otherwise permitted by applicable law. Unless otherwise provided in a limited liability company agreement, a consent transmitted by electronic transmission by a member or by a person or persons authorized to act for a member shall be deemed to be written and signed for purposes of this subsection. For purposes of this subsection, the term "electronic transmission" means any form of communication not directly involving the physical transmission of paper including the use, or participation in, 1 or more electronic networks or databases (including 1 or more distributed electronic networks or databases), that creates a record that may be retained, retrieved and reviewed by a recipient thereof and that may be directly reproduced in paper form by such a recipient through an automated process.

(e) If a limited liability company agreement provides for the manner in which it may be amended, including by requiring the approval of a person who is not a party to the limited liability company agreement or the satisfaction of conditions, it may be amended only in that manner or as otherwise permitted by law, including as permitted by § 18–209(f) of this title (provided that the approval of any person may be waived by such person and that any such conditions may be waived by all persons for whose benefit such conditions were intended). Unless otherwise provided in a limited liability company agreement, a super-majority amendment provision shall only apply to provisions of the limited liability company agreement that are expressly included in the limited liability company agreement. As used in this section, "supermajority amendment provision" means any amendment provision set forth in a limited liability company agreement requiring that an amendment to a provision of the limited liability company agreement be adopted by no less than the vote or consent required to take action under such latter provision.

(f) If a limited liability company agreement does not provide for the manner in which it may be amended, the limited liability company agreement may be amended with the approval of all of the members or as otherwise permitted by law, including as permitted by § 18–209(f) of this title. This subsection shall only apply to a limited liability company whose original certificate of formation was filed with the Secretary of State on or after January 1, 2012.

§ 18–303.   Liability to Third Parties

(a) Except as otherwise provided by this chapter, the debts, obligations and liabilities of a limited liability company, whether arising in contract, tort or otherwise, shall be solely the debts, obligations and liabilities of the limited liability company, and no member or manager of a limited liability company shall be obligated personally for any such debt, obligation or liability of the limited liability company solely by reason of being a member or acting as a manager of the limited liability company.

(b) Notwithstanding the provisions of Section 18–303(a) of this chapter, under a limited liability company agreement or under another agreement, a member or manager may agree to be obligated personally for any or all of the debts, obligations and liabilities of the limited liability company.

§ 18–304.   Events of Bankruptcy

A person ceases to be a member of a limited liability company upon the happening of any of the following events:

(1) Unless otherwise provided in a limited liability company agreement, or with the consent of all members, a member:

a. Makes an assignment for the benefit of creditors;

b. Files a voluntary petition in bankruptcy;

c. Is adjudged a bankrupt or insolvent, or has entered against him an order for relief, in any bankruptcy or insolvency proceeding;

d. Files a petition or answer seeking for himself any reorganization, arrangement, composition, readjustment, liquidation, dissolution or similar relief under any statute, law or regulation;

e. Files an answer or other pleading admitting or failing to contest the material allegations of a petition filed against him in any proceeding of this nature;

　　f. Seeks, consents to or acquiesces in the appointment of a trustee, receiver or liquidator of the member or of all or any substantial part of his properties; or

　　(2) Unless otherwise provided in a limited liability company agreement, or with the written consent of all members, 120 days after the commencement of any proceeding against the member seeking reorganization, arrangement, composition, readjustment, liquidation, dissolution or similar relief under any statute, law or regulation, if the proceeding has not been dismissed, or if within 90 days after the appointment without his consent or acquiescence of a trustee, receiver or liquidator of the member or of all or any substantial part of his properties, the appointment is not vacated or stayed, or within 90 days after the expiration of any such stay, the appointment is not vacated.

§ 18–305.　　Access to and Confidentiality of Information; Records

　　(a) Each member of a limited liability company, in person or by attorney or other agent, has the right, subject to such reasonable standards (including standards governing what information and documents are to be furnished at what time and location and at whose expense) as may be set forth in a limited liability company agreement or otherwise established by the manager or, if there is no manager, then by the members, to obtain from the limited liability company from time to time upon reasonable demand for any purpose reasonably related to the member's interest as a member of the limited liability company:

　　(1) True and full information regarding the status of the business and financial condition of the limited liability company;

　　(2) Promptly after becoming available, a copy of the limited liability company's federal, state and local income tax returns for each year;

　　(3) A current list of the name and last known business, residence or mailing address of each member and manager;

　　(4) A copy of any written limited liability company agreement and certificate of formation and all amendments thereto, together with executed copies of any written powers of attorney pursuant to which the limited liability company agreement and any certificate and all amendments thereto have been executed;

　　(5) True and full information regarding the amount of cash and a description and statement of the agreed value of any other property or services contributed by each member and which each member has agreed to contribute in the future, and the date on which each became a member; and

　　(6) Other information regarding the affairs of the limited liability company as is just and reasonable.

　　(b) Each manager shall have the right to examine all of the information described in subsection (a) of this section for a purpose reasonably related to his position as a manager.

　　(c) The manager of a limited liability company shall have the right to keep confidential from the members, for such period of time as the manager deems reasonable, any information which the manager reasonably believes to be in the nature of trade secrets or other information the disclosure of which the manager in good faith believes is not in the best interest of the limited liability company or could damage the limited liability company or its business or which the limited liability company is required by law or by agreement with a third party to keep confidential.

　　(d) A limited liability company may maintain its records in other than a written form, including on, by means of, or in the form of any information storage device, method, or 1 or more electronic network or databases (including 1 or more distributed electronic networks or databases), if such form is capable of conversion into written form within a reasonable time.

　　(e) Any demand by a member under this section shall be in writing and shall state the purpose of such demand. In every instance where an attorney or other agent shall be the person who seeks the right to obtain the information described in subsection (a) of this section, the demand shall be accompanied by a power of attorney or such other writing which authorizes the attorney or other agent to so act on behalf of the member.

(f) Any action to enforce any right arising under this section shall be brought in the Court of Chancery. If the limited liability company refuses to permit a member, or attorney or other agent acting for the member, to obtain or a manager to examine the information described in subsection (a) of this section or does not reply to the demand that has been made within 5 business days (or such shorter or longer period of time as is provided for in a limited liability company agreement but not longer than 30 business days) after the demand has been made, the demanding member or manager may apply to the Court of Chancery for an order to compel such disclosure. The Court of Chancery is hereby vested with exclusive jurisdiction to determine whether or not the person seeking such information is entitled to the information sought. The Court of Chancery may summarily order the limited liability company to permit the demanding member to obtain or manager to examine the formation described in subsection (a) of this section and to make copies or abstracts therefrom, or the Court of Chancery may summarily order the limited liability company to furnish to the demanding member or manager the information described in subsection (a) of this section on the condition that the demanding member or manager first pay to the limited liability company the reasonable cost of obtaining and furnishing such information and on such other conditions as the Court of Chancery deems appropriate. When a demanding member seeks to obtain or a manager seeks to examine the information described in subsection (a) of this section, the demanding member or manager shall first establish:

(1) that the demanding member or manager has complied with the provisions of this section respecting the form and manner of making demand for obtaining or examining of such information, and

(2) that the information the demanding member or manager seeks is reasonably related to the member's interest as a member or the manager's position as a manager, as the case may be. The Court of Chancery may, in its discretion, prescribe any limitations or conditions with reference to the obtaining or examining of information, or award such other or further relief as the Court of Chancery may deem just and proper. The Court of Chancery may order books, documents and records, pertinent extracts therefrom, or duly authenticated copies thereof, to be brought within the State of Delaware and kept in the State of Delaware upon such terms and conditions as the order may prescribe.

(g) The rights of a member or manager to obtain information as provided in this section may be restricted in an original limited liability company agreement or in any subsequent amendment approved or adopted by all of the members or in compliance with any applicable requirements of the limited liability company agreement. The provisions of this subsection shall not be construed to limit the ability to impose restrictions on the rights of a member or manager to obtain information by any other means permitted under this chapter.

(h) A limited liability company shall maintain a current record that identifies the name and last known business, residence or mailing address of each member and manager.

§ 18–306.   Remedies for Breach of Limited Liability Company Agreement by Member

A limited liability company agreement may provide that:

(1) A member who fails to perform in accordance with, or to comply with the terms and conditions of, the limited liability company agreement shall be subject to specified penalties or specified consequences; and

(2) At the time or upon the happening of events specified in the limited liability company agreement, a member shall be subject to specified penalties or specified consequences.

Such specified penalties or specified consequences may include and take the form of any penalty or consequence set forth in § 18–502(c) of this chapter.

SUBCHAPTER IV. MANAGERS

§ 18–401.   Admission of Managers

A person may be named or designated as a manager of the limited liability company as provided in § 18–101(10) of this title.

§ 18–402.　　Management of Limited Liability Company

Unless otherwise provided in a limited liability company agreement, the management of a limited liability company shall be vested in its members in proportion to the then current percentage or other interest of members in the profits of the limited liability company owned by all of the members, the decision of members owning more than 50 percent of the said percentage or other interest in the profits controlling; provided however, that if a limited liability company agreement provides for the management, in whole or in part, of a limited liability company by a manager, the management of the limited liability company, to the extent so provided, shall be vested in the manager who shall be chosen in the manner provided in the limited liability company agreement. The manager shall also hold the offices and have the responsibilities accorded to the manager by or in the manner provided in a limited liability company agreement. Subject to § 18–602 of this title, a manager shall cease to be a manager as provided in a limited liability company agreement. A limited liability company may have more than 1 manager. Unless otherwise provided in a limited liability company agreement, each member and manager has the authority to bind the limited liability company.

§ 18–403.　　Contributions by a Manager

A manager of a limited liability company may make contributions to the limited liability company and share in the profits and losses of, and in distributions from, the limited liability company as a member. A person who is both a manager and a member has the rights and powers, and is subject to the restrictions and liabilities, of a manager and, except as provided in a limited liability company agreement, also has the rights and powers, and is subject to the restrictions and liabilities, of a member to the extent of his participation in the limited liability company as a member.

§ 18–404.　　Classes and Voting

(a) A limited liability company agreement may provide for classes or groups of managers having such relative rights, powers and duties as the limited liability company agreement may provide, and may make provision for the future creation in the manner provided in the limited liability company agreement of additional classes or groups of managers having such relative rights, powers and duties as may from time to time be established, including rights, powers and duties senior to existing classes and groups of managers. A limited liability company agreement may provide for the taking of an action, including the amendment of the limited liability company agreement, without the vote or approval of any manager or class or group of managers, including an action to create under the provisions of the limited liability company agreement a class or group of limited liability company interests that was not previously outstanding.

(b) A limited liability company agreement may grant to all or certain identified managers or a specified class or group of the managers the right to vote, separately or with all or any class or group of managers or members, on any matter. Voting by managers may be on a per capita, number, financial interest, class, group or any other basis.

(c) A limited liability company agreement may set forth provisions relating to notice of the time, place or purpose of any meeting at which any matter is to be voted on by any manager or class or group of managers, waiver of any such notice, action by consent without a meeting, the establishment of a record date, quorum requirements, voting in person or by proxy, or any other matter with respect to the exercise of any such right to vote.

(d) Unless otherwise provided in a limited liability company agreement, meetings of managers may be held by means of conference telephone or other communications equipment by means of which all persons participating in the meeting can hear each other, and participation in a meeting pursuant to this subsection shall constitute presence in person at the meeting. Unless otherwise provided in a limited liability company agreement, on any matter that is to be voted on, consented to or approved by managers, the managers may take such action without a meeting, without prior notice and without a vote if consented to or approved, in writing, by electronic transmission or by any other means permitted by law, by managers having not less than the minimum number of votes that would be necessary to authorize or take such action at a meeting at which all managers entitled to vote thereon were present and voted. Unless otherwise provided in a limited liability company agreement, if a person (whether or not then a manager) consenting as a manager to any matter provides that such consent will be effective at a future time (including a time determined upon the happening of an event), then such person shall be deemed to have consented as a manager at such future time so long as such person is then a manager. Unless otherwise provided in a limited liability company agreement, on any matter that is to be voted on by managers, the managers may vote in person or by proxy, and such proxy may be granted in writing, by means of electronic transmission or as otherwise permitted by applicable law. Unless otherwise provided in a limited liability company agreement, a consent transmitted by electronic transmission by a manager or by a person or persons authorized to act for a manager shall be deemed to be written and signed for purposes of this subsection. For purposes of this subsection, the term "electronic transmission" means any form of communication not directly involving the physical transmission of paper, including the use of, or participation in, 1 or more electronic networks or databases (including 1 or more distributed networks or databases), that creates a record that may be retained, retrieved and reviewed by a recipient thereof and that may be directly reproduced in paper form by such a recipient through an automated process.

§ 18–405. Remedies for Breach of Limited Liability Company Agreement by Manager

A limited liability company agreement may provide that:

(1) A manager who fails to perform in accordance with, or to comply with the terms and conditions of, the limited liability company agreement shall be subject to specified penalties or specified consequences; and

(2) At the time or upon the happening of events specified in the limited liability company agreement, a manager shall be subject to specified penalties or specified consequences.

§ 18–406. Reliance on Reports and Information by Member or Manager

A member, manager or liquidating trustee of a limited liability company shall be fully protected in relying in good faith upon the records of the limited liability company and upon information, opinions, reports or statements presented by another manager, member or liquidating trustee, an officer or employee of the limited liability company, or committees of the limited liability company, members or managers, or by any other person as to matters the member, manager or liquidating trustees reasonably believes are within such other person's professional or expert competence, including information, opinions, reports or statements as to the value and amount of the assets, liabilities, profits or losses of the limited liability company, or the value and amount of assets or reserves or contracts, agreements or other undertakings that would be sufficient to pay claims and obligations of the limited liability company or to make reasonable provision to pay such claims and obligations, or any other facts pertinent to the existence and amount of assets from which distributions to members or creditors might properly be paid.

§ 18–407. Delegation of Rights and Powers to Manage

Unless otherwise provided in the limited liability company agreement, a member or manager of limited liability company has the power and authority to delegate to one or more other persons the member's or manager's, as the case may be, rights and powers to manage and control the business and affairs of the limited liability company, including to delegate to agents, officers and employees of a member or manager [of] the limited liability company, and to delegate by a management agreement or another agreement with, or otherwise to, other persons. Unless otherwise provided in the limited liability company agreement, such delegation by a member or manager shall be irrevocable if it states that it is irrevocable. Unless otherwise provided in the limited liability company agreement, such delegation by a member or manager of a limited liability company shall not cause the member or manager to cease to be a member or manager, as the case may be, of the limited liability company or cause the person to whom any such rights and powers have been delegated to be a member or manager, as the case may be, of the limited liability company.

SUBCHAPTER V. FINANCE

§ 18–501.   Form of Contribution

The contribution of a member to a limited liability company may be in cash, property or services rendered, or a promissory note or other obligation to contribute cash or property or to perform services.

§ 18–502.   Liability for Contribution

(a) Except as provided in a limited liability company agreement, a member is obligated to a limited liability company to perform any promise to contribute cash or property or to perform services, even if he is unable to perform because of death, disability or any other reason. If a member does not make the required contribution of property or services, he is obligated at the option of the limited liability company to contribute cash equal to that portion of the agreed value (as stated in the records of the limited liability company) of the contribution that has not been made. The foregoing option shall be in addition to, and not in lieu of, any other rights, including the right to specific performance, that the limited liability company may have against such member under the limited liability company agreement or applicable law.

(b) Unless otherwise provided in a limited liability company agreement, the obligation of a member to make a contribution or return money or other property paid or distributed in violation of this chapter may be compromised only by consent of all the members. Notwithstanding the compromise, a creditor of a limited liability company who extends credit, after the entering into of a limited liability company agreement or an amendment thereto which, in either case, reflects the obligation, and before the amendment thereof to reflect the compromise, may enforce the original obligation to the extent that, in extending credit, the creditor reasonably relied on the obligation of a member to make a contribution or return. A conditional obligation of a member to make a contribution or return money or other property to a limited liability company may not be enforced unless the conditions of the obligation have been satisfied or waived as to or by such member. Conditional obligations include contributions payable upon a discretionary call of a limited liability company prior to the time the call occurs.

(c) A limited liability company agreement may provide that the interest of any member who fails to make any contribution that he is obligated to make shall be subject to specified penalties for, or specified consequences of, such failure. Such penalty or consequence may take the form of reducing or eliminating the defaulting member's proportionate interest in a limited liability company, subordinating his limited liability company interest to that of nondefaulting members, a forced sale of his limited liability company interest, forfeiture of his limited liability company interest, the lending by other members of the amount necessary to meet his commitment, a fixing of the value of his limited liability company interest by appraisal or by formula and redemption or sale of his limited liability company interest at such value, or other penalty or consequence.

§ 18–503.   Allocation of Profits and Losses

The profits and losses of a limited liability company shall be allocated among the members, and among classes or groups of members, in the manner provided in a limited liability company agreement. If the limited liability company agreement does not so provide, profits and losses shall be allocated on the basis of the agreed value (as stated in the records of the limited liability company) of the contributions made by each member to the extent they have been received by the limited liability company and have not been returned.

§ 18–504.   Allocation of Distributions

Distributions of cash or other assets of a limited liability company shall be allocated among the members, and among classes or groups of members, in the manner provided in a limited liability company agreement. If the limited liability company agreement does not so provide, distributions shall be made on the basis of the agreed value (as stated in the records of the limited liability company) of the contributions made by each member to the extent they have been received by the limited liability company and have not been returned.

SUBCHAPTER VI. DISTRIBUTIONS AND RESIGNATION

§ 18–601. Interim Distributions

Except as provided in this subchapter, to the extent and at the times or upon the happening of the events specified in a limited liability company agreement, a member is entitled to receive from a limited liability company distributions before his resignation from the limited liability company and before the dissolution and winding up thereof.

§ 18–602. Resignation of Manager

A manager may resign as a manager of a limited liability company at the time or upon the happening of events specified in a limited liability company agreement and in accordance with the limited liability company agreement. A limited liability company agreement may provide that a manager shall not have the right to resign as a manager of a limited liability company. Notwithstanding that a limited liability company agreement provides that a manager does not have the right to resign as a manager of a limited liability company, a manager may resign as a manager of a limited liability company at any time by giving written notice to the members and other managers. If the resignation of a manager violates a limited liability company agreement, in addition to any remedies otherwise available under applicable law, a limited liability company may recover from the resigning manager damages for breach of the limited liability company agreement and offset the damages against the amount otherwise distributable to the resigning manager.

§ 18–603. Resignation of Member

A member may resign from a limited liability company only at the time or upon the happening of events specified in a limited liability company agreement and in accordance with the limited liability company agreement. Notwithstanding anything to the contrary under applicable law, unless a limited liability company agreement provides otherwise, a member may not resign from a limited liability company prior to the dissolution and winding up of the limited liability company. Notwithstanding anything to the contrary under applicable law, a limited liability company agreement may provide that a limited liability company interest may not be assigned prior to the dissolution and winding up of the limited liability company. . . . .

§ 18–604. Distribution Upon Resignation

Except as provided in this subchapter, upon resignation any resigning member is entitled to receive any distribution to which such member is entitled under a limited liability company agreement and, if not otherwise provided in a limited liability company agreement, such member is entitled to receive, within a reasonable time after resignation, the fair value of such member's limited liability company interest as of the date of resignation based upon such member's right to share in distributions from the limited liability company.

§ 18–605. Distribution in Kind

Except as provided in a limited liability company agreement, a member, regardless of the nature of the member's contribution, has no right to demand and receive any distribution from a limited liability company in any form other than cash. Except as provided in a limited liability company agreement, a member may not be compelled to accept a distribution of any asset in kind from a limited liability company to the extent that the percentage of the asset distributed exceeds a percentage of that asset which is equal to the percentage in which the member shares in distributions from the limited liability company. Except as provided in the limited liability company agreement, a member may be compelled to accept a distribution of any asset in kind from a limited liability company to the extent that the percentage of the asset distributed to him is equal to a percentage of that asset which is equal to the percentage in which the member shares in distributions from the limited liability company.

§ 18–606. Right to Distribution

Subject to §§ 18–607 and 18–804 of this title, and unless otherwise provided in a limited liability company agreement, at the time a member becomes entitled to receive a distribution, he has the status of, and is entitled to all remedies available to, a creditor of a limited liability company with respect to the distribution. A limited liability company agreement may provide for the establishment of a record date with respect to allocations and distributions by a limited liability company.

§ 18–607.   Limitations on Distribution

(a) A limited liability company shall not make a distribution to a member to the extent that at the time of the distribution, after giving effect to the distribution, all liabilities of the limited liability company, other than liabilities to members on account of their limited liability company interests and liabilities for which the recourse of creditors is limited to specified property of the limited liability company, exceed the fair value of the assets of the limited liability company, except that the fair value of property that is subject to a liability for which the recourse of creditors is limited shall be included in the assets of the limited liability company only to the extent that the fair value of that property exceeds that liability. For purposes of this subsection (a), the term "distribution" shall not include amounts constituting reasonable compensation for present or past services or reasonable payments made in the ordinary course of business pursuant to a bona fide retirement plan or other benefits program.

(b) A member who receives a distribution in violation of subsection (a) of this section, and who knew at the time of the distribution that the distribution violated subsection (a) of this section, shall be liable to a limited liability company for the amount of the distribution. A member who receives a distribution in violation of subsection (a) of this section, and who did not know at the time of the distribution that the distribution violated subsection (a) of this section, shall not be liable for the amount of the distribution. Subject to subsection (c) of this section, this subsection shall not affect any obligation or liability of a member under agreement or other applicable law for the amount of a distribution.

(c) Unless otherwise agreed, a member who receives a distribution from a limited liability company shall have no liability under this chapter or other applicable law for the amount of the distribution after the expiration of 3 years from the date of the distribution unless an action to recover the distribution from such member is commenced prior to the expiration of the said 3-year period and an adjudication of liability against such member is made in the said action.

SUBCHAPTER VII. ASSIGNMENT OF LIMITED LIABILITY COMPANY INTERESTS

§ 18–701.   Nature of Limited Liability Company Interest

A limited liability company interest is personal property. A member has no interest in specific limited liability company property.

§ 18–702.   Assignment of Limited Liability Company Interest

(a) A limited liability company interest is assignable in whole or in part except as provided in a limited liability company agreement. The assignee of a member's limited liability company interest shall have no right to participate in the management of the business and affairs of a limited liability company except as provided in a limited liability company agreement or, unless otherwise provided in the limited liability agreement, upon the vote or consent of all of the members of the limited liability company.

(b) Unless otherwise provided in a limited liability company agreement:

(1) An assignment of a limited liability company interest does not entitle the assignee to become or to exercise any rights or powers of a member;

(2) An assignment of a limited liability company interest entitles the assignee to share in such profits and losses, to receive such distribution or distributions, and to receive such allocation of income, gain, loss, deduction, or credit or similar item to which the assignor was entitled, to the extent assigned; and

(3) A member ceases to be a member and to have the power to exercise any rights or powers of a member upon assignment of all of his limited liability company interest. Unless otherwise provided in a limited liability company agreement, the pledge of, or granting of a security interest, lien or other

encumbrance in or against, any or all of the limited liability company interest of a member shall not cause the member to cease to be a member or to have the power to exercise any rights or powers of a member.

(c) Unless otherwise provided in a limited liability company agreement, a member's interest in a limited liability company may be evidenced by a certificate of limited liability company interest issued by the limited liability company. A limited liability company agreement may provide for the assignment or transfer of any limited liability company interest represented by such a certificate and make other provisions with respect to such certificates. A limited liability company shall not have the power to issue a certificate of limited liability company interest in bearer form.

(d) Unless otherwise provided in a limited liability company agreement and except to the extent assumed by agreement, until an assignee of a limited liability company interest becomes a member, the assignee shall have no liability as a member solely as a result of the assignment.

(e) Unless otherwise provided in the limited liability company agreement, a limited liability company may acquire, by purchase, redemption or otherwise, any limited liability company interest or other interest of a member or manager in the limited liability company. Unless otherwise provided in the limited liability company agreement, any such interest so acquired by the limited liability company shall be deemed canceled.

§ 18–703. Member's Limited Liability Company Interest Subject to Charging Order

(a) On application by a judgment creditor of a member or of a member's assignee, a court having jurisdiction may charge the limited liability company interest of the judgment debtor to satisfy the judgment. To the extent so charged, the judgment creditor has only the right to receive any distribution or distributions to which the judgment debtor would otherwise have been entitled in respect of such limited liability company interest.

(b) A charging order constitutes a lien on the judgment debtor's limited liability company interest.

(c) This chapter does not deprive a member or member's assignee of a right under exemption laws with respect to the judgment debtor's limited liability company interest.

(d) The entry of a charging order is the exclusive remedy by which a judgment creditor of a member or of a member's assignee may satisfy a judgment out of the judgment debtor's limited liability company interest and attachment, garnishment, foreclosure or other legal or equitable remedies are not available to the judgment creditor whether the limited liability company has one member or more than one member.

(e) No creditor of a member or of a member's assignee shall have any right to obtain possession of, or otherwise exercise legal or equitable remedies with respect to, the property of the limited liability company.

(f) The Court of Chancery shall have jurisdiction to hear and determine any matter relating to any such charging order.

§ 18–704. Right of Assignee to Become Member

(a) An assignee of a limited liability company interest becomes a member:

(1) As provided in the limited liability company agreement;

(2) Unless otherwise provided in the limited liability company agreement, upon the affirmative vote or written consent of all of the members of the limited liability company.

(3) Unless otherwise provided in the limited liability company agreement by a specific reference to this subsection or otherwise provided in connection with the assignment, upon the voluntary assignment by the sole member of the limited liability company of all the limited liability company interests in the limited liability company to a single assignee. An assignment will be voluntary for purposes of this subsection if it is consented to by the member at the time of the assignment and is not effected by foreclosure or other similar legal process.

(b) An assignee who has become a member has, to the extent assigned, the rights and powers, and is subject to the restrictions and liabilities, of a member under a limited liability company agreement and this chapter. Notwithstanding the foregoing, unless otherwise provided in a limited liability company agreement, an assignee who becomes a member is liable for the obligations of his assignor to make contributions as provided in § 18–502 of this title, but shall not be liable for the obligations of his assignor under subchapter VI of this chapter. However, the assignee is not obligated for liabilities, including the obligations of his assignor to make contributions as provided in § 18–502 of this title, unknown to the assignee at the time he became a member and which could not be ascertained from a limited liability company agreement.

(c) Whether or not an assignee of a limited liability company interest becomes a member, the assignor is not released from his liability to a limited liability company under subchapters V and VI of this chapter.

§ 18–705. Powers of Estate of Deceased or Incompetent Member

If a member who is an individual dies or a court of competent jurisdiction adjudges him to be incompetent to manage his person or his property, the member's personal representative may exercise all of the member's rights for the purpose of settling his estate or administering his property, including any power under a limited liability company agreement of an assignee to become a member. If a member is a corporation, trust or other entity and is dissolved or terminated, the powers of that member may be exercised by its personal representative.

SUBCHAPTER VIII. DISSOLUTION

§ 18–801. Dissolution

(a) A limited liability company is dissolved and its affairs shall be wound up upon the first to occur of the following:

(1) At the time specified in a limited liability company agreement, but if no such time is set forth in the limited liability company agreement, then the limited liability company shall have a perpetual existence;

(2) Upon the happening of events specified in a limited liability company agreement;

(3) Unless otherwise provided in the limited liability company agreement, upon the affirmative vote or written consent of members who own more than two-thirds of the then-current percentage or other interest in the profits of the limited liability company owned by all of the members;

(4) At any time there are no members; provided that the limited liability company is not dissolved and is not required to be wound up if, (i) unless otherwise provided in a limited liability company agreement, within 90 days or such other period as is provided for in the limited liability company agreement after the occurrence of the event that terminated the continued membership of the last remaining member, the personal representative of the last remaining member agrees to continue the limited liability company and to the admission of the personal representative of such member or its nominee or designee to the limited liability company as a member, effective as of the occurrence of the event that terminated the continued membership of the last remaining member; provided that a limited liability company agreement may provide that the personal representative of the last remaining member shall be obligated to agree in writing to continue the limited liability company and to the admission of the personal representative of such member or its nominee or designee to the limited liability company as a member, effective as of the occurrence of the event that terminated the continued membership of the last remaining member, or, (ii) a member is admitted to the limited liability company in the manner provided for in the limited liability company agreement, effective as of the occurrence of the event that terminated the continued membership of the last remaining member, within 90 days or such other period as is provided for in the limited liability company agreement after the occurrence of the event that terminated the continued membership of the last remaining member, pursuant to a provision of the limited liability company agreement that specifically provides for the admission of a member to the limited liability company after there is no longer a remaining member of the limited liability company.

(5) The entry of a decree of judicial dissolution under § 18–802 of this title.

Unless otherwise provided in a limited liability company agreement, a limited liability company whose original certificate of formation was filed with the Secretary of State and effective on or prior to July 15, 2015, shall continue to be governed by paragraph (3) of this subsection as in effect on July 15, 2015 (except that "affirmative" and "written" shall be deleted from such paragraph (a)(3)).

(b) Unless otherwise provided in a limited liability company agreement, the death, retirement, resignation, expulsion, bankruptcy or dissolution of any member or the occurrence of an event that terminates the continued membership of any member shall not cause the limited liability company to be dissolved or its affairs to be wound up, and upon the occurrence of any such event, the limited liability company shall be continued without dissolution.

§ 18–802.   Judicial Dissolution

On application by or for a member or manager the Court of Chancery may decree dissolution of a limited liability company whenever it is not reasonably practicable to carry on the business in conformity with a limited liability company agreement.

§ 18–803.   Winding Up

(a) Unless otherwise provided in a limited liability company agreement, a manager who has not wrongfully dissolved a limited liability company or, if none, the members or a person approved by the members, in either case, by members who own more than 50 percent of the then current percentage or other interest in the profits of the limited liability company owned by all of the members, may wind up the limited liability company's affairs; but the Court of Chancery, upon cause shown, may wind up the limited liability company's affairs upon application of any member or manager, or the member's personal representative or assignee, and in connection therewith, may appoint a liquidating trustee. Unless otherwise provided in a limited liability company agreement, a limited liability company whose original certificate of formation was filed with the Secretary of State and effective on or prior to July 15, 2015, shall continue to be governed by this subsection as in effect on July 15, 2015.

(b) Upon dissolution of a limited liability company and until the filing of a certificate of cancellation as provided in § 18–203 of this title, the persons winding up the limited liability company's affairs may, in the name of, and for and on behalf of, the limited liability company, prosecute and defend suits, whether civil, criminal or administrative, gradually settle and close the limited liability company's business, dispose of and convey the limited liability company's property, discharge or make reasonable provision for the limited liability company's liabilities, and distribute to the members any remaining assets of the limited liability company, all without affecting the liability of members and managers and without imposing liability on a liquidating trustee.

§ 18–804.   Distribution of Assets

(a) Upon the winding up of a limited liability company, the assets shall be distributed as follows:

(1) To creditors, including members and managers who are creditors, to the extent otherwise permitted by law, in satisfaction of liabilities of the limited liability company (whether by payment or the making of reasonable provision for payment thereof) other than liabilities for which reasonable provision for payment has been made and liabilities for distributions to members and former members under § 18–601 or § 18–604 of this title;

(2) Unless otherwise provided in a limited liability company agreement, to members and former members in satisfaction of liabilities for distributions under § 18–601 or § 18–604 of this title; and

(3) Unless otherwise provided in a limited liability company agreement, to members first for the return of their contributions and second respecting their limited liability company interests, in the proportions in which the members share in distributions.

(b) A limited liability company which has dissolved (i) shall pay or make reasonable provision to pay all claims and obligations, including all contingent, conditional or unmatured contractual claims, known to the limited liability company, (ii) shall make such provision as will be reasonably likely to be sufficient to provide compensation for any claim against the limited liability company which is the subject of a pending action, suit or proceeding to which the limited liability company is a party and (iii) shall make such provision as will be reasonably likely to be sufficient to provide compensation for claims that have not been made known to the limited liability company or that have not arisen but that, based on facts known to the limited liability company, are likely to arise or to become known to the limited liability company within 10 years after the date of dissolution. If there are sufficient assets, such claims and obligations shall be paid in full and any such provision for payment made shall be made in full. If there are insufficient assets, such claims and obligations shall be paid or provided for according to their priority and, among claims of equal priority, ratably to the extent of assets available therefor. Unless otherwise provided in the limited liability company agreement, any remaining assets shall be distributed as provided in this chapter. Any liquidating trustee winding up a limited liability company's affairs who has complied with this section shall not be personally liable to the claimants of the dissolved limited liability company by reason of such person's actions in winding up the limited liability company.

(c) A member who receives a distribution in violation of subsection (a) of this section, and who knew at the time of the distribution that the distribution violated subsection (a) of this section, shall be liable to the limited liability company for the amount of the distribution. For purposes of the immediately preceding sentence, the term "distribution" shall not include amounts constituting reasonable compensation for present or past services or reasonable payments made in the ordinary course of business pursuant to a bona fide retirement plan or other benefits program. A member who receives a distribution in violation of subsection (a) of this section, and who did not know at the time of the distribution that the distribution violated subsection (a) of this section, shall not be liable for the amount of the distribution. Subject to subsection (d) of this section, this subsection shall not affect any obligation or liability of a member under an agreement or other applicable law for the amount of a distribution.

(d) Unless otherwise agreed, a member who receives a distribution from a limited liability company to which this section applies shall have no liability under this chapter or other applicable law for the amount of the distribution after the expiration of 3 years from the date of the distribution unless an action to recover the distribution from such member is commenced prior to the expiration of the said 3-year period and an adjudication of liability against such member is made in the said action.

(e) Section 18–607 of this title shall not apply to a distribution to which this section applies.

§ 18–806.   Revocation of Dissolution

If a limited liability company agreement provides the manner in which a dissolution may be revoked, it may be revoked in that manner and, unless a limited liability company agreement prohibits revocation of dissolution, then notwithstanding the occurrence of an event set forth in § 18–801(a)(1), (2), (3) or (4) of this title, the limited liability company shall not be dissolved and its affairs shall not be wound up if, prior to the filing of a certificate of cancellation in the office of the Secretary of State, the limited liability company is continued, effective as of the occurrence of such event, (i) in the case of dissolution effected by the vote or consent of the members or other persons, pursuant to such vote or consent (and the approval of any members or other persons whose approval is required under the limited liability company agreement to revoke a dissolution contemplated by this clause), (ii) in the case of dissolution under § 18–801(a)(1) or (2) (other than a dissolution effected by the vote or consent of the members or other persons or the occurrence of an event that causes the last remaining member to cease to be a member), pursuant to such vote or consent that, pursuant to the terms of the limited liability company agreement, is required to amend the provision of the limited liability company agreement effecting such dissolution (and the approval of any members or other persons whose approval is required under the limited liability company agreement to revoke a dissolution contemplated by this clause), and (iii) in the case of dissolution effected by the occurrence of an event that causes the last remaining member to cease to be a member, pursuant to the vote or consent of the personal representative of the last remaining member of the limited liability company or the assignee of all of the limited liability company interests in the limited liability company (and the approval of any other persons whose approval is required under the limited liability company agreement to revoke a dissolution contemplated by this clause). If there is no remaining member of the limited liability company and the personal representative of the last remaining member or the assignee of all of the limited liability company interests in the limited liability company votes in favor of or consents to the continuation of the limited liability company, such personal representative or such assignee, as applicable, shall be required to agree to the admission of its a nominee or designee to as a member, effective as of the occurrence of the event that terminated the continued membership of the last remaining member. The provisions of this section shall not be construed to limit the accomplishment of a revocation of dissolution by other means permitted by law.

SUBCHAPTER IX. FOREIGN LIMITED LIABILITY COMPANIES

§ 18–901.　Law Governing

(a) Subject to the Constitution of the State of Delaware:

(1) The laws of the state, territory, possession, or other jurisdiction or country under which a foreign limited liability company is organized govern its organization and internal affairs and the liability of its members and managers; and

(2) A foreign limited liability company may not be denied registration by reason of any difference between those laws and the laws of the State of Delaware.

(b) A foreign limited liability company shall be subject to § 18–106 of this title.

§ 18–902.　Registration Required; Application

Before doing business in the State of Delaware, a foreign limited liability company shall register with the Secretary of State. . . .

§ 18–912.　Activities Not Constituting Doing Business

(a) Activities of a foreign limited liability company in the State of Delaware that do not constitute doing business for the purpose of this subchapter include:

(1) Maintaining, defending or settling an action or proceeding;

(2) Holding meetings of its members or managers or carrying on any other activity concerning its internal affairs;

(3) Maintaining bank accounts;

(4) Maintaining offices or agencies for the transfer, exchange or registration of the limited liability company's own securities or maintaining trustees or depositories with respect to those securities;

(5) Selling through independent contractors;

(6) Soliciting or obtaining orders, whether by mail or through employees or agents or otherwise, if the orders require acceptance outside the State of Delaware before they become contracts;

(7) Selling, by contract consummated outside the State of Delaware, and agreeing, by the contract, to deliver into the State of Delaware, machinery, plants or equipment, the construction, erection or installation of which within the State of Delaware requires the supervision of technical engineers or skilled employees performing services not generally available, and as part of the contract of sale agreeing to furnish such services, and such services only, to the vendee at the time of construction, erection or installation;

(8) Creating, as borrower or lender, or acquiring indebtedness with or without a mortgage or other security interest in property;

(9) Collecting debts or foreclosing mortgages or other security interests in property securing the debts, and holding, protecting and maintaining property so acquired;

(10) Conducting an isolated transaction that is not one in the course of similar transactions;

(11) Doing business in interstate commerce; and

(12) Doing business in the State of Delaware as an insurance company.

(b) A person shall not be deemed to be doing business in the State of Delaware solely by reason of being a member or manager of a domestic limited liability company or a foreign limited liability company.

(c) This section does not apply in determining whether a foreign limited liability company is subject to service of process, taxation or regulation under any other law of the State of Delaware.

SUBCHAPTER X. DERIVATIVE ACTIONS

§ 18–1001.   Right to Bring Action

A member or an assignee of a limited liability company interest may bring an action in the Court of Chancery in the right of a limited liability company to recover a judgment in its favor if managers or members with authority to do so have refused to bring the action or if an effort to cause those managers or members to bring the action is not likely to succeed.

§ 18–1002.   Proper Plaintiff

In a derivative action, the plaintiff must be a member or an assignee of a limited liability company interest at the time of bringing the action and:

(1) At the time of the transaction of which he complains; or

(2) His status as a member or an assignee of a limited liability company interest had devolved upon him by operation of law or pursuant to the terms of a limited liability company agreement from a person who was a member or an assignee of a limited liability company interest at the time of the transaction.

§ 18–1003.   Complaint

In a derivative action, the complaint shall set forth with particularity the effort, if any, of the plaintiff to secure initiation of the action by a manager or member or the reasons for not making the effort.

§ 18–1004.   Expenses

If a derivative action is successful, in whole or in part, as a result of a judgment, compromise or settlement of any such action, the court may award the plaintiff reasonable expenses, including reasonable attorney's fees, from any recovery in any such action or from a limited liability company.

SUBCHAPTER XI. MISCELLANEOUS

§ 18–1101.   Construction and Application of Chapter and Limited Liability Company Agreement

(a) The rule that statutes in derogation of the common law are to be strictly construed shall have no application to this chapter.

(b) It is the policy of this chapter to give the maximum effect to the principle of freedom of contract and to the enforceability of limited liability company agreements.

(c) To the extent that, at law or in equity, a member or manager or other person has duties (including fiduciary duties) to a limited liability company or to another member or manager or to another person that is a party to or is otherwise bound by a limited liability company agreement, the member's or manager's or other person's duties may be expanded or restricted or eliminated by provisions in the limited liability company agreement; provided that the limited liability company agreement may not eliminate the implied contractual covenant of good faith and fair dealing.

(d) Unless otherwise provided in a limited liability company agreement, a member or manager or other person shall not be liable to a limited liability company or to another member or manager or to another person that is a party to or is otherwise bound by a limited liability company agreement for breach of fiduciary duty for the member's or manager's or other person's good faith reliance on the provisions of the limited liability company agreement.

(e) A limited liability company agreement may provide for the limitation or elimination of any and all liabilities for breach of contract and breach of duties (including fiduciary duties) of a member, manager or other person to a limited liability company or to another member or manager or to another person that is a party to or is otherwise bound by a limited liability company agreement; provided that a limited liability company agreement may not limit or eliminate liability for any act or omission that constitutes a bad faith violation of the implied contractual covenant of good faith and fair dealing.

(f) Unless the context otherwise requires, as used herein, the singular shall include the plural and the plural may refer to only the singular. The use of any gender shall be applicable to all genders. The captions contained herein are for purposes of convenience only and shall not control or affect the construction of this chapter.

(g) Sections 9–406 and 9–408 of this title do not apply to any interest in a limited liability company, including all rights, powers and interests arising under a limited liability company agreement or this chapter. This provision prevails over §§ 9–406 and 9–408 of this title.

(h) Action validly taken pursuant to one provision of this chapter shall not be deemed invalid solely because it is identical or similar in substance to an action that could have been taken pursuant to some other provision of this chapter but fails to satisfy one or more requirements prescribed by such other provision.

(i) A limited liability company agreement that provides for the application of Delaware law shall be governed by and construed under the laws of the State of Delaware in accordance with its terms.

(j) The provisions of this chapter shall apply whether a limited liability company has one member or more than one member.

§ 18–1102.   Short Title

This chapter may be cited as the "Delaware Limited Liability Company Act."

§ 18–1104.   Cases Not Provided for in This Chapter

In any case not provided for in this chapter, the rules of law and equity, including the rules of law and equity relating to fiduciary duties and the law merchant, shall govern.

§ 18–1106.   Reserved Power of State of Delaware to Alter or Repeal Chapter

All provisions of this chapter may be altered from time to time or repealed and all rights of members and managers are subject to this reservation. Unless expressly stated to the contrary in this chapter, all amendments of this chapter shall apply to limited liability companies and members and managers whether or not existing as such at the time of the enactment of any such amendment.

§ 18–1107.   Taxation of Limited Liability Companies

(a) For purposes of any tax imposed by the State of Delaware or any instrumentality, agency or political subdivision of the State of Delaware, a limited liability company formed under this chapter or qualified to do business in the State of Delaware as a foreign limited liability company shall be classified as a partnership unless classified otherwise for federal income tax purposes, in which case the limited liability company shall be classified in the same manner as it is classified for federal income tax purposes. . . .

DELAWARE STATUTORY PUBLIC BENEFIT LIABILITY COMPANIES

TABLE OF CONTENTS
DEL. CODE ANN. TITLE 6, CHAPTER 18

SUBCHAPTER XII. STATUTORY PUBLIC BENEFIT LIMITED LIABILITY COMPANIES

Sec.		Page
18–1201.	Law Applicable to Statutory Public Benefit Limited Liability Companies; How Formed	271
18–1202.	Statutory Public Benefit Limited Liability Company Defined; Contents of Certificate of Formation and Limited Liability Company Agreement	271
18–1203.	Certain Amendments and Mergers; Votes Required	272
18–1204.	Duties of Members or Managers	272
18–1205.	Periodic Statements and Third-Party Certification	272
18–1206.	Derivative Suits	273
18–1207.	No Effect on Other Limited Liability Companies	273
18–1208.	Accomplishment by Other Means	273

SUBCHAPTER XII. STATUTORY PUBLIC BENEFIT LIMITED LIABILITY COMPANIES

§ 18–1201. Law Applicable to Statutory Public Benefit Limited Liability Companies; How Formed

This subchapter applies to all statutory public benefit limited liability companies, as defined in § 18–1202 of this title. If a limited liability company elects to become a statutory public benefit limited liability company under this subchapter in the manner prescribed in this subchapter, it shall be subject in all respects to the provisions of this chapter, except to the extent this subchapter imposes additional or different requirements, in which case such requirements shall apply, and notwithstanding § 18–1101 or any other provision of this title, such requirements imposed by this subchapter may not be altered in the limited liability company agreement.

§ 18–1202. Statutory Public Benefit Limited Liability Company Defined; Contents of Certificate of Formation and Limited Liability Company Agreement

(a) A "statutory public benefit limited liability company" is a for-profit limited liability company formed under and subject to the requirements of this chapter that is intended to produce a public benefit or public benefits and to operate in a responsible and sustainable manner. To that end, a statutory public benefit limited liability company shall be managed in a manner that balances the members' pecuniary interests, the best interests of those materially affected by the limited liability company's conduct, and the public benefit or public benefits set forth in its certificate of formation. A statutory public benefit limited liability company shall state in the heading of its certificate of formation that it is a statutory public benefit limited liability company and shall set forth one or more specific public benefits to be promoted by the limited liability company in its certificate of formation. The limited liability company agreement of a statutory public benefit limited liability company may not contain any provision inconsistent with this subchapter.

(b) "Public benefit" means a positive effect (or reduction of negative effects) on one or more categories of persons, entities, communities or interests (other than members in their capacities as members) including, but not limited to, effects of an artistic, charitable, cultural, economic, educational, environmental, literary, medical, religious, scientific or technological nature. "Public benefit provisions" means the provisions of a limited liability company agreement contemplated by this subchapter.

§ 18-1203.   Certain Amendments and Mergers; Votes Required

Notwithstanding any other provision of this chapter, a statutory public benefit limited liability company may not, without the approval of members who own at least 2/3 of the then-current percentage or other interest in the profits of the limited liability company owned by all members:

(1) Amend its certificate of formation to delete or amend a provision required by § 18-1202(a) of this title;

(2) Merge or consolidate with or into another entity or divide into two or more domestic limited liability companies if, as a result of such merger, consolidation or division, the limited liability company interests in such limited liability company would become, or be converted into or exchanged for the right to receive, limited liability company interests or other equity interests in a domestic or foreign limited liability company or other entity that is not a statutory public benefit limited liability company or similar entity, the certificate of formation or limited liability company agreement (or similar governing document) of which does not contain provisions identifying a public benefit or public benefits comparable in all material respects to those set forth in the certificate of formation of such limited liability company as contemplated by § 18-1202(a) of this title; or

(3) Cease to be a statutory public benefit limited liability company under the provisions of this subchapter.

§ 18-1204.   Duties of Members or Managers

(a) The members or managers or other persons with authority to manage or direct the business and affairs of a statutory public benefit limited liability company shall manage or direct the business and affairs of the statutory public benefit limited liability company in a manner that balances the pecuniary interests of the members, the best interests of those materially affected by the limited liability company's conduct, and the specific public benefit or public benefits set forth in its certificate of formation. Unless otherwise provided in a limited liability company agreement, no member, manager or other person with authority to manage or direct the business and affairs of the statutory public benefit limited liability company shall have any liability for monetary damages for the failure to manage or direct the business and affairs of the statutory public benefit limited liability company as provided in this subsection.

(b) A member or manager of a statutory public benefit limited liability company or any other person with authority to manage or direct the business and affairs of the statutory public benefit limited liability company shall not, by virtue of the public benefit provisions or § 18-1202(a) of this title, have any duty to any person on account of any interest of such person in the public benefit or public benefits set forth in its certificate of formation or on account of any interest materially affected by the limited liability company's conduct and, with respect to a decision implicating the balance requirement in subsection (a) of this section, will be deemed to satisfy such person's fiduciary duties to members and the limited liability company if such person's decision is both informed and disinterested and not such that no person of ordinary, sound judgment would approve.

§ 18-1205.   Periodic Statements and Third-Party Certification

A statutory public benefit limited liability company shall no less than biennially provide its members with a statement as to the limited liability company's promotion of the public benefit or public benefits set forth in its certificate of formation and as to the best interests of those materially affected by the limited liability company's conduct. The statement shall include:

(1) The objectives that have been established to promote such public benefit or public benefits and interests;

(2) The standards that have been adopted to measure the limited liability company's progress in promoting such public benefit or public benefits and interests;

(3) Objective factual information based on those standards regarding the limited liability company's success in meeting the objectives for promoting such public benefit or public benefits and interests; and

(4) An assessment of the limited liability company's success in meeting the objectives and promoting such public benefit or public benefits and interests.

§ 18–1206.   Derivative Suits

Members of a statutory public benefit limited liability company or assignees of limited liability company interests in a statutory public benefit limited liability company owning individually or collectively, as of the date of instituting such derivative suit, at least 2% of the then-current percentage or other interest in the profits of the limited liability company or, in the case of a limited liability company with limited liability company interests listed on a national securities exchange, the lesser of such percentage or limited liability company interests of at least $2,000,000 in market value, may maintain a derivative lawsuit to enforce the requirements set forth in § 18–1204(a) of this title.

§ 18–1207.   No Effect on Other Limited Liability Companies

This subchapter shall not affect a statute or rule of law that is applicable to a limited liability company that is not a statutory public benefit limited liability company.

§ 18–1208.   Accomplishment by Other Means

The provisions of this subchapter shall not be construed to limit the accomplishment by any other means permitted by law of the formation or operation of a limited liability company that is formed or operated for a public benefit (including a limited liability company that is designated as a public benefit limited liability company) that is not a statutory public benefit limited liability company.

UNIFORM LIMITED LIABILITY COMPANY ACT (2006)

(Last Amended 2013)

Drafted by the

NATIONAL CONFERENCE OF COMMISSIONERS
ON UNIFORM STATE LAWS

and by it

APPROVED AND RECOMMENDED FOR ENACTMENT
IN ALL THE STATES

at its

ANNUAL CONFERENCE

MEETING IN ITS ONE-HUNDRED-AND-TWENTY-SECOND YEAR
BOSTON, MASSACHUSETTS
JULY 6 - JULY 12, 2013

WITH PREFATORY NOTE AND COMMENTS

COPYRIGHT © 2014
By
NATIONAL CONFERENCE OF COMMISSIONERS
ON UNIFORM STATE LAWS

August 19, 2015

ABOUT ULC

The **Uniform Law Commission** (ULC), also known as National Conference of Commissioners on Uniform State Laws (NCCUSL), now in its 123rd year, provides states with non-partisan, well-conceived and well-drafted legislation that brings clarity and stability to critical areas of state statutory law.

ULC members must be lawyers, qualified to practice law. They are practicing lawyers, judges, legislators and legislative staff and law professors, who have been appointed by state governments as well as the District of Columbia, Puerto Rico, and the U.S. Virgin Islands to research, draft, and promote enactment of uniform state laws in areas of state law where uniformity is desirable and practical.

- ULC strengthens the federal system by providing rules and procedures that are consistent from state to state but that also reflect the diverse experience of the states.

- ULC statutes are representative of state experience, because the organization is made up of representatives from each state, appointed by state government.

- ULC keeps state law up-to-date by addressing important and timely legal issues.

- ULC's efforts reduce the need for individuals and businesses to deal with different laws as they move and do business in different states.

- ULC's work facilitates economic development and provides a legal platform for foreign entities to deal with U.S. citizens and businesses.

- Uniform Law Commissioners donate thousands of hours of their time and legal and drafting expertise every year as a public service, and receive no salary or compensation for their work.

- ULC's deliberative and uniquely open drafting process draws on the expertise of commissioners, but also utilizes input from legal experts, and advisors and observers representing the views of other legal organizations or interests that will be subject to the proposed laws.

ULC is a state-supported organization that represents true value for the states, providing services that most states could not otherwise afford or duplicate.

DRAFTING COMMITTEE ON REVISIONS TO
UNIFORM LIMITED LIABILITY COMPANY ACT (2006)

The Committee appointed by and representing the National Conference of Commissioners on Uniform State Laws in revising this Act consisted of the following individuals:

DAVID S. WALKER, Drake University Law School, 2507 University Ave., Des Moines, IA 50311, Chair

REX BLACKBURN, 1673 West Shoreline Dr., Suite 200, P.O. Box 7808, Boise, ID 83707

ANN E. CONAWAY, Widener University, School of Law, 4601 Concord Pike, Wilmington, DE 19803

DONALD K. DENSBORN, 8888 Keystone Crossing, Suite 1400, Indianapolis, IN 46240-4609

STEVEN G. FROST, 111 W. Monroe St., Suite 1500, Chicago, IL 60603-4080

HARRY J. HAYNSWORTH, IV, 2200 IDS Center, Minneapolis, MN 55402

MICHAEL HOUGHTON, P.O. Box 1347, 1201 N. Market St., 18th Floor, Wilmington, DE 19899

HARRIET LANSING, 313 Judicial Center, 25 Rev. Dr. Martin Luther King Jr. Blvd., St. Paul, MN 55155

EDWIN E. SMITH, 150 Federal St., 21st Floor, Boston, MA 02110-1726

CARTER G. BISHOP, Suffolk University Law School, 120 Tremont St., Boston, MA 02108-4977, Co-Reporter

DANIEL S. KLEINBERGER, 1818 Twin Circle Drive, Mendota Heights, MN 55118-4140, Co-Reporter

EX OFFICIO

HOWARD J. SWIBEL, 120 S. Riverside Plaza, Suite 1200, Chicago, IL 60606, *President*

DALE G. HIGER, 1302 Warm Springs Ave., Boise, ID 83712, *Division Chair*

AMERICAN BAR ASSOCIATION ADVISOR

ROBERT R. KEATINGE, 555 17th St., Suite 3200, Denver, CO 80202-3979

AMERICAN BAR ASSOCIATION SECTION ADVISORS

WILLIAM J. CALLISON, 370 17th St., 2500 Republic Plaza, Denver, CO 80202, *ABA Business Law Section Advisor*

WILLIAM H. CLARK, JR., One Logan Square, 18th and Cherry Streets, Philadelphia, PA 19103-6996, *ABA Business Law Section Advisor*

THOMAS EARL GEU, University of South Dakota, School of Law, 414 Clark St., Suite 214, Vermillion, SD 57069-2390, *ABA Real Property, Probate and Trust Law Section Advisor*

JON T. HIRSCHOFF, One Landmark Square, Suite 1400, Stamford, CT 06901, *ABA Business Law Section Advisor*

ROBERT KRAPF, One Rodney Square, 920 King St., P.O. Box 551, Wilmington, DE 19899, *ABA Real Property, Probate and Trust Law Section Advisor*

PAUL L. LION, III, 755 Page Mill Rd., Palo Alto, CA 94304-1018, *ABA Business Law Section Advisor, California State Bar*

SCOTT E. LUDWIG, 200 Clinton Ave. W., Suite 900, Huntsville, AL 35801-4900, *ABA Business Law Section Advisor*

JOHN R. MAXFIELD, 555 17th St., Suite 3200, P.O. Box 8749, Denver, CO 80201, *ABA Tax Section Advisor*

ELIZABETH STONE MILLER, Baylor Law School, 1114 S. University Parks Dr., 1 Bear Pl #97288, Waco, TX 76706, *ABA Business Law Section Advisor*

UNIFORM LIMITED LIABILITY COMPANY ACT (2006)

SANDRA K. MILLER, Widener University School of Business Administration, One University Place, Chester, PA 19013-5792, *ABA Business Law Section Advisor*

BARRY B. NEKRITZ, 8000 Sears Tower, 233 S. Wacker Dr., Chicago, IL 60606, *ABA Real Property, Probate and Trust Law Section Advisor*

THOMAS E. RUTLEDGE, 2000 PNC Plaza, 500 W. Jefferson St., Louisville, KY 40202-2874, *ABA Business Law Section Advisor*

EXECUTIVE DIRECTOR

WILLIAM H. HENNING, University of Alabama School of Law, Box 870382, Tuscaloosa, AL 35487-0382, *Executive Director*

DRAFTING COMMITTEE ON HARMONIZATION OF BUSINESS ENTITY ACTS

The Committee appointed by and representing the National Conference of Commissioners on Uniform State Laws in preparing the harmonized uniform unincorporated entity acts consists of the following individuals:

HARRY J. HAYNSWORTH, 108 Addingtons, Williamsburg, VA 23188, *Chair*

WILLIAM H. CLARK, JR., One Logan Square, 18th and Cherry Sts., Philadelphia, PA 19103-6996, *Vice-Chair*

ANN E. CONAWAY, 302 High Ridge Rd., Greeneville, DE 19807

THOMAS E. GEU, University of South Dakota School of Law, 414 Clark St., Suite 214, Vermillion, SD 57069-2390

DALE G. HIGER, 1302 Warm Springs Ave., Boise, ID 83712

JAMES C. MCKAY, JR., Office of the Attorney General for the District of Columbia, 441 Fourth St. NW, 6th Floor S., Washington, DC 20001

MARILYN E. PHELAN, 306 Peninsula Ct., Granbury, TX 76048

WILLIAM J. QUINLAN, Two First National Plaza, 20 S. Clark St., Suite 2900, Chicago, IL 60603

KEVIN P. SUMIDA, 735 Bishop St., Suite 411, Honolulu, HI 96813

JUSTIN L. VIGDOR, 350 Linden Oaks, Suite 310, Rochester, NY 14625-2825

DAVID S. WALKER, Drake University Law School, 2507 University Ave., Des Moines, IA 50311

CARTER G. BISHOP, Suffolk University Law School, 120 Tremont St., Boston, MA 02108-4977, *Co-Reporter*

DANIEL S. KLEINBERGER, 1818 Twin Circle Dr., Mendota Heights, MN 55118-4140, *Co-Reporter*

EX OFFICIO

ROBERT A. STEIN, University of Minnesota Law School, 229 19th Ave. S., Minneapolis, MN 55455, *President*

MARILYN E. PHELAN, 306 Peninsula Ct., Granbury, TX 76048, *Division Chair*

AMERICAN BAR ASSOCIATION ADVISORS

ROBERT R. KEATINGE, 555 17th St., Suite 3200, Denver, CO 80202-3979, *ABA Advisor*

WILLIAM J. CALLISON, 3200 Wells Fargo Center, 1700 Lincoln St., Denver, CO 80203, *ABA Section Advisor*

ALLAN G. DONN, Wells Fargo Center, 440 Monticello Ave., Suite 2200, Norfolk, VA 23510-2243, *ABA Section Advisor*

WILLIAM S. FORSBERG, 150 S. Fifth St., Suite 2300, Minneapolis, MN 55402-4238, *ABA Section Advisor*

BARRY B. NEKRITZ, 311 S. Wacker Dr., Suite 4400, Chicago, IL 60606, *ABA Section Advisor*

UNIFORM LIMITED LIABILITY COMPANY ACT (2006)

JAMES J. WHEATON, 1716 Corporate Landing Pkwy., Virginia Beach, VA 23454, *ABA Section Advisor*

EXECUTIVE DIRECTOR

JOHN A. SEBERT, 111 N. Wabash Ave., Suite 1010, Chicago, IL 60602, Executive Director

Copies of this Act may be obtained from:

NATIONAL CONFERENCE OF COMMISSIONERS
ON UNIFORM STATE LAWS

111 N. Wabash Ave., Suite 1010
Chicago, Illinois 60602
312/450-6600

www.uniformlaws.org

UNIFORM LIMITED LIABILITY
COMPANY ACT (2006)

(*Last Amended* 2013)

TABLE OF CONTENTS

Prefatory Note to ULLCA (2006) 282
Prefatory Note to 2011 And 2013 Amendments 285
Explanatory Note on the Revised Comments 286

[ARTICLE] 1
GENERAL PROVISIONS

Sec.

101.	Short Title.	287
102.	Definitions.	287
103.	Knowledge; Notice.	294
104.	Governing Law.	295
105.	Operating Agreement; Scope, Function, and Limitations.	297
106.	Operating Agreement; Effect on Limited Liability Company and Person Becoming Member; Preformation Agreement.	308
107.	Operating Agreement; Effect on Third Parties and Relationship to Records Effective on Behalf of Limited Liability Company.	309
108.	Nature, Purpose, and Duration of Limited Liability Company.	311
109.	Powers.	312
110.	Application to Existing Relationships.	312
111.	Supplemental Principles of Law.	313
112.	Permitted Names.	313
113.	Reservation of Name.	314
114.	Registration of Name.	315
115.	Registered Agent.	315
116.	Change of Registered Agent or Address for Registered Agent by Limited Liability Company.	316
117.	Resignation of Registered Agent.	316
118.	Change of Name or Address by Registered Agent.	317
119.	Service of Process, Notice, or Demand.	318
120.	Delivery of Record.	319

121.   Reservation of Power to Amend or Repeal. 319

[ARTICLE] 2
FORMATION; CERTIFICATE OF ORGANIZATION
AND OTHER FILINGS

201.   Formation of Limited Liability Company; Certificate of Organization.................... 320
202.   Amendment or Restatement of Certificate of
       Organization. 321
203.   Signing of Records to Be Delivered for Filing to
       [Secretary of State]. 322
204.   Signing and Filing Pursuant to Judicial Order. 322
205.   Liability for Inaccurate Information In Filed Record. 323
206.   Filing Requirements. 324
207.   Effective Date and Time. 325
208.   Withdrawal of Filed Record Before Effectiveness. 326
209.   Correcting Filed Record. 326
210.   Duty of [Secretary of State] to File; Review of Refusal to File; Delivery of Record by
       [Secretary of State]. 327
211.   Certificate of Good Standing or Registration. 328
212.   [Annual] [Biennial] Report for [Secretary of State]. 330

[ARTICLE] 3
RELATIONS OF MEMBERS AND MANAGERS TO PERSONS
DEALING WITH LIMITED LIABILITY COMPANY

301.   No Agency Power of Member As Member.. 330
302.   Statement of Limited Liability Company Authority. 332
303.   Statement of Denial. 336
304.   Liability of Members and Managers. 336

[ARTICLE] 4
RELATIONS OF MEMBERS TO EACH OTHER
AND TO LIMITED LIABILITY COMPANY

401.   Becoming Member. 339
402.   Form of Contribution. 340
403.   Liability for Contributions. 341
404.   Sharing of and Right to Distributions Before Dissolution. 341
405.   Limitations on Distributions. 342
406.   Liability for Improper Distributions. 344
407.   Management of Limited Liability Company.. 346
408.   Reimbursement; Indemnification; Advancement; and Insurance. 350
409.   Standards of Conduct for Members and Managers. 352
410.   Rights to Information of Member, Manager, and Person Dissociated As Member. 357

[ARTICLE] 5
TRANSFERABLE INTERESTS AND RIGHTS
OF TRANSFEREES AND CREDITORS

501.   Nature of Transferable Interest. 360
502.   Transfer of Transferable Interest. 361
503.   Charging Order. 363
504.   Power of Legal Representative of Deceased Member................................. 367

[ARTICLE] 6
DISSOCIATION

601. Power to Dissociate As Member; Wrongful Dissociation. 367
602. Events Causing Dissociation. 368
603. Effect of Dissociation. 371

[ARTICLE] 7
DISSOLUTION AND WINDING UP

701. Events Causing Dissolution. 373
702. Winding Up. 376
703. Rescinding Dissolution. 378
704. Known Claims Against Dissolved Limited Liability Company. 379
705. Other Claims Against Dissolved Limited Liability Company. 379
706. Court Proceedings. 380
707. Disposition of Assets In Winding Up. 380
708. Administrative Dissolution. 381
709. Reinstatement. 382
710. Judicial Review of Denial of Reinstatement. 383

[ARTICLE] 8
ACTIONS BY MEMBERS

801. Direct Action by Member. 383
802. Derivative Action. 384
803. Proper Plaintiff. 385
804. Pleading. 385
805. Special Litigation Committee. 385
806. Proceeds and Expenses. 387

[ARTICLE] 9
FOREIGN LIMITED LIABILITY COMPANIES

901. Governing Law. 387
902. Registration to Do Business In This State. 388
903. Foreign Registration Statement. 389
904. Amendment of Foreign Registration Statement 389
905. Activities Not Constituting Doing Business. 390
906. Noncomplying Name of Foreign Limited Liability Company. 391
907. Withdrawal Deemed on Conversion to Domestic Filing Entity or Domestic Limited
      Liability Partnership. 392
908. Withdrawal on Dissolution or Conversion to Nonfiling Entity Other Than Limited
      Liability Partnership. 392
909. Transfer of Registration. 393
910. Termination of Registration. 393
911. Withdrawal of Registration of Registered Foreign Limited Liability Company. 394
912. Action by [Attorney General]. 394

[ARTICLE] 10
MERGER, INTEREST EXCHANGE, CONVERSION, AND DOMESTICATION

[PART] 1
GENERAL PROVISIONS

1001. Definitions. 395

1002.   Relationship of [Article] to Other Laws. 404
1003.   Required Notice or Approval. 405
1004.   Nonexclusivity. 406
1005.   Reference to External Facts. 406
1006.   Appraisal Rights. 406
[1007.   Excluded Entities and Transactions.] 406

[PART] 2
MERGER

1021.   Merger Authorized. 407
1022.   Plan of Merger. 408
1023.   Approval of Merger. 409
1024.   Amendment or Abandonment of Plan of Merger. 410
1025.   Statement of Merger; Effective Date of Merger. 410
1026.   Effect of Merger. 412

[PART] 3
INTEREST EXCHANGE

1031.   Interest Exchange Authorized. 415
1032.   Plan of Interest Exchange. 416
1033.   Approval of Interest Exchange. 417
1034.   Amendment or Abandonment of Plan of Interest Exchange. 418
1035.   Statement of Interest Exchange; Effective Date of Interest Exchange. ... 418
1036.   Effect of Interest Exchange. 419

[PART] 4
CONVERSION

1041.   Conversion Authorized. 420
1042.   Plan of Conversion. 421
1043.   Approval of Conversion. 422
1044.   Amendment or Abandonment of Plan of Conversion. 422
1045.   Statement of Conversion; Effective Date of Conversion. 423
1046.   Effect of Conversion. 424

[PART] 5
DOMESTICATION

1051.   Domestication Authorized. 426
1052.   Plan of Domestication. 427
1053.   Approval of Domestication. 427
1054.   Amendment or Abandonment of Plan of Domestication. 428
1055.   Statement of Domestication; Effective Date of Domestication. 429
1056.   Effect of Domestication. 430

[ARTICLE] 11
MISCELLANEOUS PROVISIONS

1101.   Uniformity of Application and Construction. 432
1102.   Relation to Electronic Signatures In Global and National Commerce Act. 432
1103.   Savings Clause. 432
[1104.   Severability Clause.] 432
1105.   Repeals. 432
1106.   Effective Date. 433

UNIFORM LIMITED LIABILITY COMPANY ACT (2006)

(Last Amended 2013)
PREFATORY NOTE TO ULLCA (2006)

Background to this Act:

Developments since the Conference Considered and Approved the Original
Uniform Limited Liability Company Act (ULLCA)

The Uniform Limited Liability Company Act ("ULLCA") was conceived in 1992 and first adopted by the Conference in 1994. By that time nearly every state had adopted an LLC statute, and those statutes varied considerably in both form and substance. Many of those early statutes were based on the first version of the ABA Model Prototype LLC Act.

ULLCA's drafting relied substantially on the then recently adopted Revised Uniform Partnership Act ("RUPA"), and this reliance was especially heavy with regard to member-managed LLCs. ULLCA's provisions for manager-managed LLCs comprised an amalgam fashioned from the 1985 Revised Uniform Limited Partnership Act ("RULPA") and the Model Business Corporation Act ("MBCA"). ULLCA's provisions were also significantly influenced by the then-applicable federal tax classification regulations, which classified an unincorporated organization as a corporation if the organization more nearly resembled a corporation than a partnership. Those same regulations also made the tax classification of single-member LLCs problematic.

Much has changed. All states and the District of Columbia have adopted LLC statutes, and many LLC statutes have been substantially amended several times. LLC filings are significant in every U.S. jurisdiction, and in many states new LLC filings approach or even outnumber new corporate filings on an annual basis. Manager-managed LLCs have become a significant factor in non-publicly traded capital markets, and increasing numbers of states provide for mergers and conversions involving LLCs and other unincorporated entities.

In 1997 the tax classification context changed radically, when the IRS' "check-the-box" regulations became effective. Under these regulations, an "unincorporated" business entity is taxed either as a partnership or disregarded entity (depending upon the number of owners) unless it elects to be taxed as a corporation. Exceptions exist (*e.g.*, entities whose interests are publicly traded), but, in general, tax classification concerns no longer constrain the structure of LLCs and the content of LLC statutes. Single-member LLCs, once suspect because of novel and uncertain tax status, are now popular both for sole proprietorships and as corporate subsidiaries.

In 1995 the Conference amended RUPA to add "full-shield" LLP provisions, and today every state has some form of LLP legislation (either through a RUPA adoption or shield-related revisions to a UPA-based statute). While some states still provide only a "partial shield" for LLPs, many states have adopted "full shield" LLP provisions. In full-shield jurisdictions, LLPs and member-managed LLCs offer entrepreneurs very similar attributes and, in the case of professional service organizations, LLPs may dominate the field.

ULLCA was revised in 1996 in anticipation of the "check the box" regulations and has been adopted in a number of states. In many non-ULLCA states, the LLC statute includes RUPA-like provisions. However, state LLC laws are far from uniform.

Eighteen years have passed since the IRS issued its gate-opening Revenue Ruling 88–76, declaring that a Wyoming LLC would be taxed as a partnership despite the entity's corporate-like liability shield. More than eight years have passed since the IRS opened the gate still further with the "check the box" regulations. It is an opportune moment to identify the best elements of the myriad "first generation" LLC statutes and to infuse those elements into a new, "second generation" uniform act.

UNIFORM LIMITED LIABILITY COMPANY ACT (2006)

Noteworthy Provisions of the 2006 Act

The Revised Uniform Limited Company Act is drafted to replace a state's current LLC statute, whether or not that statute is based on ULLCA. The new Act's noteworthy provisions concern:

- the operating agreement
- fiduciary duty
- the ability to "pre-file" a certificate of organization without having a member at the time of the filing
- the power of a member or manager to bind the limited liability company
- default rules on management structure
- charging orders
- a remedy for oppressive conduct
- derivative claims and special litigation committees
- organic transactions—mergers, conversions, and domestications

The Operating Agreement: Like the partnership agreement in a general or limited partnership, an LLC's operating agreement serves as the foundational contract among the entity's owners. RUPA pioneered the notion of centralizing all statutory provisions pertaining to the foundational contract, and—like ULLCA and ULPA (2001)—the new Act continues that approach. However, because an operating agreement raises issues too numerous and complex to include easily in a single section, the new Act uses three related sections to address the operating agreement:

- Section 110—scope, function, and limitations;
- Section 111—effect on limited liability company and persons becoming members; preformation agreement; and
- Section 112—effect on third parties and relationship to records effective on behalf of limited liability company.

The new Act also contains a number of substantive innovations concerning the operating agreement, including:

- better delineating the extent to which the operating agreement can define, alter, or even eliminate aspects of fiduciary duty;
- expressly authorizing the operating agreement to relieve members and managers from liability for money damages arising from breach of duty, subject to specific limitations; and
- stating specific rules for applying the statutory phrase "manifestly unreasonable" and thereby providing clear guidance for courts considering whether to invalidate operating agreement provisions that address fiduciary duty and other sensitive matters.

Fiduciary Duty: RUPA also pioneered the idea of codifying partners' fiduciary duties in order to protect the partnership agreement from judicial second-guessing. This approach—to "cabin in" (or corral) fiduciary duty—was followed in ULLCA and ULPA (2001). In contrast, the new Act recognizes that, at least in the realm of limited liability companies:

- the "cabin in" approach creates more problems than it solves (*e.g.*, by putting inordinate pressure on the concept of "good faith and fair dealing"); and
- the better way to protect the operating agreement from judicial second-guessing is to:

  o increase and clarify the power of the operating agreement to define or re-shape fiduciary duties (including the power to eliminate aspects of fiduciary duties); and

  o provide some guidance to courts when a person seeks to escape an agreement by claiming its provisions are "manifestly unreasonable."

Accordingly, the new Act codifies major fiduciary duties but does not purport to do so exhaustively. *See* Section 409.

The Ability to "Pre-File" a Certificate of Organization: The Comments to Section 201 explain in detail how the new Act resolves the difficult question of the "shelf LLC" (*i.e.,* an LLC formed without having at least one member upon formation). In short, the Act: (i) permits an organizer to file a certificate of organization without a person "waiting in the wings" to become a member upon formation; but (ii) provides that the LLC is not formed until and unless at least one person becomes a member and the organizer makes a second filing stating that the LLC has at least one member.

The Power of a Member or Manager to Bind the Limited Liability Company: In 1914 the original Uniform Partnership Act codified a particular type of apparent authority by position, providing that "[t]he act of every partner . . . for apparently carrying on in the usual way the business of the partnership binds the partnership. . . ." This concept of "statutory apparent authority" applies by linkage in the 1916 Uniform Limited Partnership Act and the 1976/85 Revised Uniform Limited Partnership Act and appears in RUPA, ULLCA, ULPA (2001), and almost every LLC statute in the United States.

The concept makes good sense for general and limited partnerships. A third party dealing with either type of partnership can know by the formal name of the entity and by a person's status as general or limited partner whether the person has the power to bind the entity.

The concept does not make sense for modern LLC law, because: (i) an LLC's status as member-managed or manager-managed is not apparent from the LLC's name (creating traps for unwary third parties); and (ii) although most LLC statutes provide templates for member-management and manager-management, variability of management structure is a key strength of the LLC as a form of business organization.

The new Act recognizes that "statutory apparent authority" is an attribute of partnership formality that does not belong in an LLC statute. Section 301(a) provides that "a member is not an agent of the limited liability company solely by reason of being a member." Other law—most especially the law of agency—will handle power-to-bind questions.

Although conceptually innovative, this approach will not significantly alter the commercial reality that exists between limited liability companies and third parties, because:

1. The vast majority of interactions between limited liability companies and "third parties" are quotidian and transpire without agency law issues being recognized by the parties, let alone disputed.

2. When a limited liability company enters into a major transaction with a sophisticated third party, the third party never relies on statutory apparent authority to determine that the person purporting to act for the limited liability company has the authority to do so;

3. Most LLCs use employees to carry out most of the LLC's dealings with third parties. In that context, the agency power of members and managers is usually irrelevant (if an employee's authority is contested and the employee "reports to" a member or manager, the member's or manager's authority will be relevant to determining the employee's authority. However, in that situation, agency law principles will suffice to delineate the manager or member's supervisory authority);

4. Very few current LLC statutes contain rules for attributing to an LLC the wrongful acts of the LLC's members or managers. *Compare* RUPA § 305. In this realm, this Act merely acknowledges pre-existing reality;

5. As explained in detail in the Comments to Sections 301 and 407(c), agency law principles are well-suited to the tasks resulting from the "de-codification" of apparent authority by position.

The moment is opportune for this reform. The newly issued Restatement (Third) of Agency gives substantial attention to the power of an enterprise's participants to bind the enterprise. In addition, the new Act has "souped up" RUPA's statement of authority to permit an LLC to publicly file a statement of authority for a position (not merely a particular person). Statements of authority will enable LLCs to provide reliable documentation of authority to enter into transactions without having to disclose to third parties the entirety of the operating agreement. (The new Act also has eliminated prolix provisions that sought to restate agency law rules on notice and knowledge.)

<u>Default Rules on Management Structure</u>: The new Act retains the manager-managed and member-managed constructs as options for members to use in configuring their *inter se* relationship, and the operating agreement is the vehicle by which the members make and state their choice of management structure. Given the elimination of statutory apparent authority, it is unnecessary and could be confusing to require the articles of organization to state the members' determination on this point.

<u>Charging Orders</u>: The charging order mechanism: (i) dates back to the 1914 Uniform Partnership Act and the English Partnership Act of 1890, and (ii) is an essential part of the "pick your partner" approach that is fundamental to the law of unincorporated businesses. The new Act continues the charging order mechanism, but modernizes the statutory language so that the language (and its protections against outside interference in an LLC's activities) can be readily understood.

<u>A Remedy for Oppressive Conduct</u>: Reflecting case law developments around the country, the new Act permits a member (but not a transferee) to seek a court order "dissolving the company on the grounds that the managers or those members in control of the company . . . have acted or are acting in a manner that is oppressive and was, is, or will be directly harmful to the [member]." Section 701(5)(B). This provision is necessary given the perpetual duration of an LLC formed under this Act, Section 104(c), and this Act's elimination of the "put right" provided by ULLCA § 701.

<u>Derivative Claims and Special Litigation Committees</u>: The new Act contains modern provisions addressing derivative litigation, including a provision authorizing special litigation committees, and subjecting their composition and conduct to judicial review.

<u>Organic Transactions—Mergers, Conversions, and Domestications</u>: The new Act has comprehensive, self-contained provisions for these transactions, including "inter-species" transactions.

PREFATORY NOTE TO 2011 AND 2013 HARMONIZATION AMENDMENTS

From 2009 to 2013, the Uniform Law Conference undertook an intensive effort to harmonize, to the extent possible, all uniform acts pertaining to unincorporated organizations. As part of that effort, the Uniform Limited Liability Company Act ("ULLCA") underwent four types of changes: substantive; major improvements in language; minor revisions in language for the sake of harmonization; and relocation within this particular "spoke" of provisions that are part of the "HUB" in the new Uniform Business Organizations Code ("UBOC").

Substantive Changes

The three most significant substantive changes are:

- eliminating the possibility of a shelf LLC (with the attendant, complex provision requiring two filings with the filing office) and providing instead that "[a] limited liability company is formed when the company's certificate of organization becomes effective and at least one person becomes a member," Section 201(d);

- replacing the "ordinary care/business judgment rule" standard with the duty to "refrain from engaging in grossly negligent or reckless conduct, willful or intentional misconduct, or knowing violation of law," Section 409(c);

- recognizing that, when an LLC has only one member, the "pick your partner" concept is inapposite and providing that, in that situation, the foreclosure of a charging order pertains to the entire ownership interest, not just the economic rights, Section 503(f).

Other substantive changes include: (i) providing a narrow exception to the rule that the amendments to the operating agreement control the rights of person dissociated as a members and of persons that had previously become transferees, Section 107(b)(2); (ii) eliminating the requirement that a domestic LLC designate and maintain an in-state office, Section 201; (iii) requiring that the annual report list the name of at least one member if the LLC is member-managed and one manager if the LLC is manger-managed,

Section 212(a)(4) and (5); and (iv) expressly authorizing a limited liability company to provide advancements to a person entitled to indemnification, Section 408(c).

Substantial Improvements to Language

The most significant improvements in language appear in Section 105 (formerly Section 110), the first of three sections addressing the operating agreement. The structure of Section 105 is far less complicated than the structure of former Section 110.

Harmonization-Based Language Changes

Minor changes in language for the sake of harmonization appear throughout the act. For example, Section 202(b) is revised as follows:

(b) To amend its certificate of organization, a limited liability company must deliver to the [Secretary of State] for filing an amendment stating:

(1) the name of the company;

(2) the date of filing of its initial certificate of organization; and

(3) ~~the changes~~ the text of the amendment ~~makes to the certificate as most recently amended or restated~~.

Relocation and Renumbering of HUB-Based Provisions

The Harmonization Project included both the harmonization of various stand-alone acts and the compilation of UBOC, which comprises a "HUB" (somewhat analogous to Article 1 of the Uniform Commercial Code) and various spokes. Each spoke pertains to a different type of organization (*e.g.*, limited liability company, statutory trust entity). Naturally, spokes in UBOC do not repeat the provisions from the HUB. In contrast, each stand-alone act includes provisions that appear in the HUB in the Code.

So that the section numbers of this "spoke" correspond with the spoke provisions in the Code, "HUB"-based provisions of this Act have been renumbered to appear at the end of articles. *See, e.g.*, Sections 112–21.

The Drafting Committee on Harmonization of Business Entity Acts was greatly assisted in its work by the very substantial and knowledgeable contributions of the following Observers who diligently attended and actively participated in its meetings:

ELIZABETH K. BABSON, One Logan Square, 18th & Cherry Sts., Philadelphia, PA 19103

LISA R. JACOBS, One Liberty Place, 1650 Market St., Philadelphia, PA 19103

GARTH JACOBSON, 520 Pike St., Seattle, WA 98101

JULIE M. KARAVAS, 1248 O St., Lincoln, NE 68508

DAVID MARTIN, 333W. Wyoming, St. Paul, MN 55107

SANDRA K. MILLER, One University Place, Chester, PA 19013

JOHN A. SINGER, Federal Trade Commission, Washington, D.C.

ROBERT H. SITKOFF, 1575 Massachusetts Ave., Cambridge, MA 02138

SARAH STEINBECK, Colorado Secretary of State, Denver, CO

KEVIN P. WALSH, One Logan Square, 18th & Cherry Sts., Philadelphia, PA 19103

HOWARD P. WALTHALL, Cumberland School of Law, Birmingham, AL 35229

EXPLANATORY NOTE ON THE REVISED COMMENTS

As part of the Harmonization Project, the Conference substantially revised the Comments to the Uniform Limited Liability Company Act. Professor Daniel S. Kleinberger was the principal drafter of the revised comments.

To distinguish among the current and prior versions of uniform business organization acts, the Harmonization comments use the following references.

The phrase "this act" refers to the Harmonized act—*i.e.*, the Uniform Limited Liability Company Act (2006) (Last Amended 2013).

"ULLCA (2006)" refers to the Revised Uniform Limited Liability Company Act as promulgated in 2006.

"ULLCA (1996)" refers to the original Uniform Limited Liability Company Act as promulgated in 1996.

"ULPA (2001) (Last Amended 2013)" refers to the Uniform Limited Partnership Act (2001) as harmonized.

"ULPA (2001) refers to the Uniform Limited Partnership Act as promulgated in 2001.

"ULPA (1976/1985)" refers to the Revised Uniform Limited Partnership Act as promulgated in 1976 and substantially revised in 1985.

"ULPA (1976)" refers to the Revised Uniform Limited Partnership Act as promulgated in 1976.

"ULPA (1916)" refers to the Uniform Limited Partnership Act as promulgated in 1916.

"UPA (1997) (Last Amended 2013)" refers to the Uniform Partnership Act (1997) as harmonized.

"UPA (1997)" refers to the version of the Uniform Partnership Act originally promulgated in 1994, with all amendments through 1997.

"UPA (1914)" refers to the original Uniform Partnership Act as promulgated in 1914.

"MBCA" refers to the Model Business Corporation Act.

UNIFORM LIMITED LIABILITY COMPANY ACT (2006)

(Last Amended 2013)

[ARTICLE] 1

GENERAL PROVISIONS

§ 101.   SHORT TITLE.

This [act] may be cited as the Uniform Limited Liability Company Act.

Comment

This Act is drafted to replace a state's current limited liability company statute, regardless of whether that statute is based on ULLCA (1996), ULLCA (2006), or other source. Section 110 contains transition provisions.

§ 102.   DEFINITIONS.

In this [act]:

(1) "Certificate of organization" means the certificate required by Section 201. The term includes the certificate as amended or restated.

(2) "Contribution", except in the phrase "right of contribution", means property or a benefit described in Section 402 which is provided by a person to a limited liability company to become a member or in the person's capacity as a member.

(3) "Debtor in bankruptcy" means a person that is the subject of:

(A) an order for relief under Title 11 of the United States Code or a comparable order under a successor statute of general application; or

(B) a comparable order under federal, state, or foreign law governing insolvency.

(4) "Distribution" means a transfer of money or other property from a limited liability company to a person on account of a transferable interest or in the person's capacity as a member. The term:

(A) includes:

(i) a redemption or other purchase by a limited liability company of a transferable interest; and

(ii) a transfer to a member in return for the member's relinquishment of any right to participate as a member in the management or conduct of the company's activities and affairs or to have access to records or other information concerning the company's activities and affairs; and

(B) does not include amounts constituting reasonable compensation for present or past service or payments made in the ordinary course of business under a bona fide retirement plan or other bona fide benefits program.

(5) "Foreign limited liability company" means an unincorporated entity formed under the law of a jurisdiction other than this state which would be a limited liability company if formed under the law of this state.

(6) "Jurisdiction", used to refer to a political entity, means the United States, a state, a foreign county, or a political subdivision of a foreign country.

(7) "Jurisdiction of formation" means the jurisdiction whose law governs the internal affairs of an entity.

(8) "Limited liability company", except in the phrase "foreign limited liability company" and in [Article] 10, means an entity formed under this [act] or which becomes subject to this [act] under [Article] 10 or Section 110.

(9) "Manager" means a person that under the operating agreement of a manager- managed limited liability company is responsible, alone or in concert with others, for performing the management functions stated in Section 407(c).

(10) "Manager-managed limited liability company" means a limited liability company that qualifies under Section 407(a).

(11) "Member" means a person that:

(A) has become a member of a limited liability company under Section 401 or was a member in a company when the company became subject to this [act] under Section 110; and

(B) has not dissociated under Section 602.

(12) "Member-managed limited liability company" means a limited liability company that is not a manager-managed limited liability company.

(13) "Operating agreement" means the agreement, whether or not referred to as an operating agreement and whether oral, implied, in a record, or in any combination thereof, of all the members of a limited liability company, including a sole member, concerning the matters described in Section 105(a). The term includes the agreement as amended or restated.

(14) "Organizer" means a person that acts under Section 201 to form a limited liability company.

(15) "Person" means an individual, business corporation, nonprofit corporation, partnership, limited partnership, limited liability company, [general cooperative association,] limited cooperative association, unincorporated nonprofit association, statutory trust, business trust, common-law business trust, estate, trust, association, joint venture, public corporation, government or governmental subdivision, agency, or instrumentality, or any other legal or commercial entity.

(16) "Principal office" means the principal executive office of a limited liability company or foreign limited liability company, whether or not the office is located in this state.

(17) "Property" means all property, whether real, personal, or mixed or tangible or intangible, or any right or interest therein.

(18) "Record", used as a noun, means information that is inscribed on a tangible medium or that is stored in an electronic or other medium and is retrievable in perceivable form.

(19) "Registered agent" means an agent of a limited liability company or foreign limited liability company which is authorized to receive service of any process, notice, or demand required or permitted by law to be served on the company.

(20) "Registered foreign limited liability company" means a foreign limited liability company that is registered to do business in this state pursuant to a statement of registration filed by the [Secretary of State].

(21) "Sign" means, with present intent to authenticate or adopt a record:

(A) to execute or adopt a tangible symbol; or

(B) to attach to or logically associate with the record an electronic symbol, sound, or process.

(22) "State" means a state of the United States, the District of Columbia, Puerto Rico, the United States Virgin Islands, or any territory or insular possession subject to the jurisdiction of the United States.

(23) "Transfer" includes:

(A) an assignment;

(B) a conveyance;

(C) a sale;

(D) a lease;

(E) an encumbrance, including a mortgage or security interest;

(F) a gift; and

(G) a transfer by operation of law.

(24) "Transferable interest" means the right, as initially owned by a person in the person's capacity as a member, to receive distributions from a limited liability company, whether or not the person remains a member or continues to own any part of the right. The term applies to any fraction of the interest, by whomever owned.

(25) "Transferee" means a person to which all or part of a transferable interest has been transferred, whether or not the transferor is a member. The term includes a person that owns a transferable interest under Section 603(a)(3).

Comment

This Section contains definitions for terms used throughout the act, while Section 1001 contains definitions specific to Article 10's provisions on mergers, conversions, interest exchanges, and domestications.

"Certificate of organization" [(1)]—The original ULLCA and most other LLC statutes use "articles of organization" rather than "certificate of organization." This act purposely uses the latter term to signal that the certificate: (i) merely reflects the existence of an LLC (rather than being the locus for important governance rules); and (ii) is significantly different from articles of *incorporation*, which have a substantially greater power to affect *inter se* rules for the corporate entity and its owners. For the relationship between the certificate of organization and the operating agreement, see Section 107(d).

"Contribution" [(2)]—This definition serves to distinguish capital contributions from other circumstances under which a member or would-be member might provide benefits to a limited liability company (*e.g.*, providing services to the LLC as an employee or independent contractor, leasing property to the LLC).

This definition also distinguishes "contributions" from capital raised from transferees who invest; to be a contribution, the property or benefit must be "provided by a person . . . to become a partner or in the person's capacity as a partner." This distinction is ubiquitous in the law of unincorporated business organizations. *See, e.g.,* N.Y. LTD. LIAB. CO. LAW § 102(f) (McKinney 2013) (" 'Contribution' means any cash, property, services rendered, or a promissory note or other binding obligation to contribute cash or property or to render services that a member contributes to a limited liability company in his or her capacity as a member."); DEL. CODE ANN. tit. 6, § 17–101(2) (West 2013) (" 'Contribution' means any cash, property, services rendered or a promissory note or other obligation to contribute cash or property or to perform services, which a person contributes to a limited liability company in the person's capacity as a partner.").

In contrast, operating agreements sometimes provide for contributions from transferees. In such circumstances, the default rules for liquidating distributions should be altered accordingly. *See* Section 707(b)(1) (referring to distributions to be made "to each person owning a transferable interest that reflects *contributions* made and not previously returned") (emphasis added).

"Distribution" [(4)(A)—redemptions included]—This provision specifically refers to transactions between a limited liability company and one of its members, which in the corporate context would be labeled a "redemption." The paragraph has subparts because ownership interests in an LLC are conceptually bifurcated into economic rights ("transferable interest") and governance and information rights.

Under Section 404(a), "[a]ny distribution made by a limited liability company before its dissolution and winding up must be in equal shares among members and persons dissociated as members. . . ." Since a redemption is a distribution, absent authorization in the operating agreement an LLC may not redeem the interest of one member or transferee without redeeming (or at least offering to redeem) the interests of all other members and transferees to a comparable extent.

The law of close corporations has flirted with a similar notion. *See, e.g., Donahue v. Rodd Electrotype Co. of New England, Inc.,* 367 Mass. 578, 598, 328 N.E.2d 505, 518 (1975) (stating, with regard to closely held corporations, "if the stockholder whose shares were purchased was a member of the controlling group, the controlling stockholders must cause the corporation to offer each stockholder an equal opportunity to sell a ratable number of his shares to the corporation at an identical price"); *Toner v. Baltimore Envelope Co.,* 304 Md. 256, 273, 498 A.2d 642, 650 (1985) (rejecting the "per se breach of duty" approach); *Wilkes v. Springside Nursing Home, Inc.,* 370 Mass. 842, 850, 353 N.E.2d 657, 663 (1976) (stating that "untempered application of the strict good faith standard enunciated in *Donahue* to . . . will result in the imposition of limitations on legitimate action by the controlling group in a close corporation which will unduly hamper its effectiveness in managing the corporation in the best interests of all concerned").

An operating agreement can override Section 404(a)'s equal treatment requirement without specifically mentioning redemptions.

Example: Ryan, LLC is a manager-managed limited liability company whose operating agreement: (i) includes a list (the "protected list") of decisions or actions that may be taken only with the consent of all members; and (ii) provides that all other decisions and acts may be taken as the manager determines. The protected list does not include redemptions. The operating agreement overrides the Section 404(a)'s equal treatment requirement.

[(4)(B)—exclusion]—This exclusion affects the reach of: (i) the charging order remedy under Section 503; and (ii) Section 405's clawback provision. The effect on the clawback provision reflects the law in several states, *see, e.g.,* DEL. CODE ANN., tit. 6, § 18–607(b) (2012) and VA. CODE ANN. § 13.1–1036 (2012), and makes sense conceptually and as a matter of policy. *See In re Tri-River Trading, LLC,* 329 B.R. 252, 266 (B.A.P. 8th Cir. 2005), *aff'd,* 452 F.3d 756 (8th Cir. 2006) ("We know of no principle of law which suggests that a manager of a company is required to give up agreed upon salary to pay creditors when business turns bad.").

"Foreign limited liability company" [(5)]—Some statutes have elaborate definitions addressing the question of whether an entity organized under the law of another jurisdiction is a "foreign limited liability company." The New York statute, for example, defines a "foreign limited liability company" as:

an unincorporated organization formed under the laws of any jurisdiction, including any foreign country, other than the laws of this state (i) that is not authorized to do business in this state under any other law of this state and (ii) of which some or all of the persons who are entitled (A) to receive a distribution of the assets thereof upon the dissolution of the organization or otherwise or (B) to exercise voting rights with respect to an interest in the organization have, or are entitled or authorized to have, under the laws of such other jurisdiction, limited liability for the contractual obligations or other liabilities of the organization.

N.Y. LTD. LIAB. CO. LAW § 102(k) (McKinney 2012). In contrast, Delaware takes a succinct and entirely formalistic approach. DEL. CODE ANN. tit. 6, § 18–101(4) (2012) (stating that the foreign limited liability company is one that is "denominated as such").

This definition, in contrast, intends a flexible, comparative approach. If a particular type of foreign entity has key legal characteristics that approximate the essential legal characteristics of a domestic limited liability company, that particular type of foreign entity is a foreign limited liability company under this act.

"Jurisdiction of formation" [(7)]—This definition is not limited to United States jurisdictions.

"Limited liability company" [(8)]—This definition makes no reference to a limited liability company having members upon formation, but Section 201(d) does.

"Manager" [(9)]—The act uses "manager" as a term of art, whose applicability under this act is confined to manager-managed LLCs. The phrase "manager-managed" is itself a term of art, referring only to an LLC whose operating agreement refers to the LLC as such. *See* Paragraph 10 (defining "manager-managed limited liability company"). Thus, for purposes of this act, if the members of a *member*-managed LLC delegate plenipotentiary management authority to one person (whether or not a member), this act's references to "manager" do not apply to that person, even if the members or their operating agreement refers to the person as a "manager."

This approach has the potential for confusion, but confusion around the term "manager" is common to all LLC statutes. The confusion stems from the choice to define "manager" as a term of art in a way that can be at odds with other, common usages of the word. For example, a member-managed LLC might well have an "office manager" or a "property manager." Moreover, in a manager-managed LLC, the "property manager" is not likely to be a manager as the term is used in many LLC statutes. For this nomenclature problem, the best solution is to have the operating agreement carefully delineate who is and is not a manager as this act uses that label.

For cases exemplifying the complexity and problems, *see, e.g.*, *In re Weddle*, 353 BR 892, 895 n.2 (Bankr. D. Idaho 2006) ("Plaintiff appears to argue that Debtors were managers of the LLC. However, Plaintiff's use of the term 'managers' to describe Debtors' duties under their employment agreement is not synonymous with 'manager' of the LLC within the use of that term in the operating agreement, the articles of incorporation, or chapter 6 of title 53 of the Idaho Code. The court views Debtors' 'management' role in the daily operation of the lodge as separate and distinct from management of the LLC."); *Brown v. MR Group, LLC*, 693 N.W.2d 138, 143 (Wis. App. 2005) (declining to use the dictionary definition of "manager" in determining coverage of a policy applicable to a limited liability company and its "managers" and relying instead on the meaning of the term under the Wisconsin LLC act); *Old Nat'l Villages, LLC v. Lenox Pine,' LLC*, 659 S.E. 2d 891, 893 (Ga. Ct. App. 2008) (treating the label "general manager" as a manager "under Georgia's LLC statute").

Under this act, the category of "person" is not limited to individuals. Therefore, a "manager" need not be a natural person. For example, one limited liability company can serve as the manager of another limited liability company.

After a person ceases to be a manager, the term "manager" continues to apply to the person's conduct while a manager. *See* Section 407(c)(6).

"Manager-managed limited liability company" [(10)]—This act authorizes a private agreement (the operating agreement) rather than a public document (certificate or articles of organization) to establish an LLC's status as a manager-managed limited liability company, thereby departing from most existing LLC statutes. Using the operating agreement makes sense, because under this act managerial structure creates no statutory power to bind the entity. *See* Section 301 (eliminating statutory apparent authority).

The only direct consequences of manager-managed status are *inter se*—principally the triggering of a set of rules concerning management structure, fiduciary duty, and information rights. *See* Sections 407–410. The rules on management structure are entirely default provisions—subject to change in whole or in part by the operating agreement. The operating agreement can also significantly affect the provisions on fiduciary duty and information rights. *See* Section 105.

An LLC that is "manager-managed" under this definition does not change its management structure simply because the members fail to designate anyone to act as a manager. In that situation, absent additional facts, the LLC is manager-managed and the manager position is vacant. Non-manager members who exercise managerial functions during the vacancy (or at any other time) will have duties as determined by other law, most particularly the law of agency.

"Member" [(11)]—After a person has been dissociated as a member under Section 602, the term "member" continues to apply to the person's conduct while a member. *See* Section 603(b).

"Member-managed limited liability company" [(12)]—Under this act, member-management is the default mode. *See* Section 407(a).

Some member-managed LLCs give important managerial responsibilities to one or more members. Because "manager" is a term of art under this act and applies only to manager-managed LLC, referring to such members as "managers" risks confusion. *See* the comment to Paragraph 9 (Manager). In contrast, "managing member" or some other designation such as Chief Executive Officer avoids the defined term of "manager" and thereby avoids confusion.

"Operating agreement" [(13)]—This definition must be read in conjunction with Sections 105 through 107, which further describe the operating agreement. In particular, although this definition refers to "the agreement . . . of all the members," the limited liability company itself is bound by and may enforce the agreement. Section 106(a).

An operating agreement is a contract, and therefore all statutory language pertaining to the operating agreement must be understood in the context of the law of contracts.

The definition in Paragraph 13 is very broad and recognizes a wide scope of authority for the operating agreement: "the matters described in Section 105(a)." Those matters include not only all relations *inter se* the members and the limited liability company but also all "activities and affairs of the company and the conduct of those activities and affairs." Section 105(a)(3). Moreover, the definition puts no limits on the form of the operating agreement. To the contrary, the definition contains the phrase "whether oral, implied, in a record, or in any combination thereof."

Unless the operating agreement itself provides otherwise:

- an operating agreement may comprise a number of separate documents (or records), however denominated; and

- subject to Section 106(b) (deeming new members to assent to the then-existing operating agreement), a document, record, understanding, etc. can be part of the operating agreement only with the assent of all persons then members.

An agreement among less than all members might well be enforceable among those members as parties, but would not be part of the operating agreement. However, under Section 105(a)(4), an amendment to an operating agreement can be made with less than unanimous consent if the operating agreement itself so provides.

An agreement to form an LLC is not itself an operating agreement. The term "operating agreement" presupposes at least one "member," and a person cannot be a member of an LLC before the LLC exists. However, as soon as a limited liability company has any members, the limited liability company perforce has an operating agreement. For example, suppose: (i) two persons orally and informally agree to join their activities in some way through the mechanism of an LLC; (ii) they form the LLC or cause it to be formed; and (iii) without further ado or agreement, they become the LLC's initial members. An operating agreement exists. In the words of Paragraph 13, "all the members" have agreed on who the members are, and that agreement—no matter how informal or rudimentary—is an agreement "concerning the matters described in Section 105(a)." To the extent the agreement does not provide the *inter se* "rules of the game," this act "fills in the gaps." Section 105(b).

The result is the same when a person becomes the sole initial member of an LLC, so long as the person has any understanding or intention with regard to the LLC. Any such understanding or intention constitutes an "agreement of all the members of the limited liability company, including a sole member." Paragraph 13.

It may seem oxymoronic to refer an "agreement of . . . a sole member," but this approach is common in LLC statutes. *See, e.g.,* ARIZ. REV. STAT. ANN. § 29–601 (14)(b) (2012) (defining operating agreement to mean "[i]n the case of a limited liability company that has a single member, any written or oral statement of the member made in good faith purporting to govern the affairs of a limited liability company or the conduct of its business as of the effective time of the statement"); WASH. REV. CODE ANN. § 25.15.005 (5) (2012) (defining limited liability company agreement to include "any written statement of the sole member").

This re-definition of "agreement" is a function of "path dependence." LLC statutes initially required an LLC to have at least two members, and almost all LLC statutes contemplated an agreement among members as an LLC's key organic document. Because LLC statutes make the operating agreement the principal way to override statutory default rules, the advent of single member LLCs made it necessary to provide that a sole member could make an operating agreement.

This act states no rule as to whether the statute of frauds applies to operating agreements. Case law suggests that the answer is yes. *Olson v. Halvorsen*, 986 A.2d 1150, 1161 (Del. 2009) ("The legislative history of the LLC Act does not demonstrate the General Assembly's intent to place LLC agreements outside of the statute of frauds.") (applying the one-year provision to an alleged oral buy-out agreement), *negated by* 2010 DEL. LAWS, ch. 287 (H.B. 372), §§ 1, 31 (pertaining to statutes of fraud generally).

The Delaware court decision is consistent with partnership cases.

> Partnership agreements, like other contracts, are subject to the Statute of Frauds. A contract of partnership for a term exceeding one year is within the Statute of Frauds and is void unless it is in writing [and signed by the party to be bound]; however, a contract establishing a partnership terminable at the will of any partner is generally held to be capable of performance by its terms within one year of its making and, therefore, to be outside the Statute of Frauds.

Abbott v. Hurst, 643 So. 2d 589, 592 (Ala. 1994) (citations omitted).

Likewise, the land provision of the statute of frauds:

> applies to an oral contract to transfer or convey partnership real property, and the interest of the other partners therein, to one partner as an individual, as well as to a parol contract by one of the parties to convey certain land owned by him individually to the partnership, or to another partner, or to put it into the partnership stock.

Froiseth v. Nowlin, 156 Wash. 314, 316, 287 P. 55, 56 (Wash. 1930) (quoting 27 C.J.S. § 220); *see also E. Piedmont 120 Associates, L.P. v. Sheppard*, 209 Ga. App. 664, 665, 434 S.E.2d 101, 102 (1993) (same, stating that "the fact that promises covered by the Statute of Frauds are made in the context of a partnership or joint venture agreement does not render the statute inapplicable"); *Filippi v. Filippi*, 818 A.2d 608, 618 (R.I. 2003) (applying the statute of frauds to an alleged oral agreement to transfer land owned by a limited partnership to one of its partners).

In contrast, the land provision does not apply to a member's ownership interest in an LLC, no matter how much the LLC owns or deals in real property. Interests in a limited liability company are personal property and reflect no direct interest in the entity's assets. *See* Sections 102(24), 501. Thus, the real property issues pertaining to the LLC's ownership of land do not "flow through" to the members and membership interests. *See, e.g., Wooten v. Marshall*, 153 F. Supp. 759, 763–64 (S.D. N.Y. 1957) (involving an "oral agreement for a joint venture concerning the purchase, exploitation and eventual disposition of this 160 acre tract" and stating "[t]he real property acquired and dealt with by the venturers takes on the character of personal property as between the partners in the enterprise, and hence is not covered by [the Statute of Frauds]"); *see also Wade v. DeHart*, 1926 WL 2944 (Ohio Com. Pl. 1926), *aff'd sub nom., Wade v. De Hart*, 26 Ohio App. 177, 159 N.E. 838 (1927) (same).

On the question of how far a written (or "in a record") operating agreement can go to prevent oral or implied-in-fact terms, see Section 105(a)(4), comment. For the effect of a pre-formation agreement, see Section 106(c). For the limited liability company's status viz-a-viz the operating agreement, see Section 106(a).

"Organizer" [(14)]—An organizer need not be a prospective member of the limited liability company. Unless the organizer will be the sole initial member of the limited liability company, as a matter of agency law and Section 401(a) and (b), the organizer is acting on behalf of the person or persons who have agreed to become the initial member or members of the limited liability company. The organizer does not act on behalf of the limited liability company, because a person cannot be an agent of an organization that does not yet exist. RESTATEMENT (THIRD) OF AGENCY § 4.04, cmt. c (2006) (Nonexistent Principals).

"Property" [(16)]—This definition encompasses every form of property.

"Transfer" [(23)]—The term "transfer" is broadly defined to include all types of conveyances of interests in property. The reference to "transfer by operation of law" is significant in connection with Section 502 (Transfer of Transferable Interest). That section severely restricts a transferee's rights (absent the consent of the members), and this definition makes those restrictions applicable, for example, to transfers ordered by a family court as part of a divorce proceeding and transfers resulting from the death of a member. The restrictions also apply to transfers in the context of a member's bankruptcy, except to the extent that bankruptcy law supersedes this act.

"Transferable interest" [(24)]—Absent a contrary provision in the operating agreement or the consent of the members, a "transferable interest" is the only interest in an LLC which can be transferred to a non-member. *See* the comment to Section 502.

This paragraph defines "transferable interest" as an interest "initially owned by a person in the person's capacity as a member," because this act does not contemplate an LLC directly creating interests that comprise only economic rights. *See* Sections 401 (addressing how a person becomes a member), 502 (addressing how a person becomes a transferee).

"Transferee" [(25)]—This definition should be read in light of Section 603(a)(3), which subject to limited exceptions provides that "any transferable interest owned by the person in the person's capacity as a member immediately before dissociation as a member is owned by the person solely as a transferee."

§ 103.   KNOWLEDGE; NOTICE.

(a) A person knows a fact if the person:

(1) has actual knowledge of it; or

(2) is deemed to know it under subsection (d)(1) or law other than this [act].

(b) A person has notice of a fact if the person:

(1) has reason to know the fact from all the facts known to the person at the time in question; or

(2) is deemed to have notice of the fact under subsection (d)(2).

(c) Subject to Section 210(f), a person notifies another person of a fact by taking steps reasonably required to inform the other person in ordinary course, whether or not those steps cause the other person to know the fact.

(d) A person not a member is deemed:

(1) to know of a limitation on authority to transfer real property as provided in Section 302(g); and

(2) to have notice of a limited liability company's:

(A) dissolution 90 days after a statement of dissolution under Section 702(b)(2)(A) becomes effective;

(B) termination 90 days after a statement of termination under Section 702(b)(2)(F) becomes effective; and

(C) participation in a merger, interest exchange, conversion, or domestication, 90 days after articles of merger, interest exchange, conversion, or domestication under [Article] 10 become effective.

Comment

This section is substantially slimmer than the corresponding provisions of previous uniform acts pertaining to business organizations: UPA (1997), ULLCA (1996), and ULPA (2001). Each of those acts borrowed heavily from the comparable Uniform Commercial Code provision. This act relies instead on generally applicable principles of agency law, *see* Section 111; therefore, this section is confined mostly to rules specifically tailored to this act.

Several facets of this section warrant particular note. First, and most fundamentally, because this act does not provide for "statutory apparent authority," Section 301, this section contains no special rules for attributing to an LLC information possessed, communicated to, or communicated by a member or manager.

Second, the section contains no generally applicable provisions determining when an organization is charged with knowledge or notice, because those imputation rules: (i) comprise core topics within the law of agency; (ii) are very complicated; (iii) should not have any different content under this act than in other circumstances; and (iv) are the subject of considerable attention in the Restatement (Third) of Agency (2006).

Third, this act does not define "notice" to include "knowledge." Although conceptualizing the latter as giving the former makes logical sense and has a long pedigree, that conceptualization is counter-intuitive for the uninitiated. In ordinary usage, notice has a meaning separate from knowledge. This act follows ordinary usage and therefore contains some references to "knowledge or notice."

Subsection (a)(2)—In this context, the most important source of "law other than this [act]" is the common law of agency.

Subsection (b)(1)—The "facts known to the person at the time in question" include facts the person is deemed to know under Subsection (a)(2).

Subsection (c)—If a person "notifies" another person of a fact, the other person has "reason to know" the fact and therefore has notice under Subsection (b)(1). However, a person can have "notice" of a fact without having been "notifie[d]" of the fact.

Section 210(f) pertains to delivery of records *by* the filing office.

Subsection (d)—This subsection provides constructive notice of facts stated in specified filed public records.

Subsection (d)(2)—Under this act, the power to bind a limited liability company to a third party is primarily a matter of agency law. Section 301, cmt. The constructive notice provided under this paragraph will be relevant if a third party makes a claim under agency law that someone who purported to act on behalf of a limited liability company had the apparent authority to do so.

§ 104.   GOVERNING LAW.

The law of this state governs:

(1) the internal affairs of a limited liability company; and

(2) the liability of a member as member and a manager as manager for a debt, obligation, or other liability of a limited liability company.

Comment

Paragraph (1)—Like any other legal concept, "internal affairs" may be indeterminate at its edges. However, the concept certainly includes interpretation and enforcement of the operating agreement, relations among the members as members, relations between the limited liability company and a member as a member, relations between a manager-managed limited liability company and a manager, and relations between a manager of a manager-managed limited liability company and the members as members. *Compare* Paragraph 1, *with* RESTATEMENT (SECOND) OF CONFLICT OF LAWS § 302, cmt. a (1971) (defining "internal affairs" with reference to a corporation as "the relations inter se of the corporation, its shareholders, directors, officers or agents").

"Internal affairs" do not encompass the power *vel non* of a person to bind a limited liability company. RESTATEMENT (SECOND) OF CONFLICT OF LAWS § 292(2) (1971) ("The principal will be held bound by the agent's action if he would so be bound under the local law of the state where the agent dealt with the third person, provided at least that the principal had authorized the agent to act on his behalf in that state or had led the third person reasonably to believe that the agent had such authority."); *Id.* § 295(1) ("Whether a partnership is bound by action taken on its behalf by an agent in dealing with a third person is determined by the local law of the state selected by application of the rule of § 292."); RESTATEMENT (FIRST) OF CONFLICT OF LAWS § 345, cmt. c (1934) (Law Governing Effect of Act of Agent or Partner) ("If. . . the principal or partner sends the agent or other partner into a state to act on his behalf, he assumes the risk of liability not only for authorized but for unauthorized conduct of the agent or partner in accordance with the law of that state."). *See also Farm & Ranch Services, Ltd. v. LT Farm & Ranch, L.L.C.*, 779 F. Supp. 2d 949, 960 (S.D. Iowa 2011).

The operating agreement cannot alter this section. *See* Section 105(c)(1). This approach comports with the law of other businesses entities whose formation or legal status depends at least in part on a publicly-filed record. *See, e.g.,* ULPA (2001) (Last Amended 2013) § 104 (stating that the law of the state of formation is the domestic entity's governing law) and ULLCA (2006) (Last Amended 2013) § 104 (same).

However, an operating agreement may lawfully incorporate by reference the provisions of another state's LLC statute. If done correctly, this incorporation makes the foreign statutory language part of the operating agreement, and the incorporated terms (together with the rest of the operating agreement) then govern the members (and those claiming through the members) to the extent not prohibited by this act. *See* Section 105. This approach: (i) does *not* switch the limited liability company's governing law to that of another state; (ii) instead takes the provisions of another state's law and incorporates them by reference into the contract among the members; (iii) raises complex drafting issues—*e.g.,* how to address subsequent changes to the incorporated law (whether occurring by statutory amendment or court decision); and (iv) thus is rarely, if ever, a good idea.

Paragraph (2)—This paragraph obviously encompasses Section 304 (the liability shield) but does not necessarily encompass a claim that a member or manager is liable to a third party for: (i) having purported inaccurately to have the actual authority to bind a limited liability company to the third party; or (ii) having committed a tort against the third party while acting on the limited liability company's behalf or in the course of the company's business. That liability is not by status (*i.e.,* not "as member . . . [or] as manager") but rather results from function or conduct. *Compare* Paragraph 2, *with* Section 301(b) (stating that, although this act does not make a member as member the agent of a limited liability company, other law may make an LLC liable for the conduct of a member).

"Internal affairs" and the "liability of a member as a member" are mentioned separately because it can be argued that the liability of members and managers to third parties is not an internal affair. *See, e.g.,* RESTATEMENT (SECOND) OF CONFLICT OF LAWS § 307 (1971) (treating shareholders' liability separately from the internal affairs doctrine). A few cases subsume owner/manager liability into internal affairs, but many do not. *See, e.g., Kalb, Voorhis & Co. v. Am. Fin. Corp.*, 8 F.3d 130, 132 (2nd Cir. 1993) (holding that the corporation's "primary purpose is to insulate shareholders from legal liability" and therefore "the state of incorporation has the greater interest in determining when and if that insulation is to be stripped away") (quoting *Soviet Pan Am Travel Effort v. Travel Comm., Inc.*, 756 F. Supp. 126, 131 (S.D.N.Y. 1991) (internal quotation marks omitted).

In any event, most (if not all) LLC statutes follow the rule stated in this paragraph. *See, e.g.,* Ariz. Rev. Stat. Ann. § 29–801(A)(1) (2013) (stating that "[t]he laws of the state or another jurisdiction under which a foreign limited liability company is organized govern its organization and internal affairs and the liability of its members"); Ga. Code Ann. § 14–11–701 (West 2013)(a) (stating that "[t]he laws of the jurisdiction under which a foreign limited liability company is organized govern its organization and internal affairs and the liability of its managers, members, and other owners"); N.Y. Ltd. Liab. Co. Law § 801(a) (McKinney 2013) (stating that "[t]he laws of the jurisdiction under which a foreign limited liability company is formed govern its organization and internal affairs and the liability of its members and managers").

Moreover, in the case law, "[t]he general rule is that a plaintiff's alter ego theory is governed by the law of the state in which the business at issue is organized." *Rual Trade Ltd. v. Viva Trade L.L.C.*, 549 F. Supp. 2d 1067, 1077 (E.D. Wis. 2008); *see also In re Gulf Fleet Holdings, Inc.*, 491 B.R. 747, 787 (Bankr. W.D. La. 2013) (stating both conceptual and policy rationales for choosing the law of the state of formation); *In re Saba Enterprises, Inc.*, 421 B.R. 626, 648–51 (Bankr. S.D.N.Y. 2009) (examining the issue in detail and applying the state of formation rule).

§ 105. OPERATING AGREEMENT; SCOPE, FUNCTION, AND LIMITATIONS.

(a) Except as otherwise provided in subsections (c) and (d), the operating agreement governs:

(1) relations among the members as members and between the members and the

limited liability company;

(2) the rights and duties under this [act] of a person in the capacity of manager;

(3) the activities and affairs of the company and the conduct of those activities and affairs; and

(4) the means and conditions for amending the operating agreement.

(b) To the extent the operating agreement does not provide for a matter described in subsection (a), this [act] governs the matter.

(c) An operating agreement may not:

(1) vary the law applicable under Section 104;

(2) vary a limited liability company's capacity under Section 109 to sue and be sued in its own name;

(3) vary any requirement, procedure, or other provision of this [act] pertaining to:

(A) registered agents; or

(B) the [Secretary of State], including provisions pertaining to records authorized or required to be delivered to the [Secretary of State] for filing under this [act];

(4) vary the provisions of Section 204;

(5) alter or eliminate the duty of loyalty or the duty of care, except as otherwise provided in subsection (d);

(6) eliminate the contractual obligation of good faith and fair dealing under Section 409(d), but the operating agreement may prescribe the standards, if not manifestly unreasonable, by which the performance of the obligation is to be measured;

(7) relieve or exonerate a person from liability for conduct involving bad faith, willful or intentional misconduct, or knowing violation of law;

(8) unreasonably restrict the duties and rights under Section 410, but the operating agreement may impose reasonable restrictions on the availability and use of information obtained under that section and may define appropriate remedies, including liquidated damages, for a breach of any reasonable restriction on use;

(9) vary the causes of dissolution specified in Section 701(a)(4);

(10) vary the requirement to wind up the company's activities and affairs as specified in Section 702(a), (b)(1), and (e);

(11) unreasonably restrict the right of a member to maintain an action under [Article] 8;

(12) vary the provisions of Section 805, but the operating agreement may provide that the company may not have a special litigation committee;

(13) vary the right of a member to approve a merger, interest exchange, conversion, or domestication under Section 1023(a)(2), 1033(a)(2), 1043(a)(2), or 1053(a)(2);

(14) vary the required contents of a plan of merger under Section 1022(a), plan of interest exchange under Section 1032(a), plan of conversion under Section 1042(a), or plan of domestication under Section 1052(a); or

(15) except as otherwise provided in Sections 106 and 107(b), restrict the rights under this [act] of a person other than a member or manager.

(d) Subject to subsection (c)(7), without limiting other terms that may be included in an operating agreement, the following rules apply:

(1) The operating agreement may:

(A) specify the method by which a specific act or transaction that would otherwise violate the duty of loyalty may be authorized or ratified by one or more disinterested and independent persons after full disclosure of all material facts; and

(B) alter the prohibition in Section 405(a)(2) so that the prohibition requires only that the company's total assets not be less than the sum of its total liabilities.

(2) To the extent the operating agreement of a member-managed limited liability company expressly relieves a member of a responsibility that the member otherwise would have under this [act] and imposes the responsibility on one or more other members, the agreement also may eliminate or limit any fiduciary duty of the member relieved of the responsibility which would have pertained to the responsibility.

(3) If not manifestly unreasonable, the operating agreement may:

(A) alter or eliminate the aspects of the duty of loyalty stated in Section 409(b) and (i);

(B) identify specific types or categories of activities that do not violate the duty of loyalty;

(C) alter the duty of care, but may not authorize conduct involving bad faith, willful or intentional misconduct, or knowing violation of law; and

(D) alter or eliminate any other fiduciary duty.

(e) The court shall decide as a matter of law whether a term of an operating agreement is manifestly unreasonable under subsection (c)(6) or (d)(3). The court:

(1) shall make its determination as of the time the challenged term became part of the operating agreement and by considering only circumstances existing at that time; and

(2) may invalidate the term only if, in light of the purposes, activities, and affairs of the limited liability company, it is readily apparent that:

(A) the objective of the term is unreasonable; or

(B) the term is an unreasonable means to achieve the term's objective.

Comment

Principal Provisions of the Act Concerning the Operating Agreement

The operating agreement is pivotal to a limited liability company, and Sections 105 through 107 are pivotal to this act. They must be read together, along with Section 102(13) (defining the operating agreement).

This section performs five essential functions. Subsection (a) establishes the primacy of the operating agreement in establishing relations *inter se* the limited liability company, its member or members, and any manager. Subsection (b) recognizes this act as comprising mostly default rules— *i.e.,* gap fillers for issues as to which the operating agreement provides no rule. Subsection (c) lists the few mandatory provisions of the act. Subsection (d) lists some provisions frequently found in operating agreements, authorizing some unconditionally and others so long as "not manifestly unreasonable." Subsection (e) delineates in detail both the meaning of "not manifestly unreasonable" and the information relevant to a determining a claim that a provision of an operating agreement is manifestly unreasonable.

Section 106 details the effect of an operating agreement on the limited liability company and on persons becoming members of an LLC. Section 107 concerns the effect of an operating agreement on third parties.

Role and Inevitability of Operating Agreement

A limited liability company is as much a creature of contract as of statute, *TravelCenters of Am., L.L.C. v. Brog*, CIV.A. 3516-CC, 2008 WL 1746987, at *1 (Del. Ch. Apr. 3, 2008) (stating that "limited liability companies are creatures of contract"); *Gottsacker v. Monnier*, 281 Wis. 2d 361, 370, 697 N.W.2d 436, 440 (2005) (stating that "from the partnership form, the LLC borrows . . . internal governance by contract"), and Section 102(13) delineates a very broad scope for "operating agreement." As a result, once an LLC comes into existence and has a member, the LLC necessarily has an operating agreement. *See* the comment to Section 102(13). Accordingly, this act refers to "the operating agreement" rather than "an operating agreement." This phrasing should not, however, be read to require a limited liability company or its members to take any formal action to adopt an operating agreement.

The operating agreement is the exclusive consensual process for modifying this act's various default rules pertaining to relationships *inter se* the members and between the members and the limited liability company. Section 105(b). The operating agreement also has power over "the rights and duties under this [act] of a person in the capacity of manager," Subsection (a)(2), and "the obligations of a limited liability company and its members to a person in the person's capacity as a transferee or person dissociated as a member," Section 107(b). For the relationship between the operating agreement and certificate of formation, see Section 107(d).

The Operating Agreement and the Fiduciary and Other Duties of Those Who Manage

One of the most complex questions in the law of unincorporated business organizations is the extent to which an agreement among the organization's owners can affect the fiduciary and other duties of those who manage the organization (*e.g.,* members in a member-managed LLC; managers in a manager-managed LLC). As explained in detail in the comment to Subsection (d)(3), this act rejects the notion that a contract can completely transform an inherently fiduciary relationship into a merely arm's length association. Within that limitation, however, this section provides substantial power to the operating agreement to reshape, limit, and eliminate fiduciary and other managerial duties.

Subsection (a) recognizes that the operating agreement is the map to the parties' deal and that any claim by a member of managerial misconduct must be assessed first under the relevant terms of the operating agreement. Subsection (d) specifically validates arrangements commonly used to reshape managerial duties and limit the consequences of breaching those duties. Subsection (c) contains relevant limitations, but those limitations: (i) must be read together with subsection (d); and (ii) do not preclude the operating agreement fundamentally redesigning the duties applicable to those who manage the organization. For the act's design of those duties, see Sections 409 and 410.

Subsection (a)—This section describes the very broad scope of a limited liability company's operating agreement, which includes all matters constituting "internal affairs." *Compare* Subsection (a), *with* Section 104(1) (using the phrase "internal affairs" in stating a choice of law rule). This broad grant of authority is subject to the restrictions stated in Subsection (c), including the broad restriction stated in Paragraph (c)(15) (concerning the rights of third parties under this act).

Subsection (a)(1)—This paragraph encompasses all the rights and duties of each member, including rights and duties pertaining to transactions under Article 10.

Subsection (a)(2)—Under this paragraph, the operating agreement has the power to affect the rights and duties of managers (including non-member managers). Because the term "[o]perating agreement . . . includes the agreement as amended or restated," Section 102(13), this paragraph gives the members the ongoing power to define the role of an LLC's managers. Power is not the same as right, however, and exercising the power provided by this paragraph might constitute a breach of a separate contract between the LLC and the manager. A non-member manager might also have rights under Section 107(a).

Subsection (a)(4)—Under this provision, the operating agreement can control both the quantum of consent required (*e.g.,* majority of members) and the means by which the consent is manifested (*e.g.,* prohibiting modifications except when consented to in writing). *See* the comment to Section 107(a).

If the operating agreement does not address the issue, this act provides the rule. Section 407(b)(4)(C) and 407(c)(3)(C) each require the affirmative vote or consent of all the members. Under Section 111 (supplemental principles of law), the parol evidence rule will apply to a written operating agreement when appropriate under contract law.

Subsection (b)—To the extent the operating agreement does not determine an *inter se* matter, this act determines the matter. The operating agreement may vary any provision of this act pertaining to *inter se* matters, except as provided in Subsections (c) and (d).

Sometimes—but not always—the Comments to this act refer to a variable provision as a "default rule" and a non-waivable provision as "mandatory." These references are merely to draw attention to the default/mandatory distinction in particular contexts and have neither the intent nor the power to affect the default/mandatory status of provisions of this act whose comments lack a comparable reference.

Subsection (c)—This subsection lists provisions of this act whose respective effects cannot be varied or may be varied subject to a stated limitation. For historical reasons, this subsection uses the words "vary" and "alter" interchangeably. No difference in meaning is intended.

If a person claims that a term of the operating agreement violates this subsection, as a matter of ordinary procedural law the burden of proof is on the person making the claim.

Subsection (c)(1)—Section 104 states that this act provides the law applicable to: (i) the internal affairs of an LLC formed under this act; and (ii) the liability of members and managers for obligations of the LLC. The organizers of an LLC make this choice of law by choosing to form an LLC under this act. Domestication to another jurisdiction will re-set the choice of law, *see* Sections 1051–56, but the operating agreement cannot, *see* the comment to Section 104(1).

Subsection (c) contains no parallel prohibition on varying Section 901 (stating the governing law for foreign limited liability companies), because a prohibition is unnecessary. As a matter of fundamental contract law, an agreement among members of one limited liability company is powerless to govern the affairs of another limited liability company.

Subsection (c)(2)—Under this act, a limited liability company is emphatically an entity, and the members lack the power to alter that characteristic.

Subsection (c)(3)—This prohibition is arguably implicit in Subsection (c)(15) (affecting rights of third parties under this act) but is specifically noted to avoid doubt.

Subsection (c)(4)—This provision means that the operating agreement cannot affect the right of an "aggrieved" person to seek the court's help when "a person required by this [act] to sign a record or deliver a record to the [Secretary of State] for filing under this [act] does not do so." Section 204(a).

Subsection (c)(5)—This limitation is less powerful than might first appear, because Subsection (d) specifically authorizes substantial alterations to the duties of loyalty and care, including restricting and substantially eliminating those duties.

Subsection (c)(6)—Section 409(d) refers to the "contractual obligation of good faith and fair dealing," which contract law implies in every contract. The operating agreement cannot eliminate this obligation, neither in whole (*i.e.,* generally) nor in part (*i.e.,* as applicable to specified situations).

However, an operating agreement may "prescribe the standards . . . by which the performance of the obligation is to be measured."

Example: The operating agreement of a manager-managed LLC gives the manager the discretion to cause the LLC to enter into contracts with affiliates of the manager (so-called "Conflict Transactions"). The agreement further provides: "When causing the Company to enter into a Conflict Transaction, the manager complies with Section 409(d) of [this act] if a disinterested person, knowledgeable in the subject matter, states in writing that the terms and conditions of the Conflict Transaction are equivalent to the terms and conditions that would be agreed to by persons at arm's length in comparable circumstances." This provision "prescribe[s] the standards by which the performance of the [Section 409(d)] obligation is to be measured."

Example: Same facts as the previous example, except that, during the performance of a Conflict Transaction, the manager causes the LLC to waive material protections under the applicable contract. The standard stated in the previous example is inapposite to this conduct. Section 409(d) therefore applies to the conduct without any direct contractual delineation. (However, other terms of the agreement may be relevant to determining whether the conduct violates Section 409(d). *See* the comment to Section 409(d).)

Example: The operating agreement of a manager-managed LLC gives the manager "sole discretion" to make various decisions. The agreement further provides: "Whenever this agreement requires or permits a manager to make a decision that has the potential to benefit one class of members to the detriment of another class, the manager complies with Section 409(d) of [this act] if the manager makes the decision with:

    a.   the honest belief that the decision:

        i.   serves the best interests of the LLC; or

        ii.   at least does not injure or otherwise disserve those interests; and

    b.   the reasonable belief that the decision breaches no member's rights under this agreement."

This provision "prescribe[s] the standards by which the performance of the [Section 409(d)] obligation is to be measured." *Compare* Section 105(c)(6), *with Nemec v. Shrader*, 991 A.2d 1120 (Del. 2010) (considering such a situation in the context of the right to call preferred stock and deciding by a 3–2 vote that exercising the call did not breach the implied covenant of good faith and fair dealing).

An operating agreement that seeks to prescribe standards for measuring the contractual obligation of good faith and fair dealing under Section 409(d) should expressly refer to the obligation. *See Gerber v. Enter. Prods. Hldgs., L.L.C.*, 67 A.3d 400, 418 (Del. 2013) (distinguishing between the implied contractual covenant and an express contractual obligation of "good faith" as stated in a limited partnership agreement).

For an explanation of the function and role of the covenant of good faith and fair dealing, see Section 409(d), comment. For the rules delimiting the "not manifestly unreasonable" requirement, see Subsection (e).

Subsection (c)(7)—These restrictions are ubiquitous in the law of business entities and, in conjunction with other provisions of this section, control the otherwise very broad power of an operating agreement to affect fiduciary and other duties. The restrictions are central to the raft of exculpatory provisions that sprung up in corporate statutes in response to *Smith v. Van Gorkum*, 488 A.2d 858 (Del. 1985), *overruled on other grounds by Gantler v. Stephens*, 965 A.2d 695 (Del. 2009). Delaware led the response with DEL. CODE ANN. tit. 8, § 102(b)(7), and a number of LLC statutes have similar provisions. *E.g.*, GA. CODE ANN. § 14–11–305(4)(A) (2011). For an extreme example, *see* VA. CODE ANN. § 13.1–1025 (B) (2012). In this context, "conduct" includes both acts and omissions. BLACK'S LAW DICTIONARY (9th ed. 2009) (defining conduct as "[p]ersonal behavior, whether by action or inaction").

The term "bad faith" has multiple meanings, and the context determines which meaning applies. In the context of the duty of loyalty, "bad faith" includes conduct motivated by ill will or other intent purposely to harm another person. The concept also includes conduct from which a person derives an improper personal benefit. *See, e.g., Mroz v. Hoaloha Na Eha, Inc.*, 410 F. Supp. 2d 919, 936–37 (D. Haw. 2005) (denying a motion to dismiss a claim that "the Majority Partners" were personally liable for the partnership's wrongful termination of the plaintiff; quoting the complaint as alleging that "the Majority Partners, individually and as a group, acted with malice and/or ill will, and/or with an intent to serve their own personal interests and/or without an intent to serve company interests, and/or outside of the scope of their authority and/or without justification"); *BOGNC, L.L.C. v. Cornelius NC Self-Storage L.L.C.*, 10 CVS 19072, 2013 WL 1867065, at *9 (N.C. Super. [Business Court] May 1, 2013) (noting that "no . . . [exculpatory] provision may limit a manager's liability for acts known to be in conflict with the interests of the limited liability company, or for acts from which the manager derived an improper personal benefit") (citing N.C. GEN. STAT. § 57C–3–32(b)); *Lasica v. Savers Grp. of Minn., L.L.C.*, A12-0092, 2012 WL 3553246, at *2 (Minn. Ct. App. Aug. 20, 2012) (noting that an "individual seeking indemnification [under statute providing for indemnification] must have acted in good faith and must not have received an improper personal benefit") (citing MINN. STAT. § 322B.699, subdivs. 2(a)(2), (3) (2010)).

In the context of the duty of care, the concept of bad faith comes primarily from corporate law and means an extreme breach of the duty (*i.e.*, "the failure to exercise "*honest judgment* in the lawful and legitimate furtherance of corporate purposes." *Deblinger v. Sani-Pine Products Co., Inc.*, 107 A.D.3d 659, 661, 967 N.Y.S.2d 394 (2013) (quoting Auerbach v. Bennett, 47 N.Y.2d 619, 629, 393 N.E.2d 994 (1979) (emphasis added) (internal quotation marks omitted).

Thus, when a plaintiff alleges bad faith as pertaining to the duty of care, "[t]he burden . . . is to show irrationality: a plaintiff must demonstrate that no reasonable business person could possibly authorize the action in good faith. Put positively, the decision must go so far beyond the bounds of reasonable business judgment that its only explanation is bad faith." *In re Tower Air, Inc.*, 416 F.3d 229, 238 (3d Cir. 2005) (discussing then prevailing Delaware law) (citation omitted); *see also KDW Restructuring & Liquidation Servs. LLC v. Greenfield*, 874 F. Supp. 2d 213, 226 (S.D.N.Y. 2012) (referring to a lack of "a rationale corporate purpose" and "a disregard for the duty to examine all available information—*information that was readily at hand*") (emphasis added).

With regard to both the duty of loyalty and the duty of care, "bad faith" is entirely distinct from the meaning of "good faith" in the contractual covenant of good faith and fair dealing. *See* the comment to Section 409(d).

Subsection (c)(7) pertains to indirect as well as direct efforts to "relieve or exonerate" and thus limits how far an operating agreement can go in providing for indemnification. *See* Section 408(b) (stating a default rule for indemnification). Also, in accordance with this paragraph, an exculpatory provision cannot shield against a member's claim of oppression. *See* Section 701(a)(4)(C).

Although this paragraph does not expressly address contracts between an LLC and a member or manager, the stated constraints must also apply to such contracts. If not, those constraints are effectively meaningless.

Example: A manager-managed LLC enters into a management contract with its sole manager, and the contract provides the manager exoneration for liability to the LLC even for willful and intentional misconduct. Most likely, contract law will treat the provision as against public policy and therefore unenforceable. RESTATEMENT (SECOND) OF CONTRACTS § 195(1) (1981) ("A term exempting a party from tort liability for harm caused intentionally or recklessly is unenforceable on grounds of public policy."). If not, a court should hold the provision unenforceable to avoid evisceration of Subsection (c)(7). (Or, the court could invoke the policy expressed in Subsection (c)(7) as grounds for holding the provision unenforceable under contract law.)

Subsection (c)(8)—Although phrased as a restriction, this provision grants substantial power to the operating agreement.

Example: A law firm operates as a limited liability company, and the operating agreement provides that a "Compensation Committee" periodically decides each member's compensation. The agreement also states that only members who are on the Compensation Committee may have access to the Committee's compensation decisions pertaining to other members. This restriction is reasonable.

The act also empowers the LLC "as a matter within the ordinary course of its activities and affairs [to] impose reasonable restrictions and conditions on access to and use of information" obtained under Section 410. *See* Section 410(h).

In determining whether a restriction is reasonable, a court might consider: (i) the danger or other problem the restriction seeks to avoid; (ii) the purpose for which the information is sought; and (iii) whether, in light of both the problem and the purpose, the restriction is reasonably tailored. In addition, a restriction that is reasonable viz-a-viz a non-managing member in a manager-managed LLC might be unreasonable viz-a-viz a managing member or in the context of a member-managed LLC.

Subsection (c)(9)—The operating agreement may not change the stated grounds for judicial dissolution but may determine the forum in which a claim for dissolution under Section 701(a)(4) is determined. For example, arbitration and forum selection clauses are commonplace in business relationships in general and in operating agreements in particular.

The approach of this paragraph differs from the law of Delaware. *Huatuco v. Satellite Healthcare*, CV 8465-VCG, 2013 WL 6460898, at *1, n.2 (Del. Ch. Dec. 9, 2013) (stating that "the right to judicial dissolution is a default right which the parties may eschew by contract" but reserving the question of "[w]hether the parties may, by contract, divest this Court of its authority to order a dissolution in all circumstances, even where it appears manifest that equity so requires—leaving, for instance, irreconcilable members locked away together forever like some alternative entity version of Sartre's *Huis Clos*").

Subsection (c)(10)—The cited provisions comprise the non-waivable aspects of winding up a dissolved limited liability company. The other provisions of Section 702 are default rules.

Subsection (c)(11)—Article 8 delineates a member's rights to bring direct and derivative actions. It would be unreasonable to frustrate these rights but not unreasonable to channel their exercise. For example, the operating agreement might select a forum, require pre-suit mediation, provide for arbitration of both direct and derivative claims, or override Section 802 and require "universal demand" in all derivative cases. Similarly, it is not unreasonable to provide for liquidated damages consonant with the law of contracts. In contrast, it would be unreasonable for an operating agreement to both: (i) require a would-be derivative plaintiff to make demand regardless of futility; and (ii) bar taking the claim to court no matter how long the management group ponders the demand.

Subsection (c)(12)—An operating agreement may not alter the act's rules for a special litigation committee but may preclude entirely the use of such a committee.

Subsection (c)(13)—Section 1023(a)(1), 1033(a)(1), 1043(a)(1), and 1053(a)(1) each requires the consent or the affirmative vote of all members. The operating agreement may modify these requirements. In contrast, under the sections stated in this subsection:

- each member is protected from being merged, exchanged, converted, or domesticated "into" the status of a partner in a general partnership that is not a limited liability partnership (or a comparable "unshielded" position in some other organization) without the member having *directly* consented to either:

  o the merger, interest exchange, conversion, or domestication; or

  o an operating agreement provision that permits such transactions to occur with less than unanimous consent of the members; and

- merely consenting to an operating agreement provision that permits amendment of the agreement with less than unanimous consent of the members does not qualify as the requisite direct consent.

Subsection (c)(14)—Because these plans are the basic "deal documents" for each of the organic transactions contemplated in Article 10, the operating agreement may not vary the contents of these plans.

Subsection (c)(15)—This limitation pertains only to "the rights under this [act] of" third parties other than members and managers. Moreover, the limitation is subject to two substantial exceptions: Section 106 (pertaining to the operating agreement's relationship to the limited liability company itself and to persons becoming members) and Section 107(b) (pertaining to the operating agreement's power over the rights of transferees).

Subsection (d)—The operating agreement has plenipotentiary power over the matters described in Subsection (a), except as specifically limited by Subsections (c) and (d)(3). However, for the convenience of practitioners and the courts. Paragraphs 1 and 2 list various terms often found in operating agreements. No negative inference should be drawn about terms not listed; the listing is provided "without limiting other terms that may be included in an operating agreement."

Paragraph 3 lists terms subject to the "not manifestly unreasonable" standard. Subsection (e) delineates that standard. The same standard applies to terms of an operating agreement which seek to "prescribe the standards . . . by which the performance of the [Section 409(d)] obligation [of good faith and fair dealing] is to be measured." Subsection (c)(6).

Subsection (d)(1)(A)—An arrangement *not* involving "one or more disinterested and independent persons" acting "after full disclosure of all material facts" would "alter . . . the aspects of the duty of loyalty stated in Section 409(b) and (i)" and would therefore be subject to the "not manifestly unreasonable standard" of Subsection (d)(3)(A).

For the meaning of "material" as applied to information, see Section 409(f), comment.

Subsection (d)(1)(B)—Section 405(a)(2) prohibits distributions:

- *not merely* when, after the distribution, "the company's total assets would be less than the sum of its total liabilities,"

- *but also* when, after the distribution, the assets would less than the total liabilities "plus the amount that would be needed, if the company were to be dissolved and wound up at the time of the distribution, to satisfy the preferential rights upon dissolution and winding up of members and transferees whose preferential rights are superior to those of persons receiving the distribution."

The second part of the solvency test pertains to preferential rights to distributions, is thus a matter *inter se* the members and any transferees, and is therefore subject to change in the operating agreement.

In contrast, the first part of the solvency test protects third parties—creditors of the LLC—and therefore cannot be changed by the operating agreement. Subsection (c)(15). Likewise, the operating agreement cannot change the solvency test stated in Section 405(a)(1) (providing that "the company would not be able to pay its debts as they become due in the ordinary course of the company's activities and affairs").

Subsection (d)(2)—This provision is limited to member-managed limited liability companies on the premise that: (i) managers are collectively responsible; and (ii) managers may properly delegate a duty but the delegation does not discharge the duty. However, in a manager-managed LLC (as well as in a member-managed LLC), subject to Subsection (d)(3) the operating agreement may alter or even eliminate fiduciary duties.

Example: ABC LLC ("ABC") is a member-managed LLC. ABC has two entirely separate lines of business, the Alpha business and the Beta business. Under ABC's operating agreement:

- Member 1's responsibilities pertain exclusively to the Alpha business, while responsibility for:

   - the Beta business is allocated exclusively to Member 2; and

   - ABC's overall operations is allocated exclusively to Member 3.

- Member 2's responsibilities pertain exclusively to the Beta business, while responsibility for:

   - the Alpha business is allocated exclusively to Member 1; and o   ABC's overall operations is allocated exclusively to Member 3.

- Member 1 has no fiduciary duties pertaining to the Beta business.

- Member 2 has no fiduciary duties pertaining to the Alpha business.

The elimination of Member 1's fiduciary duties with regard to the Beta business and Member 2's fiduciary duties with regard to the Alpha business are enforceable, without regard to the "manifestly unreasonable" standard of Subsection (d)(3).

Subsection (d)(3)—This act rejects the ultra-contractarian notion that fiduciary duty within a business organization is merely a set of default rules and seeks instead to balance the virtues of "freedom of contract" against the dangers that inescapably exist when some persons have power over the interests of others. *Cf.* Leo E. Strine, Jr. J. Travis Laster, *The Siren Song of Unlimited Contractual Freedom*, ELGAR HANDBOOK ON ALTERNATIVE ENTITIES (Eds. Mark Lowenstein and Robert Hillman), forthcoming 2014,, Edward Elgar Publishing 2014) (noting that an "argument often made in favor of [Delaware] alternative entity statutes is that they allow for the elimination of fiduciary duties and the establishment of a purely contractual relationship between entity managers and investors" and stating that "[a]s judges who have seen our fair share of alternative entity disputes, we do not immediately grasp why this would be seen as a compelling advantage"); available at SSRN: http://ssrn.com/abstract=2481039, at 9–10 (footnote omitted).

Under this act, a properly drafted operating agreement may substantially alter and even eliminate fiduciary duties. However, two important limitations exist.

First, arrangements subject to this subsection may not be "manifestly unreasonable." *See* Subsection (e) (delineating this standard).

Second, the operating agreement may not transform the relationship *inter se* members, managers, and the LLC into an entirely arm's length arrangement. For example, displacement of fiduciary duties is effective only to the extent that the displacement is stated clearly and with particularity. This rule is fundamental in the jurisprudence of fiduciary duty. *See, e.g., Paige Capital Mgmt, L.L.C. v. Lerner Master Fund, L.L.C.*, Civ. A. No. 5502-CS, 2011 WL 3505355, at *31 (Del. Ch. Aug. 8, 2011) (Del. Ch. 2011) (stating that, even under a statute that "permits the waiver of fiduciary duties . . . such waivers must be set forth clearly"); *Kelly v. Blum*, Civ. A. No. 4516-VCP, 2010 WL 629850, at *10, n.70 (Del. Ch. Feb. 24, 2010) ("Having been granted great contractual freedom by the LLC Act, drafters of or parties to an LLC agreement should be expected to provide . . . clear and unambiguous provisions when they desire to expand, restrict or eliminate the operation of traditional fiduciary duties"). It would therefore be manifestly unreasonable for an operating agreement to negate this rule.

Although Subsection (d)(3) does not expressly address contracts between an LLC and a member or manager, the stated constraints must also apply to such contracts. If not, those constraints are effectively meaningless.

Example: A manager-managed LLC enters into a management contract with its sole manager, and the contract provides that the duties of loyalty stated in Section 409(b) and (i) are entirely eliminated. If the operating agreement were to so provide, the provision would be subject to the "manifestly unreasonable standard." Section 105(d)(3)(A). Absent the authorization provided by Section 105(d)(3)(A), the management contract's attempt to waive fiduciary duties may be unenforceable as a matter of public policy and contract law. *See Neubauer v. Goldfarb*, 108 Cal. App. 4th 47, 57, 133 Cal. Rptr. 2d 218 (2003) (stating that "waiver of corporate directors' and majority shareholders' fiduciary duties to minority shareholders in private close corporations is against public policy and a contract provision in a buy-sell agreement purporting to effect such a waiver is void"). If not, a court should hold the provision unenforceable nonetheless so as to avoid eviscerating Subsection (d)(3).

Subsection (d)(3)(A)—Subject to the "not manifestly unreasonable" standard, this paragraph empowers the operating agreement to eliminate *all* aspects of the duty of loyalty listed in Section 409(b). The obligation of good faith and fair dealing, Section 409(d), would remain. See Subsection (c)(6). As to any other, uncodified aspects of the duty of loyalty, see Subsection (d)(3)(D) (empowering the operating agreement to "alter or eliminate any other fiduciary duty").

Example: Joint Venture LLC ("JV") is a manager-managed limited liability company, with two members, Kappa, Inc. ("Kappa") and Lambda, LLC ("Lambda"). The operating agreement provides that:

- JV is managed by a "board of managers" consisting of one person appointed by Kappa and one person appointed by Lambda;

- each appointee:

  - owes fiduciary and any other duties exclusively to the member that made the appointment; and

  - owes no duties to the other member and the limited liability company.

The "not manifestly unreasonable" standard applies to these provisions under Subsection (d)(3)(A) and (D), and the provisions are not manifestly unreasonable. Note that the provisions do not affect the duties of Kappa and Lambda to:

- the limited liability company, under applicable case law (pertaining to the obligations of owners of an entity who control the entity indirectly); and

- each other, under applicable case law and Section 701(a)(4)(C)(ii) (providing for judicial dissolution when "the managers or those members in control of the company . . . have acted or are acting in a manner that is oppressive and was, is, or will be directly harmful to the [member seeking dissolution").

Example: ABC LLC ("ABC") is a manager-managed limited liability company with three managers and two entirely separate lines of business, the Alpha business and the Beta business. Under ABC's operating agreement:

- Manager 1's responsibilities pertain exclusively to the Alpha business; responsibility for:

  - the Beta business is allocated exclusively to Manager 2; and

  - ABC's overall operations is allocated exclusively to Manager 3.

- Manager 2's responsibilities pertain exclusively to the Beta business; responsibility for:

  - the Alpha business is allocated exclusively to Manager 1; and

  - ABC's overall operations is allocated exclusively to Manager 3.

- Manager 1 has no fiduciary duties pertaining to the Beta business.

- Manager 2 has no fiduciary duties pertaining to the Alpha business.

The "not manifestly unreasonable" standard applies to these provisions under Subsection (d)(3)(A) and (D), and the provisions are not manifestly unreasonable.

Subsection (d)(3)(B)—Under this paragraph, an operating agreement might provide that an affiliate of a manager of a manager-managed LLC will provide compensated services to the LLC at a price not exceeding market price, or that the manager may pursue opportunities that otherwise would be company opportunities. Such arrangements are commonplace and permissible.

Subsection (d)(3)(C)—In this context, "conduct" includes both acts and omissions. BLACK'S LAW DICTIONARY (9th ed. 2009) (defining conduct as "[p]ersonal behavior, whether by action or inaction"). Subject to the "not manifestly unreasonable" standard and the bedrock requirements stated here and in Subsection (c)(7), the operating agreement can reduce the duty of care substantially. In particular, the operating agreement can eliminate the aspects of the duty of care pertaining to gross negligence and recklessness.

This provision replicates in a particular context the general rule stated in Subsection (c)(7). For the meaning of "bad faith" in the context of the duty of care, see Subsection (c)(7), comment.

Subsection (e)—The "not manifestly unreasonable" concept became part of uniform business entity statutes when UPA (1997) imported the concept from the Uniform Commercial Code. (In the current version of the Uniform Commercial Code, the concept appears in Section 1–302(b).)

This subsection provides rules for applying the concept, specifying:

- who decides the issue of "manifestly unreasonable"
  - "the court . . . as a matter of law," Subsection (e);
- the framework for determining the issue
- determination to be made "in light of the purposes, activities, and affairs of the limited liability company," Subsection (e)(2);
  - the temporal setting for determining the issue
- "determination [to be made] as of the time the challenged term became part of the operating agreement," Subsection (e)(1); and
  - what information is admissible for determining the issue
- "only circumstances existing" when "the challenged term became part of the operating agreement," Subsection (e)(1).

The subsection also provides a very demanding standard for persons claiming that a term of an operating agreement is "manifestly unreasonable." "The court . . . may invalidate the term only if, in light of the purposes, activities, and affairs of the limited liability company, it is *readily apparent* that: (A) the objective of the term is unreasonable; or (B) the term is an unreasonable means to achieve the term's objective." Subsection (e)(2) (emphasis added).

Subsection (e) is fundamental to this act, because: (i) this act generally defers to the agreement among the members; and (ii) Subsection (e) safeguards the operating agreement in at least four ways:

- Determining manifest unreasonableness *inter se* owners of an organization is a different task than doing so in a commercial context, where concepts like "usages of trade" are available to inform the analysis. Each business organization must be understood in its own terms and context.

- If loosely applied, the concept of "manifestly unreasonable" would permit a court to rewrite the members' agreement, which would destroy the balance this act seeks to establish between freedom of contract and fiduciary duty.

- Case law has not adequately delineated the concept. *See, e.g., In re Brobeck, Phleger & Harrison L.L.P.*, 408 B.R. 318, 335 (Bankr. N.D. Cal. 2009) ("RUPA [UPA (1997)] does not define what is 'manifestly unreasonable' and the parties have not cited, nor can the court locate, a decision that defines the term. Absent case law or even a dictionary definition, the court must rely on its common sense to recognize something as manifestly unreasonable.").

- In the context of statutes permitting stock transfer restrictions unless "manifestly unreasonable," courts have often ignored the word "manifestly." *See, e.g., Brandt v. Somerville*, 692 N.W.2d 144, 152 (N.D. 2005) (stating that "in close corporations, a majority of courts have sustained restrictions that are determined to be reasonable in light of the relevant circumstances"); *Roof Depot, Inc. v. Ohman*, 638 N.W.2d 782, 786 (Minn. Ct. App. 2002) (stating that "the restrictions [on share transfer] are not 'manifestly unreasonable' because they are reasonable means to ensure that the management and control of the business remains in the group of investors or with people well known to them"); *Castriota v. Castriota*, 633 A.2d 1024, 1027–28 (App. Div. 1993) ("We are obliged to apply the statute in a manner consonant with its essential purpose to permit reasonable restrictions upon alienation.").

Subsection (e)(1)—The significance of the phrase "as of the time the term as challenged became part of the operating agreement" is best shown by example.

Example: When a particular manager-managed LLC comes into existence, its business plan is quite unusual and its success depends on the willingness of a particular individual to serve as the LLC's sole manager. This individual has a rare combination of skills, experiences, and contacts, which are particularly appropriate for the LLC's start-up. In order to induce the individual to accept the position of sole manager, the members are willing to have the operating agreement significantly limit the manager's fiduciary duties. Several years later, when the LLC's operations have turned prosaic and the manager's talents and background are not nearly so crucial, a member challenges the fiduciary duty limitations as manifestly unreasonable. The relevant time under Subsection (e)(1) is when the LLC began. Subsequent developments are not relevant, except as they might inferentially bear on the circumstances in existence at the relevant time.

Example: As initially adopted, an operating agreement identifies a category of decisions ordinarily subject to the duty of loyalty and provides that "the manager's sole, reasonable discretion" satisfies the duty. A year later, the agreement is amended to delete the word "reasonable." Later, a member claims that, without the word "reasonable," the provision is manifestly unreasonable. The relevant time under Subsection (e)(1) is when the agreement was amended, not when the agreement was initially adopted.

Subsection (e)(2)—If a person claims that a term of the operating agreement is manifestly unreasonable under Subsections (c)(6) or (d)(3), as a matter of ordinary procedural law the person making the claim has the burden of proof.

§ 106. OPERATING AGREEMENT; EFFECT ON LIMITED LIABILITY COMPANY AND PERSON BECOMING MEMBER; PREFORMATION AGREEMENT.

(a) A limited liability company is bound by and may enforce the operating agreement, whether or not the company has itself manifested assent to the operating agreement.

(b) A person that becomes a member is deemed to assent to the operating agreement.

(c) Two or more persons intending to become the initial members of a limited liability company may make an agreement providing that upon the formation of the company the agreement will become the operating agreement. One person intending to become the initial member of a limited liability company may assent to terms providing that upon the formation of the company the terms will become the operating agreement.

Comment

Subsection (a)—This subsection resolves twin questions that have troubled some courts—namely, whether an unincorporated entity that has not signed its foundational agreement nonetheless is bound by and may enforce the agreement. The questions have been particularly troubling in the context of agreements to arbitrate. *See, e.g., Elkjer v. Scheef & Stone, L.L.P.*, 3:13-CV-1655-K, ___ F. Supp.2d ___, 2014 WL 1255844 at *5–6 (N.D. Tex. Mar. 27, 2014) (concluding that a limited liability partnership "is a party to the Partnership Agreement," even though the partnership itself never signed or otherwise assented to the agreement; enforcing arbitration provision to the benefit of the LLP). *Contra Trover v. 419 OCR, Inc.*, 397 Ill. App. 3d 403, 409, 921 N.E.2d 1249, 1255 (2010) (finding that "neither FODG [an LLC] nor the Golf Club [a related LLC] was a party to the operating agreements and that they are therefore not bound by the arbitration clauses therein").

Developments pertaining to the Virginia LLC Act further illustrate the difficulties. In *Mission Residential, L.L.C. v. Triple Net Properties, L.L.C.*, 654 S.E.2d 888, 891 (2008), the Virginia Supreme Court held that a member's derivative claim was not subject to the arbitration provision in the operating agreement, because: (i) the LLC was "the real party in interest"; (ii) the LLC had not signed the operating agreement; and (iii) requiring the claim to be arbitrated would "ignore[ ] the separate existence of Holdings [the LLC]." The Virginia legislature promptly disagreed and amended the LLC act to state: "A limited liability company is bound by its operating agreement whether or not the limited liability company executes the operating agreement." VA. CODE ANN. § 13.1–1023.A.1 (2012). The legislature left open the question of a limited liability company's power to enforce an operating agreement that the company has not executed.

This subsection answers the twin questions, categorically and in the affirmative.

This subsection does not consider whether a limited liability company is an indispensable party to a suit concerning the operating agreement. That question is one of procedural law, and the answer can determine whether federal diversity jurisdiction exists.

Subsection (b)—Given the possibility of oral and implied-in-fact terms in the operating agreement, a person becoming a member of an existing limited liability company should take precautions to ascertain fully the contents of the operating agreement. *See* the comment to Section 105(a)(4).

Subsection (c)—The second sentence refers to "assent to terms" rather than "make an agreement" because, under venerable principles of contract law, an agreement presupposes at least two parties, and Section 102(13) specifically contemplates an operating agreement in a single member LLC.

A pre-formation arrangement is not an operating agreement. An operating agreement presupposes at least one member, and, under this act, the earliest a person can become a member is upon the formation of the limited liability company. *See* Section 401.

§ 107. OPERATING AGREEMENT; EFFECT ON THIRD PARTIES AND RELATIONSHIP TO RECORDS EFFECTIVE ON BEHALF OF LIMITED LIABILITY COMPANY.

(a) An operating agreement may specify that its amendment requires the approval of a person that is not a party to the agreement or the satisfaction of a condition. An amendment is ineffective if its adoption does not include the required approval or satisfy the specified condition.

(b) The obligations of a limited liability company and its members to a person in the person's capacity as a transferee or a person dissociated as a member are governed by the operating agreement. Subject only to a court order issued under Section 503(b)(2) to effectuate a charging order, an amendment to the operating agreement made after a person becomes a transferee or is dissociated as a member:

(1) is effective with regard to any debt, obligation, or other liability of the limited liability company or its members to the person in the person's capacity as a transferee or person dissociated as a member; and

(2) is not effective to the extent the amendment imposes a new debt, obligation, or other liability on the transferee or person dissociated as a member.

(c) If a record delivered by a limited liability company to the [Secretary of State] for filing becomes effective and contains a provision that would be ineffective under Section 105(c) or (d)(3) if contained in the operating agreement, the provision is ineffective in the record.

(d) Subject to subsection (c), if a record delivered by a limited liability company to the [Secretary of State] for filing becomes effective and conflicts with a provision of the operating agreement:

(1) the agreement prevails as to members, persons dissociated as members, transferees, and managers; and

(2) the record prevails as to other persons to the extent they reasonably rely on the record.

Comment

Subsection (a)—This subsection, derived from DEL. CODE ANN. tit. 6, § 18–302(e), permits the operating agreement to: (i) accord a non-member veto rights over amendments to the agreement; and (ii) establish other preconditions for amendments. An amendment made in derogation of a veto right or precondition is ineffective.

Veto rights are likely to be sought by lenders but may also be attractive to non-member managers.

Example: A non-member manager enters into a management contract with an LLC, and that agreement provides in part that the LLC may remove the manager without cause only with the consent of members holding 2/3 of the profits interests. The operating agreement contains a parallel provision (the "operating agreement's quantum provision"), but the non-member manager is not a party to the operating agreement. Later, the LLC members amend the operating agreement's quantum provision to reduce the quantum to a simple majority of profits interests and thereafter purport to remove the manager without cause. Although the LLC has undoubtedly breached its contract with the manager and subjected itself to a damage claim, the LLC has the *power* under Section 105(a)(2) to effect the removal—unless the operating agreement provides the manager a veto right over changes in the operating agreement's quantum provision.

This subsection does not refer to member veto rights because, unless otherwise provided in the operating agreement, the consent of each member is necessary to effect an amendment. *See* Section 407(b)(4)(B), (c)(3)(B).

Because "[a]n operating agreement may specify that its amendment requires . . . the satisfaction of a condition," an operating agreement can require that any amendment be made through a writing or a record signed by each member. *See* Section 105(a)(4) (empowering the operating agreement to determine "the means and conditions for amending the operating agreement").

Subsection (b)—The law of unincorporated business organizations is only beginning to grapple in a modern way with the tension between the rights of an organization's owners to carry on their activities as they see fit (or have agreed) and the rights of transferees of the organization's economic interests. Such transferees can include the heirs of business founders as well as former owners who are "locked in" as transferees of their own interests. *See* Section 603(a)(3).

If the law categorically favors the owners, there is a serious risk of expropriation and other abuse. On the other hand, if the law grants former owners and other transferees the right to seek judicial protection, that specter can "freeze the deal" as of the moment an owner leaves the enterprise or a third party obtains an economic interest.

There is little case law in this area, and almost all of it pertains to limited partnerships rather than LLCs. The partnership case law clearly favors the remaining owners over former owners and other transferees. *See, e.g., Bauer v. Blomfield Co./Holden Joint Venture*, 849 P.2d 1365, 1367, n.2 (Alaska 1993) (holding that a mere assignee "was not entitled to complain about a decision made with the consent of all the partners" and stating "[w]e are unwilling to hold that partners owe a duty of good faith and fair dealing to assignees of a partner's interest"); *Bynum v. Frisby*, 73 Nev. 145, 149–50, 311 P.2d 972, 975 (1957) ("[A]n assignment of a partnership interest from one partner to a stranger does not bring that stranger into fiduciary relationship with the remaining partners nor require them to resort to dissolution in order to prevent such a relationship from arising. The stranger remains a stranger entitled only to share in the partnership's worth and to demand an accounting upon dissolution.") (applying UPA (1914) § 27, pertaining to rights of an assignee). *See generally* Daniel S. Kleinberger, *The Plight of the Bare Naked Assignee*, 42 Suffolk L. Rev. 587 (2009).

This subsection follows *Bauer* and other cases by expressly subjecting transferees (including a person dissociated as a member) to operating agreement amendments made after the transfer or dissociation, except amendments that increase obligations on transferees. For example, an amendment might extend the duration of a limited liability company but may not institute a new capital call obligation on transferees.

The question of whether, in extreme and sufficiently harsh circumstances, transferees might be able to claim some type of duty or obligation to protect against expropriation awaits development in the case law. An unreported LLC case suggests the answer might be yes, but the decision rests primarily on the wording of the LLC's operating agreement. In *Kohannim v. Katoli*, 08-11-00155-CV, 2013 WL 3943078, at *10–11 (Tex. App. July 24, 2013), the court: (i) noted that the LLC's "Regulations provide[ ] for the distribution of 'available cash' to members quarterly provided that the available cash is not needed for a reasonable working capital reserve"; (ii) also noted that "Jacob [the defendant member] paid himself $100,000 for management services that were not performed and failed to make any profit distributions to Mike [former member and ex-spouse of the plaintiff Parvaneh] or Parvaneh [ex-spouse of Mike, who became Mike's transferee as part of their divorce proceeding] even though more than $250,000 in undistributed profit had accumulated in the company's accounts since the mortgage on the property had been paid off in February 2007"; and (iii) concluded that "more than a scintilla of evidence supports the trial court's finding that Jacob failed to make profit distributions to Parvaneh." In essence, the court upheld a finding that Jacob had breached (or caused the LLC to breach) a contractual obligation to make distributions. But the court went further: "We also agree with the trial court's conclusion that the established facts demonstrated Jacob engaged in wrongful conduct and exhibited a lack of fair dealing in the company's affairs to the prejudice of Parvaneh." *Id.* at *11.

For the very limited rights of transferees, see Section 502.

Subsection (b)(1)—This provision is inapposite when "a member or transferee becomes entitled to receive a distribution." Section 404(d). In that circumstance:

- "the member or transferee has the status of . . . a creditor of the limited liability company with respect to the distribution," *Id.*; and

- the relevant obligation is not owed to "a person in the person's capacity as a transferee or person dissociated as a member," Subsection (b), but rather to the person in the person's capacity as a creditor.

Subsection (c)—This provision precludes using the certificate of organization to make an end run around the strictures of Section 105(c) and (d)(3).

Subsection (d)—It will be possible, albeit improvident, for a limited liability company's operating agreement to be inconsistent with the certificate of organization or other public filings pertaining to the company. For those circumstances, this subsection provides rules for determining which source of information prevails:

- For members, managers and transferees, the operating agreement is paramount.

- Third parties may invoke the public record upon a showing of reasonable reliance, which presupposes actual knowledge—*i.e.*, deemed knowledge under Section 103(d) does not suffice.

The mere fact that a term is present in a publicly filed record and not in the operating agreement, or *vice versa*, does not automatically establish a conflict. This subsection does not expressly cover a situation in which: (i) one of the specified filed records contains information in addition to, but not inconsistent with, the operating agreement; and (ii) a person, other than a member or transferee, reasonably relies on the additional information. However, the policy reflected in this subsection seems equally applicable to that situation. Moreover, to argue that the operating agreement prevails over the filed record is to argue that the additional term does conflict with the operating agreement, at least in effect.

Section 105(a)(4) might also be relevant to the subject matter of this subsection. Absent a contrary provision in the operating agreement, language in an LLC's certificate of organization or other record delivered to the filing office for filing on behalf of the LLC might be evidence of the members' agreement and might thereby constitute or at least imply a term of the operating agreement.

This subsection does not apply to records delivered to the filing office for filing on behalf of a person other than a limited liability company.

§ 108. NATURE, PURPOSE, AND DURATION OF LIMITED LIABILITY COMPANY.

(a) A limited liability company is an entity distinct from its member or members.

(b) A limited liability company may have any lawful purpose, regardless of whether for profit.

(c) A limited liability company has perpetual duration.

Comment

Subsection (a)—The "separate entity" characteristic is fundamental to a limited liability company and is inextricably connected to both the liability shield, Section 304, and the inability of creditors of a member or transferee to reach the assets of the limited liability company absent a "reverse pierce" or a claim of fraudulent transfer. *See, e.g., Litchfield Asset Mgmt Corp. v. Howell*, 799 A2d 298 (Conn. Ct. App. 2002) (applying an "outside reverse pierce" to allow judgment creditor of member to reach assets of LLC) (overruled on other grounds by *Robinson v. Coughlin*, 830 A2d 1114 (Conn. 2003)); *Egle v. Egle*, 817 So. 2d 136, 140 (La. Ct. App. 2002) (allowing plaintiff to proceed with claims that transfers made by her ex-spouse inter alia to an LLC were sham transactions).

Subsection (b)—Although some LLC statutes continue to require a business purpose, this act follows the current trend and takes a more expansive approach. The phrase "any lawful purpose, regardless of whether for profit" encompasses even charitable activities, but this act does not include any comprehensive protections pertaining to charitable assets and purposes. Section 1004(b) does contain a "nondiversion" provision, but the provision applies only to the organic transactions contemplated by Article 10. Comprehensive protections must be (and typically are) found in other law, although sometimes that "other law" appears within a state's non-profit corporation statute. *See, e.g.,* MINN. STAT. § 317A.811 (2012) (providing restrictions on charitable organizations that seek to "dissolve, merge, or consolidate, or to transfer all or substantially all of their assets" but imposing those restrictions only on "corporations," which are elsewhere defined as corporations incorporated under the non-profit corporation act).

Subsection (c)—The word "perpetual" is a misnomer, albeit one commonplace in LLC statutes. In this context, "perpetual" means merely that the act: (i) does not require a definite term; and (ii) creates no nexus between the dissociation of a member and the dissolution of the entity.

Moreover, the public record pertaining to a limited liability company will not necessarily reveal whether the company actually has a perpetual duration or has in fact dissolved, because: (i) this act, like all LLC statutes, provides several consent-based methods to dissolve a limited liability company; and (ii) none of those methods involve a public filing. For example, dissolution and winding up of a limited liability company may result from a term specified in the operating agreement or the affirmative vote or consent of all members. *See* Sections 701 (events causing dissolution) and 702 (winding up required upon dissolution). An operating agreement is not a publicly filed document, and a member vote to dissolve a limited liability company is not a public event. A dissolved limited partnership may deliver to the filing office for filing a statement of dissolution, Section 702(b)(2)(A), and later a statement of termination, Section 702(b)(2)(F), or both, but the filing of such statements is permissive rather than mandatory, *id.*

Likewise, the public record will not reveal when (or even whether) a limited liability company has come into existence. *See* Section 201(d) ("A limited liability company is formed when the company's certificate of becomes effective and at least one person becomes a member.").

§ 109.   POWERS.

A limited liability company has the capacity to sue and be sued in its own name and the power to do all things necessary or convenient to carry on its activities and affairs.

Comment

Continuing the approach initiated in ULPA (2001) § 105, this act omits as unnecessary any detailed list of specific powers.

The operating agreement cannot vary a limited liability company's capacity to sue and be sued. Section 105(c)(2). An LLC's standing to enforce the operating agreement is a separate matter, which is covered by Section 106(a) (stating, as a default rule, that the limited liability company "may enforce the operating agreement").

§ 110.   APPLICATION TO EXISTING RELATIONSHIPS.

(a) Before [all-inclusive date], this [act] governs only:

(1) a limited liability company formed on or after [the effective date of this [act]];

and

(2) except as otherwise provided in subsection (c), a limited liability company formed before [the effective date of this [act]] which elects, in the manner provided in its operating agreement or by law for amending the operating agreement, to be subject to this [act].

(b) Except as otherwise provided in subsection (c), on and after [all-inclusive date] this [act] governs all limited liability companies.

(c) For purposes of applying this [act] to a limited liability company formed before [the effective date of this [act]]:

(1) the company's articles of organization are deemed to be the company's certificate of organization; and

(2) for purposes of applying Section 102(10) and subject to Section 107(d), language in the company's articles of organization designating the company's management structure operates as if that language were in the operating agreement.

Legislative Note:

For states that have previously enacted ULLCA (2006): *For these states this section is unnecessary. There is no need for a delayed effective date, even with regard to pre-existing limited liability companies.*

For states that have not previously enacted ULLCA (2006):

Each enacting jurisdiction should consider whether: (i) this act makes material changes to the "default" (or "gap filler") rules of a predecessor statute; and (ii) if so, whether Subsection (c) should carry forward any of those rules for pre-existing limited liability companies. In this assessment, the focus is on pre-existing limited liability companies that have left default rules in place, whether advisedly or not. The central question is whether, for such limited liability companies, expanding Subsection (c) is necessary to prevent material changes to the members' "deal."

Section 301 (de-codifying statutory apparent authority) does not require any special transition provisions, because: (i) applying the law of agency, as explained in the Comments to Sections 301 and 407, will produce appropriate results; and (ii) the notion of "lingering apparent authority" will protect any third party that has previously relied on the statutory apparent authority of a member of a particular member-managed LLC or a manager of a particular manager-managed LLC. RESTATEMENT (THIRD) OF AGENCY § 3.11, cmt. c (2006).

It is recommended that the "all-inclusive" date should be at least one year after the effective date of this act, Section 1106, but no more than two years.

Comment

Subsection (c)—When a pre-existing limited liability company becomes subject to this act, the company ceases to be governed by the predecessor act, including whatever requirements that act might have imposed for the contents of the articles of organization.

§ 111. SUPPLEMENTAL PRINCIPLES OF LAW.

Unless displaced by particular provisions of this [act], the principles of law and equity supplement this [act].

Comment

For this act, the common law rules of contract and agency are among the most important supplemental "principles of law." With regard to transactions under Article 10, noteworthy principles include the rights of creditors following leveraged buyouts, spinoffs, asset purchases, or other similar transactions; and creditors' rights under other laws.

§ 112. PERMITTED NAMES.

(a) The name of a limited liability company must contain the phrase "limited liability company" or "limited company" or the abbreviation "L.L.C.", "LLC", "L.C.", or "LC". "Limited" may be abbreviated as "Ltd.", and "company" may be abbreviated as "Co.".

(b) Except as otherwise provided in subsection (d), the name of a limited liability company, and the name under which a foreign limited liability company may register to do business in this state, must be distinguishable on the records of the [Secretary of State] from any:

(1) name of an existing person whose formation required the filing of a record by the [Secretary of State] and which is not at the time administratively dissolved;

(2) name of a limited liability partnership whose statement of qualification is in effect;

(3) name under which a person is registered to do business in this state by the filing of a record by the [Secretary of State];

(4) name reserved under Section 113 or other law of this state providing for the reservation of a name by the filing of a record by the [Secretary of State];

(5) name registered under Section 114 or other law of this state providing for the registration of a name by the filing of a record by the [Secretary of State]; and

(6) name registered under [this state's assumed or fictitious name statute].

(c) If a person consents in a record to the use of its name and submits an undertaking in a form satisfactory to the [Secretary of State] to change its name to a name that is distinguishable on the records of the [Secretary of State] from any name in any category of names in subsection (b), the name of the consenting person may be used by the person to which the consent was given.

(d) Except as otherwise provided in subsection (e), in determining whether a name is the same as or not distinguishable on the records of the [Secretary of State] from the name of another person, words, phrases, or abbreviations indicating a type of person, such as "corporation", "corp.", "incorporated", "Inc.", "professional corporation", "P.C.", "PC", "professional association", "P.A.", "PA", "Limited", "Ltd.", "limited partnership", "L.P.", "LP", "limited liability partnership", "L.L.P.", "LLP", "registered limited liability partnership", "R.L.L.P.", "RLLP", "limited liability limited partnership", "L.L.L.P.", "LLLP", "registered limited liability limited partnership", "R.L.L.L.P.", "RLLLP", "limited liability company", "L.L.C.", "LLC", "limited cooperative association", "limited cooperative", or "L.C.A.", or "LCA" may not be taken into account.

(e) A person may consent in a record to the use of a name that is not distinguishable on the records of the [Secretary of State] from its name except for the addition of a word, phrase, or abbreviation indicating the type of person as provided in subsection (d). In such a case, the person need not change its name pursuant to subsection (c).

(f) The name of a limited liability company or foreign limited liability company may not contain the words [insert prohibited word or words that may be used only with approval by an appropriate state agency].

(g) A limited liability company or foreign limited liability company may use a name that is not distinguishable from a name described in subsection (b)(1) through (6) if the company delivers to the [Secretary of State] a certified copy of a final judgment of a court of competent jurisdiction establishing the right of the company to use the name in this state.

Comment

This section adopts the "distinguishable on the records" test for name availability and rejects the "deceptively similar" test widely used in the past.

For name requirements for foreign limited liability companies, see Section 906.

§ 113.   RESERVATION OF NAME.

(a) A person may reserve the exclusive use of a name that complies with Section 112 by delivering an application to the [Secretary of State] for filing. The application must state the name and address of the applicant and the name to be reserved. If the [Secretary of State] finds that the name is available, the [Secretary of State] shall reserve the name for the applicant's exclusive use for [120] days.

(b) The owner of a reserved name may transfer the reservation to another person by delivering to the [Secretary of State] a signed notice in a record of the transfer which states the name and address of the person to which the reservation is being transferred.

Comment

This section does not provide for the renewal of a name reservation for successive 120-day periods. A new reservation may be filed upon the expiration of a reservation, but by requiring a new filing this section creates the possibility that another party may timely submit a reservation for the same name. It was considered appropriate to allow for that possibility so that the procedure in this section cannot be used to block a name indefinitely. *Compare* Section 113, *with* Section 114(d) (authorizing a renewable registration of certain names).

§ 114.   REGISTRATION OF NAME.

(a) A foreign limited liability company not registered to do business in this state under [Article] 9 may register its name, or an alternate name adopted pursuant to Section 906, if the name is distinguishable on the records of the [Secretary of State] from the names that are not available under Section 112.

(b) To register its name or an alternate name adopted pursuant to Section 906, a foreign limited liability company must deliver to the [Secretary of State] for filing an application stating the company's name, the jurisdiction and date of its formation, and any alternate name adopted pursuant to Section 906. If the [Secretary of State] finds that the name applied for is available, the [Secretary of State] shall register the name for the applicant's exclusive use.

(c) The registration of a name under this section is effective for [one year] after the date of registration.

(d) A foreign limited liability company whose name registration is effective may renew the registration for successive [one-year] periods by delivering, not earlier than [three months] before the expiration of the registration, to the [Secretary of State] for filing a renewal application that complies with this section. When filed, the renewal application renews the registration for a succeeding [one-year] period.

(e) A foreign limited liability company whose name registration is effective may register as a foreign limited liability company under the registered name or consent in a signed record to the use of that name by another person that is not an individual.

Comment

Unlike the reservation of a name under Section 113, a registration of a name under this section may be renewed for successive periods thus permitting a name to be protected for a period longer than the initial registration period. Use of the procedure in this section is limited, however, to the names of foreign limited liability companies that are not registered to do business in the state. The purpose of this section is to permit a foreign entity to make sure its name will be available if the entity should choose to register in the state in the future.

§ 115.   REGISTERED AGENT.

(a) Each limited liability company and each registered foreign limited liability company shall designate and maintain a registered agent in this state. The designation of a registered agent is an affirmation of fact by the limited liability company or registered foreign limited liability company that the agent has consented to serve.

(b) A registered agent for a limited liability company or registered foreign limited liability company must have a place of business in this state.

(c) The only duties under this [act] of a registered agent that has complied with this [act] are:

(1) to forward to the limited liability company or registered foreign limited liability company at the address most recently supplied to the agent by the company or foreign company any process, notice, or demand pertaining to the company or foreign company which is served on or received by the agent;

(2) if the registered agent resigns, to provide the notice required by Section 117(c) to the company or foreign company at the address most recently supplied to the agent by the company or foreign company; and

(3) to keep current the information with respect to the agent in the certificate of organization or foreign registration statement.

Comment

This section is limited to prescribing the duties of a registered agent under this act. The operating agreement cannot vary this section. Section 105(c)(3)(A). However, an agent may undertake other responsibilities to a represented limited liability company or foreign limited liability company, such as by contract or course of dealing, but those duties will be determined under other law.

§ 116. CHANGE OF REGISTERED AGENT OR ADDRESS FOR REGISTERED AGENT BY LIMITED LIABILITY COMPANY.

(a) A limited liability company or registered foreign limited liability company may change its registered agent or the address of its registered agent by delivering to the [Secretary of State] for filing a statement of change that states:

(1) the name of the company or foreign company; and

(2) the information that is to be in effect as a result of the filing of the statement of change.

(b) The members or managers of a limited liability company need not approve the delivery to the [Secretary of State] filing of:

(1) a statement of change under this section; or

(2) a similar filing changing the registered agent or registered office, if any, of the company in any other jurisdiction.

(c) A statement of change under this section designating a new registered agent is an affirmation of fact by the limited liability company or registered foreign limited liability company that the agent has consented to serve.

(d) As an alternative to using the procedure in this section, a limited liability company may amend its certificate of organization.

Comment

A change in the identity of the registered agent of a LLC or foreign LLC or a change of the office address of a company's registered agent are usually routine matters that do not affect the rights of the members of the represented LLC. This section permits those changes to be made without: (i) amendment of an LLC's certificate of organization; (ii) formal approval by an LLC's managers (if any); and (iii) any approval by an LLC's members. For the registered agent's power to resign, see Section 117. For the registered agent's power to change its name, address, or both, see Section 118.

Subsection (c)—This subsection avoids the need to file with a statement of change consent of the new registered agent being designated.

Subsection (d)—This subsection makes clear that the procedures in this section are not exclusive. A common way in which a limited liability company changes its registered agent is to include the change in an amendment of its certificate of organization or in its annual/biennial report. *See* Section 212(e).

§ 117. RESIGNATION OF REGISTERED AGENT.

(a) A registered agent may resign as an agent for a limited liability company or registered foreign limited liability company by delivering to the [Secretary of State] for filing a statement of resignation that states:

(1) the name of the company or foreign company;

(2) the name of the agent;

(3) that the agent resigns from serving as registered agent for the company or foreign company; and

(4) the address of the company or foreign company to which the agent will send the notice required by subsection (c).

(b) A statement of resignation takes effect on the earlier of:

(1) the 31st day after the day on which it is filed by the [Secretary of State]; or

(2) the designation of a new registered agent for the limited liability company or registered foreign limited liability company.

(c) A registered agent promptly shall furnish to the limited liability company or registered foreign limited liability company notice in a record of the date on which a statement of resignation was filed.

(d) When a statement of resignation takes effect, the registered agent ceases to have responsibility under this [act] for any matter thereafter tendered to it as agent for the limited liability company or registered foreign limited liability company. The resignation does not affect any contractual rights the company or foreign company has against the agent or that the agent has against the company or foreign company.

(e) A registered agent may resign with respect to a limited liability company or registered foreign limited liability company whether or not the company or foreign company is in good standing.

Comment

Resignation under this section may be accomplished solely by action of the registered agent and does not require the cooperation or consent of the represented LLC or foreign LLC. Whether a resignation violates a contract between the registered agent and the company is beyond the scope of this act, and Subsection (d) preserves whatever claims a represented LLC may have against its registered agent for a wrongful termination. Even if a resignation were to violate such a contract, the resignation would still be effective if the provisions of this section were followed.

Subsection (b)—This subsection delays the effectiveness of a statement of resignation for thirty-one days to allow the notice of the resignation that must be sent under Subsection (c) to reach the represented LLC or registered foreign LLC and to allow the represented LLC to arrange for a substitute registered agent.

Subsection (e)—This subsection makes clear that a registered agent may resign with respect to LLC or registered foreign LLC that is not in good standing and supersedes the contrary administrative practice in some states of refusing to accept any filings with respect to an entity that is not in good standing until the problem with the entity's standing is cured.

§ 118.   CHANGE OF NAME OR ADDRESS BY REGISTERED AGENT.

(a) If a registered agent changes its name or address, the agent may deliver to the [Secretary of State] for filing a statement of change that states:

(1) the name of the limited liability company or registered foreign limited liability company represented by the registered agent;

(2) the name of the agent as currently shown in the records of the [Secretary of State] for the company or foreign company;

(3) if the name of the agent has changed, its new name; and

(4) if the address of the agent has changed, its new address.

(b) A registered agent promptly shall furnish notice to the represented limited liability company or registered foreign limited liability company of the filing by the [Secretary of State] of the statement of change and the changes made by the statement.

Legislative Note: *Many registered agents act in that capacity for many entities, and the Model Registered Agents Act (2006) (Last Amended 2013) provides a streamlined method through which a commercial registered agent can make a single filing to change its information for all represented entities. The single filing does not prevent an enacting state from assessing filing fees on the basis of the number of entity records affected. Alternatively the fees can be set on an incremental sliding fee or capitated amount based upon potential economies of costs for a bulk filing.*

Comment

This section permits a registered agent to change the name and address of the agent that appears in the registered agent filing of an LLC or foreign LLC represented by the agent. This act does not provide for commercial registered agents. *Cf.* UBOC (2011) (Last Amended 2013) §§ 1–405, 1–406, 1–409. As a result, a registered agent will need to make a separate filing under this section for each LLC and foreign LLC represented by the agent, unless, if authorized by rule or administrative policy, the filing office establishes procedures for a bulk filing with one filing listing the names of all the registered agent's represented entities.

§ 119.　SERVICE OF PROCESS, NOTICE, OR DEMAND.

(a) A limited liability company or registered foreign limited liability company may be served with any process, notice, or demand required or permitted by law by serving its registered agent.

(b) If a limited liability company or registered foreign limited liability company ceases to have a registered agent, or if its registered agent cannot with reasonable diligence be served, the company or foreign company may be served by registered or certified mail, return receipt requested, or by similar commercial delivery service, addressed to the company or foreign company at its principal office. The address of the principal office must be as shown on the company's or foreign company's most recent [annual] [biennial] report filed by the [Secretary of State]. Service is effected under this subsection on the earliest of:

(1) the date the company or foreign company receives the mail or delivery by the commercial delivery service;

(2) the date shown on the return receipt, if signed by the company or foreign company; or

(3) five days after its deposit with the United States Postal Service, or with the commercial delivery service, if correctly addressed and with sufficient postage or payment.

(c) If process, notice, or demand cannot be served on a limited liability company or registered foreign limited liability company pursuant to subsection (a) or (b), service may be made by handing a copy to the individual in charge of any regular place of business or activity of the company or foreign company if the individual served is not a plaintiff in the action.

(d) Service of process, notice, or demand on a registered agent must be in a written record.

(e) Service of process, notice, or demand may be made by other means under law other than this [act].

Comment

Subsection (b)—This subsection offers three alternative methods for establishing the date service is effected, a date important for determining the time within which an LLC or registered foreign LLC must respond to the process, notice, or demand served. Under Subsection (b)(1), service is effected on the date of receipt by the company of the mail or commercial delivery. Under Subsection (b)(2), service is effected on the date shown on the return receipt, if signed on behalf of the company. Under Subsection (b)(3), service is effected five days after it is deposited with the Postal Service or with a similar commercial delivery service, if correctly addressed and with correct postage or payment. Service is effective at the earliest of the three listed circumstances.

However, for the party effecting service there are difficulties of proof under the first two circumstances. Under Subsection (b)(1) the exact date of the receipt by the LLC or foreign LLC of mail or commercial delivery is peculiarly within the knowledge of the company. Under Subsection (b)(2) the return receipt must be signed on behalf of the company. That requirement is designed to assure that the service is actually received by the company, but the signature on the return receipt may not always show unambiguously that the signer was acting for the company and was authorized to do so. As a practical matter, therefore, parties effecting service under Subsection (b) may find it most convenient to rely on subsection (3) and to maintain their own records so that the date of deposit in the mails or with a commercial delivery service can easily be established.

Subsection (c)—This subsection provides a means for serving process on an LLC or foreign LLC that cannot be served under Subsection (a) or (b). Some LLC statutes require or permit service of process in that circumstance be made on the filing office

Subsection (e)—*See, e.g.,* Fed. R. Civ. P. 4(h)(1)(B) (authorizing service on "a domestic or foreign corporation, or a partnership or other unincorporated association that is subject to suit under a common name" to be made on "an officer, a managing or general agent, or any other agent authorized by appointment or by law to receive service of process").

§ 120. DELIVERY OF RECORD.

(a) Except as otherwise provided in this [act], permissible means of delivery of a record include delivery by hand, mail, conventional commercial practice, and electronic transmission.

(b) Delivery to the [Secretary of State] is effective only when a record is received by the [Secretary of State].

Comment

Subsection (a)—Permissible means of delivery are not limited to those listed in this subsection, because this subsection by its terms is a non-exclusive list. Conventional commercial practice includes the use of private delivery or courier services. What constitutes conventional commercial practice may change over time.

Subsection (b)—This section lists permissible means of delivery but, except for delivery to the filing office, does not determine when delivery occurs. Delivery to the filing office is effective only upon actual receipt.

§ 121. RESERVATION OF POWER TO AMEND OR REPEAL.

The [legislature of this state] has power to amend or repeal all or part of this [act] at any time, and all limited liability companies and foreign limited liability companies subject to this [act] are governed by the amendment or repeal.

Comment

Provisions similar to this section have their genesis in *Trustees of Dartmouth College v. Woodward*, 17 U.S. (4 Wheat) 518 (1819), which held that the United States Constitution prohibited the application of newly enacted statutes to existing corporations while suggesting the efficacy of a reservation of power similar to this section. This section is a generalized form of the type of provision found in many entity organic laws, the purpose of which is to avoid any possible argument that an entity has contractual or vested rights in any specific statutory provision of its organic law and to ensure that the state may in the future modify its entity statutes as it deems appropriate and require existing entities to comply with the statutes as modified.

This section applies to changes in mandatory provisions of this act; the section does not pertain to changes in default rules.

Example: Having enacted this act, State A later amends Section 401(c)(3) (affirmative vote or consent of all members required for a person for a person to become a member) to reduce, as a default rule, the necessary quantum of consent to consent from members owning in the aggregate at least two-third of the interests in current profits owned by members at the time of the consent. XYZ, LLC is a limited liability company formed under State A's act before the amendment. XYZ's operating agreement is silent on this issue, leaving in place the act's default rule. Whether the act's amended default rule applies depends on whether the members initially: (i) agreed (whether expressly or implicitly) to accept the then-applicable default rule requiring unanimous consent; (ii) agreed (whether expressly or implicitly) to adopt whatever rule the act provided; or (iii) never considered the issue. In short, the change in a default rule occasions an inquiry into the members' express or implied agreement as to the role of the default rule in their mutual understanding. In the first instance, the old rule would continue in effect. In the second and third instances, the new rule would apply.

[ARTICLE] 2

FORMATION; CERTIFICATE OF ORGANIZATION AND OTHER FILINGS

§ 201. FORMATION OF LIMITED LIABILITY COMPANY; CERTIFICATE OF ORGANIZATION.

(a) One or more persons may act as organizers to form a limited liability company by delivering to the [Secretary of State] for filing a certificate of organization.

(b) A certificate of organization must state:

(1) the name of the limited liability company, which must comply with Section 112;

(2) the street and mailing addresses of the company's principal office; and

(3) the name and street and mailing addresses in this state of the company's registered agent.

(c) A certificate of organization may contain statements as to matters other than those required by subsection (b), but may not vary or otherwise affect the provisions specified in Section 105(c) and (d) in a manner inconsistent with that section. However, a statement in a certificate of organization is not effective as a statement of authority.

(d) A limited liability company is formed when the certificate of organization becomes effective and at least one person has become a member.

Comment

For a limited liability company to be formed (*i.e.*, to come into existence), two conditions must be met: (i) a certificate of organization must become effective; and (ii) at least one person must become a member.

By definition, the earliest a person can become a member is when the certificate of organization takes effect. *See* Section 102(11) (defining "member" as a person that "has become a member of a limited liability company"). However, a certificate of organization can take effect long before any person becomes a member, and the act does not require any public filing to indicate that a person has become a member. Therefore, the public record will not reflect when (and even whether) a limited liability company has come into existence. *See also* the comment to Section 211.

Subsection (b)—Consistent with the modern trend, this act requires only the most "bare bones" of disclosure.

Unlike many LLC statutes, this act does not require that the certificate of organization state whether the limited liability company is manager-managed or member-managed. Placing that information in a public record pertains primarily to "statutory apparent authority," which this act has eschewed. *See* the comment to Section 301(a). Under this act, the manager-managed and member-managed characterizations pertain principally to *inter se* relations, and the act therefore looks to the operating agreement to make the characterization. *See* Sections 102(10) and (12); Section 407(a).

Subsection (c)—This provision permits the certificate of organization to contain information beyond that required in Subsection (b). An LLC should have good reason, however, before choosing to include additional information. Such information: (i) is available to the public (including competitors); (ii) increases the chances of a conflict between the certificate of organization and the operating agreement, *see* Section 107(d); (iii) permits the argument that the additional information is part of the operating agreement, *see* the comment to Section 102(13) (stating that "[u]nless the operating agreement itself provides otherwise . . . an operating agreement may comprise a number of separate documents (or records), however denominated"); and (iv) can be confusing to the extent the information appears to delineate the power of persons to act for the LLC. (Subsection (c) states explicitly that information in a certificate of formation "is not effective as a statement of authority."). In any event, placing additional information in the certificate of formation does not enable an LLC to "end run" the provisions of Section 105(c) (limiting the power of the operating agreement to vary specified provisions of this act).

Subsection (d)—ULLCA (2006) flirted with the concept of a "shelf" LLC—*i.e.*, a limited liability company duly formed without having at least one member upon formation. As the Prefatory Note to ULLCA (2006) explains:

[T]he Act: (i) permits an organizer to file a certificate of organization without a person "waiting in the wings" to become a member upon formation; but (ii) provides that the LLC is not formed until and unless at least one person becomes a member and the organizer makes a second filing stating that the LLC has at least one member.

Prefatory Note, *The Ability to "Pre-File" a Certificate of Organization.*

Subsection (d) clearly precludes a "shelf" LLC, which is consistent with ULPA (2001) (Last Amended 2013) Section 201(d) (providing that a limited partnership is formed when the certificate of limited partnership becomes effective, at least two persons have become partners, at least one person has become a general partner, and at least one person has become a limited partner).

§ 202. AMENDMENT OR RESTATEMENT OF CERTIFICATE OF ORGANIZATION.

(a) A certificate of organization may be amended or restated at any time.

(b) To amend its certificate of organization, a limited liability company must deliver to the [Secretary of State] for filing an amendment stating:

(1) the name of the company;

(2) the date of filing of its initial certificate; and

(3) the text of the amendment.

(c) To restate its certificate of organization, a limited liability company must deliver to the [Secretary of State] for filing a restatement, designated as such in its heading.

(d) If a member of a member-managed limited liability company, or a manager of a manager-managed limited liability company, knows that any information in a filed certificate of organization was inaccurate when the certificate was filed or has become inaccurate due to changed circumstances, the member or manager shall promptly:

(1) cause the certificate to be amended; or

(2) if appropriate, deliver to the [Secretary of State] for filing a statement of change under Section 116 or a statement of correction under Section 209.

Comment

Like other provisions of the act requiring records to be delivered to the filing officer for filing, this section is not subject to change by the operating agreement. See Section 105(c)(3). Except for Subsection (d), this section is essentially mechanical.

Subsection (d)—This subsection imposes an obligation directly on the members and managers rather than on the limited liability company. A member's or manager's failure to meet the obligation exposes the member or manager to liability to third parties under Section 205(a)(2) and might constitute a breach of the member or manager's duties under Section 409(c) and (i). In addition, an aggrieved person may seek a remedy under Sections 204 (Signing and Filing Pursuant to Judicial Order) and 205 (Liability for Inaccurate Information in Filed Record).

Like other provisions of the act requiring records to be delivered to the filing officer for filing, this section is not subject to change by the operating agreement. *See* Section 105(c)(3).

§ 203.   SIGNING OF RECORDS TO BE DELIVERED FOR FILING TO [SECRETARY OF STATE].

(a) A record delivered to the [Secretary of State] for filing pursuant to this [act] must be signed as follows:

(1) Except as otherwise provided in paragraphs (2) and (3), a record signed by a limited liability company must be signed by a person authorized by the company.

(2) A company's initial certificate of organization must be signed by at least one person acting as an organizer.

(3) A record delivered on behalf of a dissolved company that has no member must be signed by the person winding up the company's activities and affairs under Section 702(c) or a person appointed under Section 702(d) to wind up the activities and affairs.

(4) A statement of denial by a person under Section 303 must be signed by that person.

(5) Any other record delivered on behalf of a person to the [Secretary of State] for filing must be signed by that person.

(b) A record delivered for filing under this [act] may be signed by an agent. Whenever this [act] requires a particular individual to sign a record and the individual is deceased or incompetent, the record may be signed by a legal representative of the individual.

(c) A person that signs a record as an agent or legal representative affirms as a fact that the person is authorized to sign the record.

Comment

Subsection (a)—Section 102(21) defines "sign" broadly, including "an electronic symbol, sound, or process."

Subsection (a)(1)—From the perspective of the filing office, it is not necessary that a record delivered for filing on behalf of a limited liability company be signed by a member or, in the case of a manager-managed LLC, a manager. The operating agreement can impose such a requirement as an *inter se* matter, but the requirement would not affect this provision. See Section 105(c)(3)(B) (stating that the operating agreement may not "vary any requirement, procedure, or other provision of this [act] pertaining to . . . the [Secretary of State], including provisions pertaining to records authorized or required to be delivered to the [Secretary of State] for filing under this [act]").

The filing office will not check whether a person who purports to be authorized to sign a record on behalf of an LLC actually has that authority, even if a statement of authority pertaining to the matter is in effect. Indeed, even if the filing office somehow "knows" of a statement limiting authority, the office lacks the authority to reject a record on that basis. *See* the comment to Section 206(a) (stating the requirements for filing and noting that the filing office's review is ministerial and limited to information pertaining to the stated requirements) and the comment to Section 302(c) (explaining why such a statement of authority does not affect the filing office).

Subsection (b)—The filing office will not check the bona fides of a person purporting to have signed a record in a representative capacity. This subsection expressly authorizes taking action through an agent so as to provide context for Subsection (c) and for the avoidance of doubt. No negative inference should be drawn about using agents to take other action under this act.

Subsection (c)—As a matter of agency law, a person who signs in a representative capacity gives a "warranty of authority." RESTATEMENT (THIRD) OF AGENCY § 6.10 (2006) (Agent's Implied Warranty of Authority). This subsection has criminal law implications.

§ 204.   SIGNING AND FILING PURSUANT TO JUDICIAL ORDER.

(a) If a person required by this [act] to sign a record or deliver a record to the [Secretary of State] for filing under this [act] does not do so, any other person that is aggrieved may petition [the appropriate court] to order:

(1) the person to sign the record;

(2) the person to deliver the record to the [Secretary of State] for filing; or

(3) the [Secretary of State] to file the record unsigned.

(b) If a petitioner under subsection (a) is not the limited liability company or foreign limited liability company to which the record pertains, the petitioner shall make the company or foreign company a party to the action.

(c) A record filed under subsection (a)(3) is effective without being signed.

Comment

This section gives the court the flexibility to order either that a record be signed or that the record be filed by the filing office unsigned. The latter circumstance may arise, for example, in a situation where the person who should sign the record is not subject to the jurisdiction of the court. This section also makes clear that the court may order a person with control over a record that has been signed to deliver the record to the filing office for filing.

§ 205.   LIABILITY FOR INACCURATE INFORMATION IN FILED RECORD.

(a) If a record delivered to the [Secretary of State] for filing under this [act] and filed by the [Secretary of State] contains inaccurate information, a person that suffers loss by reliance on the information may recover damages for the loss from:

(1) a person that signed the record, or caused another to sign it on the person's behalf, and knew the information to be inaccurate at the time the record was signed; and

(2) subject to subsection (b), a member of a member-managed limited liability company or a manager of a manager-managed limited liability company if:

(A) the record was delivered for filing on behalf of the company; and

(B) the member or manager knew or had notice of the inaccuracy for a reasonably sufficient time before the information was relied upon so that, before the reliance, the member or manager reasonably could have:

(i) effected an amendment under Section 202;

(ii) filed a petition under Section 204; or

(iii) delivered to the [Secretary of State] for filing a statement of change under Section 116 or a statement of correction under Section 209.

(b) To the extent the operating agreement of a member-managed limited liability company expressly relieves a member of responsibility for maintaining the accuracy of information contained in records delivered on behalf of the company to the [Secretary of State] for filing under this [act] and imposes that responsibility on one or more other members, the liability stated in subsection (a)(2) applies to those other members and not to the member that the operating agreement relieves of the responsibility.

(c) An individual who signs a record authorized or required to be filed under this [act] affirms under penalty of perjury that the information stated in the record is accurate.

Comment

Subsection (a)—This subsection relates to liability to third parties for inaccurate information in a filed record. Paragraph 1 requires actual knowledge because the paragraph can inculpate a person who is neither a member of a member-managed limited liability company nor a manager of a manager-managed limited liability company. Under Paragraph 2(B), notice suffices, because: (i) the provision applies only to members of a member-managed LLC and managers of a manager-managed LLC; (ii) by status these persons have overall management authority; and (iii) therefore it is reasonable to impose liability when a person either knows or "has reason to know . . . from all the facts known to the person at the time in question." Section 103(b)(1) (defining notice). For the same reason, Paragraph 1 applies only to "information [known] to be inaccurate at the time the record was signed," while Paragraph 2 applies whenever a "member or manager knew or had notice of the inaccuracy for a reasonably sufficient time before the information was relied upon so that, before the reliance, the member or manager reasonably could have [taken corrective action]." Paragraph (2)(B).

Subsection (a)(2)—Although this act establishes the avoidance of gross negligence as the standard of care for those who manage a limited liability company, this provision encompasses liability to third parties. Accordingly, the standard here is more demanding. The phrases "reasonably sufficient time" and "reasonably could have" indicate a standard of ordinary care. "[N]otice of the inaccuracy" involves "reason to know." Section 103(b)(1).

Subsection (b)—Section 105(d)(2) authorizes the operating agreement to establish an analogous rule *inter se* the members. This subsection goes where the operating agreement cannot reach and affects the rights of third parties.

Subsection (c)—This subsection provides criminal liability. The elements of perjury are a matter for the criminal law of the jurisdiction.

§ 206.   FILING REQUIREMENTS.

(a) To be filed by the [Secretary of State] pursuant to this [act], a record must be received by the [Secretary of State], comply with this [act], and satisfy the following:

(1) The filing of the record must be required or permitted by this [act].

(2) The record must be physically delivered in written form unless and to the extent the [Secretary of State] permits electronic delivery of records.

(3) The words in the record must be in English, and numbers must be in Arabic or Roman numerals, but the name of an entity need not be in English if written in English letters or Arabic or Roman numerals.

(4) The record must be signed by a person authorized or required under this [act] to sign the record.

(5) The record must state the name and capacity, if any, of each individual who signed it, either on behalf of the individual or the person authorized or required to sign the record, but need not contain a seal, attestation, acknowledgment, or verification.

(b) If law other than this [act] prohibits the disclosure by the [Secretary of State] of information contained in a record delivered to the [Secretary of State] for filing, the [Secretary of State] shall file the record if the record otherwise complies with this [act] but may redact the information.

(c) When a record is delivered to the [Secretary of State] for filing, any fee required under this [act] and any fee, tax, interest, or penalty required to be paid under this [act] or law other than this [act] must be paid in a manner permitted by the [Secretary of State] or by that law.

(d) The [Secretary of State] may require that a record delivered in written form be accompanied by an identical or conformed copy.

(e) The [Secretary of State] may provide forms for filings required or permitted to be made by this [act], but, except as otherwise provided in subsection (f), their use is not required.

(f) The [Secretary of State] may require that a cover sheet for a filing be on a form prescribed by the [Secretary of State].

Comment

The filing office's duty under this section is ministerial, Section 210(a), and the office's assessment of a record delivered for filing is limited to conformity with this section. The filing office *must* file a record delivered for filing if the record contains the information required by this act and is accompanied by the required filing fee. The filing office is authorized to provide forms but not require their use, and, as a result, may not reject records delivered for filing on the basis of form (except to the very limited extent permitted by Subsections (d) and (f)).

In view of the very limited discretion granted to the filing office under this section and Section 210(a), "[t]he filing of . . . a record does not create a presumption that the information contained in the record is correct. . . ." Section 210(e).

Subsection (a)—The first requisite for having a record filed is to cause the record actually to be received by the filing office. Section 120(b) reiterates this point.

Subsection (a)(2)—A record delivered for filing must be in typewritten or printed form unless the filing office permits delivery by electronic transmission. The types of electronic transmission that may be used will be determined by the filing office and is intended to include the evolving methods of electronic delivery, including facsimile transmissions, electronic transmissions between computers, and filings through delivery of storage media.

Subsection (a)(3)—The text of an entity filing must be in the English language, except to the limited extent permitted by this paragraph.

Subsection (a)(4)—To be filed a record must be signed by the appropriate person. *See* Section 102(21) (defining "sign" and manner in which a record may be "signed"). Who is an appropriate person is determined under Section 203, but the filing office will not check to determine whether a person purportedly authorized to sign is in fact authorized. *See* the comment to Section 203(a)–(c).

The requirement in some state statutes that records delivered for filing on behalf of an entity must be acknowledged or verified as a condition for filing has been rejected. These requirements serve little purpose in connection with entity filings. On the other hand, many organizations, like lenders or title companies, may desire that specific records include acknowledgements, verifications, or seals; Subsection (a)(4) does not prohibit the addition of these forms of execution and their use does not affect the eligibility of the record for filing.

Subsection (b)—Under this subsection, a confidentiality obligation does not affect the filing office's duty to file, and the filing office is authorized but not required to redact. This act does not affect any confidentiality-related obligations the filing office may have under other law.

§ 207.   EFFECTIVE DATE AND TIME.

Except as otherwise provided in Section 208 and subject to Section 209(d), a record filed under this [act] is effective:

(1) on the date and at the time of its filing by the [Secretary of State], as provided in Section 210(b);

(2) on the date of filing and at the time specified in the record as its effective time, if later than the time under paragraph (1);

(3) at a specified delayed effective date and time, which may not be more than 90 days after the date of filing; or

(4) if a delayed effective date is specified, but no time is specified, at 12:01 a.m. on the date specified, which may not be more than 90 days after the date of filing.

Comment

Records accepted for filing become effective at the date and time of filing as recorded by the filing office, or at another specified time on that date, unless a permissible delayed effective date is stated in the record.

Section 210(b) requires the filing office to maintain some means of recording the date and time of delivery of a record and requires that office to record that date and time as the date and time of filing. That provision gives express statutory authority to the common practice of most filing offices of ignoring processing time and treating a record as filed as of the date and time it is delivered for filing even though it may not be reviewed and accepted for filing until several days after delivery. That section contemplates that time of delivery, as well as the date, will be routinely recorded.

Paragraph (1)—In the absence of provision for a delayed effective date, a record delivered for filing becomes effective on the date and time of filing by the filing office. Since under 210(b) the date and time of filing is the recorded date and time of delivery of the record to the filing office (which under

Section 210(b) is the date and time of actual receipt), together these provisions eliminate any doubt about situations involving same-day transactions in which a record, for example, a statement of merger, is delivered for filing on the morning of the day the merger is to become effective.

Paragraph (3)—This paragraph does not authorize or contemplate the retroactive establishment of an effective date before the date of filing.

Paragraphs (3) and (4)—A record that states an effective date beyond the 90-day limit is not a record that "satisfies this [act]," Section 210(a), and will properly be rejected by the filing office.

§ 208.   WITHDRAWAL OF FILED RECORD BEFORE EFFECTIVENESS.

(a) Except as otherwise provided in Sections 1024, 1034, 1044, and 1054, a record delivered to the [Secretary of State] for filing may be withdrawn before it takes effect by delivering to the [Secretary of State] for filing a statement of withdrawal.

(b) A statement of withdrawal must:

(1) be signed by each person that signed the record being withdrawn, except as otherwise agreed by those persons;

(2) identify the record to be withdrawn; and

(3) if signed by fewer than all the persons that signed the record being withdrawn, state that the record is withdrawn in accordance with the agreement of all the persons that signed the record.

(c) On filing by the [Secretary of State] of a statement of withdrawal, the action or transaction evidenced by the original record does not take effect.

Comment

Only records that have not yet taken effect may be withdrawn under this section. If a record has taken effect, it may be corrected under Section 209 if the requirements of that section are satisfied. Otherwise, the record must be amended in accordance with this act or, if the record is a certificate of organization, the resulting limited liability company may be dissolved and terminated in accordance with Article 7.

Subsection (b)(1)—This provision is subject to Section 203(b) ("Whenever this [act] requires a particular individual to sign a record and the individual is deceased or incompetent, the record may be signed by a legal representative of the individual.").

§ 209.   CORRECTING FILED RECORD.

(a) A person on whose behalf a filed record was delivered to the [Secretary of State] for filing may correct the record if:

(1) the record at the time of filing was inaccurate;

(2) the record was defectively signed; or

(3) the electronic transmission of the record to the [Secretary of State] was defective.

(b) To correct a filed record, a person on whose behalf the record was delivered to the [Secretary of State] must deliver to the [Secretary of State] for filing a statement of correction.

(c) A statement of correction:

(1) may not state a delayed effective date;

(2) must be signed by the person correcting the filed record;

(3) must identify the filed record to be corrected;

(4) must specify the inaccuracy or defect to be corrected; and

(5) must correct the inaccuracy or defect.

(d) A statement of correction is effective as of the effective date of the filed record that it corrects except for purposes of Section 103(d) and as to persons relying on the uncorrected filed record and adversely affected by the correction. For those purposes and as to those persons, the statement of correction is effective when filed.

Comment

This section permits making corrections in filed records without re-submitting the entire record.

Subsection (a)(1) and (2)—A filed record may be corrected because it contains an inaccuracy or because it was defectively signed (including defects in optional forms of execution that do not affect the eligibility of the original record for filing).

Subsection (a)(3)—In addition, a filed record may be corrected if its electronic transmission was defective—*i.e.*, where an electronic delivery is made but, due to a defect in transmission, the filed record is later discovered to be inconsistent with the record intended to be filed. If no delivery is made because of a defect in transmission, a statement of correction may not be used to effect a retroactive filing. Therefore, a limited liability company making an electronic delivery should take steps to confirm that the transmission was received by the filing office.

Subsection (c)—A provision in a filed record setting an effective date may be corrected under this section, but the corrected effective date must comply with Section 207, which limits delayed effective dates to within ninety days after filing. A corrected effective date is thus measured from the date of the original filing of the record being corrected, *i.e.*, it cannot be before the date of filing of the record or more than ninety days thereafter.

Subsection (d)—The correction relates back to the original effective date of the record being corrected, except as to persons relying on the original entity filing and adversely affected by the correction. As to these persons, the effective date of the statement of correction is the date the statement is filed.

§ 210. DUTY OF [SECRETARY OF STATE] TO FILE; REVIEW OF REFUSAL TO FILE; DELIVERY OF RECORD BY [SECRETARY OF STATE].

(a) The [Secretary of State] shall file a record delivered to the [Secretary of State] for filing which satisfies this [act]. The duty of the [Secretary of State] under this section is ministerial.

(b) When the [Secretary of State] files a record, the [Secretary of State] shall record it as filed on the date and at the time of its delivery. After filing a record, the [Secretary of State] shall deliver to the person that submitted the record a copy of the record with an acknowledgment of the date and time of filing and, in the case of a statement of denial, also to the limited liability company to which the statement pertains.

(c) If the [Secretary of State] refuses to file a record, the [Secretary of State] shall, not later than [15] business days after the record is delivered:

(1) return the record or notify the person that submitted the record of the refusal; and

(2) provide a brief explanation in a record of the reason for the refusal.

(d) If the [Secretary of State] refuses to file a record, the person that submitted the record may petition [the appropriate court] to compel filing of the record. The record and the explanation of the [Secretary of State] of the refusal to file must be attached to the petition. The court may decide the matter in a summary proceeding.

(e) The filing of or refusal to file a record does not:

(1) affect the validity or invalidity of the record in whole or in part; or

(2) create a presumption that the information contained in the record is correct or incorrect.

(f) Except as otherwise provided by Section 119 or by law other than this [act], the [Secretary of State] may deliver any record to a person by delivering it:

(1) in person to the person that submitted it;

327

(2) to the address of the person's registered agent;

(3) to the principal office of the person; or

(4) to another address the person provides to the [Secretary of State] for delivery.

Comment

Subsection (a)—Under this subsection the filing office is required to file a record if it "satisfies this [act]." The purpose of this language is to limit the discretion of the filing office to a ministerial role in reviewing the contents of records. If the record submitted is in the form prescribed, contains the information required by this act, and the appropriate filing fee is tendered, the filing office must file the record. Consistent with this approach, this subsection states explicitly that the filing duty of the filing office is ministerial. *See also* Subsection (e) (pertaining to presumptions not created).

Subsection (b)—This subsection provides that when the filing office files a record, the filing office records it as filed on the date and time of delivery to the filing office, retains the original record for the office's records, and delivers a copy of the record to the person who delivered the record for filing with an acknowledgement of the date and time of filing. In the case of a statement of denial, Section 303, the filing office will also send a copy of the record and acknowledgment to the limited liability company.

In the case of a record transmitted electronically to the filing office, that office may make delivery by electronic transmission. The copy returned will be the exact or conformed copy if one has been required by the filing office, or will be a copy made by the filing office if an exact or conformed copy was not required.

Under this subsection the acceptance of a filing is evidenced merely by the filing office's delivery of a copy of the record with an acknowledgment of the date and time of filing. The act does not provide for the filing office to issue a formal certificate of filing. A copy of the filed record together with an acknowledgment of the date and time of filing should sufficiently indicate that the filing has been accepted for filing and been filed.

Subsection (c)—Because of the simplification of formal filing requirements and the limited discretion granted to the filing office by this act, it is probable that rejection of records delivered to the filing office for filing will occur only rarely. This subsection provides that if the filing office does reject a record delivered for filing, the filing office must return the record to the person that submitted the filing within fifteen days together with a brief written explanation of the reason for rejection. In the case of a record delivered by electronic transmission, rejection of the record may be made electronically by the filing office or by a mailing to the person that submitted the record.

Subsection (e)—This subsection provides that the filing of a record by the filing office does not affect the validity or invalidity of any provision contained in the record and does not create any presumption with respect to any information in the record. Likewise, the refusal of the filing office to file a record creates no presumption that any of the information in the record is incorrect. Persons adversely affected by a statement in a filed record may contest the statement in a proceeding appropriate for that purpose, including a damage action under Section 205.

§ 211.　CERTIFICATE OF GOOD STANDING OR REGISTRATION.

(a) On request of any person, the [Secretary of State] shall issue a certificate of good standing for a limited liability company or a certificate of registration for a registered foreign limited liability company.

(b) A certificate under subsection (a) must state:

(1) the limited liability company's name or the registered foreign limited liability company's name used in this state;

(2) in the case of a limited liability company:

(A) that a certificate of organization has been filed and has taken effect;

(B) the date the certificate became effective;

(C) the period of the company's duration if the records of the [Secretary of State] reflect that its period of duration is less than perpetual; and

(D) that:

(i) no statement of dissolution, statement of administrative dissolution, or statement of termination has been filed;

(ii) the records of the [Secretary to State] do not otherwise reflect that the company has been dissolved or terminated; and

(iii) a proceeding is not pending under Section 708;

(3) in the case of a registered foreign limited liability company, that it is registered to do business in this state;

(4) that all fees, taxes, interest, and penalties owed to this state by the limited liability company or foreign limited liability company and collected through the [Secretary of State] have been paid, if:

(A) payment is reflected in the records of the [Secretary of State]; and

(B) nonpayment affects the good standing or registration of the company or foreign company;

(5) that the most recent [annual] [biennial] report required by Section 212 has been delivered to the [Secretary of State] for filing; and

(6) other facts reflected in the records of the [Secretary of State] pertaining to the limited liability company or foreign limited liability company which the person requesting the certificate reasonably requests.

(c) Subject to any qualification stated in the certificate, a certificate issued by the [Secretary of State] under subsection (a) may be relied on as conclusive evidence of the facts stated in the certificate.

Comment

This section establishes a procedure by which anyone may obtain a conclusive certificate from the filing office that, among other things, the records of the filing office either (i) do not indicate that a particular domestic limited liability company has ceased to exist; or (ii) indicate that a particular foreign limited liability company is registered to do business in the state. The certificate will probably be a standardized form. The filing office is to make those determinations from public records only and is neither expected nor permitted to make a more extensive investigation.

Thus, the certificate of good standing will state whether a certificate has been filed and become effective but not that the limited liability company has been formed. For two reasons, a certificate concerning a domestic limited liability company can never conclusively indicate whether the LLC has actually been formed and, if formed, whether the LLC has been dissolved. Formation depends in part on the occurrence of an act "not of record." *See* Section 201(d) ("A limited liability company is formed when the company's certificate of organization becomes effective and at least one person becomes a member."). Similarly, causes of dissolution are typically "not of record." *See* Section 701. A dissolved limited liability company may deliver for filing a statement of dissolution, Section 702(b)(2)(A), and the filing of such a statement would preclude the issuance of a certificate of good standing, Subsection (b)(2)(D)(i). However a statement of dissolution is permissive; so too is a statement of termination. *See* Section 702(b)(2)(F).

Subsection (b)(4)(B)—This provision refers only to fees, taxes, interest, and penalties collected by the filing office. In some states other agencies may report to the filing office that franchise or other taxes have been paid; in those states, this information may be included in the certificate. In states where this procedure does not unduly delay the issuance of certificates, this section may be revised appropriately. Subsection (b)(4)(B) limits the scope of the statement in the certificate that all fees, taxes, interest, and penalties have been paid to those where nonpayment affects the existence or authorization to do business of the entity.

§ 212.   [ANNUAL] [BIENNIAL] REPORT FOR [SECRETARY OF STATE].

(a) A limited liability company or registered foreign limited liability company shall deliver to the [Secretary of State] for filing [an annual] [a biennial] report that states:

(1) the name of the company or foreign company;

(2) the name and street and mailing addresses of its registered agent in this state;

(3) the street and mailing addresses of its principal office;

(4) if the company is member managed, the name of at least one member;

(5) if the company is manager managed, the name of at least one manager; and

(6) in the case of a foreign company, its jurisdiction of formation and any alternate name adopted under Section 906(a).

(b) Information in the [annual] [biennial] report must be current as of the date the report is signed by the limited liability company or registered foreign limited liability company.

(c) The first [annual] [biennial] report must be delivered to the [Secretary of State] for filing after [January 1] and before [April 1] of the year following the calendar year in which the limited liability company's certificate of organization became effective or the registered foreign limited liability company registered to do business in this state. Subsequent [annual] [biennial] reports must be delivered to the [Secretary of State] for filing after [January 1] and before [April 1] of each [second] calendar year thereafter.

(d) If [an annual] [a biennial] report does not contain the information required by this section, the [Secretary of State] promptly shall notify the reporting limited liability company or registered foreign limited liability company in a record and return the report for correction.

(e) If [an annual] [a biennial] report contains the name or address of a registered agent which differs from the information shown in the records of the [Secretary of State] immediately before the report becomes effective, the differing information in the report is considered a statement of change under Section 116.

Comment

In some states, an annual or biennial report by a limited liability company or registered foreign limited liability company will be a new requirement.

Subsection (a)(4) and (5)—The requirement that the report include the name of at least one member of a member-managed LLC and one manager of a manager-managed LLC will be a new requirement in some states. There has been increasing pressure from law enforcement agencies for access to more information about the ownership and control of legal entities. This requirement will enable law enforcement to contact a person with some knowledge about the affairs of the limited liability company. Members of the public will also have that ability.

[ARTICLE] 3

RELATIONS OF MEMBERS AND MANAGERS TO PERSONS DEALING WITH LIMITED LIABILITY COMPANY

§ 301.   NO AGENCY POWER OF MEMBER AS MEMBER.

(a) A member is not an agent of a limited liability company solely by reason of being a member.

(b) A person's status as a member does not prevent or restrict law other than this [act] from imposing liability on a limited liability company because of the person's conduct.

Comment

Subsection (a)—Most LLC statutes, including the original ULLCA (1996), provide for what might be termed "statutory apparent authority" for members in a member-managed limited liability company and managers in a manager-managed limited liability company. This approach codifies the common law notion of apparent authority by position and dates back at least to the original Uniform

Partnership Act. UPA (1914) § 9 provided that "the act of every partner . . . for apparently carrying on in the usual way the business of the partnership . . . binds the partnership," and that formulation has been essentially followed by UPA (1997) § 301, ULLCA (1996) § 301, ULPA (2001) § 402, and myriad state LLC statutes.

This act rejects the statutory apparent authority approach, for reasons summarized in a "Progress Report on the Revised Uniform Limited Liability Company Act," published in the March 2006 issue of the newsletter of the ABA Committee on Partnerships and Unincorporated Business Organizations:

> The concept [of statutory apparent authority] still makes sense both for general and limited partnerships. A third party dealing with either type of partnership can know by the formal name of the entity and by a person's status as general or limited partner whether the person has the power to bind the entity.
>
> Most LLC statutes have attempted to use the same approach but with a fundamentally important (and problematic) distinction. An LLC's status as member-managed or manager-managed determines whether members or managers have the statutory power to bind. But an LLC's status as member- or manager-managed is not apparent from the LLC's name. A third party must check the public record, which may reveal that the LLC is manager-managed, which in turn means a member as member has no power to bind the LLC. As a result, a provision that originated in 1914 as a protection for third parties can, in the LLC context, easily function as a trap for the unwary. The problem is exacerbated by the almost infinite variety of management structures permissible in and used by LLCs.
>
> The new Act cuts through this problem by simply eliminating statutory apparent authority.

PUBOGRAM, Vol. XXIII, no. 2 at 9–10.

Codifying power to bind according to position makes sense only for organizations that have well-defined, well-known, and almost paradigmatic management structures. Because:

- flexibility of management structure is a hallmark of the limited liability company; and
- an LLC's name gives no signal as to the organization's structure,

it makes no sense to:

- require each LLC to publicly select between two statutorily preordained structures (*i.e.*, manager-managed/member-managed); and then
- link a "statutory power to bind" to each of those two structures.

Under this act, other law—most especially the law of agency—will handle power-to-bind questions. Thus, LLCs formed under this act and corporations are subject to the same principles for attributing to the entity the conduct of those who act or purport to act on the entity's behalf. *See* RESTATEMENT (THIRD) AGENCY §§ 1.03, cmt. c (manifestations of authority by organizations); 2.01, cmt. e (actual authority); 2.03, cmts. (c)—(e) (apparent authority) (2006). Section 407 provides the default rules on the actual authority of those who manage an LLC.

This subsection does not address the power to bind of a manager in a manager-managed LLC, although this act does consider a manager's management responsibilities. *See* Section 407(c) (allocating management authority, subject to the operating agreement). For a discussion of how agency law will approach the actual and apparent authority of managers, see Section 407(c), comment.

Subsection (b)—As the "flip side" to Subsection (a), this subsection expressly preserves the power of other law to hold an LLC directly or vicariously liable on account of conduct by a person who happens to be a member. For example, given the proper set of circumstances: (i) a member might have actual or apparent authority to bind an LLC to a contract; (ii) the doctrine of *respondeat superior* might make an LLC liable for the tortious conduct of a member (*i.e.*, in some circumstances a member acts analogously to a "servant" or "employee" of the LLC); and (iii) an LLC might be liable for negligently supervising a member who is acting on behalf of the LLC. A person's status as a member does not weigh against these or any other relevant theories of law.

Moreover, subsection (a) does not prevent member status from being relevant to one or more elements of an "other law" theory. *See* Section 111. The most likely "other law" theory is the agency doctrine of apparent authority. Of course, if a member lacking actual authority binds an LLC through conduct within the member's apparent authority, the LLC has a claim against the member. RESTATEMENT (THIRD) OF AGENCY § 8.09 (2006) (Duty to Act Only Within Scope of Actual Authority and to Comply with Principal's Lawful Instructions). In contrast, if the member lacked even the power to bind the LLC, the member him, her, or itself will be liable to the vendor as a matter of agency law. RESTATEMENT (THIRD) OF AGENCY § 6.10 (2006) (Agent's Implied Warranty of Authority).

For example, the common law of agency will determine the apparent authority of a member to bind a member-managed LLC. In that analysis what the particular third party knows or has reason to know about the management structure and business practices of the particular LLC will always be relevant. RESTATEMENT (THIRD) OF AGENCY § 3.03, cmt. b (2006) ("A principal may also make a manifestation by placing an agent in a defined position in an organization. . . . Third parties who interact with the principal through the agent will naturally and reasonably assume that the agent has authority to do acts consistent with the agent's position . . . unless they have notice of facts suggesting that this may not be so.")

Under Section 301(a), however, the mere fact that a person is a member of a member-managed limited liability company cannot *by itself* establish apparent authority by position. A course of dealing, however, may easily change the analysis:

Example: David is a one of two members of DS, LLC, a member-managed LLC. David orders paper clips on behalf of the LLC, signing the purchase agreement, "David, as a member of DS, LLC." Absent further facts, David has no apparent authority to bind the LLC.

However, the vendor accepts the order, sends an invoice to the LLC's address, and in due course receives a check drawn on the LLC's bank account. When David next places an order with the vendor, the LLC's payment of the first order is a manifestation that the vendor may use in asserting that David had apparent authority to place the second order. A successful apparent authority claim also presupposes that: (i) the vendor believed that David was authorized; and (ii) the belief was reasonable. RESTATEMENT (THIRD) OF AGENCY § 3.03 (2006) (Creation of Apparent Authority).

In general, a member's actual authority to act for an LLC will depend fundamentally on the operating agreement. *See* the comment to Section 407(b).

§ 302.   STATEMENT OF LIMITED LIABILITY COMPANY AUTHORITY.

(a) A limited liability company may deliver to the [Secretary of State] for filing a statement of authority. The statement:

(1) must include the name of the company and the name and street and mailing addresses of its registered agent;

(2) with respect to any position that exists in or with respect to the company, may state the authority, or limitations on the authority, of all persons holding the position to:

(A) sign an instrument transferring real property held in the name of the company; or

(B) enter into other transactions on behalf of, or otherwise act for or bind, the company; and

(3) may state the authority, or limitations on the authority, of a specific person to:

(A) sign an instrument transferring real property held in the name of the company; or

(B) enter into other transactions on behalf of, or otherwise act for or bind, the company.

(b) To amend or cancel a statement of authority filed by the [Secretary of State], a limited liability company must deliver to the [Secretary of State] for filing an amendment or cancellation stating:

(1) the name of the company;

(2) the name and street and mailing addresses of the company's registered agent;

(3) the date the statement being affected became effective; and

(4) the contents of the amendment or a declaration that the statement is canceled.

(c) A statement of authority affects only the power of a person to bind a limited liability company to persons that are not members.

(d) Subject to subsection (c) and Section 103(d), and except as otherwise provided in subsections (f), (g), and (h), a limitation on the authority of a person or a position contained in an effective statement of authority is not by itself evidence of any person's knowledge or notice of the limitation.

(e) Subject to subsection (c), a grant of authority not pertaining to transfers of real property and contained in an effective statement of authority is conclusive in favor of a person that gives value in reliance on the grant, except to the extent that when the person gives value:

(1) the person has knowledge to the contrary;

(2) the statement has been canceled or restrictively amended under subsection (b); or

(3) a limitation on the grant is contained in another statement of authority that became effective after the statement containing the grant became effective.

(f) Subject to subsection (c), an effective statement of authority that grants authority to transfer real property held in the name of the limited liability company, a certified copy of which statement is recorded in the office for recording transfers of the real property, is conclusive in favor of a person that gives value in reliance on the grant without knowledge to the contrary, except to the extent that when the person gives value:

(1) the statement has been canceled or restrictively amended under subsection (b), and a certified copy of the cancellation or restrictive amendment has been recorded in the office for recording transfers of the real property; or

(2) a limitation on the grant is contained in another statement of authority that became effective after the statement containing the grant became effective, and a certified copy of the later-effective statement is recorded in the office for recording transfers of the real property.

(g) Subject to subsection (c), if a certified copy of an effective statement containing a limitation on the authority to transfer real property held in the name of a limited liability company is recorded in the office for recording transfers of that real property, all persons are deemed to know of the limitation.

(h) Subject to subsection (i), an effective statement of dissolution or termination is a cancellation of any filed statement of authority for the purposes of subsection (f) and is a limitation on authority for the purposes of subsection (g).

(i) After a statement of dissolution becomes effective, a limited liability company may deliver to the [Secretary of State] for filing and, if appropriate, may record a statement of authority that is designated as a post-dissolution statement of authority. The statement operates as provided in subsections (f) and (g).

(j) Unless earlier canceled, an effective statement of authority is canceled by operation of law five years after the date on which the statement, or its most recent amendment, becomes effective. This cancellation operates without need for any recording under subsection (f) or (g).

(k) An effective statement of denial operates as a restrictive amendment under this section and may be recorded by certified copy for purposes of subsection (f)(1).

Comment

This section is derived from and builds on UPA (1997) § 303, which was refined in ULLCA (2006) and further refined in the Harmonization Project. This section is conceptually divided into two realms: statements pertaining to the power to transfer interests in the LLC's real property and statements pertaining to other matters. In the latter realm, statements are filed only in the records of the filing office and operate only to the extent the statements are actually known and relied on by a third party. Section 302(d) and (e).

As to interests in real property, in contrast, this section: (i) requires double-filing—with the filing office and in the appropriate land records; and (ii) provides for constructive knowledge of statements limiting authority. Thus, a properly filed and recorded statement can protect the limited liability company, Section 302(g), and, in order for a statement pertaining to real property to be a sword in the hands of a third party, the statement must have been both filed and properly recorded. Section 302(f). Experience suggests that statements of authority will most often be used in connection with transactions in real estate.

By its terms, this section applies only to domestic limited liability companies. A foreign LLC cannot make use of this section even as to real property located in this state. The section refers throughout to "limited liability company," which this act defines as a domestic limited liability company. *See* Section 102(8) (" 'Limited liability company'. . . means an entity formed under this [act] or which becomes subject to this [act]"). *Cf. Fannie Mae v. Heather Apartments Ltd. P'ship*, A13-0562, 2013 WL 6223564 at *6 (Minn. Ct. App. Dec. 2, 2013) (considering the remedies available to a judgment creditor with respect to the judgment debtor's interest in a Cook Islands LLC; rejecting the debtor's argument that the creditor's "only remedy is to obtain a charging order under" [the Minnesota LLC statute]; explaining that "this argument fails because that statute only applies to Minnesota limited liability companies" which the Minnesota LLC statute "defines . . . as 'a limited liability company, other than a foreign limited liability company, *organized or governed by this chapter*' ") (emphasis added; statutory citations omitted).

Subsection (a)(2)—This paragraph permits a statement to designate authority by position (or office) rather than by specific person, thus avoiding the need to file anew whenever a new person assumes the position or the office. This type of a statement will enable LLCs to provide evidence of ongoing power to enter into transactions without having to disclose to third parties the entirety of the operating agreement.

Subsection (a)(2)(A) and (a)(3)(A)—The authority to "sign" an instrument includes the authority to commit the partnership to the transfer reflected in the agreement. *See* Subsection (f) (referring not merely to signing but also to "an effective statement of authority that grants authority to transfer real property").

Here and elsewhere in the section, the phrase "real property" includes all interests in real property, such as mortgages, easements, etc.

Subsection (c)—This subsection expresses a very important limitation—*i.e.*, that this section's rules do not operate viz-a-viz members. For members, the operating agreement is controlling. Section 107(d). However, like any other record delivered for filing on behalf of an LLC, a statement of authority might be some evidence of the contents of the operating agreement. *See* the comment to Section 107(d).

Another important limitation exists. The filing office is not affected by a statement of authority that purports to delineate the authority of persons to sign documents to be delivered for filing of behalf of a limited liability company. The act does define "[p]erson" to include a "government or governmental subdivision, agency, or instrumentality," Section 102(15), but "a limitation on the authority of a person or a position contained in an effective statement of authority is not by itself evidence of knowledge or notice of the limitation by any person." Subsection (d).

Moreover, even if an employee of the filing office happened to see that a statement of authority purported to delineate the authority of persons to sign records to be delivered on behalf of an LLC, that information would not pertain to a "fact [that] is material to the agent's duties to the principal" and therefore would not be attributed to the filing office. RESTATEMENT (THIRD) OF AGENCY § 5.03 (2006).

Subsection (d)—The phrase "by itself" is important, because the existence of a limitation of authority could be evidence if, for example, the person in question reviewed the public record at a time when the limitation was of record.

Subsection (e)(1)—What happens if a statement of authority conflicts with the contents of an LLC's certificate of organization? The contents of the certificate are not statements of authority, Section 201(c), so the information in the certificate does not directly figure into the operation of this section. However, if the person claiming to rely on a statement of authority had read the certificate's conflicting information before giving value, that fact might be evidence that person gave value with "knowledge to the contrary" of the statement.

Subsection (e)(2)—This paragraph by its terms does not affect a claim of lingering apparent authority. A person could: (i) assert knowledge of a statement of authority as the statement existed before a cancellation or restrictive amendment; and (ii) characterize the original statement as a manifestation of authority traceable to the limited liability company. RESTATEMENT (THIRD) OF AGENCY § 3.03, cmt. b (2006) ("Apparent authority is present only when a third party's belief is traceable to manifestations of the principal.").

However, for apparent authority to exist, the purported agent must *reasonably* appear to be authorized. RESTATEMENT (THIRD) OF AGENCY § 2.03 (2006) (stating that apparent authority can only exist when "a third party reasonably believes the actor has authority to act on behalf of the principal"). Given the possibility of cancellation or restrictive amendment, it might not be reasonable for a person to know of a statement of authority, let time pass, and then rely on the statement without re-checking the public record.

Subsections (f) through (h)—These subsections: (i) pertain to transactions in real property; (ii) provide a mechanism by which authority to transfer an LLC's real property can be made to appear in the real estate records; and (iii) thus address the principal concerns (raised by real estate lawyers) that led the drafters of UPA (1997) to provide for statements of authority.

Subsection (f)—This subsection provides a sword for a vendee of real property. If the vendee has "give[n] value in reliance on the grant without knowledge to the contrary," the statement of authority protects the vendee against claims that contradict the grant.

Subsection (f)(1) and (2)—As a claim of lingering apparent authority, see the comment to Section (e)(2). The analysis stated there applies even more strongly in the context of customary practices involving land transfers.

Subsection (g)—This subsection provides a shield for the limited liability company as alleged vendor. If a vendee's claim contradicts the stated limitation, constructive knowledge ("deemed to know") defeats the claim even if the vendee gave value and lacked actual knowledge.

Subsection (h)—This subsection integrates statements of dissolution and termination, Section 702, into the operation of this section.

The effect of a statement of dissolution depends on the circumstances.

Example: ABC, LLC has in effect a properly filed and recorded statement of authority authorizing ABC's CEO to transfer real estate owned by the LLC. The proper filing and recording by ABC of a statement of dissolution cancels the statement of authority. Subsequently, Buyer gives value in return for a deed signed by the CEO on behalf of ABC. Due to Subsections (h) and (f)(1), Subsection (f) does not protect Buyer. Moreover, under Subsections (g) and (h), Buyer is "deemed to know" of the dissolution. Whether that deemed knowledge functions to deprive the CEO of authority to bind ABC depends on agency law and additional facts. For example, the CEO might have had actual or apparent authority to transfer the real estate despite the dissolution of the LLC.

If properly filed with the filing office and properly recorded in the office for land records, a statement of termination eliminates the power of any person to transfer real property owned in the name of the LLC. No one can have the authority to act for a non-existent entity. *Cf.* RESTATEMENT (THIRD) OF AGENCY § 4.04(1)(a) (2006) (precluding ratification by a principal that did not exist at the time of the unauthorized act).

Subsection (i)—This provision permits an LLC to use statements of authority during winding up. As an additional protection for third parties, a statement must be "designated as a post-dissolution statement of authority" to be effective under this provision.

Subsection (k)—Presumably, when real property is involved, a person who obtains the filing of a statement of denial under Section 303 will cause a certified copy of the statement to be "recorded by certified copy for purposes of subsection (f)(1)" [undercutting constructive notice as to authority to transfer real property]. However, nothing in this subsection prevents the limited liability company from causing a certified copy to appear in the land records; due the section's use of the passive voice ("may be recorded"), the act does not delimit who has the authority to act under this subsection.

§ 303.　STATEMENT OF DENIAL.

A person named in a filed statement of authority granting that person authority may deliver to the [Secretary of State] for filing a statement of denial that:

(1) provides the name of the limited liability company and the caption of the statement of authority to which the statement of denial pertains; and

(2) denies the grant of authority.

Comment

A person whose powers are delineated in the public record by another person should have the right to dissent from that delineation. This section takes an "all or nothing" approach; a person may not deny in part and confirm in part. For the effect of a statement of denial, see Section 302(k).

§ 304.　LIABILITY OF MEMBERS AND MANAGERS.

(a) A debt, obligation, or other liability of a limited liability company is solely the debt, obligation, or other liability of the company. A member or manager is not personally liable, directly or indirectly, by way of contribution or otherwise, for a debt, obligation, or other liability of the company solely by reason of being or acting as a member or manager. This subsection applies regardless of the dissolution of the company.

(b) The failure of a limited liability company to observe formalities relating to the exercise of its powers or management of its activities and affairs is not a ground for imposing liability on a member or manager for a debt, obligation, or other liability of the company.

Comment

Derivation—ULLCA (2006) derived this section from UPA (1997) § 306, which was also the source for ULPA (2001) § 404. The Harmonization Project brought the two partnership acts and the limited liability company act into accord to the extent the three acts overlap.

Subsection (a)—This subsection provides a corporate-like liability shield to members and managers, protecting them against (and only against) the debts, obligations and liabilities of the limited liability company—*i.e.*, against a member's or manager's alleged vicarious liability for the obligations of the entity. The shield "applies regardless of the dissolution of the company" and thus continues in effect through the completion of winding up (*i.e.*, termination). The shield applies regardless of the law giving rise to a claim against a limited liability company.

Shield Applicable Regardless of the Identity of the Plaintiff

What makes the shield relevant is the nature of the claim. If the complaint seeks to hold a member vicariously liability for the LLC's obligations, the shield applies. If not, not. Thus, there is no distinction between a claim arising from an LLC's debt to a commercial creditor, a member's claim that the LLC has failed to return a contribution as required by the operating agreement, and a claim by a former member that the LLC has failed to follow through on a buy-out agreement. *See Rappaport v. Gelfand*, 197 Cal. App.4th 1213, 1230–1232, 129 Cal. Rptr. 3d 670, 682–84 (Cal. App. 2 Dist. 2011) (involving a claim by a former partner). *Accord Ederer v. Gursky*, 9 N.Y.3d 514, 526, 881 N.E.2d 204, 212–213 (N.Y. 2007) (Smith, J., dissenting).

Shield Inapposite for Claims Arising from a Member's or Manager's Own Conduct

Because the member or manager liability at issue is solely vicarious, the shield is irrelevant to claims seeking to hold a member or manager directly liable on account of the member's or manager's own conduct. Put another way, "[t]here is no question" that "the member-manager of a limited liability company who causes his business to breach common law and statutory duties may be held independently liable for his personal torts." *Dep't of Agric. v. Appletree Mktg., L.L.C.*, 485 Mich. 1, 4, 18, 779 N.W.2d 237, 239, 247 (2010).

A few judges have failed to understand this point. *See Puleo v. Topel*, 368 Ill. App. 3d 63, 68–69, 856 N.E.2d 1152, 1157 (Ill. App. Ct. 2006) (basing its holding on a legislative amendment that "removed . . . language which explicitly provided that a member or manager of an LLC could be held personally liable for his or her own actions or for the actions of the LLC to the same extent as a shareholder or director of a corporation could be held personally liable").

This mistaken view: (i) ignores the actual words of LLC shield provisions (which protect members and managers only against liability for obligations *of* an LLC and make no reference to direct obligations of a member or manager); and (ii) flouts public policy (which recoils from the idea of immunizing a person's misconduct solely because the person acts on behalf of an organization). Moreover, the mistaken view is contrary to the overwhelming weight of the case law. *See, e.g., Mbahaba v. Morgan*, 163 N.H. 561, 565, 44 A.3d 472, 476 (2012) ("When ... a member or manager commits or participates in the commission of a tort, whether or not he acts on behalf of his LLC, he is liable to third persons injured thereby."); *Sturm v. Harb Dev., LLC*, 298 Conn. 124, 138, 2 A.3d 859, 870 (2010) (holding that the liability shield of an LLC is subject to "the common-law tort exception ... [for] individual claims against LLC members); *Allen v. Dackman*, 413 Md. 132, 154, 991 A.2d 1216, 1229 (2010) ("An LLC member is liable for torts he or she personally commits, inspires, or participates in because he or she personally committed a wrong, not 'solely' because he or she is a member of the LLC."); *Weber v. U.S. Sterling Sec., Inc.*, 282 Conn. 722, 732–34, 924 A2d 816, 824–25 (2007) (stating that the Delaware LLC Act "does not preclude individual liability for members of a limited liability company if that liability is not based simply on the member's affiliation with the company" and holding, in particular, that the Act "does not bar the defendants' liability for tortious conduct").

Example: A manager personally guarantees a debt of a limited liability company. Subsection (a) is irrelevant to the manager's liability as guarantor.

Example: A member purports to bind a limited liability company while lacking any agency law power to do so. The limited liability company is not bound, but the member is liable for having breached the "warranty of authority" (an agency law doctrine). Subsection (a) does not apply. The liability is not *for* a debt, obligation, or other liability of the [limited liability] company, but rather is the member's own, direct liability. Indeed, the liability exists because the limited liability company is *not* indebted, obligated or liable. RESTATEMENT (THIRD) OF AGENCY § 6.10 (2006).

Example: A manager of a limited liability company defames a third party in circumstances that render the limited liability company vicariously liable under agency law. Under Subsection (a), the third party cannot hold the manager accountable for the *company's* liability, but that protection is immaterial. The manager is the tortfeasor and in that role is directly liable to the third party.

Example: A limited liability company provides professional services, and one of its members commits malpractice. The liability shield is irrelevant to the member's direct liability in tort. However, if the member's malpractice liability is attributed to the LLC under agency law principles, the liability shield will protect the other members of the LLC against a claim that they must make good on the LLC's liability.

Example: A single member limited liability company enters into a contract to build a home, and the member performs substantial amounts of the work. The homeowner sues both the LLC and the member for allegedly defective work, but the complaint sounds in contract rather than in tort. The LLC may be liable, but the member is not. *See Ogea v. Merritt* ___ So.3d ___, 2013 WL 6439355 at *24–25 (La. 2013).

Subsection (a) pertains only to claims based on the LLC's liability and is irrelevant to claims by a limited liability company against a member or manager and *vice versa. E.g.*, Sections 408 (pertaining to a limited liability company's obligation to indemnify a member or manager), 409 (pertaining to management duties) and 801 (pertaining to a member's rights to bring a direct claim against a limited liability company).

Shield Inapposite to Role Liability Claims

Provisions of regulatory law may impose liability on a member or manager due to a role the person plays in the LLC. *See, e.g., Food Team Intern., Ltd. v. Unilink, LLC*, 872 F. Supp. 2d 405, 424 (E.D Pa. 2012) (holding several individuals "subject to secondary individual liability under PACA [Perishable Agricultural Commodities Act]" because their roles within the LLC enabled them to control the relevant assets) (citing *Bear Mountain Orchards, Inc. v. Mich-Kim, Inc.*, 623 F.3d 163, 172 (3d Cir. 2010)).

The Shield and Dissolution.

The rule stated here is inherent in the nature of LLC dissolution. "[D]issolution does not end a limited liability company's existence but rather changes the purpose of that existence." Section 701, cmt. "A dissolved limited liability company shall wind up its activities and affairs and . . . continues after dissolution . . . for the purpose of winding up." Section 702(a). Put another way: dissolution and winding up are part of the life cycle of a limited liability company—sometimes the most complicated part. There is no logical reason to remove the shield during the last part of an LLC's life cycle.

This subsection makes this point expressly, because it is possible to misinterpret some outlying LLP cases as holding to the contrary. *See, e.g., Carolina Cas. Ins. Co. v. L.M. Ross Law Grp., LLP*, 151 Cal. Rptr. 3d 628, 635 (2012) (affirming the trial court's decision to hold an LLP's named partner liable for a judgment against his limited ability partnership; noting that "[c]entral to the decision to amend the judgment to add Ross [the named partner] as a judgment debtor . . . is the trial court's finding that Ross Law Group dissolved"; recognizing, however, that, before the partnership incurred the liability, Ross had signed and filed with the California Secretary of State a form stating that the law firm had "cease[d] to be a registered limited liability partnership and is hereby filing this notice with the California Secretary of State that [it] is no longer a registered limited partnership") (quotation marks omitted).

The Shield and Termination

This subsection does not expressly provide that, when a limited liability company's existence terminates, the liability shield remains in place as to any debt, obligation, or other liability of the LLC incurred before the termination. However, the point follows ineluctably from Subsection 304(a), which provides that the shield applies to any "debt, obligation, or other liability of a limited liability company." A debt, obligation or other liability of an LLC does not disappear merely because the LLC has terminated.

Moreover, any other result would: (i) create huge holes in the shield; (ii) put the law of unincorporated businesses at odds with the law of corporations; (iii) render surplus this act's distribution recapture provision, Section 406; and (iv) render nonsensical the otherwise logical extension of the equitable trust fund theory to limited liability companies. *Cf. Velasquez v. Franz*, 589 A.2d 143, 146 (N.J. 1991) (explaining that "the trust-fund doctrine. . . renders shareholders who receive distributed assets of the corporation liable as 'trustees' for claims of the corporation's creditors").

Dangers of Indemnification Provisions Inter Se the Members

Despite the phrase "by way of contribution or otherwise," the LLC shield has no effect on contribution or indemnification requirements running directly from member to member or from members to a manager. These obligations are not obligations of the LLC but rather personal to each member. Indirectly they pose a risk to the shield as to liability arising from the misconduct of a member or manager.

Example: A law firm operates as a professional limited liability company. One practice area (the "Practice Area") brings in large fees but also exposes its practitioners (the "Practitioners") to liability risks substantially higher than the risks faced by other lawyers in the firm. Fees in the Practice Area are episodic, so it makes sense for the Practitioners to share profits with the rest of the firm, where returns are lower but more regular.

The firm carries liability insurance, and the operating agreement provides broad indemnification rights to all the firm's lawyers. However, the Practitioners are mindful that the LLC liability shield sets a practical limit to the firm's indemnification obligations and that policies of insurance have limits. The Practitioners obtain a provision in the operating agreement by which each member of the LLC makes a personal promise of indemnification (subject to a cap).

The tortious conduct of one of the Practitioners (the "Tortfeasor") results in a substantial judgment against the Tortfeasor and, per Section 305(a), against the LLC. For unrelated reasons, the LLC has become insolvent and its liability coverage is "maxed out." The Tortfeasor's right to indemnification from fellow members is an asset of the Tortfeasor. The judgment creditor can levy on that asset, thereby defeating the liability shield in effect if not in form.

Subsection (b)—This subsection pertains to the equitable doctrine of "piercing the veil"—*i.e.*, conflating an entity and its owners to hold one liable for the obligations of the other. The doctrine of "piercing the corporate veil" is well-established, and courts regularly (and sometimes almost reflexively) apply that doctrine to limited liability companies. In the corporate realm, "disregard of corporate formalities" is a key factor in the piercing analysis. In the realm of LLCs, that factor is inappropriate, because informality of organization and operation is both common and desired. *See, e.g., In re Packer*, Bankruptcy No. 13–41304, 2014 WL 5100095 (Bankr. E.D. Tex. Oct. 10, 2014) (noting the informality of LLC governance, recognizing that "the disregard of corporate formalities . . . [is] one of the key factors in [corporate] veil-piercing determinations"; but holding that " 'it makes no sense to imperil the shield simply because the members do not undergo meaningless formalities such as formal meetings' ") (citing Carter G. Bishop & Daniel S. Kleinberger, LIMITED LIABILITY COMPANIES: TAX AND BUSINESS LAW ¶ 6.03 at *3 (Thomson Reuters Tax and Accounting 2014)).

The formalities at issue are the process formalities of governance—both those few created by this act and however few or many might be created by the operating agreement.

Example: The operating agreement of a three-member, member-managed limited liability company requires formal monthly meetings of the members. Each of the members works in the LLC's business, and they consult each other regularly. They have forgotten or ignore the requirement of monthly meetings. Under Subsection (b), that fact is irrelevant to a piercing claim.

In contrast, this subsection is inapposite to another key piercing factor—disregard of the separateness between entity and owner. *E.g., Vanderford Co. v. Knudson*, 165 P.3d 261, 271 (Idaho 2007) (noting that managing member and "his accountant testified that the LLC's checking account was so confusing that the accountant could not be sure whose money was in the account at what times"); *Utzler v. Braca*, 972 A.2d 743 (Conn. App. 2009) (holding that veil piercing was appropriate under alter-ego theory when owner deposited LLC funds into a commingled bank account from which he made withdrawals for personal needs and unrelated projects).

Example: The sole owner of a limited liability company uses a car titled in the company's name for personal purposes and writes checks on the company's account to pay for personal expenses. These facts are relevant to a piercing claim; they pertain to economic separateness, not Subsection (b) formalities.

This subsection also is inapposite to a member's claim of oppression under Section 701(a)(4)(C)(ii). In some circumstances, disregard of agreed-upon formalities can be a "freeze out" mechanism. Likewise, this subsection has no relevance to a member's claim that the disregard of agreed-upon formalities is a breach of the operating agreement.

This subsection addresses claims to "impos[e] liability on a member or manager for a debt, obligation, or other liability of the company"—*i.e.*, for what is sometimes termed a "direct pierce." Whether the same approach should apply to claims for a "reverse pierce" is a question for the courts. *See Comm'r of Envtl. Prot. v. State Five Indus. Park, Inc.*, 304 Conn. 128, 140, 37 A.3d 724, 732–33 (2012) (stating that "[a]lthough some courts have adopted reverse veil piercing with little distinction as a logical corollary of traditional veil piercing, because the two share the same equitable goals, others wisely have recognized important differences between them").

[ARTICLE] 4

RELATIONS OF MEMBERS TO EACH OTHER AND TO LIMITED LIABILITY COMPANY

§ 401. BECOMING MEMBER.

(a) If a limited liability company is to have only one member upon formation, the person becomes a member as agreed by that person and the organizer of the company. That person and the organizer may be, but need not be, different persons. If different, the organizer acts on behalf of the initial member.

(b) If a limited liability company is to have more than one member upon formation, those persons become members as agreed by the persons before the formation of the company. The organizer acts on behalf of the persons in forming the company and may be, but need not be, one of the persons.

(c) After formation of a limited liability company, a person becomes a member:

(1) as provided in the operating agreement;

(2) as the result of a transaction effective under [Article] 10;

(3) with the affirmative vote or consent of all the members; or

(4) as provided in Section 701(a)(3).

(d) A person may become a member without:

(1) acquiring a transferable interest; or

(2) making or being obligated to make a contribution to the limited liability company.

Comment

Most LLC statutes address in separate provisions: (i) how an LLC obtains its initial member or members; and (ii) how additional persons might later become members. This act follows that approach.

Subsections (a) and (b)—These subsections make explicit the agency relationship between the person acting as organizer and the initial member or members.

Subsection (c)(3)—A limited liability company being in part a creature of contract, consent is determined on an objective basis (*i.e.,* contract law's "reasonable person" standard). Depending on the terms of an LLC's operating agreement, the members' manifestation of consent might involve detailed formalities, entirely informal activities, or anything in between. Moreover, the operating agreement might reduce the quantum of consent necessary or shift the consent right to a manager.

A limited liability company being a voluntary association, a person cannot become a member without manifesting consent to do so. That consent also is judged objectively.

Under Section 106(b), "[a] person that becomes a member of a limited liability company is deemed to assent to the operating agreement," and the agreement binds the member regardless of whether the member has actually indicated assent in any way.

Subsection (d)(1)—To accommodate business practices and also because a limited liability company need not have a business purpose, this provision permits so-called "non-economic members."

§ 402.   FORM OF CONTRIBUTION.

A contribution may consist of property transferred to, services performed for, or another benefit provided to the limited liability company or an agreement to transfer property to, perform services for, or provide another benefit to the company.

Comment

This section is intentionally quite broad, encompassing past, present, and promised benefits. Comparable language exists in most, if not all, LLC statutes, and case law recognizes the intended broadness of this approach. *See, e.g., Belgard v. Manchac Technologies, LLC*, 92 So.3d 660, 664 (La.App. 3 Cir. 2012) (stating that "the creation of an obligation to establish a $1.8 million line of credit was valid consideration for the transfer of 24% of the membership interest in Manchac"); *In re Eight of Swords, LLC*, 96 A.D.3d 839, 840, 946 N.Y.S.2d 248, 249 (N.Y.A.D. 2 Dept. 2012) (referring to "the petitioner's contributions to the LLC, which overwhelmingly consisted of services rendered to the LLC in the form of preparing and filing start-up documentation and performing activities associated with the renovation of the business's premises").

This act does not contain a statute of frauds specifically applicable to promised contributions. Generally applicable statutes of fraud might apply, however. For example, a promise to contribute land to the LLC would be subject to the statute of frauds pertaining to land transfers. Likewise, a promise that by its terms requires performance that extends beyond one year from the making of the contract would be subject to the one-year provision of the statute of frauds. *See* the comment to Section 102(13).

§ 403. LIABILITY FOR CONTRIBUTIONS.

(a) A person's obligation to make a contribution to a limited liability company is not excused by the person's death, disability, termination, or other inability to perform personally.

(b) If a person does not fulfill an obligation to make a contribution other than money, the person is obligated at the option of the limited liability company to contribute money equal to the value of the part of the contribution which has not been made.

(c) The obligation of a person to make a contribution may be compromised only by the affirmative vote or consent of all the members. If a creditor of a limited liability company extends credit or otherwise acts in reliance on an obligation described in subsection (a) without knowledge or notice of a compromise under this subsection, the creditor may enforce the obligation.

Comment

Subsection (a)—Under common law principles of impracticability, an individual's death or incapacity will sometimes discharge a duty to render performance. RESTATEMENT (SECOND) OF CONTRACTS §§ 261 (Discharge by Supervening Impracticability), 262 (Death or Incapacity of Person Necessary For Performance). This subsection overrides those principles. Moreover, the reference to "perform personally" is not limited to individuals but rather may refer to any legal person (including an entity) that has a non-delegable duty.

Subsection (b)—This subsection is a statutory liquidated damage provision, exercisable at the option of the limited liability company, with the damage amount set according to the value of the promised, non-monetary contribution.

Example: In order to become a member, a person promises to contribute to the limited liability company various assets "free and clear," which the operating agreement values at $150,000. In return for the person's promise, and in light of the agreed value, the limited liability company admits the person as a member with a right to receive 25% of the LLC's distributions.

However, the promised assets are subject to a security agreement, and, before the member can contribute the assets, the secured party forecloses on the security interest and sells the assets at a public sale for $75,000. Even if the $75,000 reflects the actual fair market value of the assets, under this subsection the limited liability company has a claim against the member for "money equal to the value of the part of the contribution which has not been made"—*i.e.*, $150,000.

Example: Same facts as the previous example, except that the public sale brings $225,000. The limited liability company is neither obliged to invoke this subsection nor limited to the $150,000. The LLC may instead sue for breach of the promise to make the contribution, asserting the $225,000 figure as evidence of the actual loss suffered as a result of the breach.

Subsection (c)—The unanimity requirement expressed in the first sentence might indirectly benefit creditors, but the requirement is nonetheless a default rule and therefore may be varied by operating agreement. The right of each member to consent is not a "right[ ] under this [act] of a person other than a member or manager." *See* Section 105(c)(15) (preventing the operating agreement from affecting such rights). In contrast, the creditor right stated in the second sentence fits squarely within Section 105(c)(15) and therefore may not be varied by the operating agreement.

§ 404. SHARING OF AND RIGHT TO DISTRIBUTIONS BEFORE DISSOLUTION.

(a) Any distribution made by a limited liability company before its dissolution and winding up must be in equal shares among members and persons dissociated as members, except to the extent necessary to comply with a transfer effective under Section 502 or charging order in effect under Section 503.

(b) A person has a right to a distribution before the dissolution and winding up of a limited liability company only if the company decides to make an interim distribution. A person's dissociation does not entitle the person to a distribution.

(c) A person does not have a right to demand or receive a distribution from a limited liability company in any form other than money. Except as otherwise provided in Section 707(d), a company may distribute an asset in kind only if each part of the asset is fungible with each other part and each person receives a percentage of the asset equal in value to the person's share of distributions.

(d) If a member or transferee becomes entitled to receive a distribution, the member or transferee has the status of, and is entitled to all remedies available to, a creditor of the limited liability company with respect to the distribution. However, the company's obligation to make a distribution is subject to offset for any amount owed to the company by the member or a person dissociated as a member on whose account the distribution is made.

Comment

Past uniform unincorporated entity acts and many current LLC acts provide default rules for allocation of profits, and UPA (1997) even provided a default structure for maintaining capital accounts. For the following reasons, this act, incorporating changes made by the Harmonization Project, provides a default rule only for rights to share in distributions:

- Capital accounts are maintained for one purpose, to determine how distributions will be made to members. The rules for maintenance of capital accounts can be very complex. Generally, however, profits increase capital account balances (and increase the amounts that will be distributed to the members) and losses reduce capital account balances (and reduce the amounts that will be distributed to the members). If the statute has a simple default rule for how distributions are to be made to the members, providing an additional set of default profit and loss allocation provisions and capital account rules will be, at best, duplicative and, at worse, inconsistent with the distribution rules.

- Some argue that capital account rules and profit and loss allocation provisions are necessary to comply with tax requirements. Tax income or loss is allocated to "partners" (including members of an LLC taxed as a partnership) according to the partners' economic interests in the LLC, and these interests are based on distributions that would be made to partners on liquidation of the LLC. By including default distribution provisions, the act includes the information necessary to make these tax determinations. To the extent the tax law allows partners to make further tax elections or satisfy alternative safe harbors, the partners may look to the tax law for guidance and include necessary provisions in their agreements.

Subsection (a)—The rule stated applies to redemptions as well as operating distributions but is a default rule in both contexts. *See* the comment to Section 102(4)(A).

Subsection (b)—The second sentence of this subsection accords with Section 603(a)(3)—upon dissociation a person is treated as a mere transferee of its own transferable interest. Like most *inter se* rules in this act, this one is subject change by the operating agreement. *See* the comment to Section 603(a)(3).

Subsection (d)—*See also* Section 405(d) (pertaining to the rights of members and transferees that receive a distribution in the form of indebtedness) and 405(e) (pertaining to solvency testing for payments on indebtedness issued to redeem an interest).

§ 405. LIMITATIONS ON DISTRIBUTIONS.

(a) A limited liability company may not make a distribution, including a distribution under Section 707, if after the distribution:

(1) the company would not be able to pay its debts as they become due in the ordinary course of the company's activities and affairs; or

(2) the company's total assets would be less than the sum of its total liabilities plus the amount that would be needed, if the company were to be dissolved and wound up at the time of the distribution, to satisfy the preferential rights upon dissolution and winding up of members and transferees whose preferential rights are superior to the rights of persons receiving the distribution.

(b) A limited liability company may base a determination that a distribution is not prohibited under subsection (a) on:

(1) financial statements prepared on the basis of accounting practices and principles that are reasonable in the circumstances; or

(2) a fair valuation or other method that is reasonable under the circumstances.

(c) Except as otherwise provided in subsection (e), the effect of a distribution under subsection (a) is measured:

(1) in the case of a distribution as defined in Section 102(4)(A), as of the earlier of:

(A) the date money or other property is transferred or debt is incurred by the limited liability company; or

(B) the date the person entitled to the distribution ceases to own the interest or right being acquired by the company in return for the distribution;

(2) in the case of any other distribution of indebtedness, as of the date the indebtedness is distributed; and

(3) in all other cases, as of the date:

(A) the distribution is authorized, if the payment occurs not later than 120 days after that date; or

(B) the payment is made, if the payment occurs more than 120 days after the distribution is authorized.

(d) A limited liability company's indebtedness to a member or transferee incurred by reason of a distribution made in accordance with this section is at parity with the company's indebtedness to its general, unsecured creditors, except to the extent subordinated by agreement.

(e) A limited liability company's indebtedness, including indebtedness issued as a distribution, is not a liability for purposes of subsection (a) if the terms of the indebtedness provide that payment of principal and interest is made only if and to the extent that payment of a distribution could then be made under this section. If the indebtedness is issued as a distribution, each payment of principal or interest is treated as a distribution, the effect of which is measured on the date the payment is made.

(f) In measuring the effect of a distribution under Section 707, the liabilities of a dissolved limited liability company do not include any claim that has been disposed of under Section 704, 705, or 706.

Comment

Both this section and Section 406 were derived essentially from the Model Business Corporation. Act section 6.40. Both sections are necessary and appropriate because a limited liability company provides its members and managers a corporate-like liability shield. With the exception noted in the comment to Subsection (a)(2), the provisions of this section are non-waivable. Section 105(c)(15).

"Distribution" does not include "amounts constituting reasonable compensation for present or past service or payments made in the ordinary course of business under a bona fide retirement plan or other bona fide benefits program." Section 102(4)(B).

Subsection (a)—Insolvency is a fundamental issue under this section, and this subsection provides two tests of insolvency. The tests are disjunctive; a distribution violates this section if after the distribution the LLC fails either of the tests. The subsection applies both to interim and liquidating distributions.

Solvency is also a fundamental issue under bankruptcy and fraudulent transfer law, which provide their own respective definitions of the concept.

Subsection (a)(2)—The reference to "preferential rights upon dissolution and winding up" is a default rule, because removing this protection for preferred members or transferees is an *inter se* matter. *See* Section 105(d)(1)(B). The rest of the section is not subject to change in the operating agreement. Section 105(c)(15).

Subsection (b)—This subsection states a standard of ordinary care, in contrast with the generally-applicable standard stated in Section 409(c) (gross negligence).

Subsection (b)(2)—This alternative valuation provision is likely to be both useful and fair when the limited liability company has appreciated assets but for accounting purposes these assets are valued at book value less depreciation.

Subsection (c)—This subsection provides three alternative rules for determining the point(s) in time of as which to apply the Subsection (a) solvency tests. The timing depends on which of three categories encompasses a distribution: (i) a distribution in the nature of a redemption (regardless of whether the distribution includes a distribution of indebtedness); (ii) any distribution of indebtedness other than a distribution in the nature of a redemption; and (iii) any distribution that involves neither a redemption nor a distribution of indebtedness. A requirement for additional solvency testing pertaining to distributions of indebtedness appears in Subsection (e).

Subsection (c)(1)—Section 102(4)(A) encompasses distributions in the nature of a redemption.

Subsection (c)(1)(A) and (B)—Under Subparagraph (A), any beginning of payment activity triggers the rule and sets the date as of when to apply the solvency tests. Under Subparagraph (B), the LLC's complete acquisition of the rights is necessary to trigger the rule.

Subsection (c)(2)—This provision states the general rule for distributions in the form of debt which are not connected with a redemption.

Subsection (c)(3)—This provision states alternative rules for all distributions of money or property (*i.e.*, not debt). The measuring date depends on the length of time between the authorization and payment of the distribution.

Subsection (d)—*Compare* Subsection (d), *with* Section 404(d) (characterizing as a creditor a person who has become entitled to receive a distribution).

Subsection (e)—This subsection contains two rules pertaining to indebtedness issued as part of a distribution and the solvency tests of Subsection (a). The first sentence states the sensible rule that indebtedness that is essentially subordinated to the solvency requirement—*i.e.*, not payable if making payment would transgress that requirement—is not counted in determining liabilities for purposes of the solvency tests. The second sentence applies the solvency tests to each payment of principal and interest on any indebtedness issued as a distribution, in addition to any previous testing required by Subsection (c)(1)(A) or (c)(2).

Example: An LLC and one of its members agree that the LLC will buy out the member's entire ownership interest in the LLC in return for a promissory note from the LLC, payable in installments. Under the redemption agreement, the member surrenders all its interests and rights on January 15 and the LLC signs and delivers the note to the person dissociated as a member on February 15. Under the note, payment of interest is due monthly beginning March 15, with a balloon payment of the principal due December 30.

Under Subsection (c)(1)(B), the solvency tests are applied as of January 15. Under Subsection (e), the solvency tests are again applied on the March 15, April 15, etc., and again on December 30.

Subsection (f)—The cited sections provide methods for extinguishing or limiting the debts of an LLC that is winding up its affairs and activities and thus any debt affected by any of the cited sections is irrelevant for purposes of solvency testing.

§ 406.   LIABILITY FOR IMPROPER DISTRIBUTIONS.

(a) Except as otherwise provided in subsection (b), if a member of a member-managed limited liability company or manager of a manager-managed limited liability company consents to a distribution made in violation of Section 405 and in consenting to the distribution fails to comply with Section 409, the member or manager is personally liable to the company for the amount of the distribution which exceeds the amount that could have been distributed without the violation of Section 405.

(b) To the extent the operating agreement of a member-managed limited liability company expressly relieves a member of the authority and responsibility to consent to distributions and imposes that authority and responsibility on one or more other members, the liability stated in subsection (a) applies to the other members and not the member that the operating agreement relieves of the authority and responsibility.

(c) A person that receives a distribution knowing that the distribution violated Section 405 is personally liable to the limited liability company but only to the extent that the distribution received by the person exceeded the amount that could have been properly paid under Section 405.

(d) A person against which an action is commenced because the person is liable under subsection (a) may:

(1) implead any other person that is liable under subsection (a) and seek to enforce a right of contribution from the person; and

(2) implead any person that received a distribution in violation of subsection (c) and seek to enforce a right of contribution from the person in the amount the person received in violation of subsection (c).

(e) An action under this section is barred unless commenced not later than two years after the distribution.

Comment

This section and Section 405 were derived essentially from Model Business Corporation Act section 6.40. As with Section 405, this section is appropriate and necessary due to the liability shield of a limited liability company. The provisions of this section are non-waivable. Section 105(c)(15).

This section contemplates two categories of liability: liability of those who have authorized improper distributions, Subsection (a), and the liability of those who have received improper distributions, Subsection (c). Liability that has accrued under this section is not affected by a person subsequently ceasing to be a member, manager or transferee.

The liability is to the LLC, not to the creditors of an insolvent LLC. *Weinstein v. Colborne Foodbotics, LLC*, 302 P.3d 263, 268 (2013); *Rev O, Inc. v. Woo*, 725 S.E.2d 45, 52 (N.C. Ct. App. 2012).

This section does not preclude or interfere with claims for fraudulent transfer. *See* the comment to Subsection (e).

Subsection (a)—The liability is not strict liability but rather attaches only to the extent a decision maker has failed to comply with the duties stated in Section 409. To the extent those duties have been permissibly revised by the operating agreement, the revised standards apply to this subsection. *See also* Section 405(b)(1) (permitting reasonable reliance on specified financial information).

Subsection (b)—*Compare* Subsection (b), *with* Section 105(d)(2) (generally permitting provisions of this type).

Subsection (c)—Actual knowledge is necessary to impose liability. Reason to know does not suffice. *Compare* Subsection (c), *with* Section 103(a)–(b).

Subsections (c) and (d)(2)—Liability could apply to a person who receives a distribution under a charging order, but only if the person meets the knowledge requirement. That situation is very unlikely unless the person with the charging order is also a member or manager.

Subsection (e)—When the distribution is in the form of indebtedness, the distribution may occur on several different dates. *See* the comment to Section 405(e).

This statute of limitations applies only to actions "under this section" and does not affect claims under other applicable law, which most often is fraudulent transfer law. For a different approach, see DEL. CODE ANN. tit. 6, § 17–607(c) (West 2013) (applying a 3-year statute of limitations to claims "under this chapter or other applicable law"); NY LTD. LIAB. CO. § 508(c) (McKinney 2013) (same). *But see, e.g.*, *In re The Heritage Org., LLC*, 413 BR 438, 461 (Bankr. ND Tex. 2009) (invoking the Texas Uniform Fraudulent Act [TUFTA] to recover distributions made by a Delaware LLC headquartered in Texas;

rejecting DEL. CODE ANN. tit. 6, § 18–607(c) on choice of law grounds; stating that "the Delaware legislature cannot limit the reach of TUFTA").

§ 407.   MANAGEMENT OF LIMITED LIABILITY COMPANY.

(a) A limited liability company is a member-managed limited liability company unless the operating agreement:

    (1) expressly provides that:

        (A) the company is or will be "manager-managed";

        (B) the company is or will be "managed by managers"; or

        (C) management of the company is or will be "vested in managers"; or

    (2) includes words of similar import.

(b) In a member-managed limited liability company, the following rules apply:

    (1) Except as expressly provided in this [act], the management and conduct of the company are vested in the members.

    (2) Each member has equal rights in the management and conduct of the company's activities and affairs.

    (3) A difference arising among members as to a matter in the ordinary course of the activities and affairs of the company may be decided by a majority of the members.

    (4) The affirmative vote or consent of all the members is required to:

        (A) undertake an act outside the ordinary course of the activities and affairs of the company; or

        (B) amend the operating agreement.

(c) In a manager-managed limited liability company, the following rules apply:

    (1) Except as expressly provided in this [act], any matter relating to the activities and affairs of the company is decided exclusively by the manager, or, if there is more than one manager, by a majority of the managers.

    (2) Each manager has equal rights in the management and conduct of the company's activities and affairs.

    (3) The affirmative vote or consent of all members is required to:

        (A) undertake an act outside the ordinary course of the company's activities and affairs; or

        (B) amend the operating agreement.

    (4) A manager may be chosen at any time by the affirmative vote or consent of a majority of the members and remains a manager until a successor has been chosen, unless the manager at an earlier time resigns, is removed, or dies, or, in the case of a manager that is not an individual, terminates. A manager may be removed at any time by the affirmative vote or consent of a majority of the members without notice or cause.

    (5) A person need not be a member to be a manager, but the dissociation of a member that is also a manager removes the person as a manager. If a person that is both a manager and a member ceases to be a manager, that cessation does not by itself dissociate the person as a member.

    (6) A person's ceasing to be a manager does not discharge any debt, obligation, or other liability to the limited liability company or members which the person incurred while a manager.

(d) An action requiring the vote or consent of members under this [act] may be taken without a meeting, and a member may appoint a proxy or other agent to vote, consent, or otherwise act for the member by signing an appointing record, personally or by the member's agent.

(e) The dissolution of a limited liability company does not affect the applicability of this section. However, a person that wrongfully causes dissolution of the company loses the right to participate in management as a member and a manager.

(f) A limited liability company shall reimburse a member for an advance to the company beyond the amount of capital the member agreed to contribute.

(g) A payment or advance made by a member which gives rise to a limited liability company obligation under subsection (f) or Section 408(a) constitutes a loan to the company which accrues interest from the date of the payment or advance.

(h) A member is not entitled to remuneration for services performed for a member-managed limited liability company, except for reasonable compensation for services rendered in winding up the activities of the company.

Comment

Subsection (a)—This subsection follows implicitly from the definitions of "manager-managed" and "member-managed" limited liability companies, Section 102(10) and (12), but is included here for the sake of clarity. Although this act has eliminated the link between management structure and statutory apparent authority, the act retains the manager-managed and member-managed constructs as options for members to use to structure their *inter se* relationship. *See also* the comments to Sections 301 (No Agency Power of Member as Member), and 409 (Standards of Conduct).

Subsection (b)—The subsection follows essentially the long-standing default paradigm for management rights of general partners. *See* UPA (1914) § 18; UPA (1997) (Last Amended 2013) § 401. The stated rules are subject to change by the operating agreement. Section 105.

In general, a member's actual authority to act for an LLC will depend fundamentally on the operating agreement.

Example: Rachael and Sam, who have known each other for years, decide to go into business arranging musical tours. They fill out and electronically sign a one page form available on the website of the filing office and become the organizers of MMT, LLC. They are the only members of the LLC, and their understanding of who will do what in managing the enterprise is based on several lengthy, late-night conversations that preceded the LLC's formation. Sam is to "get the acts," and Rachael is to manage the tour logistics. There is no written operating agreement.

In the terminology of this act, MMT, LLC is member-managed, Section 407(a), and the understanding reached in the late night conversations has become part of the LLC's operating agreement, Section 102(13). In the terminology of agency law, the operating agreement constitutes a manifestation by the LLC to Rachael and Sam concerning the scope of their respective authority to act on behalf of the LLC. RESTATEMENT (THIRD) OF AGENCY § 2.01, cmt. c (2006) (explaining that a person's actual authority depends first on some manifestation attributable to the principal and stating: "[a]ctual authority is a consequence of a principal's expressive conduct toward an agent, through which the principal manifests assent to be affected by the agent's action, and the agent's reasonable understanding of the principal's manifestation").

Circumstances outside the operating agreement can also be relevant to determining the scope of a member's actual authority.

Example: Homeworks, LLC is a manager-managed LLC with three members. The LLC's written operating agreement:

- specifies in considerable detail the management responsibilities of Margaret, the LLC's manager-member, and also states that Margaret is responsible for "the day-to-day operations" of the company;

- puts Garrett, a non-manager member, in charge of the LLC's transportation department; and

- specifies no management role for Brooksley, the third member.

When the LLC's chief financial officer quits suddenly, Margaret asks Brooksley, a CPA, to "step in until we can hire a replacement."

Under the operating agreement, Margaret's request to Brooksley is within Margaret's actual authority and is a manifestation attributable to the LLC. If Brooksley manifests assent to Margaret's request, Brooksley will have the actual authority to act as the LLC's chief financial officer.

In the unlikely event that two or more people form a member-managed LLC without any understanding of how to allocate management responsibility, agency law, operating in the context the act's "gap fillers" on management responsibility, will produce the following result:

A single member of a multi-member, member-managed LLC:

- has no actual authority to bind the LLC to any matter "outside the ordinary course of the activities of the company," Section 407(b)(3); and

- has the actual authority to bind the LLC to any matter "in the management and conduct of the company's [ordinary course of] activities and affairs," Section 407(b)(2), unless the member has reason to know that other members might disagree or the member has some other reason to know that consultation with fellow members is appropriate.

For an explanation of this result, see Section 407(c), comment, which provides a detailed analysis in the context of a multi-manager LLC whose operating agreement is silent on the analogous question.

For a discussion of the apparent authority of a member to bind an LLC, see Section 301(b), comment.

Subsection (b)(4)—This list is not exhaustive. Other approval rights appear in the context of the provisions to which the rights apply. *E.g.*, Section 401(c)(3) (providing that "[a]fter formation of a limited liability company, a person becomes a member . . . with the affirmative vote or consent of all the members"); Section 703(b)(1) requiring "the affirmative vote or consent of each member" to rescind dissolution); Sections 1023, 1033, 1043, 1053 (same with regard to Article 10 transactions).

Subsection (c)—Like Subsection (b), this subsection states default rules that, under Section 105, are subject to the operating agreement. For example, a limited liability company's operating agreement might state "This company is manager-managed," Sections 102(10) and 407(a), while providing that managers must submit specified ordinary matters for review by the members.

The actual authority of an LLC's manager or managers is a question of agency law and depends fundamentally on the contents of the operating agreement and any separate management contract between the LLC and its manager or managers. These agreements are the primary source of the manifestations of the LLC (as principal) from which a manager (as agent) will form the reasonable beliefs that delimit the scope of the manager's actual authority. RESTATEMENT (THIRD) OF AGENCY § 3.01 (2006). *See also* RESTATEMENT (SECOND) OF AGENCY §§ 15, 26 (1958).

Other information may be relevant as well, such as the course of dealing within the LLC, unless the operating agreement effectively precludes consideration of that information. *See* the comment to Section 105(a)(4) (stating that the operating agreement governs "the means and conditions for amending the operating agreement").

If the operating agreement and a management contract conflict, the reasonable manager will know that the operating agreement controls the extent of the manager's rightful authority to act for the LLC—despite any contract claims the manager might have. *See* the comment to Section 105(a)(2) (stating that the operating agreement governs "the rights and duties under this [act] of a person in the capacity of manager"). *See also* RESTATEMENT (THIRD) OF AGENCY § 8.13, cmt. b (2006) and RESTATEMENT (SECOND) OF AGENCY § 432, cmt. b (1958) (stating that, when a principal's instructions to an agent contravene a contract between the principal and agent, the agent may have a breach of contract claim but has no right to act contrary to the principal's instructions).

If: (i) an LLC's operating agreement merely states that the LLC is manager-managed and does not further specify the managerial responsibilities; and (ii) the LLC has only one manager, the actual authority analysis is simple. In that situation, this subsection:

- serves as "gap filler" to the operating agreement; and thereby

- constitutes the LLC's manifestation to the manager as to the scope of the manager's authority; and thereby

- delimits the manager's actual authority, subject to whatever subsequent manifestations the LLC may make to the manager (*e.g.,* by a vote of the members, or an amendment of the operating agreement).

If the operating agreement states only that the LLC is manager-managed and the LLC has more than one manager, the question of actual authority has an additional aspect. It is necessary to determine what actual authority any one manager has to act alone.

Paragraphs (c)(1)–(3), combine to provide the answer. A single manager of a multi-manager LLC:

- has no actual authority to commit the LLC to any matter encompassed in Paragraph (c)(3) or for which this act elsewhere requires unanimity;

- has the actual authority to commit the LLC to usual and customary matters, unless the manager has reason to know that: (i) other managers might disagree; or (ii) for some other reason consultation with fellow managers is appropriate; and

- has no actual authority to take unusual or non-customary actions that will have a substantial effect on the LLC.

The first point follows self-evidently from the language of Paragraph (c)(3) and other provisions requiring the affirmative vote or consent of the members, which reserves specified matters to the members. Given that language, no manager could reasonably believe to the contrary (unless the operating agreement provided otherwise).

The second point follows because:

Subsection (c) serves as the gap-filler manifestation from the LLC to its managers and does *not* require managers of a multi-manager LLC to act *only* in concert or after consultation. To the contrary, subject to the operating agreement Subsection (c)(2) expressly provides that "each manager has equal rights in the management and conduct of the company's activities and affairs."

- It would be impractical to require collective action on even the smallest of decisions.

- However, to the extent a manager has reason to know of a possible difference of opinion among the managers, Paragraph (c)(1) requires decision by "a majority of the managers."

The third point is a matter of common sense. The more serious the matter, the less likely it is that a manager has actual authority to act unilaterally. *Cf.* RESTATEMENT (THIRD) OF AGENCY § 3.03, cmt. c (2006) (noting the unreasonableness of believing, without more facts, that an individual has "an unusual degree of unilateral authority over a matter fraught with enduring consequences for the institution" and stating that "[t]he gravity of the matter from the standpoint of the organization is relevant to whether a third party could reasonably believe that the manager has authority to proceed unilaterally").

The common law of agency will also determine the apparent authority of an LLC's manager or managers, and in that analysis what the particular third party knows or has reason to know about the management structure and business practices of the particular LLC will always be relevant. RESTATEMENT (THIRD) OF AGENCY § 3.03, cmt. d (2006) ("The nature of an organization's business or activity is relevant to whether a third party could reasonably believe that a [manager] is authorized to commit the organization to a particular transaction.").

As a general matter, absent countervailing facts, courts may see the position of manager as clothing its occupants with the apparent authority to take actions that reasonably appear within the ordinary course of the company's business. The actual authority analysis stated above supports that proposition; absent a reason to believe to the contrary, a third party could reasonably believe that a manager possesses the authority contemplated by the gap-fillers of this act. *But see* the comment to Section 102(9) (stating that "confusion around the term 'manager' is common to almost all LLC statutes").

Subsection (c)(1)—For limited liability companies that have more than one manager, this act provides that in most circumstances a "matter relating to the activities and affairs of the company is decided . . . by a majority of the managers." However, unlike corporate statutes, this act does not provide a rule for the quantum of participation necessary to constitute "a majority." *Cf., e.g.,* MINN. STAT. § 302A.237 (2014) (providing rules for determining the votes need to constitute "an act of the board"). If a manager-managed LLC has more than one manager, the operating agreement should consider what "a majority" means in the event a manager position is vacant.

Subsection (c)(3)—This list is not exhaustive. *See* the comment to Subsection (b)(4).

Subsection (c)(4)—Under the default rule stated in this paragraph, dissolution of an entity that is a manager of an LLC does not end the entity's status as manager. Likewise, dissolution of entity that is a member does not cause the entity to dissociate. *See* Section 602(11) (providing that termination of such an entity causes dissociation).

An LLC does not cease to be "manager-managed" simply because no managers are in place. In that situation, absent additional facts, the LLC is manager-managed and the manager position is vacant. Non-manager members who exercise managerial functions during the vacancy (or at any other time) will have duties as determined by other law, most particularly the law of agency.

Subsection (c)(6)—For example, the obligation to safeguard trade secrets and other confidential or propriety information learned when the person is a manager remains in force after the person ceases to be a manager.

Subsection (d)—In this context, the doctrine of *noscitur a sociis* limits the authorized extent of a proxy holder or other agent. (The doctrine of *noscitur a sociis* holds "that the meaning of an unclear word or phrase should be determined by the words immediately surrounding it." BLACK'S LAW DICTIONARY (9th ed. 2009).

In particular, unless the operating agreement so provides, neither a proxy nor other agent may be used to circumvent the transfer restrictions that are fundamental to the law of limited liability companies. *See* Article 5 and RESTATEMENT (SECOND) OF CONTRACTS § 318(2) (1981) (stating that "a promise requires performance by a particular person . . . to the extent that the obligee has a substantial interest in having that person perform or control the acts promised").

Subsection (e), second sentence—The default rules of this act do not contemplate a person wrongfully causing dissolution, as distinguished from wrongfully dissociating. *Compare* Section 701, *with* Section 601(b). However, the operating agreement might contemplate wrongful dissolution, and then the second sentence of this subsection would apply unless the operating agreement provided otherwise.

Subsection (h)—This provision traces back to the UPA (1914) § 18(f) and is included to avoid its absence being misinterpreted as implying a contrary rule.

This act does not provide for remuneration to a manager of a manager-managed LLC. That issue is for the operating agreement, or a separate agreement between the LLC and the manager. A manager may also have a common law right to compensation. RESTATEMENT (THIRD) AGENCY § 8.13, cmt. d (2006) ("Unless an agreement between a principal and an agent indicates otherwise, a principal has a duty to pay compensation to an agent for services that the agent provides.").

§ 408. REIMBURSEMENT; INDEMNIFICATION; ADVANCEMENT; AND INSURANCE.

(a) A limited liability company shall reimburse a member of a member-managed company or the manager of a manager-managed company for any payment made by the member or manager in the course of the member's or manager's activities on behalf of the company, if the member or manager complied with Sections 405, 407, and 409 in making the payment.

(b) A limited liability company shall indemnify and hold harmless a person with respect to any claim or demand against the person and any debt, obligation, or other liability incurred by the person by reason of the person's former or present capacity as a member or manager, if the claim, demand, debt, obligation, or other liability does not arise from the person's breach of Section 405, 407, or 409.

(c) In the ordinary course of its activities and affairs, a limited liability company may advance reasonable expenses, including attorney's fees and costs, incurred by a person in connection with a claim or demand against the person by reason of the person's former or present capacity as a member or manager, if the person promises to repay the company if the person ultimately is determined not to be entitled to be indemnified under subsection (b).

(d) A limited liability company may purchase and maintain insurance on behalf of a member or manager against liability asserted against or incurred by the member or manager in that capacity or arising from that status even if, under Section 105(c)(7), the operating agreement could not eliminate or limit the person's liability to the company for the conduct giving rise to the liability.

Comment

Subsections (a) and (b)—A limited liability company's obligation, if any, to reimburse or indemnify others (*e.g.*, employees, independent contractors, other agents) is a question for other law, including the law of agency, contract and restitution. The fact a person has dissociated as a member or ceased to be a manager does not affect any obligations incurred by the limited liability company under these subsections for conduct occurring before the dissociation or cessation.

Subsection (a)—The reimbursement obligation stated here is a default rule and roughly parallels a rule of agency law. RESTATEMENT (THIRD) OF AGENCY § 8.14(2)(a) (2006) (stating that "[a] principal has a duty to indemnify an agent . . . when the agent makes a payment (i) within the scope of the agent's actual authority, or (ii) that is beneficial to the principal, unless the agent acts officiously in making the payment").

This subsection applies only to managers of manager-managed limited liability companies and members of member-managed companies. The definite article in the phrase "the member or manager'" and "the member's" refers back to the original phrase: "A limited liability company shall reimburse a member of a member-managed company or the manager of a manger-managed company. . . .'"

A limited liability company's obligation, if any, to reimburse others (including LLC employees and non-managing members of a manager-managed LLC) is a question for other law, including the law of agency and restitution. The fact a person has ceased to be a member of a member-managed LLC or a manager of a manager-managed LLC does not affect any obligations incurred by the LLC under this subsection for payments made before the cessation.

To the extent an operating agreement modifies or displaces the default rules stated in Sections 407 and 409, the agreement should also address this section. For example, if the operating agreement establishes a duty of ordinary care (modifying Section 409(c)), the agreement should specify which level of care is necessary to satisfy this subsection. It is not necessary that the levels of care be the same, only that the operating agreement make the situation clear and thereby avoid difficult issues of interpretation.

Subsection (b)—This subsection provides for indemnification but only as a default rule. Subject only to Section 105(c)(7), the operating agreement can relax these preconditions substantially. The agreement can also impose stricter preconditions.

The rule's eligibility requirements correspond to the default rules on management duties, which is appropriate because otherwise the statutory default rule on indemnification could undercut or even vitiate the statutory default rules on duty. To the extent an operating agreement modifies or displaces the default rules stated in Sections 405, 407, or 409, the agreement should also address this section. *See* the comment to Subsection (a).

Although referring broadly to any "person," this subsection is actually limited to present and former members or managers. The indemnification obligation applies only to a "debt, obligation, or other liability incurred by the person by reason of the person's former or present capacity as a member or manager." Thus, by its terms this subsection does not apply to a person in the capacity of an "officer," unless being an officer constitutes being a manager. For a discussion of the vagaries of the term "manager," see Section 102(9), comment.

Of course, the operating agreement may mandate indemnification to officers, employees, and other persons providing services to or acting for the limited liability company. Within the limitations

351

stated in Section 105(c)(7), the operating agreement may obligate an LLC to indemnify a person even when the person has breached a managerial duty or the operating agreement itself.

Subsection (c)—This subsection authorizes but does not require a limited liability company to provide advances to cover expenses. *Cf. Majkowski v. American Imaging Mgmt. Servs., LLC*, 913 A.2d 572, 589 (Del. Ch. 2006) ("Because rights to indemnification and advancement differ in important ways, our courts have refused to recognize claims for advancement not granted in specific language clearly suggesting such rights."). The phrase "hold harmless" likewise does not encompass advances. *Id.* The authorization applies only to those persons eligible for indemnification under Subsection (b), but the operating agreement certainly can authorize a broader scope and also make advances obligatory.

The reference to "ordinary course" pertains to Section 407(b)(3) (stating that any "difference arising among members [in a member-managed LLC] as to a matter in the ordinary course of the activities of the company may be decided by a majority of the members"). As for a manager-managed LLC, see Section 407(c)(1) ("Except as expressly provided in this [act], *any* matter relating to the activities and affairs of the [manager-managed] company is decided exclusively by the manager, or, if there is more than one manager, by a majority of the managers.") (emphasis added).

Subsection (d)—This subsection's language is very broad and authorizes an LLC to purchase insurance to cover, *e.g.,* a manager's intentional misconduct. It is unlikely that such insurance would be available. In contrast to Subsection (a), this subsection encompasses all members, not just members in a member-managed LLC. This authorization comes from the act, not the operating agreement, and therefore is not subject to Section 105(c)(7).

§ 409.   STANDARDS OF CONDUCT FOR MEMBERS AND MANAGERS.

(a) A member of a member-managed limited liability company owes to the company and, subject to Section 801, the other members the duties of loyalty and care stated in subsections (b) and (c).

(b) The fiduciary duty of loyalty of a member in a member-managed limited liability company includes the duties:

(1) to account to the company and hold as trustee for it any property, profit, or benefit derived by the member:

(A) in the conduct or winding up of the company's activities and affairs;

(B) from a use by the member of the company's property; or

(C) from the appropriation of a company opportunity;

(2) to refrain from dealing with the company in the conduct or winding up of the company's activities and affairs as or on behalf of a person having an interest adverse to the company; and

(3) to refrain from competing with the company in the conduct of the company's activities and affairs before the dissolution of the company.

(c) The duty of care of a member of a member-managed limited liability company in the conduct or winding up of the company's activities and affairs is to refrain from engaging in grossly negligent or reckless conduct, willful or intentional misconduct, or knowing violation of law.

(d) A member shall discharge the duties and obligations under this [act] or under the operating agreement and exercise any rights consistently with the contractual obligation of good faith and fair dealing.

(e) A member does not violate a duty or obligation under this [act] or under the operating agreement solely because the member's conduct furthers the member's own interest.

(f) All the members of a member-managed limited liability company or a manager-managed limited liability company may authorize or ratify, after full disclosure of all material facts, a specific act or transaction that otherwise would violate the duty of loyalty.

(g) It is a defense to a claim under subsection (b)(2) and any comparable claim in equity or at common law that the transaction was fair to the limited liability company.

(h) If, as permitted by subsection (f) or (i)(6) or the operating agreement, a member enters into a transaction with the limited liability company which otherwise would be prohibited by subsection (b)(2), the member's rights and obligations arising from the transaction are the same as those of a person that is not a member.

(i) In a manager-managed limited liability company, the following rules apply:

(1) Subsections (a), (b), (c), and (g) apply to the manager or managers and not the members.

(2) The duty stated under subsection (b)(3) continues until winding up is completed.

(3) Subsection (d) applies to managers and members.

(4) Subsection (e) applies only to members.

(5) The power to ratify under subsection (f) applies only to the members.

(6) Subject to subsection (d), a member does not have any duty to the company or to any other member solely by reason of being a member.

Comment

This section states some of the core aspects of the fiduciary duty of loyalty, provides a duty of care, and incorporates the contractual obligation of good faith and fair dealing. The section follows the structure of many LLC acts, first stating the duties of members in a member-managed limited liability company and then using that statement and a "switching" mechanism, Subsection (i), to allocate duties in a manager-managed company. The duties stated in this section are subject to the operating agreement, but Section 105(c) and (d) contain important limitations on the power of the operating agreement to affect fiduciary and other duties and the obligation of good faith and fair dealing.

For the effect of dissociation on a person's duties under this section, see Section 603(a)(2).

Subsection (a)—This subsection recognizes two core managerial duties but, unlike some earlier uniform acts, does not purport to state all managerial duties. Indeed, many cases characterize a manager's duty to disclose as a fiduciary duty. *E.g., Salm v. Feldstein*, 20 A.D.3d 469, 470, 799 N.Y.S.2d 104, 105 (N.Y. App. Div. 2005) (stating that, "[a]s the managing member of the [limited liability] company and as a co-member with the plaintiff, the defendant owed the plaintiff a fiduciary duty to make full disclosure of all material facts"); *Metro Commc'n Corp. BVI v. Advanced Mobilecomm Technologies Inc.*, 854 A.2d 121, 156 n. 78 (Del. Ch. 2004) (referring to "certain standards governing the disclosure-related duties of the fiduciaries of Delaware business entities;" noting that "[t]hese standards have been mostly articulated in the corporate context but the corporate standards often serve as the default rule in the alternative entity context").

Subsection (b)—This subsection states three core aspects of the fiduciary duty of loyalty: (i) not "usurping" company opportunities or otherwise wrongly benefiting from the company's operations or property; (ii) avoiding conflict of interests in dealing with the company (whether directly or on behalf of another); and (iii) refraining from competing with the company. Essentially the same duties exist in agency law and under the law of all types of business organizations.

The subsection applies beginning with "the conduct of the company's activities and affairs," which by definition cannot exist before the company exists; thus the stated duties do not apply to pre-formation activities. In some circumstances, comparable duties might arise from other law, particular the law of agency. *See, e.g.,* Section 401(a) and (b) (stating that the organizer acts "on behalf of others").

The stated duties comprise a default rule. Under Section 105(d)(3)(A): "If not manifestly unreasonable, the operating agreement may . . . alter or eliminate the aspects of the duty of loyalty stated in Section 409(b)."

Subsection (b)(1)—The phrase "hold as trustee" dates back to UPA (1914) § 21 and reflects the availability of disgorgement remedies, such as a constructive trust. In contrast to an actual trustee, a person subject to this duty does not: (i) face the special obstacles to consent characteristic of trust law; or (ii) enjoy protection for decisions taken in reliance on the governing instrument and other sources of information. *Cf.* UNIFORM STATUTORY TRUST ENTITY ACT (2009) (Last Amended 2013) § 506 ("A trustee [of a statutory trust]. . . is not liable to the trust or to a beneficial owner for breach of any duty, *including a fiduciary duty*, to the extent the breach results from reasonable reliance on: (i) a term of the governing instrument; (ii) a record of the statutory trust; or (iii) an opinion, report, or statement of another person that the person to which the opinion, report, or statement is made or delivered reasonably believes is within the other person's professional or expert competence and is made or delivered to the trustee. . . .") (emphasis added).

Subsection (b)(1)(A)—This provision is consistent with a basic principle of agency law—namely, that an agent may not benefit at all from the performance of the agency unless the principal consents. RESTATEMENT (THIRD) OF AGENCY § 8.06, cmt. c (2006). Typically, however, the operating agreement will legitimize particular benefits—*e.g.*, a management fee paid to a managing member in addition to that member's share of distributions. Also, an agreed allocation of distributions takes those benefits outside the reach of this provision.

Subsection (b)(1)(B)—For the expansive meaning of "property," see Section 102(17). The term includes confidential information.

Subsection (b)(1)(C)—This act does not specify what constitutes "a company opportunity," but ample case law exists. *See, e.g.*, *Ebenezer United Methodist Church v. Riverwalk Development Phase, II, LLC*, 45 A.3d 883, 887 (Md. App. 2012) (discussing the "interest or reasonable expectancy test"); *In re McCook Metals, L.L.C.*, 319 B.R. 570, 596 (Bkrtcy. N.D.Ill. 2005) (discussing the "line of business test").

This duty continues through winding up, although in that context the scope of company opportunities inevitably narrows.

In most, if not all, situations, usurping a company opportunity also breaches the duty not to compete, Paragraph (b)(3), but not *vice versa*.

Subsection (b)(2)—In this context, the phrase "adverse interest" is a term of art, meaning "to be on the other side of the table" in some dealing with the limited liability company. Absent informed consent by the LLC, this duty is breached by the mere existence of the conflict of interest; the LLC need not prove that the outcome of the dealing was adverse to the LLC. *But see* Subsection (g) (permitting the defense of fairness). This duty continues through winding up.

Subsection (b)(3)—Although competition is often thought of in terms of potential customers, this duty applies equally to competition for resources, including employees. The duty not to compete continues longer in a manager-managed LLC. *See* Subsection (i)(2).

Subsection (c)—ULLCA (2006) § 409(c) stated a different rule: "Subject to the business judgment rule, the duty of care of a member of a member-managed limited liability company in the conduct and winding up of the company's activities is to act with the care that a person in a like position would reasonably exercise under similar circumstances and in a manner the member reasonably believes to be in the best interests of the company." As part of the Harmonization Project, the ULLCA duty of care was conformed to the duty of care stated in ULPA (2001) and UPA (1997).

Neither this act nor the two harmonized partnership acts refer to the duty of care as a fiduciary duty, because: (i) the duty of care applies in many non-fiduciary situations; and (ii) breach of the duty of care is remediable only in damages while breach of a fiduciary duty gives rise also to equitable remedies, including disgorgement, constructive trust, and rescission. *See* ULPA (2001) (Last Amended 2013) § 409(c) and UPA (1997) (Last Amended 2013) § 409(c).

The change in label is consistent with the RESTATEMENT (THIRD) OF AGENCY § 8.02 (2006), which refers to the agent's "fiduciary duty to act loyally, but eschews the word "fiduciary" when stating the agent's duties of "care, competence, and diligence." *Id.* § 8.08. However, the change in label is merely semantics; no change in the law is intended.

The operating agreement can raise the standard of care, or subject to Sections 105(c)(7) and (d)(3)(C), lower it. A person's practical exposure for breaching the duty of care involves not only the standard of care but also any operating agreement provision that: (i) exonerates the person from liability for breach of the duty of care, Section 105(c)(7); or (ii) entitles the person to indemnification despite such breach, Section 408(b), comment.

Subsection (d)—This subsection refers to the "*contractual* obligation of good faith and fair dealing" (emphasis added) and thereby invokes the implied obligation that exists in every contract. *See* RESTATEMENT (SECOND) CONTRACTS § 205 (1981) ("Every contract imposes upon each party a duty of good faith and fair dealing in its performance and its enforcement."). The adjective ("contractual") should help avoid decisions like *Phelps v. Frampton*, 2007 MT 263, 339 Mont. 330, 342–43, 170 P.3d 474, 483 (2007) (holding that Montana's version of UPA (1997) creates a statutory obligation of good faith and fair dealing separate from the implied contractual covenant).

At first glance, it may seem strange to apply a contractual obligation to statutory duties and rights—*i.e.*, duties and rights "under this [act]." However, for the most part those duties and rights apply to relationships *inter se* the members and the LLC and function only to the extent not displaced by the operating agreement. These statutory default rules are intended in essence to function like a contract; applying the contractual notion of good faith and fair dealing therefore makes sense.

The contractual obligation of "good faith" has nothing to do with the corporate concept of good faith that for years bedeviled courts and attorneys trying to understand: (i) Delaware's famous corporate law exoneration provision; and (ii) that provision's exception "for acts or omissions not in good faith." DEL. CODE ANN. tit. 8, § 102(b)(7) (2012). In that context, good faith is an aspect of the duty of loyalty. *See Stone ex rel. AmSouth Bancorporation v. Ritter*, 911 A.2d 362, 369–70 (Del. 2006).

Likewise, the contractual obligation of good faith and fair dealing has nothing to do with the "utmost good faith" sometimes used to describe the fiduciary duties that owners of closely held businesses owe each other. *See, e.g., Meinhard v. Salmon*, 249 N.Y. 458, 477, 164 N.E. 545, 551 (1928) ("[W]here parties engage in a joint enterprise each owes to the other the duty of the utmost good faith in all that relates to their common venture. Within its scope they stand in a fiduciary relationship."); *Donahue v. Rodd Electrotype Co. of New England, Inc.*, 367 Mass. 578, 593, 328 N.E.2d 505, 515 (1975) ("[S]tockholders in the close corporation owe one another substantially the same fiduciary duty in the operation of the enterprise1 that partners owe to one another. In our previous decisions, we have defined the standard of duty owed by partners to one another as the utmost good faith and loyalty.") (footnotes omitted) (citations omitted) (internal quotations omitted).

To the contrary, the contractual obligation of good faith and fair dealing is not a fiduciary duty, does not command altruism or self-abnegation, and does not prevent a member from acting in the member's own self-interest:

> "Fair dealing" is not akin to the fair process component of entire fairness, *i.e.*, whether the fiduciary acted fairly when engaging in the challenged transaction as measured by duties of loyalty and care. . . . It is rather a commitment to deal "fairly" in the sense of consistently with the terms of the parties' agreement and its purpose. Likewise "good faith" does not envision loyalty to the contractual counterparty, but rather faithfulness to the scope, purpose, and terms of the parties' contract. Both necessarily turn on the contract itself and what the parties would have agreed upon had the issue arisen when they were bargaining originally.

Gerber v. Enter. Products Holdings, LLC, 67 A.3d 400, 418–19 (Del. 2013) (quoting *ASB Allegiance Real Estate Fund v. Scion Breckenridge Managing Member, LLC*, 50 A.3d 434, 440–42 (Del. Ch. 2012), *aff'd in part, rev'd in part on other grounds*, 68 A.3d 665 (Del. 2013)) (footnotes omitted) (citations omitted) (internal quotations omitted without ellipsis by *Gerber*). *See also* Subsection (e).

Courts should not use the contractual obligation to change *ex post facto* the parties' or this act's allocation of risk and power. To the contrary, the obligation should be used only to protect agreed-upon arrangements from conduct that is manifestly beyond what a reasonable person could have contemplated when the arrangements were made.

The operating agreement or this act may grant discretion to a member or manager, and the contractual obligation of good faith and fair dealing is especially salient when discretion is at issue. However, a member or manager may properly exercise discretion even though another member suffers as a consequence. Conduct does not violate the obligation of good faith and fair dealing merely because that conduct substantially prejudices a party. Indeed, parties allocate risk precisely because prejudice may occur.

The exercise of discretion constitutes a breach of the obligation of good faith and fair dealing only when the party claiming breach shows that the conduct has no honestly-held purpose that legitimately comports with the parties' agreed-upon arrangements:

An implied covenant claim . . . looks to the past. It is not a free-floating duty unattached to the underlying legal documents. It does not ask what duty the law should impose on the parties given their relationship at the time of the wrong, but *rather what the parties would have agreed to themselves had they considered the issue in their original bargaining positions at the time of contracting.*

Gerber v. Enter. Prods. Holdings, LLC, 67 A.3d 400, 418 (Del. 2013) (quoting *ASB Allegiance Real Estate Fund v. Scion Breckenridge Managing Member, LLC*, 50 A.3d 434, 440–42 (Del. Ch. 2012), *aff'd in part, rev'd in part on other grounds*, 68 A.3d 665 (Del. 2013)) (emphasis added) (footnotes omitted) (citations omitted) (internal quotations omitted without ellipsis by *Gerber*).

In sum, the purpose of the contractual obligation of good faith and fair dealing is to protect the arrangement the members have chosen for themselves, not to restructure that arrangement under the guise of safeguarding it.

As to the power of the operating agreement to affect the contractual obligation of good faith and fair dealing, see Section 105(c)(6) (prohibiting elimination but allowing the agreement to "prescribe standards, if not manifestly unreasonable, by which the performance of the obligation is to be measured"). For examples, see Section 105(c)(6), comment. As to whether the obligation stated in this subsection applies to transferees, see Section 107(b), comment.

Subsection (e)—A member in a member-managed LLC has at least two different roles: (i) as a party to the operating agreement, with rights and obligations under that agreement; and (ii) as manager or co-manager of the enterprise. This provision pertains to the first role. A member's exercise of rights under the operating agreement is subject to the obligation of good faith and fair dealing, Subsection (d), but a person does not breach that contractual obligation "solely because the [person's exercise of rights] furthers the [person's] own interest." In contrast, this provision is ineffective with regard to a member's duties as manager or co-manager. For example, a member's liability under Section 409(b)(3) (prohibiting competition) is not "solely because the member's conduct furthers the member's own interest." Rather, the liability results from the breach of a specific obligation—*i.e.*, the codified aspect of the duty of loyalty that prohibits competition.

With regard to a manager-managed LLC: (i) the same analysis applies to a member that is a manager; and (ii) with regard to a non-managing member the analysis as to contractual rights applies and the analysis as to managerial duties is inapposite.

Subsection (f)—Here and elsewhere in this act, information "is material if there is a substantial likelihood that a reasonable [decision maker] would consider it important in deciding how to vote" or take other action under this act or the operating agreements. *TSC Industries, Inc. v. Northway, Inc.*, 426 U.S. 438, 449, 96 S.Ct. 2126, 2132 (1976).

The operating agreement can provide additional or different methods of authorization or ratification, subject to the strictures of Section 105(c)(5), (d)(1), and (d)(3)(A)(B) and (D).

Subsection (g)—This subsection codifies judge-made law applicable to all business entities. *See, e.g., Gottsacker v. Monnier*, 281 Wis. 2d 361, 379, 697 N.W.2d 436, 444 (Wisc. 2005) (referring to "a willful failure to deal fairly with the LLC or its other members"); *Lonergan v. EPE Holdings, LLC*, 5 A.3d 1008, 1019 (Del. Ch. 2010) (discussing "entire fairness" in the context of a limited partnership"); *Kahn v. Lynch Commc'n Sys., Inc.*, 638 A.2d 1110, 1116 (Del. 1994) (discussing "entire fairness" in the context of a corporation's merger with an affiliate); *Lonergan v. EPE Holdings, LLC*, 5 A.3d 1008, 1019 (Del. Ch. 2010) (discussing "entire fairness" in the context of a limited partnership").

Subsection (h)—This subsection is the modern, reformulated version of a language that sought to overturn the now-defunct notion that debts to owners were categorically inferior to debts to non-owner creditors. *See, e.g.*, ULPA (2001) § 112 ("A partner may lend money to and transact other business with the limited partnership and has the same rights and obligations with respect to the loan or other transaction as a person that is not a partner."). The reformulation makes clear that this provision has nothing to do with the fiduciary duty pertaining to conflict of interests. *See BT-I v. Equitable Life Assurance Soc'y of the United States*, 75 Cal. App. 4th 1406, 1415, 89 Cal. Rptr. 2d 811 (1999) (examining the prior formulation, explaining its history and stating "[w]e cannot discern anything in the purpose of [the prior formulation] that suggests an intent to affect a general partner's fiduciary duty to limited partners").

This subsection states a default rule. The operating agreement may provide that debt to a member (or members generally) is subordinate to other limited liability company obligations. The agreement that creates the debt may do likewise.

Subsection (i)—This is the "switching" mechanism, referred to in the introduction to this comment. The list does not include Subsection (h).

Subsection (i)(1)—This provision switches most managerial duties to the managers and away from members. Of course, if a member is a manager, the duties apply to the member-manager in the person's capacity of manager.

Subsection (i)(2)—On the assumption that the members of a manager-managed LLC are dependent on the manager, this paragraph extends the duty not to compete longer than in a member-managed LLC.

Subsection (i)(3)—The contractual obligation of good faith and fair dealing applies to members regardless of whether they are managers; non-managing members have rights and perhaps duties under the operating agreement and under this act. As to non-member managers, the operating agreement (and the corresponding obligation of good faith and fair dealing) are relevant regardless of whether the manager is party to the agreement. *See* Section 105(a)(2) (stating that the operating agreement "governs . . . the rights and duties under this [act] of a person in the capacity of manager"). Also, non-member managers will have rights and obligations under this act, which per Subsection (d) are also subject to the obligation of good faith and fair dealing.

Subsection (i)(4)—As explained in the comment to Subsection (e), that provision does not apply to the managerial function.

Subsection (i)(5)—The power to ratify belongs to the entity's owners; thus Subsection (f) does not switch from members to managers.

Subsection (i)(6)—This paragraph merely negates a claim of fiduciary duty that is exclusively status-based and does not immunize misconduct.

Example: Although a limited liability company is manager-managed, one member who is not a manager owns a controlling interest and effectively, albeit indirectly, controls the company's activities. A member owning a minority interest brings an action for dissolution under Section 701(a)(4)(C)(ii) (oppression by "the managers or those members in control of the company"). This paragraph does not prevent the court from construing the claim as alleging a breach of fiduciary duty by the controlling member.

§ 410. RIGHTS TO INFORMATION OF MEMBER, MANAGER, AND PERSON DISSOCIATED AS MEMBER.

(a) In a member-managed limited liability company, the following rules apply:

(1) On reasonable notice, a member may inspect and copy during regular business hours, at a reasonable location specified by the company, any record maintained by the company regarding the company's activities, affairs, financial condition, and other circumstances, to the extent the information is material to the member's rights and duties under the operating agreement or this [act].

(2) The company shall furnish to each member:

(A) without demand, any information concerning the company's activities, affairs, financial condition, and other circumstances which the company knows and is material to the proper exercise of the member's rights and duties under the operating agreement or this [act], except to the extent the company can establish that it reasonably believes the member already knows the information; and

(B) on demand, any other information concerning the company's activities, affairs, financial condition, and other circumstances, except to the extent the demand for the information demanded is unreasonable or otherwise improper under the circumstances.

(3) The duty to furnish information under paragraph (2) also applies to each member to the extent the member knows any of the information described in paragraph (2).

(b) In a manager-managed limited liability company, the following rules apply:

(1) The informational rights stated in subsection (a) and the duty stated in subsection (a)(3) apply to the managers and not the members.

(2) During regular business hours and at a reasonable location specified by the company, a member may inspect and copy information regarding the activities, affairs, financial condition, and other circumstances of the company as is just and reasonable if:

(A) the member seeks the information for a purpose **reasonably related** to the member's interest as a member;

(B) the member makes a demand in a record received by the company, describing with reasonable particularity the information sought and the purpose for seeking the information; and

(C) the information sought is directly connected to the member's purpose.

(3) Not later than 10 days after receiving a demand pursuant to paragraph (2)(B), the company shall inform in a record the member that made the demand of:

(A) what information the company will provide in response to the demand and when and where the company will provide the information; and

(B) the company's reasons for declining, if the company declines to provide any demanded information.

(4) Whenever this [act] or an operating agreement provides for a member to vote on or give or withhold consent to a matter, before the vote is cast or consent is given or withheld, the company shall, without demand, provide the member with all information that is known to the company and is material to the member's decision.

(c) Subject to subsection (h), on 10 days' demand made in a record received by a limited liability company, a person dissociated as a member may have access to the information to which the person was entitled while a member if:

(1) the information pertains to the period during which the person was a member;

(2) the person seeks the information in good faith; and

(3) the person satisfies the requirements imposed on a member by subsection (b)(2).

(d) A limited liability company shall respond to a demand made pursuant to subsection (c) in the manner provided in subsection (b)(3).

(e) A limited liability company may charge a person that makes a demand under this section the reasonable costs of copying, limited to the costs of labor and material.

(f) A member or person dissociated as a member may exercise the rights under this section through an agent or, in the case of an individual under legal disability, a legal representative. Any restriction or condition imposed by the operating agreement or under subsection (h) applies both to the agent or legal representative and to the member or person dissociated as a member.

(g) Subject to Section 504, the rights under this section do not extend to a person as transferee.

(h) In addition to any restriction or condition stated in its operating agreement, a limited liability company, as a matter within the ordinary course of its activities and affairs, may impose reasonable restrictions and conditions on access to and use of information to be furnished under this section, including designating information confidential and imposing nondisclosure and safeguarding obligations on the recipient. In a dispute concerning the reasonableness of a restriction under this subsection, the company has the burden of proving reasonableness.

Comment

This section is derived from the Uniform Limited Partnership Act (2001) §§ 304 (rights to information of limited partners and former limited partners) and 407 (rights to information of general partners and former general partners). The rules stated here are what might be termed "quasi-default rules"—subject to some change by the operating agreement. *See* Section 105(c)(8) (prohibiting unreasonable restrictions on the information rights stated in this section).

Although the rights and duties stated in this section are extensive, they are not necessarily all-inclusive. This act's statement of fiduciary duties is not exhaustive, *see* the comment to Section 409(a), and some cases characterize owners' information rights as reflecting a fiduciary duty of those with management power. *E.g., Bakerman v. Sidney Frank Importing Co., Inc.*, No. Civ.A. 1844-N, 2006 WL 3927242 at *14 (Del. Ch. Oct. 16, 2006) (holding that an LLC manager owed "certain duties to members of the LLC" and stating that "[w]hen fiduciaries communicate with their beneficiaries in the context of asking the beneficiary to make a discretionary decision—such as whether to consent to a sale of substantially all the assets of an LLC—the fiduciary has a duty to disclose all material facts bearing on the decision at issue") (citing *Loudon v. Archer-Daniels-Midland Co.*, 700 A.2d 135, 137 (Del.1997)). Also, the rights stated in this section are in addition to whatever discovery rights a party has in a civil suit.

Subsection (a)—Paragraph 1 states the rule pertaining to information memorialized in "any record maintained by the company." Paragraph 2 applies to information not in such a record. Appropriately, Paragraph (2) sets a more demanding standard for those seeking such information.

Subsection (a)(2) and (3)—In appropriate circumstances, violation of either or both of these provisions might cause a court to enjoin or even rescind action taken by the LLC, especially when the violation has interfered with an approval or veto mechanism involving member consent. *E.g., Blue Chip Emerald LLC v. Allied Partners Inc.*, 299 A.D.2d 278, 279–80 (N.Y. App. Div. 2002) (invoking partnership law precedent as reflecting a duty of full disclosure and holding that "[a]bsent such full disclosure, the transaction is voidable").

Subsection (a)(2)—This paragraph imposes a duty on the limited liability company, not the members who manage the LLC. However, a member could be liable in damages if the member were to: (i) breach a duty under Section 409 or the operating agreement; and (ii) in doing so cause or suffer the LLC to breach the duty stated in this paragraph.

Subsection (a)(2)(A)—For the meaning of "material" as applied to information, see Section 409(f), comment.

Subsection (a)(3)—This paragraph imposes a duty directly on each member. Therefore, a member's violation of this paragraph is actionable in damages without need to show a violation of a duty stated in Section 409.

Subsection (b)(1)—This is a switching provision. The comments to Paragraph (a)(2) and (3) apply here by analogy.

Subsection (b)(2)—This paragraph refers to "information" rather than "records maintained by the company" so in some circumstances the company might have an obligation to memorialize information. *Compare* Subsection (b)(2), *with* Subsection (a). Such circumstances will likely be rare or at least unusual. This section generally concerns providing existing information, not creating it. In any event, a member does not trigger the company's obligation under this paragraph merely by satisfying Subparagraphs (A) through (C). The member must also satisfy the "just and reasonable" requirement.

Subsection (b)(4)—For the meaning of "material" as applied to information, see Section 409(f), comment.

Subsection (c)—When a member dies, Section 504 provides information rights to the legal representative of the deceased member.

Subsection (c)(1)—A person dissociated as a member has information rights in that capacity only as to the period during which the person was a member. To the extent that further information is accessible under Section 504(2) (providing access to the legal representative of a deceased partner), that access is limited both in purpose ("for purposes of settling the estate") and in scope ("the rights the deceased partner had under Section 410").

Subsection (f)—Some old cases involved conflicts over whether a shareholder could exercise inspection rights through another person. *White v. Coeur D'Alene Big Creek Mining Co.*, 55 P.2d 720, 723 (Idaho 1936) (stating that "[t]he refusal to permit respondent [shareholder] to appoint his own attorney or agent to make the examination [of the corporation's books] was in effect a denial of his right" of inspection); *State v. Monida & Yellowstone Stage Co.*, 124 N.W. 971, 972 (Minn. 1910) (upholding a trial court's mandamus order, "which shall provide that [the shareholder complainant], or such attorney or agent as he may select, . . . shall be allowed to inspect the books, records, and papers of the defendant [corporation]"). In light of that history, for the avoidance of doubt, this subsection expressly authorizes taking action through an agent. No negative inference should be drawn about using agents to take other action under this act.

Subsection (h)—This provision provides fallback protection for gaps in the operating agreement. For example, those managing an LLC may protect trade secrets from disclosure prohibit various misuses of confidential information even if the operating agreement omits to do so.

The reference to "ordinary course" pertains to Section 407(b)(3) (stating that any "difference arising among members [in a member-managed LLC] as to a matter in the ordinary course of the activities of the company may be decided by a majority of the members"). As for a manager-managed LLC, see Section 407(c)(1) ("Except as expressly provided in this [act], *any* matter relating to the activities and affairs of the [manager-managed] company is decided exclusively by the manager, or, if there is more than one manager, by a majority of the managers.") (emphasis added). This approach is necessary, lest a requesting member (or manager-member) have the power to block imposition of a reasonable restriction or condition needed to prevent the requestor from abusing the LLC.

The burden of persuasion under this subsection contrasts with the burden of persuasion under Section 105(c)(8) (prohibiting unreasonable limitations on the information rights provided by this section). Under that subsection, as a matter of ordinary procedural law the burden is on the person making the claim.

[ARTICLE] 5

TRANSFERABLE INTERESTS AND RIGHTS OF TRANSFEREES AND CREDITORS

§ 501.   NATURE OF TRANSFERABLE INTEREST.

A transferable interest is personal property.

Comment

For the definition of transferable interest, see Section 102(24). Absent a contrary provision in the operating agreement or the consent of the members, a "transferable interest" is the only interest in an LLC which can be transferred to a person who is not already a member. *See* Section 502. As to whether a member may transfer governance rights to a fellow member, the question is moot absent a provision in the operating agreement changing the default rule, *see* Section 407(b)(2) (allocating governance rights *per capita*). In the default mode, a member's transfer of governance rights to another member: (i) does not increase the transferee's governance rights; (ii) eliminates the transferor's governance rights; and (iii) thereby changes that denominator but not the numerator in calculating governance rights.

Example: LCN Company, LLC is a member-managed limited liability company with three members, Laura, Charles, and Nora. The operating agreement does not displace this act's default rule on the allocation of governance rights among members. Thus, each member has 1/3 of those rights. Laura transfers her entire ownership interest to Charles. The transfer does not increase Charles's governance rights but does eliminate Laura's. After the transfer, Laura has no governance rights (regardless of whether Charles and Nora agree to expel Laura under Section 602(5)(B)). As a result, Charles and Nora each have 1/2 of the governance rights.

Whether a transferable interest pledged as security is governed by Article 8 or 9 of the Uniform Commercial Code depends on the rules stated in those articles.

§ 502.   TRANSFER OF TRANSFERABLE INTEREST.

(a) Subject to Section 503(f), a transfer, in whole or in part, of a transferable interest:

(1) is permissible;

(2) does not by itself cause a person's dissociation as a member or a dissolution and winding up of the limited liability company's activities and affairs; and

(3) subject to Section 504, does not entitle the transferee to:

(A) participate in the management or conduct of the company's activities and affairs; or

(B) except as otherwise provided in subsection (c), have access to records or other information concerning the company's activities and affairs.

(b) A transferee has the right to receive, in accordance with the transfer, distributions to which the transferor would otherwise be entitled.

(c) In a dissolution and winding up of a limited liability company, a transferee is entitled to an account of the company's transactions only from the date of dissolution.

(d) A transferable interest may be evidenced by a certificate of the interest issued by a limited liability company in a record, and, subject to this section, the interest represented by the certificate may be transferred by a transfer of the certificate.

(e) A limited liability company need not give effect to a transferee's rights under this section until the company knows or has notice of the transfer.

(f) A transfer of a transferable interest in violation of a restriction on transfer contained in the operating agreement is ineffective if the intended transferee has knowledge or notice of the restriction at the time of transfer.

(g) Except as otherwise provided in Section 602(5)(B), if a member transfers a transferable interest, the transferor retains the rights of a member other than the transferable interest transferred and retains all the duties and obligations of a member.

(h) If a member transfers a transferable interest to a person that becomes a member with respect to the transferred interest, the transferee is liable for the member's obligations under Sections 403 and 406 known to the transferee when the transferee becomes a member.

Comment

One of the most fundamental characteristics of LLC law is its fidelity to the "pick your partner" principle. *See, e.g., Bynum v. Frisby*, 73 Nev. 145, 149–50, 311 P.2d 972, 975 (1957) (stating that (i) "the assignment of a partnership interest from one partner to a stranger does not bring that stranger into fiduciary relationship with the remaining partners" and (ii) absent consent by the remaining partners "[t]he stranger remains a stranger" with no rights to management or even information).

This section is the core of the act's provisions reflecting and protecting that principle. A member's rights in a limited liability company are bifurcated into economic rights (the transferable interest) and governance rights (including management rights, consent rights, rights to information, rights to seek judicial intervention). Unless the operating agreement otherwise provides, a member acting without the consent of all other members lacks both the power and the right to: (i) bestow membership on a non-member, Section 401(d); or (ii) transfer to a non-member anything other than some or all of the member's transferable interest, Section 502(a)(3). The rights of a mere transferee are quite limited— *i.e.*, to receive distributions, Section 502(b), and, if the LLC dissolves and winds up, to receive specified information pertaining to the LLC from the date of dissolution. Section 502(c).

This section applies regardless of whether the transferor is a member, a transferee of a member, a transferee of a transferee, etc. *See* Section 102(24) (defining "transferable interest" in terms of a right "initially owned by a person in the person's capacity as a member" regardless of "whether or not the person remains a member or continues to own any part of the right").

This section does not directly consider whether a member may transfer governance rights to another member without obtaining consent from all the other members. As noted above, Section 501, cmt., the question is moot under this act's default rule for allocating governance rights.

However, the question can be pivotal when the operating agreement displaces the default rule on governance rights but does not determine whether transfer restrictions (whether contractual, statutory, or both) apply to transfers of governance rights from one member to another. Case law is scant but suggests that this act does not protect members from control shifts that result from transfers among members (as distinguished from transfers to non-members who seek thereby to become members). *Blythe v. Bell*, No. 11 CVS 933. 2012 WL 7807800, at ¶ 6 (N.C. Dist. Dec. 10, 2012) (holding in a case of "first impression in North Carolina" that "in the absence of articles of incorporation or an operating agreement to the contrary . . . the assignment of control (*i.e.*, governance) interests between members is effective without unanimous member consent;" *Achaian, Inc. v. Leemon Family L.L.C.*, 25 A.3d 800, 810 (Del. Ch. 2011) (Strine, Ch.) (holding that the terms of the LLC agreement did not preclude one member of a three-member LLC from transferring the member's entire interest (including governance rights) to a second member without first having the consent of the third member; stating that the third member's "argument relies on a very thinly sliced version of [the "pick-your-partner principle, the strained version being] . . . that once one chooses his initial co-members, one continues to hold a veto over how much additional voting power they may acquire;" explaining that "[t]he problem for [the third member] is that nothing in the LLC Agreement supports [that member's] reading of it that would require an already admitted Member, like [the acquirer—*i.e.*, the second member], to be become once, twice (or even three times) a Member each and every time that Member acquires an additional block of Interests").

Other law may affect the applicability of this section. *See* 11 U.S.C. § 541(c)(1) (providing that, initially at least, all property of a debtor becomes part of the bankruptcy estate regardless of restrictions on transfer); UCC §§ 9–406, 9–408 (overriding specified restrictions on assignment in specified circumstances, regardless of whether state law or a contract imposes the restrictions).

In any event, this section does not apply to the transfer of ownership interests in a member that is an entity.

Example: ABC, LLC has three members: Ralph (an individual), Alice, Inc. ("Alice"), and Norton, LLC ("Norton"). Section 502 applies to any attempt by Ralph, Alice, or Norton to transfer their respective membership interest in ABC. Section 502 is inapplicable, however, to a change in control of Alice or Norton or even a complete change in their respective membership.

Subsection (a)—The definition of "transfer," Section 102(23), and this subsection's reference to "in whole or in part" combine to mean that this section encompasses not only unconditional, permanent, and complete transfers but also temporary, contingent, and partial ones. Thus, for example, a charging order under Section 503 effects a transfer of part of the judgment debtor's transferable interest, as does the pledge of a transferable interest as collateral for a loan and the gift of a life-interest in a member's rights to distribution.

Subsection (a)(2)—The phrase "by itself" contemplates Section 602(5)(B), which creates a risk of dissociation via expulsion when a member transfers all of the member's transferable interest.

Subsection (a)(3)—Mere transferees have no right to participate in management or otherwise intrude as the members carry on the affairs of the limited liability company and their activities as members.

Because Section 102(22)(G) defines "transfer" to include "a transfer by operation of law," this section affects the power of other law to effect transfers of a member's ownership interest. For example, a divorce court lacks the power to award a member's spouse anything beyond the member's transferable interest. Nor does the member have the power to enter into a property settlement purporting to effect any greater transfer.

For the divorce court, the best solution is to value the member's complete ownership interest (*i.e.*, the transferable interest as enhanced by the management and information rights and the standing to sue) and: (i) if possible, award the member's spouse marital property of equal value; or (ii) if not possible, award the member's spouse a money judgment and a charging order to enforce the judgment.

Granting the non-member any part of member's transferable interest is almost always imprudent; marital discord will almost inevitably carry over into the business relationship. Granting the member's ex-spouse the entire transferable interest is rarely a viable alternative. If the member is an active participant in the limited liability company, the approach is impossible. The member's transferable interest will typically constitute much or all of the member's remuneration for the partner's activity. Even if the member is essentially passive, granting the transferable interest to the ex-spouse puts him or her at great risk as a "bare naked assignee." *See* the comment to Section 107(b).

When a member dies, subject to the operating agreement other law may effect a transfer of the member's transferable interest to the member's estate or personal representative. However, for the reasons just stated, other law lacks the power to transfer anything more than a transferable interest. (Section (504) does provide extra information rights for the purposes of settling the estate of the deceased member.)

Subsection (a)(3)(B)—*See* Section 410(g) (providing that that section's information rights do not apply to transferees).

Subsection (b)—Amounts due under this subsection are of course subject to offset for any amount owed to the limited liability company by the member or person dissociated as a member on whose account the distribution is made. Section 404(d). As to whether an LLC may properly offset for claims against a transferor that was never a member is matter for other law, specifically the law of contracts dealing with assignments.

Subsection (c)—This very limited grant of information rights encompasses only transactions occurring at or after the date of the LLC's dissolution. The transferee has only the right to information as to the allocation of net assets among the LLC's creditors, members, and transferees—and only from the date of dissolution.

This subsection does not prevent a transferee from contracting with a member-transferor to require the member-transferor to disclose further information to the transferee. Whether such an agreement would breach the operating agreement, the implied contractual obligation of good faith and fair dealing, Section 409(d), or a fiduciary duty depends on the circumstances.

If a dissolved LLC rescinds its dissolution, Section 703, this subsection no longer applies.

Subsection (d)—The use of certificates can raise issues relating to Articles 8 and 9 of the Uniform Commercial Code.

Subsection (f)—This provision originated as UPA (1997) § 503(e), was then consistent with U.C.C section 9–318(3), and is now consistent with U.C.C section 9–406(a) (stating that "an account debtor . . . may discharge its obligation by paying the assignor until, but not after, the account debtor receives a notification, authenticated by the assignor or the assignee, that the amount due or to become due has been assigned and that payment is to be made to the assignee").

The term "notice" includes "reason to know," Section 103(b)(1), and ordinarily a potential transferee has reason to inquire about transfer restrictions that might be contained in the operating agreement.

Subsection (g)—Under this subsection, a member remains a member (with all attendant rights and obligations) even after permanently transferring the entirety of the transferable interest, unless: (i) the other members opt for expulsion under Section 602(5)(B); or (ii) as otherwise provided in the operating agreement.

§ 503. CHARGING ORDER.

(a) On application by a judgment creditor of a member or transferee, a court may enter a charging order against the transferable interest of the judgment debtor for the unsatisfied amount of the judgment.

Except as otherwise provided in subsection (f), a charging order constitutes a lien on a judgment debtor's transferable interest and requires the limited liability company to pay over to the person to which the charging order was issued any distribution that otherwise would be paid to the judgment debtor.

(b) To the extent necessary to effectuate the collection of distributions pursuant to a charging order in effect under subsection (a), the court may:

(1) appoint a receiver of the distributions subject to the charging order, with the power to make all inquiries the judgment debtor might have made; and

(2) make all other orders necessary to give effect to the charging order.

(c) Upon a showing that distributions under a charging order will not pay the judgment debt within a reasonable time, the court may foreclose the lien and order the sale of the transferable interest. Except as otherwise provided in subsection (f), the purchaser at the foreclosure sale obtains only the transferable interest, does not thereby become a member, and is subject to Section 502.

(d) At any time before foreclosure under subsection (c), the member or transferee whose transferable interest is subject to a charging order under subsection (a) may extinguish the charging order by satisfying the judgment and filing a certified copy of the satisfaction with the court that issued the charging order.

(e) At any time before foreclosure under subsection (c), a limited liability company or one or more members whose transferable interests are not subject to the charging order may pay to the judgment creditor the full amount due under the judgment and thereby succeed to the rights of the judgment creditor, including the charging order.

(f) If a court orders foreclosure of a charging order lien against the sole member of a limited liability company:

(1) the court shall confirm the sale;

(2) the purchaser at the sale obtains the member's entire interest, not only the member's transferable interest;

(3) the purchaser thereby becomes a member; and

(4) the person whose interest was subject to the foreclosed charging order is dissociated as a member.

(g) This [act] does not deprive any member or transferee of the benefit of any exemption law applicable to the transferable interest of the member or transferee.

(h) This section provides the exclusive remedy by which a person seeking in the capacity of judgment creditor to enforce a judgment against a member or transferee may satisfy the judgment from the judgment debtor's transferable interest.

Comment

The charging order concept dates back to the English Partnership Act of 1890 and in the United States has been a fundamental part of law of unincorporated business organizations since 1914. *See* UPA (1914) § 28. As much a remedy limitation as a remedy, the charging order is the sole method by which a person acting as judgment creditor of a member or transferee can extract value from the member's or transferee's ownership interest in a limited liability company. *See* the comment to Subsection (h).

Under this section, the judgment creditor of a member or transferee is entitled to a charging order against the relevant transferable interest. While in effect, that order entitles the judgment creditor to whatever distributions would otherwise be due to the member or transferee whose interest is subject to the order. However, the judgment creditor has no say in the timing or amount of those distributions. The charging order does not entitle the judgment creditor to accelerate any distributions or to otherwise interfere with the management and activities of the limited liability company.

By its terms, this section does not apply to foreign limited liability companies. *See* Section 102(8) (defining "[l]imited liability company" to mean "an entity *formed under this [act] or which becomes subject to this [act]*") (emphasis added); *see also Fannie Mae v. Heather Apartments Ltd. P'ship,* A13-

0562, 2013 WL 6223564, at *6 (Minn. Ct. App. Dec. 2, 2013) (considering the remedies available to a judgment creditor with respect to the judgment debtor's interest in a Cook Islands LLC; rejecting the debtor's argument that the creditor's "only remedy is to obtain a charging order under" [the Minnesota LLC statute]; explaining that "this argument fails because that statute only applies to Minnesota limited liability companies" which that statute "defines . . . as 'a limited liability company, other than a foreign limited liability company, *organized or governed by this chapter*'") (emphasis added) (statutory citations omitted).

The operating agreement has no power to alter the provisions of this section to the prejudice of third parties. Section 105(c)(15).

Subsection (a)—The phrase "judgment debtor" encompasses both members and transferees. The lien pertains only to a distribution, which excludes "amounts constituting reasonable compensation for present or past service or payments made in the ordinary course of business under a bona fide retirement plan or other bona fide benefits program." Section 102(4)(B). A judgment creditor that wishes to levy on such amounts should use the appropriate creditor's remedy, such as garnishment (which may be subject to exemptions or exclusions not relevant to a charging order). *Cf. PB Real Estate, Inc. v. Dem II Props.*, 719 A.2d 73, 76 (Conn. 1998) (rejecting the contention of an LLC's two members that "payments of $28,000 to each of them" should be treated "as expenses for wages" rather than as distributions).

Whether an application for a charging order must be served on the limited liability company, the judgment debtor, or both is a matter for other law, principally the law of remedies and civil procedure. The order itself must be served on the limited liability company. Whether the order must also be served on the judgment debtor is a matter for other law.

If a distribution consists of rights to acquire interests in a limited liability company, the charging order applies only to those rights within the definition of transferable interest. *See* Section 102(24) (defining transferable interest).

Subsection (b)—Paragraph (2) refers to "other orders" rather than "additional orders." Therefore, given appropriate circumstances, a court may invoke Paragraph (1), Paragraph (2), or both.

Subsection (b)(1)—The receiver contemplated here is emphatically not a receiver for the limited liability company, but rather a receiver for the distributions subject to the charging order. The principal advantage provided by this paragraph is an expanded right to information. However, that right goes no further than "the extent necessary to effectuate the collections of distributions pursuant to a charging order." For a correctly narrow reading of this provision, see *Wells Fargo Bank, Nat. Ass'n v. Continuous Control Solutions, Inc.*, No. 11–1285, 2012 WL 3195759 (Iowa Ct. App. Aug. 8, 2012).

Subsection (b)(2)—This paragraph must be understood in the context of: (i) the very limited nature of the charging order; and (ii) the importance of preventing overreaching on behalf of a person that is not a judgment creditor of the LLC, has no claim on the LLC's assets, and has no right to interfere in the activities, affairs, and management of the LLC. In particular, the court's power to make "all other orders" is limited to "orders necessary to give effect to the charging order."

Example: A judgment creditor with a charging order believes that the limited liability company should invest less of its surplus in operations, leaving more funds for distributions. The creditor moves the court for an order directing the limited liability company to restrict re-investment. Subsection (b)(2) does not authorize the court to grant the motion.

Example: A judgment creditor with a judgment for $10,000 against a member obtains a charging order against the member's transferable interest. Having been properly served with the order, the limited liability company nonetheless fails to comply and makes a $3000 distribution to the member. The court has the power to order the limited liability company to pay $3000 to the judgment creditor to "give effect to the charging order."

Under Subsection (b)(2), the court has the power to decide whether a particular payment is a distribution, because that decision determines whether the payment is part of a transferable interest subject to a charging order.

Example: Member A of ABC, LLC has for some years received distributions form the LLC. However, when a judgment creditor of Member A obtains a charging order against Member A's transferable interest, the LLC ceases to make distributions to Member A and instead provides a salary to Member A equivalent to former distributions. A court might deem this salary a disguised distribution. (In any event, however, the salary will be subject to garnishment.)

This act has no specific rules for determining the fate or effect of a charging order when the limited liability company undergoes a merger, conversion, interest exchange, or domestication under [Article] 10. In the proper circumstances, such an organic change might trigger an order under Subsection (b)(2).

Subsection (c)—The phrase "that distributions under the charging order will not pay the judgment debt within a reasonable period of time" comes from case law. *See, e.g., Stewart v. Lanier Park Med. Office Bldg.*, Ltd., 578 S.E.2d 572, 574 (Ga. Ct. App. 2003) ("Judicial sale may be appropriate where . . . it is apparent that distributions under the charging order will not pay the judgment debt within a reasonable amount of time."); *Nigri v. Lotz*, 453 S.E.2d 780, 783 (Ga. Ct. App. 1995). A purchaser at a foreclosure sale obtains only the very limited rights of a transferee under Section 502 and is in some ways more vulnerable and less powerful than the holder of a charging order. After foreclosure and sale, Subsection (b) no longer applies. More generally, the court is no longer involved in the matter. For the vulnerability of a transferee, see Section 107(b), comment.

Subsection (d)—This provision allows the judgment debtor to end the charging order without need for a hearing.

Subsection (e)—Traditionally, charging order provisions referred to the possibility of "redeeming" an interest subject to a charging order. That usage was confusing, leaving several important questions unanswered. This act substitutes a far simpler approach, contemplating the limited partnership or its members buying the underlying judgment and thereby dispensing with any interference the judgment creditor might seek to inflict on the partnership.

In many circumstances, buying the judgment is superior to the mechanism provided by this subsection, because: (i) this subsection requires full satisfaction of the underlying judgment; and (ii) the LLC or the other members might be able to buy the judgment for less than face value. On the other hand, this subsection operates without need for the judgment creditor's consent, so it remains a valuable protection in the event a judgment creditor seeks to do mischief to the LLC.

Whether a member-managed LLC's decision to invoke this subsection is "ordinary course" or "outside the ordinary course," Section 407(b)(3) and (4)(A), depends on the circumstances. However, the involvement of this subsection does not by itself make the decision "outside the ordinary course." For a manager-managed LLC, the distinction is irrelevant. Section 407(c)(1).

Subsection (f)—The charging order remedy—and, more particularly, the exclusiveness of the remedy—protect the "pick your partner" principle. That principle is inapposite when a limited liability company has only one member. The exclusivity of the charging order remedy was never intended to protect a judgment debtor, but rather only to protect the interests of the judgment debtor's co-owners.

Put another way, the charging order remedy was never intended as an "asset protection" device for judgment debtors. *See Olmstead v. F.T.C.*, 44 So. 3d 76, 83 (Fla. 2010) (recognizing "the full scope of a judgment creditor's rights with respect to a judgment debtor's freely alienable membership interest in a single-member LLC"); *In re Albright*, 291 B.R. 538, 540 (Bankr. D. Colo. 2003) (holding that, "[b]ecause there are no other members in the LLC, . . . the Debtor's bankruptcy filing effectively assigned her entire membership interest in the LLC to the bankruptcy estate, and the Trustee obtained all her rights, including the right to control the management of the LLC"). Accordingly, when a charging order against an LLC's sole member is foreclosed, the member's entire ownership interest is sold and the buyer replaces the judgment debtor as the LLC's sole member.

This subsection was added during the Harmonization Project but not for the purposes of harmonization. The subsection addresses an issue that does not exist with partnerships; neither a general nor a limited partnership can continue perpetually in existence with only one partner. *See* ULPA (2001) (Last Amended 2013) § 801(a)(5) (stating that dissolution is caused upon "the passage of 90 consecutive days during which the partnership has only one partner"); UPA (1997) (Last Amended

2013) § 801(6) (stating that dissolution is caused upon "the passage of 90 consecutive days during which the partnership does not have at least two partners").

Subsection (g)—This subsection preserves otherwise applicable exemptions but does not create any. *In re Foos*, 405 B.R. 604, 609 (Bankr. N.D. Ohio 2009) (interpreting the comparable provision in UPA (1997) and stating, "it is clear that [the provision] does not create an exemption").

Subsection (h)—This subsection does not override Uniform Commercial Code, Article 9, which may provide different remedies for a secured creditor acting in that capacity. A secured creditor with a judgment might decide to proceed under Article 9 alone, under this section alone, or under both Article 9 and this section. In the last-mentioned circumstance, the constraints of this section would apply to the charging order but not to the Article 9 remedies.

This subsection is not intended to prevent a court from effecting a "reverse pierce" where appropriate. In a reverse pierce, the court conflates the entity and its owner to hold the entity liable for a debt of the owner. *Litchfield Asset Mgmt. Corp. v. Howell*, 799 A.2d 298, 312 (Conn. App. Ct. 2002) (approving a reverse pierce where a judgment debtor had established a limited liability company in a patent attempt to frustrate the judgment creditor), *overruled on other grounds by, Robinson v. Coughlin*, 830 A.2d 1114 (Conn. 2003). Likewise, this subsection does not supplant fraudulent transfer law.

§ 504. POWER OF LEGAL REPRESENTATIVE OF DECEASED MEMBER.

If a member dies, the deceased member's legal representative may exercise:

(1) the rights of a transferee provided in Section 502(c); and

(2) for the purposes of settling the estate, the rights the deceased member had under Section 410.

Comment

The estate and those claiming through the estate are transferees, and as such they have very limited rights to information. This section provides temporary, additional information rights to the legal representative of the estate. Sections 410 and 502(c) pertain only to information rights.

[ARTICLE] 6

DISSOCIATION

§ 601. POWER TO DISSOCIATE AS MEMBER; WRONGFUL DISSOCIATION.

(a) A person has the power to dissociate as a member at any time, rightfully or wrongfully, by withdrawing as a member by express will under Section 602(1).

(b) A person's dissociation as a member is wrongful only if the dissociation:

(1) is in breach of an express provision of the operating agreement; or

(2) occurs before the completion of the winding up of the limited liability company and:

(A) the person withdraws as a member by express will;

(B) the person is expelled as a member by judicial order under Section 602(6);

(C) the person is dissociated under Section 602(8); or

(D) in the case of a person that is not a trust other than a business trust, an estate, or an individual, the person is expelled or otherwise dissociated as a member because it willfully dissolved or terminated.

(c) A person that wrongfully dissociates as a member is liable to the limited liability company and, subject to Section 801, to the other members for damages caused by the dissociation. The liability is in addition to any debt, obligation, or other liability of the member to the company or the other members.

Comment

This article deals with the dissociation of a person as a member. Article 7 deals with the dissolution of a limited liability company.

Subsection (a)—The operating agreement can vary this provision, even to the extent of negating a member's power to dissociate. Doing so, however, is fundamentally at odds with the concept of a limited liability company as a creature of contract. *See* the comment to Section 105 (Role and Inevitability of Operating Agreement). Only in exceptional circumstances does a party to a contract lack the power to breach, and courts will not enjoin a person to remain in an ongoing contractual relationship that involves trust and confidence. E. ALLAN FARNSWORTH, CONTRACTS § 12.7, at 781 (3d ed. 1999) ("A court will not grant specific performance of a contract to provide a service that is personal in nature. This refusal . . . is based [in part] of the undesirability of compelling the continuance of personal relations after disputes have arisen and confidence and loyalty have been shaken and the undesirability, in some instances, of imposing what might seem like involuntary servitude.") (footnote omitted). Moreover, eliminating or even substantially restricting a member's power to dissociate may have dreadful practical consequences.

Subsection (b)—This subsection list exhaustively ("only if") the dissociations that are "wrongful," but the list is a default rule. The operating agreement can expand the list; *e.g.*, by making wrongful a dissociation that beaches the implied contractual covenant of good faith and fair dealing. In theory, the operating agreement can provide for liquidated damages (subject to the requirements of contract law) and, in theory, can also contract or even eliminate the list of wrongful dissociations.

Subsection (b)(1)—The reference to "an express provision of the operating agreement" means that a person's dissociation as a member in breach of the obligation of good faith and fair dealing is not wrongful dissociation for the purposes of this section. The breach might be actionable on other grounds.

Subsection (b)(2)(C)—This subsection refers to Section 602(8), which involves *inter alia* dissociation on account of bankruptcy, which in turn is subject to bankruptcy law. *See, e.g.,* 11 U.S.C.A. § 365(e) (invalidating "ipso facto" clauses, subject to some exceptions).

Subsection (c)—A person who prematurely dissociates as a member risks liability for any resulting damages. For example, the limited liability company might incur substantial expenses in replacing the member's expertise, reputation, or creditworthiness.

In effect, this subsection equates wrongful dissociation with breach of contract. Accordingly, courts should look to contract law to determine what consequential damages are recoverable. *See Hadley v. Baxendale*, 9 Exch. 341 (1854); RESTATEMENT (SECOND) OF CONTRACTS § 351 (1981); *see also Williams v. Hildebrand*, 247 S.W.2d 356, 358 (Ark. 1952) (interpreting UPA (1914) § 38(2)(a)(II), pertaining to wrongful dissolution, and stating that "the measure of damages, when the partnership was to have continued for a fixed term, is the profits that the injured partner would have received").

§ 602.   EVENTS CAUSING DISSOCIATION.

A person is dissociated as a member when:

(1) the limited liability company knows or has notice of the person's express will to withdraw as a member, but, if the person has specified a withdrawal date later than the date the company knew or had notice, on that later date;

(2) an event stated in the operating agreement as causing the person's dissociation occurs;

(3) the person's entire interest is transferred in a foreclosure sale under Section 503(f);

(4) the person is expelled as a member pursuant to the operating agreement;

(5) the person is expelled as a member by the affirmative vote or consent of all the other members if:

(A) it is unlawful to carry on the limited liability company's activities and affairs with the person as a member;

(B) there has been a transfer of all the person's transferable interest in the company, other than:

(i) a transfer for security purposes; or

(ii) a charging order in effect under Section 503 which has not been foreclosed;

(C) the person is an entity and:

(i) the company notifies the person that it will be expelled as a member because the person has filed a statement of dissolution or the equivalent, the person has been administratively dissolved, the person's charter or the equivalent has been revoked, or the person's right to conduct business has been suspended by the person's jurisdiction of formation; and

(ii) not later than 90 days after the notification, the statement of dissolution or the equivalent has not been withdrawn, rescinded, or revoked, the person has not been reinstated, or the person's charter or the equivalent or right to conduct business has not been reinstated; or

(D) the person is an unincorporated entity that has been dissolved and whose activities and affairs are being wound up;

(6) on application by the limited liability company or a member in a direct action under Section 801, the person is expelled as a member by judicial order because the person:

(A) has engaged or is engaging in wrongful conduct that has affected adversely and materially, or will affect adversely and materially, the company's activities and affairs;

(B) has committed willfully or persistently, or is committing willfully or persistently, a material breach of the operating agreement or a duty or obligation under Section 409; or

(C) has engaged or is engaging in conduct relating to the company's activities and affairs which makes it not reasonably practicable to carry on the activities and affairs with the person as a member;

(7) in the case of an individual:

(A) the individual dies; or

(B) in a member-managed limited liability company:

(i) a guardian or general conservator for the individual is appointed; or

(ii) a court orders that the individual has otherwise become incapable of performing the individual's duties as a member under this [act] or the operating agreement;

(8) in a member-managed limited liability company, the person:

(A) becomes a debtor in bankruptcy;

(B) signs an assignment for the benefit of creditors; or

(C) seeks, consents to, or acquiesces in the appointment of a trustee, receiver, or liquidator of the person or of all or substantially all the person's property;

(9) in the case of a person that is a testamentary or inter vivos trust or is acting as a member by virtue of being a trustee of such a trust, the trust's entire transferable interest in the limited liability company is distributed;

(10) in the case of a person that is an estate or is acting as a member by virtue of being a personal representative of an estate, the estate's entire transferable interest in the limited liability company is distributed;

(11) in the case of a person that is not an individual, the existence of the person terminates;

(12) the limited liability company participates in a merger under [Article] 10 and:

(A) the company is not the surviving entity; or

(B) otherwise as a result of the merger, the person ceases to be a member;

(13) the limited liability company participates in an interest exchange under [Article] 10 and, as a result of the interest exchange, the person ceases to be a member;

(14) the limited liability company participates in a conversion under [Article] 10;

(15) the limited liability company participates in a domestication under [Article] 10 and, as a result of the domestication, the person ceases to be a member; or

(16) the limited liability company dissolves and completes winding up.

Comment

This section mostly states default rules, which the operating agreement may vary. However, it would make no sense to vary some of the rules—*e.g.,* to provide that the death of a member who is an individual does not cause the individual's dissociation as a member, Paragraph (7)(A), or that an entity remains a member even *after* the existence of the person has terminated. Paragraph (11).

Paragraph (1)—Operating agreements often require notice of dissociation to be in writing and to specify the effective date of the dissociation.

Paragraph (3)—The cited section pertains to a charging order against the transferable interest of the sole member of a limited liability company.

Paragraph (4)—Many operating agreements provide for "no cause" expulsion, and courts considering such provisions will likely look to cases addressing the issue in the context of partnerships. In that context, courts have taken somewhat different approaches. *Compare Gelder Med. Grp. v. Webber*, 363 N.E.2d 573, 576 (N.Y. 1977), *with Winston & Strawn v. Nosal*, 664 N.E.2d 239, 245 (Ill. App. Ct. 1996). *See also* the comment to Section 409(d) (stating and explaining the implied contractual covenant of good faith and fair dealing).

Paragraph (5)(B)—This paragraph permits expulsion when a member no longer has any "skin in the game." Under this paragraph (unless the operating agreement provides otherwise), a member's transferee can protect itself from the vulnerability of "bare naked assignee" status, Section 107(b), cmt., by obligating the member/transferor to retain a one-percent interest and exercise the member's governance rights (including the right to bring a derivative suit) to protect the transferee's interests.

Paragraph (6)—The reference to "a direct action under Section 801(b)" reflects the "separate entity" nature of a limited liability company. Section 801(b) limits a member's standing to bring a direct action to circumstances in which the member can "plead and prove an actual or threatened injury that is not solely the result of an injury suffered or threatened to be suffered by the limited liability company." For example, a member might invoke Paragraph (6)(B) if another member's breach of the operating agreement harmed the first member directly. If a member has suffered only indirect harm, the Paragraph (6)(B) claim belongs to the LLC and not the member. If the LLC fails to bring suit, the member may assert the claim derivatively. *See* Sections 802–06.

Although the operating agreement can revise or eliminate the possibility of judicial expulsion, doing so requires careful planning. *Cf. Huatuco v. Satellite Healthcare*, CV 8465-VCG, 2013 WL 6460898, at *1, n.2 (Del. Ch. Dec. 9, 2013) (stating that "the right to judicial dissolution is a default right which the parties may eschew by contract" while reserving the question of "[w]hether the parties may, by contract, divest this Court of its authority to order a dissolution in all circumstances, even where it appears manifest that equity so requires—leaving, for instance, irreconcilable members locked away together forever like some alternative entity version of Sartre's Huis Clos").

For examples of conduct warranting an expulsion order, see *All Saints Univ. of Med. Aruba v. Chilana*, A-2628-09T1, 2012 WL 6652510 (N.J. Super. Ct. App. Div. Dec. 24, 2012) (discussing a pattern of conduct); *Sherwood Park Bus. Ctr., L.L.C. v. Taggart*, 323 P.3d 551, 561 (Or. Ct. App. 2014) (upholding expulsion of a member who "had stolen a large amount of money from [the limited liability company], had intentionally failed to provide financial information, and had made himself unavailable to carry on the business"); *CCD, L.C. v. Millsap,* 116 P.3d 366, 373 (Utah 2005) (holding that a member's "misappropriat[ion of] trust account funds totaling at least $11,540.06 for his personal use" warranted expulsion, where the member's "misconduct continued the pattern of behavior that [had previously] resulted in losses to the company of $625,000[, where the new misconduct] . . . took place after [the member's] prior wrongdoing had been discovered and after [the limited liability company] had assented to permit [the member] to atone for his misdeeds by fulfilling the terms of the amended operating agreement").

For an analysis that helps distinguish Paragraph (6)(C) from Paragraphs (6)(A) and (B), see *All Saints Univ. of Med. Aruba v. Chilana*, A-2628-09T1, 2012 WL 6652510, at *15 (N.J. Super. Ct. App. Div. Dec. 24, 2012) (interpreting predecessor law and noting that the "not reasonably practicable standard" does not require a showing of wrongful conduct). *Cf. Dunnagan v. Watson*, 204 S.W.3d 30, 40 (Tex. Ct. App. 2006) (same issue in the context of dissolution). Where grounds exist for both dissociation and dissolution, a court has the discretion to choose between the alternatives. *Robertson v. Jacobs Cattle Co.*, 830 N.W.2d 191, 201–02 (Neb. 2013) (discussing analogous provisions of UPA (1997)). "[T]here is no textual basis for imposing a higher burden of proof for dissociation than dissolution." *Brennan v. Brennan Assocs.*, 977 A.2d 107, 121 (Conn. 2009) (general partnership).

Paragraph (6)(C)—This provision has an analog among the causes for dissolution. *See* Section 701(a)(4)(B).

Paragraph (7)(B)—This provision does not apply to a manager-managed limited liability company because, given the limited rights of non-manager members, the stated occurrences do not necessarily justify dissociation. For a parallel provision approach under the uniform limited partnership act, see ULPA §§ 601(b)(6) (2001) (Last Amended 2013) (limited partner), 603(6)(B) and (C) (general partner). As for the effect of the stated occurrences on a person's role as a manager, see Section 407(c)(4) (permitting the removal of a manager "at any time by the affirmative vote or consent of a majority of the members without notice or cause").

Paragraph 8(A)—This provision is subject to bankruptcy law. *See, e.g.,* 11 U.S.C.A. § 365(e) (invalidating "ipso facto" clauses, subject to some exceptions).

Paragraphs (9) and (10)—A change in trustee or personal representation does not cause dissociation.

Paragraph (11)—This provision is the entity analog to Paragraph (7)(A) (death of an individual). Although in theory the operating agreement could change this rule, doing so would be nonsensical. *See* the comment to Section 703(a) (noting that a terminated limited liability company cannot rescind its dissolution because "a 'dead' entity lacks both the capacity and power to bring itself back from the dead").

Paragraph (12)(A)—If a limited liability company disappears as part of a merger, no person can continue as a member of the company. When the merger takes effect, the members of the disappearing company are perforce dissociated. Depending on the plan of merger, those persons may become members of a surviving limited liability company. In those circumstances, the merger will have dissociated them from one LLC and admitted them into membership in the surviving LLC. *See* Sections 401(c)(2), 1026(c)(10).

Paragraph (12)(B)—It is possible for a plan of merger to "shuffle the equity" of the surviving entity, even to the extent of "taking out" some or all of the owners of the surviving entity. A reverse triangular merger involving a limited liability company as the surviving entity would dissociate all the members of the LLC.

Paragraph (14)—By definition, a limited liability company that converts ceases to be a limited liability company. *See* Section 1046. Thus, when the plan of conversion takes effect, all the members of the converted entity are dissociated from that entity. In many cases, those persons will all be owners of the converted entity. In some cases, the conversion will "shuffle the equity" and "take out" some of the members of the converting LLC.

Paragraph (15)—Domestication does not by itself dissociate a member, because the domesticated entity remains both a limited liability company and "the same entity without interruption as the domesticating company." Section 1056(a)(1)(B). However, an "equity shuffle" could dissociate a member.

§ 603. EFFECT OF DISSOCIATION.

(a) If a person is dissociated as a member:

(1) the person's right to participate as a member in the management and conduct of the limited liability company's activities and affairs terminates;

(2) the person's duties and obligations under Section 409 as a member end with regard to matters arising and events occurring after the person's dissociation; and

(3) subject to Section 504 and [Article] 10, any transferable interest owned by the person in the person's capacity as a member immediately before dissociation is owned by the person solely as a transferee.

(b) A person's dissociation as a member does not of itself discharge the person from any debt, obligation, or other liability to the limited liability company or the other members which the person incurred while a member.

Comment

Subsection (a)—This provision makes no reference to power-to-bind matters, because the act provides that a member *qua* member has no power to bind the LLC. Section 301.

Subsection (a)(2)—This provision establishes a dividing line, separating out "matters arising and events occurring after the person's dissociation." If the limited liability company has continuing projects with clients, ongoing relationships with clients, or both, the dividing line requires special attention with regard to non-competition and partnership opportunities duties. *See* Section 409(b)(1), (3).

Disputes involving law firms have generated much of the relevant case law. *See, e.g., Jewel v. Boxer*, 156 Cal. App. 3d 171, 175 (Cal. Ct. App. 1984); *Meehan v. Shaughnessy*, 535 N.E.2d 1255, 1257 (Mass. 1989). To a large extent, a well-drawn operating agreement can delineate the parties' respective rights and responsibilities and thereby avoid problems. However, if the company becomes insolvent, the bankruptcy court may well scrutinize the members' *inter se* arrangements. *See Geron v. Robinson & Cole L.L.P.*, 476 B.R. 732, 743 (S.D.N.Y. 2012) (considering whether a law firm had "fraudulently transferred . . . assets when its partners adopted the Jewel Waiver [releasing rights recognized by *Jewel v. Boxer*] on the eve of dissolution without consideration").

This provision applies regardless of whether the limited liability company is member-managed or manager-managed. However, in the latter case, the pre-dissociation duties will be much narrower, because in a manager-managed LLC a member *qua* member has no management duties. Section 409(i)(1). But each member remains subject to the obligation of good faith and fair dealing. Section 409(i)(3).

This provision does not determine the effect of a person's dissociation as a member on the person's future obligations or rights under the operating agreement. Some contractual obligations typically extend beyond dissociation—*e.g.*, non-competition provisions, buyout arrangements. To the extent provisions of the operating agreement continue to apply, the common law obligation of good faith continues to apply as well. *See* the comment to Section 409(d) (explaining that the subsection "invokes the implied obligation that exists in every contract" as a matter of common law).

Subsection (a)(3)—This paragraph accords with Section 404(b)—dissociation does not result in a distribution. In general, when a person dissociates as a member, the person's rights as a member disappear and the person's status degrades to that of a mere transferee—even when the dissociation takes the form of expulsion. *All Saints Univ. of Med. Aruba v. Chilana*, A-2628-09T1, 2012 WL 6652510, at *12 (N.J. Super. Ct. App. Div. Dec. 24, 2012).

Like most *inter se* rules in this act, this one is subject to the operating agreement. For example, the operating agreement has the power to provide for the buyout of a person's transferable interest in connection with the person's dissociation.

Section 504 provides additional information rights when an individual's death has caused dissociation. Article 10 covers organic transactions such as mergers and conversions.

Subsection (b)—In a member-managed limited liability company, a member's obligation to safeguard trade secrets and other confidential or proprietary information is incurred when the member learns or otherwise obtains the information. This subsection preserves the obligation post-dissociation. (In a manager-managed LLC, any obligations of a non-manager member viz-a-viz proprietary information would be a matter for the operating agreement, the obligation of good faith and fair dealing, or other law.)

[ARTICLE] 7

DISSOLUTION AND WINDING UP

§ 701. EVENTS CAUSING DISSOLUTION.

(a) A limited liability company is dissolved, and its activities and affairs must be wound up, upon the occurrence of any of the following:

(1) an event or circumstance that the operating agreement states causes dissolution;

(2) the affirmative vote or consent of all the members;

(3) the passage of 90 consecutive days during which the company has no members unless before the end of the period:

(A) consent to admit at least one specified person as a member is given by transferees owning the rights to receive a majority of distributions as transferees at the time the consent is to be effective; and

(B) at least one person becomes a member in accordance with the consent;

(4) on application by a member, the entry by [the appropriate court] of an order dissolving the company on the grounds that:

(A) the conduct of all or substantially all the company's activities and affairs is unlawful;

(B) it is not reasonably practicable to carry on the company's activities and affairs in conformity with the certificate of organization and the operating agreement; or

(C) the managers or those members in control of the company:

(i) have acted, are acting, or will act in a manner that is illegal or fraudulent; or

(ii) have acted or are acting in a manner that is oppressive and was, is, or will be directly harmful to the applicant; or

(5) the signing and filing of a statement of administrative dissolution by the [Secretary of State] under Section 708.

(b) In a proceeding brought under subsection (a)(4)(C), the court may order a remedy other than dissolution.

Comment

"Dissolution" has been a term of art in the law of unincorporated business organizations since at least the time of Roman law. JOSEPH STORY, COMMENTARIES ON THE LAW OF PARTNERSHIP § 266, at 408 (2d ed. 1850) ("The Roman law . . . declared, that partnership might be dissolved in various ways. . . ."). Dissolution does not end a limited liability company's existence but rather changes the purpose of that existence: "A dissolved limited liability company shall wind up its activities and affairs and . . . the company continues after dissolution only for the purpose of winding up." Section 702(a). The company may, but need not, filed a statement of dissolution. Section 702(b)(2)(A). The limited liability company terminates when winding up is complete. The company may, but need not, file a statement of termination. Section 702(b)(2)(F).

Except for Paragraphs (a)(4) and (5), this section comprises default rules. Paragraph 5 is fully mandatory, Section 105(c)(3)(B); Paragraph 4 is mandatory only with regard to the stated grounds for dissolution. *See* the comment to Section 105(c)(9). Moreover, an operating agreement can provide additional causes of dissolution. *See* Subsection (a)(1). Variations to the statutory causes of dissolution are commonplace.

Section 703 permits rescission of dissolution in some circumstances. In some circumstances, an amendment to the operating agreement might avert dissolution (*e.g.*, by revising an agreed-upon deadline for selling the LLC's assets and winding up the business). A retroactive amendment may also be possible. *See Kindred Ltd. P'ship v. Screen Actors Guild, Inc.*, CV082220PSGPJWX, 2009 WL 279080, at *5–6 (C.D. Cal. Feb. 3, 2009) (giving effect to an amendment that retroactively eliminated an event of dissolution; noting that UPA (1997) § 802(b) permitted a partnership to rescind dissolution).

Subsection (a)(4)—The operating agreement cannot vary the causes of dissolution stated in this provision. However, the operating agreement may contain a forum selection clause or change the forum from "the appropriate court" to binding arbitration. Section 105(c)(9), cmt.

As to whether the court of another jurisdiction can properly order dissolution of a limited liability company formed under this act, the majority rule is clearly no. "[T]he courts of several states have held that jurisdiction to dissolve a corporation rests only in the courts of the state of incorporation." *In re Blixseth*, 484 B.R. 360, 370 (B.A.P. 9th Cir. 2012) (citing cases, including a case involving an LLC). *But see In re Mercantile Guar. Co.*, 238 Cal. App. 2d 426, 430–33 (Cal. Ct. App. 1965) (explaining that "[w]e are . . . required to determine whether the courts of a state in which a foreign corporation has done business and in which its assets are there located have jurisdiction to wind up its affairs, even though the corporation was organized in another state," stating that "the question is not one of jurisdiction or power in the court of the state which is not the legal domicile of a foreign corporation, but it is a question . . . of the balance of convenience, of whether considerations of public policy, efficiency, expedience and justice to all parties interested demand that jurisdiction be retained in the foreign court, or that it be declined under the rule of forum *non conveniens*," and holding that "[t]he circumstances of the case at bench require a holding that the California courts assume jurisdiction of the winding up of [a Delaware corporation's] affairs preparatory to a dissolution").

Subsection (a)(4)(B)—The standard stated here is conventional, deriving originally from the law of limited partnerships. *See, e.g., Kirksey v. Grohmann*, 754 N.W.2d 825, 828–30 (S.D. 2008) (discussing cases and noting that "cases interpreting language similar to our statutory terminology, whether involving a partnership or a limited liability company, are instructive"). For discussion of the meaning of the standard, see *Venture Sales, L.L.C. v. Perkins*, 86 So. 3d 910, 914–15 (Miss. 2012) (discussing cases); *In re 1545 Ocean Ave., LLC*, 72 A.D.3d 121, 129–30 (N.Y. 2010) (same).

The court-ordered expulsion of a miscreant member can negate a claim for dissolution. *Dunbar Grp., LLC v. Tignor*, 267 Va. 361, 367–68, 593 S.E.2d 216, 219 (2004) ("Although Tignor's actions in [the] capacities [of member and manager of Xpert] had created numerous problems in the operation of Xpert, his expulsion as a member changed his role from one of an active participant in the management of Xpert to the more passive role of an investor in the company. The record fails to show that after this change in the daily management of Xpert, it would not be reasonably practicable for Xpert to carry on its business pursuant to its operating authority.").

However, where grounds exist for both dissociation and dissolution, a court has the discretion to choose between the alternatives. *Robertson v. Jacobs Cattle Co.*, 830 N.W.2d 191 201–02 (Neb. 2013). "[T]here is no textual basis for imposing a higher burden of proof for dissociation than dissolution." *Brennan v. Brennan Assocs.*, 977 A.2d 107, 121 (Conn. 2009) (general partnership).

This provision has an analog among the grounds for dissociation. *See* Section 602(6)(c).

Subsection (a)(4)(C)—The provision's reference to "those members in control of the company" implies that such members have a duty to avoid acting oppressively toward fellow members.

The act does not define "oppressively," but "oppression" is a concept well-grounded in the law of close corporations. *See, e.g., Kiriakides v. Atlas Food Sys. & Servs., Inc.*, 541 S.E.2d 257, 264–66 (S.C. 2001); Robert B. Thompson, *The Shareholder's Cause of Action for Oppression*, 48 Bus. Law. 69, 70 (1993) (referring to then "evolving cause of action of shareholder oppression"). In many jurisdictions the concept equates to or at least includes the frustration of the plaintiff's reasonable expectations. *Baur v. Baur Farms, Inc.*, 832 N.W.2d 663, 670 (Iowa 2013) (stating that "perhaps the most widely adopted [approach] links oppression to the frustration of the reasonable expectations of the corporation's shareholders"). (This concept of reasonable expectations is entirely separate from the "fruits of the bargain" and "reasonable expectations" language sometimes used in explaining the implied contractual obligation of good faith and fair dealing.)

Courts have extrapolated close corporation doctrine to unincorporated organizations. *See, e.g.*, *Alloy v. Wills Family Trust*, 944 A.2d 1234, 1262–64 (Md. Ct. Spec. App. 2008) (discussing cases). Indeed many cases simply conflate the two contexts. *E.g. Kohannim v. Katoli*, 08-11-00155-CV, 2013 WL 3943078, at *9 (Tex. Ct. App. July 24, 2013) ("A member oppression claim may exist when: (i) a majority shareholder's conduct substantially defeats the minority's expectations that objectively viewed, were both reasonable under the circumstances and central to the minority shareholder's decision to join the venture; or (ii) burdensome, harsh, or wrongful conduct, a lack of probity and fair dealing in the company's affairs to the prejudice of some members, or a visible departure from the standards of fair dealing, and a violation of fair play on which every shareholder who entrusts his money to a company is entitled to rely."); *Pinnacle Data Servs., Inc. v. Gillen*, 104 S.W.3d 188, 196 (Tex. Ct. App. 2003) (explaining oppression of "members" in terms of shareholder oppression).

However, applying close corporation law to limited liability companies requires some caution. Close corporation law developed in part because the standard corporate governance structure exalts majority power and does not presuppose contractual relationships among the shareholders.

In contrast, while an LLC depends on the sovereign for legal existence and the all-important liability shield, LLC governance is fundamentally contractual. Therefore, in most situations, the operating agreement should reflect and comprise members' reasonable expectations. As a result, a court considering a claim of oppression by an LLC member should consider, with regard to each reasonable expectation invoked by the plaintiff, whether the expectation: (i) contradicts any term of the operating agreement or any reasonable implication of any term of that agreement; (ii) was central to the plaintiff's decision to become a member of the limited liability company or for a substantial time has been centrally important in the member's continuing membership; (iii) was known to other members, who expressly or impliedly acquiesced in it; (iv) is consistent with the reasonable expectations of all the members, including expectations pertaining to the plaintiff's conduct; and (v) is otherwise reasonable under the circumstances. *See* the comment to Sections 102(13) ("[T]he definition [of 'operating agreement'] puts no limits on the form of the operating agreement. To the contrary, the definition contains the phrase 'whether oral, implied, in a record, or in any combination thereof.' "), Section 105(a)(4), cmt. (explaining how a written operating agreement, if properly drafted, can provide that amendments must be in writing and signed to be effective).

Example: From its formation, Work-Here, LLC has had three members, been member-managed, involved all three members in company operations, and allocated distributions in part in reference to the members' work for the company. The operating agreement is brief, informal, contains no integration clause, and makes no reference to a member's right to work for the company.

After ten years, two of the members: (i) take a vote; (ii) purport to oust the third member from any continuing role in company operations; and (iii) announce that the third member's distributions will be substantially reduced.

The ousted member has at least three theories of recovery:

- breach of an implied-in-fact term of the operating agreement, under which each member is entitled to work for the company and be compensated for the work;

- violation of Section 407(b)(4)(A) (requiring "[t]he affirmative vote or consent of all the members . . . to . . . undertake an act outside the ordinary course of the activities and affairs of the company"); and

- oppression under Section 701(4)(C)(ii).

On the limited facts stated, these theories are undoubtedly plausible, although of course not necessarily persuasive. *See* Section 409(d) (incorporating "the contractual obligation of good faith and fair dealing").

Subsection (a)(5)—The operating agreement may not vary this provision.

Subsection (b)—In the close corporation context, many courts have reached this position without express statutory authority, most often with regard to court-ordered buyouts of oppressed shareholders. *See, e.g., Kirtz v. Grossman*, 463 S.W.2d 541, 545 (Mo. Ct. App. 1971) (per curiam); *Brenner v. Berkowitz*, 634 A.2d 1019, 1031 (N.J. 1993); *N.D. ex rel. Heitkamp v. Family Life Servs.*, 616 N.W.2d 826, 838 (N.D. 2000); *Baker v. Commercial Body Builders, Inc.*, 507 P.2d 387, 394–96 (Or. 1973); *Davis v. Sheerin*, 754 S.W.2d 375, 380 (Tex. Ct. App. 1988). *Contra White v. Perkins*, 189 S.E.2d 315, 320 (Va. 1972).

This subsection saves courts and litigants the trouble of re-inventing that wheel in the LLC context. However, unlike Subsection (a)(4), Subsection (b) can be overridden by the operating agreement. Thus, the members may agree to restrict or eliminate a court's power to craft a lesser remedy, even to the extent of confining the court (and themselves) to the all-or-nothing remedy of dissolution.

§ 702.   WINDING UP.

(a) A dissolved limited liability company shall wind up its activities and affairs and, except as otherwise provided in Section 703, the company continues after dissolution only for the purpose of winding up.

(b) In winding up its activities and affairs, a limited liability company:

(1) shall discharge the company's debts, obligations, and other liabilities, settle and close the company's activities and affairs, and marshal and distribute the assets of the company; and

(2) may:

(A) deliver to the [Secretary of State] for filing a statement of dissolution stating the name of the company and that the company is dissolved;

(B) preserve the company activities, affairs, and property as a going concern for a reasonable time;

(C) prosecute and defend actions and proceedings, whether civil, criminal, or administrative;

(D) transfer the company's property;

(E) settle disputes by mediation or arbitration;

(F) deliver to the [Secretary of State] for filing a statement of termination stating the name of the company and that the company is terminated; and

(G) perform other acts necessary or appropriate to the winding up.

(c) If a dissolved limited liability company has no members, the legal representative of the last person to have been a member may wind up the activities and affairs of the company. If the person does so, the person has the powers of a sole manager under Section 407(c) and is deemed to be a manager for the purposes of Section 304(a).

(d) If the legal representative under subsection (c) declines or fails to wind up the limited liability company's activities and affairs, a person may be appointed to do so by the consent of transferees owning a majority of the rights to receive distributions as transferees at the time the consent is to be effective. A person appointed under this subsection:

(1) has the powers of a sole manager under Section 407(c) and is deemed to be a manager for the purposes of Section 304(a); and

(2) shall deliver promptly to the [Secretary of State] for filing an amendment to the company's certificate of organization stating:

(A) that the company has no members;

(B) the name and street and mailing addresses of the person; and

(C) that the person has been appointed pursuant to this subsection to wind up the company.

(e) [The appropriate court] may order judicial supervision of the winding up of a dissolved limited liability company, including the appointment of a person to wind up the company's activities and affairs:

(1) on the application of a member, if the applicant establishes good cause;

(2) on the application of a transferee, if:

(A) the company does not have any members;

(B) the legal representative of the last person to have been a member declines or fails to wind up the company's activities; and

(C) within a reasonable time following the dissolution a person has not been appointed pursuant to subsection (c); or

(3) in connection with a proceeding under Section 701(a)(4).

Comment

Under the default rules of this act, dissolution does not change governance arrangements. However, dissolution does change the context for determining, with regard to a member-managed LLC, whether a matter is in or outside "the ordinary course of the activities of the company." Section 407(b)(3), (4).

As for determining the post-dissolution power of a member or manager to bind the LLC, other law, primarily agency law, supplies the rules. Thus, dissolution does not change the applicable source of law for determining actual and apparent authority. Section 301, cmt.

Subsection (a)—*See* the comment to Section 701(a).

Subsection (b)—The particular circumstances determine how long winding up may continue without giving "good cause" for court intervention under Section 702(e). The case law is partnership law and applies by analogy. There is no "hard and fast" rule. *See, e.g., Mathis v. Meyeres*, 574 P.2d 447, 450 (Alaska 1978) (stating that we are aware of [no authority] requiring that deadlines be set in the winding up of a partnership"); *8182 Md. Assocs., Ltd. P'ship v. Sheehan*, 14 S.W.3d 576, 581 (Mo. 2000) ("The Uniform Partnership Law contemplates that dissolved partnerships may continue in business for a short, long or indefinite period of time . . . .") (quoting *Schoeller v. Schoeller*, 497 S.W.2d 860, 867 (Mo. Ct. App. 1973)).

"Winding up usually entails the time necessary for the partners to finish old business, collect and pay debts, and finally distribute remaining assets to the partners." *Gibson v. Deuth*, 270 N.W.2d 632, 635 (Iowa 1978). "Generally the best interests of the partnership will be served by winding up the partnership affairs as quickly as possible." *Doting v. Trunk*, 259 Mont. 343, 349, 856 P.2d 536, 540 (1993). However, in some circumstances, a long period of winding up is not only appropriate but necessary. *Lebanon Trotting Ass'n v. Battista*, 306 N.E.2d 769, 772 (Ohio Ct. App. 1972) ("[I]f the only means of availing the partners of the benefit of the value of the lease would be to continue to operate under such lease until its expiration, then such operation may continue as part of the winding up of the partnership affairs after dissolution. It is not necessary that a partnership, in the absence of the consent of all the partners, abandon a valuable asset upon dissolution merely because it may have no ready market value, but the value of such asset can continue to inure to the benefit of the partners through the continuation of the partnership after dissolution.")

Subsection (b)(2)(A) and (F)—For the constructive notice effect of a statement of dissolution or termination, see Sections 103(d)(2)(A) and (B) and 302(h).

Subsection (c)—Section 304 provides a shield for managers as well members against automatic, vicarious liability for an LLC's debts, obligations, and other liabilities. Section 407 provides default rules for a manager's actual authority. Some of those rules provide for consent by members. *See* Section 407(c)(3). Those rules are inapposite in the circumstances contemplated by this subsection.

Section 409 does not apply to a person appointed under this section. Such person will inevitably be an agent of the dissolved limited liability company, acting pursuant to a contract. Thus, agency and contract law will determine the person's duties.

Subsection (d)(1)—See the comment to Subsection (c).

Subsection (e)—Section 409 does not apply to a person appointed under this section. The applicable standards of conduct might come from any or all of these sources: the court order, state law pertaining to receiverships, agency law, and contract law.

Subsection (e)(1)—Managers do not have standing under this provision. If a non-member manager has so lost control of the limited liability company as to desire dissolution, the non-manager's remedy is to: (i) seek court enforcement of the relevant provisions of the operating agreement, management agreement, or both; or (ii) resign.

§ 703.   RESCINDING DISSOLUTION.

(a) A limited liability company may rescind its dissolution, unless a statement of termination applicable to the company has become effective, [the appropriate court] has entered an order under Section 701(a)(4) dissolving the company, or the [Secretary of State] has dissolved the company under Section 708.

(b) Rescinding dissolution under this section requires:

(1) the affirmative vote or consent of each member; and

(2) if the limited liability company has delivered to the [Secretary of State] for filing a statement of dissolution and:

(A) the statement has not become effective, delivery to the [Secretary of State] for filing of a statement of withdrawal under Section 208 applicable to the statement of dissolution; or

(B) if the statement of dissolution has become effective, delivery to the [Secretary of State] for filing of a statement of rescission stating the name of the company and that dissolution has been rescinded under this section.

(c) If a limited liability company rescinds its dissolution:

(1) the company resumes carrying on its activities and affairs as if dissolution had never occurred;

(2) subject to paragraph (3), any liability incurred by the company after the dissolution and before the rescission has becomes effective is determined as if dissolution had never occurred; and

(3) the rights of a third party arising out of conduct in reliance on the dissolution before the third party knew or had notice of the rescission may not be adversely affected.

Comment

The Harmonization Project added this section, which is based on UPA (1997) § 802(b)(1) permitting the partners to "waive the right to have the partnership's business wound up and the partnership terminated" after which "the partnership resumes carrying on its business as if dissolution had never occurred").

Subsection (a)—The first exclusion results inevitably from the effect of a statement of termination (*i.e.*, the limited liability company ceases to exist). A "dead" entity lacks both the capacity and power to bring itself back from the dead.

The second and third exclusions pertain to dissolutions affected by outsiders (*i.e.*, the court and the filing office).

Subsections (b)(1)—The requirement of unanimous consent protects any vested rights of, or reliance by, members. However, the operating agreement may vary this provision.

Subsection (c)(3)—This paragraph protects third parties. *E.g., Neurobehavorial Assocs., P.A. v. Cypress Creek Hosp., Inc.*, 995 S.W.2d 326, 331 (Tex. Ct. App. 1999) ("If the Hospital had the right to terminate the Agreement when it did because the Association was then dissolved, then even though the Association can revoke articles of dissolution and have that relate back to the date of dissolution, it would be grossly unfair to let the Association assert its ex post facto change as a defense. Surely the Association would be estopped from doing so, having created the very conditions that gave the Hospital the correct impression that it was then dissolved.").

§ 704. KNOWN CLAIMS AGAINST DISSOLVED LIMITED LIABILITY COMPANY.

(a) Except as otherwise provided in subsection (d), a dissolved limited liability company may give notice of a known claim under subsection (b), which has the effect provided in subsection (c).

(b) A dissolved limited liability company may in a record notify its known claimants of the dissolution. The notice must:

(1) specify the information required to be included in a claim;

(2) state that a claim must be in writing and provide a mailing address to which the claim is to be sent;

(3) state the deadline for receipt of a claim, which may not be less than 120 days after the date the notice is received by the claimant; and

(4) state that the claim will be barred if not received by the deadline.

(c) A claim against a dissolved limited liability company is barred if the requirements of subsection (b) are met and:

(1) the claim is not received by the specified deadline; or

(2) if the claim is timely received but rejected by the company:

(A) the company causes the claimant to receive a notice in a record stating that the claim is rejected and will be barred unless the claimant commences an action against the company to enforce the claim not later than 90 days after the claimant receives the notice; and

(B) the claimant does not commence the required action not later than 90 days after the claimant receives the notice.

(d) This section does not apply to a claim based on an event occurring after the date of dissolution or a liability that on that date is contingent.

Comment

Sections 704 through 706 provide rules under which a dissolved limited liability company may achieve finality with regard to claims.

This section is derived almost verbatim from Model Business Corporation Act section 14.06.

§ 705. OTHER CLAIMS AGAINST DISSOLVED LIMITED LIABILITY COMPANY.

(a) A dissolved limited liability company may publish notice of its dissolution and request persons having claims against the company to present them in accordance with the notice.

(b) A notice under subsection (a) must:

(1) be published at least once in a newspaper of general circulation in the [county] in this state in which the dissolved limited liability company's principal office is located or, if the principal office is not located in this state, in the [county] in which the office of the company's registered agent is or was last located;

(2) describe the information required to be contained in a claim, state that the claim must be in writing, and provide a mailing address to which the claim is to be sent; and

(3) state that a claim against the company is barred unless an action to enforce the claim is commenced not later than three years after publication of the notice.

(c) If a dissolved limited liability company publishes a notice in accordance with subsection (b), the claim of each of the following claimants is barred unless the claimant commences an action to enforce the claim against the company not later than three years after the publication date of the notice:

(1) a claimant that did not receive notice in a record under Section 704;

(2) a claimant whose claim was timely sent to the company but not acted on; and

(3) a claimant whose claim is contingent at, or based on an event occurring after, the date of dissolution.

(d) A claim not barred under this section or Section 704 may be enforced:

(1) against a dissolved limited liability company, to the extent of its undistributed assets; and

(2) except as otherwise provided in Section 706, if assets of the company have been distributed after dissolution, against a member or transferee to the extent of that person's proportionate share of the claim or of the company's assets distributed to the member or transferee after dissolution, whichever is less, but a person's total liability for all claims under this paragraph may not exceed the total amount of assets distributed to the person after dissolution.

Comment

This section is derived almost verbatim from Model Business Corporation Act section 14.07.

Subsection (d)(2)—Liability under this paragraph extends to those who have received distributions under a charging order. *See* the comment to Section 502(a) (explaining that the beneficiary of a charging order is a transferee). Unlike Section 406(c) (recapture of improper distributions), this paragraph contains no "knowledge" element.

§ 706.   COURT PROCEEDINGS.

(a) A dissolved limited liability company that has published a notice under Section 705 may file an application with [the appropriate court] in the [county] where the company's principal office is located or, if the principal office is not located in this state, where the office of its registered agent is or was last located, for a determination of the amount and form of security to be provided for payment of claims that are reasonably expected to arise after the date of dissolution based on facts known to the company and:

(1) at the time of application:

(A) are contingent; or

(B) have not been made known to the company; or

(2) are based on an event occurring after the date of dissolution.

(b) Security is not required for any claim that is or is reasonably anticipated to be barred under Section 705.

(c) Not later than 10 days after the filing of an application under subsection (a), the dissolved limited liability company shall give notice of the proceeding to each claimant holding a contingent claim known to the company.

(d) In a proceeding under this section, the court may appoint a guardian ad litem to represent all claimants whose identities are unknown. The reasonable fees and expenses of the guardian, including all reasonable expert witness fees, must be paid by the dissolved limited liability company.

(e) A dissolved limited liability company that provides security in the amount and form ordered by the court under subsection (a) satisfies the company's obligations with respect to claims that are contingent, have not been made known to the company, or are based on an event occurring after the date of dissolution, and such claims may not be enforced against a member or transferee on account of assets received in liquidation.

Comment

This section is derived almost verbatim from Model Business Corporation Act section 14.08.

§ 707.   DISPOSITION OF ASSETS IN WINDING UP.

(a) In winding up its activities and affairs, a limited liability company shall apply its assets to discharge the company's obligations to creditors, including members that are creditors.

(b) After a limited liability company complies with subsection (a), any surplus must be distributed in the following order, subject to any charging order in effect under Section 503:

(1) to each person owning a transferable interest that reflects contributions made and not previously returned, an amount equal to the value of the unreturned contributions; and

(2) among persons owning transferable interests in proportion to their respective rights to share in distributions immediately before the dissolution of the company.

(c) If a limited liability company does not have sufficient surplus to comply with subsection (b)(1), any surplus must be distributed among the owners of transferable interests in proportion to the value of the respective unreturned contributions.

(d) All distributions made under subsections (b) and (c) must be paid in money.

Comment

Subsection (a)—This subsection is non-waivable as to creditors who are not members. *See* Section 105(c)(15) (stating that the operating agreement may not "restrict the rights under this [act] of a person other than a member or manager"). However, if a creditor is willing, a dissolved limited liability company may certainly make agreements with the creditor specifying the terms under which the LLC will "discharge its obligations" to the creditor.

Subsections (b), (c) and (d)—For the most part, these subsections state default rules. For example, operating agreements often provide for different distribution rights upon liquidation than during operations. However, distributions under these subsections (or otherwise under the operating agreement) are subject to Section 503 (charging orders). As to the extent the operating agreement can be amended to affect the distribution rights of persons already transferees, see Section 107(b).

§ 708. ADMINISTRATIVE DISSOLUTION.

(a) The [Secretary of State] may commence a proceeding under subsection (b) to dissolve a limited liability company administratively if the company does not:

(1) pay any fee, tax, interest, or penalty required to be paid to the [Secretary of State] not later than [six months] after it is due;

(2) deliver [an annual] [a biennial] report to the [Secretary of State] not later than [six months] after it is due; or

(3) have a registered agent in this state for [60] consecutive days.

(b) If the [Secretary of State] determines that one or more grounds exist for administratively dissolving a limited liability company, the [Secretary of State] shall serve the company with notice in a record of the [Secretary of State's] determination.

(c) If a limited liability company, not later than [60] days after service of the notice under subsection (b), does not cure or demonstrate to the satisfaction of the [Secretary of State] the nonexistence of each ground determined by the [Secretary of State], the [Secretary of State] shall administratively dissolve the company by signing a statement of administrative dissolution that recites the grounds for dissolution and the effective date of dissolution. The [Secretary of State] shall file the statement and serve a copy on the company pursuant to Section 210.

(d) A limited liability company that is administratively dissolved continues in existence as an entity but may not carry on any activities except as necessary to wind up its activities and affairs and liquidate its assets under Sections 702, 704, 705, 706, and 707, or to apply for reinstatement under Section 709.

(e) The administrative dissolution of a limited liability company does not terminate the authority of its registered agent.

Comment

Many failures to comply with statutory requirements that may give rise to administrative dissolution occur because of oversight or inadvertence and are usually corrected promptly when brought to the entity's attention. Subsections (b) and (c) therefore provide a mandatory notice by the filing office to each limited liability company subject to administrative dissolution and a sixty-day grace period following the notice before the statement of administrative dissolution may be filed.

In most instances, the issue whether the limited liability company is subject to administrative dissolution will not be controverted. If a limited liability company is administratively dissolved, it may petition the filing office for reinstatement under Section 709 and, if reinstatement is denied, the company may appeal to the courts under Section 710.

As a practical matter, administrative dissolution permits the filing office to clear the record of "dead wood" and free up names.

§ 709.   REINSTATEMENT.

(a) A limited liability company that is administratively dissolved under Section 708 may apply to the [Secretary of State] for reinstatement [not later than [two] years after the effective date of dissolution]. The application must state:

(1) the name of the company at the time of its administrative dissolution and, if needed, a different name that satisfies Section 112;

(2) the address of the principal office of the company and the name and street and mailing addresses of its registered agent;

(3) the effective date of the company's administrative dissolution; and

(4) that the grounds for dissolution did not exist or have been cured.

(b) To be reinstated, a limited liability company must pay all fees, taxes, interest, and penalties that were due to the [Secretary of State] at the time of the company's administrative dissolution and all fees, taxes, interest, and penalties that would have been due to the [Secretary of State] while the company was administratively dissolved.

(c) If the [Secretary of State] determines that an application under subsection (a) contains the required information, is satisfied that the information is correct, and determines that all payments required to be made to the [Secretary of State] by subsection (b) have been made, the [Secretary of State] shall:

(1) cancel the statement of administrative dissolution and prepare a statement of reinstatement that states the [Secretary of State's] determination and the effective date of reinstatement; and

(2) file the statement of reinstatement and serve a copy on the limited liability company.

(d) When reinstatement under this section has become effective, the following rules apply:

(1) The reinstatement relates back to and takes effect as of the effective date of the administrative dissolution.

(2) The limited liability company resumes carrying on its activities and affairs as if the administrative dissolution had not occurred.

(3) The rights of a person arising out of an act or omission in reliance on the dissolution before the person knew or had notice of the reinstatement are not affected.

Comment

Some states require that reinstatement be sought within two years of administrative dissolution. Other states provide a longer time, or do not impose any time limit. Imposing no limit risks abuse by unscrupulous people seeking to reinstate and appropriate for improper ends a dormant limited liability company that has been abandoned by its members. On the other hand, reinstatement is intended as a safety net for the inattentive (*i.e.*, for people in charge of a limited liability company who have neglected to file an annual report or otherwise subjected the LLC to administrative dissolution). If the deadline comes too soon, the safety net may be gone before the inattentive even learn that administrative dissolution has occurred.

Subsection (a)(1)—This provision will apply if, before the limited liability company is reinstated, another entity has taken the company's name. *See* Section 112(b)(1).

Subsection (d)(3)—This paragraph provides an exception to the retroactive effect provided by this subsection's Paragraphs (1) and (2). The exception could preclude a reinstated LLC's use of its own name. *See* Section 112(b)(1) (indirectly permitting a limited liability company to use the name of an LLC that has been administratively dissolved). Comparable provisions exist in other uniform acts pertaining to entities. *E.g.*, UPA (1997) (Last Amended 2013) § 902(c)(2).

§ 710. JUDICIAL REVIEW OF DENIAL OF REINSTATEMENT.

(a) If the [Secretary of State] denies a limited liability company's application for reinstatement following administrative dissolution, the [Secretary of State] shall serve the company with a notice in a record that explains the reasons for the denial.

(b) A limited liability company may seek judicial review of denial of reinstatement in [the appropriate court] not later than [30] days after service of the notice of denial.

Comment

Because the grounds for administrative dissolution under Section 708 are limited and straightforward, it is unlikely there will be a dispute about whether a limited liability company has corrected the reasons for its administrative dissolution. If a dissolved limited liability company disagrees with a determination by the filing office to deny the company's application for reinstatement, this section gives the company a limited right to seek judicial review of the denial of reinstatement.

[ARTICLE] 8

ACTIONS BY MEMBERS

§ 801. DIRECT ACTION BY MEMBER.

(a) Subject to subsection (b), a member may maintain a direct action against another member, a manager, or the limited liability company to enforce the member's rights and protect the member's interests, including rights and interests under the operating agreement or this [act] or arising independently of the membership relationship.

(b) A member maintaining a direct action under this section must plead and prove an actual or threatened injury that is not solely the result of an injury suffered or threatened to be suffered by the limited liability company.

Comment

Subsection (a)—A member's rights under this subsection are subject to the rule of standing stated in Subsection (b). The phrase "otherwise protect the member's interests" pertains to remedies and creates no additional causes of action.

The last phrase of this subsection ("or arising independently . . . .") does not create any new rights, obligations, or remedies, and is included merely to emphasize that a person's membership in an LLC does not preclude the person from enforcing rights existing "independently of the membership relationship" (*e.g.*, as a creditor).

Subsection (b)—This subsection codifies the rule of standing that predominates in entity law. *See, e.g.*, *PacLink Commc'ns Int'l, Inc. v. Superior Court*, 109 Cal. Rptr. 2d 436, 441 (Cal. Ct. App. 2001) (noting that, "[i]n determining whether an individual action as opposed to a derivative action lies, a court looks at 'the gravamen of the wrong alleged in the pleadings' "; holding that "[a] contextual reading of [plaintiffs'] complaint makes clear that they are not suing based upon a claim that as members of the LLC they were entitled to a distribution which was not made, but instead are suing for financial injury caused by fraudulent transfer of the company's assets") (quoting *Nelson v. Anderson*, 84 Cal. Rptr. 2d 753. (Cal. Ct. App. 1999)); *Mallia v. PaineWebber, Inc.*, 889 F. Supp. 277, 282 (S.D. Tex. 1995) ("[T]o bring a direct representative action against a general partner, a limited partner must demonstrate either direct injury or an injury that exists independently of the partnerships.' "); *Tooley v. Donaldson, Lufkin, & Jenrette, Inc.*, 845 A.2d 1031, 1039 (Del. 2004) (expressly disapproving "both the concept of 'special injury' and the concept that a claim is necessarily derivative if it affects all stockholders equally;" stating that "a court should look to the nature of the wrong and to whom the relief should go;" requiring that any "claimed direct injury . . . be independent of any alleged injury to the [entity]"); *Tzolis v. Wolff*, 884 N.E.2d 1005, 1008 (N.Y. 2008) (holding that derivative actions exist under New York LLC law and referring to "the traditional line between direct and derivative claims"); *see also CML V, LLC v. Bax* 6 A.3d 238, 245 (Del. Ch. 2010) (noting that issues of standing viz-a-viz direct and derivative claims are comparable regardless of whether the entity is a limited partnership, a limited liability company, or a corporation), *aff'd*, 28 A.3d 1037 (Del. 2011).

The distinction between direct and derivative claims protects the operating agreement. If any member can sue directly over any management issue, the mere threat of suit can interfere with the members' agreed-upon arrangements.

Although in ordinary contractual situations it is axiomatic that each party to a contract has standing to sue for breach of that contract, within a limited liability company different circumstances typically exist. A member does not have a direct claim against a manager or another member merely because the manager or other member has breached the operating agreement. Likewise a member's violation of this act does not automatically create a direct claim for every other member. To have standing in his, her, or its own right, a member plaintiff must be able to show a harm that occurs independently of the harm caused or threatened to be caused to the limited liability company.

Example: Through grossly negligent conduct, in violation of Section 409(c), the manager of a manager-managed LLC reduces the net assets of an LLC by fifty percent, which in turns decreases the value of Member A's investment by $3,000,000. Member A has no standing to bring a direct claim; the damage is merely derivative of the damage first suffered by the LLC. Member A may, however, bring a derivative claim. Sections 802–806.

Example: Same facts, except in addition to violating Section 409(c), the manager's conduct breaches an express provision of the operating agreement to which Member A is a signatory. The analysis and the result are the same.

Example: An operating agreement defines "distributable cash" and requires the LLC to periodically distribute that cash among all members. The LLC's manager fails to distribute the cash. Each member has a direct claim against the manager and the LLC.

The reference to "threatened injury" is to encompass potential claims for preventative relief, such as a temporary restraining order or preliminary injunction.

This section's standing rule is subject to reasonable alterations by the operating agreement. *See* the comment to Section 105(c)(11).

§ 802.　　DERIVATIVE ACTION.

A member may maintain a derivative action to enforce a right of a limited liability company if:

(1) the member first makes a demand on the other members in a member-managed limited liability company, or the managers of a manager-managed limited liability company, requesting that they cause the company to bring an action to enforce the right, and the managers or other members do not bring the action within a reasonable time; or

(2) a demand under paragraph (1) would be futile.

Comment

Paragraph (1)—The demand requirement recognizes that, presumptively at least, the decision to cause a limited liability company to bring suit is a business decision, to be made by those who manage the business. Deborah A. DeMott, SHAREHOLDER DERIVATIVE ACTIONS: LAW AND PRACTICE § 5.9 (Westlaw, November 4, 2012) (Demand on directors—Rationales for demand).

Paragraph (2)—Some jurisdictions have a "universal demand" requirement, but the approach stated here is by far the majority one. Deborah A. DeMott, SHAREHOLDER DERIVATIVE ACTIONS: LAW AND PRACTICE § 5.12 (Westlaw, November 4, 2012).

§ 803. PROPER PLAINTIFF.

A derivative action to enforce a right of a limited liability company may be maintained only by a person that is a member at the time the action is commenced and:

(1) was a member when the conduct giving rise to the action occurred; or

(2) whose status as a member devolved on the person by operation of law or pursuant to the terms of the operating agreement from a person that was a member at the time of the conduct.

Comment

The rule stated here is conventional in both the law of unincorporated entities and corporate law. Persons dissociated as members have no standing to bring a derivative action. *A fortiori*, mere transferees have no standing. *See* the comments to Sections 107(b) and 502.

Paragraph (2)—This paragraph will be inapposite if the limited liability company has only two members, one of whom is the derivative plaintiff. In that limited circumstance, the plaintiff's death would cause the derivative action to abate. The "pick your partner" principal enshrined in Section 502 would prevent the decedent's heirs from succeeding to plaintiff status in the derivative action (except in the unlikely event that the remaining member consents to the heirs becoming members). The analysis and result will be the same if the derivative plaintiff is an entity whose existence terminates.

This act takes no position on whether:

- the death of member abates a direct claim against the LLC or a fellow member; and
- bringing a direct claim precludes a person from being a proper plaintiff for a derivative claim.

As to the latter issue, see, *e.g.*, *Cordts-Auth v. Crunk, L.L.C.*, 815 F. Supp. 2d 778, 793–94 (S.D.N.Y. 2011) (discussing the potential conflict of interest), *aff'd*, 479 F. App'x 375 (2d Cir. 2012).

§ 804. PLEADING.

In a derivative action, the complaint must state with particularity:

(1) the date and content of plaintiff's demand and the response to the demand by the managers or other members; or

(2) why demand should be excused as futile.

Comment

This section parallels Section 802. The pleading requirement first appeared in a uniform act in 1976. ULPA (1976) § 1003.

§ 805. SPECIAL LITIGATION COMMITTEE.

(a) If a limited liability company is named as or made a party in a derivative proceeding, the company may appoint a special litigation committee to investigate the claims asserted in the proceeding and determine whether pursuing the action is in the best interests of the company. If the company appoints a special litigation committee, on motion by the committee made in the name of the company, except for good cause shown, the court shall stay discovery for the time reasonably necessary to permit the committee to make its investigation. This subsection does not prevent the court from:

(1) enforcing a person's right to information under Section 410; or

(2) granting extraordinary relief in the form of a temporary restraining order or preliminary injunction.

(b) A special litigation committee must be composed of one or more disinterested and independent individuals, who may be members.

(c) A special litigation committee may be appointed:

(1) in a member-managed limited liability company:

(A) by the affirmative vote or consent of a majority of the members not named as parties in the proceeding; or

(B) if all members are named as parties in the proceeding, by a majority of the members named as defendants; or

(2) in a manager-managed limited liability company:

(A) by a majority of the managers not named as parties in the proceeding; or

(B) if all managers are named as parties in the proceeding, by a majority of the managers named as defendants.

(d) After appropriate investigation, a special litigation committee may determine that it is in the best interests of the limited liability company that the proceeding:

(1) continue under the control of the plaintiff;

(2) continue under the control of the committee;

(3) be settled on terms approved by the committee; or

(4) be dismissed.

(e) After making a determination under subsection (d), a special litigation committee shall file with the court a statement of its determination and its report supporting its determination and shall serve each party with a copy of the determination and report. The court shall determine whether the members of the committee were disinterested and independent and whether the committee conducted its investigation and made its recommendation in good faith, independently, and with reasonable care, with the committee having the burden of proof. If the court finds that the members of the committee were disinterested and independent and that the committee acted in good faith, independently, and with reasonable care, the court shall enforce the determination of the committee. Otherwise, the court shall dissolve the stay of discovery entered under subsection (a) and allow the action to continue under the control of the plaintiff.

Comment

Although special litigation committees are best known in the corporate field, they are no more inherently corporate than derivative litigation or the notion that an organization is a person distinct from its owners. An "SLC" can serve as an ADR mechanism, help protect an agreed upon arrangement from strike suits, protect the interests of members who are neither plaintiffs nor defendants (if any), and bring the benefits of a specially tailored business judgment to any judicial decision.

This section's approach corresponds to established law in most jurisdictions, modified to fit the typical governance structures of a limited liability company. Use of an SLC is optional. An operating agreement can preclude the use of SLCs, rendering this section inapplicable, but cannot otherwise vary this section. *See* Section 105(c)(12).

Subsection (a)(1)—Section 410 pertains to information rights. On the availability of remedies pending the SLC's investigation, *compare* Section 410, *with Kaufman v. Computer Assocs. Int'l, Inc.*, No. Civ.A. 699-N, 2005 WL 3470589, at *1 (Del. Ch. Dec. 21, 2005) (presenting "the question of whether to stay a books and records action under 8 Del. C. § 220 at the request of a special litigation committee when a derivative action encompassing substantially the same allegations of wrongdoing filed by different plaintiffs is pending in another jurisdiction"; concluding "[f]or reasons that have much to do with the light burden imposed by the plaintiff's demand in this case . . . that the special litigation committee's motion to stay the books and records action should be denied").

Subsection (e)—The standard stated for judicial review of the SLC determination follows *Auerbach v. Bennett*, 393 N.E.2d 994 (N.Y. 1979) rather than *Zapata Corp. v. Maldonado*, 430 A.2d 779 (Del. 1981), because the latter's reference to a court's business judgment has generally not been followed in other states. In essence, an SLC is intended to function as a surrogate decision-maker, allowing the limited liability company to make what is fundamentally a business decision. If a court determines that "the members of the committee were disinterested and independent and whether the committee conducted its investigation and made its recommendation in good faith, independently, and with reasonable care, with the committee having the burden of proof," it makes no sense to substitute the court's legal judgment for the business judgment of the SLC.

Houle v. Low, 556 N.E.2d 51, 58 (Mass. 1990) contains an excellent explanation of the court's role in reviewing an SLC decision:

The value of a special litigation committee is coextensive with the extent to which that committee truly exercises business judgment. In order to ensure that special litigation committees do act for the [entity]'s best interest, a good deal of judicial oversight is necessary in each case. At the same time, however, courts must be careful not to usurp the committee's valuable role in exercising business judgment. . . . [A] special litigation committee must be independent, unbiased, and act in good faith. Moreover, such a committee must conduct a thorough and careful analysis regarding the plaintiff's derivative suit. . . . The burden of proving that these procedural requirements have been met must rest, in all fairness, on the party capable of making that proof—the [entity].

For an extensive discussion of how a court should approach the question of independence, see *Einhorn v. Culea*, 612 N.W.2d 78, 91 (Wis. 2000).

§ 806. PROCEEDS AND EXPENSES.

(a) Except as otherwise provided in subsection (b):

(1) any proceeds or other benefits of a derivative action, whether by judgment, compromise, or settlement, belong to the limited liability company and not to the plaintiff; and

(2) if the plaintiff receives any proceeds, the plaintiff shall remit them immediately to the company.

(b) If a derivative action is successful in whole or in part, the court may award the plaintiff reasonable expenses, including reasonable attorney's fees and costs, from the recovery of the limited liability company.

(c) A derivative action on behalf of a limited liability company may not be voluntarily dismissed or settled without the court's approval.

Comment

Subsection (c)—This provision is intended to prevent collusion.

[ARTICLE] 9

FOREIGN LIMITED LIABILITY COMPANIES

§ 901. GOVERNING LAW.

(a) The law of the jurisdiction of formation of a foreign limited liability company governs:

(1) the internal affairs of the company;

(2) the liability of a member as member and a manager as manager for a debt, obligation, or other liability of the company; and

(3) the liability of a series of the company.

(b) A foreign limited liability company is not precluded from registering to do business in this state because of any difference between the law of its jurisdiction of formation and the law of this state.

(c) Registration of a foreign limited liability company to do business in this state does not authorize the foreign company to engage in any activities and affairs or exercise any power that a limited liability company may not engage in or exercise in this state.

Comment

Subsection (a)—This subsection provides that the laws of the jurisdiction of formation of a foreign limited liability company, rather than the laws of this state, govern both the internal affairs of the foreign LLC and the liability of its members and managers for the obligations of the LLC. An operating agreement cannot change this provision. Section 105(c)(15).

This subdivision parallels Section 104 (pertaining to the governing law for domestic LLCs). *See* the comment to Section 104.

Subsection (a)(3)—The LLC statutes of several states authorize limited liability companies to have asset-partitioning series. According to those statutes, if series are properly created, a debt, obligation, or liability associated with the property of a particular series is enforceable only against property of that series, and not against the property of the LLC generally or any other series thereof.

This act does not provide for asset-partitioning series. However, under this provision, the law of this state will respect the "internal shields" created under the series provisions of another jurisdiction's limited liability company statute. This provision does *not* address the myriad of other unsettled issues pertaining to series.

For an explanation of how the asset-partitioning concept of series differs from the traditional concept, see Section 1031, comment.

Subsections (b) and (c)—These sections together make clear that, although a foreign limited liability company may not be denied registration simply because of a difference between the laws of its jurisdiction of formation and the laws of this state, the foreign limited liability company "may not engage in any activity or exercise any power that a limited liability company may not engage in or exercise in this state." Subsection (c).

§ 902.   REGISTRATION TO DO BUSINESS IN THIS STATE.

(a) A foreign limited liability company may not do business in this state until it registers with the [Secretary of State] under this [article].

(b) A foreign limited liability company doing business in this state may not maintain an action or proceeding in this state unless it is registered to do business in this state.

(c) The failure of a foreign limited liability company to register to do business in this state does not impair the validity of a contract or act of the company or preclude it from defending an action or proceeding in this state.

(d) A limitation on the liability of a member or manager of a foreign limited liability company is not waived solely because the company does business in this state without registering to do business in this state.

(e) Section 901(a) and (b) applies even if a foreign limited liability company fails to register under this [article].

Comment

Subsection (a)—Following a long-established tradition, this act does not state what constitutes "do[ing] business in this state." Instead, Section 905 provides a non-exhaustive list of "[a]ctivities of a foreign limited liability company which do not constitute doing business in this state."

Subsection (b)—The purpose of this subsection is to induce foreign limited liability companies to register without imposing harsh or erratic sanctions. Often the failure to register is a result of inadvertence or bona fide disagreement as to the scope of Section 905, which is necessarily imprecise. Thus, the imposition of harsh sanctions in those situations is inappropriate. The sanction of closing the courts of the state to suits brought by foreign LLCs that should have registered is not a punitive one. If a foreign LLC should have registered and failed to do so, it may still enforce its contractual and other rights simply by registering.

However, if a court dismisses a case under this subsection rather than staying the proceedings pending the foreign LLC's registration, a statute of limitations problem may occur. *See Corco, Inc. v. Ledar Transport, Inc.* 946 P.2d 1009, 1010 (Kan. Ct. App. 1997) ("[T]he proper remedy was to dismiss [the unregistered entity's] counterclaim without prejudice rather than with prejudice. This would leave [the entity] the opportunity to comply with the statutes and then reassert its claim against [the defendant]. On the other hand, it would also leave the risk that the statute of limitations might run against [the entity].").

This subsection does not prevent a foreign LLC that has failed to register from "defending" an action or proceeding. The distinction between "maintaining" an action or proceeding under this subsection and "defending" an action or proceeding under Subsection (c) is determined on the basis of whether affirmative relief is sought. A nonregistered foreign LLC may interpose any defense or permissive or mandatory counterclaim to defeat a claimed recovery, but may not obtain an affirmative judgment based on the counterclaim without first registering.

Subsection (c)—In addition to permitting a non-registered foreign LLC doing business in this state to defend (but not maintain) an action or proceeding, this section makes clear that failure to register does not impair the validity of a foreign LLC's acts.

Subsection (d)—This subsection preserves the effectiveness of a foreign LLC's liability shield applicable under the LLC's governing law.

§ 903. FOREIGN REGISTRATION STATEMENT.

To register to do business in this state, a foreign limited liability company must deliver a foreign registration statement to the [Secretary of State] for filing. The statement must state:

(1) the name of the company and, if the name does not comply with Section 112, an alternate name adopted pursuant to Section 906(a);

(2) that the company is a foreign limited liability company;

(3) the company's jurisdiction of formation;

(4) the street and mailing addresses of the company's principal office and, if the law of the company's jurisdiction of formation requires the company to maintain an office in that jurisdiction, the street and mailing addresses of the required office; and

(5) the name and street and mailing addresses of the company's registered agent in this state.

Comment

The foreign registration statement provides certain basic information about the foreign limited liability company to ensure that citizens of the state have access to that information in their dealings with the foreign limited liability company. The statement also facilitates making the foreign company subject to the jurisdiction of the courts of the state.

Once registered, a foreign limited liability company must file an annual/biennial report. Section 212.

§ 904. AMENDMENT OF FOREIGN REGISTRATION STATEMENT.

A registered foreign limited liability company shall deliver to the [Secretary of State] for filing an amendment to its foreign registration statement if there is a change in:

(1) the name of the company;

(2) the company's jurisdiction of formation;

(3) an address required by Section 903(4); or

(4) the information required by Section 903(5).

Comment

This section works in tandem with the annual/biennial report required by Section 212 to keep up to date the information of record in the office of the filing office about a registered foreign limited liability company.

§ 905. ACTIVITIES NOT CONSTITUTING DOING BUSINESS.

(a) Activities of a foreign limited liability company which do not constitute doing business in this state under this [article] include:

(1) maintaining, defending, mediating, arbitrating, or settling an action or proceeding;

(2) carrying on any activity concerning its internal affairs, including holding meetings of its members or managers;

(3) maintaining accounts in financial institutions;

(4) maintaining offices or agencies for the transfer, exchange, and registration of securities of the company or maintaining trustees or depositories with respect to those securities;

(5) selling through independent contractors;

(6) soliciting or obtaining orders by any means if the orders require acceptance outside this state before they become contracts;

(7) creating or acquiring indebtedness, mortgages, or security interests in property;

(8) securing or collecting debts or enforcing mortgages or security interests in property securing the debts and holding, protecting, or maintaining property;

(9) conducting an isolated transaction that is not in the course of similar transactions;

(10) owning, without more, property; and

(11) doing business in interstate commerce.

(b) A person does not do business in this state solely by being a member or manager of a foreign limited liability company that does business in this state.

(c) This section does not apply in determining the contacts or activities that may subject a foreign limited liability company to service of process, taxation, or regulation under law of this state other than this [act].

Comment

This act does not attempt to formulate an inclusive definition of what constitutes doing business in a state. Rather, the concept is defined in a negative fashion by Subsections (a) and (b), which state that certain activities do not constitute doing business.

In general terms, any conduct more regular, systematic, or extensive than that described in Subsection (a) constitutes doing business and requires the foreign limited liability company to register to do business. Typical conduct requiring registration includes maintaining an office to conduct local intrastate business, selling personal property not in interstate commerce, entering into contracts relating to the local business or sales, and owning or using real estate for general purposes. But the passive owning of real estate for investment purposes does not constitute doing business. *See* Subsection (a)(10).

The test of "doing business" defined in a negative way in Subsections (a) and (b) applies only to the question whether a foreign limited liability company's contacts with the state are such that it must register under this section. The test is not applicable to other questions such as whether the foreign LLC is amenable to service of process under state "long-arm" statutes or liable for state or local taxes. A foreign LLC that has registered (or is required to register) will generally be subject to suit and state taxation in the state, while a foreign LLC that is subject to service of process or state taxation in a state will not necessarily be required to register.

Subsection (a)—The list of activities set forth in this subsection is not exhaustive.

Subsection (a)(1)—A foreign limited liability company is not "doing business" solely because it resorts to the courts of the state to recover an indebtedness, enforce an obligation, recover possession of personal property, obtain the appointment of a receiver, intervene in a pending proceeding, bring a petition to compel arbitration, file an appeal bond, or pursue appellate remedies. Similarly, a foreign

LLC is not required to register merely because it files a complaint with a governmental agency or participates in an administrative proceeding within the state.

Subsection (a)(2)—A foreign limited liability company does not "do business" within a state under this section merely because some of its internal affairs occur within a state. Thus, a foreign LLC may hold meetings of its managers or members within a state without first registering. A foreign LLC also may maintain offices or agencies within a state relating solely to the transfer, exchange or registration of its interests without registering. Other activities relating to the internal affairs of the foreign LLC that do not constitute doing business under this section include having officers or representatives who reside within or are physically present in the state; while there, the officers or representatives may make executive decisions relating to the internal affairs of the foreign LLC without imposing on the foreign LLC the requirement that it register, if these activities are not so regular and systematic as to cause the residence to be viewed as a business office.

Subsection (a)(5)—Under this paragraph, a foreign limited liability company need not register if it sells goods in the state through independent contractors. These transactions are viewed as transactions by the independent contractors, not by the foreign LLC itself even though the foreign LLC sets some limits or ground rules for its contractors. If these controls are sufficiently pervasive, however, the foreign LLC may be deemed to be selling for itself in intrastate commerce, and not through the independent contractors and therefore engaged in doing business in the state.

Subsection (a)(7) and (8)—The mere act of making a loan by a foreign limited liability company that is not in the business of making loans does not constitute doing business in the state in which the loan is made. On the same theory, a foreign LLC may obtain security for the repayment of a loan, and foreclose or enforce the lien or security interest to collect the loan, without being deemed to be doing business. Similarly, a refunding or "roll over" of a loan or its adjustment or compromise does not involve doing business.

Subsection (a)(9)—The concept of "doing business" involves regular, repeated, and continuing business contacts of a local nature. A single agreement or isolated transaction within a state does not constitute doing business if there is no intention to repeat the transaction or engage in similar transactions. This act does not impose the limitation found in some statutes, such as section 15.01(b)(10) of the Model Business Corporation Act, that the isolated transaction be completed within thirty days. A foreign LLC should not be required to register simply because it engages in an isolated transaction that takes longer than thirty days to complete.

Subsection (a)(11)—A foreign limited liability company is not "doing business" within the meaning of this section if it is transacting business in interstate commerce. *See* Subsection (a)(6) (stating that soliciting or obtaining orders that must be accepted outside the state before they become contracts is not "doing business" within the meaning of this section).

These exclusions reflect the provisions of the United States Constitution that grant to the United States Congress exclusive power over interstate commerce, and preclude states from imposing restrictions or conditions upon this commerce. This subsection should be construed in a manner consistent with judicial decisions under the United States Constitution. Under those decisions, a foreign entity is not required to register even though it sells goods within the state if they are shipped to the purchasers in interstate commerce. Thus, a foreign LLC need not register even if it also does work and performs acts within the state incidental to the interstate business (*e.g.*, if it takes or enforces a security interest incidental to these transactions). Nor is it required to register merely because it sends traveling salespeople or solicitors into a state so long as contracts are not made within the state. Similarly, an office may be maintained by a foreign LLC in this state without registering if the office's functions relate solely to interstate commerce. Purchases of goods may of course be in interstate commerce as readily as sales. Thus, the purchase of personal property in this state by a foreign limited liability company for shipment in interstate commerce out of the state does not require the entity to register.

§ 906. NONCOMPLYING NAME OF FOREIGN LIMITED LIABILITY COMPANY.

(a) A foreign limited liability company whose name does not comply with Section 112 may not register to do business in this state until it adopts, for the purpose of doing business in this state, an alternate name that complies with Section 112. A company that registers under an alternate name under this subsection need not comply with [this state's assumed or fictitious name statute]. After registering to do business in this state with an alternate name, a company shall do business in this state under:

(1) the alternate name;

(2) the company's name, with the addition of its jurisdiction of formation; or

(3) a name the company is authorized to use under [this state's assumed or fictitious name statute].

(b) If a registered foreign limited liability company changes its name to one that does not comply with Section 112, it may not do business in this state until it complies with subsection (a) by amending its registration to adopt an alternate name that complies with Section 112.

Comment

A foreign limited liability company must register under its true name if that name satisfies the requirements of Section 112. If the true name is unavailable because it is not distinguishable upon the records of the filing office from a name already in use or reserved or registered, the foreign LLC may use an alternate name.

A foreign limited liability company that registers to do business in the state may do business under a fictitious name to the same extent as a domestic entity.

§ 907. WITHDRAWAL DEEMED ON CONVERSION TO DOMESTIC FILING ENTITY OR DOMESTIC LIMITED LIABILITY PARTNERSHIP.

A registered foreign limited liability company that converts to a domestic limited liability partnership or to a domestic entity whose formation requires delivery of a record to the [Secretary of State] for filing is deemed to have withdrawn its registration on the effective date of the conversion.

Comment

When a registered foreign limited liability company has converted to a domestic "filing entity" or domestic limited liability partnership, information about the entity in its capacity as a domestic entity will continue to be of record in the filing office. At that point, there is no further reason for the entity to be registered as a foreign LLC, and this section automatically treats its prior registration as withdrawn.

§ 908. WITHDRAWAL ON DISSOLUTION OR CONVERSION TO NONFILING ENTITY OTHER THAN LIMITED LIABILITY PARTNERSHIP.

(a) A registered foreign limited liability company that has dissolved and completed winding up or has converted to a domestic or foreign entity whose formation does not require the public filing of a record, other than a limited liability partnership, shall deliver a statement of withdrawal to the [Secretary of State] for filing. The statement must state:

(1) in the case of a company that has completed winding up:

(A) its name and jurisdiction of formation;

(B) that the company surrenders its registration to do business in this state; and

(2) in the case of a company that has converted:

(A) the name of the converting company and its jurisdiction of formation;

(B) the type of entity to which the company has converted and its jurisdiction of formation;

(C) that the converted entity surrenders the converting company's registration to do business in this state and revokes the authority of the converting company's registered agent to act as registered agent in this state on behalf of the company or the converted entity; and

(D) a mailing address to which service of process may be made under subsection (b).

(b) After a withdrawal under this section has become effective, service of process in any action or proceeding based on a cause of action arising during the time the foreign limited liability company was registered to do business in this state may be made pursuant to Section 119.

Comment

When a registered foreign limited liability company has dissolved and completed winding up, or has converted to a "nonfiling entity" other than a limited liability partnership, there is no further reason for information about the entity to appear in the records of the filing office. This section thus requires delivery of a statement of withdrawal for the purpose of removing the foreign LLC from the rolls of registered foreign entities.

Subsection (a)—The exclusion of limited liability partnerships from this provision is merely technical; Section 907 covers conversion to a domestic LLP.

§ 909. TRANSFER OF REGISTRATION.

(a) When a registered foreign limited liability company has merged into a foreign entity that is not registered to do business in this state or has converted to a foreign entity required to register with the [Secretary of State] to do business in this state, the foreign entity shall deliver to the [Secretary of State] for filing an application for transfer of registration. The application must state:

(1) the name of the registered foreign limited liability company before the merger or conversion;

(2) that before the merger or conversion the registration pertained to a foreign limited liability company;

(3) the name of the applicant foreign entity into which the foreign limited liability company has merged or to which it has been converted and, if the name does not comply with Section 112, an alternate name adopted pursuant to Section 906(a);

(4) the type of entity of the applicant foreign entity and its jurisdiction of formation;

(5) the street and mailing addresses of the principal office of the applicant foreign entity and, if the law of the entity's jurisdiction of formation requires the entity to maintain an office in that jurisdiction, the street and mailing addresses of that office; and

(6) the name and street and mailing addresses of the applicant foreign entity's registered agent in this state.

(b) When an application for transfer of registration takes effect, the registration of the foreign limited liability company to do business in this state is transferred without interruption to the foreign entity into which the company has merged or to which it has been converted.

Comment

The purpose of this section is to clarify the status of the foreign limited liability company in the public records of the state. A filing under this section has the two-fold effect of canceling the authority of the foreign LLC to do business in the state while at the same time reregistering the former foreign LLC as the new type of foreign entity. If the reregistered foreign entity subsequently wishes to cancel its registration to do business in the state, it may do so under the statute of this state pertaining to the registration of the new type of foreign entity.

§ 910. TERMINATION OF REGISTRATION.

(a) The [Secretary of State] may terminate the registration of a registered foreign limited liability company in the manner provided in subsections (b) and (c) if the company does not:

(1) pay, not later than [60] days after the due date, any fee, tax, interest, or penalty required to be paid to the [Secretary of State] under this [act] or law other than this [act];

(2) deliver to the [Secretary of State] for filing, not later than [60] days after the due date, [an annual] [a biennial] report required under Section 212;

(3) have a registered agent as required by Section 115; or

(4) deliver to the [Secretary of State] for filing a statement of a change under Section 116 not later than [30] days after a change has occurred in the name or address of the registered agent.

(b) The [Secretary of State] may terminate the registration of a registered foreign limited liability company by:

(1) filing a notice of termination or noting the termination in the records of the [Secretary of State]; and

(2) delivering a copy of the notice or the information in the notation to the company's registered agent or, if the company does not have a registered agent, to the company's principal office.

(c) The notice must state or the information in the notation must include:

(1) the effective date of the termination, which must be at least [60] days after the date the [Secretary of State] delivers the copy; and

(2) the grounds for termination under subsection (a).

(d) The authority of a registered foreign limited liability company to do business in this state ceases on the effective date of the notice of termination or notation under subsection (b), unless before that date the company cures each ground for termination stated in the notice or notation. If the company cures each ground, the [Secretary of State] shall file a record so stating.

Comment

This section is analogous to the procedures for administrative dissolution under Section 708.

§ 911. WITHDRAWAL OF REGISTRATION OF REGISTERED FOREIGN LIMITED LIABILITY COMPANY.

(a) A registered foreign limited liability company may withdraw its registration by delivering a statement of withdrawal to the [Secretary of State] for filing. The statement of withdrawal must state:

(1) the name of the company and its jurisdiction of formation;

(2) that the company is not doing business in this state and that it withdraws its registration to do business in this state;

(3) that the company revokes the authority of its registered agent to accept service on its behalf in this state; and

(4) an address to which service of process may be made under subsection (b).

(b) After the withdrawal of the registration of a foreign limited liability company, service of process in any action or proceeding based on a cause of action arising during the time the company was registered to do business in this state may be made pursuant to Section 119.

Comment

The statement of withdrawal must set forth an address where service of process may be made on the foreign limited liability company pursuant to Section 119. There is no limit on how long the withdrawn company must keep that address up to date.

§ 912. ACTION BY [ATTORNEY GENERAL].

The [Attorney General] may maintain an action to enjoin a foreign limited liability company from doing business in this state in violation of this [article].

Comment

The authority stated here has been part of corporate law for more than a century and has been carried over into the law of unincorporated business entities. Nowadays, the authority is rarely if ever invoked in either realm of entity law.

[ARTICLE] 10

MERGER, INTEREST EXCHANGE, CONVERSION, AND DOMESTICATION

Introductory Comment

This article deals comprehensively with both same-type and cross-type mergers and interest exchanges and with conversions and domestications. For this article to apply, at least one participant organization must be a domestic limited liability company. For a foreign organization to be involved, its organic law must permit the organization's participation.

Part 1 contains definitions specific to this article as well as provisions applicable to all transactions authorized by this article.

Part 2 governs mergers and is an amalgamation of existing entity law, both unincorporated and incorporated.

Part 3 governs interest exchanges, previously a feature only of corporate law. Part 3 is derived from the share exchange provisions in chapter 11 of the Model Business Corporation Act.

Part 4 governs conversions, a one-step procedure by which an entity changes from one type of entity to another type while nonetheless continuing in existence as the same legal entity.

Part 5 governs domestications, a procedure by a domestic limited liability company can become a foreign limited liability company or vice versa, in each instance with the company remaining the same legal entity.

Part 2 sets the paradigm for Parts 3, 4, and 5, because mergers are long-established and merger rules and concepts are familiar to business lawyers. Moreover, conversions and domestications could formerly be accomplished via mergers (with a new entity), and an interest exchange produces the same result as a triangular merger. The comments to Part 2 are thus relevant to understanding Parts 3, 4, and 5.

This article contemplates transactions in which the surviving entity is neither a filing entity nor otherwise of record in the filing office (*e.g.*, the merger of an LLC into a non-LLP general partnership). As a result, a filing under this article may be the first time that a filing office takes cognizance of an entity's existence.

[PART] 1

GENERAL PROVISIONS

§ 1001. DEFINITIONS.

In this [article]:

(1) "Acquired entity" means the entity, all of one or more classes or series of interests of which are acquired in an interest exchange.

(2) "Acquiring entity" means the entity that acquires all of one or more classes or series of interests of the acquired entity in an interest exchange.

(3) "Conversion" means a transaction authorized by [Part] 4.

(4) "Converted entity" means the converting entity as it continues in existence after a conversion.

(5) "Converting entity" means the domestic entity that approves a plan of conversion pursuant to Section 1043 or the foreign entity that approves a conversion pursuant to the law of its jurisdiction of formation.

(6) "Distributional interest" means the right under an unincorporated entity's organic law and organic rules to receive distributions from the entity.

(7) "Domestic", with respect to an entity, means governed as to its internal affairs by the law of this state.

(8) "Domesticated limited liability company" means the domesticating limited liability company as it continues in existence after a domestication.

(9) "Domesticating limited liability company" means the domestic limited liability company that approves a plan of domestication pursuant to Section 1053 or the foreign limited liability company that approves a domestication pursuant to the law of its jurisdiction of formation.

(10) "Domestication" means a transaction authorized by [Part] 5.

(11) "Entity":

    (A) means:

        (i) a business corporation;

        (ii) a nonprofit corporation;

        (iii) a general partnership, including a limited liability partnership;

        (iv) a limited partnership, including a limited liability limited partnership;

        (v) a limited liability company;

        [(vi) a general cooperative association;]

        (vii) a limited cooperative association;

        (viii) an unincorporated nonprofit association;

        (ix) a statutory trust, business trust, or common-law business trust; or

        (x) any other person that has:

            (I) a legal existence separate from any interest holder of that person; or

            (II) the power to acquire an interest in real property in its own name; and

    (B) does not include:

        (i) an individual;

        (ii) a trust with a predominantly donative purpose or a charitable trust;

        (iii) an association or relationship that is not an entity listed in subparagraph A and is not a partnership under the rules stated in [Section 202(c) of the Uniform Partnership Act (1997) (Last Amended 2013)] [Section 7 of the Uniform Partnership Act (1914)] or a similar provision of the law of another jurisdiction;

        (iv) a decedent's estate; or

        (v) a government or a governmental subdivision, agency, or instrumentality.

(12) "Filing entity" means an entity whose formation requires the filing of a public organic record. The term does not include a limited liability partnership.

(13) "Foreign", with respect to an entity, means an entity governed as to its internal affairs by the law of a jurisdiction other than this state.

(14) "Governance interest" means a right under the organic law or organic rules of an unincorporated entity, other than as a governor, agent, assignee, or proxy, to:

    (A) receive or demand access to information concerning, or the books and records of, the entity;

    (B) vote for or consent to the election of the governors of the entity; or

    (C) receive notice of or vote on or consent to an issue involving the internal affairs of the entity.

(15) "Governor" means:

(A) a director of a business corporation;

(B) a director or trustee of a nonprofit corporation;

(C) a general partner of a general partnership;

(D) a general partner of a limited partnership;

(E) a manager of a manager-managed limited liability company;

(F) a member of a member-managed limited liability company;

[(G) a director of a general cooperative association;]

(H) a director of a limited cooperative association;

(I) a manager of an unincorporated nonprofit association;

(J) a trustee of a statutory trust, business trust, or common-law business trust; or

(K) any other person under whose authority the powers of an entity are exercised and under whose direction the activities and affairs of the entity are managed pursuant to the organic law and organic rules of the entity.

(16) "Interest" means:

(A) a share in a business corporation;

(B) a membership in a nonprofit corporation;

(C) a partnership interest in a general partnership;

(D) a partnership interest in a limited partnership;

(E) a membership interest in a limited liability company;

[(F) a share in a general cooperative association;]

(G) a member's interest in a limited cooperative association;

(H) a membership in an unincorporated nonprofit association;

(I) a beneficial interest in a statutory trust, business trust, or common-law business trust; or

(J) a governance interest or distributional interest in any other type of unincorporated entity.

(17) "Interest exchange" means a transaction authorized by [Part] 3.

(18) "Interest holder" means:

(A) a shareholder of a business corporation;

(B) a member of a nonprofit corporation;

(C) a general partner of a general partnership;

(D) a general partner of a limited partnership;

(E) a limited partner of a limited partnership;

(F) a member of a limited liability company;

[(G) a shareholder of a general cooperative association;]

(H) a member of a limited cooperative association;

(I) a member of an unincorporated nonprofit association;

(J) a beneficiary or beneficial owner of a statutory trust, business trust, or common-law business trust; or

(K) any other direct holder of an interest.

(19) "Interest holder liability" means:

(A) personal liability for a liability of an entity which is imposed on a person:

(i) solely by reason of the status of the person as an interest holder; or

(ii) by the organic rules of the entity which make one or more specified interest holders or categories of interest holders liable in their capacity as interest holders for all or specified liabilities of the entity; or

(B) an obligation of an interest holder under the organic rules of an entity to contribute to the entity.

(20) "Merger" means a transaction authorized by [Part] 2.

(21) "Merging entity" means an entity that is a party to a merger and exists immediately before the merger becomes effective.

(22) "Organic law" means the law of an entity's jurisdiction of formation governing the internal affairs of the entity.

(23) "Organic rules" means the public organic record and private organic rules of an entity.

(24) "Plan" means a plan of merger, plan of interest exchange, plan of conversion, or plan of domestication.

(25) "Plan of conversion" means a plan under Section 1042.

(26) "Plan of domestication" means a plan under Section 1052.

(27) "Plan of interest exchange" means a plan under Section 1032.

(28) "Plan of merger" means a plan under Section 1022.

(29) "Private organic rules" means the rules, whether or not in a record, that govern the internal affairs of an entity, are binding on all its interest holders, and are not part of its public organic record, if any. The term includes:

(A) the bylaws of a business corporation;

(B) the bylaws of a nonprofit corporation;

(C) the partnership agreement of a general partnership;

(D) the partnership agreement of a limited partnership;

(E) the operating agreement of a limited liability company;

[(F) the bylaws of a general cooperative association;]

(G) the bylaws of a limited cooperative association;

(H) the governing principles of an unincorporated nonprofit association; and

(I) the trust instrument of a statutory trust or similar rules of a business trust or common-law business trust.

(30) "Protected agreement" means:

(A) a record evidencing indebtedness and any related agreement in effect on [the effective date of this [act]];

(B) an agreement that is binding on an entity on [the effective date of this [act]];

(C) the organic rules of an entity in effect on [the effective date of this [act]]; or

(D) an agreement that is binding on any of the governors or interest holders of an entity on [the effective date of this [act]].

(31) "Public organic record" means the record the filing of which by the [Secretary of State] is required to form an entity and any amendment to or restatement of that record. The term includes:

(A) the articles of incorporation of a business corporation;

(B) the articles of incorporation of a nonprofit corporation;

(C) the certificate of limited partnership of a limited partnership;

(D) the certificate of organization of a limited liability company;

[(E) the articles of incorporation of a general cooperative association;]

(F) the articles of organization of a limited cooperative association; and

(G) the certificate of trust of a statutory trust or similar record of a business trust.

(32) "Registered foreign entity" means a foreign entity that is registered to do business in this state pursuant to a record filed by the [Secretary of State].

(33) "Statement of conversion" means a statement under Section 1045.

(34) "Statement of domestication" means a statement under Section 1055.

(35) "Statement of interest exchange" means a statement under Section 1035.

(36) "Statement of merger" means a statement under Section 1025.

(37) "Surviving entity" means the entity that continues in existence after or is created by a merger.

(38) "Type of entity" means a generic form of entity:

(A) recognized at common law; or

(B) formed under an organic law, whether or not some entities formed under that organic law are subject to provisions of that law that create different categories of the form of entity.

Comment

This section defines the terms that are used in this article. Many of the definitions describe attributes that are significant in some forms of entity and not in others. For example, the concept of separate "distributional" and "governance" interests are inherent in unincorporated entities but have no counterpart in corporations. In addition, because some statutes use different terms to describe the same transaction, the definitions are intended to be broad enough to encompass those similar transactions, regardless of how described. *See, e.g.*, Paragraph 10 (defining "domestication").

"Acquired entity" [(1)]—This definition recognizes that an interest exchange may involve only the acquisition of a particular "class" or "series" of interests in an entity. Model Business Corporation Act section 6.01 does not expressly define "classes" or "series." Because the interests of members in an unincorporated business organization often tend to be distinctive, it may be that each member's interest will comprise a separate class or series. For an explanation of a new and different meaning of the word "series," see Section 1031, introductory comment. The term "acquired entity" does not encompass series under that new meaning.

"Acquiring entity" [(2)]—An "acquiring entity" is an entity that acquires the interests of the acquired entity in an interest exchange governed by Part 3 of this article.

"Conversion" [(3)]—The term "conversion" means a transaction authorized by Part 4 pursuant to which an entity of one type is converted into an entity of another type. As used in this act, the term "conversion" does not include a transaction in which an entity changes the jurisdiction in which it is organized but does not change to a different form of entity; that type of transaction is referred to in this act as a "domestication" and is governed by Part 5.

"Converted entity" [(4)]—This term is used in Part 4 to describe the entity that results from a conversion.

"Converting entity" [(5)]—A converting entity is the entity that becomes the converted entity under Part 4.

"Distributional interest" [(6)]—This term is similar to the concept of a "transferable interest" found in this act and the organic laws of several other types of unincorporated entities, but has a broader meaning because the scope of this act includes entities in addition to those whose organic law uses the term "transferable interest."

"Domestic" [(7)]—The term "domestic", when used in this article with respect to an entity, refers to an entity whose internal affairs are governed by the organic laws of this state. Except in the case of general partnerships and unincorporated nonprofit associations, this will mean an entity that is formed, organized, or incorporated under domestic law. In the case of a general partnership organized under UPA (1997) (Last Amended 2013), the term will mean a general partnership whose governing law under UPA (1997) § 104 is the law of the adopting state. Under that section, the governing law is determined by the location of the partnership's principal office, except for limited liability partnerships whose governing law is the law of the state where the LLP's statement of qualification is filed. It is a factual question whether the activities and organization of an unincorporated nonprofit association make it a domestic or foreign entity.

"Domesticated limited liability company" [(8)]—This term is used in Part 5 and means the entity that is domesticated pursuant to Part 5. By the nature of the transaction, the domesticated entity will be of the same type as the domesticating entity (*i.e.*, an LLC).

"Domesticating limited liability company" [(9)]—This term is used in Part 5 and means the entity that is domesticated pursuant to Part 5.

"Domestication" [(10)]—The term "domestication" means a transaction of the kind authorized by Part 5 pursuant to which an entity may change its *jurisdiction* of formation *but not its type* so long as the laws of the foreign jurisdiction permit the domestication. The legal effect of the domestication of a limited liability company out of this state will be governed by the laws of both this state and the foreign jurisdiction. Some statutes include what is described in this act as "domestication" in their definition of a "conversion." *See, e.g.*, COLO. REV. STAT. § 7–90–201. It is intended that the domestication provisions of this act will apply to a transaction that may be characterized under another act as a "conversion" if the transaction meets the definition of "domestication" under this act.

"Entity" [(11)]—This definition determines the overall scope of the act because only an "entity" may participate in the transactions authorized by Parts 2 (mergers), 3 (interest exchanges), 4 (conversions), and 5 (domestications). *See* Sections 1021 (authorization of mergers), 1031(authorization of interest exchanges), 1041(authorization of conversions), 1051(authorization of domestications).

Subparagraph (A)(x) is a "catch-all" provision that includes within the definition of "entity" any type of organization recognized under the law of this state, which is not listed specifically in the preceding paragraphs of this definition. Subparagraph (A)(x) is intended to include all forms of private organizations, regardless of whether organized for profit, and artificial legal persons other than those excluded by Subparagraph (B). This definition does not exclude regulated entities such as public utilities, banks, and insurance companies. Should a state desire to exclude certain types of regulated entities or any of the entities listed in Subparagraph (A)(i)–(x) from participating in transactions permitted by this act for policy reasons, that may be done by listing those types of entities in Section 1007(a), or by permitting those type of entities to engage in transactions under this act generally but prohibiting certain types of transactions by listing those transactions in Section 1007(b).

Unincorporated nonprofit associations are treated as a type of entity in Subparagraph (A)(viii) because section 5 of the Uniform Unincorporated Nonprofit Association Act (2008) (Last Amended 2013) specifically states that an unincorporated nonprofit association is an entity. In many states, the status of a nonprofit association may not be clear. Nevertheless, in most states a nonprofit association has the power to acquire an interest in real property in its own name and therefore would qualify as an "entity" under Subparagraph (A)(x). See Section 6 of the UUNAA, which gives an unincorporated nonprofit association the power to acquire in its own name an interest in real property.

Subparagraph (B)(i) of this definition excludes a sole proprietorship from the concept of an "entity."

Trusts with a predominately donative purpose, such as inter vivos and testamentary trusts and charitable trusts, are treated in many states as having a separate legal existence, but they have been excluded from the definition of "entity" (and thus are not within the scope of this article) under Subparagraph (B)(ii) because they should not be able to engage in transactions under this act as a matter of public policy. Trusts that carry on a business, however, such as business and statutory entity trusts, are "entities." *See* Subparagraph (A)(ix).

Subparagraph (B)(iii) of this definition excludes from the concept of an "entity" any form of co-ownership of property or sharing of returns from property that is not listed in Subparagraph (A) and is not a partnership under UPA (1997). In that connection, Section 202(c) of that act provides in part:

In determining whether a partnership is formed, the following rules apply:

(1) Joint tenancy, tenancy in common, tenancy by the entireties, joint property, common property, or part ownership does not by itself establish a partnership, even if the co-owners share profits made by the use of the property.

(2) The sharing of gross returns does not by itself establish a partnership, even if the persons sharing them have a joint or common right or interest in property from which the returns are derived.

Limited liability partnerships and limited liability limited partnerships are "entities" because they are general partnerships and limited partnerships respectively that have made the additional required election claiming LLP or LLLP status. A limited liability partnership is not, therefore, a separate type of entity from the underlying general or limited partnership that has elected limited liability partnership status. Thus, for example, the election of a general partnership to become a limited liability partnership is not a conversion subject to Article 4.

Under Subparagraph (B)(iv), decedent's estates are excluded from the definition of an entity for the same policy reason as trusts with a predominately donative purpose and charitable trusts.

This same public policy rationale is the justification for the exclusion of governmental subdivisions, agencies, or instrumentalities in Subparagraph (B)(v).

"Filing entity" [(12)]—Whether an entity is a filing entity is determined by reference to whether its legal existence requires the filing of a document with the state filing officer. To fit within this definition, the filing must be necessary but need not be sufficient to form the entity. *See, e.g.*, Section 201(d) ("A limited liability company is formed when the company's certificate of organization becomes effective *and* at least one person becomes a member.") (emphasis added).

While the statute refers to the "formation" of an entity, the term is intended to encompass corporations that are "incorporated," as well as other filing entities whose statutes refer to them as being "organized." Business trusts present a special problem. In some states, a business trust could be a filing entity or a common law relationship, while in other states business trusts are only recognized at common law. A statutory trust entity formed under the Uniform Statutory Trust Entity Act (2009) (Last Amended 2013) § 201(a) is a filing entity, because a statutory trust entity is formed by the filing office filing a certificate of trust pertaining to the entity.

The term "filing entity" does not include a limited liability partnership because, while a filed document is a precondition to LLP status, that document (a statement of qualification under UPA (1997) (Last Amended 2013) § 901) does not form the underlying entity. A limited liability limited partnership, on the other hand, is a filing entity because the underlying limited partnership is formed by filing a certificate of limited partnership. ULPA (2001) (Last Amended 2013) § 201(a).

"Foreign" [(13)]—The term "foreign entity" includes any non-domestic entity of any type. Where a foreign entity is a filing entity, the entity is governed by the laws of the state of filing. A nonfiling foreign entity is governed by the laws governing its internal affairs. It is a factual question whether a general partnership whose internal affairs are governed by UPA (1914) is a domestic or foreign partnership. A UPA (1914) partnership will likely be deemed to be a domestic entity where the greatest nexus of contacts are found. The domestic or foreign characterization of partnerships under the UPA (1997) (Last Amended 2013) that have not become limited liability partnerships will be governed by Section 104(2) ("the law of the jurisdiction in which the partnership has its principal office") or the partnership agreement. (Section 104(2) is a default rule.)

"Governance interest" [(14)]—A governance interest is typically only part of the interest that a person will hold in an unincorporated entity and is usually coupled with a distributional interest (or economic rights). Memberships in some nonprofit corporations and unincorporated nonprofit associations consist solely of governance interests and memberships in other nonprofit entities may not include either governance interests or distributional interests. In some unincorporated business entities, including limited liability companies, there is a more limited right to transfer governance interests than there is to transfer distributional interests. An interest holder in such an unincorporated business entity who transfers only a distributional interest and retains the governance interest will also retain the status of an interest holder. Whether a transferee who acquires only a distributional interest will acquire the status of an interest holder is determined by the definition of "interest holder."

Governors of an entity have the kinds of rights listed in the definition of "governance interest" by reason of their position with the entity. For a governor to have a "governance interest," however, requires that the governor also have those rights for a reason other than the governor's status as such. A manager who is not a member in a limited liability company, for example, will not have a governance interest, but a manager who is a member will have a governance interest arising from the ownership of a membership interest.

"Governor" [(15)]—This term has been chosen to provide a way of referring to a person who has the authority under an entity's organic law to make management decisions regarding the entity that is different from any of the existing terms used in connection with particular types of entities. Depending on the type of entity or its organic rules, the governors of an entity may have the power to act on their own authority, or they may be organized as a board or similar group and only have the power to act collectively, and then only through a designated agent. In other words, a person having only the power to bind the organization pursuant to the instruction of the governors is not a governor. Under the organic rules, particularly those of unincorporated entities, most or all of the management decisions may be reserved to the members or partners. Thus, if a manager of a limited liability company were limited to having authority to execute management decisions made by the members and did not have any authority to make independent management decisions, the manager would not be a governor under this definition.

"Interest" [(16)]—In the usual case, the interest held by an interest holder will include both a governance interest and a distributional interest. Members in nonprofit corporations or unincorporated nonprofit associations generally do not have any distributional interest because they do not receive distributions, but they nonetheless may hold a governance interest in which case they would have the status of interest holders under this article.

"Interest exchange" [(17)]—The term "interest exchange" means a transaction authorized by Part 3 pursuant to which an entity may acquire interests in another entity. The consideration that may be provided to the interest holders whose interests are being acquired in an exchange may consist in whole or part of interests in a third party that is not one of the two parties to the exchange itself. *See* Section 1031(a).

"Interest holder" [(18)]—This act does not refer to "equity" interests or "equity" owners or holders because the term "equity" could be confusing in the case of a nonprofit entity whose members do not have an interest in the assets or results of operations of the entity but have only a right to vote on its internal affairs.

"Interest holder liability" [(19)]—This term is used to describe the vicarious liability of an interest holder, by virtue of being an interest holder, for liabilities of the entity. The term includes only personal liability of an interest holder for a debt of the entity imposed on the interest holder either by statute or by the organic rules to the extent authorized pursuant to the organic law. Liabilities that an interest holder incurs in any other fashion are not interest holder liabilities for purposes of this act. Thus, for example, if a state's business corporation law makes shareholders personally liable for unpaid wages because of their status as shareholders, that liability would be an "interest holder liability." If, on the other hand, a shareholder were to guarantee payment of an obligation of a corporation, that liability would not be an "interest holder liability" because it is a direct liability and not based on the status of being a shareholder. Similarly, the liability to return an improper distribution is not an interest holder liability because it is a direct liability of the interest holder based on receipt of the distribution.

"Merger" [(20)]—The term means a transaction in which two or more entities are combined into a single entity pursuant to a filing with the filing office. The term "merger" in this act includes the transaction known as a consolidation in which a new entity results from the combination of two or more pre-existing entities.

"Merging entity" [(21)]—The term "merging entity" refers to each entity that is in existence immediately before a merger and is a party to the merger. It will include the surviving entity if the surviving entity exists before the merger becomes effective. It does not include an entity that provides consideration to be received by interest holders if that entity is not a party to the merger.

"Organic law" [(22)]—Organic law means statutes that govern the internal affairs of an entity. For example, this act is the organic law of a limited liability company formed under this act.

Entity laws in a few states purport to require that some of their internal governance rules applicable to a domestic entity also apply to a foreign entity with significant ties to the state. *See, e.g.,* CAL. CORP. CODE § 2115 (Foreign Corporations); N.Y. NOT-FOR-PROFIT-CORP. §§ 1318–21 (Liabilities of Directors and Officers of Foreign Corporations); 15 PA. CONS. STAT. § 6145 (Applicability of Certain Safeguards to Foreign Corporations). Such a "sticky fingers" law is not included within the definition of "organic law" for purposes of this act because those laws are not part of the law of the entity's jurisdiction of formation.

"Organic rules" [(23)]—The term "organic rules" means an entity's public organic record and the private organic rules. The organic rules, together with this act, the organic law, and the common law, provide the rules governing the internal affairs of the entity. For example, this act and the operating agreement comprise the organic rules of a limited liability company formed under this act.

"Plan" [(24)]—The term "plan" is a short-hand way of referring to the plan of merger, interest exchange, conversion, or domestication, as the case may be, depending on which form of transaction is taking place. *See* Sections 1022 (plan of merger), 1032 (plan of interest exchange), 1042 (plan of conversion), 1052 (plan of domestication).

"Private organic rules" [(29)]—The term private "organic rules" is intended to include all governing rules of an entity that are binding on all of its interest holders, whether or not in record form, except for the provisions of the entity's public organic record, if any. The term is intended to include agreements in "record" form such as corporate bylaws, as well as oral partnership agreements and oral operating agreements among LLC members.

"Protected agreement" [(30)]—The term "protected agreement" refers to evidences of indebtedness and agreements binding on the entity or any of its governors or interest holders that are unpaid or executory in whole or in part on the effective date of the act. Thus, a revolving line of credit from a bank to a corporation would constitute a protected agreement even if advances were not made until after the effective date of the act. Likewise, an operating agreement in effect under this act or a predecessor to this act is a "protected agreement."

If a protected agreement has provisions that apply if an entity merges, those provisions will apply if the entity enters into an interest exchange, conversion, or domestication even though the agreement does not mention those other types of transactions. *See* Sections 1031(c) (interest exchange), 1041(c) (conversion), 1051(c) (domestication).

"Public organic record" [(31)]—A "public organic record" is a record that is filed publicly to form, organize, incorporate, or otherwise create an entity. The term does not include a statement of authority filed under UPA (1997) (Last Amended 2013) § 303 or any of the other statements that may be filed under that act since those statements do not create a new entity. The same is true for statements filed under this act.

For the same reason, a statement of qualification filed under UPA (1997) (Last Amended 2013) § 1001 is not a "public organic record." The limited liability partnership that results from the filing is the same entity as the partnership that delivered the statement to the filing office. Similarly, the term does not include a statement of authority filed under section 7 of the Revised Uniform Unincorporated Nonprofit Association Act (2008) (Last Amended 2013), a statement appointing a registered agent filed under section 31 of that act, or any of the various statements filed under this act.

In those states where a deed of trust or other instrument is publicly filed to create a business trust, that filing will constitute a public organic record. But in those states where a business trust is not created by a public filing, the deed of trust or similar record will be part of the private organic rules of the business trust.

Where a public organic document has been amended or restated, the term means the public organic document as last amended or restated.

"Registered foreign entity" [(32)]—This term refers to a foreign entity that is registered to transact business in this state pursuant to a public filing.

"Surviving entity" [(37)]—The term "surviving entity" refers to either a merging entity that survives the merger or the new entity created by the merger.

"Type of entity" [(38)]—The term "type of entity" has been developed in an attempt to distinguish different legal forms of entities. It is sometimes difficult to decide whether one is dealing with a different form of entity or a variation of the same form. For example, a limited partnership, although it has long been characterized or even defined as a partnership, is a different type of entity from a general partnership, while a limited liability partnership is not a different type of entity from a general partnership. In some states cooperatives are categories of business corporations or nonprofit corporations, while in other states cooperatives are a separate type of entity.

§ 1002. RELATIONSHIP OF [ARTICLE] TO OTHER LAWS.

(a) This [article] does not authorize an act prohibited by, and does not affect the application or requirements of, law other than this [article].

(b) A transaction effected under this [article] may not create or impair a right, duty or obligation of a person under the statutory law of this state other than this [article] relating to a change in control, takeover, business combination, control-share acquisition, or similar transaction involving a domestic merging, acquired, converting, or domesticating business corporation unless:

(1) if the corporation does not survive the transaction, the transaction satisfies any requirements of the law; or

(2) if the corporation survives the transaction, the approval of the plan is by a vote of the shareholders or directors which would be sufficient to create or impair the right, duty, or obligation directly under the law.

Comment

This section preserves existing regulatory law in an adopting state in general terms. Adopting states should consider more carefully integrating this act with their various regulatory laws. For example, in some states certain professions are limited in their use of limited liability entities. *See* Section 1003.

Laws other than this act that will apply to transactions under this act include, for example, fraudulent transfer and fraudulent conveyance acts, state insolvency statutes, federal bankruptcy law, and Articles 8 and 9 of the Uniform Commercial Code.

Subsection (b)—Many states have enacted "antitakeover" statutes intended to make it more difficult to acquire control of a publicly traded corporation. Those statutes often provide that their application to a particular corporation cannot be changed unless the corporation obtains certain specified approvals, such as a vote of disinterested directors or a supermajority vote by the shareholders. The purpose of the special requirements in this subsection on varying the application of an antitakeover statute is to protect against a hostile acquirer or group of shareholders seeking to use the act to avoid the application of the antitakeover statute.

This subsection protects the application of antitakeover statutes from being affected by a transaction under this act by requiring that the transaction be approved in a manner that would be sufficient to approve changing the application of the antitakeover statute. If a transaction is approved in that manner, there is no policy reason to prohibit the application of the antitakeover statute from being varied by a transaction under this act. If the application of an antitakeover statute cannot be varied by action of an entity subject to it, then a transaction under this act will be permissible only if the antitakeover provision continues to apply after the transaction or the transaction itself is permissible under the antitakeover statute.

§ 1003.   REQUIRED NOTICE OR APPROVAL.

(a) A domestic or foreign entity that is required to give notice to, or obtain the approval of, a governmental agency or officer of this state to be a party to a merger must give the notice or obtain the approval to be a party to an interest exchange, conversion, or domestication.

(b) Property held for a charitable purpose under the law of this state by a domestic or foreign entity immediately before a transaction under this [article] becomes effective may not, as a result of the transaction, be diverted from the objects for which it was donated, granted, devised, or otherwise transferred unless, to the extent required by or pursuant to the law of this state concerning cy pres or other law dealing with nondiversion of charitable assets, the entity obtains an appropriate order of [the appropriate court] [the Attorney General] specifying the disposition of the property.

(c) A bequest, devise, gift, grant, or promise contained in a will or other instrument of donation, subscription, or conveyance which is made to a merging entity that is not the surviving entity and which takes effect or remains payable after the merger inures to the surviving entity.

(d) A trust obligation that would govern property if transferred to a nonsurviving entity applies to property that is transferred to the surviving entity under this section.

Legislative Note: As an alternative to enacting Subsection (a), a state may identify each of its regulatory laws that requires prior approval for a merger of a regulated entity, decide whether regulatory approval should be required for an interest exchange, conversion, or domestication, and make amendments as appropriate to those laws.

As with Subsection (a), an adopting state may choose to amend its various laws with respect to the nondiversion of charitable property to cover the various transactions authorized by this act as an alternative to enacting Subsection (b).

Comment

Subsection (a)—Because at least some of the provisions of this act will be new in most states, it is likely that existing state laws that require regulatory approval of transactions by businesses such as banks, insurance companies, or public utilities may not be worded in a fashion that will include at least some of the transactions authorized by this act. The purpose of this subsection is to ensure that transactions under this act will be subject to the same regulatory approval as mergers. This subsection is based on whether a merger by a regulated entity requires prior approval because the transactions authorized by this act may be effectuated indirectly in many cases under existing law by establishing a wholly-owned subsidiary of the desired type and then merging into it.

The consequence of violating this subsection should be the same as in the case of a merger consummated without the required approval.

Subsection (b)—This act applies generally to nonprofit corporations and unincorporated nonprofit associations. As in the case of laws regulating particular industries, a state's laws governing the nondiversion of charitable property to other uses may not cover some of the transactions authorized by this act. To prevent the procedures in this act from being used to avoid restrictions on the use of charitable property held by nonprofit entities, this subsection requires approval of the effect of transactions under this act by the appropriate arm of government having supervision of nonprofit entities.

An approval or order obtained under this section may impose conditions or specify the disposition of assets or liabilities in a manner different than would otherwise be the case. In such an instance, the approval or order will control over the provisions of this act specifying the effects of a transaction. *See* Sections 1026 (effect of merger), 1036 (effect of interest exchange), 1046 (effect of conversion), 1056 (effect of domestication).

Subsection (c)—This subsection clarifies the legal effect of a merger on bequests, etc. that were originally made to an entity that does not survive the merger. This issue does not arise in an interest exchange, conversion, or domestication transaction because the entity to which the bequest, etc. was made survives in some form after the transaction.

§ 1004.   NONEXCLUSIVITY.

The fact that a transaction under this [article] produces a certain result does not preclude the same result from being accomplished in any other manner permitted by law other than this [article].

Comment

This section allows a transaction that has the same end result as one of the transactions governed by this act, but that is accomplished in a manner not within the scope of this act, to be exempt from this act. For example, a sale of assets and transfer of liabilities by two entities to a third entity followed by the liquidation of the two transferring entities can be accomplished pursuant to statutory provisions pertaining to sale of assets rather than under Part 2 of this article, even though the end result of the transaction is essentially the same as if the two entities had merged into a third entity.

§ 1005.   REFERENCE TO EXTERNAL FACTS.

A plan may refer to facts ascertainable outside the plan if the manner in which the facts will operate upon the plan is specified in the plan. The facts may include the occurrence of an event or a determination or action by a person, whether or not the event, determination, or action is within the control of a party to the transaction.

Comment

This section is based on, but more concise than, section 1.20(k) of the Model Business Corporation Act.

§ 1006.   APPRAISAL RIGHTS.

An interest holder of a domestic merging, acquired, converting, or domesticating limited liability company is entitled to contractual appraisal rights in connection with a transaction under this [article] to the extent provided in:

(1) the operating agreement; or

(2) the plan.

Comment

In corporate law, appraisal rights developed when corporate statutes were amended to permit mergers with less than unanimous consent of the shareholders. This article provides no appraisal rights, because, as a default rule, transactions under this article require the consent or affirmative vote of all the members. Where the operating agreement changes this default rule, parties may wish to consider contractual appraisal rights.

This subsection validates the grant of such contractual appraisal rights. *Cf.* 6 DEL. CODE §§ 15–120 (general partnerships), 17–212 (limited partnerships), 18–210 (limited liability companies) (validating "contractual appraisal rights"); MBCA § 13.02(5) (permitting the articles of incorporation, bylaws, or a resolution of the board of directors to confer appraisal rights in contexts in which they would otherwise not be available). Legislative authorization in this subsection of the grant of contractual appraisal rights removes any question as to whether a court would have jurisdiction to hear a case in which the parties were attempting to create jurisdiction in the court by private agreement.

In this section, the term "appraisal rights" refers to any arrangement, either in the operating agreement or the plan, providing for the buy-out of members that object to a transaction under this article.

[§ 1007.   EXCLUDED ENTITIES AND TRANSACTIONS.

(a) The following entities may not participate in a transaction under this [article]:

(1)

(2).

(b) This [article] may not be used to effect a transaction that:

(1)

(2).]

Legislative Note: *Subsection (a) may be used by states that have special statutes restricted to the organization of certain types of entities. A common example is banking statutes that prohibit banks from engaging in transactions other than pursuant to those statutes.*

Nonprofit entities may participate in transactions under this act with for-profit entities, subject to compliance with Section 1003. If a state desires, however, to exclude entities with a charitable purpose or to exclude other types of entities from the scope of this article, that may be done by referring to those entities in Subsection (a).

Subsection (b) may be used to exclude certain types of transactions governed by more specific statutes. A common example is the conversion of an insurance company from mutual to stock form. There may be other types of transactions that vary greatly among the states.

[PART] 2

MERGER

§ 1021. MERGER AUTHORIZED.

(a) By complying with this [part]:

(1) one or more domestic limited liability companies may merge with one or more domestic or foreign entities into a domestic or foreign surviving entity; and

(2) two or more foreign entities may merge into a domestic limited liability company.

(b) By complying with the provisions of this [part] applicable to foreign entities, a foreign entity may be a party to a merger under this [part] or may be the surviving entity in such a merger if the merger is authorized by the law of the foreign entity's jurisdiction of formation.

Comment

The merger transaction authorized by this act involves the combination of one or more domestic limited liability companies with or into one or more other domestic or foreign entities. It also contemplates the consolidation of two or more foreign entities into a single domestic limited liability company. Upon the effective date of the merger, all the assets and liabilities of the constituent entities vest in the surviving entity as a matter of law. As such, mergers require the existence of at least two separate entities before the transaction and only one entity may survive the merger. If independent existence of the constituent entities is desired following the conclusion of the transaction, a restructuring transaction other than a merger must be used to accomplish the transfer of assets and liabilities.

This act authorizes a merger for state entity law purposes. Federal law and other state law will independently determine how a merger transaction will be taxed.

Subsection (a)(1)—This paragraph states the general rule that subject to Subsection (b) one or more domestic limited liability companies may merge with or into a domestic or foreign surviving entity.

Subsection (a)(2)—This paragraph provides that two or more foreign entities may merge into a domestic surviving limited liability company so long as the requirements of Subsection (b) are met.

Subsection (b)—This subsection provides that a foreign entity may be a party to a merger or may be the surviving entity in a merger only if the merger is authorized by the laws of the foreign entity's jurisdiction of formation.

§ 1022.   PLAN OF MERGER.

(a) A domestic limited liability company may become a party to a merger under this [part] by approving a plan of merger. The plan must be in a record and contain:

(1) as to each merging entity, its name, jurisdiction of formation, and type of entity;

(2) if the surviving entity is to be created in the merger, a statement to that effect and the entity's name, jurisdiction of formation, and type of entity;

(3) the manner of converting the interests in each party to the merger into interests, securities, obligations, money, other property, rights to acquire interests or securities, or any combination of the foregoing;

(4) if the surviving entity exists before the merger, any proposed amendments to:

(A) its public organic record, if any; and

(B) its private organic rules that are, or are proposed to be, in a record;

(5) if the surviving entity is to be created in the merger:

(A) its proposed public organic record, if any; and

(B) the full text of its private organic rules that are proposed to be in a record;

(6) the other terms and conditions of the merger; and

(7) any other provision required by the law of a merging entity's jurisdiction of formation or the organic rules of a merging entity.

(b) In addition to the requirements of subsection (a), a plan of merger may contain any other provision not prohibited by law.

Comment

Subsection (a)—This subsection states the requirements for the plan of merger. They are similar to plan of merger provisions in corporation statutes. *See* MBCA § 11.02(c). The requirements stated in this subsection are mandatory. *See* Section 105(c)(14).

Subsection (a)(1)—This paragraph requires that the plan of merger identify the parties to the merger. The name of a merging entity as it appears in the plan of merger will be its name in its jurisdiction of formation.

Subsection (a)(3)—The language of this paragraph is similar to Model Business Corporation Act section 11.02(c)(3). What may be done under this paragraph with respect to providing for continuing interests in the surviving entity for some holders of interests of a class or series of a party to the merger while paying some other form of consideration to other holders of the same class or series of interests in that entity will vary depending on the type of entity involved and the extent to which its organic rules provide for non-uniform treatment of interest holders in a manner that is permissible under its organic law. Similarly, the ability to use a merger to reorganize the capital structure of the surviving entity will vary depending on the type of entity involved and whether the entity has appropriately adopted relevant provisions in its organic rules.

If the organic law and organic rules of an unincorporated entity permit a non-uniform "equity shuffle" to be accomplished in a merger involving the unincorporated entity, the minority owners of the unincorporated entity will not necessarily be entitled to the statutory appraisal rights currently afforded to minority stockholders in merging corporate entities. Any perceived unfairness in the shuffle would be addressed either: (i) under principles of fiduciary duties and the contractual obligations of good faith and fair dealing, assuming, of course, that such duties and obligations have not been contractually modified or eliminated to the extent permitted by the applicable organic law; or (ii) by the exercise of whatever rights the minority owners may have to veto the transaction or to withdraw or to dissociate and be paid the value of their interests.

The Model Business Corporation Act generally requires that shares of the same class or series be treated in the same manner in a merger unless the corporation has adopted an applicable provision of its articles of incorporation pursuant to section 6.01(e) of that act providing for variations in the treatment of holders of the same class or series of shares. Thus a determination of what may be done by way of an equity shuffle in the case of a corporation will require reference to its organic law and organic rules.

The consideration paid to the interest holders of the merging parties may be supplied in whole or part by a person who is not a party to the merger.

Subsection (b)—This subsection provides the statutory authority for a merging party to include a provision in a plan of merger that is not specifically listed in Subsection (a). One such possibility is contractual appraisal rights as provided in Section 1006(b).

§ 1023. APPROVAL OF MERGER.

(a) A plan of merger is not effective unless it has been approved:

(1) by a domestic merging limited liability company, by all the members of the company entitled to vote on or consent to any matter; and

(2) in a record, by each member of a domestic merging limited liability company which will have interest holder liability for debts, obligations, and other liabilities that are incurred after the merger becomes effective, unless:

(A) the operating agreement of the company provides in a record for the approval of a merger in which some or all of its members become subject to interest holder liability by the affirmative vote or consent of fewer than all the members; and

(B) the member consented in a record to or voted for that provision of the operating agreement or became a member after the adoption of that provision.

(b) A merger involving a domestic merging entity that is not a limited liability company is not effective unless the merger is approved by that entity in accordance with its organic law.

(c) A merger involving a foreign merging entity is not effective unless the merger is approved by the foreign entity in accordance with the law of the foreign entity's jurisdiction of formation.

Comment

Subsection (a)—In the uniform acts pertaining to unincorporated business organizations, unanimity is the default rule for approving a merger. The operating agreement certainly can change this rule, but care should be taken in doing so. For example, a merger can revise the operating agreement. Section 1022(a)(4). Thus, if a merger requires less-than-unanimous consent, the operating agreement is subject to amendment by the same quantum of consent. "Exit rights" also require consideration. This act does not provide appraisal rights, because such rights are inapposite when unanimous consent is required. *See* the comment to Section 1006.

Subsection (a)(2)—This provision is not a default rule, Section 105(c)(14), and deals with the situation in which a member of an LLC that is a party to a merger will have vicarious liability for the liabilities of the surviving entity that are incurred after the merger becomes effective. The special approval requirement in Subsection (a)(2) will be applicable; for example, to members of an LLC that merges into a general partnership that is not a limited liability partnership if the members become general partners of the surviving general partnership.

The consent of a member required by Subsection (a)(2)(B) may be given either by: (i) signing or agreeing generally to the terms of an operating agreement that includes the required provision permitting less than unanimous approval of a merger in which members become subject to "interest holder liability"; or (ii) voting for or consenting to an amendment to the operating agreement to add such a provision.

Subsection (b)—Where a domestic entity other than a limited liability company is a party to a merger under this act, this subsection defers to that entity's organic law for the requirements for approval of the merger by that entity.

Subsection (c)—Where a foreign entity is a party to a merger under this act, this subsection defers to the laws of the foreign jurisdiction for the requirements for approval of the merger by the foreign entity. Those laws will include the organic law of the foreign entity and other applicable laws. The laws of the foreign jurisdiction will also control the application of any special approval requirements found in the organic rules of the foreign entity.

§ 1024.　AMENDMENT OR ABANDONMENT OF PLAN OF MERGER.

(a) A plan of merger may be amended only with the consent of each party to the plan, except as otherwise provided in the plan.

(b) A domestic merging limited liability company may approve an amendment of a plan of merger:

(1) in the same manner as the plan was approved, if the plan does not provide for the manner in which it may be amended; or

(2) by its managers or members in the manner provided in the plan, but a member that was entitled to vote on or consent to approval of the merger is entitled to vote on or consent to any amendment of the plan that will change:

(A) the amount or kind of interests, securities, obligations, money, other property, rights to acquire interests or securities, or any combination of the foregoing, to be received by the interest holders of any party to the plan;

(B) the public organic record, if any, or private organic rules of the surviving entity that will be in effect immediately after the merger becomes effective, except for changes that do not require approval of the interest holders of the surviving entity under its organic law or organic rules; or

(C) any other terms or conditions of the plan, if the change would adversely affect the member in any material respect.

(c) After a plan of merger has been approved and before a statement of merger becomes effective, the plan may be abandoned as provided in the plan. Unless prohibited by the plan, a domestic merging limited liability company may abandon the plan in the same manner as the plan was approved.

(d) If a plan of merger is abandoned after a statement of merger has been delivered to the [Secretary of State] for filing and before the statement becomes effective, a statement of abandonment, signed by a party to the plan, must be delivered to the [Secretary of State] for filing before the statement of merger becomes effective. The statement of abandonment takes effect on filing, and the merger is abandoned and does not become effective. The statement of abandonment must contain:

(1) the name of each party to the plan of merger;

(2) the date on which the statement of merger was filed by the [Secretary of State]; and

(3) a statement that the merger has been abandoned in accordance with this section.

Comment

This section sets out the requirements for amending or abandoning the plan of merger. They are similar to provisions for amending or abandoning mergers found in existing corporation merger statutes. *See* MBCA §§ 11.02(e), 11.08.

§ 1025.　STATEMENT OF MERGER; EFFECTIVE DATE OF MERGER.

(a) A statement of merger must be signed by each merging entity and delivered to the [Secretary of State] for filing.

(b) A statement of merger must contain:

(1) the name, jurisdiction of formation, and type of entity of each merging entity that is not the surviving entity;

(2) the name, jurisdiction of formation, and type of entity of the surviving entity;

(3) a statement that the merger was approved by each domestic merging entity, if any, in accordance with this [part] and by each foreign merging entity, if any, in accordance with the law of its jurisdiction of formation;

(4) if the surviving entity exists before the merger and is a domestic filing entity, any amendment to its public organic record approved as part of the plan of merger;

(5) if the surviving entity is created by the merger and is a domestic filing entity, its public organic record, as an attachment; and

(6) if the surviving entity is created by the merger and is a domestic limited liability partnership, its statement of qualification, as an attachment.

(c) In addition to the requirements of subsection (b), a statement of merger may contain any other provision not prohibited by law.

(d) If the surviving entity is a domestic entity, its public organic record, if any, must satisfy the requirements of the law of this state, except that the public organic record does not need to be signed.

(e) A plan of merger that is signed by all the merging entities and meets all the requirements of subsection (b) may be delivered to the [Secretary of State] for filing instead of a statement of merger and on filing has the same effect. If a plan of merger is filed as provided in this subsection, references in this [article] to a statement of merger refer to the plan of merger filed under this subsection.

(f) If the surviving entity is a domestic limited liability company, the merger becomes effective when the statement of merger is effective. In all other cases, the merger becomes effective on the later of:

(1) the date and time provided by the organic law of the surviving entity; and

(2) when the statement is effective.

Comment

The filing of a statement of merger makes the transaction a matter of public record.

Subsection (a)—This subsection pertains to all merging entities involved in a merger, not merely any merging domestic limited liability company. Other filings may be required by the organic law of other entities participating in the merger.

Subsection (b)(1) and (2)—The names of foreign entities set forth in the statement of merger will generally be their names in their jurisdiction of formation, except that if a foreign entity has been required to adopt a different name in order to register to do business in this state, the foreign qualification statute will likely require that, when the entity does business in this state, the entity must use the name adopted for the purposes of registering to do business. Engaging in a merger under this act will be part of the business done by the entity in this state and the name of the entity set forth in the statement of merger will thus need to be the name under which the entity has registered to do business. Use of the name under which the entity has registered to do business will allow the records in the filing office to associate the registration of the entity to do business with the statement of merger.

Subsection (b)(3)—*See* the comment to Subsection (f).

Subsection (b)(4)—The statement in this paragraph that the plan of merger was approved by each entity in accordance with this article necessarily presupposes that the plan was approved in accordance with any valid, special requirements in the organic rules of each merging entity.

Subsection (b)(5) and (6)—The public organic record of a domestic surviving entity created by the merger that is attached to the statement of merger becomes the original, officially filed text of the public organic record of the surviving entity when the statement of merger takes effect. It is not necessary, or appropriate, to make any other filing to create the surviving entity.

Similarly, a statement of qualification for a domestic limited liability partnership created by the merger that is attached to the statement of merger does not need to be filed separately.

Subsection (d)—Organic laws typically require that an initial filing that creates an entity be signed by the person serving as the incorporator or other organizer. This subsection, however, provides that the public organic record of the surviving entity does not need to be signed since the record is attached to a signed record.

This subsection also permits the public organic record of the surviving entity to omit any provision that is not required to be included in a restatement of the public organic record. Pursuant to this provision, for example, the public organic record of a business corporation created as the surviving entity in the merger would not need to state the name and address of each incorporator even though that information would be required by the Model Business Corporation Act section 2.02(a)(4) if the corporation were being incorporated outside the context of the merger.

Subsection (e)—A plan of merger that contains all the information required in the statement of merger may be filed instead of the statement of merger. The plan must be in a record and signed by each merging party.

Subsection (f)—A merger in which the surviving entity is a domestic limited liability company takes effect when the statement of merger takes effect. A merger in which the surviving entity is a foreign entity will usually also take effect when the statement of merger takes effect because the practice is to coordinate the filings that need to be made when a merger involves both a domestic entity and also a foreign entity so that the filings in each jurisdiction take effect at the same time.

However, when the surviving limited liability company is a foreign limited liability company, it is possible that the filing in the foreign jurisdiction will take effect at a different time. For that reason, this subsection provides that the merger will take effect at the later of: (i) when the statement of merger takes effect; and (ii) when the merger takes effect under the law of the foreign jurisdiction. This rule avoids the possibility that the merger will take effect in this state before it takes effect in the foreign jurisdiction, which would produce the undesirable result that the merging domestic limited liability company would cease to appear as an active entity on the records of this state before the records of the foreign jurisdiction reflect a completed merger.

It is only necessary for the filing office to record the effective date of the statement of merger and the filing office does not need to be concerned with the effective date of the merger itself. Persons wishing to determine the effective date of a merger involving both a domestic and foreign entity will be able to do so by consulting the records of the filing offices in each jurisdiction.

§ 1026. EFFECT OF MERGER.

(a) When a merger becomes effective:

(1) the surviving entity continues or comes into existence;

(2) each merging entity that is not the surviving entity ceases to exist;

(3) all property of each merging entity vests in the surviving entity without transfer, reversion, or impairment;

(4) all debts, obligations, and other liabilities of each merging entity are debts, obligations, and other liabilities of the surviving entity;

(5) except as otherwise provided by law or the plan of merger, all the rights, privileges, immunities, powers, and purposes of each merging entity vest in the surviving entity;

(6) if the surviving entity exists before the merger:

(A) all its property continues to be vested in it without transfer, reversion, or impairment;

(B) it remains subject to all its debts, obligations, and other liabilities; and

(C) all its rights, privileges, immunities, powers, and purposes continue to be vested in it;

(7) the name of the surviving entity may be substituted for the name of any merging entity that is a party to any pending action or proceeding;

(8) if the surviving entity exists before the merger:

(A) its public organic record, if any, is amended to the extent provided in the statement of merger; and

(B) its private organic rules that are to be in a record, if any, are amended to the extent provided in the plan of merger;

(9) if the surviving entity is created by the merger, its private organic rules are effective and:

(A) if it is a filing entity, its public organic record becomes effective; and

(B) if it is a limited liability partnership, its statement of qualification becomes effective; and

(10) the interests in each merging entity which are to be converted in the merger are converted, and the interest holders of those interests are entitled only to the rights provided to them under the plan of merger and to any appraisal rights they have under Section 1006 and the merging entity's organic law.

(b) Except as otherwise provided in the organic law or organic rules of a merging entity, the merger does not give rise to any rights that an interest holder, governor, or third party would have upon a dissolution, liquidation, or winding up of the merging entity.

(c) When a merger becomes effective, a person that did not have interest holder liability with respect to any of the merging entities and becomes subject to interest holder liability with respect to a domestic entity as a result of the merger has interest holder liability only to the extent provided by the organic law of that entity and only for those debts, obligations, and other liabilities that are incurred after the merger becomes effective.

(d) When a merger becomes effective, the interest holder liability of a person that ceases to hold an interest in a domestic merging limited liability company with respect to which the person had interest holder liability is subject to the following rules:

(1) The merger does not discharge any interest holder liability under this [act] to the extent the interest holder liability was incurred before the merger became effective.

(2) The person does not have interest holder liability under this [act] for any debt, obligation, or other liability that is incurred after the merger becomes effective.

(3) This [act] continues to apply to the release, collection, or discharge of any interest holder liability preserved under paragraph (1) as if the merger had not occurred.

(4) The person has whatever rights of contribution from any other person as are provided by this [act], law other than this [act], or the operating agreement of the domestic merging limited liability company with respect to any interest holder liability preserved under paragraph (1) as if the merger had not occurred.

(e) When a merger becomes effective, a foreign entity that is the surviving entity may be served with process in this state for the collection and enforcement of any debts, obligations, or other liabilities of a domestic merging limited liability company as provided in Section 119.

(f) When a merger becomes effective, the registration to do business in this state of any foreign merging entity that is not the surviving entity is canceled.

Comment

With the exception of Subsections (c) and (d), this section is similar to statutory provisions on the effect of a merger of a corporation with a corporation. *See* MBCA § 11.07.

Subsection (a)—This subsection states the general understanding that in a merger the assets and liabilities of the merging entities automatically vest in the surviving entity. The surviving entity becomes the owner of all real and personal property of the merged entities and is subject to all debts, obligations, and liabilities of the merging entities. A merger does not constitute a transfer, assignment, or conveyance of any property held by the merging entities before the merger. A merger also does not give rise to a claim that a contract with a merging entity is no longer in effect on the ground of nonassignability, unless the contract specifically provides that it does not survive a merger. The contract rights that are vested in the surviving entity include the right to enforce subscription agreements for interests and obligations to make capital contributions entered into or incurred before the merger. *See* Section 1003(c) (dealing with the surviving entity's rights in trust obligations of a nonsurviving party in a merger and transactions such as bequests made to a nonsurviving party to a merger that take effect after the merger).

After a merger becomes effective, the law of the surviving entity's jurisdiction of formation governs the surviving entity.

Sections 1003(a) and (b), modify the provisions of this section with respect to the effects of a merger to the extent a regulatory law provides otherwise or any of the parties holds property committed to charitable purposes.

Subsection (a)(2)—A merger cannot have the effect of making an interest holder of a domestic merging entity subject to interest holder liability for the debts, obligations, or other liabilities of any other person or entity unless the interest holder has signed a separate written consent to become subject to such liability or previously agreed to the effectuation of a transaction having that effect without the interest holder's consent. The operating agreement cannot change this provision. Section 105(c)(14).

Subsection (a)(7)—All pending proceedings involving either the survivor or a party whose separate existence ceased as a result of the merger are continued. Under this paragraph, the name of the survivor may be, but need not be, substituted in any pending proceeding for the name of a party to the merger whose separate existence ceased as a result of the merger. The substitution may be made whether the survivor is a complainant or a respondent, and may be made at the instance of either the survivor or an opposing party. Such a substitution has no substantive effect because, whether or not the survivor's name is substituted, the survivor succeeds to the claims, and is subject to the liabilities, of any party to the merger whose separate existence ceased as a result of the merger.

Subsection (a)(8)(B)—The private organic rules of an unincorporated entity typically may be either oral or written. The plan of merger is not required to set forth amendments to oral provisions of the private organic rules of the surviving entity, and thus this provision is limited in scope to amendments to the private organic rules that are to be in a record, if any.

Subsection (a)(10)—*See* the comments to Section 1006.

Subsections (c) and (d)—These subsections set forth rules for two circumstances that typically do not exist in a merger where all the entities involved are corporations. Subsection (c) deals with the situation where an interest holder that does not have vicarious liability for the obligations of a merging entity before the merger has interest holder liability after the merger. An example would be a corporate shareholder who agrees to be the general partner in a limited partnership that is the surviving entity in a merger between a corporation and a limited partnership that is not a limited liability limited partnership. Subsection (d) deals with the situation where an interest holder has vicarious liability for the obligations of one of the merging parties before the merger but ceases to have any interest holder liability for the obligations of the surviving entity after the merger becomes effective. An example would be a general partner in a general partnership that merges into a corporation.

The effects of Subsections (c) and (d) will depend on when a liability is incurred, which is determined by other law. For a discussion of the issue in a related context, see UPA (1997) (Last Amended 2013) § 306(c), cmt. (The Temporal Nexus—When Claim Incurred).

These subsections apply not only to merging domestic limited liability companies but also to any other domestic entity involved in the merger.

Subsection (c)—This subsection sets forth the general rule that an interest holder that was not liable for the liabilities of a merging entity before the merger but will have personal liability for the obligations of the surviving entity after the merger will be personally liable only for the liabilities of a domestic surviving entity that are incurred after the effective date of a merger. When a liability is incurred will be determined by other applicable law.

Subsection (d)—This subsection provides four rules with respect to an interest holder who ceases to have interest holder liability after the effective date of the merger:

(1)   the interest holder remains personally liable for any obligations that were incurred before the effective date of the merger;

(2)   the interest holder does not have any personal liability for obligations of the surviving entity;

(3)   the pre-existing personal liability of the interest holder is enforced against the interest holder on the same basis as if the merger had not taken place; and

(4)   the interest holder has the same rights of contribution from other interest holders of the merging entity as the interest holder would have had if the merger had not occurred.

See the comment to Section 1046(d).

Subsection (e)—When a merger becomes effective, this subsection provides that a foreign entity that is the surviving entity may be served with process in this state. The proceedings covered by this subsection include a proceeding to enforce the rights of any interest holders of each domestic merging entity who are entitled to and exercise appraisal rights. One of the liabilities that a foreign surviving entity succeeds to is the obligation of a merging entity to pay the amount, if any, to which its interest holders who assert appraisal rights are entitled.

[PART] 3

INTEREST EXCHANGE

§ 1031.   INTEREST EXCHANGE AUTHORIZED.

(a) By complying with this [part]:

(1) a domestic limited liability company may acquire all of one or more classes or series of interests of another domestic entity or a foreign entity in exchange for interests, securities, obligations, money, other property, rights to acquire interests or securities, or any combination of the foregoing; or

(2) all of one or more classes or series of interests of a domestic limited liability company may be acquired by another domestic entity or a foreign entity in exchange for interests, securities, obligations, money, other property, rights to acquire interests or securities, or any combination of the foregoing.

(b) By complying with the provisions of this [part] applicable to foreign entities, a foreign entity may be the acquiring or acquired entity in an interest exchange under this [part] if the interest exchange is authorized by the law of the foreign entity's jurisdiction of formation.

(c) If a protected agreement contains a provision that applies to a merger of a domestic limited liability company but does not refer to an interest exchange, the provision applies to an interest exchange in which the domestic limited liability company is the acquired entity as if the interest exchange were a merger until the provision is amended after [the effective date of this [act]].

Comment

An interest exchange is the same type of transaction as the share exchange provided for in section 11.03 of the Model Business Corporation Act. The effect of an interest exchange is that: (i) the separate existence of the acquired entity is not affected; and (ii) the acquiring entity acquires all of the interests of one or more classes of the acquired entity. An interest exchange also allows an indirect acquisition through the use of consideration in the exchange that is not provided by the acquiring entity (*e.g.,* consideration from another or related entity).

Neither share exchanges nor interest exchanges are universally recognized in either corporation or unincorporated entity laws. The effect of an interest exchange can be achieved through a triangular merger in which the acquiring entity forms a new subsidiary and the acquired entity is then merged into the new subsidiary. Part 3 allows the interest exchange to be accomplished directly in a single step, rather than indirectly through the triangular merger route.

The "series" referenced in Subsection (a) are not the series contemplated by the Uniform Statutory Entity Trust Act §§ 401–05 and some LLC statutes. *See, e.g.,* DEL. CODE ANN. tit. 6, § 18–215 (2012); 805 ILL. COMP. STAT. 180/37–40 (2012). Instead, in this context "series" refers to a subset of a class, which is a meaning commonly found in corporation law. *See, e.g.*, MBCA § 6.02. Specific provisions authorizing classes and series are less common in unincorporated entity law but do exist. *See, e.g.*, MINN. STAT. § 322B.155 (2012). In any event, an operating agreement certainly has the power to create classes and series as contemplated by this section.

Subsection (a)—For this section to apply, a domestic limited liability company must be either the acquiring or acquired entity.

The acquiring entity is not required to acquire all of the interests in the acquired entity. For example, assume that an LLC with three classes of membership interests enters into an interest exchange with an acquiring entity. The acquiring entity need only acquire all of the ownership interests of one or more classes of the LLC membership interests.

Subsection (b)—This subsection allows a foreign entity to effectuate an interest exchange with a domestic limited liability company if the interest exchange is authorized by the organic law of the foreign entity.

Subsection (c)—This subsection deals with rights of parties to protected agreements (defined in Section 1001(30)) when an interest exchange takes place. Because the concept of an interest exchange is relatively new, a person contracting with a domestic limited liability company or loaning it money who drafted and negotiated special rights relating to the transaction before the enactment of this article should not be charged with the consequences of not having dealt with the concept of an interest exchange in the context of those special rights. Similarly, when the governance structure of an entity has been negotiated before the enactment of this act, the concept of an interest exchange may not have been reflected in any special governance arrangements; for example, special approval rights may have been provided for fundamental transactions, but those rights fail to include language that would make them applicable to an interest exchange.

Accordingly, this subsection provides a transitional rule that is intended to protect such special rights. If, for example, a limited liability company is a party to a contract that provides that the company cannot participate in a merger without the consent of the other party to the contract, the requirement to obtain the consent of the other party will also apply to an interest exchange in which the entity is the acquired entity. If the limited liability company fails to obtain the consent, the result will be that the other party will have the same rights it would have had if the entity were to participate in a merger without the required consent.

The transitional rule in this subsection ceases to make sense at such time as the provisions of the agreement giving rise to the special rights are first amended after the effective date of this article because at that time the provision may be amended to address expressly an interest exchange. The transitional rule will continue to apply, however, if a provision other than the specific provisions giving rise to the special rights is amended.

§ 1032. PLAN OF INTEREST EXCHANGE.

(a) A domestic limited liability company may be the acquired entity in an interest exchange under this [part] by approving a plan of interest exchange. The plan must be in a record and contain:

(1) the name of the acquired entity;

(2) the name, jurisdiction of formation, and type of entity of the acquiring entity;

(3) the manner of converting the interests in the acquired entity into interests, securities, obligations, money, other property, rights to acquire interests or securities, or any combination of the foregoing;

(4) any proposed amendments to:

(A) the certificate of organization of the acquired entity; and

(B) the operating agreement of the acquired entity that are, or are proposed to be, in a record;

(5) the other terms and conditions of the interest exchange; and

(6) any other provision required by the law of this state or the operating agreement of the acquired entity.

(b) In addition to the requirements of subsection (a), a plan of interest exchange may contain any other provision not prohibited by law.

Comment

This section sets forth the requirements for the plan of interest exchange, which must be approved by the acquired entity in accordance with Section 1031. The content of the plan of interest exchange is similar to the content of a plan of merger. *See* Section 1022.

The plan of interest exchange may, but need not, be filed instead of the statement of interest exchange, Section 1035, so long as the plan contains all the information required to be in the statement and is delivered to the filing office for filing after the plan has been adopted and approved. *See* Section 1035(d).

Subsection (a)—The requirements stated in this subsection are mandatory. *See* Section 105(c)(14).

Subsection (a)(3)—Under this paragraph, interest holders in the acquired entity may receive interests or securities of the acquiring entity or of a party other than the acquiring entity, obligations, rights to acquire interests or securities, cash, or other property. *See* the comment to Section 1022(a)(3).

Subsection (b)—This subsection authorizes the plan to contain any other provision the parties wish to include, unless the provision is prohibited by law.

§ 1033. APPROVAL OF INTEREST EXCHANGE.

(a) A plan of interest exchange is not effective unless it has been approved:

(1) by all the members of a domestic acquired limited liability company entitled to vote on or consent to any matter; and

(2) in a record, by each member of the domestic acquired limited liability company that will have interest holder liability for debts, obligations, and other liabilities that are incurred after the interest exchange becomes effective, unless:

(A) the operating agreement of the company provides in a record for the approval of an interest exchange or a merger in which some or all of its members become subject to interest holder liability by the affirmative vote or consent of fewer than all the members; and

(B) the member consented in a record to or voted for that provision of the operating agreement or became a member after the adoption of that provision.

(b) An interest exchange involving a domestic acquired entity that is not a limited liability company is not effective unless it is approved by the domestic entity in accordance with its organic law.

(c) An interest exchange involving a foreign acquired entity is not effective unless it is approved by the foreign entity in accordance with the law of the foreign entity's jurisdiction of formation.

(d) Except as otherwise provided in its organic law or organic rules, the interest holders of the acquiring entity are not required to approve the interest exchange.

Comment

This section sets forth the required approval of an interest exchange. An interest exchange transaction governed by this article only requires approval by the acquired entity, unless the applicable organic law or the organic rules of the acquiring entity otherwise provide, Subsection (d), a condition that rarely exists.

Subsection (a)(2)—For an explanation of this interest holder liability provision, see Section 1023(a)(2), comment.

§ 1034.   AMENDMENT OR ABANDONMENT OF PLAN OF INTEREST EXCHANGE.

(a) A plan of interest exchange may be amended only with the consent of each party to the plan, except as otherwise provided in the plan.

(b) A domestic acquired limited liability company may approve an amendment of a plan of interest exchange:

(1) in the same manner as the plan was approved, if the plan does not provide for the manner in which it may be amended; or

(2) by its managers or members in the manner provided in the plan, but a member that was entitled to vote on or consent to approval of the interest exchange is entitled to vote on or consent to any amendment of the plan that will change:

(A) the amount or kind of interests, securities, obligations, money, other property, rights to acquire interests or securities, or any combination of the foregoing, to be received by any of the members of the acquired company under the plan;

(B) the certificate of organization or operating agreement of the acquired company that will be in effect immediately after the interest exchange becomes effective, except for changes that do not require approval of the members of the acquired company under this [act] or the operating agreement; or

(C) any other terms or conditions of the plan, if the change would adversely affect the member in any material respect.

(c) After a plan of interest exchange has been approved and before a statement of interest exchange becomes effective, the plan may be abandoned as provided in the plan. Unless prohibited by the plan, a domestic acquired limited liability company may abandon the plan in the same manner as the plan was approved.

(d) If a plan of interest exchange is abandoned after a statement of interest exchange has been delivered to the [Secretary of State] for filing and before the statement becomes effective, a statement of abandonment, signed by the acquired limited liability company, must be delivered to the [Secretary of State] for filing before the statement of interest exchange becomes effective. The statement of abandonment takes effect on filing, and the interest exchange is abandoned and does not become effective. The statement of abandonment must contain:

(1) the name of the acquired company;

(2) the date on which the statement of interest exchange was filed by the [Secretary of State]; and

(3) a statement that the interest exchange has been abandoned in accordance with this section.

Comment

This section parallels provisions in Parts 2 (mergers), 4 (conversions), and 5 (domestications). *See* Sections 1024 (mergers), 1044 (conversions), 1054 (domestications).

§ 1035.   STATEMENT OF INTEREST EXCHANGE; EFFECTIVE DATE OF INTEREST EXCHANGE.

(a) A statement of interest exchange must be signed by a domestic acquired limited liability company and delivered to the [Secretary of State] for filing.

(b) A statement of interest exchange must contain:

(1) the name of the acquired limited liability company;

(2) the name, jurisdiction of formation, and type of entity of the acquiring entity;

(3) a statement that the plan of interest exchange was approved by the acquired company in accordance with this [part]; and

(4) any amendments to the acquired company's certificate of organization approved as part of the plan of interest exchange.

(c) In addition to the requirements of subsection (b), a statement of interest exchange may contain any other provision not prohibited by law.

(d) A plan of interest exchange that is signed by a domestic acquired limited liability company and meets all the requirements of subsection (b) may be delivered to the [Secretary of State] for filing instead of a statement of interest exchange and on filing has the same effect. If a plan of interest exchange is filed as provided in this subsection, references in this [article] to a statement of interest exchange refer to the plan of interest exchange filed under this subsection.

(e) An interest exchange becomes effective when the statement of interest exchange is effective.

Comment

This section applies only when the acquired entity is a domestic limited liability company. The filing makes the transaction a matter of public record.

This act has no filing requirement when the only domestic limited liability company involved is the acquiring entity.

Subsection (b)—This subsection states the requirements for a statement of interest exchange, which are essentially the same as the requirements for a statement of merger under Section 1025(b).

Subsection (d)—A plan of interest exchange can be used as a substitute for the statement of interest exchange so long as the plan satisfies the requirements in Subsection (b).

Subsection (e)—This subsection applies when the acquiring entity is a domestic limited liability company, and Section 207 determines when a record delivered for filing under this act becomes effective. A statement of interest exchange may specify a delayed effective time and date, subject to the ninety-day limit stated in Section 207(3) and (4).

If the acquiring entity is not a domestic limited liability company, the effectiveness of the interest exchange will occur when provided by the law of the jurisdiction of formation of the acquiring entity.

§ 1036. EFFECT OF INTEREST EXCHANGE.

(a) When an interest exchange in which the acquired entity is a domestic limited liability company becomes effective:

(1) the interests in the acquired company which are the subject of the interest exchange are converted, and the members holding those interests are entitled only to the rights provided to them under the plan of interest exchange and to any appraisal rights they have under Section 1006;

(2) the acquiring entity becomes the interest holder of the interests in the acquired company stated in the plan of interest exchange to be acquired by the acquiring entity;

(3) the certificate of organization of the acquired company is amended to the extent provided in the statement of interest exchange; and

(4) the provisions of the operating agreement of the acquired company that are to be in a record, if any, are amended to the extent provided in the plan of interest exchange.

(b) Except as otherwise provided in the operating agreement of a domestic acquired limited liability company, the interest exchange does not give rise to any rights that a member, manager, or third party would have upon a dissolution, liquidation, or winding up of the acquired company.

(c) When an interest exchange becomes effective, a person that did not have interest holder liability with respect to a domestic acquired limited liability company and becomes subject to interest holder liability with respect to a domestic entity as a result of the interest exchange has interest holder liability only to the extent provided by the organic law of the entity and only for those debts, obligations, and other liabilities that are incurred after the interest exchange becomes effective.

(d) When an interest exchange becomes effective, the interest holder liability of a person that ceases to hold an interest in a domestic acquired limited liability company with respect to which the person had interest holder liability is subject to the following rules:

(1) The interest exchange does not discharge any interest holder liability under this [act] to the extent the interest holder liability was incurred before the interest exchange became effective.

(2) The person does not have interest holder liability under this [act] for any debt, obligation, or other liability that is incurred after the interest exchange becomes effective.

(3) This [act] continues to apply to the release, collection, or discharge of any interest holder liability preserved under paragraph (1) as if the interest exchange had not occurred.

(4) The person has whatever rights of contribution from any other person as are provided by this [act], law other than this [act], or the operating agreement of the acquired company with respect to any interest holder liability preserved under paragraph (1) as if the interest exchange had not occurred.

Comment

This section applies only when the *acquired* entity is a domestic limited liability company, and this part states no rule for the effect of an interest exchange when the only domestic limited liability company involved is the *acquiring* entity. For that situation, the other provisions of this act must be consulted, because this act is the organic law of the acquiring entity.

Subsection (a)—In contrast to a merger, an interest exchange does not in and of itself affect the separate existence of the parties, vest in the acquiring entity the assets of the acquired entity, or render the acquiring entity liable for the liabilities of the acquired entity. Thus, Subsection (a) is significantly simpler than Section 1026(a) with respect to the effects of a merger.

When an interest exchange becomes effective: (i) the interests of the acquired domestic limited liability company are exchanged, converted, or canceled as provided in the plan; (ii) the only rights of the former members and transferees of the acquired LLC whose interests are affected by the interest exchange are those rights related to the exchange, conversion, or cancellation; (iii) the acquiring entity becomes the owner of the acquired LLC's interests as provided in the plan; (iv) the certificate of organization of the acquired LLC is amended as provided in the statement of interest exchange, thus obviating the need for repetitive filings (*i.e.*, a filing as to the entity interest exchange and another filing to reflect amendments to certificate); and (v) the provisions of the operating agreement of the acquired LLC that are to be in a record, if any, are amended to the extent provided in the plan of interest exchange.

Subsection (c)—This subsection provides the rule for future interest holder liability pertaining to domestic entities and parallels analogous provisions in Parts 2 (mergers), 4 (conversions), and 5 (domestications). *See* the comment to Section 1026.

Subsection (d)—This subsection provides the rule for past interest holder liability and parallels analogous provisions in Parts 2 (mergers), 4 (conversions), and 5 (domestications). *See* the comments to Sections 1026(d) and 1046(d).

[PART] 4

CONVERSION

§ 1041. CONVERSION AUTHORIZED.

(a) By complying with this [part], a domestic limited liability company may become:

(1) a domestic entity that is a different type of entity; or

(2) a foreign entity that is a different type of entity, if the conversion is authorized by the law of the foreign entity's jurisdiction of formation.

(b) By complying with the provisions of this [part] applicable to foreign entities, a foreign entity that is not a foreign limited liability company may become a domestic limited liability company if the conversion is authorized by the law of the foreign entity's jurisdiction of formation.

(c) If a protected agreement contains a provision that applies to a merger of a domestic limited liability company but does not refer to a conversion, the provision applies to a conversion of the company as if the conversion were a merger until the provision is amended after [the effective date of this [act]].

Comment

This part of Article 10 permits an entity to change to a different type of entity in its jurisdiction of formation or in a foreign jurisdiction. A transaction in which an entity changes its jurisdiction of organization but does not change its type is a domestication and is the subject of Part 5.

Subsection (a)(2)—For this provision to apply, this type of conversion must be authorized by the law of the foreign jurisdiction. If this is not the case, it may be possible to achieve the same result by forming an entity of the type desired in the foreign jurisdiction and then merging the domestic entity into the new foreign entity under Part 2 of Article 10.

Subsection (b)—This subsection allows a foreign entity to effectuate a conversion into a domestic limited liability company, but only if the conversion is permitted by the laws of the foreign entity's jurisdiction of formation. When a foreign entity becomes a domestic limited liability company pursuant to this part of Article 10, the effect of the conversion will be as provided in Section 1046. The procedures by which the conversion is approved, however, will be determined by the laws of the foreign entity's jurisdiction of formation. *See* Section 102(7) (defining "jurisdiction of formation").

Subsection (c)—*See* the comment to Section 1031(c).

§ 1042. PLAN OF CONVERSION.

(a) A domestic limited liability company may convert to a different type of entity under this [part] by approving a plan of conversion. The plan must be in a record and contain:

(1) the name of the converting limited liability company;

(2) the name, jurisdiction of formation, and type of entity of the converted entity;

(3) the manner of converting the interests in the converting limited liability company into interests, securities, obligations, money, other property, rights to acquire interests or securities, or any combination of the foregoing;

(4) the proposed public organic record of the converted entity if it will be a filing entity;

(5) the full text of the private organic rules of the converted entity which are proposed to be in a record;

(6) the other terms and conditions of the conversion; and

(7) any other provision required by the law of this state or the operating agreement of the converting limited liability company.

(b) In addition to the requirements of subsection (a), a plan of conversion may contain any other provision not prohibited by law.

Comment

This section sets forth the requirements for the plan of conversion, which must be approved by the converting entity in accordance with Section 1043. The content of a plan of conversion is similar to the content of a plan of merger. *See* Section 1022.

Subsection (a)—The requirements stated in this subsection are mandatory. *See* Section 105(c)(14).

Subsection (a)(3)—Interest holders in the converting entity may receive interests or other securities of the converted entity or of any other person, obligations, rights to acquire interests or other securities, cash, or other property. *See* Sections 1022(a)(3) (mergers), 1032(a)(3) (interest exchanges), 1052(a)(3) (domestications).

Subsection (b)—This subsection authorizes the plan to contain any other provision the parties wish to include, unless the provision is prohibited by law.

§ 1043. APPROVAL OF CONVERSION.

(a) A plan of conversion is not effective unless it has been approved:

(1) by a domestic converting limited liability company, by all the members of the limited liability company entitled to vote on or consent to any matter; and

(2) in a record, by each member of a domestic converting limited liability company which will have interest holder liability for debts, obligations, and other liabilities that are incurred after the conversion becomes effective, unless:

(A) the operating agreement of the company provides in a record for the approval of a conversion or a merger in which some or all of its members become subject to interest holder liability by the affirmative vote or consent of fewer than all the members; and

(B) the member voted for or consented in a record to that provision of the operating agreement or became a member after the adoption of that provision.

(b) A conversion involving a domestic converting entity that is not a limited liability company is not effective unless it is approved by the domestic converting entity in accordance with its organic law.

(c) A conversion of a foreign converting entity is not effective unless it is approved by the foreign entity in accordance with the law of the foreign entity's jurisdiction of formation.

Comment

Subsection (a)(1)—This provision is a default rule, subject to change in the operating agreement.

Subsection (a)(2)—This provision is not a default rule. Section 105(c)(14). For an explanation of this interest holder liability provision, see Section 1023(a)(2), comment.

§ 1044. AMENDMENT OR ABANDONMENT OF PLAN OF CONVERSION.

(a) A plan of conversion of a domestic converting limited liability company may be amended:

(1) in the same manner as the plan was approved, if the plan does not provide for the manner in which it may be amended; or

(2) by its managers or members in the manner provided in the plan, but a member that was entitled to vote on or consent to approval of the conversion is entitled to vote on or consent to any amendment of the plan that will change:

(A) the amount or kind of interests, securities, obligations, money, other property, rights to acquire interests or securities, or any combination of the foregoing, to be received by any of the members of the converting company under the plan;

(B) the public organic record, if any, or private organic rules of the converted entity which will be in effect immediately after the conversion becomes effective, except for changes that do not require approval of the interest holders of the converted entity under its organic law or organic rules; or

(C) any other terms or conditions of the plan, if the change would adversely affect the member in any material respect.

(b) After a plan of conversion has been approved by a domestic converting limited liability company and before a statement of conversion becomes effective, the plan may be abandoned as provided in the plan. Unless prohibited by the plan, a domestic converting limited liability company may abandon the plan in the same manner as the plan was approved.

(c) If a plan of conversion is abandoned after a statement of conversion has been delivered to the [Secretary of State] for filing and before the statement becomes effective, a statement of abandonment, signed by the converting entity, must be delivered to the [Secretary of State] for filing before the statement of conversion becomes effective. The statement of abandonment takes effect on filing, and the conversion is abandoned and does not become effective. The statement of abandonment must contain:

(1) the name of the converting limited liability company;

(2) the date on which the statement of conversion was filed by the [Secretary of State]; and

(3) a statement that the conversion has been abandoned in accordance with this section.

Comment

This section parallels analogous provisions in Parts 2 (mergers), 3 (interest exchanges), and 5 (domestications). *See* Sections 1024 (mergers), 1034 (interest exchanges), 1054 (domestications).

§ 1045. STATEMENT OF CONVERSION; EFFECTIVE DATE OF CONVERSION.

(a) A statement of conversion must be signed by the converting entity and delivered to the [Secretary of State] for filing.

(b) A statement of conversion must contain:

(1) the name, jurisdiction of formation, and type of entity of the converting entity;

(2) the name, jurisdiction of formation, and type of entity of the converted entity;

(3) if the converting entity is a domestic limited liability company, a statement that the plan of conversion was approved in accordance with this [part] or, if the converting entity is a foreign entity, a statement that the conversion was approved by the foreign entity in accordance with the law of its jurisdiction of formation;

(4) if the converted entity is a domestic filing entity, its public organic record, as an attachment; and

(5) if the converted entity is a domestic limited liability partnership, its statement of qualification, as an attachment.

(c) In addition to the requirements of subsection (b), a statement of conversion may contain any other provision not prohibited by law.

(d) If the converted entity is a domestic entity, its public organic record, if any, must satisfy the requirements of the law of this state, except that the public organic record does not need to be signed.

(e) A plan of conversion that is signed by a domestic converting limited liability company and meets all the requirements of subsection (b) may be delivered to the [Secretary of State] for filing instead of a statement of conversion and on filing has the same effect. If a plan of conversion is filed as provided in this subsection, references in this [article] to a statement of conversion refer to the plan of conversion filed under this subsection.

(f) If the converted entity is a domestic limited liability company, the conversion becomes effective when the statement of conversion is effective. In all other cases, the conversion becomes effective on the later of:

(1) the date and time provided by the organic law of the converted entity; and

(2) when the statement is effective.

Comment

This section applies regardless of whether a domestic limited liability company is the converting or converted entity. A foreign entity seeking to convert to a domestic LLC must therefore comply with this section.

If either the converting or converted entity is a foreign entity, the organic law of the foreign entity's jurisdiction must also be consulted.

The filing of a statement of conversion makes the transaction a matter of public record.

Subsection (b)—This subsection sets forth the requirements for a statement of conversion. They are essentially the same as the requirements for a statement of merger in Section 1025.

Subsection (e)—A plan of conversion can be used as a substitute for the statement of conversion so long as the plan satisfies the requirements in Subsection (b).

Subsection (f)—Section 207 determines when a record delivered for filing under this act becomes effective. A statement of conversion may specify a delayed effective time and date, subject to the ninety-day limit stated in Section 207(3) and (4).

When the statement of conversion becomes effective under this subsection, the conversion transaction occurs if the converted entity is a domestic limited liability company. A conversion in which the converted entity is a foreign entity will usually also take effect when the statement of conversion takes effect because the best practice will be to coordinate the filings that need to be made when a conversion involves both a domestic entity and also a foreign entity so that the filings in each jurisdiction take effect at the same time.

However, when the converting limited liability company is a foreign limited liability company, it is possible that the filing in the foreign jurisdiction will take effect at a different time. For that reason, this subsection provides that the conversion will take effect at the later of: (i) when the statement of conversion takes effect; and (ii) when the conversion takes effect under the law of the foreign jurisdiction. This rule avoids the possibility that the conversion will take effect in this state before it takes effect in the foreign jurisdiction, which would produce the undesirable result that the converting domestic limited liability company would cease to appear as an active entity on the records of this state before appearing as its active, converted self on the records of the foreign jurisdiction.

It is only necessary for the filing office to record the effective date of the statement of conversion and the filing office does not need to be concerned with the effective date of the conversion itself. Persons wishing to determine the effective date of a conversion involving both a domestic limited liability company and a foreign entity will be able to do so by consulting the records of the filing offices in each jurisdiction.

§ 1046.   EFFECT OF CONVERSION.

(a) When a conversion becomes effective:

　　(1) the converted entity is:

　　　　(A) organized under and subject to the organic law of the converted entity; and

　　　　(B) the same entity without interruption as the converting entity;

　　(2) all property of the converting entity continues to be vested in the converted entity without transfer, reversion, or impairment;

　　(3) all debts, obligations, and other liabilities of the converting entity continue as debts, obligations, and other liabilities of the converted entity;

　　(4) except as otherwise provided by law or the plan of conversion, all the rights, privileges, immunities, powers, and purposes of the converting entity remain in the converted entity;

　　(5) the name of the converted entity may be substituted for the name of the converting entity in any pending action or proceeding;

　　(6) the certificate of organization of the converted entity becomes effective;

　　(7) the provisions of the operating agreement of the converted entity which are to be in a record, if any, approved as part of the plan of conversion become effective; and

　　(8) the interests in the converting entity are converted, and the interest holders of the converting entity are entitled only to the rights provided to them under the plan of conversion and to any appraisal rights they have under Section 1006.

(b) Except as otherwise provided in the operating agreement of a domestic converting limited liability company, the conversion does not give rise to any rights that a member, manager, or third party would have upon a dissolution, liquidation, or winding up of the converting entity.

(c) When a conversion becomes effective, a person that did not have interest holder liability with respect to the converting entity and becomes subject to interest holder liability with respect to a domestic entity as a result of the conversion has interest holder liability only to the extent provided by the organic law of the entity and only for those debts, obligations, and other liabilities that are incurred after the conversion becomes effective.

(d) When a conversion becomes effective, the interest holder liability of a person that ceases to hold an interest in a domestic converting limited liability company with respect to which the person had interest holder liability is subject to the following rules:

(1) The conversion does not discharge any interest holder liability under this [act] to the extent the interest holder liability was incurred before the conversion became effective;

(2) The person does not have interest holder liability under this [act] for any debt, obligation, or other liability that arises after the conversion becomes effective.

(3) This [act] continues to apply to the release, collection, or discharge of any interest holder liability preserved under paragraph (1) as if the conversion had not occurred.

(4) The person has whatever rights of contribution from any other person as are provided by this [act], law other than this [act], or the organic rules of the converting entity with respect to any interest holder liability preserved under paragraph (1) as if the conversion had not occurred.

(e) When a conversion becomes effective, a foreign entity that is the converted entity may be served with process in this state for the collection and enforcement of any of its debts, obligations, and other liabilities as provided in Section 119.

(f) If the converting entity is a registered foreign entity, its registration to do business in this state is canceled when the conversion becomes effective.

(g) A conversion does not require the entity to wind up its affairs and does not constitute or cause the dissolution of the entity.

Comment

A converted entity is the same entity as it was before the conversion; the entity just has a different legal form.

Subsection (a)—This subsection states the principal legal effects of a conversion. The converted entity remains the owner of all real and personal property and remains subject to all the liabilities, actual or contingent, of the converted entity. A conversion is not a conveyance, transfer, or assignment. A conversion does not give rise to: (i) claims of reverter or impairment of title based on a prohibited conveyance or transfer; or (ii) to a claim that a contract with the converting entity is no longer in effect on the ground of nonassignability, unless the contract specifically provides that it does not survive a conversion. The contract rights that remain in the converted entity include, without limitation, the right to enforce subscription agreements for interests and obligations to make capital contributions entered into or incurred before the conversion.

When a conversion becomes effective, the internal affairs of the converting entity are no longer governed by its former organic law but instead by the organic law of the converted entity. As a result, filings that may have been made under the organic law of the converting entity, such as the following, will no longer be effective: a statement of qualification as a limited liability partnership under UPA (1997) (Last Amended 2013) § 901, a statement of partnership authority under section 303 of that act, a statement of authority under ULLCA (2006) (Last Amended 2013) § 302, or under Uniform Unincorporated Nonprofit Association Act (2008) (Last Amended 2013) § 7.

Subsection (a)(5)—All pending proceedings involving the converting entity are continued. The name of the converted entity may be, but need not be, substituted in any pending proceeding for the name of the converting entity.

Subsection (c)—This subsection provides the rule for future interest holder liability and parallels provisions in Parts 2 (mergers), 3 (interest exchanges), and 5 (domestications). *See* the comment to Section 1026(c).

Subsection (d)—Subsection (d) provides the rule for past interest holder liability and parallels analogous provisions in Parts 2 (mergers), 3 (interest exchanges), and 5 (domestications). *See* the comment to Section 1026(d).

At first glance, this subsection might seem to apply to the null set; members of an LLC typically do not have interest holder liability. However, the definition of interest holder liability also includes "personal liability for a liability of an entity which is imposed on a person . . . by the organic rules of the entity which make one or more specified interest holders or categories of interest holders liable in their capacity as interest holders for all or specified liabilities of the entity." Section 1001(19)(A)(ii).

Subsection (e)—For this provision to apply, the converting entity must have been a domestic limited liability company. When a domestic LLC becomes a foreign entity as a result of a conversion, some mechanism is needed to facilitate the enforcement of claims by the creditors and interest holders of the converting LLC. This subsection, which parallels analogous provisions in Parts 2 (mergers) and 5 (domestications), authorizes service of process for all such claims in this state.

Subsection (g)—When a conversion takes effect, the entity continues to exist—simply in a different form. This subsection thus makes clear that the conversion does not require the entity to wind up its affairs and does not constitute or cause the dissolution of the entity.

[PART] 5

DOMESTICATION

§ 1051. DOMESTICATION AUTHORIZED.

(a) By complying with this [part], a domestic limited liability company may become a foreign limited liability company if the domestication is authorized by the law of the foreign jurisdiction.

(b) By complying with the provisions of this [part] applicable to foreign limited liability companies, a foreign limited liability company may become a domestic limited liability company if the domestication is authorized by the law of the foreign limited liability company's jurisdiction of formation.

(c) If a protected agreement contains a provision that applies to a merger of a domestic limited liability company but does not refer to a domestication, the provision applies to a domestication of the limited liability company as if the domestication were a merger until the provision is amended after [the effective date of this [act]].

Comment

A domestication authorized by Part 5 of Article 10 differs from a conversion in that a domestication requires that the domesticating entity be the same type of entity as the domesticated entity. In a conversion, by contrast, the converting entity changes its type.

As with a conversion, all rights and privileges, debts, obligations and other liabilities, and actions or proceedings of a domesticating entity vest unimpaired in the domesticated entity. A domestication is not a sale, transfer, assignment, or conveyance and does not give rise to a claim of reverter or impairment of title.

Part 5 of Article 10 governs the legal effect of a foreign limited liability company domesticating in this state. On the other hand, the organic laws of the foreign jurisdiction, and not Part 5, will govern the legal effect of most aspects of a domestication of a domestic limited liability company in another jurisdiction. In the latter scenario, Part 5 authorizes the domestication of the domestic entity in the foreign jurisdiction, but Part 5 does not create a right in the domestic entity to be received in the foreign jurisdiction. Similarly, this section does not provide a right on the part of a foreign limited liability company to become a domestic limited liability company if the domestication is not authorized by the laws of the foreign jurisdiction. If the foreign jurisdiction does not authorize a domestication transaction, the same results can be accomplished by forming a new limited liability company in this state and merging the existing foreign limited liability company into the new domestic limited liability company.

Subsection (c)—*See* Section 1031(c).

§ 1052. PLAN OF DOMESTICATION.

(a) A domestic limited liability company may become a foreign limited liability company in a domestication by approving a plan of domestication. The plan must be in a record and contain:

(1) the name of the domesticating limited liability company;

(2) the name and jurisdiction of formation of the domesticated limited liability company;

(3) the manner of converting the interests in the domesticating limited liability company into interests, securities, obligations, money, other property, rights to acquire interests or securities, or any combination of the foregoing;

(4) the proposed certificate of organization of the domesticated limited liability company;

(5) the full text of the provisions of the operating agreement of the domesticated limited liability company that are proposed to be in a record;

(6) the other terms and conditions of the domestication; and

(7) any other provision required by the law of this state or the operating agreement of the domesticating limited liability company.

(b) In addition to the requirements of subsection (a), a plan of domestication may contain any other provision not prohibited by law.

Comment

This section sets forth the requirements for the plan of domestication for a domestic limited liability company seeking to become a limited liability company existing under the law of another jurisdiction. For a foreign limited liability company seeking to become a domestic limited liability company, the organic law of the foreign limited liability company governs the requirements for a plan of domestication. The content of a plan of domestication is similar to the content of a plan of merger. *See* Section 1022.

Subsection (a)—The requirements stated in this subsection are mandatory. *See* Section 105(c)(14).

Subsection (a)(3)—Interest holders in the domesticating limited liability company may receive interests or other securities of the domesticated limited liability company or any other entity, obligations, rights to acquire interests or other securities, cash, or other property. *See* the comment to Section 1022(a)(3).

Subsection (b)—This subsection authorizes the plan to contain any other provision the parties wish to include, unless the provision is prohibited by law.

§ 1053. APPROVAL OF DOMESTICATION.

(a) A plan of domestication of a domestic domesticating limited liability company is not effective unless it has been approved:

(1) by all the members entitled to vote on or consent to any matter; and

(2) in a record, by each member that will have interest holder liability for debts, obligations, and other liabilities that are incurred after the domestication becomes effective, unless:

(A) the operating agreement of the domesticating company in a record provides for the approval of a domestication or merger in which some or all of its members become subject to interest holder liability by the affirmative vote or consent of fewer than all the members; and

(B) the member voted for or consented in a record to that provision of the operating agreement or became a member after the adoption of that provision.

(b) A domestication of a foreign domesticating limited liability company is not effective unless it is approved in accordance with the law of the foreign limited liability company's jurisdiction of formation.

Comment

Subsection (a)(1)—This provision is a default rule, subject to change in the operating agreement.

Subsection (a)(2)—This provision is mandatory. Section 105(c)(14). For an explanation of the provision, see Section 1023(a)(2), comment.

Subsection (b)—In the case of a foreign limited liability company that is domesticating in this state, this subsection provides that the required approval is determined by the laws of the foreign limited liability company's jurisdiction of formation.

§ 1054. AMENDMENT OR ABANDONMENT OF PLAN OF DOMESTICATION.

(a) A plan of domestication of a domestic domesticating limited liability company may be amended:

(1) in the same manner as the plan was approved, if the plan does not provide for the manner in which it may be amended; or

(2) by its managers or members in the manner provided in the plan, but a member that was entitled to vote on or consent to approval of the domestication is entitled to vote on or consent to any amendment of the plan that will change:

(A) the amount or kind of interests, securities, obligations, money, other property, rights to acquire interests or securities, or any combination of the foregoing, to be received by any of the members of the domesticating limited liability company under the plan;

(B) the certificate of organization or operating agreement of the domesticated limited liability company that will be in effect immediately after the domestication becomes effective, except for changes that do not require approval of the members of the domesticated limited liability company under its organic law or operating agreement; or

(C) any other terms or conditions of the plan, if the change would adversely affect the member in any material respect.

(b) After a plan of domestication has been approved by a domestic domesticating limited liability company and before a statement of domestication becomes effective, the plan may be abandoned as provided in the plan. Unless prohibited by the plan, a domestic domesticating limited liability company may abandon the plan in the same manner as the plan was approved.

(c) If a plan of domestication is abandoned after a statement of domestication has been delivered to the [Secretary of State] for filing and before the statement becomes effective, a statement of abandonment, signed by the domesticating limited liability company, must be delivered to the [Secretary of State] for filing before the statement of domestication becomes effective. The statement of abandonment takes effect on filing, and the domestication is abandoned and does not become effective. The statement of abandonment must contain:

(1) the name of the domesticating limited liability company;

(2) the date on which the statement of domestication was filed by the [Secretary of State]; and

(3) a statement that the domestication has been abandoned in accordance with this section.

Comment

This section parallels provisions in Parts 2 (mergers), 3 (interest exchanges), and 4 (conversions). *See* Sections 1024 (mergers), 1034 (interest exchanges), 1044 (conversions).

§ 1055. STATEMENT OF DOMESTICATION; EFFECTIVE DATE OF DOMESTICATION.

(a) A statement of domestication must be signed by the domesticating limited liability company and delivered to the [Secretary of State] for filing.

(b) A statement of domestication must contain:

(1) the name and jurisdiction of formation of the domesticating limited liability company;

(2) the name and jurisdiction of formation of the domesticated limited liability company;

(3) if the domesticating limited liability company is a domestic limited liability company, a statement that the plan of domestication was approved in accordance with this [part] or, if the domesticating limited liability company is a foreign limited liability company, a statement that the domestication was approved in accordance with the law of its jurisdiction of formation; and

(4) the certificate of organization of the domesticated limited liability company, as an attachment.

(c) In addition to the requirements of subsection (b), a statement of domestication may contain any other provision not prohibited by law.

(d) The certificate of organization of a domestic domesticated limited liability company must satisfy the requirements of this [act], but the certificate does not need to be signed.

(e) A plan of domestication that is signed by a domesticating domestic limited liability company and meets all the requirements of subsection (b) may be delivered to the [Secretary of State] for filing instead of a statement of domestication and on filing has the same effect. If a plan of domestication is filed as provided in this subsection, references in this [article] to a statement of domestication refer to the plan of domestication filed under this subsection.

(f) If the domesticated entity is a domestic limited liability company, the domestication becomes effective when the statement of domestication is effective. If the domesticated entity is a foreign limited liability company, the domestication becomes effective on the later of:

(1) the date and time provided by the organic law of the domesticated entity; and

(2) when the statement is effective.

Comment

Regardless of whether a domestic limited liability company is the domesticating or domesticated entity:

- This section applies and, therefore, a foreign limited liability company seeking to domesticate and thereby become a domestic LLC must comply with this section.

- The organic law of the foreign LLC's jurisdiction must also be consulted.

The filing of a statement of domestication makes the transaction a matter of public record.

Subsection (b)—This subsection sets forth the requirements for a statement of domestication. They are essentially the same as the requirements for a statement of merger in Section 1025.

Subsection (e)—A plan of domestication can be used as a substitute for the statement of domestication so long as the plan satisfies the requirements in Subsection (b).

Subsection (f)—Section 207 determines when a record delivered for filing under this act becomes effective. A statement of domestication may specify a delayed effective time and date, subject to the ninety-day limit stated in Section 207(3) and (4).

When the statement of domestication becomes effective under this subsection, the domestication transaction occurs if the domesticated entity is a domestic limited liability company. A domestication in which the domesticated entity is a foreign limited liability company will usually also take effect when the statement of domestication takes effect because the best practice will be to coordinate the filings that need to be made in each jurisdiction so that they take effect at the same time.

However, when the domesticated limited liability company is a foreign limited liability company, it is possible that the filing in the foreign jurisdiction will take effect at a different time. For that reason, this subsection provides that the domestication will take effect at the later of: (i) when the statement of domestication takes effect; and (ii) when the domestication takes effect under the law of the foreign jurisdiction. This rule avoids the possibility that the domestication will take effect in this state before it takes effect in the foreign jurisdiction, which would produce the undesirable result that the domesticating domestic limited liability company would cease to appear as an active entity on the records of this state before appearing as its active, domesticated self on the records of the foreign jurisdiction.

It is only necessary for the filing office to record the effective date of the statement of domestication and the filing office does not need to be concerned with the effective date of the domestication itself. Persons wishing to determine the effective date of a domestication will be able to do so by consulting the records of the filing offices in each jurisdiction.

§ 1056. EFFECT OF DOMESTICATION.

(a) When a domestication becomes effective:

(1) the domesticated entity is:

(A) organized under and subject to the organic law of the domesticated entity; and

(B) the same entity without interruption as the domesticating entity;

(2) all property of the domesticating entity continues to be vested in the domesticated entity without transfer, reversion, or impairment;

(3) all debts, obligations, and other liabilities of the domesticating entity continue as debts, obligations, and other liabilities of the domesticated entity;

(4) except as otherwise provided by law or the plan of domestication, all the rights, privileges, immunities, powers, and purposes of the domesticating entity remain in the domesticated entity;

(5) the name of the domesticated entity may be substituted for the name of the domesticating entity in any pending action or proceeding;

(6) the certificate of organization of the domesticated entity becomes effective;

(7) the provisions of the operating agreement of the domesticated entity that are to be in a record, if any, approved as part of the plan of domestication become effective; and

(8) the interests in the domesticating entity are converted to the extent and as approved in connection with the domestication, and the members of the domesticating entity are entitled only to the rights provided to them under the plan of domestication and to any appraisal rights they have under Section 1006.

(b) Except as otherwise provided in the organic law or operating agreement of the domesticating limited liability company, the domestication does not give rise to any rights that a member, manager, or third party would otherwise have upon a dissolution, liquidation, or winding up of the domesticating company.

(c) When a domestication becomes effective, a person that did not have interest holder liability with respect to the domesticating limited liability company and becomes subject to interest holder liability with respect to a domestic company as a result of the domestication has interest holder liability only to the extent provided by this [act] and only for those debts, obligations, and other liabilities that are incurred after the domestication becomes effective.

(d) When a domestication becomes effective, the interest holder liability of a person that ceases to hold an interest in a domestic domesticating limited liability company with respect to which the person had interest holder liability is subject to the following rules:

(1) The domestication does not discharge any interest holder liability under this [act] to the extent the interest holder liability was incurred before the domestication became effective.

(2) A person does not have interest holder liability under this [act] for any debt, obligation, or other liability that is incurred after the domestication becomes effective.

(3) This [act] continues to apply to the release, collection, or discharge of any interest holder liability preserved under paragraph (1) as if the domestication had not occurred.

(4) A person has whatever rights of contribution from any other person as are provided by this [act], law other than this [act], or the operating agreement of the domestic domesticating limited liability company with respect to any interest holder liability preserved under paragraph (1) as if the domestication had not occurred.

(e) When a domestication becomes effective, a foreign limited liability company that is the domesticated company may be served with process in this state for the collection and enforcement of any of its debts, obligations, and other liabilities as provided in Section 119.

(f) If the domesticating limited liability company is a registered foreign entity, the registration of the company is canceled when the domestication becomes effective.

(g) A domestication does not require a domestic domesticating limited liability company to wind up its affairs and does not constitute or cause the dissolution of the company.

Comment

Subsection (a)(1)—The domesticated entity is the same entity as the domesticating entity; it has merely changed its jurisdiction of formation.

Subsection (a)(2)—A domestication is not a sale, conveyance, transfer, or assignment and does not give rise to claims of reverter or impairment of title that may be based on a prohibition on transfer, assignment, or conveyance.

Subsection (a)(4)—All pending proceedings involving the domesticating entity are continued. The name of the domesticated entity may be, but need not be, substituted in any pending proceeding for the name of the domesticating entity.

Subsection (a)(8)—The interests of the domesticating limited liability company are reclassified into whatever rights were negotiated in the domestication and the members and transferees of the domesticating LLC are only entitled to those rights. Paragraph 8, on its face, allows for certain members of the domesticating LLC to be entitled to a continuing equity interest in the domesticated LLC whereas other members of the domesticating LLC may be cashed out as a result of the transaction.

Subsection (c)—This subsection provides the rule for future interest holder liability and parallels analogous provisions in Parts 2 (mergers), 3 (interest exchanges), and 4 (conversions). *See* the comment to Section 1026(c).

Subsection (d)—This subsection provides the rule for past interest holder liability and parallels analogous provisions in Parts 2 (mergers), 3 (interest exchanges), and 4 (conversions). *See* the comments to Sections 1026(d) and 1046(d).

Subsection (e)—When a domestic domesticating limited liability company becomes a foreign LLC as a result of a domestication, some mechanism is needed to facilitate the enforcement of claims by the creditors and interest holders of the domesticating LLC. This subsection, which parallels analogous provisions in Parts 2 (mergers) and 4 (conversions), authorizes service of process for all such claims in this state.

Subsection (g)—When a domestication takes effect, the entity continues to exist—simply as a domestic entity under the laws of a different state. This subsection thus makes clear that the domestication does not require the limited liability company to wind up its affairs and does not constitute or cause the dissolution of the limited liability company.

[ARTICLE] 11

MISCELLANEOUS PROVISIONS

§ 1101. UNIFORMITY OF APPLICATION AND CONSTRUCTION.

In applying and construing this uniform act, consideration must be given to the need to promote uniformity of the law with respect to its subject matter among states that enact it.

§ 1102. RELATION TO ELECTRONIC SIGNATURES IN GLOBAL AND NATIONAL COMMERCE ACT.

This [act] modifies, limits, and supersedes the Electronic Signatures in Global and National Commerce Act, 15 U.S.C. Section 7001 et seq., but does not modify, limit, or supersede Section 101(c) of that act, 15 U.S.C. Section 7001(c), or authorize electronic delivery of any of the notices described in Section 103(b) of that act, 15 U.S.C. Section 7003(b).

Comment

This section responds to specific language of the Electronic Signatures in Global and National Commerce Act and is designed to avoid preemption of state law under that federal legislation.

§ 1103. SAVINGS CLAUSE.

This [act] does not affect an action commenced, proceeding brought, or right accrued before [the effective date of this [act]].

Comment

This section continues prior law after the effective date of this act with respect to rights accrued and proceedings. But for this section, the new law of this act would displace the old laws in some circumstances. The power of a new act to displace the old statute with respect to conduct occurring before the new act's enactment is substantial. Millard H. Ruud, *The Savings Clause—Some Problems in Construction and Drafting*, 33 TEX. L. REV. 285, 286–93 (1955). A court generally applies the law that exists at the time it acts.

Eventually, this act will apply all to pre-existing limited liability companies—whether by choice under Section 110(a)(2) (permitting an early opt-in), or without choice on the "all-inclusive date." Section 110(b). In this context, the phrase "before [the effective date of this [act]]" should be understood as referring to the date upon which this act became applicable to the particular limited liability company at issue.

[§ 1104. SEVERABILITY CLAUSE.

If any provision of this [act] or its application to any person or circumstance is held invalid, the invalidity does not affect other provisions or applications of this [act] which can be given effect without the invalid provision or application, and to this end the provisions of this [act] are severable.]

Legislative Note: Include this section only if this state lacks a general severability statute or decision by the highest court of this state stating a general rule of severability.

§ 1105. REPEALS.

The following are repealed:

(1) [the state limited liability company act, as [amended, and as] in effect immediately before [the effective date of this [act]];

(2) . . . .

(3) . . . .

§ 1106. EFFECTIVE DATE.

This [act] takes effect. . . .

Comment

For the effect of the act's effective date on pre-existing limited liability companies, see Section 110.

LIMITED LIABILITY COMPANY
AGREEMENT—SHORT-FORM

Short-Form Limited Liability Company Agreement—Member-Managed (Portfolio 67: Limited Liability Companies: Legal Aspects of Organization, Operation, and Dissolution)

THE UNDERSIGNED are executing this Limited Liability Company Agreement ("Agreement") for the purpose of forming a limited liability company (the "Company") pursuant to the provisions of the Delaware Limited Liability Company Act, 6 *Del. C.* §§ 18–101 *et seq.* (the "Delaware Act"), and do hereby certify and agree as follows:

1. *Name; Formation.* The name of the Company shall be _____, L.L.C., or such other name as the Members may from time to time hereafter designate. The Company shall be formed upon the execution and filing by any Member (each of which is hereby authorized to take such action) of a certificate of formation of the Company with the Secretary of State of the State of Delaware setting forth the information required by Section 18–201 of the Delaware Act.

2. *Definitions; Rules of Construction.* In addition to terms otherwise defined herein, the following terms are used herein as defined below:

"Capital Contribution" means, with respect to any Member, the amount of capital contributed by such Member to the Company in accordance with Section 8 hereof.

"Event of Withdrawal" means the occurrence of any event that terminates the continued membership of a Member in the Company.

"Initial Members" mean _____, a(n) _____, and _____, a(n) _____.

"Interest" means the ownership interest of a Member in the Company (which shall be considered personal property for all purposes), consisting of (i) such Member's Percentage Interest in profits, losses, allocations, and distributions, (ii) such Member's right to vote or grant or withhold consents with respect to Company matters as provided herein or in the Delaware Act, and (iii) such Member's other rights and privileges as herein provided.

"Majority in Interest of the Members" means Members whose Percentage Interests aggregate to greater than 50 percent of the Percentage Interests of all Members.

"Members" means the Initial Members and all other persons or entities admitted as additional or substituted Members pursuant to this Agreement, so long as they remain Members. Reference to a "Member" means any one of the Members.

"Percentage Interest" means a Member's share of the profits and losses of the Company and the Member's percentage right to receive distributions of the Company's assets. The Percentage Interest of each Member shall initially be the percentage set forth opposite such Member's name on Schedule I hereto, as such Schedule shall be amended from time to time in accordance with the provisions hereof. The combined Percentage Interest of all Members shall at all times equal 100 percent.

Words used herein, regardless of the number and gender used, shall be deemed and construed to include any other number, singular or plural, and any other gender, masculine, feminine, or neuter, as the context requires, and, as used herein, unless the context clearly requires otherwise, the words "hereof," "herein," and "hereunder" and words of similar import shall refer to this Agreement as a whole and not to any particular provisions hereof.

3. *Purpose.* The purpose of the Company shall be to engage in any lawful business that may be engaged in by a limited liability company organized under the Delaware Act, as such business activities may be determined by the Members from time to time.

4.   *Offices.*

(a)   The principal office of the Company, and such additional offices as the Members may determine to establish, shall be located at such place or places inside or outside the State of Delaware as the Members may designate from time to time.

(b)   The registered office of the Company in the State of Delaware is located at _____. The registered agent of the Company for service of process at such address is _____.

5.   *Members.* The name and business or residence address of each Member of the Company are as set forth on Schedule I attached hereto, as the same may be amended from time to time.

6.   *Term.* The Company shall continue until dissolved and terminated in accordance with Section 14 of this Agreement.

7.   *Management of the Company.*

(a)   The Members shall have the right to manage the business of the Company, and shall have all powers and rights necessary, appropriate, or advisable to effectuate and carry out the purposes and business of the Company. The Members may appoint, employ, or otherwise contract with any persons or entities for the transaction of the business of the Company or the performance of services for or on behalf of the Company, and the Members may delegate to any such person (who may be designated an officer of the Company) or entity such authority to act on behalf of the Company as the Members may from time to time deem appropriate.

(b)   Except as to actions herein specified to be taken by all the Members or by the Members acting unanimously, the duties and powers of the Members may be exercised by a Majority in Interest of the Members (or by any Member acting pursuant to authority delegated by a Majority in Interest of the Members).

(c)   Any Member, authorized by all Members, may execute and file on behalf of the Company with the Secretary of State of the State of Delaware any certificates of correction of, or certificates of amendment to, the Company's certificate of formation, one or more restated certificates of formation and certificates of merger or consolidation and, upon the dissolution and completion of winding up of the Company, or as otherwise required by the Delaware Act, a certificate of cancellation canceling the Company's certificate of formation.

8.   *Capital Contributions; Capital Accounts; Administrative Matters.*

(a)   The Initial Members have contributed to the Company in cash the respective amounts set forth on Schedule I hereto. Except as otherwise agreed by all Members, the Initial Members shall have no obligation to make any further capital contributions to the Company. Persons or entities hereafter admitted as Members of the Company shall make such contributions of cash (or promissory obligations), property, or services to the Company as shall be determined by the Members, acting unanimously, at the time of each such admission.

(b)   A single, separate capital account shall be maintained for each Member. Each Member's capital account shall be credited with the amount of money and the fair market value of property (net of any liabilities secured by such contributed property that the Company assumes or takes subject to) contributed by that Member to the Company; the amount of any Company liabilities assumed by such Member (other than in connection with a distribution of Company property), and such Member's distributive share of Company profits (including tax exempt income). Each Member's capital account shall be debited with the amount of money and the fair market value of property (net of any liabilities that such Member assumes or takes subject to) distributed to such Member; the amount of any liabilities of such Member assumed by the Company (other than in connection with a contribution); and such Member's distributive share of Company losses (including items that may be neither deducted nor capitalized for federal income tax purposes).

(c)   Notwithstanding any provision of this Agreement to the contrary, each Member's capital account shall be maintained and adjusted in accordance with the Internal Revenue Code of 1986, as amended (the "Internal Revenue Code"), and the regulations thereunder (the "Regulations"), including, without limitation, (i) the adjustments permitted or required by Internal Revenue Code

Section 704(b) and, to the extent applicable, the principles expressed in Internal Revenue Code Section 704(c) and (ii) adjustments required to maintain capital accounts in accordance with the "substantial economic effect test" set forth in the Regulations under Internal Revenue Code Section 704(b).

(d)   Any Member, including any substitute Member, who shall receive an Interest (or whose Interest shall be increased) by means of a transfer to him of all or a part of the Interest of another Member, shall have a capital account that reflects the capital account associated with the transferred Interest (or the applicable percentage thereof in case of a transfer of a part of an Interest).

(e)   The Company hereby designates _____ as "Tax Matters Partner" for purposes of Internal Revenue Code Section 6231 and the Regulations promulgated thereunder. The Tax Matters Partner shall promptly advise each Member of any audit proceedings proposed to be conducted with respect to the Company.

(f)   It is the intention of the Members that the Company shall be taxed as a "partnership" for federal, state, local, and foreign income tax purposes. The Members agree to take all reasonable actions, including the amendment of this Agreement and the execution of other documents, as may reasonably be required in order for the Company to qualify for and receive "partnership" treatment for federal, state, local, and foreign income tax purposes.

(g)   The fiscal year of the Company shall be a calendar year. The books and records of the Company shall be maintained in accordance with generally accepted accounting principles and Section 704(b) of the Internal Revenue Code and the Regulations.

(h)   All items of Company income, gain, loss, deduction, credit, or the like shall be allocated among the Members in accordance with their respective Percentage Interests as set forth in Schedule I.

9.   *Assignments of Company Interest.*

(a)   No Member may sell, assign, pledge, or otherwise transfer or encumber (collectively "transfer") all or any part of its interest in the Company, and no transferee of all or any part of the interest of a Member shall be admitted as a substituted Member, without, in either event, having obtained the prior written consent of all other Members.

(b)   The Members shall amend Schedule I hereto from time to time to reflect transfers made in accordance with, and as permitted under, this Section 9. Any purported transfer in violation of this Section 9 shall be null and void and shall not be recognized by the Company.

10.   *Withdrawal.* No Member shall have the right to withdraw from the Company except with the consent of all of the other Members and upon such terms and conditions as may be specifically agreed upon between such other Members and the withdrawing Member. The provisions hereof with respect to distributions upon withdrawal are exclusive and no Member shall be entitled to claim any further or different distribution upon withdrawal under Section 18–604 of the Delaware Act or otherwise.

11.   *Additional Members.* The Members, acting unanimously, shall have the right to admit additional Members upon such terms and conditions, at such time or times, and for such Capital Contributions as shall be determined by all of the Members; and in connection with any such admission, the Members shall amend Schedule I hereof to reflect the name, address, and Capital Contribution of the additional Member and any agreed upon changes in Percentage Interests.

12.   *Distributions.* Distributions of cash or other assets of the Company shall be made at such times and in such amounts as the Members acting unanimously may determine. Distributions shall be made to (and profits and losses shall be allocated among) Members pro rata in accordance with their respective Percentage Interests.

13.   *Return of Capital.* No Member shall have any liability for the return of any Member's Capital Contribution which Capital Contribution shall be payable solely from the assets of the Company at the absolute discretion of the Members, subject to the requirements of the Delaware Act.

14. *Dissolution.* Subject to the provisions of Section 15 of this Agreement, the Company shall be dissolved and its affairs wound up and terminated upon the first to occur of the following: (a) December 31, _____; (b) The determination of all of the Members to dissolve the Company; or (c) The occurrence of any other event causing a dissolution of the Company under Section 18–801 of the Delaware Act.

15. *Continuation of the Company.* Notwithstanding the provisions of Section 14(c) hereof, the occurrence of an Event of Withdrawal of the last remaining Member shall not dissolve the Company if within ninety (90) days after the occurrence of such Event of Withdrawal, the business of the Company is continued as provided in the Delaware Act.

16. *Limitation on Liability.* The debts, obligations, and liabilities of the Company, whether arising in contract, tort, or otherwise, shall be solely the debts, obligations, and liabilities of the Company, and no Member of the Company shall be obligated personally for any such debt, obligation, or liability of the Company solely by reason of being a Member.

17. *Standard of Care; Indemnification of Managers, Officers, Employees, and Agents.*

(a)   No Member shall have any personal liability whatsoever to the Company or any other Member on account of such Member's status as a Member or by reason of such Member's acts or omissions in connection with the conduct of the business of the Company; provided, however, that nothing contained herein shall protect any Member against any liability to the Company or the Members to which such Member would otherwise be subject by reason of (i) any act or omission of such Manager or officer that involves actual fraud or willful misconduct or (ii) any transaction from which such Member derived improper personal benefit.

(b)   The Company shall indemnify and hold harmless each Member and the affiliates of any Member (each an "Indemnified Person") against any and all losses, claims, damages, expenses, and liabilities (including, but not limited to, any investigation, legal and other reasonable expenses incurred in connection with, and any amounts paid in settlement of, any action, suits, proceeding, or claim) of any kind or nature whatsoever that such Indemnified Person may at any time become subject to or liable for by reason of the formation, operation, or termination of the Company, or the Indemnified Person's acting as a Member under this Agreement, or the authorized actions of such Indemnified Person in connection with the conduct of the affairs of the Company (including, without limitation, indemnification against negligence, gross negligence, or breach of duty); provided, however, that no Indemnified Person shall be entitled to indemnification if and to the extent that the liability otherwise to be indemnified for results from (i) any act or omission of such Indemnified Person that involves actual fraud or willful misconduct or (ii) any transaction from which such Indemnified Person derived improper personal benefit. The indemnities provided hereunder shall survive termination of the Company and this Agreement. Each Indemnified Person shall have a claim against the property and assets of the Company for payment of any indemnity amounts from time to time due hereunder, which amounts shall be paid or properly reserved for prior to the making of distributions by the Company to Members. Costs and expenses that are subject to indemnification hereunder shall, at the request of any Indemnified Person, be advanced by the Company to or on behalf of such Indemnified Person prior to final resolution of a matter, so long as such Indemnified Person shall have provided the Company with a written undertaking to reimburse the Company for all amounts so advanced if it is ultimately determined that the Indemnified Person is not entitled to indemnification hereunder.

(c)   The contract rights to indemnification and to the advancement of expenses conferred in this Section 17 shall not be exclusive of any other right that any person may have or hereafter acquire under any statute, agreement, vote of the Members, or otherwise.

(d)   The Company may maintain insurance, at its expense, to protect itself and any Member, employee, or agent of the Company, or another limited liability company, corporation, partnership, joint venture, trust, or other enterprise against any expense, liability, or loss, whether or not the Company would have the power to indemnify such person against such expense, liability, or loss under the Delaware Act.

(e)   The Company may, to the extent authorized from time to time by the Members, grant rights to indemnification and to advancement of expenses to any employee or agent of the Company to the fullest extent of the provisions of this Section 17 with respect to the indemnification and advancement of expenses of Members of the Company.

18.   *Amendments.* This Agreement may be amended only upon the written consent of all Members.

19.   *Governing Law.* This Agreement shall be governed by and construed in accordance with the domestic laws of the State of Delaware without giving effect to any choice of law or conflict of law provision or rule (whether of the State of Delaware or any other jurisdiction) that would cause the application of the laws of any jurisdiction other than the State of Delaware.

IN WITNESS WHEREOF, the undersigned have duly executed this Agreement as of _____, _____.

MEMBER

[ENTITY NAME]

_____

By: _____

Title: _____

MEMBER

[ENTITY NAME]

_____

By: _____

Title: _____

SCHEDULE I

Name & Address	Capital Contribution	Percentage Interest
	$	%
	$	%
Total	$	%

Contact us at http://www.bna.com/contact-us or call 1-800-372-1033   ISSN 2330-6963

DELAWARE GENERAL CORPORATION LAW

TABLE OF CONTENTS

SUBCHAPTER I. FORMATION

Sec.		Page
101.	Incorporators; How Corporation Formed; Purposes	446
102.	Contents of Certificate of Incorporation	446
103.	Execution, Acknowledgment, Filing, Recording and Effective Date of Original Certificate of Incorporation and Other Instruments; Exceptions	450
104.	Certificate of Incorporation; Definition	453
105.	Certificate of Incorporation and Other Certificates; Evidence	453
106.	Commencement of Corporate Existence	453
107.	Powers of Incorporators	453
108.	Organization Meeting of Incorporators or Directors Named in Certificate of Incorporation	453
109.	Bylaws	454
110.	Emergency Bylaws and Other Powers in Emergency	454
111.	Jurisdiction to Interpret, Apply, Enforce or Determine the Validity of Corporate Instruments and Provisions of This Title	454
112.	Access to Proxy Solicitation Materials	455
113.	Proxy Expense Reimbursement	455
114.	Application of Chapter to Nonstock Corporations*	
115.	Forum Selection Provisions	456

SUBCHAPTER II. POWERS

121.	General Powers	456
122.	Specific Powers	456
123.	Powers Respecting Securities of Other Corporations or Entities	457
124.	Effect of Lack of Corporate Capacity or Power; Ultra Vires	457
125.	Conferring Academic or Honorary Degrees*	
126.	Banking Power Denied*	
127.	Private Foundations; Powers and Duties*	

SUBCHAPTER III. REGISTERED OFFICE AND REGISTERED AGENT

131.	Registered Office in State; Principal Office or Place of Business in State	458
132.	Registered Agent in State; Resident Agent	458
133.	Change of Location of Registered Office; Change of Registered Agent*	
134.	Change of Address or Name of Registered Agent*	
135.	Resignation of Registered Agent Coupled with Appointment of Successor*	
136.	Resignation of Registered Agent Not Coupled with Appointment of Successor*	

SUBCHAPTER IV. DIRECTORS AND OFFICERS

141.	Board of Directors; Powers; Number, Qualifications, Terms and Quorum; Committees; Classes of Directors; . . . Reliance upon Books; Action Without Meeting; Removal	461
142.	Officers; Titles, Duties, Selection, Term; Failure to Elect; Vacancies	464
143.	Loans to Employees and Officers; Guaranty of Obligations of Employees and Officers	464
144.	Interested Directors; Quorum	464
145.	Indemnification of Officers, Directors, Employees and Agents; Insurance	465
146.	Submission of Matters for Stockholder Vote	466

---

* Omitted.

SUBCHAPTER V.   STOCK AND DIVIDENDS

151.	Classes and Series of Stock; Redemption; Rights	467
152.	Issuance of Stock, Lawful Consideration; Fully Paid Stock	469
153.	Consideration for Stock	469
154.	Determination of Amount of Capital; Capital, Surplus and Net Assets Defined	469
155.	Fractions of Shares	470
156.	Partly Paid Shares	470
157.	Rights and Options Respecting Stock	470
158.	Stock Certificates; Uncertificated Shares	471
159.	Shares of Stock; Personal Property, Transfer and Taxation*	
160.	Corporation's Powers Respecting Ownership, Voting, etc. of Its Own Stock; Rights of Stock Called for Redemption	471
161.	Issuance of Additional Stock; When and by Whom	472
162.	Liability of Stockholder or Subscriber for Stock Not Paid in Full	472
163.	Payment for Stock Not Paid in Full	472
164.	Failure to Pay for Stock; Remedies	473
165.	Revocability of Preincorporation Subscriptions	473
166.	Formalities Required of Stock Subscriptions	473
167.	Lost, Stolen or Destroyed Stock Certificates; Issuance of New Certificate or Uncertificated Shares*	
168.	Judicial Proceedings to Compel Issuance of New Certificate or Uncertificated Shares*	
169.	Situs of Ownership of Stock	473
170.	Dividends; Payment; Wasting Asset Corporations	473
171.	Special Purpose Reserves*	
172.	Liability of Directors and Committee Members as to Dividends or Stock Redemption	474
173.	Declaration and Payment of Dividends	474
174.	Liability of Directors for Unlawful Payment of Dividend or Unlawful Stock Purchase or Redemption; Exoneration from Liability; Contribution Among Directors; Subrogation	474

SUBCHAPTER VI.   STOCK TRANSFERS

201.	Transfer of Stock, Stock Certificates and Uncertificated Stock	475
202.	Restriction on Transfer and Ownership of Securities	475
203.	Business Combinations with Interested Stockholders	476
204.	Ratification of Defective Corporate Acts and Stock	480
205.	Proceedings Regarding Validity of Defective Corporate Acts and Stock	485

SUBCHAPTER VII.   MEETINGS, ELECTIONS, VOTING AND NOTICE

211.	Meetings of Stockholders	486
212.	Voting Rights of Stockholders; Proxies; Limitations	487
213.	Fixing Date for Determination of Stockholders of Record	488
214.	Cumulative Voting	489
215.	Voting Rights of Members of Nonstock Corporations; Quorum; Proxies*	
216.	Quorum and Required Vote for Stock Corporations	489
217.	Voting Rights of Fiduciaries, Pledgors and Joint Owners of Stock	489
218.	Voting Trusts and Other Voting Agreements	490
219.	List of Stockholders Entitled to Vote; Penalty for Refusal to Produce; Stock Ledger	490
220.	Inspection of Books and Records	491
221.	Voting, Inspection and Other Rights of Bondholders and Debenture Holders	492
222.	Notice of Meetings and Adjourned Meetings	493
223.	Vacancies and Newly Created Directorships	493
224.	Form of Records*	
225.	Contested Election of Directors; Proceedings to Determine Validity	494

---

* Omitted.

226. Appointment of Custodian or Receiver of Corporation on Deadlock or for Other Cause 495
227. Powers of Court in Elections of Directors 495
228. Consent of Stockholders or Members in Lieu of Meeting 495
229. Waiver of Notice 496
230. Exception to Requirements of Notice*
231. Voting Procedures and Inspectors of Election 496
232. Notice by Electronic Transmission 497
233. Notice to Stockholders Sharing an Address*

SUBCHAPTER VIII.   AMENDMENT OF CERTIFICATE OF INCORPORATION; CHANGES IN CAPITAL AND CAPITAL STOCK

241. Amendment of Certificate of Incorporation Before Receipt of Payment for Stock 498
242. Amendment of Certificate of Incorporation After Receipt of Payment for Stock; Nonstock Corporations 498
243. Retirement of Stock 500
244. Reduction of Capital 501
245. Restated Certificate of Incorporation 501

SUBCHAPTER IX.   MERGER, CONSOLIDATION, OR CONVERSION

251. Merger or Consolidation of Domestic Corporations 502
252. Merger or Consolidation of Domestic and Foreign Corporations; Service of Process upon Surviving or Resulting Corporation 507
253. Merger of Parent Corporation and Subsidiary Corporation or Corporations 509
254. Merger or Consolidation of Domestic Corporations and Joint-Stock or Other Associations*
255. Merger or Consolidation of Domestic Nonstock Corporations*
256. Merger or Consolidation of Domestic and Foreign Nonstock Corporations; Service of Process upon Surviving or Resulting Corporation*
257. Merger or Consolidation of Domestic Stock and Nonstock Corporations*
258. Merger or Consolidation of Domestic and Foreign Stock and Nonstock Corporations*
259. Status, Rights, Liabilities, of Constituent and Surviving or Resulting Corporations Following Merger or Consolidation 510
260. Powers of Corporation Surviving or Resulting from Merger or Consolidation; Issuance of Stock, Bonds or Other Indebtedness 511
261. Effect of Merger upon Pending Actions 511
262. Appraisal Rights 511
263. Merger or Consolidation of Domestic Corporations and Partnerships; Service of Process upon Surviving or Resulting Corporation or Partnership 515
264. Merger or Consolidation of Domestic Corporations and Limited Liability Companies; Service of Process upon Surviving or Resulting Corporation or Limited Liability Company 517
265. Conversion of Other Entities to a Domestic Corporation 520
266. Conversion of a Domestic Corporation to Other Entities 521
267. Merger of Parent Entity and Subsidiary Corporation or Corporations 523

SUBCHAPTER X.   SALE OF ASSETS, DISSOLUTION AND WINDING UP

271. Sale, Lease or Exchange of Assets; Consideration; Procedure 524
272. Mortgage or Pledge of Assets 524
273. Dissolution of Joint Venture Corporation Having 2 Stockholders 524
274. Dissolution Before Issuance of Shares or Beginning of Business; Procedure*
275. Dissolution Generally; Procedure 525
276. Dissolution of Nonstock Corporation; Procedure*
277. Payment of Franchise Taxes Before Dissolution, Merger, Transfer or Conversion*

---

* Omitted.

278. Continuation of Corporation After Dissolution for Purposes of Suit and Winding Up Affairs... 526
279. Trustees or Receivers for Dissolved Corporations; Appointment; Powers; Duties.............. 526
280. Notice to Claimants; Filing of Claims.. 526
281. Payment and Distribution to Claimants and Stockholders... 528
282. Liability of Stockholders of Dissolved Corporations 529
283. Jurisdiction 529
284. Revocation or Forfeiture of Charter; Proceedings... 529
285. Dissolution or Forfeiture of Charter by Decree of Court; Filing*

SUBCHAPTER XI.   INSOLVENCY; RECEIVERS AND TRUSTEES*

291. Receivers for Insolvent Corporations; Appointment and Powers*
292. Title to Property; Filing Order of Appointment; Exception*
293. Notices to Stockholders and Creditors*
294. Receivers or Trustees; Inventory; List of Debts and Reports*
295. Creditors' Proofs of Claims; when Barred; Notice*
296. Adjudication of Claims; Appeal*
297. Sale of Perishable or Deteriorating Property*
298. Compensation, Costs and Expenses of Receiver or Trustee*
299. Substitution of Trustee or Receiver as Party; Abatement of Actions*
300. Employee's Lien for Wages when Corporation Insolvent*
301. Discontinuance of Liquidation*
302. Compromise or Arrangement Between Corporation and Creditors or Stockholders*
303. Proceeding Under the Federal Bankruptcy Code of the United States; Effectuation*

SUBCHAPTER XII.   RENEWAL, REVIVAL, EXTENSION AND RESTORATION OF CERTIFICATE OF INCORPORATION OR CHARTER*

311. Revocation of Voluntary Dissolution; Restoration of Expired Certificate of Incorporation*
312. Revival of Certificate of Incorporation*
313. Revival of Certificate of Incorporation or Charter of Exempt Corporations*
314. Status of Corporation*

SUBCHAPTER XIII.   SUITS AGAINST CORPORATIONS, DIRECTORS, OFFICERS OR STOCKHOLDERS

321. Service of Process on Corporations*
322. Failure of Corporation to Obey Order of Court; Appointment of Receiver*
323. Failure of Corporation to Obey Writ of Mandamus; Quo Warranto Proceedings for Forfeiture of Charter*
324. Attachment of Shares of Stock or Any Option, Right or Interest Therein; Procedure; Sale; Title upon Sale; Proceeds*
325. Actions Against Officers, Directors or Stockholders to Enforce Liability of Corporation; Unsatisfied Judgment Against Corporation.. 530
326. Action by Officer, Director or Stockholder Against Corporation for Corporate Debt Paid*
327. Stockholder's Derivative Action; Allegation of Stock Ownership................................ 530
328. Effect of Liability of Corporation on Impairment of Certain Transactions 530
329. Defective Organization of Corporation as Defense 530
330. Usury; Pleading by Corporation*

SUBCHAPTER XIV.   CLOSE CORPORATIONS; SPECIAL PROVISIONS

341. Law Applicable to Close Corporation 530
342. Close Corporation Defined; Contents of Certificate of Incorporation 530
343. Formation of a Close Corporation... 531

---

* Omitted

344. Election of Existing Corporation to Become a Close Corporation 531
345. Limitations on Continuation of Close Corporation Status 531
346. Voluntary Termination of Close Corporation Status by Amendment of Certificate of Incorporation; Vote Required 531
347. Issuance or Transfer of Stock of a Close Corporation in Breach of Qualifying Conditions........ 532
348. Involuntary Termination of Close Corporation Status; Proceeding to Prevent Loss of Status 532
349. Corporate Option Where a Restriction on Transfer of a Security Is Held Invalid 533
350. Agreements Restricting Discretion of Directors... 533
351. Management by Stockholders.. 533
352. Appointment of Custodian for Close Corporation 534
353. Appointment of a Provisional Director in Certain Cases 534
354. Operating Corporation as Partnership... 534
355. Stockholders' Option to Dissolve Corporation.. 535
356. Effect of This Subchapter on Other Laws 535

SUBCHAPTER XV.   PUBLIC BENEFIT CORPORATIONS

361. Law Applicable to Public Benefit Corporations; How Formed 535
362. Public Benefit Corporation Defined; Contents of Certificate of Incorporation. 535
363. Certain Amendments and Mergers; Votes Required; Appraisal Rights 536
364. Stock Certificates; Notices Regarding Uncertificated Stock... 537
365. Duties of Directors... 537
366. Periodic Statements and Third-Party Certification 537
367. Derivative Suits 538
368. No Effect on Other Corporations 538

SUBCHAPTER XVI.   FOREIGN CORPORATIONS

371. Definition; Qualification to Do Business in State; Procedure 538
372. Additional Requirements in Case of Change of Name, Change of Business Purpose or Merger or Consolidation*
373. Exceptions to Requirements*
374. Annual Report*
375. Failure to File Report*
376. Service of Process upon Qualified Foreign Corporations*
377. Change of Registered Agent*
378. Penalties For Noncompliance*
379. Banking Powers Denied*
380. Foreign Corporation as Fiduciary in this State*
381. Withdrawal of Foreign Corporation from State; Procedure; Service of Process on Secretary of State*
382. Service of Process on Nonqualifying Foreign Corporations*
383. Actions by and Against Unqualified Foreign Corporations... 539
384. Foreign Corporations Doing Business Without Having Qualified; Injunctions*
385. Filing of Certain Instruments with Recorder of Deeds Not Required*

SUBCHAPTER XVII.   DOMESTICATION AND TRANSFER

388. Domestication of Non-United States Entities*
389. Temporary Transfer of Domicile into this State*
390. Transfer, Domestication or Continuance of Domestic Corporations.. 539

---

* Omitted.

SUBCHAPTER XVIII. MISCELLANEOUS PROVISIONS

391.   Amounts Payable to Secretary of State upon Filing Certificate or Other Paper*
393.   Rights, Liabilities and Duties under Prior Statutes*
394.   Reserved Power of State to Amend or Repeal Chapter; Chapter Part of Corporation's
        Charter or Certificate of Incorporation.. 542
395.   Corporations Using "Trust" in Name, Advertisements and Otherwise; Restrictions;
        Violations and Penalties; Exceptions*
396.   Publication of Chapter by Secretary of State; Distribution*
397.   Penalty for Unauthorized Publication of Chapter*
398.   Short Title*

SUBCHAPTER I. FORMATION

§ 101.   Incorporators; How Corporation Formed; Purposes

(a) Any person, partnership, association or corporation, singly or jointly with others, and without regard to such person's or entity's residence, domicile or state of incorporation, may incorporate or organize a corporation under this chapter by filing with the Division of Corporations in the Department of State a certificate of incorporation which shall be executed, acknowledged and filed in accordance with § 103 of this title.

(b) A corporation may be incorporated or organized under this chapter to conduct or promote any lawful business or purposes, except as may otherwise be provided by the Constitution or other law of this State.

(c) Corporations for constructing, maintaining and operating public utilities, whether in or outside of this State, may be organized under this chapter, but corporations for constructing, maintaining and operating public utilities within this State shall be subject to, in addition to this chapter, the special provisions and requirements of Title 26 applicable to such corporations.

§ 102.   Contents of Certificate of Incorporation

(a) The certificate of incorporation shall set forth:

(1) The name of the corporation, which (i) shall contain 1 of the words "association," "company," "corporation," "club," "foundation," "fund," "incorporated," "institute," "society," "union," "syndicate," or "limited," (or abbreviations thereof, with or without punctuation), or words (or abbreviations thereof, with or without punctuation) of like import of foreign countries or jurisdictions (provided they are written in roman characters or letters); provided, however, that the Division of Corporations in the Department of State may waive such requirement (unless it determines that such name is, or might otherwise appear to be, that of a natural person) if such corporation executes, acknowledges and files with the Secretary of State in accordance with § 103 of this title a certificate stating that its total assets, as defined in § 503(i) of this title, are not less than $10,000,000, or, in the sole discretion of the Division of Corporations in the Department of State, if the corporation is both a nonprofit nonstock corporation and an association of professionals, (ii) shall be such as to distinguish it upon the records in the office of the Division of Corporations in the Department of State from the names that are reserved on such records and from the names on such records of each other corporation, partnership, limited partnership, limited liability company, registered series of a limited liability company or statutory trust organized or registered as a domestic or foreign corporation, partnership, limited partnership, limited liability company, registered series of a limited liability company or statutory trust under the laws of this State, except with the written consent of the person who has reserved such name or such other foreign corporation or domestic or foreign partnership, limited partnership, limited liability company, registered series of a limited liability company or statutory trust, executed, acknowledged and filed with the Secretary of State in accordance with § 103 of this title, or except that, without prejudicing any rights of the person who has reserved such name or such other foreign

---

*   Omitted.

corporation or domestic or foreign partnership, limited partnership, limited liability company, registered series of a limited liability company or statutory trust, the Division of Corporations in the Department of State may waive such requirement if the corporation demonstrates to the satisfaction of the Secretary of State that the corporation or a predecessor entity previously has made substantial use of such name or a substantially similar name, that the corporation has made reasonable efforts to secure such written consent, and that such waiver is in the interest of the State, (iii) except as permitted by § 395 of this title, shall not contain the word "trust," and (iv) shall not contain the word "bank," or any variation thereof, except for the name of a bank reporting to and under the supervision of the State Bank Commissioner of this State or a subsidiary of a bank or savings association (as those terms are defined in the Federal Deposit Insurance Act, as amended, at 12 U.S.C. § 1813), or a corporation regulated under the Bank Holding Company Act of 1956, as amended, 12 U.S.C. § 1841 et seq., or the Home Owners' Loan Act, as amended, 12 U.S.C. § 1461 et seq.; provided, however, that this section shall not be construed to prevent the use of the word "bank," or any variation thereof, in a context clearly not purporting to refer to a banking business or otherwise likely to mislead the public about the nature of the business of the corporation or to lead to a pattern and practice of abuse that might cause harm to the interests of the public or the State as determined by the Division of Corporations in the Department of State;

(2) The address (which shall be stated in accordance with § 131(c) of this title) of the corporation's registered office in this State, and the name of its registered agent at such address;

(3) The nature of the business or purposes to be conducted or promoted. It shall be sufficient to state, either alone or with other businesses or purposes, that the purpose of the corporation is to engage in any lawful act or activity for which corporations may be organized under the General Corporation Law of Delaware, and by such statement all lawful acts and activities shall be within the purposes of the corporation, except for express limitations, if any;

(4) If the corporation is to be authorized to issue only 1 class of stock, the total number of shares of stock which the corporation shall have authority to issue and the par value of each of such shares, or a statement that all such shares are to be without par value. If the corporation is to be authorized to issue more than 1 class of stock, the certificate of incorporation shall set forth the total number of shares of all classes of stock which the corporation shall have authority to issue and the number of shares of each class and shall specify each class the shares of which are to be without par value and each class the shares of which are to have par value and the par value of the shares of each such class. The certificate of incorporation shall also set forth a statement of the designations and the powers, preferences and rights, and the qualifications, limitations or restrictions thereof, which are permitted by § 151 of this title in respect of any class or classes of stock or any series of any class of stock of the corporation and the fixing of which by the certificate of incorporation is desired, and an express grant of such authority as it may then be desired to grant to the board of directors to fix by resolution or resolutions any thereof that may be desired but which shall not be fixed by the certificate of incorporation. The foregoing provisions of this paragraph shall not apply to nonstock corporations. In the case of nonstock corporations, the fact that they are not authorized to issue capital stock shall be stated in the certificate of incorporation. The conditions of membership, or other criteria for identifying members, of nonstock corporations shall likewise be stated in the certificate of incorporation or the bylaws. Nonstock corporations shall have members, but failure to have members shall not affect otherwise valid corporate acts or work a forfeiture or dissolution of the corporation. Nonstock corporations may provide for classes or groups of members having relative rights, powers and duties, and may make provision for the future creation of additional classes or groups of members having such relative rights, powers and duties as may from time to time be established, including rights, powers and duties senior to existing classes and groups of members. Except as otherwise provided in this chapter, nonstock corporations may also provide that any member or class or group of members shall have full, limited, or no voting rights or powers, including that any member or class or group of members shall have the right to vote on a specified transaction even if that member or class or group of members does not have the right to vote for the election of the members of the governing body of the corporation. Voting by members of a nonstock corporation may be on a per capita, number, financial interest, class, group, or any other basis set forth. The provisions referred to in the 3 preceding sentences may be set forth in the certificate of incorporation or the bylaws. If neither the certificate of incorporation nor the bylaws of a nonstock corporation state the conditions of membership, or other

criteria for identifying members, the members of the corporation shall be deemed to be those entitled to vote for the election of the members of the governing body pursuant to the certificate of incorporation or bylaws of such corporation or otherwise until thereafter otherwise provided by the certificate of incorporation or the bylaws;

(5) The name and mailing address of the incorporator or incorporators;

(6) If the powers of the incorporator or incorporators are to terminate upon the filing of the certificate of incorporation, the names and mailing addresses of the persons who are to serve as directors until the first annual meeting of stockholders or until their successors are elected and qualify.

(b) In addition to the matters required to be set forth in the certificate of incorporation by subsection (a) of this section, the certificate of incorporation may also contain any or all of the following matters:

(1) Any provision for the management of the business and for the conduct of the affairs of the corporation, and any provision creating, defining, limiting and regulating the powers of the corporation, the directors, and the stockholders, or any class of the stockholders, or the governing body, members, or any class or group of members of a nonstock corporation; if such provisions are not contrary to the laws of this State. Any provision which is required or permitted by any section of this chapter to be stated in the bylaws may instead be stated in the certificate of incorporation;

(2) The following provisions, in haec verba, (i), for a corporation other than a nonstock corporation, viz:

"Whenever a compromise or arrangement is proposed between this corporation and its creditors or any class of them and/or between this corporation and its stockholders or any class of them, any court of equitable jurisdiction within the State of Delaware may, on the application in a summary way of this corporation or of any creditor or stockholder thereof or on the application of any receiver or receivers appointed for this corporation under § 291 of Title 8 of the Delaware Code or on the application of trustees in dissolution or of any receiver or receivers appointed for this corporation under § 279 of Title 8 of the Delaware Code order a meeting of the creditors or class of creditors, and/or of the stockholders or class of stockholders of this corporation, as the case may be, to be summoned in such manner as the said court directs. If a majority in number representing three fourths in value of the creditors or class of creditors, and/or of the stockholders or class of stockholders of this corporation, as the case may be, agree to any compromise or arrangement and to any reorganization of this corporation as consequence of such compromise or arrangement, the said compromise or arrangement and the said reorganization shall, if sanctioned by the court to which the said application has been made, be binding on all the creditors or class of creditors, and/or on all the stockholders or class of stockholders, of this corporation, as the case may be, and also on this corporation"; or

(ii), for a nonstock corporation, viz:

"Whenever a compromise or arrangement is proposed between this corporation and its creditors or any class of them and/or between this corporation and its members or any class of them, any court of equitable jurisdiction within the State of Delaware may, on the application in a summary way of this corporation or of any creditor or member thereof or on the application of any receiver or receivers appointed for this corporation under § 291 of Title 8 of the Delaware Code or on the application of trustees in dissolution or of any receiver or receivers appointed for this corporation under § 279 of Title 8 of the Delaware Code order a meeting of the creditors or class of creditors, and/or of the members or class of members of this corporation, as the case may be, to be summoned in such manner as the said court directs. If a majority in number representing three fourths in value of the creditors or class of creditors, and/or of the members or class of members of this corporation, as the case may be, agree to any compromise or arrangement and to any reorganization of this corporation as consequence of such compromise or arrangement, the said compromise or arrangement and the said reorganization shall, if sanctioned by the court to which the said application has been made, be binding on all the creditors or class of creditors, and/or on all the members or class of members, of this corporation, as the case may be, and also on this corporation";

(3) Such provisions as may be desired granting to the holders of the stock of the corporation, or the holders of any class or series of a class thereof, the preemptive right to subscribe to any or all additional issues of stock of the corporation of any or all classes or series thereof, or to any securities of the corporation convertible into such stock. No stockholder shall have any preemptive right to subscribe to an additional issue of stock or to any security convertible into such stock unless, and except to the extent that, such right is expressly granted to such stockholder in the certificate of incorporation. All such rights in existence on July 3, 1967, shall remain in existence unaffected by this paragraph unless and until changed or terminated by appropriate action which expressly provides for the change or termination;

(4) Provisions requiring for any corporate action, the vote of a larger portion of the stock or of any class or series thereof, or of any other securities having voting power, or a larger number of the directors, than is required by this chapter;

(5) A provision limiting the duration of the corporation's existence to a specified date; otherwise, the corporation shall have perpetual existence;

(6) A provision imposing personal liability for the debts of the corporation on its stockholders to a specified extent and upon specified conditions; otherwise, the stockholders of a corporation shall not be personally liable for the payment of the corporation's debts except as they may be liable by reason of their own conduct or acts;

(7) A provision eliminating or limiting the personal liability of a director to the corporation or its stockholders for monetary damages for breach of fiduciary duty as a director, provided that such provision shall not eliminate or limit the liability of a director: (i) For any breach of the director's duty of loyalty to the corporation or its stockholders; (ii) for acts or omissions not in good faith or which involve intentional misconduct or a knowing violation of law; (iii) under § 174 of this title; or (iv) for any transaction from which the director derived an improper personal benefit. No such provision shall eliminate or limit the liability of a director for any act or omission occurring prior to the date when such provision becomes effective. All references in this paragraph to a director shall also be deemed to refer to such other person or persons, if any, who, pursuant to a provision of the certificate of incorporation in accordance with § 141(a) of this title, exercise or perform any of the powers or duties otherwise conferred or imposed upon the board of directors by this title.

(c) It shall not be necessary to set forth in the certificate of incorporation any of the powers conferred on corporations by this chapter.

(d) Except for provisions included pursuant to paragraphs (a)(1), (a)(2), (a)(5), (a)(6), (b)(2), (b)(5), (b)(7) of this section, and provisions included pursuant to paragraph (a)(4) of this section specifying the classes, number of shares, and par value of shares a corporation other than a nonstock corporation is authorized to issue, any provision of the certificate of incorporation may be made dependent upon facts ascertainable outside such instrument, provided that the manner in which such facts shall operate upon the provision is clearly and explicitly set forth therein. The term "facts," as used in this subsection, includes, but is not limited to, the occurrence of any event, including a determination or action by any person or body, including the corporation.

(e) The exclusive right to the use of a name that is available for use by a domestic or foreign corporation may be reserved by or on behalf of:

(1) Any person intending to incorporate or organize a corporation with that name under this chapter or contemplating such incorporation or organization;

(2) Any domestic corporation or any foreign corporation qualified to do business in the State of Delaware, in either case, intending to change its name or contemplating such a change;

(3) Any foreign corporation intending to qualify to do business in the State of Delaware and adopt that name or contemplating such qualification and adoption; and

(4) Any person intending to organize a foreign corporation and have it qualify to do business in the State of Delaware and adopt that name or contemplating such organization, qualification and adoption.

The reservation of a specified name may be made by filing with the Secretary of State an application, executed by the applicant, certifying that the reservation is made by or on behalf of a domestic corporation, foreign corporation or other person described in paragraphs (e)(1)–(4) of this section above, and specifying the name to be reserved and the name and address of the applicant. If the Secretary of State finds that the name is available for use by a domestic or foreign corporation, the Secretary shall reserve the name for the use of the applicant for a period of 120 days. The same applicant may renew for successive 120-day periods a reservation of a specified name by filing with the Secretary of State, prior to the expiration of such reservation (or renewal thereof), an application for renewal of such reservation, executed by the applicant, certifying that the reservation is renewed by or on behalf of a domestic corporation, foreign corporation or other person described in paragraphs (e)(1)–(4) of this section above and specifying the name reservation to be renewed and the name and address of the applicant. The right to the exclusive use of a reserved name may be transferred to any other person by filing in the office of the Secretary of State a notice of the transfer, executed by the applicant for whom the name was reserved, specifying the name reservation to be transferred and the name and address of the transferee. The reservation of a specified name may be cancelled by filing with the Secretary of State a notice of cancellation, executed by the applicant or transferee, specifying the name reservation to be cancelled and the name and address of the applicant or transferee. Unless the Secretary of State finds that any application, application for renewal, notice of transfer, or notice of cancellation filed with the Secretary of State as required by this subsection does not conform to law, upon receipt of all filing fees required by law the Secretary of State shall prepare and return to the person who filed such instrument a copy of the filed instrument with a notation thereon of the action taken by the Secretary of State. A fee as set forth in § 391 of this title shall be paid at the time of the reservation of any name, at the time of the renewal of any such reservation and at the time of the filing of a notice of the transfer or cancellation of any such reservation.

(f) The certificate of incorporation may not contain any provision that would impose liability on a stockholder for the attorneys' fees or expenses of the corporation or any other party in connection with an internal corporate claim, as defined in § 115 of this title.

§ 103. Execution, Acknowledgment, Filing, Recording and Effective Date of Original Certificate of Incorporation and Other Instruments; Exceptions

(a) Whenever any instrument is to be filed with the Secretary of State or in accordance with this section or chapter, such instrument shall be executed as follows:

(1) The certificate of incorporation, and any other instrument to be filed before the election of the initial board of directors if the initial directors were not named in the certificate of incorporation, shall be signed by the incorporator or incorporators (or, in the case of any such other instrument, such incorporator's or incorporators' successors and assigns). If any incorporator is not available then any such other instrument may be signed, with the same effect as if such incorporator had signed it, by any person for whom or on whose behalf such incorporator, in executing the certificate of incorporation, was acting directly or indirectly as employee or agent, provided that such other instrument shall state that such incorporator is not available and the reason therefor, that such incorporator in executing the certificate of incorporation was acting directly or indirectly as employee or agent for or on behalf of such person, and that such person's signature on such instrument is otherwise authorized and not wrongful.

(2) All other instruments shall be signed:

a. By any authorized officer of the corporation; or

b. If it shall appear from the instrument that there are no such officers, then by a majority of the directors or by such directors as may be designated by the board; or

c. If it shall appear from the instrument that there are no such officers or directors, then by the holders of record, or such of them as may be designated by the holders of record, of a majority of all outstanding shares of stock; or

d. By the holders of record of all outstanding shares of stock.

(b) Whenever this chapter requires any instrument to be acknowledged, such requirement is satisfied by either:

(1) The formal acknowledgment by the person or 1 of the persons signing the instrument that it is such person's act and deed or the act and deed of the corporation, and that the facts stated therein are true. Such acknowledgment shall be made before a person who is authorized by the law of the place of execution to take acknowledgments of deeds. If such person has a seal of office such person shall affix it to the instrument.

(2) The signature, without more, of the person or persons signing the instrument, in which case such signature or signatures shall constitute the affirmation or acknowledgment of the signatory, under penalties of perjury, that the instrument is such person's act and deed or the act and deed of the corporation, and that the facts stated therein are true.

(c) Whenever any instrument is to be filed with the Secretary of State or in accordance with this section or chapter, such requirement means that:

(1) The signed instrument shall be delivered to the office of the Secretary of State;

(2) All taxes and fees authorized by law to be collected by the Secretary of State in connection with the filing of the instrument shall be tendered to the Secretary of State; and

(3) Upon delivery of the instrument, the Secretary of State shall record the date and time of its delivery. Upon such delivery and tender of the required taxes and fees, the Secretary of State shall certify that the instrument has been filed in the Secretary of State's office by endorsing upon the signed instrument the word "Filed", and the date and time of its filing. This endorsement is the "filing date" of the instrument, and is conclusive of the date and time of its filing in the absence of actual fraud. The Secretary of State shall file and index the endorsed instrument. Except as provided in paragraph (c)(4) of this section and in subsection (i) of this section, such filing date of an instrument shall be the date and time of delivery of the instrument.

(4) Upon request made upon or prior to delivery, the Secretary of State may, to the extent deemed practicable, establish as the filing date of an instrument a date and time after its delivery. If the Secretary of State refuses to file any instrument due to an error, omission or other imperfection, the Secretary of State may hold such instrument in suspension, and in such event, upon delivery of a replacement instrument in proper form for filing and tender of the required taxes and fees within 5 business days after notice of such suspension is given to the filer, the Secretary of State shall establish as the filing date of such instrument the date and time that would have been the filing date of the rejected instrument had it been accepted for filing. The Secretary of State shall not issue a certificate of good standing with respect to any corporation with an instrument held in suspension pursuant to this subsection. The Secretary of State may establish as the filing date of an instrument the date and time at which information from such instrument is entered pursuant to paragraph (c)(8) of this section if such instrument is delivered on the same date and within 4 hours after such information is entered.

(5) The Secretary of State, acting as agent for the recorders of each of the counties, shall collect and deposit in a separate account established exclusively for that purpose a county assessment fee with respect to each filed instrument and shall thereafter weekly remit from such account to the recorder of each of the said counties the amount or amounts of such fees as provided for in paragraph (c)(6) of this section or as elsewhere provided by law. Said fees shall be for the purposes of defraying certain costs incurred by the counties in merging the information and images of such filed documents with the document information systems of each of the recorder's offices in the counties and in retrieving, maintaining and displaying such information and images in the offices of the recorders and at remote locations in each of such counties. In consideration for its acting as the agent for the recorders with respect to the collection and payment of the county assessment fees, the Secretary of State shall retain and pay over to the General Fund of the State an administrative charge of 1 percent of the total fees collected.

(6) The assessment fee to the counties shall be $24 for each 1-page instrument filed with the Secretary of State in accordance with this section and $9.00 for each additional page for instruments with more than 1 page. The recorder's office to receive the assessment fee shall be the recorder's office in the county in which the corporation's registered office in this State is, or is to be, located, except that an assessment fee shall not be charged for either a certificate of dissolution qualifying for treatment under § 391(a)(5)b. of this title or a document filed in accordance with subchapter XVI of this chapter.

(7) The Secretary of State, acting as agent, shall collect and deposit in a separate account established exclusively for that purpose a courthouse municipality fee with respect to each filed instrument and shall thereafter monthly remit funds from such account to the treasuries of the municipalities designated in § 301 of Title 10. Said fees shall be for the purposes of defraying certain costs incurred by such municipalities in hosting the primary locations for the Delaware courts. The fee to such municipalities shall be $20 for each instrument filed with the Secretary of State in accordance with this section. The municipality to receive the fee shall be the municipality designated in § 301 of Title 10 in the county in which the corporation's registered office in this State is, or is to be, located, except that a fee shall not be charged for a certificate of dissolution qualifying for treatment under § 391(a)(5)b. of this title, a resignation of agent without appointment of a successor under § 136 of this title, or a document filed in accordance with subchapter XVI of this chapter.

(8) The Secretary of State shall cause to be entered such information from each instrument as the Secretary of State deems appropriate into the Delaware Corporation Information System or any system which is a successor thereto in the office of the Secretary of State, and such information and a copy of each such instrument shall be permanently maintained as a public record on a suitable medium. The Secretary of State is authorized to grant direct access to such system to registered agents subject to the execution of an operating agreement between the Secretary of State and such registered agent. Any registered agent granted such access shall demonstrate the existence of policies to ensure that information entered into the system accurately reflects the content of instruments in the possession of the registered agent at the time of entry.

(d) Any instrument filed in accordance with subsection (c) of this section shall be effective upon its filing date. Any instrument may provide that it is not to become effective until a specified time subsequent to the time it is filed, but such time shall not be later than a time on the ninetieth day after the date of its filing. If any instrument filed in accordance with subsection (c) of this section provides for a future effective date or time and if the transaction is terminated or its terms are amended to change the future effective date or time prior to the future effective date or time, the instrument shall be terminated or amended by the filing, prior to the future effective date or time set forth in such instrument, of a certificate of termination or amendment of the original instrument, executed in accordance with subsection (a) of this section, which shall identify the instrument which has been terminated or amended and shall state that the instrument has been terminated or the manner in which it has been amended.

(e) If another section of this chapter specifically prescribes a manner of executing, acknowledging or filing a specified instrument or a time when such instrument shall become effective which differs from the corresponding provisions of this section, then such other section shall govern.

(f) Whenever any instrument authorized to be filed with the Secretary of State under any provision of this title, has been so filed and is an inaccurate record of the corporate action therein referred to, or was defectively or erroneously executed, sealed or acknowledged, the instrument may be corrected by filing with the Secretary of State a certificate of correction of the instrument which shall be executed, acknowledged and filed in accordance with this section. The certificate of correction shall specify the inaccuracy or defect to be corrected and shall set forth the portion of the instrument in corrected form. In lieu of filing a certificate of correction the instrument may be corrected by filing with the Secretary of State a corrected instrument which shall be executed, acknowledged and filed in accordance with this section. The corrected instrument shall be specifically designated as such in its heading, shall specify the inaccuracy or defect to be corrected, and shall set forth the entire instrument in corrected form. An instrument corrected in accordance with this section shall be effective as of the date the original instrument was filed, except as to those persons who are substantially and adversely affected by the correction and as to those persons the instrument as corrected shall be effective from the filing date.

(g) Notwithstanding that any instrument authorized to be filed with the Secretary of State under this title is when filed inaccurately, defectively or erroneously executed, sealed or acknowledged, or otherwise defective in any respect, the Secretary of State shall have no liability to any person for the preclearance for filing, the acceptance for filing or the filing and indexing of such instrument by the Secretary of State.

(h) Any signature on any instrument authorized to be filed with the Secretary of State under this title may be a facsimile, a conformed signature or an electronically transmitted signature. . . .

§ 104. Certificate of Incorporation; Definition

The term "certificate of incorporation," as used in this chapter, unless the context requires otherwise, includes not only the original certificate of incorporation filed to create a corporation but also all other certificates, agreements of merger or consolidation, plans of reorganization, or other instruments, howsoever designated, which are filed pursuant to § 102, §§ 133–136, § 151, §§ 241–243, § 245, §§ 251–258, §§ 263–264, § 267, § 303, §§ 311–313, or any other section of this title, and which have the effect of amending or supplementing in some respect a corporation's certificate of incorporation.

§ 105. Certificate of Incorporation and Other Certificates; Evidence

A copy of a certificate of incorporation, or a restated certificate of incorporation, or of any other certificate which has been filed in the office of the Secretary of State as required by any provision of this title shall, when duly certified by the Secretary of State, be received in all courts, public offices and official bodies as prima facie evidence of:

(1) Due execution, acknowledgment and filing of the instrument;

(2) Observance and performance of all acts and conditions necessary to have been observed and performed precedent to the instrument becoming effective; and

(3) Any other facts required or permitted by law to be stated in the instrument.

§ 106. Commencement of Corporate Existence

Upon the filing with the Secretary of State of the certificate of incorporation, executed and acknowledged in accordance with § 103 of this title, the incorporator or incorporators who signed the certificate, and such incorporator's or incorporators' successors and assigns, shall, from the date of such filing, be and constitute a body corporate, by the name set forth in the certificate, subject to § 103(d) of this title and subject to dissolution or other termination of its existence as provided in this chapter.

§ 107. Powers of Incorporators

If the persons who are to serve as directors until the first annual meeting of stockholders have not been named in the certificate of incorporation, the incorporator or incorporators, until the directors are elected, shall manage the affairs of the corporation and may do whatever is necessary and proper to perfect the organization of the corporation, including the adoption of the original bylaws of the corporation and the election of directors.

§ 108. Organization Meeting of Incorporators or Directors Named in Certificate of Incorporation

(a) After the filing of the certificate of incorporation an organization meeting of the incorporator or incorporators, or of the board of directors if the initial directors were named in the certificate of incorporation, shall be held, either within or without this State, at the call of a majority of the incorporators or directors, as the case may be, for the purposes of adopting bylaws, electing directors (if the meeting is of the incorporators) to serve or hold office until the first annual meeting of stockholders or until their successors are elected and qualify, electing officers if the meeting is of the directors, doing any other or further acts to perfect the organization of the corporation, and transacting such other business as may come before the meeting.

(b) The persons calling the meeting shall give to each other incorporator or director, as the case may be, at least 2 days' written notice thereof by any usual means of communication, which notice shall state the time, place and purposes of the meeting as fixed by the persons calling it. Notice of the meeting need not be given to anyone who attends the meeting or who signs a waiver of notice either before or after the meeting.

(c) Any action permitted to be taken at the organization meeting of the incorporators or directors, as the case may be, may be taken without a meeting if each incorporator or director, where there is more than 1, or the sole incorporator or director where there is only 1, signs an instrument which states the action so taken.

(d) If any incorporator is not available to act, then any person for whom or on whose behalf the incorporator was acting directly or indirectly as employee or agent, may take any action that such incorporator would have been authorized to take under this section or § 107 of this title; provided that any instrument signed by such other person, or any record of the proceedings of a meeting in which such person participated, shall state that such incorporator is not available and the reason therefor, that such incorporator was acting directly or indirectly as employee or agent for or on behalf of such person, and that such person's signature on such instrument or participation in such meeting is otherwise authorized and not wrongful.

§ 109.   Bylaws

(a) The original or other bylaws of a corporation may be adopted, amended or repealed by the incorporators, by the initial directors of a corporation other than a nonstock corporation or initial members of the governing body of a nonstock corporation if they were named in the certificate of incorporation, or, before a corporation other than a nonstock corporation has received any payment for any of its stock, by its board of directors. After a corporation other than a nonstock corporation has received any payment for any of its stock, the power to adopt, amend or repeal bylaws shall be in the stockholders entitled to vote. In the case of a nonstock corporation, the power to adopt, amend or repeal bylaws shall be in its members entitled to vote. Notwithstanding the foregoing, any corporation may, in its certificate of incorporation, confer the power to adopt, amend or repeal bylaws upon the directors or, in the case of a nonstock corporation, upon its governing body. The fact that such power has been so conferred upon the directors or governing body, as the case may be, shall not divest the stockholders or members of the power, nor limit their power to adopt, amend or repeal bylaws.

(b) The bylaws may contain any provision, not inconsistent with law or with the certificate of incorporation, relating to the business of the corporation, the conduct of its affairs, and its rights or powers or the rights or powers of its stockholders, directors, officers or employees. The bylaws may not contain any provision that would impose liability on a stockholder for the attorneys' fees or expenses of the corporation or any other party in connection with an internal corporate claim, as defined in § 115 of this title.

§ 110.   Emergency Bylaws and Other Powers in Emergency

(a) The board of directors of any corporation may adopt emergency bylaws, subject to repeal or change by action of the stockholders, which shall notwithstanding any different provision elsewhere in this chapter or in Chapters 3 [repealed] and 5 [repealed] of Title 26, or in Chapter 7 of Title 5, or in the certificate of incorporation or bylaws, be operative during any emergency resulting from an attack on the United States or on a locality in which the corporation conducts its business or customarily holds meetings of its board of directors or its stockholders, or during any nuclear or atomic disaster, or during the existence of any catastrophe, or other similar emergency condition, as a result of which a quorum of the board of directors or a standing committee thereof cannot readily be convened for action. The emergency bylaws may make any provision that may be practical and necessary for the circumstances of the emergency . . .

§ 111.   Jurisdiction to Interpret, Apply, Enforce or Determine the Validity of Corporate Instruments and Provisions of This Title

(a) Any civil action to interpret, apply, enforce or determine the validity of the provisions of:

(1) The certificate of incorporation or the bylaws of a corporation;

(2) Any instrument, document or agreement (i) by which a corporation creates or sells, or offers to create or sell, any of its stock, or any rights or options respecting its stock, or (ii) to which a corporation and 1 or more holders of its stock are parties, and pursuant to which any such holder or holders sell or offer to sell any of such stock, or (iii) by which a corporation agrees to sell, lease or exchange any of its property or assets, and which by its terms provides that 1 or more holders of its stock approve of or consent to such sale, lease or exchange;

(3) Any written restrictions on the transfer, registration of transfer or ownership of securities under § 202 of this title;

(4) Any proxy under § 212 or § 215 of this title;

(5) Any voting trust or other voting agreement under § 218 of this title;

(6) Any agreement, certificate of merger or consolidation, or certificate of ownership and merger governed by §§ 251–253, §§ 255–258, §§ 263–264, or § 267 of this title;

(7) Any certificate of conversion under § 265 or § 266 of this title;

(8) Any certificate of domestication, transfer or continuance under § 388, § 389 or § 390 of this title; or

(9) Any other instrument, document, agreement, or certificate required by any provision of this title;

may be brought in the Court of Chancery, except to the extent that a statute confers exclusive jurisdiction on a court, agency or tribunal other than the Court of Chancery.

(b) Any civil action to interpret, apply or enforce any provision of this title may be brought in the Court of Chancery.

§ 112. Access to Proxy Solicitation Materials

The bylaws may provide that if the corporation solicits proxies with respect to an election of directors, it may be required, to the extent and subject to such procedures or conditions as may be provided in the bylaws, to include in its proxy solicitation materials (including any form of proxy it distributes), in addition to individuals nominated by the board of directors, 1 or more individuals nominated by a stockholder. Such procedures or conditions may include any of the following:

(1) A provision requiring a minimum record or beneficial ownership, or duration of ownership, of shares of the corporation's capital stock, by the nominating stockholder, and defining beneficial ownership to take into account options or other rights in respect of or related to such stock;

(2) A provision requiring the nominating stockholder to submit specified information concerning the stockholder and the stockholder's nominees, including information concerning ownership by such persons of shares of the corporation's capital stock, or options or other rights in respect of or related to such stock;

(3) A provision conditioning eligibility to require inclusion in the corporation's proxy solicitation materials upon the number or proportion of directors nominated by stockholders or whether the stockholder previously sought to require such inclusion;

(4) A provision precluding nominations by any person if such person, any nominee of such person, or any affiliate or associate of such person or nominee, has acquired or publicly proposed to acquire shares constituting a specified percentage of the voting power of the corporation's outstanding voting stock within a specified period before the election of directors;

(5) A provision requiring that the nominating stockholder undertake to indemnify the corporation in respect of any loss arising as a result of any false or misleading information or statement submitted by the nominating stockholder in connection with a nomination; and

(6) Any other lawful condition.

§ 113. Proxy Expense Reimbursement

(a) The bylaws may provide for the reimbursement by the corporation of expenses incurred by a stockholder in soliciting proxies in connection with an election of directors, subject to such procedures or conditions as the bylaws may prescribe, including:

(1) Conditioning eligibility for reimbursement upon the number or proportion of persons nominated by the stockholder seeking reimbursement or whether such stockholder previously sought reimbursement for similar expenses;

(2) Limitations on the amount of reimbursement based upon the proportion of votes cast in favor of 1 or more of the persons nominated by the stockholder seeking reimbursement, or upon the amount spent by the corporation in soliciting proxies in connection with the election;

(3) Limitations concerning elections of directors by cumulative voting pursuant to § 214 of this title; or

(4) Any other lawful condition.

(b) No bylaw so adopted shall apply to elections for which any record date precedes its adoption.

§ 115.　　Forum Selection Provisions

The certificate of incorporation or the bylaws may require, consistent with applicable jurisdictional requirements, that any or all internal corporate claims shall be brought solely and exclusively in any or all of the courts in this State, and no provision of the certificate of incorporation or the bylaws may prohibit bringing such claims in the courts of this State. "Internal corporate claims" means claims, including claims in the right of the corporation, (i) that are based upon a violation of a duty by a current or former director or officer or stockholder in such capacity, or (ii) as to which this title confers jurisdiction upon the Court of Chancery.

SUBCHAPTER II.　POWERS

§ 121.　　General Powers

(a) In addition to the powers enumerated in § 122 of this title, every corporation, its officers, directors and stockholders shall possess and may exercise all the powers and privileges granted by this chapter or by any other law or by its certificate of incorporation, together with any powers incidental thereto, so far as such powers and privileges are necessary or convenient to the conduct, promotion or attainment of the business or purposes set forth in its certificate of incorporation.

(b) Every corporation shall be governed by the provisions and be subject to the restrictions and liabilities contained in this chapter.

§ 122.　　Specific Powers

Every corporation created under this chapter shall have power to:

(1) Have perpetual succession by its corporate name, unless a limited period of duration is stated in its certificate of incorporation;

(2) Sue and be sued in all courts and participate, as a party or otherwise, in any judicial, administrative, arbitrative or other proceeding, in its corporate name;

(3) Have a corporate seal, which may be altered at pleasure, and use the same by causing it or a facsimile thereof, to be impressed or affixed or in any other manner reproduced;

(4) Purchase, receive, take by grant, gift, devise, bequest or otherwise, lease, or otherwise acquire, own, hold, improve, employ, use and otherwise deal in and with real or personal property, or any interest therein, wherever situated, and to sell, convey, lease, exchange, transfer or otherwise dispose of, or mortgage or pledge, all or any of its property and assets, or any interest therein, wherever situated;

(5) Appoint such officers and agents as the business of the corporation requires and to pay or otherwise provide for them suitable compensation;

(6) Adopt, amend and repeal bylaws;

(7) Wind up and dissolve itself in the manner provided in this chapter;

(8) Conduct its business, carry on its operations and have offices and exercise its powers within or without this State;

(9) Make donations for the public welfare or for charitable, scientific or educational purposes, and in time of war or other national emergency in aid thereof;

(10) Be an incorporator, promoter or manager of other corporations of any type or kind;

(11) Participate with others in any corporation, partnership, limited partnership, joint venture or other association of any kind, or in any transaction, undertaking or arrangement which the participating corporation would have power to conduct by itself, whether or not such participation involves sharing or delegation of control with or to others;

(12) Transact any lawful business which the corporation's board of directors shall find to be in aid of governmental authority;

(13) Make contracts, including contracts of guaranty and suretyship, incur liabilities, borrow money at such rates of interest as the corporation may determine, issue its notes, bonds and other obligations, and secure any of its obligations by mortgage, pledge or other encumbrance of all or any of its property, franchises and income, and make contracts of guaranty and suretyship which are necessary or convenient to the conduct, promotion or attainment of the business of (a) a corporation all of the outstanding stock of which is owned, directly or indirectly, by the contracting corporation, or (b) a corporation which owns, directly or indirectly, all of the outstanding stock of the contracting corporation, or (c) a corporation all of the outstanding stock of which is owned, directly or indirectly, by a corporation which owns, directly or indirectly, all of the outstanding stock of the contracting corporation, which contracts of guaranty and suretyship shall be deemed to be necessary or convenient to the conduct, promotion or attainment of the business of the contracting corporation, and make other contracts of guaranty and suretyship which are necessary or convenient to the conduct, promotion or attainment of the business of the contracting corporation;

(14) Lend money for its corporate purposes, invest and reinvest its funds, and take, hold and deal with real and personal property as security for the payment of funds so loaned or invested;

(15) Pay pensions and establish and carry out pension, profit sharing, stock option, stock purchase, stock bonus, retirement, benefit, incentive and compensation plans, trusts and provisions for any or all of its directors, officers and employees, and for any or all of the directors, officers and employees of its subsidiaries;

(16) Provide insurance for its benefit on the life of any of its directors, officers or employees, or on the life of any stockholder for the purpose of acquiring at such stockholder's death shares of its stock owned by such stockholder.

(17) Renounce, in its certificate of incorporation or by action of its board of directors, any interest or expectancy of the corporation in, or in being offered an opportunity to participate in, specified business opportunities or specified classes or categories of business opportunities that are presented to the corporation or 1 or more of its officers, directors or stockholders.

§ 123. Powers Respecting Securities of Other Corporations or Entities

Any corporation organized under the laws of this State may guarantee, purchase, take, receive, subscribe for or otherwise acquire; own, hold, use or otherwise employ; sell, lease, exchange, transfer or otherwise dispose of; mortgage, lend, pledge or otherwise deal in and with, bonds and other obligations of, or shares or other securities or interests in, or issued by, any other domestic or foreign corporation, partnership, association or individual, or by any government or agency or instrumentality thereof. A corporation while owner of any such securities may exercise all the rights, powers and privileges of ownership, including the right to vote.

§ 124. Effect of Lack of Corporate Capacity or Power; Ultra Vires

No act of a corporation and no conveyance or transfer of real or personal property to or by a corporation shall be invalid by reason of the fact that the corporation was without capacity or power to do such act or to make or receive such conveyance or transfer, but such lack of capacity or power may be asserted:

(1) In a proceeding by a stockholder against the corporation to enjoin the doing of any act or acts or the transfer of real or personal property by or to the corporation. If the unauthorized acts or transfer sought to be enjoined are being, or are to be, performed or made pursuant to any contract to which the corporation is a party, the court may, if all of the parties to the contract are parties to the proceeding and if it deems the same to be equitable, set aside and enjoin the performance of such contract, and in

so doing may allow to the corporation or to the other parties to the contract, as the case may be, such compensation as may be equitable for the loss or damage sustained by any of them which may result from the action of the court in setting aside and enjoining the performance of such contract, but anticipated profits to be derived from the performance of the contract shall not be awarded by the court as a loss or damage sustained;

(2) In a proceeding by the corporation, whether acting directly or through a receiver, trustee or other legal representative, or through stockholders in a representative suit, against an incumbent or former officer or director of the corporation, for loss or damage due to such incumbent or former officer's or director's unauthorized act;

(3) In a proceeding by the Attorney General to dissolve the corporation, or to enjoin the corporation from the transaction of unauthorized business.

SUBCHAPTER III. REGISTERED OFFICE AND REGISTERED AGENT

§ 131.   Registered Office in State; Principal Office or Place of Business in State

(a) Every corporation shall have and maintain in this State a registered office which may, but need not be, the same as its place of business.

(b) Whenever the term "corporation's principal office or place of business in this State" or "principal office or place of business of the corporation in this State," or other term of like import, is or has been used in a corporation's certificate of incorporation, or in any other document, or in any statute, it shall be deemed to mean and refer to, unless the context indicates otherwise, the corporation's registered office required by this section; and it shall not be necessary for any corporation to amend its certificate of incorporation or any other document to comply with this section.

(c) As contained in any certificate of incorporation or other document filed with the Secretary of State under this chapter, the address of a registered office shall include the street, number, city, county and postal code.

§ 132.   Registered Agent in State; Resident Agent

(a) Every corporation shall have and maintain in this State a registered agent, which agent may be any of:

(1) The corporation itself;

(2) An individual resident in this State;

(3) A domestic corporation (other than the corporation itself), a domestic partnership (whether general (including a limited liability partnership) or limited (including a limited liability limited partnership)), a domestic limited liability company or a domestic statutory trust; or

(4) A foreign corporation, a foreign partnership (whether general (including a limited liability partnership) or limited (including a limited liability limited partnership)), a foreign limited liability company or a foreign statutory trust.

(b) Every registered agent for a domestic corporation or a foreign corporation shall:

(1) If an entity, maintain a business office in this State which is generally open, or if an individual, be generally present at a designated location in this State, at sufficiently frequent times to accept service of process and otherwise perform the functions of a registered agent;

(2) If a foreign entity, be authorized to transact business in this State;

(3) Accept service of process and other communications directed to the corporations for which it serves as registered agent and forward same to the corporation to which the service or communication is directed;

(4) Forward to the corporations for which it serves as registered agent the annual report required by § 502 of this title or an electronic notification of same in a form satisfactory to the Secretary of State ("Secretary"); and

(5) Satisfy and adhere to regulations established by the Secretary regarding the verification of both the identity of the entity's contacts and individuals for which the registered agent maintains a record for the reduction of risk of unlawful business purposes.

(c) Any registered agent who at any time serves as registered agent for more than 50 entities (a "commercial registered agent"), whether domestic or foreign, shall satisfy and comply with the following qualifications.

(1) A natural person serving as a commercial registered agent shall:

a. Maintain a principal residence or a principal place of business in this State;

b. Maintain a Delaware business license;

c. Be generally present at a designated location within this State during normal business hours to accept service of process and otherwise perform the functions of a registered agent as specified in subsection (b) of this section;

d. Provide the Secretary upon request with such information identifying and enabling communication with such commercial registered agent as the Secretary shall require; and

e. Satisfy and adhere to regulations established by the Secretary regarding the verification of both the identity of the entity's contacts and individuals for which the natural person maintains a record for the reduction of risk of unlawful business purposes.

(2) A domestic or foreign corporation, a domestic or foreign partnership (whether general (including a limited liability partnership) or limited (including a limited liability limited partnership)), a domestic or foreign limited liability company, or a domestic or foreign statutory trust serving as a commercial registered agent shall:

a. Have a business office within this State which is generally open during normal business hours to accept service of process and otherwise perform the functions of a registered agent as specified in subsection (b) of this section;

b. Maintain a Delaware business license;

c. Have generally present at such office during normal business hours an officer, director or managing agent who is a natural person;

d. Provide the Secretary upon request with such information identifying and enabling communication with such commercial registered agent as the Secretary shall require; and

e. Satisfy and adhere to regulations established by the Secretary regarding the verification of both the identity of the entity's contacts and individuals for which it maintains a record for the reduction of risk of unlawful business purposes.

(3) For purposes of this subsection and paragraph (f)(2)a. of this section, a commercial registered agent shall also include any registered agent which has an officer, director or managing agent in common with any other registered agent or agents if such registered agents at any time during such common service as officer, director or managing agent collectively served as registered agents for more than 50 entities, whether domestic or foreign.

(d) Every corporation formed under the laws of this State or qualified to do business in this State shall provide to its registered agent and update from time to time as necessary the name, business address and business telephone number of a natural person who is an officer, director, employee, or designated agent of the corporation, who is then authorized to receive communications from the registered agent. Such person shall be deemed the communications contact for the corporation. Every registered agent shall retain (in paper or electronic form) the above information concerning the current communications contact for each corporation for which he, she or it serves as a registered agent. If the corporation fails to provide the registered agent with a current communications contact, the registered agent may resign as the registered agent for such corporation pursuant to § 136 of this title.

(e) The Secretary is fully authorized to issue such regulations as may be necessary or appropriate to carry out the enforcement of subsections (b), (c) and (d) of this section, and to take actions reasonable and necessary to assure registered agents' compliance with subsections (b), (c) and (d) of this section. Such actions may include refusal to file documents submitted by a registered agent, including the refusal to file any documents regarding an entity's formation.

(f) Upon application of the Secretary, the Court of Chancery may enjoin any person or entity from serving as a registered agent or as an officer, director or managing agent of a registered agent.

(1) Upon the filing of a complaint by the Secretary pursuant to this section, the Court may make such orders respecting such proceeding as it deems appropriate, and may enter such orders granting interim or final relief as it deems proper under the circumstances.

(2) Any one or more of the following grounds shall be a sufficient basis to grant an injunction pursuant to this section:

a. With respect to any registered agent who at any time within 1 year immediately prior to the filing of the Secretary's complaint is a commercial registered agent, failure after notice and warning to comply with the qualifications set forth in subsection (b) of this section and/or the requirements of subsection (c) or (d) of this section above;

b. The person serving as a registered agent, or any person who is an officer, director or managing agent of an entity registered agent, has been convicted of a felony or any crime which includes an element of dishonesty or fraud or involves moral turpitude;

c. The registered agent has engaged in conduct in connection with acting as a registered agent that is intended to or likely to deceive or defraud the public.

(3) With respect to any order the court enters pursuant to this section with respect to an entity that has acted as a registered agent, the court may also direct such order to any person who has served as an officer, director, or managing agent of such registered agent. Any person who, on or after January 1, 2007, serves as an officer, director, or managing agent of an entity acting as a registered agent in this State shall be deemed thereby to have consented to the appointment of such registered agent as agent upon whom service of process may be made in any action brought pursuant to this section, and service as an officer, director, or managing agent of an entity acting as a registered agent in this State shall be a signification of the consent of such person that any process when so served shall be of the same legal force and validity as if served upon such person within this State, and such appointment of the registered agent shall be irrevocable.

(4) Upon the entry of an order by the Court enjoining any person or entity from acting as a registered agent, the Secretary shall mail or deliver notice of such order to each affected corporation at the address of its principal place of business as specified in its most recent franchise tax report or other record of the Secretary. If such corporation is a domestic corporation and fails to obtain and designate a new registered agent within 30 days after such notice is given, the Secretary shall declare the charter of such corporation forfeited. If such corporation is a foreign corporation, and fails to obtain and designate a new registered agent within 30 days after such notice is given, the Secretary shall forfeit its qualification to do business in this State. If the court enjoins a person or entity from acting as a registered agent as provided in this section and no new registered agent shall have been obtained and designated in the time and manner aforesaid, service of legal process against the corporation for which the registered agent had been acting shall thereafter be upon the Secretary in accordance with § 321 of this title. The Court of Chancery may, upon application of the Secretary on notice to the former registered agent, enter such orders as it deems appropriate to give the Secretary access to information in the former registered agent's possession in order to facilitate communication with the corporations the former registered agent served.

(g) The Secretary is authorized to make a list of registered agents available to the public, and to establish such qualifications and issue such rules and regulations with respect to such listing as the Secretary deems necessary or appropriate.

(h) Whenever the term "resident agent" or "resident agent in charge of a corporation's principal office or place of business in this State," or other term of like import which refers to a corporation's agent required by statute to be located in this State, is or has been used in a corporation's certificate of incorporation, or in any other document, or in any statute, it shall be deemed to mean and refer to, unless the context indicates otherwise, the corporation's registered agent required by this section; and it shall not be necessary for any corporation to amend its certificate of incorporation or any other document to comply with this section.

SUBCHAPTER IV. DIRECTORS AND OFFICERS

§ 141. Board of Directors; Powers; Number, Qualifications, Terms and Quorum; Committees; Classes of Directors; . . . Reliance upon Books; Action Without Meeting; Removal

(a) The business and affairs of every corporation organized under this chapter shall be managed by or under the direction of a board of directors, except as may be otherwise provided in this chapter or in its certificate of incorporation. If any such provision is made in the certificate of incorporation, the powers and duties conferred or imposed upon the board of directors by this chapter shall be exercised or performed to such extent and by such person or persons as shall be provided in the certificate of incorporation.

(b) The board of directors of a corporation shall consist of 1 or more members, each of whom shall be a natural person. The number of directors shall be fixed by, or in the manner provided in, the bylaws, unless the certificate of incorporation fixes the number of directors, in which case a change in the number of directors shall be made only by amendment of the certificate. Directors need not be stockholders unless so required by the certificate of incorporation or the bylaws. The certificate of incorporation or bylaws may prescribe other qualifications for directors. Each director shall hold office until such director's successor is elected and qualified or until such director's earlier resignation or removal. Any director may resign at any time upon notice given in writing or by electronic transmission to the corporation. A resignation is effective when the resignation is delivered unless the resignation specifies a later effective date or an effective date determined upon the happening of an event or events. A resignation which is conditioned upon the director failing to receive a specified vote for reelection as a director may provide that it is irrevocable. A majority of the total number of directors shall constitute a quorum for the transaction of business unless the certificate of incorporation or the bylaws require a greater number. Unless the certificate of incorporation provides otherwise, the bylaws may provide that a number less than a majority shall constitute a quorum which in no case shall be less than ⅓ of the total number of directors. The vote of the majority of the directors present at a meeting at which a quorum is present shall be the act of the board of directors unless the certificate of incorporation or the bylaws shall require a vote of a greater number.

(c)(1) All corporations incorporated prior to July 1, 1996, shall be governed by this paragraph (c)(1) of this section, provided that any such corporation may by a resolution adopted by a majority of the whole board elect to be governed by paragraph (c)(2) of this section, in which case this paragraph (c)(1) of this section shall not apply to such corporation. All corporations incorporated on or after July 1, 1996, shall be governed by paragraph (c)(2) of this section. The board of directors may, by resolution passed by a majority of the whole board, designate 1 or more committees, each committee to consist of 1 or more of the directors of the corporation. The board may designate 1 or more directors as alternate members of any committee, who may replace any absent or disqualified member at any meeting of the committee. The bylaws may provide that in the absence or disqualification of a member of a committee, the member or members present at any meeting and not disqualified from voting, whether or not the member or members present constitute a quorum, may unanimously appoint another member of the board of directors to act at the meeting in the place of any such absent or disqualified member. Any such committee, to the extent provided in the resolution of the board of directors, or in the bylaws of the corporation, shall have and may exercise all the powers and authority of the board of directors in the management of the business and affairs of the corporation, and may authorize the seal of the corporation to be affixed to all papers which may require it; but no such committee shall have the power or authority in reference to amending the certificate of incorporation (except that a committee may, to the extent authorized in the resolution or resolutions providing for the issuance of shares of stock adopted by the board of directors as provided in § 151(a) of this title, fix the designations and any of the preferences or rights of such shares relating to dividends, redemption, dissolution, any distribution of assets of the corporation or the conversion into, or the exchange of such shares for, shares of any other class or classes or any other series of the same or any other class or classes of stock of the corporation or fix the number of shares of any series of stock or authorize the increase or decrease of the shares of any series), adopting an agreement of merger or consolidation under § 251, § 252, § 254, § 255, § 256, § 257, § 258, § 263 or § 264 of this title, recommending to the stockholders the sale, lease or exchange of all or substantially all of the corporation's property and assets, recommending to the stockholders a dissolution of the corporation or a revocation of a dissolution, or amending the bylaws of the corporation; and, unless the resolution, bylaws or certificate of incorporation expressly so provides, no such committee shall have the power or authority to declare a dividend, to authorize the issuance of stock or to adopt a certificate of ownership and merger pursuant to § 253 of this title.

(2) The board of directors may designate 1 or more committees, each committee to consist of 1 or more of the directors of the corporation. The board may designate 1 or more directors as alternate members of any committee, who may replace any absent or disqualified member at any meeting of the committee. The bylaws may provide that in the absence or disqualification of a member of a committee, the member or members present at any meeting and not disqualified from voting, whether or not such member or members constitute a quorum, may unanimously appoint another member of the board of directors to act at the meeting in the place of any such absent or disqualified member. Any such committee, to the extent provided in the resolution of the board of directors, or in the bylaws of the corporation, shall have and may exercise all the powers and authority of the board of directors in the management of the business and affairs of the corporation, and may authorize the seal of the corporation to be affixed to all papers which may require it; but no such committee shall have the power or authority in reference to the following matter: (i) approving or adopting, or recommending to the stockholders, any action or matter (other than the election or removal of directors) expressly required by this chapter to be submitted to stockholders for approval or (ii) adopting, amending or repealing any bylaw of the corporation.

(3) Unless otherwise provided in the certificate of incorporation, the bylaws or the resolution of the board of directors designating the committee, a committee may create 1 or more subcommittees, each subcommittee to consist of 1 or more members of the committee, and delegate to a subcommittee any or all of the powers and authority of the committee. Except for references to committees and members of committees in subsection (c) of this section, every reference in this chapter to a committee of the board of directors or a member of a committee shall be deemed to include a reference to a subcommittee or member of a subcommittee.

(4) A majority of the directors then serving on a committee of the board of directors or on a subcommittee of a committee shall constitute a quorum for the transaction of business by the committee or subcommittee, unless the certificate of incorporation, the bylaws, a resolution of the board of directors or a resolution of a committee that created the subcommittee requires a greater or lesser number, provided that in no case shall a quorum be less than ⅓ of the directors then serving on the committee or subcommittee. The vote of the majority of the members of a committee or subcommittee present at a meeting at which a quorum is present shall be the act of the committee or subcommittee, unless the certificate of incorporation, the bylaws, a resolution of the board of directors or a resolution of a committee that created the subcommittee requires a greater number.

(d) The directors of any corporation organized under this chapter may, by the certificate of incorporation or by an initial bylaw, or by a bylaw adopted by a vote of the stockholders, be divided into 1, 2 or 3 classes; the term of office of those of the first class to expire at the first annual meeting held after such classification becomes effective; of the second class 1 year thereafter; of the third class 2 years thereafter; and at each annual election held after such classification becomes effective, directors shall be chosen for a full term, as the case may be, to succeed those whose terms expire. The certificate of incorporation or bylaw provision dividing the directors into classes may authorize the board of directors to assign members of the board already in office to such classes at the time such classification becomes effective. The certificate of incorporation may confer upon holders of any class or series of stock the right to elect 1 or more directors who shall serve for such term, and have such voting powers as shall be stated in the certificate of incorporation. The terms of office and voting powers of the directors elected separately by the holders of any class or series of stock may be greater than or less than those of any other director or class of directors. In addition, the certificate of incorporation may confer upon 1 or more directors, whether or not elected separately by the holders of any class or series of stock, voting powers greater than or less than those of other directors. Any such provision conferring greater or lesser voting power shall apply to voting in any committee, unless otherwise provided in the certificate of incorporation or bylaws. If the certificate of incorporation provides that 1 or more directors shall have more or less than 1 vote per director on any matter, every reference in this chapter to a majority or other proportion of the directors shall refer to a majority or other proportion of the votes of the directors.

(e) A member of the board of directors, or a member of any committee designated by the board of directors, shall, in the performance of such member's duties, be fully protected in relying in good faith upon the records of the corporation and upon such information, opinions, reports or statements presented to the corporation by any of the corporation's officers or employees, or committees of the board of directors, or by any other person as to matters the member reasonably believes are within such other person's professional or expert competence and who has been selected with reasonable care by or on behalf of the corporation.

(f) Unless otherwise restricted by the certificate of incorporation or bylaws, any action required or permitted to be taken at any meeting of the board of directors or of any committee thereof may be taken without a meeting if all members of the board or committee, as the case may be, consent thereto in writing, or by electronic transmission and the writing or writings or electronic transmission or transmissions are filed with the minutes of proceedings of the board, or committee. Such filing shall be in paper form if the minutes are maintained in paper form and shall be in electronic form if the minutes are maintained in electronic form. Any person (whether or not then a director) may provide, whether through instruction to an agent or otherwise, that a consent to action will be effective at a future time (including a time determined upon the happening of an event), no later than 60 days after such instruction is given or such provision is made and such consent shall be deemed to have been given for purposes of this subsection at such effective time so long as such person is then a director and did not revoke the consent prior to such time. Any such consent shall be revocable prior to its becoming effective.

(g) Unless otherwise restricted by the certificate of incorporation or bylaws, the board of directors of any corporation organized under this chapter may hold its meetings, and have an office or offices, outside of this State.

(h) Unless otherwise restricted by the certificate of incorporation or bylaws, the board of directors shall have the authority to fix the compensation of directors.

(i) Unless otherwise restricted by the certificate of incorporation or bylaws, members of the board of directors of any corporation, or any committee designated by the board, may participate in a meeting of such board, or committee by means of conference telephone or other communications equipment by means of which all persons participating in the meeting can hear each other, and participation in a meeting pursuant to this subsection shall constitute presence in person at the meeting.

(j) The certificate of incorporation of any nonstock corporation may provide that less than $1/3$ of the members of the governing body may constitute a quorum thereof and may otherwise provide that the business and affairs of the corporation shall be managed in a manner different from that provided in this section. Except as may be otherwise provided by the certificate of incorporation, this section shall apply to such a corporation, and when so applied, all references to the board of directors, to members thereof, and to stockholders shall be deemed to refer to the governing body of the corporation, the members thereof and the members of the corporation, respectively; and all references to stock, capital stock, or shares thereof shall be deemed to refer to memberships of a nonprofit nonstock corporation and to membership interests of any other nonstock corporation.

(k) Any director or the entire board of directors may be removed, with or without cause, by the holders of a majority of the shares then entitled to vote at an election of directors, except as follows:

(1) Unless the certificate of incorporation otherwise provides, in the case of a corporation whose board is classified as provided in subsection (d) of this section, stockholders may effect such removal only for cause; or

(2) In the case of a corporation having cumulative voting, if less than the entire board is to be removed, no director may be removed without cause if the votes cast against such director's removal would be sufficient to elect such director if then cumulatively voted at an election of the entire board of directors, or, if there be classes of directors, at an election of the class of directors of which such director is a part.

Whenever the holders of any class or series are entitled to elect 1 or more directors by the certificate of incorporation, this subsection shall apply, in respect to the removal without cause of a director or directors so elected, to the vote of the holders of the outstanding shares of that class or series and not to the vote of the outstanding shares as a whole.

§ 142.   Officers; Titles, Duties, Selection, Term; Failure to Elect; Vacancies

(a) Every corporation organized under this chapter shall have such officers with such titles and duties as shall be stated in the bylaws or in a resolution of the board of directors which is not inconsistent with the bylaws and as may be necessary to enable it to sign instruments and stock certificates which comply with §§ 103(a)(2) and 158 of this title. One of the officers shall have the duty to record the proceedings of the meetings of the stockholders and directors in a book to be kept for that purpose. Any number of offices may be held by the same person unless the certificate of incorporation or bylaws otherwise provide.

(b) Officers shall be chosen in such manner and shall hold their offices for such terms as are prescribed by the bylaws or determined by the board of directors or other governing body. Each officer shall hold office until such officer's successor is elected and qualified or until such officer's earlier resignation or removal. Any officer may resign at any time upon written notice to the corporation.

(c) The corporation may secure the fidelity of any or all of its officers or agents by bond or otherwise.

(d) A failure to elect officers shall not dissolve or otherwise affect the corporation.

(e) Any vacancy occurring in any office of the corporation by death, resignation, removal or otherwise, shall be filled as the bylaws provide. In the absence of such provision, the vacancy shall be filled by the board of directors or other governing body.

§ 143.   Loans to Employees and Officers; Guaranty of Obligations of Employees and Officers

Any corporation may lend money to, or guarantee any obligation of, or otherwise assist any officer or other employee of the corporation or of its subsidiary, including any officer or employee who is a director of the corporation or its subsidiary, whenever, in the judgment of the directors, such loan, guaranty or assistance may reasonably be expected to benefit the corporation. The loan, guaranty or other assistance may be with or without interest, and may be unsecured, or secured in such manner as the board of directors shall approve, including, without limitation, a pledge of shares of stock of the corporation. Nothing in this section contained shall be deemed to deny, limit or restrict the powers of guaranty or warranty of any corporation at common law or under any statute.

§ 144.   Interested Directors; Quorum

(a) No contract or transaction between a corporation and 1 or more of its directors or officers, or between a corporation and any other corporation, partnership, association, or other organization in which 1 or more of its directors or officers, are directors or officers, or have a financial interest, shall be void or voidable solely for this reason, or solely because the director or officer is present at or participates in the meeting of the board or committee which authorizes the contract or transaction, or solely because any such director's or officer's votes are counted for such purpose, if:

(1) The material facts as to the director's or officer's relationship or interest and as to the contract or transaction are disclosed or are known to the board of directors or the committee, and the board or committee in good faith authorizes the contract or transaction by the affirmative votes of a majority of the disinterested directors, even though the disinterested directors be less than a quorum; or

(2) The material facts as to the director's or officer's relationship or interest and as to the contract or transaction are disclosed or are known to the stockholders entitled to vote thereon, and the contract or transaction is specifically approved in good faith by vote of the stockholders; or

(3) The contract or transaction is fair as to the corporation as of the time it is authorized, approved or ratified, by the board of directors, a committee or the stockholders.

(b) Common or interested directors may be counted in determining the presence of a quorum at a meeting of the board of directors or of a committee which authorizes the contract or transaction.

§ 145.   Indemnification of Officers, Directors, Employees and Agents; Insurance

(a) A corporation shall have power to indemnify any person who was or is a party or is threatened to be made a party to any threatened, pending or completed action, suit or proceeding, whether civil, criminal, administrative or investigative (other than an action by or in the right of the corporation) by reason of the fact that the person is or was a director, officer, employee or agent of the corporation, or is or was serving at the request of the corporation as a director, officer, employee or agent of another corporation, partnership, joint venture, trust or other enterprise, against expenses (including attorneys' fees), judgments, fines and amounts paid in settlement actually and reasonably incurred by the person in connection with such action, suit or proceeding if the person acted in good faith and in a manner the person reasonably believed to be in or not opposed to the best interests of the corporation, and, with respect to any criminal action or proceeding, had no reasonable cause to believe the person's conduct was unlawful. The termination of any action, suit or proceeding by judgment, order, settlement, conviction, or upon a plea of nolo contendere or its equivalent, shall not, of itself, create a presumption that the person did not act in good faith and in a manner which the person reasonably believed to be in or not opposed to the best interests of the corporation, and, with respect to any criminal action or proceeding, had reasonable cause to believe that the person's conduct was unlawful.

(b) A corporation shall have power to indemnify any person who was or is a party or is threatened to be made a party to any threatened, pending or completed action or suit by or in the right of the corporation to procure a judgment in its favor by reason of the fact that the person is or was a director, officer, employee or agent of the corporation, or is or was serving at the request of the corporation as a director, officer, employee or agent of another corporation, partnership, joint venture, trust or other enterprise against expenses (including attorneys' fees) actually and reasonably incurred by the person in connection with the defense or settlement of such action or suit if the person acted in good faith and in a manner the person reasonably believed to be in or not opposed to the best interests of the corporation and except that no indemnification shall be made in respect of any claim, issue or matter as to which such person shall have been adjudged to be liable to the corporation unless and only to the extent that the Court of Chancery or the court in which such action or suit was brought shall determine upon application that, despite the adjudication of liability but in view of all the circumstances of the case, such person is fairly and reasonably entitled to indemnity for such expenses which the Court of Chancery or such other court shall deem proper.

(c) To the extent that a present or former director or officer of a corporation has been successful on the merits or otherwise in defense of any action, suit or proceeding referred to in subsections (a) and (b) of this section, or in defense of any claim, issue or matter therein, such person shall be indemnified against expenses (including attorneys' fees) actually and reasonably incurred by such person in connection therewith.

(d) Any indemnification under subsections (a) and (b) of this section (unless ordered by a court) shall be made by the corporation only as authorized in the specific case upon a determination that indemnification of the present or former director, officer, employee or agent is proper in the circumstances because the person has met the applicable standard of conduct set forth in subsections (a) and (b) of this section. Such determination shall be made, with respect to a person who is a director or officer of the corporation at the time of such determination:

   (1) By a majority vote of the directors who are not parties to such action, suit or proceeding, even though less than a quorum; or

   (2) By a committee of such directors designated by majority vote of such directors, even though less than a quorum; or

   (3) If there are no such directors, or if such directors so direct, by independent legal counsel in a written opinion; or

   (4) By the stockholders.

(e) Expenses (including attorneys' fees) incurred by an officer or director of the corporation in defending any civil, criminal, administrative or investigative action, suit or proceeding may be paid by the corporation in advance of the final disposition of such action, suit or proceeding upon receipt of an undertaking by or on behalf of such director or officer to repay such amount if it shall ultimately be determined that such person is not entitled to be indemnified by the corporation as authorized in this section. Such expenses (including attorneys' fees) incurred by former directors and officers or other employees and agents of the corporation or by persons serving at the request of the corporation as directors, officers, employees or agents of another corporation, partnership, joint venture, trust or other enterprise may be so paid upon such terms and conditions, if any, as the corporation deems appropriate.

(f) The indemnification and advancement of expenses provided by, or granted pursuant to, the other subsections of this section shall not be deemed exclusive of any other rights to which those seeking indemnification or advancement of expenses may be entitled under any bylaw, agreement, vote of stockholders or disinterested directors or otherwise, both as to action in such person's official capacity and as to action in another capacity while holding such office. A right to indemnification or to advancement of expenses arising under a provision of the certificate of incorporation or a bylaw shall not be eliminated or impaired by an amendment to the certificate of incorporation or the bylaws after the occurrence of the act or omission that is the subject of the civil, criminal, administrative or investigative action, suit or proceeding for which indemnification or advancement of expenses is sought, unless the provision in effect at the time of such act or omission explicitly authorizes such elimination or impairment after such action or omission has occurred.

(g) A corporation shall have power to purchase and maintain insurance on behalf of any person who is or was a director, officer, employee or agent of the corporation, or is or was serving at the request of the corporation as a director, officer, employee or agent of another corporation, partnership, joint venture, trust or other enterprise against any liability asserted against such person and incurred by such person in any such capacity, or arising out of such person's status as such, whether or not the corporation would have the power to indemnify such person against such liability under this section.

(h) For purposes of this section, references to "the corporation" shall include, in addition to the resulting corporation, any constituent corporation (including any constituent of a constituent) absorbed in a consolidation or merger which, if its separate existence had continued, would have had power and authority to indemnify its directors, officers, and employees or agents, so that any person who is or was a director, officer, employee or agent of such constituent corporation, or is or was serving at the request of such constituent corporation as a director, officer, employee or agent of another corporation, partnership, joint venture, trust or other enterprise, shall stand in the same position under this section with respect to the resulting or surviving corporation as such person would have with respect to such constituent corporation if its separate existence had continued.

(i) For purposes of this section, references to "other enterprises" shall include employee benefit plans; references to "fines" shall include any excise taxes assessed on a person with respect to any employee benefit plan; and references to "serving at the request of the corporation" shall include any service as a director, officer, employee or agent of the corporation which imposes duties on, or involves services by, such director, officer, employee or agent with respect to an employee benefit plan, its participants or beneficiaries; and a person who acted in good faith and in a manner such person reasonably believed to be in the interest of the participants and beneficiaries of an employee benefit plan shall be deemed to have acted in a manner "not opposed to the best interests of the corporation" as referred to in this section.

(j) The indemnification and advancement of expenses provided by, or granted pursuant to, this section shall, unless otherwise provided when authorized or ratified, continue as to a person who has ceased to be a director, officer, employee or agent and shall inure to the benefit of the heirs, executors and administrators of such a person.

(k) The Court of Chancery is hereby vested with exclusive jurisdiction to hear and determine all actions for advancement of expenses or indemnification brought under this section or under any bylaw, agreement, vote of stockholders or disinterested directors, or otherwise. The Court of Chancery may summarily determine a corporation's obligation to advance expenses (including attorneys' fees).

§ 146.   Submission of Matters for Stockholder Vote

A corporation may agree to submit a matter to a vote of its stockholders whether or not the board of directors determines at any time subsequent to approving such matter that such matter is no longer advisable and recommends that the stockholders reject or vote against the matter.

SUBCHAPTER V. STOCK AND DIVIDENDS

§ 151. Classes and Series of Stock; Redemption; Rights

(a) Every corporation may issue 1 or more classes of stock or 1 or more series of stock within any class thereof, any or all of which classes may be of stock with par value or stock without par value and which classes or series may have such voting powers, full or limited, or no voting powers, and such designations, preferences and relative, participating, optional or other special rights, and qualifications, limitations or restrictions thereof, as shall be stated and expressed in the certificate of incorporation or of any amendment thereto, or in the resolution or resolutions providing for the issue of such stock adopted by the board of directors pursuant to authority expressly vested in it by the provisions of its certificate of incorporation. Any of the voting powers, designations, preferences, rights and qualifications, limitations or restrictions of any such class or series of stock may be made dependent upon facts ascertainable outside the certificate of incorporation or of any amendment thereto, or outside the resolution or resolutions providing for the issue of such stock adopted by the board of directors pursuant to authority expressly vested in it by its certificate of incorporation, provided that the manner in which such facts shall operate upon the voting powers, designations, preferences, rights and qualifications, limitations or restrictions of such class or series of stock is clearly and expressly set forth in the certificate of incorporation or in the resolution or resolutions providing for the issue of such stock adopted by the board of directors. The term "facts," as used in this subsection, includes, but is not limited to, the occurrence of any event, including a determination or action by any person or body, including the corporation. The power to increase or decrease or otherwise adjust the capital stock as provided in this chapter shall apply to all or any such classes of stock.

(b) Any stock of any class or series may be made subject to redemption by the corporation at its option or at the option of the holders of such stock or upon the happening of a specified event; provided however, that immediately following any such redemption the corporation shall have outstanding 1 or more shares of 1 or more classes or series of stock, which share, or shares together, shall have full voting powers. Notwithstanding the limitation stated in the foregoing proviso:

(1) Any stock of a regulated investment company registered under the Investment Company Act of 1940 [15 U.S.C. § 80 a–1 et seq.], as heretofore or hereafter amended, may be made subject to redemption by the corporation at its option or at the option of the holders of such stock.

(2) Any stock of a corporation which holds (directly or indirectly) a license or franchise from a governmental agency to conduct its business or is a member of a national securities exchange, which license, franchise or membership is conditioned upon some or all of the holders of its stock possessing prescribed qualifications, may be made subject to redemption by the corporation to the extent necessary to prevent the loss of such license, franchise or membership or to reinstate it.

Any stock which may be made redeemable under this section may be redeemed for cash, property or rights, including securities of the same or another corporation, at such time or times, price or prices, or rate or rates, and with such adjustments, as shall be stated in the certificate of incorporation or in the resolution or resolutions providing for the issue of such stock adopted by the board of directors pursuant to subsection (a) of this section.

(c) The holders of preferred or special stock of any class or of any series thereof shall be entitled to receive dividends at such rates, on such conditions and at such times as shall be stated in the certificate of incorporation or in the resolution or resolutions providing for the issue of such stock adopted by the board of directors as hereinabove provided, payable in preference to, or in such relation to, the dividends payable on any other class or classes or of any other series of stock, and cumulative or noncumulative as shall be so stated and expressed. When dividends upon the preferred and special stocks, if any, to the extent of the preference to which such stocks are entitled, shall have been paid or declared and set apart for payment, a dividend on the remaining class or classes or series of stock may then be paid out of the remaining assets of the corporation available for dividends as elsewhere in this chapter provided.

(d) The holders of the preferred or special stock of any class or of any series thereof shall be entitled to such rights upon the dissolution of, or upon any distribution of the assets of, the corporation as shall be stated in the certificate of incorporation or in the resolution or resolutions providing for the issue of such stock adopted by the board of directors as hereinabove provided.

(e) Any stock of any class or of any series thereof may be made convertible into, or exchangeable for, at the option of either the holder or the corporation or upon the happening of a specified event, shares of any other class or classes or any other series of the same or any other class or classes of stock of the corporation, at such price or prices or at such rate or rates of exchange and with such adjustments as shall be stated in the certificate of incorporation or in the resolution or resolutions providing for the issue of such stock adopted by the board of directors as hereinabove provided.

(f) If any corporation shall be authorized to issue more than 1 class of stock or more than 1 series of any class, the powers, designations, preferences and relative, participating, optional, or other special rights of each class of stock or series thereof and the qualifications, limitations or restrictions of such preferences and/or rights shall be set forth in full or summarized on the face or back of the certificate which the corporation shall issue to represent such class or series of stock, provided that, except as otherwise provided in § 202 of this title, in lieu of the foregoing requirements, there may be set forth on the face or back of the certificate which the corporation shall issue to represent such class or series of stock, a statement that the corporation will furnish without charge to each stockholder who so requests the powers, designations, preferences and relative, participating, optional, or other special rights of each class of stock or series thereof and the qualifications, limitations or restrictions of such preferences and/or rights. Within a reasonable time after the issuance or transfer of uncertificated stock, the registered owner thereof shall be given a notice, in writing or by electronic transmission, containing the information required to be set forth or stated on certificates pursuant to this section or § 156, § 202(a), § 218(a) or § 364 of this title or with respect to this section a statement that the corporation will furnish without charge to each stockholder who so requests the powers, designations, preferences and relative participating, optional or other special rights of each class of stock or series thereof and the qualifications, limitations or restrictions of such preferences and/or rights. Except as otherwise expressly provided by law, the rights and obligations of the holders of uncertificated stock and the rights and obligations of the holders of certificates representing stock of the same class and series shall be identical.

(g) When any corporation desires to issue any shares of stock of any class or of any series of any class of which the powers, designations, preferences and relative, participating, optional or other rights, if any, or the qualifications, limitations or restrictions thereof, if any, shall not have been set forth in the certificate of incorporation or in any amendment thereto but shall be provided for in a resolution or resolutions adopted by the board of directors pursuant to authority expressly vested in it by the certificate of incorporation or any amendment thereto, a certificate of designations setting forth a copy of such resolution or resolutions and the number of shares of stock of such class or series as to which the resolution or resolutions apply shall be executed, acknowledged, filed and shall become effective, in accordance with § 103 of this title. Unless otherwise provided in any such resolution or resolutions, the number of shares of stock of any such series to which such resolution or resolutions apply may be increased (but not above the total number of authorized shares of the class) or decreased (but not below the number of shares thereof then outstanding) by a certificate likewise executed, acknowledged and filed setting forth a statement that a specified increase or decrease therein had been authorized and directed by a resolution or resolutions likewise adopted by the board of directors. In case the number of such shares shall be decreased the number of shares so specified in the certificate shall resume the status which they had prior to the adoption of the first resolution or resolutions. When no shares of any such class or series are outstanding, either because none were issued or because no issued shares of any such class or series remain outstanding, a certificate setting forth a resolution or resolutions adopted by the board of directors that none of the authorized shares of such class or series are outstanding, and that none will be issued subject to the certificate of designations previously filed with respect to such class or series, may be executed, acknowledged and filed in accordance with § 103 of this title and, when such certificate becomes effective, it shall have the effect of eliminating from the certificate of incorporation all matters set forth in the certificate of designations with respect to such class or series of stock. Unless otherwise provided in the certificate of incorporation, if no shares of stock have been issued of a class or series of stock established by a resolution of the board of directors, the voting powers, designations, preferences and relative, participating, optional or other rights, if any, or the qualifications, limitations or restrictions thereof, may be amended by a resolution or resolutions adopted by the board of directors. A certificate which:

(1) States that no shares of the class or series have been issued;

(2) Sets forth a copy of the resolution or resolutions; and

(3) If the designation of the class or series is being changed, indicates the original designation and the new designation,

shall be executed, acknowledged and filed and shall become effective, in accordance with § 103 of this title. When any certificate filed under this subsection becomes effective, it shall have the effect of amending the certificate of incorporation; except that neither the filing of such certificate nor the filing of a restated certificate of incorporation pursuant to § 245 of this title shall prohibit the board of directors from subsequently adopting such resolutions as authorized by this subsection.

§ 152. Issuance of Stock; Lawful Consideration; Fully Paid Stock

The consideration, as determined pursuant to § 153(a) and (b) of this title, for subscriptions to, or the purchase of, the capital stock to be issued by a corporation shall be paid in such form and in such manner as the board of directors shall determine. The board of directors may authorize capital stock to be issued for consideration consisting of cash, any tangible or intangible property or any benefit to the corporation, or any combination thereof. The resolution authorizing the issuance of capital stock may provide that any stock to be issued pursuant to such resolution may be issued in 1 or more transactions in such numbers and at such times as are set forth in or determined by or in the manner set forth in the resolution, which may include a determination or action by any person or body, including the corporation, provided the resolution fixes a maximum number of shares that may be issued pursuant to such resolution, a time period during which such shares may be issued and a minimum amount of consideration for which such shares may be issued. The board of directors may determine the amount of consideration for which shares may be issued by setting a minimum amount of consideration or approving a formula by which the amount or minimum amount of consideration is determined. The formula may include or be made dependent upon facts ascertainable outside the formula, provided the manner in which such facts shall operate upon the formula is clearly and expressly set forth in the formula or in the resolution approving the formula. In the absence of actual fraud in the transaction, the judgment of the directors as to the value of such consideration shall be conclusive. The capital stock so issued shall be deemed to be fully paid and nonassessable stock upon receipt by the corporation of such consideration; provided, however, nothing contained herein shall prevent the board of directors from issuing partly paid shares under § 156 of this title.

§ 153. Consideration for Stock

(a) Shares of stock with par value may be issued for such consideration, having a value not less than the par value thereof, as determined from time to time by the board of directors, or by the stockholders if the certificate of incorporation so provides.

(b) Shares of stock without par value may be issued for such consideration as is determined from time to time by the board of directors, or by the stockholders if the certificate of incorporation so provides.

(c) Treasury shares may be disposed of by the corporation for such consideration as may be determined from time to time by the board of directors, or by the stockholders if the certificate of incorporation so provides.

(d) If the certificate of incorporation reserves to the stockholders the right to determine the consideration for the issue of any shares, the stockholders shall, unless the certificate requires a greater vote, do so by a vote of a majority of the outstanding stock entitled to vote thereon.

§ 154. Determination of Amount of Capital; Capital, Surplus and Net Assets Defined

Any corporation may, by resolution of its board of directors, determine that only a part of the consideration which shall be received by the corporation for any of the shares of its capital stock which it shall issue from time to time shall be capital; but, in case any of the shares issued shall be shares having a par value, the amount of the part of such consideration so determined to be capital shall be in excess of the aggregate par value of the shares issued for such consideration having a par value, unless all the shares issued shall be shares having a par value, in which case the amount of the part of such consideration so determined to be capital need be only equal to the aggregate par value of such shares. In each such case the board of directors shall specify in dollars the part of such consideration which shall be capital. If the board of directors shall not have determined (1) at the time of issue of any shares of the capital stock of the corporation issued for cash or (2) within 60 days after the issue of any shares of the capital stock of the corporation issued for consideration other than cash what part of the consideration for such shares shall be capital, the capital of the corporation in respect of such shares shall be an amount equal to the aggregate par value of such shares having a par value, plus the amount of the consideration for such shares without par value. The amount of the consideration so determined to be capital in respect of any shares without par value shall be the stated capital of such shares. The capital of the corporation may be increased from time to time by resolution of the board of directors directing that a portion of the net assets of the corporation in excess of the amount so determined to be capital be transferred to the capital account. The board of directors may direct that the portion of such net assets so transferred shall be treated as capital in respect of any shares of the corporation of any designated class or classes. The excess, if any, at any given time, of the net assets of the corporation over the amount so determined to be capital shall be surplus. Net assets means the amount by which total assets exceed total liabilities. Capital and surplus are not liabilities for this purpose. Notwithstanding anything in this section to the contrary, for purposes of this section and §§ 160 and 170 of this title, the capital of any nonstock corporation shall be deemed to be zero.

§ 155.   Fractions of Shares

A corporation may, but shall not be required to, issue fractions of a share. If it does not issue fractions of a share, it shall (1) arrange for the disposition of fractional interests by those entitled thereto, (2) pay in cash the fair value of fractions of a share as of the time when those entitled to receive such fractions are determined or (3) issue scrip or warrants in registered form (either represented by a certificate or uncertificated) or in bearer form (represented by a certificate) which shall entitle the holder to receive a full share upon the surrender of such scrip or warrants aggregating a full share. A certificate for a fractional share or an uncertificated fractional share shall, but scrip or warrants shall not unless otherwise provided therein, entitle the holder to exercise voting rights, to receive dividends thereon and to participate in any of the assets of the corporation in the event of liquidation. The board of directors may cause scrip or warrants to be issued subject to the conditions that they shall become void if not exchanged for certificates representing the full shares or uncertificated full shares before a specified date, or subject to the conditions that the shares for which scrip or warrants are exchangeable may be sold by the corporation and the proceeds thereof distributed to the holders of scrip or warrants, or subject to any other conditions which the board of directors may impose.

§ 156.   Partly Paid Shares

Any corporation may issue the whole or any part of its shares as partly paid and subject to call for the remainder of the consideration to be paid therefor. Upon the face or back of each stock certificate issued to represent any such partly paid shares, or upon the books and records of the corporation in the case of uncertificated partly paid shares, the total amount of the consideration to be paid therefor and the amount paid thereon shall be stated. Upon the declaration of any dividend on fully paid shares, the corporation shall declare a dividend upon partly paid shares of the same class, but only upon the basis of the percentage of the consideration actually paid thereon.

§ 157.   Rights and Options Respecting Stock

(a) Subject to any provisions in the certificate of incorporation, every corporation may create and issue, whether or not in connection with the issue and sale of any shares of stock or other securities of the corporation, rights or options entitling the holders thereof to acquire from the corporation any shares of its capital stock of any class or classes, such rights or options to be evidenced by or in such instrument or instruments as shall be approved by the board of directors.

(b) The terms upon which, including the time or times which may be limited or unlimited in duration, at or within which, and the consideration (including a formula by which such consideration may be determined) for which any such shares may be acquired from the corporation upon the exercise of any such right or option, shall be such as shall be stated in the certificate of incorporation, or in a resolution adopted by the board of directors providing for the creation and issue of such rights or options, and, in every case, shall be set forth or incorporated by reference in the instrument or instruments evidencing such rights or options. A formula by which such consideration may be determined may include or be made dependent upon facts ascertainable outside the formula, provided the manner in which such facts shall operate upon the formula is clearly and expressly set forth in the formula or in the resolution approving the formula. In the absence of actual fraud in the transaction, the judgment of the directors as to the consideration for the issuance of such rights or options and the sufficiency thereof shall be conclusive.

(c) The board of directors may, by a resolution adopted by the board, authorize 1 or more officers of the corporation to do 1 or both of the following: (i) designate officers and employees of the corporation or of any of its subsidiaries to be recipients of such rights or options created by the corporation, and (ii) determine the number of such rights or options to be received by such officers and employees; provided, however, that the resolution so authorizing such officer or officers shall specify the total number of rights or options such officer or officers may so award. The board of directors may not authorize an officer to designate himself or herself as a recipient of any such rights or options.

(d) In case the shares of stock of the corporation to be issued upon the exercise of such rights or options shall be shares having a par value, the consideration so to be received therefor shall have a value not less than the par value thereof. In case the shares of stock so to be issued shall be shares of stock without par value, the consideration therefor shall be determined in the manner provided in § 153 of this title.

§ 158.   Stock Certificates; Uncertificated Shares

The shares of a corporation shall be represented by certificates, provided that the board of directors of the corporation may provide by resolution or resolutions that some or all of any or all classes or series of its stock shall be uncertificated shares. Any such resolution shall not apply to shares represented by a certificate until such certificate is surrendered to the corporation. Every holder of stock represented by certificates shall be entitled to have a certificate signed by, or in the name of, the corporation by any 2 authorized officers of the corporation representing the number of shares registered in certificate form. Any or all the signatures on the certificate may be a facsimile. In case any officer, transfer agent or registrar who has signed or whose facsimile signature has been placed upon a certificate shall have ceased to be such officer, transfer agent or registrar before such certificate is issued, it may be issued by the corporation with the same effect as if such person were such officer, transfer agent or registrar at the date of issue. A corporation shall not have power to issue a certificate in bearer form.

§ 160.   Corporation's Powers Respecting Ownership, Voting, etc., of Its Own Stock; Rights of Stock Called for Redemption

(a) Every corporation may purchase, redeem, receive, take or otherwise acquire, own and hold, sell, lend, exchange, transfer or otherwise dispose of, pledge, use and otherwise deal in and with its own shares; provided, however, that no corporation shall:

(1) Purchase or redeem its own shares of capital stock for cash or other property when the capital of the corporation is impaired or when such purchase or redemption would cause any impairment of the capital of the corporation, except that a corporation other than a nonstock corporation may purchase or redeem out of capital any of its own shares which are entitled upon any distribution of its assets, whether by dividend or in liquidation, to a preference over another class or series of its stock, or, if no shares entitled to such a preference are outstanding, any of its own shares, if such shares will be retired upon their acquisition and the capital of the corporation reduced in accordance with §§ 243 and 244 of this title. Nothing in this subsection shall invalidate or otherwise affect a note, debenture or other obligation of a corporation given by it as consideration for its acquisition by purchase, redemption or exchange of its shares of stock if at the time such note, debenture or obligation was delivered by the corporation its capital was not then impaired or did not thereby become impaired;

(2) Purchase, for more than the price at which they may then be redeemed, any of its shares which are redeemable at the option of the corporation; or

(3)

. . . [R]edeem any of its shares, unless their redemption is authorized by § 151(b) of this title and then only in accordance with such section and the certificate of incorporation . . .

(b) Nothing in this section limits or affects a corporation's right to resell any of its shares theretofore purchased or redeemed out of surplus and which have not been retired, for such consideration as shall be fixed by the board of directors.

(c) Shares of its own capital stock belonging to the corporation or to another corporation, if a majority of the shares entitled to vote in the election of directors of such other corporation is held, directly or indirectly, by the corporation, shall neither be entitled to vote nor be counted for quorum purposes. Nothing in this section shall be construed as limiting the right of any corporation to vote stock, including but not limited to its own stock, held by it in a fiduciary capacity.

(d) Shares which have been called for redemption shall not be deemed to be outstanding shares for the purpose of voting or determining the total number of shares entitled to vote on any matter on and after the date on which written notice of redemption has been sent to holders thereof and a sum sufficient to redeem such shares has been irrevocably deposited or set aside to pay the redemption price to the holders of the shares upon surrender of certificates therefor.

§ 161.   Issuance of Additional Stock; When and by Whom

The directors may, at any time and from time to time, if all of the shares of capital stock which the corporation is authorized by its certificate of incorporation to issue have not been issued, subscribed for, or otherwise committed to be issued, issue or take subscriptions for additional shares of its capital stock up to the amount authorized in its certificate of incorporation.

§ 162.   Liability of Stockholder or Subscriber for Stock Not Paid in Full

(a) When the whole of the consideration payable for shares of a corporation has not been paid in, and the assets shall be insufficient to satisfy the claims of its creditors, each holder of or subscriber for such shares shall be bound to pay on each share held or subscribed for by such holder or subscriber the sum necessary to complete the amount of the unpaid balance of the consideration for which such shares were issued or are to be issued by the corporation.

(b) The amounts which shall be payable as provided in subsection (a) of this section may be recovered as provided in § 325 of this title, after a writ of execution against the corporation has been returned unsatisfied as provided in said § 325.

(c) Any person becoming an assignee or transferee of shares or of a subscription for shares in good faith and without knowledge or notice that the full consideration therefor has not been paid shall not be personally liable for any unpaid portion of such consideration, but the transferor shall remain liable therefor.

(d) No person holding shares in any corporation as collateral security shall be personally liable as a stockholder but the person pledging such shares shall be considered the holder thereof and shall be so liable. No executor, administrator, guardian, trustee or other fiduciary shall be personally liable as a stockholder, but the estate or funds held by such executor, administrator, guardian, trustee or other fiduciary in such fiduciary capacity shall be liable.

(e) No liability under this section or under § 325 of this title shall be asserted more than 6 years after the issuance of the stock or the date of the subscription upon which the assessment is sought.

(f) In any action by a receiver or trustee of an insolvent corporation or by a judgment creditor to obtain an assessment under this section, any stockholder or subscriber for stock of the insolvent corporation may appear and contest the claim or claims of such receiver or trustee.

§ 163.   Payment for Stock Not Paid in Full

The capital stock of a corporation shall be paid for in such amounts and at such times as the directors may require. The directors may, from time to time, demand payment, in respect of each share of stock not fully paid, of such sum of money as the necessities of the business may, in the judgment of the board of directors, require, not exceeding in the whole the balance remaining unpaid on said stock, and such sum so demanded shall be paid to the corporation at such times and by such installments as the directors shall direct. The directors shall give written notice of the time and place of such payments, which notice shall be mailed at least 30 days before the time for such payment, to each holder of or subscriber for stock which is not fully paid at such holder's or subscriber's last known post-office address.

§ 164. Failure to Pay for Stock; Remedies

When any stockholder fails to pay any installment or call upon such stockholder's stock which may have been properly demanded by the directors, at the time when such payment is due, the directors may collect the amount of any such installment or call or any balance thereof remaining unpaid, from the said stockholder by an action at law, or they shall sell at public sale such part of the shares of such delinquent stockholder as will pay all demands then due from such stockholder with interest and all incidental expenses, and shall transfer the shares so sold to the purchaser, who shall be entitled to a certificate therefor.

Notice of the time and place of such sale and of the sum due on each share shall be given by advertisement at least 1 week before the sale, in a newspaper of the county in this State where such corporation's registered office is located, and such notice shall be mailed by the corporation to such delinquent stockholder at such stockholder's last known post-office address, at least 20 days before such sale.

If no bidder can be had to pay the amount due on the stock, and if the amount is not collected by an action at law, which may be brought within the county where the corporation has its registered office, within 1 year from the date of the bringing of such action at law, the said stock and the amount previously paid in by the delinquent stockholder on the stock shall be forfeited to the corporation.

§ 165. Revocability of Preincorporation Subscriptions

Unless otherwise provided by the terms of the subscription, a subscription for stock of a corporation to be formed shall be irrevocable, except with the consent of all other subscribers or the corporation, for a period of 6 months from its date.

§ 166. Formalities Required of Stock Subscriptions

A subscription for stock of a corporation, whether made before or after the formation of a corporation, shall not be enforceable against a subscriber, unless in writing and signed by the subscriber or by such subscriber's agent.

§ 169. Situs of Ownership of Stock

For all purposes of title, action, attachment, garnishment and jurisdiction of all courts held in this State, but not for the purpose of taxation, the situs of the ownership of the capital stock of all corporations existing under the laws of this State, whether organized under this chapter or otherwise, shall be regarded as in this State.

§ 170. Dividends; Payment; Wasting Asset Corporations

(a) The directors of every corporation, subject to any restrictions contained in its certificate of incorporation, may declare and pay dividends upon the shares of its capital stock either:

(1) Out of its surplus, as defined in and computed in accordance with §§ 154 and 244 of this title; or

(2) In case there shall be no such surplus, out of its net profits for the fiscal year in which the dividend is declared and/or the preceding fiscal year.

If the capital of the corporation, computed in accordance with §§ 154 and 244 of this title, shall have been diminished by depreciation in the value of its property, or by losses, or otherwise, to an amount less than the aggregate amount of the capital represented by the issued and outstanding stock of all classes having a preference upon the distribution of assets, the directors of such corporation shall not declare and pay out of such net profits any dividends upon any shares of any classes of its capital stock until the deficiency in the amount of capital represented by the issued and outstanding stock of all classes having a preference upon the distribution of assets shall have been repaired. Nothing in this subsection shall invalidate or otherwise affect a note, debenture or other obligation of the corporation paid by it as a dividend on shares of its stock, or any payment made thereon, if at the time such note, debenture or obligation was delivered by the corporation, the corporation had either surplus or net profits as provided in (a)(1) or (2) of this section from which the dividend could lawfully have been paid.

(b) Subject to any restrictions contained in its certificate of incorporation, the directors of any corporation engaged in the exploitation of wasting assets (including but not limited to a corporation engaged in the exploitation of natural resources or other wasting assets, including patents, or engaged primarily in the liquidation of specific assets) may determine the net profits derived from the exploitation of such wasting assets or the net proceeds derived from such liquidation without taking into consideration the depletion of such assets resulting from lapse of time, consumption, liquidation or exploitation of such assets.

§ 172. Liability of Directors and Committee Members as to Dividends or Stock Redemption

A member of the board of directors, or a member of any committee designated by the board of directors, shall be fully protected in relying in good faith upon the records of the corporation and upon such information, opinions, reports or statements presented to the corporation by any of its officers or employees, or committees of the board of directors, or by any other person as to matters the director reasonably believes are within such other person's professional or expert competence and who has been selected with reasonable care by or on behalf of the corporation, as to the value and amount of the assets, liabilities and/or net profits of the corporation or any other facts pertinent to the existence and amount of surplus or other funds from which dividends might properly be declared and paid, or with which the corporation's stock might properly be purchased or redeemed.

§ 173. Declaration and Payment of Dividends

No corporation shall pay dividends except in accordance with this chapter. Dividends may be paid in cash, in property, or in shares of the corporation's capital stock. If the dividend is to be paid in shares of the corporation's theretofore unissued capital stock the board of directors shall, by resolution, direct that there be designated as capital in respect of such shares an amount which is not less than the aggregate par value of par value shares being declared as a dividend and, in the case of shares without par value being declared as a dividend, such amount as shall be determined by the board of directors. No such designation as capital shall be necessary if shares are being distributed by a corporation pursuant to a split-up or division of its stock rather than as payment of a dividend declared payable in stock of the corporation.

§ 174. Liability of Directors for Unlawful Payment of Dividend or Unlawful Stock Purchase or Redemption; Exoneration from Liability; Contribution Among Directors; Subrogation

(a) In case of any wilful or negligent violation of § 160 or § 173 of this title, the directors under whose administration the same may happen shall be jointly and severally liable, at any time within 6 years after paying such unlawful dividend or after such unlawful stock purchase or redemption, to the corporation, and to its creditors in the event of its dissolution or insolvency, to the full amount of the dividend unlawfully paid, or to the full amount unlawfully paid for the purchase or redemption of the corporation's stock, with interest from the time such liability accrued. Any director who may have been absent when the same was done, or who may have dissented from the act or resolution by which the same was done, may be exonerated from such liability by causing his or her dissent to be entered on the books containing the minutes of the proceedings of the directors at the time the same was done, or immediately after such director has notice of the same.

(b) Any director against whom a claim is successfully asserted under this section shall be entitled to contribution from the other directors who voted for or concurred in the unlawful dividend, stock purchase or stock redemption.

(c) Any director against whom a claim is successfully asserted under this section shall be entitled, to the extent of the amount paid by such director as a result of such claim, to be subrogated to the rights of the corporation against stockholders who received the dividend on, or assets for the sale or redemption of, their stock with knowledge of facts indicating that such dividend, stock purchase or redemption was unlawful under this chapter, in proportion to the amounts received by such stockholders respectively.

SUBCHAPTER VI. STOCK TRANSFERS

§ 201. Transfer of Stock, Stock Certificates and Uncertificated Stock

Except as otherwise provided in this chapter, the transfer of stock and the certificates of stock which represent the stock or uncertificated stock shall be governed by Article 8 of subtitle I of Title 6. To the extent that any provision of this chapter is inconsistent with any provision of subtitle I of Title 6, this chapter shall be controlling.

§ 202. Restrictions on Transfer and Ownership of Securities

(a) A written restriction or restrictions on the transfer or registration of transfer of a security of a corporation, or on the amount of the corporation's securities that may be owned by any person or group of persons, if permitted by this section and noted conspicuously on the certificate or certificates representing the security or securities so restricted or, in the case of uncertificated shares, contained in the notice or notices given pursuant to § 151(f) of this title, may be enforced against the holder of the restricted security or securities or any successor or transferee of the holder including an executor, administrator, trustee, guardian or other fiduciary entrusted with like responsibility for the person or estate of the holder. Unless noted conspicuously on the certificate or certificates representing the security or securities so restricted or, in the case of uncertificated shares, contained in the notice or notices given pursuant to § 151(f) of this title, a restriction, even though permitted by this section, is ineffective except against a person with actual knowledge of the restriction.

(b) A restriction on the transfer or registration of transfer of securities of a corporation, or on the amount of a corporation's securities that may be owned by any person or group of persons, may be imposed by the certificate of incorporation or by the bylaws or by an agreement among any number of security holders or among such holders and the corporation. No restrictions so imposed shall be binding with respect to securities issued prior to the adoption of the restriction unless the holders of the securities are parties to an agreement or voted in favor of the restriction.

(c) A restriction on the transfer or registration of transfer of securities of a corporation or on the amount of such securities that may be owned by any person or group of persons is permitted by this section if it:

(1) Obligates the holder of the restricted securities to offer to the corporation or to any other holders of securities of the corporation or to any other person or to any combination of the foregoing, a prior opportunity, to be exercised within a reasonable time, to acquire the restricted securities; or

(2) Obligates the corporation or any holder of securities of the corporation or any other person or any combination of the foregoing, to purchase the securities which are the subject of an agreement respecting the purchase and sale of the restricted securities; or

(3) Requires the corporation or the holders of any class or series of securities of the corporation to consent to any proposed transfer of the restricted securities or to approve the proposed transferee of the restricted securities, or to approve the amount of securities of the corporation that may be owned by any person or group of persons; or

(4) Obligates the holder of the restricted securities to sell or transfer an amount of restricted securities to the corporation or to any other holders of securities of the corporation or to any other person or to any combination of the foregoing, or causes or results in the automatic sale or transfer of an amount of restricted securities to the corporation or to any other holders of securities of the corporation or to any other person or to any combination of the foregoing; or

(5) Prohibits or restricts the transfer of the restricted securities to, or the ownership of restricted securities by, designated persons or classes of persons or groups of persons, and such designation is not manifestly unreasonable.

(d) Any restriction on the transfer or the registration of transfer of the securities of a corporation, or on the amount of securities of a corporation that may be owned by a person or group of persons, for any of the following purposes shall be conclusively presumed to be for a reasonable purpose:

(1) Maintaining any local, state, federal or foreign tax advantage to the corporation or its stockholders, including without limitation:

a. Maintaining the corporation's status as an electing small business corporation under subchapter S of the United States Internal Revenue Code [26 U.S.C. § 1371 et seq.], or

b. Maintaining or preserving any tax attribute (including without limitation net operating losses), or

c. Qualifying or maintaining the qualification of the corporation as a real estate investment trust pursuant to the United States Internal Revenue Code or regulations adopted pursuant to the United States Internal Revenue Code, or

(2) Maintaining any statutory or regulatory advantage or complying with any statutory or regulatory requirements under applicable local, state, federal or foreign law.

(e) Any other lawful restriction on transfer or registration of transfer of securities, or on the amount of securities that may be owned by any person or group of persons, is permitted by this section.

§ 203. Business Combinations with Interested Stockholders

(a) Notwithstanding any other provisions of this chapter, a corporation shall not engage in any business combination with any interested stockholder for a period of 3 years following the time that such stockholder became an interested stockholder, unless:

(1) Prior to such time the board of directors of the corporation approved either the business combination or the transaction which resulted in the stockholder becoming an interested stockholder;

(2) Upon consummation of the transaction which resulted in the stockholder becoming an interested stockholder, the interested stockholder owned at least 85% of the voting stock of the corporation outstanding at the time the transaction commenced, excluding for purposes of determining the voting stock outstanding (but not the outstanding voting stock owned by the interested stockholder) those shares owned (i) by persons who are directors and also officers and (ii) employee stock plans in which employee participants do not have the right to determine confidentially whether shares held subject to the plan will be tendered in a tender or exchange offer; or

(3) At or subsequent to such time the business combination is approved by the board of directors and authorized at an annual or special meeting of stockholders, and not by written consent, by the affirmative vote of at least $66^{2}/_{3}$% of the outstanding voting stock which is not owned by the interested stockholder.

(b) The restrictions contained in this section shall not apply if:

(1) The corporation's original certificate of incorporation contains a provision expressly electing not to be governed by this section;

(2) The corporation, by action of its board of directors, adopts an amendment to its bylaws within 90 days of February 2, 1988, expressly electing not to be governed by this section, which amendment shall not be further amended by the board of directors;

(3) The corporation, by action of its stockholders, adopts an amendment to its certificate of incorporation or bylaws expressly electing not to be governed by this section; provided that, in addition to any other vote required by law, such amendment to the certificate of incorporation or bylaws must be adopted by the affirmative vote of a majority of the outstanding stock entitled to vote thereon. In the case of a corporation that both (i) has never had a class of voting stock that falls within any of the 2 categories set out in paragraph (b)(4) of this section, and (ii) has not elected by a provision in its original certificate of incorporation or any amendment thereto to be governed by this section, such amendment shall become effective upon (i) in the case of an amendment to the certificate of incorporation, the date and time at which the certificate filed in accordance with § 103 of this title

becomes effective thereunder or (ii) in the case of an amendment to the bylaws, the date of the adoption of such amendment. In all other cases, an amendment adopted pursuant to this paragraph shall become effective (i) in the case of an amendment to the certificate of incorporation, 12 months after the date and time at which the certificate filed in accordance with § 103 of this title becomes effective thereunder or (ii) in the case of an amendment to the bylaws, 12 months after the date of the adoption of such amendment, and, in either case, the election not to be governed by this section shall not apply to any business combination between such corporation and any person who became an interested stockholder of such corporation on or before (A) in the case of an amendment to the certificate of incorporation, the date and time at which the certificate filed in accordance with § 103 of this title becomes effective thereunder; or (B) in the case of an amendment to the bylaws, the date of the adoption of such amendment. A bylaw amendment adopted pursuant to this paragraph shall not be further amended by the board of directors;

(4) The corporation does not have a class of voting stock that is: (i) Listed on a national securities exchange; or (ii) held of record by more than 2,000 stockholders, unless any of the foregoing results from action taken, directly or indirectly, by an interested stockholder or from a transaction in which a person becomes an interested stockholder;

(5) A stockholder becomes an interested stockholder inadvertently and (i) as soon as practicable divests itself of ownership of sufficient shares so that the stockholder ceases to be an interested stockholder; and (ii) would not, at any time within the 3-year period immediately prior to a business combination between the corporation and such stockholder, have been an interested stockholder but for the inadvertent acquisition of ownership;

(6) The business combination is proposed prior to the consummation or abandonment of and subsequent to the earlier of the public announcement or the notice required hereunder of a proposed transaction which (i) constitutes 1 of the transactions described in the second sentence of this paragraph; (ii) is with or by a person who either was not an interested stockholder during the previous 3 years or who became an interested stockholder with the approval of the corporation's board of directors or during the period described in paragraph (b)(7) of this section; and (iii) is approved or not opposed by a majority of the members of the board of directors then in office (but not less than 1) who were directors prior to any person becoming an interested stockholder during the previous 3 years or were recommended for election or elected to succeed such directors by a majority of such directors. The proposed transactions referred to in the preceding sentence are limited to (x) a merger or consolidation of the corporation (except for a merger in respect of which, pursuant to § 251(f) of this title, no vote of the stockholders of the corporation is required); (y) a sale, lease, exchange, mortgage, pledge, transfer or other disposition (in 1 transaction or a series of transactions), whether as part of a dissolution or otherwise, of assets of the corporation or of any direct or indirect majority-owned subsidiary of the corporation (other than to any direct or indirect wholly-owned subsidiary or to the corporation) having an aggregate market value equal to 50% or more of either that aggregate market value of all of the assets of the corporation determined on a consolidated basis or the aggregate market value of all the outstanding stock of the corporation; or (z) a proposed tender or exchange offer for 50% or more of the outstanding voting stock of the corporation. The corporation shall give not less than 20 days' notice to all interested stockholders prior to the consummation of any of the transactions described in clause (x) or (y) of the second sentence of this paragraph; or

(7) The business combination is with an interested stockholder who became an interested stockholder at a time when the restrictions contained in this section did not apply by reason of any of paragraphs (b)(1) through (4) of this section, provided, however, that this paragraph (b)(7) shall not apply if, at the time such interested stockholder became an interested stockholder, the corporation's certificate of incorporation contained a provision authorized by the last sentence of this subsection (b).

Notwithstanding paragraphs (b)(1), (2), (3) and (4) of this section, a corporation may elect by a provision of its original certificate of incorporation or any amendment thereto to be governed by this section; provided that any such amendment to the certificate of incorporation shall not apply to restrict a business combination between the corporation and an interested stockholder of the corporation if the interested stockholder became such before the date and time at which the certificate filed in accordance with § 103 of this title becomes effective thereunder.

(c) As used in this section only, the term:

(1) "Affiliate" means a person that directly, or indirectly through 1 or more intermediaries, controls, or is controlled by, or is under common control with, another person.

(2) "Associate," when used to indicate a relationship with any person, means: (i) Any corporation, partnership, unincorporated association or other entity of which such person is a director, officer or partner or is, directly or indirectly, the owner of 20% or more of any class of voting stock; (ii) any trust or other estate in which such person has at least a 20% beneficial interest or as to which such person serves as trustee or in a similar fiduciary capacity; and (iii) any relative or spouse of such person, or any relative of such spouse, who has the same residence as such person.

(3) "Business combination," when used in reference to any corporation and any interested stockholder of such corporation, means:

(i) Any merger or consolidation of the corporation or any direct or indirect majority-owned subsidiary of the corporation with (A) the interested stockholder, or (B) with any other corporation, partnership, unincorporated association or other entity if the merger or consolidation is caused by the interested stockholder and as a result of such merger or consolidation subsection (a) of this section is not applicable to the surviving entity;

(ii) Any sale, lease, exchange, mortgage, pledge, transfer or other disposition (in 1 transaction or a series of transactions), except proportionately as a stockholder of such corporation, to or with the interested stockholder, whether as part of a dissolution or otherwise, of assets of the corporation or of any direct or indirect majority-owned subsidiary of the corporation which assets have an aggregate market value equal to 10% or more of either the aggregate market value of all the assets of the corporation determined on a consolidated basis or the aggregate market value of all the outstanding stock of the corporation;

(iii) Any transaction which results in the issuance or transfer by the corporation or by any direct or indirect majority-owned subsidiary of the corporation of any stock of the corporation or of such subsidiary to the interested stockholder, except: (A) Pursuant to the exercise, exchange or conversion of securities exercisable for, exchangeable for or convertible into stock of such corporation or any such subsidiary which securities were outstanding prior to the time that the interested stockholder became such; (B) pursuant to a merger under § 251(g) of this title; (C) pursuant to a dividend or distribution paid or made, or the exercise, exchange or conversion of securities exercisable for, exchangeable for or convertible into stock of such corporation or any such subsidiary which security is distributed, pro rata to all holders of a class or series of stock of such corporation subsequent to the time the interested stockholder became such; (D) pursuant to an exchange offer by the corporation to purchase stock made on the same terms to all holders of said stock; or (E) any issuance or transfer of stock by the corporation; provided however, that in no case under items (C)–(E) of this subparagraph shall there be an increase in the interested stockholder's proportionate share of the stock of any class or series of the corporation or of the voting stock of the corporation;

(iv) Any transaction involving the corporation or any direct or indirect majority-owned subsidiary of the corporation which has the effect, directly or indirectly, of increasing the proportionate share of the stock of any class or series, or securities convertible into the stock of any class or series, of the corporation or of any such subsidiary which is owned by the interested stockholder, except as a result of immaterial changes due to fractional share adjustments or as a result of any purchase or redemption of any shares of stock not caused, directly or indirectly, by the interested stockholder; or

(v) Any receipt by the interested stockholder of the benefit, directly or indirectly (except proportionately as a stockholder of such corporation), of any loans, advances, guarantees, pledges or other financial benefits (other than those expressly permitted in paragraphs (c)(3)(i)–(iv) of this section) provided by or through the corporation or any direct or indirect majority-owned subsidiary.

(4) "Control," including the terms "controlling," "controlled by" and "under common control with," means the possession, directly or indirectly, of the power to direct or cause the direction of the

management and policies of a person, whether through the ownership of voting stock, by contract or otherwise. A person who is the owner of 20% or more of the outstanding voting stock of any corporation, partnership, unincorporated association or other entity shall be presumed to have control of such entity, in the absence of proof by a preponderance of the evidence to the contrary; Notwithstanding the foregoing, a presumption of control shall not apply where such person holds voting stock, in good faith and not for the purpose of circumventing this section, as an agent, bank, broker, nominee, custodian or trustee for 1 or more owners who do not individually or as a group have control of such entity.

(5) "Interested stockholder" means any person (other than the corporation and any direct or indirect majority-owned subsidiary of the corporation) that (i) is the owner of 15% or more of the outstanding voting stock of the corporation, or (ii) is an affiliate or associate of the corporation and was the owner of 15% or more of the outstanding voting stock of the corporation at any time within the 3-year period immediately prior to the date on which it is sought to be determined whether such person is an interested stockholder, and the affiliates and associates of such person; provided, however, that the term "interested stockholder" shall not include (x) any person who (A) owned shares in excess of the 15% limitation set forth herein as of, or acquired such shares pursuant to a tender offer commenced prior to, December 23, 1987, or pursuant to an exchange offer announced prior to the aforesaid date and commenced within 90 days thereafter and either (I) continued to own shares in excess of such 15% limitation or would have but for action by the corporation or (II) is an affiliate or associate of the corporation and so continued (or so would have continued but for action by the corporation) to be the owner of 15% or more of the outstanding voting stock of the corporation at any time within the 3-year period immediately prior to the date on which it is sought to be determined whether such a person is an interested stockholder or (B) acquired said shares from a person described in item (A) of this paragraph by gift, inheritance or in a transaction in which no consideration was exchanged; or (y) any person whose ownership of shares in excess of the 15% limitation set forth herein is the result of action taken solely by the corporation; provided that such person shall be an interested stockholder if thereafter such person acquires additional shares of voting stock of the corporation, except as a result of further corporate action not caused, directly or indirectly, by such person. For the purpose of determining whether a person is an interested stockholder, the voting stock of the corporation deemed to be outstanding shall include stock deemed to be owned by the person through application of paragraph (9) of this subsection but shall not include any other unissued stock of such corporation which may be issuable pursuant to any agreement, arrangement or understanding, or upon exercise of conversion rights, warrants or options, or otherwise.

(6) "Person" means any individual, corporation, partnership, unincorporated association or other entity.

(7) "Stock" means, with respect to any corporation, capital stock and, with respect to any other entity, any equity interest.

(8) "Voting stock" means, with respect to any corporation, stock of any class or series entitled to vote generally in the election of directors and, with respect to any entity that is not a corporation, any equity interest entitled to vote generally in the election of the governing body of such entity. Every reference to a percentage of voting stock shall refer to such percentage of the votes of such voting stock.

(9) "Owner," including the terms "own" and "owned," when used with respect to any stock, means a person that individually or with or through any of its affiliates or associates:

(i) Beneficially owns such stock, directly or indirectly; or

(ii) Has (A) the right to acquire such stock (whether such right is exercisable immediately or only after the passage of time) pursuant to any agreement, arrangement or understanding, or upon the exercise of conversion rights, exchange rights, warrants or options, or otherwise; provided, however, that a person shall not be deemed the owner of stock tendered pursuant to a tender or exchange offer made by such person or any of such person's affiliates or associates until such tendered stock is accepted for purchase or exchange; or (B) the right to vote such stock pursuant to any agreement, arrangement or understanding; provided, however, that a person shall not be deemed the owner of any stock because of such person's right to vote such stock if the agreement, arrangement or understanding to vote such stock arises solely from a revocable proxy or consent given in response to a proxy or consent solicitation made to 10 or more persons; or

(iii) Has any agreement, arrangement or understanding for the purpose of acquiring, holding, voting (except voting pursuant to a revocable proxy or consent as described in item (B) of subparagraph (ii) of this paragraph), or disposing of such stock with any other person that beneficially owns, or whose affiliates or associates beneficially own, directly or indirectly, such stock.

(d) No provision of a certificate of incorporation or bylaw shall require, for any vote of stockholders required by this section, a greater vote of stockholders than that specified in this section.

(e) The Court of Chancery is hereby vested with exclusive jurisdiction to hear and determine all matters with respect to this section.

§ 204.   Ratification of Defective Corporate Acts and Stock

(a) Subject to subsection (f) of this section, no defective corporate act or putative stock shall be void or voidable solely as a result of a failure of authorization if ratified as provided in this section or validated by the Court of Chancery in a proceeding brought under § 205 of this title.

(b)(1) In order to ratify 1 or more defective corporate acts pursuant to this section (other than the ratification of an election of the initial board of directors pursuant to paragraph (b)(2) of this section), the board of directors of the corporation shall adopt resolutions stating:

(A) The defective corporate act or acts to be ratified;

(B) The date of each defective corporate act or acts;

(C) If such defective corporate act or acts involved the issuance of shares of putative stock, the number and type of shares of putative stock issued and the date or dates upon which such putative shares were purported to have been issued;

(D) The nature of the failure of authorization in respect of each defective corporate act to be ratified; and

(E) That the board of directors approves the ratification of the defective corporate act or acts.

Such resolutions may also provide that, at any time before the validation effective time in respect of any defective corporate act set forth therein, notwithstanding the approval of the ratification of such defective corporate act by stockholders, the board of directors may abandon the ratification of such defective corporate act without further action of the stockholders. The quorum and voting requirements applicable to the ratification by the board of directors of any defective corporate act shall be the quorum and voting requirements applicable to the type of defective corporate act proposed to be ratified at the time the board adopts the resolutions ratifying the defective corporate act; provided that if the certificate of incorporation or bylaws of the corporation, any plan or agreement to which the corporation was a party or any provision of this title, in each case as in effect as of the time of the defective corporate act, would have required a larger number or portion of directors or of specified directors for a quorum to be present or to approve the defective corporate act, such larger number or portion of such directors or such specified directors shall be required for a quorum to be present or to adopt the resolutions to ratify the defective corporate act, as applicable, except that the presence or approval of any director elected, appointed or nominated by holders of any class or series of which no shares are then outstanding, or by any person that is no longer a stockholder, shall not be required.

(2) In order to ratify a defective corporate act in respect of the election of the initial board of directors of the corporation pursuant to § 108 of this title, a majority of the persons who, at the time the resolutions required by this paragraph (b)(2) of this section are adopted, are exercising the powers of directors under claim and color of an election or appointment as such may adopt resolutions stating:

(A) The name of the person or persons who first took action in the name of the corporation as the initial board of directors of the corporation;

(B) The earlier of the date on which such persons first took such action or were purported to have been elected as the initial board of directors; and

(C) That the ratification of the election of such person or persons as the initial board of directors is approved.

(c) Each defective corporate act ratified pursuant to paragraph (b)(1) of this section shall be submitted to stockholders for approval as provided in subsection (d) of this section, unless:

(1)(A) No other provision of this title, and no provision of the certificate of incorporation or bylaws of the corporation, or of any plan or agreement to which the corporation is a party, would have required stockholder approval of such defective corporate act to be ratified, either at the time of such defective corporate act or at the time the board of directors adopts the resolutions ratifying such defective corporate act pursuant to paragraph (b)(1) of this section; and

(B) Such defective corporate act did not result from a failure to comply with § 203 of this title; or

(2) As of the record date for determining the stockholders entitled to vote on the ratification of such defective corporate act, there are no shares of valid stock outstanding and entitled to vote thereon, regardless of whether there then exist any shares of putative stock.

(d) If the ratification of a defective corporate act is required to be submitted to stockholders for approval pursuant to subsection (c) of this section, due notice of the time, place, if any, and purpose of the meeting shall be given at least 20 days before the date of the meeting to each holder of valid stock and putative stock, whether voting or nonvoting, at the address of such holder as it appears or most recently appeared, as appropriate, on the records of the corporation. The notice shall also be given to the holders of record of valid stock and putative stock, whether voting or nonvoting, as of the time of the defective corporate act (or, in the case of any defective corporate act that involved the establishment of a record date for notice of or voting at any meeting of stockholders, for action by written consent of stockholders in lieu of a meeting, or for any other purpose, the record date for notice of or voting at such meeting, the record date for action by written consent, or the record date for such other action, as the case may be), other than holders whose identities or addresses cannot be determined from the records of the corporation. The notice shall contain a copy of the resolutions adopted by the board of directors pursuant to paragraph (b)(1) of this section or the information required by paragraphs (b)(1)(A) through (E) of this section and a statement that any claim that the defective corporate act or putative stock ratified hereunder is void or voidable due to the failure of authorization, or that the Court of Chancery should declare in its discretion that a ratification in accordance with this section not be effective or be effective only on certain conditions must be brought within 120 days from the applicable validation effective time. At such meeting, the quorum and voting requirements applicable to ratification of such defective corporate act shall be the quorum and voting requirements applicable to the type of defective corporate act proposed to be ratified at the time of the approval of the ratification, except that:

(1) If the certificate of incorporation or bylaws of the corporation, any plan or agreement to which the corporation was a party or any provision of this title in effect as of the time of the defective corporate act would have required a larger number or portion of stock or of any class or series thereof or of specified stockholders for a quorum to be present or to approve the defective corporate act, the presence or approval of such larger number or portion of stock or of such class or series thereof or of such specified stockholders shall be required for a quorum to be present or to approve the ratification of the defective corporate act, as applicable, except that the presence or approval of shares of any class or series of which no shares are then outstanding, or of any person that is no longer a stockholder, shall not be required;

(2) The approval by stockholders of the ratification of the election of a director shall require the affirmative vote of the majority of shares present at the meeting and entitled to vote on the election of such director, except that if the certificate of incorporation or bylaws of the corporation then in effect or in effect at the time of the defective election require or required a larger number or portion of stock or of any class or series thereof or of specified stockholders to elect such director, the affirmative vote of such larger number or portion of stock or of any class or series thereof or of such specified stockholders shall be required to ratify the election of such director, except that the presence or approval of shares of any class or series of which no shares are then outstanding, or of any person that is no longer a stockholder, shall not be required; and

(3) In the event of a failure of authorization resulting from failure to comply with the provisions of § 203 of this title, the ratification of the defective corporate act shall require the vote set forth in § 203(a)(3) of this title, regardless of whether such vote would have otherwise been required.

Shares of putative stock on the record date for determining stockholders entitled to vote on any matter submitted to stockholders pursuant to subsection (c) of this section (and without giving effect to any ratification that becomes effective after such record date) shall neither be entitled to vote nor counted for quorum purposes in any vote to ratify any defective corporate act.

(e) If a defective corporate act ratified pursuant to this section would have required under any other section of this title the filing of a certificate in accordance with § 103 of this title, then, whether or not a certificate was previously filed in respect of such defective corporate act and in lieu of filing the certificate otherwise required by this title, the corporation shall file a certificate of validation with respect to such defective corporate act in accordance with § 103 of this title. A separate certificate of validation shall be required for each defective corporate act requiring the filing of a certificate of validation under this section, except that (i) 2 or more defective corporate acts may be included in a single certificate of validation if the corporation filed, or to comply with this title would have filed, a single certificate under another provision of this title to effect such acts, and (ii) 2 or more overissues of shares of any class, classes or series of stock may be included in a single certificate of validation, provided that the increase in the number of authorized shares of each such class or series set forth in the certificate of validation shall be effective as of the date of the first such overissue. The certificate of validation shall set forth:

(1) Each defective corporate act that is the subject of the certificate of validation (including, in the case of any defective corporate act involving the issuance of shares of putative stock, the number and type of shares of putative stock issued and the date or dates upon which such putative shares were purported to have been issued), the date of such defective corporate act, and the nature of the failure of authorization in respect of such defective corporate act;

(2) A statement that such defective corporate act was ratified in accordance with this section, including the date on which the board of directors ratified such defective corporate act and the date, if any, on which the stockholders approved the ratification of such defective corporate act; and

(3) Information required by 1 of the following paragraphs:

a. If a certificate was previously filed under § 103 of this title in respect of such defective corporate act and no changes to such certificate are required to give effect to such defective corporate act in accordance with this section, the certificate of validation shall set forth (x) the name, title and filing date of the certificate previously filed and of any certificate of correction thereto and (y) a statement that a copy of the certificate previously filed, together with any certificate of correction thereto, is attached as an exhibit to the certificate of validation;

b. If a certificate was previously filed under § 103 of this title in respect of the defective corporate act and such certificate requires any change to give effect to the defective corporate act in accordance with this section (including a change to the date and time of the effectiveness of such certificate), the certificate of validation shall set forth (x) the name, title and filing date of the certificate so previously filed and of any certificate of correction thereto, (y) a statement that a certificate containing all of the information required to be included under the applicable section or sections of this title to give effect to the defective corporate act is attached as an exhibit to the certificate of validation, and (z) the date and time that such certificate shall be deemed to have become effective pursuant to this section; or

c. If a certificate was not previously filed under § 103 of this title in respect of the defective corporate act and the defective corporate act ratified pursuant to this section would have required under any other section of this title the filing of a certificate in accordance with § 103 of this title, the certificate of validation shall set forth (x) a statement that a certificate containing all of the information required to be included under the applicable section or sections of this title to give effect to the defective corporate act is attached as an exhibit to the certificate of validation, and (y) the date and time that such certificate shall be deemed to have become effective pursuant to this section.

A certificate attached to a certificate of validation pursuant to paragraph (e)(3)b. or c. of this section need not be separately executed and acknowledged and need not include any statement required by any other section of this title that such instrument has been approved and adopted in accordance with the provisions of such other section.

(f) From and after the validation effective time, unless otherwise determined in an action brought pursuant to § 205 of this title:

(1) Subject to the last sentence of subsection (d) of this section, each defective corporate act ratified in accordance with this section shall no longer be deemed void or voidable as a result of the failure of authorization described in the resolutions adopted pursuant to subsection (b) of this section and such effect shall be retroactive to the time of the defective corporate act; and

(2) Subject to the last sentence of subsection (d) of this section, each share or fraction of a share of putative stock issued or purportedly issued pursuant to any such defective corporate act shall no longer be deemed void or voidable and shall be deemed to be an identical share or fraction of a share of outstanding stock as of the time it was purportedly issued.

(g) In respect of each defective corporate act ratified by the board of directors pursuant to subsection (b) of this section, prompt notice of the ratification shall be given to all holders of valid stock and putative stock, whether voting or nonvoting, as of the date the board of directors adopts the resolutions approving such defective corporate act, or as of a date within 60 days after such date of adoption, as established by the board of directors, at the address of such holder as it appears or most recently appeared, as appropriate, on the records of the corporation. The notice shall also be given to the holders of record of valid stock and putative stock, whether voting or nonvoting, as of the time of the defective corporate act, other than holders whose identities or addresses cannot be determined from the records of the corporation. The notice shall contain a copy of the resolutions adopted pursuant to subsection (b) of this section or the information specified in paragraphs (b)(1)(A) through (E) or paragraphs (b)(2)(A) through (C) of this section, as applicable, and a statement that any claim that the defective corporate act or putative stock ratified hereunder is void or voidable due to the failure of authorization, or that the Court of Chancery should declare in its discretion that a ratification in accordance with this section not be effective or be effective only on certain conditions must be brought within 120 days from the later of the validation effective time or the time at which the notice required by this subsection is given. Notwithstanding the foregoing, (i) no such notice shall be required if notice of the ratification of the defective corporate act is to be given in accordance with subsection (d) of this section, and (ii) in the case of a corporation that has a class of stock listed on a national securities exchange, the notice required by this subsection and the second sentence of subsection (d) of this section may be deemed given if disclosed in a document publicly filed by the corporation with the Securities and Exchange Commission pursuant to § 13, § 14 or § 15(d) (15 U.S.C. § 78m, § 77n or § 78o(d)) of the Securities Exchange Act of 1934, as amended, and the rules and regulations promulgated thereunder, or the corresponding provisions of any subsequent United States federal securities laws, rules or regulations. If any defective corporate act has been approved by stockholders acting pursuant to § 228 of this title, the notice required by this subsection may be included in any notice required to be given pursuant to § 228(e) of this title and, if so given, shall be sent to the stockholders entitled thereto under § 228(e) and to all holders of valid and putative stock to whom notice would be required under this subsection if the defective corporate act had been approved at a meeting other than any stockholder who approved the action by consent in lieu of a meeting pursuant to § 228 of this title or any holder of putative stock who otherwise consented thereto in writing. Solely for purposes of subsection (d) of this section and this subsection, notice to holders of putative stock, and notice to holders of valid stock and putative stock as of the time of the defective corporate act, shall be treated as notice to holders of valid stock for purposes of §§ 222 and 228, 229, 230, 232 and 233 of this title.

(h) As used in this section and in § 205 of this title only, the term:

(1) "Defective corporate act" means an overissue, an election or appointment of directors that is void or voidable due to a failure of authorization, or any act or transaction purportedly taken by or on behalf of the corporation that is, and at the time such act or transaction was purportedly taken would have been, within the power of a corporation under subchapter II of this chapter (without regard to the failure of authorization identified in § 204(b)(1)(D) of this title), but is void or voidable due to a failure of authorization;

(2) "Failure of authorization" means: (i) the failure to authorize or effect an act or transaction in compliance with (A) the provisions of this title, (B) the certificate of incorporation or bylaws of the corporation, or (C) any plan or agreement to which the corporation is a party or the disclosure set forth in any proxy or consent solicitation statement, if and to the extent such failure would render such act or transaction void or voidable; or (ii) the failure of the board of directors or any officer of the corporation to authorize or approve any act or transaction taken by or on behalf of the corporation that would have required for its due authorization the approval of the board of directors or such officer;

(3) "Overissue" means the purported issuance of:

a. Shares of capital stock of a class or series in excess of the number of shares of such class or series the corporation has the power to issue under § 161 of this title at the time of such issuance; or

b. Shares of any class or series of capital stock that is not then authorized for issuance by the certificate of incorporation of the corporation;

(4) "Putative stock" means the shares of any class or series of capital stock of the corporation (including shares issued upon exercise of options, rights, warrants or other securities convertible into shares of capital stock of the corporation, or interests with respect thereto that were created or issued pursuant to a defective corporate act) that:

a. But for any failure of authorization, would constitute valid stock; or

b. Cannot be determined by the board of directors to be valid stock;

(5) "Time of the defective corporate act" means the date and time the defective corporate act was purported to have been taken;

(6) "Validation effective time" with respect to any defective corporate act ratified pursuant to this section means the latest of:

a. The time at which the defective corporate act submitted to the stockholders for approval pursuant to subsection (c) of this section is approved by such stockholders or if no such vote of stockholders is required to approve the ratification of the defective corporate act, the time at which the board of directors adopts the resolutions required by paragraph (b)(1) or (b)(2) of this section;

b. Where no certificate of validation is required to be filed pursuant to subsection (e) of this section, the time, if any, specified by the board of directors in the resolutions adopted pursuant to paragraph (b)(1) or (b)(2) of this section, which time shall not precede the time at which such resolutions are adopted; and

c. The time at which any certificate of validation filed pursuant to subsection (e) of this section shall become effective in accordance with § 103 of this title.

(7) "Valid stock" means the shares of any class or series of capital stock of the corporation that have been duly authorized and validly issued in accordance with this title.

In the absence of actual fraud in the transaction, the judgment of the board of directors that shares of stock are valid stock or putative stock shall be conclusive, unless otherwise determined by the Court of Chancery in a proceeding brought pursuant to § 205 of this title.

(i) Ratification under this section or validation under § 205 of this title shall not be deemed to be the exclusive means of ratifying or validating any act or transaction taken by or on behalf of the corporation, including any defective corporate act, or any issuance of stock, including any putative stock, or of adopting or endorsing any act or transaction taken by or in the name of the corporation prior to the commencement of its existence, and the absence or failure of ratification in accordance with either this section or validation under § 205 of this title shall not, of itself, affect the validity or effectiveness of any act or transaction or the issuance of any stock properly ratified under common law or otherwise, nor shall it create a presumption that any such act or transaction is or was a defective corporate act or that such stock is void or voidable.

§ 205. Proceedings Regarding Validity of Defective Corporate Acts and Stock

(a) Subject to subsection (f) of this section, upon application by the corporation, any successor entity to the corporation, any member of the board of directors, any record or beneficial holder of valid stock or putative stock, any record or beneficial holder of valid or putative stock as of the time of a defective corporate act ratified pursuant to § 204 of this title, or any other person claiming to be substantially and adversely affected by a ratification pursuant to § 204 of this title, the Court of Chancery may:

(1) Determine the validity and effectiveness of any defective corporate act ratified pursuant to § 204 of this title;

(2) Determine the validity and effectiveness of the ratification of any defective corporate act pursuant to § 204 of this title;

(3) Determine the validity and effectiveness of any defective corporate act not ratified or not ratified effectively pursuant to § 204 of this title;

(4) Determine the validity of any corporate act or transaction and any stock, rights or options to acquire stock; and

(5) Modify or waive any of the procedures set forth in § 204 of this title to ratify a defective corporate act.

(b) In connection with an action under this section, the Court of Chancery may:

(1) Declare that a ratification in accordance with and pursuant to § 204 of this title is not effective or shall only be effective at a time or upon conditions established by the Court;

(2) Validate and declare effective any defective corporate act or putative stock and impose conditions upon such validation by the Court;

(3) Require measures to remedy or avoid harm to any person substantially and adversely affected by a ratification pursuant to § 204 of this title or from any order of the Court pursuant to this section, excluding any harm that would have resulted if the defective corporate act had been valid when approved or effectuated;

(4) Order the Secretary of State to accept an instrument for filing with an effective time specified by the Court, which effective time may be prior or subsequent to the time of such order, provided that the filing date of such instrument shall be determined in accordance with § 103(c)(3) of this title;

(5) Approve a stock ledger for the corporation that includes any stock ratified or validated in accordance with this section or with § 204 of this title;

(6) Declare that shares of putative stock are shares of valid stock or require a corporation to issue and deliver shares of valid stock in place of any shares of putative stock;

(7) Order that a meeting of holders of valid stock or putative stock be held and exercise the powers provided to the Court under § 227 of this title with respect to such a meeting;

(8) Declare that a defective corporate act validated by the Court shall be effective as of the time of the defective corporate act or at such other time as the Court shall determine;

(9) Declare that putative stock validated by the Court shall be deemed to be an identical share or fraction of a share of valid stock as of the time originally issued or purportedly issued or at such other time as the Court shall determine; and

(10) Make such other orders regarding such matters as it deems proper under the circumstances.

(c) Service of the application under subsection (a) of this section upon the registered agent of the corporation shall be deemed to be service upon the corporation, and no other party need be joined in order for the Court of Chancery to adjudicate the matter. In an action filed by the corporation, the Court may require notice of the action be provided to other persons specified by the Court and permit such other persons to intervene in the action.

(d) In connection with the resolution of matters pursuant to subsections (a) and (b) of this section, the Court of Chancery may consider the following:

(1) Whether the defective corporate act was originally approved or effectuated with the belief that the approval or effectuation was in compliance with the provisions of this title, the certificate of incorporation or bylaws of the corporation;

(2) Whether the corporation and board of directors has treated the defective corporate act as a valid act or transaction and whether any person has acted in reliance on the public record that such defective corporate act was valid;

(3) Whether any person will be or was harmed by the ratification or validation of the defective corporate act, excluding any harm that would have resulted if the defective corporate act had been valid when approved or effectuated;

(4) Whether any person will be harmed by the failure to ratify or validate the defective corporate act; and

(5) Any other factors or considerations the Court deems just and equitable.

(e) The Court of Chancery is hereby vested with exclusive jurisdiction to hear and determine all actions brought under this section.

(f) Notwithstanding any other provision of this section, no action asserting:

(1) That a defective corporate act or putative stock ratified in accordance with § 204 of this title is void or voidable due to a failure of authorization identified in the resolution adopted in accordance with 204(b) of this title; or

(2) That the Court of Chancery should declare in its discretion that a ratification in accordance with § 204 of this title not be effective or be effective only on certain conditions,

may be brought after the expiration of 120 days from the later of the validation effective time and the time notice, if any, that is required to be given pursuant to § 204(g) of this title is given with respect to such ratification, except that this subsection shall not apply to an action asserting that a ratification was not accomplished in accordance with § 204 of this title or to any person to whom notice of the ratification was required to have been given pursuant to § 204(d) or (g) of this title, but to whom such notice was not given.

SUBCHAPTER VII. MEETINGS, ELECTIONS, VOTING AND NOTICE

§ 211.   Meetings of Stockholders

(a)(1) Meetings of stockholders may be held at such place, either within or without this State as may be designated by or in the manner provided in the certificate of incorporation or bylaws, or if not so designated, as determined by the board of directors. If, pursuant to this paragraph or the certificate of incorporation or the bylaws of the corporation, the board of directors is authorized to determine the place of a meeting of stockholders, the board of directors may, in its sole discretion, determine that the meeting shall not be held at any place, but may instead be held solely by means of remote communication as authorized by paragraph (a)(2) of this section.

(2) If authorized by the board of directors in its sole discretion, and subject to such guidelines and procedures as the board of directors may adopt, stockholders and proxyholders not physically present at a meeting of stockholders may, by means of remote communication:

a. Participate in a meeting of stockholders; and

b. Be deemed present in person and vote at a meeting of stockholders, whether such meeting is to be held at a designated place or solely by means of remote communication, provided that (i) the corporation shall implement reasonable measures to verify that each person deemed present and permitted to vote at the meeting by means of remote communication is a stockholder or proxyholder, (ii) the corporation shall implement reasonable measures to provide such stockholders and proxyholders a reasonable opportunity to participate in the meeting and to vote on matters submitted to the stockholders, including an opportunity to read or hear the proceedings of the meeting substantially concurrently with such proceedings, and (iii) if any stockholder or proxyholder votes or takes other action at the meeting by means of remote communication, a record of such vote or other action shall be maintained by the corporation.

(b) Unless directors are elected by written consent in lieu of an annual meeting as permitted by this subsection, an annual meeting of stockholders shall be held for the election of directors on a date and at a time designated by or in the manner provided in the bylaws. Stockholders may, unless the certificate of incorporation otherwise provides, act by written consent to elect directors; provided, however, that, if such consent is less than unanimous, such action by written consent may be in lieu of holding an annual meeting only if all of the directorships to which directors could be elected at an annual meeting held at the effective time of such action are vacant and are filled by such action. Any other proper business may be transacted at the annual meeting.

(c) A failure to hold the annual meeting at the designated time or to elect a sufficient number of directors to conduct the business of the corporation shall not affect otherwise valid corporate acts or work a forfeiture or dissolution of the corporation except as may be otherwise specifically provided in this chapter. If the annual meeting for election of directors is not held on the date designated therefor or action by written consent to elect directors in lieu of an annual meeting has not been taken, the directors shall cause the meeting to be held as soon as is convenient. If there be a failure to hold the annual meeting or to take action by written consent to elect directors in lieu of an annual meeting for a period of 30 days after the date designated for the annual meeting, or if no date has been designated, for a period of 13 months after the latest to occur of the organization of the corporation, its last annual meeting or the last action by written consent to elect directors in lieu of an annual meeting, the Court of Chancery may summarily order a meeting to be held upon the application of any stockholder or director. The shares of stock represented at such meeting, either in person or by proxy, and entitled to vote thereat, shall constitute a quorum for the purpose of such meeting, notwithstanding any provision of the certificate of incorporation or bylaws to the contrary. The Court of Chancery may issue such orders as may be appropriate, including, without limitation, orders designating the time and place of such meeting, the record date or dates for determination of stockholders entitled to notice of the meeting and to vote thereat, and the form of notice of such meeting.

(d) Special meetings of the stockholders may be called by the board of directors or by such person or persons as may be authorized by the certificate of incorporation or by the bylaws.

(e) All elections of directors shall be by written ballot unless otherwise provided in the certificate of incorporation; if authorized by the board of directors, such requirement of a written ballot shall be satisfied by a ballot submitted by electronic transmission, provided that any such electronic transmission must either set forth or be submitted with information from which it can be determined that the electronic transmission was authorized by the stockholder or proxy holder.

§ 212. Voting Rights of Stockholders; Proxies; Limitations

(a) Unless otherwise provided in the certificate of incorporation and subject to § 213 of this title, each stockholder shall be entitled to 1 vote for each share of capital stock held by such stockholder. If the certificate of incorporation provides for more or less than 1 vote for any share, on any matter, every reference in this chapter to a majority or other proportion of stock, voting stock or shares shall refer to such majority or other proportion of the votes of such stock, voting stock or shares.

(b) Each stockholder entitled to vote at a meeting of stockholders or to express consent or dissent to corporate action in writing without a meeting may authorize another person or persons to act for such stockholder by proxy, but no such proxy shall be voted or acted upon after 3 years from its date, unless the proxy provides for a longer period.

(c) Without limiting the manner in which a stockholder may authorize another person or persons to act for such stockholder as proxy pursuant to subsection (b) of this section, the following shall constitute a valid means by which a stockholder may grant such authority:

(1) A stockholder may execute a writing authorizing another person or persons to act for such stockholder as proxy. Execution may be accomplished by the stockholder or such stockholder's authorized officer, director, employee or agent signing such writing or causing such person's signature to be affixed to such writing by any reasonable means including, but not limited to, by facsimile signature.

(2) A stockholder may authorize another person or persons to act for such stockholder as proxy by transmitting or authorizing the transmission of a telegram, cablegram, or other means of electronic transmission to the person who will be the holder of the proxy or to a proxy solicitation firm, proxy support service organization or like agent duly authorized by the person who will be the holder of the proxy to receive such transmission, provided that any such telegram, cablegram or other means of electronic transmission must either set forth or be submitted with information from which it can be determined that the telegram, cablegram or other electronic transmission was authorized by the stockholder. If it is determined that such telegrams, cablegrams or other electronic transmissions are valid, the inspectors or, if there are no inspectors, such other persons making that determination shall specify the information upon which they relied.

(d) Any copy, facsimile telecommunication or other reliable reproduction of the writing or transmission created pursuant to subsection (c) of this section may be substituted or used in lieu of the original writing or transmission for any and all purposes for which the original writing or transmission could be used, provided that such copy, facsimile telecommunication or other reproduction shall be a complete reproduction of the entire original writing or transmission.

(e) A duly executed proxy shall be irrevocable if it states that it is irrevocable and if, and only as long as, it is coupled with an interest sufficient in law to support an irrevocable power. A proxy may be made irrevocable regardless of whether the interest with which it is coupled is an interest in the stock itself or an interest in the corporation generally.

§ 213. Fixing Date for Determination of Stockholders of Record

(a) In order that the corporation may determine the stockholders entitled to notice of any meeting of stockholders or any adjournment thereof, the board of directors may fix a record date, which record date shall not precede the date upon which the resolution fixing the record date is adopted by the board of directors, and which record date shall not be more than 60 nor less than 10 days before the date of such meeting. If the board of directors so fixes a date, such date shall also be the record date for determining the stockholders entitled to vote at such meeting unless the board of directors determines, at the time it fixes such record date, that a later date on or before the date of the meeting shall be the date for making such determination. If no record date is fixed by the board of directors, the record date for determining stockholders entitled to notice of and to vote at a meeting of stockholders shall be at the close of business on the day next preceding the day on which notice is given, or, if notice is waived, at the close of business on the day next preceding the day on which the meeting is held. A determination of stockholders of record entitled to notice of or to vote at a meeting of stockholders shall apply to any adjournment of the meeting; provided, however, that the board of directors may fix a new record date for determination of stockholders entitled to vote at the adjourned meeting, and in such case shall also fix as the record date for stockholders entitled to notice of such adjourned meeting the same or an earlier date as that fixed for determination of stockholders entitled to vote in accordance with the foregoing provisions of this subsection (a) at the adjourned meeting.

(b) In order that the corporation may determine the stockholders entitled to consent to corporate action in writing without a meeting, the board of directors may fix a record date, which record date shall not precede the date upon which the resolution fixing the record date is adopted by the board of directors, and which date shall not be more than 10 days after the date upon which the resolution fixing the record date is adopted by the board of directors. If no record date has been fixed by the board of directors, the record date for determining stockholders entitled to consent to corporate action in writing without a meeting, when no prior action by the board of directors is required by this chapter, shall be the first date on which a signed written consent setting forth the action taken or proposed to be taken is delivered to the corporation by delivery to its registered office in this State, its principal place of business or an officer or agent of the corporation having custody of the book in which proceedings of meetings of stockholders are recorded. Delivery made to a corporation's registered office shall be by hand or by certified or registered mail, return receipt requested. If no record date has been fixed by the board of directors and prior action by the board of directors is required by this chapter, the record date for determining stockholders entitled to consent to corporate action in writing without a meeting shall be at the close of business on the day on which the board of directors adopts the resolution taking such prior action.

(c) In order that the corporation may determine the stockholders entitled to receive payment of any dividend or other distribution or allotment of any rights or the stockholders entitled to exercise any rights in respect of any change, conversion or exchange of stock, or for the purpose of any other lawful action, the board of directors may fix a record date, which record date shall not precede the date upon which the resolution fixing the record date is adopted, and which record date shall be not more than 60 days prior to such action. If no record date is fixed, the record date for determining stockholders for any such purpose shall be at the close of business on the day on which the board of directors adopts the resolution relating thereto.

§ 214. Cumulative Voting

The certificate of incorporation of any corporation may provide that at all elections of directors of the corporation, or at elections held under specified circumstances, each holder of stock or of any class or classes or of a series or series thereof shall be entitled to as many votes as shall equal the number of votes which (except for such provision as to cumulative voting) such holder would be entitled to cast for the election of directors with respect to such holder's shares of stock multiplied by the number of directors to be elected by such holder, and that such holder may cast all of such votes for a single director or may distribute them among the number to be voted for, or for any 2 or more of them as such holder may see fit.

§ 216. Quorum and Required Vote for Stock Corporations

Subject to this chapter in respect of the vote that shall be required for a specified action, the certificate of incorporation or bylaws of any corporation authorized to issue stock may specify the number of shares and/or the amount of other securities having voting power the holders of which shall be present or represented by proxy at any meeting in order to constitute a quorum for, and the votes that shall be necessary for, the transaction of any business, but in no event shall a quorum consist of less than $1/3$ of the shares entitled to vote at the meeting, except that, where a separate vote by a class or series or classes or series is required, a quorum shall consist of no less than $1/3$ of the shares of such class or series or classes or series. In the absence of such specification in the certificate of incorporation or bylaws of the corporation:

(1) A majority of the shares entitled to vote, present in person or represented by proxy, shall constitute a quorum at a meeting of stockholders;

(2) In all matters other than the election of directors, the affirmative vote of the majority of shares present in person or represented by proxy at the meeting and entitled to vote on the subject matter shall be the act of the stockholders;

(3) Directors shall be elected by a plurality of the votes of the shares present in person or represented by proxy at the meeting and entitled to vote on the election of directors; and

(4) Where a separate vote by a class or series or classes or series is required, a majority of the outstanding shares of such class or series or classes or series, present in person or represented by proxy, shall constitute a quorum entitled to take action with respect to that vote on that matter and, in all matters other than the election of directors, the affirmative vote of the majority of shares of such class or series or classes or series present in person or represented by proxy at the meeting shall be the act of such class or series or classes or series.

A bylaw amendment adopted by stockholders which specifies the votes that shall be necessary for the election of directors shall not be further amended or repealed by the board of directors.

§ 217. Voting Rights of Fiduciaries, Pledgors and Joint Owners of Stock

(a) Persons holding stock in a fiduciary capacity shall be entitled to vote the shares so held. Persons whose stock is pledged shall be entitled to vote, unless in the transfer by the pledgor on the books of the corporation such person has expressly empowered the pledgee to vote thereon, in which case only the pledgee, or such pledgee's proxy, may represent such stock and vote thereon.

(b) If shares or other securities having voting power stand of record in the names of 2 or more persons, whether fiduciaries, members of a partnership, joint tenants, tenants in common, tenants by the entirety or otherwise, or if 2 or more persons have the same fiduciary relationship respecting the same shares, unless the secretary of the corporation is given written notice to the contrary and is furnished with a copy of the instrument or order appointing them or creating the relationship wherein it is so provided, their acts with respect to voting shall have the following effect:

    (1) If only 1 votes, such person's act binds all;

    (2) If more than 1 vote, the act of the majority so voting binds all;

    (3) If more than 1 vote, but the vote is evenly split on any particular matter, each faction may vote the securities in question proportionally, or any person voting the shares, or a beneficiary, if any, may apply to the Court of Chancery or such other court as may have jurisdiction to appoint an additional person to act with the persons so voting the shares, which shall then be voted as determined by a majority of such persons and the person appointed by the Court. If the instrument so filed shows that any such tenancy is held in unequal interests, a majority or even split for the purpose of this subsection shall be a majority or even split in interest.

§ 218.   Voting Trusts and Other Voting Agreements

→ agreement of voting trust

    (a) One stockholder or 2 or more stockholders may by agreement in writing deposit capital stock of an original issue with or transfer capital stock to any person or persons, or entity or entities authorized to act as trustee, for the purpose of vesting in such person or persons, entity or entities, who may be designated voting trustee, or voting trustees, the right to vote thereon for any period of time determined by such agreement, upon the terms and conditions stated in such agreement. The agreement may contain any other lawful provisions not inconsistent with such purpose. After delivery of a copy of the agreement to the registered office of the corporation in this State or the principal place of business of the corporation, which copy shall be open to the inspection of any stockholder of the corporation or any beneficiary of the trust under the agreement daily during business hours, certificates of stock or uncertificated stock shall be issued to the voting trustee or trustees to represent any stock of an original issue so deposited with such voting trustee or trustees, and any certificates of stock or uncertificated stock so transferred to the voting trustee or trustees shall be surrendered and cancelled and new certificates or uncertificated stock shall be issued therefore to the voting trustee or trustees. In the certificate so issued, if any, it shall be stated that it is issued pursuant to such agreement, and that fact shall also be stated in the stock ledger of the corporation. The voting trustee or trustees may vote the stock so issued or transferred during the period specified in the agreement. Stock standing in the name of the voting trustee or trustees may be voted either in person or by proxy, and in voting the stock, the voting trustee or trustees shall incur no responsibility as stockholder, trustee or otherwise, except for their own individual malfeasance. In any case where 2 or more persons or entities are designated as voting trustees, and the right and method of voting any stock standing in their names at any meeting of the corporation are not fixed by the agreement appointing the trustees, the right to vote the stock and the manner of voting it at the meeting shall be determined by a majority of the trustees, or if they be equally divided as to the right and manner of voting the stock in any particular case, the vote of the stock in such case shall be divided equally among the trustees.

    (b) Any amendment to a voting trust agreement shall be made by a written agreement, a copy of which shall be delivered to the registered office of the corporation in this State or principal place of business of the corporation.

→ general agreement of stockholders

    (c) An agreement between 2 or more stockholders, if in writing and signed by the parties thereto, may provide that in exercising any voting rights, the shares held by them shall be voted as provided by the agreement, or as the parties may agree, or as determined in accordance with a procedure agreed upon by them.

    (d) This section shall not be deemed to invalidate any voting or other agreement among stockholders or any irrevocable proxy which is not otherwise illegal.

§ 219.   List of Stockholders Entitled to Vote; Penalty for Refusal to Produce; Stock Ledger

    (a) The corporation shall prepare, at least 10 days before every meeting of stockholders, a complete list of the stockholders entitled to vote at the meeting; provided, however, if the record date for determining the stockholders entitled to vote is less than 10 days before the meeting date, the list shall reflect the stockholders entitled to vote as of the tenth day before the meeting date, arranged in alphabetical order, and showing the address of each stockholder and the number of shares registered in the name of each stockholder. Nothing contained in this section shall require the corporation to include electronic mail addresses or other electronic contact information on such list. Such list shall be open to the examination of any stockholder for any purpose germane to the meeting for a period of at least 10 days prior to the meeting: (i) on a reasonably accessible electronic network, provided that the information required to gain access to such list is provided with the notice of the meeting, or (ii) during ordinary business hours, at the principal place of business of the corporation. In the event that the corporation determines to make the list available on an electronic network, the corporation may take reasonable steps to ensure that such information is available only to stockholders of the corporation. If the meeting is to be held at a place, then a list of stockholders entitled to vote at the meeting shall be produced and kept at the time and place of the meeting during the whole time thereof and may be examined by any stockholder who is present. If the meeting is to be held solely by means of remote communication, then such list shall also be open to the examination of any stockholder during the whole time of the meeting on a reasonably accessible electronic network, and the information required to access such list shall be provided with the notice of the meeting.

(b) If the corporation, or an officer or agent thereof, refuses to permit examination of the list by a stockholder, such stockholder may apply to the Court of Chancery for an order to compel the corporation to permit such examination. The burden of proof shall be on the corporation to establish that the examination such stockholder seeks is for a purpose not germane to the meeting. The Court may summarily order the corporation to permit examination of the list upon such conditions as the Court may deem appropriate, and may make such additional orders as may be appropriate, including, without limitation, postponing the meeting or voiding the results of the meeting.

(c) For purposes of this chapter, "stock ledger" means 1 or more records administered by or on behalf of the corporation in which the names of all of the corporation's stockholders of record, the address and number of shares registered in the name of each such stockholder, and all issuances and transfers of stock of the corporation are recorded in accordance with § 224 of this title. The stock ledger shall be the only evidence as to who are the stockholders entitled by this section to examine the list required by this section or to vote in person or by proxy at any meeting of stockholders.

§ 220. Inspection of Books and Records

(a) As used in this section:

(1) "Stockholder" means a holder of record of stock in a stock corporation, or a person who is the beneficial owner of shares of such stock held either in a voting trust or by a nominee on behalf of such person.

(2) "Subsidiary" means any entity directly or indirectly owned, in whole or in part, by the corporation of which the stockholder is a stockholder and over the affairs of which the corporation directly or indirectly exercises control, and includes, without limitation, corporations, partnerships, limited partnerships, limited liability partnerships, limited liability companies, statutory trusts and/or joint ventures.

(3) "Under oath" includes statements the declarant affirms to be true under penalty of perjury under the laws of the United States or any state.

(b) Any stockholder, in person or by attorney or other agent, shall, upon written demand under oath stating the purpose thereof, have the right during the usual hours for business to inspect for any proper purpose, and to make copies and extracts from:

(1) The corporation's stock ledger, a list of its stockholders, and its other books and records; and

(2) A subsidiary's books and records, to the extent that:

a. The corporation has actual possession and control of such records of such subsidiary; or

b. The corporation could obtain such records through the exercise of control over such subsidiary, provided that as of the date of the making of the demand:

1. The stockholder inspection of such books and records of the subsidiary would not constitute a breach of an agreement between the corporation or the subsidiary and a person or persons not affiliated with the corporation; and

2. The subsidiary would not have the right under the law applicable to it to deny the corporation access to such books and records upon demand by the corporation.

In every instance where the stockholder is other than a record holder of stock in a stock corporation, or a member of a nonstock corporation, the demand under oath shall state the person's status as a stockholder, be accompanied by documentary evidence of beneficial ownership of the stock, and state that such documentary evidence is a true and correct copy of what it purports to be. A proper purpose shall mean a purpose reasonably related to such person's interest as a stockholder. In every instance where an attorney or other agent shall be the person who seeks the right to inspection, the demand under oath shall be accompanied by a power of attorney or such other writing which authorizes the attorney or other agent to so act on behalf of the stockholder. The demand under oath shall be directed to the corporation at its registered office in this State or at its principal place of business.

(c) If the corporation, or an officer or agent thereof, refuses to permit an inspection sought by a stockholder or attorney or other agent acting for the stockholder pursuant to subsection (b) of this section or does not reply to the demand within 5 business days after the demand has been made, the stockholder may apply to the Court of Chancery for an order to compel such inspection. The Court of Chancery is hereby vested with exclusive jurisdiction to determine whether or not the person seeking inspection is entitled to the inspection sought. The Court may summarily order the corporation to permit the stockholder to inspect the corporation's stock ledger, an existing list of stockholders, and its other books and records, and to make copies or extracts therefrom; or the Court may order the corporation to furnish to the stockholder a list of its stockholders as of a specific date on condition that the stockholder first pay to the corporation the reasonable cost of obtaining and furnishing such list and on such other conditions as the Court deems appropriate. Where the stockholder seeks to inspect the corporation's books and records, other than its stock ledger or list of stockholders, such stockholder shall first establish that:

(1) Such stockholder is a stockholder;

(2) Such stockholder has complied with this section respecting the form and manner of making demand for inspection of such documents; and

(3) The inspection such stockholder seeks is for a proper purpose.

Where the stockholder seeks to inspect the corporation's stock ledger or list of stockholders and establishes that such stockholder is a stockholder and has complied with this section respecting the form and manner of making demand for inspection of such documents, the burden of proof shall be upon the corporation to establish that the inspection such stockholder seeks is for an improper purpose. The Court may, in its discretion, prescribe any limitations or conditions with reference to the inspection, or award such other or further relief as the Court may deem just and proper. The Court may order books, documents and records, pertinent extracts therefrom, or duly authenticated copies thereof, to be brought within this State and kept in this State upon such terms and conditions as the order may prescribe.

(d) Any director shall have the right to examine the corporation's stock ledger, a list of its stockholders and its other books and records for a purpose reasonably related to the director's position as a director. The Court of Chancery is hereby vested with the exclusive jurisdiction to determine whether a director is entitled to the inspection sought. The Court may summarily order the corporation to permit the director to inspect any and all books and records, the stock ledger and the list of stockholders and to make copies or extracts therefrom. The burden of proof shall be upon the corporation to establish that the inspection such director seeks is for an improper purpose. The Court may, in its discretion, prescribe any limitations or conditions with reference to the inspection, or award such other and further relief as the Court may deem just and proper.

§ 221.   Voting, Inspection and Other Rights of Bondholders and Debenture Holders

Every corporation may in its certificate of incorporation confer upon the holders of any bonds, debentures or other obligations issued or to be issued by the corporation the power to vote in respect to the corporate affairs and management of the corporation to the extent and in the manner provided in the certificate of incorporation and may confer upon such holders of bonds, debentures or other obligations the same right of inspection of its books, accounts and other records, and also any other rights, which the stockholders of the corporation have or may have by reason of this chapter or of its certificate of incorporation. If the certificate of incorporation so provides, such holders of bonds, debentures or other obligations shall be deemed to be stockholders, and their bonds, debentures or other obligations shall be deemed to be shares of stock, for the purpose of any provision of this chapter which requires the vote of stockholders as a prerequisite to any corporate action and the certificate of incorporation may divest the holders of capital stock, in whole or in part, of their right to vote on any corporate matter whatsoever, except as set forth in § 242(b)(2) of this title.

§ 222. Notice of Meetings and Adjourned Meetings

(a) Whenever stockholders are required or permitted to take any action at a meeting, a written notice of the meeting shall be given which shall state the place, if any, date and hour of the meeting, the means of remote communications, if any, by which stockholders and proxy holders may be deemed to be present in person and vote at such meeting, the record date for determining the stockholders entitled to vote at the meeting, if such date is different from the record date for determining stockholders entitled to notice of the meeting, and, in the case of a special meeting, the purpose or purposes for which the meeting is called.

(b) Unless otherwise provided in this chapter, the written notice of any meeting shall be given not less than 10 nor more than 60 days before the date of the meeting to each stockholder entitled to vote at such meeting as of the record date for determining the stockholders entitled to notice of the meeting. If mailed, notice is given when deposited in the United States mail, postage prepaid, directed to the stockholder at such stockholder's address as it appears on the records of the corporation. An affidavit of the secretary or an assistant secretary or of the transfer agent or other agent of the corporation that the notice has been given shall, in the absence of fraud, be prima facie evidence of the facts stated therein.

(c) When a meeting is adjourned to another time or place, unless the bylaws otherwise require, notice need not be given of the adjourned meeting if the time, place, if any, thereof, and the means of remote communications, if any, by which stockholders and proxy holders may be deemed to be present in person and vote at such adjourned meeting are announced at the meeting at which the adjournment is taken. At the adjourned meeting the corporation may transact any business which might have been transacted at the original meeting. If the adjournment is for more than 30 days, a notice of the adjourned meeting shall be given to each stockholder of record entitled to vote at the meeting. If after the adjournment a new record date for stockholders entitled to vote is fixed for the adjourned meeting, the board of directors shall fix a new record date for notice of such adjourned meeting in accordance with § 213(a) of this title, and shall give notice of the adjourned meeting to each stockholder of record entitled to vote at such adjourned meeting as of the record date fixed for notice of such adjourned meeting.

§ 223. Vacancies and Newly Created Directorships

(a) Unless otherwise provided in the certificate of incorporation or bylaws:

(1) Vacancies and newly created directorships resulting from any increase in the authorized number of directors elected by all of the stockholders having the right to vote as a single class may be filled by a majority of the directors then in office, although less than a quorum, or by a sole remaining director;

(2) Whenever the holders of any class or classes of stock or series thereof are entitled to elect 1 or more directors by the certificate of incorporation, vacancies and newly created directorships of such class or classes or series may be filled by a majority of the directors elected by such class or classes or series thereof then in office, or by a sole remaining director so elected.

If at any time, by reason of death or resignation or other cause, a corporation should have no directors in office, then any officer or any stockholder or an executor, administrator, trustee or guardian of a stockholder, or other fiduciary entrusted with like responsibility for the person or estate of a stockholder, may call a special meeting of stockholders in accordance with the certificate of incorporation or the bylaws, or may apply to the Court of Chancery for a decree summarily ordering an election as provided in § 211 or § 215 of this title.

(b) In the case of a corporation the directors of which are divided into classes, any directors chosen under subsection (a) of this section shall hold office until the next election of the class for which such directors shall have been chosen, and until their successors shall be elected and qualified.

(c) If, at the time of filling any vacancy or any newly created directorship, the directors then in office shall constitute less than a majority of the whole board (as constituted immediately prior to any such increase), the Court of Chancery may, upon application of any stockholder or stockholders holding at least 10 percent of the voting stock at the time outstanding having the right to vote for such directors, summarily order an election to be held to fill any such vacancies or newly created directorships, or to replace the directors chosen by the directors then in office as aforesaid, which election shall be governed by § 211 or § 215 of this title as far as applicable.

(d) Unless otherwise provided in the certificate of incorporation or bylaws, when 1 or more directors shall resign from the board, effective at a future date, a majority of the directors then in office, including those who have so resigned, shall have power to fill such vacancy or vacancies, the vote thereon to take effect when such resignation or resignations shall become effective, and each director so chosen shall hold office as provided in this section in the filling of other vacancies.

§ 225.   Contested Election of Directors; Proceedings to Determine Validity

(a) Upon application of any stockholder or director, or any officer whose title to office is contested, the Court of Chancery may hear and determine the validity of any election, appointment, removal or resignation of any director or officer of any corporation, and the right of any person to hold or continue to hold such office, and, in case any such office is claimed by more than 1 person, may determine the person entitled thereto; and to that end make such order or decree in any such case as may be just and proper, with power to enforce the production of any books, papers and records of the corporation relating to the issue. In case it should be determined that no valid election has been held, the Court of Chancery may order an election to be held in accordance with § 211 or § 215 of this title. In any such application, service of copies of the application upon the registered agent of the corporation shall be deemed to be service upon the corporation and upon the person whose title to office is contested and upon the person, if any, claiming such office; and the registered agent shall forward immediately a copy of the application to the corporation and to the person whose title to office is contested and to the person, if any, claiming such office, in a postpaid, sealed, registered letter addressed to such corporation and such person at their post-office addresses last known to the registered agent or furnished to the registered agent by the applicant stockholder. The Court may make such order respecting further or other notice of such application as it deems proper under the circumstances.

(b) Upon application of any stockholder or upon application of the corporation itself, the Court of Chancery may hear and determine the result of any vote of stockholders upon matters other than the election of directors or officers. Service of the application upon the registered agent of the corporation shall be deemed to be service upon the corporation, and no other party need be joined in order for the Court to adjudicate the result of the vote. The Court may make such order respecting notice of the application as it deems proper under the circumstances.

(c) If 1 or more directors has been convicted of a felony in connection with the duties of such director or directors to the corporation, or if there has been a prior judgment on the merits by a court of competent jurisdiction that 1 or more directors has committed a breach of the duty of loyalty in connection with the duties of such director or directors to that corporation, then, upon application by the corporation, or derivatively in the right of the corporation by any stockholder, in a subsequent action brought for such purpose, the Court of Chancery may remove from office such director or directors if the Court determines that the director or directors did not act in good faith in performing the acts resulting in the prior conviction or judgment and judicial removal is necessary to avoid irreparable harm to the corporation. In connection with such removal, the Court may make such orders as are necessary to effect such removal. In any such application, service of copies of the application upon the registered agent of the corporation shall be deemed to be service upon the corporation and upon the director or directors whose removal is sought; and the registered agent shall forward immediately a copy of the application to the corporation and to such director or directors, in a postpaid, sealed, registered letter addressed to such corporation and such director or directors at their post office addresses last known to the registered agent or furnished to the registered agent by the applicant. The Court may make such order respecting further or other notice of such application as it deems proper under the circumstances.

§ 226. Appointment of Custodian or Receiver of Corporation on Deadlock or for Other Cause

(a) The Court of Chancery, upon application of any stockholder, may appoint 1 or more persons to be custodians, and, if the corporation is insolvent, to be receivers, of and for any corporation when:

(1) At any meeting held for the election of directors the stockholders are so divided that they have failed to elect successors to directors whose terms have expired or would have expired upon qualification of their successors; or

(2) The business of the corporation is suffering or is threatened with irreparable injury because the directors are so divided respecting the management of the affairs of the corporation that the required vote for action by the board of directors cannot be obtained and the stockholders are unable to terminate this division; or

(3) The corporation has abandoned its business and has failed within a reasonable time to take steps to dissolve, liquidate or distribute its assets.

(b) A custodian appointed under this section shall have all the powers and title of a receiver appointed under § 291 of this title, but the authority of the custodian is to continue the business of the corporation and not to liquidate its affairs and distribute its assets, except when the Court shall otherwise order and except in cases arising under paragraph (a)(3) of this section or § 352(a)(2) of this title. . . .

§ 227. Powers of Court in Elections of Directors

(a) The Court of Chancery, in any proceeding instituted under § 211, § 215 or § 225 of this title may determine the right and power of persons claiming to own stock to vote at any meeting of the stockholders.

(b) The Court of Chancery may appoint a Master to hold any election provided for in § 211, § 215 or § 225 of this title under such orders and powers as it deems proper; and it may punish any officer or director for contempt in case of disobedience of any order made by the Court; and, in case of disobedience by a corporation of any order made by the Court, may enter a decree against such corporation for a penalty of not more than $5,000.

§ 228. Consent of Stockholders or Members in Lieu of Meeting

(a) Unless otherwise provided in the certificate of incorporation, any action required by this chapter to be taken at any annual or special meeting of stockholders of a corporation, or any action which may be taken at any annual or special meeting of such stockholders, may be taken without a meeting, without prior notice and without a vote, if a consent or consents in writing, setting forth the action so taken, shall be signed by the holders of outstanding stock having not less than the minimum number of votes that would be necessary to authorize or take such action at a meeting at which all shares entitled to vote thereon were present and voted and shall be delivered to the corporation by delivery to its registered office in this State, its principal place of business or an officer or agent of the corporation having custody of the book in which proceedings of meetings of stockholders are recorded. Delivery made to a corporation's registered office shall be by hand or by certified or registered mail, return receipt requested.

(b) Unless otherwise provided in the certificate of incorporation, any action required by this chapter to be taken at a meeting of the members of a nonstock corporation, or any action which may be taken at any meeting of the members of a nonstock corporation, may be taken without a meeting, without prior notice and without a vote, if a consent or consents in writing, setting forth the action so taken, shall be signed by members having not less than the minimum number of votes that would be necessary to authorize or take such action at a meeting at which all members having a right to vote thereon were present and voted and shall be delivered to the corporation by delivery to its registered office in this State, its principal place of business or an officer or agent of the corporation having custody of the book in which proceedings of meetings of members are recorded. Delivery made to a corporation's registered office shall be by hand or by certified or registered mail, return receipt requested.

(c) No written consent shall be effective to take the corporate action referred to therein unless written consents signed by a sufficient number of holders or members to take action are delivered to the corporation in the manner required by this section within 60 days of the first date on which a written consent is so delivered to the corporation. Any person executing a consent may provide, whether through instruction to an agent or otherwise, that such a consent will be effective at a future time (including a time determined upon the happening of an event), no later than 60 days after such instruction is given or such provision is made, if evidence of such instruction or provision is provided to the corporation. Unless otherwise provided, any such consent shall be revocable prior to its becoming effective.

(d)(1) A telegram, cablegram or other electronic transmission consenting to an action to be taken and transmitted by a stockholder, member or proxyholder, or by a person or persons authorized to act for a stockholder, member or proxyholder, shall be deemed to be written and signed for the purposes of this section, provided that any such telegram, cablegram or other electronic transmission sets forth or is delivered with information from which the corporation can determine (A) that the telegram, cablegram or other electronic transmission was transmitted by the stockholder, member or proxyholder or by a person or persons authorized to act for the stockholder, member or proxyholder and (B) the date on which such stockholder, member or proxyholder or authorized person or persons transmitted such telegram, cablegram or electronic transmission. No consent given by telegram, cablegram or other electronic transmission shall be deemed to have been delivered until such consent is reproduced in paper form and until such paper form shall be delivered to the corporation by delivery to its registered office in this State, its principal place of business or an officer or agent of the corporation having custody of the book in which proceedings of meetings of stockholders or members are recorded. Delivery made to a corporation's registered office shall be made by hand or by certified or registered mail, return receipt requested. Notwithstanding the foregoing limitations on delivery, consents given by telegram, cablegram or other electronic transmission, may be otherwise delivered to the principal place of business of the corporation or to an officer or agent of the corporation having custody of the book in which proceedings of meetings of stockholders or members are recorded if, to the extent and in the manner provided by resolution of the board of directors or governing body of the corporation.

(2) Any copy, facsimile or other reliable reproduction of a consent in writing may be substituted or used in lieu of the original writing for any and all purposes for which the original writing could be used, provided that such copy, facsimile or other reproduction shall be a complete reproduction of the entire original writing.

(e) Prompt notice of the taking of the corporate action without a meeting by less than unanimous written consent shall be given to those stockholders or members who have not consented in writing and who, if the action had been taken at a meeting, would have been entitled to notice of the meeting if the record date for notice of such meeting had been the date that written consents signed by a sufficient number of holders or members to take the action were delivered to the corporation as provided in this section. In the event that the action which is consented to is such as would have required the filing of a certificate under any other section of this title, if such action had been voted on by stockholders . . . at a meeting thereof, the certificate filed under such other section shall state, in lieu of any statement required by such section concerning any vote of stockholders . . . , that written consent has been given in accordance with this section.

§ 229.   Waiver of Notice

Whenever notice is required to be given under any provision of this chapter or the certificate of incorporation or bylaws, a written waiver, signed by the person entitled to notice, or a waiver by electronic transmission by the person entitled to notice, whether before or after the time stated therein, shall be deemed equivalent to notice. Attendance of a person at a meeting shall constitute a waiver of notice of such meeting, except when the person attends a meeting for the express purpose of objecting at the beginning of the meeting, to the transaction of any business because the meeting is not lawfully called or convened. Neither the business to be transacted at, nor the purpose of, any regular or special meeting of the stockholders, directors or members of a committee of directors need be specified in any written waiver of notice or any waiver by electronic transmission unless so required by the certificate of incorporation or the bylaws.

§ 231.   Voting Procedures and Inspectors of Elections

(a) The corporation shall, in advance of any meeting of stockholders, appoint 1 or more inspectors to act at the meeting and make a written report thereof. The corporation may designate 1 or more persons as alternate inspectors to replace any inspector who fails to act. If no inspector or alternate is able to act at a meeting of stockholders, the person presiding at the meeting shall appoint 1 or more inspectors to act at the meeting. Each inspector, before entering upon the discharge of the duties of inspector, shall take and sign an oath faithfully to execute the duties of inspector with strict impartiality and according to the best of such inspector's ability.

(b) The inspectors shall:

(1) Ascertain the number of shares outstanding and the voting power of each;

(2) Determine the shares represented at a meeting and the validity of proxies and ballots;

(3) Count all votes and ballots;

(4) Determine and retain for a reasonable period a record of the disposition of any challenges made to any determination by the inspectors; and

(5) Certify their determination of the number of shares represented at the meeting, and their count of all votes and ballots.

The inspectors may appoint or retain other persons or entities to assist the inspectors in the performance of the duties of the inspectors.

(c) The date and time of the opening and the closing of the polls for each matter upon which the stockholders will vote at a meeting shall be announced at the meeting. No ballot, proxies or votes, nor any revocations thereof or changes thereto, shall be accepted by the inspectors after the closing of the polls unless the Court of Chancery upon application by a stockholder shall determine otherwise.

(d) In determining the validity and counting of proxies and ballots, the inspectors shall be limited to an examination of the proxies, any envelopes submitted with those proxies, any information provided in accordance with § 211(e) or § 212(c)(2) of this title, or any information provided pursuant to § 211(a)(2)b.(i) or (iii) of this title, ballots and the regular books and records of the corporation, except that the inspectors may consider other reliable information for the limited purpose of reconciling proxies and ballots submitted by or on behalf of banks, brokers, their nominees or similar persons which represent more votes than the holder of a proxy is authorized by the record owner to cast or more votes than the stockholder holds of record. If the inspectors consider other reliable information for the limited purpose permitted herein, the inspectors at the time they make their certification pursuant to paragraph (b)(5) of this section shall specify the precise information considered by them including the person or persons from whom they obtained the information, when the information was obtained, the means by which the information was obtained and the basis for the inspectors' belief that such information is accurate and reliable.

(e) Unless otherwise provided in the certificate of incorporation or bylaws, this section shall not apply to a corporation that does not have a class of voting stock that is:

(1) Listed on a national securities exchange;

(2) Authorized for quotation on an interdealer quotation system of a registered national securities association; or

(3) Held of record by more than 2,000 stockholders.

§ 232. Notice by Electronic Transmission

(a) Without limiting the manner by which notice otherwise may be given effectively to stockholders, any notice to stockholders given by the corporation under any provision of this chapter, the certificate of incorporation, or the bylaws shall be effective if given by a form of electronic transmission consented to by the stockholder to whom the notice is given. Any such consent shall be revocable by the stockholder by written notice to the corporation. Any such consent shall be deemed revoked if (1) the corporation is unable to deliver by electronic transmission 2 consecutive notices given by the corporation in accordance with such consent and (2) such inability becomes known to the secretary or an assistant secretary of the corporation or to the transfer agent, or other person responsible for the giving of notice; provided, however, the inadvertent failure to treat such inability as a revocation shall not invalidate any meeting or other action.

(b) Notice given pursuant to subsection (a) of this section shall be deemed given:

(1) If by facsimile telecommunication, when directed to a number at which the stockholder has consented to receive notice;

(2) If by electronic mail, when directed to an electronic mail address at which the stockholder has consented to receive notice;

(3) If by a posting on an electronic network together with separate notice to the stockholder of such specific posting, upon the later of (A) such posting and (B) the giving of such separate notice; and

(4) If by any other form of electronic transmission, when directed to the stockholder.

An affidavit of the secretary or an assistant secretary or of the transfer agent or other agent of the corporation that the notice has been given by a form of electronic transmission shall, in the absence of fraud, be prima facie evidence of the facts stated therein.

(c) For purposes of this chapter, "electronic transmission" means any form of communication, not directly involving the physical transmission of paper, including the use of, or participation in, 1 or more electronic networks or databases (including 1 or more distributed electronic networks or databases), that creates a record that may be retained, retrieved and reviewed by a recipient thereof, and that may be directly reproduced in paper form by such a recipient through an automated process.

(d) [Repealed.]

(e) This section shall not apply to § 164, § 296, § 311, § 312, or § 324 of this title.

SUBCHAPTER VIII. AMENDMENT OF CERTIFICATE OF INCORPORATION; CHANGES IN CAPITAL AND CAPITAL STOCK

§ 241. Amendment of Certificate of Incorporation Before Receipt of Payment for Stock

(a) Before a corporation has received any payment for any of its stock, it may amend its certificate of incorporation at any time or times, in any and as many respects as may be desired, so long as its certificate of incorporation as amended would contain only such provisions as it would be lawful and proper to insert in an original certificate of incorporation filed at the time of filing the amendment.

(b) The amendment of a certificate of incorporation authorized by this section shall be adopted by a majority of the incorporators, if directors were not named in the original certificate of incorporation or have not yet been elected, or, if directors were named in the original certificate of incorporation or have been elected and have qualified, by a majority of the directors. A certificate setting forth the amendment and certifying that the corporation has not received any payment for any of its stock, or that the corporation has no members, as applicable, and that the amendment has been duly adopted in accordance with this section shall be executed, acknowledged and filed in accordance with § 103 of this title. Upon such filing, the corporation's certificate of incorporation shall be deemed to be amended accordingly as of the date on which the original certificate of incorporation became effective, except as to those persons who are substantially and adversely affected by the amendment and as to those persons the amendment shall be effective from the filing date.

(c) This section will apply to a nonstock corporation before such a corporation has any members; provided, however, that all references to directors shall be deemed to be references to members of the governing body of the corporation.

§ 242. Amendment of Certificate of Incorporation After Receipt of Payment for Stock; Nonstock Corporations

(a) After a corporation has received payment for any of its capital stock, or after a nonstock corporation has members, it may amend its certificate of incorporation, from time to time, in any and as many respects as may be desired, so long as its certificate of incorporation as amended would contain only such provisions as it would be lawful and proper to insert in an original certificate of incorporation filed at the time of the filing of the amendment; and, if a change in stock or the rights of stockholders, or an exchange, reclassification, subdivision, combination or cancellation of stock or rights of stockholders is to be made, such provisions as may be necessary to effect such change, exchange, reclassification, subdivision, combination or cancellation. In particular, and without limitation upon such general power of amendment, a corporation may amend its certificate of incorporation, from time to time, so as:

(1) To change its corporate name; or

(2) To change, substitute, enlarge or diminish the nature of its business or its corporate powers and purposes; or

(3) To increase or decrease its authorized capital stock or to reclassify the same, by changing the number, par value, designations, preferences, or relative, participating, optional, or other special rights of the shares, or the qualifications, limitations or restrictions of such rights, or by changing shares with par value into shares without par value, or shares without par value into shares with par value either with or without increasing or decreasing the number of shares, or by subdividing or combining the outstanding shares of any class or series of a class of shares into a greater or lesser number of outstanding shares; or

(4) To cancel or otherwise affect the right of the holders of the shares of any class to receive dividends which have accrued but have not been declared; or

(5) To create new classes of stock having rights and preferences either prior and superior or subordinate and inferior to the stock of any class then authorized, whether issued or unissued; or

(6) To change the period of its duration; or

(7) To delete:

a. Such provisions of the original certificate of incorporation which named the incorporator or incorporators, the initial board of directors and the original subscribers for shares; and

b. Such provisions contained in any amendment to the certificate of incorporation as were necessary to effect a change, exchange, reclassification, subdivision, combination or cancellation of stock, if such change, exchange, reclassification, subdivision, combination or cancellation has become effective.

Any or all such changes or alterations may be effected by 1 certificate of amendment.

(b) Every amendment authorized by subsection (a) of this section shall be made and effected in the following manner:

(1) If the corporation has capital stock, its board of directors shall adopt a resolution setting forth the amendment proposed, declaring its advisability, and either calling a special meeting of the stockholders entitled to vote in respect thereof for the consideration of such amendment or directing that the amendment proposed be considered at the next annual meeting of the stockholders; provided, however, that unless otherwise expressly required by the certificate of incorporation, no meeting or vote of stockholders shall be required to adopt an amendment that effects only changes described in paragraph (a)(1) or (7) of this section. Such special or annual meeting shall be called and held upon notice in accordance with § 222 of this title. The notice shall set forth such amendment in full or a brief summary of the changes to be effected thereby unless such notice constitutes a notice of internet availability of proxy materials under the rules promulgated under the Securities Exchange Act of 1934 [15 U.S.C. § 78a et seq.]. At the meeting a vote of the stockholders entitled to vote thereon shall be taken for and against any proposed amendment that requires adoption by stockholders. If no vote of stockholders is required to effect such amendment, or if a majority of the outstanding stock entitled to vote thereon, and a majority of the outstanding stock of each class entitled to vote thereon as a class has been voted in favor of the amendment, a certificate setting forth the amendment and certifying that such amendment has been duly adopted in accordance with this section shall be executed, acknowledged and filed and shall become effective in accordance with § 103 of this title.

(2) The holders of the outstanding shares of a class shall be entitled to vote as a class upon a proposed amendment, whether or not entitled to vote thereon by the certificate of incorporation, if the amendment would increase or decrease the aggregate number of authorized shares of such class, increase or decrease the par value of the shares of such class, or alter or change the powers, preferences,

or special rights of the shares of such class so as to affect them adversely. If any proposed amendment would alter or change the powers, preferences, or special rights of 1 or more series of any class so as to affect them adversely, but shall not so affect the entire class, then only the shares of the series so affected by the amendment shall be considered a separate class for the purposes of this paragraph. The number of authorized shares of any such class or classes of stock may be increased or decreased (but not below the number of shares thereof then outstanding) by the affirmative vote of the holders of a majority of the stock of the corporation entitled to vote irrespective of this subsection, if so provided in the original certificate of incorporation, in any amendment thereto which created such class or classes of stock or which was adopted prior to the issuance of any shares of such class or classes of stock, or in any amendment thereto which was authorized by a resolution or resolutions adopted by the affirmative vote of the holders of a majority of such class or classes of stock.

(3) If the corporation is a nonstock corporation, then the governing body thereof shall adopt a resolution setting forth the amendment proposed and declaring its advisability. If a majority of all the members of the governing body shall vote in favor of such amendment, a certificate thereof shall be executed, acknowledged and filed and shall become effective in accordance with § 103 of this title. The certificate of incorporation of any nonstock corporation may contain a provision requiring any amendment thereto to be approved by a specified number or percentage of the members or of any specified class of members of such corporation in which event such proposed amendment shall be submitted to the members or to any specified class of members of such corporation in the same manner, so far as applicable, as is provided in this section for an amendment to the certificate of incorporation of a stock corporation; and in the event of the adoption thereof by such members, a certificate evidencing such amendment shall be executed, acknowledged and filed and shall become effective in accordance with § 103 of this title.

(4) Whenever the certificate of incorporation shall require for action by the board of directors of a corporation other than a nonstock corporation or by the governing body of a nonstock corporation, by the holders of any class or series of shares or by the members, or by the holders of any other securities having voting power the vote of a greater number or proportion than is required by any section of this title, the provision of the certificate of incorporation requiring such greater vote shall not be altered, amended or repealed except by such greater vote.

(c) The resolution authorizing a proposed amendment to the certificate of incorporation may provide that at any time prior to the effectiveness of the filing of the amendment with the Secretary of State, notwithstanding authorization of the proposed amendment by the stockholders of the corporation or by the members of a nonstock corporation, the board of directors or governing body may abandon such proposed amendment without further action by the stockholders or members.

§ 243. Retirement of Stock

(a) A corporation, by resolution of its board of directors, may retire any shares of its capital stock that are issued but are not outstanding.

(b) Whenever any shares of the capital stock of a corporation are retired, they shall resume the status of authorized and unissued shares of the class or series to which they belong unless the certificate of incorporation otherwise provides. If the certificate of incorporation prohibits the reissuance of such shares, or prohibits the reissuance of such shares as a part of a specific series only, a certificate stating that reissuance of the shares (as part of the class or series) is prohibited identifying the shares and reciting their retirement shall be executed, acknowledged and filed and shall become effective in accordance with § 103 of this title. When such certificate becomes effective, it shall have the effect of amending the certificate of incorporation so as to reduce accordingly the number of authorized shares of the class or series to which such shares belong or, if such retired shares constitute all of the authorized shares of the class or series to which they belong, of eliminating from the certificate of incorporation all reference to such class or series of stock.

(c) If the capital of the corporation will be reduced by or in connection with the retirement of shares, the reduction of capital shall be effected pursuant to § 244 of this title.

§ 244. Reduction of Capital

(a) A corporation, by resolution of its board of directors, may reduce its capital in any of the following ways:

(1) By reducing or eliminating the capital represented by shares of capital stock which have been retired;

(2) By applying to an otherwise authorized purchase or redemption of outstanding shares of its capital stock some or all of the capital represented by the shares being purchased or redeemed, or any capital that has not been allocated to any particular class of its capital stock;

(3) By applying to an otherwise authorized conversion or exchange of outstanding shares of its capital stock some or all of the capital represented by the shares being converted or exchanged, or some or all of any capital that has not been allocated to any particular class of its capital stock, or both, to the extent that such capital in the aggregate exceeds the total aggregate par value or the stated capital of any previously unissued shares issuable upon such conversion or exchange; or

(4) By transferring to surplus (i) some or all of the capital not represented by any particular class of its capital stock; (ii) some or all of the capital represented by issued shares of its par value capital stock, which capital is in excess of the aggregate par value of such shares; or (iii) some of the capital represented by issued shares of its capital stock without par value.

(b) Notwithstanding the other provisions of this section, no reduction of capital shall be made or effected unless the assets of the corporation remaining after such reduction shall be sufficient to pay any debts of the corporation for which payment has not been otherwise provided. No reduction of capital shall release any liability of any stockholder whose shares have not been fully paid.

§ 245. Restated Certificate of Incorporation

(a) A corporation may, whenever desired, integrate into a single instrument all of the provisions of its certificate of incorporation which are then in effect and operative as a result of there having theretofore been filed with the Secretary of State 1 or more certificates or other instruments pursuant to any of the sections referred to in § 104 of this title, and it may at the same time also further amend its certificate of incorporation by adopting a restated certificate of incorporation.

(b) If the restated certificate of incorporation merely restates and integrates but does not further amend the certificate of incorporation, as theretofore amended or supplemented by any instrument that was filed pursuant to any of the sections mentioned in § 104 of this title, it may be adopted by the board of directors without a vote of the stockholders, or it may be proposed by the directors and submitted by them to the stockholders for adoption, in which case the procedure and vote required, if any, by § 242 of this title for amendment of the certificate of incorporation shall be applicable. If the restated certificate of incorporation restates and integrates and also further amends in any respect the certificate of incorporation, as theretofore amended or supplemented, it shall be proposed by the directors and adopted by the stockholders in the manner and by the vote prescribed by § 242 of this title or, if the corporation has not received any payment for any of its stock, in the manner and by the vote prescribed by § 241 of this title.

(c) A restated certificate of incorporation shall be specifically designated as such in its heading. It shall state, either in its heading or in an introductory paragraph, the corporation's present name, and, if it has been changed, the name under which it was originally incorporated, and the date of filing of its original certificate of incorporation with the Secretary of State. A restated certificate shall also state that it was duly adopted in accordance with this section. If it was adopted by the board of directors without a vote of the stockholders (unless it was adopted pursuant to § 241 of this title or without a vote of members pursuant to 242(b)(3) of this title), it shall state that it only restates and integrates and does not further amend (except, if applicable, as permitted under § 242(a)(1) and § 242(b)(1) of this title) the provisions of the corporation's certificate of incorporation as theretofore amended or supplemented, and that there is no discrepancy between those provisions and the provisions of the restated certificate. A restated certificate of incorporation may omit (a) such provisions of the original certificate of incorporation which named the incorporator or incorporators, the initial board of directors and the original subscribers for shares, and (b) such provisions contained in any amendment to the certificate of incorporation as were necessary to effect a change, exchange, reclassification, subdivision, combination or cancellation of stock, if such change, exchange, reclassification, subdivision, combination or cancellation has become effective. Any such omissions shall not be deemed a further amendment.

(d) A restated certificate of incorporation shall be executed, acknowledged and filed in accordance with § 103 of this title. Upon its filing with the Secretary of State, the original certificate of incorporation, as theretofore amended or supplemented, shall be superseded; thenceforth, the restated certificate of incorporation, including any further amendments or changes made thereby, shall be the certificate of incorporation of the corporation, but the original date of incorporation shall remain unchanged.

(e) Any amendment or change effected in connection with the restatement and integration of the certificate of incorporation shall be subject to any other provision of this chapter, not inconsistent with this section, which would apply if a separate certificate of amendment were filed to effect such amendment or change.

SUBCHAPTER IX. MERGER, CONSOLIDATION OR CONVERSION

§ 251.   Merger or Consolidation of Domestic Corporations

(a) Any 2 or more corporations of this State may merge into a single surviving corporation, which may be any 1 of the constituent corporations or may consolidate into a new resulting corporation formed by the consolidation, pursuant to an agreement of merger or consolidation, as the case may be, complying and approved in accordance with this section.

(b) The board of directors of each corporation which desires to merge or consolidate shall adopt a resolution approving an agreement of merger or consolidation and declaring its advisability. The agreement shall state:

(1) The terms and conditions of the merger or consolidation;

(2) The mode of carrying the same into effect;

(3) In the case of a merger, such amendments or changes in the certificate of incorporation of the surviving corporation as are desired to be effected by the merger (which amendments or changes may amend and restate the certificate of incorporation of the surviving corporation in its entirety), or, if no such amendments or changes are desired, a statement that the certificate of incorporation of the surviving corporation shall be its certificate of incorporation;

(4) In the case of a consolidation, that the certificate of incorporation of the resulting corporation shall be as is set forth in an attachment to the agreement;

(5) The manner, if any, of converting the shares of each of the constituent corporations into shares or other securities of the corporation surviving or resulting from the merger or consolidation, or of cancelling some or all of such shares, and, if any shares of any of the constituent corporations are not to remain outstanding, to be converted solely into shares or other securities of the surviving or resulting corporation or to be cancelled, the cash, property, rights or securities of any other corporation or entity which the holders of such shares are to receive in exchange for, or upon conversion of such shares and the surrender of any certificates evidencing them, which cash, property, rights or securities of any other corporation or entity may be in addition to or in lieu of shares or other securities of the surviving or resulting corporation; and

(6) Such other details or provisions as are deemed desirable, including, without limiting the generality of the foregoing, a provision for the payment of cash in lieu of the issuance or recognition of fractional shares, rights or other securities of the surviving or resulting corporation or of any other corporation or entity the shares, rights or other securities of which are to be received in the merger or consolidation, or for any other arrangement with respect thereto, consistent with § 155 of this title.

The agreement so adopted shall be executed and acknowledged in accordance with § 103 of this title. Any of the terms of the agreement of merger or consolidation may be made dependent upon facts ascertainable outside of such agreement, provided that the manner in which such facts shall operate upon the terms of the agreement is clearly and expressly set forth in the agreement of merger or consolidation. The term "facts," as used in the preceding sentence, includes, but is not limited to, the occurrence of any event, including a determination or action by any person or body, including the corporation.

(c) The agreement required by subsection (b) of this section shall be submitted to the stockholders of each constituent corporation at an annual or special meeting for the purpose of acting on the agreement. Due notice of the time, place and purpose of the meeting shall be mailed to each holder of stock, whether voting or nonvoting, of the corporation at the stockholder's address as it appears on the records of the corporation, at least 20 days prior to the date of the meeting. The notice shall contain a copy of the agreement or a brief summary thereof. At the meeting, the agreement shall be considered and a vote taken for its adoption or rejection. If a majority of the outstanding stock of the corporation entitled to vote thereon shall be voted for the adoption of the agreement, that fact shall be certified on the agreement by the secretary or assistant secretary of the corporation, provided that such certification on the agreement shall not be required if a certificate of merger or consolidation is filed in lieu of filing the agreement. If the agreement shall be so adopted and certified by each constituent corporation, it shall then be filed and shall become effective, in accordance with § 103 of this title. In lieu of filing the agreement of merger or consolidation required by this section, the surviving or resulting corporation may file a certificate of merger or consolidation, executed in accordance with § 103 of this title, which states:

(1) The name and state of incorporation of each of the constituent corporations;

(2) That an agreement of merger or consolidation has been approved, adopted, executed and acknowledged by each of the constituent corporations in accordance with this section;

(3) The name of the surviving or resulting corporation;

(4) In the case of a merger, such amendments or changes in the certificate of incorporation of the surviving corporation as are desired to be effected by the merger (which amendments or changes may amend and restate the certificate of incorporation of the surviving corporation in its entirety), or, if no such amendments or changes are desired, a statement that the certificate of incorporation of the surviving corporation shall be its certificate of incorporation;

(5) In the case of a consolidation, that the certificate of incorporation of the resulting corporation shall be as set forth in an attachment to the certificate;

(6) That the executed agreement of consolidation or merger is on file at an office of the surviving or resulting corporation, stating the address thereof; and

(7) That a copy of the agreement of consolidation or merger will be furnished by the surviving or resulting corporation, on request and without cost, to any stockholder of any constituent corporation.

(d) Any agreement of merger or consolidation may contain a provision that at any time prior to the time that the agreement (or a certificate in lieu thereof) filed with the Secretary of State becomes effective in accordance with § 103 of this title, the agreement may be terminated by the board of directors of any constituent corporation notwithstanding approval of the agreement by the stockholders of all or any of the constituent corporations; in the event the agreement of merger or consolidation is terminated after the filing of the agreement (or a certificate in lieu thereof) with the Secretary of State but before the agreement (or a certificate in lieu thereof) has become effective, a certificate of termination or merger or consolidation shall be filed in accordance with § 103 of this title. Any agreement of merger or consolidation may contain a provision that the boards of directors of the constituent corporations may amend the agreement at any time prior to the time that the agreement (or a certificate in lieu thereof) filed with the Secretary of State becomes effective in accordance with § 103 of this title, provided that an amendment made subsequent to the adoption of the agreement by the stockholders of any constituent corporation shall not (1) alter or change the amount or kind of shares, securities, cash, property and/or rights to be received in exchange for or on conversion of all or any of the shares of any class or series thereof of such constituent corporation, (2) alter or change any term of the certificate of incorporation of the surviving corporation to be effected by the merger or consolidation, or (3) alter or change any of the terms and conditions of the agreement if such alteration or change would adversely affect the holders of any class or series thereof of such constituent corporation; in the event the agreement of merger or consolidation is amended after the filing thereof with the Secretary of State but before the agreement has become effective, a certificate of amendment of merger or consolidation shall be filed in accordance with § 103 of this title.

(e) In the case of a merger, the certificate of incorporation of the surviving corporation shall automatically be amended to the extent, if any, that changes in the certificate of incorporation are set forth in the agreement of merger.

(f) Notwithstanding the requirements of subsection (c) of this section, unless required by its certificate of incorporation, no vote of stockholders of a constituent corporation surviving a merger shall be necessary to authorize a merger if (1) the agreement of merger does not amend in any respect the certificate of incorporation of such constituent corporation, (2) each share of stock of such constituent corporation outstanding immediately prior to the effective date of the merger is to be an identical outstanding or treasury share of the surviving corporation after the effective date of the merger, and (3) either no shares of common stock of the surviving corporation and no shares, securities or obligations convertible into such stock are to be issued or delivered under the plan of merger, or the authorized unissued shares or the treasury shares of common stock of the surviving corporation to be issued or delivered under the plan of merger plus those initially issuable upon conversion of any other shares, securities or obligations to be issued or delivered under such plan do not exceed 20% of the shares of common stock of such constituent corporation outstanding immediately prior to the effective date of the merger. No vote of stockholders of a constituent corporation shall be necessary to authorize a merger or consolidation if no shares of the stock of such corporation shall have been issued prior to the adoption by the board of directors of the resolution approving the agreement of merger or consolidation. If an agreement of merger is adopted by the constituent corporation surviving the merger, by action of its board of directors and without any vote of its stockholders pursuant to this subsection, the secretary or assistant secretary of that corporation shall certify on the agreement that the agreement has been adopted pursuant to this subsection and, (1) if it has been adopted pursuant to the first sentence of this subsection, that the conditions specified in that sentence have been satisfied, or (2) if it has been adopted pursuant to the second sentence of this subsection, that no shares of stock of such corporation were issued prior to the adoption by the board of directors of the resolution approving the agreement of merger or consolidation, provided that such certification on the agreement shall not be required if a certificate of merger or consolidation is filed in lieu of filing the agreement. The agreement so adopted and certified shall then be filed and shall become effective, in accordance with § 103 of this title. Such filing shall constitute a representation by the person who executes the agreement that the facts stated in the certificate remain true immediately prior to such filing.

(g) Notwithstanding the requirements of subsection (c) of this section, unless expressly required by its certificate of incorporation, no vote of stockholders of a constituent corporation shall be necessary to authorize a merger with or into a single direct or indirect wholly-owned subsidiary of such constituent corporation if: (1) such constituent corporation and the direct or indirect wholly-owned subsidiary of such constituent corporation are the only constituent entities to the merger; (2) each share or fraction of a share of the capital stock of the constituent corporation outstanding immediately prior to the effective time of the merger is converted in the merger into a share or equal fraction of share of capital stock of a holding company having the same designations, rights, powers and preferences, and the qualifications, limitations and restrictions thereof, as the share of stock of the constituent corporation being converted in the merger; (3) the holding company and the constituent corporation are corporations of this State and the direct or indirect wholly-owned subsidiary that is the other constituent entity to the merger is a corporation or limited liability company of this State; (4) the certificate of incorporation and by-laws of the holding company immediately following the effective time of the merger contain provisions identical to the certificate of incorporation and by-laws of the constituent corporation immediately prior to the effective time of the merger (other than provisions, if any, regarding the incorporator or incorporators, the corporate name, the registered office and agent, the initial board of directors and the initial subscribers for shares and such provisions contained in any amendment to the certificate of incorporation as were necessary to effect a change, exchange, reclassification, subdivision, combination or cancellation of stock, if such change, exchange, reclassification, subdivision, combination, or cancellation has become effective); (5) as a result of the merger the constituent corporation or its successor becomes or remains a direct or indirect wholly-owned subsidiary of the holding company; (6) the directors of the constituent corporation become or remain the directors of the holding company upon the effective time of the merger; (7) the organizational documents of the surviving entity immediately following the effective time of the merger contain provisions identical to the certificate of incorporation of the constituent corporation immediately prior to the effective time of the merger (other than provisions, if any, regarding the incorporator or incorporators, the corporate or entity name, the registered office and agent, the initial board of directors and the initial subscribers for shares, references to members

504

rather than stockholders or shareholders, references to interests, units or the like rather than stock or shares, references to managers, managing members or other members of the governing body rather than directors and such provisions contained in any amendment to the certificate of incorporation as were necessary to effect a change, exchange, reclassification, subdivision, combination or cancellation of stock, if such change, exchange, reclassification, subdivision, combination or cancellation has become effective); provided, however, that (i) if the organizational documents of the surviving entity do not contain the following provisions, they shall be amended in the merger to contain provisions requiring that (A) any act or transaction by or involving the surviving entity, other than the election or removal of directors or managers, managing members or other members of the governing body of the surviving entity, that requires for its adoption under this chapter or its organizational documents the approval of the stockholders or members of the surviving entity shall, by specific reference to this subsection, require, in addition, the approval of the stockholders of the holding company (or any successor by merger), by the same vote as is required by this chapter and/or by the organizational documents of the surviving entity; provided, however, that for purposes of this clause (i)(A), any surviving entity that is not a corporation shall include in such amendment a requirement that the approval of the stockholders of the holding company be obtained for any act or transaction by or involving the surviving entity, other than the election or removal of directors or managers, managing members or other members of the governing body of the surviving entity, which would require the approval of the stockholders of the surviving entity if the surviving entity were a corporation subject to this chapter; (B) any amendment of the organizational documents of a surviving entity that is not a corporation, which amendment would, if adopted by a corporation subject to this chapter, be required to be included in the certificate of incorporation of such corporation, shall, by specific reference to this subsection, require, in addition, the approval of the stockholders of the holding company (or any successor by merger), by the same vote as is required by this chapter and/or by the organizational documents of the surviving entity; and (C) the business and affairs of a surviving entity that is not a corporation shall be managed by or under the direction of a board of directors, board of managers or other governing body consisting of individuals who are subject to the same fiduciary duties applicable to, and who are liable for breach of such duties to the same extent as, directors of a corporation subject to this chapter; and (ii) the organizational documents of the surviving entity may be amended in the merger (A) to reduce the number of classes and shares of capital stock or other equity interests or units that the surviving entity is authorized to issue and (B) to eliminate any provision authorized by § 141(d) of this title; and (8) the stockholders of the constituent corporation do not recognize gain or loss for United States federal income tax purposes as determined by the board of directors of the constituent corporation. Neither paragraph (g)(7)(i) of this section nor any provision of a surviving entity's organizational documents required by paragraph (g)(7)(i) of this section shall be deemed or construed to require approval of the stockholders of the holding company to elect or remove directors or managers, managing members or other members of the governing body of the surviving entity. The term "organizational documents", as used in paragraph (g)(7) of this section and in the preceding sentence, shall, when used in reference to a corporation, mean the certificate of incorporation of such corporation, and when used in reference to a limited liability company, mean the limited liability company agreement of such limited liability company.

As used in this subsection only, the term "holding company" means a corporation which, from its incorporation until consummation of a merger governed by this subsection, was at all times a direct or indirect wholly-owned subsidiary of the constituent corporation and whose capital stock is issued in such merger. From and after the effective time of a merger adopted by a constituent corporation by action of its board of directors and without any vote of stockholders pursuant to this subsection: (i) to the extent the restrictions of § 203 of this title applied to the constituent corporation and its stockholders at the effective time of the merger, such restrictions shall apply to the holding company and its stockholders immediately after the effective time of the merger as though it were the constituent corporation, and all shares of stock of the holding company acquired in the merger shall for purposes of § 203 of this title be deemed to have been acquired at the time that the shares of stock of the constituent corporation converted in the merger were acquired, and provided further that any stockholder who immediately prior to the effective time of the merger was not an interested stockholder within the meaning of § 203 of this title shall not solely by reason of the merger become an interested stockholder of the holding company, (ii) if the corporate name of the holding company immediately following the effective time of the merger is the same as the corporate name of the constituent corporation immediately prior to the effective time of the merger, the shares of capital stock of the holding company into which the shares of capital stock of the constituent corporation are converted in the merger shall be represented by the stock certificates that previously represented shares of capital stock of the constituent corporation and (iii) to the extent a stockholder of the constituent corporation immediately prior to the merger had standing to institute or maintain derivative litigation on behalf of the constituent corporation, nothing in this section shall be deemed to limit or extinguish such standing. If an agreement of merger is adopted by a constituent corporation by action of its board of directors and without any vote of stockholders pursuant to this subsection, the secretary or assistant secretary of the constituent corporation shall certify on the agreement that the agreement has been adopted pursuant to this subsection and that the conditions specified in the first sentence of this subsection have been satisfied, provided that such certification on the agreement shall not be required if a certificate of merger or consolidation is filed in lieu of filing the agreement. The agreement so adopted and certified shall then be filed and become effective, in accordance with § 103 of this title. Such filing shall constitute a representation by the person who executes the agreement that the facts stated in the certificate remain true immediately prior to such filing.

(h) Notwithstanding the requirements of subsection (c) of this section, unless expressly required by its certificate of incorporation, no vote of stockholders of a constituent corporation that has a class or series of stock that is listed on a national securities exchange or held of record by more than 2,000 holders immediately prior to the execution of the agreement of merger by such constituent corporation shall be necessary to authorize a merger if:

(1) The agreement of merger expressly:

a. Permits or requires such merger to be effected under this subsection; and

b. Provides that such merger shall be effected as soon as practicable following the consummation of the offer referred to in paragraph (h)(2) of this section if such merger is effected under this subsection;

(2) A corporation consummates an offer for all of the outstanding stock of such constituent corporation on the terms provided in such agreement of merger that, absent this subsection, would be entitled to vote on the adoption or rejection of the agreement of merger; provided, however, that such offer may be conditioned on the tender of a minimum number or percentage of shares of the stock of such constituent corporation, or of any class or series thereof, and such offer may exclude any excluded stock and provided further that the corporation may consummate separate offers for separate classes or series of the stock of such constituent corporation;

a.–d. [Repealed.]

(3) Immediately following the consummation of the offer referred to in paragraph (h)(2) of this section, the stock irrevocably accepted for purchase or exchange pursuant to such offer and received by the depository prior to expiration of such offer, together with the stock otherwise owned by the consummating corporation or its affiliates and any rollover stock, equals at least such percentage of the shares of stock of such constituent corporation, and of each class or series thereof, that, absent this subsection, would be required to adopt the agreement of merger by this chapter and by the certificate of incorporation of such constituent corporation;

(4) The corporation consummating the offer referred to in paragraph (h)(2) of this section merges with or into such constituent corporation pursuant to such agreement; and

(5) Each outstanding share (other than shares of excluded stock) of each class or series of stock of such constituent corporation that is the subject of and is not irrevocably accepted for purchase or exchange in the offer referred to in paragraph (h)(2) of this section is to be converted in such merger into, or into the right to receive, the same amount and kind of cash, property, rights or securities to be paid for shares of such class or series of stock of such constituent corporation irrevocably accepted for purchase or exchange in such offer.

(6) As used in this section only, the term:

a. "Affiliate" means, in respect of the corporation making the offer referred to in paragraph (h)(2) of this section, any person that (i) owns, directly or indirectly, all of the outstanding stock of such corporation or (ii) is a direct or indirect wholly-owned subsidiary of such corporation or of any person referred to in clause (i) of this definition;

b. "Consummates" (and with correlative meaning, "consummation" and "consummating") means irrevocably accepts for purchase or exchange stock tendered pursuant to an offer;

c. "Depository" means an agent, including a depository, appointed to facilitate consummation of the offer referred to in paragraph (h)(2) of this section;

d. "Excluded stock" means (i) stock of such constituent corporation that is owned at the commencement of the offer referred to in paragraph (h)(2) of this section by such constituent corporation, the corporation making the offer referred to in paragraph (h)(2) of this section, any person that owns, directly or indirectly, all of the outstanding stock of the corporation making such offer, or any direct or indirect wholly-owned subsidiary of any of the foregoing and (ii) rollover stock;

e. "Person" means any individual, corporation, partnership, limited liability company, unincorporated association or other entity;

f. "Received" (solely for purposes of paragraph (h)(3) of this section) means (a) with respect to certificated shares, physical receipt of a stock certificate accompanied by an executed letter of transmittal, (b) with respect to uncertificated shares held of record by a clearing corporation as nominee, transfer into the depository's account by means of an agent's message, and (c) with respect to uncertificated shares held of record by a person other than a clearing corporation as nominee, physical receipt of an executed letter of transmittal by the depository; provided, however, that shares shall cease to be "received" (i) with respect to certificated shares, if the certificate representing such shares was canceled prior to consummation of the offer referred to in paragraph (h)(2) of this section, or (ii) with respect to uncertificated shares, to the extent such uncertificated shares have been reduced or eliminated due to any sale of such shares prior to consummation of the offer referred to in paragraph (h)(2) of this section; and

g. "Rollover stock" means any shares of stock of such constituent corporation that are the subject of a written agreement requiring such shares to be transferred, contributed or delivered to the consummating corporation or any of its affiliates in exchange for stock or other equity interests in such consummating corporation or an affiliate thereof; *provided, however*, that such shares of stock shall cease to be rollover stock for purposes of paragraph (h)(3) of this section if, immediately prior to the time the merger becomes effective under this chapter, such shares have not been transferred, contributed or delivered to the consummating corporation or any of its affiliates pursuant to such written agreement.

If an agreement of merger is adopted without the vote of stockholders of a corporation pursuant to this subsection, the secretary or assistant secretary of the surviving corporation shall certify on the agreement that the agreement has been adopted pursuant to this subsection and that the conditions specified in this subsection (other than the condition listed in paragraph (h)(4) of this section) have been satisfied; provided that such certification on the agreement shall not be required if a certificate of merger is filed in lieu of filing the agreement. The agreement so adopted and certified shall then be filed and shall become effective, in accordance with § 103 of this title. Such filing shall constitute a representation by the person who executes the agreement that the facts stated in the certificate remain true immediately prior to such filing.

§ 252. Merger or Consolidation of Domestic and Foreign Corporations; Service of Process upon Surviving or Resulting Corporation

(a) Any 1 or more corporations of this State may merge or consolidate with 1 or more foreign corporations, unless the laws of the jurisdiction or jurisdictions under which such foreign corporation or corporations are organized prohibit such merger or consolidation. The constituent corporations may merge into a single surviving corporation, which may be any 1 of the constituent corporations, or they may consolidate into a new resulting corporation formed by the consolidation, which may be a corporation of the jurisdiction of organization of any 1 of the constituent corporations, pursuant to an agreement of merger or consolidation, as the case may be, complying and approved in accordance with this section.

(b) All the constituent corporations shall enter into an agreement of merger or consolidation. The agreement shall state:

(1) The terms and conditions of the merger or consolidation;

(2) The mode of carrying the same into effect;

(3) In the case of a merger in which the surviving corporation is a corporation of this State, such amendments or changes in the certificate of incorporation of the surviving corporation as are desired to be effected by the merger (which amendments or changes may amend and restate the certificate of incorporation of the surviving corporation in its entirety), or, if no such amendments or changes are desired, a statement that the certificate of incorporation of the surviving corporation shall be its certificate of incorporation;

(4) In the case of a consolidation in which the resulting corporation is a corporation of this State, that the certificate of incorporation of the resulting corporation shall be as is set forth in an attachment to the agreement;

(5) The manner, if any, of converting the shares of each of the constituent corporations into shares or other securities of the corporation surviving or resulting from the merger or consolidation, or of cancelling some or all of such shares, and, if any shares of any of the constituent corporations are not to remain outstanding, to be converted solely into shares or other securities of the surviving or resulting corporation or to be cancelled, the cash, property, rights or securities of any other corporation or entity which the holders of such shares are to receive in exchange for, or upon conversion of, such shares and the surrender of any certificates evidencing them, which cash, property, rights or securities of any other corporation or entity may be in addition to or in lieu of the shares or other securities of the surviving or resulting corporation;

(6) Such other details or provisions as are deemed desirable, including, without limiting the generality of the foregoing, a provision for the payment of cash in lieu of the issuance or recognition of fractional shares, rights or other securities of the surviving or resulting corporation or of any other corporation or entity the shares, rights or other securities of which are to be received in the merger or consolidation, or for some other arrangement with respect thereto, consistent with § 155 of this title; and

(7) Such other provisions or facts as shall be required to be set forth in an agreement of merger or consolidation (including any provision for amendment of the certificate of incorporation (or equivalent document) of a surviving or resulting foreign corporation) by the laws of each jurisdiction under which any of the foreign corporations are organized.

Any of the terms of the agreement of merger or consolidation may be made dependent upon facts ascertainable outside of such agreement, provided that the manner in which such facts shall operate upon the terms of the agreement is clearly and expressly set forth in the agreement of merger or consolidation. The term "facts," as used in the preceding sentence, includes, but is not limited to, the occurrence of any event, including a determination or action by any person or body, including the corporation.

(c) The agreement shall be adopted, approved, certified, executed and acknowledged by each of the constituent corporations in accordance with the laws under which it is organized, and, in the case of a corporation of this State, in the same manner as is provided in § 251 of this title. The agreement shall be filed and shall become effective for all purposes of the laws of this State when and as provided in § 251 of this title with respect to the merger or consolidation of corporations of this State. In lieu of filing the agreement of merger or consolidation, the surviving or resulting corporation may file a certificate of merger or consolidation, executed in accordance with § 103 of this title, which states:

(1) The name and jurisdiction of organization of each of the constituent corporations;

(2) That an agreement of merger or consolidation has been approved, adopted, certified, executed and acknowledged by each of the constituent corporations in accordance with this subsection;

(3) The name of the surviving or resulting corporation;

(4) In the case of a merger in which the surviving corporation is a corporation of this State, such amendments or changes in the certificate of incorporation of the surviving corporation as are desired to be effected by the merger (which amendments or changes may amend and restate the certificate of incorporation of the surviving corporation in its entirety), or, if no such amendments or changes are desired, a statement that the certificate of incorporation of the surviving corporation shall be its certificate of incorporation;

(5) In the case of a consolidation in which the resulting corporation is a corporation of this State, that the certificate of incorporation of the resulting corporation shall be as is set forth in an attachment to the certificate;

(6) That the executed agreement of consolidation or merger is on file at an office of the surviving or resulting corporation and the address thereof;

(7) That a copy of the agreement of consolidation or merger will be furnished by the surviving or resulting corporation, on request and without cost, to any stockholder of any constituent corporation;

(8) If the corporation surviving or resulting from the merger or consolidation is a corporation of this State, the authorized capital stock of each constituent corporation which is not a corporation of this State; and

(9) The agreement, if any, required by subsection (d) of this section.

(d) If the corporation surviving or resulting from the merger or consolidation is a foreign corporation, it shall agree that it may be served with process in this State in any proceeding for enforcement of any obligation of any constituent corporation of this State, as well as for enforcement of any obligation of the surviving or resulting corporation arising from the merger or consolidation, including any suit or other proceeding to enforce the right of any stockholders as determined in appraisal proceedings pursuant to § 262 of this title, and shall irrevocably appoint the Secretary of State as its agent to accept service of process in any such suit or other proceedings and shall specify the address to which a copy of such process shall be mailed by the Secretary of State. Process may be served upon the Secretary of State under this subsection by means of electronic transmission but only as prescribed by the Secretary of State. The Secretary of State is authorized to issue such rules and regulations with respect to such service as the Secretary of State deems necessary or appropriate. In the event of such service upon the Secretary of State in accordance with this subsection, the Secretary of State shall forthwith notify such surviving or resulting corporation thereof by letter, directed to such surviving or resulting corporation at its address so specified, unless such surviving or resulting corporation shall have designated in writing to the Secretary of State a different address for such purpose, in which case it shall be mailed to the last address so designated. Such letter shall be sent by a mail or courier service that includes a record of mailing or deposit with the courier and a record of delivery evidenced by the signature of the recipient. Such letter shall enclose a copy of the process and any other papers served on the Secretary of State pursuant to this subsection. It shall be the duty of the plaintiff in the event of such service to serve process and any other papers in duplicate, to notify the Secretary of State that service is being effected pursuant to this subsection and to pay the Secretary of State the sum of $50 for the use of the State, which sum shall be taxed as part of the costs in the proceeding, if the plaintiff shall prevail therein. The Secretary of State shall maintain an alphabetical record of any such service setting forth the name of the plaintiff and the defendant, the title, docket number and nature of the proceeding in which process has been served, the fact that service has been effected pursuant to this subsection, the return date thereof, and the day and hour service was made. The Secretary of State shall not be required to retain such information longer than 5 years from receipt of the service of process.

(e) Section 251(d) of this title shall apply to any merger or consolidation under this section; § 251(e) of this title shall apply to a merger under this section in which the surviving corporation is a corporation of this State; and § 251(f) and (h) of this title shall apply to any merger under this section.

§ 253. Merger of Parent Corporation and Subsidiary Corporation or Corporations

(a) In any case in which: (1)at least 90% of the outstanding shares of each class of the stock of a corporation or corporations (other than a corporation which has in its certificate of incorporation the provision required by § 251(g)(7)(i) of this title), of which class there are outstanding shares that, absent this subsection, would be entitled to vote on such merger, is owned by a corporation of this State or a foreign corporation, and (2) 1 or more of such corporations is a corporation of this State, unless the laws of the jurisdiction or jurisdictions under which the foreign corporation or corporations are organized prohibit such merger, the parent corporation may either merge the subsidiary corporation or corporations into itself and assume all of its or their obligations, or merge itself, or itself and 1 or more of such other subsidiary corporations, into 1 of the subsidiary corporations by executing, acknowledging and filing, in accordance with § 103 of this title, a certificate of such ownership and merger setting forth a copy of the resolution of its board of directors to so merge and the date of the adoption; provided, however, that in case the parent corporation shall not own all the outstanding stock of all the subsidiary corporations, parties to a merger as aforesaid, the resolution of the board of directors of the parent corporation shall state the terms and conditions of the merger, including the securities, cash, property, or rights to be issued, paid, delivered or granted by the surviving corporation upon surrender of each share of the subsidiary corporation or corporations not owned by the parent corporation, or the cancellation of some or all of such shares. Any of the terms of the resolution of the board of directors to so merge may be made dependent upon facts ascertainable outside of such resolution, provided that the manner in which such facts shall operate upon the terms of the resolution is clearly and expressly set forth in the resolution. The term "facts," as used in the preceding sentence, includes, but is not limited to, the occurrence of any event, including a determination or action by any person or body, including the corporation. If the parent corporation be not the surviving corporation, the resolution shall include provision for the pro rata issuance of stock of the surviving corporation to the holders of the stock of the parent corporation on surrender of any certificates therefor, and the certificate of ownership and merger shall state that the proposed merger has been approved by a majority of the outstanding stock of the parent corporation entitled to vote thereon at a meeting duly called and held after 20 days' notice of the purpose of the meeting mailed to each such stockholder at the stockholder's address as it appears on the records of the corporation if the parent corporation is a corporation of this State or state that the proposed merger has been adopted, approved, certified, executed and acknowledged by the parent corporation in accordance with the laws under which it is organized if the parent corporation is a foreign corporation. If the surviving corporation is a foreign corporation:

(1) Section 252(d) of this title or § 258(c) of this title, as applicable, shall also apply to a merger under this section; and

(2) The terms and conditions of the merger shall obligate the surviving corporation to provide the agreement, and take the actions, required by § 252(d) of this title or § 258(c) of this title, as applicable.

(b) If the surviving corporation is a Delaware corporation, it may change its corporate name by the inclusion of a provision to that effect in the resolution of merger adopted by the directors of the parent corporation and set forth in the certificate of ownership and merger, and upon the effective date of the merger, the name of the corporation shall be so changed.

(c) Section § 251(d) of this title shall apply to a merger under this section, and § 251(e) of this title shall apply to a merger under this section in which the surviving corporation is the subsidiary corporation and is a corporation of this State. References to "agreement of merger" in § 251(d) and (e) of this title shall mean for purposes of this subsection the resolution of merger adopted by the board of directors of the parent corporation. Any merger which effects any changes other than those authorized by this section or made applicable by this subsection shall be accomplished under § 251, § 252, § 257, or § 258 of this title. Section 262 of this title shall not apply to any merger effected under this section, except as provided in subsection (d) of this section.

(d) In the event all of the stock of a subsidiary Delaware corporation party to a merger effected under this section is not owned by the parent corporation immediately prior to the merger, the stockholders of the subsidiary Delaware corporation party to the merger shall have appraisal rights as set forth in § 262 of this title.

(e) This section shall apply to nonstock corporations if the parent corporation is such a corporation and is the surviving corporation of the merger; provided, however, that references to the directors of the parent corporation shall be deemed to be references to members of the governing body of the parent corporation, and references to the board of directors of the parent corporation shall be deemed to be references to the governing body of the parent corporation.

(f) Nothing in this section shall be deemed to authorize the merger of a corporation with a charitable nonstock corporation, if the charitable status of such charitable nonstock corporation would thereby be lost or impaired.

§ 259.   Status, Rights, Liabilities, of Constituent and Surviving or Resulting Corporations Following Merger or Consolidation

(a) When any merger or consolidation shall have become effective under this chapter, for all purposes of the laws of this State the separate existence of all the constituent corporations, or of all such constituent corporations except the one into which the other or others of such constituent corporations have been merged, as the case may be, shall cease and the constituent corporations shall become a new corporation, or be merged into 1 of such corporations, as the case may be, possessing all the rights, privileges, powers and franchises as well of a public as of a private nature, and being subject to all the restrictions, disabilities and duties of each of such corporations so merged or consolidated; and all and singular, the rights, privileges, powers and franchises of each of said corporations, and all property, real, personal and mixed, and all debts due to any of said constituent corporations on whatever account, as well for stock subscriptions as all other things in action or belonging to each of such corporations shall be vested in the corporation surviving or resulting from such merger or consolidation; and all property, rights, privileges, powers and franchises, and all and every other interest shall be thereafter as effectually the property of the surviving or resulting corporation as they were of the several and respective constituent corporations, and the title to any real estate vested by deed or otherwise, under the laws of this State, in any of such constituent corporations, shall not revert or be in any way impaired by reason of this chapter; but all rights of creditors and all liens upon any property of any of said constituent corporations shall be preserved unimpaired, and all debts, liabilities and duties of the respective constituent corporations shall thenceforth attach to said surviving or resulting corporation, and may be enforced against it to the same extent as if said debts, liabilities and duties had been incurred or contracted by it. . . .

§ 260. Powers of Corporation Surviving or Resulting from Merger or Consolidation; Issuance of Stock, Bonds or Other Indebtedness

When 2 or more corporations are merged or consolidated, the corporation surviving or resulting from the merger may issue bonds or other obligations, negotiable or otherwise, and with or without coupons or interest certificates thereto attached, to an amount sufficient with its capital stock to provide for all the payments it will be required to make, or obligations it will be required to assume, in order to effect the merger or consolidation. For the purpose of securing the payment of any such bonds and obligations, it shall be lawful for the surviving or resulting corporation to mortgage its corporate franchise, rights, privileges and property, real, personal or mixed. The surviving or resulting corporation may issue certificates of its capital stock or uncertificated stock if authorized to do so and other securities to the stockholders of the constituent corporations in exchange or payment for the original shares, in such amount as shall be necessary in accordance with the terms of the agreement of merger or consolidation in order to effect such merger or consolidation in the manner and on the terms specified in the agreement.

§ 261. Effect of Merger upon Pending Actions

Any action or proceeding, whether civil, criminal or administrative, pending by or against any corporation which is a party to a merger or consolidation shall be prosecuted as if such merger or consolidation had not taken place, or the corporation surviving or resulting from such merger or consolidation may be substituted in such action or proceeding.

§ 262. Appraisal Rights

(a) Any stockholder of a corporation of this State who holds shares of stock on the date of the making of a demand pursuant to subsection (d) of this section with respect to such shares, who continuously holds such shares through the effective date of the merger or consolidation, who has otherwise complied with subsection (d) of this section and who has neither voted in favor of the merger or consolidation nor consented thereto in writing pursuant to § 228 of this title shall be entitled to an appraisal by the Court of Chancery of the fair value of the stockholder's shares of stock under the circumstances described in subsections (b) and (c) of this section. As used in this section, the word "stockholder" means a holder of record of stock in a corporation; the words "stock" and "share" mean and include what is ordinarily meant by those words; and the words "depository receipt" mean a receipt or other instrument issued by a depository representing an interest in 1 or more shares, or fractions thereof, solely of stock of a corporation, which stock is deposited with the depository.

(b) Appraisal rights shall be available for the shares of any class or series of stock of a constituent corporation in a merger or consolidation to be effected pursuant to § 251 (other than a merger effected pursuant to § 251(g) of this title), § 252, § 254, § 255, § 256, § 257, § 258, § 263 or § 264 of this title:

(1) Provided, however, that, except as expressly provided in § 363(b) of this title, no appraisal rights under this section shall be available for the shares of any class or series of stock, which stock, or depository receipts in respect thereof, at the record date fixed to determine the stockholders entitled to receive notice of the meeting of stockholders to act upon the agreement of merger or consolidation (or, in the case of a merger pursuant to § 251(h), as of immediately prior to the execution of the agreement of merger), were either: (i) listed on a national securities exchange or (ii) held of record by more than 2,000 holders; and further provided that no appraisal rights shall be available for any shares of stock of the constituent corporation surviving a merger if the merger did not require for its approval the vote of the stockholders of the surviving corporation as provided in § 251(f) of this title.

(2) Notwithstanding paragraph (b)(1) of this section, appraisal rights under this section shall be available for the shares of any class or series of stock of a constituent corporation if the holders thereof are required by the terms of an agreement of merger or consolidation pursuant to §§ 251, 252, 254, 255, 256, 257, 258, 263 and 264 of this title to accept for such stock anything except:

a. Shares of stock of the corporation surviving or resulting from such merger or consolidation, or depository receipts in respect thereof;

b. Shares of stock of any other corporation, or depository receipts in respect thereof, which shares of stock (or depository receipts in respect thereof) or depository receipts at the effective date of the merger or consolidation will be either listed on a national securities exchange or held of record by more than 2,000 holders;

c. Cash in lieu of fractional shares or fractional depository receipts described in the foregoing paragraphs (b)(2)a. and b. of this section; or

d. Any combination of the shares of stock, depository receipts and cash in lieu of fractional shares or fractional depository receipts described in the foregoing paragraphs (b)(2)a., b. and c. of this section.

(3) In the event all of the stock of a subsidiary Delaware corporation party to a merger effected under § 253 or § 267 of this title is not owned by the parent immediately prior to the merger, appraisal rights shall be available for the shares of the subsidiary Delaware corporation.

(4) In the event of an amendment to a corporation's certificate of incorporation contemplated by § 363(a) of this title, appraisal rights shall be available as contemplated by § 363(b) of this title, and the procedures of this section, including those set forth in subsections (d) and (e) of this section, shall apply as nearly as practicable, with the word "amendment" substituted for the words "merger or consolidation," and the word "corporation" substituted for the words "constituent corporation" and/or "surviving or resulting corporation."

(c) Any corporation may provide in its certificate of incorporation that appraisal rights under this section shall be available for the shares of any class or series of its stock as a result of an amendment to its certificate of incorporation, any merger or consolidation in which the corporation is a constituent corporation or the sale of all or substantially all of the assets of the corporation. If the certificate of incorporation contains such a provision, the provisions of this section, including those set forth in subsections (d),(e), and (g) of this section, shall apply as nearly as is practicable.

(d) Appraisal rights shall be perfected as follows:

(1) If a proposed merger or consolidation for which appraisal rights are provided under this section is to be submitted for approval at a meeting of stockholders, the corporation, not less than 20 days prior to the meeting, shall notify each of its stockholders who was such on the record date for notice of such meeting (or such members who received notice in accordance with § 255(c) of this title) with respect to shares for which appraisal rights are available pursuant to subsection (b) or (c) of this section that appraisal rights are available for any or all of the shares of the constituent corporations, and shall include in such notice a copy of this section and, if 1 of the constituent corporations is a nonstock corporation, a copy of § 114 of this title. Each stockholder electing to demand the appraisal of such stockholder's shares shall deliver to the corporation, before the taking of the vote on the merger or consolidation, a written demand for appraisal of such stockholder's shares. Such demand will be sufficient if it reasonably informs the corporation of the identity of the stockholder and that the

stockholder intends thereby to demand the appraisal of such stockholder's shares. A proxy or vote against the merger or consolidation shall not constitute such a demand. A stockholder electing to take such action must do so by a separate written demand as herein provided. Within 10 days after the effective date of such merger or consolidation, the surviving or resulting corporation shall notify each stockholder of each constituent corporation who has complied with this subsection and has not voted in favor of or consented to the merger or consolidation of the date that the merger or consolidation has become effective; or

(2) If the merger or consolidation was approved pursuant to § 228, § 251(h), § 253, or § 267 of this title, then either a constituent corporation before the effective date of the merger or consolidation or the surviving or resulting corporation within 10 days thereafter shall notify each of the holders of any class or series of stock of such constituent corporation who are entitled to appraisal rights of the approval of the merger or consolidation and that appraisal rights are available for any or all shares of such class or series of stock of such constituent corporation, and shall include in such notice a copy of this section and, if 1 of the constituent corporations is a nonstock corporation, a copy of § 114 of this title. Such notice may, and, if given on or after the effective date of the merger or consolidation, shall, also notify such stockholders of the effective date of the merger or consolidation. Any stockholder entitled to appraisal rights may, within 20 days after the date of mailing of such notice or, in the case of a merger approved pursuant to § 251(h) of this title, within the later of the consummation of the offer contemplated by § 251(h) of this title and 20 days after the date of mailing of such notice, demand in writing from the surviving or resulting corporation the appraisal of such holder's shares. Such demand will be sufficient if it reasonably informs the corporation of the identity of the stockholder and that the stockholder intends thereby to demand the appraisal of such holder's shares. If such notice did not notify stockholders of the effective date of the merger or consolidation, either (i) each such constituent corporation shall send a second notice before the effective date of the merger or consolidation notifying each of the holders of any class or series of stock of such constituent corporation that are entitled to appraisal rights of the effective date of the merger or consolidation or (ii) the surviving or resulting corporation shall send such a second notice to all such holders on or within 10 days after such effective date; provided, however, that if such second notice is sent more than 20 days following the sending of the first notice or, in the case of a merger approved pursuant to § 251(h) of this title, later than the later of the consummation of the offer contemplated by § 251(h) of this title and 20 days following the sending of the first notice, such second notice need only be sent to each stockholder who is entitled to appraisal rights and who has demanded appraisal of such holder's shares in accordance with this subsection. An affidavit of the secretary or assistant secretary or of the transfer agent of the corporation that is required to give either notice that such notice has been given shall, in the absence of fraud, be prima facie evidence of the facts stated therein. For purposes of determining the stockholders entitled to receive either notice, each constituent corporation may fix, in advance, a record date that shall be not more than 10 days prior to the date the notice is given, provided, that if the notice is given on or after the effective date of the merger or consolidation, the record date shall be such effective date. If no record date is fixed and the notice is given prior to the effective date, the record date shall be the close of business on the day next preceding the day on which the notice is given.

(e) Within 120 days after the effective date of the merger or consolidation, the surviving or resulting corporation or any stockholder who has complied with subsections (a) and (d) of this section hereof and who is otherwise entitled to appraisal rights, may commence an appraisal proceeding by filing a petition in the Court of Chancery demanding a determination of the value of the stock of all such stockholders. Notwithstanding the foregoing, at any time within 60 days after the effective date of the merger or consolidation, any stockholder who has not commenced an appraisal proceeding or joined that proceeding as a named party shall have the right to withdraw such stockholder's demand for appraisal and to accept the terms offered upon the merger or consolidation. Within 120 days after the effective date of the merger or consolidation, any stockholder who has complied with the requirements of subsections (a) and (d) of this section hereof, upon written request, shall be entitled to receive from the corporation surviving the merger or resulting from the consolidation a statement setting forth the aggregate number of shares not voted in favor of the merger or consolidation (or, in the case of a merger approved pursuant to § 251(h) of this title, the aggregate number of shares (other than any excluded stock (as defined in § 251(h)(6)d. of this title)) that were the subject of, and were not tendered into, and accepted for purchase or exchange in, the offer referred to in § 251(h)(2)), and, in either case, with respect to which demands for appraisal have been received and the aggregate number of holders of such shares. Such written statement shall be mailed to the stockholder within 10 days after such stockholder's written request for such a statement is received by the surviving or resulting corporation or within 10 days after expiration of the period for delivery of demands for appraisal under subsection (d) of this section hereof, whichever is later. Notwithstanding subsection (a) of this section, a person who is the beneficial owner of shares of such stock held either in a voting trust or by a nominee on behalf of such person may, in such person's own name, file a petition or request from the corporation the statement described in this subsection.

(f) Upon the filing of any such petition by a stockholder, service of a copy thereof shall be made upon the surviving or resulting corporation, which shall within 20 days after such service file in the office of the Register in Chancery in which the petition was filed a duly verified list containing the names and addresses of all stockholders who have demanded payment for their shares and with whom agreements as to the value of their shares have not been reached by the surviving or resulting corporation. If the petition shall be filed by the surviving or resulting corporation, the petition shall be accompanied by such a duly verified list. The Register in Chancery, if so ordered by the Court, shall give notice of the time and place fixed for the hearing of such petition by registered or certified mail to the surviving or resulting corporation and to the stockholders shown on the list at the addresses therein stated. Such notice shall also be given by 1 or more publications at least 1 week before the day of the hearing, in a newspaper of general circulation published in the City of Wilmington, Delaware or such publication as the Court deems advisable. The forms of the notices by mail and by publication shall be approved by the Court, and the costs thereof shall be borne by the surviving or resulting corporation.

(g) At the hearing on such petition, the Court shall determine the stockholders who have complied with this section and who have become entitled to appraisal rights. The Court may require the stockholders who have demanded an appraisal for their shares and who hold stock represented by certificates to submit their certificates of stock to the Register in Chancery for notation thereon of the pendency of the appraisal proceedings; and if any stockholder fails to comply with such direction, the Court may dismiss the proceedings as to such stockholder. If immediately before the merger or consolidation the shares of the class or series of stock of the constituent corporation as to which appraisal rights are available were listed on a national securities exchange, the Court shall dismiss the proceedings as to all holders of such shares who are otherwise entitled to appraisal rights unless (1) the total number of shares entitled to appraisal exceeds 1% of the outstanding shares of the class or series eligible for appraisal, (2) the value of the consideration provided in the merger or consolidation for such total number of shares exceeds $1 million, or (3) the merger was approved pursuant to § 253 or § 267 of this title.

(h) After the Court determines the stockholders entitled to an appraisal, the appraisal proceeding shall be conducted in accordance with the rules of the Court of Chancery, including any rules specifically governing appraisal proceedings. Through such proceeding the Court shall determine the fair value of the shares exclusive of any element of value arising from the accomplishment or expectation of the merger or consolidation, together with interest, if any, to be paid upon the amount determined to be the fair value. In determining such fair value, the Court shall take into account all relevant factors. Unless the Court in its discretion determines otherwise for good cause shown, and except as provided in this subsection, interest from the effective date of the merger through the date of payment of the judgment shall be compounded quarterly and shall accrue at 5% over the Federal Reserve discount rate (including any surcharge) as established from time to time during the period between the effective date of the merger and the date of payment of the judgment. At any time before the entry of judgment in the proceedings, the surviving corporation may pay to each stockholder entitled to appraisal an amount in cash, in which case interest shall accrue thereafter as provided herein only upon the sum of (1) the difference, if any, between the amount so paid and the fair value of the shares as determined by the Court, and (2) interest theretofore accrued, unless paid at that time. Upon application by the surviving or resulting corporation or by any stockholder entitled to participate in the appraisal proceeding, the Court may, in its discretion, proceed to trial upon the appraisal prior to the final determination of the stockholders entitled to an appraisal. Any stockholder whose name appears on the list filed by the surviving or resulting corporation pursuant to subsection (f) of this section and who has submitted such stockholder's certificates of stock to the Register in Chancery, if such is required, may participate fully in all proceedings until it is finally determined that such stockholder is not entitled to appraisal rights under this section.

(i) The Court shall direct the payment of the fair value of the shares, together with interest, if any, by the surviving or resulting corporation to the stockholders entitled thereto. Payment shall be so made to each such stockholder, in the case of holders of uncertificated stock forthwith, and the case of holders of shares represented by certificates upon the surrender to the corporation of the certificates representing such stock. The Court's decree may be enforced as other decrees in the Court of Chancery may be enforced, whether such surviving or resulting corporation be a corporation of this State or of any state.

(j) The costs of the proceeding may be determined by the Court and taxed upon the parties as the Court deems equitable in the circumstances. Upon application of a stockholder, the Court may order all or a portion of the expenses incurred by any stockholder in connection with the appraisal proceeding, including, without limitation, reasonable attorney's fees and the fees and expenses of experts, to be charged pro rata against the value of all the shares entitled to an appraisal.

(k) From and after the effective date of the merger or consolidation, no stockholder who has demanded appraisal rights as provided in subsection (d) of this section shall be entitled to vote such stock for any purpose or to receive payment of dividends or other distributions on the stock (except dividends or other distributions payable to stockholders of record at a date which is prior to the effective date of the merger or consolidation); provided, however, that if no petition for an appraisal shall be filed within the time provided in subsection (e) of this section, or if such stockholder shall deliver to the surviving or resulting corporation a written withdrawal of such stockholder's demand for an appraisal and an acceptance of the merger or consolidation, either within 60 days after the effective date of the merger or consolidation as provided in subsection (e) of this section or thereafter with the written approval of the corporation, then the right of such stockholder to an appraisal shall cease. Notwithstanding the foregoing, no appraisal proceeding in the Court of Chancery shall be dismissed as to any stockholder without the approval of the Court, and such approval may be conditioned upon such terms as the Court deems just; provided, however that this provision shall not affect the right of any stockholder who has not commenced an appraisal proceeding or joined that proceeding as a named party to withdraw such stockholder's demand for appraisal and to accept the terms offered upon the merger or consolidation within 60 days after the effective date of the merger or consolidation, as set forth in subsection (e) of this section.

(*l*) The shares of the surviving or resulting corporation to which the shares of such objecting stockholders would have been converted had they assented to the merger or consolidation shall have the status of authorized and unissued shares of the surviving or resulting corporation.

§ 263. Merger or Consolidation of Domestic Corporations and Partnerships; Service of Process upon Surviving or Resulting Corporation or Partnership

(a) Any 1 or more corporations of this State may merge or consolidate with 1 or more partnerships (whether general (including a limited liability partnership) or limited (including a limited liability limited partnership)), unless the laws of the jurisdiction or jurisdictions under which such partnership or partnerships are formed prohibit such merger or consolidation. Such corporation or corporations and such 1 or more partnerships may merge with or into a surviving corporation, which may be any 1 of such corporations, or they may merge with or into a surviving partnership, which may be any 1 of such partnerships, or they may consolidate into a new resulting corporation, which corporation shall be a corporation of this State, or a partnership formed pursuant to an agreement of merger or consolidation, as the case may be, complying and approved in accordance with this section. The term "partnership" as used in this section includes any partnership (whether general (including a limited liability partnership) or limited (including a limited liability limited partnership)) formed under the laws of this State or the laws of any other jurisdiction.

(b) Each such corporation and partnership shall enter into a written agreement of merger or consolidation. The agreement shall state:

(1) The terms and conditions of the merger or consolidation;

(2) The mode of carrying the same into effect;

(3) In the case of a merger in which the surviving entity is a corporation of this State, such amendments or changes in the certificate of incorporation of the surviving corporation as are desired to be effected by the merger (which amendments or changes may amend and restate the certificate of

incorporation of the surviving corporation in its entirety), or, if no such amendments or changes are desired, a statement that the certificate of incorporation of the surviving corporation shall be its certificate of incorporation;

(4) In the case of a consolidation in which the resulting entity is a corporation of this State, that the certificate of incorporation of the resulting corporation shall be as is set forth in an attachment to the agreement;

(5) The manner, if any, of converting the shares of stock of each such corporation and the partnership interests of each such partnership into shares, partnership interests or other securities of the entity surviving or resulting from such merger or consolidation or of cancelling some or all of such shares or interests, and if any shares of any such corporation or any partnership interests of any such partnership are not to remain outstanding, to be converted solely into shares, partnership interests or other securities of the entity surviving or resulting from such merger or consolidation or to be cancelled, the cash, property, rights or securities of any other corporation or entity which the holders of such shares or partnership interests are to receive in exchange for, or upon conversion of such shares or partnership interests and the surrender of any certificates evidencing them, which cash, property, rights or securities of any other corporation or entity may be in addition to or in lieu of shares, partnership interests or other securities of the entity surviving or resulting from such merger or consolidation;

(6) Such other details or provisions as are deemed desirable, including, without limiting the generality of the foregoing, a provision for the payment of cash in lieu of the issuance or recognition of fractional shares, rights, other securities or interests of the surviving or resulting corporation or partnership or of any other corporation or entity the shares, rights, other securities or interests of which are to be received in the merger or consolidation, or for some other arrangement with respect thereto, consistent with § 155 of this title; and

(7) Such other provisions or facts as shall be required to be set forth in an agreement of merger or consolidation (including any provision for amendment of the partnership agreement and statement of partnership existence or certificate of limited partnership (or equivalent documents) of the surviving partnership) by the laws of each jurisdiction under which any of the partnerships are formed.

Any of the terms of the agreement of merger or consolidation may be made dependent upon facts ascertainable outside of such agreement, provided that the manner in which such facts shall operate upon the terms of the agreement is clearly and expressly set forth in the agreement of merger or consolidation. The term "facts," as used in the preceding sentence, includes, but is not limited to, the occurrence of any event, including a determination or action by any person or body, including the corporation.

(c) The agreement required by subsection (b) of this section shall be adopted, approved, certified, executed and acknowledged by each of the corporations in the same manner as is provided in § 251 or § 255 of this title and, in the case of the partnerships, in accordance with their partnership agreements and in accordance with the laws of the jurisdiction under which they are formed. If the surviving or resulting entity is a partnership, in addition to any other approvals, each stockholder of a merging corporation who will become a general partner of the surviving or resulting partnership must approve the agreement of merger or consolidation. The agreement shall be filed and shall become effective for all purposes of the laws of this State when and as provided in § 251 or § 255 of this title with respect to the merger or consolidation of corporations of this State. In lieu of filing the agreement of merger or consolidation, the surviving or resulting corporation or partnership may file a certificate of merger or consolidation, executed in accordance with § 103 of this title, if the surviving or resulting entity is a corporation, or by a general partner, if the surviving or resulting entity is a partnership, which states:

(1) The name, jurisdiction of formation or organization and type of entity of each of the constituent entities;

(2) That an agreement of merger or consolidation has been approved, adopted, certified, executed and acknowledged by each of the constituent entities in accordance with this subsection;

(3) The name of the surviving or resulting corporation or partnership;

(4) In the case of a merger in which a corporation is the surviving entity, such amendments or changes in the certificate of incorporation of the surviving corporation as are desired to be effected by the merger (which amendments or changes may amend and restate the certificate of incorporation of the surviving corporation in its entirety), or, if no such amendments or changes are desired, a statement that the certificate of incorporation of the surviving corporation shall be its certificate of incorporation;

(5) In the case of a consolidation in which a corporation is the resulting entity, that the certificate of incorporation of the resulting corporation shall be as is set forth in an attachment to the certificate;

(6) That the executed agreement of consolidation or merger is on file at an office of the surviving or resulting corporation or partnership and the address thereof;

(7) That a copy of the agreement of consolidation or merger will be furnished by the surviving or resulting entity, on request and without cost, to any stockholder of any constituent corporation or any partner of any constituent partnership; and

(8) The agreement, if any, required by subsection (d) of this section.

(d) If the entity surviving or resulting from the merger or consolidation is a partnership formed under the laws of a jurisdiction other than this State, it shall agree that it may be served with process in this State in any proceeding for enforcement of any obligation of any constituent corporation or partnership of this State, as well as for enforcement of any obligation of the surviving or resulting corporation or partnership arising from the merger or consolidation, including any suit or other proceeding to enforce the right of any stockholders as determined in appraisal proceedings pursuant to § 262 of this title, and shall irrevocably appoint the Secretary of State as its agent to accept service of process in any such suit or other proceedings and shall specify the address to which a copy of such process shall be mailed by the Secretary of State. Process may be served upon the Secretary of State under this subsection by means of electronic transmission but only as prescribed by the Secretary of State. The Secretary of State is authorized to issue such rules and regulations with respect to such service as the Secretary of State deems necessary or appropriate. In the event of such service upon the Secretary of State in accordance with this subsection, the Secretary of State shall forthwith notify such surviving or resulting corporation or partnership thereof by letter, directed to such surviving or resulting corporation or partnership at its address so specified, unless such surviving or resulting corporation or partnership shall have designated in writing to the Secretary of State a different address for such purpose, in which case it shall be mailed to the last address so designated. Such letter shall be sent by a mail or courier service that includes a record of mailing or deposit with the courier and a record of delivery evidenced by the signature of the recipient. Such letter shall enclose a copy of the process and any other papers served on the Secretary of State pursuant to this subsection. It shall be the duty of the plaintiff in the event of such service to serve process and any other papers in duplicate, to notify the Secretary of State that service is being effected pursuant to this subsection and to pay the Secretary of State the sum of $50 for the use of the State, which sum shall be taxed as part of the costs in the proceeding, if the plaintiff shall prevail therein. The Secretary of State shall maintain an alphabetical record of any such service setting forth the name of the plaintiff and the defendant, the title, docket number and nature of the proceeding in which process has been served upon the Secretary of State, the fact that service has been effected pursuant to this subsection, the return date thereof, and the day and hour service was made. The Secretary of State shall not be required to retain such information longer than 5 years from receipt of the service of process.

(e) Sections 251(d)–(f), 255(c) (second sentence) and (d)–(f), 259–261 and 328 of this title shall, insofar as they are applicable, apply to mergers or consolidations between corporations and partnerships. . . .

§ 264. Merger or Consolidation of Domestic Corporations and Limited Liability Companies; Service of Process upon Surviving or Resulting Corporation or Limited Liability Company

(a) Any 1 or more corporations of this State may merge or consolidate with 1 or more limited liability companies, unless the laws of the jurisdiction or jurisdictions under which such limited liability company or limited liability companies are formed prohibit such merger or consolidation. Such corporation or corporations and such 1 or more limited liability companies may merge with or into a surviving corporation, which may be any 1 of such corporations, or they may merge with or into a surviving limited liability company, which may be any 1 of such limited liability companies, or they may consolidate into a new resulting corporation, which corporation shall be a corporation of this State, or a limited liability company formed pursuant to an agreement of merger or consolidation, as the case may be, complying and approved in accordance with this section. The term "limited liability company" as used in this section includes any limited liability company formed under the laws of this State or the laws of any other jurisdiction.

(b) Each such corporation and limited liability company shall enter into a written agreement of merger or consolidation. The agreement shall state:

(1) The terms and conditions of the merger or consolidation;

(2) The mode of carrying the same into effect;

(3) In the case of a merger in which the surviving entity is a corporation of this State, such amendments or changes in the certificate of incorporation of the surviving corporation as are desired to be effected by the merger (which amendments or changes may amend and restate the certificate of incorporation of the surviving corporation in its entirety), or, if no such amendments or changes are desired, a statement that the certificate of incorporation of the surviving corporation shall be its certificate of incorporation;

(4) In the case of a consolidation in which the resulting entity is a corporation of this State, that the certificate of incorporation of the resulting corporation shall be as is set forth in an attachment to the agreement;

(5) The manner, if any, of converting the shares of stock of each such corporation and the limited liability company interests of each such limited liability company into shares, limited liability company interests or other securities of the entity surviving or resulting from such merger or consolidation or of cancelling some or all of such shares or interests, and if any shares of any such corporation or any limited liability company interests of any such limited liability company are not to remain outstanding, to be converted solely into shares, limited liability company interests or other securities of the entity surviving or resulting from such merger or consolidation or to be cancelled, the cash, property, rights or securities of any other corporation or entity which the holders of such shares or limited liability company interests are to receive in exchange for, or upon conversion of such shares or limited liability company interests and the surrender of any certificates evidencing them, which cash, property, rights or securities of any other corporation or entity may be in addition to or in lieu of shares, limited liability company interests or other securities of the entity surviving or resulting from such merger or consolidation;

(6) Such other details or provisions as are deemed desirable, including, without limiting the generality of the foregoing, a provision for the payment of cash in lieu of the issuance or recognition of fractional shares, rights, other securities or interests of the surviving or resulting corporation or limited liability company or of any other corporation or entity the shares, rights, other securities or interests of which are to be received in the merger or consolidation, or for some other arrangement with respect thereto, consistent with § 155 of this title; and

(7) Such other provisions or facts as shall be required to be set forth in an agreement of merger or consolidation (including any provision for amendment of the limited liability company agreement and certificate of formation (or equivalent documents) of the surviving limited liability company) by the laws of each jurisdiction under which any of the limited liability companies are formed.

Any of the terms of the agreement of merger or consolidation may be made dependent upon facts ascertainable outside of such agreement, provided that the manner in which such facts shall operate upon the terms of the agreement is clearly and expressly set forth in the agreement of merger or consolidation. The term "facts," as used in the preceding sentence, includes, but is not limited to, the occurrence of any event, including a determination or action by any person or body, including the corporation.

(c) The agreement required by subsection (b) of this section shall be adopted, approved, certified, executed and acknowledged by each of the corporations in the same manner as is provided in § 251 or § 255 of this title and, in the case of the limited liability companies, in accordance with their limited liability company agreements and in accordance with the laws of the jurisdiction under which they are formed. The agreement shall be filed and shall become effective for all purposes of the laws of this State when and as provided in § 251 or § 255 of this title with respect to the merger or consolidation of corporations of this State. In lieu of filing the agreement of merger or consolidation, the surviving or resulting corporation or limited liability company may file a certificate of merger or consolidation, executed in accordance with § 103 of this title, if the surviving or resulting entity is a corporation, or by an authorized person, if the surviving or resulting entity is a limited liability company, which states:

(1) The name and jurisdiction of formation or organization of each of the constituent entities;

(2) That an agreement of merger or consolidation has been approved, adopted, certified, executed and acknowledged by each of the constituent entities in accordance with this subsection;

(3) The name of the surviving or resulting corporation or limited liability company;

(4) In the case of a merger in which a corporation is the surviving entity, such amendments or changes in the certificate of incorporation of the surviving corporation as are desired to be effected by the merger (which amendments or changes may amend and restate the certificate of incorporation of the surviving corporation in its entirety), or, if no such amendments or changes are desired, a statement that the certificate of incorporation of the surviving corporation shall be its certificate of incorporation;

(5) In the case of a consolidation in which a corporation is the resulting entity, that the certificate of incorporation of the resulting corporation shall be as is set forth in an attachment to the certificate;

(6) That the executed agreement of consolidation or merger is on file at an office of the surviving or resulting corporation or limited liability company and the address thereof;

(7) That a copy of the agreement of consolidation or merger will be furnished by the surviving or resulting entity, on request and without cost, to any stockholder of any constituent corporation or any member of any constituent limited liability company; and

(8) The agreement, if any, required by subsection (d) of this section.

(d) If the entity surviving or resulting from the merger or consolidation is a limited liability company formed under the laws of a jurisdiction other than this State, it shall agree that it may be served with process in this State in any proceeding for enforcement of any obligation of any constituent corporation or limited liability company of this State, as well as for enforcement of any obligation of the surviving or resulting corporation or limited liability company arising from the merger or consolidation, including any suit or other proceeding to enforce the right of any stockholders as determined in appraisal proceedings pursuant to the provisions of § 262 of this title, and shall irrevocably appoint the Secretary of State as its agent to accept service of process in any such suit or other proceedings and shall specify the address to which a copy of such process shall be mailed by the Secretary of State. Process may be served upon the Secretary of State under this subsection by means of electronic transmission but only as prescribed by the Secretary of State. The Secretary of State is authorized to issue such rules and regulations with respect to such service as the Secretary of State deems necessary or appropriate. In the event of such service upon the Secretary of State in accordance with this subsection, the Secretary of State shall forthwith notify such surviving or resulting corporation or limited liability company thereof by letter, directed to such surviving or resulting corporation or limited liability company at its address so specified, unless such surviving or resulting corporation or limited liability company shall have designated in writing to the Secretary of State a different address for such purpose, in which case it shall be mailed to the last address so designated. Such letter shall be sent by a mail or courier service that includes a record of mailing or deposit with the courier and a record of delivery evidenced by the signature of the recipient. Such letter shall enclose a copy of the process and any other papers served on the Secretary of State pursuant to this subsection. It shall be the duty of the plaintiff in the event of such service to serve process and any other papers in duplicate, to notify the Secretary of State that service is being effected pursuant to this subsection and to pay the Secretary of State the sum of $50 for the use of the State, which sum shall be taxed as part of the costs in the proceeding, if the plaintiff shall prevail therein. The Secretary of State shall maintain an alphabetical record of any such service setting forth the name of the plaintiff and the defendant, the title, docket number and nature of the proceeding in which process has been served upon the Secretary of State, the fact that service has been effected pursuant to this subsection, the return date thereof, and the day and hour service was made. The Secretary of State shall not be required to retain such information longer than 5 years from receipt of the service of process.

(e) Sections 251(d)–(f), 255(c) (second sentence) and (d)–(f), 259–261 and 328 of this title shall, insofar as they are applicable, apply to mergers or consolidations between corporations and limited liability companies. . . .

§ 265.   Conversion of Other Entities to a Domestic Corporation

(a) As used in this section, the term "other entity" means a limited liability company, statutory trust, business trust or association, real estate investment trust, common-law trust or any other unincorporated business including a partnership (whether general (including a limited liability partnership) or limited (including a limited liability limited partnership)), or a foreign corporation.

(b) Any other entity may convert to a corporation of this State by complying with subsection (h) of this section and filing in the office of the Secretary of State:

(1) A certificate of conversion to corporation that has been executed in accordance with subsection (i) of this section and filed in accordance with § 103 of this title; and

(2) A certificate of incorporation that has been executed, acknowledged and filed in accordance with § 103 of this title.

Each of the certificates required by this subsection (b) shall be filed simultaneously in the office of the Secretary of State and, if such certificates are not to become effective upon their filing as permitted by § 103(d) of this title, then each such certificate shall provide for the same effective date or time in accordance with § 103(d) of this title.

(c) The certificate of conversion to corporation shall state:

(1) The date on which and jurisdiction where the other entity was first created, incorporated, formed or otherwise came into being and, if it has changed, its jurisdiction immediately prior to its conversion to a domestic corporation;

(2) The name and type of entity of the other entity immediately prior to the filing of the certificate of conversion to corporation; and

(3) The name of the corporation as set forth in its certificate of incorporation filed in accordance with subsection (b) of this section.

(4) [Repealed.]

(d) Upon the effective time of the certificate of conversion to corporation and the certificate of incorporation, the other entity shall be converted to a corporation of this State and the corporation shall thereafter be subject to all of the provisions of this title, except that notwithstanding § 106 of this title, the existence of the corporation shall be deemed to have commenced on the date the other entity commenced its existence in the jurisdiction in which the other entity was first created, formed, incorporated or otherwise came into being.

(e) The conversion of any other entity to a corporation of this State shall not be deemed to affect any obligations or liabilities of the other entity incurred prior to its conversion to a corporation of this State or the personal liability of any person incurred prior to such conversion.

(f) When an other entity has been converted to a corporation of this State pursuant to this section, the corporation of this State shall, for all purposes of the laws of the State of Delaware, be deemed to be the same entity as the converting other entity. When any conversion shall have become effective under this section, for all purposes of the laws of the State of Delaware, all of the rights, privileges and powers of the other entity that has converted, and all property, real, personal and mixed, and all debts due to such other entity, as well as all other things and causes of action belonging to such other entity, shall remain vested in the domestic corporation to which such other entity has converted and shall be the property of such domestic corporation and the title to any real property vested by deed or otherwise in such other entity shall not revert or be in any way impaired by reason of this chapter; but all rights of creditors and all liens upon any property of such other entity shall be preserved unimpaired, and all debts, liabilities and duties of the other entity that has converted shall remain attached to the corporation of this State to which such other entity has converted, and may be enforced against it to the same extent as if said debts, liabilities and duties had originally been incurred or contracted by it in its capacity as a corporation of this State. The rights, privileges, powers and interests in property of the other entity, as well as the debts, liabilities and duties of the other entity, shall not be deemed, as a consequence of the conversion, to have been transferred to the domestic corporation to which such other entity has converted for any purpose of the laws of the State of Delaware.

(g) Unless otherwise agreed for all purposes of the laws of the State of Delaware or as required under applicable non-Delaware law, the converting other entity shall not be required to wind up its affairs or pay its liabilities and distribute its assets, and the conversion shall not be deemed to constitute a dissolution of such other entity and shall constitute a continuation of the existence of the converting other entity in the form of a corporation of this State.

(h) Prior to filing a certificate of conversion to corporation with the office of the Secretary of State, the conversion shall be approved in the manner provided for by the document, instrument, agreement or other writing, as the case may be, governing the internal affairs of the other entity and the conduct of its business or by applicable law, as appropriate, and a certificate of incorporation shall be approved by the same authorization required to approve the conversion.

(i) The certificate of conversion to corporation shall be signed by any person who is authorized to sign the certificate of conversion to corporation on behalf of the other entity.

(j) In connection with a conversion hereunder, rights or securities of, or interests in, the other entity which is to be converted to a corporation of this State may be exchanged for or converted into cash, property, or shares of stock, rights or securities of such corporation of this State or, in addition to or in lieu thereof, may be exchanged for or converted into cash, property, or shares of stock, rights or securities of or interests in another domestic corporation or other entity or may be cancelled.

§ 266.   Conversion of a Domestic Corporation to Other Entities

(a) A corporation of this State may, upon the authorization of such conversion in accordance with this section, convert to a limited liability company, statutory trust, business trust or association, real estate investment trust, common-law trust or any other unincorporated business including a partnership (whether general (including a limited liability partnership) or limited (including a limited liability limited partnership)) or a foreign corporation.

(b) The board of directors of the corporation which desires to convert under this section shall adopt a resolution approving such conversion, specifying the type of entity into which the corporation shall be converted and recommending the approval of such conversion by the stockholders of the corporation. Such resolution shall be submitted to the stockholders of the corporation at an annual or special meeting. Due notice of the time, and purpose of the meeting shall be mailed to each holder of stock, whether voting or nonvoting, of the corporation at the address of the stockholder as it appears on the records of the corporation, at least 20 days prior to the date of the meeting. At the meeting, the resolution shall be considered and a vote taken for its adoption or rejection. If all outstanding shares of stock of the corporation, whether voting or nonvoting, shall be voted for the adoption of the resolution, the conversion shall be authorized.

(1)–(4) [Repealed.]

(c) If a corporation shall convert in accordance with this section to another entity organized, formed or created under the laws of a jurisdiction other than the State of Delaware, the corporation shall file with the Secretary of State a certificate of conversion executed in accordance with § 103 of this title, which certifies:

(1) The name of the corporation, and if it has been changed, the name under which it was originally incorporated;

(2) The date of filing of its original certificate of incorporation with the Secretary of State;

(3) The name and jurisdiction of the entity to which the corporation shall be converted;

(4) That the conversion has been approved in accordance with the provisions of this section;

(5) The agreement of the corporation that it may be served with process in the State of Delaware in any action, suit or proceeding for enforcement of any obligation of the corporation arising while it was a corporation of this State, and that it irrevocably appoints the Secretary of State as its agent to accept service of process in any such action, suit or proceeding; and

(6) The address to which a copy of the process referred to in paragraph (c)(5) of this section shall be mailed to it by the Secretary of State. Process may be served upon the Secretary of State in accordance with paragraph (c)(5) of this section by means of electronic transmission but only as prescribed by the Secretary of State. The Secretary of State is authorized to issue such rules and regulations with respect to such service as the Secretary of State deems necessary or appropriate. In the event of such service upon the Secretary of State in accordance with paragraph (c)(5) of this section, the Secretary of State shall forthwith notify such corporation that has converted out of the State of Delaware by letter, directed to such corporation that has converted out of the State of Delaware at the address so specified, unless such corporation shall have designated in writing to the Secretary of State a different address for such purpose, in which case it shall be mailed to the last address designated. Such letter shall be sent by a mail or courier service that includes a record of mailing or deposit with the courier and a record of delivery evidenced by the signature of the recipient. Such letter shall enclose a copy of the process and any other papers served on the Secretary of State pursuant to this subsection. It shall be the duty of the plaintiff in the event of such service to serve process and any other papers in duplicate, to notify the Secretary of State that service is being effected pursuant to this subsection and to pay the Secretary of State the sum of $50 for the use of the State, which sum shall be taxed as part of the costs in the proceeding, if the plaintiff shall prevail therein. The Secretary of State shall maintain an alphabetical record of any such service setting forth the name of the plaintiff and the defendant, the title, docket number and nature of the proceeding in which process has been served, the fact that service has been effected pursuant to this subsection, the return date thereof, and the day and hour service was made. The Secretary of State shall not be required to retain such information longer than 5 years from receipt of the service of process.

(d) Upon the filing in the Office of the Secretary of State of a certificate of conversion to non-Delaware entity in accordance with subsection (c) of this section or upon the future effective date or time of the certificate of conversion to non-Delaware entity and payment to the Secretary of State of all fees prescribed under this title, the Secretary of State shall certify that the corporation has filed all documents and paid all fees required by this title, and thereupon the corporation shall cease to exist as a corporation of this State at the time the certificate of conversion becomes effective in accordance with § 103 of this title. Such certificate of the Secretary of State shall be prima facie evidence of the conversion by such corporation out of the State of Delaware.

(e) The conversion of a corporation out of the State of Delaware in accordance with this section and the resulting cessation of its existence as a corporation of this State pursuant to a certificate of conversion to non-Delaware entity shall not be deemed to affect any obligations or liabilities of the corporation incurred prior to such conversion or the personal liability of any person incurred prior to such conversion, nor shall it be deemed to affect the choice of law applicable to the corporation with respect to matters arising prior to such conversion.

(f) Unless otherwise provided in a resolution of conversion adopted in accordance with this section, the converting corporation shall not be required to wind up its affairs or pay its liabilities and distribute its assets, and the conversion shall not constitute a dissolution of such corporation.

(g) In connection with a conversion of a domestic corporation to another entity pursuant to this section, shares of stock, of the corporation of this State which is to be converted may be exchanged for or converted into cash, property, rights or securities of, or interests in, the entity to which the corporation of this State is being converted or, in addition to or in lieu thereof, may be exchanged for or converted into cash, property, shares of stock, rights or securities of, or interests in, another domestic corporation or other entity or may be cancelled.

(h) When a corporation has been converted to another entity or business form pursuant to this section, the other entity or business form shall, for all purposes of the laws of the State of Delaware, be deemed to be the same entity as the corporation. When any conversion shall have become effective under this section, for all purposes of the laws of the State of Delaware, all of the rights, privileges and powers of the corporation that has converted, and all property, real, personal and mixed, and all debts due to such corporation, as well as all other things and causes of action belonging to such corporation, shall remain vested in the other entity or business form to which such corporation has converted and shall be the property of such other entity or business form, and the title to any real property vested by deed or otherwise in such corporation shall not revert or be in any way impaired by reason of this chapter; but all rights of creditors and all liens upon any property of such corporation shall be preserved unimpaired, and all debts, liabilities and duties of the corporation that has converted shall remain attached to the other entity or business form to which such corporation has converted, and may be enforced against it to the same extent as if said debts, liabilities and duties had originally been incurred or contracted by it in its capacity as such other entity or business form. The rights, privileges, powers and interest in property of the corporation that has converted, as well as the debts, liabilities and duties of such corporation, shall not be deemed, as a consequence of the conversion, to have been transferred to the other entity or business form to which such corporation has converted for any purpose of the laws of the State of Delaware.

(i) No vote of stockholders of a corporation shall be necessary to authorize a conversion if no shares of the stock of such corporation shall have been issued prior to the adoption by the board of directors of the resolution approving the conversion. . . .

§ 267.   Merger of Parent Entity and Subsidiary Corporation or Corporations

(a) In any case in which: (1) at least 90% of the outstanding shares of each class of the stock of a corporation or corporations (other than a corporation which has in its certificate of incorporation the provision required by § 251(g)(7)(i) of this title), of which class there are outstanding shares that, absent this subsection, would be entitled to vote on such merger, is owned by an entity, and (2) 1 or more of such corporations is a corporation of this State, unless the laws of the jurisdiction or jurisdictions under which such entity or such foreign corporations are formed or organized prohibit such merger, the entity having such stock ownership may either merge the corporation or corporations into itself and assume all of its or their obligations, or merge itself, or itself and 1 or more of such corporations, into 1 of the other corporations by (a) authorizing such merger in accordance with such entity's governing documents and the laws of the jurisdiction under which such entity is formed or organized and (b) acknowledging and filing with the Secretary of State, in accordance with § 103 of this title, a certificate of such ownership and merger certifying (i) that such merger was authorized in accordance with such entity's governing documents and the laws of the jurisdiction under which such entity is formed or organized, such certificate executed in accordance with such entity's governing documents and in accordance with the laws of the jurisdiction under which such entity is formed or organized and (ii) the type of entity of each constituent entity to the merger; provided, however, that in case the entity shall not own all the outstanding stock of all the corporations, parties to a merger as aforesaid, (A) the certificate of ownership and merger shall state the terms and conditions of the merger, including the securities, cash, property, or rights to be issued, paid, delivered or granted by the surviving constituent party upon surrender of each share of the corporation or corporations not owned by the entity, or the cancellation of some or all of such shares and (B) such terms and conditions of the merger may not result in a holder of stock in a corporation becoming a general partner in a surviving entity that is a partnership (other than a limited liability partnership or a limited liability limited partnership). Any of the terms of the merger may be made dependent upon facts ascertainable outside of the certificate of ownership and merger, provided that the manner in which such facts shall operate upon the terms of the merger is clearly and expressly set forth in the certificate of ownership and merger. The term "facts," as used in the preceding sentence, includes, but is not limited to, the occurrence of any event, including a determination or action by any person or body, including the entity. If the surviving constituent party is an entity formed or organized under the laws of a jurisdiction other than this State, (1) § 252(d) of this title shall also apply to a merger under this section; if the surviving constituent party is the entity, the word "corporation" where applicable, as used in § 252(d) of this title, shall be deemed to include an entity as defined herein; and (2) the terms and conditions of the merger shall obligate the surviving constituent party to provide the agreement, and take the actions, required by § 252(d) of this title.

(b) Sections 259, 261, and 328 of this title shall, insofar as they are applicable, apply to a merger under this section, and §§ 260 and 251(e) of this title shall apply to a merger under this section in which the surviving constituent party is a corporation of this State. For purposes of this subsection, references to "agreement of merger" in § 251(e) of this title shall mean the terms and conditions of the merger set forth in the certificate of ownership and merger, and references to "corporation" in §§ 259–261 of this title, and § 328 of this title shall be deemed to include the entity, as applicable. Section 262 of this title shall not apply to any merger effected under this section, except as provided in subsection (c) of this section.

(c) In the event all of the stock of a Delaware corporation party to a merger effected under this section is not owned by the entity immediately prior to the merger, the stockholders of such Delaware corporation party to the merger shall have appraisal rights as set forth in § 262 of this title.

(d) As used in this section only, the term:

(1) "Constituent party" means an entity or corporation to be merged pursuant to this section;

(2) "Entity" means a partnership (whether general (including a limited liability partnership) or limited (including a limited liability limited partnership)), limited liability company, any association of the kind commonly known as a joint-stock association or joint-stock company and any unincorporated association, trust or enterprise having members or having outstanding shares of stock or other evidences of financial or beneficial interest therein, whether formed or organized by agreement or under statutory authority or otherwise and whether formed or organized under the laws of this State or the laws of any other jurisdiction; and

(3) "Governing documents" means a partnership agreement, limited liability company agreement, articles of association or any other instrument containing the provisions by which an entity is formed or organized.

SUBCHAPTER X. SALE OF ASSETS, DISSOLUTION AND WINDING UP

§ 271.   Sale, Lease or Exchange of Assets; Consideration; Procedure

(a) Every corporation may at any meeting of its board of directors or governing body sell, lease or exchange all or substantially all of its property and assets, including its goodwill and its corporate franchises, upon such terms and conditions and for such consideration, which may consist in whole or in part of money or other property, including shares of stock in, and/or other securities of, any other corporation or corporations, as its board of directors or governing body deems expedient and for the best interests of the corporation, when and as authorized by a resolution adopted by the holders of a majority of the outstanding stock of the corporation entitled to vote thereon or, if the corporation is a nonstock corporation, by a majority of the members having the right to vote for the election of the members of the governing body and any other members entitled to vote thereon under the certificate of incorporation or the bylaws of such corporation, at a meeting duly called upon at least 20 days' notice. The notice of the meeting shall state that such a resolution will be considered.

(b) Notwithstanding authorization or consent to a proposed sale, lease or exchange of a corporation's property and assets by the stockholders or members, the board of directors or governing body may abandon such proposed sale, lease or exchange without further action by the stockholders or members, subject to the rights, if any, of third parties under any contract relating thereto.

(c) For purposes of this section only, the property and assets of the corporation include the property and assets of any subsidiary of the corporation. As used in this subsection, "subsidiary" means any entity wholly-owned and controlled, directly or indirectly, by the corporation and includes, without limitation, corporations, partnerships, limited partnerships, limited liability partnerships, limited liability companies, and/or statutory trusts. Notwithstanding subsection (a) of this section, except to the extent the certificate of incorporation otherwise provides, no resolution by stockholders or members shall be required for a sale, lease or exchange of property and assets of the corporation to a subsidiary.

§ 272.   Mortgage or Pledge of Assets

The authorization or consent of stockholders to the mortgage or pledge of a corporation's property and assets shall not be necessary, except to the extent that the certificate of incorporation otherwise provides.

§ 273.   Dissolution of Joint Venture Corporation Having 2 Stockholders

(a) If the stockholders of a corporation of this State, having only 2 stockholders each of which own 50% of the stock therein, shall be engaged in the prosecution of a joint venture and if such stockholders shall be unable to agree upon the desirability of discontinuing such joint venture and disposing of the assets used in such venture, either stockholder may, unless otherwise provided in the certificate of incorporation of the corporation or in a written agreement between the stockholders, file with the Court of Chancery a petition stating that it desires to discontinue such joint venture and to dispose of the assets used in such venture in accordance with a plan to be agreed upon by both stockholders or that, if no such plan shall be agreed upon by both stockholders, the corporation be dissolved. Such petition shall have attached thereto a copy of the proposed plan of discontinuance and distribution and a certificate stating that copies of such petition and plan have been transmitted in writing to the other stockholder and to the directors and officers of such corporation. The petition and certificate shall be executed and acknowledged in accordance with § 103 of this title.

(b) Unless both stockholders file with the Court of Chancery:

(1) Within 3 months of the date of the filing of such petition, a certificate similarly executed and acknowledged stating that they have agreed on such plan, or a modification thereof, and

(2) Within 1 year from the date of the filing of such petition, a certificate similarly executed and acknowledged stating that the distribution provided by such plan had been completed,

the Court of Chancery may dissolve such corporation and may by appointment of 1 or more trustees or receivers with all the powers and title of a trustee or receiver appointed under § 279 of this title, administer and wind up its affairs. Either or both of the above periods may be extended by agreement of the stockholders, evidenced by a certificate similarly executed, acknowledged and filed with the Court of Chancery prior to the expiration of such period.

(c) In the case of a charitable nonstock corporation, the petitioner shall provide a copy of any petition referred to in subsection (a) of this section to the Attorney General of the State of Delaware within 1 week of its filing with the Court of Chancery.

§ 275.   Dissolution Generally; Procedure

(a) If it should be deemed advisable in the judgment of the board of directors of any corporation that it should be dissolved, the board, after the adoption of a resolution to that effect by a majority of the whole board at any meeting called for that purpose, shall cause notice of the adoption of the resolution and of a meeting of stockholders to take action upon the resolution to be mailed to each stockholder entitled to vote thereon as of the record date for determining the stockholders entitled to notice of the meeting.

(b) At the meeting a vote shall be taken upon the proposed dissolution. If a majority of the outstanding stock of the corporation entitled to vote thereon shall vote for the proposed dissolution, a certification of dissolution shall be filed with the Secretary of State pursuant to subsection (d) of this section.

(c) Dissolution of a corporation may also be authorized without action of the directors if all the stockholders entitled to vote thereon shall consent in writing and a certificate of dissolution shall be filed with the Secretary of State pursuant to subsection (d) of this section.

(d) If dissolution is authorized in accordance with this section, a certificate of dissolution shall be executed, acknowledged and filed, and shall become effective, in accordance with § 103 of this title. Such certificate of dissolution shall set forth:

(1) The name of the corporation;

(2) The date dissolution was authorized;

(3) That the dissolution has been authorized by the board of directors and stockholders of the corporation, in accordance with subsections (a) and (b) of this section, or that the dissolution has been authorized by all of the stockholders of the corporation entitled to vote on a dissolution, in accordance with subsection (c) of this section;

(4) The names and addresses of the directors and officers of the corporation; and

(5) The date of filing of the corporation's original certificate of incorporation with the Secretary of State.

(e) The resolution authorizing a proposed dissolution may provide that notwithstanding authorization or consent to the proposed dissolution by the stockholders, or the members of a nonstock corporation pursuant to § 276 of this title, the board of directors or governing body may abandon such proposed dissolution without further action by the stockholders or members.

(f) Upon a certificate of dissolution becoming effective in accordance with § 103 of this title, the corporation shall be dissolved.

§ 278. Continuation of Corporation After Dissolution for Purposes of Suit and Winding Up Affairs

All corporations, whether they expire by their own limitation or are otherwise dissolved, shall nevertheless be continued, for the term of 3 years from such expiration or dissolution or for such longer period as the Court of Chancery shall in its discretion direct, bodies corporate for the purpose of prosecuting and defending suits, whether civil, criminal or administrative, by or against them, and of enabling them gradually to settle and close their business, to dispose of and convey their property, to discharge their liabilities and to distribute to their stockholders any remaining assets, but not for the purpose of continuing the business for which the corporation was organized. With respect to any action, suit or proceeding begun by or against the corporation either prior to or within 3 years after the date of its expiration or dissolution, the action shall not abate by reason of the dissolution of the corporation; the corporation shall, solely for the purpose of such action, suit or proceeding, be continued as a body corporate beyond the 3-year period and until any judgments, orders or decrees therein shall be fully executed, without the necessity for any special direction to that effect by the Court of Chancery.

Sections 279 through 282 of this title shall apply to any corporation that has expired by its own limitation, and when so applied, all references in those sections to a dissolved corporation or dissolution shall include a corporation that has expired by its own limitation and to such expiration, respectively.

§ 279. Trustees or Receivers for Dissolved Corporations; Appointment; Powers; Duties

When any corporation organized under this chapter shall be dissolved in any manner whatever, the Court of Chancery, on application of any creditor, stockholder or director of the corporation, or any other person who shows good cause therefor, at any time, may either appoint 1 or more of the directors of the corporation to be trustees, or appoint 1 or more persons to be receivers, of and for the corporation, to take charge of the corporation's property, and to collect the debts and property due and belonging to the corporation, with power to prosecute and defend, in the name of the corporation, or otherwise, all such suits as may be necessary or proper for the purposes aforesaid, and to appoint an agent or agents under them, and to do all other acts which might be done by the corporation, if in being, that may be necessary for the final settlement of the unfinished business of the corporation. The powers of the trustees or receivers may be continued as long as the Court of Chancery shall think necessary for the purposes aforesaid.

§ 280. Notice to Claimants; Filing of Claims

(a)(1) After a corporation has been dissolved in accordance with the procedures set forth in this chapter, the corporation or any successor entity may give notice of the dissolution, requiring all persons having a claim against the corporation other than a claim against the corporation in a pending action, suit or proceeding to which the corporation is a party to present their claims against the corporation in accordance with such notice. Such notice shall state:

   a. That all such claims must be presented in writing and must contain sufficient information reasonably to inform the corporation or successor entity of the identity of the claimant and the substance of the claim;

   b. The mailing address to which such a claim must be sent;

   c. The date by which such a claim must be received by the corporation or successor entity, which date shall be no earlier than 60 days from the date thereof; and

   d. That such claim will be barred if not received by the date referred to in paragraph (a)(1)c. of this section; and

e. That the corporation or a successor entity may make distributions to other claimants and the corporation's stockholders or persons interested as having been such without further notice to the claimant; and

f. The aggregate amount, on an annual basis, of all distributions made by the corporation to its stockholders for each of the 3 years prior to the date the corporation dissolved.

Such notice shall also be published at least once a week for 2 consecutive weeks in a newspaper of general circulation in the county in which the office of the corporation's last registered agent in this State is located and in the corporation's principal place of business and, in the case of a corporation having $10,000,000 or more in total assets at the time of its dissolution, at least once in all editions of a daily newspaper with a national circulation. On or before the date of the first publication of such notice, the corporation or successor entity shall mail a copy of such notice by certified or registered mail, return receipt requested, to each known claimant of the corporation including persons with claims asserted against the corporation in a pending action, suit or proceeding to which the corporation is a party.

(2) Any claim against the corporation required to be presented pursuant to this subsection is barred if a claimant who was given actual notice under this subsection does not present the claim to the dissolved corporation or successor entity by the date referred to in paragraph (a)(1)c. of this section.

(3) A corporation or successor entity may reject, in whole or in part, any claim made by a claimant pursuant to this subsection by mailing notice of such rejection by certified or registered mail, return receipt requested, to the claimant within 90 days after receipt of such claim and, in all events, at least 150 days before the expiration of the period described in § 278 of this title; provided however, that in the case of a claim filed pursuant to § 295 of this title against a corporation or successor entity for which a receiver or trustee has been appointed by the Court of Chancery the time period shall be as provided in § 296 of this title, and the 30-day appeal period provided for in § 296 of this title shall be applicable. A notice sent by a corporation or successor entity pursuant to this subsection shall state that any claim rejected therein will be barred if an action, suit or proceeding with respect to the claim is not commenced within 120 days of the date thereof, and shall be accompanied by a copy of §§ 278–283 of this title and, in the case of a notice sent by a court-appointed receiver or trustee and as to which a claim has been filed pursuant to § 295 of this title, copies of §§ 295 and 296 of this title.

(4) A claim against a corporation is barred if a claimant whose claim is rejected pursuant to paragraph (a)(3) of this section does not commence an action, suit or proceeding with respect to the claim no later than 120 days after the mailing of the rejection notice.

(b)(1) A corporation or successor entity electing to follow the procedures described in subsection (a) of this section shall also give notice of the dissolution of the corporation to persons with contractual claims contingent upon the occurrence or nonoccurrence of future events or otherwise conditional or unmatured, and request that such persons present such claims in accordance with the terms of such notice. Provided however, that as used in this section and in § 281 of this title, the term "contractual claims" shall not include any implied warranty as to any product manufactured, sold, distributed or handled by the dissolved corporation. Such notice shall be in substantially the form, and sent and published in the same manner, as described in paragraph (a)(1) of this section.

(2) The corporation or successor entity shall offer any claimant on a contract whose claim is contingent, conditional or unmatured such security as the corporation or successor entity determines is sufficient to provide compensation to the claimant if the claim matures. The corporation or successor entity shall mail such offer to the claimant by certified or registered mail, return receipt requested, within 90 days of receipt of such claim and, in all events, at least 150 days before the expiration of the period described in § 278 of this title. If the claimant offered such security does not deliver in writing to the corporation or successor entity a notice rejecting the offer within 120 days after receipt of such offer for security, the claimant shall be deemed to have accepted such security as the sole source from which to satisfy the claim against the corporation.

(c)(1) A corporation or successor entity which has given notice in accordance with subsection (a) of this section shall petition the Court of Chancery to determine the amount and form of security that will be reasonably likely to be sufficient to provide compensation for any claim against the corporation which is the subject of a pending action, suit or proceeding to which the corporation is a party other than a claim barred pursuant to subsection (a) of this section.

(2) A corporation or successor entity which has given notice in accordance with subsections (a) and (b) of this section shall petition the Court of Chancery to determine the amount and form of security that will be sufficient to provide compensation to any claimant who has rejected the offer for security made pursuant to paragraph (b)(2) of this section.

(3) A corporation or successor entity which has given notice in accordance with subsection (a) of this section shall petition the Court of Chancery to determine the amount and form of security which will be reasonably likely to be sufficient to provide compensation for claims that have not been made known to the corporation or that have not arisen but that, based on facts known to the corporation or successor entity, are likely to arise or to become known to the corporation or successor entity within 5 years after the date of dissolution or such longer period of time as the Court of Chancery may determine not to exceed 10 years after the date of dissolution. The Court of Chancery may appoint a guardian ad litem in respect of any such proceeding brought under this subsection. The reasonable fees and expenses of such guardian, including all reasonable expert witness fees, shall be paid by the petitioner in such proceeding.

(d) The giving of any notice or making of any offer pursuant to this section shall not revive any claim then barred or constitute acknowledgment by the corporation or successor entity that any person to whom such notice is sent is a proper claimant and shall not operate as a waiver of any defense or counterclaim in respect of any claim asserted by any person to whom such notice is sent.

(e) As used in this section, the term "successor entity" shall include any trust, receivership or other legal entity governed by the laws of this State to which the remaining assets and liabilities of a dissolved corporation are transferred and which exists solely for the purposes of prosecuting and defending suits, by or against the dissolved corporation, enabling the dissolved corporation to settle and close the business of the dissolved corporation, to dispose of and convey the property of the dissolved corporation, to discharge the liabilities of the dissolved corporation and to distribute to the dissolved corporation's stockholders any remaining assets, but not for the purpose of continuing the business for which the dissolved corporation was organized.

(f) The time periods and notice requirements of this section shall, in the case of a corporation or successor entity for which a receiver or trustee has been appointed by the Court of Chancery, be subject to variation by, or in the manner provided in, the Rules of the Court of Chancery. . . .

§ 281.   Payment and Distribution to Claimants and Stockholders

(a) A dissolved corporation or successor entity which has followed the procedures described in § 280 of this title:

(1) Shall pay the claims made and not rejected in accordance with § 280(a) of this title,

(2) Shall post the security offered and not rejected pursuant to § 280(b)(2) of this title,

(3) Shall post any security ordered by the Court of Chancery in any proceeding under § 280(c) of this title, and

(4) Shall pay or make provision for all other claims that are mature, known and uncontested or that have been finally determined to be owing by the corporation or such successor entity.

Such claims or obligations shall be paid in full and any such provision for payment shall be made in full if there are sufficient assets. If there are insufficient assets, such claims and obligations shall be paid or provided for according to their priority, and, among claims of equal priority, ratably to the extent of assets legally available therefor. Any remaining assets shall be distributed to the stockholders of the dissolved corporation; provided, however, that such distribution shall not be made before the expiration of 150 days from the date of the last notice of rejections given pursuant to § 280(a)(3) of this title. In the absence of actual fraud, the judgment of the directors of the dissolved corporation or the governing persons of such successor entity as to the provision made for the payment of all obligations under paragraph (a)(4) of this section shall be conclusive.

(b) A dissolved corporation or successor entity which has not followed the procedures described in § 280 of this title shall, prior to the expiration of the period described in § 278 of this title, adopt a plan of distribution pursuant to which the dissolved corporation or successor entity (i) shall pay or make reasonable provision to pay all claims and obligations, including all contingent, conditional or unmatured contractual claims known to the corporation or such successor entity, (ii) shall make such provision as will be reasonably likely to be sufficient to provide compensation for any claim against the corporation which is the subject of a pending action, suit or proceeding to which the corporation is a party and (iii) shall make such provision as will be reasonably likely to be sufficient to provide compensation for claims that have not been made known to the corporation or that have not arisen but that, based on facts known to the corporation or successor entity, are likely to arise or to become known to the corporation or successor entity within 10 years after the date of dissolution. The plan of distribution shall provide that such claims shall be paid in full and any such provision for payment made shall be made in full if there are sufficient assets. If there are insufficient assets, such plan shall provide that such claims and obligations shall be paid or provided for according to their priority and, among claims of equal priority, ratably to the extent of assets legally available therefor. Any remaining assets shall be distributed to the stockholders of the dissolved corporation.

(c) Directors of a dissolved corporation or governing persons of a successor entity which has complied with subsection (a) or (b) of this section shall not be personally liable to the claimants of the dissolved corporation.

(d) As used in this section, the term "successor entity" has the meaning set forth in § 280(e) of this title.

(e) The term "priority," as used in this section, does not refer either to the order of payments set forth in paragraph (a)(1)–(4) of this section or to the relative times at which any claims mature or are reduced to judgment. . . .

§ 282. Liability of Stockholders of Dissolved Corporations

(a) A stockholder of a dissolved corporation the assets of which were distributed pursuant to § 281(a) or (b) of this title shall not be liable for any claim against the corporation in an amount in excess of such stockholder's pro rata share of the claim or the amount so distributed to such stockholder, whichever is less.

(b) A stockholder of a dissolved corporation the assets of which were distributed pursuant to § 281(a) of this title shall not be liable for any claim against the corporation on which an action, suit or proceeding is not begun prior to the expiration of the period described in § 278 of this title.

(c) The aggregate liability of any stockholder of a dissolved corporation for claims against the dissolved corporation shall not exceed the amount distributed to such stockholder in dissolution.

§ 283. Jurisdiction

The Court of Chancery shall have jurisdiction of any application prescribed in this subchapter and of all questions arising in the proceedings thereon, and may make such orders and decrees and issue injunctions therein as justice and equity shall require.

§ 284. Revocation or Forfeiture of Charter; Proceedings

(a) Upon motion by the Attorney General, the Court of Chancery shall have jurisdiction to revoke or forfeit the charter of any corporation for abuse, misuse or nonuse of its corporate powers, privileges or franchises. The Attorney General shall proceed for this purpose by complaint in the Court of Chancery.

(b) The Court of Chancery shall have power, by appointment of trustees, receivers or otherwise, to administer and wind up the affairs of any corporation whose charter shall be revoked or forfeited by the Court of Chancery under this section, and to make such orders and decrees with respect thereto as shall be just and equitable respecting its affairs and assets and the rights of its stockholders and creditors.

(c) No proceeding shall be instituted under this section for nonuse of any corporation's powers, privileges or franchises during the first 2 years after its incorporation.

SUBCHAPTER XIII. SUITS AGAINST CORPORATIONS, DIRECTORS, OFFICERS OR STOCKHOLDERS

§ 325. Actions Against Officers, Directors or Stockholders to Enforce Liability of Corporation; Unsatisfied Judgment Against Corporation

(a) When the officers, directors or stockholders of any corporation shall be liable by the provisions of this chapter to pay the debts of the corporation, or any part thereof, any person to whom they are liable may have an action, at law or in equity, against any 1 or more of them, and the complaint shall state the claim against the corporation, and the ground on which the plaintiff expects to charge the defendants personally.

(b) No suit shall be brought against any officer, director or stockholder for any debt of a corporation of which such person is an officer, director or stockholder, until judgment be obtained therefor against the corporation and execution thereon returned unsatisfied.

§ 327. Stockholder's Derivative Action; Allegation of Stock Ownership

In any derivative suit instituted by a stockholder of a corporation, it shall be averred in the complaint that the plaintiff was a stockholder of the corporation at the time of the transaction of which such stockholder complains or that such stockholder's stock thereafter devolved upon such stockholder by operation of law.

§ 328. Effect of Liability of Corporation on Impairment of Certain Transactions

The liability of a corporation of this State, or the stockholders, directors or officers thereof, or the rights or remedies of the creditors thereof, or of persons doing or transacting business with the corporation, shall not in any way be lessened or impaired by the sale of its assets, or by the increase or decrease in the capital stock of the corporation, or by its merger or consolidation with 1 or more corporations or by any change or amendment in its certificate of incorporation.

§ 329. Defective Organization of Corporation as Defense

(a) No corporation of this State and no person sued by any such corporation shall be permitted to assert the want of legal organization as a defense to any claim.

(b) This section shall not be construed to prevent judicial inquiry into the regularity or validity of the organization of a corporation, or its lawful possession of any corporate power it may assert in any other suit or proceeding where its corporate existence or the power to exercise the corporate rights it asserts is challenged, and evidence tending to sustain the challenge shall be admissible in any such suit or proceeding.

SUBCHAPTER XIV. CLOSE CORPORATIONS; SPECIAL PROVISIONS

§ 341. Law Applicable to Close Corporation

(a) This subchapter applies to all close corporations, as defined in § 342 of this title. Unless a corporation elects to become a close corporation under this subchapter in the manner prescribed in this subchapter, it shall be subject in all respects to this chapter, except this subchapter.

(b) This chapter shall be applicable to all close corporations, as defined in § 342 of this title, except insofar as this subchapter otherwise provides.

§ 342. Close Corporation Defined; Contents of Certificate of Incorporation

(a) A close corporation is a corporation organized under this chapter whose certificate of incorporation contains the provisions required by § 102 of this title and, in addition, provides that:

(1) All of the corporation's issued stock of all classes, exclusive of treasury shares, shall be represented by certificates and shall be held of record by not more than a specified number of persons, not exceeding 30; and

(2) All of the issued stock of all classes shall be subject to 1 or more of the restrictions on transfer permitted by § 202 of this title; and

(3) The corporation shall make no offering of any of its stock of any class which would constitute a "public offering" within the meaning of the United States Securities Act of 1933 [15 U.S.C. § 77a et seq.] as it may be amended from time to time.

(b) The certificate of incorporation of a close corporation may set forth the qualifications of stockholders, either by specifying classes of persons who shall be entitled to be holders of record of stock of any class, or by specifying classes of persons who shall not be entitled to be holders of stock of any class or both.

(c) For purposes of determining the number of holders of record of the stock of a close corporation, stock which is held in joint or common tenancy or by the entireties shall be treated as held by 1 stockholder.

§ 343. Formation of a Close Corporation

A close corporation shall be formed in accordance with §§ 101, 102 and 103 of this title, except that:

(1) Its certificate of incorporation shall contain a heading stating the name of the corporation and that it is a close corporation; and

(2) Its certificate of incorporation shall contain the provisions required by § 342 of this title.

§ 344. Election of Existing Corporation to Become a Close Corporation

Any corporation organized under this chapter may become a close corporation under this subchapter by executing, acknowledging and filing, in accordance with § 103 of this title, a certificate of amendment of its certificate of incorporation which shall contain a statement that it elects to become a close corporation, the provisions required by § 342 of this title to appear in the certificate of incorporation of a close corporation, and a heading stating the name of the corporation and that it is a close corporation. Such amendment shall be adopted in accordance with the requirements of § 241 or 242 of this title, except that it must be approved by a vote of the holders of record of at least $2/3$ of the shares of each class of stock of the corporation which are outstanding.

§ 345. Limitations on Continuation of Close Corporation Status

A close corporation continues to be such and to be subject to this subchapter until:

(1) It files with the Secretary of State a certificate of amendment deleting from its certificate of incorporation the provisions required or permitted by § 342 of this title to be stated in the certificate of incorporation to qualify it as a close corporation; or

(2) Any 1 of the provisions or conditions required or permitted by § 342 of this title to be stated in a certificate of incorporation to qualify a corporation as a close corporation has in fact been breached and neither the corporation nor any of its stockholders takes the steps required by § 348 of this title to prevent such loss of status or to remedy such breach.

§ 346. Voluntary Termination of Close Corporation Status by Amendment of Certificate of Incorporation; Vote Required

(a) A corporation may voluntarily terminate its status as a close corporation and cease to be subject to this subchapter by amending its certificate of incorporation to delete therefrom the additional provisions required or permitted by § 342 of this title to be stated in the certificate of incorporation of a close corporation. Any such amendment shall be adopted and shall become effective in accordance with § 242 of this title, except that it must be approved by a vote of the holders of record of at least $2/3$ of the shares of each class of stock of the corporation which are outstanding.

(b) The certificate of incorporation of a close corporation may provide that on any amendment to terminate its status as a close corporation, a vote greater than $2/3$ or a vote of all shares of any class shall be required; and if the certificate of incorporation contains such a provision, that provision shall not be amended, repealed or modified by any vote less than that required to terminate the corporation's status as a close corporation.

§ 347. Issuance or Transfer of Stock of a Close Corporation in Breach of Qualifying Conditions

(a) If stock of a close corporation is issued or transferred to any person who is not entitled under any provision of the certificate of incorporation permitted by § 342(b) of this title to be a holder of record of stock of such corporation, and if the certificate for such stock conspicuously notes the qualifications of the persons entitled to be holders of record thereof, such person is conclusively presumed to have notice of the fact of such person's ineligibility to be a stockholder.

(b) If the certificate of incorporation of a close corporation states the number of persons, not in excess of 30, who are entitled to be holders of record of its stock, and if the certificate for such stock conspicuously states such number, and if the issuance or transfer of stock to any person would cause the stock to be held by more than such number of persons, the person to whom such stock is issued or transferred is conclusively presumed to have notice of this fact.

(c) If a stock certificate of any close corporation conspicuously notes the fact of a restriction on transfer of stock of the corporation, and the restriction is one which is permitted by § 202 of this title, the transferee of the stock is conclusively presumed to have notice of the fact that such person has acquired stock in violation of the restriction, if such acquisition violates the restriction.

(d) Whenever any person to whom stock of a close corporation has been issued or transferred has, or is conclusively presumed under this section to have, notice either:

(1) That such person is a person not eligible to be a holder of stock of the corporation, or

(2) That transfer of stock to such person would cause the stock of the corporation to be held by more than the number of persons permitted by its certificate of incorporation to hold stock of the corporation, or

(3) That the transfer of stock is in violation of a restriction on transfer of stock,

the corporation may, at its option, refuse to register transfer of the stock into the name of the transferee.

(e) Subsection (d) of this section shall not be applicable if the transfer of stock, even though otherwise contrary to subsection (a), (b) or (c) of this section has been consented to by all the stockholders of the close corporation, or if the close corporation has amended its certificate of incorporation in accordance with § 346 of this title.

(f) The term "transfer," as used in this section, is not limited to a transfer for value.

(g) The provisions of this section do not in any way impair any rights of a transferee regarding any right to rescind the transaction or to recover under any applicable warranty express or implied.

§ 348. Involuntary Termination of Close Corporation Status; Proceeding to Prevent Loss of Status

(a) If any event occurs as a result of which 1 or more of the provisions or conditions included in a close corporation's certificate of incorporation pursuant to § 342 of this title to qualify it as a close corporation has been breached, the corporation's status as a close corporation under this subchapter shall terminate unless:

(1) Within 30 days after the occurrence of the event, or within 30 days after the event has been discovered, whichever is later, the corporation files with the Secretary of State a certificate, executed and acknowledged in accordance with § 103 of this title, stating that a specified provision or condition included in its certificate of incorporation pursuant to § 342 of this title to qualify it as a close corporation has ceased to be applicable, and furnishes a copy of such certificate to each stockholder; and

(2) The corporation concurrently with the filing of such certificate takes such steps as are necessary to correct the situation which threatens its status as a close corporation, including, without limitation, the refusal to register the transfer of stock which has been wrongfully transferred as provided by § 347 of this title, or a proceeding under subsection (b) of this section.

(b) The Court of Chancery, upon the suit of the corporation or any stockholder, shall have jurisdiction to issue all orders necessary to prevent the corporation from losing its status as a close corporation, or to restore its status as a close corporation by enjoining or setting aside any act or threatened act on the part of the corporation or a stockholder which would be inconsistent with any of the provisions or conditions required or permitted by § 342 of this title to be stated in the certificate of incorporation of a close corporation, unless it is an act approved in accordance with § 346 of this title. The Court of Chancery may enjoin or set aside any transfer or threatened transfer of stock of a close corporation which is contrary to the terms of its certificate of incorporation or of any transfer restriction permitted by § 202 of this title, and may enjoin any public offering, as defined in § 342 of this title, or threatened public offering of stock of the close corporation.

§ 349. Corporate Option Where a Restriction on Transfer of a Security Is Held Invalid

If a restriction on transfer of a security of a close corporation is held not to be authorized by § 202 of this title, the corporation shall nevertheless have an option, for a period of 30 days after the judgment setting aside the restriction becomes final, to acquire the restricted security at a price which is agreed upon by the parties, or if no agreement is reached as to price, then at the fair value as determined by the Court of Chancery. In order to determine fair value, the Court may appoint an appraiser to receive evidence and report to the Court such appraiser's findings and recommendation as to fair value.

§ 350. Agreements Restricting Discretion of Directors

A written agreement among the stockholders of a close corporation holding a majority of the outstanding stock entitled to vote, whether solely among themselves or with a party not a stockholder, is not invalid, as between the parties to the agreement, on the ground that it so relates to the conduct of the business and affairs of the corporation as to restrict or interfere with the discretion or powers of the board of directors. The effect of any such agreement shall be to relieve the directors and impose upon the stockholders who are parties to the agreement the liability for managerial acts or omissions which is imposed on directors to the extent and so long as the discretion or powers of the board in its management of corporate affairs is controlled by such agreement.

§ 351. Management by Stockholders

The certificate of incorporation of a close corporation may provide that the business of the corporation shall be managed by the stockholders of the corporation rather than by a board of directors. So long as this provision continues in effect:

(1) No meeting of stockholders need be called to elect directors;

(2) Unless the context clearly requires otherwise, the stockholders of the corporation shall be deemed to be directors for purposes of applying provisions of this chapter; and

(3) The stockholders of the corporation shall be subject to all liabilities of directors.

Such a provision may be inserted in the certificate of incorporation by amendment if all incorporators and subscribers or all holders of record of all of the outstanding stock, whether or not having voting power, authorize such a provision. An amendment to the certificate of incorporation to delete such a provision shall be adopted by a vote of the holders of a majority of all outstanding stock of the corporation, whether or not otherwise entitled to vote. If the certificate of incorporation contains a provision authorized by this section, the existence of such provision shall be noted conspicuously on the face or back of every stock certificate issued by such corporation.

§ 352. Appointment of Custodian for Close Corporation

(a) In addition to § 226 of this title respecting the appointment of a custodian for any corporation, the Court of Chancery, upon application of any stockholder, may appoint 1 or more persons to be custodians, and, if the corporation is insolvent, to be receivers, of any close corporation when:

(1) Pursuant to § 351 of this title the business and affairs of the corporation are managed by the stockholders and they are so divided that the business of the corporation is suffering or is threatened with irreparable injury and any remedy with respect to such deadlock provided in the certificate of incorporation or bylaws or in any written agreement of the stockholders has failed; or

(2) The petitioning stockholder has the right to the dissolution of the corporation under a provision of the certificate of incorporation permitted by § 355 of this title.

(b) In lieu of appointing a custodian for a close corporation under this section or § 226 of this title the Court of Chancery may appoint a provisional director, whose powers and status shall be as provided in § 353 of this title if the Court determines that it would be in the best interest of the corporation. Such appointment shall not preclude any subsequent order of the Court appointing a custodian for such corporation.

§ 353. Appointment of a Provisional Director in Certain Cases

(a) Notwithstanding any contrary provision of the certificate of incorporation or the bylaws or agreement of the stockholders, the Court of Chancery may appoint a provisional director for a close corporation if the directors are so divided respecting the management of the corporation's business and affairs that the votes required for action by the board of directors cannot be obtained with the consequence that the business and affairs of the corporation can no longer be conducted to the advantage of the stockholders generally.

(b) An application for relief under this section must be filed (1) by at least one half of the number of directors then in office, (2) by the holders of at least one third of all stock then entitled to elect directors, or, (3) if there be more than 1 class of stock then entitled to elect 1 or more directors, by the holders of two thirds of the stock of any such class; but the certificate of incorporation of a close corporation may provide that a lesser proportion of the directors or of the stockholders or of a class of stockholders may apply for relief under this section.

(c) A provisional director shall be an impartial person who is neither a stockholder nor a creditor of the corporation or of any subsidiary or affiliate of the corporation, and whose further qualifications, if any, may be determined by the Court of Chancery. A provisional director is not a receiver of the corporation and does not have the title and powers of a custodian or receiver appointed under §§ 226 and 291 of this title. A provisional director shall have all the rights and powers of a duly elected director of the corporation, including the right to notice of and to vote at meetings of directors, until such time as such person shall be removed by order of the Court of Chancery or by the holders of a majority of all shares then entitled to vote to elect directors or by the holders of two thirds of the shares of that class of voting shares which filed the application for appointment of a provisional director. A provisional director's compensation shall be determined by agreement between such person and the corporation subject to approval of the Court of Chancery, which may fix such person's compensation in the absence of agreement or in the event of disagreement between the provisional director and the corporation.

(d) Even though the requirements of subsection (b) of this section relating to the number of directors or stockholders who may petition for appointment of a provisional director are not satisfied, the Court of Chancery may nevertheless appoint a provisional director if permitted by § 352(b) of this title.

§ 354. Operating Corporation as Partnership

No written agreement among stockholders of a close corporation, nor any provision of the certificate of incorporation or of the bylaws of the corporation, which agreement or provision relates to any phase of the affairs of such corporation, including but not limited to the management of its business or declaration and payment of dividends or other division of profits or the election of directors or officers or the employment of stockholders by the corporation or the arbitration of disputes, shall be invalid on the ground that it is an attempt by the parties to the agreement or by the stockholders of the corporation to treat the corporation as if it were a partnership or to arrange relations among the stockholders or between the stockholders and the corporation in a manner that would be appropriate only among partners.

§ 355. Stockholders' Option to Dissolve Corporation

(a) The certificate of incorporation of any close corporation may include a provision granting to any stockholder, or to the holders of any specified number or percentage of shares of any class of stock, an option to have the corporation dissolved at will or upon the occurrence of any specified event or contingency. Whenever any such option to dissolve is exercised, the stockholders exercising such option shall give written notice thereof to all other stockholders. After the expiration of 30 days following the sending of such notice, the dissolution of the corporation shall proceed as if the required number of stockholders having voting power had consented in writing to dissolution of the corporation as provided by § 228 of this title.

(b) If the certificate of incorporation as originally filed does not contain a provision authorized by subsection (a) of this section, the certificate may be amended to include such provision if adopted by the affirmative vote of the holders of all the outstanding stock, whether or not entitled to vote, unless the certificate of incorporation specifically authorizes such an amendment by a vote which shall be not less than $2/3$ of all the outstanding stock whether or not entitled to vote.

(c) Each stock certificate in any corporation whose certificate of incorporation authorizes dissolution as permitted by this section shall conspicuously note on the face thereof the existence of the provision. Unless noted conspicuously on the face of the stock certificate, the provision is ineffective.

§ 356. Effect of This Subchapter on Other Laws

This subchapter shall not be deemed to repeal any statute or rule of law which is or would be applicable to any corporation which is organized under this chapter but is not a close corporation.

SUBCHAPTER XV. PUBLIC BENEFIT CORPORATIONS

§ 361. Law Applicable to Public Benefit Corporations; How Formed

This subchapter applies to all public benefit corporations, as defined in § 362 of this title. If a corporation elects to become a public benefit corporation under this subchapter in the manner prescribed in this subchapter, it shall be subject in all respects to the provisions of this chapter, except to the extent this subchapter imposes additional or different requirements, in which case such requirements shall apply.

§ 362. Public Benefit Corporation Defined; Contents of Certificate of Incorporation

(a) A "public benefit corporation" is a for-profit corporation organized under and subject to the requirements of this chapter that is intended to produce a public benefit or public benefits and to operate in a responsible and sustainable manner. To that end, a public benefit corporation shall be managed in a manner that balances the stockholders' pecuniary interests, the best interests of those materially affected by the corporation's conduct, and the public benefit or public benefits identified in its certificate of incorporation. In the certificate of incorporation, a public benefit corporation shall:

(1) Identify within its statement of business or purpose pursuant to § 102(a)(3) of this title 1 or more specific public benefits to be promoted by the corporation; and

(2) State within its heading that it is a public benefit corporation.

(b) "Public benefit" means a positive effect (or reduction of negative effects) on 1 or more categories of persons, entities, communities or interests (other than stockholders in their capacities as stockholders) including, but not limited to, effects of an artistic, charitable, cultural, economic, educational, environmental, literary, medical, religious, scientific or technological nature. "Public benefit provisions" means the provisions of a certificate of incorporation contemplated by this subchapter.

(c) The name of the public benefit corporation may contain the words "public benefit corporation," or the abbreviation "P.B.C.," or the designation "PBC," which shall be deemed to satisfy the requirements of § 102(a)(*l*)(i) of this title. If the name does not contain such language, the corporation shall, prior to issuing unissued shares of stock or disposing of treasury shares, provide notice to any person to whom such stock is issued or who acquires such treasury shares that it is a public benefit corporation; provided that such notice need not be provided if the issuance or disposal is pursuant to an offering registered under the Securities Act of 1933 [15 U.S.C. § 77r et seq.] or if, at the time of issuance or disposal, the corporation has a class of securities that is registered under the Securities Exchange Act of 1934 [15 U.S.C. § 78a et seq.].

§ 363.   Certain Amendments and Mergers; Votes Required; Appraisal Rights

(a) Notwithstanding any other provisions of this chapter, a corporation that is not a public benefit corporation, may not, without the approval of ²/₃ of the outstanding stock of the corporation entitled to vote thereon:

(1) Amend its certificate of incorporation to include a provision authorized by § 362(a)(1) of this title; or

(2) Merge or consolidate with or into another entity if, as a result of such merger or consolidation, the shares in such corporation would become, or be converted into or exchanged for the right to receive, shares or other equity interests in a domestic or foreign public benefit corporation or similar entity.

The restrictions of this section shall not apply prior to the time that the corporation has received payment for any of its capital stock, or in the case of a nonstock corporation, prior to the time that it has members.

(b) Any stockholder of a corporation that is not a public benefit corporation that holds shares of stock of such corporation immediately prior to the effective time of:

(1) An amendment to the corporation's certificate of incorporation to include a provision authorized by § 362(a)(1) of this title; or

(2) A merger or consolidation that would result in the conversion of the corporation's stock into or exchange of the corporation's stock for the right to receive shares or other equity interests in a domestic or foreign public benefit corporation or similar entity;

and has neither voted in favor of such amendment or such merger or consolidation nor consented thereto in writing pursuant to § 228 of this title, shall be entitled to an appraisal by the Court of Chancery of the fair value of the stockholder's shares of stock; provided, however, that no appraisal rights under this section shall be available for the shares of any class or series of stock, which stock, or depository receipts in respect thereof, at the record date fixed to determine the stockholders entitled to receive notice of the meeting of stockholders to act upon the agreement of merger or consolidation, or amendment, were either: (i) listed on a national securities exchange or (ii) held of record by more than 2,000 holders, unless, in the case of a merger or consolidation, the holders thereof are required by the terms of an agreement of merger or consolidation to accept for such stock anything except (A) shares of stock of any other corporation, or depository receipts in respect thereof, which shares of stock (or depository receipts in respect thereof) or depository receipts at the effective date of the merger or consolidation will be either listed on a national securities exchange or held of record by more than 2,000 holders; (B) cash in lieu of fractional shares or fractional depository receipts described in the foregoing clause (A); or (C) any combination of the shares of stock, depository receipts and cash in lieu of fractional shares or fractional depository receipts described in the foregoing clauses (A) and (B).

(c) Notwithstanding any other provisions of this chapter, a corporation that is a public benefit corporation may not, without the approval of ²/₃ of the outstanding stock of the corporation entitled to vote thereon:

(1) Amend its certificate of incorporation to delete or amend a provision authorized by § 362(a)(1) or § 366(c) of this title; or

(2) Merge or consolidate with or into another entity if, as a result of such merger or consolidation, the shares in such corporation would become, or be converted into or exchanged for the right to receive, shares or other equity interests in a domestic or foreign corporation that is not a public benefit corporation or similar entity and the certificate of incorporation (or similar governing instrument) of which does not contain the identical provisions identifying the public benefit or public benefits pursuant to § 362(a) of this title or imposing requirements pursuant to § 366(c) of this title.

(d) Notwithstanding the foregoing, a nonprofit nonstock corporation may not be a constituent corporation to any merger or consolidation governed by this section.

§ 364. Stock Certificates; Notices Regarding Uncertificated Stock

Any stock certificate issued by a public benefit corporation shall note conspicuously that the corporation is a public benefit corporation formed pursuant to this subchapter. Any notice given by a public benefit corporation pursuant to § 151(f) of this title shall state conspicuously that the corporation is a public benefit corporation formed pursuant to this subchapter.

§ 365. Duties of Directors

(a) The board of directors shall manage or direct the business and affairs of the public benefit corporation in a manner that balances the pecuniary interests of the stockholders, the best interests of those materially affected by the corporation's conduct, and the specific public benefit or public benefits identified in its certificate of incorporation.

(b) A director of a public benefit corporation shall not, by virtue of the public benefit provisions or § 362(a) of this title, have any duty to any person on account of any interest of such person in the public benefit or public benefits identified in the certificate of incorporation or on account of any interest materially affected by the corporation's conduct and, with respect to a decision implicating the balance requirement in subsection (a) of this section, will be deemed to satisfy such director's fiduciary duties to stockholders and the corporation if such director's decision is both informed and disinterested and not such that no person of ordinary, sound judgment would approve.

(c) The certificate of incorporation of a public benefit corporation may include a provision that any disinterested failure to satisfy this section shall not, for the purposes of § 102(b)(7) or § 145 of this title, constitute an act or omission not in good faith, or a breach of the duty of loyalty.

§ 366. Periodic Statements and Third-Party Certification

(a) A public benefit corporation shall include in every notice of a meeting of stockholders a statement to the effect that it is a public benefit corporation formed pursuant to this subchapter.

(b) A public benefit corporation shall no less than biennially provide its stockholders with a statement as to the corporation's promotion of the public benefit or public benefits identified in the certificate of incorporation and of the best interests of those materially affected by the corporation's conduct. The statement shall include:

(1) The objectives the board of directors has established to promote such public benefit or public benefits and interests;

(2) The standards the board of directors has adopted to measure the corporation's progress in promoting such public benefit or public benefits and interests;

(3) Objective factual information based on those standards regarding the corporation's success in meeting the objectives for promoting such public benefit or public benefits and interests; and

(4) An assessment of the corporation's success in meeting the objectives and promoting such public benefit or public benefits and interests.

(c) The certificate of incorporation or bylaws of a public benefit corporation may require that the corporation:

(1) Provide the statement described in subsection (b) of this section more frequently than biennially;

(2) Make the statement described in subsection (b) of this section available to the public; and/or

(3) Use a third-party standard in connection with and/or attain a periodic third-party certification addressing the corporation's promotion of the public benefit or public benefits identified in the certificate of incorporation and/or the best interests of those materially affected by the corporation's conduct.

§ 367.   Derivative Suits

Stockholders of a public benefit corporation owning individually or collectively, as of the date of instituting such derivative suit, at least 2% of the corporation's outstanding shares or, in the case of a corporation with shares listed on a national securities exchange, the lesser of such percentage or shares of at least $2,000,000 in market value, may maintain a derivative lawsuit to enforce the requirements set forth in § 365(a) of this title.

§ 368.   No Effect on Other Corporations

This subchapter shall not affect a statute or rule of law that is applicable to a corporation that is not a public benefit corporation, except as provided in § 363 of this title.

SUBCHAPTER XVI. FOREIGN CORPORATIONS

§ 371.   Definition; Qualification to Do Business in State; Procedure

(a) As used in this chapter, the words "foreign corporation" mean a corporation organized under the laws of any jurisdiction other than this State.

(b) No foreign corporation shall do any business in this State, through or by branch offices, agents or representatives located in this State, until it shall have paid to the Secretary of State of this State for the use of this State, $80, and shall have filed in the office of the Secretary of State:

(1) A certificate, as of a date not earlier than 6 months prior to the filing date, issued by an authorized officer of the jurisdiction of its incorporation evidencing its corporate existence. If such certificate is in a foreign language, a translation thereof, under oath of the translator, shall be attached thereto;

(2) A statement executed by an authorized officer of each corporation setting forth (i) the name and address of its registered agent in this State, which agent may be any of the foreign corporation itself, an individual resident in this State, a domestic corporation, a domestic partnership (whether general (including a limited liability partnership) or limited (including a limited liability limited partnership)), a domestic limited liability company, a domestic statutory trust, a foreign corporation (other than the foreign corporation itself), a foreign partnership (whether general (including a limited liability partnership) or limited (including a limited liability limited partnership)), a foreign limited liability company or a foreign statutory trust, (ii) a statement, as of a date not earlier than 6 months prior to the filing date, of the assets and liabilities of the corporation, and (iii) the business it proposes to do in this State, and a statement that it is authorized to do that business in the jurisdiction of its incorporation. The statement shall be acknowledged in accordance with § 103 of this title.

(c) The certificate of the Secretary of State, under seal of office, of the filing of the certificates required by subsection (b) of this section, shall be delivered to the registered agent upon the payment to the Secretary of State of the fee prescribed for such certificates, and the certificate shall be prima facie evidence of the right of the corporation to do business in this State; provided, that the Secretary of State shall not issue such certificate unless the name of the corporation is such as to distinguish it upon the records in the office of the Division of Corporations in the Department of State from the names that are reserved on such records and from the names on such records of each other corporation, partnership, limited partnership, limited liability company or statutory trust organized or registered as a domestic or foreign corporation, partnership, limited partnership, limited liability company or statutory trust under the laws of this State, except with the written consent of the person who has reserved such name or such other corporation, partnership, limited partnership, limited liability company or statutory trust, executed, acknowledged and filed with the Secretary of State in accordance with § 103 of this title. If the name of the foreign corporation conflicts with the name of a corporation, partnership, limited partnership, limited liability company or statutory trust organized under the laws of this State, or a name reserved for a corporation, partnership, limited partnership, limited liability company or statutory trust to be organized under the laws of this State, or a name reserved or registered as that of a foreign corporation, partnership, limited partnership, limited liability company or statutory trust under the laws of this State, the foreign corporation may qualify to do business if it adopts an assumed name which shall be used when doing business in this State as long as the assumed name is authorized for use by this section.

§ 383. Actions by and Against Unqualified Foreign Corporations

(a) A foreign corporation which is required to comply with §§ 371 and 372 of this title and which has done business in this State without authority shall not maintain any action or special proceeding in this State unless and until such corporation has been authorized to do business in this State and has paid to the State all fees, penalties and franchise taxes for the years or parts thereof during which it did business in this State without authority. This prohibition shall not apply to any successor in interest of such foreign corporation.

(b) The failure of a foreign corporation to obtain authority to do business in this State shall not impair the validity of any contract or act of the foreign corporation or the right of any other party to the contract to maintain any action or special proceeding thereon, and shall not prevent the foreign corporation from defending any action or special proceeding in this State.

SUBCHAPTER XVII. DOMESTICATION AND TRANSFER

§ 390. Transfer, Domestication or Continuance of Domestic Corporations

(a) Upon compliance with the provisions of this section, any corporation existing under the laws of this State may transfer to or domesticate or continue in any foreign jurisdiction and, in connection therewith, may elect to continue its existence as a corporation of this State. As used in this section, the term:

(1) "Foreign jurisdiction" means any foreign country, or other foreign jurisdiction (other than the United States, any state, the District of Columbia, or any possession or territory of the United States); and

(2) "Resulting entity" means the entity formed, incorporated, created or otherwise coming into being as a consequence of the transfer of the corporation to, or its domestication or continuance in, a foreign jurisdiction pursuant to this section.

(b) The board of directors of the corporation which desires to transfer to or domesticate or continue in a foreign jurisdiction shall adopt a resolution approving such transfer, domestication or continuance specifying the foreign jurisdiction to which the corporation shall be transferred or in which the corporation shall be domesticated or continued and, if applicable, that in connection with such transfer, domestication or continuance the corporation's existence as a corporation of this State is to continue and recommending the approval of such transfer or domestication or continuance by the stockholders of the corporation. Such resolution shall be submitted to the stockholders of the corporation at an annual or special meeting. Due notice of the time, place and purpose of the meeting shall be mailed to each holder of stock, whether voting or nonvoting, of the corporation at the address of the stockholder as it appears on the records of the corporation, at least 20 days prior to the date of the meeting. At the meeting, the resolution shall be considered and a vote taken for its adoption or rejection. If all outstanding shares of stock of the corporation, whether voting or nonvoting, shall be voted for the adoption of the resolution, the corporation shall file with the Secretary of State a certificate of transfer if its existence as a corporation of this State is to cease or a certificate of transfer and domestic continuance if its existence as a corporation of this State is to continue, executed in accordance with § 103 of this title, which certifies:

(1) The name of the corporation, and if it has been changed, the name under which it was originally incorporated.

(2) The date of filing of its original certificate of incorporation with the Secretary of State.

(3) The foreign jurisdiction to which the corporation shall be transferred or in which it shall be domesticated or continued and the name of the resulting entity.

(4) That the transfer, domestication or continuance of the corporation has been approved in accordance with the provisions of this section.

(5) In the case of a certificate of transfer, (i) that the existence of the corporation as a corporation of this State shall cease when the certificate of transfer becomes effective, and (ii) the agreement of the corporation that it may be served with process in this State in any proceeding for enforcement of any obligation of the corporation arising while it was a corporation of this State which shall also irrevocably appoint the Secretary of State as its agent to accept service of process in any such proceeding and specify the address (which may not be that of the corporation's registered agent without the written consent of the corporation's registered agent, such consent to be filed along with the certificate of transfer) to which a copy of such process shall be mailed by the Secretary of State. Process may be served upon the Secretary of State under this subsection by means of electronic transmission but only as prescribed by the Secretary of State. The Secretary of State is authorized to issue such rules and regulations with respect to such service as the Secretary of State deems necessary or appropriate. In the event of service upon the Secretary of State in accordance with this subsection, the Secretary of State shall forthwith notify such corporation that has transferred out of the State of Delaware by letter, directed to such corporation that has transferred out of the State of Delaware at the address so specified, unless such corporation shall have designated in writing to the Secretary of State a different address for such purpose, in which case it shall be mailed to the last address designated. Such letter shall be sent by a mail or courier service that includes a record of mailing or deposit with the courier and a record of delivery evidenced by the signature of the recipient. Such letter shall enclose a copy of the process and any other papers served on the Secretary of State pursuant to this subsection. It shall be the duty of the plaintiff in the event of such service to serve process and any other papers in duplicate, to notify the Secretary of State that service is being effected pursuant to this subsection and to pay the Secretary of State the sum of $50 for the use of the State, which sum shall be taxed as part of the costs in the proceeding, if the plaintiff shall prevail therein. The Secretary of State shall maintain an alphabetical record of any such service setting forth the name of the plaintiff and the defendant, the title, docket number and nature of the proceeding in which process has been served, the fact that service has been effected pursuant to this subsection, the return date thereof, and the day and hour service was made. The Secretary of State shall not be required to retain such information longer than 5 years from receipt of the service of process.

(6) In the case of a certificate of transfer and domestic continuance, that the corporation will continue to exist as a corporation of this State after the certificate of transfer and domestic continuance becomes effective.

(c) Upon the filing of a certificate of transfer in accordance with subsection (b) of this section and payment to the Secretary of State of all fees prescribed under this title, the Secretary of State shall certify that the corporation has filed all documents and paid all fees required by this title, and thereupon the corporation shall cease to exist as a corporation of this State at the time the certificate of transfer becomes effective in accordance with § 103 of this title. Such certificate of the Secretary of State shall be prima facie evidence of the transfer, domestication or continuance by such corporation out of this State.

(d) The transfer, domestication or continuance of a corporation out of this State in accordance with this section and the resulting cessation of its existence as a corporation of this State pursuant to a certificate of transfer shall not be deemed to affect any obligations or liabilities of the corporation incurred prior to such transfer, domestication or continuance, the personal liability of any person incurred prior to such transfer, domestication or continuance, or the choice of law applicable to the corporation with respect to matters arising prior to such transfer, domestication or continuance. Unless otherwise agreed or otherwise provided in the certificate of incorporation, the transfer, domestication or continuance of a corporation out of the State of Delaware in accordance with this section shall not require such corporation to wind up its affairs or pay its liabilities and distribute its assets under this title and shall not be deemed to constitute a dissolution of such corporation.

(e) If a corporation files a certificate of transfer and domestic continuance, after the time the certificate of transfer and domestic continuance becomes effective, the corporation shall continue to exist as a corporation of this State, and the law of the State of Delaware, including this title, shall apply to the corporation to the same extent as prior to such time. So long as a corporation continues to exist as a corporation of the State of Delaware following the filing of a certificate of transfer and domestic continuance, the continuing corporation and the resulting entity shall, for all purposes of the laws of the State of

Delaware, constitute a single entity formed, incorporated, created or otherwise having come into being, as applicable, and existing under the laws of the State of Delaware and the laws of the foreign jurisdiction.

(f) When a corporation has transferred, domesticated or continued pursuant to this section, for all purposes of the laws of the State of Delaware, the resulting entity shall be deemed to be the same entity as the transferring, domesticating or continuing corporation and shall constitute a continuation of the existence of such corporation in the form of the resulting entity. When any transfer, domestication or continuance shall have become effective under this section, for all purposes of the laws of the State of Delaware, all of the rights, privileges and powers of the corporation that has transferred, domesticated or continued, and all property, real, personal and mixed, and all debts due to such corporation, as well as all other things and causes of action belonging to such corporation, shall remain vested in the resulting entity (and also in the corporation that has transferred, domesticated or continued, if and for so long as such corporation continues its existence as a corporation of this State) and shall be the property of such resulting entity (and also of the corporation that has transferred, domesticated or continued, if and for so long as such corporation continues its existence as a corporation of this State), and the title to any real property vested by deed or otherwise in such corporation shall not revert or be in any way impaired by reason of this title; but all rights of creditors and all liens upon any property of such corporation shall be preserved unimpaired, and all debts, liabilities and duties of such corporation shall remain attached to the resulting entity (and also to the corporation that has transferred, domesticated or continued, if and for so long as such corporation continues its existence as a corporation of this State), and may be enforced against it to the same extent as if said debts, liabilities and duties had originally been incurred or contracted by it in its capacity as such resulting entity. The rights, privileges, powers and interests in property of the corporation, as well as the debts, liabilities and duties of the corporation, shall not be deemed, as a consequence of the transfer, domestication or continuance, to have been transferred to the resulting entity for any purpose of the laws of the State of Delaware.

(g) In connection with a transfer, domestication or continuance under this section, shares of stock of the transferring, domesticating or continuing corporation may be exchanged for or converted into cash, property, or shares of stock, rights or securities of, or interests in, the resulting entity or, in addition to or in lieu thereof, may be exchanged for or converted into cash, property, or shares of stock, rights or securities of, or interests in, another corporation or other entity or may be cancelled.

(h) No vote of the stockholders of a corporation shall be necessary to authorize a transfer, domestication or continuance if no shares of the stock of such corporation shall have been issued prior to the adoption by the board of directors of the resolution approving the transfer, domestication or continuance.

(i) Whenever it shall be desired to transfer to or domesticate or continue in any foreign jurisdiction any nonstock corporation, the governing body shall perform all the acts necessary to effect a transfer, domestication or continuance which are required by this section to be performed by the board of directors of a corporation having capital stock. If the members of a nonstock corporation are entitled to vote for the election of members of its governing body or are entitled under the certificate of incorporation or the bylaws of such corporation to vote on such transfer, domestication or continuance or on a merger, consolidation, or dissolution of the corporation, they, and any other holder of any membership interest in the corporation, shall perform all the acts necessary to effect a transfer, domestication or continuance which are required by this section to be performed by the stockholders of a corporation having capital stock. If there is no member entitled to vote thereon, nor any other holder of any membership interest in the corporation, the transfer, domestication or continuance of the corporation shall be authorized at a meeting of the governing body, upon the adoption of a resolution to transfer or domesticate or continue by the vote of a majority of members of its governing body then in office. In all other respects, the method and proceedings for the transfer, domestication or continuance of a nonstock corporation shall conform as nearly as may be to the proceedings prescribed by this section for the transfer, domestication or continuance of corporations having capital stock. In the case of a charitable nonstock corporation, due notice of the corporation's intent to effect a transfer, domestication or continuance shall be mailed to the Attorney General of the State of Delaware 10 days prior to the date of the proposed transfer, domestication or continuance.

SUBCHAPTER XVIII. MISCELLANEOUS PROVISIONS

§ 394.   Reserved Power of State to Amend or Repeal Chapter; Chapter Part of Corporation's Charter or Certificate of Incorporation

This chapter may be amended or repealed, at the pleasure of the General Assembly, but any amendment or repeal shall not take away or impair any remedy under this chapter against any corporation or its officers for any liability which shall have been previously incurred. This chapter and all amendments thereof shall be a part of the charter or certificate of incorporation of every corporation except so far as the same are inapplicable and inappropriate to the objects of the corporation.

MODEL BUSINESS CORPORATION ACT

(2016 Revision)

TABLE OF CONTENTS

CHAPTER 1. GENERAL PROVISIONS

Subchapter A. Short Title and Reservation of Power

Sec.		Page
1.01.	Short Title	550
1.02.	Reservation of Power to Amend or Repeal	550

Subchapter B. Filing Documents

1.20.	Requirements for Documents; Extrinsic Facts	550
1.21.	Forms	552
1.22.	Filing, Service, and Copying Fees*	
1.23.	Effective Date of Filed Document	552
1.24.	Correcting Filed Document	552
1.25.	Filing Duty of Secretary of State	552
1.26.	Appeal from Secretary of State's Refusal to File Document*	
1.27.	Evidentiary Effect of Certified Copy of Filed Document	553
1.28.	Certificate of Existence or Registration*	
1.29.	Penalty for Signing False Document*	

Subchapter C. Secretary of State

1.30.	Powers*	

Subchapter D. Definitions

1.40.	Act Definitions	553
1.41.	Notices and Other Communications	559
1.42.	Number of Shareholders	561
1.43.	Qualified Director	562
1.44.	Householding	564

Subchapter E. Ratification of Defective Corporate Actions

1.45.	Definitions	565
1.46.	Defective Corporate Actions	565
1.47.	Ratification of Defective Corporate Actions	566
1.48.	Action on Ratification	567
1.49.	Notice Requirements	568
1.50.	Effect of Ratification	568
1.51.	Filings	568
1.52.	Judicial Proceedings Regarding Validity of Corporate Actions	569

CHAPTER 2. INCORPORATION

2.01.	Incorporators	570
2.02.	Articles of Incorporation	570
2.03.	Incorporation	574

---

* Omitted.

proba corp yet

2.04.   Liability for Preincorporation Transactions ...(promoters).. 574
2.05.   Organization of Corporation 575
2.06.   Bylaws 575
2.07.   Emergency Bylaws 576
2.08.   Forum Selection Provisions 576

CHAPTER 3.   PURPOSES AND POWERS

3.01.   Purposes 578
3.02.   General Powers 578
3.03.   Emergency Powers 579
3.04.   Lack of Power to Act 579

CHAPTER 4.   NAME

4.01.   Corporate Name 580
4.02.   Reserved Name 580
4.03.   Registered Name 581

CHAPTER 5.   OFFICE AND AGENT

5.01.   Registered Office and Agent of Domestic and Registered Foreign Corporations 581
5.02.   Change of Registered Office or Registered Agent*
5.03.   Resignation of Registered Agent*
5.04.   Service on Corporation*

CHAPTER 6.   SHARES AND DISTRIBUTIONS

Subchapter A.   Shares

6.01.   Authorized Shares 581
6.02.   Terms of Class or Series Determined by Board of Directors 584
6.03.   Issued and Outstanding Shares 585
6.04.   Fractional Shares 585

Subchapter B.   Issuance of Shares

6.20.   Subscription for Shares before Incorporation 586
6.21.   Issuance of Shares 586
6.22.   Liability of Shareholders 590
6.23.   Share Dividends 590
6.24.   Share Rights, Options, Warrants and Awards 590
6.25.   Form and Content of Certificates 591
6.26.   Shares Without Certificates 592
6.27.   Restriction on Transfer of Shares 592

Subchapter C.   Subsequent Acquisition of Shares by Shareholders and Corporation

6.30.   Shareholders' Preemptive Rights 593
6.31.   Corporation's Acquisition of Its Own Shares 594

Subchapter D.   Distributions

6.40.   Distributions to Shareholders 594

---

*   Omitted.

CHAPTER 7.   SHAREHOLDERS

Subchapter A.   Meetings

7.01.	Annual Meeting	597
7.02.	Special Meeting	598
7.03.	Court-Ordered Meeting	598
7.04.	Action Without Meeting	599
7.05.	Notice of Meeting	600
7.06.	Waiver of Notice	601
7.07.	Record Date for Meeting	602
7.08.	Conduct of Meeting	603
7.09.	Remote Participation in Shareholders' Meetings	603

Subchapter B.   Voting

7.20.	Shareholders' List for Meeting	604
7.21.	Voting Entitlement of Shares	605
7.22.	Proxies	606
7.23.	Shares Held by Intermediaries and Nominees	607
7.24.	Acceptance of Votes and Other Instruments	608
7.25.	Quorum and Voting Requirements for Voting Groups	609
7.26.	Action by Single and Multiple Voting Groups	610
7.27.	Modifying Quorum or Voting Requirements	612
7.28.	Voting for Directors; Cumulative Voting	612
7.29.	Inspectors of Election	612

Subchapter C.   Voting Trusts and Agreements

7.30.	Voting Trusts	614
7.31.	Voting Agreements	614
7.32.	Shareholder Agreements	614

Subchapter D.   Derivative Proceedings

7.40.	Subchapter Definitions	618
7.41.	Standing	618
7.42.	Demand	618
7.43.	Stay of Proceedings	619
7.44.	Dismissal	619
7.45.	Discontinuance or Settlement	620
7.46.	Payment of Expenses	621
7.47.	Applicability to Foreign Corporations	621

Subchapter E.   Judicial Proceedings

7.48.	Shareholder Action to Appoint a Custodian or Receiver	621
7.49.	Judicial Determination of Corporate Offices and Review of Elections and Shareholder Votes	622

CHAPTER 8.   DIRECTORS AND OFFICERS

Subchapter A.   Board of Directors

8.01.	Requirement for and Functions of Board of Directors	624
8.02.	Qualifications of Directors	625
8.03.	Number and Election of Directors	627
8.04.	Election of Directors by Certain Classes or Series of Shares	627

8.05. Terms of Directors Generally 628
8.06. Staggered Terms for Directors 628
8.07. Resignation of Directors 629
8.08. Removal of Directors by Shareholders 629
8.09. Removal of Directors by Judicial Proceeding 630
8.10. Vacancy on Board of Directors 630
8.11. Compensation of Directors 631

Subchapter B. Meetings and Action of the Board

8.20. Meetings 631
8.21. Action Without Meeting 631
8.22. Notice of Meeting 631
8.23. Waiver of Notice 632
8.24. Quorum and Voting 632
8.25. Committees of the Board 632
8.26. Submission of Matters for Shareholder Vote 633

Subchapter C. Directors

8.30. Standards of Conduct for Directors 634
8.31. Standards of Liability for Directors 639
8.32. Directors' Liability for Unlawful Distributions 644

Subchapter D. Officers

8.40. Officers 644
8.41. Functions of Officers 645
8.42. Standards of Conduct for Officers 645
8.43. Resignation and Removal of Officers 647
8.44. Contract Rights of Officers 648

Subchapter E. Indemnification and Advance for Expenses

8.50. Subchapter Definitions 649
8.51. Permissible Indemnification 650
8.52. Mandatory Indemnification 653
8.53. Advance for Expenses 653
8.54. Court-Ordered Indemnification and Advance for Expenses 655
8.55. Determination and Authorization of Indemnification 656
8.56. Indemnification of Officers 657
8.57. Insurance 659
8.58. Variation by Corporate Action; Application of Subchapter 659
8.59. Exclusivity of Subchapter 661

Subchapter F. Directors' Conflicting Interest Transactions

8.60. Subchapter Definitions 663
8.61. Judicial Action 667
8.62. Directors' Action 668
8.63. Shareholders' Action 670

Subchapter G. Business Opportunities

8.70. Business Opportunities 672

MODEL BUSINESS CORPORATION ACT

CHAPTER 9.   DOMESTICATION AND CONVERSION

Subchapter A.   Preliminary Provisions

9.01.   Definitions.. 674
9.02.   Excluded Transactions [optional] 675
9.03.   Required Approvals [optional] 676
9.04.   Relationship of Chapter to Other Laws [optional] 676

Subchapter B.   Domestication

9.20.   Domestication 676
9.21.   Action on a Plan of Domestication 678
9.22.   Articles of Domestication; Effectiveness.................................. 679
9.23.   Amendment of Plan of Domestication; Abandonment 680
9.24.   Effect of Domestication... 680

Subchapter C.   Conversion

9.30.   Conversion 682
9.31.   Plan of Conversion.. 683
9.32.   Action on a Plan of Conversion 683
9.33.   Articles of Conversion; Effectiveness....................................... 684
9.34.   Amendment of Plan of Conversion; Abandonment 685
9.35.   Effect of Conversion.. 686

CHAPTER 10.   AMENDMENT OF ARTICLES OF INCORPORATION AND BYLAWS

Subchapter A.   Amendment of Articles of Incorporation

10.01.   Authority to Amend.. 688
10.02.   Amendment Before Issuance of Shares 688
10.03.   Amendment by Board of Directors and Shareholders 688
10.04.   Voting on Amendments by Voting Groups................................ 690
10.05.   Amendment by Board of Directors.. 691
10.06.   Articles of Amendment... 692
10.07.   Restated Articles of Incorporation 692
10.08.   Amendment Pursuant to Reorganization 693
10.09.   Effect of Amendment.. 693

Subchapter B.   Amendment of Bylaws

10.20.   Authority to Amend.. 694
10.21.   Bylaw Increasing Quorum or Voting Requirements for Directors..... 695
10.22.   Bylaw Provisions Relating to the Election of Directors............ 695

CHAPTER 11.   MERGERS AND SHARE EXCHANGES

11.01.   Definitions... 698
11.02.   Merger... 698
11.03.   Share Exchange 700
11.04.   Action on a Plan of Merger or Share Exchange 702
11.05.   Merger Between Parent and Subsidiary or Between Subsidiaries......... 706
11.06.   Articles of Merger or Share Exchange...................................... 707
11.07.   Effect of Merger or Share Exchange... 708
11.08.   Abandonment of a Merger of Share Exchange......................... 710

MODEL BUSINESS CORPORATION ACT

CHAPTER 12.   DISPOSITION OF ASSETS

12.01.   Disposition of Assets Not Requiring Shareholder Approval.................................... 711
12.02.   Shareholder Approval of Certain Dispositions.. 712

CHAPTER 13.   APPRAISAL RIGHTS

Subchapter A.   Right to Appraisal and Payment for Shares

13.01.   Definitions... 714
13.02.   Right to Appraisal 717
13.03.   Assertion of Rights by Nominees and Beneficial Shareholders 720

Subchapter B.   Procedure for Exercise of Appraisal Rights

13.20.   Notice of Appraisal Rights 721
13.21.   Notice of Intent to Demand Payment and Consequences of Voting or Consenting.... 722
13.22.   Appraisal Notice and Form 722
13.23.   Perfection of Rights; Right to Withdraw 723
13.24.   Payment... 724
13.25.   After-Acquired Shares.. 725
13.26.   Procedure if Shareholder Dissatisfied with Payment or Offer................... 725

Subchapter C.   Judicial Appraisal of Shares

13.30.   Court Action.. 726
13.31.   Court Costs and Expenses... 726

Subchapter D.   Other Remedies

13.40.   Other Remedies Limited 727

CHAPTER 14.   DISSOLUTION

Subchapter A.   Voluntary Dissolution

14.01.   Dissolution by Incorporators or Initial Directors.................................... 728
14.02.   Dissolution by Board of Directors and Shareholders................................ 729
14.03.   Articles of Dissolution 730
14.04.   Revocation of Dissolution 730
14.05.   Effect of Dissolution 730
14.06.   Known Claims Against Dissolved Corporation 731
14.07.   Other Claims Against Dissolved Corporation 732
14.08.   Court Proceedings... 733
14.09.   Director Duties 734

Subchapter B.   Administrative Dissolution

14.20.   Grounds for Administrative Dissolution 734
14.21.   Procedure for and Effect of Administrative Dissolution*
14.22.   Reinstatement Following Administrative Dissolution*
14.23.   Appeal From Denial of Reinstatement*

Subchapter C.   Judicial Dissolution

14.30.   Grounds for Judicial Dissolution 734
14.31.   Procedure for Judicial Dissolution... 736

---

*   Omitted.

14.32. Receivership or Custodianship.. 736
14.33. Decree of Dissolution 737
14.34. Election to Purchase in Lieu of Dissolution 737

Subchapter D. Miscellaneous

14.40. Deposit with State Treasurer.. 739

CHAPTER 15.   FOREIGN CORPORATIONS

15.01. Governing Law.. 740
15.02. Registration to Do Business in This State 740
15.03. Foreign Registration Statement 740
15.04. Amendment of Foreign Registration Statement 740
15.05. Activities Not Constituting Doing Business... 741
15.06. Noncomplying Name of Foreign Corporation*
15.07. Withdrawal of Registration of Registered Foreign Corporation.......... 742
15.08. Deemed Withdrawal upon Domestication or Conversion to Certain Domestic Entities*
15.09. Withdrawal upon Dissolution or Conversion to Certain Nonfiling Entities*
15.10. Transfer of Registration*
15.11. Administrative Termination of Registration*
15.12. Action by [Attorney General]*

CHAPTER 16.   RECORDS AND REPORTS

Subchapter A. Records

16.01. Corporate Records 743
16.02. Inspection Rights of Shareholders 744
16.03. Scope of Inspection Right 745
16.04. Court-Ordered Inspection 746
16.05. Inspection Rights of Directors... 746

Subchapter B. Reports

16.20. Financial Statements for Shareholders.. 747
16.21. Annual Report for Secretary of State 749

CHAPTER 17.   TRANSITION PROVISIONS

17.01. Application to Existing Domestic Corporations 751
17.02. Application to Existing Foreign Corporations...................................... 751
17.03. Saving Provisions 751
17.04. Severability 751
17.06. Repeal*

---

* Omitted.

Chapter 1

GENERAL PROVISIONS

Subchapter A

Short Title and Reservation of Power

§ 1.01. Short Title

This Act shall be known and may be cited as the "[name of state] Business Corporation Act."

§ 1.02. Reservation of Power to Amend or Repeal

The [name of state legislature] has power to amend or repeal all or part of this Act at any time and all domestic and foreign corporations subject to this Act are governed by the amendment or repeal.

Official Comment

The purpose of section 1.02 is to avoid any possible argument that a corporation has contractual or vested rights in any specific statutory provision and to ensure that the state may in the future modify its corporation statutes as it deems appropriate and require existing corporations to comply with the statutes as modified.

All articles of incorporation and foreign registration statements are subject to the reservation of power set forth in section 1.02. Further, corporations "governed" by this Act—which includes all corporations formed or qualified or registered under earlier general incorporation statutes that contain such a reservation of power—are also subject to the reservation of power of section 1.02 and bound by subsequent amendments to the Act.

Subchapter B

Filing Documents

§ 1.20. Requirements for Documents; Extrinsic Facts

(a) A document must satisfy the requirements of this section, and of any other section that adds to or varies these requirements, to be entitled to filing by the secretary of state.

(b) This Act must require or permit filing the document in the office of the secretary of state.

(c) The document must contain the information required by this Act and may contain other information.

(d) The document must be typewritten or printed or, if electronically transmitted, it must be in a format that can be retrieved or reproduced in typewritten or printed form.

(e) The document must be in the English language. A corporate name need not be in English if written in English letters or Arabic or Roman numerals.

(f) The document must be signed:

(1) by the chairman of the board of directors of a domestic or foreign corporation, by its president, or by another of its officers;

(2) if directors have not been selected or the corporation has not been formed, by an incorporator; or

(3) if the corporation is in the hands of a receiver, trustee, or other court-appointed fiduciary, by that fiduciary.

(g) The person executing the document shall sign it and state beneath or opposite the person's signature the person's name and the capacity in which the document is signed. The document may but need not contain a corporate seal, attestation, acknowledgment, or verification.

(h) If the secretary of state has prescribed a mandatory form for the document under section 1.21(a), the document must be in or on the prescribed form.

(i) The document must be delivered to the office of the secretary of state for filing. Delivery may be made by electronic transmission if and to the extent permitted by the secretary of state. If it is filed in typewritten or printed form and not transmitted electronically, the secretary of state may require one exact or conformed copy to be delivered with the document.

(j) When the document is delivered to the office of the secretary of state for filing, the correct filing fee, and any franchise tax, license fee, or penalty required by this Act or other law to be paid at the time of delivery for filing must be paid or provision for payment made in a manner permitted by the secretary of state.

(k) Whenever a provision of this Act permits any of the terms of a plan or a filed document to be dependent on facts objectively ascertainable outside the plan or filed document, the following provisions apply:

(1) The manner in which the facts will operate upon the terms of the plan or filed document must be set forth in the plan or filed document.

(2) The facts may include:

(i) any of the following that is available in a nationally recognized news or information medium either in print or electronically: statistical or market indices, market prices of any security or group of securities, interest rates, currency exchange rates, or similar economic or financial data;

(ii) a determination or action by any person or body, including the corporation or any other party to a plan or filed document; or

(iii) the terms of, or actions taken under, an agreement to which the corporation is a party, or any other agreement or document.

(3) As used in this subsection (k):

(i) "filed document" means a document filed by the secretary of state under any provision of this Act except chapter 15 or section 16.21; and

(ii) "plan" means a plan of domestication, conversion, merger, or share exchange.

(4) The following provisions of a plan or filed document may not be made dependent on facts outside the plan or filed document:

(i) the name and address of any person required in a filed document;

(ii) the registered office of any entity required in a filed document;

(iii) the registered agent of any entity required in a filed document;

(iv) the number of authorized shares and designation of each class or series of shares;

(v) the effective date of a filed document; and

(vi) any required statement in a filed document of the date on which the underlying transaction was approved or the manner in which that approval was given.

(5) If a provision of a filed document is made dependent on a fact ascertainable outside of the filed document, and that fact is neither ascertainable by reference to a source described in subsection (k)(2)(i) or a document that is a matter of public record, nor have the affected shareholders received notice of the fact from the corporation, then the corporation shall file with the secretary of state articles of amendment to the filed document setting forth the fact promptly after the time when the fact referred to is first ascertainable or thereafter changes. Articles of amendment under this subsection (k)(5) are deemed to be authorized by the authorization of the original filed document to which they relate and may be filed by the corporation without further action by the board of directors or the shareholders.

§ 1.21.   Forms

(a) The secretary of state may prescribe and furnish on request forms for: (i) an application for a certificate of existence or certificate of registration, (ii) a foreign corporation's registration statement, (iii) a foreign corporation's statement of withdrawal, (iv) a foreign corporation's transfer of registration statement, and (v) the annual report. If the secretary of state so requires, use of these forms is mandatory.

(b) The secretary of state may prescribe and furnish on request forms for other documents required or permitted to be filed by this Act but their use is not mandatory.

§ 1.23.   Effective Date of Filed Document

(a) Except to the extent otherwise provided in section 1.24(c) and subchapter E of this chapter, a document accepted for filing is effective:

    (1) on the date and at the time of filing, as provided in section 1.25(b);

    (2) on the date of filing and at the time specified in the document as its effective time if later than the time under subsection (a)(1);

    (3) at a specified delayed effective date and time which may not be more than 90 days after filing; or

    (4) if a delayed effective date is specified, but no time is specified, at 12:01 a.m. on the date specified, which may not be more than 90 days after the date of filing.

(b) If a filed document does not specify the time zone or place at which a date or time or both is to be determined, the date or time or both at which it becomes effective shall be those prevailing at the place of filing in this state.

§ 1.24.   Correcting Filed Document

(a) A document filed by the secretary of state pursuant to this Act may be corrected if (i) the document contains an inaccuracy, (ii) the document was defectively signed, attested, sealed, verified, or acknowledged, or (iii) the electronic transmission was defective.

(b) A document is corrected:

    (1) by preparing articles of correction that

        (i) describe the document (including its filing date) or attach a copy of it to the articles of correction,

        (ii) specify the inaccuracy or defect to be corrected, and

        (iii) correct the inaccuracy or defect; and

    (2) by delivering the articles of correction to the secretary of state for filing.

(c) Articles of correction are effective on the effective date of the document they correct except as to persons relying on the uncorrected document and adversely affected by the correction. As to those persons, articles of correction are effective when filed.

§ 1.25.   Filing Duty of Secretary of State

(a) If a document delivered to the office of the secretary of state for filing satisfies the requirements of section 1.20, the secretary of state shall file it.

(b) The secretary of state files a document by recording it as filed on the date and time of receipt. After filing a document, the secretary of state shall return to the person who delivered the document for filing a copy of the document with an acknowledgement of the date and time of filing.

(c) If the secretary of state refuses to file a document, it shall be returned to the person who delivered the document for filing within five days after the document was delivered, together with a brief, written explanation of the reason for the refusal.

(d) The secretary of state's duty to file documents under this section is ministerial. The secretary of state's filing or refusing to file a document does not create a presumption that: (i) the document does or does not conform to the requirements of the Act; or (ii) the information contained in the document is correct or incorrect.

§ 1.27. Evidentiary Effect of Certified Copy of Filed Document

A certificate from the secretary of state delivered with a copy of a document filed by the secretary of state is conclusive evidence that the original document is on file with the secretary of state.

Subchapter D
Definitions

§ 1.40. Act Definitions

In this Act, unless otherwise specified:

"Articles of incorporation" means the articles of incorporation described in section 2.02, all amendments to the articles of incorporation, and any other documents permitted or required to be delivered for filing by a domestic business corporation with the secretary of state under any provision of this Act that modify, amend, supplement, restate or replace the articles of incorporation. After an amendment of the articles of incorporation or any other document filed under this Act that restates the articles of incorporation in their entirety, the articles of incorporation shall not include any prior documents. When used with respect to a foreign corporation or a domestic or foreign nonprofit corporation, the "articles of incorporation" of such an entity means the document of such entity that is equivalent to the articles of incorporation of a domestic business corporation.

"Authorized shares" means the shares of all classes a domestic or foreign corporation is authorized to issue.

"Beneficial shareholder" means a person who owns the beneficial interest in shares, which may be a record shareholder or a person on whose behalf shares are registered in the name of an intermediary or nominee.

"Conspicuous" means so written, displayed, or presented that a reasonable person against whom the writing is to operate should have noticed it.

"Corporation," "domestic corporation," "business corporation" or "domestic business corporation" means a corporation for profit, which is not a foreign corporation, incorporated under this Act.

"Deliver" or "delivery" means any method of delivery used in conventional commercial practice, including delivery by hand, mail, commercial delivery, and, if authorized in accordance with section 1.41, by electronic transmission.

"Distribution" means a direct or indirect transfer of cash or other property (except a corporation's own shares) or incurrence of indebtedness by a corporation to or for the benefit of its shareholders in respect of any of its shares. A distribution may be in the form of a payment of a dividend; a purchase, redemption, or other acquisition of shares; a distribution of indebtedness; a distribution in liquidation; or otherwise.

"Document" means (i) any tangible medium on which information is inscribed, and includes handwritten, typed, printed or similar instruments, and copies of such instruments, or (ii) an electronic record.

"Domestic," with respect to an entity, means an entity governed as to its internal affairs by the law of this state.

"Effective date," when referring to a document accepted for filing by the secretary of state, means the time and date determined in accordance with section 1.23.

"Electronic" means relating to technology having electrical, digital, magnetic, wireless, optical, electromagnetic, or similar capabilities.

"Electronic record" means information that is stored in an electronic or other nontangible medium and is retrievable in paper form through an automated process used in conventional commercial practice, unless otherwise authorized in accordance with section 1.41(j).

"Electronic transmission" or "electronically transmitted" means any form or process of communication not directly involving the physical transfer of paper or another tangible medium, which (i) is suitable for the retention, retrieval, and reproduction of information by the recipient, and (ii) is retrievable in paper form by the recipient through an automated process used in conventional commercial practice, unless otherwise authorized in accordance with section 1.41(j).

"Eligible entity" means a domestic or foreign unincorporated entity or a domestic or foreign nonprofit corporation.

"Eligible interests" means interests or memberships.

"Employee" includes an officer but not a director. A director may accept duties that make the director also an employee.

"Entity" includes domestic and foreign business corporation; domestic and foreign nonprofit corporation; estate; trust; domestic and foreign unincorporated entity; and state, United States, and foreign government.

"Expenses" means reasonable expenses of any kind that are incurred in connection with a matter.

"Filing entity" means an unincorporated entity, other than a limited liability partnership, that is of a type that is created by filing a public organic record or is required to file a public organic record that evidences its creation.

"Foreign," with respect to an entity, means an entity governed as to its internal affairs by the organic law of a jurisdiction other than this state.

"Foreign corporation" or "foreign business corporation" means a corporation incorporated under a law other than the law of this state which would be a business corporation if incorporated under the law of this state.

"Foreign nonprofit corporation" means a corporation incorporated under a law other than the law of this state which would be a nonprofit corporation if incorporated under the law of this state.

"Foreign registration statement" means the foreign registration statement described in section 15.03.

"Governmental subdivision" includes authority, county, district, and municipality.

"Governor" means any person under whose authority the powers of an entity are exercised and under whose direction the activities and affairs of the entity are managed pursuant to the organic law governing the entity and its organic rules.

"Includes" and "including" denote a partial definition or a nonexclusive list.

"Individual" means a natural person.

"Interest" means either or both of the following rights under the organic law governing an unincorporated entity:

    (i) the right to receive distributions from the entity either in the ordinary course or upon liquidation; or

    (ii) the right to receive notice or vote on issues involving its internal affairs, other than as an agent, assignee, proxy or person responsible for managing its business and affairs.

"Interest holder" means a person who holds of record an interest.

"Interest holder liability" means:

    (i) personal liability for a debt, obligation, or other liability of a domestic or foreign corporation or eligible entity that is imposed on a person:

        (A) solely by reason of the person's status as a shareholder, member or interest holder; or

(B) by the articles of incorporation of the domestic corporation or the organic rules of the eligible entity or foreign corporation that make one or more specified shareholders, members, or interest holders, or categories of shareholders, members, or interest holders, liable in their capacity as shareholders, members, or interest holders for all or specified liabilities of the corporation or eligible entity; or

(ii) an obligation of a shareholder, member, or interest holder under the articles of incorporation of a domestic corporation or the organic rules of an eligible entity or foreign corporation to contribute to the entity.

For purposes of the foregoing, except as otherwise provided in the articles of incorporation of a domestic corporation or the organic law or organic rules of an eligible entity or a foreign corporation, interest holder liability arises under clause (i) when the corporation or eligible entity incurs the liability.

"Jurisdiction of formation" means the state or country the law of which includes the organic law governing a domestic or foreign corporation or eligible entity.

"Means" denotes an exhaustive definition.

"Membership" means the rights of a member in a domestic or foreign nonprofit corporation.

"Merger" means a transaction pursuant to section 11.02.

"Nonfiling entity" means an unincorporated entity that is of a type that is not created by filing a public organic record.

"Nonprofit corporation" or "domestic nonprofit corporation" means a corporation incorporated under the laws of this state and subject to the provisions of the [name of state] Nonprofit Corporation Act.

"Organic law" means the statute governing the internal affairs of a domestic or foreign business or nonprofit corporation or unincorporated entity.

"Organic rules" means the public organic record and private organic rules of a domestic or foreign corporation or eligible entity.

"Person" includes an individual and an entity.

"Principal office" means the office (in or out of this state) so designated in the annual report or foreign registration statement where the principal executive offices of a domestic or foreign corporation are located.

"Private organic rules" means (i) the bylaws of a domestic or foreign business or nonprofit corporation or (ii) the rules, regardless of whether in writing, that govern the internal affairs of an unincorporated entity, are binding on all its interest holders, and are not part of its public organic record, if any. Where private organic rules have been amended or restated, the term means the private organic rules as last amended or restated.

"Proceeding" includes civil suit and criminal, administrative, and investigatory action.

"Public organic record" means (i) the articles of incorporation of a domestic or foreign business or nonprofit corporation or (ii) the document, if any, the filing of which is required to create an unincorporated entity, or which creates the unincorporated entity and is required to be filed. Where a public organic record has been amended or restated, the term means the public organic record as last amended or restated.

"Record date" means the date fixed for determining the identity of the corporation's shareholders and their shareholdings for purposes of this Act. Unless another time is specified when the record date is fixed, the determination shall be made as of the close of business at the principal office of the corporation on the date so fixed.

"Record shareholder" means (i) the person in whose name shares are registered in the records of the corporation or (ii) the person identified as the beneficial owner of shares in a beneficial ownership certificate pursuant to section 7.23 on file with the corporation to the extent of the rights granted by such certificate.

"Registered foreign corporation" means a foreign corporation registered to do business in the state pursuant to chapter 15.

"Secretary" means the corporate officer to whom the board of directors has delegated responsibility under section 8.40(c) to maintain the minutes of the meetings of the board of directors and of the shareholders and for authenticating records of the corporation.

"Share exchange" means a transaction pursuant to section 11.03.

"Shareholder" means a record shareholder.

"Shares" means the units into which the proprietary interests in a domestic or foreign corporation are divided.

"Sign" or "signature" means, with present intent to authenticate or adopt a document:

(i) to execute or adopt a tangible symbol to a document, and includes any manual, facsimile, or conformed signature; or

(ii) to attach to or logically associate with an electronic transmission an electronic sound, symbol, or process, and includes an electronic signature in an electronic transmission.

"State," when referring to a part of the United States, includes a state and commonwealth (and their agencies and governmental subdivisions) and a territory and insular possession (and their agencies and governmental subdivisions) of the United States.

"Subscriber" means a person who subscribes for shares in a corporation, whether before or after incorporation.

"Type of entity" means a generic form of entity:

(i) recognized at common law; or

(ii) formed under an organic law, regardless of whether some entities formed under that law are subject to provisions of that law that create different categories of the form of entity.

"Unincorporated entity" means an organization or artificial legal person that either has a separate legal existence or has the power to acquire an estate in real property in its own name and that is not any of the following: a domestic or foreign business or nonprofit corporation, a series of a limited liability company or of another type of entity, an estate, a trust, a state, United States, or foreign government. The term includes a general partnership, limited liability company, limited partnership, business trust, joint stock association and unincorporated nonprofit association.

"United States" includes district, authority, bureau, commission, department, and any other agency of the United States.

"Unrestricted voting trust beneficial owner" means, with respect to any shareholder rights, a voting trust beneficial owner whose entitlement to exercise the shareholder right in question is not inconsistent with the voting trust agreement.

"Voting group" means all shares of one or more classes or series that under the articles of incorporation or this Act are entitled to vote and be counted together collectively on a matter at a meeting of shareholders. All shares entitled by the articles of incorporation or this Act to vote generally on the matter are for that purpose a single voting group.

"Voting power" means the current power to vote in the election of directors.

"Voting trust beneficial owner" means an owner of a beneficial interest in shares of the corporation held in a voting trust established pursuant to section 7.30(a).

"Writing" or "written" means any information in the form of a document.

Official Comment

Section 1.40 contains definitions of terms used generally throughout the Act. Other subchapters and sections of the Act contain specialized definitions that are applicable only to those subchapters or sections.

Beneficial Shareholder

. . .

When shares of a public corporation are held, as explained in the Official Comment to section 7.23, indirectly in street name with a broker-dealer or other financial institution, which may in turn have the shares on deposit with Depository Trust Company ("DTC") as a clearing agency, a reference to shares in this Act is technically a reference to a "securities entitlement" under section 8–102(a)(17) of the Uniform Commercial Code, which is an undivided interest in a mass of shares held by the financial intermediary or on deposit with DTC. Nevertheless, the Act continues for convenience to refer to the interests as "shares," and thus references to shares should be read to include securities entitlements with respect to those shares. . . .

Distribution

Section 1.40 defines "distribution" to include all transfers of cash or other property made by a corporation to any shareholder in respect of the corporation's shares, except mere changes in the unit of interest such as share dividends and share splits. Thus, a "distribution" includes the payment of a dividend, a purchase by a corporation of its own shares, a distribution of evidences of indebtedness or promissory notes of the corporation, and a distribution in voluntary or involuntary liquidation. If a corporation incurs indebtedness to shareholders in connection with a distribution (as in the case of a distribution of a debt instrument or an installment purchase of shares), the creation, incurrence, or distribution of the indebtedness is the event which constitutes the distribution rather than the subsequent payment of the debt by the corporation, except in the situation addressed in section 6.40(g).

The term "indirect" in the definition of "distribution" is intended to address transactions like the repurchase of parent company shares by a subsidiary whose actions are controlled by the parent. It also is intended to address any other transaction in which the substance is clearly the same as a typical dividend or share repurchase, no matter how structured or labeled. . . .

Electronic Transmission

The terms "electronic," "electronic record," "electronic transmission" and "electronically transmitted" incorporate into the Act terminology from the Uniform Electronic Transmissions Act ("UETA") and the federal Electronic Signatures in Global and National Commerce Act ("E-Sign"). See Official Comment to section 1.41, Note on the Relationship Between Act Provisions on Electronic Technology and UETA and E-Sign. Electronic records and transmissions are intended to be broadly construed.

Entity

The term "entity," defined in section 1.40, appears in the definition of "person" in section 1.40 and covers all types of artificial persons. Estates and trusts and general partnerships are included even though they may not, in some jurisdictions, be considered artificial persons. "Trust," by itself, means a nonbusiness trust, such as a traditional testamentary or inter vivos trust. The term "entity" is broader than the term "unincorporated entity" which is also defined in section 1.40. See also the definitions in section 1.40 of "governmental subdivision," "state," and "United States." A form of co-ownership of property or sharing of returns from property that is not a partnership under the Uniform Partnership Act will not be an "unincorporated entity." . . .

Membership

"Membership" is defined in section 1.40 to refer only to the rights of a member in a nonprofit corporation. Although the owners of a limited liability company are generally referred to as "members," for purposes of the Act they are referred to as "interest holders" and what they own in the limited liability company is referred to in the Act as an "interest."

Organic Rules, Public Organic Record and Private Organic Rules

The term "organic rules" in section 1.40 includes both public organic records and private organic rules. The term "public organic record" includes such documents as the articles of incorporation of a business or nonprofit corporation, the certificate of limited partnership of a limited partnership, the articles of organization or certificate of formation of a limited liability company, the deed of trust of a business trust and comparable documents, however denominated, that are publicly filed to create other types of unincorporated entities. An election of limited liability partnership status is not of itself a public organic record because it does not create the underlying general or limited partnership by filing the election, although the election may be made part of the public organic record of the partnership by its organic law. The term "private organic rules" includes corporate bylaws, a partnership agreement of a general or limited partnership, an operating agreement of a limited liability company and comparable agreements, however denominated, of unincorporated types of other entities. Private organic rules of unincorporated entities are not required by the Act to be in writing, and therefore would include oral partnership agreements and oral operating agreements. . . .

Principal Office

Many corporations maintain numerous offices, but there is usually one office, sometimes colloquially referred to as the home office or headquarters, where the principal corporate officers are located. The corporation must designate its principal office address in the annual report required by section 16.21, and a foreign corporation must also do so in its foreign registration statement. To clarify which corporate office is the principal office, the Act defines the office designated by the corporation in the annual report (or foreign registration statement) as the principal office of the corporation. . . .

Shareholder and Record Shareholder

The term "shareholder" is usually used in the Act to mean a "record shareholder" as defined in section 1.40, but section 1.40 contemplates that definitions may be expanded or limited by the Act for purposes of specific provisions. The definition of "record shareholder" in section 1.40 includes a beneficial owner of shares named in a beneficial ownership certificate under section 7.23, but only to the extent of the rights granted the beneficial owner in the certificate—for example, the right to receive notice of, and vote at, shareholders' meetings. Various substantive sections of the Act also permit holders of voting trust certificates or beneficial owners of shares (not subject to a beneficial ownership certificate under section 7.23) to exercise some of the rights of a "shareholder." See, for example, section 7.40, which relates to derivative proceedings. Separate definitions of "voting trust beneficial owner," "unrestricted voting trust beneficial owner" and "beneficial shareholder" also appear in section 1.40.

Sign or Signature

The definition of "sign" or "signature" incorporates into the Act concepts and terminology from UETA and the federal E-Sign. Thus, the terms "sign" and "signature" include not only traditional forms of signing, such as manual, facsimile, or conformed signatures, but also electronic signatures in electronic transmissions. The intent of the Act is that any manifestation of an intention to sign or authenticate a document be accepted, although electronic transmissions having electronic signatures must comply with the requirements in the definition of "electronic transmission," including being retrievable in paper form by the recipient through an automated process unless otherwise authorized in accordance with section 1.41(j).

Unincorporated Entity

The term "unincorporated entity" is a subset of the broader term "entity" and includes an unincorporated nonprofit association. The Uniform Unincorporated Nonprofit Association Act gives an unincorporated nonprofit association the power to acquire an estate in real property and thus an unincorporated nonprofit association organized in a state that has adopted that act will be an "unincorporated entity." At common law, an unincorporated nonprofit association was not a legal entity and did not have the power to acquire real property.

As used in the definition of unincorporated entity, "business trust" includes any trust carrying on a business, such as a Massachusetts business trust, real estate investment trust, or other common law or statutory business trust. The term "unincorporated entity" (and thus the term "eligible entity") expressly excludes series of limited liability companies or of other types of entities, and estates and trusts (*i.e.*, trusts that are not business trusts), regardless of whether they would be considered artificial persons under the governing jurisdiction's law, to make it clear that they are not eligible to participate in a conversion under chapter 9 or a merger or share exchange under chapter 11.

Voting Group

Section 1.40 defines "voting group" for purposes of the Act as a matter of convenient reference. When the definition refers to shares entitled to vote "generally" on a matter, it signifies all shares entitled to vote together on the matter by the articles of incorporation or the Act, regardless of whether they also have the right to be counted or tabulated separately. "Voting groups" are thus the basic units of collective voting by shareholders, and voting by voting groups may provide essential protection to one or more classes or series of shares against actions that are detrimental to the rights or interests of that class or series.

The determination of which shares form part of a single voting group must be made from the provisions of the articles of incorporation and of the Act. In a few instances under the Act, the board of directors may establish the right to vote by voting groups. On most matters to be voted on by shareholders, only a single voting group, consisting of a class of voting or common shares, will be involved, and action on such a matter is effective when approved by that voting group pursuant to section 7.25. In other circumstances, the vote of multiple groups may be required. See sections 7.25 and 7.26.

Voting Power

Application of the definition of "voting power" turns on whether the relevant shares carry the power to vote in the election of directors as of the time for voting on the relevant transaction. If shares carry the power to vote in the election of directors only under a certain contingency, as is often the case with preferred stock, the shares would not carry voting power within the meaning of section 1.40 unless the contingency has occurred, and then only during the period when the voting rights are in effect. Shares that carry the power to vote for any directors as of the time to vote on the relevant transaction have the current power to vote in the election of directors within the meaning of the definition, even if the shares do not carry the power to vote for all directors. . . .

Writing or Written

"Writing" or "written" means information in the form of a "document," which in turn means any tangible medium on which information is inscribed, such as a paper instrument, as well as an electronic record. Thus, under the Act a written consent of shareholders under section 7.04, for example, may be in the form of paper or an electronic record.

§ 1.41.   Notices and Other Communications

(a) A notice under this Act must be in writing unless oral notice is reasonable in the circumstances. Unless otherwise agreed between the sender and the recipient, words in a notice or other communication under this Act must be in English.

(b) A notice or other communication may be given by any method of delivery, except that electronic transmissions must be in accordance with this section. If the methods of delivery are impracticable, a notice or other communication may be given by means of a broad non-exclusionary distribution to the public (which may include a newspaper of general circulation in the area where published; radio, television, or other form of public broadcast communication; or other methods of distribution that the corporation has previously identified to its shareholders).

(c) A notice or other communication to a domestic corporation or to a foreign corporation registered to do business in this state may be delivered to the corporation's registered agent at its registered office or to the secretary at the corporation's principal office shown in its most recent annual report or, in the case of a foreign corporation that has not yet delivered an annual report, in its foreign registration statement.

(d) A notice or other communications may be delivered by electronic transmission if consented to by the recipient or if authorized by subsection (j).

(e) Any consent under subsection (d) may be revoked by the person who consented by written or electronic notice to the person to whom the consent was delivered. Any such consent is deemed revoked if (i) the corporation is unable to deliver two consecutive electronic transmissions given by the corporation in accordance with such consent, and (ii) such inability becomes known to the secretary or an assistant secretary or to the transfer agent, or other person responsible for the giving of notice or other communications; provided, however, the inadvertent failure to treat such inability as a revocation shall not invalidate any meeting or other action.

(f) Unless otherwise agreed between the sender and the recipient, an electronic transmission is received when:

(1) it enters an information processing system that the recipient has designated or uses for the purposes of receiving electronic transmissions or information of the type sent, and from which the recipient is able to retrieve the electronic transmission; and

(2) it is in a form capable of being processed by that system.

(g) Receipt of an electronic acknowledgement from an information processing system described in subsection (f)(1) establishes that an electronic transmission was received but, by itself, does not establish that the content sent corresponds to the content received.

(h) An electronic transmission is received under this section even if no person is aware of its receipt.

(i) A notice or other communication, if in a comprehensible form or manner, is effective at the earliest of the following:

(1) if in a physical form, the earliest of when it is actually received, or when it is left at:

(i) a shareholder's address shown on the corporation's record of shareholders maintained by the corporation under section 16.01(d);

(ii) a director's residence or usual place of business; or

(iii) the corporation's principal office;

(2) if mailed postage prepaid and correctly addressed to a shareholder, upon deposit in the United States mail;

(3) if mailed by United States mail postage prepaid and correctly addressed to a recipient other than a shareholder, the earliest of when it is actually received, or:

(i) if sent by registered or certified mail, return receipt requested, the date shown on the return receipt signed by or on behalf of the addressee; or

(ii) five days after it is deposited in the United States mail;

(4) if an electronic transmission, when it is received as provided in subsection (f); and

(5) if oral, when communicated.

(j) A notice or other communication may be in the form of an electronic transmission that cannot be directly reproduced in paper form by the recipient through an automated process used in conventional commercial practice only if (i) the electronic transmission is otherwise retrievable in perceivable form, and (ii) the sender and the recipient have consented in writing to the use of such form of electronic transmission.

(k) If this Act prescribes requirements for notices or other communications in particular circumstances, those requirements govern. If articles of incorporation or bylaws prescribe requirements for notices or other communications, not inconsistent with this section or other provisions of this Act, those requirements govern. The articles of incorporation or bylaws may authorize or require delivery of notices of meetings of directors by electronic transmission.

(*l*) In the event that any provisions of this Act are deemed to modify, limit, or supersede the federal Electronic Signatures in Global and National Commerce Act, 15 U.S.C. §§ 7001 *et seq.*, the provisions of this Act shall control to the maximum extent permitted by section 102(a)(2) of that federal act.

Official Comment

. . .

Note on the Relationship Between Act Provisions on Electronic Technology and UETA and E-Sign

The provisions of the Act relating to electronic records, electronic transmissions and related matters, found principally in the definitions in section 1.40, are set against the backdrop of the Uniform Electronic Transmissions Act ("UETA") and the federal Electronic Signatures in Global and National Commerce Act ("E-Sign"). A brief description of certain aspects of UETA and E-Sign is useful to understand the Act's electronic technology provisions.

UETA adopted definitions for the terms electronic, electronic records, electronic signatures, records, transactions, and the like, as well as provisions governing the use of those terms. UETA applies to "transactions," which are defined to mean actions between two or more persons "relating to the conduct of business [or] commercial ... affairs." UETA §§ 2(16) and 3(a). The reach of the term "transactions" in the context of a comprehensive business corporation act is unclear. For example, although obtaining a proxy from a shareholder that is voting on a cash-out merger would likely constitute a "transaction," the unilateral act by a corporation of sending notice of an annual meeting at which no significant action is proposed might not.

If UETA applies, it establishes certain statutory norms for the validity of electronic signatures, electronic records, etc. However, UETA also provides that it applies only to transactions between parties each of which has agreed to conduct transactions by electronic means, and that such agreement is determined from the context and surrounding circumstances, including the parties' conduct. *Id.* § 5(b).

560

E-Sign, codified at 15 U.S.C. §§ 7001 *et seq.*, in turn adopted the substance of UETA's principal definitions, including electronic, electronic signature, record, and transaction, as well as many of the operative provisions of UETA. The applicability of E-Sign, like UETA, turns on whether a "transaction" is involved. *Id.* § 7001(a). Like UETA, E-Sign's applicability also depends upon the parties consenting to transact business by electronic means. *Id.* § 7001(b)(2).

Importantly, E-Sign contains a federal preemption provision that itself excepts certain state adoptions of UETA. Thus, in general terms, section 7002(a) of E-Sign allows a state statute to modify, limit, or supersede the provisions of E-Sign section 7001 only if (i) it is a state enactment of the version of UETA approved in 1999, and (ii) the state's enactment of UETA does not contain any state exceptions, or "carve outs," other than those contained in the 1999 version of UETA § 3(b)(4). If, for example, a state enactment of UETA carved out that state's general business corporation law from the applicability of UETA, a carve out that is not contained in the 1999 version of UETA § 3(b)(4), and that business corporation law was deemed to be inconsistent with E-Sign, the offending provisions of the business corporation law would be preempted. *Id.* § 7002(a)(1).

Note one aspect of the definition of "record" in both UETA and E-Sign: they both provide that information that is stored in an electronic medium must simply be "retrievable in perceivable form." This is in contrast to states that require not only that an electronic transmission may be retained, retrieved, and reviewed but also requires that it "may be directly reproduced in paper form by [the] recipient through an automated process." The former would include, *e.g.*, a voicemail, a text message, and an electronic page, although the latter would not.

Against that backdrop, the Act's electronic technology provisions align, in all material respects, with the terminology and concepts of UETA and E-Sign. However, the Act does not adopt wholesale the vocabulary and concepts of UETA and E-Sign . . .

The Act instead adopts an approach that involves incorporating into the definitions in section 1.40, the principal electronic technology vocabulary and concepts of UETA and E-Sign, in ways that do not require substantial changes throughout the Act.

Thus, the Act's electronic technology provisions:

- define "document" "writing" and "written," to include electronic records;

- define "deliver" and "delivery" to include electronic transmissions if properly authorized;

- use definitions of "electronic" and "electronic record" that borrow heavily from UETA and E-Sign;

- define "electronic transmission" and "electronically transmitted" to incorporate UETA and E-Sign vocabulary and concepts;

- require that electronic records and electronic transmissions be retrievable in paper form through an automated process used in conventional commercial practice, unless specifically authorized in accordance with section 1.41(j), thereby establishing the default rule that, until they are used in conventional commercial practice, voicemails and text messages are not generally recognized as valid, absent a specific consent (parties may, however, consent to their use); and

- define "sign" or "signature" to incorporate technical E-Sign and UETA terminology, while retaining common terminology such as "any manual, facsimile, or conformed signature."

This approach is pragmatic, addresses the vast majority of recurring questions involving electronic transmissions and records, and yet enables parties who wish to do so to consent specifically to use electronic records or transmissions that are merely "retrievable in perceivable form."

As for the preemption issue under E-Sign, the Act's electronic technology provisions are consistent in all material respects with E-Sign and UETA. . . .

§ 1.42. Number of Shareholders

(a) For purposes of this Act, the following identified as a shareholder in a corporation's current record of shareholders constitutes one shareholder:

(1) three or fewer co-owners;

(2) a corporation, partnership, trust, estate, or other entity; and

(3) the trustees, guardians, custodians, or other fiduciaries of a single trust, estate, or account.

(b) For purposes of this Act, shareholdings registered in substantially similar names constitute one shareholder if it is reasonable to believe that the names represent the same person.

§ 1.43. Qualified Director

(a) A "qualified director" is a director who, at the time action is to be taken under:

(1) section 2.02(b)(6), is not a director (i) to whom the limitation or elimination of the duty of an officer to offer potential business opportunities to the corporation would apply, or (ii) who has a material relationship with any other person to whom the limitation or elimination would apply;

(2) section 7.44, does not have (i) a material interest in the outcome of the proceeding, or (ii) a material relationship with a person who has such an interest;

(3) section 8.53 or 8.55, (i) is not a party to the proceeding, (ii) is not a director as to whom a transaction is a director's conflicting interest transaction or who sought a disclaimer of the corporation's interest in a business opportunity under section 8.70, which transaction or disclaimer is challenged in the proceeding, and (iii) does not have a material relationship with a director described in either clause (i) or clause (ii) of this subsection (a)(3);

(4) section 8.62, is not a director (i) as to whom the transaction is a director's conflicting interest transaction, or (ii) who has a material relationship with another director as to whom the transaction is a director's conflicting interest transaction; or

(5) section 8.70, is not a director who (i) pursues or takes advantage of the business opportunity, directly, or indirectly through or on behalf of another person, or (ii) has a material relationship with a director or officer who pursues or takes advantage of the business opportunity, directly, or indirectly through or on behalf of another person.

(b) For purposes of this section:

(1) "material relationship" means a familial, financial, professional, employment or other relationship that would reasonably be expected to impair the objectivity of the director's judgment when participating in the action to be taken; and

(2) "material interest" means an actual or potential benefit or detriment (other than one which would devolve on the corporation or the shareholders generally) that would reasonably be expected to impair the objectivity of the director's judgment when participating in the action to be taken.

(c) The presence of one or more of the following circumstances shall not automatically prevent a director from being a qualified director:

(1) nomination or election of the director to the current board by any director who is not a qualified director with respect to the matter (or by any person that has a material relationship with that director), acting alone or participating with others;

(2) service as a director of another corporation of which a director who is not a qualified director with respect to the matter (or any individual who has a material relationship with that director), is or was also a director; or

(3) with respect to action to be taken under section 7.44, status as a named defendant, as a director against whom action is demanded, or as a director who approved the conduct being challenged.

Official Comment

. . .

Although the term "qualified director" embraces the concept of independence, it does so only in relation to the director's interest or involvement in the specific situations to which the definition applies. The judicial decisions that have examined the qualifications of directors for such purposes have generally required that directors be both *disinterested,* in the sense of not having exposure to an actual or potential benefit or detriment arising out of the action being taken (as opposed to an actual or potential benefit or detriment to the corporation or all shareholders generally), and *independent,* in the sense of having no personal or other relationship with an interested director (*e.g.,* a director who is a party to a transaction with the corporation) that presents a reasonable likelihood that the director's objectivity will be impaired. The "qualified director" concept embraces both of those requirements, and its application is situation-specific; that is, "qualified director" determinations will depend upon the directly relevant facts and circumstances, and the disqualification of a director to act arises from factors that would reasonably be expected to impair the objectivity of the director's judgment. On the other hand, the concept does not suggest that a "qualified director" has or should have special expertise to act on the matter in question. . . .

1. Disqualification Due to Conflicting Interest

The "qualified director" concept prescribes significant disqualifications, depending upon the purpose for which a director might be considered eligible to participate in the action to be taken. These disqualifications include the following:

- In the case of action under a provision adopted under the authority of section 2.02(b)(6) to limit or eliminate any duty of an officer to offer the corporation business opportunities, the definition excludes any director who is also an officer and to whom the provision would apply.

- In the case of action on dismissal of a derivative proceeding under section 7.44, the definition excludes any director who has a material interest in the outcome of the proceeding, such as where the proceeding involves a challenge to the validity of a transaction in which the director has a material financial interest.

- In the case of action to approve indemnification or advance of funds for expenses, the definition excludes any director who is a party to the proceeding (see section 8.50 for the definition of "party" and for the definition of "proceeding").

- In the case of action to approve a director's conflicting interest transaction, the definition excludes any director whose interest, knowledge or status results in the transaction being treated as a "director's conflicting interest transaction." See section 8.60 for the definition of "director's conflicting interest transaction."

- In the case of action under section 8.70(a) to disclaim corporate interest in a business opportunity, the definition excludes any director who directly or indirectly pursues or takes advantage of the business opportunity, or who has a material relationship with another director or officer who does so.

Whether a director has a material interest in the outcome of a proceeding in which the director does not have a conflicting personal interest is heavily fact-dependent. At one end of the spectrum, if a claim against a director is clearly frivolous or is not supported by particularized and well-pleaded facts, the director should not be deemed to have a "material interest in the outcome of the proceeding" within the meaning of section 1.43(a)(2), even though the director is named as a defendant. At the other end of the spectrum, a director normally should be deemed to have a "material interest in the outcome of the proceeding" within the meaning of section 1.43(a)(2) if a claim against the director is supported by particularized and well-pleaded facts which, if true, would be likely to give rise to a significant adverse outcome against the director.

2. Disqualification Due to Relationships with Interested Persons

In each context in which the "qualified director" definition applies, it also excludes any director who has a "material relationship" with another director (or, with respect to a provision applying to an officer under section 2.02(b)(6) or section 8.70, a "material relationship" with that officer) who is not disinterested for one or more of the reasons outlined in the preceding paragraph. Any relationship with such a person, whether the relationship is familial, financial, professional, employment or otherwise, is a "material relationship," as that term is defined in section 1.43(b)(1), if it would reasonably be expected to impair the objectivity of the director's judgment when voting or otherwise participating in action to be taken on a matter referred to in section 1.43(a). The determination of whether there is a "material relationship" should be based on the practicalities of the situation rather than on formalistic considerations. For example, a director employed by a corporation controlled by another director should be regarded as having an employment relationship with that director. On the other hand, a casual social acquaintance with another director should not be regarded as a disqualifying relationship.

The term "qualified director" is distinct from the generic term "independent director," which is not used in the Act. As a result, a director who might typically be viewed as an "independent director" may in some circumstances not be a "qualified director," and vice versa. See also the Official Comment to section 8.01.

3. Elimination of Automatic Disqualification in Certain Circumstances

Section 1.43(c) addresses three categories of circumstances that, if present alone or together, do not automatically prevent a director from being a qualified director:

- Subsection (c)(1) makes it clear that the participation of nonqualified directors (or interested shareholders or other interested persons) in the nomination or election of a director does not automatically prevent the director so nominated or elected from being qualified. Special litigation committees acting with regard to derivative litigation often consist of directors nominated or elected (after the alleged wrongful acts) by directors named as defendants in the action. In other settings, directors who are seeking indemnification, or who are interested in a director's conflicting interest transaction, may have participated in the nomination or election of an individual director who is otherwise a "qualified director."

- Subsection (c)(2) provides, in a similar fashion, that the mere fact that an individual director is or was a director of another corporation—on the board of which a director who is not a "qualified director" also serves or has served—does not automatically prevent qualification to act.

- Subsection (c)(3) confirms a number of decisions, involving dismissal of derivative proceedings, in which the court rejected a disqualification claim predicated on the mere fact that a director had been named as a defendant, was an individual against whom action has been demanded, or had approved the action being challenged. These cases have held that, where a director's approval of the challenged action is at issue, approval does not automatically make the director ineligible to act. On the other hand, for example, director approval of a challenged transaction, in combination with other particularized facts showing that the director's ability to act objectively on a proposal to dismiss a derivative proceeding is impaired by a material conflicting personal interest in the transaction, disqualifies a director from acting on the proposal to dismiss the proceeding.

The effect of section 1.43(c), while significant, is limited. It merely precludes an automatic inference of director disqualification from the circumstances specified in that subsection.

§ 1.44.   Householding

(a) A corporation has delivered written notice or any other report or statement under this Act, the articles of incorporation or the bylaws to all shareholders who share a common address if:

(1) the corporation delivers one copy of the notice, report or statement to the common address;

(2) the corporation addresses the notice, report or statement to those shareholders either as a group or to each of those shareholders individually or to the shareholders in a form to which each of those shareholders has consented; and

(3) each of those shareholders consents to delivery of a single copy of such notice, report or statement to the shareholders' common address.

(b) Any such consent described in subsections (a)(2) or (a)(3) shall be revocable by any of such shareholders who deliver written notice of revocation to the corporation. If such written notice of revocation is delivered, the corporation shall begin providing individual notices, reports or other statements to the revoking shareholder no later than 30 days after delivery of the written notice of revocation.

(c) Any shareholder who fails to object by written notice to the corporation, within 60 days of written notice by the corporation of its intention to deliver single copies of notices, reports or statements to shareholders who share a common address as permitted by subsection (a), shall be deemed to have consented to receiving such single copy at the common address; provided that the notice of intention explains that consent may be revoked and the method for revoking.

Official Comment

The proxy rules under the Securities Exchange Act of 1934 permit publicly held corporations to meet their obligation to deliver proxy statements and annual reports to shareholders who share a common address by delivery of a single copy of such materials to the common address under certain conditions. This practice is known as "householding." This section permits a corporation comparable flexibility to household the written notice of shareholders' meetings as well as any other written notices, reports or statements required to be delivered to shareholders under the Act or the corporation's articles of incorporation or bylaws. Ability to household such notices, reports or statements would not, of course, eliminate the practical necessity of delivering to a common address sufficient copies of any accompanying document requiring individual shareholder signature or other action, such as a proxy card or consent. . . .

Subchapter E

Ratification of Defective Corporate Actions

§ 1.45. Definitions

In this subchapter:

"Corporate action" means any action taken by or on behalf of the corporation, including any action taken by the incorporator, the board of directors, a committee of the board of directors, an officer or agent of the corporation or the shareholders.

"Date of the defective corporate action" means the date (or the approximate date, if the exact date is unknown) the defective corporate action was purported to have been taken.

"Defective corporate action" means (i) any corporate action purportedly taken that is, and at the time such corporate action was purportedly taken would have been, within the power of the corporation, but is void or voidable due to a failure of authorization, and (ii) an overissue.

"Failure of authorization" means the failure to authorize, approve or otherwise effect a corporate action in compliance with the provisions of this Act, the articles of incorporation or bylaws, a corporate resolution or any plan or agreement to which the corporation is a party, if and to the extent such failure would render such corporate action void or voidable.

"Overissue" means the purported issuance of:

(i) shares of a class or series in excess of the number of shares of a class or series the corporation has the power to issue under section 6.01 at the time of such issuance; or

(ii) shares of any class or series that is not then authorized for issuance by the articles of incorporation.

"Putative shares" means the shares of any class or series (including shares issued upon exercise of rights, options, warrants or other securities convertible into shares of the corporation, or interests with respect to such shares) that were created or issued as a result of a defective corporate action, that (i) but for any failure of authorization would constitute valid shares, or (ii) cannot be determined by the board of directors to be valid shares.

"Valid shares" means the shares of any class or series that have been duly authorized and validly issued in accordance with this Act, including as a result of ratification or validation under this subchapter.

"Validation effective time" with respect to any defective corporate action ratified under this subchapter means the later of:

(i) the time at which the ratification of the defective corporate action is approved by the shareholders, or if approval of shareholders is not required, the time at which the notice required by section 1.49 becomes effective in accordance with section 1.41; and

(ii) the time at which any articles of validation filed in accordance with section 1.51 become effective.

The validation effective time shall not be affected by the filing or pendency of a judicial proceeding under section 1.52 or otherwise, unless otherwise ordered by the court.

§ 1.46. Defective Corporate Actions

(a) A defective corporate action shall not be void or voidable if ratified in accordance with section 1.47 or validated in accordance with section 1.52.

(b) Ratification under section 1.47 or validation under section 1.52 shall not be deemed to be the exclusive means of ratifying or validating any defective corporate action, and the absence or failure of ratification in accordance with this subchapter shall not, of itself, affect the validity or effectiveness of any corporate action properly ratified under common law or otherwise, nor shall it create a presumption that any such corporate action is or was a defective corporate action or void or voidable.

(c) In the case of an overissue, putative shares shall be valid shares effective as of the date originally issued or purportedly issued upon:

(1) the effectiveness under this subchapter and under chapter 10 of an amendment to the articles of incorporation authorizing, designating or creating such shares; or

(2) the effectiveness of any other corporate action under this subchapter ratifying the authorization, designation or creation of such shares.

Official Comment

Subchapter E provides a statutory ratification procedure for corporate actions that may not have been properly authorized and shares that may have been improperly issued. The statutory ratification procedure is designed to supplement common law ratification. Corporate actions ratified under this subchapter remain subject to equitable review.

Examples of defective corporate actions subject to ratification include the failure of the incorporator to validly appoint an initial board of directors, corporate action taken in the absence of board resolutions authorizing the action, the failure to obtain the requisite shareholder approval of a corporate action, issuance of shares in the absence of evidence that consideration payable to the corporation for shares was received, the failure to comply with appraisal requirements and the issuance of shares without complying with preemptive rights. The ratification procedure is intended to be available only where there is objective evidence that a corporate action was defectively implemented. For example, subchapter E would permit ratification of shares previously issued but subsequently determined to have been issued improperly. It would not permit the corporation to issue shares retroactively as of an earlier date, however, where there is no objective evidence that those shares had previously been issued. Objective evidence may include resolutions, issuance of share certificates, subscription or share purchase agreements, entries in a share ledger or other correspondence indicating that shares were issued or intended to have been issued.

Section 1.46(a) does not distinguish between void and voidable actions. Instead it provides that any defective corporate action that is ratified in accordance with section 1.47 or validated under section 1.52 shall not be void or voidable. Section 1.47 is not the exclusive means by which a defective corporate action may be ratified. Thus, the general common law doctrine of ratification, as applied to a board of directors' adoption of actions taken by officers who may not have had the actual authority to take such actions, continues to be an effective mode of ratification. Section 1.46(b) makes clear that the corporation's ratification of a defective corporate action that is voidable but not void using common law methods of ratification rather than under section 1.47 will not, standing alone, affect the validity of the action or create a presumption that the action is not valid. In addition, ratification under subchapter E is distinct from correction of an already filed document under section 1.24.

Section 1.46(c) provides that an overissue can be remedied by the adoption of articles of amendment or other corporate action that has the effect of authorizing, designating or creating shares of a series or class, such that the putative shares that resulted in the overissue are deemed to be validly issued from the date of original issuance. This provision enables a corporation to cure an overissue occurring when shares have been duly authorized but are issued before articles of amendment are filed. It also permits a corporation to remedy an overissue even if it cannot specifically identify the putative shares.

§ 1.47.   Ratification of Defective Corporate Actions

(a) To ratify a defective corporate action under this section (other than the ratification of an election of the initial board of directors under subsection (b)), the board of directors shall take action ratifying the action in accordance with section 1.48, stating:

(1) the defective corporate action to be ratified and, if the defective corporate action involved the issuance of putative shares, the number and type of putative shares purportedly issued;

(2) the date of the defective corporate action;

(3) the nature of the failure of authorization with respect to the defective corporate action to be ratified; and

(4) that the board of directors approves the ratification of the defective corporate action.

(b) In the event that a defective corporate action to be ratified relates to the election of the initial board of directors of the corporation under section 2.05(a)(2), a majority of the persons who, at the time of the ratification, are exercising the powers of directors may take an action stating:

(1) the name of the person or persons who first took action in the name of the corporation as the initial board of directors of the corporation;

(2) the earlier of the date on which such persons first took such action or were purported to have been elected as the initial board of directors; and

(3) that the ratification of the election of such person or persons as the initial board of directors is approved.

(c) If any provision of this Act, the articles of incorporation or bylaws, any corporate resolution or any plan or agreement to which the corporation is a party in effect at the time action under subsection (a) is taken requires shareholder approval or would have required shareholder approval at the date of the occurrence of the defective corporate action, the ratification of the defective corporate action approved in the action taken by the directors under subsection (a) shall be submitted to the shareholders for approval in accordance with section 1.48.

(d) Unless otherwise provided in the action taken by the board of directors under subsection (a), after the action by the board of directors has been taken and, if required, approved by the shareholders, the board of directors may abandon the ratification at any time before the validation effective time without further action of the shareholders.

§ 1.48. Action on Ratification

(a) The quorum and voting requirements applicable to a ratifying action by the board of directors under section 1.47(a) shall be the quorum and voting requirements applicable to the corporate action proposed to be ratified at the time such ratifying action is taken.

(b) If the ratification of the defective corporate action requires approval by the shareholders under section 1.47(c), and if the approval is to be given at a meeting, the corporation shall notify each holder of valid and putative shares, regardless of whether entitled to vote, as of the record date for notice of the meeting and as of the date of the occurrence of defective corporate action, provided that notice shall not be required to be given to holders of valid or putative shares whose identities or addresses for notice cannot be determined from the records of the corporation. The notice must state that the purpose, or one of the purposes, of the meeting, is to consider ratification of a defective corporate action and must be accompanied by (i) either a copy of the action taken by the board of directors in accordance with section 1.47(a) or the information required by sections 1.47(a)(1) through (a)(4), and (ii) a statement that any claim that the ratification of such defective corporate action and any putative shares issued as a result of such defective corporate action should not be effective, or should be effective only on certain conditions, shall be brought within 120 days from the applicable validation effective time.

(c) Except as provided in subsection (d) with respect to the voting requirements to ratify the election of a director, the quorum and voting requirements applicable to the approval by the shareholders required by section 1.47(c) shall be the quorum and voting requirements applicable to the corporate action proposed to be ratified at the time of such shareholder approval.

(d) The approval by shareholders to ratify the election of a director requires that the votes cast within the voting group favoring such ratification exceed the votes cast opposing such ratification of the election at a meeting at which a quorum is present.

(e) Putative shares on the record date for determining the shareholders entitled to vote on any matter submitted to shareholders under section 1.47(c) (and without giving effect to any ratification of putative shares that becomes effective as a result of such vote) shall neither be entitled to vote nor counted for quorum purposes in any vote to approve the ratification of any defective corporate action.

(f) If the approval under this section of putative shares would result in an overissue, in addition to the approval required by section 1.47, approval of an amendment to the articles of incorporation under chapter 10 to increase the number of shares of an authorized class or series or to authorize the creation of a class or series of shares so there would be no overissue shall also be required.

§ 1.49.   Notice Requirements

(a) Unless shareholder approval is required under section 1.47(c), prompt notice of an action taken under section 1.47 shall be given to each holder of valid and putative shares, regardless of whether entitled to vote, as of (i) the date of such action by the board of directors and (ii) the date of the defective corporate action ratified, provided that notice shall not be required to be given to holders of valid and putative shares whose identities or addresses for notice cannot be determined from the records of the corporation.

(b) The notice must contain (i) either a copy of the action taken by the board of directors in accordance with section 1.47(a) or (b) or the information required by sections 1.47(a)(1) through (a)(4) or sections 1.47(b)(1) through (b)(3), as applicable, and (ii) a statement that any claim that the ratification of the defective corporate action and any putative shares issued as a result of such defective corporate action should not be effective, or should be effective only on certain conditions, shall be brought within 120 days from the applicable validation effective time.

(c) No notice under this section is required with respect to any action required to be submitted to shareholders for approval under section 1.47(c) if notice is given in accordance with section 1.48(b).

(d) A notice required by this section may be given in any manner permitted by section 1.41 and, for any corporation subject to the reporting requirements of Section 13 or 15(d) of the Securities Exchange Act of 1934, may be given by means of a filing or furnishing of such notice with the United States Securities and Exchange Commission.

§ 1.50.   Effect of Ratification

From and after the validation effective time, and without regard to the 120-day period during which a claim may be brought under section 1.52:

(a) Each defective corporate action ratified in accordance with section 1.47 shall not be void or voidable as a result of the failure of authorization identified in the action taken under section 1.47(a) or (b) and shall be deemed a valid corporate action effective as of the date of the defective corporate action;

(b) The issuance of each putative share or fraction of a putative share purportedly issued pursuant to a defective corporate action identified in the action taken under section 1.47 shall not be void or voidable, and each such putative share or fraction of a putative share shall be deemed to be an identical share or fraction of a valid share as of the time it was purportedly issued; and

(c) Any corporate action taken subsequent to the defective corporate action ratified in accordance with this subchapter in reliance on such defective corporate action having been validly effected and any subsequent defective corporate action resulting directly or indirectly from such original defective corporate action shall be valid as of the time taken.

§ 1.51.   Filings

(a) If the defective corporate action ratified under this subchapter would have required under any other section of this Act a filing in accordance with this Act, then, regardless of whether a filing was previously made in respect of such defective corporate action and in lieu of a filing otherwise required by this Act, the corporation shall file articles of validation in accordance with this section, and such articles of validation shall serve to amend or substitute for any other filing with respect to such defective corporate action required by this Act.

(b) The articles of validation must set forth:

    (1) the defective corporate action that is the subject of the articles of validation (including, in the case of any defective corporate action involving the issuance of putative shares, the number and type of putative shares issued and the date or dates upon which such putative shares were purported to have been issued);

    (2) the date of the defective corporate action;

    (3) the nature of the failure of authorization in respect of the defective corporate action;

(4) a statement that the defective corporate action was ratified in accordance with section 1.47, including the date on which the board of directors ratified such defective corporate action and the date, if any, on which the shareholders approved the ratification of such defective corporate action; and

(5) the information required by subsection (c).

(c) The articles of validation must also contain the following information:

(1) if a filing was previously made in respect of the defective corporate action and no changes to such filing are required to give effect to the ratification of such defective corporate action in accordance with section 1.47, the articles of validation must set forth (i) the name, title and filing date of the filing previously made and any articles of correction to that filing and (ii) a statement that a copy of the filing previously made, together with any articles of correction to that filing, is attached as an exhibit to the articles of validation;

(2) if a filing was previously made in respect of the defective corporate action and such filing requires any change to give effect to the ratification of such defective corporate action in accordance with section 1.47, the articles of validation must set forth (i) the name, title and filing date of the filing previously made and any articles of correction to that filing and (ii) a statement that a filing containing all of the information required to be included under the applicable section or sections of the Act to give effect to such defective corporate action is attached as an exhibit to the articles of validation, and (iii) the date and time that such filing is deemed to have become effective; or

(3) if a filing was not previously made in respect of the defective corporate action and the defective corporate action ratified under section 1.47 would have required a filing under any other section of the Act, the articles of validation must set forth (i) a statement that a filing containing all of the information required to be included under the applicable section or sections of the Act to give effect to such defective corporate action is attached as an exhibit to the articles of validation, and (ii) the date and time that such filing is deemed to have become effective.

§ 1.52. Judicial Proceedings Regarding Validity of Corporate Actions

(a) Upon application by the corporation, any successor entity to the corporation, a director of the corporation, any shareholder, beneficial shareholder or unrestricted voting trust beneficial owner of the corporation, including any such shareholder, beneficial shareholder or unrestricted voting trust beneficial owner as of the date of the defective corporate action ratified under section 1.47, or any other person claiming to be substantially and adversely affected by a ratification under section 1.47, the [name or describe court] may:

(1) determine the validity and effectiveness of any corporate action or defective corporate action;

(2) determine the validity and effectiveness of any ratification under section 1.47;

(3) determine the validity of any putative shares; and

(4) modify or waive any of the procedures specified in section 1.47 or 1.48 to ratify a defective corporate action.

(b) In connection with an action under this section, the court may make such findings or orders, and take into account any factors or considerations, regarding such matters as it deems proper under the circumstances.

(c) Service of process of the application under subsection (a) on the corporation may be made in any manner provided by statute of this state or by rule of the applicable court for service on the corporation, and no other party need be joined in order for the court to adjudicate the matter. In an action filed by the corporation, the court may require notice of the action be provided to other persons specified by the court and permit such other persons to intervene in the action.

(d) Notwithstanding any other provision of this section or otherwise under applicable law, any action asserting that the ratification of any defective corporate action and any putative shares issued as a result of such defective corporate action should not be effective, or should be effective only on certain conditions, shall be brought within 120 days of the validation effective time.

Chapter 2

INCORPORATION

§ 2.01. Incorporators

One or more persons may act as the incorporator or incorporators of a corporation by delivering articles of incorporation to the secretary of state for filing.

§ 2.02. Articles of Incorporation

(a) The articles of incorporation must set forth:

(1) a corporate name for the corporation that satisfies the requirements of section 4.01;

(2) the number of shares the corporation is authorized to issue;

(3) the street and mailing addresses of the corporation's initial registered office and the name of its initial registered agent at that office; and

(4) the name and address of each incorporator.

(b) The articles of incorporation may set forth:

(1) the names and addresses of the individuals who are to serve as the initial directors;

(2) provisions not inconsistent with law regarding:

(i) the purpose or purposes for which the corporation is organized;

(ii) managing the business and regulating the affairs of the corporation;

(iii) defining, limiting, and regulating the powers of the corporation, its board of directors, and shareholders;

(iv) a par value for authorized shares or classes of shares; or

(v) the imposition of interest holder liability on shareholders;

(3) any provision that under this Act is required or permitted to be set forth in the bylaws;

(4) a provision eliminating or limiting the liability of a director to the corporation or its shareholders for money damages for any action taken, or any failure to take any action, as a director, except liability for (i) the amount of a financial benefit received by a director to which the director is not entitled; (ii) an intentional infliction of harm on the corporation or the shareholders; (iii) a violation of section 8.32; or (iv) an intentional violation of criminal law;

(5) a provision permitting or making obligatory indemnification of a director for liability as defined in section 8.50 to any person for any action taken, or any failure to take any action, as a director, except liability for (i) receipt of a financial benefit to which the director is not entitled, (ii) an intentional infliction of harm on the corporation or its shareholders, (iii) a violation of section 8.32, or (iv) an intentional violation of criminal law; and

(6) a provision limiting or eliminating any duty of a director or any other person to offer the corporation the right to have or participate in any, or one or more classes or categories of, business opportunities, before the pursuit or taking of the opportunity by the director or other person; provided that any application of such a provision to an officer or a related person of that officer (i) also requires approval of that application by the board of directors, subsequent to the effective date of the provision, by action of qualified directors taken in compliance with the same procedures as are set forth in section 8.62, and (ii) may be limited by the authorizing action of the board.

(c) The articles of incorporation need not set forth any of the corporate powers enumerated in this Act.

(d) Provisions of the articles of incorporation may be made dependent upon facts objectively ascertainable outside the articles of incorporation in accordance with section 1.20(k).

(e) As used in this section, "related person" has the meaning specified in section 8.60.

Official Comment

1. Introduction

A corporation will have perpetual duration unless a special provision is included in its articles of incorporation providing for a shorter period. See section 3.02. Similarly, a corporation with articles of incorporation which do not contain a purpose clause will have the purpose of engaging in any lawful business under section 3.01(a). . . .

3. Optional Provisions . . .

B. CORPORATE POWERS

Section 2.02(c) makes it unnecessary to set forth any corporate powers in the articles of incorporation in view of the broad grant of power in section 3.02. This grant of power, however, may be overbroad for particular corporations; if so, it may be qualified or narrowed by appropriate provisions in the articles of incorporation.

. . .

D. SHAREHOLDER LIABILITY

The basic tenet of corporation law is that shareholders are not liable for the corporation's liabilities by reason of their status as shareholders. Section 2.02(b)(2)(v) nevertheless permits a corporation to impose that liability under specified circumstances if that is desirable. If no provision of this type is included, shareholders have no liability for corporate liabilities except to the extent they become liable by reason of their own conduct or acts. See section 6.22(b).

E. LIMITATIONS OF DIRECTOR LIABILITY

Section 2.02(b)(4) authorizes the inclusion of a provision in the articles of incorporation eliminating or limiting, with certain exceptions, the liability of the directors to the corporation or its shareholders for money damages. This section is optional rather than self-executing and does not apply to equitable relief. Likewise, nothing in section 2.02(b)(4) in any way affects the right of the shareholders to remove directors, under section 8.08(a), with or without cause. The phrase "as a director" emphasizes that section 2.02(b)(4) applies to a director's actions or failures to take action in the director's capacity as a director and not in any other capacity, such as officer, employee or controlling shareholder. However, it is not intended to exclude coverage of conduct by individuals, even though they are also officers, employees or controlling shareholders, to the extent they are acting in their capacity as directors.

Shareholders are given considerable latitude in limiting directors' liability for money damages. The statutory exceptions to permitted limitations of director liability are few and narrow and are discussed below.

Financial Benefit

Corporate law subjects transactions from which a director could benefit personally to special scrutiny. The financial benefits exception is limited to the amount of the benefit actually received. Thus, liability for punitive damages could be eliminated, except in cases of intentional infliction of harm or for violation of criminal law (as described below) where, in a particular case (for example, theft), punitive damages may be available. The benefit must be financial rather than in less easily measured and more conjectural forms, such as business goodwill, personal reputation, or social ingratiation. The phrase "received by a director" is not intended to be a "bright line." As a director's conduct moves toward the edge of what may be exculpated, the director should bear the risk of miscalculation. Depending upon the circumstances, a director may be deemed to have received a benefit that the director caused to be directed to another person, for example, a relative, friend, or affiliate.

What constitutes a financial benefit "to which the director is not entitled" is left to judicial development. For example, a director is entitled to reasonable compensation for the performance of services or to an increase in the value of stock or stock options held by the director; on the other hand, a director is not entitled to a bribe, a kick-back, or the profits from a corporate opportunity improperly taken by the director. See section 8.70 as to procedures for disclaiming the corporation's interest in a business opportunity by action of qualified directors or shareholders. See section 2.02(b)(6) for optional provisions permitted in the articles of incorporation to limit or eliminate, in advance, any duty of directors and others to bring business opportunities to the corporation. If the corporation declines the opportunity after it has been presented to the corporation by the director in accordance with the provisions of section 8.70(a)(1)(i) or (ii), or if a provision under section 2.02(b)(6) limits or eliminates the duty to bring the particular opportunity to the corporation, the corporation will have no right to participate in any financial benefit arising from the opportunity if the director pursues or takes the opportunity.

Intentional Infliction of Harm

There may be situations in which a director intentionally causes harm to the corporation even though the director does not receive any improper benefit. The use of the word "intentional," rather than a less precise term such as "knowing," is meant to refer to the specific intent to perform, or fail to perform, the acts with actual knowledge that the director's action, or failure to act, will cause harm, rather than a general intent to perform the acts which cause the harm.

Unlawful Distributions

Section 8.32(a) indicates a strong policy in favor of liability for unlawful distributions approved by directors who have not complied with the standards of conduct of section 8.30. Accordingly, the exception in section 2.02(b)(4)(iii) prohibits the shareholders from eliminating or limiting the liability of directors for a violation of section 8.32.

Intentional Violation of Criminal Law

Even though a director committing a crime may intend to benefit the corporation, the shareholders should not be permitted to exculpate the director for any harm caused by an intentional violation of criminal law, including, for example, fines and legal expenses of the corporation in defending a criminal prosecution. The use of the word "intentional," rather than a less precise term such as "knowing," is meant to refer to the specific intent to perform, or fail to perform, the acts with actual knowledge that the director's action, or failure to act, constitutes a violation of criminal law.

. . .

G.   BUSINESS OPPORTUNITIES

Section 2.02 (b)(6) authorizes the inclusion of a provision in the articles of incorporation to limit or eliminate, in advance, the duty of a director or other person to bring a business opportunity to the corporation. The limitation or elimination may be blanket in nature and apply to any business opportunities, or it may extend only to one or more specified classes or categories of business opportunities. The adoption of such a provision constitutes a curtailment of the duty of loyalty which includes the doctrine of corporate opportunity. If such a provision is included in the articles, taking advantage of a business opportunity covered by the provision of the articles without offering it to the corporation will not expose the director or other person to whom it is made applicable either to monetary damages or to equitable or any other relief in favor of the corporation upon compliance with the requirements of section 2.02(b)(6).

This provision may be useful, for example, in the context of a private equity investor that wishes to have a nominee on the board but conditions its investment on an advance limitation or elimination of the corporate opportunity doctrine because of the uncertainty over the application of the corporate opportunity doctrine inherent when investments are made in multiple enterprises in specific industries. Another example is a joint venture in corporate form where the participants in the joint venture want to be sure that the corporate opportunity doctrine would not apply to their activities outside the joint venture.

The focus of the advance limitation or elimination is on the duty of the director which extends indirectly to the investor through the application of the related party definition in section 8.60. This provision also permits extension of the limitation or elimination of the duty to any other persons who might be deemed to have a duty to offer business opportunities to the corporation. For example, courts have held that the corporate opportunity doctrine extends to officers of the corporation. Although officers may be included in a provision under this subsection, the limitation or elimination of corporate opportunity obligations of officers must be addressed by the board of directors in specific cases or by the directors' authorizing provisions in employment agreements or other contractual arrangements with such officers. Accordingly, section 2.02(b)(6) requires that the application of an advance limitation or elimination of the duty to offer a business opportunity to the corporation to any person who is an officer of the corporation or a related person of an officer also requires action by the board of directors acting through qualified directors. This action must be taken subsequent to the inclusion of the provision in the articles of incorporation and may limit the application. This means that if the advance limitation or elimination of the duty of an officer to offer business opportunities to the corporation is included in the articles by an amendment recommended by the directors and approved by the shareholders, that recommendation of the directors does not serve as the required authorization by qualified directors; rather, separate authorization by qualified directors after the amendment is included in the articles is necessary to apply the provision to a particular officer or any related person of that officer. See sections 1.43(a)(1) and 8.60 for the definition of "qualified directors" and "related persons," respectively.

Whether a provision for advance limitation or elimination of duty in the articles of incorporation should be a broad "blanket" provision or one more tailored to specific categories or classes of transactions deserves careful consideration given the particular circumstances of the corporation.

Limitation or elimination of the duty of a director or officer to present a business opportunity to the corporation does not limit or eliminate the director's or officer's duty not to make unauthorized use of corporate property or information or to compete unfairly with the corporation.

4. *List of Options in the Act That May Be Elected Only in the Articles of Incorporation*

    A. OPTIONS WITH RESPECT TO DIRECTORS

    - Board of directors may be dispensed with entirely, § 7.32, or its functions may be restricted, § 8.01.
    - Power to compensate directors may be restricted or eliminated, § 8.11.
    - Election of directors by cumulative voting may be authorized, § 7.28.
    - Election of directors by greater than plurality vote may be authorized, § 7.28.
    - Directors may be elected by classes or series of shares, § 8.04.
    - Director's term may be limited by failure to receive specified vote for election, § 8.05.
    - Power to remove directors without cause may be restricted or eliminated, § 8.08.
    - Terms of directors may be staggered so that all directors are not elected in the same year, § 8.06.
    - Power to fill vacancies may be limited to the shareholders, § 8.10.
    - Power to indemnify directors, officers, and employees may be limited, §§ 8.50 through 8.59.
    - Prohibition on adoption of bylaw provision under § 10.22.

    B. OPTIONS WITH RESPECT TO SHAREHOLDERS

    - Action by shareholders may be taken without a meeting, § 7.04.
    - Special voting groups of shareholders may be authorized, § 7.25.
    - Elimination or restriction of separate voting groups for mergers and share exchanges, § 11.04, and for domestications, § 9.21.
    - Quorum for voting groups of shareholders may be increased or reduced, §§ 7.25, 7.26, and 7.27.
    - Quorum for voting by voting groups of shareholders may be prescribed, see § 7.26.
    - Greater than majority vote may be required for action by voting groups of shareholders, § 7.27.

    C. OPTIONS WITH RESPECT TO SHARES

    - Shares may be divided into classes and classes into series, §§ 6.01 and 6.02.
    - Cumulative voting for directors may be permitted, § 7.28.
    - Distributions may be restricted, § 6.40.
    - Share dividends may be restricted, § 6.23.
    - Voting rights of classes or series of shares may be limited or denied, § 6.01.
    - Classes or series of shares may be given more or less than one vote per share, § 7.21.
    - Terms of a class or series of shares may vary among holders of the same class or series, so long as such variations are expressly set forth in the articles, § 6.01.
    - The board of directors may allocate authorized but unissued shares of a class or series of shares to another class or series without shareholder approval, § 6.02.
    - Shares may be redeemed at the option of the corporation or the shareholder, § 6.01.
    - Reissue of acquired or redeemed shares may be prohibited, § 6.31.

- Shareholders may be given preemptive rights to acquire unissued shares, § 6.30.
- Redemption preferences may be ignored in determining lawfulness of distributions, § 6.40.

5. *List of Options in the Act That May Be Elected Either in the Articles of Incorporation or in the Bylaws*

   A. OPTIONS WITH RESPECT TO DIRECTORS

   - Number of directors may be fixed or changed within limits, § 8.03.
   - Qualifications for directors may be prescribed, § 8.02.
   - Notice of regular or special meetings of board of directors may be prescribed, § 8.22.
   - Power of board of directors to act without meeting may be restricted, § 8.21.
   - Quorum for meeting of board of directors may be increased or decreased (down to one-third) from majority, § 8.24.
   - Action at meeting of board of directors may require a greater than majority vote, § 8.24.
   - Power of directors to participate in meeting without being physically present may be prohibited, § 8.20.
   - Board of directors may create board committees and specify their powers, § 8.25.
   - Board of directors may create safe harbor for consideration of corporate opportunities, § 8.70.
   - Power of board of directors to amend bylaws may be restricted, §§ 10.20 and 10.21.
   - Election of directors may be governed by the optional rules under section 10.22.

   B. OPTIONS WITH RESPECT TO SHARES

   - Shares may be issued without certificates, § 6.26.
   - Procedure for treating beneficial owner of street name shares as record owner may be prescribed, § 7.23.
   - Transfer of shares may be restricted, § 6.27.

§ 2.03. Incorporation

(a) Unless a delayed effective date is specified, the corporate existence begins when the articles of incorporation are filed.

(b) The secretary of state's filing of the articles of incorporation is conclusive proof that the incorporators satisfied all conditions precedent to incorporation except in a proceeding by the state to cancel or revoke the incorporation or involuntarily dissolve the corporation.

§ 2.04. Liability for Preincorporation Transactions *(Promoters)*

All persons purporting to act as or on behalf of a corporation, knowing there was no incorporation under this Act, are jointly and severally liable for all liabilities created while so acting.

Official Comment

Ordinarily, only the filing of articles of incorporation should create the privilege of limited liability. Situations may arise, however, in which the protection of limited liability arguably should be recognized even though the simple incorporation process established by the Act has not been completed.

As a result, the Act imposes liability only on persons who act as or on behalf of corporations "knowing" that no corporation exists. In addition, section 2.04 does not foreclose the possibility that persons who urge defendants to execute contracts in the corporate name knowing that no steps to incorporate have been taken may be estopped to impose personal liability on individual defendants. This estoppel may be based on the inequity perceived when persons, unwilling or reluctant to enter into a commitment under their own name, are persuaded to use the name of a nonexistent corporation, and then are sought to be held personally liable under section 2.04 by the party advocating execution in the name of the corporation.

*[handwritten notes: * promoters owe fiduciary duties to one another and to future corp — during pre-incorporation they owe duties of joint venturers to future corp sometimes to investors]*

§ 2.05.   Organization of Corporation

(a) After incorporation:

(1) if initial directors are named in the articles of incorporation, the initial directors shall hold an organizational meeting, at the call of a majority of the directors, to complete the organization of the corporation by appointing officers, adopting bylaws, and carrying on any other business brought before the meeting; or

(2) if initial directors are not named in the articles of incorporation, the incorporator or incorporators shall hold an organizational meeting at the call of a majority of the incorporators:

(i) to elect initial directors and complete the organization of the corporation; or

(ii) to elect a board of directors who shall complete the organization of the corporation.

(b) Action required or permitted by this Act to be taken by incorporators at an organizational meeting may be taken without a meeting if the action taken is evidenced by one or more written consents describing the action taken and signed by each incorporator.

(c) An organizational meeting may be held in or out of this state.

§ 2.06.   Bylaws

(a) The incorporators or board of directors of a corporation shall adopt initial bylaws for the corporation.

(b) The bylaws of a corporation may contain any provision that is not inconsistent with law or the articles of incorporation.

(c) The bylaws may contain one or both of the following provisions:

(1) a requirement that if the corporation solicits proxies or consents with respect to an election of directors, the corporation include in its proxy statement and any form of its proxy or consent, to the extent and subject to such procedures or conditions as are provided in the bylaws, one or more individuals nominated by a shareholder in addition to individuals nominated by the board of directors; and

(2) a requirement that the corporation reimburse the expenses incurred by a shareholder in soliciting proxies or consents in connection with an election of directors, to the extent and subject to such procedures and conditions as are provided in the bylaws, provided that no bylaw so adopted shall apply to elections for which any record date precedes its adoption.

(d) Notwithstanding section 10.20(b)(2), the shareholders in amending, repealing, or adopting a bylaw described in subsection (c) may not limit the authority of the board of directors to amend or repeal any condition or procedure set forth in or to add any procedure or condition to such a bylaw to provide for a reasonable, practical, and orderly process.

Official Comment

The responsibility for adopting the original bylaws is placed on the person or persons completing the organization of the corporation. Section 2.06(b) permits any bylaw provision that is not inconsistent with law or the articles of incorporation. This limitation precludes bylaw provisions that limit the managerial authority of directors established by section 8.01(b). . . .

The power to amend or repeal bylaws, or adopt new bylaws after the organization of the corporation is completed, is addressed in sections 10.20, 10.21 and 10.22.

Section 2.06(c) expressly authorizes bylaws that require the corporation to include individuals nominated by shareholders for election as directors in its proxy statement and proxy cards (or consents) and that require the reimbursement by the corporation of expenses incurred by a shareholder in soliciting proxies (or consents) in an election of directors, in each case subject to such procedures or conditions as may be provided in the bylaws. Expenses reimbursed under section 2.06(c)(2) must be reasonable as contemplated in the definition of expenses set forth in section 1.40.

Examples of the procedures and conditions that may be included in bylaws contemplated by section 2.06(c) include provisions that relate to the ownership of shares (including requirements as to the duration of ownership); informational requirements; restrictions on the number of directors to be nominated or on the use of the provisions by shareholders seeking to acquire control; provisions requiring the nominating shareholder to indemnify the corporation; limitations on reimbursement based on the amount spent by the corporation or the proportion of votes cast for the nominee; and limitations concerning the election of directors by cumulative voting.

Section 2.06(c) clarifies that proxy access and expense reimbursement provisions do not infringe upon the scope of authority granted to the board of directors of a corporation under section 8.01(b). Section 2.06(c) underscores the model of corporate governance embodied by the Act and reflected in section 8.01, but recognizes that different corporations may wish to grant shareholders varying rights in selecting directors through the election process.

Section 2.06(d) limits the rule set forth in section 10.20(b)(2) that shareholder adopted bylaws may limit the authority of directors to amend bylaws, by specifying that such a limit will not apply absolutely to conditions and procedures set forth in access or reimbursement bylaws authorized by section 2.06(c). Section 2.06(d) allows directors to ensure that such bylaws adequately provide for a reasonable, practical, and orderly process, but is not intended to allow the board of directors to frustrate the purpose of a shareholder-adopted proxy access or expense reimbursement provision.

§ 2.07. Emergency Bylaws

(a) Unless the articles of incorporation provide otherwise, the board of directors may adopt bylaws to be effective only in an emergency defined in subsection (d). The emergency bylaws, which are subject to amendment or repeal by the shareholders, may make all provisions necessary for managing the corporation during the emergency, including:

(1) procedures for calling a meeting of the board of directors;

(2) quorum requirements for the meeting; and

(3) designation of additional or substitute directors.

(b) All provisions of the regular bylaws not inconsistent with the emergency bylaws remain effective during the emergency. The emergency bylaws are not effective after the emergency ends.

(c) Corporate action taken in good faith in accordance with the emergency bylaws:

(1) binds the corporation; and

(2) may not be used to impose liability on a director, officer, employee, or agent of the corporation.

(d) An emergency exists for purposes of this section if a quorum of the board of directors cannot readily be assembled because of some catastrophic event.

Official Comment

. . .

The definition of "emergency" adopted by section 2.07(d) includes any catastrophic event that makes it difficult or impossible for a quorum of the board of directors to be assembled. To encourage corporations to adopt emergency bylaws, section 2.07(c) broadly validates all corporate actions taken "in good faith" pursuant to them and immunizes all directors, officers, employees, and agents of the corporation from liability as a result of these actions. The phrase "action taken in good faith in accordance with the emergency bylaws" is designed to conform to the standard for immunity elsewhere in the Act.

A corporation that does not adopt emergency bylaws under this section may nevertheless exercise the powers described in section 3.03 in the event of an emergency as defined in section 2.07(d).

§ 2.08. Forum Selection Provisions

(a) The articles of incorporation or the bylaws may require that any or all internal corporate claims shall be brought exclusively in any specified court or courts of this state and, if so specified, in any additional courts in this state or in any other jurisdictions with which the corporation has a reasonable relationship.

(b) A provision of the articles of incorporation or bylaws adopted under subsection (a) shall not have the effect of conferring jurisdiction on any court or over any person or claim, and shall not apply if none of the courts specified by such provision has the requisite personal and subject matter jurisdiction. If the court or courts of this state specified in a provision adopted under subsection (a) do not have the requisite personal and subject matter jurisdiction and another court of this state does have such jurisdiction, then the internal corporate claim may be brought in such other court of this state, notwithstanding that such other court of this state is not specified in such provision, and in any other court specified in such provision that has the requisite jurisdiction.

(c) No provision of the articles of incorporation or the bylaws may prohibit bringing an internal corporate claim in the courts of this state or require such claims to be determined by arbitration.

(d) "Internal corporate claim" means, for the purposes of this section, (i) any claim that is based upon a violation of a duty under the laws of this state by a current or former director, officer, or shareholder in such capacity, (ii) any derivative action or proceeding brought on behalf of the corporation, (iii) any action asserting a claim arising pursuant to any provision of this Act or the articles of incorporation or bylaws, or (iv) any action asserting a claim governed by the internal affairs doctrine that is not included in (i) through (iii) above.

Official Comment

Section 2.08(a) authorizes a provision in either the articles of incorporation or the bylaws creating an exclusive forum or forums for the adjudication of internal corporate claims. Under section 2.08(a), the provision must specify at least one court of this state (*i.e.*, a state court rather than a federal court). The provision may also include additional specified courts or all courts of this state or courts in this state (such as federal courts) or in one or more additional jurisdictions with a reasonable relationship to the corporation. In addition, the provision may prioritize among the specified courts. For example, the provision may specify that the claim shall be brought exclusively in a particular court of this state unless such court does not have the requisite personal and subject matter jurisdiction, in which case the claim shall be brought in other specified courts.

Under the last sentence of section 2.08(b), an internal corporate claim will always be permitted to be brought in at least one court of this state unless there is no court of this state that has the requisite personal and subject matter jurisdiction. For example, if the articles of incorporation or the bylaws provide that an internal corporate claim may only be brought in a specified court of this state and in the courts of another state with a reasonable relationship to the corporation, and the specified court of this state does not have the requisite personal and subject matter jurisdiction, then the claim can be brought in any other court of this state that does have the requisite jurisdiction or in the courts of the specified other state (so long as those courts have the requisite jurisdiction). Similarly, if the articles of incorporation or the bylaws provide that an internal corporate claim may only be brought in a specified court of this state and in the federal courts in this state, and the specified court of this state does not have the requisite personal and subject matter jurisdiction, then the claim can be brought in any other court of this state that does have the requisite jurisdiction or in the federal courts in this state (so long as the federal court has the requisite jurisdiction). In each of the foregoing examples, (i) if the specified court of this state does have the requisite personal and subject matter jurisdiction, then such court would be the only court of this state in which the internal corporate claim could be brought, and (ii) if no court of this state has the requisite personal and subject matter jurisdiction, then the courts of the other state (in the first example) or the federal courts in this state (in the second example) would become the exclusive forum for such internal corporate claim, in each case so long as such court has the requisite jurisdiction.

If no court of this state has the requisite personal and subject matter jurisdiction, and none of the other courts, if any, specified in the provision of the articles of incorporation or the bylaws has the requisite jurisdiction, then the provision will have no effect and the internal corporate claim may be brought in any court that does have the requisite jurisdiction.

Chapter 3
PURPOSES AND POWERS

§ 3.01. Purposes

(a) Every corporation incorporated under this Act has the purpose of engaging in any lawful business unless a more limited purpose is set forth in the articles of incorporation.

(b) A corporation engaging in a business that is subject to regulation under another statute of this state may incorporate under this Act only if permitted by, and subject to all limitations of, the other statute.

§ 3.02. General Powers

Unless its articles of incorporation provide otherwise, every corporation has perpetual duration and succession in its corporate name and has the same powers as an individual to do all things necessary or convenient to carry out its business and affairs, including power:

(a) to sue and be sued, complain and defend in its corporate name;

(b) to have a corporate seal, which may be altered at will, and to use it, or a facsimile of it, by impressing or affixing it or in any other manner reproducing it;

(c) to make and amend bylaws, not inconsistent with its articles of incorporation or with the laws of this state, for managing the business and regulating the affairs of the corporation;

(d) to purchase, receive, lease, or otherwise acquire, and own, hold, improve, use, and otherwise deal with, real or personal property, or any legal or equitable interest in property, wherever located;

(e) to sell, convey, mortgage, pledge, lease, exchange, and otherwise dispose of all or any part of its property;

(f) to purchase, receive, subscribe for, or otherwise acquire, own, hold, vote, use, sell, mortgage, lend, pledge, or otherwise dispose of, and deal in and with shares or other interests in, or obligations of, any other entity;

(g) to make contracts and guarantees, incur liabilities, borrow money, issue its notes, bonds, and other securities and obligations (which may be convertible into or include the option to purchase other securities of the corporation), and secure any of its obligations by mortgage or pledge of any of its property, franchises, or income;

(h) to lend money, invest and reinvest its funds, and receive and hold real and personal property as security for repayment;

(i) to be a promoter, partner, member, associate, or manager of any partnership, joint venture, trust, or other entity;

(j) to conduct its business, locate offices, and exercise the powers granted by this Act within or without this state;

(k) to elect directors and appoint officers, employees, and agents of the corporation, define their duties, fix their compensation, and lend them money and credit;

(*l*) to pay pensions and establish pension plans, pension trusts, profit sharing plans, share bonus plans, share option plans, and benefit or incentive plans for any or all of its current or former directors, officers, employees, and agents;

(m) to make donations for the public welfare or for charitable, scientific, or educational purposes;

(n) to transact any lawful business that will aid governmental policy; and

(o) to make payments or donations, or do any other act, not inconsistent with law, that furthers the business and affairs of the corporation.

Official Comment

The general philosophy of section 3.02 is that corporations formed under the Act should be automatically authorized to engage in all acts and have all powers that an individual may have. . . .

The powers of a corporation under the Act exist independently of whether a corporation has a broad or narrow purpose clause. A corporation with a narrow purpose clause nevertheless has the same powers as an individual to do all things necessary or convenient to carry out its business. . . . For example, a corporation may generally make charitable contributions without regard to the purpose for which the charity will use the funds or may invest money in shares of other corporations without regard to whether the corporate purpose of the other corporation is broader or narrower than the limited purpose clause of the investing corporation. . . .

§ 3.03. Emergency Powers

(a) In anticipation of or during an emergency defined in subsection (d), the board of directors of a corporation may:

(1) modify lines of succession to accommodate the incapacity of any director, officer, employee, or agent; and

(2) relocate the principal office, designate alternative principal offices or regional offices, or authorize the officers to do so.

(b) During an emergency defined in subsection (d), unless emergency bylaws provide otherwise:

(1) notice of a meeting of the board of directors need be given only to those directors whom it is practicable to reach and may be given in any practicable manner; and

(2) one or more officers of the corporation present at a meeting of the board of directors may be deemed to be directors for the meeting, in order of rank and within the same rank in order of seniority, as necessary to achieve a quorum.

(c) Corporate action taken in good faith during an emergency under this section to further the ordinary business affairs of the corporation:

(1) binds the corporation; and

(2) may not be used to impose liability on a director, officer, employee, or agent.

(d) An emergency exists for purposes of this section if a quorum of the board of directors cannot readily be assembled because of some catastrophic event.

Official Comment

Section 3.03 should be read in conjunction with section 2.07, which authorizes a corporation to adopt emergency bylaws. Section 3.03 grants every corporation limited powers to act in an emergency even though it has failed to adopt emergency bylaws under section 2.07.

§ 3.04. Lack of Power to Act

(a) Except as provided in subsection (b), the validity of corporate action may not be challenged on the ground that the corporation lacks or lacked power to act.

(b) A corporation's power to act may be challenged:

(1) in a proceeding by a shareholder against the corporation to enjoin the act;

(2) in a proceeding by the corporation, directly, derivatively, or through a receiver, trustee, or other legal representative, against an incumbent or former director, officer, employee, or agent of the corporation; or

(3) in a proceeding by the attorney general under section 14.30.

(c) In a shareholder's proceeding under subsection (b)(1) to enjoin an unauthorized corporate act, the court may enjoin or set aside the act, if equitable and if all affected persons are parties to the proceeding, and may award damages for loss (other than anticipated profits) suffered by the corporation or another party because of enjoining the unauthorized act.

Official Comment

Under section 3.04, it is unnecessary for persons dealing with a corporation to inquire into limitations on its purpose or powers that may appear in its articles of incorporation. A person who is unaware of these limitations when dealing with the corporation is not bound by them. The phrase in section 3.04(a) that the "validity of corporate action may not be challenged on the ground that the corporation lacks or lacked power to act" applies equally to the use of the doctrine as a sword or as a shield: a third person may no more avoid an undesired contract with a corporation on the ground the corporation was without authority to make the contract than a corporation may defend a suit on a contract on the ground that the contract is ultra vires.

The language of section 3.04 extends beyond contracts and conveyances of property; "corporate action" of any kind cannot be challenged on the ground of ultra vires. For this reason it makes no difference whether a limitation in articles of incorporation is considered to be a limitation on a purpose or a limitation on a power; both are equally subject to section 3.04. Corporate action also includes inaction or refusal to act. The common law of ultra vires distinguished between executory contracts, partially executed contracts, and fully executed ones; section 3.04 treats all corporate action the same—except to the extent described in section 3.04(b)—and the same rules apply to all contracts no matter at what stage of performance.

Section 3.04, however, does not validate corporate conduct that is made illegal or unlawful by statute or common law decision. This conduct is subject to whatever sanction, criminal or civil, that is provided by the statute or decision. Whether illegal corporate conduct is voidable or rescindable depends on the applicable statute or substantive law and is not affected by section 3.04. . . .

Section 3.04(b) permits challenges to the corporation's lack of power in three limited classes of cases:

- In a suit by a shareholder against the corporation to enjoin an ultra vires act. This suit, however, is subject to the requirements of section 3.04(c). Section 3.04(c) authorizes a court to enjoin or set aside an ultra vires act or grant other relief that may be necessary to protect the interests of all affected persons, including the interests of third persons who deal with the corporation. Under this subsection an ultra vires act may be enjoined only if all "affected parties" are parties to the suit. The requirement that the action be "equitable" generally means that only third persons dealing with a corporation while specifically aware that the corporation's action was ultra vires will be enjoined. The general phrase "if equitable" is used because of the possibility that other circumstances may exist in which it may be equitable to refuse to enforce an ultra vires contract. Further, if enforcement of the contract is enjoined, either the third person or the corporation may in the discretion of the court be awarded damages from the other for loss (excluding anticipated profits). . . .

Chapter 4

NAME

§ 4.01. Corporate Name

(a) A corporate name:

(1) must contain the word "corporation," "incorporated," "company," or "limited," or the abbreviation "corp.," "inc.," "co.," or "ltd.," or words or abbreviations of like import in another language; and

(2) may not contain language stating or implying that the corporation is organized for a purpose other than that permitted by section 3.01 and its articles of incorporation. . . .

§ 4.02. Reserved Name

(a) A person may reserve the exclusive use of a corporate name, including a fictitious or alternate name for a foreign corporation whose corporate name is not available, by delivering an application to the secretary of state for filing. The application must set forth the name and address of the applicant and the name proposed to be reserved. If the secretary of state finds that the corporate name applied for is available, the secretary of state shall reserve the name for the applicant's exclusive use for a nonrenewable 120-day period.

(b) The owner of a reserved corporate name may transfer the reservation to another person by delivering to the secretary of state a signed notice of the transfer that states the name and address of the transferee.

§ 4.03. Registered Name

(a) A foreign corporation may register its corporate name (or its corporate name with the addition of any word or abbreviation listed in section 4.01(a)(1) if necessary for the corporate name to comply with section 4.01(a)(1)) if the name is distinguishable upon the records of the secretary of state from the corporate names that are not available under section 4.01(b). . . .

Chapter 5

OFFICE AND AGENT

§ 5.01. Registered Office and Agent of Domestic and Registered Foreign Corporations

(a) Each corporation shall continuously maintain in this state:

(1) a registered office that may be the same as any of its places of business; and

(2) a registered agent, which may be:

(i) an individual who resides in this state and whose business office is identical with the registered office; or

(ii) a domestic or foreign corporation or eligible entity whose business office is identical with the registered office and, in the case of a foreign corporation or foreign eligible entity, is registered to do business in this state.

(b) As used in this chapter, "corporation" means both a domestic corporation and a registered foreign corporation.

Chapter 6

SHARES AND DISTRIBUTIONS

Subchapter A

Shares

§ 6.01. Authorized Shares

(a) The articles of incorporation must set forth any classes of shares and series of shares within a class, and the number of shares of each class and series, that the corporation is authorized to issue. If more than one class or series of shares is authorized, the articles of incorporation must prescribe a distinguishing designation for each class or series and, before the issuance of shares of a class or series, describe the terms, including the preferences, rights, and limitations, of that class or series. Except to the extent varied as permitted by this section, all shares of a class or series must have terms, including preferences, rights, and limitations, that are identical with those of other shares of the same class or series.

(b) The articles of incorporation must authorize:

(1) one or more classes or series of shares that together have full voting rights, and

(2) one or more classes or series of shares (which may be the same class, classes or series as those with voting rights) that together are entitled to receive the net assets of the corporation upon dissolution.

(c) The articles of incorporation may authorize one or more classes or series of shares that:

(1) have special, conditional, or limited voting rights, or no right to vote, except to the extent otherwise provided by this Act;

(2) are redeemable or convertible as specified in the articles of incorporation:

    (i) at the option of the corporation, the shareholder, or another person or upon the occurrence of a specified event;

    (ii) for cash, indebtedness, securities, or other property; and

    (iii) at prices and in amounts specified or determined in accordance with a formula;

(3) entitle the holders to distributions calculated in any manner, including dividends that may be cumulative, noncumulative, or partially cumulative; or

(4) have preference over any other class or series of shares with respect to distributions, including distributions upon the dissolution of the corporation.

(d) Terms of shares may be made dependent upon facts objectively ascertainable outside the articles of incorporation in accordance with section 1.20(k).

(e) Any of the terms of shares may vary among holders of the same class or series so long as such variations are expressly set forth in the articles of incorporation.

(f) The description of the preferences, rights, and limitations of classes or series of shares in subsection (c) is not exhaustive.

Official Comment

1. Section 6.01(a)

Section 6.01(a) requires that the articles of incorporation prescribe the classes and series of shares and the number of shares of each class and series that the corporation is authorized to issue. If the articles of incorporation authorize the issue of only one class of shares, no designation or description of the shares is required, it being understood that these shares have both the power to vote and the power to receive the net assets of the corporation upon dissolution. See section 6.01(b). Shares with both of these characteristics are usually referred to as "common shares" but no specific designation is required by the Act. The articles of incorporation may set forth the number of shares authorized and permit the board of directors under section 6.02 to allocate the authorized shares among designated classes or series of shares.

The preferences, rights and limitations of each class or series of shares constitute the "contract" of the holders of those classes and series of shares with respect to the holders' interest in the corporation and must be set forth in sufficient detail reasonably to define their interest. The terms, including the preferences, rights and limitations, of shares with one or more special or preferential rights which may be authorized are further described in section 6.01(c).

If more than one class or series is authorized (or if only one class or series is originally authorized but at some future time one or more other classes or series of shares are added by amendment), the terms, including the preferences, rights and limitations of each class, classes or series of shares, including the class, classes or series that possess the fundamental characteristics of voting and residual equity financial interests, must be described before shares of those classes or series are issued. If both fundamental characteristics are placed exclusively in a single class of shares, that class may be described simply as "common shares" or by statements such as the "shares have the general distribution and voting rights," the "shares have all the rights of common shares," or the "shares have all rights not granted to the class A shares."

If the articles of incorporation create classes or series of shares that divide these fundamental rights among two or more classes or series of shares, it is necessary that the rights be clearly allocated among the classes and series. Specificity is required only to the extent necessary to differentiate the relative rights of the respective classes and series. For example, where one class or series has a liquidation preference over another, it is necessary to specify only the preferential liquidation right of that class or series; in the absence of a contrary provision in the articles of incorporation, the remaining class or series would be entitled to receive the net assets remaining after the liquidation preference has been satisfied. More than one class or series of shares may be designated as "common shares;" however, each must have a "distinguishing designation" under section 6.01(a), *e.g.*, "nonvoting common shares" or "class A common shares," and the rights of the classes and series must be described. For example, if a corporation authorizes two classes of shares with equal rights to share in all distributions and with identical voting rights except that one class is entitled exclusively to elect one director and the second class is entitled exclusively to elect a second director, the two classes may be designated, *e.g.*, as "Class A common" and "Class B common." What is required is language that makes the allocation of these rights clear.

Rather than describing the terms of each class or series of shares in the articles of incorporation, the corporation may delegate to the board of directors under section 6.02 the power to establish the terms of a class of shares or a series within a class if no shares of that class or series have previously been issued. Those terms, however, must be set forth in an amendment to the articles of incorporation that is effective before the shares are issued.

2. Section 6.01(b)

Section 6.01(b) requires that every corporation authorize one or more classes or series of shares that in the aggregate have the two fundamental characteristics of full voting rights and the right to receive the net assets of the corporation upon its dissolution. The phrase "full voting rights" refers to the right to vote on all matters for which voting is required by either the Act or the articles of incorporation.

The two fundamental characteristics need not be placed in a single class or series of shares but may be divided as desired. It is nevertheless essential that the corporation always have authorized shares having in the aggregate these two characteristics, and section 6.03 requires that shares having in the aggregate these characteristics always be outstanding.

3. Section 6.01(c)

Section 6.01(c) provides a non-exhaustive list of the principal features that are customarily incorporated into classes or series of shares.

A. In general

Section 6.01(c) authorizes creation of classes or series of shares with a range of preferences, rights and limitations as further described below. The Act permits the creation of shares convertible into, or redeemable in exchange for, cash, other property, or shares or debt securities of the corporation ranking senior to the shares, at the option of either the holder or the corporation. Such a conversion or redemption is subject to the restrictions on distributions under section 6.40.

B. Voting of shares

Any class or series of shares may be granted multiple or fractional votes per share without limitation. See section 7.21. Shares of any class or series may also be made nonvoting "except to the extent otherwise provided by this Act." This "except" clause refers to the provisions in the Act that permit shares which are designated to be nonvoting to vote as separate voting groups on amendments to articles of incorporation and other organic changes in the corporation that directly affect that class or series (see sections 7.26 and 10.04). In addition, shares may be given voting rights that are limited or conditional (*e.g.*, voting rights triggered by the failure to pay specified dividends).

C. Redemption and conversion of shares

Section 6.01(c)(2) permits redemption for any class or series of shares and thereby permits the creation of redeemable or callable shares without limitation (subject only to the provisions that the class, classes or series of shares described in section 6.01(b) must always be authorized and that at least one or more shares which together have those rights must be outstanding under section 6.03).

The prices to be paid upon the redemption of shares under section 6.01(c)(2) and the amounts to be redeemed may be fixed in the articles of incorporation or "determined in accordance with a formula." The formula could be self contained or, pursuant to the provisions of section 6.01(d), could be determined by reference to extrinsic data or events. This permits the redemption price and the amounts to be redeemed to be established on the basis of matters external to the corporation, such as the purchase price of other shares, the level of market reference rates, the effective interest rate at which the corporation may obtain short or long-term financing, the consumer price index or a designated currency ratio.

All redemptions of shares are subject to the restrictions on distributions set forth in section 6.40. See section 6.03(b).

Section 6.01(c)(2) also permits shares of any class or series to be made convertible into shares of any other class or series or into cash, indebtedness, securities, or other property of the corporation or another person.

D.   Extrinsic facts

Section 6.01(d) permits the creation of classes or series of shares with terms that are dependent upon facts objectively ascertainable outside the articles of incorporation. See section 1.20(k) and the related Official Comment for an explanation of the meaning of the phrase "facts objectively ascertainable" and the requirement for the filing of articles of amendment under the circumstances set forth in that section. Terms that depend upon reference to extrinsic facts may include dividend rates that vary according to some external index or event. Because such a "variable rate" class or series of shares would be intended to respond to current market conditions, it would most often be used with "blank check" provisions in the articles of incorporation with the terms of shares set by the board of directors immediately before issuance. See the Official Comment to section 6.02. Note that section 6.21 requires the board to determine the adequacy of consideration received or to be received by the corporation before issuing shares. If shares with terms to be determined by reference to extrinsic facts are to be authorized for issuance, the board should take care to establish appropriately defined parameters for such terms.

E.   Variation among holders

Section 6.01(e) permits the creation of classes or series of shares with terms that may vary among holders of the same class or series of shares. An example of such variation would be a provision that shares held by a bank or bank holding company in excess of a certain percentage would not have voting rights. In addition, section 6.24(b) expressly permits the issuance of rights, options or warrants for the purchase of shares or other securities of the corporation that contain terms and conditions which vary the rights of the holders of such rights, warrants or options based on a holder's ownership of, or offer to acquire, a specified number or percentage of the outstanding shares or other securities of the corporation.

4.   Examples of Classes or Series of Shares Permitted by Section 6.01

Section 6.01 is enabling rather than restrictive given that corporations often find it necessary to create new classes or series of shares for a variety of reasons, for instance in connection with raising debt or equity capital. Classes or series of shares may also be used in connection with desired control relationships among the participants in a venture. Under section 7.21, only securities classified as "shares" in the articles of incorporation can have the power to vote.

Examples of such classes and series of shares include:

- Shares of one class or series may be authorized to elect a specified number of directors while shares of a second class or series may be authorized to elect the same or a different number of directors.

- Shares of one class or series may be entitled to vote as a separate voting group on certain transactions, but shares of two or more classes or series may be only entitled to vote together as a single voting group on the election of directors and other matters.

- Shares of one class or series may be nonvoting or may be given multiple or fractional votes per share.

- Shares of one class or series may be entitled to different dividend rights or rights on dissolution than shares of another class or series.

- Shares of one class or series may be created to include some characteristics of debt securities.

A corporation has power to issue debt securities under section 3.02. Although 6.01 authorizes the creation of interests that usually will be classed as "equity" rather than "debt," it is permissible to create classes or series of securities under section 6.01 that have some of the characteristics of debt securities. These securities are often referred to as "hybrid securities." Section 6.01 does not limit the development of hybrid securities, and equity securities may be created under the Act that embody any characteristics of debt. As noted above, however, the Act restricts the power to vote to securities classified as "shares" in the articles of incorporation.

§ 6.02.   Terms of Class or Series Determined by Board of Directors

(a) If the articles of incorporation so provide, the board of directors is authorized, without shareholder approval, to:

    (1) classify any unissued shares into one or more classes or into one or more series within a class;

    (2) reclassify any unissued shares of any class into one or more classes or into one or more series within one or more classes; or

(3) reclassify any unissued shares of any series of any class into one or more classes or into one or more series within a class.

(b) If the board of directors acts pursuant to subsection (a), it shall determine the terms, including the preferences, rights, and limitations, to the same extent permitted under section 6.01, of:

(1) any class of shares before the issuance of any shares of that class, or

(2) any series within a class before the issuance of any shares of that series.

(c) Before issuing any shares of a class or series created under this section, the corporation shall deliver to the secretary of state for filing articles of amendment setting forth the terms determined under subsection (a).

Official Comment

Section 6.02 permits the board of directors, if authority to do so is contained in the articles of incorporation, to determine the terms of a class of shares or of a series of shares within a class to meet corporate needs, including current requirements of the securities markets or the flexibility needed for acquisitions, without the necessity of holding a shareholders' meeting to amend the articles of incorporation. If given that authority, the board of directors may create new series within a class and may also determine the terms of a class or series if there are no outstanding shares of that class or series.

A provision in the articles of incorporation authorizing shares to be issued in different classes or series with terms to be set by the board of directors is sometimes referred to as a "blank check" provision. The power to make the terms of shares so created dependent on facts objectively ascertainable outside the articles of incorporation and to vary their terms among holders of the same class or series extends to all the permitted provisions set forth in section 6.01(c).

Sections 6.02(a) and (b) make it clear that the board of directors has the same broad flexibility with regard to setting the terms of a class or series under this section as is permitted under section 6.01(c). Section 6.02(c) requires a filing to amend the articles of incorporation so there will be a public record of the class or series which the corporation intends to issue. The amendment does not require shareholder action. See section 10.05(h).

§ 6.03.   Issued and Outstanding Shares

(a) A corporation may issue the number of shares of each class or series authorized by the articles of incorporation. Shares that are issued are outstanding shares until they are reacquired, redeemed, converted, or cancelled.

(b) The reacquisition, redemption, or conversion of outstanding shares is subject to the limitations of subsection (c) and to section 6.40.

(c) At all times that shares of the corporation are outstanding, one or more shares that together have full voting rights and one or more shares that together are entitled to receive the net assets of the corporation upon dissolution must be outstanding.

§ 6.04.   Fractional Shares

(a) A corporation may issue fractions of a share or in lieu of doing so may:

(1) pay in cash the value of fractions of a share;

(2) issue scrip in registered or bearer form entitling the holder to receive a full share upon surrendering enough scrip to equal a full share; or

(3) arrange for disposition of fractional shares by the holders of such shares.

(b) Each certificate representing scrip must be conspicuously labeled "scrip" and must contain the information required by section 6.25(b).

(c) The holder of a fractional share is entitled to exercise the rights of a shareholder, including the rights to vote, to receive dividends and to receive distributions upon dissolution. The holder of scrip is not entitled to any of these rights unless the scrip provides for them.

(d) The board of directors may authorize the issuance of scrip subject to any condition, including that:

(1) the scrip will become void if not exchanged for full shares before a specified date; and

(2) the shares for which the scrip is exchangeable may be sold and the proceeds paid to the scripholders.

Subchapter B

Issuance of Shares

§ 6.20. Subscription for Shares Before Incorporation

(a) A subscription for shares entered into before incorporation is irrevocable for six months unless the subscription agreement provides a longer or shorter period or all the subscribers agree to revocation.

(b) The board of directors may determine the payment terms of subscriptions for shares that were entered into before incorporation, unless the subscription agreement specifies them. A call for payment by the board of directors must be uniform so far as practicable as to all shares of the same class or series, unless the subscription agreement specifies otherwise.

(c) Shares issued pursuant to subscriptions entered into before incorporation are fully paid and nonassessable when the corporation receives the consideration specified in the subscription agreement.

(d) If a subscriber defaults in payment of cash or property under a subscription agreement entered into before incorporation, the corporation may collect the amount owed as any other debt. Alternatively, unless the subscription agreement provides otherwise, the corporation may rescind the agreement and may sell the shares if the debt remains unpaid for more than 20 days after the corporation delivers a written demand for payment to the subscriber.

Official Comment

Because of the uncertainty of the legal enforceability of preincorporation agreements to purchase shares, section 6.20 provides a simple set of rules applicable to the enforcement of preincorporation subscriptions by the corporation after its formation. It does not address the extent to which preincorporation subscriptions may constitute a contract between or among subscribers, and other subscribers may enforce whatever contract rights they have without regard to section 6.20.

Section 6.20(a) provides as a default that preincorporation subscriptions are irrevocable for six months but the subscription agreement may provide otherwise or all the subscribers to shares may agree otherwise. If the corporation accepts the subscription during the period of irrevocability, the subscription becomes a contract binding on both the subscribers and the corporation. The terms of this contract are set forth in sections 6.20(b) and (d).

Section 6.20(c) provides that shares issued pursuant to preincorporation subscriptions are fully paid and nonassessable when the corporation receives the subscription price. The liability of the subscriber to pay the purchase price is addressed in section 6.22. Section 6.20 does not address the liability of transferees of shares for any unpaid subscription price, or the power of the corporation to cancel for nonpayment shares that have been issued before payment of the full subscription price. Issued shares represented by unpaid subscriptions are subject to cancellation for nonpayment to the same extent as shares issued for promissory notes or shares issued before the consideration therefor is paid. See the Official Comment to sections 6.21 and 6.22.

§ 6.21. Issuance of Shares

(a) The powers granted in this section to the board of directors may be reserved to the shareholders by the articles of incorporation.

(b) The board of directors may authorize shares to be issued for consideration consisting of any tangible or intangible property or benefit to the corporation, including cash, promissory notes, services performed, contracts for services to be performed, or other securities of the corporation.

(c) Before the corporation issues shares, the board of directors shall determine that the consideration received or to be received for shares to be issued is adequate. That determination by the board of directors

586

is conclusive insofar as the adequacy of consideration for the issuance of shares relates to whether the shares are validly issued, fully paid, and nonassessable.

(d) When the corporation receives the consideration for which the board of directors authorized the issuance of shares, the shares issued therefor are fully paid and nonassessable.

(e) The corporation may place in escrow shares issued for a contract for future services or benefits or a promissory note, or make other arrangements to restrict the transfer of the shares, and may credit distributions in respect of the shares against their purchase price, until the services are performed, the benefits are received, or the note is paid. If the services are not performed, the benefits are not received, or the note is not paid, the shares escrowed or restricted and the distributions credited may be cancelled in whole or part.

(f)(1) An issuance of shares or other securities convertible into or rights exercisable for shares in a transaction or a series of integrated transactions requires approval of the shareholders, at a meeting at which a quorum consisting of a majority (or such greater number as the articles of incorporation may prescribe) of the votes entitled to be cast on the matter exists, if:

(i) the shares, other securities, or rights are to be issued for consideration other than cash or cash equivalents, and

(ii) the voting power of shares that are issued and issuable as a result of the transaction or series of integrated transactions will comprise more than 20% of the voting power of the shares of the corporation that were outstanding immediately before the transaction.

(2) In this subsection:

(i) For purposes of determining the voting power of shares issued and issuable as a result of a transaction or series of integrated transactions, the voting power of shares or other securities convertible into or rights exercisable for shares shall be the greater of (A) the voting power of the shares to be issued, or (B) the voting power of the shares that would be outstanding after giving effect to the conversion of convertible shares and other securities and the exercise of rights to be issued.

(ii) A series of transactions is integrated only if consummation of one transaction is made contingent on consummation of one or more of the other transactions.

Official Comment

Because a statutory structure embodying "par value" and "stated capital" concepts does not protect creditors and senior security holders from payments to junior security holders, section 6.21 does not use these concepts.

1. Consideration

Because shares need not have a par value under section 6.21, there is no minimum price at which shares must be issued. Section 6.21(b) specifically validates "any tangible or intangible property or benefit to the corporation," as consideration for the present issue of shares, specifically including contracts for future services (including promoters' services) and promissory notes. The term "benefit" should be broadly construed also to include, for example, a reduction of a liability, a release of a claim, or intangible gain obtained by a corporation. Business judgment should determine what kind of property or benefit should be obtained for shares, and a determination by the directors meeting the requirements of section 8.30 to accept a specific kind of property or benefit for shares should be accepted and not circumscribed by artificial or arbitrary rules.

2. Board Determination of Adequacy

Protection of shareholders against abuse of the power granted to the board of directors to determine that shares should be issued for intangible property or benefit is provided by the requirements of section 8.30 applicable to a determination that the consideration received for shares is adequate.

In many instances, property or benefit received by the corporation will be of uncertain value; if the board of directors determines that the issuance of shares for the property or benefit is an appropriate transaction, that is sufficient under section 6.21. The board of directors does not have to make an explicit "adequacy" determination by formal resolution; that determination may be inferred from a determination to authorize the issuance of shares for a specified consideration. Likewise, section 6.21 does not require the board of directors to determine an exact value of the consideration to be entered on the books of the corporation.

The second sentence of section 6.21(c) describes the effect of the determination by the board of directors that consideration is adequate for the issuance of shares. That determination, without more, is conclusive to the extent that adequacy is relevant to the question whether the shares are validly issued, fully paid, and nonassessable. Whether shares are validly issued may depend on compliance with corporate procedural requirements, such as issuance within the amount authorized in the articles of incorporation or holding a directors' meeting upon proper notice and with a quorum present. The Act does not address the remedies that may be available for issuances that are subject to challenge. See subchapter E of chapter 1 regarding ratification of defective issuance of shares.

The Act also does not address whether validly issued shares may thereafter be cancelled on the grounds of fraud or bad faith if the shares are in the hands of the original shareholder or other persons who were aware of the circumstances under which they were issued when they acquired the shares. It also leaves to the Uniform Commercial Code other questions relating to the rights of persons other than the person acquiring the shares from the corporation. See the Official Comment to section 6.22.

Section 6.21(e) permits shares issued for contracts for future services or benefits or for promissory notes to be placed in escrow, or their transfer otherwise restricted, until the services are performed, the benefits are received or the notes are paid. In addition, any distributions on such shares may be credited against payment, or other agreed performance, of the consideration for the shares. Under section 6.21(e), if the corporation has restricted the transfer of the shares or placed them in escrow, it may cancel the shares and any credited distributions, in whole or in part, in the event of a failure of performance. This remedy is in the nature of a partial or complete rescission, and therefore rescission principles would be applicable.

Section 6.21 addresses only the corporation's cancellation remedy. It does not address whether other remedies may be available to the corporation, including a right to a deficiency against the nonperforming shareholder, or whether the shareholder may have any rights where the value of the shares subject to cancellation exceeds the value of the obligation remaining unperformed.

If the shares are issued without being restricted as provided in section 6.21(e), they are validly issued in so far as the adequacy of consideration is concerned. See section 6.22 and its Official Comment.

Section 6.24(c) provides express authority for delegation by the board of directors to officers for the issuance of shares as compensatory awards within limitations established by the board.

3. Shareholder Approval Requirement for Certain Issuances

The shareholder approval requirement of section 6.21(f) is generally patterned after the listing standards of national securities exchanges. The calculation of the 20% compares the maximum number of votes entitled to be cast by the shares to be issued or that could be outstanding after giving effect to the conversion of convertible securities and the exercise of rights being issued, with the actual number of votes entitled to be cast by outstanding shares before the transaction.

In making the 20% determination under section 6.21(f), shares that are issuable in a transaction of any kind, including a merger, share exchange, or acquisition of assets, on a contingent basis are counted as shares or securities to be issued as a result of the transaction. On the other hand, shares that are issuable under antidilution clauses, such as those designed to take account of future share splits or share dividends, are not counted as shares or securities to be issued as a result of the transaction, because they are issuable only as a result of a later corporate action authorizing the split or dividend. If a transaction involves an earn-out provision, under which the total amount of shares or securities to be issued will depend on future earnings or other performance measures, the maximum amount of shares or securities that can be issued under the earn-out must be included in the determination.

If the number of shares to be issued or issuable is not fixed, but is subject to a formula, the application of the test in section 6.21(f)(2)(i) requires a calculation of the maximum amount that could be issued under the formula, whether stated as a range or otherwise, in the governing agreement. Even if ultimate issuance of the maximum amount is unlikely, a vote will be required if the maximum amount would result in an issuance of more than 20% of the voting power of shares outstanding immediately before the transaction.

Shares that have or would have only contingent voting rights when issued or issuable are not shares that carry voting power for purposes of the calculation under section 6.21(f).

The vote required to approve issuances that fall within section 6.21(f) is the basic voting rule under the Act, set forth in section 7.25, that more shares must be voted in favor of the issuance than are voted against. This is the same voting rule that applies under chapter 9 for domestications and conversions, chapter 10 for amendments of the articles of incorporation, chapter 11 for mergers and share exchanges, chapter 12 for dispositions of assets that require shareholder approval, and chapter 14 for voluntary dissolutions. The quorum rule under section 6.21(f) is also the same as the quorum rule under chapters 9, 10, 11, 12, and 14.

Section 6.21(f) does not apply to an issuance for cash or cash equivalents, regardless of whether in connection with a public offering. "Cash equivalents" are generally short-term investments that are both readily convertible to known amounts of cash and present insignificant risk of changes in interest rates. Shares that are issued partly for cash or cash equivalents and partly for other consideration are "issued for consideration other than cash or cash equivalents" within the meaning of section 6.21(f).

The term "rights" in section 6.21(f) includes warrants, options, and rights of exchange, whether at the option of the holder, the corporation, or another person. The term "voting power" is defined in section 1.40 as the current power to vote in the election of directors. See also the Official Comment to that section. Because transactions are integrated within the meaning of section 6.21(f) only where consummation of one transaction is made contingent on consummation of one or more of the other transactions, transactions are not integrated for purposes of section 6.21(f) merely because they are proximate in time or because the kind of consideration for which the corporation issues shares is similar in each transaction.

Section 6.21(f) only applies to issuances for consideration. Accordingly, section 6.21(f) does not require shareholder approval for share dividends or for shareholder rights plans. See section 6.23 and its Official Comment.

Illustrations of the application of section 6.21(f) follow:

1. C corporation, which has 2,000,000 shares of Class A voting common stock outstanding (carrying one vote per share), proposes to issue 600,000 shares of authorized but unissued Class B nonvoting common stock in exchange for a business owned by D Corporation. The proposed issuance does not require shareholder approval under section 6.21(f) because the Class B shares do not carry voting power.

2. The facts being otherwise as stated in Illustration 1, C proposes to issue 600,000 additional shares of its Class A voting common stock. The proposed issuance requires shareholder approval under section 6.21(f) because the voting power carried by the shares to be issued will comprise more than 20% of the voting power of C's shares outstanding immediately before the issuance.

3. The facts being otherwise as stated in Illustration 1, C proposes to issue 400,000 shares of authorized but unissued voting preferred stock, each share of which carries one vote and is convertible into 1.5 shares of Class A voting common stock. The proposed issuance requires shareholder approval under section 6.21(f). Although the voting power of the preferred shares to be issued will not comprise more than 20% of the voting power of C's shares outstanding immediately before the issuance, the voting power of the shares issuable upon conversion of the preferred shares will carry more than 20% of such voting power.

4. The facts being otherwise as stated in Illustration 1, C proposes to issue 200,000 shares of its Class A voting common stock, and 100,000 shares of authorized but unissued nonvoting preferred stock, each share of which is convertible into 2.5 shares of C's Class A voting common stock. The proposed issuance requires shareholder approval under section 6.21(f) because the voting power of the Class A shares to be issued, after giving effect to the common stock that is issuable upon conversion of the preferred shares, would comprise more than 20% of the voting power of C's outstanding shares immediately before the issuance.

5. The facts being otherwise as stated in Illustration 4, each share of the preferred stock is convertible into 1.2 shares of the Class A voting common stock. The proposed issuance does not require shareholder approval under section 6.21(f) because neither the voting power of the shares to be issued at the outset (200,000) nor the voting power of the shares that would be outstanding after giving effect to the common stock issuable upon conversion of the preferred shares (a total of 320,000) constitutes more than 20% of the voting power of C's outstanding shares immediately before the issuance.

6. The facts being otherwise as stated in Illustration 1, C proposes to acquire businesses from Corporations G, H, and I for 200,000, 300,000, and 400,000 shares of Class A voting common stock, respectively, within a short period of time. None of the transactions is conditioned on the negotiation or completion of the other transactions. The proposed issuance of voting shares does not require shareholder approval, because the three transactions are not integrated within the meaning of section 6.21(f), and none of the transactions individually involves the issuance of more than 20% of the voting power of C's outstanding shares immediately before each issuance.

§ 6.22.　Liability of Shareholders

(a) A purchaser from a corporation of the corporation's own shares is not liable to the corporation or its creditors with respect to the shares except to pay the consideration for which the shares were authorized to be issued or specified in the subscription agreement.

(b) A shareholder of a corporation is not personally liable for any liabilities of the corporation (including liabilities arising from acts of the corporation) except (i) to the extent provided in a provision of the articles of incorporation permitted by section 2.02(b)(2)(v), and (ii) that a shareholder may become personally liable by reason of the shareholder's own acts or conduct.

Official Comment

The sole obligation of a purchaser of shares from the corporation is to pay the consideration determined by the board of directors (or the consideration specified in the subscription agreement, in the case of preincorporation subscriptions). Upon the transfer to the corporation of the consideration so determined or specified, the shareholder has no further responsibility to the corporation or its creditors "with respect to the shares," although the shareholder may have continuing obligations under a contract or promissory note entered into in connection with the acquisition of shares.

Section 6.22(a) deals only with the responsibility for payment by the purchaser of shares from the corporation. The Act leaves to the Uniform Commercial Code questions with respect to the rights of subsequent purchasers of shares if the consideration is not paid when due. See sections 8–202 and 8–302 of the Uniform Commercial Code.

Section 6.22(b) sets forth the basic rule of nonliability of shareholders for corporate acts or debts that underlies corporation law. Unless such liability is provided for in the articles of incorporation (see section 2.02(b)(2)(v)), shareholders are not liable for corporate obligations, although the last clause of section 6.22(b) recognizes that such liability may be assumed voluntarily or by other conduct.

§ 6.23.　Share Dividends

(a) Unless the articles of incorporation provide otherwise, shares may be issued pro rata and without consideration to the corporation's shareholders or to the shareholders of one or more classes or series of shares. An issuance of shares under this subsection is a share dividend.

(b) Shares of one class or series may not be issued as a share dividend in respect of shares of another class or series unless (i) the articles of incorporation so authorize, (ii) a majority of the votes entitled to be cast by the class or series to be issued approve the issue, or (iii) there are no outstanding shares of the class or series to be issued.

(c) The board of directors may fix the record date for determining shareholders entitled to a share dividend, which date may not be retroactive. If the board of directors does not fix the record date for determining shareholders entitled to a share dividend, the record date is the date the board of directors authorizes the share dividend.

Official Comment

A share dividend is solely a paper transaction: no assets are received by the corporation for the shares and any "dividend" paid in shares does not involve the distribution of property by the corporation to its shareholders. Section 6.23 therefore recognizes that such a transaction involves the issuance of shares "without consideration," and section 1.40 excludes it from the definition of a "distribution."

§ 6.24.　Share Rights, Options, Warrants and Awards

(a) A corporation may issue rights, options, or warrants for the purchase of shares or other securities of the corporation. The board of directors shall determine (i) the terms and conditions upon which the rights, options, or warrants are issued and (ii) the terms, including the consideration for which the shares or other securities are to be issued. The authorization by the board of directors for the corporation to issue such rights, options, or warrants constitutes authorization of the issuance of the shares or other securities for which the rights, options or warrants are exercisable.

(b) The terms and conditions of such rights, options or warrants may include restrictions or conditions that:

(1) preclude or limit the exercise, transfer or receipt of such rights, options or warrants by any person or persons owning or offering to acquire a specified number or percentage of the outstanding shares or other securities of the corporation or by any transferee or transferees of any such person or persons, or

(2) invalidate or void such rights, options, or warrants held by any such person or persons or any such transferee or transferees.

(c) The board of directors may authorize one or more officers to (i) designate the recipients of rights, options, warrants, or other equity compensation awards that involve the issuance of shares and (ii) determine, within an amount and subject to any other limitations established by the board of directors and, if applicable, the shareholders, the number of such rights, options, warrants, or other equity compensation awards and the terms of such rights, options, warrants or awards to be received by the recipients, provided that an officer may not use such authority to designate himself or herself or any other persons as the board of directors may specify as a recipient of such rights, options, warrants, or other equity compensation awards.

Official Comment

Section 6.24 specifically authorizes the creation of rights, options and warrants and confirms the broad discretion of the board of directors in determining the consideration to be received by the corporation for their issuance, including the creation of compensation plans for directors, officers, agents, and employees.

Section 6.24(a) does not require shareholder approval of rights, options, warrants or compensation plans. Of course, prior shareholder approval may be sought as a discretionary matter, or required to comply with the rules of national securities exchanges or to acquire federal income tax benefits that may be conditioned upon shareholder approval of such plans.

Section 6.24(b) confirms that the issuance of rights, options or warrants as part of a shareholder rights plan is permitted. The permissible scope of shareholder rights plans may, however, be limited by the courts.

Section 6.24(c) provides express authority for the delegation to officers of the designation of recipients of compensatory awards involving the issuance of shares, either directly or upon exercise of rights to acquire shares, and the determination of the amount and other terms of the awards, subject to any applicable limitations established by the board of directors or the shareholders. A board of directors (or a board committee with authority delegated to it under section 8.25, typically a compensation committee) may decide whether to exercise the authority under section 6.24(c) and, to the extent it does so, the board must specify the total amount that may be awarded and may impose any other limits it desires as part of the board's oversight of the award process. A board or committee delegating authority under section 6.24(c) would typically include appropriate limits. These limits might include, for example, the amount or range of shares to be awarded to different classes of employees, the timing and pricing of awards, and the vesting terms or other variable provisions of awards.

§ 6.25.   Form and Content of Certificates

(a) Shares may, but need not, be represented by certificates. Unless this Act or another statute expressly provides otherwise, the rights and obligations of shareholders are identical regardless of whether their shares are represented by certificates.

(b) At a minimum each share certificate must state on its face:

(1) the name of the corporation and that it is organized under the law of this state;

(2) the name of the person to whom issued; and

(3) the number and class of shares and the designation of the series, if any, the certificate represents.

(c) If the corporation is authorized to issue different classes of shares or series of shares within a class, the front or back of each certificate must summarize (i) the preferences, rights, and limitations applicable to each class and series, (ii) any variations in preferences, rights, and limitations among the holders of the same class or series, and (iii) the authority of the board of directors to determine the terms of future classes or series. Alternatively, each certificate may state conspicuously on its front or back that the corporation will furnish the shareholder this information on request in writing and without charge.

(d) Each share certificate must be signed by two officers designated in the bylaws.

(e) If the person who signed a share certificate no longer holds office when the certificate is issued, the certificate is nevertheless valid.

§ 6.26. Shares Without Certificates

(a) Unless the articles of incorporation or bylaws provide otherwise, the board of directors of a corporation may authorize the issuance of some or all of the shares of any or all of its classes or series without certificates. The authorization does not affect shares already represented by certificates until they are surrendered to the corporation.

(b) Within a reasonable time after the issuance or transfer of shares without certificates, the corporation shall deliver to the shareholder a written statement of the information required on certificates by sections 6.25(b) and (c), and, if applicable, section 6.27. ment that this information be delivered to purchasers of shares without certificates before purchase.

§ 6.27. Restriction on Transfer of Shares → Freely transferable unless a restriction

(a) The articles of incorporation, the bylaws, an agreement among shareholders, or an agreement between shareholders and the corporation may impose restrictions on the transfer or registration of transfer of shares of the corporation. A restriction does not affect shares issued before the restriction was adopted unless the holders of the shares are parties to the restriction agreement or voted in favor of the restriction.

(b) A restriction on the transfer or registration of transfer of shares is valid and enforceable against the holder or a transferee of the holder if the restriction is authorized by this section and its existence is noted conspicuously on the front or back of the certificate or is contained in the information statement required by section 6.26(b). Unless so noted or contained, a restriction is not enforceable against a person without knowledge of the restriction.

(c) A restriction on the transfer or registration of transfer of shares is authorized:

(1) to maintain the corporation's status when it is dependent on the number or identity of its shareholders;

(2) to preserve exemptions under federal or state securities law; or

(3) for any other reasonable purpose.

(d) A restriction on the transfer or registration of transfer of shares may:

(1) obligate the shareholder first to offer the corporation or other persons (separately, consecutively, or simultaneously) an opportunity to acquire the restricted shares;

(2) obligate the corporation or other persons (separately, consecutively, or simultaneously) to acquire the restricted shares;

(3) require the corporation, the holders of any class or series of its shares, or other persons to approve the transfer of the restricted shares, if the requirement is not manifestly unreasonable; or

(4) prohibit the transfer of the restricted shares to designated persons or classes of persons, if the prohibition is not manifestly unreasonable.

(e) For purposes of this section, "shares" includes a security convertible into or carrying a right to subscribe for or acquire shares.

Subchapter C
Subsequent Acquisition of Shares by Shareholders and Corporation

§ 6.30.   Shareholders' Preemptive Rights

(a) The shareholders of a corporation do not have a preemptive right to acquire the corporation's unissued shares except to the extent the articles of incorporation so provide.

(b) A statement included in the articles of incorporation that "the corporation elects to have preemptive rights" (or words of similar effect) means that the following principles apply except to the extent the articles of incorporation expressly provide otherwise:

(1) The shareholders of the corporation have a preemptive right, granted on uniform terms and conditions prescribed by the board of directors to provide a fair and reasonable opportunity to exercise the right, to acquire proportional amounts of the corporation's unisssued shares upon the decision of the board of directors to issue them.

(2) A preemptive right may be waived by a shareholder. A waiver evidenced by a writing is irrevocable even though it is not supported by consideration.

(3) There is no preemptive right with respect to:

(i) shares issued as compensation to directors, officers, employees or agents of the corporation, its subsidiaries or affiliates;

(ii) shares issued to satisfy conversion or option rights created to provide compensation to directors, officers, employees or agents of the corporation, its subsidiaries or affiliates;

(iii) shares authorized in the articles of incorporation that are issued within six months from the effective date of incorporation; or

(iv) shares sold otherwise than for cash.

(4) Holders of shares of any class or series without voting power but with preferential rights to distributions have no preemptive rights with respect to shares of any class or series.

(5) Holders of shares of any class or series with voting power but without preferential rights to distributions have no preemptive rights with respect to shares of any class or series with preferential rights to distributions unless the shares with preferential rights are convertible into or carry a right to subscribe for or acquire the shares without preferential rights.

(6) Shares subject to preemptive rights that are not acquired by shareholders may be issued to any person for a period of one year after being offered to shareholders at a consideration set by the board of directors that is not lower than the consideration set for the exercise of preemptive rights. An offer at a lower consideration or after the expiration of one year is subject to the shareholders' preemptive rights.

(c) For purposes of this section, "shares" includes a security convertible into or carrying a right to subscribe for or acquire shares.

Official Comment

Section 6.30(a) adopts an "opt in" provision for preemptive rights: unless an affirmative reference to these rights appears in the articles of incorporation, no preemptive rights exist. . . .

Preemptive rights can protect the voting power and equity participation of shareholders. This combination of functions creates no problem in a corporation that has authorized only a single class of shares but may occasionally create problems in corporations with more complex capital structures. In many capital structures, the issuance of additional shares of one class or series typically does not adversely affect other classes or series. For example, the issuance of additional shares with voting power but without preferential rights normally does not affect either the limited voting power or equity participation of holders of shares with preferential rights; holders of shares with preferential equity participation rights but without voting power should therefore have no preemptive rights with respect to shares with voting power but without preferential rights. See sections 6.30(b)(4) and (b)(5). Classes or series of shares that may give rise to possible conflict between the protection of voting interests and equity participation when the board of directors desires to issue additional shares include classes or series of nonvoting shares without preferential rights and classes or series of shares with both voting power and preferential rights to distributions. These conflicts can be dealt with by specific provisions in the articles of incorporation.

§ 6.31. Corporation's Acquisition of Its Own Shares

(a) A corporation may acquire its own shares, and shares so acquired constitute authorized but unissued shares.

(b) If the articles of incorporation prohibit the reissue of the acquired shares, the number of authorized shares is reduced by the number of shares acquired.

Official Comment

Shares that are acquired by the corporation become authorized but unissued shares under section 6.31 unless the articles of incorporation prohibit reissue, in which event the shares are cancelled and the number of authorized shares is automatically reduced.

If the number of authorized shares of a class is reduced as a result of the operation of section 6.31(b), the board of directors should amend the articles of incorporation under section 10.05(f) to reflect that reduction. If there are no remaining authorized shares in a class as a result of the operation of section 6.31, the board should amend the articles of incorporation under section 10.05(g) to delete the class from the classes of shares authorized by the articles of incorporation.

Subchapter D
Distributions

§ 6.40. Distributions to Shareholders

(a) A board of directors may authorize and the corporation may make distributions to its shareholders subject to restriction by the articles of incorporation and the limitation in subsection (c).

(b) The board of directors may fix the record date for determining shareholders entitled to a distribution, which date may not be retroactive. If the board of directors does not fix a record date for determining shareholders entitled to a distribution (other than one involving a purchase, redemption, or other acquisition of the corporation's shares), the record date is the date the board of directors authorizes the distribution.

(c) No distribution may be made if, after giving it effect:

(1) the corporation would not be able to pay its debts as they become due in the usual course of business; or

(2) the corporation's total assets would be less than the sum of its total liabilities plus (unless the articles of incorporation permit otherwise) the amount that would be needed, if the corporation were to be dissolved at the time of the distribution, to satisfy the preferential rights upon dissolution of shareholders whose preferential rights are superior to those receiving the distribution.

(d) The board of directors may base a determination that a distribution is not prohibited under subsection (c) either on financial statements prepared on the basis of accounting practices and principles that are reasonable in the circumstances or on a fair valuation or other method that is reasonable in the circumstances.

(e) Except as provided in subsection (g), the effect of a distribution under subsection (c) is measured:

(1) in the case of distribution by purchase, redemption, or other acquisition of the corporation's shares, as of the earlier of (i) the date cash or other property is transferred or debt to a shareholder is incurred by the corporation or (ii) the date the shareholder ceases to be a shareholder with respect to the acquired shares;

(2) in the case of any other distribution of indebtedness, as of the date the indebtedness is distributed; and

(3) in all other cases, as of (i) the date the distribution is authorized if the payment occurs within 120 days after the date of authorization or (ii) the date the payment is made if it occurs more than 120 days after the date of authorization.

(f) A corporation's indebtedness to a shareholder incurred by reason of a distribution made in accordance with this section is at parity with the corporation's indebtedness to its general, unsecured creditors except to the extent subordinated by agreement.

(g) Indebtedness of a corporation, including indebtedness issued as a distribution, is not considered a liability for purposes of determinations under subsection (c) if its terms provide that payment of principal and interest are made only if and to the extent that payment of a distribution to shareholders could then be made under this section. If such indebtedness is issued as a distribution, each payment of principal or interest is treated as a distribution, the effect of which is measured on the date the payment is actually made.

(h) This section shall not apply to distributions in liquidation under chapter 14.

Official Comment

1. The Scope of Section 6.40

Section 6.40 imposes a single, uniform test on all distributions other than distributions in liquidation under chapter 14. Section 1.40 defines "distribution" broadly to include transfers of cash and other property (excluding a corporation's own shares) to a shareholder in respect of the corporation's shares. Examples of such transfers are cash or property dividends, payments by a corporation to purchase its own shares, and distributions of promissory notes or indebtedness. The financial provisions of the Act do not use the concept of surplus but do have restrictions on distributions built around both equity insolvency and balance sheet tests.

2. Equity Insolvency Test → if this then look @ 8.30(d)

In most cases involving a corporation operating as a going concern in the normal course, it will be apparent from information generally available that no particular inquiry concerning the equity insolvency test in section 6.40(c)(1) is needed. Although neither a balance sheet nor an income statement can be conclusive as to this test, the existence of significant shareholders' equity and normal operating conditions are of themselves a strong indication that no issue should arise under that test. In the case of a corporation having regularly audited financial statements, the absence of any qualification in the most recent auditor's opinion as to the corporation's status as a "going concern," coupled with a lack of subsequent adverse events, would normally be decisive.

It is only when circumstances indicate that the corporation is encountering difficulties or is in an uncertain position concerning its liquidity and operations that the board of directors or, more commonly, the officers or others upon whom they may place reliance under section 8.30(d), may need to address the issue. Because of the overall judgment required in evaluating the equity insolvency test, no "bright line" test is provided. However, in determining whether the equity insolvency test has been met, certain judgments or assumptions as to the future course of the corporation's business are customarily justified, absent clear evidence to the contrary. These include the likelihood that (i) based on existing and contemplated demand for the corporation's products or services, it will be able to generate funds over a period of time sufficient to satisfy its existing and reasonably anticipated obligations as they mature, and (ii) indebtedness which matures in the near-term will be refinanced where, on the basis of the corporation's financial condition and future prospects and the general availability of credit to businesses similarly situated, it is reasonable to assume that such refinancing may be accomplished. To the extent that the corporation may be subject to asserted or unasserted contingent liabilities, reasonable judgments as to the likelihood, amount, and time of any recovery against the corporation, after giving consideration to the extent to which the corporation is insured or otherwise protected against loss, may be utilized. There may be occasions when it would be useful to consider a cash flow analysis, based on a business forecast and budget, covering a sufficient period of time to permit a conclusion that known obligations of the corporation can reasonably be expected to be satisfied over the period of time that they will mature.

In exercising their judgment, the directors are entitled to rely, as provided in section 8.30(e), on information, opinions, reports, and statements prepared by others. Ordinarily, they should not be expected to become involved in the details of the various analyses or market or economic projections that may be relevant.

3. Balance Sheet Test → if this then look @ 8.30(e)

The determination of a corporation's assets and liabilities for purposes of the balance sheet test of section 6.40(c)(2) and the choice of the permissible basis on which to do so are left to the judgment of its board of directors.

In making a judgment under section 6.40(d), the board may rely as provided in section 8.30(e) upon information, opinions, reports, and statements, including financial statements and other financial data, prepared or presented by public accountants or others.

Section 6.40 does not utilize particular accounting terminology of a technical nature or specify particular accounting concepts. In making determinations under this section, the board of directors may make judgments about accounting matters.

In a corporation with subsidiaries, the board of directors may rely on unconsolidated statements prepared on the basis of the equity method of accounting as to the corporation's investee corporations, including corporate joint ventures and subsidiaries, although other evidence would be relevant in the total determination. The board of directors is entitled to rely as provided by section 8.30(e) upon reasonably current financial statements in determining whether the balance sheet test of section 6.40(c)(2) has been met, unless the board has knowledge that makes such reliance unwarranted. Section 6.40 does not mandate the use of generally accepted accounting principles; it only requires the use of accounting practices and principles that are reasonable in the circumstances. Although corporations subject to registration under the Securities Exchange Act of 1934 must, and many other corporations in fact do, use financial statements prepared on the basis of generally accepted accounting principles, a great number of smaller or closely held corporations do not. Some of these corporations maintain records solely on a tax accounting basis and their financial statements are of necessity prepared on that basis. Others prepare financial statements that substantially reflect generally accepted accounting principles but may depart from them in some respects (*e.g.*, footnote disclosure). A statutory standard of reasonableness, rather than stipulating generally accepted accounting principles as the normative standard, is appropriate to achieve a reasonable degree of flexibility and to accommodate the needs of the many different types of business corporations which might be subject to these provisions, including in particular closely held corporations.

Section 6.40(d) specifically permits determinations to be made under section 6.40(c)(2) on the basis of a fair valuation or other method that is reasonable in the circumstances. The statute authorizes departures from historical cost accounting and permits the use of appraisal and current value methods to determine the amount available for distribution. No particular method of valuation is prescribed in the statute, as different methods may have validity depending upon the circumstances, including the type of enterprise and the purpose for which the determination is made. In most cases, a fair valuation method or a going concern basis would be appropriate if it is believed that the enterprise will continue as a going concern.

Ordinarily a corporation should not selectively revalue assets. It should consider the value of all of its material assets, regardless of whether they are reflected in the financial statements (*e.g.*, a valuable executory contract). Likewise, all of a corporation's material obligations should be considered and revalued to the extent appropriate and possible. In any event, section 6.40(d) calls for the application under section 6.40(c)(2) of a method of determining the aggregate amount of assets and liabilities that is reasonable in the circumstances.

The phrase "other method that is reasonable in the circumstances means that under section 6.40(c)(2) a wide variety of methods may be considered reasonable in a particular case even if any such method might not be a "fair valuation" or "current value" method.

4. Relationship to the Federal Bankruptcy Code and Other Fraudulent Conveyance Statutes

The Act establishes the validity of distributions from the corporate law standpoint under section 6.40 and determines the potential liability of directors for improper distributions under sections 8.30 and 8.32. The federal bankruptcy laws and state fraudulent conveyance statutes, on the other hand, are designed to enable the trustee or other representative to recapture for the benefit of creditors funds distributed to others in some circumstances. Accordingly, the tests of section 6.40 are different from the tests for insolvency under those statutes.

5. Preferential Dissolution Rights and the Balance Sheet Test

Section 6.40(c)(2) treats preferential dissolution rights of shares for distribution purposes as if they were liabilities for the sole purpose of determining the amount available for distributions. In making the calculation of the amount that must be added to the liabilities of the corporation to reflect the preferential dissolution rights, the assumption should be made that the preferential dissolution rights are to be established pursuant to the articles of incorporation as of the date of the distribution or proposed distribution. The amount so determined must include arrearages in preferential dividends if the articles of incorporation require that they be paid upon the dissolution of the corporation. In the case of shares having both preferential rights upon dissolution and other nonpreferential rights, only the preferential rights should be taken into account. The treatment of preferential dissolution rights of classes or series of shares set forth in section 6.40(c)(2) is applicable only to the balance sheet test and is not applicable to the equity insolvency test of section 6.40(c)(1). The treatment of preferential rights mandated by section 6.40(c)(2) may always be eliminated by an appropriate provision in the articles of incorporation.

6. Application to Acquisition of Shares

In an acquisition of its shares, a corporation may transfer property or incur debt to the former holder of the shares. Share repurchase agreements involving payment for shares over a period of time are of special importance in closely held corporations. Section 6.40(e) provides a clear rule for this situation: the legality of the distribution must be measured at the time of the issuance or incurrence of the debt, not at a later date when the debt is actually paid, except as provided in section 6.40(g).

Section 6.40(g) provides that indebtedness need not be taken into account as a liability in determining whether the tests of section 6.40(c) have been met if the terms of the indebtedness provide that payments of principal or interest can be made only if and to the extent that payment of a distribution could then be made under section 6.40. This has the effect of making the holder of the indebtedness junior to all other creditors but senior to the holders of shares, not only during the time the corporation is operating but also upon dissolution and liquidation. It should be noted that the creation of such indebtedness, and the related limitations on payments of principal and interest, may create tax problems or raise other legal questions.

Although section 6.40(g) is applicable to all indebtedness meeting its tests, regardless of the circumstances of its issuance, it is anticipated that it will apply most frequently to permit the reacquisition of shares of the corporation at a time when the deferred purchase price exceeds the net worth of the corporation. This type of reacquisition may be necessary in the case of businesses in early stages of development or service businesses whose value derives principally from existing or prospective net income or cash flow rather than from net asset value. In such situations, net worth will usually be anticipated to grow over time from operations so that when payments in respect of the indebtedness are to be made the two insolvency tests will be satisfied. In the meantime, the fact that the indebtedness is outstanding will not prevent distributions that could be made under section 6.40(c) if the indebtedness were not counted in making the determination.

Chapter 7

SHAREHOLDERS

Subchapter A

Meetings

§ 7.01. Annual Meeting

(a) Unless directors are elected by written consent in lieu of an annual meeting as permitted by section 7.04, a corporation shall hold a meeting of shareholders annually at a time stated in or fixed in accordance with the bylaws at which directors shall be elected.

(b) Annual meetings may be held in or out of this state at the place stated in or fixed in accordance with the bylaws. If no place is so stated or fixed, annual meetings shall be held at the corporation's principal office.

(c) The failure to hold an annual meeting at the time stated in or fixed in accordance with a corporation's bylaws does not affect the validity of any corporate action.

Official Comment

The principal action to be taken at the annual meeting is the election of directors pursuant to section 8.03, but the purposes of the annual meeting are not limited by the Act. The requirement of section 7.01(a) that an annual meeting be held is phrased in mandatory terms to ensure that every shareholder entitled to participate in an annual meeting has the unqualified rights to (i) demand that an annual meeting be held and (ii) compel the holding of the meeting under section 7.03 if the corporation does not promptly hold the meeting and if the shareholders have not elected directors by written consent.

Many corporations, such as nonpublic subsidiaries and closely held corporations, do not regularly hold annual meetings and, if no shareholder objects or action has been taken by written consent, that practice creates no problem under section 7.01, because section 7.01(c) provides that failure to hold an annual meeting does not affect the validity of any corporate action. The shareholders may act by unanimous written consent under section

7.04 (or by less than unanimous written consent if the articles of incorporation so provide). Directors, once duly elected, remain in office until their successors are elected or they resign or are removed. See sections 8.05 and 8.07 through 8.09. . . .

§ 7.02.   Special Meeting

(a) A corporation shall hold a special meeting of shareholders:

(1) on call of its board of directors or the person or persons authorized to do so by the articles of incorporation or bylaws; or

(2) if shareholders holding at least 10% of all the votes entitled to be cast on an issue proposed to be considered at the proposed special meeting sign, date, and deliver to the corporation one or more written demands for the meeting describing the purpose or purposes for which it is to be held, provided that the articles of incorporation may fix a lower percentage or a higher percentage not exceeding 25% of all the votes entitled to be cast on any issue proposed to be considered. Unless otherwise provided in the articles of incorporation, a written demand for a special meeting may be revoked by a writing to that effect received by the corporation before the receipt by the corporation of demands sufficient in number to require the holding of a special meeting.

(b) If not otherwise fixed under section 7.03 or 7.07, the record date for determining shareholders entitled to demand a special meeting shall be the first date on which a signed shareholder demand is delivered to the corporation. No written demand for a special meeting shall be effective unless, within 60 days of the earliest date on which such a demand delivered to the corporation as required by this section was signed, written demands signed by shareholders holding at least the percentage of votes specified in or fixed in accordance with subsection (a)(2) have been delivered to the corporation.

(c) Special meetings of shareholders may be held in or out of this state at the place stated in or fixed in accordance with the bylaws. If no place is so stated or fixed, special meetings shall be held at the corporation's principal office.

(d) Only business within the purpose or purposes described in the meeting notice required by section 7.05(c) may be conducted at a special meeting of shareholders.

§ 7.03.   Court-Ordered Meeting

(a) The [name or describe court] may summarily order a meeting to be held:

(1) on application of any shareholder of the corporation if an annual meeting was not held or action by written consent in lieu of an annual meeting did not become effective within the earlier of six months after the end of the corporation's fiscal year or 15 months after its last annual meeting; or

(2) on application of one or more shareholders who signed a demand for a special meeting valid under section 7.02, if:

(i) notice of the special meeting was not given within 30 days after the first day on which the requisite number of such demands have been delivered to the corporation; or

(ii) the special meeting was not held in accordance with the notice.

(b) The court may fix the time and place of the meeting, determine the shares entitled to participate in the meeting, specify a record date or dates for determining shareholders entitled to notice of and to vote at the meeting, prescribe the form and content of the meeting notice, fix the quorum required for specific matters to be considered at the meeting (or direct that the shares represented at the meeting constitute a quorum for action on those matters), and enter other orders necessary to accomplish the purpose or purposes of the meeting.

(c) For purposes of subsection (a)(1), "shareholder" means a record shareholder, a beneficial shareholder, and an unrestricted voting trust beneficial owner.

Official Comment

. . .

1. The Discretion of the Court to Order a Meeting

The court has broad discretion under section 7.03 whether to order that a meeting be held, since the language of the statute is that the court "may summarily order" that a meeting be held. A court, for example, may refuse to order a special meeting if the specified purpose is repetitive of the purpose of a special meeting held in the recent past. Alternatively, the court may view the demand as a good faith request for reconsideration of an action taken in the recent past and may order a meeting to be held. Similarly, even though a demand for an annual meeting is not a formal prerequisite for an application for a summary order under this section, the court may withhold setting a time and date for the annual meeting for a reasonably short period to permit the corporation to do so. . . .

§ 7.04. Action Without Meeting

(a) Action required or permitted by this Act to be taken at a shareholders' meeting may be taken without a meeting if the action is taken by all the shareholders entitled to vote on the action. The action must be evidenced by one or more written consents bearing the date of signature and describing the action taken, signed by all the shareholders entitled to vote on the action and delivered to the corporation for filing by the corporation with the minutes or corporate records.

(b) The articles of incorporation may provide that any action required or permitted by this Act to be taken at a shareholders' meeting may be taken without a meeting, and without prior notice, if consents in writing setting forth the action so taken are signed by the holders of outstanding shares having not less than the minimum number of votes that would be required to authorize or take the action at a meeting at which all shares entitled to vote on the action were present and voted; provided, however, that if a corporation's articles of incorporation authorize shareholders to cumulate their votes when electing directors pursuant to section 7.28, directors may not be elected by less than unanimous written consent. A written consent must bear the date of signature of the shareholder who signs the consent and be delivered to the corporation for filing by the corporation with the minutes or corporate records.

(c) If not otherwise fixed under section 7.07 and if prior action by the board of directors is not required respecting the action to be taken without a meeting, the record date for determining the shareholders entitled to take action without a meeting shall be the first date on which a signed written consent is delivered to the corporation. If not otherwise fixed under section 7.07 and if prior action by the board of directors is required respecting the action to be taken without a meeting, the record date shall be the close of business on the day the resolution of the board of directors taking such prior action is adopted. No written consent shall be effective to take the corporate action referred to therein unless, within 60 days of the earliest date on which a consent delivered to the corporation as required by this section was signed, written consents signed by sufficient shareholders to take the action have been delivered to the corporation. A written consent may be revoked by a writing to that effect delivered to the corporation before unrevoked written consents sufficient in number to take the corporate action have been delivered to the corporation.

(d) A consent signed pursuant to the provisions of this section has the effect of a vote taken at a meeting and may be described as such in any document. Unless the articles of incorporation, bylaws or a resolution of the board of directors provides for a reasonable delay to permit tabulation of written consents, the action taken by written consent shall be effective when written consents signed by sufficient shareholders to take the action have been delivered to the corporation.

(e) If this Act requires that notice of a proposed action be given to nonvoting shareholders and the action is to be taken by written consent of the voting shareholders, the corporation shall give its nonvoting shareholders written notice of the action not more than 10 days after (i) written consents sufficient to take the action have been delivered to the corporation, or (ii) such later date that tabulation of consents is completed pursuant to an authorization under subsection (d). The notice must reasonably describe the action taken and contain or be accompanied by the same material that, under any provision of this Act, would have been required to be sent to nonvoting shareholders in a notice of a meeting at which the proposed action would have been submitted to the shareholders for action.

(f) If action is taken by less than unanimous written consent of the voting shareholders, the corporation shall give its nonconsenting voting shareholders written notice of the action not more than 10 days after (i) written consents sufficient to take the action have been delivered to the corporation, or (ii) such later date that tabulation of consents is completed pursuant to an authorization under subsection (d). The notice must reasonably describe the action taken and contain or be accompanied by the same material that, under any provision of this Act, would have been required to be sent to voting shareholders in a notice of a meeting at which the action would have been submitted to the shareholders for action.

(g) The notice requirements in subsections (e) and (f) shall not delay the effectiveness of actions taken by written consent, and a failure to comply with such notice requirements shall not invalidate actions taken by written consent, provided that this subsection shall not be deemed to limit judicial power to fashion any appropriate remedy in favor of a shareholder adversely affected by a failure to give such notice within the required time period.

Official Comment

Section 7.04(a) permits shareholders to act by unanimous written consent without holding a meeting. This applies to any shareholder action, including election of directors, approval of mergers, domestications, conversions, sales of the corporation's assets requiring shareholder approval, amendments of articles of incorporation, and dissolution. Unanimous written consent is generally obtainable only for matters on which there are relatively few shareholders entitled to vote and is thus generally not used by public corporations. Under section 7.04(b), however, a corporation may include in its articles of incorporation a provision that permits shareholder action by less than unanimous written consent except with respect to the election of directors by written consent where cumulative voting applies. See section 7.28. If the articles of incorporation permit action by less than unanimous written consent, they may also limit or otherwise specify the shareholder actions that may be approved by less than unanimous consent.

1.   Form of Written Consent

To be effective, consents must be in writing, dated and sent to the corporation in any manner authorized by section 1.41, including electronic transmission if the applicable conditions of section 1.41 are met.

A shareholder or proxy may use an electronic transmission to consent to an action. If an electronic transmission is used to consent to an action, the corporation must be able to determine from the transmission the date of the signature and that the consent was authorized by the shareholder or a person authorized to act for the shareholder. See sections 1.40 ("electronic," "sign," and "signature") and 1.41(d).

In some cases, more votes may be required to approve an action by less than unanimous written consent than would be required to approve the same action at a meeting that is not attended by all shareholders. For example, for a corporation with 1,000 shares eligible to vote, unrevoked consents from the holders of at least 501 shares are necessary to take action by written consent under the default quorum and voting requirement provisions of section 7.25. In contrast, at a meeting at which the minimum quorum is present, the same action could be taken with the vote of the holders of 251 shares, or even fewer if not all shares present are voted. Where the Act or a corporation's articles of incorporation provide for a greater voting requirement, however, the number of shares required to consent to an action may be the same as the number of shares required to approve the action at a meeting of shareholders.

The phrase "one or more written consents" in section 7.04 makes it clear that shareholders do not need to sign the same document. To minimize the possibility that action by written consent will be authorized by action of persons who may no longer be shareholders at the time the action is taken, section 7.04(c) requires that all consents be signed within 60 days of the earliest signature date of the consents delivered to the corporation.

2.   Notice to Nonconsenting Shareholders

. . . By requiring notice only after shareholder action has been taken, the Act preserves the practical utility of the less than unanimous written consent when action needs to be taken quickly, without the delay that would result from a mandatory prior notice requirement. A corporation may provide for advance notice in its articles of incorporation. . . .

§ 7.05.   Notice of Meeting

(a) A corporation shall notify shareholders of the date, time, and place of each annual and special shareholders' meeting no fewer than 10 nor more than 60 days before the meeting date. If the board of directors has authorized participation by means of remote communication pursuant to section 7.09 for holders of any class or series of shares, the notice to the holders of such class or series of shares must describe the means of remote communication to be used. The notice must include the record date for determining the shareholders entitled to vote at the meeting, if such date is different from the record date for determining shareholders entitled to notice of the meeting. Unless this Act or the articles of incorporation require otherwise, the corporation is required to give notice only to shareholders entitled to vote at the meeting as of the record date for determining the shareholders entitled to notice of the meeting.

(b) Unless this Act or the articles of incorporation require otherwise, the notice of an annual meeting of shareholders need not include a description of the purpose or purposes for which the meeting is called.

(c) Notice of a special meeting of shareholders must include a description of the purpose or purposes for which the meeting is called.

(d) If not otherwise fixed under section 7.03 or 7.07, the record date for determining shareholders entitled to notice of and to vote at an annual or special shareholders' meeting is the day before the first notice is delivered to shareholders.

(e) Unless the bylaws require otherwise, if an annual or special shareholders' meeting is adjourned to a different date, time, or place, notice need not be given of the new date, time, or place if the new date, time, or place is announced at the meeting before adjournment. If a new record date for the adjourned meeting is or must be fixed under section 7.07, however, notice of the adjourned meeting shall be given under this section to shareholders entitled to vote at such adjourned meeting as of the record date fixed for notice of such adjourned meeting.

Official Comment

The Act does not require that the notice of an annual meeting refer to any specific purpose or purposes, and any matter appropriate for shareholder action may be considered. Section 7.05(b) recognizes, however, that other provisions of the Act or the corporation's articles of incorporation may require that specific reference to a proposed action appear in the notice of meeting. See sections 9.21, 9.32, 10.03, 11.04, 12.02, and 14.02. In addition, as a condition to relying upon shareholder action to establish the safe harbor protection of section 8.61(b), section 8.63 requires notice to shareholders providing information regarding any director's conflict of interest in a transaction. If the board of directors chooses, a notice of an annual meeting may contain references to purposes or proposals not required by statute. If a notice of an annual meeting refers specifically to one or more purposes, the meeting is not limited to those purposes. Although the corporation is not required to give notice of the purpose or purposes of an annual meeting unless the Act or the articles of incorporation so provide, a shareholder, in order to raise a matter at an annual meeting (for example, to nominate an individual for election as a director or to propose a resolution for adoption), may have to comply with any advance notice provisions in the corporation's articles of incorporation or bylaws. Such provisions might include requirements that shareholder nominations for election to the board of directors or resolutions intended to be voted on at the annual meeting be submitted in writing and received by the corporation a prescribed number of days in advance of the meeting.

The selection of the day before the notice is delivered as the catch-all record date under section 7.05(d) is intended to permit the corporation to deliver notices to shareholders on a given day without regard to any requests for transfer that may have been received during that day. For this reason, this section is consistent with the general principle set forth in section 7.07(b) that the board of directors may not fix a retroactive record date.

Section 7.05(e) provides rules for adjourned meetings and determines whether new notice must be given to shareholders. If a new record date is or must be fixed under section 7.07, the 10- to 60-day notice requirement and all other requirements of section 7.05 must be complied with because notice must be given to the persons who are shareholders as of the new record date. In such circumstances, a new quorum for the adjourned meeting must also be established. See section 7.25, which provides that if a quorum exists for a meeting, it is deemed to continue to exist automatically for an adjourned meeting unless a new record date is or must be set for the adjourned meeting.

§ 7.06. Waiver of Notice

(a) A shareholder may waive any notice required by this Act or the articles of incorporation or bylaws, before or after the date and time stated in the notice. The waiver must be in writing, be signed by the shareholder entitled to the notice, and be delivered to the corporation for filing by the corporation with the minutes or corporate records.

(b) A shareholder's attendance at a meeting:

(1) waives objection to lack of notice or defective notice of the meeting, unless the shareholder at the beginning of the meeting objects to holding the meeting or transacting business at the meeting; and

(2) waives objection to consideration of a particular matter at the meeting that is not within the purpose or purposes described in the meeting notice, unless the shareholder objects to considering the matter when it is presented.

§ 7.07.   Record Date for Meeting

(a) The bylaws may fix or provide the manner of fixing the record date or dates for one or more voting groups to determine the shareholders entitled to notice of a shareholders' meeting, to demand a special meeting, to vote, or to take any other action. If the bylaws do not fix or provide for fixing a record date, the board of directors may fix the record date.

(b) A record date fixed under this section may not be more than 70 days before the meeting or action requiring a determination of shareholders and may not be retroactive.

(c) A determination of shareholders entitled to notice of or to vote at a shareholders' meeting is effective for any adjournment of the meeting unless the board of directors fixes a new record date or dates, which it shall do if the meeting is adjourned to a date more than 120 days after the date fixed for the original meeting.

(d) If a court orders a meeting adjourned to a date more than 120 days after the date fixed for the original meeting, it may provide that the original record date or dates continues in effect or it may fix a new record date or dates.

(e) The record dates for a shareholders' meeting fixed by or in the manner provided in the bylaws or by the board of directors shall be the record date for determining shareholders entitled both to notice of and to vote at the shareholders' meeting, unless in the case of a record date fixed by the board of directors and to the extent not prohibited by the bylaws, the board, at the time it fixes the record date for shareholders entitled to notice of the meeting, fixes a later record date on or before the date of the meeting to determine the shareholders entitled to vote at the meeting.

Official Comment

Section 7.07 authorizes the board of directors to fix record dates for determining shareholders entitled to take any action unless the bylaws themselves fix or otherwise provide for the fixing of a record date. A separate record date may be established for each voting group entitled to vote separately on a matter at a meeting, or a single record date may be established for all voting groups entitled to participate in the meeting. If neither the bylaws nor the board of directors fixes a record date for a specific action, the section of the Act that deals with that action itself fixes the record date. For example, section 7.05(d), relating to giving notice of a meeting, provides that the record date for determining who is entitled to notice of and to vote at a meeting (if not fixed by the directors or the bylaws) is the close of business on the day before the date the corporation first gives notice to shareholders of the meeting.

After a record date is fixed, if a new record date subsequently is or must be fixed under section 7.07, section 7.05 requires that new notice be given to the persons who are shareholders as of the new record date, and section 7.25 requires that a quorum be reestablished for that meeting.

Section 7.07(e) provides a board of directors with flexibility to align shareholders' voting and economic interests and addresses, in part, concerns over the separation of ownership and voting by permitting a board of directors to set a record date for voting closer to the meeting date. This provision does not restrict how close a record date for voting can be to the meeting date, but a board of directors would need to consider the practical issues in fixing the voting record date, including the requirement of section 7.20(c) that a list of shareholders entitled to vote be available at the meeting. The board may fix a separate record date for voting only at the time it fixes the record date for notice, and, as provided in section 7.05, notice of the separate record date must be included in the notice of meeting. If the board fixes separate record dates, section 16.02(e) provides for shareholders entitled to vote at the meeting who were not shareholders on the record date for notice to have access to the information provided by the corporation to shareholders in connection with the meeting. If the board does not fix separate record dates, the normal provisions for fixing a single record date for notice and voting will apply.

§ 7.08.   Conduct of Meeting

(a) At each meeting of shareholders, a chair shall preside. The chair shall be appointed as provided in the bylaws or, in the absence of such provision, by the board of directors.

(b) The chair, unless the articles of incorporation or bylaws provide otherwise, shall determine the order of business and shall have the authority to establish rules for the conduct of the meeting.

(c) Any rules adopted for, and the conduct of, the meeting shall be fair to shareholders.

(d) The chair of the meeting shall announce at the meeting when the polls close for each matter voted upon. If no announcement is made, the polls shall be deemed to have closed upon the final adjournment of the meeting. After the polls close, no ballots, proxies or votes nor any revocations or changes to such ballots, proxies or votes may be accepted.

Official Comment

Section 7.08 provides that, at any meeting of the shareholders, there shall be a chair who shall preside over the meeting. Inherent in the chair's power in section 7.08(b) to establish rules for the conduct of the meeting is the authority to require that the order of business be observed and that any discussion or comments from shareholders or their proxies be confined to the business item under discussion. The rules for conduct of the meeting may cover such subjects as the proper means for obtaining the floor, who shall have the right to address the meeting, the manner in which shareholders will be recognized to speak, time limits per speaker, the number of times a shareholder may address the meeting, and the person to whom questions should be addressed. The chair should be fair in determining the order of business and in establishing rules for the conduct of the meeting so as not to unfairly foreclose the right of shareholders—subject to the Act, the articles of incorporation and the bylaws—to raise items which are properly a subject for shareholder discussion or action at some point in the meeting before adjournment. . . .

§ 7.09.   Remote Participation in Shareholders' Meetings

(a) Shareholders of any class or series of shares may participate in any meeting of shareholders by means of remote communication to the extent the board of directors authorizes such participation for such class or series. Participation as a shareholder by means of remote communication shall be subject to such guidelines and procedures as the board of directors adopts, and shall be in conformity with subsection (b).

(b) Shareholders participating in a shareholders' meeting by means of remote communication shall be deemed present and may vote at such a meeting if the corporation has implemented reasonable measures:

(1) to verify that each person participating remotely as a shareholder is a shareholder; and

(2) to provide such shareholders a reasonable opportunity to participate in the meeting and to vote on matters submitted to the shareholders, including an opportunity to communicate, and to read or hear the proceedings of the meeting, substantially concurrently with such proceedings.

Official Comment

Section 7.09 permits shareholders to participate in annual and special shareholders' meetings by means of remote communication, such as over the Internet or through telephone conference calls, subject to the conditions set forth in section 7.09(b) and any other guidelines and procedures that the board of directors adopts. This would include the use of electronic ballots to the extent authorized by the board of directors. This authorization extends as well to anyone to whom such shareholder has granted a proxy appointment. Section 7.09(a) ensures that the board of directors has the sole discretion to determine whether to allow shareholders to participate by means of remote communication.

Section 7.09 allows the board of directors to limit participation by means of remote communication to all shareholders of a particular class or series, but does not permit the board of directors to limit such participation to particular shareholders within a class or series.

Section 7.09 is not intended to expand the rights to participate in meetings or otherwise alter the ability of the board of directors or the chair to conduct meetings, pursuant to section 7.08, in a manner that is fair. For example, many corporations limit shareholder comments and, if such practice is fair to shareholders consistent with section 7.08, such practice is not changed by section 7.09. The two requirements under section 7.09(b) reflect the minimum deemed necessary to safeguard the integrity of the shareholders' meeting. Section 7.09 specifically gives the board of directors the flexibility and discretion to adopt additional guidelines and procedures for allowing shareholders to participate in a meeting by means of remote communication.

To give corporations the flexibility to choose the most efficient means of remote communication, under section 7.09(a), the board of directors may require that shareholders communicate their desire to participate by a certain date and condition the provision of remote communication or the form of communication to be used on the affirmative response of a certain number or proportion of shareholders eligible to participate. If the board of directors authorizes shareholder participation by means of remote communication pursuant to this section, such authorization and the process for participating by remote means of communication must be included in the meeting notice required by section 7.05.

Subchapter B

Voting

§ 7.20.　Shareholders' List for Meeting

(a) After fixing a record date for a meeting, a corporation shall prepare an alphabetical list of the names of all its shareholders who are entitled to notice of a shareholders' meeting. If the board of directors fixes a different record date under section 7.07(e) to determine the shareholders entitled to vote at the meeting, a corporation also shall prepare an alphabetical list of the names of all its shareholders who are entitled to vote at the meeting. A list must be arranged by voting group (and within each voting group by class or series of shares) and show the address of and number of shares held by each shareholder. Nothing contained in this subsection shall require the corporation to include on such list the electronic mail address or other electronic contact information of a shareholder.

(b) The shareholders' list for notice shall be available for inspection by any shareholder, beginning two business days after notice of the meeting is given for which the list was prepared and continuing through the meeting, at the corporation's principal office or at a place identified in the meeting notice in the city where the meeting will be held. A shareholders' list for voting shall be similarly available for inspection promptly after the record date for voting. A shareholder, or the shareholder's agent or attorney, is entitled on written demand to inspect and, subject to the requirements of section 16.02(c), to copy a list, during regular business hours and at the shareholder's expense, during the period it is available for inspection.

(c) The corporation shall make the list of shareholders entitled to vote available at the meeting, and any shareholder, or the shareholder's agent or attorney, is entitled to inspect the list at any time during the meeting or any adjournment.

(d) If the corporation refuses to allow a shareholder, or the shareholder's agent or attorney, to inspect a shareholders' list before or at the meeting (or copy a list as permitted by subsection (b)), the [name or describe court], on application of the shareholder, may summarily order the inspection or copying at the corporation's expense and may postpone the meeting for which the list was prepared until the inspection or copying is complete.

(e) Refusal or failure to prepare or make available the shareholders' list does not affect the validity of action taken at the meeting.

Official Comment

. . .

5.　*The Right to Obtain a Copy of the List*

Section 7.20(b) permits shareholders to inspect the list without limitation, but permits the shareholder to copy the list only if the shareholder complies with the requirement of section 16.02(c) that the demand be made in good faith and for a proper purpose. The right to copy the list may be satisfied at the corporation's option, if reasonable, by furnishing to the shareholder a copy of the list upon payment of a reasonable charge. See sections 16.03(b) and (c). The distinction between inspection and copying set forth in section 7.20(b) reflects an accommodation between competing considerations of permitting shareholders access to the list before a meeting and possible misuse of the list.

6. Relationship to Right to Inspect Corporate Records Generally

Section 7.20 creates a right of shareholders to inspect a list of shareholders in advance of and at a meeting that is independent of the right of shareholders to inspect corporate records under chapter 16. A shareholder may obtain the right to inspect the list of shareholders as provided in chapter 16 without regard to the provisions relating to the pendency of a meeting in section 7.20, and similarly the limitations of chapter 16 are not applicable to the right of inspection created by section 7.20 except to the extent the shareholder seeks to copy the list in advance of the meeting.

The right to inspect under chapter 16 is also broader in the sense that the shareholder may make or receive copies of the documents the shareholder is entitled to inspect. See section 16.03.

§ 7.21. Voting Entitlement of Shares

(a) Except as provided in subsections (b) and (d) or unless the articles of incorporation provide otherwise, each outstanding share, regardless of class or series, is entitled to one vote on each matter voted on at a shareholders' meeting. Only shares are entitled to vote.

(b) Shares of a corporation are not entitled to vote if they are owned by or otherwise belong to the corporation directly, or indirectly through an entity of which a majority of the voting power is held directly or indirectly by the corporation or which is otherwise controlled by the corporation.

(c) Shares held by the corporation in a fiduciary capacity for the benefit of any person are entitled to vote unless they are held for the benefit of, or otherwise belong to, the corporation directly, or indirectly through an entity of which a majority of the voting power is held directly or indirectly by the corporation or which is otherwise controlled by the corporation.

(d) Redeemable shares are not entitled to vote after delivery of written notice of redemption is effective and a sum sufficient to redeem the shares has been deposited with a bank, trust company, or other financial institution under an irrevocable obligation to pay the holders the redemption price on surrender of the shares.

(e) For purposes of this section, "voting power" means the current power to vote in the election of directors of a corporation or to elect, select or appoint governors of another entity.

Official Comment

1. Voting Power of Shares

Section 7.21(a) provides that each outstanding share, regardless of class or series, is entitled to one vote per share unless otherwise provided in the articles of incorporation. The articles of incorporation may provide for multiple or fractional votes per share and may provide that some classes or series of shares are nonvoting on some or all matters, or that some classes or series have a single vote per share or different multiple or fractional votes per share, or that some classes or series constitute one or more separate voting groups and are entitled to vote separately on the matter. To reflect the possibility that shares may have multiple or fractional votes per share, the provisions relating to quorums, voting, and similar matters in the Act are phrased in terms of votes represented by shares.

2. Voting Power of Nonshareholders

Under the last sentence of section 7.21(a), the power to vote may only be vested in shares. For example, bondholders may not be given the direct power to vote under the Act. They may, however, be given the power to vote by issuing them special classes or series of shares. See the Official Comment to section 7.22.

3. Circular Holdings

The purpose of the prohibition in section 7.21(b) is to prevent a board of directors or management from using a corporate investment to perpetuate itself in power. While shares acquired by a corporation cease to be outstanding under section 6.31, except as provided in that section, and therefore are not entitled to vote, other arrangements may be devised seeking to obtain the benefits of ownership without actually acquiring the shares at all or not acquiring the shares at the time the right to vote is determined. The concept of shares that "otherwise belong to" is included in addition to "owned by" to ensure that courts will have the flexibility to apply public policy considerations to arrangements under which shares are not technically "owned," or under which shares may or will be owned at a later time, but which have a similar effect. For example, if the corporation or a controlled entity has entered into a forward purchase contract for shares with the right to vote or direct the vote of the shares, a court could find that the shares belong to the corporation and are not entitled to be voted under section 7.21. Similarly, if the voting power is exercised by someone acting on behalf of the corporation or by a member of management of the corporation, a court could find that the shares otherwise belong to the corporation, and are not entitled to vote under section 7.21. Section 7.21(c), however, makes the prohibition of section 7.21(b) against voting of shares inapplicable to shares held in a fiduciary capacity where the beneficiaries are persons other than the corporation directly or through an entity controlled by the corporation.

4. Redeemable Shares

Redeemable shares are often redeemed in connection with a transaction such as a merger or the issuance of a new senior class or series of shares that requires shareholder approval. Section 7.21(d) avoids subjecting a transaction to approval by a class or series of redeemable shares that will be redeemed as a result of the transaction if adequate provision has been made to ensure that the holders of the redeemable shares will in fact receive the amount payable to them on redemption.

§ 7.22. Proxies

(a) A shareholder may vote the shareholder's shares in person or by proxy.

(b) A shareholder, or the shareholder's agent or attorney-in-fact, may appoint a proxy to vote or otherwise act for the shareholder by signing an appointment form, or by an electronic transmission. An electronic transmission must contain or be accompanied by information from which the recipient can determine the date of the transmission and that the transmission was authorized by the sender or the sender's agent or attorney-in-fact.

(c) An appointment of a proxy is effective when a signed appointment form or an electronic transmission of the appointment is received by the inspector of election or the officer or agent of the corporation authorized to count votes. An appointment is valid for the term provided in the appointment form, and, if no term is provided, is valid for 11 months unless the appointment is irrevocable under subsection (d).

(d) An appointment of a proxy is revocable unless the appointment form or electronic transmission states that it is irrevocable and the appointment is coupled with an interest. Appointments coupled with an interest include the appointment of:

> (1) a pledgee;

> (2) a person who purchased or agreed to purchase the shares;

> (3) a creditor of the corporation who extended it credit under terms requiring the appointment;

> (4) an employee of the corporation whose employment contract requires the appointment; or

> (5) a party to a voting agreement created under section 7.31.

(e) The death or incapacity of the shareholder appointing a proxy does not affect the right of the corporation to accept the proxy's authority unless notice of the death or incapacity is received by the secretary or other officer or agent authorized to tabulate votes before the proxy exercises authority under the appointment.

(f) An appointment made irrevocable under subsection (d) is revoked when the interest with which it is coupled is extinguished.

(g) Unless it otherwise provides, an appointment made irrevocable under subsection (d) continues in effect after a transfer of the shares and a transferee takes subject to the appointment, except that a transferee for value of shares subject to an irrevocable appointment may revoke the appointment if the transferee did not know of its existence when acquiring the shares and the existence of the irrevocable appointment was not noted conspicuously on the certificate representing the shares or on the information statement for shares without certificates.

(h) Subject to section 7.24 and to any express limitation on the proxy's authority stated in the appointment form or electronic transmission, a corporation is entitled to accept the proxy's vote or other action as that of the shareholder making the appointment.

Official Comment

1. Nomenclature

The word "proxy" is often used ambiguously, sometimes referring to the grant of authority to vote, sometimes to the document granting the authority, and sometimes to the person to whom the authority is granted. In the Act, the word "proxy" is used only in the last sense; the terms "proxy appointment," "appointment form" and "electronic transmission" are used to describe the document or communication appointing the proxy; and the word "appointment" is used to describe the grant of authority to vote. . . .

§ 7.23. Shares Held by Intermediaries and Nominees

(a) A corporation's board of directors may establish a procedure under which a person on whose behalf shares are registered in the name of an intermediary or nominee may elect to be treated by the corporation as the record shareholder by filing with the corporation a beneficial ownership certificate. The terms, conditions, and limitations of this treatment shall be specified in the procedure. To the extent such person is treated under such procedure as having rights or privileges that the record shareholder otherwise would have, the record shareholder shall not have those rights or privileges.

(b) The procedure must specify:

(1) the types of intermediaries or nominees to which it applies;

(2) the rights or privileges that the corporation recognizes in a person with respect to whom a beneficial ownership certificate is filed;

(3) the manner in which the procedure is selected which must include that the beneficial ownership certificate be signed or assented to by or on behalf of the record shareholder and the person on whose behalf the shares are held;

(4) the information that must be provided when the procedure is selected;

(5) the period for which selection of the procedure is effective;

(6) requirements for notice to the corporation with respect to the arrangement; and

(7) the form and contents of the beneficial ownership certificate.

(c) The procedure may specify any other aspects of the rights and duties created by the filing of a beneficial ownership certificate.

Official Comment

Traditionally, a corporation recognizes only the person in whose name shares are registered as the owner of the shares. It is a common practice for persons purchasing shares of a public company to hold them in "street name" through a broker-dealer or other financial institution. In addition, a securities depository system exists under which financial institutions deposit securities with the depository, whose nominee becomes the registered owner of the shares or the "record shareholder." Transfers between depository participants are accomplished by book entry of the depository. As a result, there may be several entities interposed between the corporation and the beneficial owner. . . .

The signature or assent of the record shareholder and the person or persons on whose behalf the shares are held, as required by section 7.23(b)(3), can be provided on behalf of any such person by another person authorized to do so. In a typical situation where the record shareholder is Cede & Co., the nominee of Depository Trust Company, and the shares are ultimately beneficially owned by a shareholder who has an account with a broker-dealer that is a participant in the Depository Trust Company, a beneficial ownership certificate could be signed by both the ultimate beneficial owner and the broker-dealer shown on the position list of Depository Trust Company, acting under authority granted to it by Cede & Co., as the record shareholder. The statute does not prescribe the notices that must be provided to the corporation, but provides that the procedure shall specify whatever notice provisions will be required. For example, the corporation may wish to include provisions for notice to it by the ultimate beneficial owner and the broker-dealer upon the sale or other disposition of the shares, which normally should be accompanied by notice to the corporation of termination or modification of the effect of the beneficial ownership certificate. . . .

The definition of "record shareholder" in section 1.40 includes beneficial owners to the extent they obtain the rights of record shareholders through the filing of a beneficial ownership certificate pursuant to the procedure authorized by section 7.23.

§ 7.24. Acceptance of Votes and Other Instruments

(a) If the name signed on a vote, ballot, consent, waiver, shareholder demand, or proxy appointment corresponds to the name of a shareholder, the corporation, if acting in good faith, is entitled to accept the vote, ballot, consent, waiver, shareholder demand, or proxy appointment and give it effect as the act of the shareholder.

(b) If the name signed on a vote, ballot, consent, waiver, shareholder demand, or proxy appointment does not correspond to the name of its shareholder, the corporation, if acting in good faith, is nevertheless entitled to accept the vote, ballot, consent, waiver, shareholder demand, or proxy appointment and give it effect as the act of the shareholder if:

(1) the shareholder is an entity and the name signed purports to be that of an officer or agent of the entity;

(2) the name signed purports to be that of an administrator, executor, guardian, or conservator representing the shareholder and, if the corporation requests, evidence of fiduciary status acceptable to the corporation has been presented with respect to the vote, ballot, consent, waiver, shareholder demand, or proxy appointment;

(3) the name signed purports to be that of a receiver or trustee in bankruptcy of the shareholder and, if the corporation requests, evidence of this status acceptable to the corporation has been presented with respect to the vote, ballot, consent, waiver, shareholder demand, or proxy appointment;

(4) the name signed purports to be that of a pledgee, beneficial owner, or attorney-in-fact of the shareholder and, if the corporation requests, evidence acceptable to the corporation of the signatory's authority to sign for the shareholder has been presented with respect to the vote, ballot, consent, waiver, shareholder demand, or proxy appointment; or

(5) two or more persons are the shareholder as co-tenants or fiduciaries and the name signed purports to be the name of at least one of the co-owners and the person signing appears to be acting on behalf of all the co-owners.

(c) The corporation is entitled to reject a vote, ballot, consent, waiver, shareholder demand, or proxy appointment if the person authorized to accept or reject such instrument, acting in good faith, has reasonable basis for doubt about the validity of the signature on it or about the signatory's authority to sign for the shareholder.

(d) Neither the corporation or any person authorized by it, nor an inspector of election appointed under section 7.29, that accepts or rejects a vote, ballot, consent, waiver, shareholder demand, or proxy appointment in good faith and in accordance with the standards of this section 7.24 or section 7.22(b) is liable in damages to the shareholder for the consequences of the acceptance or rejection.

(e) Corporate action based on the acceptance or rejection of a vote, ballot, consent, waiver, shareholder demand, or proxy appointment under this section is valid unless a court of competent jurisdiction determines otherwise.

(f) If an inspector of election has been appointed under section 7.29, the inspector of election also has the authority to request information and make determinations under subsections (a), (b), and (c). Any determination made by the inspector of election under those subsections is controlling.

Official Comment

Corporations are often asked to accept a written instrument as evidence of action by a shareholder. These instruments usually involve appointment forms for a proxy to vote the shares, but may also include ballots, waivers of notice, consents to action without a meeting, demands for a special meeting of shareholders, and other demands by shareholders. Usually the corporation or its officers will have no personal knowledge of the circumstances under which the instrument was executed and no way of verifying whether the signature on the instrument is in fact the signature of the shareholder. This problem is particularly acute in public corporations.

Section 7.24 establishes general rules permitting the corporation and any inspector of election appointed under section 7.29 to accept these instruments if they appear to be signed by the shareholder or by a person who has authority to sign the instrument for the shareholder and they are accompanied by whatever authenticating evidence is requested. Section 7.24 also establishes general rules for rejecting these instruments. The rules set forth in this section are not exclusive and may be supplemented by additional rules established by the corporation pursuant to section 2.06(b). . . .

§ 7.25.   Quorum and Voting Requirements for Voting Groups

(a) Shares entitled to vote as a separate voting group may take action on a matter at a meeting only if a quorum of those shares exists with respect to that matter. Unless the articles of incorporation provide otherwise, shares representing a majority of the votes entitled to be cast on the matter by the voting group constitutes a quorum of that voting group for action on that matter. Whenever this Act requires a particular quorum for a specified action, the articles of incorporation may not provide for a lower quorum.

(b) Once a share is represented for any purpose at a meeting, it is deemed present for quorum purposes for the remainder of the meeting and for any adjournment of that meeting unless a new record date is or must be fixed for that adjourned meeting.

(c) If a quorum exists, action on a matter (other than the election of directors) by a voting group is approved if the votes cast within the voting group favoring the action exceed the votes cast opposing the action, unless the articles of incorporation require a greater number of affirmative votes.

(d) An amendment of the articles of incorporation adding, changing, or deleting a quorum or voting requirement for a voting group greater than specified in subsection (a) or (c) is governed by section 7.27.

(e) The election of directors is governed by section 7.28.

(f) Whenever a provision of this Act provides for voting of classes or series as separate voting groups, the rules provided in section 10.04(c) for amendments of the articles of incorporation apply to that provision.

Official Comment

Section 7.25 establishes general quorum and voting requirements for voting groups for purposes of the Act. As defined in section 1.40, a "voting group" consists of all shares of one or more classes or series that under the articles of incorporation or the Act are entitled to vote and be counted together collectively on a matter. Shares entitled to vote "generally" on a matter (that is, all shares entitled to vote on the matter by the articles of incorporation or the Act that do not expressly have the right to be counted separately) are a single voting group. On most matters coming before shareholders' meetings, only a single voting group, consisting of a class of voting shares, will be involved, and action on such a matter is effective when approved by that voting group pursuant to section 7.25. See section 7.26(a). . . .

1.   *Determination of Voting Groups under the Act*

Under the Act, classes or series of shares are generally not entitled to vote separately by voting group except to the extent specifically authorized by the articles of incorporation. But sections 9.21, 9.32, 10.04, and 11.04 of the Act grant classes or series of shares the right to vote separately when fundamental changes are proposed that may adversely affect that class or series. Section 10.04(c) further provides that when two or more classes or series are affected by an amendment covered by section 10.04 in essentially the same way, the classes or series are grouped together and must vote as a single voting group rather than as multiple voting groups on the matter, unless otherwise provided in the articles of incorporation or required by the board of directors. Section 7.25(f) provides that the group voting rule of section 10.04(c), including the ability to vary that rule in the articles of incorporation or by action of the board of directors, also applies to the group voting provisions in sections 9.21, 9.32, and 11.04. Under the Act even a class or series of shares that is expressly described as nonvoting under the articles of incorporation may be entitled to vote separately on an amendment to the articles of incorporation that affects the class or series in a designated way. See section 10.04(d).

In addition to the provisions of the Act, separate voting by voting group may be authorized by the articles of incorporation (except that the statutory privilege of voting by separate voting groups cannot be diluted or reduced). On some matters, the board of directors may condition its submission of matters to shareholders on their approval by specific voting groups designated by the board of directors. Sections 7.25 and 7.26 establish the mechanics by which all voting by single or multiple voting groups is carried out.

In some situations, shares of a single class or series may be entitled to vote in two different voting groups. See the Official Comment to section 7.26.

2. Quorum and Voting Requirements in General

A corporation's determination of the voting groups entitled to vote, and the quorum and voting requirements applicable to that determination, should be determined separately for each matter coming before a meeting. As a result, different quorum and voting requirements may be applicable to different portions of a meeting, depending on the matter being considered. In the normal case where only a single voting group is entitled to vote on all matters coming before a meeting of shareholders, a single quorum and voting requirement will usually be applicable to the entire meeting. To reflect the possibility that shares may have multiple or fractional votes per share, the provisions relating to quorums are phrased in terms of votes represented by shares.

3. Quorum Requirements for Action by Voting Group

Under Section 7.25(b), once a share is present at a meeting, it is deemed present for quorum purposes throughout the meeting. Thus, a voting group may continue to act despite the withdrawal of persons having the power to vote one or more shares.

The shares owned by a shareholder who comes to the meeting to object on grounds of lack of notice are considered present for purposes of determining the presence of a quorum. Similarly, shares owned by a shareholder who attends a meeting solely for purposes of raising the objection that a quorum is not present are considered present for purposes of determining the presence of a quorum. Attendance at a meeting, however, does not constitute a waiver of other objections to the meeting such as the lack of notice. Such waivers are governed by section 7.06(b).

If a new record date is set, new notice must be given to holders of shares of a voting group and a quorum must be established from within the holders of shares of that voting group as of the new record date.

4. Voting Requirements for Approval by Voting Group

Section 7.25(c) provides that an action (other than the election of directors, which is governed by section 7.28) is approved by a voting group at a meeting at which a quorum is present if the votes cast in favor of the action exceed the votes cast opposing the action, unless the articles of incorporation require a greater number of votes. This default rule differs from a formulation appearing in some state statutes that an action is approved at a meeting at which a quorum is present if it receives the affirmative vote of a majority of the shares represented at that meeting. That formulation in effect treats abstentions as negative votes; the Act treats them truly as abstentions. For example, if a corporation (that has not, through the articles of incorporation, modified quorum and voting requirements) has 1,000 shares of a single class outstanding, each share entitled to cast one vote, a quorum consists of 501 shares; if 600 shares are represented at the meeting and the vote on a proposed action is 280 in favor, 225 opposed, and 95 abstaining, the action would not be approved in a state following the formulation that treats abstentions as negative votes because fewer than a majority of the 600 shares attending voted in favor of the action. Under section 7.25(c) the action would be approved and not be defeated by the 95 abstaining votes.

5. Modification of Standard Requirements

The articles of incorporation may modify the quorum and voting requirements of section 7.25 for a single voting group or for all voting groups entitled to vote on any matter. The articles of incorporation may increase the quorum and voting requirements to any extent desired up to and including unanimity, subject to section 7.27. They may also require that shares of different classes or series are entitled to vote separately or together on specific issues or provide that actions are approved only if they receive the favorable vote of a majority of the shares of a voting group present at a meeting at which a quorum is present. The articles may also decrease the quorum requirement as desired, subject to section 7.25(a) and section 7.27.

§ 7.26.   Action by Single and Multiple Voting Groups

(a) If the articles of incorporation or this Act provide for voting by a single voting group on a matter, action on that matter is taken when voted upon by that voting group as provided in section 7.25.

(b) If the articles of incorporation or this Act provide for voting by two or more voting groups on a matter, action on that matter is taken only when voted upon by each of those voting groups counted separately as provided in section 7.25. Action may be taken by different voting groups on a matter at different times.

Official Comment

. . . In most instances, a single voting group will consist of all the shares of the class or classes or series entitled to vote by the articles of incorporation. Voting by two or more voting groups as contemplated by section 7.26(b) is the exceptional case.

Implicit in section 7.26(b) are the concepts that (i) different quorum and voting requirements may be applicable to different matters considered at a single meeting and (ii) different quorum and voting requirements may be applicable to different voting groups voting on the same matter. See the Official Comment to section 7.25. Each group entitled to vote must independently meet the quorum and voting requirements established by section 7.25. If a quorum is present for one or more voting groups but not for all voting groups, section 7.26(b) provides that the voting groups for which a quorum is present may vote upon the matter, even though their vote alone will not be sufficient for the matter to be approved.

A single meeting, furthermore, may consider matters on which action by several voting groups is required and also matters on which only a single voting group may act. Action may be taken on the matters on which the single voting group may act even though no quorum is present to take action on other matters. For example, in a corporation with one class of nonvoting shares with preferential rights ("preferred shares") and one class of general voting shares without preferential rights ("common shares"), a matter to be considered at the annual meeting might be a proposed amendment to the articles of incorporation that reduces the cumulative dividend right of the preferred shares (a matter on which the preferred shares have a statutory right to vote as a separate voting group). Other matters to be considered might include the election of directors and the ratification of the appointment of an auditor, both matters on which the preferred shares may have no vote. If a quorum of the voting group consisting of the common shares but no quorum of the voting group consisting of the preferred shares is present, the common shares may proceed to elect directors and ratify the appointment of the auditor. The common shares voting group may also vote to approve the proposed amendment to the articles of incorporation, but that amendment will not be approved until the preferred shares voting group also votes to approve the amendment, which could occur at a different time.

Normally, each class or series of shares will participate in only a single voting group. But because holders of shares entitled by the articles of incorporation to vote generally on a matter are always entitled to vote in the voting group consisting of the general voting shares, in some instances classes or series of shares may be entitled to be counted in two voting groups. This will occur whenever a class or series of shares entitled to vote generally on a matter under the articles of incorporation is affected by the matter in a way that gives rise to the right to have its vote counted separately as an independent voting group under the Act. For example, assume that corporation Y has outstanding one class of common shares, 500 shares issued and outstanding, and one class of preferred shares, 100 shares issued and outstanding, that also have full voting rights under the articles of incorporation, *i.e.*, the preferred may vote for election of directors and on all other matters on which common may vote. The preferred and the common therefore are part of the general voting group. The directors propose to amend the articles of incorporation to change the preferential dividend rights of the preferred from cumulative to noncumulative. All shares are present at the meeting and they divide as follows on the proposal to adopt the amendment.

Yes	Common	230
	Preferred	80
No	Common	270
	Preferred	20

Both the preferred and the common are entitled to vote on the amendment to the articles of incorporation because they are part of a general voting group pursuant to the articles. But the vote of the preferred is also entitled to be counted separately on the proposal by section 10.04(a)(3). The result is that the proposal passes by a vote of 310 to 290 in the voting group consisting of the shares entitled to vote generally and 80 to 20 in the voting group consisting solely of the preferred shares.

In this situation, in the absence of a special quorum requirement, a meeting could approve the proposal to amend the articles of incorporation if—and only if—a quorum of each voting group is present, *i.e.*, at least 51 shares of preferred and 301 shares of common and preferred were represented at the meeting.

§ 7.27.　Modifying Quorum or Voting Requirements

An amendment to the articles of incorporation that adds, changes, or deletes a quorum or voting requirement shall meet the same quorum requirement and be adopted by the same vote and voting groups required to take action under the quorum and voting requirements then in effect or proposed to be adopted, whichever is greater.

Official Comment

Section 7.27 permits the articles of incorporation to change the quorum or voting requirements for approval of an action by shareholders up to any desired amount so long as the change is adopted in accordance with the requirements of section 7.27. For example, a supermajority provision that requires an 80% affirmative vote of all eligible votes of a voting group present at the meeting may not be removed from the articles of incorporation or reduced in any way except by an 80% affirmative vote. If the 80% requirement is coupled with a quorum requirement for a voting group that shares representing two-thirds of the total votes must be present in person or by proxy, both the 80% voting requirement and the two-thirds quorum requirement are immune from reduction except at a meeting of the voting group at which the two-thirds quorum requirement is met and the reduction is approved by an 80% affirmative vote. If the proposal is to increase the 80% voting requirement to 90%, that proposal must be approved by a 90% affirmative vote at a meeting of the voting group at which the two-thirds quorum requirement is met; if the proposal is to increase the two-thirds quorum requirement to three-quarters without changing the 80% voting requirement, that proposal must be approved by an 80% affirmative vote at a meeting of the voting group at which a three-quarters quorum requirement is met.

§ 7.28.　Voting for Directors; Cumulative Voting

(a) Unless otherwise provided in the articles of incorporation, directors are elected by a plurality of the votes cast by the shares entitled to vote in the election at a meeting at which a quorum is present.

(b) Shareholders do not have a right to cumulate their votes for directors unless the articles of incorporation so provide.

(c) A statement included in the articles of incorporation that "[all] [a designated voting group of] shareholders are entitled to cumulate their votes for directors" (or words of similar import) means that the shareholders designated are entitled to multiply the number of votes they are entitled to cast by the number of directors for whom they are entitled to vote and cast the product for a single candidate or distribute the product among two or more candidates.

(d) Shares otherwise entitled to vote cumulatively may not be voted cumulatively at a particular meeting unless:

　　(1) the meeting notice or proxy statement accompanying the notice states conspicuously that cumulative voting is authorized; or

　　(2) a shareholder who has the right to cumulate the shareholder's votes gives notice to the corporation not less than 48 hours before the time set for the meeting of the shareholder's intent to cumulate votes during the meeting, and if one shareholder gives this notice all other shareholders in the same voting group participating in the election are entitled to cumulate their votes without giving further notice.

§ 7.29.　Inspectors of Election

(a) A corporation that has a class of equity securities registered pursuant to section 12 of the Securities Exchange Act of 1934 shall, and any other corporation may, appoint one or more inspectors to act at a meeting of shareholders in connection with determining voting results. Each inspector shall verify in writing that the inspector will faithfully execute the duties of inspector with strict impartiality and according to the best of the inspector's ability. An inspector may be an officer or employee of the corporation. The inspectors may appoint or retain other persons to assist the inspectors in the performance of the duties of inspector under subsection (b), and may rely on information provided by such persons and other persons, including those appointed to tabulate votes, unless the inspectors believe reliance is unwarranted.

(b) The inspectors shall:

(1) ascertain the number of shares outstanding and the voting power of each;

(2) determine the shares represented at a meeting;

(3) determine the validity of proxy appointments and ballots;

(4) count the votes; and

(5) make a written report of the results.

(c) In performing their duties, the inspectors may examine (i) the proxy appointment forms and any other information provided in accordance with section 7.22(b), (ii) any envelope or related writing submitted with those appointment forms, (iii) any ballots, (iv) any evidence or other information specified in section 7.24 and (v) the relevant books and records of the corporation relating to its shareholders and their entitlement to vote, including any securities position list provided by a depository clearing agency.

(d) The inspectors also may consider other information that they believe is relevant and reliable for the purpose of performing any of the duties assigned to them pursuant to subsection (b), including for the purpose of evaluating inconsistent, incomplete or erroneous information and reconciling information submitted on behalf of banks, brokers, their nominees or similar persons that indicates more votes being cast than a proxy authorized by the record shareholder is entitled to cast. If the inspectors consider other information allowed by this subsection, they shall in their report under subsection (b) specify the information considered by them, including the purpose or purposes for which the information was considered, the person or persons from whom they obtained the information, when the information was obtained, the means by which the information was obtained, and the basis for the inspectors' belief that such information is relevant and reliable.

(e) Determinations of law by the inspectors of election are subject to de novo review by a court in a proceeding under section 7.49 or other judicial proceeding.

Official Comment

"Street name" holdings, the use of a securities depository system and the involvement of intermediaries complicate the vote counting process. See Official Comment to section 7.23. This complexity limits the role of inspectors of election in the case of corporations subject to the federal proxy rules. Such inspectors have a limited role because federal law requires multiple steps to be taken by various parties before shares are voted. The inspectors may not have access to information pertaining to each of those steps or from each of the parties involved in the process, such as the voting instruction forms given by beneficial shareholders that lead to voting by the record shareholders. For these reasons, section 7.29 generally permits inspectors to rely on information provided by others.

The selection of inspectors of election should usually be made by responsible officers or by the directors, as authorized either generally or specifically in the corporation's bylaws. . . . The requirement of a written report is to facilitate judicial review of determinations made by inspectors. . . .

In the case of corporations subject to the federal proxy rules, inspectors should generally be independent persons who are neither employees nor officers if there is a contested matter to be considered. The use of independent inspectors in these circumstances enhances shareholder perception of the fairness of the voting process, and the report of independent inspectors can be expected to be given greater evidentiary weight by any court reviewing a contested vote.

To determine the validity of proxy appointments and ballots, depending on the issues presented, the inspectors of election may be required to determine whether appointment forms have been validly executed by the record shareholder, to identify the latest executed appointment form and to determine whether the proxy cast more votes than the record shareholder was entitled to cast. The inspectors are expected to apply the provisions of chapter 7 . . . [and] the court should give such weight to determinations of fact by the inspectors as it deems appropriate, taking into account the relationship of the inspectors, if any, to the management of the company and other persons interested in the outcome of the vote, the evidence available to inspectors, whether their determinations appear to be consistent and reasonable, and such other circumstances as the court regards as relevant. As provided in section 7.29(e), the court may review de novo all determinations of law made by the inspectors.

Section 7.29(d) gives the inspectors broad discretion with respect to the information they may consider but does not require that they take any specific action with respect to such information other than to specify in their report the information they considered and the other details listed in section 7.29(d).

Subchapter C
Voting Trusts and Agreements

§ 7.30.   Voting Trusts

(a) One or more shareholders may create a voting trust, conferring on a trustee the right to vote or otherwise act for them, by signing an agreement setting out the provisions of the trust (which may include anything consistent with its purpose) and transferring their shares to the trustee. When a voting trust agreement is signed, the trustee shall prepare a list of the names and addresses of all voting trust beneficial owners, together with the number and class of shares each transferred to the trust, and deliver copies of the list and agreement to the corporation at its principal office.

(b) A voting trust becomes effective on the date the first shares subject to the trust are registered in the trustee's name.

(c) Limits, if any, on the duration of a voting trust shall be as set forth in the voting trust. A voting trust that became effective when this Act provided a 10-year limit on its duration remains governed by the provisions of this section concerning duration then in effect, unless the voting trust is amended to provide otherwise by unanimous agreement of the parties to the voting trust.

§ 7.31.   Voting Agreements

(a) Two or more shareholders may provide for the manner in which they will vote their shares by signing an agreement for that purpose. A voting agreement created under this section is not subject to the provisions of section 7.30.

(b) A voting agreement created under this section is specifically enforceable.

Official Comment

Section 7.31(a) explicitly recognizes agreements among two or more shareholders as to the voting of shares and makes clear that these agreements are not subject to the rules relating to a voting trust. The only formal requirements are that they be in writing and signed by all the participating shareholders. In other respects their validity is to be judged like any other contract.

A voting agreement may provide its own enforcement mechanism, as by the appointment of a proxy to vote all shares subject to the agreement; the appointment may be made irrevocable under section 7.22. If no enforcement mechanism is provided, a court may order specific enforcement of the agreement and order the votes cast as the agreement contemplates. Section 7.31(b) recognizes that damages are not likely to be an appropriate remedy for breach of a voting agreement.

§ 7.32.   Shareholder Agreements

(a) An agreement among the shareholders of a corporation that complies with this section is effective among the shareholders and the corporation even though it is inconsistent with one or more other provisions of this Act in that it:

(1) eliminates the board of directors or restricts the discretion or powers of the board of directors;

(2) governs the authorization or making of distributions, regardless of whether they are in proportion to ownership of shares, subject to the limitations in section 6.40;

(3) establishes who shall be directors or officers of the corporation, or their terms of office or manner of selection or removal;

(4) governs, in general or in regard to specific matters, the exercise or division of voting power by or between the shareholders and directors or by or among any of them, including use of weighted voting rights or director proxies;

(5) establishes the terms and conditions of any agreement for the transfer or use of property or the provision of services between the corporation and any shareholder, director, officer or employee of the corporation or among any of them;

(6) transfers to one or more shareholders or other persons all or part of the authority to exercise the corporate powers or to manage the business and affairs of the corporation, including the resolution of any issue about which there exists a deadlock among directors or shareholders;

(7) requires dissolution of the corporation at the request of one or more of the shareholders or upon the occurrence of a specified event or contingency; or

(8) otherwise governs the exercise of the corporate powers or the management of the business and affairs of the corporation or the relationship among the shareholders, the directors and the corporation, or among any of them, and is not contrary to public policy.

(b) An agreement authorized by this section shall be:

(1) as set forth (i) in the articles of incorporation or bylaws and approved by all persons who are shareholders at the time of the agreement, or (ii) in a written agreement that is signed by all persons who are shareholders at the time of the agreement and is made known to the corporation; and

(2) subject to amendment only by all persons who are shareholders at the time of the amendment, unless the agreement provides otherwise.

(c) The existence of an agreement authorized by this section shall be noted conspicuously on the front or back of each certificate for outstanding shares or on the information statement required by section 6.26(b). If at the time of the agreement the corporation has shares outstanding represented by certificates, the corporation shall recall the outstanding certificates and issue substitute certificates that comply with this subsection. The failure to note the existence of the agreement on the certificate or information statement shall not affect the validity of the agreement or any action taken pursuant to it. Any purchaser of shares who, at the time of purchase, did not have knowledge of the existence of the agreement shall be entitled to rescission of the purchase. A purchaser shall be deemed to have knowledge of the existence of the agreement if its existence is noted on the certificate or information statement for the shares in compliance with this subsection and, if the shares are not represented by a certificate, the information statement is delivered to the purchaser at or before the time of purchase of the shares. An action to enforce the right of rescission authorized by this subsection shall be commenced within the earlier of 90 days after discovery of the existence of the agreement or two years after the time of purchase of the shares.

(d) If the agreement ceases to be effective for any reason, the board of directors may, if the agreement is contained or referred to in the corporation's articles of incorporation or bylaws, adopt an amendment to the articles of incorporation or bylaws, without shareholder action, to delete the agreement and any references to it.

(e) An agreement authorized by this section that limits the discretion or powers of the board of directors shall relieve the directors of, and impose upon the person or persons in whom such discretion or powers are vested, liability for acts or omissions imposed by law on directors to the extent that the discretion or powers of the directors are limited by the agreement.

(f) The existence or performance of an agreement authorized by this section shall not be a ground for imposing personal liability on any shareholder for the acts or debts of the corporation even if the agreement or its performance treats the corporation as if it were a partnership or results in failure to observe the corporate formalities otherwise applicable to the matters governed by the agreement.

(g) Incorporators or subscribers for shares may act as shareholders with respect to an agreement authorized by this section if no shares have been issued when the agreement is made.

(h) Limits, if any, on the duration of an agreement authorized by this section must be set forth in the agreement. An agreement that became effective when this Act provided for a 10-year limit on duration of shareholder agreements, unless the agreement provided otherwise, remains governed by the provisions of this section concerning duration then in effect.

Official Comment

Shareholders of some corporations, especially those that are closely held, frequently enter into agreements that govern the operation of the enterprise.

Section 7.32 provides, within the context of the traditional corporate structure, legal certainty to such agreements that embody various aspects of the business arrangement established by the shareholders to meet their business and personal needs. The subject matter of these arrangements includes governance of the entity, allocation of the economic return from the business, and other aspects of the relationships among shareholders, directors, and the corporation which are part of the business arrangement. Section 7.32 also recognizes that many of the corporate norms contained in the Act were designed with an eye towards corporations whose management and share ownership are distinct. These functions are often conjoined in some corporations, such as the close corporation. Thus, section 7.32 validates agreements among shareholders even when the agreements are inconsistent with the statutory norms contained in the Act.

Importantly, section 7.32 only addresses the parties to the shareholder agreement, their transferees, and the corporation, and does not have any binding legal effect on the state, creditors, or other third persons.

Section 7.32 supplements the other provisions of the Act. If an agreement is not in conflict with another section of the Act, no resort need be made to section 7.32 with its requirement of unanimity. For example, special provisions may be included in the articles of incorporation or bylaws with less than unanimous shareholder agreement so long as such provisions are not in conflict with other provisions of the Act. Similarly, section 7.32 would not have to be relied upon to validate typical buy-sell agreements among two or more shareholders or the covenants and other terms of a stock purchase agreement entered into in connection with the issuance of shares by a corporation.

1. Section 7.32(a)

An agreement authorized by section 7.32 is "not inconsistent with law" within the meaning of sections 2.02(b)(2) and 2.06(b) of the Act.

The range of agreements validated by section 7.32(a) is expansive though not unlimited. Section 7.32 defines the types of agreements that can be validated largely by illustration. The seven specific categories that are listed are designed to cover some of the most frequently used arrangements. There are numerous other arrangements that may be made, and section 7.32(a)(8) provides an additional category for any provisions that, in a manner inconsistent with any other provision of the Act, otherwise govern the exercise of the corporate powers or the management of the business and affairs of the corporation or the relationship between and among the shareholders, the directors, and the corporation or any of them, and are not contrary to public policy.

Section 7.32(a) validates virtually all types of shareholder agreements that, in practice, normally concern shareholders and their advisors. Given that breadth, any provision that may be contained in the articles of incorporation with a majority vote under sections 2.02(b)(2)(ii) and (iii), as well as under section 2.02(b)(4), may also be effective if contained in a shareholder agreement that complies with section 7.32.

The provisions of a shareholder agreement authorized by section 7.32(a) will often, in operation, conflict with the language of more than one section of the Act, and courts should in such cases construe all related sections of the Act flexibly and in a manner consistent with the underlying intent of the shareholder agreement. Thus, for example, in the case of an agreement that provides for weighted voting by directors, every reference in the Act to a majority or other proportion of directors should be construed to refer to a majority or other proportion of the votes of the directors.

Although the limits of section 7.32(a)(8) are left uncertain, there are provisions of the Act that may not be overridden if they reflect core principles of public policy with respect to corporate affairs. For example, a provision of a shareholder agreement that purports to eliminate all of the standards of conduct established under section 8.30 might be viewed as contrary to public policy and thus not validated under section 7.32(a)(8). Similarly, a provision that exculpates directors from liability more broadly than permitted by section 2.02(b)(4), or indemnifies them more broadly than permitted by section 2.02(b)(5), might not be validated under section 7.32 because of strong public policy reasons for the statutory limitations on the right to exculpate directors from liability and to indemnify them. The validity of some provisions may depend upon the circumstances. For example, a provision of a shareholder agreement that limited inspection rights under section 16.02 or the right to financial statements under section 16.20 might, as a general matter, be valid, but that provision might not be given effect if it prevented shareholders from obtaining information necessary to determine whether directors of the corporation have satisfied the standards of conduct under section 8.30. The foregoing are examples and are not intended to be exclusive.

As noted above, shareholder agreements otherwise validated by section 7.32 are not legally binding on the state, on creditors, or on other third parties. For example, . . . an agreement among shareholders that provides that only the president has authority to enter into contracts for the corporation would not, without more, be binding against third parties, and ordinary principles of agency, including the concept of apparent authority, would continue to apply.

2. Section 7.32(b)

. . .

Section 7.32(b) requires unanimous shareholder approval of the shareholder agreement regardless of entitlement to vote. Unanimity is required because an agreement authorized by section 7.32 can effect material organic changes in the corporation's operation and structure, and in the rights and obligations of shareholders. . . .

3. Section 7.32(c)

Section 7.32(c) addresses the effect of a shareholder agreement on subsequent purchasers or transferees of shares. Typically, corporations with shareholder agreements also have restrictions on the transferability of the shares as authorized by section 6.27, thus lessening the practical effects of the problem in the context of voluntary transferees. Transferees of shares without knowledge of the agreement or those acquiring shares upon the death of an original participant in a close corporation may, however, be heavily affected. Weighing the burdens on transferees against the burdens on the remaining shareholders in the enterprise, section 7.32(c) affirms the continued validity of the shareholder agreement on all transferees, whether by purchase, gift, operation of law, or otherwise. Unlike restrictions on transfer, it may be impossible to enforce a shareholder agreement against less than all of the shareholders. Thus, under section 7.32, one who inherits shares subject to a shareholder agreement must continue to abide by the agreement. If that is not the desired result, care must be exercised at the initiation of the shareholder agreement to ensure a different outcome, such as providing for a buy-back upon death.

Where shares are transferred to a purchaser without knowledge of a shareholder agreement, the validity of the agreement is similarly unaffected, but the purchaser is afforded a rescission remedy against the seller. Under section 7.32(c), the time at which notice to a purchaser is relevant for purposes of determining entitlement to rescission is the time when a purchaser acquires the shares rather than when a commitment is made to acquire the shares. If the purchaser learns of the agreement after committing to purchase but before acquiring the shares, the purchaser may not proceed with the purchase and still obtain the benefit of the remedies in section 7.32(c). Under contract principles and the securities laws, a failure to disclose the existence of a shareholder agreement may constitute the omission of a material fact and may excuse performance of the commitment to purchase. . . .

Consistent with this dichotomy, the rights and remedies available to purchasers under section 7.32(c) are independent of those provided by contract law, Article 8 of the Uniform Commercial Code, the securities laws, and other laws outside the Act.

With respect to the related subject of restrictions on transferability of shares, note that section 7.32 does not directly address or validate such restrictions, which are governed instead by section 6.27 of the Act. However, if such restrictions are adopted as a part of a shareholder agreement that complies with the requirements of section 7.32, a court should apply the concept of reasonableness under section 6.27 in determining the validity of such restrictions. . . .

If the shares are certificated and duly legended, a purchaser is charged with notice of the shareholder agreement even if the purchaser never saw the certificate. In the case of uncertificated shares, however, the purchaser is not charged with notice of the shareholder agreement unless a duly-legended information statement is delivered to the purchaser at or before the time of purchase. This different rule for uncertificated shares is intended to provide an additional safeguard to protect innocent purchasers, and is necessary because section 6.26(b) of the Act and Article 8 of the Uniform Commercial Code permit delivery of statements after a transfer of shares. . . .

6. Section 7.32(h)

Section 7.32 does not limit the duration of a shareholder agreement. This approach is consistent with the wide freedom of contract provided to participants in such enterprises. . . .

Subchapter D
Derivative Proceedings

§ 7.40. Subchapter Definitions

In this subchapter:

"Derivative proceeding" means a civil suit in the right of a domestic corporation or, to the extent provided in section 7.47, in the right of a foreign corporation.

"Shareholder" means a record shareholder, a beneficial shareholder, and an unrestricted voting trust beneficial owner.

Official Comment

The definition of "shareholder," for purposes of chapter 7D, extends the right to bring a derivative proceeding to a beneficial shareholder and an unrestricted voting trust beneficial owner. The inclusion of beneficial shareholder and unrestricted voting trust beneficial owner recognizes that these persons have or hold on behalf of others an economic interest in the shares.

§ 7.41. Standing

A shareholder may not commence or maintain a derivative proceeding unless the shareholder (i) was a shareholder of the corporation at the time of the act or omission complained of or became a shareholder through transfer by operation of law from one who was a shareholder at that time and (ii) fairly and adequately represents the interests of the corporation in enforcing the right of the corporation.

Official Comment

Section 7.41 requires (i) the plaintiff to be a shareholder and therefore does not permit, for example, creditors or holders of options, warrants, or conversion rights to commence a derivative proceeding, and (ii) that the plaintiff fairly and adequately represent the interests of *the corporation,* rather than *shareholders similarly situated* as provided in some rules of procedure, because the reference to the corporation more clearly reflects the nature of the derivative suit.

The introductory language of section 7.41 refers both to the commencement and maintenance of the proceeding to make it clear that the proceeding should be dismissed if, after commencement, the plaintiff ceases to be a shareholder or a fair and adequate representative. The latter would occur, for example, if the plaintiff were using the proceeding for personal advantage. If a plaintiff no longer has standing, courts have in a number of instances provided an opportunity for one or more other shareholders to intervene.

§ 7.42. Demand

No shareholder may commence a derivative proceeding until (i) a written demand has been made upon the corporation to take suitable action and (ii) 90 days have expired from the date delivery of the demand was made unless the shareholder has earlier been notified that the demand has been rejected by the corporation or unless irreparable injury to the corporation would result by waiting for the expiration of the 90-day period.

Official Comment

Section 7.42 requires a written demand for two reasons. First, even though no director may be "qualified" (see section 1.43), the demand will give the corporation the opportunity to re-examine the act complained of in the light of a potential lawsuit and take corrective action. Second, the provision eliminates the time and expense of litigating whether demand is required. Requiring a demand in all cases does not impose an onerous burden given the relatively short waiting period and that this period may be shortened if irreparable injury to the corporation would result by waiting for the expiration of the 90-day period.

1.   Form of Demand

Section 7.42 specifies only that the demand shall be in writing. Detailed pleading is not required given that the corporation can contact the shareholder for clarification if there are any questions, and cases have noted that a demand which sets forth the facts concerning share ownership and is sufficiently specific should apprise the corporation of the action sought to be taken and the grounds for that action so that the demand can be evaluated.

2. *Upon Whom Demand Should Be Made*

To ensure that the demand reaches the appropriate person for review, it should be addressed to the board of directors, chief executive officer, or secretary at the corporation's principal office. In most cases the board of directors will be the appropriate body to review the demand but there may be instances, such as a decision to sue a third party for an injury to the corporation, in which the taking of, or refusal to take, action would fall within the authority of an officer of the corporation.

3. *The 90-Day Period . . .*

Two exceptions are provided to the 90-day waiting period. The first exception is the situation where the shareholder has been notified of the rejection of the demand before the end of the 90 days. The standard under the second exception for irreparable injury to the corporation is intended to be the same as that governing the entry of a preliminary injunction. Other factors may also be considered, such as the possible expiration of the statute of limitations, although this would depend on the period of time during which the shareholder was aware of the grounds for the proceeding.

The shareholder bringing suit does not necessarily have to be the person making the demand. Only one demand need be made in order for the corporation to consider whether to take corrective action.

4. *Response by the Corporation*

There is no obligation on the part of the corporation to respond to the demand. However, if the corporation, after receiving the demand, decides to institute litigation or, after a derivative proceeding has commenced, decides to assume control of the litigation, the shareholder's right to commence or control the proceeding normally ends unless it can be shown that the corporation will not adequately pursue the matter.

§ 7.43. Stay of Proceedings

If the corporation commences an inquiry into the allegations made in the demand or complaint, the court may stay any derivative proceeding for such period as the court deems appropriate.

Official Comment

A stay may be appropriate where, for example, the complaint is filed 90 days after demand but the inquiry into matters raised by the demand has not been completed or where a demand has not been investigated but the corporation commences the inquiry after the complaint has been filed. In any case, the court will likely monitor the course of the inquiry to ensure that the corporation is proceeding expeditiously and in good faith.

§ 7.44. Dismissal

(a) A derivative proceeding shall be dismissed by the court on motion by the corporation if one of the groups specified in subsection (b) or subsection (e) has determined in good faith, after conducting a reasonable inquiry upon which its conclusions are based, that the maintenance of the derivative proceeding is not in the best interests of the corporation.

(b) Unless a panel is appointed pursuant to subsection (e), the determination in subsection (a) shall be made by:

(1) a majority vote of qualified directors present at a meeting of the board of directors if the qualified directors constitute a quorum; or

(2) a majority vote of a committee consisting of two or more qualified directors appointed by majority vote of qualified directors present at a meeting of the board of directors, regardless of whether such qualified directors constitute a quorum.

(c) If a derivative proceeding is commenced after a determination has been made rejecting a demand by a shareholder, the complaint shall allege with particularity facts establishing either (1) that a majority of the board of directors did not consist of qualified directors at the time the determination was made or (2) that the requirements of subsection (a) have not been met.

(d) If a majority of the board of directors consisted of qualified directors at the time the determination was made, the plaintiff shall have the burden of proving that the requirements of subsection (a) have not been met; if not, the corporation shall have the burden of proving that the requirements of subsection (a) have been met.

(e) Upon motion by the corporation, the court may appoint a panel of one or more individuals to make a determination whether the maintenance of the derivative proceeding is in the best interests of the corporation. In such case, the plaintiff shall have the burden of proving that the requirements of subsection (a) have not been met.

Official Comment

The procedures set forth in section 7.44 are not intended to be exclusive. Discretion is left with the courts to determine when a derivative action should be dismissed under circumstances other than those set forth in section 7.44. For example, as noted in the comment to section 7.42, there may be instances where a decision to commence an action falls within the authority of an officer of the corporation, depending upon the amount of the claim and the identity of the potential defendants.

1. The Persons Making the Determination and Timing

The determination under section 7.44(b) that the maintenance of the proceeding is not in the best interests of the corporation can be made before commencement of the derivative action in response to a demand or after commencement of the action upon examination of the allegations of the complaint. Section 7.44(b) allows the determination to be made by "qualified directors" as defined in section 1.43. These provisions parallel the mechanics for authorizing an officer's pursuit of a business opportunity pursuant to a provision in the articles of incorporation (section 2.02(b)(6)), for determining entitlement to indemnification (section 8.55), for authorizing directors' conflicting interest transactions (section 8.62), and for renunciation of the corporation's interests in a business opportunity (section 8.70). Section 7.44(e) provides for the appointment of a panel only upon motion by the corporation. This would not, however, prevent the court on its own initiative from appointing a special master if permitted under applicable state rules of procedure.

This panel procedure may be desirable in a number of circumstances, particularly if there are no qualified directors available. In addition, even if there are qualified directors, they may not be in a position to conduct the inquiry.

2. Standards to Be Applied

Section 7.44(a) contemplates that the court will examine the "good faith" of the persons making the determination. Both the determination and the inquiry in section 7.44(a) must be made in "good faith." Section 7.44(a) does not authorize the court to review the reasonableness of the determination to reject a demand or seek a dismissal. The "good faith" standard, which is also found in section 8.30 (general standards of conduct for directors) and 8.51 (authority to indemnify), is a subjective one, meaning "honestly or in an honest manner."

The word "inquiry"—rather than "investigation"—has been used to make it clear that the scope of the inquiry will depend upon the issues raised and the knowledge of the group making the determination with respect to those issues. In some cases, the issues may be within the knowledge of the group so that extensive additional investigation is not necessary. In other cases, the group may need to engage counsel and possibly other professionals to conduct an investigation and assist the group in its evaluation of the issues.

The phrase "upon which its conclusions are based" requires that the conclusions follow logically from the inquiry. The burden of convincing the court about this issue lies with whichever party has the burden under section 7.44(d). This phrase does not require the persons making the determination to prepare a written report that sets forth their determination and its bases, as circumstances will vary as to the need for such a report.

Section 7.44 is not intended to modify the general standards of conduct for directors set forth in section 8.30 but rather to make those standards more explicit in the derivative proceeding context. In this regard, the qualified directors making the determination would be entitled to rely on information and reports from other persons in accordance with section 8.30.

§ 7.45. Discontinuance or Settlement

A derivative proceeding may not be discontinued or settled without the court's approval. If the court determines that a proposed discontinuance or settlement will substantially affect the interests of the corporation's shareholders or a class or series of shareholders, the court shall direct that notice be given to the shareholders affected.

Official Comment

Section 7.45's requirement that all proposed settlements and discontinuances receive judicial approval supports the proposition that a derivative suit is brought for the benefit of all shareholders and thus should not be settled privately.

By requiring that notice be given to all affected shareholders if the court determines that the proposed settlement may substantially affect their interests, section 7.45 permits the court to decide whether notice to shareholders (or holders of a class or series of shares) need be given. For example, the court may decide not to require notice of dismissal if, in the court's judgment, the proceeding is frivolous or has become moot. . . .

§ 7.46. Payment of Expenses

On termination of the derivative proceeding the court may:

(1) order the corporation to pay the plaintiff's expenses incurred in the proceeding if it finds that the proceeding has resulted in a substantial benefit to the corporation;

(2) order the plaintiff to pay any defendant's expenses incurred in defending the proceeding if it finds that the proceeding was commenced or maintained without reasonable cause or for an improper purpose; or

(3) order a party to pay an opposing party's expenses incurred because of the filing of a pleading, motion or other paper, if it finds that the pleading, motion or other paper (i) was not well grounded in fact, after reasonable inquiry, or warranted by existing law or a good faith argument for the extension, modification or reversal of existing law or (ii) was interposed for an improper purpose, such as to harass or cause unnecessary delay or needless increase in the cost of litigation.

Official Comment

. . .

The standard under section 7.46(b) for the court to require the plaintiff to pay the defendants' expenses if the action was commenced without reasonable cause or for an improper purpose is intended to discourage proceedings brought for the sole purpose of obtaining early settlement payments by defendants to avoid significant defense costs, while also protecting plaintiffs whose suits have a reasonable foundation. This test is similar to but not identical to the test utilized in section 13.31, relating to dissenters' rights, where the standard for award of expenses is that dissenters "acted arbitrarily, vexatiously or not in good faith" in demanding a judicial appraisal of their shares. The derivative action situation is sufficiently different from the dissenters' rights situation to justify a different and less onerous test for imposing costs on the plaintiff. . . .

§ 7.47. Applicability to Foreign Corporations

In any derivative proceeding in the right of a foreign corporation, the matters covered by this subchapter shall be governed by the laws of the jurisdiction of incorporation of the foreign corporation except for sections 7.43, 7.45, and 7.46.

Subchapter E
Judicial Proceedings

§ 7.48. Shareholder Action to Appoint a Custodian or Receiver

(a) The [name or describe court] may appoint one or more persons to be custodians, or, if the corporation is insolvent, to be receivers, of and for a corporation in a proceeding by a shareholder where it is established that:

(1) the directors are deadlocked in the management of the corporate affairs, the shareholders are unable to break the deadlock, and irreparable injury to the corporation is threatened or being suffered; or

(2) the directors or those in control of the corporation are acting fraudulently and irreparable injury to the corporation is threatened or being suffered.

(b) The court:

(1) may issue injunctions, appoint a temporary custodian or temporary receiver with all the powers and duties the court directs, take other action to preserve the corporate assets wherever located, and carry on the business of the corporation until a full hearing is held;

(2) shall hold a full hearing, after notifying all parties to the proceeding and any interested persons designated by the court, before appointing a custodian or receiver; and

(3) has jurisdiction over the corporation and all of its property, wherever located.

(c) The court may appoint an individual or domestic or foreign corporation (registered to do business in this state) as a custodian or receiver and may require the custodian or receiver to post bond, with or without sureties, in an amount the court directs.

(d) The court shall describe the powers and duties of the custodian or receiver in its appointing order, which may be amended from time to time. Among other powers:

(1) a custodian may exercise all of the powers of the corporation, through or in place of its board of directors, to the extent necessary to manage the business and affairs of the corporation; and

(2) a receiver (i) may dispose of all or any part of the assets of the corporation wherever located, at a public or private sale, if authorized by the court; and (ii) may sue and defend in the receiver's own name as receiver in all courts of this state.

(e) The court during a custodianship may redesignate the custodian a receiver, and during a receivership may redesignate the receiver a custodian, if doing so is in the best interests of the corporation.

(f) The court from time to time during the custodianship or receivership may order compensation paid and expense disbursements or reimbursements made to the custodian or receiver from the assets of the corporation or proceeds from the sale of its assets.

(g) In this section, "shareholder" means a record shareholder, a beneficial shareholder, and an unrestricted voting trust beneficial owner.

§ 7.49. Judicial Determination of Corporate Offices and Review of Elections and Shareholder Votes

(1) the result or validity of the election, appointment, removal or resignation of a director or officer of the corporation;

(2) the right of an individual to hold the office of director or officer of the corporation;

(3) the result or validity of any vote by the shareholders of the corporation;

(4) the right of a director to membership on a committee of the board of directors; and

(5) the right of a person to nominate or an individual to be nominated as a candidate for election or appointment as a director of the corporation, and any right under a bylaw adopted pursuant to section 2.06(c) or any comparable right under any provision of the articles of incorporation, contract, or applicable law.

(b) An application or proceeding pursuant to subsection (a) of this section may be filed or commenced by any of the following persons:

(1) the corporation;

(2) any record shareholder, beneficial shareholder or unrestricted voting trust beneficial owner of the corporation;

(3) a director of the corporation, an individual claiming the office of director, or a director whose membership on a committee of the board of directors is contested, in each case who is seeking a determination of his or her right to such office or membership;

(4) an officer of the corporation or an individual claiming to be an officer of the corporation, in each case who is seeking a determination of his or her right to such office; and

(5) a person claiming a right covered by subsection (a)(5) and who is seeking a determination of such right.

(c) In connection with any application or proceeding under subsection (a), the following shall be named as defendants, unless such person made the application or commenced the proceeding:

(1) the corporation;

(2) any individual whose right to office or membership on a committee of the board of directors is contested;

(3) any individual claiming the office or membership at issue; and

(4) any person claiming a right covered by subsection (a)(5) that is at issue.

(d) In connection with any application or proceeding under subsection (a), service of process may be made upon each of the persons specified in subsection (c) either by:

(1) service of process on the corporation addressed to such person in any manner provided by statute of this state or by rule of the applicable court for service on the corporation; or

(2) service of process on the person in any manner provided by statute of this state or by rule of the applicable court.

(e) When service of process is made upon a person other than the corporation by service upon the corporation pursuant to subsection (d)(1), the plaintiff and the corporation or its registered agent shall promptly provide written notice of such service, together with copies of all process and the application or complaint, to the person at the person's last known residence or business address, or as permitted by statute of this state or by rule of the applicable court.

(f) In connection with any application or proceeding under subsection (a), the court shall dispose of the application or proceeding on an expedited basis and also may:

(1) order such additional or further notice as the court deems proper under the circumstances;

(2) order that additional persons be joined as parties to the proceeding if the court determines that such joinder is necessary for a just adjudication of matters before the court;

(3) order an election or meeting be held in accordance with the provisions of section 7.03(b) or otherwise;

(4) appoint a master to conduct an election or meeting;

(5) enter temporary, preliminary or permanent injunctive relief;

(6) resolve solely for the purpose of this proceeding any legal or factual issues necessary for the resolution of any of the matters specified in subsection (a), including the right and power of persons claiming to own shares to vote at any meeting of the shareholders; and

(7) order such other relief as the court determines is equitable, just and proper.

(g) It is not necessary to make shareholders a party to a proceeding or application pursuant to this section unless the shareholder is a required defendant under subsection (c)(4), relief is sought against the shareholder individually, or the court orders joinder pursuant to subsection (f)(2).

(h) Nothing in this section limits, restricts, or abolishes the subject matter jurisdiction or powers of the court as existed before the enactment of this section, and an application or proceeding pursuant to this section is not the exclusive remedy or proceeding available with respect to the matters specified in subsection (a).

Official Comment

Section 7.49 establishes a procedure for judicial resolution of disputes with respect to the identity of the corporation's directors or officers, the identity of the members of any committee of its board of directors, the validity of nominations for director or the results or validity of shareholder votes. It confers subject matter jurisdiction on the specified court to resolve these disputes. That jurisdiction may be exercised either in a new proceeding or by an application made in an already pending proceeding. . . .

Chapter 8

DIRECTORS AND OFFICERS

Subchapter A

Board of Directors

§ 8.01. Requirement for and Functions of Board of Directors

(a) except as may be provided in an agreement authorized under section 7.32, each corporation shall have a board of directors.

(b) Except as may be provided in an agreement authorized under section 7.32, and subject to any limitation in the articles of incorporation permitted by section 2.02(b), all corporate powers shall be exercised by or under the authority of the board of directors, and the business and affairs of the corporation shall be managed by or under the direction, and subject to the oversight, of the board of directors.

Official Comment

As provided in Section 8.01(a), the board of directors is the traditional form of governance, but the shareholders of a corporation may, in an agreement that satisfies the requirements of section 7.32, dispense with a board of directors and structure the corporation's management and governance to address specific needs of the enterprise.

In section 8.01(b), the phrase "by or under the direction, and subject to the oversight, of" encompasses the varying functions of boards of directors of different corporations. In some corporations, particularly closely held corporations, the board of directors may be involved in the day-to-day business and affairs and it may be reasonable to describe management as being "by" the board of directors. In many other corporations, including most public corporations, the business and affairs are managed "under the direction, and subject to the oversight, of" the board of directors, and operational management is delegated to executive officers and other professional managers.

Section 8.01(b) often is considered to constitute the heart of the governance provisions of the Act. Giving the board of directors the power, and the responsibility, to oversee and direct the business of the corporation permits separation of ownership of the corporation from control of its oversight and direction. The Act's broad grant of authority and responsibility to the board of directors constitutes the rejection of the concept that the directors, having been elected by the shareholders, merely serve as agents to implement the will of the shareholders. See section 8.30.

Section 8.01(b), in providing for corporate powers to be exercised under the direction of the board of directors, allows the board of directors to delegate to appropriate officers, employees or agents of the corporation authority to exercise powers and perform functions not required by law to be exercised or performed by the board of directors itself. Although such delegation does not relieve the board of directors from its responsibility to oversee the business and affairs of the corporation, directors are not personally responsible for actions or omissions of officers, employees, or agents of the corporation so long as the directors have relied reasonably and in good faith upon these officers, employees, or agents. See sections 8.30 and 8.31 and their Official Comments.

The scope of the board's oversight responsibility will vary depending on the nature of the corporation and its business. At least for public corporations, the board's responsibilities generally include oversight of the following:

- business performance, plans and strategy;
- management's assessment of major risks to which the corporation is or may be exposed;
- the performance and compensation of executive officers;
- policies and practices to foster the corporation's compliance with law and ethical conduct;
- management's preparation of the corporation's financial statements;
- management's design and assessment of effectiveness of the corporation's internal controls;

- plans for the succession of the chief executive officer and other executive officers;

- the composition of the board and of board committees; and

- whether the corporation has information and reporting systems in place to provide directors with appropriate information in a timely manner.

In giving attention to the composition of the board, directors of public corporations should consider the corporation's processes for obtaining and evaluating the views of shareholders, including processes for considering individuals proposed by shareholders as nominees for election as directors. Directors of public corporations also should take into account the important role of independent directors. When ownership is separated from responsibility for oversight and direction, as is the case with public corporations, having nonmanagement independent directors who participate actively in the board's oversight functions increases the likelihood that actions taken by the board, if challenged, will be given deference by the courts. The listing standards of most public securities markets have requirements for independent directors to serve on boards; in many cases, they must constitute a majority of the board, and certain board committees must be composed entirely of independent directors. The listing standards have differing rules as to what constitutes an independent director. The Act does not attempt to define "independent director." Ordinarily, an independent director may not be a present or recent member of senior management and must be free of significant professional, financial or similar relationships with the corporation, and the director and members of the director's immediate family must be free of similar relationships with the corporation's senior management. Judgment is required to determine independence in light of the particular circumstances, subject to any specific requirements of a listing standard. The qualifications for disinterestedness required of directors for specific purposes under the Act are similar, but not necessarily identical, to those that are prerequisites to independence. For the requirements for a director to be considered disinterested and qualified to act in those specified situations, see section 1.43. An individual who is an independent director may not be eligible to act in a particular case under those other provisions of the Act. Conversely, a director who is not independent (for example, a member of management) may be disinterested and qualified to act in a particular case.

Section 8.01(b) recognizes that the powers of the board of directors may be limited by express provisions in the articles of incorporation and in an agreement among all shareholders under section 7.32. In an agreement under section 7.32, board powers also may be assigned to others. Because all of the shareholders must approve a section 7.32 agreement, the only restriction on limiting or assigning board powers is that any limitation or assignment must be provided for in sections 7.32(a)(1) through (a)(7) or must not be contrary to public policy under section 7.32(a)(8). In contrast, as is provided in section 2.02(b)(2), any limitation on board powers in the articles of incorporation cannot be "inconsistent with law." As a result of this difference in standards, any such limitation under section 2.02 should not, for example, be inconsistent with requirements of section 8.30 regarding standards of conduct for directors or otherwise preclude the directors from fulfilling their duties to the corporation.

§ 8.02. Qualifications of Directors → Delaware title 8 § 141

(a) The articles of incorporation or bylaws may prescribe qualifications for directors or for nominees for directors. Qualifications must be reasonable as applied to the corporation and be lawful.

(b) A requirement that is based on a past, prospective, or current action, or expression of opinion, by a nominee or director that could limit the ability of a nominee or director to discharge his or her duties as a director is not a permissible qualification under this section. Notwithstanding the foregoing, qualifications may include not being or having been subject to specified criminal, civil, or regulatory sanctions or not having been removed as a director by judicial action or for cause.

(c) A director need not be a resident of this state or a shareholder unless the articles of incorporation or bylaws so prescribe.

(d) A qualification for nomination for director prescribed before a person's nomination shall apply to such person at the time of nomination. A qualification for nomination for director prescribed after a person's nomination shall not apply to such person with respect to such nomination.

(e) A qualification for director prescribed before a director has been elected or appointed may apply only at the time an individual becomes a director or may apply during a director's term. A qualification prescribed after a director has been elected or appointed shall not apply to that director before the end of that director's term.

Official Comment

Some corporations have adopted qualifications for individuals to be directors or to be nominated as directors. One use of qualifications may be by closely held corporations, to ensure representation and voting power on the board of directors. Other provisions of the Act also are designed to accomplish these purposes. See, for example, section 7.32 providing for shareholder agreements. See also section 2.02(b).

Qualifications may apply to all board members or to a specified percentage or number of directors. An example of a qualification applying to fewer than all directors would be a requirement that at least two directors must have specified business or professional experience or a particular educational degree or background. Careful consideration should be given to the intended effect of the application of any qualification that applies to fewer than all directors in the context of an election contest in which only some of the nominees satisfy this qualification. In the event that specified qualifications for some or all directors are not satisfied, remedial steps could be addressed in the articles of incorporation or bylaws, or can be left to other mechanisms available to a corporation and its board and shareholders, such as the provisions permitting changes in the number of directors and providing for the filling of vacancies on the board. See sections 8.03 and 8.10.

The purpose of section 8.02(a) is to permit qualifications that may benefit the corporation by enhancing the board's ability to perform its role effectively. However, this needs to be balanced against the risk that qualifications could be misused for entrenchment purposes by incumbents or for other improper purposes. To address these concerns, section 8.02(a) requires that qualifications must be reasonable as applied to the corporation and must be lawful. For example, a qualification that seeks to favor incumbent directors or distinguish between a director elected from the slate nominated by a corporation's board and a director elected as the result of being nominated by one or more shareholders, including under a bylaw adopted pursuant to section 2.06(c), would not ordinarily be reasonable and thus not ordinarily authorized by section 8.02(a). An example of a qualification that would not be lawful would be a requirement that is impermissibly discriminatory under the Civil Rights Act of 1964.

1. *Scope of Permitted Qualifications*

Examples of qualifications that may be permissible under section 8.02 are eligibility requirements based on residence, shareholdings, age, length of service, experience, expertise, and professional licenses or certifications.

Under section 8.02(b) a qualification that is based on a past, current, or prospective action, or expression of opinion, by a nominee or director that could limit the ability of a nominee or director to discharge his or her duties as a director is not a permissible qualification. The discharge of duties of a director is referenced in section 8.30. A requirement based on a director's having voted for or against, or expressed an intent to vote for or against, a particular type of resolution, such as a resolution in favor of or against a bylaw pursuant to section 2.06(c) or a resolution in favor of or against a shareholder rights plan, would be impermissible.

A shareholder agreement that meets the requirements of section 7.32 could override the terms of section 8.02, including with respect to the requirement of reasonableness in section 8.02(a) and the limitation on permitted qualifications in section 8.02(b).

2. *Timing and Applicability of Qualifications*

Sections 8.02(d) and (e) prohibit "springing" qualifications. A qualification for a director that is prescribed during the term of that director shall, assuming it remains in effect, apply to that director upon the start of any additional term of that director.

To avoid ambiguity as to whether a qualification for director only applies at the start of a term or applies during the term, a qualification provision should provide clearly when it applies. In the event that a qualification provision does not so specify, customary principles of interpretation and construction will apply. Examples of qualifications the nature of which would generally indicate an intent that they apply throughout a term would be a citizenship or residence qualification or a qualification that a director have a particular license or government clearance.

A director who ceases to meet a qualification that applies during a term will not satisfy that qualification at that time. For example, if a bylaw provision that is in effect at the start of a director's term requires that all directors be residents of state X during their terms, and that director at the start of his or her term is a resident of state X but during the term becomes a resident of state Y, then that director would cease to satisfy the qualification and, therefore, cease to be a director at the time the director becomes a resident of state Y.

§ 8.03. Number and Election of Directors

(a) A board of directors shall consist of one or more individuals, with the number specified in or fixed in accordance with the articles of incorporation or bylaws.

(b) The number of directors may be increased or decreased from time to time by amendment to, or in the manner provided in, the articles of incorporation or bylaws.

(c) Directors are elected at the first annual shareholders' meeting and at each annual shareholders' meeting thereafter unless elected by written consent in lieu of an annual meeting as permitted by section 7.04 or unless their terms are staggered under section 8.06.

Official Comment

Section 8.03 prescribes rules for (i) the determination of the size of the board of directors of corporations, and (ii) changes in the number of directors once the board's size has been established.

1. Number of Directors

Under section 8.03(a), the size of the board of directors may be fixed initially in one or more of the fundamental corporate documents, or the decision as to the size of the initial board of directors may be made thereafter in the manner authorized in those documents.

2. Changes in the Size of the Board of Directors

Section 8.03(b) provides a corporation with the freedom to design its articles of incorporation and bylaw provisions relating to the size of its board with a view to achieving the combination of flexibility for the board of directors and protection for shareholders that it deems appropriate. The articles of incorporation could provide for a specified number of directors or a board size within a range from a minimum to a maximum, or an unlimited size not fewer than one as determined by the board or the shareholders. If the shareholders or the board of directors want to change the specified size of the board, to change the range established for the size of the board or to change from a board size within a range or of unlimited size to a specified board size or vice versa, board of directors and shareholder action would be required to make those changes by amending the articles of incorporation. Alternatively, the bylaws could provide for a specified number of directors or a size within a stated range or unlimited size, with the number to be fixed by the board of directors. Any change would be made in the manner provided by the bylaws. The bylaws could permit amendment by the board of directors or the bylaws could require that any amendment, in whole or in part, be made only by the shareholders in accordance with section 10.20(a). Typically, the board of directors would be permitted to change the board size within the established range. If a corporation wishes to ensure that any change in the number of directors be approved by shareholders, then an appropriate restriction would have to be included in the articles of incorporation or bylaws.

The board's power to change the number of directors, like all other board powers, is subject to compliance with applicable standards governing director conduct. In particular, it may be inappropriate to change the size of the board for the primary purpose of maintaining control or defeating particular candidates for the board.

In many closely held corporations, shareholder approval for a change in the size of the board of directors may be readily accomplished if that is desired. In many closely held corporations a board of directors of a fixed size may be an essential part of a control arrangement. In these situations, an increase or decrease in the size of the board of directors by even a single member may significantly affect control. To maintain control arrangements dependent on a board of directors of a fixed size, the power of the board of directors to change its own size must be negated. This may be accomplished by fixing the size of the board of directors in the articles of incorporation or by expressly negating the power of the board of directors to change the size of the board, whether by amendment of the bylaws or otherwise. See section 10.20(a).

§ 8.04. Election of Directors by Certain Classes or Series of Shares

If the articles of incorporation or action by the board of directors pursuant to section 6.02 authorize dividing the shares into classes or series, the articles of incorporation may also authorize the election of all or a specified number of directors by the holders of one or more authorized classes or series of shares. A class or series (or multiple classes or series) of shares entitled to elect one or more directors is a separate voting group for purposes of the election of directors.

Official Comment

Provisions allowing separate classes or series of shares each to elect a specified number of directors are often used in corporations to effect an agreed upon allocation of control, for example, to ensure representation on the board of directors by particular shareholders by issuing to those shareholders a class or series of shares entitled to elect one or more directors. Each class or series (or multiple classes or series) entitled to elect separately one or more directors constitutes a separate voting group for this purpose, and the quorum and voting requirements must be separately met by each voting group as provided in sections 7.25, 7.26 and 7.28.

§ 8.05.　Terms of Directors Generally

(a) The terms of the initial directors of a corporation expire at the first shareholders' meeting at which directors are elected.

(b) The terms of all other directors expire at the next, or if their terms are staggered in accordance with section 8.06, at the applicable second or third, annual shareholders' meeting following their election, except to the extent (i) provided in section 10.22 if a bylaw electing to be governed by that section is in effect, or (ii) a shorter term is specified in the articles of incorporation in the event of a director nominee failing to receive a specified vote for election.

(c) A decrease in the number of directors does not shorten an incumbent director's term.

(d) The term of a director elected to fill a vacancy expires at the next shareholders' meeting at which directors are elected.

(e) Except to the extent otherwise provided in the articles of incorporation or under section 10.22 if a bylaw electing to be governed by that section is in effect, despite the expiration of a director's term, the director continues to serve until the director's successor is elected and qualifies or there is a decrease in the number of directors.

Official Comment

Section 8.05 provides for the annual election of directors at the annual shareholders' meeting with the single exception that terms may be staggered as permitted in section 8.06.

Under section 8.05(d), if terms are staggered, the term of a director elected to fill a vacant term with more than a year to run is shorter than the term of the director's predecessor. The board of directors may take appropriate steps, by designation of short terms or otherwise, to return the rotation of election of directors to the original staggered terms established or fixed by the articles of incorporation or bylaws.

Section 8.05(e), with two exceptions, provides for "holdover" directors so that directorships do not automatically become vacant at the expiration of their terms. This means that the power of the board of directors to act continues uninterrupted even if an annual shareholders' meeting is not held or the shareholders are deadlocked or otherwise do not elect directors at the meeting. The articles of incorporation may modify or eliminate this holdover concept. Also, if a bylaw is adopted invoking section 10.22, the effect will be that directors who are elected by a plurality vote but receive more votes against than for their election will not hold over past the abbreviated 90-day term of office specified in section 10.22.

§ 8.06.　Staggered Terms for Directors

The articles of incorporation may provide for staggering the terms of directors by dividing the total number of directors into two or three groups, with each group containing half or one-third of the total, as near as may be practicable. In that event, the terms of directors in the first group expire at the first annual shareholders' meeting after their election, the terms of the second group expire at the second annual shareholders' meeting after their election, and the terms of the third group, if any, expire at the third annual shareholders' meeting after their election. At each annual shareholders' meeting held thereafter, directors shall be elected for a term of two years or three years, as the case may be, to succeed those whose terms expire.

Official Comment

Section 8.06 permits the practice of "classifying" the board or "staggering" the terms of directors. The requirement that these provisions be in the articles of incorporation ensures that, unless included in the corporation's original articles, a staggered board may only be implemented with shareholder approval.

§ 8.07. Resignation of Directors

(a) A director may resign at any time by delivering a written notice of resignation to the board of directors or its chair, or to the secretary.

(b) A resignation is effective as provided in section 1.41(i) unless the resignation provides for a delayed effectiveness, including effectiveness determined upon a future event or events. A resignation that is conditioned upon failing to receive a specified vote for election as a director may provide that it is irrevocable.

Official Comment

In addition to permitting resignations effective at a date later than the date of delivery of the resignation, section 8.07(b) permits a director resignation to be conditioned upon "future events," which might include the director failing to achieve a specified vote for reelection, *e.g.*, more votes "for" than "against" coupled with board acceptance of the resignation. Corporations and individual directors may thus give effect, in a manner subsequently enforceable by the corporation, to voting standards for the election of directors that exceed the plurality default standard in section 7.28. Section 8.07(b) also makes it clear that such arrangements do not contravene public policy. . . .

Under section 8.10, a vacancy that will occur at a specific later date by reason of a resignation effective at a later date may be filled before the vacancy occurs, but the new director may not take office until the vacancy occurs. Because the individual tendering that resignation is still a member of the board, he or she may participate in all decisions until the specified date, including the choice of his or her successor under section 8.10.

§ 8.08. Removal of Directors by Shareholders

(a) The shareholders may remove one or more directors with or without cause unless the articles of incorporation provide that directors may be removed only for cause.

(b) If a director is elected by a voting group of shareholders, only the shareholders of that voting group may participate in the vote to remove that director.

(c) A director may be removed if the number of votes cast to remove exceeds the number of votes cast not to remove the director, except to the extent the articles of incorporation or bylaws require a greater number; provided that if cumulative voting is authorized, a director may not be removed if, in the case of a meeting, the number of votes sufficient to elect the director under cumulative voting is voted against removal and, if action is taken by less than unanimous written consent, voting shareholders entitled to the number of votes sufficient to elect the director under cumulative voting do not consent to the removal.

(d) A director may be removed by the shareholders only at a meeting called for the purpose of removing the director and the meeting notice must state that removal of the director is a purpose of the meeting.

Official Comment

Section 8.08(a) provides a default rule that shareholders have the power to change the directors at will. However, that section permits the power to remove directors without cause to be eliminated by a provision in the articles of incorporation. Section 8.08(c) assures that a minority faction with sufficient votes to guarantee the election of a director under cumulative voting will be able to protect that director from removal by the remaining shareholders. In computing whether a director elected by cumulative voting is protected from removal under that section, the votes should be counted as though (i) the vote to remove the director occurred in an election to elect the number of directors normally elected by the relevant voting group along with the director whose removal is sought, (ii) the number of votes cast cumulatively against removal had been cast for election of the director, and (iii) all votes cast for removal of the director had been cast cumulatively in an efficient pattern for the election of a sufficient number of candidates so as to deprive the director whose removal is being sought of the director's office.

Although sections 8.08(b) and (c) have specific requirements with respect to removal of directors elected by particular voting groups or by cumulative voting, such directors nevertheless may be removed by court proceeding under section 8.09. Section 8.08(d) acknowledges the seriousness of director removal by requiring the meeting notice to state that removal of specific directors will be proposed. Section 8.08(d) governs removal of directors at a meeting of shareholders, but does not preclude removal by means of shareholder action by written consent under section 7.04. Unless cumulative voting is authorized, and in the absence of a greater vote requirement in the articles of incorporation or bylaws, removal of a director by less than unanimous written consent would require that a majority of the outstanding shares of the relevant voting group consent to the removal.

§ 8.09. Removal of Directors by Judicial Proceeding

(a) The [name or describe court] may remove a director from office or may order other relief, including barring the director from reelection for a period prescribed by the court, in a proceeding commenced by or in the right of the corporation if the court finds that (i) the director engaged in fraudulent conduct with respect to the corporation or its shareholders, grossly abused the position of director, or intentionally inflicted harm on the corporation; and (ii) considering the director's course of conduct and the inadequacy of other available remedies, removal or such other relief would be in the best interest of the corporation.

(b) A shareholder proceeding on behalf of the corporation under subsection (a) shall comply with all of the requirements of subchapter 7D, except clause (i) of section 7.41.

Official Comment

Section 8.09 is designed to operate in the limited circumstance where other remedies are inadequate to address serious misconduct by a director and it is impracticable for shareholders to invoke removal under section 8.08. A proceeding under section 8.09 may be brought by the corporation or by a shareholder suing derivatively. If an action is brought derivatively, all of the provisions of chapter 7D, including dismissal under section 7.44, are applicable to the action with the exception of the contemporaneous ownership requirement of clause (i) of section 7.41. This extraordinary remedy of judicial removal is only for the kind of misconduct described in clause (i) of section 8.09(a) and does not reach matters falling within an individual director's lawful exercise of business judgment.

The court may determine that the director's continuation in office is inimical to the best interest of the corporation. Judicial removal might be the most appropriate remedy if shareholder removal under section 8.08 is impracticable because of situations such as the following:

- The director charged with serious misconduct personally owns or controls sufficient shares to block removal.

- The director was elected by voting group or cumulative voting, and the shareholders with voting power to prevent removal will exercise that power despite the director's serious misconduct and without regard to what the court deems to be the best interest of the corporation.

- A shareholders' meeting to consider removal under section 8.08 will entail considerable expense and a period of delay that will be contrary to the corporation's best interest.

§ 8.10. Vacancy on Board of Directors

(a) Unless the articles of incorporation provide otherwise, if a vacancy occurs on a board of directors, including a vacancy resulting from an increase in the number of directors:

(1) the shareholders may fill the vacancy;

(2) the board of directors may fill the vacancy; or

(3) if the directors remaining in office are less than a quorum, they may fill the vacancy by the affirmative vote of a majority of all the directors remaining in office.

(b) If the vacant office was held by a director elected by a voting group of shareholders, only the holders of shares of that voting group are entitled to vote to fill the vacancy if it is filled by the shareholders, and only the remaining directors elected by that voting group, even if less than a quorum, are entitled to fill the vacancy if it is filled by the directors.

(c) A vacancy that will occur at a specific later date (by reason of a resignation effective at a later date under section 8.07(b) or otherwise) may be filled before the vacancy occurs but the new director may not take office until the vacancy occurs.

Official Comment

Section 8.10(a)(3) allows the directors remaining in office to fill director vacancies even though they do not constitute a quorum. The test for the exercise of this power is whether the directors remaining in office are less than a quorum, not whether the directors seeking to act are less than a quorum. For example, on a board of six directors where a quorum is four, if there are two vacancies, they may not be filled under section 8.10(a)(3) at a "meeting" attended by only three directors. Even though the three directors are less than a quorum, section 8.10(a)(3) is not applicable because the number of directors remaining in office—four—is not less than a quorum. . . .

Under section 8.10(c), the director in the office that will become vacant may participate in the selection of a successor. Such a vacancy typically arises when there is a resignation by a director that is effective at a later date; it may also arise in connection with retirements or with prospective amendments to bylaws. In a closely held corporation with a balance of power on the board of directors that was reached by agreement, a prospective resignation followed by the appointment of a successor under this section permits the board to act on the replacement before the change in balance of power the resignation would otherwise cause.

§ 8.11.   Compensation of Directors

Unless the articles of incorporation or bylaws provide otherwise, the board of directors may fix the compensation of directors.

Subchapter B

Meetings and Action of the Board

§ 8.20.   Meetings

(a) The board of directors may hold regular or special meetings in or out of this state.

(b) Unless restricted by the articles of incorporation or bylaws, any or all directors may participate in any meeting of the board of directors through the use of any means of communication by which all directors participating may simultaneously hear each other during the meeting. A director participating in a meeting by this means is deemed to be present in person at the meeting.

§ 8.21.   Action Without Meeting

(a) Except to the extent that the articles of incorporation or bylaws require that action by the board of directors be taken at a meeting, action required or permitted by this Act to be taken by the board of directors may be taken without a meeting if each director signs a consent describing the action to be taken and delivers it to the corporation.

(b) Action taken under this section is the act of the board of directors when one or more consents signed by all the directors are delivered to the corporation. The consent may specify a later time as the time at which the action taken is to be effective. A director's consent may be withdrawn by a revocation signed by the director and delivered to the corporation before delivery to the corporation of unrevoked written consents signed by all the directors.

(c) A consent signed under this section has the effect of action taken at a meeting of the board of directors and may be described as such in any document.

§ 8.22.   Notice of Meeting

(a) Unless the articles of incorporation or bylaws provide otherwise, regular meetings of the board of directors may be held without notice of the date, time, place, or purpose of the meeting.

(b) Unless the articles of incorporation or bylaws provide for a longer or shorter period, special meetings of the board of directors shall be preceded by at least two days' notice of the date, time, and place of the meeting. The notice need not describe the purpose of the special meeting unless required by the articles of incorporation or bylaws. → *special meetings of shareholders requires purpose*

§ 8.23.   Waiver of Notice

(a) A director may waive any notice required by this Act, the articles of incorporation or the bylaws before or after the date and time stated in the notice. Except as provided by subsection (b), the waiver must be in writing, signed by the director entitled to the notice and delivered to the corporation for filing by the corporation with the minutes or corporate records.

(b) A director's attendance at or participation in a meeting waives any required notice to the director of the meeting unless the director at the beginning of the meeting (or promptly upon arrival) objects to holding the meeting or transacting business at the meeting and does not after objecting vote for or assent to action taken at the meeting.

§ 8.24.   Quorum and Voting

(a) Unless the articles of incorporation or bylaws provide for a greater or lesser number or unless otherwise expressly provided in this Act, a quorum of a board of directors consists of a majority of the number of directors specified in or fixed in accordance with the articles of incorporation or bylaws.

(b) The quorum of the board of directors specified in or fixed in accordance with the articles of incorporation or bylaws may not consist of less than one-third of the specified or fixed number of directors.

(c) If a quorum is present when a vote is taken, the affirmative vote of a majority of directors present is the act of the board of directors unless the articles of incorporation or bylaws require the vote of a greater number of directors or unless otherwise expressly provided in this Act.

(d) A director who is present at a meeting of the board of directors or a committee when corporate action is taken is deemed to have assented to the action taken unless: (i) the director objects at the beginning of the meeting (or promptly upon arrival) to holding it or transacting business at the meeting; (ii) the dissent or abstention from the action taken is entered in the minutes of the meeting; or (iii) the director delivers written notice of the director's dissent or abstention to the presiding officer of the meeting before its adjournment or to the corporation immediately after adjournment of the meeting. The right of dissent or abstention is not available to a director who votes in favor of the action taken.

CROSS-REFERENCES

Action without meeting, see § 8.21.

Committees of board of directors, see § 8.25.

Meetings of board of directors, see § 8.20.

Notices and other communications, see § 1.41.

Number of directors, see § 8.03.

Quorum for determination of advance for expenses, see § 8.53.

Quorum for determination and authorization of indemnification, see § 8.55.

§ 8.25.   Committees of the Board *(Delegation)*

(a) Unless this Act, the articles of incorporation or the bylaws provide otherwise, a board of directors may establish one or more board committees composed exclusively of one or more directors to perform functions of the board of directors.

(b) The establishment of a board committee and appointment of members to it shall be approved by the greater of (i) a majority of all the directors in office when the action is taken or (ii) the number of directors required by the articles of incorporation or bylaws to take action under section 8.24, unless, in either case, this Act or the articles of incorporation provide otherwise.

(c) Sections 8.20 through 8.24 apply to board committees and their members.

(d) A board committee may exercise the powers of the board of directors under section 8.01, to the extent specified by the board of directors or in the articles of incorporation or bylaws, except that a board committee may not:

(1) authorize or approve distributions, except according to a formula or method, or within limits, prescribed by the board of directors;

(2) approve or propose to shareholders action that this Act requires be approved by shareholders;

(3) fill vacancies on the board of directors or, subject to subsection (e), on any board committees; or

(4) adopt, amend, or repeal bylaws.

(e) The board of directors may appoint one or more directors as alternate members of any board committee to replace any absent or disqualified member during the member's absence or disqualification. If the articles of incorporation, the bylaws, or the resolution creating the board committee so provide, the member or members present at any board committee meeting and not disqualified from voting may, by unanimous action, appoint another director to act in place of an absent or disqualified member during that member's absence or disqualification.

Official Comment

Section 8.25 deals only with board committees authorized to perform functions of the board of directors. The board of directors or management, independently of section 8.25, may establish non-board committees composed in whole or in part of directors, employees, or others to address matters in ways that do not constitute performing functions required to be performed by the board of directors under section 8.01, including acting in an advisory capacity.

Under section 8.25(a), except as otherwise provided by the Act, the articles of incorporation or the bylaws, a board committee may consist of a single director. This accommodates situations in which only one director may be present or available to make a decision on short notice, as well as situations in which it is unnecessary or inconvenient to have more than one member on a board committee or where only one board member is disinterested or independent with respect to a matter. Various other sections of the Act require the participation or approval of at least two qualified directors in order for the decision of the board or committee to have effect. (For the definition of "qualified director," see section 1.43.) These include a determination that maintenance of a derivative suit is not in the corporation's best interests (section 7.44(b)(2)), a determination that indemnification is permissible (section 8.55(b)(1)), an approval of a director's conflicting interest transaction (section 8.62(a)), and disclaimer of the corporation's interest in a business opportunity (section 8.70(a)). . . .

The limitations in section 8.25(d)(1) through (4) are based on the principle that the listed actions so substantially affect the rights of shareholders or are so fundamental to the governance of the corporation that they should be determined by the full board and not delegated to a committee. On the other hand, section 8.25(d) allows board committees to take many actions that may be material, such as the authorization of long-term debt and capital investment or the issuance of shares. . . .

Section 8.25(e) is a rule of convenience that permits the board of directors or the other board committee members to replace an absent or disqualified member during the time that the member is absent or disqualified. Unless otherwise provided or unless a quorum is no longer present, replacement of an absent or disqualified member of a committee is not necessary to permit the other committee members to continue to perform their duties.

§ 8.26.   Submission of Matters for Shareholder Vote

A corporation may agree to submit a matter to a vote of its shareholders even if, after approving the matter, the board of directors determines it no longer recommends the matter.

Official Comment

Section 8.26 authorizes a corporation to enter into an agreement, such as a merger agreement, containing a provision that requires a shareholder vote on the matter despite a subsequent change in the recommendation of the board of directors. Otherwise, a board is not required to submit a matter to the shareholders, even if it has been approved by the board. Section 8.26 also applies to the provisions of the Act that require the board of directors to approve a matter before recommending that the shareholders vote to approve it. Section 8.26 does not change the standards of conduct or liability applicable when considering whether to authorize such agreement by the corporation.

Subchapter C
Directors

§ 8.30.   Standards of Conduct for Directors

(a) Each member of the board of directors, when discharging the duties of a director, shall act: (i) in good faith, and (ii) in a manner the director reasonably believes to be in the best interests of the corporation.

(b) The members of the board of directors or a board committee, when becoming informed in connection with their decision-making function or devoting attention to their oversight function, shall discharge their duties with the care that a person in a like position would reasonably believe appropriate under similar circumstances.

(c) In discharging board or board committee duties, a director shall disclose, or cause to be disclosed, to the other board or committee members information not already known by them but known by the director to be material to the discharge of their decision-making or oversight functions, except that disclosure is not required to the extent that the director reasonably believes that doing so would violate a duty imposed under law, a legally enforceable obligation of confidentiality, or a professional ethics rule.

(d) In discharging board or board committee duties, a director who does not have knowledge that makes reliance unwarranted is entitled to rely on the performance by any of the persons specified in subsection (f)(1) or subsection (f)(3) to whom the board may have delegated, formally or informally by course of conduct, the authority or duty to perform one or more of the board's functions that are delegable under applicable law.

(e) In discharging board or board committee duties, a director who does not have knowledge that makes reliance unwarranted is entitled to rely on information, opinions, reports, or statements, including financial statements and other financial data, prepared or presented by any of the persons specified in subsection (f).

(f) A director is entitled to rely, in accordance with subsection (d) or (e), on:

(1) one or more officers or employees of the corporation whom the director reasonably believes to be reliable and competent in the functions performed or the information, opinions, reports or statements provided;

(2) legal counsel, public accountants, or other persons retained by the corporation as to matters involving skills or expertise the director reasonably believes are matters (i) within the particular person's professional or expert competence, or (ii) as to which the particular person merits confidence; or

(3) a board committee of which the director is not a member if the director reasonably believes the committee merits confidence.

Official Comment

Section 8.30 sets standards of conduct for directors that focus on the manner in which directors make their decisions, not the correctness of the decisions made. Section 8.30 should be read in light of the basic role of directors set forth in section 8.01(b), which provides that the "business and affairs of a corporation shall be managed by or under the direction and subject to the oversight of the board of directors," as supplemented by various provisions of the Act assigning specific powers or responsibilities to the board. The standards of conduct for directors established by section 8.30 are analogous to those generally articulated by courts in evaluating director conduct, often referred to as the duties of care and loyalty.

Section 8.30 addresses standards of conduct—the level of performance expected of directors undertaking the role and responsibilities of the office of director. The section does not address the liability of a director, although exposure to liability may result from a failure to honor the standards of conduct required to be observed. The issue of director liability is addressed in sections 8.31 and 8.32. Section 8.30 does, however, play an important role in evaluating a director's conduct and the effectiveness of board action. It has relevance in assessing, under section

8.31, the reasonableness of a director's belief. Similarly, it has relevance in assessing a director's timely attention to appropriate inquiry when particular facts and circumstances of significant concern materialize. It also serves as a frame of reference for determining, under section 8.32(a), liability for an unlawful distribution. Finally, section 8.30 compliance may influence a court's analysis where injunctive relief against a transaction is being sought. Directors act both individually and collectively as a board in performing their functions and discharging their duties. Section 8.30 addresses actions in both capacities.

Under the standards of section 8.30, the board may delegate or assign to appropriate officers or employees of the corporation the authority or duty to exercise powers that the law does not require the board to retain. Because the directors are entitled to rely on these persons absent knowledge making reliance unwarranted, the directors will not be in breach of the standards under section 8.30 as a result of their delegatees' actions or omissions so long as the board acted in good faith and complied with the other standards of conduct set forth in section 8.30 in delegating responsibility and, where appropriate, monitoring performance of the duties delegated. In addition, subsections (d), (e) and (f) permit a director to rely on enumerated third parties for specified purposes, although reliance is prohibited when a director has knowledge that makes reliance unwarranted. Section 8.30(a)'s standards of good faith and reasonable belief in the best interests of the corporation also apply to a director's reliance under subsections (d), (e) and (f).

1. *Section 8.30(a)*

Section 8.30(a) establishes the basic standards of conduct for all directors and its mandate governs all aspects of directors' conduct, including the requirements in other subsections. It includes concepts courts have used in defining the duty of loyalty. Two of the phrases used in section 8.30(a) deserve further comment:

- The phrase "reasonably believes" is both subjective and objective in character. Its first level of analysis is geared to what the particular director, acting in good faith, actually believes—not what objective analysis would lead another director (in a like position and acting in similar circumstances) to conclude. The second level of analysis is focused specifically on "reasonably." Although a director has wide discretion in gathering information and reaching conclusions, whether a director's belief is reasonable (*i.e.*, could—not would—a reasonable person in a like position and acting in similar circumstances, taking into account that director's knowledge and experience, have arrived at that belief) ultimately involves an overview that is objective in character.

- The phrase "best interests of the corporation" is key to an understanding of a director's duties. The term "corporation" is a surrogate for the business enterprise as well as a frame of reference encompassing the shareholder body. In determining the corporation's "best interests," the director has wide discretion in deciding how to weigh near-term opportunities versus long-term benefits as well as in making judgments where the interests of various groups of shareholders or other corporate constituencies may differ.

Section 8.30 operates as a "baseline" principle governing director conduct in circumstances uncomplicated by self-interest. The Act recognizes, however, that directors' personal interests may not always align with the corporation's best interests and provides procedures by which situations and transactions involving conflicts of interest can be processed. See subchapter D (derivative proceedings) of chapter 7 and subchapters E (indemnification and advance for expenses), F (directors' conflicting interest transactions), and G (business opportunities) of this chapter 8. Those procedures generally contemplate that the interested director will provide appropriate disclosure and will not be involved in taking action on the matter giving rise to the conflict of interest.

2. *Section 8.30(b)*

Section 8.30(b) establishes a general standard of care for directors in the context of their dealing with the board's decision-making and oversight functions. Although certain aspects will involve individual conduct (*e.g.*, preparation for meetings), these functions are generally performed by the board of directors through collective action, as recognized by the reference in subsection (b) to board and committee "members" and "their duties." In contrast with section 8.30(a)'s individual conduct mandate, section 8.30(b) has a two-fold thrust: it provides a standard of conduct for individual action and, more broadly, it states a conduct obligation—"shall discharge their duties"—concerning the degree of care to be used collectively by the directors when performing those functions. The standard is not what care a particular director might believe appropriate in the circumstances but what a person—in a like position and acting under similar circumstances—would reasonably believe to be appropriate. Thus, the degree of care that directors should employ under section 8.30(b) involves an objective standard.

The process by which a director becomes informed, in carrying out the decision-making and oversight functions, will vary. The directors' decision-making function is reflected in various sections of the Act, including:

the issuance of shares (section 6.21); distributions (section 6.40); dismissal of derivative proceedings (section 7.44); indemnification (section 8.55); conflict of interest transaction authorization (section 8.62); articles of incorporation amendments (sections 10.02 and 10.03); bylaw amendments (section 10.20); mergers and share exchanges (section 11.04); asset dispositions (section 12.02); and dissolution (section 14.02). The directors' oversight function is established under section 8.01. In discharging the section 8.01 duties associated with the board's oversight function, the standard of care entails primarily a requirement of attention. In contrast with the board's decision-making function, which generally involves informed action at a point in time, the oversight function is concerned with a continuum and the attention of the directors accordingly involves participatory performance over a period of time.

Several of the phrases chosen to define the standard of conduct in section 8.30(b) deserve specific mention:

- The phrase "becoming informed," in the context of the decision—making function, refers to the process of gaining sufficient familiarity with the background facts and circumstances to make an informed judgment. Unless the circumstances would permit a reasonable director to conclude that he or she is already sufficiently informed, the standard of care requires every director to take steps to become informed about the background facts and circumstances before taking action on the matter at hand. The process typically involves review of written materials provided before or at the meeting and attention to or participation in the deliberations leading up to a vote. In addition to considering information and data on which a director is expressly entitled to rely under section 8.30(e), "becoming informed" can also involve consideration of information and data generated by other persons, for example, review of industry studies or research articles prepared by third parties. It can also involve direct communications, outside of the boardroom, with members of management or other directors. There is no one way for "becoming informed," and both the method and measure—"how to" and "how much"—are matters of reasonable judgment for the director to exercise.

- The phrase "devoting attention," in the context of the oversight function, refers to considering such matters as the corporation's information and reporting systems generally and not to an independent investigation into particular system inadequacies or noncompliance. Although directors typically give attention to future plans and trends as well as current activities, they should not be expected to anticipate any particular problems which the corporation may face except in those circumstances where something has occurred to make it obvious to the board that the corporation should be addressing a particular problem. The standard of care associated with the oversight function involves gaining assurances from management and advisers that appropriate systems have been established, such as those concerned with legal compliance, risk assessment or internal controls. Such assurances also should cover establishment of ongoing monitoring of the systems in place, with appropriate follow-up responses when alerted to the issues requiring attention.

- The reference to "person," without embellishment, is intended to avoid implying any qualifications, such as specialized expertise or experience requirements, beyond the basic attributes of common sense, practical wisdom, and informed judgment (however, see the last bullet below).

- The phrase "reasonably believe appropriate" refers to the array of possible options that a person possessing the basic attributes of common sense, practical wisdom and informed judgment would recognize to be available, in terms of the degree of care that might be appropriate, and from which a choice by such person would be made. The measure of care that such person might determine to be appropriate, in a given instance, would normally involve a selection from the range of options and any choice within the realm of reason would be an appropriate decision under the standard of care called for under section 8.30(b). However, a decision that is so removed from the realm of reason, or is so unreasonable, that it falls outside the permissible bounds of sound discretion, and thus is an abuse of discretion, will not satisfy the standard.

- The phrase "in a like position" recognizes that the "care" under consideration is that which would be used by the "person" if he or she were a director of the particular corporation.

- The combined phrase "in a like position . . . under similar circumstances" is intended to recognize that (i) the nature and extent of responsibilities will vary, depending upon such factors as the size, complexity, urgency, and location of activities carried on by the particular corporation, (ii) decisions must be made on the basis of the information known to the directors without the benefit of hindsight, and (iii) the special background, qualifications, and oversight responsibilities of a particular director may be relevant in evaluating that director's compliance with the standard of care.

3. Section 8.30(c)

A requirement to disclose to other directors information that a director knows to be material to the decision-making or oversight functions of the board of directors or a board committee is implicit in the standards of conduct set forth in sections 8.30(a) and (b), but section 8.30(c) makes this explicit. Thus, for example, when a member of the board of directors knows information that the director recognizes is material to a decision by the board but is not known to the other directors, the director is obligated to disclose that information to the other members of the board. Such disclosure can occur through direct statements in meetings of the board, or by any other timely means, including, for example, communicating the information to the chairman of the board or the chairman of a committee, or to the corporation's general counsel, and requesting that the recipient inform the other board or committee members of the information.

Section 8.30(c) recognizes that a duty of confidentiality to a third party can override a director's obligation to share with other directors information pertaining to a current corporate matter. In some circumstances, a duty of confidentiality to a third party may even prohibit disclosure of the nature or the existence of the duty itself. Ordinarily, however, a director who withholds material information based on a reasonable belief that a duty of confidentiality to a third party prohibits disclosure should advise the other directors of the existence and nature of that duty. Under the standards of conduct set forth in section 8.30(a), the withholding of material information may, depending on the nature of the material information and of the matter before the board of directors or a board committee, require that a director abstain or recuse himself or herself from all or a portion of the other directors' deliberation or vote on the matter to which the undisclosed information is material, or even resign as a director. See Official Comment to section 8.62.

In connection with a director's conflicting interest transaction, the required disclosure (as defined in section 8.60) that must be made under section 8.62(a) and the exceptions to the required disclosure in that context under section 8.62(b) have elements that parallel the disclosure obligation of directors under section 8.30(c). The demands of section 8.62, however, are more detailed and specific. They apply to just one situation—a director's conflicting interest transaction—while the requirements of section 8.30(c) apply generally to all other decision-making and oversight functions. For example, the specific requirements of section 8.62(a)(1) for deliberation and a vote outside the presence of the conflicted director are not imposed universally for all decision-making matters or for oversight matters that do not involve decisions. Although they may be different from the generally applicable provisions of section 8.30(c), the specific provisions of subchapter 8F control and are exclusive with respect to director conflicting interest transactions.

The requirement that a director disclose information to other directors as set forth in section 8.30(c) is different from any common law duty the board may have to cause the corporation to make disclosures to shareholders under certain circumstances. The Act does not seek to codify such a duty of disclosure, but leaves its existence and scope, the circumstances for its application, and the consequences of any failure to satisfy it, to be developed by courts on a case-by-case basis.

4. Section 8.30(d)

The delegation of authority and responsibility described in section 8.30(d) may take a variety of forms, including (i) formal action through a board resolution, (ii) implicit action through the election of corporate officers (*e.g.*, chief financial officer or controller) or the appointment of corporate managers (*e.g.*, credit manager), or (iii) informal action through a course of conduct (*e.g.*, involvement through corporate officers and managers in the management of a significant 50%-owned joint venture). Under section 8.30(d), a director may properly rely on those to whom authority has been delegated pursuant to section 8.30(d) respecting particular matters calling for specific action or attention in connection with the directors' decision-making function as well as matters on the board's continuing agenda, such as legal compliance and internal controls, in connection with the directors' oversight function. Delegation should be carried out in accordance with the standard of care set forth in section 8.30(b).

By identifying those persons upon whom a director may rely in connection with the discharge of duties, section 8.30(d) does not limit the ability of directors to delegate their powers under section 8.01(b) except where delegation is expressly prohibited by the Act or otherwise by applicable law. See section 8.25 and its Official Comment for discussion of delegation to committees of the authority of the board under section 8.01. By employing the concept of delegation, the Act does not limit the ability of directors to establish baseline principles as to management responsibilities. Specifically, section 8.01(b) provides that "all corporate powers shall be exercised by or under the authority of" the board, and a basic board function involves the allocation of management responsibilities and the related assignment (or delegation) of corporate powers. For example, a board can properly decide to retain a third party to assume responsibility for the administration of designated aspects of risk management for the corporation (*e.g.*, health insurance or disability claims).

Although the board of directors may delegate the authority or duty to perform one or more of its functions, delegation and reliance under section 8.30(d) may not alone constitute compliance with sections 8.30(a) and (b) and the action taken by the delegatee may not alone satisfy the directors or a noncommittee board member's section 8.01 responsibilities. On the other hand, failure of the board committee or the corporate officer or employee performing the function delegated to meet section 8.30(b)'s standard of care will not automatically result in violation by the board of section 8.01. Factors to be considered in determining whether a violation of section 8.01 has occurred will include the care used in the delegation to and supervision over the delegatee, and the amount of knowledge regarding the particular matter which is reasonably available to the particular director. Care in delegation and supervision includes appraisal of the capabilities and diligence of the delegatee in light of the subject and its relative importance and may be satisfied, in the usual case, by receipt of reports concerning the delegatee's activities. The enumeration of these factors is intended to emphasize that directors may not abdicate their responsibilities and avoid accountability simply by delegating authority to others. Rather, a director who is accountable for the acts of delegatees will fulfill the director's duties if the standards contained in section 8.30 are met.

5.   *Section 8.30(e)*

Reliance under section 8.30(e) on a report, statement, opinion, or other information is permitted only if the director has read or heard orally presented the information, opinion, report or statement in question, or took other steps to become generally familiar with it. A director must comply with the general standard of care of section 8.30(b) in making a judgment as to the reliability and competence of the source of information upon which the director proposes to rely or, as appropriate, that it otherwise merits confidence.

6.   *Section 8.30(f)*

In determining whether a corporate officer or employee is "reliable," for purposes of section 8.30(f)(1), the director would typically consider (i) the individual's background experience and scope of responsibility within the corporation in gauging the individual's familiarity and knowledge respecting the subject matter and (ii) the individual's record and reputation for honesty, care and ability in discharging responsibilities which he or she undertakes. In determining whether a person is "competent," the director would normally take into account the same considerations and, if expertise should be relevant, the director would consider the individual's technical skills as well. Recognition of the right of one director to rely on the expertise and experience of another director, in the context of board or committee deliberations, is unnecessary, for reliance on shared experience and wisdom of other board members is an implicit underpinning of collective board conduct. In relying on another member of the board, a director would quite properly take advantage of the colleague's knowledge and experience in becoming informed about the matter at hand before taking action; however, the director would be expected to exercise independent judgment when it comes time to vote.

Advisers on whom a director may rely under section 8.30(f)(2) include not only licensed professionals, such as lawyers, accountants, and engineers, but also those in other fields involving special experience and skills, such as investment bankers, geologists, management consultants, actuaries, and appraisers. The adviser could be an individual or an organization, such as a law or investment banking firm. Reliance on a nonmanagement director, who is specifically engaged (and, normally, additionally compensated) to undertake a special assignment or a particular consulting role, would fall within this outside adviser frame of reference. The concept of "expert competence" embraces a wide variety of qualifications and is not limited to the more precise and narrower recognition of experts under the Securities Act of 1933. In addition, a director may also rely on outside advisers where skills or expertise of a technical nature is not a prerequisite, or where the person's professional or expert competence has not been established, so long as the director reasonably believes the person merits confidence. For example, a board might choose to engage a private investigator to inquire into a particular matter (*e.g.*, follow up on rumors about a senior executive's alleged misconduct) and properly rely on the private investigator's report.

Section 8.30(f)(3) permits reliance on a board committee when it is submitting recommendations for action by the full board of directors as well as when it is performing supervisory or other functions in instances where neither the full board of directors nor the committee takes dispositive action. For example, the compensation committee typically reviews proposals and makes recommendations for action by the full board of directors. There also might be reliance upon an investigation undertaken by a board committee and reported to the full board, which forms the basis for a decision by the board of directors not to take dispositive action. Another example is reliance on a board committee, such as an audit committee with respect to the board's ongoing role of oversight of the accounting and auditing functions of the corporation. In addition, where reliance on information or materials prepared or presented by a board committee is not involved in connection with board action, a director may properly rely on oversight monitoring or dispositive action by a board committee (of which the director is not a member) empowered to act pursuant to authority delegated under section 8.25 or acting with the acquiescence of the board of directors. See the Official Comment to section 8.25. In parallel with section 8.30(f)(2)(ii), the concept of "confidence" is used instead of "competence" to avoid any inference that technical skills are a prerequisite. In the usual case, the appointment of committee members or the reconstitution of the membership of a standing committee (*e.g.*, the audit committee), following an annual shareholders' meeting, would alone manifest the noncommittee members' belief that the committee "merits confidence." Depending on the circumstances, the reliance contemplated by section 8.30(f)(3) is geared to the point in time when the board takes action or the period of time over which a committee is engaged in an oversight function; consequently, the judgment to be made (*i.e.*, whether a committee "merits confidence") will arise at varying points in time. Ordinarily, after making an initial judgment that a committee (of which a director is not a member) merits confidence, a director may continue to rely on that committee so long as the director has no reason to believe that confidence is no longer warranted.

7. *Application to Officers*

Section 8.30 generally deals only with directors. Section 8.42 and its Official Comment explain the extent to which the principles set forth in section 8.30 apply to officers.

§ 8.31. Standards of Liability for Directors

(a) A director shall not be liable to the corporation or its shareholders for any decision to take or not to take action, or any failure to take any action, as a director, unless the party asserting liability in a proceeding establishes that:

(1) no defense interposed by the director based on (i) any provision in the articles of incorporation authorized by section 2.02(b)(4) or by section 2.02(b)(6), (ii) the protection afforded by section 8.61 (for action taken in compliance with section 8.62 or section 8.63), or (iii) the protection afforded by section 8.70, precludes liability; and

(2) the challenged conduct consisted or was the result of:

(i) action not in good faith; or

(ii) a decision

(A) which the director did not reasonably believe to be in the best interests of the corporation, or

(B) as to which the director was not informed to an extent the director reasonably believed appropriate in the circumstances; or

(iii) a lack of objectivity due to the director's familial, financial or business relationship with, or a lack of independence due to the director's domination or control by, another person having a material interest in the challenged conduct,

(A) which relationship or which domination or control could reasonably be expected to have affected the director's judgment respecting the challenged conduct in a manner adverse to the corporation, and

(B) after a reasonable expectation to such effect has been established, the director shall not have established that the challenged conduct was reasonably believed by the director to be in the best interests of the corporation; or

(iv) a sustained failure of the director to devote attention to ongoing oversight of the business and affairs of the corporation, or a failure to devote timely attention, by making (or causing to be made) appropriate inquiry, when particular facts and circumstances of significant concern materialize that would alert a reasonably attentive director to the need for such inquiry; or

(v) receipt of a financial benefit to which the director was not entitled or any other breach of the director's duties to deal fairly with the corporation and its shareholders that is actionable under applicable law.

(b) The party seeking to hold the director liable:

(1) for money damages, shall also have the burden of establishing that:

(i) harm to the corporation or its shareholders has been suffered, and

(ii) the harm suffered was proximately caused by the director's challenged conduct; or

(2) for other money payment under a legal remedy, such as compensation for the unauthorized use of corporate assets, shall also have whatever persuasion burden may be called for to establish that the payment sought is appropriate in the circumstances; or

(3) for other money payment under an equitable remedy, such as profit recovery by or disgorgement to the corporation, shall also have whatever persuasion burden may be called for to establish that the equitable remedy sought is appropriate in the circumstances.

(c) Nothing contained in this section shall (i) in any instance where fairness is at issue, such as consideration of the fairness of a transaction to the corporation under section 8.61(b)(3), alter the burden of proving the fact or lack of fairness otherwise applicable, (ii) alter the fact or lack of liability of a director under another section of this Act, such as the provisions governing the consequences of an unlawful distribution under section 8.32 or a transactional interest under section 8.61, or (iii) affect any rights to which the corporation or a shareholder may be entitled under another statute of this state or the United States.

Official Comment

Boards of directors and corporate managers make numerous decisions that involve the balancing of risks and benefits for the enterprise. Although some decisions turn out to have been unwise or the result of a mistake of judgment, it is not reasonable to impose liability for an informed decision made in good faith which with the benefit of hindsight turns out to be wrong or unwise. Therefore, as a general rule, a director is not exposed to personal liability for injury or damage caused by an unwise decision and conduct conforming with the standards of section 8.30 will almost always be protected regardless of the end result. Moreover, the fact that a director's performance fails to meet the standards of section 8.30 does not in itself establish personal liability for damages that the corporation or its shareholders may have suffered as a consequence. Nevertheless, a director can be held liable for misfeasance or nonfeasance in performing his or her duties. Section 8.31 sets forth the standards of liability of directors as distinct from the standards of conduct set forth in section 8.30.

Courts have developed the broad common law concept of the business judgment rule. Although formulations vary, in basic principle, a board of directors generally enjoys a presumption of sound business judgment and its decisions will not be disturbed by a court substituting its own notions of what is or is not sound business judgment if the board's decisions can be attributed to any rational business purpose. It is also presumed that, in making a business decision, directors act in good faith, on an informed basis, and in the honest belief that the action taken is in the best interests of the corporation. The elements of the business judgment rule and the circumstances for its application continue to be developed and refined by courts. Accordingly, it would not be desirable to freeze the concept in a statute. Thus, section 8.31 does not codify the business judgment rule as a whole, although certain of its principal elements, relating to personal liability issues, are reflected in section 8.31(a)(2).

* * * * *

Note on Directors' Liability

A director's exposure to financial liability (*e.g.*, in a lawsuit for money damages suffered by the corporation or its shareholders claimed to have resulted from misfeasance or nonfeasance in connection with the performance of the director's duties) can be analyzed as follows:

- *Articles of incorporation limitations.* If the corporation's articles of incorporation contain a provision eliminating its directors' liability to the corporation or its shareholders for money damages, adopted pursuant to section 2.02(b)(4), there is no liability unless the director's conduct involves one of the exceptions prescribed in that section that preclude the elimination of liability. If the matter involves a director's taking of a business opportunity and an articles of incorporation provision has been adopted under section 2.02(b)(6) eliminating directors' duties with respect to those opportunities, there also will be no liability. See section 2.02 and its Official Comment.

- *Director's conflicting interest transaction safe harbor.* If the matter at issue involves a director's conflicting interest transaction (as defined in section 8.60) and a safe harbor procedure under section 8.61 involving action taken in compliance with section 8.62 or 8.63 has been properly implemented, there is no liability for the interested director arising out of the transaction. See subchapter 8F.

- *Business opportunities safe harbors.* Similarly, if the matter involves a director's pursuit or taking of a business opportunity, there is no liability for that director if (i) an applicable limitation or elimination of any duty to offer that business opportunity has been adopted pursuant to section 2.02(b)(6), or (ii) a safe harbor procedure under section 8.70 has been properly implemented, even if the articles of incorporation contain no provision under section 2.02(b)(6). See subchapter 8G.

- *Business judgment rule.* If a provision in the articles of incorporation adopted pursuant to section 2.02(b)(4) or (6) or a safe harbor procedure under section 8.61 or 8.70 does not shield the director's conduct from liability, the presumptions, standards of judicial review and procedural matters related to the business judgment rule may insulate the director from liability for conduct in connection with a corporate decision.

- *Damages and proximate cause.* If the business judgment rule does not shield the directors' decision-making from liability, as a general rule it must be established that money damages were suffered by the corporation or its shareholders and those damages resulted from and were legally caused by the challenged act or omission of the director.

- *Other liability for money payment.* Aside from a claim for damages, the director may have monetary liability for other reasons, for example, if corporate resources have been used without proper authorization, or a claim for disgorgement of short-swing trading profits under section 16(b) of the Securities Exchange Act of 1934.

- *Equitable profit recovery or disgorgement.* An equitable remedy compelling the disgorgement of the director's improper financial gain or entitling the corporation to profit recovery, where directors' duties have been breached, may require the payment of money by the director to the corporation.

- *Corporate indemnification.* If the director is monetarily liable, the director may be indemnified by the corporation for any payments made and expenses incurred, depending upon the circumstances. See subchapter 8E.

- *Insurance.* To the extent that corporate indemnification is not available, the director may be reimbursed for the money damages for which the director is accountable, together with proceeding-related expenses, if the claim and grounds for liability come within the coverage under directors' and officers' liability insurance that has been purchased by the corporation as authorized under section 8.57.

* * * * *

1. *Section 8.31(a)*

A.   SECTION 8.31(A)(1)—AFFIRMATIVE DEFENSES

Under section 8.31(a)(1), if a provision in the articles of incorporation (i) (adopted pursuant to section 2.02(b)(4)) shelters the director from liability for money damages, or (ii) (adopted pursuant to section 2.02(b)(6)) limits or eliminates any duty to offer the particular business opportunity to the corporation, or if a safe harbor procedure under sections 8.61(b)(1) or (b)(2) or section 8.70(a)(1) shelters the director's conduct in connection with a conflicting interest transaction or the pursuit or taking of a business opportunity, and such defense applies to all claims in plaintiff's complaint, there is no need to consider further the application of section 8.31's standards of liability. In that event, the court would presumably grant the defendant director's motion for dismissal or summary judgment (or the equivalent) and the proceeding would be ended. If the defense applies to some but not all of plaintiff's claims, dismissal or summary judgment would presumably be granted with respect to those claims. Termination of the proceeding or dismissal of claims on the basis of a provision in the articles of incorporation or a safe harbor procedure will not automatically follow, however, if the party challenging the director's conduct can assert any of the valid bases for contesting the availability of the liability shelter. Absent such a challenge, the relevant shelter provision is self-executing and the individual director's exoneration from liability is automatic. Further, under both sections 8.61 and 8.70, the directors approving the conflicting interest transaction or approving a director's taking of the business opportunity will presumably be protected as well, because compliance with the relevant standards of conduct under section 8.30 is important for their action to be effective and because, as noted above, conduct meeting section 8.30's standards will almost always be protected.

If a claim of liability arising out of a challenged act or omission of a director is not resolved and disposed of under section 8.31(a)(1), section 8.31(a)(2) provides the basis for evaluating whether the conduct in question can be challenged. One of the elements in section 8.31(a)(2) must be established for a director to have liability under section 8.31.

B.　SECTION 8.31(A)(2)(I)—GOOD FAITH

It is a basic standard under section 8.31(a)(2)(i) that a director's conduct in performing his or her duties be in good faith. If a director's conduct can be successfully challenged pursuant to other clauses of section 8.31(a)(2), there is a substantial likelihood that the conduct in question will also present an issue of good faith implicating section 8.31(a)(2)(i). Similarly, if section 8.31(a)(2) included only subsection (i), much of the conduct with which the other clauses are concerned could still be considered under that subsection, on the basis that such conduct evidenced the director's lack of good faith. Where conduct has not been found deficient on other grounds, decision-making outside the bounds of reasonable judgment can give rise to an inference of bad faith. That form of conduct, sometimes characterized as "reckless indifference" or "deliberate disregard," giving rise to an inference of bad faith can also raise a question whether the director could have reasonably believed that the best interests of the corporation would be served. These issues could arise, for example, in approval of conflicting interest transactions. See the Official Comment to section 8.61.

C.　SECTION 8.31(A)(2)(II)—REASONABLE BELIEF

Liability under section 8.31(a)(2)(ii) turns on a director's reasonable belief with respect to the nature of his or her decision and the degree to which he or she has become informed. In each case, the director must have an actual subjective belief and, so long as it is his or her honest and good faith belief, a director has wide discretion. There is also an objective element to be met, in that the director's belief must also be reasonable. The inquiry is similar to that in section 8.30(a)—could a reasonable person in a like position and acting in similar circumstances have arrived at that belief? In the rare case where a decision respecting the corporation's best interests is so removed from the realm of reason (*e.g.*, corporate waste), or a belief as to the sufficiency of the director's preparation to make an informed judgment is so unreasonable as to fall outside the permissible bounds of sound discretion (*e.g.*, if the director has undertaken no preparation and is completely uninformed), the director's judgment will not be sustained.

D.　SECTION 8.31(A)(2)(III)—LACK OF OBJECTIVITY OR INDEPENDENCE

If the matter at issue involves a director's transactional interest, such as a "director's conflicting interest transaction" in which a "related person" is involved (see section 8.60), it will be governed by section 8.61; otherwise, a lack of objectivity due to a relationship's influence on the director's judgment will be evaluated, in the context of the pending challenge of director conduct, under section 8.31. If the matter at issue involves lack of independence, the proof of domination or control and its influence on the director's judgment will typically entail different (and perhaps more convincing) evidence than what may be involved in a lack of objectivity case. The variables are manifold, and the facts must be sorted out and weighed on a case-by-case basis. For example, the closeness or nature of the relationship with the person allegedly exerting influence on the director could be a factor. If the director is required under section 8.31(a)(2)(iii)(B) to establish that the action taken by him or her was reasonably believed to be in the best interests of the corporation, the inquiry will involve the elements of actual subjective belief and objective reasonableness similar to those found in section 8.31(a)(2)(ii) and section 8.30(a).

To call into question the director's objectivity or independence on the basis of a person's relationship with, or exertion of dominance over, the director, the person must have a material interest in the challenged conduct. In the typical case, analysis of another's interest would first consider the materiality of the transaction or conduct at issue—in most cases, any transaction or other action involving the attention of the board of directors or a board committee will cross the materiality threshold, but not always—and would then consider the materiality of that person's interest in the matter. The possibility that a director's judgment would be adversely affected by another's interest in a transaction or conduct that is not material, or another's immaterial interest in a transaction or conduct, is sufficiently remote that it should not be made subject to judicial review.

In situations where there may be a lack of objectivity, domination, a conflict of interest or divided loyalty, or even where there may be grounds for the issue to be raised, the better course to follow where board or committee action is required is usually for the director to disclose the facts and circumstances posing the possible issue, and then to withdraw from the meeting (or, in the alternative, to abstain from the deliberations and voting). The board members free of any possible taint may then take appropriate action as contemplated by section 8.30 (or section 8.61 if applicable). If this course is followed, the director's conduct respecting the matter in question should be beyond challenge.

E. SECTION 8.31(A)(2)(IV)—FAILURE TO DEVOTE ATTENTION

The director's role involves two fundamental components: the decision-making function and the oversight function. In contrast with the decision-making function, which generally involves action taken at a point in time, the oversight function under section 8.01(b) involves ongoing monitoring of the corporation's business and affairs over a period of time. Although the facts will be outcome-determinative, deficient conduct involving a sustained failure to exercise oversight—where found actionable—has typically been characterized by the courts in terms of abdication and continued neglect by a director to devote attention, not a brief distraction or temporary interruption. Also embedded in the oversight function is the need to inquire when suspicions are aroused. This need to inquire is not a component of ongoing oversight, and does not entail proactive vigilance, but arises under section 8.31(a)(2)(iv) when, and only when, particular facts and circumstances of material concern (*e.g.*, evidence of embezzlement at a high level or the discovery of significant inventory shortages) surface.

F. SECTION 8.31(A)(2)(V)—IMPROPER FINANCIAL BENEFIT AND OTHER BREACHES OF DUTIES

Subchapter 8F deals in detail with directors' transactional interests. Its coverage of those interests is exclusive and its safe harbor procedures for director's conflicting interest transactions (as defined)—providing shelter from legal challenges based on interest conflicts, when properly observed—will establish a director's entitlement to any financial benefit gained from the transactional event. A director's conflicting interest transaction that is not protected by the fairness standard set forth in section 8.61(b)(3), pursuant to which the conflicted director may establish the transaction to have been fair to the corporation, would often involve receipt of a financial benefit to which the director was not entitled (*i.e.*, the transaction was not "fair" to the corporation). Unauthorized use of corporate assets, such as aircraft or hotel suites, would also provide a basis for the proper challenge of a director's conduct. There can be other forms of improper financial benefit not involving a transaction with the corporation or use of its facilities, such as where a director profits from unauthorized use of proprietary information.

There is no materiality threshold that applies to a financial benefit to which a director is not properly entitled. The Act observes this principle in several places, for example, the exception to liability elimination prescribed in section 2.02(b)(4)(i) and the indemnification restriction in section 8.51(d)(2), as well as the liability standard in section 8.31(a)(2)(v).

The second clause of section 8.31(a)(2)(v) is, in part, a catchall provision that implements the intention to make section 8.31 a generally inclusive provision but, at the same time, to recognize the existence of other breaches of common-law principles that can give rise to liability for directors. As developed in the case law, these actionable breaches may include unauthorized use of corporate property or information (which as noted above, might also be characterized as receipt of an improper financial benefit), unfair competition with the corporation or the taking of a corporate opportunity. In the case of corporate opportunity, if the director is alleged to have wrongfully diverted a business opportunity as to which the corporation had a prior right, the Act provides two possible safe harbors. First, any duty to offer the business opportunity to the corporation may have been limited or eliminated pursuant to a provision in the articles of incorporation authorized by section 2.02(b)(6). Second, section 8.70(a)(1) provides a safe harbor procedure for a director who wishes to pursue or take advantage of a business opportunity, regardless of whether such opportunity would be characterized as a "corporate opportunity" under existing case law. Note that section 8.70(b) provides that the fact that a director did not employ the safe harbor procedure of section 8.70(a)(1) does not create an implication that the opportunity should have first been presented to the corporation or alter the burden of proof otherwise applicable to establish a breach of the director's duty to the corporation.

2. *Section 8.31(b)*

Whether a corporation or its shareholders have suffered harm and whether a particular director's conduct was the proximate cause of that harm may be affected by the collective nature of board action. Proper performance of the relevant duty through the action taken by the director's colleagues can overcome the consequences of his or her deficient conduct. For example, where a director's conduct can be challenged under section 8.31(a)(2)(ii)(B) by reason of having been uninformed about the decision or not reading the materials distributed before the meeting, or arriving late at the board meeting just in time for the vote but, nonetheless, voting in favor solely because the others were in favor—the favorable action by a quorum of properly informed directors would ordinarily protect the director against liability, either because there was no harm or the offending director's actions were not the proximate cause of the harm. Although the concept of "proximate cause" is a term of art that is basic to tort law, for purposes of section 8.31(b)(1), a useful approach for the concept's application would be that the challenged conduct must have been a "substantial factor in producing the harm."

3.   Section 8.31(c)

Section 8.31(c) expressly disclaims any shift of the burden of proof otherwise applicable where the question of the fairness of a transaction or other challenged conduct is at issue. This is the case whether the question of fairness arises under another section of the Act, such as section 8.61, under existing case law, under a judicial requirement in a particular instance or otherwise. Similarly, section 8.31 does not affect liability under other sections of the Act. It also does not foreclose any rights of the corporation or its shareholders under other laws, for example, rights of shareholders or the corporation under applicable federal securities laws. In addition, directors can have liability to persons other than the corporation and its shareholders, such as liability to employee benefit plan participants and beneficiaries (who may or may not be shareholders), if the directors are determined to be fiduciaries under other applicable laws, to government agencies for regulatory violations or to individuals claiming damages for injury governed by tort-law concepts (*e.g.*, libel or slander). Section 8.31 is not intended to change the standards applicable under these other laws or legal principles.

§ 8.32.   Directors' Liability for Unlawful Distributions

(a) A director who votes for or assents to a distribution in excess of what may be authorized and made pursuant to section 6.40(a) or 14.09(a) is personally liable to the corporation for the amount of the distribution that exceeds what could have been distributed without violating section 6.40(a) or 14.09(a) if the party asserting liability establishes that when taking the action the director did not comply with section 8.30.

(b) A director held liable under subsection (a) for an unlawful distribution is entitled to:

    (1) contribution from every other director who could be held liable under subsection (a) for the unlawful distribution; and

    (2) recoupment from each shareholder of the pro-rata portion of the amount of the unlawful distribution the shareholder accepted, knowing the distribution was made in violation of section 6.40(a) or 14.09(a).

(c) A proceeding to enforce:

    (1) the liability of a director under subsection (a) is barred unless it is commenced within two years after the date (i) on which the effect of the distribution was measured under section 6.40(e) or (g), (ii) as of which the violation of section 6.40(a) occurred as the consequence of disregard of a restriction in the articles of incorporation, or (iii) on which the distribution of assets to shareholders under section 14.09(a) was made; or

    (2) contribution or recoupment under subsection (b) is barred unless it is commenced within one year after the liability of the claimant has been finally adjudicated under subsection (a).

Official Comment

A director whose conduct, in voting for or assenting to a distribution, is challenged under section 8.32 will have no liability unless the complaining party establishes a breach of the relevant standards of section 8.30, for example a failure to act with the care required by section 8.30(b) or reliance on persons or information unwarranted under section 8.30(d) or (e). A shareholder (other than a director) who receives a payment not knowing of its invalidity is not subject to recoupment under subsection (b)(2). Although no attempt has been made in the Act to work out in detail the relationship between the right of recoupment from shareholders under subsection (b)(2) and the right of contribution from directors under subsection (b)(1), a court may equitably apportion the obligations and benefits arising from the application of the principles set forth in section 8.32. . . .

Subchapter D
Officers

§ 8.40.   Officers

(a) A corporation has the officers described in its bylaws or appointed by the board of directors in accordance with the bylaws.

(b) The board of directors may elect individuals to fill one or more offices of the corporation. An officer may appoint one or more officers if authorized by the bylaws or the board of directors.

(c) The bylaws or the board of directors shall assign to an officer responsibility for maintaining and authenticating the records of the corporation required to be kept under section 16.01(a).

(d) The same individual may simultaneously hold more than one office in a corporation.

Official Comment

Section 8.40 permits every corporation to designate the officers it will have. No particular officers are required.

The board of directors, as well as duly authorized officers, employees or agents, may also appoint other agents for the corporation. In addition, a board of directors has the intrinsic power to organize its own internal affairs, including designating officers of the board.

The officer who has the responsibility to maintain the minutes and authenticate the corporate records referred to in section 16.01(a) is referred to as the "secretary" of the corporation throughout the Act. See section 1.40. The person so designated has authority to bind the corporation by that officer's authentication under this section. This assignment of authority, traditionally vested in the corporate "secretary," allows third persons to rely on authenticated records without inquiry as to their truth or accuracy.

§ 8.41. Functions of Officers

Each officer has the authority and shall perform the functions set forth in the bylaws or, to the extent consistent with the bylaws, the functions prescribed by the board of directors or by direction of an officer authorized by the board of directors to prescribe the functions of other officers.

Official Comment

The methods of investing officers with formal authority in section 8.41 do not exhaust the sources of an officer's actual or apparent authority. Specific officers, particularly the chief executive officer, may have implied authority to take certain actions on behalf of a corporation merely by virtue of their positions. Officers may also be vested with apparent authority by reason of corporate conduct on which third persons reasonably rely.

In addition to express, implied, or apparent authority, a corporation is bound by unauthorized acts of officers if they are ratified by the board of directors. Generally, ratification may extend only to acts that could have been authorized as an original matter. Ratification may itself be express or implied and may in some cases serve as the basis of apparent authority.

§ 8.42. Standards of Conduct for Officers

(a) An officer, when performing in such capacity, has the duty to act:

(1) in good faith;

(2) with the care that a person in a like position would reasonably exercise under similar circumstances; and

(3) in a manner the officer reasonably believes to be in the best interests of the corporation.

(b) The duty of an officer includes the obligation:

(1) to inform the superior officer to whom, or the board of directors or the board committee to which, the officer reports of information about the affairs of the corporation known to the officer, within the scope of the officer's functions, and known to the officer to be material to such superior officer, board or committee; and

(2) to inform his or her superior officer, or another appropriate person within the corporation, or the board of directors, or a board committee, of any actual or probable material violation of law involving the corporation or material breach of duty to the corporation by an officer, employee, or agent of the corporation, that the officer believes has occurred or is likely to occur.

(c) In discharging his or her duties, an officer who does not have knowledge that makes reliance unwarranted is entitled to rely on:

(1) the performance of properly delegated responsibilities by one or more employees of the corporation whom the officer reasonably believes to be reliable and competent in performing the responsibilities delegated; or

(2) information, opinions, reports or statements, including financial statements and other financial data, prepared or presented by one or more employees of the corporation whom the officer reasonably believes to be reliable and competent in the matters presented or by legal counsel, public accountants, or other persons retained by the corporation as to matters involving skills or expertise the officer reasonably believes are matters (i) within the particular person's professional or expert competence or (ii) as to which the particular person merits confidence.

(d) An officer shall not be liable to the corporation or its shareholders for any decision to take or not to take action, or any failure to take any action, as an officer, if the duties of the office are performed in compliance with this section. Whether an officer who does not comply with this section shall have liability will depend in such instance on applicable law, including those principles of section 8.31 that have relevance.

Official Comment

Under section 8.42(a), an officer, when performing in such officer's official capacity, has to meet standards of conduct generally specified for directors under section 8.30. This section is not intended to modify, diminish or qualify the duties or standards of conduct that may be imposed upon specific officers by other law or regulation.

Common law has generally recognized a duty on the part of officers and key employees to disclose to their superiors material information relevant to the affairs of the corporation. This duty is implicit in, and embraced under, the broader standard of section 8.42(a), but section 8.42(b) sets forth this disclosure obligation explicitly. Section 8.42(b)(1) specifies that business information shall be transmitted through the officer's regular reporting channels. Section 8.42(b)(2) specifies the reporting responsibility differently with respect to actual or probable material violations of law or material breaches of duty. The use of the term "appropriate" in subsection (b)(2) accommodates any normative standard that the corporation may have prescribed for reporting potential violations of law or duty to a specified person, such as an ombudsperson, ethics officer, internal auditor, general counsel or the like, as well as situations where there is no designated person but the officer's immediate superior is not appropriate (for example, because the officer believes that individual is complicit in the unlawful activity or breach of duty).

Section 8.42(b)(1) should not be interpreted so broadly as to discourage efficient delegation of functions. It addresses the flow of information to the board of directors and to superior officers necessary to enable them to perform their decision-making and oversight functions. See the Official Comment to section 8.31. The officer's duties under subsection (b) may not be negated by agreement; however, their scope under section 8.42(b)(1) may be shaped by prescribing the scope of an officer's functional responsibilities.

With respect to the duties under section 8.42(b)(2), codes of conduct or codes of ethics may prescribe the circumstances in which and mechanisms by which officers and employees may discharge their duty to report material information to superior officers or the board of directors, or to other designated persons.

The term "material" modifying violations of law or breaches of duty in section 8.42(b)(2) denotes a qualitative as well as quantitative standard. It relates not only to the potential direct financial impact on the corporation, but also to the nature of the violation or breach. For example, an embezzlement of $10,000, or even less, would be material because of the seriousness of the offense, even though the amount involved would ordinarily not be material to the financial position or results of operations of the corporation.

The duty under section 8.42(b)(2) is triggered by an officer's subjective belief that a material violation of law or breach of duty actually or probably has occurred or is likely to occur. This duty is not triggered by objective knowledge concepts, such as whether the officer should have concluded that such misconduct was occurring. The subjectivity of the trigger under subsection (b)(2), however, does not excuse officers from their obligations under subsection (a) to act in good faith and with due care in the performance of the functions assigned to them, including oversight duties within their respective areas of responsibility. There may be occasions when the principles applicable under section 8.30(c) limiting the duty of disclosure by directors where a duty of confidentiality is overriding may also apply to officers. See the Official Comment to section 8.30(c).

An officer's ability to rely on others in meeting the standards prescribed in section 8.42 may be more limited, depending upon the circumstances of the particular case, than the measure and scope of reliance permitted a director under section 8.30, in view of the greater obligation the officer may have to be familiar with the affairs of the corporation. The proper delegation of responsibilities by an officer, separate and apart from the exercise of judgment as to the delegatee's reliability and competence, is concerned with the procedure employed. This will involve, in the usual case, sufficient communication such that the delegatee understands the scope of the assignment and, in turn, manifests to the officer a willingness and commitment to undertake its performance. The entitlement to rely upon employees assumes that a delegating officer will maintain a sufficient level of communication with the officer's subordinates to fulfill his or her supervisory responsibilities. The definition of "employee" in section 1.40 includes an officer; accordingly, section 8.42 contemplates the delegation of responsibilities to other officers as well as to non-officer employees.

Although under section 8.42(d), performance meeting that section's standards of conduct will eliminate an officer's exposure to any liability to the corporation or its shareholders, failure by an officer to meet that section's standards will not automatically result in liability. Deficient performance of duties by an officer, depending upon the facts and circumstances, will normally be dealt with through intracorporate disciplinary procedures, such as reprimand, compensation adjustment, delayed promotion, demotion or discharge. These procedures may be subject to (and limited by) the terms of an officer's employment agreement. See section 8.44.

In some cases, failure to observe relevant standards of conduct can give rise to an officer's liability to the corporation or its shareholders. A court review of challenged conduct will involve an evaluation of the particular facts and circumstances in light of applicable law. In this connection, section 8.42(d) recognizes that relevant principles of section 8.31, such as duties to deal fairly with the corporation and its shareholders and the challenger's burden of establishing proximately caused harm, should be taken into account. In addition, the business judgment rule will normally apply to decisions within an officer's discretionary authority. Liability to others can also arise from an officer's own acts or omissions (*e.g.*, violations of law or tort claims) and, in some cases, an officer with supervisory responsibilities can have risk exposure in connection with the acts or omissions of others.

The Official Comment to section 8.30 supplements this Official Comment to the extent that it can be appropriately viewed as generally applicable to officers as well as directors.

§ 8.43. Resignation and Removal of Officers

(a) An officer may resign at any time by delivering a written notice to the board of directors, or its chair, or to the appointing officer or the secretary. A resignation is effective as provided in section 1.41(i) unless the notice provides for a delayed effectiveness, including effectiveness determined upon a future event or events. If effectiveness of a resignation is stated to be delayed and the board of directors or the appointing officer accepts the delay, the board of directors or the appointing officer may fill the pending vacancy before the delayed effectiveness but the new officer may not take office until the vacancy occurs.

(b) An officer may be removed at any time with or without cause by (i) the board of directors; (ii) the appointing officer, unless the bylaws or the board of directors provide otherwise; or (iii) any other officer if authorized by the bylaws or the board of directors.

(c) In this section, "appointing officer" means the officer (including any successor to that officer) who appointed the officer resigning or being removed.

Official Comment

In part because of the unlimited power of removal under section 8.43(b), a corporation may enter into an employment agreement with the holder of an office that gives the officer rights in the event of removal or failure to be reelected or reappointed to office. This type of contract is binding on the corporation even if the articles of incorporation or bylaws provide that officers are elected for a term shorter than the period of the employment contract. Such an employment agreement does not override the removal power set forth in section 8.43(b) and may give the officer the right to damages, but not specific performance, if employment is terminated before the end of the contract term.

Section 8.43(b) provides the corporation with the flexibility to determine when, if ever, an officer will be permitted to remove another officer. To the extent that the corporation wishes to permit an officer, other than the appointing officer, to remove another officer, the bylaws or a board resolution should set forth clearly the persons having removal authority.

A person may be removed from office irrespective of contract rights or the presence or absence of "cause" in a legal sense.

§ 8.44.   Contract Rights of Officers

(a) The election or appointment of an officer does not itself create contract rights.

(b) An officer's removal does not affect the officer's contract rights, if any, with the corporation. An officer's resignation does not affect the corporation's contract rights, if any, with the officer.

Subchapter E

Indemnification and Advance for Expenses

Introductory Comment

1.   *Policy Issues Raised by Indemnification and Advance for Expenses*

Indemnification (including advance for expenses) provides financial protection by the corporation for its directors against exposure to expenses and liabilities that may be incurred by them in connection with legal proceedings based on an alleged breach of duty in their service to or on behalf of the corporation.

The concept of indemnification recognizes that there will be situations in which even though the director does not satisfy all of the elements of the standard of conduct set forth in section 8.30(a) or the requirements of some other applicable law, the corporation should nevertheless be permitted (or required) to absorb the economic costs incurred by the director in any ensuing litigation.

Subchapter 8E is an integrated treatment of indemnification and advance for expenses and strikes a balance among important public policies. It would be difficult to persuade responsible persons to serve as directors if they were compelled to bear personally the cost of vindicating the propriety of their conduct in every instance in which it might be challenged. If permitted too broadly, however, indemnification may violate equally basic tenets of public policy. For example, a director who intentionally inflicts harm on the corporation should not expect to receive assistance from the corporation for legal or other expenses and should be required to satisfy from his or her personal assets not only any adverse judgment but also expenses incurred in connection with the proceeding. A similar policy issue is raised in connection with indemnification against liabilities or sanctions imposed under state or federal civil or criminal statutes. A shift of the economic cost of these liabilities from the individual director to the corporation by way of indemnification may in some instances frustrate the public policy of those statutes.

Some of the same policy considerations apply to the indemnification of officers and, in many cases, employees and agents. The indemnification of officers, whose duties are specified in section 8.42, is dealt with separately in section 8.56. The indemnification of employees and agents, whose duties are prescribed by sources of law other than corporation law (*e.g.*, contract and agency law), is beyond the scope of this subchapter. Section 8.58(d), however, makes clear that subchapter E does not limit a corporation's power to indemnify or advance expenses to employees and agents in accordance with applicable law.

2.   *Relationship of Indemnification to Other Policies Established in the Act*

Indemnification is closely related to the standards of conduct for directors and officers established elsewhere in chapter 8. The structure of the Act is based on the assumption that if a director acts consistently with the standards of conduct described in section 8.30 or with the standards of a liability-limitation provision in the articles of incorporation (as authorized by section 2.02(b)(4)), the director will not have exposure to liability to the corporation or to shareholders and any expenses necessary to establish a defense will be borne by the corporation (under section 8.52). The converse, however, is not necessarily true. The basic standards for indemnification set forth in section 8.51 for a civil action, in the absence of an indemnification provision in the articles of incorporation (as authorized by section 2.02(b)(5)), are good faith and reasonable belief that the conduct was in or not opposed to the best interests of the corporation. In some circumstances, a director or officer may be found to have violated a statutory or common law duty and yet be able to establish eligibility for indemnification under these standards of conduct. In addition, subchapter E permits a director or officer who is held liable for violating a statutory or common law duty, but who does not meet the relevant standard of conduct, to petition a court to order indemnification under section 8.54 if the court determines that it would be fair and reasonable to do so.

§ 8.50. Subchapter Definitions

In this subchapter:

"Corporation" includes any domestic or foreign predecessor entity of a corporation in a merger.

"Director" or "officer" means an individual who is or was a director or officer, respectively, of a corporation or who, while a director or officer of the corporation, is or was serving at the corporation's request as a director, officer, manager, partner, trustee, employee, or agent of another entity or employee benefit plan. A director or officer is considered to be serving an employee benefit plan at the corporation's request if the individual's duties to the corporation also impose duties on, or otherwise involve services by, the individual to the plan or to participants in or beneficiaries of the plan. "Director" or "officer" includes, unless the context requires otherwise, the estate or personal representative of a director or officer.

"Liability" means the obligation to pay a judgment, settlement, penalty, fine (including an excise tax assessed with respect to an employee benefit plan), or expenses incurred with respect to a proceeding.

"Official capacity" means: (i) when used with respect to a director, the office of director in a corporation; and (ii) when used with respect to an officer, as contemplated in section 8.56, the office in a corporation held by the officer. "Official capacity" does not include service for any other domestic or foreign corporation or any joint venture, trust, employee benefit plan, or other entity.

"Party" means an individual who was, is, or is threatened to be made, a defendant or respondent in a proceeding.

"Proceeding" means any threatened, pending, or completed action, suit, or proceeding, whether civil, criminal, administrative, arbitrative, or investigative and whether formal or informal.

Official Comment

The definitions set forth in section 8.50 apply only to subchapter E and have no application elsewhere in the Act, except for the use of "liability" in section 2.02(b)(5). The term "qualified director," which is used in sections 8.53 and 8.55, is defined in section 1.43.

1. Corporation

Subchapter E's definition of "corporation" includes predecessor entities that have been absorbed in mergers to negate any argument that a different result might be reached under section 11.07(a), which provides for the assumption of liabilities by operation of law upon a merger. The express responsibility of successor entities for the liabilities of their predecessors under this subchapter is broader than under section 11.07(a) and may impose liability on a successor although section 11.07(a) does not. The definition of "corporation" in section 8.50 is thus an essential aspect of the protection provided by this subchapter for persons eligible for indemnification.

2. Director and Officer

A special definition of "director" and "officer" is included in subchapter E to cover individuals who are made parties to proceedings because they are or were directors or officers or, while serving as directors or officers, also serve or served at the corporation's request in another capacity for another entity. The purpose of the latter part of this definition is to give directors and officers the benefits of the protection of this subchapter while serving at the corporation's request in a responsible position for employee benefit plans, trade associations, nonprofit or charitable entities, domestic or foreign entities, or other kinds of profit or nonprofit ventures. To avoid misunderstanding, it is good practice from both the corporation's and director's or officer's viewpoint for this type of request to be evidenced by resolution, memorandum or other writing.

Even without such a formal action, the second sentence of the definition of "director" or "officer" in section 8.50 addresses the question of liabilities arising under the Employee Retirement Income Security Act of 1974 (ERISA). It makes clear that a director or officer who is serving as a fiduciary of an employee benefit plan is automatically viewed for purposes of this subchapter as having been requested by the corporation to act in that capacity. Special treatment is believed necessary because of ERISA's broad definition of "fiduciary" and the requirement that a "fiduciary" must discharge his or her duties "solely in the interest" of the participants and beneficiaries of the employee benefit plan. Decisions by a director or officer, who is serving as a fiduciary under the plan on questions regarding, for example, (i) eligibility for benefits, (ii) investment decisions, or (iii) interpretation of plan provisions respecting (a) qualifying service, (b) years of service, or (c) retroactivity, are all subject to the protections of this subchapter. See also the definition of "official capacity" in section 8.50.

In the last sentence of the definition of "director" or "officer" in section 8.50, the phrase "unless the context requires otherwise" is intended to clarify that the estate or personal representative does not have the right to participate in decisions by directors authorized in this subchapter.

3. *Liability*

"Liability" is defined for convenience to avoid repeated references to recoverable items throughout the subchapter. Even though the definition of "liability" includes amounts paid in settlement or to satisfy a judgment, indemnification against certain types of settlements and judgments is not allowed under several provisions of subchapter E. For example, indemnification in suits brought by or in the right of the corporation is limited to expenses (see section 8.51(d)(1)), unless indemnification for a settlement is ordered by a court under section 8.54(a)(3).

The definition of "liability" permits the indemnification of "expenses." The definition of "expenses" in section 1.40 limits expenses to those that are reasonable. The result is that any portion of expenses which is not reasonable should not be advanced or indemnified. In contrast, amounts paid to settle or satisfy substantive claims are not subject to a reasonableness test. Since payment of these amounts is permissive—mandatory indemnification is available under section 8.52 only where the defendant is "wholly successful"—a limitation of "reasonableness" for settlements is inappropriate.

The definition of "liability" is intended to cover every type of monetary obligation that may be imposed upon a director, including civil penalties, restitution, and the levy of excise taxes under the Internal Revenue Code pursuant to ERISA.

4. *Official Capacity*

The term "official capacity" is used in determining which of the two alternative standards of conduct set forth in section 8.51(a)(1)(ii) applies: If the action was taken in an "official capacity," the individual to be indemnified must have reasonably believed that he or she was acting in the best interests of the corporation. In contrast, if the action in question was not taken in an "official capacity," the individual need only have reasonably believed that the conduct was not opposed to the best interests of the corporation. See also the Official Comment to section 8.51(a).

5. *Party*

The definition of "party" includes present and former parties in addition to individuals currently or formerly threatened with being made a party. An individual who is only called as a witness is not a "party" within this definition, but as specifically provided in section 8.58(e) payment or reimbursement of witness expenses is not limited by this subchapter.

6. *Proceeding*

The broad definition of "proceeding" ensures that the benefits of this subchapter will be available to directors in new and unexpected, as well as traditional, types of litigation or other adversarial matters, whether civil, criminal, administrative, or investigative. It also includes arbitration and other dispute resolution proceedings, appeals and petitions to review administrative actions.

§ 8.51. Permissible Indemnification

(a) Except as otherwise provided in this section, a corporation may indemnify an individual who is a party to a proceeding because the individual is a director against liability incurred in the proceeding if:

    (1)(i) the director conducted himself or herself in good faith; and

        (ii) the director reasonably believed:

            (A) in the case of conduct in an official capacity, that his or her conduct was in the best interests of the corporation; and

            (B) in all other cases, that his or her conduct was at least not opposed to the best interests of the corporation; and

(iii) in the case of any criminal proceeding, the director had no reasonable cause to believe his or her conduct was unlawful; or

(2) the director engaged in conduct for which broader indemnification has been made permissible or obligatory under a provision of the articles of incorporation (as authorized by section 2.02(b)(5)).

(b) A director's conduct with respect to an employee benefit plan for a purpose the director reasonably believed to be in the interests of the participants in, and the beneficiaries of, the plan is conduct that satisfies the requirement of subsection (a)(1)(ii)(B).

(c) The termination of a proceeding by judgment, order, settlement, or conviction, or upon a plea of nolo contendere or its equivalent, is not, of itself, determinative that the director did not meet the relevant standard of conduct described in this section.

(d) Unless ordered by a court under section 8.54(a)(3), a corporation may not indemnify a director:

(1) in connection with a proceeding by or in the right of the corporation, except for expenses incurred in connection with the proceeding if it is determined that the director has met the relevant standard of conduct under subsection (a); or

(2) in connection with any proceeding with respect to conduct for which the director was adjudged liable on the basis of receiving a financial benefit to which he or she was not entitled, regardless of whether it involved action in the director's official capacity.

Official Comment

1. Section 8.51(a)

The standards for indemnification of directors contained in section 8.51(a) define the limits of the conduct for which discretionary indemnification is permitted under the Act, except to the extent that court-ordered indemnification is available under section 8.54(a)(3). Conduct that falls within these limits does not automatically entitle directors to indemnification, although a corporation may obligate itself to indemnify directors to the maximum extent permitted by applicable law. See section 8.58(a). Absent such an obligatory provision, section 8.52 defines much narrower circumstances in which directors are entitled as a matter of right to indemnification.

The standards of conduct in section 8.51(a) are not dependent on the type of proceeding in which the claim arises. These standards are closely related, but not identical, to the standards of conduct imposed by section 8.30 on directors when discharging the duties of a director: good faith, reasonable belief that the best interests of the corporation are being served, and appropriate care (*i.e.*, that which a person in a like position would reasonably believe appropriate under similar circumstances). As in the case of section 8.30, where the concept of good faith is also used, section 8.51 provides no definition for that term. The concept involves a subjective test, which would permit indemnification for an unwise decision or "a mistake of judgment," even though made negligently by objective standards. Section 8.51 also requires, as does section 8.30, a "reasonable" belief that conduct when acting in the director's official capacity was in the corporation's best interests. It then adds a provision, not found in section 8.30, relating to criminal proceedings that requires the director to have had no "reasonable cause" to believe that the conduct was unlawful. These both involve objective standards applicable to the director's belief concerning the effect of the conduct in question. Conduct includes both acts and omissions.

In section 8.51(a)(1)(ii)(B), the words "at least" qualify "not opposed to" and make clear that this standard is for conduct other than in an official capacity. Although this provision deals with indemnification by the corporation, a director serving another entity at the request of the corporation remains subject to the provisions of the law governing service to that other entity, including provisions dealing with conflicts of interest. Compare sections 8.60 through 8.63. Should indemnification from the requesting corporation be sought by a director for acts done while serving another entity, which acts involved breach of a duty owed to that other entity, nothing in section 8.51(a)(1)(ii)(B) would preclude the requesting corporation from considering, in assessing its own best interests, whether the fact that its director had engaged in a violation of the duty owed to the other entity was in fact "opposed to" the interests of the indemnifying corporation.

If the relevant standards are met, section 8.51 also permits indemnification in connection with a proceeding involving an alleged failure to satisfy legal standards other than the standards of conduct in section 8.30, *e.g.*, violations of antitrust, environmental or securities laws.

In addition to indemnification under section 8.51(a)(1), section 8.51(a)(2) permits indemnification under the standard of conduct set forth in a provision of the articles of incorporation adopted pursuant to section 2.02(b)(5).

Based on such a provision, section 8.51(a)(2) permits indemnification in connection with claims by third parties and, through section 8.56, applies to officers as well as directors. (This goes beyond the scope of a provision of the articles of incorporation adopted pursuant to section 2.02(b)(4), which can only limit liability of directors against claims by the corporation or its shareholders.) Section 8.51(a)(2) is subject to the prohibition of subsection (d)(1) against indemnification of settlements and judgments in derivative suits, except as ordered by a court under section 8.54(a)(3). It is also subject to the prohibition of subsection (d)(2) against indemnification for receipt of an improper financial benefit; however, this prohibition is already subsumed in the exception contained in section 2.02(b)(5)(i).

2.   *Section 8.51(b)*

As discussed in the Official Comment to the definition of "director" or "officer" in section 8.50, ERISA requires that a "fiduciary" (as defined in ERISA) discharge the fiduciary's duties "solely in the interest" of the participants in and beneficiaries of an employee benefit plan. The standard in section 8.51(b) for indemnification of a director who is serving as a trustee or fiduciary for an employee benefit plan under ERISA is arguably an exception to the more general standard that conduct not in an official corporate capacity is indemnifiable if it is "at least not opposed to" the best interests of the corporation. However, a corporation that causes a director to undertake fiduciary duties in connection with an employee benefit plan should expect the director to act in the best interests of the plan's beneficiaries or participants. Thus, subsection (b) establishes and provides a standard for indemnification that is consistent with the statutory policies embodied in ERISA. See Official Comment to section 8.50(2).

3.   *Section 8.51(c)*

Section 8.51(c) rejects the argument that indemnification is automatically improper whenever a proceeding has been concluded on a basis that does not exonerate the director claiming indemnification. However, any judicial determination of substantive liability should be taken into account in determining whether the standards of section 8.51(a) were met. By the same token, it is clear that the termination of a proceeding by settlement or plea of no contest should not of itself create a presumption either that conduct met or did not meet the relevant standard of subsection (a) since a settlement or nolo plea may be agreed to for many reasons unrelated to the merits of the claim. On the other hand, a final determination of non-liability (including one based on a liability-limitation provision adopted under section 2.02(b)(4)) or an acquittal in a criminal case automatically entitles the director to indemnification of expenses under section 8.52.

4.   *Section 8.51(d)*

Section 8.51(d) does not permit indemnification of settlements and judgments in derivative proceedings which would give rise to a circularity in which the corporation receiving payment of damages by the director in the settlement or judgment (less attorneys' fees) would then immediately return the same amount to the director (including attorneys' fees) as indemnification. Thus, the corporation would be in a poorer economic position than if there had been no proceeding. Further, in many cases a director may be protected by a provision in the articles of incorporation under section 2.02(b)(4) limiting liability or because a proceeding was dismissed under section 7.44. The prohibition on indemnification of a settlement or a judgment in a derivative proceeding, however, does not extend to the related expenses incurred in the proceeding so long as the director meets the relevant standard of conduct set forth in section 8.51(a). In addition, indemnification and advance of expenses may be ordered by a court under section 8.54(a)(3) even if the relevant standard was not met.

Indemnification under section 8.51 is also prohibited if there has been an adjudication that a director received a financial benefit to which the director is not entitled, even if, for example, the director acted in a manner not opposed to the best interests of the corporation. For example, improper use of inside information for financial benefit should not be an action for which the corporation may elect to provide indemnification, even if the corporation was not thereby harmed. Given the express language of section 2.02(b)(5) establishing the limit of an indemnification provision contained in the articles of incorporation, a director found to have received an improper financial benefit would not be permitted indemnification under section 8.51(a)(2). Although it is unlikely that a director found to have received an improper financial benefit could meet the standard in section 8.51(a)(1)(ii)(B), this limitation is made explicit in section 8.51(d)(2). Section 8.54(a)(3) permits a director found liable in a proceeding referred to in section 8.51(d)(2) to petition a court for a judicial determination of entitlement to indemnification for expenses. The language of section 8.51(d)(2) parallels sections 2.02(b)(4)(i) and 2.02(b)(5)(i), and thus, the same standards should be used in interpreting the application of all three provisions. Although a settlement may create an obligation to pay money, it should not be construed for purposes of this subchapter as an adjudication of liability.

§ 8.52. Mandatory Indemnification

A corporation shall indemnify a director who was wholly successful, on the merits or otherwise, in the defense of any proceeding to which the director was a party because he or she was a director of the corporation against expenses incurred by the director in connection with the proceeding.

Official Comment

Section 8.52 creates a right of indemnification in favor of the director who meets its requirements. Enforcement of this right by judicial proceeding is specifically contemplated by section 8.54(a)(1). Section 8.54(b) gives the director a right to recover expenses incurred in enforcing the director's right to indemnification under section 8.52.

The basic standard for mandatory indemnification is that the director has been "wholly successful, on the merits or otherwise," in the defense of the proceeding. A defendant is "wholly successful" only if the entire proceeding is disposed of on a basis which does not involve a finding of liability. A director who is precluded from mandatory indemnification by this requirement may still be entitled to permissible indemnification under section 8.51(a) or court-ordered indemnification under section 8.54(a)(3).

Although the standard "on the merits or otherwise" may result in an occasional defendant becoming entitled to indemnification because of procedural defenses not related to the merits, *e.g.*, the statute of limitations or disqualification of the plaintiff, it is unreasonable to require a defendant with a valid procedural defense to undergo a possibly prolonged and expensive trial on the merits to establish eligibility for mandatory indemnification.

§ 8.53. Advance for Expenses

(a) A corporation may, before final disposition of a proceeding, advance funds to pay for or reimburse expenses incurred in connection with the proceeding by an individual who is a party to the proceeding because that individual is a director if the director delivers to the corporation a signed written undertaking of the director to repay any funds advanced if (i) the director is not entitled to mandatory indemnification under section 8.52 and (ii) it is ultimately determined under section 8.54 or section 8.55 that the director is not entitled to indemnification.

(b) The undertaking required by subsection (a) must be an unlimited general obligation of the director but need not be secured and may be accepted without reference to the financial ability of the director to make repayment.

(c) Authorizations under this section shall be made:

(1) by the board of directors:

(i) if there are two or more qualified directors, by a majority vote of all the qualified directors (a majority of whom shall for such purpose constitute a quorum) or by a majority of the members of a committee consisting solely of two or more qualified directors appointed by such a vote; or

(ii) if there are fewer than two qualified directors, by the vote necessary for action by the board of directors in accordance with section 8.24(c), in which authorization directors who are not qualified directors may participate; or

(2) by the shareholders, but shares owned by or voted under the control of a director who at the time is not a qualified director may not be voted on the authorization.

Official Comment

Section 8.53 authorizes, but does not require, a corporation to advance or reimburse a director's reasonable expenses, subject to the delivery of the repayment undertaking required by subsection (a) and any limitations set forth in the articles of incorporation pursuant to section 8.58(d). The repayment undertaking required by section 8.53 is also required in connection with obligatory advancement pursuant to section 8.58(a).

Section 8.53 recognizes an important difference between indemnification and an advance for expenses: indemnification is retrospective and, therefore, enables the persons determining whether to indemnify to do so on the basis of known facts, including the outcome of the proceeding. Indemnification may include reimbursement for non-advanced expenses. Advance for expenses is necessarily prospective and, in situations where advancement is not obligatory, the individuals making the decision whether to authorize expense advancement generally have fewer known facts on which to base their decision.

Section 8.53 reflects a determination that it is sound public policy to permit the corporation to advance (by direct payment or by reimbursement) the defense expenses of a director so long as the director agrees to repay any amounts advanced if it is ultimately determined that the director is not entitled to indemnification. This policy is based upon the view that a person who serves an entity in a representative capacity should not be required to finance his or her own defense of actions taken in that capacity. Moreover, adequate legal representation often involves substantial expenses during the course of the proceeding and many individuals are willing to serve as directors only if they have the assurance that the corporation will advance these expenses. Accordingly, many corporations enter into contractual obligations (*e.g.*, by a provision in the articles of incorporation or bylaws or by individual agreements) to advance expenses for directors. See section 8.58(a).

A single written undertaking by the director pursuant to section 8.53(a) may cover all funds advanced from time to time in connection with a proceeding. The theory underlying section 8.53(b) is that wealthy directors should not be favored over directors whose financial resources are modest. The undertaking must be made by the director and not by a third party. If the director or the corporation wishes some third party to be responsible for the director's obligation in this regard, either is free to make those arrangements separately with the third party.

If advancement is not obligatory, the standards of section 8.30 should, in general, govern the decision of directors acting on a request for advancement. In making such a decision, the directors may consider any matters they deem appropriate and may condition the advance of expenses on compliance with any requirements they believe are appropriate, including, for example, an affirmation of a requesting director's good faith belief that he or she is entitled to indemnification under section 8.51.

A corporation may obligate itself pursuant to section 8.58(a) to advance for expenses under section 8.53 by means of a provision set forth in the articles of incorporation or bylaws, by a resolution of its board of directors or shareholders, or by an agreement. Unless provided otherwise, section 8.58(a) deems a general obligatory provision requiring indemnification to the fullest extent permitted by law to include advance for expenses to the fullest extent permitted by law, even if not specifically mentioned, subject to providing the required repayment undertaking. No other procedures are required or contemplated although obligatory arrangements may include notice and any other requirements that the directors believe are appropriate.

If advancement is not obligatory, the decision to advance expenses is required to be made only one time with respect to each proceeding rather than each time a request for payment of expenses is received by the corporation. However, the directors are free to reconsider the decision at any time (*e.g.*, upon a change in the financial ability of the corporation to pay the amounts in question). The decision as to the reasonableness of any expenses may be made by any officer or agent of the corporation duly authorized to do so.

The procedures set forth in section 8.53(c) for authorizing an advance for expenses parallel the procedures set forth in section 8.55(b) for selecting the person or persons to make the determination that indemnification is permissible. If the advance for expenses is not authorized by the shareholders under section 8.53(c)(2), the applicable procedure specified in subsection (c)(1) must be used.

Under subsection (c)(1)(ii), which is available only if subsection (c)(1)(i) is not available, the action of the board of directors must be taken in accordance with section 8.20 or section 8.21, as the case may be, and directors who are not qualified directors may participate in the vote. Allowing directors who at the time are not qualified directors to participate in the authorization decision, if there is no or only one qualified director, is based on the concept that, if there are not at least two qualified directors, then it is preferable to return the power to make the decision to the full board (even though it includes non-qualified directors) than to leave it with one qualified director.

Illustration 1: The board consists of 15 directors, four of whom are non-qualified directors. Of the 11 qualified directors, nine are present at the meeting at which the authorization is to be made (or the committee is to be appointed). Under subsection (c)(1)(i), a quorum is present and at least six of the nine qualified directors present at the board meeting must authorize any advance for expenses because six is an absolute majority of the 11 qualified directors. Alternatively, six of the nine qualified directors present at the board meeting may appoint a committee of two or more of the qualified directors (up to all 11) to decide whether to authorize the advance. Action by the committee would require a majority of the committee.

Illustration 2: The board consists of 15 directors, only one of whom is a qualified director. Subsection (c)(1)(i) is not available because the number of qualified directors is less than two. Accordingly, the decision must be made by the board under subsection (c)(1)(ii) (or, as is always permitted, by the shareholders under subsection (c)(2)).

With respect to shareholder authorizations under section 8.53(c)(2), the prohibition on voting shares owned by or voted under the control of directors who at the time are not qualified directors does not affect general rules as to the required presence of a quorum at the meeting.

The fact that there has been an advance for expenses does not determine whether a director is entitled to indemnification. A proceeding will often terminate without a judicial or other determination as to whether the director's conduct met the applicable standard of conduct in section 8.51. Nevertheless, the board of directors should make, or cause to be made, an affirmative determination of entitlement to indemnification at the conclusion of the proceeding. This decision should be made in accordance with the procedures set forth in section 8.55.

Judicial enforcement of rights granted by or pursuant to section 8.53 is specifically contemplated by section 8.54.

§ 8.54. Court-Ordered Indemnification and Advance for Expenses

(a) A director who is a party to a proceeding because he or she is a director may apply for indemnification or an advance for expenses to the court conducting the proceeding or to another court of competent jurisdiction. After receipt of an application and after giving any notice it considers necessary, the court shall:

(1) order indemnification if the court determines that the director is entitled to mandatory indemnification under section 8.52;

(2) order indemnification or advance for expenses if the court determines that the director is entitled to indemnification or advance for expenses pursuant to a provision authorized by section 8.58(a); or

(3) order indemnification or advance for expenses if the court determines, in view of all the relevant circumstances, that it is fair and reasonable (i) to indemnify the director, or (ii) to advance expenses to the director, even if, in the case of (i) or (ii), he or she has not met the relevant standard of conduct set forth in section 8.51(a), failed to comply with section 8.53 or was adjudged liable in a proceeding referred to in section 8.51(d)(1) or (d)(2), but if the director was adjudged so liable indemnification shall be limited to expenses incurred in connection with the proceeding.

(b) If the court determines that the director is entitled to indemnification under subsection (a)(1) or to indemnification or advance for expenses under subsection (a)(2), it shall also order the corporation to pay the director's expenses incurred in connection with obtaining court-ordered indemnification or advance for expenses. If the court determines that the director is entitled to indemnification or advance for expenses under subsection (a)(3), it may also order the corporation to pay the director's expenses to obtain court-ordered indemnification or advance for expenses.

Official Comment

In determining whether indemnification or expense advance would be "fair and reasonable" under section 8.54(a)(3), a court should give appropriate deference to an informed decision of a board of directors or committee made in good faith and based upon full information. Ordinarily, a court should not determine that it is "fair and reasonable" to order indemnification or expense advance where the director has not met conditions and procedures to which he or she agreed. A director seeking court-ordered indemnification or expense advance under section 8.54(a)(3) must show that there are facts peculiar to his or her situation that make it fair and reasonable to both the corporation and to the director to override an intra-corporate declination or any otherwise applicable statutory prohibition against indemnification, *e.g.*, sections 8.51(a) or (d).

Apart from the provisions of section 8.54(a)(3), there are no statutory outer limits on the court's power to order indemnification under that subsection. In an appropriate case, a court may wish to refer to the provisions of section 2.02(b)(4) establishing the outer limits of a liability-limiting provision in the articles of incorporation. It would be unusual for a court to provide indemnification going beyond the limits of section 2.02(b)(4), but the court is permitted to do so.

Among the factors a court may want to consider under section 8.54(a)(3) are the gravity of the offense, the financial impact upon the corporation, the occurrence of a change in control or, in the case of an advance for expenses, the inability of the director to finance a defense. A court may want to give special attention to certain other issues. For example, has the corporation joined in the application to the court for indemnification or an advance for expenses? This factor may be particularly important where under section 8.51(d) indemnification is not permitted for an amount paid in settlement of a proceeding brought by or in the right of the corporation. Also, in a case where indemnification would have been available under section 8.51(a)(2) if the corporation had adopted a provision authorized by section 2.02(b)(5), was the decision to adopt such a provision presented to and rejected by the shareholders and, if not, would exculpation of the director's conduct have resulted under a section 2.02(b)(4) provision? Additionally, in connection with considering indemnification for expenses under section 8.51(d)(2) in a proceeding in which a director was adjudged liable for receiving a financial benefit to which he or she was not entitled, was the financial benefit insubstantial—particularly in relation to the other aspects of the transaction involved—and what was the degree of the director's involvement in the transaction and the corporate decision to participate?

Under section 8.54(b), if a director successfully sues to enforce the right to indemnification under subsection (a)(1) or to indemnification or advance for expenses under subsection (a)(2), the court is required to order the corporation to pay the director's expenses in the enforcement proceeding. However, if a director successfully sues for indemnification or expense advancement under subsection (a)(3), the court may (but is not required to) order the corporation to pay those expenses. The basis for the distinction is that the corporation breached its obligation in the first two cases but not in the third.

Application for indemnification under section 8.54 may be made either to the court in which the proceeding was heard or to another court of appropriate jurisdiction. For example, a defendant in a criminal proceeding who has been convicted but believes that indemnification would be proper could apply either to the court which heard the criminal proceeding or bring an action against the corporation in another forum.

A decision by the board of directors not to oppose a request for indemnification is governed by the general standards of conduct of section 8.30. Even if the corporation does not oppose the request, the court must satisfy itself that the person seeking indemnification is entitled to or otherwise deserving of receiving it under section 8.54.

As provided in section 8.58(d), a corporation may limit the rights of a director under section 8.54 by a provision in the articles of incorporation. In the absence of such a provision, the court has general power to exercise the authority granted under this section.

§ 8.55.   Determination and Authorization of Indemnification

(a) A corporation may not indemnify a director under section 8.51 unless authorized for a specific proceeding after a determination has been made that indemnification is permissible because the director has met the relevant standard of conduct set forth in section 8.51.

(b) The determination shall be made:

(1) if there are two or more qualified directors, by the board of directors by a majority vote of all the qualified directors (a majority of whom shall for such purpose constitute a quorum), or by a majority of the members of a committee of two or more qualified directors appointed by such a vote;

(2) by special legal counsel:

(i) selected in the manner prescribed in subsection (b)(1); or

(ii) if there are fewer than two qualified directors, selected by the board of directors (in which selection directors who are not qualified directors may participate); or

(3) by the shareholders, but shares owned by or voted under the control of a director who at the time is not a qualified director may not be voted on the determination.

(c) Authorization of indemnification shall be made in the same manner as the determination that indemnification is permissible except that if there are fewer than two qualified directors, or if the determination is made by special legal counsel, authorization of indemnification shall be made by those entitled to select special legal counsel under subsection (b)(2)(ii).

Official Comment

Section 8.55 distinguishes between a "determination" that indemnification is permissible and an "authorization" of indemnification. A "determination" involves a decision by individuals or groups described in section 8.55(b) whether, under the circumstances, the person seeking indemnification has met the relevant standard of conduct under section 8.51 and is therefore eligible for indemnification. After a favorable determination has been made, the corporation must decide whether to authorize indemnification except to the extent that an obligatory provision under section 8.58(a) is applicable. Although special legal counsel may make the determination of eligibility for indemnification, counsel may not authorize the indemnification. A pre-existing obligation under section 8.58(a) to indemnify if the director is eligible for indemnification dispenses with the second-step decision to authorize indemnification.

Section 8.55(b) establishes procedures for selecting the person or persons who will make the determination of permissibility of indemnification. The committee of qualified directors referred to in subsection (b)(1) may include a committee to which has been delegated the power to determine whether to indemnify a director so long as the appointment and composition of the committee members comply with subsection (b)(1). In selecting special legal counsel under subsection (b)(2), directors who are parties to the proceeding may participate in the decision if there are insufficient qualified directors to satisfy subsection (b)(1). Directors who are not eligible to act as qualified directors may also participate in the decision to authorize indemnification on the basis of a favorable determination if necessary to permit action by the board of directors. The authorization of indemnification is the decision that results in payment of any amounts to be indemnified. This limited participation of non-qualified directors in the authorization decision is justified by the principle of necessity.

Under section 8.55(b)(*l*), the vote required when the qualified directors act as a group is an absolute majority of their number. A majority of the qualified directors constitutes a quorum for board action for this purpose. If there are not at least two qualified directors, then the determination of entitlement to indemnification must be made by special legal counsel or by the shareholders.

The phrase "special legal counsel" is not defined in the Act, and it is important that the process be sufficiently flexible to permit selection of counsel in light of the particular circumstances. In many instances, however, it may be important that "special legal counsel" be counsel having no prior professional relationship with those seeking indemnification, be retained for the specific purpose, and not be or have been either inside counsel or regular outside counsel to the corporation. Among other factors that may be considered are whether special legal counsel has any familial, financial or other relationship with any of those seeking indemnification that would, in the circumstances, reasonably be expected to exert an influence on counsel in making the determination.

In determinations of eligibility for indemnification by shareholders under section 8.55(b)(3), shares owned by or voted under the control of directors who at the time are not qualified directors may not be voted on the determination. This does not affect general rules as to the required presence of a quorum at the meeting in order for the determination to be made.

Section 8.55 is subject to section 8.58(a), which authorizes an arrangement obligating the corporation in advance to provide indemnification or to advance expenses. Although such an arrangement may effectively provide an authorization of indemnification, the determination requirements of sections 8.55(a) and (b) must still be satisfied.

§ 8.56. Indemnification of Officers

(a) A corporation may indemnify and advance expenses under this subchapter to an officer who is a party to a proceeding because he or she is an officer

    (1) to the same extent as a director; and

    (2) if he or she is an officer but not a director, to such further extent as may be provided by the articles of incorporation or the bylaws, or by a resolution adopted or a contract approved by the board of directors or shareholders, except for

        (i) liability in connection with a proceeding by or in the right of the corporation other than for expenses incurred in connection with the proceeding, or

        (ii) liability arising out of conduct that constitutes

            (A) receipt by the officer of a financial benefit to which he or she is not entitled,

(B) an intentional infliction of harm on the corporation or the shareholders, or

(C) an intentional violation of criminal law.

(b) Subsection (a)(2) shall apply to an officer who is also a director if he or she is made a party to the proceeding based on an act or omission solely as an officer.

(c) An officer who is not a director is entitled to mandatory indemnification under section 8.52, and may apply to a court under section 8.54 for indemnification or an advance for expenses, in each case to the same extent to which a director may be entitled to indemnification or advance for expenses under those sections.

Official Comment

Section 8.56 correlates the general legal principles relating to the indemnification of officers of the corporation with the limitations on indemnification in subchapter E. This correlation may be summarized in general terms as follows.

- An officer of a corporation who is *not* a director may be indemnified by the corporation on a discretionary basis to the same extent as though he or she were a director, and, in addition, may have additional indemnification rights apart from subchapter E, subject to the limits set forth in section 8.56(a)(2).

- An officer who is *also* a director is entitled to the indemnification rights of a director, and if the conduct that is the subject of the proceeding was solely in his or her capacity as an officer, also to any of the rights of an officer who is not a director. See preceding bullet.

- An *officer* who is not a director has the right of mandatory indemnification granted to directors under section 8.52 and the right to apply for court-ordered indemnification under section 8.54. See section 8.56(c).

Section 8.56 does not deal with indemnification of employees and agents because the concerns of self-dealing that arise when directors provide for their own indemnification and expense advance (and sometimes for senior executive officers) are not present when directors (or officers) provide for indemnification and expense advance for employees and agents who are not directors or officers.

Although subchapter E is silent with respect to such employees and agents, they may be indemnified using broad grants of powers to corporations under section 3.02, including powers to make contracts, appoint and fix the compensation of employees and agents and to make payments furthering the business and affairs of the corporation. Many corporations use these powers to provide for employees and agents in the same provisions in the articles, bylaws or otherwise in which they provide for expense advance and indemnification for directors and officers. Indemnification may also be provided to protect employees or agents from liabilities incurred while serving at a corporation's request as a director, officer, partner, trustee, or agent of another commercial, charitable, or nonprofit venture.

Although employees and agents are not covered by subchapter E, the principles and procedures set forth in the subchapter for indemnification and advance for expenses for directors and officers may be helpful to counsel and courts in dealing with indemnification and expense advance for employees and agents.

Careful consideration should be given to extending mandatory maximum indemnification and expense advance to employees and agents. The same considerations that may favor mandatory maximum indemnification for directors and officers—*e.g.*, encouraging qualified individuals to serve—may not be present in the cases of employees and agents. Many corporations may prefer to retain the discretion to decide, on a case-by-case basis, whether to indemnify and advance expenses to employees and agents (and perhaps even officers, especially nonexecutive officers) rather than binding themselves in advance to do so.

1.   *Officers Who Are Not Directors*

Although section 8.56 does not prescribe the standards governing the rights of officers to indemnification, subsection (a) does set outer limits beyond which the corporation may not indemnify. These limits for officers are substantially the same as the outer limits on the corporation's power to indemnify directors. Since officers are held to substantially the same standards of conduct as directors (see section 8.42), there does not appear to be any reasoned basis for granting officers greater indemnification rights as a substantive matter. Procedurally, however, there is an important difference. To permit greater flexibility, officers may be indemnified (within the above-mentioned limits) with respect to conduct that does not meet the standards set by section 8.51(a)(1) simply by authorization of the board of directors, whereas directors' indemnification can reach beyond those standards, as contemplated by section 8.51(a)(2), only with a provision included in the articles of incorporation pursuant to section 2.02(b)(5). This procedural difference reflects the reduced risk of self-dealing as to officers.

The broad authority in section 8.56(a)(2) to grant indemnification may be limited by appropriate provisions in the articles of incorporation. See section 8.58(c).

2.   Officers Who Are Also Directors

Section 8.56(b) provides, in effect, that an officer of the corporation who is also a director is subject to the same standards of indemnification as other directors and cannot avail himself or herself of the provisions of subsection (a) unless the act or omission that is the subject of the proceeding was committed solely in the capacity as an officer. Thus, a vice president for sales who is also a director and whose actions failed to meet section 8.51(a) standards could be indemnified provided that the conduct was within the limits of section 8.56(a)(2) and involved only his or her officer capacity.

This more flexible approach for situations where the individual is not acting as a director seems appropriate as a matter of fairness. There are many instances where officers who also serve as directors assume responsibilities and take actions in their non-director capacities for which indemnification may be appropriate.

For a director-officer to be indemnified under section 8.51 for conduct in the capacity as a director when he or she has not satisfied the standards of section 8.51(a), a provision in the articles of incorporation under section 2.02(b)(5) is required. If such a provision is included in the articles, the standards for indemnification are those specified in the articles of incorporation, subject to the limitations in section 2.02(b)(5). For a director-officer to be indemnified for conduct solely in the capacity as an officer, even though the director-officer has not satisfied the standards of section 8.56(a), only a bylaw or a resolution of the board of directors authorizing such indemnification is required, rather than a provision in the articles of incorporation. If such a bylaw or resolution is adopted, the standards for indemnification are those specified in section 8.56(a)(2). However, when a director-officer seeks indemnification or expense advance under sections 8.56(b) and (a)(2) on the basis of having acted solely in the capacity as an officer, indemnification or expense advance must be approved through the same procedures as set forth in section 8.55 or 8.53(c), as the case may be, for approval of indemnification or expense advance for a director when acting in the capacity of a director.

§ 8.57.   Insurance

A corporation may purchase and maintain insurance on behalf of an individual who is a director or officer of the corporation, or who, while a director or officer of the corporation, serves at the corporation's request as a director, officer, partner, trustee, employee, or agent of another domestic or foreign corporation or a joint venture, trust, employee benefit plan, or other entity, against liability asserted against or incurred by the individual in that capacity or arising from the individual's status as a director or officer, regardless of whether the corporation would have power to indemnify or advance expenses to the individual against the same liability under this subchapter.

Official Comment

In authorizing a corporation to purchase and maintain insurance on behalf of directors and officers, section 8.57 sets no limits on the type of insurance which a corporation may maintain or the type of persons who are covered. Insurance is not limited to claims against which a corporation is entitled to indemnify under this subchapter. Such insurance can provide protection to directors and officers in addition to the rights of indemnification created by or pursuant to subchapter E (as well as typically protecting the individual insureds against the corporation's failure to pay indemnification required or permitted by this subchapter) and can also provide a source of reimbursement for a corporation that indemnifies its directors and others for conduct covered by the insurance. On the other hand, policies typically do not cover uninsurable matters, such as actions involving dishonesty, self-dealing, bad faith, knowing violations of the securities laws, or other willful misconduct.

Although section 8.57 does not include employees and agents for the reasons stated in the Official Comment to section 8.58, the corporation has the power under section 3.02 to purchase and maintain insurance on their behalf. This power is confirmed in section 8.58(f).

§ 8.58.   Variation by Corporate Action; Application of Subchapter

(a) A corporation may, by a provision in its articles of incorporation or bylaws or in a resolution adopted or a contract approved by the board of directors or shareholders, obligate itself in advance of the act or omission giving rise to a proceeding to provide indemnification in accordance with section 8.51 or advance funds to pay for or reimburse expenses in accordance with section 8.53. Any such obligatory provision shall be deemed to satisfy the requirements for authorization referred to in section 8.53(c) and in section 8.55(c). Any such provision that obligates the corporation to provide indemnification to the fullest extent permitted by law shall be deemed to obligate the corporation to advance funds to pay for or reimburse expenses in accordance with section 8.53 to the fullest extent permitted by law, unless the provision expressly provides otherwise.

(b) A right of indemnification or to advances for expenses created by this subchapter or under subsection (a) and in effect at the time of an act or omission shall not be eliminated or impaired with respect to such act or omission by an amendment of the articles of incorporation or bylaws or a resolution of the board of directors or shareholders, adopted after the occurrence of such act or omission, unless, in the case of a right created under subsection (a), the provision creating such right and in effect at the time of such act or omission explicitly authorizes such elimination or impairment after such act or omission has occurred.

(c) Any provision pursuant to subsection (a) shall not obligate the corporation to indemnify or advance expenses to a director of a predecessor of the corporation, pertaining to conduct with respect to the predecessor, unless otherwise expressly provided. Any provision for indemnification or advance for expenses in the articles of incorporation or bylaws, or a resolution of the board of directors or shareholders of a predecessor of the corporation in a merger or in a contract to which the predecessor is a party, existing at the time the merger takes effect, shall be governed by section 11.07(a)(4).

(d) Subject to subsection (b), a corporation may, by a provision in its articles of incorporation, limit any of the rights to indemnification or advance for expenses created by or pursuant to this subchapter.

(e) This subchapter does not limit a corporation's power to pay or reimburse expenses incurred by a director or an officer in connection with appearing as a witness in a proceeding at a time when he or she is not a party.

(f) This subchapter does not limit a corporation's power to indemnify, advance expenses to or provide or maintain insurance on behalf of an employee or agent.

Official Comment

Section 8.58(a) authorizes a corporation to make obligatory the permissive provisions of subchapter E in advance of the conduct giving rise to the request for indemnification or advance for expenses. An obligatory provision satisfies the requirements for authorization in sections 8.53(c) and 8.55(c), but the requirements for determination of eligibility for indemnification in subsections (a) and (b) of those sections must still be met.

If a corporation provides for obligatory indemnification and not for obligatory advance for expenses, the provision should be reviewed to ensure that it properly reflects the intent in view of the third sentence of section 8.58(a). Also, a corporation should consider whether obligatory expense advance is intended for direct suits by the corporation as well as for derivative suits by shareholders in the right of the corporation. In the former case, assuming compliance with sections 8.53(a) and (b), the corporation could be required to fund the defense of a defendant director even where the board of directors has already concluded that the director has engaged in significant wrongdoing. See Official Comment to section 8.53.

Although section 8.58(d) permits a corporation to limit the right of the corporation to indemnify or advance expenses by a provision in its articles of incorporation, as provided in section 10.09, no such limitation will affect rights in existence when the provision becomes effective pursuant to section 1.23.

Subchapter E does not regulate the power of the corporation to indemnify or advance expenses to employees and agents. That subject is governed by the law of agency and related principles and frequently by contractual arrangements between the corporation and the employee or agent. Section 8.58(f) makes clear that, although indemnification, advance for expenses, and insurance for employees and agents are beyond the scope of subchapter E, the elaboration in subchapter E of standards and procedures for indemnification, expense advance, and insurance for directors and officers is not in any way intended to cast doubt on the power of the corporation to indemnify or advance expenses to or purchase and maintain insurance for employees and agents under section 3.02 or otherwise.

§ 8.59. Exclusivity of Subchapter

A corporation may provide indemnification or advance expenses to a director or an officer only as permitted by this subchapter.

Official Comment

Subchapter E is the exclusive source for the power of a corporation to indemnify or advance expenses to a director or an officer.

Section 8.59 does not preclude provisions in the articles of incorporation, the bylaws, resolutions, or contracts designed to provide procedural machinery in addition to (but not inconsistent with) that provided by subchapter E. For example, a corporation may properly obligate the board of directors to consider and act expeditiously on an application for indemnification or advance for expenses or to cooperate in the procedural steps required to obtain a judicial determination under section 8.54.

Subchapter F

Director's Conflicting Interest Transactions

Introductory Comment

1. *Overview.*

There are four basic elements in subchapter F.

First, subchapter F defines, with bright-line rules, the transactions that are to be treated as director's conflicting interest transactions.

Second, subchapter F provides that a director's transaction that is not within the statutory definition of a director's conflicting interest transaction is not subject to judicial review for fairness on the ground that it involved a conflict of interest (although circumstances that fall outside the statutory definition may afford the basis for a legal attack on the transaction on some other ground), even if the transaction involves some sort of conflict lying outside the statutory definition, such as a remote familial relationship.

Third, subchapter F provides that if a director's conflicting interest transaction is properly approved by disinterested (or "qualified") directors or shareholders, the transaction is insulated from judicial review for fairness (although, again, it might be open to attack on some basis other than the conflict).

Fourth, subchapter F also provides that if a director's conflicting interest transaction is properly approved by disinterested (or "qualified") directors or shareholders, the conflicted director may not be subject to an award of damages or other sanctions (although the director could be subject to claims on some basis other than the conflict).

Bright-line provisions of any kind represent a trade-off between the benefits of certainty and the danger that some transactions or conduct that fall outside the area circumscribed by the bright-lines may be so similar to the transactions and conduct that fall within the area that different treatment may seem anomalous. Subchapter F reflects the judgment that in corporate matters, where planning is critical, the clear and important efficiency gains that result from certainty through defining director's conflicting interest transactions exceed any potential and uncertain efficiency losses that might follow from excluding other director's transactions from judicial review for fairness on conflict-of-interest grounds.

2. *Scope of Subchapter F*

Subchapter F addresses legal challenges based on director conflicts of interest only. Subchapter F does not undertake to define, regulate, or provide any form of procedure regarding other possible claims. For example, subchapter F does not address a claim that a controlling shareholder has violated a duty owed to the corporation or minority shareholders. So, although transactions between a corporation and a parent corporation or other controlling shareholder who owns less than all of its shares may give rise to the possibility of abuse of power by the controlling shareholder, subchapter F does not address proceedings brought on that basis because section 8.61 concerns only proceedings that are brought on the ground that a "director has an interest respecting the transaction."

Subchapter F applies only when there is a "transaction" by or with the corporation. For purposes of subchapter F, "transaction" generally connotes negotiations or consensual arrangements between the corporation and another party or parties that concern their respective and differing economic rights or interests—not a unilateral action by the corporation or a director. Whether safe harbor procedures of some kind might be available to the director and the corporation with respect to non-transactional matters is discussed in numbered part 3 of this Introductory Comment.

Subchapter F does not preclude the assertion of defenses, such as statute of limitations or failure of a condition precedent, that are based on grounds other than the defenses set forth in this subchapter.

The voting procedures and conduct standards prescribed in subchapter F deal solely with the complicating element presented by the director's conflicting interest in a transaction. A transaction that receives favorable directors' or shareholders' action complying with subchapter F may still fail to satisfy a different quorum requirement or to achieve a different vote than may be needed for substantive approval of the transaction under other applicable statutory provisions or under the articles of incorporation, and vice versa. (Under the Act, a corporation may set higher voting requirements and different quorum requirements in the articles of incorporation. See sections 2.02(b)(2) and 7.27). In addition, subchapter F does not shield misbehavior by a director or other person that is actionable under other provisions of the Act, such as section 8.31, or under other legal rules, regardless of whether the misbehavior is incident to a transaction with the corporation and regardless of whether the rule is one of corporate law.

Finally, certain corporate transactions or arrangements in which directors inherently have a special personal interest are of a unique character and are regulated by special procedural provisions of the Act. See sections 8.51 and 8.52 dealing with indemnification arrangements, and section 7.44 dealing with termination of derivative proceedings by board action. Any corporate transactions or arrangements affecting directors that are governed by such regulatory sections of the Act are not governed by subchapter F.

3. *Nontransactional Situations Involving Interest Conflicts*

A. CORPORATE OR BUSINESS OPPORTUNITY

Subchapter F does not apply by its terms to corporate or business opportunities because no transaction between the corporation and the director is involved in the taking of an opportunity. However, subchapter 8G provides, in effect, that the safe harbor procedures of section 8.62 or 8.63 may be employed, at the interested director's election, to protect the taking of a business opportunity that might be challenged under the corporate opportunity doctrine. Also, section 2.02(b)(6) permits a corporation to include in its articles of incorporation a provision that limits or eliminates the duty to present a business opportunity to the corporation.

B. OTHER SITUATIONS

Many other kinds of situations can give rise to divergent economic interests between a director and the corporation. For example, a director's personal financial interests can be affected by a nontransactional policy decision of the board of directors, such as where it decides to establish a divisional headquarters in the director's small hometown. In other situations, simple inaction by a board might work to a director's personal advantage, or a flow of ongoing business relationships between a director and the corporation may, without centering upon any discrete "transaction," raise questions of possible favoritism, unfair dealing, or undue influence. If a director decides to engage in business activity that directly competes with the corporation's own business, the economic interest in that competing activity ordinarily will conflict with the best interests of the corporation and put in issue the breach of the director's duties to the corporation. Basic conflicts and improprieties can also arise out of a director's personal appropriation of corporate assets or improper use of corporate proprietary or inside information.

The circumstances in which such nontransactional conflict situations should be brought to the board of directors or shareholders for clearance, and the legal effect, if any, of such clearance, are matters for development under the common law and lie outside the ambit of subchapter F. Although these nontransactional situations are not covered by the provisions of subchapter F, a court may well recognize that the subchapter F procedures provide a useful analogy for dealing with such situations.

* * * * *

Note on Terms in Official Comments

In the Official Comments to subchapter F, the director who has a conflicting interest is for convenience referred to as "the director" or "D," and the corporation of which he or she is a director is referred to as "the corporation" or "X Co." A subsidiary of the corporation is referred to as "S Co." Another corporation dealing with X Co. is referred to as "Y Co."

§ 8.60. Subchapter Definitions

In this subchapter:

"Control" (including the term "controlled by") means (i) having the power, directly or indirectly, to elect or remove a majority of the members of the board of directors or other governing body of an entity, whether through the ownership of voting shares or interests, by contract, or otherwise, or (ii) being subject to a majority of the risk of loss from the entity's activities or entitled to receive a majority of the entity's residual returns.

"Director's conflicting interest transaction" means a transaction effected or proposed to be effected by the corporation (or by an entity controlled by the corporation)

> (i) to which, at the relevant time, the director is a party;

> (ii) respecting which, at the relevant time, the director had knowledge and a material financial interest known to the director; or

> (iii) respecting which, at the relevant time, the director knew that a related person was a party or had a material financial interest.

"Fair to the corporation" means, for purposes of section 8.61(b)(3), that the transaction as a whole was beneficial to the corporation, taking into appropriate account whether it was (i) fair in terms of the director's dealings with the corporation, and (ii) comparable to what might have been obtainable in an arm's length transaction, given the consideration paid or received by the corporation.

"Material financial interest" means a financial interest in a transaction that would reasonably be expected to impair the objectivity of the director's judgment when participating in action on the authorization of the transaction.

"Related person" means:

> (i) the individual's spouse;

> (ii) a child, stepchild, grandchild, parent, step parent, grandparent, sibling, step sibling, half sibling, aunt, uncle, niece or nephew (or spouse of any such person) of the individual or of the individual's spouse;

> (iii) a natural person living in the same home as the individual;

> (iv) an entity (other than the corporation or an entity controlled by the corporation) controlled by the individual or any person specified above in this definition;

> (v) a domestic or foreign (A) business or nonprofit corporation (other than the corporation or an entity controlled by the corporation) of which the individual is a director, (B) unincorporated entity of which the individual is a general partner or a member of the governing body, or (C) individual, trust or estate for whom or of which the individual is a trustee, guardian, personal representative or like fiduciary; or

> (vi) a person that is, or an entity that is controlled by, an employer of the individual.

"Relevant time" means (i) the time at which directors' action respecting the transaction is taken in compliance with section 8.62, or (ii) if the transaction is not brought before the board of directors (or a committee) for action under section 8.62, at the time the corporation (or an entity controlled by the corporation) becomes legally obligated to consummate the transaction.

"Required disclosure" means disclosure of (i) the existence and nature of the director's conflicting interest, and (ii) all facts known to the director respecting the subject matter of the transaction that a director free of such conflicting interest would reasonably believe to be material in deciding whether to proceed with the transaction.

Official Comment

The definitions set forth in section 8.60 apply only to subchapter F and section 2.02(b)(6) and, where relevant to subchapter G. They have no application elsewhere in the Act. (For the meaning and use of certain terms used below, such as "D," "X Co." and "Y Co.," see the Note on Terms at the end of the Introductory Comment of subchapter F.)

1. Director's Conflicting Interest Transaction

The definition of "director's conflicting interest transaction" in section 8.60 is the core concept underlying subchapter F. The definition operates preclusively in that, as used in section 8.61, it denies the power of a court to invalidate transactions or otherwise to remedy conduct on the ground that the director has a conflict of interest if it falls outside the statutory definition of "director's conflicting interest transaction."

A. TRANSACTION

For purposes of subchapter F, "transaction" requires a bilateral (or multilateral) arrangement to which the corporation or an entity controlled by the corporation is a party. Subchapter F does not apply to transactions to which no such entity is a party. For example, a purchase or sale by the director of the corporation's shares on the open market or from or to a third party is not a "director's conflicting interest transaction" within the meaning of subchapter F.

B. PARTY TO THE TRANSACTION—THE CORPORATION OR A CONTROLLED ENTITY

In the usual case, the transaction would be effected by X Co. Assume, however, that X Co. controls the vote for directors of S Co. D wishes to sell a building D owns to X Co. and X Co. is willing to buy it. As a business matter, it makes no difference to X Co. whether it takes the title directly or indirectly through its subsidiary S Co. or some other entity that X Co. controls. The applicability of subchapter F does not depend upon that formal distinction, because the subchapter includes within its operative framework transactions by entities controlled by X Co. Thus, subchapter F would apply to a sale of the building by D to S Co.

C. PARTY TO THE TRANSACTION—THE DIRECTOR OR A RELATED PERSON

D can have a conflicting interest in only two ways.

First, a conflicting interest can arise under either clause (i) or (ii) of the definition of "director's conflicting interest transaction." This will be the case if, under clause (i), the transaction is between D and X Co. A conflicting interest also will arise under clause (ii) if D is not a party to the transaction, but knows about it and knows that he or she has a material financial interest in it. The personal economic stake of the director must be in the transaction itself—that is, the director's gain must flow directly from the transaction. A remote gain (for example, a future reduction in tax rates in the local community) is not enough to give rise to a conflicting interest under clause (ii) of the definition.

Second, a conflicting interest for D can arise under clause (iii) of the definition from the involvement in the transaction of a "related person" of D that is either a party to the transaction or has a "material financial interest" in it. "Related person" is defined in section 8.60.

Circumstances may arise where a director could have a conflicting interest under more than one clause of the definition. For example, if Y Co. is a party to or interested in the transaction with X Co. and Y Co. is a related person of D, the matter would fall under clause (iii), but D also may have a conflicting interest under clause (ii) if D's economic interest in Y Co. is sufficiently material and if the importance of the transaction to Y Co. is sufficiently material.

A director may have relationships and connections to persons and institutions that are not specified in clause (iii) of the definition. Such relationships and connections fall outside subchapter F because the categories of persons described in clause (iii) constitute the exclusive universe for purposes of subchapter F. For example, in a challenged transaction between X Co. and Y Co., suppose the court confronts the argument that D also is a major creditor of Y Co. and that creditor status in Y Co. gives D a conflicting interest. The court should rule that D's creditor status in Y Co. does not fit any category of the definition; and therefore, the conflict of interest claim must be rejected by reason of section 8.61(a). The result would be different if Y Co.'s debt to D were of such economic significance to D that it would either fall under clause (ii) of the definition or, if it placed D in control of Y Co., it would fall under clause (iii) (because Y Co. is a related person of D under clause (iv) of the definition). To explore the example further, if D is also a shareholder of Y Co., but D does not have a material financial interest in the transaction and does not control Y Co., no director's conflicting interest transaction arises and the transaction cannot be challenged on conflict of interest grounds. To avoid any appearance of impropriety, D, nonetheless, could consider recusal from the other directors' deliberations and voting on the transaction between X Co. and Y Co.

Any director's interest in a transaction that meets the criteria of the definition renders the transaction a "director's conflicting interest transaction." If the director's interest satisfies those criteria, subchapter F draws no distinction between a director's interest that clashes with the interests of the corporation and a director's interest that coincides with, or is parallel to, or even furthers the interests of the corporation.

Routine business transactions frequently occur between companies with overlapping directors. If X Co. and Y Co. have routine, frequent business dealings with terms dictated by competitive market forces, then even if a director of X Co. has a relevant relationship with Y Co., the transactions would almost always be defensible, regardless of approval by disinterested directors or shareholders, on the ground that they are "fair." For example, a common transaction involves a purchase of the corporation's products or services by Y Co., or perhaps by D or a related person, at prices normally charged by the corporation. In such circumstances, it usually will not be difficult for D to show that the transaction was on arms-length terms and was fair. Even a purchase by D of a product of X Co. at a usual "employee's discount," although technically assailable as a conflicting interest transaction, would customarily be viewed as a routine incident of the office of director and, thus, "fair" to the corporation.

2. Control

The definition of "control" in section 8.60 contains two independent clauses. The first clause addresses the ability to elect or remove a majority of the members of an entity's governing body. That power can arise, for example, from articles of incorporation or a shareholders' agreement. The second clause addresses economic interest in the entity and may include, among other circumstances, financial structures that do not have voting interests or a governing body in the traditional sense, such as special purpose entities.

3. Relevant Time

The definition of director's conflicting interest transaction requires that, except where he or she is a party, the director know of the transaction at the "relevant time" as defined in section 8.60. Where the director lacks such knowledge, the risk to the corporation that the director's judgment might be improperly influenced, or the risk of unfair dealing by the director, is not present. In a corporation of significant size, routine transactions in the ordinary course of business, which typically involve decision making at lower management levels, normally will not be known to the director and, if that is the case, will not meet the "knowledge" requirement of clauses (ii) or (iii) of the definition of director's conflicting interest transaction.

4. Material Financial Interest

The "interest" of a director or a related person in a transaction can be direct or indirect (*e.g.*, as an owner of an entity or a beneficiary of a trust or estate), but it must be financial for there to exist a "director's conflicting interest transaction." Thus, for example, an interest in a transaction between X Co. and a director's alma mater, or any other transaction involving X Co. and a party with which D might have emotional involvement but no financial interest, would not give rise to a director's conflicting interest transaction. Moreover, whether a financial interest is material does not turn on any assertion by the possibly conflicted director that the interest in question would not impair his or her objectivity if called upon to vote on the authorization of the transaction. Instead, assuming a court challenge asserting the materiality of the financial interest, the standard calls upon the trier of fact to determine whether the objectivity of the director would reasonably be expected to have been impaired by the financial interest when voting on the matter. Thus, the standard is objective, not subjective.

Under clause (ii) of the definition of "director's conflicting interest transaction," at the relevant time a director must have knowledge of his or her financial interest in the transaction in addition to knowing about the transaction itself. As a practical matter, a director could not be influenced by a financial interest about which that director had no knowledge. For example, the possibly conflicted director might know about X Co.'s transaction with Y Co., but might not know that his or her money manager recently established a significant position in Y Co. stock for the director's portfolio. In such circumstances, the transaction with Y Co. would not fall within clause (ii), notwithstanding the portfolio investment's significance. If the director did not know about the Y Co. portfolio investment, it could not reasonably be expected to impair the objectivity of that director's judgment.

Similarly, under clause (iii) of that definition, a director must know about his or her related person's financial interest in the transaction for the matter to give rise to a "material financial interest" as defined in section 8.60. If there is such knowledge and "interest" (*i.e.*, the financial interest could reasonably be expected to influence the director's judgment), then the matter involves a director's conflicting interest transaction.

5. Related Person

Six categories of "related person" of the director are set out in the definition of that term. These categories are specific, exclusive and preemptive.

The first three categories involve closely related family, or near-family, individuals as specified in clauses (i) through (iii). These clauses are exclusive insofar as family relationships are concerned and include adoptive relationships. The references to a "spouse" include a common law spouse. Clause (iii) covers personal, as opposed to business, relationships; for example, clause (iii) does not cover a lessee.

Regarding the subcategories of persons described in clause (v) from the perspective of X Co., certain of D's relationships with other entities and D's fiduciary relationships are always a sensitive concern, separate and apart from whether D has a financial interest in the transaction. Clause (v) reflects the policy judgment that D cannot escape D's legal obligation to act in the best interests of another person for whom D has such a relationship and, accordingly, that such a relationship (without regard to any financial interest on D's part) should cause the relevant entity to have "related person" status.

The term "employer" as used in clause (vi) is not separately defined but should be interpreted in light of the purpose of subchapter F. The relevant inquiry is whether D, because of an employment relationship with an employer who has a significant stake in the outcome of the transaction, is likely to be influenced to act in the interest of that employer rather than in the interest of X Co.

References in the foregoing to "director" or "D" include the term "officer" where relevant in section 2.02(b)(6) and section 8.70.

6. Fair to the Corporation

The term "fair" to the corporation in subchapter F has a special meaning. The transaction, viewed as a whole, must have been beneficial to the corporation.

In considering the "fairness" of the transaction, the court will be required to consider not only the market fairness of the terms of the deal—whether it is comparable to what might have been obtainable in an arm's length transaction—but also (as the board of directors would have been required to do) whether the transaction was one that was reasonably likely to yield favorable results (or reduce detrimental results). Thus, if a manufacturing company that lacks sufficient working capital allocates some of its scarce funds to purchase at a market price a sailing yacht owned by one of its directors, it will not be easy to persuade the court that the transaction was "fair" in the sense that it was reasonably made to further the business interests of the corporation. The fact that the price paid for the yacht was a "fair" market price, and that the full measure of disclosures made by the director is beyond challenge, may still not be enough to defend and uphold the transaction.

A.   CONSIDERATION AND OTHER TERMS OF THE TRANSACTION

The fairness of the consideration and other transaction terms are to be judged at the relevant time. See section 8.61(b)(3). The relevant inquiry is whether the consideration paid or received by the corporation or the benefit expected to be realized by the corporation was adequate in relation to the obligations assumed or received or other consideration provided by or to the corporation. If the issue in a transaction is the "fairness" of a price, "fair" is not to be taken to imply that there is one single "fair" price, all others being "unfair." Generally a "fair" price is any price within a range that an unrelated party might have been willing to pay or willing to accept, as the case may be, for the relevant property, asset, service or commitment, following a normal arm's-length business negotiation. The same approach applies not only to gauging the fairness of price, but also to the fairness evaluation of any other key term of the deal.

Although the "fair" criterion used to assess the consideration under section 8.61(b)(3) is also a range rather than a point, the width of that range may be narrower than would be the case in an arm's-length transaction. For example, the quality and completeness of disclosures, if any, made by the conflicted director that bear upon the consideration in question are relevant in determining whether the consideration paid or received by the corporation, although otherwise commercially reasonable, was "fair" for purposes of section 8.61(b)(3).

B.   PROCESS OF DECISION AND THE DIRECTOR'S CONDUCT

In some circumstances, the behavior of the director having the conflicting interest may affect the finding and content of "fairness." Fair dealing requires that the director make "required disclosure" at the "relevant time" (both as defined) even if the director plays no role in arranging or negotiating the terms of the transaction. One illustration of unfair dealing is the director's failure to disclose fully the director's interest or hidden defects known to the director regarding the transaction. Another illustration would be the exertion by the director of improper pressure upon the other directors or other parties that might be involved with the transaction. Whether a transaction can be successfully challenged by reason of deficient or improper conduct, notwithstanding the fairness of the economic terms, will turn on the court's evaluation of the conduct and its impact on the transaction.

7. *Required Disclosure*

An important element of subchapter F's safe harbor procedures is that those acting for the corporation be able to make an informed judgment. As an example of "required disclosure" (as defined), if D knows that the land the corporation is proposing to buy from D is sinking into an abandoned coal mine, D must disclose not only D's interest in the transaction but also that the land is subsiding. As a director of X Co., D may not invoke the "buyer beware" doctrine. On the other hand, D does not have any obligation to reveal the price that D paid for the property 10 years ago, or the fact that D inherited the property, because that information is not material to the board's evaluation of the property and its business decision whether to proceed with the transaction. Further, although material facts respecting the subject of the transaction must be disclosed, D is not required to reveal personal or subjective information that bears upon D's negotiating position (such as, for example, D's urgent need for cash, or the lowest price D would be willing to accept). This is true even though such information would be highly relevant to the corporation's decision-making in that, if the information were known to the corporation, it could enable the corporation to hold out for more favorable terms.

§ 8.61. Judicial Action

(a) A transaction effected or proposed to be effected by the corporation (or by an entity controlled by the corporation) may not be the subject of equitable relief, or give rise to an award of damages or other sanctions against a director of the corporation, in a proceeding by a shareholder or by or in the right of the corporation, on the ground that the director has an interest respecting the transaction, if it is not a director's conflicting interest transaction.

(b) A director's conflicting interest transaction may not be the subject of equitable relief, or give rise to an award of damages or other sanctions against a director of the corporation, in a proceeding by a shareholder or by or in the right of the corporation, on the ground that the director has an interest respecting the transaction, if:

(1) directors' action respecting the transaction was taken in compliance with section 8.62 at any time; or

(2) shareholders' action respecting the transaction was taken in compliance with section 8.63 at any time; or

(3) the transaction, judged according to the circumstances at the relevant time, is established to have been fair to the corporation.

Official Comment

Section 8.61 is the operational section of subchapter F, as it prescribes the judicial consequences of the other sections. In general terms:

- If the section 8.62 or 8.63 procedures are complied with, or if it is established that at the relevant time a director's conflicting interest transaction was fair to the corporation, then a director's conflicting interest transaction is immune from attack by a shareholder or the corporation on the ground of an interest of the director. However, if the transaction is vulnerable to attack on some other ground, observance of subchapter F's procedures does not make it less so.

- If a transaction is *not* a director's conflicting interest transaction as defined in section 8.60, then the transaction may *not* be enjoined, rescinded, or made the basis of other sanction on the ground of a conflict of interest of a director, regardless of whether it went through the procedures of subchapter F. In that sense, subchapter F is specifically intended to be both comprehensive and exclusive.

- If a director's conflicting interest transaction that was not at any time the subject of action taken in compliance with section 8.62 or 8.63 is challenged on grounds of the director's conflicting interest, and is not shown to be fair to the corporation, then the court may take such remedial action as it considers appropriate under the applicable law of the jurisdiction.

1. *Section 8.61(a)*

Section 8.61(a) makes clear that the bright-line definition of "director's conflicting interest transaction" is exclusive with respect to a court's review of a director's interest in a transaction. So, for example, a transaction will not constitute a director's conflicting interest transaction and, therefore, will not be subject to judicial review on the ground that a director had an interest in the transaction, where the transaction is made with a relative of a director who is not one of the relatives specified in the definition of "related person," or on the ground of an alleged interest other than a material financial interest, such as a financial interest of the director that is not material, as defined in section 8.60, or a nonfinancial interest. If, however, there is reason to believe that the fairness of a transaction involving D could be questioned, D should subject the transaction to the safe harbor procedures of subchapter F. The procedures of section 8.62 (and, to a lesser extent, section 8.63) may be used for many transactions that lie outside the definitions of section 8.60.

2.   *Section 8.61(b)*

Section 8.61(b)(1) provides a defense in a proceeding challenging a director's conflicting interest transaction if the procedures of section 8.62 have been properly followed.

The plaintiff may challenge the availability of that defense based on a failure to meet the specific requirements of section 8.62 or to conform with general standards of director conduct. For example, a challenge addressed to section 8.62 compliance might question whether the acting directors were "qualified directors" or might dispute the quality and completeness of the disclosures made by D to the qualified directors. If such a challenge is successful, the board action is ineffective for purposes of section 8.61(b)(1) and both D and the transaction may be subject to the full range of remedies that might apply, absent the safe harbor, unless the fairness of the transaction can be established under section 8.61(b)(3). The fact that a transaction has been nominally passed through safe harbor procedures does not preclude a subsequent challenge based on any failure to meet the requirements of section 8.62. A challenge to the effectiveness of board action for purposes of section 8.61(b)(1) might also assert that, although the conflicted director's conduct in connection with the process of approval by qualified directors may have been consistent with the statute's expectations, the qualified directors dealing with the matter did not act in good faith or on reasonable inquiry. The kind of relief that may be appropriate when qualified directors have approved a transaction but have not acted in good faith or have failed to become reasonably informed—and, again, where the fairness of the transaction has not been established under section 8.61(b)(3)—will depend heavily on the facts of the individual case.

Section 8.61(b)(2) regarding shareholders' approval of the transaction is the matching piece to section 8.61(b)(1) regarding directors' approval.

The language "at any time" in these provisions permits the directors or the shareholders to ratify a director's conflicting interest transaction after the fact for purposes of subchapter F.

Section 8.61(b)(3) permits a showing that a director's conflicting interest transaction was fair to the corporation even if there was no compliance with section 8.62 or 8.63. Under section 8.61(b)(3) the interested director has the burden of establishing that the transaction was fair.

* * * * *

Note on Directors' Compensation

Although directors' fees and other forms of director compensation are typically set by the board of directors and are specifically authorized by section 8.11 of the Act, they do involve a director's conflicting interest transaction in which most if not all of the directors may not be qualified directors. Therefore, board action on directors' compensation and benefits would be subject to judicial sanction if they are not favorably acted upon by shareholders pursuant to section 8.63 or if they are not in the circumstances fair to the corporation pursuant to section 8.61(b)(3).

§ 8.62.   Directors' Action

(a) Directors' action respecting a director's conflicting interest transaction is effective for purposes of section 8.61(b)(1) if the transaction has been authorized by the affirmative vote of a majority (but no fewer than two) of the qualified directors who voted on the transaction, after required disclosure by the conflicted director of information not already known by such qualified directors, or after modified disclosure in compliance with subsection (b), provided that:

(1) the qualified directors have deliberated and voted outside the presence of and without the participation by any other director; and

(2) where the action has been taken by a board committee, all members of the committee were qualified directors, and either (i) the committee was composed of all the qualified directors on the board of directors or (ii) the members of the committee were appointed by the affirmative vote of a majority of the qualified directors on the board of directors.

(b) Notwithstanding subsection (a), when a transaction is a director's conflicting interest transaction only because a related person described in clause (v) or (vi) of the definition of "related person" in section 8.60 is a party to or has a material financial interest in the transaction, the conflicted director is not obligated to make required disclosure to the extent that the director reasonably believes that doing so would violate a duty imposed under law, a legally enforceable obligation of confidentiality, or a professional ethics rule, provided that the conflicted director discloses to the qualified directors voting on the transaction:

    (1) all information required to be disclosed that is not so violative,

    (2) the existence and nature of the director's conflicting interest, and

    (3) the nature of the conflicted director's duty not to disclose the confidential information.

(c) A majority (but no fewer than two) of all the qualified directors on the board of directors, or on the board committee, constitutes a quorum for purposes of action that complies with this section.

(d) Where directors' action under this section does not satisfy a quorum or voting requirement applicable to the authorization of the transaction by reason of the articles of incorporation or bylaws or a provision of law, independent action to satisfy those authorization requirements shall be taken by the board of directors or a board committee, in which action directors who are not qualified directors may participate.

Official Comment

Section 8.62 provides the procedure for action by the board of directors or by a board committee under subchapter F. In the normal course this section, together with section 8.61(b), will be the key method for addressing directors' conflicting interest transactions. Any discussion of section 8.62 must have in mind the requirements that directors act in good faith and on reasonable inquiry. See section 8.30. Director action that does not comply with those requirements, even if otherwise in compliance with section 8.62, will be subject to challenge and not be given effect under section 8.62. See the Official Comment to section 8.61(b).

1. *Section 8.62(a)*

The definition of "qualified director" in section 1.43(a)(4) excludes not only a director who is conflicted directly or because of a person specified in the categories of the "related person" definition in section 8.60, but also any director with a familial, financial, employment, professional or other relationship with *another director for whom the transaction is a director's conflicting interest transaction* that would be likely to impair the objectivity of the first director's judgment when participating in a vote on the transaction.

Action under section 8.62 may take the form of committee action meeting the requirements of subsection (a)(2). The requirements for effective committee action are intended to preclude the appointment as committee members of a favorably inclined minority from among all the qualified directors. With respect to required disclosure under subsection (a), if there is more than one conflicted director interested in the transaction, the need for required disclosure would apply to each.

2. *Section 8.62(b)*

Section 8.62(b) accommodates situations where a director who has a conflicting interest is not able to comply fully with the disclosure requirement of subsection (a) because of an extrinsic duty of confidentiality that such director reasonably believes to exist. The director may, for example, be prohibited from making full disclosure because of legal restrictions that happen to apply to the transaction (*e.g.*, grand jury seal or national security statute) or professional ethics rule (*e.g.*, attorney-client confidentiality). The most frequent use of subsection (b), however, will likely involve directors who have conflicting fiduciary obligations. If D is also a director of Y Co., D may have acquired confidential information from one or both directorships relevant to a transaction between X Co. and Y Co., that D cannot reveal to one without violating a fiduciary duty owed to the other. In such circumstances, subsection (b) enables the conflicting interest complication to be presented for consideration under subsection (a), and thereby enables X Co. (and Y Co.) and D to secure for the transaction the protection afforded by subchapter F even though D cannot, by reason of applicable law, confidentiality strictures or a professional ethics rule, make the full disclosure otherwise required.

To comply with section 8.62(b), D must meet all three requirements set forth in clauses (1), (2) and (3). D must then play no personal role in the board's (or committee's) ultimate deliberations or action. The purpose of subsection (b) is to make it clear that the provisions of subchapter F may be employed to "safe harbor" a transaction in circumstances where a conflicted director cannot, because of enforced fiduciary silence, disclose all the known facts. A director could, of course, encounter the same problem of mandated silence with regard to any matter that comes before the board; that is, the problem of forced silence is not linked at all to the problems of transactions involving a conflicting interest of a director. It could happen that at the same board meeting of X Co. at which D invokes subsection (b), another director who has no financial interest in the transaction might conclude that under applicable law he or she is bound to silence (because of attorney-client confidentiality, for example) and would under general principles of sound director conduct withdraw from participation in the board's deliberations and action. Of course, if D invokes subsection (b) and does not make disclosures that would otherwise be required under subsection (a) before leaving the meeting, the qualified directors may decline to act on the transaction out of concern that D knows (or may know) something they do not. On the other hand, if D is subject to an extrinsic duty of confidentiality but has no knowledge of material facts that should otherwise be disclosed, D would normally state just that and subsection (b) would be irrelevant. Having disclosed the existence and nature of the conflicting interest, D would thereby comply with the "required disclosure" as defined under section 8.60.

Although section 8.62(b) will apply to the recurring situation where transacting corporations have common directors (or where a director of one party is an officer of the other), it should not otherwise be read as attempting to address the scope, or mandate the consequences, of various silence-privileges.

Section 8.62(b) is available to D if a transaction is a director's conflicting interest transaction only because a related person described in clauses (v) or (vi) of the definition of that term in section 8.60 is a party to or has a material financial interest in the transaction. Its availability is so limited because in those instances a director owes a fiduciary duty to such a related person. If D or a related person of D other than a related person described in clauses (v) or (vi) of the definition of is a party to or has a material financial interest in the transaction, D's only options are satisfying the required disclosure obligation on an unrestricted basis, abandoning the transaction, or accepting the risk of establishing fairness under section 8.61(b)(3), if the transaction is challenged in a court proceeding.

Whenever a conflicted director proceeds in the manner provided in subsection (b), the other directors should recognize that the conflicted director may have information that, but for the narrow exception set forth in subsection (b), D would be required to reveal to the qualified directors who are acting on the transaction— information that could well indicate that the transaction would be either favorable or unfavorable for X Co.

3. *Section 8.62(d)*

Subsection 8.62(d) underscores the fact that the directors' voting procedures and requirements set forth in subsections (a) through (c) address only the director's conflicting interest. Thus, in any case where the quorum or voting requirements for substantive approval of a transaction differ from the quorum or voting requirements for "safe harbor" protection under section 8.62, the directors may find it necessary to conduct (and record in the minutes of the proceedings) two separate votes—one for section 8.62 purposes and the other for substantive approval purposes.

§ 8.63. Shareholders' Action

(a) Shareholders' action respecting a director's conflicting interest transaction is effective for purposes of section 8.61(b)(2) if a majority of the votes cast by the holders of all qualified shares are in favor of the transaction after (i) notice to shareholders describing the action to be taken respecting the transaction, (ii) provision to the corporation of the information referred to in subsection (b), and (iii) communication to the shareholders entitled to vote on the transaction of the information that is the subject of required disclosure, to the extent the information is not known by them. In the case of shareholders' action at a meeting, the shareholders entitled to vote shall be determined as of the record date for notice of the meeting.

(b) A director who has a conflicting interest respecting the transaction shall, before the shareholders' vote, inform the secretary or other officer or agent of the corporation authorized to tabulate votes, in writing, of the number of shares that the director knows are not qualified shares under subsection (c), and the identity of the holders of those shares.

(c) For purposes of this section: (i) "holder" means and "held by" refers to shares held by a record shareholder, a beneficial shareholder, and an unrestricted voting trust beneficial owner; and (ii) "qualified shares" means all shares entitled to be voted with respect to the transaction except for shares that the secretary or other officer or agent of the corporation authorized to tabulate votes either knows, or under subsection (b) is notified, are held by (A) a director who has a conflicting interest respecting the transaction or (B) a related person of the director (excluding a person described in clause (vi) of the definition of "related person" in section 8.60).

(d) A majority of the votes entitled to be cast by the holders of all qualified shares constitutes a quorum for purposes of compliance with this section. Subject to the provisions of subsection (e), shareholders' action that otherwise complies with this section is not affected by the presence of holders, or by the voting, of shares that are not qualified shares.

(e) If a shareholders' vote does not comply with subsection (a) solely because of a director's failure to comply with subsection (b), and if the director establishes that the failure was not intended to influence and did not in fact determine the outcome of the vote, the court may take such action respecting the transaction and the director, and may give such effect, if any, to the shareholders' vote, as the court considers appropriate in the circumstances.

(f) Where shareholders' action under this section does not satisfy a quorum or voting requirement applicable to the authorization of the transaction by reason of the articles of incorporation or the bylaws or a provision of law, independent action to satisfy those authorization requirements shall be taken by the shareholders, in which action shares that are not qualified shares may participate.

Official Comment

Section 8.63 provides the machinery for shareholders' action that confers safe harbor protection for a director's conflicting interest transaction, just as section 8.62 provides the machinery for directors' action that confers subchapter F safe harbor protection for such a transaction.

1. Section 8.63(a)

Section 8.63(a) specifies the procedure required to confer effective safe harbor protection for a director's conflicting interest transaction through a vote of shareholders. In advance of the vote, three steps must be taken: (i) shareholders must be given timely and adequate notice describing the transaction; (ii) D must disclose the information called for in subsection (b); and (iii) required disclosure (as defined in section 8.60) must be made to the shareholders entitled to vote. Shareholder action that complies with subsection (a) may be taken at any time, before or after the corporation becomes legally obligated to complete the transaction.

Section 8.63 does not contain a "limited disclosure" provision that is comparable to section 8.62(b). Thus, the safe harbor protection of subchapter F is not available through shareholder action under section 8.63 in a case where D either remains silent or makes less than required disclosure because of an extrinsic duty of confidentiality

2. Section 8.63(b)

In many circumstances, the secretary or other person charged with counting votes on behalf of X Co. will have no way to know which of X Co.'s outstanding shares should be excluded from the vote. Section 8.63(b) (together with subsection (c)) therefore obligates a director who has a conflicting interest respecting the transaction, as a prerequisite to safe harbor protection by shareholder action, to provide information known to the director with respect to the shares that are not qualified.

If the person counting the votes knows, or is notified under subsection (b), that particular shares should be excluded but for some reason fails to exclude them from the count and their inclusion in the vote does not affect its outcome, the shareholders' vote will stand. If the improper inclusion determines the outcome, the shareholders' vote fails because it does not comply with subsection (a). Subsection (e) permits the court to take the appropriate action in cases where the notification under subsection (b) is defective but not determinative of the outcome of the vote.

3. Section 8.63(c)

The definition of "qualified shares" in section 8.63(c) does not exclude shares held by entities or persons described in clause (vi) of the definition of "related person" in section 8.60, *i.e.*, a person that is, or is an entity that is controlled by, an employer of D. If D is an employee of Y Co., that fact does not prevent Y Co. from exercising its usual rights to vote any shares it may hold in X Co. D may be unaware of, and would not necessarily monitor, whether his or her employer holds X Co. shares. Moreover, D will typically have no control over his or her employer and how it may vote its X Co. shares.

4. Section 8.63(e)

If D did not provide the information required under section 8.63(b), on its face the shareholders' action is not in compliance with subsection (a) and D has no safe harbor under subsection (a). In the absence of that safe harbor, D can be put to the burden of establishing the fairness of the transaction under section 8.61(b)(3).

That result is proper where D's failure to inform was determinative of the vote results or, worse, was part of a deliberate effort on D's part to influence the outcome. If, however, D's omission was not motivated by D's effort to influence the integrity of the voting process (for example, it was the result of D's negligence), and the voting of the unreported shares was not determinative of the outcome of the vote, then the court should be free to fashion an appropriate response to the situation in light of all the considerations at the time of its decision.

Despite the presumption of regularity customarily accorded the secretary's record, a plaintiff may go behind the secretary's record for purposes of subsection (e).

5.   *Section 8.63(f)*

Section 8.63(f) underscores that the shareholders' voting procedures and requirements set forth in subsections (a) through (e) treat only the director's conflicting interest. A transaction that receives a shareholders' vote that complies with subchapter F may well fail to achieve a different vote or quorum that may be required for substantive approval of the transaction under other applicable statutory provisions or provisions contained in X Co.'s articles of incorporation or bylaws, and vice versa. Thus, in any case where the quorum or voting requirements for substantive approval of a transaction differ from the quorum or voting requirements for "safe harbor" protection under section 8.63, the corporation may find it necessary to conduct (and record in the minutes of the proceedings) two separate shareholder votes—one for section 8.63 purposes and the other for substantive approval purposes (or, if appropriate, conduct two separate tabulations of one vote).

Subchapter G

Business Opportunities

§ 8.70.   Business Opportunities

(a) If a director or officer pursues or takes advantage of a business opportunity directly, or indirectly through or on behalf of another person, that action may not be the subject of equitable relief, or give rise to an award of damages or other sanctions against the director, officer or other person, in a proceeding by or in the right of the corporation on the ground that the opportunity should have first been offered to the corporation, if

(1) before the director, officer or other person becomes legally obligated respecting the opportunity the director or officer brings it to the attention of the corporation and either:

(i) action by qualified directors disclaiming the corporation's interest in the opportunity is taken in compliance with the same procedures as are set forth in section 8.62, or

(ii) shareholders' action disclaiming the corporation's interest in the opportunity is taken in compliance with the procedures set forth in section 8.63, in either case as if the decision being made concerned a director's conflicting interest transaction, except that, rather than making "required disclosure" as defined in section 8.60, the director or officer shall have made prior disclosure to those acting on behalf of the corporation of all material facts concerning the business opportunity known to the director or officer; or

(2) the duty to offer the corporation the business opportunity has been limited or eliminated pursuant to a provision of the articles of incorporation adopted (and where required, made effective by action of qualified directors) in accordance with section 2.02(b)(6).

(b) In any proceeding seeking equitable relief or other remedies based upon an alleged improper pursuit or taking advantage of a business opportunity by a director or officer, directly, or indirectly through or on behalf of another person, the fact that the director or officer did not employ the procedure described in subsection (a)(1)(i) or (ii) before pursuing or taking advantage of the opportunity shall not create an implication that the opportunity should have been first presented to the corporation or alter the burden of proof otherwise applicable to establish that the director or officer breached a duty to the corporation in the circumstances.

Official Comment

Section 8.70(a)(1) provides a safe harbor for a director or officer weighing possible involvement with a prospective business opportunity that might constitute a "corporate opportunity." The phrase "directly, or indirectly through or on behalf of another person" recognizes the need to cover transactions pursued or effected either directly by the director or officer or indirectly through or on behalf of another person, which might be a related person as defined in section 8.60 or a person which is not a related person. By action of the board of directors or shareholders of the corporation under section 8.70(a)(1), the director or officer can obtain a disclaimer of the corporation's interest in the matter before proceeding with such involvement. In the alternative, the corporation may, among other things, (i) decline to disclaim its interest, (ii) delay a decision respecting granting a disclaimer pending receipt from the director or officer of additional information (or for any other reason), or (iii) attach conditions to the disclaimer it grants under section 8.70(a)(1).

The safe harbor provided under section 8.70(a)(1) may be utilized only for a specific business opportunity. A broader advance safe harbor for any, or one or more classes or categories of, business opportunities must meet the requirements of section 2.02(b)(6). Section 8.70(a)(2) confirms that if the duty of an officer or director to present an opportunity has been limited or eliminated by a provision in the articles of incorporation under section 2.02(b)(6) (and, in the case of officers, appropriate action by qualified directors as required by that section), a safe harbor exists in connection with the pursuit or taking of the opportunity. The common law doctrine of "corporate opportunity" has long been recognized as a part of the director's duty of loyalty and, under court decisions, extends to officers. See section 8.30(a) and its Official Comment. The doctrine recognizes that the corporation has a right prior to that of its directors or officers to act on certain business opportunities that come to the attention of the directors or officers. In such situations, a director or officer who acts on the opportunity for the benefit of the director or officer or another person without having first presented it to the corporation can be held to have "usurped" or "intercepted" a right of the corporation. A defendant director or officer who is found by a court to have violated the duty of loyalty in this regard, as well as related or other persons involved in the transaction, may be subject to damages or possible equitable remedies, including injunction, disgorgement or the imposition of a constructive trust in favor of the corporation. Although the doctrine's concept is easily described, whether it will be found to apply in a given case depends on the facts and circumstances of the particular situation and is thus frequently unpredictable.

In recognition that the corporation need not pursue every business opportunity of which it becomes aware, an opportunity coming within the doctrine's criteria that has been properly presented to and declined by the corporation may then be pursued or taken by the presenting director or officer without breach of the duty of loyalty.

The fact-intensive nature of the corporate opportunity doctrine resists statutory definition. Instead, subchapter G employs the broader notion of "business opportunity" that encompasses any opportunity, without regard to whether it would come within the judicial definition of a "corporate opportunity," as it may have been developed by courts in a jurisdiction. When properly employed, subchapter G provides a safe-harbor mechanism enabling a director or officer to pursue an opportunity directly, or indirectly through or on behalf of another person, free of possible challenge claiming conflict with the director's or officer's duty on the ground that the opportunity should first have been offered to the corporation. Section 8.70 is modeled on the safe-harbor and approval procedures of subchapter F pertaining to directors' conflicting interest transactions with, however, some modifications necessary to accommodate differences in the two matters addressed.

1.   *Section 8.70(a)(1)*

Section 8.70(a)(1) describes the safe harbor available to a director or officer who elects to subject a business opportunity, regardless of whether the opportunity would be classified as a "corporate opportunity," to the disclosure and approval procedures set forth in that section. The safe harbor provided is as broad as that provided for a director's conflicting interest transaction in section 8.61. If the director or officer makes the prescribed disclosure of the facts specified and the corporation's interest in the opportunity is disclaimed by director action under subsection (a)(1)(i) or shareholder action under subsection (a)(1)(ii), the director or officer has foreclosed any claimed breach of the duty of loyalty and may not be subject to equitable relief, damages or other sanctions if the director or officer thereafter pursues or takes the opportunity for his or her own account or through or for the benefit of another person. As a general proposition, disclaimer by director action under subsection (a)(1)(i) must meet all of the requirements provided in section 8.62 with respect to a director's conflicting interest transaction and disclaimer by shareholder action under subsection (a)(1)(ii) must likewise meet all of the requirements for shareholder action under section 8.63. Note, however, several important differences.

First, in contrast to director or shareholder action under sections 8.62 and 8.63, which may be taken at any time, section 8.70(a)(1) requires that the director or officer present the opportunity and secure director or shareholder action disclaiming it *before* the director of officer or other person involved through or on behalf of the director or officer becomes legally obligated respecting the opportunity. The safe harbor concept contemplates that the corporation's decision maker will have full freedom of action in deciding whether the corporation should take over a proffered opportunity or disclaim the corporation's interest in it. If the director or officer could seek ratification after the legal obligation respecting the opportunity arises, the option of taking over the opportunity would, in most cases, be foreclosed to the corporation. The safe harbor's benefit is available only when the corporation can entertain the opportunity in a fully objective way.

The second difference relates to the necessary disclosure. Instead of employing section 8.60's definition of "required disclosure" which is incorporated in sections 8.62 and 8.63 and includes "the existence and nature of the director's conflicting interest," the disclosure obligation of section 8.70(a)(1) requires only that the director or officer reveal all material facts concerning the business opportunity known to the director or officer. The safe harbor procedure shields the director or officer even if a material fact regarding the business opportunity is not disclosed, so long as the proffering director or officer had no knowledge of that fact.

2.　*Section 8.70(b)*

Section 8.70(b) reflects a fundamental difference between the coverage of subchapters F and G. Because subchapter F provides an exclusive definition of "director's conflicting interest transaction," any transaction meeting the definition that is not approved in accordance with the provisions of subchapter F is not entitled to its safe harbor. Unless the interested director can, upon challenge, establish the transaction's fairness, the director's conduct is presumptively actionable and subject to the full range of remedies that might otherwise be awarded by a court. In contrast, the concept of "business opportunity" under section 8.70 is not defined but is intended to be broader than what might be regarded as an actionable "corporate opportunity." This approach reflects the fact-intensive nature of the corporate opportunity doctrine, with the result that a director or officer may be inclined to seek safe harbor protection under section 8.70 before pursuing an opportunity that may or may not be a "corporate opportunity." Likewise, a director or officer may conclude that a business opportunity is not a "corporate opportunity" under applicable law and choose to pursue it without seeking a disclaimer by the corporation under subsection (a)(1). Accordingly, subsection (b) provides that a decision not to seek the safe harbor offered by subsection (a)(1) neither creates a negative implication nor alters the burden of proof in any subsequent proceeding seeking damages or equitable relief based upon an alleged improper taking of a "corporate opportunity."

Chapter 9

DOMESTICATION AND CONVERSION

Introductory Comment

This chapter provides procedures by which a domestic corporation may become a foreign corporation or a different form of domestic or foreign entity and, conversely, a foreign corporation or an eligible entity may become a domestic corporation. These procedures are:

- **Domestication.** The procedures in subchapter 9B permit a corporation to change its state of incorporation, thus allowing a domestic corporation to become a foreign corporation or a foreign corporation to become a domestic corporation.

- **Conversion.** The procedures in subchapter 9C permit a domestic corporation to become a domestic or foreign eligible entity and also permit a domestic or foreign eligible entity to become a domestic corporation.

The provisions of this chapter apply only if a domestic corporation is present either immediately before or immediately after a domestication or conversion.

Note on Adoption: Some states may wish to generalize the provisions of this chapter so that they are not limited to transactions involving a domestic business corporation. For example, a state may wish to permit a domestic limited partnership to become a domestic limited liability company. The Model Entity Transactions Act prepared by the Uniform Law Commission is such a generalized statute. Some states have elected to include transactions that are described in chapter 9 as domestications in their definition of conversions and not to refer to domestication separately.

Subchapter A

Preliminary Provisions

§ 9.01.　Definitions

As used in this chapter:

"Conversion" means a transaction pursuant to subchapter C.

"Converted entity" means the converting entity as it continues in existence after a conversion.

"Converting entity" means the domestic corporation or eligible entity that approves a plan of conversion pursuant to section 9.32 or the foreign eligible entity that approves a conversion pursuant to the organic law of the eligible entity.

"Domesticated corporation" means the domesticating corporation as it continues in existence after a domestication.

"Domesticating corporation" means the domestic corporation that approves a plan of domestication pursuant to section 9.21 or the foreign corporation that approves a domestication pursuant to the organic law of the foreign corporation.

"Domestication" means a transaction pursuant to subchapter B.

"Protected agreement" means:

(i) a document evidencing indebtedness of a domestic corporation or eligible entity and any related agreement in effect immediately before the enactment date;

(ii) an agreement that is binding on a domestic corporation or eligible entity immediately before the enactment date;

(iii) the articles of incorporation or bylaws of a domestic corporation or the organic rules of a domestic eligible entity, in each case in effect immediately before the enactment date; or

(iv) an agreement that is binding on any of the shareholders, members, interest holders, directors or other governors of a domestic corporation or eligible entity, in their capacities as such, immediately before the enactment date.

For purposes of this definition and sections 9.20 and 9.30, "enactment date" means the first date on which the law of this state authorized a transaction having the effect of a domestication or a conversion, as applicable.

Note on adoption: When adopting the definition of "protected agreement," a state could consider setting out in the last sentence of the definition the actual dates when domestication and conversion statutes were first enacted in the state so those dates would be apparent on the face of the statute.

Official Comment

Section 9.01 sets out definitions used in the Act's provisions on domestication and conversion. It defines "protected agreement" as those specified documents and agreements which were in effect before the laws of the state first provided for domestication or conversion transactions. A person contracting with a corporation or loaning it money, or which drafted and negotiated special rights relating to mergers or similar transactions, before the enactment of this chapter (or any similar predecessor law) should not be charged with the consequences of not having dealt with domestications and conversions. Sections 9.20(f) and 9.30(d) provide special rules dealing with protected agreements.

§ 9.02. Excluded Transactions [optional]

This chapter may not be used to effect a transaction that:

(a) [converts a company organized on the mutual principle to one organized on the basis of share ownership]; or

(b) [other examples]

Note on adoption: A state should use this section to list those situations in which the state has enacted specific legislation governing the domestication or conversion of domestic corporations that engage in particular types of activities or that do business in a regulated industry. Mutual to share conversions (for instance, of an insurance company, bank, savings institution or credit union) are examples of such transactions.

The purpose of this section is to prohibit certain transactions that are subject to a separate statutory or legal framework from being effected under this chapter.

§ 9.03.   Required Approvals [optional]

If a domestic or foreign corporation or eligible entity may not be a party to a merger without the approval of the [attorney general], the [department of banking], the [department of insurance] or the [public utility commission], and the applicable statutes or regulations do not specifically deal with transactions under this chapter but do require such approval for mergers, a corporation or eligible entity shall not be a party to a transaction under this chapter without the prior approval of that agency or official.

Note on adoption: *Section 9.03 is an optional provision that should be considered in states where corporations or other entities that conduct regulated activities, such as banking, insurance or the provision of public utility services, are incorporated or organized under general laws instead of under special laws applicable only to entities conducting the regulated activity. If this section is used, the list of officials and agencies should be conformed to the laws of the enacting state.*

Official Comment

The purpose of section 9.03 is to ensure that transactions under chapter 9 will be effected only if required state governmental approvals have been obtained. If other state laws require such approvals in the case of mergers, but do not address approvals in the case of domestications and conversions, then section 9.03 requires that transactions under chapter 9 obtain the same regulatory approvals as mergers.

§ 9.04.   Relationship of Chapter to Other Laws [optional]

A transaction effected under this chapter may not create or impair a right, duty or obligation of a person under the statutory law of this state other than this chapter relating to a change in control, business combination, control-share acquisition, or similar transaction involving a domesticating or converting domestic corporation, unless the approval of the plan of domestication or conversion is by a vote of the shareholders or the board of directors which would be sufficient to create or impair the right, duty or obligation directly under that law.

Official Comment

This section protects the application of change of control statutes from being affected by a transaction under this chapter by requiring that the transaction be approved in a manner that would be sufficient to approve changing the application of the change of control statute. If a domestication or conversion is approved in that manner, there is no policy reason to prohibit the application of the change of control statute from being varied for the transaction. If the application of a change of control statute cannot be varied by action of an entity subject to it, then a transaction under this chapter will be permissible only if the change of control provision continues to apply after the transaction or the transaction itself is permissible under the change of control statute.

Subchapter B

Domestication

§ 9.20.   Domestication

(a) By complying with the provisions of this subchapter applicable to foreign corporations, a foreign corporation may become a domestic corporation if the domestication is permitted by the organic law of the foreign corporation.

(b) By complying with the provisions of this subchapter, a domestic corporation may become a foreign corporation pursuant to a plan of domestication if the domestication is permitted by the organic law of the foreign corporation.

(c) The plan of domestication must include:

(1) the name of the domesticating corporation;

(2) the name and jurisdiction of formation of the domesticated corporation;

(3) the manner and basis of reclassifying the shares of the domesticating corporation into shares or other securities, obligations, rights to acquire shares or other securities, cash, other property, or any combination of the foregoing;

(4) the proposed articles of incorporation and bylaws of the domesticated corporation; and

(5) the other terms and conditions of the domestication.

(d) In addition to the requirements of subsection (c), a plan of domestication may contain any other provision not prohibited by law.

(e) The terms of a plan of domestication may be made dependent upon facts objectively ascertainable outside the plan in accordance with section 1.20(k).

(f) If a protected agreement of a domestic domesticating corporation in effect immediately before the domestication becomes effective contains a provision applying to a merger of the corporation and the agreement does not refer to a domestication of the corporation, the provision applies to a domestication of the corporation as if the domestication were a merger until such time as the provision is first amended after the enactment date.

Official Comment

1. Applicability

This subchapter authorizes a foreign corporation to become a domestic corporation and a domestic corporation to become a foreign corporation. In each case, the domestication is authorized only if the laws of the foreign jurisdiction permit it. Whether and on what terms a foreign corporation is authorized to domesticate in this state are issues governed by the organic law of the foreign corporation, not by this subchapter. A foreign corporation is not required to have a valid registration to do business in this state under chapter 15 to domesticate in this state.

2. Terms and Conditions of Domestication

This subchapter imposes no restrictions or limitations on the terms and conditions of a domestication, except for those set forth in section 9.23(a) with respect to certain amendments to the plan of domestication. The list in section 9.20(c) of required provisions in a plan of domestication is not exhaustive. Unlike a domestic corporation, a foreign corporation is not required to have a plan of domestication, although it must comply with the provisions of this subchapter applicable to foreign corporations.

3. Articles of Incorporation

Under section 9.20(c)(4), a domestic corporation's plan of domestication must include that corporation's proposed articles of incorporation and bylaws, which should comply with the organic law of the foreign jurisdiction into which it is domesticating. In the case of a domestic corporation domesticating into a foreign jurisdiction, the Act places no separate limitations on the provisions that the proposed articles of incorporation and bylaws may contain, and they may be substantially identical to or completely different from those of the domesticating corporation. However, the content of the proposed articles may affect the approvals required for the plan of domestication. See the approval requirements in section 9.21(f) with respect to certain changes in the articles of incorporation, and section 9.21(g) with respect to interest holder liability with respect to the domesticated corporation.

4. Appraisal Rights

This subchapter does not require that a shareholder in the domesticating corporation receive the same type or amount, or even any, shares of the domesticated corporation. However, a shareholder of a domestic corporation that domesticates into a foreign jurisdiction has appraisal rights if the shareholder does not receive shares in the domesticated corporation having terms as favorable to the shareholder in all material respects, and representing at least the same percentage interest of the total voting rights of the outstanding shares of the domesticated corporation, as the shares held by the shareholder before the domestication. See section 13.02(a)(6).

5. Protected Agreements

Section 9.20(f) provides special rules for "protected agreements"—certain documents and agreements in effect before the date (defined as the "enactment date") of this chapter (or any similar predecessor statute).

§ 9.21.   Action On a Plan of Domestication

In the case of a domestication of a domestic corporation into a foreign jurisdiction, the plan of domestication shall be adopted in the following manner:

(a) The plan of domestication shall first be adopted by the board of directors.

(b) The plan of domestication shall then be approved by the shareholders. In submitting the plan of domestication to the shareholders for approval, the board of directors shall recommend that the shareholders approve the plan, unless (i) the board of directors makes a determination that because of conflicts of interest or other special circumstances it should not make such a recommendation or (ii) section 8.26 applies. If either (i) or (ii) applies, the board shall inform the shareholders of the basis for its so proceeding.

(c) The board of directors may set conditions for approval of the plan of domestication by the shareholders or the effectiveness of the plan of domestication.

(d) If the approval of the shareholders is to be given at a meeting, the corporation shall notify each shareholder, regardless of whether entitled to vote, of the meeting of shareholders at which the plan of domestication is to be submitted for approval. The notice must state that the purpose, or one of the purposes, of the meeting is to consider the plan of domestication and must contain or be accompanied by a copy or summary of the plan. The notice must include or be accompanied by a copy of the articles of incorporation and the bylaws as they will be in effect immediately after the domestication.

(e) Unless the articles of incorporation, or the board of directors acting pursuant to subsection (c), require a greater vote or a greater quorum, approval of the plan of domestication requires (i) the approval of the shareholders at a meeting at which a quorum exists consisting of a majority of the votes entitled to be cast on the plan, and, (ii) except as provided in subsection (f), the approval of each class or series of shares voting as a separate voting group at a meeting at which a quorum of the voting group exists consisting of a majority of the votes entitled to be cast on the plan by that voting group.

(f) The articles of incorporation may expressly limit or eliminate the separate voting rights provided in subsection (e)(ii) as to any class or series of shares, except when the articles of incorporation of the foreign corporation resulting from the domestication include what would be in effect an amendment that would entitle the class or series to vote as a separate group under section 10.04 if it were a proposed amendment of the articles of incorporation of the domestic domesticating corporation.

(g) If as a result of a domestication one or more shareholders of a domestic domesticating corporation would become subject to interest holder liability, approval of the plan of domestication shall require the signing in connection with the domestication, by each such shareholder, of a separate written consent to become subject to such interest holder liability, unless in the case of a shareholder that already has interest holder liability with respect to the domesticating corporation, the terms and conditions of the interest holder liability with respect to the domesticated corporation are substantially identical to those of the existing interest holder liability (other than for changes that eliminate or reduce such interest holder liability).

Official Comment

1.   *In General*

Section 9.21 sets forth the rules for adoption and approval of a plan of domestication of a domestic corporation into a foreign jurisdiction. The manner in which the domestication of a foreign corporation into this state must be adopted and approved will be controlled by the organic law of the foreign corporation.

When submitting a plan of domestication to shareholders, the board of directors must recommend the transaction, subject to two exceptions in section 9.21(b). The board might exercise the exception under clause (i) where the number of directors having a conflicting interest makes it inadvisable for the board to recommend the domestication or where the board is evenly divided as to the merits of the domestication but is able to agree that shareholders should be permitted to consider it. Alternatively, the board of directors might exercise the exception under clause (ii), which recognizes that, under section 8.26, a board of directors may agree to submit a plan to a vote of shareholders even if, after approving the plan, the board of directors determines that it no longer recommends the plan.

Section 9.21(c) permits the board of directors to condition its submission of a plan of domestication to the shareholders or the effectiveness of the plan of domestication. Among the conditions that a board of directors might impose are that the plan will not be deemed approved (i) unless it is approved by a specified vote of the shareholders, or by one or more specified classes or series of shares, voting as a separate voting group, or by a specified percentage of disinterested shareholders or (ii) if shareholders holding more than a specified fraction of the outstanding shares assert appraisal rights.

Section 9.21(d) provides a notice requirement if a plan of domestication is to be considered by the shareholders at a meeting. Requirements concerning the timing and content of a notice of meeting are in section 7.05. Section 9.21(d) does not address the notice to be given to nonvoting or nonconsenting shareholders where the plan is approved without a meeting by written consent. However, that requirement is imposed by section 7.04. . . .

3. Personal Liability of Shareholders

Section 9.21(g) applies only in situations where a shareholder of a domestic corporation is becoming subject to "interest holder liability," as defined in section 1.40, with respect to the domesticated corporation. Approval of a domestication that would have such a result generally requires the written consent of each such shareholder who becomes subject to such interest holder liability. The exception is the limited case where the shareholder has interest holder liability with respect to the domesticating corporation, and the terms and conditions of the shareholder's interest holder liability with respect to the domesticated corporation are substantially identical to those existing prior to the domestication. If, for example, a shareholder before the domestication has interest holder liability for certain borrowings and after the domestication would have interest holder liability for unpaid wages, the terms and conditions of the interest holder liability are not substantially identical, and the shareholder's written consent to become subject to that liability would be required for the domestication to be approved.

§ 9.22. Articles of Domestication; Effectiveness

(a) After (i) a plan of domestication of a domestic corporation has been adopted and approved as required by this Act, or (ii) a foreign corporation that is the domesticating corporation has approved a domestication as required under its organic law, articles of domestication shall be signed by the domesticating corporation. The articles must set forth:

(1) the name of the domesticating corporation and its jurisdiction of formation;

(2) the name and jurisdiction of formation of the domesticated corporation; and

(3) if the domesticating corporation is a domestic corporation, a statement that the plan of domestication was approved in accordance with this chapter or, if the domesticating corporation is a foreign corporation, a statement that the domestication was approved in accordance with its organic law.

(b) If the domesticated corporation is a domestic corporation, the articles of domestication must attach articles of incorporation of the domesticated corporation that satisfy the requirements of section 2.02. Provisions that would not be required to be included in restated articles of incorporation may be omitted from the articles of incorporation attached to the articles of domestication.

(c) The articles of domestication shall be delivered to the secretary of state for filing, and shall take effect at the effective date determined in accordance with section 1.23.

(d) If the domesticated corporation is a domestic corporation, the domestication becomes effective when the articles of domestication are effective. If the domesticated corporation is a foreign corporation, the domestication becomes effective on the later of (i) the date and time provided by the organic law of the domesticated corporation, and (ii) when the articles of domestication are effective.

(e) If the domesticating corporation is a foreign corporation that is registered to do business in this state under chapter 15, its registration statement shall be cancelled automatically when the domestication becomes effective.

§ 9.23. Amendment of Plan of Domestication; Abandonment

(a) A plan of domestication of a domestic corporation may be amended:

(1) in the same manner as the plan was approved, if the plan does not provide for the manner in which it may be amended; or

(2) in the manner provided in the plan, except that a shareholder that was entitled to vote on or consent to approval of the plan is entitled to vote on or consent to any amendment of the plan that will change:

(i) the amount or kind of shares or other securities, obligations, rights to acquire shares or other securities, cash, other property, or any combination of the foregoing, to be received by any of the shareholders of the domesticating corporation under the plan;

(ii) the articles of incorporation or bylaws of the domesticated corporation that will be in effect immediately after the domestication becomes effective, except for changes that do not require approval of the shareholders of the domesticated corporation under its organic law or its proposed articles of incorporation or bylaws as set forth in the plan; or

(iii) any of the other terms or conditions of the plan, if the change would adversely affect the shareholder in any material respect.

(b) After a plan of domestication has been adopted and approved by a domestic corporation as required by this subchapter, and before the articles of domestication have become effective, the plan may be abandoned by the corporation without action by its shareholders in accordance with any procedures set forth in the plan or, if no such procedures are set forth in the plan, in the manner determined by the board of directors.

(c) If a domestication is abandoned after the articles of domestication have been delivered to the secretary of state for filing but before the articles of domestication have become effective, articles of abandonment, signed by the domesticating corporation, must be delivered to the secretary of state for filing before the articles of domestication become effective. The articles of abandonment take effect upon filing, and the domestication shall be deemed abandoned and shall not become effective. The articles of abandonment must contain:

(1) the name of the domesticating corporation;

(2) the date on which the articles of domestication were filed by the secretary of state; and

(3) a statement that the domestication has been abandoned in accordance with this section.

§ 9.24. Effect of Domestication

(a) When a domestication becomes effective:

(1) all property owned by, and every contract right possessed by, the domesticating corporation are the property and contract rights of the domesticated corporation without transfer, reversion or impairment;

(2) all debts, obligations and other liabilities of the domesticating corporation are the debts, obligations and other liabilities of the domesticated corporation;

(3) the name of the domesticated corporation may but need not be substituted for the name of the domesticating corporation in any pending proceeding;

(4) the articles of incorporation and bylaws of the domesticated corporation become effective;

(5) the shares of the domesticating corporation are reclassified into shares or other securities, obligations, rights to acquire shares or other securities, cash or other property in accordance with the terms of the domestication, and the shareholders of the domesticating corporation are entitled only to the rights provided to them by those terms and to any appraisal rights they may have under the organic law of the domesticating corporation; and

(6) the domesticated corporation is:

(i) incorporated under and subject to the organic law of the domesticated corporation;

(ii) the same corporation without interruption as the domesticating corporation; and

(iii) deemed to have been incorporated on the date the domesticating corporation was originally incorporated.

(b) When a domestication of a domestic corporation into a foreign jurisdiction becomes effective, the domesticated corporation is deemed to:

(1) appoint the secretary of state as its agent for service of process in a proceeding to enforce the rights of shareholders who exercise appraisal rights in connection with the domestication; and

(2) agree that it will promptly pay the amount, if any, to which such shareholders are entitled under chapter 13.

(c) Except as otherwise provided in the organic law or organic rules of a domesticating foreign corporation, the interest holder liability of a shareholder in a foreign corporation that is domesticated into this state who had interest holder liability in respect of such domesticating corporation before the domestication becomes effective shall be as follows:

(1) The domestication does not discharge that prior interest holder liability with respect to any interest holder liabilities that arose before the domestication becomes effective.

(2) The provisions of the organic law of the domesticating corporation shall continue to apply to the collection or discharge of any interest holder liabilities preserved by subsection (c)(1), as if the domestication had not occurred.

(3) The shareholder shall have such rights of contribution from other persons as are provided by the organic law of the domesticating corporation with respect to any interest holder liabilities preserved by subsection (c)(1), as if the domestication had not occurred.

(4) The shareholder shall not, by reason of such prior interest holder liability, have interest holder liability with respect to any interest holder liabilities that are incurred after the domestication becomes effective.

(d) A shareholder who becomes subject to interest holder liability in respect of the domesticated corporation as a result of the domestication shall have such interest holder liability only in respect of interest holder liabilities that arise after the domestication becomes effective.

(e) A domestication does not constitute or cause the dissolution of the domesticating corporation.

(f) Property held for charitable purposes under the laws of this state by a domestic or foreign corporation immediately before a domestication shall not, as a result of the transaction, be diverted from the objects for which it was donated, granted, devised, or otherwise transferred except and to the extent permitted by or pursuant to the laws of this state addressing cy près or dealing with nondiversion of charitable assets.

(g) A bequest, devise, gift, grant, or promise contained in a will or other instrument of donation, subscription, or conveyance which is made to the domesticating corporation and which takes effect or remains payable after the domestication inures to the domesticated corporation.

(h) A trust obligation that would govern property if transferred to the domesticating corporation applies to property that is transferred to the domesticated corporation after the domestication takes effect.

Official Comment

The domesticated corporation is the same entity as the domesticating corporation, and it continues without interruption. It becomes a business corporation in the resulting jurisdiction with the same status as if it had been originally incorporated there. The domesticated corporation will have all of the powers, privileges and rights granted to corporations originally incorporated in that jurisdiction and will be subject to all of the duties, liabilities and limitations imposed on business corporations in that jurisdiction. Thus, a domestication is not a conveyance, transfer or assignment. It does not give rise to claims of reverter or impairment of title based on a prohibited conveyance, transfer or assignment. Nor does it give rise to a claim that a contract with the corporation is no longer in effect on the ground of nonassignability, unless the contract specifically provides that it does not survive domestication. See, however, section 9.20(f) and its Official Comment with respect to special rules regarding protected agreements. All pending proceedings involving the domesticating corporation are continued.

A domestic corporation domesticating into a foreign jurisdiction remains obligated to its shareholders who exercise appraisal rights to pay them the amount, if any, to which they are entitled under chapter 13. For this purpose, under section 9.24(b) the domesticated corporation is deemed to appoint the secretary of state as its agent for service of process in proceedings to enforce those rights.

Section 9.24(c) preserves the interest holder liability of shareholders of the domesticating foreign corporation only for interest holder liabilities to the extent they arise before the domestication becomes effective. Interest holder liability is not preserved for subsequent changes in an underlying liability, regardless of whether a change is voluntary or involuntary. Section 9.24(d) similarly provides that interest holder liability with respect to the domesticated corporation only relates to interest holder liabilities that arise after the domestication.

Subchapter C

Conversion

§ 9.30. Conversion

(a) By complying with this chapter, a domestic corporation may become (i) a domestic eligible entity or (ii) a foreign eligible entity if the conversion is permitted by the organic law of the foreign entity.

(b) By complying with this subchapter and applicable provisions of its organic law, a domestic eligible entity may become a domestic corporation. If procedures for the approval of a conversion are not provided by the organic law or organic rules of a domestic eligible entity, the conversion shall be adopted and approved in the same manner as a merger of that eligible entity. If the organic law or organic rules of a domestic eligible entity do not provide procedures for the approval of either a conversion or a merger, a plan of conversion may nonetheless be adopted and approved by the unanimous consent of all the interest holders of such eligible entity. In either such case, the conversion thereafter may be effected as provided in the other provisions of this subchapter; and for purposes of applying this chapter in such a case:

(1) the eligible entity, its members or interest holders, eligible interests and organic rules taken together, shall be deemed to be a domestic business corporation, shareholders, shares and articles of incorporation, respectively and vice versa, as the context may require; and

(2) if the business and affairs of the eligible entity are managed by a person or persons that are not identical to the members or interest holders, that person or persons shall be deemed to be the board of directors.

(c) By complying with the provisions of this subchapter applicable to foreign entities, a foreign eligible entity may become a domestic corporation if the organic law of the foreign eligible entity permits it to become a business corporation in another jurisdiction.

(d) If a protected agreement of a domestic converting corporation in effect immediately before the conversion becomes effective contains a provision applying to a merger of the corporation that is a converting entity and the agreement does not refer to a conversion of the corporation, the provision applies to a conversion of the corporation as if the conversion were a merger, until such time as the provision is first amended after the enactment date.

Official Comment

1.   Applicability

This subchapter authorizes a domestic corporation to become a domestic eligible entity. It also authorizes a domestic corporation to become a foreign eligible entity, but only if the conversion is permitted by the laws under which the foreign eligible entity will be organized. Further, this subchapter authorizes a domestic or foreign eligible entity to become a domestic corporation. Whether and on what terms a foreign eligible entity is authorized to convert is governed by its organic law. If a foreign eligible entity is so authorized, it must comply with the provisions of this subchapter applicable to foreign entities. For example, it must file articles of conversion under section 9.33(a), and section 9.33(b) requires its articles of incorporation to meet the requirements of section 2.02.

682

With respect to a domestic eligible entity, if the law under which it is organized does not expressly authorize it to convert to a domestic corporation, section 9.30(b) provides procedures for such an entity to adopt and effect a plan of conversion.

2. *Protected Agreements*

Section 9.30(d) provides special rules about "protected agreements"—certain documents and agreements in effect before the date (defined as the "enactment date") of this chapter (or any similar predecessor statute).

§ 9.31. Plan of Conversion

(a) A domestic corporation may convert to a domestic or foreign eligible entity under this subchapter by approving a plan of conversion. The plan of conversion must include:

(1) the name of the converting corporation;

(2) the name, jurisdiction of formation and type of entity of the converted entity;

(3) the manner and basis of converting the shares of the domestic corporation into eligible interests or other securities, obligations, rights to acquire eligible interests or other securities, cash, other property, or any combination of the foregoing;

(4) the other terms and conditions of the conversion; and

(5) the full text, as it will be in effect immediately after the conversion becomes effective, of the organic rules of the converted entity which are to be in writing.

(b) In addition to the requirements of subsection (a), a plan of conversion may contain any other provision not prohibited by law.

(c) The terms of a plan of conversion may be made dependent upon facts objectively ascertainable outside the plan in accordance with section 1.20(k).

§ 9.32. Action On a Plan of Conversion

In the case of a conversion of a domestic corporation to a domestic or foreign eligible entity, the plan of conversion shall be adopted in the following manner:

(a) The plan of conversion shall first be adopted by the board of directors.

(b) The plan of conversion shall then be approved by the shareholders. In submitting the plan of conversion to the shareholders for their approval, the board of directors must recommend that the shareholders approve the plan, unless (i) the board of directors makes a determination that because of conflicts of interest or other special circumstances it should not make such a recommendation, or (ii) section 8.26 applies. If either (i) or (ii) applies, the board of directors shall inform the shareholders of the basis for its so proceeding.

(c) The board of directors may set conditions for approval of the plan of conversion by the shareholders or the effectiveness of the plan of conversion.

(d) If the approval of the shareholders is to be given at a meeting, the corporation shall notify each shareholder, regardless of whether entitled to vote, of the meeting of shareholders at which the plan of conversion is to be submitted for approval. The notice must state that the purpose, or one of the purposes, of the meeting is to consider the plan of conversion and must contain or be accompanied by a copy or summary of the plan. The notice must include or be accompanied by a copy of the organic rules of the converted entity which are to be in writing as they will be in effect immediately after the conversion.

(e) Unless the articles of incorporation, or the board of directors acting pursuant to subsection (c), require a greater vote or a greater quorum, approval of the plan of conversion requires (i) the approval of the shareholders at a meeting at which a quorum exists consisting of a majority of the votes entitled to be cast on the plan, and (ii) the approval of each class or series of shares voting as a separate voting group at a meeting at which a quorum of the voting group exists consisting of a majority of the votes entitled to be cast on the plan by that voting group.

(f) If as a result of the conversion one or more shareholders of the converting domestic corporation would become subject to interest holder liability, approval of the plan of conversion shall require the signing in connection with the transaction, by each such shareholder, of a separate written consent to become subject to such interest holder liability.

Official Comment

1.   In General

This section sets forth the rules for adoption and approval of a plan of conversion by a domestic corporation. The manner in which the conversion of a foreign eligible entity to a domestic corporation must be adopted and approved will be controlled by the organic law of the foreign jurisdiction. The manner in which the conversion of a domestic eligible entity to a domestic corporation must be adopted and approved will be controlled by the organic law of the eligible entity, as supplemented by section 9.30(b), if applicable.

When submitting a plan of conversion to shareholders, the board of directors must recommend the transaction, subject to two exceptions in section 9.32(b). The board might exercise the exception under clause (i) where the number of directors having a conflicting interest makes it inadvisable for the board to recommend the conversion or where the board is evenly divided as to the merits of the conversion but is able to agree that shareholders should be permitted to consider it. Alternatively, the board of directors might exercise the exception in clause (ii), which recognizes that, under section 8.26, a board of directors may agree to submit a plan to a vote of shareholders even if, after approving the plan, the board of directors determines that it no longer recommends the plan.

Section 9.32(c) permits the board of directors to condition its submission of a plan of conversion to the shareholders or the effectiveness of the plan of conversion. Among the conditions that a board of directors might impose are that the plan will not be deemed approved (i) unless it is approved by a specified vote of the shareholders, or by one or more specified classes or series of shares, voting as a separate voting group, or by a specified percentage of disinterested shareholders or (ii) if shareholders holding more than a specified percentage of the outstanding shares assert appraisal rights.

Section 9.32(d) provides a notice requirement if a plan of conversion is to be considered by the shareholders at a meeting. Requirements concerning the timing and content of a notice of meeting are in section 7.05. Section 9.32(d) does not address the notice to be given to nonvoting or nonconsenting shareholders where the plan is approved without a meeting by written consent. However, that requirement is imposed by section 7.04.

2.   Quorum and Voting

Section 9.32(e) sets forth quorum and voting requirements applicable to a shareholder vote to approve a plan of conversion. It requires both the vote of the shareholders entitled to vote on the plan, and the vote of each class or series of shares voting as a separate voting group. See sections 7.25(f) and 10.04(c) for rules governing when separate classes or series vote together as a single voting group. In lieu of approval at a meeting, shareholder approval may be by written consent under the procedures set forth in section 7.04.

3.   Personal Liability of Shareholders

Section 9.32(f) applies only in situations where a shareholder of a domestic corporation is becoming subject to "interest holder liability," as defined in section 1.40, with respect to the converted entity. Approval of a conversion that would have such a result requires the written consent of each such shareholder who becomes subject to such interest holder liability.

§ 9.33.   Articles of Conversion; Effectiveness

(a) After (i) a plan of conversion of a domestic corporation has been adopted and approved as required by this Act, or (ii) a domestic or foreign eligible entity that is the converting entity has approved a conversion as required under its organic law, articles of conversion shall be signed by the converting entity and must:

(1) state the name, jurisdiction of formation, and type of entity of the converting entity;

(2) state the name, jurisdiction of formation, and type of entity of the converted entity;

(3) if the converting entity is (i) a domestic corporation, state that the plan of conversion was approved in accordance with this subchapter; or (ii) an eligible entity, (A) state that the conversion was approved by the eligible entity in accordance with its organic law or (B) if the converting entity is a

684

domestic eligible entity the organic law of which does not provide for approval of the conversion, state that the conversion was approved by the domestic eligible entity in accordance with this subchapter; and

(4) if the converted entity is (i) a domestic business corporation, or a domestic nonprofit corporation or filing entity, have attached the public organic record of the converted entity, except that provisions that would not be required to be included in a restated public organic record may be omitted; or (ii) a domestic limited liability partnership, have attached the filing required to become a limited liability partnership.

(b) If the converted entity is a domestic corporation, its articles of incorporation must satisfy the requirements of section 2.02, except that provisions that would not be required to be included in restated articles of incorporation may be omitted from the articles of incorporation. If the converted entity is a domestic eligible entity, its public organic record, if any, must satisfy the requirements of the organic law of this state, except that the public organic record does not need to be signed.

(c) The articles of conversion shall be delivered to the secretary of state for filing, and shall take effect at the effective date determined in accordance with section 1.23.

(d) If a converted entity is a domestic entity, the conversion becomes effective when the articles of conversion are effective. With respect to a conversion in which the converted entity is a foreign eligible entity, the conversion itself shall become effective at the later of (i) the date and time provided by the organic law of that eligible entity, and (ii) when the articles of conversion become effective.

(e) Articles of conversion under this section may be combined with any required conversion filing under the organic law of a domestic eligible entity that is the converting entity or converted entity if the combined filing satisfies the requirements of both this section and the other organic law.

(f) If the converting entity is a foreign eligible entity that is registered to do business in this state under a provision of law similar to chapter 15, its registration statement or other type of foreign qualification shall be cancelled automatically on the effective date of its conversion.

§ 9.34. Amendment of Plan of Conversion; Abandonment

(a) A plan of conversion of a converting entity that is a domestic corporation may be amended:

(1) in the same manner as the plan was approved, if the plan does not provide for the manner in which it may be amended; or

(2) in the manner provided in the plan, except that shareholders that were entitled to vote on or consent to approval of the plan are entitled to vote on or consent to any amendment of the plan that will change:

(i) the amount or kind of eligible interests or other securities, obligations, rights to acquire eligible interests or other securities, cash, other property, or any combination of the foregoing, to be received by any of the shareholders of the converting corporation under the plan;

(ii) the organic rules of the converted entity that will be in effect immediately after the conversion becomes effective, except for changes that do not require approval of the eligible interest holders of the converted entity under its organic law or organic rules; or

(iii) any other terms or conditions of the plan, if the change would adversely affect such shareholders in any material respect.

(b) After a plan of conversion has been approved by a converting entity that is a domestic corporation in the manner required by this subchapter and before the articles of conversion become effective, the plan may be abandoned by the corporation without action by its shareholders in accordance with any procedures set forth in the plan or, if no such procedures are set forth in the plan, in the manner determined by the board of directors.

(c) If a conversion is abandoned after the articles of conversion have been delivered to the secretary of state for filing and before the articles of conversion become effective, articles of abandonment, signed by the converting entity, must be delivered to the secretary of state for filing before the articles of conversion become effective. The articles of abandonment take effect on filing, and the conversion is abandoned and does not become effective. The articles of abandonment must contain:

(1) the name of the converting entity;

(2) the date on which the articles of conversion were filed by the secretary of state; and

(3) a statement that the conversion has been abandoned in accordance with this section.

§ 9.35. Effect of Conversion

(a) When a conversion becomes effective:

(1) all property owned by, and every contract right possessed by, the converting entity remain the property and contract rights of the converted entity without transfer, reversion or impairment;

(2) all debts, obligations and other liabilities of the converting entity remain the debts, obligations and other liabilities of the converted entity;

(3) the name of the converted entity may but need not be substituted for the name of the converting entity in any pending action or proceeding;

(4) if the converted entity is a filing entity or a domestic business corporation or a domestic or foreign nonprofit corporation, its public organic record and its private organic rules become effective;

(5) if the converted entity is a nonfiling entity, its private organic rules become effective;

(6) if the converted entity is a limited liability partnership, the filing required to become a limited liability partnership and its private organic rules become effective;

(7) the shares or eligible interests of the converting entity are reclassified into shares, eligible interests or other securities, obligations, rights to acquire shares, eligible interests or other securities, cash, or other property in accordance with the terms of the conversion, and the shareholders or interest holders of the converting entity are entitled only to the rights provided to them by those terms and to any appraisal rights they may have under the organic law of the converting entity; and

(8) the converted entity is:

(i) incorporated or organized under and subject to the organic law of the converted entity;

(ii) the same entity without interruption as the converting entity; and

(iii) deemed to have been incorporated or otherwise organized on the date that the converting entity was originally incorporated or organized.

(b) When a conversion of a domestic corporation to a foreign eligible entity becomes effective, the converted entity is deemed to:

(1) appoint the secretary of state as its agent for service of process in a proceeding to enforce the rights of shareholders who exercise appraisal rights in connection with the conversion; and

(2) agree that it will promptly pay the amount, if any, to which such shareholders are entitled under chapter 13.

(c) Except as otherwise provided in the articles of incorporation of a domestic corporation or the organic law or organic rules of a foreign corporation or a domestic or foreign eligible entity, a shareholder or eligible interest holder who becomes subject to interest holder liability in respect of a domestic corporation or eligible entity as a result of the conversion shall have such interest holder liability only in respect of interest holder liabilities that arise after the conversion becomes effective.

(d) Except as otherwise provided in the organic law or the organic rules of the eligible entity, the interest holder liability of an interest holder in a converting eligible entity that converts to a domestic corporation who had interest holder liability in respect of such converting eligible entity before the conversion becomes effective shall be as follows:

(1) The conversion does not discharge that prior interest holder liability with respect to any interest holder liabilities that arose before the conversion became effective.

(2) The provisions of the organic law of the eligible entity shall continue to apply to the collection or discharge of any interest holder liabilities preserved by subsection (d)(1), as if the conversion had not occurred.

(3) The eligible interest holder shall have such rights of contribution from other persons as are provided by the organic law of the eligible entity with respect to any interest holder liabilities preserved by subsection (d)(1), as if the conversion had not occurred.

(4) The eligible interest holder shall not, by reason of such prior interest holder liability, have interest holder liability with respect to any interest holder liabilities that arise after the conversion becomes effective.

(e) A conversion does not require the converting entity to wind up its affairs and does not constitute or cause the dissolution or termination of the entity.

(f) Property held for charitable purposes under the laws of this state by a corporation or a domestic or foreign eligible entity immediately before a conversion shall not, as a result of the transaction, be diverted from the objects for which it was donated, granted, devised, or otherwise transferred except and to the extent permitted by or pursuant to the laws of this state addressing cy près or dealing with nondiversion of charitable assets.

(g) A bequest, devise, gift, grant, or promise contained in a will or other instrument of donation, subscription, or conveyance which is made to the converting entity and which takes effect or remains payable after the conversion inures to the converted entity.

(h) A trust obligation that would govern property if transferred to the converting entity applies to property that is transferred to the converted entity after the conversion takes effect.

Official Comment

The converted entity is the same entity as the converting entity, and it continues without interruption. It becomes the new type of entity in the specified jurisdiction of formation with the same status as if it had been originally incorporated or organized there. The converted entity will be subject to the organic law for that entity in that jurisdiction and will be subject to all of the duties, liabilities and limitations imposed on such entities in that jurisdiction. Thus, a conversion is not a conveyance, transfer or assignment. It does not give rise to claims of reverter or impairment of title based on a prohibited conveyance, transfer or assignment. Nor does it give rise to a claim that a contract with the converting entity is no longer in effect on the ground of nonassignability, unless the contract specifically provides that it does not survive a conversion. See, however, section 9.30(d) and its Official Comment with respect to special rules regarding protected agreements. All pending proceedings involving the converting entity are continued.

A domestic corporation converting to a foreign entity remains obligated to its shareholders who exercise appraisal rights to pay them the amount, if any, to which they are entitled under chapter 13. For this purpose, under section 9.35(b)(1) that entity is deemed to appoint the secretary of state as its agent for service of process in proceedings to enforce those rights. Where the converted entity is a domestic other entity, it will be similarly liable to the shareholders of a domestic converting corporation pursuant to section 9.35(a)(2).

Section 9.35(c) provides that interest holder liability with respect to a domestic corporation or eligible entity that is the converted entity only relates to interest holder liabilities that arise after the conversion. Section 9.35(d) similarly preserves the interest holder liability of interest holders in an eligible entity that converts to a domestic corporation only for interest holder liabilities to the extent they arise before the conversion becomes effective. Interest holder liability is not preserved for subsequent changes in an underlying liability, regardless of whether a change is voluntary or involuntary.

Chapter 10

AMENDMENT OF ARTICLES OF INCORPORATION AND BYLAWS

Subchapter A

Amendment of Articles of Incorporation

§ 10.01. Authority to Amend

(a) A corporation may amend its articles of incorporation at any time to add or change a provision that is required or permitted in the articles of incorporation as of the effective date of the amendment or to delete a provision that is not required to be contained in the articles of incorporation.

(b) A shareholder of the corporation does not have a vested property right resulting from any provision in the articles of incorporation, including provisions relating to management, control, capital structure, dividend entitlement, or purpose or duration of the corporation.

Official Comment

Under section 10.01(a), the sole test for the permissibility of an amendment to the corporation's articles of incorporation is whether the provision could lawfully have been included in (or in the case of a deletion, omitted from) the articles of incorporation on the effective date of the amendment. The articles of incorporation need not make any reference to, or reserve, the express power to amend the articles of incorporation. Under the Act, a provision in the articles of incorporation is subject to amendment under section 10.01 even though the provision is described, referred to, or stated in a share certificate, a written information statement, or other document issued by the corporation that reflects provisions of the articles of incorporation. Certain amendments or liabilities, however, may not be enforceable against all shareholders without their consent. See, *e.g.*, section 6.27(a) with respect to transfer restrictions and section 9.32(e) with respect to interest holder liability after a conversion, section 10.03(f) with respect to new interest holder liability after an amendment of the articles of incorporation, and section 11.04(i) with respect to new interest holder liability after a merger or share exchange.

Section 10.01 does not override contracts by a corporation outside of its articles of incorporation. For example, a corporation might contract with a shareholder or a third party that it would not make particular amendments to its articles. If the corporation made such an amendment, it would be in breach of the contract even if the amendment were otherwise permitted by this section. A shareholder may also obtain protection against amendments by establishing procedures in the articles of incorporation or bylaws that limit the power of amendment without that shareholder's consent.

Section 10.01(b) expressly rejects the concept that an otherwise lawful amendment to the articles of incorporation might be restricted or invalidated because it modified particular rights conferred on shareholders by the original or prior version of the articles of incorporation. Similarly, under section 1.02, corporations and their shareholders are subject to subsequent amendments of the Act.

§ 10.02. Amendment Before Issuance of Shares

If a corporation has not yet issued shares, its board of directors, or its incorporators if it has no board of directors, may adopt one or more amendments to the corporation's articles of incorporation.

§ 10.03. Amendment by Board of Directors and Shareholders

If a corporation has issued shares, an amendment to the articles of incorporation shall be adopted in the following manner:

(a) The proposed amendment shall first be adopted by the board of directors.

(b) Except as provided in sections 10.05, 10.07, and 10.08, the amendment shall then be approved by the shareholders. In submitting the proposed amendment to the shareholders for approval, the board of directors shall recommend that the shareholders approve the amendment, unless (i) the board of directors makes a determination that because of conflicts of interest or other special circumstances it should not make such a recommendation, or (ii) section 8.26 applies. If either (i) or (ii) applies, the board must inform the shareholders of the basis for its so proceeding.

(c) The board of directors may set conditions for the approval of the amendment by the shareholders or the effectiveness of the amendment.

(d) If the amendment is required to be approved by the shareholders, and the approval is to be given at a meeting, the corporation shall notify each shareholder, regardless of whether entitled to vote, of the meeting of shareholders at which the amendment is to be submitted for approval. The notice must state that the purpose, or one of the purposes, of the meeting is to consider the amendment. The notice must contain or be accompanied by a copy of the amendment.

(e) Unless the articles of incorporation, or the board of directors acting pursuant to subsection (c), require a greater vote or a greater quorum, approval of the amendment requires the approval of the shareholders at a meeting at which a quorum consisting of a majority of the votes entitled to be cast on the amendment exists, and, if any class or series of shares is entitled to vote as a separate group on the amendment, except as provided in section 10.04(c), the approval of each such separate voting group at a meeting at which a quorum of the voting group exists consisting of a majority of the votes entitled to be cast on the amendment by that voting group.

(f) If as a result of an amendment of the articles of incorporation one or more shareholders of a domestic corporation would become subject to new interest holder liability, approval of the amendment requires the signing in connection with the amendment, by each such shareholder, of a separate written consent to become subject to such new interest holder liability, unless in the case of a shareholder that already has interest holder liability the terms and conditions of the new interest holder liability (i) are substantially identical to those of the existing interest holder liability, or (ii) are substantially identical to those of the existing interest holder liability (other than changes that eliminate or reduce such interest holder liability).

(g) For purposes of subsection (f) and section 10.09, "new interest holder liability" means interest holder liability of a person resulting from an amendment of the articles of incorporation if (i) the person did not have interest holder liability before the amendment becomes effective, or (ii) the person had interest holder liability before the amendment becomes effective, the terms and conditions of which are changed when the amendment becomes effective.

Official Comment

Section 10.03 governs amendments to the articles of incorporation after shares have been issued. Most such amendments will require a shareholder vote. When submitting an amendment to the articles of incorporation to shareholders, the board of directors must recommend the amendment, subject to two exceptions in section 10.03(b). The board might exercise the exception under clause (i) where the number of directors having a conflicting interest makes it inadvisable for the board to recommend the amendment or where the board is evenly divided as to the merits of the amendment but is able to agree that shareholders should be permitted to consider it. Alternatively, the board of directors might exercise the exception under clause (ii), which recognizes that, under section 8.26, a board of directors may agree to submit an amendment to a vote of shareholders even if, after approving the amendment, the board of directors determines that it no longer recommends the amendment.

Section 10.03(c) permits the board of directors to set conditions for its submission of an amendment to the shareholders or effectiveness of an amendment. Examples of conditions that a board might impose are that the amendment will not be deemed approved (i) unless it is approved by a specified vote of the shareholders, or by one or more specified classes or series of shares, voting as a separate voting group, or by a specified percentage of votes of disinterested shareholders, or (ii) if shareholders holding more than a specified number or percentage of outstanding shares assert appraisal rights.

Section 10.03(e) specifies quorum and voting requirements applicable to a shareholder vote to approve an amendment to the articles of incorporation. If the prescribed quorum exists, then under sections 7.25 and 7.26 the amendment will be approved if more votes are cast in favor of the amendment than against it by the voting group or separate voting groups entitled to vote on the amendment, unless the articles of incorporation or the board of directors acting pursuant to section 10.03(c) require a greater vote. In lieu of approval at a meeting, shareholder approval may be by written consent under the procedures set forth in section 7.04.

If an amendment would affect the voting or quorum requirements on future amendments, it must also be approved by the vote required by section 7.27.

§ 10.04. Voting on Amendments by Voting Groups

(a) The holders of the outstanding shares of a class are entitled to vote as a separate voting group (if shareholder voting is otherwise required by this Act) on a proposed amendment to the articles of incorporation if the amendment would:

(1) effect an exchange or reclassification of all or part of the shares of the class into shares of another class;

(2) effect an exchange or reclassification, or create the right of exchange, of all or part of the shares of another class into shares of the class;

(3) change the rights, preferences, or limitations of all or part of the shares of the class;

(4) change the shares of all or part of the class into a different number of shares of the same class;

(5) create a new class of shares having rights or preferences with respect to distributions that are prior or superior to the shares of the class;

(6) increase the rights, preferences, or number of authorized shares of any class that, after giving effect to the amendment, have rights or preferences with respect to distributions that are prior or superior to the shares of the class;

(7) limit or deny an existing preemptive right of all or part of the shares of the class; or

(8) cancel or otherwise affect rights to distributions that have accumulated but not yet been authorized on all or part of the shares of the class.

(b) If a proposed amendment would affect a series of a class of shares in one or more of the ways described in subsection (a), the holders of shares of that series are entitled to vote as a separate voting group on the proposed amendment.

(c) If a proposed amendment that entitles the holders of two or more classes or series of shares to vote as separate voting groups under this section would affect those two or more classes or series in the same or a substantially similar way, the holders of shares of all the classes or series so affected shall vote together as a single voting group on the proposed amendment, unless otherwise provided in the articles of incorporation or added as a condition by the board of directors pursuant to section 10.03(c).

(d) A class or series of shares is entitled to the voting rights granted by this section even if the articles of incorporation provide that the shares are nonvoting shares.

Official Comment

Section 10.04(a) requires separate approval by voting groups for certain types of amendments to the articles of incorporation where the corporation has more than one class or series of shares outstanding. Even if a class or series of shares is described as "nonvoting" or the articles purport to make that class or series nonvoting "for all purposes," that class or series nonetheless has the voting rights provided by this section. Likewise, shares are entitled to vote as separate voting groups under this section even though the articles of incorporation purport to allow other classes or series of shares to vote as part of the same voting group. However, an amendment that does not require shareholder approval does not trigger the right to vote by voting groups under this section. This would include a determination by the board, pursuant to authority granted in the articles of incorporation, of the rights, preferences and limitations of any class before the issuance of any shares of that class, or of one or more series within a class before the issuance of any shares of that series. See sections 6.02(a) and (b).

The right to vote as a separate voting group provides a major protection for classes or series of shares with preferential rights, or classes or series of limited or nonvoting shares, against amendments that affect that class or series. This section, however, does not make the right to vote by a separate voting group dependent on an evaluation of whether the amendment is detrimental to that class or series; if the amendment is one of those described in section 10.04(a), the class or series is automatically entitled to vote as a separate voting group on the amendment.

An amendment that changes the number of shares owned by one or more shareholders of a class into a fraction of a share, through a "reverse split," falls within subsection (a)(4) and therefore requires approval by the class, voting as a separate voting group, whether the fractional share is to be issued or otherwise paid in cash under section 6.04. Sections 10.04(a)(5) and (6) refer to preferences with respect to distributions, including distributions in liquidation or dissolution. See section 1.40 and the Official Comment to section 1.40 under "Distributions."

Sections 7.25 and 7.26 set forth the mechanics of voting by multiple voting groups. Section 10.04(b) extends the privilege of voting as a separate voting group to a series of a class of shares if the series is affected in one or more of the ways described in subsection (a). Any distinguishing feature of a series, which an amendment affects or alters, should trigger the right of voting as a separate voting group for that series. However, if a proposed amendment that affects two or more classes or series of shares in the same or a substantially similar way, under subsection (c), the shares of all the class or series so affected must vote together, as a single voting group, unless otherwise provided in the articles of incorporation or a condition set by the board of directors pursuant to section 10.03(c).

The application of sections 10.04(b) and (c) may best be illustrated by the following examples, all of which assume there is no provision in the articles of incorporation providing otherwise and that the board has not set an additional voting condition.

First, assume there is a class of shares comprised of three series, each with different preferential dividend rights. A proposed amendment would reduce the rate of dividend applicable to the "Series A" shares and would change the dividend right of the "Series B" shares from a cumulative to a noncumulative right. The amendment would not affect the preferential dividend right of the "Series C" shares. Both Series A and B would be entitled to vote as separate voting groups on the proposed amendment; the holders of the Series C shares, not directly affected by the amendment, would not be entitled to vote unless the Series C shares are voting shares under the articles of incorporation, in which case the Series C shares would not vote as a separate voting group but would vote in the voting group consisting of all shares in the class, as well as in the voting group consisting of all shares with general voting rights under the articles of incorporation.

Second, if the proposed amendment would reduce the dividend right of Series A and change the dividend right of both Series B and C from a cumulative to a noncumulative right, the holders of Series A would be entitled to vote as a single voting group, and the holders of Series B and C would be required to vote together as a single, separate voting group.

Third, assume that a corporation has common stock and two classes of preferred stock. A proposed amendment would create a new class of senior preferred that would have priority in distribution rights over both the common stock and the existing classes of preferred stock. Because the creation of the new senior preferred would affect all three classes of stock in the same or a substantially similar way, all three classes would vote together as a single voting group on the proposed amendment.

§ 10.05. Amendment by Board of Directors

Unless the articles of incorporation provide otherwise, a corporation's board of directors may adopt amendments to the corporation's articles of incorporation without shareholder approval:

(a) to extend the duration of the corporation if it was incorporated at a time when limited duration was required by law;

(b) to delete the names and addresses of the initial directors;

(c) to delete the name and address of the initial registered agent or registered office, if a statement of change is on file with the secretary of state;

(d) if the corporation has only one class of shares outstanding:

(1) to change each issued and unissued authorized share of the class into a greater number of whole shares of that class; or

(2) to increase the number of authorized shares of the class to the extent necessary to permit the issuance of shares as a share dividend;

(e) to change the corporate name by substituting the word "corporation," "incorporated," "company," "limited," or the abbreviation "corp.," "inc.," "co.," or "ltd.," for a similar word or abbreviation in the name, or by adding, deleting, or changing a geographical attribution for the name;

(f) to reflect a reduction in authorized shares, as a result of the operation of section 6.31(b), when the corporation has acquired its own shares and the articles of incorporation prohibit the reissue of the acquired shares;

(g) to delete a class of shares from the articles of incorporation, as a result of the operation of section 6.31(b), when there are no remaining shares of the class because the corporation has acquired all shares of the class and the articles of incorporation prohibit the reissue of the acquired shares; or

(h) to make any change expressly permitted by section 6.02(a) or (b) to be made without shareholder approval.

Official Comment

The amendments described in subsections (a) through (h) are so routine and ministerial in nature as not to require approval by shareholders. None affects the substantive rights of shareholders in any meaningful way. Although the board of directors' designation of the preferences, rights and limitations of a new class or series of shares under section 6.02 may have substantive effects, amendments of the articles of incorporation to set forth the terms of a new class or series are already permitted by section 6.02(c). Amendments provided for in this section may be included in restated articles of incorporation under section 10.07 or in articles of merger under chapter 11.

§ 10.06. Articles of Amendment

(a) After an amendment to the articles of incorporation has been adopted and approved in the manner required by this Act and by the articles of incorporation, the corporation shall deliver to the secretary of state for filing articles of amendment, which must set forth:

(1) the name of the corporation;

(2) the text of each amendment adopted, or the information required by section 1.20(k)(5);

(3) if an amendment provides for an exchange, reclassification, or cancellation of issued shares, provisions for implementing the amendment if not contained in the amendment itself, (which may be made dependent upon facts objectively ascertainable outside the articles of amendment in accordance with section 1.20(k)(5);

(4) the date of each amendment's adoption; and

(5) if an amendment:

(i) was adopted by the incorporators or board of directors without shareholder approval, a statement that the amendment was duly adopted by the incorporators or by the board of directors, as the case may be, and that shareholder approval was not required;

(ii) required approval by the shareholders, a statement that the amendment was duly approved by the shareholders in the manner required by this Act and by the articles of incorporation; or

(iii) is being filed pursuant to section 1.20(k)(5), a statement to that effect.

(b) Articles of amendment shall take effect at the effective date determined in accordance with section 1.23.

Official Comment

Section 10.06(a)(3) requires the articles of amendment to contain a statement of the manner in which an exchange, reclassification, or cancellation of issued shares is to be put into effect if not set forth in the amendment itself. This requirement avoids confusion as to how the amendment is to be put into effect and also permits the amendment itself to be limited to provisions of permanent applicability, with transitional provisions having no long-range effect appearing only in the articles of amendment. If such transitional provisions are not part of the amendment itself, they are not required to be in a restatement of the articles of incorporation pursuant to section 10.07.

§ 10.07. Restated Articles of Incorporation

(a) A corporation's board of directors may restate its articles of incorporation at any time, without shareholder approval, to consolidate all amendments into a single document.

(b) If the restated articles include one or more new amendments that require shareholder approval, the amendments shall be adopted and approved as provided in section 10.03.

(c) A corporation that restates its articles of incorporation shall deliver to the secretary of state for filing articles of restatement setting forth:

(1) the name of the corporation;

(2) the text of the restated articles of incorporation;

(3) a statement that the restated articles consolidate all amendments into a single document; and

(4) if a new amendment is included in the restated articles, the statements required under section 10.06 with respect to the new amendment.

(d) Duly adopted restated articles of incorporation supersede the original articles of incorporation and all amendments to the articles of incorporation.

(e) The secretary of state may certify restated articles of incorporation as the articles of incorporation currently in effect, without including the statements required by subsection (c)(4).

Official Comment

Restated articles of incorporation permit articles of incorporation that have been amended over time, or are being concurrently amended, to be consolidated into a single document. A restatement of a corporation's articles of incorporation is not an amendment, but only a consolidation of amendments. A corporation that is restating its articles may concurrently amend the articles, and include the new amendments in the restated articles. In such a case, the provisions of this chapter that govern amendments of the articles of incorporation would apply to the new amendments. If it is unclear whether a provision of a restatement of the articles of incorporation might be deemed to be an amendment, rather than a consolidation, the prudent course for the corporation is to treat that provision as an amendment, and follow the procedures that apply to amendments under this chapter.

§ 10.08. Amendment Pursuant to Reorganization

(a) A corporation's articles of incorporation may be amended without action by the board of directors or shareholders to carry out a plan of reorganization ordered or decreed by a court of competent jurisdiction under the authority of a law of the United States.

(b) The individual or individuals designated by the court shall deliver to the secretary of state for filing articles of amendment setting forth:

(1) the name of the corporation;

(2) the text of each amendment approved by the court;

(3) the date of the court's order or decree approving the articles of amendment;

(4) the title of the reorganization proceeding in which the order or decree was entered; and

(5) a statement that the court had jurisdiction of the proceeding under federal statute.

(c) This section does not apply after entry of a final decree in the reorganization proceeding even though the court retains jurisdiction of the proceeding for limited purposes unrelated to consummation of the reorganization plan.

Official Comment

Section 10.08 provides a simplified method of conforming corporate documents filed under state law with the federal statutes relating to corporate reorganization. If a federal court confirms a plan of reorganization that requires articles of amendment to be filed, those amendments may be prepared and filed by the persons designated by the court and the approval of neither the shareholders nor the board of directors is required.

§ 10.09. Effect of Amendment

(a) An amendment to the articles of incorporation does not affect a cause of action existing against or in favor of the corporation, a proceeding to which the corporation is a party, or the existing rights of persons other than the shareholders. An amendment changing a corporation's name does not affect a proceeding brought by or against the corporation in its former name.

(b) A shareholder who becomes subject to new interest holder liability in respect of the corporation as a result of an amendment to the articles of incorporation shall have that new interest holder liability only in respect of interest holder liabilities that arise after the amendment becomes effective.

(c) Except as otherwise provided in the articles of incorporation of the corporation, the interest holder liability of a shareholder who had interest holder liability in respect of the corporation before the amendment becomes effective and has new interest holder liability after the amendment becomes effective shall be as follows:

(1) The amendment does not discharge that prior interest holder liability with respect to any interest holder liabilities that arose before the amendment becomes effective.

(2) The provisions of the articles of incorporation of the corporation relating to interest holder liability as in effect immediately prior to the amendment shall continue to apply to the collection or discharge of any interest holder liabilities preserved by subsection (c)(1), as if the amendment had not occurred.

(3) The shareholder shall have such rights of contribution from other persons as are provided by the articles of incorporation relating to interest holder liability as in effect immediately prior to the amendment with respect to any interest holder liabilities preserved by subsection (c)(1), as if the amendment had not occurred.

(4) The shareholder shall not, by reason of such prior interest holder liability, have interest holder liability with respect to any interest holder liabilities that arise after the amendment becomes effective.

Subchapter B

Amendment of Bylaws

§ 10.20. Authority to Amend

(a) A corporation's shareholders may amend or repeal the corporation's bylaws.

(b) A corporation's board of directors may amend or repeal the corporation's bylaws, unless:

(1) the articles of incorporation, section 10.21 or, if applicable, section 10.22 reserve that power exclusively to the shareholders in whole or part; or

(2) except as provided in section 2.06(d), the shareholders in amending, repealing, or adopting a bylaw expressly provide that the board of directors may not amend, repeal, or adopt that bylaw.

(c) A shareholder of the corporation does not have a vested property right resulting from any provision in the bylaws.

Official Comment

The power to amend or repeal bylaws is shared by the board of directors and the shareholders, unless that power is reserved exclusively to the shareholders by an appropriate provision in the articles of incorporation. Section 10.20(b)(1) permits the reservation of amendment power to the shareholders to be limited to specific articles or sections of the bylaws or to specific subjects or topics addressed in the bylaws.

The authority granted to the shareholders in section 10.20(b)(2) to prevent the board of directors from further changing a bylaw which the shareholders have amended, repealed, or adopted is expressly subject to section 2.06(d), which limits the authority of shareholders to restrict board action on bylaws with regard to procedures or conditions set forth in certain bylaws regulating the election of directors. See the Official Comment to section 2.06. . . .

Similar to section 10.01(b), section 10.21(c) expressly confirms that an amendment to the bylaws may not be restricted or invalidated because it modifies particular rights conferred on shareholders by the original or a prior version of the bylaws.

694

§ 10.21. Bylaw Increasing Quorum or Voting Requirement for Directors

(a) A bylaw that increases a quorum or voting requirement for the board of directors may be amended or repealed:

(1) if originally adopted by the shareholders, only by the shareholders, unless the bylaw otherwise provides; or

(2) if adopted by the board of directors, either by the shareholders or by the board of directors.

(b) A bylaw adopted or amended by the shareholders that increases a quorum or voting requirement for the board of directors may provide that it can be amended or repealed only by a specified vote of either the shareholders or the board of directors.

(c) Action by the board of directors under subsection (a) to amend or repeal a bylaw that changes a quorum or voting requirement for the board of directors shall meet the same quorum requirement and be adopted by the same vote required to take action under the quorum and voting requirement then in effect or proposed to be adopted, whichever is greater.

§ 10.22. Bylaw Provisions Relating to the Election of Directors

(a) Unless the articles of incorporation (i) specifically prohibit the adoption of a bylaw pursuant to this section, (ii) alter the vote specified in section 7.28(a), or (iii) provide for cumulative voting, a corporation may elect in its bylaws to be governed in the election of directors as follows:

(1) each vote entitled to be cast may be voted for or against up to that number of candidates that is equal to the number of directors to be elected, or a shareholder may indicate an abstention, but without cumulating the votes;

(2) to be elected, a nominee shall have received a plurality of the votes cast by holders of shares entitled to vote in the election at a meeting at which a quorum is present, provided that a nominee who is elected but receives more votes against than for election shall serve as a director for a term that shall terminate on the date that is the earlier of (i) 90 days from the date on which the voting results are determined pursuant to section 7.29(b)(5) or (ii) the date on which an individual is selected by the board of directors to fill the office held by such director, which selection shall be deemed to constitute the filling of a vacancy by the board to which section 8.10 applies. Subject to subsection (a)(3), a nominee who is elected but receives more votes against than for election shall not serve as a director beyond the 90-day period referenced above; and

(3) the board of directors may select any qualified individual to fill the office held by a director who received more votes against than for election.

(b) Subsection (a) does not apply to an election of directors by a voting group if (i) at the expiration of the time fixed under a provision requiring advance notification of director candidates, or (ii) absent such a provision, at a time fixed by the board of directors which is not more than 14 days before notice is given of the meeting at which the election is to occur, there are more candidates for election by the voting group than the number of directors to be elected, one or more of whom are properly proposed by shareholders. An individual shall not be considered a candidate for purposes of this subsection if the board of directors determines before the notice of meeting is given that such individual's candidacy does not create a bona fide election contest.

(c) A bylaw electing to be governed by this section may be repealed:

(1) if originally adopted by the shareholders, only by the shareholders, unless the bylaw otherwise provides;

(2) if adopted by the board of directors, by the board of directors or the shareholders.

Official Comment

Section 10.22 is effective only if a corporation elects in a bylaw to be governed by its terms. The provisions of section 10.22 effectively modify the term and holdover provisions of section 8.05 pursuant to a limited exception for section 10.22 that is recognized in section 8.05. Accordingly, a bylaw provision that would seek to alter the term and holdover provision of section 8.05 that varied in any manner from section 10.22 would not be effective.

1.   *Section 10.22(a)*

The rule in subsection (a) is straightforward if the nominees for director equal the number of directorships up for election. In that case, and by way of example, the holder of a single share could vote either for or against each director. In the unusual case that section 10.22(a) were applicable to a contested election notwithstanding the provisions of section 10.22(b) (*e.g.*, in the absence of an advance notice bylaw, a contest arises as a result of candidates for director being proposed subsequent to the determination date under section 10.22(b)), the holder of a share would have to choose whether to indicate opposition to a slate by voting in favor of a candidate on the preferred slate or by voting against a candidate on the disfavored slate, or to abstain. Because it would be in the interests of all contestants to explain in their proxy materials that against votes would not be counted in favor of any candidate in a contested election, the rational voter in a contested election might be expected to vote in favor of all candidates on the preferred slate to promote a simple plurality victory rather than voting against candidates on the disfavored slate. Nothing in section 10.22 would prevent the holder of more than one share from voting differently with respect to each share held.

Section 10.22(a) specifically contemplates that a corporate ballot for the election of directors would provide for "against" votes. Although there is no prohibition in the Act against a corporation offering shareholders the opportunity to vote "against" candidates at any time, unless the corporation elects to be governed by section 10.22 or the articles of incorporation are amended to make such a vote meaningful, an "against" vote is given no effect under the Act.

Section 10.22(a)(2) does not conflict with or alter the plurality voting default standard. However, because section 10.22 shortens the term of a director who is elected but receives more votes against election than in favor of election, a vacancy will exist if no action is taken to fill the vacancy before the expiration of the shortened term. As contemplated by section 8.10, that vacancy may be filled by shareholders or by the board of directors, unless the articles of incorporation provide otherwise. In the alternative, action could be taken by amendment to, or in the manner provided in, the articles of incorporation or bylaws to reduce the size of the board of directors. See section 8.03.

Under section 8.05(d), the director appointed to fill the vacancy would be up for reelection at the next annual meeting, even if the term for that directorship would otherwise have been for more than one year, as in the case of a staggered board.

There is also no limitation in section 10.22 or elsewhere in the Act on the power of either the board of directors or shareholders to fill a vacancy with the person who held such directorship before the vacancy arose.

2.   *Section 10.22(b)*

Under section 10.22(b), when there are more candidates for election as directors by a voting group (as defined in section 1.40) than director positions to be filled, the resulting election contest would not be subject to the voting regime under section 10.22(a). Instead, it would be conducted by means of a plurality vote under section 7.28(a). Such plurality voting is appropriate in that circumstance because shareholders will have a choice between competing candidates.

The timing provided in clauses (i) and (ii) of subsection (b) for determining when section 10.22(a) does not apply to an election assures that the voting regime that will apply will be known in advance of the giving of notice, and that the disclosure of the voting rules and the proxy appointment form will be clear and reflect the applicable voting regime. The determination of how many candidates there are to fill the number of director positions up for election may be made by the board of directors. The board's determination of whether an individual shall not be considered a candidate for purposes of section 10.22(b) because the candidacy does not create a bona fide election contest must be made before notice of the meeting is given. The board of directors might choose, for example, to exercise this authority to preserve the voting regime under section 10.22(a) when it is clear that an individual has designated himself or herself as a candidate without intending to solicit votes or for the purpose of frustrating the availability of the section 10.22(a) voting regime.

The contested or uncontested nature of the election can change following the date for determining the voting regime that will apply. For example, an election that is contested at that date could become uncontested if a candidate withdraws. Conversely, unless the bylaws require advance notice of director nomination, an uncontested election could become contested before the vote is taken but after notice of the meeting has been given because there is no limitation on the ability of shareholders to nominate candidates for directorships up until the time nominations are closed at the meeting. Section 10.22(b) does not authorize changing the voting regime in those circumstances.

Chapter 11

MERGERS AND SHARE EXCHANGES

Introductory Comment

Transactions Permitted

Chapter 11 deals with mergers and share exchanges. A merger is the traditional form for combining entities by operation of law, and the range of merger transactions chapter 11 permits is broad. In a merger, a domestic business corporation may merge with one or more of the following domestic or foreign entities: (i) business corporations; (ii) unincorporated entities (including limited liability companies, general and limited partnerships and business trusts); and (iii) nonprofit corporations (which are defined together with unincorporated entities as "eligible entities;" neither is included in the defined term "corporation"). These and other relevant terms used in this chapter are defined in sections 1.40 and 11.01.

The entity resulting from the merger may be one of the parties to the merger, or a new corporation or eligible entity created by the merger. Chapter 11 therefore may apply to a merger in which none of the parties is a domestic corporation, as long as the resulting entity (defined in section 11.01 as the "survivor") is a new domestic corporation. In the case of any merger involving a corporation or eligible entity organized under the laws of a foreign jurisdiction, the Act recognizes that whether and how those foreign entities may merge are matters governed by the law of the foreign jurisdiction.

Chapter 11 also permits share exchanges in which either (i) a domestic corporation acquires all of the shares or eligible interests of one or more classes or series of another domestic or foreign corporation or eligible entity, or (ii) all of the shares of one of more classes or series of a domestic corporation are acquired by another domestic or foreign corporation or eligible entity. As a result, in a share exchange, the existence of the acquired entity (the entity whose shares are acquired) continues. If enough shares or eligible interests are acquired, the acquired entity may become a subsidiary of the acquiring entity. Each of these transactions is a share exchange, even if it involves no shares and only "eligible interests" (which are defined in section 1.40 as specified rights in unincorporated entities and memberships in nonprofit corporations). A foreign corporation or eligible entity may only be the acquired entity in a share exchange if it is permitted by the law governing the foreign corporation or eligible entity.

Other chapters of the Act permit transactions that once could only be effected by merger. For example, chapter 9 provides for domestications, in which corporations can reincorporate in another jurisdiction, and conversions, in which corporations may convert to eligible entities. The Act's approach is generally to provide similar procedures for effecting any of these types of transactions and certain other fundamental actions, such as amendments to the articles of incorporation under chapter 10 and sales of assets outside the usual and regular course of business under chapter 12.

Requirements and Effects

Section 11.02 generally authorizes mergers and sets out requirements for their approval. For a domestic corporation, the requirements usually include a plan of merger, adopted by the board of directors and recommended by the board of directors to the shareholders, and approved by the shareholders. Section 11.03 has similar provisions for share exchanges and plans of share exchange. These sections permit the holders of shares or eligible interests of a party to a merger or of an acquired class or series in a share exchange to receive a broad range of consideration for their shares or interests. Section 11.04 sets out the approval requirements for domestic corporations that are parties to mergers or acquired entities in share exchanges, although section 11.05 has special rules for certain parent-subsidiary transactions. Section 11.06 relates to the preparation and filing of articles of merger and share exchange, and section 11.07 states the effects of those transactions. Finally, section 11.08 provides how mergers and share exchanges may be abandoned after they are adopted and approved. Dissenting shareholders in certain mergers and share exchanges and certain other fundamental actions have appraisal rights under chapter 13.

§ 11.01. Definitions

As used in this chapter:

"Acquired entity" means the domestic or foreign corporation or eligible entity that will have all of one or more classes or series of its shares or eligible interests acquired in a share exchange.

"Acquiring entity" means the domestic or foreign corporation or eligible entity that will acquire all of one or more classes or series of shares or eligible interests of the acquired entity in a share exchange.

"New interest holder liability" means interest holder liability of a person, resulting from a merger or share exchange, that is (i) in respect of an entity which is different from the entity in which the person held shares or eligible interests immediately before the merger or share exchange became effective; or (ii) in respect of the same entity as the one in which the person held shares or eligible interests immediately before the merger or share exchange became effective if (A) the person did not have interest holder liability immediately before the merger or share exchange became effective, or (B) the person had interest holder liability immediately before the merger or share exchange became effective, the terms and conditions of which were changed when the merger or share exchange became effective.

"Party to a merger" means any domestic or foreign corporation or eligible entity that will merge under a plan of merger but does not include a survivor created by the merger.

"Survivor" in a merger means the domestic or foreign corporation or eligible entity into which one or more other corporations or eligible entities are merged.

Official Comment

Section 11.01 defines the parties to a merger as the entities that merge. Thus the parties to a merger do not include, for example, a new corporation or entity created by the merger that is the survivor, even though it results from the merger, or a parent corporation or entity that issues its securities as part of the merger consideration but does not itself merge. The definition of "survivor" contemplates the possibility that the survivor may not exist prior to the merger, and not be a party to the merger, but rather be created by the merger of two or more other corporations or entities. In that case, the survivor will need to be specified as a new corporation or entity in the plan of merger.

Share exchange is defined in section 1.40 by reference to section 11.03, and the range of parties and types of consideration permitted in a transaction under that section is broad. It could include, for example, the acquisition by a corporation of eligible interests in a partnership for cash. While that transaction would not involve either the acquisition or issuance of a corporation's shares, it nevertheless falls within the definition of share exchange.

§ 11.02. Merger

(a) By complying with this chapter:

(1) one or more domestic business corporations may merge with one or more domestic or foreign business corporations or eligible entities pursuant to a plan of merger, resulting in a survivor; and

(2) two or more foreign business corporations or domestic or foreign eligible entities may merge, resulting in a survivor that is a domestic business corporation created in the merger.

(b) By complying with the provisions of this chapter applicable to foreign entities, a foreign business corporation or a foreign eligible entity may be a party to a merger with a domestic business corporation, or may be created as the survivor in a merger in which a domestic business corporation is a party, but only if the merger is permitted by the organic law of the foreign business corporation or eligible entity.

(c) If the organic law or organic rules of a domestic eligible entity do not provide procedures for the approval of a merger, a plan of merger may nonetheless be adopted and approved by the unanimous consent of all of the interest holders of such eligible entity, and the merger may thereafter by effected as provided in the other provisions of this chapter; and for the purposes of applying this chapter in such a case:

(1) the eligible entity, its members or interest holders, eligible interests and articles of incorporation or other organic rules taken together shall be deemed to be a domestic business corporation, shareholders, shares and articles of incorporation, respectively and vice versa as the context may require; and

(2) if the business and affairs of the eligible entity are managed by a person or persons that are not identical to the members or interest holders, that group shall be deemed to be the board of directors.

(d) The plan of merger must include:

(1) as to each party to the merger, its name, jurisdiction of formation, and type of entity;

(2) the survivor's name, jurisdiction of formation, and type of entity, and, if the survivor is to be created in the merger, a statement to that effect;

(3) the terms and conditions of the merger;

(4) the manner and basis of converting the shares of each merging domestic or foreign business corporation and eligible interests of each merging domestic or foreign eligible entity into shares or other securities, eligible interests, obligations, rights to acquire shares, other securities or eligible interests, cash, other property, or any combination of the foregoing;

(5) the articles of incorporation of any domestic or foreign business or nonprofit corporation, or the public organic record of any domestic or foreign unincorporated entity, to be created by the merger, or if a new domestic or foreign business or nonprofit corporation or unincorporated entity is not to be created by the merger, any amendments to the survivor's articles of incorporation or other public organic record; and

(6) any other provisions required by the laws under which any party to the merger is organized or by which it is governed, or by the articles of incorporation or organic rules of any such party.

(e) In addition to the requirements of subsection (d), a plan of merger may contain any other provision not prohibited by law.

(f) Terms of a plan of merger may be made dependent on facts objectively ascertainable outside the plan in accordance with section 1.20(k).

(g) A plan of merger may be amended only with the consent of each party to the merger, except as provided in the plan. A domestic party to a merger may approve an amendment to a plan:

(1) in the same manner as the plan was approved, if the plan does not provide for the manner in which it may be amended; or

(2) in the manner provided in the plan, except that shareholders, members, or interest holders that were entitled to vote on or consent to approval of the plan are entitled to vote on or consent to any amendment of the plan that will change:

(i) the amount or kind of shares or other securities, eligible interests, obligations, rights to acquire shares, other securities or eligible interests, cash, or other property to be received under the plan by the shareholders, members, or interest holders of any party to the merger;

(ii) the articles of incorporation of any domestic or foreign business or nonprofit corporation, or the organic rules of any unincorporated entity, that will be the survivor of the merger, except for changes permitted by section 10.05 or by comparable provisions of the organic law of any such foreign corporation or domestic or foreign nonprofit corporation or unincorporated entity; or

(iii) any of the other terms or conditions of the plan if the change would adversely affect such shareholders, members, or interest holders in any material respect.

Official Comment

1. In General

Section 11.02 authorizes domestic corporations to merge with each other. It also authorizes one or more domestic corporations to merge with one or more foreign corporations or domestic or foreign eligible entities (such as limited liability companies or partnerships). In addition, it provides for the merger of two or more foreign corporations or foreign or domestic eligible entities, even if no domestic business corporation is a party to the merger, but only if the survivor is a domestic business corporation created by the merger.

2. Applicability to Foreign Corporations and Eligible Entities and to Domestic Eligible Entities

A foreign corporation or a foreign eligible entity may be a party to or be the survivor in a merger authorized by chapter 11 only if the merger is permitted by the laws under which the foreign corporation or eligible entity is organized. Whether and on what terms a foreign corporation or a foreign eligible entity is authorized to merge is governed by those laws. If a foreign corporation or eligible entity is so authorized, it must comply with the applicable provisions of chapter 11 in addition to the requirements of its own governing laws. For example, section 11.02(d) sets forth certain requirements for the contents of a plan of merger with a domestic corporation, and section 11.07(d) provides that upon a merger becoming effective, a foreign corporation or foreign eligible entity that is the survivor is deemed to appoint the secretary of state as its agent for service of process in a proceeding to enforce appraisal rights of shareholders of each domestic corporation that is a party to the merger.

With respect to a domestic eligible entity, if the law under which it is organized does not expressly authorize it to be a party to or survive a merger under chapter 11, section 11.02(c) provides procedures for such an entity to adopt and effect a plan of merger.

3. Terms and Conditions of Merger

Chapter 11 imposes no restrictions or limitations on the terms or conditions of a merger, except for those set forth in section 11.02(g). The list in section 11.02(d) of provisions in a plan of merger is not exhaustive.

4. Amendments of Articles of Incorporation

Under section 11.02, a corporation's articles of incorporation may be amended by a merger, and section 11.02(d)(5) provides that a plan of merger must include any such amendments. If the plan of merger is approved and the survivor is a domestic entity, section 11.07 provides that the amendments will become effective with the merger. If the plan includes amendments to the articles of incorporation of a surviving domestic corporation, section 11.04(f)(1)(ii), by reference to the voting requirements of section 10.04 relating to amendments of the articles of incorporation, may impose voting requirements by separate voting groups that would not otherwise apply.

Although the plan of merger must include any amendments to the articles of incorporation or public organic record of the survivor, the survivor's articles of incorporation or public organic record are not required to be included in the plan unless the survivor is created by the merger. However, if approval of the plan of merger by the shareholders of a domestic corporation is required under section 11.04, section 11.04(d) requires that its shareholders be furnished with a copy or summary of the articles of incorporation or public organic record of the survivor in connection with voting on approval.

§ 11.03. Share Exchange

(a) By complying with this chapter:

(1) a domestic corporation may acquire all of the shares of one or more classes or series of shares of another domestic or foreign corporation, or all of the eligible interests of one or more classes or series of interests of a domestic or foreign eligible entity, in exchange for shares or other securities, eligible interests, obligations, rights to acquire shares or other securities or eligible interests, cash, other property, or any combination of the foregoing, pursuant to a plan of share exchange; or

(2) all of the shares of one or more classes or series of shares of a domestic corporation may be acquired by another domestic or foreign corporation or eligible entity, in exchange for shares or other securities, eligible interests, obligations, rights to acquire shares or other securities or eligible interests, cash, other property, or any combination of the foregoing, pursuant to a plan of share exchange.

(b) A foreign corporation or eligible entity may be the acquired entity in a share exchange only if the share exchange is permitted by the organic law of that corporation or other entity.

(c) If the organic law or organic rules of a domestic eligible entity do not provide procedures for the approval of a share exchange, a plan of share exchange may be adopted and approved, and the share exchange effected, in accordance with the procedures, if any, for a merger. If the organic law or organic rules of a domestic eligible entity do not provide procedures for the approval of either a share exchange or a merger, a plan of share exchange may nonetheless be adopted and approved by the unanimous consent of all of the interest holders of such eligible entity whose interests will be exchanged under the plan of share exchange, and the share exchange may thereafter be effected as provided in the other provisions of this chapter; and for purposes of applying this chapter in such a case:

(1) the eligible entity, its interest holders, interests and articles of incorporation or other organic rules taken together shall be deemed to be a domestic business corporation, shareholders, shares and articles of incorporation, respectively and vice versa as the context may require; and

(2) if the business and affairs of the eligible entity are managed by a person or persons that are not identical to the members or interest holders, that person or those persons shall be deemed to be the board of directors.

(d) The plan of share exchange must include:

(1) the name of each domestic or foreign corporation or other eligible entity the shares or eligible interests of which will be acquired and the name of the domestic or foreign corporation or eligible entity that will acquire those shares or eligible interests;

(2) the terms and conditions of the share exchange;

(3) the manner and basis of exchanging shares of a domestic or foreign corporation or eligible interests in a domestic or foreign eligible entity the shares or eligible interests of which will be acquired under the share exchange for shares or other securities, eligible interests, obligations, rights to acquire shares, other securities, or eligible interests, cash, other property, or any combination of the foregoing; and

(4) any other provisions required by the organic law governing the acquired entity or its articles of incorporation or organic rules.

(e) Terms of a plan of share exchange may be made dependent on facts objectively ascertainable outside the plan in accordance with section 1.20(k).

(f) A plan of share exchange may be amended only with the consent of each party to the share exchange, except as provided in the plan. A domestic entity may approve an amendment to a plan:

(1) in the same manner as the plan was approved, if the plan does not provide for the manner in which it may be amended; or

(2) in the manner provided in the plan, except that shareholders, members, or interest holders that were entitled to vote on or consent to approval of the plan are entitled to vote on or consent to any amendment of the plan that will change:

(i) the amount or kind of shares or other securities, eligible interests, obligations, rights to acquire shares, other securities or eligible interests, cash, or other property to be received under the plan by the shareholders, members or interest holders of the acquired entity; or

(ii) any of the other terms or conditions of the plan if the change would adversely affect such shareholders, members or interest holders in any material respect.

Official Comment

1. In General

It is often desirable to structure a corporate combination so that the separate existence of one or more parties to the combination does not cease although another corporation or other entity obtains ownership of the shares or interests of those parties. This objective is often particularly important in the formation of insurance and bank holding companies, but is not limited to those contexts. In the absence of the procedure authorized in section 11.03, this kind of result often can be accomplished only by a reverse triangular merger, which involves the formation by a corporation, A, of a new subsidiary, followed by a merger of that subsidiary into another party to the merger, B, effected through the exchange of A's securities for securities of B. Section 11.03 authorizes a more straightforward procedure to accomplish the same result.

Section 11.03 authorizes a share exchange—a transaction in which the acquiring entity acquires all of the shares or eligible interests of one or more classes or series of shares or eligible interests of the acquired entity. The shares or eligible interests of one or more other classes or series of the acquired entity may be excluded from the share exchange or may be included on different bases. Shares or eligible interests of the affected class or series of the acquired entity owned at the effective time of the share exchange by the acquiring entity (or any parent of the acquiring entity or by any wholly owned subsidiary of the acquiring entity or of any such parent, each as defined in section 11.04(k)), may also be excluded from the share exchange.

After the plan of share exchange is adopted and approved as required by section 11.04, it is binding on all holders of the shares or eligible interests of the class or series to be acquired. Section 11.03 does not limit the power of a domestic corporation to acquire shares of another corporation or interests in another entity in a transaction other than a share exchange. In contrast to mergers, the articles of incorporation or public organic record of a party to a share exchange may not be amended by a plan of share exchange. Such an amendment to the articles of incorporation may, however, be effected under chapter 10 as a separate element of a corporate combination that involves a share exchange.

2. *Applicability to Foreign Corporations and Foreign and Domestic Eligible Entities*

A foreign corporation or a foreign eligible entity may be an acquired entity in a share exchange authorized by chapter 11 only if the share exchange is permitted by the organic law of the foreign corporation or eligible entity. Whether and on what terms a foreign corporation or a foreign eligible entity is authorized to be a party to a share exchange is governed by its organic law. If a foreign corporation or eligible entity is so authorized, it must also comply with the applicable terms of chapter 11 in addition to the requirements of its organic law. For example, section 11.03(d) sets forth certain requirements for the content of a plan of share exchange.

With respect to a domestic eligible entity, if the law under which it is organized does not expressly authorize it to be a party to a share exchange under chapter 11, section 11.03(a) is intended to provide the necessary authority. In that case, section 11.03(c) provides procedures for adopting, approving and effecting a plan of share exchange.

3. *Terms and Conditions of Share Exchange*

Chapter 11 imposes no restrictions or limitations on the terms or conditions of a share exchange, except for those contained in section 11.03(f), and the requirement in section 11.03(a) that the acquiring entity must acquire all the shares or eligible interests of the acquired class or series of shares or eligible interests. However, shares or interests of the acquired class or series owned at the effective time of the share exchange by the acquiring entity or any of its parents or their wholly owned subsidiaries may be excluded from the exchange. The list in section 11.03(d) of provisions in a plan of share exchange is not exhaustive.

§ 11.04. Action on a Plan of Merger or Share Exchange

In the case of a domestic corporation that is a party to a merger or the acquired entity in a share exchange, the plan of merger or share exchange shall be adopted in the following manner:

(a) The plan of merger or share exchange shall first be adopted by the board of directors.

(b) Except as provided in subsections (h), (j) and (*l*) and in section 11.05, the plan of merger or share exchange shall then be approved by the shareholders. In submitting the plan of merger or share exchange to the shareholders for approval, the board of directors shall recommend that the shareholders approve the plan or, in the case of an offer referred to in subsection (j)(2), that the shareholders tender their shares to the offeror in response to the offer, unless (i) the board of directors makes a determination that because of conflicts of interest or other special circumstances it should not make such a recommendation or (ii) section 8.26 applies. If either (i) or (ii) applies, the board shall inform the shareholders of the basis for its so proceeding.

(c) The board of directors may set conditions for the approval of the plan of merger or share exchange by the shareholders or the effectiveness of the plan of merger or share exchange.

(d) If the plan of merger or share exchange is required to be approved by the shareholders, and if the approval is to be given at a meeting, the corporation shall notify each shareholder, regardless of whether entitled to vote, of the meeting of shareholders at which the plan is to be submitted for approval. The notice must state that the purpose, or one of the purposes, of the meeting is to consider the plan and must contain or be accompanied by a copy or summary of the plan. If the corporation is to be merged into an existing foreign or domestic corporation or eligible entity, the notice must also include or be accompanied by a copy or summary of the articles of incorporation and bylaws or the organic rules of that corporation or eligible entity. If the corporation is to be merged with a domestic or foreign corporation or eligible entity and a new domestic or foreign corporation or eligible entity is to be created pursuant to the merger, the notice must include or be accompanied by a copy or a summary of the articles of incorporation and bylaws or the organic rules of the new corporation or eligible entity.

(e) Unless the articles of incorporation, or the board of directors acting pursuant to subsection (c), require a greater vote or a greater quorum, approval of the plan of merger or share exchange requires the approval of the shareholders at a meeting at which a quorum exists consisting of a majority of the votes entitled to be cast on the plan, and, if any class or series of shares is entitled to vote as a separate group on the plan of merger or share exchange, the approval of each such separate voting group at a meeting at which a quorum of the voting group is present consisting of a majority of the votes entitled to be cast on the merger or share exchange by that voting group.

(f) Subject to subsection (g), separate voting by voting groups is required:

(1) on a plan of merger, by each class or series of shares that:

(i) are to be converted under the plan of merger into shares, other securities, eligible interests, obligations, rights to acquire shares, other securities or eligible interests, cash, other property, or any combination of the foregoing; or

(ii) are entitled to vote as a separate group on a provision in the plan that constitutes a proposed amendment to the articles of incorporation of a surviving corporation that requires action by separate voting groups under section 10.04;

(2) on a plan of share exchange, by each class or series of shares included in the exchange, with each class or series constituting a separate voting group; and

(3) on a plan of merger or share exchange, if the voting group is entitled under the articles of incorporation to vote as a voting group to approve a plan of merger or share exchange, respectively.

(g) The articles of incorporation may expressly limit or eliminate the separate voting rights provided in subsections (f)(1)(i) and (f)(2) as to any class or series of shares, except when the plan of merger or share exchange (i) includes what is or would be in effect an amendment subject to subsection (f)(1)(ii), and (ii) will not effect a substantive business combination.

(h) Unless the articles of incorporation otherwise provide, approval by the corporation's shareholders of a plan of merger is not required if:

(1) the corporation will survive the merger;

(2) except for amendments permitted by section 10.05, its articles of incorporation will not be changed;

(3) each shareholder of the corporation whose shares were outstanding immediately before the effective date of the merger or share exchange will hold the same number of shares, with identical preferences, rights and limitations, immediately after the effective date of the merger; and

(4) the issuance in the merger of shares or other securities convertible into or rights exercisable for shares does not require a vote under section 6.21(f).

(i) If as a result of a merger or share exchange one or more shareholders of a domestic corporation would become subject to new interest holder liability, approval of the plan of merger or share exchange requires the signing in connection with the transaction, by each such shareholder, of a separate written consent to become subject to such new interest holder liability, unless in the case of a shareholder that already has interest holder liability with respect to such domestic corporation, (i) the new interest holder liability is with respect to a domestic or foreign corporation (which may be a different or the same domestic corporation in which the person is a shareholder), and (ii) the terms and conditions of the new interest holder liability are substantially identical to those of the existing interest holder liability (other than for changes that eliminate or reduce such interest holder liability).

(j) Unless the articles of incorporation otherwise provide, approval by the shareholders of a plan of merger or share exchange is not required if:

(1) the plan of merger or share exchange expressly (i) permits or requires the merger or share exchange to be effected under this subsection and (ii) provides that, if the merger or share exchange is

to be effected under this subsection, the merger or share exchange will be effected as soon as practicable following the satisfaction of the requirement set forth in subsection (j)(6);

(2) another party to the merger, the acquiring entity in the share exchange, or a parent of another party to the merger or the acquiring entity in the share exchange, makes an offer to purchase, on the terms provided in the plan of merger or share exchange, any and all of the outstanding shares of the corporation that, absent this subsection, would be entitled to vote on the plan of merger or share exchange, except that the offer may exclude shares of the corporation that are owned at the commencement of the offer by the corporation, the offeror, or any parent of the offeror, or by any wholly owned subsidiary of any of the foregoing;

(3) the offer discloses that the plan of merger or share exchange provides that the merger or share exchange will be effected as soon as practicable following the satisfaction of the requirement set forth in subsection (j)(6) and that the shares of the corporation that are not tendered in response to the offer will be treated as set forth in subsection (j)(8);

(4) the offer remains open for at least 10 days;

(5) the offeror purchases all shares properly tendered in response to the offer and not properly withdrawn;

(6) the shares listed below are collectively entitled to cast at least the minimum number of votes on the merger or share exchange that, absent this subsection, would be required by this chapter and by the articles of incorporation for the approval of the merger or share exchange by the shareholders and by any other voting group entitled to vote on the merger or share exchange at a meeting at which all shares entitled to vote on the approval were present and voted:

(i) shares purchased by the offeror in accordance with the offer;

(ii) shares otherwise owned by the offeror or by any parent of the offeror or any wholly owned subsidiary of any of the foregoing; and

(iii) shares subject to an agreement that they are to be transferred, contributed or delivered to the offeror, any parent of the offeror, or any wholly owned subsidiary of any of the foregoing in exchange for shares or eligible interests in such offeror, parent or subsidiary;

(7) the offeror or a wholly owned subsidiary of the offeror merges with or into, or effects a share exchange in which it acquires shares of, the corporation; and

(8) each outstanding share of each class or series of shares of the corporation that the offeror is offering to purchase in accordance with the offer, and that is not purchased in accordance with the offer, is to be converted in the merger into, or into the right to receive, or is to be exchanged in the share exchange for, or for the right to receive, the same amount and kind of securities, eligible interests, obligations, rights, cash, or other property to be paid or exchanged in accordance with the offer for each share of that class or series of shares that is tendered in response to the offer, except that shares of the corporation that are owned by the corporation or that are described in clause (ii) or (iii) of subsection (j)(6) need not be converted into or exchanged for the consideration described in this subsection (j)(8).

(k) As used in subsection (j):

(1) "offer" means the offer referred to in subsection (j)(2);

(2) "offeror" means the person making the offer;

(3) "parent" of an entity means a person that owns, directly or indirectly (through one or more wholly owned subsidiaries), all of the outstanding shares of or eligible interests in that entity;

(4) shares tendered in response to the offer shall be deemed to have been "purchased" in accordance with the offer at the earliest time as of which (i) the offeror has irrevocably accepted those shares for payment and (ii) either (A) in the case of shares represented by certificates, the offeror, or the offeror's designated depository or other agent, has physically received the certificates representing those shares or (B) in the case of shares without certificates, those shares have been transferred into the account of the offeror or its designated depository or other agent, or an agent's message relating to those shares has been received by the offeror or its designated depository or other agent; and

(5) "wholly owned subsidiary" of a person means an entity of or in which that person owns, directly or indirectly (through one or more wholly owned subsidiaries), all of the outstanding shares or eligible interests.

(*l*) Unless the articles of incorporation otherwise provide,

(1) approval of a plan of share exchange by the shareholders of a domestic corporation is not required if the corporation is the acquiring entity in the share exchange; and

(2) shares not to be exchanged under the plan of share exchange are not entitled to vote on the plan.

Official Comment

1. In General

Subject to the exceptions set forth in section 11.04(b), a plan of merger must always be approved by the shareholders of a corporation that is a party to a merger and a plan of share exchange must always be approved by shareholders of the class or series that is being acquired in a share exchange. Under section 11.04(h) approval of a plan of merger by the shareholders of a surviving corporation is not required if the conditions stated in that section are satisfied. Under section 11.04(j), shareholder action by selling shares in a tender offer or exchange offer is accepted as an alternative to the traditional consent by voting if the conditions specified in section 11.04(j) are met.

Section 11.04(g), together with the appraisal rights provisions of chapter 13, is designed to assure that in transactions or actions that may occur under chapters 9, 10, 11 and 12, a shareholder has either a group voting right or an appraisal right.

Under section 10.04(c), and therefore under section 11.04(f)(1)(ii), if a change that requires voting by separate voting groups affects two or more classes or two or more series in the same or a substantially similar way, the relevant classes or series vote together, rather than separately, on the change, unless otherwise provided in the articles of incorporation or required by the board of directors. If separate voting by voting groups is required for a merger or a share exchange under section 11.04(f), it will not fall within the exception to shareholder approval provided by section 11.04(h). For the mechanics of voting where voting by voting groups is required under section 11.04(f), see sections 7.25 and 7.26 and the Official Comments to those sections.

If a merger would amend the articles of incorporation of a survivor that is a domestic corporation in such a way as to affect the voting requirements on future amendments, the transaction must also be approved by the vote required by section 7.27.

2. Submission to the Shareholders

When submitting a plan of merger or share exchange to shareholders, the board of directors must recommend the transaction, subject to two exceptions in section 11.04(b). The board might exercise the exception under clause (i) where the number of directors having a conflicting interest makes it inadvisable for them to recommend the transaction or where the board is evenly divided as to the merits of the transaction but is able to agree that shareholders should be permitted to consider the transaction. Alternatively, the board of directors might exercise the exception in clause (ii), which recognizes that, under section 8.26, a board of directors may include a "force the vote" clause in a plan of merger or share exchange, agreeing to submit the plan to shareholders even if, after approving the plan, the board of directors determines that it no longer recommends the plan. Section 11.04(c) permits the board of directors to condition its submission of a plan of merger or share exchange to the shareholders or the effectiveness of a plan of merger or share exchange. Among the conditions that a board of directors might impose are that the plan will not be deemed approved (i) unless it is approved by a specified vote of the shareholders, or by one or more specified classes or series of shares, voting as a separate voting group, or by a specified percentage of disinterested shareholders or (ii) if shareholders holding more than a specified fraction of the outstanding shares assert appraisal rights.

Section 11.04(d) sets forth the notice requirements if a plan of merger or share exchange is to be considered by the shareholders at a meeting. Requirements concerning the timing and content of a notice of meeting are set out in section 7.05. Section 11.04(d) does not address the notice to be given to nonvoting or nonconsenting shareholders where the merger or share exchange is approved, without a meeting, by written consent. However, that requirement is imposed by section 7.04.

3. *Quorum and Voting*

Section 11.04(e) sets forth quorum and voting requirements applicable to a shareholder vote to approve a plan of merger or share exchange. See sections 7.25(f) and 10.04(c) for rules governing when separate classes or series vote together as a single voting group. If a quorum is present, and subject to any greater vote required by the articles of incorporation or the board of directors pursuant to section 11.04(c), under sections 7.25 and 7.26 the plan will be approved if more votes are cast in favor of the plan than against it by the voting group or each separate voting group, as the case may be, entitled to vote on the plan. In lieu of action at a meeting, shareholder approval may be by written consent under the procedures set forth in section 7.04.

Section 11.04(g) authorizes limiting or eliminating separate voting as a voting group for a class or series of shares in a merger or share exchange by an express provision in the articles of incorporation. The authorization, however, does not apply to a plan of merger that includes amendments to the articles of incorporation of the survivor for which, under section 11.04(f)(1)(ii), a separate vote under section 10.04 is required. The authorization also would not apply if a plan of merger that is subject to section 11.04(f)(1)(i) or a share exchange that is subject to section 11.04(f)(2) has the same effect as an amendment to which section 10.04 would apply and the transaction has no substantive business combination effect, such as a reincorporation or recapitalization where there is no significant change in the enterprise on a consolidated basis. For example, if a corporation with preferred and common shares merges into a wholly-owned subsidiary with all shares being exchanged for common shares of the subsidiary, the authorization to eliminate the separate group vote of the preferred shares would not apply because the transaction would be in effect an amendment of the preferred stock without separate substance as a business combination. On the other hand, if the subsidiary (assuming it was significant) was only 60% owned and the holders of the remaining 40% were being cashed out in the merger, elimination of the separate group vote would be effective because the merger would have substance as a business combination. The requirement that a provision limiting or eliminating group voting rights on a merger or share exchange be "express" is meant to avoid any ambiguity that might arise from a provision that generally denies voting rights.

4. *Two-Step Transactions*

Section 11.04(j) authorizes a two-step transaction meeting the requirements of that section to proceed without the shareholder vote that would otherwise be required by section 11.04(b). The first step is an offer to the shareholders to tender their shares in response to which enough shareholders tender so that, upon consummation of the offer, the offering party (and any parent or wholly owned subsidiary) owns or has the right to acquire shares with sufficient voting power to satisfy the shareholder approval that would otherwise be required to approve the plan of merger or share exchange pursuant to section 11.04. The second step is a merger or share exchange providing the remaining shareholders the same consideration as was offered to their class or series in the first step offer. The shareholder action in selling in response to the offer provides the necessary consent for the transaction, in lieu of a shareholder vote, if the other conditions set forth in section 11.04(j) are met. The requirements of section 11.04(j), together with sections 11.04(b), 13.20, 13.21 and 13.22, are intended to ensure that shareholders are not disadvantaged by the absence of a vote, and that they receive the same protection in terms of timing, director duties and appraisal rights that they would in a transaction approved by a shareholder vote. For example, section 11.04(b) requires, subject to limited exceptions, that the board of directors make a recommendation with respect to the offer that shareholders tender their shares. This ensures that there is a corporate action implicated by the offer, and that the same director duties will apply to the recommendation to tender into the offer as to conversion or exchange pursuant to a plan of merger or share exchange.

5. *Personal Liability of Shareholders*

The approval provisions of section 11.04(i) apply only in situations where a shareholder is becoming subject to "new interest holder liability" as defined in section 11.01, for example, where a corporation is merging into a general partnership or a cap on the shareholder's interest holder liability is increased. The effect of a merger or share exchange on interest holder liability will be determined as provided in section 11.07(e).

§ 11.05. Merger Between Parent and Subsidiary or Between Subsidiaries

(a) A domestic or foreign parent entity that owns shares of a domestic corporation which carry at least 90% of the voting power of each class and series of the outstanding shares of the subsidiary that has voting power may (i) merge the subsidiary into itself (if it is a domestic or foreign corporation or eligible entity) or into another domestic or foreign corporation or eligible entity in which the parent entity owns at least 90% of the voting power of each class and series of the outstanding shares or eligible interests which have voting power, or (ii) merge itself (if it is a domestic or foreign corporation or eligible entity) into such subsidiary, in either case without the approval of the board of directors or shareholders of the subsidiary, unless the articles of incorporation or organic rules of the parent entity or the articles of incorporation of the subsidiary corporation otherwise provide. Section 11.04(i) applies to a merger under this section. The articles of merger relating to a merger under this section do not need to be signed by the subsidiary.

(b) A parent entity shall, within 10 days after the effective date of a merger approved under subsection (a), notify each of the subsidiary's shareholders that the merger has become effective.

(c) Except as provided in subsections (a) and (b), a merger between a parent entity and a domestic subsidiary corporation shall be governed by the provisions of chapter 11 applicable to mergers generally.

§ 11.06. Articles of Merger or Share Exchange

(a) After (i) a plan of merger has been adopted and approved as required by this Act, or (ii) if the merger is being effected under section 11.02(a)(2), the merger has been approved as required by the organic law governing the parties to the merger, then articles of merger shall be signed by each party to the merger except as provided in section 11.05(a). The articles must set forth:

(1) the name, jurisdiction of formation, and type of entity of each party to the merger;

(2) the name, jurisdiction of formation, and type of entity of the survivor;

(3) if the survivor of the merger is a domestic corporation and its articles of incorporation are amended, or if a new domestic corporation is created as a result of the merger:

(i) the amendments to the survivor's articles of incorporation; or

(ii) the articles of incorporation of the new corporation;

(4) if the survivor of the merger is a domestic eligible entity and its public organic record is amended, or if a new domestic eligible entity is created as a result of the merger:

(i) the amendments to the public organic record of the survivor; or

(ii) the public organic record of the new eligible entity;

(5) if the plan of merger required approval by the shareholders of a domestic corporation that is a party to the merger, a statement that the plan was duly approved by the shareholders and, if voting by any separate voting group was required, by each such separate voting group, in the manner required by this Act and the articles of incorporation;

(6) if the plan of merger or share exchange did not require approval by the shareholders of a domestic corporation that is a party to the merger, a statement to that effect;

(7) as to each foreign corporation that is a party to the merger, a statement that the participation of the foreign corporation was duly authorized as required by its organic law;

(8) as to each domestic or foreign eligible entity that is a party to the merger, a statement that the merger was approved in accordance with its organic law or section 11.02(c); and

(9) if the survivor is created by the merger and is a domestic limited liability partnership, the filing required to become a limited liability partnership, as an attachment.

(b) After a plan of share exchange in which the acquired entity is a domestic corporation or eligible entity has been adopted and approved as required by this Act, articles of share exchange shall be signed by the acquired entity and the acquiring entity. The articles shall set forth:

(1) the name of the acquired entity;

(2) the name, jurisdiction of formation, and type of entity of the domestic or foreign corporation or eligible entity that is the acquiring entity; and

(3) a statement that the plan of share exchange was duly approved by the acquired entity by:

(i) the required vote or consent of each class or series of shares or eligible interests included in the exchange; and

(ii) the required vote or consent of each other class or series of shares or eligible interests entitled to vote on approval of the exchange by the articles of incorporation or organic rules of the acquired entity or section 11.03(c).

(c) In addition to the requirements of subsection (a) or (b), articles of merger or share exchange may contain any other provision not prohibited by law.

(d) The articles of merger or share exchange shall be delivered to the secretary of state for filing and, subject to subsection (e), the merger or share exchange shall take effect at the effective date determined in accordance with section 1.23.

(e) With respect to a merger in which one or more foreign entities is a party or a foreign entity created by the merger is the survivor, the merger itself shall become effective at the later of:

(1) when all documents required to be filed in foreign jurisdictions to effect the merger have become effective, or

(2) when the articles of merger take effect.

(f) Articles of merger filed under this section may be combined with any filing required under the organic law governing any domestic eligible entity involved in the transaction if the combined filing satisfies the requirements of both this section and the other organic law.

Official Comment

The filing of articles of merger or share exchange makes the transaction a matter of public record. The requirements of filing are set forth in section 1.20. Under section 1.23, the articles are effective on the date and at the time of filing unless a later effective date is specified in the articles within the limits provided in section 1.23 under the authority of section 11.06(c). Under section 1.23, a delayed effective date may not be later than the 90th day after the date the document is filed.

If a merger involves a domestic eligible entity whose organic law also requires a filing to effect the transaction, section 11.06(f) permits the filings under that organic law and this section to be combined so that only one document need be delivered to the secretary of state for filing.

§ 11.07. Effect of Merger or Share Exchange

(a) When a merger becomes effective:

(1) the domestic or foreign corporation or eligible entity that is designated in the plan of merger as the survivor continues or comes into existence, as the case may be;

(2) the separate existence of every domestic or foreign corporation or eligible entity that is a party to the merger, other than the survivor, ceases;

(3) all property owned by, and every contract right possessed by, each domestic or foreign corporation or eligible entity that is a party to the merger, other than the survivor, are the property and contract rights of the survivor without transfer, reversion or impairment;

(4) all debts, obligations and other liabilities of each domestic or foreign corporation or eligible entity that is a party to the merger, other than the survivor, are debts, obligations or liabilities of the survivor;

(5) the name of the survivor may, but need not be, substituted in any pending proceeding for the name of any party to the merger whose separate existence ceased in the merger;

(6) if the survivor is a domestic entity, the articles of incorporation and bylaws or the organic rules of the survivor are amended to the extent provided in the plan of merger;

(7) the articles of incorporation and bylaws or the organic rules of a survivor that is a domestic entity and is created by the merger become effective;

(8) the shares of each domestic or foreign corporation that is a party to the merger, and the eligible interests in an eligible entity that is a party to a merger, that are to be converted in accordance with the terms of the merger into shares or other securities, eligible interests, obligations, rights to acquire

shares, other securities, or eligible interests, cash, other property, or any combination of the foregoing, are converted, and the former holders of such shares or eligible interests are entitled only to the rights provided to them by those terms or to any rights they may have under chapter 13 or the organic law governing the eligible entity or foreign corporation;

(9) except as provided by law or the terms of the merger, all the rights, privileges, franchises, and immunities of each entity that is a party to the merger, other than the survivor, are the rights, privileges, franchises, and immunities of the survivor; and

(10) if the survivor exists before the merger:

(i) all the property and contract rights of the survivor remain its property and contract rights without transfer, reversion, or impairment;

(ii) the survivor remains subject to all its debts, obligations, and other liabilities; and

(iii) except as provided by law or the plan of merger, the survivor continues to hold all of its rights, privileges, franchises, and immunities.

(b) When a share exchange becomes effective, the shares or eligible interests in the acquired entity that are to be exchanged for shares or other securities, eligible interests, obligations, rights to acquire shares, other securities or eligible interests, cash, other property, or any combination of the foregoing, are entitled only to the rights provided to them in the plan of share exchange or to any rights they may have under chapter 13 or under the organic law governing the acquired entity.

(c) Except as otherwise provided in the articles of incorporation of a domestic corporation or the organic law governing or organic rules of a foreign corporation or a domestic or foreign eligible entity, the effect of a merger or share exchange on interest holder liability is as follows:

(1) A person who becomes subject to new interest holder liability in respect of an entity as a result of a merger or share exchange shall have that new interest holder liability only in respect of interest holder liabilities that arise after the merger or share exchange becomes effective.

(2) If a person had interest holder liability with respect to a party to the merger or the acquired entity before the merger or share exchange becomes effective with respect to shares or eligible interests of such party or acquired entity which were (i) exchanged in the merger or share exchange, (ii) were cancelled in the merger or (iii) the terms and conditions of which relating to interest holder liability were amended pursuant to the merger:

(i) The merger or share exchange does not discharge that prior interest holder liability with respect to any interest holder liabilities that arose before the merger or share exchange becomes effective.

(ii) The provisions of the organic law governing any entity for which the person had that prior interest holder liability shall continue to apply to the collection or discharge of any interest holder liabilities preserved by subsection (c)(2)(i), as if the merger or share exchange had not occurred.

(iii) The person shall have such rights of contribution from other persons as are provided by the organic law governing the entity for which the person had that prior interest holder liability with respect to any interest holder liabilities preserved by subsection (c)(2)(i), as if the merger or share exchange had not occurred.

(iv) The person shall not, by reason of such prior interest holder liability, have interest holder liability with respect to any interest holder liabilities that arise after the merger or share exchange becomes effective.

(3) If a person has interest holder liability both before and after a merger becomes effective with unchanged terms and conditions with respect to the entity that is the survivor by reason of owning the same shares or eligible interests before and after the merger becomes effective, the merger has no effect on such interest holder liability.

(4) A share exchange has no effect on interest holder liability related to shares or eligible interests of the acquired entity that were not exchanged in the share exchange.

(d) Upon a merger becoming effective, a foreign corporation, or a foreign eligible entity, that is the survivor of the merger is deemed to:

(1) appoint the secretary of state as its agent for service of process in a proceeding to enforce the rights of shareholders of each domestic corporation that is a party to the merger who exercise appraisal rights; and

(2) agree that it will promptly pay the amount, if any, to which such shareholders are entitled under chapter 13.

(e) Except as provided in the organic law governing a party to a merger or in its articles of incorporation or organic rules, the merger does not give rise to any rights that an interest holder, governor, or third party would have upon a dissolution, liquidation, or winding up of that party. The merger does not require a party to the merger to wind up its affairs and does not constitute or cause its dissolution or termination.

(f) Property held for a charitable purpose under the law of this state by a domestic or foreign corporation or eligible entity immediately before a merger becomes effective may not, as a result of the transaction, be diverted from the objects for which it was donated, granted, devised, or otherwise transferred except and to the extent permitted by or pursuant to the laws of this state addressing cy près or dealing with nondiversion of charitable assets.

(g) A bequest, devise, gift, grant, or promise contained in a will or other instrument of donation, subscription, or conveyance which is made to an entity that is a party to a merger that is not the survivor and which takes effect or remains payable after the merger inures to the survivor.

(h) A trust obligation that would govern property if transferred to a nonsurviving entity applies to property that is transferred to the survivor after a merger becomes effective.

Official Comment

Under section 11.07(a), in a merger the parties that merge become one. The survivor automatically becomes the owner of all real and personal property and becomes subject to all the liabilities, actual or contingent, of each other party to the merger. A merger is not a conveyance, transfer, or assignment. It does not give rise to claims of reverter or impairment of title based on a prohibited conveyance, transfer, or assignment. It does not give rise to a claim that a contract with a party to the merger is no longer in effect on the ground of nonassignability, unless the contract specifically addresses that issue. All pending proceedings involving either the survivor or a party whose separate existence ceased as a result of the merger are continued.

In contrast to a merger, a share exchange does not vest in the acquiring entity the assets of the acquired entity, or render the acquiring entity liable for the liabilities of the acquired entity. The statements in sections 11.07(a)(8) and 11.07(b) regarding the rights of former holders of shares or eligible interests are not intended to preclude an otherwise proper question concerning the validity of the merger or share exchange, or to override or otherwise affect any provisions of chapter 13 concerning the exclusiveness of rights under that chapter.

The deemed appointment and agreement in section 11.07(d) by a foreign survivor is based on the implied consent of such a foreign corporation, or foreign eligible entity, to the terms of chapter 11 by reason of entering into an agreement that is governed by this chapter.

Section 11.07(e) sets forth the impact of mergers and share exchanges on interest holder liability. Section 11.04(i) sets forth when approval of a merger or share exchange requires the consent of shareholders who would otherwise become subject to new interest holder liability.

§ 11.08. Abandonment of a Merger or Share Exchange

(a) After a plan of merger or share exchange has been adopted and approved as required by this chapter, and before articles of merger or share exchange have become effective, the plan may be abandoned by a domestic business corporation that is a party to the plan without action by its shareholders in accordance with any procedures set forth in the plan of merger or share exchange or, if no such procedures are set forth in the plan, in the manner determined by the board of directors.

(b) If a merger or share exchange is abandoned under subsection (a) after articles of merger or share exchange have been delivered to the secretary of state for filing but before the merger or share exchange has become effective, a statement of abandonment signed by all the parties that signed the articles of merger or share exchange shall be delivered to the secretary of state for filing before the articles of merger or share exchange become effective. The statement shall take effect on filing and the merger or share exchange shall be deemed abandoned and shall not become effective. The statement of abandonment must contain:

> (1) the name of each party to the merger or the names of the acquiring and acquired entities in a share exchange;

> (2) the date on which the articles of merger or share exchange were filed by the secretary of state; and

> (3) a statement that the merger or share exchange has been abandoned in accordance with this section.

CROSS-REFERENCES

Approval of merger or share exchange, see § 11.04.

"Corporation" and "domestic business corporation" defined, see § 1.40.

Effective time and date of filing, see § 1.23.

Filing requirements, see § 1.20.

Official Comment

. . . The power to abandon a transaction does not affect any contract rights that other parties may have. The power of a foreign business corporation or a domestic or foreign eligible entity to abandon a transaction will be determined by the organic law of the corporation or eligible entity, except as provided in sections 11.02(c) and 11.03(c).

Chapter 12

DISPOSITION OF ASSETS

§ 12.01. Disposition of Assets Not Requiring Shareholder Approval

No approval of the shareholders is required, unless the articles of incorporation otherwise provide:

(a) to sell, lease, exchange, or otherwise dispose of any or all of the corporation's assets in the usual and regular course of business;

(b) to mortgage, pledge, dedicate to the repayment of indebtedness (whether with or without recourse), or otherwise encumber any or all of the corporation's assets, regardless of whether in the usual and regular course of business;

(c) to transfer any or all of the corporation's assets to one or more domestic or foreign corporations or other entities all of the shares or interests of which are owned by the corporation; or

(d) to distribute assets pro rata to the holders of one or more classes or series of the corporation's shares.

Official Comment . . .

Examples of dispositions in the usual and regular course of business under section 12.01(a) include the sale of a building that was the corporation's only major asset where the corporation was formed for the purpose of constructing and selling that building, the sale by a corporation of its only major business where the corporation was formed to buy and sell businesses and the proceeds of the sale are to be reinvested in the purchase of a new business, or sales of assets by an open- or closed-end investment company the portfolio of which turns over many times in short periods.

No shareholder approval is required for a transaction involving a pro rata distribution because it comes within section 12.01(d). An example is a spin-off in which shares of a subsidiary are distributed pro rata to the holders of one or more classes or series of shares. On the other hand, a non pro rata distribution—for example, a split-off in which shares of a subsidiary are distributed only to some shareholders in exchange for some or all of their shares—would require shareholder approval under section 12.02(a) if the disposition would leave the corporation without a significant continuing business activity. When the transaction involves a distribution in liquidation—for example, when two or more subsidiaries (whether they have existed previously or are newly formed) representing all of a dissolved corporation's business activities are distributed to shareholders (sometimes referred to as a split-up)—the transaction will be governed by chapter 14 (dissolution), not by chapter 12.

§ 12.02. Shareholder Approval of Certain Dispositions

(a) A sale, lease, exchange, or other disposition of assets, other than a disposition described in section 12.01, requires approval of the corporation's shareholders if the disposition would leave the corporation without a significant continuing business activity. A corporation will conclusively be deemed to have retained a significant continuing business activity if it retains a business activity that represented, for the corporation and its subsidiaries on a consolidated basis, at least (i) 25% of total assets at the end of the most recently completed fiscal year, and (ii) either 25% of either income from continuing operations before taxes or 25% of revenues from continuing operations, in each case for the most recently completed fiscal year.

(b) To obtain the approval of the shareholders under subsection (a) the board of directors shall first adopt a resolution authorizing the disposition. The disposition shall then be approved by the shareholders. In submitting the disposition to the shareholders for approval, the board of directors shall recommend that the shareholders approve the disposition, unless (i) the board of directors makes a determination that because of conflicts of interest or other special circumstances it should not make such a recommendation, or (ii) section 8.26 applies. If either (i) or (ii) applies, the board shall inform the shareholders of the basis for its so proceeding.

(c) The board of directors may set conditions for the approval by the shareholders of a disposition or the effectiveness of the disposition.

(d) If a disposition is required to be approved by the shareholders under subsection (a), and if the approval is to be given at a meeting, the corporation shall notify each shareholder, regardless of whether entitled to vote, of the meeting of shareholders at which the disposition is to be submitted for approval. The notice must state that the purpose, or one of the purposes, of the meeting is to consider the disposition and must contain a description of the disposition, including the terms and conditions of the disposition and the consideration to be received by the corporation.

(e) Unless the articles of incorporation or the board of directors acting pursuant to subsection (c) require a greater vote or a greater quorum, the approval of a disposition by the shareholders shall require the approval of the shareholders at a meeting at which a quorum exists consisting of a majority of the votes entitled to be cast on the disposition.

(f) After a disposition has been approved by the shareholders under this chapter, and at any time before the disposition has been consummated, it may be abandoned by the corporation without action by the shareholders, subject to any contractual rights of other parties to the disposition.

(g) A disposition of assets in the course of dissolution under chapter 14 is not governed by this section.

(h) The assets of a direct or indirect consolidated subsidiary shall be deemed to be the assets of the parent corporation for the purposes of this section.

Official Comment

1.   In General

Section 12.02(a) requires shareholder approval for a sale, lease, exchange or other disposition of assets by a corporation that would leave the corporation without a significant continuing business activity, other than as provided in section 12.01. Whether a disposition leaves a corporation with a significant continuing business activity, within the meaning of section 12.02(a), depends on whether the corporation's remaining business activity is significant when compared to the corporation's business before the disposition. The 25% safe harbor provides a measure of certainty in making this determination. The safe-harbor test is applied to assets and to revenue or income for the fiscal year ended immediately before the decision by the board of directors to make the disposition in question.

If a corporation disposes of assets for the purpose of reinvesting the proceeds of the disposition in substantially the same business in a somewhat different form (for example, by selling the corporation's only plant for the purpose of buying or building a replacement plant), the disposition and reinvestment should be treated together, so that the transaction should not be deemed to leave the corporation without a significant continuing business activity.

In determining whether a disposition would leave a corporation without a significant continuing business activity, the test combines a parent corporation with subsidiaries that are or should be consolidated with it under applicable accounting principles. For example, if a corporation's only significant business is owned by a consolidated subsidiary, a sale of that business requires approval of the parent's shareholders under section 12.02. Correspondingly, if a corporation owns one significant business directly, and several other significant businesses through one or more wholly or almost wholly owned subsidiaries, a sale by the corporation of the single business it owns directly does not require shareholder approval under section 12.02 (for example, the 25% retention tests of section 12.02(a) are met).

If all or a large part of a corporation's assets are held for investment, the corporation actively manages those assets, and it has no other significant business, for purposes of chapter 12 the corporation should be considered to be in the business of investing in assets, so that a sale of most of those assets without a reinvestment should be considered a sale that would leave the corporation without a significant continuing business activity. In applying the 25% tests of section 12.02(a), an issue could arise if a corporation had more than one business activity, one or more of which might be traditional operating activities, such as manufacturing or distribution, and another of which might be considered managing investments in other securities or enterprises. If the activity constituting the management of investments is to be a continuing business activity as a result of the active engagement of the management of the corporation in that process and the 25% retention tests were met upon the disposition of the other businesses, shareholder approval would not be required.

A board of directors may determine that a retained continuing business falls within the 25% bright-line tests of the safe harbor in section 12.02(a) based either on accounting principles and practices that are reasonable in the circumstances or (in applying the asset test) on a fair valuation or other method that is reasonable in the circumstances in a manner similar to that described in section 6.40(d) and the Official Comment 4 to that section.

The use of the term "significant" and the specific 25% safe harbor test for purposes of this section do not imply a standard for the test of significance or materiality for any other purposes under the Act or otherwise.

2. Submission to Shareholders

When submitting a proposal to shareholders for a disposition of assets, the board of directors must recommend the disposition, subject to two exceptions in section 12.02(b). The board might exercise the exception under clause (i) where the number of directors having a conflicting interest makes it inadvisable for the board to recommend the disposition or where the board is evenly divided as to the merits of the proposal but is able to agree that shareholders should be permitted to consider it. Alternatively, the board of directors might exercise the exception under clause (ii), which recognizes that, under section 8.26, a board of directors may agree to submit a proposal for a disposition to a vote of shareholders even if, after approving the proposal, the board of directors determines that it no longer recommends the proposal.

Section 12.02(c) permits the board of directors to condition its submission to the shareholders of a proposal for a disposition of assets or the effectiveness of the disposition. Among the conditions that a board of directors might impose are that the proposal will not be deemed approved: (i) unless it is approved by a specified percentage of the shareholders, or by one or more specified classes or series of shares, voting as a separate voting group, or by a specified percentage of disinterested shareholders; or (ii) if shareholders holding more than a specified fraction of the outstanding shares exercise appraisal rights.

3. Quorum and Voting

Requirements concerning the timing and content of a notice of meeting, as required by section 12.02(d), are set out in section 7.05. Section 12.02(d) does not address the notice to be given to nonvoting or nonconsenting shareholders where the proposal is approved without a meeting by written consent. That requirement is imposed by section 7.04.

Section 12.02(e) sets forth quorum and voting requirements applicable to a shareholder vote to approve a disposition. In lieu of approval at a meeting, shareholder approval may be by written consent under the procedures set forth in section 7.04.

The Act does not mandate separate voting by voting groups on dispositions, because after a disposition under this chapter the rights of all classes or series of shares remain the same. Separate voting by voting groups may nevertheless be required if provided for in the articles of incorporation or by the board of directors, acting pursuant to section 12.02(c). Appraisal may be available to shareholders entitled to vote on the disposition. See chapter 13.

Chapter 13

APPRAISAL RIGHTS

Subchapter A

Right to Appraisal and Payment for Shares

§ 13.01. Definitions

In this chapter:

"Affiliate" means a person that directly or indirectly through one or more intermediaries controls, is controlled by, or is under common control with another person or is a senior executive of such person. For purposes of section 13.02(b)(4), a person is deemed to be an affiliate of its senior executives.

"Corporation" means the domestic corporation that is the issuer of the shares held by a shareholder demanding appraisal and, for matters covered in sections 13.22 through 13.31, includes the survivor of a merger.

"Fair value" means the value of the corporation's shares determined:

(i) immediately before the effectiveness of the corporate action to which the shareholder objects;

(ii) using customary and current valuation concepts and techniques generally employed for similar businesses in the context of the transaction requiring appraisal; and

(iii) without discounting for lack of marketability or minority status except, if appropriate, for amendments to the articles of incorporation pursuant to section 13.02(a)(4).

"Interest" means interest from the date the corporate action becomes effective until the date of payment, at the rate of interest on judgments in this state on the effective date of the corporate action.

"Interested transaction" means a corporate action described in section 13.02(a), other than a merger pursuant to section 11.05, involving an interested person in which any of the shares or assets of the corporation are being acquired or converted. As used in this definition:

(i) "Interested person" means a person, or an affiliate of a person, who at any time during the one-year period immediately preceding approval by the board of directors of the corporate action:

(A) was the beneficial owner of 20% or more of the voting power of the corporation, other than as owner of excluded shares;

(B) had the power, contractually or otherwise, other than as owner of excluded shares, to cause the appointment or election of 25% or more of the directors to the board of directors of the corporation; or

(C) was a senior executive or director of the corporation or a senior executive of any affiliate of the corporation, and that senior executive or director will receive, as a result of the corporate action, a financial benefit not generally available to other shareholders as such, other than:

(I) employment, consulting, retirement, or similar benefits established separately and not as part of or in contemplation of the corporate action;

(II) employment, consulting, retirement, or similar benefits established in contemplation of, or as part of, the corporate action that are not more favorable than those existing before the corporate action or, if more favorable, that have been approved on behalf of the corporation in the same manner as is provided in section 8.62; or

(III) in the case of a director of the corporation who will, in the corporate action, become a director or governor of the acquiror or any of its affiliates, rights and benefits as a director

714

or governor that are provided on the same basis as those afforded by the acquiror generally to other directors or governors of such entity or such affiliate.

(ii) "Beneficial owner" means any person who, directly or indirectly, through any contract, arrangement, or understanding, other than a revocable proxy, has or shares the power to vote, or to direct the voting of, shares; except that a member of a national securities exchange is not deemed to be a beneficial owner of securities held directly or indirectly by it on behalf of another person if the member is precluded by the rules of the exchange from voting without instruction on contested matters or matters that may affect substantially the rights or privileges of the holders of the securities to be voted. When two or more persons agree to act together for the purpose of voting their shares of the corporation, each member of the group formed thereby is deemed to have acquired beneficial ownership, as of the date of the agreement, of all shares having voting power of the corporation beneficially owned by any member of the group.

(iii) "Excluded shares" means shares acquired pursuant to an offer for all shares having voting power if the offer was made within one year before the corporate action for consideration of the same kind and of a value equal to or less than that paid in connection with the corporate action.

"Preferred shares" means a class or series of shares whose holders have preference over any other class or series of shares with respect to distributions.

"Senior executive" means the chief executive officer, chief operating officer, chief financial officer, and any individual in charge of a principal business unit or function.

"Shareholder" means a record shareholder, a beneficial shareholder, and a voting trust beneficial owner.

Official Comment

1.   Overview

Chapter 13 proceeds from the premise that judicial appraisal should be provided by statute only when two conditions co-exist. First, a proposed corporate action as approved by a majority will result in a fundamental change in the shares to be affected by the action. Second, uncertainty concerning the fair value of the affected shares may cause reasonable persons to differ about the fairness of the terms of the corporate action. Uncertainty is reduced, however, in the case of publicly traded shares. This explains both the market exception described below and the limits provided to that exception.

When these two conditions exist in connection with domestications and conversions under chapter 9, mergers and share exchanges under chapter 11, and dispositions of assets requiring shareholder approval under chapter 12, chapter 13 provides for appraisal rights. Each of these actions will result in a fundamental change in the shares that a disapproving shareholder may believe was not adequately compensated by the terms approved by the majority. Shareholders are not entitled to appraisal, however, if the change will not alter the terms of the class or series of securities that they hold. For example, statutory appraisal rights are not available for shares of any class or series of the surviving corporation in a merger that are not being changed in the merger or for shares of any class or series that is not included in a share exchange. Appraisal is also not triggered by a voluntary dissolution under chapter 14 because the dissolution does not affect liquidation rights of the shares of any class or series.

With the exception of reverse stock splits that result in cashing out some of the shares of a class or series, chapter 13 does not grant appraisal rights in connection with amendments to the articles of incorporation. This does not reflect a judgment that an amendment changing the terms of a particular class or series may not have significant economic effects. Rather, it reflects a judgment that distinguishing among different types of amendments for the purposes of statutory appraisal is necessarily arbitrary. Chapter 13 delineates in section 13.02(a)(5) a list of actions for which the corporation may voluntarily choose to provide appraisal. It also allows, under section 13.02(c), a provision in the articles of incorporation that eliminates, in whole or in part, statutory appraisal rights for preferred shares, subject to certain conditions.

Chapter 13 provides an exception to appraisal rights for publicly traded shares, referred to as the "market exception." This exception is available in those situations when shareholders are likely to receive fair value if they sell their shares in the market after the announcement of an appraisal-triggering transaction. For the market exception to apply under chapter 13, there must be a liquid market for the shares. The market exception does not apply where the appraisal-triggering action is a conflict transaction.

2. Definitions

Section 13.01 contains specialized definitions applicable only to chapter 13.

A. CORPORATION

The definition of "corporation" in section 13.01 includes, for purposes of the post-transaction matters covered in sections 13.22 through 13.31, a successor entity in a merger where the corporation is not the surviving entity. The definition does not include an acquiring entity in a share exchange or disposition of assets because the corporation whose shares or assets were acquired continues in existence in both of these instances and remains responsible for the appraisal obligations. Whether a foreign corporation or other form of domestic or foreign entity is subject to appraisal rights in connection with any of these transactions depends upon the applicable law of the relevant jurisdiction.

B. FAIR VALUE

Clause (i) of the definition of "fair value" in section 13.01 specifies that fair value is to be determined immediately before the effectiveness of the corporate action, which will be after the shareholder vote. Accordingly, section 13.01 permits consideration of changes in the value of the corporation's shares after the shareholder vote but before the effectiveness of the transaction, to the extent such changes are relevant. Similarly, in a two-step transaction culminating in a merger, fair value is determined immediately before the second step merger, taking into account any interim changes in value.

Clause (ii) of the definition of "fair value" in section 13.01 adopts the view that different transactions and different contexts may warrant different valuation methodologies. Customary valuation concepts and techniques will typically take into account numerous relevant factors, and will normally result in a range of values, not a particular single value. A court determining fair value under chapter 13 should give great deference to the aggregate consideration accepted or approved by a disinterested board of directors for an appraisal-triggering transaction.

Valuation discounts for lack of marketability or minority status are inappropriate in most appraisal actions, both because most transactions that trigger appraisal rights affect the corporation as a whole and because such discounts may give the majority the opportunity to take advantage of minority shareholders who have been forced against their will to accept the appraisal-triggering transaction. Clause (iii) of the definition of "fair value" adopts the view that appraisal should generally award a shareholder his or her proportional interest in the corporation after valuing the corporation as a whole, rather than the value of the shareholder's shares when valued alone.

C. INTEREST

The specification of the rate of interest on judgments, rather than a more subjective rate, eliminates a possible issue of contention and should facilitate voluntary settlements. Other state law determines whether interest is compound or simple.

D. INTERESTED TRANSACTION

The term "interested transaction" addresses two groups of conflict transactions: those in subsections (i)(A) and (B) of the definition, which involve large shareholders; and those in subsection (i)(C), which involve senior executives and directors. The phrase "involving an interested person" as applied to subsections (i)(A) and (B) denotes participation beyond merely voting or participating on the same basis as other holders of securities of the same or a similar class or series. When a transaction fits within the definition of an interested transaction there are two consequences: the market exception will not be applicable, and the exclusion of other remedies under section 13.40 will not be applicable unless certain disinterested approvals have been obtained.

The definition of "beneficial owner" in subsection (ii) of the definition of "interested transaction" is used to identify possible conflict situations by deeming each member of a group that agrees to vote in concert to be a beneficial owner of all the voting shares owned by the members of the group. (In contrast, the term "beneficial shareholder," as defined in section 1.40, is used to identify those persons entitled to appraisal rights.) When an acquisition is effected in two steps (a tender offer followed by a merger) within one year, and the consideration in the merger is of the same kind and of at least the same value as that in the tender offer, the two-step acquisition is properly considered a single transaction for purposes of identifying conflict transactions, regardless of whether the second-step merger is governed by section 11.04 or 11.05. Therefore the shares acquired in such an offer (defined as "excluded shares" in subsection (iii)) are excluded in subsections (i)(A) and (B) from the determination of whether a person is an "interested person" for purposes of the second-step merger.

A reverse split in which small shareholders are cashed out will constitute an interested transaction if there is an affiliate of the corporation who satisfies the test in subsections (i)(A) or (B). In that case, the corporation itself will be considered an affiliate of the large shareholder and fall within the definition of "interested person," such that when the corporation acquires and cashes out the shares of the small shareholders the acquisition will be an interested transaction.

Subsection (i)(C) applies to management buyouts because management's participation in the buyout group is itself "a financial benefit not generally available to other shareholders." It also applies to transactions involving other types of economic benefits (excluding benefits afforded to shareholders generally) afforded to senior executives (as defined in section 13.01) and directors in specified conflict situations, unless specific objective or procedural standards are met. It would also apply to less common situations, such as where the vote of a director is manipulated by providing the director with special consideration to secure his or her vote in favor of the transaction. Section 13.01 specifically defines the term "affiliate" to include an entity of which a person is a senior executive. As a result of this definition, if a senior executive of the corporation is to continue and is to receive enumerated employment and other financial benefits after the transaction, exempting the transaction from the category of "interested transactions" will depend on meeting one of the three conditions specified in subsection (i)(C), for example:

- If an individual has an arrangement under which benefits will be triggered on a "change of control," such as accelerated vesting of options, retirement benefits, deferred compensation and similar items, or is afforded the opportunity to retire or leave the employ of the enterprise with more favorable economic results than would be the case absent a change of control, the existence of these arrangements would not mean that the transaction is an interested transaction if the arrangements had been established as a general condition of the individual's employment or continued employment, rather than in contemplation of the particular transaction.

- If such arrangements are established as part of, or as a condition of, the transaction, the transaction will still not be considered an interested transaction if the arrangements are either not more favorable to the officer or director than those already in existence or, if they treat the director or officer more favorably, are approved by "qualified" directors (*i.e.*, meeting the standard specified in section 1.43), in the same manner as provided for conflicting interest transactions generally with the corporation under section 8.62. This category would include arrangements with the corporation that have been negotiated as part of, or as a condition to, the transaction or arrangements with the acquiring company or one or more of its other subsidiaries.

- If a person who is a director of the corporation and, in connection with the transaction, is to become a director of the acquiror or its parent, or to continue as a director of the corporation when it becomes a subsidiary of the acquiror, the transaction will not be considered an interested transaction as long as that person will not be treated more favorably as a director than are other persons who are serving in the same director positions.

E.   SENIOR EXECUTIVE

The definition of "senior executive" in section 13.01 encompasses the group of individuals in control of corporate information and the corporation's day-to-day operations. An employee of a subsidiary organization is a "senior executive" of the parent if the employee is "in charge of a principal business unit or function" of the parent and its subsidiaries on a combined or consolidated basis.

F.   SHAREHOLDER

The definition of "shareholder" in section 13.01 encompasses beneficial shareholders and voting trust beneficial owners. This recognizes that these persons have or hold on behalf of others an economic interest in the shares. Use of the term "beneficial shareholder" for this purpose is to be contrasted with the use of the term "beneficial owner" in subsection (ii) of the definition of "interested transaction" to identify possible conflict situations. The distinction between "record shareholder" and "beneficial shareholder" appears primarily in section 13.03, which establishes the manner in which beneficial shareholders, and record shareholders who are acting on behalf of beneficial shareholders, perfect appraisal rights.

§13.02. Right to Appraisal

(a) A shareholder is entitled to appraisal rights, and to obtain payment of the fair value of that shareholder's shares, in the event of any of the following corporate actions:

(1) consummation of a merger to which the corporation is a party (i) if shareholder approval is required for the merger by section 11.04, or would be required but for the provisions of section 11.04(j), except that appraisal rights shall not be available to any shareholder of the corporation with respect

to shares of any class or series that remain outstanding after consummation of the merger, or (ii) if the corporation is a subsidiary and the merger is governed by section 11.05;

(2) consummation of a share exchange to which the corporation is a party the shares of which will be acquired, except that appraisal rights shall not be available to any shareholder of the corporation with respect to any class or series of shares of the corporation that is not acquired in the share exchange;

(3) consummation of a disposition of assets pursuant to section 12.02 if the shareholder is entitled to vote on the disposition, except that appraisal rights shall not be available to any shareholder of the corporation with respect to shares of any class or series if (i) under the terms of the corporate action approved by the shareholders there is to be distributed to shareholders in cash the corporation's net assets, in excess of a reasonable amount reserved to meet claims of the type described in sections 14.06 and 14.07, (A) within one year after the shareholders' approval of the action and (B) in accordance with their respective interests determined at the time of distribution, and (ii) the disposition of assets is not an interested transaction;

(4) an amendment of the articles of incorporation with respect to a class or series of shares that reduces the number of shares of a class or series owned by the shareholder to a fraction of a share if the corporation has the obligation or right to repurchase the fractional share so created;

(5) any other merger, share exchange, disposition of assets or amendment to the articles of incorporation, in each case to the extent provided by the articles of incorporation, bylaws or a resolution of the board of directors;

(6) consummation of a domestication pursuant to section 9.20 if the shareholder does not receive shares in the foreign corporation resulting from the domestication that have terms as favorable to the shareholder in all material respects, and represent at least the same percentage interest of the total voting rights of the outstanding shares of the foreign corporation, as the shares held by the shareholder before the domestication;

(7) consummation of a conversion of the corporation to a nonprofit corporation pursuant to section 9.30; or

(8) consummation of a conversion of the corporation to an unincorporated entity pursuant to section 9.30.

(b) Notwithstanding subsection (a), the availability of appraisal rights under subsections (a)(1), (2), (3), (4), (6) and (8) shall be limited in accordance with the following provisions:

(1) Appraisal rights shall not be available for the holders of shares of any class or series of shares which is:

(i) a covered security under section 18(b)(1)(A) or (B) of the Securities Act of 1933;

(ii) traded in an organized market and has at least 2,000 shareholders and a market value of at least $20 million (exclusive of the value of such shares held by the corporation's subsidiaries, senior executives and directors and by any beneficial shareholder and any voting trust beneficial owner owning more than 10% of such shares); or

(iii) issued by an open end management investment company registered with the Securities and Exchange Commission under the Investment Company Act of 1940 and which may be redeemed at the option of the holder at net asset value.

(2) The applicability of subsection (b)(1) shall be determined as of:

(i) the record date fixed to determine the shareholders entitled to receive notice of the meeting of shareholders to act upon the corporate action requiring appraisal rights or, in the case of an offer made pursuant to section 11.04(j), the date of such offer; or

(ii) if there is no meeting of shareholders and no offer made pursuant to section 11.04(j), the day before the consummation of the corporate action or effective date of the amendment of the articles of incorporation, as applicable.

(3) Subsection (b)(1) shall not be applicable and appraisal rights shall be available pursuant to subsection (a) for the holders of any class or series of shares (i) who are required by the terms of the corporate action requiring appraisal rights to accept for such shares anything other than cash or shares of any class or any series of shares of any corporation, or any other proprietary interest of any other entity, that satisfies the standards set forth in subsection (b)(1) at the time the corporate action becomes effective, or (ii) in the case of the consummation of a disposition of assets pursuant to section 12.02, unless the cash, shares, or proprietary interests received in the disposition are, under the terms of the corporate action approved by the shareholders, to be distributed to the shareholders, as part of a distribution to shareholders of the net assets of the corporation in excess of a reasonable amount to meet claims of the type described in sections 14.06 and 14.07, (A) within one year after the shareholders' approval of the action, and (B) in accordance with their respective interests determined at the time of the distribution.

(4) Subsection (b)(1) shall not be applicable and appraisal rights shall be available pursuant to subsection (a) for the holders of any class or series of shares where the corporate action is an interested transaction.

(c) Notwithstanding any other provision of section 13.02, the articles of incorporation as originally filed or any amendment to the articles of incorporation may limit or eliminate appraisal rights for any class or series of preferred shares, except that (i) no such limitation or elimination shall be effective if the class or series does not have the right to vote separately as a voting group (alone or as part of a group) on the action or if the action is a conversion under section 9.30, or a merger having a similar effect as a conversion in which the converted entity is an eligible entity, and (ii) any such limitation or elimination contained in an amendment to the articles of incorporation that limits or eliminates appraisal rights for any of such shares that are outstanding immediately before the effective date of such amendment or that the corporation is or may be required to issue or sell thereafter pursuant to any conversion, exchange or other right existing immediately before the effective date of such amendment shall not apply to any corporate action that becomes effective within one year after the effective date of such amendment if such action would otherwise afford appraisal rights.

Official Comment

1. Transactions Requiring Appraisal Rights

Section 13.02(a) establishes the scope of appraisal rights by identifying those transactions that afford this right. Statutory appraisal is made available only for corporate actions that will result in a fundamental change in the shares to be affected by the action and then only when uncertainty concerning the fair value of the affected shares may cause reasonable differences about the fairness of the terms of the corporate action. The transactions that satisfy both of these criteria are set forth in section 13.02(a), subject to the exceptions set forth in section 13.02(b). In a two-step transaction authorized by section 11.04(j), shareholders at the time of the second step merger could have appraisal rights even though there is no shareholder vote. Shareholders who tender in response to the offer in the first step of such a transaction would not have appraisal rights; their tendering in response to the offer has the same effect on appraisal rights as if they had voted for the transaction.

Under section 13.02(b)(4), the reasons for granting appraisal rights in a reverse stock split in which shares are cashed out are similar to those for granting such rights in cases of cash-out mergers, as both transactions could compel affected shareholders to accept cash for their investment in an amount established by the corporation. Appraisal is afforded only for those shareholders of a class or series whose interest is so affected by the amendment. As provided in section 12.02(g), a disposition of assets by a corporation in the course of dissolution under chapter 14 is governed by that chapter, not chapter 12, and thus does not implicate appraisal rights.

An express grant of voluntary appraisal rights under section 13.02(a)(5) overrides any of the exceptions to the availability of appraisal rights in section 13.02(a). Any voluntary grant of appraisal rights by the corporation to the holders of one or more of its classes or series of shares in connection with a corporate action will automatically make all of the provisions of chapter 13 applicable to the corporation and such holders regarding that corporate action.

2. Market Exception to Appraisal Rights

Chapter 13 provides a limited exception to appraisal rights for those situations where shareholders may either accept the appraisal-triggering corporate action or sell their shares in an organized market described in section 13.02(b)(1). For purposes of this chapter, the market exception is provided for a class or series of shares if two tests are satisfied: the market in which the shares are traded must be liquid, as described in section 13.02(b)(1), and the value of the shares established by the appraisal-triggering event must be the result of a process reasonably calculated to arrive at a price reflective of an arm's length transaction.

Because section 13.02(b)(3)(i) excludes from the market exception those transactions that require shareholders to accept anything other than cash or securities that also meet the liquidity tests of section 13.02(b)(1), shareholders are assured of receiving either appraisal rights, cash from the transaction, or shares or other proprietary interests in the survivor entity that are liquid. Section 13.02(b)(2) specifies the date on which the corporation must satisfy the requirements of section 13.02(b)(1) for the market exception to be applicable. Section 13.02(b)(4) recognizes that the market price of, or consideration for, shares of a corporation that proposes to engage in an interested transaction of the type listed in section 13.02(a) may be subject to influences where a corporation's management, controlling shareholders or directors have conflicting interests that could, if not dealt with appropriately, adversely affect the consideration that otherwise could have been expected. Section 13.02(b)(4) thus provides that the market exception will not apply in those instances where the transaction constitutes an interested transaction (as defined in section 13.01).

3.   *Elimination of Appraisal Rights for Preferred Shares*

Section 13.02(c) permits the corporation to eliminate or limit appraisal rights that would otherwise be available for the holders of one or more series or classes of preferred shares provided that the standards in that section are met. Chapter 13 does not permit the corporation to eliminate or limit the appraisal rights of common shares.

§ 13.03. Assertion of Rights by Nominees and Beneficial Shareholders

(a) A record shareholder may assert appraisal rights as to fewer than all the shares registered in the record shareholder's name but owned by a beneficial shareholder or a voting trust beneficial owner only if the record shareholder objects with respect to all shares of a class or series owned by the beneficial shareholder or the voting trust beneficial owner and notifies the corporation in writing of the name and address of each beneficial shareholder or voting trust beneficial owner on whose behalf appraisal rights are being asserted. The rights of a record shareholder who asserts appraisal rights for only part of the shares held of record in the record shareholder's name under this subsection shall be determined as if the shares as to which the record shareholder objects and the record shareholder's other shares were registered in the names of different record shareholders.

(b) A beneficial shareholder and a voting trust beneficial owner may assert appraisal rights as to shares of any class or series held on behalf of the shareholder only if such shareholder:

(1) submits to the corporation the record shareholder's written consent to the assertion of such rights no later than the date referred to in section 13.22(b)(2)(ii); and

(2) does so with respect to all shares of the class or series that are beneficially owned by the beneficial shareholder or the voting trust beneficial owner.

Official Comment

Section 13.03 addresses the relationship between those who are entitled to assert appraisal rights and the widespread practice of nominee or street name ownership of publicly traded shares. Generally, a shareholder must demand appraisal for all the shares of a class or series which the shareholder owns. If a record shareholder is a nominee for several beneficial shareholders, some of whom wish to demand appraisal and some of whom do not, section 13.03(a) permits the record shareholder to assert appraisal rights with respect to a portion of the shares held of record by the record shareholder but only with respect to all the shares beneficially owned by a single person. The same rule applies to shares held by voting trustees. A shareholder who owns shares in more than one class or series, however, may assert appraisal rights for only some rather than all classes or series that the shareholder owns.

Voting trustees hold shares on behalf of voting trust beneficial owners and may want to or be required to pass the decision on asserting appraisal rights on to the voting trust beneficial owners. To make appraisal rights effective without burdening record shareholders, beneficial shareholders and voting trust beneficial owners are allowed to assert their own claims as provided in section 13.03(b). After the corporation has received the form of consent required by section 13.03(b)(1), the corporation must deal with the beneficial shareholder, or, in the case of a voting trust, the voting trust beneficial owner.

Subchapter B

Procedure for Exercise of Appraisal Rights

§ 13.20. Notice of Appraisal Rights

(a) Where any corporate action specified in section 13.02(a) is to be submitted to a vote at a shareholders' meeting, the meeting notice (or where no approval of such action is required pursuant to section 11.04(j), the offer made pursuant to section 11.04(j)), must state that the corporation has concluded that appraisal rights are, are not or may be available under this chapter. If the corporation concludes that appraisal rights are or may be available, a copy of this chapter must accompany the meeting notice or offer sent to those record shareholders entitled to exercise appraisal rights.

(b) In a merger pursuant to section 11.05, the parent entity shall notify in writing all record shareholders of the subsidiary who are entitled to assert appraisal rights that the corporate action became effective. Such notice shall be sent within 10 days after the corporate action became effective and include the materials described in section 13.22.

(c) Where any corporate action specified in section 13.02(a) is to be approved by written consent of the shareholders pursuant to section 7.04:

(1) written notice that appraisal rights are, are not or may be available shall be sent to each record shareholder from whom a consent is solicited at the time consent of such shareholder is first solicited and, if the corporation has concluded that appraisal rights are or may be available, the notice must be accompanied by a copy of this chapter; and

(2) written notice that appraisal rights are, are not or may be available must be delivered together with the notice to nonconsenting and nonvoting shareholders required by sections 7.04(e) and (f), may include the materials described in section 13.22 and, if the corporation has concluded that appraisal rights are or may be available, must be accompanied by a copy of this chapter.

(d) Where corporate action described in section 13.02(a) is proposed, or a merger pursuant to section 11.05 is effected, the notice referred to in subsection (a) or (c), if the corporation concludes that appraisal rights are or may be available, and in subsection (b) must be accompanied by:

(1) financial statements of the corporation that issued the shares that may be subject to appraisal, consisting of a balance sheet as of the end of a fiscal year ending not more than 16 months before the date of the notice, an income statement for that year, and a cash flow statement for that year; provided that, if such financial statements are not reasonably available, the corporation shall provide reasonably equivalent financial information; and

(2) the latest interim financial statements of such corporation, if any.

(e) The right to receive the information described in subsection (d) may be waived in writing by a shareholder before or after the corporate action.

Official Comment

The notices required by sections 13.20(a), (b) and (c) are necessary because many shareholders do not know what appraisal rights they may have or how to assert them. Because appraisal is an "opt in" remedy, shareholders otherwise entitled to an appraisal of their shares by reason of corporate actions specified in section 13.02 must elect whether to seek that remedy or accept the results of that action.

Section 13.20(d) specifies certain disclosure requirements for corporate actions for which appraisal rights are provided. Disclosure of additional information may be necessary under common law disclosure duties.

By specifying certain disclosure requirements, section 13.20(d) reduces the risk, in the transactions to which it applies, of an uninformed shareholder decision whether to exercise appraisal rights. Section 13.31(b)(1) provides that a corporation may be liable for the fees and expenses of counsel and experts for the respective parties for failure to comply substantially with sections 13.20 and 13.24.

§ 13.21. Notice of Intent to Demand Payment and Consequences of Voting or Consenting

(a) If a corporate action specified in section 13.02(a) is submitted to a vote at a shareholders' meeting, a shareholder who wishes to assert appraisal rights with respect to any class or series of shares:

(1) shall deliver to the corporation, before the vote is taken, written notice of the shareholder's intent to demand payment if the proposed action is effectuated; and

(2) shall not vote, or cause or permit to be voted, any shares of such class or series in favor of the proposed action.

(b) If a corporate action specified in section 13.02(a) is to be approved by written consent, a shareholder who wishes to assert appraisal rights with respect to any class or series of shares shall not sign a consent in favor of the proposed action with respect to that class or series of shares.

(c) If a corporate action specified in section 13.02(a) does not require shareholder approval pursuant to section 11.04(j), a shareholder who wishes to assert appraisal rights with respect to any class or series of shares (i) shall deliver to the corporation before the shares are purchased pursuant to the offer written notice of the shareholder's intent to demand payment if the proposed action is effected; and (ii) shall not tender, or cause or permit to be tendered, any shares of such class or series in response to such offer.

(d) A shareholder who fails to satisfy the requirements of subsection (a), (b) or (c) is not entitled to payment under this chapter.

Official Comment

Section 13.21 applies to all transactions requiring appraisal, except short-form mergers under section 11.05 in which shareholders of the subsidiary do not vote on the transaction but are nevertheless entitled to appraisal.

The notice from the shareholder required by section 13.21(a) enables the corporation, among other things, to estimate how much of a cash payment may be required by reference to the maximum number of shares for which appraisal may be sought. It also limits the number of persons to whom the corporation must give further notice during the remainder of the appraisal process.

§ 13.22. Appraisal Notice and Form

(a) If a corporate action requiring appraisal rights under section 13.02(a) becomes effective, the corporation shall deliver a written appraisal notice and form required by subsection (b) to all shareholders who satisfy the requirements of sections 13.21(a), (b) or (c). In the case of a merger under section 11.05, the parent shall deliver an appraisal notice and form to all record shareholders who may be entitled to assert appraisal rights.

(b) The appraisal notice shall be delivered no earlier than the date the corporate action specified in section 13.02(a) became effective, and no later than 10 days after such date, and must:

(1) supply a form that (i) specifies the first date of any announcement to shareholders made before the date the corporate action became effective of the principal terms of the proposed corporate action, and (ii) if such announcement was made, requires the shareholder asserting appraisal rights to certify whether beneficial ownership of those shares for which appraisal rights are asserted was acquired before that date, and (iii) requires the shareholder asserting appraisal rights to certify that such shareholder did not vote for or consent to the transaction as to the class or series of shares for which appraisal is sought;

(2) state:

(i) where the form shall be sent and where certificates for certificated shares shall be deposited and the date by which those certificates must be deposited, which date may not be earlier than the date by which the corporation must receive the required form under subsection (b)(2)(ii);

(ii) a date by which the corporation shall receive the form, which date may not be fewer than 40 nor more than 60 days after the date the subsection (a) appraisal notice is sent, and state that the shareholder shall have waived the right to demand appraisal with respect to the shares unless the form is received by the corporation by such specified date;

(iii) the corporation's estimate of the fair value of the shares;

(iv) that, if requested in writing, the corporation will provide, to the shareholder so requesting, within 10 days after the date specified in subsection (b)(2)(ii) the number of shareholders who return the forms by the specified date and the total number of shares owned by them; and

(v) the date by which the notice to withdraw under section 13.23 shall be received, which date shall be within 20 days after the date specified in subsection (b)(2)(ii); and

(3) be accompanied by a copy of this chapter.

Official Comment

The purpose of section 13.22 is to require the corporation to provide shareholders with information and a form for perfecting appraisal rights.

Section 13.22(b)(1) requires that the corporation specify the date of the first announcement of the terms of the proposed corporate action. This date determines the rights of shareholder-transferees. Persons who became shareholders before that date are entitled to full appraisal rights, while persons who became shareholders on or after that date are entitled only to the more limited rights provided by section 13.25. See the Official Comments to sections 13.23 and 13.25. The date the principal terms of the transaction were announced by the corporation to shareholders may be the day the terms were communicated directly to the shareholders, included in a public filing with the Securities and Exchange Commission, published in a newspaper of general circulation that can be expected to reach the financial community, or any earlier date on which such terms were first announced by any other person or entity to such persons or sources. Any announcement to news media or to shareholders that relates to the proposed transaction but does not contain the principal terms of the transaction to be authorized at the shareholders' meeting is not considered to be an announcement for the purposes of section 13.22. If a corporation or other person does not make a public announcement of the terms of a proposed corporation action, the requirement of section 13.22(b)(1) is not applicable.

The information required by sections 13.22(b)(2)(iii) and (iv) is intended to help shareholders assess whether they wish to demand payment or to withdraw their demand for appraisal, although the information under section 13.22(b)(2)(iv) is required to be sent only to those shareholders from whom the corporation has received a written request.

§ 13.23. Perfection of Rights; Right to Withdraw

(a) A shareholder who receives notice pursuant to section 13.22 and who wishes to exercise appraisal rights shall sign and return the form sent by the corporation and, in the case of certificated shares, deposit the shareholder's certificates in accordance with the terms of the notice by the date referred to in the notice pursuant to section 13.22(b)(2)(ii). In addition, if applicable, the shareholder shall certify on the form whether the beneficial owner of such shares acquired beneficial ownership of the shares before the date required to be set forth in the notice pursuant to section 13.22(b)(1)(i). If a shareholder fails to make this certification, the corporation may elect to treat the shareholder's shares as after-acquired shares under section 13.25. Once a shareholder deposits that shareholder's certificates or, in the case of uncertificated shares, returns the signed forms, that shareholder loses all rights as a shareholder, unless the shareholder withdraws pursuant to subsection (b).

(b) A shareholder who has complied with subsection (a) may nevertheless decline to exercise appraisal rights and withdraw from the appraisal process by so notifying the corporation in writing by the date set forth in the appraisal notice pursuant to section 13.22(b)(2)(v). A shareholder who fails to so withdraw from the appraisal process may not thereafter withdraw without the corporation's written consent.

(c) A shareholder who does not sign and return the form and, in the case of certificated shares, deposit that shareholder's share certificates where required, each by the date set forth in the notice described in section 13.22(b), shall not be entitled to payment under this chapter.

Official Comment

In the case of a transaction involving a vote by shareholders, returning the signed form and, in the case of certificated shares, depositing the shares are the shareholder's confirmation of the intention expressed earlier under section 13.21(a) to pursue appraisal rights. In the case of a merger of a subsidiary under section 11.05, the form required by section 13.23 is the shareholder's first statement of this intention.

Information on the appraisal form regarding whether the beneficial shareholder acquired beneficial ownership of the shares before, on or after the date the transaction was announced permits the corporation to exercise its right under section 13.25 to defer payment of compensation for certain shares. The corporation may elect to proceed under section 13.25 with respect to those shareholders who were required to make the certification but did not do so.

Once a shareholder deposits that shareholder's shares as required by section 13.23(a), that shareholder loses all rights as a shareholder unless the shareholder withdraws from the appraisal process pursuant to section 13.23(b).

Under section 13.23(c), a shareholder who fails to comply with the requirements of section 13.23(a) loses all rights to pursue appraisal and obtain payment under this chapter. If a beneficial shareholder wishes to assert appraisal rights in place of the record shareholder, the beneficial shareholder must also comply with section 13.03(b).

§ 13.24. Payment

(a) Except as provided in section 13.25, within 30 days after the form required by section 13.22(b)(2)(ii) is due, the corporation shall pay in cash to those shareholders who complied with section 13.23(a) the amount the corporation estimates to be the fair value of their shares, plus interest.

(b) The payment to each shareholder pursuant to subsection (a) must be accompanied by:

(1)(i) financial statements of the corporation that issued the shares to be appraised, consisting of a balance sheet as of the end of a fiscal year ending not more than 16 months before the date of payment, an income statement for that year, and a cash flow statement for that year; provided that, if such annual financial statements are not reasonably available, the corporation shall provide reasonably equivalent financial information, and (ii) the latest interim financial statements of such corporation, if any;

(2) a statement of the corporation's estimate of the fair value of the shares, which estimate shall equal or exceed the corporation's estimate given pursuant to section 13.22(b)(2)(iii); and

(3) a statement that shareholders described in subsection (a) have the right to demand further payment under section 13.26 and that if any such shareholder does not do so within the time period specified in section 13.26(b), such shareholder shall be deemed to have accepted the payment under subsection (a) in full satisfaction of the corporation's obligations under this chapter.

Official Comment

Section 13.24 is applicable to shareholders who have complied with section 13.23(a) and to shareholders described in section 13.25(a) if the corporation so chooses. The corporation must, however, elect to treat all shareholders described in section 13.25(a) either under section 13.24 or under section 13.25; it may not treat some shareholders described in section 13.25(a) under section 13.24 but treat others under section 13.25.

The requirement of section 13.24 that the corporation pay its estimate of the fair value of the stock plus interest reflects a judgment that a difference of opinion over the total amount to be paid should not delay payment of the amount that is undisputed. Because a former shareholder must decide whether to accept that payment in full satisfaction, the corporation must include with the payment the information specified in section 13.24(b), which includes a reminder of the former shareholder's further rights.

Even though the information specified in section 13.24(b) was previously furnished under section 13.20(d) at the time notice of appraisal rights was given, it must still be furnished under section 13.24(b) at the time of payment. That information may need to be updated to satisfy the requirements of section 13.24(b).

§ 13.25. After-Acquired Shares

(a) A corporation may elect to withhold payment required by section 13.24 from any shareholder who was required to, but did not certify that beneficial ownership of all of the shareholder's shares for which appraisal rights are asserted was acquired before the date set forth in the appraisal notice sent pursuant to section 13.22(b)(1).

(b) If the corporation elected to withhold payment under subsection (a), it shall, within 30 days after the form required by section 13.22(b)(2)(ii) is due, notify all shareholders who are described in subsection (a):

(1) of the information required by section 13.24(b)(1);

(2) of the corporation's estimate of fair value pursuant to section 13.24(b)(2);

(3) that they may accept the corporation's estimate of fair value, plus interest, in full satisfaction of their demands or demand appraisal under section 13.26;

(4) that those shareholders who wish to accept such offer shall so notify the corporation of their acceptance of the corporation's offer within 30 days after receiving the offer; and

(5) that those shareholders who do not satisfy the requirements for demanding appraisal under section 13.26 shall be deemed to have accepted the corporation's offer.

(c) Within 10 days after receiving the shareholder's acceptance pursuant to subsection (b)(4), the corporation shall pay in cash the amount it offered under subsection (b)(2) plus interest to each shareholder who agreed to accept the corporation's offer in full satisfaction of the shareholder's demand.

(d) Within 40 days after delivering the notice described in subsection (b), the corporation shall pay in cash the amount it offered to pay under subsection (b)(2) plus interest to each shareholder described in subsection (b)(5).

Official Comment

If a public announcement of the proposed corporate action is made, section 13.25(a) gives the corporation the option not to make payment under section 13.24(a) to holders of shares acquired on or after the date of that announcement or to holders of shares who are required to but do not certify under section 13.23(a) when they acquired beneficial ownership. Instead, the corporation may give these shareholders an offer of payment which is conditioned on their agreement to accept it in full satisfaction of their claim.

The date used as a cut-off for determining the application of this section is when "the principal terms" of the proposed transaction are first announced to shareholders. See the Official Comment to section 13.22. The cut-off is not set at an earlier date, such as when the first public statement that the corporate action was under consideration was made, because the goal of this section is to discourage use of appraisal rights as a speculative device only after the principal terms of the proposed transaction are announced.

A shareholder may accept the offered payment in full satisfaction of that shareholder's claim; alternatively, a shareholder may reject the corporation's offer and demand a judicial determination under section 13.26 and payment of the amount so determined at the termination of the proceeding. A shareholder who does not satisfy the requirements of section 13.26 shall be deemed to have accepted the corporation's offer.

§ 13.26. Procedure if Shareholder Dissatisfied with Payment or Offer

(a) A shareholder paid pursuant to section 13.24 who is dissatisfied with the amount of the payment shall notify the corporation in writing of that shareholder's estimate of the fair value of the shares and demand payment of that estimate (less any payment under section 13.24) plus interest. A shareholder offered payment under section 13.25 who is dissatisfied with that offer shall reject the offer and demand payment of the shareholder's stated estimate of the fair value of the shares plus interest.

(b) A shareholder who fails to notify the corporation in writing of that shareholder's demand to be paid the shareholder's stated estimate of the fair value plus interest under subsection (a) within 30 days after receiving the corporation's payment or offer of payment under section 13.24 or section 13.25, respectively, waives the right to demand payment under this section and shall be entitled only to the payment made or offered pursuant to those respective sections.

Official Comment

A shareholder who is not content with the corporation's remittance under section 13.24, or offer of remittance under section 13.25, and wishes to pursue appraisal rights further must state in writing the amount the shareholder is willing to accept. A shareholder whose demand is deemed arbitrary, unreasonable or not in good faith, however, runs the risk of being assessed litigation expenses under section 13.31. These provisions are designed to encourage settlement without a judicial proceeding.

A shareholder to whom the corporation has made payment (or who has been offered payment under section 13.25) must make a supplemental demand within 30 days after receipt of the payment or offer of payment to permit the corporation to make an early decision on initiating appraisal proceedings. A failure to make such demand causes the shareholder to relinquish under section 13.26(b) anything beyond the amount the corporation paid or offered to pay.

Subchapter C
Judicial Appraisal of Shares

§ 13.30. Court Action

(a) If a shareholder makes demand for payment under section 13.26 which remains unsettled, the corporation shall commence a proceeding within 60 days after receiving the payment demand and petition the court to determine the fair value of the shares and accrued interest. If the corporation does not commence the proceeding within the 60-day period, it shall pay in cash to each shareholder the amount the shareholder demanded pursuant to section 13.26 plus interest.

(b) The corporation shall commence the proceeding in the [name or describe court].

(c) The corporation shall make all shareholders (regardless of whether they are residents of this state) whose demands remain unsettled parties to the proceeding as in an action against their shares, and all parties shall be served with a copy of the petition. Nonresidents may be served by registered or certified mail or by publication as provided by law.

(d) The jurisdiction of the court in which the proceeding is commenced under subsection (b) is plenary and exclusive. The court may appoint one or more persons as appraisers to receive evidence and recommend a decision on the question of fair value. The appraisers shall have the powers described in the order appointing them, or in any amendment to it. The shareholders demanding appraisal rights are entitled to the same discovery rights as parties in other civil proceedings. There shall be no right to a jury trial.

(e) Each shareholder made a party to the proceeding is entitled to judgment (i) for the amount, if any, by which the court finds the fair value of the shareholder's shares exceeds the amount paid by the corporation to the shareholder for such shares, plus interest, or (ii) for the fair value, plus interest, of the shareholder's shares for which the corporation elected to withhold payment under section 13.25.

Official Comment

Section 13.30 provides for judicial appraisal as the ultimate means of determining fair value. All demands for payment made under section 13.26 are to be resolved in a single proceeding brought in the court specified by section 13.30(b). All shareholders making demands under section 13.26 must be made parties, with service by publication authorized if necessary. Because the nature of the proceeding is similar to a proceeding in equity or for an accounting, section 13.30(d) provides that there is no right to a jury trial. The final judgment establishes not only the fair value of the shares in the abstract but also determines how much each shareholder who made a section 13.26 demand should receive.

§ 13.31. Court Costs and Expenses

(a) The court in an appraisal proceeding commenced under section 13.30 shall determine all court costs of the proceeding, including the reasonable compensation and expenses of appraisers appointed by the court. The court shall assess the court costs against the corporation, except that the court may assess court costs against all or some of the shareholders demanding appraisal, in amounts which the court finds equitable, to the extent the court finds such shareholders acted arbitrarily, vexatiously, or not in good faith with respect to the rights provided by this chapter.

(b) The court in an appraisal proceeding may also assess the expenses of the respective parties in amounts the court finds equitable:

(1) against the corporation and in favor of any or all shareholders demanding appraisal if the court finds the corporation did not substantially comply with the requirements of sections 13.20, 13.22, 13.24, or 13.25; or

(2) against either the corporation or a shareholder demanding appraisal, in favor of any other party, if the court finds the party against whom expenses are assessed acted arbitrarily, vexatiously, or not in good faith with respect to the rights provided by this chapter.

(c) If the court in an appraisal proceeding finds that the expenses incurred by any shareholder were of substantial benefit to other shareholders similarly situated and that such expenses should not be assessed against the corporation, the court may direct that such expenses be paid out of the amounts awarded the shareholders who were benefited.

(d) To the extent the corporation fails to make a required payment pursuant to sections 13.24, 13.25, or 13.26, the shareholder may sue directly for the amount owed, and to the extent successful, shall be entitled to recover from the corporation all expenses of the suit.

Official Comment

The purpose of the grants of discretion to the court under section 13.31 with respect to expenses of appraisal proceedings is to increase the incentives of both sides to proceed in good faith under this chapter to attempt to resolve their disagreement without the need of a formal judicial appraisal of the value of shares.

While subsections (a) through (c) allocate court costs and expenses in an appraisal proceeding, subsection (d) covers the situation where the corporation was obligated to make payment and did not meet this obligation.

Subchapter D
Other Remedies

§ 13.40. Other Remedies Limited

(a) The legality of a proposed or completed corporate action described in section 13.02(a) may not be contested, nor may the corporate action be enjoined, set aside or rescinded, in a legal or equitable proceeding by a shareholder after the shareholders have approved the corporate action.

(b) Subsection (a) does not apply to a corporate action that:

(1) was not authorized and approved in accordance with the applicable provisions of:

(i) chapter 9, 10, 11, or 12;

(ii) the articles of incorporation or bylaws; or

(iii) the resolution of the board of directors authorizing the corporate action;

(2) was procured as a result of fraud, a material misrepresentation, or an omission of a material fact necessary to make statements made, in light of the circumstances in which they were made, not misleading;

(3) is an interested transaction, unless it has been recommended by the board of directors in the same manner as is provided in section 8.62 and has been approved by the shareholders in the same manner as is provided in section 8.63 as if the interested transaction were a director's conflicting interest transaction; or

(4) is approved by less than unanimous consent of the voting shareholders pursuant to section 7.04 if:

(i) the challenge to the corporate action is brought by a shareholder who did not consent and as to whom notice of the approval of the corporate action was not effective at least 10 days before the corporate action was effected; and

(ii) the proceeding challenging the corporate action is commenced within 10 days after notice of the approval of the corporate action is effective as to the shareholder bringing the proceeding.

Official Comment

The principle underlying section 13.40 generally is that when the holders of a majority of the shares have approved a corporate change, the corporation should be permitted to proceed even if a minority considers the change unwise or disadvantageous. The existence of an appraisal remedy recognizes that shareholders may disagree about the financial consequences that a corporate action may have and that some may hold such strong views that they will want to vindicate them in a judicial proceeding. Accordingly, if an appraisal proceeding results in an award of additional consideration to the shareholders who pursued appraisal, no inference should be drawn that the judgment of the majority was wrong or that compensation is now owed to shareholders who did not seek appraisal. The limitations are not confined to cases where appraisal is available. The liquidity and reliability considerations that justify the market exception also justify imposing the same limitation on post-shareholder approval remedies that apply when appraisal is available.

Section 13.40 permits proceedings contesting the legality of a transaction, or seeking to enjoin, rescind or set aside the corporate action after the action has been approved by shareholders under the four circumstances described in section 13.40(b)(1). In the case of a corporate action that is an interested transaction, the same reasoning that supports the provision of appraisal rights in situations where the market exception would otherwise apply under section 13.02(b) also supports the approach in section 13.40(b)(3) not to preclude judicial review or relief in connection with such transactions, unless other strong safeguards are present. Those safeguards are drawn from the treatment of director conflicting interest transactions in sections 8.60 through 8.63. In those sections, a conflict of interest transaction may be protected if either qualified director or disinterested shareholder approval is obtained after required disclosure. Here, the protection is made available only if both those requirements are met. Absent compliance with those safeguards, the standard of review to be applied, and the extent of the relief that may be available is not addressed by this section.

The scope of section 13.40(b) is limited and does not otherwise affect applicable state law. Section 13.40(b) does not create any cause of action; it merely removes the bar to the types of post-transaction claims provided in section 13.40(a). Even then, whether the specific facts of a transaction subject to section 13.40(b) warrant invalidation or rescission is left to the discretion of the court. Similarly, section 13.40 leaves to applicable state law the question of remedies, such as injunctive relief, that may be available before the corporate action is approved by shareholders in light of other remedies that may be available after the transaction is approved or completed. Where post-shareholder approval claims outside the scope of section 13.40 are asserted, the availability of judicial review, the remedies (such as damages) that shareholders may have, and questions relating to election of remedies, will be determined by applicable state law. Section 13.40 addresses challenges only to the corporate action and does not address remedies, if any, that shareholders may have against directors or other persons as a result of the corporate action, even where subsection (b)(4) applies. See section 8.31 and the related Official Comment and the introductory Official Comment to chapter 8F under the heading "Scope of Subchapter F."

Chapter 14

DISSOLUTION

Subchapter A

Voluntary Dissolution

§ 14.01. Dissolution by Incorporators or Initial Directors

A majority of the incorporators or initial directors of a corporation that has not issued shares or has not commenced business may dissolve the corporation by delivering to the secretary of state for filing articles of dissolution that set forth:

(a) the name of the corporation;

(b) the date of its incorporation;

(c) either (i) that none of the corporation's shares has been issued or (ii) that the corporation has not commenced business;

(d) that no debt of the corporation remains unpaid;

(e) that the net assets of the corporation remaining after winding up have been distributed to the shareholders, if shares were issued; and

(f) that a majority of the incorporators or initial directors authorized the dissolution.

§14.02. Dissolution by Board of Directors and Shareholders

(a) The board of directors may propose dissolution for submission to the shareholders by first adopting a resolution authorizing the dissolution.

(b) For a proposal to dissolve to be adopted, it shall then be approved by the shareholders. In submitting the proposal to dissolve to the shareholders for approval, the board of directors shall recommend that the shareholders approve the dissolution, unless (i) the board of directors determines that because of conflict of interest or other special circumstances it should make no recommendation or (ii) section 8.26 applies. If either (i) or (ii) applies, the board shall inform the shareholders of the basis for its so proceeding.

(c) The board of directors may set conditions for the approval of the proposal for dissolution by shareholders or the effectiveness of the dissolution.

(d) If the approval of the shareholders is to be given at a meeting, the corporation shall notify each shareholder, regardless of whether entitled to vote, of the meeting of shareholders at which the dissolution is to be submitted for approval. The notice must state that the purpose, or one of the purposes, of the meeting is to consider dissolving the corporation.

(e) Unless the articles of incorporation or the board of directors acting pursuant to subsection (c) require a greater vote, a greater quorum, or a vote by voting groups, adoption of the proposal to dissolve shall require the approval of the shareholders at a meeting at which a quorum exists consisting of a majority of the votes entitled to be cast on the proposal to dissolve.

Official Comment

When submitting a proposal to dissolve to shareholders, the board of directors must recommend the dissolution, subject to two exceptions in section 14.02(b). The board might exercise the exception under clause (i) where the number of directors having a conflicting interest makes it inadvisable for the board to recommend the proposal or where the board is evenly divided as to the merits of the proposal but is able to agree that shareholders should be permitted to consider it. Alternatively, the board of directors might exercise the exception under clause (ii), which recognizes that, under section 8.26, a board of directors may agree to submit a proposal to dissolve to a vote of shareholders even if, after approving the proposal, the board of directors determines that it no longer recommends the proposal.

Section 14.02(c) permits the board of directors to condition its submission to the shareholders of a proposal for dissolution or the effectiveness of the dissolution. Among the conditions that a board might impose are that the proposal will not be deemed approved unless it is approved by a specified percentage of the shareholders, or by one or more specified classes or series of shares, voting as a separate voting group, or by a specified percentage of disinterested shareholders.

Requirements concerning the timing and content of a notice of meeting, as required by section 14.02(d), are set out in section 7.05. Section 14.02(d) does not address the notice to be given to nonvoting or nonconsenting shareholders where the proposal is approved, without a meeting, by written consent. However, that requirement is imposed by section 7.04.

Section 14.02(e) sets forth the quorum and voting requirements applicable to a shareholder vote to approve a dissolution. In lieu of approval at a meeting, shareholder approval may be by written consent under the procedures set forth in section 7.04.

The Act does not mandate separate voting by voting groups or appraisal rights in relation to dissolution proposals because upon dissolution, the rights of all classes or series of shares are fixed by the articles of incorporation. Separate voting by voting groups may nevertheless be required if provided for in the articles of incorporation or by the board of directors, acting pursuant to section 14.02(c).

§ 14.03. Articles of Dissolution

(a) At any time after dissolution is authorized, the corporation may dissolve by delivering to the secretary of state for filing articles of dissolution setting forth:

(1) the name of the corporation;

(2) the date that dissolution was authorized; and

(3) if dissolution was approved by the shareholders, a statement that the proposal to dissolve was duly approved by the shareholders in the manner required by this Act and by the articles of incorporation.

(b) The articles of dissolution shall take effect at the effective date determined in accordance with section 1.23. A corporation is dissolved upon the effective date of its articles of dissolution.

(c) For purposes of this subchapter, "dissolved corporation" means a corporation whose articles of dissolution have become effective and includes a successor entity to which the remaining assets of the corporation are transferred subject to its liabilities for purposes of liquidation.

§ 14.04. Revocation of Dissolution

(a) A corporation may revoke its dissolution within 120 days after its effective date.

(b) Revocation of dissolution shall be authorized in the same manner as the dissolution was authorized unless that authorization permitted revocation by action of the board of directors alone, in which event the board of directors may revoke the dissolution without shareholder action.

(c) After the revocation of dissolution is authorized, the corporation may revoke the dissolution by delivering to the secretary of state for filing articles of revocation of dissolution, together with a copy of its articles of dissolution, that set forth:

(1) the name of the corporation;

(2) the effective date of the dissolution that was revoked;

(3) the date that the revocation of dissolution was authorized;

(4) if the corporation's board of directors (or incorporators) revoked the dissolution, a statement to that effect;

(5) if the corporation's board of directors revoked a dissolution as authorized by the shareholders, a statement that revocation was permitted by action by the board of directors alone pursuant to that authorization; and

(6) if shareholder action was required to revoke the dissolution, a statement that the revocation was duly approved by the shareholders in the manner required by this Act and by the articles of incorporation.

(d) The articles of revocation of dissolution shall take effect at the effective date determined in accordance with section 1.23. Revocation of dissolution is effective upon the effective date of the articles of revocation of dissolution.

(e) When the revocation of dissolution is effective, it relates back to and takes effect as of the effective date of the dissolution and the corporation resumes carrying on its business as if dissolution had never occurred.

§ 14.05. Effect of Dissolution

(a) A corporation that has dissolved continues its corporate existence but the dissolved corporation may not carry on any business except that appropriate to wind up and liquidate its business and affairs, including:

(1) collecting its assets;

(2) disposing of its properties that will not be distributed in kind to its shareholders;

(3) discharging or making provision for discharging its liabilities;

(4) making distributions of its remaining assets among its shareholders according to their interests; and

(5) doing every other act necessary to wind up and liquidate its business and affairs.

(b) Dissolution of a corporation does not:

(1) transfer title to the corporation's property;

(2) prevent transfer of its shares or securities;

(3) subject its directors or officers to standards of conduct different from those prescribed in chapter 8;

(4) change (i) quorum or voting requirements for its board of directors or shareholders; (ii) provisions for selection, resignation, or removal of its directors or officers or both; or (iii) provisions for amending its bylaws;

(5) prevent commencement of a proceeding by or against the corporation in its corporate name;

(6) abate or suspend a proceeding pending by or against the corporation on the effective date of dissolution; or

(7) terminate the authority of the registered agent of the corporation.

(c) A distribution in liquidation under this section may only be made by a dissolved corporation. For purposes of determining the shareholders entitled to receive a distribution in liquidation, the board of directors may fix a record date for determining shareholders entitled to a distribution in liquidation, which date may not be retroactive. If the board of directors does not fix a record date for determining shareholders entitled to a distribution in liquidation, the record date is the date the board of directors authorizes the distribution in liquidation.

Official Comment

Although section 14.05(a) provides that dissolution does not terminate the corporate existence, it does require the corporation to wind up its affairs and liquidate its assets. After dissolution, the corporation may not carry on its business except as may be appropriate for winding up. Because distributions in liquidation that occur after dissolution are distinct from the pre-dissolution distributions governed by section 6.40, section 14.05(c) sets forth a separate provision for establishing a record date for determining shareholders entitled to receive a distribution in liquidation.

§ 14.06. Known Claims Against Dissolved Corporation

(a) A dissolved corporation may dispose of the known claims against it by notifying its known claimants in writing of the dissolution at any time after its effective date.

(b) The written notice must:

(1) describe information that must be included in a claim;

(2) provide a mailing address where a claim may be sent;

(3) state the deadline, which may not be fewer than 120 days after the written notice is effective, by which the dissolved corporation shall receive the claim; and

(4) state that the claim will be barred if not received by the deadline.

(c) A claim against the dissolved corporation is barred:

(1) if a claimant who was given written notice under subsection (b) does not deliver the claim to the dissolved corporation by the deadline; or

(2) if a claimant whose claim was rejected by the dissolved corporation does not commence a proceeding to enforce the claim within 90 days after the rejection notice is effective.

(d) For purposes of this section, "claim" does not include a contingent liability or a claim based on an event occurring after the effective date of dissolution.

Official Comment

Sections 14.06 and 14.07 provide a simplified system for handling claims against a dissolved corporation. Section 14.06 deals solely with known claims while section 14.07 deals with unknown or subsequently arising claims. Known claims may be unliquidated, but a claim that is contingent or has not yet matured (or in certain cases has matured but has not been asserted) is not a "claim" for purposes of section 14.06(d). For example, an unmatured liability under a guarantee, a potential default under a lease, or an unasserted claim based upon a defective product manufactured by the dissolved corporation would not be a "claim" under section 14.06.

Known claims are handled in section 14.06 through a process of written notice to claimants, which must provide the information described in section 14.06(b). See section 1.41 with respect to notices and communications generally. Section 14.06(c) then provides fixed deadlines by which known claims are barred under various circumstances. Section 14.06(c), however, does not bar a claim if the dissolved corporation does not act on it or fails to notify the claimant of the rejection of the claim. Section 14.07 bars certain claims not covered by section 14.06.

The principles of sections 14.06 and 14.07 do not lengthen statutes of limitation applicable under general state law. Thus, claims that are not barred under the foregoing rules—for example, if the corporation does not give notice to the claimant under section 14.06(a) or does not act on a claim—will nevertheless be subject to the general statute of limitations applicable to claims of that type. The Act does not require that a dissolved corporation take the actions set out in sections 14.06 and 14.07, but if it does not do so the protections those sections provide are not available to it.

§ 14.07. Other Claims Against Dissolved Corporation

(a) A dissolved corporation may publish notice of its dissolution and request that persons with claims against the dissolved corporation present them in accordance with the notice.

(b) The notice must:

(1) be published (i) one time in a newspaper of general circulation in the county where the dissolved corporation's principal office (or, if none in this state, its registered office) is or was last located or (ii) be posted conspicuously for at least 30 days on the dissolved corporation's website;

(2) describe the information that must be included in a claim and provide a mailing address where the claim may be sent; and

(3) state that a claim against the dissolved corporation will be barred unless a proceeding to enforce the claim is commenced within three years after the publication of the notice.

(c) If the dissolved corporation publishes a notice in accordance with subsection (b), the claim of each of the following claimants is barred unless the claimant commences a proceeding to enforce the claim against the dissolved corporation within three years after the publication date of the notice:

(1) a claimant who was not given written notice under section 14.06;

(2) a claimant whose claim was timely sent to the dissolved corporation but not acted on by the corporation;

(3) a claimant whose claim is contingent or based on an event occurring after the effective date of dissolution.

(d) A claim that is not barred by section 14.06(c) or section 14.07(c) may be enforced:

(1) against the dissolved corporation, to the extent of its undistributed assets; or

(2) except as provided in section 14.08(d), if the assets have been distributed in liquidation, against a shareholder of the dissolved corporation to the extent of the shareholder's pro rata share of the claim or the corporate assets distributed to the shareholder in liquidation, whichever is less, but a shareholder's total liability for all claims under this section may not exceed the total amount of assets distributed to the shareholder.

Official Comment

Section 14.07 addresses the problems created by possible claims that might arise long after the dissolution process is completed and the corporate assets distributed to shareholders. One example would be claims based on personal injuries occurring after dissolution but caused by allegedly defective products sold before dissolution. The problems raised by such claims are difficult. On one hand, the application of a mechanical limitation period to a claim for injury that occurs after the period has expired may involve injustice to the plaintiff. On the other hand, to permit these suits generally makes it impossible ever to complete the winding up of the corporation, make suitable provision for creditors, and distribute the balance of the corporate assets to the shareholders.

The approach adopted in section 14.07 is to continue the liability of a dissolved corporation for subsequent claims for a period of three years after it publishes notice of dissolution. The three-year cut-off, although arbitrary, provides a reasonable compromise between the competing interests of potential injured plaintiffs, the ability of dissolved corporations to distribute remaining assets free of all claims, and the interests of shareholders in receiving those assets secure in the knowledge that they may not be reclaimed.

Directors must generally discharge or make provision for discharging the corporation's liabilities before distributing the remaining assets to the shareholders. See section 14.09(a). Under section 14.07(d)(1), unbarred claimants will continue to have recourse to the remaining assets of the dissolved corporation. Further, where unbarred claims arise after distributions have been made to shareholders in liquidation, section 14.07(d)(2) authorizes recovery against the shareholders receiving those distributions. That section limits recovery, however, to the smaller of the recipient shareholder's pro rata share of the claim or the total amount of assets received as liquidating distributions by the shareholder from the corporation. The provision encourages claimants seeking to recover distributions from shareholders to try to recover from the entire class of shareholders rather than concentrating only on the larger shareholders and protects the limited liability of shareholders. Shareholders also may be liable to directors for recoupment under section 8.32(b)(2).

§ 14.08. Court Proceedings

(a) A dissolved corporation that has published a notice under section 14.07 may file an application with the [name or describe court] for a determination of the amount and form of security to be provided for payment of claims that are contingent or have not been made known to the dissolved corporation or that are based on an event occurring after the effective date of dissolution but that, based on the facts known to the dissolved corporation, are reasonably estimated to arise after the effective date of dissolution. Provision need not be made for any claim that is or is reasonably anticipated to be barred under section 14.07(c).

(b) Within 10 days after the filing of the application, notice of the proceeding shall be given by the dissolved corporation to each claimant holding a contingent claim whose contingent claim is shown on the records of the dissolved corporation.

(c) The court may appoint a guardian ad litem to represent all claimants whose identities are unknown in any proceeding brought under this section. The reasonable fees and expenses of such guardian, including all reasonable expert witness fees, shall be paid by the dissolved corporation.

(d) Provision by the dissolved corporation for security in the amount and the form ordered by the court under section 14.08(a) shall satisfy the dissolved corporation's obligations with respect to claims that are contingent, have not been made known to the dissolved corporation or are based on an event occurring after the effective date of dissolution, and such claims may not be enforced against a shareholder who received assets in liquidation.

Official Comment

Section 14.08 allows a dissolved corporation to initiate a court proceeding to establish the provision that should be made for contingent or unknown claims that are not reasonably expected to be barred after the three-year period in section 14.07(c). By following this procedure, a corporation removes the risk of director and shareholder liability for inadequate provision for claims.

Section 14.08 is designed to permit the court to adopt procedures appropriate to the circumstances. Estimates for contingent or unknown claims, such as product liability injury claims that might arise after dissolution, need only be made for those claims that the court determines are reasonably anticipated to be asserted within three years after dissolution.

The notice required by section 14.08(b) would include notice to holders of guarantees made by the corporation.

If the dissolved corporation provides for security for claims as set forth in section 14.08(d), that section protects shareholders who receive distributions against those claims, and section 14.09(b) similarly protects directors from liability for those distributions.

§ 14.09. Director Duties

(a) Directors shall cause the dissolved corporation to discharge or make reasonable provision for the payment of claims and make distributions in liquidation of assets to shareholders after payment or provision for claims.

(b) Directors of a dissolved corporation which has disposed of claims under section 14.06, 14.07, or 14.08 shall not be liable for breach of section 14.09(a) with respect to claims against the dissolved corporation that are barred or satisfied under section 14.06, 14.07 or 14.08.

Subchapter B

Administrative Dissolution

§ 14.20. Grounds for Administrative Dissolution

The secretary of state may commence a proceeding under section 14.21 to dissolve a corporation administratively if:

(a) the corporation does not pay within 60 days after they are due any fees, taxes, interest or penalties imposed by this Act or other laws of this state;

(b) the corporation does not deliver its annual report to the secretary of state within 60 days after it is due;

(c) the corporation is without a registered agent or registered office in this state for 60 days or more;

(d) the secretary of state has not been notified within 60 days that the corporation's registered agent or registered office has been changed, that its registered agent has resigned, or that its registered office has been discontinued; or

(e) the corporation's period of duration stated in its articles of incorporation expires.

Official Comment

Under the Act, actual or threatened administrative dissolution is an effective enforcement mechanism for a variety of statutory obligations. The advantages of administrative dissolution in the circumstances outlined in this section are compelling: it not only reduces the number of records maintained by the secretary of state, but also avoids futile attempts to compel compliance by abandoned corporations and returns corporate names promptly to the status of available names. It is also less costly and requires fewer legal resources than judicial dissolution.

Subchapter C

Judicial Dissolution

§ 14.30. Grounds for Judicial Dissolution

(a) The [name or describe court or courts] may dissolve a corporation:

(1) in a proceeding by the attorney general if it is established that:

(i) the corporation obtained its articles of incorporation through fraud; or

(ii) the corporation has continued to exceed or abuse the authority conferred upon it by law;

(2) in a proceeding by a shareholder if it is established that:

(i) the directors are deadlocked in the management of the corporate affairs, the shareholders are unable to break the deadlock, and irreparable injury to the corporation is threatened or being suffered, or the business and affairs of the corporation can no longer be conducted to the advantage of the shareholders generally, because of the deadlock;

(ii) the directors or those in control of the corporation have acted, are acting, or will act in a manner that is illegal, oppressive, or fraudulent;

(iii) the shareholders are deadlocked in voting power and have failed, for a period that includes at least two consecutive annual meeting dates, to elect successors to directors whose terms have expired; or

(iv) the corporate assets are being misapplied or wasted;

(3) in a proceeding by a creditor if it is established that:

(i) the creditor's claim has been reduced to judgment, the execution on the judgment returned unsatisfied, and the corporation is insolvent; or

(ii) the corporation has admitted in writing that the creditor's claim is due and owing and the corporation is insolvent;

(4) in a proceeding by the corporation to have its voluntary dissolution continued under court supervision; or

(5) in a proceeding by a shareholder if the corporation has abandoned its business and has failed within a reasonable time to liquidate and distribute its assets and dissolve.

(b) Subsection (a)(2) shall not apply in the case of a corporation that, on the date of the filing of the proceeding, has a class or series of shares which is:

(i) a covered security under section 18(b)(1)(A) or (B) of the Securities Act of 1933; or

(ii) not a covered security, but is held by at least 300 shareholders and the shares outstanding have a market value of at least $20 million (exclusive of the value of such shares held by the corporation's subsidiaries, senior executives, directors and beneficial shareholders and voting trust beneficial owners owning more than 10% of such shares).

(c) In subsection (a), "shareholder" means a record shareholder, a beneficial shareholder, and an unrestricted voting trust beneficial owner, and in subsection (b), "shareholder" means a record shareholder, a beneficial shareholder, and a voting trust beneficial owner.

Official Comment

Section 14.30 provides grounds for the judicial dissolution of a corporation at the request of the state, a shareholder, a creditor, or when a corporation that has commenced voluntary dissolution seeks judicial oversight. Judicial oversight may be useful to protect the corporation from suits by creditors or shareholders. Under this section, the court has discretion as to whether dissolution is appropriate even though the specified grounds for judicial dissolution exist.

1. Involuntary Dissolution by State

Section 14.30(a)(1) provides a means by which the state may ensure compliance with the fundamentals of corporate existence and prevent abuse. That section limits the power of the state in this regard to grounds that are reasonably related to this objective.

2. Involuntary Dissolution by Shareholders

Section 14.30(a)(2) provides for involuntary dissolution at the request of a shareholder under circumstances involving deadlock or significant abuse of power by controlling shareholders or directors. Section 14.30(c) extends the ability to seek judicial dissolution under section 14.30(a)(2) to beneficial shareholders and unrestricted voting trust beneficial owners, as these persons have, or hold on behalf of others, an economic interest in the shares. The remedy of judicial dissolution is available only for shareholders of corporations that do not meet the tests in section 14.30(b). Even for those corporations to which section 14.30(a)(2) applies, however, the court can take into account the number of shareholders and the nature of the trading market for the shares in deciding whether to exercise its discretion to order dissolution. Shareholders of corporations that meet the tests of section 14.30(b) may often have the ability to sell their shares if they are dissatisfied with current management or may seek other remedies under the Act. See, for example, sections 7.48(a) and 8.09. The grounds for dissolution under section 14.30(a)(2) are broader than those required to be shown for the appointment of a custodian or receiver under section 7.48(a). The difference is attributable to the different focus of the two proceedings. Although some of the circumstances listed in 14.30(a)(2), such as deadlock, may implicate the welfare of the corporation as a whole, the primary focus is on the effect of actions by those in control on the value of the complaining shareholder's individual investment. For example, "oppressive" behavior in section 14.30(a)(2)(ii) generally describes action directed against a particular shareholder. In contrast, the focus of protection in an action to appoint a custodian or receiver under section 7.48(a) is the corporate entity, and the remedy is intended to protect the interests of all shareholders, creditors and others who may have an interest therein. In other instances, action that is "illegal" or "fraudulent" under section 14.30(a)(2)(ii) may be severely prejudicial to the interests of an individual shareholder, whereas conduct that is illegal with respect to the entire corporation may be remedied by other causes of action under the Act.

Section 14.30(a)(5) provides a basis for a shareholder to obtain involuntary dissolution in the event the corporation has abandoned its business, but those in control of the corporation have delayed unreasonably in either liquidating and distributing its assets or completing the necessary procedures to dissolve the corporation

3. Involuntary Dissolution by Creditors

Creditors may obtain involuntary dissolution only when the corporation is insolvent and only in the limited circumstances set forth in section 14.30(a)(3). Typically, a proceeding under the federal bankruptcy laws is an alternative in these situations.

4. Judicial Supervision of Dissolution

A corporation that has commenced voluntary dissolution may petition a court to supervise its dissolution. Such an action may be appropriate to permit the orderly liquidation of the corporate assets and to protect the corporation from a multitude of creditors' suits or suits by dissatisfied shareholders.

§ 14.31. Procedure for Judicial Dissolution

(a) Venue for a proceeding by the attorney general to dissolve a corporation lies in [name or describe court]. Venue for a proceeding brought by any other party named in section 14.30(a) lies in [name or describe court].

(b) It is not necessary to make shareholders parties to a proceeding to dissolve a corporation unless relief is sought against them individually.

(c) A court in a proceeding brought to dissolve a corporation may issue injunctions, appoint a receiver or custodian during the proceeding with all powers and duties the court directs, take other action required to preserve the corporate assets wherever located, and carry on the business of the corporation until a full hearing can be held.

(d) Within 10 days of the commencement of a proceeding to dissolve a corporation under section 14.30(a)(2), the corporation shall deliver to all shareholders, other than the petitioner, a notice stating that the shareholders are entitled to avoid the dissolution of the corporation by electing to purchase the petitioner's shares under section 14.34 and accompanied by a copy of section 14.34.

§ 14.32. Receivership or Custodianship

(a) Unless an election to purchase has been filed under section 14.34, a court in a judicial proceeding brought to dissolve a corporation may appoint one or more receivers to wind up and liquidate, or one or more custodians to manage, the business and affairs of the corporation. The court shall hold a hearing, after notifying all parties to the proceeding and any interested persons designated by the court, before appointing a receiver or custodian. The court appointing a receiver or custodian has jurisdiction over the corporation and all of its property wherever located.

(b) The court may appoint an individual or a domestic or foreign corporation or eligible entity as a receiver or custodian, which, if a foreign corporation or foreign eligible entity, must be registered to do business in this state. The court may require the receiver or custodian to post bond, with or without sureties, in an amount the court directs.

(c) The court shall describe the powers and duties of the receiver or custodian in its appointing order, which may be amended from time to time. Among other powers:

(1) the receiver (i) may dispose of all or any part of the assets of the corporation wherever located, at a public or private sale; and (ii) may sue and defend in the receiver's own name as receiver of the corporation in all courts of this state;

(2) the custodian may exercise all of the powers of the corporation, through or in place of its board of directors, to the extent necessary to manage the affairs of the corporation in the best interests of its shareholders and creditors.

The receiver or custodian shall have such other powers and duties as the court may provide in the appointing order, which may be amended from time to time.

(d) The court during a receivership may redesignate the receiver a custodian and during a custodianship may redesignate the custodian a receiver.

(e) The court from time to time during the receivership or custodianship may order compensation paid and expenses paid or reimbursed to the receiver or custodian from the assets of the corporation or proceeds from the sale of the assets.

§ 14.33. Decree of Dissolution

(a) If after a hearing the court determines that one or more grounds for judicial dissolution described in section 14.30 exist, it may enter a decree dissolving the corporation and specifying the effective date of the dissolution, and the clerk of the court shall deliver a certified copy of the decree to the secretary of state for filing.

(b) After entering the decree of dissolution, the court shall direct the winding-up and liquidation of the corporation's business and affairs in accordance with section 14.05 and the notification of claimants in accordance with sections 14.06 and 14.07.

§ 14.34. Election to Purchase in Lieu of Dissolution

(a) In a proceeding under section 14.30(a)(2) to dissolve a corporation, the corporation may elect or, if it fails to elect, one or more shareholders may elect to purchase all shares owned by the petitioning shareholder at the fair value of the shares. An election pursuant to this section shall be irrevocable unless the court determines that it is equitable to set aside or modify the election.

(b) An election to purchase pursuant to this section may be filed with the court at any time within 90 days after the filing of the petition under section 14.30(a)(2) or at such later time as the court in its discretion may allow. If the election to purchase is filed by one or more shareholders, the corporation shall, within 10 days thereafter, give written notice to all shareholders, other than the petitioner. The notice must state the name and number of shares owned by the petitioner and the name and number of shares owned by each electing shareholder and must advise the recipients of their right to join in the election to purchase shares in accordance with this section. Shareholders who wish to participate shall file notice of their intention to join in the purchase no later than 30 days after the effectiveness of the notice to them. All shareholders who have filed an election or notice of their intention to participate in the election to purchase thereby become parties to the proceeding and shall participate in the purchase in proportion to their ownership of shares as of the date the first election was filed, unless they otherwise agree or the court otherwise directs. After an election has been filed by the corporation or one or more shareholders, the proceeding under section 14.30(a)(2) may not be discontinued or settled, nor may the petitioning shareholder sell or otherwise dispose of his or her shares, unless the court determines that it would be equitable to the corporation and the shareholders, other than the petitioner, to permit such discontinuance, settlement, sale, or other disposition.

(c) If, within 60 days of the filing of the first election, the parties reach agreement as to the fair value and terms of purchase of the petitioner's shares, the court shall enter an order directing the purchase of the petitioner's shares upon the terms and conditions agreed to by the parties.

(d) If the parties are unable to reach an agreement as provided for in subsection (c), the court, upon application of any party, shall stay the proceedings under section 14.30(a)(2) and determine the fair value of the petitioner's shares as of the day before the date on which the petition under section 14.30(a)(2) was filed or as of such other date as the court deems appropriate under the circumstances.

(e) Upon determining the fair value of the shares, the court shall enter an order directing the purchase upon such terms and conditions as the court deems appropriate, which may include payment of the purchase price in installments, where necessary in the interests of equity, provision for security to assure payment of the purchase price and any additional expenses as may have been awarded, and, if the shares are to be purchased by shareholders, the allocation of shares among them. In allocating the petitioner's shares among holders of different classes or series of shares, the court should attempt to preserve the existing distribution of voting rights among holders of different classes or series insofar as practicable and may direct that holders of a specific class or classes or series shall not participate in the purchase. Interest may be allowed at the rate and from the date determined by the court to be equitable, but if the court finds that the refusal of the petitioning shareholder to accept an offer of payment was arbitrary or otherwise not in good faith, no interest shall be allowed. If the court finds that the petitioning shareholder had probable grounds for relief under sections 14.30(a)(2)(ii) or (iv), it may award expenses to the petitioning shareholder.

(f) Upon entry of an order under subsections (c) or (e), the court shall dismiss the petition to dissolve the corporation under section 14.30(a)(2), and the petitioning shareholder shall no longer have any rights or status as a shareholder of the corporation, except the right to receive the amounts awarded by the order of the court which shall be enforceable in the same manner as any other judgment.

(g) The purchase ordered pursuant to subsection (e) shall be made within 10 days after the date the order becomes final.

(h) Any payment by the corporation pursuant to an order under subsections (c) or (e), other than an award of expenses pursuant to subsection (e), is subject to the provisions of section 6.40.

Official Comment

It is not always necessary to dissolve a corporation and liquidate its assets to provide relief for the situations covered in section 14.30(a)(2). Section 14.34 provides an alternative by means of which a dissolution proceeding under section 14.30(a)(2) can be terminated upon payment of the fair value of the petitioner's shares, allowing the corporation to continue in existence for the benefit of the remaining shareholders.

1. *Availability*

There are two prerequisites to filing an election to purchase under section 14.34. First, a proceeding to dissolve the corporation under section 14.30(a)(2) must have been commenced. Second, the election may be made only by the corporation or by shareholders other than the shareholder who is seeking to dissolve the corporation under section 14.30(a)(2).

2. *Effect of Filing*

The election to purchase is wholly voluntary, but it may only be made as a matter of right within 90 days after the filing of the petition under section 14.30(a)(2). After 90 days, leave of court is required to make an election to purchase.

Sections 14.34(a) and (b) include provisions with respect to the irrevocability of an election and the inability to discontinue a dissolution proceeding or dispose of shares following the filing of an election. These provisions are intended to reduce the risk that either the dissolution proceeding or the buyout election will be used other than in good faith, because under section 14.34 a petitioner using section 14.30(a)(2) becomes irrevocably committed to sell these shares pursuant to section 14.34 once an election is filed. The petitioning shareholder may not thereafter discontinue the dissolution proceeding or dispose of the petitioner's shares without permission of the court, which is specifically directed to consider whether such action would be equitable from the standpoint of the corporation and the other shareholders.

If the corporation or the other shareholders fail to elect to purchase the petitioner's shares within the first 90 days, they run the risk that the court will decline to accept a subsequent election and will, instead, allow the dissolution proceeding to go forward. The dissolution proceeding is not affected by the filing of an election; it will be stayed only upon an application to the court to determine the fair value of the petitioner's shares filed after the expiration of the 60-day negotiating period provided for in section 14.34(c).

Once an election is filed, it may be set aside or modified only for reasons that the court finds equitable. If the court sets aside the election, the corporation or the electing shareholders are released from their obligation to purchase the petitioner's shares. Under section 14.34(a), the court also has discretion to "modify" the election by releasing one or more electing shareholders without releasing the others.

3. *Election by Corporation or Shareholders*

Because any change in the allocation of shareholdings may upset control or other arrangements that have been previously negotiated by the parties, the corporation's election to purchase is given preference during the 90-day period provided for in section 14.34(b). This preference does not affect the order of filing, and any shareholder may file an election (thus triggering the provisions of subsection (b)) as soon as the dissolution proceeding is commenced. If the corporation thereafter files an election within the 90-day period, its election takes precedence over any previously filed election by shareholders. An election by the corporation after 90 days may be filed only with the court's approval. Section 14.34 does not affect an agreement between the corporation and the other shareholders to participate jointly in the purchase of the petitioner's shares.

Section 14.34(b) requires the corporation to notify all other shareholders of their right to join in the purchase "in proportion to their ownership of shares as of the date the first election was filed." This may raise the question of whether shareholders of a class different from the class of shares owned by the petitioner may participate in the purchase. Given the wide variety of capital structures adopted by corporations, it is not possible to state a general rule that would be appropriate in all cases. Any allocation that is agreed to by the electing shareholders controls regardless of whether the other terms and conditions of the purchase are set by the parties' agreement pursuant to subsection (c) or are determined by the court pursuant to subsection (e). If electing shareholders cannot agree, the court, under subsection (e), must determine an allocation.

4. *Court Order*

If the parties come to terms within the 60-day negotiating period provided for in section 14.34(c), their agreement will be incorporated in an order of the court and will thereafter be enforceable as such. If the parties are unable to reach agreement, any party may apply to the court to determine the fair value of the shares. After the court makes that determination, section 14.34(e) requires it to enter an order directing the sale on such terms as the court finds appropriate. Section 14.34(e) does place some limitations on when the court may provide for installment payments or award interest or expenses and does state that the court should attempt to preserve the distribution of certain voting rights. Otherwise, the contents of the order under subsection (e) are subject to the court's discretion.

The entry of an order under section 14.34(c) or (e) requires the court to dismiss the dissolution proceeding under section 14.30(a)(2) and terminates all rights of the petitioner as a shareholder. Thus, the order also terminates all claims that the petitioner may have had in his or her capacity as a shareholder, and the value of such claims must either be asserted as part of the "fair value" of the petitioner's shares or forever lost. Under subsection (f), claims asserted by the petitioner in any nonshareholder capacity, such as claims for back wages or indemnification, are not affected by the entry of an order nor does the order affect any rights the petitioner may have as a creditor with respect to shares pledged as security for the purchase price. Otherwise, the order is enforceable only in the same manner as any other judgment, and the petitioner may not seek to reopen the proceedings in the event of a default.

After the entry of an order under section 14.34(c) or (e), the petitioner is a creditor with respect to the electing shareholders who participate in the purchase, but any payments to be made by the corporation, other than expenses awarded under section 14.34(e), fall within the definition of "distribution" and are subject to section 6.40.

Subchapter D

Miscellaneous

§ 14.40. Deposit with State Treasurer

Assets of a dissolved corporation that should be transferred to a creditor, claimant, or shareholder of the corporation who cannot be found or who is not competent to receive them shall be reduced to cash and deposited with the state treasurer or other appropriate state official for safekeeping. When the creditor, claimant, or shareholder furnishes satisfactory proof of entitlement to the amount deposited, the state treasurer or other appropriate state official shall pay such person or his or her representative that amount.

Official Comment

Section 14.40 is a deposit provision, not an escheat provision. It does not provide for ultimate disposition of unclaimed funds. The handling and ultimate disposition of unclaimed funds by the state treasurer or other appropriate state official is to be determined by state law other than the Act.

Chapter 15

FOREIGN CORPORATIONS

§ 15.01. Governing Law

(a) The law of the jurisdiction of formation of a foreign corporation governs:

(1) the internal affairs of the foreign corporation; and

(2) the interest holder liability of its shareholders.

(b) A foreign corporation is not precluded from registering to do business in this state because of any difference between the law of the foreign corporation's jurisdiction of formation and the law of this state.

(c) Registration of a foreign corporation to do business in this state does not permit the foreign corporation to engage in any business or affairs or exercise any power that a domestic corporation may not engage in or exercise in this state.

§ 15.02. Registration to Do Business in This State

(a) A foreign corporation may not do business in this state until it registers with the secretary of state under this chapter.

(b) A foreign corporation doing business in this state may not maintain a proceeding in any court of this state until it is registered to do business in this state.

(c) The failure of a foreign corporation to register to do business in this state does not impair the validity of a contract or act of the foreign corporation or preclude it from defending a proceeding in this state.

(d) A limitation on the liability of a shareholder or director of a foreign corporation is not waived solely because the foreign corporation does business in this state without registering.

(e) Section 15.01(a) applies even if a foreign corporation fails to register under this chapter.

§ 15.03. Foreign Registration Statement

To register to do business in this state, a foreign corporation shall deliver a foreign registration statement to the secretary of state for filing. The registration statement must be signed by the foreign corporation and state:

(a) the corporate name of the foreign corporation and, if the name does not comply with section 4.01, an alternate name as required by section 15.06;

(b) the foreign corporation's jurisdiction of formation;

(c) the street and mailing addresses of the foreign corporation's principal office and, if the law of the foreign corporation's jurisdiction of formation requires the foreign corporation to maintain an office in that jurisdiction, the street and mailing addresses of that office;

(d) the street and mailing addresses of the foreign corporation's registered office in this state and the name of its registered agent at that office;

(e) the names and business addresses of its directors and principal officers; and

(f) a brief description of the nature of its business to be conducted in this state.

§ 15.04. Amendment of Foreign Registration Statement

A registered foreign corporation shall sign and deliver to the secretary of state for filing an amendment to its foreign registration statement if there is a change in:

(a) its name or alternate name;

(b) its jurisdiction of formation, unless its registration is deemed to have been withdrawn under section 15.08 or transferred under section 15.10; or

(c) an address required by section 15.03(c).

§ 15.05. Activities Not Constituting Doing Business

(a) Activities of a foreign corporation that do not constitute doing business in this state for purposes of this chapter include:

(1) maintaining, defending, mediating, arbitrating, or settling a proceeding;

(2) carrying on any activity concerning the internal affairs of the foreign corporation, including holding meetings of its shareholders or board of directors;

(3) maintaining accounts in financial institutions;

(4) maintaining offices or agencies for the transfer, exchange, and registration of securities of the foreign corporation or maintaining trustees or depositories with respect to those securities;

(5) selling through independent contractors;

(6) soliciting or obtaining orders by any means if the orders require acceptance outside this state before they become contracts;

(7) creating or acquiring indebtedness, mortgages, or security interests in property;

(8) securing or collecting debts or enforcing mortgages or security interests in property securing the debts, and holding, protecting, or maintaining property so acquired;

(9) conducting an isolated transaction that is not in the course of similar transactions;

(10) owning, protecting and maintaining property; and

(11) doing business in interstate commerce.

(b) This section does not apply in determining the contacts or activities that may subject a foreign corporation to service of process, taxation, or regulation under the laws of this state other than this Act.

Official Comment

The Act does not attempt to formulate an exclusive definition of what constitutes doing business in this state. Rather, the concept is illustrated in a negative fashion by the non-exclusive list of examples in section 15.05(a) of activities that do not constitute doing business. In general terms, any conduct more regular, systematic, or extensive than that described in subsection (a) constitutes doing business and requires the foreign corporation to register to do business. Typical conduct requiring registration includes maintaining an office to conduct local intrastate business, selling personal property not in interstate commerce, entering into contracts relating to the local business or sales, and owning or using real estate for general purposes. The passive owning of real estate for investment purposes does not constitute doing business. See sections 15.05(a)(8) and (a)(10).

The description of "doing business" set forth in section 15.05(a) applies only under this chapter, and only to the question whether the foreign corporation's activities in this state are such that it must register under the Act. It is not applicable to other questions, such as whether the foreign corporation is amenable to service of process under state "long-arm" statutes or liable for state or local taxes. A foreign corporation that has registered (or is required to register) will generally be subject to suit and state taxation in this state, while a foreign corporation that is subject to service of process or state taxation in this state will not necessarily be required to register.

The following provides additional guidance with respect to some of the activities listed in section 15.05(a) that will not, in and of themselves, constitute doing business in this state.

1. Engaging in Litigation and Other Proceedings

Under section 15.05(a)(1), a foreign corporation is not doing business by maintaining, defending, mediating, arbitrating, or settling a proceeding, which as defined in section 1.40 includes civil suits and criminal, administrative, and investigatory actions. Accordingly, a foreign corporation is not doing business solely because it resorts to the courts of this state to, for example, collect indebtedness, enforce an obligation, recover possession of personal property, obtain the appointment of a receiver, intervene in a pending proceeding, bring a petition to compel arbitration, file an appeal bond, or pursue appellate remedies. Similarly, a foreign corporation is not required to register merely because it files a complaint with a governmental agency or participates in an administrative proceeding within this state.

2. Internal Affairs

As provided in section 15.05(a)(2), a foreign corporation does not do business in this state merely because it holds meetings of its shareholders or board of directors within this state. It also may maintain offices or agencies within this state relating solely to the transfer, exchange or registration of its securities without registering. Other activities relating to the internal affairs of the foreign corporation that do not constitute doing business under this section include having officers or representatives who reside within or are physically present in this state. While there, the officers or representatives may make executive decisions without imposing on the foreign corporation the requirement that it register, if these activities are not so regular and systematic as to cause the residence to be viewed as a business office.

3. Sales through Independent Contractors

Under section 15.05(a)(5), a foreign corporation need not register if it sells goods in this state through independent contractors. These transactions are viewed as transactions by the independent contractors, not by the foreign corporation itself, even if the foreign corporation sets some limits or rules for its contractors. If these limits or rules are sufficiently pervasive, however, the foreign corporation may be deemed to be selling for itself in intrastate commerce, and not through the independent contractors and therefore doing business in this state.

4. Creating, Acquiring, or Collecting Debts

The mere act of making a loan by a foreign corporation does not constitute doing business in the state in which the loan is made. On the same theory a foreign corporation may obtain security for the repayment of a loan, and foreclose or enforce the lien or security interest to collect the loan, without being deemed to be doing business. Similarly, a refunding or "roll over" of a loan or its adjustment or compromise does not involve doing business.

5. Isolated Transactions

The concept of doing business involves regular, repeated, and continuing business activities in this state. A single agreement or isolated transaction within the state does not constitute doing business. An isolated transaction does not constitute "doing business" regardless of how long the transaction takes to complete.

6. Interstate Transactions

A foreign corporation is not doing business within the meaning of this chapter if it is transacting business in interstate commerce (section 15.05 (a)(11)) or soliciting or obtaining orders that must be accepted outside this state before they become contracts (section 15.05(a)(6)). These limitations reflect the provisions of the United States Constitution that grant to the United States Congress exclusive power over interstate commerce, and preclude states from imposing restrictions or conditions upon this commerce.

7. Other Activities

Among other activities that do not give rise to the requirement that a registration statement be filed by a foreign corporation are the ownership of all the shares of a corporation that is engaged in activities in the state or as a limited partner in a limited partnership engaged in activities in the state, or taking ministerial actions such as filing financing statements or registering trademarks.

§ 15.07. Withdrawal of Registration of Registered Foreign Corporation

(a) A registered foreign corporation may withdraw its registration by delivering a statement of withdrawal to the secretary of state for filing. The statement of withdrawal must be signed by the foreign corporation and state:

(1) the name of the foreign corporation and its jurisdiction of formation;

(2) that the foreign corporation is not doing business in this state and that it withdraws its registration to do business in this state;

(3) that the foreign corporation revokes the authority of its registered agent in this state; and

(4) an address to which process on the foreign corporation may be sent by the secretary of state under section 5.04(c).

(b) After the withdrawal of the registration of a foreign corporation, service of process in any proceeding based on a cause of action arising during the time the entity was registered to do business in this state may be made as provided in section 5.04.

Chapter 16

RECORDS AND REPORTS

Subchapter A

Records

§ 16.01. Corporate Records

(a) A corporation shall maintain the following records:

(1) its articles of incorporation as currently in effect;

(2) any notices to shareholders referred to in section 1.20(k)(5) specifying facts on which a filed document is dependent if those facts are not included in the articles of incorporation or otherwise available as specified in section 1.20(k)(5);

(3) its bylaws as currently in effect;

(4) all written communications within the past three years to shareholders generally;

(5) minutes of all meetings of, and records of all actions taken without a meeting by, its shareholders, its board of directors, and board committees established under section 8.25;

(6) a list of the names and business addresses of its current directors and officers; and

(7) its most recent annual report delivered to the secretary of state under section 16.21.

(b) A corporation shall maintain all annual financial statements prepared for the corporation for its last three fiscal years (or such shorter period of existence) and any audit or other reports with respect to such financial statements.

(c) A corporation shall maintain accounting records in a form that permits preparation of its financial statements.

(d) A corporation shall maintain a record of its current shareholders in alphabetical order by class or series of shares showing the address of, and the number and class or series of shares held by, each shareholder. Nothing contained in this subsection shall require the corporation to include in such record the electronic mail address or other electronic contact information of a shareholder.

(e) A corporation shall maintain the records specified in this section in a manner so that they may be made available for inspection within a reasonable time.

CROSS-REFERENCES

Annual report of corporation, see § 16.21.

Articles of incorporation, see § 2.02.

Articles of amendment, see § 10.06.

Bylaws, see § 2.06 and ch. 10B.

Committees of board of directors, see § 8.25.

Directors' action without meeting, see § 8.21.

Inspection of corporate records, see §§ 16.02 and 16.04.

Meetings of board of directors, see § 8.20.

Officers, see § 8.40.

Restated articles of incorporation, see § 10.07.

Series of shares, see §§ 6.01 and 6.02.

Shareholders' action without meeting, see § 7.04.

Shareholders' meeting, see §§ 7.01 through 7.03.

Shareholders' voting list, see § 7.20.

Official Comment

1. *Records to be Maintained*

Section 16.01(a) requires certain basic records to be maintained by the corporation. The Act does not generally specify how records must be maintained (other than in a manner so that they may be made available for inspection within a reasonable time), where they must be located or, with the exception of section 16.02(a), where they must be available. They may be maintained in one or more offices within or without the state and in some cases, such as shareholder records, may be maintained by agents of the corporation; indeed, in the case of records in intangible form, it may be impossible to determine where they are located.

2. *Minutes and Related Documents*

Section 16.01(a) does not address the amount of detail that should appear in minutes or written actions. Minutes of meetings customarily include the formalities of notice, the time and place of the meeting, those in attendance, and the results of any votes. Minutes of meetings and written actions without a meeting show formal action taken. The extent to which further detail is included is a matter of judgment which may depend upon the circumstances. Section 7.04, which addresses written actions taken by shareholders, requires that written consents by shareholders be delivered to the corporation for filing with corporate records.

3. *Financial Statements and Accounting Records*

The Act does not provide normative standards for the financial statements and accounting records to be prepared or maintained. The financial statements to be maintained under section 16.01(b) are those that the corporation prepares in the operation of its business, including in response to third party requirements. The form of the financial statements prepared by a corporation depends to some extent on the nature and complexity of the corporation's business and third party requirements such as those governing the preparation and filing of tax returns with applicable tax authorities. To accommodate the needs of the many different types of business corporations that may be subject to these provisions, including closely held corporations, the Act does not require that the corporation prepare and maintain financial statements on the basis of generally accepted accounting principles ("GAAP") if it is not otherwise required to prepare GAAP financial statements. The Act does not define what accounting records must be maintained or mandate how long they must be maintained. The accounting records to be maintained under section 16.01(c) depend upon the form of the corporation's financial statements. For example, annual tax returns filed with the relevant taxing authorities may be the only annual financial statements prepared by small businesses operating on a cash basis and, in those instances, the requisite accounting records to be maintained might consist of only a check register, vouchers and receipts.

4. *Shareholders' Lists*

Section 16.01(d) requires the corporation to maintain such records of its shareholders as will permit it to compile a list of current shareholders when required. These records may vary from stubs from which certificates have been detached in the case of corporations with a few shareholders to elaborate electronic data in the case of large corporations whose shares are publicly traded. The record may be maintained by the corporation or an agent, who traditionally is the transfer agent but may be another agent. A corporation may maintain additional information regarding its shareholders, such as a list of nominees and nonobjecting beneficial owners if its shares are publicly traded.

§ 16.02. Inspection Rights of Shareholders

(a) A shareholder of a corporation is entitled to inspect and copy, during regular business hours at the corporation's principal office, any of the records of the corporation described in section 16.01(a), excluding minutes of meetings of, and records of actions taken without a meeting by, the corporation's board of directors and board committees established under section 8.25, if the shareholder gives the corporation a signed written notice of the shareholder's demand at least five business days before the date on which the shareholder wishes to inspect and copy.

(b) A shareholder of a corporation is entitled to inspect and copy, during regular business hours at a reasonable location specified by the corporation, any of the following records of the corporation if the shareholder meets the requirements of subsection (c) and gives the corporation a signed written notice of the shareholder's demand at least five business days before the date on which the shareholder wishes to inspect and copy:

(1) the financial statements of the corporation maintained in accordance with section 16.01(b);

(2) accounting records of the corporation;

(3) excerpts from minutes of any meeting of, or records of any actions taken without a meeting by, the corporation's board of directors and board committees maintained in accordance with section 16.01(a); and

(4) the record of shareholders maintained in accordance with section 16.01(d).

(c) A shareholder may inspect and copy the records described in subsection (b) only if:

(1) the shareholder's demand is made in good faith and for a proper purpose;

(2) the shareholder's demand describes with reasonable particularity the shareholder's purpose and the records the shareholder desires to inspect; and

(3) the records are directly connected with the shareholder's purpose.

(d) The corporation may impose reasonable restrictions on the confidentiality, use or distribution of records described in subsection (b).

(e) For any meeting of shareholders for which the record date for determining shareholders entitled to vote at the meeting is different than the record date for notice of the meeting, any person who becomes a shareholder subsequent to the record date for notice of the meeting and is entitled to vote at the meeting is entitled to obtain from the corporation upon request the notice and any other information provided by the corporation to shareholders in connection with the meeting, unless the corporation has made such information generally available to shareholders by posting it on its website or by other generally recognized means. Failure of a corporation to provide such information does not affect the validity of action taken at the meeting.

(f) The right of inspection granted by this section may not be abolished or limited by a corporation's articles of incorporation or bylaws.

(g) This section does not affect:

(1) the right of a shareholder to inspect records under section 7.20 or, if the shareholder is in litigation with the corporation, to the same extent as any other litigant; or

(2) the power of a court, independently of this Act, to compel the production of corporate records for examination and to impose reasonable restrictions as provided in section 16.04(c), provided that, in the case of production of records described in subsection (b) of this section at the request of a shareholder, the shareholder has met the requirements of subsection (c).

(h) For purposes of this section, "shareholder" means a record shareholder, a beneficial shareholder, and an unrestricted voting trust beneficial owner.

§ 16.03. Scope of Inspection Right

(a) A shareholder may appoint an agent or attorney to exercise the shareholder's inspection and copying rights under section 16.02.

(b) The corporation may, if reasonable, satisfy the right of a shareholder to copy records under section 16.02 by furnishing to the shareholder copies by photocopy or other means chosen by the corporation, including furnishing copies through an electronic transmission.

(c) The corporation may comply at its expense with a shareholder's demand to inspect the record of shareholders under section 16.02(b)(4) by providing the shareholder with a list of shareholders that was compiled no earlier than the date of the shareholder's demand.

(d) The corporation may impose a reasonable charge to cover the costs of providing copies of documents to the shareholder, which may be based on an estimate of such costs.

§ 16.04. Court-Ordered Inspection

(a) If a corporation does not allow a shareholder who complies with section 16.02(a) to inspect and copy any records required by that section to be available for inspection, the [name or describe court] may summarily order inspection and copying of the records demanded at the corporation's expense upon application of the shareholder.

(b) If a corporation does not within a reasonable time allow a shareholder who complies with section 16.02(b) to inspect and copy the records required by that section, the shareholder who complies with section 16.02(c) may apply to the [name or describe court] for an order to permit inspection and copying of the records demanded. The court shall dispose of an application under this subsection on an expedited basis.

(c) If the court orders inspection and copying of the records demanded under section 16.02(b), it may impose reasonable restrictions on their confidentiality, use or distribution by the demanding shareholder and it shall also order the corporation to pay the shareholder's expenses incurred to obtain the order unless the corporation establishes that it refused inspection in good faith because the corporation had:

> (1) a reasonable basis for doubt about the right of the shareholder to inspect the records demanded; or

> (2) required reasonable restrictions on the confidentiality, use or distribution of the records demanded to which the demanding shareholder had been unwilling to agree.

Official Comment . . .

If the right of inspection under section 16.02(a) is invoked and the corporation refuses to grant inspection, the shareholder may seek a summary order compelling inspection at the corporation's expense. A summary order is appropriate since the right of inspection under section 16.02(a) is either automatic or subject only to a determination that the person is in fact a shareholder of the corporation. By contrast, if inspection is demanded under section 16.02(b), a number of matters may be at issue, including the shareholder's good faith and proper purpose for demands under section 16.02(c) or the reasonableness of the restrictions required by the corporation on the confidentiality, use or distribution of the records. Accordingly, section 16.04(b) directs the court to handle the proceeding "on an expedited basis" instead of in a summary proceeding. The purpose of this phrase is to discourage dilatory tactics to avoid or delay inspection without requiring the court to resolve these issues on a summary basis.

The principal sanction against unreasonable delay or refusal to grant inspection is provided by section 16.04(c), which imposes on the corporation the shareholder's expenses to obtain the order unless the corporation establishes that it refused inspection in good faith on the grounds specified in section 16.04(c)(1) or (2). For example, a corporation may point to conduct of the shareholder involving improper use of information obtained from the corporation in the past as indicating that reasonable doubt existed as to the shareholder's present purpose or by showing that the corporation refused inspection because the shareholder had been unwilling to agree to reasonable restrictions on the confidentiality, use or distribution of records demanded under section 16.02(b).

§ 16.05. Inspection Rights of Directors

(a) A director of a corporation is entitled to inspect and copy the books, records and documents of the corporation at any reasonable time to the extent reasonably related to the performance of the director's duties as a director, including duties as a member of a board committee, but not for any other purpose or in any manner that would violate any duty to the corporation.

(b) The [name or describe court] may order inspection and copying of the books, records and documents at the corporation's expense, upon application of a director who has been refused such inspection rights, unless the corporation establishes that the director is not entitled to such inspection rights. The court shall dispose of an application under this subsection on an expedited basis.

(c) If an order is issued, the court may include provisions protecting the corporation from undue burden or expense, and prohibiting the director from using information obtained upon exercise of the inspection rights in a manner that would violate a duty to the corporation, and may also order the corporation to reimburse the director for the director's expenses incurred in connection with the application.

Subchapter B

Reports

§ 16.20. Financial Statements for Shareholders

(a) Upon the written request of a shareholder, a corporation shall deliver or make available to such requesting shareholder by posting on its website or by other generally recognized means annual financial statements for the most recent fiscal year of the corporation for which annual financial statements have been prepared for the corporation. If financial statements have been prepared for the corporation on the basis of generally accepted accounting principles for such specified period, the corporation shall deliver or make available such financial statements to the requesting shareholder. If the annual financial statements to be delivered or made available to the requesting shareholder are audited or otherwise reported upon by a public accountant, the report shall also be delivered or made available to the requesting shareholder.

(b) A corporation shall deliver, or make available and provide written notice of availability of, the financial statements required under subsection (a) to the requesting shareholder within five business days of delivery of such written request to the corporation.

(c) A corporation may fulfill its responsibilities under this section by delivering the specified financial statements, or otherwise making them available, in any manner permitted by the applicable rules and regulations of the United States Securities and Exchange Commission.

(d) Notwithstanding the provisions of subsections (a), (b) and (c) of this section:

(1) as a condition to delivering or making available financial statements to a requesting shareholder, the corporation may require the requesting shareholder to agree to reasonable restrictions on the confidentiality, use and distribution of such financial statements; and

(2) the corporation may, if it reasonably determines that the shareholder's request is not made in good faith or for a proper purpose, decline to deliver or make available such financial statements to that shareholder.

(e) If a corporation does not respond to a shareholder's request for annual financial statements pursuant to this section in accordance with subsection (b) within five business days of delivery of such request to the corporation:

(1) The requesting shareholder may apply to the [name or describe court] for an order requiring delivery of or access to the requested financial statements. The court shall dispose of an application under this subsection on an expedited basis.

(2) If the court orders delivery or access to the requested financial statements, it may impose reasonable restrictions on their confidentiality, use or distribution.

(3) In such proceeding, if the corporation has declined to deliver or make available such financial statements because the shareholder had been unwilling to agree to restrictions proposed by the corporation on the confidentiality, use and distribution of such financials statements, the corporation shall have the burden of demonstrating that the restrictions proposed by the corporation were reasonable.

(4) In such proceeding, if the corporation has declined to deliver or make available such financial statements pursuant to section 16.20(d)(2), the corporation shall have the burden of demonstrating that it had reasonably determined that the shareholder's request was not made in good faith or for a proper purpose.

(5) If the court orders delivery or access to the requested financial statements it shall order the corporation to pay the shareholder's expenses incurred to obtain such order unless the corporation establishes that it had refused delivery or access to the requested financial statements because the shareholder had refused to agree to reasonable restrictions on the confidentiality, use or distribution

of the financial statements or that the corporation had reasonably determined that the shareholder's request was not made in good faith or for a proper purpose.

Official Comment

1.   *Section 16.20(a)*

Although section 16.20 requires a corporation, upon the written request of a shareholder, to deliver or make available annual financial statements that have been prepared, it does not require a corporation to prepare financial statements. This recognizes that many small, closely held corporations do not regularly prepare formal financial statements unless required by banks, suppliers or other third parties.

Section 16.20 does not limit the financial statements to be delivered or made available to shareholders to financial statements prepared on the basis of generally accepted accounting principles. Many small corporations have never prepared financial statements on the basis of GAAP. "Cash basis" financial statements (often used in preparing the tax returns of small corporations) do not comply with GAAP. Smaller corporations that keep accrual basis records, and file their federal income tax returns on that basis, frequently do not make the adjustments that may be required to present their financial statements on a GAAP basis. Internally or externally prepared financial statements prepared on the basis of other accounting practices and principles that are reasonable in the circumstances, including tax returns filed with the U.S. Internal Revenue Service (if that is all that is prepared), will suffice for these types of corporations and they may satisfy their obligations under section 16.20 by delivering or making available the requested financial statements in whatever form that they have been prepared for other purposes. If a corporation does prepare financial statements on a GAAP basis for any purpose for the particular year, however, it must send or make available those statements to the requesting shareholder as provided by section 16.20(a).

The last sentence of section 16.20(a) requires that if the financial statements to be delivered or made available have been reported upon by a public accountant, that report must be furnished. Section 16.20(a) refers to a "public accountant." The same terminology is used in section 8.30 (standards of conduct for directors). In various states different terms are employed to identify those persons who are permitted under the state licensing requirements to act as professional accountants. Phrases like "independent public accountant," "certified public accountant," "public accountant," and others may be used. In adopting the term "public accountant," the Act uses the words in a general sense to refer to any class or classes of persons who, under the applicable requirements of a particular jurisdiction, are professionally entitled to practice accountancy.

Failure to comply with the requirements of section 16.20 does not adversely affect the existence or good standing of the corporation. Rather, failure to comply gives an aggrieved shareholder rights to compel compliance or to obtain damages, if they can be established, under general principles of law.

A shareholder may also seek access to the financial statements of the corporation through the inspection rights established in section 16.02.

2.   *Section 16.20(d)*

In establishing restrictions with respect to confidentiality, use or distribution that are reasonable under the circumstances, a corporation may consider a number of factors, including the potential competitive harm to the corporation and its other shareholders that could result if the confidential financial information were used to compete with the corporation or disclosed to third parties such as competitors. As provided in section 16.20(d)(2), a corporation may withhold delivery or making available its financial statements to a requesting shareholder if it reasonably determines that the shareholder's request is not made in good faith and for a proper purpose.

3.   *Section 16.20(e)*

If a corporation fails to comply with section 16.20(b) in a timely manner the judicial remedy of 16.20(e) directs the court to handle the proceeding on an expedited basis to discourage dilatory tactics to avoid or delay delivery or access to financial statements, but does not require the court to resolve these issues on a summary basis. Section 16.20(e), like section 16.04, establishes a sanction against unreasonable delay or refusal to deliver or provide access to financial statements by imposing on the corporation the shareholder's expenses in obtaining the court's order unless the corporation can establish that the shareholder had been unwilling to agree to reasonable restrictions on the confidentiality, use or distribution of the requested financial statements or the corporation had reasonably determined that the shareholder's request was not made in good faith or for a proper purpose.

§ 16.21. Annual Report for Secretary of State

(a) Each domestic corporation shall deliver to the secretary of state for filing an annual report that sets forth:

(1) the name of the corporation;

(2) the street and mailing address of its registered office and the name of its registered agent at that office in this state;

(3) the street and mailing address of its principal office;

(4) the names and business addresses of its directors and principal officers;

(5) a brief description of the nature of its business;

(6) the total number of authorized shares, itemized by class and series, if any, within each class; and

(7) the total number of issued and outstanding shares, itemized by class and series, if any, within each class.

(b) Each foreign corporation registered to do business in this state shall deliver to the secretary of state for filing an annual report that sets forth:

(1) the name of the foreign corporation and, if the name does not comply with section 4.01, an alternate name as required by section 15.06;

(2) the foreign corporation's jurisdiction of formation;

(3) the street and mailing addresses of the foreign corporation's principal office and, if the law of the foreign corporation's jurisdiction of formation requires the foreign corporation to maintain an office in that jurisdiction, the street and mailing addresses of that office;

(4) the street and mailing addresses of the foreign corporation's registered office in this state and the name of its registered agent at that office;

(5) the names and business addresses of its directors and principal officers; and

(6) a brief description of the nature of its business conducted in this state.

(c) Information in the annual report must be current as of the date the annual report is signed on behalf of the corporation.

(d) The first annual report shall be delivered to the secretary of state between January 1 and April 1 of the year following the calendar year in which a domestic corporation was incorporated or a foreign corporation was registered to do business. Subsequent annual reports shall be delivered to the secretary of state between January 1 and April 1 of the following calendar years.

(e) If an annual report does not contain the information required by this section, the secretary of state shall promptly notify the reporting domestic or foreign corporation in writing and return the report to it for correction. If the report is corrected to contain the information required by this section and delivered to the secretary of state within 30 days after the notice from the secretary of state becomes effective as determined in accordance with section 1.41, it is deemed to be timely filed.

Official Comment

The purpose of the annual report by a domestic corporation is to show the location of the principal office of the corporation, the names and business addresses of its directors and principal officers, the general nature of the corporation's business, and its capital structure. It permits members of the general public to ascertain the identity of the corporation and communicate directly with it. It also establishes the alternative to the registered office for service of process and related matters. The "principal office" of the corporation is defined in section 1.40 as the location of its principal executive offices as set forth in its annual report or foreign registration statement.

The reference to "principal officers" in sections 16.21(a)(4) and (b)(5) simplifies reporting requirements of corporations with very large numbers of employees who have some managerial responsibility and who, for business reasons, are designated as officers. The "principal officers" of a corporation include at least the chair of the board of directors, the chief executive officer, and the officers performing the traditional functions performed by the secretary and treasurer, no matter what their designation.

An annual report is also required of foreign corporations registered to do business in the state, and serves functions similar to those served with respect to domestic corporations. For both domestic and foreign corporations, the failure to file an annual report, like the failure to satisfy other mandatory requirements of the Act, is a ground for administrative dissolution of a domestic corporation or termination of the registration of a foreign corporation to do business. See sections 14.20 and 15.11.

Chapter 17

TRANSITION PROVISIONS

Note on Adoption of the Act

Chapter 17 addresses various transitional and interpretational issues that merit consideration by the legislature adopting the Act, especially as an entirety. This Note summarizes and explains some of those issues. Each adopting state will need to consider the differences between the Act and its existing corporation statute to determine if additional transitional provisions will be necessary.

Special Circumstances Warranting Delayed Effectiveness

The Act has been drafted to apply to domestic business corporations in existence on its effective date. See section 17.01. To the extent that some of the provisions of the Act differ in significant respects from earlier laws, it may be appropriate to delay the effective date of such provisions to give existing corporations adequate time to revise controlling corporate documents to take into account the provisions of the Act, or in unusual circumstances, to allow existing corporations to continue to be governed by a preexisting law until a later election to be governed by the pertinent provision of the Act. Two examples of such transitional problems are discussed below.

- Changes in Voting Requirements

The Act, unlike some corporation statutes, requires by virtue of section 7.25 only that votes cast in favor exceed votes cast against, in a meeting at which a quorum is present, to approve transactions such as mergers, sale of assets outside the usual and regular course of business, important amendments to the articles of incorporation, and dissolution. When considering adoption of the Act's voting requirements, it is important to recognize that specific control arrangements may have been established on the assumption that the existing statutory voting requirements would not be reduced. Rather than defeat those reasonable assumptions by effectively eliminating a shareholder's power to veto changes when there was a higher statutory vote requirement, a state that adopts the Act's lesser voting requirement may wish to consider "grandfathering" existing corporations and afford them an option to elect to be governed by the new requirement.

- Increased Power of the Board of Directors

The Act generally grants the board of directors authority to increase or decrease its own size without specific authority (section 8.03) unless the articles of incorporation restrict this power. Some corporation statutes do not grant this power to the board of directors unless express provision is made in the articles or bylaws. Corporations that have not granted this express power to the board of directors may in effect do so when they become subject to the Act, and a delayed effective date therefore may be appropriate.

Foreign Corporations

Although chapter 15 of the Act may change the rules applicable to foreign corporations in some states, these changes are not of a type that requires a transition period. It is therefore recommended that only a single effective date be provided for the application of the Act to foreign corporations and that delayed effective dates for specific provisions in this regard are unnecessary. See section 17.02.

Savings and Severability Provisions

The Act contains its own savings and severability provisions, in sections 17.03 and 17.04, respectively. If the state has a savings statute of general application, however, it may be unnecessary to adopt section 17.03. Likewise, if the state has a severability provision of general application, or if the state's highest court has established a general rule of severability, it may be unnecessary to adopt section 17.04.

Repeal

Although section 17.05 provides for repeal of previously enacted general corporation statutes that are specified, such repeal is generally unnecessary with regard to statutes providing special incorporation and regulatory provisions for corporations engaged in specific businesses, like banking and insurance. If these specialized statutes expressly incorporate by reference provisions from the general business corporation act, however, these statutes should be amended to refer specifically to the present Act rather than to an earlier statute; an appropriate provision would apply this Act to all these corporations except to the extent the specialized statute expressly provides that a different principle should apply.

§ 17.01. Application to Existing Domestic Corporations

This Act applies to all domestic corporations in existence on its effective date that were incorporated under any general statute of this state providing for incorporation of corporations for profit if power to amend or repeal the statute under which the corporation was incorporated was reserved.

Official Comment

The Act's application to all domestic corporations in existence on the effective date of the Act, as well as to all new domestic corporations formed after that date, avoids a confusing coexistence of different and overlapping rules of corporation law. The Act does not, however, supersede statutes governing nonprofit corporations or associations, nor does it apply to corporations formed for the purpose of engaging in a business for which the state has provided a separate incorporation procedure.

Section 17.01 applies the Act to all corporations to which that application is constitutionally permissible. In view of the universal adoption of "reservation of power" clauses in all states for more than a century, there are very few active domestic corporations to which the Act will not be applicable under this section.

§ 17.02. Application to Existing Foreign Corporations

A foreign corporation registered or authorized to do business in this state on the effective date of this Act is subject to this Act, is deemed to be registered to do business in this state, and is not required to file a foreign registration statement under this Act.

Official Comment

Section 17.02 makes the Act applicable on its effective date to all foreign corporations that are registered or authorized to do business in the state on that date without action by the foreign corporation.

§ 17.03. Saving Provisions

(a) Except as to procedural provisions, this Act does not affect a pending action or proceeding or a right accrued before the effective date of this Act, and a pending civil action or proceeding may be completed, and a right accrued may be enforced, as if this Act had not become effective.

(b) If a penalty or punishment for violation of a statute or rule is reduced by this Act, the penalty, if not already imposed, shall be imposed in accordance with this Act.

§ 17.04. Severability

If any provision of this Act or its application to any person or circumstance is held invalid by a court of competent jurisdiction, the invalidity does not affect other provisions or applications of this Act that can be given effect without the invalid provision or application.

CALIFORNIA CORPORATIONS CODE
(SELECTED PROVISIONS)

TABLE OF CONTENTS

GENERAL PROVISIONS

Sec.		Page
20.	Electronic transmission by the corporation defined	759
21.	Electronic transmission to the corporation defined	759

TITLE 1

CORPORATIONS

Division 1

GENERAL CORPORATION LAW

Chapter 1

GENERAL PROVISIONS AND DEFINITIONS

114.	Financial Statements or Comparable Statements or Items	760
150.	Affiliate; Affiliated	760
151.	Approved by (or Approval of) the Board	760
152.	Approved by (or Approval of) the Outstanding Shares	760
153.	Approved by (or Approval of) the Shareholders	760
158.	Close Corporation	760
160.	Control	761
161.	Constituent Corporation	761
161.7	Constituent Other Business Entity	761
161.9	Conversion	761
163.1	Cumulative Dividends in Arrears	762
165.	Disappearing Corporation	762
166.	Distribution to Its Shareholders	762
167.8	Disappearing Other Business Entity	762
168.	Equity Security	762
171.1	Initial Transaction Statement	762
171.08	Social Purpose Corporation	763
172.	Liquidation Price; Liquidation Preference	763
174.5	Other Business Entity	763
175.	Parent	763
180.	Redemption Price	763
181.	Reorganization	763
183.5	Share Exchange Tender Offer	763
186.	Shareholders' Agreement	764
187.	Short Form Merger	764
189.	Subsidiary	764
190.	Surviving Corporation	764
190.5	Surviving Limited Partnership	764
190.7	Surviving Other Business Entity	764
194.	Vote	764
194.5	Voting Power	764
194.7	Voting Shift	764

195.   Written; In Writing... 765

Chapter 2

ORGANIZATION AND BYLAWS

202.   Contents of Articles of Incorporation 765
204.   Articles of Incorporation; Optional Provisions 765
212.   Bylaws; Contents 766

Chapter 3

DIRECTORS AND MANAGEMENT

300.   Powers of Board; Delegation; Close Corporations; Shareholders' Agreements;
        Validity; Liability; Failure to Observe Formalities... 767
301.   Directors; Election; Term 768
301.3   Female Directors on Boards of Publicly Held Corporations; Requirements 768
301.5   Listed Corporations; Classes of Directors; Cumulative Voting; Election of Directors;
        Amendment of Articles and Bylaws 769
302.   Directors; Vacancy; Grounds for Declaration 770
303.   Directors; Removal Without Cause 770
304.   Removal for Cause; Shareholders Suit 771
305.   Filling Vacancies; Special Meeting of Shareholders; Notice of Opposition; Resignation 771
307.   Meetings; Time and Place of Regular Meetings; Notice; Adjournment; Meetings
        May Be Within or Without the State; Participation via Electronic Means; Quorum;
        Acts or Decisions of Board 772
308.   Deadlock on Board With Even Number of Directors; Provisional Director; Appointment;
        Powers 773
309.   Performance of Duties by Director; Liability... 773
310.   Contracts in Which Director Has Material Financial Interest; Validity 774
312.   Officers; Election; Term; Resignation 774
313.   Instrument in Writing and Assignment or Endorsement Thereof; Signatures; Validity........ 775
316.   Corporate Actions Subjecting Directors to Joint and Several Liability; Actions; Damages.... 775
317.   Indemnification of Agent of Corporation in Proceedings or Actions 776

Chapter 4

SHARES AND SHARE CERTIFICATES

407.   Fractional Shares... 778
418.   Certificates or Initial Transaction Statements; Required Contents of Statements on Face
        of Documents; Failure to State; Enforceability; Close Corporations; Validity of Transfers.... 778

Chapter 5

DIVIDENDS AND REACQUISITIONS OF SHARES

500.   Distributions; Retained Earnings or Assets Remaining After Completion 779
501.   Inability to Meet Liabilities as They Mature; Prohibition of Distribution 780
503.   Purchase or Redemption of Shares of Deceased Shareholder from Insurance Proceeds;
        Application of Provisions Relating to Prohibited Distributions 780
506.   Receipt of Prohibited Dividend; Liability of Shareholder; Suit by Creditors or Other
        Shareholders; Fraudulent Transfers 781
510.   Acquisition of Own Shares; Status; Prohibition of Reissue by Articles; Reduction in
        Authorized Shares; Amendment of Articles; Filing 781

SELECTED PROVISIONS

Chapter 6

SHAREHOLDERS' MEETINGS AND CONSENTS

602. Quorum; Votes; Withdrawal During Meeting Leaving Less Than Quorum 782
604. Proxies or Written Consents; Contents; Form 783

Chapter 7

VOTING OF SHARES

703. Shares in Name of Other Corporations, [Shares Owned by] Subsidiary or Held in Fiduciary Capacity by Issuing Corporation 783
705. Proxies; Validity; Expiration; Revocation; Irrevocable Proxies 784
706. Agreement Between Two or More Shareholders of a Corporation; Voting Trust Agreements 784
708. Directors; Cumulative Voting; Election by Ballot 785
708.5 Director Election; Approval of Shareholders Required; Term of Incumbent Director When Not Approved in Uncontested Election; Board Vacancy 786
710. Supermajority Vote Requirement; Approval 786
711. Maintenance by Holding Legal Owners and Disclosure to Persons on Whose Behalf Shares Are Voted; Charges; Actions to Enforce Section; Payment of Costs and Attorney's Fees 787

Chapter 8

SHAREHOLDER DERIVATIVE ACTIONS

800. Conditions; Security; Motion for Order; Determination 788

Chapter 9

AMENDMENT OF ARTICLES

900. Authorization 789

Chapter 10

SALES OF ASSETS

1001. Sale, Lease, Exchange, etc. . . . . ; of Property or Assets; Approval; Abandonment; Terms, Conditions and Consideration 790

Chapter 11

MERGER

1100. Authorization 790
1101. Agreement of Merger; Approval of Boards; Contents 790
1111. Approval Where Disappearing Corporation in a Merger Is Close Corporation and Surviving Corporation Is Not 791
1112.5 Merger into Social Purpose Corporation; Approval Required 791

Chapter 11.5

CONVERSIONS

1152. Plan of Conversion 791

CALIFORNIA CORPORATIONS CODE

Chapter 12

REORGANIZATIONS

1200. Approval by Board 792
1201. Approval of Shareholders; Abandonment by Board; Actions to Attack Validity if Party Directly or Indirectly Controlled by Other Party 792
1201.5 Share Exchange Tender Offer; Approval of Principal Terms 793
1202. Terms of Merger Reorganization or Sale-of-Assets Reorganization; Approval by Shareholders; Foreign Corporations 794
1203. Interested Party Proposal or Tender Offer to Shareholders; Affirmative Opinion; Delivery; Approval; Later Proposal or Tender Offer; Withdrawal of Vote, Consent, or Proxy; Procedures 794

Chapter 13

DISSENTERS' RIGHTS

1300. Reorganization or Short-Form Merger; Dissenting Shares; Corporate Purchase at Fair Market Value; Definitions 795
1311. Exempt Shares 796
1312. Right of Dissenting Shareholder to Attack, Set Aside or Rescind Merger or Reorganization; Restraining Order or Injunction; Conditions 796

Chapter 15

RECORDS AND REPORTS

1501. Annual Report; Time of Sending to Shareholders; Contents; Quarterly Financial Statements; Written Request; Inspection; Expenses in Actions 797
1502. Statement of Information; Timing and Contents of Filing; Additional Contents for Publicly Traded Companies; Agent for Service of Process; Updated Information; Public Inspection; Certification 798
1502.1 Statement of Information Pertaining to Independent Auditors, Members of the Board of Directors, and Executive Officers; Definitions; Public Inspection; Certification 799

Chapter 16

RIGHTS OF INSPECTION

1600. List of Shareholders' Names, Addresses and Shareholdings; Time for Compliance After Demand; Delay; Postponement of Shareholders' Meeting; Inspection and Copying 801
1601. Accounting Books and Records and Minutes of Meetings; Inspection upon Demand by Shareholder or Holder of Voting Trust Certificate; Nature of Right 801
1602. Directors 802
1603. Action to Enforce Right; Appointment of Inspector or Accountant; Report; Penalty for Failure to Produce Records; Expenses of Suit 802

Chapter 18

INVOLUNTARY DISSOLUTION

1800. Verified Complaint; Plaintiffs; Grounds; Intervention by Shareholder or Creditor; Exempt Corporations 802
1802. Provisional Director; Appointment; Deadlocked Board 803
1804. Decree for Winding Up and Dissolution; Other Judicial Relief 803

SELECTED PROVISIONS

Chapter 19

VOLUNTARY DISSOLUTION

1900.   Election by Shareholders; Required Vote; Election by Board; Grounds 803

Chapter 20

GENERAL PROVISIONS RELATING TO DISSOLUTION

2000.   Avoidance of Dissolution by Purchase of Plaintiffs' Shares; Valuation; Vote Required;
         Stay of Dissolution Proceedings; Appraisal Under Court Order; Confirmation by Court;
         Appeal.. 804

Chapter 21

FOREIGN CORPORATIONS

2115.   Foreign Corporations Subject to Corporate Laws of State; Tests to Determine Subject
         Corporations; Laws Applicable; Time of Application 805
2117.   Statement of Information; Timing and Contents of Filing; Additional Contents for Publicly
         Traded Companies; Agent for Service of Process; Public Inspection; Notice of Change of
         Information 806
2117.1   Statement of Information Pertaining to Independent Auditors, Members of the Board of
         Directors, and Executive Officers; Definitions; Public Inspection; Certification.................... 807

Chapter 22

CRIMES AND PENALTIES

2200.   Neglect, Failure or Refusal to Keep Record of Shareholders or Books of Account or Prepare
         or Submit Financial Statements; Penalty; Payment to Shareholder....................................... 808
2207.   Liability of Corporation for Civil Penalty for Failure to Notify Attorney General or
         Appropriate Government Agency and Shareholders or Investors With Respect to
         Knowledge of Certain Enumerated Acts 809

Division 15

SOCIAL PURPOSE CORPORATIONS ACT

2501.   Application of Provisions of Division 1 811
2502.   Application of Division 811
2602.   Contents of Articles of Incorporation... 811
2604.   Authorized Business Activities 813
2800.   Certification Requirements 813
3202.   Plan of Conversion.. 813
3500.   Annual Report.. 813
3501.   Special Purpose Current Report 814
3502.   Provision of Information in Reports... 815

CALIFORNIA CORPORATIONS CODE

Division 3

CORPORATIONS FOR SPECIFIC PURPOSES

Part 13

BENEFIT CORPORATIONS

Chapter 1

PRELIMINARY PROVISIONS

14600. Application of Part..816
14601. Definitions..816
14602. Formation of Benefit Corporation..818
14603. Amendment of Corporation's Articles to Become Benefit Corporation; Surviving Corporations in Merger Reorganization or Acquired Corporations to Be Benefit Corporation; Domestic Other Business Entity as Party to Merger Reorganization or Converting Entity; Minimum Status Vote Requirement...818
14604. Termination of Status as Benefit Corporation by Amendment of Corporation's Articles or Reorganization; Benefit Corporation as Converting Corporation in Conversion; Transaction Regarding All or Substantially All Assets of Benefit Corporation; Minimum Status Vote Requirement. 819

Chapter 2

CORPORATE PURPOSES

14610. Purpose of Benefit Corporation; General and Specific Public Benefit; Amendment of Articles to Add, Amend, or Delete Specific Public Benefit......................................819

Chapter 3

ACCOUNTABILITY

14620. Performance of Duties by Director; Requirements of Board of Directors, Committees of the Board, and Individual Directors When Discharging Duties; Liability of Director; Fiduciary Duty of Director; Director of Foreign Corporation 820
14621. Statement in Annual Benefit Report of Whether Benefit Corporation Failed to Pursue Benefit Purpose...821
14622. Officers of Benefit Corporations; Consideration of Interests and Factors Described in § 14620; Liability; Fiduciary Duty...821
14623. Benefit Enforcement Proceeding; Liability of Benefit Corporation for Monetary Damages; Attorney Fees and Expenses 822

Chapter 4

TRANSPARENCY

14630. Annual Benefit Report..822
14631. Share Certificates; Required Language..823

TITLE 4

SECURITIES

25402. Purchase or Sale of Securities by Person Having Access to Material Information Not Available to Public Through Special Relationship With Issuer 823
25502. Violation of Section 25402; Damages.. 823
25502.5 Liability to Issuer of Violator of Insider Trading Prohibitions; Allegation by Shareholder; Consideration by Board 823

TITLE 1

CORPORATIONS

CORPORATIONS CODE
GENERAL PROVISIONS

§ 20. Electronic transmission by the corporation defined

"Electronic transmission by the corporation" means a communication (a) delivered by (1) facsimile telecommunication or electronic mail when directed to the facsimile number or electronic mail address, respectively, for that recipient on record with the corporation, (2) posting on an electronic message board or network which the corporation has designated for those communications, together with a separate notice to the recipient of the posting, which transmission shall be validly delivered upon the later of the posting or delivery of the separate notice thereof, or (3) other means of electronic communication, (b) to a recipient who has provided an unrevoked consent to the use of those means of transmission for communications under or pursuant to this code, and (c) that creates a record that is capable of retention, retrieval, and review, and that may thereafter be rendered into clearly legible tangible form. However, an electronic transmission under this code by a corporation to an individual shareholder or member of the corporation who is a natural person, and if an officer or director of the corporation, only if communicated to the recipient in that person's capacity as a shareholder or member, is not authorized unless, in addition to satisfying the requirements of this section, the consent to the transmission has been preceded by or includes a clear written statement to the recipient as to (a) any right of the recipient to have the record provided or made available on paper or in nonelectronic form, (b) whether the consent applies only to that transmission, to specified categories of communications, or to all communications from the corporation, and (c) the procedures the recipient must use to withdraw consent.

§ 21. Electronic transmission to the corporation defined

"Electronic transmission to the corporation" means a communication (a) delivered by (1) facsimile telecommunication or electronic mail when directed to the facsimile number or electronic mail address, respectively, which the corporation has provided from time to time to shareholders or members and directors for sending communications to the corporation, (2) posting on an electronic message board or network which the corporation has designated for those communications, and which transmission shall be validly delivered upon the posting, or (3) other means of electronic communication, (b) as to which the corporation has placed in effect reasonable measures to verify that the sender is the shareholder or member (in person or by proxy) or director purporting to send the transmission, and (c) that creates a record that is capable of retention, retrieval, and review, and that may thereafter be rendered into clearly legible tangible form.

Chapter 1

GENERAL PROVISIONS AND DEFINITIONS

§ 114.   Financial Statements or Comparable Statements or Items

All references in this division to financial statements, balance sheets, income statements, and statements of cashflows, and all references to assets, liabilities, earnings, retained earnings, and similar accounting items of a corporation mean those financial statements or comparable statements or items prepared or determined in conformity with generally accepted accounting principles then applicable, fairly presenting in conformity with generally accepted accounting principles the matters that they purport to present, subject to any specific accounting treatment required by a particular section of this division. Unless otherwise expressly stated, all references in this division to financial statements mean, in the case of a corporation that has subsidiaries, consolidated statements of the corporation and each of its subsidiaries as are required to be included in the consolidated statements under generally accepted accounting principles then applicable and all references to accounting items mean the items determined on a consolidated basis in accordance with the consolidated financial statements. Financial statements other than annual statements may be condensed or otherwise presented as permitted by authoritative accounting pronouncements.

§ 150.   Affiliate; Affiliated

A corporation is an "affiliate" of, or a corporation is "affiliated" with, another specified corporation if it directly, or indirectly through one or more intermediaries, controls, is controlled by or is under common control with the other specified corporation.

§ 151.   Approved by (or Approval of) the Board

"Approved by (or approval of) the board" means approved or ratified by the vote of the board or by the vote of a committee authorized to exercise the powers of the board. . . .

§ 152.   Approved by (or Approval of) the Outstanding Shares

"Approved by (or approval of) the outstanding shares" means approved by the affirmative vote of a majority of the outstanding shares entitled to vote. Such approval shall include the affirmative vote of a majority of the outstanding shares of each class or series entitled, by any provision of the articles or of this division, to vote as a class or series on the subject matter being voted upon and shall also include the affirmative vote of such greater proportion (including all) of the outstanding shares of any class or series if such greater proportion is required by the articles or this division.

§ 153.   Approved by (or Approval of) the Shareholders

"Approved by (or approval of) the shareholders" means approved or ratified by the affirmative vote of a majority of the shares . . . represented and voting at a duly held meeting at which a quorum is present (which shares voting affirmatively also constitute at least a majority of the required quorum) or by the written consent of shareholders . . . or by the affirmative vote or written consent of such greater proportion (including all) of the shares of any class or series as may be provided in the articles or in this division for all or any specified shareholder action.

§ 158.   Close Corporation

(a) "Close corporation" means a corporation, including a social purpose corporation, whose articles contain, in addition to the provisions required by Section 202 [Articles of Incorporation; Required Provisions], a provision that all of the corporation's issued shares of all classes shall be held of record by not more than a specified number of persons, not exceeding 35, and a statement "This corporation is a close corporation."

(b) The special provisions referred to in subdivision (a) may be included in the articles by amendment, but if such amendment is adopted after the issuance of shares only by the affirmative vote of all of the issued and outstanding shares of all classes.

(c) The special provisions referred to in subdivision (a) may be deleted from the articles by amendment, or the number of shareholders specified may be changed by amendment, but if such amendment is adopted after the issuance of shares only by the affirmative vote of at least two-thirds of each class of the outstanding shares; provided, however, that the articles may provide for a lesser vote, but not less than a majority of the outstanding shares, or may deny a vote to any class, or both.

(d) In determining the number of shareholders for the purposes of the provision in the articles authorized by this section, spouses and the personal representative of either shall be counted as one regardless of how shares may be held by either or both of them, a trust or personal representative of a decedent holding shares shall be counted as one regardless of the number of trustees or beneficiaries and a partnership or corporation or business association holding shares shall be counted as one (except that any such trust or entity the primary purpose of which was the acquisition or voting of the shares shall be counted according to the number of beneficial interests therein).

(e) A corporation shall cease to be a close corporation upon the filing of an amendment to its articles pursuant to subdivision (c) or if it shall have more than the maximum number of holders of record of its shares specified in its articles as a result of an inter vivos transfer of shares which is not void under subdivision (d) of Section 418, the transfer of shares on distribution by will or pursuant to the laws of descent and distribution, the dissolution of a partnership or corporation or business association or the termination of a trust which holds shares, by court decree upon dissolution of a marriage or otherwise by operation of law. Promptly upon acquiring more than the specified number of holders of record of its shares, a close corporation shall execute and file an amendment to its articles deleting the special provisions referred to in subdivision (a) and deleting any other provisions not permissible for a corporation which is not a close corporation, which amendment shall be promptly approved and filed by the board and need not be approved by the outstanding shares.

(f) Nothing contained in this section shall invalidate any agreement among the shareholders to vote for the deletion from the articles of the special provisions referred to in subdivision (a) upon the lapse of a specified period of time or upon the occurrence of a certain event or condition or otherwise. . . .

(g) The following sections contain specific references to close corporations: Sections 186, . . . 204, 300, 418 . . . 1201, 1800. . . .

§ 160. Control

(a) Except as provided in subdivision (b), "control" means the possession, direct or indirect, of the power to direct or cause the direction of the management and policies of a corporation.

(b) "Control" in Sections 181, 1001 and 1200 means the ownership directly or indirectly of shares or equity securities possessing more than 50 percent of the voting power of a domestic corporation, a foreign corporation, or an other business entity.

§ 161. Constituent Corporation

"Constituent corporation" means a corporation which is merged with or into one or more other corporations or one or more other business entities and includes a surviving corporation.

§ 161.7 Constituent Other Business Entity

"Constituent other business entity" means an other business entity that is merged with or into one or more corporations and includes the surviving other business entity.

§ 161.9 Conversion

"Conversion" means a conversion pursuant to Chapter 11.5. . . .

§ 163.1   Cumulative Dividends in Arrears

For purposes of subdivision (b) of Section 500 and subdivision (b) of Section 506, "cumulative dividends in arrears" means only cumulative dividends that have not been paid as required on a scheduled payment date set forth in, or determined pursuant to, the articles of incorporation, regardless of whether those dividends had been declared prior to that scheduled payment date.

§ 165.   Disappearing Corporation

"Disappearing corporation" means a constituent corporation which is not the surviving corporation.

§ 166.   Distribution to Its Shareholders

"Distribution to its shareholders" means the transfer of cash or property by a corporation to its shareholders without consideration, whether by way of dividend or otherwise, except a dividend in shares of the corporation, or the purchase or redemption of its shares for cash or property, including the transfer, purchase, or redemption by a subsidiary of the corporation. The time of any distribution by way of dividend shall be the date of declaration thereof and the time of any distribution by purchase or redemption of shares shall be the date cash or property is transferred by the corporation, whether or not pursuant to a contract of an earlier date; provided, that where a debt obligation that is a security (as defined in Section 8102 of the Commercial Code) is issued in exchange for shares the time of the distribution is the date when the corporation acquires the shares in the exchange. In the case of a sinking fund payment, cash or property is transferred within the meaning of this section at the time that it is delivered to a trustee for the holders of preferred shares to be used for the redemption of the shares or physically segregated by the corporation in trust for that purpose. "Distribution to its shareholders" shall not include (a) satisfaction of a final judgment of a court or tribunal of appropriate jurisdiction ordering the rescission of the issuance of shares, (b) the rescission by a corporation of the issuance of its shares, if the board determines (with any director who is, or would be, a party to the transaction not being entitled to vote) that (1) it is reasonably likely that the holder or holders of the shares in question could legally enforce a claim for the rescission, (2) that the rescission is in the best interests of the corporation, and (3) the corporation is likely to be able to meet its liabilities (except those for which payment is otherwise adequately provided) as they mature, or (c) the repurchase by a corporation of its shares issued by it pursuant to Section 408 [Employee Stock Purchase or Stock Option Plans], if the board determines (with any director who is, or would be, a party to the transaction not being entitled to vote) that (1) the repurchase is in the best interests of the corporation and that (2) the corporation is likely to be able to meet its liabilities (except those for which payment is otherwise adequately provided) as they mature.

§ 167.8   Disappearing Other Business Entity

"Disappearing other business entity" means a constituent other business entity that is not the surviving other business entity.

§ 168.   Equity Security

"Equity security" in Sections 181, 1001, 1113, 1200, and 1201 means any share or membership of a domestic or foreign corporation; any partnership interest, membership interest, or equivalent equity interest in an other business entity; and any security convertible with or without consideration into, shares or any warrant or right to subscribe to or purchase, any of the foregoing.

§ 171.1   Initial Transaction Statement

"Initial transaction statement" means a statement signed by or on behalf of the issuer sent to the new registered owner or registered pledgee, and "written statements," when used in connection with uncertificated securities, means the written statements that are periodically, or at the request of the registered owner or registered pledgee, sent by the issuer to the registered owner or registered pledgee describing the issue of which the uncertificated security is a part.

§ 171.08. Social Purpose Corporation

"Social purpose corporation" means any social purpose corporation formed under Division 1.5 (commencing with Section 2500).

§ 172. Liquidation Price; Liquidation Preference

"Liquidation price" or "liquidation preference" means amounts payable on shares of any class upon voluntary or involuntary dissolution, winding up or distribution of the entire assets of the corporation, including any cumulative dividends accrued and unpaid, in priority to shares of another class or classes.

§ 174.5 Other Business Entity

"Other business entity" means a domestic or foreign limited liability company, limited partnership, [or] general partnership. . . .

§ 175. Parent

Except as used in Sections 1001, 1101, and 1113, a "parent" of a specified corporation is an affiliate in control (Section 160(a)) of that corporation directly or indirectly through one or more intermediaries. In Sections 1001, 1101, and 1113, "parent" means a person in control (Section 160(b)) of a domestic corporation, a foreign corporation, or an other business entity.

§ 180. Redemption Price

"Redemption price" means the amount or amounts (in cash, property or securities, or any combination thereof) payable on shares of any class or series upon the redemption of the shares. Unless otherwise expressly provided, the redemption price is payable in cash.

§ 181. Reorganization

"Reorganization" means either:

(a) A merger pursuant to Chapter 11 (commencing with Section 1100) other than a short-form merger (a "merger reorganization").

(b) The acquisition by one domestic corporation, foreign corporation, or other business entity in exchange, in whole or in part, for its equity securities (or the equity securities of a domestic corporation, a foreign corporation, or an other business entity which is in control of the acquiring entity) of equity securities of another domestic corporation, foreign corporation, or other business entity if, immediately after the acquisition, the acquiring entity has control of the other entity (an "exchange reorganization").

(c) The acquisition by one domestic corporation, foreign corporation, or other business entity in exchange in whole or in part for its equity securities (or the equity securities of a domestic corporation, a foreign corporation, or an other business entity which is in control of the acquiring entity) or for its debt securities (or debt securities of a domestic corporation, foreign corporation, or other business entity which is in control of the acquiring entity) which are not adequately secured and which have a maturity date in excess of five years after the consummation of the reorganization, or both, of all or substantially all of the assets of another domestic corporation, foreign corporation, or other business entity (a "sale-of-assets reorganization").

§ 183.5 Share Exchange Tender Offer

"Share exchange tender offer" means any acquisition by one corporation in exchange in whole or in part for its equity securities (or the equity securities of a corporation which is in control of the acquiring corporation) of shares of another corporation, other than an exchange reorganization (subdivision (b) of Section 181).

§ 186.   Shareholders' Agreement

"Shareholders' agreement" means a written agreement among all of the shareholders of a close corporation, or if a close corporation has only one shareholder between such shareholder and the corporation, as authorized by subdivision (b) of Section 300.

§ 187.   Short Form Merger

"Short-form merger" means a merger pursuant to Section 1110.

§ 189.   Subsidiary

(a) Except as provided in subdivision (b), "subsidiary" of a specified corporation means a corporation shares of which possessing more than 50 percent of the voting power are owned directly or indirectly through one or more subsidiaries by the specified corporation.

(b) For the purpose of Section 703, "subsidiary" of a specified corporation means a corporation shares of which possessing more than 25 percent of the voting power are owned directly or indirectly through one or more subsidiaries as defined in subdivision (a) by the specified corporation.

§ 190.   Surviving Corporation

"Surviving corporation" means a corporation into which one or more other corporations or one or more other business entities are merged.

§ 190.5   Surviving Limited Partnership

"Surviving limited partnership" means a limited partnership into which one or more other limited partnerships or one or more corporations are merged.

§ 190.7   Surviving Other Business Entity

"Surviving other business entity" means an other business entity into which one or more other business entities or one or more corporations are merged.

§ 194.   Vote

"Vote" includes authorization by written consent, subject to the provisions of subdivision (b) of Section 307 and subdivision (d) of Section 603.*

§ 194.5   Voting Power

"Voting power" means the power to vote for the election of directors at the time any determination of voting power is made and does not include the right to vote upon the happening of some condition or event which has not yet occurred. In any case where different classes of shares are entitled to vote as separate classes for different members of the board, the determination of percentage of voting power shall be made on the basis of the percentage of the total number of authorized directors which the shares in question (whether of one or more classes) have the power to elect in an election at which all shares then entitled to vote for the election of any directors are voted.

§ 194.7   Voting Shift

"Voting shift" means a change, pursuant to or by operation of a provision of the articles, in the relative rights of the holders of one or more classes or series of shares, voting as one or more separate classes or series, to elect one or more directors.

---

*   Section 603(d) provides that directors may not be elected by written consent except by unanimous written consent. (Footnote by ed.)

§ 195. Written; In Writing

"Written" or "in writing" includes facsimile, telegraphic, and other electronic communication when authorized by this code, including an electronic transmission by a corporation that satisfies the requirements of Section 20.

Chapter 2

ORGANIZATION AND BYLAWS

§ 202. Contents of Articles of Incorporation

The articles of incorporation shall set forth:

(a) The name of the corporation; provided, however, that in order for the corporation to be subject to the provisions of this division applicable to a close corporation (Section 158), the name of the corporation must contain the word "corporation," "incorporated," or "limited" or an abbreviation of one of such words.

(b)(1) The applicable one of the following statements:

(A) The purpose of the corporation is to engage in any lawful act or activity for which a corporation may be organized under the General Corporation Law of California other than the banking business, the trust company business or the practice of a profession permitted to be incorporated by the California Corporations Code. . . .

§ 204. Articles of Incorporation; Optional Provisions

The articles of incorporation may set forth:

(a) Any or all of the following provisions, which shall not be effective unless expressly provided in the articles:

(1) Granting, with or without limitations, the power to levy assessments upon the shares or any class of shares.

(2) Granting to shareholders preemptive rights to subscribe to any or all issues of shares or securities.

(3) Special qualifications of persons who may be shareholders.

(4) A provision limiting the duration of the corporation's existence to a specified date.

(5) A provision requiring, for any or all corporate actions (except as provided in Section 303, subdivision (b) of Section 402.5, subdivision (c) of Section 708 and Section 1900) the vote of a larger proportion or of all of the shares of any class or series, or the vote or quorum for taking action of a larger proportion or of all of the directors, than is otherwise required by this division.

(6) A provision limiting or restricting the business in which the corporation may engage or the powers which the corporation may exercise or both.

(7) A provision conferring upon the holders of any evidences of indebtedness, issued or to be issued by the corporation, the right to vote in the election of directors and on any other matters on which shareholders may vote.

(8) A provision conferring upon shareholders the right to determine the consideration for which shares shall be issued.

(9) A provision requiring the approval of the shareholders (Section 153) or the approval of the outstanding shares (Section 152) for any corporate action, even though not otherwise required by this division.

(10) Provisions eliminating or limiting the personal liability of a director for monetary damages in an action brought by or in the right of the corporation for breach of a director's duties to the corporation and its shareholders, as set forth in Section 309, provided, however, that (A) such a provision may not eliminate or limit the liability of directors (i) for acts or omissions that involve intentional misconduct or a knowing

and culpable violation of law, (ii) for acts or omissions that a director believes to be contrary to the best interests of the corporation or its shareholders or that involve the absence of good faith on the part of the director, (iii) for any transaction from which a director derived an improper personal benefit, (iv) for acts or omissions that show a reckless disregard for the director's duty to the corporation or its shareholders in circumstances in which the director was aware, or should have been aware, in the ordinary course of performing a director's duties, of a risk of serious injury to the corporation or its shareholders, (v) for acts or omissions that constitute an unexcused pattern of inattention that amounts to an abdication of the director's duty to the corporation or its shareholders, (vi) under Section 310, or (vii) under Section 316, (B) no such provision shall eliminate or limit the liability of a director for any act or omission occurring prior to the date when the provision becomes effective, and (C) no such provision shall eliminate or limit the liability of an officer for any act or omission as an officer, notwithstanding that the officer is also a director or that his or her actions, if negligent or improper, have been ratified by the directors.

(11) A provision authorizing, whether by bylaw, agreement, or otherwise, the indemnification of agents (as defined in Section 317) in excess of that expressly permitted by Section 317 for those agents of the corporation for breach of duty to the corporation and its stockholders, provided, however, that the provision may not provide for indemnification of any agent for any acts or omissions or transactions from which a director may not be relieved of liability as set forth in the exception to paragraph (10) or as to circumstances in which indemnity is expressly prohibited by Section 317.

Notwithstanding this subdivision, in the case of a close corporation any of the provisions referred to above may be validly included in a shareholders' agreement. Notwithstanding this subdivision, bylaws may require for all or any actions by the board the affirmative vote of a majority of the authorized number of directors. Nothing contained in this subdivision shall affect the enforceability, as between the parties thereto, of any lawful agreement not otherwise contrary to public policy.

(b) Reasonable restrictions upon the right to transfer or hypothecate shares of any class or classes or series, but no restriction shall be binding with respect to shares issued prior to the adoption of the restriction unless the holders of such shares voted in favor of the restriction.

(c) The names and addresses of the persons appointed to act as initial directors.

(d) Any other provision, not in conflict with law, for the management of the business and for the conduct of the affairs of the corporation, including any provision which is required or permitted by this division to be stated in the bylaws.

§ 212.   Bylaws; Contents

(a) The bylaws shall set forth (unless such provision is contained in the articles, in which case it may only be changed by an amendment of the articles) the number of directors of the corporation; or that the number of directors shall be not less than a stated minimum nor more than a stated maximum (which in no case shall be greater than two times the stated minimum minus one), with the exact number of directors to be fixed, within the limits specified, by approval of the board or the shareholders (Section 153) in the manner provided in the bylaws, subject to paragraph (5) of subdivision (a) of Section 204. The number or minimum number of directors shall not be less than three; provided, however, that (1) before shares are issued, the number may be one, (2) before shares are issued, the number may be two, (3) so long as the corporation has only one shareholder, the number may be one, (4) so long as the corporation has only one shareholder, the number may be two, and (5) so long as the corporation has only two shareholders, the number may be two. After the issuance of shares, a bylaw specifying or changing a fixed number of directors or the maximum or minimum number or changing from a fixed to a variable board or vice versa may only be adopted by approval of the outstanding shares (Section 152); provided, however that a bylaw or amendment of the articles reducing the fixed number or the minimum number of directors to a number less than five cannot be adopted if the votes cast against its adoption at a meeting or the shares not consenting in the case of action by written consent are equal to more than 16⅔ percent of the outstanding shares entitled to vote.

(b) The bylaws may contain any provision, not in conflict with law or the articles for the management of the business and for the conduct of the affairs of the corporation, including but not limited to:

(1) Any provision referred to in subdivision (b), (c) or (d) of Section 204.

(2) The time, place and manner of calling, conducting and giving notice of shareholders', directors' and committee meetings.

(3) The manner of execution, revocation and use of proxies.

(4) The qualifications, duties and compensation of directors; the time of their annual election; and the requirements of a quorum for directors' and committee meetings.

(5) The appointment and authority of committees of the board.

(6) The appointment, duties, compensation and tenure of officers.

(7) The mode of determination of holders of record of its shares.

(8) The making of annual reports and financial statements to the shareholders.

. . .

Chapter 3

DIRECTORS AND MANAGEMENT

§ 300. **Powers of Board; Delegation; Close Corporations; Shareholders' Agreements; Validity; Liability; Failure to Observe Formalities**

(a) Subject to the provisions of this division and any limitations in the articles relating to action required to be approved by the shareholders (Section 153) or by the outstanding shares (Section 152), or by a less than majority vote of a class or series of preferred shares (Section 402.5), the business and affairs of the corporation shall be managed and all corporate powers shall be exercised by or under the direction of the board. The board may delegate the management of the day-to-day operation of the business of the corporation to a management company or other person provided that the business and affairs of the corporation shall be managed and all corporate powers shall be exercised under the ultimate direction of the board.

(b) Notwithstanding subdivision (a) or any other provision of this division, but subject to subdivision (c), no shareholders' agreement, which relates to any phase of the affairs of a close corporation, including but not limited to management of its business, division of its profits or distribution of its assets on liquidation, shall be invalid as between the parties thereto on the ground that it so relates to the conduct of the affairs of the corporation as to interfere with the discretion of the board or that it is an attempt to treat the corporation as if it were a partnership or to arrange their relationships in a manner that would be appropriate only between partners. A transferee of shares covered by such an agreement which is filed with the secretary of the corporation for inspection by any prospective purchaser of shares, who has actual knowledge thereof or notice thereof by a notation on the certificate pursuant to Section 418, is bound by its provisions and is a party thereto for the purposes of subdivision (d). Original issuance of shares by the corporation to a new shareholder who does not become a party to the agreement terminates the agreement, except that if the agreement so provides it shall continue to the extent it is enforceable apart from this subdivision. The agreement may not be modified, extended or revoked without the consent of such a transferee, subject to any provision of the agreement permitting modification, extension or revocation by less than unanimous agreement of the parties. A transferor of shares covered by such an agreement ceases to be a party thereto upon ceasing to be a shareholder of the corporation unless the transferor is a party thereto other than as a shareholder. An agreement made pursuant to this subdivision shall terminate when the corporation ceases to be a close corporation, except that if the agreement so provides it shall continue to the extent it is enforceable apart from this subdivision. This subdivision does not apply to an agreement authorized by subdivision (a) of Section 706.

(c) No agreement entered into pursuant to subdivision (b) may alter or waive any of the provisions of Sections 158, 417, 418, 500, 501, and 1111, subdivision (e) of Section 1201, Sections 2009, 2010, and 2011, or of Chapters 15 (commencing with Section 1500), 16 (commencing with Section 1600), 18 (commencing with Section 1800), and 22 (commencing with Section 2200). All other provisions of this division may be altered or waived as between the parties thereto in a shareholders' agreement, except the required filing of any document with the Secretary of State.

(d) An agreement of the type referred to in subdivision (b) shall, to the extent and so long as the discretion or powers of the board in its management of corporate affairs is controlled by such agreement, impose upon each shareholder who is a party thereto liability for managerial acts performed or omitted by such person pursuant thereto that is otherwise imposed by this division upon directors, and the directors shall be relieved to that extent from such liability.

(e) The failure of a close corporation to observe corporate formalities relating to meetings of directors or shareholders in connection with the management of its affairs, pursuant to an agreement authorized by subdivision (b), shall not be considered a factor tending to establish that the shareholders have personal liability for corporate obligations.

§ 301. Directors; Election; Term

(a) Except as provided in Section 301.5, at each annual meeting of shareholders, directors shall be elected to hold office until the next annual meeting. However, to effectuate a voting shift (Section 194.7) the articles may provide that directors hold office for a shorter term. The articles may provide for the election of one or more directors by the holders of the shares of any class or series voting as a class or series.

(b) Each director, including a director elected to fill a vacancy, shall hold office until the expiration of the term for which elected and until a successor has been elected and qualified.

§ 301.3 Female Directors on Boards of Publicly Held Corporations; Requirements

(a) No later than the close of the 2019 calendar year, a publicly held domestic or foreign corporation whose principal executive offices, according to the corporation's SEC 10-K form, are located in California shall have a minimum of one female director on its board. A corporation may increase the number of directors on its board to comply with this section.

(b) No later than the close of the 2021 calendar year, a publicly held domestic or foreign corporation whose principal executive offices, according to the corporation's SEC 10-K form, are located in California shall comply with the following:

(1) If its number of directors is six or more, the corporation shall have a minimum of three female directors.

(2) If its number of directors is five, the corporation shall have a minimum of two female directors.

(3) If its number of directors is four or fewer, the corporation shall have a minimum of one female director.

(c) No later than July 1, 2019, the Secretary of State shall publish a report on its Internet Web site documenting the number of domestic and foreign corporations whose principal executive offices, according to the corporation's SEC 10-K form, are located in California and who have at least one female director.

(d) No later than March 1, 2020, and annually thereafter, the Secretary of State shall publish a report on its Internet Web site regarding, at a minimum, all of the following:

(1) The number of corporations subject to this section that were in compliance with the requirements of this section during at least one point during the preceding calendar year.

(2) The number of publicly held corporations that moved their United States headquarters to California from another state or out of California into another state during the preceding calendar year.

(3) The number of publicly held corporations that were subject to this section during the preceding year, but are no longer publicly traded.

(e)(1) The Secretary of State may adopt regulations to implement this section. The Secretary of State may impose fines for violations of this section as follows:

(A) For failure to timely file board member information with the Secretary of State pursuant to a regulation adopted pursuant to this paragraph, the amount of one hundred thousand dollars ($100,000).

(B) For a first violation, the amount of one hundred thousand dollars ($100,000).

(C) For a second or subsequent violation, the amount of three hundred thousand dollars ($300,000).

(2) For the purposes of this subdivision, each director seat required by this section to be held by a female, which is not held by a female during at least a portion of a calendar year, shall count as a violation.

(3) For purposes of this subdivision, a female director having held a seat for at least a portion of the year shall not be a violation.

(4) Fines collected pursuant to this section shall be available, upon appropriation by the Legislature, for use by the Secretary of State to offset the cost of administering this section.

(f) For purposes of this section, the following definitions apply:

(1) "Female" means an individual who self-identifies her gender as a woman, without regard to the individual's designated sex at birth.

(2) "Publicly held corporation" means a corporation with outstanding shares listed on a major United States stock exchange.

§ 301.5 Listed Corporations; Classes of Directors; Cumulative Voting; Election of Directors; Amendment of Articles and Bylaws

(a) A listed corporation may, by amendment of its articles or bylaws, adopt provisions to divide the board of directors into two or three classes to serve for terms of two or three years respectively, or to eliminate cumulative voting, or both. After the issuance of shares, a corporation that is not a listed corporation may, by amendment of its articles or bylaws, adopt provisions to be effective when the corporation becomes a listed corporation to divide the board of directors into two or three classes to serve for terms of two or three years respectively, or to eliminate cumulative voting, or both. An article or bylaw amendment providing for division of the board of directors into classes, or any change in the number of classes, or the elimination of cumulative voting may only be adopted by the approval of the board and the outstanding shares (Section 152) voting as a single class. . . .

(b) If the board of directors is divided into two classes pursuant to subdivision (a), the authorized number of directors shall be no less than six and one-half of the directors or as close an approximation as possible shall be elected at each annual meeting of shareholders. If the board of directors is divided into three classes, the authorized number of directors shall be no less than nine and one-third of the directors or as close an approximation as possible shall be elected at each annual meeting of shareholders. Directors of a listed corporation may be elected by classes at a meeting of shareholders at which an amendment to the articles or bylaws described in subdivision (a) is approved, but the extended terms for directors are contingent on that approval, and in the case of an amendment to the articles, the filing of any necessary amendment to the articles. . . .

(c) If directors for more than one class are to be elected by the shareholders at any one meeting of shareholders and the election is by cumulative voting pursuant to Section 708, votes may be cumulated only for directors to be elected within each class.

(d) For purposes of this section, a "listed corporation" means a corporation with outstanding shares listed on the New York Stock Exchange, the NYSE Amex, the NASDAQ Global Market, or the NASDAQ Capital Market.

(e) Subject to subdivision (h), if a listed corporation having a board of directors divided into classes pursuant to subdivision (a) ceases to be a listed corporation for any reason, unless the articles of incorporation or bylaws of the corporation provide for the elimination of classes of directors at an earlier date or dates, the board of directors of the corporation shall cease to be divided into classes as to each class of directors on the date of the expiration of the term of the directors in that class and the term of each director serving at the time the corporation ceases to be a listed corporation (and the term of each director elected to fill a vacancy resulting from the death, resignation, or removal of any of those directors) shall continue until its expiration as if the corporation had not ceased to be a listed corporation.

(f) Subject to subdivision (h), if a listed corporation having a provision in its articles or bylaws eliminating cumulative voting pursuant to subdivision (a) or permitting noncumulative voting in the election of directors pursuant to that subdivision, or both, ceases to be a listed corporation for any reason, the shareholders shall be entitled to cumulate their votes pursuant to Section 708 at any election of directors occurring while the corporation is not a listed corporation notwithstanding that provision in its articles of incorporation or bylaws.

(g) Subject to subdivision (i), if a corporation that is not a listed corporation adopts amendments to its articles of incorporation or bylaws to divide its board of directors into classes or to eliminate cumulative voting, or both, pursuant to subdivision (a) and then becomes a listed corporation, unless the articles of incorporation or bylaws provide for those provisions to become effective at some other time and, in cases where classes of directors are provided for, identify the directors who, or the directorships that, are to be in each class or the method by which those directors or directorships are to be identified, the provisions shall become effective for the next election of directors after the corporation becomes a listed corporation at which all directors are to be elected.

(h) If a corporation ceases to be a listed corporation on or after the record date for a meeting of shareholders and prior to the conclusion of the meeting, including the conclusion of the meeting after an adjournment or postponement that does not require or result in the setting of a new record date, then, solely for purposes of subdivisions (e) and (f), the corporation shall not be deemed to have ceased to be a listed corporation until the conclusion of the meeting of shareholders.

(i) If a corporation becomes a listed corporation on or after the record date for a meeting of shareholders and prior to the conclusion of the meeting, including the conclusion of the meeting after an adjournment or postponement that does not require or result in the setting of a new record date, then, solely for purposes of subdivision (g), the corporation shall not be deemed to have become a listed corporation until the conclusion of the meeting of shareholders.

(j) If an article amendment referred to in subdivision (a) is adopted by a listed corporation, the certificate of amendment shall include a statement of the facts showing that the corporation is a listed corporation within the meaning of subdivision (d). If an article or bylaw amendment referred to in subdivision (a) is adopted by a corporation which is not a listed corporation, the provision as adopted, shall include the following statement or the substantial equivalent: "This provision shall become effective only when the corporation becomes a listed corporation within the meaning of Section 301.5 of the Corporations Code."

§ 302. Directors; Vacancy; Grounds for Declaration

The board may declare vacant the office of a director who has been declared of unsound mind by an order of court or convicted of a felony.

§ 303. Directors; Removal Without Cause

(a) Any or all of the directors may be removed without cause if such removal is approved by the outstanding shares (Section 152), subject to the following:

(1) Except for a corporation to which paragraph (3) is applicable, no director may be removed (unless the entire board is removed) when the votes cast against removal, or not consenting in writing to the removal, would be sufficient to elect the director if voted cumulatively at an election at which the same total number of votes were cast (or, if the action is taken by written consent, all shares entitled to vote were voted) and the entire number of directors authorized at the time of the director's most recent election were then being elected.

(2) When by the provisions of the articles the holders of the shares of any class or series, voting as a class or series, are entitled to elect one or more directors, any director so elected may be removed only by the applicable vote of the holders of the shares of that class or series.

(3) A director of a corporation whose board of directors is classified pursuant to Section 301.5 may not be removed if the votes cast against removal of the director, or not consenting in writing to the removal, would be sufficient to elect the director if voted cumulatively (without regard to whether shares may otherwise be voted cumulatively) at an election at which the same total number of votes were cast (or, if the action is taken by written consent, all shares entitled to vote were voted) and either the number of directors elected at the most recent annual meeting of shareholders, or if greater, the number of directors for whom removal is being sought, were then being elected.

(b) Any reduction of the authorized number of directors or amendment reducing the number of classes of directors does not remove any director prior to the expiration of such director's term of office.

(c) Except as provided in this section and Sections 302 and 304, a director may not be removed prior to the expiration of the director's term of office.

§ 304. Removal for Cause; Shareholders Suit

The superior court of the proper county may, at the suit of shareholders holding at least 10 percent of the number of outstanding shares of any class, remove from office any director in case of fraudulent or dishonest acts or gross abuse of authority or discretion with reference to the corporation and may bar from reelection any director so removed for a period prescribed by the court. The corporation shall be made a party to such action.

§ 305. Filling Vacancies; Special Meeting of Shareholders; Notice of Opposition; Resignation

(a) Unless otherwise provided in the articles or bylaws and except for a vacancy created by the removal of a director, vacancies on the board may be filled by approval of the board (Section 151) or, if the number of directors then in office is less than a quorum, by (1) the unanimous written consent of the directors then in office, (2) the affirmative vote of a majority of the directors then in office at a meeting held pursuant to notice or waivers of notice complying with Section 307 or (3) a sole remaining director. Unless the articles or a bylaw adopted by the shareholders provide that the board may fill vacancies occurring in the board by reason of the removal of directors, such vacancies may be filled only by approval of the shareholders (Section 153).

(b) The shareholders may elect a director at any time to fill any vacancy not filled by the directors. Any such election by written consent other than to fill a vacancy created by removal, which requires the unanimous consent of all shares entitled to vote for the election of directors, requires the consent of a majority of the outstanding shares entitled to vote.

(c) If, after the filling of any vacancy by the directors, the directors then in office who have been elected by the shareholders shall constitute less than a majority of the directors then in office, then both of the following shall be applicable:

(1) Any holder or holders of an aggregate of 5 percent or more of the total number of shares at the time outstanding having the right to vote for those directors may call a special meeting of shareholders, or

(2) The superior court of the proper county shall, upon application of such shareholder or shareholders, summarily order a special meeting of shareholders, to be held to elect the entire board. The term of office of any director shall terminate upon that election of a successor.

The hearing on any application filed pursuant to this subdivision shall be held on not less than 10 business days notice to the corporation. If the corporation intends to oppose the application, it shall file with the court a notice of opposition not later than five business days prior to the date set for the hearing. The application and any notice of opposition shall be supported by appropriate affidavits and the court's determination shall be made on the basis of the papers in the record; but, for good cause shown, the court may receive and consider at the hearing additional evidence, oral or documentary, and additional points and authorities. The hearing shall take precedence over all other matters not of a similar nature pending on the date set for the hearing.

(d) Any director may resign effective upon giving written notice to the chairperson of the board, the president, the secretary or the board of directors of the corporation, unless the notice specifies a later time for the effectiveness of such resignation. If the resignation is effective at a future time, a successor may be elected to take office when the resignation becomes effective.

§ 307. Meetings; Time and Place of Regular Meetings; Notice; Adjournment; Meetings May Be Within or Without the State; Participation via Electronic Means; Quorum; Acts or Decisions of Board

(a) Unless otherwise provided in the articles or, subject to paragraph (5) of subdivision (a) of Section 204, in the bylaws, all of the following apply:

(1) Meetings of the board may be called by the chairperson of the board or the president or any vice president or the secretary or any two directors.

(2) Regular meetings of the board may be held without notice if the time and place of the meetings are fixed by the bylaws or the board. Special meetings of the board shall be held upon four days' notice by mail or 48 hours' notice delivered personally or by telephone, including a voice messaging system or by electronic transmission by the corporation (Section 20). The articles or bylaws may not dispense with notice of a special meeting. A notice, or waiver of notice, need not specify the purpose of any regular or special meeting of the board.

(3) Notice of a meeting need not be given to a director who provides a waiver of notice or a consent to holding the meeting or an approval of the minutes thereof in writing, whether before or after the meeting, or who attends the meeting without protesting, prior thereto or at its commencement, the lack of notice to that director. These waivers, consents and approvals shall be filed with the corporate records or made a part of the minutes of the meeting.

(4) A majority of the directors present, whether or not a quorum is present, may adjourn any meeting to another time and place. If the meeting is adjourned for more than 24 hours, notice of an adjournment to another time or place shall be given prior to the time of the adjourned meeting to the directors who were not present at the time of the adjournment.

(5) Meetings of the board may be held at a place within or without the state that has been designated in the notice of the meeting or, if not stated in the notice or there is no notice, designated in the bylaws or by resolution of the board.

(6) Members of the board may participate in a meeting through use of conference telephone, electronic video screen communication, or electronic transmission by and to the corporation (Sections 20 and 21). Participation in a meeting through use of conference telephone or electronic video screen communication pursuant to this subdivision constitutes presence in person at that meeting as long as all members participating in the meeting are able to hear one another. Participation in a meeting through electronic transmission by and to the corporation (other than conference telephone and electronic video screen communication), pursuant to this subdivision constitutes presence in person at that meeting if both of the following apply:

(A) Each member participating in the meeting can communicate with all of the other members concurrently.

(B) Each member is provided the means of participating in all matters before the board, including, without limitation, the capacity to propose, or to interpose an objection to, a specific action to be taken by the corporation.

(7) A majority of the authorized number of directors constitutes a quorum of the board for the transaction of business. The articles or bylaws may not provide that a quorum shall be less than one-third the authorized number of directors or less than two, whichever is larger, unless the authorized number of directors is one, in which case one director constitutes a quorum.

(8) An act or decision done or made by a majority of the directors present at a meeting duly held at which a quorum is present is the act of the board, subject to the provisions of Section 310 and subdivision (e) of Section 317. The articles or bylaws may not provide that a lesser vote than a majority of the directors present at a meeting is the act of the board. A meeting at which a quorum is initially present may continue to transact business notwithstanding the withdrawal of directors, if any action taken is approved by at least a majority of the required quorum for that meeting.

(b) An action required or permitted to be taken by the board may be taken without a meeting, if all members of the board shall individually or collectively consent in writing to that action and if the number of members of the board serving at the time constitutes a quorum. The written consent or consents shall be filed with the minutes of the proceedings of the board. For purposes of this subdivision only, "all members of the board" shall include an "interested director" as described in subdivision (a) of Section 310 or a "common director" as described in subdivision (b) of Section 310 who abstains in writing from providing consent, where the disclosures required by Section 310 have been made to the noninterested or noncommon directors, as applicable, prior to their execution of the written consent or consents, the specified disclosures are conspicuously included in the written consent or consents executed by the noninterested or noncommon directors, and the noninterested or noncommon directors, as applicable, approve the action by a vote that is sufficient without counting the votes of the interested or common directors. If written consent is provided by the directors in accordance with the immediately preceding sentence and the disclosures made regarding the action that is the subject of the consent do not comply with the requirements of Section 310, the action that is the subject of the consent shall be deemed approved, but in any suit brought to challenge the action, the party asserting the validity of the action shall have the burden of proof in establishing that the action was just and reasonable to the corporation at the time it was approved.

(c) This section applies also to committees of the board and incorporators and action by those committees and incorporators, mutatis mutandis.

§ 308. Deadlock on Board With Even Number of Directors; Provisional Director; Appointment; Powers

(a) If a corporation has an even number of directors who are equally divided and cannot agree as to the management of its affairs, so that its business can no longer be conducted to advantage or so that there is danger that its property and business will be impaired or lost, the superior court of the proper county may, notwithstanding any provisions of the articles or bylaws and whether or not an action is pending for an involuntary winding up or dissolution of the corporation, appoint a provisional director pursuant to this section. Action for such appointment may be brought by any director or by the holders of not less than 33⅓ percent of the voting power.

(b) If the shareholders of a corporation are deadlocked so that they cannot elect the directors to be elected at an annual meeting of shareholders, the superior court of the proper county may, notwithstanding any provisions of the articles or bylaws, upon petition of a shareholder or shareholders holding 50 percent of the voting power, appoint a provisional director or directors pursuant to this section or order such other equitable relief as the court deems appropriate.

(c) A provisional director shall be an impartial person, who is neither a shareholder nor a creditor of the corporation, nor related by consanguinity or affinity within the third degree according to the common law to any of the other directors of the corporation or to any judge of the court by which such provisional director is appointed. A provisional director shall have all the rights and powers of a director until the deadlock in the board or among shareholders is broken or until such provisional director is removed by order of the court or by approval of the outstanding shares (Section 152). Such person shall be entitled to such compensation as shall be fixed by the court unless otherwise agreed with the corporation. . . .

§ 309. Performance of Duties by Director; Liability

(a) A director shall perform the duties of a director, including duties as a member of any committee of the board upon which the director may serve, in good faith, in a manner such director believes to be in the best interests of the corporation and its shareholders and with such care, including reasonable inquiry, as an ordinarily prudent person in a like position would use under similar circumstances.

(b) In performing the duties of a director, a director shall be entitled to rely on information, opinions, reports or statements, including financial statements and other financial data, in each case prepared or presented by any of the following:

(1) One or more officers or employees of the corporation whom the director believes to be reliable and competent in the matters presented.

(2) Counsel, independent accountants or other persons as to matters which the director believes to be within such person's professional or expert competence.

(3) A committee of the board upon which the director does not serve, as to matters within its designated authority, which committee the director believes to merit confidence, so long as, in any such case, the director acts in good faith, after reasonable inquiry when the need therefor is indicated by the circumstances and without knowledge that would cause such reliance to be unwarranted.

(c) A person who performs the duties of a director in accordance with subdivisions (a) and (b) shall have no liability based upon any alleged failure to discharge the person's obligations as a director. In addition, the liability of a director for monetary damages may be eliminated or limited in a corporation's articles to the extent provided in paragraph (10) of subdivision (a) of Section 204.

§ 310.   Contracts in Which Director Has Material Financial Interest; Validity

(a) No contract or other transaction between a corporation and one or more of its directors, or between a corporation and any corporation, firm or association in which one or more of its directors has a material financial interest, is either void or voidable because such director or directors or such other corporation, firm or association are parties or because such director or directors are present at the meeting of the board or a committee thereof which authorizes, approves or ratifies the contract or transaction, if

(1) The material facts as to the transaction and as to such director's interest are fully disclosed or known to the shareholders and such contract or transaction is approved by the shareholders (Section 153) in good faith, with the shares owned by the interested director or directors not being entitled to vote thereon, or

(2) The material facts as to the transaction and as to such director's interest are fully disclosed or known to the board or committee, and the board or committee authorizes, approves or ratifies the contract or transaction in good faith by a vote sufficient without counting the vote of the interested director or directors and the contract or transaction is just and reasonable as to the corporation at the time it is authorized, approved or ratified, or

(3) As to contracts or transactions not approved as provided in paragraph (1) or (2) of this subdivision, the person asserting the validity of the contract or transaction sustains the burden of proving that the contract or transaction was just and reasonable as to the corporation at the time it was authorized, approved or ratified.

A mere common directorship does not constitute a material financial interest within the meaning of this subdivision. A director is not interested within the meaning of this subdivision in a resolution fixing the compensation of another director as a director, officer or employee of the corporation, notwithstanding the fact that the first director is also receiving compensation from the corporation.

(b) No contract or other transaction between a corporation and any corporation or association of which one or more of its directors are directors is either void or voidable because such director or directors are present at the meeting of the board or a committee thereof which authorizes, approves or ratifies the contract or transaction, if

(1) The material facts as to the transaction and as to such director's other directorship are fully disclosed or known to the board or committee, and the board or committee authorizes, approves or ratifies the contract or transaction in good faith by a vote sufficient without counting the vote of the common director or directors or the contract or transaction is approved by the shareholders (Section 153) in good faith, or

(2) As to contracts or transactions not approved as provided in paragraph (1) of this subdivision, the contract or transaction is just and reasonable as to the corporation at the time it is authorized, approved or ratified.

This subdivision does not apply to contracts or transactions covered by subdivision (a).

(c) Interested or common directors may be counted in determining the presence of a quorum at a meeting of the board or a committee thereof which authorizes, approves or ratifies a contract or transaction.

§ 312.   Officers; Election; Term; Resignation

(a) A corporation shall have (1) a chairperson of the board, who may be given the title of chair of the board, chairperson of the board, chairman of the board, or chairwoman of the board, or a president or both,

(2) a secretary, (3) a chief financial officer, and (4) such other officers with such titles and duties as shall be stated in the bylaws or determined by the board and as may be necessary to enable it to sign instruments and share certificates. The president, or if there is no president the chairperson of the board, is the general manager and chief executive officer of the corporation, unless otherwise provided in the articles or bylaws. Any number of offices may be held by the same person unless the articles or bylaws provide otherwise.

(b) Except as otherwise provided by the articles or bylaws, officers shall be chosen by the board and serve at the pleasure of the board, subject to the rights, if any, of an officer under any contract of employment. Any officer may resign at any time upon written notice to the corporation without prejudice to the rights, if any, of the corporation under any contract to which the officer is a party.

§ 313. Instrument in Writing and Assignment or Endorsement Thereof; Signatures; Validity

Subject to the provisions of subdivision (a) of Section 208, any note, mortgage, evidence of indebtedness, contract, share certificate, initial transaction statement or written statement, conveyance, or other instrument in writing, and any assignment or endorsement thereof, executed or entered into between any corporation and any other person, when signed by the chairperson of the board, the president or any vice president and the secretary, any assistant secretary, the chief financial officer or any assistant treasurer of such corporation, is not invalidated as to the corporation by any lack of authority of the signing officers in the absence of actual knowledge on the part of the other person that the signing officers had no authority to execute the same.

§ 316. Corporate Actions Subjecting Directors to Joint and Several Liability; Actions; Damages

(a) Subject to the provisions of Section 309, directors of a corporation who approve any of the following corporate actions shall be jointly and severally liable to the corporation for the benefit of all of the creditors or shareholders entitled to institute an action under subdivision (c):

(1) The making of any distribution to its shareholders to the extent that it is contrary to the provisions of Sections 500 to 503, inclusive.

(2) The distribution of assets to shareholders after institution of dissolution proceedings of the corporation, without paying or adequately providing for all known liabilities of the corporation, excluding any claims not filed by creditors within the time limit set by the court in a notice given to creditors under Chapters 18 (commencing with Section 1800), 19 (commencing with Section 1900) and 20 (commencing with Section 2000).

(3) The making of any loan or guaranty contrary to Section 315 [Loans or guarantees of obligations of directors, officers, or other persons].

(b) A director who is present at a meeting of the board, or any committee thereof, at which action specified in subdivision (a) is taken and who abstains from voting shall be considered to have approved the action.

(c) Suit may be brought in the name of the corporation to enforce the liability (1) under paragraph (1) of subdivision (a) against any or all directors liable by the persons entitled to sue under subdivision (b) of Section 506, (2) under paragraph (2) or (3) of subdivision (a) against any or all directors liable by any one or more creditors of the corporation whose debts or claims arose prior to the time of any of the corporate actions specified in paragraph (2) or (3) of subdivision (a) and who have not consented to the corporate action, whether or not they have reduced their claims to judgment, or (3) under paragraph (3) of subdivision (a) against any or all directors liable by any one or more holders of shares outstanding at the time of any corporate action specified in paragraph (3) of subdivision (a) who have not consented to the corporate action, without regard to the provisions of Section 800.

(d) The damages recoverable from a director under this section shall be the amount of the illegal distribution (or if the illegal distribution consists of property, the fair market value of that property at the time of the illegal distribution) plus interest thereon from the date of the distribution at the legal rate on judgments until paid, together with all reasonably incurred costs of appraisal or other valuation, if any, of that property or loss suffered by the corporation as a result of the illegal loan or guaranty, as the case may be, but not exceeding the liabilities of the corporation owed to nonconsenting creditors at the time of the violation and the injury suffered by nonconsenting shareholders, as the case may be.

(e) Any director sued under this section may implead all other directors liable and may compel contribution, either in that action or in an independent action against directors not joined in that action.

(f) Directors liable under this section shall also be entitled to be subrogated to the rights of the corporation:

(1) With respect to paragraph (1) of subdivision (a), against shareholders who received the distribution.

(2) With respect to paragraph (2) of subdivision (a), against shareholders who received the distribution of assets.

(3) With respect to paragraph (3) of subdivision (a), against the person who received the loan or guaranty. Any director sued under this section may file a cross-complaint against the person or persons who are liable to the director as a result of the subrogation provided for in this subdivision or may proceed against them in an independent action.

§ 317.   Indemnification of Agent of Corporation in Proceedings or Actions

(a) For the purposes of this section, "agent" means any person who is or was a director, officer, employee or other agent of the corporation, or is or was serving at the request of the corporation as a director, officer, employee or agent of another foreign or domestic corporation, partnership, joint venture, trust or other enterprise, or was a director, officer, employee or agent of a foreign or domestic corporation which was a predecessor corporation of the corporation or of another enterprise at the request of the predecessor corporation; "proceeding" means any threatened, pending or completed action or proceeding, whether civil, criminal, administrative or investigative; and "expenses" includes without limitation attorneys' fees and any expenses of establishing a right to indemnification under subdivision (d) or paragraph (4) of subdivision (e).

(b) A corporation shall have power to indemnify any person who was or is a party or is threatened to be made a party to any proceeding (other than an action by or in the right of the corporation to procure a judgment in its favor) by reason of the fact that the person is or was an agent of the corporation, against expenses, judgments, fines, settlements, and other amounts actually and reasonably incurred in connection with the proceeding if that person acted in good faith and in a manner the person reasonably believed to be in the best interests of the corporation and, in the case of a criminal proceeding, had no reasonable cause to believe the conduct of the person was unlawful. The termination of any proceeding by judgment, order, settlement, conviction, or upon a plea of nolo contendere or its equivalent shall not, of itself, create a presumption that the person did not act in good faith and in a manner which the person reasonably believed to be in the best interests of the corporation or that the person had reasonable cause to believe that the person's conduct was unlawful.

(c) A corporation shall have power to indemnify any person who was or is a party or is threatened to be made a party to any threatened, pending, or completed action by or in the right of the corporation to procure a judgment in its favor by reason of the fact that the person is or was an agent of the corporation, against expenses actually and reasonably incurred by that person in connection with the defense or settlement of the action if the person acted in good faith, in a manner the person believed to be in the best interests of the corporation and its shareholders.

No indemnification shall be made under this subdivision for any of the following:

(1) In respect of any claim, issue or matter as to which the person shall have been adjudged to be liable to the corporation in the performance of that person's duty to the corporation and its shareholders, unless and only to the extent that the court in which the proceeding is or was pending shall determine upon application that, in view of all the circumstances of the case, the person is fairly and reasonably entitled to indemnity for expenses and then only to the extent that the court shall determine.

(2) Of amounts paid in settling or otherwise disposing of a pending action without court approval.

(3) Of expenses incurred in defending a pending action which is settled or otherwise disposed of without court approval.

(d) To the extent that an agent of a corporation has been successful on the merits in defense of any proceeding referred to in subdivision (b) or (c) or in defense of any claim, issue, or matter therein, the agent shall be indemnified against expenses actually and reasonably incurred by the agent in connection therewith.

(e) Except as provided in subdivision (d), any indemnification under this section shall be made by the corporation only if authorized in the specific case, upon a determination that indemnification of the agent is proper in the circumstances because the agent has met the applicable standard of conduct set forth in subdivision (b) or (c), by any of the following:

(1) A majority vote of a quorum consisting of directors who are not parties to such proceeding.

(2) If such a quorum of directors is not obtainable, by independent legal counsel in a written opinion.

(3) Approval of the shareholders (Section 153), with the shares owned by the person to be indemnified not being entitled to vote thereon.

(4) The court in which the proceeding is or was pending upon application made by the corporation or the agent or the attorney or other person rendering services in connection with the defense, whether or not the application by the agent, attorney or other person is opposed by the corporation.

(f) Expenses incurred in defending any proceeding may be advanced by the corporation prior to the final disposition of the proceeding upon receipt of an undertaking by or on behalf of the agent to repay that amount if it shall be determined ultimately that the agent is not entitled to be indemnified as authorized in this section. The provisions of subdivision (a) of Section 315 do not apply to advances made pursuant to this subdivision.

(g) The indemnification authorized by this section shall not be deemed exclusive of any additional rights to indemnification for breach of duty to the corporation and its shareholders while acting in the capacity of a director or officer of the corporation to the extent the additional rights to indemnification are authorized in an article provision adopted pursuant to paragraph (11) of subdivision (a) of Section 204. The indemnification provided by this section for acts, omissions, or transactions while acting in the capacity of, or while serving as, a director or officer of the corporation but not involving breach of duty to the corporation and its shareholders shall not be deemed exclusive of any other rights to which those seeking indemnification may be entitled under any bylaw, agreement, vote of shareholders or disinterested directors, or otherwise, to the extent the additional rights to indemnification are authorized in the articles of the corporation. An article provision authorizing indemnification "in excess of that otherwise permitted by Section 317" or "to the fullest extent permissible under California law" or the substantial equivalent thereof shall be construed to be both a provision for additional indemnification for breach of duty to the corporation and its shareholders as referred to in, and with the limitations required by, paragraph (11) of subdivision (a) of Section 204 and a provision for additional indemnification as referred to in the second sentence of this subdivision. The rights to indemnity hereunder shall continue as to a person who has ceased to be a director, officer, employee, or agent and shall inure to the benefit of the heirs, executors, and administrators of the person. Nothing contained in this section shall affect any right to indemnification to which persons other than the directors and officers may be entitled by contract or otherwise.

(h) No indemnification or advance shall be made under this section, except as provided in subdivision (d) or paragraph (4) of subdivision (e), in any circumstance where it appears:

(1) That it would be inconsistent with a provision of the articles, bylaws, a resolution of the shareholders, or an agreement in effect at the time of the accrual of the alleged cause of action asserted in the proceeding in which the expenses were incurred or other amounts were paid, which prohibits or otherwise limits indemnification.

(2) That it would be inconsistent with any condition expressly imposed by a court in approving a settlement.

(i) A corporation shall have power to purchase and maintain insurance on behalf of any agent of the corporation against any liability asserted against or incurred by the agent in that capacity or arising out of the agent's status as such whether or not the corporation would have the power to indemnify the agent against that liability under this section. The fact that a corporation owns all or a portion of the shares of the company issuing a policy of insurance shall not render this subdivision inapplicable if either of the following conditions are satisfied: (1) if the articles authorize indemnification in excess of that authorized in this section and the insurance provided by this subdivision is limited as indemnification is required to be limited by paragraph (11) of subdivision (a) of Section 204; or (2)(A) the company issuing the insurance policy is organized, licensed, and operated in a manner that complies with the insurance laws and regulations applicable to its jurisdiction of organization, (B) the company issuing the policy provides procedures for processing claims that do not permit that company to be subject to the direct control of the corporation that purchased that policy, and (C) the policy issued provides for some manner of risk sharing between the issuer and purchaser of the policy, on one hand, and some unaffiliated person or persons, on the other, such as by providing for more than one unaffiliated owner of the company issuing the policy or by providing that a portion of the coverage furnished will be obtained from some unaffiliated insurer or reinsurer.

(j) This section does not apply to any proceeding against any trustee, investment manager, or other fiduciary of an employee benefit plan in that person's capacity as such, even though the person may also be an agent as defined in subdivision (a) of the employer corporation. A corporation shall have power to indemnify such a trustee, investment manager or other fiduciary to the extent permitted by subdivision (f) of Section 207 [corporate powers].

Chapter 4

SHARES AND SHARE CERTIFICATES

§ 407.   Fractional Shares

A corporation may, but is not required to, issue fractions of a share originally or upon transfer. If it does not issue fractions of a share, it shall in connection with any original issuance of shares (a) arrange for the disposition of fractional interests by those entitled thereto, (b) pay in cash the fair value of fractions of a share as of the time when those entitled to receive those fractions are determined or (c) issue scrip or warrants in registered form, as certificated securities or uncertificated securities, or [in] bearer form as certificated securities, which shall entitle the holder to receive a certificate for a full share upon the surrender of such script or warrants aggregating a full share; provided, however, that if the fraction of a share that any person would otherwise be entitled to receive in a merger, conversion, or reorganization is less than one-half of 1 percent of the total shares that person is entitled to receive, a merger, conversion, or reorganization agreement may provide that fractions of a share will be disregarded or that shares issuable in the merger will be rounded off to the nearest whole share; and provided, further, that a corporation may not pay cash for fractional shares if that action would result in the cancellation of more than 10 percent of the outstanding shares of any class. A determination by the board of the fair value of fractions of a share shall be conclusive in the absence of fraud. A certificate for a fractional share shall, but scrip or warrants shall not unless otherwise provided therein, entitle the holder to exercise voting rights, to receive dividends thereon and to participate in any of the assets of the corporation in the event of liquidation. The board may cause scrip or warrants to be issued subject to the condition that they shall become void if not exchanged for full shares before a specified date or that the shares for which scrip or warrants are exchangeable may be sold by the corporation and the proceeds thereof distributed to the holder of the scrip or warrants or any other condition that the board may impose.

§ 418.   Certificates or Initial Transaction Statements; Required Contents of Statements on Face of Documents; Failure to State; Enforceability; Close Corporations; Validity of Transfers

(a) There shall also appear on the certificate, the initial transaction statement, and written statements (unless stated or summarized under subdivision (a) or (b) of Section 417) the statements required by all of the following clauses to the extent applicable:

(1) The fact that the shares are subject to restrictions upon transfer.

(2) If the shares are assessable or are not fully paid, a statement that they are assessable or the statements required by subdivision (d) of Section 409 if they are not fully paid.

(3) The fact that the shares are subject to a voting agreement under subdivision (a) of Section 706 or an irrevocable proxy under subdivision (e) of Section 705 or restrictions upon voting rights contractually imposed by the corporation.

(4) The fact that the shares are redeemable.

(5) The fact that the shares are convertible and the period for conversion.

Any such statement or reference thereto (Section 174) on the face of the certificate, the initial transaction statement, and written statements required by paragraph (1) or (2) shall be conspicuous.

(b) Unless stated on the certificate, the initial transaction statement, and written statements as required by subdivision (a), no restriction upon transfer, no right of redemption and no voting agreement under subdivision (a) of Section 706, no irrevocable proxy under subdivision (e) of Section 705, and no voting restriction imposed by the corporation shall be enforceable against a transferee of the shares without actual knowledge of such restriction, right, agreement of proxy. With regard only to liability to assessment or for the unpaid portion of the subscription price, unless stated on the certificate as required by subdivision (a), that liability shall not be enforceable against a transferee of the shares. For the purpose of this subdivision, "transferee" includes a purchaser from the corporation.

(c) All certificates representing shares of a close corporation shall contain in addition to any other statements required by this section, the following conspicuous legend on the face thereof: "This corporation is a close corporation. The number of holders of record of its shares of all classes cannot exceed _____ [a number not in excess of 35]. Any attempted voluntary inter vivos transfer which would violate this requirement is void. Refer to the articles, bylaws and any agreements on file with the secretary of the corporation for further restrictions."

(d) Any attempted voluntary inter vivos transfer of the shares of a close corporation which would result in the number of holders of record of its shares exceeding the maximum number specified in its articles is void if the certificate contains the legend required by subdivision (c).

Chapter 5

DIVIDENDS AND REACQUISITIONS OF SHARES

§ 500.   Distributions; Retained Earnings or Assets Remaining After Completion . . .

(a) Neither a corporation nor any of its subsidiaries shall make any distribution to the corporation's shareholders (Section 166) unless the board of directors has determined in good faith either of the following:

(1) The amount of retained earnings of the corporation immediately prior to the distribution equals or exceeds the sum of (A) the amount of the proposed distribution plus (B) the preferential dividends arrears amount.

(2) Immediately after the distribution, the value of the corporation's assets would equal or exceed the sum of its total liabilities plus the preferential rights amount.

(b) For the purpose of applying paragraph (a) of subdivision (a) to a distribution by a corporation, "preferential dividends arrears amount" means the amount, if any, of cumulative dividends in arrears on all shares having a preference with respect to payment of dividends over the class or series to which the applicable distribution is being made, provided that if the articles of incorporation provide that a distribution can be made without regard to preferential dividends arrears amount, then the preferential dividends arrears amount shall be zero. For the purpose of applying paragraph (2) of subdivision (a) to a distribution by a corporation, "preferential rights amount" means the amount that would be needed if the corporation were to be dissolved at the time of the distribution to satisfy the preferential rights, including accrued but unpaid dividends, of other shareholders upon dissolution that are superior to the rights of the shareholders receiving the distribution, provided that if the articles of incorporation provide that a distribution can be made without regard to any preferential rights, then the preferential rights amount shall be zero. In the case of a distribution of cash or property in payment by the corporation in connection with the purchase of its shares, (1) there shall be added to retained earnings all amounts that had been previously deducted therefrom with respect to obligations incurred in connection with the corporation's repurchase of its shares and reflected on the corporation's balance sheet, but not in excess of the principal of the obligations that remain unpaid immediately prior to the distribution and (2) there shall be deducted from liabilities all amounts that had been previously added thereto with respect to the obligations incurred in connection with the corporation's repurchase of its shares and reflected on the corporation's balance sheet, but not in excess of the principal of the obligations that will remain unpaid after the distribution, provided that no addition to retained earnings or deduction from liabilities under this subdivision shall occur on account of any obligation that is a distribution to the corporation's shareholders (Section 166) at the time the obligation is incurred.

(c) The board of directors may base a determination that a distribution is not prohibited under subdivision (a) or under Section 501 on any of the following:

(1) Financial statements prepared on the basis of accounting practices and principles that are reasonable under the circumstances.

(2) A fair valuation.

(3) Any other method that is reasonable under the circumstances.

(d) The effect of a distribution under paragraph (1) or (2) of subdivision (a) is measured as of the date the distribution is authorized if the payment occurs within 120 days after the date of authorization.

(e) (1) If terms of indebtedness provide that payment of principal and interest is to be made only if, and to the extent that, payment of a distribution to shareholders could then be made under this section, indebtedness of a corporation, including indebtedness issued as a distribution, is not a liability for purposes of determinations made under paragraph (2) of subdivision (a).

(2) If indebtedness is issued as a distribution, each payment of principal or interest on the indebtedness shall be treated as a distribution, the effect of which is measured on the date the payment of the indebtedness is actually made. . . .

§ 501.   Inability to Meet Liabilities as They Mature; Prohibition of Distribution

Neither a corporation nor any of its subsidiaries shall make any distribution to the corporation's shareholders (Section 166) if the corporation or the subsidiary making the distribution is, or as a result thereof would be, likely to be unable to meet its liabilities (except those whose payment is otherwise adequately provided for) as they mature.

§ 503.   Purchase or Redemption of Shares of Deceased Shareholder from Insurance Proceeds; Application of Provisions Relating to Prohibited Distributions

(a) The provisions of Sections 500 and 501 shall not apply to a purchase or redemption of shares of a deceased shareholder from the proceeds of insurance on the life of that shareholder in excess of the total amount of all premiums paid by the corporation for that insurance, in order to carry out the provisions of an agreement between the corporation and that shareholder to purchase or redeem those shares upon the death of the shareholder.

(b) The provisions of Sections 500 and 501 shall not apply to the purchase or redemption of shares of a disabled shareholder from the proceeds of disability insurance applicable to the disabled shareholder in excess of the total amount of all premiums paid by the corporation for the insurance, in order to carry out the provisions of an agreement between the corporation and the shareholder to purchase or redeem shares upon the disability of the shareholder as defined within that policy. For the purposes of this subdivision, "disability insurance" means an agreement of indemnification against the insured's loss of the ability to work due to accident or illness.

§ 506. Receipt of Prohibited Dividend; Liability of Shareholder; Suit by Creditors or Other Shareholders; Fraudulent Transfers

(a) Any shareholder who receives any distribution prohibited by this chapter with knowledge of facts indicating the impropriety thereof is liable to the corporation for the benefit of all of the creditors or shareholders entitled to institute an action under subdivision (b) for the amount so received by the shareholder with interest thereon at the legal rate on judgments until paid, but not exceeding the liabilities of the corporation owed to nonconsenting creditors at the time of the violation and the injury suffered by nonconsenting shareholders, as the case may be. For purposes of determining the value of any noncash property received in a distribution described in the preceding sentence, the shareholder receiving that illegal distribution shall be liable to the corporation for an amount equal to the fair market value of the property at the time of the illegal distribution plus interest thereon from the date of the distribution at the legal rate on judgments until paid, together with all reasonably incurred costs of appraisal or other valuation, if any, of that property, but not exceeding the liabilities of the corporation owed to nonconsenting creditors at the time of the violation and the injury suffered by nonconsenting shareholders, as the case may be.

(b) Suit may be brought in the name of the corporation to enforce the liability (1) to creditors arising under subdivision (a) for a violation of Section 500 or 501 against any or all shareholders liable by any one or more creditors of the corporation whose debts or claims arose prior to the time of the distribution to shareholders and who have not consented thereto, whether or not they have reduced their claims to judgment, or (2) to shareholders arising under subdivision (a) for a violation of Section 500 against any or all shareholders liable by one or more holders of shares having preferential rights with respect to cumulative dividends in arrears, in the case of a violation of paragraph (1) of subdivision (a) of Section 500, or upon dissolution, in the case of a violation of paragraph (2) of subdivision (a) of Section 500, in each case who have not consented to the applicable distribution, without regard to the provisions in Section 800, and in each case to the extent the applicable shares with preferential rights were outstanding at the time of the distribution; provided that holders of shares of preferential rights shall not have the right to bring suit in the name of the corporation under this subdivision unless the preferential dividends arrears amount, in the case of a violation of paragraph (1) of subdivision (a) of Section 500, or the preferential rights amount, in the case of a violation of paragraph (2) of subdivision (a) of Section 500, was greater than zero. A cause of action with respect to an obligation to return a distribution pursuant to this section shall be extinguished unless the action is brought within four years after the date the distribution is made.

(c) Any shareholder sued under this section may implead all other shareholders liable under this section and may compel contribution, either in that action or in an independent action against shareholders not joined in that action. . . .

(d) Nothing contained in this section affects any liability which any shareholder may have under Chapter 1 (commencing with Section 3439) of Title 2 of Part 2 of Division 4 of the Civil Code [Uniform Fraudulent Transfer Act].

§ 510. Acquisition of Own Shares; Status; Prohibition of Reissue by Articles; Reduction in Authorized Shares; Amendment of Articles; Filing

(a) When a corporation reacquires its own shares, those shares are restored to the status of authorized but unissued shares, unless the articles prohibit the reissuance thereof.

(b) When a corporation reacquires authorized shares of a class or series and the articles prohibit the reissuance of those shares:

(1) If all of the authorized shares of that class or series, as the case may be, are reacquired, then (A) that class or series is automatically eliminated, (B) in the case of reacquisition of all of the authorized shares of a series, the authorized number of shares of the class to which the shares belonged is reduced by the number of shares so reacquired, and (C) the articles shall be amended to eliminate any statement of rights, preferences, privileges, and restrictions relating solely to that class or series.

(2) If less than all of the authorized shares but all of the issued and outstanding shares of that class or series, as the case may be, are reacquired, the authorized number of shares of the class or series is automatically reduced by the number of shares so reacquired, and the board shall determine either (A) to eliminate that class or series, whereupon the articles shall be amended to eliminate any statement of rights,

preferences, privileges, and restrictions relating solely to that class or series, or (B) not to eliminate that class or series, whereupon the articles shall be amended to reflect that reduction of the number of authorized shares of that class or series by the shares so reacquired.

(3) If less than all of the authorized shares and less than all of the issued and outstanding shares of a class or series, as the case may be, are reacquired, the authorized number of shares of that class or series shall be automatically reduced by the number of shares reacquired, and the articles shall be amended to reflect that reduction.

(c) When a corporation reacquires authorized shares of a series of shares and the articles only prohibit the reissuance of those shares as shares of the same series:

(1) If all of the authorized shares of that series are reacquired, then that series is automatically eliminated, the articles shall be amended to eliminate any statement of rights, preferences, privileges, and restrictions relating solely to that series, and the board shall determine either (A) to return those shares to the status of authorized but undesignated shares of the class to which they belong or (B) to eliminate those shares entirely, whereupon the articles in either case shall be amended to reflect the reduction in the authorized shares of that series and the effect, if any, on the class to which that series belongs.

(2) If all of the issued and outstanding shares of that series (but less than all of the authorized shares of that series) are reacquired, the board shall determine either (A) to eliminate that series, whereupon the articles shall be amended to eliminate any statement of rights, preferences, privileges, and restrictions relating solely to that series, or (B) not to eliminate that series, whereupon the articles shall be amended to reflect the return of the reacquired shares to the status of authorized but undesignated shares of the class to which they belong.

(3) If less than all of the issued and outstanding shares of that series are reacquired, the authorized number of shares of that series shall be automatically reduced by the number of shares reacquired, and the board shall determine either (A) to return those shares to the status of authorized but undesignated shares of the class to which they belong, or (B) to eliminate those shares entirely, whereupon the articles in either case shall be amended to reflect the reduction in the authorized shares of that series and the effect, if any, on the class to which that series belongs.

(d) "Reacquires" as used in this section means that a corporation purchases, redeems, acquires by way of conversion to another class or series, or otherwise acquires its own shares or that issued and outstanding shares cease to be outstanding.

(e) The provisions of this section are subject to any contrary or inconsistent provision in the articles.

(f) A certificate of amendment shall be filed in accordance with the requirements of Chapter 9. (commencing with Section 900) reflecting any elimination or reduction of authorized shares set forth in subdivisions (b) and (c), and any related elimination from the articles of the designation and the rights, preferences, privileges, and restrictions of any series or class of stock that is eliminated, except that approval by the outstanding shares (Section 152) shall not be required to adopt any such amendment. . . .

Chapter 6

SHAREHOLDERS' MEETINGS AND CONSENTS

§ 602.　　Quorum; Votes; Withdrawal During Meeting Leaving Less Than Quorum

(a) Unless otherwise provided in the articles, a majority of the shares entitled to vote, represented in person or by proxy, shall constitute a quorum at a meeting of the shareholders, but in no event shall a quorum consist of less than one-third . . . of the shares entitled to vote at the meeting or, except in the case of a close corporation, of more than a majority of the shares entitled to vote at the meeting. Except as provided in subdivision (b), the affirmative vote of a majority of the shares represented and voting at a duly held meeting at which a quorum is present (which shares voting affirmatively also constitute at least a majority of the required quorum) shall be the act of the shareholders, unless the vote of a greater number or voting by classes is required by this division or the articles.

(b) The shareholders present at a duly called or held meeting at which a quorum is present may continue to transact business until adjournment notwithstanding the withdrawal of enough shareholders to leave less than a quorum, if any action taken (other than adjournment) is approved by at least a majority of the shares required to constitute a quorum or, if required by this division or the articles, the vote of a greater number or voting by class.

(c) In the absence of a quorum, any meeting of shareholders may be adjourned from time to time by the vote of a majority of the shares represented either in person or by proxy, but no other business may be transacted, except as provided in subdivision (b).

§ 604. Proxies or Written Consents; Contents; Form

(a) Any form of proxy or written consent distributed to 10 or more shareholders of a corporation with outstanding shares held of record by 100 or more persons shall afford an opportunity on the proxy or form of written consent to specify a choice between approval and disapproval of each matter or group of related matters intended to be acted upon at the meeting for which the proxy is solicited or by such written consent, other than elections to office, and shall provide, subject to reasonable specified conditions, that where the person solicited specifies a choice with respect to any such matter the shares will be voted in accordance therewith.

(b) In any election of directors, any form of proxy in which the directors to be voted upon are named therein as candidates and which is marked by a shareholder "withhold" or otherwise marked in a manner indicating that the authority to vote for the election of directors is withheld shall not be voted for the election of a director.

(c) Failure to comply with this section shall not invalidate any corporate action taken, but may be the basis for challenging any proxy at a meeting and the superior court may compel compliance therewith at the suit of any shareholder.

(d) This section does not apply to any corporation with an outstanding class of securities registered under Section 12 of the Securities Exchange Act of 1934 or whose securities are exempted from such registration by Section 12(g)(2) of that act.

Chapter 7

VOTING OF SHARES

§ 703. Shares in Name of Other Corporations, [Shares Owned by] Subsidiary or Held in Fiduciary Capacity by Issuing Corporation

(a) Shares standing in the name of another corporation, domestic or foreign, may be voted by an officer, agent, or proxyholder as the bylaws of the other corporation may prescribe or, in the absence of such provision, as the board of the other corporation may determine or, in the absence of that determination, by the chairperson of the board, president or any vice president of the other corporation, or by any other person authorized to do so by the chairperson of the board, president, or any vice president of the other corporation. Shares which are purported to be voted or any proxy purported to be executed in the name of a corporation (whether or not any title of the person signing is indicated) shall be presumed to be voted or the proxy executed in accordance with the provisions of this subdivision, unless the contrary is shown.

(b) Shares of a corporation owned by its subsidiary shall not be entitled to vote on any matter.

(c) Shares held by the issuing corporation in a fiduciary capacity, and shares of an issuing corporation held in a fiduciary capacity by its subsidiary, shall not be entitled to vote on any matter, except as follows:

(1) To the extent that the settlor or beneficial owner possesses and exercises a right to vote or to give the corporation binding instructions as to how to vote such shares.

(2) Where there are one or more cotrustees who are not affected by the prohibition of this subdivision, in which case the shares may be voted by the cotrustees as if it or they are the sole trustee.

§ 705.   Proxies; Validity; Expiration; Revocation; Irrevocable Proxies

(a) Every person entitled to vote shares may authorize another person or persons to act by proxy with respect to such shares. Any proxy purporting to be executed in accordance with the provisions of this division shall be presumptively valid.

(b) No proxy shall be valid after the expiration of 11 months from the date thereof unless otherwise provided in the proxy. Every proxy continues in full force and effect until revoked by the person executing it prior to the vote pursuant thereto, except as otherwise provided in this section. Such revocation may be effected by a writing delivered to the corporation stating that the proxy is revoked or by a subsequent proxy executed by the person executing the prior proxy and presented to the meeting, or as to any meeting by attendance at such meeting and voting in person by the person executing the proxy. The dates contained on the forms of proxy presumptively determine the order of execution, regardless of the postmark dates on the envelopes in which they are mailed.

(c) A proxy is not revoked by the death or incapacity of the maker unless, before the vote is counted, written notice of such death or incapacity is received by the corporation.

(d) Except when other provision shall have been made by written agreement between the parties, the recordholder of shares which such person holds as pledgee or otherwise as security or which belong to another shall issue to the pledgor or to the owner of such shares, upon demand therefor and payment of necessary expenses thereof, a proxy to vote or take other action thereon.

(e) A proxy which states that it is irrevocable is irrevocable for the period specified therein (notwithstanding subdivision (c)) when it is held by any of the following or a nominee of any of the following:

(1) A pledgee.

(2) A person who has purchased or agreed to purchase or holds an option to purchase the shares or a person who has sold a portion of such person's shares in the corporation to the maker of the proxy.

(3) A creditor or creditors of the corporation or the shareholder who extended or continued credit to the corporation or the shareholder in consideration of the proxy if the proxy states that it was given in consideration of such extension or continuation of credit and the name of the person extending or continuing credit.

(4) A person who has contracted to perform services as an employee of the corporation, if a proxy is required by the contract of employment and if the proxy states that it was given in consideration of such contract of employment, the name of the employee and the period of employment contracted for.

(5) A person designated by or under an agreement under Section 706.

(6) A beneficiary of a trust with respect to shares held by the trust.

Notwithstanding the period of irrevocability specified, the proxy becomes revocable when the pledge is redeemed, the option or agreement to purchase is terminated or the seller no longer owns any shares of the corporation or dies, the debt of the corporation or the shareholder is paid, the period of employment provided for in the contract of employment has terminated, the agreement under Section 706 has terminated, or the person ceases to be a beneficiary of the trust. In addition to the foregoing clauses (1) through (5), a proxy may be made irrevocable (notwithstanding subdivision (c)) if it is given to secure the performance of a duty or to protect a title, either legal or equitable, until the happening of events which, by its terms, discharge the obligations secured by it.

(f) A proxy may be revoked, notwithstanding a provision making it irrevocable, by a transferee of shares without knowledge of the existence of the provision unless the existence of the proxy and its irrevocability appears, in the case of certificated securities, on the certificate representing such shares, or in the case of uncertificated securities, on the initial transaction statement and written statements.

§ 706.   Agreement Between Two or More Shareholders of a Corporation; Voting Trust Agreements

(a) Notwithstanding any other provision of this division, an agreement between two or more shareholders of a corporation, if in writing and signed by the parties thereto, may provide that in exercising any voting rights the shares held by them shall be voted as provided by the agreement, or as the parties may agree or as determined in accordance with a procedure agreed upon by them, and the parties may but need not transfer the shares covered by such an agreement to a third party or parties with authority to vote them in accordance with the terms of the agreement. Such an agreement shall not be denied specific performance by a court on the ground that the remedy at law is adequate or on other grounds relating to the jurisdiction of a court of equity.

(b) Shares in any corporation may be transferred by written agreement to trustees in order to confer upon them the right to vote and otherwise represent the shares for such period of time, not exceeding 10 years, as may be specified in the agreement. The validity of a voting trust agreement, otherwise lawful, shall not be affected during a period of 10 years from the date when it was created or last extended as hereinafter provided by the fact that under its terms it will or may last beyond such 10-year period. At any time within two years prior to the time of expiration of any voting trust agreement as originally fixed or as last extended as provided in this subdivision, one or more beneficiaries under the voting trust agreement may, by written agreement and with the written consent of the voting trustee or trustees, extend the duration of the voting trust agreement with respect to their shares for an additional period not exceeding 10 years from the expiration date of the trust as originally fixed or as last extended as provided in this subdivision. A duplicate of the voting trust agreement and any extension thereof shall be filed with the secretary of the corporation and shall be open to inspection by a shareholder, a holder of a voting trust certificate or the agent of either, upon the same terms as the record of shareholders of the corporation is open to inspection.

(c) No agreement made pursuant to subdivision (a) shall be held to be invalid or unenforceable on the ground that it is a voting trust that does not comply with subdivision (b) or that it is a proxy that does not comply with Section 705.

(d) This section shall not invalidate any voting or other agreement among shareholders or any irrevocable proxy complying with subdivision (e) of Section 705, which agreement or proxy is not otherwise illegal.

§ 708.   Directors; Cumulative Voting; Election by Ballot

(a) Except as provided in Sections 301.5 and 708.5, every shareholder complying with subdivision (b) and entitled to vote at any election of directors may cumulate such shareholder's votes and give one candidate a number of votes equal to the number of directors to be elected multiplied by the number of votes to which the shareholder's shares are normally entitled, or distribute the shareholder's votes on the same principle among as many candidates as the shareholder thinks fit.

(b) No shareholder shall be entitled to cumulate votes (i.e., cast for any candidate a number of votes greater than the number of votes that the shareholder normally is entitled to cast) unless the candidate or candidates' names have been placed in nomination prior to the voting and the shareholder has given notice at the meeting prior to the voting of the shareholder's intention to cumulate the shareholder's votes. If any one shareholder has given that notice, all shareholders may cumulate their votes for candidates in nomination.

(c) Except as provided in Section 708.5, in any election of directors, the candidates receiving the highest number of affirmative votes of the shares entitled to be voted for them up to the number of directors to be elected by those shares are elected; votes against the director and votes withheld shall have no legal effect.

(d) Subdivision (a) applies to the shareholders of any mutual water company organized or existing for the purpose of delivering water to its shareholders at cost on lands located within the boundaries of one or more reclamation districts now or hereafter legally existing in this state and created by or formed under the provisions of any statute of this state, but does not otherwise apply to the shareholders of mutual water companies unless their articles or bylaws so provide.

(e) Elections for directors need not be by ballot unless a shareholder demands election by ballot at the meeting and before the voting begins or unless the bylaws so require.

§ 708.5   Director Election; Approval of Shareholders Required; Term of Incumbent Director When Not Approved in Uncontested Election; Board Vacancy

(a) For purposes of this section, the following definitions shall apply:

(1) "Uncontested election" means an election of directors in which, at the expiration of the time fixed under the articles of incorporation or bylaws requiring advance notification of director candidates or, absent such a provision in the articles of incorporation or bylaws, at a time fixed by the board of directors that is not more than 14 days before notice is given of the meeting at which the election is to occur, the number of candidates for election does not exceed the number of directors to be elected by the shareholders at that election.

(2) "Listed corporation" means a domestic corporation that qualifies as a listed corporation under subdivision (d) of Section 301.5.

(b) Notwithstanding paragraph (5) of subdivision (a) of Section 204, a listed corporation that has eliminated cumulative voting pursuant to subdivision (a) of Section 301.5 may amend its articles of incorporation or bylaws to provide that, in an uncontested election, approval of the shareholders, as specified in Section 153, shall be required to elect a director.

(c) Notwithstanding subdivision (b) of Section 301, if an incumbent director fails to be elected by approval of the shareholders (Section 153) in an uncontested election of a listed corporation that has amended its articles of incorporation or bylaws pursuant to subdivision (b), then, unless the incumbent director has earlier resigned, the term of the incumbent director shall end on the date that is the earlier of 90 days after the date on which the voting results are determined pursuant to Section 707 or the date on which the board of directors selects a person to fill the office held by that director pursuant to subdivision (d).

(d) Any vacancy on the board of directors resulting from any failure of a candidate to be elected by approval of the shareholders (Section 153) in an uncontested election of a listed corporation that has amended its articles of incorporation or bylaws pursuant to subdivision (b) shall be filled in accordance with the procedures set forth in Section 305.

§ 710.   Supermajority Vote Requirement; Approval

(a) This section applies to a corporation with outstanding shares held of record by 100 or more persons (determined as provided in Section 605) that files an amendment of articles or certificate of determination containing a "supermajority vote" provision on or after January 1, 1989. This section shall not apply to a corporation that files an amendment of articles or certificate of determination on or after January 1, 1994, if, at the time of filing, the corporation has (1) outstanding shares of more than one class or series of stock, (2) no class of equity securities registered under Section 12(b) or 12(g) of the Securities Exchange Act of 1934, and (3) outstanding shares held of record by fewer than 300 persons determined as provided by Section 605.

(b) A "supermajority vote" is a requirement set forth in the articles or in a certificate of determination authorized under any provision of this division that specified corporate action or actions be approved by a larger proportion of the outstanding shares than a majority, or by a larger proportion of the outstanding shares of a class or series than a majority, but no supermajority vote that is subject to this section shall require a vote in excess of 66 2/3 percent of the outstanding shares or 66 2/3 percent of the outstanding shares of any class or series of those shares.

(c) An amendment of the articles or a certificate of determination that includes a supermajority vote requirement shall be approved by at least as large a proportion of the outstanding shares (Section 152) as is required pursuant to that amendment or certificate of determination for the approval of the specified corporate action or actions. . . .

§ 711. Maintenance by Holding Legal Owners and Disclosure to Persons on Whose Behalf Shares Are Voted; Charges; Actions to Enforce Section; Payment of Costs and Attorney's Fees . . .

(a) The Legislature finds and declares that:

Many of the residents of this state are the legal and beneficial owners or otherwise the ultimate beneficiaries of shares of stock of domestic and foreign corporations, title to which may be held by a variety of intermediate owners as defined in subdivision (b). The informed and active involvement of such beneficial owners and beneficiaries in holding legal owners and, through them, management, accountable in their exercise of corporate power is essential to the interest of those beneficiaries and beneficial owners and to the economy and well-being of this state.

The purpose of this section is to serve the public interest by ensuring that voting records are maintained and disclosed as provided in this section. In the event that by statute or regulation pursuant to the federal Employee Retirement Income Security Act of 1974 (29 U.S.C. Sec. 1001 et seq.), there are imposed upon investment managers as defined in Sec. 2(38) thereof, duties substantially the same as those set forth in this section, compliance with those statutory or regulatory requirements by persons subject to this section shall be deemed to fulfill the obligations contained in this section.

This section shall be construed liberally to achieve that purpose.

(b) For purposes of this section, a person on whose behalf shares are voted includes, but is not limited to:

(1) A participant or beneficiary of an employee benefit plan with regard to shares held for the benefit of the participant or beneficiary.

(2) A shareholder, beneficiary, or contract owner of any entity (or of any portfolio of any entity) as defined in Section 3(a) of the federal Investment Company Act of 1940 (15 U.S.C. Sec. 80a–1 et seq.), as amended, to the extent the entity (or portfolio) holds the shares for which the record is requested.

(c) For the purposes of this section, a person on whose behalf shares are voted does not include:

(1) A person who possesses the right to terminate or withdraw from the shareholder, contract owner, participant, or beneficiary relationship with any entity (or any portfolio of any entity) defined in subdivision (b). This exclusion does not apply in the event the right of termination or withdrawal cannot be exercised without automatic imposition of a tax penalty. The right to substitute a relationship with an entity or portfolio, the shares of which are voted by or subject to the direction of the investment adviser (as defined in Section 2 of the federal Investment Company Act of 1940 (15 U.S.C. Sec. 80a–1 et seq.), as amended), of the prior entity or portfolio, or an affiliate of the investment adviser, shall not be deemed to be a right of termination or withdrawal within the meaning of this subdivision.

(2) A person entitled to receive information about a trust pursuant to Section 16061 of the Probate Code.

(3) A beneficiary, participant, contract owner, or shareholder whose interest is funded through the general assets of a life insurance company authorized to conduct business in this state.

(d) Every person possessing the power to vote shares of stock on behalf of another shall maintain a record of the manner in which the shares were voted. The record shall be maintained for a period of 12 consecutive months from the effective date of the vote.

(e) Upon a reasonable written request, the person possessing the power to vote shares of stock on behalf of another, or a designated agent, shall disclose the voting record with respect to any matter involving a specific security or securities in accordance with the following procedures:

(1) Except as set forth in paragraph (2), disclosure shall be made to the person making the request. The person making the disclosure may require identification sufficient to identify the person making the request as a person on whose behalf the shares were voted. A request for identification, if made, shall be reasonable, shall be made promptly, and may include a request for the person's social security number.

(2) If the person possessing the power to vote shares on behalf of another holds that power pursuant to an agreement entered into with a party other than the person making the request for disclosure, the

person maintaining and disclosing the record pursuant to this section may, instead, make the requested disclosure to that party. Disclosure to that party shall be deemed compliance with the disclosure requirement of this section. If disclosure is made to that party and not to the person making the request, subdivision (i) shall not apply. However, nothing herein shall prohibit that party and the person possessing the power to vote on shares from entering into an agreement between themselves for the payment or assessment of a reasonable charge to defray expenses of disclosing the record.

(f) Where the entity subject to the requirements of this section is organized as a unit investment trust as defined in Section 4(2) of the federal Investment Company Act of 1940 (15 U.S.C. Sec. 80a–1 et seq.), the open-ended investment companies underlying the unit investment trust shall promptly make available their proxy voting records to the unit investment trust upon evidence of a bona fide request for voting record information pursuant to subdivision (e).

(g) Signing a proxy on another's behalf and forwarding it for disposition or receiving voting instructions does not constitute the power to vote. A person forwarding proxies or receiving voting instructions shall disclose the identity of the person having the power to vote shares upon reasonable written request by a person entitled to request a voting record under subdivision (c).

(h) For purposes of this section, if one or more persons has the power to vote shares on behalf of another, unless a governing instrument provides otherwise, the person or persons may designate an agent who shall maintain and disclose the record in accordance with subdivisions (b) and (c).

(i) Except as provided in paragraph (2) of subdivision (e), or as otherwise provided by law or a governing instrument, a person maintaining and disclosing a record pursuant to this section may assess a reasonable charge to the requesting person in order to defray expenses of disclosing the record in accordance with subdivision (e). Disclosure shall be made within a reasonable period after payment is received.

(j) Upon the petition of any person who successfully brings an action pursuant to or to enforce this section, the court may award costs and reasonable attorney's fees if the court finds that the defendant willfully violated this section. . . .

Chapter 8

SHAREHOLDER DERIVATIVE ACTIONS

§ 800.   Conditions; Security; Motion for Order; Determination . . .

(b) No action may be instituted or maintained in right of any domestic or foreign corporation by any holder of shares or of voting trust certificates of . . . the corporation unless both of the following conditions exist:

(1) The plaintiff alleges in the complaint that plaintiff was a shareholder, of record or beneficially, or the holder of voting trust certificates at the time of the transaction or any part thereof of which plaintiff complains or that plaintiff's shares or voting trust certificates thereafter devolved upon plaintiff by operation of law from a holder who was a holder at the time of the transaction or any part thereof complained of; provided, that any shareholder who does not meet . . . these requirements may nevertheless be allowed in the discretion of the court to maintain . . . the action on a preliminary showing to and determination by the court, by motion and after a hearing, at which the court shall consider such evidence, by affidavit or testimony, as it deems material, that (i) there is a strong prima facie case in favor of the claim asserted on behalf of the corporation, (ii) no other similar action has been or is likely to be instituted, (iii) the plaintiff acquired the shares before there was disclosure to the public or to the plaintiff of the wrongdoing of which plaintiff complains, (iv) unless the action can be maintained the defendant may retain a gain derived from defendant's willful breach of a fiduciary duty, and (v) the requested relief will not result in unjust enrichment of the corporation or any shareholder of the corporation; and

(2) The plaintiff alleges in the complaint with particularity plaintiff's efforts to secure from the board such action as plaintiff desires, or the reasons for not making such effort, and alleges further that plaintiff has either informed the corporation or the board in writing of the ultimate facts of each cause of action against each defendant or delivered to the corporation or the board a true copy of the complaint which plaintiff proposes to file.

(c) In any action referred to in subdivision (b), at any time within 30 days after service of summons upon the corporation or upon any defendant who is an officer or director of the corporation, or held such office at the time of the acts complained of, the corporation or . . . the defendant may move the court for an order, upon notice and hearing, requiring the plaintiff to furnish . . . a bond as hereinafter provided. The motion shall be based upon one or both of the following grounds:

(1) That there is no reasonable possibility that the prosecution of the cause of action alleged in the complaint against the moving party will benefit the corporation or its shareholders.

(2) That the moving party, if other than the corporation, did not participate in the transaction complained of in any capacity.

The court on application of the corporation or any defendant may, for good cause shown, extend the 30-day period for an additional period or periods not exceeding 60 days.

(d) At the hearing upon any motion pursuant to subdivision (c), the court shall consider such evidence, written or oral, by witnesses or affidavit, as may be material (1) to the ground or grounds upon which the motion is based, or (2) to a determination of the probable reasonable expenses, including attorneys' fees, of the corporation and the moving party which will be incurred in the defense of the action. If the court determines, after hearing the evidence adduced by the parties, that the moving party has established a probability in support of any of the grounds upon which the motion is based, the court shall fix the . . . amount of the bond, not to exceed fifty thousand dollars ($50,000), to be furnished by the plaintiff for reasonable expenses, including attorneys' fees, which may be incurred by the moving party and the corporation in connection with the action, including expenses for which the corporation may become liable pursuant to Section 317 [Indemnification]. A ruling by the court on the motion shall not be a determination of any issue in the action or of the merits thereof. . . . If the court, upon the motion, makes a determination that . . . a bond shall be furnished by the plaintiff as to any one or more defendants, the action shall be dismissed as to . . . the defendant or defendants, unless the bond required by the court . . . has been furnished within such reasonable time as may be fixed by the court. . . .

(e) If the plaintiff shall, either before or after a motion is made pursuant to subdivision (c), or any order or determination pursuant to . . . the motion, . . . furnish a bond in the aggregate amount of fifty thousand dollars ($50,000) to secure the reasonable expenses of the parties entitled to make the motion, the plaintiff has complied with the requirements of this section and with any order for . . . a bond theretofore made . . . , and any such motion then pending shall be dismissed and no further or additional bond . . . shall be required.

(f) If a motion is filed pursuant to subdivision (c), no pleadings need be filed by the corporation or any other defendant and the prosecution of the action shall be stayed until 10 days after the motion has been disposed of.

Chapter 9

AMENDMENT OF ARTICLES

§900.   Authorization . . .

(a) By complying with the provisions of this chapter, a corporation may amend its articles from time to time, in any and as many respects as may be desired, so long as its articles as amended contain only such provisions as it would be lawful to insert in original articles filed at the time of the filing of the amendment and, if a change in shares or the rights of shareholders or an exchange, reclassification or cancellation of shares or rights of shareholders is to be made, such provisions as may be necessary to effect such change, exchange, reclassification or cancellation. It is the intent of the Legislature in adopting this section to exercise to the fullest extent the reserve power of the state over corporations and to authorize any amendment of the articles covered by the preceding sentence regardless of whether any provision contained in the amendment was permissible at the time of the original incorporation of the corporation. . . .

Chapter 10

SALES OF ASSETS

§ 1001. Sale, Lease, Exchange, etc....; of Property or Assets; Approval; Abandonment; Terms, Conditions and Consideration

(a) A corporation may sell, lease, convey, exchange, transfer or otherwise dispose of all or substantially all of its assets when the principal terms are approved by the board, and, unless the transaction is in the usual and regular course of its business, approved by the outstanding shares (Section 152), either before or after approval by the board and before or after the transaction. A transaction constituting a reorganization (Section 181) is subject to the provisions of Chapter 12 (commencing with Section 1200) and not this section (other than subdivision (d)). A transaction constituting a conversion (Section 161.9) is subject to the provisions of Chapter 11.5 (commencing with Section 1150) and not this section.

(b) Notwithstanding approval of the outstanding shares (Section 152), the board may abandon the proposed transaction without further action by the shareholders, subject to the contractual rights, if any, of third parties.

(c) The sale, lease, conveyance, exchange, transfer or other disposition may be made upon those terms and conditions and for that consideration as the board may deem in the best interests of the corporation. The consideration may be money, securities, or other property.

(d) If the acquiring party in a transaction pursuant to subdivision (a) of this section or subdivision (g) of Section 2001 [sale of assets in dissolution] is in control of or under common control with the dissolving corporation, the principal terms of the sale must be approved by at least 90 percent of the voting power of the disposing corporation unless the disposition is to a domestic or foreign corporation or other business entity in consideration of the nonredeemable common shares or nonredeemable equity securities of the acquiring party or its parent.

(e) Subdivision (d) does not apply to any transaction if the Commissioner of Corporations, the Commissioner of Financial Institutions, the Insurance Commissioner or the Public Utilities Commission has approved the terms and conditions....

Chapter 11

MERGER

§ 1100. Authorization

Any two or more corporations may be merged into one of those corporations. A corporation may merge with one or more domestic corporations (Section 167), social purpose corporations (Section 171.08), foreign corporations (Section 171), or other business entities (Section 174.5) pursuant to this chapter.... [M]ergers in which a social purpose corporation but no other business entity is a constituent party are governed by Section 1112.5....

§ 1101. Agreement of Merger; Approval of Boards; Contents

The board of each corporation which desires to merge shall approve an agreement of merger. The constituent corporations shall be parties to the agreement of merger and other persons, including a parent party (Section 1200), may be parties to the agreement of merger. The agreement shall state all of the following:

(a) The terms and conditions of the merger.

(b) The amendments ... to the articles of the surviving corporation to be effected by the merger, if any. If any amendment changes the name of the surviving corporation the new name may be the same as or similar to the name of a disappearing domestic or foreign corporation....

(c) The name and place of incorporation of each constituent corporation and which of the constituent corporations is the surviving corporation.

(d) The manner of converting the shares of each of the constituent corporations into shares or other securities of the surviving corporation and, if any shares of any of the constituent corporations are not to be converted solely into shares or other securities of the surviving corporation, the cash, rights, securities, or other property which the holders of those shares are to receive in exchange for the shares, which cash, rights, securities, or other property may be in addition to or in lieu of shares or other securities of the surviving corporation, or that the shares are cancelled without consideration.

(e) Other details or provisions as are desired, if any, including, without limitation, a provision for the payment of cash in lieu of fractional shares or for any other arrangement with respect thereto consistent with the provisions of Section 407.

Each share of the same class or series of any constituent corporation (other than the cancellation of shares held by a constituent corporation or its parent or a wholly owned subsidiary of either in another constituent corporation) shall, unless all shareholders of the class or series consent and except as provided in Section 407, be treated equally with respect to any distribution of cash, rights, securities, or other property. Notwithstanding subdivision (d), except in a short-form merger, and in the merger of a corporation into its subsidiary in which it owns at least 90 percent of the outstanding shares of each class, the nonredeemable common shares or nonredeemable equity securities of a constituent corporation may be converted only into nonredeemable common shares of the surviving party or a parent party if a constituent corporation or its parent owns, directly or indirectly, prior to the merger, shares of another constituent corporation representing more than 50 percent of the voting power of the other constituent corporation prior to the merger, unless all of the shareholders of the class consent and except as provided in Section 407.

§ 1111. Approval Where Disappearing Corporation in a Merger Is Close Corporation and Surviving Corporation Is Not

If any disappearing corporation in a merger is a close corporation and the surviving corporation is not a close corporation, the merger shall be approved by the affirmative vote of at least two-thirds of each class of the outstanding shares of such disappearing corporation; provided, however, that the articles or a shareholders' agreement may provide for a lesser vote, but not less than a majority of the outstanding shares of each class.

§ 1112.5 Merger into Social Purpose Corporation; Approval Required

If a disappearing corporation in a merger is a corporation governed by this division and the surviving corporation is a social purpose corporation, both of the following shall apply:

(a) The merger shall be approved by the affirmative vote of at least two-thirds of each class, or a greater vote if required in the articles, of the outstanding shares (Section 152) of the disappearing corporation, notwithstanding any provision of Chapter 12 (commencing with Section 1200).

(b) The shareholders of the disappearing corporation shall have all of the rights under Chapter 13 (commencing with Section 1300) of the shareholders of a corporation involved in a reorganization requiring the approval of its outstanding shares (Section 152), and the disappearing corporation shall have all of the obligations under Chapter 13 (commencing with Section 1300) of a corporation involved in the reorganization.

Chapter 11.5

CONVERSIONS

§ 1152. Plan of Conversion

(a) A corporation that desires to convert to a domestic other business entity shall approve a plan of conversion. . . .

(b) The plan of conversion shall be approved by the board of the converting corporation (Section 151), and the principal terms of the plan of the conversion shall be approved by the outstanding shares (Section 152) of each class of the converting corporation. The approval of the outstanding shares may be given before or after approval by the board. Notwithstanding the foregoing, if a converting corporation is a close corporation, the conversion shall be approved by the affirmative vote of at least two-thirds of each class, or a greater vote if required in the articles, of outstanding shares (Section 152) of that converting corporation; provided, however, that the articles may provide for a lesser vote, but not less than a majority of the outstanding shares of each class.

(c) If the corporation is converting into a general or limited partnership or into a limited liability company, then in addition to the approval of the shareholders set forth in subdivision (b), the plan of conversion shall be approved by each shareholder who will become a general partner or manager, as applicable, of the converted entity pursuant to the plan of conversion unless the shareholders have dissenters' rights pursuant to Section 1159 and Chapter 13 (commencing with Section 1300). . . .

Chapter 12

REORGANIZATIONS

§ 1200. Approval by Board

A reorganization (Section 181) or a share exchange tender offer (Section 183.5) shall be approved by the board of:

(a) Each constituent corporation in a merger reorganization;

(b) The acquiring corporation in an exchange reorganization;

(c) The acquiring corporation and the corporation whose property and assets are acquired in a sale-of-assets reorganization;

(d) The acquiring corporation in a share exchange tender offer (Section 183.5); and

(e) The corporation in control of any constituent or acquiring domestic or foreign corporation or other business entity under subdivision (a), (b) or (c) and whose equity securities are issued, transferred, or exchanged in the reorganization (a "parent party").

Legislative Committee Comment . . .

Under the new law, various methods of corporate fusion are treated as different means to the same end for the purpose of codifying the "de facto merger" doctrine.

As a basis for this approach, "reorganization" is defined to encompass the three basic methods of combination. . . . This section generally requires a reorganization to be approved by the board of each party, as well as the board of any "parent party" to the transaction. Taken together, these provisions specify the transactions (including the so-called "upside-down" and "triangular" transactions) in which § 1201 may require shareholder approval and, in turn, § 1300 may require dissenters' rights.

§ 1201. Approval of Shareholders; Abandonment by Board; Actions to Attack Validity if Party Directly or Indirectly Controlled by Other Party

(a) The principal terms of a reorganization shall be approved by the outstanding shares (Section 152) of each class of each corporation the approval of whose board is required under Section 1200, except as provided in subdivision (b) and except that (unless otherwise provided in the articles) no approval of any class of outstanding preferred shares of the surviving or acquiring corporation or parent party shall be required if the rights, preferences, privileges and restrictions granted to or imposed upon that class of shares remain unchanged (subject to the provisions of subdivision (c)). For the purpose of this subdivision, two classes of common shares differing only as to voting rights shall be considered as a single class of shares.

(b) No approval of the outstanding shares (Section 152) is required by subdivision (a) in the case of any corporation if that corporation, or its shareholders immediately before the reorganization, or both, shall own (immediately after the reorganization) equity securities, other than any warrant or right to subscribe to or purchase those equity securities, of the surviving or acquiring corporation or a parent party (subdivision (d)of Section 1200) possessing more than five-sixths of the voting power of the surviving or acquiring corporation or parent party. In making the determination of ownership by the shareholders of a corporation, immediately after the reorganization, of equity securities pursuant to the preceding sentence, equity securities which they owned immediately before the reorganization as shareholders of another party to the transaction shall be disregarded. For the purpose of this section only, the voting power of a corporation shall be calculated by assuming the conversion of all equity securities convertible (immediately or at some future time) into shares entitled to vote but not assuming the exercise of any warrant or right to subscribe to or purchase those shares.

(c) Notwithstanding subdivision (b), the principal terms of a reorganization shall be approved by the outstanding shares (Section 152) of the surviving corporation in a merger reorganization if any amendment is made to its articles which would otherwise require that approval.

(d) Notwithstanding subdivision (b), the principal terms of a reorganization shall be approved by the outstanding shares (Section 152) of any class of a corporation that is a party to a merger or sale-of-assets reorganization if holders of shares of that class receive shares of the surviving or acquiring corporation or parent party having different rights, preferences, privileges or restrictions than those surrendered. Shares in a foreign corporation received in exchange for shares in a domestic corporation have different rights, preferences, privileges and restrictions within the meaning of the preceding sentence.

(e) Notwithstanding subdivisions (a) and (b), the principal terms of a reorganization shall be approved by the affirmative vote of at least two-thirds of each class, or a greater vote if required in the articles, of the outstanding shares of any social purpose corporation that is a close social purpose corporation if the reorganization would result in the holders receiving shares or other interests of a corporation or other business entity that is not a close social purpose corporation. The articles may provide for a lesser vote, but not less than a majority of the outstanding shares of each class.

(f) Notwithstanding subdivisions (a) and (b), the principal terms of a reorganization shall be approved by at least two-thirds of each class, or a greater vote if required in the articles, of the outstanding shares (Section 152) of a corporation that is a party to a merger reorganization if holders of shares receive shares of a surviving social purpose corporation in the merger.

(g) Notwithstanding subdivisions (a) and (b), the principal terms of a reorganization shall be approved by the outstanding shares (Section 152) of any class of a corporation which is a party to a merger reorganization if holders or shares of that class receive interests of a surviving other business entity [§ 174.5] in the merger.

(h) Notwithstanding subdivisions (a) and (b), the principal terms of a reorganization shall be approved by all shareholders of any class or series if, as a result of the reorganization, the holders of that class or series become personally liable for any obligations of a party to the reorganization, unless all holders of that class or series have the dissenters' rights provided in Chapter 13 (commencing with Section 1300).

(i) Any approval required by this section may be given before or after the approval by the board. Notwithstanding approval required by this section, the board may abandon the proposed reorganization without further action by the shareholders, subject to the contractual rights, if any, of third parties.

§ 1201.5 Share Exchange Tender Offer; Approval of Principal Terms

(a) The principal terms of a share exchange tender offer (Section 183.5) shall be approved by the outstanding shares (Section 152) of each class of the corporation making the tender offer or whose shares are to be used in the tender offer, except as provided in subdivision (b) and except that (unless otherwise provided in the articles) no approval of any class of outstanding preferred shares of either corporation shall be required, if the rights, preferences, privileges, and restrictions granted to or imposed upon that class of shares remain unchanged. For the purpose of this subdivision, two classes of common shares differing only as to voting rights shall be considered as a single class of shares.

(b) No approval of the outstanding shares (Section 152) is required by subdivision (a) in the case of any corporation if the corporation, or its shareholders immediately before the tender offer, or both, shall own (immediately after the completion of the share exchange proposed in the tender offer) equity securities, (other than any warrant or right to subscribe to or purchase the equity securities), of the corporation making the tender offer or of the corporation whose shares were used in the tender offer, possessing more than five-sixths of the voting power of either corporation. In making the determination of ownership by the shareholders of a corporation, immediately after the tender offer, of equity securities pursuant to the preceding sentence, equity securities which they owned immediately before the tender offer as shareholders of another party to the transaction shall be disregarded. For the purpose of this section only, the voting power of a corporation shall be calculated by assuming the conversion of all equity securities convertible (immediately or at some future time) into shares entitled to vote but not assuming the exercise of any warrant or right to subscribe to, or purchase, shares.

§ 1202. Terms of Merger Reorganization or Sale-of-Assets Reorganization; Approval by Shareholders; Foreign Corporations

(a) In addition to the requirements of Section 1201, the principal terms of a merger reorganization shall be approved by all the outstanding shares of a corporation if the agreement of merger provides that all the outstanding shares of that corporation are canceled without consideration in the merger.

(b) In addition to the requirements of Section 1201, if the terms of a merger reorganization or sale-of-assets reorganization provide that a class or series of preferred shares is to have distributed to it a lesser amount than would be required by applicable article provisions, the principal terms of the reorganization shall be approved by the same percentage of outstanding shares of that class or series which would be required to approve an amendment of the article provisions to provide for the distribution of that lesser amount.

(c) If a parent party within the meaning of Section 1200 is a foreign corporation (other than a foreign corporation to which subdivision (a) of Section 2115 is applicable), any requirement or lack of a requirement for approval by the outstanding shares of the foreign corporation shall be based, not on the application of Sections 1200 and 1201, but on the application of the laws of the state or place of incorporation of the foreign corporation.

§ 1203. Interested Party Proposal or Tender Offer to Shareholders; Affirmative Opinion; Delivery; Approval; Later Proposal or Tender Offer; Withdrawal of Vote, Consent, or Proxy; Procedures

(a) If a tender offer, including a share exchange tender offer (Section 183.5), or a written proposal for approval of a reorganization subject to Section 1200 or for a sale of assets subject to subdivision (a) of Section 1001 is made to some or all of a corporation's shareholders by an interested party (herein referred to as an "Interested Party Proposal"), an affirmative opinion in writing as to the fairness of the consideration to the shareholders of that corporation shall be delivered as follows:

(1) If no shareholder approval or acceptance is required for the consummation of the transaction, the opinion shall be delivered to the corporation's board of directors not later than the time that consummation of the transaction is authorized and approved by the board of directors.

(2) If a tender offer is made to the corporation's shareholders, the opinion shall be delivered to the shareholders at the time that the tender offer is first made in writing to the shareholders. However, if the tender offer is commenced by publication and tender offer materials are subsequently mailed or otherwise distributed to the shareholders, the opinion may be omitted in that publication if the opinion is included in the materials distributed to the shareholders.

(3) If a shareholders' meeting is to be held to vote on approval of the transaction, the opinion shall be delivered to the shareholders with the notice of the meeting (Section 601).

(4) If consents of all shareholders entitled to vote are solicited in writing (Section 603), the opinion shall be delivered at the same time as that solicitation.

(5) If the consents of all shareholders are not solicited in writing, the opinion shall be delivered to each shareholder whose consent is solicited prior to that shareholder's consent being given, and to all other shareholders at the time they are given the notice required by subdivision (b) of Section 603.

For purposes of this section, the term "interested party" means a person who is a party to the transaction and (A) directly or indirectly controls the corporation that is the subject of the tender offer or proposal, (B) is, or is directly or indirectly controlled by, an officer or director of the subject corporation, or (C) is an entity in which a material financial interest (subdivision (a) of Section 310) is held by any director or executive officer of the subject corporation. For purposes of the preceding sentence, "any executive officer" means the president, any vice president in charge of a principal business unit, division, or function such as sales, administration, research or development, or finance, and any other officer or other person who performs a policymaking function or has the same duties as those of a president or vice president. The opinion required by this subdivision shall be provided by a person who is not affiliated with the offeror and who, for compensation, engages in the business of advising others as to the value of properties, businesses, or securities. The fact that the opining person previously has provided services to the offeror or a related entity or is simultaneously engaged in providing advice or assistance with respect to the proposed transaction in a manner which makes its compensation contingent on the success of the proposed transaction shall not, for those reasons, be deemed to affiliate the opining person with the offeror. Nothing in this subdivision shall limit the applicability of the standards of review of the transaction in the event of a challenge thereto under Section 310 or subdivision (c) of Section 1312.

This subdivision shall not apply to an Interested Party Proposal if the corporation that is the subject thereof does not have shares held of record by 100 or more persons . . . , or if the transaction has been qualified under Section 25113 [Qualification by permit; application; contents; effective date] or 25120 [Necessity of qualification of security or exemption of security or transaction] and no order under Section 25140 [Issuance of stop orders affecting qualification of securities; refusal to issue or suspension or revocation of permits; grounds] or subdivision (a) of Section 25143 [Postponement or suspension of effectiveness of qualification; notice; hearing] is in effect with respect to that qualification.

(b) If a tender of shares or a vote or written consent is being sought pursuant to an Interested Party Proposal and a later tender offer or written proposal for a reorganization subject to Section 1200 or sale of assets subject to subdivision (a) of Section 1001 that would require a vote or written consent of shareholders is made to the corporation or its shareholders (herein referred to as a "Later Proposal") by any other person at least 10 days prior to the date for acceptance of the tendered shares or the vote or notice of shareholder approval on the Interested Party Proposal, then each of the following shall apply:

(1) The shareholders shall be informed of the Later Proposal and any written material provided for this purpose by the later offeror shall be forwarded to the shareholders at that offeror's expense.

(2) The shareholders shall be afforded a reasonable opportunity to withdraw any vote, consent, or proxy previously given before the vote or written consent on the Interested Party Proposal becomes effective, or a reasonable time to withdraw any tendered shares before the purchase of the shares pursuant to the Interested Party Proposal. For purposes of this subdivision, a delay of 10 days from the notice or publication of the Later Proposal shall be deemed to provide a reasonable opportunity or time to effect that withdrawal.

Chapter 13

DISSENTERS' RIGHTS

§ 1300. Reorganization or Short-Form Merger; Dissenting Shares; Corporate Purchase at Fair Market Value; Definitions

(a) If the approval of the outstanding shares (Section 152) of a corporation is required for a reorganization under subdivisions (a) and (b) or subdivision (e) or (f) of Section 1201, each shareholder of the corporation entitled to vote on the transaction and each shareholder of a subsidiary corporation in a short-form merger may, by complying with this chapter, require the corporation in which the shareholder holds shares to purchase for cash at their fair market value the shares owned by the shareholder which are dissenting shares as defined in subdivision (b). The fair market value shall be determined as of the day of, and immediately prior to, the first announcement of the terms of the proposed reorganization or short-form merger, excluding any appreciation or depreciation in consequence of the proposed reorganization or short-form merger, as adjusted for any stock split, reverse stock split or share dividend that becomes effective thereafter.

(b) As used in this chapter, "dissenting shares" means shares to which all of the following apply:

(1) That were not immediately prior to the reorganization or short-form merger listed on any national securities exchange certified by the Commissioner of Corporations under subdivision (*o*) of Section 25100, and the notice of meeting of shareholders to act upon the reorganization summarizes this section and Sections 1301, 1302, 1303 and 1304; provided, however, that this provision does not apply to any shares with respect to which there exists any restriction on transfer imposed by the corporation or by any law or regulation; and provided, further, that this provision does not apply to shares where the holder of those shares is required, by the terms of the reorganization or short-form merger, to accept for the shares anything except: (A) shares of any other corporation, which shares, at the time the reorganization or short-form merger is effective, are listed on any national securities exchange certified by the Commissioner of Corporations under subdivision (*o*) of Section 25100; (B) cash in lieu of fractional shares described in the foregoing subparagraph (A); or (C) any combination of the shares and cash in lieu of fractional shares described in the foregoing subparagraphs (A) and (B).

(2) That were outstanding on the date for the determination of shareholders entitled to vote on the reorganization and (A) were not voted in favor of the reorganization or, (B) if described in paragraph (1), were voted against the reorganization, or were held of record on the effective date of a short-form merger; provided, however, that subparagraph (A) rather than subparagraph (B) of this paragraph applies in any case where the approval required by Section 1201 is sought by written consent rather than at a meeting.

(3) That the dissenting shareholder has demanded that the corporation purchase at their fair market value, in accordance with Section 1301.

(4) That the dissenting shareholder has submitted for endorsement, in accordance with Section 1302.

(c) As used in this chapter, "dissenting shareholder" means the recordholder of dissenting shares and includes a transferee of record.

§ 1311. Exempt Shares

This chapter, except Section 1312, does not apply to classes of shares whose terms and provisions specifically set forth the amount to be paid in respect to such shares in the event of a reorganization or merger.

§ 1312. Right of Dissenting Shareholder to Attack, Set Aside or Rescind Merger or Reorganization; Restraining Order or Injunction; Conditions

(a) No shareholder of a corporation who has a right under this chapter to demand payment of cash for the shares held by the shareholder shall have any right at law or in equity to attack the validity of the reorganization or short-form merger, or to have the reorganization or short-form merger set aside or rescinded, except in an action to test whether the number of shares required to authorize or approve the reorganization have been legally voted in favor thereof; but any holder of shares of a class whose terms and provisions specifically set forth the amount to be paid in respect to them in the event of a reorganization or short-form merger is entitled to payment in accordance with those terms and provisions, or, if the principal terms of the reorganization are approved pursuant to subdivision (b) or Section 1202, is entitled to payment in accordance with the terms and provisions of the approved reorganization.

(b) If one of the parties to a reorganization or short-form merger is directly or indirectly controlled by, or under common control with, another party to the reorganization or short-form merger, subdivision (a) shall not apply to any shareholder of such party who has not demanded payment of cash for such shareholder's shares pursuant to this chapter; but if the shareholder institutes any action to attack the validity of the reorganization or short-form merger or to have the reorganization or short-form merger set aside or rescinded, the shareholder shall not thereafter have any right to demand payment of cash for the shareholder's shares pursuant to this chapter. The court in any action attacking the validity of the reorganization or short-form merger or to have the reorganization or short-form merger set aside or rescinded shall not restrain or enjoin the consummation of the transaction except upon 10 days' prior notice to the corporation and upon a determination by the court that clearly no other remedy will adequately protect the complaining shareholder or the class of shareholders of which such shareholder is a member.

(c) If one of the parties to a reorganization or short-form merger is directly or indirectly controlled by, or under common control with, another party to the reorganization or short-form merger, in any action to attack the validity of the reorganization or short-form merger or to have the reorganization or short-form merger set aside or rescinded, (1) a party to a reorganization or short-form merger which controls another party to the reorganization or short-form merger shall have the burden of proving that the transaction is just and reasonable as to the shareholders of the controlled party, and (2) a person who controls two or more parties to a reorganization shall have the burden of proving that the transaction is just and reasonable as to the shareholders of any party so controlled.

Chapter 15

RECORDS AND REPORTS

§ 1501. Annual Report; Time of Sending to Shareholders; Contents; Quarterly Financial Statements; Written Request; Inspection; Expenses in Actions

(a)(1) The board shall cause an annual report to be sent to the shareholders not later than 120 days after the close of the fiscal year, unless in the case of a corporation with less than 100 holders of record of its shares . . . this requirement is expressly waived in the bylaws. Unless otherwise provided by the articles or bylaws and if approved by the board of directors, that report and any accompanying material sent pursuant to this section may be sent by electronic transmission by the corporation (Section 20). This report shall contain a balance sheet as of the end of that fiscal year and an income statement and a statement of cash flows for that fiscal year, accompanied by any report thereon of independent accountants or, if there is no report, the certificate of an authorized officer of the corporation that the statements were prepared without audit from the books and records of the corporation.

(2) Unless so waived, the report specified in paragraph (1) shall be sent to the shareholders at least 15 (or, if sent by third-class mail, 35) days prior to the annual meeting of shareholders to be held during the next fiscal year, but this requirement shall not limit the requirement for holding an annual meeting as required by Section 600.

(3) Notwithstanding Section 114, the financial statements of any corporation with fewer than 100 holders of record of its shares . . . required to be furnished by this subdivision and subdivision (c) . . . are not required to be prepared in conformity with generally accepted accounting principles if they reasonably set forth the assets and liabilities and the income and expense of the corporation and disclose the accounting basis used in their preparation.

(4) The requirements described in paragraphs (1) and (2) shall be satisfied if a corporation with an outstanding class of securities registered under Section 12 of the Securities Exchange Act of 1934 complies with Section 240.14a–16 of Title 17 of the Code of Federal Regulations, as it may be amended from time to time, with respect to the obligation of a corporation to furnish an annual report to shareholders pursuant to Section 240.14a–3(b) of Title 17 of the Code of Federal Regulations.

(b) In addition to the financial statements required by subdivision (a), the annual report of any corporation having 100 or more holders of record of its shares . . . either not subject to the reporting requirements of Section 13 of the Securities Exchange Act of 1934, or exempted from those reporting requirements by Section 12(g)(2) of that act, shall also describe briefly both of the following:

(1) Any transaction (excluding compensation of officers and directors) during the previous fiscal year involving an amount in excess of forty thousand dollars ($40,000) (other than contracts let at competitive bid or services rendered at prices regulated by law) to which the corporation or its parent or subsidiary was a party and in which any director or officer of the corporation or of a subsidiary or (if known to the corporation or its parent or subsidiary) any holder of more than 10 percent of the outstanding voting shares of the corporation had a direct or indirect material interest, naming the person and stating the person's relationship to the corporation, the nature of the person's interest in the transaction and, where practicable, the amount of the interest; provided . . . that in the case of a transaction with a partnership of which the person is a partner, only the interest of the partnership need be stated; and provided . . . further that no report need be made in the case of any transaction approved by the shareholders (Section 153).

(2) The amount and circumstances of any indemnification or advances aggregating more than ten thousand dollars ($10,000) paid during the fiscal year to any officer or director of the corporation . . . ; provided . . . that no report need be made in the case of indemnification approved by the shareholders. . . .

(c) If no annual report for the last fiscal year has been sent to shareholders, the corporation shall, upon the written request of any shareholder made more than 120 days after the close of that fiscal year, deliver or mail to the person making the request within 30 days thereafter the financial statements required by subdivision (a) for that year. A shareholder or shareholders holding at least 5 percent of the outstanding shares of any class of a corporation may make a written request to the corporation for an income statement of the corporation for the three-month, six-month or nine-month period of the current fiscal year ended more than 30 days prior to the date of the request and a balance sheet of the corporation as of the end of the period and, in addition, if no annual report for the last fiscal year has been sent to shareholders, the statements referred to in subdivision (a) for the last fiscal year. The statements shall be delivered or mailed to the person making the request within 30 days thereafter. A copy of the statements shall be kept on file in the principal office of the corporation for 12 months and it shall be exhibited at all reasonable times to any shareholder demanding an examination of the statements or a copy shall be mailed to the shareholder.

(d) The quarterly income statements and balance sheets referred to in this section shall be accompanied by the report thereon, if any, of any independent accountants engaged by the corporation or the certificate of an authorized officer of the corporation that the financial statements were prepared without audit from the books and records of the corporation.

(e) In addition to the [financial] penalties provided for in Section 2200, the superior court of the proper county shall enforce the duty of making and mailing or delivering the information and financial statements required by this section and, for good cause shown, may extend the time therefor.

(f) In any action or proceeding under this section, if the court finds the failure of the corporation to comply with the requirements of this section to have been without justification, the court may award an amount sufficient to reimburse the shareholder for the reasonable expenses incurred by the shareholder, including attorney's fees, in connection with the action or proceeding.

(g) This section applies to any domestic corporation and also to a foreign corporation having its principal executive office in this state or customarily holding meetings of its board in this state.

§ 1502. Statement of Information; Timing and Contents of Filing; Additional Contents for Publicly Traded Companies; Agent for Service of Process; Updated Information; Public Inspection; Certification

(a) Every corporation shall file, within 90 days after the filing of its original articles and annually thereafter during the applicable filing period, on a form prescribed by the Secretary of State, a statement containing all of the following:

(1) The name of the corporation and the Secretary of State's file number.

(2) The names and complete business or residence addresses of its incumbent directors.

(3) The number of vacancies on the board, if any.

(4) The names and complete business or residence addresses of its chief executive officer, secretary, and chief financial officer.

(5) The street address of its principal executive office.

(6) The mailing address of the corporation, if different from the street address of its principal executive office.

(7) If the address of its principal executive office is not in this state, the street address of its principal business office in this state, if any.

(8) If the corporation chooses to receive renewal notices and any other notifications from the Secretary of State by electronic mail instead of by United States mail, the corporation shall include a valid electronic mail address for the corporation or for the corporation's designee to receive those notices.

(9) A statement of the general type of business that constitutes the principal business activity of the corporation (for example, manufacturer of aircraft; wholesale liquor distributor; or retail department store).

(b) The statement required by subdivision (a) shall also designate, as the agent of the corporation for the purpose of service of process, a natural person residing in this state or a corporation that has complied with Section 1505 and whose capacity to act as an agent has not terminated. If a natural person is designated, the statement shall set forth that person's complete business or residence street address. If a corporate agent is designated, no address for it shall be set forth.

(c) If there has been no change in the information in the last filed statement of the corporation on file in the Secretary of State's office, the corporation may, in lieu of filing the statement required by subdivisions (a) and (b), advise the Secretary of State, on a form prescribed by the Secretary of State, that no changes in the required information have occurred during the applicable filing period.

(d) For the purposes of this section, the applicable filing period for a corporation shall be the calendar month during which its original articles were filed and the immediately preceding five calendar months. The Secretary of State shall provide a notice to each corporation to comply with this section approximately three months prior to the close of the applicable filing period. The notice shall state the due date for compliance and shall be sent to the last address of the corporation according to the records of the Secretary of State or to the last electronic mail address according to the records of the Secretary of State if the corporation has elected to receive notices from the Secretary of State by electronic mail. The failure of the corporation to receive the notice is not an excuse for failure to comply with this section.

(e) Whenever any of the information required by subdivision (a) is changed, the corporation may file a current statement containing all the information required by subdivisions (a) and (b). In order to change its agent for service of process or the address of the agent, the corporation must file a current statement containing all the information required by subdivisions (a) and (b). Whenever any statement is filed pursuant to this section, it supersedes any previously filed statement and the statement in the articles as to the agent for service of process and the address of the agent.

(f) The Secretary of State may destroy or otherwise dispose of any statement filed pursuant to this section after it has been superseded by the filing of a new statement.

(g) This section shall not be construed to place any person dealing with the corporation on notice of, or under any duty to inquire about, the existence or content of a statement filed pursuant to this section.

(h) The statement required by subdivision (a) shall be available and open to the public for inspection. The Secretary of State shall provide access to all information contained in this statement by means of an online database.

(i) In addition to any other fees required, a corporation shall pay a five-dollar ($5) disclosure fee when filing the statement required by subdivision (a). One-half of the fee shall be utilized to further the provisions of this section, including the development and maintenance of the online database required by subdivision (h), and one-half shall be deposited into the Victims of Corporate Fraud Compensation Fund established in Section 2280.

(j) A corporation shall certify that the information it provides pursuant to subdivisions (a) and (b) is true and correct. No claim may be made against the state for inaccurate information contained in the statements.

§ 1502.1 Statement of Information Pertaining to Independent Auditors, Members of the Board of Directors, and Executive Officers; Definitions; Public Inspection; Certification

(a) In addition to the statement required pursuant to Section 1502, every publicly traded corporation shall file annually, within 150 days after the end of its fiscal year, a statement, on a form prescribed by the Secretary of State, that includes all of the following information:

(1) The name of the independent auditor that prepared the most recent auditor's report on the corporation's annual financial statements.

(2) A description of other services, if any, performed for the corporation during its two most recent fiscal years and the period between the end of its most recent fiscal year and the date of the statement by the foregoing independent auditor, by its parent corporation, or by a subsidiary or corporate affiliate of the independent auditor or its parent corporation.

(3) The name of the independent auditor employed by the corporation on the date of the statement, if different from the independent auditor listed pursuant to paragraph (1).

(4) The compensation for the most recent fiscal year of the corporation paid to each member of the board of directors and paid to each of the five most highly compensated executive officers of the corporation who are not members of the board of directors, including the number of any shares issued, options for shares granted, and similar equity-based compensation granted to each of those persons. If the chief executive officer is not among the five most highly compensated executive officers of the corporation, the compensation paid to the chief executive officer shall also be included.

(5) A description of any loan, including the amount and terms of the loan, made to any member of the board of directors by the corporation during the corporation's two most recent fiscal years at an interest rate lower than the interest rate available from unaffiliated commercial lenders generally to a similarly-situated borrower.

(6) A statement indicating whether an order for relief has been entered in a bankruptcy case with respect to the corporation, its executive officers, or members of the board of directors of the corporation during the 10 years preceding the date of the statement.

(7) A statement indicating whether any member of the board of directors or executive officer of the corporation was convicted of fraud during the 10 years preceding the date of the statement, if the conviction has not been overturned or expunged.

(8) A description of any material pending legal proceedings, other than ordinary routine litigation incidental to the business, to which the corporation or any of its subsidiaries is a party or of which any of their property is the subject, as specified by Item 103 of Regulation S–K of the Securities Exchange Commission (Section 229.103 of Title 12 of the Code of Federal Regulations). A description of any material legal proceeding during which the corporation was found legally liable by entry of a final judgment or final order that was not overturned on appeal during the five years preceding the date of the statement.

(b) For purposes of this section, the following definitions apply:

(1) "Publicly traded corporation" means a corporation, as defined in Section 162, that is an issuer as defined in Section 3 of the Securities Exchange Act of 1934, as amended (15 U.S.C. Sec. 78c), and has at least one class of securities listed or admitted for trading on a national securities exchange, on the OTC Bulletin Board, or on the electronic service operated by Pink OTC Markets, Inc.

(2) "Executive officer" means the chief executive officer, president, any vice president in charge of a principal business unit, division, or function, any other officer of the corporation who performs a policymaking function, or any other person who performs similar policymaking functions for the corporation.

(3) "Compensation" as used in paragraph (4) of subdivision (a) means all plan and nonplan compensation awarded to, earned by, or paid to the person for all services rendered in all capacities to the corporation and to its subsidiaries, as the compensation is specified by Item 402 of Regulation S–K of the Securities and Exchange Commission (Section 229.402 of Title 17 of the Code of Federal Regulations).

(4) "Loan" as used in paragraph (5) of subdivision (a) excludes an advance for expenses permitted under subdivision (d) of Section 315, the corporation's payment of life insurance premiums permitted under subdivision (e) of Section 315, and an advance of expenses permitted under Section 317.

(c) This statement shall be available and open to the public for inspection. The Secretary of State shall provide access to all information contained in this statement by means of an online database.

(d) A corporation shall certify that the information it provides pursuant to this section is true and correct. No claim may be made against the state for inaccurate information contained in statements filed under this section with the Secretary of State.

Chapter 16

RIGHTS OF INSPECTION

§ 1600. List of Shareholders' Names, Addresses and Shareholdings; Time for Compliance After Demand; Delay; Postponement of Shareholders' Meeting; Inspection and Copying

(a) A shareholder or shareholders holding at least 5 percent in the aggregate of the outstanding voting shares of a corporation or who hold at least 1 percent of those voting shares and have filed a Schedule 14A with the United States Securities and Exchange Commission . . . shall have an absolute right to do either or both of the following: (1) inspect and copy the record of shareholders' names and addresses and shareholdings during usual business hours upon five business days' prior written demand upon the corporation, or (2) obtain from the transfer agent for the corporation, upon written demand and upon the tender of its usual charges for such a list (the amount of which charges shall be stated to the shareholder by the transfer agent upon request), a list of the shareholders' names and addresses, who are entitled to vote for the election of directors, and their shareholdings, as of the most recent record date for which it has been compiled or as of a date specified by the shareholder subsequent to the date of demand. The list shall be made available on or before the later of five business days after the demand is received or the date specified therein as the date as of which the list is to be compiled. A corporation shall have the responsibility to cause its transfer agent to comply with this subdivision.

(b) Any delay by the corporation or the transfer agent in complying with a demand under subdivision (a) beyond the time limits specified therein shall give the shareholder or shareholders properly making the demand a right to obtain from the superior court, upon the filing of a verified complaint in the proper county and after a hearing, notice of which shall be given to such persons and in such manner as the court may direct, an order postponing any shareholders' meeting previously noticed for a period equal to the period of such delay. Such right shall be in addition to any other legal or equitable remedies to which the shareholder may be entitled.

(c) The record of shareholders shall also be open to inspection and copying by any shareholder or holder of a voting trust certificate at any time during usual business hours upon written demand on the corporation, for a purpose reasonably related to such holder's interests as a shareholder or holder of a voting trust certificate.

(d) Any inspection and copying under this section may be made in person or by agent or attorney. The rights provided in this section may not be limited by the articles or bylaws. This section applies to any domestic corporation and to any foreign corporation having its principal executive office in this state or customarily holding meetings of its board in this state.

§ 1601. Accounting Books and Records and Minutes of Meetings; Inspection upon Demand by Shareholder or Holder of Voting Trust Certificate; Nature of Right

(a)(1) The accounting books, records, and minutes of proceedings of the shareholders and the board and committees of the board of any domestic corporation, and of any foreign corporation keeping any records in this state or having its principal executive office in this state, or a true and accurate copy thereof if the original has been lost, destroyed, or is not normally physically located within this state shall be open to inspection at the corporation's principal office in this state, or if none, at the physical location for the corporation's registered agent for service of process in this state, upon the written demand on the corporation of any shareholder or holder of a voting trust certificate at any reasonable time during usual business hours, for a purpose reasonably related to the holder's interests as a shareholder or as the holder of a voting trust certificate.

(2) As an alternative to the procedure in subdivision (a), the shareholder or holder of a voting trust certificate may elect to request that the corporation produce the books, records, and minutes by mail or electronically, if the shareholder or holder of a voting trust certificate pays for the reasonable costs for copying or converting the requested documents to electronic format.

(3) The right of inspection created by this subdivision shall extend to the records of each subsidiary of a corporation subject to this subdivision.

(b) The inspection by a shareholder or holder of a voting trust certificate may be made in person or by agent or attorney, and the right of inspection includes the right to copy and make extracts. The right of the shareholders to inspect the corporate records may not be limited by the articles or bylaws.

§ 1602. Directors

Every director shall have the absolute right at any reasonable time to inspect and copy all books, records and documents of every kind and to inspect the physical properties of the corporation of which such person is a director and also of its subsidiary corporations, domestic or foreign. Such inspection by a director may be made in person or by agent or attorney and the right of inspection includes the right to copy and make extracts. This section applies to a director of any foreign corporation having its principal executive office in this state or customarily holding meetings of its board in this state.

§ 1603. Action to Enforce Right; Appointment of Inspector or Accountant; Report; Penalty for Failure to Produce Records; Expenses of Suit

(a) Upon refusal of a lawful demand for inspection, the superior court of the proper county, may enforce the right of inspection with just and proper conditions or may, for good cause shown, appoint one or more competent inspectors or accountants to audit the books and records kept in this state and investigate the property, funds and affairs of any domestic corporation or any foreign corporation keeping records in this state and of any subsidiary corporation thereof, domestic or foreign, keeping records in this state and to report thereon in such manner as the court may direct.

(b) All officers and agents of the corporation shall produce to the inspectors or accountants so appointed all books and documents in their custody or power, under penalty of punishment for contempt of court.

(c) All expenses of the investigation or audit shall be defrayed by the applicant unless the court orders them to be paid or shared by the corporation.

Chapter 18

INVOLUNTARY DISSOLUTION

§ 1800. Verified Complaint; Plaintiffs; Grounds; Intervention by Shareholder or Creditor; Exempt Corporations

(a) A verified complaint for involuntary dissolution of a corporation on any one or more of the grounds specified in subdivision (b) may be filed in the superior court of the proper county by any of the following persons:

(1) One-half or more of the directors in office.

(2) A shareholder or shareholders who hold shares representing not less than 33⅓ percent of (i) the total number of outstanding shares (assuming conversion of any preferred shares convertible into common shares) or (ii) the outstanding common shares or (iii) the equity of the corporation, exclusive in each case of shares owned by persons who have personally participated in any of the transactions enumerated in paragraph (4) of subdivision (b), or any shareholder or shareholders of a close corporation.

(3) Any shareholder if the ground for dissolution is that the period for which the corporation was formed has terminated without extension thereof.

(4) Any other person expressly authorized to do so in the articles.

(b) The grounds for involuntary dissolution are that:

(1) The corporation has abandoned its business for more than one year.

(2) The corporation has an even number of directors who are equally divided and cannot agree as to the management of its affairs, so that its business can no longer be conducted to advantage or so that there

is danger that its property and business will be impaired or lost, and the holders of the voting shares of the corporation are so divided into factions that they cannot elect a board consisting of an uneven number.

(3) There is internal dissension and two or more factions of shareholders in the corporation are so deadlocked that its business can no longer be conducted with advantage to its shareholders or the shareholders have failed at two consecutive annual meetings at which all voting power was exercised, to elect successors to directors whose terms have expired or would have expired upon election of their successors.

(4) Those in control of the corporation have been guilty of or have knowingly countenanced persistent and pervasive fraud, mismanagement or abuse of authority or persistent unfairness toward any shareholders or its property is being misapplied or wasted by its directors or officers.

(5) In the case of any corporation with 35 or fewer shareholders (determined as provided in Section 605), liquidation is reasonably necessary for the protection of the rights or interests of the complaining shareholder or shareholders.

(6) The period for which the corporation was formed has terminated without extension of such period.

(c) At any time prior to the trial of the action any shareholder or creditor may intervene therein.

(d) This section does not apply to any corporation subject to the Banking Law . . . , the Public Utilities Act . . . , [or] the Savings and Loan Association Law. . . .

(e) For the purposes of this section, "shareholder" includes a beneficial owner of shares who has entered into an agreement under Section 300 or 706.

§ 1802. Provisional Director; Appointment; Deadlocked Board

If the ground for the complaint for involuntary dissolution of the corporation is a deadlock in the board as set forth in subdivision (b)(2) of Section 1800, the court may appoint a provisional director. The provisions of subdivision (c) of Section 308 apply to any such provisional director so appointed.

§ 1804. Decree for Winding Up and Dissolution; Other Judicial Relief

After hearing the court may decree a winding up and dissolution of the corporation if cause therefor is shown or, with or without winding up and dissolution, may make such orders and decrees and issue such injunctions in the case as justice and equity require.

Chapter 19

VOLUNTARY DISSOLUTION

§ 1900. Election by Shareholders; Required Vote; Election by Board; Grounds

(a) Any corporation may elect voluntarily to wind up and dissolve by the vote of shareholders holding shares representing 50 percent or more of the voting power.

(b) Any corporation which comes within one of the following descriptions may elect by approval by the board to wind up and dissolve:

(1) A corporation . . . as to which an order for relief has been entered under Chapter 7 of the federal bankruptcy law.

(2) A corporation which has disposed of all its assets and has not conducted any business for a period of five years immediately preceding the adoption of the resolution electing to dissolve the corporation.

(3) A corporation which has issued no shares.

Chapter 20

GENERAL PROVISIONS RELATING TO DISSOLUTION

§ 2000.   Avoidance of Dissolution by Purchase of Plaintiffs' Shares; Valuation; Vote Required; Stay of Dissolution Proceedings; Appraisal Under Court Order; Confirmation by Court; Appeal

(a) Subject to any contrary provision in the articles, which may include a reference to a separate written agreement between two or more shareholders pertaining to the purchase of shares:

In any suit for involuntary dissolution, or in any proceeding for voluntary dissolution initiated by the vote of shareholders representing only 50 percent of the voting power, the corporation or, if it does not elect to purchase, the holders of 50 percent or more of the voting power of the corporation (the "purchasing parties") may avoid the dissolution of the corporation and the appointment of any receiver by purchasing for cash the shares owned by the plaintiffs or by the shareholders so initiating the proceeding (the "moving parties") at their fair value.

The fair value shall be determined on the basis of the liquidation value as of the valuation date but taking into account the possibility, if any, of sale of the entire business as a going concern in a liquidation. In fixing the value, the amount of any damages resulting if the initiation of the dissolution is a breach by any moving party or parties of an agreement with the purchasing party or parties may be deducted from the amount payable to the moving party or parties, unless the ground for dissolution is that specified in paragraph (4) of subdivision (b) of Section 1800. The election of the corporation to purchase may be made by the approval of the outstanding shares (Section 152) excluding shares held by the moving parties.

(b) If the purchasing parties (1) elect to purchase the shares owned by the moving parties, and (2) are unable to agree with the moving parties upon the fair value of those shares, and (3) give bond with sufficient security to pay the estimated reasonable expenses (including attorneys' fees) of the moving parties if those expenses are recoverable under subdivision (c), the court upon application of the purchasing parties, either in the pending action or in a proceeding initiated in the superior court of the proper county by the purchasing parties in the case of a voluntary election to wind up and dissolve, shall stay the winding up and dissolution proceeding and shall proceed to ascertain and fix the fair value of the shares owned by the moving parties.

(c) The court shall appoint three disinterested appraisers to appraise the fair value of the shares owned by the moving parties, and shall make an order referring the matter to the appraisers so appointed for the purpose of ascertaining the value. The order shall prescribe the time and manner of producing evidence, if evidence is required. The award of the appraisers or of a majority of them, when confirmed by the court, shall be final and conclusive upon all parties. The court shall enter a decree which shall provide in the alternative for winding up and dissolution of the corporation unless payment is made for the shares within the time specified by the decree. If the purchasing parties do not make payment for the shares within the time specified, judgment shall be entered against them and the surety or sureties on the bond for the amount of the expenses (including attorneys' fees) of the moving parties. Any shareholder aggrieved by the action of the court may appeal the court's decision.

(d) If the purchasing parties desire to prevent the winding up and dissolution, they shall pay to the moving parties the value of their shares ascertained and decreed within the time specified pursuant to this section, or, in case of an appeal, as fixed on appeal. On receiving such payment or the tender thereof, the moving parties shall transfer their shares to the purchasing parties.

(e) For the purposes of this section, "shareholder" includes a beneficial owner of shares who has entered into an agreement under Section 300 or 706.

(f) For the purposes of this section, the valuation date shall be (1) in the case of a suit for involuntary dissolution under Section 1800, the date upon which that action was commenced, or (2) in the case of a proceeding for voluntary dissolution initiated by the vote of shareholders representing only 50 percent of the voting power, the date upon which that proceeding was initiated. However, in either case the court may, upon the hearing of a motion by any party, and for good cause shown, designate some other date as the valuation date.

Chapter 21

FOREIGN CORPORATIONS

§ 2115. Foreign Corporations Subject to Corporate Laws of State; Tests to Determine Subject Corporations; Laws Applicable; Time of Application

(a) A foreign corporation (other than a foreign association or foreign nonprofit corporation but including a foreign parent corporation even though it does not itself transact intrastate business) is subject to the requirements of subdivision (b) commencing on the date specified in subdivision (d) and continuing until the date specified in subdivision (e) if:

(1) The average of the property factor, the payroll factor and the sales factor (as defined in Sections 25129, 25132 and 25134 of the Revenue and Taxation Code) with respect to it is more than 50 percent during its latest full income year and

(2) more than one-half of its outstanding voting securities are held of record by persons having addresses in this state appearing on the books of the corporation on the record date for the latest meeting of shareholders held during its latest full income year or, if no meeting was held during that year, on the last day of the latest full income year. The property factor, payroll factor and sales factor shall be those used in computing the portion of its income allocable to this state in its franchise tax return or, with respect to corporations the allocation of whose income is governed by special formulas or that are not required to file separate or any tax returns, which would have been so used if they were governed by this three-factor formula. The determination of these factors with respect to any parent corporation shall be made on a consolidated basis, including in a unitary computation (after elimination of intercompany transactions) the property, payroll and sales of the parent and all of its subsidiaries in which it owns directly or indirectly more than 50 percent of the outstanding shares entitled to vote for the election of directors, but deducting a percentage of the property, payroll and sales of any subsidiary equal to the percentage minority ownership, if any, in the subsidiary. For the purpose of this subdivision, any securities held to the knowledge of the issuer in the names of broker-dealers, nominees for broker-dealers (including clearing corporations), or banks, associations, or other entities holding securities in a nominee name or otherwise on behalf of a beneficial owner (collectively "nominee holders"), shall not be considered outstanding. However, if the foreign corporation requests all nominee holders to certify, with respect to all beneficial owners for whom securities are held, the number of shares held for those beneficial owners having addresses (as shown on the records of the nominee holder) in this state and outside of this state, then all shares so certified shall be considered outstanding and held of record by persons having addresses either in this state or outside of this state as so certified, provided that the certification so provided shall be retained with the record of shareholders and made available for inspection and copying in the same manner as provided in Section 1600 with respect to that record. A current list of beneficial owners of a foreign corporation's securities provided to the corporation by one or more Nominee Holders or their agent pursuant to the requirements of Rule 14b–1(b)(3) or 14b–2(b)(3) as adopted on January 6, 1992, promulgated under the Securities Exchange Act of 1934 shall constitute an acceptable certification with respect to beneficial owners for the purposes of this subdivision.

(b) Except as provided in subdivision (c), the following chapters and sections of this division shall apply to a foreign corporation as defined in subdivision (a) (to the exclusion of the law of the jurisdiction in which it is incorporated):

Chapter 1 (general provisions and definitions), to the extent applicable to the following provisions;

Section 301 (annual election of directors);

Section 303 (removal of directors without cause);

Section 304 (removal of directors by court proceedings);

Section 305, subdivision (c) (filing of director vacancies where less than a majority in office elected by shareholders);

Section 309 (directors' standard of care);

Section 310 (super-majority requirement);

Section 316 (excluding paragraph (3) of subdivision (a) and paragraph (3) of subdivision (f)) (liability of directors for unlawful distributions);

Section 317 (indemnification of directors, officers and others);

Sections 500 to 505, inclusive (limitations on corporate distributions in cash or property);

Section 506 (liability of shareholder who receives unlawful distribution);

Section 600, subdivisions (b) and (c) (requirement for annual shareholders' meeting and remedy if same not timely held);

Section 708, subdivisions (a), (b) and (c) (shareholder's right to cumulate votes at any election of directors);

Section 710 (supermajority vote requirement);

Section 1001, subdivision (d) (limitations on sale of assets);

Section 1101 (provisions following subdivision (e)) (limitations on mergers); . . .

Chapter 12 (commencing with Section 1200) (reorganizations);

Chapter 13 (commencing with Section 1300) (dissenters' rights);

Sections 1500 and 1501 (records and reports);

Section 1508 (action by Attorney General);

Chapter 16 (commencing with Section 1600) (rights of inspection).

(c) This section does not apply to any corporation (1) with outstanding securities listed on the New York Stock Exchange, the NYSE Amex, the NASDAQ Global Market, or the NASDAQ Capital Market, or (2) if all of its voting shares (other than directors' qualifying shares) are owned directly or indirectly by a corporation or corporations not subject to this section.

(d) For purposes of subdivision (a), the requirements of subdivision (b) shall become applicable to a foreign corporation only upon the first day of the first income year of the corporation (1) commencing on or after the 135th day of the income year immediately following the latest income year with respect to which the tests referred to in subdivision (a) have been met or (2) commencing on or after the entry of a final order by a court of competent jurisdiction declaring that those tests have been met.

(e) For purposes of subdivision (a), the requirements of subdivision (b) shall cease to be applicable to a foreign corporation (1) at the end of the first income year of the corporation immediately following the latest income year with respect to which at least one of the tests referred to in subdivision (a) is not met or (2) at the end of the income year of the corporation during which a final order has been entered by a court of competent jurisdiction declaring that one of those tests is not met, provided that a contrary order has not been entered before the end of the income year.

(f) Any foreign corporation that is subject to the requirements of subdivision (b) shall advise any shareholder of record, any officer, director, employee, or other agent . . . and any creditor of the corporation in writing, within 30 days of receipt of written request for that information, whether or not it is subject to subdivision (b) at the time the request is received. [If any party] obtains a final determination by a court of competent jurisdiction that the corporation failed to provide to the party information required to be provided by this subdivision or provided the party information of the kind required to be provided by this subdivision that was incorrect, then the court, in its discretion, shall have the power to include in its judgment recovery by the party from the corporation of all courts costs and reasonable attorneys' fees incurred in that legal proceeding to the extent they relate to obtaining that final determination.

§ 2117. Statement of Information; Timing and Contents of Filing; Additional Contents for Publicly Traded Companies; Agent for Service of Process; Public Inspection; Notice of Change of Information

(a) Every foreign corporation (other than a foreign association) qualified to transact intrastate business shall file, within 90 days after the filing of its original statement and designation of foreign corporation and annually thereafter during the applicable filing period, on a form prescribed by the Secretary of State, a statement containing the following:

(1) The name of the corporation. . . .

(2) The names and complete business or residence addresses of its chief executive officer, secretary, and chief financial officer.

(3) The street address of its principal executive office.

(4) The mailing address of the corporation, if different from the street address of its principal executive office.

(5) The street address of its principal business office in this state, if any.

(6) If the corporation chooses to receive renewal notices and any other notification from the Secretary of State by electronic mail instead of by United States mail, the corporation shall include a valid electronic email address for the corporation or for the corporation's designee to receive that notice.

(7) A statement of the general type of business that constitutes the principal business activity of the corporation (for example, manufacturer of aircraft; wholesale liquor distributor; or retail department store). . . .

(b) The statement required by subdivision (a) shall also designate, as the agent of the corporation for the purpose of service of process, a natural person residing in this state or a corporation that has complied with Section 1505 and whose capacity to act as the agent has not terminated. If a natural person is designated, the statement shall set forth the person's complete business or residence street address. If a corporate agent is designated, no address for it shall be set forth.

(c) The statement required by subdivision (a) shall be available and open to the public for inspection. The Secretary of State shall provide access to all information contained in the statement by means of an online database. . . .

§ 2117.1 Statement of Information Pertaining to Independent Auditors, Members of the Board of Directors, and Executive Officers; Definitions; Public Inspection; Certification

(a) In addition to the statement required pursuant to Section 2117, every publicly traded foreign corporation shall file annually, within 150 days after the end of its fiscal year, on a form prescribed by the Secretary of State, a statement that includes all of the following information:

(1) The name of the independent auditor that prepared the most recent auditor's report on the publicly traded foreign corporation's annual financial statements.

(2) A description of other services, if any, performed for the publicly traded foreign corporation during its two most recent fiscal years and the period between the end of its most recent fiscal year and the date of the statement by the foregoing independent auditor, by its parent corporation, or by a subsidiary or corporate affiliate of the independent auditor or its parent corporation.

(3) The name of the independent auditor employed by the foreign corporation on the date of the statement, if different from the independent auditor listed pursuant to paragraph (1).

(4) The compensation for the most recent fiscal year of the publicly traded foreign corporation paid to each member of the board of directors and paid to each of the five most highly compensated executive officers of the foreign corporation who are not members of the board of directors, including the number of any shares issued, options for shares granted, and similar equity-based compensation granted to each of those persons. If the chief executive officer is not among the five most highly compensated executive officers of the corporation, the compensation paid to the chief executive officer shall also be included.

(5) A description of any loan, including the amount and terms of the loans, made to any member of the board of directors by the publicly traded foreign corporation during the foreign corporation's two most recent fiscal years at an interest rate lower than the interest rate available from unaffiliated commercial lenders generally to a similarly situated borrower.

(6) A statement indicating whether an order for relief has been entered in a bankruptcy case with respect to the foreign corporation, its executive officers, or members of the board of directors of the foreign corporation during the 10 years preceding the date of the statement.

(7) A statement indicating whether any member of the board of directors or executive officer of the publicly traded foreign corporation was convicted of fraud during the 10 years preceding the date of the statement, which conviction has not been overturned or expunged.

(8) A description of any material pending legal proceedings, other than ordinary routine litigation incidental to the business, to which the corporation or any of its subsidiaries is a party or of which any of their property is the subject, as specified by Item 103 of Regulation S–K of the Securities Exchange Commission (Section 229.103 of Title 12 of the Code of Federal Regulations). A description of any material legal proceeding during which the corporation was found legally liable by entry of a final judgment or final order that was not overturned on appeal during the five years preceding the date of the statement.

(b) For purposes of this section, the following definitions apply:

(1) "Publicly traded foreign corporation" means a foreign corporation, as defined in Section 171, that is an issuer as defined in Section 3 of the Securities Exchange Act of 1934, as amended (15 U.S.C. Sec. 78c), and has at least one class of securities listed or admitted for trading on the OTC-Bulletin Board, or on the electronic service operated by Pink OTC Markets Inc.

(2) "Executive officer" means the chief executive officer, president, any vice president in charge of a principal business unit, division, or function, any other officer of the corporation who performs a policymaking function, or any other person who performs similar policymaking functions for the corporation.

(3) "Compensation" as used in paragraph (4) of subdivision (a) means all plan and nonplan compensation awarded to, earned by, or paid to the person for all services rendered in all capacities to the corporation and to its subsidiaries, as the compensation is specified by Item 402 of Regulation S–K of the Securities and Exchange Commission (Section 229.402 of Title 17 of the Code of Federal Regulations).

(4) "Loan" as used in paragraph (5) of subdivision (a) excludes an advance for expenses, the foreign corporation's payment of life insurance premiums, and an advance of litigation expenses, in each instance as permitted according to the applicable law of the state or place of incorporation or organization of the foreign corporation.

(c) This statement shall be available and open to the public for inspection. The Secretary of State shall provide access to all information contained in this statement by means of an online database.

(d) A foreign corporation shall certify that the information it provides pursuant to this section is true and correct. No claim may be made against the state for inaccurate information contained in statements filed under this section with the Secretary of State.

Chapter 22

CRIMES AND PENALTIES

§ 2200. Neglect, Failure or Refusal to Keep Record of Shareholders or Books of Account or Prepare or Submit Financial Statements; Penalty; Payment to Shareholder

Every corporation that neglects, fails, or refuses: (a) to keep or cause to be kept or maintained the record of shareholders or books of account required by this division to be kept or maintained, (b) to prepare or cause to be prepared or submitted the financial statements required by this division to be prepared or submitted, or (c) to give any shareholder of record the advice required by subdivision (f) of Section 2215, is subject to penalty as provided in this section.

The penalty shall be twenty-five dollars ($25) for each day that the failure or refusal continues, up to a maximum of one thousand five hundred dollars ($1,500), beginning 30 days after the receipt of the written request that the duty be performed from one entitled to make the request, except that, in the case of a failure to give advice required by subdivision (f) of Section 2115, the 30-day period shall run from the date of receipt of the request made pursuant to subdivision (f) of Section 2115, and no additional request is required by this section.

The penalty shall be paid to the shareholder or shareholders jointly making the request for performance of the duty, and damaged by the neglect, failure, or refusal, if suit therefor is commenced within 90 days after the written request is made, including any request made pursuant to subdivision (f) of Section 2115; but the maximum daily penalty because of failure to comply with any number of separate requests made on any one day or for the same act shall be two hundred fifty dollars ($250).

§ 2207. Liability of Corporation for Civil Penalty for Failure to Notify Attorney General or Appropriate Government Agency and Shareholders or Investors With Respect to Knowledge of Certain Enumerated Acts

(a) A corporation is liable for a civil penalty in an amount not exceeding one million dollars ($1,000,000) if the corporation does both of the following:

(1) Has actual knowledge that an officer, director, manager, or agent of the corporation does any of the following:

(A) Makes, publishes, or posts, or has made, published, or posted either generally or privately to the shareholders or other persons either of the following:

(i) An oral, written, or electronically transmitted report, exhibit, notice, or statement of its affairs or pecuniary condition that includes a material statement or omission that is false and intended to give the shares of stock in the corporation a materially greater or a materially less apparent market value than they really possess.

(ii) An oral, written, or electronically transmitted report, prospectus, account, or statement of operations, values, business, profits, or expenditures, that includes a material false statement or omission intended to give the shares of stock in the corporation a materially greater or a materially less apparent market value than they really possess.

(B) Refuses or has refused to make any book entry or post any notice required by law in the manner required by law.

(C) Misstates or conceals or has misstated or concealed from a regulatory body a material fact in order to deceive a regulatory body to avoid a statutory or regulatory duty, or to avoid a statutory or regulatory limit or prohibition.

(2) Within 30 days after actual knowledge is acquired of the actions described in paragraph (1), the corporation knowingly fails to do both of the following:

(A) Notify the Attorney General or appropriate government agency in writing, unless the corporation has actual knowledge that the Attorney General or appropriate government agency has been notified.

(B) Notify its shareholders in writing, unless the corporation has actual knowledge that the shareholders have been notified.

(b) The requirement for notification under this section does not apply if the action taken or about to be taken by the corporation, or by an officer, director, manager, or agent of the corporation under paragraph (1) of subdivision (a) is abated within the time prescribed for reporting, unless the appropriate government agency requires disclosure by regulation.

(c) If the action reported to the Attorney General pursuant to this section implicates the government authority of an agency other than the Attorney General, the Attorney General shall promptly forward the written notice to that agency.

(d) If the Attorney General was not notified pursuant to subparagraph (A) of paragraph (2) of subdivision (a), but the corporation reasonably and in good faith believed that it had complied with the notification requirements of this section by notifying a government agency listed in paragraph (4) of subdivision (e), no penalties shall apply.

(e) For purposes of this section:

(1) "Manager" means a person having both of the following:

(A) Management authority over a business entity.

(B) Significant responsibility for an aspect of a business that includes actual authority for the financial operations or financial transactions of the business.

(2) "Agent" means a person or entity authorized by the corporation to make representations to the public about the corporation's financial condition and who is acting within the scope of the agency when the representations are made.

(3) "Shareholder" means a person or entity that is a shareholder of the corporation at the time the disclosure is required pursuant to subparagraph (B) of paragraph (2) of subdivision (a).

(4) "Notify its shareholders" means to give sufficient description of an action taken or about to be taken that would constitute acts or omissions as described in paragraph (1) of subdivision (a). A notice or report filed by a corporation with the United States Securities and Exchange Commission that relates to the facts and circumstances giving rise to an obligation under paragraph (1) of subdivision (a) shall satisfy all notice requirements arising under paragraph (2) of subdivision (a), but is not the exclusive means of satisfying the notice requirements, if the Attorney General or appropriate agency is informed in writing that the filing has been made together with a copy of the filing or an electronic link where it is available online without charge.

(5) "Appropriate government agency" means an agency on the following list that has regulatory authority with respect to the financial operations of a corporation:

(A) Department of Business Oversight.

(B) Department of Insurance.

(C) Department of Financial Institutions.

(D) Department of Managed Health Care.

(E) United States Securities and Exchange Commission.

(6) "Actual knowledge of the corporation" means the knowledge an officer or director of a corporation actually possesses or does not consciously avoid possessing, based on an evaluation of information provided pursuant to the corporation's disclosure controls and procedures.

(7) "Refuse to make a book entry" means the intentional decision not to record an accounting transaction when all of the following conditions are satisfied:

(A) The independent auditors required recordation of an accounting transaction during the course of an audit.

(B) The corporation's audit committee has not approved the independent auditor's recommendation.

(C) The decision is made for the primary purpose of rendering the financial statements materially false or misleading.

(8) "Refuse to post any notice required by law" means an intentional decision not to post a notice required by law when all of the following conditions exist:

(A) The decision not to post the notice has not been approved by the corporation's audit committee.

(B) The decision is intended to give the shares of stock in the corporation a materially greater or a materially less apparent market value than they really possess.

(9) "Misstate or conceal material facts from a regulatory body" means an intentional decision not to disclose material facts when all of the following conditions exist:

(A) The decision not to disclose material facts has not been approved by the corporation's audit committee.

(B) The decision is intended to give the shares of stock in the corporation a materially greater or a materially less apparent market value than they really possess.

(10) "Material false statement or omission" means an untrue statement of material fact or an omission to state a material fact necessary in order to make the statements made under the circumstances under which they were made not misleading.

(11) "Officer" means any person as set forth in Rule 16a–1 promulgated under the Securities Exchange Act of 1934 or any successor regulation thereto, except an officer of a subsidiary corporation who is not also an officer of the parent corporation.

(f) This section only applies to corporations that are issuers, as defined in Section 2 of the Sarbanes-Oxley Act of 2002 (15 U.S.C. Sec. 7201 et. seq.).

(g) An action to enforce this section may only be brought by the Attorney General or a district attorney or city attorney in the name of the people of the state.

Division 15

SOCIAL PURPOSE CORPORATIONS ACT

§ 2501. Application of Provisions of Division 1

Except as otherwise expressly stated, the provisions of Division 1 (commencing with Section 100) shall apply to corporations organized under this division, and references in that division to the terms "close corporation," "constituent corporation," "corporation," "disappearing corporation," "domestic corporation," "foreign corporation," "surviving corporation," and similar terms shall be read to apply, in the same manner, to include the similar "social purpose corporation."

§ 2502. Application of Division

This division applies only to social purpose corporations organized expressly under this division whether organized or existing under this division or amended, merged or converted into a social purpose corporation in accordance with Chapter 9 (commencing with Section 900) of Division 1, Chapter 11 (commencing with Section 1100) of Division 1 or Chapter 11.5 (commencing with Section 1150) of Division 1, including all flexible purpose corporations formed under this division prior to January 1, 2015, and now existing except as provided in paragraph (2) of subdivision (b) of Section 2601 and paragraph (3) of subdivision (b) of Section 2602.

§ 2602. Contents of Articles of Incorporation

The articles of incorporation shall set forth:

(a) The name of the social purpose corporation that shall contain the words "social purpose corporation" or an abbreviation of those words.

(b)(1) Either of the following statements, as applicable:

(A) "The purpose of this social purpose corporation is to engage in any lawful act or activity for which a social purpose corporation may be organized under Division 1.5 of the California Corporations Code, other than the banking business, the trust company business or the practice of a profession permitted to be incorporated by the California Corporations Code, for the benefit of the overall interests of the social purpose corporation and its shareholders and in furtherance of the following enumerated purposes _____."

(B) "The purpose of this social purpose corporation is to engage in the profession of _____ (with the insertion of a profession permitted to be incorporated by the California Corporations Code) and any other lawful activities, other than the banking or trust company business, not prohibited to a social purpose corporation engaging in that profession by applicable laws and regulations, for the benefit of the overall interests of the social purpose corporation and its shareholders and in furtherance of the following enumerated purposes _____."

(2) A statement that a purpose of the social purpose corporation, in addition to the purpose stated pursuant to paragraph (1), is to engage in one or more of the following enumerated purposes, as also specified in the statement set forth pursuant to paragraph (1):

(A) One or more charitable or public purpose activities that a nonprofit public benefit corporation is authorized to carry out.

(B) The purpose of promoting positive effects of, or minimizing adverse effects of, the social purpose corporation's activities upon any of the following, provided that the corporation consider the purpose in addition to or together with the financial interests of the shareholders and compliance with legal obligations, and take action consistent with that purpose:

(i) The social purpose corporation's employees, suppliers, customers, and creditors.

(ii) The community and society.

(iii) The environment.

(3)(A) For any corporation organized under this division before January 1, 2015, that has not elected to change its status to a social purpose corporation, a statement that the corporation is organized as a flexible purpose corporation under the Corporate Flexibility Act of 2011. Such a corporation is not required to revise the statements required in paragraphs (1) and (2) to conform to the changes made by the act adding this subparagraph.

(B) For any corporation organized under this division on and after January 1, 2015, or that has elected to change its status to a social purpose corporation pursuant to paragraph (2) of subdivision (b) of Section 2601, a statement that the corporation is organized as a social purpose corporation under the Social Purpose Corporations Act. . . .

(7) If the social purpose corporation is a close social purpose corporation, a statement as required by subdivision (a) of Section 158.

(c) The name and street address in this state of the social purpose corporation's initial agent for service of process in accordance with subdivision (b) of Section 1502.

(d) The initial street address of the corporation.

(e) The initial mailing address of the corporation, if different from the initial street address.

(f) If the social purpose corporation is authorized to issue only one class of shares, the total number of shares that the social purpose corporation is authorized to issue.

(g) If the social purpose corporation is authorized to issue more than one class of shares, or if any class of shares is to have two or more series, the articles shall state:

(1) The total number of shares of each class that the social purpose corporation is authorized to issue and the total number of shares of each series that the social purpose corporation is authorized to issue or that the board is authorized to fix the number of shares of any such series.

(2) The designation of each class and the designation of each series or that the board may determine the designation of any such series.

(3) The rights, preferences, privileges, and restrictions granted to or imposed upon the respective classes or series of shares or the holders thereof, or that the board, within any limits and restrictions stated, may determine or alter the rights, preferences, privileges, and restrictions granted to or imposed upon any wholly unissued class of shares or any wholly unissued series of any class of shares. As to any series the number of shares of which is authorized to be fixed by the board, the articles may also authorize the board, within the limits and restrictions stated in the article or in any resolution or resolutions of the board originally fixing the number of shares constituting any series, to increase or decrease, but not below the number of shares of such series then outstanding, the number of shares of any series subsequent to the issue of shares of that series. If the number of shares of any series shall be so decreased, the shares constituting that decrease shall resume the status which they had prior to the adoption of the resolution originally fixing the number of shares of that series.

§ 2604. Authorized Business Activities

Subject to any limitation contained in the articles, to compliance with any other applicable laws, and to consistency with the special purpose of the social purpose corporation, any social purpose corporation other than a social purpose corporation subject to the Banking Law or a professional social purpose corporation may engage in any business activity. . . .

§ 2800. Certification Requirements

(a) All certificates representing shares of a social purpose corporation shall contain, in addition to any other statements required by this section, the following conspicuous language on the face of the certificate:

"This entity is a social purpose corporation organized under Division 1.5 of the California Corporations Code. The articles of this corporation state one or more purposes required by law. Refer to the articles on file with the Secretary of State, and the bylaws and any agreements on file with the secretary of the corporation, for further information." . . .

(d) All certificates representing shares of a close social purpose corporation shall contain, in addition to any other statements required by this section, the following conspicuous legend on the face thereof:

"This social purpose corporation is a close social purpose corporation. The number of holders of record of its shares of all classes cannot exceed ____ (a number not in excess of 25). Any attempted voluntary inter vivos transfer which would violate this requirement is void. Refer to the articles, bylaws and any agreements on file with the secretary of the social purpose corporation for further restrictions." . . .

§ 3202. Plan of Conversion

If a disappearing social purpose corporation in a merger is a social purpose corporation governed by this division and the surviving corporation is a nonprofit public benefit corporation, a nonprofit mutual benefit corporation, or a nonprofit religious corporation, the merger shall be approved by all of the outstanding shares of all classes of the disappearing social purpose corporation, regardless of limitations or restrictions on their voting rights, notwithstanding any provision of Chapter 10 (commencing with Section 3400).

§ 3500. Annual Report

(a) The board of a social purpose corporation shall cause an annual report to be sent to the shareholders not later than 120 days after the close of the fiscal year. The annual report shall contain (1) a balance sheet as of the end of that fiscal year and an income statement and a statement of cashflows for that fiscal year, accompanied by any report thereon of independent accountants or, if there is no report, the certificate of an authorized officer of the social purpose corporation that the statements were prepared without audit from the books and records of the corporation, and (2) the information required by subdivision (b).

(b) The board shall cause to be provided with the annual report, a management discussion and analysis (special purpose MD & A) concerning the social purpose corporation's stated purpose or purposes as set forth in its articles pursuant to paragraph (2) of subdivision (b) of Section 2602, and, to the extent consistent with reasonable confidentiality requirements, shall cause the special purpose MD & A to be made publicly available by posting it on the social purpose corporation's Internet Web site or providing it through similar electronic means. The special purpose MD & A shall include the information specified in this subdivision and any other information that the social purpose corporation's officers and directors believe to be reasonably necessary or appropriate to an understanding of the social purpose corporation's efforts in connection with its special purpose or purposes. The special purpose MD & A shall also include the following information:

(1) Identification and discussion of the overall objectives of the social purpose corporation relating to its special purpose or purposes, and an identification and explanation of any changes made in those special purpose objectives during the fiscal year.

(2) Identification and discussion of the material actions taken by the social purpose corporation during the fiscal year to achieve its special purpose objectives, the impact of those actions, including the causal

relationships between the actions and the reported outcomes, and the extent to which those actions achieved the special purpose objectives for the fiscal year.

(3) Identification and discussion of material actions, including the intended impact of those actions, that the social purpose corporation expects to take in the short term and long term with respect to achievement of its special purpose objectives.

(4) A description of the process for selecting, and an identification and description of, the financial, operating, and other measures used by the social purpose corporation during the fiscal year for evaluating its performance in achieving its special purpose objectives, including an explanation of why the social purpose corporation selected those measures and identification and discussion of the nature and rationale for any material changes in those measures made during the fiscal year.

(5) Identification and discussion of any material operating and capital expenditures incurred by the social purpose corporation during the fiscal year in furtherance of achieving the special purpose objectives, a good faith estimate of any additional material operating or capital expenditures the social purpose corporation expects to incur over the next three fiscal years in order to achieve its special purpose objectives, and other material expenditures of resources incurred by the social purpose corporation during the fiscal year, including employee time, in furtherance of achieving the special purpose objectives, including a discussion of the extent to which that capital or use of other resources serves purposes other than and in addition to furthering the achievement of the special purpose objectives.

(c) Except as may otherwise be excused pursuant to subdivision (h) of Section 1501.5, the reports specified in subdivisions (a) and (b) shall be sent to the shareholders at least 15 days, or, if sent by bulk mail, 35 days, prior to the annual meeting of shareholders to be held during the next fiscal year. This requirement shall not limit the requirement for holding an annual meeting as required by Section 600.

(d) If no annual report for the last fiscal year has been sent to shareholders, the social purpose corporation shall, upon the written request of any shareholder made more than 120 days after the end of that fiscal year, deliver or mail to the person making the request within 30 days following the request, the statements required by subdivisions (a) and (b) for that fiscal year.

(e) A shareholder or shareholders holding at least 5 percent of the outstanding shares of any class of a social purpose corporation may make a written request to the social purpose corporation for an income statement of the social purpose corporation for the three-month, six-month, or nine-month period of the current fiscal year ended more than 30 days prior to the date of the request and a balance sheet of the social purpose corporation as at the end of that period and, in addition, if no annual report for the most recent fiscal year has been sent to the shareholders, the statements referred to in subdivisions (a) and (b) relating to that fiscal year. The statements shall be delivered or mailed to the person making the request within 30 days following the request. A copy of the statements shall be kept on file in the principal office of the social purpose corporation for 12 months and shall be exhibited at all reasonable times to any shareholder demanding an examination of the statements or a copy shall be mailed to the shareholder. The quarterly income statements and balance sheets referred to in this subdivision shall be accompanied by the report thereon, if any, of any independent accountants engaged by the social purpose corporation or the certificate of an authorized officer of the social purpose corporation that the financial statements were prepared without audit from the books and records of the social purpose corporation.

§ 3501. Special Purpose Current Report

(a) The board shall cause a special purpose current report to be sent to the shareholders not later than 45 days following the occurrence of any one or more of the events specified in subdivision (b) or (c), and, to the extent consistent with reasonable confidentiality requirements, shall cause the special purpose current report to be made publicly available by posting it on the social purpose corporation's Internet Web site or providing it through similar electronic means.

(b) Unless previously reported in the most recent annual report, the special purpose current report shall identify and discuss, in reasonable detail, any expenditure or group of related or planned expenditures, excluding compensation of officers and directors, made in furtherance of the special purpose objectives, whether an operating expenditure, a capital expenditure, or some other expenditure of corporate resources, including, but not limited to, employee time, whether the expenditure was direct or indirect, and whether the expenditure was categorized as overhead or otherwise where the expenditure has or is likely to have a material adverse impact on the social purpose corporation's results of operations or financial condition for a quarterly or annual fiscal period.

(c) Unless previously reported in the most recent annual report, the special purpose current report shall identify and discuss, in reasonable detail, any decision by the board or action by management to do either of the following:

(1) Withhold expenditures or a group of related or planned expenditures, whether temporarily or permanently, that were to have been made in furtherance of the special purpose as contemplated in the most recent annual report, whether those planned expenditures were an operating expenditure, a capital expenditure, or some other expenditure of corporate resources, including, but not limited to, employee time, whether the planned expenditure was direct or indirect, and whether the planned expenditure to be made would have been categorized as overhead or otherwise, in any case, where the planned expenditure was likely to have had a material positive impact on the social purpose corporation's impact in furtherance of its special purpose objectives, as contemplated in the most recent annual report.

(2) Determine that the special purpose has been satisfied or should no longer be pursued, whether temporarily or permanently.

§ 3502. Provision of Information in Reports

(a) Nothing contained in Sections 3500 or 3501 shall require a detailing or itemization of every relevant expenditure incurred, or planned or action taken or planned, by the corporation. Management and the board shall use their discretion in providing that information, including the reasonable detail that a reasonable investor would consider important in understanding the corporation's objectives, actions, impacts, measures, rationale, and results of operations as they relate to the nature and achievement of the special purpose objectives.

(b) Where best practices emerge for providing the information required by Sections 3500 or 3501, use of those best practices shall create a presumption that the social purpose corporation caused all the information required by those provisions to be provided. This presumption can only be rebutted by showing that the reporting contained either a misstatement of a material fact or omission of a material fact.

(c) Notwithstanding Sections 3500 and 3501, under no circumstances shall the social purpose corporation be required to provide information that would result in a violation of state or federal securities laws or other applicable laws.

(d) The social purpose corporation and its officers and directors are expressly excluded from liability for any and all forward looking statements supplied in the report required by Section 3500s and 3501, so long as those statements are supplied in good faith. Statements are deemed to be forward looking as that term is defined in the federal securities laws.

(e) The special purpose MD & A and any special purpose current report shall be written in plain English and shall be provided in an efficient and understandable manner, avoiding repetition and disclosure of immaterial information.

(f) Unless otherwise provided by the articles or bylaws, and if approved by the board of directors, the reports specified in Sections 3500 and 3501 and any accompanying material sent pursuant to this section may be sent by electronic transmission by the corporation.

(g) The financial statements of any social purpose corporation with fewer than 100 holders of record of its shares, determined as provided in Section 605, required to be furnished by Sections 3500 and 3501 are not required to be prepared in conformity with generally accepted accounting principles if they reasonably set forth the assets and liabilities and the income and expense of the social purpose corporation and disclose the accounting basis used in their preparation.

(h) The requirements described in Section 3500 shall be satisfied if a corporation with an outstanding class of securities registered under Section 12 of the Securities Exchange Act of 1934 both complies with Section 240.14a–16 of Title 17 of the Code of Federal Regulations, as amended from time to time, with respect to the obligation of a corporation to furnish an annual report to shareholders pursuant to Section

240.14a–3(b) of Title 17 of the Code of Federal Regulations, and includes the information required by subdivision (b) of Section 3500 in the annual report.

(i) The requirements described in Section 3501 shall be satisfied if a corporation with an outstanding class of securities registered under Section 12 of the Securities Exchange Act of 1934 both complies with Section 240.13a–13 of Title 17 of the Code of Federal Regulations, as amended from time to time, with respect to the obligation of a corporation to furnish a quarterly report to shareholders, and includes the information required by subdivision (b) of Section 3501 in the quarterly report.

(j) In addition to the penalties provided for in this division, the superior court of the proper county shall enforce the duty of making and mailing or delivering the information and financial statements required by Sections 3500 and 3501 and, for good cause shown, may extend the time therefor.

(k) In any action or proceeding with respect to Section 3500 or 3501, if the court finds the failure of the social purpose corporation to comply with the requirements of those sections to have been without justification, the court may award an amount sufficient to reimburse the shareholder for the reasonable expenses incurred by the shareholder, including attorney's fees, in connection with the action or proceeding.

(*l*) Subdivision (b) of Section 3500 and Section 3501 apply to any domestic social purpose corporation and also to a foreign social purpose corporation having its principal executive office in this state or customarily holding meetings of its board in this state.

(m) All reports and notices required by Sections 3500 and 3501 shall be maintained by the social purpose corporation, in an electronic form for a period of not less than 10 years.

Division 3

CORPORATIONS FOR SPECIFIC PURPOSES

Part 13

BENEFIT CORPORATIONS

Chapter 1

PRELIMINARY PROVISIONS

§ 14600. Application of Part

(a) This part shall be applicable to all benefit corporations.

(b) The existence of a provision of this part shall not of itself create any implication that a contrary or different rule of law is or would be applicable to a business corporation that is not a benefit corporation. This part shall not affect any statute or rule of law that is or would be applicable to a corporation that is not a benefit corporation.

(c) The provisions of the General Corporation Law (Division 1 (commencing with Section 100)) shall apply to benefit corporations, except where those provisions are in conflict with or inconsistent with the provisions of this part.

§ 14601. Definitions

As used in this part:

(a) "Benefit corporation" means a corporation organized under the General Corporation Law that has elected to become subject to this part and whose status as a benefit corporation has not been terminated as provided in this part.

(b) "Benefit enforcement proceeding" means a claim or action relating to any of the following:

(1) Failure to pursue the general public benefit purpose of the benefit corporation or any specific public benefit purpose set forth in its articles.

(2) Violation of a duty or standard of conduct imposed on a director pursuant to this part.

(3) Failure of the benefit corporation to deliver or post an annual benefit report as required by Section 14630.

(c) "General public benefit" means a material positive impact on society and the environment, taken as a whole, as assessed against a third-party standard, from the business and operations of a benefit corporation.

(d) "Minimum status vote" means that:

(1) In the case of a corporation, in addition to any other approval or vote required by Division 1 (commencing with Section 100) or the articles of incorporation, both of the following shall apply:

(A) The shareholders of every class or series shall be entitled to vote on the corporate action regardless of any limitation stated in the articles or bylaws on the voting rights of any class or series.

(B) The corporate action shall be approved by the outstanding shares of each class or series by at least two-thirds of the votes, or greater vote if required in the articles of incorporation, that all shareholders of the class or series are entitled to cast on that action.

(2) In the case of a domestic other business entity (Section 167.7), both of the following shall apply in addition to any other approval, vote, or consent required by the statutory law, if any, that principally governs the internal affairs of the entity or any provision of the publicly filed record or document required to form the entity, if any, or of any agreement binding some or all of the holders of equity interests in the entity:

(A) The holders of every class or series of interest in the entity that are entitled to receive a distribution of any kind from the entity regardless of any otherwise applicable limitation on the voting rights of the interest.

(B) The action shall be approved by the vote or consent of the holders described in subparagraph (A) by at least two-thirds of the votes or consents, or greater vote or consent if required in the articles of incorporation, of those holders.

(e) "Specific public benefit" includes all of the following:

(1) Providing low-income or underserved individuals or communities with beneficial products or services.

(2) Promoting economic opportunity for individuals or communities beyond the creation of jobs in the ordinary course of business.

(3) Preserving the environment.

(4) Improving human health.

(5) Promoting the arts, sciences, or advancement of knowledge.

(6) Increasing the flow of capital to entities with a public benefit purpose.

(7) The accomplishment of any other particular benefit for society or the environment.

(f) "Subsidiary" of a person means an entity in which the person owns beneficially or of record 50 percent or more of the outstanding equity interests. For purposes of this definition, a percentage of ownership in an entity shall be calculated as if all outstanding rights to acquire equity interests in the entity had been exercised.

(g) "Third-party standard" means a standard for defining, reporting, and assessing overall corporate social and environmental performance to which all of the following apply:

(1) The standard is a comprehensive assessment of the impact of the business and the business's operations upon the considerations listed in paragraphs (2) to (5), inclusive, of subdivision (b) of Section 14620.

(2) The standard is developed by an entity that has no material financial relationship with the benefit corporation or any of its subsidiaries and that satisfies both of the following requirements:

(A) Not more than one-third of the members of the governing body of the entity are representatives of any of the following:

(i) Associations of businesses operating in a specific industry, the performance of whose members is measured by the standard.

(ii) Businesses from a specific industry or an association of businesses in that industry.

(iii) Businesses whose performance is assessed against the standard.

(B) The entity is not materially financed by an association or business described in subparagraph (A).

(3) The standard is developed by an entity that does both of the following:

(A) Accesses necessary and appropriate expertise to assess overall corporate social and environmental performance.

(B) Uses a balanced multistakeholder approach, including a public comment period of at least 30 days to develop the standard.

(4) All of the following information regarding the standard is publicly available:

(A) The criteria considered when measuring the overall social and environmental performance of a business.

(B) The relative weightings assigned to the criteria described in subparagraph (A).

(C) The identity of the directors, officers, any material owners, and the governing body of the entity that developed, and controls revisions to, the standard.

(D) The process by which revisions to the standard and changes to the membership of the governing body described in subparagraph (C) are made.

(E) An accounting of the sources of financial support for the entity, with sufficient detail to disclose any relationships that could reasonably be considered to present a potential conflict of interest.

§ 14602. Formation of Benefit Corporation

A benefit corporation shall be formed in accordance with Chapter 2 (commencing with Section 200) of Division 1 except that the articles shall also state that the corporation is a benefit corporation and shall identify any specific public benefit adopted pursuant to Section 14610.

§ 14603. Amendment of Corporation's Articles to Become Benefit Corporation; Surviving Corporations in Merger Reorganization or Acquired Corporations to Be Benefit Corporation; Domestic Other Business Entity as Party to Merger Reorganization or Converting Entity; Minimum Status Vote Requirement

(a) A corporation may become a benefit corporation under this part by amending the corporation's articles so that the articles contain a statement that the corporation is a benefit corporation. The amendment shall not be effective unless it is adopted by at least the minimum status vote. If the amendment is adopted, a shareholder of the corporation may, by complying with Chapter 13 (commencing with Section 1300) of Division 1, require the corporation to purchase at their fair market value the shares owned by the shareholder which are dissenting shares as defined in subdivision (b) of Section 1300 in accordance with the procedures in that chapter, as if the adoption of the amendment were a reorganization to which that chapter applies.

(b) If a corporation that is not a benefit corporation is a constituent corporation in a merger reorganization or is the acquired corporation in an exchange reorganization, and the surviving corporation in the merger reorganization is to be a benefit corporation or the articles of the acquired corporation are to be amended in the exchange reorganization to provide that it will be a benefit corporation, then the reorganization shall not be effective unless the reorganization is approved by the corporation or domestic other business entity by at least the minimum status vote.

(c) If a domestic other business entity is a party to a merger reorganization and the surviving corporation in the reorganization is to be a benefit corporation, then the reorganization shall not be effective unless the reorganization is approved by the domestic other business entity by at least the minimum status vote.

(d) If a domestic other business entity is the converting entity (subdivision (d) of Section 1150) in a conversion in which the converted corporation (subdivision (a) of Section 1150) is a benefit corporation, the conversion shall not be effective unless the conversion is approved by the domestic other business entity by at least the minimum status vote.

§ 14604. Termination of Status as Benefit Corporation by Amendment of Corporation's Articles or Reorganization; Benefit Corporation as Converting Corporation in Conversion; Transaction Regarding All or Substantially All Assets of Benefit Corporation; Minimum Status Vote Requirement

(a) A benefit corporation may terminate its status as a benefit corporation and cease to be subject to this part by amending the corporation's articles to delete the provision required by Section 14602. The amendment shall not be effective unless the amendment is adopted by at least the minimum status vote. If the amendment is adopted, a shareholder of the corporation may, by complying with Chapter 13 (commencing with Section 1300) of Division 1, require the corporation to purchase at their fair market value the shares owned by the shareholder which are dissenting shares as defined in subdivision (b) of Section 1300 in accordance with the procedures in that chapter.

(b) If a reorganization (Section 181) would have the effect of terminating the status of a corporation as a benefit corporation, the reorganization shall not be effective unless the reorganization is approved by at least the minimum status vote.

(c) If a benefit corporation is the converting corporation (Section 1150) in a conversion (Section 161.9), the conversion shall not be effective unless the conversion is approved by at least the minimum status vote.

(d) A sale, lease, conveyance, exchange, transfer, or other disposition of all or substantially all of the assets of a benefit corporation, unless the transaction is in the usual and ordinary course of business of the benefit corporation, shall not be effective unless the transaction is approved by at least the minimum status vote. If the transaction is approved, a shareholder of the corporation may, by complying with Chapter 13 (commencing with Section 1300) of Division 1, require the corporation to purchase at their fair market value the shares owned by the shareholder which are dissenting shares as defined in subdivision (b) of Section 1300 in accordance with the procedures in that chapter, as if the transaction were a reorganization to which that chapter applies.

Chapter 2

CORPORATE PURPOSES

§ 14610. Purpose of Benefit Corporation; General and Specific Public Benefit; Amendment of Articles to Add, Amend, or Delete Specific Public Benefit

(a) A benefit corporation shall have the purpose of creating general public benefit. This purpose is in addition to, and may be a limitation on, the corporation's purpose under Section 206 and any specific purpose set forth in its articles in accordance with subdivision (b).

(b) In addition to the provisions required by Section 202, the articles of incorporation of a benefit corporation shall contain the following statement: "This corporation is a benefit corporation." Notwithstanding subdivision (b) of Section 202, the articles of a benefit corporation may identify one or more specific public benefits that shall be the purpose or purposes of the benefit corporation. The identification of a specific public benefit under this subdivision does not limit the obligation of a benefit corporation to create general public benefit.

(c) The creation of general and specific public benefit as provided in subdivisions (a) and (b) shall be deemed to be in the best interests of the benefit corporation.

(d) A benefit corporation may amend its articles to add, amend, or delete the identification of a specific public benefit that shall be the purpose of the benefit corporation to create. The amendment shall not be effective unless the amendment is adopted by at least the minimum status vote.

Chapter 3

ACCOUNTABILITY

§ 14620. Performance of Duties by Director; Requirements of Board of Directors, Committees of the Board, and Individual Directors When Discharging Duties; Liability of Director; Fiduciary Duty of Director; Director of Foreign Corporation

(a) A director shall perform the duties of a director including duties as a member of any committee of the board upon which the director may serve, in good faith, in a manner the director believes to be in the best interests of the benefit corporation and with that care, including reasonable inquiry, as an ordinarily prudent person in a like position would use under similar circumstances.

(b) In discharging their respective duties, and in considering the best interests of the benefit corporation, the board of directors, committees of the board, and individual directors of a benefit corporation shall consider the impacts of any action or proposed action upon all of the following:

(1) The shareholders of the benefit corporation.

(2) The employees and workforce of the benefit corporation and its subsidiaries and suppliers.

(3) The interests of customers of the benefit corporation as beneficiaries of the general or specific public benefit purposes of the benefit corporation.

(4) Community and societal considerations, including those of any community in which offices or facilities of the benefit corporation or its subsidiaries or suppliers are located.

(5) The local and global environment.

(6) The short-term and long-term interests of the benefit corporation, including benefits that may accrue to the benefit corporation from its long-term plans and the possibility that these interests may be best served by retaining control of the benefit corporation rather than selling or transferring control to another entity.

(7) The ability of the benefit corporation to accomplish its general, and any specific, public benefit purpose.

(c) In discharging their respective duties, the persons described in subdivision (b) may consider any of the following:

(1) The resources, intent, and conduct, including past, stated, and potential conduct, of any person seeking to acquire control of the corporation.

(2) Any other pertinent factors or the interests of any other person or group.

(d) In discharging their respective duties, the persons described in subdivision (a) shall not be required to give priority to any particular factor or the interests of any particular person or group referred to in subdivision (b) or (c) over any other factor or the interests of any other person or group unless the benefit corporation has stated its intention to give priority to a specific public benefit purpose identified in the articles.

(e) In performing the duties of a director, a director shall be entitled to rely on information, opinions, reports, or statements, including financial statements and other financial data, in each case prepared or presented by any of the following:

(1) One or more officers or employees of the benefit corporation whom the director believes to be reliable and competent in the matters presented.

(2) Counsel, independent accountants, or other persons as to matters that the director believes to be within those persons' professional or expert competence.

(3) A committee of the board upon which the director does not serve, as to matters within its designated authority, which committee the director believes to merit confidence, so long as, in any of those cases, the director acts in good faith, after reasonable inquiry when the need therefor is indicated by the circumstances and without knowledge that would cause that reliance to be unwarranted.

(f) A director shall not be liable for monetary damages under this part for any failure of the benefit corporation to create a general or specific public benefit.

(g) A person who performs the duties of a director in accordance with this part shall not be liable for monetary damages for any alleged failure to discharge the person's obligations as a director.

(h) In addition to the limitations provided in subdivisions (f) and (g), the liability of a director for monetary damages may be eliminated or limited in a benefit corporation's articles to the extent provided in paragraph (10) of subdivision (a) of Section 204.

(i) A director shall not have a fiduciary duty to a person that is a beneficiary of the general or specific public benefit purposes of a benefit corporation arising from the status of the person as a beneficiary.

(j) A director of a foreign corporation that is subject to Section 2115 shall not be subject to Section 309 and shall be subject instead to this section if the director of the foreign corporation is subject to duties under its articles of incorporation, bylaws, or the law of its jurisdiction of incorporation similar to the duties of directors under this section.

§ 14621. Statement in Annual Benefit Report of Whether Benefit Corporation Failed to Pursue Benefit Purpose

(a) The board of directors of a benefit corporation shall prepare for inclusion in the annual benefit report to shareholders required by Section 14630, a statement indicating whether, in the opinion of the board of directors, the benefit corporation failed to pursue its general, and any specific, public benefit purpose in all material respects during the period covered by the report.

(b) If, in the opinion of the board of directors, the benefit corporation failed to pursue its general, and any specific, public benefit purpose, the statement required by subdivision (a) shall include a description of the ways in which the benefit corporation failed to pursue its general, and any specific, public benefit purpose.

§ 14622. Officers of Benefit Corporations; Consideration of Interests and Factors Described in § 14620; Liability; Fiduciary Duty

(a) Each officer of a benefit corporation shall consider the interests and factors described in Section 14620 in the manner provided in that section when either of the following applies:

(1) The officer has discretion to act with respect to a matter.(2) It reasonably appears to the officer that the matter may have a material effect on any of the following:

(A) The creation of a general or specific public benefit by the benefit corporation.

(B) Any of the interests or factors referred to in subdivision (b) of Section 14620.

(b) The consideration by an officer of interests and factors in the manner described in subdivision (a) shall not constitute a violation of the duties of the officer.

(c) An officer shall not be liable for monetary damages under this part for any of the following:

(1) Any action taken as an officer if the officer performed the duties of the position in compliance with this section.

(2) Any failure of the benefit corporation to create a general or specific public benefit.

(d) An officer shall not have a fiduciary duty to a person that is a beneficiary of the general or specific public benefit purposes of a benefit corporation arising from the status of the person as a beneficiary.

§ 14623. Benefit Enforcement Proceeding; Liability of Benefit Corporation for Monetary Damages; Attorney Fees and Expenses

(a) No person may bring an action or assert a claim against a benefit corporation or its directors or officers under this chapter except in a benefit enforcement proceeding.

(b) A benefit enforcement proceeding may be commenced or maintained only as follows:

(1) Directly by the benefit corporation.

(2) Derivatively by any of the following:

(A) A shareholder.

(B) A director.

(C) A person or group of persons that owns beneficially or of record 5 percent or more of the equity interests in an entity of which the benefit corporation is a subsidiary.

(D) Other persons as have been specified in the articles or bylaws of the benefit corporation.

(c) A benefit corporation shall not be liable for monetary damages under this part for any failure of the benefit corporation to create a general or specific public benefit.

(d) If the court in a benefit enforcement proceeding finds that a failure to comply with this part was without justification, the court may award an amount sufficient to reimburse the plaintiff for the reasonable expenses incurred by the plaintiff, including attorney's fees and expenses, in connection with the benefit enforcement proceeding.

Chapter 4

TRANSPARENCY

§ 14630. Annual Benefit Report

(a) A benefit corporation shall deliver to each shareholder an annual benefit report including all of the following:

(1) A narrative description of all of the following:

(A) The process and rationale for selecting the third-party standard used to prepare the benefit report.

(B) The ways in which the benefit corporation pursued a general public benefit during the applicable year and the extent to which that general public benefit was created.

(C) The ways in which the benefit corporation pursued any specific public benefit that the articles state it is the purpose of the benefit corporation to create and the extent to which that specific public benefit was created.

(D) Any circumstances that have hindered the creation by the benefit corporation of a general or specific public benefit.

(2) An assessment of the overall social and environmental performance of the benefit corporation, prepared in accordance with a third-party standard applied consistently with any application of that standard in prior benefit reports or accompanied by an explanation of the reasons for any inconsistent application. The assessment does not need to be audited or certified by a third party.

(3) The name of each person that owns 5 percent or more of the outstanding shares of the benefit corporation, either beneficially, to the extent known to the benefit corporation without independent investigation, or of record.

(4) The statement required by Section 14621.

(5) A statement of any connection between the entity that established the third-party standard, or its directors, officers, or material owners, and the benefit corporation, or its directors, officers, and material

owners, including any financial or governance relationship that might materially affect the credibility of the objective assessment of the third-party standard.

(b) The benefit report shall be sent annually to each shareholder within 120 days following the end of the fiscal year of the benefit corporation or at the same time that the benefit corporation delivers any other annual report to its shareholders.

(c) A benefit corporation shall post all of its benefit reports on the public portion of its Internet Web site, if any, except that the compensation paid to directors and any financial or proprietary information included in the benefit report may be omitted from the benefit report as posted on the Internet Web site.

(d)(1) If a benefit corporation does not have an Internet Web site, the benefit corporation shall provide a copy of its most recent benefit report, without charge, to any person that requests a copy.

(2) The benefit corporation may omit any proprietary or financial information, including, but not limited to, compensation paid to directors, from the copy of a benefit report that the benefit corporation provides pursuant to paragraph (1).

§ 14631. Share Certificates; Required Language

All certificates representing shares of a benefit corporation shall contain, in addition to any other statements required by the General Corporation Law (Division 1 (commencing with Section 100)), the following conspicuous language on the face of the certificate:

"This entity is a benefit corporation organized under Part 13 (commencing with Section 14600) of Division 3 of Title 1 of the California Corporations Code."

TITLE 4

SECURITIES

§ 25402. Purchase or Sale of Securities by Person Having Access to Material Information Not Available to Public Through Special Relationship With Issuer

It is unlawful for an issuer or any person who is an officer, director or controlling person of an issuer or any other person whose relationship to the issuer gives him access, directly or indirectly, to material information about the issuer not generally available to the public, to purchase or sell any security of the issuer in this state at a time when he knows material information about the issuer gained from such relationship which would significantly affect the market price of that security and which is not generally available to the public, and which he knows is not intended to be so available, unless he has reason to believe that the person selling to or buying from him is also in possession of the information.

§ 25502. Violation of Section 25402; Damages

Any person who violates Section 25402 shall be liable to the person who purchases a security from him or sells a security to him, for damages equal to the difference between the price at which such security was purchased or sold and the market value which such security would have had at the time of the purchase or sale if the information known to the defendant had been publicly disseminated prior to that time and a reasonable time had elapsed for the market to absorb the information, plus interest at the legal rate, unless the defendant proves that the plaintiff knew the information or that the plaintiff would have purchased or sold at the same price even if the information had been revealed to him.

§ 25502.5 Liability to Issuer of Violator of Insider Trading Prohibitions; Allegation by Shareholder; Consideration by Board

(a) Any person other than the issuer who violates Section 25402 shall be liable to the issuer of the security purchased or sold in violation of Section 25402 for damages in an amount up to three times the difference between the price at which the security was purchased or sold and the market value which the security would have had at the time of the purchase or sale if the information known to the defendant had been publicly disseminated prior to that time and a reasonable time had elapsed for the market to absorb the information and shall be liable to the issuer of the security or to a person who institutes an action under this section in the right of the issuer of the security for reasonable costs and attorney's fees.

(b) The amounts recoverable under this section by the issuer shall be reduced by any amount paid by the defendant in a proceeding brought by the Securities and Exchange Commission with respect to the same transaction or transactions under the federal Insider Trading Sanctions Act of 1984 (15 U.S.C. Secs. 78a, 78c, 78o, 78t, 78u, and 78ff) or any other act regardless of whether the amount was paid pursuant to a judgment or settlement or paid before or after the filing of an action by the plaintiff against the defendant. If a proceeding has been commenced by the Securities and Exchange Commission but has not been finally resolved, the court shall delay entering a judgment for the plaintiff under this section until that proceeding is resolved.

(c) If any shareholder of an issuer alleges to the board that there has been a violation of this section, the board shall be required to consider the allegation in good faith, and if the allegation involves misconduct by any director, that director shall not be entitled to vote on any matter involving the allegation. However, that director may be counted in determining the presence of a quorum at a meeting of the board or a committee of the board.

(d) This section shall only apply to issuers who have total assets in excess of one million dollars ($1,000,000) and have a class of equity security held of record by 500 or more persons.

CONNECTICUT GENERAL STATUTES ANN. § 33–756

§ 33–756.   General standards of conduct for directors

(a) Each member of the board of directors, when discharging the duties of a director, shall act: (1) In good faith; and (2) in a manner the director reasonably believes to be in the best interests of the corporation.

(b) The members of the board of directors or a board committee, when becoming informed in connection with their decision-making function or devoting attention to their oversight function, shall discharge their duties with the care that a person in a like position would reasonably believe appropriate under similar circumstances.

(c) In discharging board or committee duties, a director shall disclose, or cause to be disclosed, to the other board or committee members information not already known by them but known by the director to be material to the discharge of their decision-making or oversight functions, except that disclosure is not required to the extent that the director reasonably believes that doing so would violate a duty imposed under law, a legally enforceable obligation of confidentiality, or a professional ethics rule.

(d) In discharging board or committee duties, a director who does not have knowledge that makes reliance unwarranted is entitled to rely on the performance by any of the persons specified in subdivision (1) or (3) of subsection (f) of this section to whom the board may have delegated, formally or informally by course of conduct, the authority or duty to perform one or more of the board's functions that are delegable under applicable law.

(e) In discharging board or committee duties, a director who does not have knowledge that makes reliance unwarranted is entitled to rely on information, opinions, reports or statements, including financial statements and other financial data, prepared or presented by any of the persons specified in subsection (f) of this section.

(f) A director is entitled to rely, in accordance with subsection (d) or (e) of this section, on: (1) One or more officers or employees of the corporation whom the director reasonably believes to be reliable and competent in the functions performed or the information, opinions, reports or statements provided; (2) legal counsel, public accountants or other persons retained by the corporation as to matters involving skills or expertise the director reasonably believes are matters (A) within the particular person's professional or expert competence, or (B) as to which the particular person merits confidence; or (3) a board committee of which the director is not a member if the director reasonably believes the committee merits confidence.

(g) For the purposes of sections 33–817, 33–830, 33–831, 33–841 and 33–844, a director of a corporation that has a class of voting stock registered pursuant to Section 12 of the Securities Exchange Act of 1934, as the same has been or hereafter may be amended from time to time, in addition to complying with the provisions of subsections (a) to (c), inclusive, of this section, may consider, in determining what the director reasonably believes to be in the best interests of the corporation, (1) the long-term as well as the short-term interests of the corporation, (2) the interests of the shareholders, long-term as well as short-term, including the possibility that those interests may be best served by the continued independence of the corporation, (3) the interests of the corporation's employees, customers, creditors and suppliers, and (4) community and societal considerations, including those of any community in which any office or other facility of the corporation is located. A director may also consider, in the discretion of such director, any other factors the director reasonably considers appropriate in determining what the director reasonably believes to be in the best interests of the corporation.

IND. CODE ANN. TITLE 23

[Standards of Conduct for Directors;
Control Share Acquisitions]

Chapter 35

STANDARDS OF CONDUCT FOR DIRECTORS

§ 23–1–35–1   Standards of conduct; liability; reaffirmation of corporate governance rules; presumption

(a) A director shall, based on facts then known to the director, discharge the duties as a director, including the director's duties as a member of a committee:

(1) in good faith;

(2) with the care an ordinarily prudent person in a like position would exercise under similar circumstances; and

(3) in a manner the director reasonably believes to be in the best interests of the corporation.

(b) In discharging the director's duties a director is entitled to rely on information, opinions, reports, or statements, including financial statements and other financial data, if prepared or presented by:

(1) one (1) or more officers or employees of the corporation whom the director reasonably believes to be reliable and competent in the matters presented;

(2) legal counsel, public accountants, or other persons as to matters the director reasonably believes are within the person's professional or expert competence; or

(3) a committee of the board of directors of which the director is not a member if the director reasonably believes the committee merits confidence.

(c) A director is not acting in good faith if the director has knowledge concerning the matter in question that makes reliance otherwise permitted by subsection (b) unwarranted.

(d) A director may, in considering the best interests of a corporation, consider the effects of any action on shareholders, employees, suppliers, and customers of the corporation, and communities in which offices or other facilities of the corporation are located, and any other factors the director considers pertinent.

(e) A director is not liable for any action taken as a director regardless of the nature of the alleged breach of duty, including alleged breaches of the duty of care, the duty of loyalty, and the duty of good faith, or any failure to take any action, unless:

(1) the director has breached or failed to perform the duties of the director's office in compliance with this section; and

(2) the breach or failure to perform constitutes willful misconduct or recklessness.

(f) In enacting this article, the general assembly established corporate governance rules for Indiana corporations, including in this chapter, the standards of conduct applicable to directors of Indiana corporations, and the corporate constituent groups and interests that a director may take into account in exercising the director's business judgment. The general assembly intends to reaffirm certain of these corporate governance rules to ensure that the directors of Indiana corporations, in exercising their business judgment, are not required to approve a proposed corporate action if the directors in good faith determine, after considering and weighing as they deem appropriate the effects of such action on the corporation's constituents, that such action is not in the best interests of the corporation. In making such determination, directors are not required to consider the effects of a proposed corporate action on any particular corporate constituent group or interest as a dominant or controlling factor. Without limiting the generality of the foregoing, directors are not required to render inapplicable any of the provisions of [§ 23–1–43 [business combinations], to redeem any rights under or to render inapplicable a shareholder rights plan adopted pursuant to [§] 23-1-26-5 [rights, options or warrants], or to take or decline to take any other action under this article, solely because of the effect such action might have on a proposed acquisition of control of the corporation or the amounts that might be paid to shareholders under such an acquisition. Certain judicial decisions in Delaware and other jurisdictions, which might otherwise be looked to for guidance in interpreting Indiana corporate law, including decisions relating to potential change of control transactions that impose a different or higher degree of scrutiny on actions taken by directors in response to a proposed acquisition of control of the corporation, are inconsistent with the proper application of the business judgment rule under this article. Therefore, the general assembly intends:

(1) to reaffirm that this section allows directors the full discretion to weigh the factors enumerated in subsection (d) as they deem appropriate; and

(2) to protect both directors and the validity of corporate action taken by them in the good faith exercise of their business judgment after reasonable investigation.

(g) In taking or declining to take any action, or in making or declining to make any recommendation to the shareholders of the corporation with respect to any matter, a board of directors may, in its discretion, consider both the short term and long term best interests of the corporation, taking into account, and weighing as the directors deem appropriate, the effects thereof on the corporation's shareholders and the other corporate constituent groups and interests listed or described in subsection (d), as well as any other factors deemed pertinent by the directors under subsection (d). If a determination is made with respect to the foregoing with the approval of a majority of the disinterested directors of the board of directors, that determination shall conclusively be presumed to be valid unless it can be demonstrated that the determination was not made in good faith after reasonable investigation.

(h) For the purposes of subsection (g), a director is disinterested if:

(1) the director does not have a conflict of interest, within the meaning of section 2 of this chapter [conflict-of-interest transactions], in connection with the action or recommendation in question;

(2) in connection with matters described in [§] 23-1-32 [derivative actions] the director is disinterested (as defined in [§] 23-1-32-4(d));

(3) in connection with any matter involving or otherwise affecting:

(A) a control share acquisition (as defined in [§] 23-1-42-2) or any matter related to a control share acquisition . . . ;

(B) a business combination (as defined in [§] 23-1-43-5) or any matter related to a business combination . . . ;

(C) any transaction that may result in a change of control (as defined in [§] 23-1-22-4) of the corporation;

the director is not an employee of the corporation; and

(4) in connection with any matter involving or otherwise affecting:

(A) a control share acquisition (as defined in [§] 23-1-42-2) or any matter related to a control share acquisition . . . ;

(B) a business combination (as defined in [§] 23-1-43-5) or any matter related to a business combination . . . ;

(C) any transaction that may result in a change of control (as defined in [§] 23-1-22-4) of the corporation;

the director is not an affiliate or associate of, or was not nominated or designated as a director by, a person proposing any of the transactions described in clause (A), (B), or (C).

(i) A person may be disinterested under this section even though the person is a director or shareholder of the corporation. . . .

Chapter 42

CONTROL SHARE ACQUISITIONS

Sec.		Page
23–1–42–1	"Control shares" defined	829
23–1–42–2	"Control share acquisition" defined	829
23–1–42–3	"Interested shares" defined	830
23–1–42–4	"Issuing public corporation" defined	830
23–1–42–5	Voting rights under [§] 23–1–42–9	830
23–1–42–6	Acquiring person statement	830
23–1–42–7	Special meeting of shareholders	831
23–1–42–8	Notice	831
23–1–42–9	Voting rights of acquired control shares; resolution	831
23–1–42–10	Redemption of acquired control shares	832
23–1–42–11	Dissenters' rights; "fair value" defined	832

§ 23–1–42–1 "Control shares" defined

As used in this chapter, "control shares" means shares that, except for this chapter, would have voting power with respect to shares of an issuing public corporation that, when added to all other shares of the issuing public corporation owned by a person or in respect to which that person may exercise or direct the exercise of voting power, would entitle that person, immediately after acquisition of the shares (directly or indirectly, alone or as a part of a group), to exercise or direct the exercise of the voting power of the issuing public corporation in the election of directors within any of the following ranges of voting power:

(1) One-fifth (1/5) or more but less than one-third (⅓) of all voting power.

(2) One-third (⅓) or more but less than a majority of all voting power.

(3) A majority or more of all voting power.

§ 23–1–42–2 "Control share acquisition" defined

(a) As used in this chapter, "control share acquisition" means the acquisition (directly or indirectly) by any person of ownership of, or the power to direct the exercise of voting power with respect to, issued and outstanding control shares.

(b) For purposes of this section, shares acquired within ninety (90) days or shares acquired pursuant to a plan to make a control share acquisition are considered to have been acquired in the same acquisition.

(c) For purposes of this section, a person who acquires shares in the ordinary course of business for the benefit of others in good faith and not for the purpose of circumventing this chapter has voting power only of shares in respect of which that person would be able to exercise or direct the exercise of votes without further instruction from others.

(d) The acquisition of any shares of an issuing public corporation does not constitute a control share acquisition if the acquisition is consummated in any of the following circumstances: . . .

(3) Pursuant to the laws of descent and distribution.

(4) Pursuant to the satisfaction of a pledge or other security interest created in good faith and not for the purpose of circumventing this chapter.

(5) Pursuant to a merger or plan of share exchange effected in compliance with [Indiana Code] 23–1–40 [merger and share exchange] if the issuing public corporation is a party to the agreement of merger or plan of share exchange.

(e) The acquisition of shares of an issuing public corporation in good faith and not for the purpose of circumventing this chapter by or from:

(1) any person whose voting rights had previously been authorized by shareholders in compliance with this chapter; or

(2) any person whose previous acquisition of shares of an issuing public corporation would have constituted a control share acquisition but for subsection (d);

does not constitute a control share acquisition, unless the acquisition entitles any person (directly or indirectly, alone or as a part of a group) to exercise or direct the exercise of voting power of the corporation in the election of directors in excess of the range of the voting power otherwise authorized.

§ 23–1–42–3   "Interested shares" defined

As used in this chapter, "interested shares" means the shares of an issuing public corporation in respect of which any of the following persons may exercise or direct the exercise of the voting power of the corporation in the election of directors:

(1) An acquiring person or member of a group with respect to a control share acquisition.

(2) Any officer of the issuing public corporation.

(3) Any employee of the issuing public corporation who is also a director of the corporation.

§ 23–1–42–4   "Issuing public corporation" defined

(a) As used in this chapter, "issuing public corporation" means a corporation that has:

(1) one hundred (100) or more shareholders;

(2) its principal place of business or its principal office in Indiana, or that owns or controls assets within Indiana having a fair market value of more than one million dollars ($1,000,000); and

(3) either:

(A) more than ten percent (10%) of its shareholders resident in Indiana;

(B) more than ten percent (10%) of its shares owned of record or beneficially owned by Indiana residents; or

(C) one thousand (1,000) shareholders resident in Indiana.

(b) The residence of a record shareholder is presumed to be the address appearing in the records of the corporation.*

§ 23–1–42–5   Voting rights under [§] 23–1–42–9

Unless the corporation's articles of incorporation or bylaws provide that this chapter does not apply to control share acquisitions of shares of the corporation before the control share acquisition, control shares of an issuing public corporation acquired in a control share acquisition have only such voting rights as are conferred by section 9 of this chapter.

§ 23–1–42–6   Acquiring person statement

Any person who proposes to make or has made a control share acquisition may at the person's election deliver an acquiring person statement to the issuing public corporation at the issuing public corporation's principal office. The acquiring person statement must set forth all of the following:

(1) The identity of the acquiring person and each other member of any group of which the person is a part for purposes of determining control shares.

(2) A statement that the acquiring person statement is given pursuant to this chapter.

(3) The number of shares of the issuing public corporation owned (directly or indirectly) by the acquiring person and each other member of the group.

---

*   Under § 23–1–20–5, "corporation" means a corporation incorporated in Indiana. (Footnote by ed.)

(4) The range of voting power under which the control share acquisition falls or would, if consummated, fall.

(5) If the control share acquisition has not taken place:

    (A) a description in reasonable detail of the terms of the proposed control share acquisition; and

    (B) representations of the acquiring person, together with a statement in reasonable detail of the facts upon which they are based, that the proposed control share acquisition, if consummated, will not be contrary to law, and that the acquiring person has the financial capacity to make the proposed control share acquisition.

§ 23–1–42–7   Special meeting of shareholders

(a) If the acquiring person so requests at the time of delivery of an acquiring person statement and gives an undertaking to pay the corporation's expenses of a special meeting, within ten (10) days thereafter, the directors of the issuing public corporation shall call a special meeting of shareholders of the issuing public corporation for the purpose of considering the voting rights to be accorded the shares acquired or to be acquired in the control share acquisition.

(b) Unless the acquiring person agrees in writing to another date, the special meeting of shareholders shall be held within fifty (50) days after receipt by the issuing public corporation of the request.

(c) If no request is made, the voting rights to be accorded the shares acquired in the control share acquisition shall be presented to the next special or annual meeting of shareholders.

(d) If the acquiring person so requests in writing at the time of delivery of the acquiring person statement, the special meeting must not be held sooner than thirty (30) days after receipt by the issuing public corporation of the acquiring person statement.

§ 23–1–42–8   Notice

(a) If a special meeting is requested, notice of the special meeting of shareholders shall be given as promptly as reasonably practicable by the issuing public corporation to all shareholders of record as of the record date set for the meeting, whether or not entitled to vote at the meeting.

(b) Notice of the special or annual shareholder meeting at which the voting rights are to be considered must include or be accompanied by both of the following:

    (1) A copy of the acquiring person statement delivered to the issuing public corporation pursuant to this chapter.

    (2) A statement by the board of directors of the corporation, authorized by its directors, of its position or recommendation, or that it is taking no position or making no recommendation, with respect to the proposed control share acquisition.

§ 23–1–42–9   Voting rights of acquired control shares; resolution

(a) Control shares acquired in a control share acquisition have the same voting rights as were accorded the shares before the control share acquisition only to the extent granted by resolution approved by the shareholders of the issuing public corporation.

(b) To be approved under this section, the resolution must be approved by:

    (1) each voting group entitled to vote separately on the proposal by a majority of all the votes entitled to be cast by that voting group, with the holders of the outstanding shares of a class being entitled to vote as a separate voting group if the proposed control share acquisition would, if fully carried out, result in any of the changes described in [Indiana Code] 23–1–38–4(a) [class voting on amendments]; and

    (2) each voting group entitled to vote separately on the proposal by a majority of all the votes entitled to be cast by that group, excluding all interested shares.

§ 23–1–42–10   Redemption of acquired control shares

(a) If authorized in a corporation's articles of incorporation or bylaws before a control share acquisition has occurred, control shares acquired in a control share acquisition with respect to which no acquiring person statement has been filed with the issuing public corporation may, at any time during the period ending sixty (60) days after the last acquisition of control shares by the acquiring person, be subject to redemption by the corporation at the fair value thereof pursuant to the procedures adopted by the corporation.

(b) Control shares acquired in a control share acquisition are not subject to redemption after an acquiring person statement has been filed unless the shares are not accorded full voting rights by the shareholders as provided in section 9 of this chapter.

§ 23–1–42–11   Dissenters' rights; "fair value" defined

(a) Unless otherwise provided in a corporation's articles of incorporation or bylaws before a control share acquisition has occurred, in the event control shares acquired in a control share acquisition are accorded full voting rights and the acquiring person has acquired control shares with a majority or more of all voting power, all shareholders of the issuing public corporation have dissenters' rights as provided in this chapter.

(b) As soon as practicable after such events have occurred, the board of directors shall cause a notice to be sent to all shareholders of the corporation advising them of the facts and that they have dissenters' rights to receive the fair value of their shares pursuant to [Indiana Code] 23–1–44 [dissenters' rights].

(c) As used in this section, "fair value" means a value not less than the highest price paid per share by the acquiring person in the control share acquisition.

MARYLAND ANN. CODE
CORPORATIONS AND ASSOCIATIONS,
TITLE 4

[Close Corporations]

TABLE OF CONTENTS

Subtitle 1. Definitions; General Provisions.

Sec.		Page
4–101.	Definitions	833
4–102.	Execution of documents	834

Subtitle 2. Election to Be a Close Corporation.

4–201.	Statement of election	834
4–202.	Required references to close corporation status	834
4–203.	Removal of statement from charter	834

Subtitle 3. Board of Directors.

4–301.	At least one director required initially	834
4–302.	Election to have no board of directors	834
4–303.	Effect of election to have no board of directors	835

Subtitle 4. Stockholders.

4–401.	Unanimous stockholders' agreement	835
4–402.	Stockholders' annual meeting	836
4–403.	Stockholders' right of inspection	836
4–404.	Statement of affairs	836

Subtitle 5. Stock Restrictions.

4–501.	Restriction on issuance or sale of stock	837
4–502.	Certain securities and stock options prohibited	837
4–503.	Restrictions on transfer of stock	837
4–504.	Denial or restriction of voting rights; unanimous stockholder vote	837

Subtitle 6. Termination of Existence.

4–601.	Consolidation, merger, share exchange, or transfer of assets	838
4–602.	Involuntary dissolution	838
4–603.	Avoidance of dissolution by purchase of petitioner's stock	838

Subtitle 1. Definitions; General Provisions.

§ 4–101. Definitions

(a) *In general.*—In this title the following words have the meanings indicated.

(b) *Close corporation.*—"Close corporation" means a corporation which elects to be a close corporation in accordance with § 4–201 of this title.

(c) *Unanimous stockholders' agreement.*—"Unanimous stockholders' agreement" means an agreement to which every stockholder of a close corporation actually has assented and which is contained in its charter or bylaws or in a written instrument signed by all the stockholders.

§ 4–102. Execution of documents

Notwithstanding any contrary provision of law, an individual who holds more than one office in a close corporation may act in more than one capacity to execute, acknowledge, or verify any instrument required to be executed, acknowledged, or verified by more than one officer.

Subtitle 2.   Election to Be a Close Corporation.

§ 4–201. Statement of election

(a) *Statement to be contained in charter.*—A corporation may elect to be a close corporation under this title by including in its charter a statement that it is a close corporation.

(b) *Procedure.*—The statement that a corporation is a close corporation shall be:

(1) Contained in the articles of incorporation originally filed with the Department; or

(2) Added to the charter by an amendment which is approved:

(i) Under the provisions of § 2–603 [Charter amendment—No stock outstanding or subscribed for] of this article, if at the time of the adoption of the amendment no stock of the corporation is either outstanding or subscribed for; or

(ii) By the affirmative vote of every stockholder and every subscriber for stock of the corporation.

§ 4–202. Required references to close corporation status

(a) *Clear reference required.*—Clear reference to the fact that the corporation is a close corporation shall appear prominently:

(1) At the head of the charter document in which the election to be a close corporation is made;

(2) In each subsequent charter document of the corporation; and

(3) On each certificate representing outstanding stock of the corporation.

(b) *Absence of reference.*—The status of a corporation as a close corporation is not affected by the failure of any charter document or stock certificate to contain the reference required by this section.

§ 4–203. Removal of statement from charter

The charter of a close corporation may be amended to remove the statement of election to be a close corporation, but only by the affirmative vote of every stockholder and every subscriber for stock of the corporation.

Subtitle 3.   Board of Directors.

§ 4–301. At least one director required initially

A close corporation shall have at least one director until an election by the corporation in its charter to have no board of directors becomes effective.

§ 4–302. Election to have no board of directors

(a) *Effective time of election.*—An election to have no board of directors becomes effective at the later of:

(1) The time that the organization meeting of directors and the issuance of at least one share of stock of the corporation are completed;

(2) The time the charter document in which the election is made becomes effective; or

(3) The time specified in the charter document in which the election is made.

(b) *Cessation of director's status.*—A director automatically ceases to be a director when an election to have no board of directors becomes effective.

§ 4–303. Effect of election to have no board of directors

If there is an election to have no board of directors:

(1) The stockholders may exercise all powers of directors, and the business and affairs of the corporation shall be managed under their direction;

(2) The stockholders of the corporation are responsible for taking any action required by law to be taken by the board of directors;

(3) Action by stockholders shall be taken by the voting of shares of stock as provided in this article;

(4) The stockholders may take any action for which this article otherwise would require both a resolution of directors and a vote of stockholders;

(5) By the affirmative vote of a majority of all the votes entitled to be cast, the stockholders may take any action for which this article otherwise would require a vote of a majority of the entire board of directors;

(6) A statement that the corporation is a close corporation which has no board of directors satisfies any requirement that an instrument filed with the Department contain a statement that a specified action was taken by the board of directors;

(7) The special liabilities imposed on directors by § 2–312(a) of this article and the provisions of §§ 2–312(b) and 2–410 of this article apply to the stockholders of the corporation and, for this purpose, "present" in § 2–410 of this article means present in person or by proxy*; and

(8) A stockholder is not liable for any action taken as a result of a vote of the stockholders, unless he was entitled to vote on the action.

Subtitle 4. Stockholders.

§ 4–401. Unanimous stockholders' agreement

(a) *Governing the corporation.*—Under a unanimous stockholders' agreement, the stockholders of a close corporation may regulate any aspect of the affairs of the corporation or the relations of the stockholders, including:

(1) The management of the business and affairs of the corporation;

(2) Restrictions on the transfer of stock;

(3) The right of one or more stockholders to dissolve the corporation at will or on the occurrence of a specified event or contingency;

(4) The exercise or division of voting power;

(5) The terms and conditions of employment of an officer or employee of the corporation, without regard to the period of his employment;

(6) The individuals who are to be directors and officers of the corporation; and

(7) The payment of dividends or the division of profits.

(b) *Amending unanimous stockholders' agreement.*—A unanimous stockholders' agreement may be amended, but only by the unanimous written consent of the stockholders then parties to the agreement.

---

* Section 2–312 concerns the liability of directors. Section 2–410 concerns the dissent of a director to an action of the board. (Footnote by ed.)

(c) *Acquisition of stock subject to unanimous stockholders' agreement.*—A stockholder who acquires his stock after a unanimous stockholders' agreement becomes effective is considered to have actually assented to the agreement and is a party to it:

(1) Whether or not he has actual knowledge of the existence of the agreement at the time he acquires the stock, if acquired by gift or bequest from a person who was a party to the agreement; and

(2) If he has actual knowledge of the existence of the agreement at the time he acquires the stock, if acquired in any other manner.

(d) *Enforcement of unanimous stockholders' agreement.*—(1) A court of equity may enforce a unanimous stockholders' agreement by injunction or by any other relief which the court in its discretion determines to be fair and appropriate in the circumstances.

(2) As an alternative to the granting of an injunction or other equitable relief, on motion of a party to the proceeding, the court may order dissolution of the corporation under the provisions of Subtitle 6 of this title.

(e) *Inapplicability of section to other agreements.*—This section does not affect any otherwise valid agreement among stockholders of a close corporation or of any other corporation.

§ 4–402. Stockholders' annual meeting

(a) *General rule.*—The bylaws of a close corporation shall provide for an annual meeting of stockholders in accordance with Title 2 of this article, but the meeting need not be held unless requested by a stockholder.

(b) *Written request for annual meeting.*—A request for an annual meeting shall be in writing and delivered to the president or secretary of the corporation:

(1) At least 30 days before the date specified in the bylaws for the meeting; or

(2) If the bylaws specify a period during which the date for the meeting may be set, at least 30 days before the beginning of that period.

§ 4–403. Stockholders' right of inspection

A stockholder of a close corporation or his agent may inspect and copy during usual business hours any records or documents of the corporation relevant to its business and affairs, including any:

(1) Bylaws;

(2) Minutes of the proceedings of the stockholders and directors;

(3) Annual statement of affairs;

(4) Stock ledger; and

(5) Books of account.

§ 4–404. Statement of affairs

(a) *Stockholders' right to request.*—Once during each calendar year, each stockholder of a close corporation may present to any officer of the corporation a written request for a statement of its affairs.

(b) *Duty to prepare and file; verification.*—Within 20 days after a request is made for a statement of a close corporation's affairs, the corporation shall prepare and have available on file at its principal office a statement verified under oath by its president or treasurer or one of its vice-presidents or assistant treasurers which sets forth in reasonable detail the corporation's assets and liabilities as of a reasonably current date.

Subtitle 5. Stock Restrictions.

§ 4–501. Restriction on issuance or sale of stock

If there is any stock of a close corporation outstanding, the corporation may not issue or sell any of its stock, including treasury stock, unless the issuance or sale is:

(1) Approved by the affirmative vote of the holders of all outstanding stock; or

(2) Permitted by a unanimous stockholders' agreement.

§ 4–502. Certain securities and stock options prohibited

A close corporation may not have outstanding any:

(1) Securities which are convertible into its stock;

(2) Voting securities other than stock; or

(3) Options, warrants, or other rights to subscribe for or purchase any of its stock, unless they are nontransferable.

§ 4–503. Restrictions on transfer of stock

(a) *"Transfer" defined.*—(1) In this section, "transfer" means the transfer of any interest in the stock of a close corporation, except:

(i) A transfer by operation of law to a personal representative, trustee in bankruptcy, receiver, guardian, or similar legal representative;

(ii) The acquisition of a lien or power of sale by an attachment, levy, or similar procedure; or

(iii) The creation or assignment of a security interest.

(2) A foreclosure sale or other transfer by a person who acquired his interest or power in a transaction described in paragraph (1) of this subsection is a transfer subject to all the provisions of this section. For purposes of the transfer, the person effecting the foreclosure sale or other transfer shall be treated as and have the rights of a holder of the stock under this section and § 4–602(b) of this title.

(b) *Enumeration of restrictions.*—A transfer of the stock of a close corporation is invalid unless:

(1) Every stockholder of the corporation consents to the transfer in writing within the 90 days before the date of the transfer; or

(2) The transfer is made under a provision of a unanimous stockholders' agreement permitting the transfer to the corporation or to or in trust for the principal benefit of:

(i) One or more of the stockholders or security holders of the corporation or their wives, children, or grandchildren; or

(ii) One or more persons named in the agreement.

§ 4–504. Denial or restriction of voting rights; unanimous stockholder vote

(a) *Denial or restriction of voting rights.*—A close corporation may deny or restrict the voting rights of any of its stock as provided in this article. Notwithstanding any denial or restriction, all stock has voting rights on any matter required by this title to be authorized by the affirmative vote of every stockholder or every subscriber for stock of a close corporation.

(b) *Unanimous stockholder vote.*—Notwithstanding the provisions of § 2–104(b)(5)* of this article, the charter of a close corporation may not lower the proportion of votes required to approve any action for which

---

* Section 2–104(b)(5) provides that the articles of incorporation may include certain provisions that reduce the shareholder note that would otherwise be required. (Footnote by ed.)

this title requires the affirmative vote or assent of every stockholder or every subscriber for stock of the corporation.

Subtitle 6.   Termination of Existence.

§ 4–601. Consolidation, merger, share exchange, or transfer of assets

A consolidation, merger, share exchange, or transfer of assets of a close corporation shall be made in accordance with the provisions of Title 3 of this article [Extraordinary Actions]. However, approval of a proposed consolidation or merger, a transfer of its assets, or an acquisition of its stock in a share exchange requires the affirmative vote of every stockholder of the corporation.

§ 4–602. Involuntary dissolution

(a) *Dissolution by stockholder generally.*—Any stockholder of a close corporation may petition a court of equity for dissolution of the corporation on the grounds set forth in § 3–413 of this article [Grounds for petition for involuntary dissolution] or on the ground that there is such internal dissension among the stockholders of the corporation that the business and affairs of the corporation can no longer be conducted to the advantage of the stockholders generally.

(b) *Dissolution by stockholder desiring to transfer stock.*—(1) Unless a unanimous stockholders' agreement provides otherwise, a stockholder of a close corporation has the right to require dissolution of the corporation if:

      (i) The stockholder made a written request for consent to a proposed bona fide transfer of his stock in accordance with the provisions of § 4–503(b)(1) of this title, specifying the proposed transferee and consideration, and the consent was not received by him within 30 days after the date of the request; or

      (ii) Another party to a unanimous stockholders' agreement defaulted in an obligation, set forth in or arising under the agreement, to purchase or cause to be purchased stock of the stockholder, and the default was not remedied within 30 days after the date for performance of the obligation.

      (2) A petition for dissolution under this subsection shall be filed within 60 days after the date of the request or the default, as the case may be.

(c) *Proceeding to be in accordance with § 3–414.*—A proceeding for dissolution authorized by this section shall be in accordance with the provisions of § 3–414 of this article [Appointment of receiver in involuntary dissolution].

§ 4–603. Avoidance of dissolution by purchase of petitioner's stock

(a) *Stockholder's right to avoid dissolution.*—Any one or more stockholders who desire to continue the business of a close corporation may avoid the dissolution of the corporation or the appointment of a receiver by electing to purchase the stock owned by the petitioner at a price equal to its fair value.

(b) *Court to determine fair value of stock.*—(1) If a stockholder who makes the election is unable to reach an agreement with the petitioner as to the fair value of the stock, then, if the electing stockholder gives bond or other security sufficient to assure payment to the petitioner of the fair value of the stock, the court shall stay the proceeding and determine the fair value of the stock.

      (2) Fair value shall be determined in accordance with the procedure set forth in Title 3, Subtitle 2 of this article [Rights of Objecting Shareholders], as of the close of business on the day on which the petition for dissolution was filed.

(c) *Court order.*—After the fair value of the stock is determined, the order of the court directing the purchase shall set the purchase price and the time within which payment shall be made. The court may order other appropriate terms and conditions of sale, including:

      (1) Payment of the purchase price in installments; and

      (2) The allocation of shares of stock among electing stockholders.

(d) *Interest on purchase price; cessation of other rights.*—The petitioner:

 (1) Is entitled to interest on the purchase price of his stock from the date the petition is filed; and

 (2) Ceases to have any other rights with respect to the stock, except the right to receive payment of its fair value.

(e) *Costs of proceeding.*—The costs of the proceeding, as determined by the court, shall be divided between the petitioner and the purchasing stockholder. The costs shall include the reasonable compensation and expenses of appraisers, but may not include fees and expenses of counsel or of other experts retained by a party.

(f) *Transfer of stock.*—The petitioner shall transfer his shares of stock to the purchasing stockholder:

 (1) At a time set by the court; or

 (2) If the court sets no time, at the time the purchase price is paid in full.

MICH. COMP. LAWS § 450.1489

§ 450.1489. Shareholders' actions; relief; exclusions

Sec. 489. (1) A shareholder may bring an action in the circuit court of the county in which the principal place of business or registered office of the corporation is located to establish that the acts of the directors or those in control of the corporation are illegal, fraudulent, or willfully unfair and oppressive to the corporation or to the shareholder. If the shareholder establishes grounds for relief, the circuit court may make an order or grant relief as it considers appropriate, including, without limitation, an order providing for any of the following:

(a) The dissolution and liquidation of the assets and business of the corporation.

(b) The cancellation or alteration of a provision contained in the articles of incorporation, an amendment of the articles of incorporation, or the bylaws of the corporation.

(c) The cancellation, alteration, or injunction against a resolution or other act of the corporation.

(d) The direction or prohibition of an act of the corporation or of shareholders, directors, officers, or other persons party to the action.

(e) The purchase at fair value of the shares of a shareholder, either by the corporation or by the officers, directors, or other shareholders responsible for the wrongful acts.

(f) *An award of damages to the corporation or a shareholder*. An action seeking an award of damages must be commenced within 3 years after the cause of action under this section has accrued, or within 2 years after the shareholder discovers or reasonably should have discovered the cause of action under this section, whichever occurs first.

(2) No action under this section shall be brought by a shareholder whose shares are listed on a national securities exchange or regularly traded in a market maintained by 1 or more members of a national or affiliated securities association.

(3) As used in this section, "willfully unfair and oppressive conduct" means a continuing course of conduct or a significant action or series of actions that substantially interferes with the interests of the shareholder as a shareholder. Willfully unfair an oppressive conduct may include the termination of employment or limitations on employment benefits to the extent that the actions interfere with distributions or other shareholder interests disproportionately as to the affected shareholder. The term does not include conduct or actions that are permitted by an agreement, the articles of incorporation, the bylaws, or a consistently applied written corporate policy or procedure.

MINNESOTA STATS. ANN. § 302A.751

§ 302A.751. Judicial intervention; equitable remedies or dissolution

Subdivision 1. When permitted. A court may grant any equitable relief it deems just and reasonable in the circumstances or may dissolve a corporation and liquidate its assets and business:

(a) In a supervised voluntary dissolution pursuant to section 302A.741;

(b) In an action by a shareholder when it is established that:

(1) the directors or the persons having the authority otherwise vested in the board are deadlocked in the management of the corporate affairs and the shareholders are unable to break the deadlock;

(2) the directors or those in control of the corporation have acted fraudulently or illegally toward one or more shareholders in their capacities as shareholders or directors, or as officers or employees of a closely held corporation;

(3) the directors or those in control of the corporation have acted in a manner unfairly prejudicial toward one or more shareholders in their capacities as shareholders or directors of a corporation that is not a publicly held corporation, or as officers or employees of a closely held corporation;

(4) the shareholders of the corporation are so divided in voting power that, for a period the includes the time when two consecutive regular meetings were held, they have failed to elect successors to directors whose terms have expired or would have expired upon the election and qualification of their successors;

(5) the corporate assets are being misapplied or wasted; or

(6) the period of duration as provided in the articles has expired. . . .

Subd. 2. Buy-out on motion. In an action under subdivision 1, clause (b), involving a corporation that is not a publicly held corporation at the time the action is commenced and in which one or more of the circumstances described in that clause is established, the court may, upon motion of a corporation or a shareholder or beneficial owner of shares of the corporation, order the sale by plaintiff or a defendant of all shares of the corporation held by the plaintiff or defendant to either the corporation or the moving shareholders, whichever is specified in the motion, if the court determines in its discretion that an order would be fair and equitable to all parties under all of the circumstances of the case.

The purchase price of any shares so sold shall be the fair value of the shares as of the date of the commencement of the action or as of another date found equitable by the court, provided that, if the shares in question are then subject to sale and purchase pursuant to the bylaws of the corporation, a shareholder control agreement, the terms of the shares, or otherwise, the court shall order the sale for the price and on the terms set forth in them, unless the court determines that the price or terms are unreasonable under all the circumstances of the case.

Within five days after the entry of the order, the corporation shall provide each selling shareholder or beneficial owner with the information it is required to provide under section 302A.473, subdivision 5, paragraph (a).

If the parties are unable to agree on fair value within 40 days of entry of the order, the court shall determine the fair value of the shares under the provisions of section 302A.473, subdivision 7, and may allow interest or costs as provided in section 302A.473, subdivisions 1 and 8.

The purchase price shall be paid in one or more installments as agreed on by the parties, or, if no agreement can be reached within 40 days of entry of the order, as ordered by the court. Upon entry of an order for the sale of shares under this subdivision and provided that the corporation or the moving shareholders post a bond in adequate amount with sufficient sureties or otherwise satisfy the court that the full purchase price of the shares, plus such additional costs, expenses, and fees as may be awarded, will be paid when due and payable, the selling shareholders shall no longer have any rights or status as shareholders, officers, or directors, except the right to receive the fair value of their shares plus such other amounts as might be awarded.

Subd. 3. Condition of corporation. In determining whether to order equitable relief, dissolution, or a buy-out, the court shall take into consideration the financial condition of the corporation but shall not refuse to order equitable relief, dissolution, or a buy-out solely on the ground that the corporation has accumulated or current operating profits.

Subd. 3a. Considerations in granting relief involving closely held corporations. In determining whether to order equitable relief, dissolution, or a buy-out, the court shall take into consideration the duty which all shareholders in a closely held corporation owe one another to act in an honest, fair, and reasonable manner in the operation of the corporation and the reasonable expectations of all shareholders as they exist at the inception and develop during the course of the shareholders' relationship with the corporation and with each other. For purposes of this section, any written agreements, including employment agreements and buy-sell agreements, between or among shareholders or between or among one or more shareholders and the corporation are presumed to reflect the parties' reasonable expectations concerning matters dealt with in the agreements.

Subd. 3b. Dissolution as remedy. In deciding whether to order dissolution, the court shall consider whether lesser relief suggested by one or more parties, such as any form of equitable relief, a buy-out, or a partial liquidation, would be adequate to permanently relieve the circumstances established under subdivision 1, clause (b) or (c). Lesser relief may be ordered in any case where it would be appropriate under all the facts and circumstances of the case.

Subd. 4. Expenses. If the court finds that a party to a proceeding brought under this section has acted arbitrarily, vexatiously, or otherwise not in good faith, it may in its discretion award reasonable expenses, including attorneys' fees and disbursements, to any of the other parties.

Subd. 5. Venue; parties. Proceedings under this section shall be brought in a court within the county in which the registered office of the corporation is located. It is not necessary to make shareholders parties to the action or proceeding unless relief is sought against them personally.

NEV. REV. STAT. § 78.138

§ 78.138.   **Directors and officers: Fiduciary duties; exercise of powers; performance of duties; presumptions and considerations; liability to corporation and stockholders.**

1. The fiduciary duties of directors and officers are to exercise their respective powers in good faith and with a view to the interests of the corporation.

2. In exercising their respective powers, directors and officers may, and are entitled to, rely on information, opinions, reports, books of account or statements, including financial statements and other financial data, that are prepared or presented by:

(a) One or more directors, officers or employees of the corporation reasonably believed to be reliable and competent in the matters prepared or presented;

(b) Counsel, public accountants, financial advisers, valuation advisers, investment bankers or other persons as to matters reasonably believed to be within the preparer's or presenter's professional or expert competence; or

(c) A committee on which the director or officer relying thereon does not serve, established in accordance with NRS 78.125, as to matters within the committee's designated authority and matters on which the committee is reasonably believed to merit confidence, but a director or officer is not entitled to rely on such information, opinions, reports, books of account or statements if the director or officer has knowledge concerning the matter in question that would cause reliance thereon to be unwarranted.

3. Except as otherwise provided in subsection 1 of NRS 78.139, directors and officers, in deciding upon matters of business, are presumed to act in good faith, on an informed basis and with a view to the interests of the corporation. A director or officer is not individually liable for damages as a result of an act or failure to act in his or her capacity as a director or officer except under circumstances described in subsection 7.

4. Directors and officers, in exercising their respective powers with a view to the interests of the corporation, may:

(a) Consider all relevant facts, circumstances, contingencies or constituencies, including, without limitation:

(1) The interests of the corporation's employees, suppliers, creditors or customers;

(2) The economy of the State or Nation;

(3) The interests of the community or of society;

(4) The long-term or short-term interests of the corporation, including the possibility that these interests may be best served by the continued independence of the corporation; or

(5) The long-term or short-term interests of the corporation's stockholders, including the possibility that these interests may be best served by the continued independence of the corporation.

(b) Consider or assign weight to the interests of any particular person or group, or to any other relevant facts, circumstances, contingencies or constituencies.

5. Directors and officers are not required to consider, as a dominant factor, the effect of a proposed corporate action upon any particular group or constituency having an interest in the corporation.

6. The provisions of subsections 4 and 5 do not create or authorize any causes of action against the corporation or its directors or officers.

7. Except as otherwise provided in NRS 35.230, 90.660, 91.250, 452.200, 452.270, 668.045 and 694A.030, or unless the articles of incorporation or an amendment thereto, in each case filed on or after October 1, 2003, provide for greater individual liability, a director or officer is not individually liable to the

corporation or its stockholders or creditors for any damages as a result of any act or failure to act in his or her capacity as a director or officer unless:

(a) The trier of fact determines that the presumption established by subsection 3 has been rebutted; and

(b) It is proven that:

(1) The director's or officer's act or failure to act constituted a breach of his or her fiduciary duties as a director or officer; and

(2) Such breach involved intentional misconduct, fraud or a knowing violation of law.

8. This section applies to all cases, circumstances and matters unless otherwise provided in the articles of incorporation, or an amendment thereto, including, without limitation, any change or potential change in control of the corporation.

NEW YORK BUSINESS CORPORATION LAW (SELECTED PROVISIONS)

TABLE OF CONTENTS

ARTICLE 1.   SHORT TITLE; DEFINITIONS; APPLICATION; CERTIFICATES; MISCELLANEOUS

Sec.		Page
102.	Definitions	849

ARTICLE 2.   CORPORATE PURPOSES AND POWERS

201.	Purposes	850
202.	General Powers	850
203.	Defense of Ultra Vires	851

ARTICLE 4.   FORMATION OF CORPORATIONS

401.	Incorporations	851
402.	Certificate of Incorporation; Contents	851
403.	Certificate of Incorporation; Effect	852

ARTICLE 5.   CORPORATE FINANCE

501.	Authorized Shares	853
502.	Issue of Any Class of Preferred Shares in Series	853
503.	Subscription for Shares; Time for Payment, Forfeiture for Default	854
504.	Consideration and Payment for Shares	855
505.	Rights and Options to Purchase Shares; Issue of Rights and Options to Directors, Officers and Employees	855
506.	Determination of Stated Capital	857
510.	Dividends or Other Distributions in Cash or Property	857
511.	Share Distributions and Changes	857
512.	Redeemable Shares	858
513.	Purchase, Redemption and Certain Other Transactions by a Corporation With Respect to Its Own Shares	859
514.	Agreements for Purchase by a Corporation of Its Own Shares	859
515.	Reacquired Shares	860
516.	Reduction of Stated Capital in Certain Cases	860
518.	Corporate Bonds	860
520.	Liability for Failure to Disclose Required Information	861

ARTICLE 6.   SHAREHOLDERS

601.	By-Laws	861
602.	Meetings of Shareholders	861
603.	Special Meeting for Election of Directors	862
604.	Fixing Record Date	862
605.	Notice of Meetings of Shareholders	862
606.	Waivers of Notice	863
607.	List of Shareholders at Meetings	863
608.	Quorum of Shareholders	863
609.	Proxies	864
614.	Vote of Shareholders	865

615. Written Consent of Shareholders, Subscribers or Incorporators Without a Meeting 865
616. Greater Requirement as to Quorum and Vote of Shareholders 866
617. Voting by Class or Classes of Shares 866
619. Powers of Supreme Court Respecting Elections 866
620. Agreements as to Voting; Provision in Certificate of Incorporation as to Control of Directors 867
621. Voting Trust Agreements 867
622. Preemptive Rights 868
623. Procedure to Enforce Shareholder's Right to Receive Payment for Shares 870
624. Books and Records; Right of Inspection, Prima Facie Evidence 871
626. Shareholders' Derivative Action Brought in the Right of the Corporation to Procure a Judgment in Its Favor 872
627. Security for Expenses in Shareholders' Derivative Action Brought in the Right of the Corporation to Procure a Judgment in Its Favor 872
628. Liability of Subscribers and Shareholders 873
629. Certain Transfers or Assignments by Shareholders or Subscribers; Effect 873
630. Liability of Shareholders for Wages Due to Laborers, Servants or Employees 873

ARTICLE 7.   DIRECTORS AND OFFICERS

701. Board of Directors 874
702. Number of Directors 874
703. Election and Term of Directors 874
704. Classification of Directors 874
705. Newly Created Directorships and Vacancies 875
706. Removal of Directors 875
707. Quorum of Directors 876
708. Action by the Board 876
709. Greater Requirement as to Quorum and Vote of Directors 876
712. Executive Committee and Other Committees 877
713. Interested Directors 877
714. Loans to Directors 878
715. Officers 878
716. Removal of Officers 879
717. Duty of Directors 879
719. Liability of Directors in Certain Cases 880
720. Action Against Directors and Officers for Misconduct 881
721. Nonexclusivity of Statutory Provisions for Indemnification of Directors and Officers 881
722. Authorization for Indemnification of Directors and Officers 881
723. Payment of Indemnification Other Than by Court Award 882
724. Indemnification of Directors and Officers by a Court 883
725. Other Provisions Affecting Indemnification of Directors and Officers 883
726. Insurance for Indemnification of Directors and Officers 884

ARTICLE 8.   AMENDMENTS AND CHANGES

801. Right to Amend Certificate of Incorporation 884
802. Reduction of Stated Capital by Amendment 885
804. Class Voting on Amendment 886

ARTICLE 9.   MERGER OR CONSOLIDATION; GUARANTEE; DISPOSITION OF ASSETS

912. Requirements Relating to Certain Business Combinations 886

ARTICLE 10.   NON-JUDICIAL DISSOLUTION

1001. Authorization of Dissolution 891
1002. Dissolution Under Provision in Certificate of Incorporation 891

ARTICLE 11.   JUDICIAL DISSOLUTION

1101. Attorney-General's Action for Judicial Dissolution 892
1102. Directors' Petition for Judicial Dissolution 892
1103. Shareholders' Petition for Judicial Dissolution 892
1104. Petition in Case of Deadlock Among Directors or Shareholders 892
1104–a. Petition for Judicial Dissolution Under Special Circumstances 893
1111. Judgment or Final Order of Dissolution 893
1118. Purchase of Petitioner's Shares; Valuation 894

ARTICLE 13.   FOREIGN CORPORATIONS

1315. Record of Shareholders 894
1317. Liabilities of Directors and Officers of Foreign Corporations 895
1318. Liability of Foreign Corporations for Failure to Disclose Required Information 895
1319. Applicability of Other Provisions 896
1320. Exemption From Certain Provisions 896

ARTICLE 17.   BENEFIT CORPORATIONS

1701. Application and Effect of Article 896
1702. Definitions 896
1703. Formation of Benefit Corporations 898
1704. Election of an Existing Business Corporation to Become a Benefit Corporation 898
1705. Termination of Benefit Corporation Status 898
1706. Corporate Purposes 898
1707. Standard of Conduct for Directors and Officers 899
1708. Annual Benefit Report 899
1709. Conspicuous Language on the Face of Certificates 900

ARTICLE 1

SHORT TITLE; DEFINITIONS; APPLICATION; CERTIFICATES; MISCELLANEOUS

§ 102.   Definitions

(a) As used in this chapter, unless the context otherwise requires, the term. . . .

(8) "Insolvent" means being unable to pay debts as they become due in the usual course of the debtor's business.

(9) "Net assets" means the amount by which the total assets exceed the total liabilities. Stated capital and surplus are not liabilities. . . .

(12) "Stated capital" means the sum of (A) the par value of all shares with par value that have been issued, (B) the amount of the consideration received for all shares without par value that have been issued, except such part of the consideration therefor as may have been allocated to surplus in a manner permitted by law, and (C) such amounts not included in clauses (A) and (B) as have been transferred to stated capital, whether upon the distribution of shares or otherwise, minus all reductions from such sums as have been effected in a manner permitted by law.

(13) "Surplus" means the excess of net assets over stated capital.

(14) "Treasury shares" means shares which have been issued, have been subsequently acquired, and are retained uncancelled by the corporation. Treasury shares are issued shares, but not outstanding shares, and are not assets. . . .

ARTICLE 2

CORPORATE PURPOSES AND POWERS

§ 201.   Purposes

(a) A corporation may be formed under this chapter for any lawful business purpose or purposes except to do in this state any business for which formation is permitted under any other statute of this state unless such statute permits formation under this chapter. If, immediately prior to the effective date of this chapter, a statute of this state permitted the formation of a corporation under the stock corporation law for a purpose or purposes specified in such other statute, such statute shall be deemed and construed to permit formation of such corporation under this chapter, and any conditions, limitations or restrictions in such other statute upon the formation of such corporation under the stock corporation law shall apply to the formation thereof under this chapter. . . .

(c) In time of war or other national emergency, a corporation may do any lawful business in aid thereof, notwithstanding the purpose or purposes set forth in its certificate of incorporation, at the request or direction of any competent governmental authority. . . .

§ 202.   General Powers

(a) Each corporation, subject to any limitations provided in this chapter or any other statute of this state or its certificate of incorporation, shall have power in furtherance of its corporate purposes:

(1) To have perpetual duration.

(2) To sue and be sued in all courts and to participate in actions and proceedings, whether judicial, administrative, arbitrative or otherwise, in like cases as natural persons.

(3) To have a corporate seal, and to alter such seal at pleasure, and to use it by causing it or a facsimile to be affixed or impressed or reproduced in any other manner.

(4) To purchase, receive, take by grant, gift, devise, bequest or otherwise, lease, or otherwise acquire, own, hold, improve, employ, use and otherwise deal in and with, real or personal property, or any interest therein, wherever situated.

(5) To sell, convey, lease, exchange, transfer or otherwise dispose of, or mortgage or pledge, or create a security interest in, all or any of its property, or any interest therein, wherever situated.

(6) To purchase, take, receive, subscribe for, or otherwise acquire, own, hold, vote, employ, sell, lend, lease, exchange, transfer, or otherwise dispose of, mortgage, pledge, use and otherwise deal in and with, bonds and other obligations, shares, or other securities or interests issued by others, whether engaged in similar or different business, governmental, or other activities.

(7) To make contracts, give guarantees and incur liabilities, borrow money at such rates of interest as the corporation may determine, issue its notes, bonds and other obligations, and secure any of its obligations by mortgage or pledge of all or any of its property or any interest therein, wherever situated.

(8) To lend money, invest and reinvest its funds, and take and hold real and personal property as security for the payment of funds so loaned or invested.

(9) To do business, carry on its operations, and have offices and exercise the powers granted by this chapter in any jurisdiction within or without the United States.

(10) To elect or appoint officers, employees and other agents of the corporation, define their duties, fix their compensation and the compensation of directors, and to indemnify corporate personnel.

(11) To adopt, amend or repeal by-laws, including emergency by-laws made pursuant to subdivision seventeen of section twelve of the state defense emergency act, relating to the business of the corporation, the conduct of its affairs, its rights or powers or the rights or powers of its shareholders, directors or officers.

(12) To make donations, irrespective of corporate benefit, for the public welfare or for community fund, hospital, charitable, educational, scientific, civic or similar purposes, and in time of war or other national emergency in aid thereof.

(13) To pay pensions, establish and carry out pension, profit-sharing, share bonus, share purchase, share option, savings, thrift and other retirement, incentive and benefit plans, trusts and provisions for any or all of its directors, officers and employees.

(14) To purchase, receive, take, or otherwise acquire, own, hold, sell, lend, exchange, transfer or otherwise dispose of, pledge, use and otherwise deal in and with its own shares.

(15) To be a promoter, partner, member, associate or manager of other business enterprises or ventures, or to the extent permitted in any other jurisdiction to be an incorporator of other corporations of any type or kind.

(16) To have and exercise all powers necessary or convenient to effect any or all of the purposes for which the corporation is formed.

(b) No corporation shall do business in New York state under any name, other than that appearing in its certificate of incorporation, without compliance with the filing provisions of section one hundred thirty of the general business law governing the conduct of business under an assumed name.

§ 203. Defense of Ultra Vires

(a) No act of a corporation and no transfer of real or personal property to or by a corporation, otherwise lawful, shall be invalid by reason of the fact that the corporation was without capacity or power to do such act or to make or receive such transfer, but such lack of capacity or power may be asserted:

(1) In an action by a shareholder against the corporation to enjoin the doing of any act or the transfer of real or personal property by or to the corporation. If the unauthorized act or transfer sought to be enjoined is being, or is to be, performed or made under any contract to which the corporation is a party, the court may, if all of the parties to the contract are parties to the action and if it deems the same to be equitable, set aside and enjoin the performance of such contract, and in so doing may allow to the corporation or to the other parties to the contract, as the case may be, such compensation as may be equitable for the loss or damage sustained by any of them from the action of the court in setting aside and enjoining the performance of such contract; provided that anticipated profits to be derived from the performance of the contract shall not be awarded by the court as a loss or damage sustained.

(2) In an action by or in the right of the corporation to procure a judgment in its favor against an incumbent or former officer or director of the corporation for loss or damage due to his unauthorized act.

(3) In an action or special proceeding by the attorney-general to annul or dissolve the corporation or to enjoin it from the doing of unauthorized business.

ARTICLE 4

FORMATION OF CORPORATIONS

§ 401. Incorporations

One or more natural persons of the age of eighteen years or over may act as incorporators of a corporation to be formed under this chapter.

§ 402. Certificate of Incorporation; Contents

(a) A certificate, entitled "Certificate of incorporation of _____ (name of corporation) under section 402 of the Business Corporation Law", shall be signed by each incorporator, with his name and address included in such certificate[,] and delivered to the department of state. It shall set forth:

(1) The name of the corporation.

(2) The purpose or purposes for which it is formed, it being sufficient to state, either alone or with other purposes, that the purpose of the corporation is to engage in any lawful act or activity for which corporations may be organized under this chapter, provided that it also state that it is not formed to engage in any act or activity requiring the consent or approval of any state official, department, board, agency or other body without such consent or approval first being obtained. By such statement all lawful acts and activities shall be within the purposes of the corporation, except for express limitations therein or in this chapter, if any.

(3) The county within this state in which the office of the corporation is to be located.

(4) The aggregate number of shares which the corporation shall have the authority to issue; if such shares are to consist of one class only, the par value of the shares or a statement that the shares are without par value; or, if the shares are to be divided into classes, the number of shares of each class and the par value of the shares having par value and a statement as to which shares, if any, are without par value.

(5) If the shares are to be divided into classes, the designation of each class and a statement of the relative rights, preferences and limitations of the shares of each class.

(6) If the shares of any preferred class are to be issued in series, the designation of each series and a statement of the variations in the relative rights, preferences and limitations as between series insofar as the same are to be fixed in the certificate of incorporation, a statement of any authority to be vested in the board to establish and designate series and to fix the variations in the relative rights, preferences and limitations as between series and a statement of any limit on the authority of the board of directors to change the number of shares of any series of preferred shares as provided in paragraph (e) of section 502 (Issue of any class of preferred shares in series).

(7) A designation of the secretary of state as agent of the corporation upon whom process against it may be served and the post office address within or without this state to which the secretary of state shall mail a copy of any process against it served upon him.

(8) If the corporation is to have a registered agent, his name and address within this state and a statement that the registered agent is to be the agent of the corporation upon whom process against it may be served.

(9) The duration of the corporation if other than perpetual.

(b) The certificate of incorporation may set forth a provision eliminating or limiting the personal liability of directors to the corporation or its shareholders for damages for any breach of duty in such capacity, provided that no such provision shall eliminate or limit:

(1) the liability of any director if a judgment or other final adjudication adverse to him establishes that his acts or omissions were in bad faith or involved intentional misconduct or a knowing violation of law or that he personally gained in fact a financial profit or other advantage to which he was not legally entitled or that his acts violated section 719, or

(2) the liability of any director for any act or omission prior to the adoption of a provision authorized by this paragraph.

(c) The certificate of incorporation may set forth any provision, not inconsistent with this chapter or any other statute of this state, relating to the business of the corporation, its affairs, its rights or powers, or the rights or powers of its shareholders, directors or officers including any provision relating to matters which under this chapter are required or permitted to be set forth in the by-laws. It is not necessary to set forth in the certificate of incorporation any of the powers enumerated in this chapter.

§ 403. Certificate of Incorporation; Effect

Upon the filing of the certificate of incorporation by the department of state, the corporate existence shall begin, and such certificate shall be conclusive evidence that all conditions precedent have been fulfilled and that the corporation has been formed under this chapter, except in an action or special proceeding brought by the attorney-general. Notwithstanding the above, a certificate of incorporation may set forth a date subsequent to filing, not to exceed ninety days after filing, upon which date corporate existence shall begin.

ARTICLE 5

CORPORATE FINANCE

§ 501. Authorized Shares

(a) Every corporation shall have power to create and issue the number of shares stated in its certificate of incorporation. Such shares may be all of one class or may be divided into two or more classes. Each class shall consist of either shares with par value or shares without par value, having such designation and such relative voting, dividend, liquidation and other rights, preferences and limitations, consistent with this chapter, as shall be stated in the certificate of incorporation. The certificate of incorporation may deny, limit or otherwise define the voting rights and may limit or otherwise define the dividend or liquidation rights of shares of any class, but no such denial, limitation or definition of voting rights shall be effective unless at the time one or more classes of outstanding shares or bonds, singly or in the aggregate, are entitled to full voting rights, and no such limitation or definition of dividend or liquidation rights shall be effective unless at the time one or more classes of outstanding shares, singly or in the aggregate, are entitled to unlimited dividend and liquidation rights.

(b) If the shares are divided into two or more classes, the shares of each class shall be designated to distinguish them from the shares of all other classes. Shares which are entitled to preference in the distribution of dividends or assets shall not be designated as common shares. Shares which are not entitled to preference in the distribution of dividends or assets shall be common shares, even if identified by a class or other designation, and shall not be designated as preferred shares.

(c) Subject to the designations, relative rights, preferences and limitations applicable to separate series and except as otherwise permitted by subparagraph two of paragraph (a) of section five hundred five of this article, each share shall be equal to every other share of the same class. . . .

§ 502. Issue of Any Class of Preferred Shares in Series

(a) If the certificate of incorporation so provides, a corporation may issue any class of preferred shares in series. Shares of each such series when issued, shall be designated to distinguish them from shares of all other series.

(b) The number of shares included in any or all series of any classes of preferred shares and any or all of the designations, relative rights, preferences and limitations of any or all such series may be fixed in the certificate of incorporation, subject to the limitation that, unless the certificate of incorporation provides otherwise, if the stated dividends and amounts payable on liquidation are not paid in full, the shares of all series of the same class shall share ratably in the payment of dividends including accumulations, if any, in accordance with the sums which would be payable on such shares if all dividends were declared and paid in full, and in any distribution of assets other than by way of dividends in accordance with the sums which would be payable on such distribution if all sums payable were discharged in full.

(c) If any such number of shares or any such designation, relative right, preference or limitation of the shares of any series is not fixed in the certificate of incorporation, it may be fixed by the board, to the extent authorized by the certificate of incorporation. Unless otherwise provided in the certificate of incorporation, the number of preferred shares of any series so fixed by the board may be increased (but not above the total number of authorized shares of the class) or decreased (but not below the number of shares thereof then outstanding) by the board. In case the number of such shares shall be decreased, the number of shares by which the series is decreased shall, unless eliminated pursuant to paragraph (e) of this section, resume the status which they had prior to being designated as part of a series of preferred shares.

(d) Before the issue of any shares of a series established by the board, a certificate of amendment under section 805 (Certificate of amendment; contents) shall be delivered to the department of state. Such certificate shall set forth:

(1) The name of the corporation, and, if it has been changed, the name under which it was formed.

(2) The date the certificate of incorporation was filed by the department of state.

(3) That the certificate of incorporation is thereby amended by the addition of a provision stating the number, designation, relative rights, preferences, and limitations of the shares of the series as fixed by the board, setting forth in full the text of such provision.

(e) Action by the board to increase or decrease the number of preferred shares of any series pursuant to paragraph (c) of this section shall become effective by delivering to the department of state a certificate of amendment under section 805 (Certificate of amendment; contents) which shall set forth:

(1) The name of the corporation, and, if it has been changed, the name under which it was formed.

(2) The date its certificate of incorporation was filed with the department of state.

(3) That the certificate of incorporation is thereby amended to increase or decrease, as the case may be, the number of preferred shares of any series so fixed by the board, setting forth the specific terms of the amendment and the number of shares so authorized following the effectiveness of the amendment.

When no shares of any such series are outstanding, either because none were issued or because no issued shares of any such series remain outstanding, the certificate of amendment under section 805 may also set forth a statement that none of the authorized shares of such series are outstanding and that none will be issued subject to the certificate of incorporation, and, when such certificate becomes accepted for filing, it shall have the effect of eliminating from the certificate of incorporation all matter set forth therein with respect to such series of preferred shares.

§ 503.   Subscription for Shares; Time of Payment, Forfeiture for Default

(a) Unless otherwise provided by the terms of the subscription, a subscription for shares of a corporation to be formed shall be irrevocable, except with the consent of all other subscribers or the corporation, for a period of three months from its date.

(b) A subscription, whether made before or after the formation of a corporation, shall not be enforceable unless in writing and signed by the subscriber.

(c) Unless otherwise provided by the terms of the subscription, subscriptions for shares, whether made before or after the formation of a corporation, shall be paid in full at such time, or in such installments and at such times, as shall be determined by the board. Any call made by the board for payment on subscriptions shall be uniform as to all shares of the same class or of the same series. If a receiver of the corporation has been appointed, all unpaid subscriptions shall be paid at such times and in such installments as such receiver or the court may direct.

(d) In the event of default in the payment of any installment or call when due, the corporation may proceed to collect the amount due in the same manner as any debt due the corporation or the board may declare a forfeiture of the subscriptions. The subscription agreement may prescribe other penalties, not amounting to forfeiture, for failure to pay installments or calls that may become due. No forfeiture of the subscription shall be declared as against any subscriber unless the amount due thereon shall remain unpaid for a period of thirty days after written demand has been made therefor. If mailed, such written demand shall be deemed to be made when deposited in the United States mail in a sealed envelope addressed to the subscriber at his last post office address known to the corporation, with postage thereon prepaid. Upon forfeiture of the subscription, if at least fifty percent of the subscription price has been paid, the shares subscribed for shall be offered for sale for cash or a binding obligation to pay cash at a price at least sufficient to pay the full balance owed by the delinquent subscriber plus the expenses incidental to such sale, and any excess of net proceeds realized over the amount owed on such shares shall be paid to the delinquent subscriber or to his legal representative. If no prospective purchaser offers a cash price or binding obligation to pay cash sufficient to pay the full balance owed by the delinquent subscriber plus the expenses incidental to such sale, or if less than fifty percent of the subscription price has been paid, the shares subscribed for shall be cancelled and restored to the status of authorized but unissued shares and all previous payments thereon shall be forfeited to the corporation and transferred to capital surplus.

(e) Notwithstanding the provisions of paragraph (d) of this section, in the event of default in payment or other performance under the instrument evidencing a subscriber's binding obligation to pay a portion of the subscription price or perform services, the corporation may pursue such remedies as are provided in such instrument or a related agreement or under law.

§ 504. Consideration and Payment for Shares

(a) Consideration for the issue of shares shall consist of money or other property, tangible or intangible; labor or services actually received by or performed for the corporation or for its benefit or in its formation or reorganization; a binding obligation to pay the purchase price or the subscription price in cash or other property; a binding obligation to perform services having an agreed value; or a combination thereof. In the absence of fraud in the transaction, the judgment of the board or shareholders, as the case may be, as to the value of the consideration received for shares shall be conclusive. . . .

(c) Shares with par value may be issued for such consideration, not less than the par value thereof, as is fixed from time to time by the board.

(d) Shares without par value may be issued for such consideration as is fixed from time to time by the board unless the certificate of incorporation reserves to the shareholders the right to fix the consideration. If such right is reserved as to any shares, a vote of the shareholders shall either fix the consideration to be received for the shares or authorize the board to fix such consideration.

(e) Treasury shares may be disposed of by a corporation on such terms and conditions as are fixed from time to time by the board.

(f) Upon distribution of authorized but unissued shares to shareholders, that part of the surplus of a corporation which is concurrently transferred to stated capital shall be the consideration for the issue of such shares.

(g) In the event of a conversion of bonds or shares into shares, or in the event of an exchange of bonds or shares for shares, with or without par value, the consideration for the shares so issued in exchange or conversion shall be the sum of (1) either the principal sum of, and accrued interest on, the bonds so exchanged or converted, or the stated capital then represented by the shares so exchanged or converted, plus (2) any additional consideration paid to the corporation for the new shares, plus (3) any stated capital not theretofore allocated to any designated class or series which is thereupon allocated to the new shares, plus (4) any surplus thereupon transferred to stated capital and allocated to the new shares.

(h) Certificates for shares may not be issued until the amount of the consideration therefor determined to be stated capital pursuant to section 506 (Determination of stated capital) has been paid in the form of cash, services rendered, personal or real property or a combination thereof and consideration for the balance (if any) complying with paragraph (a) of this section has been provided, except as provided in paragraphs (e) and (f) of section 505 (Rights and options to purchase shares; issue of rights and options to directors, officers and employees).

(i) When the consideration for shares has been provided in compliance with paragraph (h) of this section, the subscriber shall be entitled to all the rights and privileges of a holder of such shares and to a certificate representing his shares, and such shares shall be fully paid and nonassessable.

(j) Notwithstanding that such shares may be fully paid and nonassessable, the corporation may place in escrow shares issued for a binding obligation to pay cash or other property or to perform future services, or make other arrangements to restrict the transfer of the shares, and may credit distributions in respect of the shares against the obligation, until the obligation is performed. If the obligation is not performed in whole or in part, the corporation may pursue such remedies as are provided in the instrument evidencing the obligation or a related agreement or under law.

§ 505. Rights and Options to Purchase Shares; Issue of Rights and Options to Directors, Officers and Employees

(a)(1) Except as otherwise provided in this section or in the certificate of incorporation, a corporation may create and issue, whether or not in connection with the issue and sale of any of its shares or bonds, rights or options entitling the holders thereof to purchase from the corporation, upon such consideration, terms and conditions as may be fixed by the board, shares of any class or series, whether authorized but unissued shares, treasury shares or shares to be purchased or acquired or assets of the corporation.

(2)(i) In the case of a domestic corporation that has a class of voting stock registered with the Securities and Exchange Commission pursuant to section twelve of the Exchange Act, the terms and conditions of such rights or options may include, without limitation, restrictions or conditions that preclude or limit the exercise, transfer or receipt of such rights or options by an interested shareholder or any transferee of any such interested shareholder or that invalidate or void such rights or options held by any such interested shareholder or any such transferee. For the purposes of this subparagraph, the terms "voting stock", "Exchange Act" and "interested shareholder" shall have the same meanings as set forth in section nine hundred twelve of this chapter.

(ii) Determinations of the board of directors whether to impose, enforce or waive or otherwise render ineffective such limitations or conditions as are permitted by clause (i) of this subparagraph shall be subject to judicial review in an appropriate proceeding in which the courts formulate or apply appropriate standards in order to insure that such limitations or conditions are imposed, enforced or waived in the best long-term interests and short-term interests of the corporation and its shareholders considering, without limitation, the prospects for potential growth, development, productivity and profitability of the corporation.

(b) The consideration for shares to be purchased under any such right or option shall comply with the requirements of section 504 (Consideration and payment for shares).

(c) The terms and conditions of such rights or options, including the time or times at or within which and the price or prices at which they may be exercised and any limitations upon transferability, shall be set forth or incorporated by reference in the instrument or instruments evidencing such rights or options.

(d) The issue of such rights or options to one or more directors, officers or employees of the corporation or a subsidiary or affiliate thereof, as an incentive to service or continued service with the corporation, a subsidiary or affiliate thereof, or to a trustee on behalf of such directors, officers or employees, shall be authorized as required by the policies of all stock exchanges or automated quotation systems on which the corporation's shares are listed or authorized for trading, or if the corporation's shares are not so listed or authorized, by a majority of the votes cast at a meeting of shareholders by the holders of shares entitled to vote thereon, or authorized by and consistent with a plan adopted by such vote of shareholders. If, under the certificate of incorporation, there are preemptive rights to any of the shares to be thus subject to rights or options to purchase, either such issue or such plan, if any shall also be approved by the vote or written consent of the holders of a majority of the shares entitled to exercise preemptive rights with respect to such shares and such vote or written consent shall operate to release the preemptive rights with respect thereto of the holders of all the shares that were entitled to exercise such preemptive rights.

In the absence of preemptive rights, nothing in this paragraph shall require shareholder approval for the issuance of rights or options to purchase shares of the corporation in substitution for, or upon the assumption of, rights or options issued by another corporation, if such substitution or assumption is in connection with such other corporation's merger or consolidation with, or the acquisition of its shares or all or part of its assets by, the corporation or its subsidiary.

(e) A plan adopted by the shareholders for the issue of rights or options to directors, officers or employees shall include the material terms and conditions upon which such rights or options are to be issued, such as, but without limitation thereof, any restrictions on the number of shares that eligible individuals may have the right or option to purchase, the method of administering the plan, the terms and conditions of payment for shares in full or in installments, the issue of certificates for shares to be paid for in installments, any limitations upon the transferability of such shares and the voting and dividend rights to which the holders of such shares may be entitled, though the full amount of the consideration therefor has not been paid; provided that under this section no certificate for shares shall be delivered to a shareholder, prior to full payment therefor, unless the fact that the shares are partly paid is noted conspicuously on the face or back of such certificate.

(f) If there is shareholder approval for the issue of rights or options to individual directors, officers or employees, but not under an approved plan under paragraph (e), the terms and conditions of issue set forth in paragraph (e) shall be permissible except that the grantees of such rights or options shall not be granted voting or dividend rights until the consideration for the shares to which they are entitled under such rights or options has been fully paid.

(g) If there is shareholder approval for the issue of rights and options, such approval may provide that the board is authorized by certificate of amendment under section 805 (Certificate of amendment; contents) to increase the authorized shares of any class or series to such number as will be sufficient, when added to the previously authorized but unissued shares of such class or series, to satisfy any such rights or options entitling the holders thereof to purchase from the corporation authorized but unissued shares of such class or series.

(h) In the absence of fraud in the transaction, the judgment of the board shall be conclusive as to the adequacy of the consideration, tangible or intangible, received or to be received by the corporation for the issue of rights or options for the purchase from the corporation of its shares.

(i) The provisions of this section are inapplicable to the rights of the holders of convertible shares or bonds to acquire shares upon the exercise of conversion privileges under section 519 (Convertible shares and bonds).

§ 506.   Determination of Stated Capital

(a) Upon issue by a corporation of shares with a par value, the consideration received therefor shall constitute stated capital to the extent of the par value of such shares.

(b) Upon issue by a corporation of shares without par value, the entire consideration received therefor shall constitute stated capital unless the board within a period of sixty days after issue allocates to surplus a portion, but not all, of the consideration received for such shares. No such allocation shall be made of any portion of the consideration received for shares without par value having a preference in the assets of the corporation upon involuntary liquidation except all or part of the amount, if any, of such consideration in excess of such preference, nor shall such allocation be made of any portion of the consideration for the issue of shares without par value which is fixed by the shareholders pursuant to a right reserved in the certificate of incorporation, unless such allocation is authorized by vote of the shareholders.

(c) The stated capital of a corporation may be increased from time to time by resolution of the board transferring all or part of the surplus of the corporation to stated capital. The board may direct that the amount so transferred shall be stated capital in respect of any designated class or series of shares.

§ 510.   Dividends or Other Distributions in Cash or Property

(a) A corporation may declare and pay dividends or make other distributions in cash or its bonds or its property, including the shares or bonds of other corporations, on its outstanding shares, except when currently the corporation is insolvent or would thereby be made insolvent, or when the declaration, payment or distribution would be contrary to any restrictions contained in the certificate of incorporation.

(b) Dividends may be declared or paid and other distributions may be made either (1) out of surplus, so that the net assets of the corporation remaining after such declaration, payment or distribution shall at least equal the amount of its stated capital, or (2) in case there shall be no such surplus, out of its net profits for the fiscal year in which the dividend is declared and/or the preceding fiscal year. If the capital of the corporation shall have been diminished by depreciation in the value of its property or by losses or otherwise to an amount less than the aggregate amount of the stated capital represented by the issued and outstanding shares of all classes having a preference upon the distribution of assets, the directors of such corporation shall not declare and pay out of such net profits any dividends upon any shares until the deficiency in the amount of stated capital represented by the issued and outstanding shares of all classes having a preference upon the distribution of assets shall have been repaired. A corporation engaged in the exploitation of natural resources or other wasting assets, including patents, or formed primarily for the liquidation of specific assets, may declare and pay dividends or make other distributions in excess of its surplus, computed after taking due account of depletion and amortization, to the extent that the cost of the wasting or specific assets has been recovered by depletion reserves, amortization or sale, if the net assets remaining after such dividends or distributions are sufficient to cover the liquidation preferences of shares having such preferences in involuntary liquidation.

§ 511.   Share Distributions and Changes

(a) A corporation may make pro rata distributions of its authorized but unissued shares to holders of any class or series of its outstanding shares, subject to the following conditions:

(1) If a distribution of shares having a par value is made, such shares shall be issued at not less than the par value thereof and there shall be transferred to stated capital at the time of such distribution an amount of surplus equal to the aggregate par value of such shares.

(2) If a distribution of shares without par value is made, the amount of stated capital to be represented by each such share shall be fixed by the board, unless the certificate of incorporation reserves to the shareholders the right to fix the consideration for the issue of such shares, and there shall be transferred to stated capital at the time of such distribution an amount of surplus equal to the aggregate stated capital represented by such shares.

(3) A distribution of shares of any class or series may be made to holders of the same or any other class or series of shares unless the certificate of incorporation provides otherwise, provided, however, that in the case of a corporation incorporated prior to [February 22, 1998] then so long as any shares of such class remain outstanding a distribution of shares of any class or series of shares of such corporation may be made only to holders of the same class or series of shares unless the certificate of incorporation permits distribution to holders of another class or series, or unless such distribution is approved by the affirmative vote or the written consent of the holders of a majority of the outstanding shares of the class or series to be distributed.

(4) A distribution of any class or series of shares shall be subject to the preemptive rights, if any, applicable to such shares pursuant to this chapter.

(b) A corporation making a pro rata distribution of authorized but unissued shares to the holders of any class or series of outstanding shares may at its option make an equivalent distribution upon treasury shares of the same class or series, and any shares so distributed shall be treasury shares.

(c) A change of issued shares of any class which increases the stated capital represented by those shares may be made if the surplus of the corporation is sufficient to permit the transfer, and a transfer is concurrently made, from surplus to stated capital, of an amount equal to such increase.

(d) No transfer from surplus to stated capital need be made by a corporation making a distribution of its treasury shares to holders of any class of outstanding shares; nor upon a split up or division of issued shares of any class into a greater number of shares of the same class, or a combination of issued shares of any class into a lesser number of shares of the same class, if there is no increase in the aggregate stated capital represented by them.

(e) Nothing in this section shall prevent a corporation from making other transfers from surplus to stated capital in connection with share distributions or otherwise.

(f) Every distribution to shareholders of certificates representing a share distribution or a change of shares which affects stated capital or surplus shall be accompanied by a written notice (1) disclosing the amounts by which such distribution or change affects stated capital and surplus, or (2) if such amounts are not determinable at the time of such notice, disclosing the approximate effect of such distribution or change upon stated capital and surplus and stating that such amounts are not yet determinable.

(g) When issued shares are changed in any manner which affects stated capital or surplus, and no distribution to shareholders of certificates representing any shares resulting from such change is made, disclosure of the effect of such change upon the stated capital and surplus shall be made in the next financial statement covering the period in which such change is made that is furnished by the corporation to holders of shares of the class or series so changed or, if practicable, in the first notice of dividend or share distribution or change that is furnished to such shareholders between the date of the change of shares and the next such financial statement, and in any event within six months of the date of such change.

§ 512.   Redeemable Shares

(a) Subject to the restrictions contained in section 513 (Purchase, redemption and certain other transactions by a corporation with respect to its own shares) and paragraph (b) of this section, a corporation may provide in its certificate of incorporation for one or more classes or series of shares which are redeemable, in whole or in part, at the option of the corporation the holder or another person or upon the happening of a specified event.

(b) No redeemable common shares, other than shares of an open-end investment company, as defined in an act of congress entitled "Investment Company Act of 1940", as amended, or of a member corporation of a national securities exchange registered under a statute of the United States such as the Securities Exchange Act of 1934, as amended, or of a corporation described in this paragraph, shall be issued or redeemed unless the corporation at the time has outstanding a class of common shares that is not subject to redemption. Any common shares of a corporation which directly or through a subsidiary has a license or franchise to conduct its business, which license or franchise is conditioned upon some or all of the holders of such corporation's common shares possessing prescribed qualifications, may be made subject to redemption by the corporation to the extent necessary to prevent the loss of, or to reinstate, such license or franchise.

(c) Shares of any class or series which may be made redeemable under this section may be redeemed for cash, other property, indebtedness or other securities of the same or another corporation, at such time or times, price or prices, or rate or rates, and with such adjustments, as shall be stated in the certificate of incorporation.

(d) Nothing in this section shall prevent a corporation from creating sinking funds for the redemption or purchase of its shares to the extent permitted by section 513 (Purchase, redemption and certain other transactions by a corporation with respect to its own shares).

§ 513. Purchase, Redemption and Certain Other Transactions by a Corporation With Respect to Its Own Shares

(a) Notwithstanding any authority contained in the certificate of incorporation, the shares of a corporation may not be purchased by the corporation, or, if redeemable, convertible or exchangeable shares, may not be redeemed, converted or exchanged, in each case for or into cash, other property, indebtedness or other securities of the corporation (other than shares of the corporation and rights to acquire such shares) if the corporation is then insolvent or would thereby be made insolvent. Shares may be purchased or redeemed only out of surplus.

(b) When its redeemable, convertible or exchangeable shares are purchased by the corporation within the period during which such shares may be redeemed, converted or exchanged at the option of the corporation, the purchase price thereof shall not exceed the applicable redemption, conversion or exchange price stated in the certificate of incorporation. Upon a redemption, conversion or exchange, the amount payable by the corporation for shares having a cumulative preference on dividends may include the stated redemption, conversion or exchange price plus accrued dividends to the next dividend date following the date of redemption, conversion or exchange of such shares.

(c) No domestic corporation which is subject to the provisions of section nine hundred twelve of this chapter shall purchase or agree to purchase more than ten percent of the stock of the corporation from a shareholder for more than the market value thereof unless such purchase or agreement to purchase is approved by the affirmative vote of the board of directors and a majority of the votes of all outstanding shares entitled to vote thereon at a meeting of shareholders unless the certificate of incorporation requires a greater percentage of the votes of the outstanding shares to approve.

The provisions of this paragraph shall not apply when the corporation offers to purchase shares from all holders of stock or for stock which the holder has been the beneficial owner of for more than two years.

The terms "stock", "beneficial owner", and "market value" shall be as defined in section nine hundred twelve of this chapter.

§ 514. Agreements for Purchase by a Corporation of Its Own Shares

(a) An agreement for the purchase by a corporation of its own shares shall be enforceable by the shareholder and the corporation to the extent such purchase is permitted at the time of purchase by section 513 (Purchase or redemption by a corporation of its own shares).

(b) The possibility that a corporation may not be able to purchase its shares under section 513 shall not be a ground for denying to either party specific performance of an agreement for the purchase by a corporation of its own shares, if at the time for performance the corporation can purchase all or part of such shares under section 513.

§ 515.   Reacquired Shares

(a) Shares that have been issued and have been purchased, redeemed or otherwise reacquired by a corporation shall be cancelled if they are reacquired out of stated capital, or if they are converted shares, or if the certificate of incorporation requires that such shares be cancelled upon reacquisition.

(b) Any shares reacquired by the corporation and not required to be cancelled may be either retained as treasury shares or cancelled by the board at the time of reacquisition or at any time thereafter.

(c) Neither the retention of reacquired shares as treasury shares, nor their subsequent distribution to shareholders or disposition for a consideration shall change the stated capital. When treasury shares are disposed of for a consideration, the surplus shall be increased by the full amount of the consideration received.

(d) Shares cancelled under this section are restored to the status of authorized but unissued shares. However, if the certificate of incorporation prohibits the reissue of any shares required or permitted to be cancelled under this section, the board by certificate of amendment under section 805 (Certificate of amendment; contents) shall reduce the number of authorized shares accordingly.

§ 516.   Reduction of Stated Capital in Certain Cases

(a) Except as otherwise provided in the certificate of incorporation, the board may at any time reduce the stated capital of a corporation in any of the following ways:

(1) by eliminating from stated capital any portion of amounts previously transferred by the board from surplus to stated capital and not allocated to any designated class or series of shares;

(2) by reducing or eliminating any amount of stated capital represented by issued shares having a par value which exceeds the aggregate par value of such shares;

(3) by reducing the amount of stated capital represented by issued shares without par value; or

(4) by applying to an otherwise authorized purchase, redemption, conversion or exchange of outstanding shares some or all of the stated capital represented by the shares being purchased, redeemed, converted or exchanged, or some or all of any stated capital that has been allocated to any particular shares, or both. Notwithstanding the foregoing, if the consideration for the issue of shares without par value was fixed by the shareholders under section 504 (Consideration and payment for shares), the board shall not reduce the stated capital represented by such shares except to the extent, if any, that the board was authorized by the shareholders to allocate any portion of such consideration to surplus.

(b) No reduction of stated capital shall be made under this section unless after such reduction the stated capital exceeds the aggregate preferential amounts payable upon involuntary liquidation upon all issued shares having preferential rights in the assets plus the par value of all other issued shares with par value.

(c) When a reduction of stated capital has been effected under this section, the amount of such reduction shall be disclosed in the next financial statement covering the period in which such reduction is made that is furnished by the corporation to all its shareholders or, if practicable, in the first notice of dividend or share distribution that is furnished to the holders of each class or series of its shares between the date of such reduction and the next such financial statement, and in any event to all its shareholders within six months of the date of such reduction.

§ 518.   Corporate Bonds

(a) No corporation shall issue bonds except for money or other property, tangible or intangible, or labor or services actually received by or performed for the corporation or for its benefit or in its formation or reorganization; a binding obligation to pay the purchase price thereof in cash or other property; a binding obligation to perform services having an agreed value; or a combination thereof. In the absence of fraud in the transaction, the judgment of the board as to the value of the consideration received shall be conclusive.

(b) If a distribution of its own bonds is made by a corporation to holders of any class or series of its outstanding shares, there shall be concurrently transferred to the liabilities of the corporation in respect of such bonds an amount of surplus equal to the principal amount of, and any accrued interest on, such bonds. The amount of the surplus so transferred shall be the consideration for the issue of such bonds.

(c) A corporation may, in its certificate of incorporation, confer upon the holders of any bonds issued or to be issued by the corporation, rights to inspect the corporate books and records and to vote in the election of directors and on any other matters on which shareholders of the corporation may vote.

§ 520. Liability for Failure to Disclose Required Information

Failure of the corporation to comply in good faith with the notice or disclosure provisions of paragraphs (f) and (g) of section 511 (Share distributions and changes), or paragraph (c) of section 516 (Reduction of stated capital in certain cases), shall make the corporation liable for any damage sustained by any shareholder in consequence thereof.

ARTICLE 6

SHAREHOLDERS

§ 601. By-Laws

(a) The initial by-laws of a corporation shall be adopted by its incorporator or incorporators at the organization meeting. Thereafter, subject to section 613 (Limitations on right to vote), by-laws may be adopted, amended or repealed by a majority of the votes cast by the shares at the time entitled to vote in the election of any directors. When so provided in the certificate of incorporation or a by-law adopted by the shareholders, by-laws may also be adopted, amended or repealed by the board by such vote as may be therein specified, which may be greater than the vote otherwise prescribed by this chapter, but any by-law adopted by the board may be amended or repealed by the shareholders entitled to vote thereon as herein provided. Any reference in this chapter to a "by-law adopted by the shareholders" shall include a by-law adopted by the incorporator or incorporators.

(b) The by-laws may contain any provision relating to the business of the corporation, the conduct of its affairs, its rights or powers or the rights or powers of its shareholders, directors or officers, not inconsistent with this chapter or any other statute of this state or the certificate of incorporation.

§ 602. Meetings of Shareholders

(a) Meetings of shareholders may be held at such place, within or without this state, as may be fixed by or under the by-laws, or if not so fixed, at the office of the corporation in this state.

(b) A meeting of shareholders shall be held annually for the election of directors and the transaction of other business on a date fixed by or under the by-laws. A failure to hold the annual meeting on the date so fixed or to elect a sufficient number of directors to conduct the business of the corporation shall not work a forfeiture or give cause for dissolution of the corporation, except as provided in paragraph (c) of section 1104 (Petition in case of deadlock among directors or shareholders).

(c) Special meetings of the shareholders may be called by the board and by such person or persons as may be so authorized by the certificate of incorporation or the by-laws. At any such special meeting only such business may be transacted which is related to the purpose or purposes set forth in the notice required by section 605 (Notice of meetings of shareholders).

(d) Except as otherwise required by this chapter, the by-laws may designate reasonable procedures for the calling and conduct of a meeting of shareholders, including but not limited to specifying: (i) who may call and who may conduct the meeting, (ii) the means by which the order of business to be conducted shall be established, (iii) the procedures and requirements for the nomination of directors, (iv) the procedures with respect to the making of shareholder proposals, and (v) the procedures to be established for the adjournment of any meeting of shareholders. No amendment of the by-laws pertaining to the election of directors or the procedures for the calling and conduct of a meeting of shareholders shall affect the election of directors or the procedures for the calling or conduct in respect of any meeting of shareholders unless adequate notice thereof is given to the shareholders in a manner reasonably calculated to provide shareholders with sufficient time to respond thereto prior to such meeting.

§ 603.   Special Meeting for Election of Directors

(a) If, for a period of one month after the date fixed by or under the by-laws for the annual meeting of shareholders, or if no date has been so fixed, for a period of thirteen months after the formation of the corporation or the last annual meeting, there is a failure to elect a sufficient number of directors to conduct the business of the corporation, the board shall call a special meeting for the election of directors. If such special meeting is not called by the board within two weeks after the expiration of such period or if it is so called but there is a failure to elect such directors for a period of two months after the expiration of such period, holders of ten percent of the votes of the shares entitled to vote in an election of directors may, in writing, demand the call of a special meeting for the election of directors specifying the date and month thereof, which shall not be less than sixty nor more than ninety days from the date of such written demand. The secretary of the corporation upon receiving the written demand shall promptly give notice of such meeting, or if he fails to do so within five business days thereafter, any shareholder signing such demand may give such notice. The meeting shall be held at the place fixed in the by-laws or, if not so fixed, at the office of the corporation.

(b) At any such special meeting called on demand of shareholders, notwithstanding section 608 (Quorum of shareholders), the shareholders attending, in person or by proxy, and entitled to vote in an election of directors shall constitute a quorum for the purpose of electing directors, but not for the transaction of any other business.

§ 604.   Fixing Record Date

(a) For the purpose of determining the shareholders entitled to notice of or to vote at any meeting of shareholders or any adjournment thereof, or to express consent to or dissent from any proposal without a meeting, or for the purpose of determining shareholders entitled to receive payment of any dividend or the allotment of any rights, or for the purpose of any other action, the by-laws may provide for fixing or, in the absence of such provision, the board may fix, in advance, a date as the record date for any such determination of shareholders. Such date shall not be more than sixty nor less than ten days before the date of such meeting, nor more than sixty days prior to any other action.

(b) If no record date is fixed:

(1) The record date for the determination of shareholders entitled to notice of or to vote at a meeting of shareholders shall be at the close of business on the day next preceding the day on which notice is given, or, if no notice is given, the day on which the meeting is held.

(2) The record date for determining shareholders for any purpose other than that specified in subparagraph (1) shall be at the close of business on the day on which the resolution of the board relating thereto is adopted.

(c) When a determination of shareholders of record entitled to notice of or to vote at any meeting of shareholders has been made as provided in this section, such determination shall apply to any adjournment thereof, unless the board fixes a new record date under this section for the adjourned meeting.

§ 605.   Notice of Meetings of Shareholders

(a) Whenever under the provisions of this chapter shareholders are required or permitted to take any action at a meeting, notice shall be given stating the place, date and hour of the meeting and, unless it is the annual meeting, indicating that it is being issued by or at the direction of the person or persons calling the meeting. Notice of a special meeting shall also state the purpose or purposes for which the meeting is called. Notice of any meeting of shareholders may be written or electronic. If, at any meeting, action is proposed to be taken which would, if taken, entitle shareholders fulfilling the requirements of section 623 (Procedure to enforce shareholder's right to receive payment for shares) to receive payment for their shares, the notice of such meeting shall include a statement of that purpose and to that effect and shall be accompanied by a copy of section 623 or an outline of its material terms. Notice of any meeting shall be given not fewer than ten nor more than sixty days before the date of the meeting, provided, however, that such notice may be given by third class mail not fewer than twenty-four nor more than sixty days before the date of the meeting, to each shareholder entitled to vote at such meeting. If mailed, such notice is given when deposited in the United States mail, with postage thereon prepaid, directed to the shareholder at the shareholder's address as it appears on the record of shareholders, or, if the shareholder shall have filed with the secretary of the corporation a request that notices to the shareholder be mailed to some other address, then directed to him at such other address. If transmitted electronically, such notice is given when directed to the shareholder's electronic mail address as supplied by the shareholder to the secretary of the corporation or as otherwise directed pursuant to the shareholder's authorization or instructions. An affidavit of the secretary or other person giving the notice or of a transfer agent of the corporation that the notice required by this section has been given shall, in the absence of fraud, be prima facie evidence of the facts therein stated.

(b) When a meeting is adjourned to another time or place, it shall not be necessary, unless the by-laws require otherwise, to give any notice of the adjourned meeting if the time and place to which the meeting is adjourned are announced at the meeting at which the adjournment is taken, and at the adjourned meeting any business may be transacted that might have been transacted on the original date of the meeting. However, if after the adjournment the board fixes a new record date for the adjourned meeting, a notice of the adjourned meeting shall be given to each shareholder of record on the new record date entitled to notice under paragraph (a).

§ 606. Waivers of Notice

Notice of meeting need not be given to any shareholder who submits a waiver of notice whether before or after the meeting. Waiver of notice may be written or electronic. If written, the waiver must be executed by the shareholder or the shareholder's authorized officer, director, employee or agent by signing such waiver or causing his or her signature to be affixed to such waiver by any reasonable means, including, but not limited to, facsimile signature. If electronic, the transmission of the waiver must either set forth or be submitted with information from which it can reasonably be determined that the transmission was authorized by the shareholder. The attendance of any shareholder at a meeting, in person or by proxy, without protesting prior to the conclusion of the meeting the lack of notice of such meeting, shall constitute a waiver of notice by such shareholder.

§ 607. List of Shareholders at Meetings

A list of shareholders as of the record date, certified by the corporate officer responsible for its preparation or by a transfer agent, shall be produced at any meeting of shareholders upon the request there at or prior thereto of any shareholder. If the right to vote at any meeting is challenged, the inspectors of election, or person presiding thereat, shall require such list of shareholders to be produced as evidence of the right of the persons challenged to vote at such meeting, and all persons who appear from such list to be shareholders entitled to vote thereat may vote at such meeting.

§ 608. Quorum of Shareholders

(a) The holders of a majority of the votes of shares entitled to vote thereat shall constitute a quorum at a meeting of shareholders for the transaction of any business, provided that when a specified item of business is required to be voted on by a particular class or series of shares, voting as a class, the holders of a majority of the votes of shares of such class or series shall constitute a quorum for the transaction of such specified item of business.

(b) The certificate of incorporation or by-laws may provide for any lesser quorum not less than one-third of the votes of shares entitled to vote, and the certificate of incorporation may, under section 616 (Greater requirement as to quorum and vote of shareholders), provide for a greater quorum.

(c) When a quorum is once present to organize a meeting, it is not broken by the subsequent withdrawal of any shareholders.

(d) The shareholders present may adjourn the meeting despite the absence of a quorum.

§ 609.   Proxies

(a) Every shareholder entitled to vote at a meeting of shareholders or to express consent or dissent without a meeting may authorize another person or persons to act for him by proxy.

(b) No proxy shall be valid after the expiration of eleven months from the date thereof unless otherwise provided in the proxy. Every proxy shall be revocable at the pleasure of the shareholder executing it, except as otherwise provided in this section.

(c) The authority of the holder of a proxy to act shall not be revoked by the incompetence or death of the shareholder who executed the proxy unless, before the authority is exercised, written notice of an adjudication of such incompetence or of such death is received by the corporate officer responsible for maintaining the list of shareholders.

(d) Except when other provision shall have been made by written agreement between the parties, the record holder of shares which he holds as pledgee or otherwise as security or which belong to another, shall issue to the pledgor or to such owner of such shares, upon demand therefor and payment of necessary expenses thereof, a proxy to vote or take other action thereon.

(e) A shareholder shall not sell his vote or issue a proxy to vote to any person for any sum of money or anything of value, except as authorized in this section and section 620 (Agreements as to voting; provision in certificate of incorporation as to control of directors), provided, however, that this paragraph shall not apply to votes, proxies or consents given by holders of preferred shares in connection with a proxy or consent solicitation made available on identical terms to all holders of shares of the same class or series and remaining open for acceptance for at least twenty business days.

(f) A proxy which is entitled "irrevocable proxy" and which states that it is irrevocable, is irrevocable when it is held by any of the following or a nominee of any of the following:

(1) A pledgee;

(2) A person who has purchased or agreed to purchase the shares;

(3) A creditor or creditors of the corporation who extend or continue credit to the corporation in consideration of the proxy if the proxy states that it was given in consideration of such extension or continuation of credit, the amount thereof, and the name of the person extending or continuing credit;

(4) A person who has contracted to perform services as an officer of the corporation, if a proxy is required by the contract of employment, if the proxy states that it was given in consideration of such contract of employment, the name of the employee and the period of employment contracted for;

(5) A person designated by or under an agreement under paragraph (a) of section 620.

(g) Notwithstanding a provision in a proxy, stating that it is irrevocable, the proxy becomes revocable after the pledge is redeemed, or the debt of the corporation is paid, or the period of employment provided for in the contract of employment has terminated, or the agreement under paragraph (a) of section 620 has terminated; and, in a case provided for in subparagraphs (f)(3) or (4), becomes revocable three years after the date of the proxy or at the end of the period, if any, specified therein, whichever period is less, unless the period of irrevocability is renewed from time to time by the execution of a new irrevocable proxy as provided in this section. This paragraph does not affect the duration of a proxy under paragraph (b).

(h) A proxy may be revoked, notwithstanding a provision making it irrevocable, by a purchaser of shares without knowledge of the existence of the provision unless the existence of the proxy and its irrevocability is noted conspicuously on the face or back of the certificate representing such shares.

(i) Without limiting the manner in which a shareholder may authorize another person or persons to act for him as proxy pursuant to paragraph (a) of this section, the following shall constitute a valid means by which a shareholder may grant such authority.

(1) A shareholder may execute a writing authorizing another person or persons to act from him as proxy. Execution may be accomplished by the shareholder or the shareholder's authorized officer, director, employee or agent signing such writing or causing his or her signature to be affixed to such writing by any reasonable means including, but not limited to, by facsimile signature.

(2) A shareholder may authorize another person or persons to act for the shareholder as proxy by transmitting or authorizing the transmission of a telegram, cablegram or other means of electronic transmission to the person who will be the holder of the proxy or to a proxy solicitation firm, proxy support service organization or like agent duly authorized by the person who will be the holder of the proxy to receive such transmission, provided that any such telegram, cablegram or other means of electronic transmission must either set forth or be submitted with information from which it can be reasonably determined that the telegram, cablegram or other electronic transmission was authorized by the shareholder. If it is determined that such telegrams, cablegrams or other electronic transmissions are valid, the inspectors or, if there are no inspectors, such other persons making that determination shall specify the nature of the information upon which they relied.

(j) Any copy, facsimile telecommunication or other reliable reproduction of the writing or transmission created pursuant to paragraph (i) of this section may be substituted or used in lieu of the original writing or transmission for any and all purposes for which the original writing or transmission could be used, provided that such copy, facsimile telecommunication or other reproduction shall be a complete reproduction of the entire original writing or transmission.

§ 614. Vote of Shareholders

(a) Directors shall, except as otherwise required by this chapter or by the by-laws or certificate of incorporation as permitted by this chapter, be elected by a plurality of the votes cast at a meeting of shareholders by the holders of shares entitled to vote in the election.

(b) Whenever any corporate action, other than the election of directors, is to be taken under this chapter by vote of the shareholders, it shall, except as otherwise required by this chapter or by the certificate of incorporation as permitted by this chapter or by the specific provisions of a by-law adopted by the shareholders, be authorized by a majority of the votes cast in favor of or against such action at a meeting of shareholders by the holders of shares entitled to vote thereon. Except as otherwise provided in the certificate of incorporation or the specific provision of a by-law adopted by the shareholders, an abstention shall not constitute a vote cast.

§ 615. Written Consent of Shareholders, Subscribers or Incorporators Without a Meeting

(a) Whenever under this chapter shareholders are required or permitted to take any action by vote, such action may be taken without a meeting on written consent, setting forth the action so taken, signed by the holders of all outstanding shares entitled to vote thereon or, if the certificate of incorporation so permits, signed by the holders of outstanding shares having not less than the minimum number of votes that would be necessary to authorize or take such action at a meeting at which all shares entitled to vote thereon were present and voted. In addition, this paragraph shall not be construed to alter or modify the provisions of any section or any provision in a certificate of incorporation not inconsistent with this chapter under which the written consent of the holders of less than all outstanding shares is sufficient for corporate action.

(b) No written consent shall be effective to take the corporate action referred to therein unless, within sixty days of the earliest dated consent delivered in the manner required by this paragraph to the corporation, written consents signed by a sufficient number of holders to take action are delivered to the corporation by delivery to its registered office in this state, its principal place of business, or an officer or agent of the corporation having custody of the book in which proceedings of meetings of shareholders are recorded. Delivery made to a corporation's registered office shall be by hand or by certified or registered mail, return receipt requested.

(c) Prompt notice of the taking of the corporate action without a meeting by less than unanimous written consent shall be given to those shareholders who have not consented in writing.

(d) Written consent thus given by the holders of such number of shares as is required under paragraph (a) of this section shall have the same effect as a valid vote of holders of such number of shares, and any certificate with respect to the authorization or taking of any such action which is to be delivered to the department of state shall recite that written consent has been given in accordance with this section and that written notice has been given as and to the extent required by this section.

(e) When there are no shareholders of record, such action may be taken on the written consent signed by a majority in interest of the subscribers for shares whose subscriptions have been accepted or their successors in interest or, if no subscription has been accepted, on the written consent signed by the incorporator or a majority of the incorporators. When there are two or more incorporators, if any dies or is for any reason unable to act, the other or others may act. If there is no incorporator able to act, any person for whom an incorporator was acting as agent may act in his stead, or if such other person also dies or is for any reason unable to act, his legal representative may act.

§ 616.   Greater Requirement as to Quorum and Vote of Shareholders

(a) The certificate of incorporation may contain provisions specifying either or both of the following:

(1) That the proportion of votes of shares, or the proportion of votes of shares of any class or series thereof, the holders of which shall be present in person or by proxy at any meeting of shareholders . . . in order to constitute a quorum for the transaction of any business or of any specified item of business, including amendments to the certificate of incorporation, shall be greater than the proportion prescribed by this chapter in the absence of such provision.

(2) That the proportion of votes of shares, or votes of shares of a particular class or series of shares, that shall be necessary at any meeting of shareholders for the transaction of any business or of any specified item of business, including amendments to the certificate of incorporation, shall be greater than the proportion prescribed by this chapter in the absence of such provision.

(b) An amendment of the certificate of incorporation which changes or strikes out a provision permitted by this section, shall be authorized at a meeting of shareholders by two-thirds of the votes of the shares entitled to vote thereon, or of such greater proportion of votes of shares, or votes of shares of a particular class or series of shares, as may be provided specifically in the certificate of incorporation for changing or striking out a provision permitted by this section.

(c) If the certificate of incorporation of any corporation contains a provision authorized by this section, the existence of such provision shall be noted conspicuously on the face or back of every certificate for shares issued by such corporation, except that this requirement shall not apply to any corporation having any class of any equity security registered pursuant to Section twelve of the Securities Exchange Act of 1934, as amended.

§ 617.   Voting by Class or Classes of Shares

(a) The certificate of incorporation may contain provisions specifying that any class or classes of shares or of any series thereof shall vote as a class in connection with the transaction of any business or of any specified item of business at a meeting of shareholders, including amendments to the certificate of incorporation.

(b) Where voting as a class is provided in the certificate of incorporation, it shall be by the proportionate vote so provided or, if no proportionate vote is provided, in the election of directors, by a plurality of the votes cast at such meeting by the holders of shares of such class entitled to vote in the election, or for any other corporate action, by a majority of the votes cast at such meeting by the holders of shares of such class entitled to vote thereon.

(c) Such voting by class shall be in addition to any other vote, including vote by class, required by this chapter and by the certificate of incorporation as permitted by this chapter.

§ 619.   Powers of Supreme Court Respecting Elections

Upon the petition of any shareholder aggrieved by an election, and upon notice to the persons declared elected thereat, the corporation and such other persons as the court may direct, the supreme court at a special term held within the judicial district where the office of the corporation is located shall forthwith hear the proofs and allegations of the parties, and confirm the election, order a new election, or take such other action as justice may require.

§ 620. Agreements as to Voting; Provision in Certificate of Incorporation as to Control of Directors

(a) An agreement between two or more shareholders, if in writing and signed by the parties thereto, may provide that in exercising any voting rights, the shares held by them shall be voted as therein provided, or as they may agree, or as determined in accordance with a procedure agreed upon by them.

(b) A provision in the certificate of incorporation otherwise prohibited by law because it improperly restricts the board in its management of the business of the corporation, or improperly transfers to one or more shareholders or to one or more persons or corporations to be selected by him or them, all or any part of such management otherwise within the authority of the board under this chapter, shall nevertheless be valid:

(1) If all the incorporators or holders of record of all outstanding shares, whether or not having voting power, have authorized such provision in the certificate of incorporation or an amendment thereof; and

(2) If, subsequent to the adoption of such provision, shares are transferred or issued only to persons who had knowledge or notice thereof or consented in writing to such provision.

(c) A provision authorized by paragraph (b) shall be valid only so long as no shares of the corporation are listed on a national securities exchange or regularly quoted in an over-the-counter market by one or more members of a national or affiliated securities association.

(d)(1) Except as provided in paragraph (e), an amendment to strike out a provision authorized by paragraph (b) shall be authorized at a meeting of shareholders by (A)(i) for any corporation in existence on [February 22, 1998], two-thirds of the votes of the shares entitled to vote thereon and (ii) for any corporation in existence on the effective date of this clause the certificate of incorporation of which expressly provides such and for any corporation incorporated after the effective date of subparagraph (2) of this paragraph, a majority of the votes of the shares entitled to vote thereon or (B) in either case, by such greater proportion of votes of shares as may be required by the certificate of incorporation for that purpose.

(2) Any corporation may adopt an amendment of the certificate of incorporation in accordance with the applicable clause or subclause of paragraph (1) of this paragraph to provide that any further amendment of the certificate of incorporation that strikes out a provision authorized by paragraph (b) of this section shall be authorized at a meeting of the shareholders by a specified proportion of votes of the shares, or votes of a particular class or series of shares, entitled to vote thereon, provided that such proportion may not be less than a majority.

(e) Alternatively, if a provision authorized by paragraph (b) shall have ceased to be valid under this section, the board may authorize a certificate of amendment under section 805 (Certificate of amendment; contents) striking out such provision. Such certificate shall set forth the event by reason of which the provision ceased to be valid.

(f) The effect of any such provision authorized by paragraph (b) shall be to relieve the directors and impose upon the shareholders authorizing the same or consenting thereto the liability for managerial acts or omissions that is imposed on directors by this chapter to the extent that and so long as the discretion or powers of the board in its management of corporate affairs is controlled by any such provision.

(g) If the certificate of incorporation of any corporation contains a provision authorized by paragraph (b), the existence of such provision shall be noted conspicuously on the face or back of every certificate for shares issued by such corporation.

§ 621. Voting Trust Agreements

(a) Any shareholder or shareholders, under an agreement in writing, may transfer his or their shares to a voting trustee or trustees for the purpose of conferring the right to vote thereon for a period not exceeding ten years upon the terms and conditions therein stated. The certificates for shares so transferred shall be surrendered and cancelled and new certificates therefor issued to such trustee or trustees stating that they are issued under such agreement, and in the entry of such ownership in the record of the corporation that fact shall also be noted, and such trustee or trustees may vote the shares so transferred during the term of such agreement.

(b) The trustee or trustees shall keep available for inspection by holders of voting trust certificates at his or their office or at a place designated in such agreement or of which the holders of voting trust certificates have been notified in writing, correct and complete books and records of account relating to the trust, and a record containing the names and addresses of all persons who are holders of voting trust certificates and the number and class of shares represented by the certificates held by them and the dates when they became the owners thereof. The record may be in written form or any other form capable of being converted into written form within a reasonable time.

(c) A duplicate of every such agreement shall be filed in the office of the corporation and it and the record of voting trust certificate holders shall be subject to the same right of inspection by a shareholder of record or a holder of a voting trust certificate, in person or by agent or attorney, as are the records of the corporation under section 624 (Books and records; right of inspection, prima facie evidence). The shareholder or holder of a voting trust certificate shall be entitled to the remedies provided in that section.

(d) At any time within six months before the expiration of such voting trust agreement as originally fixed or as extended one or more times under this paragraph, one or more holders of voting trust certificates may, by agreement in writing, extend the duration of such voting trust agreement, nominating the same or substitute trustee or trustees, for an additional period not exceeding ten years. Such extension agreement shall not affect the rights or obligations of persons not parties thereto and shall in every respect comply with and be subject to all the provisions of this section applicable to the original voting trust agreement.

§ 622.   Preemptive Rights

(a) As used in this section, the term:

(1) "Unlimited dividend rights" means the right without limitation as to amount either to all or to a share of the balance of current or liquidating dividends after the payment of dividends on any shares entitled to a preference.

(2) "Equity shares" means shares of any class, whether or not preferred as to dividends or assets, which have unlimited dividend rights.

(3) "Voting rights" means the right to vote for the election of one or more directors, excluding a right so to vote which is dependent on the happening of an event specified in the certificate of incorporation which would change the voting rights of any class of shares.

(4) "Voting shares" means shares of any class which have voting rights, but does not include bonds on which voting rights are conferred under section 518 (Corporate bonds).

(5) "Preemptive right" means the right to purchase shares or other securities to be issued or subject to rights or options to purchase, as such right is defined in this section.

(b)(1) With respect to any corporation incorporated prior to [February 22, 1998], except as otherwise provided in the certificate of incorporation, and except as provided in this section, the holders of equity shares of any class, in case of the proposed issuance by the corporation of, or the proposed granting by the corporation of rights or options to purchase, its equity shares of any class or any shares or other securities convertible into or carrying rights or options to purchase its equity shares of any class, shall, if the issuance of the equity shares proposed to be issued or issuable upon exercise of such rights or options or upon conversion of such other securities would adversely affect the unlimited dividend rights of such holders, have the right during a reasonable time and on reasonable conditions, both to be fixed by the board, to purchase such shares or other securities in such proportions as shall be determined as provided in this section.

(2) With respect to any corporation incorporated on or after [February 22, 1998], the holders of such shares shall not have any preemptive right, except as otherwise expressly provided in the certificate of incorporation.

(c) Except as otherwise provided in the certificate of incorporation, and except as provided in this section, the holders of voting shares of any class having any preemptive right under this paragraph on the date immediately prior to [February 22, 1998], in case of the proposed issuance by the corporation of, or the proposed granting by the corporation of rights or options to purchase, its voting shares of any class or any shares or other securities convertible into or carrying rights or options to purchase its voting shares of any class, shall, if the issuance of the voting shares proposed to be issued or issuable upon exercise of such rights or options or upon conversion of such other securities would adversely affect the voting rights of such holders, have the right during a reasonable time and on reasonable conditions, both to be fixed by the board, to purchase such shares or other securities in such proportions as shall be determined as provided in this section.

(d) The preemptive right provided for in paragraphs (b) and (c) shall entitle shareholders having such rights to purchase the shares or other securities to be offered or optioned for sale as nearly as practicable in such proportions as would, if such preemptive right were exercised, preserve the relative unlimited dividend rights and voting rights of such holders and at a price or prices not less favorable than the price or prices at which such shares or other securities are proposed to be offered for sale to others, without deduction of such reasonable expenses of and compensation for the sale, underwriting or purchase of such shares or other securities by underwriters or dealers as may lawfully be paid by the corporation. In case each of the shares entitling the holders thereof to preemptive rights does not confer the same unlimited dividend right or voting right, the board shall apportion the shares or other securities to be offered or optioned for sale among the shareholders having preemptive rights to purchase them in such proportions as in the opinion of the board shall preserve as far as practicable the relative unlimited dividend rights and voting rights of the holders at the time of such offering. The apportionment made by the board shall, in the absence of fraud or bad faith, be binding upon all shareholders.

(e) Unless otherwise provided in the certificate of incorporation, shares or other securities offered for sale or subjected to rights or options to purchase shall not be subject to preemptive rights under paragraph (b) or (c) of this section if they:

(1) Are to be issued by the board to effect a merger or consolidation or offered or subjected to rights or options for consideration other than cash;

(2) Are to be issued or subjected to rights or options under paragraph (d) of section 505 (Rights and options to purchase shares; issue of rights and options to directors, officers and employees);

(3) Are to be issued to satisfy conversion or option rights theretofore granted by the corporation;

(4) Are treasury shares;

(5) Are part of the shares or other securities of the corporation authorized in its original certificate of incorporation and are issued, sold or optioned within two years from the date of filing such certificate; or

(6) Are to be issued under a plan of reorganization approved in a proceeding under any applicable act of congress relating to reorganization of corporations.

(f) Shareholders of record entitled to preemptive rights on the record date fixed by the board under section 604 (Fixing record date), or, if no record date is fixed, then on the record date determined under section 604, and no others shall be entitled to the right defined in this section.

(g) The board shall cause to be given to each shareholder entitled to purchase shares or other securities in accordance with this section, a notice directed to him in the manner provided in section 605 (Notice of meetings of shareholders) setting forth the time within which and the terms and conditions upon which the shareholder may purchase such shares or other securities and also the apportionment made of the right to purchase among the shareholders entitled to preemptive rights. Such notice shall be given personally or by mail at least fifteen days prior to the expiration of the period during which the shareholder shall have the right to purchase. All shareholders entitled to preemptive rights to whom notice shall have been given as aforesaid shall be deemed conclusively to have had a reasonable time in which to exercise their preemptive rights.

(h) Shares or other securities which have been offered to shareholders having preemptive rights to purchase and which have not been purchased by them within the time fixed by the board may thereafter, for a period of not exceeding one year following the expiration of the time during which shareholders might have exercised such preemptive rights, be issued, sold or subjected to rights or options to any other person or persons at a price, without deduction of such reasonable expenses of and compensation for the sale, underwriting or purchase of such shares by underwriters or dealers as may lawfully be paid by the corporation, not less than that at which they were offered to such shareholders. Any such shares or other securities not so issued, sold or subjected to rights or options to others during such one year period shall thereafter again be subject to the preemptive rights of shareholders.

(i) Except as otherwise provided in the certificate of incorporation and except as provided in this section, no holder of any shares of any class shall as such holder have any preemptive right to purchase any other shares or securities of any class which at any time may be sold or offered for sale by the corporation. Unless otherwise provided in the certificate of incorporation, holders of bonds on which voting rights are conferred under section 518 shall have no preemptive rights.

§ 623. Procedure to Enforce Shareholder's Right to Receive Payment for Shares

(a) A shareholder intending to enforce his right under a section of this chapter to receive payment for his shares if the proposed corporate action referred to therein is taken shall file with the corporation, before the meeting of shareholders at which the action is submitted to a vote, or at such meeting but before the vote, written objection to the action. . . .

(c) Within twenty days after the giving of notice to him, any shareholder from whom written objection was not required and who elects to dissent shall file with the corporation a written notice of such election, stating his name and residence address, the number and classes of shares as to which he dissents and a demand for payment of the fair value of his shares. . . .

(g) Within fifteen days after the expiration of the period within which shareholders may file their notices of election to dissent, or within fifteen days after the proposed corporate action is consummated, whichever is later (but in no case later than ninety days from the shareholders' authorization date), the corporation or, in the case of a merger or consolidation, the surviving or new corporation, shall make a written offer by registered mail to each shareholder who has filed such notice of election to pay for his shares at a specified price which the corporation considers to be their fair value. Such offer shall be accompanied by a statement setting forth the aggregate number of shares with respect to which notices of election to dissent have been received and the aggregate number of holders of such shares. If the corporate action has been consummated, such offer shall also be accompanied by (1) advance payment to each such shareholder who has submitted the certificates representing his shares to the corporation, as provided in paragraph (f), of an amount equal to eighty percent of the amount of such offer, or (2) as to each shareholder who has not yet submitted his certificates a statement that advance payment to him of an amount equal to eighty percent of the amount of such offer will be made by the corporation promptly upon submission of his certificates. If the corporate action has not been consummated at the time of the making of the offer, such advance payment or statement as to advance payment shall be sent to each shareholder entitled thereto forthwith upon consummation of the corporate action. Every advance payment or statement as to advance payment shall include advice to the shareholder to the effect that acceptance of such payment does not constitute a waiver of any dissenters' rights. . . .

(h) The following procedure shall apply if the corporation fails to make such offer within such period of fifteen days, or if it makes the offer and any dissenting shareholder or shareholders fail to agree with it within the period of thirty days thereafter upon the price to be paid for their shares:

(1) The corporation shall, within twenty days after the expiration of whichever is applicable of the two periods last mentioned, institute a special proceeding in the supreme court in the judicial district in which the office of the corporation is located to determine the rights of dissenting shareholders and to fix the fair value of their shares. If, in the case of merger or consolidation, the surviving or new corporation is a foreign corporation without an office in this state, such proceeding shall be brought in the county where the office of the domestic corporation, whose shares are to be valued, was located.

(2) If the corporation fails to institute such proceeding within such period of twenty days, any dissenting shareholder may institute such proceeding for the same purpose not later than thirty days after the expiration of such twenty day period. If such proceeding is not instituted within such thirty day period, all dissenter's rights shall be lost unless the supreme court, for good cause shown, shall otherwise direct.

(3) All dissenting shareholders, excepting those who, as provided in paragraph (g), have agreed with the corporation upon the price to be paid for their shares, shall be made parties to such proceeding, which shall have the effect of an action quasi in rem against their shares. The corporation shall serve a copy of the petition in such proceeding upon each dissenting shareholder who is a resident of this state in the manner

provided by law for the service of a summons, and upon each nonresident dissenting shareholder either by registered mail and publication, or in such other manner as is permitted by law. The jurisdiction of the court shall be plenary and exclusive.

(4) The court shall determine whether each dissenting shareholder, as to whom the corporation requests the court to make such determination, is entitled to receive payment for his shares. If the corporation does not request any such determination or if the court finds that any dissenting shareholder is so entitled, it shall proceed to fix the value of the shares, which, for the purposes of this section, shall be the fair value as of the close of business on the day prior to the shareholders' authorization date. In fixing the fair value of the shares, the court shall consider the nature of the transaction giving rise to the shareholder's right to receive payment for shares and its effects on the corporation and its shareholders, the concepts and methods then customary in the relevant securities and financial markets for determining fair value of shares of a corporation engaging in a similar transaction under comparable circumstances and all other relevant factors. The court shall determine the fair value of the shares without a jury and without referral to an appraiser or referee. Upon application by the corporation or by any shareholder who is a party to the proceeding, the court may, in its discretion, permit pretrial disclosure, including, but not limited to, disclosure of any expert's reports relating to the fair value of the shares whether or not intended for use at the trial in the proceeding. . . .

§ 624.   Books and Records; Right of Inspection, Prima Facie Evidence

(a) Each corporation shall keep correct and complete books and records of account and shall keep minutes of the proceedings of its shareholders, board and executive committee, if any, and shall keep at the office of the corporation in this state or at the office of its transfer agent or registrar in this state, a record containing the names and addresses of all shareholders, the number and class of shares held by each and the dates when they respectively became the owners of record thereof. Any of the foregoing books, minutes or records may be in written form or in any other form capable of being converted into written form within a reasonable time.

(b) Any person who shall have been a shareholder of record of a corporation upon at least five days' written demand shall have the right to examine in person or by agent or attorney, during usual business hours, its minutes of the proceedings of its shareholders and record of shareholders and to make extracts therefrom for any purpose reasonably related to such person's interest as a shareholder. Holders of voting trust certificates representing shares of the corporation shall be regarded as shareholders for the purpose of this section. Any such agent or attorney shall be authorized in a writing that satisfies the requirements of a writing under paragraph (b) of section 609 (Proxies). A corporation requested to provide information pursuant to this paragraph shall make available such information in written form and in any format in which such information is maintained by the corporation and shall not be required to provide such information in any other format. If a request made pursuant to this paragraph includes a request to furnish information regarding beneficial owners, the corporation shall make available such information in its possession regarding beneficial owners as is provided to the corporation by a registered broker or dealer or a bank, association or other entity that exercises fiduciary powers in connection with the forwarding of information to such owners. The corporation shall not be required to obtain information about beneficial owners not in its possession.

(c) An inspection authorized by paragraph (b) may be denied to such shareholder or other person upon his refusal to furnish to the corporation, its transfer agent or registrar an affidavit that such inspection is not desired for a purpose which is in the interest of a business or object other than the business of the corporation and that he has not within five years sold or offered for sale any list of shareholders of any corporation of any type or kind, whether or not formed under the laws of this state, or aided or abetted any person in procuring any such record of shareholders for any such purpose.

(d) Upon refusal by the corporation or by an officer or agent of the corporation to permit an inspection of the minutes of the proceedings of its shareholders or of the record of shareholders as herein provided, the person making the demand for inspection may apply to the supreme court in the judicial district where the office of the corporation is located, upon such notice as the court may direct, for an order directing the corporation, its officer or agent to show cause why an order should not be granted permitting such inspection by the applicant. Upon the return day of the order to show cause, the court shall hear the parties summarily, by affidavit or otherwise, and if it appears that the applicant is qualified and entitled to such inspection, the court shall grant an order compelling such inspection and awarding such further relief as to the court may seem just and proper.

(e) Upon the written request of any shareholder the corporation shall give or mail to such shareholder an annual balance sheet and profit and loss statement for the preceding fiscal year, and, if any interim balance sheet or profit and loss statement has been distributed to its shareholders or otherwise made available to the public, the most recent such interim balance sheet or profit and loss statement. The corporation shall be allowed a reasonable time to prepare such annual balance sheet and profit and loss statement.

(f) Nothing herein contained shall impair the power of courts to compel the production for examination of the books and records of a corporation.

(g) The books and records specified in paragraph (a) shall be prima facie evidence of the facts therein stated in favor of the plaintiff in any action or special proceeding against such corporation or any of its officers, directors or shareholders.

§ 626. Shareholders' Derivative Action Brought in the Right of the Corporation to Procure a Judgment in Its Favor

(a) An action may be brought in the right of a domestic or foreign corporation to procure a judgment in its favor, by a holder of shares or of voting trust certificates of the corporation or of a beneficial interest in such shares or certificates.

(b) In any such action, it shall be made to appear that the plaintiff is such a holder at the time of bringing the action and that he was such a holder at the time of the transaction of which he complains, or that his shares or his interest therein devolved upon him by operation of law.

(c) In any such action, the complaint shall set forth with particularity the efforts of the plaintiff to secure the initiation of such action by the board or the reasons for not making such effort.

(d) Such action shall not be discontinued, compromised or settled, without the approval of the court having jurisdiction of the action. If the court shall determine that the interests of the shareholders or any class or classes thereof will be substantially affected by such discontinuance, compromise, or settlement, the court, in its discretion, may direct that notice, by publication or otherwise, shall be given to the shareholders or class or classes thereof whose interest it determines will be so affected; if notice is so directed to be given, the court may determine which one or more of the parties to the action shall bear the expense of giving the same, in such amount as the court shall determine and find to be reasonable in the circumstances, and the amount of such expense shall be awarded as special costs of the action and recoverable in the same manner as statutory taxable costs.

(e) If the action on behalf of the corporation was successful, in whole or in part, or if anything was received by the plaintiff or plaintiffs or a claimant or claimants as the result of a judgment, compromise or settlement of an action or claim, the court may award the plaintiff or plaintiffs, claimant or claimants, reasonable expenses, including reasonable attorney's fees, and shall direct him or them to account to the corporation for the remainder of the proceeds so received by him or them. This paragraph shall not apply to any judgment rendered for the benefit of injured shareholders only and limited to a recovery of the loss or damage sustained by them.

§ 627. Security for Expenses in Shareholders' Derivative Action Brought in the Right of the Corporation to Procure a Judgment in Its Favor

In any action specified in section 626 (Shareholders' derivative action brought in the right of the corporation to procure a judgment in its favor), unless the plaintiff or plaintiffs hold five percent or more of any class of the outstanding shares or hold voting trust certificates or a beneficial interest in shares representing five percent or more of any class of such shares, or the shares, voting trust certificates and beneficial interest of such plaintiff or plaintiffs have a fair value in excess of fifty thousand dollars, the corporation in whose right such action is brought shall be entitled at any stage of the proceedings before final judgment to require the plaintiff or plaintiffs to give security for the reasonable expenses, including attorney's fees, which may be incurred by it in connection with such action and by the other parties defendant in connection therewith for which the corporation may become liable under this chapter, under any contract or otherwise under law, to which the corporation shall have recourse in such amount as the court having jurisdiction of such action shall determine upon the termination of such action. The amount of such security may thereafter from time to time be increased or decreased in the discretion of the court having jurisdiction of such action upon showing that the security provided has or may become inadequate or excessive.

§ 628. Liability of Subscribers and Shareholders

(a) A holder of or subscriber for shares of a corporation shall be under no obligation to the corporation for payment for such shares other than the obligation to pay the unpaid portion of his subscription which in no event shall be less than the amount of the consideration for which such shares could be issued lawfully.

(b) Any person becoming an assignee or transferee of shares or of a subscription for shares in good faith and without knowledge or notice that the full consideration therefor has not been paid shall not be personally liable for any unpaid portion of such consideration, but the transferor shall remain liable therefor.

(c) No person holding shares in any corporation as collateral security shall be personally liable as a shareholder but the person pledging such shares shall be considered the holder thereof and shall be so liable. No executor, administrator, guardian, trustee or other fiduciary shall be personally liable as a shareholder, but the estate and funds in the hands of such executor, administrator, guardian, trustee or other fiduciary shall be liable.

§ 629. Certain Transfers or Assignments by Shareholders or Subscribers; Effect

Any transfer or assignment by a shareholder of his shares, or by a subscriber for shares of his interest in the corporation, shall not relieve him of any liability as a shareholder or subscriber if at the time of such transfer or assignment the aggregate of the corporation's property, exclusive of any property which it may have conveyed, transferred, concealed, removed, or permitted to be concealed or removed, with intent to defraud, hinder or delay its creditors, is not at a fair valuation sufficient in amount to pay its debts, or if such condition is imminent.

§ 630. Liability of Shareholders for Wages Due to Laborers, Servants or Employees

(a) The ten largest shareholders, as determined by the fair value of their beneficial interest as of the beginning of the period during which the unpaid services referred to in this section are performed, of every domestic corporation or of any foreign corporation, when the unpaid services were performed in the state, no shares of which are listed on a national securities exchange or regularly quoted in an over-the-counter market by one or more members of a national or an affiliated securities association, shall jointly and severally be personally liable for all debts, wages or salaries due and owing to any of its laborers, servants or employees other than contractors, for services performed by them for such corporation. Before such laborer, servant or employee shall charge such shareholder for such services, he shall give notice in writing to such shareholder that he intends to hold him liable under this section. Such notice shall be given within one hundred and eighty days after termination of such services, except that if, within such period, the laborer, servant or employee demands an examination of the record of shareholders under paragraph (b) of section 624 (Books and records; right of inspection, prima facie evidence), such notice may be given within sixty days after he has been given the opportunity to examine the record of shareholders. An action to enforce such liability shall be commenced within ninety days after the return of an execution unsatisfied against the corporation upon a judgment recovered against it for such services. The provisions of this paragraph shall not apply to an investment company registered as such under an act of congress entitled "Investment Company Act of 1940."

(b) For the purposes of this section, wages or salaries shall mean all compensation and benefits payable by an employer to or for the account of the employee for personal services rendered by such employee. These shall specifically include but not be limited to salaries, overtime, vacation, holiday and severance pay; employer contributions to or payments of insurance or welfare benefits; employer contributions to pension or annuity funds; and any other moneys properly due or payable for services rendered by such employee.

(c) A shareholder who has paid more than his pro rata share under this section shall be entitled to contribution pro rata from the other shareholders liable under this section with respect to the excess so paid, over and above his pro rata share, and may sue them jointly or severally or any number of them to recover the amount due from them. Such recovery may be had in a separate action. As used in this paragraph, "pro rata" means in proportion to beneficial share interest. Before a shareholder may claim contribution from other shareholders under this paragraph, he shall, unless they have been given notice by a laborer, servant or employee under paragraph (a), give them notice in writing that he intends to hold them so liable to him. Such notice shall be given by him within twenty days after the date that notice was given to him by a laborer, servant or employee under paragraph (a).

ARTICLE 7

DIRECTORS AND OFFICERS

§ 701.   Board of Directors

Subject to any provision in the certificate of incorporation authorized by paragraph (b) of section 620 (Agreements as to voting; provision in certificate of incorporation as to control of directors) or by paragraph (b) of section 715 (Officers), the business of a corporation shall be managed under the direction of its board of directors, each of whom shall be at least eighteen years of age. The certificate of incorporation or the by-laws may prescribe other qualifications for directors.

§ 702.   Number of Directors

(a) The board of directors shall consist of one or more members. The number of directors constituting the board may be fixed by the by-laws, or by action of the shareholders or of the board under the specific provisions of a by-law adopted by the shareholders. If not otherwise fixed under this paragraph, the number shall be one. As used in this article, "entire board" means the total number of directors which the corporation would have if there were no vacancies.

(b) The number of directors may be increased or decreased by amendment of the by-laws, or by action of the shareholders or of the board under the specific provisions of a by-law adopted by the shareholders, subject to the following limitations.

(1) If the board is authorized by the by-laws to change the number of directors, whether by amending the by-laws or by taking action under the specific provisions of a by-law adopted by the shareholders, such amendment or action shall require the vote of a majority of the entire board.

(2) No decrease shall shorten the term of any incumbent director.

§ 703.   Election and Term of Directors

(a) At each annual meeting of shareholders, directors shall be elected to hold office until the next annual meeting except as authorized by section 704 (Classification of directors). The certificate of incorporation may provide for the election of one or more directors by the holders of the shares of any class or series, or by the holders of bonds entitled to vote in the election of directors pursuant to section 518 (Corporate bonds), voting as a class.

(b) Each director shall hold office until the expiration of the term for which he is elected, and until his successor has been elected and qualified.

§ 704.   Classification of Directors

(a) The certificate of incorporation or the specific provisions of a by-law adopted by the shareholders may provide that the directors be divided into either two, three or four classes. All classes shall be as nearly equal in number as possible. The terms of office of the directors initially classified shall be as follows: that of the first class shall expire at the next annual meeting of shareholders, the second class at the second succeeding annual meeting, the third class, if any, at the third succeeding annual meeting, and the fourth class, if any, at the fourth succeeding annual meeting.

(b) At each annual meeting after such initial classification, directors to replace those whose terms expire at such annual meeting shall be elected to hold office until the second succeeding annual meeting if there are two classes, the third succeeding annual meeting if there are three classes, or the fourth succeeding annual meeting if there are four classes.

(c) If directors are classified and the number of directors is thereafter changed:

(1) Any newly created directorships or any decrease in directorships shall be so apportioned among the classes as to make all classes as nearly equal in number as possible.

(2) When the number of directors is increased by the board and any newly created directorships are filled by the board, there shall be no classification of the additional directors until the next annual meeting of shareholders.

§ 705. Newly Created Directorships and Vacancies

(a) Newly created directorships resulting from an increase in the number of directors and vacancies occurring in the board for any reason except the removal of directors without cause may be filled by vote of the board. If the number of the directors then in office is less than a quorum, such newly created directorships and vacancies may be filled by vote of a majority of the directors then in office. Nothing in this paragraph shall affect any provision of the certificate of incorporation or the by-laws which provides that such newly created directorships or vacancies shall be filled by vote of the shareholders, or any provision of the certificate of incorporation specifying greater requirements as permitted under section 709 (Greater requirements as to quorum and vote of directors).

(b) Unless the certificate of incorporation or the specific provisions of a by-law adopted by the shareholders provide that the board may fill vacancies occurring in the board by reason of the removal of directors without cause, such vacancies may be filled only by vote of the shareholders.

(c) A director elected to fill a vacancy, unless elected by the shareholders, shall hold office until the next meeting of shareholders at which the election of directors is in the regular order of business, and until his successor has been elected and qualified.

(d) Unless otherwise provided in the certificate of incorporation or by-laws, notwithstanding the provisions of paragraphs (a) and (b) of this section, whenever the holders of any class or classes of shares or series thereof are entitled to elect one or more directors by the certificate of incorporation, any vacancy that may be filled by the board or a majority of the directors then in office, as the case may be, shall be filled by a majority of the directors elected by such class or classes or series thereof then in office, or, if no such director is in office, then as provided in paragraph (a) or (b) of this section, as the case may be.

§ 706. Removal of Directors

(a) Any or all of the directors may be removed for cause by vote of the shareholders. The certificate of incorporation or the specific provisions of a by-law adopted by the shareholders may provide for such removal by action of the board, except in the case of any director elected by cumulative voting, or by the holders of the shares of any class or series, or holders of bonds, voting as a class, when so entitled by the provisions of the certificate of incorporation.

(b) If the certificate of incorporation or the by-laws so provide, any or all of the directors may be removed without cause by vote of the shareholders.

(c) The removal of directors, with or without cause, as provided in paragraphs (a) and (b) is subject to the following:

(1) In the case of a corporation having cumulative voting, no director may be removed when the votes cast against his removal would be sufficient to elect him if voted cumulatively at an election at which the same total number of votes were cast and the entire board, or the entire class of directors of which he is a member, were then being elected; and

(2) When by the provisions of the certificate of incorporation the holders of the shares of any class or series, or holders of bonds, voting as a class, are entitled to elect one or more directors, any director so elected

may be removed only by the applicable vote of the holders of the shares of that class or series, or the holders of such bonds, voting as a class.

(d) An action to procure a judgment removing a director for cause may be brought by the attorney-general or by the holders of ten percent of the outstanding shares, whether or not entitled to vote. The court may bar from re-election any director so removed for a period fixed by the court.

§ 707.   Quorum of Directors

Unless a greater proportion is required by the certificate of incorporation, a majority of the entire board shall constitute a quorum for the transaction of business or of any specified item of business, except that the certificate of incorporation or the by-laws may fix the quorum at less than a majority of the entire board but not less than one-third thereof.

§ 708.   Action by the Board

(a) Except as otherwise provided in this chapter, any reference in this chapter to corporate action to be taken by the board shall mean such action at a meeting of the board.

(b) Unless otherwise restricted by the certificate of incorporation or the by-laws, any action required or permitted to be taken by the board or any committee thereof may be taken without a meeting if all members of the board or the committee consent in writing to the adoption of a resolution authorizing the action. The resolution and the written consents thereto by the members of the board or committee shall be filed with the minutes of the proceedings of the board or committee.

(c) Unless otherwise restricted by the certificate of incorporation or the by-laws, any one or more members of the board or any committee thereof may participate in a meeting of such board or committee by means of a conference telephone or similar communications equipment allowing all persons participating in the meeting to hear each other at the same time. Participation by such means shall constitute presence in person at a meeting.

(d) Except as otherwise provided in this chapter, the vote of a majority of the directors present at the time of the vote, if a quorum is present at such time, shall be the act of the board.

§ 709.   Greater Requirement as to Quorum and Vote of Directors

(a) The certificate of incorporation may contain provisions specifying either or both of the following:

(1) That the proportion of directors that shall constitute a quorum for the transaction of business or of any specified item of business shall be greater than the proportion prescribed by this chapter in the absence of such provision.

(2) That the proportion of votes of directors that shall be necessary for the transaction of business or of any specified item of business shall be greater than the proportion prescribed by this chapter in the absence of such provision.

(b)(1) An amendment of the certificate of incorporation which changes or strikes out a provision permitted by this section shall be authorized at a meeting of shareholders by (A)(i) for any corporation in existence on [February 22, 1998], two-thirds of the votes of all outstanding shares entitled to vote thereon, and (ii) for any corporation in existence on [February 22, 1998], the certificate of incorporation of which expressly provides such and for any corporation incorporated after the effective date of subparagraph (2) of this paragraph, a majority of the votes of all outstanding shares entitled to vote thereon or (B) in either case, such greater proportion of votes of shares, or votes of a class or series of shares, as may be provided specifically in the certificate of incorporation for changing or striking out a provision permitted by the section.

(2) Any corporation may adopt an amendment of the certificate of incorporation in accordance with any applicable clause or subclause of subparagraph (1) of this paragraph to provide that any further amendment of the certificate of incorporation that changes or strikes out a provision permitted by this section shall be authorized at a meeting of the shareholders by a specified proportion of the votes of shares, or particular

class or series of shares, entitled to vote thereon, provided that such proportion may not be less than a majority.

§ 712. Executive Committee and Other Committees

(a) If the certificate of incorporation or the by-laws so provide, the board, by resolution adopted by a majority of the entire board, may designate from among its members an executive committee and other committees, each consisting of one or more directors, and each of which, to the extent provided in the resolution or in the certificate of incorporation or by-laws, shall have all the authority of the board, except that no such committee shall have authority as to the following matters:

(1) The submission to shareholders of any action that needs shareholders' approval under this chapter.

(2) The filling of vacancies in the board of directors or in any committee.

(3) The fixing of compensation of the directors for serving on the board or on any committee.

(4) The amendment or repeal of the by-laws, or the adoption of new by-laws.

(5) The amendment or repeal of any resolution of the board which by its terms shall not be so amendable or repealable.

(b) The board may designate one or more directors as alternate members of any such committee, who may replace any absent or disqualified member or members at any meeting of such committee.

(c) Each such committee shall serve at the pleasure of the board. The designation of any such committee, the delegation thereto of authority, or action by any such committee pursuant to such authority shall not alone constitute performance by any member of the board who is not a member of the committee in question, of his duty to the corporation under section 717 (Duty of directors).

§ 713. Interested Directors

(a) No contract or other transaction between a corporation and one or more of its directors, or between a corporation and any other corporation, firm, association or other entity in which one or more of its directors are directors or officers, or have a substantial financial interest, shall be either void or voidable for this reason alone or by reason alone that such director or directors are present at the meeting of the board, or of a committee thereof, which approves such contract or transaction, or that his or their votes are counted for such purpose:

(1) If the material facts as to such director's interest in such contract or transaction and as to any such common directorship, officership or financial interest are disclosed in good faith or known to the board or committee, and the board or committee approves such contract or transaction by a vote sufficient for such purpose without counting the vote of such interested director or, if the votes of the disinterested directors are insufficient to constitute an act of the board as defined in section 708 (Action by the board), by unanimous vote of the disinterested directors; or

(2) If the material facts as to such director's interest in such contract or transaction and as to any such common directorship, officership or financial interest are disclosed in good faith or known to the shareholders entitled to vote thereon, and such contract or transaction is approved by vote of such shareholders.

(b) If a contract or other transaction between a corporation and one or more of its directors, or between a corporation and any other corporation, firm, association or other entity in which one or more of its directors are directors or officers, or have a substantial financial interest, is not approved in accordance with paragraph (a), the corporation may avoid the contract or transaction unless the party or parties thereto shall establish affirmatively that the contract or transaction was fair and reasonable as to the corporation at the time it was approved by the board, a committee or the shareholders.

(c) Common or interested directors may be counted in determining the presence of a quorum at a meeting of the board or of a committee which approves such contract or transaction.

(d) The certificate of incorporation may contain additional restrictions on contracts or transactions between a corporation and its directors and may provide that contracts or transactions in violation of such restrictions shall be void or voidable by the corporation.

(e) Unless otherwise provided in the certificate of incorporation or the by-laws, the board shall have authority to fix the compensation of directors for services in any capacity.

§ 714.   Loans to Directors

(a) A corporation may not lend money to or guarantee the obligation of a director of the corporation unless:

(1) the particular loan or guarantee is approved by the shareholders, with the holders of a majority of the votes of the shares entitled to vote thereon constituting a quorum, but shares held of record or beneficially by directors who are benefitted by such loan or guarantee shall not be entitled to vote or to be included in the determination of a quorum; or

(2) with respect to any corporation in existence on the effective date of this subparagraph (2) the certificate of incorporation of which expressly provides such and with respect to any corporation incorporated after the effective date of this subparagraph (2), the board determines that the loan or guarantee benefits the corporation and either approves the specific loan or guarantee or a general plan authorizing loans and guarantees.

(b) The fact that a loan or guarantee is made in violation of this section does not affect the borrower's liability on the loan.

§ 715.   Officers

(a) The board may elect or appoint a president, one or more vice-presidents, a secretary and a treasurer, and such other officers as it may determine, or as may be provided in the by-laws.

(b) The certificate of incorporation may provide that all officers or that specified officers shall be elected by the shareholders instead of by the board.

(c) Unless otherwise provided in the certificate of incorporation or the by-laws, all officers shall be elected or appointed to hold office until the meeting of the board following the next annual meeting of shareholders or, in the case of officers elected by the shareholders, until the next annual meeting of shareholders.

(d) Each officer shall hold office for the term for which he is elected or appointed, and until his successor has been elected or appointed and qualified.

(e) Any two or more offices may be held by the same person. When all of the issued and outstanding stock of the corporation is owned by one person, such person may hold all or any combination of offices.

(f) The board may require any officer to give security for the faithful performance of his duties.

(g) All officers as between themselves and the corporation shall have such authority and perform such duties in the management of the corporation as may be provided in the by-laws or, to the extent not so provided, by the board.

(h) An officer shall perform his duties as an officer in good faith and with that degree of care which an ordinarily prudent person in a like position would use under similar circumstances. In performing his duties, an officer shall be entitled to rely on information, opinions, reports or statements including financial statements and other financial data, in each case prepared or presented by:

(1) one or more other officers or employees of the corporation or of any other corporation of which at least fifty percentum of the outstanding shares of stock entitling the holders thereof to vote for the election of directors is owned directly or indirectly by the corporation, whom the officer believes to be reliable and competent in the matters presented, or

(2) counsel, public accountants or other persons as to matters which the officer believes to be within such person's professional or expert competence, so long as in so relying he shall be acting in good faith and with such degree of care, but he shall not be considered to be acting in good faith if he has knowledge

concerning the matter in question that would cause such reliance to be unwarranted. A person who so performs his duties shall have no liability by reason of being or having been an officer of the corporation.

§ 716. Removal of Officers

(a) Any officer elected or appointed by the board may be removed by the board with or without cause. An officer elected by the shareholders may be removed, with or without cause, only by vote of the shareholders, but his authority to act as an officer may be suspended by the board for cause.

(b) The removal of an officer without cause shall be without prejudice to his contract rights, if any. The election or appointment of an officer shall not of itself create contract rights.

(c) An action to procure a judgment removing an officer for cause may be brought by the attorney-general or by ten percent of the votes of the outstanding shares, whether or not entitled to vote. The court may bar from re-election or reappointment any officer so removed for a period fixed by the court.

§ 717. Duty of Directors

(a) A director shall perform his duties as a director, including his duties as a member of any committee of the board upon which he may serve, in good faith and with that degree of care which an ordinarily prudent person in a like position would use under similar circumstances. In performing his duties, a director shall be entitled to rely on information, opinions, reports or statements including financial statements and other financial data, in each case prepared or presented by:

(1) one or more officers or employees of the corporation or of any other corporation of which at least fifty percentum of the outstanding shares of stock entitling the holders thereof to vote for the election of directors is owned directly or indirectly by the corporation, whom the director believes to be reliable and competent in the matters presented,

(2) counsel, public accountants or other persons as to matters which the director believes to be within such person's professional or expert competence, or

(3) a committee of the board upon which he does not serve, duly designated in accordance with a provision of the certificate of incorporation or the by-laws, as to matters within its designated authority, which committee the director believes to merit confidence, so long as in so relying he shall be acting in good faith and with such degree of care, but he shall not be considered to be acting in good faith if he has knowledge concerning the matter in question that would cause such reliance to be unwarranted. A person who so performs his duties shall have no liability by reason of being or having been a director of the corporation.

(b) In taking action, including, without limitation, action which may involve or relate to a change or potential change in the control of the corporation, a director shall be entitled to consider, without limitation, (1) both the long-term and the short-term interests of the corporation and its shareholders and (2) the effects that the corporation's actions may have in the short-term or in the long-term upon any of the following:

(i) the prospects for potential growth, development, productivity and profitability of the corporation;

(ii) the corporation's current employees;

(iii) the corporation's retired employees and other beneficiaries receiving or entitled to receive retirement, welfare or similar benefits from or pursuant to any plan sponsored, or agreement entered into, by the corporation;

(iv) the corporation's customers and creditors; and

(v) the ability of the corporation to provide, as a going concern, goods, services, employment opportunities and employment benefits and otherwise to contribute to the communities in which it does business.

Nothing in this paragraph shall create any duties owed by any director to any person or entity to consider or afford any particular weight to any of the foregoing or abrogate any duty of the directors, either statutory or recognized by common law or court decisions.

For purposes of this paragraph, "control" shall mean the possession, directly or indirectly, of the power to direct or cause the direction of the management and policies of the corporation, whether through the ownership of voting stock, by contract, or otherwise.

§ 719.   Liability of Directors in Certain Cases

(a) Directors of a corporation who vote for or concur in any of the following corporate actions shall be jointly and severally liable to the corporation for the benefit of its creditors or shareholders, to the extent of any injury suffered by such persons, respectively, as a result of such action:

(1) The declaration of any dividend or other distribution to the extent that it is contrary to the provisions of paragraphs (a) and (b) of section 510 (Dividends or other distributions in cash or property).

(2) The purchase of the shares of the corporation to the extent that it is contrary to the provisions of section 513 (Purchase or redemption by a corporation of its own shares).

(3) The distribution of assets to shareholders after dissolution of the corporation without paying or adequately providing for all known liabilities of the corporation, excluding any claims not filed by creditors within the time limit set in a notice given to creditors under articles 10 (Non-judicial dissolution) or 11 (Judicial dissolution).

(4) The making of any loan contrary to section 714 (Loans to directors).

(b) A director who is present at a meeting of the board, or any committee thereof, when action specified in paragraph (a) is taken shall be presumed to have concurred in the action unless his dissent thereto shall be entered in the minutes of the meeting, or unless he shall submit his written dissent to the person acting as the secretary of the meeting before the adjournment thereof, or shall deliver or send by registered mail such dissent to the secretary of the corporation promptly after the adjournment of the meeting. Such right to dissent shall not apply to a director who voted in favor of such action. A director who is absent from a meeting of the board, or any committee thereof, when such action is taken shall be presumed to have concurred in the action unless he shall deliver or send by registered mail his dissent thereto to the secretary of the corporation or shall cause such dissent to be filed with the minutes of the proceedings of the board or committee within a reasonable time after learning of such action.

(c) Any director against whom a claim is successfully asserted under this section shall be entitled to contribution from the other directors who voted for or concurred in the action upon which the claim is asserted.

(d) Directors against whom a claim is successfully asserted under this section shall be entitled, to the extent of the amounts paid by them to the corporation as a result of such claims:

(1) Upon payment to the corporation of any amount of an improper dividend or distribution, to be subrogated to the rights of the corporation against shareholders who received such dividend or distribution with knowledge of facts indicating that it was not authorized by section 510, in proportion to the amounts received by them respectively.

(2) Upon payment to the corporation of any amount of the purchase price of an improper purchase of shares, to have the corporation rescind such purchase of shares and recover for their benefit, but at their expense, the amount of such purchase price from any seller who sold such shares with knowledge of facts indicating that such purchase of shares by the corporation was not authorized by section 513.

(3) Upon payment to the corporation of the claim of any creditor by reason of a violation of subparagraph (a)(3), to be subrogated to the rights of the corporation against shareholders who received an improper distribution of assets.

(4) Upon payment to the corporation of the amount of any loan made contrary to section 714, to be subrogated to the rights of the corporation against a director who received the improper loan.

(e) A director shall not be liable under this section if, in the circumstances, he performed his duty to the corporation under paragraph (a) of section 717.

(f) This section shall not affect any liability otherwise imposed by law upon any director.

§ 720. Action Against Directors and Officers for Misconduct

(a) An action may be brought against one or more directors or officers of a corporation to procure a judgment for the following relief:

(1) Subject to any provision of the certificate of incorporation authorized pursuant to paragraph (b) of section 402, to compel the defendant to account for his official conduct in the following cases:

(A) The neglect of, or failure to perform, or other violation of his duties in the management and disposition of corporate assets committed to his charge.

(B) The acquisition by himself, transfer to others, loss or waste of corporate assets due to any neglect of, or failure to perform, or other violation of his duties.

(C) In the case of directors or officers of a benefit corporation organized under article seventeen of this chapter: (i) the failure to pursue the general public benefit purpose of a benefit corporation or any specific public benefit set forth in its certificate of incorporation; (ii) the failure by a benefit corporation to deliver or post an annual report as required by section seventeen hundred eight of article seventeen of this chapter; or (iii) the neglect of, or failure to perform, or other violation of his or her duties or standard of conduct under article seventeen of this chapter.

(2) To set aside an unlawful conveyance, assignment or transfer of corporate assets, where the transferee knew of its unlawfulness.

(3) To enjoin a proposed unlawful conveyance, assignment or transfer of corporate assets, where there is sufficient evidence that it will be made.

(b) An action may be brought for the relief provided in this section, and in paragraph (a) of section 719 (Liability of directors in certain cases) by a corporation, or a receiver, trustee in bankruptcy, officer, director or judgment creditor thereof, or, under section 626 (Shareholders' derivative action brought in the right of the corporation to procure a judgment in its favor), by a shareholder, voting trust certificate holder, or the owner of a beneficial interest in shares thereof.

(c) This section shall not affect any liability otherwise imposed by law upon any director or officer.

§ 721. Nonexclusivity of Statutory Provisions for Indemnification of Directors and Officers

The indemnification and advancement of expenses granted pursuant to, or provided by, this article shall not be deemed exclusive of any other rights to which a director or officer seeking indemnification or advancement of expenses may be entitled, whether contained in the certificate of incorporation or the by-laws or, when authorized by such certificate of incorporation or by-laws, (i) a resolution of shareholders, (ii) a resolution of directors, or (iii) an agreement providing for such indemnification, provided that no indemnification may be made to or on behalf of any director or officer if a judgment or other final adjudication adverse to the director or officer establishes that his acts were committed in bad faith or were the result of active and deliberate dishonesty and were material to the cause of action so adjudicated, or that he personally gained in fact a financial profit or other advantage to which he was not legally entitled. Nothing contained in this article shall affect any rights to indemnification to which corporate personnel other than directors and officers may be entitled by contract or otherwise under law.

§ 722. Authorization for Indemnification of Directors and Officers

(a) A corporation may indemnify any person made, or threatened to be made, a party to an action or proceeding (other than one by or in the right of the corporation to procure a judgment in its favor), whether civil or criminal, including an action by or in the right of any other corporation of any type or kind, domestic or foreign, or any partnership, joint venture, trust, employee benefit plan or other enterprise, which any director or officer of the corporation served in any capacity at the request of the corporation, by reason of the fact that he, his testator or intestate, was a director or officer of the corporation, or served such other corporation, partnership, joint venture, trust, employee benefit plan or other enterprise in any capacity, against judgments, fines, amounts paid in settlement and reasonable expenses, including attorneys' fees actually and necessarily incurred as a result of such action or proceeding, or any appeal therein, if such director or officer acted, in good faith, for a purpose which he reasonably believed to be in, or, in the case of service for any other corporation or any partnership, joint venture, trust, employee benefit plan or other enterprise, not opposed to, the best interests of the corporation and, in criminal actions or proceedings, in addition, had no reasonable cause to believe that his conduct was unlawful.

(b) The termination of any such civil or criminal action or proceeding by judgment, settlement, conviction or upon a plea of nolo contendere, or its equivalent, shall not in itself create a presumption that any such director or officer did not act, in good faith, for a purpose which he reasonably believed to be in, or, in the case of service for any other corporation or any partnership, joint venture, trust, employee benefit plan or other enterprise, not opposed to, the best interests of the corporation or that he had reasonable cause to believe that his conduct was unlawful.

(c) A corporation may indemnify any person made, or threatened to be made, a party to an action by or in the right of the corporation to procure a judgment in its favor by reason of the fact that he, his testator or intestate, is or was a director or officer of the corporation, or is or was serving at the request of the corporation as a director or officer of any other corporation of any type or kind, domestic or foreign, [or] of any partnership, joint venture, trust, employee benefit plan or other enterprise, against amounts paid in settlement and reasonable expenses, including attorneys' fees, actually and necessarily incurred by him in connection with the defense or settlement of such action, or in connection with an appeal therein, if such director or officer acted, in good faith, for a purpose which he reasonably believed to be in, or, in the case of service for any other corporation or any partnership, joint venture, trust, employee benefit plan or other enterprise, not opposed to, the best interests of the corporation, except that no indemnification under this paragraph shall be made in respect of (1) a threatened action, or a pending action which is settled or otherwise disposed of, or (2) any claim, issue or matter as to which such person shall have been adjudged to be liable to the corporation, unless and only to the extent that the court in which the action was brought, or, if no action was brought, any court of competent jurisdiction, determines upon application that, in view of all the circumstances of the case, the person is fairly and reasonably entitled to indemnity for such portion of the settlement amount and expenses as the court deems proper.

(d) For the purpose of this section, a corporation shall be deemed to have requested a person to serve an employee benefit plan where the performance by such person of his duties to the corporation also imposes duties on, or otherwise involves services by, such person to the plan or participants or beneficiaries of the plan; excise taxes assessed on a person with respect to an employee benefit plan pursuant to applicable law shall be considered fines; and action taken or omitted by a person with respect to an employee benefit plan in the performance of such person's duties for a purpose reasonably believed by such person to be in the interest of the participants and beneficiaries of the plan shall be deemed to be for a purpose which is not opposed to the best interests of the corporation.

§ 723.   Payment of Indemnification Other Than by Court Award

(a) A person who has been successful, on the merits or otherwise, in the defense of a civil or criminal action or proceeding of the character described in section 722 shall be entitled to indemnification as authorized in such section.

(b) Except as provided in paragraph (a), any indemnification under section 722 or otherwise permitted by section 721, unless ordered by a court under section 724 (Indemnification of directors and officers by a court), shall be made by the corporation, only if authorized in the specific case:

(1) By the board acting by a quorum consisting of directors who are not parties to such action or proceeding upon a finding that the director or officer has met the standard of conduct set forth in section 722 or established pursuant to section 721, as the case may be, or,

(2) If a quorum under subparagraph (1) is not obtainable or, even if obtainable, a quorum of disinterested directors so directs;

(A) By the board upon the opinion in writing of independent legal counsel that indemnification is proper in the circumstances because the applicable standard of conduct set forth in such sections has been met by such director or officer, or

(B) By the shareholders upon a finding that the director or officer has met the applicable standard of conduct set forth in such sections.

(C) Expenses incurred in defending a civil or criminal action or proceeding may be paid by the corporation in advance of the final disposition of such action or proceeding upon receipt of an undertaking by or on behalf of such director or officer to repay such amount as, and to the extent, required by paragraph (a) of section 725.

§ 724. Indemnification of Directors and Officers by a Court

(a) Notwithstanding the failure of a corporation to provide indemnification, and despite any contrary resolution of the board or of the shareholders in the specific case under section 723 (Payment of indemnification other than by court award), indemnification shall be awarded by a court to the extent authorized under section 722 (Authorization for indemnification of directors and officers), and paragraph (a) of section 723. Application therefor may be made, in every case, either:

(1) In the civil action or proceeding in which the expenses were incurred or other amounts were paid, or

(2) To the supreme court in a separate proceeding, in which case the application shall set forth the disposition of any previous application made to any court for the same or similar relief and also reasonable cause for the failure to make application for such relief in the action or proceeding in which the expenses were incurred or other amounts were paid.

(b) The application shall be made in such manner and form as may be required by the applicable rules of court or, in the absence thereof, by direction of a court to which it is made. Such application shall be upon notice to the corporation. The court may also direct that notice be given at the expense of the corporation to the shareholders and such other persons as it may designate in such manner as it may require.

(c) Where indemnification is sought by judicial action, the court may allow a person such reasonable expenses, including attorneys' fees, during the pendency of the litigation as are necessary in connection with his defense therein, if the court shall find that the defendant has by his pleadings or during the course of the litigation raised genuine issues of fact or law.

§ 725. Other Provisions Affecting Indemnification of Directors and Officers

(a) All expenses incurred in defending a civil or criminal action or proceeding which are advanced by the corporation under paragraph (c) of section 723 (Payment of indemnification other than by court award) or allowed by a court under paragraph (c) of section 724 (Indemnification of directors and officers by a court) shall be repaid in case the person receiving such advancement or allowance is ultimately found, under the procedure set forth in this article, not to be entitled to indemnification or, where indemnification is granted, to the extent the expenses so advanced by the corporation or allowed by the court exceed the indemnification to which he is entitled.

(b) No indemnification, advancement or allowance shall be made under this article in any circumstance where it appears:

(1) That the indemnification would be inconsistent with the law of the jurisdiction of incorporation of a foreign corporation which prohibits or otherwise limits such indemnification;

(2) That the indemnification would be inconsistent with a provision of the certificate of incorporation, a by-law, a resolution of the board or of the shareholders, an agreement or other proper corporate action, in effect at the time of the accrual of the alleged cause of action asserted in the threatened or pending action or proceeding in which the expenses were incurred or other amounts were paid, which prohibits or otherwise limits indemnification; or

(3) If there has been a settlement approved by the court, that the indemnification would be inconsistent with any condition with respect to indemnification expressly imposed by the court in approving the settlement.

(c) If any expenses or other amounts are paid by way of indemnification, otherwise than by court order or action by the shareholders, the corporation shall, not later than the next annual meeting of shareholders unless such meeting is held within three months from the date of such payment, and, in any event, within fifteen months from the date of such payment, mail to its shareholders of record at the time entitled to vote for the election of directors a statement specifying the persons paid, the amounts paid, and the nature and status at the time of such payment of the litigation or threatened litigation.

(d) If any action with respect to indemnification of directors and officers is taken by way of amendment of the by-laws, resolution of directors, or by agreement, then the corporation shall, not later than the next annual meeting of shareholders, unless such meeting is held within three months from the date of such action, and, in any event, within fifteen months from the date of such action, mail to its shareholders of record at the time entitled to vote for the election of directors a statement specifying the action taken. . . .

(f) The provisions of this article relating to indemnification of directors and officers and insurance therefor shall apply to domestic corporations and foreign corporations doing business in this state, except as provided in section 1320 (Exemption from certain provisions).

§ 726.   Insurance for Indemnification of Directors and Officers

(a) Subject to paragraph (b), a corporation shall have power to purchase and maintain insurance:

(1) To indemnify the corporation for any obligation which it incurs as a result of the indemnification of directors and officers under the provisions of this article, and

(2) To indemnify directors and officers in instances in which they may be indemnified by the corporation under the provisions of this article, and

(3) To indemnify directors and officers in instances in which they may not otherwise be indemnified by the corporation under the provisions of this article provided the contract of insurance covering such directors and officers provides, in a manner acceptable to the superintendent of financial services, for a retention amount and for co-insurance.

(b) No insurance under paragraph (a) may provide for any payment, other than cost of defense, to or on behalf of any director or officer:

(1) if a judgment or other final adjudication adverse to the insured director or officer establishes that his acts of active and deliberate dishonesty were material to the cause of action so adjudicated, or that he personally gained in fact a financial profit or other advantage to which he was not legally entitled, or

(2) in relation to any risk the insurance of which is prohibited under the insurance law of this state.

(c) Insurance under any or all subparagraphs of paragraph (a) may be included in a single contract or supplement thereto. Retrospective rated contracts are prohibited.

(d) The corporation shall, within the time and to the persons provided in paragraph (c) of section 725 (Other provisions affecting indemnification of directors or officers), mail a statement in respect of any insurance it has purchased or renewed under this section, specifying the insurance carrier, date of the contract, cost of the insurance, corporate positions insured, and a statement explaining all sums, not previously reported in a statement to shareholders, paid under any indemnification insurance contract.

(e) This section is the public policy of this state to spread the risk of corporate management, notwithstanding any other general or special law of this state or of any other jurisdiction including the federal government.

ARTICLE 8

AMENDMENTS AND CHANGES

§ 801.   Right to Amend Certificate of Incorporation

(a) A corporation may amend its certificate of incorporation, from time to time, in any and as many respects as may be desired, if such amendment contains only such provisions as might be lawfully contained in an original certificate of incorporation filed at the time of making such amendment.

(b) In particular, and without limitation upon such general power of amendment, a corporation may amend its certificate of incorporation, from time to time, so as:

(1) To change its corporate name.

(2) To enlarge, limit or otherwise change its corporate purposes.

(3) To specify or change the location of the office of the corporation.

(4) To specify or change the post office address to which the secretary of state shall mail a copy of any process against the corporation served upon him.

(5) To make, revoke or change the designation of a registered agent, or to specify or change the address of its registered agent.

(6) To extend the duration of the corporation or, if the corporation ceased to exist because of the expiration of the duration in its certificate of incorporation, to revive its existence.

(7) To increase or decrease the aggregate number of shares, or shares of any class or series, with or without par value, which the corporation shall have to issue.

(8) To remove from authorized shares any class of shares, or any shares of any class, whether issued or unissued.

(9) To increase the par value of any authorized shares of any class with par value, whether issued or unissued.

(10) To reduce the par value of any authorized shares of any class with par value, whether issued or unissued.

(11) To change any authorized shares, with or without par value, whether issued or unissued, into a different number of shares of the same class or into the same or a different number of shares of any one or more classes or any series thereof, either with or without par value.

(12) To fix, change or abolish the designation of any authorized class or any series thereof or any of the relative rights, preferences and limitations of any shares of any authorized class or any series thereof, whether issued or unissued, including any provisions in respect of any undeclared dividends, whether or not cumulative or accrued, or the redemption of any shares, or any sinking fund for the redemption or purchase of any shares, or any preemptive right to acquire shares or other securities.

(13) As to the shares of any preferred class, then or theretofore authorized, which may be issued in series, to grant authority to the board or to change or revoke the authority of the board to establish and designate series and to fix the number of shares and the relative rights, preferences and limitation as between series.

(14) To strike out, change or add any provision, not inconsistent with this chapter or any other statute, relating to the business of the corporation, its affairs, its rights or powers, or the rights or powers of its shareholders, directors or officers, including any provision which under this chapter is required or permitted to be set forth in the by-laws, except that a certificate of amendment may not be filed wherein the duration of the corporation shall be reduced.

(c) A corporation created by special act may accomplish any or all amendments permitted in this article, in the manner and subject to the conditions in this article.

§ 802. Reduction of Stated Capital by Amendment

(a) A corporation may reduce its stated capital by an amendment of its certificate of incorporation under section 801 (Right to amend certificate of incorporation) which:

(1) Reduces the par value of any issued shares with par value.

(2) Changes issued shares under subparagraph (b)(11) of section 801 that results in a reduction of stated capital.

(3) Removes from authorized shares, shares that have been issued, reacquired and cancelled by the corporation.

(b) This section shall not prevent a corporation from reducing its stated capital in any other manner permitted by this chapter.

§ 804.   Class Voting on Amendment

(a) Notwithstanding any provision in the certificate of incorporation, the holders of shares of a class shall be entitled to vote and to vote as a class upon the authorization of an amendment and, in addition to the authorization of the amendment by a majority of the votes of all outstanding shares entitled to vote thereon, the amendment shall be authorized by a majority of the votes of all outstanding shares of the class when a proposed amendment would:

(1) Exclude or limit their right to vote on any matter, except as such right may be limited by voting rights given to new shares then being authorized of any existing or new class or series.

(2) Change their shares under subparagraphs (b) (10), (11) or (12) of section 801 (Right to amend certificate of incorporation) or provide that their shares may be converted into shares of any other class or into shares of any other series of the same class, or alter the terms or conditions upon which their shares are convertible or change the shares issuable upon conversion of their shares, if such action would adversely affect such holders, or

(3) Subordinate their rights, by authorizing shares having preferences which would be in any respect superior to their rights.

(b) If any proposed amendment referred to in paragraph (a) would adversely affect the rights of the holders of shares of only one or more series of any class, but not the entire class, then only the holders of those series whose rights would be affected shall be considered a separate class for the purposes of this section.

ARTICLE 9

MERGER OR CONSOLIDATION; GUARANTEE; DISPOSITION OF ASSETS

§ 912.   Requirements Relating to Certain Business Combinations

(a) For the purposes of this section:

(1) "Affiliate" means a person that directly, or indirectly through one or more intermediaries, controls, or is controlled by, or is under common control with, a specified person.

(2) "Announcement date", when used in reference to any business combination, means the date of the first public announcement of the final, definitive proposal for such business combination.

(3) "Associate", when used to indicate a relationship with any person, means (A) any corporation or organization of which such person is an officer or partner or is, directly or indirectly, the beneficial owner of ten percent or more of any class of voting stock, (B) any trust or other estate in which such person has a substantial beneficial interest or as to which such person serves as trustee or in a similar fiduciary capacity, and (C) any relative or spouse of such person, or any relative of such spouse, who has the same home as such person.

(4) "Beneficial owner", when used with respect to any stock, means a person:

(A) that, individually or with or through any of its affiliates or associates, beneficially owns such stock, directly or indirectly; or

(B) that, individually or with or through any of its affiliates or associates, has (i) the right to acquire such stock (whether such right is exercisable immediately or only after the passage of time), pursuant to any agreement, arrangement or understanding (whether or not in writing), or upon the exercise of conversion rights, exchange rights, warrants or options, or otherwise; provided, however, that a person shall not be deemed the beneficial owner of stock tendered pursuant to a tender or exchange offer made by such person or any of such person's affiliates or associates until such tendered stock is accepted for purchase or exchange; or (ii) the right to vote such stock pursuant to any agreement, arrangement or understanding (whether or not in writing); provided, however, that a person shall not be deemed the beneficial owner of any stock under this item if the agreement, arrangement or understanding to vote such stock (X) arises solely from a revocable proxy or consent given in response to a proxy or consent solicitation made in accordance with the applicable rules and regulations under the Exchange Act and (Y) is not then reportable on a Schedule 13D under the Exchange Act (or any comparable or successor report); or

(C) that has any agreement, arrangement or understanding (whether or not in writing), for the purpose of acquiring, holding, voting (except voting pursuant to a revocable proxy or consent as described in item (ii) of clause (B) of this subparagraph), or disposing of such stock with any other person that beneficially owns, or whose affiliates or associates beneficially own, directly or indirectly, such stock.

(5) "Business combination", when used in reference to any domestic corporation and any interested shareholder of such corporation, means:

(A) any merger or consolidation of such corporation or any subsidiary of such corporation with (i) such interested shareholder or (ii) any other corporation (whether or not itself an interested shareholder of such corporation) which is, or after such merger or consolidation would be, an affiliate or associate of such interested shareholder;

(B) any sale, lease, exchange, mortgage, pledge, transfer or other disposition (in one transaction or a series of transactions) to or with such interested shareholder or any affiliate or associate of such interested shareholder of assets of such corporation or any subsidiary of such corporation (i) having an aggregate market value equal to ten percent or more of the aggregate market value of all the assets, determined on a consolidated basis, of such corporation, (ii) having an aggregate market value equal to ten percent or more of the aggregate market value of all the outstanding stock of such corporation, or (iii) representing ten percent or more of the earning power or net income, determined on a consolidated basis, of such corporation;

(C) the issuance or transfer by such corporation or any subsidiary of such corporation (in one transaction or a series of transactions) of any stock of such corporation or any subsidiary of such corporation which has an aggregate market value equal to five percent or more of the aggregate market value of all the outstanding stock of such corporation to such interested shareholder or any affiliate or associate of such interested shareholder except pursuant to the exercise of warrants or rights to purchase stock offered, or a dividend or distribution paid or made, pro rata to all shareholders of such corporation;

(D) the adoption of any plan or proposal for the liquidation or dissolution of such corporation proposed by, or pursuant to any agreement, arrangement or understanding (whether or not in writing) with, such interested shareholder or any affiliate or associate of such interested shareholder;

(E) any reclassification of securities (including, without limitation, any stock split, stock dividend, or other distribution of stock in respect of stock, or any reverse stock split), or recapitalization of such corporation, or any merger or consolidation of such corporation with any subsidiary of such corporation, or any other transaction (whether or not with or into or otherwise involving such interested shareholder), proposed by, or pursuant to any agreement, arrangement or understanding (whether or not in writing) with, such interested shareholder or any affiliate or associate of such interested shareholder, which has the effect, directly or indirectly, of increasing the proportionate share of the outstanding shares of any class or series of voting stock or securities convertible into voting stock of such corporation or any subsidiary of such corporation which is directly or indirectly owned by such interested shareholder or any affiliate or associate of such interested shareholder, except as a result of immaterial changes due to fractional share adjustments; or

(F) any receipt by such interested shareholder or any affiliate or associate of such interested shareholder of the benefit, directly or indirectly (except proportionately as a shareholder of such corporation) of any loans, advances, guarantees, pledges or other financial assistance or any tax credits or other tax advantages provided by or through such corporation.

(6) "Common stock" means any stock other than preferred stock.

(7) "Consummation date", with respect to any business combination, means the date of consummation of such business combination, or, in the case of a business combination as to which a shareholder vote is taken, the later of the business day prior to the vote or twenty days prior to the date of consummation of such business combination.

(8) "Control", including the terms "controlling", "controlled by" and "under common control with", means the possession, directly or indirectly, of the power to direct or cause the direction of the management and policies of a person, whether through the ownership of voting stock, by contract, or otherwise. A person's

beneficial ownership of ten percent or more of a corporation's outstanding voting stock shall create a presumption that such person has control of such corporation. Notwithstanding the foregoing, a person shall not be deemed to have control of a corporation if such person holds voting stock, in good faith and not for the purpose of circumventing this section, as an agent, bank, broker, nominee, custodian or trustee for one or more beneficial owners who do not individually or as a group have control of such corporation.

(9) "Exchange Act" means the Act of Congress known as the Securities Exchange Act of 1934, as the same has been or hereafter may be amended from time to time.

(10) "Interested shareholder", when used in reference to any domestic corporation, means any person (other than such corporation or any subsidiary of such corporation) that

(A)(i) is the beneficial owner, directly or indirectly, of twenty percent or more of the outstanding voting stock of such corporation; or

(ii) is an affiliate or associate of such corporation and at any time within the five-year period immediately prior to the date in question was the beneficial owner, directly or indirectly, of twenty percent or more of the then outstanding voting stock of such corporation; provided that

(B) for the purpose of determining whether a person is an interested shareholder, the number of shares of voting stock of such corporation deemed to be outstanding shall include shares deemed to be beneficially owned by the person through application of subparagraph four of this paragraph but shall not include any other unissued shares of voting stock of such corporation which may be issuable pursuant to any agreement, arrangement or understanding, or upon exercise of conversion rights, warrants or options, or otherwise.

(11) "Market value", when used in reference to stock or property of any domestic corporation, means:

(A) in the case of stock, the highest closing sale price during the thirty-day period immediately preceding the date in question of a share of such stock on the composite tape for New York stock exchange-listed stocks, or, if such stock is not quoted on such composite tape or if such stock is not listed on such exchange, on the principal United States securities exchange registered under the Exchange Act on which such stock is listed, or, if such stock is not listed on any such exchange, the highest closing bid quotation with respect to a share of such stock during the thirty-day period preceding the date in question on the National Association of Securities Dealers, Inc. Automated Quotations System or any system then in use, or if no such quotations are available, the fair market value on the date in question of a share of such stock as determined by the board of directors of such corporation in good faith; and

(B) in the case of property other than cash or stock, the fair market value of such property on the date in question as determined by the board of directors of such corporation in good faith.

(12) "Preferred stock" means any class or series of stock of a domestic corporation which under the by-laws or certificate of incorporation of such corporation is entitled to receive payment of dividends prior to any payment of dividends on some other class or series of stock, or is entitled in the event of any voluntary liquidation, dissolution or winding up of the corporation to receive payment or distribution of a preferential amount before any payments or distributions are received by some other class or series of stock. . . .

(14) "Stock" means:

(A) any stock or similar security, any certificate of interest, any participation in any profit sharing agreement, any voting trust certificate, or any certificate of deposit for stock; and

(B) any security convertible, with or without consideration, into stock, or any warrant, call or other option or privilege of buying stock without being bound to do so, or any other security carrying any right to acquire, subscribe to or purchase stock.

(15) "Stock acquisition date", with respect to any person and any domestic corporation, means the date that such person first becomes an interested shareholder of such corporation.

(16) "Subsidiary" of any person means any other corporation of which a majority of the voting stock is owned, directly or indirectly, by such person.

(17) "Voting stock" means shares of capital stock of a corporation entitled to vote generally in the election of directors.

(b) Notwithstanding anything to the contrary contained in this chapter (except the provisions of paragraph (d) of this section), no domestic corporation shall engage in any business combination with any interested shareholder of such corporation for a period of five years following such interested shareholder's stock acquisition date unless such business combination or the purchase of stock made by such interested shareholder on such interested shareholder's stock acquisition date is approved by the board of directors of such corporation prior to such interested shareholder's stock acquisition date. If a good faith proposal is made in writing to the board of directors of such corporation regarding a business combination, the board of directors shall respond, in writing, within thirty days or such shorter period, if any, as may be required by the Exchange Act, setting forth its reasons for its decision regarding such proposal. If a good faith proposal to purchase stock is made in writing to the board of directors of such corporation, the board of directors, unless it responds affirmatively in writing within thirty days or such shorter period, if any, as may be required by the Exchange Act, shall be deemed to have disapproved such stock purchase.

(c) Notwithstanding anything to the contrary contained in this chapter (except the provisions of paragraphs (b) and (d) of this section), no domestic corporation shall engage at any time in any business combination with any interested shareholder of such corporation other than a business combination specified in any one of subparagraph (1), (2) or (3):

(1) A business combination approved by the board of directors of such corporation prior to such interested shareholder's stock acquisition date, or where the purchase of stock made by such interested shareholder on such interested shareholder's stock acquisition date had been approved by the board of directors of such corporation prior to such interested shareholder's stock acquisition date.

(2) A business combination approved by the affirmative vote of the holders of a majority of the outstanding voting stock not beneficially owned by such interested shareholder or any affiliate or associate of such interested shareholder at a meeting called for such purpose no earlier than five years after such interested shareholder's stock acquisition date.

(3) A business combination that meets all of the following conditions:

(A) The aggregate amount of the cash and the market value as of the consummation date of consideration other than cash to be received per share by holders of outstanding shares of common stock of such corporation in such business combination is [at] least equal to the higher of the following:

(i) the highest per share price paid by such interested shareholder at a time when he was the beneficial owner, directly or indirectly, of five percent or more of the outstanding voting stock of such corporation, for any shares of common stock of the same class or series acquired by it (X) within the five-year period immediately prior to the announcement date with respect to such business combination, or (Y) within the five-year period immediately prior to, or in, the transaction in which such interested shareholder became an interested shareholder, whichever is higher; plus, in either case, interest compounded annually from the earliest date on which such highest per share acquisition price was paid through the consummation date at the rate for one-year United States treasury obligations from time to time in effect; less the aggregate amount of any cash dividends paid, and the market value of any dividends paid other than in cash, per share of common stock since such earliest date, up to the amount of such interest; and

(ii) the market value per share of common stock on the announcement date with respect to such business combination or on such interested shareholder's stock acquisition date, whichever is higher; plus interest compounded annually from such date through the consummation date at the rate for one-year United States treasury obligations from time to time in effect; less the aggregate amount of any cash dividends paid, and the market value of any dividends paid other than in cash, per share of common stock since such date, up to the amount of such interest.

(B) The aggregate amount of the cash and the market value as of the consummation date of consideration other than cash to be received per share by holders of outstanding shares of any class or series of stock, other than common stock, of such corporation is at least equal to the highest of the following (whether or not such interested shareholder has previously acquired any shares of such class or series of stock):

(i) the highest per share price paid by such interested shareholder at a time when he was the beneficial owner, directly or indirectly, of five percent or more of the outstanding voting stock of such corporation, for any shares of such class or series of stock acquired by it (X) within the five-year period immediately prior to the announcement date with respect to such business combination, or (Y) within the five-year period immediately prior to, or in, the transaction in which such interested shareholder became an interested shareholder, whichever is higher; plus, in either case, interest compounded annually from the earliest date on which such highest per share acquisition price was paid through the consummation date at the rate for one-year United States treasury obligations from time to time in effect; less the aggregate amount of any cash dividends paid, and the market value of any dividends paid other than in cash, per share of such class or series of stock since such earliest date, up to the amount of such interest;

(ii) the highest preferential amount per share to which the holders of shares of such class or series of stock are entitled in the event of any voluntary liquidation, dissolution or winding up of such corporation, plus the aggregate amount of any dividends declared or due as to which such holders are entitled prior to payment of dividends on some other class or series of stock (unless the aggregate amount of such dividends is included in such preferential amount); and

(iii) the market value per share of such class or series of stock on the announcement date with respect to such business combination or on such interested shareholder's stock acquisition date, whichever is higher; plus interest compounded annually from such date through the consummation date at the rate for one-year United States treasury obligations from time to time in effect; less the aggregate amount of any cash dividends paid, and the market value of any dividends paid other than in cash, per share of such class or series of stock since such date, up to the amount of such interest.

(C) The consideration to be received by holders of a particular class or series of outstanding stock (including common stock) of such corporation in such business combination is in cash or in the same form as the interested shareholder has used to acquire the largest number of shares of such class or series of stock previously acquired by it, and such consideration shall be distributed promptly.

(D) The holders of all outstanding shares of stock of such corporation not beneficially owned by such interested shareholder immediately prior to the consummation of such business combination are entitled to receive in such business combination cash or other consideration for such shares in compliance with clauses (A), (B) and (C) of this subparagraph.

(E) After such interested shareholder's stock acquisition date and prior to the consummation date with respect to such business combination, such interested shareholder has not become the beneficial owner of any additional shares of voting stock of such corporation except:

(i) as part of the transaction which resulted in such interested shareholder becoming an interested shareholder;

(ii) by virtue of proportionate stock splits, stock dividends or other distributions of stock in respect of stock not constituting a business combination under clause (E) of subparagraph five of paragraph (a) of this section;

(iii) through a business combination meeting all of the conditions of paragraph (b) of this section and this paragraph; or

(iv) through purchase by such interested shareholder at any price which, if such price had been paid in an otherwise permissible business combination the announcement date and consummation date of which were the date of such purchase, would have satisfied the requirements of clauses (A), (B) and (C) of this subparagraph.

(d) The provisions of this section shall not apply:

(1) to any business combination of a domestic corporation that does not have a class of voting stock registered with the Securities and Exchange Commission pursuant to section twelve of the Exchange Act, unless the certificate of incorporation provides otherwise; or

(2) to any business combination of a domestic corporation whose certificate of incorporation has been amended to provide that such corporation shall be subject to the provisions of this section, which did not have a class of voting stock registered with the Securities and Exchange Commission pursuant to section twelve of the Exchange Act on the effective date of such amendment, and which is a business combination with an interested shareholder whose stock acquisition date is prior to the effective date of such amendment; or

(3) to any business combination of a domestic corporation (i) the original certificate of incorporation of which contains a provision expressly electing not to be governed by this section, or (ii) which adopts an amendment to such corporation's by-laws prior to March thirty-first, nineteen hundred eighty-six, expressly electing not to be governed by this section, or (iii) which adopts an amendment to such corporation's by-laws, approved by the affirmative vote of a majority of votes of the outstanding voting stock of such corporation, excluding the voting stock of interested shareholders and their affiliates and associates, expressly electing not to be governed by this section, provided that such amendment to the by-laws shall not be effective until eighteen months after such vote of such corporation's shareholders and shall not apply to any business combination of such corporation with an interested shareholder whose stock acquisition date is on or prior to the effective date of such amendment; or

(4) to any business combination of a domestic corporation with an interested shareholder of such corporation which became an interested shareholder inadvertently, if such interested shareholder (i) as soon as practicable, divests itself of a sufficient amount of the voting stock of such corporation so that it no longer is the beneficial owner, directly or indirectly, of twenty percent or more of the outstanding voting stock of such corporation, and (ii) would not at any time within the five-year period preceding the announcement date with respect to such business combination have been an interested shareholder but for such inadvertent acquisition; or

(5) to any business combination with an interested shareholder who was the beneficial owner, directly or indirectly, of five per cent or more of the outstanding voting stock of such corporation on October thirtieth, nineteen hundred eighty-five, and remained so to such interested shareholder's stock acquisition date.

ARTICLE 10

NON-JUDICIAL DISSOLUTION

§ 1001. Authorization of Dissolution

(a) A corporation may be dissolved under this article. Such dissolution shall be authorized at a meeting of shareholders by (i) for corporations the certificate of incorporation of which expressly provides such or corporations incorporated after [February 22, 1998], a majority of the votes of all outstanding shares entitled to vote thereon or (ii) for other corporations, two-thirds of the votes of all outstanding shares entitled to vote thereon, except, in either case, as otherwise provided under section 1002 (Dissolution under provision in certificate of incorporation).

(b) Any corporation may adopt an amendment of the certificate of incorporation providing that such dissolution shall be authorized at a meeting of shareholders by a specified proportion of votes of all outstanding shares entitled to vote thereon, provided that such proportion may not be less than a majority.

§ 1002. Dissolution Under Provision in Certificate of Incorporation

(a) The certificate of incorporation may contain a provision that any shareholder, or the holders of any specified number or proportion of shares or votes of shares, or of any specified number or proportion of shares or votes of shares of any class or series thereof, may require the dissolution of the corporation at will or upon the occurrence of a specified event. If the certificate of incorporation contains such a provision, a certificate of dissolution under section 1003 (Certificate of dissolution; contents) may be signed, verified and delivered to the department of state as provided in section 104 (Certificate; requirements, signing, filing, effectiveness) when authorized by a holder or holders of the number or proportion of shares or votes of shares specified in such provision, given in such manner as may be specified therein, or if no manner is specified therein, when authorized on written consent signed by such holder or holders; or such certificate may be signed, verified and delivered to the department by such holder or holders or by such of them as are designated by them.

(b) An amendment of the certificate of incorporation which adds a provision permitted by this section, or which changes or strikes out such a provision, shall be authorized at a meeting of shareholders by vote of all outstanding shares, whether or not otherwise entitled to vote on any amendment, or of such lesser proportion of shares and of such class or series of shares, but not less than a majority of all outstanding shares entitled to vote on any amendment, as may be provided specifically in the certificate of incorporation for adding, changing or striking out a provision permitted by this section.

(c) If the certificate of incorporation of any corporation contains a provision authorized by this section, the existence of such provision shall be noted conspicuously on the face or back of every certificate for shares issued by such corporation.

ARTICLE 11

JUDICIAL DISSOLUTION

§ 1101. Attorney-General's Action for Judicial Dissolution

(a) The attorney-general may bring an action for the dissolution of a corporation upon one or more of the following grounds:

(1) That the corporation procured its formation through fraudulent misrepresentation or concealment of a material fact.

(2) That the corporation has exceeded the authority conferred upon it by law, or has violated any provision of law whereby it has forfeited its charter, or carried on, conducted or transacted its business in a persistently fraudulent or illegal manner, or by the abuse of its powers contrary to the public policy of the state has become liable to be dissolved. . . .

§ 1102. Directors' Petition for Judicial Dissolution

If a majority of the board adopts a resolution that finds that the assets of a corporation are not sufficient to discharge its liabilities or that a dissolution will be beneficial to the shareholders, it may present a petition for its dissolution.

§ 1103. Shareholders' Petition for Judicial Dissolution

(a) If the shareholders of a corporation adopt a resolution stating that they find that its assets are not sufficient to discharge its liabilities, or that they deem a dissolution to be beneficial to the shareholders, the shareholders or such of them as are designated for that purpose in such resolution may present a petition for its dissolution.

(b) A shareholders' meeting to consider such a resolution may be called, notwithstanding any provision in the certificate of incorporation, by the holders of shares representing ten percent of the votes of all outstanding shares entitled to vote thereon, or if the certificate of incorporation authorizes a lesser proportion of votes of shares to call the meeting, by such lesser proportion. A meeting under this paragraph may not be called more often than once in any period of twelve consecutive months.

(c) Such a resolution may be adopted at a meeting of shareholders by vote of a majority of the votes of all outstanding shares entitled to vote thereon or if the certificate of incorporation requires a greater proportion of votes to adopt such a resolution, by such greater proportion.

§ 1104. Petition in Case of Deadlock Among Directors or Shareholders

(a) Except as otherwise provided in the certificate of incorporation under section 613 (Limitations on right to vote), the holders of shares representing one-half of the votes of all outstanding shares of a corporation entitled to vote in an election of directors may present a petition for dissolution on one or more of the following grounds:

(1) That the directors are so divided respecting the management of the corporation's affairs that the votes required for action by the board cannot be obtained.

(2) That the shareholders are so divided that the votes required for the election of directors cannot be obtained.

(3) That there is internal dissension and two or more factions of shareholders are so divided that dissolution would be beneficial to the shareholders.

(b) If the certificate of incorporation provides that the proportion of votes required for action by the board, or the proportion of votes of shareholders required for election of directors, shall be greater than that otherwise required by this chapter, such a petition may be presented by the holders of shares representing more than one-third of the votes of all outstanding shares entitled to vote on non-judicial dissolution under section 1001 (Authorization of dissolution).

(c) Notwithstanding any provision in the certificate of incorporation, any holder of shares entitled to vote at an election of directors of a corporation, may present a petition for its dissolution on the ground that the shareholders are so divided that they have failed, for a period which includes at least two consecutive annual meeting dates, to elect successors to directors whose terms have expired or would have expired upon the election and qualification of their successors.

§ 1104–a.   Petition for Judicial Dissolution Under Special Circumstances

(a) The holders of shares representing twenty percent or more of the votes of all outstanding shares of a corporation, other than a corporation registered as an investment company under an act of congress entitled "Investment Company Act of 1940", no shares of which are listed on a national securities exchange or regularly quoted in an over-the-counter market by one or more members of a national or an affiliated securities association, entitled to vote in an election of directors may present a petition of dissolution on one or more of the following grounds:

(1) The directors or those in control of the corporation have been guilty of illegal, fraudulent or oppressive actions toward the complaining shareholders;

(2) The property or assets of the corporation are being looted, wasted, or diverted for non-corporate purposes by its directors, officers or those in control of the corporation.

(b) The court, in determining whether to proceed with involuntary dissolution pursuant to this section, shall take into account:

(1) Whether liquidation of the corporation is the only feasible means whereby the petitioners may reasonably expect to obtain a fair return on their investment; and

(2) Whether liquidation of the corporation is reasonably necessary for the protection of the rights and interests of any substantial number of shareholders or of the petitioners.

(c) In addition to all other disclosure requirements, the directors or those in control of the corporation, no later than thirty days after the filing of a petition hereunder, shall make available for inspection and copying to the petitioners under reasonable working conditions the corporate financial books and records for the three preceding years.

(d) The court may order stock valuations be adjusted and may provide for a surcharge upon the directors or those in control of the corporation upon a finding of wilful or reckless dissipation or transfer of assets or corporate property without just or adequate compensation therefor.

§ 1111.   Judgment or Final Order of Dissolution

(a) In an action or special proceeding under this article if, in the court's discretion, it shall appear that the corporation should be dissolved, it shall make a judgment or final order dissolving the corporation.

(b) In making its decision, the court shall take into consideration the following criteria:

(1) In an action brought by the attorney-general, the interest of the public is of paramount importance.

(2) In a special proceeding brought by directors or shareholders, the benefit to the shareholders of a dissolution is of paramount importance.

(3) In a special proceeding brought under section 1104 (Petition in case of deadlock among directors or shareholders) or section 1104–a (Petition for judicial dissolution under special circumstances) dissolution is not to be denied merely because it is found that the corporate business has been or could be conducted at a profit.

(c) If the judgment or final order shall provide for a dissolution of the corporation, the court may, in its discretion, provide therein for the distribution of the property of the corporation to those entitled thereto according to their respective rights.

(d) The clerk of the court or such other person as the court may direct shall transmit certified copies of the judgment or final order of dissolution to the department of state and to the clerk of the county in which the office of the corporation was located at the date of the judgment or order. Upon filing by the department of state, the corporation shall be dissolved.

(e) The corporation shall promptly thereafter transmit a certified copy of the judgment or final order to the clerk of each other county in which its certificate of incorporation was filed.

§ 1118.   Purchase of Petitioner's Shares; Valuation

(a) In any proceeding brought pursuant to section eleven hundred four-a of this chapter, any other shareholder or shareholders or the corporation may, at any time within ninety days after the filing of such petition or at such later time as the court in its discretion may allow, elect to purchase the shares owned by the petitioners at their fair value and upon such terms and conditions as may be approved by the court, including the conditions of paragraph (c) herein. An election pursuant to this section shall be irrevocable unless the court, in its discretion, for just and equitable considerations, determines that such election be revocable.

(b) If one or more shareholders or the corporation elect to purchase the shares owned by the petitioner but are unable to agree with the petitioner upon the fair value of such shares, the court, upon the application of such prospective purchaser or purchasers or the petitioner, may stay the proceedings brought pursuant to section 1104–a of this chapter and determine the fair value of the petitioner's shares as of the day prior to the date on which such petition was filed, exclusive of any element of value arising from such filing but giving effect to any adjustment or surcharge found to be appropriate in the proceeding under section 1104–a of this chapter. In determining the fair value of the petitioner's shares, the court, in its discretion, may award interest from the date the petition is filed to the date of payment for the petitioner's share at an equitable rate upon judicially determined fair value of his shares.

(c) In connection with any election to purchase pursuant to this section:

(1) If such election is made beyond ninety days after the filing of the petition, and the court allows such petition, the court, in its discretion, may award the petitioner his reasonable expenses incurred in the proceeding prior to such election, including reasonable attorneys' fees;

(2) The court, in its discretion, may require, at any time prior to the actual purchase of petitioner's shares, the posting of a bond or other acceptable security in an amount sufficient to secure petitioner for the fair value of his shares.

ARTICLE 13

FOREIGN CORPORATIONS

§ 1315.   Record of Shareholders

(a) Any resident of this state who shall have been a shareholder of record of a foreign corporation doing business in this state upon at least five days' written demand may require such foreign corporation to produce a record of its shareholders setting forth the names and addresses of all shareholders, the number and class of shares held by each and the dates when they respectively became the owners of record thereof and shall have the right to examine in person or by agent or attorney at the office of the foreign corporation in this state or at the office of its transfer agent or registrar in this state or at such other place in the county in this state in which the foreign corporation is doing business as may be designated by the foreign corporation, during the usual business hours, the record of shareholders or an exact copy thereof certified as correct by the corporate officer or agent responsible for keeping or producing such record and to make extracts therefrom. Resident holders of voting trust certificates representing shares of the foreign corporation shall for the purpose of this section be regarded as shareholders. Any such agent or authority shall be authorized in a writing that satisfies the requirements of a writing under paragraph (b) of section

609 (proxies). A corporation requested to provide information pursuant to this paragraph shall make available such information in the format in which such information is maintained by the corporation and shall not be required to provide such information in any other format. If a request made pursuant to this paragraph includes a request to furnish information regarding beneficial owners, the corporation shall make available such information in its possession regarding beneficial owners as is provided to the corporation by a registered broker or dealer or a bank, association or other entity that exercises fiduciary powers in connection with the forwarding of information to such owners. The corporation shall not be required to obtain information about beneficial owners not in its possession.

(b) An examination authorized by paragraph (a) may be denied to such shareholder or other person upon his refusal to furnish to the foreign corporation or its transfer agent or registrar an affidavit that such inspection is not desired for a purpose which is in the interest of a business or object other than the business of the foreign corporation and that such shareholder or other person has not within five years sold or offered for sale any list of shareholders of any corporation of any type or kind, whether or not formed under the laws of this state, or aided or abetted any person in procuring any such record of shareholders for any such purpose.

(c) Upon refusal by the foreign corporation or by an officer or agent of the foreign corporation to produce for examination or to permit an examination of the record of shareholders as herein provided, the person making the demand for production and examination may apply to the supreme court in the judicial district where the office of the foreign corporation within this state is located, upon such notice as the court may direct, for an order directing the foreign corporation, its officer or agent, to show cause why an order should not be granted directing such production and permitting such examination by the applicant. Upon the return day of the order to show cause, the court shall hear the parties summarily, by affidavit or otherwise, and if its appears that the applicant is qualified and entitled to such examination, the court shall grant an order compelling such production for examination and awarding such further relief as to the court may seem just and proper.

(d) Nothing herein contained shall impair the power of courts to compel the production for examination of the books of a foreign corporation. The record of shareholders specified in paragraph (a) shall be prima facie evidence of the facts therein stated in favor of the plaintiff in any action or special proceeding against such foreign corporation or any of its officers, directors or shareholders.

§ 1317. Liabilities of Directors and Officers of Foreign Corporations

(a) Except as otherwise provided in this chapter, the directors and officers of a foreign corporation doing business in this state are subject, to the same extent as directors and officers of a domestic corporation, to the provisions of:

(1) Section 719 (Liability of directors in certain cases) except subparagraph (a)(3) thereof, and

(2) Section 720 (Action against directors and officers for misconduct.)

(b) Any liability imposed by paragraph (a) may be enforced in, and such relief granted by, the courts in this state, in the same manner as in the case of a domestic corporation.

§ 1318. Liability of Foreign Corporations for Failure to Disclose Required Information

A foreign corporation doing business in this state shall, in the same manner as a domestic corporation, disclose to its shareholders of record who are residents of this state the information required under paragraph (c) of section 510 (Dividends or other distributions in cash or property), paragraphs (f) and (g) of section 511 (Share distributions and changes), paragraph (d) of section 515 (Reacquired shares), paragraph (c) of section 516 (Reduction of stated capital in certain cases), and shall be liable as provided in section 520 (Liability for failure to disclose required information) for failure to comply in good faith with these requirements.

§ 1319. Applicability of Other Provisions

(a) In addition to articles 1 (Short title; definitions; application; certificates; miscellaneous) and 3 (Corporate name and service of process) and the other sections of article 13, the following provisions, to the extent provided therein, shall apply to a foreign corporation doing business in this state, its directors, officers and shareholders:

(1) Section 623 (Procedure to enforce shareholder's right to receive payment for shares).

(2) Section 626 (Shareholders' derivative action brought in the right of the corporation to procure a judgment in its favor).

(3) Section 627 (Security for expenses in shareholders' derivative action brought in the right of the corporation to procure a judgment in its favor).

(4) Sections 721 (Exclusivity of statutory provisions for indemnification of directors and officers) through 727 (Insurance for indemnification of directors and officers), inclusive.

(5) Section 808 (Reorganization under act of congress).

(6) Section 907 (Merger or consolidation of domestic and foreign corporations).

§ 1320. Exemption From Certain Provisions

(a) Notwithstanding any other provision of this chapter, a foreign corporation doing business in this state which is authorized under this article, its directors, officers and shareholders, shall be exempt from the provisions of paragraph (e) of section 1316 (Voting trust records), subparagraph (a)(1) of section 1317 (Liabilities of directors and officers of foreign corporations), section 1318 (Liability of foreign corporations for failure to disclose required information) and subparagraph (a)(4) of section 1319 (Applicability of other provisions) if when such provision would otherwise apply:

(1) Shares of such corporation were listed on a national securities exchange, or

(2) Less than one-half of the total of its business income for the preceding three fiscal years, or such portion thereof as the foreign corporation was in existence, was allocable to this state for franchise tax purposes under the tax law.

ARTICLE 17

BENEFIT CORPORATIONS

§ 1701. Application and Effect of Article

(a) This article shall be applicable to all benefit corporations.

(b) The existence of a provision of this article shall not of itself create any implication that a contrary or different rule of law is or would be applicable to a business corporation that is not a benefit corporation. This article shall not affect any statute or rule of law that is or would be applicable to a business corporation that is not a benefit corporation.

(c) Except as otherwise provided in this article, this chapter shall be applicable to all benefit corporations. The specific provisions of this article shall control over the general provisions of this chapter.

(d) A provision of the certificate of incorporation or bylaws of a benefit corporation may not relax, be inconsistent with or supersede any provision of this article.

§ 1702. Definitions

As used in this article, unless the context otherwise requires, the term:

(a) "Benefit corporation" means a business corporation incorporated under this article and whose status as a benefit corporation has not been terminated as provided in this article.

(b) "General public benefit" means a material positive impact on society and the environment, taken as a whole, assessed against a third-party standard, from the business and operations of a benefit corporation.

(c) "Independent" means that a person has no material relationship with a benefit corporation or any of its subsidiaries. A material relationship between a person and a benefit corporation or any of its subsidiaries will be conclusively presumed to exist if:

(1) the person is, or has been within the last three years, an employee of the benefit corporation or any of its subsidiaries;

(2) an immediate family member of the person is, or has been within the last three years, an executive officer of the benefit corporation or any of its subsidiaries; or

(3) the person, or an entity of which the person is a director, officer or other manager or in which the person owns beneficially or of record five percent or more of the equity interests, owns beneficially or of record five percent or more of the shares of the benefit corporation. A percentage of ownership in an entity shall be calculated as if all outstanding rights to acquire equity interests in the entity had been exercised.

(d) "Minimum status vote" means that, in addition to any other approval or vote required by this chapter, the certificate of incorporation or a bylaw adopted by the shareholders:

(1) The holders of shares of every class or series that are entitled to vote on the corporate action shall be entitled to vote as a class on the corporate action; and

(2) The corporate action must be approved by vote of the shareholders of each class or series entitled to cast at least three-quarters of the votes that all shareholders of the class or series are entitled to cast thereon.

(e) "Specific public benefit," includes:

(1) providing low-income or underserved individuals or communities with beneficial products or services;

(2) promoting economic opportunity for individuals or communities beyond the creation of jobs in the normal course of business;

(3) preserving the environment;

(4) improving human health;

(5) promoting the arts, sciences or advancement of knowledge;

(6) increasing the flow of capital to entities with a public benefit purpose; and

(7) the accomplishment of any other particular benefit for society or the environment.

(f) "Subsidiary" means an entity in which a person owns beneficially or of record fifty percent or more of the equity interests. A percentage of ownership in an entity shall be calculated as if all outstanding rights to acquire equity interests in the entity had been exercised.

(g) "Third-party standard" means a recognized standard for defining, reporting and assessing general public benefit that is:

(1) developed by a person that is independent of the benefit corporation; and

(2) transparent because the following information about the standard is publicly available:

(A) the factors considered when measuring the performance of a business;

(B) the relative weightings of those factors; and

(C) the identity of the persons who developed and control changes to the standard and the process by which those changes are made.

§ 1703. Formation of Benefit Corporations

A benefit corporation shall be formed in accordance with this chapter except that its certificate of incorporation shall also state that it is a benefit corporation.

§ 1704. Election of an Existing Business Corporation to Become a Benefit Corporation

(a) A business corporation may become a benefit corporation under this article by amending its certificate of incorporation so that it contains a statement that the corporation is a benefit corporation. The amendment shall not be effective unless it is adopted by at least the minimum status vote.

(b) Any corporation that is not a benefit corporation that is a party to a merger or consolidation in which the surviving or consolidated corporation will be a benefit corporation must approve the plan of merger or consolidation by at least the minimum status vote in addition to any other vote required by this chapter, the certificate of incorporation or the bylaws.

(c) Any corporation that is not a benefit corporation that is party to a merger or consolidation in which shares of stock of such corporation will be converted into a right to receive shares of stock of a benefit corporation must approve the plan of merger or consolidation by at least the minimum status vote in addition to any other vote required by this chapter, the certificate of incorporation or the bylaws.

§ 1705. Termination of Benefit Corporation Status

(a) A benefit corporation may terminate its status as such and cease to be subject to this article by amending its certificate of incorporation to delete the statement that the corporation is a benefit corporation. The amendment shall not be effective unless it is adopted by at least the minimum status vote.

(b) If a benefit corporation is a party to a merger or consolidation in which the surviving or new corporation will not be a benefit corporation, the plan of merger or consolidation shall not be effective unless it is adopted by at least the minimum status vote in addition to any other vote required by this chapter, the certificate of incorporation or the bylaws.

(c) Any benefit corporation that is party to a merger or consolidation in which shares of stock of such benefit corporation will be converted into a right to receive shares of stock of a corporation that is not a benefit corporation must approve the plan of merger or consolidation by at least the minimum status vote in addition to any other vote required by this chapter, the certificate of incorporation or the bylaws.

(d) A sale, lease, conveyance, exchange, transfer, or other disposition of all or substantially all of the assets of a benefit corporation, unless the transaction is in the usual and regular course of business of the benefit corporation, shall not be effective unless the transaction is approved by at least the minimum status vote in addition to any other vote required by this chapter, the certificate of incorporation or the bylaws.

§ 1706. Corporate Purposes

(a) Every benefit corporation shall have a purpose of creating general public benefit. This purpose is in addition to its purposes under section two hundred one of this chapter and any specific purpose set forth in its certificate of incorporation under paragraph (b) of this section. The purpose to create general public benefit shall be a limitation on the other purposes of the benefit corporation, and shall control over any inconsistent purpose of the benefit corporation.

(b) The certificate of incorporation of a benefit corporation may identify one or more specific public benefits that it is the purpose of the benefit corporation to create in addition to its purposes under section two hundred one of this chapter and paragraph (a) of this section. The identification of a specific public benefit under this paragraph does not limit the obligation of a benefit corporation to create general public benefit.

(c) The creation of general and specific public benefits as provided in paragraphs (a) and (b) of this section is in the best interests of the benefit corporation.

(d) A benefit corporation may amend its certificate of incorporation to add, amend or delete the identification of a specific public benefit that it is the purpose of the benefit corporation to create. The amendment shall not be effective unless it is adopted by at least the minimum status vote.

§ 1707. Standard of Conduct for Directors and Officers

(a) In discharging the duties of their respective positions, the board of directors, committees of the board and individual directors and officers of a benefit corporation:

(1) shall consider the effects of any action upon:

(A) the ability for the benefit corporation to accomplish its general and any specific public benefit purpose;

(B) the shareholders of the benefit corporation;

(C) the employees and workforce of the benefit corporation and its subsidiaries and suppliers;

(D) the interests of customers as beneficiaries of the general or specific public benefit purposes of the benefit corporation;

(E) community and societal considerations, including those of any community in which offices or facilities of the benefit corporation or its subsidiaries or suppliers are located;

(F) the local and global environment; and

(G) the short-term and long-term interests of the benefit corporation, including benefits that may accrue to the benefit corporation from its long-term plans and the possibility that these interests may be best served by the continued independence of the benefit corporation;

(2) may consider:

(A) the resources, intent and conduct (past, stated and potential) of any person seeking to acquire control of the corporation; and

(B) any other pertinent factors or the interests of any other group that they deem appropriate; and

(3) shall not be required to give priority to the interests of any particular person or group referred to in subparagraphs one and two of this paragraph over the interests of any other person or group unless the benefit corporation has stated its intention to give priority to interests related to a specific public benefit purpose identified in its certificate of incorporation.

(b) The consideration of interests and factors in the manner required by paragraph (a) of this section:

(1) shall not constitute a violation of the provisions of sections seven hundred fifteen or seven hundred seventeen of this chapter; and

(2) is in addition to the ability of directors to consider interests and factors as provided in section seven hundred seventeen of this chapter.

(c) A director does not have a fiduciary duty to a person that is a beneficiary of the general or specific public benefit purposes of a benefit corporation arising from the status of the person as a beneficiary, unless otherwise stated in the certificate of incorporation or the bylaws of the benefit corporation.

§ 1708. Annual Benefit Report

(a) A benefit corporation must deliver to each shareholder an annual benefit report including:

(1) a narrative description of:

(A) the process and rationale for selecting the third party standard used to prepare the benefit report;

(B) the ways in which the benefit corporation pursued general public benefit during the year and the extent to which general public benefit was created;

(C) the ways in which the benefit corporation pursued any specific public benefit that the certificate of incorporation states it is the purpose of the benefit corporation to create and the extent to which that specific public benefit was created; and

(D) any circumstances that have hindered the creation by the benefit corporation of general or specific public benefit;

(2) an assessment of the performance of the benefit corporation, relative to its general public benefit purpose assessed against a third-party standard applied consistently with any application of that standard in prior benefit reports or accompanied by an explanation of the reasons for any inconsistent application and, if applicable, assessment of the performance of the benefit corporation, relative to its specific public benefit purpose or purposes;

(3) the compensation paid by the benefit corporation during the year to each director in that capacity; and

(4) the name of each person that owns beneficially or of record five percent or more of the outstanding shares of the benefit corporation.

(b) The benefit report must be sent annually to each shareholder within one hundred twenty days following the end of the fiscal year of the benefit corporation. Delivery of a benefit report to shareholders is in addition to any other requirement to deliver an annual report to shareholders.

(c) A benefit corporation must post its most recent benefit report on the public portion of its website, if any, except that the compensation paid to directors and any financial or proprietary information included in the benefit report may be omitted from the benefit report as posted.

(d) Concurrently with the delivery of the benefit report to shareholders pursuant to paragraph (b) of this section, the benefit corporation must deliver a copy of the benefit report to the department for filing, except that the compensation paid to directors and any financial or proprietary information included in the benefit report may be omitted from the benefit report as filed under this section.

(e) The annual benefit report shall be in addition to all other reporting requirements under this chapter.

§ 1709. Conspicuous Language on the Face of Certificates

All certificates representing shares of a benefit corporation shall contain, in addition to any other statements required by the business corporation law, the following conspicuous language on the face of the certificate:

"This entity is a benefit corporation organized under article seventeen of the New York business corporation law."

NORTH DAKOTA PUBLICLY TRADED CORPORATIONS ACT

TABLE OF SECTIONS

Sec.		Page
10–35–01.	Citation	901
10–35–02.	Definitions	901
10–35–03.	Application and Effect of Chapter	903
10–35–04.	Application of Chapter 10–19.1	903
10–35–05.	Amendment of the Bylaws	903
10–35–06.	Board of Directors	903
10–35–07.	Nomination of Directors	904
10–35–08.	Access to Corporation's Proxy Statement	904
10–35–09.	Election of Directors	905
10–35–10.	Reimbursement of Proxy Expenses	906
10–35–11.	Supermajority Provisions Prohibited	906
10–35–12.	Regular Meeting of Shareholders	906
10–35–13.	Call of Special Meeting of Shareholders	906
10–35–14.	Shareholder Proposals of Business at a Regular Meeting	907
10–35–15.	Shareholder Proposals of Amendment of the Articles	907
10–35–16.	Requirements for Convening Shareholder Meetings	908
10–35–17.	Approval of Certain Issuances of Shares	908
10–35–18.	Preemptive Rights	909
10–35–19.	Conduct and Business of Shareholder Meetings	909
10–35–20.	Action by Shareholders Without a Meeting	909
10–35–21.	Financial Statements	909
10–35–22.	Duration of Poison Pills Limited	909
10–35–23.	Protection of Power of Current Directors Over Poison [Pills]	910
10–35–24.	Minimum Share Ownership Triggering Level for Poison Pills	910
10–35–25.	Optional Restrictions or Prohibitions on Poison Pills	910
10–35–26.	Adoption of Antitakeover Provisions	911
10–35–27.	Liberal Construction	912

---

§ 10–35–01. Citation.

This chapter may be cited as the "North Dakota Publicly Traded Corporations Act".

§ 10–35–02. Definitions.

For purposes of this chapter, unless the context otherwise requires:

1. "Beneficial owner", "owns beneficially", and similar terms have the same meaning as in the rules and regulations of the commission under section 13 of the Exchange Act.

2. "Commission" means the United States securities and exchange commission.

3. "Exchange Act" means the Securities Exchange Act of 1934, as amended [15 U.S.C. section 78a et seq.].

4. "Executive officer" has the same meaning as in the rules and regulations of the commission under the Exchange Act.

5. "Poison pill" means a security created or issued by a publicly traded corporation that precludes or limits a person or group of persons from owning beneficially or of record, or from exercising, converting, transferring, or receiving, the security on the same terms as other shareholders or which is intended to have the effect of diluting disproportionately from the shareholders generally the interest of the person or group of persons in the corporation or a successor to the corporation or otherwise discouraging the person or group of persons from acquiring beneficial ownership of shares of the corporation or a successor to the corporation. For the purposes of this subsection:

    a. A security may constitute a poison pill whether or not it trades separately or together with other securities of the corporation and whether or not it is evidenced by a separate certificate or by a certificate for other securities of the corporation.

    b. "Poison pill" includes any form of security created or issued by a corporation, or any agreement or arrangement entered into by a corporation, regardless of the name by which it is known, that is designed or intended to operate as or that has the effect of what is commonly referred to, either on July 1, 2007, or at any time thereafter, as a "poison pill" or "shareholder rights plan".

    c. A security is not a poison pill if it would otherwise be a poison pill solely because it contains restrictions on ownership or acquisition of shares of the corporation that are necessary:

        (1) To maintain the tax status of the corporation; or

        (2) For the corporation to comply with a statute, rule, or regulation that regulates a business in which the corporation is engaged.

    d. "Security" includes:

        (1) An investment contract, warrant, option right, conversion right, or any other form of right or obligation;

        (2) A "security" within the meaning of that term in the Exchange Act, the Securities Act of 1933, as amended [15 U.S.C. section 77a et seq.], the rules and regulations of the commission, or judicial interpretations under any of the foregoing;

        (3) Any other ownership interest or right to acquire an ownership interest;

        (4) Any other instrument commonly known as a "security"; and

        (5) Any instrument or contract right created or issued by a publicly traded corporation, whether or not the instrument or contract right is a security under any other provision of law.

6. "Publicly traded corporation" or "corporation" means a corporation as defined in section 10–19.1–01 [North Dakota Business Corporation Act—General Provisions]:

    a. That becomes governed by chapter 10–19.1 after July 1, 2007; and

    b. The articles of which state that the corporation is governed by this chapter. . . .

8. "Qualified shareholder" means a person or group of persons acting together that satisfies the following requirements:

    a. The person or group owns beneficially in the aggregate more than five percent of the outstanding shares of the publicly traded corporation that are entitled to vote generally for the election of directors; and

    b. The person or each member of the group has beneficially owned the shares that are used for purposes of determining the ownership threshold in subdivision a continuously for at least two years.

9. "Required vote" means approval of a provision of the articles or bylaws, at a time when the publicly traded corporation has a class of voting shares registered under the Exchange Act, by at least the affirmative vote of both:

    a. A majority of the directors in office who are not executive officers of the corporation; and

    b. Two-thirds of the voting power of the outstanding shares entitled to vote generally for the election of directors that are not owned beneficially or of record by directors or executive officers of the corporation.

§ 10–35–03. Application and Effect of Chapter.

1. This chapter applies only to a publicly traded corporation meeting the definition of a "publicly traded corporation" in section 10–35–02 during such time as its articles state that it is governed by this chapter.

2. The existence of a provision of this chapter does not of itself create any implication that a contrary or different rule of law is or would be applicable to a corporation that is not a publicly traded corporation. This chapter does not affect any statute or rule of law as it applies to a corporation that is not a publicly traded corporation.

3. A provision of the articles or bylaws of a publicly traded corporation may not be inconsistent with any provision of this chapter.

4. The computation of a percentage of shares owned beneficially or of record by a person or group of persons for purposes of this chapter or chapter 10–19.1 shall be based on the number of outstanding shares of the publicly traded corporation shown most recently in a filing by the corporation with the commission under the Exchange Act.

§ 10–35–04. Application of Chapter 10–19.1.

1. Chapter 10–19.1 applies generally to all publicly traded corporations, except that the provisions of this chapter control over any inconsistent provision of chapter 10–19.1.

2. A publicly traded corporation is a "publicly held corporation" as that term is used in chapter 10–19.1.

3. The definitions in section 10–19.1–01 apply to the use in this chapter of the terms defined in that section.

§ 10–35–05. Amendment of the Bylaws.

1. Any shareholder of a publicly traded corporation may propose the adoption, amendment, or repeal of a bylaw.

2. Subdivision c of subsection 3 of section 10–19.1–31 [Bylaws] shall not apply to a publicly traded corporation except that a provision of the articles or bylaws authorized by section 10–35–14 may apply to a proposal to adopt, amend, or repeal a bylaw.

§ 10–35–06. Board of Directors.

1. The articles or bylaws of a publicly traded corporation may not fix a term for directors longer than one year.

2. The articles or bylaws of a publicly traded corporation may not stagger the terms of directors into groups whose terms end at different times.

3. The size of the board of a publicly traded corporation may not be changed at a time when:

a. The board has notice that there will be a contested election of directors at the next regular or special meeting of the shareholders; or

b. The shareholders do not have the right to nominate candidates for election at the next regular meeting of the shareholders under a provision of the articles or bylaws adopted pursuant to section 10–35–07.

4. The board of a publicly traded corporation must elect one of its members as the chair of the board who shall preside at meetings of the board and perform such other functions as may be provided in the articles or bylaws or by resolution of the board. The chair of the board may not serve as an executive officer of the corporation.

§ 10–35–07. Nomination of Directors.

1. A publicly traded corporation may not require a shareholder or beneficial owner of shares to provide notice of an intention to nominate a candidate for election as a director except as provided in a provision of the articles or bylaws that satisfies the requirements of this section.

2. A provision of the articles or bylaws of a publicly traded corporation requiring a shareholder or beneficial owner to provide notice of an intention to nominate a candidate for election as a director may not require the notice to include more than:

   a. The name of the shareholder or beneficial owner;

   b. A statement that the shareholder or beneficial owner is the beneficial owner of one or more shares in the corporation and reasonable evidence of that ownership; and

   c. The number of candidates the shareholder or beneficial owner intends to nominate.

3. Any deadline fixed by the articles or bylaws for submission by a shareholder or beneficial owner of a notice of intention to nominate a candidate for election as a director may not be earlier than:

   a. In the case of a meeting held within five business days before or after the anniversary of the previous year's regular meeting, ninety days before the anniversary date of the prior regular meeting; or

   b. In the case of a meeting not held within five business days before or after the anniversary of the previous year's regular meeting ninety days before the date of the meeting.

4. A provision of the articles or bylaws requiring a shareholder or beneficial owner to provide notice of an intention to nominate a candidate for election as a director must provide a period of at least twenty days during which the shareholder or beneficial owner may submit the notice to the public corporation.

5. The adoption or amendment of a bylaw requiring advance notice of nominations may not take effect in the one hundred twenty-day period before the next meeting of shareholders, unless the adoption or amendment of the bylaw has been approved by the shareholders.

§ 10–35–08. Access to Corporation's Proxy Statement.

1. If a qualified shareholder provides notice of an intention to nominate one or more candidates for election to the board of directors that satisfies both section 10–35–07 and this section, the publicly traded corporation must:

   a. Include the name of each nominee and a statement not longer than five hundred words without counting the information required under subdivisions a through e of subsection 2 supplied by the qualified shareholder in support of each nominee in the corporation's proxy statement; and

   b. Make provision for a shareholder to vote on each nominee on the form of proxy solicited on behalf of the corporation.

2. The publicly traded corporation may not require the notice from the qualified shareholder to include more than:

   a. The name of the person or the names of the members of the group;

   b. A statement that the person or group satisfies the definition of a qualified shareholder in subsection 8 of section 10–35–02 and reasonable evidence of the required ownership of shares by the person or group;

   c. A statement that the person or group does not have knowledge that the candidacy or, if elected, board membership of any of its nominees would violate controlling state or federal law or rules other than rules regarding director independence of a national securities exchange or national securities association applicable to the corporation;

   d. The information regarding each nominee that is required to be included in the corporation's proxy statement by the rules and regulations adopted by the commission under the Exchange Act;

e. A statement from each nominee that the nominee consents to be named in the corporation's proxy statement and form of proxy and, if elected, to serve on the board of directors of the corporation, for inclusion in the corporation's proxy statement; and

f. The supporting statement permitted by subdivision a of subsection 1.

3. If the qualified shareholder does not own at least five percent of the outstanding shares of the publicly traded corporation entitled to vote generally for the election of directors on the date of the meeting, the qualified shareholder is not entitled to nominate the candidates named in the notice provided under subsection 1.

§ 10–35–09. Election of Directors.

1. After a quorum is established at a meeting of the shareholders of a publicly traded corporation at which directors are to be elected, the polls must be opened for the election of directors before the meeting may be recessed or adjourned. If the polls have not been previously closed, the polls close for the election of directors upon the first recess or adjournment of the meeting.

2. Except as provided in subsection 3, if the articles of a publicly traded corporation provide that the shareholders do not have the right to cumulate their votes in an election of directors:

a. Each share in the corporation entitled to vote on the election of directors shall be entitled to vote noncumulatively for or against, or to abstain with respect to, each candidate for election.

b. To be elected, a candidate must receive the affirmative vote of at least a majority of the votes cast for or against the candidate's election.

c. An individual who is not elected under subdivision b may not be appointed by the board of directors to fill a vacancy on the board at any time thereafter unless the individual is subsequently elected as a director by the shareholders.

d. If a director who was a candidate for reelection is not elected under subdivision b, the director may continue to serve under subdivision b of subsection 1 of section 10–19.1–35 [Terms of directors] for not longer than ninety days after the date of the first public announcement of the results of the election.

e. If no directors are elected under subdivision b, the current directors continue to serve under subdivision b of subsection 1 of section 10–19.1–35, and another meeting of the shareholders for the election of directors must be held not later than eighty-nine days after the date of the first public announcement of the results of the election.

3. Subsection 2 does not apply to an election of directors by a voting group if there are more candidates for election by the voting group than the number of directors to be elected by the voting group and one or more of the candidates has been properly nominated by the shareholders. An individual is not counted as a candidate for election under this subsection if the board of directors reasonably determines before the notice of meeting is given that the individual's candidacy does not create a bona fide election contest. The determination of the number of candidates for purposes of this subsection shall be made as of:

a. The expiration of the time fixed by the articles or bylaws for advance notice by a shareholder of an intention to nominate directors; or

b. Absent such a provision at a time publicly announced by the board of directors which is not more than fourteen days before notice is given of the meeting at which the election is to occur.

4. A publicly traded corporation may not compensate an individual, directly or indirectly, as a result of the fact, in whole or in part, that the individual is not elected or reelected as a director, and without regard to whether the compensation would be paid to the individual as a director or officer or on any other basis.

5. The shareholders of a publicly traded corporation may act by consent in a record to elect directors, but the consent will be in lieu of a regular meeting of shareholders only if:

a. The shareholders are not entitled to vote cumulatively for the election of directors;

b. The election by consent takes effect within the one hundred twenty-day period before the anniversary of the most recent regular meeting; and

c. The full board is elected by the consent.

§ 10-35-10.   Reimbursement of Proxy Expenses.

1. A shareholder of a publicly traded corporation who nominates one or more candidates for election as directors who are not nominated by management or the board of directors must be reimbursed by the corporation for the reasonable actual costs of solicitation of proxies incurred by the shareholder in an amount equal to the shareholder's total reasonable actual costs of solicitation multiplied by a fraction, the numerator of which is the number of candidates nominated by the shareholder who are elected, and the denominator of which is the total number of candidates nominated by the shareholder.

2. As used in this section, "actual costs of solicitation" means amounts paid to third parties relating to the solicitation, including lawyers, proxy solicitors, public relations firms, printers, the United States postal service, and media outlets.

§ 10-35-11.   Supermajority Provisions Prohibited.

Neither the articles nor the bylaws of a publicly traded corporation may provide a quorum or voting requirement:

1. For the board or a committee of the board that is greater than a majority of the number of directors that would constitute the full board or committee assuming there are no vacancies; or

2. For shareholders that is greater than a majority of the voting power of the shares entitled to vote on the item of business or, in the case of a class or series entitled to vote as a separate group, a majority of the voting power of the outstanding shares of the class or series.

§ 10-35-12.   Regular Meeting of Shareholders.

1. Unless directors are elected by consent in lieu of a regular meeting as provided in subsection 5 of section 10-35-09, a publicly traded corporation must hold a meeting of shareholders annually for the election of directors and the conduct of such other business as may be properly brought before the meeting by the board or the shareholders.

2. The articles or bylaws of a publicly traded corporation must state the latest date in each calendar year by which the regular meeting of shareholders must be held. The date so fixed by the articles or bylaws may not be later than one hundred eighty days after the end of the prior fiscal year of the corporation.

3. Any shareholder of a publicly traded corporation may demand a regular meeting of shareholders under subsection 2 of section 10-19.1-71 [Regular meetings of shareholders] or apply for an order of court directing the holding of a regular meeting of shareholders under section 10-19.1-72.1 [Court-ordered meetings of shareholders], in each case without regard to the percentage of the voting power held by the shareholder.

4. An amendment of the bylaws of a publicly traded corporation that changes the latest date by which the regular meeting of shareholders must be held may not take effect until after the regular meeting has been held for the year during which the amendment is adopted, unless the amendment has been approved by the shareholders.

5. The committee of the board of a publicly traded corporation that has authority to set the compensation of executive officers must report to the shareholders at each regular meeting of shareholders on the compensation of the corporation's executive officers. The shareholders that are entitled to vote for the election of directors shall also be entitled to vote on an advisory basis on whether they accept the report of the committee.

§ 10-35-13.   Call of Special Meeting of Shareholders.

1. A publicly traded corporation shall hold a special meeting of shareholders upon the demand of its shareholders as provided in section 10-19.1-72, except that, regardless of the purpose for the meeting, the

shareholders demanding the meeting must own beneficially ten percent or more of the voting power of all shares entitled to vote on each issue proposed to be considered at the special meeting.

2. The articles or bylaws of a publicly traded corporation may not restrict:

a. The period during which shareholders may call a special meeting of shareholders; or

b. The business that may be conducted at a special meeting.

§ 10–35–14. Shareholder Proposals of Business at a Regular Meeting.

1. A publicly traded corporation may not require a shareholder or beneficial owner to provide notice of an intention to propose a matter for consideration or a vote at a regular meeting of shareholders except as provided in a provision of the article or bylaws that satisfies the requirements of this section.

2. A provision of the articles or bylaws requiring a shareholder or beneficial owner to provide notice of an intention to propose a matter for consideration or a vote by the shareholders may not require the notice to include more than:

a. The name of the shareholder or beneficial owner;

b. A statement that the shareholder or beneficial owner is the beneficial owner of one or more shares in the corporation and reasonable evidence of that ownership; and

c. The general nature of the business to be proposed.

3. Any deadline fixed by the articles or bylaws for submission by a shareholder or beneficial owner of a notice of intention to propose a matter for consideration or a vote by the shareholders may not be earlier than:

a. In the case of a meeting held within five business days before or after the anniversary of the previous year's regular meeting, ninety days before the anniversary date of the prior regular meeting; or

b. In the case of a meeting not held within five business days before or after the anniversary of the previous year's regular meeting ninety days before the date of the meeting.

4. A provision of the articles or bylaws requiring a shareholder or beneficial owner to provide notice of an intention to propose a matter for consideration or a vote by the shareholders must provide a period of at least twenty days during which the shareholder or beneficial owner may submit the notice to the publicly traded corporation.

5. The adoption or amendment of a bylaw requiring advance notice of business to be proposed by a shareholder or beneficial owner may not take effect in the one hundred twenty-day period before the next regular meeting of shareholders, unless the adoption or amendment of the bylaw has been approved by the shareholders.

6. This section does not apply to the proposal by a shareholder or beneficial owner of an amendment of the articles of a publicly traded corporation.

§ 10–35–15. Shareholder Proposals of Amendment of the Articles.

1. A proposal of an amendment of the articles of a publicly traded corporation by a shareholder or shareholders under subsection 2 of section 10–19.1–19 need not include more than:

a. The name of the shareholder or the names of the members of the group of shareholders;

b. A statement of the number of shares of each class owned beneficially or of record by the shareholder or group of shareholders and reasonable evidence of that ownership; and

c. The text of the proposed amendment.

2. The articles or bylaws of a publicly traded corporation may not impose any requirements on the proposal of an amendment of the articles by a shareholder.

3. An amendment proposed by a shareholder or shareholders pursuant to subsection 1 and approved by the shareholders does not need to approved by the board to be adopted and become effective.

§ 10–35–16. Requirements for Convening Shareholder Meetings.

1. If the articles or bylaws of a publicly traded corporation have a provision for advance notice authorized by section 10–35–07 or 10–35–14, a regular meeting of shareholders of the corporation may not be convened unless the corporation has announced the date of the meeting in the body of a public filing, and not solely in an exhibit or attachment to a filing, regardless of whether the exhibit or attachment has been incorporated by reference into the body of the filing, with the commission under the Exchange Act at least twenty-five days before the deadline in the articles or bylaws for a shareholder to give the advance notice.

2. If a proxy is given authority by a shareholder of a publicly traded corporation to vote on less than all items of business considered at a meeting of shareholders, the shareholder is considered to be present and entitled to vote by the proxy on all items of business to be considered at the meeting for purposes of determining the existence of a quorum under section 10–19.1–76. A proxy who is given authority by a shareholder who abstains with respect to an item of business is considered to have authority to vote on the item of business for purposes of this subsection.

§ 10–35–17. Approval of Certain Issuances of Shares.

1. An issuance by a publicly traded corporation of shares, or other securities convertible into or rights exercisable for shares, in a transaction or a series of integrated transactions, requires approval of the shareholders if the voting power of the shares that are issued or issuable as a result of the transaction or series of integrated transactions will exceed twenty percent of the voting power of the shares of the corporation which were outstanding immediately before the transaction.

2. Subsection 1 does not apply to:

a. A public offering solely for cash, cash equivalents or a combination of cash and cash equivalents; or

b. A bona fide private financing, solely for cash, cash equivalents or a combination of cash and cash equivalents, of:

(1) Shares at a price equal to at least the greater of the book or market value of the corporation's common shares; or

(2) Other securities or rights if the conversion or exercise price is equal to at least the greater of the book or market value of the corporation's common shares.

3. For purposes of this section:

a. The voting power of shares issued and issuable as a result of a transaction or series of integrated transactions shall be the greater of:

(1) The voting power of the shares to be issued; or

(2) The voting power of the shares that would be outstanding after giving effect to the conversion of convertible shares and other securities and the exercise of rights to be issued.

b. A series of transactions is integrated if consummation of one transaction is made contingent on consummation of one or more of the other transactions.

c. "Bona fide private financing" means a sale in which:

(1) A registered broker-dealer purchases the shares, other securities, or rights from the publicly traded corporation with a view to their private sale to one or more purchasers; or

(2) The corporation sells the shares, other securities, or rights to multiple purchasers, and no one purchaser or group of related purchasers acquires, or has the right to acquire, more than five percent of the voting power of shares issued or issuable in the transaction or series of integrated transactions.

§ 10–35–18. Preemptive Rights.

Unless otherwise provided in the articles, a shareholder of a publicly traded corporation does not have the preemptive rights provided in section 10–19.1–65.

§ 10–35–19. Conduct and Business of Shareholder Meetings.

1. There must be a presiding officer at every meeting of the shareholders of a publicly traded corporation. The presiding officer must be appointed in the manner provided in the articles or bylaws or, in the absence of such a provision, by the board before the meeting or by the shareholders at the meeting. If the articles or bylaws are silent on the appointment of a presiding officer and the board and the shareholders fail to designate a presiding officer, the president is the presiding officer.

2. Except as otherwise provided in the articles or bylaws or, in the absence of such a provision, by the board before the meeting, the presiding officer determines the order of business and has the authority to establish rules for the conduct of the meeting.

3. The order of business and rules for the conduct of a meeting and any action by the presiding officer must:

    a. Be reasonable;

    b. Be fair to all of the shareholders; and

    c. May not favor or disadvantage the proponent of any action to be taken at the meeting.

4. The presiding officer may announce at the meeting when the polls close for each matter voted upon. If no announcement is made, the polls close upon the final adjournment of the meeting, except as provided in subsection 1 of section 10–35–09. After the polls close, ballots, proxies, and votes may not be accepted, and changes and revocations of ballots, proxies, or votes may not be made.

§ 10–35–20. Action by Shareholders Without a Meeting.

1. An action required or permitted to be taken at a meeting of the shareholders of a publicly traded corporation may be taken without a meeting by one or more records signed by shareholders who own voting power equal to the voting power that would be required to take the same action at a meeting of the shareholders at which all shareholders were present.

2. Action may not be taken by a publicly traded corporation by ballot of its shareholders without a meeting.

§ 10–35–21. Financial Statements.

Section 10–19.1–85 [Financial statements] does not apply to a publicly traded corporation.

§ 10–35–22. Duration of Poison Pills Limited.

1. If a publicly traded corporation adopts, creates, or issues a poison pill without a vote of its shareholders authorizing that action, the poison pill must expire or be redeemed and will otherwise be of no further force or effect not later than the earlier of:

    a. One year after the date of its adoption, creation, or issuance; or

    b. Ninety days after the first public announcement that a number of shares have been tendered into an offer to purchase any and all shares of the corporation, which number of shares tendered represents at least a majority of the outstanding shares of each class or series of shares entitled to vote generally for the election of directors when added to those shares owned beneficially or of record by the person or group of persons making the offer or by any affiliates of that person or group of persons.

2. If authorized by a vote of its shareholders, a publicly traded corporation may:

    a. Adopt, create, or issue a poison pill that will be in effect for a period not longer than the shorter of:

(1) Two years; and

(2) The period set forth in subdivision b of subsection 1; or

b. Extend the period during which a poison pill adopted, created, or issued pursuant to subsection 1 will be in effect to not longer in the aggregate than the period set forth in subdivision a.

3. A publicly traded corporation may not adopt, create, or issue a poison pill without the approval of its shareholders until after it has held a regular meeting of shareholders after its most recent prior poison pill has expired or been redeemed and otherwise ceased to be of any force or effect. The date of the regular meeting of shareholders must:

a. Comply with section 10–35–12:

b. Be at least ninety days after the date on which the prior poison pill expired, was redeemed, or otherwise ceased to be of any force or effect; and

c. If the corporation has an advance notice requirement adopted pursuant to section 10–35–07, give the shareholders the full period of time required by subsection 4 of section 10–35–07 in which to provide notice to the corporation of an intention to nominate candidates for election at the meeting.

§ 10–35–23.　Protection of Power of Current Directors Over Poison [Pills].

A poison pill adopted, created, or issued by a publicly traded corporation, with or without the approval of its shareholders, may not include a provision that limits in any way the power of the board of directors, as it may be constituted at any point in time, to take any action at any time with respect to the poison pill, including without limitation what is commonly referred to as a "dead hand", "no hand", or "slow hand" provision.

§ 10–35–24.　Minimum Share Ownership Triggering Level for Poison Pills.

A poison pill adopted, created, or issued by a publicly traded corporation, with or without the approval of its shareholders, may not provide that beneficial ownership or announcement of an intention to seek beneficial ownership by a person or group of persons of shares equal to less than twenty percent of the total number of outstanding shares of all classes and series of shares of the corporation will result, either immediately or after the passage of a period of time, in:

1. A distribution or distribution date for rights certificates or other securities as defined in subdivision d of subsection 5 of section 10–35–02;

2. The person or group of persons becoming what is commonly referred to as an "acquiring person" or "adverse person" or otherwise having the status of a person intended to be diluted or subject to dilution by the poison pill;

3. What is commonly referred to as a "flip-in" or "flip-over" event or the poison pill otherwise being triggered or becoming operative; or

4. The poison pill otherwise having a dilutive, discriminatory, or other adverse effect on the person or group of persons.

§ 10–35–25.　Optional Restrictions or Prohibitions on Poison Pills.

1. A provision of the articles or bylaws of a publicly traded corporation may restrict or prohibit the corporation from adopting, creating, or issuing a poison pill. Such a provision may provide for the effect it has on a poison pill in force at the time of the provision's adoption.

2. A provision of the articles or bylaws adopted pursuant to subsection 1 at a time when a publicly traded corporation has a poison pill in effect must be adopted by the affirmative vote of a majority of the outstanding shares entitled to vote on adoption of the provision. In every other instance, a provision of the articles or bylaws adopted pursuant to subsection 1 must be adopted by the affirmative vote of a majority of the votes cast by holders of shares entitled to vote on adoption of the provision.

§ 10–35–26. Adoption of Antitakeover Provisions.

1. The articles or bylaws of a publicly traded corporation may not contain an antitakeover provision unless it has been approved by the required vote.

2. As used in this section:

a. Except as provided in subdivision b, "antitakeover provision" means a provision that:

(1) Would block an acquisition by any person or group of persons of beneficial ownership of any shares of the corporation or a change in control of the corporation absent compliance with the provision;

(2) Restricts the price that may be paid by any person or group of persons in an acquisition of beneficial ownership of any shares of the corporation;

(3) Restricts the terms of a transaction after the occurrence of a change in control of the corporation or limits the price that may be paid in such a transaction, when it may be conducted, or how it must be approved by the directors or shareholders;

(4) Requires an approval of the directors or shareholders in addition to, or in a different manner from, whatever approvals are required under this chapter and chapter 10–19.1 for a transaction involving an acquisition by any person or group of persons of beneficial ownership of any shares of the corporation or a change in control of the corporation;

(5) Requires the approval of a nongovernmental third party for an acquisition by any person or group of persons of beneficial ownership of any shares of the corporation or a transaction that would involve a change in control of the corporation;

(6) Requires the corporation, directly or indirectly, to take an action that it would not have been required to take if it had not been the subject of an acquisition by any person or group of persons of beneficial ownership of any of its shares or a transaction that would involve a change in control of the corporation;

(7) Limits, directly or indirectly, the power of the corporation if it is the subject of an acquisition by any person or group of persons of beneficial ownership of any of its shares or a transaction that would involve a change in control of the corporation to take an action that the corporation would have had the power to take, without that limit, if the acquisition of beneficial ownership or transaction had not occurred;

(8) Changes or limits the voting rights of any shares of the corporation following a transaction involving an acquisition by any person or group of persons of beneficial ownership of any shares of the corporation or a change in control of the corporation;

(9) Would give any beneficial or record owner of shares of the corporation a direct right of action against a person or group of persons with respect to the acquisition by the person or group of persons of beneficial ownership of any shares in the corporation or control of the corporation; or

(10) Is designed or intended to operate as, or that has the effect of, what is commonly referred to, either on July 1, 2007, or at any time thereafter, as a "business combination", "control share acquisition", "control share cash out", "freeze out", "fair price", "disgorgement", or other "antitakeover" provision.

b. "Antitakeover provision" does not include a provision in the terms of a class or series of shares:

(1) If the shares are issuable upon the exercise of a poison pill, but only so long as the shares of the class or series are not issued by the corporation except pursuant to the exercise of a poison pill; or

(2) Which serves to protect dividend, interest, sinking fund, conversion, exchange, or other rights of the shares, or to protect against the issuance of additional securities that would be on a parity with or superior to the shares.

　　c. "Control" has the same meaning as in the rules and regulations of the commission under the Exchange Act.

§ 10–35–27.　Liberal Construction.

　　The provisions of this chapter and of chapter 10–19.1 must be liberally construed to protect and enhance the rights of shareholders in publicly traded corporations. . . .

PENNSYLVANIA CONSOL. STATS. ANN.
TITLE 15 (EXCERPTS)

TITLE 15

CORPORATIONS AND UNINCORPORATED ASSOCIATIONS

PART II

CORPORATIONS

TABLE OF CONTENTS

Sec.		Page
511.	Application and effect of subchapter	914
512.	Standard of care and justifiable reliance	914
513.	Personal liability of directors	915
515.	Exercise of powers generally	915
516.	Alternative standard	916
517.	Limitation on standing	917

ARTICLE C

DOMESTIC CORPORATION ANCILLARIES

Chapter 25

REGISTERED CORPORATIONS

Subchapter A

Preliminary Provisions

2502.	Registered corporation status	917

Subchapter F

Business Combinations

2552.	Definitions	917

Subchapter G

Control-Share Acquisitions

2562.	Definitions	918
2563.	Acquiring person safe harbor	918

Subchapter H

Disgorgement by Certain Controlling Shareholders Following Attempts to Acquire Control

2571. Application and effect of subchapter 919
2572. Policy and purpose.. 920
2573. Definitions.. 921
2574. Controlling person or group safe harbor.. 922
2575. Ownership by corporation of profits resulting from certain transactions...................... 923
2576. Enforcement actions.. 923

Subchapter I

Severance Compensation for Employees Terminated Following Certain Control-Share Acquisitions

2581. Definitions.. 924
2582. Severance compensation 925
2583. Enforcement and remedies.. 926

Subchapter J

Business Combination Transactions—Labor Contracts

2585. Application and effect of subchapter 926
2586. Definitions.. 926
2587. Labor contracts preserved in business combination transactions.................................. 927
2588. Civil remedies 927

---

§ 511.   Application and effect of subchapter

(a) **General rule.**—This subchapter shall apply to and the terms "corporation" or "domestic corporation" in this subchapter shall mean a domestic corporation except:

(1) A business corporation as defined in section 1103 (relating to definitions).

(2) A nonprofit corporation as defined in section 5103 (relating to definitions).

(b) **Alternative provisions.**—Section 516 (relating to alternative standard) shall not be applicable to any corporation to which section 515 (relating to exercise of powers generally) is applicable. Section 515 shall be applicable to any corporation except a corporation:

(1) the bylaws of which, by amendment adopted by the board of directors on or before July 26, 1990, and not subsequently rescinded by an articles amendment, explicitly provide that section 515 or corresponding provisions of prior law shall not be applicable to the corporation; or

(2) the articles of which explicitly provide that section 515 or corresponding provisions of prior law shall not be applicable to the corporation.

§ 512.   Standard of care and justifiable reliance

(a) **Directors.**—A director of a domestic corporation shall stand in a fiduciary relation to the corporation and shall perform his duties as a director, including his duties as a member of any committee of the board upon which he may serve, in good faith, in a manner he reasonably believes to be in the best interests of the corporation and with such care, including reasonable inquiry, skill and diligence, as a person of ordinary prudence would use under similar circumstances. In performing his duties, a director shall be entitled to rely in good faith on information, opinions, reports or statements, including financial statements and other financial data, in each case prepared or presented by any of the following:

(1) One or more officers or employees of the corporation whom the director reasonably believes to be reliable and competent in the matters presented.

(2) Counsel, public accountants or other persons as to matters which the director reasonably believes to be within the professional or expert competence of such person.

(3) A committee of the board upon which he does not serve, duly designated in accordance with law, as to matters within its designated authority, which committee the director reasonably believes to merit confidence.

(b) Effect of actual knowledge.—A director shall not be considered to be acting in good faith if he has knowledge concerning the matter in question that would cause his reliance to be unwarranted.

(c) Officers.—Except as otherwise provided in the articles, an officer shall perform his duties as an officer in good faith, in a manner he reasonably believes to be in the best interests of the corporation and with such care, including reasonable inquiry, skill and diligence, as a person of ordinary prudence would use under similar circumstances. A person who so performs his duties shall not be liable by reason of having been an officer of the corporation.

§ 513. Personal liability of directors

(a) General rule.—If a bylaw adopted by the shareholders entitled to vote or members entitled to vote of a domestic corporation so provides, a director shall not be personally liable, as such, for monetary damages for any action taken unless:

(1) the director has breached or failed to perform the duties of his office under this subchapter; and

(2) the breach or failure to perform constitutes self-dealing, willful misconduct or recklessness.

(b) Exceptions.—

Subsection (a) shall not apply to:

(1) the responsibility or liability of a director pursuant to any criminal statute; or

(2) the liability of a director for the payment of taxes pursuant to Federal, State or local law.

. . .

§ 515. Exercise of powers generally

(a) General rule.—In discharging the duties of their respective positions, the board of directors, committees of the board and individual directors of a business corporation may, in considering the best interests of the corporation, consider to the extent they deem appropriate:

(1) The effects of any action upon any or all groups affected by such action, including shareholders, employees, suppliers, customers and creditors of the corporation, and upon communities in which offices or other establishments of the corporation are located.

(2) The short-term and long-term interests of the corporation, including benefits that may accrue to the corporation from its long-term plans and the possibility that these interests may be best served by the continued independence of the corporation.

(3) The resources, intent and conduct (past, stated and potential) of any person seeking to acquire control of the corporation.

(4) All other pertinent factors.

(b) Consideration of interests and factors.—The board of directors, committees of the board and individual directors shall not be required, in considering the best interests of the corporation or the effects of any action, to regard any corporate interest or the interests of any particular group affected by such action as a dominant or controlling interest or factor. The consideration of interests and factors in the manner described in this subsection and in subsection (a) shall not constitute a violation of section 512 (relating to standard of care and justifiable reliance).

(c) Specific applications.—In exercising the powers vested in the corporation, and in no way limiting the discretion of the board of directors, committees of the board and individual directors pursuant to subsections (a) and (b), the fiduciary duty of directors shall not be deemed to require them to act as the board of directors, a committee of the board or an individual director solely because of the effect such action might have on an acquisition or potential or proposed acquisition of control of the corporation or the consideration that might be offered or paid to shareholders or members in such an acquisition.

(d) Presumption.—Absent breach of fiduciary duty, lack of good faith or self-dealing, any act as the board of directors, a committee of the board or an individual director shall be presumed to be in the best interests of the corporation. In assessing whether the standard set forth in section 512 has been satisfied, there shall not be any greater obligation to justify, or higher burden of proof with respect to, any act as the board of directors, any committee of the board or any individual director relating to or affecting an acquisition or potential or proposed acquisition of control of the corporation than is applied to any other act as a board of directors, any committee of the board or any individual director. Notwithstanding the preceding provisions of this subsection, any act as the board of directors, a committee of the board or an individual director relating to or affecting an acquisition or potential or proposed acquisition of control to which a majority of the disinterested directors shall have assented shall be presumed to satisfy the standard set forth in section 512, unless it is proven by clear and convincing evidence that the disinterested directors did not assent to such act in good faith after reasonable investigation.

(e) Definition.—The term "disinterested director" as used in subsection (d) and for no other purpose means:

(1) A director of the corporation other than:

(i) A director who has a direct or indirect financial or other interest in the person acquiring or seeking to acquire control of the corporation or who is an affiliate or associate, as defined in section 2552 (relating to definitions), of, or was nominated or designated as a director by, a person acquiring or seeking to acquire control of the corporation.

(ii) Depending on the specific facts surrounding the director and the act under consideration, an officer or employee or former officer or employee of the corporation.

(2) A person shall not be deemed to be other than a disinterested director solely by reason of any or all of the following:

(i) The ownership by the director of shares of the corporation.

(ii) The receipt as a holder of any class or series of any distribution made to all owners of shares of that class or series.

(iii) The receipt by the director of director's fees or other consideration as a director.

(iv) Any interest the director may have in retaining the status or position of director.

(v) The former business or employment relationship of the director with the corporation.

(vi) Receiving or having the right to receive retirement or deferred compensation from the corporation due to service as a director, officer or employee.

(f) Cross reference.—See section 1711 (relating to alternative provisions).

§ 516.   Alternative standard

(a) General rule.—In discharging the duties of their respective positions, the board of directors, committees of the board and individual directors of a business corporation may, in considering the best interests of the corporation, consider the effects of any action upon employees, upon suppliers and customers of the corporation and upon communities in which offices or other establishments of the corporation are located, and all other pertinent factors. The consideration of those factors shall not constitute a violation of section 512 (relating to standard of care and justifiable reliance).

(b) Presumption.—Absent breach of fiduciary duty, lack of good faith or self-dealing, actions taken as a director shall be presumed to be in the best interests of the corporation.

(c) Cross reference.—See section 511 (relating to alternative provisions).

§ 517. Limitation on standing

The duty of the board of directors, committees of the board and individual directors under section 512 (relating to standard of care and justifiable reliance) is solely to the domestic corporation and may be enforced directly by the corporation or may be enforced by a shareholder or member, as such, by an action in the right of the corporation, and may not be enforced directly by a shareholder, member or by any other person or group. Notwithstanding the preceding sentence, sections 515(a) and (b) (relating to exercise of powers generally) and 516(a) (relating to alternative standard) do not impose upon the board of directors, committees of the board and individual directors any legal or equitable duties, obligations or liabilities or create any right or cause of action against, or basis for standing to sue, the board of directors, committees of the board and individual directors.

ARTICLE C

DOMESTIC CORPORATION ANCILLARIES

Chapter 25

REGISTERED CORPORATIONS

Subchapter A

Preliminary Provisions

§ 2502. Registered corporation status

Subject to additional definitions contained in subsequent provisions of this chapter which are applicable to specific subchapters of this chapter, as used in this chapter, the term "registered corporation" shall mean:

(1) A domestic business corporation:

(i) that:

(A) has a class or series of shares entitled to vote generally in the election of directors of the corporation registered under the [Exchange Act]; or . . .

(ii) that is:

(A) subject to the reporting obligations imposed by section 15(d) of the Exchange Act by reason of having filed a registration statement which has become effective under the Securities Act of 1933 relating to shares of a class or series of its equity securities entitled to vote generally in the election of directors. . . .

A corporation which satisfies both subparagraphs (i) and (ii) shall be deemed to be described solely in subparagraph (i) for the purposes of this chapter.

(2) A domestic business corporation all of the shares of which are owned, directly or indirectly, by one or more registered corporations. . . .

Subchapter F

Business Combinations

§ 2552. Definitions

The following words and phrases when used in this subchapter shall have the meanings given to them in this section unless the context clearly indicates otherwise: . . .

"Beneficial owner." When used with respect to any shares, a person:

(1) that, individually or with or through any of its affiliates or associates, beneficially owns such shares, directly or indirectly;

(2) that, individually or with or through any of its affiliates or associates, has:

(i) the right to acquire such shares (whether the right is exercisable immediately or only after the passage of time), pursuant to any agreement, arrangement or understanding (whether or not in writing), or upon the exercise of conversion rights, exchange rights, warrants or options, or otherwise, except that a person shall not be deemed the beneficial owner of shares tendered pursuant to a tender or exchange offer made by such person or the affiliates or associates of any such person until the tendered shares are accepted for purchase or exchange; or

(ii) the right to vote such shares pursuant to any agreement, arrangement or understanding (whether or not in writing), except that a person shall not be deemed the beneficial owner of any shares under this subparagraph if the agreement, arrangement or understanding to vote such shares:

(A) arises solely from a revocable proxy or consent given in response to a proxy or consent solicitation made in accordance with the applicable rules and regulations under the Exchange Act; and

(B) is not then reportable on a Schedule 13D under the Exchange Act, (or any comparable or successor report); or

(3) that has any agreement, arrangement or understanding (whether or not in writing), for the purpose of acquiring, holding, voting (except voting pursuant to a revocable proxy or consent as described in paragraph (2)(ii)), or disposing of such shares with any other person that beneficially owns, or whose affiliates or associates beneficially own, directly or indirectly, such shares. . . .

"Voting shares." Shares of a corporation entitled to vote generally in the election of directors.

Subchapter G

Control-Share Acquisitions

§ 2562. Definitions

The following words and phrases when used in this subchapter shall have the meanings given to them in this section unless the context clearly indicates otherwise. . . .

"Publicly disclosed or caused to be disclosed." Includes, but is not limited to, any disclosure (whether or not required by law) that becomes public made by a person:

(1) with the intent or expectation that such disclosure become public; or

(2) to another where the disclosing person knows, or reasonably should have known, that the receiving person was not under an obligation to refrain from making such disclosure, directly or indirectly, to the public and such receiving person does make such disclosure, directly or indirectly, to the public. . . .

§ 2563. Acquiring person safe harbor

(a) Nonparticipant.—For the purposes of this subchapter, a person shall not be deemed an acquiring person, absent significant other activities indicating that a person should be deemed an acquiring person, by reason of voting or giving a proxy or consent as a shareholder of the corporation if the person is one who:

(1) did not acquire any voting shares of the corporation with the purpose of changing or influencing control of the corporation, seeking to acquire control of the corporation or influencing the outcome of a vote of shareholders under section 2564 (relating to voting rights of shares acquired in a control-share acquisition) or in connection with or as a participant in any agreement, arrangement, relationship, understanding or otherwise having any such purpose;

(2) if the control-share acquisition were consummated, would not be a person that has control over the corporation and will not receive, directly or indirectly, any consideration from a person that has control over the corporation other than consideration offered proportionately to all holders of voting shares of the corporation; and

(3) if a proxy or consent is given, executes a revocable proxy or consent given without consideration in response to a proxy or consent solicitation made in accordance with the applicable rules and regulations under the Exchange Act under circumstances not then reportable on Schedule 13d under the Exchange Act (or any comparable or successor report) by the person who gave the proxy or consent.

(b) Certain holders.—For the purpose of this subchapter, a person shall not be deemed an acquiring person if such person holds voting power within any of the ranges specified in the definition of "control-share acquisition":

(1) in good faith and not for the purpose of circumventing this subchapter, as an agent, bank, broker, nominee or trustee for one or more beneficial owners who do not individually or, if they are a group acting in concert, as a group have the voting power specified in any of the ranges in the definition of "control-share acquisition";

(2) in connection with the solicitation of proxies or consents by or on behalf of the corporation in connection with shareholder meetings or actions of the corporation;

(3) as a result of the solicitation of revocable proxies or consents with respect to voting shares if such proxies or consents both:

(i) are given without consideration in response to a proxy or consent solicitation made in accordance with the applicable rules and regulations under the Exchange Act; and

(ii) do not empower the holder thereof, whether or not this power is shared with any other person, to vote such shares except on the specific matters described in such proxy or consent and in accordance with the instructions of the giver of such proxy or consent; or

(4) to the extent of voting power arising from a contingent right of the holders of one or more classes or series of preference shares to elect one or more members of the board of directors upon or during the continuation of a default in the payment of dividends on such shares or another similar contingency.

Subchapter H

Disgorgement by Certain Controlling Shareholders Following Attempts to Acquire Control

§ 2571. Application and effect of subchapter

(a) General rule.—Except as otherwise provided in this section, this subchapter shall apply to every registered corporation.

(b) Exceptions.—This subchapter shall not apply to any transfer of an equity security:

(1) Of a registered corporation described in section 2502(1)(ii) or (2) (relating to registered corporation status).

(2) Of a corporation:

(i) the bylaws of which explicitly provide that this subchapter shall not be applicable to the corporation by amendment adopted by the board of directors on or before July 26, 1990, in the case of a corporation:

(A) which on April 27, 1990, was a registered corporation described in section 2502(1)(i); and

(B) did not on that date have outstanding one or more classes or series of preference shares entitled, upon the occurrence of a default in the payment of dividends or another similar contingency, to elect a majority of the members of the board of directors (a bylaw adopted on or before July 26, 1990, by a corporation excluded from the scope of this subparagraph by this clause shall be ineffective unless ratified under subparagraph (ii));

(ii) the bylaws of which explicitly provide that this subchapter shall not be applicable to the corporation by amendment ratified by the board of directors on or after December 19, 1990, and on or before March 19, 1991, in the case of a corporation:

(A) which on April 27, 1990, was a registered corporation described in section 2502(1)(i);

(B) which on that date had outstanding one or more classes or series of preference shares entitled, upon the occurrence of a default in the payment of dividends or another similar contingency, to elect a majority of the members of the board of directors; and

(C) the bylaws of which on that date contained a provision described in subparagraph (i); or

(iii) in any other case, the articles of which explicitly provide that this subchapter shall not be applicable to the corporation by a provision included in the original articles, or by an articles amendment adopted at any time while it is a corporation other than a registered corporation described in section 2502(1)(i) or on or before 90 days after the corporation first becomes a registered corporation described in section 2502(1)(i). . . .

(6) Consummated by:

(i) The corporation or any of its subsidiaries.

(ii) Any savings, stock ownership, stock option or other benefit plan of the corporation or any of its subsidiaries, or any fiduciary with respect to any such plan when acting in such capacity, or by any participant in any such plan with respect to any equity security acquired pursuant to any such plan or any equity security acquired as a result of the exercise or conversion of any equity security (specifically including any options, warrants or rights) issued to such participant by the corporation pursuant to any such plan. . . .

(7)(i) where the acquisition of the equity security has been approved by a resolution adopted prior to the acquisition of the equity security; or

(ii) where the disposition of the equity security has been approved by a resolution adopted prior to the disposition of the equity security if the equity security at the time of the adoption of the resolution is beneficially owned by a person or group that is or was a controlling person or group with respect to the corporation and is in control of the corporation if:

the resolution in either subparagraph (i) or (ii) is approved by the board of directors and ratified by the affirmative vote of the shareholders entitled to cast at least a majority of the votes which all shareholders are entitled to cast thereon and identifies the specific person or group that proposes such acquisition or disposition, the specific purpose of such acquisition or disposition and the specific number of equity securities that are proposed to be acquired or disposed of by such person or group. . . .

(d) Formation of group.—For the purposes of this subchapter, if there is no change in the beneficial ownership of an equity security held by a person, then the formation of or participation in a group involving the person shall not be deemed to constitute an acquisition of the beneficial ownership of such equity security by the group.

§ 2572. Policy and purpose

(a) General rule.—The purpose of this subchapter is to protect certain registered corporations and legitimate interests of various groups related to such corporations from certain manipulative and coercive actions. Specifically, this subchapter seeks to:

(1) Protect registered corporations from being exposed to and paying "greenmail."

(2) Promote a stable relationship among the various parties involved in registered corporations, including the public whose confidence in the future of a corporation tends to be undermined when a corporation is put "in play."

(3) Ensure that speculators who put registered corporations "in play" do not misappropriate corporate values for themselves at the expense of the corporation and groups affected by corporate actions.

(4) Discourage such speculators from putting registered corporations "in play" through any means, including, but not limited to, offering to purchase at least 20% of the voting shares of the corporation or threatening to wage or waging a proxy contest in connection with or as a means toward or part of a plan to acquire control of the corporation, with the effect of reaping short-term speculative profits.

Moreover, this subchapter recognizes the right and obligation of the Commonwealth to regulate and protect the corporations it creates from abuses resulting from the application of its own laws affecting generally corporate governance and particularly director obligations, mergers and related matters. Such laws, and the obligations imposed on directors or others thereunder, should not be the vehicles by which registered corporations are manipulated in certain instances for the purpose of obtaining short-term profits.

(b) Limitations.—The purpose of this subchapter is not to affect legitimate shareholder activity that does not involve putting a corporation "in play" or involve seeking to acquire control of the corporation. Specifically, the purpose of this subchapter is not to:

(1) curtail proxy contests on matters properly submitted for shareholder action under applicable State or other law, including, but not limited to, certain elections of directors, corporate governance matters such as cumulative voting or staggered boards, or other corporate matters such as environmental issues or conducting business in a particular country if, in any such instance, such proxy contest is not utilized in connection with or as a means toward or part of a plan to put the corporation "in play" or to seek to acquire control of the corporation; or

(2) affect the solicitation of proxies or consents by or on behalf of the corporation in connection with shareholder meetings or actions of the corporation.

§ 2573. Definitions

The following words and phrases when used in this subchapter shall have the meanings given to them in this section unless the context clearly indicates otherwise:

"Beneficial owner." The term shall have the meaning specified in section 2552 (relating to definitions).

"Control." The power, whether or not exercised, to direct or cause the direction of the management and policies of a person, whether through the ownership of voting shares, by contract or otherwise.

"Controlling person or group."

(1)(i) A person or group who has acquired, offered to acquire or, directly or indirectly, publicly disclosed or caused to be disclosed (other than for the purpose of circumventing the intent of this subchapter) the intention of acquiring voting power over voting shares of a registered corporation that would entitle the holder thereof to cast at least 20% of the votes that all shareholders would be entitled to cast in an election of directors of the corporation; or

(ii) a person or group who has otherwise, directly or indirectly, publicly disclosed or caused to be disclosed (other than for the purpose of circumventing the intent of this subchapter) that it may seek to acquire control of a corporation through any means.

(2) Two or more persons acting in concert, whether or not pursuant to an express agreement, arrangement, relationship or understanding, including as a partnership, limited partnership, syndicate, or through any means of affiliation whether or not formally organized, for the purpose of acquiring, holding, voting or disposing of equity securities of a corporation shall be deemed a group for

purposes of this subchapter. Notwithstanding any other provision of this subchapter to the contrary, and regardless of whether a group has been deemed to acquire beneficial ownership of an equity security under this subchapter, each person who participates in a group, where such group is a controlling person or group as defined in this subchapter, shall also be deemed to be a controlling person or group for the purposes of this subchapter. . . .

"Equity security." Any security, including all shares, stock or similar security, and any security convertible into (with or without additional consideration) or exercisable for any such shares, stock or similar security, or carrying any warrant, right or option to subscribe to or purchase such shares, stock or similar security or any such warrant, right, option or similar instrument. . . .

"Profit." The positive value, if any, of the difference between:

(1) the consideration received from the disposition of equity securities less only the usual and customary broker's commissions actually paid in connection with such disposition; and

(2) the consideration actually paid for the acquisition of such equity securities plus only the usual and customary broker's commissions actually paid in connection with such acquisition.

"Proxy." Includes any proxy, consent or authorization.

"Proxy solicitation" or **"solicitation of proxies."** Includes any solicitation of a proxy, including a solicitation of a revocable proxy of the nature and under the circumstances described in section 2574(b)(3) (relating to controlling person or group safe harbor).

"Publicly disclosed or caused to be disclosed." The term shall have the meaning specified in section 2562 (relating to definitions).

"Transfer." Acquisition or disposition.

"Voting shares." The term shall have the meaning specified in section 2552 (relating to definitions).

§ 2574. Controlling person or group safe harbor

(a) **Nonparticipant.**—For the purpose of this subchapter, a person or group shall not be deemed a controlling person or group, absent significant other activities indicating that a person or group should be deemed a controlling person or group, by reason of voting or giving a proxy or consent as a shareholder of the corporation if the person or group is one who or which:

(1) did not acquire any voting shares of the corporation with the purpose of changing or influencing control of the corporation or seeking to acquire control of the corporation or in connection with or as a participant in any agreement, arrangement, relationship, understanding or otherwise having any such purpose;

(2) if control were acquired, would not be a person or group or a participant in a group that has control over the corporation and will not receive, directly or indirectly, any consideration from a person or group that has control over the corporation other than consideration offered proportionately to all holders of voting shares of the corporation; and

(3) if a proxy or consent is given, executes a revocable proxy or consent given without consideration in response to a proxy or consent solicitation made in accordance with the applicable rules and regulations under the Exchange Act under circumstances not then reportable on Schedule 13D under the Exchange Act (or any comparable or successor report) by the person or group who gave the proxy or consent.

(b) **Certain holders.**—For the purpose of this subchapter, a person or group shall not be deemed a controlling person or group under subparagraph (1)(i) of the definition of "controlling person or group" in section 2573 (relating to definitions) if such person or group holds voting power:

(1) in good faith and not for the purpose of circumventing this subchapter, as an agent, bank, broker, nominee or trustee for one or more beneficial owners who do not individually or, if they are a group acting in concert, as a group have the voting power specified in subparagraph (1)(i) of the definition of "controlling person or group" in section 2573;

(2) in connection with the solicitation of proxies or consents by or on behalf of the corporation in connection with shareholder meetings or actions of the corporation; or

(3) in the amount specified in subparagraph (1)(i) of the definition of "controlling person or group" in section 2573 as a result of the solicitation of revocable proxies or consents with respect to voting shares if such proxies or consents both:

(i) are given without consideration in response to a proxy or consent solicitation made in accordance with the applicable rules and regulations under the exchange act; and

(ii) do not empower the holder thereof, whether or not this power is shared with any other person, to vote such shares except on the specific matters described in such proxy or consent and in accordance with the instructions of the giver of such proxy or consent. . . .

§ 2575. Ownership by corporation of profits resulting from certain transactions

Any profit realized by any person or group who is or was a controlling person or group with respect to a registered corporation from the disposition of any equity security of the corporation to any person . . . including, without limitation, to the corporation . . . or to another member of the controlling person or group, shall belong to and be recoverable by the corporation where the profit is realized by such person or group:

(1) from the disposition of the equity security within 18 months after the person or group obtained the status of a controlling person or group; and

(2) the equity security had been acquired by the controlling person or group within 24 months prior to or 18 months subsequent to the obtaining by the person or group of the status of a controlling person or group.

Any transfer by a controlling person or group of the ownership of any equity security may be suspended on the books of the corporation, and certificates representing such securities may be duly legended, to enforce the rights of the corporation under this subchapter.

§ 2576. Enforcement actions

(a) **Venue.**—Actions to recover any profit due under this subchapter may be commenced in any court of competent jurisdiction by the registered corporation issuing the equity security or by any holder of any equity security of the corporation in the name and on behalf of the corporation if the corporation fails or refuses to bring the action within 60 days after written request by a holder or shall fail to prosecute the action diligently. If a judgment requiring the payment of any such profits is entered, the party bringing such action shall recover all costs, including reasonable attorney fees, incurred in connection with enforcement of this subchapter.

(b) **Jurisdiction.**—By engaging in the activities necessary to become a controlling person or group and thereby becoming a controlling person or group, the person or group and all persons participating in the group consent to personal jurisdiction in the courts of this Commonwealth for enforcement of this subchapter. Courts of this Commonwealth may exercise personal jurisdiction over any controlling person or group in actions to enforce this subchapter. . . . Service of process may be made upon such persons outside this Commonwealth in accordance with the procedures specified by 42 Pa.C.S. § 5323 (relating to service of process on persons outside this Commonwealth).

(c) **Limitation.**—Any action to enforce this subchapter shall be brought within two years from the date any profit recoverable by the corporation was realized.

Subchapter I

Severance Compensation for Employees Terminated Following Certain Control-Share Acquisitions

§ 2581. Definitions

The following words and phrases when used in this subchapter shall have the meanings given to them in this section unless the context clearly indicates otherwise:

"Acquiring person." The term shall have the meaning specified in section 2562 (relating to definitions).

"Control-share acquisition." The term shall have the meaning specified in section 2562.

"Control-share approval."

(1) The occurrence of both:

(i) a control-share acquisition to which Subchapter G (relating to control-share acquisitions) applies with respect to a registered corporation described in section 2502(1)(i) (relating to registered corporation status) by an acquiring person; and

(ii) the according by such registered corporation of voting rights pursuant to section 2564(a) (relating to voting rights of shares acquired in a control-share acquisition) in connection with such control-share acquisition to control shares of the acquiring person.

(2) The term shall also include a control-share acquisition effected by an acquiring person, other than a control-share acquisition described in section 2561(b)(3), (4) or (5) (other than subparagraph 2561(b)(5)(vii)) (relating to application and effect of subchapter) if the control-share acquisition:

(i)(A) occurs primarily in response to the actions of another acquiring person where Subchapter G (relating to control-share acquisitions) applies to a control-share acquisition or proposed control-share acquisition by such other acquiring person; and

(B) either:

(I) pursuant to an agreement or plan [of merger, consolidation, or share exchange] described in section 2561(b)(5)(vii);

(II) after adoption of an amendment to the articles of the registered corporation [which provide that Subchapter G shall not be applicable to the corporation] pursuant to section 2561(b)(2)(iii); or

(III) after reincorporation of the registered corporation in another jurisdiction;

if the agreement or plan is approved or the amendment or reincorporation is adopted by the board of directors of the corporation during the period commencing after the satisfaction by such other acquiring person of the requirements of section 2565(a) or (b) (relating to procedure for establishing voting rights of control shares) and ending 90 days after the date such issue is voted on by the shareholders, is withdrawn from consideration or becomes moot; or

(ii) is consummated in any manner by a person who satisfied, within two years prior to such acquisition, the requirements of section 2565(a) or (b).

"Control shares." The term shall have the meaning specified in section 2562.

"Eligible employee." Any employee of a registered corporation (or any subsidiary thereof) if:

(1) the registered corporation was the subject of a control-share approval;

(2) the employee was an employee of such corporation (or any subsidiary thereof) within 90 days before or on the day of the control-share approval and had been so employed for at least two years prior thereto; and

(3) the employment of the employee is in this Commonwealth.

"Employee." Any person lawfully employed by an employer.

"Employment in this Commonwealth."

(1) The entire service of an employee, performed inside and outside of this Commonwealth, if the service is localized in this Commonwealth.

(2) Service shall be deemed to be localized in this Commonwealth if:

(i) the service is performed entirely inside this Commonwealth; or

(ii) the service is performed both inside and outside of this Commonwealth but the service performed outside of this Commonwealth is incidental to the service of the employee inside this Commonwealth, as where such service is temporary or transitory in nature or consists of isolated transactions.

(3) Employment in this Commonwealth shall also include service of the employee, performed inside and outside of this Commonwealth, if the service is not localized in any state, but some of the service is performed in this Commonwealth, and:

(i) the base of operations of the employee is in this Commonwealth;

(ii) there is no base of operations, and the place from which such service is directed or controlled is in this Commonwealth; or

(iii) the base of operations of the employee or place from which such service is directed or controlled is not in any state in which some part of the service is performed, but the residence of the employee is in this Commonwealth.

"Minimum severance amount." With respect to an eligible employee, the weekly compensation of the employee multiplied by the number of the completed years of service of the employee, up to a maximum of 26 times the weekly compensation of the employee.

"Subsidiary." The term shall have the meaning specified in section 2552 (relating to definitions).

"Termination of employment." The layoff of at least six months, or the involuntary termination of an employee, except that any employee employed in a business operation who is continued or employed or offered employment (within 60 days) by the purchaser of such business operation, on substantially the same terms (including geographic location) as those pursuant to which the employee was employed in such business operation, shall not be deemed to have been laid off or involuntarily terminated for the purposes of this subchapter by such transfer of employment to the purchaser, but the purchaser shall make the lump-sum payment under this subchapter in the event of a layoff of at least six months or the involuntary termination of the employee within the period specified in section 2582 (relating to severance compensation).

"Weekly compensation." The average regular weekly compensation of an employee based on normal schedule of hours in effect for such employee over the last three months preceding the control-share approval.

"Year of service." Each full year during which the employee has been employed by the employer.

§ 2582. Severance compensation

(a) **General rule.**—Any eligible employee whose employment is terminated, other than for willful misconduct connected with the work of the employee, within 90 days before the control-share approval with respect to the registered corporation if such termination was pursuant to an agreement, arrangement or understanding, whether formal or informal, with the acquiring person whose control shares were accorded voting rights in connection with such control-share approval or within 24 calendar months after the control-share approval with respect to the registered corporation shall receive a one-time, lump-sum payment from the employer equal to:

(1) the minimum severance amount with respect to the employee; less

(2) any payments made to the employee by the employer due to termination of employment, whether pursuant to any contract, policy, plan or otherwise, but not including any final wage payments to the employee or payments to the employee under pension, savings, retirement or similar plans.

(b) Limitation.—If the amount specified in subsection (a)(2) is at least equal to the amount specified in subsection (a)(1), no payment shall be required to be made under this subchapter.

(c) Due date of payment.—Severance compensation under this subchapter to eligible employees shall be made within one regular pay period after the last day of work of the employee, in the case of a layoff known at such time to be at least six months or an involuntary termination and in all other cases within 30 days after the eligible employee first becomes entitled to compensation under this subchapter.

§ 2583. Enforcement and remedies

(a) Notice.—Within 30 days of the control-share approval, the employer shall provide written notice to each eligible employee and to the collective bargaining representative, if any, of the rights of eligible employees under this subchapter.

(b) Remedies.—In the event any eligible employee is denied a lump-sum payment in violation of this subchapter or the employer fails to provide the notice required by subsection (a), the employee on his or her own behalf or on behalf of other employees similarly situated, or the collective bargaining representative, if any, on the behalf of the employee, may, in addition to all other remedies available at law or in equity, bring an action to remedy such violation. In any such action, the court may order such equitable or legal relief as it deems just and proper.

(c) Civil penalty.—In the case of violations of subsection (a), the court may order the employer to pay to each employee who was subject to a termination of employment and entitled to severance compensation under this subchapter a civil penalty not to exceed $75 per day for each business day that notice was not provided to such employee.

(d) Successor liability.—The rights under this subchapter of any individual who was an eligible employee at the time of the control-share approval shall vest at that time, and, in any action based on a violation of this subchapter, recovery may be secured against:

(1) a merged, consolidated or resulting domestic or foreign corporation or other successor employer; or

(2) the corporation after its status as a registered corporation has terminated;

notwithstanding any provision of law to the contrary.

Subchapter J

Business Combination Transactions—Labor Contracts

§ 2585. Application and effect of subchapter

(a) General rule.—Except as otherwise provided in this section, this subchapter shall apply to every business combination transaction relating to a business operation if such business operation was owned by a registered corporation (or any subsidiary thereof) at the time of a control-share approval with respect to the corporation (regardless of the fact, if such be the case, that such operation after the control-share approval is owned by the registered corporation or any other person).

(b) Exceptions.—This subchapter shall not apply to:

(1) Any business combination transaction occurring more than five years after the control-share approval of the registered corporation.

(2) Any business operation located other than in this Commonwealth.

§ 2586. Definitions

The following words and phrases when used in this subchapter shall have the meanings given to them in this section unless the context clearly indicates otherwise:

"Business combination transaction." Any merger or consolidation, sale, lease, exchange or other disposition, in one transaction or a series of transactions, whether affecting all or substantially all the property and assets, including its good will, of the business operation that is the subject of the labor contract referred to in section 2587 (relating to labor contracts preserved in business combination transactions) or any transfer of a controlling interest in such business operation.

"**Control-share approval.**" The term shall have the meaning specified in section 2581 (relating to definitions).

"**Covered labor contract.**" Any labor contract if such contract:

(1) covers persons engaged in employment in this Commonwealth;

(2) was negotiated by a labor organization or by a collective bargaining agent or other representative;

(3) relates to a business operation that was owned by the registered corporation (or any subsidiary thereof) at the time of the control-share approval with respect to such corporation; and

(4) was in effect and covered such business operation and such employees at the time of such control-share approval.

"**Employee**" and "**employment in this Commonwealth.**" The terms shall have the meanings specified in section 2581.

"**Subsidiary.**" The term shall have the meaning specified in section 2552 (relating to definitions).

§ 2587. Labor contracts preserved in business combination transactions

No business combination transaction shall result in the termination or impairment of the provisions of any covered labor contract, and the contract shall continue in effect pursuant to its terms until it is terminated pursuant to any termination provision contained therein or until otherwise agreed upon by the parties to such contract or their successors.

§ 2588. Civil remedies

(a) **General rule.**—In the event that an employee is denied or fails to receive wages, benefits or wage supplements or suffers any contractual loss as a result of a violation of this subchapter, the employee on his or her own behalf or on behalf of other employees similarly situated, or the labor organization or collective bargaining agent party to the labor contract, may, in addition to all other remedies available at law or in equity, bring an action in any court of competent jurisdiction to recover such wages, benefits, wage supplements or contractual losses and to enjoin the violation of this subchapter.

(b) **Successor liability.**—The rights under this subchapter of any employee at the time of the control-share approval shall vest at that time, and, in any action based on a violation of this subchapter, recovery may be secured against:

(1) a merged, consolidated or resulting domestic or foreign corporation or other successor employer; or

(2) the corporation after its status as a registered corporation has terminated;

notwithstanding any provision of law to the contrary.

VIRGINIA CORPORATIONS CODE
§§ 13.1–690, 13.1–692.1

§ 13.1–690   General standards of conduct for director

A.   A director shall discharge his duties as a director, including his duties as a member of a committee, in accordance with his good faith business judgment of the best interests of the corporation.

B.   Unless he has knowledge or information concerning the matter in question that makes reliance unwarranted, a director is entitled to rely on information, opinions, reports or statements, including financial statements and other financial data, if prepared or presented by:

1.   One or more officers or employees of the corporation whom the director believes, in good faith, to be reliable and competent in the matters presented;

2.   Legal counsel, public accountants, or other persons as to matters the director believes, in good faith, are within the person's professional or expert competence; or

3.   A committee of the board of directors of which he is not a member if the director believes, in good faith, that the committee merits confidence.

C.   A director is not liable for any action taken as a director, or any failure to take any action, if he performed the duties of his office in compliance with this section.

D.   A person alleging a violation of this section has the burden of proving the violation.

§ 13.1–692.1 Limitation on liability of officers and directors: exception

A.   In any proceeding brought by or in the right of a corporation or brought by or on behalf of shareholders of the corporation, the damages assessed against an officer or director arising out of a single transaction, occurrence or course of conduct shall not exceed the lesser of:

1.   The monetary amount, including the elimination of liability, specified in the articles of incorporation or, if approved by the shareholders, in the bylaws as a limitation on or elimination of the liability of the officer or director; or

2.   The greater of (i) $100,000 or (ii) the amount of cash compensation received by the officer or director from the corporation during the twelve months immediately preceding the act or omission for which liability was imposed.

B.   The liability of an officer or director shall not be limited as provided in this section if the officer or director engaged in willful misconduct or a knowing violation of the criminal law or of any federal or state securities law, including, without limitation, any claim of unlawful insider trading or manipulation of the market for any security.

C.   No limitation on or elimination of liability adopted pursuant to this section may be affected by any amendment of the articles of incorporation or bylaws with respect to any act or omission occurring before such amendment.

§ 8–204.   Effect of Issuer's Restriction on Transfer

A restriction on transfer of a security imposed by the issuer, even if otherwise lawful, is ineffective against a person without knowledge of the restriction unless:

(1) the security is certificated and the restriction is noted conspicuously on the security certificate; or

(2) the security is uncertificated and the registered owner has been notified of the restriction.

Official Comment

1.   Restrictions on transfer of securities are imposed by issuers in a variety of circumstances and for a variety of purposes, such as to retain control of a close corporation or to ensure compliance with federal securities laws. Other law determines whether such restrictions are permissible. This section deals only with the consequences of failure to note the restriction on a security certificate.

This section imposes no bar to enforcement of a restriction on transfer against a person who has actual knowledge of it.

2.   A restriction on transfer of a certificated security is ineffective against a person without knowledge of the restriction unless the restriction is noted conspicuously on the certificate. The word "noted" is used to make clear that the restriction need not be set forth in full text. Refusal by an issuer to register a transfer on the basis of an unnoted restriction would be a violation of the issuer's duty to register under Section 8–401 [Duty of Issuer to Register Transfer].

3.   . . . A purchaser who takes delivery of a certificated security is entitled to rely on the terms stated on the certificate. That policy obviously does not apply to uncertificated securities. For uncertificated securities, this section requires only that the registered owner has been notified of the restriction. Suppose, for example, that A is the registered owner of an uncertificated security, and that the issuer has notified A of a restriction on transfer. A agrees to sell the security to B, in violation of the restriction. A completes a written instruction directing the issuer to register transfer to B, and B pays A for the security at the time A delivers the instruction to B. A does not inform B of the restriction, and B does not otherwise have notice or knowledge of it at the time B pays and receives the instruction. B presents the instruction to the issuer, but the issuer refuses to register the transfer on the grounds that it would violate the restriction. The issuer has complied with this section, because it did notify the registered owner A of the restriction. The issuer's refusal to register transfer is not wrongful. B has an action against A for breach of transfer warranty. . . . B's mistake was treating an uncertificated security transaction in the fashion appropriate only for a certificated security. The mechanism for transfer of uncertificated securities is registration of transfer on the books of the issuer; handing over an instruction only initiates the process. The purchaser should make arrangements to ensure that the price is not paid until it knows that the issuer has or will register transfer.

4.   In the indirect holding system, investors neither take physical delivery of security certificates nor have uncertificated securities registered in their names. So long as the requirements of this section have been satisfied at the level of the relationship between the issuer and the securities intermediary that is a direct holder, this section does not preclude the issuer from enforcing a restriction on transfer. . . .

5.   This section deals only with restrictions imposed by the issuer. Restrictions imposed by statute are not affected. See Quiner v. Marblehead Social Co., 10 Mass. 476 (1813); Madison Bank v. Price, 79 Kan. 289, 100 P. 280 (1909); Healey v. Steele Center Creamery Ass'n, 115 Minn. 451, 133 N.W. 69 (1911). Nor does it deal with private agreements between stockholders containing restrictive covenants as to the sale of the security.

FEDERAL RULES OF CIVIL PROCEDURE, RULES 11, 23, 23.1

TABLE OF CONTENTS

Rule		Page
11.	Signing of Pleadings, Motions, and Other Papers; Representations to Court; Sanctions	933
23.	Class Actions	934
23.1	Derivative Actions by Shareholders	938

Rule 11. Signing of Pleadings, Motions, and Other Papers; Representations to Court; Sanctions

(a) Signature. Every pleading, written motion, and other paper must be signed by at least one attorney of record in the attorney's name—or by a party personally if the party is unrepresented. The paper must state the signer's address, e-mail address, and telephone number. Unless a rule or statute specifically states otherwise, a pleading need not be verified or accompanied by an affidavit. The court must strike an unsigned paper unless the omission is promptly corrected after being called to the attorney's or party's attention.

(b) Representations to the Court. By presenting to the court a pleading, written motion, or other paper—whether by signing, filing, submitting, or later advocating it—an attorney or unrepresented party certifies that to the best of the person's knowledge, information, and belief, formed after an inquiry reasonable under the circumstances:

(1) it is not being presented for any improper purpose, such as to harass, cause unnecessary delay, or needlessly increase the cost of litigation;

(2) the claims, defenses, and other legal contentions are warranted by existing law or by a nonfrivolous argument for extending, modifying, or reversing existing law or for establishing new law;

(3) the factual contentions have evidentiary support or, if specifically so identified, will likely have evidentiary support after a reasonable opportunity for further investigation or discovery; and

(4) the denials of factual contentions are warranted on the evidence or, if specifically so identified, are reasonably based on belief or a lack of information.

(c) Sanctions.

(1) In General. If, after notice and a reasonable opportunity to respond, the court determines that Rule 11(b) has been violated, the court may impose an appropriate sanction on any attorney, law firm, or party that violated the rule or is responsible for the violation. Absent exceptional circumstances, a law firm must be held jointly responsible for a violation committed by its partner, associate, or employee.

(2) Motion for Sanctions. A motion for sanctions must be made separately from any other motion and must describe the specific conduct that allegedly violates Rule 11(b). The motion must be served under Rule 5, but it must not be filed or be presented to the court if the challenged paper, claim, defense, contention, or denial is withdrawn or appropriately corrected within 21 days after service or within another time the court sets. If warranted, the court may award to the prevailing party the reasonable expenses, including attorney's fees, incurred for the motion.

(3) On the Court's Initiative. On its own, the court may order an attorney, law firm, or party to show cause why conduct specifically described in the order has not violated Rule 11(b).

(4) Nature of a Sanction. A sanction imposed under this rule must be limited to what suffices to deter repetition of the conduct or comparable conduct by others similarly situated. The sanction may include nonmonetary directives; an order to pay a penalty into court; or, if imposed on motion and warranted for effective deterrence, an order directing payment to the movant of part or all of the reasonable attorney's fees and other expenses directly resulting from the violation.

(5) Limitations on Monetary Sanctions. The court must not impose a monetary sanction:

    (A) against a represented party for violating Rule 11(b)(2); or

    (B) on its own, unless it issued the show-cause order under Rule 11(c)(3) before voluntary dismissal or settlement of the claims made by or against the party that is, or whose attorneys are, to be sanctioned.

(6) Requirements for an Order. An order imposing a sanction must describe the sanctioned conduct and explain the basis for the sanction.

(d) Inapplicability to Discovery. This rule does not apply to disclosures and discovery requests, responses, objections, and motions under Rules 26 through 37.

Rule 23.   Class Actions

(a) Prerequisites. One or more members of a class may sue or be sued as representative parties on behalf of all members only if:

    (1) the class is so numerous that joinder of all members is impracticable;

    (2) there are questions of law or fact common to the class;

    (3) the claims or defenses of the representative parties are typical of the claims or defenses of the class; and

    (4) the representative parties will fairly and adequately protect the interests of the class.

(b) Types of Class Actions. A class action may be maintained if Rule 23(a) is satisfied and if:

    (1) prosecuting separate actions by or against individual class members would create a risk of:

        (A) inconsistent or varying adjudications with respect to individual class members that would establish incompatible standards of conduct for the party opposing the class; or

        (B) adjudications with respect to individual class members that, as a practical matter, would be dispositive of the interests of the other members not parties to the individual adjudications or would substantially impair or impede their ability to protect their interests;

    (2) the party opposing the class has acted or refused to act on grounds that apply generally to the class, so that final injunctive relief or corresponding declaratory relief is appropriate respecting the class as a whole; or

    (3) the court finds that the questions of law or fact common to class members predominate over any questions affecting only individual members, and that a class action is superior to other available methods for fairly and efficiently adjudicating the controversy. The matters pertinent to these findings include:

        (A) the class members' interests in individually controlling the prosecution or defense of separate actions;

        (B) the extent and nature of any litigation concerning the controversy already begun by or against class members;

        (C) the desirability or undesirability of concentrating the litigation of the claims in the particular forum; and

        (D) the likely difficulties in managing a class action.

(c) Certification Order; Notice to Class Members; Judgment; Issues Classes; Subclasses.

    (1) *Certification Order.*

        (A) Time to Issue. At an early practicable time after a person sues or is sued as a class representative, the court must determine by order whether to certify the action as a class action.

(B) *Defining the Class; Appointing Class Counsel.* An order that certifies a class action must define the class and the class claims, issues, or defenses, and must appoint class counsel under Rule 23(g).

(C) *Altering or Amending the Order.* An order that grants or denies class certification may be altered or amended before final judgment.

(2) *Notice.*

(A) *For (b)(1) or (b)(2) Classes.* For any class certified under Rule 23(b)(1) or (b)(2), the court may direct appropriate notice to the class.

(B) *For (b)(3) Classes.* For any class certified under Rule 23(b)(3)—or upon ordering notice under Rule 23(e)(1) to a class proposed to be certified for purposes of settlement under Rule 23(b)(3)—the court must direct to class members the best notice that is practicable under the circumstances, including individual notice to all members who can be identified through reasonable effort. The notice may be by one or more of the following: United States mail, electronic means, or other appropriate means. The notice must clearly and concisely state in plain, easily understood language:

(i) the nature of the action;

(ii) the definition of the class certified;

(iii) the class claims, issues, or defenses;

(iv) that a class member may enter an appearance through an attorney if the member so desires;

(v) that the court will exclude from the class any member who requests exclusion;

(vi) the time and manner for requesting exclusion; and

(vii) the binding effect of a class judgment on members under Rule 23(c)(3).

(3) *Judgment.* Whether or not favorable to the class, the judgment in a class action must:

(A) for any class certified under Rule 23(b)(1) or (b)(2), include and describe those whom the court finds to be class members; and

(B) for any class certified under Rule 23(b)(3), include and specify or describe those to whom the Rule 23(c)(2) notice was directed, who have not requested exclusion, and whom the court finds to be class members.

(4) *Particular Issues.* When appropriate, an action may be brought or maintained as a class action with respect to particular issues.

(5) *Subclasses.* When appropriate, a class may be divided into subclasses that are each treated as a class under this rule.

(d) Conducting the Action.

(1) *In General.* In conducting an action under this rule, the court may issue orders that:

(A) determine the course of proceedings or prescribe measures to prevent undue repetition or complication in presenting evidence or argument;

(B) require—to protect class members and fairly conduct the action—giving appropriate notice to some or all class members of:

(i) any step in the action;

(ii) the proposed extent of the judgment; or

(iii) the members' opportunity to signify whether they consider the representation fair and adequate, to intervene and present claims or defenses, or to otherwise come into the action;

(C) impose conditions on the representative parties or on intervenors;

(D) require that the pleadings be amended to eliminate allegations about representation of absent persons and that the action proceed accordingly; or

(E) deal with similar procedural matters.

(2) *Combining and Amending Orders.* An order under Rule 23(d)(1) may be altered or amended from time to time and may be combined with an order under Rule 16.

(e) Settlement, Voluntary Dismissal, or Compromise. The claims, issues, or defenses of a certified class—or a class proposed to be certified for purposes of settlement—may be settled, voluntarily dismissed, or compromised only with the court's approval. The following procedures apply to a proposed settlement, voluntary dismissal, or compromise:

(1) *Notice to the Class.*

(A) Information That Parties Must Provide to the Court. The parties must provide the court with information sufficient to enable it to determine whether to give notice of the proposal to the class.

(B) Grounds for a Decision to Give Notice. The court must direct notice in a reasonable manner to all class members who would be bound by the proposal if giving notice is justified by the parties' showing that the court will likely be able to:

(i) approve the proposal under Rule 23(e)(2); and

(ii) certify the class for purposes of judgment on the proposal.

(2) *Approval of the Proposal.* If the proposal would bind class members, the court may approve it only after a hearing and only on finding that it is fair, reasonable, and adequate after considering whether:

(A) the class representatives and class counsel have adequately represented the class;

(B) the proposal was negotiated at arm's length;

(C) the relief provided for the class is adequate, taking into account:

(i) the costs, risks, and delay of trial and appeal;

(ii) the effectiveness of any proposed method of distributing relief to the class, including the method of processing class-member claims;

(iii) the terms of any proposed award of attorney's fees, including timing of payment; and

(iv) any agreement required to be identified under Rule 23(e)(3); and

(D) the proposal treats class members equitably relative to each other.

(3) *Identifying Agreements.* The parties seeking approval must file a statement identifying any agreement made in connection with the proposal.

(4) *New Opportunity to Be Excluded.* If the class action was previously certified under Rule 23(b)(3), the court may refuse to approve a settlement unless it affords a new opportunity to request exclusion to individual class members who had an earlier opportunity to request exclusion but did not do so.

(5) *Class-Member Objections.*

(A) In General. Any class member may object to the proposal if it requires court approval under this subdivision (e). The objection must state whether it applies only to the objector, to a specific subset of the class, or to the entire class, and also state with specificity the grounds for the objection.

(B) Court Approval Required for Payment in Connection with an Objection. Unless approved by the court after a hearing, no payment or other consideration may be provided in connection with:

(i) forgoing or withdrawing an objection, or

(ii) forgoing, dismissing, or abandoning an appeal from a judgment approving the proposal.

(C) *Procedure for Approval After an Appeal.* If approval under Rule 23(e)(5)(B) has not been obtained before an appeal is docketed in the court of appeals, the procedure of Rule 62.1 applies while the appeal remains pending.

(f) Appeals. A court of appeals may permit an appeal from an order granting or denying class-action certification under this rule, but not from an order under Rule 23(e)(1). A party must file a petition for permission to appeal with the circuit clerk within 14 days after the order is entered or within 45 days after the order is entered if any party is the United States, a United States agency, or a United States officer or employee sued for an act or omission occurring in connection with duties performed on the United States' behalf. An appeal does not stay proceedings in the district court unless the district judge or the court of appeals so orders.

(g) Class Counsel.

(1) *Appointing Class Counsel.* Unless a statute provides otherwise, a court that certifies a class must appoint class counsel. In appointing class counsel, the court:

(A) must consider:

(i) the work counsel has done in identifying or investigating potential claims in the action;

(ii) counsel's experience in handling class actions, other complex litigation, and the types of claims asserted in the action;

(iii) counsel's knowledge of the applicable law; and

(iv) the resources that counsel will commit to representing the class;

(B) may consider any other matter pertinent to counsel's ability to fairly and adequately represent the interests of the class;

(C) may order potential class counsel to provide information on any subject pertinent to the appointment and to propose terms for attorney's fees and nontaxable costs;

(D) may include in the appointing order provisions about the award of attorney's fees or nontaxable costs under Rule 23(h); and

(E) may make further orders in connection with the appointment.

(2) *Standard for Appointing Class Counsel.* When one applicant seeks appointment as class counsel, the court may appoint that applicant only if the applicant is adequate under Rule 23(g)(1) and (4). If more than one adequate applicant seeks appointment, the court must appoint the applicant best able to represent the interests of the class.

(3) *Interim Counsel.* The court may designate interim counsel to act on behalf of a putative class before determining whether to certify the action as a class action.

(4) *Duty of Class Counsel.* Class counsel must fairly and adequately represent the interests of the class.

(h) Attorney's Fees and Nontaxable Costs. In a certified class action, the court may award reasonable attorney's fees and nontaxable costs that are authorized by law or by the parties' agreement. The following procedures apply:

(1) A claim for an award must be made by motion under Rule 54(d)(2), subject to the provisions of this subdivision (h), at a time the court sets. Notice of the motion must be served on all parties and, for motions by class counsel, directed to class members in a reasonable manner.

(2) A class member, or a party from whom payment is sought, may object to the motion.

(3) The court may hold a hearing and must find the facts and state its legal conclusions under Rule 52(a).

(4) The court may refer issues related to the amount of the award to a special master or a magistrate judge, as provided in Rule 54(d)(2)(D).

Rule 23.1   Derivative Actions by Shareholders

(a) Prerequisites. This rule applies when one or more shareholders or members of a corporation or an unincorporated association bring a derivative action to enforce a right that the corporation or association may properly assert but has failed to enforce. The derivative action may not be maintained if it appears that the plaintiff does not fairly and adequately represent the interests of shareholders or members who are similarly situated in enforcing the right of the corporation or association.

(b) Pleading Requirements. The complaint must be verified and must:

(1) allege that the plaintiff was a shareholder or member at the time of the transaction complained of, or that the plaintiff's share or membership later devolved on it by operation of law;

(2) allege that the action is not a collusive one to confer jurisdiction that the court would otherwise lack; and

(3) state with particularity:

   (A) any effort by the plaintiff to obtain the desired action from the directors or comparable authority and, if necessary, from the shareholders or members; and

   (B) the reasons for not obtaining the action or not making the effort.

(c) Settlement, Dismissal, and Compromise. A derivative action may be settled, voluntarily dismissed, or compromised only with the court's approval. Notice of a proposed settlement, voluntary dismissal, or compromise must be given to shareholders or members in the manner that the court orders.

UNIFORM FRAUDULENT TRANSFER ACT (SELECTED PROVISIONS)

TABLE OF CONTENTS

Sec.		Page
1.	Definitions	939
2.	Insolvency	940
4.	Transfers Fraudulent as to Present and Future Creditors	940
5.	Transfers Fraudulent as to Present Creditors	941
7.	Remedies of Creditors	941
8.	Defenses, Liability, and Protection of Transferee	941
9.	Extinguishment of [Claim for Relief] [Cause of Action]	941

---

§ 1. Definitions . . .

As used in this [Act]:

(1) "Affiliate" means:

(i) a person who directly or indirectly owns, controls, or holds with power to vote, 20 percent or more of the outstanding voting securities of the debtor, other than a person who holds the securities,

(A) as a fiduciary or agent without sole discretionary power to vote the securities; or

(B) solely to secure a debt, if the person has not exercised the power to vote;

(ii) a corporation 20 percent or more of whose outstanding voting securities are directly or indirectly owned, controlled, or held with power to vote, by the debtor or a person who directly or indirectly owns, controls, or holds, with power to vote, 20 percent or more of the outstanding voting securities of the debtor, other than a person who holds the securities,

(A) as a fiduciary or agent without sole power to vote the securities; or

(B) solely to secure a debt, if the person has not in fact exercised the power to vote;

(iii) a person whose business is operated by the debtor under a lease or other agreement, or a person substantially all of whose assets are controlled by the debtor; or

(iv) a person who operates the debtor's business under a lease or other agreement or controls substantially all of the debtor's assets. . . .

(7) "Insider" includes . . .

(ii) if the debtor is a corporation,

(A) a director of the debtor;

(B) an officer of the debtor;

(C) a person in control of the debtor;

(D) a partnership in which the debtor is a general partner;

(E) a general partner in a partnership described in clause (D); or

(F) a relative of a general partner, director, officer, or person in control of the debtor;

(iii) if the debtor is a partnership,

(A) a general partner in the debtor;

939

(B) a relative of a general partner in, a general partner of, or a person in control of the debtor;

(C) another partnership in which the debtor is a general partner;

(D) a general partner in a partnership described in clause (C); or

(E) a person in control of the debtor;

(iv) an affiliate, or an insider of an affiliate as if the affiliate were the debtor; and

(v) a managing agent of the debtor. . . .

(12) "Transfer" means every mode, direct or indirect, absolute or conditional, voluntary or involuntary, of disposing of or parting with an asset or an interest in an asset, and includes payment of money, release, lease, and creation of a lien or other encumbrance.

§ 2. Insolvency

(a) A debtor is insolvent if the sum of the debtor's debts is greater than all of the debtor's assets at a fair valuation. . . .

(b) A debtor who is generally not paying his [or her] debts as they become due is presumed to be insolvent.

(c) A partnership is insolvent under subsection (a) if the sum of the partnership's debts is greater than the aggregate, at a fair valuation, of all of the partnership's assets and the sum of the excess of the value of each general partner's nonpartnership assets over the partner's nonpartnership debts. . . .

§ 4. Transfers Fraudulent as to Present and Future Creditors

(a) A transfer made or obligation incurred by a debtor is fraudulent as to a creditor, whether the creditor's claim arose before or after the transfer was made or the obligation was incurred, if the debtor made the transfer or incurred the obligation:

(1) with actual intent to hinder, delay, or defraud any creditor of the debtor; or

(2) without receiving a reasonably equivalent value in exchange for the transfer or obligation, and the debtor:

(i) was engaged or was about to engage in a business or a transaction for which the remaining assets of the debtor were unreasonably small in relation to the business or transaction; or

(ii) intended to incur, or believed or reasonably should have believed that he [or she] would incur, debts beyond his [or her] ability to pay as they became due.

(b) In determining actual intent under subsection (a)(1), consideration may be given, among other factors, to whether:

(1) the transfer or obligation was to an insider;

(2) the debtor retained possession or control of the property transferred after the transfer; . . .

(8) the value of the consideration received by the debtor was reasonably equivalent to the value of the asset transferred or the amount of the obligation incurred;

(9) the debtor was insolvent or became insolvent shortly after the transfer was made or the obligation was incurred;

(10) the transfer occurred shortly before or shortly after a substantial debt was incurred; and

(11) the debtor transferred the essential assets of the business to a lienor who transferred the assets to an insider of the debtor.

§ 5. Transfers Fraudulent as to Present Creditors

(a) A transfer made or obligation incurred by a debtor is fraudulent as to a creditor whose claim arose before the transfer was made or the obligation was incurred if the debtor made the transfer or incurred the obligation without receiving a reasonably equivalent value in exchange for the transfer or obligation and the debtor was insolvent at that time or the debtor became insolvent as a result of the transfer or obligation.

(b) A transfer made by a debtor is fraudulent as to a creditor whose claim arose before the transfer was made if the transfer was made to an insider for an antecedent debt, the debtor was insolvent at that time, and the insider had reasonable cause to believe that the debtor was insolvent.

§ 7. Remedies of Creditors

(a) In an action for relief against a transfer or obligation under this [Act], a creditor . . . may obtain:

(1) avoidance of the transfer or obligation to the extent necessary to satisfy the creditor's claim . . .

. . .

(3) subject to applicable principles of equity and in accordance with applicable rules of civil procedure,

(i) an injunction against further disposition by the debtor or a transferee, or both, of the asset transferred or of other property;

(ii) appointment of a receiver to take charge of the asset transferred or of other property of the transferee; or

(iii) any other relief the circumstances may require.

(b) If a creditor has obtained a judgment on a claim against the debtor, the creditor, if the court so orders, may levy execution on the asset transferred or its proceeds.

§ 8. Defenses, Liability, and Protection of Transferee

(a) A transfer or obligation is not voidable under Section 4(a)(1) against a person who took in good faith and for a reasonably equivalent value or against any subsequent transferee or obligee.

(b) Except as otherwise provided in this section, to the extent a transfer is voidable in an action by a creditor under Section 7(a)(1), the creditor may recover judgment for the value of the asset transferred [at the time of the transfer, subject to adjustment as the equities may require], or the amount necessary to satisfy the creditor's claim, whichever is less. The judgment may be entered against:

(1) the first transferee of the asset or the person for whose benefit the transfer was made; or

(2) any subsequent transferee other than a good faith transferee who took for value or from any subsequent transferee. . . .

(d) Notwithstanding voidability of a transfer or an obligation under this [Act], a good-faith transferee or obligee is entitled, to the extent of the value given the debtor for the transfer or obligation, to

(1) a lien on or a right to retain any interest in the asset transferred;

(2) enforcement of any obligation incurred; or

(3) a reduction in the amount of the liability on the judgment. . . .

§ 9. Extinguishment of [Claim for Relief] [Cause of Action]

A [claim for relief] [cause of action] with respect to a fraudulent transfer or obligation under this [Act] is extinguished unless action is brought. . . .

(b) under Section 4(a)(2) or 5(a), within 4 years after the transfer was made or the obligation was incurred. . . .

BANKRUPTCY CODE
11 U.S.C.A. §§ 101(32), 548(a)

TABLE OF CONTENTS

Sec.		Page
101.	Definitions	943
548.	Fraudulent Transfers and Obligations	943

§ 101.   Definitions . . .

(32) "insolvent" means—

(A) with reference to an entity other than a partnership . . . financial condition such that the sum of such entity's debts is greater than all of such entity's property, at a fair valuation. . . .

Historical and Revision Notes

The definition of "insolvent" is . . . the traditional bankruptcy balance sheet test of insolvency.

§ 548.   Fraudulent Transfers and Obligations

(a)(1) The trustee [in bankruptcy] may avoid any transfer (including any transfer to or for the benefit of an insider under an employment contract) of an interest of the debtor in property, or any obligation (including any obligation to or for the benefit of an insider under an employment contract) incurred by the debtor, that was made or incurred on or within two years before the date of the filing of the petition, if the debtor voluntarily or involuntarily—

(A) made such transfer or incurred such obligation with actual intent to hinder, delay, or defraud any entity to which the debtor was or became, on or after the date that such transfer was made or such obligation was incurred, indebted; or

(B)(i) received less than a reasonably equivalent value in exchange for such transfer or obligation; and

(B)(ii)(I) was insolvent on the date that such transfer was made or such obligation was incurred, or became insolvent as a result of such transfer or obligation;

(II) was engaged in business or a transaction, or was about to engage in business or a transaction, for which any property remaining with the debtor was an unreasonably small capital;

(III) intended to incur, or believed that the debtor would incur, debts that would be beyond the debtor's ability to pay as such debts matured; or

(IV) made such transfer to or for the benefit of an insider, or incurred such obligation to or for the benefit of an insider, under an employment contract and not in the ordinary course of business.

NEW YORK STOCK EXCHANGE LISTED
COMPANY MANUAL (EXCERPTS)

TABLE OF CONTENTS

Para.		Page
202.01	Internal Handling of Confidential Corporate Matters	945
202.02	Relationship Between Company Officials and Others	946
202.03	Dealing With Rumors or Unusual Market Activity	946
202.04	Exchange Market Surveillance	947
202.05	Timely Disclosure of Material News Developments	947
202.06	Procedure for Public Release of Information; Trading Halts	947
302.00	Annual Meetings	948
303A.	Corporate Governance Standards	948
303A.00	Introduction	948
303A.01	Independent Directors	948
303A.02	Independence Tests	948
303A.03	Executive Sessions	950
303A.04	Nominating/Corporate Governance Committee	951
303A.05	Compensation Committee	952
303A.06	Audit Committee	953
303A.07	Audit Committee Additional Requirements	954
303A.08	Shareholder Approval of Equity Compensation Plans	956
303A.09	Corporate Governance Guidelines	959
303A.10	Code of Business Conduct and Ethics	960
303A.11	Foreign Private Issuer Disclosure	961
303A.12	Certification Requirements	961
303A.13	Public Reprimand Letter	962
304.00	Classified Boards of Directors	962
312.00	Shareholder Approval Policy	962
312.03	Shareholder Approval	962
312.04	For the Purpose of Para. 312.03	963
312.05	Exceptions	964
312.07	Where Shareholder	965
313.00	Voting Rights	965

¶ 202.01   Internal Handling of Confidential Corporate Matters

Unusual market activity or a substantial price change has on occasion occurred in a company's securities shortly before the announcement of an important corporate action or development. Such incidents are extremely embarrassing and damaging to both the company and the Exchange since the public may quickly conclude that someone acted on the basis of inside information.

Negotiations leading to mergers and acquisitions, stock splits, the making of arrangements preparatory to an exchange or tender offer, changes in dividend rates or earnings, calls for redemption, and new contracts, products, or discoveries are the type of developments where the risk of untimely and inadvertent disclosure of corporate plans are most likely to occur. Frequently, these matters require extensive discussion and study by corporate officials before final decisions can be made. Accordingly, extreme care must be used in order to keep the information on a confidential basis.

Where it is possible to confine formal or informal discussions to a small group of the top management of the company or companies involved, and their individual confidential advisors where adequate security can be maintained, premature public announcement may properly be avoided. In this regard, the market action of a company's securities should be closely watched at a time when consideration is being given to important corporate matters. If unusual market activity should arise, the company should be prepared to make an immediate public announcement of the matter.

At some point it usually becomes necessary to involve other persons to conduct preliminary studies or assist in other preparations for contemplated transactions, e.g., business appraisals, tentative financing arrangements, attitude of large outside holders, availability of major blocks of stock, engineering studies and market analyses and surveys. Experience has shown that maintaining security at this point is virtually impossible. Accordingly, fairness requires that the company make an immediate public announcement as soon as disclosures relating to such important matters are made to outsiders.

The extent of the disclosures will depend upon the stage of discussions, studies, or negotiations. So far as possible, public statements should be definite as to price, ratio, timing and/or any other pertinent information necessary to permit a reasonable evaluation of the matter. As a minimum, they should include those disclosures made to outsiders. Where an initial announcement cannot be specific or complete, it will need to be supplemented from time to time as more definitive or different terms are discussed or determined.

Corporate employees, as well as directors and officers, should be regularly reminded as a matter of policy that they must not disclose confidential information they may receive in the course of their duties and must not attempt to take advantage of such information themselves.

In view of the importance of this matter and the potential difficulties involved, the Exchange suggests that a periodic review be made by each company of the manner in which confidential information is being handled within its own organization. A reminder notice of the company's policy to those in sensitive areas might also be helpful.

A sound corporate disclosure policy is essential to the maintenance of a fair and orderly securities market. It should minimize the occasions where the Exchange finds it necessary to temporarily halt trading in a security due to information leaks or rumors in connection with significant corporate transactions.

While the procedures are directed primarily at situations involving two or more companies, they are equally applicable to major corporate developments involving a single company.

¶ 202.02   Relationship Between Company Officials and Others

(A) Security Analysts, Institutional Investors, Etc.

Security analysts play an increasingly important role in the evaluation and interpretation of the financial affairs of listed companies. Annual reports, quarterly reports, and interim releases cannot by their nature provide all of the financial and statistical data that should be available to the investing public. The Exchange recommends that companies observe an "open door" policy in their relations with security analysts, financial writers, shareholders, and others who have legitimate investment interest in the company's affairs.

A company should not give information to one inquirer which it would not give to another, nor should it reveal information it would not willingly give or has not given to the press for publication. Thus, for companies to give advance earnings, dividend, stock split, merger, or tender information to analysts, whether representing an institution, brokerage house, investment advisor, large shareholder, or anyone else, would clearly violate Exchange policy. On the other hand, it should not withhold information in which analysts or other members of the investment public have a warrantable interest.

If during the course of a discussion with analysts substantive material not previously published is disclosed, that material should be simultaneously released to the public. The various security analysts societies usually have a regular procedure to be followed where formal presentations are made. The company should follow these same precautions when dealing with groups of industry analysts in small or closed meetings. . . .

¶ 202.03   Dealing With Rumors or Unusual Market Activity

The market activity of a company's securities should be closely watched at a time when consideration is being given to significant corporate matters. If rumors or unusual market activity indicate that information on impending developments has leaked out, a frank and explicit announcement is clearly required. If rumors are in fact false or inaccurate, they should be promptly denied or clarified. A statement to the effect that the company knows of no corporate developments to account for the unusual market activity can have a salutary effect. It is obvious that if such a public statement is contemplated, management should be checked prior to any public comment so as to avoid any embarrassment or potential criticism. If rumors are correct or there are developments, an immediate candid statement to the public as to the state of negotiations or of development of corporate plans in the rumored area must be made directly and openly. Such statements are essential despite the business inconvenience which may be caused and even though the matter may not as yet have been presented to the company's Board of Directors for consideration.

The Exchange recommends that its listed companies contact their Exchange representative if they become aware of rumors circulating about their company. Exchange Rule 435 provides that no member, member organization or allied member shall circulate in any manner rumors of a sensational character which might reasonably be expected to affect market conditions on the Exchange. Information provided concerning rumors will be promptly investigated.

¶ 202.04   Exchange Market Surveillance

The Exchange maintains a continuous market surveillance program through its Market Surveillance and Evaluation Division. An "on-line" computer system has been developed which monitors the price movement of every listed stock—on a trade-to-trade basis—throughout the trading session. The program is designed to closely review the markets in those securities in which unusual price and volume changes occur or where there is a large unexplained influx of buy or sell orders. If the price movement of a stock exceeds a predetermined guideline, it is immediately "flagged" and review of the situation is immediately undertaken to seek the causes of the exceptional activity. Under these circumstances, the company may be called by its Exchange representative to inquire about any company developments which have not been publicly announced but which could be responsible for unusual market activity. Where the market appears to reflect undisclosed information, the company will normally be requested to make the information public immediately. Occasionally it may be necessary to carry out a review of the trading after the fact, and the Exchange may request such information from the company as may be necessary to complete the inquiry.

The Listing Agreement provides that a company must furnish the Exchange with such information concerning the company as the Exchange may reasonably require. . . .

¶ 202.05   Timely Disclosure of Material News Developments

A listed company is expected to release quickly to the public any news or information which might reasonably be expected to materially affect the market for its securities. This is one of the most important and fundamental purposes of the listing agreement which the company enters into with the Exchange.

A listed company should also act promptly to dispel unfounded rumors which result in unusual market activity or price variations. . . .

¶ 202.06   Procedure for Public Release of Information; Trading Halts

(A) Immediate Release Policy

Information required to be released quickly to the public under Section 202.05 above should be disclosed by means of any Regulation FD compliant method (or combination of methods). While foreign private issuers are not required to comply with Regulation FD, foreign private issuers must comply with the timely alert policy set forth in Section 202.05 and may do so by any method (or combination of methods) that would constitute compliance with Regulation FD for a domestic U.S. issuer. While not requiring them to do so, the Exchange encourages listed companies to comply with the immediate release policy by issuing press releases.

The spirit of the immediate release policy is not considered to be violated on weekends where a "Hold for Sunday or Monday A.M.'s" is used to obtain a broad public release of the news. This procedure facilitates the combination of a press release with a mailing to shareholders.

Annual and quarterly earnings, dividend announcements, mergers, acquisitions, tender offers, stock splits, major management changes, and any substantive items of unusual or non-recurrent nature are examples of news items that should be handled on an immediate release basis. News of major new products, contract awards, expansion plans, and discoveries very often fall into the same category. Unfavorable news should be reported as promptly and candidly as favorable news. Reluctance or unwillingness to release a negative story or an attempt to disguise unfavorable news endangers management's reputation for integrity. Changes in accounting methods to mask such occurrences can have a similar impact. . . .

¶ 302.00   Annual Meetings

Listed companies are required to hold an annual shareholders' meeting during each fiscal year.

¶ 303A.   Corporate Governance Standards . . .

¶ 303A.00 Introduction

General Application

Companies listed on the Exchange must comply with certain standards regarding corporate governance as codified in this Section 303A. Consistent with the NYSE's traditional approach, as well as the requirements of the Sarbanes-Oxley Act of 2002, certain provisions of Section 303A are applicable to some listed companies but not to others.

Equity Listings

Section 303A applies in full to all companies listing common equity securities, with the following exceptions:

Controlled Companies

A listed company of which more than 50% of the voting power for the election of directors is held by an individual, a group or another company is not required to comply with the requirements of Sections 303A.01, 303A.04 or 303A.05. Controlled companies must comply with the remaining provisions of Section 303A.

Disclosure Requirement

A controlled company that chooses to take advantage of any or all of these exemptions must comply with the disclosure requirements set forth in Instruction 1 to Item 407(a) of Regulation S–K.

Limited Partnerships and Companies in Bankruptcy

Due to their unique attributes, limited partnerships and companies in bankruptcy proceedings are not required to comply with the requirements of Sections 303A.01, 303A.04 or 303A.05. However, all limited partnerships (at the general partner level) and companies in bankruptcy proceedings must comply with the remaining provisions of Section 303A. . . .

¶ 303A.01 Independent Directors

Listed companies must have a majority of independent directors.

Commentary: Effective boards of directors exercise independent judgment in carrying out their responsibilities. Requiring a majority of independent directors will increase the quality of board oversight and lessen the possibility of damaging conflicts of interest.

¶ 303A.02 Independence Tests

In order to tighten the definition of "independent director" for purposes of these standards:

(a)(i) No director qualifies as "independent" unless the board of directors affirmatively determines that the director has no material relationship with the listed company (either directly or as a partner, shareholder or officer of an organization that has a relationship with the company).

(ii) In addition, in affirmatively determining the independence of any director who will serve on the compensation committee of the listed company's board of directors, the board of directors must consider all factors specifically relevant to determining whether a director has a relationship to the listed company which is material to that director's ability to be independent from management in connection with the duties of a compensation committee member, including, but not limited to:

(A) the source of compensation of such director, including any consulting, advisory or other compensatory fee paid by the listed company to such director; and

(B) whether such director is affiliated with the listed company, a subsidiary of the listed company or an affiliate of a subsidiary of the listed company.

Commentary: It is not possible to anticipate, or explicitly to provide for, all circumstances that might signal potential conflicts of interest, or that might bear on the materiality of a director's relationship to a listed company (references to "listed company" would include any parent or subsidiary in a consolidated group with the listed company). Accordingly, it is best that boards making "independence" determinations broadly consider all relevant facts and circumstances. In particular, when assessing the materiality of a director's relationship with the listed company, the board should consider the issue not merely from the standpoint of the director, but also from that of persons or organizations with which the director has an affiliation. Material relationships can include commercial, industrial, banking, consulting, legal, accounting, charitable and familial relationships, among others. However, as the concern is independence from management, the Exchange does not view ownership of even a significant amount of stock, by itself, as a bar to an independence finding.

When considering the sources of a director's compensation in determining his independence for purposes of compensation committee service, the board should consider whether the director receives compensation from any person or entity that would impair his ability to make independent judgments about the listed company's executive compensation. Similarly, when considering any affiliate relationship a director has with the company, a subsidiary of the company, or an affiliate of a subsidiary of the company, in determining his independence for purposes of compensation committee service, the board should consider whether the affiliate relationship places the director under the direct or indirect control of the listed company or its senior management, or creates a direct relationship between the director and members of senior management, in each case of a nature that would impair his ability to make independent judgments about the listed company's executive compensation.

Disclosure Requirement: The listed company must comply with the disclosure requirements set forth in Item 407(a) of Regulation S–K.

(b) In addition, a director is not independent if:

(i) The director is, or has been within the last three years, an employee of the listed company, or an immediate family member is, or has been within the last three years, an executive officer, 1 of the listed company.

Commentary: Employment as an interim Chairman or CEO or other executive officer shall not disqualify a director from being considered independent following that employment.

(ii) The director has received, or has an immediate family member who has received, during any twelve-month period within the last three years, more than $120,000 in direct compensation from the listed company, other than director and committee fees and pension or other forms of deferred compensation for prior service (provided such compensation is not contingent in any way on continued service).

Commentary: Compensation received by a director for former service as an interim Chairman or CEO or other executive officer need not be considered in determining independence under this test. Compensation received by an immediate family member for service as an employee of the listed company (other than an executive officer) need not be considered in determining independence under this test.

(iii) (A) The director is a current partner or employee of a firm that is the listed company's internal or external auditor; (B) the director has an immediate family member who is a current partner of such a firm; (C) the director has an immediate family member who is a current employee of such a firm and personally works on the listed company's audit; or (D) the director or an immediate family member was within the last three years a partner or employee of such a firm and personally worked on the listed company's audit within that time.

(iv) The director or an immediate family member is, or has been with the last three years, employed as an executive officer of another company where any of the listed company's present executive officers at the same time serves or served on that company's compensation committee.

(v) The director is a current employee, or an immediate family member is a current executive officer, of a company that has made payments to, or received payments from, the listed company for property or services in an amount which, in any of the last three fiscal years, exceeds the greater of $1 million, or 2% of such other company's consolidated gross revenues.

Commentary: In applying the test in Section 303A.02(b)(v), both the payments and the consolidated gross revenues to be measured shall be those reported in the last completed fiscal year of such other company. The look-back provision for this test applies solely to the financial relationship between the listed company and the director or immediate family member's current employer; a listed company need not consider former employment of the director or immediate family member.

Disclosure Requirement: Contributions to tax exempt organizations shall not be considered payments for purposes of Section 303A.02(b)(v), provided however that a listed company shall disclose either on or through its website or in its annual proxy statement, or if the listed company does not file an annual proxy statement, in the listed company's annual report on Form 10-K filed with the SEC, any such contributions made by the listed company to any tax exempt organization in which any independent director serves as an executive officer if, within the preceding three years, contributions in any single fiscal year from the listed company to the organization exceeded the greater of $1 million, or 2% of such tax exempt organization's consolidated gross revenues. If this disclosure is made on or through the listed company's website, the listed company must disclose that fact in its annual proxy statement or annual report, as applicable, and provide the website address. Listed company boards are reminded of their obligations to consider the materiality of any such relationship in accordance with Section 303A.02(a) above.

General Commentary to Section 303A.02(b): An "immediate family member" includes a person's spouse, parents, children, siblings, mothers and fathers-in-law, sons and daughters-in-law, brothers and sisters-in-law, and anyone (other than domestic employees) who shares such person's home. When applying the look-back provisions in Section 303A.02(b), listed companies need not consider individuals who are no longer immediate family members as a result of legal separation or divorce, or those who have died or become incapacitated.

In addition, references to the "listed company" or "company" include any parent or subsidiary in a consolidated group with the listed company or such other company as is relevant to any determination under the independent standards set forth in this Section 303A.02(b).[1]

¶ 303A.03 Executive Sessions

To empower non-management directors to serve as a more effective check on management, the non-management directors of each listed company must meet at regularly scheduled executive sessions without management.

Commentary: To promote open discussion among the non-management directors, companies must schedule regular executive sessions in which those directors meet without management participation. "Non-management" directors are all those who are not executive officers, and includes such directors who are not independent by virtue of a material relationship, former status or family membership, or for any other reason.

Regular scheduling of such meetings is important not only to foster better communication among non-management directors, but also to prevent any negative inference from attaching to the calling of executive sessions. A non-management director must preside over each executive session, although the same director is not required to preside at all executive sessions. . . .

While this Section 303A.03 refers to meetings of non-management directors, listed companies may instead choose to hold regular executive sessions of independent directors only. An independent

---

[1] For purposes of Section 303A, the term "executive officer" has the same meaning specified for the term "officer" in Rule 16a–1(f) under the Securities Exchange Act of 1934.

director must preside over each executive session of the independent directors, although the same director is not required to preside at all executive sessions of the independent directors.

If a listed company chooses to hold regular meetings of all non-management directors, such listed company should hold an executive session including only independent directors at least once a year.

Disclosure Requirements: If one director is chosen to preside at all of these executive sessions, his or her name must be disclosed either on or through the listed company's website or in its annual proxy statement or, if the listed company does not file an annual proxy statement, in its annual report on Form 10-K filed with the SEC. If this disclosure is made on or through the listed company's website, the listed company must disclose that fact in its annual proxy statement or annual report, as applicable, and provide the website address. Alternatively, if the same individual is not the presiding director at every meeting, a listed company must disclose the procedure by which a presiding director is selected for each executive session. For example, a listed company may wish to rotate the presiding position among the chairs of board committees.

In order that all interested parties (not just shareholders) may be able to make their concerns known to the non-management or independent directors, a listed company must also disclose a method for such parties to communicate directly with the presiding director or with those directors as a group either on or through the listed company's website or in its annual proxy statement or, if the listed company does not file an annual proxy statement, in its annual report on Form 10-K filed with the SEC. If this disclosure is made on or through the listed company's website, the listed company must disclose that fact in its annual proxy statement or annual report, as applicable, and provide the website address. Companies may, if they wish, utilize for this purpose the same procedures they have established to comply with the requirement of Rule 10A–3(b)(3) under the Exchange Act regarding complaints to the audit committee, as applied to listed companies through Section 303A.06.

¶ 303A.04 Nominating/Corporate Governance Committee

(a) Listed companies must have a nominating/corporate governance committee composed entirely of independent directors.

(b) The nominating/corporate governance committee must have a written charter that addresses:

(i) the committee's purpose and responsibilities—which, at minimum, must be to: identify individuals qualified to become board members, consistent with criteria approved by the board, and to select, or to recommend that the board select, the director nominees for the next annual meeting of shareholders; develop and recommend to the board a set of corporate governance guidelines applicable to the corporation; and oversee the evaluation of the board and management; and

(ii) an annual performance evaluation of the committee.

Commentary: A nominating/corporate governance committee is central to the effective functioning of the board. New director and board committee nominations are among a board's most important functions. Placing this responsibility in the hands of an independent nominating/corporate governance committee can enhance the independence and quality of nominees. The committee is also responsible for taking a leadership role in shaping the corporate governance of a corporation.

If a listed company is legally required by contract or otherwise to provide third parties with the ability to nominate directors (for example, preferred stock rights to elect directors upon a dividend default, shareholder agreements, and management agreements), the selection and nomination of such directors need not be subject to the nominating committee process.

The nominating/corporate governance committee charter should also address the following items: committee member qualifications; committee member appointment and removal; committee structure and operations (including authority to delegate to subcommittees); and committee reporting to the board. In addition, the charter should give the nominating/corporate governance committee sole authority to retain and terminate any search firm to be used to identify director candidates, including sole authority to approve the search firm's fees and other retention terms.

Boards may allocate the responsibilities of the nominating/corporate governance committee to committees of their own denomination, provided that the committees are composed entirely of independent directors. Any such committee must have a committee charter.

Website Posting Requirement: A listed company must make its nominating/corporate governance committee charter available on or through its website. . . .

¶ 303A.05 Compensation Committee

(a) Listed companies must have a compensation committee composed entirely of independent directors. Compensation committee members must satisfy the additional independence requirements specific to compensation committee membership set forth in Section 303A.02(a)(ii).

(b) The compensation committee must have a written charter that addresses:

(i) the committee's purpose and responsibilities—which, at minimum, must be to have direct responsibility to:

(A) review and approve corporate goals and objectives relevant to CEO compensation, evaluate the CEO's performance in light of those goals and objectives, and, either as a committee or together with the other independent directors (as directed by the board), determine and approve the CEO's compensation level based on this evaluation;

(B) make recommendations to the board with respect to non-CEO executive officer compensation, and incentive-compensation and equity-based plans that are subject to board approval; and

(C) prepare the disclosure required by Item 407(e)(5) of Regulation S–K;

(ii) an annual performance evaluation of the compensation committee.

(iii) The rights and responsibilities of the compensation committee set forth in Section 303A.05(c).

Commentary: In determining the long-term incentive component of CEO compensation, the committee should consider the listed company's performance and relative shareholder return, the value of similar incentive awards to CEOs at comparable companies, and the awards given to the listed company's CEO in past years. To avoid confusion, note that the compensation committee is not precluded from approving awards (with or without ratification of the board) as may be required to comply with applicable tax laws (i.e., Rule 162(m)). Note also that nothing in Section 303A.05(b)(i)(B) is intended to preclude the board from delegating its authority over such matters to the compensation committee.

The compensation committee charter should also address the following items: committee member qualifications; committee member appointment and removal; committee structure and operations (including authority to delegate to subcommittees); and committee reporting to the board.

Boards may allocate the responsibilities of the compensation committee to committees of their own denomination, provided that the committees are composed entirely of independent directors. Any such committee must have a committee charter.

Nothing in this provision should be construed as precluding discussion of CEO compensation with the board generally, as it is not the intent of this standard to impair communication among members of the board.

Website Posting Requirement: A listed company must make its compensation committee charter available on or through its website. If any function of the compensation committee has been delegated to another committee, the charter of that committee must also be made available on or through the listed company's website.

Disclosure Requirements: A listed company must disclose in its annual proxy statement or, if it does not file an annual proxy statement, in its annual report on Form 10-K filed with the SEC that its compensation committee charter is available on or through its website and provide the website address.

(c)(i) The compensation committee may, in its sole discretion, retain or obtain the advice of a compensation consultant, independent legal counsel or other adviser.

(ii) The compensation committee shall be directly responsible for the appointment, compensation and oversight of the work of any compensation consultant, independent legal counsel or other adviser retained by the compensation committee.

(iii) The listed company must provide for appropriate funding, as determined by the compensation committee, for payment of reasonable compensation to a compensation consultant, independent legal counsel or any other adviser retained by the compensation committee.

(iv) The compensation committee may select a compensation consultant, legal counsel or other adviser to the compensation committee only after taking into consideration, all factors relevant to that person's independence from management, including the following:

(A) The provision of other services to the listed company by the person that employs the compensation consultant, legal counsel or other adviser;

(B) The amount of fees received from the listed company by the person that employs the compensation consultant, legal counsel or other adviser, as a percentage of the total revenue of the person that employs the compensation consultant, legal counsel or other adviser;

(C) The policies and procedures of the person that employs the compensation consultant, legal counsel or other adviser that are designed to prevent conflicts of interest;

(D) Any business or personal relationship of the compensation consultant, legal counsel or other adviser with a member of the compensation committee;

(E) Any stock of the listed company owned by the compensation consultant, legal counsel or other adviser; and

(F) Any business or personal relationship of the compensation consultant, legal counsel, other adviser or the person employing the adviser with an executive officer of the listed company.

Commentary: Nothing in this Section 303A.05(c) shall be construed: (A) to require the compensation committee to implement or act consistently with the advice or recommendations of the compensation consultant, independent legal counsel or other adviser to the compensation committee; or (B) to affect the ability or obligation of the compensation committee to exercise its own judgment in fulfillment of the duties of the compensation committee.

The compensation committee is required to conduct the independence assessment outlined in Section 303A.05(c)(iv) with respect to any compensation consultant, legal counsel or other adviser that provides advice to the compensation committee, other than (i) in-house legal counsel; and (ii) any compensation consultant, legal counsel or other adviser whose role is limited to the following activities for which no disclosure would be required under Item 407(e)(3)(iii) of Regulation S–K: consulting on any broad-based plan that does not discriminate in scope, terms, or operation, in favor of executive officers or directors of the listed company, and that is available generally to all salaried employees; or providing information that either is not customized for a particular company or that is customized based on parameters that are not developed by the compensation consultant, and about which the compensation consultant does not provide.

Nothing in this Section 303A.05(c) requires a compensation consultant, legal counsel or other compensation adviser to be independent, only that the compensation committee consider the enumerated independence factors before selecting or receiving advice from a compensation adviser. The compensation committee may select or receive advice from any compensation adviser they prefer including ones that are not independent, after considering the six independence factors outlined in Section 303A.05(c)(iv)(A)–(F).

¶ 303A.06 Audit Committee

Listed companies must have an audit committee that satisfies the requirements of Rule 10A–3 under the Exchange Act. . . .

¶ 303A.07   Audit Committee Additional Requirements

(a) The audit committee must have a minimum of three members. All audit committee members must satisfy the requirements for independence set out in Section 303A.02 and, in the absence of an applicable exemption, Rule 10A–3(b)(1).

Commentary: Each member of the audit committee must be financially literate, as such qualification is interpreted by the listed company's board in its business judgment, or must become financially literate within a reasonable period of time after his or her appointment to the audit committee. In addition, at least one member of the audit committee must have accounting or related financial management expertise, as the listed company's board interprets such qualification in its business judgment. While the Exchange does not require that a listed company's audit committee include a person who satisfies the definition of audit committee financial expert set out in Item 407(d)(5)(ii) of Regulation S–K, a board may presume that such a person has accounting or related financial management expertise.

Because of the audit committee's demanding role and responsibilities, and the time commitment attendant to committee membership, each prospective audit committee member should evaluate carefully the existing demands on his or her time before accepting this important assignment.

Disclosure Requirement: If an audit committee member simultaneously serves on the audit committees of more than three public companies, the board must determine that such simultaneous service would not impair the ability of such member to effectively serve on the listed company's audit committee and must disclose such determination either on or through the listed company's website or in its annual proxy statement or, if the listed company does not file an annual proxy statement, in its annual report on Form 10-K filed with the SEC. . . .

(c) The audit committee must have a written charter that addresses:

(i) the committee's purpose—which, at minimum, must be to:

(A) assist board oversight of (1) the integrity of the listed company's financial statements, (2) the listed company's compliance with legal and regulatory requirements, (3) the independent auditor's qualifications and independence, and (4) the performance of the listed company's internal audit function and independent auditors; and

(B) prepare the disclosure required by Item 407(d)(3)(i) of Regulation S–K;

(ii) an annual performance evaluation of the audit committee; and

(iii) the duties and responsibilities of the audit committee—which, at a minimum, must include those set out in Rule 10A–3(b)(2), (3), (4) and (5) of the Exchange Act, as well as to:

(A) at least annually, obtain and review a report by the independent auditor describing: the firm's internal quality-control procedures; any material issues raised by the most recent internal quality-control review, or peer review, of the firm, or by any inquiry or investigation by governmental or professional authorities, within the preceding five years, respecting one or more independent audits carried out by the firm, and any steps taken to deal with any such issues; and (to assess the auditor's independence) all relationships between the independent auditor and the listed company;

Commentary: After reviewing the foregoing report and the independent auditor's work throughout the year, the audit committee will be in a position to evaluate the auditor's qualifications, performance and independence. This evaluation should include the review and evaluation of the lead partner of the independent auditor. In making its evaluation, the audit committee should take into account the opinions of management and the listed company's internal auditors (or other personnel responsible for the internal audit function). In addition to assuring the regular rotation of the lead audit partner as required by law, the audit committee should further consider whether, in order to assure continuing auditor independence, there should be regular rotation of the audit firm itself. The audit committee should present its conclusions with respect to the independent auditor to the full board.

(B) meet to review and discuss the listed company's annual audited financial statements and quarterly financial statements with management and the independent auditor, including reviewing the listed company's specific disclosures under "Management's Discussion and Analysis of Financial Condition and Results of Operations"; . . .

(C) discuss the listed company's earnings press releases, as well as financial information and earnings guidance provided to analysts and rating agencies;

Commentary: The audit committee's responsibility to discuss earnings releases, as well as financial information and earnings guidance, may be done generally (i.e., discussion of the types of information to be disclosed and the type of presentation to be made). The audit committee need not discuss in advance each earnings release or each instance in which a listed company may provide earnings guidance.

(D) discuss policies with respect to risk assessment and risk management;

Commentary: While it is the job of the CEO and senior management to assess and manage the listed company's exposure to risk, the audit committee must discuss guidelines and policies to govern the process by which this is handled. The audit committee should discuss the listed company's major financial risk exposures and the steps management has taken to monitor and control such exposures. The audit committee is not required to be the sole body responsible for risk assessment and management, but, as stated above, the committee must discuss guidelines and policies to govern the process by which risk assessment and management is undertaken. Many companies, particularly financial companies, manage and assess their risk through mechanisms other than the audit committee. The processes these companies have in place should be reviewed in a general manner by the audit committee, but they need not be replaced by the audit committee.

(E) meet separately, periodically, with management, with internal auditors (or other personnel responsible for the internal audit function) and with independent auditors;

Commentary: To perform its oversight functions most effectively, the audit committee must have the benefit of separate sessions with management, the independent auditors and those responsible for the internal audit function. As noted herein, all listed companies must have an internal audit function. These separate sessions may be more productive than joint sessions in surfacing issues warranting committee attention.

(F) review with the independent auditor any audit problems or difficulties and management's response;

Commentary: The audit committee must regularly review with the independent auditor any difficulties the auditor encountered in the course of the audit work, including any restrictions on the scope of the independent auditor's activities or on access to requested information, and any significant disagreements with management. Among the items the audit committee may want to review with the auditor are: any accounting adjustments that were noted or proposed by the auditor but were "passed" (as immaterial or otherwise); any communications between the audit team and the audit firm's national office respecting auditing or accounting issues presented by the engagement; and any "management" or "internal control" letter issued, or proposed to be issued, by the audit firm to the listed company. The review should also include discussion of the responsibilities, budget and staffing of the listed company's internal audit function.

(G) set clear hiring policies for employees or former employees of the independent auditors; and

Commentary: Employees or former employees of the independent auditor are often valuable additions to corporate management. Such individuals' familiarity with the business, and personal rapport with the employees, may be attractive qualities when filling a key opening. However, the audit committee should set hiring policies taking into account the pressures that may exist for auditors consciously or subconsciously seeking a job with the listed company they audit.

(H) report regularly to the board of directors.

Commentary: The audit committee should review with the full board any issues that arise with respect to the quality or integrity of the listed company's financial statements, the company's compliance with legal or regulatory requirements, the performance and independence of the company's independent auditors, or the performance of the internal audit function.

General Commentary to Section 303A.07(b): While the fundamental responsibility for the listed company's financial statements and disclosures rests with management and the independent auditor, the audit committee must review: (A) major issues regarding accounting principles and financial statement presentations, including any significant changes in the listed company's selection or application of accounting principles, and major issues as to the adequacy of the listed company's internal controls and any special audit steps adopted in light of material control deficiencies; (B) analyses prepared by management and/or the independent auditor setting forth significant financial reporting issues and judgments made in connection with the preparation of the financial statements, including analyses of the effects of alternative GAAP methods on the financial statements; (C) the effect of regulatory and accounting initiatives, as well as off-balance sheet structures, on the financial statements of the listed company; and (D) the type and presentation of information to be included in earnings press releases (paying particular attention to any use of "pro forma," or "adjusted" non-GAAP, information), as well as review any financial information and earnings guidance provided to analysts and rating agencies. . . .

(c) Each listed company must have an internal audit function.

Commentary: Listed companies must maintain an internal audit function to provide management and the audit committee with ongoing assessments of the company's risk management processes and system of internal control. A listed company may choose to outsource this function to a third party service provider other than its independent auditor.

General Commentary to Section 303A.07: To avoid any confusion, note that the audit committee functions specified in Section 303A.07 are the sole responsibility of the audit committee and may not be allocated to a different committee.

¶ 303A.08   Shareholder Approval of Equity Compensation Plans

Shareholders must be given the opportunity to vote on all equity-compensation plans and material revisions thereto, with limited exemptions explained below.

Equity-compensation plans can help align shareholder and management interests, and equity-based awards are often very important components of employee compensation. To provide checks and balances on the potential dilution resulting from the process of earmarking shares to be used for equity-based awards, the Exchange requires that all equity-compensation plans, and any material revisions to the terms of such plans, be subject to shareholder approval, with the limited exemptions explained below.

Definition of Equity-Compensation Plan

An "equity-compensation plan" is a plan or other arrangement that provides for the delivery of equity securities (either newly issued or treasury shares) of the listed company to any employee, director or other service provider as compensation for services. Even a compensatory grant of options or other equity securities that is not made under a plan is, nonetheless, an "equity-compensation plan" for these purposes.

However, the following are not "equity-compensation plans" even if the brokerage and other costs of the plan are paid for by the listed company:

- Plans that are made available to shareholders generally, such as a typical dividend reinvestment plan.

- Plans that merely allow employees, directors or other service providers to elect to buy shares on the open market or from the listed company for their current fair market value, regardless of whether:

—the shares are delivered immediately or on a deferred basis; or

—the payments for the shares are made directly or by giving up compensation that is otherwise due (for example, through payroll deductions).

Material Revisions

A "material revision" of an equity-compensation plan includes (but is not limited to), the following:

- A material increase in the number of shares available under the plan (other than an increase solely to reflect a reorganization, stock split, merger, spinoff or similar transaction).

—If a plan contains a formula for automatic increases in the shares available (sometimes called an "evergreen formula") or for automatic grants pursuant to a formula, each such increase or grant will be considered a revision requiring shareholder approval *unless* the plan has a term of not more than ten years.

This type of plan (regardless of its term) is referred to below as a "formula plan." Examples of automatic grants pursuant to a formula are (1) annual grants to directors of restricted stock having a certain dollar value, and (2) "matching contributions," whereby stock is credited to a participant's account based upon the amount of compensation the participant elects to defer.

—If a plan contains no limit on the number of shares available and is not a formula plan, then each grant under the plan will require separate shareholder approval *regardless* of whether the plan has a term of not more than ten years.

This type of plan is referred to below as a "discretionary plan." A requirement that grants be made out of treasury shares or repurchased shares will not, in itself, be considered a limit or pre-established formula so as to prevent a plan from being considered a discretionary plan.

- An expansion of the types of awards available under the plan.
- A material expansion of the class of employees, directors or other service providers eligible to participate in the plan.
- A material extension of the term of the plan.
- A material change to the method of determining the strike price of options under the plan.

—A change in the method of determining "fair market value" from the closing price on the date of grant to the average of the high and low price on the date of grant is an example of a change that the Exchange would not view as material.

- The deletion or limitation of any provision prohibiting repricing of options. See the next section for details.

Note that an amendment will not be considered a "material revision" if it curtails rather than expands the scope of the plan in question.

Repricings

A plan that does not contain a provision that specifically *permits* repricing of options will be considered for purposes of this listing standard as *prohibiting* repricing. Accordingly any actual repricing of options will be considered a material revision of a plan even if the plan itself is not revised. This consideration will not apply to a repricing through an exchange offer that commenced before the date this listing standard became effective.

"Repricing" means any of the following or any other action that has the same effect:

- Lowering the strike price of an option after it is granted.
- Any other action that is treated as a repricing under generally accepted accounting principles.
- Canceling an option at a time when its strike price exceeds the fair market value of the underlying stock, in exchange for another option, restricted stock, or other equity, unless the cancellation and exchange occurs in connection with a merger, acquisition, spin-off or other similar corporate transaction.

Exemptions

This listing standard does not require shareholder approval of employment inducement awards, certain grants, plans and amendments in the context of mergers and acquisitions, and certain specific types of plans, all as described below. However, these exempt grants, plans and amendments may be made only with the approval of the company's independent compensation committee or the approval of a majority of the company's independent directors. Companies must also notify the Exchange in writing when they use one of these exemptions.

Employment Inducement Awards

An employment inducement award is a grant of options or other equity-based compensation as a material inducement to a person or persons being hired by the listed company or any of its subsidiaries, or being rehired following a bona fide period of interruption of employment. Inducement awards include grants to new employees in connection with a merger or acquisition. Promptly following a grant of any inducement award in reliance on this exemption, the listed company must disclose in a press release the material terms of the award, including the recipient(s) of the award and the number of shares involved.

Mergers and Acquisitions

Two exemptions apply in the context of corporate acquisitions and mergers.

First, shareholder approval will not be required to convert, replace or adjust outstanding options or other equity-compensation awards to reflect the transaction.

Second, shares available under certain plans acquired in corporate acquisitions and mergers may be used for certain post-transaction grants without further shareholder approval.

This exemption applies to situations where a party that is not a listed company following the transaction has shares available for grant under pre-existing plans that were previously approved by shareholders. A plan adopted in contemplation of the merger or acquisition transaction would not be considered "pre-existing" for purposes of this exemption.

Shares available under such a pre-existing plan may be used for post-transaction grants of options and other awards with respect to equity of the entity that is the listed company after the transaction, either under the pre-existing plan or another plan, without further shareholder approval, so long as:

- the number of shares available for grants is appropriately adjusted to reflect the transaction;
- the time during which those shares are available is not extended beyond the period when they would have been available under the pre-existing plan, absent the transaction; and
- the options and other awards are not granted to individuals who were employed, immediately before the transaction, by the post-transaction listed company or entities that were its subsidiaries immediately before the transaction.

Any shares reserved for listing in connection with a transaction pursuant to either of these exemptions would be counted by the Exchange in determining whether the transaction involved the issuance of 20% or more of the company's outstanding common stock and thus required shareholder approval under Listed Company Manual Section 312.03(c).

These merger-related exemptions will not result in any increase in the aggregate potential dilution of the combined enterprise. Further, mergers or acquisitions are not routine occurrences, and are not likely to be abused. Therefore, the Exchange considers both of these exemptions to be consistent with the fundamental policy involved in this standard.

Qualified Plans, Parallel Excess Plans and Section 423 Plans

The following types of plans (and material revisions thereto) are exempt from the shareholder approval requirement:

- plans intended to meet the requirements of Section 401(a) of the Internal Revenue Code (e.g., ESOPs);
- plans intended to meet the requirements of Section 423 of the Internal Revenue Code; and

- "parallel excess plans" as defined below.

Section 401(a) plans and Section 423 plans are already regulated under the Internal Revenue Code and Treasury regulations. Section 423 plans, which are stock purchase plans under which an employee can purchase no more than $25,000 worth of stock per year at a plan-specified discount capped at 15%, are also required by the Internal Revenue Code to receive shareholder approval. While Section 401(a) plans and parallel excess plans are not required to be approved by shareholders, U.S. GAAP requires that the shares issued under these plans be "expensed" (i.e., treated as a compensation expense on the income statement) by the company issuing the shares.

An equity-compensation plan that provides non-U.S. employees with substantially the same benefits as a comparable Section 401(a) plan, Section 423 plan or parallel excess plan that the listed company provides to its U.S. employees, but for features necessary to comply with applicable foreign tax law, are also exempt from shareholder approval under this section.

The term "parallel excess plan" means a plan that is a "pension plan" within the meaning of the Employee Retirement Income Security Act ("ERISA") that is designed to work in parallel with a plan intended to be qualified under Internal Revenue Code Section 401(a) to provide benefits that exceed the limits set forth in Internal Revenue Code Section 402(g) (the section that limits an employee's annual pre-tax contributions to a 401(k) plan), Internal Revenue Code Section 401(a)(17) (the section that limits the amount of an employee's compensation that can be taken into account for plan purposes) and/or Internal Revenue Code Section 415 (the section that limits the contributions and benefits under qualified plans) and/or any successor or similar limitations that may hereafter be enacted. A plan will not be considered a parallel excess plan unless (1) it covers all or substantially all employees of an employer who are participants in the related qualified plan whose annual compensation is in excess of the limit of Code Section 401(a)(17) (or any successor or similar limits that may hereafter be enacted); (2) its terms are substantially the same as the qualified plan that it parallels except for the elimination of the limits described in the preceding sentence and the limitation described in clause (3); and (3) no participant receives employer equity contributions under the plan in excess of 25% of the participant's cash compensation. . . .

¶ 303A.09   Corporate Governance Guidelines

Listed companies must adopt and disclose corporate governance guidelines.

Commentary: No single set of guidelines would be appropriate for every listed company, but certain key areas of universal importance include director qualifications and responsibilities, responsibilities of key board committees, and director compensation.

The following subjects must be addressed in the corporate governance guidelines:

- **Director qualification standards.** These standards should, at minimum, reflect the independence requirements set forth in Sections 303A.01 and 303A.02. Companies may also address other substantive qualification requirements, including policies limiting the number of boards on which a director may sit, and director tenure, retirement and succession.

- **Director responsibilities.** These responsibilities should clearly articulate what is expected from a director, including basic duties and responsibilities with respect to attendance at board meetings and advance review of meeting materials.

- **Director access to management and, as necessary and appropriate, independent advisors.**

- **Director compensation.** Director compensation guidelines should include general principles for determining the form and amount of director compensation (and for reviewing those principles, as appropriate). The board should be aware that questions as to directors' independence may be raised when directors' fees and emoluments exceed what is customary. Similar concerns may be raised when the listed company makes substantial charitable contributions to organizations in which a director is affiliated, or enters into consulting contracts with (or provides other indirect forms of compensation to) a director. The board should critically evaluate each of these matters when determining the form and amount of director compensation, and the independence of a director.

- **Director orientation and continuing education.**

- **Management succession.** Succession planning should include policies and principles for CEO selection and performance review, as well as policies regarding succession in the event of an emergency or the retirement of the CEO.

- **Annual performance evaluation of the board.** The board should conduct a self-evaluation at least annually to determine whether it and its committees are functioning effectively.

Website Posting Requirement: A listed company must make its corporate governance guidelines available on or through its website.

Disclosure Requirements: A listed company must disclose in its annual proxy statement or, if it does not file an annual proxy statement, in its annual report on Form 10-K filed with the SEC that its corporate governance guidelines are available on or through its website and provide the website address.

¶ 303A.10   Code of Business Conduct and Ethics

Listed companies must adopt and disclose a code of business conduct and ethics for directors, officers and employees, and promptly disclose any waivers of the code for directors or executive officers.

Commentary: No code of business conduct and ethics can replace the thoughtful behavior of an ethical director, officer or employee. However, such a code can focus the board and management on areas of ethical risk, provide guidance to personnel to help them recognize and deal with ethical issues, provide mechanisms to report unethical conduct, and help to foster a culture of honesty and accountability.

Each code of business conduct and ethics must require that any waiver of the code for executive officers or directors may be made only by the board or a board committee.

Each code of business conduct and ethics must also contain compliance standards and procedures that will facilitate the effective operation of the code. These standards should ensure the prompt and consistent action against violations of the code.

Each listed company may determine its own policies, but all listed companies should address the most important topics, including the following:

- **Conflicts of interest.** A "conflict of interest" occurs when an individual's private interest interferes in any way—or even appears to interfere—with the interests of the corporation as a whole. A conflict situation can arise when an employee, officer or director takes actions or has interests that may make it difficult to perform his or her company work objectively and effectively. Conflicts of interest also arise when an employee, officer or director, or a member of his or her family, receives improper personal benefits as a result of his or her position in the company. Loans to, or guarantees of obligations of, such persons are of special concern. The listed company should have a policy prohibiting such conflicts of interest, and providing a means for employees, officers and directors to communicate potential conflicts to the listed company.

- **Corporate opportunities.** Employees, officers and directors should be prohibited from (a) taking for themselves personally opportunities that are discovered through the use of corporate property, information or position; (b) using corporate property, information, or position for personal gain; and (c) competing with the company. Employees, officers and directors owe a duty to the company to advance its legitimate interests when the opportunity to do so arises.

- **Confidentiality.** Employees, officers and directors should maintain the confidentiality of information entrusted to them by the listed company or its customers, except when disclosure is authorized or legally mandated. Confidential information includes all non-public information that might be of use to competitors, or harmful to the company or its customers, if disclosed.

- **Fair dealing.** Each employee, officer and director should endeavor to deal fairly with the company's customers, suppliers, competitors and employees. None should take unfair advantage of anyone through manipulation, concealment, abuse of privileged information, misrepresentation of material facts, or any other unfair-dealing practice. Listed companies may write their codes in a manner that does not alter existing legal rights and obligations of companies and their employees, such as "at will" employment arrangements.

- **Protection and proper use of listed company assets.** All employees, officers and directors should protect the listed company's assets and ensure their efficient use. Theft, carelessness and waste have a direct impact on the listed company's profitability. All listed company assets should be used for legitimate business purposes.

- **Compliance with laws, rules and regulations (including insider trading laws).** The listed company should proactively promote compliance with laws, rules and regulations, including insider trading laws. Insider trading is both unethical and illegal, and should be dealt with decisively.

- **Encouraging the reporting of any illegal or unethical behavior.** The listed company should proactively promote ethical behavior. The listed company should encourage employees to talk to supervisors, managers or other appropriate personnel when in doubt about the best course of action in a particular situation. Additionally, employees should report violations of laws, rules, regulations or the code of business conduct to appropriate personnel. To encourage employees to report such violations, the listed company must ensure that employees know that the listed company will not allow retaliation for reports made in good faith.

Website Posting Requirement: A listed company must make its code of business conduct and ethics available on or through its website.

Disclosure Requirements: A listed company must disclose in its annual proxy statement or, if it does not file an annual proxy statement, in its annual report on Form 10-K filed with the SEC that its code of business conduct and ethics is available on or through its website and provide the website address.

To the extent that a listed company's board or a board committee determines to grant any waiver of the code of business conduct and ethics for an executive officer or director, the waiver must be disclosed to shareholders within four business days of such determination. Disclosure must be made by distributing a press release, providing website disclosure, or by filing a current report on Form 8-K with the SEC.

¶ 303A.11 Foreign Private Issuer Disclosure

Listed foreign private issuers must disclose any significant ways in which their corporate governance practices differ from those followed by domestic companies under NYSE listing standards.

Commentary: Foreign private issuers must make their U.S. investors aware of the significant ways in which their corporate governance practices differ from those required of domestic companies under NYSE listing standards. However, foreign private issuers are not required to present a detailed, item-by-item analysis of these differences. Such a disclosure would be long and unnecessarily complicated. Moreover, this requirement is not intended to suggest that one country's corporate governance practices are better or more effective than another. The Exchange believes that U.S. shareholders should be aware of the significant ways that the governance of a listed foreign private issuer differs from that of a U.S. listed company. The Exchange underscores that what is required is a brief, general summary of the significant differences, not a cumbersome analysis. . . .

¶ 303A.12 Certification Requirements

(a) Each listed company CEO must certify to the NYSE each year that he or she is not aware of any violation by the listed company of NYSE corporate governance listing standards, qualifying the certification to the extent necessary.

Commentary: The CEO's annual certification regarding the NYSE's corporate governance listing standards will focus the CEO and senior management on the listed company's compliance with the listing standards.

(b) Each listed company CEO must promptly notify the NYSE in writing after any executive officer of the listed company becomes aware of any non-compliance with any applicable provisions of this Section 303A.

(c) Each listed company must submit an executed Written Affirmation annually to the NYSE. In addition, each listed company must submit an interim Written Affirmation as and when required by the interim Written Affirmation form specified by the NYSE.

¶ 303A.13 Public Reprimand Letter

The NYSE may issue a public reprimand letter to any listed company that violates a NYSE listing standard.

Commentary: Suspending trading in or delisting a listed company can be harmful to the very shareholders that the NYSE listing standards seek to protect; the NYSE must therefore use these measures sparingly and judiciously. For this reason it is appropriate for the NYSE to have the ability to apply a lesser sanction to deter companies from violating its corporate governance (or other) listing standards. Accordingly, the NYSE may issue a public reprimand letter to any listed company, regardless of type of security listed or country of incorporation that it determines has violated a NYSE listing standard. For companies that repeatedly or flagrantly violate NYSE listing standards, suspension and delisting remain the ultimate penalties. For clarification, this lesser sanction is not intended for use in the case of companies that fall below the financial and other continued listing standards provided in Chapter 8 of the Listed Company Manual or that fail to comply with the audit committee standards set out in Section 303A.06. The processes and procedures provided for in Chapter 8 govern the treatment of companies falling below those standards. . . .

¶ 304.00 Classified Boards of Directors.

The Exchange expects that Boards of Directors will be elected by all of the shareholders entitled to vote as a class except where special representation is required by the default provisions of a class or classes of preferred stock.

The Exchange will refuse to authorize listing where the Board of Directors is divided into more than three classes. Where classes are provided, they should be of approximately equal size and tenure and directors' terms of office should not exceed three years.

¶ 312.00 Shareholder Approval Policy . . .

¶ 312.03 Shareholder Approval

Shareholder approval is a prerequisite to issuing securities in the following situations:

(a) Shareholder approval is required for equity compensation plans. See Section 303A.08.

(b) Shareholder approval is required prior to the issuance of common stock, or of securities convertible into or exercisable for common stock, in any transaction or series of related transactions, to:

(1) a director, officer or substantial security holder of the company (each a "Related Party");

(2) a subsidiary, affiliate or other closely-related person of a Related Party; or

(3) any company or entity in which a Related Party has a substantial direct or indirect interest; if the number of shares of common stock to be issued, or if the number of shares of common stock into which the securities may be convertible or exercisable, exceeds either one percent of the number of shares of common stock or one percent of the voting power outstanding before the issuance.

However, if the Related Party involved in the transaction is classified as such solely because such person is a substantial security holder, and if the issuance relates to a sale of stock for cash at a price at least as great as the Minimum Price, then shareholder approval will not be required unless the number of shares of common stock to be issued, or unless the number of shares of common stock into which the securities may be convertible or exercisable, exceeds either five percent of the number of shares of common stock or five percent of the voting power outstanding before the issuance.

In addition, the provisions of this Section 312.03(b) will not apply to the sale of stock for cash by an Early Stage Company to (i) a Related Party, (ii) a subsidiary, affiliate or other closely-related person of a Related Party; or (iii) any company or entity in which a Related Party has a substantial direct or indirect interest, provided that the Early Stage Company's audit committee or a comparable committee comprised solely of independent directors reviews and approves of all such transactions prior to their completion.

The exemption in the preceding paragraph will not be applicable to a sale of securities by the listed company to any person subject to the provisions of this Section 312.03(b) in a transaction, or series of transactions, whose proceeds will be used to fund an acquisition of stock or assets of another company where such person has a direct or indirect interest in the company or assets to be acquired or in the consideration to be paid for such acquisition.

The sale of stock to a Related Party that is an employee, director or service provider is subject to the equity compensation rules in Section 303A.08 of the Manual. For example, a sale of stock by an Early Stage Company to any of such parties at a discount to the then market price would be treated as equity compensation under Section 303A.08 notwithstanding the exemption from shareholder approval provided under Section 312.03(b). Consequently, the company would be required to either: (i) obtain shareholder approval of such sale, or (ii) issue such shares under an equity compensation plan that had previously been approved by shareholders and for which shareholder approval under Section 303A.08 is not otherwise required. Moreover, shareholder approval is required if any of the subparagraphs of Section 312.03 require such approval, notwithstanding the fact that the transaction does not require approval under this subparagraph or one or more of the other subparagraphs. (See Section 312.04(a).)

(c) Shareholder approval is required prior to the issuance of common stock, or of securities convertible into or exercisable for common stock, in any transaction or series of related transactions if:

(1) the common stock has, or will have upon issuance, voting power equal to or in excess of 20 percent of the voting power outstanding before the issuance of such stock or of securities convertible into or exercisable for common stock; or

(2) the number of shares of common stock to be issued is, or will be upon issuance, equal to or in excess of 20 percent of the number of shares of common stock outstanding before the issuance of the common stock or of securities convertible into or exercisable for common stock.

However, shareholder approval will not be required for any such issuance involving:

- any public offering for cash;
- any bona fide private financing, if such financing involves a sale of:
- common stock, for cash, at a price at least as great as the Minimum Price; or
- securities convertible into or exercisable for common stock, for cash, if the conversion or exercise price is at least as great as the Minimum Price.

(d) Shareholder approval is required prior to an issuance that will result in a change of control of the issuer.

(e) Sections 312.03 (b), (c) and (d) shall not apply to issuances by limited partnerships.

¶ 312.04   For the Purpose of Para. 312.03

For the purpose of Section 312.03:

(a) Shareholder approval is required if any of the subparagraphs of Section 312.03 require such approval, notwithstanding the fact that the transaction does not require approval under one or more of the other subparagraphs.

(b) Pursuant to Sections 312.03 (b) and (c), shareholder approval is required for the issuance of securities convertible into or exercisable for common stock if the stock that can be issued upon conversion or exercise exceeds the applicable percentages. This is the case even if such convertible or exchangeable securities are not to be listed on the Exchange.

(c) The Exchange's policy regarding the need to apply to list common stock reserved for issuance on the conversion or the exercise of other securities is described in Section 703.07.

(d) Only shares actually issued and outstanding (excluding treasury shares or shares held by a subsidiary) are to be used in making any calculation provided for in Sections 312.03 (b) and (c). Shares reserved for issuance upon conversion of securities or upon exercise of options or warrants will not be regarded as outstanding.

(e) An interest consisting of less than either five percent of the number of shares of common stock or five percent of the voting power outstanding of a company or entity shall not be considered a substantial interest or cause the holder of such an interest to be regarded as a substantial security holder.

(f) "Voting power outstanding" refers to the aggregate number of votes that may be cast by holders of those securities outstanding that entitle the holders thereof to vote generally on all matters submitted to the company's security holders for a vote.

(g) "Bona fide private financing" refers to a sale in which either:

- a registered broker-dealer purchases the securities from the issuer with a view to the private sale of such securities to one or more purchasers; or

- the issuer sells the securities to multiple purchasers, and no one such purchaser, or group of related purchasers, acquires, or has the right to acquire upon exercise or conversion of the securities, more than five percent of the shares of the issuer's common stock or more than five percent of the issuer's voting power before the sale.

(h) "Officer" has the same meaning as defined by the Securities and Exchange Commission in Rule 16a–1(f) under the Securities Exchange Act of 1934, or any successor rule.

(i) "Minimum Price" means a price that is the lower of: (i) the Official Closing Price immediately preceding the signing of the binding agreement; or (ii) the average Official Closing Price for the five trading days immediately preceding the signing of the binding agreement.

(j) "Official Closing Price" of the issuer's common stock means the official closing price on the Exchange as reported to the Consolidated Tape immediately preceding the signing of a binding agreement to issue the securities. For example, if the transaction is signed after the close of the regular session at 4:00 pm Eastern Standard Time on a Tuesday, then Tuesday's official closing price is used. If the transaction is signed at any time between the close of the regular session on Monday and the close if the regular session on Tuesday, then Monday's official closing price is used.

(k) The issuance of shares from treasury is considered an issuance of shares for purposes of Section 312.03. (See Section 703.01, Part 1, of the Listed Company Manual regarding required notice to the Exchange of issuance of shares from treasury.)

(*l*) "Early Stage Company" means a company that has not reported revenues greater than $20 million in any two consecutive fiscal years since its incorporation and any Early Stage Company will lose that designation at any time after listing on the Exchange that it files an annual report with the SEC in which it reports two consecutive fiscal years in which it has revenues greater than $20 million in each year.

¶ 312.05   Exceptions

Exceptions may be made to the shareholder approval policy in Para. 312.03 upon application to the Exchange when (1) the delay in securing stockholder approval would seriously jeopardize the financial viability of the enterprise and (2) reliance by the company on this exception is expressly approved by the Audit Committee of the Board.

A company relying on this exception must mail to all shareholders not later than 10 days before issuance of the securities a letter alerting them to its omission to seek the shareholder approval that would otherwise be required under the policy of the Exchange and indicating that the Audit Committee of the Board has expressly approved the exception.

¶ 312.07   Where Shareholder

Where shareholder approval is a prerequisite to the listing of any additional or new securities of a listed company, the minimum vote which will constitute shareholder approval for listing purposes is defined as approval by a majority of votes cast on a proposal in a proxy bearing on the particular matter.

¶ 313.00   Voting Rights

(A) Voting Rights Policy. . . .

Voting rights of existing shareholders of publicly traded common stock under Section 12 of the Exchange Act cannot be disparately reduced or restricted through any corporate action or issuance. Examples of such corporate action or issuance include, but are not limited to, the adoption of time phased voting plans, the adoption of capped voting rights plans, the issuance of super voting stock, or the issuance of stock with voting rights less than the per share voting rights of the existing common stock through an exchange offer.

Supplementary Material:

.10 Companies with Dual Class Structures—The restriction against the issuance of super voting stock is primarily intended to apply to the issuance of a new class of stock, and companies with existing dual class capital structures would generally be permitted to issue additional shares of the existing super voting stock without conflict with this Policy.

.20 Consultation with the Exchange—Violation of the Exchange's Voting Rights Policy could result in the loss of an Issuers's Exchange market or public trading market. The Policy can apply to a variety of corporate actions and securities issuances, not just super voting or so-called "time phase" voting common stock. . . .

(B) Non-Voting Common Stock

The Exchange's voting rights policy permits the listing of the voting common stock of a company which also has outstanding a non-voting common stock as well as the listing of non-voting common stock. However, certain safeguards must be provided to holders of a listed non-voting common stock:

(1) Any class of non-voting common stock that is listed on the Exchange must meet all original listing standards. The rights of the holders of the non-voting common stock should, except for voting rights, be substantially the same as those of the holders of the company's voting common stock.

(2) The requirement that listed companies publish at least once a year and submit to shareholders an annual report . . . applies equally to holders of voting common stock and to holders of listed non-voting common stock.

(3) In addition, although the holders of shares of listed non-voting common stock are not entitled to vote generally on matters submitted for shareholder action, holders of any listed non-voting common stock must receive all communications, including proxy material, sent generally to the holders of the voting securities of the listed company.

(C) Preferred Stock, Minimum Voting Rights Required

Preferred stock, voting as a class, should have the right to elect a minimum of two directors upon default of the equivalent of six quarterly dividends. The right to elect directors should accrue regardless of whether defaulted dividends occurred in consecutive periods.

The right to elect directors should remain in effect until cumulative dividends have been paid in full or until non-cumulative dividends have been paid regularly for at least a year. The preferred stock quorum should be low enough to ensure that the right to elect directors can be exercised as soon as it accrues. In no event should the quorum exceed the percentage required for a quorum of the common stock required for the election of directors. The Exchange prefers that no quorum requirement be fixed in respect of the right of a preferred stock, voting as a class, to elect directors when dividends are in default. . . .

NEW YORK STOCK EXCHANGE RULES
AND CONSTITUTION—OPERATION
OF MEMBER ORGANIZATIONS

PROXIES

Rule 452.   GIVING PROXIES BY MEMBER ORGANIZATION

A member organization shall give or authorize the giving of a proxy for stock registered in its name, or in the name of its nominee, at the direction of the beneficial owner. . . .

Voting procedure without instructions

A member organization which has transmitted proxy soliciting material to the beneficial owner of stock or to an investment adviser, . . . and which has not received instructions from the beneficial owner . . . by the date specified in the statement accompanying such material, may give or authorize the giving of a proxy to vote such stock, provided the person in the member organization giving or authorizing the giving of the proxy has no knowledge of any contest as to the action to be taken at the meeting and provided such action is adequately disclosed to stockholders and does not include authorization for a merger, consolidation or any other matter which may affect substantially the rights or privileges of such stock. . . .

Supplementary Material:

Giving a Proxy to Vote Stock

.11 *When member organization may not vote without customer instructions.*—In the list of meetings of stockholders appearing in the Weekly Bulletin, after proxy material has been reviewed by the Exchange, each meeting will be designated by an appropriate symbol to indicate either (a) that members may vote a proxy without instructions of beneficial owners, (b) that members may not vote specific matters on the proxy, or (c) that members may not vote the entire proxy.

Generally speaking, a member organization may not give a proxy to vote without instructions from beneficial owners when the matter to be voted upon:

(1) is not submitted to stockholders by means of a proxy statement comparable to that specified in Schedule 14-A of the Securities and Exchange Commission;

(2) is the subject of a counter-solicitation, or is part of a proposal made by a stockholder which is being opposed by management (i.e., a contest);

(3) relates to a merger or consolidation (except when the company's proposal is to merge with its own wholly owned subsidiary, provided its shareholders dissenting thereto do not have rights of appraisal);

(4) involves right of appraisal;

(5) authorizes mortgaging of property;

(6) authorizes or creates indebtedness or increases the authorized amount of indebtedness;

(7) authorizes or creates a preferred stock or increases the authorized amount of an existing preferred stock;

(8) alters the terms or conditions of existing stock or indebtedness;

(9) involves waiver or modification of preemptive rights (except when the company's proposal is to waive such rights with respect to shares being offered pursuant to stock option or purchase plans involving the additional issuance of not more than 5% of the company's outstanding common shares (see Item 12));

(10) changes existing quorum requirements with respect to stockholder meetings;

(11) alters voting provisions or the proportionate voting power of a stock, or the number of its votes per share (except where cumulative voting provisions govern the number of votes per share for election of

directors and the company's proposal involves a change in the number of its directors by not more than 10% or not more than one);

(12) authorizes the implementation of any equity compensation plan, or any material revision to the terms of any existing equity compensation plan (whether or not stockholder approval of such plan is required by subsection 8 of Section 303A of the Exchange's Listed Company Manual);

(13) authorizes

a.   a new profit-sharing or special remuneration plan, or a new retirement plan, the annual cost of which will amount to more than 10% of average annual income before taxes for the preceding five years, or

b.   the amendment of an existing plan which would bring its cost above 10% of such average annual income before taxes.

Exceptions may be made in cases of

a.   retirement plans based on agreement or negotiations with labor unions (or which have been or are to be approved by such unions); and

b.   any related retirement plan for benefit of non-union employees having terms substantially equivalent to the terms of such union-negotiated plan, which is submitted for action of stockholders concurrently with such union-negotiated plan;

(14) changes the purposes or powers of a company to an extent which would permit it to change to a materially different line of business and it is the company's stated intention to make such a change;

(15) authorizes the acquisition of property, assets, or a company, where the consideration to be given has a fair value approximating 20% or more of the market value of the previously outstanding shares;

(16) authorizes the sale or other disposition of assets or earning power approximating 20% or more of those existing prior to the transaction.

(17) authorizes a transaction not in the ordinary course of business in which an officer, director or substantial security holder has a direct or indirect interest;

(18) reduces earned surplus by 51% or more, or reduces earned surplus to an amount less than the aggregate of three years' common stock dividends computed at the current dividend rate; or

(19) is the election of directors. . . .

ABA MODEL RULES OF PROFESSIONAL CONDUCT, RULES 1.6, 1.7, 1.13

Rule 1.6. Confidentiality of Information

(a) A lawyer shall not reveal information relating to the representation of a client unless the client gives informed consent, the disclosure is impliedly authorized in order to carry out the representation or the disclosure is permitted by paragraph (b).

(b) A lawyer may reveal information relating to the representation of a client to the extent the lawyer reasonably believes necessary:

(1) to prevent reasonably certain death or substantial bodily harm;

(2) to prevent the client from committing a crime or fraud that is reasonably certain to result in substantial injury to the financial interests or property of another and in furtherance of which the client has used or is using the lawyer's services;

(3) to prevent, mitigate or rectify substantial injury to the financial interests or property of another that is reasonably certain to result or has resulted from the client's commission of a crime or fraud in furtherance of which the client has used the lawyer's services;

(4) to secure legal advice about the lawyer's compliance with these Rules;

(5) to establish a claim or defense on behalf of the lawyer in a controversy between the lawyer and the client, to establish a defense to a criminal charge or civil claim against the lawyer based upon conduct in which the client was involved, or to respond to allegations in any proceeding concerning the lawyer's representation of the client; or

(6) to comply with other law or a court order. . . .

Comment . . .

Disclosure Adverse to Client

[6]   Although the public interest is usually best served by a strict rule requiring lawyers to preserve the confidentiality of information relating to the representation of their clients, the confidentiality rule is subject to limited exceptions. Paragraph (b)(1) recognizes the overriding value of life and physical integrity and permits disclosure reasonably necessary to prevent reasonably certain death or substantial bodily harm. Such harm is reasonably certain to occur if it will be suffered imminently or if there is a present and substantial threat that a person will suffer such harm at a later date if the lawyer fails to take action necessary to eliminate the threat. Thus, a lawyer who knows that a client has accidentally discharged toxic waste into a town's water supply may reveal this information to the authorities if there is a present and substantial risk that a person who drinks the water will contract a life-threatening or debilitating disease and the lawyer's disclosure is necessary to eliminate the threat or reduce the number of victims.

[7]   Paragraph (b)(2) is a limited exception to the rule of confidentiality that permits the lawyer to reveal information to the extent necessary to enable affected persons or appropriate authorities to prevent the client from committing a crime or fraud . . . that is reasonably certain to result in substantial injury to the financial or property interests of another and in furtherance of which the client has used or is using the lawyer's services. Such a serious abuse of the client-lawyer relationship by the client forfeits the protection of this Rule. The client can, of course, prevent such disclosure by refraining from the wrongful conduct. Although paragraph (b)(2) does not require the lawyer to reveal the client's misconduct, the lawyer may not counsel or assist the client in conduct the lawyer knows is criminal or fraudulent. See Rule 1.2(d). See also Rule 1.16 with respect to the lawyer's obligation or right to withdraw from the representation of the client in such circumstances, and Rule 1.13(c), which permits the lawyer, where the client is an organization, to reveal information relating to the representation in limited circumstances.

[8]   Paragraph (b)(3) addresses the situation in which the lawyer does not learn of the client's crime or fraud until after it has been consummated. Although the client no longer has the option of preventing disclosure by refraining from the wrongful conduct, there will be situations in which the loss suffered by the

affected person can be prevented, rectified or mitigated. In such situations, the lawyer may disclose information relating to the representation to the extent necessary to enable the affected persons to prevent or mitigate reasonably certain losses or to attempt to recoup their losses. Paragraph (b)(3) does not apply when a person who has committed a crime or fraud thereafter employs a lawyer for representation concerning that offense. . . .

Rule 1.7.   Conflict of Interest: Current Clients

(a) Except as provided in paragraph (b), a lawyer shall not represent a client if the representation involves a concurrent conflict of interest. A concurrent conflict of interest exists if:

(1) the representation of one client will be directly adverse to another client; or

(2) there is a significant risk that the representation of one or more clients will be materially limited by the lawyer's responsibilities to another client, a former client or a third person or by a personal interest of the lawyer.

(b) Notwithstanding the existence of a concurrent conflict of interest under paragraph (a), a lawyer may represent a client if:

(1) the lawyer reasonably believes that the lawyer will be able to provide competent and diligent representation to each affected client;

(2) the representation is not prohibited by law;

(3) the representation does not involve the assertion of a claim by one client against another client represented by the lawyer in the same litigation or other proceeding before a tribunal; and

(4) each affected client gives informed consent, confirmed in writing.

Comment . . .

Organizational Clients

[34] A lawyer who represents a corporation or other organization does not, by virtue of that representation, necessarily represent any constituent or affiliated organization, such as a parent or subsidiary. See Rule 1.13(a). Thus, the lawyer for an organization is not barred from accepting representation adverse to an affiliate in an unrelated matter, unless the circumstances are such that the affiliate should also be considered a client of the lawyer, there is an understanding between the lawyer and the organizational client that the lawyer will avoid representation adverse to the client's affiliates, or the lawyer's obligations to either the organizational client or the new client are likely to limit materially the lawyer's representation of the other client.

[35] A lawyer for a corporation or other organization who is also a member of its board of directors should determine whether the responsibilities of the two roles may conflict. The lawyer may be called on to advise the corporation in matters involving actions of the directors. Consideration should be given to the frequency with which such situations may arise, the potential intensity of the conflict, the effect of the lawyer's resignation from the board and the possibility of the corporation's obtaining legal advice from another lawyer in such situations. If there is material risk that the dual role will compromise the lawyer's independence of professional judgment, the lawyer should not serve as a director or should cease to act as the corporation's lawyer when conflicts of interest arise. The lawyer should advise the other members of the board that in some circumstances matters discussed at board meetings while the lawyer is present in the capacity of director might not be protected by the attorney-client privilege and that conflict of interest considerations might require the lawyer's recusal as a director or might require the lawyer and the lawyer's firm to decline representation of the corporation in a matter.

Rule 1.13.   Organization as Client

(a) A lawyer employed or retained by an organization represents the organization acting through its duly authorized constituents.

(b) If a lawyer for an organization knows that an officer, employee or other person associated with the organization is engaged in action, intends to act or refuses to act in a matter related to the representation that is a violation of a legal obligation to the organization, or a violation of law that reasonably might be imputed to the organization, and that is likely to result in substantial injury to the organization, then the lawyer shall proceed as is reasonably necessary in the best interest of the organization. Unless the lawyer reasonably believes that it is not necessary in the best interest of the organization to do so, the lawyer shall refer the matter to higher authority in the organization, including, if warranted by the circumstances, to the highest authority that can act on behalf of the organization as determined by applicable law.

(c) Except as provided in paragraph (d), if

(1) despite the lawyer's efforts in accordance with paragraph (b) the highest authority that can act on behalf of the organization insists upon or fails to address in a timely and appropriate manner an action or a refusal to act, that is clearly a violation of law, and

(2) the lawyer reasonably believes that the violation is reasonably certain to result in substantial injury to the organization,

then the lawyer may reveal information relating to the representation whether or not Rule 1.6 permits such disclosure, but only if and to the extent the lawyer reasonably believes necessary to prevent substantial injury to the organization.

(d) Paragraph (c) shall not apply with respect to information relating to a lawyer's representation of an organization to investigate an alleged violation of law, or to defend the organization or an officer, employee or other constituent associated with the organization against a claim arising out of an alleged violation of law.

(e) A lawyer who reasonably believes that he or she has been discharged because of the lawyer's actions taken pursuant to paragraphs (b) or (c), or who withdraws under circumstances that require or permit the lawyer to take action under either of those paragraphs, shall proceed as the lawyer reasonably believes necessary to assure that the organization's highest authority is informed of the lawyer's discharge or withdrawal.

(f) In dealing with an organization's directors, officers, employees, members, shareholders or other constituents, a lawyer shall explain the identity of the client when the lawyer knows or reasonably should know that the organization's interests are adverse to those of the constituents with whom the lawyer is dealing.

(g) A lawyer representing an organization may also represent any of its directors, officers, employees, members, shareholders or other constituents, subject to the provisions of Rule 1.7. If the organization's consent to the dual representation is required by Rule 1.7, the consent shall be given by an appropriate official of the organization other than the individual who is to be represented, or by the shareholders.

Comment

The Entity as the Client

[1]   An organizational client is a legal entity, but it cannot act except through its officers, directors, employees, shareholders and other constituents. Officers, directors, employees and shareholders are the constituents of the corporate organizational client. The duties defined in this Comment apply equally to unincorporated associations. "Other constituents" as used in this Comment means the positions equivalent to officers, directors, employees and shareholders held by persons acting for organizational clients that are not corporations.

[2]   When one of the constituents of an organizational client communicates with the organization's lawyer in that person's organizational capacity, the communication is protected by Rule 1.6. Thus, by way of example, if an organizational client requests its lawyer to investigate allegations of wrongdoing, interviews made in the course of that investigation between the lawyer and the client's employees or other constituents are covered by Rule 1.6. This does not mean, however, that constituents of an organizational client are the clients of the lawyer. The lawyer may not disclose to such constituents information relating to the representation except for disclosures explicitly or impliedly authorized by the organizational client in order to carry out the representation or as otherwise permitted by Rule 1.6.

[3]   When constituents of the organization make decisions for it, the decisions ordinarily must be accepted by the lawyer even if their utility or prudence is doubtful. Decisions concerning policy and

operations, including ones entailing serious risk, are not as such in the lawyer's province. Paragraph (b) makes clear, however, that when the lawyer knows that the organization is likely to be substantially injured by action of an officer or other constituent that violates a legal obligation to the organization or is in violation of law [and] that might be imputed to the organization, the lawyer must proceed as is reasonably necessary in the best interest of the organization. . . . [K]nowledge can be inferred from circumstances, and a lawyer cannot ignore the obvious.

[4]   In determining how to proceed under paragraph (b), the lawyer should give due consideration to the seriousness of the violation and its consequences, the responsibility in the organization and the apparent motivation of the person involved, the policies of the organization concerning such matters, and any other relevant considerations. Ordinarily, referral to a higher authority would be necessary. In some circumstances, however, it may be appropriate for the lawyer to ask the constituent to reconsider the matter; for example, if the circumstances involve a constituent's innocent misunderstanding of law and subsequent acceptance of the lawyer's advice, the lawyer may reasonably conclude that the best interest of the organization does not require that the matter be referred to higher authority. If a constituent persists in conduct contrary to the lawyer's advice, it will be necessary for the lawyer to take steps to have the matter reviewed by a higher authority in the organization. If the matter is of sufficient seriousness and importance or urgency to the organization, referral to higher authority in the organization may be necessary even if the lawyer has not communicated with the constituent. Any measures taken should, to the extent practicable, minimize the risk of revealing information relating to the representation to persons outside the organization. Even in circumstances where a lawyer is not obligated by Rule 1.13 to proceed, a lawyer may bring to the attention of an organizational client, including its highest authority, matters that the lawyer reasonably believes to be of sufficient importance to warrant doing so in the best interest of the organization.

[5]   Paragraph (b) also makes clear that when it is reasonably necessary to enable the organization to address the matter in a timely and appropriate manner, the lawyer must refer the matter to higher authority, including, if warranted by the circumstances, the highest authority that can act on behalf of the organization under applicable law. The organization's highest authority to whom a matter may be referred ordinarily will be the board of directors or similar governing body. However, applicable law may prescribe that under certain conditions the highest authority reposes elsewhere, for example, in the independent directors of a corporation.

Relation to Other Rules

[6]   The authority and responsibility provided in this Rule are concurrent with the authority and responsibility provided in other Rules. . . . Paragraph (c) of this Rule supplements Rule 1.6(b) by providing an additional basis upon which the lawyer may reveal information relating to the representation, but does not modify, restrict, or limit the provisions of Rule 1.6(b)(1)–(6). Under Paragraph (c) the lawyer may reveal such information only when the organization's highest authority insists upon or fails to address threatened or ongoing action that is clearly a violation of law, and then only to the extent the lawyer reasonably believes necessary to prevent reasonably certain substantial injury to the organization. It is not necessary that the lawyer's services be used in furtherance of the violation, but it is required that the matter be related to the lawyer's representation of the organization. If the lawyer's services are being used by an organization to further a crime or fraud by the organization, Rules 1.6(b)(2) and 1.6(b)(3) may permit the lawyer to disclose confidential information. . . .

[7]   Paragraph (d) makes clear that the authority of a lawyer to disclose information relating to a representation in circumstances described in paragraph (c) does not apply with respect to information relating to a lawyer's engagement by an organization to investigate an alleged violation of law or to defend the organization or an officer, employee or other person associated with the organization against a claim arising out of an alleged violation of law. This is necessary in order to enable organizational clients to enjoy the full benefits of legal counsel in conducting an investigation or defending against a claim.

[8]   A lawyer who reasonably believes that he or she has been discharged because of the lawyer's actions taken pursuant to Paragraph (b) or (c), or who withdraws in circumstances that require or permit the lawyer to take action under either of these Paragraphs, must proceed as the lawyer reasonably believes necessary to assure that the organization's highest authority is informed of the lawyer's discharge or withdrawal, and what the lawyer reasonably believes is the basis for his or her discharge or withdrawal.

Government Agency

[9]   The duty defined in this Rule applies to governmental organizations. Defining precisely the identity of the client and prescribing the resulting obligations of such lawyers may be more difficult in the government context and is a matter beyond the scope of these Rules. . . . Although in some circumstances the client may be a specific agency, it may also be a branch of government, such as the executive branch, or the government as a whole. For example, if the action or failure to act involves the head of a bureau, either the department of which the bureau is a part or the relevant branch of government may be the client for purposes of this Rule. Moreover, in a matter involving the conduct of government officials, a government lawyer may have authority under applicable law to question such conduct more extensively than that of a lawyer for a private organization in similar circumstances. Thus, when the client is a governmental organization, a different balance may be appropriate between maintaining confidentiality and assuring that the wrongful act is prevented or rectified, for public business is involved. In addition, duties of lawyers employed by the government or lawyers in military service may be defined by statutes and regulation. This Rule does not limit that authority. . . .

Clarifying the Lawyer's Role

[10]   There are times when the organization's interest may be or become adverse to those of one or more of its constituents. In such circumstances the lawyer should advise any constituent, whose interest the lawyer finds adverse to that of the organization of the conflict or potential conflict of interest, that the lawyer cannot represent such constituent, and that such person may wish to obtain independent representation. Care must be taken to assure that the individual understands that, when there is such adversity of interest, the lawyer for the organization cannot provide legal representation for that constituent individual, and that discussions between the lawyer for the organization and the individual may not be privileged.

[11]   Whether such a warning should be given by the lawyer for the organization to any constituent individual may turn on the facts of each case.

Dual Representation

[12]   Paragraph (g) recognizes that a lawyer for an organization may also represent a principal officer or major shareholder.

Derivative Actions

[13]   Under generally prevailing law, the shareholders or members of a corporation may bring suit to compel the directors to perform their legal obligations in the supervision of the organization. Members of unincorporated associations have essentially the same right. Such an action may be brought nominally by the organization, but usually is, in fact, a legal controversy over management of the organization.

[14]   The question can arise whether counsel for the organization may defend such an action. The proposition that the organization is the lawyer's client does not alone resolve the issue. Most derivative actions are a normal incident of an organization's affairs, to be defended by the organization's lawyer like any other suit. However, if the claim involves serious charges of wrongdoing by those in control of the organization, a conflict may arise between the lawyer's duty to the organization and the lawyer's relationship with the board. In those circumstances, Rule 1.7 governs who should represent the directors and the organization.

AMERICAN LAW INSTITUTE PRINCIPLES OF CORPORATE GOVERNANCE: ANALYSIS AND RECOMMENDATIONS (1994)

TABLE OF CONTENTS

PART I

DEFINITIONS

Sec.		Page
1.01	Effect of Definitions	979
1.02	Approved by the Shareholders	979
1.03	Associate	979
1.04	Business Organization	979
1.05	Charter Documents	980
1.06	Closely Held Corporation	980
1.07	Commercial Payment	980
1.08	Control	980
1.09	Control Group	980
1.10	Controlling Shareholder	980
1.11	Corporate Decisionmaker	981
1.12	Corporation	981
1.13	Director	981
1.14	Disclosure	981
1.15	Disinterested Directors	981
1.16	Disinterested Shareholders	981
1.17	Eligible Holder	981
1.18	Employee-Owned Corporation*	
1.19	Equity Interest	982
1.20	Equity Security	982
1.21	Family Group	982
1.22	Holder	982
1.23	Interested	982
1.24	Large Publicly Held Corporation	983
1.25	Material Fact	983
1.26	Member of the Immediate Family	983
1.27	Officer	983
1.28	Person	983
1.29	Principal Manager	983
1.30	Principal Senior Executive	983
1.31	Publicly Held Corporation	983
1.32	Record Holder	984
1.33	Senior Executive	984
1.34	Significant Relationship	984
1.35	Small Publicly Held Corporation	985
1.36	Standard of the Corporation	985
1.37	Total Assets	985
1.38	Transaction in Control	985
1.39	Unsolicited Tender Offer	985
1.40	Voting Equity Security	985

---

* Omitted.

1.41   Voting Security 985
1.42   Waste of Corporate Assets 986

PART II

THE OBJECTIVE AND CONDUCT OF THE CORPORATION

2.01   The Objective and Conduct of the Corporation 986

PART III

CORPORATE STRUCTURE: FUNCTIONS AND POWERS OF DIRECTORS AND OFFICERS; AUDIT COMMITTEE IN LARGE PUBLICLY HELD CORPORATIONS

3.01   Management of the Corporation's Business: Functions and Powers of Principal Senior Executives and Other Officers 989
3.02   Functions and Powers of the Board of Directors 989
3.03   Directors' Informational Rights 990
3.04   Right of Directors Who Have No Significant Relationship With the Corporation's Senior Executives to Retain Outside Experts 990
3.05   Audit Committee in Large Publicly Held Corporations 990

PART III-A

RECOMMENDATIONS OF CORPORATE PRACTICE CONCERNING THE BOARD AND THE PRINCIPAL OVERSIGHT COMMITTEES

3A.01   Composition of the Board in Publicly Held Corporations 991
3A.02   Audit Committee in Small Publicly Held Corporations 991
3A.03   Functions and Powers of Audit Committees 991
3A.04   Nominating Committee in Publicly Held Corporations: Composition, Powers, and Functions 992
3A.05   Compensation Committee in Large Publicly Held Corporations: Composition, Powers, and Functions 992

PART IV

DUTY OF CARE AND THE BUSINESS JUDGMENT RULE

4.01   Duty of Care of Directors and Officers; the Business Judgment Rule 993
4.02   Reliance on Directors, Officers, Employees, Experts, and Other Persons 995
4.03   Reliance on a Committee of the Board 995

PRINCIPLES OF CORPORATE GOVERNANCE

PART V

DUTY OF FAIR DEALING

CHAPTER 1

GENERAL PRINCIPLE

5.01   Duty of Fair Dealing of Directors, Senior Executives, and Controlling Shareholders 996

CHAPTER 2

DUTY OF FAIR DEALING OF DIRECTORS AND SENIOR EXECUTIVES

5.02   Transactions With the Corporation 996
5.03   Compensation of Directors and Senior Executives 998
5.04   Use by a Director or Senior Executive of Corporate Property, Material Non-public
        Corporate Information, or Corporate Position 998
5.05   Taking of Corporate Opportunities by Directors or Senior Executives........................... 999
5.06   Competition With the Corporation 1000
5.07   Transactions Between Corporations With Common Directors or Senior Executives............. 1000
5.08   Conduct on Behalf of Associates of Directors or Senior Executives 1001
5.09   Effect of a Standard of the Corporation.. 1001

CHAPTER 3

DUTY OF FAIR DEALING OF CONTROLLING SHAREHOLDERS

5.10   Transactions by a Controlling Shareholder With the Corporation 1001
5.11   Use by a Controlling Shareholder of Corporate Property, Material Non-public Corporate
        Information, or Corporate Position.. 1002
5.12   Taking of Corporate Opportunities by a Controlling Shareholder................................ 1002
5.13   Conduct on Behalf of Associates of a Controlling Shareholder 1002
5.14   Effect of a Standard of the Corporation*

CHAPTER 4

TRANSFER OF CONTROL

5.15   Transfer of Control in Which a Director or Principal Senior Executive Is Interested 1003
5.16   Disposition of Voting Equity Securities by a Controlling Shareholder to Third Parties 1003

PART VI

ROLE OF DIRECTORS AND SHAREHOLDERS IN TRANSACTIONS
IN CONTROL AND TENDER OFFERS

6.01   Role of Directors and Holders of Voting Equity Securities With Respect to Transactions in
        Control Proposed to the Corporation 1004
6.02   Action of Directors That Has the Foreseeable Effect of Blocking Unsolicited Tender
        Offers... 1004

---

*   Omitted.

PART VII

REMEDIES

CHAPTER 1

THE DERIVATIVE ACTION

7.01	Direct and Derivative Actions Distinguished	1006
7.02	Standing to Commence and Maintain a Derivative Action	1007
7.03	Exhaustion of Intracorporate Remedies: The Demand Rule	1007
7.04	Pleading, Demand Rejection, Procedure, and Costs in a Derivative Action	1008
7.05	Board or Committee Authority in Regard to a Derivative Action	1009
7.06	Authority of Court to Stay a Derivative Action	1009
7.07	Dismissal of a Derivative Action Based on a Motion Requesting Dismissal by the Board or a Committee: General Statement	1009
7.08	Dismissal of a Derivative Action Against Directors, Senior Executives, Controlling Persons, or Associates Based on a Motion Requesting Dismissal by the Board or a Committee	1010
7.09	Procedures for Requesting Dismissal of a Derivative Action	1010
7.10	Standard of Judicial Review With Regard to a Board or Committee Motion Requesting Dismissal of a Derivative Action Under § 7.08	1011
7.11	Dismissal of a Derivative Action Based Upon Action by the Shareholders	1012
7.12	Special Panel or Special Committee Members	1012
7.13	Judicial Procedures on Motions to Dismiss a Derivative Action Under § 7.08 or § 7.11	1012
7.14	Settlement of a Derivative Action by Agreement Between the Plaintiff and a Defendant	1013
7.15	Settlement of a Derivative Action Without the Agreement of the Plaintiff	1013
7.16	Disposition of Recovery in a Derivative Action	1014
7.17	Plaintiff's Attorney's Fees and Expenses	1014

CHAPTER 2

RECOVERY FOR BREACH OF DUTY

7.18	Recovery Resulting From a Breach of Duty: General Rules	1015
7.19	Limitation on Damages for Certain Violations of the Duty of Care	1016

CHAPTER 3

INDEMNIFICATION AND INSURANCE

7.20	Indemnification and Insurance	1016

CHAPTER 4

THE APPRAISAL REMEDY

7.21	Corporate Transactions Giving Rise to Appraisal Rights	1018
7.22	Standards for Determining Fair Value	1019
7.23	Procedural Standards	1019
7.24	Transactions in Control Involving Corporate Combinations in Which Directors, Principal Senior Executives, and Controlling Shareholders Are Not Interested	1020
7.25	Transactions in Control Involving Corporate Combinations to Which a Majority Shareholder Is a Party	1020

PART I

DEFINITIONS

§ 1.01 Effect of Definitions

The definitions in Part I apply for the purposes of Parts I–VII unless the context requires otherwise.

§ 1.02 Approved by the Shareholders

(a) "Approved by the shareholders" means approval by a majority of the voting shares, unless a greater percentage is required by the corporation's charter documents [§ 1.05] pursuant to Subsection (b).

(b) Any provision in a charter document (other than a fair-price provision) that increases the percentage of shares whose approval is required to more than a majority shall be approved by the same vote as is set forth in the provision.

(c) A change in the corporation's charter documents that affects shareholders' rights or control [§ 1.08] of the corporation that is made by the board of directors is to be considered as having been approved by the shareholders if the shareholders have clearly empowered the board of directors to adopt the change or provision.

§ 1.03 Associate

(a) "Associate" means:

(1)(A) The spouse (or a parent or sibling thereof) of a director [§ 1.13], senior executive [§ 1.33], or shareholder, or a child, grandchild, sibling, or parent (or the spouse of any thereof) of a director, senior executive, or shareholder, or an individual having the same home as a director, senior executive, or shareholder, or a trust or estate of which an individual specified in this Subsection (A) is a substantial beneficiary; or

(B) a trust, estate, incompetent, conservatee, or minor of which a director, senior executive, or shareholder is a fiduciary; or

(2) A person [§ 1.28] with respect to whom a director, senior executive, or shareholder has a business, financial, or similar relationship that would reasonably be expected to affect the person's judgment with respect to the transaction or conduct in question in a manner adverse to the corporation.

(b) Notwithstanding § 1.03(a)(2), a business organization [§ 1.04] is not an associate of a director, senior executive, or shareholder solely because the director, senior executive, or shareholder is a director or principal manager [§ 1.29] of the business organization. A business organization in which a director, senior executive, or shareholder is the beneficial or record holder of not more than 10 percent of any class of equity interest [§ 1.19] is not presumed to be an associate of the holder by reason of the holding, unless the value of the interest to the holder would reasonably be expected to affect the holder's judgment with respect to the transaction in question in a manner adverse to the corporation. A business organization in which a director, senior executive, or shareholder is the beneficial or record holder (other than in a custodial capacity) of more than 10 percent of any class of equity interest is presumed to be an associate of the holder by reason of the holding, unless the value of the interest to the holder would not reasonably be expected to affect the holder's judgment with respect to the transaction or conduct in question in a manner adverse to the corporation.

§ 1.04 Business Organization

"Business organization" means an organization of any form (other than an agency or instrumentality of government) that is primarily engaged in business, including a corporation, a partnership or any other form of association, a sole proprietorship, or any form of trust or estate.

§ 1.05   Charter Documents

"Charter documents" means the articles or certificate of incorporation; documents supplementary thereto that set forth the rights, preferences, and privileges of equity securities [§ 1.20] and any limitations thereon; and the bylaws of the corporation.

§ 1.06   Closely Held Corporation

"Closely held corporation" means a corporation the equity securities [§ 1.20] of which are owned by a small number of persons, and for which securities no active trading market exists.

§ 1.07   Commercial Payment

"Commercial payment" means any payment except the following: a payment of interest on securities, a pro rata distribution to a class of shareholders, a payment to a corporation for its stock, a loan, a repayment of principal, a payment by an insurer on account of an insured loss, a payment to a public utility at a regulated rate, a director's fee, or a payment on behalf of a third party.

§ 1.08   Control

(a) "Control" means the power, directly or indirectly, either alone or pursuant to an arrangement or understanding with one or more other persons [§ 1.28], to exercise a controlling influence over the management or policies of a business organization [§ 1.04], through the ownership of or power to vote equity interests [§ 1.19], through one or more intermediary persons, by contract, or otherwise.

(b) A person who, either alone or pursuant to an arrangement or understanding with one or more other persons, owns or has the power to vote more than 25 percent of the equity interests in a business organization is presumed to be in control of the organization, unless some other person, either alone or pursuant to an arrangement or understanding with one or more other persons, owns or has the power to vote a greater percentage of equity interests. A person who does not, either alone or pursuant to an arrangement or understanding with one or more other persons, own or have the power to vote more than 25 percent of the equity interests in a business organization is not presumed to be in control of the business organization by virtue solely of ownership of or power to vote equity interests in that organization.

(c) A person is not in control of a business organization solely because the person is a director [§ 1.13] or principal manager [§ 1.29] of the organization.

§ 1.09   Control Group

"Control group" means a group of persons [§ 1.28] who act in concert to exercise a controlling influence over the management or policies of a business organization [§ 1.04] pursuant to an arrangement or understanding with each other.

§ 1.10   Controlling Shareholder

(a) A "controlling shareholder" means a person [§ 1.28] who, either alone or pursuant to an arrangement or understanding with one or more other persons:

(1) Owns and has the power to vote more than 50 percent of the outstanding voting equity securities [§ 1.40] of a corporation; or

(2) Otherwise exercises a controlling influence over the management or policies of the corporation or the transaction or conduct in question by virtue of the person's position as a shareholder.

(b) A person who, either alone or pursuant to an arrangement or understanding with one or more other persons, owns or has the power to vote more than 25 percent of the outstanding voting equity securities of a corporation is presumed to exercise a controlling influence over the management or policies of the corporation, unless some other person, either alone or pursuant to an arrangement or understanding with one or more other persons, owns or has the power to vote a greater percentage of the voting equity securities. A person who does not, either alone or pursuant to an arrangement with one or more other persons, own or have the power to vote more than 25 percent of the outstanding voting equity securities of a corporation is not presumed to be in control of the corporation by virtue solely of ownership of or power to vote voting equity securities.

§ 1.11 Corporate Decisionmaker

"Corporate decisionmaker" means that corporate official or body with the authority to make a particular decision for the corporation.

§ 1.12 Corporation

(a) A "corporation" means a corporation incorporated under a business corporation law or an analogue thereof.

(b) For purposes of the obligations imposed upon a corporation under § 7.23(c)–(e) (procedural standards for appraisal), including the obligation to pay fair value on the occurrence of the events specified in § 7.21 (Corporate Transactions Giving Rise to Appraisal Rights), "corporation" includes the surviving, successor, or acquiring entity in the case of a business combination that gives rise to appraisal rights under that section.

§ 1.13 Director

"Director" means an individual designated as a director by the corporation or an individual who acts in place of a director under applicable law or a standard of the corporation [§ 1.36].

§ 1.14 Disclosure

(a) *Disclosure Concerning a Conflict of Interest.* A director [§ 1.13], senior executive [§ 1.33], or controlling shareholder [§ 1.10] makes "disclosure concerning a conflict of interest" if the director, senior executive, or controlling shareholder discloses to the corporate decisionmaker [§ 1.11] who authorizes in advance or ratifies the transaction in question the material facts [§ 1.25] known to the director, senior executive, or controlling shareholder concerning the conflict of interest, or if the corporate decisionmaker knows of those facts at the time the transaction is authorized or ratified.

(b) *Disclosure Concerning a Transaction.* A director, senior executive, or controlling shareholder makes "disclosure concerning a transaction" if the director, senior executive, or controlling shareholder discloses to the corporate decisionmaker who authorizes in advance or ratifies the transaction in question the material facts known to the director, senior executive, or controlling shareholder concerning the transaction, or if the corporate decisionmaker knows of those facts at the time the transaction is authorized or ratified.

§ 1.15 Disinterested Directors

A provision that gives a specified effect to action by "disinterested directors" requires the affirmative vote of a majority, but not less than two, of the directors on the board or on an appropriate committee who are not interested [§ 1.23] in the transaction or conduct in question.

§ 1.16 Disinterested Shareholders

A provision that gives a specified effect to action by "disinterested shareholders" requires approval by a majority of the votes cast by shareholders who are not interested [§ 1.23] in the transaction or conduct in question. In the case of § 5.15 (Transfer of Control in Which a Director or Principal Senior Executive Is Interested), such approval shall be deemed to have been given when there has been a tender offer and it has been accepted by a majority of the shares for which the tender offer has been made.

§ 1.17 Eligible Holder

(a) "Eligible holder" means the holder [§ 1.22] of one or more shares, whether common or preferred, that (1) carry voting rights with respect to the election of directors, (2) are entitled to share in all or any portion of current or liquidating dividends after the payment of dividends on any shares entitled to a preference, or (3) are adversely affected by an amendment of the certificate of incorporation as described in

§ 7.21(d), in each case as of the date of the shareholder vote or other corporate action under § 7.21 (Corporate Transactions Giving Rise to Appraisal Rights).

(b) No person shall be deemed an eligible holder if (1) the shares owned by such person were voted in favor of the proposed transaction or provision, (2) the person fails to elect appraisal with respect to all shares of the class owned by the person, or (3) in the case of a beneficial owner who is not the record holder [§ 1.32] of the shares, the beneficial owner fails to submit to the corporation the record holder's written consent to the beneficial owner's dissent not later than 20 days after the date of the corporate action giving rise to appraisal rights (or such later date on which notice thereof is first given to shareholders).

§ 1.19   Equity Interest

"Equity interest" means an equity security [§ 1.20] in a corporation, or a beneficial interest in any other form of business organization [§ 1.04].

§ 1.20   Equity Security

"Equity security" means (a) a share in a corporation or similar security, or (b) a security convertible, with or without consideration, into such a security, or carrying a warrant or right to subscribe for or buy such a security, if the warrant or right or convertible security is issued by the issuer of that security.

§ 1.21   Family Group

"Family group" means a group of persons [§ 1.28], all of whom act in concert concerning the corporation's affairs and who are either individuals related by blood, marriage, or adoption, or trusts or other organizations created or acting primarily for the benefit of such individuals.

§ 1.22   Holder

A "holder" is a person [§ 1.28] having a legal or substantial beneficial interest in an equity security [§ 1.20].

§ 1.23   Interested

(a) A director [§ 1.13] or officer [§ 1.27] is "interested" in a transaction or conduct if either:

(1) The director or officer, or an associate [§ 1.03] of the director or officer, is a party to the transaction or conduct;

(2) The director or officer has a business, financial, or familial relationship with a party to the transaction or conduct, and that relationship would reasonably be expected to affect the director's or officer's judgment with respect to the transaction or conduct in a manner adverse to the corporation;

(3) The director or officer, an associate of the director or officer, or a person with whom the director or officer has a business, financial, or familial relationship, has a material pecuniary interest in the transaction or conduct (other than usual and customary directors' fees and benefits) and that interest and (if present) that relationship would reasonably be expected to affect the director's or officer's judgment in a manner adverse to the corporation; or

(4) The director or officer is subject to a controlling influence by a party to the transaction or conduct or a person who has a material pecuniary interest in the transaction or conduct, and that controlling influence could reasonably be expected to affect the director's or officer's judgment with respect to the transaction or conduct in a manner adverse to the corporation.

(b) A shareholder is interested in a transaction or conduct if either the shareholder or, to the shareholder's knowledge, an associate of the shareholder is a party to the transaction or conduct, or the shareholder is also an interested director or officer with respect to the same transaction or conduct.

(c) A director is interested in an action within the meaning of Part VII, Chapter 1 (The Derivative Action), but not elsewhere in these Principles, if:

(1) The director is interested, within the meaning of Subsection (a), in the transaction or conduct that is the subject of the action, or

(2) The director is a defendant in the action, except that the fact a director is named as a defendant does not make the director interested under this section if the complaint against the director:

(A) is based only on the fact that the director approved of or acquiesced in the transaction or conduct that is the subject of the action, and

(B) does not otherwise allege with particularity facts that, if true, raise a significant prospect that the director would be adjudged liable to the corporation or its shareholders.

§ 1.24 Large Publicly Held Corporation

"Large publicly held corporation" means a corporation that as of the record date for its most recent annual shareholders' meeting had both 2,000 or more record holders [§ 1.32] of its equity securities [§ 1.20] and $100 million or more of total assets [§ 1.37]; but a corporation shall not cease to be a large publicly held corporation because its total assets fall below $100 million unless total assets remain below $100 million for *two* consecutive fiscal years.

§ 1.25 Material Fact

A fact is "material" if there is a substantial likelihood that a reasonable person would consider it important under the circumstances in determining the person's course of action.

§ 1.26 Member of the Immediate Family

"Member of the immediate family" of an individual means a spouse (or a parent or sibling thereof) of the individual, or a child, grandchild, sibling, parent (or spouse of any thereof) of the individual, or a natural person having the same home as the individual.

§ 1.27 Officer

"Officer" means (a) the chief executive, operating, financial, legal, and accounting officers of a corporation; (b) to the extent not encompassed by the foregoing, the chairman of the board of directors (unless the chairman neither performs a policymaking function other than as a director nor receives a material amount of compensation in excess of director's fees), president, treasurer, and secretary, and a vice-president or vice-chairman who is in charge of a principal business unit, division, or function (such as sales, administration, or finance) or performs a major policymaking function for the corporation; and (c) any other individual designated by the corporation as an officer.

§ 1.28 Person

"Person" means (a) an individual, (b) any form of organization, including a corporation, a partnership or any other form of association, any form of trust or estate, a government or any political subdivision, or an agency or instrumentality of government, or (c) any other legal or commercial entity.

§ 1.29 Principal Manager

"Principal manager" means a senior executive [§ 1.33] of a corporation, a general partner of a partnership, a person holding a comparable position in any other business organization [§ 1.04], or a trustee of a trust.

§ 1.30 Principal Senior Executive

"Principal senior executive" means an officer described in Subsection (a) of § 1.27 (Officer).

§ 1.31 Publicly Held Corporation

"Publicly held corporation" means a corporation that as of the record date for its most recent annual shareholders' meeting had both 500 or more record holders [§ 1.32] of its equity securities [§ 1.20] and $5 million or more of total assets [§ 1.37]; but a corporation shall not cease to be a publicly held corporation because its total assets fall below $5 million, unless total assets remain below $5 million for *two* consecutive fiscal years.

§ 1.32 Record Holder

A "record holder" of equity securities [§ 1.20] means a person [§ 1.28] identified as the owner of such securities on the record of security holders maintained by or on behalf of the corporation, except that: (a) a group of persons holding as co-owners or co-fiduciaries shall be treated as a single person; and (b) for purposes of §§ . . . , 1.24 (Large Publicly Held Corporation), 1.31 (Publicly Held Corporation), and 1.35 (Small Publicly Held Corporation), there shall be included as record holders the number of beneficial owners of equity securities held in the name of a voting trustee, trustee of an employee stock ownership trust, stock depository, stockbroker, or nominee, and the number of owners of equity securities held in bearer form, that the corporation has a reasonable basis for estimating.

§ 1.33 Senior Executive

"Senior executive" means an officer described in Subsection (a) or (b) of § 1.27 (Officer).

§ 1.34 Significant Relationship

(a) Except as provided in § 1.34(b), a director has a "significant relationship" with the senior executives [§ 1.33] of a corporation if, as of the end of the corporation's last fiscal year, either:

(1) The director is employed by the corporation, or was so employed within the *two* preceding years;

(2) The director is a member of the immediate family [§ 1.26] of an individual who (A) is employed by the corporation as an officer [§ 1.27], or (B) was employed by the corporation as a senior executive within the *two* preceding years;

(3) The director has made to or received from the corporation during either of its *two* preceding years, commercial payments [§ 1.07] which exceeded *$200,000,* or the director owns or has power to vote an equity interest [§ 1.19] in a business organization [§ 1.04] to which the corporation made, or from which the corporation received, during either of its *two* preceding years, commercial payments that, when multiplied by the director's percentage equity interest in the organization, exceeded *$200,000;*

(4) The director is a principal manager [§ 1.29] of a business organization to which the corporation made, or from which the corporation received, during either of the organization's *two* preceding years, commercial payments that exceeded *five percent* of the organization's consolidated gross revenues for that year, or *$200,000,* whichever is more; or

(5) The director is affiliated in a professional capacity with a law firm that was the primary legal adviser to the corporation with respect to general corporate or securities law matters, or with an investment banking firm that was retained by the corporation in an advisory capacity or acted as a managing underwriter in an issue of the corporation's securities, within the *two* preceding years, or was so affiliated with such a law or investment banking firm when it was so retained or so acted.

(b) A director shall not be deemed to have a significant relationship with the senior executives under § 1.34(a)(3)–(5) if, on the basis of countervailing or other special circumstances, it could not reasonably be believed that the judgment of a person in the director's position would be affected by the relationship under § 1.34(a)(3)–(5) in a manner adverse to the corporation.

(c) For purposes of § 1.34 (and § 1.27, to the extent it is incorporated in § 1.34 by reference) the term "the corporation" includes any corporation that controls [§ 1.08] the corporation, and any subsidiary or other business organization that is controlled by the corporation.

§ 1.35 Small Publicly Held Corporation

A "small publicly held corporation" is a publicly held corporation [§ 1.31] other than a large publicly held corporation [§ 1.24].

§ 1.36 Standard of the Corporation

"Standard of the corporation" means a valid certificate or bylaw provision or board of directors or shareholder resolution.

§ 1.37 Total Assets

A corporation's "total assets" means the total assets shown on the balance sheet for its most recent fiscal year-end.

§ 1.38 Transaction in Control

(a) Subject to Subsection (b), a "transaction in control" with respect to a corporation means:

(1) A business combination effected through (i) a merger, (ii) a consolidation, (iii) an issuance of voting equity securities [§ 1.40] to effect an acquisition of the assets of another corporation that would constitute a transaction in control under Subsection (a)(2) with respect to the other corporation, or (iv) an issuance of voting equity securities in exchange for at least a majority of the voting equity securities of another corporation, in each case whether effected directly or by means of a subsidiary;

(2) A sale of assets that would leave the corporation without a significant continuing business; or

(3) An issuance of securities or any other transaction by the corporation (other than pursuant to a transaction described in Subsection (a)(1)) that, alone or in conjunction with other transactions or circumstances, would cause a change in control [§ 1.08] of the corporation;

(b) A transaction is not a transaction in control within § 1.38(a) if the transaction consists of:

(1) The issuance of voting equity securities (other than pursuant to a transaction described in Subsection (a)(1)) in a widely distributed offering;

(2) The issuance of debt or equity securities that would constitute a transaction in control only because the securities carry the right to approve transactions in control, and such right serves to protect dividend, interest, sinking fund, conversion, exchange, or other rights of the securities, or to protect against the issuance of additional securities that would be on a parity with or superior to the securities; or

(3) A transaction described in Subsection (a)(1) if those persons [§ 1.28] who were the holders of voting equity securities in the corporation immediately before the transaction would own immediately after the transaction at least 75 percent of the surviving corporation's voting equity securities, in substantially the same proportions in relation to other preexisting shareholders of the corporation.

§ 1.39 Unsolicited Tender Offer

"Unsolicited tender offer" means an offer to purchase or invitation to tender made to holders of voting equity securities [§ 1.40] of a corporation, without the approval of the corporation's board of directors, to effect a change in control [§ 1.08] of the corporation by purchasing the holders' securities for cash, securities, other consideration, or any combination thereof.

§ 1.40 Voting Equity Security

"Voting equity security" means an equity security [§ 1.20] that is a voting security [§ 1.41].

§ 1.41 Voting Security

(a) "Voting security" means a security that currently entitles its record holder [§ 1.32] to vote for the election of directors.

(b) A specified percentage of the voting securities of a corporation means whatever amount of its outstanding voting securities entitles the record holders to cast that specified percentage of the aggregate votes that the record holders of all the outstanding voting securities are entitled to cast in the election of directors.

§ 1.42   Waste of Corporate Assets

A transaction constitutes a "waste of corporate assets" if it involves an expenditure of corporate funds or a disposition of corporate assets for which no consideration is received in exchange and for which there is no rational business purpose, or, if consideration is received in exchange, the consideration the corporation receives is so inadequate in value that no person of ordinary sound business judgment would deem it worth that which the corporation has paid.

PART II

THE OBJECT AND CONDUCT OF THE CORPORATION

§ 2.01   The Objective and Conduct of the Corporation

(a) Subject to the provisions of Subsection (b) and § 6.02 (Action of Directors That Has the Foreseeable Effect of Blocking Unsolicited Tender Offers), a corporation [§ 1.12] should have as its objective the conduct of business activities with a view to enhancing corporate profit and shareholder gain.

(b) Even if corporate profit and shareholder gain are not thereby enhanced, the corporation, in the conduct of its business:

(1) Is obliged, to the same extent as a natural person, to act within the boundaries set by law;

(2) May take into account ethical considerations that are reasonably regarded as appropriate to the responsible conduct of business; and

(3) May devote a reasonable amount of resources to public welfare, humanitarian, educational, and philanthropic purposes.

Comment . . .

f.   The economic objective. In very general terms, Subsection (a) may be thought of as a broad injunction to enhance economic returns, while Subsection (b) makes clear that certain kinds of conduct must or may be pursued whether or not they enhance such returns (that is, even if the conduct either yields no economic return or entails a net economic loss). In most cases, however, the kinds of conduct described in Subsection (b) could be pursued even under the principle embodied in Subsection (a). Such conduct will usually be consistent with economic self-interest, because the principle embodied in Subsection (a)—that the objective of the corporation is to conduct business activities with a view to enhancing corporate profit and shareholder gain—does not mean that the objective of the corporation must be to realize corporate profit and shareholder gain in the short run. . . .

Illustrations:

1.   Corporation A is a publicly held corporation with annual earnings in the range of $2–3 million. A has entered into a contract that is unenforceable against it under the Statute of Frauds. Performance of the contract will involve a loss of $70,000. A performs the contract, because the relevant corporate decisionmaker makes a judgment, in a manner that meets the standards of § 4.01 (Duty of Care of Directors and Officers; the Business Judgment Rule), that the loss is likely to be exceeded by long-run profits from preserving confidence in A's willingness to honor its commitments. A's action does not involve a departure from the economic objective stated in § 2.01(a).

2.   B Corporation is a publicly held corporation with annual earnings in the range of $6–8 million. White, a long-time middle-manager of B, is forced to retire because of serious injuries sustained in an automobile accident. B has a pension plan covering White, but the plan was installed only recently, and White's benefits are only 30 percent vested. B purchases an annuity for White at a cost of $50,000 to bring White's retirement income up to a reasonable amount, because the relevant

corporate decisionmaker makes a judgment, in a manner that meets the standards of § 4.01, that the cost of the annuity will be exceeded by long-run economic benefits from improving the morale of B's remaining employees. B's action does not involve a departure from the economic objective stated in § 2.01(a). . . .

g. *Compliance with legal rules.* Under § 2.01(b)(1), the corporation is obliged, to the same extent as a natural person, to act within the boundaries set by law. It is sometimes maintained that whether a corporation should adhere to a given legal rule may properly depend on a kind of cost-benefit analysis, in which probable corporate gains are weighed against either probable social costs, measured by the dollar liability imposed for engaging in such conduct, or probable corporate losses, measured by potential dollar liability discounted for likelihood of detection. Section 2.01 does not adopt this position. With few exceptions, dollar liability is not a "price" that can properly be paid for the privilege of engaging in legally wrongful conduct. Cost-benefit analysis may have a place in the state's determination whether a given type of conduct should be deemed legally wrongful. Once that determination has been made, however, the resulting legal rule normally represents a community decision that the conduct is wrongful as such, so that cost-benefit analysis whether to obey the rule is out of place. . . .

Illustrations:

7. F Corporation is a publicly held corporation with annual earnings in the range of $3–5 million. F hopes to be awarded a supply contract by P, a large publicly held corporation. The anticipated profits on the contract are $5 million over a two-year period. A vice-president of P has approached Brown, the relevant corporate decisionmaker of F, with the suggestion that if F pays the vice-president $20,000, F will be awarded the contract. Brown knows such a payment would be illegal, but correctly regards the risk of detection as extremely small. After carefully weighing that risk and the consequences of detection, Brown causes F to pay the $20,000. F's action involves a departure from the principle stated in § 2.01(b)(1).

8. G Corporation owns and operates 15 plants that were traditionally non-union. For the last several years, Union U has been attempting to organize G's workers, and has won elections at three of G's plants. Although G does not have a good faith belief that the elections were invalid, it adopts a strategy of refusing to bargain at these three plants and harassing members, adherents, and supporters of U at G's other 12 plants. The relevant corporate decisionmaker knows that the conduct violates the National Labor Relations Act, but believes that a long time will elapse before sanctions are imposed, and that the profit from this conduct will far exceed the cost of possible sanctions. G's action involves a departure from the principle stated in § 2.01(b)(1). . . .

h. *Ethical considerations.* Section 2.01(b)(2) provides that a corporation may take into account ethical considerations that are reasonably regarded as appropriate to the responsible conduct of business. . . . [O]bservation suggests that corporate decisions are not infrequently made on the basis of ethical considerations even when doing so would not enhance corporate profit or shareholder gain. Such behavior is not only appropriate, but desirable. Corporate officials are not less morally obliged than any other citizens to take ethical considerations into account, and it would be unwise social policy to preclude them from doing so.

This does not mean that corporate officials can properly take into account any ethical consideration, no matter how idiosyncratic. Because such officials are dealing with other people's money, they will act properly in taking ethical principles into account only where those considerations are reasonably regarded as appropriate to the responsible conduct of business. In this connection, however, it should be recognized that new principles may emerge over time. A corporate official therefore should be permitted to take into account emerging ethical principles, reasonably regarded as appropriate to the responsible conduct of business, that have significant support although less-than-universal acceptance. . . .

Illustrations:

11. The facts being otherwise as stated in Illustration 1, A is about to be dissolved. A nevertheless honors the contract, because ethical considerations that it reasonably regards as appropriate to the responsible conduct of business suggest that seriously made business promises should be kept even if there is a technical excuse for nonperformance. A's action can be justified under § 2.01(b)(2), and therefore does not involve a departure from the principles stated in § 2.01. . . .

    i.   Public welfare, humanitarian, educational, and philanthropic purposes. Section 2.01(b)(3) permits the corporation to devote a reasonable amount of resources to public welfare, humanitarian, educational, and philanthropic purposes, even if corporate profit and shareholder gain are not thereby enhanced. As in the case of ethical considerations, conduct that appears to be based on public welfare, humanitarian, educational, or philanthropic considerations may be intended to enhance corporate profit and shareholder gain. For example, a donation to public television may be made for reasons comparable to those for sponsoring a commercial, and a contribution to local Red Cross or Community Chest activities may be made for reasons of employee well-being and morale. . . .

    Section 2.01(b)(3) goes beyond these justifications and allows corporate resources to be devoted to public welfare, humanitarian, educational, and philanthropic purposes even without a showing of expected profits or ethical norms. . . . Social policy . . . favors humane behavior by major social institutions. [Social policy also] favors the maintenance of diversity in educational and philanthropic activity, and this objective would be more difficult to achieve if corporations, which control a great share of national resources, were not allowed to devote a portion of those resources to those ends. However, corporate activity that is justified solely by social considerations should be subject to a limit of reasonableness. . . .

Illustrations:

    13.   The facts being otherwise as stated in Illustration 2, B is about to liquidate. Accordingly, it will have no remaining employees and therefore cannot justify the purchase of an annuity for White on the basis of long-term profitability. B's assets net of liabilities are $30 million. White is the only employee whom the liquidation will leave without retirement security. The relevant decisionmaker causes B to purchase an annuity, at a cost of $50,000, to bring White's retirement income up to a reasonable amount, partly for humanitarian reasons, and partly because ethical considerations that B reasonably regards as appropriate to the responsible conduct of business suggest that a business should make reasonable provision for a faithful long-term employee who has made a contribution to the business, and is forced by ill health to retire while in the corporation's employ. B's action can be justified under both § 2.01(b)(2) and § 2.01(b)(3), and therefore does not involve a departure from the principles stated in § 2.01. . . .

    19.   O, a publicly held corporation, has assets of $100 million and annual earnings in the range of $13–15 million. O owns three aluminum plants, which are profitable, and one plastics plant, which is losing $4 million a year. The plastics plant shows no sign of ever becoming profitable, because of its very high operating costs, and there is no evidence that the plant and the underlying real estate will increase in value. O decides to sell the plastics plant. The only bidder for the plant is Gold, who intends to use the plant for a new purpose, introduce automation, and replace all existing employees. O turns down Gold's bid and keeps the plastics plant operating indefinitely for the purpose of preserving the employees' jobs. O's action involves a departure from the principles stated in § 2.01. The action is for a humanitarian purpose, but cannot be justified under § 2.01(b)(3), because the expenditures involved are unreasonable in amount in relation to earnings. It cannot be justified under § 2.01(b)(2), because a corporation is not ethically obliged to continue indefinitely the operation of a business that is losing large amounts of money, equal to more than one fourth of the corporation's earnings, for the purpose of keeping workers employed. The action cannot be justified under § 2.01(a), because the action is not motivated by profit considerations, and on the facts it would not be within the realm of business judgment to conclude that the action will result in short- or long-term profits exceeding the costs involved.

    20.   The facts being otherwise as stated in Illustration 19, the only person who bids on the plant is a real-estate developer who plans to close the plant and hold the land for investment. The developer is agreeable to leasing the plant back to O at a moderate rent for up to 12 months. O enters into a three-month lease, and continues to operate the plant during that period, at a loss of $500,000, so as to provide the employees at the plant a period of adjustment prior to its closing. This action is taken partly out of humanitarian considerations, and partly because ethical considerations that are reasonably regarded as appropriate to the responsible conduct of business suggest that an enterprise should make reasonable provision to cushion the transition of long-term employees who are about to be discharged. O's action can be justified under § 2.01(b)(2) and § 2.01(b)(3), and therefore does not involve a departure from the principles stated in § 2.01. . . .

PART III

CORPORATE STRUCTURE: FUNCTIONS AND POWERS OF DIRECTORS AND OFFICERS; AUDIT COMMITTEE IN LARGE PUBLICLY HELD CORPORATIONS

§ 3.01 Management of the Corporation's Business: Functions and Powers of Principal Senior Executives and Other Officers

The management of the business of a publicly held corporation [§ 1.31] should be conducted by or under the supervision of such principal senior executives [§ 1.30] as are designated by the board of directors, and by those other officers [§ 1.27] and employees to whom the management function is delegated by the board or those executives, subject to the functions and powers of the board under § 3.02.

§ 3.02 Functions and Powers of the Board of Directors

Except as otherwise provided by statute:

(a) The board of directors of a publicly held corporation [§ 1.31] should perform the following functions:

(1) Select, regularly evaluate, fix the compensation of, and, where appropriate, replace the principal senior executives [§ 1.30];

(2) Oversee the conduct of the corporation's business to evaluate whether the business is being properly managed;

(3) Review and, where appropriate, approve the corporation's financial objectives and major corporate plans and actions;

(4) Review and, where appropriate, approve major changes in, and determinations of other major questions of choice respecting, the appropriate auditing and accounting principles and practices to be used in the preparation of the corporation's financial statements;

(5) Perform such other functions as are prescribed by law, or assigned to the board under a standard of the corporation [§ 1.36].

(b) A board of directors also has power to:

(1) Initiate and adopt corporate plans, commitments, and actions;

(2) Initiate and adopt changes in accounting principles and practices;

(3) Provide advice and counsel to the principal senior executives;

(4) Instruct any committee, principal senior executive, or other officer [§ 1.27], and review the actions of any committee, principal senior executive, or other officer;

(5) Make recommendations to shareholders;

(6) Manage the business of the corporation;

(7) Act as to all other corporate matters not requiring shareholder approval.

(c) Subject to the board's ultimate responsibility for oversight under Subsection (a)(2), the board may delegate to its committees authority to perform any of its functions and exercise any of its powers.

Comment . . .

d.   The oversight function. In the publicly held corporation, the management function is normally vested in the principal senior executives. A basic function of the board is to select these executives and to oversee their performance (using the term "oversee" to refer to general observation and oversight, not active supervision or day-to-day scrutiny) to determine whether the business is being properly managed, having in mind the objective and conduct of the corporation under § 2.01. This oversight function is usually performed, not directly by actively supervising the principal senior executives, but indirectly by evaluating the performance of those executives and replacing any who are not meeting reasonable expectations concerning job performance. . . .

§ 3.03   Directors' Informational Rights

(a) Every director has the right, within the limits of § 3.03(b) (and subject to other applicable law), to inspect and copy all books, records, and documents of every kind, and to inspect the physical properties, of the corporation and of its subsidiaries, domestic or foreign, at any reasonable time, in person or by an attorney or other agent.

(b)(1) A judicial order to enforce such right should be granted unless the corporation establishes that the information to be obtained by the exercise of the right is not reasonably related to the performance of directorial functions and duties, or that the director or the director's agent is likely to use the information in a manner that would violate the director's fiduciary obligation to the corporation.

(2) An application for such an order should be decided expeditiously and may be decided on the basis of affidavits.

(3) Such an order may contain provisions protecting the corporation from undue burden or expense, and prohibiting the director from using the information in a manner that would violate the director's fiduciary obligation to the corporation.

(4) A director who makes an application for such an order after the corporation has denied a request should, if successful, be reimbursed by the corporation for expenses (including attorney's fees) reasonably incurred in connection with the application.

§ 3.04   Right of Directors Who Have No Significant Relationship With the Corporation's Senior Executives to Retain Outside Experts

The directors of a publicly held corporation [§ 1.31] who have no significant relationship [§ 1.34] with the corporation's senior executives [§ 1.33] should be entitled, acting as a body by the vote of a majority of such directors, to retain legal counsel, accountants, or other experts, at the corporation's expense, to advise them on problems arising in the exercise of their functions and powers (§ 3.02), if:

(a) Payment of such expense is authorized by the board; or

(b) A court approves an application for the payment of such expense upon a finding that the board had been requested to authorize the payment of such expense and had declined to do so, and the directors who have no relationship with the corporation's senior executives reasonably believed that (i) retention of an outside expert was required for the proper performance of the directors' functions and powers, (ii) the amount involved was reasonable in relation to both the importance of the problem and the corporation's assets and income, and (iii) assistance by corporate staff or corporate counsel was inappropriate or inadequate.

§ 3.05   Audit Committee in Large Publicly Held Corporations

Every large publicly held corporation [§ 1.24] should have an audit committee to implement and support the oversight function of the board (§ 3.02) by reviewing on a periodic basis the corporation's processes for producing financial data, its internal controls, and the independence of the corporation's external auditor. The audit committee should consist of at least three members, and should be composed exclusively of directors who are neither employed by the corporation nor were so employed within the two preceding years, including at least a majority of members who have no significant relationship [§ 1.34] with the corporation's senior executives.

Comment:

a.   *Comparison with present law and practice.* An audit committee is not required as a matter of state law, except in Connecticut. However, the New York Stock Exchange requires listed companies to establish and maintain an audit committee "comprised solely of directors independent of management and free from any relationship that, in the opinion of its Board of Directors, would interfere with the exercise of independent judgment as a committee member." . . . The American Stock Exchange and NASDAQ also recommend or require audit committees, and the employment of such committees in publicly held corporations is now prevalent practice. . . .

PART III-A

RECOMMENDATIONS OF CORPORATE PRACTICE CONCERNING THE BOARD AND THE PRINCIPAL OVERSIGHT COMMITTEES

§ 3A.01 Composition of the Board in Publicly Held Corporations

It is recommended as a matter of corporate practice that:

(a) The board of every large publicly held corporation [§ 1.24] should have a majority of directors who are free of any significant relationship [§ 1.34] with the corporation's senior executives [§ 1.33], unless a majority of the corporation's voting securities [§ 1.41] are owned by a single person [§ 1.28], a family group [§ 1.21], or a control group [§ 1.09].

(b) The board of a publicly held corporation [§ 1.31] that does not fall within Subsection (a) should have at least three directors who are free of any significant relationship with the corporation's senior executives.

Reporter's Note. . . .

3. Data from various sources show that the concepts embodied in § 3A.01 have taken firm hold in practice. A 1991 study by Korn/Ferry reported that the boards of responding corporations had an average number of three inside and nine outside directors. Korn/Ferry, *Board of Directors* 5, 15 (1991). In 1985, Korn/Ferry had found that the comparable average was 10 outside directors and four inside directors; in 1975, the average had been eight outside directors and five inside directors. Id. at 3, 5. The 1990 Korn/Ferry study predicts that in the next decade, the number of insiders on the board will drop even further, from three to two, and that increasingly the only insiders on the board will be the chief executive officer and the chief operating officer. Id. at 3. Two studies by Heidrick & Struggles in the 1980s, using different samples, found that "independent" directors (defined as those who were neither management nor affiliated nonmanagement directors) made up 61 percent of the boards of responding companies in one sample, and 59 percent in the other. Heidrick & Struggles, *The Changing Board* 3 (1983); Heidrick & Struggles, *Director Data* 1.

§ 3A.02 Audit Committee in Small Publicly Held Corporations

It is recommended as a matter of corporate practice that every small publicly held corporation [§ 1.35] should have an audit committee to implement and support the oversight function of the board (§ 3.02) by reviewing on a periodic basis the corporation's processes for producing financial data, its internal controls, and the independence of the corporation's external auditor. The audit committee should consist of at least three members, and should be composed exclusively of directors who are neither employed by the corporation nor were so employed within the previous two years, including a majority of members who have no significant relationship [§ 1.34] with the corporation's senior executives.

§ 3A.03 Functions and Powers of Audit Committees

It is recommended as a matter of corporate practice that:

The audit committee of a publicly held corporation established under §§ 3.05 (Audit Committee in Large Publicly Held Corporations) or 3A.02 (Audit Committee in Small Publicly Held Corporations) should:

(a) Recommend the firm to be employed as the corporation's external auditor and review the proposed discharge of any such firm;

(b) Review the external auditor's compensation, the proposed terms of its engagement, and its independence;

(c) Review the appointment and replacement of the senior internal auditing executive, if any;

(d) Serve as a channel of communication between the external auditor and the board and between the senior internal auditing executive, if any, and the board;

(e) Review the results of each external audit of the corporation, the report of the audit, any related management letter, management's responses to recommendations made by the external auditor in connection with the audit, reports of the internal auditing department that are material to the corporation as a whole, and management's responses to those reports;

(f) Review the corporation's annual financial statements, any certification, report, opinion, or review rendered by the external auditor in connection with those financial statements, and any significant disputes between management and the external auditor that arose in connection with the preparation of those financial statements;

(g) Consider, in consultation with the external auditor and the senior internal auditing executive, if any, the adequacy of the corporation's internal controls;

(h) Consider major changes and other major questions of choice respecting the appropriate auditing and accounting principles and practices to be used in the preparation of the corporation's financial statements, when presented by the external auditor, a principal senior executive [§ 1.30], or otherwise.

§ 3A.04   Nominating Committee in Publicly Held Corporations: Composition, Powers, and Functions

It is recommended as a matter of corporate practice that:

(a) Every publicly held corporation [§ 1.31], except corporations a majority of whose voting securities are owned by a single person [§ 1.28], a family group [§ 1.21], or a control group [§ 1.09], should establish a nominating committee composed exclusively of directors who are not officers [§ 1.27] or employees of the corporation, including at least a majority of members who have no significant relationship [§ 1.34] with the corporation's senior executives [§ 1.33].

(b) The nominating committee should:

    (1) Recommend to the board candidates for all directorships to be filled by the shareholders or the board.

    (2) Consider, in making its recommendations, candidates for directorships proposed by the chief executive officer and, within the bounds of practicability, by any other senior executive or any director or shareholder.

    (3) Recommend to the board directors to fill the seats on board committees.

Reporter's Note

. . . A 1990 study by Heidrick & Struggles, based on 1989 data, reported that 60 percent of the respondents had nominating committees. . . . A 1990 study by Korn/Ferry, based on 1989 data, reported that 57 percent of the respondents had nominating committees. . . .

§ 3A.05   Compensation Committee in Large Publicly Held Corporations: Composition, Powers, and Functions

It is recommended as a matter of corporate practice that:

(a) Every large publicly held corporation [§ 1.24] should establish a compensation committee to implement and support the oversight function of the board in the area of compensation. The committee should be composed exclusively of directors who are not officers [§ 1.27] or employees of the corporation, including at least a majority of members who have no significant relationship [§ 1.34] with the corporation's senior executives [§ 1.33].

(b) The compensation committee should:

    (1) Review and recommend to the board, or determine, the annual salary, bonus, stock options, and other benefits, direct and indirect, of the senior executives.

(2) Review new executive compensation programs; review on a periodic basis the operation of the corporation's executive compensation programs to determine whether they are properly coordinated; establish and periodically review policies for the administration of executive compensation programs; and take steps to modify any executive compensation programs that yield payments and benefits that are not reasonably related to executive performance.

(3) Establish and periodically review policies in the area of management perquisites.

Reporter's Note

... A 1990 study by Heidrick & Struggles, based on 1989 data, reported that 93 percent of the respondents had compensation committees. ... A 1990 study by Korn/Ferry, based on 1989 data, reported that 91 percent of the respondents had compensation committees. ...

PART IV

DUTY OF CARE AND THE BUSINESS JUDGMENT RULE

§ 4.01   Duty of Care of Directors and Officers; the Business Judgment Rule

(a) A director or officer has a duty to the corporation to perform the director's or officer's functions in good faith, in a manner that he or she reasonably believes to be in the best interests of the corporation, and with the care that an ordinarily prudent person would reasonably be expected to exercise in a like position and under similar circumstances. This Subsection (a) is subject to the provisions of Subsection (c) (the business judgment rule) where applicable.

(1) The duty in Subsection (a) includes the obligation to make, or cause to be made, an inquiry when, but only when, the circumstances would alert a reasonable director or officer to the need therefor. The extent of such inquiry shall be such as the director or officer reasonably believes to be necessary.

(2) In performing any of his or her functions (including oversight functions), a director or officer is entitled to rely on materials and persons in accordance with §§ 4.02 and 4.03 (reliance on directors, officers, employees, experts, other persons, and committees of the board).

(b) Except as otherwise provided by statute or by a standard of the corporation [§ 1.36] and subject to the board's ultimate responsibility for oversight, in performing its functions (including oversight functions), the board may delegate, formally or informally by course of conduct, any function (including the function of identifying matters requiring the attention of the board) to committees of the board or to directors, officers, employees, experts, or other persons; a director may rely on such committees and persons in fulfilling the duty under this Section with respect to any delegated function if the reliance is in accordance with §§ 4.02 and 4.03.

(c) A director or officer who makes a business judgment in good faith fulfills the duty under this Section if the director or officer:

(1) is not interested [§ 1.23] in the subject of the business judgment;

(2) is informed with respect to the subject of the business judgment to the extent the director or officer reasonably believes to be appropriate under the circumstances; and

(3) rationally believes that the business judgment is in the best interests of the corporation.

(d) A person challenging the conduct of a director or officer under this Section has the burden of proving a breach of the duty of care, including the inapplicability of the provisions as to the fulfillment of duty under Subsection (b) or (c), and, in a damage action, the burden of proving that the breach was the legal cause of damage suffered by the corporation.

Comment to § 4.01(a), first paragraph: . . .

Illustrations:

6.   C, who is rich and charming, has been a director of Y Corporation for several years. C's only significant contribution to Y has been a willingness to entertain important customers. C has said: "I do not have the capacity to oversee Y's business," and has made no attempt to oversee it. Y Corporation has gone into bankruptcy because of mismanagement. C, as a result of the failure to oversee the conduct of Y's business, has committed a breach of the duty of care. The fact that C may not have the capacity of an "ordinarily prudent person" is no defense. C will be held to an objective standard. . . .

Comment to § 4.01(a)(1)–(a)(2):

Illustrations . . .

1.   Last year X Corporation, which had annual sales of $900,000,000 and a wide distribution system for its consumer products, was fined $1 million for horizontal price fixing, a criminal violation of the Sherman Act. It also had to settle a number of civil antitrust actions by paying an aggregate of $16.8 million. The directors of X Corporation have never been concerned with the existence of an antitrust compliance program, and X Corporation still has no company statement on antitrust policy and no compliance program. A new horizontal price-fixing violation has just occurred. It is clear, however, that the directors of X Corporation had no knowledge of the new antitrust violation. The directors of X Corporation may well have violated their duty of care. The recent antitrust violations, the size of X Corporation, and its wide distribution system should have made compliance with the antitrust laws a particularly prominent concern. Unless other facts were present, such as the delegation of antitrust law compliance functions to the general counsel and proper reliance on the general counsel in accordance with § 4.01(b), the failure of the directors of X Corporation to be reasonably concerned with the existence of an antitrust compliance program would constitute a breach of the directors' duty of care.

2.   The facts being otherwise as stated in Illustration 1, after the $1 million fine was paid, X Corporation did in fact install an antitrust compliance program which required X's local staff attorneys to refer all antitrust questions—and report all suspicious circumstances—to a designated staff attorney at company headquarters. An attorney in one regional office has, however, failed to report questionable conduct that may constitute a *per se* antitrust violation. X's directors have not failed to meet their duty of care due to an isolated breakdown in the compliance program. No violation of § 4.01(a) has occurred. . . .

Comment to § 4.01(c) . . .

c.   *Prerequisite of a conscious exercise of judgment.* Section 4.01(c) affords protection only to a "business judgment." This means that to be afforded protection a decision must have been consciously made and judgment must, in fact, have been exercised. For efficiency reasons, corporate decisionmakers should be permitted to act decisively and with relative freedom from a judge's or jury's subsequent second-guessing. It is desirable to encourage directors and officers to enter new markets, develop new products, innovate, and take other business risks.

There is, however, no reason to provide special protection where no business decisionmaking is to be found. If, for example, directors have failed to oversee the conduct of the corporation's business (§ 3.02(a)(2)) by not even considering the need for an effective audit process, and this permits an executive to abscond with corporate funds, business judgment rule protection would be manifestly undesirable. The same would be true where a director received but did not read basic financial information, over a period of time, and thus allowed his corporation to be looted. Cf. Hoye v. Meek, 795 F.2d 893 (10th Cir.1986); DePinto v. Provident Security Life Insur. Co., 374 F.2d 37 (9th Cir.1967), cert. denied 389 U.S. 822, 88 S.Ct. 48, 19 L.Ed.2d 74 (1967); Francis v. United Jersey Bank, 87 N.J. 15, 432 A.2d 814 (1981). In these and other "omission" situations, the director or officer would be judged under the reasonable care standards of § 4.01(a) and not protected by § 4.01(c). See, e.g., Aronson v. Lewis, 473 A.2d 805, 813 (Del.1984) ("the business judgment rule operates only in the context of director action. . . . [I]t has no role where directors have either abdicated their functions, or absent a conscious decision, failed to act."); Arsht, The Business Judgment Rule Revisited, 8 Hofstra L.Rev. 93, 112 (1979); Block & Prussin, The Business Judgment Rule and Shareholder Derivative Actions: Viva

Zapata?, 37 Bus.Law. 27, 33 (1981) ("The [business judgment] rule does not apply where the director has in fact made no decision"). . . .

   e.   Prerequisite of an informed decision. The great weight of case law and commentator authority supports the proposition that an informed decision (made, for example, on the basis of explanatory information presented to the board) is a prerequisite to the legal insulation afforded by the business judgment rule. In a much quoted statement, the court in Casey v. Woodruff, 49 N.Y.S.2d 625, 643 (1944), observed: "When courts say that they will not interfere in matters of business judgment, it is presupposed that judgment—reasonable diligence—has in fact been exercised." See . . . Arsht, The Business Judgment Rule Revisited, 8 Hofstra L.Rev. 93, 111 (1979) (the business judgment rule should not be available to directors who do "not exercise due care to ascertain the relevant and available facts before voting"). . . .

   f.   The "rationally believes" requirement. If the requirements of "good faith" and § 4.01(c)(1)–(c)(2) are met, § 4.01(c)(3) will protect a director or officer from liability for a business judgment if the director or officer "rationally believes that the business judgment is in the best interests of the corporation." The term "rationally believes" has both an objective and a subjective content. A director or officer must actually believe that the business judgment is in the best interests of the corporation and that belief must be rational. . . .

   There have been varying approaches taken in the cases and by commentators to the proper standard for judicial review of business judgments. Some courts have stated that a director's or officer's business judgment must be "reasonable" to be upheld. . . . On the other hand, a few cases have simply said that a director's or officer's judgment would be upheld if made with disinterest, in an informed manner, and in good faith. . . .

   Sound public policy dictates that directors and officers be given greater protection than courts and commentators using a "reasonableness" test would afford. . . .

   On the other hand, courts that have articulated only a "good faith" test may, depending on the court's meaning, provide too much legal insulation for directors and officers. A "good faith" test could be interpreted broadly to achieve the same result as the "rationally believes" standard. For example, in Sam Wong & Son v. New York Mercantile Exchange, 735 F.2d 653, 671, 678 n. 32 (2d Cir.1984), Judge Friendly held that the rationality of a decision by the Board of Governors of the Mercantile Exchange was relevant in determining whether the Board had acted in good faith, and concluded that "[a]bsent some basis in reason, action could hardly be in good faith even apart from ulterior motive.". . . . Serious problems arise, however, if the phrase "good faith" is interpreted narrowly to mean only the absence of subjective "bad motives." There is no reason to insulate an objectively irrational business decision—one so removed from the realm of reason that it should not be sustained—solely on the basis that it was made in subjective good faith. . . .

§ 4.02   Reliance on Directors, Officers, Employees, Experts, and Other Persons

   In performing his or her duties and functions, a director or officer who acts in good faith, and reasonably believes that reliance is warranted, is entitled to rely on information, opinions, reports, statements (including financial statements and other financial data), decisions, judgments, and performance (including decisions, judgments, and performance within the scope of § 4.01(b)) prepared, presented, made, or performed by:

   (a) One or more directors, officers, or employees of the corporation, or of a business organization [§ 1.04] under joint control or common control [§ 1.08] with the corporation, who the director or officer reasonably believes merit confidence; or

   (b) Legal counsel, public accountants, engineers, or other persons who the director or officer reasonably believes merit confidence.

§ 4.03   Reliance on a Committee of the Board

   In performing his or her duties and functions, a director who acts in good faith, and reasonably believes that reliance is warranted, is entitled to rely on:

(a) The decisions, judgments, and performance (including decisions, judgments, and performance within the scope of § 4.01(b)), of a duly authorized committee of the board upon which the director does not serve, with respect to matters delegated to that committee, provided that the director reasonably believes the committee merits confidence.

(b) Information, opinions, reports, and statements (including financial statements and other financial data), prepared or presented by a duly authorized committee of the board upon which the director does not serve, provided that the director reasonably believes the committee merits confidence.

PART V

DUTY OF FAIR DEALING

Chapter 1

GENERAL PRINCIPLE

§ 5.01   Duty of Fair Dealing of Directors, Senior Executives, and Controlling Shareholders

Directors [§ 1.13], senior executives [§ 1.33], and controlling shareholders [§ 1.10], when interested [§ 1.23] in a matter affecting the corporation, are under a duty of fair dealing, which may be fulfilled as set forth in Chapters 2 and 3 of Part V. This duty includes the obligation to make appropriate disclosure as provided in such Chapters.

Chapter 2

DUTY OF FAIR DEALING OF DIRECTORS AND SENIOR EXECUTIVES

§ 5.02   Transactions With the Corporation

(a) *General Rule.* A director [§ 1.13] or senior executive [§ 1.33] who enters into a transaction with the corporation (other than a transaction involving the payment of compensation) fulfills the duty of fair dealing with respect to the transaction if:

(1) Disclosure concerning the conflict of interest [§ 1.14(a)] and the transaction [§ 1.14(b)] is made to the corporate decisionmaker [§ 1.11] who authorizes in advance or ratifies the transaction; and

(2) either:

(A) The transaction is fair to the corporation when entered into;

(B) The transaction is authorized in advance, following disclosure concerning the conflict of interest and the transaction, by disinterested directors [§ 1.15], or in the case of a senior executive who is not a director by a disinterested superior, who could reasonably have concluded that the transaction was fair to the corporation at the time of such authorization;

(C) The transaction is ratified, following such disclosure, by disinterested directors who could reasonably have concluded that the transaction was fair to the corporation at the time it was entered into, provided (i) a corporate decisionmaker who is not interested [§ 1.23] in the transaction acted for the corporation in the transaction and could reasonably have concluded that the transaction was fair to the corporation; (ii) the interested director or senior executive made disclosure to such decisionmaker pursuant to Subsection (a)(1) to the extent he or she then knew of the material facts; (iii) the interested director or senior executive did not act unreasonably in failing to seek advance authorization of the transaction by disinterested directors or a disinterested superior; and (iv) the failure to obtain advance authorization of the transaction by disinterested directors or a disinterested superior did not adversely affect the interests of the corporation in a significant way; or

(D) the transaction is authorized in advance or ratified, following such disclosure, by disinterested shareholders [§ 1.16], and does not constitute a waste of corporate assets [§ 1.42] at the time of the shareholder action.

(b) *Burden of Proof.* A party who challenges a transaction between a director or senior executive and the corporation has the burden of proof, except that if such party establishes that none of Subsections (a)(2)(B), (a)(2)(C), or (a)(2)(D) is satisfied, the director or senior executive has the burden of proving that the transaction was fair to the corporation.

(c) *Ratification of Disclosure or Nondisclosure.* The disclosure requirements of § 5.02(a)(1) will be deemed to be satisfied if at any time (but no later than a reasonable time after suit is filed challenging the transaction) the transaction is ratified, following such disclosure, by the directors, the shareholders, or the corporate decisionmaker who initially approved the transaction or the decisionmaker's successor.

Comment to § 5.02(a)(1) . . .

A director or senior executive may not deal with the corporation as a stranger at arm's length. Even where the conflict of interest is made known, there is a relationship of "trust and confidence" with the corporation, so as to require disclosure of "material matters," rather than the relationship of a stranger to the corporation with a much more limited duty of disclosure. Compare Restatement, Second, Torts § 551(2)(a) with Restatement, Second, Torts § 551(2)(e). See also Restatement, Second, Torts § 551, Comments *e, f* and *k*. The duty of one who occupies a relationship of trust and confidence to disclose material facts is widely recognized. See, e.g., Restatement, Second, Contracts § 161, Comment *f*; Restatement, Second, Agency § 390; Restatement of Restitution § 191, Comment on Clause (b). A director or senior executive owes a duty to the corporation not only to avoid misleading it by misstatements or omissions, but affirmatively to disclose the material facts known to the director or senior executive. The interested director or senior executive also has an obligation to explain the implications of a transaction, when he or she is in a position to realize those implications and the disinterested superior or director reviewing the transaction is not in a position to do so. See Globe Woolen Co. v. Utica Gas & Elec. Co., 224 N.Y. 483, 121 N.E. 378 (1918).

Section 1.14 sets forth the required elements of disclosure and § 1.25 sets forth the definition of material facts which are required to be disclosed. Under § 5.02, a director or senior executive who fails to make required disclosure has failed to fulfill the duty of fair dealing, even if the terms of the transaction are fair. A contract price might be fair in the sense that it corresponds to market price, and yet the corporation might have refused to make the contract if a given material fact had been disclosed. See, e.g., Illustrations 4 and 6. Furthermore, as pointed out in paragraph d of the Introductory Note, fairness is often a range, rather than a point, and disclosure of a material fact might have induced the corporation to bargain the price down lower in the range. . . .

Illustrations . . .

4.   X Corporation is seeking a new headquarters building. D, a vice president of X Corporation, owns all the stock of R Corporation, which owns an office building. D causes a real estate agent to offer R Corporation's building to X Corporation, but does not disclose his ownership of R Corporation. X Corporation's board of directors agrees to purchase the building for a fair price. Two weeks later, X Corporation learns of D's interest in R Corporation. D has not fulfilled his duty to the corporation under [§] 5.02(a)(1). . . .

6.   The facts being otherwise as stated in Illustration 4, D discloses to X Corporation, prior to the acquisition, his interest in R Corporation. D fails to disclose, however, that he has information, not publicly available, that the State Highway Department has formally decided to run a highway through the property on which R Corporation's building stands, and to condemn the building under its power of eminent domain. The price paid by X Corporation is fair, even taking the proposed condemnation into account, since the condemnation award is likely to equal or exceed the price. Two weeks after the acquisition, X Corporation learns of the Highway Department's decision. D has not fulfilled his duty to the corporation under § 5.02(a)(1). . . .

Illustrations [to Section 5.02(a)(2)(B)] . . .

9.   Corporation C is engaged in commercial agriculture. C's Board consists of L, its president, and N, O, and P, who own other types of agricultural businesses. C is potentially in the market for a new headquarters building. L recently inherited a commercial building that is somewhat rundown and only partially rented. Although L has no experience in real estate, she is convinced that with a $1 million renovation the building will be worth $9 million. L offered the building to a number of sophisticated buyers, whose bids ranged between $3 and 5 million. Subsequently, L listed the building with a commercial real estate broker for six months at a price of $7.5 million, but received no offers. L then offered the building to C's board for $7.5 million, making full disclosure, but arguing that this was a bargain price. N, O, and P, who are disinterested within the meaning of § 1.15, consulted a real estate expert, who advised that the building might conceivably be worth $7.5 million, but this was an extremely high price, and the expert would not pay it. The board nevertheless accepted L's offer. N, O, and P did not act irrationally, since real estate cannot be precisely valued, and the value that will be added to a building by renovation is always somewhat problematic. However, the $7.5 million price could not reasonably be regarded as fair, considering that the building had been extensively marketed to sophisticated real estate investors who were aware of the possibility of renovation; that none of these investors was willing to pay more than $5 million; and that N, O, and P were not themselves experts in real estate. The transaction fails to meet the standard of § 5.02(a)(2)(B), and an action may be brought against L to rescind the transaction. However, N, O, and P are protected from liability as individuals since they meet the standard of the business judgment rule [§ 4.01(c)]. . . .

§ 5.03   Compensation of Directors and Senior Executives

(a) *General Rule.* A director [§ 1.13] or senior executive [§ 1.33] who receives compensation from the corporation for services in that capacity fulfills the duty of fair dealing with respect to the compensation if either:

(1) The compensation is fair to the corporation when approved;

(2) The compensation is authorized in advance by disinterested directors [§ 1.15] or, in the case of a senior executive who is not a director, authorized in advance by a disinterested superior, in a manner that satisfies the standards of the business judgment rule [§ 4.01(c)];

(3) The compensation is ratified by disinterested directors [§ 1.15] who satisfy the requirements of the business judgment rule [§ 4.01(c)], provided (i) a corporate decisionmaker who was not interested [§ 1.23] in receipt of the compensation acted for the corporation in determining the compensation and satisfied the requirements of the business judgment rule; (ii) the interested director or senior executive did not act unreasonably in failing to seek advance authorization of the compensation by disinterested directors or a disinterested superior; and (iii) the failure to obtain advance authorization of the compensation by disinterested directors or a disinterested superior did not adversely affect the interests of the corporation in a significant way; or

(4) The compensation is authorized in advance or ratified by disinterested shareholders [§ 1.16], and does not constitute a waste of corporate assets [§ 1.42] at the time of the shareholder action.

(b) *Burden of Proof.* A party who challenges a transaction involving the payment of compensation to a director or senior executive has the burden of proof, except that if such party establishes that the requirements of neither Subsections (a)(2), (a)(3), nor (a)(4) are met, the director or the senior executive has the burden of proving that the transaction was fair to the corporation.

§ 5.04   Use by a Director or Senior Executive of Corporate Property, Material Non-public Corporate Information, or Corporate Position

(a) *General Rule.* A director [§ 1.13] or senior executive [§ 1.33] may not use corporate property, material non-public corporate information, or corporate position to secure a pecuniary benefit, unless either:

(1) Value is given for the use and the transaction meets the standards of § 5.02 (Transactions with the Corporation);

(2) The use constitutes compensation and meets the standards of § 5.03 (Compensation of Directors and Senior Executives);

(3) The use is solely of corporate information, and is not in connection with trading of the corporation's securities, is not a use of proprietary information of the corporation, and does not harm the corporation;

(4) The use is subject neither to § 5.02 nor § 5.03 but is authorized in advance or ratified by disinterested directors [§ 1.15] or disinterested shareholders [§ 1.16], and meets the requirements and standards of disclosure and review set forth in § 5.02 as if that Section were applicable to the use; or

(5) The benefit is received as a shareholder and is made proportionately available to all other similarly situated shareholders,

and the use is not otherwise unlawful.

(b) *Burden of Proof.* A party who challenges the conduct of a director or senior executive under Subsection (a) has the burden of proof, except that if value was given for the benefit, the burden of proving whether the value was fair should be allocated as provided in § 5.02 in the case of a transaction with the corporation.

(c) *Special Rule on Remedies.* A director or senior executive is subject to liability under this Section only to the extent of any improper benefit received and retained, except to the extent that any foreseeable harm caused by the conduct of the director or senior executive exceeds the value of the benefit received, and multiple liability based on receipt of the same benefit is not to be imposed.

§ 5.05 Taking of Corporate Opportunities by Directors or Senior Executives

(a) *General Rule.* A director [§ 1.13] or senior executive [§ 1.33] may not take advantage of a corporate opportunity unless:

(1) The director or senior executive first offers the corporate opportunity to the corporation and makes disclosure concerning the conflict of interest [§ 1.14(a)] and the corporate opportunity [§ 1.14(b)];

(2) The corporate opportunity is rejected by the corporation; and

(3) either:

(A) The rejection of the opportunity is fair to the corporation;

(B) The opportunity is rejected in advance, following such disclosure, by disinterested directors [§ 1.15], or, in the case of a senior executive who is not a director, by a disinterested superior, in a manner that satisfies the standards of the business judgment rule [§ 4.01(c)]; or

(C) The rejection is authorized in advance or ratified, following such disclosure, by disinterested shareholders [§ 1.16], and the rejection is not equivalent to a waste of corporate assets [§ 1.42].

(b) *Definition of a Corporate Opportunity.* For purposes of this Section, a corporate opportunity means:

(1) Any opportunity to engage in a business activity of which a director or senior executive becomes aware, either:

(A) In connection with the performance of functions as a director or senior executive, or under circumstances that should reasonably lead the director or senior executive to believe that the person offering the opportunity expects it to be offered to the corporation; or

(B) Through the use of corporate information or property, if the resulting opportunity is one that the director or senior executive should reasonably be expected to believe would be of interest to the corporation; or

(2) Any opportunity to engage in a business activity of which a senior executive becomes aware and knows is closely related to a business in which the corporation is engaged or expects to engage.

(c) *Burden of Proof.* A party who challenges the taking of a corporate opportunity has the burden of proof, except that if such party establishes that the requirements of Subsection (a)(3)(B) or (C) are not met, the director or the senior executive has the burden of proving that the rejection and the taking of the opportunity were fair to the corporation.

(d) *Ratification of Defective Disclosure.* A good faith but defective disclosure of the facts concerning the corporate opportunity may be cured if at any time (but no later than a reasonable time after suit is filed challenging the taking of the corporate opportunity) the original rejection of the corporate opportunity is ratified, following the required disclosure, by the board, the shareholders, or the corporate decisionmaker who initially approved the rejection of the corporate opportunity, or such decisionmaker's successor.

(e) *Special Rule Concerning Delayed Offering of Corporate Opportunities.* Relief based solely on failure to first offer an opportunity to the corporation under Subsection (a)(1) is not available if: (1) such failure resulted from a good faith belief that the business activity did not constitute a corporate opportunity, and (2) not later than a reasonable time after suit is filed challenging the taking of the corporate opportunity, the corporate opportunity is to the extent possible offered to the corporation and rejected in a manner that satisfies the standards of Subsection (a).

§ 5.06 Competition With the Corporation

(a) *General Rule.* Directors [§ 1.13] and senior executives [§ 1.33] may not advance their pecuniary interests by engaging in competition with the corporation unless either:

(1) Any reasonably foreseeable harm to the corporation from such competition is outweighed by the benefit that the corporation may reasonably be expected to derive from allowing the competition to take place, or there is no reasonably foreseeable harm to the corporation from such competition;

(2) The competition is authorized in advance or ratified, following disclosure concerning the conflict of interest [§ 1.14(a)] and the competition [§ 1.14(b)], by disinterested directors [§ 1.15], or in the case of a senior executive who is not a director, is authorized in advance by a disinterested superior, in a manner that satisfies the standards of the business judgment rule [§ 4.01(c)]; or

(3) The competition is authorized in advance or ratified, following such disclosure, by disinterested shareholders [§ 1.16], and the shareholders' action is not equivalent to a waste of corporate assets [§ 1.42].

(b) *Burden of Proof.* A party who challenges a director or senior executive for advancing the director's or senior executive's pecuniary interest by competing with the corporation has the burden of proof, except that if such party establishes that neither Subsection (a)(2) nor (3) is satisfied, the director or the senior executive has the burden of proving that any reasonably foreseeable harm to the corporation from such competition is outweighed by the benefit that the corporation may reasonably be expected to derive from allowing the competition to take place, or that there is no reasonably foreseeable harm to the corporation.

§ 5.07 Transactions Between Corporations With Common Directors or Senior Executives

(a) A transaction between two corporations is not to be treated as a transaction subject to the provisions of § 5.02 (Transactions With the Corporation) solely on the ground that the same person is a director [§ 1.13] or senior executive [§ 1.33] of both corporations unless:

(1) The director or senior executive participates personally and substantially in negotiating the transaction for either of the corporations; or

(2) The transaction is approved by the board of either corporation, and a director on that board who is also a director or senior executive of the other corporation casts a vote that is necessary to approve the transaction.

(b) If a transaction falls within Subsection (a)(1) or (a)(2), it will be reviewed under § 5.02.

§ 5.08 Conduct on Behalf of Associates of Directors or Senior Executives

A director [§ 1.13] or senior executive [§ 1.33] fails to fulfill the duty of fair dealing to the corporation if the director or senior executive knowingly advances the pecuniary interest of an associate [§ 1.03] in a manner that would fail to comply with the provisions of this Chapter 2 had the director or senior executive acted for himself or herself.

§ 5.09 Effect of a Standard of the Corporation

If a director [§ 1.13] or senior executive [§ 1.33] acts in reliance upon a standard of the corporation [§ 1.36] that authorizes a director or senior executive to either:

(a) Enter into a transaction with the corporation that is of a specified type and that could be expected to recur in the ordinary course of business of the corporation;

(b) Use corporate position or corporate property in a specified manner that is not unlawful and that could be expected to recur in the ordinary course of business of the corporation;

(c) Take advantage of a specified type of corporate opportunity of which the director or senior executive becomes aware other than (i) in connection with the performance of directorial or executive functions, or (ii) under circumstances that should reasonably lead the director or senior executive to believe that the person [§ 1.28] offering the opportunity expected it to be offered to the corporation, or (iii) through the use of corporate information or property; or

(d) Engage in competition of a specified type;

and the standard was authorized in advance by disinterested directors [§ 1.15] or disinterested shareholders [§ 1.16], following disclosure concerning the effect of the standard and of the type of transaction or conduct intended to be covered by the standard, then the standard is to be deemed equivalent to an authorization of the action in advance by disinterested directors or shareholders under §§ 5.02 (Transactions with the Corporation), 5.03 (Compensation of Directors and Senior Executives), 5.04 (Use by a Director or Senior Executive of Corporate Property, Material Non-Public Corporate Information, or Corporate Position), 5.05 (Taking of Corporate Opportunities by Directors or Senior Executives), or 5.06 (Competition with the Corporation), as the case may be.

Chapter 3

DUTY OF FAIR DEALING OF CONTROLLING SHAREHOLDERS

§ 5.10 Transactions by a Controlling Shareholder With the Corporation

(a) *General Rule.* A controlling shareholder [§ 1.10] who enters into a transaction with the corporation fulfills the duty of fair dealing to the corporation with respect to the transaction if:

(1) The transaction is fair to the corporation when entered into; or

(2) The transaction is authorized in advance or ratified by disinterested shareholders [§ 1.16], following disclosure concerning the conflict of interest [§ 1.14(a)] and the transaction [§ 1.14(b)], and does not constitute a waste of corporate assets [§ 1.42] at the time of the shareholder action.

(b) *Burden of Proof.* If the transaction was authorized in advance by disinterested directors [§ 1.15], or authorized in advance or ratified by disinterested shareholders, following such disclosure, the party challenging the transaction has the burden of proof. The party challenging the transaction also has the burden of proof if the transaction was ratified by disinterested directors and the failure to obtain advance authorization did not adversely affect the interests of the corporation in a significant way. If the transaction was not so authorized or ratified, the controlling shareholder has the burden of proof, except to the extent otherwise provided in Subsection (c).

(c) *Transactions in the Ordinary Course of Business.* In the case of a transaction between a controlling shareholder and the corporation that was in the ordinary course of the corporation's business, a party who challenges the transaction has the burden of coming forward with evidence that the transaction was unfair, whether or not the transaction was authorized in advance or ratified by disinterested directors or disinterested shareholders.

§ 5.11   Use by a Controlling Shareholder of Corporate Property, Material Non-public Corporate Information, or Corporate Position

(a) *General Rule.* A controlling shareholder may not use corporate property, its controlling position, or (when trading in the corporation's securities) material non-public corporate information to secure a pecuniary benefit, unless:

(1) Value is given for the use and the transaction meets the standards of § 5.10 (Transactions by a Controlling Shareholder with the Corporation), or

(2) Any resulting benefit to the controlling shareholder either is made proportionally available to the other similarly situated shareholders or is derived only from the use of controlling position and is not unfair to other shareholders,

and the use is not otherwise unlawful.

(b) *Burden of Proof.* A party who challenges the conduct of a controlling shareholder under Subsection (a) has the burden of proof, except that if value was given for the benefit, the burden of proving whether the value was fair should be determined as provided in § 5.10 in the case of a transaction with the corporation.

(c) *Special Rule on Remedies.* A controlling shareholder is subject to liability under this section only to the extent of any improper benefit received and retained, except to the extent that any foreseeable harm caused by the shareholder's conduct exceeds the value of the benefit received, and multiple liability based on receipt of the same benefit is not to be imposed.

§ 5.12   Taking of Corporate Opportunities by a Controlling Shareholder

(a) *General Rule.* A controlling shareholder [§ 1.10] may not take advantage of a corporate opportunity unless:

(1) The taking of the opportunity is fair to the corporation; or

(2) The taking of the opportunity is authorized in advance or ratified by disinterested shareholders [§ 1.16], following disclosure concerning the conflict of interest [§ 1.14(a)] and the corporate opportunity [§ 1.14(b)], and the taking of the opportunity is not equivalent to a waste of corporate assets [§ 1.42].

(b) *Definition of a Corporate Opportunity.* For purposes of this Section, a corporate opportunity means any opportunity to engage in a business activity that:

(1) Is developed or received by the corporation, or comes to the controlling shareholder primarily by virtue of its relationship to the corporation; or

(2) Is held out to shareholders of the corporation by the controlling shareholder, or by the corporation with the consent of the controlling shareholder, as being a type of business activity that will be within the scope of the business in which the corporation is engaged or expects to engage and will not be within the scope of the controlling shareholder's business.

(c) *Burden of Proof.* A party who challenges the taking of a corporate opportunity has the burden of proof, except that the controlling shareholder has the burden of proving that the taking of the opportunity is fair to the corporation if the taking of the opportunity was not authorized in advance or ratified by disinterested directors or disinterested shareholders, following the disclosure required by Subsection (a)(2).

§ 5.13   Conduct on Behalf of Associates of a Controlling Shareholder

A controlling shareholder [§ 1.10] fails to fulfill the duty of fair dealing to the corporation if it knowingly advances the pecuniary interest of an associate [§ 1.03] of the controlling shareholder in a manner that would fail to comply with the provisions of this Chapter 3 had the controlling shareholder acted for itself.

Chapter 4

TRANSFER OF CONTROL

§ 5.15 Transfer of Control in Which a Director or Principal Senior Executive Is Interested

(a) If directors or principal senior executives [§ 1.30] of a corporation are interested [§ 1.23] in a transaction in control [§ 1.38] or a tender offer that results in a transfer of control [§ 1.08] of the corporation to another person [§ 1.28], then those directors or principal senior executives have the burden of proving that the transaction was fair to the shareholders of the corporation unless (1) the transaction involves a transfer by a controlling shareholder [§ 1.10] or (2) the conditions of Subsection (b) are satisfied.

(b) If in connection with a transaction described in Subsection (a) involving a publicly held corporation [§ 1.31]:

(1) Public disclosure of the proposed transaction is made;

(2) Responsible persons who express an interest are provided relevant information concerning the corporation and given a reasonable opportunity to submit a competing proposal;

(3) The transaction is authorized in advance by disinterested directors [§ 1.15] after the procedures set forth in Subsections (1) and (2) have been complied with; and

(4) The transaction is authorized or ratified by disinterested shareholders [§ 1.16] (or, if the transaction is effected by a tender offer, the offer is accepted by disinterested shareholders), after disclosure concerning the conflict of interest [§ 1.14(a)] and the transaction [§ 1.14(b)] has been made;

then a party challenging the transaction has the burden of proving that the terms of the transaction are equivalent to a waste of corporate assets [§ 1.42].

(c) The fact that holders of equity securities are entitled to an appraisal remedy reflecting the general principles embodied in §§ 7.21–7.23 with respect to a transaction specified in Subsection (a) does not make an appraisal proceeding the exclusive remedy of a shareholder who proposes to challenge the transaction, unless the transaction falls within § 7.25 (Transactions in Control Involving Corporate Combinations to Which a Majority Shareholder Is a Party).

§ 5.16 Disposition of Voting Equity Securities by a Controlling Shareholder to Third Parties

A controlling shareholder [§ 1.10] has the same right to dispose of voting equity securities [§ 1.40] as any other shareholder, including the right to dispose of those securities for a price that is not made proportionally available to other shareholders, but the controlling shareholder does not satisfy the duty of fair dealing to the other shareholders if:

(a) The controlling shareholder does not make disclosure concerning the transaction [§ 1.14(b)] to other shareholders with whom the controlling shareholder deals in connection with the transaction; or

(b) It is apparent from the circumstances that the purchaser is likely to violate the duty of fair dealing under Part V in such a way as to obtain a significant financial benefit for the purchaser or an associate [§ 1.03].

PART VI

ROLE OF DIRECTORS AND SHAREHOLDERS IN TRANSACTIONS IN CONTROL AND TENDER OFFERS

§ 6.01 Role of Directors and Holders of Voting Equity Securities With Respect to Transactions in Control Proposed to the Corporation

(a) The board of directors, in the exercise of its business judgment [§ 4.01(c)], may approve, reject, or decline to consider a proposal to the corporation to engage in a transaction in control [§ 1.38].

(b) A transaction in control of the corporation to which the corporation is a party should require approval by the shareholders [§ 1.02].

§ 6.02 Action of Directors That Has the Foreseeable Effect of Blocking Unsolicited Tender Offers

(a) The board of directors may take an action that has the foreseeable effect of blocking an unsolicited tender offer [§ 1.39], if the action is a reasonable response to the offer.

(b) In considering whether its action is a reasonable response to the offer:

(1) The board may take into account all factors relevant to the best interests of the corporation and shareholders, including, among other things, questions of legality and whether the offer, if successful, would threaten the corporation's essential economic prospects; and

(2) The board may, in addition to the analysis under § 6.02(b)(1), have regard for interests or groups (other than shareholders) with respect to which the corporation has a legitimate concern if to do so would not significantly disfavor the long-term interests of shareholders.

(c) A person who challenges an action of the board on the ground that it fails to satisfy the standards of Subsection (a) has the burden of proof that the board's action is an unreasonable response to the offer.

(d) An action that does not meet the standards of Subsection (a) may be enjoined or set aside, but directors who authorize such an action are not subject to liability for damages if their conduct meets the standard of the business judgment rule [§ 4.01(c)].

PART VII

REMEDIES

INTRODUCTION...

Reporter's Note

1.   *The empirical evidence.* Critiques of the derivative action are not new. In the 1940s, the Chamber of Commerce of the State of New York sponsored a study by Franklin Wood that examined 1400 derivative actions filed between 1936 and 1942 in New York City. Wood reported a consistent pattern in which (1) the plaintiff's stockholdings were generally nominal, (2) the plaintiff seldom secured a litigated victory, and (3) private settlements (in which the corporation often received nothing) were common. F. Wood, Survey and Report Regarding Stockholders' Derivative Suits, 32 (1944) (the "Wood Report"). He concluded that the benefits of the action were outweighed by its costs. Partly as a result of the Wood Report and similar commentary, and partly because of the bar's uneasiness with an action in which the attorney was frequently the real party in interest, the derivative action was frequently derided as a "strike suit" that served no interests other than those of the plaintiff's attorney.

In response, legislative treatment of the action was generally skeptical and constraining: statutes requiring security for expenses' bonds were enacted, common law defenses were tightened, and an extraordinary procedural complexity developed around such questions as jurisdiction, alignment of the parties, demand on the board and shareholders, and settlement and dismissal. Later, other commentators re-analyzed Wood's data and, after excluding those cases that were still pending or in which the disposition was unknown, concluded that the overall rate of plaintiff's "success" (i.e., cases in which some recovery was secured) was about 44 percent, and thus compared favorably with the rate of plaintiff's success in similar forms of civil litigation. See Conard, A Behavioral Analysis of Directors' Liability for Negligence, 1972 Duke L.J. 895, 901 n.21; Hornstein, The Death Knell of Stockholders' Derivative Suits in New York, 32 Calif.L.Rev. 123, 127–28 (1944).

Important empirical work has been done in this area since the time of the original Wood study, but an overall evaluation of the derivative action remains difficult to reach. One such effort casts some partial light on the disputed benefits of the derivative action. An eight-year study followed 531 derivative and class action suits brought against the officers or directors of 205 publicly held corporations between 1971 and 1978. See Jones, An Empirical Examination of the Resolution of Shareholder Derivative and Class Action Lawsuits, 60 B.U.L.Rev. 542 (1980). The following results of that study seem salient:

(1) In roughly 75 percent of the cases, plaintiffs obtained some form of relief, typically by way of settlement (70%), but in less than one percent did plaintiffs win a litigated judgment. Although this study concluded that "the notion that shareholder plaintiffs rarely obtain relief is clearly a myth" (Id. at 545), it is uncertain at what price this relief came. Because data were not collected with respect to the size or adequacy of the settlement funds in these actions, and because direct and derivative actions were not carefully distinguished, it remains an open question whether these actions yielded a net compensatory benefit to their corporations.

(2) The incidence of "primary" shareholder litigation (i.e., litigation directed at corporate officials personally) did not significantly rise over the period from 1971 to 1978, and, if adjustment is made for a sudden spurt of "illegal payments" cases in the mid-1970s, probably fell slightly over this period.

(3) Derivative ligation tended to focus on self-dealing transactions and duty of loyalty issues and only infrequently involved challenges to arm's-length business decisions.

(4) Only a minority of publicly held corporations experienced such litigation. About 30 percent of the large publicly held corporations surveyed were involved in any form of shareholder litigation, direct or derivative, during the eight-year period. Once the impact of multiple suits arising out of the same event or transaction was adjusted for, the study concluded that the typical publicly held firm would be involved in such a suit only once every 17.6 years on average. See Jones, An Empirical Evaluation of the Incidence of Shareholder Derivative and Class Action Lawsuits, 1971–1978, 60 B.U.L.Rev. 306, 312–13 (1980).

Recently, social scientists have reanalyzed the data collected in the foregoing study. Although they found important information to be lacking from much of the sample, they still noted that, when the amount of the recovery was indicated, "one-third of the total reported settlements involved no monetary relief, and six of the fifteen cases in which attorney fees were reported involved only 'procedural changes,' but significant attorney fees." This pattern suggests the existence of a substantial conflict of interest may exist between the plaintiff's attorney and his nominal clients, the shareholders. See Garth, Nagel and Plager, The Role of Empirical Research in Assessing the Efficacy of the Shareholders' Derivative Suit: Promise and Potential, 48 Law and Contemp.Probs. 137, 146–47 (1985). See also Rosenfeld, An Empirical Test of Class Action Settlements, 5 J.Legal Stud. 113, 119 (1976); Coffee, The Unfaithful Champion: The Plaintiff as Monitor in Shareholder Litigation, 48 Law and Contemp.Probs. 5, 26–33 (1985).

The most recent study of shareholder litigation examined a random sample of 535 public corporations over a period extending from the late 1960s to 1987. See Romano, The Shareholder Suit: Litigation Without Foundation?, 7 J.Law, Econ., & Org. 55 (1991). Its findings underline the relative infrequency of derivative actions and the centrality of the settlement stage. Only 19 percent of the corporations in the sample experienced a derivative suit, but some corporations attracted recurrent litigation, and there was an increase in litigation frequency during the 1980s. Although very few judgments for plaintiffs were obtained, the most striking fact about derivative litigation in this study was the high rate of settlement. Eighty-three out of 128 actions resolved during this period (or roughly 65%) were settled. Id. at 60. Yet, only half of the settlements (46 out of 83) involved any monetary recovery; however, the vast majority (75 out of 83) involved fee awards to the plaintiffs' attorneys. In another 25 cases, the settlement afforded non-pecuniary structural relief (there was also a monetary recovery in four of the suits). In those cases where the settlement fund could be valued (39 out of 83), the average recovery was $9 million, but there was substantial variation within this class (as the median recovery was only $2 million). Interestingly, the average recovery in derivative actions was found to be about half that in class actions. Id. at 61. These results can be interpreted in various ways. Some would explain them on the hypothesis that a significant percentage of shareholder litigation is without merit; another hypothesis is that plaintiffs' attorneys in such actions have serious conflicts of interest that lead them not to maximize the possible recovery to their class. Yet, a paradox arises here: another recent study has found that securities class actions tend to settle at 25 percent of the asserted potential damages. See Alexander, Do the Merits Matter? A Study of Settlements in Securities Class Actions, 43 Stan.L.Rev. 497, 500 (1991). Although such findings can similarly be interpreted to show an excessive incentive to litigate and to settle, the puzzle is that the two contexts are closely related. Indeed, typically, the same plaintiffs' attorneys are suing similarly situated defendants in both types of actions. In this light, the difference in outcomes between class and derivative actions (and the greater recoveries in the former) may reflect the greater legal barriers surrounding the derivative action. Overbroad rules that deny standing to plaintiffs in derivative actions in which the underlying allegations have legal merit could explain the lesser apparent settlement value of legal claims in the derivative action context.

Some preliminary efforts have been made to use econometric techniques to study the impact of the termination of derivative actions on the stock prices of companies in whose name the action was brought. Early results have reported a marginally negative market reaction to the suit's termination, but one that was statistically insignificant. See Fischel and Bradley, The Role of Liability Rules and the Derivative Suit in Corporate Law: A Theoretical and Empirical Analysis, 71 Cornell L.Rev. 261, 277–83 (1986). However, both because the methodology underlying these studies makes questionable assumptions about the stock market's sensitivity to the prospect of relatively small recoveries and because there is no evidence that the market's expectation was frustrated by the suit's termination (i.e., the market may assume that most suits will be terminated, whatever their merit), little reliance is here placed on such data. Even if reliable data that showed an insignificant or negative trend in the wake of an action's filing were available, the interpretation that should be placed on such data would remain open to debate. Stock market indifference to derivative litigation could be explained as based on the expectation that such actions were likely to result in collusive or cosmetic settlements in which any recovery would be consumed by costly attorneys' fees and other expenses. In addition, if the principal benefit of such actions lies in their general deterrent effect on all corporate managements, the stock price reaction of any single corporation would not reveal this benefit.

The existing state of the empirical data does not answer many important questions. First, it does not tell us whether derivative actions yield on average a net compensatory benefit for the corporation (after appropriate deduction is made for the cost of attorneys' fees and indemnification). Second, although the data shows little evidence of any recent explosion in the rate of shareholder litigation and suggests that such litigation only infrequently concerns business decisions not complicated by an alleged conflict of interest, it is possible that directors' perception of such litigation may be very different, and it is the perceived threat that may shape their willingness to serve on boards. Finally, recent institutional changes—such as the decreased availability of liability insurance and the change in incidence of takeover contests—may not be reflected in historical data. Still, the empirical evidence does clearly highlight the centrality of the settlement stage and the possibility that the conflicts of interest attending this stage may weaken the ability of derivative litigation to serve shareholders' interests.

Chapter 1

THE DERIVATIVE ACTION

§ 7.01 Direct and Derivative Actions Distinguished

(a) A derivative action may be brought in the name or right of a corporation by a holder [§ 1.22], as provided in § 7.02 (Standing to Commence and Maintain a Derivative Action), to redress an injury sustained by, or enforce a duty owed to, a corporation. An action in which the holder can prevail only by showing an injury or breach of duty to the corporation should be treated as a derivative action.

(b) A direct action may be brought in the name and right of a holder to redress an injury sustained by, or enforce a duty owed to, the holder. An action in which the holder can prevail without showing an injury or breach of duty to the corporation should be treated as a direct action that may be maintained by the holder in an individual capacity.

(c) If a transaction gives rise to both direct and derivative claims, a holder may commence and maintain direct and derivative actions simultaneously, and any special restrictions or defenses pertaining to the maintenance, settlement, or dismissal of either action should not apply to the other.

(d) In the case of a closely held corporation [§ 1.06], the court in its discretion may treat an action raising derivative claims as a direct action, exempt it from those restrictions and defenses applicable only to derivative actions, and order an individual recovery, if it finds that to do so will not (i) unfairly expose the corporation or the defendants to a multiplicity of actions, (ii) materially prejudice the interests of creditors of the corporation, or (iii) interfere with a fair distribution of the recovery among all interested persons.

§ 7.02   Standing to Commence and Maintain a Derivative Action

(a) A holder [§ 1.22] of an equity security [§ 1.20] has standing to commence and maintain a derivative action if the holder:

(1) Acquired the equity security either (A) before the material facts relating to the alleged wrong were publicly disclosed or were known by, or specifically communicated to, the holder, or (B) by devolution of law, directly or indirectly, from a prior holder who acquired the security as described in the preceding Clause (A);

(2) Continues to hold the equity security until the time of judgment, unless the failure to do so is the result of corporate action in which the holder did not acquiesce, and either (A) the derivative action was commenced prior to the corporate action terminating the holder's status, or (B) the court finds that the holder is better able to represent the interests of the shareholders than any other holder who has brought suit;

(3) Has complied with the demand requirement of § 7.03 (Exhaustion of Intracorporate Remedies: The Demand Rule) or was excused by its terms; and

(4) Is able to represent fairly and adequately the interests of the shareholders.

(b) On a timely motion, a holder of an equity security should be permitted to intervene in a derivative action, unless the court finds that the interests to be represented by the intervenor are already fairly and adequately represented or that the intervenor is unable to represent fairly and adequately the interests of the shareholders.

(c) A director [§ 1.13] of a corporation has standing to commence and maintain a derivative action unless the court finds that the director is unable to represent fairly and adequately the interests of the shareholders.

§ 7.03   Exhaustion of Intracorporate Remedies: The Demand Rule

(a) Before commencing a derivative action, a holder [§ 1.22] or a director [§ 1.13] should be required to make a written demand upon the board of directors of the corporation, requesting it to prosecute the action or take suitable corrective measures, unless demand is excused under § 7.03(b). The demand should give notice to the board, with reasonable specificity, of the essential facts relied upon to support each of the claims made therein.

(b) Demand on the board should be excused only if the plaintiff makes a specific showing that irreparable injury to the corporation would otherwise result, and in such instances demand should be made promptly after commencement of the action.

(c) Demand on shareholders should not be required.

(d) Except as provided in § 7.03(b), the court should dismiss a derivative action that is commenced prior to the response of the board or a committee thereof to the demand required by § 7.03(a), unless the board or committee fails to respond within a reasonable time.

§ 7.04   Pleading, Demand Rejection, Procedure, and Costs in a Derivative Action

The legal standards applicable to a derivative action should provide that:

(a) *Particularity; Demand Rejection.*

(1) *In General.* The complaint shall plead with particularity facts that, if true, raise a significant prospect that the transaction or conduct complained of did not meet the applicable requirements of Parts IV (Duty of Care and the Business Judgment Rule), V (Duty of Fair Dealing), or VI (Role of Directors and Shareholders in Transactions in Control and Tender Offers), in light of any approvals of the transaction or conduct communicated to the plaintiff by the corporation.

(2) *Demand Rejection.* If a corporation rejects the demand made on the board pursuant to § 7.03, and if, at or following the rejection, the corporation delivers to the plaintiff a written reply to the demand which states that the demand was rejected by directors who were not interested [§ 1.23] in the transaction or conduct described in and forming the basis for the demand and that such directors constituted a majority of the entire board and were capable as a group of objective judgment in the circumstances, and provides specific reasons for those statements, then the complaint shall also plead with particularity facts that, if true, raise a significant prospect that either:

(A) The statements in the reply are not correct;

(B) If Part IV, V, or VI provides that the underlying transaction or conduct would be reviewed under the standard of the business judgment rule, that the rejection did not satisfy the requirements of the business judgment rule as specified in § 4.01(c); or

(C) If Part IV, V, or VI provides that the underlying transaction or conduct would be reviewed under a standard other than the business judgment rule, either (i) that the disinterested directors who rejected the demand did not satisfy the good faith and informational requirements (§ 4.01(c)(2)) of the business judgment rule or (ii) that disinterested directors could not reasonably have determined that rejection of the demand was in the best interests of the corporation.

If the complaint fails to set forth sufficiently such particularized facts, defendants shall be entitled to dismissal of the complaint prior to discovery.

(b) *Attorney's Certification.* Each party's attorney of record shall sign every pleading, motion, and other paper filed on behalf of the party, and such signature shall constitute the attorney's certification that (i) to the best of the attorney's knowledge, information, and belief, formed after reasonable inquiry, the pleading, motion, or other paper is well grounded in fact and is warranted by existing law or by a good faith argument for the extension, modification, or reversal of existing law, and (ii) the pleading, motion, or other paper is not interposed for any improper purpose, such as to harass or to cause unnecessary delay or needless increase in the cost of litigation.

(c) *Security for Expenses.* Except as authorized by statute or judicial rule applicable to civil actions generally, no bond, undertaking, or other security for expenses shall be required.

(d) *Award of Costs.* The court may award applicable costs, including reasonable attorney's fees and expenses, against a party, or a party's counsel:

(1) At any time, if the court finds that any specific claim for relief or defense was asserted or any pleading, motion, request for discovery, or other action was made or taken in bad faith or without reasonable cause; or

(2) Upon final judgment, if the court finds, in light of all the evidence, and considering both the state and trend of the substantive law, that the action taken as a whole was brought, prosecuted, or defended in bad faith or in an unreasonable manner.

Comment . . .

d.   *Section 7.04(a)(2)* . . .

Section 7.04(a)(1) and § 7.04(a)(2) state separate tests, so both are required to be met. There is nevertheless an interrelationship between the two tests. In applying § 7.04(a), a court should balance the strength and seriousness of the case set out by the particularized pleading of the plaintiff, as tested under

§ 7.04(a)(1), with that required under § 7.04(a)(2). The stronger and more serious the case set out by the plaintiff's particularized pleading, as tested under § 7.04(a)(1), the less the complaint must allege with particularity to establish under § 7.04(a)(2) that there is a significant prospect the directors could not have satisfied the business judgment rule under § 7.04(a)(2)(B), or could not reasonably have determined that rejection of the demand was in the best interests of the corporation under § 7.04(a)(2)(C).

§ 7.05 Board or Committee Authority in Regard to a Derivative Action

(a) The board of a corporation in whose name or right a derivative action is brought has standing on behalf of the corporation to:

(1) Move to dismiss the action on account of the plaintiff's lack of standing under § 7.02 (Standing to Commence and Maintain a Derivative Action) or the plaintiff's failure to comply with § 7.03 (Exhaustion of Intracorporate Remedies: The Demand Rule) or § 7.04(a) or (b) (Pleading, Demand Rejection, Procedure, and Costs in a Derivative Action) or move for dismissal of the complaint or for summary judgment;

(2) Move for a stay of the action, including discovery, as provided by § 7.06 (Authority of Court to Stay a Derivative Action);

(3) Move to dismiss the action as contrary to the best interests of the corporation, as provided in §§ 7.07–7.12 (dismissal of a derivative action based on a motion requesting dismissal by the board, a board committee, the shareholders, or a special panel);

(4) Oppose injunctive or other relief materially affecting the corporation's interests;

(5) Adopt or pursue the action in the corporation's right;

(6) Comment on, object to, or recommend any proposed settlement, discontinuance, compromise, or voluntary dismissal by agreement between the plaintiff and any defendant under § 7.14 (Settlement of a Derivative Action by Agreement Between the Plaintiff and a Defendant), or any award of attorney's fees and other expenses under § 7.17 (Plaintiff's Attorney's Fees and Expenses); and

(7) Seek to settle the action without agreement of the plaintiff under § 7.15 (Settlement of a Derivative Action Without the Agreement of the Plaintiff).

Except as provided above, the corporation may not otherwise defend the action in the place of, or raise defenses on behalf of, other defendants.

(b) The board of a corporation in whose name or right a derivative action is brought may:

(1) Delegate its authority to take any action specified in § 7.05(a) to a committee of directors; or

(2) Request the court to appoint a special panel in lieu of a committee of directors, or a special member of a committee, under § 7.12 (Special Panel or Special Committee Members).

§ 7.06 Authority of Court to Stay a Derivative Action

In the absence of special circumstances, the court should stay discovery and all further proceedings by the plaintiff in a derivative action on the motion of the corporation and upon such conditions as the court deems appropriate pending the court's determination of any motion made by the corporation under § 7.04(a)(2) and the completion within a reasonable period of any review and evaluation undertaken and diligently pursued pursuant to § 7.09 (Procedures for Requesting Dismissal of a Derivative Action). On the same basis, the court may stay discovery and further proceedings pending (a) the resolution of a related action or (b) such other event or development as the interests of justice may require.

§ 7.07 Dismissal of a Derivative Action Based on a Motion Requesting Dismissal by the Board or a Committee: General Statement

(a) The court having jurisdiction over a derivative action should dismiss the action as against one or more of the defendants based on a motion by the board or a properly delegated committee requesting dismissal of the action as in the best interests of the corporation, if:

(1) In the case of an action against a person [§ 1.28] other than a director [§ 1.13], senior executive [§ 1.33], or person in control [§ 1.08] of the corporation, or an associate [§ 1.03] of any such person, the determinations of the board or committee underlying the motion satisfy the requirements of the business judgment rule as specified in § 4.01;

(2) In the case of an action against a director, senior executive, or person in control of the corporation, or an associate of any such person, the conditions specified in § 7.08 (Dismissal of a Derivative Action Against Directors, Senior Executives, Controlling Persons, or Associates Based on a Motion Requesting Dismissal by the Board or a Committee) are satisfied; or

(3) In any case, the shareholders approve a resolution requesting dismissal of the action in the manner provided in § 7.11 (Dismissal of a Derivative Action Based Upon Action by the Shareholders).

(b) Regardless of whether a corporation chooses to proceed under § 7.08 or § 7.11, it is free to make any other motion available to it under the law, including a motion to dismiss the complaint or for summary judgment.

§ 7.08   Dismissal of a Derivative Action Against Directors, Senior Executives, Controlling Persons, or Associates Based on a Motion Requesting Dismissal by the Board or a Committee

The court should, subject to the provisions of § 7.10(b) (retention of significant improper benefit), dismiss a derivative action against a defendant who is a director [§ 1.13], a senior executive [§ 1.33], or a person [§ 1.28] in control [§ 1.08] of the corporation, or an associate [§ 1.03] of any such person, if:

(a) The board of directors or a properly delegated committee thereof (either in response to a demand or following commencement of the action) has determined that the action is contrary to the best interests of the corporation and has requested dismissal of the action;

(b) The procedures specified in § 7.09 (Procedures for Requesting Dismissal of a Derivative Action) for the conduct of a review and evaluation of the action were substantially complied with (either in response to a demand or following commencement of the action), or any material departures therefrom were justified under the circumstances; and

(c) The determinations of the board or committee satisfy the applicable standard of review set forth in § 7.10(a) (Standard of Judicial Review with Regard to a Board or Committee Motion Requesting Dismissal of a Derivative Action Under § 7.08).

§ 7.09   Procedures for Requesting Dismissal of a Derivative Action

(a) The following procedural standards should apply to the review and evaluation of a derivative action by the board or committee under § 7.08 (Dismissal of a Derivative Action Against Directors, Senior Executives, Controlling Persons, or Associates Based on a Motion Requesting Dismissal by the Board or a Committee) or § 7.11 (Dismissal of a Derivative Action Based Upon Action by the Shareholders):

(1) The board or committee should be composed of two or more persons, no participating member of which was interested [§ 1.23] in the action, and should as a group be capable of objective judgment in the circumstances;

(2) The board or committee should be assisted by counsel of its choice and such other agents as it reasonably considers necessary;

(3) The determinations of the board or committee should be based upon a review and evaluation that was sufficiently informed to satisfy the standards applicable under § 7.10(a); and

(4) If the board or committee determines to request dismissal of the derivative action, it shall prepare and file with the court a report or other written submission setting forth its determinations in a manner sufficient to enable the court to conduct the review required under § 7.10 (Standard of Judicial Review with Regard to a Board or Committee Motion Requesting Dismissal of a Derivative Action Under § 7.08).

(b) If the court is unwilling to grant a motion to dismiss under § 7.08 or § 7.11 because the procedures followed by the board or committee departed materially from the standards specified in § 7.09(a), the court should permit the board or committee to supplement its procedures, and make such further reports or other written submissions, as will satisfy the standards specified in § 7.09(a), unless the court decides that (i) the board or committee did not act on the basis of a good faith belief that its procedures and report were justified in the circumstances; (ii) unreasonable delay or prejudice would result; or (iii) there is no reasonable prospect that such further steps would support dismissal of the action.

§ 7.10 Standard of Judicial Review With Regard to a Board or Committee Motion Requesting Dismissal of a Derivative Action Under § 7.08

(a) *Standard of Review.* In deciding whether an action should be dismissed under § 7.08 (Dismissal of a Derivative Action Against Directors, Senior Executives, Controlling Persons, or Associates Based on a Motion Requesting Dismissal by the Board or a Committee), the court should apply the following standards of review:

(1) If the gravamen of the claim is that the defendant violated a duty set forth in Part IV (Duty of Care and the Business Judgment Rule), other than by committing a knowing and culpable violation of law that is alleged with particularity, or if the underlying transaction or conduct would be reviewed under the business judgment rule under § 5.03, § 5.04, § 5.05, § 5.06, § 5.08, or § 6.02, the court should dismiss the claim unless it finds that the board's or committee's determinations fail to satisfy the requirements of the business judgment rule as specified in § 4.01(c).

(2) In other cases governed by Part V (Duty of Fair Dealing) or Part VI (Role of Directors and Shareholders in Transactions in Control and Tender Offers), or to which the business judgment rule is not applicable, including cases in which the gravamen of the claim is that defendant committed a knowing and culpable violation of law in breach of Part IV, the court should dismiss the action if the court finds, in light of the applicable standards under Part IV, V, or VI that the board or committee was adequately informed under the circumstances and reasonably determined that dismissal was in the best interests of the corporation, based on grounds that the court deems to warrant reliance.

(3) In cases arising under either Subsection (a)(1) or (a)(2), the court may substantively review and determine any issue of law.

(b) *Retention of Significant Improper Benefit.* The court shall not dismiss an action if the plaintiff establishes that dismissal would permit a defendant, or an associate [§ 1.03], to retain a significant improper benefit where:

(1) The defendant, either alone or collectively with others who are also found to have received a significant improper benefit arising out of the same transaction, possesses control [§ 1.08] of the corporation; or

(2) Such benefit was obtained:

(A) As the result of a knowing and material misrepresentation or omission or other fraudulent act; or

(B) Without advance authorization or the requisite ratification of such benefit by disinterested directors [§ 1.15] (or, in the case of a non-director senior executive, advance authorization by a disinterested superior), or authorization or ratification by disinterested shareholders [§ 1.16], and in breach of § 5.02 (Transactions with the Corporation) or § 5.04 (Use by a Director or Senior Executive of Corporate Property, Material Non-Public Corporate Information, or Corporate Position);

unless the court determines, in light of specific reasons advanced by the board or committee, that the likely injury to the corporation from continuation of the action convincingly outweighs any adverse impact on the public interest from dismissal of the action.

(c) *Subsequent Developments.* In determining whether the standards of § 7.10(a) are satisfied or whether § 7.10(b) or any of the exceptions set forth therein are applicable, the court may take into account considerations set forth by the board or committee (or otherwise brought to the court's attention) that reflect material developments subsequent to the time of the underlying transaction or conduct or to the time of the motion by the board or committee requesting dismissal.

§ 7.11   Dismissal of a Derivative Action Based Upon Action by the Shareholders

The court should dismiss a derivative action against any defendant upon approval by the shareholders of a resolution requesting dismissal of the action as in the best interests of the corporation if the court finds that:

(a) A resolution recommending such dismissal to the shareholders was adopted by the board of directors, or a properly delegated committee thereof, after a review and evaluation that substantially complied with the procedures specified in § 7.09(a)(1)–(3) (Procedures for Requesting Dismissal of a Derivative Action) or in which any material departures from those procedures were justified under the circumstances;

(b) Disclosure was made to the shareholders of all material facts [§ 1.25] concerning the derivative action and the board's resolution recommending its dismissal to the shareholders and, if requested by plaintiff, the disclosure statement included a brief statement by the plaintiff summarizing the plaintiff's views of the action and of the board's or committee's resolutions;

(c) The resolution was approved by a vote of disinterested shareholders [§ 1.16]; and

(d) Dismissal would not constitute a waste of corporate assets [§ 1.42].

§ 7.12   Special Panel or Special Committee Members

(a) On motion made by a corporation in whose name or right a derivative action is brought or upon which a demand has been made, the court may appoint one or more individuals to serve as a panel in lieu of a committee of directors for purposes of § 7.08 (Dismissal of a Derivative Action Against Directors, Senior Executives, Controlling Persons, or Associates Based on a Motion Requesting Dismissal by the Board or a Committee) or § 7.11 (Dismissal of a Derivative Action Based Upon Action by the Shareholders), none of whom should be interested [§ 1.23] in the action or have a significant relationship [§ 1.34] with a senior executive [§ 1.33] of the corporation or a similar relationship with any defendant or plaintiff. The panel so appointed should conduct a review and evaluation and prepare a report or other written submission as to the advisability of terminating the action, in compliance with the procedures specified in § 7.09 (Procedures for Requesting Dismissal of a Derivative Action). Any report or other written submission so prepared should have the same status under § 7.08, § 7.10, § 7.11, or § 7.13 (Judicial Procedures on Motions to Dismiss a Derivative Action Under § 7.08 or § 7.11) as a report or other written submission of the board or a properly delegated committee thereof. The costs of the inquiry and report or other written submission should be borne by the corporation, unless the court directs otherwise.

(b) In lieu of the appointment of a panel under § 7.12(a), the court on motion of a corporation may appoint one or more individuals who are not directors of the corporation and who meet the qualifications specified in § 7.12(a) to serve on a committee established by the corporation under § 7.05(b)(1).

§ 7.13   Judicial Procedures on Motions to Dismiss a Derivative Action Under § 7.08 or § 7.11

(a) *Filing of Report or Other Written Submission.* Upon a motion to dismiss an action under § 7.08 (Dismissal of a Derivative Action Against Directors, Senior Executives, Controlling Persons, or Associates Based on a Motion Requesting Dismissal by the Board or a Committee) or § 7.11 (Dismissal of a Derivative Action Based Upon Action by the Shareholders), the corporation shall file with the court a report or other written submission setting forth the procedures and determinations of the board or committee, or the resolution of the shareholders. A copy of the report or other written submission, including any supporting documentation filed by the corporation, shall be given to the plaintiff's counsel.

(b) *Protective Order.* The court may issue a protective order concerning such materials, where appropriate.

(c) *Discovery.* Subject to § 7.06 (Authority of Court to Stay a Derivative Action), if the plaintiff has demonstrated that a substantial issue exists whether the applicable standards of § 7.08, § 7.09, § 7.10, § 7.11, or § 7.12 have been satisfied and if the plaintiff is unable without undue hardship to obtain the information by other means, the court may order such limited discovery or limited evidentiary hearing, as to issues specified by the court, as the court finds to be (i) necessary to enable it to render a decision on the motion under the applicable standards of § 7.08, § 7.09, § 7.10, § 7.11, or § 7.12, and (ii) consistent with an expedited resolution of the motion. In the absence of special circumstances, the court should limit on a similar basis any discovery that is sought by the plaintiff in response to a motion for summary judgment by the corporation or any defendant to those facts likely to be in dispute. The results of any such discovery may be made subject to a protective order on the same basis as under § 7.13(b).

(d) *Burdens of Proof.* The plaintiff has the burden of proof in the case of a motion (1) under § 7.08 where the standard of judicial review is determined under § 7.10(a)(1) because the basis of the claim involves a breach of a duty set forth in Part IV (Duty of Care and the Business Judgment Rule) or because the underlying transaction would be reviewed under the business judgment rule, or (2) under § 7.07(a)(1) (suits against third parties and lesser corporate officials). The corporation has the burden of proof in the case of a motion under § 7.08 where the standard of judicial review is determined under § 7.10(a)(2) because the underlying transaction would be reviewed under a standard other than the business judgment rule, except that the plaintiff retains the burden of proof in all cases to show (i) that a defendant's conduct involved a knowing and culpable violation of law, (ii) that the board or committee as a group was not capable of objective judgment in the circumstances as required by § 7.09(a)(1), and (iii) that dismissal of the action would permit a defendant or an associate [§ 1.03] thereof to retain a significant improper benefit under § 7.10(b). The corporation shall also have the burden of proving under § 7.10(b) that the likely injury to the corporation from continuation of the action convincingly outweighs any adverse impact on the public interest from dismissal of the action. In the case of a motion under § 7.11 (Dismissal of a Derivative Action Based Upon Action by the Shareholders), the plaintiff has the burden of proof with respect to § 7.11(b), (c), and (d), and the corporation has the burden of proof with respect to § 7.11(a).

(e) *Privilege.* The plaintiff's counsel should be furnished a copy of related legal opinions received by the board or committee if any opinion is tendered to the court under § 7.13(a). Subject to that requirement, communications, both oral and written, between the board or committee and its counsel with respect to the subject matter of the action do not forfeit their privileged character, and documents, memoranda, or other material qualifying as attorney's work product do not become subject to discovery, on the grounds that the action is derivative or that the privilege was waived by the production to the plaintiff or the filing with the court of a report, other written submission, or supporting documents pursuant to § 7.13.

§ 7.14 Settlement of a Derivative Action by Agreement Between the Plaintiff and a Defendant

(a) A derivative action should not be settled, discontinued, compromised, or voluntarily dismissed by agreement between the plaintiff and a defendant, except with the approval of the court.

(b) The court should approve a proposed settlement or other disposition if the balance of corporate interests warrants approval and the settlement or other disposition is consistent with public policy. In evaluating a proposed settlement, the court should place special weight on the net benefit, including pecuniary and non-pecuniary elements, to the corporation.

(c) In the absence of circumstances leading the court to find that the interests of the shareholders will not be substantially affected by the settlement or other disposition, the court's approval should be preceded by notice (which should be on an individual basis to the extent practicable) to, and an opportunity of a hearing for, affected shareholders. At such a hearing, objecting shareholders should have a reasonable opportunity to contest a proposed settlement or other disposition, including an opportunity with the court's approval to present and to cross-examine witnesses, and the court may allow, upon good cause shown, reasonable discovery consistent with avoiding undue delay.

§ 7.15 Settlement of a Derivative Action Without the Agreement of the Plaintiff

(a) Once a derivative action is commenced, the board or a properly delegated committee, without the agreement of a plaintiff, may with the approval of the court enter into a settlement with, or grant a release to, a director [§ 1.13], a senior executive [§ 1.33], or a person [§ 1.28] in control [§ 1.08] of the corporation, or an associate [§ 1.03] of any such person, with respect to any claim raised on behalf of the corporation in the action. The court should approve the settlement or release if it finds, in response to a motion made on behalf of the corporation by its board of directors or a properly delegated committee, that the following conditions are satisfied:

(1) The board or a properly delegated committee, whose participating members in either case were not interested [§ 1.23] in the action, entered into the proposed settlement after conducting an adequately informed review and evaluation, and filed with the court a report or other written submission that was substantially in conformity with the requirements applicable to a motion requesting dismissal by the board or a committee under § 7.09 (Procedures for Requesting Dismissal of a Derivative Action), or any material departures from those procedures were justified in the circumstances.

(2) The provisions of § 7.14 (Settlement of a Derivative Action by Agreement Between the Plaintiff and a Defendant) applicable to notice and an opportunity for a hearing to affected shareholders in the case of a settlement between the plaintiff and a defendant were substantially complied with.

(3) On the basis of the entire record, the balance of corporate interests warrants approval and the settlement or release is consistent with public policy. In evaluating a proposed settlement, the court should place special weight on the net benefit, including pecuniary and nonpecuniary elements, to the corporation.

(b) Any settlement or release entered into in accordance with § 7.15(a) constitutes a valid affirmative defense with respect to the claims and liabilities covered to the same extent as a settlement entered into with the plaintiff and approved pursuant to § 7.14.

(c) In lieu of a report or other written submission from the board or a committee, the court may consider and rely upon the determinations and conclusions of a special panel appointed under procedures that were substantially in conformity with the procedures of § 7.12 (Special Panel or Special Committee Members) applicable to a panel appointed to consider whether a derivative action should be dismissed.

§ 7.16   Disposition of Recovery in a Derivative Action

Except in the special circumstances specified in § 7.18(e) (pro-rata recovery), the recovery in a derivative action should accrue exclusively to the corporation. Any plaintiff or attorney who brings (or threatens to bring) an action in the name or right of the corporation and who receives property or money (including reimbursement for expenses) from the corporation or any defendant, as a result of the settlement, compromise, discontinuance, or dismissal of an actual or threatened derivative action, should be required to account to the corporation therefor, unless such money or property was received pursuant to a judicial order or a judicially approved settlement.

§ 7.17   Plaintiff's Attorney's Fees and Expenses

A successful plaintiff in a derivative action should be entitled to recover reasonable attorney's fees and other reasonable litigation expenses from the corporation, as determined by the court having jurisdiction over the action, but in no event should the attorney's fee award exceed a reasonable proportion of the value of the relief (including nonpecuniary relief) obtained by the plaintiff for the corporation.

Comment . . .

. . . Because individual shareholders would find it infeasible to organize and tax themselves the costs necessary for a successful action, the well-established rule that a successful plaintiff in a derivative action may look to the corporation for reimbursement of attorney's fees and expenses is a precondition to an effective litigation remedy. In effect, this rule represents the common law's efficient solution to the well-recognized "free rider" problem that arises whenever an individual must incur costs to benefit a group of which the individual is a member. Unless some mechanism exists by which to allocate these costs among the group in proportion to the respective benefits to be received, the individual (here, the plaintiff shareholder) has an inadequate incentive to proceed.

Although the foregoing logic is widely accepted, there is less agreement as to the appropriate formula by which to determine the amount of the fee. Two basic approaches exist. Under the traditional "salvage value" approach, courts have calculated counsel fees by awarding a percentage of the total recovery. . . . The alternative approach, recommended by the Manual for Complex Litigation, Second § 24.12 (1986), and prevalent among federal courts, focuses principally on the value of the attorney's time at the attorney's customary hourly rate, and then adjusts this "lodestar figure" upward (or downward) to reflect the risk assumed by the attorney and the quality of the work done. . . . Recently, there appears to have been a trend toward greater use of the percentage method, and in some Circuits a 30 percent fee award has now become presumptive. . . . Other courts have expressly used high multipliers under the lodestar formula in order to achieve the same desired percentage of the recovery. . . .

Both the lodestar and the percentage-of-the-recovery approaches have well-recognized deficiencies if they are applied literally and without a sense of their impact upon the incentives held out to the plaintiff's attorney. Because a time-based formula, such as the "lodestar" method, compensates attorneys for the hours they expend, a number of commentators have suggested that such a formula gives rise to an incentive to expend unnecessary time and engage in dilatory tactics in order to maximize the attorney's recovery. Such an incentive is unfortunate not only because it delays the progress of the litigation, but also because it aggravates a latent conflict of interest between the attorney and the class he or she represents; the greater the fee, the smaller the net recovery will typically be for the shareholders. In addition, if the defendant strategically delays any settlement offer until just before the moment of trial or judgment, the defendant can further exacerbate this conflict, because at this point an inadequate settlement offer should produce nearly the same attorney's fee under a time-based formula as would a highly successful litigated victory. Thus, the plaintiff's attorney may have an incentive to accept an offer that is not in the best interests of the client in order to avoid the risk of trial and an adverse decision.

In contrast, a percentage-of-the-recovery formula avoids these problems (because the attorney's fee grows only in proportion to the recovery), but encounters others. First, a percentage formula may sometimes encourage premature settlements that are not in the best interests of the class. . . . Second, a percentage formula clearly does not work with respect to nonpecuniary recoveries, such as injunctive or equitable relief, where the value of the benefit conferred cannot be easily quantified. Finally, such a formula may produce windfall profits (such as where a case is settled immediately), which may evoke public criticism and erode respect for the law. Accordingly, § 7.17 proposes a compromise that attempts to retain the best of both formulas while avoiding their deficiencies. Section 7.17 permits the use of the percentage-of-the-recovery formula, but does not require it. Where it is not employed as the measure of the fee award, however, it should set a ceiling on the maximum fee allowable under any formula. The effect is to reduce the incentive to expend time needlessly, to minimize the danger of collusive settlements, and to align better the attorney's self-interest with that of the client; in addition, the danger of unjustified "windfall" profits is better avoided.

Chapter 2

RECOVERY FOR BREACH OF DUTY

§ 7.18   Recovery Resulting From a Breach of Duty: General Rules

(a) Except as otherwise provided in § 7.19 (Limitation on Damages for Certain Violations of the Duty of Care), a defendant who violates the standards of conduct set forth in Part IV (Duty of Care and the Business Judgment Rule), Part V (Duty of Fair Dealing), or Part VI (Role of Directors and Shareholders in Transactions in Control and Tender Offers) is subject to liability for the losses to the corporation (or, to the extent that a direct action lies under § 7.01 (Direct and Derivative Actions Distinguished), to its shareholders) of which the violation is a legal cause, and, in the case of a violation of the standards set forth in Part V, for any additional gains derived by the defendant or an associate [§ 1.03] to the extent necessary to make equitable restitution.

(b) A violation of the standards of conduct set forth in Part IV, Part V, or Part VI is the legal cause of loss if the plaintiff proves that (i) satisfaction of the applicable standard would have been a substantial factor in averting the loss, and (ii) the likelihood of injury would have been foreseeable to an ordinarily prudent person in like position to that of the defendant and in similar circumstances. It is not a defense to liability in such cases that damage to the corporation would not have resulted but for the acts or omissions of other individuals.

(c) A plaintiff bears the burden of proving causation and the amount of damages suffered by, or other recovery due to, the corporation or the shareholders as the result of a defendant's violation of a standard of conduct set forth in Part IV, Part V, or Part VI. The court may permit a defendant to offset against such liability any gains to the corporation that the defendant can establish arose out of the same transaction and whose recognition in this manner is not contrary to public policy.

(d) The losses deemed to be legally caused by a knowing violation of a standard of conduct set forth in Part V include the costs and expenses to which the corporation was subjected as a result of the violation, including the counsel fees and expenses of a successful plaintiff in a derivative action, except to the extent the court determines that inclusion of some or all of such costs and expenses would be inequitable in the circumstances.

(e) The court having jurisdiction over a derivative action may direct that all or a portion of the award be paid directly to individual shareholders, on a pro-rata basis, when such a payment is equitable in the circumstances and adequate provision has been made for the creditors of the corporation.

§ 7.19   Limitation on Damages for Certain Violations of the Duty of Care

Except as otherwise provided by statute, if a failure by a director [§ 1.13] or an officer [§ 1.27] to meet the standard of conduct specified in Part IV (Duty of Care and the Business Judgment Rule) did not either:

(1) Involve a knowing and culpable violation of law by the director or officer;

(2) Show a conscious disregard for the duty of the director or officer to the corporation under circumstances in which the director or officer was aware that the conduct or omission created an unjustified risk of serious injury to the corporation; or

(3) Constitute a sustained and unexcused pattern of inattention that amounted to an abdication of the defendant's duty to the corporation;

and the director or officer, or an associate [§ 1.03], did not receive a benefit that was improper under Part V (Duty of Fair Dealing), then a provision in a certificate of incorporation that limits damages against an officer or a director for such failure to an amount not less than such person's annual compensation from the corporation should be given effect, if the provision is adopted by a vote of disinterested shareholders [§ 1.16] after disclosure [§ 1.14(b)] concerning the provision, may be repealed by the shareholders at any annual meeting without prior action by the board, and does not reduce liability with respect to pending actions or losses incurred prior to its adoption.

Chapter 3

INDEMNIFICATION AND INSURANCE

§ 7.20   Indemnification and Insurance

(a) *General Rule.* Subject to the limitations set forth in Subsection (b):

(1) A corporation should have the power to indemnify a person who is or was a director [§ 1.13] or officer [§ 1.27] for liabilities and reasonable expenses incurred in connection with any threatened, pending, or completed action, suit, or other proceeding, formal or informal, whether civil, criminal, administrative, or investigative, to which the director or officer is or may be made a party or in connection with which the director or officer is or may be otherwise required to appear:

(A) Because such person was acting in his or her capacity as a director or officer of the corporation, or acting in some capacity on behalf of a third party at the request of the corporation, if such person was acting in good faith or otherwise engaged in good faith conduct in such capacity, or

(B) Solely because of the fact that such person is or was a director or officer.

(2) A corporation should have the power to pay expenses incurred by a person who is or was a director or officer in connection with a proceeding described in Subsection (a)(1) in advance of the final disposition of such proceeding, upon receipt of an undertaking by or on behalf of the director or officer to repay such expenses, if it is ultimately determined that the person is not entitled to be indemnified by the corporation.

(3) A corporation should be obligated to indemnify a person who is or was a director or officer for liabilities and reasonable expenses incurred in connection with a proceeding described in Subsection (a)(1) if:

(A) the director or officer was wholly successful, on the merits or otherwise, in the defense of such proceeding, or

(B) the corporation properly obligates itself to so indemnify the director or officer, to the extent permitted by this Section, by a provision in its charter documents or by contract.

(4) A corporation should have the power to purchase insurance on behalf of a person who is or was a director or officer against liability asserted against or expenses incurred by the person in connection with a proceeding described in Subsection (a)(1), whether or not the corporation would have the power to indemnify the person against the same liability or expenses.

(b) *Limitations on Indemnification and Insurance*

(1) A corporation should not have the power or be obligated to indemnify a director or officer for liabilities and reasonable expenses incurred in connection with a proceeding described in Subsection (a)(1):

(A) If the conduct for which indemnification is sought directly involved a knowing and culpable violation of law or a significant pecuniary benefit was obtained to which the director or officer was not legally entitled;

(B) To the extent that the indemnification would involve any amount paid in satisfaction of a fine, civil penalty, or similar judgment as a result of violation of statutory law, the policy of which clearly precludes indemnification;

(C) If the indemnification would involve any amount paid in settlement of the proceeding and the conduct directly involved a violation of statutory law, the policy of which clearly precludes indemnification; or

(D) To the extent that the indemnification would involve amounts paid (i) in satisfaction of a judgment or in settlement of an action that was brought by or in the right of the corporation, or (ii) for expenses incurred in any such proceeding in which the director or officer was adjudged liable to the corporation, except as provided in Subsection (c).

In the absence of a judicial determination, the applicability of Subsection (b)(1) may be determined by disinterested directors, disinterested shareholders, or independent counsel, but if a determination so made is adverse to the director or officer, the director or officer should have standing to seek a de novo court determination thereof.

(2) A corporation should not be entitled to purchase insurance pursuant to Subsection (a)(4), to the extent that the insurance would furnish protection against liability for conduct directly involving a knowing and culpable violation of law or involving a significant pecuniary benefit obtained by an insured person to which the person is not legally entitled.

(c) *Court-Ordered Indemnification*

(1) A court should order the payment of indemnification in the circumstances described in Subsection (a)(3) and should also order the corporation to pay the reasonable expenses incurred by the director or officer in successfully obtaining court-ordered indemnification.

(2) A court may order the indemnification of amounts paid in settlement of an action brought by or in the right of the corporation (other than amounts paid in settlement of an action in which the court determines that there was a substantial likelihood that the director or officer received a significant pecuniary benefit to which the director or officer was not legally entitled), or for expenses in any proceeding referred to in Subsection (b)(1)(A) or (D), if it determines that indemnification is fair and reasonable, in whole or in part, in view of all the circumstances.

(d) *Report to Shareholders Concerning Indemnification in Derivative Actions.* If a corporation indemnifies or advances expenses to a director or officer in connection with a proceeding by or in the right of the corporation, the corporation should report the indemnification or advance to the shareholders at or before the time notice of the next shareholders' meeting is sent.

(e) *Nonexclusivity of Indemnification Provisions.* Subject to the limitations set forth in Subsection (b): (1) a corporation should have the power to provide indemnification and the payment of expenses under a standard of the corporation [§ 1.36], agreement, or otherwise, and (2) this Section should not be deemed exclusive of any other rights to which a director or officer seeking indemnification or the payment of expenses may be entitled.

(f) *Legal Successors.* The power or obligation to indemnify or pay expenses under this section shall extend to executors, administrators, trustees, and other successors in interest of directors and officers against whom liabilities are threatened or asserted.

Chapter 4

THE APPRAISAL REMEDY

§ 7.21   Corporate Transactions Giving Rise to Appraisal Rights

An eligible holder [§ 1.17] of the corporation [§ 1.12(b)] should be entitled on demand to be paid in cash the fair value of the shares owned by the eligible holder as provided in §§ 7.22 (Standards for Determining Fair Value) and 7.23 (Procedural Standards) in the event of:

(a) A merger, a consolidation, a mandatory share exchange, or an exchange by the corporation of its stock for substantial assets or equity securities [§ 1.20] of another corporation (hereinafter collectively referred to as a "business combination"), whether effected directly or by means of a subsidiary, unless those persons who were shareholders of the corporation immediately before the combination own 60 percent or more of the total voting power of the surviving or issuing corporation immediately thereafter, in approximately the same proportions (in relation to the other preexisting shareholders) as before the combination;

(b) Any business combination, amendment of the corporation's charter documents [§ 1.05], or other corporate act or transaction that has the effect of involuntarily eliminating the eligible holder's equity interest [§ 1.19] (other than the elimination of less than a round lot in a publicly traded corporation or a similar elimination of a comparably insignificant interest in a non-publicly traded corporation);

(c) A sale, lease, exchange, or other disposition of substantial assets by the corporation that

(1) Falls within § 5.15(a) (Transfer of Control in Which a Director or Principal Senior Executive Is Interested) and the assets so disposed of would account for a majority of the corporation's earnings or total assets [§ 1.37] as of the end of its most recent fiscal year, unless (A) the procedures specified in § 5.15(b)(1)–(3) are complied with, and (B) at least one class of equity securities [§ 1.20] of the corporation is listed on a national securities exchange or is included within NASDAQ's National Market System; or

(2) Leaves the corporation without a significant continuing business, unless the sale (A) is in the ordinary course of business, or (B) is for cash or for cash equivalents that are to be liquidated for cash or used to satisfy corporate obligations, and is pursuant to a plan of complete dissolution by which all or substantially all of the net assets will be distributed to the shareholders within one year after the date of such transaction;

(d) An amendment of the charter documents [§ 1.05], whether accomplished directly or through a merger or consolidation, whose effect is to (1) materially and adversely alter or abolish a preferential, preemptive, redemption, or conversion right applicable to the eligible holder's shares, (2) reduce the number of shares owned by the eligible holder (other than a holder of less than a round lot in a publicly traded corporation or a similar holder of a comparably insignificant interest in a non-publicly traded corporation) to a fraction of a share or less, (3) create a right to redeem the eligible holder's shares, or (4) exclude or limit the voting rights of shares with respect to any matter, other than simply through the authorization of new shares of an existing or new class or the elimination of cumulative voting rights; or

(e) Any corporate action as to which the charter documents, other than the bylaws, provide that eligible holders have applicable appraisal rights.

§ 7.22 Standards for Determining Fair Value

(a) The fair value of shares under § 7.21 (Corporate Transactions Giving Rise to Appraisal Rights) should be the value of the eligible holder's [§ 1.17] proportionate interest in the corporation, without any discount for minority status or, absent extraordinary circumstances, lack of marketability. Subject to Subsections (b) and (c), fair value should be determined using the customary valuation concepts and techniques generally employed in the relevant securities and financial markets for similar businesses in the context of the transaction giving rise to appraisal.

(b) In the case of a business combination that gives rise to appraisal rights, but does not fall within § 5.10 (Transactions by a Controlling Shareholder with the Corporation), § 5.15 (Transfer of Control in Which a Director or Principal Senior Executive Is Interested), or § 7.25 (Transactions in Control Involving Corporate Combinations to Which a Majority Shareholder Is a Party), the aggregate price accepted by the board of directors of the subject corporation should be presumed to represent the fair value of the corporation, or of the assets sold in the case of an asset sale, unless the plaintiff can prove otherwise by clear and convincing evidence.

(c) If the transaction giving rise to appraisal falls within § 5.10, § 5.15, or § 7.25, the court generally should give substantial weight to the highest realistic price that a willing, able, and fully informed buyer would pay for the corporation as an entirety. In determining what such a buyer would pay, the court may include a proportionate share of any gain reasonably to be expected to result from the combination, unless special circumstances would make such an allocation unreasonable.

§ 7.23 Procedural Standards

(a) *Notice.* A corporation that proposes to engage in a transaction giving rise to appraisal rights under § 7.21 (Corporate Transactions Giving Rise to Appraisal Rights) should:

(i) Notify each record holder [§ 1.32] as of the record date set for the shareholder vote, and attempt in good faith to notify each other beneficial holder [§ 1.22] of shares as of such date who is known to it, of the right to exercise appraisal reasonably in advance of the date on which the transaction is to be voted upon by the shareholders, or, if no shareholder vote is required, the date on which the corporate action giving rise to appraisal is to be taken;

(ii) Describe the method for exercising the right, including the procedures in § 7.23(f);

(iii) Disclose the material facts [§ 1.25] concerning the transaction or other action and furnish copies of the corporation's financial statements; and

(iv) Provide a reasonable means by which eligible holders [§ 1.17] can easily and effectively indicate their election to dissent.

(b) *Shareholder Response.* To perfect a right to dissent, an eligible holder should be required only to utilize the means provided for under § 7.23(a)(iv), or otherwise deliver a written instrument expressing an election to dissent, at or before the shareholders' meeting, or, if no shareholder vote is to be taken, on or before the day preceding the date on which the corporate action giving rise to the right to appraisal is to be taken; provided, however, that eligible holders should have a reasonable period in which to elect to dissent from the time notice is first sent by the corporation pursuant to § 7.23(a)(i). Any eligible holder who so responds should be deemed a "dissenting holder" for purposes of § 7.23. If notice is not given as required under § 7.23(a), any eligible holder may initiate an appraisal proceeding without taking any other action.

(c) *Mandatory Prepayment.* Promptly after the transaction that gives rise to appraisal under § 7.21 is consummated and upon the tender of the dissenting holder's shares to the corporation's transfer agent for the notation of an appropriate legend to reflect the payment required under this § 7.23(c), the corporation should pay to such dissenting holder the amount in cash that it reasonably estimates to be the fair value of the shares plus any interest due. Acceptance of such prepayment shall not constitute a waiver of the dissenting holder's rights under § 7.21.

(d) *Costs and Expenses.* If payment of the amount required under § 7.23(c) is not made within *30* days after the later of the date on which the transaction is consummated or the date on which shares are tendered under § 7.23(c), or if the amount so paid is materially less than the amount ultimately determined by the court to constitute fair value, the corporation should be required to pay all costs and expenses of the appraisal proceeding, including such dissenting holder's reasonable attorney's and experts' fees. In all other circumstances, the costs and expenses of the action shall be assessed or apportioned as the court deems equitable, except that the corporation's attorney's fees may be assessed or apportioned against a shareholder only where the court finds the shareholder's action to have been arbitrary, vexatious, or not in good faith.

(e) *Interest.* Interest on the amount awarded by the court (less the amount of prepayment) should be paid at the time of the payment of the award and should be computed from the time the relevant transaction is consummated at an appropriate market rate for the corporation.

(f) *Consolidation.* If there are any dissenting holders, the corporation should commence a consolidated proceeding in the state of incorporation under § 7.21 to fix fair value and determine eligibility to dissent. All dissenting holders should be made parties to the action. If such a consolidated action is not commenced by the corporation within a reasonable time after consummation of the transaction that gives rise to the appraisal right, it may be commenced by any dissenting holder. The court may appoint a lead counsel or steering committee to coordinate discovery and the trial of the proceeding and to represent any dissenting holders who have not secured other counsel. The court should also require the corporation to provide it with the names and addresses of all dissenting holders known to the corporation, and, subject to appropriate restrictions, such list should be available for inspection by dissenting holders or their agents.

§ 7.24   Transactions in Control Involving Corporate Combinations in Which Directors, Principal Senior Executives, and Controlling Shareholders Are Not Interested

(a) An appraisal proceeding is the exclusive remedy of an eligible holder [§ 1.17] to challenge a transaction in control [§ 1.38] involving a corporate combination that requires shareholder approval and is not subject to § 5.10 (Transactions by a Controlling Shareholder with the Corporation), § 5.15 (Transfer of Control in Which a Director or Principal Senior Executive Is Interested), or § 7.25 (Transactions in Control Involving Corporate Combinations to Which a Majority Shareholder Is a Party), if:

(1) Disclosure concerning the transaction [§ 1.14(b)] is made to the shareholders who are entitled to authorize the transaction;

(2) The transaction is approved pursuant to, and is otherwise in accordance with, applicable provisions of law and the corporation's charter documents [§ 1.05]; and

(3) Eligible holders who are entitled to but do not vote to approve the transaction are entitled to an appraisal remedy reflecting the general principles embodied in §§ 7.22 (Standards for Determining Fair Value) and 7.23 (Procedural Standards).

(b) A party who challenges a transaction subject to this Section has the burden of proving failure to comply with Subsections (a)(1)–(3).

(c) If Subsections (a)(1) and (a)(2) are satisfied, but Subsection (a)(3) is not, the transaction may be challenged on the ground that it constituted a waste of corporate assets [§ 1.42].

(d) The availability of an appraisal remedy does not preclude a proceeding against a director, officer, controlling shareholder, or an associate of any of the foregoing, for a violation of Part V (Duty of Fair Dealing).

§ 7.25   Transactions in Control Involving Corporate Combinations to Which a Majority Shareholder Is a Party

(a) An appraisal proceeding is the exclusive remedy of an eligible holder [§ 1.17] to challenge a transaction in control [§ 1.38] involving a corporate combination to which a shareholder who holds sufficient voting shares of a corporation to approve the corporate combination under the law of the relevant jurisdiction, or its associate [§ 1.03], is a party if:

(1) The directors who approve the transaction on behalf of the corporation (or the directors of the shareholder if the directors of the corporation are not required by law to approve the transaction) have an adequate basis, grounded on substantial objective evidence, for believing that the consideration offered to the minority shareholders in the transaction constitutes fair value for their shares, as determined in accordance with the standards provided in § 7.22 (Standards for Determining Fair Value);

(2) Disclosure concerning the transaction [§ 1.14(b)] (including representations of the directors' belief with respect to the fair value of minority shares and the basis for such belief) and the conflict of interest [§ 1.14(a)] is made to the minority shareholders, as contemplated by § 7.23(a);

(3) The transaction is approved pursuant to, and is otherwise in accordance with, applicable provisions of law and the corporation's charter documents [§ 1.05]; and

(4) Holders of equity securities who do not vote to approve the transaction are entitled to an appraisal remedy reflecting the general principles embodied in §§ 7.22 (Standards for Determining Fair Value) and 7.23 (Procedural Standards).

(b) A party who challenges a transaction that is subject to this Section has the burden of proving a failure to comply with Subsections (a)(1)–(4) if the transaction was authorized in advance by disinterested directors [§ 1.15] and authorized in advance or ratified by disinterested shareholders [§ 1.16], following the disclosure set forth in Subsection (a)(2); otherwise, the burden is on the majority shareholder to prove compliance with Subsections (a)(1)–(4).

(c) If Subsections (a)(1)–(3) are satisfied but Subsection (a)(4) is not, then:

(1) If the transaction was approved by disinterested shareholders following the disclosure required by Subsection (a)(2), it may be challenged on the ground that it was not fair, with the burden on the challenging party to prove that the transaction was unfair to the minority shareholders; and

(2) If the transaction was not so approved, it may be challenged on the ground that it was not fair, with the burden on the majority shareholder to prove that the transaction was fair to the minority shareholders.

(d) The exclusivity provisions of this Section are not applicable to closely held corporations [§ 1.06].

CORPORATE FORMS

TABLE OF CONTENTS

Form	Page
Simple Form of Certificate of Incorporation	1025
Form of By-Laws	1027
Form of Minutes of Organization Meeting	1033
Selected ISS United States Proxy Voting Guidelines	1037
Form of Stock Certificate	1057
Form of Proxy Statement and Form of Proxy	1059
Richards, Layton & Finger, P.A. Forum Selection Bylaw	1111
Agreement Between Activist Investor and Public Company	1113
Wachtell, Lipton, Rosen & Katz, Share Purchase Rights Plan	1125
Form of Chubb's Directors and Officers Liability Policy	1155

SIMPLE FORM OF CERTIFICATE OF INCORPORATION

[From 3 R. Balotti & J. Finkelstein, The Delaware Law of
Corporations and Business Organizations,
Form 1.5 (3d ed. 1998).]

CERTIFICATE OF INCORPORATION OF _____ CORPORATION

I, the undersigned, for the purpose of incorporating and organizing a corporation under the General Corporation Law of the State of Delaware, do execute this Certificate of Incorporation and do hereby certify as follows:

FIRST. The name of the corporation is _____.

SECOND. The address of the corporation's registered office in the State of Delaware is One Rodney Square, 10th Floor, Tenth and King Streets, in the City of Wilmington, County of New Castle, 19801. The name of its registered agent at such address is RL&F Service Corp.

THIRD. The purpose of the corporation is to engage in any lawful act or activity for which corporations may be organized under the General Corporation Law of the State of Delaware.

FOURTH. The total number of shares of stock which the corporation shall have authority to issue is _____. All such shares are to be Common Stock, par value of $_____ per share and are to be of one class.

FIFTH. The incorporator of the corporation is _____, whose mailing address is One Rodney Square, P.O. Box 551, Wilmington, Delaware 19899.

SIXTH. Unless and except to the extent that the by-laws of the corporation shall so require, the election of directors of the corporation need not be by written ballot.

SEVENTH. In furtherance and not in limitation of the powers conferred by the laws of the State of Delaware, the Board of Directors of the corporation is expressly authorized to make, alter and repeal the by-laws of the corporation, subject to the power of the stockholders of the corporation to alter or repeal any by-law whether adopted by them or otherwise.

EIGHTH. A director of the corporation shall not be liable to the corporation or its stockholders for monetary damages for breach of fiduciary duty as a director, except to the extent such exemption from liability or limitation thereof is not permitted under the General Corporation Law of the State of Delaware as the same exists or may hereafter be amended. Any amendment, modification or repeal of the foregoing sentence shall not adversely affect any right or protection of a director of the corporation hereunder in respect of any act or omission occurring prior to the time of such amendment, modification or repeal.

NINTH. The corporation reserves the right at any time, and from time to time, to amend, alter, change or repeal any provision contained in this Certificate of Incorporation, and other provisions authorized by the laws of the State of Delaware at the time in force may be added or inserted, in the manner now or hereafter prescribed by law; and all rights, preferences and privileges of whatsoever nature conferred upon stockholders, directors or any other persons whomsoever by and pursuant to this Certificate of Incorporation in its present form or as hereafter amended are granted subject to the rights reserved in this article.

TENTH. The powers of the incorporator are to terminate upon the filing of this Certificate of Incorporation. The name and mailing address of the person who is to serve as the initial director of the corporation until the first annual meeting of stockholders of the corporation, or until his successor is elected and qualifies, is: _____.

The undersigned incorporator hereby acknowledges that the foregoing certificate of incorporation is his act and deed on this _____ day of _____ 2___.

_____
Incorporator

FORM OF BY-LAWS

[From 3 R. Balotti & J. Finkelstein, The Delaware Law of
Corporations and Business Organizations,
Form 1.17 (3d ed. 1998).]

BY-LAWS OF _____ CORPORATION

ARTICLE I

Stockholders

Section 1.1. *Annual Meetings.* An annual meeting of stockholders shall be held for the Section election of directors at such date, time and place, either within or without the State of Delaware, as may be designated by resolution of the Board of Directors from time to time. Any other proper business may be transacted at the annual meeting.

Section 1.2. *Special Meetings.* Special meetings of stockholders for any purpose or purposes may be called at any time by the Board of Directors, or by a committee of the Board of Directors that has been duly designated by the Board of Directors and whose powers and authority, as expressly provided in a resolution of the Board of Directors, include the power to call such meetings, but such special meetings may not be called by any other person or persons.

Section 1.3. *Notice of Meetings.* Whenever stockholders are required or permitted to take any action at a meeting, a written notice of the meeting shall be given that shall state the place, date and hour of the meeting and, in the case of a special meeting, the purpose or purposes for which the meeting is called. Unless otherwise provided by law, the certificate of incorporation or these by-laws, the written notice of any meeting shall be given not less than ten nor more than sixty days before the date of the meeting to each stockholder entitled to vote at such meeting. If mailed, such notice shall be deemed to be given when deposited in the United States mail, postage prepaid, directed to the stockholder at his address as it appears on the records of the corporation.

Section 1.4. *Adjournments.* Any meeting of stockholders, annual or special, may adjourn from time to time to reconvene at the same or some other place, and notice need not be given of any such adjourned meeting if the time and place thereof are announced at the meeting at which the adjournment is taken. At the adjourned meeting the corporation may transact any business which might have been transacted at the original meeting. If the adjournment is for more than thirty days, or if after the adjournment a new record date is fixed for the adjourned meeting, notice of the adjourned meeting shall be given to each stockholder of record entitled to vote at the meeting.

Section 1.5. *Quorum.* Except as otherwise provided by law, the certificate of incorporation or these by-laws, at each meeting of stockholders the presence in person or by proxy of the holders of shares of stock having a majority of the votes which could be cast by the holders of all outstanding shares entitled to vote at the meeting shall be necessary and sufficient to constitute a quorum. In the absence of a quorum, the stockholders so present may, by majority vote, adjourn the meeting from time to time in the manner provided in Section 1.4 of these by-laws until a quorum shall attend. Shares of its own stock belonging to the corporation or to another corporation, if a majority of the shares entitled to vote in the election of directors of such other corporation is held, directly or indirectly, by the corporation, shall neither be entitled to vote nor be counted for quorum purposes; provided, however, that the foregoing shall not limit the right of the corporation to vote stock, including but not limited to its own stock, held by it in a fiduciary capacity.

Section 1.6. *Organization.* Meetings of stockholders shall be presided over by the Chairman of the Board, if any, or in his absence by the Vice Chairman of the Board, if any, or in his absence by the President, or in his absence by a Vice President, or in the absence of the foregoing persons by a chairman designated by the Board of Directors, or in the absence of such designation by a chairman chosen at the meeting. The Secretary shall act as secretary of the meeting, but in his absence the chairman of the meeting may appoint any person to act as secretary of the meeting. The chairman of the meeting shall announce at the meeting of stockholders the date and time of the opening and the closing of the polls for each matter upon which the stockholders will vote.

Section 1.7.   *Voting; Proxies.* Except as otherwise provided by the certificate of incorporation, each stockholder entitled to vote at any meeting of stockholders shall be entitled to one vote for each share of stock held by him which has voting power upon the matter in question. Each stockholder entitled to vote at a meeting of stockholders or to express consent or dissent to corporate action in writing without a meeting may authorize another person or persons to act for him by proxy, but no such proxy shall be voted or acted upon after three years from its date, unless the proxy provides for a longer period. A proxy shall be irrevocable if it states that it is irrevocable and if, and only as long as, it is coupled with an interest sufficient in law to support an irrevocable power. A stockholder may revoke any proxy which is not irrevocable by attending the meeting and voting in person or by filing an instrument in writing revoking the proxy or by delivering a proxy in accordance with applicable law bearing a later date to the Secretary of the corporation. Voting at meetings of stockholders need not be by written ballot and, unless otherwise required by law, need not be conducted by inspectors of election unless so determined by the holders of shares of stock having a majority of the votes which could be cast by the holders of all outstanding shares of stock entitled to vote thereon which are present in person or by proxy at such meeting. At all meetings of stockholders for the election of directors a plurality of the votes cast shall be sufficient to elect. All other elections and questions shall, unless otherwise provided by law, the certificate of incorporation or these by-laws, be decided by the vote of the holders of shares of stock having a majority of the votes which could be cast by the holders of all shares of stock outstanding and entitled to vote thereon.

Section 1.8.   *Fixing Date for Determination of Stockholders of Record.* In order that the corporation may determine the stockholders entitled to notice of or to vote at any meeting of stockholders or any adjournment thereof, or to express consent to corporate action in writing without a meeting, or entitled to receive payment of any dividend or other distribution or allotment of any rights, or entitled to exercise any rights in respect of any change, conversion or exchange of stock or for the purpose of any other lawful action, the Board of Directors may fix a record date, which record date shall not precede the date upon which the resolution fixing the record date is adopted by the Board of Directors and which record date: (1) in the case of determination of stockholders entitled to vote at any meeting of stockholders or adjournment thereof, shall, unless otherwise required by law, not be more than sixty nor less than ten days before the date of such meeting; (2) in the case of determination of stockholders entitled to express consent to corporate action in writing without a meeting, shall not be more than ten days from the date upon which the resolution fixing the record date is adopted by the Board of Directors; and (3) in the case of any other action, shall not be more than sixty days prior to such other action. If no record date is fixed: (1) the record date for determining stockholders entitled to notice of or to vote at a meeting of stockholders shall be at the close of business on the day next preceding the day on which notice is given, or, if notice is waived, at the close of business on the day next preceding the day on which the meeting is held; (2) the record date for determining stockholders entitled to express consent to corporate action in writing without a meeting when no prior action of the Board of Directors is required by law, shall be the first date on which a signed written consent setting forth the action taken or proposed to be taken is delivered to the corporation in accordance with applicable law, or, if prior action by the Board of Directors is required by law, shall be at the close of business on the day on which the Board of Directors adopts the resolution taking such prior action; and (3) the record date for determining stockholders for any other purpose shall be at the close of business on the day on which the Board of Directors adopts the resolution relating thereto. A determination of stockholders of record entitled to notice of or to vote at a meeting of stockholders shall apply to any adjournment of the meeting; provided, however, that the Board of Directors may fix a new record date for the adjourned meeting.

Section 1.9.   *List of Stockholders Entitled to Vote.* The Secretary shall prepare and make, at least ten days before every meeting of stockholders, a complete list of the stockholders entitled to vote at the meeting, arranged in alphabetical order, and showing the address of each stockholder and the number of shares registered in the name of each stockholder. Such list shall be open to the examination of any stockholder, for any purpose germane to the meeting, during ordinary business hours, for a period of at least ten days prior to the meeting, either at a place within the city where the meeting is to be held, which place shall be specified in the notice of the meeting, or if not so specified, at the place where the meeting is to be held. The list shall also be produced and kept at the time and place of the meeting during the whole time thereof and may be inspected by any stockholder who is present. Upon the willful neglect or refusal of the directors to produce such a list at any meeting for the election of directors, they shall be ineligible for election to any office at such meeting. The stock ledger shall be the only evidence as to who are the stockholders entitled to examine the stock ledger, the list of stockholders or the books of the corporation, or to vote in person or by proxy at any meeting of stockholders.

Section 1.10. *Action By Consent of Stockholders.* Unless otherwise restricted by the certificate of incorporation, any action required or permitted to be taken at any annual or special meeting of the stockholders may be taken without a meeting, without prior notice and without a vote, if a consent or consents in writing, setting forth the action so taken, shall be signed by the holders of outstanding stock having not less than the minimum number of votes that would be necessary to authorize or take such action at a meeting at which all shares entitled to vote thereon were present and voted and shall be delivered (by hand or by certified or registered mail, return receipt requested) to the corporation by delivery to its registered office in the State of Delaware, its principal place of business, or an officer or agent of the corporation having custody of the book in which proceedings of minutes of stockholders are recorded. Prompt notice of the taking of the corporate action without a meeting by less than unanimous written consent shall be given to those stockholders who have not consented in writing.

Section 1.11. *Conduct of Meetings.* The Board of Directors of the corporation may adopt by resolution such rules and regulations for the conduct of the meeting of stockholders as it shall deem appropriate. Except to the extent inconsistent with such rules and regulations as adopted by the Board of Directors, the chairman of any meeting of stockholders shall have the right and authority to prescribe such rules, regulations and procedures and to do all such acts as, in the judgment of such chairman, are appropriate for the proper conduct of the meeting. Such rules, regulations or procedures, whether adopted by the Board of Directors or prescribed by the chairman of the meeting, may include, without limitation, the following: (i) the establishment of an agenda or order of business for the meeting; (ii) rules and procedures for maintaining order at the meeting and the safety of those present; (iii) limitations on attendance at or participation in the meeting to stockholders of record of the corporation, their duly authorized and constituted proxies or such other persons as the chairman of the meeting shall determine; (iv) restrictions on entry to the meeting after the time fixed for the commencement thereof; and (v) limitations on the time allotted to questions or comments by participants. Unless and to the extent determined by the Board of Directors or the chairman of the meeting, meetings of stockholders shall not be required to be held in accordance with the rules of parliamentary procedure.

ARTICLE II

Board of Directors

Section 2.1. *Number; Qualifications.* The Board of Directors shall consist of one or more members, the number thereof to be determined from time to time by resolution of the Board of Directors. Directors need not be stockholders.

Section 2.2. *Election: Resignation: Removal: Vacancies.* The Board of Directors shall initially consist of the persons named as directors by the incorporator, and each director so elected shall hold office until the first annual meeting of stockholders or until his successor is elected and qualified. At the first annual meeting of stockholders and at each annual meeting thereafter, the stockholders shall elect directors each of whom shall hold office for a term of one year or until his successor is elected and qualified. Any director may resign at any time upon written notice to the corporation. Any newly created directorship or any vacancy occurring in the Board of Directors for any cause may be filled by a majority of the remaining members of the Board of Directors, although such majority is less than a quorum, or by a plurality of the votes cast at a meeting of stockholders, and each director so elected shall hold office until the expiration of the term of office of the director whom he has replaced or until his successor is elected and qualified.

Section 2.3. *Regular Meetings.* Regular meetings of the Board of Directors may be held at such places within or without the State of Delaware and at such times as the Board of Directors may from time to time determine, and if so determined notices thereof need not be given.

Section 2.4. *Special Meetings.* Special meetings of the Board of Directors may be held at any time or place within or without the State of Delaware whenever called by the President, any Vice President, the Secretary, or by any member of the Board of Directors. Notice of a special meeting of the Board of Directors shall be given by the person or persons calling the meeting at least twenty-four hours before the special meeting.

Section 2.5.   *Telephonic Meetings Permitted.* Members of the Board of Directors, or any committee designated by the Board of Directors, may participate in a meeting thereof by means of conference telephone or similar communications equipment by means of which all persons participating in the meeting can hear each other, and participation in a meeting pursuant to this by-law shall constitute presence in person at such meeting.

Section 2.6.   *Quorum: Vote Required for Action.* At all meetings of the Board of Directors a majority of the whole Board of Directors shall constitute a quorum for the transaction of business. Except in cases in which the certificate of incorporation or these by-laws otherwise provide, the vote of a majority of the directors present at a meeting at which a quorum is present shall be the act of the Board of Directors.

Section 2.7.   *Organization.* Meetings of the Board of Directors shall be presided over by the Chairman of the Board, if any, or in his absence by the Vice Chairman of the Board, if any, or in his absence by the President, or in their absence by a chairman chosen at the meeting. The Secretary shall act as secretary of the meeting, but in his absence the chairman of the meeting may appoint any person to act as secretary of the meeting.

Section 2.8.   *Informal Action by Directors.* Unless otherwise restricted by the certificate of incorporation or these by-laws, any action required or permitted to be taken at any meeting of the Board of Directors, or of any committee thereof, may be taken without a meeting if all members of the Board of Directors or such committee, as the case may be, consent thereto in writing, and the writing or writings are filed with the minutes of proceedings of the Board of Directors or such committee.

ARTICLE III

Committees

Section 3.1.   *Committees.* The Board of Directors may, by resolution passed by a majority of the whole Board of Directors, designate one or more committees, each committee to consist of one or more of the directors of the corporation. The Board of Directors may designate one or more directors as alternate members of any committee, who may replace any absent or disqualified member at any meeting of the committee. In the absence or disqualification of a member of the committee, the member or members thereof present at any meeting and not disqualified from voting, whether or not he or they constitute a quorum, may unanimously appoint another member of the Board of Directors to act at the meeting in place of any such absent or disqualified member. Any such committee, to the extent permitted by law and to the extent provided in the resolution of the Board of Directors, shall have and may exercise all the powers and authority of the Board of Directors in the management of the business and affairs of the corporation, and may authorize the seal of the corporation to be affixed to all papers which may require it.

Section 3.2.   *Committee Rules.* Unless the Board of Directors otherwise provides, each committee designated by the Board of Directors may make, alter and repeal rules for the conduct of its business. In the absence of such rules each committee shall conduct its business in the same manner as the Board of Directors conducts its business pursuant to Article II of these by-laws.

ARTICLE IV

Officers

Section 4.1.   *Executive Officers; Election; Qualifications; Term of Office; Resignation; Removal; Vacancies.* The Board of Directors shall elect a President and Secretary, and it may, if it so determines, choose a Chairman of the Board and a Vice Chairman of the Board from among its members. The Board of Directors may also choose one or more Vice Presidents, one or more Assistant Secretaries, a Treasurer and one or more Assistant Treasurers. Each such officer shall hold office until the first meeting of the Board of Directors after the annual meeting of stockholders next succeeding his election, and until his successor is elected and qualified or until his earlier resignation or removal. Any officer may resign at any time upon written notice to the corporation. The Board of Directors may remove any officer with or without cause at any time, but such removal shall be without prejudice to the contractual rights of such officer, if any, with the corporation. Any number of offices may be held by the same person. Any vacancy occurring in any office of the corporation by death, resignation, removal or otherwise may be filled for the unexpired portion of the term by the Board of Directors at any regular or special meeting.

Section 4.2.   *Powers and Duties of Executive Officers.* The officers of the corporation shall have such powers and duties in the management of the corporation as may be prescribed in a resolution by the Board of Directors and, to the extent not so provided, as generally pertain to their respective offices, subject to the control of the Board of Directors. The Board of Directors may require any officer, agent or employee to give security for the faithful performance of his duties.

ARTICLE V

Stock

Section 5.1.   Certificates. Every holder of stock shall be entitled to have a certificate signed by or in the name of the corporation by the Chairman or Vice Chairman of the Board of Directors, if any, or the President or a Vice President, and by the Treasurer or an Assistant Treasurer, or the Secretary or an Assistant Secretary, of the corporation certifying the number of shares owned by him in the corporation. Any of or all the signatures on the certificate may be a facsimile. In case any officer, transfer agent or registrar who has signed or whose facsimile signature has been placed upon a certificate shall have ceased to be such officer, transfer agent, or registrar before such certificate is issued, it may be issued by the corporation with the same effect as if he were such officer, transfer agent, or registrar at the date of issue.

Section 5.2.   *Lost, Stolen or Destroyed Stock Certificates; Issuance of New Certificates.* The corporation may issue a new certificate of stock in the place of any certificate theretofore issued by it, alleged to have been lost, stolen or destroyed, and the corporation may require the owner of the lost, stolen or destroyed certificate, or his legal representative, to give the corporation a bond sufficient to indemnify it against any claim that may be made against it on account of the alleged loss, theft or destruction of any such certificate or the issuance of such new certificate.

ARTICLE VI

Indemnification

Section 6.1.   Right to Indemnification. The corporation shall indemnify and hold harmless, to the fullest extent permitted by applicable law as it presently exists or may hereafter be amended, any person who was or is made or is threatened to be made a party or is otherwise involved in any action, suit or proceeding, whether civil, criminal, administrative or investigative (a "proceeding") by reason of the fact that he, or a person for whom he is the legal representative, is or was a director or officer of the corporation or is or was serving at the request of the corporation as a director, officer, employee or agent of another corporation or of a partnership, joint venture, trust, enterprise or nonprofit entity, including service with respect to employee benefit plans, against all liability and loss suffered and expenses (including attorneys' fees) reasonably incurred by such person. The corporation shall be required to indemnify a person in connection with a proceeding (or part thereof) initiated by such person only if the proceeding (or part thereof) was authorized by the Board of Directors of the corporation.

Section 6.2.   *Prepayment of Expenses.* The corporation may, in its discretion, pay the expenses (including attorneys' fees) incurred in defending any proceeding in advance of its final disposition, provided, however, that the payment of expenses incurred by a director or officer in advance of the final disposition of the proceeding shall be made only upon receipt of an undertaking by the director or officer to repay all amounts advanced if it should be ultimately determined that the director or officer is not entitled to be indemnified under this Article or otherwise.

Section 6.3.   *Claims.* If a claim for indemnification or payment of expenses under this Article is not paid in full within sixty days after a written claim therefor has been received by the corporation, the claimant may file suit to recover the unpaid amount of such claim and, if successful in whole or in part, shall be entitled to be paid the expense of prosecuting such claim. In any such action the corporation shall have the burden of proving that the claimant was not entitled to the requested indemnification or payment of expenses under applicable law.

Section 6.4.   *Non-Exclusivity of Rights.* The rights conferred on any person by this Article VI shall not be exclusive of any other rights which such person may have or hereafter acquire under any statute, provision of the certificate of incorporation, these by-laws, agreement, vote of stockholders or disinterested directors or otherwise.

Section 6.5.   *Other Indemnification.* The corporation's obligation, if any, to indemnify any person who was or is serving at its request as a director, officer, employee or agent of another corporation, partnership, joint venture, trust, enterprise or nonprofit entity shall be reduced by any amount such person may collect as indemnification from such other corporation, partnership, joint venture, trust, enterprise or nonprofit enterprise.

Section 6.6.   *Amendment or Repeal.* Any repeal or modification of the foregoing provisions of this Article VI shall not adversely affect any right or protection hereunder of any person in respect of any act or omission occurring prior to the time of such repeal or modification.

ARTICLE VII

Miscellaneous

Section 7.1.   *Fiscal Year.* The fiscal year of the corporation shall be determined by resolution of the Board of Directors.

Section 7.2.   *Seal.* The corporate seal shall have the name of the corporation inscribed thereon and shall be in such form as may be approved from time to time by the Board of Directors.

Section 7.3.   *Waiver of Notice of Meetings of Stockholders, Directors and Committees.* Any written waiver of notice, signed by the person entitled to notice, whether before or after the time stated therein, shall be deemed equivalent to notice. Attendance of a person at a meeting shall constitute a waiver of notice of such meeting, except when the person attends a meeting for the express purpose of objecting, at the beginning of the meeting, to the transaction of any business because the meeting is not lawfully called or convened. Neither the business to be transacted at nor the purpose of any regular or special meeting of the stockholders, directors, or members of a committee of directors need be specified in any written waiver of notice.

Section 7.4.   *Interested Directors; Quorum.* No contract or transaction between the corporation and one or more of its directors or officers, or between the corporation and any other corporation, partnership, association, or other organization in which one or more of its directors or officers are directors or officers, or have a financial interest, shall be void or voidable solely for this reason, or solely because the director or officer is present at or participates in the meeting of the Board of Directors or committee thereof which authorizes the contract or transaction, or solely because his or their votes are counted for such purpose, if: (1) the material facts as to his relationship or interest and as to the contract or transaction are disclosed or are known to the Board of Directors or the committee, and the Board of Directors or committee in good faith authorizes the contract or transaction by the affirmative votes of a majority of the disinterested directors, even though the disinterested directors be less than a quorum; or (2) the material facts as to his relationship or interest and as to the contract or transaction are disclosed or are known to the stockholders entitled to vote thereon, and the contract or transaction is specifically approved in good faith by vote of the stockholders; or (3) the contract or transaction is fair as to the corporation as of the time it is authorized, approved or ratified, by the Board of Directors, a committee thereof, or the stockholders. Common or interested directors may be counted in determining the presence of a quorum at a meeting of the Board of Directors or of a committee which authorizes the contract or transaction.

Section 7.5.   *Form of Records.* Any records maintained by the corporation in the regular course of its business, including its stock ledger, books of account, and minute books, may be kept on, or be in the form of, punch cards, magnetic tape, photographs, microphotographs, or any other information storage device, provided that the records so kept can be converted into clearly legible form within a reasonable time.

Section 7.6.   *Amendment of By-Laws.* These by-laws may be altered or repealed, and new by-laws made, by the Board of Directors, but the stockholders may make additional by-laws and may alter and repeal any by-laws whether adopted by them or otherwise.

FORM OF MINUTES OF
ORGANIZATION MEETING

[From 3 R. Balotti & J. Finkelstein, The Delaware Law of
Corporations and Business Organizations,
Form 1.24 (3d ed. 1998).]

MINUTES OF THE FIRST MEETING OF THE BOARD OF DIRECTORS OF _____

The first meeting of the Board of Directors of _____, a Delaware corporation (the "Corporation"), was held on _____, 2___ at _____ __.m., at _____. Present were _____, _____ and _____, being a majority of the Directors and a quorum. Present by invitation were _____.

By unanimous vote, _____ was chosen Chairman of the meeting, and _____ was chosen Secretary of the meeting. The Secretary presented a Waiver of Notice of the meeting signed by all of the Directors of the Corporation. The Chairman directed that the original of such Waiver be prefixed to the Minutes of this meeting.

The Secretary presented a certified copy of the Certificate of Incorporation, and upon motion made and duly carried, it was:

RESOLVED, that the original Certificate of Incorporation of this Corporation, filed in the office of the Secretary of State of the State of Delaware on _____, 2___, is hereby approved.

RESOLVED, FURTHER, that all of the actions taken by the incorporator of this Corporation to effect the incorporation of this Corporation are hereby approved, ratified, confirmed and adopted by and on behalf of this Corporation.

The Secretary presented a form of By-laws for the regulation of the affairs of the Corporation. Upon motion made and duly carried, it was:

RESOLVED, FURTHER, that the By-laws for the regulation of the affairs of this Corporation, attached hereto as Exhibit A and incorporated herein by reference, are hereby ratified, adopted and approved as the By-laws of this Corporation and shall be filed with the minutes of the Corporation.

RESOLVED, FURTHER, that pursuant to Section 2.1 of the By-laws of this Corporation, the Board of Directors shall consist of _____ members.

The Secretary submitted to the meeting a seal proposed to be used as the corporate seal of the Corporation. Upon motion made and duly carried, it was:

RESOLVED, FURTHER, that the form of corporate seal, an impression of which is imprinted at the margin of this Consent, is adopted as the official corporate seal of the Corporation.

The Secretary presented to the meeting a proposed form of certificate for the Corporation's Common stock. The Chairman directed that a specimen of such form of certificate be annexed to the Minutes of this meeting. Upon motion made and duly carried, it was:

RESOLVED, FURTHER, that the form of stock certificate representing shares of Common Stock, par value _____ ($___) per share, a specimen of which is attached hereto as Exhibit B, is adopted as the form of stock certificate for the Common Stock of the Corporation.

The following persons were nominated to hold the offices of the Corporation set forth opposite their respective names. Upon motion made and duly adopted, it was:

RESOLVED, FURTHER, that the following persons be and each of them hereby is elected to serve in the offices of the Corporation set opposite their respective names, each to hold such offices until his respective successor is duly elected and qualified or until his earlier resignation or removal:

FORM—MINUTES OF ORGANIZATION MEETING

Name	Office
1	Chief Executive Officer
2	President
3	Executive Vice President
4	Vice President
5	Secretary
6	Assistant Secretary
7	Treasurer
8	Assistant Treasurer

The Chairman stated that the Corporation had received an offer from _____ to purchase _____ shares of the Corporation's common stock for a purchase price of _____. Upon motion made and duly carried, it was:

RESOLVED, FURTHER, that in consideration of $_____ in cash paid to the Corporation by _____, such consideration being at least equal to the par value of such shares, the Corporation shall immediately issue _____ shares of its Common Stock to _____, which shares shall be fully paid, nonassessable Common Stock of the Corporation.

RESOLVED, FURTHER, that the President and the Secretary of the Corporation be and each of them hereby is authorized to issue to _____ a stock certificate or certificates evidencing the ownership of _____ shares of Common Stock of the Corporation.

RESOLVED, FURTHER, that of the $_____ in cash to be received in exchange for the issuance of shares of Common Stock of the Corporation to _____ pursuant to the foregoing resolution, $_____ ($___ per share) is hereby designated and specified as the stated capital of such shares, and said amount shall constitute the capital of the Corporation in respect of such shares.

RESOLVED, FURTHER, that of the $_____ in cash to be received in exchange for the issuance of shares of Common Stock of the Corporation to _____ pursuant to the foregoing resolution, $_____ ($___ per share) is hereby accepted as a capital surplus contribution from _____, and the Treasurer of this Corporation is hereby authorized and directed to cause this capital surplus contribution to be reflected in the accounting books and records of this Corporation.

The Chairman stated that the Corporation may wish to qualify to do business in other jurisdictions in order to carry on the business of the Corporation. Upon motion made and duly carried, it was:

RESOLVED, FURTHER, that for the purpose of authorizing the Corporation to do business in any jurisdiction in which it is necessary or expedient for the Corporation to transact business, the officers of the Corporation be and each of them hereby is authorized to appoint and substitute all necessary agents or attorneys for service of process, to designate and change the location of all necessary statutory offices and under the corporate seal if required, to make and file all necessary certificates, reports, powers of attorney and other instruments as may be required by the laws of such jurisdiction to authorize the Corporation to transact business therein, and whenever it is expedient for the Corporation to cease doing business therein and withdraw therefrom, to revoke any appointment of agent or attorney for service of process and to file such certificates, reports, revocations of appointment, or surrenders of authority as may be necessary to terminate the authority of the Corporation to do business in any such jurisdiction.

The Chairman next stated that it would be desirable to designate a depository of the funds of the Corporation. The Secretary presented to the meeting a form of resolutions supplied by the bank with respect to establishing one or more accounts with the bank. Upon motion made and duly carried, it was:

RESOLVED, FURTHER, that the Chairman of the Board of Directors, the President and the Treasurer of the Corporation (the "Designated Officers") be and each of them hereby is authorized for and on behalf of the Corporation to designate from time to time one or more banks, trust companies or other banking institutions (any thereof being hereinafter referred to as a "bank") to act as depository or depositories for the funds of the Corporation for and during such period as he may from time to time deem necessary or desirable in the interests of the Corporation and to open or close out from time to time accounts in any such depository so selected or reselected.

RESOLVED, FURTHER, that the proper officers of the Corporation be and each of them hereby is authorized and directed, in the name and on behalf of the Corporation, to take any and all action that they may deem necessary or advisable in order to establish bank accounts at _____ from time to time for the efficient conduct of the Corporation's business.

RESOLVED, FURTHER, that the form of resolutions supplied by _____ for the establishment of the Corporation's checking account, attached hereto as Exhibit C and incorporated herein by reference, are hereby adopted as the resolutions of this Board of Directors.

RESOLVED, FURTHER, that the President of the Corporation be and he hereby is authorized to designate those officers or agents of the Corporation who may be authorized from time to time to sign checks on any of such bank accounts.

The Chairman suggested that the Treasurer of the Corporation be authorized to pay all expenses and reimburse all persons for expenditures made in connection with the organization of the Corporation, and that the Secretary and the Treasurer be authorized to procure proper books for the maintenance of the records of the Corporation. Upon motion made and duly carried, it was:

RESOLVED, FURTHER, that the President, any Vice President, Secretary and Treasurer be, and each of them hereby is, authorized and directed, for and on behalf of the Corporation, to pay all charges and expenses incident to or arising out of the incorporation of the Corporation and to reimburse the persons who have made any disbursements therefor.

RESOLVED, FURTHER, that the officers of the Corporation be and each of them hereby is authorized and empowered on behalf of the Corporation to pay any other such fees and expenses and to do such other acts and things as they may deem necessary or advisable in connection with the carrying out of any of the matters or purposes set forth in the foregoing resolutions.

RESOLVED, FURTHER, that the Secretary and the Treasurer of this Corporation be and hereby are authorized and directed to procure all appropriate corporate books, books of account and stock books that may be deemed necessary or appropriate in connection with the business of this Corporation.

The Chairman suggested that the Corporation adopt a fiscal year end and set a date for the annual meeting of the Stockholders and Directors of the Corporation. Upon motion made and duly carried, it was:

RESOLVED, FURTHER, that the date for the annual meeting of the Corporation be and the same hereby is fixed as the day of _____ of _____ each year, with the first such meeting to be held _____, 2___, at _____.

RESOLVED, FURTHER, that the fiscal year of the Corporation shall commence on the _____ day of _____ and shall end on the day of _____ of each year.

The Chairman indicated that the Stockholder of the Corporation desired the Corporation to be qualified with the Internal Revenue Service as an S Corporation. Upon motion made and duly carried, it was:

RESOLVED, FURTHER, that the appropriate officers of this Corporation be and each of them hereby is authorized and directed to take any action deemed necessary or advisable to qualify this Corporation as an S Corporation under Section 1361 of the Internal Revenue Code.

There being no further business to come before the meeting, upon motion made and duly carried, the meeting was adjourned.

_____

Secretary of the Meeting

1035

United States

Proxy Voting Guidelines

Benchmark Policy Recommendations

Effective for Meetings on or after February 1, 2019

Published December 6, 2018

Table of Contents

COVERAGE... 8

1. BOARD OF DIRECTORS.. 9
   VOTING ON DIRECTOR NOMINEES IN UNCONTESTED ELECTIONS..................................... 9
   Independence 9
      ISS Classification of Directors – U.S. 10
   Composition 12
   Responsiveness 13
   Accountability 13
   VOTING ON DIRECTOR NOMINEES IN CONTESTED ELECTIONS... 17
   Vote-No Campaigns 17
   Proxy Contests/Proxy Access — Voting for Director Nominees in Contested Elections 17
   OTHER BOARD-RELATED PROPOSALS 17
   Adopt Anti-Hedging/Pledging/Speculative Investments Policy 17
   Age/Term Limits 17
   Board Size 18
   Classification/Declassification of the Board 18
   CEO Succession Planning 18
   Cumulative Voting 18
   Director and Officer Indemnification and Liability Protection 18
   Establish/Amend Nominee Qualifications 19
   Establish Other Board Committee Proposals 19
   Filling Vacancies/Removal of Directors 19
   Independent Chair (Separate Chair/CEO) 19
   Majority of Independent Directors/Establishment of Independent Committees 20
   Majority Vote Standard for the Election of Directors 20
   Proxy Access 21
   Require More Nominees than Open Seats 21
   Shareholder Engagement Policy (Shareholder Advisory Committee) 21

2. AUDIT-RELATED 22
   Auditor Indemnification and Limitation of Liability 22
   Auditor Ratification 22
   Shareholder Proposals Limiting Non-Audit Services 22
   Shareholder Proposals on Audit Firm Rotation 23

3. SHAREHOLDER RIGHTS & DEFENSES 24
   Advance Notice Requirements for Shareholder Proposals/Nominations 24
   Amend Bylaws without Shareholder Consent 24
   Control Share Acquisition Provisions 24
   Control Share Cash-Out Provisions 24
   Disgorgement Provisions 25
   Fair Price Provisions 25

Freeze-Out Provisions 25
Greenmail 25
Litigation Rights (including Exclusive Venue and Fee-Shifting Bylaw Provisions) 25
Net Operating Loss (NOL) Protective Amendments 26
POISON PILLS (SHAREHOLDER RIGHTS PLANS) **26**
Shareholder Proposals to Put Pill to a Vote and/or Adopt a Pill Policy 26
Management Proposals to Ratify a Poison Pill 27
Management Proposals to Ratify a Pill to Preserve Net Operating Losses (NOLs) 27
Proxy Voting Disclosure, Confidentiality, and Tabulation 27
Ratification Proposals: Management Proposals to Ratify Existing Charter or Bylaw Provisions 28
Reimbursing Proxy Solicitation Expenses 28
Reincorporation Proposals 28
Shareholder Ability to Act by Written Consent 28
Shareholder Ability to Call Special Meetings 29
Stakeholder Provisions 29
State Antitakeover Statutes 29
Supermajority Vote Requirements 29

4. **CAPITAL/RESTRUCTURING** **31**
   CAPITAL **31**
   Adjustments to Par Value of Common Stock 31
   Common Stock Authorization 31
   Dual Class Structure 32
   Issue Stock for Use with Rights Plan 32
   Preemptive Rights 32
   Preferred Stock Authorization 32
   Recapitalization Plans 33
   Reverse Stock Splits 33
   Share Repurchase Programs 33
   Stock Distributions: Splits and Dividends 33
   Tracking Stock 33
   RESTRUCTURING **34**
   Appraisal Rights 34
   Asset Purchases 34
   Asset Sales 34
   Bundled Proposals 34
   Conversion of Securities 34
   Corporate Reorganization/Debt Restructuring/Prepackaged Bankruptcy Plans/Reverse Leveraged Buyouts/Wrap Plans 35
   Formation of Holding Company 35
   Going Private and Going Dark Transactions (LBOs and Minority Squeeze-outs) 35
   Joint Ventures 36
   Liquidations 36

   Mergers and Acquisitions 36

Private Placements/Warrants/Convertible Debentures 37
Reorganization/Restructuring Plan (Bankruptcy) 38
Special Purpose Acquisition Corporations (SPACs) 38
Special Purpose Acquisition Corporations (SPACs) - Proposals for Extensions 39
Spin-offs 39
Value Maximization Shareholder Proposals 39

5. COMPENSATION 40
    EXECUTIVE PAY EVALUATION 40
    Advisory Votes on Executive Compensation—Management Proposals (Management Say-on-Pay) ... 40
        Pay-for-Performance Evaluation 41
        Problematic Pay Practices 41
        Compensation Committee Communications and Responsiveness 42
    Frequency of Advisory Vote on Executive Compensation ("Say When on Pay") 43
    Voting on Golden Parachutes in an Acquisition, Merger, Consolidation, or Proposed Sale .. 43
    EQUITY-BASED AND OTHER INCENTIVE PLANS 44
        Shareholder Value Transfer (SVT) 45
        Three-Year Burn Rate 45
    Egregious Factors 45
        Liberal Change in Control Definition 45
        Repricing Provisions 45
        Problematic Pay Practices or Significant Pay-for-Performance Disconnect 46
    Amending Cash and Equity Plans (including Approval for Tax Deductibility (162(m)) 46
    Specific Treatment of Certain Award Types in Equity Plan Evaluations 47
        Dividend Equivalent Rights 47
        Operating Partnership (OP) Units in Equity Plan Analysis of Real Estate Investment Trusts (REITs) ... 47
    OTHER COMPENSATION PLANS 47
    401(k) Employee Benefit Plans 47
    Employee Stock Ownership Plans (ESOPs) 47
    Employee Stock Purchase Plans—Qualified Plans 47
    Employee Stock Purchase Plans—Non-Qualified Plans 47
    Option Exchange Programs/Repricing Options 48
    Stock Plans in Lieu of Cash 48
    Transfer Stock Option (TSO) Programs 49
    DIRECTOR COMPENSATION 49
    Shareholder Ratification of Director Pay Programs 49
    Equity Plans for Non-Employee Directors 50
    Non-Employee Director Retirement Plans 50
    SHAREHOLDER PROPOSALS ON COMPENSATION 50
    Bonus Banking/Bonus Banking "Plus" 50
    Compensation Consultants—Disclosure of Board or Company's Utilization 50
    Disclosure/Setting Levels or Types of Compensation for Executives and Directors 51

    Golden Coffins/Executive Death Benefits 51

Hold Equity Past Retirement or for a Significant Period of Time 51
Non-Deductible Compensation 51
Pay Disparity 51
Pay for Performance/Performance-Based Awards 52
Pay for Superior Performance 52
Pre-Arranged Trading Plans (10b5-1 Plans) 53
Prohibit Outside CEOs from Serving on Compensation Committees 53
Recoupment of Incentive or Stock Compensation in Specified Circumstances 53
Severance Agreements for Executives/Golden Parachutes 53
Share Buyback Proposals 54
Supplemental Executive Retirement Plans (SERPs) 54
Tax Gross-Up Proposals 54
Termination of Employment Prior to Severance Payment/Eliminating Accelerated Vesting of Unvested Equity 54

6. ROUTINE/MISCELLANEOUS 56
Adjourn Meeting 56
Amend Quorum Requirements 56
Amend Minor Bylaws 56
Change Company Name 56
Change Date, Time, or Location of Annual Meeting 56
Other Business 56

7. SOCIAL AND ENVIRONMENTAL ISSUES 57
GLOBAL APPROACH 57
ENDORSEMENT OF PRINCIPLES 57
ANIMAL WELFARE 57
Animal Welfare Policies 57
Animal Testing 58
Animal Slaughter 58
CONSUMER ISSUES 58
Genetically Modified Ingredients 58
Reports on Potentially Controversial Business/Financial Practices 58
Pharmaceutical Pricing, Access to Medicines, and Prescription Drug Reimportation 59
Product Safety and Toxic/Hazardous Materials 59
Tobacco-Related Proposals 59
CLIMATE CHANGE 60
Climate Change/Greenhouse Gas (GHG) Emissions 60
Energy Efficiency 61
Renewable Energy 61
DIVERSITY 61
Board Diversity 61
Equality of Opportunity 62
Gender Identity, Sexual Orientation, and Domestic Partner Benefits 62

Gender Pay Gap 62

SELECTED ISS UNITED STATES PROXY VOTING GUIDELINES

ENVIRONMENT AND SUSTAINABILITY **62**
Facility and Workplace Safety 62
General Environmental Proposals and Community Impact Assessments 63
Hydraulic Fracturing 63
Operations in Protected Areas 63
Recycling 63
Sustainability Reporting 64
Water Issues 64
GENERAL CORPORATE ISSUES **64**
Charitable Contributions 64
Data Security, Privacy, and Internet Issues 64
Environmental, Social, and Governance (ESG) Compensation-Related Proposals 64
HUMAN RIGHTS, LABOR ISSUES, AND INTERNATIONAL OPERATIONS **65**
Human Rights Proposals 65
Operations in High Risk Markets 65
Outsourcing/Offshoring 66
Weapons and Military Sales 66
POLITICAL ACTIVITIES **66**
Lobbying 66
Political Contributions 66
Political Ties 67
8. **MUTUAL FUND PROXIES** **68**
Election of Directors 68
Converting Closed-end Fund to Open-end Fund 68
Proxy Contests 68
Investment Advisory Agreements 68
Approving New Classes or Series of Shares 68
Preferred Stock Proposals 68
1940 Act Policies 69
Changing a Fundamental Restriction to a Nonfundamental Restriction 69
Change Fundamental Investment Objective to Nonfundamental 69
Name Change Proposals 69
Change in Fund's Subclassification 69
Business Development Companies—Authorization to Sell Shares of Common Stock at a Price below Net Asset Value 69
Disposition of Assets/Termination/Liquidation 70
Changes to the Charter Document 70
Changing the Domicile of a Fund 70
Authorizing the Board to Hire and Terminate Subadvisers Without Shareholder Approval 70
Distribution Agreements 71
Master-Feeder Structure 71

Mergers 71
SHAREHOLDER PROPOSALS FOR MUTUAL FUNDS **71**

Establish Director Ownership Requirement..71
Reimburse Shareholder for Expenses Incurred..71
Terminate the Investment Advisor...71

COVERAGE

The U.S. research team provides proxy analyses and voting recommendations for common shareholder meetings of publicly - traded U.S. - incorporated companies that are held in our institutional investor clients' portfolios and includes all S&P 1500 and Russell 3000 companies that are considered U.S. Domestic Issuers by the SEC. Coverage generally includes corporate actions for common equity holders, such as written consents and bankruptcies. ISS' U.S. coverage includes investment companies (including open-end funds, closed-end funds, exchange-traded funds, and unit investment trusts), limited partnerships ("LPs"), master limited partnerships ("MLPs"), limited liability companies ("LLCs"), and business development companies. ISS reviews its universe of coverage on an annual basis, and the coverage is subject to change based on client need and industry trends.

The U.S. research team also produces, for subscribing clients, research and recommendations for fixed income meetings, and meetings of certain preferred securities, including Auction Rate Preferred Securities ("ARPS") and Variable Rate Municipal Term Preferred securities ("VMTPs")....

1. BOARD OF DIRECTORS

Voting on Director Nominees in Uncontested Elections . . .

General Recommendation: Generally vote for director nominees, except under the following circumstances:

Independence

Vote against[1] or withhold from non-independent directors (Executive Directors and Non-Independent Non-Executive Directors per ISS' Classification of Directors) when:

› Independent directors comprise 50 percent or less of the board;
› The non-independent director serves on the audit, compensation, or nominating committee;
› The company lacks an audit, compensation, or nominating committee so that the full board functions as that committee; or
› The company lacks a formal nominating committee, even if the board attests that the independent directors fulfill the functions of such a committee.

---

[1] In general, companies with a plurality vote standard use "Withhold" as the contrary vote option in director elections; companies with a majority vote standard use "Against". However, it will vary by company and the proxy must be checked to determine the valid contrary vote option for the particular company.

Composition

Attendance at Board and Committee Meetings: Generally vote against or withhold from directors (except new nominees, who should be considered case-by-case) who attend less than 75 percent of the aggregate of their board and committee meetings for the period for which they served, unless an acceptable reason for absences is disclosed in the proxy or another SEC filing. Acceptable reasons for director absences are generally limited to the following:

> Medical issues/illness;
> Family emergencies; and
> Missing only one meeting (when the total of all meetings is three or fewer).

In cases of chronic poor attendance without reasonable justification, in addition to voting against the director(s) with poor attendance, generally vote against or withhold from appropriate members of the nominating/governance committees or the full board.

If the proxy disclosure is unclear and insufficient to determine whether a director attended at least 75 percent of the aggregate of his/her board and committee meetings during his/her period of service, vote against or withhold from the director(s) in question.

Overboarded Directors: Generally vote against or withhold from individual directors who:

> Sit on more than five public company boards; or
> Are CEOs of public companies who sit on the boards of more than two public companies besides their own—withhold only at their outside boards.

Diversity: Highlight boards with no gender diversity. For 2019 meetings, no adverse vote recommendations will be made due to a lack of gender diversity.

For companies in the Russell 3000 or S&P 1500 indices, effective for meetings on or after Feb. 1, 2020, generally vote against or withhold from the chair of the nominating committee (or other directors on a case-by-case basis) at companies when there are no women on the company's board. Mitigating factors include:

> A firm commitment, as stated in the proxy statement, to appoint at least one female to the board in the near term;
> The presence of a female on the board at the preceding annual meeting; or
> Other relevant factors as applicable.

Responsiveness

Vote case-by-case on individual directors, committee members, or the entire board of directors as appropriate if:

> The board failed to act on a shareholder proposal that received the support of a majority of the shares cast in the previous year or failed to act on a management proposal seeking to ratify an existing charter/bylaw provision that received opposition of a majority of the shares cast in the previous year. Factors that will be considered are:
>> Disclosed outreach efforts by the board to shareholders in the wake of the vote;
>> Rationale provided in the proxy statement for the level of implementation;
>> The subject matter of the proposal;
>> The level of support for and opposition to the resolution in past meetings;
>> Actions taken by the board in response to the majority vote and its engagement with shareholders;

- › The continuation of the underlying issue as a voting item on the ballot (as either shareholder or management proposals); and
- › Other factors as appropriate.
- › The board failed to act on takeover offers where the majority of shares are tendered;
- › At the previous board election, any director received more than 50 percent withhold/against votes of the shares cast and the company has failed to address the issue(s) that caused the high withhold/against vote.

Vote case-by-case on Compensation Committee members (or, in exceptional cases, the full board) and the Say on Pay proposal if:

- › The company's previous say-on-pay received the support of less than 70 percent of votes cast. Factors that will be considered are:
  - › The company's response, including:
    - › Disclosure of engagement efforts with major institutional investors, including the frequency and timing of engagements and the company participants (including whether independent directors participated);
    - › Disclosure of the specific concerns voiced by dissenting shareholders that led to the say-on-pay opposition;
    - › Disclosure of specific and meaningful actions taken to address shareholders' concerns;
  - › Other recent compensation actions taken by the company;
  - › Whether the issues raised are recurring or isolated;
  - › The company's ownership structure; and
  - › Whether the support level was less than 50 percent, which would warrant the highest degree of responsiveness.
- › The board implements an advisory vote on executive compensation on a less frequent basis than the frequency that received the plurality of votes cast.

Accountability

Vote against or withhold from the entire board of directors (except new nominees, who should be considered case-by-case) for the following:

Problematic Takeover Defenses/Governance Structure

Poison Pills: Vote against or withhold from all nominees (except new nominees, who should be considered case-by-case) if:

- › The company has a poison pill that was not approved by shareholders[5]. However, vote case-by-case on nominees if the board adopts an initial pill with a term of one year or less, depending on the disclosed rationale for the adoption, and other factors as relevant (such as a commitment to put any renewal to a shareholder vote).
- › The board makes a material adverse modification to an existing pill, including, but not limited to, extension, renewal, or lowering the trigger, without shareholder approval.

Classified Board Structure: The board is classified, and a continuing director responsible for a problematic governance issue at the board/committee level that would warrant a withhold/against vote recommendation is not up for election. All appropriate nominees (except new) may be held accountable.

Removal of Shareholder Discretion on Classified Boards: The company has opted into, or failed to opt out of, state laws requiring a classified board structure.

Director Performance Evaluation: The board lacks mechanisms to promote accountability and oversight, coupled with sustained poor performance relative to peers. Sustained poor performance is measured by one-, three-, and five-year

---

[5] Public shareholders only, approval prior to a company's becoming public is insufficient.

total shareholder returns in the bottom half of a company's four-digit GICS industry group (Russell 3000 companies only). Take into consideration the company's operational metrics and other factors as warranted. Problematic provisions include but are not limited to:

›   A classified board structure;
›   A supermajority vote requirement;
›   Either a plurality vote standard in uncontested director elections, or a majority vote standard in contested elections;
›   The inability of shareholders to call special meetings;
›   The inability of shareholders to act by written consent;
›   A multi-class capital structure; and/or
›   A non-shareholder-approved poison pill.

Unilateral Bylaw/Charter Amendments and Problematic Capital Structures: Generally vote against or withhold from directors individually, committee members, or the entire board (except new nominees, who should be considered case-by-case) if the board amends the company's bylaws or charter without shareholder approval in a manner that materially diminishes shareholders' rights or that could adversely impact shareholders, considering the following factors:

›   The board's rationale for adopting the bylaw/charter amendment without shareholder ratification;
›   Disclosure by the company of any significant engagement with shareholders regarding the amendment;
›   The level of impairment of shareholders' rights caused by the board's unilateral amendment to the bylaws/charter;
›   The board's track record with regard to unilateral board action on bylaw/charter amendments or other entrenchment provisions;
›   The company's ownership structure;
›   The company's existing governance provisions;
›   The timing of the board's amendment to the bylaws/charter in connection with a significant business development; and
›   Other factors, as deemed appropriate, that may be relevant to determine the impact of the amendment on shareholders.

Unless the adverse amendment is reversed or submitted to a binding shareholder vote, in subsequent years vote case-by-case on director nominees. Generally vote against (except new nominees, who should be considered case-by-case) if the directors:
›   Classified the board;
›   Adopted supermajority vote requirements to amend the bylaws or charter; or
›   Eliminated shareholders' ability to amend bylaws.

Problematic Governance Structure - Newly public companies: For newly public companies, generally vote against or withhold from directors individually, committee members, or the entire board (except new nominees, who should be considered case-by-case) if, prior to or in connection with the company's public offering, the company or its board adopted bylaw or charter provisions materially adverse to shareholder rights, or implemented a multi-class capital structure in which the classes have unequal voting rights considering the following factors:

›   The level of impairment of shareholders' rights;
›   The disclosed rationale;
›   The ability to change the governance structure (e.g., limitations on shareholders' right to amend the bylaws or charter, or supermajority vote requirements to amend the bylaws or charter);
›   The ability of shareholders to hold directors accountable through annual director elections, or whether the company has a classified board structure;
›   Any reasonable sunset provision; and
›   Other relevant factors.

Unless the adverse provision and/or problematic capital structure is reversed or removed, vote case-by-case on director nominees in subsequent years. . . .

Voting on Director Nominees in Contested Elections

Vote-No Campaigns

▶ **General Recommendation:** In cases where companies are targeted in connection with public "vote-no" campaigns, evaluate director nominees under the existing governance policies for voting on director nominees in uncontested elections. Take into consideration the arguments submitted by shareholders and other publicly available information.

Proxy Contests/Proxy Access — Voting for Director Nominees in Contested Elections

▶ **General Recommendation:** Vote case-by-case on the election of directors in contested elections, considering the following factors:

› Long-term financial performance of the company relative to its industry;
› Management's track record;
› Background to the contested election;
› Nominee qualifications and any compensatory arrangements;
› Strategic plan of dissident slate and quality of the critique against management;
› Likelihood that the proposed goals and objectives can be achieved (both slates); and
› Stock ownership positions.

In the case of candidates nominated pursuant to proxy access, vote case-by-case considering any applicable factors listed above or additional factors which may be relevant, including those that are specific to the company, to the nominee(s) and/or to the nature of the election (such as whether there are more candidates than board seats).

Other Board-Related Proposals

Adopt Anti-Hedging/Pledging/Speculative Investments Policy

▶ **General Recommendation:** Generally vote for proposals seeking a policy that prohibits named executive officers from engaging in derivative or speculative transactions involving company stock, including hedging, holding stock in a margin account, or pledging stock as collateral for a loan. However, the company's existing policies regarding responsible use of company stock will be considered.

Age/Term Limits

▶ **General Recommendation:** Vote against management and shareholder proposals to limit the tenure of outside directors through mandatory retirement ages.

---

[6] Examples of failure of risk oversight include but are not limited to: bribery; large or serial fines or sanctions from regulatory bodies; significant adverse legal judgments or settlement; or hedging of company stock.

Vote against management proposals to limit the tenure of outside directors through term limits. However, scrutinize boards where the average tenure of all directors exceeds 15 years for independence from management and for sufficient turnover to ensure that new perspectives are being added to the board.

Board Size

▶ **General Recommendation:** Vote for proposals seeking to fix the board size or designate a range for the board size.

Vote against proposals that give management the ability to alter the size of the board outside of a specified range without shareholder approval.

Classification/Declassification of the Board

▶ **General Recommendation:** Vote against proposals to classify (stagger) the board.
Vote for proposals to repeal classified boards and to elect all directors annually.

CEO Succession Planning

▶ **General Recommendation:** Generally vote for proposals seeking disclosure on a CEO succession planning policy, considering, at a minimum, the following factors:
) The reasonableness/scope of the request; and
) The company's existing disclosure on its current CEO succession planning process.

Cumulative Voting

▶ **General Recommendation:** Generally vote against management proposals to eliminate cumulate voting, and for shareholder proposals to restore or provide for cumulative voting, unless:

) The company has proxy access[7], thereby allowing shareholders to nominate directors to the company's ballot; and
) The company has adopted a majority vote standard, with a carve-out for plurality voting in situations where there are more nominees than seats, and a director resignation policy to address failed elections.

Vote for proposals for cumulative voting at controlled companies (insider voting power > 50%).

Filling Vacancies/Removal of Directors

▶ **General Recommendation:** Vote against proposals that provide that directors may be removed only for cause.
Vote for proposals to restore shareholders' ability to remove directors with or without cause.
Vote against proposals that provide that only continuing directors may elect replacements to fill board vacancies.
Vote for proposals that permit shareholders to elect directors to fill board vacancies.

Independent Chair (Separate Chair/CEO)

▶ **General Recommendation:** Generally vote for shareholder proposals requiring that the chairman's position be filled by an independent director, taking into consideration the following:

) The scope of the proposal;
) The company's current board leadership structure;
) The company's governance structure and practices;

> Company performance; and
> Any other relevant factors that may be applicable.

Regarding the scope of the proposal, consider whether the proposal is precatory or binding and whether the proposal is seeking an immediate change in the chairman role or the policy can be implemented at the next CEO transition.

Under the review of the company's board leadership structure, ISS may support the proposal under the following scenarios absent a compelling rationale: the presence of an executive or non-independent chair in addition to the CEO; a recent recombination of the role of CEO and chair; and/or departure from a structure with an independent chair. ISS will also consider any recent transitions in board leadership and the effect such transitions may have on independent board leadership as well as the designation of a lead director role.

When considering the governance structure, ISS will consider the overall independence of the board, the independence of key committees, the establishment of governance guidelines, board tenure and its relationship to CEO tenure, and any other factors that may be relevant. Any concerns about a company's governance structure will weigh in favor of support for the proposal.

The review of the company's governance practices may include, but is not limited to, poor compensation practices, material failures of governance and risk oversight, related-party transactions or other issues putting director independence at risk, corporate or management scandals, and actions by management or the board with potential or realized negative impact on shareholders. Any such practices may suggest a need for more independent oversight at the company thus warranting support of the proposal. . . .

Majority of Independent Directors/Establishment of Independent Committees

General Recommendation: Vote for shareholder proposals asking that a majority or more of directors be independent unless the board composition already meets the proposed threshold by ISS' definition of Independent Director (See ISS' Classification of Directors.)

Vote for shareholder proposals asking that board audit, compensation, and/or nominating committees be composed exclusively of independent directors unless they currently meet that standard.

Majority Vote Standard for the Election of Directors

General Recommendation: Generally vote for management proposals to adopt a majority of votes cast standard for directors in uncontested elections. Vote against if no carve-out for a plurality vote standard in contested elections is included.

Generally vote for precatory and binding shareholder resolutions requesting that the board change the company's bylaws to stipulate that directors need to be elected with an affirmative majority of votes cast, provided it does not conflict with the state law where the company is incorporated. Binding resolutions need to allow for a carve-out for a plurality vote standard when there are more nominees than board seats.

Companies are strongly encouraged to also adopt a post-election policy (also known as a director resignation policy) that will provide guidelines so that the company will promptly address the situation of a holdover director.

Proxy Access

► **General Recommendation:** Generally vote for management and shareholder proposals for proxy access with the following provisions:

› **Ownership threshold:** maximum requirement not more than three percent (3%) of the voting power;
› **Ownership duration:** maximum requirement not longer than three (3) years of continuous ownership for each member of the nominating group;
› **Aggregation:** minimal or no limits on the number of shareholders permitted to form a nominating group;
› **Cap:** cap on nominees of generally twenty-five percent (25%) of the board.

Review for reasonableness any other restrictions on the right of proxy access.
Generally vote against proposals that are more restrictive than these guidelines. . . .

Shareholder Engagement Policy (Shareholder Advisory Committee)

► **General Recommendation:** Generally vote for shareholder proposals requesting that the board establish an internal mechanism/process, which may include a committee, in order to improve communications between directors and shareholders, unless the company has the following features, as appropriate:

› Established a communication structure that goes beyond the exchange requirements to facilitate the exchange of information between shareholders and members of the board;
› Effectively disclosed information with respect to this structure to its shareholders;
› Company has not ignored majority-supported shareholder proposals or a majority withhold vote on a director nominee; and
› The company has an independent chairman or a lead director, according to ISS' definition. This individual must be made available for periodic consultation and direct communication with major shareholders.

3. SHAREHOLDER RIGHTS & DEFENSES

Advance Notice Requirements for Shareholder Proposals/Nominations

► **General Recommendation:** Vote case-by-case on advance notice proposals, giving support to those proposals which allow shareholders to submit proposals/nominations as close to the meeting date as reasonably possible and within the broadest window possible, recognizing the need to allow sufficient notice for company, regulatory, and shareholder review.

To be reasonable, the company's deadline for shareholder notice of a proposal/nominations must not be more than 60 days prior to the meeting, with a submittal window of at least 30 days prior to the deadline. The submittal window is the period under which a shareholder must file his proposal/nominations prior to the deadline.

In general, support additional efforts by companies to ensure full disclosure in regard to a proponent's economic and voting position in the company so long as the informational requirements are reasonable and aimed at providing shareholders with the necessary information to review such proposals.

Amend Bylaws without Shareholder Consent

► **General Recommendation:** Vote against proposals giving the board exclusive authority to amend the bylaws.

Vote case-by-case on proposals giving the board the ability to amend the bylaws in addition to shareholders, taking into account the following:

> Any impediments to shareholders' ability to amend the bylaws (i.e. supermajority voting requirements);
> The company's ownership structure and historical voting turnout;
> Whether the board could amend bylaws adopted by shareholders; and
> Whether shareholders would retain the ability to ratify any board-initiated amendments. . . .

Litigation Rights (including Exclusive Venue and Fee-Shifting Bylaw Provisions)

Bylaw provisions impacting shareholders' ability to bring suit against the company may include exclusive venue provisions, which provide that the state of incorporation shall be the sole venue for certain types of litigation, and fee-shifting provisions that require a shareholder who sues a company unsuccessfully to pay all litigation expenses of the defendant corporation.

General Recommendation: Vote case-by-case on bylaws which impact shareholders' litigation rights, taking into account factors such as:

> The company's stated rationale for adopting such a provision;
> Disclosure of past harm from shareholder lawsuits in which plaintiffs were unsuccessful or shareholder lawsuits outside the jurisdiction of incorporation;
> The breadth of application of the bylaw, including the types of lawsuits to which it would apply and the definition of key terms; and
> Governance features such as shareholders' ability to repeal the provision at a later date (including the vote standard applied when shareholders attempt to amend the bylaws) and their ability to hold directors accountable through annual director elections and a majority vote standard in uncontested elections.

Generally vote against bylaws that mandate fee-shifting whenever plaintiffs are not completely successful on the merits (i.e., in cases where the plaintiffs are partially successful)....

Poison Pills (Shareholder Rights Plans)

Shareholder Proposals to Put Pill to a Vote and/or Adopt a Pill Policy

▶ **General Recommendation:** Vote for shareholder proposals requesting that the company submit its poison pill to a shareholder vote or redeem it unless the company has: (1) A shareholder approved poison pill in place; or (2) The company has adopted a policy concerning the adoption of a pill in the future specifying that the board will only adopt a shareholder rights plan if either:
> Shareholders have approved the adoption of the plan; or
> The board, in its exercise of its fiduciary responsibilities, determines that it is in the best interest of shareholders under the circumstances to adopt a pill without the delay in adoption that would result from seeking stockholder approval (i.e., the "fiduciary out" provision). A poison pill adopted under this fiduciary out will be put to a shareholder ratification vote within 12 months of adoption or expire. If the pill is not approved by a majority of the votes cast on this issue, the plan will immediately terminate.

If the shareholder proposal calls for a time period of less than 12 months for shareholder ratification after adoption, vote for the proposal, but add the caveat that a vote within 12 months would be considered sufficient implementation.

Management Proposals to Ratify a Poison Pill

▶ **General Recommendation:** Vote case-by-case on management proposals on poison pill ratification, focusing on the features of the shareholder rights plan. Rights plans should contain the following attributes:
> No lower than a 20 percent trigger, flip-in or flip-over;
> A term of no more than three years;
> No dead-hand, slow-hand, no-hand, or similar feature that limits the ability of a future board to redeem the pill;
> Shareholder redemption feature (qualifying offer clause); if the board refuses to redeem the pill 90 days after a qualifying offer is announced, 10 percent of the shares may call a special meeting or seek a written consent to vote on rescinding the pill.

In addition, the rationale for adopting the pill should be thoroughly explained by the company. In examining the request for the pill, take into consideration the company's existing governance structure, including: board independence, existing takeover defenses, and any problematic governance concerns.....

Proxy Voting Disclosure, Confidentiality, and Tabulation

▶ **General Recommendation:** Vote case-by-case on proposals regarding proxy voting mechanics, taking into consideration whether implementation of the proposal is likely to enhance or protect shareholder rights. Specific issues covered under the policy include, but are not limited to, confidential voting of individual proxies and ballots, confidentiality of running vote tallies, and the treatment of abstentions and/or broker non-votes in the company's vote-counting methodology.

While a variety of factors may be considered in each analysis, the guiding principles are: transparency, consistency, and fairness in the proxy voting process. The factors considered, as applicable to the proposal, may include:

› The scope and structure of the proposal;
› The company's stated confidential voting policy (or other relevant policies) and whether it ensures a "level playing field" by providing shareholder proponents with equal access to vote information prior to the annual meeting;
› The company's vote standard for management and shareholder proposals and whether it ensures consistency and fairness in the proxy voting process and maintains the integrity of vote results;
› Whether the company's disclosure regarding its vote counting method and other relevant voting policies with respect to management and shareholder proposals are consistent and clear;
› Any recent controversies or concerns related to the company's proxy voting mechanics;
› Any unintended consequences resulting from implementation of the proposal; and
› Any other factors that may be relevant. . . .

Reimbursing Proxy Solicitation Expenses

▶ **General Recommendation:** Vote case-by-case on proposals to reimburse proxy solicitation expenses.

When voting in conjunction with support of a dissident slate, vote for the reimbursement of all appropriate proxy solicitation expenses associated with the election.

Generally vote for shareholder proposals calling for the reimbursement of reasonable costs incurred in connection with nominating one or more candidates in a contested election where the following apply:

› The election of fewer than 50 percent of the directors to be elected is contested in the election;
› One or more of the dissident's candidates is elected;
› Shareholders are not permitted to cumulate their votes for directors; and
› The election occurred, and the expenses were incurred, after the adoption of this bylaw. . . .

Shareholder Ability to Act by Written Consent

▶ **General Recommendation:** Generally vote against management and shareholder proposals to restrict or prohibit shareholders' ability to act by written consent.

Generally vote for management and shareholder proposals that provide shareholders with the ability to act by written consent, taking into account the following factors:

> Shareholders' current right to act by written consent;
> The consent threshold;
> The inclusion of exclusionary or prohibitive language;
> Investor ownership structure; and
> Shareholder support of, and management's response to, previous shareholder proposals.

Vote case-by-case on shareholder proposals if, in addition to the considerations above, the company has the following governance and antitakeover provisions:

> An unfettered[8] right for shareholders to call special meetings at a 10 percent threshold;
> A majority vote standard in uncontested director elections;
> No non-shareholder-approved pill; and
> An annually elected board.

Shareholder Ability to Call Special Meetings

▶ **General Recommendation:** Vote against management or shareholder proposals to restrict or prohibit shareholders' ability to call special meetings.

Generally vote for management or shareholder proposals that provide shareholders with the ability to call special meetings taking into account the following factors:

> Shareholders' current right to call special meetings;
> Minimum ownership threshold necessary to call special meetings (10 percent preferred);
> The inclusion of exclusionary or prohibitive language;
> Investor ownership structure; and
> Shareholder support of, and management's response to, previous shareholder proposals.

Stakeholder Provisions

▶ **General Recommendation:** Vote against proposals that ask the board to consider non-shareholder constituencies or other non-financial effects when evaluating a merger or business combination.

State Antitakeover Statutes

▶ **General Recommendation:** Vote case-by-case on proposals to opt in or out of state takeover statutes (including fair price provisions, stakeholder laws, poison pill endorsements, severance pay and labor contract provisions, and anti-greenmail provisions).

Supermajority Vote Requirements

▶ **General Recommendation:** Vote against proposals to require a supermajority shareholder vote.

---

[8] "Unfettered" means no restrictions on agenda items, no restrictions on the number of shareholders who can group together to reach the 10 percent threshold, and only reasonable limits on when a meeting can be called: no greater than 30 days after the last annual meeting and no greater than 90 prior to the next annual meeting.

Vote for management or shareholder proposals to reduce supermajority vote requirements. However, for companies with shareholder(s) who have significant ownership levels, vote case-by-case, taking into account:

› Ownership structure;
› Quorum requirements; and
› Vote requirements.

FORM OF STOCK CERTIFICATE

[From 3 R. Balotti & J. Finkelstein, The Delaware Law of
Corporations and Business Organizations,
Form 5.1 (2d ed. 1990).]

COMMON STOCK CERTIFICATE

FORM—STOCK CERTIFICATE

The corporation will furnish without charge to each stockholder who so requests the powers, designations, preferences and relative, participating, optional or other special rights of each class of stock or series thereof of the corporation, and the qualifications, limitations or restrictions of such preferences and/or rights. Such request may be made to the corporation or the transfer agent.

The following abbreviations, when used in the inscription on the face of this certificate, shall be construed as though they were written out in full according to applicable laws or regulations:

TEN COM   —   as tenants in common

TEN ENT   —   as tenants by the entireties

JT TEN   —   as joint tenants with right of survivorship and

                  not as tenants in common

UNIF GIFT MIN ACT—_____ Custodian _____

                       (Cust)   (Minor)

           under Uniform Gifts to Minors Act

_____

                                     (State)

Additional abbreviations may also be used though not in the above list.

For value received, _____ hereby sell, assign and transfer unto

          Please insert social security or other
          <u>identifying number of assignee</u>

          _____

(Please print or typewrite name and address, including zip code, of assignee)
_____
_____

_____ Shares of the capital stock represented by the within Certificate, and do hereby irrevocably constitute and appoint

_____ Attorney to transfer the said stock on the books of the within named Corporation with full power of substitution in the premises.

Dated: _____

                                  _____

                                  Notice: The signature to this assignment must correspond with the name as written upon the face of the certificate in every particular, without alteration or enlargement or any change whatever.

FORM OF PROXY STATEMENT
AND FORM OF PROXY

DEF 14A 1 d334778ddef14a.htm DEF 14A

UNITED STATES
SECURITIES AND EXCHANGE COMMISSION
WASHINGTON, D.C. 20549

SCHEDULE 14A

**PROXY STATEMENT PURSUANT TO SECTION 14(a)
OF THE SECURITIES EXCHANGE ACT OF 1934
(AMENDMENT NO.   )**

Filed by the Registrant ☒   Filed by a Party other than the Registrant ☐

Check the appropriate box:

- ☐ Preliminary Proxy Statement
- ☐ **Confidential, for Use of the Commission Only (as permitted by Rule 14a-6(e)(2))**
- ☒ Definitive Proxy Statement
- ☐ Definitive Additional Materials
- ☐ Soliciting Material under §240.14a-12

AMAZON.COM, INC.
(NAME OF REGISTRANT AS SPECIFIED IN ITS CHARTER)

(NAME OF PERSON(S) FILING PROXY STATEMENT, IF OTHER THAN THE REGISTRANT)

Payment of Filing Fee (Check the appropriate box):

- ☒ No fee required.
- ☐ Fee computed on table below per Exchange Act Rules 14a-6(i)(1) and 0-11.

    (1) Title of each class of securities to which transaction applies:
    _____

    (2) Aggregate number of securities to which transaction applies:
    _____

    (3) Per unit price or other underlying value of transaction computed pursuant to Exchange Act Rule 0-11 (set forth the amount on which the filing fee is calculated and state how it was determined):
    _____

    (4) Proposed maximum aggregate value of transaction:
    _____

    (5) Total fee paid:
    _____

- ☐ Fee paid previously with preliminary materials.
- ☐ Check box if any part of the fee is offset as provided by Exchange Act Rule 0-11(a)(2) and identify the filing for which the offsetting fee was paid previously. Identify the previous filing by registration statement number, or the Form or Schedule and the date of its filing.

    (1) Amount Previously Paid:
    _____

    (2) Form, Schedule or Registration Statement No.:
    _____

    (3) Filing Party:
    _____

(4)   Date Filed:

FORM OF PROXY STATEMENT AND FORM OF PROXY

amazon.com

NOTICE OF 2017 ANNUAL MEETING OF SHAREHOLDERS
To Be Held on Tuesday, May 23, 2017

The 2017 Annual Meeting of Shareholders of Amazon.com, Inc. (the "Annual Meeting") will be held at 9:00 a.m., Pacific Time, on Tuesday, May 23, 2017, at Fremont Studios, 155 N. 35th Street, Seattle, Washington 98103, for the following purposes:

1. To elect the ten directors named in the Proxy Statement to serve until the next Annual Meeting of Shareholders or until their respective successors are elected and qualified;

2. To ratify the appointment of Ernst & Young LLP as our independent auditors for the fiscal year ending December 31, 2017;

3. To conduct an advisory vote to approve our executive compensation;

4. To conduct an advisory vote on the frequency of future advisory votes on executive compensation;

5. To approve our 1997 Stock Incentive Plan, as amended and restated (the "1997 Plan");

6. To consider and act upon three shareholder proposals, if properly presented at the Annual Meeting; and

7. To transact such other business as may properly come before the meeting or any adjournment or postponement thereof.

Our Board of Directors recommends you vote (i) "FOR" the election of each of the nominees to the Board; (ii) "FOR" the ratification of the appointment of Ernst & Young LLP as independent auditors; (iii) "FOR" approval, on an advisory basis, of our executive compensation as described in the Proxy Statement; (iv) on an advisory basis, to conduct future advisory votes on executive compensation every "THREE YEARS"; (v) "FOR" approval of the 1997 Plan; and (vi) "AGAINST" each of the three shareholder proposals.

The Board of Directors has fixed March 29, 2017 as the record date for determining shareholders entitled to receive notice of, and to vote at, the Annual Meeting or any adjournment or postponement thereof. Only shareholders of record at the close of business on that date will be entitled to notice of, and to vote at, the Annual Meeting.

By Order of the Board of Directors

David A. Zapolsky
Secretary

Seattle, Washington
April 12, 2017

Important Notice Regarding the Availability of Proxy Materials for the Amazon.com, Inc. Shareholder Meeting to be Held on May 23, 2017
The Proxy Statement and our 2016 Annual Report are available at www.envisionreports.com/amzn.

FORM OF PROXY STATEMENT AND FORM OF PROXY

AMAGON.COM, INC.

PROXY STATEMENT

ANNUAL MEETING OF SHAREHOLDERS
To Be Held on Tuesday, May 23, 2017

General

The enclosed proxy is solicited by the Board of Directors of Amazon.com, Inc. (the "Company") for use at the Annual Meeting of Shareholders to be held at 9:00 a.m., Pacific Time, on Tuesday, May 23, 2017, at Fremont Studios, 155 N. 35ᵗʰ Street, Seattle, Washington 98103, and at any adjournment or postponement thereof. Our principal offices are located at 410 Terry Avenue North, Seattle, Washington 98109. This Proxy Statement is first being made available to our shareholders on or about April 12, 2017.

Outstanding Securities and Quorum

Only holders of record of our common stock, par value $0.01 per share, at the close of business on March 29, 2017, the record date, will be entitled to notice of, and to vote at, the Annual Meeting. On that date, we had 477,948,433 shares of common stock outstanding and entitled to vote. Each share of common stock is entitled to one vote for each director nominee and one vote for each other item to be voted on at the Annual Meeting.

A majority of the outstanding shares of common stock entitled to vote, present in person or represented by proxy, constitutes a quorum for the transaction of business at the Annual Meeting. Abstentions and broker nonvotes will be included in determining the presence of a quorum at the Annual Meeting.

Internet Availability of Proxy Materials

We are furnishing proxy materials to some of our shareholders via the Internet by mailing a Notice of Internet Availability of Proxy Materials, instead of mailing or e-mailing copies of those materials. The Notice of Internet Availability of Proxy Materials directs shareholders to a website where they can access our proxy materials, including our proxy statement and our annual report, and view instructions on how to vote via the Internet, mobile device, or by telephone. If you received a Notice of Internet Availability of Proxy Materials and would prefer to receive a paper copy of our proxy materials, please follow the instructions included in the Notice of Internet Availability of Proxy Materials. If you have previously elected to receive our proxy materials via e-mail, you will continue to receive access to those materials electronically unless you elect otherwise.

Proxy Voting

Shares that are properly voted via the Internet, mobile device, or by telephone or for which proxy cards are properly executed and returned will be voted at the Annual Meeting in accordance with the directions given or, in the absence of directions, will be voted in accordance with the Board's recommendations as follows: "FOR" the election of each of the nominees to the Board named herein; "FOR" the ratification of the appointment of our independent auditors; "FOR" approval, on an advisory basis, of our executive compensation as described in this Proxy Statement; on an advisory basis, to conduct future advisory votes on executive compensation every "THREE YEARS"; "FOR" approval of the 1997 Plan; and "AGAINST" each of the shareholder proposals. It is not expected that any additional matters will be brought before the Annual Meeting, but if other matters are properly presented, the persons named as proxies in the proxy card or their substitutes will vote in their discretion on such matters.

FORM OF PROXY STATEMENT AND FORM OF PROXY

The manner in which your shares may be voted depends on how your shares are held. If you own shares of record, meaning that your shares are represented by certificates or book entries in your name so that you appear as a shareholder on the records of Computershare, our stock transfer agent, you may vote by proxy, meaning you authorize individuals named in the proxy card to vote your shares. You may provide this authorization by voting via the Internet, mobile device, by telephone, or (if you have received paper copies of our proxy materials) by returning a proxy card. In these circumstances, if you do not vote by proxy or in person at the Annual Meeting, your shares will not be voted. If you own shares in street name, meaning that your shares are held by a bank, brokerage firm, or other nominee, you may instruct that institution on how to vote your shares. You may provide these instructions by voting via the Internet, mobile device, by telephone, or (if you have received paper copies of proxy materials through your bank, brokerage firm, or other nominee) by returning a voting instruction form received from that institution. In these circumstances, if you do not provide voting instructions, the institution may nevertheless vote your shares on your behalf with respect to the ratification of the appointment of Ernst & Young LLP as our independent auditors for the fiscal year ending December 31, 2017, but cannot vote your shares on any other matters being considered at the meeting.

Voting Standard

A nominee for director shall be elected to the Board if the votes cast for such nominee's election exceed the votes cast against such nominee's election. If the votes cast for any nominee do not exceed the votes cast against the nominee, the Board will consider whether to accept or reject such director's resignation, which is tendered to the Board pursuant to the Board of Directors Guidelines on Significant Corporate Governance Issues. Abstentions and broker nonvotes will have no effect on the outcome of the election. Broker nonvotes occur when a person holding shares in street name, such as through a brokerage firm, does not provide instructions as to how to vote those shares and the broker does not then vote those shares on the shareholder's behalf.

For all other matters proposed for a vote at the Annual Meeting, the affirmative vote of a majority of the outstanding shares of common stock present in person or represented by proxy and entitled to vote on the matter is required to approve the matter. For these matters, abstentions are not counted as affirmative votes on a matter but are counted as present at the Annual Meeting and entitled to vote, and broker nonvotes, if any, will have no effect on the outcome of these matters.

Voting via the Internet, mobile device, or by telephone helps save money by reducing postage and proxy tabulation costs. To vote by any of these methods, read this Proxy Statement, have your Notice of Internet Availability of Proxy Materials, proxy card, or voting instruction form in hand, and follow the instructions below for your preferred method of voting. Each of these voting methods is available 24 hours per day, seven days per week.

We encourage you to cast your vote by one of the following methods:		
VOTE BY INTERNET **Shares Held of Record:** *http://www.envisionreports.com/amzn* **Shares Held in Street Name:** *http://www.proxyvote.com*	**VOTE BY QR CODE** **Shares Held of Record:** Scan the QR code above with your mobile device. **Shares Held in Street Name:** *See Voting Instruction Form*	**VOTE BY TELEPHONE** **Shares Held of Record:** 800-652-VOTE **Shares Held in Street Name:** *See Voting Instruction Form*

We encourage you to register to receive all future shareholder communications electronically, instead of in print. This means that access to the annual report, proxy statement, and other correspondence will be delivered to you via e-mail.

FORM OF PROXY STATEMENT AND FORM OF PROXY

Voting at the Annual Meeting

If you own common stock of record, you may attend the Annual Meeting and vote in person, regardless of whether you have previously voted by proxy card, via the Internet, mobile device, or by telephone. If you own common stock in street name, you may attend the Annual Meeting, but in order to vote your shares at the meeting you must obtain a "legal proxy" from the bank, brokerage firm, or other nominee that holds your shares. You should contact your bank or brokerage account representative to learn how to obtain a legal proxy. We encourage you to vote your shares in advance of the Annual Meeting by one of the methods described above, even if you plan on attending the Annual Meeting. If you have already voted prior to the meeting, you may nevertheless change or revoke your vote at the Annual Meeting as described below.

Revocation

If you own common stock of record, you may revoke your proxy or change your voting instructions at any time before your shares are voted at the Annual Meeting by delivering to the Secretary of Amazon.com, Inc. a written notice of revocation or a duly executed proxy (via the Internet, mobile device, or telephone or by returning a proxy card) bearing a later date or by attending the Annual Meeting and voting in person. A shareholder owning common stock in street name may revoke or change voting instructions by contacting the bank, brokerage firm, or other nominee holding the shares or by obtaining a legal proxy from such institution and voting in person at the Annual Meeting.

Attending the Annual Meeting

Only shareholders as of the record date (March 29, 2017) are entitled to attend the Annual Meeting in person. If you own common stock of record, your name will be on a list and you will be able to gain entry with a government-issued photo identification, such as a driver's license, state-issued ID card, or passport. If you own common stock in street name, in order to gain entry you must present a government-issued photo identification and proof of beneficial stock ownership as of the record date, such as your Notice of Internet Availability of Proxy Materials, a copy of your proxy card or voting instruction form if you received one, or an account or brokerage statement or other similar evidence showing stock ownership as of the record date. If you are a representative of an entity that owns common stock of the Company, you must present a government-issued photo identification, evidence that you are the entity's authorized representative or proxyholder, and, if the entity is a street name owner, proof of the entity's beneficial stock ownership as of the record date.

If you are not a shareholder, you will be entitled to admission only if you have a valid legal proxy from a record holder and a government-issued photo identification. Each shareholder may appoint only one proxyholder or representative to attend on his or her behalf.

You can find directions to the Annual Meeting at *www.amazon.com/ir*. Cameras, recording devices, and other electronic devices are prohibited at the meeting.

ITEM 1—ELECTION OF DIRECTORS

In accordance with our Bylaws, the Board has fixed the number of directors constituting the Board at ten. The Board, based on the recommendation of the Nominating and Corporate Governance Committee, proposed that the following ten nominees be elected at the Annual Meeting, each of whom will hold office until the next Annual Meeting of Shareholders or until his or her successor shall have been elected and qualified:

- Jeffrey P. Bezos
- Tom A. Alberg
- John Seely Brown
- Jamie S. Gorelick
- Daniel P. Huttenlocher
- Judith A. McGrath
- Jonathan J. Rubinstein
- Thomas O. Ryder
- Patricia Q. Stonesifer
- Wendell P. Weeks

Each of the nominees is currently a director of Amazon.com, Inc. and has been elected to hold office until the 2017 Annual Meeting or until his or her successor has been elected and qualified. Mr. Huttenlocher was elected as a director by the Board of Directors on September 7, 2016 and the other nominees were most recently elected at the 2016 Annual Meeting. Biographical and related information on each nominee is set forth below.

Although the Board expects that the ten nominees will be available to serve as directors, if any of them should be unwilling or unable to serve, the Board may decrease the size of the Board or may designate substitute nominees, and the proxies will be voted in favor of any such substitute nominees.

THE BOARD OF DIRECTORS RECOMMENDS A VOTE "FOR" EACH NOMINEE.

Director Nominees' Biographical and Related Information

In evaluating the nominees for the Board of Directors, the Board and the Nominating and Corporate Governance Committee took into account the qualities they seek for directors, as discussed below under "Corporate Governance" and "Board Meetings and Committees," and the directors' individual qualifications, skills, and background that enable the directors to effectively and productively contribute to the Board's oversight of Amazon. These individual qualifications and skills are included below in each nominee's biography.

Biographical Information

Jeffrey P. Bezos, age 53, has been Chairman of the Board since founding the Company in 1994 and Chief Executive Officer since May 1996. Mr. Bezos served as President from founding until June 1999 and again from October 2000 to the present. Mr. Bezos' individual qualifications and skills as a director include his customer-focused point of view, his willingness to encourage invention, his long-term perspective, and his on-going contributions as founder and CEO.

Tom A. Alberg, age 77, has been a director since June 1996. Mr. Alberg has been a managing director of Madrona Venture Group, LLC, a venture capital firm, since September 1999, and a principal in Madrona Investment Group, LLC, a private investment firm, since January 1996. Prior to co-founding Madrona Investment Group, Mr. Alberg served as president of LIN Broadcasting Corporation, Executive Vice President of McCaw Cellular Communications, Inc., and Executive Vice President of AT&T Wireless Services. Previously, he was chair of the Executive Committee and Partner at Perkins Coie, the Northwest's largest law firm. Mr. Alberg has served as a director of Impinj, Inc. since September 2000. Mr. Alberg's individual qualifications and skills as a director include his experience as a venture capitalist investing in technology companies, through which he gained experience with emerging technologies, his experience as a lawyer, his knowledge of Amazon from having served as a director since 1996, as well as his customer experience skills and skills relating to financial statement and accounting matters.

John Seely Brown, age 76, has been a director since June 2004. Mr. Brown has served as a Visiting Scholar and Advisor to the Provost at the University of Southern California ("USC") since 1996 and as Independent Co-Chairman of the Deloitte Center for the Edge since 2006. He held various scientific research positions at Xerox Corporation, from 1978 until 2002, including Chief Scientist until April 2002 and director of the Xerox Palo Alto Research Center ("PARC") until June 2000. Mr. Brown served as a director of Corning Incorporated from February 1996 to April 2014, and served as a director of Varian Medical Systems, Inc. from February 1998 to February 2013. Mr. Brown's individual qualifications and skills as a director include his experience in senior positions with USC, a leading university, and Xerox PARC, a technology research facility, his role as Chief Scientist at Xerox Corporation, a global technology company, through which he gained experience with emerging technologies, as well as his customer experience skills.

Jamie S. Gorelick, age 66, has been a director since February 2012. Ms. Gorelick has been a partner with the law firm Wilmer Cutler Pickering Hale and Dorr LLP since July 2003. She has held numerous positions in the

U.S. government, serving as Deputy Attorney General of the United States, General Counsel of the Department of Defense, Assistant to the Secretary of Energy, and a member of the bipartisan National Commission on Terrorist Threats Upon the United States. Ms. Gorelick has served as a director of VeriSign, Inc. since January 2015, a director of United Technologies Corporation from February 2000 to December 2014, and a director of Schlumberger Limited from April 2002 to June 2010. Ms. Gorelick's individual qualifications and skills as a director include her experience as a lawyer, her leadership experience in senior governmental positions, including experience with regulatory and compliance matters, as well as her customer experience skills and skills relating to public policy and financial statement and accounting matters.

Daniel P. Huttenlocher, age 58, has been a director since September 2016. Mr. Huttenlocher has been Dean and Vice Provost, Cornell Tech at Cornell University since 2012, and has worked for Cornell University since 1988 in various positions. Mr. Huttenlocher has served as a director of Corning Incorporated since February 2015. Mr. Huttenlocher's individual qualifications and skills as a director include his experience in senior positions at Cornell University, a leading university, Cornell Tech, a research, technology commercialization, and graduate-level educational facility, and Xerox PARC, a technology research facility, through which he gained experience with emerging technologies, as well as his customer experience skills.

Judith A. McGrath, age 64, has been a director since July 2014. Ms. McGrath has been the President of Astronauts Wanted * No experience necessary, a multimedia joint venture between Ms. McGrath and Sony Music Entertainment, since June 2013. Ms. McGrath served as Chair and Chief Executive Officer of MTV Networks Company, a subsidiary of Viacom, Inc., from July 2004 until May 2011. Ms. McGrath's individual qualifications and skills as a director include her leadership and multimedia operations experience as a senior executive of MTV Networks Company through which she gained experience with media and entertainment companies, entrepreneurial experience in her role at Astronauts Wanted * No experience necessary, as well as her customer experience skills.

Jonathan J. Rubinstein, age 60, has been a director since December 2010. Mr. Rubinstein was co-CEO of Bridgewater Associates, LP, a global investment management firm, from May 2016 to April 2017. Previously, Mr. Rubinstein was Senior Vice President, Product Innovation, for the Personal Systems Group at the Hewlett-Packard Company ("HP"), a multinational information technology company, from July 2011 to January 2012, and served as Senior Vice President and General Manager, Palm Global Business Unit, at HP from July 2010 to July 2011. Mr. Rubinstein was Chief Executive Officer and President of Palm, Inc., a smartphone manufacturer, from June 2009 until its acquisition by HP in July 2010, and Chairman of the Board of Palm, Inc. from October 2007 through the acquisition. Prior to joining Palm, Mr. Rubinstein was a Senior Vice President at Apple Inc., also serving as the General Manager of the iPod Division. Mr. Rubinstein served as a director of Qualcomm Incorporated from May 2013 to May 2016. Mr. Rubinstein's individual qualifications and skills as a director include his leadership and technology experience as a senior executive at large financial and technology companies, through which he gained experience with hardware devices and emerging technologies, as well as his customer experience skills and skills relating to financial statement and accounting matters.

Thomas O. Ryder, age 72, has been a director since November 2002. Mr. Ryder was Chairman of the Reader's Digest Association, Inc. from April 1998 to December 2006, and was Chief Executive Officer from April 1998 to December 2005. From 1984 to 1998, Mr. Ryder worked in several roles at American Express, including as President of American Express Travel Related Services International. Mr. Ryder has been a director of RPX Corporation since December 2009, a director of Quad/Graphics, Inc. since July 2010, and a director of Interval Leisure Group, Inc. since May 2016. He was a director of Starwood Hotels & Resorts Worldwide, Inc. from April 2001 to September 2016 and Chairman of the Board of Directors at Virgin Mobile USA, Inc. from October 2007 to November 2009. Mr. Ryder's individual qualifications and skills as a director include his leadership experience as a senior executive of Reader's Digest, a large media and publishing company, and American Express, a large financial services company, through which he gained experience with intellectual property, media, enterprise sales, payments, and international operations, as well as his customer experience skills and skills relating to financial statement and accounting matters.

Patricia Q. Stonesifer, age 60, has been a director since February 1997. Ms. Stonesifer has served as the President and CEO of Martha's Table, a non-profit, since April 2013. She served as Chair of the Board of Regents of the Smithsonian Institution from January 2009 to January 2012 and as Vice Chair from January 2012 to January 2013. From September 2008 to January 2012, she served as senior advisor to the Bill and Melinda Gates Foundation, a private philanthropic organization, where she was Chief Executive Officer from January 2006 to September 2008 and President and Co-chair from June 1997 to January 2006. Since September 2009, she has also served as a private philanthropy advisor. From 1988 to 1997, she worked in many roles at Microsoft Corporation, including as a Senior Vice President of the Interactive Media Division, and also served as the Chairwoman of the Gates Learning Foundation from 1997 to 1999. Ms. Stonesifer's individual qualifications and skills as a director include her leadership experience as a senior executive at the Bill and Melinda Gates Foundation and at Microsoft, through which she gained experience with emerging technologies and consumer-focused product development and marketing issues, her knowledge of Amazon from having served as a director since 1997, as well as her customer experience skills and skills relating to public policy and financial statement and accounting matters.

Wendell P. Weeks, age 57, has been a director since February 2016. Mr. Weeks has been the Chief Executive Officer of Corning Incorporated, a materials science and specialty glass company, since April 2005 and President since December 2010, where he has also served as the Chairman of its board of directors since April 2007. Mr. Weeks has served in various roles at Corning Incorporated since 1983. Mr. Weeks has served as a director of Merck & Co., Inc. since February 2004. Mr. Weeks' individual qualifications and skills as a director include his leadership and operations experience as a senior executive at a large corporation with international operations, experience with product development, as well as his customer experience skills and skills relating to financial statement and accounting matters.

Corporate Governance

General

Board Leadership. The Board is responsible for the control and direction of the Company. The Board represents the shareholders and its primary purpose is to build long-term shareholder value. The Chair of the Board is selected by the Board and currently is the CEO, Jeff Bezos. The Board believes that this leadership structure is appropriate given Mr. Bezos' role in founding Amazon and his significant ownership stake. The Board believes that this leadership structure improves the Board's ability to focus on key policy and operational issues and helps the Company operate in the long-term interests of shareholders. In addition, the independent directors on the Board have appointed a lead director from the Board's independent directors, currently Patricia Q. Stonesifer, in order to promote independent leadership of the Board. The lead director presides over the executive sessions of the independent directors, chairs Board meetings in the Chair's absence, and provides direction on agendas, schedules, information, and materials for Board meetings that will be most helpful to the independent directors. In addition, the lead director confers from time to time with the Chair of the Board and the independent directors and reviews, as appropriate, the annual schedule of regular Board meetings and major Board meeting agenda topics. The guidance and direction provided by the lead director reinforce the Board's independent oversight of management and contribute to communication among members of the Board.

Director Independence. The Board has determined that the following directors are independent as defined by Nasdaq rules: Mr. Alberg, Mr. Brown, Ms. Gorelick, Mr. Huttenlocher, Ms. McGrath, Mr. Rubinstein, Mr. Ryder, Ms. Stonesifer, and Mr. Weeks. In addition, the Board determined that Alain Monié, who served as a director through May 2016, and William B. Gordon, who served as a director through March 2017, were independent during the time each served as a director. In assessing directors' independence, the Board took into account certain transactions, relationships, and arrangements involving some of the directors and concluded that such transactions, relationships, and arrangements did not impair the independence of the director. For Messrs. Monié and Weeks, the Board considered payments in the past three years in the ordinary course of business between the Company and Ingram Micro, Inc. and Corning Incorporated, respectively, or their affiliates.

For Mr. Rubinstein, the Board considered payments in the past year in the ordinary course of business to Bridgewater Associates, LP, or its affiliates. All such payments were not significant for any of these companies. For Messrs. Alberg and Gordon, the Board considered that Amazon and its executive officers have in the past and may in the future invest in investment funds managed by entities where Messrs. Alberg or Gordon are managing directors or partners or in companies in which those funds invest, and that Amazon has in the past and may in the future engage in transactions with companies in which these funds have invested. For Mr. Ryder, the Board considered that his son-in-law has been employed with Amazon since 2008 in a non-officer and non-strategic position, as disclosed in "Certain Relationships and Related Person Transactions."

Risk Oversight. As part of regular Board and committee meetings, the directors oversee executives' management of risks relevant to the Company. While the full Board has overall responsibility for risk oversight, the Board has delegated responsibility related to certain risks to the Audit Committee and the Leadership Development and Compensation Committee. The Audit Committee is responsible for overseeing management of risks related to our financial statements and financial reporting process, data privacy and security, business continuity, and operational risks, the qualifications, independence, and performance of our independent auditors, the performance of our internal audit function, and our compliance with legal and regulatory requirements. The Leadership Development and Compensation Committee is responsible for overseeing management of risks related to succession planning and compensation for our executive officers and our overall compensation program, including our equity-based compensation plans. The full Board regularly reviews reports from management on various aspects of our business, including related risks and tactics and strategies for addressing them. At least annually, the Board reviews our CEO succession planning as described in our Board of Directors Guidelines on Significant Corporate Governance Issues.

Corporate Governance Documents. Please visit our investor relations website at *www.amazon.com/ir*, "Corporate Governance," for additional information on our corporate governance, including:

- our Certificate of Incorporation and Bylaws;
- the Board of Directors Guidelines on Significant Corporate Governance Issues, which includes policies on shareholder communications with the Board, director attendance at our annual meetings, director resignations to facilitate our majority vote standard, director stock ownership guidelines, and succession planning;
- the charters approved by the Board for the Audit Committee, the Leadership Development and Compensation Committee, and the Nominating and Corporate Governance Committee;
- the Code of Business Conduct and Ethics; and
- our Political Expenditures Statement.

In addition, we provide information regarding our sustainability and environmental activities on our Sustainability website at *www.amazon.com/sustainability*.

Board Meetings and Committees

The Board meets regularly during the year, and holds special meetings and acts by unanimous written consent whenever circumstances require. During 2016, there were four meetings of the Board. All incumbent directors attended at least 75% of the aggregate of the meetings of the Board and committees on which they served occurring during 2016. All directors then serving attended the 2016 Annual Meeting of Shareholders.

The Board has established an Audit Committee, a Leadership Development and Compensation Committee, and a Nominating and Corporate Governance Committee, each of which is comprised entirely of directors who meet the applicable independence requirements of the Nasdaq rules. The Committees keep the Board informed of their actions and provide assistance to the Board in fulfilling its oversight responsibility to shareholders. The table below provides current membership information as well as meeting information for the last fiscal year.

Name	Audit Committee	Leadership Development and Compensation Committee	Nominating and Corporate Governance Committee
Jeffrey P. Bezos			
Tom A. Alberg	X		
John Seely Brown			X
Jamie S. Gorelick			X*
Daniel P. Huttenlocher(1)		X	
Judith A. McGrath		X	
Jonathan J. Rubinstein		X*	
Thomas O. Ryder	X*		
Patricia Q. Stonesifer			X
Wendell P. Weeks(2)	X		
Total Meetings in 2016	**6**	**3**	**4**

*   Committee Chair
(1) Mr. Huttenlocher joined the Leadership Development and Compensation Committee on September 7, 2016.
(2) Mr. Weeks joined the Audit Committee on February 10, 2016.

The functions performed by these Committees, which are set forth in more detail in their charters, are summarized below.

Audit Committee.   The Audit Committee represents and assists the Board in fulfilling its oversight responsibility relating to our financial statements and financial reporting process, the qualifications, independence, and performance of our independent auditors, the performance of our internal audit function, and our compliance with legal and regulatory requirements. The Board has designated each of Messrs. Alberg, Ryder, and Weeks as an Audit Committee Financial Expert, as defined by Securities and Exchange Commission ("SEC") rules. During the past year, the Audit Committee met with management and reviewed matters that included the Company's risk assessment and compliance functions, information security, business continuity, accounting industry issues, the reappointment of our independent auditor, and pending litigation. The Audit Committee also met with the auditors to review the scope and results of the auditor's annual audit and quarterly reviews of the Company's financial statements.

Leadership Development and Compensation Committee.   The Leadership Development and Compensation Committee evaluates our programs and practices relating to leadership development, reviews and establishes compensation of the Company's executive officers, and oversees management of risks for succession planning and our overall compensation program, including our equity-based compensation plans, all with a view toward maximizing long-term shareholder value. The Committee may engage compensation consultants but did not do so in 2016. Additional information on the Committee's processes and procedures for considering and determining executive compensation is contained in the "Compensation Discussion and Analysis" section of this Proxy Statement. During the past year, the Leadership Development and Compensation Committee met with management and reviewed matters that included the design, amounts, and effectiveness of the Company's compensation of senior executives, management succession planning, the Company's benefit and compensation programs, and feedback from the Company's shareholder engagement.

Nominating and Corporate Governance Committee.   The Nominating and Corporate Governance Committee reviews and assesses the composition of the Board, assists in identifying potential new candidates for director, recommends candidates for election as director, and provides a leadership role with respect to our corporate governance. The Nominating and Corporate Governance Committee also recommends to the Board compensation for newly elected directors and reviews director compensation as necessary. During the past year, the Nominating and Corporate Governance Committee met with management and reviewed matters that included the Board's composition, diversity, and skills in the context of identifying and evaluating new director candidates to join the Board, the Board's recruitment and self-evaluation processes, consideration of feedback from the Company's shareholder engagement, including the adoption of a proxy access right for shareholders, and corporate governance developments.

Director Nominations.   The Nominating and Corporate Governance Committee considers candidates for director who are recommended by its members, by other Board members, by shareholders, and by management, as well as those identified by a third party search firm retained to assist in identifying and evaluating possible candidates. Mr. Huttenlocher was initially recommended to the Nominating and Corporate Governance Committee by other non-management directors. The Board recruited Mr. Huttenlocher because, as a professor of computer science and Dean and Vice Provost of Cornell Tech, the Board believes Mr. Huttenlocher will help the Company as it pursues innovations in computer science, including machine learning across its businesses, and will also help attract and retain computer scientists, technologists, and academics. The Nominating and Corporate Governance Committee annually reviews the tenure, performance, and contributions of existing Board members to the extent they are candidates for re-election, and considers all aspects of each candidate's qualifications and skills in the context of the Company's needs at that point in time and, as stated in the Board of Directors Guidelines on Significant Corporate Governance Issues, seeks out candidates with a diversity of experience and perspectives. When considering candidates as potential Board members, the Board and the Nominating and Corporate Governance Committee evaluate the candidates' ability to contribute to such diversity. The Board assesses its effectiveness in this regard as part of its annual Board and director evaluation process. Currently, one-third of our independent directors are women. Our Board's composition also represents a balanced approach to director tenure, allowing the Board to benefit from the experience of longer-serving directors combined with fresh perspectives from newer directors (with three new directors on-boarding and two directors leaving in the last three years). The current tenure range of our Board is as follows:

Tenure on Board	Number of Director Nominees
More than 10 years	5
6-10 years	1
1-5 years	4

Among the qualifications and skills of a candidate considered important by the Nominating and Corporate Governance Committee are: a commitment to representing the long-term interests of shareholders; customer experience skills; Internet savvy; an inquisitive and objective perspective; the willingness to take appropriate risks; leadership ability; personal and professional ethics, integrity, and values; practical wisdom and sound judgment; and business and professional experience in fields such as operations, technology, finance/accounting, product development, intellectual property, law, multimedia entertainment, and marketing. When evaluating re-nomination of existing directors, the Committee also considers the nominees' past and ongoing effectiveness on the Board and, with the exception of Mr. Bezos, who is an employee, their independence. The Nominating and Corporate Governance Committee believes that each of the director nominees for the Annual Meeting possesses these attributes.

The Nominating and Corporate Governance Committee evaluates director candidates recommended by shareholders in the same way that it evaluates candidates recommended by its members, other members of the

Board, or other persons. Shareholders wishing to submit recommendations for director candidates for consideration by the Nominating and Corporate Governance Committee must provide the following information in writing to the attention of the Secretary of Amazon.com, Inc. by certified or registered mail:

- the name, address, and biography of the candidate, and an indication of whether the candidate has expressed a willingness to serve;
- the name, address, and phone number of the shareholder or group of shareholders making the recommendation; and
- the number of shares of common stock beneficially owned by the shareholder or group of shareholders making the recommendation, the length of time held, and to the extent any shareholder is not a registered holder of such securities, proof of such ownership.

To be considered by the Nominating and Corporate Governance Committee for the 2018 Annual Meeting of Shareholders, a director candidate recommendation must be received by the Secretary of Amazon.com, Inc. by December 13, 2017.

Our Bylaws provide a proxy access right for shareholders, pursuant to which a shareholder, or group of up to 20 shareholders, may include director nominees (representing up to 20% of the number of directors in office) in our proxy materials for annual meetings of our shareholders. To be eligible to utilize these proxy access provisions, the shareholder or group must have owned at least 3% of the aggregate of the issued and outstanding shares of our common stock continuously for at least the prior three years and must satisfy the additional eligibility, procedural, and disclosure requirements set forth in our Bylaws.

Compensation of Directors

Our directors do not receive cash compensation for their services as directors or as members of committees of the Board, but we pay reasonable expenses incurred for attending meetings. At the discretion of the Board, directors are eligible to receive stock-based awards under the 1997 Plan. Based on the Nominating and Corporate Governance Committee's recommendation, in February 2016, the Board approved a restricted stock unit award for 1,365 shares to Mr. Weeks, vesting in three equal annual installments on February 15, 2017, February 15, 2018, and February 15, 2019. Based on the Nominating and Corporate Governance Committee's recommendation, in September 2016, the Board approved a restricted stock unit award for 1,131 shares to Mr. Huttenlocher, vesting in three equal annual installments on November 15, 2017, November 15, 2018, and November 15, 2019. Based on the Nominating and Corporate Governance Committee's recommendation, in November 2016, the Board approved restricted stock unit awards for 1,077 shares each to Messrs. Alberg, Rubinstein, and Ryder and Ms. Stonesifer, each vesting in three equal annual installments, with the first vest date occurring approximately one year after the final vest under the director's previous restricted stock unit award. The February 2016 award was designed to provide approximately $270,000 in compensation annually, and the September and November 2016 awards were designed to provide approximately $288,000 in compensation annually, in each case based on an assumed value of the restricted stock units vesting in each year, which compensation represents the 50th percentile for annual director compensation among a group of peer companies. When determining the amount and vesting schedule for directors' restricted stock unit awards, the Nominating and Corporate Governance Committee and Board have not varied awards based on specific committee service.

The following table sets forth for the year ended December 31, 2016 all compensation reportable for directors who served during 2016, as determined by SEC rules.

Director Compensation for 2016

Name	Stock Awards(1)
Jeffrey P. Bezos(2)	$ —
Tom A. Alberg(3)	793,087
John Seely Brown(4)	—
William B. Gordon(5)	—
Jamie Gorelick(4)	—
Daniel P. Huttenlocher(6)	890,730
Judith A. McGrath(7)	—
Alain Monié(8)	—
Jonathan J. Rubinstein(3)	793,087
Thomas O. Ryder(3)	793,087
Patricia Q. Stonesifer(3)	793,087
Wendell P. Weeks(9)	676,125

(1) Stock awards are reported at aggregate grant date fair value in the year granted, as determined under applicable accounting standards. Grant date fair value for restricted stock units is determined based on the number of shares granted multiplied by the average of the high and the low trading price of common stock of the Company on the grant date, without regard to the fact that the grants vest over a number of years. See Note 1, *"Description of Business and Accounting Policies—Stock-Based Compensation,"* in Item 8, "Financial Statements and Supplementary Data," in our 2016 Annual Report on Form 10-K.

(2) Mr. Bezos does not receive any compensation for his services as a director in addition to his compensation as Chief Executive Officer.

(3) Messrs. Alberg, Rubinstein, and Ryder and Ms. Stonesifer each held 1,077 unvested restricted stock units as of December 31, 2016.

(4) Mr. Brown and Ms. Gorelick each held 1,758 unvested restricted stock units as of December 31, 2016.

(5) Mr. Gordon held 870 unvested restricted stock units as of December 31, 2016. These unvested restricted stock units were cancelled in March 2017 when Mr. Gordon ceased to serve as a director.

(6) Mr. Huttenlocher held 1,131 unvested restricted stock units as of December 31, 2016.

(7) Ms. McGrath held 840 unvested restricted stock units as of December 31, 2016.

(8) Mr. Monié's unvested restricted stock units were cancelled in May 2016 when he ceased to serve as a director.

(9) Mr. Weeks held 1,365 unvested restricted stock units as of December 31, 2016.

ITEM 2—RATIFICATION OF APPOINTMENT OF ERNST & YOUNG LLP

Under the rules and regulations of the SEC and Nasdaq, the Audit Committee is directly responsible for the appointment, compensation, retention, and oversight of our independent auditors. In addition, the Audit Committee considers the independence of our independent auditors and participates in the selection of the independent auditor's lead engagement partner. The Audit Committee has appointed, and, as a matter of good corporate governance, is requesting ratification by the shareholders of the appointment of, the registered public accounting firm of Ernst & Young LLP ("E&Y") to serve as independent auditors for the fiscal year ending December 31, 2017. E&Y has served as our independent auditor since 1997. The Audit Committee considered a number of factors in determining whether to re-engage E&Y as the Company's independent registered public accounting firm, including the length of time the firm has served in this role, the firm's professional qualifications and resources, the firm's past performance, and the firm's capabilities in handling the breadth and complexity of our business, as well as the potential impact of changing independent auditors.

The Board of Directors and the Audit Committee believe that the continued retention of E&Y as the Company's independent auditor is in the best interests of the Company and its shareholders. If shareholders do not ratify the selection of E&Y, the Audit Committee will evaluate the shareholder vote when considering the selection of a registered public accounting firm for the audit engagement for the 2018 fiscal year. In addition, if shareholders ratify the selection of E&Y as independent auditors, the Audit Committee may nevertheless periodically request proposals from the major registered public accounting firms and as a result of such process may select E&Y or another registered public accounting firm as our independent auditors.

THE BOARD OF DIRECTORS RECOMMENDS A VOTE "FOR" RATIFICATION OF THE APPOINTMENT OF E&Y AS OUR INDEPENDENT AUDITORS FOR THE FISCAL YEAR ENDING DECEMBER 31, 2017.

AUDITORS

Representatives of E&Y are expected to attend the Annual Meeting and will have an opportunity to make a statement and to respond to appropriate questions from shareholders.

Audit Fees

Audit fees include the aggregate fees for the audit of our annual consolidated financial statements and internal controls, and the reviews of each of the quarterly consolidated financial statements included in our Forms 10-Q. These fees also include statutory and other audit work performed with respect to certain of our subsidiaries. The aggregate audit fees billed and expected to be billed by E&Y for the fiscal year ended December 31, 2016 were $15,146,000. The aggregate audit fees we were billed by E&Y for the fiscal year ended December 31, 2015 were $11,783,000.

Audit-Related Fees

Audit-related fees include accounting advisory services related to the accounting treatment of transactions or events, including acquisitions, and to the adoption of new accounting standards, as well as additional procedures related to accounting records performed to comply with regulatory reporting requirements and to provide certain attest reports. The aggregate audit-related fees billed and expected to be billed by E&Y for services rendered during the fiscal year ended December 31, 2016 were $1,214,000. The aggregate audit-related fees we were billed by E&Y for services rendered during the fiscal year ended December 31, 2015 were $1,086,000.

Tax Fees

Tax fees were for tax compliance services and assistance with federal and provincial tax-related matters for certain international entities. The aggregate tax fees billed and expected to be billed by E&Y for services rendered during the fiscal year ended December 31, 2016 were $0. The aggregate tax fees we were billed by E&Y for services rendered during the fiscal year ended December 31, 2015 were $0.

All Other Fees

All other fees were for advisory services related to compliance with regulatory reporting requirements. The aggregate other fees billed and expected to be billed by E&Y for services rendered during the fiscal year ended December 31, 2016 were $61,000. The aggregate other fees we were billed by E&Y for services rendered during the fiscal year ended December 31, 2015 were $65,000.

Pre-Approval Policies and Procedures

All of the fees described above were approved by the Audit Committee. The Audit Committee is responsible for overseeing the audit fee negotiations associated with the retention of E&Y to perform the audit of our annual consolidated financial statements and internal controls. The Audit Committee has adopted a pre-approval policy under which the Audit Committee approves in advance all audit and non-audit services to be performed by our independent auditors. As part of its pre-approval policy, the Audit Committee considers whether the provision of any proposed non-audit services is consistent with the SEC's rules on auditor independence. In accordance with the pre-approval policy, the Audit Committee has pre-approved certain specified audit and non-audit services to be provided by E&Y if they are initiated within 18 months after the date of the pre-approval (or within such other period from the date of pre-approval as may be provided). If there are any additional services to be provided, a request for pre-approval must be submitted by management to the Audit Committee for its consideration under the policy. Finally, in accordance with the pre-approval policy, the Audit Committee has delegated pre-approval authority to each of its members. Any member who exercises this authority must report any pre-approval decisions to the Audit Committee at its next meeting.

Audit Committee Report

The Audit Committee is composed solely of independent directors meeting the applicable requirements of the Nasdaq rules. The Audit Committee reviews the Company's financial reporting process on behalf of the Board. Management has the primary responsibility for establishing and maintaining adequate internal control over financial reporting, for preparing the financial statements, and for the reporting process. The Audit Committee members do not serve as professional accountants or auditors, and their functions are not intended to duplicate or to certify the activities of management and the independent registered public accounting firm. The Company's independent auditors are engaged to audit and report on the conformity of the Company's financial statements to accounting principles generally accepted in the United States and the effectiveness of the Company's internal control over financial reporting.

In this context, the Audit Committee reviewed and discussed with management and the independent auditors the audited financial statements for the year ended December 31, 2016 (the "Audited Financial Statements"), management's assessment of the effectiveness of the Company's internal control over financial reporting, and the independent auditors' evaluation of the Company's system of internal control over financial reporting. The Audit Committee has discussed with Ernst & Young LLP, the Company's independent auditors, the matters required to be discussed by Public Company Accounting Oversight Board ("PCAOB") Auditing Standard 1301, *Communications with Audit Committees*. In addition, the Audit Committee has received the written disclosures and the letter from the independent auditors required by applicable requirements of the PCAOB regarding the independent auditors' communications with the Audit Committee concerning independence, and has discussed with the independent auditors the independent auditors' independence.

Based upon the reviews and discussions referred to above, the Audit Committee recommended to the Board that the Audited Financial Statements be included in the Company's Annual Report on Form 10-K for the year ended December 31, 2016, for filing with the Securities and Exchange Commission.

The Audit Committee

Tom A. Alberg
Thomas O. Ryder
Wendell P. Weeks

ITEM 3—ADVISORY VOTE TO APPROVE EXECUTIVE COMPENSATION

We are asking shareholders to approve, on an advisory basis, the compensation of our named executive officers as disclosed in the Compensation Discussion and Analysis, the Summary Compensation Table, and the related compensation tables and narrative. Our executive compensation programs are designed to support our long-term success. As described in the "Compensation Discussion and Analysis" section of this Proxy Statement, the Leadership Development and Compensation Committee has structured our executive compensation program to tie total compensation to long-term shareholder value, as reflected primarily in our stock price.

We note that our stock price has increased approximately 88% between January 2014 and December 2016. In addition, the total number of restricted stock units granted to our named executive officers during 2016 represented only (i) 1.73% of the total number of restricted stock units granted to all employees during 2016 and (ii) 0.03% of the weighted-average number of shares outstanding for 2016. The total number of restricted stock units granted to our named executive officers during the three-year period from 2014 to 2016 represented only (i) 0.97% of the total number of restricted stock units granted to all employees during the same three-year period and (ii) 0.02% of the weighted-average number of shares outstanding for the same three-year period. For more information, shareholders should read the "Compensation Discussion and Analysis," which describes how our executive compensation policies and procedures operate and are designed to achieve our compensation objectives, as well as the Summary Compensation Table and related compensation tables and narrative, which provide detailed information on the compensation of our named executive officers. The Leadership Development and Compensation Committee and the Board believe that the policies and procedures articulated in the "Compensation Discussion and Analysis" are effective in achieving our goals and that the compensation of our named executive officers reported in this Proxy Statement has supported and contributed to our success.

At our 2011 Annual Meeting of Shareholders, our shareholders approved, on an advisory basis, a frequency of every three years for casting advisory votes approving our executive compensation. After the 2017 Annual Meeting, our next advisory vote on executive compensation will occur at our 2020 Annual Meeting of Shareholders unless the Company announces otherwise following the Board of Directors' consideration of the advisory vote provided in Item 4 of this Proxy Statement regarding the frequency of future advisory votes on executive compensation.

This item is being presented pursuant to Section 14A of the Securities Exchange Act of 1934, as amended (the "Exchange Act"). Although this advisory vote is not binding, the Leadership Development and Compensation Committee will consider the voting results when evaluating our executive compensation program.

THE BOARD OF DIRECTORS RECOMMENDS A VOTE "FOR" APPROVAL, ON AN ADVISORY BASIS, OF OUR EXECUTIVE COMPENSATION AS DESCRIBED IN THIS PROXY STATEMENT.

ITEM 4—ADVISORY VOTE ON THE FREQUENCY OF FUTURE ADVISORY VOTES ON EXECUTIVE COMPENSATION

Pursuant to Section 14A of the Exchange Act, we are asking shareholders to cast an advisory vote on the frequency of future advisory votes on executive compensation. Shareholders may specify whether they prefer such votes to occur every year, every two years, or every three years, or they may abstain. The Board recommends that such vote occur every three years, because the Company takes a long-term view of employee compensation, including executive compensation. Because of the unique nature of our executive compensation program, where a substantial portion of employee compensation is in the form of restricted stock units that are granted periodically and typically vest over five years or more, we believe that it is more appropriate to evaluate our executive compensation by comparing amounts received by our executives and our total shareholder return over a three-year period, instead of evaluating our executive compensation based on the total grant date fair value of restricted stock unit awards granted each year.

Although the shareholders' vote on this proposal is not binding, the Board will consider the voting results in determining the frequency of future advisory votes. Notwithstanding the Board's recommendation and the outcome of the shareholder vote, the Board may in the future decide to conduct advisory votes on a more or less frequent basis and may vary its practice based on factors such as discussions with shareholders and the adoption of material changes to compensation programs.

At our 2011 Annual Meeting of Shareholders, our shareholders approved, on an advisory basis, a frequency of every three years for casting advisory votes approving our executive compensation. The Board of Directors recommends that future advisory votes on executive compensation continue to occur once every three years. Because our executive compensation programs are designed to reward long-term performance and operate over a period of years, shareholders should evaluate how our programs perform over the long term. Also, an advisory vote every three years provides an appropriate period for the Leadership Development and Compensation Committee and the Board to evaluate the results of the most recent advisory vote on executive compensation and to develop and implement any appropriate adjustments to our executive compensation programs. Conducting an advisory vote every three years provides shareholders a meaningful opportunity to provide regular feedback and sufficient time for us to respond to it. Our last two advisory votes to approve executive compensation were approved by more than 97% of the outstanding shares of common stock present in person or represented by proxy and entitled to vote at the respective annual meetings of our shareholders.

THE BOARD OF DIRECTORS RECOMMENDS SHAREHOLDERS VOTE, ON AN ADVISORY BASIS, TO CONDUCT FUTURE ADVISORY VOTES ON EXECUTIVE COMPENSATION EVERY "THREE YEARS."

ITEM 5—APPROVAL OF THE COMPANY'S 1997 STOCK INCENTIVE PLAN, AS AMENDED AND RESTATED

The Board of Directors recommends that shareholders approve the 1997 Plan, including the material terms of the performance goals set forth in the 1997 Plan. Approval of the material terms of the performance goals is a condition for certain awards made under the 1997 Plan to qualify as tax-deductible performance-based compensation under Section 162 (m) of the Internal Revenue Code. In addition, approval of the 1997 Plan is intended to satisfy shareholder approval requirements for making certain tax-qualified awards under the 1997 Plan to our French employees. Each of these aspects of the 1997 Plan, along with a summary of other significant terms of the 1997 Plan, is set forth in Appendix A to this Proxy Statement, which is incorporated herein by reference.

Shareholder approval of this proposal does not increase the number of shares of Amazon common stock reserved for grant pursuant to awards issued under the 1997 Plan. The discussion below and the summary of the 1997 Plan attached as Appendix A to this Proxy Statement are qualified by reference to the text of the 1997 Plan. A copy of the 1997 Plan was included as an exhibit to our Form 10-Q filed on April 26, 2013 and can be obtained upon request from the Secretary of the Company.

Section 162(m)

Section 162(m) places a limit of $1 million on the amount the Company may deduct in any one year for compensation paid to a "covered employee," which means any person who as of the last day of the fiscal year is the chief executive officer or one of the Company's three highest compensated executive officers other than the CFO, as determined under SEC rules. There is, however, an exception to this limit on deductibility for compensation that satisfies certain conditions for "qualified performance-based compensation" set forth under Section 162(m). One of the conditions requires shareholder approval every five years of the material terms of the performance goals of the plan under which the compensation will be paid. As noted above, the Company's shareholders most recently approved the material terms of the performance goals of the 1997 Plan at the

Company's 2012 Annual Meeting. The list of business criteria on which performance goals may be based remains unchanged and the Company is asking shareholders to approve the material terms of the performance goals under the 1997 Plan.

For purposes of Section 162(m), the material terms of the performance goals include (i) the employees eligible to receive compensation under the 1997 Plan, (ii) a description of the business criteria on which the performance goal is based, and (iii) the maximum amount of compensation that can be paid to an employee under the performance goal. Each of these aspects of the 1997 Plan is discussed in Appendix A to this Proxy Statement.

The Board believes that it is in the best interests of the Company and its shareholders to enable the Company to implement compensation arrangements that qualify as fully tax deductible performance-based compensation in the 1997 Plan. The Board is therefore asking shareholders to approve, for Section 162(m) purposes, the material terms of the performance goals as set forth in Appendix A to this Proxy Statement. However, shareholder approval of the 1997 Plan is only one of several requirements under Section 162(m) that must be satisfied for amounts realized under the 1997 Plan to qualify for the "performance-based" compensation exemption under Section 162(m), and submission of the material terms of the 1997 Plan's performance goals for shareholder approval should not be viewed as a guarantee that the Company can deduct all compensation under the 1997 Plan. Nothing in this proposal precludes the Company or the Leadership Development and Compensation Committee from making any payment or granting awards that do not qualify for tax deductibility under Section 162(m), nor is there any guarantee that awards intended to qualify for tax deductibility under Section 162(m) will ultimately be viewed as so qualifying by the Internal Revenue Service.

French Tax-Qualified RSU Grants

France adopted a Finance Act in December 2016 (the "Finance Law"), which, along with another law adopted in August 2015 (Loi Macron), introduced changes to the terms under which French tax-qualified restricted stock units ("RSUs"), including performance-based RSUs, may be granted to employees of our subsidiaries in France. One of the conditions for granting French tax-qualified RSUs under the Finance Law is that the RSUs are granted pursuant to an equity incentive plan approved by shareholders on or after December 31, 2016. Shareholder approval of this proposal will satisfy one of the requirements of the Finance Law for granting tax-qualified RSUs to employees of our subsidiaries in France. Under the Finance Law, French tax-qualified RSUs granted to employees of our French subsidiaries may benefit from certain French income and social tax treatment, provided certain conditions are met. Following shareholder approval of this proposal, we will determine whether or not to seek to satisfy the other requirements to grant tax-qualified RSUs in France.

THE BOARD OF DIRECTORS RECOMMENDS A VOTE "FOR" APPROVAL OF THE COMPANY'S 1997 STOCK INCENTIVE PLAN, AS AMENDED AND RESTATED

ITEM 6—SHAREHOLDER PROPOSAL REGARDING A REPORT ON USE OF CRIMINAL BACKGROUND CHECKS IN HIRING DECISIONS

AFL-CIO Reserve Fund, 815 16th Street, NW, Washington, DC 20006, a beneficial owner of 232 shares of common stock of the Company, has notified us that it intends to present the following resolution at the Annual Meeting. Zevin Asset Management, LLC, 11 Beacon Street, Suite 1125, Boston, Massachusetts 02108, acting on behalf of Emma Creighton Irrevocable Trust, a beneficial owner of 7 shares of common stock of the Company, is a co-sponsor of the AFL-CIO Reserve Fund proposal. THE BOARD RECOMMENDS A VOTE "AGAINST" THIS SHAREHOLDER PROPOSAL.

Beginning of Shareholder Proposal and Statement of Support by AFL-CIO Reserve Fund:

RESOLVED: Shareholders of Amazon.com (the "Company") request that the Board of Directors prepare a report on the use of criminal background checks in hiring and employment decisions for the Company's employees, independent contractors, and subcontracted workers. The report shall evaluate the risk of racial discrimination that may result from the use of criminal background checks in hiring and employment decisions. The report shall be prepared at reasonable cost and omit proprietary information, and shall be made available on the Company's website no later than the 2018 annual meeting of shareholders.

SUPPORTING STATEMENT:

Approximately one third of US adults have a criminal record according to the National Employment Law Project (http://www.nelp.org/campaign/ensuring-fair-chance-to-work/). Because the criminal justice system disproportionately affects minorities, the use of arrest and conviction records in employment decisions may violate the Civil Rights Act of 1964 and the Equal Employment Opportunity Commission's guidelines if such policies are not job related for the position in question and consistent with business necessity (https://www.eeoc.gov/laws/guidance/arrest_conviction.cfm).

Our Company is a large and growing employer who also subcontracts with staffing agencies and uses independent contractors for various positions including warehouse jobs and delivery drivers. Like at many companies, criminal background checks are used in hiring decisions for these positions. In our opinion, excluding individuals who have had previous contact with the criminal justice system may hurt our Company's competitiveness in attracting and retaining top talent.

The disparate impact that such practices may have on people of color may also work against our Company's commitment to diversity. While it may be appropriate to disqualify certain individuals with relevant criminal records from specific positions, an overly restrictive ban on employing all individuals with any criminal record in effect imposes a second sentence. We believe that previously incarcerated individuals who have paid their debt to society deserve a chance to achieve gainful employment.

On October 12, 2016, the Lawyers' Committee for Civil Rights and Economic Justice wrote to our Company's CEO Jeff Bezos to express concern about a purported new Company directive that requires delivery companies that our Company contracts with to institute more stringent background check procedures. The letter alleges that dozens of primarily black and Latino delivery drivers in the Boston area were terminated as a result of this change (http://lawyerscom.org/lawyers-committee-urges-amazon-to-halt-employment-practices-that-harm-communities-of-color/).

This proposal urges the Board of Directors to prepare a report on the Company's criminal background check practices and policies and the risk that racial discrimination may result. In our view, the use of criminal background checks for employment decisions creates significant legal, reputational and operational risks. Accordingly, we believe that the Board of Directors has an obligation to adequately inform itself of and manage these material risks to the Company.

For these reasons, we urge shareholders to vote FOR this proposal.

End of Shareholder Proposal and Statement of Support by AFL-CIO Reserve Fund

Recommendation of the Board of Directors on Item 6

The Board of Directors recommends that you vote against this proposal.

We are strongly committed to providing an equal opportunity in all aspects of employment and will not tolerate any illegal discrimination or harassment of any kind. Additionally, our process for performing background checks on prospective employees and contracted service providers serves significant public safety and business purposes.

FORM OF PROXY STATEMENT AND FORM OF PROXY

The nature of our business requires that we implement certain controls to protect our customers, employees, and the public and serve the interests of our shareholders. For example, our contracted delivery drivers operate largely independently in the field without direct supervision. They are in contact with customers and other members of the public, including children and vulnerable adults, often face-to-face at the customer's doorstep and, in some cases, after dark. In this context, it is critically important to managing our reputational, operational, and legal risks that background checks are performed. Accordingly, taking into account the nature of a conviction, the time that has elapsed, and the nature of the job for which an individual is being considered, we do consider certain types of serious criminal convictions to be disqualifying.

Our processes for conducting background checks involve complex considerations that are designed to be fair, reasonable, and lawful and to achieve the primary goal of protecting employees, customers, and the public. Further, we believe our targeted screening process is well-tailored to protecting public safety and our business interests. We do not allow or condone racial discrimination of any kind, in the background checking process or otherwise; we are strongly committed to providing an equal opportunity in all aspects of employment; and we are proud of the diverse population of drivers who serve our customers. Diversity is a cornerstone of our continued success, and we benefit from the diverse perspectives of our employees that come from many sources, including gender, race, age, national origin, sexual orientation, disability, culture, education, as well as professional and life experience.

Given our commitment to equality and the nature of our business, the Board believes that the preparation of the report requested by the proposal would not be an effective and prudent use of the Company's time and resources.

THE BOARD RECOMMENDS THAT YOU VOTE "AGAINST" THIS PROPOSAL REGARDING A REPORT ON USE OF CRIMINAL BACKGROUND CHECKS IN HIRING DECISIONS.

ITEM 7—SHAREHOLDER PROPOSAL REGARDING SUSTAINABILITY AS AN EXECUTIVE COMPENSATION PERFORMANCE MEASURE

Mercy For Animals, 8033 Sunset Boulevard, Suite 864, Los Angeles, California 90046, a beneficial owner of 10 shares of common stock of the Company, has notified us that it intends to present the following resolution at the Annual Meeting. THE BOARD RECOMMENDS A VOTE "AGAINST" THIS SHAREHOLDER PROPOSAL.

Beginning of Shareholder Proposal and Statement of Support by Mercy For Animals:

RESOLVED: That the shareholders of Amazon.com request the Board's Compensation Committee, when setting senior executive compensation, include sustainability as one of the performance measures for senior executives under the Company's incentive plans. Sustainability is defined as how environmental and social considerations, and related financial impacts, are integrated into corporate strategy over the long term.

SUPPORTING STATEMENT: We believe that the long-term interests of shareholders, as well as other important constituents, are best served by companies that operate their businesses in a sustainable manner focused on long-term value creation. As the recent financial crisis demonstrates, those boards of directors and management that operate their companies with integrity and a focus on the long term are much more likely to prosper than ones that are dominated by a short-term focus.

The best means of demonstrating a company's commitment to the concept of sustainability is through incorporating it as a performance measure in the Company's annual and/or long-term incentive plans. We believe that the current failure to do so represents a serious shortcoming.

Examples of sustainability metrics include evaluation of how its operations may affect environmental pollution, natural resource depletion, the social and environmental impact of industrial agriculture and manufacturing, and other appropriate issues of corporate social responsibility and sustainability.

Several studies within the past few years show that businesses incorporating environmental and social considerations into their corporate governance strategies are better able to mitigate risk in legal, regulatory, and reputational areas and thus increase overall performance and efficiency.

According to a UN Global Compact and Accenture study entitled *CEO Study on Sustainability 2013*, 76 percent of executives believe that including sustainability in fundamental corporate strategy will drive revenue growth and increase opportunities; 93 percent believe sustainability is a major factor for organizational success, and 86 percent believe sustainability should be a factor discussed when determining compensation (67 percent reported that they already do).

A Harvard Business School study from 2012 determined that organizations that embraced progressive environmental and social programs outperformed those that did not in both the stock market as well as accounting performance.

Further, in 2014, a report entitled *Greening the Green 2014: Linking Executive Pay to Sustainability* from Glass Lewis found that a "mounting body of research showing that firms that operate in a more responsible manner may perform better financially... Moreover, these companies were also more likely to tip top executive incentives to sustainability metrics."

Finally, a report published by the United Nations Principles for Responsible Investment and the UN Global Compact found that including "Environmental, Social and Governance (ESG) issues within executive management goals and incentive schemes" is an essential factor in determining long-term shareholder worth.

Determining which specific metrics to utilize rests within the discretion of the board and its compensation committee.

End of Shareholder Proposal and Statement of Support by Mercy For Animals

Recommendation of the Board of Directors on Item 7

The Board of Directors recommends that you vote against this proposal.

While the Board recognizes the importance of good corporate citizenship and is committed to sustainability and social responsibility, it does not believe that making sustainability a performance measure for senior executives is necessary or in the best interests of shareholders. We already regularly consider environmental, social, and governance issues in our business and continue to develop and improve our sustainability practices. In May 2016, the Company launched its sustainability website (see *www.amazon.com/sustainability*) to report on its sustainability and social responsibility efforts. Our current areas of focus include renewable energy procurement, energy efficiency programs in our operations, waste minimization for our operations (including for our packaging), and responsible supply chain management in the provision of our products and services. Here is a sample of some of our sustainability initiatives:

Sustainability

- At the end of 2016, more than 40% of the power consumed by Amazon Web Services' ("AWS") global infrastructure came from renewable energy sources. We have set a new goal for AWS to be powered by 50% renewable energy by the end of 2017, and our long term commitment is to achieve 100% renewable energy usage for AWS' global infrastructure footprint.

- In 2016, we announced construction of new wind farms in Ohio and Texas and five new solar farms in Virginia that will bring renewable energy capacity onto the grid before the end of 2017. These farms join our four existing projects—Amazon Wind Farm Fowler Ridge, Amazon Solar Farm US East, Amazon Wind Farm US East, Amazon Wind Farm US Central—which started producing power in 2016.

- Under the 2014 Amazon Climate Research Grant Program, we announced the availability of grants for up to 50 million core hours of AWS services to accelerate research to improve our understanding of the scope and effect of climate change. We are currently working with a number of grant recipients under this program.

- Our corporate headquarters in Seattle consists of sustainable, energy-efficient buildings. The buildings' interiors feature salvaged and locally-sourced woods, energy-efficient lighting, and composting and recycling alternatives, as well as public plazas and pockets of open green space outside of the buildings. The U.S. Green Building Council has awarded six of our buildings with LEED Gold certification for sustainable design and construction methods. Our newest buildings in the Denny Triangle area of Seattle are heated through an innovative, and energy efficient, "district energy" system that recycles heat generated at a neighboring data center.

- We have joined a number of business roundtables and working groups on sustainability, including the Corporate Eco Forum, an invitation-only membership group for large companies that demonstrate a serious commitment to sustainability as a business strategy issue, the American Council on Renewable Energy ("ACORE"), the U.S. Partnership for Renewable Energy Finance, a program of ACORE, and the Business Renewables Center run by Rocky Mountain Institute. We have also become a signatory on a number of sustainability commitments, including the Buyers' Principles for Renewable Energy and the American Business Act on Climate Pledge (a way for companies to express support for action on climate change), sponsored by the White House. In 2016, Amazon also joined an amicus brief with three other tech companies in support of the continued implementation of the U.S. Environmental Protection Agency's Clean Power Plan.

Sustainable Packaging and Recycling

- We continue to pursue multi-year waste reduction initiatives—preparation-free packaging, Ships in Own Container, and Amazon Frustration-Free Packaging—to promote the use of 100% recyclable packaging that is easy to open and eliminates hard plastic "clamshell" cases, plastic-coated wire ties commonly used in toy packaging, all packing foams, and additional shipping boxes. These initiatives have eliminated more than 110 million pounds of excess packaging just in 2016, a 54% increase over 2015. Further, with all Amazon-branded devices and electronic accessories meeting these requirements, we set a very high bar with our own products.

- We have helped lead the industry on waste-reduction and sustainable packing materials and packaging through our promotion of two recently-adopted testing standards with the International Safe Transit Association for their certification processes, and through our work with testing labs and packaging design firms to help others meet these standards.

- In 2016, we launched a partnership with Give Back Box to make it easier for Amazon customers to reuse their Amazon shipping boxes and donate to charity. Customers can reuse their Amazon shipping box, fill it with household items to donate, print a free shipping label at *www.amazon.com/givebackbox*, and ship the box to the nearest participating charitable organization.

- We support the responsible disposal and recycling of electronics products. To encourage our customers to recycle their Amazon devices, we offer free shipping for this purpose. We also cover the costs associated with Amazon device recycling, which is performed by licensed recycling facilities. We are an industry steward participant and financial supporter of Call2Recycle. As part of this program, customers can drop off Amazon Basics rechargeable batteries at more than 30,000 collection sites throughout the

U.S. and Canada. Additionally, we offer the Amazon Trade-In program, which promotes the reuse, resale, or responsible recycling of hundreds of thousands of eligible items in working or non-working condition. Through the program, customers can trade in an array of eligible items, including electronics, with the convenience of free shipping. In exchange, the program offers Amazon Gift Card value which can be used toward anything Amazon offers.

- Our North American fulfillment network is working on initiatives to minimize the amount of food going to landfills and has been helping local communities by donating food to local food banks. In 2016, these facilities donated enough food to provide over 3.5 million meals for local communities.

Socially-Responsible and Ethical Sourcing

- We are strongly committed to social responsibility in our operations and supply chain. We are also strongly committed to conducting our business in a lawful and ethical manner, both in our own operations and through engagement with suppliers that are committed to the same principles. Our products must be manufactured in a manner that meets or exceeds the expectations of Amazon and our customers as reflected in our Supplier Code of Conduct (see http://www.amazon.com/gp/help/customer/display.html?nodeId=200885140). These are some of the key areas we focus on:

  - Health and safety in production areas and any living quarters.

  - The right to legal wages and benefits.

  - Appropriate working hours and overtime pay.

  - Prevention of child labor or forced labor.

  - Fair and ethical treatment, including non-discrimination.

- In 2016, we joined the Electronic Industry Citizenship Coalition, a nonprofit coalition of companies committed to supporting the rights and well-being of workers and communities worldwide affected by the global electronics supply chain.

- We also offer fulfillment center tours in eight countries, including six locations in the U.S., which allow the public an opportunity to view the working conditions and operations at our facilities first-hand.

The Board further believes that the Leadership Development and Compensation Committee, which is made up of independent directors, should maintain the ability to develop executive compensation principles and practices as it sees fit. The Board believes that it is appropriate for the Leadership Development and Compensation Committee to determine the performance measures against which executives are measured. The executive compensation program currently in place, as developed by the Leadership Development and Compensation Committee, promotes the long-term interests of shareholders in how it incentivizes executives. Our compensation program provides strong long-term incentives to align our employees' interests with our shareholders' interests. Consistent with our philosophy that total compensation should be tied to long-term shareholder value, the primary component of each executive officer's total compensation is stock-based. As a result, we believe that the success of our substantial sustainability efforts is already included in the long-term view of creating shareholder value through our stock price, and is already a part of our executive compensation incentive structure, and the Board believes that making sustainability an explicit executive compensation performance measure is not necessary.

THE BOARD RECOMMENDS THAT YOU VOTE "AGAINST" THIS PROPOSAL REGARDING SUSTAINABILITY AS AN EXECUTIVE COMPENSATION PERFORMANCE MEASURE.

ITEM 8—SHAREHOLDER PROPOSAL REGARDING VOTE-COUNTING PRACTICES FOR SHAREHOLDER PROPOSALS

Investor Voice, SPC, 111 Queen Anne Avenue N, Suite 500, Seattle, Washington 98109, acting on behalf of Bryce A. Mathern, a beneficial owner of 15 shares of common stock of the Company, has notified us that it intends to present the following resolution at the Annual Meeting. THE BOARD RECOMMENDS A VOTE "AGAINST" THIS SHAREHOLDER PROPOSAL.

Beginning of Shareholder Proposal and Statement of Support by Investor Voice:

RESOLVED: Amazon.com, Inc. ("Amazon") shareholders ask the Board to take or initiate steps to amend Company governing documents to provide that all non-binding matters presented by shareholders shall be decided by a simple majority of the votes cast FOR and AGAINST an item. This policy would apply to all such matters unless shareholders have approved higher thresholds, or applicable laws or stock exchange regulations dictate otherwise.

SUPPORTING STATEMENT:

This proposal seeks greater transparency, clarity, and understanding around how informed stockholders vote on shareholder proposals. In voting, the meaning of "Abstain" is defined by the Oxford English dictionary as:

To formally decline to vote either FOR or AGAINST a proposal or motion.

A "simple majority" formula, therefore, includes votes cast FOR and AGAINST but not abstentions. It provides the most democratic, clear, and accurate picture of the intent of shareowners who are both informed and decided, while not including in the formula the votes of abstaining voters who, by definition, have declined to express an opinion.

When abstaining voters choose to mark ABSTAIN (whether they are confused, disinterested, or lack time to become fully informed), it is apparent that their votes should be regarded as neither FOR nor AGAINST an item.

In contrast, Amazon unilaterally counts ABSTAIN votes as if AGAINST every shareholder sponsored proposal.

- **Is it reasonable for Amazon to assert it knows the will of undecided voters (and to artificially construe abstentions in favor of management)?**

Companies often imply they have no choice but to use the Delaware "default standard" (which includes abstentions). However, this nominal 'standard' is not mandated – it is what Delaware assigns to companies that do not proactively choose "simple majority" voting.

Research has demonstrated that the so-called 'default standard' systematically disadvantages shareholders: http://bit.ly/Voting-Research_Corporate-Secretary.

How? It does this by:

- **Depressing the appearance of support for shareholder concerns.**

    The math is simple: When abstaining shareholders elect to not express an opinion but then are treated as if they voted AGAINST a proposal, the tally is lowered and management benefits (because they routinely oppose stockholder proposals).

- **Subverting vote outcomes.**

   Historically, these practices have allowed companies to describe numerous true majority votes on shareholder items as, instead, having 'failed'.

- **Distorting communication.**

   Annual meeting votes offer the sole opportunity for most shareholders to communicate with Boards. Counting abstentions as de facto votes AGAINST shareholder proposals, management changes how outcomes are reported and how the public perceives support for shareholder concerns.

In contrast to how shareholder items are treated, we see that Amazon's Director Election (where management benefits from the appearance of strong support), does not count abstentions. **Thus, management items and shareholder items do <u>not</u> receive equal treatment**; though the Company has complete discretion to cure such inconsistencies in its voting policies.

To avert discrepancies like these, the Council of Institutional Investors has declared: "...abstentions should be counted only for purposes of a quorum."

THEREFORE: Support accuracy, fairness, and good governance at Amazon by voting FOR simple majority vote-counting on shareholder-sponsored proposals.

End of Shareholder Proposal and Statement of Support by Investor Voice

Recommendation of the Board of Directors on Item 8

The Board of Directors recommends that you vote against this proposal.

The Board regularly reviews the Company's corporate governance practices, including the methodologies for how votes are cast. The Board has undertaken several steps to improve the Company's governance practices, including adopting proxy access and majority voting for directors. The Board does not, however, believe that the actions requested by the proposal represent a necessary change to the Company's governance practices.

Our vote-counting practices are consistent with Delaware law

The Company's vote-counting methodology is consistent with Delaware law, which applies to the Company by virtue of its incorporation in that state. Section 216 of the Delaware General Corporation Law provides, as a default, that in all matters other than the election of directors, the affirmative vote of the majority of shares present in person or represented by proxy at the meeting and entitled to vote on the subject matter shall be the act of the shareholders. Because shares that vote to abstain are present and entitled to vote, under this Delaware law standard any shares present at the meeting that abstain from voting are essentially counted as votes against the matter.

Our vote-counting practices are fair and consistent with practices of peer companies

The vote-counting methodology used by the Company does not inherently favor proposals submitted by the Board over proposals submitted by shareholders, as the vote-counting standard for approving any proposal other than for the election of directors is identical. Thus, the Company applies the same vote counting standard to its own advisory votes on executive compensation, for example, as it does to a shareholder proposal. In addition, the vote-counting methodology used by the Company is the standard applied by a majority of our peers incorporated in Delaware and, according to a 2013 study by GMI Ratings, by a majority of S&P 500 companies.

Changing our vote-counting practices would not be in the best interests of the Company

All shares present in person or represented by proxy at our Annual Meeting are entitled to vote on each shareholder proposal included in the Proxy Statement. The Board believes that it is the responsibility of any person putting a proposal forward for shareholders to approve—regardless of whether the Company or a shareholder proponent—to persuade shareholders owning a majority of the shares that vote to support the proposal. Abstentions reflect the fact that a shareholder has reviewed and evaluated a proposal but has not been persuaded to support the proposal. Further, shareholders are clearly told the effect of an abstaining vote. As opposed to ignoring shareholders who abstain, as the proposal would do, we believe it appropriate to count abstentions as present at the Annual Meeting and entitled to vote, and thus as relevant in determining whether a majority of the shares present have voted in favor of a proposal. The effect of changing the Company's vote-counting methodology to completely remove abstentions from the results of a vote would be to disenfranchise those voters who chose to abstain from voting. It would remove one of the voter's three options, as a vote to abstain, itself, is a position taken by a shareholder and is an opinion expressed to the Board.

Changing our vote-counting practices is not necessary

Changing the manner in which abstentions are counted in shareholder votes would not have been determinative in any of the proposals voted on by the Company's shareholders since the Company went public in 1997. Over that time, if the proponent's proposed vote-counting methodology had been used, it would never have increased the voting results for a proposal by more than 4%, and would never have resulted in a different outcome in terms of whether a proposal passed or failed to pass.

The Company's vote-counting methodology is both consistent with Delaware law and fair to shareholders. The Board believes that it is important to recognize the voices of all shareholders, including those who choose to abstain from voting on a particular proposal. Therefore, the Board does not believe that changing the Company's vote-counting methodology is in the best interests of the Company.

THE BOARD RECOMMENDS THAT YOU VOTE "AGAINST" THIS PROPOSAL REGARDING VOTE-COUNTING PRACTICES FOR SHAREHOLDER PROPOSALS.

BENEFICIAL OWNERSHIP OF SHARES

The following table sets forth certain information regarding the beneficial ownership of our common stock as of February 17, 2017 (except as otherwise indicated) by (i) each person or entity known by us to beneficially own more than 5% of our common stock, (ii) each director, (iii) each executive officer for whom compensation information is given in the Summary Compensation Table in this Proxy Statement, and (iv) all directors and executive officers as a group. Except as otherwise indicated, and subject to any interests of the reporting person's spouse, we believe that the beneficial owners of common stock listed below, based on information furnished by such owners, have sole voting and investment power with respect to such shares. As of February 17, 2017 we had 477,614,699 shares of common stock outstanding.

Name and Address of Beneficial Owner	Amount and Nature of Beneficial Ownership	Percent of Class
Jeffrey P. Bezos	80,897,696	16.9%
410 Terry Avenue North, Seattle, WA 98109		
The Vanguard Group, Inc.	25,136,813(1)	5.3%
100 Vanguard Blvd, Malvern, PA 19355		
Tom A. Alberg	30,115(2)	*
John Seely Brown	13,565	*
Jamie S. Gorelick	5,362	*
Daniel P. Huttenlocher	—	*
Judith A. McGrath	1,680	*
Jonathan J. Rubinstein	7,775	*
Thomas O. Ryder	17,523	*
Patricia Q. Stonesifer	12,268	*
Wendell P. Weeks	455	*
Brian T. Olsavsky	1,063	*
Jeffrey M. Blackburn	67,560(3)	*
Andrew R. Jassy	74,995	*
Diego Piacentini	79,146	*
Jeffrey A. Wilke	86,126(4)	*
All directors and executive officers as a group (16 persons)	81,225,330(5)	17.0%

*   Less than 1%.
(1) As of December 31, 2016, based on information provided in a Schedule 13G filed February 9, 2017. The Vanguard Group has sole voting power with respect to 618,806 of the reported shares, shared voting power with respect to 73,153 of the reported shares, sole investment power with respect to 24,450,846 of the reported shares, and shared investment power with respect to 685,967 of the reported shares.
(2) Includes 7,000 shares held by a charitable trust of which Mr. Alberg is a trustee and as to which he shares voting and investment power. Mr. Alberg disclaims beneficial ownership of such shares.
(3) Includes 20,000 shares as to which Mr. Blackburn shares or may be deemed to share voting and investment power. Mr. Blackburn disclaims beneficial ownership of such shares.
(4) Includes 24,831 shares as to which Mr. Wilke shares or may be deemed to share voting and investment power. Mr. Wilke disclaims beneficial ownership of such shares.
(5) Includes 9,148 shares beneficially owned by other executive officers not individually listed in the table.

EXECUTIVE COMPENSATION

Compensation Discussion and Analysis

Compensation Philosophy. As stated in the Company's 1997 letter to shareholders, we believe that a fundamental measure of our success will be the shareholder value we create over the long term. As a result, we may make decisions and weigh tradeoffs differently than some companies. For example, under our compensation philosophy, we have prioritized stock-based compensation that vests over an extended period of time. In addition, we believe granting stock-based compensation to employees at all levels across the Company results in motivated, customer-centric people who think and act like owners because they are owners.

Our compensation philosophy for our "named executive officers" identified in the "Summary Compensation Table" below is the same as for all of our employees and is governed by the following principles. First, our compensation program is designed to attract and retain the highest caliber employees by providing above industry-average compensation assuming stock price performance. Second, our compensation program provides strong long-term incentives to align our employees' interests with our shareholders' interests. Third, our compensation program emphasizes performance and potential to contribute to our long-term success as a basis for compensation increases, as opposed to rewarding solely for length of service. Finally, our compensation program reinforces and reflects our core values, including customer obsession, innovation, bias for action, acting like owners and thinking long term, a high hiring bar, and frugality.

For our named executive officers, who are employed on an at-will basis, we provide few perquisites and generally do not provide cash bonuses other than in a new-hire context. We do not maintain nonqualified deferred compensation plans, supplemental executive retirement plan benefits, cash severance programs, or change-in-control benefits for our executive officers. Additionally, except as noted below for Rule 162(m) purposes, we do not provide cash or equity incentives tied to performance criteria, which could cause employees to focus solely on short-term returns at the expense of long-term growth and innovation. We believe that investing in the creation of long-term value, without the use of performance measures or specific indices, is optimal for Amazon employees, particularly at the executive level, and for shareholders.

We believe that the best measure of our performance is how we are valued over the long term. To help align our employees with long-term value creation, we compensate our employees with restricted stock unit awards that have long vesting periods. Over time, employees will have multiple restricted stock unit awards that vest over many years, and thus provide a greater amount of potential compensation in later years than the current year. This encourages employees, including executives, to seek out, develop, and pursue initiatives that focus on serving our customers and reflect a long-term view for thinking about our operations holistically and contributing to initiatives across the Company.

As a company that relentlessly pursues invention across a wide range of opportunities, we believe it would be inappropriate to utilize a few discrete or short term financial or operational performance measures that may narrowly focus our executives on the success of only isolated initiatives, instead of on the long-term success of the Company as a whole. For example, in 1997, we could have adopted performance measures appropriate for an Internet bookseller, but those performance measures may have discouraged our employees from investing their time and energy into initiatives that later became AWS, Kindle, and Alexa. Other examples of long-term focus include the development of our third-party seller business, which was aided by the lessons learned from our unsuccessful efforts to build an auctions marketplace, and when we experimented with adding services other than fast shipping to our Prime membership program. A performance goal assumes some level of success by a prescribed measure, but to have a culture that relentlessly pursues invention, we have to encourage experimentation and long-term thinking, which, by definition, means we do not know in advance whether it will work.

In addition, given the unique nature of Amazon and our many initiatives, standardized industry indices are either too broad or too narrow to serve as relevant comparisons for benchmarking performance. For example, if we had tied compensation to our performance relative to a retail index, we might never have pursued our AWS business since executives would have been penalized for making the early investments in cloud technology and infrastructure that AWS required. Similarly, if we tied compensation to our performance relative to a technology index, we might not have built our own devices, developed our own movies and TV shows, or innovated shipping and delivery methods. A customized index locks in a business profile at a point in time and may deter employees from considering or pursuing initiatives that do not fit into that mold. Thus, we think the best stock market comparison we can make is measuring our own success: can we continue to grow our share value over the long term?

As a result, we believe the best performance measure for our company is stock price performance over the long term. Therefore, when we set our executives' target compensation, we assume a fixed annual increase in the stock price (currently 15%) so that our executives will be directly impacted if our stock price is flat or declines. This approach has worked well over the past three years, as our stock price has increased approximately 88% between January 2014 and December 2016.

Base Salaries. Consistent with our philosophy that total compensation should be tied to long-term shareholder value, base salaries for named executive officers are designed to provide a minimum level of cash compensation and to be significantly less than those paid to senior leadership at similarly situated companies. Base salaries ranged from $81,840 for Mr. Bezos to $175,000 for Messrs. Blackburn, Jassy, Piacentini, and Wilke. Due to Mr. Bezos' substantial ownership in Amazon, Mr. Bezos again requested not to receive additional compensation in 2016 and has never received annual cash compensation in excess of his current amount.

Stock-Based Compensation. The primary component of a named executive officer's total compensation is stock-based compensation in order to closely tie total compensation to long-term shareholder value. Accordingly, named executive officers receive sizeable stock-based awards at the time of hire and are also eligible for stock-based awards on a periodic basis. Because our compensation program is designed to reward long-term performance and operate over a period of years, named executive officers may not necessarily receive stock-based awards every year. For example, because annual total compensation as reported in the Summary Compensation Table below includes the entire fair value as of the grant date of a stock award granted in that year, without regard to the fact that the grant vests over a number of years, a named executive officer's total compensation as reported will be higher in years in which he or she receives a grant compared to years in which he or she does not receive a grant. Due to Mr. Bezos' substantial stock ownership, he believes he is appropriately incentivized and his interests are appropriately aligned with shareholders' interests. Mr. Bezos has never received any stock-based compensation from Amazon.

Since late 2002, we have used restricted stock units as our primary stock-based compensation vehicle. We believe that restricted stock units align the long-term interests of named executive officers and shareholders and help efficiently manage overall shareholder dilution from stock awards. Restricted stock unit grant amounts and vesting for named executive officers, whether for new hire or subsequent grants, are established by the Leadership Development and Compensation Committee after receiving recommendations from the Senior Vice President of Human Resources and the Chief Executive Officer. These restricted stock unit grants generally vest over a period of five or six years. Vesting does not accelerate as a result of termination of employment or upon a change-in-control (unless the Leadership Development and Compensation Committee determines that the acquiring company will not be assuming or substituting the awards).

For new hire grants and grants made in connection with internal promotions, the Senior Vice President of Human Resources, the Chief Executive Officer, and the Leadership Development and Compensation Committee consider a variety of factors, including past compensation from the named executive officer's former employer, future compensation from such former employer that will be forfeited upon joining the Company, the compensation of similarly situated senior executives at Amazon, the named executive officer's expected level of responsibility and expected contributions to our future success, and the compensation of similarly situated executives at other retail, Internet, and technology companies.

For periodic grants, the Senior Vice President of Human Resources, the Chief Executive Officer, and the Leadership Development and Compensation Committee consider a variety of factors, including the named executive officer's level of responsibility, past contributions to our performance, including our core values, and expected contributions to our future success, as well as the compensation of similarly situated executives at other retail, Internet, and technology companies. Generally, the Leadership Development and Compensation Committee considers whether to make periodic grants to executive officers in connection with our annual performance and compensation review process, which normally occurs between January and April.

For both new hire and periodic restricted stock unit grants, the Senior Vice President of Human Resources and Chief Executive Officer develop grant recommendations by subjectively evaluating the factors above to set a total compensation target for each named executive officer and then designing restricted stock unit grants to help meet those total compensation targets based on stock price appreciation assumptions, taking into account the named executive officer's cash compensation and the estimated value of pre-existing stock-based compensation vesting in subsequent years, if any. In this process, the Senior Vice President of Human Resources and Chief Executive Officer view projected total compensation for a given year as cash compensation expected to be earned in that year plus an assumed value of stock-based compensation vesting in that year. Because we focus on total compensation over time and take into account existing compensation, periodic grants for a smaller number of shares do not necessarily reflect lower total compensation.

In April 2016, Messrs. Olsavsky, Blackburn, Jassy, and Wilke received restricted stock unit awards with vesting beginning in May 2017, assuming continued employment, as follows:

- Mr. Olsavsky received a restricted stock unit award for 7,458 shares. In making this grant, the Leadership Development and Compensation Committee considered the factors discussed above with respect to periodic grants, including Mr. Olsavsky's experience and skill as Chief Financial Officer, his performance in the year preceding the grant, and his expected future contributions.

- Mr. Blackburn received a restricted stock unit award for 37,362 shares. In making this grant, the Leadership Development and Compensation Committee considered the factors discussed above with respect to periodic grants, including Mr. Blackburn's experience and skill in managing the Company's business development projects, his sustained performance over time in years preceding the grant, and his expected future contributions.

- Mr. Jassy received a restricted stock unit award for 30,118 shares. In making this grant, the Leadership Development and Compensation Committee considered the factors discussed above with respect to periodic grants, including Mr. Jassy's experience and skill in managing web services and cloud computing operations, his sustained performance over time in years preceding the grant, and his expected future contributions.

- Mr. Wilke received a restricted stock unit award for 25,619 shares. In making this grant, the Leadership Development and Compensation Committee considered the factors discussed above with respect to periodic grants, including Mr. Wilke's experience and skill in managing Worldwide Consumer operations, his sustained performance over time in years preceding the grant, and his expected future contributions.

In setting these amounts, the Leadership Development and Compensation Committee considered the vesting schedule of existing equity awards as well as aggregated information from third party surveys, including compensation data for retail, Internet, technology, and media companies including Alphabet, Apple, AT&T, Best Buy, Cisco, eBay, Facebook, General Electric, Honeywell, IBM, Intel, Microsoft, Oracle, Starbucks, Target, Wal-Mart, and The Walt Disney Company. The Leadership Development and Compensation Committee exercises discretion in determining executive officers' compensation and does not require that compensation be set at a specific level relative to what is reflected in the survey data.

In addition, Messrs. Jassy and Wilke each received an additional restricted stock unit award for 30,000 shares, which vest 45% in 2019, 15% in 2020, 30% in 2022, and 10% in 2023, in connection with being named CEO Amazon Web Services and CEO Worldwide Consumer, respectively. These grants were designed to encourage long-term retention, and were given in recognition of their level of responsibility and expected contribution to our future success over the long term.

The total number of restricted stock units granted to our named executive officers during 2016 represented only (i) 1.73% of the total number of restricted stock units granted to all employees during 2016 and (ii) 0.03% of the weighted-average number of shares outstanding for 2016. The total number of restricted stock units granted to our named executive officers during the three-year period from 2014 to 2016 represented only (i) 0.97% of the total number of restricted stock units granted to all employees during the same three-year period and (ii) 0.02% of the weighted-average number of shares outstanding for the same three-year period.

At the time of grant we impose additional vesting conditions on certain stock-based awards issued to named executive officers so that the awards may qualify as tax-deductible compensation under Section 162(m)(4)(c) of the Internal Revenue Code. However, the Company or the Leadership Development and Compensation Committee may grant awards that do not qualify for tax deductibility under Section 162(m), and there is no guarantee that awards intended to qualify for tax deductibility under Section 162(m) will ultimately be viewed as so qualifying by the Internal Revenue Service.

New Hire Cash Bonuses.   None of the named executive officers received a new hire cash bonus in 2016.

Other Compensation and Benefits.   Named executive officers receive additional compensation in the form of vacation, medical, 401(k), relocation, and other benefits generally available to all of our employees. We provide security for Mr. Bezos, including security in addition to that provided at business facilities and during business-related travel. We believe that all Company-incurred security costs are reasonable and necessary and for the Company's benefit, and that the amount of the reported security expenses is especially reasonable in light of Mr. Bezos' low salary and the fact that he has never received any stock-based compensation. The Leadership Development and Compensation Committee periodically reviews the amount and nature of Mr. Bezos' security expenses. Reportable security expenses, along with Mr. Piacentini's expatriation benefits, including a cost of living and housing allowance, are included in the "All Other Compensation" column of the Summary Compensation Table. We do not provide any other perquisites or other personal benefits to our named executive officers.

Shareholder Advisory Vote to Approve Executive Compensation.   At our 2014 Annual Meeting of Shareholders, our shareholders overwhelmingly approved the compensation of our named executive officers, with more than 97% of the votes cast for approval of our executive compensation on an advisory basis. The Leadership Development and Compensation Committee evaluated the results of the 2014 advisory vote approving the compensation of our named executive officers as well as discussions we have had in recent years with our shareholders and the other factors discussed in this Compensation Discussion and Analysis when evaluating our executive compensation and compensation policies and practices. While each of these factors informed the Leadership Development and Compensation Committee's decisions regarding our executive compensation program, the Leadership Development and Compensation Committee did not implement changes to our executive compensation program as a result of the shareholder advisory vote.

Leadership Development and Compensation Committee Report

The Leadership Development and Compensation Committee, which is composed solely of independent members of the Board of Directors, assists the Board in fulfilling its oversight responsibility relating to, among other things, establishing and reviewing compensation of the Company's executive officers. The Leadership Development and Compensation Committee reviewed and discussed with management the Company's Compensation Discussion and Analysis and, based on the review and discussion, recommended to the Board that the Compensation Discussion and Analysis be included in this Proxy Statement.

> The Leadership Development and
> Compensation Committee
>
> Daniel P. Huttenlocher
> Judith A. McGrath
> Jonathan J. Rubinstein

Compensation of Named Executive Officers

The following table sets forth for the year ended December 31, 2016 the compensation reportable for the named executive officers, as determined by SEC rules.

2016 Summary Compensation Table

Name And Principal Position	Year	Salary	Stock Awards(1)	All Other Compensation	Total
Jeffrey P. Bezos	2016	$ 81,840	$ —	$ 1,600,000(2)	$ 1,681,840
Chief Executive Officer	2015	81,840	—	1,600,000	1,681,840
	2014	81,840	—	1,600,000	1,681,840
Brian T. Olsavsky	2016	160,000	4,395,447	3,200(3)	4,558,647
SVP and Chief Financial Officer(4)	2015	160,000	7,623,373	3,200	7,786,573
Jeffrey M. Blackburn	2016	171,250	22,019,668	3,425(3)	22,194,343
SVP, Business Development(4)					
Andrew R. Jassy	2016	175,000	35,431,144(5)	3,500(3)	35,609,644
CEO Amazon Web Services	2015	171,250	—	3,425	174,675
	2014	160,000	7,501,668	3,200	7,664,868
Diego Piacentini	2016	110,326	23,585,138(7)	35,166(8)	23,730,630
SVP, International Consumer					
Business(6)	2015	175,000	—	55,905	230,905
	2014	175,000	6,635,459	55,905	6,866,364
Jeffrey A. Wilke	2016	175,000	32,779,614(9)	3,500(3)	32,958,114
CEO Worldwide Consumer	2015	172,509	—	3,450	175,959
	2014	165,000	8,347,749	3,300	8,516,049

(1) Stock awards are reported at aggregate grant date fair value in the year granted, as determined under applicable accounting standards. Grant date fair value for restricted stock units is determined based on the number of shares granted multiplied by the average of the high and the low trading price of common stock of the Company on the grant date, without regard to the fact that the grants vest over a number of years. See Note 1, *"Description of Business and Accounting Policies—Stock-Based Compensation,"* in Item 8, "Financial Statements and Supplementary Data," in our 2016 Annual Report on Form 10-K.

(2) Represents the approximate aggregate incremental cost to Amazon of security arrangements for Mr. Bezos in addition to security arrangements provided at business facilities and for business travel. We believe that all Company-incurred security costs are reasonable and necessary and for the Company's benefit.

(3) Represents the value of cash and/or shares of common stock we contributed to the named executive officer's account in our 401(k) plan.

(4) Mr. Olsavsky became a named executive officer in 2015 and Mr. Blackburn became a named executive officer in 2016.

(5) In addition to receiving a periodic stock grant, Mr. Jassy also received an additional restricted stock unit award for 30,000 shares in connection with being named CEO Amazon Web Services. In making this grant, the Leadership Development and Compensation Committee considered the factors discussed in the "Compensation Discussion and Analysis" section of this Proxy Statement above in relation to this grant.

(6) On February 10, 2016, the Board approved a leave of absence for Diego Piacentini, Senior Vice President, International Consumer Business, for two years beginning in August 2016.

(7) In connection with Mr. Piacentini's leave of absence, the Board's Leadership Development and Compensation Committee approved suspending forfeiture of Mr. Piacentini's restricted stock unit awards under the 1997 Plan for the duration of his leave of absence. The amount reported reflects the incremental fair value of his previously-granted restricted stock unit awards as a result of modification of the forfeiture terms and not a new award grant.

(8) Represents expatriation benefits, including a cost of living and housing allowance in the amount of $35,166. Mr. Piacentini's 2000 employment offer letter, which provided for an initial annual salary of $175,000 and has no specified term, also provides for certain expatriation benefits, including a cost of living and housing allowance.

(9) In addition to receiving a periodic stock grant, Mr. Wilke also received an additional restricted stock unit award for 30,000 shares in connection with being named CEO Worldwide Consumer operations. In making this grant, the Leadership Development and Compensation Committee considered the factors discussed in the "Compensation Discussion and Analysis" section of this Proxy Statement above in relation to this grant.

The following table supplements the disclosure in the Summary Compensation Table with respect to stock awards made to the named executive officers in 2016.

Grants of Plan-Based Awards in Fiscal Year 2016

Name	Grant Date	All Other Stock Awards: Number of Shares of Stock or Units	Grant Date Fair Value of Stock Awards(1)
Jeffrey P. Bezos		—	$ —
Brian T. Olsavsky	4/5/2016	7,458(2)(3)	4,395,447
Jeffrey M. Blackburn	4/5/2016	37,362(2)(4)	22,019,668
Andrew R. Jassy	4/5/2016	30,118(2)(5)	17,750,344
	4/5/2016	30,000(2)(6)	17,680,800
Diego Piacentini	2/10/2016	47,615(7)	23,585,138
Jeffrey A. Wilke	4/5/2016	25,619(2)(8)	15,098,814
	4/5/2016	30,000(2)(9)	17,680,800

(1) Stock awards are reported at aggregate grant date fair value, as determined under applicable accounting standards. Grant date fair value for restricted stock units is determined based on the number of shares granted multiplied by the average of the high and the low trading price of common stock of the Company on the grant date, without regard to the fact that the grants vest over a number of years. The holder of the restricted stock unit award does not have any voting, dividend, or other ownership rights in the shares of common stock subject to the award unless and until the award vests and the shares are issued.

(2) The vesting schedule reflects total compensation targets for future years based on the number of shares vesting and stock price assumptions for each future year.

(3) This award vests based upon the following vesting schedule and the satisfaction of certain business criteria intended to qualify the award as tax-deductible compensation under Section 162(m) of the Internal Revenue Code: 150 shares on each of May 15, 2017, August 15, 2017, and November 15, 2017; 151 shares on

February 15, 2018; 130 shares on each of May 15, 2018 and August 15, 2018; 131 shares on each of November 15, 2018 and February 15, 2019; 284 shares on May 15, 2019; 285 shares on each of August 15, 2019, November 15, 2019, and February 15, 2020; 239 shares on each of May 15, 2020, August 15, 2020, November 15, 2020, and February 15, 2021; and 1,060 shares on each of May 15, 2021, August 15, 2021, November 15, 2021, and February 15, 2022.

(4) This award vests based upon the following vesting schedule and the satisfaction of certain business criteria intended to qualify the award as tax-deductible compensation under Section 162(m) of the Internal Revenue Code: 1,036 shares on each of May 15, 2017 and August 15, 2017; 1,037 shares on each of November 15, 2017 and February 15, 2018; 1,667 shares on each of May 15, 2018 and August 15, 2018; 1,668 shares on each of November 15, 2018 and February 15, 2019; 1,692 shares on each of May 15, 2019, August 15, 2019, November 15, 2019, and February 15, 2020; 2,791 shares on each of May 15, 2020, August 15, 2020, and November 15, 2020; 2,792 shares on February 15, 2021; 2,153 shares on each of May 15, 2021, August 15, 2021, and November 15, 2021; and 2,154 shares on February 15, 2022.

(5) This award vests based upon the following vesting schedule and the satisfaction of certain business criteria intended to qualify the award as tax-deductible compensation under Section 162(m) of the Internal Revenue Code: 494 shares on each of May 15, 2017, August 15, 2017, and November 15, 2017; 495 shares on February 15, 2018; 952 shares on each of May 15, 2018, August 15, 2018, November 15, 2018, and February 15, 2019; 1,138 shares on May 15, 2019; 1,139 shares on each of August 15, 2019, November 15, 2019, and February 15, 2020; 2,791 shares on each of May 15, 2020, August 15, 2020, and November 15, 2020; 2,792 shares on February 15, 2021; 2,153 shares on each of May 15, 2021, August 15, 2021, and November 15, 2021; and 2,154 shares on February 15, 2022.

(6) In addition to receiving a periodic stock grant, Mr. Jassy also received an additional restricted stock unit award for 30,000 shares in connection with being named CEO Amazon Web Services. In making this grant, the Leadership Development and Compensation Committee considered the factors discussed in the "Compensation Discussion and Analysis" section of this Proxy Statement above in relation to this grant. This award vests based upon the following vesting schedule and the satisfaction of certain business criteria intended to qualify the award as tax-deductible compensation under Section 162(m) of the Internal Revenue Code: 4,500 shares on each of May 15, 2019, August 15, 2019, November 15, 2019, and February 15, 2020; and 3,000 shares on each of May 15, 2022, August 15, 2022, November 15, 2022, and February 15, 2023.

(7) In connection with Mr. Piacentini's leave of absence, the Board's Leadership Development and Compensation Committee approved suspending forfeiture of Mr. Piacentini's restricted stock unit awards under the 1997 Plan for the duration of his leave of absence. The amount reported reflects the incremental fair value of his previously granted restricted stock unit awards as a result of modification of the forfeiture terms and not a new award grant.

(8) This award vests based upon the following vesting schedule and the satisfaction of certain business criteria intended to qualify the award as tax-deductible compensation under Section 162(m) of the Internal Revenue Code: 596 shares on each of May 15, 2018, August 15, 2018, and November 15, 2018; 597 shares on February 15, 2019; 864 shares on each of May 15, 2019, August 15, 2019, November 15, 2019, and February 15, 2020; 2,791 shares on each of May 15, 2020, August 15, 2020, and November 15, 2020; 2,792 shares on February 15, 2021; 2,153 shares on each of May 15, 2021, August 15, 2021, and November 15, 2021; and 2,154 shares on February 15, 2022.

(9) In addition to receiving a periodic stock grant, Mr. Wilke also received an additional restricted stock unit award for 30,000 shares in connection with being named CEO Worldwide Consumer operations. In making this grant, the Leadership Development and Compensation Committee considered the factors discussed in the "Compensation Discussion and Analysis" section of this Proxy Statement above in relation to this grant. This award vests based upon the following vesting schedule and the satisfaction of certain business criteria intended to qualify the award as tax-deductible compensation under Section 162(m) of the Internal Revenue Code: 4,500 shares on each of May 15, 2019, August 15, 2019, November 15, 2019, and February 15, 2020; and 3,000 shares on each of May 15, 2022, August 15, 2022, November 15, 2022, and February 15, 2023.

Outstanding Equity Awards at 2016 Fiscal Year-End and Stock Vested in 2016

The following table sets forth information concerning the outstanding stock awards held at December 31, 2016 by the named executive officers.

Outstanding Equity Awards at 2016 Fiscal Year-End

Name	Number of Shares or Units of Stock That Have Not Vested	Market Value of Shares or Units of Stock That Have Not Vested(1)
Jeffrey P. Bezos	—	$ —
Brian T. Olsavsky		
Restricted stock units	35,767(2)	26,820,600
Jeffrey M. Blackburn		
Restricted stock units	74,188(3)	55,631,356
Andrew R. Jassy		
Restricted stock units	104,890(4)	78,653,864
Diego Piacentini		
Restricted stock units	47,615(5)	35,705,060
Jeffrey A. Wilke		
Restricted stock units	108,638(6)	81,464,377

(1) Reflects the closing market price of our common stock on December 30, 2016, $749.87, multiplied by the number of restricted stock units that were not vested as of December 31, 2016.

(2) Reflects shares of our common stock subject to: (a) a restricted stock unit award that vested as to 297 shares on February 15, 2017; and vesting as follows, assuming continued employment: 747 shares on May 15, 2017; 748 shares on each of August 15, 2017, November 15, 2017, and February 15, 2018; 781 shares on each of May 15, 2018 and August 15, 2018; 782 shares on each of November 15, 2018 and February 15, 2019; 1,479 shares on May 15, 2019; 1,480 shares on each of August 15, 2019, November 15, 2019, and February 15, 2020; 1,137 shares on May 15, 2020; and 1,138 shares on each of August 15, 2020, November 15, 2020, and February 15, 2021; (b) a restricted stock unit award vesting as follows, assuming continued employment: 73 shares on each of May 15, 2017, August 15, 2017, November 15, 2017, and February 15, 2018; and 1,117 shares on each of May 15, 2018, August 15, 2018, November 15, 2018, and February 15, 2019; (c) a restricted stock unit award vesting as follows, assuming continued employment: 1,363 shares on each of May 15, 2017, August 15, 2017, and November 15, 2017; and 1,361 shares on February 15, 2018; (d) a restricted stock unit award that vested as to 1,215 shares on February 15, 2017; and (e) a restricted stock unit award vesting as follows, assuming continued employment: 150 shares on each of May 15, 2017, August 15, 2017, and November 15, 2017; 151 shares on February 15, 2018; 130 shares on each of May 15, 2018 and August 15, 2018; 131 shares on each of November 15, 2018 and February 15, 2019; 284 shares on May 15, 2019; 285 shares on each of August 15, 2019, November 15, 2019, and February 15, 2020; 239 shares on each of May 15, 2020, August 15, 2020, November 15, 2020, and February 15, 2021; and 1,060 shares on each of May 15, 2021, August 15, 2021, November 15, 2021, and February 15, 2022.

(3) Reflects shares of our common stock subject to: (a) a restricted stock unit award that vested as to 4,787 shares on February 15, 2017; and vesting as follows, assuming continued employment: 3,689 shares on May 15, 2017; and 3,688 shares on each of August 15, 2017, November 15, 2017, and February 15, 2018; (b) a restricted stock unit award vesting as follows, assuming continued employment: 2,441 shares on each of May 15, 2018, August 15, 2018, November 15, 2018, and February 15, 2019; 1,880 shares on each of May 15, 2019 and August 15, 2019; and 1,881 shares on each of November 15, 2019 and February 15,

2020; and (c) a restricted stock unit award vesting as follows, assuming continued employment: 1,036 shares on each of May 15, 2017 and August 15, 2017; 1,037 shares on each of November 15, 2017 and February 15, 2018; 1,667 shares on each of May 15, 2018 and August 15, 2018; 1,668 shares on each of November 15, 2018 and February 15, 2019; 1,692 shares on each of May 15, 2019, August 15, 2019, November 15, 2019, and February 15, 2020; 2,791 shares on each of May 15, 2020, August 15, 2020, and November 15, 2020; 2,792 shares on February 15, 2021; 2,153 shares on each of May 15, 2021, August 15, 2021, and November 15, 2021; and 2,154 shares on February 15, 2022.

(4) Reflects shares of our common stock subject to: (a) a restricted stock unit award vesting as follows, assuming continued employment: 3,156 shares on May 15, 2018 and August 15, 2018; 3,157 shares on November 15, 2018 and February 15, 2019; 2,433 shares on May 15, 2019; and 2,434 shares on August 15, 2019 and quarterly thereafter through February 15, 2020; (b) a restricted stock unit award that vested as to 5,489 shares on February 15, 2017; and vesting as follows, assuming continued employment: 4,231 shares on May 15, 2017 and August 15, 2017; and 4,230 shares on November 15, 2017 and February 15, 2018; (c) a restricted stock unit award vesting as follows, assuming continued employment: 494 shares on each of May 15, 2017, August 15, 2017, and November 15, 2017; 495 shares on February 15, 2018; 952 shares on each of May 15, 2018, August 15, 2018, November 15, 2018, and February 15, 2019; 1,138 shares on May 15, 2019; 1,139 shares on each of August 15, 2019, November 15, 2019, and February 15, 2020; 2,791 shares on each of May 15, 2020, August 15, 2020, and November 15, 2020; 2,792 shares on February 15, 2021; 2,153 shares on each of May 15, 2021, August 15, 2021, and November 15, 2021; and 2,154 shares on February 15, 2022; and (d) a restricted stock unit award vesting as follows, assuming continued employment: 4,500 shares on each of May 15, 2019, August 15, 2019, November 15, 2019, and February 15, 2020; and 3,000 shares on each of May 15, 2022, August 15, 2022, November 15, 2022, and February 15, 2023.

(5) On February 10, 2016, the Board approved a leave of absence for Diego Piacentini, Senior Vice President, International Consumer Business, for two years beginning in August 2016. In connection with Mr. Piacentini's leave of absence, the Board's Leadership Development and Compensation Committee approved suspending forfeiture of Mr. Piacentini's restricted stock unit awards under the 1997 Plan for the duration of his leave of absence, with vesting dates to be extended for a period corresponding to the term of his leave of absence. Prior to that modification, the vesting terms of Mr. Piacentini's restricted stock units that were scheduled to vest following the date his leave of absence commenced were as follows: (a) 2,792 shares on May 15, 2018; 2,793 shares on August 15, 2018 and quarterly thereafter through February 15, 2019; 2,152 shares on May 15, 2019 and quarterly thereafter through February 15, 2020; and (b) 5,477 shares on November 15, 2016 and February 15, 2017; 4,221 shares on May 15, 2017 and August 15, 2017; and 4,220 shares on November 15, 2017 and February 15, 2018.

(6) Reflects shares of our common stock subject to: (a) a restricted stock unit award vesting as follows, assuming continued employment: 3,512 shares on May 15, 2018 and quarterly thereafter through November 15, 2018; 3,513 shares on February 15, 2019; 2,708 shares on May 15, 2019 and August 15, 2019; and 2,709 shares on November 15, 2019 and February 15, 2020; (b) a restricted stock unit award that vested as to 6,888 shares on February 15, 2017; and vesting as follows, assuming continued employment: 5,312 shares on May 15, 2017 and quarterly thereafter through February 15, 2018; (c) a restricted stock unit award vesting as follows, assuming continued employment: 596 shares on each of May 15, 2018, August 15, 2018, and November 15, 2018; 597 shares on February 15, 2019; 864 shares on each of May 15, 2019, August 15, 2019, November 15, 2019, and February 15, 2020; 2,791 shares on each of May 15, 2020, August 15, 2020, and November 15, 2020; 2,792 shares on February 15, 2021; 2,153 shares on each of May 15, 2021, August 15, 2021, and November 15, 2021; and 2,154 shares on February 15, 2022; and (d) a restricted stock unit award vesting as follows, assuming continued employment: 4,500 shares on each of May 15, 2019, August 15, 2019, November 15, 2019, and February 15, 2020; and 3,000 shares on each of May 15, 2022, August 15, 2022, November 15, 2022, and February 15, 2023.

Stock Vested in 2016

The following table sets forth information concerning stock awards that vested during the last fiscal year with respect to the named executive officers.

	Stock Awards	
	Number of Shares Acquired on Vesting	Value Realized on Vesting(1)
Jeffrey P. Bezos	—	$ —
Brian T. Olsavsky	10,629	7,258,969
Jeffrey M. Blackburn	20,495	13,745,670
Andrew R. Jassy	23,496	15,758,902
Diego Piacentini	17,971	11,655,635
Jeffrey A. Wilke	29,484	19,775,635

(1) Amount is the number of shares of stock acquired upon vesting multiplied by the closing market price of our common stock on the vesting date (or the preceding trading day if the vesting date was not a trading day).

Potential Payments Upon Termination of Employment or Change-in-Control

Termination and Change-in-Control Agreements or Arrangements.   We do not have any contracts, agreements, or arrangements with any of our named executive officers providing for additional benefits or payments in connection with a termination of employment, change in job responsibility, or change-in-control. Upon termination of employment for any reason, all unvested restricted stock units expire.

Change-in-Control Provisions of 1997 Plan.   In the event of (i) the merger or consolidation in which we are not the surviving corporation pursuant to which shares of common stock are converted into cash, securities, or other property (other than a merger in which holders of common stock immediately before the merger have the same proportionate ownership of the capital stock of the surviving corporation immediately after the merger), (ii) the sale, lease, exchange, or other transfer of all or substantially all of our assets (other than a transfer to a majority-owned subsidiary), or (iii) the approval by the holders of common stock of any plan or proposal for our liquidation or dissolution (each a "Corporate Transaction"), the Leadership Development and Compensation Committee will determine whether provision will be made in connection with the Corporate Transaction for the assumption of stock-based awards under the 1997 Plan or the substitution of appropriate new awards covering the stock of the successor corporation or an affiliate of the successor corporation. If the Leadership Development and Compensation Committee determines that no such assumption or substitution will be made, vesting of outstanding awards under the 1997 Plan will automatically accelerate so that such awards become 100% vested immediately before the Corporate Transaction. On a hypothetical basis, assuming the Leadership Development and Compensation Committee had made such a determination in a Corporate Transaction that closed on December 31, 2016, the dollar value of the unvested stock-based awards held by named executive officers that would have vested based on the closing price of our common stock of $749.87 on December 30, 2016 is set forth in the "Outstanding Equity Awards at 2016 Fiscal Year-End" table.

SECURITIES AUTHORIZED FOR ISSUANCE UNDER EQUITY COMPENSATION PLANS

The following table sets forth information concerning our equity compensation plans as of December 31, 2016:

Plan Category	Number of Securities to be Issued Upon Exercise of Outstanding Options, Warrants, and Rights	Weighted-average Exercise Price of Outstanding Options, Warrants, and Rights	Number of Securities Remaining Available for Future Issuance Under Equity Compensation Plans
Equity compensation plans approved by shareholders	19,770,488(1)	$ —	104,297,334(2)
Equity compensation plans not approved by shareholders	—	—	18,812,972
Total	19,770,488(3)		123,110,306

(1) Includes 19,770,488 shares issuable pursuant to restricted stock unit awards, which awards may be granted only under our shareholder-approved 1997 Plan. There is no exercise price associated with a restricted stock unit award.
(2) The 1997 Plan authorizes the issuance of options and restricted stock unit awards.
(3) Excludes 131,004 shares of common stock issuable upon exercise of stock options having a weighted-average exercise price of $23.69 and 3,312 shares of common stock issuable upon vesting of restricted stock units under equity plans assumed by Amazon as a result of acquisitions.

Equity Compensation Plans Not Approved By Security Holders. The Board adopted the 1999 Nonofficer Employee Stock Option Plan (the "1999 Plan") to enable the grant of nonqualified stock options to employees, consultants, agents, advisors, and independent contractors of Amazon and its subsidiaries who are not officers or directors of Amazon. Restricted stock units, our primary form of stock-based compensation since 2002, are not granted from the 1999 Plan. The 1999 Plan, which does not have a fixed expiration date, has not been approved by our shareholders. The Leadership Development and Compensation Committee is the administrator of the 1999 Plan, and as such determines all matters relating to options granted under the 1999 Plan, including the selection of the recipients, the size of the grants, and the conditions to vesting and exercisability. The Leadership Development and Compensation Committee has delegated authority to make grants under the 1999 Plan to another committee of the Board and to certain officers, subject to specified limitations on the size and terms of such grants. A maximum of 40 million shares of common stock were reserved for issuance under the 1999 Plan.

CERTAIN RELATIONSHIPS AND RELATED PERSON TRANSACTIONS

Justin Burks, an employee of Amazon, is the son-in-law of Thomas O. Ryder, a director. In 2016, Mr. Burks earned $159,650 in salary. He was also granted a restricted stock unit award with respect to 194 shares, vesting over 2.2 years. His compensation is consistent with the total compensation provided to other employees of the same level with similar responsibilities.

Jeff Bezos, our President, CEO, and Chairman, owns entities that publish The Washington Post, with which we do business in the ordinary course. In 2016, Amazon purchased approximately $1.1 million of advertising from and paid approximately $2.9 million related to digital content to such entities, and such entities were obligated to pay Amazon approximately $174,000 for subscriber services in 2016, all on terms negotiated on an arms-length basis.

On March 14, 2017, William B. Gordon resigned as a director of the Company in order to provide consulting services to us for two years, which includes being available as a non-voting Board observer. Under the consulting agreement, Mr. Gordon was granted a restricted stock unit award for 3,100 shares, vesting over two years.

The Audit Committee reviews and, as appropriate, approves and ratifies "related person" transactions, defined as any transaction, arrangement, or relationship (including any indebtedness or guarantee of indebtedness), or any series of similar transactions, arrangements, or relationships, in which (a) the aggregate amount involved will or may be expected to exceed $120,000, (b) Amazon is a participant, and (c) any Related Person has or will have a direct or indirect material interest (other than solely as a result of being a director or trustee (or any similar position) or a less than 10 percent beneficial owner of another entity). A "Related Person" is any (a) person who is an executive officer, director, or nominee for election as a director of Amazon, (b) greater than 5 percent beneficial owner of our outstanding common stock, or (c) Immediate Family Member of any of the foregoing. An "Immediate Family Member" is any child, stepchild, parent, stepparent, spouse, sibling, mother-in-law, father-in-law, son-in-law, daughter-in-law, brother-in-law, or sister-in-law, and any person (other than a tenant or employee) sharing the household of a person. We do not have written policies or procedures for related person transactions but rely on the Audit Committee's exercise of business judgment, consistent with Delaware law, in reviewing such transactions.

SECTION 16(a) BENEFICIAL OWNERSHIP REPORTING COMPLIANCE

To our knowledge, based solely on a review of the copies of such reports furnished to us and written representations that no other reports were required, we believe that during the year ended December 31, 2016, our officers, directors, and greater-than-10% shareholders timely filed all reports required by Section 16(a) of the Securities Exchange Act of 1934.

EXPENSES OF SOLICITATION

The accompanying proxy is solicited by and on behalf of the Board of Directors, and the cost of such solicitation will be borne by Amazon. Georgeson Inc. will distribute proxy materials to banks, brokers, and other nominees for forwarding to beneficial owners, may solicit proxies by personal interview, mail, telephone, and electronic communications, and will request brokerage houses and other custodians, nominees, and fiduciaries to forward soliciting materials to the beneficial owners of the common stock held on the record date by such persons. We will pay Georgeson Inc. $13,500 plus variable amounts for additional proxy solicitation services. We will also reimburse Georgeson Inc. for payments made to brokers and other nominees for their expenses in forwarding solicitation materials. Solicitations also may be made by personal interview, mail, telephone, and electronic communications by directors, officers, and other Amazon employees without additional compensation.

OTHER MATTERS

As of the date of this Proxy Statement there are no other matters that we intend to present, or have reason to believe others will present, at the Annual Meeting. If, however, other matters properly come before the Annual Meeting, the accompanying proxy authorizes the persons named as proxies or their substitutes to vote on such matters as they determine appropriate.

PROPOSALS OF SHAREHOLDERS

To be considered for inclusion in the proxy statement and proxy card for the 2018 Annual Meeting, proposals of shareholders pursuant to Rule 14a-8 under the Securities Exchange Act of 1934 and shareholder director nominations pursuant to the proxy access provisions of the Bylaws must be submitted in writing to the Corporate Secretary of Amazon.com, Inc., at Amazon.com, Inc., 410 Terry Avenue North, Seattle, Washington 98109, and must be received no later than 6:00 p.m., Pacific Time, on Wednesday December 13, 2017 and, in the case of a proxy access nomination, no earlier than November 13, 2017. The submission of a shareholder proposal or proxy access nomination does not guarantee that it will be included in our proxy statement.

Our Bylaws include separate advance notice provisions applicable to shareholders desiring to bring nominations for directors before an annual shareholders meeting other than pursuant to the Bylaws' proxy access provisions or to bring proposals before an annual shareholders meeting other than pursuant to Rule 14a-8. These advance notice provisions require that, among other things, shareholders give timely written notice to the Secretary of Amazon.com, Inc. regarding such nominations or proposals and provide the information and satisfy the other requirements set forth in the Bylaws. To be timely, a shareholder who intends to present nominations or a proposal at the 2018 Annual Meeting of Shareholders other than pursuant to the Bylaws' proxy access provisions or Rule 14a-8 must provide the information set forth in the Bylaws to the Secretary of Amazon.com, Inc. no earlier than January 23, 2018 and no later than February 22, 2018. However, if we hold the 2018 Annual Meeting of Shareholders more than 30 days before, or more than 60 days after, the anniversary of the 2017 Annual Meeting date, then the information must be received no earlier than the 120th day prior to the 2018 Annual Meeting date, and not later than (i) the 90th day prior to the 2018 Annual Meeting date or (ii) the tenth day after public disclosure of the 2018 Annual Meeting date, whichever is later. If a shareholder fails to meet these deadlines and fails to satisfy the requirements of Rule 14a-4 under the Securities Exchange Act of 1934, we may exercise discretionary voting authority under proxies we solicit to vote on any such proposal as we determine appropriate.

We reserve the right to reject, rule out of order, or take other appropriate action with respect to any nomination or proposal that does not comply with these and other applicable requirements.

HOUSEHOLDING; AVAILABILITY OF ANNUAL REPORT ON FORM 10-K AND PROXY STATEMENT

A copy of our combined Annual Report to Shareholders and Annual Report on Form 10-K for the year ended December 31, 2016 (the "2016 Annual Report") accompanies this Proxy Statement. If you and others who share your mailing address own common stock in street name, meaning through a bank, brokerage firm, or other nominee, you may have received a notice that your household will receive only one annual report and proxy statement, or Notice of Internet Availability of Proxy Materials, as applicable, from each company whose stock is held in such accounts. This practice, known as "householding," is designed to reduce the volume of duplicate information and reduce printing and postage costs. Unless you responded that you did not want to participate in householding, you were deemed to have consented to it, and a single copy of this Proxy Statement and the 2016 Annual Report (and/or a single copy of our Notice of Internet Availability of Proxy Materials) has been sent to your address. Each street name shareholder receiving this Proxy Statement by mail will continue to receive a separate voting instruction form.

If you would like to revoke your consent to householding and in the future receive your own set of proxy materials (or your own Notice of Internet Availability of Proxy Materials, as applicable), or if your household is currently receiving multiple copies of the same items and you would like in the future to receive only a single copy at your address, please contact Householding Department by mail at 51 Mercedes Way, Edgewood, New York 11717, or by calling 1-800-542-1061, and indicate your name, the name of each of your brokerage firms or banks where your shares are held, and your account numbers. The revocation of a consent to householding will be effective 30 days following its receipt. You will also have an opportunity to opt in or opt out of householding by contacting your bank or broker.

FORM OF PROXY STATEMENT AND FORM OF PROXY

If you would like an additional copy of the 2016 Annual Report, this Proxy Statement, or the Notice of Internet Availability of Proxy Materials, these documents are available in digital form for download or review by visiting "Annual Reports, Proxies and Shareholder Letters" at *www.amazon.com/ir*. Alternatively, we will promptly send a copy of these documents to you without charge upon request by mail to Investor Relations, Amazon.com, Inc., P.O. Box 81226, Seattle, Washington 98108-1226, or by calling 1-800-426-6825. Please note, however, that if you did not receive a printed copy of our proxy materials and you wish to receive a paper proxy card or voting instruction form or other proxy materials for the purposes of the Annual Meeting, you should follow the instructions included in your Notice of Internet Availability of Proxy Materials.

If you own shares in street name, you can also register to receive all future shareholder communications electronically, instead of in print. This means that links to the annual report, proxy statement, and other correspondence will be delivered to you via e-mail. Holders in street name can register for electronic delivery at *http://www.icsdelivery.com/amzn*. Electronic delivery of shareholder communications helps save Amazon money by reducing printing and postage costs.

FORM OF PROXY STATEMENT AND FORM OF PROXY

SUMMARY OF THE 1997 STOCK INCENTIVE PLAN

Material Terms of 1997 Plan Performance Goals for Purposes of 162(m)

Eligibility and Participation

Awards may be granted under the 1997 Plan to those officers, directors, and employees of the Company and its subsidiaries as the plan administrator from time to time selects. The plan administrator for the 1997 Plan is the Leadership Development and Compensation Committee. Awards may also be granted to consultants, agents, advisors, and independent contractors who provide services to the Company and its subsidiaries. As of March 31, 2017, the approximate number of persons eligible to participate under the 1997 Plan was 298,977, including approximately 4,627 employees of the Company's French subsidiaries who could qualify for French tax-qualified awards under the 1997 Plan if all of the requirements of the Finance Law (as described in more detail below) for granting such awards are satisfied.

Performance Goals

Under the 1997 Plan, for awards made in the form of or denominated in common stock, the business criteria on which performance goals can be based are: (i) profits or loss, revenue or profit growth or loss reduction, profit or loss related return ratios, or other balance sheet or income statement targets or ratios; (ii) market share, including targets, ratios, or other objective measures of sessions, units, orders, customers, sales, and other comparable metrics related to the various businesses conducted by the Company; or (iii) cash flow, share price appreciation, dilution, or total stockholder return, as the plan administrator shall determine, in its sole discretion. Such performance goals may be stated in absolute terms or relative to comparison companies.

Maximum 162(m) Grants

The plan administrator has the authority in its sole discretion to determine the type or types of awards made under the 1997 Plan. Such awards may include, but are not limited to, stock options and awards made or denominated in shares of common stock. Awards may be granted singly or in combination. Not more than 4,500,000 shares of common stock may be made subject to awards under the 1997 Plan to any individual in the aggregate in any one fiscal year of the Company, except that the Company may make additional one-time grants of up to 18,000,000 shares to newly hired or newly promoted individuals. The foregoing share limitations will be proportionately adjusted by the plan administrator in the event that a stock dividend, stock split, spin-off, combination or exchange of shares, recapitalization, merger, consolidation, distribution to shareholders other than a normal cash dividend, or other change in the Company's corporate or capital structure results in the Company's outstanding shares (or any securities exchanged therefor or received in their place) being exchanged for a different number or class of securities of the Company or of any other corporation or new, different, or additional securities of the Company or of any other corporation being received by the holders of shares of the Company's common stock.

Description of Other Significant Terms of the 1997 Plan

The 1997 Plan provides a means whereby employees, directors, officers, consultants, agents, advisors and independent contractors of the Company and its subsidiaries may be granted stock awards, incentive stock options ("ISOs") or nonqualified stock options ("NSOs") to acquire shares of common stock.

The plan administrator is authorized to make awards of common stock on such terms and conditions and subject to such restrictions, if any (whether based on performance standards, periods of service or otherwise) as the plan administrator may determine. Restrictions may include repurchase or forfeiture rights in favor of the Company.

A-1

The number of shares available for issuance under the 1997 Plan was initially 80,000,000 shares, subject to an annual increase on the first day of each fiscal year through January 1, 2010. As of March 31, 2017, 88,622,067 shares remained available for grant under the 1997 Plan. As of that date, approximately 19,506,562 shares were subject to outstanding grants under the 1997 Plan, all of which represent outstanding restricted stock units. No stock options were outstanding under the 1997 Plan as of March 31, 2017. Information regarding the number of awards held by each of our directors and named executive officers that were granted under the 1997 Plan is set forth on pages 11 and 33 of this Proxy Statement, and as of March 31, 2017, all directors and executives as a group hold restricted stock units covering 356,383 shares. On March 31, 2017, the average of the high and low sale prices of the common stock was $883.50 per share, as reported by the Nasdaq Global Select Market.

The maximum number of shares that may be issued pursuant to options that are intended to qualify as ISOs is 251,025,075 shares. The share limitations described in this and the preceding paragraph will be proportionately adjusted by the plan administrator in the event that a stock dividend, stock split, spin-off, combination or exchange of shares, recapitalization, merger, consolidation, distribution to shareholders other than a normal cash dividend, or other change in the Company's corporate or capital structure results in the Company's outstanding shares (or any securities exchanged therefore or received in their place) being exchanged for a different number or class of securities of the Company or of any other corporation or new, different or additional securities of the Company or of any other corporation being received by the holders of shares of common stock of the Company.

Subject to the terms of the 1997 Plan, the plan administrator is authorized to make awards of restricted stock units, restricted stock and other awards of common stock or denominated in units of common stock, in each case on such terms and conditions and subject to such restrictions, if any as the plan administrator shall determine. The terms of such awards may be based on continuous service with the Company or the achievement of performance goals specified by the plan administrator. The plan administrator may in its discretion waive the forfeiture period and any other terms, conditions or restrictions on any such award, except that the plan administrator may not adjust performance goals for any such award intended to be exempt under Section 162(m) of the Internal Revenue Code in such a manner as would increase the amount otherwise payable to a participant.

Subject to the terms of the 1997 Plan, the plan administrator determines the terms and conditions of stock options granted under the plan, including the exercise price of options granted under the plan. The 1997 Plan provides that the plan administrator must establish an exercise price for ISOs that is not less than the fair market value per share at the date of grant. Each ISO must expire within ten years of the date of grant. However, if ISOs are granted to persons owning more than 10% of the voting stock of the Company, the 1997 Plan and the tax laws pertaining to ISOs provide that the exercise price may not be less than 110% of the fair market value per share at the date of grant. Unless approved by shareholders, the plan administrator cannot decrease the exercise price of outstanding options and cannot allow the exchange of underwater options for the grant of a new option with a lower exercise price, the grant of another award, or cash.

The option exercise price may be paid in cash or by check, by tendering shares of common stock that the optionee has owned for at least six months, by a broker-assisted cashless exercise, by any combination of the foregoing, or with such other consideration as the plan administrator may permit. Unless otherwise established by the plan administrator, the term of each option is ten years from the date of grant, except that if ISOs are granted to persons owning more than 10% of the Company's voting stock, the term may not exceed five years. Unless otherwise provided by the plan administrator, options granted under the 1997 Plan vest over five years, at a rate of 20% per year for two years, then an additional 5% for each three months of employment completed thereafter.

The 1997 Plan provides that the plan administrator may adopt sub-plans as it determines necessary or desirable to ensure that awards benefit participants employed in foreign countries and to meet the objectives of the 1997 Plan, which includes a sub-plan under which RSUs, including performance-based RSUs, may be granted that are intended to satisfy the requirements of the Finance Law for employees of our subsidiaries in

A-2

France. Consistent with the requirements of the Finance Law, the aggregate number of shares of common stock underlying French-Qualified RSUs may not exceed 10% of the Company's share capital.

No stock award or option may be transferred by the optionee other than by will or the laws of descent or distribution, except for certain transfers that may be permitted by the plan administrator. Unless otherwise established by the plan administrator, an optionee whose relationship with the Company or any related corporation ceases for any reason (other than termination for cause, retirement, death or disability, as such terms are defined in the 1997 Plan) may exercise options, to the extent vested on the date of termination, in the three-month period following such cessation (unless such options terminate or expire sooner by their terms). In the event the optionee is terminated for cause, the options terminate upon the first notification to the optionee of such termination. In the event the optionee retires, dies or becomes permanently and totally disabled, options vested as of the date of retirement, death or disability may be exercised prior to the earlier of the option's specified expiration date and one year from the date of the optionee's retirement, death or disability.

In the event of a Corporate Transaction (as defined in the 1997 Plan), the plan administrator will determine whether provisions will be made in connection with the Corporate Transaction for the assumption of the options under the 1997 Plan or substitution of appropriate new options covering the stock of the successor corporation or an affiliate of the successor corporation. If the plan administrator determines that no such assumption or substitution will be made, each outstanding option under the 1997 Plan will automatically accelerate so that it will become 100% vested and exercisable immediately before the Corporate Transaction.

The 1997 Plan does not have a fixed expiration date. No ISOs may be granted under the 1997 Plan, however, more than ten years after the later of (i) the plan's adoption by the Board and (ii) the adoption by the Board of any amendment to the plan that constitutes the adoption of a new plan for purposes of Section 422 of the Internal Revenue Code.

Because benefits under the 1997 Plan depend on the plan administrator's actions and the fair market value of shares of common stock at various future dates, it is not possible to determine the benefits that will be received by officers and other employees, including French employees, under the 1997 Plan.

Income Tax Consequences

The material U.S. federal income tax consequences to the Company and to any person granted a stock award or an option under the 1997 Plan who is subject to taxation in the United States under existing applicable provisions of the Internal Revenue Code and underlying Treasury Regulations are substantially as follows. The following summary does not address state, local or foreign tax consequences and it is based on present law and regulations as in effect as of the date hereof.

NSOs. No income will be recognized by an optionee upon the grant of an NSO. Upon the exercise of an NSO, the optionee will recognize taxable ordinary income in an amount equal to the excess of the fair market value at the time of exercise of the shares acquired over the exercise price. Upon a later sale of those shares, the optionee will have capital gain or loss equal to the difference between the amount realized on such sale and the tax basis of the shares sold. Furthermore, this capital gain or loss will be long-term capital gain or loss if the shares are held for more than one year before they are sold. If payment of the option price is made entirely in cash, the tax basis of the shares will be equal to their fair market value on the exercise date (but not less than the exercise price), and the shares' holding period will begin on the day after the exercise date.

If the optionee uses already-owned shares to pay the exercise price of an NSO in whole or in part, the transaction will not be considered to be a taxable disposition of the already-owned shares. The optionee's tax basis and holding period of the already-owned shares will be carried over to the equivalent number of shares received upon exercise. The tax basis of the additional shares received upon exercise will be the fair market value of the shares on the exercise date (but not less than the amount of cash, if any, used in payment), and the holding period for such additional shares will begin on the day after the exercise date.

A-3

ISOs.   No income will be recognized by an optionee upon the grant of an ISO. The rules for the tax treatment of an NSO also apply to an ISO that is exercised more than three months after the optionee's termination of employment (or more than 12 months thereafter in the case of permanent and total disability, as defined in the 1997 Plan).

Upon the exercise of an ISO during employment or within three months after the optionee's termination of employment (12 months in the case of permanent and total disability), for regular tax purposes the optionee will recognize no ordinary income at the time of exercise (although the optionee will have income for alternative minimum income tax purposes at that time equal to the excess of the fair market value of the shares over the exercise price). If the acquired shares are sold or exchanged after the later of (i) one year from the date of exercise of the option and (ii) two years from the date of grant of the option, the difference between the amount realized by the optionee on that sale or exchange and the option exercise price will be taxed to the optionee as long-term capital gain or loss. If the shares are disposed of in an arms' length sale before such holding period requirements are satisfied, then the optionee will recognize taxable ordinary income in the year of disposition in an amount equal to the excess of the fair market value of the shares received on the exercise date over the exercise price (or, if less, the excess of the amount realized on the sale of the shares over the exercise price), and the optionee will have short-term or long-term capital gain or loss, as the case may be, in an amount equal to the difference between (i) the amount realized by the optionee upon the disposition of the shares and (ii) the exercise price paid by the optionee increased by the amount of ordinary income, if any, so recognized by the optionee.

Company Deduction.   In all the foregoing cases, the Company will be entitled to a deduction at the same time and in the same amount as the participant recognizes ordinary income, subject to certain limitations. Among these limitations is Section 162(m) of the Internal Revenue Code. As discussed above, certain performance-based compensation is not subject to the Section 162(m) limitation on deductibility. Stock options and restricted stock and performance share awards can qualify for this performance-based exception if they meet the requirements set forth in Section 162(m) and Treasury Regulations promulgated thereunder. The 1997 Plan has been drafted to allow, but not require, compliance with those performance-based criteria.

Finance Law.   If shareholders approve the 1997 Plan and the grant of RSUs otherwise qualify under the Finance Law, grants of qualifying RSUs to French-resident employees subject to the French social regime will be subject to (i) 15.5% social taxes on the value of the RSUs at the time of vesting to the extent such value is below EUR 300,000 and (ii) 18% social taxes on the value of the RSUs at the time of vesting to the extent such value exceeds EUR 300,000, such taxes being imposed at the time of sale of the shares underlying the RSUs. The vesting gain continues to be subject to progressive income tax rates that employees pay upon ultimate sale of shares received under such RSUs but under the Finance Law can be reduced by 50% or more if the shares are held for a specified number of years for the portion of the RSUs having a value at the time of vesting below EUR 300,000. In addition, under the Finance Law, the employing company will be subject to a 30% social tax upon vesting of qualifying RSUs, in contrast to the current 30% social tax that is imposed upon grant of RSUs and is not refunded if RSUs are subsequently forfeited before vesting. The tax consequences of qualifying RSUs to French-resident employees may vary with respect to individual situations; income tax laws, regulations and interpretations thereof change frequently. Participants should rely upon their own tax advisors for advice concerning the specific tax consequences applicable to them, including the applicability and effect of state, local, and foreign tax laws.

A-4

amazon.com

IMPORTANT ANNUAL MEETING INFORMATION

Electronic Voting Instructions

Available 24 hours a day, 7 days a week!

Instead of mailing your proxy, you may choose one of the voting methods outlined below to vote your proxy.

VALIDATION DETAILS ARE LOCATED BELOW IN THE TITLE BAR.

Proxies submitted by the Internet or telephone must be received by 11:59 P.M. Eastern Time on May 22, 2017.

Vote by Internet

- Go to www.envisionreports.com/amzn
- Or scan the QR code with your smartphone
- Follow the steps outlined on the secure website

Vote by telephone

- Call toll free 1-800-652-VOTE (8683) within the USA, US territories & Canada on a touch tone telephone
- Follow the instructions provided by the recorded message

Using a **black ink** pen, mark your votes with an **X** as shown in this example. Please do not write outside the designated areas. [X]

Annual Meeting Proxy Card

▼ IF YOU HAVE NOT VOTED VIA THE INTERNET **OR** TELEPHONE, FOLD ALONG THE PERFORATION, DETACH AND RETURN THE BOTTOM PORTION IN THE ENCLOSED ENVELOPE. ▼

A Proposals — The Board of Directors recommends a vote **FOR** all the nominees listed in Proposal 1, **FOR** Proposals 2 and 3, for every **3 YEARS** for Proposal 4, **FOR** Proposal 5, and **AGAINST** Proposals 6, 7, and 8.

1. ELECTION OF DIRECTORS:

	For	Against	Abstain		For	Against	Abstain		For	Against	Abstain
1a - Jeffrey P. Bezos	☐	☐	☐	1b - Tom A. Alberg	☐	☐	☐	1c - John Seely Brown	☐	☐	☐
1d - Jamie S. Gorelick	☐	☐	☐	1e - Daniel P. Huttenlocher	☐	☐	☐	1f - Judith A. McGrath	☐	☐	☐
1g - Jonathan J. Rubinstein	☐	☐	☐	1h - Thomas O. Ryder	☐	☐	☐	1i - Patricia Q. Stonesifer	☐	☐	☐
1j - Wendell P. Weeks	☐	☐	☐								

	For	Against	Abstain			For	Against	Abstain
2. RATIFICATION OF THE APPOINTMENT OF ERNST & YOUNG LLP AS INDEPENDENT AUDITORS	☐	☐	☐		6. SHAREHOLDER PROPOSAL REGARDING A REPORT ON USE OF CRIMINAL BACKGROUND CHECKS IN HIRING DECISIONS	☐	☐	☐
3. ADVISORY VOTE TO APPROVE EXECUTIVE COMPENSATION	☐	☐	☐		7. SHAREHOLDER PROPOSAL REGARDING SUSTAINABILITY AS AN EXECUTIVE COMPENSATION PERFORMANCE MEASURE	☐	☐	☐

	3 Years	2 Years	1 Year	Abstain			For	Against	Abstain
4. ADVISORY VOTE ON THE FREQUENCY OF FUTURE ADVISORY VOTES ON EXECUTIVE COMPENSATION	☐	☐	☐	☐		8. SHAREHOLDER PROPOSAL REGARDING VOTE-COUNTING PRACTICES FOR SHAREHOLDER PROPOSALS	☐	☐	☐

	For	Against	Abstain
5. APPROVAL OF THE COMPANY'S 1997 STOCK INCENTIVE PLAN, AS AMENDED AND RESTATED	☐	☐	☐

IF VOTING BY MAIL, PLEASE COMPLETE SECTIONS A - C ON BOTH SIDES OF THIS CARD.

1 U P X

02IQ0H

FORM OF PROXY STATEMENT AND FORM OF PROXY

You can view the Annual Report and Proxy Statement on the Internet at http://www.envisionreports.com/amzn

▼ IF YOU HAVE NOT VOTED VIA THE INTERNET OR TELEPHONE, FOLD ALONG THE PERFORATION, DETACH AND RETURN THE BOTTOM PORTION IN THE ENCLOSED ENVELOPE. ▼

amazon.com

Proxy — AMAZON.COM, INC.

Annual Meeting of Shareholders — May 23, 2017
THIS PROXY IS SOLICITED BY THE BOARD OF DIRECTORS OF THE COMPANY

The undersigned shareholder of Amazon.com, Inc., a Delaware corporation (the "Company"), hereby appoints Jeffrey P. Bezos, Brian T. Olsavsky, and David A. Zapolsky, or any one of them, with full power of substitution in each, as proxies to cast all votes that the undersigned is entitled to cast at the Annual Meeting of Shareholders (the "Annual Meeting") of the Company to be held at 9:00 a.m., Pacific Time, on May 23, 2017 at Fremont Studios, 155 N. 35th Street, Seattle, Washington 98103, or any adjournment or postponement thereof, with authority to vote upon the matters set forth on the reverse side of this Proxy Card and in their discretion upon such other matters as may be properly presented at the meeting.

THIS PROXY, WHEN PROPERLY EXECUTED, WILL BE VOTED IN THE MANNER DIRECTED HEREIN BY THE UNDERSIGNED SHAREHOLDER AND IN ACCORDANCE WITH THE DIRECTION OF THE PROXIES AS TO ANY OTHER MATTERS THAT ARE PROPERLY PRESENTED. IF DIRECTION IS NOT GIVEN, THIS PROXY WILL BE VOTED AS THE BOARD OF DIRECTORS RECOMMENDS.

(Continued and to be marked on the other side)

B **Authorized Signatures — This section must be completed for your vote to be counted. — Date and Sign Below**

NOTE: Please sign as name appears hereon. Joint owners should each sign. When signing as attorney, executor, administrator, trustee or guardian, please give full title as such.

Date (mm/dd/yyyy) — Please print date below.	Signature 1 — Please keep signature within the box.	Signature 2 — Please keep signature within the box.
/ /		

C **Non-Voting Items**

Change of Address — Please print your new address below.	Comments — Please print your comments below.	Meeting Attendance
		Mark the box to the right if you plan to attend the Annual Meeting. Proof of ownership and photo ID required for attendance. ☐

IF VOTING BY MAIL, PLEASE COMPLETE SECTIONS A - C ON BOTH SIDES OF THIS CARD.

1106

amazon.com

IMPORTANT ANNUAL MEETING INFORMATION

Electronic Voting Instructions

Available 24 hours a day, 7 days a week!

Instead of mailing your proxy, you may choose one of the voting methods outlined below to vote your proxy.

VALIDATION DETAILS ARE LOCATED BELOW IN THE TITLE BAR.

Proxies submitted by the Internet or telephone must be received by 11:59 P.M. Eastern Time on May 18, 2017.

Vote by Internet

- Go to www.envisionreports.com/amzn
- Or scan the QR code with your smartphone
- Follow the steps outlined on the secure website

Vote by telephone

- Call toll free 1-800-652-VOTE (8683) within the USA, US territories & Canada on a touch tone telephone
- Follow the instructions provided by the recorded message

Using a **black ink** pen, mark your votes with an **X** as shown in this example. Please do not write outside the designated areas. | X |

Annual Meeting Proxy Card

▼ IF YOU HAVE NOT VOTED VIA THE INTERNET **OR** TELEPHONE, FOLD ALONG THE PERFORATION, DETACH AND RETURN THE BOTTOM PORTION IN THE ENCLOSED ENVELOPE. ▼

A Proposals — The Board of Directors recommends a vote **FOR** all the nominees listed in Proposal 1, **FOR** Proposals 2 and 3, for every **3 YEARS** for Proposal 4, **FOR** Proposal 5, and **AGAINST** Proposals 6, 7, and 8.

1. ELECTION OF DIRECTORS:

	For	Against	Abstain		For	Against	Abstain		For	Against	Abstain
1a - Jeffrey P. Bezos	☐	☐	☐	1b - Tom A. Alberg	☐	☐	☐	1c - John Seely Brown	☐	☐	☐
1d - Jamie S. Gorelick	☐	☐	☐	1e - Daniel P. Huttenlocher	☐	☐	☐	1f - Judith A. McGrath	☐	☐	☐
1g - Jonathan J. Rubinstein	☐	☐	☐	1h - Thomas O. Ryder	☐	☐	☐	1i - Patricia Q. Stonesifer	☐	☐	☐
1j - Wendell P. Weeks	☐	☐	☐								

	For	Against	Abstain		For	Against	Abstain
2. RATIFICATION OF THE APPOINTMENT OF ERNST & YOUNG LLP AS INDEPENDENT AUDITORS	☐	☐	☐	6. SHAREHOLDER PROPOSAL REGARDING A REPORT ON USE OF CRIMINAL BACKGROUND CHECKS IN HIRING DECISIONS	☐	☐	☐
3. ADVISORY VOTE TO APPROVE EXECUTIVE COMPENSATION	☐	☐	☐	7. SHAREHOLDER PROPOSAL REGARDING SUSTAINABILITY AS AN EXECUTIVE COMPENSATION PERFORMANCE MEASURE	☐	☐	☐

	3 Years	2 Years	1 Year	Abstain		For	Against	Abstain
4. ADVISORY VOTE ON THE FREQUENCY OF FUTURE ADVISORY VOTES ON EXECUTIVE COMPENSATION	☐	☐	☐	☐	8. SHAREHOLDER PROPOSAL REGARDING VOTE-COUNTING PRACTICES FOR SHAREHOLDER PROPOSALS	☐	☐	☐

	For	Against	Abstain
5. APPROVAL OF THE COMPANY'S 1997 STOCK INCENTIVE PLAN, AS AMENDED AND RESTATED	☐	☐	☐

IF VOTING BY MAIL, PLEASE COMPLETE SECTIONS A - C ON BOTH SIDES OF THIS CARD.

■ 1 U P X +

02IQ6H

FORM OF PROXY STATEMENT AND FORM OF PROXY

▼ IF YOU HAVE NOT VOTED VIA THE INTERNET OR TELEPHONE, FOLD ALONG THE PERFORATION, DETACH AND RETURN THE BOTTOM PORTION IN THE ENCLOSED ENVELOPE. ▼

amazon.com

Proxy — AMAZON.COM, INC.

Annual Meeting of Shareholders — May 23, 2017
THIS PROXY IS SOLICITED BY THE BOARD OF DIRECTORS OF THE COMPANY

The undersigned participant in the Amazon.com Company Stock Fund of the Amazon.com 401(k) Plan hereby directs Vanguard Fiduciary Trust Company, the trustee of the Amazon.com 401(k) Plan, to vote his or her Amazon.com Company Stock Fund shares as indicated on the reverse side of this Proxy Card, or if not so indicated, in accordance with the Amazon.com 401(k) Plan document (generally, in the same proportion as the shares for which the trustee received timely voting instructions).

(Continued and to be marked on the other side)

B Authorized Signatures — This section must be completed for your vote to be counted. — Date and Sign Below

NOTE: Please sign as name appears hereon. Joint owners should each sign. When signing as attorney, executor, administrator, trustee or guardian, please give full title as such.

Date (mm/dd/yyyy) — Please print date below.	Signature 1 — Please keep signature within the box.	Signature 2 — Please keep signature within the box.
/ /		

C Non-Voting Items

Change of Address — Please print your new address below.	Comments — Please print your comments below.	Meeting Attendance
		Mark the box to the right if you plan to attend the Annual Meeting. Proof of ownership and photo ID required for attendance. ☐

IF VOTING BY MAIL, PLEASE COMPLETE SECTIONS A - C ON BOTH SIDES OF THIS CARD.

1108

amazon.com

April 12, 2017

**Re: Important Notice Regarding the Availability of Proxy Materials for the
Amazon.com, Inc. Shareholder Meeting to be Held on May 23, 2017**

Dear 401(k) Plan Participant:

Enclosed are the 2016 Annual Report for Amazon.com, Inc. (the "Company") and a Proxy Statement and proxy card for the Company's 2017 Annual Meeting of Shareholders. You can view the Annual Report and Proxy Statement on the Internet at http://www.envisionreports.com/amzn.

The Amazon.com 401(k) Plan allows each plan participant to direct the voting of the shares of common stock of the Company that are allocated to the participant's 401(k) plan account. By following the instructions for Internet, mobile device, or telephone voting on the enclosed proxy card, or by marking, signing, and mailing the proxy card in the envelope provided, you may instruct Vanguard Fiduciary Trust Company, the trustee of the Amazon.com 401(k) Plan, how to vote the shares of the common stock of the Company allocated to your 401(k) plan account on the matters presented at the Company's 2017 Annual Meeting. The trustee will vote as you have directed. All shares for which voting instructions are not timely received will be voted by the trustee on each matter in the same proportion as the shares for which the trustee received timely voting instructions, except in the case where to do so would be inconsistent with applicable law. Your vote will be kept confidential except to the extent necessary to comply with applicable law.

Votes will be tabulated by the Company's transfer agent, Computershare. To be timely, your voting instructions must be received by Computershare no later than 11:59 PM Eastern Time on May 18, 2017.

VOTING VIA THE INTERNET, MOBILE DEVICE, OR BY TELEPHONE IS FAST AND CONVENIENT, AND YOUR VOTE IS IMMEDIATELY CONFIRMED AND TABULATED. USING THE INTERNET, MOBILE DEVICE, OR TELEPHONE HELPS SAVE YOUR COMPANY MONEY BY REDUCING POSTAGE AND PROXY TABULATION COSTS.

RICHARDS, LAYTON & FINGER, P.A.
FORUM SELECTION BYLAW

Section [_____]. <u>Forum Selection Bylaw</u>. Unless the Corporation consents in writing to the selection of an alternative forum, the Court of Chancery of the State of Delaware shall, to the fullest extent permitted by law, be the sole and exclusive forum for (1) any derivative action or proceeding brought on behalf of the Corporation, (2) any action asserting a claim of breach of a fiduciary duty owed by any current or former director, officer or stockholder of the Corporation to the Corporation or the Corporation's stockholders, (3) any action asserting a claim arising pursuant to any provision of the General Corporation Law of the State of Delaware, the Certificate of Incorporation or these Bylaws or as to which the General Corporation Law of the State of Delaware confers jurisdiction on the Court of Chancery of the State of Delaware, or (4) any action asserting a claim governed by the internal affairs doctrine. Any person or entity purchasing or otherwise acquiring or holding any interest in shares of capital stock of the Corporation shall be deemed to have notice of and consented to the provisions of this Section [_____].

AGREEMENT BETWEEN ACTIVIST INVESTOR AND PUBLIC COMPANY

SUPPORT AGREEMENT

This Support Agreement, dated November 20, 2014 (this "Agreement"), is by and among (i) Third Point LLC, Third Point Partners Qualified L.P., Third Point Partners L.P., Third Point Offshore Master Fund L.P., Third Point Ultra Master Fund L.P. and Third Point Reinsurance Co. Ltd. (collectively, "Third Point", and each individually, a "member" of Third Point) and (ii) The Dow Chemical Company (the "Company").

WHEREAS, Third Point and its Affiliates beneficially own 27,500,000 shares of common stock of the Company, par value $2.50 (the "Common Stock") of the Common Stock issued and outstanding on the date hereof; and

WHEREAS, the Company has determined that it is in the best interests of the Company and its stockholders and Third Point has determined that it is in its best interests to come to an agreement with respect to the election of members of the Company's Board of Directors (the "Board") at the Company's 2015 Annual Meeting of Stockholders (the "2015 Annual Meeting") and certain other matters, as provided in this Agreement.

NOW, THEREFORE, in consideration of and reliance upon the mutual covenants and agreements contained herein, and for other good and valuable consideration, the receipt and sufficiency of which is hereby acknowledged, the parties hereto agree as follows:

1. Board Representation and Board Matters.

(a) The Company and Third Point agree as follows:

(i) the Board shall take all action necessary (A) to increase the size of the Board by three directors to 13 directors, effective as of January 1, 2015, and (B) to appoint each of Robert Steven Miller and Raymond J. Milchovich (collectively, the "Designees") and Mark Loughridge to serve as directors of the Company, effective as of January 1, 2015, until the later of (1) the 2015 Annual Meeting and (2) the date that their successors are duly elected and qualified, subject to the terms of this Agreement;

(ii) the Company's slate of nominees for election as directors of the Company at the Company's 2015 Annual Meeting shall include (A) the Designees, (B) Mark Loughridge, (C) Richard Davis, who will replace a then-current director, other than the Designees and Mark Loughridge, and (D) no more than nine other nominees identified and approved by the Governance Committee and the Board;

(iii) the Company will use its reasonable best efforts to cause the election of each of the Designees to the Company's Board at the 2015 Annual Meeting (including recommending that the Company's stockholders vote in favor of the election of the Designees (along with all other Company nominees) and otherwise supporting each of them for election in a manner no less rigorous and favorable than the manner in which the Company supports its other nominees in the aggregate);

(iv) the Company shall take all action necessary to decrease the size of the Board to 12 directors by the completion of the Company's 2016 Annual Meeting of Shareholders (the "2016 Annual Meeting");

(v) that no later than the date of this Agreement, Third Point will provide to the Company an executed letter in the form attached hereto as Exhibit A, which includes a consent from each Designee to be named as a nominee in the Company's proxy statement for the 2015 Annual Meeting and to serve as a director if so elected (the "Nominee Letter");

(vi) that for so long as the following Designees serve on the Board, such Designee shall be offered the opportunity to become a member of the committees of the Board as follows:

(1) Robert Steven Miller, Governance Committee; and

(2) Raymond J. Milchovich, Compensation and Leadership Development Committee; and

(vii) at all times prior to completion of the 2016 Annual Meeting and provided that at least one Designee remains a member of the Board, at least one Designee shall be offered the opportunity to be a member of each committee of the Board which may be created by the Board following execution hereof, and upon election to become such a member the Board shall effect such change in committee composition immediately (and no less than two business days following such election), assuming the absence of conflicts of interest involving such Designee relevant to such committee's activities.

2. <u>Certain Other Matters</u>.

(a) Each Designee shall be entitled to resign from the Board at any time in his discretion. For purposes of this Agreement, the "<u>Standstill Period</u>" shall mean the period from the date of this Agreement until 12:01 a.m. on the forty-fifth (45th) day prior to the advance notice deadline for making director nominations at the Company's 2016 Annual Meeting. If any Designee agrees to be included as a director nominee for election at any Stockholders Meeting other than as a director nominated by the Board for election at such Stockholders Meeting, the irrevocable resignation provision set forth in the Nominee Letter previously provided by such Designee shall become effective.

(b) The Company agrees that for so long as any of the Designees are on the Board, Third Point may request notice from the Company as to whether the Board intends to nominate each Designee for election at the 2016 Annual Meeting and the Company shall notify Third Point in writing of its then-current intentions with respect to the nomination of such Designee for election at the 2016 Annual Meeting (which written notice from the Company shall be delivered to Third Point by the later of forty-five (45) days prior to the advance notice deadline for making director nominations at the Company's 2016 Annual Meeting or ten business days following the Company's receipt of such request from Third Point). In the event that the Company's notifies Third Point pursuant to the immediately preceding sentence of its intent to nominate a Designee for election at the 2016 Annual Meeting, the Company shall so nominate such Designee (including recommending that the Company's stockholders vote in favor of the election of the Designees (along with all other Company nominees) and otherwise supporting each of them for election in a manner no less rigorous and favorable than the manner in which the Company supports its other nominees in the aggregate), unless (i) the Board determines, based on the advice of outside counsel, that it is required as a result of its fiduciary duties not to make such nomination, (ii) such Designee resigns from his position as a director of the Company or (iii) Third Point or any Third Point Affiliate takes any of the actions referenced in Section 2(c)(i), (iv) and, solely as it relates to the action referenced in clause (i) or (iv), clause (iii).

(c) During the Standstill Period, no member of Third Point shall, directly or indirectly (it being understood that any actions taken by Daniel S. Loeb shall be deemed to be actions taken by Third Point), and each member of Third Point shall cause each Third Point Affiliate (as defined below) it controls and Daniel S. Loeb not to, directly or indirectly:

(i) solicit proxies or written consents of stockholders or conduct any other type of referendum (binding or non-binding) with respect to, or from the holders of, the Voting Securities (as defined below), or become a "participant" (as such term is defined in Instruction 3 to Item 4 of Schedule 14A promulgated under the Securities Exchange Act of 1934, as amended (the "Exchange Act")) in or assist any person or entity not a party to this agreement (a "Third Party") in any "solicitation" of any proxy, consent or other authority (as such terms are defined under the Exchange Act) to vote any shares of the Voting Securities (other than such encouragement, advice or influence that is consistent with Company management's recommendation in connection with such matter);

(ii) encourage, advise or influence any other person or assist any Third Party in so encouraging, assisting or influencing any person with respect to the giving or withholding of any proxy, consent or other authority to vote or in conducting any type of referendum (other than such encouragement, advice or influence that is consistent with Company management's recommendation in connection with such matter);

(iii) form or join in a partnership, limited partnership, syndicate or other group, including a "group" as defined under Section 13(d) of the Exchange Act, with respect to the Voting Securities (for the avoidance of doubt, excluding any group composed solely of Third Point and their Affiliates) or otherwise support or participate in any effort by a Third Party with respect to the matters set forth in clauses (i), (vii) or (ix) herein;

(iv) present at any annual meeting or any special meeting of the Company's stockholders any proposal for consideration for action by stockholders or seek the removal of any member of the Board or propose any nominee for election to the Board or seek representation on the Board;

(v) other than in market transactions where the identity of the purchaser is not known and in underwritten widely dispersed public offerings, sell, offer or agree to sell directly or indirectly, through swap or hedging transactions or otherwise, the securities of the Company or any rights decoupled from the underlying securities held by Third Point to any Third Party unless (A) such Third Party is a passive investor that has not filed a Schedule 13D and would not as a result of the purchase of the securities of the Company be required to file a Schedule 13D and (B) such sale, offer, or agreement to sell would not knowingly result in such Third Party, together with its Affiliates, owning, controlling or otherwise having any beneficial or other ownership interest in the aggregate of 9.9% or more of the shares of Common Stock outstanding at such time or would increase the beneficial or other ownership interest of any Third Party who, together with its Affiliates, has a beneficial or other ownership interest in the aggregate of 9.9% or more of the shares of Common Stock outstanding at such time, except in each case in a transaction approved by the Board;

(vi) grant any proxy, consent or other authority to vote with respect to any matters (other than to the named proxies included in the Company's proxy card for any annual meeting or special meeting of stockholders) or deposit any Voting Securities of the Company in a voting trust or subject them to a voting agreement or other arrangement of similar effect with respect to any annual meeting except as provided in Section 2(d) below, special meeting of stockholders or action by written consent (excluding customary brokerage accounts, margin accounts, prime brokerage accounts and the like);

(vii) make any request for stocklist materials or other books and records of the Company under Section 220 of the Delaware General Corporation Law or otherwise;

(viii) make, or cause to be made, any statement or announcement that relates to and constitutes an ad hominem attack on, or relates to and otherwise disparages, the Company or its business, operations or financial performance, its officers or its directors or any person who has served as an officer or director of the Company in the past, or who serves on or following the date of this Agreement as an officer, director or agent of the Company: (A) in any document or report filed with or furnished to the SEC or any other governmental agency, (B) in any press release or other publicly available format, or (C) to any analyst, journalist or member of the media (including without limitation, in a television, radio, internet, newspaper or magazine interview) (and the Company agrees that this Section 2(c)(viii) shall apply mutatis mutandis to the Company and its directors and officers with respect to Third Point);

(ix) institute, solicit or join, as a party, any litigation, arbitration or other proceeding against the Company or any of its current or former directors or officers (including derivative actions), other than (A) litigation by Third Point to enforce the provisions of this Agreement, (B) counterclaims with respect to any proceeding initiated by, or on behalf of, the Company or its Affiliates against Third Point or a Designee and (C) the exercise of statutory appraisal rights; provided that the foregoing shall not prevent any member of Third Point from responding to or complying with a validly issued legal process (and the Company agrees that this Section 2(c)(ix) shall apply mutatis mutandis to the Company and its directors and officers with respect to Third Point);

(x) without the prior written approval of the Board, separately or in conjunction with any other person or entity in which it is or proposes to be either a principal, partner or financing source or is acting or proposes to act as broker or agent for compensation, propose (publicly, privately or to the Company) or effect any tender offer or exchange offer, merger, acquisition, reorganization, restructuring, recapitalization or other business combination involving the Company or a material amount of the assets or businesses of the Company or actively encourage, initiate or support any other Third Party in any such activity;

(xi) purchase or cause to be purchased or otherwise acquire or agree to acquire Beneficial Ownership of any Voting Securities, if in any such case, immediately after the taking of such action, Third Point would, in the aggregate, collectively beneficially own, or have an economic interest in, an amount that would exceed 4.99% of the then outstanding shares of Common Stock;

(xii) enter into any negotiations, agreements, arrangements or understandings with any Third Party with respect to the matters set forth in this Section 2; or

(xiii) request, directly or indirectly, any amendment or waiver of the foregoing in a manner that would be reasonably likely to require public disclosure by Third Point or the Company.

As used in this Agreement, the term "Voting Securities" shall mean the Common Stock, and any other securities of the Company entitled to vote in the election of directors, or securities convertible into, or exercisable or exchangeable for Common Stock or other securities, whether or not subject to the passage of time or other contingencies.

As used in this Agreement, the term "Beneficial Ownership" of "Voting Securities" means ownership of: (i) Voting Securities and (ii) rights or options to own or acquire any Voting Securities (whether such right or option is exercisable immediately or only after the passage of time or upon the satisfaction of one or more conditions (whether or not within the control of such person), compliance with regulatory requirements or otherwise). For purposes of this Section 2, no Person shall be, or be deemed to be, the "Beneficial Owner" of, or to "beneficially own," any securities beneficially owned by any director of the Company to the extent such securities were acquired directly from the Company by such director as or pursuant to director compensation for serving as a director of the Company.

(d) Until the end of the Standstill Period, Third Point together with all controlled Affiliates of the members of Third Point (such controlled Affiliates, collectively and individually, the "Third Point Affiliates") shall cause all Voting Securities owned by them directly or indirectly, whether owned of record or Beneficially Owned, as of the record date for any annual or special meeting of stockholders or in connection with any solicitation of stockholder action by written consent (each a "Stockholders Meeting") within the Standstill Period, in each case that are entitled to vote at any such Stockholders Meeting, to be present for quorum purposes and to be voted, at all such Stockholders Meetings or at any adjournments or postponements thereof, (i) for all directors nominated by the Board for election at such Stockholders Meeting and (ii) in accordance with the recommendation of the Board on any precatory or non-binding proposals and any non-transaction-related proposals that come before any Stockholder Meeting.

3. Public Announcements. Promptly following the execution of this Agreement, (a) the Company and Third Point shall announce this Agreement by means of a jointly issued press release in the form attached hereto as Exhibit B (the "Joint Press Release") and (b) the Company shall announce the agreement to appoint four new directors to the Board by means of a press release in the form attached hereto as Exhibit C (the "Dow Release"). Neither the Company (and the Company shall cause each of its Affiliates, directors and officers not to) nor Third Point (it being understood that any actions taken by Daniel S. Loeb shall be deemed to be actions taken by Third Point) or any Third Point Affiliate shall make or cause to be made any public announcement or statement with respect to the subject of this Agreement that is contrary to the statements made in the Press Release and the Dow Release, except as required by law or the rules of any stock exchange or with the prior written consent of the other party.

4. Representations and Warranties of All Parties. Each of the parties represents and warrants to the other party that: (a) such party has all requisite power and authority to execute and deliver this Agreement and to perform its obligations hereunder; (b) this Agreement has been duly and validly authorized, executed and delivered by it and is a valid and binding obligation of such party, enforceable against such party in accordance with its terms; and (c) this Agreement will not result in a violation of any terms or conditions of any agreements to which such person is a party or by which such party may otherwise be bound or of any law, rule, license, regulation, judgment, order or decree governing or affecting such party.

5. Representations and Warranties of Third Point. Each member of Third Point jointly represents and warrants that, as of the date of this Agreement, (a) Third Point, together with all of the Third Point Affiliates, collectively Beneficially Own, an aggregate of 27,500,000 shares of Common Stock, (b) except for such ownership, no member of Third Point, individually or in the aggregate with all other members of Third Point and the Third Point Affiliates, has any other Beneficial Ownership of any Voting Securities and (c) Third Point, collectively with the Third Point Affiliates, have a Net Long Position of 18,250,000 shares of Common Stock. The term "Net Long Position" shall mean: such shares of Common Stock Beneficially Owned, directly or indirectly, that constitute such person's net long position as defined in Rule 14e–4 under the Exchange Act mutatis mutandis, provided that "Net Long Position" shall not include any shares as to which such person does not have the right to vote or direct the vote; and the terms "person" or "persons" shall mean any individual, corporation (including not-for-profit), general or limited partnership, limited liability or unlimited liability company, joint venture, estate, trust, association, organization or other entity of any kind or nature.

6. <u>Miscellaneous</u>. The parties hereto recognize and agree that if for any reason any of the provisions of this Agreement are not performed in accordance with their specific terms or are otherwise breached, immediate and irreparable harm or injury would be caused for which money damages would not be an adequate remedy. Accordingly, each party agrees that in addition to other remedies the other party shall be entitled to at law or equity, the other party shall be entitled to seek an injunction or injunctions to prevent breaches of this Agreement and to enforce specifically the terms and provisions of this Agreement exclusively in the Court of Chancery or other federal or state courts of the State of Delaware. Furthermore, each of the parties hereto (a) consents to submit itself to the personal jurisdiction of the Court of Chancery or other federal or state courts of the State of Delaware in the event any dispute arises out of this Agreement or the transactions contemplated by this Agreement, (b) agrees that it shall not attempt to deny or defeat such personal jurisdiction by motion or other request for leave from any such court, (c) agrees that it shall not bring any action relating to this Agreement or the transactions contemplated by this Agreement in any court other than the Court of Chancery or other federal or state courts of the State of Delaware, and each of the parties irrevocably waives the right to trial by jury and (d) irrevocably consents to service of process by a reputable overnight mail delivery service, signature requested, to the address of such party's principal place of business or as otherwise provided by applicable law. THIS AGREEMENT SHALL BE GOVERNED IN ALL RESPECTS, INCLUDING VALIDITY, INTERPRETATION AND EFFECT, BY THE LAWS OF THE STATE OF DELAWARE APPLICABLE TO CONTRACTS EXECUTED AND TO BE PERFORMED WHOLLY WITHIN SUCH STATE WITHOUT GIVING EFFECT TO THE CHOICE OF LAW PRINCIPLES OF SUCH STATE.

7. <u>No Waiver</u>. Any waiver by any party of a breach of any provision of this Agreement shall not operate as or be construed to be a waiver of any other breach of such provision or of any breach of any other provision of this Agreement. The failure of a party to insist upon strict adherence to any term of this Agreement on one or more occasions shall not be considered a waiver or deprive that party of the right thereafter to insist upon strict adherence to that term or any other term of this Agreement.

8. <u>Entire Agreement</u>. This Agreement contains the entire understanding of the parties with respect to the subject matter hereof and may be amended only by an agreement in writing executed by the parties hereto.

9. <u>Notices</u>. All notices, consents, requests, instructions, approvals and other communications provided for herein and all legal process in regard hereto shall be in writing and shall be deemed validly given, made or served, if (a) given by email, when such email is sent to the email address set forth below during normal business hours and the appropriate confirmation is received or (b) if given by any other means, when actually received during normal business hours at the address specified in this subsection:

If to the Company:	The Dow Chemical Company
	2030 Dow Center
	Midland, Michigan 48674
	Attention: Charles J. Kalil, General Counsel,
	Corporate Secretary, Executive Vice President
	Email: CJKalil@dow.com
	and
	Attention: Howard I. Ungerleider, Chief Financial Officer,
	Executive Vice President
	Email: HIUngerleider@dow.com

With a copy to (which shall not constitute notice):

Weil, Gotshal & Manges LLP

767 Fifth Avenue

New York, New York 10153

Attention: Michael J. Aiello

Email: michael.aiello@weil.com

If to Third Point: c/o Third Point LLC

390 Park Avenue, 18th Floor

New York, New York 10022

Attention: Josh Targoff,

Chief Operating Officer and

General Counsel

Email: jtargoff@thirdpoint.com

With a copy to (which shall not constitute notice):

Willkie Farr & Gallagher LLP

787 Seventh Avenue, 34th Floor

New York, New York 10019

Attention: Steven J. Gartner

Morgan D. Elwyn

Email: sgartner@willkie.com

melwyn@willkie.com

10. Severability. If at any time subsequent to the date hereof, any provision of this Agreement shall be held by any court of competent jurisdiction to be illegal, void or unenforceable, such provision shall be of no force and effect, but the illegality or unenforceability of such provision shall have no effect upon the legality or enforceability of any other provision of this Agreement.

11. Counterparts. This Agreement may be executed in two or more counterparts which together shall constitute a single agreement.

12. Successors and Assigns. This Agreement shall not be assignable by any of the parties to this Agreement. This Agreement, however, shall be binding on successors of the parties hereto.

13. No Third Party Beneficiaries. This Agreement is solely for the benefit of the parties hereto and is not enforceable by any other persons.

14. Fees and Expenses. Each party to this Agreement shall bear and pay all fees, costs and expenses that have been incurred or that are incurred in the future by such party in connection with, relating to or resulting from such party's efforts and actions, and any preparations therefor, prior to the execution and delivery of this Agreement, including, without limitation, communications between Third Point, on the one hand, and the Board and the Company's management, on the other hand, Third Point's Schedule 14A and Hart-Scott-Rodino filings, and such party's preparation of soliciting materials and this Agreement.

15. Interpretation and Construction. Each of the parties hereto acknowledges that it has been represented by counsel of its choice throughout all negotiations that have preceded the execution of this Agreement, and that it has executed the same with the advice of said independent counsel. Each party and its counsel cooperated and participated in the drafting and preparation of this Agreement and the documents referred to herein, and any and all drafts relating thereto exchanged among the parties shall be deemed the work product of all of the parties and may not be construed against any party by reason of its drafting or preparation. Accordingly, any rule of law or any legal decision that would require interpretation of any ambiguities in this Agreement against any party that drafted or prepared it is of no application and

is hereby expressly waived by each of the parties hereto, and any controversy over interpretations of this Agreement shall be decided without regards to events of drafting or preparation. The section headings contained in this Agreement are for reference purposes only and shall not affect in any way the meaning or interpretation of this Agreement. The term "including" shall be deemed to mean "including without limitation" in all instances.

16. <u>Liability Several and Not Joint</u>. Notwithstanding anything contained herein to the contrary, the obligations of the members of Third Point hereunder are several and not joint or collective.

[Signature Pages Follow]

IN WITNESS WHEREOF, each of the parties hereto has executed this Agreement, or caused the same to be executed by its duly authorized representative as of the date first above written.

THE DOW CHEMICAL COMPANY

By: /s/ Charles J. Kalil

Name: Charles J. Kalil

Title: General Counsel, Corporate Secretary and Executive Vice President

THIRD POINT LLC

By: /s/ Josh Targoff

Name: Josh Targoff

Title: Chief Operating Officer and General Counsel

THIRD POINT PARTNERS L.P.

By: Third Point LLC, its investment manager

By: /s/ Josh Targoff

Name: Josh Targoff

Title: Chief Operating Officer and General Counsel

THIRD POINT PARTNERS QUALIFIED L.P.

By: Third Point LLC, its investment manager

By: /s/ Josh Targoff

Name: Josh Targoff

Title: Chief Operating Officer and General Counsel

THIRD POINT OFFSHORE MASTER FUND L.P.

By: Third Point LLC, its investment manager

By: /s/ Josh Targoff

Name: Josh Targoff

Title: Chief Operating Officer and General Counsel

AGREEMENT BETWEEN ACTIVIST INVESTOR
AND PUBLIC COMPANY

THIRD POINT ULTRA MASTER FUND L.P.

By: Third Point LLC, its investment manager

By: /s/ Josh Targoff

Name: Josh Targoff

Title: Chief Operating Officer and General Counsel

THIRD POINT REINSURANCE CO. LTD.

By: Third Point LLC, its investment manager

By: /s/ Josh Targoff

Name: Josh Targoff

Title: Chief Operating Officer and General Counsel

SIGNATURE PAGE TO SUPPORT AGREEMENT

EXHIBIT A

FORM OF NOMINEE LETTER

November 20, 2014

Attention: Board of Directors

The Dow Chemical Company

2030 Dow Center

Midland, MI 48674

Re: Consent and Resignation

Ladies and Gentlemen:

This letter is delivered pursuant to Sections 1(a)(v) and 2(a) of the Support Agreement, dated as of November 20, 2014 (the "Agreement"), by and among The Dow Chemical Company and Third Point (as defined therein). Capitalized terms used herein but not defined shall have the meaning set forth in the Agreement.

In connection with the Agreement, I hereby consent to (i) serve as a director of the Company effective January 1, 2015, (ii) be named as a nominee for the position of director of the Company in the Company's proxy statement for the 2015 Annual Meeting and (iii) serve as a director if I am so elected at the 2015 Annual Meeting. I also agree that, after the date hereof, I will provide to the Company, as requested by the Company from time to time, such information as the Company is entitled to reasonably receive from other members of the Board and as is required to be disclosed in proxy statements under applicable law.

Consistent with existing Company policies and the treatment of all other directors of the Company and assuming the absence of conflicts of interest involving me relevant to such committee's activities, at all times that I am a director of the Company, regardless of whether a member of such committee, I shall be entitled to attend any meeting of any committee of the Board and participate as a non-voting member (if not a committee member), including the right to receive any materials distributed to any committee members.

At all times while serving as a member of the Board, I agree to comply with all policies, procedures, processes, codes, rules, standards and guidelines applicable to Board members, including the Company's code of business conduct and ethics, securities trading policies, anti-hedging policies, Regulation FD-related policies, director confidentiality policies, related party transaction policy and Corporate Governance Guidelines, in each case that have been identified to me, and preserve the confidentiality of Company business and information, including discussions or matters considered in meetings of the Board or Board committees.

AGREEMENT BETWEEN ACTIVIST INVESTOR
AND PUBLIC COMPANY

Following January 1, 2015, effective only upon, and subject to, such time as I agree to be included as a director nominee for election at any Stockholders Meeting, other than as a director nominated by the Board for election at such Stockholders Meeting, I hereby resign from my position as a director of the Company and from any and all committees of the Board on which I serve.

This resignation may not be withdrawn by me at any time during which it is effective.

Sincerely,

_____

Name:

EXHIBIT B

JOINT PRESS RELEASE

The Dow Chemical Company and Third Point Reach Agreement

MIDLAND, Michigan and NEW YORK, NY—November 21, 2014

(BUSINESS WIRE)—The Dow Chemical Company (NYSE: DOW) and Third Point LLC (NYSE: TPRE) today announced a comprehensive agreement to add four new, independent directors to Dow's Board. [link to Board announcement] Mark Loughridge, Ray Milchovich and R. "Steve" Miller will join the Board on January 1, 2015. Richard Davis will join in May 2015 following the 2015 Annual Meeting of Shareholders.

The agreement also provides that:

- The four independent directors will be included in Dow's nominees for election at the 2015 Annual Meeting.

- Third Point will vote in favor of the company's nominees at the 2015 Annual Meeting.

- Thirteen directors will stand for election at the 2015 Annual Meeting. However, Dow has agreed to reduce the size of its Board to twelve members before its Annual Meeting in 2016.

- Third Point has agreed to a one year customary standstill and voting agreement.

Dow and Third Point will be making no further public comment on the matter and both are pleased to have resolved the matter amicably and to have arrived at an agreeable path forward.

The complete agreement between Dow and Third Point will be included as an exhibit to a Current Report on Form 8-K, which will be filed with the Securities and Exchange Commission.

###

Dow Contact:

Rebecca Bentley

+1 989 638 8568

rmbentley@dow.com

About Dow

Dow (NYSE: DOW) combines the power of science and technology to passionately innovate what is essential to human progress. The Company is driving innovations that extract value from the intersection of chemical, physical and biological sciences to help address many of the world's most challenging problems such as the need for clean water, clean energy generation and conservation, and increasing agricultural productivity. Dow's integrated, market-driven, industry-leading portfolio of specialty chemical, advanced materials, agrosciences and plastics businesses delivers a broad range of technology-based products and solutions to customers in approximately 180 countries and in high growth sectors such as packaging, electronics, water, coatings and agriculture. In 2013, Dow had annual sales of more than $57 billion and employed approximately 53,000 people worldwide. The Company's more than 6,000 products are manufactured at 201 sites in 36 countries across the globe. References to "Dow" or the "Company" mean The Dow Chemical Company and its consolidated subsidiaries unless otherwise expressly noted. More information about Dow can be found at www.dow.com.

About Third Point LLC: Third Point LLC is an SEC-registered investment adviser headquartered in New York, managing over $17 billion in assets. Founded in 1995, Third Point follows an event-driven approach to investing globally.

Contact:

Elissa Doyle

Managing Director of Communications

edoyle@thirdpoint.com

(212) 715-4907

EXHIBIT C

COMPANY RELEASE

Dow to Add New Independent Directors to Its Board

MIDLAND, Michigan—November 21, 2014

(BUSINESS WIRE)—The Dow Chemical Company (NYSE: DOW) today announced it will add four new independent directors to its Board:

- Mr. Richard Davis, Chairman, President and CEO of U.S. Bancorp
- Mr. Mark Loughridge, former Chief Financial Officer of IBM
- Mr. Raymond J. Milchovich, Lead Director of Nucor and former Chairman and CEO of Foster Wheeler AG
- Mr. Robert S. (Steve) Miller, non-executive Chairman of the Board of American International Group (AIG); Former Chief Executive Officer, Hawker Beechcraft, Inc.; Former Executive Chairman, Delphi

All four individuals will be included in Dow's nominations for election at the 2015 Annual Meeting of Shareholders.

Loughridge, Milchovich and Miller will join the Board effective January 1, 2015, and Davis will join the Board in May 2015, following Dow's 2015 Annual Meeting.

As a result of today's announcement, Dow's Board will increase from 10 to 13 members, as of January 1, 2015.

* * *

Mr. Mark Loughridge

Former SVP and CFO, IBM

Mr. Mark Loughridge was named IBM's Senior Vice President and Chief Financial Officer in May 2004. He was given the additional responsibility for Enterprise Transformation in July 2010 to lead IBM's ongoing integration and transformation as well as continue in his role as CFO. Loughridge retired from this position in December 2013 after 36 years with IBM. He joined the company in 1977, where he started as a development engineer in the Office Products Division in Lexington, KY.

He holds a Master of Business Administration degree from the University of Chicago Booth School of Business, a bachelor's degree in mechanical engineering from Stanford University and completed studies at Ecole Nationale Superieure de Mecaniquein Nantes, France.

In 2010, Loughridge was rated by the buy-side analysts as the top rated CFO in the IT Hardware Sector by Institutional Investor. In 2012, he was ranked the #1 CFO in America by the Wall Street Journal, and named the "Executive Dream Team" CFO by Fortune Magazine, and the "Best CFO" in the IT hardware category by Institutional Investor.

Loughridge serves on the Board of Directors of The Vanguard Group. He is also a member of the Council on Chicago Booth.

AGREEMENT BETWEEN ACTIVIST INVESTOR
AND PUBLIC COMPANY

Raymond J. Milchovich

Lead Director, Nucor Corp; Former Chief Executive Officer, Chairman and President, Foster Wheeler AG

Mr. Milchovich has served as the Lead Director of Nucor since September 2013. Mr. Milchovich served as non-executive Chairman of the board of directors of, and a consultant to, Foster Wheeler AG, a Switzerland-based global engineering and construction company serving primarily the energy infrastructure markets, from 2010 until his retirement in 2011. Previously, Mr. Milchovich served as the Chairman and Chief Executive Officer of Foster Wheeler from 2001 to 2010 and as President from 2001 to 2007. Prior to that, Mr. Milchovich served as Chairman, President and Chief Executive Officer of Kaiser Aluminum & Chemical Corporation, a producer and marketer of alumina, aluminum and aluminum fabricated products, from 1999 to 2001, and as President and Chief Operating Officer from 1997 to 1999.

Mr. Milchovich began his career in the steel industry, holding a variety of operating management positions for Wisconsin Steel Corporation and Wheeling-Pittsburgh Steel Corporation. From 2002 to 2007, Mr. Milchovich served as a director of Nucor and voluntarily resigned from such position to devote more time to his position as Chief Executive Officer of Foster Wheeler. Mr. Milchovich was also a director of Delphi Corporation from 2005 through 2009. In serving as Chief Executive Officer of two different companies for more than ten years, Mr. Milchovich developed strong leadership and strategic management skills. Mr. Milchovich has more than 30 years of experience in the metals industry.

At Nucor, Mr. Milchovich is the Chairman of the Governance & Nominating Committee and a member of the Audit Committee and the Compensation & Executive Development Committee.

Mr. Milchovich holds a Bachelor of Science from the California University of Pennsylvania and Advanced Management Program from Harvard University.

Robert S. Miller

Non-Executive Chairman of the Board, AIG, Inc.; Former Chief Executive Officer, Hawker Beechcraft, Inc. Former Executive Chairman, Delphi

Mr. Miller is Chairman of the Board of American International Group (AIG), and Chairman of MidOcean Partners, a private equity firm specializing in leveraged buyouts, recapitalizations and growth capital investments in middle-market companies.

Mr. Miller served as Chief Executive Officer of Hawker Beechcraft, an aircraft manufacturing company, from February 2012 to February 2013. He served as Executive Chairman of Delphi Corporation from January 2007 until November 2009 and as Chairman and Chief Executive Officer from July 2005 until January 2007. From January 2004 to June 2005, Mr. Miller was non-executive Chairman of Federal Mogul Corporation. From September 2001 until December 2003, Mr. Miller was Chairman and Chief Executive Officer of Bethlehem Steel Corporation. Prior to joining Bethlehem Steel, Mr. Miller served as Chairman and Chief Executive Officer on an interim basis upon the departure of Federal Mogul's top executive in September 2000.

Mr. Miller began his career in 1968 at Ford Motor Company and after more than a decade there joined Chrysler Corporation where he worked for 13 years, eventually serving as Vice Chairman. While at Chrysler, corporate staffs, financial services, international automotive operations, and non-automotive operations all reported to him. Mr. Miller led the financial negotiations with 400 bank lenders and the Federal government, which resulted in the Loan Guarantee Act bailout package in 1980 that saved Chrysler.

Mr. Miller currently serves as a Director of Symantec (NASDAQ: SYMC) and WL Ross Holding Corp. (NASDAQ: WLRH). Mr. Miller has previously served as a director of a variety of companies, including United Airlines Corporation, Reynolds American, Inc., U.S. Bancorp, and Waste Management, Inc.

Mr. Miller earned a degree in economics from Stanford University, a law degree from Harvard Law School and a master's of business administration, majoring in finance from Stanford Business School.

Mr. Richard Davis

Chairman, President and CEO, U.S. Bancorp

Mr. Richard Davis is Chairman, President and Chief Executive Officer of Minneapolis-based U.S. Bancorp, the fifth largest bank in the United States. Mr. Davis has served as Chairman of U.S. Bancorp since

December 2007, Chief Executive Officer since December 2006, and President since October 2004. He also served as Chief Operating Officer from October 2004 until December 2006.

Mr. Davis was also an Executive Vice President at Bank of America and Security Pacific Bank prior to joining Star Banc Corporation, which was one of U S Bancorp's legacy companies.

Mr. Davis brings extensive leadership skills and financial services industry experience and knowledge to the Board. During his career, he has served as Chairman of the Financial Services Roundtable, Chairman of the Consumer Bankers Association, Chairman of The Clearing House, and representative for the Ninth District of the Federal Reserve, where he was President of its Financial Advisory Committee. Additionally, his service as lead director of the Xcel Energy board of directors broadens his experience of overseeing management in an industry subject to extensive regulation.

Mr. Davis also currently serves on the board of directors of the National American Red Cross, The Itasca Project, the Minnesota Business Partnership, The Minnesota Institute of Arts, the Twin Cities YMCA, and the University of San Diego. He was also one of three executive co-Chairs that made the presentation to the NFL to secure the Super Bowl coming to Minneapolis in 2018. He continues to serve on the 2018 Super Bowl Host Committee.

* * *

Dow Contact:

Rebecca Bentley

+1 989 638 8568

rmbentley@dow.com

About Dow

Dow (NYSE: DOW) combines the power of science and technology to passionately innovate what is essential to human progress. The Company is driving innovations that extract value from the intersection of chemical, physical and biological sciences to help address many of the world's most challenging problems such as the need for clean water, clean energy generation and conservation, and increasing agricultural productivity. Dow's integrated, market-driven, industry-leading portfolio of specialty chemical, advanced materials, agrosciences and plastics businesses delivers a broad range of technology-based products and solutions to customers in approximately 180 countries and in high growth sectors such as packaging, electronics, water, coatings and agriculture. In 2013, Dow had annual sales of more than $57 billion and employed approximately 53,000 people worldwide. The Company's more than 6,000 products are manufactured at 201 sites in 36 countries across the globe. References to "Dow" or the "Company" mean The Dow Chemical Company and its consolidated subsidiaries unless otherwise expressly noted. More information about Dow can be found at www.dow.com.

WACHTELL, LIPTON, ROSEN & KATZ, SHARE PURCHASE RIGHTS PLAN

Wachtell, Lipton, Rosen & Katz
Share Purchase Rights Plan

[COMPANY]

and

[RIGHTS AGENT]

Rights Agreement

Dated as of _____, ____

TABLE OF CONTENTS

Sec.		Page
Section 1.	Definitions	1126
Section 2.	Appointment of Rights Agent	1129
Section 3.	Issue of Right Certificates	1129
Section 4.	Form of Right Certificates	1130
Section 5.	Countersignature and Registration	1131
Section 6.	Transfer, Split Up, Combination and Exchange of Right Certificates; Mutilated, Destroyed, Lost or Stolen Right Certificates	1131
Section 7.	Exercise of Rights; Purchase Price; Expiration Date of Rights	1131
Section 8.	Cancellation and Destruction of Right Certificates	1132
Section 9.	Availability of Preferred Shares	1132
Section 10.	Preferred Shares Record Date	1132
Section 11.	Adjustment of Purchase Price, Number of Shares or Number of Rights	1132
Section 12.	Certificate of Adjusted Purchase Price or Number of Shares	1135
Section 13.	Consolidation, Merger or Sale or Transfer of Assets or Earning Power	1136
Section 14.	Fractional Rights and Fractional Shares	1136
Section 15.	Rights of Action	1137
Section 16.	Agreement of Right Holders	1137
Section 17.	Right Certificate Holder Not Deemed a Stockholder	1137

Section 18. Concerning the Rights Agent 1137

Section 19. Merger or Consolidation or Change of Name of Rights Agent 1138

Section 20. Duties of Rights Agent 1138

Section 21. Change of Rights Agent 1138

Section 22. Issuance of New Right Certificates 1139

Section 23. Redemption 1139

Section 24. Exchange 1139

Section 25. Notice of Certain Events 1140

Section 26. Notices 1140

Section 27. Supplements and Amendments 1140

Section 28. Successors 1141

Section 29. Benefits of this Agreement 1141

Section 30. Severability 1141

Section 31. Governing Law 1141

Section 32. Counterparts 1141

Section 33. Descriptive Headings 1141

Section 34. Customer Identification Program (omitted)

Section 35. Force Majeure 1141

Exhibit A. Form of Certificate of Designations 1143

Exhibit B. Form of Right Certificate 1147

Exhibit C. Summary of Rights to Purchase Preferred Shares 1151

Rights Agreement, dated as of _____, _____, between _____, a Delaware corporation (the "Company"), and _____, as rights agent (the "Rights Agent").

The Board of Directors of the Company has authorized and declared a dividend of one preferred share purchase right (a "Right") for each Common Share (as hereinafter defined) of the Company outstanding as of [the close of business] on _____, 20__ (the "Record Date"), each Right representing the right to purchase one one-hundredth of a Preferred Share (as hereinafter defined), upon the terms and subject to the conditions herein set forth, and has further authorized and directed the issuance of one Right with respect to each Common Share that shall become outstanding between the Record Date and the earliest of the Distribution Date, the Redemption Date and the Final Expiration Date (as such terms are hereinafter defined).

Accordingly, in consideration of the premises and the mutual agreements herein set forth, the parties hereby agree as follows:

Section 1. Definitions. For purposes of this Agreement, the following terms have the meanings indicated:

(a) "Acquiring Person" shall mean any Person who or which, together with all Affiliates and Associates of such Person, shall be the Beneficial Owner of [10]% or more of the Common Shares of the Company then outstanding, but shall not include the Company, any Subsidiary of the Company, any employee benefit plan of the Company or any Subsidiary of the Company, or any entity holding Common Shares for or pursuant to the terms of any such plan. [For Bifurcated/Higher Threshold for .13G Institutional Investors w/ 60-Day selldown grace period for 13G–13D switch and grandfathering—would be incorporated into the ancillary documents as well: provided, however, that no Person which, together with

1126

all Affiliates and Associates of such Person, is the Beneficial Owner of Common Shares of the Company representing less than [20]% of the Common Shares of the Company then outstanding, and which is entitled to file, and files, a statement on Schedule 13G ("Schedule 13G") pursuant to Rule 13d–1(b) or Rule 13d–1(c) of the General Rules and Regulations under the Exchange Act as in effect at the time of the public announcement of the declaration of the Rights dividend with respect to the Common Shares Beneficially Owned by such Person (a "13G Investor"), shall be deemed to be an "Acquiring Person"; provided, further, however, that a Person who was deemed a 13G Investor shall no longer be deemed such if it files a statement on Schedule 13D pursuant to Rule 13d–1(a), 13d–1(e), 13d–1(f) or 13d–1(g) of the General Rules and Regulations under the Exchange Act as in effect at the time of the public announcement of the declaration of the Rights dividend with respect to the Common Shares Beneficially Owned by such Person, and shall be deemed an Acquiring Person if it is the Beneficial Owner of [10]% or more of the Common Shares of the Company then outstanding at any point from the time it first files such a statement on Schedule 13D provided that if at such time such Person's Beneficial Ownership is not less than [10]%, then such Person shall have 60 days from such time to reduce its Beneficial Ownership (together with all Affiliates and Associates of such Person) to below [10]% of the Common Shares of the Company before being deemed an "Acquiring Person" but shall be deemed an "Acquiring Person" if after reducing its Beneficial Ownership to below [10]% it subsequently becomes the Beneficial Owner of [10]% or more of the Common Shares of the Company or if, prior to reducing its Beneficial Ownership to below [10]%, it increases (or makes any offer or takes any other action that would increase) its Beneficial Ownership of the then-outstanding Common Shares of the Company (other than as a result of an acquisition of Common Shares by the Company) above the lowest Beneficial Ownership of such Person at any time during such 60-day period.] [*Non-Entity Specific Grandfathering w/ Bifurcated Thresholds*: Notwithstanding the foregoing, (i) no Person who is not a 13G Investor and who Beneficially Owns, each as of the time of the first public announcement of the declaration of the Rights dividend, [10]% or more of the Common Shares of the Company then outstanding and (ii) no Person who is a 13G Investor and who Beneficially Owns, each as of at the time of the first public announcement of the declaration of the Rights dividend, [20]% or more of the Common Shares of the Company then outstanding, shall become an Acquiring Person unless such Person shall, after the time of the public announcement of the declaration of the Rights dividend, increase its Beneficial Ownership of the then-outstanding Common Shares (other than as a result of an acquisition of Common Shares by the Company) to an amount equal to or greater than the greater of (x) [10]% (in the case of a Person who is not then a 13G Investor) or [20]% (in the case of a Person who is then a 13G Investor) or (y) the sum of (i) the lowest Beneficial Ownership of such Person as a percentage of the outstanding Common Shares as of any time from and after the time of the public announcement of the declaration of the Rights dividend plus (ii) 0.001%. Notwithstanding the foregoing, no Person shall become an "Acquiring Person" as the result of an acquisition of Common Shares by the Company that, by reducing the number of Common Shares of the Company outstanding, increases the proportionate number of Common Shares of the Company Beneficially Owned by such Person to [10]% ([20]% in the case of a 13G Investor) or more of the Common Shares of the Company then outstanding; provided, however, that, if a Person shall become the Beneficial Owner of [10]% ([20]% in the case of a 13G Investor) or more of the Common Shares of the Company then outstanding by reason of share purchases by the Company and shall, after the public announcement of such share purchases by the Company, become the Beneficial Owner of any additional Common Shares of the Company, then such Person shall be deemed to be an "Acquiring Person." Notwithstanding the foregoing, if the Board of Directors of the Company determines in good faith that a Person who would otherwise be an "Acquiring Person," as defined pursuant to the foregoing provisions of this paragraph (a), has become such inadvertently, and such Person divests as promptly as practicable a sufficient number of Common Shares so that such Person would no longer be an "Acquiring Person," as defined pursuant to the foregoing provisions of this paragraph (a), then such Person shall not be deemed to be an "Acquiring Person" for any purposes of this Agreement. Notwithstanding the foregoing, if a bona fide swaps dealer who would otherwise be an "Acquiring Person" has become so as a result of its actions in the ordinary course of its business that the Board of Directors of the Company determines, in its sole discretion, were taken without the intent or effect of evading or assisting any other Person to evade the purposes and intent of this Agreement, or otherwise seeking to control or influence the management or policies of the Company, then, and unless and until the Board of Directors shall otherwise determine, such Person shall not be deemed to be an "Acquiring Person" for any purposes of this Agreement.

(b)   "Affiliate" shall have the meaning ascribed to such term in Rule 12b–2 of the General Rules and Regulations under the Exchange Act as in effect on the date of this Agreement.

(c)   "Associate" shall have the meaning ascribed to such term in Rule 12b–2 of the General Rules and Regulations under the Exchange Act as in effect on the date of this Agreement.

(d)   A Person shall be deemed the "Beneficial Owner" of and shall be deemed to "Beneficially Own" any securities:

(i)   which such Person or any of such Person's Affiliates or Associates beneficially owns, directly or indirectly;

(ii)   which such Person or any of such Person's Affiliates or Associates has (A) the right or the obligation to acquire (whether such right is exercisable, or such obligation is required to be performed, immediately or only after the passage of time) pursuant to any agreement, arrangement or understanding (other than customary agreements with and between underwriters and selling group members with respect to a bona fide public offering of securities), or upon the exercise of conversion rights, exchange rights, rights (other than these Rights), warrants or options, or otherwise; provided, however, that a Person shall not be deemed the Beneficial Owner of, or to Beneficially Own, securities tendered pursuant to a tender or exchange offer made by or on behalf of such Person or any of such Person's Affiliates or Associates until such tendered securities are accepted for purchase or exchange; or (B) the right to vote pursuant to any agreement, arrangement or understanding; provided, however, that a Person shall not be deemed the Beneficial Owner of, or to Beneficially Own, any security if the agreement, arrangement or understanding to vote such security (1) arises solely from a revocable proxy or consent given to such Person in response to a public proxy or consent solicitation made pursuant to, and in accordance with, the applicable rules and regulations promulgated under the Exchange Act and (2) is not also then reportable on Schedule 13D under the Exchange Act (or any comparable or successor report);

(iii)   which are beneficially owned, directly or indirectly, by any other Person with which such Person or any of such Person's Affiliates or Associates has any agreement, arrangement or understanding (other than customary agreements with and between underwriters and selling group members with respect to a bona fide public offering of securities) for the purpose of acquiring, holding, voting (except to the extent contemplated by the proviso to Section 1(d)(ii)(B) hereof) or disposing of any securities of the Company; or

(iv)   which are beneficially owned, directly or indirectly, by a Counterparty (or any of such Counterparty's Affiliates or Associates) under any Derivatives Contract (without regard to any short or similar position under the same or any other Derivatives Contract) to which such Person or any of such Person's Affiliates or Associates is a Receiving Party (as such terms are defined in the immediately following paragraph); provided, however, that the number of Common Shares that a Person is deemed to Beneficially Own pursuant to this clause (iv) in connection with a particular Derivatives Contract shall not exceed the number of Notional Common Shares with respect to such Derivatives Contract; provided, further, that the number of securities beneficially owned by each Counterparty (including its Affiliates and Associates) under a Derivatives Contract shall for purposes of this clause (iv) be deemed to include all securities that are beneficially owned, directly or indirectly, by any other Counterparty (or any of such other Counterparty's Affiliates or Associates) under any Derivatives Contract to which such first Counterparty (or any of such first Counterparty's Affiliates or Associates) is a Receiving Party, with this proviso being applied to successive Counterparties as appropriate.

A "Derivatives Contract" is a contract between two parties (the "Receiving Party" and the "Counterparty") that is designed to produce economic benefits and risks to the Receiving Party that correspond substantially to the ownership by the Receiving Party of a number of Common Shares specified or referenced in such contract (the number corresponding to such economic benefits and risks, the "Notional Common Shares"), regardless of whether obligations under such contract are required or permitted to be settled through the delivery of cash, Common Shares or other property, without regard to any short position under the same or any other Derivatives Contract. For the avoidance of doubt, interests in broad-based index options, broad-based index futures and broad-based publicly traded market baskets of stocks approved for trading by the appropriate federal governmental authority shall not be deemed to be Derivatives Contracts.

Notwithstanding anything in this definition of Beneficial Ownership to the contrary, the phrase "then outstanding," when used with reference to a Person's Beneficial Ownership of securities of the Company, shall mean the number of such securities then issued and outstanding together with the number of such securities not then actually issued and outstanding which are issuable by the Company and which such Person would be deemed to Beneficially Own hereunder.

(e) "Book Entry" shall mean an uncertificated book entry for any Common Share or Preferred Share.

(f) "Business Day" shall mean any day other than a Saturday, a Sunday, or a day on which banking institutions in [State of Rights Agent] are authorized or obligated by law or executive order to close.

(g) "Close of Business" on any given date shall mean 5:00 P.M., [City of Rights Agent] time, on such date; provided, however, that, if such date is not a Business Day, it shall mean 5:00 P.M., [City of Rights Agent] time, on the next succeeding Business Day.

(h) "Common Shares" when used with reference to the Company shall mean the shares of common stock, par value $__ per share, of the Company. "Common Shares" when used with reference to any Person other than the Company shall mean the capital stock (or equity interest) with the greatest voting power of such other Person or, if such other Person is a Subsidiary of another Person, the Person or Persons which ultimately control such first-mentioned Person. . . .

(o) "Ownership Statements" means, with respect to any Book Entry Common Share, current ownership statements issued to the record holders thereof in lieu of a certificate representing such Common Share.

(p) "Person" shall mean any individual, partnership, firm, corporation, limited liability company, association, trust, limited liability partnership, joint venture, unincorporated organization or other entity, and shall include any successor (by merger or otherwise) of such entity, as well as any group under Rule 13d–5(b)(1) of the Exchange Act.

(q) "Preferred Shares" shall mean shares of Series A Junior Participating Preferred Stock, par value $__ per share, of the Company having the rights and preferences set forth in the Form of Certificate of Designations attached to this Agreement as Exhibit A. . . .

(u) "Redemption Price" shall have the meaning set forth in Section 23(a) hereof.

(v) "Right" shall have the meaning set forth in the second paragraph hereof.

(w) "Right Certificate" shall have the meaning set forth in Section 3(a) hereof.

(x) "Shares Acquisition Date" shall mean the first date of public announcement by the Company or an Acquiring Person that an Acquiring Person has become such.

(y) "Subsidiary" of any Person shall mean any corporation or other entity of which a majority of the voting power of the voting equity securities or equity interest is owned, directly or indirectly, by such Person.

(z) "Summary of Rights" shall have the meaning set forth in Section 3(b) hereof.

(aa) "Trading Day" shall have the meaning set forth in Section 11(d) hereof.

Section 2. Appointment of Rights Agent. The Company hereby appoints the Rights Agent to act as agent for the Company in accordance with the express terms and conditions (and no implied terms and conditions) hereof, and the Rights Agent hereby accepts such appointment. . . .

Section 3. Issue of Right Certificates. (a) Until the tenth (10th) day after the Shares Acquisition Date (including any such date that is after the date of this Agreement and prior to the issuance of the Rights; the "Distribution Date"), (x) the Rights will be evidenced (subject to the provisions of Section 3(b) hereof) by the certificates for Common Shares of the Company (or by Book Entry Common Shares of the Company) registered in the names of the holders thereof (which certificates shall also be deemed to be Right Certificates) and not by separate Right Certificates or book entry, and (y) the Rights Certificates and the right to receive Right Certificates will be transferable only in connection with the transfer of Common Shares of the Company. As soon as practicable after the Distribution Date, the Company will prepare and execute, and upon written request of the Company, the Rights Agent will countersign, and the Company will send or cause to be sent (and the Rights Agent will, if requested and provided with all necessary information and documents at the expense of the Company, send) by first-class, insured, postage-prepaid mail, to each record holder of Common Shares of the Company as of the Close of Business on the Distribution Date (other than any Acquiring Person or any Associate or Affiliate of an Acquiring Person), at the address of such holder shown on the records of the Company, a Right Certificate, in substantially the form of Exhibit B hereto (a "Right Certificate"), evidencing one Right for each Common Share so held, subject to adjustment as provided herein; provided, however, that notwithstanding anything to the contrary herein, the Company may choose to use book entry in lieu of physical certificates, in which case "Rights Certificates" shall be deemed to mean the uncertificated book entry representing the related Rights. As of and after the Distribution Date, the Rights will be evidenced solely by such Right Certificates. The Company shall promptly notify the Rights Agent in writing upon the occurrence of the Distribution Date, the Redemption Date and/or the Final Expiration Date and, if such notification is given orally, the Company shall confirm same in writing on or prior to the Business Day next following. Until such written notice is received by the Rights Agent, the Rights Agent may presume conclusively for all purposes that none of the Distribution Date, the Redemption Date or the Final Expiration Date has occurred.

(b)   On the Record Date, or as soon as practicable thereafter, the Company will send (directly, or at the expense of the Company, upon the written request of the Company and after providing all necessary information and documents, through the Rights Agent or the Company's transfer agent for the Common Shares) a copy of a Summary of Rights to Purchase Preferred Shares, in substantially the form of Exhibit C hereto (the "Summary of Rights"), by first-class, postage-prepaid mail, to each record holder of Common Shares as of the Close of Business on the Record Date (other than any Acquiring Person or any Associate or Affiliate of an Acquiring Person), at the address of such holder shown on the records of the Company.... Until the Distribution Date (or the earlier of the Redemption Date or the Final Expiration Date), the surrender for transfer of any certificate for Common Shares or the transfer of any Book Entry Common Shares of the Company outstanding on the Record Date, with or without a copy of the Summary of Rights attached thereto, shall also constitute the transfer of the Rights associated with the Common Shares of the Company represented thereby.

(c)   Certificates for Common Shares (or Book Entry Common Shares) that become outstanding (including, without limitation, reacquired Common Shares referred to in the last sentence of this Section 3(c)) after the Record Date but prior to the earliest of the Distribution Date, the Redemption Date or the Final Expiration Date shall have impressed on, printed on, written on or otherwise affixed to them a legend in substantially the following form:

> This certificate also evidences and entitles the holder hereof to certain rights as set forth in an Agreement between _____ and _____, dated as of _____, ___, as it may be amended from time to time (the "Agreement"), the terms of which are hereby incorporated herein by reference and a copy of which is on file at the principal executive offices of _____. Under certain circumstances, as set forth in the Agreement, such Rights (as defined in the Agreement) will be evidenced by separate certificates and will no longer be evidenced by this certificate. _____ will mail to the holder of this certificate a copy of the Agreement without charge after receipt of a written request therefor. As set forth in the Agreement, Rights that are or were acquired or Beneficially Owned (as defined in the Agreement) by any Person (as defined in the Agreement) who becomes an Acquiring Person (as defined in the Agreement) or an Associate or Affiliate (each as defined in the Agreement) thereof become null and void.

With respect to any Book Entry Common Share of the Company, such legend shall be included in the Ownership Statement in respect of such Common Share or in a notice to the record holder of such Common Share in accordance with applicable law. With respect to such certificates containing the foregoing legend, or any Ownership Statement or notice containing the foregoing legend delivered to holders of Book Entry Common Shares, until the earliest of the Distribution Date, the Redemption Date or the Final Expiration Date, the Rights associated with the Common Shares of the Company represented by such certificates or such Book Entry Common Shares shall be evidenced by such certificates or such Book Entry Common Shares (including any Ownership Statement) alone, and the surrender for transfer of any such certificate or the transfer of any Book Entry Common Share shall also constitute the transfer of the Rights associated with the Common Shares of the Company represented thereby....

Section 4. Form of Right Certificates. The Right Certificates (and the forms of election to purchase Preferred Shares and of assignment to be printed on the reverse thereof) shall be substantially the same as

Exhibit B hereto, and may have such marks of identification or designation and such legends, summaries or endorsements printed thereon as the Company may deem appropriate (but which do not materially and adversely affect the rights, duties, liabilities or responsibilities of the Rights Agent) and as are not inconsistent with the provisions of this Agreement, or as may be required to comply with any applicable law or with any applicable rule or regulation made pursuant thereto or with any applicable rule or regulation of any stock exchange or the Financial Industry Regulatory Authority, or to conform to usage. Subject to the provisions of Section 22 hereof, the Right Certificates shall entitle the holders thereof to purchase such number of one one-hundredths of a Preferred Share as shall be set forth therein at the price per one one-hundredth of a Preferred Share set forth therein (the "Purchase Price"), but the number of such one one-hundredths of a Preferred Share and the Purchase Price shall be subject to adjustment as provided herein.

Section 5. <u>Countersignature and Registration</u>. The Right Certificates shall be executed on behalf of the Company by its Chairman of the Board, its Chief Executive Officer, its President, any of its Vice Presidents or its Treasurer, either manually or by facsimile signature, shall have affixed thereto the Company's seal or a facsimile thereof, and shall be attested by the Secretary or an Assistant Secretary of the Company, either manually or by facsimile signature. . . .

Following the Distribution Date, receipt by the Rights Agent of notice to that effect and all other relevant information and documents referred to in Section 3(a), the Rights Agent will keep or cause to be kept, at its principal office, books for registration and transfer of the Right Certificates issued hereunder. Such books shall show the names and addresses of the respective holders of the Right Certificates, the number of Rights evidenced on its face by each of the Right Certificates and the date of each of the Right Certificates.

Section 6. <u>Transfer, Split Up, Combination and Exchange of Right Certificates; Mutilated, Destroyed, Lost or Stolen Right Certificates</u>. . . . Any registered holder desiring to transfer, split up, combine or exchange any Right Certificate or Right Certificates shall make such request in writing delivered to the Rights Agent, and shall surrender the Right Certificate or Right Certificates to be transferred, split up, combined or exchanged at the principal office of the Rights Agent. . . .

Notwithstanding any other provisions hereof, the Company and the Rights Agent may amend this Rights Agreement to provide for uncertificated Rights in addition to or in place of Rights evidenced by Rights Certificates.

Section 7. <u>Exercise of Rights; Purchase Price; Expiration Date of Rights</u>. (a) The registered holder of any Right Certificate may exercise the Rights evidenced thereby (except as otherwise provided herein), in whole or in part, at any time after the Distribution Date, upon surrender of the Right Certificate, with the form of election to purchase on the reverse side thereof properly completed and duly executed, to the Rights Agent at the principal office of the Rights Agent, together with payment of the Purchase Price for each one one-hundredth of a Preferred Share as to which the Rights are exercised, at or prior to the earliest of (i) the Close of Business on _____, _____ (the "Final Expiration Date"), (ii) the time at which the Rights are redeemed as provided in Section 23 hereof (the "Redemption Date"), or (iii) the time at which such Rights are exchanged as provided in Section 24 hereof. From such time as the Rights are no longer exercisable hereunder, the Rights Agent shall have no further duties, obligations or liabilities hereunder except as expressly stated herein.

(b)   The Purchase Price for each one one-hundredth of a Preferred Share purchasable pursuant to the exercise of a Right shall initially be $__, and shall be subject to adjustment from time to time as provided in Section 11 or 13 hereof, and shall be payable in lawful money of the United States of America in accordance with paragraph (c) below.

(c)   Upon receipt of a Right Certificate representing exercisable Rights, with the form of election to purchase properly completed and duly executed, accompanied by payment of the Purchase Price for the shares to be purchased and an amount equal to any applicable transfer tax required to be paid by the holder of such Right Certificate in accordance with Section 9 hereof by cash or by certified check, cashier's check or money order payable to the order of the Company, the Rights Agent shall thereupon promptly (i) (A) requisition from any transfer agent of the Preferred Shares (or make available if the Rights Agent is the Transfer Agent) certificates for the number of Preferred Shares to be purchased and the Company hereby irrevocably authorizes any such transfer agent to comply with all such requests, or (B) requisition from the depositary agent depositary receipts representing such number of one one-hundredths of a Preferred Share as are to be purchased (in which case certificates for the Preferred Shares represented by such receipts shall be deposited by the transfer agent of the Preferred Shares with such depositary agent) and the Company hereby directs such depositary agent to comply with such request; (ii) when appropriate, requisition from the Company the amount of cash to be paid in lieu of issuance of fractional shares in accordance with Section 14 hereof; (iii) after receipt of such certificates or depositary receipts, cause the same to be delivered to or upon the order of the registered holder of such Right Certificate, registered in such name or names as may be designated by such holder; and (iv) when appropriate, after receipt, deliver such cash to or upon the order of the registered holder of such Right Certificate. In the event that the Company is obligated to issue securities of the Company other than Preferred Shares (including Common Shares) of the Company pursuant to Section 11(a) hereof, the Company will make all arrangements necessary so that such other securities are available for distribution by the Rights Agent. . . .

Section 8. <u>Cancellation and Destruction of Right Certificates</u>. All Right Certificates surrendered for the purpose of exercise, transfer, split up, combination or exchange shall, if surrendered to the Company or to any of its agents, be delivered to the Rights Agent for cancellation or in cancelled form, or, if delivered or surrendered to the Rights Agent, shall be cancelled by it, and no Right Certificates shall be issued in lieu thereof except as expressly permitted by any of the provisions of this Agreement. . . .

Section 9. <u>Availability of Preferred Shares</u>. The Company covenants and agrees that it will cause to be reserved and kept available out of its authorized and unissued Preferred Shares or any Preferred Shares held in its treasury the number of Preferred Shares that will be sufficient to permit the exercise in full of all outstanding Rights in accordance with Section 7 hereof. The Company covenants and agrees that it will take all such action as may be necessary to ensure that all Preferred Shares (or Common Shares and other securities as the case may be) delivered upon exercise of Rights shall, at the time of delivery of the certificates for such Preferred Shares (or Common Shares and other securities, as the case may be) (subject to payment of the Purchase Price), be duly and validly authorized and issued and fully paid and nonassessable shares. . . .

Section 10. <u>Preferred Shares Record Date</u>. Each Person in whose name any certificate for Preferred Shares or other securities is issued upon the exercise of Rights shall for all purposes be deemed to have become the holder of record of the Preferred Shares or other securities represented thereby on, and such certificate shall be dated, the date upon which the Right Certificate evidencing such Rights was duly surrendered with the forms of election and certification properly completed and duly executed and payment of the Purchase Price (and any applicable transfer taxes) was made; <u>provided</u>, <u>however</u>, that, if the date of such surrender and payment is a date upon which the Preferred Shares or other securities transfer books of the Company are closed, such Person shall be deemed to have become the record holder of such shares on, and such certificate shall be dated, the next succeeding Business Day on which the Preferred Shares or other securities transfer books of the Company are open. Prior to the exercise of the Rights evidenced thereby, the holder of a Right Certificate shall not be entitled to any rights of a holder of Preferred Shares for which the Rights shall be exercisable, including, without limitation, the right to vote, to receive dividends or other distributions or to exercise any preemptive rights, and shall not be entitled to receive any notice of any proceedings of the Company, except as provided herein.

Section 11. <u>Adjustment of Purchase Price, Number of Shares or Number of Rights</u>. The Purchase Price, the number of Preferred Shares covered by each Right and the number of Rights outstanding are subject to adjustment from time to time as provided in this Section 11.

(a)(i) In the event the Company shall at any time after the date of this Agreement (A) declare a dividend on the Preferred Shares payable in Preferred Shares, (B) subdivide the outstanding Preferred Shares, (C) combine the outstanding Preferred Shares into a smaller number of Preferred Shares or (D) issue any shares of its capital stock in a reclassification of the Preferred Shares (including any such reclassification in connection with a share exchange, consolidation or merger in which the Company is the continuing or surviving corporation), except as otherwise provided in this Section 11(a), the Purchase Price in effect at the time of the record date for such dividend or of the effective date of such subdivision, combination or reclassification, and the number and kind of shares of capital stock issuable on such date, shall be proportionately adjusted so that the holder of any Right exercised after such time shall be entitled to receive the aggregate number and kind of shares of capital stock which, if such Right had been exercised immediately prior to such date and at a time when the Preferred Shares transfer books of the Company were open, such holder would have owned upon such exercise and been entitled to receive by virtue of such dividend, subdivision, combination or reclassification; provided, however, that in no event shall the consideration to be paid upon the exercise of one Right be less than the aggregate par value of the shares of capital stock of the Company issuable upon exercise of one Right.

(ii)   Subject to Section 24 hereof, in the event any Person becomes an Acquiring Person, each holder of a Right shall thereafter have a right to receive, upon exercise thereof at a price equal to the then current Purchase Price multiplied by the number of one one-hundredths of a Preferred Share for which a Right is then exercisable, in accordance with the terms of this Agreement and in lieu of Preferred Shares, such number of Common Shares of the Company as shall equal the result obtained by (A) multiplying the then current Purchase Price by the number of one one-hundredths of a Preferred Share for which a Right is then exercisable and dividing that product by (B) 50% of the then current per share market price of the Common Shares of the Company (determined pursuant to Section 11(d) hereof) on the date of the occurrence of such event. In the event that any Person shall become an Acquiring Person and the Rights shall then be outstanding, the Company shall not take any action that would eliminate or diminish the benefits intended to be afforded by the Rights.

From and after the occurrence of such event, any Rights that are or were acquired or Beneficially Owned by any Acquiring Person (or any Associate or Affiliate of such Acquiring Person) shall be null and void without any further action, and any holder of such Rights shall thereafter have no right to exercise such Rights under any provision of this Agreement or otherwise. Neither the Company nor the Rights Agent shall have liability to any holder of Right Certificates or other Person as a result of the Company's or the Rights Agent's failure to make any determinations with respect to an Acquiring Person or its Affiliates, Associates or transferees hereunder. No Right Certificate shall be issued pursuant to Section 3 hereof that represents Rights Beneficially Owned by an Acquiring Person whose Rights would be null and void pursuant to the preceding sentence or any Associate or Affiliate thereof; no Right Certificate shall be issued at any time upon the transfer of any Rights to an Acquiring Person whose Rights would be null and void pursuant to the preceding sentence or any Associate or Affiliate thereof or to any nominee of such Acquiring Person, Associate or Affiliate or with respect to any Common Shares otherwise deemed to be Beneficially Owned by any of the foregoing; and any Right Certificate delivered to the Rights Agent for transfer to an Acquiring Person or other Person whose Rights would be null and void pursuant to the preceding sentence shall be cancelled. The Company shall give the Rights Agent written notice of the identity of any such Acquiring Person, Associate or Affiliate, or the nominee of any of the foregoing, and the Rights Agent may rely on such written notice in carrying out its duties under this Agreement and shall be deemed not to have any knowledge of the identity of any such Acquiring Person, Associate or Affiliate, or the nominee of any of the foregoing, unless and until it shall have received such written notice.

(iii)   In the event that there shall not be sufficient Common Shares issued but not outstanding or authorized but unissued to permit the exercise in full of the Rights in accordance with subparagraph (ii) above, the Company shall take all such action as may be necessary to authorize additional Common Shares for issuance upon exercise of the Rights. . . .

(b)   In case the Company shall fix a record date for the issuance of rights, options or warrants to all holders of Preferred Shares entitling them (for a period expiring within 45 calendar days after such record date) to subscribe for or purchase Preferred Shares (or shares having the same rights, privileges and preferences as the Preferred Shares ("equivalent preferred shares")) or securities convertible into Preferred Shares or equivalent preferred shares at a price per Preferred Share or equivalent preferred share (or having a conversion price per share, if a security convertible into Preferred Shares or equivalent preferred shares) less than the then current per share market price of the Preferred Shares (as defined in Section 11(d)) on such record date, the Purchase Price to be in effect after such record date shall be determined by multiplying the Purchase Price in effect immediately prior to such record date by a fraction, the numerator of which shall be the number of Preferred Shares outstanding on such record date plus the number of Preferred Shares which the aggregate offering price of the total number of Preferred Shares and/or equivalent preferred shares so to be offered (and/or the aggregate initial conversion price of the convertible securities so to be offered) would purchase at such current market price and the denominator of which shall be the number of Preferred Shares outstanding on such record date plus the number of additional Preferred Shares and/or equivalent preferred shares to be offered for subscription or purchase (or into which the convertible securities so to be offered are initially convertible); provided, however, that in no event shall the consideration to be paid upon the exercise of one Right be less than the aggregate par value of the shares of capital stock of the Company issuable upon exercise of one Right. In case such subscription price may be paid in a consideration part or all of which shall be in a form other than cash, the value of such consideration shall be as determined in good faith by the Board of Directors of the Company, whose determination shall be described in a written statement filed with the Rights Agent and shall be binding on the Rights Agent and holders of the Rights. Preferred Shares owned by or held for the account of the Company or any Subsidiary of the Company shall not be deemed outstanding for the purpose of any such computation. Such adjustment shall be made successively whenever such a record date is fixed; and, in the event that such rights, options or warrants are not so issued, the Purchase Price shall be adjusted to be the Purchase Price which would then be in effect if such record date had not been fixed.

(c) In case the Company shall fix a record date for the making of a distribution to all holders of the Preferred Shares (including any such distribution made in connection with a share exchange, consolidation or merger in which the Company is the continuing or surviving corporation) of evidences of indebtedness or assets (other than a regular quarterly cash dividend or a dividend payable in Preferred Shares) or subscription rights or warrants (excluding those referred to in Section 11(b) hereof), the Purchase Price to be in effect after such record date shall be determined by multiplying the Purchase Price in effect immediately prior to such record date by a fraction, the numerator of which shall be the then-current per share market price of the Preferred Shares on such record date, less the fair market value (as determined in good faith by the Board of Directors of the Company, whose determination shall be described in a written statement filed with the Rights Agent and shall be binding on the Rights Agent and holders of the Rights) of the portion of the assets or evidences of indebtedness so to be distributed or of such subscription rights or warrants applicable to one Preferred Share and the denominator of which shall be such then-current per share market price of the Preferred Shares on such record date; provided, however, that in no event shall the consideration to be paid upon the exercise of one Right be less than the aggregate par value of the shares of capital stock of the Company to be issued upon exercise of one Right. Such adjustments shall be made successively whenever such a record date is fixed; and, in the event that such distribution is not so made, the Purchase Price shall again be adjusted to be the Purchase Price which would then be in effect if such record date had not been fixed.

(d)(i) For the purpose of any computation hereunder, the "current per share market price" of any security (a "Security" for the purpose of this Section 11(d)(i)) on any date shall be deemed to be the average of the daily closing prices per share of such Security for the 30 consecutive Trading Days immediately prior to but not including such date; . . .

(ii) For the purpose of any computation hereunder, the "current per share market price" of the Preferred Shares shall be determined in accordance with the method set forth in Section 11(d)(i). If the Preferred Shares are not publicly traded, the "current per share market price" of the Preferred Shares shall be conclusively deemed to be the current per share market price of the Common Shares as determined pursuant to Section 11(d)(i) hereof (appropriately adjusted to reflect any stock split, stock dividend or similar transaction occurring after the date hereof), multiplied by one hundred. If neither the Common Shares nor the Preferred Shares are publicly held or so listed or traded, "current per share market price" shall mean the fair value per share as determined in good faith by the Board of Directors of the Company, whose determination shall be described in a written statement filed with the Rights Agent. . . .

(h) Unless the Company shall have exercised its election as provided in Section 11(i) hereof, upon each adjustment of the Purchase Price as a result of the calculations made in Sections 11(b) and (c) hereof, each Right outstanding immediately prior to the making of such adjustment shall thereafter evidence the right to purchase, at the adjusted Purchase Price, that number of one one-hundredths of a Preferred Share (calculated to the nearest one one-millionth of a Preferred Share) obtained by (A) multiplying (x) the number of one one-hundredths of a share covered by a Right immediately prior to this adjustment by (y) the Purchase Price in effect immediately prior to such adjustment of the Purchase Price and (B) dividing the product so obtained by the Purchase Price in effect immediately after such adjustment of the Purchase Price.

(i) The Company may elect, on or after the date of any adjustment of the Purchase Price, to adjust the number of Rights in substitution for any adjustment in the number of one one-hundredths of a Preferred Share purchasable upon the exercise of a Right. Each of the Rights outstanding after such adjustment of the number of Rights shall be exercisable for the number of one one-hundredths of a Preferred Share for which a Right was exercisable immediately prior to such adjustment. Each Right held of record prior to such adjustment of the number of Rights shall become that number of Rights (calculated to the nearest one ten-thousandth) obtained by dividing the Purchase Price in effect immediately prior to adjustment of the Purchase Price by the Purchase Price in effect immediately after adjustment of the Purchase Price. . . . If Right Certificates have been issued, upon each adjustment of the number of Rights pursuant to this Section 11(i), the Company shall, as promptly as practicable, cause to be distributed to holders of record of Right Certificates on such record date Right Certificates evidencing, subject to Section 14 hereof, the additional Rights to which such holders shall be entitled as a result of such adjustment, or, at the option of the Company, shall cause to be distributed to such holders of record in substitution and replacement for the Right Certificates held by such holders prior to the date of adjustment, and upon surrender thereof, if required by the Company, new Right Certificates evidencing all the Rights to which such holders shall be entitled after such adjustment. Right Certificates so to be distributed shall be issued, executed and countersigned in the manner provided for herein, and shall be registered in the names of the holders of record of Right Certificates on the record date specified in the public announcement. . . .

(*l*)　In any case in which this Section 11 shall require that an adjustment in the Purchase Price be made effective as of a record date for a specified event, the Company may elect to defer (with prompt written notice thereof to the Rights Agent) until the occurrence of such event the issuing to the holder of any Right exercised after such record date of the Preferred Shares and other capital stock or securities of the Company, if any, issuable upon such exercise over and above the Preferred Shares and other capital stock or securities of the Company, if any, issuable upon such exercise on the basis of the Purchase Price in effect prior to such adjustment; provided, however, that the Company shall deliver to such holder a due bill or other appropriate instrument evidencing such holder's right to receive such additional shares upon the occurrence of the event requiring such adjustment.

(m)　Anything in this Section 11 to the contrary notwithstanding, the Company shall be entitled to make such reductions in the Purchase Price, in addition to those adjustments expressly required by this Section 11, as and to the extent that it, in its sole discretion, shall determine to be advisable in order that any consolidation or subdivision of the Preferred Shares, issuance wholly for cash of any Preferred Shares at less than the current market price, issuance wholly for cash of Preferred Shares or securities which by their terms are convertible into or exchangeable for Preferred Shares, dividends on Preferred Shares payable in Preferred Shares or issuance of rights, options or warrants referred to in Section 11(b) hereof, hereafter made by the Company to holders of the Preferred Shares shall not be taxable to such stockholders.

(n)　In the event that, at any time after the date of this Agreement and prior to the Distribution Date, the Company shall (i) declare or pay any dividend on the Common Shares payable in Common Shares, or (ii) effect a subdivision, combination or consolidation of the Common Shares (by reclassification or otherwise than by payment of dividends in Common Shares) into a greater or lesser number of Common Shares, then, in any such case, (A) the number of one one-hundredths of a Preferred Share purchasable after such event upon proper exercise of each Right shall be determined by multiplying the number of one one-hundredths of a Preferred Share so purchasable immediately prior to such event by a fraction, the numerator of which is the number of Common Shares outstanding immediately before such event and the denominator of which is the number of Common Shares outstanding immediately after such event, and (B) each Common Share outstanding immediately after such event shall have issued with respect to it that number of Rights which each Common Share outstanding immediately prior to such event had issued with respect to it. The adjustments provided for in this Section 11(n) shall be made successively whenever such a dividend is declared or paid or such a subdivision, combination or consolidation is effected.

Section 12. Certificate of Adjusted Purchase Price or Number of Shares. Whenever an adjustment is made or there is any event affecting the Rights or their exercisability (including without limitation an event that causes Rights to become null and void) as provided in Section 11 or 13 hereof, the Company shall promptly (a) prepare a certificate setting forth such adjustment or describing such event and a brief statement of the facts accounting for such adjustment or describing such event, (b) file with the Rights Agent and with each transfer agent for the Common Shares or the Preferred Shares a copy of such certificate and (c) if such adjustment occurs at any time after the Distribution Date, mail a brief summary thereof to each holder of a Right Certificate in accordance with Section 25 hereof. . . .

Section 13. <u>Consolidation, Merger or Sale or Transfer of Assets or Earning Power</u>. In the event, directly or indirectly, at any time after a Person has become an Acquiring Person, (a) the Company shall effect a share exchange, consolidate with, or merge with and into, any other Person, (b) any Person shall effect a share exchange, consolidate with the Company, or merge with and into the Company and the Company shall be the continuing or surviving corporation of such share exchange or merger and, in connection with such merger, all or part of the Common Shares shall be changed into or exchanged for stock or other securities of any other Person (or the Company) or cash or any other property, or (c) the Company shall sell or otherwise transfer (or one or more of its Subsidiaries shall sell or otherwise transfer), in one or more transactions, assets or earning power aggregating 50% or more of the assets or earning power of the Company and its Subsidiaries (taken as a whole) to any other Person other than the Company or one or more of its wholly-owned Subsidiaries, then, and in each such case, proper provision shall be made so that (i) each holder of a Right (except as otherwise provided herein) shall thereafter have the right to receive, upon the exercise thereof at a price equal to the then current Purchase Price multiplied by the number of one one-hundredths of a Preferred Share for which a Right is then exercisable, in accordance with the terms of this Agreement and in lieu of Preferred Shares, such number of Common Shares of such other Person (including the Company as successor thereto or as the surviving corporation) as shall equal the result obtained by (A) multiplying the then current Purchase Price by the number of one one-hundredths of a Preferred Share for which a Right is then exercisable and dividing that product by (B) 50% of the then current per share market price of the Common Shares of such other Person (determined pursuant to Section 11(d) hereof) on the date of consummation of such consolidation, merger, sale or transfer; (ii) the issuer of such Common Shares shall thereafter be liable for, and shall assume, by virtue of such consolidation, merger, sale or transfer, all the obligations and duties of the Company pursuant to this Agreement; (iii) the term "Company" shall thereafter be deemed to refer to such issuer; and (iv) such issuer shall take such steps (including, but not limited to, the reservation of a sufficient number of its Common Shares in accordance with Section 9 hereof) in connection with such consummation as may be necessary to assure that the provisions hereof shall thereafter be applicable, as nearly as reasonably may be, in relation to the Common Shares of the Company thereafter deliverable upon the exercise of the Rights. The Company shall not consummate any such consolidation, merger, sale or transfer unless, prior thereto, the Company and such issuer shall have executed and delivered to the Rights Agent a supplemental agreement so providing. The Company shall not enter into any transaction of the kind referred to in this Section 13 if at the time of such transaction there are any rights, warrants, instruments or securities outstanding or any agreements or arrangements which, as a result of the consummation of such transaction, would eliminate or substantially diminish the benefits intended to be afforded by the Rights. The provisions of this Section 13 shall similarly apply to successive mergers, share exchanges, or consolidations or sales or other transfers.

Section 14. <u>Fractional Rights and Fractional Shares</u>. (The Company shall not be required to issue fractions of Rights or to distribute Right Certificates which evidence fractional Rights. In lieu of such fractional Rights, there shall be paid to the registered holders of the Right Certificates with regard to which such fractional Rights would otherwise be issuable, an amount in cash equal to the same fraction of the current market value of a whole Right. . . .

(b)   The Company shall not be required to issue fractions of Preferred Shares (other than fractions which are integral multiples of one one-hundredth of a Preferred Share) upon exercise of the Rights or to distribute certificates which evidence fractional Preferred Shares (other than fractions which are integral multiples of one one-hundredth of a Preferred Share). Fractions of Preferred Shares in integral multiples of one one-hundredth of a Preferred Share may, at the election of the Company, be evidenced by depositary receipts, pursuant to an appropriate agreement between the Company and a depositary selected by it; <u>provided</u> that such agreement shall provide that the holders of such depositary receipts shall have all the rights, privileges and preferences to which they are entitled as beneficial owners of the Preferred Shares represented by such depositary receipts. In lieu of fractional Preferred Shares that are not integral multiples of one one-hundredth of a Preferred Share, the Company shall pay to the registered holders of Right Certificates at the time such Rights are exercised as herein provided an amount in cash equal to the same fraction of the current market value of one Preferred Share. For the purposes of this Section 14(b), the current market value of a Preferred Share shall be the closing price of a Preferred Share (as determined pursuant to the second sentence of Section 11(d)(i) hereof) for the Trading Day immediately prior to the date of such exercise.

(c)   The holder of a Right, by the acceptance of the Right, expressly waives such holder's right to receive any fractional Rights or any fractional shares upon exercise of a Right (except as provided above). . . .

Section 15. Rights of Action. All rights of action in respect of this Agreement, excepting the rights of action given to the Rights Agent under Section 18 hereof, are vested in the respective registered holders of the Right Certificates (and, prior to the Distribution Date, the registered holders of the Common Shares); and any registered holder of any Right Certificate (or, prior to the Distribution Date, of the Common Shares), without the consent of the Rights Agent or of the holder of any other Right Certificate (or, prior to the Distribution Date, of the Common Shares), may, in such holder's own behalf and for such holder's own benefit, enforce, and may institute and maintain any suit, action or proceeding against the Company to enforce, or otherwise act in respect of, such holder's right to exercise the Rights evidenced by such Right Certificate in the manner provided in such Right Certificate and in this Agreement. Without limiting the foregoing or any remedies available to the holders of Rights, it is specifically acknowledged that the holders of Rights would not have an adequate remedy at law for any breach of this Agreement, and will be entitled to specific performance of the obligations under, and injunctive relief against actual or threatened violations of the obligations of any Person subject to, this Agreement. . . .

Section 16. Agreement of Right Holders. Every holder of a Right, by accepting the same, consents and agrees with the Company and the Rights Agent and with every other holder of a Right that:

(a)   prior to the Distribution Date, the Rights will be transferable only in connection with the transfer of the Common Shares;

(b)   after the Distribution Date, the Right Certificates are transferable (subject to the provisions of this Agreement) only on the registry books maintained by the Rights Agent if surrendered at the principal office of the Rights Agent, duly endorsed or accompanied by a proper instrument of transfer with a completed form of certification; and

(c)   the Company and the Rights Agent may deem and treat the person in whose name the Right Certificate (or, prior to the Distribution Date, the associated Common Shares certificate (or Book Entry Common Share)) is registered as the absolute owner thereof and of the Rights evidenced thereby (notwithstanding any notations of ownership or writing on the Right Certificate or the associated Common Shares certificate (or Ownership Statements or other notices provided to holders of Book Entry Common Shares) made by anyone other than the Company or the Rights Agent) for all purposes whatsoever, and neither the Company nor the Rights Agent shall be affected by any notice to the contrary.

Section 17. Right Certificate Holder Not Deemed a Stockholder. No holder, as such, of any Right Certificate shall be entitled to vote, receive dividends or be deemed for any purpose the holder of the Preferred Shares or any other securities of the Company which may at any time be issuable on the exercise or exchange of the Rights represented thereby, nor shall anything contained herein or in any Right Certificate be construed to confer upon the holder of any Right Certificate, as such, any of the rights of a stockholder of the Company or any right to vote for the election of directors or upon any matter submitted to stockholders at any meeting thereof, or to give or withhold consent to any corporate action, or to receive notice of meetings or other actions affecting stockholders (except as provided in Section 25 hereof), or to receive dividends or subscription rights, or otherwise, until the Right or Rights evidenced by such Right Certificate shall have been exercised or exchanged in accordance with the provisions hereof.

Section 18. Concerning the Rights Agent. The Company agrees to pay to the Rights Agent reasonable compensation for all services rendered by it hereunder, and, from time to time, on demand of the Rights Agent, its reasonable expenses and counsel fees and other disbursements incurred in the preparation, negotiation, delivery, amendment, administration and execution of this Agreement and the exercise and performance of its duties hereunder. . . .

The Rights Agent shall be protected and shall incur no liability for, or in respect of any action taken, suffered or omitted by it in connection with, its administration of this Agreement in reliance upon any Right Certificate or certificate for the Preferred Shares or Common Shares or for other securities of the Company, instrument of assignment or transfer, power of attorney, endorsement, affidavit, letter, notice, direction, consent, certificate, statement, or other paper or document believed by it to be genuine and to be signed, executed and, where necessary, verified or acknowledged, by the proper person or persons, or otherwise upon the advice of counsel as set forth in Section 20 hereof. Notwithstanding anything in this Agreement to the contrary, in no event will the Rights Agent be liable for special, punitive, indirect, incidental or consequential loss or damage of any kind whatsoever (including but not limited to lost profits), even if the Rights Agent has been advised of the likelihood of such loss or damage and regardless of the form of action. The Rights Agent shall not be deemed to have knowledge of any event of which it was supposed to receive notice thereof hereunder, and the Rights Agent shall be fully protected and shall incur no liability for failing to take any action in connection therewith, unless and until it has received such notice. . . .

Section 19. Merger or Consolidation or Change of Name of Rights Agent. Any Person into which the Rights Agent or any successor Rights Agent may be merged or with which it may effect a share exchange, be consolidated, or any Person resulting from any merger, share exchange, or consolidation to which the Rights Agent or any successor Rights Agent shall be a party, or any Person succeeding to the stock transfer or corporate trust powers of the Rights Agent or any successor Rights Agent, shall be the successor to the Rights Agent under this Agreement without the execution or filing of any paper or document or any further act on the part of any of the parties hereto; . . . .

Section 20. Duties of Rights Agent. The Rights Agent undertakes to perform only the duties and obligations imposed by this Agreement and no implied duties or obligations shall be read into this Agreement against the Rights Agent. . . .

(b)   Whenever in the performance of its duties under this Agreement the Rights Agent shall deem it necessary or desirable that any fact or matter (including, without limitation, the identity of an Acquiring Person and the determination of the current per share market price of any security) be proved or established by the Company prior to taking or suffering any action hereunder, such fact or matter (unless other evidence in respect thereof be herein specifically prescribed) may be deemed to be conclusively proved and established by a certificate signed by any one of the Chairman of the Board, the Chief Executive Officer, the President, any Vice President, the Treasurer, the Secretary or any Assistant Secretary of the Company and delivered to the Rights Agent; and such certificate shall be full and complete authorization and protection to the Rights Agent and the Rights Agent shall incur no liability for any action taken or suffered in good faith by it under the provisions of this Agreement in reliance upon such a certificate.

(c)   The Rights Agent shall be liable hereunder to the Company and any other Person only for its own gross negligence, bad faith or willful misconduct (each as determined by a final, nonappealable judgment of a court of competent jurisdiction). Any liability of the Rights Agent shall be limited to three times the amount of aggregate annual fees paid by the Company to the Rights Agent. . . .

(f)   The Company agrees that it will perform, execute, acknowledge and deliver or cause to be performed, executed, acknowledged and delivered all such further and other acts, instruments and assurances as may reasonably be required by the Rights Agent for the carrying out or performing by the Rights Agent of the provisions of this Agreement.

(g)   The Rights Agent is hereby authorized and directed to accept instructions with respect to the performance of its duties hereunder from any one of the Chairman of the Board, the Chief Executive Officer, the President, any Vice President, the Secretary, any Assistant Secretary, the Treasurer or any Assistant Treasurer of the Company, and to apply to such officers for advice or instructions in connection with its duties, and it shall not be liable for any action taken or suffered by it in good faith in accordance with instructions of any such officer or for any delay in acting while waiting for those instructions. The Rights Agent shall be fully authorized and protected in relying upon the most recent instructions received by any such officer. . . .

Section 21. Change of Rights Agent. The Rights Agent or any successor Rights Agent may resign and be discharged from its duties under this Agreement upon 30 days' notice in writing mailed to the Company and, in the event that the Rights Agent or one of its Affiliates is not also the transfer agent for the Company, to each transfer agent of the Common Shares or Preferred Shares by registered or certified mail. In the event the transfer agency relationship in effect between the Company and the Rights Agent terminates, the Rights Agent will be deemed to have resigned automatically and be discharged from its duties as Rights Agent under this Agreement as of the effective date of such termination, and the Company shall be responsible for sending any required notice. The Company may remove the Rights Agent or any successor Rights Agent (with or without cause) upon 30 days' notice in writing, mailed to the Rights Agent or successor Rights Agent, as the case may be, and to each transfer agent of the Common Shares or Preferred Shares by registered or certified mail, and to the holders of the Right Certificates by first-class mail. If the Rights

Agent shall resign or be removed or shall otherwise become incapable of acting, the Company shall appoint a successor to the Rights Agent. . . . After appointment, the successor Rights Agent shall be vested with the same powers, rights, duties and responsibilities as if it had been originally named as Rights Agent without further act or deed; but the predecessor Rights Agent shall deliver and transfer to the successor Rights Agent any property at the time held by it hereunder, and execute and deliver any further assurance, conveyance, act or deed necessary for the purpose. Not later than the effective date of any such appointment, the Company shall file notice thereof in writing with the predecessor Rights Agent and each transfer agent of the Common Shares or Preferred Shares, and mail a notice thereof in writing to the registered holders of the Right Certificates. Failure to give any notice provided for in this Section 21, however, or any defect therein, shall not affect the legality or validity of the resignation or removal of the Rights Agent or the appointment of the successor Rights Agent, as the case may be.

Section 22. <u>Issuance of New Right Certificates</u>. Notwithstanding any of the provisions of this Agreement or of the Rights to the contrary, the Company may, at its option, issue new Right Certificates evidencing Rights in such form as may be approved by the Board of Directors of the Company to reflect any adjustment or change in the Purchase Price and the number or kind or class of shares or other securities or property purchasable under the Right Certificates made in accordance with the provisions of this Agreement.

Section 23. <u>Redemption</u>. (a) The Board of Directors of the Company may, at its option, at any time prior to such time as any Person becomes an Acquiring Person, redeem all but not less than all the then outstanding Rights at a redemption price of $0.01 per Right, appropriately adjusted to reflect any stock split, stock dividend or similar transaction occurring after the date hereof (such redemption price being hereinafter referred to as the "<u>Redemption Price</u>"). The redemption of the Rights by the Board of Directors of the Company may be made effective at such time, on such basis and with such conditions as the Board of Directors of the Company, in its sole discretion, may establish.

(b)   Immediately upon the action of the Board of Directors of the Company ordering the redemption of the Rights pursuant to paragraph (a) of this Section 23, and without any further action and without any notice, the right to exercise the Rights will terminate and the only right thereafter of the holders of Rights shall be to receive the Redemption Price. . . .

Section 24. <u>Exchange</u>. (a) The Board of Directors of the Company may, at its option, at any time after any Person becomes an Acquiring Person, exchange all or part of the then outstanding and exercisable Rights (which shall not include Rights that have become null and void pursuant to the provisions of Section 11(a)(ii) hereof) for Common Shares at an exchange ratio of one Common Share per Right, appropriately adjusted to reflect any adjustment in the number of Rights pursuant to Section 11(i) (such exchange ratio being hereinafter referred to as the "<u>Exchange Ratio</u>"). Notwithstanding the foregoing, the Board of Directors of the Company shall not be empowered to effect such exchange at any time after any Person (other than the Company, any Subsidiary of the Company, any employee benefit plan of the Company or any such Subsidiary, or any entity holding Common Shares for or pursuant to the terms of any such plan), together with all Affiliates and Associates of such Person, becomes the Beneficial Owner of 50% or more of the Common Shares then outstanding. The exchange of Rights by the Board of Directors may be made effective at such time, on such basis and with such conditions as the Board of Directors in its sole discretion may establish. Without limiting the foregoing, in connection with effecting an exchange pursuant to this Section 24, the Board of Directors may direct the Company to enter into a trust agreement in such form and with such terms as the Board of Directors shall then approve and issue to the trust created by such trust agreement all or some (as designated by the Board of Directors) of the securities to be exchanged for the Rights pursuant to this Section 24, and all Persons entitled to receive such securities pursuant to the exchange shall be entitled to receive all or some (as designated by the Board of Directors) of such securities (and any dividends or distributions made thereon after the date on which such securities are deposited in the trust) from such trust and upon compliance with the relevant terms of the trust agreement.

(b)   Immediately upon the action of the Board of Directors of the Company ordering the exchange of any Rights pursuant to paragraph (a) of this Section 24 and without any further action and without any notice, the right to exercise such Rights shall terminate and the only right thereafter of a holder of such Rights shall be to receive that number of Common Shares equal to the number of such Rights held by such holder multiplied by the Exchange Ratio. The Company shall promptly give public notice of any such exchange (with prompt written notice thereof to the Rights Agent); provided, however, that the failure to give, or any defect in, such notice shall not affect the validity of such exchange. . . .

(c) In the event that there shall not be sufficient Common Shares issued but not outstanding or authorized but unissued to permit any exchange of Rights as contemplated in accordance with this Section 24, the Company shall take all such action as may be necessary to authorize additional Common Shares for issuance upon exchange of the Rights. . . .

(d) The Company shall not be required to issue fractions of Common Shares or to distribute certificates which evidence fractional Common Shares. In lieu of such fractional Common Shares, the Company shall pay to the registered holders of the Right Certificates with regard to which such fractional Common Shares would otherwise be issuable an amount in cash equal to the same fraction of the current market value of a whole Common Share. . . .

Section 25. Notice of Certain Events. (a) In case the Company shall, at any time after the Distribution Date, propose (i) to pay any dividend payable in stock of any class to the holders of the Preferred Shares or to make any other distribution to the holders of the Preferred Shares (other than a regular quarterly cash dividend), (ii) to offer to the holders of the Preferred Shares rights or warrants to subscribe for or to purchase any additional Preferred Shares or shares of stock of any class or any other securities, rights or options, (iii) to effect any reclassification of the Preferred Shares (other than a reclassification involving only the subdivision of outstanding Preferred Shares), (iv) to effect any share exchange, consolidation or merger into or with, or to effect any sale or other transfer (or to permit one or more of its Subsidiaries to effect any sale or other transfer), in one or more transactions, of 50% or more of the assets or earning power of the Company and its Subsidiaries (taken as a whole) to, any other Person, (v) to effect the liquidation, dissolution or winding up of the Company, or (vi) to declare or pay any dividend on the Common Shares payable in Common Shares or to effect a subdivision, combination or consolidation of the Common Shares (by reclassification or otherwise than by payment of dividends in Common Shares), then, in each such case, the Company shall give to each holder of a Right Certificate, in accordance with Section 26 hereof, a notice of such proposed action, which shall specify the record date for the purposes of such stock dividend, or distribution of rights or warrants, or the date on which such share exchange, reclassification, consolidation, merger, sale, transfer, liquidation, dissolution, or winding up is to take place and the date of participation therein by the holders of the Common Shares and/or Preferred Shares, if any such date is to be fixed, and such notice shall be so given in the case of any action covered by clause (i) or (ii) above at least 10 days prior to the record date for determining holders of the Preferred Shares for purposes of such action, and, in the case of any such other action, at least 10 days prior to the date of the taking of such proposed action or the date of participation therein by the holders of the Common Shares and/or Preferred Shares, whichever shall be the earlier.

(b) In case the event set forth in Section 11(a)(ii) hereof shall occur, then the Company shall, as soon as practicable thereafter, give to the Rights Agent and each holder of a Right Certificate, in accordance with Section 26 hereof, a notice of the occurrence of such event, which notice shall describe such event and the consequences of such event to holders of Rights under Section 11(a)(ii) hereof.

Section 26. Notices. Notices or demands authorized by this Agreement to be given or made by the Rights Agent or by the holder of any Right Certificate to or on the Company shall be sufficiently given or made if sent by overnight delivery service or first-class mail, postage prepaid, addressed (until another address is filed in writing with the Rights Agent) as follows:

[Name and Address of Company]

Attention: Corporate Secretary

. . .

Section 27. Supplements and Amendments. Subject to this Section, the Company may, and the Rights Agent shall, if directed by the Company, from time to time supplement or amend this Agreement without the approval of any holders of Right Certificates in order to cure any ambiguity, to correct or supplement any provision contained herein which may be defective or inconsistent with any other provisions herein, or to make any other provisions with respect to the Rights which the Company may deem necessary or desirable, any such supplement or amendment to be evidenced by a writing signed by the Company and the Rights Agent; provided, however, that, from and after such time as any Person becomes an Acquiring

Person, this Agreement shall not be amended in any manner which would adversely affect the interests of the holders of Rights. [Without limiting the foregoing, the Company may at any time prior to such time as any Person becomes an Acquiring Person amend this Agreement to lower the thresholds set forth in Sections 1(a) and 3(a) hereof to not less than 10% (the "Reduced Threshold"); provided, however, that no Person who Beneficially Owns a number of Common Shares equal to or greater than the Reduced Threshold shall become an Acquiring Person unless such Person shall, after the public announcement of the Reduced Threshold, increase its Beneficial Ownership of the then outstanding Common Shares (other than as a result of an acquisition of Common Shares by the Company) to an amount equal to or greater than the greater of (x) the Reduced Threshold or (y) the sum of (i) the lowest Beneficial Ownership of such Person as a percentage of the outstanding Common Shares as of any date on or after the date of the public announcement of such Reduced Threshold plus (ii) 0.001%.] For the avoidance of doubt, the Company shall be entitled to adopt and implement such procedures and arrangements (including with third parties) as it may deem necessary or desirable to facilitate the exercise, exchange, trading, issuance or distribution of the Rights (and Preferred Shares) as contemplated hereby and to ensure that an Acquiring Person does not obtain the benefits thereof, and amendments in respect of the foregoing shall not be deemed to adversely affect the interests of the holders of Rights. Upon the delivery of a certificate from an appropriate officer of the Company that states that the proposed supplement or amendment is in compliance with the terms of this Section 27, the Rights Agent shall execute such supplement or amendment; provided, that notwithstanding anything in this Agreement to the contrary, the Rights Agent may, but shall not be obligated to, enter into any supplement or amendment that materially and adversely affects the Rights Agent's own rights, duties, obligations or immunities under this Agreement.

Section 28. <u>Successors</u>. All the covenants and provisions of this Agreement by or for the benefit of the Company or the Rights Agent shall bind and inure to the benefit of their respective successors and assigns hereunder.

Section 29. <u>Benefits of this Agreement</u>. Nothing in this Agreement shall be construed to give to any Person other than the Company, the Rights Agent and the registered holders of the Right Certificates (and, prior to the Distribution Date, the Common Shares) any legal or equitable right, remedy or claim under this Agreement; but this Agreement shall be for the sole and exclusive benefit of the Company, the Rights Agent and the registered holders of the Right Certificates (and, prior to the Distribution Date, the Common Shares).

Section 30. <u>Severability</u>. . . .

Section 31. <u>Governing Law</u>. This Agreement and each Right Certificate issued hereunder shall be deemed to be a contract made under the laws of the State of [●] and for all purposes shall be governed by and construed in accordance with the laws of such state applicable to contracts to be made and performed entirely within such state.

Section 32. <u>Counterparts</u>. This Agreement may be executed in any number of counterparts and each of such counterparts shall for all purposes be deemed to be an original, and all such counterparts shall together constitute but one and the same instrument. . . .

Section 33. <u>Descriptive Headings</u>. Descriptive headings of the several Sections of this Agreement are inserted for convenience only and shall not control or affect the meaning or construction of any of the provisions hereof. . . .

Section 35. <u>Force Majeure</u>. Notwithstanding anything to the contrary contained herein, the Rights Agent shall not be liable for any delays or failures in performance resulting from acts beyond its reasonable control including, without limitation, acts of God, terrorist acts, shortage of supply, breakdowns or malfunctions, interruptions or malfunctions of computer facilities, or loss of data due to power failures or mechanical difficulties with information storage or retrieval systems, labor difficulties, war, or civil unrest. The Rights Agent shall provide the Company prompt notice as soon as practicable in the event that any such delay or failure in performance occurs and keep the Company apprised of developments and mitigation effort with respect thereto.

WACHTELL, LIPTON, ROSEN & KATZ,
SHARE PURCHASE RIGHTS PLAN

IN WITNESS WHEREOF, the parties hereto have caused this Agreement to be duly executed and attested, all as of the day and year first above written.

Attest: [COMPANY]

By _____   By _____

       Name: Name:

       Title: Title:

Attest: [RIGHTS AGENT]

By _____   By _____

       Name: Name:

       Title: Title:

FORM
of
CERTIFICATE OF DESIGNATIONS
of
SERIES A JUNIOR PARTICIPATING PREFERRED STOCK
of
[_____]

(Pursuant to Section 151 of the
Delaware General Corporation Law)

_____, a corporation organized and existing under the General Corporation Law of the State of Delaware (hereinafter called the "Corporation"), hereby certifies that the following resolution was adopted by the Board of Directors of the Corporation as required by Section 151 of the General Corporation Law at a meeting duly called and held on _____, _____:

RESOLVED, that pursuant to the authority granted to and vested in the Board of Directors of this Corporation (hereinafter called the "Board of Directors" or the "Board") in accordance with the provisions of the Certificate of Incorporation, the Board of Directors hereby creates a series of Preferred Stock, par value $__ per share, of the Corporation (the "Preferred Stock"), and hereby states the designation and number of shares, and fixes the relative rights, preferences, and limitations thereof as follows:

Series A Junior Participating Preferred Stock:

Section 1. Designation and Amount. The shares of such series shall be designated as "Series A Junior Participating Preferred Stock" (the "Series A Preferred Stock") and the number of shares constituting the Series A Preferred Stock shall be _____. Such number of shares may be increased or decreased by resolution of the Board of Directors; provided that no decrease shall reduce the number of shares of Series A Preferred Stock to a number less than the number of shares then outstanding plus the number of shares reserved for issuance upon the exercise of outstanding options, rights or warrants or upon the conversion of any outstanding securities issued by the Corporation convertible into Series A Preferred Stock.

Section 2. Dividends and Distributions.

(A) Subject to the rights of the holders of any shares of any series of Preferred Stock (or any similar stock) ranking prior and superior to the Series A Preferred Stock with respect to dividends, the holders of shares of Series A Preferred Stock, in preference to the holders of Common Stock, par value $_____ per share (the "Common Stock"), of the Corporation, and of any other junior stock, shall be entitled to receive, when, as and if declared by the Board of Directors out of funds legally available for the purpose, quarterly dividends payable in cash on the first day of March, June, September and December in each year (each such date being referred to herein as a "Quarterly Dividend Payment Date"), commencing on the first Quarterly Dividend Payment Date after the first issuance of a share or fraction of a share of Series A Preferred Stock, in an amount per share (rounded to the nearest cent) equal to the greater of (a) $1 or (b) subject to the provision for adjustment hereinafter set forth, 100 times the aggregate per share amount of all cash dividends, and 100 times the aggregate per share amount (payable in kind) of all non-cash dividends or other distributions, other than a dividend payable in shares of Common Stock or a subdivision of the outstanding shares of Common Stock (by reclassification or otherwise), declared on the Common Stock since the immediately preceding Quarterly Dividend Payment Date or, with respect to the first Quarterly Dividend Payment Date, since the first issuance of any share or fraction of a share of Series A Preferred Stock. In the event the Corporation shall at any time declare or pay any dividend on the Common Stock payable in shares of Common Stock, or effect a subdivision or combination or consolidation of the outstanding shares of Common Stock (by reclassification or otherwise than by payment of a dividend in shares of Common Stock) into a greater or lesser number of shares of Common Stock, then in each such case the amount to which holders of shares of Series A Preferred Stock were entitled immediately prior to such event under clause (b) of the preceding sentence shall be adjusted by multiplying such amount by a fraction, the numerator of which is the number of shares of Common Stock outstanding immediately after such event and the denominator of which is the number of shares of Common Stock that were outstanding immediately prior to such event.

(B)   The Corporation shall declare a dividend or distribution on the Series A Preferred Stock as provided in paragraph (A) of this Section immediately after it declares a dividend or distribution on the Common Stock (other than a dividend payable in shares of Common Stock); provided that, in the event no dividend or distribution shall have been declared on the Common Stock during the period between any Quarterly Dividend Payment Date and the next subsequent Quarterly Dividend Payment Date, a dividend of $1 per share on the Series A Preferred Stock shall nevertheless be payable on such subsequent Quarterly Dividend Payment Date.

(C)   Dividends shall begin to accrue and be cumulative on outstanding shares of Series A Preferred Stock from the Quarterly Dividend Payment Date next preceding the date of issue of such shares, unless the date of issue of such shares is prior to the record date for the first Quarterly Dividend Payment Date, in which case dividends on such shares shall begin to accrue from the date of issue of such shares, or unless the date of issue is a Quarterly Dividend Payment Date or is a date after the record date for the determination of holders of shares of Series A Preferred Stock entitled to receive a quarterly dividend and before such Quarterly Dividend Payment Date, in either of which events such dividends shall begin to accrue and be cumulative from such Quarterly Dividend Payment Date. Accrued but unpaid dividends shall not bear interest. Dividends paid on the shares of Series A Preferred Stock in an amount less than the total amount of such dividends at the time accrued and payable on such shares shall be allocated pro rata on a share-by-share basis among all such shares at the time outstanding. The Board of Directors may fix a record date for the determination of holders of shares of Series A Preferred Stock entitled to receive payment of a dividend or distribution declared thereon, which record date shall be not more than 60 days prior to the date fixed for the payment thereof.

Section 3. <u>Voting Rights</u>. The holders of shares of Series A Preferred Stock shall have the following voting rights:

(A)   Subject to the provision for adjustment hereinafter set forth, each share of Series A Preferred Stock shall entitle the holder thereof to 100 votes on all matters submitted to a vote of the stockholders of the Corporation. In the event the Corporation shall at any time declare or pay any dividend on the Common Stock payable in shares of Common Stock, or effect a subdivision or combination or consolidation of the outstanding shares of Common Stock (by reclassification or otherwise than by payment of a dividend in shares of Common Stock) into a greater or lesser number of shares of Common Stock, then in each such case the number of votes per share to which holders of shares of Series A Preferred Stock were entitled immediately prior to such event shall be adjusted by multiplying such number by a fraction, the numerator of which is the number of shares of Common Stock outstanding immediately after such event and the denominator of which is the number of shares of Common Stock that were outstanding immediately prior to such event.

(B)   Except as otherwise provided herein, in any other Certificate of Designations creating a series of Preferred Stock or any similar stock, or by law, the holders of shares of Series A Preferred Stock and the holders of shares of Common Stock and any other capital stock of the Corporation having general voting rights shall vote together as one class on all matters submitted to a vote of stockholders of the Corporation.

(C)   Except as set forth herein, or as otherwise provided by law, holders of Series A Preferred Stock shall have no special voting rights and their consent shall not be required (except to the extent they are entitled to vote with holders of Common Stock as set forth herein) for taking any corporate action.

Section 4. <u>Certain Restrictions</u>.

(A)   Whenever quarterly dividends or other dividends or distributions payable on the Series A Preferred Stock as provided in Section 2 are in arrears, thereafter and until all accrued and unpaid dividends and distributions, whether or not declared, on shares of Series A Preferred Stock outstanding shall have been paid in full, the Corporation shall not:

(i)   declare or pay dividends, or make any other distributions, on any shares of stock ranking junior (either as to dividends or upon liquidation, dissolution or winding up) to the Series A Preferred Stock;

(ii)   declare or pay dividends, or make any other distributions, on any shares of stock ranking on a parity (either as to dividends or upon liquidation, dissolution or winding up) with the Series A Preferred Stock, except dividends paid ratably on the Series A Preferred Stock and all such parity stock on which dividends are payable or in arrears in proportion to the total amounts to which the holders of all such shares are then entitled;

(iii)   redeem or purchase or otherwise acquire for consideration shares of any stock ranking junior (either as to dividends or upon liquidation, dissolution or winding up) to the Series A Preferred Stock, provided that the Corporation may at any time redeem, purchase or otherwise acquire shares of any such junior stock in exchange for shares of any stock of the Corporation ranking junior (either as to dividends or upon dissolution, liquidation or winding up) to the Series A Preferred Stock; or

(iv)   redeem or purchase or otherwise acquire for consideration any shares of Series A Preferred Stock, or any shares of stock ranking on a parity with the Series A Preferred Stock, except in accordance with a purchase offer made in writing or by publication (as determined by the Board of Directors) to all holders of such shares upon such terms as the Board of Directors, after consideration of the respective annual dividend rates and other relative rights and preferences of the respective series and classes, shall determine in good faith will result in fair and equitable treatment among the respective series or classes.

(B)   The Corporation shall not permit any subsidiary of the Corporation to purchase or otherwise acquire for consideration any shares of stock of the Corporation unless the Corporation could, under paragraph (A) of this Section 4, purchase or otherwise acquire such shares at such time and in such manner.

Section 5. <u>Reacquired Shares</u>. Any shares of Series A Preferred Stock purchased or otherwise acquired by the Corporation in any manner whatsoever shall be retired and cancelled promptly after the acquisition thereof. All such shares shall upon their cancellation become authorized but unissued shares of Preferred Stock and may be reissued as part of a new series of Preferred Stock subject to the conditions and restrictions on issuance set forth herein, in the Certificate of Incorporation, or in any other Certificate of Designations creating a series of Preferred Stock or any similar stock or as otherwise required by law.

Section 6. <u>Liquidation, Dissolution or Winding Up</u>. Upon any liquidation, dissolution or winding up of the Corporation, no distribution shall be made (1) to the holders of shares of stock ranking junior (either as to dividends or upon liquidation, dissolution or winding up) to the Series A Preferred Stock unless, prior thereto, the holders of shares of Series A Preferred Stock shall have received $100 per share, plus an amount equal to accrued and unpaid dividends and distributions thereon, whether or not declared, to the date of such payment, provided that the holders of shares of Series A Preferred Stock shall be entitled to receive an aggregate amount per share, subject to the provision for adjustment hereinafter set forth, equal to 100 times the aggregate amount to be distributed per share to holders of shares of Common Stock, or (2) to the holders of shares of stock ranking on a parity (either as to dividends or upon liquidation, dissolution or winding up) with the Series A Preferred Stock, except distributions made ratably on the Series A Preferred Stock and all such parity stock in proportion to the total amounts to which the holders of all such shares are entitled upon such liquidation, dissolution or winding up. In the event the Corporation shall at any time declare or pay any dividend on the Common Stock payable in shares of Common Stock, or effect a subdivision or combination or consolidation of the outstanding shares of Common Stock (by reclassification or otherwise than by payment of a dividend in shares of Common Stock) into a greater or lesser number of shares of Common Stock, then in each such case the aggregate amount to which holders of shares of Series A Preferred Stock were entitled immediately prior to such event under the proviso in clause (1) of the preceding sentence shall be adjusted by multiplying such amount by a fraction the numerator of which is the number of shares of Common Stock outstanding immediately after such event and the denominator of which is the number of shares of Common Stock that were outstanding immediately prior to such event.

Section 7. <u>Consolidation, Merger, etc.</u> In case the Corporation shall enter into any consolidation, merger, combination or other transaction in which the shares of Common Stock are exchanged for or changed into other stock or securities, cash and/or any other property, then in any such case each share of Series A Preferred Stock shall at the same time be similarly exchanged or changed into an amount per share, subject to the provision for adjustment hereinafter set forth, equal to 100 times the aggregate amount of stock, securities, cash and/or any other property (payable in kind), as the case may be, into which or for which each share of Common Stock is changed or exchanged. In the event the Corporation shall at any time declare or pay any dividend on the Common Stock payable in shares of Common Stock, or effect a subdivision or combination or consolidation of the outstanding shares of Common Stock (by reclassification or otherwise than by payment of a dividend in shares of Common Stock) into a greater or lesser number of shares of Common Stock, then in each such case the amount set forth in the preceding sentence with respect to the exchange or change of shares of Series A Preferred Stock shall be adjusted by multiplying such amount by a fraction, the numerator of which is the number of shares of Common Stock outstanding immediately after such event and the denominator of which is the number of shares of Common Stock that were outstanding immediately prior to such event.

Section 8. No Redemption. The shares of Series A Preferred Stock shall not be redeemable.

Section 9. Rank. The Series A Preferred Stock shall rank, with respect to the payment of dividends and the distribution of assets, junior to all series of any other class of the Corporation's Preferred Stock.

Section 10. Amendment. The Certificate of Incorporation of the Corporation shall not be amended in any manner which would materially alter or change the powers, preferences or special rights of the Series A Preferred Stock so as to affect them adversely without the affirmative vote of the holders of at least two-thirds of the outstanding shares of Series A Preferred Stock, voting together as a single class.

IN WITNESS WHEREOF, this Certificate of Designations is executed on behalf of the Corporation by its Chairman of the Board and attested by its Secretary this _____ day of _____, 20__.

_____

Chairman of the Board

Attest:

_____

Secretary

Form of Right Certificate

Certificate No. R-_____ Rights

NOT EXERCISABLE AFTER _____, _____ OR EARLIER IF REDEMPTION OR EXCHANGE OCCURS. THE RIGHTS ARE SUBJECT TO REDEMPTION AT $0.01 PER RIGHT AND TO EXCHANGE ON THE TERMS SET FORTH IN THE AGREEMENT.

Right Certificate

_____

This certifies that _____, or registered assigns, is the registered owner of the number of Rights set forth above, each of which entitles the owner thereof, subject to the terms, provisions and conditions of the Agreement, dated as of _____, _____ (the "Agreement"), between _____, a Delaware corporation (the "Company"), and _____ (the "Rights Agent"), to purchase from the Company at any time after the Distribution Date (as such term is defined in the Agreement) and prior to 5:00 P.M., [City of Rights Agent] time, on _____, _____ at the principal office of the Rights Agent, or at the office of its successor as Rights Agent, one one-hundredth of a fully paid non-assessable share of Series A Junior Participating Preferred Stock, par value $___ per share, of the Company (the "Preferred Shares"), at a purchase price of $___ per one one-hundredth of a Preferred Share (the "Purchase Price"), upon presentation and surrender of this Right Certificate with the Form of Election to Purchase duly executed. The number of Rights evidenced by this Right Certificate (and the number of one one-hundredths of a Preferred Share which may be purchased upon exercise hereof) set forth above, and the Purchase Price set forth above, are the number and Purchase Price as of _____, _____, based on the Preferred Shares as constituted at such date. As provided in the Agreement, the Purchase Price and the number of one one-hundredths of a Preferred Share which may be purchased upon the exercise of the Rights evidenced by this Right Certificate are subject to modification and adjustment upon the happening of certain events.

This Right Certificate is subject to all of the terms, provisions and conditions of the Agreement, which terms, provisions and conditions are hereby incorporated herein by reference and made a part hereof and to which Agreement reference is hereby made for a full description of the rights, limitations of rights, obligations, duties and immunities hereunder of the Rights Agent, the Company and the holders of the Right Certificates. Copies of the Agreement are on file at the principal executive offices of the Company and the offices of the Rights Agent.

This Right Certificate, with or without other Right Certificates, upon surrender at the principal office of the Rights Agent, may be exchanged for another Right Certificate or Right Certificates of like tenor and date evidencing Rights entitling the holder to purchase a like aggregate number of Preferred Shares as the Rights evidenced by the Right Certificate or Right Certificates surrendered shall have entitled such holder to purchase. If this Right Certificate shall be exercised in part, the holder shall be entitled to receive upon surrender hereof another Right Certificate or Right Certificates for the number of whole Rights not exercised.

Subject to the provisions of the Agreement, the Rights evidenced by this Right Certificate (i) may be redeemed by the Company at a redemption price of $0.01 per Right or (ii) may be exchanged in whole or in part for Preferred Shares or shares of the Company's Common Stock, par value $___ per share.

No fractional Preferred Shares will be issued upon the exercise of any Right or Rights evidenced hereby (other than fractions which are integral multiples of one one-hundredth of a Preferred Share, which may, at the election of the Company, be evidenced by depositary receipts), but, in lieu thereof, a cash payment will be made, as provided in the Agreement.

No holder of this Right Certificate shall be entitled to vote or receive dividends or be deemed for any purpose the holder of the Preferred Shares or of any other securities of the Company which may at any time be issuable on the exercise hereof, nor shall anything contained in the Agreement or herein be construed to confer upon the holder hereof, as such, any of the rights of a stockholder of the Company or any right to vote for the election of directors or upon any matter submitted to stockholders at any meeting thereof, or to give or withhold consent to any corporate action, or to receive notice of meetings or other actions affecting stockholders (except as provided in the Agreement), or to receive dividends or subscription rights, or otherwise, until the Right or Rights evidenced by this Right Certificate shall have been exercised as provided in the Agreement.

This Right Certificate shall not be valid or obligatory for any purpose until it shall have been countersigned by the Rights Agent.

WITNESS the facsimile signature of the proper officers of the Company and its corporate seal. Dated as of _____, ___

Attest: [COMPANY]

By _____   By _____
    Name: Name:
    Title: Title:
Countersigned:

[Rights Agent]

By _____
    Name:
    Title:

Form of Reverse Side of Right Certificate

FORM OF ASSIGNMENT

(To be executed by the registered holder if such
holder desires to transfer the Right Certificate.)

FOR VALUE RECEIVED _____ hereby sells, assigns and transfers unto

_____

(Please print name and address of transferee)

this Right Certificate, together with all right, title and interest therein, and does hereby irrevocably
constitute and appoint _____ Attorney, to transfer the within Right Certificate on
the books of the within-named Company, with full power of substitution.

Dated: _____

_____
Signature

Signature Guaranteed:

Signatures must be guaranteed by a member or participant in the Medallion Signature Guarantee Program
at a guarantee level acceptable to the Company's Transfer Agent.

The undersigned hereby certifies that the Rights evidenced by this Right Certificate are not Beneficially
Owned by an Acquiring Person or an Affiliate or Associate thereof (as defined in the Agreement) and are
not issued with respect to Notional Common Shares related to a Derivatives Contract described in clause
(iv) of the definition of Beneficial Owner (as such terms are defined in the Agreement).

_____
Signature

WACHTELL, LIPTON, ROSEN & KATZ,
SHARE PURCHASE RIGHTS PLAN

Form of Reverse Side of Right Certificate—continued

FORM OF ELECTION TO PURCHASE

(To be executed if holder desires to exercise
Rights represented by the Right Certificate.)

To: _____

The undersigned hereby irrevocably elects to exercise _____ Rights represented by this Right Certificate to purchase the Preferred Shares issuable upon the exercise of such Rights and requests that certificates for such Preferred Shares be issued in the name of:

Please insert social security
or other identifying number

_____

_____

(Please print name and address)

If such number of Rights shall not be all the Rights evidenced by this Right Certificate, a new Right Certificate for the balance remaining of such Rights shall be registered in the name of and delivered to:

Please insert social security
or other identifying number

_____

(Please print name and address)

Dated: _____

_____
Signature

Signature Guaranteed:

Signatures must be guaranteed by a member or participant in the Medallion Signature Guarantee Program at a guarantee level acceptable to the Company's Transfer Agent.

The undersigned hereby certifies that the Rights evidenced by this Right Certificate are not Beneficially Owned by an Acquiring Person or an Affiliate or Associate thereof (as defined in the Agreement) and are not issued with respect to Notional Common Shares related to a Derivatives Contract described in clause (iv) of the definition of Beneficial Owner (as such terms are defined in the Agreement).

_____

Signature

NOTICE

The signature in the Form of Assignment or Form of Election to Purchase, as the case may be, must conform to the name as written upon the face of this Right Certificate in every particular, without alteration or enlargement or any change whatsoever.

In the event the certification set forth above in the Form of Assignment or the Form of Election to Purchase, as the case may be, is not completed, the Company and the Rights Agent will deem the Beneficial Owner of the Rights evidenced by this Right Certificate to be an Acquiring Person or an Affiliate or Associate thereof (as defined in the Agreement) and such Assignment or Election to Purchase will not be honored.

SUMMARY OF RIGHTS TO PURCHASE
PREFERRED SHARES

<u>Introduction</u>

On _____, _____, the Board of Directors of our Company, _____, a Delaware corporation, declared a dividend of one preferred share purchase right (a "Right") for each outstanding share of common stock, par value $__ per share. The dividend is payable on _____, _____ to the stockholders of record as of the close of business on _____, _____. [These rights will replace rights to purchase common stock that will expire on _____, _____.]

Our Board has adopted this Rights Agreement to protect stockholders from coercive or otherwise unfair takeover tactics. In general terms, it works by imposing a significant penalty upon any person or group that acquires [10]% [(or [20]% in the case of a "13G Investor," as defined in the Rights Agreement)] or more of our outstanding common stock without the approval of our Board. [If a stockholder's beneficial ownership of our common stock as of the time of the public announcement of the rights plan and associated dividend declaration is at or above the applicable threshold (including through entry into certain derivative positions), that stockholder's then-existing ownership percentage would be grandfathered, but the rights would become exercisable if at any time after such announcement, the stockholder increases its ownership percentage by 0.001% or more.] The Rights Agreement would not interfere with any merger or other business combination approved by our Board.

For those interested in the specific terms of the Rights Agreement as made between our Company and _____], as the Rights Agent, on _____, _____, we provide the following summary description. Please note, however, that this description is only a summary, and is not complete, and should be read together with the entire Rights Agreement, which has been filed with the Securities and Exchange Commission as an exhibit to a Registration Statement on Form 8-A dated _____, _____. A copy of the agreement is available free of charge from our Company.

The Rights. Our Board authorized the issuance of a Right with respect to each outstanding share of common stock on _____, _____. The Rights will initially trade with, and will be inseparable from, the common stock. The Rights are evidenced only by certificates that represent shares of common stock. New Rights will accompany any new shares of common stock we issue after _____, _____ until the Distribution Date described below.

Exercisability. The Rights will not be exercisable until 10 days after the public announcement that a person or group has become an "Acquiring Person" by obtaining beneficial ownership of [10]% [(or [20]% in the case of a "13G Investor")] or more of our outstanding common stock. Prior to exercise, the Right does not give its holder any dividend, voting, or liquidation rights.

We refer to the date when the Rights become exercisable as the "Distribution Date." Until that date, the common stock certificates (or, in the case of uncertificated shares, by notations in the book-entry account system) will also evidence the Rights, and any transfer of shares of common stock will constitute a transfer of Rights. After that date, the Rights will separate from the common stock and be evidenced by book-entry credits or by Rights certificates that we will mail to all eligible holders of common stock. Any Rights held by an Acquiring Person are null and void and may not be exercised.

[Our Board may reduce the threshold at which a person or group becomes an Acquiring Person from [__]% to not less than [10]% of the outstanding common stock.]

Exercise Price. Each Right will allow its holder to purchase from our Company one one-hundredth of a share of Series A Junior Participating Preferred Stock ("Preferred Share") for $__ (the "Exercise Price"), once the Rights become exercisable. This portion of a Preferred Share will give the stockholder approximately the same dividend, voting, and liquidation rights as would one share of common stock.

Beneficial Ownership. Certain synthetic interests in securities created by derivative positions—whether or not such interests are considered to be ownership of the underlying common stock or are reportable for purposes of Regulation 13D of the Securities Exchange Act—are treated as beneficial ownership of the number of shares of the company's common stock equivalent to the economic exposure created by the derivative position, to the extent actual shares of the company's common stock are directly or indirectly held by counterparties to the derivatives contracts. Swaps dealers unassociated with any control intent or intent to evade the purposes of the rights plan are excepted from such imputed beneficial ownership.

Shares held by Affiliates and Associates of an Acquiring Person, and Notional Shares held by counterparties to a Derivatives Contract with an Acquiring Person, will be deemed to be beneficially owned by the Acquiring Person.

Consequences of a Person or Group Becoming an Acquiring Person.

- *Flip In.* If a person or group becomes an Acquiring Person, all holders of Rights except the Acquiring Person may, for the Exercise Price, purchase shares of our common stock with a market value of $__, based on the market price of the common stock prior to such acquisition.

- *Exchange.* After a person or group becomes an Acquiring Person, but before an Acquiring Person owns 50% or more of our outstanding common stock, our Board may extinguish the Rights by exchanging one share of common stock or equivalent security for each Right, other than Rights held by the Acquiring Person.

- *Flip Over.* If our Company is later acquired in a merger or similar transaction after the Rights Distribution Date, all holders of Rights except the Acquiring Person may, for $__, purchase shares of the acquiring corporation with a market value of $__ based on the market price of the acquiring corporation's stock, prior to such merger.

Preferred Share Provisions.

Each one one-hundredth of a Preferred Share, if issued:

- will not be redeemable.

- will entitle holders to quarterly dividend payments of $0.01 per share, or an amount equal to the dividend paid on one share of common stock, whichever is greater.

- will entitle holders upon liquidation either to receive $1.00 per share, or an amount equal to the payment made on one share of common stock, whichever is greater.

- will have the same voting power as one share of common stock.

- if shares of our common stock are exchanged via merger, consolidation, or a similar transaction, will entitle holders to a per share payment equal to the payment made on one share of common stock.

The value of one one-hundredth interest in a Preferred Share should approximate the value of one share of common stock.

Expiration. The Rights will expire on _____, _____.

Redemption. Our Board may redeem the Rights for $0.01 per Right at any time before any person or group becomes an Acquiring Person. If our Board redeems any Rights, it must redeem all of the Rights. Once the Rights are redeemed, the only right of the holders of Rights will be to receive the redemption price of $0.01 per Right. The redemption price will be adjusted if we have a stock split or stock dividends of our common stock.

Anti-Dilution Provisions. Our Board may adjust the purchase price of the Preferred Shares, the number of Preferred Shares issuable and the number of outstanding Rights to prevent dilution that may occur from a stock dividend, a stock split, a reclassification of the Preferred Shares or common stock. No adjustments to the Exercise Price of less than 1% will be made.

Amendments. The terms of the Rights Agreement may be amended by our Board without the consent of the holders of the Rights. [However, our Board may not amend the Rights Agreement to lower the threshold at which a person or group becomes an Acquiring Person to below [10]% of our outstanding common stock.] [In addition/However], the Board may not cause a person or group to become an Acquiring Person by lowering this threshold below the percentage interest that such person or group already owns. After a person or group becomes an Acquiring Person, our Board may not amend the agreement in a way that adversely affects holders of the Rights.

FORM OF CHUBB'S DIRECTORS AND OFFICERS LIABILITY POLICY

In consideration of payment of the premium and subject to the Declarations, the General Terms and Conditions, and the limitations, conditions, provisions and other terms of this coverage section, the Company and the Insureds agree as follows:

Insuring Clauses

Executive Liability Coverage Insuring Clause 1

1. The Company shall pay, on behalf of each of the **Insured Persons**, **Loss** for which the **Insured Person** is not indemnified by the **Organization** and which the **Insured Person** becomes legally obligated to pay on account of any **Claim** first made against the **Insured Person**, individually or otherwise, during the **Policy Period** or, if exercised, during the Extended Reporting Period, for a **Wrongful Act** committed, attempted, or allegedly committed or attempted by such **Insured Person** before or during the **Policy Period**, but only if such **Claim** is reported to the Company in writing in the manner and within the time provided in Subsection 15 of this coverage section.

Executive Indemnification Coverage Insuring Clause 2

2. The Company shall pay, on behalf of the **Organization**, **Loss** for which the **Organization** grants indemnification to an **Insured Person**, as permitted or required by law, and which the **Insured Person** becomes legally obligated to pay on account of any **Claim** first made against the **Insured Person**, individually or otherwise, during the **Policy Period** or, if exercised, during the Extended Reporting Period, for a **Wrongful Act** committed, attempted, or allegedly committed or attempted by such **Insured Person** before or during the **Policy Period**, but only if such **Claim** is reported to the Company in writing in the manner and within the time provided in Subsection 15 of this coverage section.

Entity Securities Coverage Insuring Clause 3

3. The Company shall pay, on behalf of the **Organization**, **Loss** which the **Organization** becomes legally obligated to pay on account of any **Securities Claim** first made against the **Organization** during the **Policy Period** or, if exercised, during the Extended Reporting Period, for a **Wrongful Act** committed, attempted, or allegedly committed or attempted by the **Organization** or the **Insured Persons** before or during the **Policy Period**, but only if such **Securities Claim** is reported to the Company in writing in the manner and within the time provided in Subsection 15 of this coverage section.

Securityholder Derivative Demand Coverage Insuring Clause 4

4. The Company shall pay, on behalf of the **Organization**, **Investigative Costs** resulting from a **Securityholder Derivative Demand** first received by the **Organization** during the **Policy Period** or, if exercised, during the Extended Reporting Period, for a **Wrongful Act** committed, attempted, or allegedly committed or attempted before or during the **Policy Period**, but only if such **Securityholder Derivative Demand** is reported to the Company in writing in the manner and within the time provided in Subsection 15 of this coverage section.

Executive Protection Portfolio [SM]
Executive Liability and Entity Securities
Liability Coverage Section

Definitions

5.   When used in this coverage section:

Application means all signed applications, including attachments and other materials submitted therewith or incorporated therein, submitted by the **Insureds** to the Company for this coverage section or for any coverage section or policy of which this coverage section is a direct or indirect renewal or replacement.

Application shall also include, for each **Organization**, all of the following documents whether or not submitted with or attached to any such signed application: (i) the Annual Report (including financial statements) last issued to shareholders before this policy's inception date; (ii) the report last filed with the Securities and Exchange Commission on Form 10-K before this policy's inception date; (iii) the report last filed with the Securities and Exchange Commission on Form 10-Q before this policy's inception date; (iv) the proxy statement and (if different) definitive proxy statement last filed with the Securities and Exchange Commission before this policy's inception date; (v) all reports filed with the Securities and Exchange Commission on Form 8-K during the twelve months preceding this policy's inception date; and (vi) all reports filed with the Securities and Exchange Commission on Schedule 13D, with respect to any equity securities of such **Organization**, during the twelve months preceding this policy's inception date. All such applications, attachments, materials and other documents are deemed attached to, incorporated into and made a part of this coverage section.

Claim means:

(1)   when used in reference to the coverage provided by Insuring Clause 1 or 2:

(a)   a written demand for monetary damages or non-monetary relief;

(b)   a civil proceeding commenced by the service of a complaint or similar pleading; or

(c)   a formal civil administrative or civil regulatory proceeding commenced by the filing of a notice of charges or similar document or by the entry of a formal order of investigation or similar document,

against an **Insured Person** for a **Wrongful Act**, including any appeal therefrom;

(2)   when used in reference to the coverage provided by Insuring Clause 3:

(a)   a written demand for monetary damages or non-monetary relief;

(b)   a civil proceeding commenced by the service of a complaint or similar pleading; or

(c)   a formal civil administrative or civil regulatory proceeding commenced by the filing of a notice of charges or similar document or by the entry of a formal order of investigation or similar document, but only while such proceeding is also pending against an **Insured Person**,

against an **Organization** for a **Wrongful Act**, including any appeal therefrom; or

(3)   when used in reference to the coverage provided by Insuring Clause 4, a **Securityholder Derivative Demand**.

Except as may otherwise be provided in Subsection 12, Subsection 13(g),or Subsection 15(b) of this coverage section, a **Claim** will be deemed to have first been made when such **Claim** is commenced as set forth in this definition (or, in the case of a written demand, including but not limited to any **Securityholder Derivative Demand**, when such demand is first received by an **Insured**).

Defense Costs means that part of **Loss** consisting of reasonable costs, charges, fees (including but not limited to attorneys' fees and experts' fees) and expenses (other than regular or overtime wages, salaries, fees or benefits of the directors, officers or employees of the **Organization**) incurred in defending any **Claim** and the premium for appeal, attachment or similar bonds.

Domestic Partner means any natural person qualifying as a domestic partner under the provisions of any applicable federal, state or local law or under the provisions of any formal program established by the **Organization**.

Financial Impairment means the status of an **Organization** resulting from:

(a)   the appointment by any state or federal official, agency or court of any receiver, conservator, liquidator, trustee, rehabilitator or similar official to take control of, supervise, manage or liquidate such **Organization**; or

(b)   such **Organization** becoming a debtor in possession under the United States bankruptcy law or the equivalent of a debtor in possession under the law of any other country.

Insured means the **Organization** and any **Insured Person**.

Insured Capacity means the position or capacity of an **Insured Person** that causes him or her to meet the definition of **Insured Person** set forth in this coverage section. **Insured Capacity** does not include any position or capacity held by an **Insured Person** in any organization other than the **Organization**, even if the **Organization** directed or requested the **Insured Person** to serve in such position or capacity in such other organization.

Insured Person means any natural person who was, now is or shall become:

(a)   a duly elected or appointed director, officer, **Manager**, or the in-house general counsel of any **Organization** chartered in the United States of America;

(b)   a holder of a position equivalent to any position described in (a) above in an **Organization** that is chartered in any jurisdiction other than the United States of America; or

(c)   solely with respect to **Securities Claims**, any other employee of an **Organization**, provided that such other employees shall not, solely by reason of their status as employees, be **Insured Persons** for purposes of Exclusion 6(c).

Investigative Costs means reasonable costs, charges, fees (including but not limited to attorneys' fees and experts' fees) and expenses (other than regular or overtime wages, salaries, fees, or benefits of the directors, officers or employees of the **Organization**) incurred by the **Organization** (including its Board of Directors or any committee of its Board of Directors) in investigating or evaluating on behalf of the **Organization** whether it is in the best interest of the **Organization** to prosecute the claims alleged in a **Securityholder Derivative Demand**.

Loss means:

(a)   the amount that any **Insured Person** (for purposes of Insuring Clauses 1 and 2) or the **Organization** (for purposes of Insuring Clause 3) becomes legally obligated to pay on account of any covered **Claim**, including but not limited to damages (including punitive or exemplary damages, if and to the extent that such punitive or exemplary damages are insurable under the law of the jurisdiction most favorable to the insurability of such damages provided such jurisdiction has a substantial relationship to the relevant **Insureds**, to the Company, or to the **Claim** giving rise to the damages), judgments, settlements, pre-judgment and post-judgment interest and **Defense Costs**; or

(b)   for purposes of Insuring Clause 4, covered **Investigative Costs**.

Loss does not include:

(a)   any amount not indemnified by the **Organization** for which an **Insured Person** is absolved from payment by reason of any covenant, agreement or court order;

(b)   any costs incurred by the **Organization** to comply with any order for injunctive or other non-monetary relief, or to comply with an agreement to provide such relief;

(c)   any amount incurred by an **Insured** in the defense or investigation of any action, proceeding or demand that is not then a **Claim** even if (i) such amount also benefits the defense of a covered **Claim**, or (ii) such action, proceeding or demand subsequently gives rise to a **Claim**;

(d)   taxes, fines or penalties, or the multiple portion of any multiplied damage award, except as provided above with respect to punitive or exemplary damages;

(e)   any amount not insurable under the law pursuant to which this coverage section is construed, except as provided above with respect to punitive or exemplary damages;

(f)   any amount allocated to non-covered loss pursuant to Subsection 17 of this coverage section; or

(g)   any amount that represents or is substantially equivalent to an increase in the consideration paid (or proposed to be paid) by an **Organization** in connection with its purchase of any securities or assets.

Manager means any natural person who was, now is or shall become a manager, member of the Board of Managers or equivalent executive of an **Organization** that is a limited liability company.

Executive Protection Portfolio [SM]
**Executive Liability and Entity Securities
Liability Coverage Section**

Organization means, collectively, those organizations designated in Item 5 of the Declarations for this coverage section, including any such organization in its capacity as a debtor in possession under the United States bankruptcy law or in an equivalent status under the law of any other country.

Pollutants means (a) any substance located anywhere in the world exhibiting any hazardous characteristics as defined by, or identified on a list of hazardous substances issued by, the United States Environmental Protection Agency or any state, county, municipality or locality counterpart thereof, including, without limitation, solids, liquids, gaseous or thermal irritants, contaminants or smoke, vapor, soot, fumes, acids, alkalis, chemicals or waste materials, or (b) any other air emission, odor, waste water, oil or oil products, infectious or medical waste, asbestos or asbestos products or any noise.

Related Claims means all **Claims** for **Wrongful Acts** based upon, arising from, or in consequence of the same or related facts, circumstances, situations, transactions or events or the same or related series of facts, circumstances, situations, transactions or events.

Securities Claim means that portion of a **Claim** which:

    (a)   is brought by a securityholder of an **Organization**

        (i)   in his or her capacity as a securityholder of such **Organization**, with respect to his or her interest in securities of such **Organization**, and against such **Organization** or any of its **Insured Persons**; or

        (ii)   derivatively, on behalf of such **Organization**, against an **Insured Person** of such **Organization**; or

    (b)   alleges that an **Organization** or any of its **Insured Persons**

        (i)   violated a federal, state, local or foreign securities law or a rule or regulation promulgated under any such securities law; or

        (ii)   committed a **Wrongful Act** that constitutes or arises from a purchase, sale, or offer to purchase or sell securities of such **Organization**,

provided that **Securities Claim** does not include any **Claim** by or on behalf of a former, current, future or prospective employee of the **Organization** that is based upon, arising from, or in consequence of any offer, grant or issuance, or any plan or agreement relating to the offer, grant or issuance, by the **Organization** to such employee in his or her capacity as such of stock, stock warrants, stock options or other securities of the **Organization**, or any payment or instrument the amount or value of which is derived from the value of securities of the **Organization**; and provided, further, that **Securities Claim** does not include any **Securityholder Derivative Demand**.

Securityholder Derivative Demand means:

    (a)   any written demand, by a securityholder of an **Organization**, upon the Board of Directors or Board of **Managers** of such **Organization** to bring a civil proceeding in a court of law against an **Insured Person** for a **Wrongful Act**; or

    (b)   any lawsuit by a securityholder of an **Organization**, brought derivatively on behalf of such **Organization** against an **Insured Person** for a **Wrongful Act** without first making a demand as described in (a) above,

1159

provided such demand or lawsuit is brought and maintained without any active assistance or participation of, or solicitation by, any **Insured Person**.

Subsidiary, either in the singular or plural, means any organization while more than fifty percent (50%) of the outstanding securities or voting rights representing the present right to vote for election of or to appoint directors or **Managers** of such organization are owned or controlled, directly or indirectly, in any combination, by one or more **Organizations**.

Wrongful Act means:

(a) any error, misstatement, misleading statement, act, omission, neglect, or breach of duty committed, attempted, or allegedly committed or attempted by an **Insured Person** in his or her **Insured Capacity**, or for purposes of coverage under Insuring Clause 3, by the **Organization**, or

(b) any other matter claimed against an **Insured Person** solely by reason of his or her serving in an **Insured Capacity**.

Exclusions

Applicable To All Insuring Clauses

6. The Company shall not be liable for **Loss** on account of any **Claim**:

(a) based upon, arising from, or in consequence of any fact, circumstance, situation, transaction, event or **Wrongful Act** that, before the inception date set forth in Item 2 of the Declarations of the General Terms and Conditions, was the subject of any notice given under any policy or coverage section of which this coverage section is a direct or indirect renewal or replacement;

(b) based upon, arising from, or in consequence of any demand, suit or other proceeding pending against, or order, decree or judgment entered for or against any **Insured**, on or prior to the Pending or Prior Date set forth in Item 7 of the Declarations for this coverage section, or the same or substantially the same fact, circumstance or situation underlying or alleged therein;

(c) brought or maintained by or on behalf of any **Insured** in any capacity; provided that this Exclusion 6(c) shall not apply to:

(i) a **Claim** brought or maintained derivatively on behalf of the **Organization** by one or more securityholders of the **Organization**, provided such **Claim** is brought and maintained without any active assistance or participation of, or solicitation by, any **Insured Person**;

(ii) an employment **Claim** brought or maintained by or on behalf of an **Insured Person**;

(iii) a **Claim** brought or maintained by an **Insured Person** for contribution or indemnity, if such **Claim** directly results from another **Claim** covered under this coverage section; or

(iv) a **Claim** brought by an **Insured Person** who has not served in an **Insured Capacity** for at least four (4) years prior to the date such **Claim** is first made and who brings and maintains such **Claim** without any active assistance or participation of, or solicitation by, the **Organization** or any other **Insured Person** who is serving or has served in an **Insured Capacity** within such four (4) year period;

(d) based upon, arising from, or in consequence of:

(i) any actual, alleged, or threatened exposure to, or generation, storage, transportation, discharge, emission, release, dispersal, escape, treatment, removal or disposal of any **Pollutants**; or

(ii) any regulation, order, direction or request to test for, monitor, clean up, remove, contain, treat, detoxify or neutralize any **Pollutants**, or any action taken in contemplation or anticipation of any such regulation, order, direction or request,

including but not limited to any **Claim** for financial loss to the **Organization**, its securityholders or its creditors based upon, arising from, or in consequence of any matter described in clause (i) or clause (ii) of this Exclusion 6(d);

(e) for bodily injury, mental anguish, emotional distress, sickness, disease or death of any person or damage to or destruction of any tangible property including loss of use thereof whether or not it is damaged or destroyed; provided that this Exclusion 6(e) shall not apply to mental anguish or emotional distress for which a claimant seeks compensation in an employment **Claim**;

(f) for an actual or alleged violation of the responsibilities, obligations or duties imposed on fiduciaries by the Employee Retirement Income Security Act of 1974, or any amendments thereto, or any rules or regulations promulgated thereunder, or any similar provisions of any federal, state, or local statutory law or common law anywhere in the world;

(g) for **Wrongful Acts** of an **Insured Person** in his or her capacity as a director, officer, manager, trustee, regent, governor or employee of any entity other than the **Organization**, even if the **Insured Person's** service in such capacity is with the knowledge or consent or at the request of the **Organization**; or

(h) made against a **Subsidiary** or an **Insured Person** of such **Subsidiary** for any **Wrongful Act** committed, attempted, or allegedly committed or attempted during any time when such entity was not a **Subsidiary**.

Applicable To Insuring Clauses 1 and 2 Only

7. The **Company** shall not be liable under Insuring Clause 1 or 2 for **Loss** on account of any **Claim** made against any **Insured Person**:

(a) for an accounting of profits made from the purchase or sale by such **Insured Person** of securities of the **Organization** within the meaning of Section 16(b) of the Securities Exchange Act of 1934, any amendments thereto, or any similar provision of any federal, state, or local statutory law or common law anywhere in the world; or

(b)   based upon, arising from, or in consequence of:

     (i)   the committing in fact of any deliberately fraudulent act or omission or any willful violation of any statute or regulation by such **Insured Person**; or

     (ii)   such **Insured Person** having gained in fact any profit, remuneration or advantage to which such **Insured Person** was not legally entitled,

as evidenced by (A) any written statement or written document by any **Insured** or (B) any judgment or ruling in any judicial, administrative or alternative dispute resolution proceeding.

Applicable To Insuring Clause 3 Only

8.   The Company shall not be liable under Insuring Clause 3 for **Loss** on account of any **Securities Claim** made against any **Organization**:

(a)   based upon, arising from, or in consequence of:

     (i)   the committing in fact of any deliberately fraudulent act or omission or any willful violation of any statute or regulation by an **Organization** or by any past, present or future chief financial officer, in-house general counsel, president, chief executive officer or chairperson of an **Organization**; or

     (ii)   such **Organization** having gained in fact any profit, remuneration or advantage to which such **Organization** was not legally entitled,

as evidenced by (A) any written statement or written document by any **Insured** or (B) any judgment or ruling in any judicial, administrative or alternative dispute resolution proceeding; or

(b)   for any actual or alleged liability of an **Organization** under any contract or agreement that relates to the purchase, sale, or offer to purchase or sell any securities; provided that this Exclusion 8(b) shall not apply to liability that would have attached to such **Organization** in the absence of such contract or agreement.

Severability of Exclusions

9.   (a)   No fact pertaining to or knowledge possessed by any **Insured Person** shall be imputed to any other **Insured Person** for the purpose of applying the exclusions in Subsection 7 of this coverage section.

     (b)   Only facts pertaining to and knowledge possessed by any past, present, or future chief financial officer, in-house general counsel, president, chief executive officer or chairperson of an **Organization** shall be imputed to such **Organization** for the purpose of applying the exclusions in Subsection 8 of this coverage section.

Spouses, Estates and Legal Representatives

10. Subject otherwise to the General Terms and Conditions and the limitations, conditions, provisions and other terms of this coverage section, coverage shall extend to **Claims** for the **Wrongful Acts** of an **Insured Person** made against:

    (a) the estate, heirs, legal representatives or assigns of such **Insured Person** if such **Insured Person** is deceased or the legal representatives or assigns of such **Insured Person** if such **Insured Person** is incompetent, insolvent or bankrupt; or

    (b) the lawful spouse or **Domestic Partner** of such **Insured Person** solely by reason of such spouse or **Domestic Partner's** status as a spouse or **Domestic Partner**, or such spouse or **Domestic Partner's** ownership interest in property which the claimant seeks as recovery for an alleged **Wrongful Act** of such **Insured Person**.

    All terms and conditions of this coverage section, including without limitation the Retention, applicable to **Loss** incurred by the **Insured Persons**, shall also apply to loss incurred by the estates, heirs, legal representatives, assigns, spouses and **Domestic Partners** of such **Insured Persons**. The coverage provided by this Subsection 10 shall not apply with respect to any loss arising from an act or omission by an **Insured Person's** estate, heirs, legal representatives, assigns, spouse or **Domestic Partner**.

Coordination With Employment Practices Liability Coverage Section

11. Any **Loss** otherwise covered by both (i) this coverage section and (ii) any employment practices liability coverage section or policy issued by the Company or by any affiliate of the Company (an "Employment Practices Liability Coverage") first shall be covered as provided in, and shall be subject to the limit of liability, retention and coinsurance percentage applicable to such Employment Practices Liability Coverage. Any remaining **Loss** otherwise covered by this coverage section which is not paid under such Employment Practices Liability Coverage shall be covered as provided in, and shall be subject to the Limit of Liability, Retention and Coinsurance Percentage applicable to this coverage section; provided the Retention applicable to such **Loss** under this coverage section shall be reduced by the amount of **Loss** otherwise covered by this coverage section which is paid by the **Insureds** as the retention under such Employment Practices Liability Coverage.

Extended Reporting Period

12. If the Company or the **Parent Organization** terminates or does not renew this coverage section, other than termination by the Company for nonpayment of premium, the **Parent Organization** and the **Insured Persons** shall have the right, upon payment of the additional premium set forth in Item 6(B) of the Declarations for this coverage section, to an extension of the coverage granted by this coverage section for **Claims** that are (i) first made during the period set forth in Item 6(A) of the Declarations for this coverage section (the "Extended Reporting Period") following the effective date of termination or nonrenewal, and (ii) reported to the Company in writing within the time provided in Subsection 15(a) of this coverage section, but only to the extent such **Claims** are for **Wrongful Acts** committed, attempted, or allegedly committed or attempted before the earlier of the effective date of termination or nonrenewal or the date of the first merger, consolidation or acquisition event described in Subsection 21 below. The offer of renewal terms and conditions or premiums different from those in effect prior to renewal shall not constitute

refusal to renew. The right to purchase an extension of coverage as described in this Subsection shall lapse unless written notice of election to purchase the extension, together with payment of the additional premium due, is received by the Company within thirty (30) days after the effective date of termination or nonrenewal. Any **Claim** made during the Extended Reporting Period shall be deemed to have been made during the immediately preceding **Policy Period**. The entire additional premium for the Extended Reporting Period shall be deemed fully earned at the inception of such Extended Reporting Period.

Limit of Liability, Retention and Coinsurance

13. (a) The Company's maximum liability for all **Loss** on account of each **Claim**, whether covered under one or more Insuring Clauses, shall be the Limit of Liability set forth in Item 2(A) of the Declarations for this coverage section. The Company's maximum aggregate liability for all **Loss** on account of all **Claims** first made during the **Policy Period**, whether covered under one or more Insuring Clauses, shall be the Limit of Liability for each **Policy Period** set forth in Item 2(B) of the Declarations for this coverage section.

    (b) The Company's maximum aggregate liability under Insuring Clause 4 for all **Investigative Costs** on account of all **Securityholder Derivative Demands** shall be the Sublimit set forth in Item 2(C) of the Declarations for this coverage section. Such Sublimit is part of, and not in addition to, the Limits of Liability set forth in Items 2(A) and 2(B) of the Declarations.

    (c) **Defense Costs** are part of, and not in addition to, the Limits of Liability set forth in Item 2 of the Declarations for this coverage section, and the payment by the Company of **Defense Costs** shall reduce and may exhaust such applicable Limits of Liability.

    (d) The Company's liability under Insuring Clause 2 or 3 shall apply only to that part of covered **Loss** (as determined by any applicable provision in Subsection 17 of this coverage section) on account of each **Claim** which is excess of the applicable Retention set forth in Item 4 of the Declarations for this coverage section. Such Retention shall be depleted only by **Loss** otherwise covered under this coverage section and shall be borne by the **Insureds** uninsured and at their own risk. Except as otherwise provided in Subsection 14, no Retention shall apply to any **Loss** under Insuring Clause 1 or 4.

    (e) If different parts of a single **Claim** are subject to different Retentions, the applicable Retentions will be applied separately to each part of such **Claim**, but the sum of such Retentions shall not exceed the largest applicable Retention.

    (f) To the extent that **Loss** resulting from a **Securities Claim** is covered under Insuring Clause 2 or 3 (as determined by Subsection 17(a) of this coverage section) and is in excess of the applicable Retention, the **Insureds** shall bear uninsured and at their own risk that percentage of such **Loss** specified as the Coinsurance Percentage in Item 3(A) of the Declarations for this coverage section, and the Company's liability shall apply only to the remaining percentage of such **Loss**. To the extent that **Loss** resulting from a **Claim** other than a **Securities Claim** is covered under Insuring Clause 2 or 3 (as determined by Subsection 17(b) of this coverage section) and is in excess of the applicable Retention, the **Insureds** shall bear uninsured and at their own risk that percentage of such **Loss** specified as the Coinsurance Percentage in

Executive Protection Portfolio [SM]
Executive Liability and Entity Securities
Liability Coverage Section

Item 3(B) of the Declarations for this coverage section, and the Company's liability shall apply only to the remaining percentage of such **Loss**.

(g) All **Related Claims** shall be treated as a single **Claim** first made on the date the earliest of such **Related Claims** was first made, or on the date the earliest of such **Related Claims** is treated as having been made in accordance with Subsection 15(b) below, regardless of whether such date is before or during the **Policy Period**.

(h) The limit of liability available during the Extended Reporting Period (if exercised) shall be part of, and not in addition to, the Company's maximum aggregate limit of liability for all **Loss** on account of all **Claims** first made during the immediately preceding **Policy Period**.

Presumptive Indemnification

14. If the **Organization** fails or refuses, other than for reason of **Financial Impairment**, to indemnify an **Insured Person** for **Loss**, or to advance **Defense Costs** on behalf of an **Insured Person**, to the fullest extent permitted by statutory or common law, then, notwithstanding any other conditions, provisions or terms of this coverage section to the contrary, any payment by the Company of such **Defense Costs** or other **Loss** shall be subject to:

(i) the applicable Insuring Clause 2 Retention set forth in Item 4 of the Declarations for this coverage section; and

(ii) the applicable Coinsurance Percentage set forth in Item 3 of the Declarations for this coverage section.

Reporting and Notice

15. (a) The **Insureds** shall, as a condition precedent to exercising any right to coverage under this coverage section, give to the Company written notice of any **Claim** as soon as practicable, but in no event later than the earliest of the following dates:

(i) sixty (60) days after the date on which any **Organization's** chief financial officer, in-house general counsel, risk manager, president, chief executive officer or chairperson first becomes aware that the **Claim** has been made;

(ii) if this coverage section expires (or is otherwise terminated) without being renewed and if no Extended Reporting Period is purchased, sixty (60) days after the effective date of such expiration or termination; or

(iii) the expiration date of the Extended Reporting Period, if purchased;

provided that if the Company sends written notice to the **Parent Organization**, at any time before the date set forth in (i) above with respect to any **Claim**, stating that this coverage section is being terminated for nonpayment of premium, the **Insureds** shall give to the Company written notice of such **Claim** prior to the effective date of such termination.

Executive Protection Portfolio [SM]
Executive Liability and Entity Securities
Liability Coverage Section

(b)   If during the **Policy Period** an **Insured**:

(i)   becomes aware of circumstances which could give rise to a **Claim** and gives written notice of such circumstances to the Company;

(ii)   receives a written request to toll or waive a statute of limitations applicable to **Wrongful Acts** committed, attempted, or allegedly committed or attempted before or during the **Policy Period** and gives written notice of such request and of such alleged **Wrongful Acts** to the Company; or

(iii)   gives written notice to the Company of a **Securityholder Derivative Demand**,

then any **Claim** subsequently arising from the circumstances referred to in (i) above, from the **Wrongful Acts** referred to in (ii) above, or from the **Securityholder Derivative Demand** referred to in (iii) above, shall be deemed to have been first made during the **Policy Period** in which the written notice described in (i), (ii) or (iii) above was first given by an **Insured** to the Company, provided any such subsequent **Claim** is reported to the Company as set forth in Subsection 15(a) above. With respect to any such subsequent **Claim**, no coverage under this coverage section shall apply to loss incurred prior to the date such subsequent **Claim** is actually made.

(c)   The **Insureds** shall, as a condition precedent to exercising any right to coverage under this coverage section, give to the Company such information, assistance, and cooperation as the Company may reasonably require, and shall include in any notice under Subsection 15(a) or (b) a description of the **Claim**, circumstances, or **Securityholder Derivative Demand**, the nature of any alleged **Wrongful Acts**, the nature of the alleged or potential damage, the names of all actual or potential claimants, the names of all actual or potential defendants, and the manner in which such **Insured** first became aware of the **Claim**, circumstances, or **Securityholder Derivative Demand**.

Defense and Settlement

16.   (a)   It shall be the duty of the **Insureds** and not the duty of the Company to defend **Claims** made against the **Insureds**.

(b)   The **Insureds** agree not to settle or offer to settle any **Claim**, incur any **Defense Costs** or otherwise assume any contractual obligation or admit any liability with respect to any **Claim** without the Company's prior written consent. The Company shall not be liable for any element of **Loss** incurred, for any obligation assumed, or for any admission made, by any **Insured** without the Company's prior written consent. Provided the **Insureds** comply with Subsections 16(c) and (d) below, the Company shall not unreasonably withhold any such consent.

(c)   With respect to any **Claim** that appears reasonably likely to be covered in whole or in part under this coverage section, the Company shall have the right and shall be given the opportunity to effectively associate with the **Insureds**, and shall be consulted in advance by the **Insureds**, regarding the investigation, defense and settlement of such **Claim**, including but not limited to selecting appropriate defense counsel and negotiating any settlement.

(d) The **Insureds** agree to provide the Company with all information, assistance and cooperation which the Company may reasonably require and agree that in the event of a **Claim** the **Insureds** will do nothing that could prejudice the Company's position or its potential or actual rights of recovery.

(e) Any advancement of **Defense Costs** shall be repaid to the Company by the **Insureds**, severally according to their respective interests, if and to the extent it is determined that such **Defense Costs** are not insured under this coverage section.

Allocation

17. (a) If in any **Securities Claim** the **Insureds** incur both **Loss** that is covered under this coverage section and loss that is not covered under this coverage section, the **Insureds** and the Company shall allocate such amount between covered **Loss** and non-covered loss as follows:

(i) The portion, if any, of such amount that is in part covered and in part not covered under Insuring Clause 2 shall be allocated in its entirety to covered **Loss**, subject, however, to the applicable Retention and Coinsurance Percentage set forth in Items 4(C) and 3(A) of the Declarations for this coverage section, respectively; and

(ii) The portion, if any, of such amount that is in part covered and in part not covered under Insuring Clause 1 or 3 shall be allocated between covered **Loss** and non-covered loss based on the relative legal and financial exposures of the **Insureds** to covered and non-covered matters and, in the event of a settlement in such **Securities Claim**, based also on the relative benefits to the **Insureds** from settlement of the covered matters and from settlement of the non-covered matters; provided that the amount so allocated to covered **Loss** under Insuring Clause 3 shall be subject to the Retention and Coinsurance Percentage set forth in Items 4(C) and 3(A) of the Declarations for this coverage section, respectively.

The Company shall not be liable under this coverage section for the portion of such amount allocated to non-covered loss. The allocation described in (i) above shall be final and binding on the Company and the **Insureds** under Insuring Clause 2, but shall not apply to any allocation under Insuring Clauses 1 and 3.

(b) If in any **Claim** other than a **Securities Claim** the **Insured Persons** incur both **Loss** that is covered under this coverage section and loss that is not covered under this coverage section, either because such **Claim** includes both covered and non-covered matters or because such **Claim** is made against both **Insured Persons** and others (including the **Organization**), the **Insureds** and the Company shall allocate such amount between covered **Loss** and non-covered loss based on the relative legal and financial exposures of the parties to covered and non-covered matters and, in the event of a settlement in such **Claim**, based also on the relative benefits to the parties from such settlement. The Company shall not be liable under this coverage section for the portion of such amount allocated to non-covered loss.

(c) If the **Insureds** and the Company agree on an allocation of **Defense Costs**, the Company shall advance on a current basis **Defense Costs** allocated to the covered **Loss**. If the **Insureds** and the Company cannot agree on an allocation:

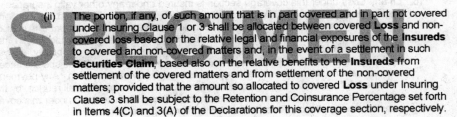

(i)   no presumption as to allocation shall exist in any arbitration, suit or other proceeding;

(ii)   the Company shall advance on a current basis **Defense Costs** which the Company believes to be covered under this coverage section until a different allocation is negotiated, arbitrated or judicially determined; and

(iii)   the Company, if requested by the **Insureds**, shall submit the dispute to binding arbitration. The rules of the American Arbitration Association shall apply except with respect to the selection of the arbitration panel, which shall consist of one arbitrator selected by the **Insureds**, one arbitrator selected by the Company, and a third independent arbitrator selected by the first two arbitrators.

(d)   Any negotiated, arbitrated or judicially determined allocation of **Defense Costs** on account of a **Claim** shall be applied retroactively to all **Defense Costs** on account of such **Claim**, notwithstanding any prior advancement to the contrary. Any allocation or advancement of **Defense Costs** on account of a **Claim** shall not apply to or create any presumption with respect to the allocation of other **Loss** on account of such **Claim**.

Other Insurance

18.   If any **Loss** under this coverage section is insured under any other valid insurance policy(ies), then this coverage section shall cover such **Loss**, subject to its limitations, conditions, provisions and other terms, only to the extent that the amount of such **Loss** is in excess of the applicable retention (or deductible) and limit of liability under such other insurance, whether such other insurance is stated to be primary, contributory, excess, contingent or otherwise, unless such other insurance is written only as specific excess insurance over the Limits of Liability provided in this coverage section. Any payment by **Insureds** of a retention or deductible under such other insurance shall reduce, by the amount of such payment which would otherwise have been covered under this coverage section, the applicable Retention under this coverage section.

Payment of Loss

19.   In the event payment of **Loss** is due under this coverage section but the amount of such **Loss** in the aggregate exceeds the remaining available Limit of Liability for this coverage section, the Company shall:

(a)   first pay such **Loss** for which coverage is provided under Insuring Clause 1 of this coverage section; then

(b)   to the extent of any remaining amount of the Limit of Liability available after payment under (a) above, pay such **Loss** for which coverage is provided under any other Insuring Clause of this coverage section.

Except as otherwise provided in this Subsection 19, the Company may pay covered **Loss** as it becomes due under this coverage section without regard to the potential for other future payment obligations under this coverage section.

Executive Protection Portfolio [SM]
Executive Liability and Entity Securities
Liability Coverage Section

Changes in Exposure

Acquisition /Creation of Another Organization

20.   If before or during the **Policy Period** any **Organization**:

(a)   acquires securities or voting rights in another organization or creates another organization, which as a result of such acquisition or creation becomes a **Subsidiary**; or

(b)   acquires another organization by merger into or consolidation with an **Organization** such that the **Organization** is the surviving entity,

such other organization and its **Insured Persons** shall be **Insureds** under this coverage section, but only with respect to **Wrongful Acts** committed, attempted, or allegedly committed or attempted after such acquisition or creation unless the Company agrees, after presentation of a complete application and all other appropriate information, to provide coverage by endorsement for **Wrongful Acts** committed, attempted, or allegedly committed or attempted by such **Insureds** before such acquisition or creation.

If the total assets of any such acquired organization or new **Subsidiary** exceed ten percent (10%) of the total assets of the **Parent Organization** (as reflected in the most recent audited consolidated financial statements of such organization and the **Parent Organization**, respectively, as of the date of such acquisition or creation), the **Parent Organization** shall give written notice of such acquisition or creation to the Company as soon as practicable, but in no event later than sixty (60) days after the date of such acquisition or creation, together with such other information as the Company may require and shall pay any reasonable additional premium required by the Company. If the **Parent Organization** fails to give such notice within the time specified in the preceding sentence, or fails to pay the additional premium required by the Company, coverage for such acquired or created organization and its **Insured Persons** shall terminate with respect to **Claims** first made more than sixty (60) days after such acquisition or creation. Coverage for any acquired or created organization described in this paragraph, and for the **Insured Persons** of such organization, shall be subject to such additional or different terms, conditions and limitations of coverage as the Company in its sole discretion may require.

Acquisition by Another Organization

21.   If:

(a)   the **Parent Organization** merges into or consolidates with another organization and the **Parent Organization** is not the surviving entity; or

(b)   another organization or person or group of organizations and/or persons acting in concert acquires securities or voting rights which result in ownership or voting control by the other organization(s) or person(s) of more than fifty percent (50%) of the outstanding securities or voting rights representing the present right to vote for the election of or to appoint directors or **Managers** of the **Parent Organization**,

coverage under this coverage section shall continue until termination of this coverage section, but only with respect to **Claims** for **Wrongful Acts** committed, attempted, or allegedly committed or attempted by **Insureds** before such merger, consolidation or

acquisition. Upon the occurrence of any event described in (a) or (b) of this Subsection 21, the entire premium for this coverage section shall be deemed fully earned.
The **Parent Organization** shall give written notice of such merger, consolidation or acquisition to the Company as soon as practicable, but in no event later than sixty (60) days after the date of such merger, consolidation or acquisition, together with such other information as the Company may require. Upon receipt of such notice and information and at the request of the **Parent Organization**, the Company shall provide to the **Parent Organization** a quotation for an extension of coverage (for such period as may be negotiated between the Company and the **Parent Organization**) with respect to **Claims** for **Wrongful Acts** committed, attempted, or allegedly committed or attempted by **Insureds** before such merger, consolidation or acquisition. Any coverage extension pursuant to such quotation shall be subject to such additional or different terms, conditions and limitations of coverage, and payment of such additional premium, as the Company in its sole discretion may require.

Cessation of Subsidiary

22. In the event an organization ceases to be a **Subsidiary** before or during the **Policy Period**, coverage with respect to such **Subsidiary** and its **Insured Persons** shall continue until termination of this coverage section, but only with respect to **Claims** for **Wrongful Acts** committed, attempted, or allegedly committed or attempted while such organization was a **Subsidiary**.

Related Entity Public Offering

23. If any **Organization** files or causes to be filed, with the United States Securities and Exchange Commission or an equivalent agency or government department in any country other than the United States of America, any registration statement in contemplation of a public offering of equity securities by any entity other than the **Parent Organization** (irrespective of whether such public offering is an initial public offering or a secondary or other offering subsequent to an initial public offering), then the Company shall not be liable for **Loss** on account of any **Claim** based upon, arising from, or in consequence of such registration statement or the sale, offer to sell, distribution or issuance of any securities pursuant to such registration statement, unless (i) the Company receives written notice at least thirty (30) days prior to the effective date of such registration statement providing full details of the contemplated offering, and (ii) the Company, in its sole discretion, agrees by written endorsement to this coverage section to provide coverage for such **Claims** upon such terms and conditions, subject to such limitations and other provisions, and for such additional premium as the Company may require. If the Company in its sole discretion agrees to provide coverage for such **Claims**, the additional premium specified by the Company shall be payable to the Company in full not later than the date on which such registration statement becomes effective.

Representations and Severability

24. In issuing this coverage section the Company has relied upon the statements, representations and information in the **Application**. All of the **Insureds** acknowledge and agree that all such statements, representations and information (i) are true and accurate, (ii) were made or provided in order to induce the Company to issue this coverage section,

and (iii) are material to the Company's acceptance of the risk to which this coverage section applies.

In the event that any of the statements, representations or information in the **Application** are not true and accurate, this coverage section shall be void with respect to (i) any **Insured** who knew as of the effective date of the **Application** the facts that were not truthfully and accurately disclosed (whether or not the **Insured** knew of such untruthful disclosure in the **Application**) or to whom knowledge of such facts is imputed, and (ii) the **Organization** under Insuring Clause 2 to the extent it indemnifies an **Insured Person** who had such actual or imputed knowledge. For purposes of the preceding sentence:

(a)   the knowledge of any **Insured Person** who is a past, present or future chief financial officer, in-house general counsel, chief executive officer, president or chairperson of an **Organization** shall be imputed to such **Organization** and its **Subsidiaries**;

(b)   the knowledge of the person(s) who signed the **Application** for this coverage section shall be imputed to all of the **Insureds**; and

(c)   except as provided in (a) above, the knowledge of an **Insured Person** who did not sign the **Application** shall not be imputed to any other **Insured**.

SPECIMEN

SECURITIES ACT OF 1933

15 U.S.C. §§ 77a et seq.

TABLE OF CONTENTS

Sec.		Page
1.	Short Title	1173
2.	Definitions; Promotion of Efficiency, Competition, and Capital Formation	1173
2A.	Swap Agreements*	
3.	Classes of Securities Under This Subchapter	1176
4.	Exempted Transactions	1179
4A.	Requirements With Respect to Certain Small Transactions	1182
5.	Prohibitions Relating to Interstate Commerce and the Mails	1186
6.	Registration of Securities	1187
7.	Information Required in Registration Statement	1187
8.	Taking Effect of Registration Statements and Amendments Thereto	1189
8A.	Cease-and-Desist Proceedings	1190
9.	Court Review of Orders	1191
10.	Information Required in Prospectus	1191
11.	Civil Liabilities on Account of False Registration Statement	1192
12.	Civil Liabilities Arising in Connection With Prospectuses and Communications	1195
13.	Limitation of Actions	1195
14.	Contrary Stipulations Void	1195
15.	Liability of Controlling Persons	1195
16.	Additional Remedies; Limitations on Remedies	1196
17.	Fraudulent Interstate Transactions	1198
18.	Exemption From State Regulation of Securities Offerings	1198
18A.	Preemption of State Law*	
19.	Special Powers of Commission	1201
20.	Injunctions and Prosecution of Offenses	1202
21.	Hearings by Commission*	
22.	Jurisdiction of Offenses and Suits	1204
23.	Unlawful Representations	1204
24.	Penalties	1204
25.	Jurisdiction of Other Government Agencies Over Securities*	
26.	Separability of Provisions*	
27.	Private Securities Litigation	1205
27A.	Application of Safe Harbor for Forward-Looking Statements	1209
28.	General Exemptive Authority	1212

Schedules of Information Required in Registration Statement*

---

§ 1. Short Title

This subchapter may be cited as the "Securities Act of 1933."

§ 2. Definitions; Promotion of Efficiency, Competition, and Capital Formation

(a) Definitions

When used in this subchapter, unless the context otherwise requires—

---

* Omitted.

(1) The term "security" means any note, stock, treasury stock, security future, bond, debenture, evidence of indebtedness, certificate of interest or participation in any profit-sharing agreement, collateral-trust certificate, preorganization certificate or subscription, transferable share, investment contract, voting-trust certificate, certificate of deposit for a security, fractional undivided interest in oil, gas, or other mineral rights, any put, call, straddle, option, or privilege on any security, certificate of deposit, or group or index of securities (including any interest therein or based on the value thereof), or any put, call, straddle, option, or privilege entered into on a national securities exchange relating to foreign currency, or, in general, any interest or instrument commonly known as a "security", or any certificate of interest or participation in, temporary or interim certificate for, receipt for, guarantee of, or warrant or right to subscribe to or purchase, any of the foregoing.

(2) The term "person" means an individual, a corporation, a partnership, an association, a joint-stock company, a trust, any unincorporated organization, or a government or political subdivision thereof. As used in this paragraph the term "trust" shall include only a trust where the interest or interests of the beneficiary or beneficiaries are evidenced by a security.

(3) The term "sale" or "sell" shall include every contract of sale or disposition of a security or interest in a security, for value. The term "offer to sell", "offer for sale", or "offer" shall include every attempt or offer to dispose of, or solicitation of an offer to buy, a security or interest in a security, for value. The terms defined in this paragraph and the term "offer to buy" as used in subsection (c) of section 5 of this title shall not include preliminary negotiations or agreements between an issuer (or any person directly or indirectly controlling or controlled by an issuer, or under direct or indirect common control with an issuer) and any underwriter or among underwriters who are or are to be in privity of contract with an issuer (or any person directly or indirectly controlling or controlled by an issuer, or under direct or indirect common control with an issuer). Any security given or delivered with, or as a bonus on account of, any purchase of securities or any other thing, shall be conclusively presumed to constitute a part of the subject of such purchase and to have been offered and sold for value. The issue or transfer of a right or privilege, when originally issued or transferred with a security, giving the holder of such security the right to convert such security into another security of the same issuer or of another person, or giving a right to subscribe to another security of the same issuer or of another person, which right cannot be exercised until some future date, shall not be deemed to be an offer or sale of such other security; but the issue or transfer of such other security upon the exercise of such right of conversion or subscription shall be deemed a sale of such other security. Any offer or sale of a security futures product by or on behalf of the issuer of the securities underlying the security futures product, an affiliate of the issuer, or an underwriter, shall constitute a contract for sale of, sale of, offer for sale, or offer to sell the underlying securities. The publication or distribution by a broker or dealer of a research report about an emerging growth company that is the subject of a proposed public offering of the common equity securities of such emerging growth company pursuant to a registration statement that the issuer proposes to file, or has filed, or that is effective shall be deemed for purposes of paragraph (10) of this subsection and section 5(c) not to constitute an offer for sale or offer to sell a security, even if the broker or dealer is participating or will participate in the registered offering of the securities of the issuer. As used in this paragraph, the term "research report" means a written, electronic, or oral communication that includes information, opinions, or recommendations with respect to securities of an issuer or an analysis of a security or an issuer, whether or not it provides information reasonably sufficient upon which to base an investment decision.

(4) The term "issuer" means every person who issues or proposes to issue any security; except that with respect to certificates of deposit, voting-trust certificates, or collateral-trust certificates, or with respect to certificates of interest or shares in an unincorporated investment trust not having a board of directors (or persons performing similar functions) or of the fixed, restricted management, or unit type, the term "issuer" means the person or persons performing the acts and assuming the duties of depositor or manager pursuant to the provisions of the trust or other agreement or instrument under which such securities are issued; except that in the case of an unincorporated association which provides by its articles for limited liability of any or all of its members, or in the case of a trust, committee, or other legal entity, the trustees or members thereof shall not be individually liable as issuers of any security issued by the association, trust, committee, or other legal entity; except that with respect to equipment-trust certificates or like securities, the term "issuer" means the person by whom the equipment or property is or is to be used; and except that with respect to fractional undivided

interests in oil, gas, or other mineral rights, the term "issuer" means the owner of any such right or of any interest in such right (whether whole or fractional) who creates fractional interests therein for the purpose of public offering.

(5) The term "Commission" means the Securities and Exchange Commission.

(6) The term "Territory" means Puerto Rico, Canal Zone, the Virgin Islands, and the insular possessions of the United States.

(7) The term "interstate commerce" means trade or commerce in securities or any transportation or communication relating thereto among the several States or between the District of Columbia or any Territory of the United States and any State or other Territory, or between any foreign country and any State, Territory, or the District of Columbia, or within the District of Columbia.

(8) The term "registration statement" means the statement provided for in section 6 of this title, and includes any amendment thereto and any report, document, or memorandum filed as part of such statement or incorporated therein by reference.

(9) The term "write" or "written" shall include printed, lithographed, or any means of graphic communication.

(10) The term "prospectus" means any prospectus, notice, circular, advertisement, letter, or communication, written or by radio or television, which offers any security for sale or confirms the sale of any security; except that (a) a communication sent or given after the effective date of the registration statement (other than a prospectus permitted under subsection (b) of section 10 of this title) shall not be deemed a prospectus if it is proved that prior to or at the same time with such communication a written prospectus meeting the requirements of subsection (a) of section 10 of this title at the time of such communication was sent or given to the person to whom the communication was made, and (b) a notice, circular, advertisement, letter, or communication in respect of a security shall not be deemed to be a prospectus if it states from whom a written prospectus meeting the requirements of section 10 of this title may be obtained and, in addition, does no more than identify the security, state the price thereof, state by whom orders will be executed, and contain such other information as the Commission, by rules or regulations deemed necessary or appropriate in the public interest and for the protection of investors, and subject to such terms and conditions as may be prescribed therein, may permit.

(11) The term "underwriter" means any person who has purchased from an issuer with a view to, or offers or sells for an issuer in connection with, the distribution of any security, or participates or has a direct or indirect participation in any such undertaking, or participates or has a participation in the direct or indirect underwriting of any such undertaking; but such term shall not include a person whose interest is limited to a commission from an underwriter or dealer not in excess of the usual and customary distributors' or sellers' commission. As used in this paragraph the term "issuer" shall include, in addition to an issuer, any person directly or indirectly controlling or controlled by the issuer, or any person under direct or indirect common control with the issuer.

(12) The term "dealer" means any person who engages either for all or part of his time, directly or indirectly, as agent, broker, or principal, in the business of offering, buying, selling, or otherwise dealing or trading in securities issued by another person.

(13) The term "insurance company" means a company which is organized as an insurance company, whose primary and predominant business activity is the writing of insurance or the reinsuring of risks underwritten by insurance companies, and which is subject to supervision by the insurance commissioner, or a similar official or agency, of a State or territory or the District of Columbia; or any receiver or similar official or any liquidating agent for such company, in his capacity as such.

(14) The term "separate account" means an account established and maintained by an insurance company pursuant to the laws of any State or territory of the United States, the District of Columbia, or of Canada or any province thereof, under which income, gains and losses, whether or not realized, from assets allocated to such account, are, in accordance with the applicable contract, credited to or charged against such account without regard to other income, gains, or losses of the insurance company.

(15) The term "accredited investor" shall mean—

(i) a bank as defined in section 3(a)(2) whether acting in its individual or fiduciary capacity; an insurance company as defined in paragraph (13) of this subsection; an investment company registered under the Investment Company Act of 1940 or a business development company as defined in section 2(a)(48) of that Act; a Small Business Investment Company licensed by the Small Business Administration; or an employee benefit plan, including an individual retirement account, which is subject to the provisions of the Employee Retirement Income Security Act of 1974, if the investment decision is made by a plan fiduciary, as defined in section 3(21) of such Act, which is either a bank, insurance company, or registered investment adviser; or

(ii) any person who, on the basis of such factors as financial sophistication, net worth, knowledge, and experience in financial matters, or amount of assets under management qualifies as an accredited investor under rules and regulations which the Commission shall prescribe.

(16) The terms "security future" . . . and "security futures product" have the same meanings as provided in section 3(a)(55) of the Securities Exchange Act of 1934. . . .

(19) The term "emerging growth company" means an issuer that had total annual gross revenues of less than $1,000,000,000 (as such amount is indexed for inflation every 5 years by the Commission to reflect the change in the Consumer Price Index for All Urban Consumers published by the Bureau of Labor Statistics, setting the threshold to the nearest 1,000,000) during its most recently completed fiscal year. An issuer that is an emerging growth company as of the first day of that fiscal year shall continue to be deemed an emerging growth company until the earliest of—

(A) the last day of the fiscal year of the issuer during which it had total annual gross revenues of $1,000,000,000 (as such amount is indexed for inflation every 5 years by the Commission to reflect the change in the Consumer Price Index for All Urban Consumers published by the Bureau of Labor Statistics, setting the threshold to the nearest 1,000,000) or more;

(B) the last day of the fiscal year of the issuer following the fifth anniversary of the date of the first sale of common equity securities of the issuer pursuant to an effective registration statement under this title;

(C) the date on which such issuer has, during the previous 3-year period, issued more than $1,000,000,000 in non-convertible debt; or

(D) the date on which such issuer is deemed to be a "large accelerated filer," as defined in Rule 12b–2 under the Securities Exchange Act.

(b) Consideration of promotion of efficiency, competition, and capital formation

Whenever pursuant to this subchapter the Commission is engaged in rulemaking and is required to consider or determine whether an action is necessary or appropriate in the public interest, the Commission shall also consider, in addition to the protection of investors, whether the action will promote efficiency, competition, and capital formation.

§ 3.   Classes of Securities Under This Subchapter

(a) Exempted securities

Except as hereinafter expressly provided, the provisions of this subchapter shall not apply to any of the following classes of securities:

(1) Any security which, prior to or within sixty days after May 27, 1933, has been sold or disposed of by the issuer or bona fide offered to the public, but this exemption shall not apply to any new offering of any such security by an issuer or underwriter subsequent to such sixty days;

(2) Any security issued or guaranteed by the United States or any territory thereof, or by the District of Columbia, or by any State of the United States, or by any political subdivision of a State or territory, or by any public instrumentality of one or more States or territories, or by any person controlled or supervised by and acting as an instrumentality of the Government of the United States

pursuant to authority granted by the Congress of the United States; or any certificate of deposit for any of the foregoing; or any security issued or guaranteed by any bank; or any security issued by or representing an interest in or a direct obligation of a Federal Reserve bank. . . .

(3) Any note, draft, bill of exchange, or banker's acceptance which arises out of a current transaction or the proceeds of which have been or are to be used for current transactions, and which has a maturity at the time of issuance of not exceeding nine months, exclusive of days of grace, or any renewal thereof the maturity of which is likewise limited;

(4) Any security issued by a person organized and operated exclusively for religious, educational, benevolent, fraternal, charitable, or reformatory purposes and not for pecuniary profit, and no part of the net earnings of which inures to the benefit of any person, private stockholder, or individual . . . ;

(5) Any security issued . . . by a savings and loan association, building and loan association, cooperative bank, homestead association, or similar institution, which is supervised and examined by State or Federal authority having supervision over any such institution . . . ;

(6) Any interest in a railroad equipment trust. For purposes of this paragraph "interest in a railroad equipment trust" means any interest in an equipment trust, lease, conditional sales contract, or other similar arrangement entered into, issued, assumed, guaranteed by, or for the benefit of, a common carrier to finance the acquisition of rolling stock, including motive power;

(7) Certificates issued by a receiver or by a trustee or debtor in possession in a case under title 11, with the approval of the court;

(8) Any insurance or endowment policy or annuity contract or optional annuity contract, issued by a corporation subject to the supervision of the insurance commissioner, bank commissioner, or any agency or officer performing like functions, of any State or Territory of the United States or the District of Columbia;

(9) Except with respect to a security exchanged in a case under title 11, any security exchanged by the issuer with its existing security holders exclusively where no commission or other remuneration is paid or given directly or indirectly for soliciting such exchange;

(10) Except with respect to a security exchanged in a case under title 11, any security which is issued in exchange for one or more bona fide outstanding securities, claims or property interests, or partly in such exchange and partly for cash, where the terms and conditions of such issuance and exchange are approved, after a hearing upon the fairness of such terms and conditions at which all persons to whom it is proposed to issue securities in such exchange shall have the right to appear, by any court, or by any official or agency of the United States, or by any State or Territorial banking or insurance commission or other governmental authority expressly authorized by law to grant such approval;

(11) Any security which is a part of an issue offered and sold only to persons resident within a single State or Territory, where the issuer of such security is a person resident and doing business within or, if a corporation, incorporated by and doing business within, such State or Territory. . . .

(b) **Additional exemptions.—**

(1) Small issues exemptive authority.—The Commission may from time to time by its rules and regulations and subject to such terms and conditions as may be prescribed therein, add any class of securities to the securities exempted as provided in this section, if it finds that the enforcement of this title with respect to such securities is not necessary in the public interest and for the protection of investors by reason of the small amount involved or the limited character of the public offering; but no issue of securities shall be exempted under this subsection where the aggregate amount at which such issue is offered to the public exceeds $5,000,000.

(2) Additional issues.—The Commission shall by rule or regulation add a class of securities to the securities exempted pursuant to this section in accordance with the following terms and conditions:

(A) The aggregate offering amount of all securities offered and sold within the prior 12-month period in reliance on the exemption added in accordance with this paragraph shall not exceed $50,000,000.

(B) The securities may be offered and sold publicly.

(C) The securities shall not be restricted securities within the meaning of the Federal securities laws and the regulations promulgated thereunder.

(D) The civil liability provision in section 12(a)(2) shall apply to any person offering or selling such securities.

(E) The issuer may solicit interest in the offering prior to filing any offering statement, on such terms and conditions as the Commission may prescribe in the public interest or for the protection of investors.

(F) The Commission shall require the issuer to file audited financial statements with the Commission annually.

(G) Such other terms, conditions, or requirements as the Commission may determine necessary in the public interest and for the protection of investors, which may include—

(i) a requirement that the issuer prepare and electronically file with the Commission and distribute to prospective investors an offering statement, and any related documents, in such form and with such content as prescribed by the Commission, including audited financial statements, a description of the issuer's business operations, its financial condition, its corporate governance principles, its use of investor funds, and other appropriate matters; and

(ii) disqualification provisions under which the exemption shall not be available to the issuer or its predecessors, affiliates, officers, directors, underwriters, or other related persons, which shall be substantially similar to the disqualification provisions contained in the regulations adopted in accordance with section 926 of the Dodd-Frank Wall Street Reform and Consumer Protection Act (15 U.S.C. 77d note).

(3) Limitation.—Only the following types of securities may be exempted under a rule or regulation adopted pursuant to paragraph (2): equity securities, debt securities, and debt securities convertible or exchangeable to equity interests, including any guarantees of such securities.

(4) Periodic disclosures.—Upon such terms and conditions as the Commission determines necessary in the public interest and for the protection of investors, the Commission by rule or regulation may require an issuer of a class of securities exempted under paragraph (2) to make available to investors and file with the Commission periodic disclosures regarding the issuer, its business operations, its financial condition, its corporate governance principles, its use of investor funds, and other appropriate matters, and also may provide for the suspension and termination of such a requirement with respect to that issuer.

(5) Adjustment.—Not later than 2 years after the date of enactment of the Small Company Capital Formation Act of 2011 and every 2 years thereafter, the Commission shall review the offering amount limitation described in paragraph (2)(A) and shall increase such amount as the Commission determines appropriate. If the Commission determines not to increase such amount, it shall report to the Committee on Financial Services of the House of Representatives and the Committee on Banking, Housing, and Urban Affairs of the Senate on its reasons for not increasing the amount.

(c)   Securities issued by small investment company

The Commission may from time to time by its rules and regulations and subject to such terms and conditions as may be prescribed therein, add to the securities exempted as provided in this section any class of securities issued by a small business investment company under the Small Business Investment Act of 1958 [15 U.S.C. 661 et seq.] if it finds, having regard to the purposes of that Act, that the enforcement of this subchapter with respect to such securities is not necessary in the public interest and for the protection of investors.

§ 4. Exempted Transactions

(a) The provisions of section 5 of this title shall not apply to—

(1) transactions by any person other than an issuer, underwriter, or dealer.

(2) transactions by an issuer not involving any public offering.

(3) transactions by a dealer (including an underwriter no longer acting as an underwriter in respect of the security involved in such transaction), except—

(A) transactions taking place prior to the expiration of forty days after the first date upon which the security was bona fide offered to the public by the issuer or by or through an underwriter,

(B) transactions in a security as to which a registration statement has been filed taking place prior to the expiration of forty days after the effective date of such registration statement or prior to the expiration of forty days after the first date upon which the security was bona fide offered to the public by the issuer or by or through an underwriter after such effective date, whichever is later (excluding in the computation of such forty days any time during which a stop order issued under section 8 of this title is in effect as to the security), or such shorter period as the Commission may specify by rules and regulations or order, and

(C) transactions as to securities constituting the whole or a part of an unsold allotment to or subscription by such dealer as a participant in the distribution of such securities by the issuer or by or through an underwriter.

With respect to transactions referred to in clause (B), if securities of the issuer have not previously been sold pursuant to an earlier effective registration statement the applicable period, instead of forty days, shall be ninety days, or such shorter period as the Commission may specify by rules and regulations or order.

(4) brokers' transactions executed upon customers' orders on any exchange or in the over-the-counter market but not the solicitation of such orders. . . .

(5) transactions involving offers or sales by an issuer solely to one or more accredited investors, if the aggregate offering price of an issue of securities offered in reliance on this paragraph does not exceed the amount allowed under section 3(b)(i) of this title, if there is no advertising or public solicitation in connection with the transaction by the issuer or anyone acting on the issuer's behalf, and if the issuer files such notice with the Commission as the Commission shall prescribe.

(6) transactions involving the offer or sale of securities by an issuer (including all entities controlled by or under common control with the issuer), provided that—

(A) the aggregate amount sold to all investors by the issuer, including any amount sold in reliance on the exemption provided under this paragraph during the 12-month period preceding the date of such transaction, is not more than $1,000,000;

(B) the aggregate amount sold to any investor by an issuer, including any amount sold in reliance on the exemption provided under this paragraph during the 12-month period preceding the date of such transaction, does not exceed—

(i) the greater of $2,000 or 5 percent of the annual income or net worth of such investor, as applicable, if either the annual income or the net worth of the investor is less than $100,000; and

(ii) 10 percent of the annual income or net worth of such investor, as applicable, not to exceed a maximum aggregate amount sold of $100,000, if either the annual income or net worth of the investor is equal to or more than $100,000;

(C) the transaction is conducted through a broker or funding portal that complies with the requirements of section 4A(a); and

(D) the issuer complies with the requirements of section 4A(b).

(7) transactions meeting the requirements of subsection (d).

(b) Offers and sales exempt under Rule 506 under the Securities Act shall not be deemed public offerings under the Federal securities laws as a result of general advertising or general solicitation.

(1) With respect to securities offered and sold in compliance with Rule 506 of Regulation D under this Act, no person who meets the conditions set forth in paragraph (2) shall be subject to registration as a broker or dealer pursuant to section 15(a)(1) of this title, solely because—

(A) that person maintains a platform or mechanism that permits the offer, sale, purchase, or negotiation of or with respect to securities, or permits general solicitations, general advertisements, or similar or related activities by issuers of such securities, whether online, in person, or through any other means;

(B) that person or any person associated with that person co-invests in such securities; or

(C) that person or any person associated with that person provides ancillary services with respect to such securities.

(2) The exemption provided in paragraph (1) shall apply to any person described in such paragraph if—

(A) such person and each person associated with that person receives no compensation in connection with the purchase or sale of such security;

(B) such person and each person associated with that person does not have possession of customer funds or securities in connection with the purchase or sale of such security; and

(C) such person is not subject to a statutory disqualification as defined in section 3(a)(39) of this title and does not have any person associated with that person subject to such a statutory disqualification.

(3) For the purposes of this subsection, the term "ancillary services" means—

(A) the provision of due diligence services, in connection with the offer, sale, purchase, or negotiation of such security, so long as such services do not include, for separate compensation, investment advice or recommendations to issuers or investors; and

(B) the provision of standardized documents to the issuers and investors, so long as such person or entity does not negotiate the terms of the issuance for and on behalf of third parties and issuers are not required to use the standardized documents as a condition of using the service.

(c)(1) With respect to securities offered and sold in compliance with Rule 506 of Regulation D under this Act [15 USCS §§ 77a et seq.], no person who meets the conditions set forth in paragraph (2) shall be subject to registration as a broker or dealer pursuant to section 15(a)(1) of this title [15 USCS § 77o(a)(1)], solely because—

(A) that person maintains a platform or mechanism that permits the offer, sale, purchase, or negotiation of or with respect to securities, or permits general solicitations, general advertisements, or similar or related activities by issuers of such securities, whether online, in person, or through any other means;

(B) that person or any person associated with that person co-invests in such securities; or

(C) that person or any person associated with that person provides ancillary services with respect to such securities.

(2) The exemption provided in paragraph (1) shall apply to any person described in such paragraph if—

(A) such person and each person associated with that person receives no compensation in connection with the purchase or sale of such security;

(B) such person and each person associated with that person does not have possession of customer funds or securities in connection with the purchase or sale of such security; and

(C) such person is not subject to a statutory disqualification as defined in section 3(a)(39) of this title [15 USCS § 78c(a)(39)] and does not have any person associated with that person subject to such a statutory disqualification.

(3) For the purposes of this subsection, the term "ancillary services" means—

(A) the provision of due diligence services, in connection with the offer, sale, purchase, or negotiation of such security, so long as such services do not include, for separate compensation, investment advice or recommendations to issuers or investors; and

(B) the provision of standardized documents to the issuers and investors, so long as such person or entity does not negotiate the terms of the issuance for and on behalf of third parties and issuers are not required to use the standardized documents as a condition of using the service.

(d) Certain accredited investor transactions. The transactions referred to in subsection (a)(7) are transactions meeting the following requirements:

(1) Accredited investor requirement. Each purchaser is an accredited investor, as that term is defined in section 230.501(a) of title 17, Code of Federal Regulations (or any successor regulation).

(2) Prohibition on general solicitation or advertising. Neither the seller, nor any person acting on the seller's behalf, offers or sells securities by any form of general solicitation or general advertising.

(3) Information requirement. In the case of a transaction involving the securities of an issuer that is neither subject to section 13 or 15(d) of the Securities Exchange Act of 1934 (15 U.S.C. 78m; 78o(d)), nor exempt from reporting pursuant to section 240.12g3–2(b) of title 17, Code of Federal Regulations, nor a foreign government (as defined in section 230.405 of title 17, Code of Federal Regulations) eligible to register securities under Schedule B, the seller and a prospective purchaser designated by the seller obtain from the issuer, upon request of the seller, and the seller in all cases makes available to a prospective purchaser, the following information (which shall be reasonably current in relation to the date of resale under this section):

(A) The exact name of the issuer and the issuer's predecessor (if any).

(B) The address of the issuer's principal executive offices.

(C) The exact title and class of the security.

(D) The par or stated value of the security.

(E) The number of shares or total amount of the securities outstanding as of the end of the issuer's most recent fiscal year.

(F) The name and address of the transfer agent, corporate secretary, or other person responsible for transferring shares and stock certificates.

(G) A statement of the nature of the business of the issuer and the products and services it offers, which shall be presumed reasonably current if the statement is as of 12 months before the transaction date.

(H) The names of the officers and directors of the issuer.

(I) The names of any persons registered as a broker, dealer, or agent that shall be paid or given, directly or indirectly, any commission or remuneration for such person's participation in the offer or sale of the securities.

(J) The issuer's most recent balance sheet and profit and loss statement and similar financial statements, which shall—

(i) be for such part of the 2 preceding fiscal years as the issuer has been in operation;

(ii) be prepared in accordance with generally accepted accounting principles or, in the case of a foreign private issuer, be prepared in accordance with generally accepted accounting principles or the International Financial Reporting Standards issued by the International Accounting Standards Board;

(iii be presumed reasonably current if—

(I) with respect to the balance sheet, the balance sheet is as of a date less than 16 months before the transaction date; and

(II) with respect to the profit and loss statement, such statement is for the 12 months preceding the date of the issuer's balance sheet; and

(iv) if the balance sheet is not as of a date less than 6 months before the transaction date, be accompanied by additional statements of profit and loss for the period from the date of such balance sheet to a date less than 6 months before the transaction date.

(K) To the extent that the seller is a control person with respect to the issuer, a brief statement regarding the nature of the affiliation, and a statement certified by such seller that they have no reasonable grounds to believe that the issuer is in violation of the securities laws or regulations.

(4) Issuers disqualified. The transaction is not for the sale of a security where the seller is an issuer or a subsidiary, either directly or indirectly, of the issuer.

(5) Bad actor prohibition. Neither the seller, nor any person that has been or will be paid (directly or indirectly) remuneration or a commission for their participation in the offer or sale of the securities, including solicitation of purchasers for the seller is subject to an event that would disqualify an issuer or other covered person under Rule 506(d)(1) of Regulation D (17 CFR 230.506(d)(1)) or is subject to a statutory disqualification described under section 3(a)(39) of the Securities Exchange Act of 1934 [15 USCS § 78c(a)(39)].

(6) Business requirement. The issuer is engaged in business, is not in the organizational stage or in bankruptcy or receivership, and is not a blank check, blind pool, or shell company that has no specific business plan or purpose or has indicated that the issuer's primary business plan is to engage in a merger or combination of the business with, or an acquisition of, an unidentified person.

(7) Underwriter prohibition. The transaction is not with respect to a security that constitutes the whole or part of an unsold allotment to, or a subscription or participation by, a broker or dealer as an underwriter of the security or a redistribution.

(8) Outstanding class requirement. The transaction is with respect to a security of a class that has been authorized and outstanding for at least 90 days prior to the date of the transaction.

(e) Additional requirements.

(1) In general. With respect to an exempted transaction described under subsection (a)(7):

(A) Securities acquired in such transaction shall be deemed to have been acquired in a transaction not involving any public offering.

(B) Such transaction shall be deemed not to be a distribution for purposes of section 2(a)(11) [15 USCS § 77b(a)(11)].

(C) Securities involved in such transaction shall be deemed to be restricted securities within the meaning of Rule 144 (17 CFR 230.144).

(2) Rule of construction. The exemption provided by subsection (a)(7) shall not be the exclusive means for establishing an exemption from the registration requirements of section 5 [15 USCS § 77e].

§ 4A. Requirements With Respect to Certain Small Transactions

(a) **Requirements on intermediaries.**—A person acting as an intermediary in a transaction involving the offer or sale of securities for the account of others pursuant to section 4(6) shall—

(1) register with the Commission as—

(A) a broker; or

(B) a funding portal (as defined in section 3(a)(80) of the Securities Exchange Act of 1934);

(2) register with any applicable self-regulatory organization (as defined in section 3(a)(26) of the Securities Exchange Act of 1934);

(3) provide such disclosures, including disclosures related to risks and other investor education materials, as the Commission shall, by rule, determine appropriate;

(4) ensure that each investor—

(A) reviews investor-education information, in accordance with standards established by the Commission, by rule:

(B) positively affirms that the investor understands that the investor is risking the loss of the entire investment, and that the investor could bear such a loss; and

(C) answers questions demonstrating—

(i) an understanding of the level of risk generally applicable to investments in startups, emerging businesses, and small issuers;

(ii) an understanding of the risk of illiquidity; and

(iii) an understanding of such other matters as the Commission determines appropriate, by rule;

(5) take such measures to reduce the risk of fraud with respect to such transactions, as established by the Commission, by rule, including obtaining a background and securities enforcement regulatory history check on each officer, director, and person holding more than 20 percent of the outstanding equity of every issuer whose securities are offered by such person;

(6) not later than 21 days prior to the first day on which securities are sold to any investor (or such other period as the Commission may establish), make available to the Commission and to potential investors any information provided by the issuer pursuant to subsection (b);

(7) ensure that all offering proceeds are only provided to the issuer when the aggregate capital raised from all investors is equal to or greater than a target offering amount, and allow all investors to cancel their commitments to invest, as the Commission shall, by rule, determine appropriate;

(8) make such efforts as the Commission determines appropriate, by rule, to ensure that no investor in a 12-month period has purchased securities offered pursuant to section 4(6) that, in the aggregate, from all issuers, exceed the investment limits set forth in section 4(6)(B);

(9) take such steps to protect the privacy of information collected from investors as the Commission shall, by rule, determine appropriate;

(10) not compensate promoters, finders, or lead generators for providing the broker or funding portal with the personal identifying information of any potential investor;

(11) prohibit its directors, officers, or partners (or any person occupying a similar status or performing a similar function) from having any financial interest in an issuer using its services; and

(12) meet such other requirements as the Commission may, by rule, prescribe, for the protection of investors and in the public interest.

(b) Requirements for issuers.—For purposes of section 4(6), an issuer who offers or sells securities shall—

(1) file with the Commission and provide to investors and the relevant broker or funding portal, and make available to potential investors—

(A) the name, legal status, physical address, and website address of the issuer;

(B) the names of the directors and officers (and any persons occupying a similar status or performing a similar function), and each person holding more than 20 percent of the shares of the issuer;

(C) a description of the business of the issuer and the anticipated business plan of the issuer;

(D) a description of the financial condition of the issuer, including, for offerings that, together with all other offerings of the issuer under section 4(6) within the preceding 12-month period, have, in the aggregate, target offering amounts of—

(i) $100,000 or less—

(I) the income tax returns filed by the issuer for the most recently completed year (if any); and

(II) financial statements of the issuer, which shall be certified by the principal executive officer of the issuer to be true and complete in all material respects;

(ii) more than $100,000, but not more than $500,000, financial statements reviewed by a public accountant who is independent of the issuer, using professional standards and procedures for such review or standards and procedures established by the Commission, by rule, for such purpose; and

(iii) more than $500,000 (or such other amount as the Commission may establish, by rule), audited financial statements;

(E) a description of the stated purpose and intended use of the proceeds of the offering sought by the issuer with respect to the target offering amount;

(F) the target offering amount, the deadline to reach the target offering amount, and regular updates regarding the progress of the issuer in meeting the target offering amount;

(G) the price to the public of the securities or the method for determining the price, provided that, prior to sale, each investor shall be provided in writing the final price and all required disclosures, with a reasonable opportunity to rescind the commitment to purchase the securities;

(H) a description of the ownership and capital structure of the issuer, including—

(i) terms of the securities of the issuer being offered and each other class of security of the issuer, including how such terms may be modified, and a summary of the differences between such securities, including how the rights of the securities being offered may be materially limited, diluted, or qualified by the rights of any other class of security of the issuer;

(ii) a description of how the exercise of the rights held by the principal shareholders of the issuer could negatively impact the purchasers of the securities being offered;

(iii) the name and ownership level of each existing shareholder who owns more than 20 percent of any class of the securities of the issuer;

(iv) how the securities being offered are being valued, and examples of methods for how such securities may be valued by the issuer in the future, including during subsequent corporate actions; and

(v) the risks to purchasers of the securities relating to minority ownership in the issuer, the risks associated with corporate actions, including additional issuances of shares, a sale of the issuer or of assets of the issuer, or transactions with related parties; and

(I) such other information as the Commission may, by rule, prescribe, for the protection of investors and in the public interest;

(2) not advertise the terms of the offering, except for notices which direct investors to the funding portal or broker;

(3) not compensate or commit to compensate, directly or indirectly, any person to promote its offerings through communication channels provided by a broker or funding portal, without taking such steps as the Commission shall, by rule, require to ensure that such person clearly discloses the receipt, past or prospective, of such compensation, upon each instance of such promotional communication;

(4) not less than annually, file with the Commission and provide to investors reports of the results of operations and financial statements of the issuer, as the Commission shall, by rule, determine appropriate, subject to such exceptions and termination dates as the Commission may establish, by rule; and

(5) comply with such other requirements as the Commission may, by rule, prescribe, for the protection of investors and in the public interest.

(c) Liability for material misstatements and omissions.—

(1) Actions authorized.—

(A) In general.—Subject to paragraph (2), a person who purchases a security in a transaction exempted by the provisions of section 4(6) may bring an action against an issuer described in paragraph (2), either at law or in equity in any court of competent jurisdiction, to recover the consideration paid for such security with interest thereon, less the amount of any income received thereon, upon the tender of such security, or for damages if such person no longer owns the security.

(B) Liability.—An action brought under this paragraph shall be subject to the provisions of section 12(b) and section 13, as if the liability were created under section 12(a)(2).

(2) Applicability.—An issuer shall be liable in an action under paragraph (1), if the issuer—

(A) by the use of any means or instruments of transportation or communication in interstate commerce or of the mails, by any means of any written or oral communication, in the offering or sale of a security in a transaction exempted by the provisions of section 4(6), makes an untrue statement of a material fact or omits to state a material fact required to be stated or necessary in order to make the statements, in the light of the circumstances under which they were made, not misleading, provided that the purchaser did not know of such untruth or omission; and

(B) does not sustain the burden of proof that such issuer did not know, and in the exercise of reasonable care could not have known, of such untruth or omission.

(3) Definition.—As used in this subsection, the term "issuer" includes any person who is a director or partner of the issuer, and the principal executive officer or officers, principal financial officer, and controller or principal accounting officer of the issuer (and any person occupying a similar status or performing a similar function) that offers or sells a security in a transaction exempted by the provisions of section 4(6), and any person who offers or sells the security in such offering.

(d) Information available to states.—The Commission shall make, or shall cause to be made by the relevant broker or funding portal, the information described in subsection (b) and such other information as the Commission, by rule, determines appropriate, available to the securities commission (or any agency or office performing like functions) of each State and territory of the United States and the District of Columbia.

(e) Restrictions on sales.—Securities issued pursuant to a transaction described in section 4(6)—

(1) may not be transferred by the purchaser of such securities during the 1-year period beginning on the date of purchase, unless such securities are transferred—

(A) to the issuer of the securities;

(B) to an accredited investor;

(C) as part of an offering registered with the Commission; or

(D) to a member of the family of the purchaser or the equivalent, or in connection with the death or divorce of the purchaser or other similar circumstance, in the discretion of the Commission; and

(2) shall be subject to such other limitations as the Commission shall, by rule, establish.

(f) Applicability.—Section 4(6) shall not apply to transactions involving the offer or sale of securities by any issuer that—

(1) is not organized under and subject to the laws of a State or territory of the United States or the District of Columbia;

(2) is subject to the requirement to file reports pursuant to section 13 or section 15(d) of the Securities Exchange Act of 1934;

(3) is an investment company . . . or

(4) the Commission, by rule or regulation, determines appropriate.

(g) Rule of construction.—Nothing in this section or section 4(6) shall be construed as preventing an issuer from raising capital through methods not described under section 4(6).

(h) Certain Calculations.—

(1) Dollar amounts.—Dollar amounts in section 4(6) and subsection (b) of this section shall be adjusted by the Commission not less frequently than once every 5 years, by notice published in the Federal Register to reflect any change in the Consumer Price Index for All Urban Consumers published by the Bureau of Labor Statistics.

(2) Income and net worth.—The income and net worth of a natural person under section 4(6)(B) shall be calculated in accordance with any rules of the Commission under this title regarding the calculation of the income and net worth, respectively, of an accredited investor.

§ 5.   Prohibitions Relating to Interstate Commerce and the Mails

(a) Sale or delivery after sale of unregistered securities

Unless a registration statement is in effect as to a security, it shall be unlawful for any person, directly or indirectly—

(1) to make use of any means or instruments of transportation or communication in interstate commerce or of the mails to sell such security through the use or medium of any prospectus or otherwise; or

(2) to carry or cause to be carried through the mails or in interstate commerce, by any means or instruments of transportation, any such security for the purpose of sale or for delivery after sale.

(b) Necessity of prospectus meeting requirements of section 10 of this title

It shall be unlawful for any person, directly or indirectly—

(1) to make use of any means or instruments of transportation or communication in interstate commerce or of the mails to carry or transmit any prospectus relating to any security with respect to which a registration statement has been filed under this subchapter, unless such prospectus meets the requirements of section 10 of this title; or

(2) to carry or cause to be carried through the mails or in interstate commerce any such security for the purpose of sale or for delivery after sale, unless accompanied or preceded by a prospectus that meets the requirements of subsection (a) of section 10 of this title.

(c) Necessity of filing registration statement

It shall be unlawful for any person, directly or indirectly, to make use of any means or instruments of transportation or communication in interstate commerce or of the mails to offer to sell or offer to buy through the use or medium of any prospectus or otherwise any security, unless a registration statement has been filed as to such security, or while the registration statement is the subject of a refusal order or stop order or (prior to the effective date of the registration statement) any public proceeding or examination under section 8 of this title. . . .

(d) Limitation.—Notwithstanding any other provision of this section, an emerging growth company or any person authorized to act on behalf of an emerging growth company may engage in oral or written communications with potential investors that are qualified institutional buyers or institutions that are accredited investors, as such terms are respectively defined in section 230.144A and section 230.501(a) of title 17, Code of Federal Regulations, or any successor thereto, to determine whether such investors might have an interest in a contemplated securities offering, either prior to or following the date of filing of a registration statement with respect to such securities with the Commission, subject to the requirement of subsection (b)(2).

(e) Notwithstanding the provisions of section 3 or 4, unless a registration statement meeting the requirements of section 10(a) is in effect as to a security-based swap, it shall be unlawful for any person, directly or indirectly, to make use of any means or instruments of transportation or communication in interstate commerce or of the mails to offer to sell, offer to buy or purchase or sell a security-based swap to any person who is not an eligible contract participant as defined in section 1a(18) of the Commodity Exchange Act (7 U.S.C. 1a(18)).

§ 6. Registration of Securities

(a) Method of registration

Any security may be registered with the Commission under the terms and conditions hereinafter provided, by filing a registration statement in triplicate, at least one of which shall be signed by each issuer, its principal executive officer or officers, its principal financial officer, its comptroller or principal accounting officer, and the majority of its board of directors or persons performing similar functions (or, if there is no board of directors or persons performing similar functions, by the majority of the persons or board having the power of management of the issuer), and in case the issuer is a foreign or Territorial person by its duly authorized representative in the United States; except that when such registration statement relates to a security issued by a foreign government, or political subdivision thereof, it need be signed only by the underwriter of such security. Signatures of all such persons when written on the said registration statements shall be presumed to have been so written by authority of the person whose signature is so affixed and the burden of proof, in the event such authority shall be denied, shall be upon the party denying the same. The affixing of any signature without the authority of the purported signer shall constitute a violation of this subchapter. A registration statement shall be deemed effective only as to the securities specified therein as proposed to be offered. . . .

(b) Emerging growth companies.—

(1) **In general.**—Any emerging growth company, prior to its initial public offering date, may confidentially submit to the Commission a draft registration statement, for confidential nonpublic review by the staff of the Commission prior to public filing, provided that the initial confidential submission and all amendments thereto shall be publicly filed with the Commission not later than 21 days before the date on which the issuer conducts a road show, as such term is defined in section 230.433(h)(4) of title 17, Code of Federal Regulations, or any successor thereto.

(2) **Confidentiality.**—Notwithstanding any other provision of this title, the Commission shall not be compelled to disclose any information provided to or obtained by the Commission pursuant to this subsection. . . . Information described in or obtained pursuant to this subsection shall be deemed to constitute confidential information for purposes of section 24(b)(2) of the Securities Exchange Act of 1934.

§ 7. Information Required in Registration Statement

(a) Information required in registration statement.—

(1) **In general.**—The registration statement, when relating to a security other than a security issued by a foreign government, or political subdivision thereof, shall contain the information, and be accompanied by the documents, specified in Schedule A of section 27 of this title, and when relating to a security issued by a foreign government, or political subdivision thereof, shall contain the information, and be accompanied by the documents, specified in Schedule B of section 27 of this title; except that the Commission may by rules or regulations provide that any such information or document need not be included in respect of any class of issuers or securities if it finds that the requirement of such information or document is inapplicable to such class and that disclosure fully adequate for the protection of investors is otherwise required to be included within the registration statement. If any accountant, engineer, or appraiser, or any person whose profession gives authority to a statement made by him, is named as having prepared or certified any part of the registration statement, or is named as having prepared or certified a report or valuation for use in connection with the registration statement, the written consent of such person shall be filed with the registration statement. If any such person is named as having prepared or certified a report or valuation (other than a public official document or statement) which is used in connection with the registration statement, but is not named as having prepared or certified such report or valuation for use in connection with the registration

statement, the written consent of such person shall be filed with the registration statement unless the Commission dispenses with such filing as impracticable or as involving undue hardship on the person filing the registration statement. Any such registration statement shall contain such other information, and be accompanied by such other documents, as the Commission may by rules or regulations require as being necessary or appropriate in the public interest or for the protection of investors.

(2) **Treatment of emerging growth companies.**—An emerging growth company—

(A) need not present more than 2 years of audited financial statements in order for the registration statement of such emerging growth company with respect to an initial public offering of its common equity securities to be effective, and in any other registration statement to be filed with the Commission, an emerging growth company need not present selected financial data in accordance with section [Item 301 of Regulation S–K], for any period prior to the earliest audited period presented in connection with its initial public offering; and

(B) may not be required to comply with any new or revised financial accounting standard until such date that a company that is not an issuer (as defined under section 2(a) of the Sarbanes-Oxley Act) is required to comply with such new or revised accounting standard, if such standard applies to companies that are not issuers.

(b)(1) The Commission shall prescribe special rules with respect to registration statements filed by any issuer that is a blank check company. Such rules may, as the Commission determines necessary or appropriate in the public interest or for the protection of investors—

(A) require such issuers to provide timely disclosure, prior to or after such statement becomes effective under section 8, of (i) information regarding the company to be acquired and the specific application of the proceeds of the offering, or (ii) additional information necessary to prevent such statement from being misleading;

(B) place limitations on the use of such proceeds and the distribution of securities by such issuer until the disclosures required under subparagraph (A) have been made; and

(C) provide a right of rescission to shareholders of such securities.

(2) The Commission may, as it determines consistent with the public interest and the protection of investors, by rule or order exempt any issuer or class of issuers from the rules prescribed under paragraph (1).

(3) For purposes of paragraph (1) of this subsection, the term "blank check company" means any development stage company that is issuing a penny stock (within the meaning of section 3(a)(51) of the Securities Exchange Act of 1934) and that—

(A) has no specific business plan or purpose; or

(B) has indicated that its business plan is to merge with an unidentified company or companies.

(c) Disclosure requirements.—

(1) **In general.**—The Commission shall adopt regulations under this subsection requiring each issuer of an asset-backed security to disclose, for each tranche or class of security, information regarding the assets backing that security.

(2) **Content of regulations.**—In adopting regulations under this subsection, the Commission shall—

(A) set standards for the format of the data provided by issuers of an asset-backed security, which shall, to the extent feasible, facilitate comparison of such data across securities in similar types of asset classes; and

(B) require issuers of asset-backed securities, at a minimum, to disclose asset-level or loan-level data, if such data are necessary for investors to independently perform due diligence, including—

(i) data having unique identifiers relating to loan brokers or originators;

(ii) the nature and extent of the compensation of the broker or originator of the assets backing the security; and

(iii) the amount of risk retention by the originator and the securitizer of such assets. . . .

§ 8. Taking Effect of Registration Statements and Amendments Thereto

(a) Effective date of registration statement

Except as hereinafter provided, the effective date of a registration statement shall be the twentieth day after the filing thereof or such earlier date as the Commission may determine, having due regard to the adequacy of the information respecting the issuer theretofore available to the public, to the facility with which the nature of the securities to be registered, their relationship to the capital structure of the issuer and the rights of holders thereof can be understood, and to the public interest and the protection of investors. If any amendment to any such statement is filed prior to the effective date of such statement, the registration statement shall be deemed to have been filed when such amendment was filed; except that an amendment filed with the consent of the Commission, prior to the effective date of the registration statement, or filed pursuant to an order of the Commission, shall be treated as a part of the registration statement.

(b) Incomplete or inaccurate registration statement

If it appears to the Commission that a registration statement is on its face incomplete or inaccurate in any material respect, the Commission may, after notice by personal service or the sending of confirmed telegraphic notice not later than ten days after the filing of the registration statement, and opportunity for hearing (at a time fixed by the Commission) within ten days after such notice by personal service or the sending of such telegraphic notice, issue an order prior to the effective date of registration refusing to permit such statement to become effective until it has been amended in accordance with such order. When such statement has been amended in accordance with such order the Commission shall so declare and the registration shall become effective at the time provided in subsection (a) of this section or upon the date of such declaration, whichever date is the later.

(c) Effective Date of Amendment to Registration Statement

An amendment filed after the effective date of the registration statement, if such amendment, upon its face, appears to the Commission not to be incomplete or inaccurate in any material respect, shall become effective on such date as the Commission may determine, having due regard to the public interest and the protection of investors.

(d) Untrue statements or omissions in registration statement

If it appears to the Commission at any time that the registration statement includes any untrue statement of a material fact or omits to state any material fact required to be stated therein or necessary to make the statements therein not misleading, the Commission may, after notice by personal service or the sending of confirmed telegraphic notice, and after opportunity for hearing (at a time fixed by the Commission) within fifteen days after such notice by personal service or the sending of such telegraphic notice, issue a stop order suspending the effectiveness of the registration statement. When such statement has been amended in accordance with such stop order, the Commission shall so declare and thereupon the stop order shall cease to be effective.

(e) Examination for issuance of stop order

The Commission is empowered to make an examination in any case in order to determine whether a stop order should issue under subsection (d) of this section. In making such examination the Commission or any officer or officers designated by it shall have access to and may demand the production of any books and papers of, and may administer oaths and affirmations to and examine, the issuer, underwriter, or any other person, in respect of any matter relevant to the examination, and may, in its discretion, require the production of a balance sheet exhibiting the assets and liabilities of the issuer, or its income statement, or both, to be certified to by a public or certified accountant approved by the Commission. If the issuer or underwriter shall fail to cooperate, or shall obstruct or refuse to permit the making of an examination, such conduct shall be proper ground for the issuance of a stop order.

(f)   Notice requirements

Any notice required under this section shall be sent to or served on the issuer, or, in case of a foreign government or political subdivision thereof, to or on the underwriter, or, in the case of a foreign or Territorial person, to or on its duly authorized representative in the United States named in the registration statement, properly directed in each case of telegraphic notice to the address given in such statement.

§ 8A.   Cease-and-Desist Proceedings

(a)   Authority of the Commission

If the Commission finds, after notice and opportunity for hearing, that any person is violating, has violated, or is about to violate any provision of this title, or any rule or regulation thereunder, the Commission may publish its findings and enter an order requiring such person, and any other person that is, was, or would be a cause of the violation, due to an act or omission the person knew or should have known would contribute to such violation, to cease and desist from committing or causing such violation and any future violation of the same provision, rule, or regulation. Such order may, in addition to requiring a person to cease and desist from committing or causing a violation, require such person to comply, or to take steps to effect compliance, with such provision, rule, or regulation, upon such terms and conditions and within such time as the Commission may specify in such order. Any such order may, as the Commission deems appropriate, require future compliance or steps to effect future compliance, either permanently or for such period of time as the Commission may specify, with such provision, rule, or regulation with respect to any security, any issuer, or any other person. . . .

(e)   Authority to enter an order requiring an accounting and disgorgement

In any cease-and-desist proceeding under subsection (a), the Commission may enter an order requiring accounting and disgorgement, including reasonable interest. The Commission is authorized to adopt rules, regulations, and orders concerning payments to investors, rates of interest, periods of accrual, and such other matters as it deems appropriate to implement this subsection.

(f)   Authority of the Commission to Prohibit Persons From Serving as Officers or Directors

In any cease-and-desist proceeding under subsection (a), the Commission may issue an order to prohibit, conditionally or unconditionally, and permanently or for such period of time as it shall determine, any person who has violated section 17(a)(*l*) or the rules or regulations thereunder, from acting as an officer or director of any issuer that has a class of securities registered pursuant to section 12 of the Securities Exchange Act of 1934, or that is required to file reports pursuant to section 15(d) of that Act, if the conduct of that person demonstrates unfitness to serve as an officer or director of any such issuer.

(g)   Authority to impose money penalties.—

(1)   **Grounds.—**In any cease-and-desist proceeding under subsection (a), the Commission may impose a civil penalty on a person if the Commission finds, on the record, after notice and opportunity for hearing, that—

(A) such person—

(i) is violating or has violated any provision of this title, or any rule or regulation issued under this title; or

(ii) is or was a cause of the violation of any provision of this title, or any rule or regulation thereunder; and

(B) such penalty is in the public interest.

(2)   **Maximum amount of penalty.—**

(A)   **First tier.—**The maximum amount of a penalty for each act or omission described in paragraph (1) shall be $7,500 for a natural person or $80,000 for any other person.

(B)   **Second tier.—**Notwithstanding subparagraph (A), the maximum amount of penalty for each such act or omission shall be $80,000 for a natural person or $400,000 for any other person, if the act or omission described in paragraph (1) involved fraud, deceit, manipulation, or deliberate or reckless disregard of a regulatory requirement.

(C) **Third tier.**—Notwithstanding subparagraphs (A) and (B), the maximum amount of penalty for each such act or omission shall be $160,000 for a natural person or $775,000 for any other person, if—

(i) the act or omission described in paragraph (1) involved fraud, deceit, manipulation, or deliberate or reckless disregard of a regulatory requirement; and

(ii) such act or omission directly or indirectly resulted in—

(I) substantial losses or created a significant risk of substantial losses to other persons; or

(II) substantial pecuniary gain to the person who committed the act or omission.

(3) **Evidence concerning ability to pay.**—In any proceeding in which the Commission may impose a penalty under this section, a respondent may present evidence of the ability of the respondent to pay such penalty. The Commission may, in its discretion, consider such evidence in determining whether such penalty is in the public interest. Such evidence may relate to the extent of the ability of the respondent to continue in business and the collectability of a penalty, taking into account any other claims of the United States or third parties upon the assets of the respondent and the amount of the assets of the respondent.

§ 9. Court Review of Orders

(a) Any person aggrieved by an order of the Commission may obtain a review of such order in the Court of Appeals of the United States, within any circuit wherein such person resides or has his principal place of business, or in the United States Court of Appeals for the District of Columbia, by filing in such court, within sixty days after the entry of such order, a written petition praying that the order of the Commission be modified or be set aside in whole or in part. A copy of such petition shall be forthwith transmitted by the clerk of the court to the Commission, and thereupon the Commission shall file in the court the record upon which the order complained of was entered, as provided in section 2112 of title 28. No objection to the order of the Commission shall be considered by the court unless such objection shall have been urged before the Commission. The finding of the Commission as to the facts, if supported by evidence, shall be conclusive. If either party shall apply to the court for leave to adduce additional evidence, and shall show to the satisfaction of the court that such additional evidence is material and that there were reasonable grounds for failure to adduce such evidence in the hearing before the Commission, the court may order such additional evidence to be taken before the Commission and to be adduced upon the hearing in such manner and upon such terms and conditions as to the court may seem proper. The Commission may modify its findings as to the facts, by reason of the additional evidence so taken, and it shall file such modified or new findings, which, if supported by evidence, shall be conclusive, and its recommendation, if any, for the modification or setting aside of the original order. The jurisdiction of the court shall be exclusive and its judgment and decree, affirming, modifying, or setting aside, in whole or in part, any order of the Commission, shall be final, subject to review by the Supreme Court of the United States upon certiorari or certification as provided in section 1254 of title 28.

(b) The commencement of proceedings under subsection (a) of this section shall not, unless specifically ordered by the court, operate as a stay of the Commission's order.

§ 10. Information Required in Prospectus

(a) Information in registration statement; documents not required

Except to the extent otherwise permitted or required pursuant to this subsection or subsections (c), (d), or (e) of this section—

(1) a prospectus relating to a security other than a security issued by a foreign government or political subdivision thereof, shall contain the information contained in the registration statement. . . .

(3) notwithstanding the provisions of paragraphs (1) and (2) of this subsection when a prospectus is used more than nine months after the effective date of the registration statement, the information

contained therein shall be as of a date not more than sixteen months prior to such use, so far as such information is known to the user of such prospectus or can be furnished by such user without unreasonable effort or expense;

(4) there may be omitted from any prospectus any of the information required under this subsection which the Commission may by rules or regulations designate as not being necessary or appropriate in the public interest or for the protection of investors.

(b) Summarizations and omissions allowed by rules and regulations

In addition to the prospectus permitted or required in subsection (a) of this section, the Commission shall by rules or regulations deemed necessary or appropriate in the public interest or for the protection of investors permit the use of a prospectus for the purposes of subsection (b)(1) of section 5 of this title which omits in part or summarizes information in the prospectus specified in subsection (a) of this section. A prospectus permitted under this subsection shall, except to the extent the Commission by rules or regulations deemed necessary or appropriate in the public interest or for the protection of investors otherwise provides, be filed as part of the registration statement but shall not be deemed a part of such registration statement for the purposes of section 11 of this title. The Commission may at any time issue an order preventing or suspending the use of a prospectus permitted under this subsection, if it has reason to believe that such prospectus has not been filed (if required to be filed as part of the registration statement) or includes any untrue statement of a material fact or omits to state any material fact required to be stated therein or necessary to make the statements therein, in the light of the circumstances under which such prospectus is or is to be used, not misleading. Upon issuance of an order under this subsection, the Commission shall give notice of the issuance of such order and opportunity for hearing by personal service or the sending of confirmed telegraphic notice. The Commission shall vacate or modify the order at any time for good cause or if such prospectus has been filed or amended in accordance with such order.

(c) Additional information required by rules and regulations

Any prospectus shall contain such other information as the Commission may by rules or regulations require as being necessary or appropriate in the public interest or for the protection of investors.

(d) Classification of prospectuses

In the exercise of its powers under subsections (a), (b), or (c) of this section, the Commission shall have authority to classify prospectuses according to the nature and circumstances of their use or the nature of the security, issue, issuer, or otherwise, and, by rules and regulations and subject to such terms and conditions as it shall specify therein, to prescribe as to each class the form and contents which it may find appropriate and consistent with the public interest and the protection of investors.

(e) Information in conspicuous part of prospectus

The statements or information required to be included in a prospectus by or under authority of subsections (a), (b), (c), or (d) of this section, when written, shall be placed in a conspicuous part of the prospectus and, except as otherwise permitted by rules or regulations, in type as large as that used generally in the body of the prospectus.

(f) Prospectus consisting of radio or television broadcast

In any case where a prospectus consists of a radio or television broadcast, copies thereof shall be filed with the Commission under such rules and regulations as it shall prescribe. The Commission may by rules and regulations require the filing with it of forms and prospectuses used in connection with the offer or sale of securities registered under this subchapter.

§ 11. Civil Liabilities on Account of False Registration Statement

(a) Persons possessing cause of action; persons liable

In case any part of the registration statement, when such part became effective, contained an untrue statement of a material fact or omitted to state a material fact required to be stated therein or necessary to make the statements therein not misleading, any person acquiring such security (unless it is proved that at the time of such acquisition he knew of such untruth or omission) may, either at law or in equity, in any court of competent jurisdiction, sue—

(1) every person who signed the registration statement;

(2) every person who was a director of (or person performing similar functions) or partner in the issuer at the time of the filing of the part of the registration statement with respect to which his liability is asserted;

(3) every person who, with his consent, is named in the registration statement as being or about to become a director, person performing similar functions, or partner;

(4) every accountant, engineer, or appraiser, or any person whose profession gives authority to a statement made by him, who has with his consent been named as having prepared or certified any part of the registration statement, or as having prepared or certified any report or valuation which is used in connection with the registration statement, with respect to the statement in such registration statement, report, or valuation, which purports to have been prepared or certified by him;

(5) every underwriter with respect to such security.

If such person acquired the security after the issuer has made generally available to its security holders an earning statement covering a period of at least twelve months beginning after the effective date of the registration statement, then the right of recovery under this subsection shall be conditioned on proof that such person acquired the security relying upon such untrue statement in the registration statement or relying upon the registration statement and not knowing of such omission, but such reliance may be established without proof of the reading of the registration statement by such person.

(b) Persons exempt from liability upon proof of issues

Notwithstanding the provisions of subsection (a) of this section no person, other than the issuer, shall be liable as provided therein who shall sustain the burden of proof—

(1) that before the effective date of the part of the registration statement with respect to which his liability is asserted (A) he had resigned from or had taken such steps as are permitted by law to resign from, or ceased or refused to act in, every office, capacity, or relationship in which he was described in the registration statement as acting or agreeing to act, and (B) he had advised the Commission and the issuer in writing that he had taken such action and that he would not be responsible for such part of the registration statement; or

(2) that if such part of the registration statement became effective without his knowledge, upon becoming aware of such fact he forthwith acted and advised the Commission, in accordance with paragraph (1) of this subsection, and, in addition, gave reasonable public notice that such part of the registration statement had become effective without his knowledge; or

(3) that (A) as regards any part of the registration statement not purporting to be made on the authority of an expert, and not purporting to be a copy of or extract from a report or valuation of an expert, and not purporting to be made on the authority of a public official document or statement, he had, after reasonable investigation, reasonable ground to believe and did believe, at the time such part of the registration statement became effective, that the statements therein were true and that there was no omission to state a material fact required to be stated therein or necessary to make the statements therein not misleading; and (B) as regards any part of the registration statement purporting to be made upon his authority as an expert or purporting to be a copy of or extract from a report or valuation of himself as an expert, (i) he had, after reasonable investigation, reasonable ground to believe and did believe, at the time such part of the registration statement became effective, that the statements therein were true and that there was no omission to state a material fact required to be stated therein or necessary to make the statements therein not misleading, or (ii) such part of the registration statement did not fairly represent his statement as an expert or was not a fair copy of or extract from his report or valuation as an expert; and (C) as regards any part of the registration statement purporting to be made on the authority of an expert (other than himself) or purporting to be a copy of or extract from a report or valuation of an expert (other than himself), he had no reasonable ground to believe and did not believe, at the time such part of the registration statement became effective, that the statements therein were untrue or that there was an omission to state a material fact required to be stated therein or necessary to make the statements therein not misleading, or that such part of the registration statement did not fairly represent the statement of the expert or was not

a fair copy of or extract from the report or valuation of the expert; and (D) as regards any part of the registration statement purporting to be a statement made by an official person or purporting to be a copy of or extract from a public official document, he had no reasonable ground to believe and did not believe, at the time such part of the registration statement became effective, that the statements therein were untrue, or that there was an omission to state a material fact required to be stated therein or necessary to make the statements therein not misleading, or that such part of the registration statement did not fairly represent the statement made by the official person or was not a fair copy of or extract from the public official document.

(c) Standard of reasonableness

In determining, for the purpose of paragraph (3) of subsection (b) of this section, what constitutes reasonable investigation and reasonable ground for belief, the standard of reasonableness shall be that required of a prudent man in the management of his own property.

(d) Effective date of registration statement with regard to underwriters

If any person becomes an underwriter with respect to the security after the part of the registration statement with respect to which his liability is asserted has become effective, then for the purposes of paragraph (3) of subsection (b) of this section such part of the registration statement shall be considered as having become effective with respect to such person as of the time when he became an underwriter.

(e) Measure of damages; undertaking for payment of costs

The suit authorized under subsection (a) of this section may be to recover such damages as shall represent the difference between the amount paid for the security (not exceeding the price at which the security was offered to the public) and (1) the value thereof as of the time such suit was brought, or (2) the price at which such security shall have been disposed of in the market before suit, or (3) the price at which such security shall have been disposed of after suit but before judgment if such damages shall be less than the damages representing the difference between the amount paid for the security (not exceeding the price at which the security was offered to the public) and the value thereof as of the time such suit was brought: *Provided,* That if the defendant proves that any portion or all of such damages represents other than the depreciation in value of such security resulting from such part of the registration statement, with respect to which his liability is asserted, not being true or omitting to state a material fact required to be stated therein or necessary to make the statements therein not misleading, such portion of or all such damages shall not be recoverable. In no event shall any underwriter (unless such underwriter shall have knowingly received from the issuer for acting as an underwriter some benefit, directly or indirectly, in which all other underwriters similarly situated did not share in proportion to their respective interests in the underwriting) be liable in any suit or as a consequence of suits authorized under subsection (a) of this section for damages in excess of the total price at which the securities underwritten by him and distributed to the public were offered to the public. In any suit under this or any other section of this subchapter the court may, in its discretion, require an undertaking for the payment of the costs of such suit, including reasonable attorney's fees, and if judgment shall be rendered against a party litigant, upon the motion of the other party litigant, such costs may be assessed in favor of such party litigant (whether or not such undertaking has been required) if the court believes the suit or the defense to have been without merit, in an amount sufficient to reimburse him for the reasonable expenses incurred by him, in connection with such suit, such costs to be taxed in the manner usually provided for taxing of costs in the court in which the suit was heard.

(f) Joint and several liability

(1) Except as provided in paragraph (2), all or any one or more of the persons specified in subsection (a) of this section shall be jointly and severally liable, and every person who becomes liable to make any payment under this section may recover contribution as in cases of contract from any person who, if sued separately, would have been liable to make the same payment, unless the person who has become liable was, and the other was not, guilty of fraudulent misrepresentation.

(2)(A) The liability of an outside director under subsection (e) of this section shall be determined in accordance with section 21D(f) of the Securities Exchange Act of 1934.

(B) For purposes of this paragraph, the term "outside director" shall have the meaning given such term by rule or regulation of the Commission.

(g) Offering price to public as maximum amount recoverable

In no case shall the amount recoverable under this section exceed the price at which the security was offered to the public.

§ 12. Civil Liabilities Arising in Connection With Prospectuses and Communications

(a) In General

Any person who—

(1) offers or sells a security in violation of section 5 of this title, or

(2) offers or sells a security (whether or not exempted by the provisions of section 3 of this title, other than paragraphs (2) and (14) of subsection (a) of said section), by the use of any means or instruments of transportation or communication in interstate commerce or of the mails, by means of a prospectus or oral communication, which includes an untrue statement of a material fact or omits to state a material fact necessary in order to make the statements, in the light of the circumstances under which they were made, not misleading (the purchaser not knowing of such untruth or omission), and who shall not sustain the burden of proof that he did not know, and in the exercise of reasonable care could not have known, of such untruth or omission,

shall be liable, subject to subsection (b), to the person purchasing such security from him, who may sue either at law or in equity in any court of competent jurisdiction, to recover the consideration paid for such security with interest thereon, less the amount of any income received thereon, upon the tender of such security, or for damages if he no longer owns the security.

(b) Loss Causation

In an action described in subsection (a)(2), if the person who offered or sold such security proves that any portion or all of the amount recoverable under subsection (a)(2) represents other than the depreciation in value of the subject security resulting from such part of the prospectus or oral communication, with respect to which the liability of that person is asserted, not being true or omitting to state a material fact required to be stated therein or necessary to make the statement not misleading, then such portion or amount, as the case may be, shall not be recoverable.

§ 13. Limitation of Actions

No action shall be maintained to enforce any liability created under section 11 or 12(a)(2) of this title unless brought within one year after the discovery of the untrue statement or the omission, or after such discovery should have been made by the exercise of reasonable diligence, or, if the action is to enforce a liability created under section 12(a)(1) of this title, unless brought within one year after the violation upon which it is based. In no event shall any such action be brought to enforce a liability created under section 11 or 12(a)(1) of this title more than three years after the security was bona fide offered to the public, or under section 12(a)(2) of this title more than three years after the sale.

§ 14. Contrary Stipulations Void

Any condition, stipulation, or provision binding any person acquiring any security to waive compliance with any provision of this subchapter or of the rules and regulations of the Commission shall be void.

§ 15. Liability of Controlling Persons

(a) Controlling Persons

Every person who, by or through stock ownership, agency, or otherwise, or who, pursuant to or in connection with an agreement or understanding with one or more other persons by or through stock ownership, agency, or otherwise, controls any person liable under sections 11 or 12 of this title, shall also be liable jointly and severally with and to the same extent as such controlled person to any person to whom such controlled person is liable, unless the controlling person had no knowledge of or reasonable ground to believe in the existence of the facts by reason of which the liability of the controlled person is alleged to exist.

(b) Prosecution of Persons Who Aid and Abet Violations

For purposes of any action brought by the Commission under subparagraph (b) or (d) of section 20, any person that knowingly or recklessly provides substantial assistance to another person in violation of a provision of this Act, or of any rule or regulation issued under this Act, shall be deemed to be in violation of such provision to the same extent as the person to whom such assistance is provided. . . .

§ 16.   Additional Remedies; Limitations on Remedies

(a) *Remedies Additional.*—Except as provided in subsection (b), the rights and remedies provided by this title shall be in addition to any and all other rights and remedies that may exist at law or in equity.

(b) *Class Action Limitations.*—No covered class action based upon the statutory or common law of any State or subdivision thereof may be maintained in any State or Federal court by any private party alleging—

(1) an untrue statement or omission of a material fact in connection with the purchase or sale of a covered security; or

(2) that the defendant used or employed any manipulative or deceptive device or contrivance in connection with the purchase or sale of a covered security.

(c) *Removal of Covered Class Actions.*—Any covered class action brought in any State court involving a covered security, as set forth in subsection (b), shall be removable to the Federal district court for the district in which the action is pending, and shall be subject to subsection (b).

(d) *Preservation of Certain Actions.*—

(1) *Actions under state law of state of incorporation.*—

(A) *Actions preserved.*—Notwithstanding subsection (b) or (c), a covered class action described in subparagraph (B) of this paragraph that is based upon the statutory or common law of the State in which the issuer is incorporated (in the case of a corporation) or organized (in the case of any other entity) may be maintained in a State or Federal court by a private party.

(B) *Permissible actions.*—A covered class action is described in this subparagraph if it involves—

(i) the purchase or sale of securities by the issuer or an affiliate of the issuer exclusively from or to holders of equity securities of the issuer; or

(ii) any recommendation, position, or other communication with respect to the sale of securities of the issuer that—

(I) is made by or on behalf of the issuer or an affiliate of the issuer to holders of equity securities of the issuer; and

(II) concerns decisions of those equity holders with respect to voting their securities, acting in response to a tender or exchange offer, or exercising dissenters' or appraisal rights.

(2) *State actions.*—

(A) *In general.*—Notwithstanding any other provision of this section, nothing in this section may be construed to preclude a State or political subdivision thereof or a State pension plan from bringing an action involving a covered security on its own behalf, or as a member of a class comprised solely of other States, political subdivisions, or State pension plans that are named plaintiffs, and that have authorized participation, in such action.

(B) *State pension plan defined.*—For purposes of this paragraph, the term "State pension plan" means a pension plan established and maintained for its employees by the government of the State or political subdivision thereof, or by any agency or instrumentality thereof.

(3) *Actions under contractual agreements between issuers and indenture trustees.*— Notwithstanding subsection (b) or (c), a covered class action that seeks to enforce a contractual

agreement between an issuer and an indenture trustee may be maintained in a State or Federal court by a party to the agreement or a successor to such party.

(4) *Remand of removed actions.*—In an action that has been removed from a State court pursuant to subsection (c), if the Federal court determines that the action may be maintained in State court pursuant to this subsection, the Federal court shall remand such action to such State court.

(e) *Preservation of State Jurisdiction.*—The securities commission (or any agency or office performing like functions) of any State shall retain jurisdiction under the laws of such State to investigate and bring enforcement actions.

(f) *Definitions.*—For purposes of this section, the following definitions shall apply:

(1) *Affiliate of the issuer.*—The term "affiliate of the issuer" means a person that directly or indirectly, through one or more intermediaries, controls or is controlled by or is under common control with, the issuer.

(2) *Covered class action.*—

(A) *In general.*—The term "covered class action" means—

(i) any single lawsuit in which—

(I) damages are sought on behalf of more than 50 persons or prospective class members, and questions of law or fact common to those persons or members of the prospective class, without reference to issues of individualized reliance on an alleged misstatement or omission, predominate over any questions affecting only individual persons or members; or

(II) one or more named parties seek to recover damages on a representative basis on behalf of themselves and other unnamed parties similarly situated, and questions of law or fact common to those persons or members of the prospective class predominate over any questions affecting only individual persons or members; or

(ii) any group of lawsuits filed in or pending in the same court and involving common questions of law or fact, in which—

(I) damages are sought on behalf of more than 50 persons; and

(II) the lawsuits are joined, consolidated, or otherwise proceed as a single action for any purpose.

(B) *Exception for derivative actions.*—Notwithstanding subparagraph (A), the term "covered class action" does not include an exclusively derivative action brought by one or more shareholders on behalf of a corporation.

(C) *Counting of certain class members.*—For purposes of this paragraph, a corporation, investment company, pension plan, partnership, or other entity, shall be treated as one person or prospective class member, but only if the entity is not established for the purpose of participating in the action.

(D) *Rule of construction.*—Nothing in this paragraph shall be construed to affect the discretion of a State court in determining whether actions filed in such court should be joined, consolidated, or otherwise allowed to proceed as a single action.

(3) *Covered security.*—The term "covered security" means a security that satisfies the standards for a covered security specified in paragraph (1) or (2) of section 18(b) at the time during which it is alleged that the misrepresentation, omission, or manipulative or deceptive conduct occurred, except that such term shall not include any debt security that is exempt from registration under this title pursuant to rules issued by the Commission under section 4(2).

§ 17.　　Fraudulent Interstate Transactions

(a)　Use of interstate commerce for purpose of fraud or deceit

It shall be unlawful for any person in the offer or sale of any securities . . . by the use of any means or instruments of transportation or communication in interstate commerce or by the use of the mails, directly or indirectly—

　　(1) to employ any device, scheme, or artifice to defraud, or

　　(2) to obtain money or property by means of any untrue statement of a material fact or any omission to state a material fact necessary in order to make the statements made, in the light of the circumstances under which they were made, not misleading, or

　　(3) to engage in any transaction, practice, or course of business which operates or would operate as a fraud or deceit upon the purchaser.

(b)　Use of interstate commerce for purpose of offering for sale

It shall be unlawful for any person, by the use of any means or instruments of transportation or communication in interstate commerce or by the use of the mails, to publish, give publicity to, or circulate any notice, circular, advertisement, newspaper, article, letter, investment service, or communication which, though not purporting to offer a security for sale, describes such security for a consideration received or to be received, directly or indirectly, from an issuer, underwriter, or dealer, without fully disclosing the receipt, whether past or prospective, of such consideration and the amount thereof.

(c)　Exemptions of section 3 not applicable to this section

The exemptions provided in section 3 of this title shall not apply to the provisions of this section. . . .

§ 18.　　Exemption From State Regulation of Securities Offerings

(a)　Scope of exemption

Except as otherwise provided in this section, no law, rule, regulation, or order, or other administrative action of any State or any political subdivision thereof—

　　(1) requiring, or with respect to, registration or qualification of securities, or registration or qualification of securities transactions, shall directly or indirectly apply to a security that—

　　　　(A) is a covered security; or

　　　　(B) will be a covered security upon completion of the transaction;

　　(2) shall directly or indirectly prohibit, limit, or impose any conditions upon the use of—

　　　　(A) with respect to a covered security described in subsection (b) of this section, any offering document that is prepared by or on behalf of the issuer; or

　　　　(B) any proxy statement, report to shareholders, or other disclosure document relating to a covered security or the issuer thereof that is required to be and is filed with the Commission or any national securities organization registered under section 15A of the Securities Exchange Act, except that this subparagraph does not apply to the laws, rules, regulations, or orders, or other administrative actions of the State of incorporation of the issuer; or

　　(3) shall directly or indirectly prohibit, limit, or impose conditions, based on the merits of such offering or issuer, upon the offer or sale of any security described in paragraph (1).

(b)　Covered securities

For purposes of this section, the following are covered securities:

　　(1) *Exclusive Federal registration of nationally traded securities*

　　A security is a covered security if such security is—

(A) listed, or authorized for listing, on the New York Stock Exchange or the American Stock Exchange, or listed, or authorized for listing, on the National Market System of the Nasdaq Stock Market (or any successor to such entities);

(B) listed, or authorized for listing, on a national securities exchange (or tier or segment thereof) that has listing standards that the Commission determines by rule (on its own initiative or on the basis of a petition) are substantially similar to the listing standards applicable to securities described in subparagraph (A); or

(C) a security of the same issuer that is equal in seniority or that is a senior security to a security described in subparagraph (A) or (B).

(2) *Exclusive Federal registration of investment companies*

A security is a covered security if such security is a security issued by an investment company that is registered, or that has filed a registration statement, under the Investment Company Act of 1940.

(3) *Sales to qualified purchasers*

A security is a covered security with respect to the offer or sale of the security to qualified purchasers, as defined by the Commission by rule. In prescribing such rule, the Commission may define the term "qualified purchaser" differently with respect to different categories of securities, consistent with the public interest and the protection of investors.

(4) *Exemption in connection with certain exempt offerings*

A security is a covered security with respect to a transaction that is exempt from registration under this subchapter pursuant to—

(A) paragraph (1) or (3) of section 4, and the issuer of such security files reports with the Commission pursuant to section 13 or 15(d) of the Securities Exchange Act;

(B) section 4(4);

(C) section 4(6);

(D) a rule or regulation adopted pursuant to section 3(b)(2) and such security is—

(i) offered or sold on a national securities exchange; or

(ii) offered or sold to a qualified purchaser, as defined by the Commission pursuant to paragraph (3) with respect to that purchase or sale;

(E) section 3(a), other than the offer or sale of a security that is exempt from such registration pursuant to paragraph (4), (10), or (11) of such section, except that a municipal security that is exempt from such registration pursuant to paragraph (2) of such section is not a covered security with respect to the offer or sale of such security in the State in which the issuer of such security is located; or

(F) Commission rules or regulations issued under section 4(2), except that this subparagraph does not prohibit a State from imposing notice filing requirements that are substantially similar to those required by rule or regulation under section 4(2) that are in effect on September 1, 1996.

(c) Preservation of authority

(1) *Fraud authority*

Consistent with this section, the securities commission (or any agency or officer performing like functions) of any State shall retain jurisdiction under the laws of such State to investigate and bring enforcement actions, in connection with securities or securities transactions

(A) with respect to—

(i) fraud or deceit; or

(ii) unlawful conduct by a broker, dealer, or funding portal; and

(B) in connection to a transaction described under section 4(6), with respect to—

    (i) fraud or deceit; or

    (ii) unlawful conduct by a broker, dealer, funding portal, or issuer.

(2) *Preservation of filing requirements*

(A) *Notice filings permitted*

Nothing in this section prohibits the securities commission (or any agency or office performing like functions) of any State from requiring the filing of any document filed with the Commission pursuant to this subchapter, together with annual or periodic reports of the value of securities sold or offered to be sold to persons located in the State (if such sales data is not included in documents filed with the Commission), solely for notice purposes and the assessment of any fee, together with a consent to service of process and any required fee.

(B) *Preservation of fees*

    (i) *In general*

Until otherwise provided by law, rule, regulation, or order, or other administrative action of any State or any political subdivision thereof, adopted after October 11, 1996, filing or registration fees with respect to securities or securities transactions shall continue to be collected in amounts determined pursuant to State law as in effect on the day before such date.

    (ii) *Schedule*

The fees required by this subparagraph shall be paid, and all necessary supporting data on sales or offers for sales required under subparagraph (A), shall be reported on the same schedule as would have been applicable had the issuer not relied on the exemption provided in subsection (a) of this section.

(C) *Availability of preemption contingent on payment of fees*

    (i) *In general*

During the period beginning on October 11, 1996, and ending 3 years after October 11, 1996, the securities commission (or any agency or office performing like functions) of any State may require the registration of securities issued by any issuer who refuses to pay the fees required by subparagraph (B).

    (ii) *Delays*

For purposes of this subparagraph, delays in payment of fees or underpayments of fees that are promptly remedied shall not constitute a refusal to pay fees.

(D) *Fees not permitted on listed securities*

Notwithstanding subparagraphs (A), (B), and (C), no filing or fee may be required with respect to any security that is a covered security pursuant to subsection (b)(1) of this section, or will be such a covered security upon completion of the transaction, or is a security of the same issuer that is equal in seniority or that is a senior security to a security that is a covered security pursuant to subsection (b)(1) of this section.

(3) *Enforcement of requirements*

Nothing in this section shall prohibit the securities commission (or any agency or office performing like functions) of any State from suspending the offer or sale of securities within such State as a result of the failure to submit any filing or fee required under law and permitted under this section. . . .

    (F) *Fees not permitted on crowdfunded securities.*—Notwithstanding subparagraphs (A), (B), and (C), no filing or fee may be required with respect to any security that is a covered security pursuant to subsection (b)(4)(B), or will be such a covered security upon completion of the transaction, except for the securities commission (or any agency or office performing like functions) of the State of the principal place of business of the issuer, or any State in which purchasers of 50 percent or greater of the aggregate amount of the issue are residents, provided that for purposes of this subparagraph, the term "State" includes the District of Columbia and the territories of the United States.

(d) Definitions

For purposes of this section, the following definitions shall apply:

(1) *Offering document*

The term "offering document"—

(A) has the meaning given the term "prospectus" in section 2(a)(10) of this title, but without regard to the provisions of subparagraphs (a) and (b) of that section; and

(B) includes a communication that is not deemed to offer a security pursuant to a rule of the Commission.

(2) *Prepared by or on behalf of the issuer*

Not later than 6 months after the date of enactment of the National Securities Market Improvement Act of 1996, the Commission shall, by rule, define the term "prepared by or on behalf of the issuer" for purposes of this section.

(3) *State*

The term "State" has the same meaning as in section 3.

(4) *Senior security*

The term "senior security" means any bond, debenture, note, or similar obligation or instrument constituting a security and evidencing indebtedness, and any stock of a class having priority over any other class as to distribution of assets or payment of dividends.

§ 19. Special Powers of Commission

(a) The Commission shall have authority from time to time to make, amend, and rescind such rules and regulations as may be necessary to carry out the provisions of this subchapter, including rules and regulations governing registration statements and prospectuses for various classes of securities and issuers, and defining accounting, technical, and trade terms used in this subchapter. Among other things, the Commission shall have authority, for the purposes of this subchapter, to prescribe the form or forms in which required information shall be set forth, the items or details to be shown in the balance sheet and earning statement, and the methods to be followed in the preparation of accounts, in the appraisal or valuation of assets and liabilities, in the determination of depreciation and depletion, in the differentiation of recurring and nonrecurring income, in the differentiation of investment and operating income, and in the preparation, where the Commission deems it necessary or desirable, of consolidated balance sheets or income accounts of any person directly or indirectly controlling or controlled by the issuer, or any person under direct or indirect common control with the issuer. The rules and regulations of the Commission shall be effective upon publication in the manner which the Commission shall prescribe. No provision of this subchapter imposing any liability shall apply to any act done or omitted in good faith in conformity with any rule or regulation of the Commission, notwithstanding that such rule or regulation may, after such act or omission, be amended or rescinded or be determined by judicial or other authority to be invalid for any reason.

(b) Recognition of accounting standards

(1) *In general.*—In carrying out its authority under subsection (a) and under section 13(b) of the Securities Exchange Act of 1934, the Commission may recognize, as "generally accepted" for purposes of the securities laws, any accounting principles established by a standard setting body—

(A) that—

(i) is organized as a private entity;

(ii) has, for administrative and operational purposes, a board of trustees (or equivalent body) serving in the public interest, the majority of whom are not, concurrent with their service on such board, and have not been during the 2-year period preceding such service, associated persons of any registered public accounting firm; . . .

(iv) has adopted procedures to ensure prompt consideration, by majority vote of its members, of changes to accounting principles necessary to reflect emerging accounting issues and changing business practices; and

(v) considers, in adopting accounting principles, the need to keep standards current in order to reflect changes in the business environment, the extent to which international convergence on high quality accounting standards is necessary or appropriate in the public interest and for the protection of investors; and

(B) that the Commission determines has the capacity to assist the Commission in fulfilling the requirements of subsection (a) and section 13(b) of the Securities Exchange Act of 1934, because, at a minimum, the standard setting body is capable of improving the accuracy and effectiveness of financial reporting and the protection of investors under the securities laws.

(2) *Annual report.*—A standard setting body described in paragraph (1) shall submit an annual report to the Commission and the public, containing audited financial statements of that standard setting body.

(c) For the purpose of all investigations which, in the opinion of the Commission, are necessary and proper for the enforcement of this subchapter, any member of the Commission or any officer or officers designated by it are empowered to administer oaths and affirmations, subpoena witnesses, take evidence, and require the production of any books, papers, or other documents which the Commission deems relevant or material to the inquiry. Such attendance of witnesses and the production of such documentary evidence may be required from any place in the United States or any Territory at any designated place of hearing. . . .

§ 20.   Injunctions and Prosecution of Offenses. . . .

(b)   Action for injunction or criminal prosecution in district court

Whenever it shall appear to the Commission that any person is engaged or about to engage in any acts or practices which constitute or will constitute a violation of the provisions of this subchapter, or of any rule or regulation prescribed under authority thereof, it may in its discretion, bring an action in any district court of the United States or United States court of any Territory, to enjoin such acts or practices, and upon a proper showing a permanent or temporary injunction or restraining order shall be granted without bond. The Commission may transmit such evidence as may be available concerning such acts or practices to the Attorney General who may, in his discretion, institute the necessary criminal proceedings under this subchapter. Any such criminal proceeding may be brought either in the district wherein the transmittal of the prospectus or security complained of begins, or in the district wherein such prospectus or security is received. . . .

(d)   Money penalties in civil actions

(1) *Authority of commission.* Whenever it shall appear to the Commission that any person has violated any provision of this title, the rules or regulations thereunder, or a cease-and-desist order entered by the Commission pursuant to section 8A of this title, other than by committing a violation subject to a penalty pursuant to section 21A of the Securities Exchange Act of 1934, the Commission may bring an action in a United States district court to seek, and the court shall have jurisdiction to impose, upon a proper showing, a civil penalty to be paid by the person who committed such violation.

(2) *Amount of penalty.*

(A) *First tier.* The amount of the penalty shall be determined by the court in light of the facts and circumstances. For each violation, the amount of the penalty shall not exceed the greater of (i) $7,500 for a natural person or $80,000 for any other person, or (ii) the gross amount of pecuniary gain to such defendant as a result of the violation.

(B) *Second tier.* Notwithstanding subparagraph (A), the amount of penalty for each such violation shall not exceed the greater of (i) $80,000 for a natural person or $400,000 for any other person, or (ii) the gross amount of pecuniary gain to such defendant as a result of the violation, if the violation described in paragraph (1) involved fraud, deceit, manipulation, or deliberate or reckless disregard of a regulatory requirement.

(C) *Third tier.* Notwithstanding subparagraphs (A) and (B), the amount of penalty for each such violation shall not exceed the greater of (i) $160,000 for a natural person or $775,000 for any other person, or (ii) the gross amount of pecuniary gain to such defendant as a result of the violation, if—

(I) the violation described in paragraph (1) involved fraud, deceit, manipulation, or deliberate or reckless disregard of a regulatory requirement; and

(II) such violation directly or indirectly resulted in substantial losses or created a significant risk of substantial losses to other persons.

(3) *Procedures for collection.*

(A) *Payment of penalty to treasury.* A penalty imposed under this section shall be payable into the Treasury of the United States, except as otherwise provided in section 308 of the Sarbanes-Oxley Act of 2002 and Section 21F of the Securities Exchange Act of 1934.

(B) *Collection of penalties.* If a person upon whom such a penalty is imposed shall fail to pay such penalty within the time prescribed in the court's order, the Commission may refer the matter to the Attorney General who shall recover such penalty by action in the appropriate United States district court.

(C) *Remedy not exclusive.* The actions authorized by this subsection may be brought in addition to any other action that the Commission or the Attorney General is entitled to bring.

(D) *Jurisdiction and venue.* For purposes of section 22 of this title, actions under this section shall be actions to enforce a liability or a duty created by this title.

(4) *Special provisions relating to a violation of a cease-and-desist order.* In an action to enforce a cease-and-desist order entered by the Commission pursuant to section 8A, each separate violation of such order shall be a separate offense, except that in the case of a violation through a continuing failure to comply with such an order, each day of the failure to comply with the order shall be deemed a separate offense.

(e) Authority of a court to prohibit persons from serving as Officers and Directors

In any proceeding under subsection (b), the court may prohibit, conditionally or unconditionally, and permanently or for such period of time as it shall determine, any person who violated section 17(a)(1) of this title from acting as an officer or director of any issuer that has a class of securities registered pursuant to section 12 of the Securities Exchange Act of 1934 or that is required to file reports pursuant to section 15(d) of such Act if the person's conduct demonstrates unfitness to serve as an officer or director of any such issuer.

(f) Prohibition of Attorneys' Fees Paid From Commission Disgorgement Funds

Except as otherwise ordered by the court upon motion by the Commission, or, in the case of an administrative action, as otherwise ordered by the Commission, funds disgorged as the result of an action brought by the Commission in Federal court, or as a result of any Commission administrative action, shall not be distributed as payment for attorneys' fees or expenses incurred by private parties seeking distribution of the disgorged funds.

(g) Authority of a court to prohibit persons from participating in an offering of penny stock

(1) *In general.*—In any proceeding under subsection (a) against any person participating in, or, at the time of the alleged misconduct, who was participating in, an offering of penny stock, the court may prohibit that person from participating in an offering of penny stock, conditionally or unconditionally, and permanently or for such period of time as the court shall determine.

(2) *Definition.*—For purposes of this subsection, the term "person participating in an offering of penny stock" includes any person engaging in activities with a broker, dealer, or issuer for purposes of issuing, trading, or inducing or attempting to induce the purchase or sale of, any penny stock. The Commission may, by rule or regulation, define such term to include other activities, and may, by rule, regulation, or order, exempt any person or class of persons, in whole or in part, conditionally or unconditionally, from inclusion in such term.

§ 22.   Jurisdiction of Offenses and Suits

(a)   Federal and State courts; venue; service of process; review; removal; costs

The district courts of the United States, and the United States courts of any Territory, shall have jurisdiction of offenses and violations under this subchapter and under the rules and regulations promulgated by the Commission in respect thereto, and, concurrent with State and Territorial courts, except as provided in section 16 with respect to covered class actions, of all suits in equity and actions at law brought to enforce any liability or duty created by this subchapter. Any such suit or action may be brought in the district wherein the defendant is found or is an inhabitant or transacts business, or in the district where the offer or sale took place, if the defendant participated therein, and process in such cases may be served in any other district of which the defendant is an inhabitant or wherever the defendant may be found. Judgments and decrees so rendered shall be subject to review as provided in sections 1254, 1291, and 1292 of title 28. Except as provided in section 16(c), no case arising under this subchapter and brought in any State court of competent jurisdiction shall be removed to any court of the United States. No costs shall be assessed for or against the Commission in any proceeding under this subchapter brought by or against it in the Supreme Court or such other courts.

(b)   Contumacy or refusal to obey subpoena: contempt

In case of contumacy or refusal to obey a subpoena issued to any person, any of the said United States courts, within the jurisdiction of which said person guilty of contumacy or refusal to obey is found or resides, upon application by the Commission may issue to such person an order requiring such person to appear before the Commission, or one of its examiners designated by it, there to produce documentary evidence if so ordered, or there to give evidence touching the matter in question; and any failure to obey such order of the court may be punished by said court as a contempt thereof.

(c)   Extraterritorial jurisdiction

The district courts of the United States and the United States courts of any Territory shall have jurisdiction of an action or proceeding brought or instituted by the Commission or the United States alleging a violation of section 17(a) involving—

(1) conduct within the United States that constitutes significant steps in furtherance of the violation, even if the securities transaction occurs outside the United States and involves only foreign investors; or

(2) conduct occurring outside the United States that has a foreseeable substantial effect within the United States.

§ 23.   Unlawful Representations

Neither the fact that the registration statement for a security has been filed or is in effect nor the fact that a stop order is not in effect with respect thereto shall be deemed a finding by the Commission that the registration statement is true and accurate on its face or that it does not contain an untrue statement of fact or omit to state a material fact, or be held to mean that the Commission has in any way passed upon the merits of, or given approval to, such security. It shall be unlawful to make, or cause to be made to any prospective purchaser any representation contrary to the foregoing provisions of this section.

§ 24.   Penalties

Any person who willfully violates any of the provisions of this subchapter, or the rules and regulations promulgated by the Commission under authority thereof, or any person who willfully, in a registration statement filed under this subchapter, makes any untrue statement of a material fact or omits to state any material fact required to be stated therein or necessary to make the statements therein not misleading, shall upon conviction be fined not more than $10,000 or imprisoned not more than five years, or both. . . .

§ 27. Private Securities Litigation

(a) Private Class Actions

(1) *In general.*—The provisions of this subsection shall apply to each private action arising under this title that is brought as a plaintiff class action pursuant to the Federal Rules of Civil Procedure.

(2) *Certification filed with complaint.*—

(A) In general.—Each plaintiff seeking to serve as a representative party on behalf of a class shall provide a sworn certification, which shall be personally signed by such plaintiff and filed with the complaint, that—

(i) states that the plaintiff has reviewed the complaint and authorized its filing;

(ii) states that the plaintiff did not purchase the security that is the subject of the complaint at the direction of plaintiff's counsel or in order to participate in any private action arising under this title;

(iii) states that the plaintiff is willing to serve as a representative party on behalf of a class, including providing testimony at deposition and trial, if necessary;

(iv) sets forth all of the transactions of the plaintiff in the security that is the subject of the complaint during the class period specified in the complaint;

(v) identifies any other action under this title, filed during the 3-year period preceding the date on which the certification is signed by the plaintiff, in which the plaintiff has sought to serve, or served, as a representative party on behalf of a class; and

(vi) states that the plaintiff will not accept any payment for serving as a representative party on behalf of a class beyond the plaintiff's pro rata share of any recovery, except as ordered or approved by the court in accordance with paragraph (4).

(B) Nonwaiver of attorney-client privilege.—The certification filed pursuant to subparagraph (A) shall not be construed to be a waiver of the attorney-client privilege.

(3) *Appointment of lead plaintiff.*—

(A) Early notice to class members.—

(i) In general.—Not later than 20 days after the date on which the complaint is filed, the plaintiff or plaintiffs shall cause to be published, in a widely circulated national business-oriented publication or wire service, a notice advising members of the purported plaintiff class—

(I) of the pendency of the action, the claims asserted therein, and the purported class period; and

(II) that, not later than 60 days after the date on which the notice is published, any member of the purported class may move the court to serve as lead plaintiff of the purported class.

(ii) Multiple actions.—If more than one action on behalf of a class asserting substantially the same claim or claims arising under this title is filed, only the plaintiff or plaintiffs in the first filed action shall be required to cause notice to be published in accordance with clause (i).

(iii) Additional notices may be required under federal rules.—Notice required under clause (i) shall be in addition to any notice required pursuant to the Federal Rules of Civil Procedure.

(B) Appointment of lead plaintiff.—

(i) In general.—Not later than 90 days after the date on which a notice is published under subparagraph (A)(i), the court shall consider any motion made by a purported class member in response to the notice, including any motion by a class member who is not individually named as a plaintiff in the complaint or complaints, and shall appoint as lead plaintiff the member or members of the purported plaintiff class that the court determines to be most capable of adequately representing the interests of class members (hereafter in this paragraph referred to as the "most adequate plaintiff") in accordance with this subparagraph.

(ii) Consolidated actions.—If more than one action on behalf of a class asserting substantially the same claim or claims arising under this title has been filed, and any party has sought to consolidate those actions for pretrial purposes or for trial, the court shall not make the determination required by clause (i) until after the decision on the motion to consolidate is rendered. As soon as practicable after such decision is rendered, the court shall appoint the most adequate plaintiff as lead plaintiff for the consolidated actions in accordance with this subparagraph.

(iii) Rebuttable presumption.—

(I) In general.—Subject to subclause (II), for purposes of clause (i), the court shall adopt a presumption that the most adequate plaintiff in any private action arising under this title is the person or group of persons that—

(aa) has either filed the complaint or made a motion in response to a notice under subparagraph (A)(i);

(bb) in the determination of the court, has the largest financial interest in the relief sought by the class; and

(cc) otherwise satisfies the requirements of Rule 23 of the Federal Rules of Civil Procedure.

(II) Rebuttal evidence.—The presumption described in subclause (I) may be rebutted only upon proof by a member of the purported plaintiff class that the presumptively most adequate plaintiff—

(aa) will not fairly and adequately protect the interests of the class; or

(bb) is subject to unique defenses that render such plaintiff incapable of adequately representing the class.

(iv) Discovery.—For purposes of this subparagraph, discovery relating to whether a member or members of the purported plaintiff class is the most adequate plaintiff may be conducted by a plaintiff only if the plaintiff first demonstrates a reasonable basis for a finding that the presumptively most adequate plaintiff is incapable of adequately representing the class.

(v) Selection of lead counsel.—The most adequate plaintiff shall, subject to the approval of the court, select and retain counsel to represent the class.

(vi) Restrictions on professional plaintiffs.—Except as the court may otherwise permit, consistent with the purposes of this section, a person may be a lead plaintiff, or an officer, director, or fiduciary of a lead plaintiff, in no more than 5 securities class actions brought as plaintiff class actions pursuant to the Federal Rules of Civil Procedure during any 3-year period.

(4) *Recovery by plaintiffs.*—The share of any final judgment or of any settlement that is awarded to a representative party serving on behalf of a class shall be equal, on a per share basis, to the portion of the final judgment or settlement awarded to all other members of the class. Nothing in this paragraph shall be construed to limit the award of reasonable costs and expenses (including lost wages) directly relating to the representation of the class to any representative party serving on behalf of the class.

(5) *Restrictions on settlements under seal.*—The terms and provisions of any settlement agreement of a class action shall not be filed under seal, except that on motion of any party to the settlement, the court may order filing under seal for those portions of a settlement agreement as to which good cause is shown for such filing under seal. For purposes of this paragraph, good cause shall exist only if publication of a term or provision of a settlement agreement would cause direct and substantial harm to any party.

(6) *Restrictions on payment of attorneys' fees and expenses.*—Total attorneys' fees and expenses awarded by the court to counsel for the plaintiff class shall not exceed a reasonable percentage of the amount of any damages and prejudgment interest actually paid to the class.

(7) *Disclosure of settlement terms to class members.*—Any proposed or final settlement agreement that is published or otherwise disseminated to the class shall include each of the following statements, along with a cover page summarizing the information contained in such statements:

(A) Statement of plaintiff recovery.—The amount of the settlement proposed to be distributed to the parties to the action, determined in the aggregate and on an average per share basis.

(B) Statement of potential outcome of case.—

(i) Agreement on amount of damages.—If the settling parties agree on the average amount of damages per share that would be recoverable if the plaintiff prevailed on each claim alleged under this title, a statement concerning the average amount of such potential damages per share.

(ii) Disagreement on amount of damages.—If the parties do not agree on the average amount of damages per share that would be recoverable if the plaintiff prevailed on each claim alleged under this title, a statement from each settling party concerning the issue or issues on which the parties disagree.

(iii) Inadmissibility for certain purposes.—A statement made in accordance with clause (i) or (ii) concerning the amount of damages shall not be admissible in any Federal or State judicial action or administrative proceeding, other than an action or proceeding arising out of such statement.

(C) Statement of attorneys' fees or costs sought.—If any of the settling parties or their counsel intend to apply to the court for an award of attorneys' fees or costs from any fund established as part of the settlement, a statement indicating which parties or counsel intend to make such an application, the amount of fees and costs that will be sought (including the amount of such fees and costs determined on an average per share basis), and a brief explanation supporting the fees and costs sought.

(D) Identification of lawyers' representatives.—The name, telephone number, and address of one or more representatives of counsel for the plaintiff class who will be reasonably available to answer questions from class members concerning any matter contained in any notice of settlement published or otherwise disseminated to the class.

(E) Reasons for settlement.—A brief statement explaining the reasons why the parties are proposing the settlement.

(F) Other information.—Such other information as may be required by the court.

(8) *Attorney conflict of interest.*—If a plaintiff class is represented by an attorney who directly owns or otherwise has a beneficial interest in the securities that are the subject of the litigation, the court shall make a determination of whether such ownership or other interest constitutes a conflict of interest sufficient to disqualify the attorney from representing the plaintiff class.

(b) Stay of Discovery; Preservation of Evidence

(1) *In general.*—In any private action arising under this title, all discovery and other proceedings shall be stayed during the pendency of any motion to dismiss, unless the court finds, upon the motion

of any party, that particularized discovery is necessary to preserve evidence or to prevent undue prejudice to that party.

(2) *Preservation of evidence.*—During the pendency of any stay of discovery pursuant to this subsection, unless otherwise ordered by the court, any party to the action with actual notice of the allegations contained in the complaint shall treat all documents, data compilations (including electronically recorded or stored data), and tangible objects that are in the custody or control of such person and that are relevant to the allegations, as if they were the subject of a continuing request for production of documents from an opposing party under the Federal Rules of Civil Procedure.

(3) *Sanction for willful violation.*—A party aggrieved by the willful failure of an opposing party to comply with paragraph (2) may apply to the court for an order awarding appropriate sanctions.

(4) *Circumvention of stay of discovery.*—Upon a proper showing, a court may stay discovery proceedings in any private action in a State court as necessary in aid of its jurisdiction, or to protect or effectuate its judgments, in an action subject to a stay of discovery pursuant to this subsection.

(c) Sanctions for Abusive Litigation

(1) *Mandatory review by court.*—In any private action arising under this title, upon final adjudication of the action, the court shall include in the record specific findings regarding compliance by each party and each attorney representing any party with each requirement of Rule 11(b) of the Federal Rules of Civil Procedure as to any complaint, responsive pleading, or dispositive motion.

(2) *Mandatory sanctions.*—If the court makes a finding under paragraph (1) that a party or attorney violated any requirement of Rule 11(b) of the Federal Rules of Civil Procedure as to any complaint, responsive pleading, or dispositive motion, the court shall impose sanctions on such party or attorney in accordance with Rule 11 of the Federal Rules of Civil Procedure. Prior to making a finding that any party or attorney has violated Rule 11 of the Federal Rules of Civil Procedure, the court shall give such party or attorney notice and an opportunity to respond.

(3) *Presumption in favor of attorneys' fees and costs.*—

(A) In general.—Subject to subparagraphs (B) and (C), for purposes of paragraph (2), the court shall adopt a presumption that the appropriate sanction—

(i) for failure of any responsive pleading or dispositive motion to comply with any requirement of Rule 11(b) of the Federal Rules of Civil Procedure is an award to the opposing party of the reasonable attorneys' fees and other expenses incurred as a direct result of the violation; and

(ii) for substantial failure of any complaint to comply with any requirement of Rule 11(b) of the Federal Rules of Civil Procedure is an award to the opposing party of the reasonable attorneys' fees and other expenses incurred in the action.

(B) Rebuttal evidence.—The presumption described in subparagraph (A) may be rebutted only upon proof by the party or attorney against whom sanctions are to be imposed that—

(i) the award of attorneys' fees and other expenses will impose an unreasonable burden on that party or attorney and would be unjust, and the failure to make such an award would not impose a greater burden on the party in whose favor sanctions are to be imposed; or

(ii) the violation of Rule 11(b) of the Federal Rules of Civil Procedure was de minimis.

(C) Sanctions.—If the party or attorney against whom sanctions are to be imposed meets its burden under subparagraph (B), the court shall award the sanctions that the court deems appropriate pursuant to Rule 11 of the Federal Rules of Civil Procedure.

(d) Defendant's Right to Written Interrogatories

In any private action arising under this title in which the plaintiff may recover money damages only on proof that a defendant acted with a particular state of mind, the court shall, when requested by a defendant, submit to the jury a written interrogatory on the issue of each such defendant's state of mind at the time the alleged violation occurred.

§ 27A. Application of Safe Harbor for Forward-Looking Statements

(a) Applicability

This section shall apply only to a forward-looking statement made by—

(1) an issuer that, at the time that the statement is made, is subject to the reporting requirements of section 13(a) or section 15(d) of the Securities Exchange Act of 1934;

(2) a person acting on behalf of such issuer;

(3) an outside reviewer retained by such issuer making a statement on behalf of such issuer; or

(4) an underwriter, with respect to information provided by such issuer or information derived from information provided by the issuer.

(b) Exclusions

Except to the extent otherwise specifically provided by rule, regulation, or order of the Commission, this section shall not apply to a forward-looking statement—

(1) that is made with respect to the business or operations of the issuer, if the issuer—

(A) during the 3-year period preceding the date on which the statement was first made—

(i) was convicted of any felony or misdemeanor described in clauses (i) through (iv) of section 15(b)(4)(B) of the Securities Exchange Act of 1934; or

(ii) has been made the subject of a judicial or administrative decree or order arising out of a governmental action that—

(I) prohibits future violations of the antifraud provisions of the securities laws;

(II) requires that the issuer cease and desist from violating the antifraud provisions of the securities laws; or

(III) determines that the issuer violated the antifraud provisions of the securities laws;

(B) makes the forward-looking statement in connection with an offering of securities by a blank check company;

(C) issues penny stock;

(D) makes the forward-looking statement in connection with a rollup transaction; or

(E) makes the forward-looking statement in connection with a going private transaction; or

(2) that is—

(A) included in a financial statement prepared in accordance with generally accepted accounting principles;

(B) contained in a registration statement of, or otherwise issued by, an investment company;

(C) made in connection with a tender offer;

(D) made in connection with an initial public offering;

(E) made in connection with an offering by, or relating to the operations of, a partnership, limited liability company, or a direct participation investment program; or

(F) made in a disclosure of beneficial ownership in a report required to be filed with the Commission pursuant to section 13(d) of the Securities Exchange Act of 1934.

(c) Safe Harbor

(1) *In general.*—Except as provided in subsection (b), in any private action arising under this title that is based on an untrue statement of a material fact or omission of a material fact necessary to make the statement not misleading, a person referred to in subsection (a) shall not be liable with respect to any forward-looking statement, whether written or oral, if and to the extent that—

(A) the forward-looking statement is—

(i) identified as a forward-looking statement, and is accompanied by meaningful cautionary statements identifying important factors that could cause actual results to differ materially from those in the forward-looking statement; or

(ii) immaterial; or

(B) the plaintiff fails to prove that the forward-looking statement—

(i) if made by a natural person, was made with actual knowledge by that person that the statement was false or misleading; or

(ii) if made by a business entity, was—

(I) made by or with the approval of an executive officer of that entity, and

(II) made or approved by such officer with actual knowledge by that officer that the statement was false or misleading.

(2) *Oral forward-looking statements.*—In the case of an oral forward-looking statement made by an issuer that is subject to the reporting requirements of section 13(a) or section 15(d) of the Securities Exchange Act of 1934, or by a person acting on behalf of such issuer, the requirement set forth in paragraph (1)(A) shall be deemed to be satisfied—

(A) if the oral forward-looking statement is accompanied by a cautionary statement—

(i) that the particular oral statement is a forward-looking statement; and

(ii) that the actual results could differ materially from those projected in the forward-looking statement; and

(B) if—

(i) the oral forward-looking statement is accompanied by an oral statement that additional information concerning factors that could cause actual results to differ materially from those in the forward-looking statement is contained in a readily available written document, or portion thereof;

(ii) the accompanying oral statement referred to in clause (i) identifies the document, or portion thereof, that contains the additional information about those factors relating to the forward-looking statement; and

(iii) the information contained in that written document is a cautionary statement that satisfies the standard established in paragraph (1)(A).

(3) *Availability.*—Any document filed with the Commission or generally disseminated shall be deemed to be readily available for purposes of paragraph (2).

(4) *Effect on other safe harbors.*—The exemption provided for in paragraph (1) shall be in addition to any exemption that the Commission may establish by rule or regulation under subsection (g).

(d)   Duty to Update

Nothing in this section shall impose upon any person a duty to update a forward-looking statement.

(e)   Dispositive Motion

On any motion to dismiss based upon subsection (c)(1), the court shall consider any statement cited in the complaint and cautionary statement accompanying the forward-looking statement, which are not subject to material dispute, cited by the defendant.

(f)   Stay Pending Decision on Motion

In any private action arising under this title, the court shall stay discovery (other than discovery that is specifically directed to the applicability of the exemption provided for in this section) during the pendency of any motion by a defendant for summary judgment that is based on the grounds that—

(1) the statement or omission upon which the complaint is based is a forward-looking statement within the meaning of this section; and

(2) the exemption provided for in this section precludes a claim for relief.

(g) Exemption Authority

In addition to the exemptions provided for in this section, the Commission may, by rule or regulation, provide exemptions from or under any provision of this title, including with respect to liability that is based on a statement or that is based on projections or other forward-looking information, if and to the extent that any such exemption is consistent with the public interest and the protection of investors, as determined by the Commission.

(h) Effect on Other Authority of Commission

Nothing in this section limits, either expressly or by implication, the authority of the Commission to exercise similar authority or to adopt similar rules and regulations with respect to forward-looking statements under any other statute under which the Commission exercises rulemaking authority.

(i) Definitions

For purposes of this section, the following definitions shall apply:

(1) *Forward-looking statement.*—The term "forward-looking statement" means—

(A) a statement containing a projection of revenues, income (including income loss), earnings (including earnings loss) per share, capital expenditures, dividends, capital structure, or other financial items;

(B) a statement of the plans and objectives of management for future operations, including plans or objectives relating to the products or services of the issuer;

(C) a statement of future economic performance, including any such statement contained in a discussion and analysis of financial condition by the management or in the results of operations included pursuant to the rules and regulations of the Commission;

(D) any statement of the assumptions underlying or relating to any statement described in subparagraph (A), (B), or (C);

(E) any report issued by an outside reviewer retained by an issuer, to the extent that the report assesses a forward-looking statement made by the issuer; or

(F) a statement containing a projection or estimate of such other items as may be specified by rule or regulation of the Commission.

(2) *Investment company.*—The term "investment company" has the same meaning as in section 3(a) of the Investment Company Act of 1940.

(3) *Penny stock.*—The term "penny stock" has the same meaning as in section 3(a)(51) of the Securities Exchange Act of 1934, and the rules and regulations, or orders issued pursuant to that section.

(4) *Going private transaction.*—The term "going private transaction" has the meaning given that term under the rules or regulations of the Commission issued pursuant to section 13(e) of the Securities Exchange Act of 1934.

(5) *Securities laws.*—The term "securities laws" has the same meaning as in section 3 of the Securities Exchange Act of 1934.

(6) *Person acting on behalf of an issuer.*—The term "person acting on behalf of an issuer" means an officer, director, or employee of the issuer.

(7) *Other terms.*—The terms "blank check company", "roll-up transaction", "partnership", "limited liability company", "executive officer of an entity" and "direct participation investment program", have the meanings given those terms by rule or regulation of the Commission.

§ 28.   General Exemptive Authority

The Commission, by rule or regulation, may conditionally or unconditionally exempt any person, security, or transaction, or any class or classes of persons, securities, or transactions, from any provision or provisions of this subchapter or of any rule or regulation issued under subchapter, to the extent that such exemption is necessary or appropriate in the public interest, and is consistent with the protection of investors.

RULES AND FORMS UNDER THE SECURITIES ACT OF 1933 (SELECTED PROVISIONS)

17 C.F.R. §§ 230.00 et seq.

TABLE OF CONTENTS

GENERAL

Rule		Page
134.	Communications Not Deemed a Prospectus	1214
135.	Notice of Proposed Registered Offerings	1217
135c.	Notice of Certain Proposed Unregistered Offerings	1218
137.	Publications or Distributions of Research Reports by Brokers or Dealers that are not Participating in an Issuer's Registered Distribution of Securities	1219
138.	Publications or Distributions of Research Reports by Brokers or Dealers About Securities Other than Those They Are Distributing	1220
139.	Publications or Distributions of Research Reports by Brokers or Dealers Distributing Securities	1220
144.	Persons Deemed Not to Be Engaged in a Distribution and Therefore Not Underwriters	1221
144A.	Private Resales of Securities to Institutions	1226
145.	Reclassification of Securities, Mergers, Consolidations and Acquisitions of Assets	1228
146.	Rules under Section 18 of the Act	1228
§ 230.147.	Intrastate Offers and Sales	1230
§ 230.147A.	Intrastate Sales Exemption	1233
153.	Definition of "Preceded by a Prospectus" as Used in Section 5(b)(2) of the Act, in Relation to Certain Transactions	1236
155.	Integration of Abandoned Offerings	1236
159.	Information Available to Purchaser at Time of Contract of Sale	1237
159A.	Certain Definitions for Purposes of Section 12(a)(2) of the Act	1237
162.	Submission of Tenders in Registered Exchange Offers	1238
163.	Exemption from Section 5(c) of the Act for Certain Communications by or on Behalf of Well-known Seasoned Issuers	1239
163A.	Exemption from Section 5(c) of the Act for Certain Communications Made by or on Behalf of Issuers More Than 30 days Before a Registration Statement is Filed	1240
164.	Post-filing Free Writing Prospectuses in Connection with Certain Registered Offerings	1241
165.	Offers Made in Connection with a Business Combination Transaction	1242
166.	Exemption from Section 5(c) for Certain Communications in Connection with Business Combination Transactions	1243
168.	Exemption from Sections 2(a)(10) and 5(c) of the Act for Certain Communications of Regularly Released Factual Business Information and Forward-looking Information	1243
169.	Exemption from Sections 2(a)(10) and 5(c) of the Act for Certain Communications of Regularly Released Factual Business Information	1244
172.	Delivery of Prospectuses	1245
173.	Notice of Registration	1246
174.	Delivery of Prospectus by Dealers; Exemptions Under Section 4(3) of the Act	1246
175.	Liability for Certain Statements by Issuers	1247
176.	Circumstances Affecting the Determination of What Constitutes Reasonable Investigation and Reasonable Grounds for Belief Under Section 11 of the Securities Act	1248
215.	Accredited Investor	1248

REGULATION A—CONDITIONAL SMALL ISSUES EXEMPTION

251.	Scope of Exemption	1249
252.	Offering Statement	1252
253.	Offering Circular	1253
254.	Preliminary Offering Circular	1254
255.	Solicitations of Interest and Other Communications	1255
256.	Definition of "Qualified Purchaser"	1256
257.	Periodic and Current Reporting; Exit Report	1256
258.	Suspension of the Exemption	1257
259.	Withdrawal or Abandonment of Offering Statements	1258
260.	Insignificant Deviations From a Term, Condition or Requirement of Regulation A	1258
261.	Definitions	1259
262.	Disqualification Provisions	1259
263.	Consent to Service of Process	1261

REGULATION C—REGISTRATION

405.	Definitions of Terms	1261
408.	Additional Information	1265
415.	Delayed or Continuous Offering and Sale of Securities	1265
421.	Presentation of Information in Prospectuses	1266
425.	Filing of Certain Prospectuses and Communications under Rule 135 in Connection with Business Combination Transactions	1267
427.	Contents of Prospectus Used After Nine Months	1268
430.	Prospectus for Use Prior to Effective Date	1268
431.	Summary Prospectuses	1268
432.	Additional Information Required to be Included in Prospectuses Relating to Tender Offers	1269
433.	Conditions to Permissible Post-filing Free Writing Prospectuses	1269
460.	Distribution of Preliminary Prospectus	1271
461.	Acceleration of Effective Date	1271

REGULATION D—RULES GOVERNING THE LIMITED OFFER AND SALE OF SECURITIES WITHOUT REGISTRATION UNDER THE SECURITIES ACT OF 1933

500.	Use of Regulation D	1272
501.	Definitions and Terms Used in Regulation D	1273
502.	General Conditions to Be Met	1276
503.	Filing of Notice of Sales	1279
504.	Exemption for Limited Offerings and Sales of Securities Not Exceeding $5,000,000	1280
506.	Exemption for Limited Offers and Sales Without Regard to Dollar Amount of Offering	1281
507.	Disqualifying Provision Relating to Exemptions Under Rule 504, Rule 505, and Rule 506	1284
508.	Insignificant Deviations From a Term, Condition or Requirement of Regulation D	1284
FORM S-1		1285
FORM S-3		1287

GENERAL

Rule 134. Communications Not Deemed a Prospectus

Except as provided in paragraphs (e) and (g) of this section, the terms "prospectus" as defined in section 2(a)(10) of the Act or "free writing prospectus" as defined in Rule 405 shall not include a communication limited to the statements required or permitted by this section, provided that the communication is published or transmitted to any person only after a registration statement relating to the offering that includes a prospectus satisfying the requirements of section 10 of the Act (except as otherwise permitted in paragraph (a) of this section) has been filed.

(a) Such communication may include any one or more of the following items of information, which need not follow the numerical sequence of this paragraph, provided that, except as to paragraphs (a)(4), (a)(5), (a)(6), and (a)(17), the prospectus included in the filed registration statement does not have to include a price range otherwise required by rule:

(1) Factual information about the legal identity and business location of the issuer limited to the following: the name of the issuer of the security, the address, phone number, and e-mail address of the issuer's principal offices and contact for investors, the issuer's country of organization, and the geographic areas in which it conducts business;

(2) The title of the security or securities and the amount or amounts being offered, which title may include a designation as to whether the securities are convertible, exercisable, or exchangeable, and as to the ranking of the securities;

(3) A brief indication of the general type of business of the issuer, limited to the following:

(i) In the case of a manufacturing company, the general type of manufacturing, the principal products or classes of products manufactured, and the segments in which the company conducts business;

(ii) In the case of a public utility company, the general type of services rendered, a brief indication of the area served, and the segments in which the company conducts business;

(iii) In the case of an asset-backed issuer, the identity of key parties, such as sponsor, depositor, issuing entity, servicer or servicers, and trustee, the asset class of the transaction, and the identity of any credit enhancement or other support; and

(iv) In the case of any other type of company, a corresponding statement;

(4) The price of the security, or if the price is not known, the method of its determination or the *bona fide* estimate of the price range as specified by the issuer or the managing underwriter or underwriters;

(5) In the case of a fixed income security, the final maturity and interest rate provisions or, if the final maturity or interest rate provisions are not known, the probable final maturity or interest rate provisions, as specified by the issuer or the managing underwriter or underwriters;

(6) In the case of a fixed income security with a fixed (non-contingent) interest rate provision, the yield or, if the yield is not known, the probable yield range, as specified by the issuer or the managing underwriter or underwriters and the yield of fixed income securities with comparable maturity and security rating as referred to in paragraph (a)(17) of this section;

(7) A brief description of the intended use of proceeds of the offering, if then disclosed in the prospectus that is part of the filed registration statement;

(8) The name, address, phone number, and e-mail address of the sender of the communication and the fact that it is participating, or expects to participate, in the distribution of the security;

(9) The type of underwriting, if then included in the disclosure in the prospectus that is part of the filed registration statement;

(10) The names of underwriters participating in the offering of the securities, and their additional roles, if any, within the underwriting syndicate;

(11) The anticipated schedule for the offering (including the approximate date upon which the proposed sale to the public will begin) and a description of marketing events (including the dates, times, locations, and procedures for attending or otherwise accessing them);

(12) A description of the procedures by which the underwriters will conduct the offering and the procedures for transactions in connection with the offering with the issuer or an underwriter or participating dealer (including procedures regarding account opening and submitting indications of interest and

conditional offers to buy), and procedures regarding directed share plans and other participation in offerings by officers, directors, and employees of the issuer;

(13) Whether, in the opinion of counsel, the security is a legal investment for savings banks, fiduciaries, insurance companies, or similar investors under the laws of any State or Territory or the District of Columbia, and the permissibility or status of the investment under the Employee Retirement Income Security Act of 1974;

(14) Whether, in the opinion of counsel, the security is exempt from specified taxes, or the extent to which the issuer has agreed to pay any tax with respect to the security or measured by the income therefrom;

(15) Whether the security is being offered through rights issued to security holders, and, if so, the class of securities the holders of which will be entitled to subscribe, the subscription ratio, the actual or proposed record date, the date upon which the rights were issued or are expected to be issued, the actual or anticipated date upon which they will expire, and the approximate subscription price, or any of the foregoing;

(16) Any statement or legend required by any state law or administrative authority;

(17) With respect to the securities being offered:

(i) Any security rating assigned, or reasonably expected to be assigned, by a *nationally recognized statistical rating organization* as defined in Rule 15c3–1(c)(2)(vi)(F) of the Securities Exchange Act of 1934 and the name or names of the nationally recognized statistical rating organization(s) that assigned or is or are reasonably expected to assign the rating(s); and

(ii) If registered on Form F-9, any security rating assigned, or reasonably expected to be assigned, by any other rating organization specified in the Instruction to paragraph A.(2) of General Instruction I of Form F-9;

(18) The names of selling security holders, if then disclosed in the prospectus that is part of the filed registration statement;

(19) The names of securities exchanges or other securities markets where any class of the issuer's securities are, or will be, listed;

(20) The ticker symbols, or proposed ticker symbols, of the issuer's securities;

(21) The CUSIP number as defined in Rule 17Ad–19(a)(5) of the Securities Exchange Act of 1934 assigned to the securities being offered; and

(22) Information disclosed in order to correct inaccuracies previously contained in a communication permissibly made pursuant to this section.

(b) Except as provided in paragraph (c) of this section, every communication used pursuant to this section shall contain the following:

(1) If the registration statement has not yet become effective, the following statement: A registration statement relating to these securities has been filed with the Securities and Exchange Commission but has not yet become effective. These securities may not be sold nor may offers to buy be accepted prior to the time the registration statement becomes effective; and

(2) The name and address of a person or persons from whom a written prospectus for the offering meeting the requirements of section 10 of the Act (other than a free writing prospectus as defined in Rule 405) including as to the identified paragraphs above a price range where required by rule, may be obtained.

(c) Any of the statements or information specified in paragraph (b) of this section may, but need not, be contained in a communication which:

(1) Does no more than state from whom and include the uniform resource locator (URL) where a written prospectus meeting the requirements of section 10 of the Act (other than a free writing prospectus as defined in Rule 405) may be obtained, identify the security, state the price thereof and state by whom orders will be executed; or

(2) Is accompanied or preceded by a prospectus or a summary prospectus, other than a free writing prospectus as defined in Rule 405, which meets the requirements of section 10 of the Act, including a price range where required by rule, at the date of such preliminary communication.

(d) A communication sent or delivered to any person pursuant to this section which is accompanied or preceded by a prospectus which meets the requirements of section 10 of the Act (other than a free writing prospectus as defined in Rule 405), including a price range where required by rule, at the date of such communication, may solicit from the recipient of the communication an offer to buy the security or request the recipient to indicate whether he or she might be interested in the security, if the communication contains substantially the following statement:

No offer to buy the securities can be accepted and no part of the purchase price can be received until the registration statement has become effective, and any such offer may be withdrawn or revoked, without obligation or commitment of any kind, at any time prior to notice of its acceptance given after the effective date.

Provided, that such statement need not be included in such a communication to a dealer.

(e) A section 10 prospectus included in any communication pursuant to this section shall remain a prospectus for all purposes under the Act.

(f) The provision in paragraphs (c)(2) and (d) of this section that a prospectus that meets the requirements of section 10 of the Act precede or accompany a communication will be satisfied if such communication is an electronic communication containing an active hyperlink to such prospectus.

(g) This section does not apply to a communication relating to an investment company registered under the Investment Company Act of 1940 or a business development company as defined in section 2(a)(48) of the Investment Company Act of 1940.

Rule 135. Notice of Proposed Registered Offerings

(a) *When notice is not an offer*. For purposes of section 5 of the Act only, an issuer or a selling security holder (and any person acting on behalf of either of them) that publishes through any medium a notice of a proposed offering to be registered under the Act will not be deemed to offer its securities for sale through that notice if:

(1) *Legend*. The notice includes a statement to the effect that it does not constitute an offer of any securities for sale; and

(2) *Limited notice content*. The notice otherwise includes no more than the following information:

(i) The name of the issuer;

(ii) The title, amount and basic terms of the securities offered;

(iii) The amount of the offering, if any, to be made by selling security holders;

(iv) The anticipated timing of the offering;

(v) A brief statement of the manner and the purpose of the offering, without naming the underwriters;

(vi) Whether the issuer is directing its offering to only a particular class of purchasers;

(vii) Any statements or legends required by the laws of any state or foreign country or administrative authority; and

(viii) In the following offerings, the notice may contain additional information, as follows:

(A) *Rights offering*. In a rights offering to existing security holders:

(1) The class of security holders eligible to subscribe;

(2) The subscription ratio and expected subscription price;

(3) The proposed record date;

(4) The anticipated issuance date of the rights; and

(5) The subscription period or expiration date of the rights offering.

(B) *Offering to employees.* In an offering to employees of the issuer or an affiliated company:

(1) The name of the employer;

(2) The class of employees being offered the securities;

(3) The offering price; and

(4) The duration of the offering period.

(C) *Exchange offer.* In an exchange offer:

(1) The basic terms of the exchange offer;

(2) The name of the subject company;

(3) The subject class of securities sought in the exchange offer.

(D) *Rule 145(a) offering.* In a Rule 145(a) offering:

(1) The name of the person whose assets are to be sold in exchange for the securities to be offered;

(2) The names of any other parties to the transaction;

(3) A brief description of the business of the parties to the transaction;

(4) The date, time and place of the meeting of security holders to vote on or consent to the transaction; and

(5) A brief description of the transaction and the basic terms of the transaction.

(b) *Corrections of misstatements about the offering.* A person that publishes a notice in reliance on this section may issue a notice that contains no more information than is necessary to correct inaccuracies published about the proposed offering.

Rule 135c.   Notice of Certain Proposed Unregistered Offerings

(a) For the purposes only of Section 5 of the Act, a notice given by an issuer required to file reports pursuant to Section 13 or 15(d) of the Securities Exchange Act of 1934 or a foreign issuer that is exempt from registration under the Securities Exchange Act of 1934 pursuant to Rule 12g3–2(b) that it proposes to make, is making or has made an offering of securities not registered or required to be registered under the Act shall not be deemed to offer any securities for sale if:

(1) Such notice is not used for the purpose of conditioning the market in the United States for any of the securities offered;

(2) Such notice states that the securities offered will not be or have not been registered under the Act and may not be offered or sold in the United States absent registration or an applicable exemption from registration requirements; and

(3) Such notice contains no more than the following additional information:

(i) The name of the issuer;

(ii) The title, amount and basic terms of the securities offered, the amount of the offering, if any, made by selling security holders, the time of the offering and a brief statement of the manner and purpose of the offering without naming the underwriters;

(iii) In the case of a rights offering to security holders of the issuer, the class of securities the holders of which will be or were entitled to subscribe to the securities offered, the subscription ratio, the record date, the date upon which the rights are proposed to be or were issued, the term or expiration date of the rights and the subscription price, or any of the foregoing;

(iv) In the case of an offering of securities in exchange for other securities of the issuer or of another issuer, the name of the issuer and the title of the securities to be surrendered in exchange for the securities offered, the basis upon which the exchange may be made, or any of the foregoing;

(v) In the case of an offering to employees of the issuer or to employees of any affiliate of the issuer, the name of the employer and class or classes of employees to whom the securities are offered, the offering price or basis of the offering and the period during which the offering is to be or was made or any of the foregoing; and

(vi) Any statement or legend required by State or foreign law or administrative authority.

(b) Any notice contemplated by this section may take the form of a news release or a written communication directed to security holders or employees, as the case may be, or other published statements.

(c) Notwithstanding the provisions of paragraphs (a) and (b) of this section, in the case of a rights offering of a security listed or subject to unlisted trading privileges on a national securities exchange or quoted on the NASDAQ inter-dealer quotation system information with respect to the interest rate, conversion ratio and subscription price may be disseminated through the facilities of the exchange, the consolidated transaction reporting system, the NASDAQ system or the Dow Jones broad tape, provided such information is already disclosed in a Form 8-K on file with the Commission, in a Form 6-K furnished to the Commission or, in the case of an issuer relying on Rule 12g3–2(b), in a submission made pursuant to that Rule to the Commission.

(d) The issuer shall file any notice contemplated by this section with the Commission under cover of Form 8-K or furnish such notice under Form 6-K, as applicable, and, if relying on Rule 12g3–2(b), shall furnish such notice to the Commission in accordance with the provisions of that exemptive Section.

Rule 137. Publications or Distributions of Research Reports by Brokers or Dealers that are not Participating in an Issuer's Registered Distribution of Securities

Under the following conditions, the terms "offers," "participates," or "participation" in section 2(a)(11) of the Act shall not be deemed to apply to the publication or distribution of research reports with respect to the securities of an issuer which is the subject of an offering pursuant to a registration statement that the issuer proposes to file, or has filed, or that is effective:

(a) The broker or dealer (and any affiliate) that has distributed the report and, if different, the person (and any affiliate) that has published the report have not participated, are not participating, and do not propose to participate in the distribution of the securities that are or will be the subject of the registered offering.

(b) In connection with the publication or distribution of the research report, the broker or dealer (and any affiliate) that has distributed the report and, if different, the person (and any affiliate) that has published the report are not receiving and have not received consideration directly or indirectly from, and are not acting under any direct or indirect arrangement or understanding with:

(1) The issuer of the securities;

(2) A selling security holder;

(3) Any participant in the distribution of the securities that are or will be the subject of the registration statement; or

(4) Any other person interested in the securities that are or will be the subject of the registration statement.

Instruction to Rule 137(b).

This paragraph (b) does not preclude payment of:

1. The regular price being paid by the broker or dealer for independent research, so long as the conditions of this paragraph (b) are satisfied; or

2. The regular subscription or purchase price for the research report.

(c) The broker or dealer publishes or distributes the research report in the regular course of its business. . . .

(e) *Definition of research report.* For purposes of this section, *research report* means a written communication, as defined in Rule 405, that includes information, opinions, or recommendations with respect to securities of an issuer or an analysis of a security or an issuer, whether or not it provides information reasonably sufficient upon which to base an investment decision.

Rule 138.   Publications or Distributions of Research Reports by Brokers or Dealers About Securities Other than Those They Are Distributing

(a) *Registered offerings.* Under the following conditions, a broker's or dealer's publication or distribution of research reports about securities of an issuer shall be deemed for purposes of sections 2(a)(10) and 5(c) of the Act not to constitute an offer for sale or offer to sell a security which is the subject of an offering pursuant to a registration statement that the issuer proposes to file, or has filed, or that is effective, even if the broker or dealer is participating or will participate in the registered offering of the issuer's securities:

(1)(i) The research report relates solely to the issuer's common stock, or debt securities, or preferred stock convertible into its common stock, and the offering involves solely the issuer's non-convertible debt securities or non-convertible, non-participating preferred stock; or

(ii) The research report relates solely to the issuer's non-convertible debt securities or non-convertible, non-participating preferred stock, and the offering involves solely the issuer's common stock, or debt securities, or preferred stock convertible into its common stock.

(2) The issuer as of the date of reliance on this section:

. . . Is required to file reports, and has filed all periodic reports required during the preceding 12 months (or such shorter time that the issuer was required to file such reports) on Forms 10-K, 10-Q, and 20-F pursuant to section 13 or section 15(d) of the Securities Exchange Act of 1934. . . .

(3) The broker or dealer publishes or distributes research reports on the types of securities in question in the regular course of its business. . . .

(b) *Rule 144A offerings.* If the conditions in paragraph (a) of this section are satisfied, a broker's or dealer's publication or distribution of a research report shall not be considered an offer for sale or an offer to sell a security or general solicitation or general advertising, in connection with an offering relying on Rule 144A.

(c) *Regulation S offerings.* If the conditions in paragraph (a) of this section are satisfied, a broker's or dealer's publication or distribution of a research report shall not:

(1) Constitute directed selling efforts as defined in Rule 902(c) for offerings under Regulation S. . . .

(d) *Definition of research report.* For purposes of this section, *research report* means a written communication, as defined in Rule 405, that includes information, opinions, or recommendations with respect to securities of an issuer or an analysis of a security or an issuer, whether or not it provides information reasonably sufficient upon which to base an investment decision.

Rule 139.   Publications or Distributions of Research Reports by Brokers or Dealers Distributing Securities

(a) *Registered offerings.* Under the conditions of paragraph (a)(1) or (a)(2) of this section, a broker's or dealer's publication or distribution of a research report about an issuer or any of its securities shall be deemed for purposes of sections 2(a)(10) and 5(c) of the Act not to constitute an offer for sale or offer to sell a security that is the subject of an offering pursuant to a registration statement that the issuer proposes to file, or has filed, or that is effective, even if the broker or dealer is participating or will participate in the registered offering of the issuer's securities:

(1) *Issuer-specific research reports.*

(i) The issuer either:

(A)(*1*) At the later of the time of filing its most recent Form S-3 . . . or the time of its most recent amendment to such registration statement for purposes of complying with section 10(a)(3) of the Act or, if no Form S-3 . . . has been filed, at the date of reliance on this section, meets the registrant requirements of such Form S-3 . . . and:

(*i*) At such date, meets the minimum float provisions of General Instruction I.B.1 of such Forms; or

(*ii*) At the date of reliance on this section, is, or if a registration statement has not been filed, will be, offering securities meeting the requirements for the offering of investment grade securities pursuant to General Instruction I.B.2 of Form S-3 . . . ; or

(*iii*) At the date of reliance on this section is a well-known seasoned issuer as defined in Rule 405, other than a majority-owned subsidiary that is a well-known seasoned issuer by virtue of paragraph (1)(ii) of the definition of well-known seasoned issuer in Rule 405; and

(*2*) As of the date of reliance on this section, has filed all periodic reports required during the preceding 12 months on Forms 10-K, 10-Q, and 20-F pursuant to section 13 or section 15(d) of the Securities Exchange Act of 1934; or

(iii) The broker or dealer publishes or distributes research reports in the regular course of its business and such publication or distribution does not represent the initiation of publication of research reports about such issuer or its securities or reinitiation of such publication following discontinuation of publication of such research reports.

(2) *Industry reports.*

(i) The issuer is required to file reports pursuant to section 13 or section 15(d) of the Securities Exchange Act of 1934 or satisfies the conditions in paragraph (a)(1)(i)(B) of this section;

(ii) The condition in paragraph (a)(1)(ii) of this section is satisfied;

(iii) The research report includes similar information with respect to a substantial number of issuers in the issuer's industry or sub-industry, or contains a comprehensive list of securities currently recommended by the broker or dealer; (iv) The analysis regarding the issuer or its securities is given no materially greater space or prominence in the publication than that given to other securities or issuers; and

(v) The broker or dealer publishes or distributes research reports in the regular course of its business and, at the time of the publication or distribution of the research report, is including similar information about the issuer or its securities in similar reports.

(b) *Rule 144A offerings.* If the conditions in paragraph (a)(1) or (a)(2) of this section are satisfied, a broker's or dealer's publication or distribution of a research report shall not be considered an offer for sale or an offer to sell a security or general solicitation or general advertising, in connection with an offering relying on Rule 144A.

(c) *Regulation S offerings.* If the conditions in paragraph (a)(1) or (a)(2) of this section are satisfied, a broker's or dealer's publication or distribution of a research report shall not:

(1) Constitute directed selling efforts as defined in Rule 902(c) for offerings under Regulation S. . . .

(d) *Definition of research report.* For purposes of this section, *research report* means a written communication, as defined in Rule 405, that includes information, opinions, or recommendations with respect to securities of an issuer or an analysis of a security or an issuer, whether or not it provides information reasonably sufficient upon which to base an investment decision.

Rule 144. Persons Deemed Not to Be Engaged in a Distribution and Therefore Not Underwriters

Preliminary Note

Certain basic principles are essential to an understanding of the registration requirements in the Securities Act of 1933 (the Act or the Securities Act) and the purposes underlying Rule 144:

1.   If any person sells a non-exempt security to any other person, the sale must be registered unless an exemption can be found for the transaction.

2. Section 4(1) of the Securities Act provides one such exemption for a transaction "by a person other than an issuer, underwriter, or dealer." Therefore, an understanding of the term "underwriter" is important in determining whether or not the Section 4(1) exemption from registration is available for the sale of the securities.

The term "underwriter" is broadly defined in Section 2(a)(11) of the Securities Act to mean any person who has purchased from an issuer with a view to, or offers or sells for an issuer in connection with, the distribution of any security, or participates, or has a direct or indirect participation in any such undertaking, or participates or has a participation in the direct or indirect underwriting of any such undertaking. The interpretation of this definition traditionally has focused on the words "with a view to" in the phrase "purchased from an issuer with a view to . . . distribution." An investment banking firm which arranges with an issuer for the public sale of its securities is clearly an "underwriter" under that section. However, individual investors who are not professionals in the securities business also may be "underwriters" if they act as links in a chain of transactions through which securities move from an issuer to the public.

Since it is difficult to ascertain the mental state of the purchaser at the time of an acquisition of securities, prior to and since the adoption of Rule 144, subsequent acts and circumstances have been considered to determine whether the purchaser took the securities "with a view to distribution" at the time of the acquisition. Emphasis has been placed on factors such as the length of time the person held the securities and whether there has been an unforeseeable change in circumstances of the holder. Experience has shown, however, that reliance upon such factors alone has led to uncertainty in the application of the registration provisions of the Act.

The Commission adopted Rule 144 to establish specific criteria for determining whether a person is not engaged in a distribution. Rule 144 creates a safe harbor from the Section 2(a)(11) definition of "underwriter." A person satisfying the applicable conditions of the Rule 144 safe harbor is deemed not to be engaged in a distribution of the securities and therefore not an underwriter of the securities for purposes of Section 2(a)(11). Therefore, such a person is deemed not to be an underwriter when determining whether a sale is eligible for the Section 4(1) exemption for "transactions by any person other than an issuer, underwriter, or dealer." If a sale of securities complies with all of the applicable conditions of Rule 144:

1. Any affiliate or other person who sells restricted securities will be deemed not to be engaged in a distribution and therefore not an underwriter for that transaction;

2. Any person who sells restricted or other securities on behalf of an affiliate of the issuer will be deemed not to be engaged in a distribution and therefore not an underwriter for that transaction; and

3. The purchaser in such transaction will receive securities that are not restricted securities.

Rule 144 is not an exclusive safe harbor. A person who does not meet all of the applicable conditions of Rule 144 still may claim any other available exemption under the Act for the sale of the securities. The Rule 144 safe harbor is not available to any person with respect to any transaction or series of transactions that, although in technical compliance with Rule 144, is part of a plan or scheme to evade the registration requirements of the Act.

(a) *Definitions.* The following definitions shall apply for the purposes of this section.

(1) An "*affiliate*" of an issuer is a person that directly, or indirectly through one or more intermediaries, controls, or is controlled by, or is under common control with, such issuer. . . .

(3) The term "*restricted securities*" means:

(i) securities that are acquired directly or indirectly from the issuer, or from an affiliate of the issuer, in a transaction or chain of transactions not involving any public offering;

(ii) securities acquired from the issuer that are subject to the resale limitations of Rule 502(d) under Regulation D . . . ;

(iii) securities acquired in a transaction or chain of transactions meeting the requirements of Rule 144A. . . .

(viii) Securities acquired from the issuer in a transaction subject to an exemption under section 4(5) of the Act.

(4) The term *debt securities* means:

(i) Any security other than an equity security as defined in Rule 405;

(ii) Non-participatory preferred stock, which is defined as non-convertible capital stock, the holders of which are entitled to a preference in payment of dividends and in distribution of assets on liquidation, dissolution, or winding up of the issuer, but are not entitled to participate in residual earnings or assets of the issuer; and

(iii) Asset-backed securities, as defined in Item 1101 of Regulation S–K.

(b) *Conditions to be met.* Subject to paragraph (i) of this section, the following conditions must be met:

(1) *Non-Affiliates.*

(i) If the issuer of the securities is, and has been for a period of at least 90 days immediately before the sale, subject to the reporting requirements of section 13 or 15(d) of the Securities Exchange Act of 1934 (the Exchange Act), any person who is not an affiliate of the issuer at the time of the sale, and has not been an affiliate during the preceding three months, who sells restricted securities of the issuer for his or her own account shall be deemed not to be an underwriter of those securities within the meaning of section 2(a)(11) of the Act if all of the conditions of paragraphs (c)(1) and (d) of this section are met. The requirements of paragraph (c)(1) of this section shall not apply to restricted securities sold for the account of a person who is not an affiliate of the issuer at the time of the sale and has not been an affiliate during the preceding three months, provided a period of one year has elapsed since the later of the date the securities were acquired from the issuer or from an affiliate of the issuer.

(ii) If the issuer of the securities is not, or has not been for a period of at least 90 days immediately before the sale, subject to the reporting requirements of section 13 or 15(d) of the Exchange Act, any person who is not an affiliate of the issuer at the time of the sale, and has not been an affiliate during the preceding three months, who sells restricted securities of the issuer for his or her own account shall be deemed not to be an underwriter of those securities within the meaning of section 2(a)(11) of the Act if the condition of paragraph (d) of this section is met.

(2) *Affiliates or persons selling on behalf of affiliates.* Any affiliate of the issuer, or any person who was an affiliate at any time during the 90 days immediately before the sale, who sells restricted securities, or any person who sells restricted or any other securities for the account of an affiliate of the issuer of such securities, or any person who sells restricted or any other securities for the account of a person who was an affiliate at any time during the 90 days immediately before the sale, shall be deemed not to be an underwriter of those securities within the meaning of section 2(a)(11) of the Act if all of the conditions of this section are met.

(c) *Current public information.* Adequate current public information with respect to the issuer of the securities must be available. Such information will be deemed to be available only if the applicable condition set forth in this paragraph is met:

(1) *Reporting Issuers.* The issuer is, and has been for a period of at least 90 days immediately before the sale, subject to the reporting requirements of section 13 or 15(d) of the Exchange Act and has filed all required reports under section 13 or 15(d) of the Exchange Act, as applicable, during the 12 months preceding such sale (or for such shorter period that the issuer was required to file such reports), other than Form 8-K reports; or

(2) *Non-reporting Issuers.* If the issuer is not subject to the reporting requirements of section 13 or 15(d) of the Exchange Act, there is publicly available the information concerning the issuer specified in paragraphs (a)(5)(i) to (xiv), inclusive, and paragraph (a)(5)(xvi) of Rule 5c2–11 of this chapter, or, if the issuer is an insurance company, the information specified in section 12(g)(2)(G)(i) of the Exchange Act.

(d) *Holding period for restricted securities.* If the securities sold are restricted securities, the following provisions apply:

(1) *General rule.*

(i) If the issuer of the securities is, and has been for a period of at least 90 days immediately before the sale, subject to the reporting requirements of section 13 or 15(d) of the Exchange Act, a minimum of six months must elapse between the later of the date of the acquisition of the securities from the issuer, or from an affiliate of the issuer, and any resale of such securities in reliance on this section for the account of either the acquiror or any subsequent holder of those securities.

(ii) If the issuer of the securities is not, or has not been for a period of at least 90 days immediately before the sale, subject to the reporting requirements of section 13 or 15(d) of the Exchange Act, a minimum of one year must elapse between the later of the date of the acquisition of the securities from the issuer, or from an affiliate of the issuer, and any resale of such securities in reliance on this section for the account of either the acquiror or any subsequent holder of those securities.

(iii) if the acquiror takes the securities by purchase, the holding period shall not begin until the until purchase price or other consideration is paid or given by the person acquiring the securities from the issuer or from an affiliate of the issuer. . . .

(e) *Limitation on amount of securities sold.* Except as hereinafter provided, the amount of securities sold for the account of an affiliate of the issuer in reliance upon this section shall be determined as follows:

(1) If any securities are sold for the account of an affiliate of the issuer, regardless of whether those securities are restricted, the amount of securities sold, together with all sales of securities of the same class sold for the account of such person within the preceding three months, shall not exceed the greatest of:

(i) One percent of the shares or other units of the class outstanding as shown by the most recent report or statement published by the issuer, or

(ii) The average weekly reported volume of trading in such securities on all national securities exchanges and/or reported through the automated quotation system of a registered securities association during the four calendar weeks preceding the filing of notice required by paragraph (h), or if no such notice is required the date of receipt of the order to execute the transaction by the broker or the date of execution of the transaction directly with a market maker, or

(iii) The average weekly volume of trading in such securities reported through the consolidated transaction reporting system contemplated by Rule 11Aa3–1 under the Securities Exchange Act of 1934 . . . during the four-week period specified in paragraph (e)(1)(ii) of this section.

(2) If the securities sold are debt securities, then the amount of debt securities sold for the account of an affiliate of the issuer, regardless of whether those securities are restricted, shall not exceed the greater of the limitation set forth in paragraph (e)(1) of this section or, together with all sales of securities of the same tranche (or class when the securities are non-participatory preferred stock) sold for the account of such person within the preceding three months, ten percent of the principal amount of the tranche (or class when the securities are non-participatory preferred stock) attributable to the securities sold. . . .

(f) *Manner of sale.*

(1) The securities shall be sold in one of the following manners:

(i) *brokers' transactions* within the meaning of section 4(4) of the Act;

(ii) transactions directly with a *market maker*, as that term is defined in section 3(a)(38) of the Exchange Act; or

(iii) *riskless principal transactions* where:

(A) the offsetting trades must be executed at the same price (exclusive of an explicitly disclosed markup or markdown, commission equivalent, or other fee);

(B) the transaction is permitted to be reported as riskless under the rules of a self-regulatory organization; and

(C) the requirements of paragraphs (g)(2)(applicable to any markup or markdown, commission equivalent, or other fee), (g)(3), and (g)(4) of this section are met.

Note to Rule 144(f)(1)i

For purposes of this paragraph, a *riskless principal transaction* means a principal transaction where, after having received from a customer an order to buy, a broker or dealer purchases the security as principal in the market to satisfy the order to buy or, after having received from a customer an order to sell, sells the security as principal to the market to satisfy the order to sell.

(2) The person selling the securities shall not:

(i) Solicit or arrange for the solicitation of orders to buy the securities in anticipation of or in connection with such transaction, or

(ii) Make any payment in connection with the offer or sale of the securities to any person other than the broker or dealer who executes the order to sell the securities.

(3) Paragraph (f) of this section shall not apply to:

(i) Securities sold for the account of the estate of a deceased person or for the account of a beneficiary of such estate provided the estate or estate beneficiary is not an affiliate of the issuer; or

(ii) Debt securities.

(g) *Brokers' transactions.* The term "brokers' transactions" in section 4(4) of the Act shall for the purposes of this rule be deemed to include transactions by a broker in which such broker:

(1) Does no more than execute the order or orders to sell the securities as agent for the person for whose account the securities are sold;

(2) Receives no more than the usual and customary broker's commission;

(3) Neither solicits nor arranges for the solicitation of customers' orders to buy the securities in anticipation of or in connection with the transaction; *provided*, that the foregoing shall not preclude:

(i) inquiries by the broker of other brokers or dealers who have indicated an interest in the securities within the preceding 60 days;

(ii) inquiries by the broker of his customers who have indicated an unsolicited bona fide interest in the securities within the preceding 10 business days;

(iii) the publication by the broker of bid and ask quotations for the security in an inter-dealer quotation system provided that such quotations are incident to the maintenance of a bona fide inter-dealer market for the security for the broker's own account and that the broker has published bona fide bid and ask quotations for the security in an inter-dealer quotation system on each of at least twelve days within the preceding thirty calendar days with no more than four business days in succession without such two-way quotations; or

(iv) the publication by the broker of bid and ask quotations for the security in an alternative trading system . . . provided that the broker has published bona fide bid and ask quotations for the security in the alternative trading system on each of the last twelve business days. . . .

(h) *Notice of proposed sale.*

(1) If the amount of securities to be sold in reliance upon this rule during any period of three months exceeds 5,000 shares or other units or has an aggregate sale price in excess of $50,000, three copies of a notice on Form 144 shall be filed with the Commission. If such securities are admitted to trading on any national securities exchange, one copy of such notice also shall be transmitted to the principal exchange on which such securities are admitted.

(2) The Form 144 shall be signed by the person for whose account the securities are to be sold and shall be transmitted for filing concurrently with either the placing with a broker of an order to execute a sale of securities in reliance upon this rule or the execution directly with a market maker of such a sale. Neither the filing of such notice nor the failure of the Commission to comment on such notice shall be deemed to preclude the Commission from taking any action that it deems necessary or appropriate with respect to the sale of the securities referred to in such notice. The person filing the notice required by this paragraph shall have a bona fide intention to sell the securities referred to in the notice within a reasonable time after the filing of such notice.

(i) *Unavailability to securities of issuers with no or nominal operations and no or nominal non-cash assets.* . . .

Rule 144A.   Private Resales of Securities to Institutions

Preliminary Notes

1.   This section relates solely to the application of Section 5 of the Act and not to antifraud or other provisions of the federal securities laws.

2.   Attempted compliance with this section does not act as an exclusive election; any seller hereunder may also claim the availability of any other applicable exemption from the registration requirements of the Act.

3.   In view of the objective of this section and the policies underlying the Act, this section is not available with respect to any transaction or series of transactions that, although in technical compliance with this section, is part of a plan or scheme to evade the registration provisions of the Act. In such cases, registration under the Act is required.

4.   Nothing in this section obviates the need for any issuer or any other person to comply with the securities registration or broker-dealer registration requirements of the Securities Exchange Act of 1934 (the "Exchange Act"), whenever such requirements are applicable.

5.   Nothing in this section obviates the need for any person to comply with any applicable state law relating to the offer or sale of securities.

6.   Securities acquired in a transaction made pursuant to the provisions of this section are deemed to be "restricted securities" within the meaning of Rule 144(a)(3).

7.   The fact that purchasers of securities from the issuer thereof may purchase such securities with a view to reselling such securities pursuant to this section will not affect the availability to such issuer of an exemption under Section 4(a)(2) of the Act, or Regulation D under the Act, from the registration requirements of the Act.

(a) *Definitions*

(1) For purposes of this section, "qualified institutional buyer" shall mean:

(i) Any of the following entities, acting for its own account or the accounts of other qualified institutional buyers, that in the aggregate owns and invests on a discretionary basis at least $100 million in securities of issuers that are not affiliated with the entity:

(A) Any *insurance company* as defined in Section 2(a)(13) of the Act;

    NOTE: A purchase by an insurance company for one or more of its separate accounts, as defined by section 2(a)(37) of the Investment Company Act of 1940 (the "Investment Company Act"), which are neither registered under section 8 of the Investment Company Act nor required to be so registered, shall be deemed to be a purchase for the account of such insurance company.

(B) Any *investment company* registered under the Investment Company Act or any *business development company* as defined in Section 2(a)(48) of that Act;

(C) Any *Small Business Investment Company* licensed by the U.S. Small Business Administration under Section 301(c) or (d) of the Small Business Investment Act of 1958;

(D) Any *plan* established and maintained by a state, its political subdivisions, or any agency or instrumentality of a state or its political subdivisions, for the benefit of its employees;

(E) Any *employee benefit plan* within the meaning of Title I of the Employee Retirement Income Security Act of 1974;

(F) Any *trust fund* whose trustee is a bank or trust company and whose participants are exclusively plans of the types identified in paragraph (a)(1)(i)(D) or (E) of this section, except trust funds that include as participants individual retirement accounts or H.R. 10 plans.

(G) Any *business development company* as defined in Section 202(a)(22) of the Investment Advisers Act of 1940;

(H) Any *organization described in Section 501(c)(3)* of the Internal Revenue Code, corporation (other than a bank as defined in Section 3(a)(2) of the Act or a savings and loan association or other institution referenced in Section 3(a)(5)(A) of the Act or a foreign bank or savings and loan association or equivalent institution), partnership, or Massachusetts or similar business trust; and

(I) Any *investment adviser* registered under the Investment Advisers Act.

(ii) Any *dealer* registered pursuant to Section 15 of the Exchange Act, acting for its own account or the accounts of other qualified institutional buyers, that in the aggregate owns and invests on a discretionary basis at least $10 million of securities of issuers that are not affiliated with the dealer, *provided that* securities constituting the whole or a part of an unsold allotment to or subscription by a dealer as a participant in a public offering shall not be deemed to be owned by such dealer;

(iii) Any *dealer* registered pursuant to Section 15 of the Exchange Act acting in a riskless principal transaction on behalf of a qualified institutional buyer . . . ;

(iv) Any investment company registered under the Investment Company Act, acting for its own account or for the accounts of other qualified institutional buyers, that is part of a *family of investment companies* which own in the aggregate at least $100 million in securities of issuers, other than issuers that are affiliated with the investment company or are part of such family of investment companies. "Family of investment companies" means any two or more investment companies registered under the Investment Company Act, except for a unit investment trust whose assets consist solely of shares of one or more registered investment companies, that have the same investment adviser (or, in the case of unit investment trusts, the same depositor) . . . ;

(v) Any entity, all of the equity owners of which are qualified institutional buyers, acting for its own account or the accounts of other qualified institutional buyers; and

(vi) Any *bank* as defined in Section 3(a)(2) of the Act, any *savings and loan association* or other institution as referenced in Section 3(a)(5)(A) of the Act, *or any foreign bank or savings and loan association or equivalent institution,* acting for its own account or the accounts of other qualified institutional buyers, that in the aggregate owns and invests on a discretionary basis at least $100 million in securities of issuers that are not affiliated with it and that has an audited net worth of at least $25 million as demonstrated in its latest annual financial statements, as of a date not more than 16 months preceding the date of sale . . . in the case of a U.S. bank or savings and loan association, and not more than 18 months preceding such date of sale for a foreign bank or savings and loan association or equivalent institution.

(2) In determining the aggregate amount of securities owned and invested on a discretionary basis by an entity, the following instruments and interests shall be excluded: bank deposit notes and certificates of deposit; loan participations; repurchase agreements; securities owned but subject to a repurchase agreement; and currency, interest rate and commodity swaps.

(3) The aggregate value of securities owned and invested on a discretionary basis by an entity shall be the cost of such securities, except where the entity reports its securities holdings in its financial statements on the basis of their market value, and no current information with respect to the cost of those securities has been published. In the latter event, the securities may be valued at market for purposes of this section. . . .

(5) For purposes of this section, "riskless principal transaction" means a transaction in which a dealer buys a security from any person and makes a simultaneous offsetting sale of such security to a qualified institutional buyer, including another dealer acting as riskless principal for a qualified institutional buyer. . . .

(b) *Sales by Persons Other Than Issuers or Dealers.* Any person, other than the issuer or a dealer, who offers or sells securities in compliance with the conditions set forth in paragraph (d) of this section shall be deemed not to be engaged in a distribution of such securities and therefore not to be an underwriter of such securities within the meaning of Sections 2(a)(11) and 4(a)(1) of the Act.

(c) *Sales by Dealers.* Any dealer who offers or sells securities in compliance with the conditions set forth in paragraph (d) of this section shall be deemed not to be a participant in a distribution of such securities within the meaning of Section 4(a)(3)(C) of the Act and not to be an underwriter of such securities within the meaning of Section 2(a)(11) of the Act, and such securities shall be deemed not to have been offered to the public within the meaning of Section 4(a)(3)(A) of the Act.

(d) *Conditions to Be Met.* To qualify for exemption under this section, an offer or sale must meet the following conditions:

(1) The securities are sold only to a qualified institutional buyer or to a purchaser that the seller and any person acting on behalf of the seller reasonably believe is a qualified institutional buyer. . . . ;

(2) The seller and any person acting on its behalf takes reasonable steps to ensure that the purchaser is aware that the seller may rely on the exemption from the provisions of Section 5 of the Act provided by this section;

(3) The securities offered or sold:

(i) Were not, when issued, of the same class as securities listed on a national securities exchange registered under Section 6 of the Exchange Act or quoted in a U.S. automated inter-dealer quotation system . . . ; and

(ii) Are not securities of an open-end investment company, unit investment trust or face-amount certificate company that is or is required to be registered under Section 8 of the Investment Company Act; and

(4)(i) In the case of securities of an issuer that is neither subject to Section 13 or 15(d) of the Exchange Act, nor exempt from reporting pursuant to Rule 12g3–2(b) under the Exchange Act, nor a foreign government as defined in Rule 405 eligible to register securities under Schedule B of the Act, the holder and a prospective purchaser designated by the holder have the right to obtain from the issuer, upon request of the holder, and the prospective purchaser has received from the issuer, the seller, or a person acting on either of their behalf, at or prior to the time of sale, upon such prospective purchaser's request to the holder or the issuer, the following information (which shall be reasonably current in relation to the date of resale under this section): a very brief statement of the nature of the business of the issuer and the products and services it offers; and the issuer's most recent balance sheet and profit and loss and retained earnings statements, and similar financial statements for such part of the two preceding fiscal years as the issuer has been in operation (the financial statements should be audited to the extent reasonably available).

(ii) The requirement that the information be "reasonably current" will be presumed to be satisfied if:

(A) the balance sheet is as of a date less than 16 months before the date of resale, the statements of profit and loss and retained earnings are for the 12 months preceding the date of such balance sheet, and if such balance sheet is not as of a date less than 6 months before the date of resale, it shall be accompanied by additional statements of profit and loss and retained earnings for the period from the date of such balance sheet to a date less than 6 months before the date of resale; and

(B) the statement of the nature of the issuer's business and its products and services offered is as of a date within 12 months prior to the date of resale; or

(C) with regard to foreign private issuers, the required information meets the timing requirements of the issuer's home country or principal trading markets.

(e) Offers and sales of securities pursuant to this section shall be deemed not to affect the availability of any exemption or safe harbor relating to any previous or subsequent offer or sale of such securities by the issuer or any prior or subsequent holder thereof.

Rule 145. Reclassification of Securities, Mergers, Consolidations and Acquisitions of Assets

Preliminary Note

Rule 145 . . . is designed to make available the protection provided by registration under the Securities Act of 1933, as amended (Act), to persons who are offered securities in a business combination of the type described in paragraphs (a)(1), (2) and (3) of the rule. The thrust of the rule is that an "offer," "offer to sell," "offer for sale," or "sale" occurs when there is submitted to security holders a plan or agreement pursuant to which such holders are required to elect, on the basis of what is in substance a new investment decision, whether to accept a new or different security in exchange for their existing security. Rule 145 embodies the Commission's determination that such transactions are subject to the registration requirements of the Act. . . .

Transactions for which statutory exemptions under the Act, including those contained in sections 3(a)(9), (10), (11) and 4(a)(2), are otherwise available are not affected by Rule 145. . . .

(a) *Transactions within this section.* An "offer," "offer to sell," "offer for sale," or "sale" shall be deemed to be involved, within the meaning of section 2(3) of the Act, so far as the security holders of a corporation or other person are concerned where, pursuant to statutory provisions of the jurisdiction under which such corporation or other person is organized, or pursuant to provisions contained in its certificate of incorporation or similar controlling instruments, or otherwise, there is submitted for the vote or consent of such security holders a plan or agreement for:

(1) *Reclassifications.* A reclassification of securities of such corporation or other person, other than a stock split, reverse stock split, or change in par value, which involves the substitution of a security for another security;

(2) *Mergers of Consolidations.* A statutory merger or consolidation or similar plan or acquisition in which securities of such corporation or other person held by such security holders will become or be exchanged for securities of any person, unless the sole purpose of the transaction is to change an issuer's domicile solely within the United States; or

(3) *Transfers of assets.* A transfer of assets of such corporation or other person, to another person in consideration of the issuance of securities of such other person or any of its affiliates, if:

(i) Such plan or agreement provides for dissolution of the corporation or other person whose security holders are voting or consenting; or

(ii) Such plan or agreement provides for a pro rata or similar distribution of such securities to the security holders voting or consenting; or

(iii) The board of directors or similar representatives of such corporation or other person, adopts resolutions relative to paragraph (a)(3)(i) or (ii) of this section within 1 year after the taking of such vote or consent; or

(iv) The transfer of assets is a part of a preexisting plan for distribution of such securities, notwithstanding paragraph (a)(3)(i), (ii), or (iii) of this section.

(b) *Communications before a Registration Statement is filed.* Communications made in connection with or relating to a transaction described in paragraph (a) of this section that will be registered under the Act may be made under Rule 135, 165 or 166.

(c) *Persons and parties deemed to be underwriters.* For purposes of this section, if any party to a transaction specified in paragraph (a) of this section is a shell company, other than a business combination related shell company, as those terms are defined in Rule 405, any party to that transaction, other than the issuer, or any person who is an affiliate of such party at the time such transaction is submitted for vote or consent, who publicly offers or sells securities of the issuer acquired in connection with any such transaction, shall be deemed to be engaged in a distribution and therefore to be an underwriter thereof within the meaning of Section 2(a)(11) of the Act.

(d) *Resale provisions for persons and parties deemed underwriters.* Notwithstanding the provisions of paragraph (c), a person or party specified in that paragraph shall not be deemed to be engaged in a distribution and therefore not to be an underwriter of securities acquired in a transaction specified in paragraph (a) that was registered under the Act if:

(1) The issuer has met the requirements applicable to an issuer of securities in paragraph (i)(2) of Rule 144; and

(2) One of the following three conditions is met:

(i) Such securities are sold by such person or party in accordance with the provisions of paragraphs (c), (e), (f), and (g) of Rule 144 and at least 90 days have elapsed since the date the securities were acquired from the issuer in such transaction; or

(ii) Such person or party is not, and has not been for at least three months, an affiliate of the issuer, and at least six months, as determined in accordance with paragraph (d) of Rule 144, have elapsed since the date the securities were acquired from the issuer in such transaction, and the issuer meets the requirements of paragraph (c) of Rule 144; or

(iii) Such person or party is not, and has not been for at least three months, an affiliate of the issuer, and at least one year, as determined in accordance with paragraph (d) of Rule 144, has elapsed since the date the securities were acquired from the issuer in such transaction.

Note to Rule 145(c) and (d)

Paragraph (d) is not available with respect to any transaction or series of transactions that, although in technical compliance with the rule, is part of a plan or scheme to evade the registration requirements of the Act.

(e) *Definitions.*

(1) The term *affiliate* as used in paragraphs (c) and (d) of this section shall have the same meaning as the definition of that term in Rule 144.

(2) The term *party* as used in paragraphs (c) and (d) of this section shall mean the corporations, business entities, or other persons, other than the issuer, whose assets or capital structure are affected by the transactions specified in paragraph (a) of this section.

(3) The term *person* as used in paragraphs (c) and (d) of this section, when used in reference to a person for whose account securities are to be sold, shall have the same meaning as the definition of that term in paragraph (a)(2) of Rule 144.

Rule 146. Rules under Section 18 of the Act . . .

(b) Covered Securities for Purposes of Section 18.

(1) For the purposes of Section 18(b) of the Act, the Commission finds that the following national securities exchanges, or segments or tiers thereof, have listing standards that are substantially similar to those of the New York Stock Exchange ("NYSE"), the American Stock Exchange ("Amex"), or the National Market System of the Nasdaq Stock Market ("Nasdaq/NGM"), and that securities listed, or authorized for listing, on such exchanges shall be deemed covered securities:

(i) Tier I of the NYSE Arca, Inc.;

(ii) Tier I of the Philadelphia Stock Exchange, Inc.;

(iii) The Chicago Board Options Exchange, Incorporated;

(iv) Options listed on the International Securities Exchange, LLC and

(v) The Nasdaq Capital Market.

(2) The designation of securities in paragraphs (b)(1)(i) through (v) of this section as covered securities is conditioned on such exchanges' listing standards (or segments or tiers thereof) continuing to be substantially similar to those of the NYSE, Amex, or Nasdaq/NGM.

§ 230.147. Intrastate Offers and Sales

(a) This section shall not raise any presumption that the exemption provided by section 3(a)(11) of the Act (15 U.S.C. 77c(a)(11)) is not available for transactions by an issuer which do not satisfy all of the provisions of this section.

(b) Manner of offers and sales. An issuer, or any person acting on behalf of the issuer, shall be deemed to conduct an offering in compliance with section 3(a)(11) of the Act (15 U.S.C. 77c(a)(11)), where offers and sales are made only to persons resident within the same state or territory in which the issuer is resident and doing business, within the meaning of section 3(a)(11) of the Act, so long as the issuer complies with the provisions of paragraphs (c), (d), and (f) through (h) of this section.

(c) Nature of the issuer. The issuer of the securities shall at the time of any offers and sales be a person resident and doing business within the state or territory in which all of the offers and sales are made.

(1) The issuer shall be deemed to be a resident of the state or territory in which:

(i) It is incorporated or organized, and it has its principal place of business, if a corporation, limited partnership, trust or other form of business organization that is organized under state or territorial law. The issuer shall be deemed to have its principal place of business in a state or territory in which the officers, partners or managers of the issuer primarily direct, control and coordinate the activities of the issuer;

(ii) It has its principal place of business, as defined in paragraph (c)(1)(i) of this section, if a general partnership or other form of business organization that is not organized under any state or territorial law;

(iii) Such person's principal residence is located, if an individual.

Instruction to paragraph (c)(1): An issuer that has previously conducted an intrastate offering pursuant to this section (§ 230.147) or Rule 147A (§ 230.147A) may not conduct another intrastate offering pursuant to this section (§ 230.147) in a different state or territory, until the expiration of the time period specified in paragraph (e) of this section (§ 230.147(e)) or paragraph (e) of Rule 147A (§ 230.147A(e)), calculated on the basis of the date of the last sale in such offering.

(2) The issuer shall be deemed to be doing business within a state or territory if the issuer satisfies at least one of the following requirements:

(i) The issuer derived at least 80% of its consolidated gross revenues from the operation of a business or of real property located in or from the rendering of services within such state or territory;

Instruction to paragraph (c)(2)(i): Revenues must be calculated based on the issuer's most recent fiscal year, if the first offer of securities pursuant to this section is made during the first six months of the issuer's current fiscal year, and based on the first six months of the issuer's current fiscal year or during the twelve-month fiscal period ending with such six-month period, if the first offer of securities pursuant to this section is made during the last six months of the issuer's current fiscal year.

(ii) The issuer had at the end of its most recent semi-annual fiscal period prior to an initial offer of securities in any offering or subsequent offering pursuant to this section, at least 80% of its assets and those of its subsidiaries on a consolidated basis located within such state or territory;

(iii) The issuer intends to use and uses at least 80% of the net proceeds to the issuer from sales made pursuant to this section (§ 230.147) in connection with the operation of a business or of real property, the purchase of real property located in, or the rendering of services within such state or territory; or

(iv) A majority of the issuer's employees are based in such state or territory.

(d) Residence of offerees and purchasers. Offers and sales of securities pursuant to this section (§ 230.147) shall be made only to residents of the state or territory in which the issuer is resident, as determined pursuant to paragraph (c) of this section, or who the issuer reasonably believes, at the time of the offer and sale, are residents of the state or territory in which the issuer is resident. For purposes of determining the residence of offerees and purchasers:

(1) A corporation, partnership, limited liability company, trust or other form of business organization shall be deemed to be a resident of a state or territory if, at the time of the offer and sale to it, it has its principal place of business, as defined in paragraph (c)(1)(i) of this section, within such state or territory.

Instruction to paragraph (d)(1): A trust that is not deemed by the law of the state or territory of its creation to be a separate legal entity is deemed to be a resident of each state or territory in which its trustee is, or trustees are, resident.

(2) Individuals shall be deemed to be residents of a state or territory if such individuals have, at the time of the offer and sale to them, their principal residence in the state or territory.

(3) A corporation, partnership, trust or other form of business organization, which is organized for the specific purpose of acquiring securities offered pursuant to this section (§ 230.147), shall not be a resident of a state or territory unless all of the beneficial owners of such organization are residents of such state or territory.

Instruction to paragraph (d): Obtaining a written representation from purchasers of in-state residency status will not, without more, be sufficient to establish a reasonable belief that such purchasers are in-state residents.

(e) Limitation on resales. For a period of six months from the date of the sale by the issuer of a security pursuant to this section (§ 230.147), any resale of such security shall be made only to persons resident within the state or territory in which the issuer was resident, as determined pursuant to paragraph (c) of this section, at the time of the sale of the security by the issuer.

Instruction to paragraph (e): In the case of convertible securities, resales of either the convertible security, or if it is converted, the underlying security, could be made during the period described in paragraph (e) only to persons resident within such state or territory. For purposes of this paragraph (e), a conversion in reliance on section 3(a)(9) of the Act (15 U.S.C. 77c(a)(9)) does not begin a new period.

(f) Precautions against interstate sales. (1) The issuer shall, in connection with any securities sold by it pursuant to this section:

(i) Place a prominent legend on the certificate or other document evidencing the security stating that: "Offers and sales of these securities were made under an exemption from registration and have not been registered under the Securities Act of 1933. For a period of six months from the date of the sale by the issuer of these securities, any resale of these securities (or the underlying securities in the case of convertible securities) shall be made only to persons resident within the state or territory of [identify the name of the state or territory in which the issuer was resident at the time of the sale of the securities by the issuer].";

(ii) Issue stop transfer instructions to the issuer's transfer agent, if any, with respect to the securities, or, if the issuer transfers its own securities, make a notation in the appropriate records of the issuer; and

(iii) Obtain a written representation from each purchaser as to his or her residence.

(2) The issuer shall, in connection with the issuance of new certificates for any of the securities that are sold pursuant to this section (§ 230.147) that are presented for transfer during the time period specified in paragraph (e), take the steps required by paragraphs (f)(1)(i) and (ii) of this section.

(3) The issuer shall, at the time of any offer or sale by it of a security pursuant to this section (§ 230.147), prominently disclose to each offeree in the manner in which any such offer is communicated and to each purchaser of such security in writing a reasonable period of time before the date of sale, the following: "Sales will be made only to residents of [identify the name of the state or territory in which the issuer was resident at the time of the sale of the securities by the issuer]. Offers and sales of these securities are made under an exemption from registration and have not been registered under the Securities Act of 1933. For a period of six months from the date of the sale by the issuer of the securities, any resale of the securities (or the underlying securities in the case of convertible securities) shall be made only to persons resident within the state or territory of [identify the name of the state or territory in which the issuer was resident at the time of the sale of the securities by the issuer]."

(g) Integration with other offerings. Offers or sales made in reliance on this section will not be integrated with:

(1) Offers or sales of securities made prior to the commencement of offers and sales of securities pursuant to this section (§ 230.147); or

(2) Offers or sales made after completion of offers and sales of securities pursuant to this section (§ 230.147) that are:

(i) Registered under the Act, except as provided in paragraph (h) of this section (§ 230.147);

(ii) Exempt from registration under Regulation A (§§ 230.251 through 230.263);

(iii) Exempt from registration under Rule 701 (§ 230.701);

(iv) Made pursuant to an employee benefit plan;

(v) Exempt from registration under Regulation S (§§ 230.901 through 230.905);

(vi) Exempt from registration under section 4(a)(6) of the Act (15 U.S.C. 77d(a)(6)); or

(vii) Made more than six months after the completion of an offering conducted pursuant to this section (§ 230.147).

Instruction to paragraph (g): If none of the safe harbors applies, whether subsequent offers and sales of securities will be integrated with any securities offered or sold pursuant to this section (§ 230.147) will depend on the particular facts and circumstances.

(h) Offerings limited to qualified institutional buyers and institutional accredited investors. Where an issuer decides to register an offering under the Act after making offers in reliance on this section (§ 230.147) limited only to qualified institutional buyers and institutional accredited investors referenced in section 5(d) of the Act, such offers will not be subject to integration with any subsequent registered offering. If the issuer makes offers in reliance on this section (§ 230.147) to persons other than qualified institutional buyers and institutional accredited investors referenced in section 5(d) of the Act, such offers will not be subject to integration if the issuer (and any underwriter, broker, dealer, or agent used by the issuer in connection with the proposed offering) waits at least 30 calendar days between the last such offer made in reliance on this section (§ 230.147) and the filing of the registration statement with the Commission.

§ 230.147A. Intrastate Sales Exemption

(a) Scope of the exemption. Offers and sales by or on behalf of an issuer of its securities made in accordance with this section (§ 230.147A) are exempt from section 5 of the Act (15 U.S.C. 77e). This exemption is not available to an issuer that is an investment company registered or required to be registered under the Investment Company Act of 1940 (15 U.S.C. 80a–1 et seq.).

(b) Manner of offers and sales. An issuer, or any person acting on behalf of the issuer, may rely on this exemption to make offers and sales using any form of general solicitation and general advertising, so long as the issuer complies with the provisions of paragraphs (c), (d), and (f) through (h) of this section.

(c) Nature of the issuer. The issuer of the securities shall at the time of any offers and sales be a person resident and doing business within the state or territory in which all of the sales are made.

(1) The issuer shall be deemed to be a resident of the state or territory in which it has its principal place of business. The issuer shall be deemed to have its principal place of business in a state or territory in which the officers, partners or managers of the issuer primarily direct, control and coordinate the activities of the issuer.

(2) The issuer shall be deemed to be doing business within a state or territory if the issuer satisfies at least one of the following requirements:

(i) The issuer derived at least 80% of its consolidated gross revenues from the operation of a business or of real property located in or from the rendering of services within such state or territory;

Instruction to paragraph (c)(2)(i): Revenues must be calculated based on the issuer's most recent fiscal year, if the first offer of securities pursuant to this section is made during the first six months of the issuer's current fiscal year, and based on the first six months of the issuer's current fiscal year or during the twelve-month fiscal period ending with such six-month period, if the first offer of securities pursuant to this section is made during the last six months of the issuer's current fiscal year.

(ii) The issuer had at the end of its most recent semi-annual fiscal period prior to an initial offer of securities in any offering or subsequent offering pursuant to this section, at least 80% of its assets and those of its subsidiaries on a consolidated basis located within such state or territory;

(iii) The issuer intends to use and uses at least 80% of the net proceeds to the issuer from sales made pursuant to this section (§ 230.147A) in connection with the operation of a business or of real property, the purchase of real property located in, or the rendering of services within such state or territory; or

(iv) A majority of the issuer's employees are based in such state or territory.

Instruction to paragraph (c): An issuer that has previously conducted an intrastate offering pursuant to this section (§ 230.147A) or Rule 147 (§ 230.147) may not conduct another intrastate offering pursuant to this section (§ 230.147A) in a different state or territory, until the expiration of the time period specified in paragraph (e) of this section (§ 230.147A(e)) or paragraph (e) of Rule 147 (§ 230.147(e)), calculated on the basis of the date of the last sale in such offering.

(d) Residence of purchasers. Sales of securities pursuant to this section (§ 230.147A) shall be made only to residents of the state or territory in which the issuer is resident, as determined pursuant to paragraph (c) of this section, or who the issuer reasonably believes, at the time of sale, are residents of the state or territory in which the issuer is resident. For purposes of determining the residence of purchasers:

(1) A corporation, partnership, limited liability company, trust or other form of business organization shall be deemed to be a resident of a state or territory if, at the time of sale to it, it has its principal place of business, as defined in paragraph (c)(1) of this section, within such state or territory.

Instruction to paragraph (d)(1): A trust that is not deemed by the law of the state or territory of its creation to be a separate legal entity is deemed to be a resident of each state or territory in which its trustee is, or trustees are, resident.

(2) Individuals shall be deemed to be residents of a state or territory if such individuals have, at the time of sale to them, their principal residence in the state or territory.

(3) A corporation, partnership, trust or other form of business organization, which is organized for the specific purpose of acquiring securities offered pursuant to this section (§ 230.147A), shall not be a resident of a state or territory unless all of the beneficial owners of such organization are residents of such state or territory.

Instruction to paragraph (d): Obtaining a written representation from purchasers of in-state residency status will not, without more, be sufficient to establish a reasonable belief that such purchasers are in-state residents.

(e) Limitation on resales. For a period of six months from the date of the sale by the issuer of a security pursuant to this section (§ 230.147A), any resale of such security shall be made only to persons resident within the state or territory in which the issuer was resident, as determined pursuant to paragraph (c) of this section, at the time of the sale of the security by the issuer.

Instruction to paragraph (e): In the case of convertible securities, resales of either the convertible security, or if it is converted, the underlying security, could be made during the period described in paragraph (e) only to persons resident within such state or territory. For purposes of this paragraph (e), a conversion in reliance on section 3(a)(9) of the Act (15 U.S.C. 77c(a)(9)) does not begin a new period.

(f) Precautions against interstate sales. (1) The issuer shall, in connection with any securities sold by it pursuant to this section:

(i) Place a prominent legend on the certificate or other document evidencing the security stating that: "Offers and sales of these securities were made under an exemption from registration and have not been registered under the Securities Act of 1933. For a period of six months from the date of the sale by the issuer of these securities, any resale of these securities (or the underlying securities in the case of convertible securities) shall be made only to persons resident within the state or territory of [identify the name of the state or territory in which the issuer was resident at the time of the sale of the securities by the issuer].";

(ii) Issue stop transfer instructions to the issuer's transfer agent, if any, with respect to the securities, or, if the issuer transfers its own securities, make a notation in the appropriate records of the issuer; and

(iii) Obtain a written representation from each purchaser as to his or her residence.

(2) The issuer shall, in connection with the issuance of new certificates for any of the securities that are sold pursuant to this section (§ 230.147A) that are presented for transfer during the time period specified in paragraph (e), take the steps required by paragraphs (f)(1)(i) and (ii) of this section.

(3) The issuer shall, at the time of any offer or sale by it of a security pursuant to this section (§ 230.147A), prominently disclose to each offeree in the manner in which any such offer is communicated and to each purchaser of such security in writing a reasonable period of time before the date of sale, the following: "Sales will be made only to residents of the state or territory of [identify the name of the state or territory in which the issuer was resident at the time of the sale of the securities by the issuer]. Offers and sales of these securities are made under an exemption from registration and have not been registered under the Securities Act of 1933. For a period of six months from the date of the sale by the issuer of the securities, any resale of the securities (or the underlying securities in the case of convertible securities) shall be made only to persons resident within the state or territory of [identify the name of the state or territory in which the issuer was resident at the time of the sale of the securities by the issuer]."

(g) *Integration with other offerings.* Offers or sales made in reliance on this section will not be integrated with:

(1) Offers or sales of securities made prior to the commencement of offers and sales of securities pursuant to this section (§ 230.147A); or

(2) Offers or sales of securities made after completion of offers and sales of securities pursuant to this section (§ 230.147A) that are:

(i) Registered under the Act, except as provided in paragraph (h) of this section (§ 230.147A);

(ii) Exempt from registration under Regulation A (§§ 230.251 through 230.263);

(iii) Exempt from registration under Rule 701 (§ 230.701);

(iv) Made pursuant to an employee benefit plan;

(v) Exempt from registration under Regulation S (§§ 230.901 through 230.905);

(vi) Exempt from registration under section 4(a)(6) of the Act (15 U.S.C. 77d(a)(6)); or

(vii) Made more than six months after the completion of an offering conducted pursuant to this section (§ 230.147A).

Instruction to paragraph (g): If none of the safe harbors applies, whether subsequent offers and sales of securities will be integrated with any securities offered or sold pursuant to this section (§ 230.147A) will depend on the particular facts and circumstances.

(h) *Offerings limited to qualified institutional buyers and institutional accredited investors.* Where an issuer decides to register an offering under the Act after making offers in reliance on this section (§ 230.147A) limited only to qualified institutional buyers and institutional accredited investors referenced in section 5(d) of the Act, such offers will not be subject to integration with any subsequent registered offering. If the issuer makes offers in reliance on this section (§ 230.147A) to persons other than qualified institutional buyers and institutional accredited investors referenced in section 5(d) of the Act, such offers will not be subject to integration if the issuer (and any underwriter, broker, dealer, or agent used by the issuer in connection with the proposed offering) waits at least 30 calendar days between the last such offer made in reliance on this section (§ 230.147A) and the filing of the registration statement with the Commission.

Rule 153.   Definition of "Preceded by a Prospectus" as Used in Section 5(b)(2) of the Act, in Relation to Certain Transactions

(a) *Definition of preceded by a prospectus.* The term preceded by a prospectus as used in section 5(b)(2) of the Act, regarding any requirement of a broker or dealer to deliver a prospectus to a broker or dealer as a result of a transaction effected between such parties on or through a national securities exchange or facility thereof, trading facility of a national securities association, or an alternative trading system, shall mean the satisfaction of the conditions in paragraph (b) of this section.

(b) *Conditions.* Any requirement of a broker or dealer to deliver a prospectus for transactions covered by paragraph (a) of this section will be satisfied if:

(1) Securities of the same class as the securities that are the subject of the transaction are trading on that national securities exchange or facility thereof, trading facility of a national securities association, or alternative trading system;

(2) The registration statement relating to the offering is effective and is not the subject of any pending proceeding or examination under section 8(d) or 8(e) of the Act;

(3) Neither the issuer, nor any underwriter or participating dealer is the subject of a pending proceeding under section 8A of the Act in connection with the offering; and

(4) The issuer has filed or will file with the Commission a prospectus that satisfies the requirements of section 10(a) of the Act.

(c) *Definitions.*

(1) The term *national securities exchange,* as used in this section, shall mean a securities exchange registered as a national securities exchange under section 6 of the Securities Exchange Act of 1934.

(2) The term *trading facility*, as used in this section, shall mean a trading facility sponsored and governed by the rules of a registered securities association or a national securities exchange.

(3) The term *alternative trading system*, as used in this section, shall mean an alternative trading system as defined in Rule 300(a) of Regulation ATS under the Securities Exchange Act of 1934 registered with the Commission pursuant to Rule 301 of Regulation ATS under the Securities Exchange Act of 1934.

Rule 155.   Integration of Abandoned Offerings

Compliance with paragraph (b) or (c) of this section provides a non-exclusive safe harbor from integration of private and registered offerings. Because of the objectives of Rule 155 and the policies underlying the Act, Rule 155 is not available to any issuer for any transaction or series of transactions that, although in technical compliance with the rule, is part of a plan or scheme to evade the registration requirements of the Act.

(a) *Definition of terms.* For the purposes of this section only, a private offering means an unregistered offering of securities that is exempt from registration under Section 4(a)(2) or 4(5) of the Act or Rule 506 of Regulation D.

(b) *Abandoned private offering followed by a registered offering.* A private offering of securities will not be considered part of an offering for which the issuer later files a registration statement if:

(1) No securities were sold in the private offering;

(2) The issuer and any person(s) acting on its behalf terminate all offering activity in the private offering before the issuer files the registration statement;

(3) The Section 10(a) final prospectus and any Section 10 preliminary prospectus used in the registered offering disclose information about the abandoned private offering, including:

(i) The size and nature of the private offering;

(ii) The date on which the issuer abandoned the private offering;

(iii) That any offers to buy or indications of interest given in the private offering were rejected or otherwise not accepted; and

(iv) That the prospectus delivered in the registered offering supersedes any offering materials used in the private offering; and

(4) The issuer does not file the registration statement until at least 30 calendar days after termination of all offering activity in the private offering, unless the issuer and any person acting on its behalf offered securities in the private offering only to persons who were (or who the issuer reasonably believes were):

(i) Accredited investors (as that term is defined in Rule 501(a)); or

(ii) Persons who satisfy the knowledge and experience standard of Rule 506(b)(2)(ii).

(c) *Abandoned registered offering followed by a private offering.* An offering for which the issuer filed a registration statement will not be considered part of a later commenced private offering if:

(1) No securities were sold in the registered offering;

(2) The issuer withdraws the registration statement under Rule 477;

(3) Neither the issuer nor any person acting on the issuer's behalf commences the private offering earlier than 30 calendar days after the effective date of withdrawal of the registration statement under Rule 477;

(4) The issuer notifies each offeree in the private offering that:

(i) The offering is not registered under the Act;

(ii) The securities will be "restricted securities" (as that term is defined in Rule 144(a)(3)) and may not be resold unless they are registered under the Act or an exemption from registration is available;

(iii) Purchasers in the private offering do not have the protection of Section 11 of the Act; and

(iv) A registration statement for the abandoned offering was filed and withdrawn, specifying the effective date of the withdrawal; and

(5) Any disclosure document used in the private offering discloses any changes in the issuer's business or financial condition that occurred after the issuer filed the registration statement that are material to the investment decision in the private offering.

Rule 159.   Information Available to Purchaser at Time of Contract of Sale

(a) For purposes of section 12(a)(2) of the Act only, and without affecting any other rights a purchaser may have, for purposes of determining whether a prospectus or oral statement included an untrue statement of a material fact or omitted to state a material fact necessary in order to make the statements, in the light of the circumstances under which they were made, not misleading at the time of sale (including, without limitation, a contract of sale), any information conveyed to the purchaser only after such time of sale (including such contract of sale) will not be taken into account.

(b) For purposes of section 17(a)(2) of the Act only, and without affecting any other rights the Commission may have to enforce that section, for purposes of determining whether a statement includes or represents any untrue statement of a material fact or any omission to state a material fact necessary in order to make the statements made, in light of the circumstances under which they were made, not misleading at the time of sale (including, without limitation, a contract of sale), any information conveyed to the purchaser only after such time of sale (including such contract of sale) will not be taken into account.

(c) For purposes of section 12(a)(2) of the Act only, knowing of such untruth or omission in respect of a sale (including, without limitation, a contract of sale), means knowing at the time of such sale (including such contract of sale).

Rule 159A.   Certain Definitions for Purposes of Section 12(a)(2) of the Act

(a) *Definition of seller for purposes of section 12(a)(2) of the Act.* For purposes of section 12(a)(2) of the Act only, in a primary offering of securities of the issuer, regardless of the underwriting method used to sell the issuer's securities, *seller* shall include the issuer of the securities sold to a person as part of the initial distribution of such securities, and the issuer shall be considered to offer or sell the securities to such person, if the securities are offered or sold to such person by means of any of the following communications:

(1) Any preliminary prospectus or prospectus of the issuer relating to the offering required to be filed pursuant to Rule 424 or Rule 497;

(2) Any free writing prospectus as defined in Rule 405 relating to the offering prepared by or on behalf of the issuer or used or referred to by the issuer and, in the case of an issuer that is an open-end management company registered under the Investment Company Act of 1940, any profile relating to the offering provided pursuant to Rule 498;

(3) The portion of any other free writing prospectus (or, in the case of an issuer that is an investment company registered under the Investment Company Act of 1940 or a business development company as defined in section 2(a)(48) of the Investment Company Act of 1940, any advertisement pursuant to Rule 482) relating to the offering containing material information about the issuer or its securities provided by or on behalf of the issuer; and

(4) Any other communication that is an offer in the offering made by the issuer to such person.

(b) *Definition of by means of for purposes of section 12(a)(2) of the Act.*

(1) For purposes of section 12(a)(2) of the Act only, an offering participant other than the issuer shall not be considered to offer or sell securities that are the subject of a registration statement by means of a free writing prospectus as to a purchaser unless one or more of the following circumstances shall exist:

(i) The offering participant used or referred to the free writing prospectus in offering or selling the securities to the purchaser;

(ii) The offering participant offered or sold securities to the purchaser and participated in planning for the use of the free writing prospectus by one or more other offering participants and such free writing prospectus was used or referred to in offering or selling securities to the purchaser by one or more of such other offering participants; or

(iii) The offering participant was required to file the free writing prospectus pursuant to the conditions to use in Rule 433.

(2) For purposes of section 12(a)(2) of the Act only, a person will not be considered to offer or sell securities by means of a free writing prospectus solely because another person has used or referred to the free writing prospectus or filed the free writing prospectus with the Commission pursuant to Rule 433.

Rule 162.   Submission of Tenders in Registered Exchange Offers

(a) Notwithstanding section 5(a) of the Act, an offeror may solicit tenders of securities in an exchange offer before a registration statement is effective as to the security offered, so long as no securities are purchased until the registration statement is effective and the tender offer has expired in accordance with the tender offer rules, and either:

(1) The exchange offer is subject to Rule 13e–4 or Rules 14d–1 through 14d–11 [under the Exchange Act]; or

(2) The offeror provides withdrawal rights to the same extent as would be required if the exchange offer were subject to the requirements of 13e–4 or 14d–1 through 14d–11; and if a material change occurs in the information published, sent or given to security holders, the offeror complies with the provisions of Rule 13e–4(e)(3) or Rule 14d–4(b) and (d) in disseminating information about the material change to security holders, and including the minimum periods during which the offer must remain open (with withdrawal rights) after notice of the change is provided to security holders.

(b) Notwithstanding Section 5(b)(2) of the Act, a prospectus that meets the requirements of Section 10(a) of the Act need not be delivered to security holders in an exchange offer that commences before the effectiveness of a registration statement in accordance with the provisions of Rule 162(a) . . . , so long as a preliminary prospectus, prospectus supplements and revised prospectuses are delivered to security holders in accordance with Rule 13e4(e)(2) or Rule 14d–4(b) of this chapter. This applies not only to exchange offers subject to those provisions, but also to exchange offers not subject to those provisions that meet the conditions in Rule 162(a)(2). . . .

Rule 163.   Exemption from Section 5(c) of the Act for Certain Communications by or on Behalf of Well-known Seasoned Issuers

Preliminary Note to Rule 163

Attempted compliance with this section does not act as an exclusive election and the issuer also may claim the availability of any other applicable exemption or exclusion. Reliance on this section does not affect the availability of any other exemption or exclusion from the requirements of section 5 of the Act.

(a) In an offering by or on behalf of a well-known seasoned issuer, as defined in Rule 405, that will be or is at the time intended to be registered under the Act, an offer by or on behalf of such issuer is exempt from the prohibitions in section 5(c) of the Act on offers to sell, offers for sale, or offers to buy its securities before a registration statement has been filed, provided that:

(1) Any written communication that is an offer made in reliance on this exemption will be a free writing prospectus as defined in Rule 405 and a prospectus under section 2(a)(10) of the Act relating to a public offering of securities to be covered by the registration statement to be filed; and

(2) The exemption from section 5(c) of the Act provided in this section for such written communication that is an offer shall be conditioned on satisfying the conditions in paragraph (b) of this section.

(b) *Conditions.*

(1) *Legend.*

(i) Every written communication that is an offer made in reliance on this exemption shall contain substantially the following legend:

The issuer may file a registration statement (including a prospectus) with the SEC for the offering to which this communication relates. Before you invest, you should read the prospectus in that registration statement and other documents the issuer has filed with the SEC for more complete information about the issuer and this offering. You may get these documents for free by visiting EDGAR on the SEC Web site at www.sec.gov. Alternatively, the company will arrange to send you the prospectus after filing if you request it by calling toll-free 1-8[xx-xxx-xxxx].

(ii) The legend also may provide an e-mail address at which the documents can be requested and may indicate that the documents also are available by accessing the issuer's Web site, and provide the Internet address and the particular location of the documents on the Web site.

(iii) An immaterial or unintentional failure to include the specified legend in a free writing prospectus required by this section will not result in a violation of section 5(c) of the Act or the loss of the ability to rely on this section so long as:

(A) A good faith and reasonable effort was made to comply with the specified legend condition;

(B) The free writing prospectus is amended to include the specified legend as soon as practicable after discovery of the omitted or incorrect legend; and

(C) If the free writing prospectus has been transmitted without the specified legend, the free writing prospectus is retransmitted with the legend by substantially the same means as, and directed to substantially the same prospective purchasers to whom, the free writing prospectus was originally transmitted.

(2) *Filing condition.*

(i) Subject to paragraph (b)(2)(ii) of this section, every written communication that is an offer made in reliance on this exemption shall be filed by the issuer with the Commission promptly upon the filing of the registration statement, if one is filed, or an amendment, if one is filed, covering the securities that have been offered in reliance on this exemption.

(ii) The condition that an issuer shall file a free writing prospectus with the Commission under this section shall not apply in respect of any communication that has previously been filed with, or furnished to, the Commission or that the issuer would not be required to file with the Commission pursuant to the conditions of Rule 433 if the communication was a free writing prospectus used after the filing of the registration statement. The condition that the issuer shall file a free writing prospectus with the

Commission under this section shall be satisfied if the issuer satisfies the filing conditions (other than timing of filing which is provided in this section) that would apply under Rule 433 if the communication was a free writing prospectus used after the filing of the registration statement.

(iii) An immaterial or unintentional failure to file or delay in filing a free writing prospectus to the extent provided in this section will not result in a violation of section 5(c) of the Act or the loss of the ability to rely on this section so long as:

(A) A good faith and reasonable effort was made to comply with the filing condition; and

(B) The free writing prospectus is filed as soon as practicable after discovery of the failure to file.

(3) *Ineligible offerings.* The exemption in paragraph (a) of this section shall not be available to:

(i) Communications relating to business combination transactions that are subject to Rule 165 or Rule 166. . . .

(c) For purposes of this section, a communication is made by or on behalf of an issuer if the issuer or an agent or representative of the issuer, other than an offering participant who is an underwriter or dealer, authorizes or approves the communication before it is made.

(d) For purposes of this section, a communication for which disclosure would be required under section 17(b) of the Act as a result of consideration given or to be given, directly or indirectly, by or on behalf of an issuer is deemed to be an offer by the issuer and, if a written communication, is deemed to be a free writing prospectus of the issuer.

(e) A communication exempt from section 5(c) of the Act pursuant to this section will not be considered to be in connection with a securities offering registered under the Securities Act for purposes of Rule 100(b)(2)(iv) of Regulation FD under the Securities Exchange Act of 1934.

Rule 163A. Exemption from Section 5(c) of the Act for Certain Communications Made by or on Behalf of Issuers More Than 30 days Before a Registration Statement is Filed

Preliminary Note to Rule 163A

Attempted compliance with this section does not act as an exclusive election and the issuer also may claim the availability of any other applicable exemption or exclusion. Reliance on this section does not affect the availability of any other exemption or exclusion from the requirements of section 5 of the Act.

(a) Except as excluded pursuant to paragraph (b) of this section, in all registered offerings by issuers, any communication made by or on behalf of an issuer more than 30 days before the date of the filing of the registration statement that does not reference a securities offering that is or will be the subject of a registration statement shall not constitute an offer to sell, offer for sale, or offer to buy the securities being offered under the registration statement for purposes of section 5(c) of the Act, provided that the issuer takes reasonable steps within its control to prevent further distribution or publication of such communication during the 30 days immediately preceding the date of filing the registration statement.

(b) The exemption in paragraph (a) of this section shall not be available with respect to the following communications:

. . . Communications relating to business combination transactions that are subject to Rule 165 or Rule 166; . . . .

(c) For purposes of this section, a communication is made by or on behalf of an issuer if the issuer or an agent or representative of the issuer, other than an offering participant who is an underwriter or dealer, authorizes or approves the communication before it is made.

(d) A communication exempt from section 5(c) of the Act pursuant to this section will not be considered to be in connection with a securities offering registered under the Securities Act for purposes of Rule 100(b)(2)(iv) of Regulation FD under the Securities Exchange Act of 1934.

Rule 164.   Post-filing Free Writing Prospectuses in Connection with Certain Registered Offerings

Preliminary Notes to Rule 164

1. This section is not available for any communication that, although in technical compliance with this section, is part of a plan or scheme to evade the requirements of section 5 of the Act.

2. Attempted compliance with this section does not act as an exclusive election and the person relying on this section also may claim the availability of any other applicable exemption or exclusion. Reliance on this section does not affect the availability of any other exemption or exclusion from the requirements of section 5 of the Act.

(a) In connection with a registered offering of an issuer meeting the requirements of this section, a free writing prospectus, as defined in Rule 405, of the issuer or any other offering participant, including any underwriter or dealer, after the filing of the registration statement will be a section 10(b) prospectus for purposes of section 5(b)(1) of the Act provided that the conditions set forth in Rule 433 are satisfied.

(b) An immaterial or unintentional failure to file or delay in filing a free writing prospectus as necessary to satisfy the filing conditions contained in Rule 433 will not result in a violation of section 5(b)(1) of the Act or the loss of the ability to rely on this section so long as:

(1) A good faith and reasonable effort was made to comply with the filing condition; and

(2) The free writing prospectus is filed as soon as practicable after discovery of the failure to file.

(c) An immaterial or unintentional failure to include the specified legend in a free writing prospectus as necessary to satisfy the legend condition contained in Rule 433 will not result in a violation of section 5(b)(1) of the Act or the loss of the ability to rely on this section so long as:

(1) A good faith and reasonable effort was made to comply with the legend condition;

(2) The free writing prospectus is amended to include the specified legend as soon as practicable after discovery of the omitted or incorrect legend; and

(3) If the free writing prospectus has been transmitted without the specified legend, the free writing prospectus must be retransmitted with the legend by substantially the same means as, and directed to substantially the same prospective purchasers to whom, the free writing prospectus was originally transmitted.

(d) Solely for purposes of this section, an immaterial or unintentional failure to retain a free writing prospectus as necessary to satisfy the record retention condition contained in Rule 433 will not result in a violation of section 5(b)(1) of the Act or the loss of the ability to rely on this section so long as a good faith and reasonable effort was made to comply with the record retention condition. Nothing in this paragraph will affect, however, any other record retention provisions applicable to the issuer or any offering participant.

(e) *Ineligible issuers* (1) This section and Rule 433 are available only if at the eligibility determination date for the offering in question, determined pursuant to paragraph (h) of this section, the issuer is not an ineligible issuer as defined in Rule 405 (or in the case of any offering participant, other than the issuer, the participant has a reasonable belief that the issuer is not an ineligible issuer);

(2) Notwithstanding paragraph (e)(1) of this section, this section and Rule 433 are available to an ineligible issuer with respect to a free writing prospectus that contains only descriptions of the terms of the securities in the offering or the offering. . . .

(g) *Excluded offerings.* This section and Rule 433 are not available if the issuer is registering a business combination transaction as defined in Rule 165(f)(1) or the issuer, other than a well-known seasoned issuer, is registering an offering on Form S-8.

(h) For purposes of this section and Rule 433, the determination date as to whether an issuer is an ineligible issuer in respect of an offering shall be:

(1) Except as provided in paragraph (h)(2) of this section, the time of filing of the registration statement covering the offering; or

(2) If the offering is being registered pursuant to Rule 415, the earliest time after the filing of the registration statement covering the offering at which the issuer, or in the case of an underwritten offering the issuer or another offering participant, makes a *bona fide* offer, including without limitation through the use of a free writing prospectus, in the offering.

Rule 165.   Offers Made in Connection with a Business Combination Transaction

Preliminary Note: This section is available only to communications relating to business combinations. The exemption does not apply to communications that may be in technical compliance with this section, but have the primary purpose or effect of conditioning the market for another transaction, such as a capital-raising or resale transaction.

(a) *Communications before a registration statement is filed.* Notwithstanding section 5(c) of the Act, the offeror of securities in a business combination transaction to be registered under the Act may make an offer to sell or solicit an offer to buy those securities from and including the first public announcement until the filing of a registration statement related to the transaction, so long as any written communication (other than non-public communications among participants) made in connection with or relating to the transaction (i.e., prospectus) is filed in accordance with Rule 425 and the conditions in paragraph (c) of this section are satisfied.

(b) *Communications after a registration statement is filed.* Notwithstanding section 5(b)(1) of the Act, any written communication (other than non-public communications among participants) made in connection with or relating to a business combination transaction (i.e., prospectus) after the filing of a registration statement related to the transaction need not satisfy the requirements of section 10 of the Act, so long as the prospectus is filed in accordance with Rule 424 or Rule 425 and the conditions in paragraph (c) of this section are satisfied.

(c) *Conditions.* To rely on paragraphs (a) and (b) of this section:

(1) Each prospectus must contain a prominent legend that urges investors to read the relevant documents filed or to be filed with the Commission because they contain important information. The legend also must explain to investors that they can get the documents for free at the Commission's web site and describe which documents are available free from the offeror; and

(2) In an exchange offer, the offer must be made in accordance with the applicable tender offer rules (Rules 14d–1 through 14e–8); and, in a transaction involving the vote of security holders, the offer must be made in accordance with the applicable proxy or information statement rules (Rules 14a–1 through 14a–101 and 14c–1 through 14c–101 [under the Securities Exchange Act]).

(d) *Applicability.* This section is applicable not only to the offeror of securities in a business combination transaction, but also to any other participant that may need to rely on and complies with this section in communicating about the transaction.

(e) *Failure to file or delay in filing.* An immaterial or unintentional failure to file or delay in filing a prospectus described in this section will not result in a violation of section 5(b)(1) or (c) of the Act, so long as:

(1) A good faith and reasonable effort was made to comply with the filing requirement; and

(2) The prospectus is filed as soon as practicable after discovery of the failure to file.

(f) *Definitions.*

(1) *A business combination transaction* means any transaction specified in Rule 145(a) or exchange offer;

(2) *A participant* is any person or entity that is a party to the business combination transaction and any persons authorized to act on their behalf; and

(3) *Public announcement* is any oral or written communication by a participant that is reasonably designed to, or has the effect of, informing the public or security holders in general about the business combination transaction.

Rule 166.   Exemption from Section 5(c) for Certain Communications in Connection with Business Combination Transactions

Preliminary Note: This section is available only to communications relating to business combinations. The exemption does not apply to communications that may be in technical compliance with this section, but have the primary purpose or effect of conditioning the market for another transaction, such as a capital-raising or resale transaction.

(a) *Communications*. In a registered offering involving a business combination transaction, any communication made in connection with or relating to the transaction before the first public announcement of the offering will not constitute an offer to sell or a solicitation of an offer to buy the securities offered for purposes of section 5(c) of the Act, so long as the participants take all reasonable steps within their control to prevent further distribution or publication of the communication until either the first public announcement is made or the registration statement related to the transaction is filed.

(b) *Definitions*. The terms business combination transaction, participant and public announcement have the same meaning as set forth in Rule 165(f).

Rule 168.   Exemption from Sections 2(a)(10) and 5(c) of the Act for Certain Communications of Regularly Released Factual Business Information and Forward-looking Information

Preliminary Notes to Rule 168.

1.   This section is not available for any communication that, although in technical compliance with this section, is part of a plan or scheme to evade the requirements of section 5 of the Act.

2.   This section provides a non-exclusive safe harbor for factual business information and forward-looking information released or disseminated as provided in this section. Attempted compliance with this section does not act as an exclusive election and the issuer also may claim the availability of any other applicable exemption or exclusion. Reliance on this section does not affect the availability of any other exemption or exclusion from the definition of prospectus in section 2(a)(10) or the requirements of section 5 of the Act.

3.   The availability of this section for a release or dissemination of a communication that contains or incorporates factual business information or forward-looking information will not be affected by another release or dissemination of a communication that contains all or a portion of the same factual business information or forward-looking information that does not satisfy the conditions of this section.

(a) For purposes of sections 2(a)(10) and 5(c) of the Act, the regular release or dissemination by or on behalf of an issuer (and, in the case of an asset-backed issuer, the other persons specified in paragraph (a)(3) of this section) of communications containing factual business information or forward-looking information shall be deemed not to constitute an offer to sell or offer for sale of a security which is the subject of an offering pursuant to a registration statement that the issuer proposes to file, or has filed, or that is effective, if the conditions of this section are satisfied by any of the following:

(1) An issuer that is required to file reports pursuant to section 13 or section 15(d) of the Securities Exchange Act of 1934. . . .

(b) *Definitions*.

(1) *Factual business information* means some or all of the following information that is released or disseminated under the conditions in paragraph (d) of this section, including, without limitation, such factual business information contained in reports or other materials filed with, furnished to, or submitted to the Commission pursuant to the Securities Exchange Act of 1934:

(i) Factual information about the issuer, its business or financial developments, or other aspects of its business;

(ii) Advertisements of, or other information about, the issuer's products or services; and

(iii) Dividend notices.

(2) *Forward-looking information* means some or all of the following information that is released or disseminated under the conditions in paragraph (d) of this section, including, without limitation, such forward-looking information contained in reports or other materials filed with, furnished to, or submitted to the Commission pursuant to the Securities Exchange Act of 1934:

(i) Projections of the issuer's revenues, income (loss), earnings (loss) per share, capital expenditures, dividends, capital structure, or other financial items;

(ii) Statements about the issuer management's plans and objectives for future operations, including plans or objectives relating to the products or services of the issuer;

(iii) Statements about the issuer's future economic performance, including statements of the type contemplated by the management's discussion and analysis of financial condition and results of operation described in Item 303 of Regulations S–B and S–K. . . .

(iv) Assumptions underlying or relating to any of the information described in paragraphs (b)(2)(i), (b)(2)(ii) and (b)(2)(iii) of this section.

(3) For purposes of this section, the release or dissemination of a communication is by or on behalf of the issuer if the issuer or an agent or representative of the issuer, other than an offering participant who is an underwriter or dealer, authorizes or approves such release or dissemination before it is made.

(4) For purposes of this section, in the case of communications of a person specified in paragraph (a)(3) of this section other than the asset-backed issuer, the release or dissemination of a communication is by or on behalf of such other person if such other person or its agent or representative, other than an underwriter or dealer, authorizes or approves such release or dissemination before it is made.

(c) *Exclusion.* A communication containing information about the registered offering or released or disseminated as part of the offering activities in the registered offering is excluded from the exemption of this section.

(d) *Conditions to exemption.* The following conditions must be satisfied:

(1) The issuer . . . has previously released or disseminated information of the type described in this section in the ordinary course of its business;

(2) The timing, manner, and form in which the information is released or disseminated is consistent in material respects with similar past releases or disseminations. . . .

Rule 169.   Exemption from Sections 2(a)(10) and 5(c) of the Act for Certain Communications of Regularly Released Factual Business Information

Preliminary Notes to Rule 169

1.   This section is not available for any communication that, although in technical compliance with this section, is part of a plan or scheme to evade the requirements of section 5 of the Act.

2.   This section provides a non-exclusive safe harbor for factual business information released or disseminated as provided in this section. Attempted compliance with this section does not act as an exclusive election and the issuer also may claim the availability of any other applicable exemption or exclusion. Reliance on this section does not affect the availability of any other exemption or exclusion from the definition of prospectus in section 2(a)(10) or the requirements of section 5 of the Act.

3.   The availability of this section for a release or dissemination of a communication that contains or incorporates factual business information will not be affected by another release or dissemination of a communication that contains all or a portion of the same factual business information that does not satisfy the conditions of this section.

(a) For purposes of sections 2(a)(10) and 5(c) of the Act, the regular release or dissemination by or on behalf of an issuer of communications containing factual business information shall be deemed not to constitute an offer to sell or offer for sale of a security by an issuer which is the subject of an offering pursuant to a registration statement that the issuer proposes to file, or has filed, or that is effective, if the conditions of this section are satisfied.

(b) *Definitions.*

(1) *Factual business information* means some or all of the following information that is released or disseminated under the conditions in paragraph (d) of this section:

(i) Factual information about the issuer, its business or financial developments, or other aspects of its business; and

(ii) Advertisement of, or other information about, the issuer's products or services.

(2) For purposes of this section, the release or dissemination of a communication is by or on behalf of the issuer if the issuer or an agent or representative of the issuer, other than an offering participant who is an underwriter or dealer, authorizes or approves such release or dissemination before it is made.

(c) *Exclusions.* A communication containing information about the registered offering or released or disseminated as part of the offering activities in the registered offering is excluded from the exemption of this section.

(d) *Conditions to exemption.* The following conditions must be satisfied:

(1) The issuer has previously released or disseminated information of the type described in this section in the ordinary course of its business;

(2) The timing, manner, and form in which the information is released or disseminated is consistent in material respects with similar past releases or disseminations;

(3) The information is released or disseminated for intended use by persons, such as customers and suppliers, other than in their capacities as investors or potential investors in the issuer's securities, by the issuer's employees or agents who historically have provided such information. . . .

Rule 172.   Delivery of Prospectuses

(a) *Sending confirmations and notices of allocations.* After the effective date of a registration statement, the following are exempt from the provisions of section 5(b)(1) of the Act if the conditions set forth in paragraph (c) of this section are satisfied:

(1) Written confirmations of sales of securities in an offering pursuant to a registration statement that contain information limited to that called for in Rule 10b–10 under the Securities Exchange Act of 1934 and other information customarily included in written confirmations of sales of securities, which may include notices provided pursuant to Rule 173; and

(2) Notices of allocation of securities sold or to be sold in an offering pursuant to the registration statement that may include information identifying the securities (including the CUSIP number) and otherwise may include only information regarding pricing, allocation and settlement, and information incidental thereto.

(b) *Transfer of the security.* Any obligation under section 5(b)(2) of the Act to have a prospectus that satisfies the requirements of section 10(a) of the Act precede or accompany the carrying or delivery of a security in a registered offering is satisfied if the conditions in paragraph (c) of this section are met.

(c) *Conditions.*

(1) The registration statement relating to the offering is effective and is not the subject of any pending proceeding or examination under section 8(d) or 8(e) of the Act;

(2) Neither the issuer, nor an underwriter or participating dealer is the subject of a pending proceeding under section 8A of the Act in connection with the offering; and

(3) The issuer has filed with the Commission a prospectus with respect to the offering that satisfies the requirements of section 10(a) of the Act or the issuer will make a good faith and reasonable effort to file such a prospectus within the time required under Rule 424 and, in the event that the issuer fails to file timely such a prospectus, the issuer files the prospectus as soon as practicable thereafter.

(4) The condition in paragraph (c)(3) of this section shall not apply to transactions by dealers requiring delivery of a final prospectus pursuant to section 4(3) of the Act.

(d) *Exclusions*. This section shall not apply to. . . .

. . . A business combination transaction as defined in Rule 165(f)(1). . . .

Rule 173.   Notice of Registration

(a) In a transaction that represents a sale by the issuer or an underwriter, or a sale where there is not an exclusion or exemption from the requirement to deliver a final prospectus meeting the requirements of section 10(a) of the Act pursuant to section 4(3) of the Act or Rule 174, each underwriter or dealer selling in such transaction shall provide to each purchaser from it, not later than two business days following the completion of such sale, a copy of the final prospectus or, in lieu of such prospectus, a notice to the effect that the sale was made pursuant to a registration statement or in a transaction in which a final prospectus would have been required to have been delivered in the absence of Rule 172.

(b) If the sale was by the issuer and was not effected by or through an underwriter or dealer, the responsibility to send a prospectus, or in lieu of such prospectus, such notice as set forth in paragraph (a) of this section, shall be the issuer's.

(c) Compliance with the requirements of this section is not a condition to reliance on Rule 172.

(d) A purchaser may request from the person responsible for sending a notice a copy of the final prospectus if one has not been sent.

(e) After the effective date of the registration statement with respect to an offering, notices as set forth in paragraph (a) of this section, are exempt from the provisions of section 5(b)(1) of the Act.

(f) *Exclusions*. This section shall not apply to any . . . 1940;

. . . business combination transaction as defined in Rule 165(f)(1). . . .

Rule 174.   Delivery of Prospectus by Dealers: Exemptions Under Section 4(3) of the Act

The obligations of a dealer (including an underwriter no longer acting as an underwriter in respect of the security involved in such transactions) to deliver a prospectus in transactions in a security as to which a registration statement has been filed taking place prior to the expiration of the 40- or 90-day period specified in section 4(3) of the Act after the effective date of such registration statement or prior to the expiration of such period after the first date upon which the security was bona fide offered to the public by the issuer or by or through an underwriter after such effective date, whichever is later, shall be subject to the following provisions. . . .

(b) No prospectus need be delivered if the issuer is subject, immediately prior to the time of filing the registration statement, to the reporting requirements of section 13 or 15(d) of the Securities Exchange Act of 1934.

(c) Where a registration statement relates to offerings to be made from time to time no prospectus need be delivered after the expiration of the initial prospectus delivery period specified in section 4(3) of the Act following the first bona fide offering of securities under such registration statement.

(d) If (1) the registration statement relates to the security of an issuer that is not subject, immediately prior to the time of filing the registration statement, to the reporting requirements of Section 13 or 15(d) of the Securities Exchange Act of 1934, and (2) as of the offering date, the security is listed on a registered national securities exchange or authorized for inclusion in an electronic interdealer quotation system sponsored and governed by the rules of a registered securities association, no prospectus need be delivered after the expiration of twenty-five calendar days after the offering date. For purposes of this provision, the term "offering date" refers to the later of the effective date of the registration statement or the first date on which the security was bona fide offered to the public.

(e) Notwithstanding the foregoing, the period during which a prospectus must be delivered by a dealer shall be:

(1) As specified in section 4(3) of the Act if the registration statement was the subject of a stop order issued under section 8 of the Act; or

(2) As the Commission may provide upon application or on its own motion in a particular case.

(f) Nothing in this section shall affect the obligation to deliver a prospectus pursuant to the provisions of section 5 of the Act by a dealer who is acting as an underwriter with respect to the securities involved or who is engaged in a transaction as to securities constituting the whole or a part of an unsold allotment to or subscription by such dealer as a participant in the distribution of such securities by the issuer or by or through an underwriter. . . .

(h) Any obligation pursuant to Section 4(3) of the Act and this section to deliver a prospectus, other than pursuant to paragraph (g) of this section, may be satisfied by compliance with the provisions of Rule 172.

Rule 175. Liability for Certain Statements by Issuers

(a) A statement within the coverage of paragraph (b) of this section which is made by or on behalf of an issuer or by an outside reviewer retained by the issuer shall be deemed not to be a fraudulent statement (as defined in paragraph (d) of this section), unless it is shown that such statement was made or reaffirmed without a reasonable basis or was disclosed other than in good faith.

(b) This rule applies to the following statements:

(1) A forward-looking statement (as defined in paragraph (c) of this section) made in a document filed with the Commission, in Part I of a quarterly report on Form 10-Q, (or in an annual report to security holders meeting the requirements of Rule 14a–3(b) and (c) or 14c–3(a) and (b) under the Securities Exchange Act of 1934), a statement reaffirming such forward-looking statement after the date the document was filed or the annual report was made publicly available, or a forward-looking statement made before the date the document was filed or the date the annual report was publicly available if such statement is reaffirmed in a filed document, in Part I of a quarterly report on Form 10-Q, or in an annual report made publicly available within a reasonable time after the making of such forward-looking statement; *Provided*, that

(i) At the time such statements are made or reaffirmed, either the issuer is subject to the reporting requirements of section 13(a) or 15(d) of the Securities Exchange Act of 1934 and has complied with the requirements of Rule 13a–1 or 15d–l thereunder, if applicable, to file its most recent annual report on Form 10-K . . . ; or if the issuer is not subject to the reporting requirements of Section 13(a) or 15(d) of the Securities Exchange Act of 1934, the statements are made in a registration statement filed under the Act, offering statement or solicitation of interest, written document or broadcast script under Regulation A or pursuant to sections 12(b) or (g) of the Securities Exchange Act of 1934; and

(ii) The statements are not made by or on behalf of an issuer that is an investment company registered under the Investment Company Act of 1940; and

(2) Information that is disclosed in a document filed with the Commission, in Part I of a quarterly report on Form 10-Q or in an annual report to shareholders meeting the requirements of Rules 14a–3 (b) and (c) or 14c–3 (a) and (b) under the Securities Exchange Act of 1934 and that relates to:

(i) The effects of changing prices on the business enterprise . . . ; or

(ii) The value of proved oil and gas reserves. . . .

(c) For the purpose of this rule, the term "forward-looking statement" shall mean and shall be limited to:

(1) A statement containing a projection of revenues, income (loss), earnings (loss) per share, capital expenditures, dividends, capital structure or other financial items;

(2) A statement of management's plans and objectives for future operations;

(3) A statement of future economic performance contained in management's discussion and analysis of financial condition and results of operations included pursuant to Item 303 of Regulation S–K . . . or

(4) Disclosed statements of the assumptions underlying or relating to any of the statements described in paragraphs (c)(1), (2), or (3) of this section.

(d) For the purpose of this rule the term "fraudulent statement" shall mean a statement which is an untrue statement of a material fact, a statement false or misleading with respect to any material fact, an omission to state a material fact necessary to make a statement not misleading, or which constitutes the employment of a manipulative, deceptive, or fraudulent device, contrivance, scheme, transaction, act, practice, course of business, or an artifice to defraud, as those terms are used in the Securities Act of 1933 or the rules or regulations promulgated thereunder.

Rule 176. Circumstances Affecting the Determination of What Constitutes Reasonable Investigation and Reasonable Grounds for Belief Under Section 11 of the Securities Act

In determining whether or not the conduct of a person constitutes a reasonable investigation or a reasonable ground for belief meeting the standard set forth in section 11(c), relevant circumstances include, with respect to a person other than the issuer.

(a) The type of issuer;

(b) The type of security;

(c) The type of person;

(d) The office held when the person is an officer;

(e) The presence or absence of another relationship to the issuer when the person is a director or proposed director;

(f) Reasonable reliance on officers, employees, and others whose duties should have given them knowledge of the particular facts (in the light of the functions and responsibilities of the particular person with respect to the issuer and the filing);

(g) When the person is an underwriter, the type of underwriting arrangement, the role of the particular person as an underwriter and the availability of information with respect to the registrant; and

(h) Whether, with respect to a fact or document incorporated by reference, the particular person had any responsibility for the fact or document at the time of the filing from which it was incorporated. . . .

Rule 215.   Accredited Investor

The term "accredited investor" as used in section 2(15)(ii) of the Securities Act of 1933 . . . shall include the following persons:

(a) Any savings and loan association or other institution specified in section 3(a)(5)(A) of the Act whether acting in its individual or fiduciary capacity; any broker or dealer registered pursuant to section 15 of the Securities Exchange Act of 1934; any plan established and maintained by a state, its political subdivisions, or any agency or instrumentality of a state or its political subdivisions, for the benefit of its employees, if such plan has total assets in excess of $5,000,000; any employee benefit plan within the meaning of Title I of the Employee Retirement Income Security Act of 1974, if the investment decision is made by a plan fiduciary, as defined in section 3(21) of such Act, which is a savings and loan association, or if the employee benefit plan has total assets in excess of $5,000,000 or, if a self-directed plan, with investment decisions made solely by persons that are accredited investors;

(b) Any private business development company as defined in section 202(a)(22) of the Investment Advisers Act of 1940;

(c) Any organization described in section 501(c)(3) of the Internal Revenue Code, corporation, Massachusetts or similar business trust, or partnership, not formed for the specific purpose of acquiring the securities offered, with total assets in excess of $5,000,000;

(d) Any director, executive officer, or general partner of the issuer of the securities being offered or sold, or any director, executive officer, or general partner of a general partner of that issuer;

(e) Any natural person whose individual net worth, or joint net worth with that person's spouse, exceeds $1,000,000; . . .

(f) Any natural person who had an individual income in excess of $200,000 in each of the two most recent years or joint income with that person's spouse in excess of $300,000 in each of those years and has a reasonable expectation of reaching the same income level in the current year;

(g) Any trust, with total assets in excess of $5,000,000, not formed for the specific purpose of acquiring the securities offered, whose purchase is directed by a sophisticated person as described in Rule 506(b)(2)(ii); and

(h) Any entity in which all of the equity owners are accredited investors.

REGULATION A—CONDITIONAL SMALL ISSUES EXEMPTION

Rule 251.   Scope of Exemption

(a) Tier 1 and Tier 2. A public offer or sale of eligible securities, as defined in Rule 261 (§ 230.261), pursuant to Regulation A shall be exempt under section 3(b) from the registration requirements of the Securities Act of 1933 (the "Securities Act") (15 U.S.C. 77a et seq.).

(1) Tier 1. Offerings pursuant to Regulation A in which the sum of all cash and other consideration to be received for the securities being offered ("aggregate offering price") plus the gross proceeds for all securities sold pursuant to other offering statements within the 12 months before the start of and during the current offering of securities ("aggregate sales") does not exceed $20,000,000, including not more than $6,000,000 offered by all selling securityholders that are affiliates of the issuer ("Tier 1 offerings").

(2) Tier 2. Offerings pursuant to Regulation A in which the sum of the aggregate offering price and aggregate sales does not exceed $50,000,000, including not more than $15,000,000 offered by all selling securityholders that are affiliates of the issuer ("Tier 2 offerings").

(3) Additional limitation on secondary sales in first year. The portion of the aggregate offering price attributable to the securities of selling securityholders shall not exceed 30% of the aggregate offering price of a particular offering in:

(i) The issuer's first offering pursuant to Regulation A; or

(ii) Any subsequent Regulation A offering that is qualified within one year of the qualification date of the issuer's first offering.

Note to paragraph (a). Where a mixture of cash and non-cash consideration is to be received, the aggregate offering price must be based on the price at which the securities are offered for cash. Any portion of the aggregate offering price or aggregate sales attributable to cash received in a foreign currency must be translated into United States currency at a currency exchange rate in effect on, or at a reasonable time before, the date of the sale of the securities. If securities are not offered for cash, the aggregate offering price or aggregate sales must be based on the value of the consideration as established by bona fide sales of that consideration made within a reasonable time, or, in the absence of sales, on the fair value as determined by an accepted standard. Valuations of non-cash consideration must be reasonable at the time made. If convertible securities or warrants are being offered and such securities are convertible, exercisable, or exchangeable within one year of the offering statement's qualification or at the discretion of the issuer, the underlying securities must also be qualified and the aggregate offering price must include the actual or maximum estimated conversion, exercise, or exchange price of such securities.

(b) Issuer. The issuer of the securities:

(1) Is an entity organized under the laws of the United States or Canada, or any State, Province, Territory or possession thereof, or the District of Columbia, with its principal place of business in the United States or Canada;

(2) [Reserved]

(3) Is not a development stage company that either has no specific business plan or purpose, or has indicated that its business plan is to merge with or acquire an unidentified company or companies;

(4) Is not an investment company registered or required to be registered under the Investment Company Act of 1940 (15 U.S.C. 80a–1 et seq.) or a business development company as defined in section 2(a)(48) of the Investment Company Act of 1940 (15 U.S.C. 80a–2(a)(48));

(5) Is not issuing fractional undivided interests in oil or gas rights, or a similar interest in other mineral rights;

(6) Is not, and has not been, subject to any order of the Commission entered pursuant to Section 12(j) (15 U.S.C. 78*l*(j)) of the Securities Exchange Act of 1934 (the "Exchange Act") (15 U.S.C. 78a et seq.) within five years before the filing of the offering statement;

(7) Has filed with the Commission all reports required to be filed, if any, pursuant to Rule 257 (§ 230.257) during the two years before the filing of the offering statement (or for such shorter period that the issuer was required to file such reports); and

(8) Is not disqualified under Rule 262 (§ 230.262).

(c) Integration with other offerings. Offers or sales made in reliance on this Regulation A will not be integrated with:

(1) Prior offers or sales of securities; or

(2) Subsequent offers or sales of securities that are:

(i) Registered under the Securities Act, except as provided in Rule 255(e) (§ 230.255(e));

(ii) Exempt from registration under Rule 701 (§ 230.701);

(iii) Made pursuant to an employee benefit plan;

(iv) Exempt from registration under Regulation S (§§ 230.901 through 203.905);

(v) Made more than six months after the completion of the Regulation A offering; or

(vi) Exempt from registration under Section 4(a)(6) of the Securities Act (15 U.S.C. 77d(a)(6)).

Note to paragraph (c). If these safe harbors do not apply, whether subsequent offers and sales of securities will be integrated with the Regulation A offering will depend on the particular facts and circumstances.

(d) Offering conditions—(1) Offers.

(i) Except as allowed by Rule 255 (§ 230.255), no offer of securities may be made unless an offering statement has been filed with the Commission.

(ii) After the offering statement has been filed, but before it is qualified:

(A) Oral offers may be made;

(B) Written offers pursuant to Rule 254 (§ 230.254) may be made; and

(C) Solicitations of interest and other communications pursuant to Rule 255 (§ 230.255) may be made.

(iii) Offers may be made after the offering statement has been qualified, but any written offers must be accompanied with or preceded by the most recent offering circular filed with the Commission for such offering.

(2) Sales. (i) No sale of securities may be made:

(A) Until the offering statement has been qualified;

(B) By issuers that are not currently required to file reports pursuant to Rule 257(b) (§ 230.257(b)), until a Preliminary Offering Circular is delivered at least 48 hours before the sale to any person that before qualification of the offering statement had indicated an interest in purchasing securities in the offering, including those persons that responded to an issuer's solicitation of interest materials; and

(C) In a Tier 2 offering of securities that are not listed on a registered national securities exchange upon qualification, unless the purchaser is either an accredited investor (as defined in Rule 501 (§ 230.501)) or the aggregate purchase price to be paid by the purchaser for the securities (including the actual or maximum estimated conversion, exercise, or exchange price for any underlying securities that have been qualified) is no more than ten percent (10%) of the greater of such purchaser's:

(1) Annual income or net worth if a natural person (with annual income and net worth for such natural person purchasers determined as provided in Rule 501 (§ 230.501)); or

(2) Revenue or net assets for such purchaser's most recently completed fiscal year end if a non-natural person.

Note to paragraph (d)(2)(i)(C). When securities underlying warrants or convertible securities are being qualified pursuant to Tier 2 of Regulation A one year or more after the qualification of an offering for which investment limitations previously applied, purchasers of the underlying securities for which investment limitations would apply at that later date may determine compliance with the ten percent (10%) investment limitation using the conversion, exercise, or exchange price to acquire the underlying securities at that later time without aggregating such price with the price of the overlying warrants or convertible securities.

(D) The issuer may rely on a representation of the purchaser when determining compliance with the ten percent (10%) investment limitation in this paragraph (d)(2)(i)(C), provided that the issuer does not know at the time of sale that any such representation is untrue.

(ii) In a transaction that represents a sale by the issuer or an underwriter, or a sale by a dealer within 90 calendar days after qualification of the offering statement, each underwriter or dealer selling in such transaction must deliver to each purchaser from it, not later than two business days following the completion of such sale, a copy of the Final Offering Circular, subject to the following provisions:

(A) If the sale was by the issuer and was not effected by or through an underwriter or dealer, the issuer is responsible for delivering the Final Offering Circular as if the issuer were an underwriter;

(B) For continuous or delayed offerings pursuant to paragraph (d)(3) of this section, the 90 calendar day period for dealers shall commence on the day of the first bona fide offering of securities under such offering statement;

(C) If the security is listed on a registered national securities exchange, no offering circular need be delivered by a dealer more than 25 calendar days after the later of the qualification date of the offering statement or the first date on which the security was bona fide offered to the public;

(D) No offering circular need be delivered by a dealer if the issuer is subject, immediately prior to the time of the filing of the offering statement, to the reporting requirements of Rule 257(b) (§ 230.257(b)); and

(E) The Final Offering Circular delivery requirements set forth in paragraph (d)(2)(ii) of this section may be satisfied by delivering a notice to the effect that the sale was made pursuant to a qualified offering statement that includes the uniform resource locator ("URL"), which, in the case of an electronic-only offering, must be an active hyperlink, where the Final Offering Circular, or the offering statement of which such Final Offering Circular is part, may be obtained on the Commission's Electronic Data Gathering, Analysis and Retrieval System ("EDGAR") and contact information sufficient to notify a purchaser where a request for a Final Offering Circular can be sent and received in response.

(3) *Continuous or delayed offerings.* (i) Continuous or delayed offerings may be made under this Regulation A, so long as the offering statement pertains only to:

(A) Securities that are to be offered or sold solely by or on behalf of a person or persons other than the issuer, a subsidiary of the issuer, or a person of which the issuer is a subsidiary;

(B) Securities that are to be offered and sold pursuant to a dividend or interest reinvestment plan or an employee benefit plan of the issuer;

(C) Securities that are to be issued upon the exercise of outstanding options, warrants, or rights;

(D) Securities that are to be issued upon conversion of other outstanding securities;

(E) Securities that are pledged as collateral; or

(F) Securities the offering of which will be commenced within two calendar days after the qualification date, will be made on a continuous basis, may continue for a period in excess of 30 calendar days from the date of initial qualification, and will be offered in an amount that, at the time the offering statement is qualified, is reasonably expected to be offered and sold within two years from the initial qualification date. These securities may be offered and sold only if not more than three years have elapsed since the initial qualification date of the offering statement under which they are being offered and sold; provided, however, that if a new offering statement has been filed pursuant to this paragraph (d)(3)(i)(F), securities covered by the prior offering statement may continue to be offered and sold until the earlier of the qualification date of the new offering statement or 180 calendar days after the third anniversary of the initial qualification date of the prior offering statement. Before the end of such three-year period, an issuer may file a new offering statement covering the securities. The new offering statement must include all the information that would be required at that time in an offering statement relating to all offerings that it covers. Before the qualification date of the new offering statement, the issuer may include as part of such new offering statement any unsold securities covered by the earlier offering statement by identifying on the cover page of the new offering circular, or the latest amendment, the amount of such unsold securities being included. The offering of securities on the earlier offering statement will be deemed terminated as of the date of qualification of the new offering statement. Securities may be sold pursuant to this paragraph (d)(3)(i)(F) only if the issuer is current in its annual and semiannual filings pursuant to Rule 257(b) (§ 230.257(b)), at the time of such sale.

(ii) At the market offerings, by or on behalf of the issuer or otherwise, are not permitted under this Regulation A. As used in this paragraph (d)(3)(ii), the term at the market offering means an offering of equity securities into an existing trading market for outstanding shares of the same class at other than a fixed price.

(e) Confidential treatment. A request for confidential treatment may be made under Rule 406 (§ 230.406) for information required to be filed, and Rule 83 (§ 200.83) for information not required to be filed.

(f) Electronic filing. Documents filed or otherwise provided to the Commission pursuant to this Regulation A must be submitted in electronic format by means of EDGAR in accordance with the EDGAR rules set forth in Regulation S-T (17 CFR part 232).

Rule 252.   Offering Statement

(a) Documents to be included. The offering statement consists of the contents required by Form 1-A (§ 239.90 of this chapter) and any other material information necessary to make the required statements, in light of the circumstances under which they are made, not misleading. . . .

(d) Non-public submission. An issuer whose securities have not been previously sold pursuant to a qualified offering statement under this Regulation A or an effective registration statement under the Securities Act may submit a draft offering statement to the Commission for non-public review by the staff of the Commission before public filing, provided that the offering statement shall not be qualified less than 21 calendar days after the public filing with the Commission of:

(1) The initial non-public submission;

(2) All non-public amendments; and

(3) All non-public correspondence submitted by or on behalf of the issuer to the Commission staff regarding such submissions (subject to any separately approved confidential treatment request under Rule 251(e) (§ 230.251(e)).

(e) Qualification. An offering statement and any amendment thereto can be qualified only at such date and time as the Commission may determine.

(f) Amendments.

(1)(i) Amendments to an offering statement must be signed and filed with the Commission in the same manner as the initial filing. Amendments to an offering statement must be filed under cover of Form 1-A and must be numbered consecutively in the order in which filed.

(ii) Every amendment that includes amended audited financial statements must include the consent of the certifying accountant to the use of such accountant's certification in connection with the amended financial statements in the offering statement or offering circular and to being named as having audited such financial statements. . . .

Rule 253.   Offering Circular

(a) Contents. An offering circular must include the information required by Form 1-A for offering circulars.

(b) Information that may be omitted. Notwithstanding paragraph (a) of this section, a qualified offering circular may omit information with respect to the public offering price, underwriting syndicate (including any material relationships between the issuer or selling securityholders and the unnamed underwriters, brokers or dealers), underwriting discounts or commissions, discounts or commissions to dealers, amount of proceeds, conversion rates, call prices and other items dependent upon the offering price, delivery dates, and terms of the securities dependent upon the offering date; provided, that the following conditions are met:

(1) The securities to be qualified are offered for cash.

(2) The outside front cover page of the offering circular includes a bona fide estimate of the range of the maximum offering price and the maximum number of shares or other units of securities to be offered or a bona fide estimate of the principal amount of debt securities offered, subject to the following conditions:

(i) The range must not exceed $2 for offerings where the upper end of the range is $10 or less or 20% if the upper end of the price range is over $10; and

(ii) The upper end of the range must be used in determining the aggregate offering price under Rule 251(a) (§ 230.251(a)).

(3) The offering statement does not relate to securities to be offered by competitive bidding.

(4) The volume of securities (the number of equity securities or aggregate principal amount of debt securities) to be offered may not be omitted in reliance on this paragraph (b).

Note to paragraph (b). A decrease in the volume of securities offered or a change in the bona fide estimate of the offering price range from that indicated in the offering circular filed as part of a qualified offering statement may be disclosed in the offering circular filed with the Commission pursuant to Rule 253(g) (§ 230.253(g)), so long as the decrease in the volume of securities offered or change in the price range would not materially change the disclosure contained in the offering statement at qualification. Notwithstanding the foregoing, any decrease in the volume of securities offered and any deviation from the low or high end of the price range may be reflected in the offering circular supplement filed with the Commission pursuant to Rule 253(g)(1) or (3) (§ 230.253(g)(1) or (3)) if, in the aggregate, the decrease in volume and/or change in price represent no more than a 20% change from the maximum aggregate offering price calculable using the information in the qualified offering statement. In no circumstances may this paragraph be used to offer securities where the maximum aggregate offering price would result in the offering exceeding the limit set forth in Rule 251(a) (§ 230.251(a)) or if the change would result in a Tier 1 offering becoming a Tier 2 offering. An offering circular supplement may not be used to increase the volume of securities being offered. Additional securities may only be offered pursuant to a new offering statement or post-qualification amendment qualified by the Commission.

(c) Filing of omitted information. The information omitted from the offering circular in reliance upon paragraph (b) of this section must be contained in an offering circular filed with the Commission pursuant to paragraph (g) of this section; except that if such offering circular is not so filed by the later of 15 business days after the qualification date of the offering statement or 15 business days after the qualification of a post-qualification amendment thereto that contains an offering circular, the information omitted in reliance upon paragraph (b) of this section must be contained in a qualified post-qualification amendment to the offering statement.

(d) Presentation of information.

(1) Information in the offering circular must be presented in a clear, concise and understandable manner and in a type size that is easily readable. Repetition of information should be avoided; cross-referencing of information within the document is permitted.

(2) Where an offering circular is distributed through an electronic medium, issuers may satisfy legibility requirements applicable to printed documents by presenting all required information in a format readily communicated to investors.

(e) Date. An offering circular must be dated approximately as of the date it was filed with the Commission.

(f) Cover page legend. The cover page of every offering circular must display the following statement highlighted by prominent type or in another manner:

The United States Securities and Exchange Commission does not pass upon the merits of or give its approval to any securities offered or the terms of the offering, nor does it pass upon the accuracy or completeness of any offering circular or other solicitation materials. These securities are offered pursuant to an exemption from registration with the Commission; however, the Commission has not made an independent determination that the securities offered are exempt from registration.

(g) Offering circular supplements.

(1) An offering circular that discloses information previously omitted from the offering circular in reliance upon Rule 253(b) (§ 230.253(b)) must be filed with the Commission no later than two business days following the earlier of the date of determination of the offering price or the date such offering circular is first used after qualification in connection with a public offering or sale.

(2) An offering circular that reflects information other than that covered in paragraph (g)(1) of this section that constitutes a substantive change from or addition to the information set forth in the last offering circular filed with the Commission must be filed with the Commission no later than five business days after the date it is first used after qualification in connection with a public offering or sale. If an offering circular filed pursuant to this paragraph (g)(2) consists of an offering circular supplement attached to an offering circular that previously had been filed or was not required to be filed pursuant to paragraph (g) of this section because it did not contain substantive changes from an offering circular that previously was filed, only the offering circular supplement need be filed under paragraph (g) of this section, provided that the cover page of the offering circular supplement identifies the date(s) of the related offering circular and any offering circular supplements thereto that together constitute the offering circular with respect to the securities currently being offered or sold.

(3) An offering circular that discloses information, facts or events covered in both paragraphs (g)(1) and (2) of this section must be filed with the Commission no later than two business days following the earlier of the date of the determination of the offering price or the date it is first used after qualification in connection with a public offering or sale.

(4) An offering circular required to be filed pursuant to paragraph (g) of this section that is not filed within the time frames specified in paragraphs (g)(1) through (3) of this section, as applicable, must be filed pursuant to this paragraph (g)(4) as soon as practicable after the discovery of such failure to file.

(5) Each offering circular filed under this section must contain in the upper right of the cover page the paragraphs of paragraphs (g)(1) through (4) of this section under which the filing is made, and the file number of the offering statement to which the offering circular relates.

Rule 254.   Preliminary Offering Circular

After the filing of an offering statement, but before its qualification, written offers of securities may be made if they meet the following requirements:

(a) Outside front cover page. The outside front cover page of the material bears the caption Preliminary Offering Circular, the date of issuance, and the following legend, which must be highlighted by prominent type or in another manner:

An offering statement pursuant to Regulation A relating to these securities has been filed with the Securities and Exchange Commission. Information contained in this Preliminary Offering Circular is subject to completion or amendment. These securities may not be sold nor may offers to buy be accepted before the offering statement filed with the Commission is qualified. This Preliminary Offering Circular shall not constitute an offer to sell or the solicitation of an offer to buy nor may there be any sales of these securities in any state in which such offer, solicitation or sale would be unlawful before registration or qualification under the laws of any such state. We may elect to satisfy our obligation to deliver a Final Offering Circular by sending you a notice within two business days after the completion of our sale to you that contains the URL where the Final Offering Circular or the offering statement in which such Final Offering Circular was filed may be obtained.

(b) Other contents. The Preliminary Offering Circular contains substantially the information required to be in an offering circular by Form 1-A (§ 239.90 of this chapter), except that certain information may be omitted under Rule 253(b) (§ 230.253(b)) subject to the conditions set forth in such rule.

(c) Filing. The Preliminary Offering Circular is filed as a part of the offering statement.

Rule 255.   Solicitations of Interest and Other Communications

(a) Solicitation of interest. At any time before the qualification of an offering statement, including before the non-public submission or public filing of such offering statement, an issuer or any person authorized to act on behalf of an issuer may communicate orally or in writing to determine whether there is any interest in a contemplated securities offering. Such communications are deemed to be an offer of a security for sale for purposes of the antifraud provisions of the federal securities laws. No solicitation or acceptance of money or other consideration, nor of any commitment, binding or otherwise, from any person is permitted until qualification of the offering statement.

(b) Conditions. The communications must:

(1) State that no money or other consideration is being solicited, and if sent in response, will not be accepted;

(2) State that no offer to buy the securities can be accepted and no part of the purchase price can be received until the offering statement is qualified, and any such offer may be withdrawn or revoked, without obligation or commitment of any kind, at any time before notice of its acceptance given after the qualification date;

(3) State that a person's indication of interest involves no obligation or commitment of any kind; and

(4) After the public filing of the offering statement:

(i) State from whom a copy of the most recent version of the Preliminary Offering Circular may be obtained, including a phone number and address of such person;

(ii) Provide the URL where such Preliminary Offering Circular, or the offering statement in which such Preliminary Offering Circular was filed, may be obtained; or

(iii) Include a complete copy of the Preliminary Offering Circular.

(c) Indications of interest. Any written communication under this rule may include a means by which a person may indicate to the issuer that such person is interested in a potential offering. This issuer may require the name, address, telephone number, and/or email address in any response form included pursuant to this paragraph (c).

(d) Revised solicitations of interest. If solicitation of interest materials are used after the public filing of the offering statement and such solicitation of interest materials contain information that is inaccurate or inadequate in any material respect, revised solicitation of interest materials must be redistributed in a substantially similar manner as such materials were originally distributed. Notwithstanding the foregoing in this paragraph (d), if the only information that is inaccurate or inadequate is contained in a Preliminary Offering Circular provided with the solicitation of interest materials pursuant to paragraphs (b)(4)(i) or (ii) of this section, no such redistribution is required in the following circumstances:

(1) in the case of paragraph (b)(4)(i) of this section, the revised Preliminary Offering Circular will be provided to any persons making new inquiries and will be recirculated to any persons making any previous inquiries; or

(2) in the case of paragraph (b)(4)(ii) of this section, the URL continues to link directly to the most recent Preliminary Offering Circular or to the offering statement in which such revised Preliminary Offering Circular was filed.

(e) Abandoned offerings. Where an issuer decides to register an offering under the Securities Act after soliciting interest in a contemplated, but subsequently abandoned, Regulation A offering, the abandoned Regulation A offering would not be subject to integration with the registered offering if the issuer engaged in solicitations of interest pursuant to this rule only to qualified institutional buyers and institutional accredited investors permitted by Section 5(d) of the Securities Act. If the issuer engaged in solicitations of interest to persons other than qualified institutional buyers and institutional accredited investors, an abandoned Regulation A offering would not be subject to integration if the issuer (and any underwriter, broker, dealer, or agent used by the issuer in connection with the proposed offering) waits at least 30 calendar days between the last such solicitation of interest in the Regulation A offering and the filing of the registration statement with the Commission.

Rule 256. Definition of "Qualified Purchaser"

For purposes of Section 18(b)(3) of the Securities Act [15 U.S.C. 77r(b)(3)], a "qualified purchaser" means any person to whom securities are offered or sold pursuant to a Tier 2 offering of this Regulation A.

Rule 257. Periodic and Current Reporting; Exit Report

(a) Tier 1: Exit report. Each issuer that has filed an offering statement for a Tier 1 offering that has been qualified pursuant to this Regulation A must file an exit report on Form 1-Z (§ 239.94 of this chapter) not later than 30 calendar days after the termination or completion of the offering.

(b) Tier 2: Periodic and current reporting. Each issuer that has filed an offering statement for a Tier 2 offering that has been qualified pursuant to this Regulation A must file with the Commission the following periodic and current reports:

(1) Annual reports. An annual report on Form 1-K (§ 239.91 of this chapter) for the fiscal year in which the offering statement became qualified and for any fiscal year thereafter, unless the issuer's obligation to file such annual report is suspended under paragraph (d) of this section. Annual reports must be filed within the period specified in Form 1-K.

(2) Special financial report. (i) A special financial report on Form 1-K or Form 1-SA if the offering statement did not contain the following:

(A) Audited financial statements for the issuer's most recent fiscal year (or for the life of the issuer if less than a full fiscal year) preceding the fiscal year in which the issuer's offering statement became qualified; or

(B) unaudited financial statements covering the first six months of the issuer's current fiscal year if the offering statement was qualified during the last six months of that fiscal year.

(ii) The special financial report described in paragraph (b)(2)(i)(A) of this section must be filed under cover of Form 1-K within 120 calendar days after the qualification date of the offering statement and must include audited financial statements for such fiscal year or other period specified in that paragraph, as the case may be. The special financial report described in paragraph (b)(2)(i)(B) of this section must be filed under cover of Form 1-SA within 90 calendar days after the qualification date of the offering statement and must include the semiannual financial statements for the first six months of the issuer's fiscal year, which may be unaudited.

(iii) A special financial report must be signed in accordance with the requirements of the form on which it is filed.

(3) Semiannual report. A semiannual report on Form 1-SA (§ 239.92 of this chapter) within the period specified in Form 1-SA. Semiannual reports must cover the first six months of each fiscal year of the issuer, commencing with the first six months of the fiscal year immediately following the most recent fiscal year for which full financial statements were included in the offering statement, or, if the offering statement included financial statements for the first six months of the fiscal year following the most recent full fiscal year, for the first six months of the following fiscal year.

(4) Current reports. Current reports on Form 1-U (§ 239.93 of this chapter) with respect to the matters and within the period specified in that form, unless substantially the same information has been previously reported to the Commission by the issuer under cover of Form 1-K or Form 1-SA.

(5) *Reporting by successor issuers.* Where in connection with a succession by merger, consolidation, exchange of securities, acquisition of assets or otherwise, securities of any issuer that is not required to file reports pursuant to paragraph (b) of this section are issued to the holders of any class of securities of another issuer that is required to file such reports, the duty to file reports pursuant to paragraph (b) of this section shall be deemed to have been assumed by the issuer of the class of securities so issued. The successor issuer must, after the consummation of the succession, file reports in accordance with paragraph (b) of this section, unless that issuer is exempt from filing such reports or the duty to file such reports is terminated or suspended under paragraph (d) of this section.

(6) *Exchange Act reporting requirements.* The duty to file reports under this rule shall be deemed to have been met if the issuer is subject to the reporting requirements of Section 13 or 15(d) of the Exchange Act (15 U.S.C. 78m or 15 U.S.C. 78o) and, as of each Form 1-K and Form 1-SA due date, has filed all reports required to be filed by Section 13 or 15(d) of the Exchange Act (15 U.S.C. 78m or 15 U.S.C. 78o) during the 12 months (or such shorter period that the registrant was required to file such reports) preceding such due date.

(c) *Amendments.* All amendments to the reports described in paragraphs (a) and (b) of this section must be filed under cover of the form amended, marked with the letter A to designate the document as an amendment, e.g., "1-K/A," and in compliance with pertinent requirements applicable to such reports. Amendments filed pursuant to this paragraph (c) must set forth the complete text of each item as amended, but need not include any items that were not amended. Amendments must be numbered sequentially and be filed separately for each report amended. Amendments must be signed on behalf of the issuer by a duly authorized representative of the issuer. An amendment to any report required to include certifications as specified in the applicable form must include new certifications by the appropriate persons.

(d) *Suspension of duty to file reports.* . . .

Rule 258. Suspension of the Exemption

(a) *Suspension.* The Commission may at any time enter an order temporarily suspending a Regulation A exemption if it has reason to believe that:

(1) No exemption is available or any of the terms, conditions or requirements of Regulation A have not been complied with;

(2) The offering statement, any sales or solicitation of interest material, or any report filed pursuant to Rule 257 (§ 230.257) contains any untrue statement of a material fact or omits to state a material fact necessary in order to make the statements made, in light of the circumstances under which they are made, not misleading;

(3) The offering is being made or would be made in violation of section 17 of the Securities Act;

(4) An event has occurred after the filing of the offering statement that would have rendered the exemption hereunder unavailable if it had occurred before such filing;

(5) Any person specified in Rule 262(a) (§ 230.262(a)) has been indicted for any crime or offense of the character specified in Rule 262(a)(1) (§ 230.262(a)(1)), or any proceeding has been initiated for the purpose of enjoining any such person from engaging in or continuing any conduct or practice of the character specified in Rule 262(a)(2) (§ 230.262(a)(2)), or any proceeding has been initiated for the purposes of Rule 262(a)(3)–(8) (§ 230.262(a)(3) through (8)); or

(6) The issuer or any promoter, officer, director, or underwriter has failed to cooperate, or has obstructed or refused to permit the making of an investigation by the Commission in connection with any offering made or proposed to be made in reliance on Regulation A.

(b) *Notice and hearing.* Upon the entry of an order under paragraph (a) of this section, the Commission will promptly give notice to the issuer, any underwriter, and any selling securityholder:

(1) That such order has been entered, together with a brief statement of the reasons for the entry of the order; and

(2) That the Commission, upon receipt of a written request within 30 calendar days after the entry of the order, will, within 20 calendar days after receiving the request, order a hearing at a place to be designated by the Commission.

(c) *Suspension order.* If no hearing is requested and none is ordered by the Commission, an order entered under paragraph (a) of this section shall become permanent on the 30th calendar day after its entry and shall remain in effect unless or until it is modified or vacated by the Commission. Where a hearing is requested or is ordered by the Commission, the Commission will, after notice of and opportunity for such hearing, either vacate the order or enter an order permanently suspending the exemption.

(d) *Permanent suspension.* The Commission may, at any time after notice of and opportunity for hearing, enter an order permanently suspending the exemption for any reason upon which it could have entered a temporary suspension order under paragraph (a) of this section. Any such order shall remain in effect until vacated by the Commission.

(e) *Notice procedures.* All notices required by this rule must be given by personal service, registered or certified mail to the addresses given by the issuer, any underwriter and any selling securityholder in the offering statement.

Rule 259.   Withdrawal or Abandonment of Offering Statements

(a) *Withdrawal.* If none of the securities that are the subject of an offering statement has been sold and such offering statement is not the subject of a proceeding under Rule 258 (§ 230.258), the offering statement may be withdrawn with the Commission's consent. The application for withdrawal must state the reason the offering statement is to be withdrawn and must be signed by an authorized representative of the issuer. Any withdrawn document will remain in the Commission's files, as well as the related request for withdrawal.

(b) *Abandonment.* When an offering statement has been on file with the Commission for nine months without amendment and has not become qualified, the Commission may, in its discretion, declare the offering statement abandoned. If the offering statement has been amended, the nine-month period shall be computed from the date of the latest amendment.

Rule 260.   Insignificant Deviations from a Term, Condition or Requirement of Regulation A

(a) *Failure to comply.* A failure to comply with a term, condition or requirement of Regulation A will not result in the loss of the exemption from the requirements of section 5 of the Securities Act for any offer or sale to a particular individual or entity, if the person relying on the exemption establishes that:

(1) The failure to comply did not pertain to a term, condition or requirement directly intended to protect that particular individual or entity;

(2) The failure to comply was insignificant with respect to the offering as a whole, provided that any failure to comply with Rule 251(a), (b), and (d)(1) and (3) (§ 230.251(a), (b), and (d)(1) and (3)) shall be deemed to be significant to the offering as a whole; and

(3) A good faith and reasonable attempt was made to comply with all applicable terms, conditions and requirements of Regulation A.

(b) *Action by Commission.* A transaction made in reliance upon Regulation A must comply with all applicable terms, conditions and requirements of the regulation. Where an exemption is established only through reliance upon paragraph (a) of this section, the failure to comply shall nonetheless be actionable by the Commission under section 20 of the Securities Act.

(c) *Suspension.* This provision provides no relief or protection from a proceeding under Rule 258 (§ 230.258).

Rule 261.   Definitions

As used in this Regulation A, all terms have the same meanings as in Rule 405 (§ 230.405), except that all references to registrant in those definitions shall refer to the issuer of the securities to be offered and sold under Regulation A. In addition, these terms have the following meanings:

(a) Affiliated issuer. An affiliate (as defined in Rule 501 (§ 230.501)) of the issuer that is issuing securities in the same offering.

(b) Business day. Any day except Saturdays, Sundays or United States federal holidays.

(c) Eligible securities. Equity securities, debt securities, and securities convertible or exchangeable to equity interests, including any guarantees of such securities, but not including asset-backed securities as such term is defined in Item 1101(c) of Regulation AB.

(d) Final order. A written directive or declaratory statement issued by a federal or state agency described in Rule 262(a)(3) (§ 230.262(a)(3)) under applicable statutory authority that provides for notice and an opportunity for hearing, which constitutes a final disposition or action by that federal or state agency.

(e) Final offering circular. The more recent of: the current offering circular contained in a qualified offering statement; and any offering circular filed pursuant to Rule 253(g) (§ 230.253(g)). If, however, the issuer is relying on Rule 253(b) ((§ 230.253(b)), the Final Offering Circular is the most recent of the offering circular filed pursuant to Rule 253(g)(1) or (3) (§ 230.253(g)(1) or (3)) and any subsequent offering circular filed pursuant to Rule 253(g) (§ 230.253(g)).

(f) Offering statement. An offering statement prepared pursuant to Regulation A.

(g) Preliminary offering circular. The offering circular described in Rule 254 (§ 230.254).

Rule 262.   Disqualification Provisions

(a) Disqualification events. No exemption under this Regulation A shall be available for a sale of securities if the issuer; any predecessor of the issuer; any affiliated issuer; any director, executive officer, other officer participating in the offering, general partner or managing member of the issuer; any beneficial owner of 20% or more of the issuer's outstanding voting equity securities, calculated on the basis of voting power; any promoter connected with the issuer in any capacity at the time of filing, any offer after qualification, or such sale; any person that has been or will be paid (directly or indirectly) remuneration for solicitation of purchasers in connection with such sale of securities; any general partner or managing member of any such solicitor; or any director, executive officer or other officer participating in the offering of any such solicitor or general partner or managing member of such solicitor:

(1) Has been convicted, within ten years before the filing of the offering statement (or five years, in the case of issuers, their predecessors and affiliated issuers), of any felony or misdemeanor:

(i) In connection with the purchase or sale of any security;

(ii) Involving the making of any false filing with the Commission; or

(iii) Arising out of the conduct of the business of an underwriter, broker, dealer, municipal securities dealer, investment adviser or paid solicitor of purchasers of securities;

(2) Is subject to any order, judgment or decree of any court of competent jurisdiction, entered within five years before the filing of the offering statement, that, at the time of such filing, restrains or enjoins such person from engaging or continuing to engage in any conduct or practice:

(i) In connection with the purchase or sale of any security;

(ii) Involving the making of any false filing with the Commission; or

(iii) Arising out of the conduct of the business of an underwriter, broker, dealer, municipal securities dealer, investment adviser or paid solicitor of purchasers of securities;

(3) Is subject to a final order (as defined in Rule 261 (§ 230.261)) of a state securities commission (or an agency or officer of a state performing like functions); a state authority that supervises or examines banks, savings associations, or credit unions; a state insurance commission (or an agency or officer of a state

performing like functions); an appropriate federal banking agency; the U.S. Commodity Futures Trading Commission; or the National Credit Union Administration that:

(i) At the time of the filing of the offering statement, bars the person from:

(A) Association with an entity regulated by such commission, authority, agency, or officer;

(B) Engaging in the business of securities, insurance or banking; or

(C) Engaging in savings association or credit union activities; or

(ii) Constitutes a final order based on a violation of any law or regulation that prohibits fraudulent, manipulative, or deceptive conduct entered within ten years before such filing of the offering statement;

(4) Is subject to an order of the Commission entered pursuant to section 15(b) or 15B(c) of the Securities Exchange Act of 1934 (15 U.S.C. 78 o (b) or 78 o–4(c)) or section 203(e) or (f) of the Investment Advisers Act of 1940 (15 U.S.C. 80b–3(e) or (f)) that, at the time of the filing of the offering statement:

(i) Suspends or revokes such person's registration as a broker, dealer, municipal securities dealer or investment adviser;

(ii) Places limitations on the activities, functions or operations of such person; or

(iii) Bars such person from being associated with any entity or from participating in the offering of any penny stock;

(5) Is subject to any order of the Commission entered within five years before the filing of the offering statement that, at the time of such filing, orders the person to cease and desist from committing or causing a violation or future violation of:

(i) Any scienter-based anti-fraud provision of the federal securities laws, including without limitation section 17(a)(1) of the Securities Act of 1933 (15 U.S.C. 77q(a)(1)), section 10(b) of the Securities Exchange Act of 1934 (15 U.S.C. 78j(b)) and 17 CFR 240.10b–5, section 15(c)(1) of the Securities Exchange Act of 1934 (15 U.S.C. 78 o (c)(1)) and section 206(1) of the Investment Advisers Act of 1940 (15 U.S.C. 80b–6(1)), or any other rule or regulation thereunder; or

(ii) Section 5 of the Securities Act of 1933 (15 U.S.C. 77e).

(6) Is suspended or expelled from membership in, or suspended or barred from association with a member of, a registered national securities exchange or a registered national or affiliated securities association for any act or omission to act constituting conduct inconsistent with just and equitable principles of trade;

(7) Has filed (as a registrant or issuer), or was or was named as an underwriter in, any registration statement or offering statement filed with the Commission that, within five years before the filing of the offering statement, was the subject of a refusal order, stop order, or order suspending the Regulation A exemption, or is, at the time of such filing, the subject of an investigation or proceeding to determine whether a stop order or suspension order should be issued; or

(8) Is subject to a United States Postal Service false representation order entered within five years before the filing of the offering statement, or is, at the time of such filing, subject to a temporary restraining order or preliminary injunction with respect to conduct alleged by the United States Postal Service to constitute a scheme or device for obtaining money or property through the mail by means of false representations.

(b) Transition, waivers, reasonable care exception. Paragraph (a) of this section shall not apply:

(1) With respect to any order under § 230.262(a)(3) or (5) that occurred or was issued before June 19, 2015;

(2) Upon a showing of good cause and without prejudice to any other action by the Commission, if the Commission determines that it is not necessary under the circumstances that an exemption be denied;

(3) If, before the filing of the offering statement, the court or regulatory authority that entered the relevant order, judgment or decree advises in writing (whether contained in the relevant judgment, order

or decree or separately to the Commission or its staff) that disqualification under paragraph (a) of this section should not arise as a consequence of such order, judgment or decree; or

(4) If the issuer establishes that it did not know and, in the exercise of reasonable care, could not have known that a disqualification existed under paragraph (a) of this section.

Note to paragraph (b)(4). An issuer will not be able to establish that it has exercised reasonable care unless it has made, in light of the circumstances, factual inquiry into whether any disqualifications exist. The nature and scope of the factual inquiry will vary based on the facts and circumstances concerning, among other things, the issuer and the other offering participants.

(c) Affiliated issuers. For purposes of paragraph (a) of this section, events relating to any affiliated issuer that occurred before the affiliation arose will be not considered disqualifying if the affiliated entity is not:

(1) In control of the issuer; or

(2) Under common control with the issuer by a third party that was in control of the affiliated entity at the time of such events.

(d) Disclosure of prior "bad actor" events. The issuer must include in the offering circular a description of any matters that would have triggered disqualification under paragraphs (a)(3) and (5) of this section but occurred before June 19, 2015. The failure to provide such information shall not prevent an issuer from relying on Regulation A if the issuer establishes that it did not know and, in the exercise of reasonable care, could not have known of the existence of the undisclosed matter or matters.

Rule 263.   Consent to Service of Process

(a) If the issuer is not organized under the laws of any of the states or territories of the United States of America, it shall furnish to the Commission a written irrevocable consent and power of attorney on Form F-X (§ 239.42 of this chapter) at the time of filing the offering statement required by Rule 252 (§ 230.252).

(b) Any change to the name or address of the agent for service of the issuer shall be communicated promptly to the Commission through amendment of the requisite form and referencing the file number of the relevant offering statement.

REGULATION C—REGISTRATION. . . .
GENERAL REQUIREMENTS. . . .

Rule 405.   Definitions of Terms

Unless the context otherwise requires, all terms used in 400 to 494, inclusive, or in the forms for registration have the same meanings as in the Act and in the general rules and regulations. In addition, the following definitions apply, unless the context otherwise requires:

Affiliate. An "affiliate" of, or person "affiliated" with, a specified person, is a person that directly, or indirectly through one or more intermediaries, controls or is controlled by, or is under common control with, the person specified. . . .

Associate. The term "associate," when used to indicate a relationship with any person, means (1) a corporation or organization (other than the registrant or a majority-owned subsidiary of the registrant) of which such person is an officer or partner or is, directly or indirectly, the beneficial owner of 10 percent or more of any class of equity securities, (2) any trust or other estate in which such person has a substantial beneficial interest or as to which such person serves as trustee or in a similar capacity, and (3) any relative or spouse of such person, or any relative of such spouse, who has the same home as such person or who is a director or officer of the registrant or any of its parents or subsidiaries. . . .

Automatic shelf registration statement. The term *automatic shelf registration statement* means a registration statement filed on Form S-3 or Form F-3 by a well-known seasoned issuer pursuant to General Instruction I.D. or I.C. of such forms, respectively. . . .

Control. The term "control" (including the terms "controlling," "controlled by" and "under common control with") means the possession, direct or indirect, of the power to direct or cause the direction of the management and policies of a person, whether through the ownership of voting securities, by contract, or otherwise. . . .

Equity security. The term "equity security" means any stock or similar security, certificate of interest or participation in any profit sharing agreement, preorganization certificate or subscription, transferable share, voting trust certificate or certificate of deposit for an equity security, limited partnership interest, interest in a joint venture, or certificate of interest in a business trust; any security future on any such security; or any security convertible, with or without consideration into such a security, or carrying any warrant or right to subscribe to or purchase such a security; or any such warrant or right; or any put, call, straddle, or other option or privilege of buying such a security from or selling such a security to another without being bound to do so.

Executive officer. The term "executive officer," when used with reference to a registrant, means its president, any vice president of the registrant in charge of a principal business unit, division or function (such as sales, administration or finance), any other officer who performs a policy making function or any other person who performs similar policy making functions for the registrant. Executive officers of subsidiaries may be deemed executive officers of the registrant if they perform such policy making functions for the registrant. . . .

Free writing prospectus. Except as otherwise specifically provided or the context otherwise requires, a *free writing prospectus* is any written communication as defined in this section that constitutes an offer to sell or a solicitation of an offer to buy the securities relating to a registered offering that is used after the registration statement in respect of the offering is filed (or, in the case of a well-known seasoned issuer, whether or not such registration statement is filed) and is made by means other than:

(1) A prospectus satisfying the requirements of section 10(a) of the Act, Rule 430, Rule 430A, Rule 430B, Rule 430C, or Rule 431;

(2) A written communication used in reliance on Rule 167 and Rule 426; or

(3) A written communication that constitutes an offer to sell or solicitation of an offer to buy such securities that falls within the exception from the definition of prospectus in clause (a) of section 2(a)(10) of the Act. . . .

Graphic communication. The term *graphic communication*, which appears in the definition of "write, written" in section 2(a)(9) of the Act and in the definition of written communication in this section, shall include all forms of electronic media, including, but not limited to, audiotapes, videotapes, facsimiles, CD-ROM, electronic mail, Internet Web sites, substantially similar messages widely distributed (rather than individually distributed) on telephone answering or voice mail systems, computers, computer networks and other forms of computer data compilation. Graphic communication shall not include a communication that, at the time of the communication, originates live, in real-time to a live audience and does not originate in recorded form or otherwise as a graphic communication, although it is transmitted through graphic means. . . .

Ineligible issuer. (1) An *ineligible issuer* is an issuer with respect to which any of the following is true as of the relevant date of determination:

(i) Any issuer that is required to file reports pursuant to section 13 or 15(d) of the Securities Exchange Act of 1934 that has not filed all reports and other materials required to be filed during the preceding 12 months (or for such shorter period that the issuer was required to file such reports pursuant to sections 13 or 15(d) of the Securities Exchange Act of 1934), other than reports on Form 8-K required solely pursuant to an item specified in General Instruction I.A.3(b) of Form S-3. . . ;

(iv) Within the past three years, a petition under the federal bankruptcy laws or any state insolvency law was filed by or against the issuer, or a court appointed a receiver, fiscal agent or similar officer with respect to the business or property of the issuer. . . .

(v) Within the past three years, the issuer or any entity that at the time was a subsidiary of the issuer was convicted of any felony or misdemeanor described in paragraphs (i) through (iv) of section 15(b)(4)(B) of the Securities Exchange Act of 1934;

(vi) Within the past three years (but in the case of a decree or order agreed to in a settlement, not before December 1, 2005), the issuer or any entity that at the time was a subsidiary of the issuer was made the subject of any judicial or administrative decree or order arising out of a governmental action that:

(A) Prohibits certain conduct or activities regarding, including future violations of, the anti-fraud provisions of the federal securities laws;

(B) Requires that the person cease and desist from violating the anti-fraud provisions of the federal securities laws; or

(C) Determines that the person violated the anti-fraud provisions of the federal securities laws;

(vii) The issuer has filed a registration statement that is the subject of any pending proceeding or examination under section 8 of the Act or has been the subject of any refusal order or stop order under section 8 of the Act within the past three years; or

(viii) The issuer is the subject of any pending proceeding under section 8A of the Act in connection with an offering.

(2) An issuer shall not be an ineligible issuer if the Commission determines, upon a showing of good cause, that it is not necessary under the circumstances that the issuer be considered an ineligible issuer. Any such determination shall be without prejudice to any other action by the Commission in any other proceeding or matter with respect to the issuer or any other person.

(3) The date of determination of whether an issuer is an ineligible issuer is as follows:

(i) For purposes of determining whether an issuer is a well-known seasoned issuer, at the date specified for purposes of such determination in paragraph (2) of the definition of well-known seasoned issuer in this section; and

(ii) For purposes of determining whether an issuer or offering participant may use free writing prospectuses in respect of an offering in accordance with the provisions of Rules 164 and 433, at the date in respect of the offering specified in paragraph (h) of Rule 164. . . .

Material. The term "material," when used to qualify a requirement for the furnishing of information as to any subject, limits the information required to those matters to which there is a substantial likelihood that a reasonable investor would attach importance in determining whether to purchase the security registered.

Officer. The term "officer" means a president, vice president, secretary, treasurer or principal financial officer, comptroller or principal accounting officer, and any person routinely performing corresponding functions with respect to any organization whether incorporated or unincorporated.

Parent. A "parent" of a specified person is an affiliate controlling such person directly, or indirectly through one or more intermediaries. . . .

Principal underwriter. The term "principal underwriter" means an underwriter in privity of contract with the issuer of the securities as to which he is underwriter, the term "issuer" having the meaning given in sections 2(4) and 2(11) of the Act.

Promoter. (1) The term "promoter" includes:

(i) Any person who, acting alone or in conjunction with one or more other persons, directly or indirectly takes initiative in founding and organizing the business or enterprise of an issuer; or

(ii) Any person who, in connection with the founding and organizing of the business or enterprise of an issuer, directly or indirectly receives in consideration of services or property, or both services and property, 10 percent or more of any class of securities of the issuer or 10 percent or more of the proceeds from the sale of any class of such securities. However, a person who receives such securities or proceeds either solely as underwriting commissions or solely in consideration of property shall not be deemed a promoter within the meaning of this paragraph if such person does not otherwise take part in founding and organizing the enterprise.

(2) All persons coming within the definition of "promoter" in paragraph (1) of this definition may be referred to as "founders" or "organizers" or by another term provided that such term is reasonably descriptive of those persons' activities with respect to the issuer. . . .

Smaller reporting company: As used in this part, the term *smaller reporting company* means an issuer that is not an investment company, an asset-backed issuer (as defined in Item 1101 of Regulation S–K), or a majority-owned subsidiary of a parent that is not a smaller reporting company and that:

(1) Had a public float of less than $75 million as of the last business day of its most recently completed second fiscal quarter, computed by multiplying the aggregate worldwide number of shares of its voting and non-voting common equity held by non-affiliates by the price at which the common equity was last sold, or the average of the bid and asked prices of common equity, in the principal market for the common equity; or

(2) In the case of an initial registration statement under the Securities Act or Exchange Act for shares of its common equity, had a public float of less than $75 million as of a date within 30 days of the date of the filing of the registration statement, computed by multiplying the aggregate worldwide number of such shares held by non-affiliates before the registration plus, in the case of a Securities Act registration statement, the number of such shares included in the registration statement by the estimated public offering price of the shares; or

(3) In the case of an issuer whose public float as calculated under paragraph (1) or (2) of this definition was zero, had annual revenues of less than $50 million during the most recently completed fiscal year for which audited financial statements are available. . . .

Subsidiary. A "subsidiary" of a specified person is an affiliate controlled by such person directly, or indirectly through one or more intermediaries. . . .

Voting securities. The term "voting securities" means securities the holders of which are presently entitled to vote for the election of directors. . . .

Well-known seasoned issuer. A *well-known seasoned issuer* is an issuer that, as of the most recent determination date determined pursuant to paragraph (2) of this definition:

(1)(i) Meets all the registrant requirements of General Instruction I.A. of Form S-3 . . . F-3 and either:

(A) As of a date within 60 days of the determination date, has a worldwide market value of its outstanding voting and non-voting common equity held by non-affiliates of $700 million or more; or

(B)(1) As of a date within 60 days of the determination date, has issued in the last three years at least $1 billion aggregate principal amount of non-convertible securities, other than common equity, in primary offerings for cash, not exchange, registered under the Act; and

(2) Will register only non-convertible securities, other than common equity, and full and unconditional guarantees permitted pursuant to paragraph (1)(ii) of this definition unless, at the determination date, the issuer also is eligible to register a primary offering of its securities relying on General Instruction I.B.1. of Form S-3. . . .

(3) Provided that as to a parent issuer only, for purposes of calculating the aggregate principal amount of outstanding non-convertible securities under paragraph (1)(i)(B)(*1*) of this definition, the parent issuer may include the aggregate principal amount of non-convertible securities, other than common equity, of its majority-owned subsidiaries issued in registered primary offerings for cash, not exchange, that it has fully and unconditionally guaranteed, within the meaning of Rule 3–10 of Regulation S–X in the last three years; or

(ii) Is a majority-owned subsidiary of a parent that is a well-known seasoned issuer pursuant to paragraph (1)(i) of this definition and, as to the subsidiaries' securities that are being or may be offered on that parent's registration statement:

(A) The parent has provided a full and unconditional guarantee, as defined in Rule 3–10 of Regulation S–X, of the payment obligations on the subsidiary's securities and the securities are non-convertible securities, other than common equity;

(B) The securities are guarantees of:

(1) Non-convertible securities, other than common equity, of its parent being registered; or

(2) Non-convertible securities, other than common equity, of another majority-owned subsidiary being registered where there is a full and unconditional guarantee, as defined in Rule 3–10 of Regulation S–X, of such non-convertible securities by the parent; or

(C) The securities of the majority-owned subsidiary meet the conditions of General Instruction I.B.2 of Form S-3. . . .

(iii) Is not an ineligible issuer as defined in this section. . . .

(2) For purposes of this definition, the determination date as to whether an issuer is a well-known seasoned issuer shall be the latest of:

(i) The time of filing of its most recent shelf registration statement; or

(ii) The time of its most recent amendment (by post-effective amendment, incorporated report filed pursuant to section 13 or 15(d) of the Securities Exchange Act of 1934, or form of prospectus) to a shelf registration statement for purposes of complying with section 10(a)(3) of the Act (or if such amendment has not been made within the time period required by section 10(a)(3) of the Act, the date on which such amendment is required); or

(iii) In the event that the issuer has not filed a shelf registration statement or amended a shelf registration statement for purposes of complying with section 10(a)(3) of the Act for sixteen months, the time of filing of the issuer's most recent annual report on Form 10-K . . . (or if such report has not been filed by its due date, such due date).

Written communication. Except as otherwise specifically provided or the context otherwise requires, a *written communication* is any communication that is written, printed, a radio or television broadcast, or a graphic communication as defined in this section.

Note to definition of "written communication." A communication that is a radio or television broadcast is a written communication regardless of the means of transmission of the broadcast.

Rule 408.   Additional Information

(a) In addition to the information expressly required to be included in a registration statement, there shall be added such further material information, if any, as may be necessary to make the required statements, in the light of the circumstances under which they are made, not misleading.

(b) Notwithstanding paragraph (a) of this section, unless otherwise required to be included in the registration statement, the failure to include in a registration statement information included in a free writing prospectus will not, solely by virtue of inclusion of the information in a free writing prospectus (as defined in Rule 405), be considered an omission of material information required to be included in the registration statement.

Rule 415.   Delayed or Continuous Offering and Sale of Securities

(a) Securities may be registered for an offering to be made on a continuous or delayed basis in the future, *Provided,* That:

(1) The registration statement pertains only to:

(i) Securities which are to be offered or sold solely by or on behalf of a person or persons other than the registrant, a subsidiary of the registrant or a person of which the registrant is a subsidiary;

(ii) Securities which are to be offered and sold pursuant to a dividend or interest reinvestment plan or an employee benefit plan of the registrant;

(iii) Securities which are to be issued upon the exercise of outstanding options, warrants or rights;

(iv) Securities which are to be issued upon conversion of other outstanding securities;

(v) Securities which are pledged as collateral . . . ;

(vii) Mortgage related securities, including such securities as mortgage backed debt and mortgage participation or pass through certificates;

(viii) Securities which are to be issued in connection with business combination transactions;

(ix) Securities the offering of which will be commenced promptly, will be made on a continuous basis and may continue for a period in excess of 30 days from the date of initial effectiveness;

(x) Securities registered (or qualified to be registered) on Form S-3 . . . which are to be offered and sold on an immediate, continuous or delayed basis by or on behalf of the registrant, a majority-owned subsidiary of the registrant or a person of which the registrant is a majority-owned subsidiary. . . .

(2) Securities in paragraph (a)(1)(viii) of this section and securities in paragraph (a)(1)(ix) of this section that are not registered on Form S-3 . . . may only be registered in an amount which, at the time the registration statement becomes effective, is reasonably expected to be offered and sold within two years from the initial effective date of the registration.

(3) The registrant furnishes the undertakings required by Item 512(a) of Regulation S–K. . . .

(4) In the case of a registration statement pertaining to an at the market offering of equity securities by or on behalf of the registrant, the offering must come within paragraph (a)(1)(x) of this section. As used in this paragraph, the term "at the market offering" means an offering of equity securities into an existing trading market for outstanding shares of the same class at other than a fixed price.

(5) Securities registered on an automatic shelf registration statement and securities described in paragraphs (a)(1)(vii), (ix), and (x) of this section may be offered and sold only if not more than three years have elapsed since the initial effective date of the registration statement under which they are being offered and sold, *provided, however,* that if a new registration statement has been filed pursuant to paragraph (a)(6) of this section:

(i) If the new registration statement is an automatic shelf registration statement, it shall be immediately effective . . . ; or

(ii) If the new registration statement is not an automatic shelf registration statement:

(A) Securities covered by the prior registration statement may continue to be offered and sold until the earlier of the effective date of the new registration statement or 180 days after the third anniversary of the initial effective date of the prior registration statement; and

(B) A continuous offering of securities covered by the prior registration statement that commenced within three years of the initial effective date may continue until the effective date of the new registration statement if such offering is permitted under the new registration statement.

(6) Prior to the end of the three-year period described in paragraph (a)(5) of this section, an issuer may file a new registration statement covering securities described in such paragraph (a)(5) of this section, which may, if permitted, be an automatic shelf registration statement. The new registration statement and prospectus included therein must include all the information that would be required at that time in a prospectus relating to all offering(s) that it covers. Prior to the effective date of the new registration statement (including at the time of filing in the case of an automatic shelf registration statement), the issuer may include on such new registration statement any unsold securities covered by the earlier registration statement by identifying on the bottom of the facing page of the new registration statement or latest amendment thereto the amount of such unsold securities being included and any filing fee paid in connection with such unsold securities, which will continue to be applied to such unsold securities. The offering of securities on the earlier registration statement will be deemed terminated as of the date of effectiveness of the new registration statement.

Rule 421.   Presentation of Information in Prospectuses. . . .

(b) You must present the information in a prospectus in a clear, concise and understandable manner. You must prepare the prospectus using the following standards:

(1) Present information in clear, concise sections, paragraphs, and sentences. Whenever possible, use short, explanatory sentences and bullet lists;

(2) Use descriptive headings and subheadings;

(3) Avoid frequent reliance on glossaries or defined terms as the primary means of explaining information in the prospectus. Define terms in a glossary or other section of the document only if the meaning is unclear from the context. Use a glossary only if it facilitates understanding of the disclosure; and

(4) Avoid legal and highly technical business terminology.

Note to Rule 421(b)

In drafting the disclosure to comply with this section, you should avoid the following:

1.   Legalistic or overly complex presentations that make the substance of the disclosure difficult to understand;

2.   Vague "boilerplate" explanations that are imprecise and readily subject to different interpretations;

3.   Complex information copied directly from legal documents without any clear and concise explanation of the provision(s); and

4.   Disclosure repeated in different sections of the document that increases the size of the document but does not enhance the quality of the information. . . .

(d)(1) To enhance the readability of the prospectus, you must use plain English principles in the organization, language, and design of the front and back cover pages, the summary, and the risk factors section.

(2) You must draft the language in these sections so that at a minimum it substantially complies with each of the following plain English writing principles:

(i) Short sentences;

(ii) Definite, concrete, everyday words;

(iii) Active voice;

(iv) Tabular presentation or bullet lists for complex material, whenever possible;

(v) No legal jargon or highly technical business terms; and

(vi) No multiple negatives.

(3) In designing these sections or other sections of the prospectus, you may include pictures, logos, charts, graphs, or other design elements so long as the design is not misleading and the required information is clear. You are encouraged to use tables, schedules, charts and graphic illustrations of the results of operations, balance sheet, or other financial data that present the data in an understandable manner. Any presentation must be consistent with the financial statements and non-financial information in the prospectus. You must draw the graphs and charts to scale. Any information you provide must not be misleading.

Rule 425.   Filing of Certain Prospectuses and Communications under Rule 135 in Connection with Business Combination Transactions

(a) All written communications made in reliance on Rule 165 are prospectuses that must be filed with the Commission under this section on the date of first use.

(b) All written communications that contain no more information than that specified in Rule 135 must be filed with the Commission on or before the date of first use except as provided in paragraph (d)(1) of this section. A communication limited to the information specified in Rule 135 will not be deemed an offer in accordance with Rule 135 even though it is filed under this section.

(c) Each prospectus or Rule 135 communication filed under this section must identify the filer, the company that is the subject of the offering and the Commission file number for the related registration statement or, if that file number is unknown, the subject company's Exchange Act or Investment Company Act file number, in the upper right corner of the cover page.

(d) Notwithstanding paragraph (a) of this section, the following need not be filed under this section:

(1) Any written communication that is limited to the information specified in Rule 135 and does not contain new or different information from that which was previously publicly disclosed and filed under this section.

(2) Any research report used in reliance on Rule 137, Rule 138 and Rule 139;

(3) Any confirmation described in Rule 10b–10 [under the Securities Exchange Act]; and

(4) Any prospectus filed under Rule 424.

Rule 427.   Contents of Prospectus Used After Nine Months

There may be omitted from any prospectus used more than 9 months after the effective date of the registration statement any information previously required to be contained in the prospectus insofar as later information covering the same subjects, including the latest available certified financial statement, as of a date not more than 16 months prior to the use of the prospectus is contained therein.

Rule 430.   Prospectus for Use Prior to Effective Date

A form of prospectus filed as a part of the registration statement shall be deemed to meet the requirements of section 10 of the Act for the purpose of section 5(b)(1) thereof prior to the effective date of the registration statement, provided such form of prospectus contains substantially the information required by the Act and the rules and regulations thereunder to be included in a prospectus meeting the requirements of section 10(a) of the Act for the securities being registered, or contains substantially that information except for the omission of information with respect to the offering price, underwriting discounts or commissions, discounts or commissions to dealers, amount of proceeds, conversion rates, call prices, or other matters dependent upon the offering price. Every such form of prospectus shall be deemed to have been filed as a part of the registration statement for the purpose of section 7 of the Act.

Rule 431.   Summary Prospectuses

(a) A summary prospectus prepared and filed as a part of a registration statement in accordance with this rule shall be deemed to be a prospectus permitted under section 10(b) of the Act for the purpose of section 5(b)(1) of the Act if the form used for registration of the securities to be offered provides for the use of a summary prospectus and, if the issuer is not a registered open-end investment company, the following conditions are met:

(1)(i) The registrant is organized under the laws of the United States or any State or Territory or the District of Columbia and has its principal business operations in the United States or its territories; or

(ii) The registrant is a foreign private issuer eligible to use Form F-2 . . . ;

(2) The registrant has a class of securities registered pursuant to section 12(b) of the Securities Exchange Act of 1934 or has a class of equity securities registered pursuant to section 12(g) of that Act or is required to file reports pursuant to section 15(d) of that Act;

(3) The registrant: (i) Has been subject to the requirements of section 12 or 15(d) of the Securities Exchange Act of 1934 and has filed all the material required to be filed pursuant to sections 13, 14 or 15(d) of that Act for a period of at least thirty-six calendar months immediately preceding the filing of the registration statement; and (ii) has filed in a timely manner all reports required to be filed during the twelve calendar months and any portion of a month immediately preceding the filing of the registration statement and . . .

(4) Neither the registrant nor any of its consolidated or unconsolidated subsidiaries has, since the end of its last fiscal year for which certified financial statements of the registrant and its consolidated subsidiaries were included in a report filed pursuant to section 13(a) or 15(d) of the Securities Exchange Act of 1934: (i) failed to pay any dividend or sinking fund installment on preferred stock; or (ii) defaulted on any

installment or installments on indebtedness for borrowed money, or on any rental on one or more long term leases, which defaults in the aggregate are material to the financial position of the registrant and its consolidated and unconsolidated subsidiaries, taken as a whole.

(b) A summary prospectus shall contain the information specified in the instructions as to summary prospectuses in the form used for registration of the securities to be offered. Such prospectus may include any other information the substance of which is contained in the registration statement except as otherwise specifically provided in the instructions as to summary prospectuses in the form used for registration. It shall not include any information the substance of which is not contained in the registration statement except that a summary prospectus may contain any information specified in Rule 134(a). . . .

(c) All information included in a summary prospectus, other than the statement required by paragraph (e) of this section, may be expressed in such condensed or summarized form as may be appropriate in the light of the circumstances under which the prospectus is to be used. The information need not follow the numerical sequence of the items of the form used for registration. Every summary prospectus shall be dated approximately as of the date of its first use.

(d) When used prior to the effective date of the registration statement, a summary prospectus shall be captioned a "Preliminary Summary Prospectus" and shall comply with the applicable requirements relating to a preliminary prospectus.

(e) A statement to the following effect shall be prominently set forth in conspicuous print at the beginning or at the end of every summary prospectus:

"Copies of a more complete prospectus may be obtained from" (Insert name(s), address(es) and telephone number(s)).

Copies of a summary prospectus filed with the Commission pursuant to paragraph (g) of this section may omit the names of persons from whom the complete prospectus may be obtained.

(f) Any summary prospectus published in a newspaper, magazine or other periodical need only be set in type at least as large as 7 point modern type. Nothing in this rule shall prevent the use of reprints of a summary prospectus published in a newspaper, magazine, or other periodical, if such reprints are clearly legible.

(g) Eight copies of every proposed summary prospectus shall be filed as a part of the registration statement, or as an amendment thereto, at least 5 days (exclusive of Saturdays, Sundays and holidays) prior to the use thereof, or prior to the release for publication by any newspaper, magazine or other person, whichever is earlier. The Commission may, however, in its discretion, authorize such use or publication prior to the expiration of the 5-day period upon a written request for such authorization. Within 7 days after the first use or publication thereof, 5 additional copies shall be filed in the exact form in which it was used or published. . . .

Rule 432. Additional Information Required to be Included in Prospectuses Relating to Tender Offers

Notwithstanding the provisions of any form for the registration of securities under the Act, any prospectus relating to securities to be offered in connection with a tender offer for, or a request or invitation for tenders of, securities subject to either Rule 13e–4 or section 14(d) of the Securities Exchange Act of 1934 must include the information required by Rule 13e–4(d)(1) or Rule 14d–6(d)(1), as applicable, in all tender offers, requests or invitations that are published, sent or given to security holders.

Rule 433. Conditions to Permissible Post-filing Free Writing Prospectuses

(a) *Scope of section.* This section applies to any free writing prospectus with respect to securities of any issuer (except as set forth in Rule 164) that are the subject of a registration statement that has been filed under the Act. Such a free writing prospectus that satisfies the conditions of this section may include information the substance of which is not included in the registration statement. Such a free writing prospectus that satisfies the conditions of this section will be a prospectus permitted under section 10(b) of the Act for purposes of sections 2(a)(10), 5(b)(1), and 5(b)(2) of the Act and will, for purposes of considering it a prospectus, be deemed to be public, without regard to its method of use or distribution, because it is related to the public offering of securities that are the subject of a filed registration statement.

(b) *Permitted use of free writing prospectus.* Subject to the conditions of this paragraph (b) and satisfaction of the conditions set forth in paragraphs (c) through (g) of this section, a free writing prospectus may be used under this section and Rule 164 in connection with a registered offering of securities:

(1) *Eligibility and prospectus conditions for seasoned issuers and well-known seasoned issuers.* Subject to the provisions of Rule 164(e), (f), and (g), the issuer or any other offering participant may use a free writing prospectus in the following offerings after a registration statement relating to the offering has been filed that includes a prospectus that, other than by reason of this section or Rule 431, satisfies the requirements of section 10 of the Act:

(i) Offerings of securities registered on Form S-3 pursuant to General Instruction I.B.1, I.B.2, I.B.5, I.C., or I.D. thereof; . . .

(iii) Any other offering not excluded from reliance on this section and Rule 164 of securities of a well-known seasoned issuer; and . . .

(2) *Eligibility and prospectus conditions for non-reporting and unseasoned issuers.* If the issuer does not fall within the provisions of paragraph (b)(1) of this section, then, subject to the provisions of Rule 164(e), (f), and (g), any person participating in the offer or sale of the securities may use a free writing prospectus as follows:

(i) If the free writing prospectus is or was prepared by or on behalf of or used or referred to by an issuer or any other offering participant, if consideration has been or will be given by the issuer or other offering participant for the dissemination (in any format) of any free writing prospectus (including any published article, publication, or advertisement), or if section 17(b) of the Act requires disclosure that consideration has been or will be given by the issuer or other offering participant for any activity described therein in connection with the free writing prospectus, then a registration statement relating to the offering must have been filed that includes a prospectus that, other than by reason of this section or Rule 431, satisfies the requirements of section 10 of the Act, including a price range where required by rule, and the free writing prospectus shall be accompanied or preceded by the most recent such prospectus; *provided, however,* that use of the free writing prospectus is not conditioned on providing the most recent such prospectus if a prior such prospectus has been provided and there is no material change from the prior prospectus reflected in the most recent prospectus; *provided, further* that after effectiveness and availability of a final prospectus meeting the requirements of section 10(a) of the Act, no such earlier prospectus may be provided in satisfaction of this condition, and such final prospectus must precede or accompany any free writing prospectus provided after such availability, whether or not an earlier prospectus had been previously provided. For purposes of paragraph (f) of this section, the prospectus included in the registration statement relating to the offering that has been filed does not have to include a price range otherwise required by rule.

(c) *Information in a free writing prospectus.*

(1) A free writing prospectus used in reliance on this section may include information the substance of which is not included in the registration statement but such information shall not conflict with:

(i) Information contained in the filed registration statement, including any prospectus or prospectus supplement that is part of the registration statement . . . and not superseded or modified; or

(ii) Information contained in the issuer's periodic and current reports filed or furnished to the Commission pursuant to section 13 or 15(d) of the Securities Exchange Act of 1934 that are incorporated by reference into the registration statement and not superseded or modified.

(2)(i) A free writing prospectus used in reliance on this section shall contain substantially the following legend:

The issuer has filed a registration statement (including a prospectus) with the SEC for the offering to which this communication relates. Before you invest, you should read the prospectus in that registration statement and other documents the issuer has filed with the SEC for more complete information about the issuer and this offering. You may get these documents for free by visiting EDGAR on the SEC Web site at www.sec.gov. Alternatively, the issuer, any underwriter or any dealer participating in the offering will arrange to send you the prospectus if you request it by calling toll-free 1-8[xx-xxx-xxxx].

(ii) The legend also may provide an e-mail address at which the documents can be requested and may indicate that the documents also are available by accessing the issuer's Web site and provide the Internet address and the particular location of the documents on the Web site. . . .

(h) *Definitions. For purposes of this section*:

(1) An *issuer free writing prospectus* means a free writing prospectus prepared by or on behalf of the issuer or used or referred to by the issuer. . . .

(2) *Issuer information* means material information about the issuer or its securities that has been provided by or on behalf of the issuer.

(3) A written communication or information is prepared or provided by or on behalf of a person if the person or an agent or representative of the person authorizes the communication or information or approves the communication or information before it is used. An offering participant other than the issuer shall not be an agent or representative of the issuer solely by virtue of its acting as an offering participant. . . .

Rule 460. Distribution of Preliminary Prospectus

(a) Pursuant to the statutory requirement that the Commission in ruling upon requests for acceleration of the effective date of a registration statement shall have due regard to the adequacy of the information respecting the issuer theretofore available to the public, the Commission may consider whether the persons making the offering have taken reasonable steps to make the information contained in the registration statement conveniently available to underwriters and dealers who it is reasonably anticipated will be invited to participate in the distribution of the security to be offered or sold.

(b) As a minimum, reasonable steps to make the information conveniently available would involve the distribution, to each underwriter and dealer who it is reasonably anticipated will be invited to participate in the distribution of the security, a reasonable time in advance of the anticipated effective date of the registration statement, of as many copies of the proposed form of preliminary prospectus permitted by Rule 430 . . . as appears to be reasonable to secure adequate distribution of the preliminary prospectus. . . .

Rule 461. Acceleration of Effective Date

(a) Requests for acceleration of the effective date of a registration statement shall be made by the registrant and the managing underwriters of the proposed issue, or, if there are no managing underwriters, by the principal underwriters of the proposed issue, and shall state the date upon which it is desired that the registration statement shall become effective. Such requests may be made in writing or orally, provided that, if an oral request is to be made, a letter indicating that fact and stating that the registrant and the managing or principal underwriters are aware of their obligations under the Act must accompany the registration statement (or a pre-effective amendment thereto) at the time of filing with the Commission. Written requests may be sent to the Commission by facsimile transmission. If by reason of the expected arrangement in connection with the offering, it is to be requested that the registration statement shall become effective at a particular hour of the day, the Commission must be advised to that effect not later than the second business day before the day which it is desired that the registration statement shall become effective. A person's request for acceleration will be considered confirmation of such person's awareness of the person's obligations under the Act. Not later than the time of filing the last amendment prior to the effective date of the registration statement, the registrant shall inform the Commission as to whether or not the amount of compensation to be allowed or paid to the underwriters and any other arrangements among the registrant, the underwriters and other broker dealers participating in the distribution, as described in the registration statement, have been reviewed to the extent required by the National Association of Securities Dealers, Inc. and such Association has issued a statement expressing no objections to the compensation and other arrangements.

(b) Having due regard to the adequacy of information respecting the registrant theretofore available to the public, to the facility with which the nature of the securities to be registered, their relationship to the capital structure of the registrant issuer and the rights of holders thereof can be understood, and to the public interest and the protection of investors, as provided in section 8(a) of the Act, it is the general policy of the Commission, upon request, as provided in paragraph (a) of this section, to permit acceleration of the effective date of the registration statement as soon as possible after the filing of appropriate amendments, if any. In determining the date on which a registration statement shall become effective, the following are included in the situations in which the Commission considers that the statutory standards of section 8(a) may not be met and may refuse to accelerate the effective date:

(1) Where there has not been a bona fide effort to make the prospectus reasonably concise, readable, and in compliance with the plain English requirements of Rule 421(d) of Regulation C in order to facilitate an understanding of the information in the prospectus.

(2) Where the form of preliminary prospectus, which has been distributed by the issuer or underwriter, is found to be inaccurate or inadequate in any material respect, until the Commission has received satisfactory assurance that appropriate correcting material has been sent to all underwriters and dealers who received such preliminary prospectus or prospectuses in quantity sufficient for their information and the information of others to whom the inaccurate or inadequate material was sent.

(3) Where the Commission is currently making an investigation of the issuer, a person controlling the issuer, or one of the underwriters, if any, of the securities to be offered, pursuant to any of the Acts administered by the Commission. . . .

(5) Where there have been transactions in securities of the registrant by persons connected with or proposed to be connected with the offering which may have artificially affected or may artificially affect the market price of the security being offered.

(6) Where the amount of compensation to be allowed or paid to the underwriters and any other arrangements among the registrant, the underwriters and other broker dealers participating in the distribution, as described in the registration statement, if required to be reviewed by the National Association of Securities Dealers, Inc. (NASD), have been reviewed by the NASD and the NASD has not issued a statement expressing no objections to the compensation and other arrangements.

(c) Insurance against liabilities arising under the Act, whether the cost of insurance is borne by the registrant, the insured or some other person, will not be considered a bar to acceleration, unless the registrant is a registered investment company or a business development company and the cost of such insurance is borne by other than an insured officer or director of the registrant. In the case of such a registrant, the Commission may refuse to accelerate the effective date of the registration statement when the registrant is organized or administered pursuant to any instrument (including a contract for insurance against liabilities arising under the Act) that protects or purports to protect any director or officer of the company against any liability to the company or its security holders to which he or she would otherwise be subject by reason of willful misfeasance, bad faith, gross negligence or reckless disregard of the duties involved in the conduct of his or her office.

REGULATION D—RULES GOVERNING THE LIMITED OFFER AND SALE OF SECURITIES WITHOUT REGISTRATION UNDER THE SECURITIES ACT OF 1933

Rule 500.   Use of Regulation D

Users of Regulation D (§§ 230.500 et seq.) should note the following:

(a) Regulation D relates to transactions exempted from the registration requirements of section 5 of the Securities Act of 1933 (the Act) (15 U.S.C.77a et seq., as amended). Such transactions are not exempt from the antifraud, civil liability, or other provisions of the federal securities laws. Issuers are reminded of their obligation to provide such further material information, if any, as may be necessary to make the information required under Regulation D, in light of the circumstances under which it is furnished, not misleading.

(b) Nothing in Regulation D obviates the need to comply with any applicable state law relating to the offer and sale of securities. Regulation D is intended to be a basic element in a uniform system of federal-state limited offering exemptions consistent with the provisions of sections 18 and 19(c) of the Act (15 U.S.C. 77r and 77(s)(c)). In those states that have adopted Regulation D, or any version of Regulation D, special attention should be directed to the applicable state laws and regulations, including those relating to registration of persons who receive remuneration in connection with the offer and sale of securities, to disqualification of issuers and other persons associated with offerings based on state administrative orders or judgments, and to requirements for filings of notices of sales.

(c) Attempted compliance with any rule in Regulation D does not act as an exclusive election; the issuer can also claim the availability of any other applicable exemption. For instance, an issuer's failure to satisfy all the terms and conditions of rule 506(b) (§ 230.506(b)) shall not raise any presumption that the exemption provided by section 4(a)(2) of the Act (15 U.S.C. 77d(2)) is not available.

(d) Regulation D is available only to the issuer of the securities and not to any affiliate of that issuer or to any other person for resales of the issuer's securities. Regulation D provides an exemption only for the transactions in which the securities are offered or sold by the issuer, not for the securities themselves.

(e) Regulation D may be used for business combinations that involve sales by virtue of rule 145(a) (§ 230.145(a)) or otherwise.

(f) In view of the objectives of Regulation D and the policies underlying the Act, Regulation D is not available to any issuer for any transaction or chain of transactions that, although in technical compliance with Regulation D, is part of a plan or scheme to evade the registration provisions of the Act. In such cases, registration under the Act is required.

(g) Securities offered and sold outside the United States in accordance with Regulation S (§ 230.901 through 905) need not be registered under the Act. See Release No. 33–6863. Regulation S may be relied upon for such offers and sales even if coincident offers and sales are made in accordance with Regulation D inside the United States. Thus, for example, persons who are offered and sold securities in accordance with Regulation S would not be counted in the calculation of the number of purchasers under Regulation D. Similarly, proceeds from such sales would not be included in the aggregate offering price. The provisions of this paragraph (g), however, do not apply if the issuer elects to rely solely on Regulation D for offers or sales to persons made outside the United States.

Rule 501. Definitions and Terms Used in Regulation D

As used in Regulation D (§ 230.500 et seq. of this chapter), the following terms shall have the meaning indicated:

(a) Accredited investor. Accredited investor shall mean any person who comes within any of the following categories, or who the issuer reasonably believes comes within any of the following categories, at the time of the sale of the securities to that person:

(1) Any bank as defined in section 3(a)(2) of the Act, or any savings and loan association or other institution as defined in section 3(a)(5)(A) of the Act whether acting in its individual or fiduciary capacity; any broker or dealer registered pursuant to section 15 of the Securities Exchange Act of 1934; any insurance company as defined in section 2(a)(13) of the Act; any investment company registered under the Investment Company Act of 1940 or a business development company as defined in section 2(a)(48) of that Act; any Small Business Investment Company licensed by the U.S. Small Business Administration under section 301(c) or (d) of the Small Business Investment Act of 1958; any plan established and maintained by a state, its political subdivisions, or any agency or instrumentality of a state or its political subdivisions, for the benefit of its employees, if such plan has total assets in excess of $5,000,000; any employee benefit plan within the meaning of the Employee Retirement Income Security Act of 1974 if the investment decision is made by a plan fiduciary, as defined in section 3(21) of such act, which is either a bank, savings and loan association, insurance company, or registered investment adviser, or if the employee benefit plan has total assets in excess of $5,000,000 or, if a self-directed plan, with investment decisions made solely by persons that are accredited investors;

(2) Any private business development company as defined in section 202(a)(22) of the Investment Advisers Act of 1940;

(3) Any organization described in section 501(c)(3) of the Internal Revenue Code, corporation, Massachusetts or similar business trust, or partnership, not formed for the specific purpose of acquiring the securities offered, with total assets in excess of $5,000,000;

(4) Any director, executive officer, or general partner of the issuer of the securities being offered or sold, or any director, executive officer, or general partner of a general partner of that issuer;

(5) Any natural person whose individual net worth, or joint net worth with that person's spouse, exceeds $1,000,000.

(i) Except as provided in paragraph (a)(5)(ii) of this section, for purposes of calculating net worth under this paragraph (a)(5):

(A) The person's primary residence shall not be included as an asset;

(B) Indebtedness that is secured by the person's primary residence, up to the estimated fair market value of the primary residence at the time of the sale of securities, shall not be included as a liability (except that if the amount of such indebtedness outstanding at the time of sale of securities exceeds the amount outstanding 60 days before such time, other than as a result of the acquisition of the primary residence, the amount of such excess shall be included as a liability); and

(C) Indebtedness that is secured by the person's primary residence in excess of the estimated fair market value of the primary residence at the time of the sale of securities shall be included as a liability;

(ii) Paragraph (a)(5)(i) of this section will not apply to any calculation of a person's net worth made in connection with a purchase of securities in accordance with a right to purchase such securities, provided that:

(A) Such right was held by the person on July 20, 2010;

(B) The person qualified as an accredited investor on the basis of net worth at the time the person acquired such right; and

(C) The person held securities of the same issuer, other than such right, on July 20, 2010.

(6) Any natural person who had an individual income in excess of $200,000 in each of the two most recent years or joint income with that person's spouse in excess of $300,000 in each of those years and has a reasonable expectation of reaching the same income level in the current year;

(7) Any trust, with total assets in excess of $5,000,000, not formed for the specific purpose of acquiring the securities offered, whose purchase is directed by a sophisticated person as described in § 230.506(b)(2)(ii); and

(8) Any entity in which all of the equity owners are accredited investors.

(b) *Affiliate.* An affiliate of, or person affiliated with, a specified person shall mean a person that directly, or indirectly through one or more intermediaries, controls or is controlled by, or is under common control with, the person specified.

(c) *Aggregate offering price.* Aggregate offering price shall mean the sum of all cash, services, property, notes, cancellation of debt, or other consideration to be received by an issuer for issuance of its securities. Where securities are being offered for both cash and non-cash consideration, the aggregate offering price shall be based on the price at which the securities are offered for cash. Any portion of the aggregate offering price attributable to cash received in a foreign currency shall be translated into United States currency at the currency exchange rate in effect at a reasonable time prior to or on the date of the sale of the securities. If securities are not offered for cash, the aggregate offering price shall be based on the value of the consideration as established by bona fide sales of that consideration made within a reasonable time, or, in the absence of sales, on the fair value as determined by an accepted standard. Such valuations of non-cash consideration must be reasonable at the time made.

(d) *Business combination.* Business combination shall mean any transaction of the type specified in paragraph (a) of Rule 145 under the Act (17 CFR 230.145) and any transaction involving the acquisition by one issuer, in exchange for all or a part of its own or its parent's stock, of stock of another issuer if, immediately after the acquisition, the acquiring issuer has control of the other issuer (whether or not it had control before the acquisition).

(e) [Effective until May 22, 2017.] *Calculation of number of purchasers.* For purposes of calculating the number of purchasers under §§ 230.505(b) and 230.506(b) only, the following shall apply:

(e) [Effective May 22, 2017.] Calculation of number of purchasers. For purposes of calculating the number of purchasers under § 230.506(b) only, the following shall apply:

(1) The following purchasers shall be excluded:

(i) Any relative, spouse or relative of the spouse of a purchaser who has the same primary residence as the purchaser;

(ii) Any trust or estate in which a purchaser and any of the persons related to him as specified in paragraph (e)(1)(i) or (e)(1)(iii) of this section collectively have more than 50 percent of the beneficial interest (excluding contingent interests);

(iii) Any corporation or other organization of which a purchaser and any of the persons related to him as specified in paragraph (e)(1)(i) or (e)(1)(ii) of this section collectively are beneficial owners of more than 50 percent of the equity securities (excluding directors' qualifying shares) or equity interests; and

(iv) Any accredited investor.

(2) A corporation, partnership or other entity shall be counted as one purchaser. If, however, that entity is organized for the specific purpose of acquiring the securities offered and is not an accredited investor under paragraph (a)(8) of this section, then each beneficial owner of equity securities or equity interests in the entity shall count as a separate purchaser for all provisions of Regulation D (§§ 230.501–230.508), except to the extent provided in paragraph (e)(1) of this section.

(3) A non-contributory employee benefit plan within the meaning of Title I of the Employee Retirement Income Security Act of 1974 shall be counted as one purchaser where the trustee makes all investment decisions for the plan.

NOTE: The issuer must satisfy all the other provisions of Regulation D for all purchasers whether or not they are included in calculating the number of purchasers. Clients of an investment adviser or customers of a broker or dealer shall be considered the "purchasers" under Regulation D regardless of the amount of discretion given to the investment adviser or broker or dealer to act on behalf of the client or customer.

(f) Executive officer. Executive officer shall mean the president, any vice president in charge of a principal business unit, division or function (such as sales, administration or finance), any other officer who performs a policy making function, or any other person who performs similar policy making functions for the issuer. Executive officers of subsidiaries may be deemed executive officers of the issuer if they perform such policy making functions for the issuer.

(g) Final order. Final order shall mean a written directive or declaratory statement issued by a federal or state agency described in § 230.506(d)(1)(iii) under applicable statutory authority that provides for notice and an opportunity for hearing, which constitutes a final disposition or action by that federal or state agency.

(h) Issuer. The definition of the term issuer in section 2(a)(4) of the Act shall apply, except that in the case of a proceeding under the Federal Bankruptcy Code (11 U.S.C. 101 et seq.), the trustee or debtor in possession shall be considered the issuer in an offering under a plan or reorganization, if the securities are to be issued under the plan.

(i) Purchaser representative. Purchaser representative shall mean any person who satisfies all of the following conditions or who the issuer reasonably believes satisfies all of the following conditions:

(1) Is not an affiliate, director, officer or other employee of the issuer, or beneficial owner of 10 percent or more of any class of the equity securities or 10 percent or more of the equity interest in the issuer, except where the purchaser is:

(i) A relative of the purchaser representative by blood, marriage or adoption and not more remote than a first cousin;

(ii) A trust or estate in which the purchaser representative and any persons related to him as specified in paragraph (h)(1)(i) or (h)(1)(iii) of this section collectively have more than 50 percent of the beneficial interest (excluding contingent interest) or of which the purchaser representative serves as trustee, executor, or in any similar capacity; or

(iii) A corporation or other organization of which the purchaser representative and any persons related to him as specified in paragraph (h)(1)(i) or (h)(1)(ii) of this section collectively are the beneficial owners of more than 50 percent of the equity securities (excluding directors' qualifying shares) or equity interests;

(2) Has such knowledge and experience in financial and business matters that he is capable of evaluating, alone, or together with other purchaser representatives of the purchaser, or together with the purchaser, the merits and risks of the prospective investment;

(3) Is acknowledged by the purchaser in writing, during the course of the transaction, to be his purchaser representative in connection with evaluating the merits and risks of the prospective investment; and

(4) Discloses to the purchaser in writing a reasonable time prior to the sale of securities to that purchaser any material relationship between himself or his affiliates and the issuer or its affiliates that then exists, that is mutually understood to be contemplated, or that has existed at any time during the previous two years, and any compensation received or to be received as a result of such relationship.

NOTE 1 to § 230.501: A person acting as a purchaser representative should consider the applicability of the registration and antifraud provisions relating to brokers and dealers under the Securities Exchange Act of 1934 (Exchange Act) (15 U.S.C. 78a et seq., as amended) and relating to investment advisers under the Investment Advisers Act of 1940.

NOTE 2 to § 230.501: The acknowledgment required by paragraph (h)(3) and the disclosure required by paragraph (h)(4) of this section must be made with specific reference to each prospective investment. Advance blanket acknowledgment, such as for all securities transactions or all private placements, is not sufficient.

NOTE 3 to § 230.501: Disclosure of any material relationships between the purchaser representative or his affiliates and the issuer or its affiliates does not relieve the purchaser representative of his obligation to act in the interest of the purchaser.

Rule 502.   General Conditions to Be Met

The following conditions shall be applicable to offers and sales made under Regulation D (§ 230.500 et seq. of this chapter):

(a) Integration. All sales that are part of the same Regulation D offering must meet all of the terms and conditions of Regulation D. Offers and sales that are made more than six months before the start of a Regulation D offering or are made more than six months after completion of a Regulation D offering will not be considered part of that Regulation D offering, so long as during those six month periods there are no offers or sales of securities by or for the issuer that are of the same or a similar class as those offered or sold under Regulation D, other than those offers or sales of securities under an employee benefit plan as defined in rule 405 under the Act (17 CFR 230.405).

NOTE: The term offering is not defined in the Act or in Regulation D. If the issuer offers or sells securities for which the safe harbor rule in paragraph (a) of this § 230.502 is unavailable, the determination as to whether separate sales of securities are part of the same offering (i.e. are considered integrated) depends on the particular facts and circumstances. Generally, transactions otherwise meeting the requirements of an exemption will not be integrated with simultaneous offerings being made outside the United States in compliance with Regulation S. See Release No. 33–6863.

The following factors should be considered in determining whether offers and sales should be integrated for purposes of the exemptions under Regulation D:

(a) Whether the sales are part of a single plan of financing;

(b) Whether the sales involve issuance of the same class of securities;

(c) Whether the sales have been made at or about the same time;

(d) Whether the same type of consideration is being received; and

(e) Whether the sales are made for the same general purpose.

See Release 33–4552 (November 6, 1962) [27 FR 11316].

(b) Information requirements—(1) When information must be furnished. If the issuer sells securities under § 230.506(b) to any purchaser that is not an accredited investor, the issuer shall furnish the information specified in paragraph (b)(2) of this section to such purchaser a reasonable time prior to sale. The issuer is not required to furnish the specified information to purchasers when it sells securities under § 230.504, or to any accredited investor.

> *NOTE*: When an issuer provides information to investors pursuant to paragraph (b)(1), it should consider providing such information to accredited investors as well, in view of the anti-fraud provisions of the federal securities laws.

(2) Type of information to be furnished. (i) If the issuer is not subject to the reporting requirements of section 13 or 15(d) of the Exchange Act, at a reasonable time prior to the sale of securities the issuer shall furnish to the purchaser, to the extent material to an understanding of the issuer, its business and the securities being offered:

(A) Non-financial statement information. If the issuer is eligible to use Regulation A (§ 230.251–263), the same kind of information as would be required in Part II of Form 1-A (§ 239.90 of this chapter). If the issuer is not eligible to use Regulation A, the same kind of information as required in Part I of a registration statement filed under the Securities Act on the form that the issuer would be entitled to use.

(B) Financial statement information.

(1) Offerings up to $2,000,000. The information required in Article 8 of Regulation S-X (§ 210.8 of this chapter), except that only the issuer's balance sheet, which shall be dated within 120 days of the start of the offering, must be audited.

(2) Offerings up to $7,500,000. The financial statement information required in Form S-1 (§ 239.10 of this chapter) for smaller reporting companies. If an issuer, other than a limited partnership, cannot obtain audited financial statements without unreasonable effort or expense, then only the issuer's balance sheet, which shall be dated within 120 days of the start of the offering, must be audited. If the issuer is a limited partnership and cannot obtain the required financial statements without unreasonable effort or expense, it may furnish financial statements that have been prepared on the basis of Federal income tax requirements and examined and reported on in accordance with generally accepted auditing standards by an independent public or certified accountant.

(3) Offerings over $7,500,000. The financial statement as would be required in a registration statement filed under the Act on the form that the issuer would be entitled to use. If an issuer, other than a limited partnership, cannot obtain audited financial statements without unreasonable effort or expense, then only the issuer's balance sheet, which shall be dated within 120 days of the start of the offering, must be audited. If the issuer is a limited partnership and cannot obtain the required financial statements without unreasonable effort or expense, it may furnish financial statements that have been prepared on the basis of Federal income tax requirements and examined and reported on in accordance with generally accepted auditing standards by an independent public or certified accountant.

(C) If the issuer is a foreign private issuer eligible to use Form 20-F (§ 249.220f of this chapter), the issuer shall disclose the same kind of information required to be included in a registration statement filed under the Act on the form that the issuer would be entitled to use. The financial statements need be certified only to the extent required by paragraph (b)(2)(i) (B) (1), (2) or (3) of this section, as appropriate.

(ii) If the issuer is subject to the reporting requirements of section 13 or 15(d) of the Exchange Act, at a reasonable time prior to the sale of securities the issuer shall furnish to the purchaser the information specified in paragraph (b)(2)(ii)(A) or (B) of this section, and in either event the information specified in paragraph (b)(2)(ii)(C) of this section:

(A) The issuer's annual report to shareholders for the most recent fiscal year, if such annual report meets the requirements of Rules 14a–3 or 14c–3 under the Exchange Act (§ 240.14a–3 or § 240.14c–3 of this chapter), the definitive proxy statement filed in connection with that annual report, and if requested by the purchaser in writing, a copy of the issuer's most recent Form 10-K (§ 249.310 of this chapter) under the Exchange Act.

(B) The information contained in an annual report on Form 10-K (§ 249.310 of this chapter) under the Exchange Act or in a registration statement on Form S-1 (§ 239.11 of this chapter) or S-11 (§ 239.18 of this chapter) under the Act or on Form 10 (§ 249.210 of this chapter) under the Exchange Act, whichever filing is the most recent required to be filed.

(C) The information contained in any reports or documents required to be filed by the issuer under sections 13(a), 14(a), 14(c), and 15(d) of the Exchange Act since the distribution or filing of the report or registration statement specified in paragraphs (b)(2)(ii) (A) or (B), and a brief description of the securities being offered, the use of the proceeds from the offering, and any material changes in the issuer's affairs that are not disclosed in the documents furnished.

(D) If the issuer is a foreign private issuer, the issuer may provide in lieu of the information specified in paragraph (b)(2)(ii) (A) or (B) of this section, the information contained in its most recent filing on Form 20-F or Form F-1 (§ 239.31 of the chapter).

(iii) Exhibits required to be filed with the Commission as part of a registration statement or report, other than an annual report to shareholders or parts of that report incorporated by reference in a Form 10-K report, need not be furnished to each purchaser that is not an accredited investor if the contents of material exhibits are identified and such exhibits are made available to a purchaser, upon his or her written request, a reasonable time before his or her purchase.

(iv) At a reasonable time prior to the sale of securities to any purchaser that is not an accredited investor in a transaction under § 230.506(b), the issuer shall furnish to the purchaser a brief description in writing of any material written information concerning the offering that has been provided by the issuer to any accredited investor but not previously delivered to such unaccredited purchaser. The issuer shall furnish any portion or all of this information to the purchaser, upon his written request a reasonable time prior to his purchase.

(v) The issuer shall also make available to each purchaser at a reasonable time prior to his purchase of securities in a transaction under § 230.506(b) the opportunity to ask questions and receive answers concerning the terms and conditions of the offering and to obtain any additional information which the issuer possesses or can acquire without unreasonable effort or expense that is necessary to verify the accuracy of information furnished under paragraph (b)(2) (i) or (ii) of this section.

(vi) For business combinations or exchange offers, in addition to information required by Form S-4 (17 CFR 239.25), the issuer shall provide to each purchaser at the time the plan is submitted to security holders, or, with an exchange, during the course of the transaction and prior to sale, written information about any terms or arrangements of the proposed transactions that are materially different from those for all other security holders. For purposes of this subsection, an issuer which is not subject to the reporting requirements of section 13 or 15(d) of the Exchange Act may satisfy the requirements of Part I.B. or C. of Form S-4 by compliance with paragraph (b)(2)(i) of this § 230.502.

(vii) At a reasonable time prior to the sale of securities to any purchaser that is not an accredited investor in a transaction under § 230.506(b), the issuer shall advise the purchaser of the limitations on resale in the manner contained in paragraph (d)(2) of this section. Such disclosure may be contained in other materials required to be provided by this paragraph.

(c) Limitation on manner of offering. Except as provided in § 230.504(b)(1) or § 230.506(c), neither the issuer nor any person acting on its behalf shall offer or sell the securities by any form of general solicitation or general advertising, including, but not limited to, the following:

(1) Any advertisement, article, notice or other communication published in any newspaper, magazine, or similar media or broadcast over television or radio; and

(2) Any seminar or meeting whose attendees have been invited by any general solicitation or general advertising; Provided, however, that publication by an issuer of a notice in accordance with § 230.135c or filing with the Commission by an issuer of a notice of sales on Form D (17 CFR 239.500) in which the issuer has made a good faith and reasonable attempt to comply with the requirements of such form, shall not be deemed to constitute general solicitation or general advertising for purposes of this section; Provided further, that, if the requirements of § 230.135e are satisfied, providing any journalist with access to press conferences held outside of the United States, to meetings with issuer or selling security holder

representatives conducted outside of the United States, or to written press-related materials released outside the United States, at or in which a present or proposed offering of securities is discussed, will not be deemed to constitute general solicitation or general advertising for purposes of this section.

(d) *Limitations on resale.* Except as provided in § 230.504(b)(1), securities acquired in a transaction under Regulation D shall have the status of securities acquired in a transaction under section 4(a)(2) of the Act and cannot be resold without registration under the Act or an exemption therefrom. The issuer shall exercise reasonable care to assure that the purchasers of the securities are not underwriters within the meaning of section 2(a)(11) of the Act, which reasonable care may be demonstrated by the following:

(1) Reasonable inquiry to determine if the purchaser is acquiring the securities for himself or for other persons;

(2) Written disclosure to each purchaser prior to sale that the securities have not been registered under the Act and, therefore, cannot be resold unless they are registered under the Act or unless an exemption from registration is available; and

(3) Placement of a legend on the certificate or other document that evidences the securities stating that the securities have not been registered under the Act and setting forth or referring to the restrictions on transferability and sale of the securities.

While taking these actions will establish the requisite reasonable care, it is not the exclusive method to demonstrate such care. Other actions by the issuer may satisfy this provision. In addition, § 230.502(b)(2)(vii) requires the delivery of written disclosure of the limitations on resale to investors in certain instances.

Rule 503.   Filing of Notice of Sales

(a) *When notice of sales on Form D is required and permitted to be filed.*

(1) [Effective until May 22, 2017.] An issuer offering or selling securities in reliance on § 230.504, § 230.505, or § 230.506 must file with the Commission a notice of sales containing the information required by Form D (17 CFR 239.500) for each new offering of securities no later than 15 calendar days after the first sale of securities in the offering, unless the end of that period falls on a Saturday, Sunday or holiday, in which case the due date would be the first business day following.

(2) An issuer may file an amendment to a previously filed notice of sales on Form D at any time.

(3) An issuer must file an amendment to a previously filed notice of sales on Form D for an offering:

(i) To correct a material mistake of fact or error in the previously filed notice of sales on Form D, as soon as practicable after discovery of the mistake or error;

(ii) To reflect a change in the information provided in the previously filed notice of sales on Form D, as soon as practicable after the change, except that no amendment is required to reflect a change that occurs after the offering terminates or a change that occurs solely in the following information:

(A) The address or relationship to the issuer of a related person identified in[[Page 10616 response to Item 3 of the notice of sales on Form D;

(B) An issuer's revenues or aggregate net asset value;

(C) The minimum investment amount, if the change is an increase, or if the change, together with all other changes in that amount since the previously filed notice of sales on Form D, does not result in a decrease of more than 10%;

(D) Any address or state(s) of solicitation shown in response to Item 12 of the notice of sales on Form D;

(E) The total offering amount, if the change is a decrease, or if the change, together with all other changes in that amount since the previously filed notice of sales on Form D, does not result in an increase of more than 10%;

(F) The amount of securities sold in the offering or the amount remaining to be sold;

(G) The number of non-accredited investors who have invested in the offering, as long as the change does not increase the number to more than 35;

(H) The total number of investors who have invested in the offering; or

(I) The amount of sales commissions, finders' fees or use of proceeds for payments to executive officers, directors or promoters, if the change is a decrease, or if the change, together with all other changes in that amount since the previously filed notice of sales on Form D, does not result in an increase of more than 10%; and

(iii) Annually, on or before the first anniversary of the filing of the notice of sales on Form D or the filing of the most recent amendment to the notice of sales on Form D, if the offering is continuing at that time.

(4) An issuer that files an amendment to a previously filed notice of sales on Form D must provide current information in response to all requirements of the notice of sales on Form D regardless of why the amendment is filed.

(b) How notice of sales on Form D must be filed and signed.

(1) A notice of sales on Form D must be filed with the Commission in electronic format by means of the Commission's Electronic Data Gathering, Analysis, and Retrieval System (EDGAR) in accordance with EDGAR rules set forth in Regulation S-T (17 CFR Part 232).

(2) Every notice of sales on Form D must be signed by a person duly authorized by the issuer.

Rule 504.   Exemption for Limited Offerings and Sales of Securities Not Exceeding $5,000,000

(a) Exemption. Offers and sales of securities that satisfy the conditions in paragraph (b) of this § 230.504 by an issuer that is not:

(1) Subject to the reporting requirements of section 13 or 15(d) of the Exchange Act,;

(2) An investment company; or

(3) A development stage company that either has no specific business plan or purpose or has indicated that its business plan is to engage in a merger or acquisition with an unidentified company or companies, or other entity or person, shall be exempt from the provision of section 5 of the Act under section 3(b) of the Act.

(b) Conditions to be met. (1) General conditions. To qualify for exemption under this § 230.504, offers and sales must satisfy the terms and conditions of §§ 230.501 and 230.502 (a), (c) and (d), except that the provisions of § 230.502 (c) and (d) will not apply to offers and sales of securities under this § 230.504 that are made:

(i) Exclusively in one or more states that provide for the registration of the securities, and require the public filing and delivery to investors of a substantive disclosure document before sale, and are made in accordance with those state provisions;

(ii) In one or more states that have no provision for the registration of the securities or the public filing or delivery of a disclosure document before sale, if the securities have been registered in at least one state that provides for such registration, public filing and delivery before sale, offers and sales are made in that state in accordance with such provisions, and the disclosure document is delivered before sale to all purchasers (including those in the states that have no such procedure); or

(iii) Exclusively according to state law exemptions from registration that permit general solicitation and general advertising so long as sales are made only to "accredited investors" as defined in § 230.501(a).

(2) The aggregate offering price for an offering of securities under this § 230.504, as defined in § 230.501(c), shall not exceed $5,000,000, less the aggregate offering price for all securities sold within the twelve months before the start of and during the offering of securities under this § 230.504, in violation of section 5(a) of the Securities Act.

Instruction to paragraph (b)(2): If a transaction under § 230.504 fails to meet the limitation on the aggregate offering price, it does not affect the availability of this § 230.504 for the other transactions considered in applying such limitation. For example, if an issuer sold $5,000,000 of its securities on January 1, 2014 under this § 230.504 and an additional $500,000 of its securities on July 1, 2014, this § 230.504 would not be available for the later sale, but would still be applicable to the January 1, 2014 sale.

(3) Disqualifications. No exemption under this section shall be available for the securities of any issuer if such issuer would be subject to disqualification under § 230.506(d) on or after January 20, 2017; provided that disclosure of prior "bad actor" events shall be required in accordance with § 230.506(e).

Instruction to paragraph (b)(3): For purposes of disclosure of prior "bad actor" events pursuant to § 230.506(e), an issuer shall furnish to each purchaser, a reasonable time prior to sale, a description in writing of any matters that would have triggered disqualification under this paragraph (b)(3) but occurred before January 20, 2017.

Rule 506.   Exemption for Limited Offers and Sales Without Regard to Dollar Amount of Offering

(a) Exemption. Offers and sales of securities by an issuer that satisfy the conditions in paragraph (b) or (c) of this section shall be deemed to be transactions not involving any public offering within the meaning of section 4(a)(2) of the Act.

(b) Conditions to be met in offerings subject to limitation on manner of offering—

(1) General conditions. To qualify for an exemption under this section, offers and sales must satisfy all the terms and conditions of §§ 230.501 and 230.502.

(2) Specific Conditions—(i) Limitation on number of purchasers. There are no more than or the issuer reasonably believes that there are no more than 35 purchasers of securities from the issuer in any offering under this section.

NOTE to paragraph (b)(2)(i): See § 230.501(e) for the calculation of the number of purchasers and § 230.502(a) for what may or may not constitute an offering under paragraph (b) of this section.

(ii) Nature of purchasers. Each purchaser who is not an accredited investor either alone or with his purchaser representative(s) has such knowledge and experience in financial and business matters that he is capable of evaluating the merits and risks of the prospective investment, or the issuer reasonably believes immediately prior to making any sale that such purchaser comes within this description.

(c) Conditions to be met in offerings not subject to limitation on manner of offering—(1) General conditions. To qualify for exemption under this section, sales must satisfy all the terms and conditions of §§ 230.501 and 230.502(a) and (d).

(2) Specific conditions—(i) Nature of purchasers. All purchasers of securities sold in any offering under paragraph (c) of this section are accredited investors.

(ii) Verification of accredited investor status. The issuer shall take reasonable steps to verify that purchasers of securities sold in any offering under paragraph (c) of this section are accredited investors. The issuer shall be deemed to take reasonable steps to verify if the issuer uses, at its option, one of the following non-exclusive and non-mandatory methods of verifying that a natural person who purchases securities in such offering is an accredited investor; provided, however, that the issuer does not have knowledge that such person is not an accredited investor:

(A) In regard to whether the purchaser is an accredited investor on the basis of income, reviewing any Internal Revenue Service form that reports the purchaser's income for the two most recent years (including, but not limited to, Form W-2, Form 1099, Schedule K-1 to Form 1065, and Form 1040) and obtaining a written representation from the purchaser that he or she has a reasonable expectation of reaching the income level necessary to qualify as an accredited investor during the current year;

(B) In regard to whether the purchaser is an accredited investor on the basis of net worth, reviewing one or more of the following types of documentation dated within the prior three months and obtaining a written representation from the purchaser that all liabilities necessary to make a determination of net worth have been disclosed:

(1) With respect to assets: Bank statements, brokerage statements and other statements of securities holdings, certificates of deposit, tax assessments, and appraisal reports issued by independent third parties; and

(2) With respect to liabilities: A consumer report from at least one of the nationwide consumer reporting agencies; or

(C) Obtaining a written confirmation from one of the following persons or entities that such person or entity has taken reasonable steps to verify that the purchaser is an accredited investor within the prior three months and has determined that such purchaser is an accredited investor:

(1) A registered broker-dealer;

(2) An investment adviser registered with the Securities and Exchange Commission;

(3) A licensed attorney who is in good standing under the laws of the jurisdictions in which he or she is admitted to practice law; or

(4) A certified public accountant who is duly registered and in good standing under the laws of the place of his or her residence or principal office.

(D) In regard to any person who purchased securities in an issuer's Rule 506(b) offering as an accredited investor prior to September 23, 2013 and continues to hold such securities, for the same issuer's Rule 506(c) offering, obtaining a certification by such person at the time of sale that he or she qualifies as an accredited investor.

Instructions to paragraph (c)(2)(ii)(A) through (D) of this section:

1. The issuer is not required to use any of these methods in verifying the accredited investor status of natural persons who are purchasers. These methods are examples of the types of non-exclusive and non-mandatory methods that satisfy the verification requirement in § 230.506(c)(2)(ii).

2. In the case of a person who qualifies as an accredited investor based on joint income with that person's spouse, the issuer would be deemed to satisfy the verification requirement in § 230.506(c)(2)(ii)(A) by reviewing copies of Internal Revenue Service forms that report income for the two most recent years in regard to, and obtaining written representations from, both the person and the spouse.

3. In the case of a person who qualifies as an accredited investor based on joint net worth with that person's spouse, the issuer would be deemed to satisfy the verification requirement in § 230.506(c)(2)(ii)(B) by reviewing such documentation in regard to, and obtaining written representations from, both the person and the spouse.

(d) "Bad Actor" disqualification. (1) No exemption under this section shall be available for a sale of securities if the issuer; any predecessor of the issuer; any affiliated issuer; any director, executive officer, other officer participating in the offering, general partner or managing member of the issuer; any beneficial owner of 20% or more of the issuer's outstanding voting equity securities, calculated on the basis of voting power; any promoter connected with the issuer in any capacity at the time of such sale; any investment manager of an issuer that is a pooled investment fund; any person that has been or will be paid (directly or indirectly) remuneration for solicitation of purchasers in connection with such sale of securities; any general partner or managing member of any such investment manager or solicitor; or any director, executive officer or other officer participating in the offering of any such investment manager or solicitor or general partner or managing member of such investment manager or solicitor:

(i) Has been convicted, within ten years before such sale (or five years, in the case of issuers, their predecessors and affiliated issuers), of any felony or misdemeanor:

(A) In connection with the purchase or sale of any security;

(B) Involving the making of any false filing with the Commission; or

(C) Arising out of the conduct of the business of an underwriter, broker, dealer, municipal securities dealer, investment adviser or paid solicitor of purchasers of securities;

(ii) Is subject to any order, judgment or decree of any court of competent jurisdiction, entered within five years before such sale, that, at the time of such sale, restrains or enjoins such person from engaging or continuing to engage in any conduct or practice:

(A) In connection with the purchase or sale of any security;

(B) Involving the making of any false filing with the Commission; or

(C) Arising out of the conduct of the business of an underwriter, broker, dealer, municipal securities dealer, investment adviser or paid solicitor of purchasers of securities;

(iii) Is subject to a final order of a state securities commission (or an agency or officer of a state performing like functions); a state authority that supervises or examines banks, savings associations, or credit unions; a state insurance commission (or an agency or officer of a state performing like functions); an appropriate federal banking agency; the U.S. Commodity Futures Trading Commission; or the National Credit Union Administration that:

(A) At the time of such sale, bars the person from:

(1) Association with an entity regulated by such commission, authority, agency, or officer;

(2) Engaging in the business of securities, insurance or banking; or

(3) Engaging in savings association or credit union activities; or

(B) Constitutes a final order based on a violation of any law or regulation that prohibits fraudulent, manipulative, or deceptive conduct entered within ten years before such sale;

(iv) Is subject to an order of the Commission entered pursuant to section 15(b) or 15B(c) of the Securities Exchange Act of 1934 (15 U.S.C. 78 o (b) or 78 o–4(c)) or section 203(e) or (f) of the Investment Advisers Act of 1940 (15 U.S.C. 80b–3(e) or (f)) that, at the time of such sale:

(A) Suspends or revokes such person's registration as a broker, dealer, municipal securities dealer or investment adviser;

(B) Places limitations on the activities, functions or operations of such person; or

(C) Bars such person from being associated with any entity or from participating in the offering of any penny stock;

(v) Is subject to any order of the Commission entered within five years before such sale that, at the time of such sale, orders the person to cease and desist from committing or causing a violation or future violation of:

(A) Any scienter-based anti-fraud provision of the federal securities laws, including without limitation section 17(a)(1) of the Securities Act of 1933 (15 U.S.C. 77q(a)(1)), section 10(b) of the Securities Exchange Act of 1934 (15 U.S.C. 78j(b)) and 17 CFR 240.10b–5, section 15(c)(1) of the Securities Exchange Act of 1934 (15 U.S.C. 78 o (c)(1)) and section 206(1) of the Investment Advisers Act of 1940 (15 U.S.C. 80b–6(1)), or any other rule or regulation thereunder; or

(B) Section 5 of the Securities Act of 1933 (15 U.S.C. 77e).

(vi) Is suspended or expelled from membership in, or suspended or barred from association with a member of, a registered national securities exchange or a registered national or affiliated securities association for any act or omission to act constituting conduct inconsistent with just and equitable principles of trade;

(vii) Has filed (as a registrant or issuer), or was or was named as an underwriter in, any registration statement or Regulation A offering statement filed with the Commission that, within five years before such sale, was the subject of a refusal order, stop order, or order suspending the Regulation A exemption, or is, at the time of such sale, the subject of an investigation or proceeding to determine whether a stop order or suspension order should be issued; or

(viii) Is subject to a United States Postal Service false representation order entered within five years before such sale, or is, at the time of such sale, subject to a temporary restraining order or preliminary injunction with respect to conduct alleged by the United States Postal Service to constitute a scheme or device for obtaining money or property through the mail by means of false representations.

(2) Paragraph (d)(1) of this section shall not apply:

(i) With respect to any conviction, order, judgment, decree, suspension, expulsion or bar that occurred or was issued before September 23, 2013;

(ii) Upon a showing of good cause and without prejudice to any other action by the Commission, if the Commission determines that it is not necessary under the circumstances that an exemption be denied;

(iii) If, before the relevant sale, the court or regulatory authority that entered the relevant order, judgment or decree advises in writing (whether contained in the relevant judgment, order or decree or separately to the Commission or its staff) that disqualification under paragraph (d)(1) of this section should not arise as a consequence of such order, judgment or decree; or

(iv) If the issuer establishes that it did not know and, in the exercise of reasonable care, could not have known that a disqualification existed under paragraph (d)(1) of this section.

Instruction to paragraph (d)(2)(iv). An issuer will not be able to establish that it has exercised reasonable care unless it has made, in light of the circumstances, factual inquiry into whether any disqualifications exist. The nature and scope of the factual inquiry will vary based on the facts and circumstances concerning, among other things, the issuer and the other offering participants.

(3) For purposes of paragraph (d)(1) of this section, events relating to any affiliated issuer that occurred before the affiliation arose will be not considered disqualifying if the affiliated entity is not:

(i) In control of the issuer; or

(ii) Under common control with the issuer by a third party that was in control of the affiliated entity at the time of such events.

(e) Disclosure of prior "bad actor" events. The issuer shall furnish to each purchaser, a reasonable time prior to sale, a description in writing of any matters that would have triggered disqualification under paragraph (d)(1) of this section but occurred before September 23, 2013. The failure to furnish such information timely shall not prevent an issuer from relying on this section if the issuer establishes that it did not know and, in the exercise of reasonable care, could not have known of the existence of the undisclosed matter or matters.

Instruction to paragraph (e). An issuer will not be able to establish that it has exercised reasonable care unless it has made, in light of the circumstances, factual inquiry into whether any disqualifications exist. The nature and scope of the factual inquiry will vary based on the facts and circumstances concerning, among other things, the issuer and the other offering participants.

Rule 507. Disqualifying Provision Relating to Exemptions Under §§ 230.504 and 230.506

(a) No exemption under § 230.504 or § 230.506 shall be available for an issuer if such issuer, any of its predecessors or affiliates have been subject to any order, judgment, or decree of any court of competent jurisdiction temporarily, preliminary or permanently enjoining such person for failure to comply with § 230.503.

(b) Paragraph (a) of this section shall not apply if the Commission determines, upon a showing of good cause, that it is not necessary under the circumstances that the exemption be denied.

Rule 508. Insignificant Deviations from a Term, Condition or Requirement of Regulation D

(a) A failure to comply with a term, condition or requirement of § 230.504, § 230.505 or § 230.506 will not result in the loss of the exemption from the requirements of section 5 of the Act for any offer or sale to a particular individual or entity, if the person relying on the exemption shows:

(1) The failure to comply did not pertain to a term, condition or requirement directly intended to protect that particular individual or entity; and

(2) The failure to comply was insignificant with respect to the offering as a whole, provided that any failure to comply with paragraph (c) of § 230.502, paragraph (b)(2) of § 230.504 paragraphs (b)(2)(i) and (ii) of § 230.505 and paragraph (b)(2)(i) of § 230.506 shall be deemed to be significant to the offering as a whole; and

(3) A good faith and reasonable attempt was made to comply with all applicable terms, conditions and requirements of § 230.504, § 230.505 or § 230.506.

(b) A transaction made in reliance on § 230.504, § 230.505 or § 230.506 shall comply with all applicable terms, conditions and requirements of Regulation D. Where an exemption is established only through reliance upon paragraph (a) of this section, the failure to comply shall nonetheless be actionable by the Commission under section 20 of the Act.

———

FORM S-1

REGISTRATION STATEMENT UNDER THE SECURITIES ACT OF 1933

_____

(Exact name of registrant as specified in its charter)

_____

(State or other jurisdiction of incorporation or organization)

_____

(Primary Standard Industrial Classification Code Number)

_____

(I.R.S. Employer Identification No.)

_____

(Address, including zip code, and telephone number,
including area code, of registrant's principal executive offices)

_____

(Name, address, including zip code, and telephone number,
including area code, of agent for service)

Approximate date of commencement of proposed sale to the public _____. . . .

GENERAL INSTRUCTIONS

I.   Eligibility Requirements for Use of Form S-1

This Form shall be used for the registration under the Securities Act of 1933 ("Securities Act") of securities of all registrants for which no other form is authorized or prescribed, except that this Form shall not be used for securities of foreign governments or political subdivisions thereof. . . .

PART I—INFORMATION REQUIRED IN PROSPECTUS. . . .

Item 3.   **Summary Information, Risk Factors and Ratio of Earnings to Fixed Charges.** . . .

Item 4.   **Use of Proceeds.** . . .

Item 5.   **Determination of Offering Price.** . . .

Item 6.   **Dilution.** . . .

Item 7.   **Selling Security Holders. . . .**

Item 8.   **Plan of Distribution. . . .**

Item 9.   **Description of Securities to Be Registered. . . .**

Item 10.   **Interests of Named Experts and Counsel. . . .**

Item 11.   **Information With Respect to the Registrant.** Furnish the following information with respect to the registrant:

(a) Information required by Item 101 of Regulation S–K . . . [concerning] description of business;

(b) Information required by Item 102 of Regulation S–K . . . [concerning] description of property;

(c) Information required by Item 103 of Regulation S–K . . . [concerning] legal proceedings;

(d) Where common equity securities are being offered, information required by Item 201 of Regulation S–K . . . [concerning] market price of and dividends on the registrant's common equity and related stockholder matters;

(e) Financial statements meeting the requirements of Regulation S–X . . .

(f) Information required by Item 301 of Regulation S–K . . . [concerning] selected financial data;

(g) Information required by Item 302 of Regulation S–K . . . [concerning] supplementary financial information;

(h) Information required by Item 303 of Regulation S–K . . . [concerning] management's discussion and analysis of financial condition and results of operations;

(i) Information required by Item 304 of Regulation S–K . . . [concerning] changes in and disagreements with accountants on accounting and financial disclosure;

(j) Information required by Item 401 of Regulation S–K . . . [concerning] directors and executive officers;

(k) Information required by Item 402 of Regulation S–K . . . [concerning] executive compensation;

(l) Information required by Item 402 of Regulation S–K, [concerning] executive compensation, and information required by paragraph (e)(4) of Item 407 of Regulation S–K, [concerning] corporate governance;

(m) Information required by Item 404 of Regulation S–K . . . [concerning] certain relationships and related transactions. . . .

(n) Information required by Item 404 of Regulation S–K, [concerning] transactions with related persons, promoters and certain control persons, and Item 407(a) of Regulation S–K, [concerning] corporate governance.

Item 11A.   Material Changes.

If the registrant elects to incorporate information by reference pursuant to General Instruction VII, describe any and all material changes in the registrant's affairs that have occurred since the end of the latest fiscal year for which audited financial statements were included in the latest Form 10-K and that have not been described in a Form 10-Q or Form 8-K filed under the Exchange Act.

Item 12.   Incorporation of Certain Information by Reference.

If the registrant elects to incorporate information by reference pursuant to General Instruction VII:

(a) It must specifically incorporate by reference into the prospectus contained in the registration statement the following documents by means of a statement to that effect in the prospectus listing all such documents:

(1) The registrant's latest annual report on Form 10-K filed pursuant to Section 13(a) or Section 15(d) of the Exchange Act that contains financial statements for the registrant's latest fiscal year for which a Form 10-K was required to have been filed; and

(2) All other reports filed pursuant to Section 13(a) or 15(d) of the Exchange Act or proxy or information statements filed pursuant to Section 14 of the Exchange Act since the end of the fiscal year covered by the annual report referred to in paragraph (a)(1) above.

(b)(1) The registrant must state:

(i) That it will provide to each person, including any beneficial owner, to whom a prospectus is delivered, a copy of any or all of the reports or documents that have been incorporated by reference in the prospectus contained in the registration statement but not delivered with the prospectus;

(ii) That it will provide these reports or documents upon written or oral request;

(iii) That it will provide these reports or documents at no cost to the requester;

(iv) The name, address, telephone number, and e-mail address, if any, to which the request for these reports or documents must be made; and

(v) The registrant's Web site address, including the uniform resource locator (URL) where the incorporated reports and other documents may be accessed.

(2) The registrant must:

(i) Identify the reports and other information that it files with the SEC; and

(ii) State that the public may read and copy any materials it files with the SEC at the SEC's Public Reference Room at 100 F Street, N.E., Washington, DC 20549. State that the public may obtain information on the operation of the Public Reference Room by calling the SEC at 1-800-SEC-0330. If the registrant is an electronic filer, state that the SEC maintains an Internet site that contains reports, proxy and information statements, and other information regarding issuers that file electronically with the SEC and state the address of that site (http://www.sec.gov).

PART II—INFORMATION NOT REQUIRED IN PROSPECTUS

Item 13. Other Expenses of Issuance and Distribution. . . .

Item 14. Indemnification of Directors and Officers. . . .

Item 15. Recent Sales of Unregistered Securities. . . .

Item 16. Exhibits and Financial Statement Schedules. . . .

Item 17. Undertakings. . . .

FORM S-3

SECURITIES AND EXCHANGE COMMISSION

REGISTRATION STATEMENT UNDER THE SECURITIES ACT OF 1933

_____

(Exact name of registrant as specified in its charter)

_____

(State or other jurisdiction of incorporation or organization)

_____

(I.R.S. Employer Identification No.)

_____

(Address, including zip code, and telephone number,
including area code, of registrant's principal executive offices)

(Name, address, including zip code, and telephone number,
including area code, of agent for service)

Approximate date of commencement of proposed sale to the public _____ . . . .

GENERAL INSTRUCTIONS

I.   **Eligibility Requirements for Use of Form S-3**

This instruction sets forth registrant requirements and transaction requirements for the use of Form S-3. Any registrant which meets the requirements of I.A. below ("Registrant Requirements") may use this Form for the registration of securities under the Securities Act of 1933 ("Securities Act") which are offered in any transaction specified in I.B. below ("Transaction Requirement") provided that the requirement applicable to the specified transaction are met. . . . With respect to well-known seasoned issuers and majority-owned subsidiaries of well-known seasoned issuers, see Instruction I.D. below.

A.   *Registrant Requirements.* Registrants must meet the following conditions in order to use this Form for registration under the Securities Act of securities offered in the transactions specified in I.B. below:

1.   The registrant is organized under the laws of the United States or any State or Territory or the District of Columbia and has its principal business operations in the United States or its territories.

2.   The registrant has a class of securities registered pursuant to Section 12(b) of the Securities Exchange Act of 1934 ("Exchange Act") or a class of equity securities registered pursuant to Section 12(g) of the Exchange Act or is required to file reports pursuant to Section 15(d) of the Exchange Act.

3.   The registrant:

(a) has been subject to the requirements of Section 12 or 15(d) of the Exchange Act and has filed all the material required to be filed pursuant to Sections 13, 14 or 15(d) for a period of at least twelve calendar months immediately preceding the filing of the registration statement on this Form; and (b) has filed in a timely manner all reports required to be filed during the twelve calendar months and any portion of a month immediately preceding the filing of the registration statement, other than a report that is required solely pursuant to Item 1.01, 1.02, 2.03, 2.04, 2.05, 2.06, 4.02(a), 6.01, 6.03 or 6.05 of Form 8-K. . . .

(b) has filed in a timely manner all reports required to be filed during the twelve calendar months and any portion of a month immediately preceding the filing of the registration statement, other than a report that is required solely pursuant to Item 1.01, 4.02(a) or 5.02(e) of Form 8-K. If the registrant has used (during the twelve calendar months and any portion of a month immediately preceding the filing of the registration statement) Rule 12b–25(b) under the Exchange Act with respect to a report or a portion of a report, that report or portion thereof has actually been filed within the time period prescribed by that rule. . . .

5.   Neither the registrant nor any of its consolidated or unconsolidated subsidiaries have, since the end of the last fiscal year for which certified financial statements of the registrant and its consolidated subsidiaries were included in a report filed pursuant to Section 13(a) or 15(d) of the Exchange Act: (a) failed to pay any dividend or sinking fund installment on preferred stock; or (b) defaulted (i) on any installment or installments on indebtedness for borrowed money, or (ii) on any rental on one or more long term leases, which defaults in the aggregate are material to the financial position of the registrant and its consolidated and unconsolidated subsidiaries, taken as a whole. . . .

B.   *Transaction Requirements.* Security offerings meeting any of the following conditions and made by a registrant meeting the Registrant Requirements specified in I.A. above may be registered on this Form:

1.   *Primary Offerings by Certain Registrants.* Securities to be offered for cash by or on behalf of a registrant, or outstanding securities to be offered for cash for the account of any person other than the registrant, including securities acquired by standby underwriters in connection with the call or redemption by the registrant of warrants or a class of convertible securities; *provided* that the aggregate market value of the voting stock held by non-affiliates of the registrant is $75 million or more. . . .

2.   *Primary Offerings of Non-convertible Investment Grade Securities.* Non-convertible securities to be offered for cash by or on behalf of a registrant, provided such securities at the time of sale are "investment grade securities," as defined below. A non-convertible security is an "investment grade security" if, at the time of sale, at least one nationally recognized statistical rating organization . . . has rated the security in one of its generic rating categories which signifies investment grade; typically, the four highest rating categories (within which there may be sub-categories or gradations indicating relative standing) signify investment grade. . . .

3.   *Transactions Involving Secondary Offerings.* Outstanding securities to be offered for the account of any person other than the issuer . . . if securities of the same class are listed and registered on a national securities exchange or are quoted on the automated quotation system of a national securities association. . . .

6.   *Limited Primary Offerings by Certain Other Registrants.* Securities to be offered for cash by or on behalf of a registrant; *provided that:*

(a) the aggregate market value of securities sold by or on behalf of the registrant pursuant to this Instruction I.B.6. during the period of 12 calendar months immediately prior to, and including, the sale is no more than one-third of the aggregate market value of the voting and non-voting common equity held by non-affiliates of the registrant;

(b) the registrant is not a shell company . . . and has not been a shell company for at least 12 calendar months previously and if it has been a shell company at any time previously, has filed current Form 10 information with the Commission at least 12 calendar months previously reflecting its status as an entity that is not a shell company; and

(c) the registrant has at least one class of common equity securities listed and registered on a national securities exchange. . . .

D.   *Automatic Shelf Offerings by Well-Known Seasoned Issuers.* Any registrant that is a well-known seasoned issuer, as defined in Rule 405, at the most recent eligibility determination date specified in paragraph (2) of that definition may use this Form for registration under the Securities Act of securities offerings, other than pursuant to Rule 415(a)(1)(vii) or (viii), as follows:

1.   The securities to be offered are:

(a) Any securities to be offered pursuant to Rule 415, Rule 430A [Prospectus in a Registration Statement at the Time of Effectiveness], or Rule 430B [Prospectus in a Registration Statement After the Effective Date] by:

(i) A registrant that is a well-known seasoned issuer by reason of paragraph (1)(i)(A) of the definition in Rule 405; or

(ii) A registrant that is a well-known seasoned issuer only by reason of paragraph (1)(i)(B) of the definition in Rule 405 if the registrant also is eligible to register a primary offering of its securities pursuant to Transaction Requirement I.B.1 of this Form. . . .

II. Application of General Rules and Regulations . . .

C.   A smaller reporting company, defined in Rule 405, that is eligible to use Form S-3 shall use the disclosure items in Regulation S–K with specific attention to the scaled disclosure provided for smaller reporting companies, if any. Smaller reporting companies may provide the financial information called for by Article 8 of Regulation S–X in lieu of the financial information called for by Item 11 in this form.

IV. Registration of Additional Securities and Additional Classes of Securities . . .

B.   **Registration of Additional Securities or Classes of Securities or Additional Registrants After Effectiveness.** A well-known seasoned issuer relying on General Instruction I.D. of this Form may register additional securities or classes of securities, pursuant to Rule 413(b) [Registration of Additional Securities] by filing a post-effective amendment to the effective registration statement. The well-known seasoned issuer may add majority-owned subsidiaries as additional registrants whose securities are eligible to be sold as part of the automatic shelf registration statement by filing a post-effective amendment identifying the additional registrants, and the registrant and the additional registrants and other persons required to sign the registration statement must sign the post-effective amendment. The post-effective amendment must consist of the facing page; any disclosure required by this Form that is necessary to update the registration statement to reflect the additional securities, additional classes of securities, or additional registrants; any required opinions and consents; and the signature page. Required information, consents, or opinions may be included in the prospectus and the registration statement through a post-effective amendment or may be provided through a document incorporated or deemed incorporated by reference into the registration statement and the prospectus that is part of the registration statement, or, as to the required information only, contained in a prospectus filed pursuant to Rule 424(b) [Filing of Prospectuses] that is deemed part of and included in the registration statement and prospectus that is part of the registration statement.

PART I—INFORMATION REQUIRED IN PROSPECTUS

Item 3.   **Summary Information, Risk Factors and Ratio of Earnings to Fixed Charges.** . . .

Item 4.   **Use of Proceeds.** . . .

Item 5.   **Determination of Offering Price.** . . .

Item 6.   **Dilution.** . . .

Item 7.   **Selling Security Holders.** . . .

Item 8.   **Plan of Distribution.** . . .

Item 9.   **Description of Securities to be Registered.** . . .

Item 10.   **Interests of Named Experts and Counsel.** . . .

Item 11.   **Material Changes.**

(a) Describe any and all material changes in the registrant's affairs that have occurred since the end of the latest fiscal year for which certified financial statements were included in the latest annual report to security holders and that have not been described in a report on Form 10-Q or Form 8-K filed under the Exchange Act. . . .

PART II—INFORMATION NOT REQUIRED IN PROSPECTUS

Item 14.   **Other Expenses of Issuance and Distribution.** . . .

Item 15.   **Indemnification of Directors and Officers.** . . .

Item 16.   **Exhibits.** . . .

Item 17.   **Undertakings.** . . .

———

REGULATION CROWDFUNDING—GENERAL RULES AND REGULATIONS (SELECTED PROVISIONS)

17 C.F.R. §§ 227.100 et seq.

TABLE OF CONTENTS

SUBPART A—GENERAL

Rule		Page
100.	Crowdfunding exemption and requirements	1291

SUBPART B—REQUIREMENTS FOR ISSUERS

201.	Disclosure requirements	1293
202.	Ongoing reporting requirements	1294
203.	Filing requirements and form	1294
204.	Advertising	1295
205.	Promoter compensation	1296

SUBPART C—REQUIREMENTS FOR INTERMEDIARIES

300.	Intermediaries	1296
301.	Measures to reduce risk of fraud	1297
302.	Account opening*	
303.	Requirements with respect to transactions	1298
304.	Completion of offerings, cancellations and reconfirmations	1299
305.	Payments to third parties*	

SUBPART D—FUNDING PORTAL REGULATION

400.	Registration of funding portals*	
401.	Exemption	1300
402.	Conditional safe harbor	1300
403.	Compliance*	
404.	Records to be made and kept by funding portals*	

SUBPART E—MISCELLANEOUS PROVISIONS

501.	Restrictions on resales	1300
502.	Insignificant deviations from a term, condition or requirement of this part (Regulation Crowdfunding)	1301
503.	Disqualification provisions*	

SUBPART A—GENERAL

Rule 100. Crowdfunding exemption and requirements

(a) *Exemption.* An issuer may offer or sell securities in reliance on section 4(a)(6) of the Securities Act of 1933 (the "Securities Act") (15 U.S.C. 77d(a)(6)), provided that:

(1) The aggregate amount of securities sold to all investors by the issuer in reliance on section 4(a)(6) of the Securities Act (15 U.S.C. 77d(a)(6)) during the 12-month period preceding the date of such offer or sale, including the securities offered in such transaction, shall not exceed $1,000,000;

---

* Omitted.

(2) The aggregate amount of securities sold to any investor across all issuers in reliance on section 4(a)(6) of the Securities Act (15 U.S.C. 77d(a)(6)) during the 12-month period preceding the date of such transaction, including the securities sold to such investor in such transaction, shall not exceed:

(i) The greater of $2,000 or 5 percent of the lesser of the investor's annual income or net worth if either the investor's annual income or net worth is less than $100,000; or

(ii) 10 percent of the lesser of the investor's annual income or net worth, not to exceed an amount sold of $100,000, if both the investor's annual income and net worth are equal to or more than $100,000;

Instruction 1 to paragraph (a)(2). To determine the investment limit for a natural person, the person's annual income and net worth shall be calculated as those values are calculated for purposes of determining accredited investor status in accordance with § 230.501 of this chapter.

Instruction 2 to paragraph (a)(2). A person's annual income and net worth may be calculated jointly with that person's spouse; however, when such a joint calculation is used, the aggregate investment of the investor spouses may not exceed the limit that would apply to an individual investor at that income or net worth level.

Instruction 3 to paragraph (a)(2). An issuer offering and selling securities in reliance on section 4(a)(6) of the Securities Act (15 U.S.C. 77d(a)(6)) may rely on the efforts of an intermediary required by § 227.303(b) to ensure that the aggregate amount of securities purchased by an investor in offerings pursuant to section 4(a)(6) of the Securities Act will not cause the investor to exceed the limit set forth in section 4(a)(6) of the Securities Act and § 227.100(a)(2), *provided that* the issuer does not know that the investor has exceeded the investor limits or would exceed the investor limits as a result of purchasing securities in the issuer's offering.

(3) The transaction is conducted through an intermediary that complies with the requirements in section 4A(a) of the Securities Act (15 U.S.C. 77d–1(a)) and the related requirements in this part, and the transaction is conducted exclusively through the intermediary's platform; and

Instruction to paragraph (a)(3). An issuer shall not conduct an offering or concurrent offerings in reliance on section 4(a)(6) of the Securities Act of 1933 (15 U.S.C. 77d(a)(6)) using more than one intermediary.

(4) The issuer complies with the requirements in section 4A(b) of the Securities Act (15 U.S.C. 77d–1(b)) and the related requirements in this part; *provided, however,* that the failure to comply with §§ 227.202, 227.203(a)(3) and 227.203(b) shall not prevent an issuer from relying on the exemption provided by section 4(a)(6) of the Securities Act (15 U.S.C. 77d(a)(6)).

(b) *Applicability.* The crowdfunding exemption shall not apply to transactions involving the offer or sale of securities by any issuer that:

(1) Is not organized under, and subject to, the laws of a State or territory of the United States or the District of Columbia;

(2) Is subject to the requirement to file reports pursuant to section 13 or section 15(d) of the Securities Exchange Act of 1934 (the "Exchange Act") (15 U.S.C. 78m or 78o(d));

(3) Is an investment company, as defined in section 3 of the Investment Company Act of 1940 (15 U.S.C. 80a–3), or is excluded from the definition of investment company by section 3(b) or section 3(c) of that Act (15 U.S.C. 80a–3(b) or 80a–3(c));

(4) Is not eligible to offer or sell securities in reliance on section 4(a)(6) of the Securities Act (15 U.S.C. 77d(a)(6)) as a result of a disqualification as specified in § 227.503(a);

(5) Has sold securities in reliance on section 4(a)(6) of the Securities Act (15 U.S.C. 77d(a)(6)) and has not filed with the Commission and provided to investors, to the extent required, the ongoing annual reports required by this part during the two years immediately preceding the filing of the required offering statement; or

Instruction to paragraph (b)(5). An issuer delinquent in its ongoing reports can again rely on section 4(a)(6) of the Securities Act (15 U.S.C. 77d(a)(6)) once it has filed with the Commission and provided to investors both of the annual reports required during the two years immediately preceding the filing of the required offering statement.

(6) Has no specific business plan or has indicated that its business plan is to engage in a merger or acquisition with an unidentified company or companies.

(c) *Issuer*. For purposes of § 227.201(r), calculating aggregate amounts offered and sold in § 227.100(a) and § 227.201(t), and determining whether an issuer has previously sold securities in § 227.201(t)(3), *issuer* includes all entities controlled by or under common control with the issuer and any predecessors of the issuer.

Instruction to paragraph (c). The term *control* means the possession, direct or indirect, of the power to direct or cause the direction of the management and policies of the entity, whether through the ownership of voting securities, by contract or otherwise.

(d) *Investor*. For purposes of this part, *investor* means any investor or any potential investor, as the context requires.

SUBPART B—REQUIREMENTS FOR ISSUERS

Rule 201. Disclosure requirements

An issuer offering or selling securities in reliance on section 4(a)(6) of the Securities Act (15 U.S.C. 77d(a)(6)) and in accordance with section 4A of the Securities Act (15 U.S.C. 77d–1) and this part must file with the Commission and provide to investors and the relevant intermediary the following information:

(a) The name, legal status (including its form of organization, jurisdiction in which it is organized and date of organization), physical address and Web site of the issuer;

(b) The names of the directors and officers (and any persons occupying a similar status or performing a similar function) of the issuer, all positions and offices with the issuer held by such persons, the period of time in which such persons served in the position or office and their business experience during the past three years, including:

(1) Each person's principal occupation and employment, including whether any officer is employed by another employer; and

(2) The name and principal business of any corporation or other organization in which such occupation and employment took place.

Instruction to paragraph (b). For purposes of this paragraph (b), the term *officer* means a president, vice president, secretary, treasurer or principal financial officer, comptroller or principal accounting officer, and any person routinely performing similar functions.

(c) The name of each person, as of the most recent practicable date but no earlier than 120 days prior to the date the offering statement or report is filed, who is a beneficial owner of 20 percent or more of the issuer's outstanding voting equity securities, calculated on the basis of voting power;

(d) A description of the business of the issuer and the anticipated business plan of the issuer;

(e) The current number of employees of the issuer;

(f) A discussion of the material factors that make an investment in the issuer speculative or risky;

(g) The target offering amount and the deadline to reach the target offering amount, including a statement that if the sum of the investment commitments does not equal or exceed the target offering amount at the offering deadline, no securities will be sold in the offering, investment commitments will be cancelled and committed funds will be returned;

(h) Whether the issuer will accept investments in excess of the target offering amount and, if so, the maximum amount that the issuer will accept and how oversubscriptions will be allocated, such as on a pro-rata, first come-first served, or other basis;

(i) A description of the purpose and intended use of the offering proceeds;

Instruction to paragraph (i). An issuer must provide a reasonably detailed description of any intended use of proceeds, such that investors are provided with enough information to understand how the offering proceeds will be used. If an issuer has identified a range of possible uses, the issuer should identify and describe each probable use and the factors the issuer may consider in allocating proceeds among the potential uses. If the issuer will accept proceeds in excess of the target offering amount, the issuer must describe the purpose, method for allocating oversubscriptions, and intended use of the excess proceeds with similar specificity.

. . .

Rule 202.   Ongoing reporting requirements

(a) An issuer that has offered and sold securities in reliance on section 4(a)(6) of the Securities Act (15 U.S.C. 77d(a)(6)) and in accordance with section 4A of the Securities Act (15 U.S.C. 77d–1) and this part must file with the Commission and post on the issuer's Web site an annual report along with the financial statements of the issuer certified by the principal executive officer of the issuer to be true and complete in all material respects and a description of the financial condition of the issuer as described in § 227.201(s). If, however, an issuer has available financial statements that have either been reviewed or audited by a public accountant that is independent of the issuer, those financial statements must be provided and the certification by the principal executive officer will not be required. The annual report also must include the disclosure required by paragraphs (a), (b), (c), (d), (e), (f), (m), (p), (q), (r), and (x) of § 227.201. The report must be filed in accordance with the requirements of § 227.203 and Form C (§ 239.900 of this chapter) and no later than 120 days after the end of the fiscal year covered by the report.

Instruction 1 to paragraph (a). Instructions (3), (8), (9), (10), and (11) to paragraph (t) of § 227.201 shall apply for purposes of this section.

Instruction 2 to paragraph (a). An issuer providing financial statements that are not audited or reviewed must have its principal executive officer provide the following certification:

I, [identify the certifying individual], certify that the financial statements of [identify the issuer] included in this Form are true and complete in all material respects.

[Signature and title].

(b) An issuer must continue to comply with the ongoing reporting requirements until one of the following occurs:

(1) The issuer is required to file reports under section 13(a) or section 15(d) of the Exchange Act (15 U.S.C. 78m(a) or 78o(d));

(2) The issuer has filed, since its most recent sale of securities pursuant to this part, at least one annual report pursuant to this section and has fewer than 300 holders of record;

(3) The issuer has filed, since its most recent sale of securities pursuant to this part, the annual reports required pursuant to this section for at least the three most recent years and has total assets that do not exceed $10,000,000;

(4) The issuer or another party repurchases all of the securities issued in reliance on section 4(a)(6) of the Securities Act (15 U.S.C. 77d(a)(6)), including any payment in full of debt securities or any complete redemption of redeemable securities; or

(5) The issuer liquidates or dissolves its business in accordance with state law.

Rule 203.   Filing requirements and form

(a) Form C—Offering statement and amendments (§ 239.900 of this chapter).

(1) Offering statement. An issuer offering or selling securities in reliance on section 4(a)(6) of the Securities Act (15 U.S.C. 77d(a)(6)) and in accordance with section 4A of the Securities Act (15 U.S.C. 77d–1) and this part must file with the Commission and provide to investors and the relevant intermediary a Form C: Offering Statement (Form C) (§ 239.900 of this chapter) prior to the commencement of the offering of securities. The Form C must include the information required by § 227.201.

(2) Amendments to offering statement. An issuer must file with the Commission and provide to investors and the relevant intermediary an amendment to the offering statement filed on Form C (§ 239.900 of this chapter) to disclose any material changes, additions or updates to information that it provides to

investors through the intermediary's platform, for any offering that has not yet been completed or terminated. The amendment must be filed on Form C: Amendment (Form C/A) (§ 239.900 of this chapter), and if the amendment reflects material changes, additions or updates, the issuer shall check the box indicating that investors must reconfirm an investment commitment within five business days or the investor's commitment will be considered cancelled.

(3) *Progress updates.* (i) An issuer must file with the Commission and provide to investors and the relevant intermediary a Form C: Progress Update (Form C-U) (§ 239.900 of this chapter) to disclose its progress in meeting the target offering amount no later than five business days after each of the dates when the issuer reaches 50 percent and 100 percent of the target offering amount.

(ii) If the issuer will accept proceeds in excess of the target offering amount, the issuer must file with the Commission and provide to investors and the relevant intermediary, no later than five business days after the offering deadline, a final Form C-U (§ 239.900 of this chapter) to disclose the total amount of securities sold in the offering.

(iii) The requirements of paragraphs (a)(3)(i) and (ii) of this section shall not apply to an issuer if the relevant intermediary makes publicly available on the intermediary's platform frequent updates regarding the progress of the issuer in meeting the target offering amount; however, the issuer must still file a Form C-U (§ 239.900 of this chapter) to disclose the total amount of securities sold in the offering no later than five business days after the offering deadline.

Instruction to paragraph (a)(3). If multiple Forms C-U (§ 239.900 of this chapter) are triggered within the same five business day period, the issuer may consolidate such progress updates into one Form C-U, so long as the Form C-U discloses the most recent threshold that was met and the Form C-U is filed with the Commission and provided to investors and the relevant intermediary by the day on which the first progress update is due.

Instruction 1 to paragraph (a). An issuer would satisfy the requirement to provide to the relevant intermediary the information required by this paragraph (a) if it provides to the relevant intermediary a copy of the disclosures filed with the Commission.

Instruction 2 to paragraph (a). An issuer would satisfy the requirement to provide to investors the information required by this paragraph (a) if the issuer refers investors to the information on the intermediary's platform by means of a posting on the issuer's Web site or by email.

(b) *Form C: Annual report and termination of reporting* (§ 239.900 of this chapter). (1) *Annual reports.* An issuer that has sold securities in reliance on section 4(a)(6) of the Securities Act (15 U.S.C. 77d(a)(6)) and in accordance with section 4A of the Securities Act (15 U.S.C. 77d–1) and this part must file an annual report on Form C: Annual Report (Form C-AR) (§ 239.900 of this chapter) with the Commission no later than 120 days after the end of the fiscal year covered by the report. The annual report shall include the information required by § 227.202(a).

(2) *Amendments to annual report.* An issuer must file with the Commission an amendment to the annual report filed on Form C: Annual Report (Form C-AR) (§ 239.900 of this chapter) to make a material change to the previously filed annual report as soon as practicable after discovery of the need for the material change. The amendment must be filed on Form C: Amendment to Annual Report (Form C-AR/A) (§ 239.900 of this chapter).

(3) *Termination of reporting.* An issuer eligible to terminate its obligation to file annual reports with the Commission pursuant to § 227.202(b) must file with the Commission, within five business days from the date on which the issuer becomes eligible to terminate its reporting obligation, Form C: Termination of Reporting (Form C-TR) (§ 239.900 of this chapter) to advise investors that the issuer will cease reporting pursuant to this part.

Rule 204.   Advertising

(a) An issuer may not, directly or indirectly, advertise the terms of an offering made in reliance on section 4(a)(6) of the Securities Act (15 U.S.C. 77d(a)(6)), except for notices that meet the requirements of paragraph (b) of this section.

Instruction to paragraph (a). For purposes of this paragraph (a), *issuer* includes persons acting on behalf of the issuer.

(b) A notice may advertise any of the terms of an issuer's offering made in reliance on section 4(a)(6) of the Securities Act (15 U.S.C. 77d(a)(6)) if it directs investors to the intermediary's platform and includes no more than the following information:

(1) A statement that the issuer is conducting an offering pursuant to section 4(a)(6) of the Securities Act (15 U.S.C. 77d(a)(6)), the name of the intermediary through which the offering is being conducted and a link directing the potential investor to the intermediary's platform;

(2) The terms of the offering; and

(3) Factual information about the legal identity and business location of the issuer, limited to the name of the issuer of the security, the address, phone number and Web site of the issuer, the email address of a representative of the issuer and a brief description of the business of the issuer.

(c) Notwithstanding the prohibition on advertising any of the terms of the offering, an issuer, and persons acting on behalf of the issuer, may communicate with investors and potential investors about the terms of the offering through communication channels provided by the intermediary on the intermediary's platform, provided that an issuer identifies itself as the issuer in all communications. Persons acting on behalf of the issuer must identify their affiliation with the issuer in all communications on the intermediary's platform.

Instruction to § 227.204. For purposes of this section, *terms of the offering* means the amount of securities offered, the nature of the securities, the price of the securities and the closing date of the offering period.

Rule 205.   Promoter compensation

(a) An issuer, or person acting on behalf of the issuer, shall be permitted to compensate or commit to compensate, directly or indirectly, any person to promote the issuer's offerings made in reliance on section 4(a)(6) of the Securities Act (15 U.S.C. 77d(a)(6)) through communication channels provided by an intermediary on the intermediary's platform, but only if the issuer or person acting on behalf of the issuer, takes reasonable steps to ensure that the person promoting the offering clearly discloses the receipt, past or prospective, of such compensation with any such communication.

Instruction to paragraph (a). The disclosure required by this paragraph is required, with each communication, for persons engaging in promotional activities on behalf of the issuer through the communication channels provided by the intermediary, regardless of whether or not the compensation they receive is specifically for the promotional activities. This includes persons hired specifically to promote the offering as well as to persons who are otherwise employed by the issuer or who undertake promotional activities on behalf of the issuer.

(b) Other than as set forth in paragraph (a) of this section, an issuer or person acting on behalf of the issuer shall not compensate or commit to compensate, directly or indirectly, any person to promote the issuer's offerings made in reliance on section 4(a)(6) of the Securities Act (15 U.S.C. 77d(a)(6)), unless such promotion is limited to notices permitted by, and in compliance with, § 227.204.

SUBPART C—REQUIREMENTS FOR INTERMEDIARIES

Rule 300.   Intermediaries

(a) *Requirements.* A person acting as an intermediary in a transaction involving the offer or sale of securities in reliance on section 4(a)(6) of the Securities Act (15 U.S.C. 77d(a)(6)) must:

(1) Be registered with the Commission as a broker under section 15(b) of the Exchange Act (15 U.S.C. 78 *o* (b)) or as a funding portal in accordance with the requirements of § 227.400; and

(2) Be a member a national securities association registered under section 15A of the Exchange Act (15 U.S.C. 78 *o*–3).

(b) *Financial interests.* Any director, officer or partner of an intermediary, or any person occupying a similar status or performing a similar function, may not have a financial interest in an issuer that is offering or selling securities in reliance on section 4(a)(6) of the Securities Act (15 U.S.C. 77d(a)(6)) through the intermediary's platform, or receive a financial interest in an issuer as compensation for the services provided to or for the benefit of the issuer in connection with the offer or sale of such securities. An intermediary may not have a financial interest in an issuer that is offering or selling securities in reliance on section 4(a)(6) of the Securities Act (15 U.S.C. 77d(a)(6)) through the intermediary's platform unless:

(1) The intermediary receives the financial interest from the issuer as compensation for the services provided to, or for the benefit of, the issuer in connection with the offer or sale of the securities being offered or sold in reliance on section 4(a)(6) of the Securities Act (15 U.S.C. 77d(a)(6)) through the intermediary's platform; and

(2) the financial interest consists of securities of the same class and having the same terms, conditions and rights as the securities being offered or sold in reliance on section 4(a)(6) of the Securities Act (15 U.S.C. 77d(a)(6)) through the intermediary's platform. For purposes of this paragraph, *a financial interest in an issuer* means a direct or indirect ownership of, or economic interest in, any class of the issuer's securities.

(c) *Definitions.* For purposes of this part:

(1) *Associated person of a funding portal* or *person associated with a funding portal* means any partner, officer, director or manager of a funding portal (or any person occupying a similar status or performing similar functions), any person directly or indirectly controlling or controlled by such funding portal, or any employee of a funding portal, except that any person associated with a funding portal whose functions are solely clerical or ministerial shall not be included in the meaning of such term for purposes of section 15(b) of the Exchange Act (15 U.S.C. 78 *o* (b)) (other than paragraphs (4) and (6) of section 15(b) of the Exchange Act).

(2) *Funding portal* means a broker acting as an intermediary in a transaction involving the offer or sale of securities in reliance on section 4(a)(6) of the Securities Act (15 U.S.C. 77d(a)(6)), that does not:

(i) Offer investment advice or recommendations;

(ii) Solicit purchases, sales or offers to buy the securities displayed on its platform;

(iii) Compensate employees, agents, or other persons for such solicitation or based on the sale of securities displayed or referenced on its platform; or

(iv) Hold, manage, possess, or otherwise handle investor funds or securities.

(3) *Intermediary* means a broker registered under section 15(b) of the Exchange Act (15 U.S.C. 78 *o* (b)) or a funding portal registered under § 227.400 and includes, where relevant, an associated person of the registered broker or registered funding portal.

(4) *Platform* means a program or application accessible via the Internet or other similar electronic communication medium through which a registered broker or a registered funding portal acts as an intermediary in a transaction involving the offer or sale of securities in reliance on section 4(a)(6) of the Securities Act (15 U.S.C. 77d(a)(6)).

Instruction to paragraph (c)(4). An intermediary through which a crowdfunding transaction is conducted may engage in back office or other administrative functions other than on the intermediary's platform.

Rule 301.   Measures to reduce risk of fraud

An intermediary in a transaction involving the offer or sale of securities in reliance on section 4(a)(6) of the Securities Act (15 U.S.C. 77d(a)(6)) must:

(a) Have a reasonable basis for believing that an issuer seeking to offer and sell securities in reliance on section 4(a)(6) of the Securities Act (15 U.S.C. 77d(a)(6)) through the intermediary's platform complies with the requirements in section 4A(b) of the Act (15 U.S.C. 77d–1(b)) and the related requirements in this part. In satisfying this requirement, an intermediary may rely on the representations of the issuer concerning compliance with these requirements unless the intermediary has reason to question the reliability of those representations;

(b) Have a reasonable basis for believing that the issuer has established means to keep accurate records of the holders of the securities it would offer and sell through the intermediary's platform, provided that an intermediary may rely on the representations of the issuer concerning its means of recordkeeping unless the intermediary has reason to question the reliability of those representations. An intermediary will be deemed to have satisfied this requirement if the issuer has engaged the services of a transfer agent that is registered under Section 17A of the Exchange Act (15 U.S.C. 78q–1(c)).

(c) Deny access to its platform to an issuer if the intermediary:

(1) Has a reasonable basis for believing that the issuer or any of its officers, directors (or any person occupying a similar status or performing a similar function) or beneficial owners of 20 percent or more of the issuer's outstanding voting equity securities, calculated on the basis of voting power, is subject to a disqualification under § 227.503. In satisfying this requirement, an intermediary must, at a minimum, conduct a background and securities enforcement regulatory history check on each issuer whose securities are to be offered by the intermediary and on each officer, director or beneficial owner of 20 percent or more of the issuer's outstanding voting equity securities, calculated on the basis of voting power.

(2) Has a reasonable basis for believing that the issuer or the offering presents the potential for fraud or otherwise raises concerns about investor protection. In satisfying this requirement, an intermediary must deny access if it reasonably believes that it is unable to adequately or effectively assess the risk of fraud of the issuer or its potential offering. In addition, if an intermediary becomes aware of information after it has granted access that causes it to reasonably believe that the issuer or the offering presents the potential for fraud or otherwise raises concerns about investor protection, the intermediary must promptly remove the offering from its platform, cancel the offering, and return (or, for funding portals, direct the return of) any funds that have been committed by investors in the offering.

. . .

Rule 303.   Requirements with respect to transactions

(a) *Issuer information.* An intermediary in a transaction involving the offer or sale of securities in reliance on section 4(a)(6) of the Securities Act (15 U.S.C. 77d(a)(6)) must make available to the Commission and to investors any information required to be provided by the issuer of the securities under §§ 227.201 and 227.203(a).

(1) This information must be made publicly available on the intermediary's platform, in a manner that reasonably permits a person accessing the platform to save, download, or otherwise store the information;

(2) This information must be made publicly available on the intermediary's platform for a minimum of 21 days before any securities are sold in the offering, during which time the intermediary may accept investment commitments;

(3) This information, including any additional information provided by the issuer, must remain publicly available on the intermediary's platform until the offer and sale of securities in reliance on section 4(a)(6) of the Securities Act (15 U.S.C. 77d(a)(6)) is completed or cancelled; and

(4) An intermediary may not require any person to establish an account with the intermediary to access this information.

(b) *Investor qualification.* Each time before accepting any investment commitment (including any additional investment commitment from the same person), an intermediary must:

(1) Have a reasonable basis for believing that the investor satisfies the investment limitations established by section 4(a)(6)(B) of the Act (15 U.S.C. 77d(a)(6)(B)) and this part. An intermediary may rely on an investor's representations concerning compliance with the investment limitation requirements concerning the investor's annual income, net worth, and the amount of the investor's other investments made pursuant to section 4(a)(6) of the Securities Act (15 U.S.C. 77d(a)(6)) unless the intermediary has reason to question the reliability of the representation.

(2) Obtain from the investor:

(i) A representation that the investor has reviewed the intermediary's educational materials delivered pursuant to § 227.302(b), understands that the entire amount of his or her investment may be lost, and is in a financial condition to bear the loss of the investment; and

(ii) A questionnaire completed by the investor demonstrating the investor's understanding that:

(A) There are restrictions on the investor's ability to cancel an investment commitment and obtain a return of his or her investment;

(B) It may be difficult for the investor to resell securities acquired in reliance on section 4(a)(6) of the Securities Act (15 U.S.C. 77d(a)(6)); and

(C) Investing in securities offered and sold in reliance on section 4(a)(6) of the Securities Act (15 U.S.C. 77d(a)(6)) involves risk, and the investor should not invest any funds in an offering made in reliance on section 4(a)(6) of the Securities Act unless he or she can afford to lose the entire amount of his or her investment.

(c) *Communication channels.* An intermediary must provide on its platform communication channels by which persons can communicate with one another and with representatives of the issuer about offerings made available on the intermediary's platform, provided:

(1) If the intermediary is a funding portal, it does not participate in these communications other than to establish guidelines for communication and remove abusive or potentially fraudulent communications;

(2) The intermediary permits public access to view the discussions made in the communication channels;

(3) The intermediary restricts posting of comments in the communication channels to those persons who have opened an account with the intermediary on its platform; and

(4) The intermediary requires that any person posting a comment in the communication channels clearly and prominently disclose with each posting whether he or she is a founder or an employee of an issuer engaging in promotional activities on behalf of the issuer, or is otherwise compensated, whether in the past or prospectively, to promote the issuer's offering.

. . .

Rule 304. Completion of offerings, cancellations and reconfirmations

(a) *Generally.* An investor may cancel an investment commitment for any reason until 48 hours prior to the deadline identified in the issuer's offering materials. During the 48 hours prior to such deadline, an investment commitment may not be cancelled except as provided in paragraph (c) of this section.

(b) *Early completion of offering.* If an issuer reaches the target offering amount prior to the deadline identified in its offering materials pursuant to § 227.201(g), the issuer may close the offering on a date earlier than the deadline identified in its offering materials pursuant to § 227.201(g), *provided that:*

(1) The offering remains open for a minimum of 21 days pursuant to § 227.303(a);

(2) The intermediary provides notice to any potential investors, and gives or sends notice to investors that have made investment commitments in the offering, of:

(i) The new, anticipated deadline of the offering;

(ii) The right of investors to cancel investment commitments for any reason until 48 hours prior to the new offering deadline; and

(iii) Whether the issuer will continue to accept investment commitments during the 48-hour period prior to the new offering deadline.

(3) The new offering deadline is scheduled for and occurs at least five business days after the notice required in paragraph (b)(2) of this section is provided; and

(4) At the time of the new offering deadline, the issuer continues to meet or exceed the target offering amount.

(c) *Cancellations and reconfirmations based on material changes.* (1) If there is a material change to the terms of an offering or to the information provided by the issuer, the intermediary must give or send to any investor who has made an investment commitment notice of the material change and that the investor's investment commitment will be cancelled unless the investor reconfirms his or her investment commitment within five business days of receipt of the notice. If the investor fails to reconfirm his or her investment within those five business days, the intermediary within five business days thereafter must:

(i) Give or send the investor a notification disclosing that the commitment was cancelled, the reason for the cancellation and the refund amount that the investor is expected to receive; and

(ii) Direct the refund of investor funds.

(2) If material changes to the offering or to the information provided by the issuer regarding the offering occur within five business days of the maximum number of days that an offering is to remain open, the offering must be extended to allow for a period of five business days for the investor to reconfirm his or her investment. . . .

(d) *Return of funds if offering is not completed.* If an issuer does not complete an offering, an intermediary must within five business days:

(1) Give or send each investor a notification of the cancellation, disclosing the reason for the cancellation, and the refund amount that the investor is expected to receive;

(2) Direct the refund of investor funds; and

(3) Prevent investors from making investment commitments with respect to that offering on its platform.

SUBPART D—FUNDING PORTAL REGULATION

Rule 401. Exemption

A funding portal that is registered with the Commission pursuant to § 227.400 is exempt from the broker registration requirements of section 15(a)(1) of the Exchange Act (15 U.S.C. 78 *o* (a)(1)) in connection with its activities as a funding portal.

Rule 402. Conditional safe harbor

(a) *General.* Under section 3(a)(80) of the Exchange Act (15 U.S.C. 78c(a)(80)), a funding portal acting as an intermediary in a transaction involving the offer or sale of securities in reliance on section 4(a)(6) of the Securities Act (15 U.S.C. 77d(a)(6)) may not: offer investment advice or recommendations; solicit purchases, sales, or offers to buy the securities offered or displayed on its platform or portal; compensate employees, agents, or other persons for such solicitation or based on the sale of securities displayed or referenced on its platform or portal; hold, manage, possess, or otherwise handle investor funds or securities; or engage in such other activities as the Commission, by rule, determines appropriate. This section is intended to provide clarity with respect to the ability of a funding portal to engage in certain activities, consistent with the prohibitions under section 3(a)(80) of the Exchange Act. No presumption shall arise that a funding portal has violated the prohibitions under section 3(a)(80) of the Exchange Act or this part by reason of the funding portal or its associated persons engaging in activities in connection with the offer or sale of securities in reliance on section 4(a)(6) of the Securities Act that do not meet the conditions specified in paragraph (b) of this section. The antifraud provisions and all other applicable provisions of the federal securities laws continue to apply to the activities described in paragraph (b) of this section.

. . .

SUBPART E—MISCELLANEOUS PROVISIONS

Rule 501. Restrictions on resales

(a) Securities issued in a transaction exempt from registration pursuant to section 4(a)(6) of the Securities Act (15 U.S.C. 77d(a)(6)) and in accordance with section 4A of the Securities Act (15 U.S.C. 77d–

1) and this part may not be transferred by any purchaser of such securities during the one-year period beginning when the securities were issued in a transaction exempt from registration pursuant to section 4(a)(6) of the Securities Act (15 U.S.C. 77d(a)(6)), unless such securities are transferred:

(1) To the issuer of the securities;

(2) To an accredited investor;

(3) As part of an offering registered with the Commission; or

(4) To a member of the family of the purchaser or the equivalent, to a trust controlled by the purchaser, to a trust created for the benefit of a member of the family of the purchaser or the equivalent, or in connection with the death or divorce of the purchaser or other similar circumstance.

(b) For purposes of this § 227.501, the term *accredited investor* shall mean any person who comes within any of the categories set forth in § 230.501(a) of this chapter, or who the seller reasonably believes comes within any of such categories, at the time of the sale of the securities to that person.

(c) For purposes of this section, the term *member of the family of the purchaser* or the equivalent includes a child, stepchild, grandchild, parent, stepparent, grandparent, spouse or spousal equivalent, sibling, mother-in-law, father-in-law, son-in-law, daughter-in-law, brother-in-law, or sister-in-law of the purchaser, and shall include adoptive relationships. For purposes of this paragraph (c), the term *spousal equivalent* means a cohabitant occupying a relationship generally equivalent to that of a spouse.

Rule 502. Insignificant deviations from a term, condition or requirement of this part (Regulation Crowdfunding)

(a) A failure to comply with a term, condition, or requirement of this part will not result in the loss of the exemption from the requirements of Section 5 of the Securities Act (15 U.S.C. 77e) for any offer or sale to a particular individual or entity, if the issuer relying on the exemption shows:

(1) The failure to comply was insignificant with respect to the offering as a whole;

(2) The issuer made a good faith and reasonable attempt to comply with all applicable terms, conditions and requirements of this part; and

(3) The issuer did not know of such failure where the failure to comply with a term, condition or requirement of this part was the result of the failure of the intermediary to comply with the requirements of section 4A(a) of the Securities Act (15 U.S.C. 77d–1(a)) and the related rules, or such failure by the intermediary occurred solely in offerings other than the issuer's offering.

(b) Paragraph (a) of this section shall not preclude the Commission from bringing an enforcement action seeking any appropriate relief for an issuer's failure to comply with all applicable terms, conditions and requirements of this part.

. . .

REGULATION S–X—FORM AND CONTENT OF AND REQUIREMENTS FOR FINANCIAL STATEMENTS

17 C.F.R. Part 210

TABLE OF CONTENTS

Rule		Page
1–02.	Definitions of terms used in Regulation S–X	1303
2–01.	Qualifications of accountants	1303
2–02.	Accountants' reports and attestation reports	1314
2–02T.	Accountants' reports and attestation reports on internal control over financial reporting	1315
2–07.	Communication with audit committees	1315

Article 1—Application of Regulation S–X

Rule 1–02.   Definitions of terms used in Regulation S–X . . .

(a) . . .

(2) *Attestation report on internal control over financial reporting.*

The term *attestation report on internal control over financial reporting* means a report in which a registered public accounting firm expresses an opinion, either unqualified or adverse, as to whether the registrant maintained, in all material respects, effective internal control over financial reporting (as defined in Rule 13a–15(f) or Rule 15d–15(f) [under the Securities Exchange Act]), except in the rare circumstance of a scope limitation that cannot be overcome by the registrant or the registered public accounting firm which would result in the accounting firm disclaiming an opinion. . . .

(4) *Definitions of terms related to internal control over financial reporting.*

The term *material weakness* means a deficiency, or a combination of deficiencies, in internal control over financial reporting (as defined in Rule l3a–15(f) or Rule 15d–15(f) [under the Securities Exchange Act]) such that there is a reasonable possibility that a material misstatement of the registrant's annual or interim financial statements will not be prevented or detected on a timely basis.

The term *significant deficiency* means a deficiency, or a combination of deficiencies, in internal control over financial reporting that is less severe than a material weakness, yet important enough to merit attention by those responsible for oversight of the registrant's financial reporting. . . .

Article 2—Qualifications and Reports of Accountants

Rule 2–01.   Qualifications of accountants . . .

(a) The Commission will not recognize any person as a certified public accountant who is not duly registered and in good standing as such under the laws of the place of his residence or principal office. The Commission will not recognize any person as a public accountant who is not in good standing and entitled to practice as such under the laws of the place of his residence or principal office.

(b) The Commission will not recognize an accountant as independent, with respect to an audit client, if the accountant is not, or a reasonable investor with knowledge of all relevant facts and circumstances would conclude that the accountant is not, capable of exercising objective and impartial judgment on all issues encompassed within the accountant's engagement. In determining whether an accountant is independent, the Commission will consider all relevant circumstances, including all relationships between the accountant and the audit client, and not just those relating to reports filed with the Commission.

(c) This paragraph sets forth a non-exclusive specification of circumstances inconsistent with paragraph (b) of this section.

(1) *Financial relationships.* An accountant is not independent if, at any point during the audit and professional engagement period, the accountant has a direct financial interest or a material indirect financial interest in the accountant's audit client, such as:

(i) *Investments in audit clients.* An accountant is not independent when:

(A) The accounting firm, any covered person in the firm, or any of his or her immediate family members, has any direct investment in an audit client, such as stocks, bonds, notes, options, or other securities. The term direct investment includes an investment in an audit client through an intermediary if:

(1) The accounting firm, covered person, or immediate family member, alone or together with other persons, supervises or participates in the intermediary's investment decisions or has control over the intermediary; or

(2) The intermediary is not a diversified management investment company, as defined by section 5(b)(1) of the Investment Company Act of 1940, and has an investment in the audit client that amounts to 20% or more of the value of the intermediary's total investments.

(B) Any partner, principal, shareholder, or professional employee of the accounting firm, any of his or her immediate family members, any close family member of a covered person in the firm, or any group of the above persons has filed a Schedule 13D or 13G with the Commission indicating beneficial ownership of more than five percent of an audit client's equity securities or controls an audit client, or a close family member of a partner, principal, or shareholder of the accounting firm controls an audit client.

(C) The accounting firm, any covered person in the firm, or any of his or her immediate family members, serves as voting trustee of a trust, or executor of an estate, containing the securities of an audit client, unless the accounting firm, covered person in the firm, or immediate family member has no authority to make investment decisions for the trust or estate.

(D) The accounting firm, any covered person in the firm, any of his or her immediate family members, or any group of the above persons has any material indirect investment in an audit client. For purposes of this paragraph, the term material indirect investment does not include ownership by any covered person in the firm, any of his or her immediate family members, or any group of the above persons of 5% or less of the outstanding shares of a diversified management investment company, as defined by section 5(b)(1) of the Investment Company Act of 1940, that invests in an audit client.

(E) The accounting firm, any covered person in the firm, or any of his or her immediate family members:

(1) Has any direct or material indirect investment in an entity where:

(i) An audit client has an investment in that entity that is material to the audit client and has the ability to exercise significant influence over that entity; or

(ii) The entity has an investment in an audit client that is material to that entity and has the ability to exercise significant influence over that audit client;

(2) Has any material investment in an entity over which an audit client has the ability to exercise significant influence; or

(3) Has the ability to exercise significant influence over an entity that has the ability to exercise significant influence over an audit client.

(ii) *Other financial interests in audit client.* An accountant is not independent when the accounting firm, any covered person in the firm, or any of his or her immediate family members has:

(A) *Loans/debtor-creditor relationship.* Any loan (including any margin loan) to or from an audit client, or an audit client's officers, directors, or record or beneficial owners of more than ten percent of the audit client's equity securities, except for the following loans obtained from a financial institution under its normal lending procedures, terms, and requirements:

(1) Automobile loans and leases collateralized by the automobile;

(2) Loans fully collateralized by the cash surrender value of an insurance policy;

(3) Loans fully collateralized by cash deposits at the same financial institution; and

(4) A mortgage loan collateralized by the borrower's primary residence provided the loan was not obtained while the covered person in the firm was a covered person.

(B) *Savings and checking accounts.* Any savings, checking, or similar account at a bank, savings and loan, or similar institution that is an audit client, if the account has a balance that exceeds the amount insured by the Federal Deposit Insurance Corporation or any similar insurer, except that an accounting firm account may have an uninsured balance provided that the likelihood of the bank, savings and loan, or similar institution experiencing financial difficulties is remote.

(C) *Broker-dealer accounts.* Brokerage or similar accounts maintained with a broker-dealer that is an audit client, if:

(1) Any such account includes any asset other than cash or securities (within the meaning of "security" provided in the Securities Investor Protection Act of 1970 ("SIPA"));

(2) The value of assets in the accounts exceeds the amount that is subject to a Securities Investor Protection Corporation advance, for those accounts, under Section 9 of SIPA; or

(3) With respect to non-U.S. accounts not subject to SIPA protection, the value of assets in the accounts exceeds the amount insured or protected by a program similar to SIPA.

(D) *Futures commission merchant accounts.* Any futures, commodity, or similar account maintained with a futures commission merchant that is an audit client.

(E) *Credit cards.* Any aggregate outstanding credit card balance owed to a lender that is an audit client that is not reduced to $10,000 or less on a current basis taking into consideration the payment due date and any available grace period.

(F) *Insurance products.* Any individual policy issued by an insurer that is an audit client unless:

(1) The policy was obtained at a time when the covered person in the firm was not a covered person in the firm; and

(2) The likelihood of the insurer becoming insolvent is remote.

(G) *Investment companies.* Any financial interest in an entity that is part of an investment company complex that includes an audit client.

(iii) *Exceptions.* Notwithstanding paragraphs (c)(1)(i) and (c)(1)(ii) of this section, an accountant will not be deemed not independent if:

(A) *Inheritance and gift.* Any person acquires an unsolicited financial interest, such as through an unsolicited gift or inheritance, that would cause an accountant to be not independent under paragraph (c)(1)(i) or (c)(1)(ii) of this section, and the financial interest is disposed of as soon as practicable, but no later than 30 days after the person has knowledge of and the right to dispose of the financial interest.

(B) *New audit engagement.* Any person has a financial interest that would cause an accountant to be not independent under paragraph (c)(1)(i) or (c)(1)(ii) of this section, and:

(1) The accountant did not audit the client's financial statements for the immediately preceding fiscal year; and

(2) The accountant is independent under paragraph (c)(1)(i) and (c)(1)(ii) of this section before the earlier of:

(i) Signing an initial engagement letter or other agreement to provide audit, review, or attest services to the audit client; or

(ii) Commencing any audit, review, or attest procedures (including planning the audit of the client's financial statements).

(C) *Employee compensation and benefit plans.* An immediate family member of a person who is a covered person in the firm only by virtue of paragraphs (f)(11)(iii) or (f)(11)(iv) of this section has a financial interest that would cause an accountant to be not independent under paragraph (c)(1)(i) or (c)(1)(ii) of this section, and the acquisition of the financial interest was an unavoidable consequence of participation in his or her employer's employee compensation or benefits program, provided that the financial interest, other than unexercised employee stock options, is disposed of as soon as practicable, but no later than 30 days after the person has the right to dispose of the financial interest.

(iv) *Audit clients' financial relationships.* An accountant is not independent when:

(A) *Investments by the audit client in the accounting firm.* An audit client has, or has agreed to acquire, any direct investment in the accounting firm, such as stocks, bonds, notes, options, or other securities, or the audit client's officers or directors are record or beneficial owners of more than 5% of the equity securities of the accounting firm.

(B) *Underwriting.* An accounting firm engages an audit client to act as an underwriter, broker-dealer, market-maker, promoter, or analyst with respect to securities issued by the accounting firm.

(2) *Employment relationships.* An accountant is not independent if, at any point during the audit and professional engagement period, the accountant has an employment relationship with an audit client, such as:

(i) *Employment at audit client of accountant.* A current partner, principal, shareholder, or professional employee of the accounting firm is employed by the audit client or serves as a member of the board of directors or similar management or governing body of the audit client.

(ii) *Employment at audit client of certain relatives of accountant.* A close family member of a covered person in the firm is in an accounting role or financial reporting oversight role at an audit client, or was in such a role during any period covered by an audit for which the covered person in the firm is a covered person.

(iii) *Employment at audit client of former employee of accounting firm.*

(A) A former partner, principal, shareholder, or professional employee of an accounting firm is in an accounting role or financial reporting oversight role at an audit client, unless the individual:

(1) Does not influence the accounting firm's operations or financial policies;

(2) Has no capital balances in the accounting firm; and

(3) Has no financial arrangement with the accounting firm other than one providing for regular payment of a fixed dollar amount (which is not dependent on the revenues, profits, or earnings of the accounting firm):

(i) Pursuant to a fully funded retirement plan, rabbi trust, or, in jurisdictions in which a rabbi trust does not exist, a similar vehicle; or

(ii) In the case of a former professional employee who was not a partner, principal, or shareholder of the accounting firm and who has been disassociated from the accounting firm for more than five years, that is immaterial to the former professional employee; and

(B) A former partner, principal, shareholder, or professional employee of an accounting firm is in a financial reporting oversight role at an issuer (as defined in section 10A(f) of the Securities Exchange Act of 1934), except an issuer that is an investment company registered under section 8 of the Investment Company Act of 1940, unless the individual:

(1) Employed by the issuer was not a member of the audit engagement team of the issuer during the one year period preceding the date that audit procedures commenced for the fiscal period that included the date of initial employment of the audit engagement team member by the issuer;

(2) For purposes of paragraph (c)(2)(iii)(B)(1) of this section, the following individuals are not considered to be members of the audit engagement team:

(i) Persons, other than the lead partner and the concurring partner, who provided ten or fewer hours of audit, review, or attest services during the period covered by paragraph (c)(2)(iii)(B)(1) of this section;

(ii) Individuals employed by the issuer as a result of a business combination between an issuer that is an audit client and the employing entity, provided employment was not in contemplation of the business combination and the audit committee of the successor issuer is aware of the prior employment relationship; and

(iii) Individuals that are employed by the issuer due to an emergency or other unusual situation provided that the audit committee determines that the relationship is in the interest of investors;

(3) For purposes of paragraph (c)(2)(iii)(B)(1) of this section, audit procedures are deemed to have commenced for a fiscal period the day following the filing of the issuer's periodic annual report with the Commission covering the previous fiscal period; or

(C) A former partner, principal, shareholder, or professional employee of an accounting firm is in a financial reporting oversight role with respect to an investment company registered under section 8 of the Investment Company Act of 1940, if:

(1) The former partner, principal, shareholder, or professional employee of an accounting firm is employed in a financial reporting oversight role related to the operations and financial reporting of the registered investment company at an entity in the investment company complex, as defined in (f)(14) of this section, that includes the registered investment company; and

(2) The former partner, principal, shareholder, or professional employee of an accounting firm employed by the registered investment company or any entity in the investment company complex was a member of the audit engagement team of the registered investment company or any other registered investment company in the investment company complex during the one year period preceding the date that audit procedures commenced that included the date of initial employment of the audit engagement team member by the registered investment company or any entity in the investment company complex.

(3) For purposes of paragraph (c)(2)(iii)(C)(2) of this section, the following individuals are not considered to be members of the audit engagement team:

(i) Persons, other than the lead partner and concurring partner, who provided ten or fewer hours of audit, review or attest services during the period covered by paragraph (c)(2)(iii)(C)(2) of this section;

(ii) Individuals employed by the registered investment company or any entity in the investment company complex as a result of a business combination between a registered investment company or any entity in the investment company complex that is an audit client and the employing entity, provided employment was not in contemplation of the business combination and the audit committee of the registered investment company is aware of the prior employment relationship; and

(iii) Individuals that are employed by the registered investment company or any entity in the investment company complex due to an emergency or other unusual situation provided that the audit committee determines that the relationship is in the interest of investors.

(4) For purposes of paragraph (c)(2)(iii)(C)(2) of this section, audit procedures are deemed to have commenced the day following the filing of the registered investment company's periodic annual report with the Commission.

(iv) Employment at Accounting Firm of Former Employee of Audit Client. A former officer, director, or employee of an audit client becomes a partner, principal, shareholder, or professional employee of the accounting firm, unless the individual does not participate in, and is not in a position to influence, the audit of the financial statements of the audit client covering any period during which he or she was employed by or associated with that audit client.

(3) *Business relationships.* An accountant is not independent if, at any point during the audit and professional engagement period, the accounting firm or any covered person in the firm has any direct or material indirect business relationship with an audit client, or with persons associated with the audit client in a decision-making capacity, such as an audit client's officers, directors, or substantial stockholders. The relationships described in this paragraph do not include a relationship in which the accounting firm or covered person in the firm provides professional services to an audit client or is a consumer in the ordinary course of business.

(4) *Non-audit services.* An accountant is not independent if, at any point during the audit and professional engagement period, the accountant provides the following non-audit services to an audit client:

(i) *Bookkeeping or other services related to the accounting records or financial statements of the audit client.* Any service, unless it is reasonable to conclude that the results of these services will not be subject to audit procedures during an audit of the audit client's financial statements, including:

(A) Maintaining or preparing the audit client's accounting records;

(B) Preparing the audit client's financial statements that are filed with the Commission or that form the basis of financial statements filed with the Commission; or

(C) Preparing or originating source data underlying the audit client's financial statements.

(ii) *Financial information systems design and implementation.* Any service, unless it is reasonable to conclude that the results of these services will not be subject to audit procedures during an audit of the audit client's financial statements, including:

(A) Directly or indirectly operating, or supervising the operation of, the audit client's information system or managing the audit client's local area network; or

(B) Designing or implementing a hardware or software system that aggregates source data underlying the financial statements or generates information that is significant to the audit client's financial statements or other financial information systems taken as a whole.

(iii) Appraisal or valuation services, fairness opinions, or contribution-in-kind reports. Any appraisal service, valuation service, or any service involving a fairness opinion or contribution-in-kind report for an audit client, unless it is reasonable to conclude that the results of these services will not be subject to audit procedures during an audit of the audit client's financial statements.

(iv) *Actuarial services.* Any actuarially-oriented advisory service involving the determination of amounts recorded in the financial statements and related accounts for the audit client other than assisting a client in understanding the methods, models, assumptions, and inputs used in computing an amount, unless it is reasonable to conclude that the results of these services will not be subject to audit procedures during an audit of the audit client's financial statements.

(v) *Internal audit outsourcing services.* Any internal audit service that has been outsourced by the audit client that relates to the audit client's internal accounting controls, financial systems, or financial statements, for an audit client unless it is reasonable to conclude that the results of these services will not be subject to audit procedures during an audit of the audit client's financial statements.

(vi) *Management functions.* Acting, temporarily or permanently, as a director, officer, or employee of an audit client, or performing any decision-making, supervisory, or ongoing monitoring function for the audit client.

(vii) *Human resources.*

(A) Searching for or seeking out prospective candidates for managerial, executive, or director positions;

(B) Engaging in psychological testing, or other formal testing or evaluation programs;

(C) Undertaking reference checks of prospective candidates for an executive or director position;

(D) Acting as a negotiator on the audit client's behalf, such as determining position, status or title, compensation, fringe benefits, or other conditions of employment; or

(E) Recommending, or advising the audit client to hire, a specific candidate for a specific job (except that an accounting firm may, upon request by the audit client, interview candidates and advise the audit client on the candidate's competence for financial accounting, administrative, or control positions).

(viii) *Broker-dealer, investment adviser, or investment banking services.* Acting as a broker-dealer (registered or unregistered), promoter, or underwriter, on behalf of an audit client, making investment decisions on behalf of the audit client or otherwise having discretionary authority over an audit client's investments, executing a transaction to buy or sell an audit client's investment, or having custody of assets of the audit client, such as taking temporary possession of securities purchased by the audit client.

(ix) *Legal services.* Providing any service to an audit client that, under circumstances in which the service is provided, could be provided only by someone licensed, admitted, or otherwise qualified to practice law in the jurisdiction in which the service is provided.

(x) *Expert services unrelated to the audit.* Providing an expert opinion or other expert service for an audit client, or an audit client's legal representative, for the purpose of advocating an audit client's interests in litigation or in a regulatory or administrative proceeding or investigation. In any litigation or regulatory or administrative proceeding or investigation, an accountant's independence shall not be deemed to be impaired if the accountant provides factual accounts, including in testimony, of work performed or explains the positions taken or conclusions reached during the performance of any service provided by the accountant for the audit client.

(5) *Contingent fees.* An accountant is not independent if, at any point during the audit and professional engagement period, the accountant provides any service or product to an audit client for a contingent fee or a commission, or receives a contingent fee or commission from an audit client.

(6) *Partner rotation.*

    (i) Except as provided in paragraph (c)(6)(ii) of this section, an accountant is not independent of an audit client when:

        (A) Any audit partner as defined in paragraph (f)(7)(ii) of this section performs:

            (1) The services of a lead partner, as defined in paragraph (f)(7)(ii)(A) of this section, or concurring partner, as defined in paragraph (f)(7)(ii)(B) of this section, for more than five consecutive years; or

            (2) One or more of the services defined in paragraphs (f)(7)(ii)(C) and (D) of this section for more than seven consecutive years;

        (B) Any audit partner:

            (1) Within the five consecutive year period following the performance of services for the maximum period permitted under paragraph (c)(6)(i)(A)(1) of this section, performs for that audit client the services of a lead partner, as defined in paragraph (f)(7)(ii)(A) of this section, or concurring partner, as defined in paragraph (f)(7)(ii)(B) of this section, or a combination of those services, or

            (2) Within the two consecutive year period following the performance of services for the maximum period permitted under paragraph (c)(6)(i)(A)(2) of this section, performs one or more of the services defined in paragraph (f)(7)(ii) of this section.

    (ii) Any accounting firm with less than five audit clients that are issuers (as defined in section 10A(f) of the Securities Exchange Act of 1934 (15 U.S.C. 78j–1(f))) and less than ten partners shall be exempt from paragraph (c)(6)(i) of this section provided the Public Company Accounting Oversight Board conducts a review at least once every three years of each of the audit client engagements that would result in a lack of auditor independence under this paragraph.

    (iii) For purposes of paragraph (c)(6)(i) of this section, an audit client that is an investment company registered under section 8 of the Investment Company Act of 1940 (15 U.S.C. 80a–8), does not include an affiliate of the audit client that is an entity in the same investment company complex, as defined in paragraph (f)(14) of this section, except for another registered investment company in the same investment company complex. For purposes of calculating consecutive years of service under paragraph (c)(6)(i) of this section with respect to investment companies in an investment company complex, audits of registered investment companies with different fiscal year-ends that are performed in a continuous 12-month period count as a single consecutive year.

    (7) *Audit committee administration of the engagement.* An accountant is not independent of an issuer (as defined in section 10A(f) of the Securities Exchange Act of 1934), . . . unless:

    (i) In accordance with Section 10A(i) of the Securities Exchange Act of 1934 either:

        (A) Before the accountant is engaged by the issuer or its subsidiaries, or the registered investment company or its subsidiaries, to render audit or non-audit services, the engagement is approved by the issuer's or registered investment company's audit committee; or

        (B) The engagement to render the service is entered into pursuant to pre-approval policies and procedures established by the audit committee of the issuer or registered investment company, provided the policies and procedures are detailed as to the particular service and the audit committee is informed of each service and such policies and procedures do not include delegation of the audit committees responsibilities under the Securities Exchange Act of 1934 to management; or

        (C) With respect to the provision of services other than audit, review or attest services the pre-approval requirement is waived if:

            (1) The aggregate amount of all such services provided constitutes no more than five percent of the total amount of revenues paid by the audit client to its accountant during the fiscal year in which the services are provided;

(2) Such services were not recognized by the issuer or registered investment company at the time of the engagement to be non-audit services; and

(3) Such services are promptly brought to the attention of the audit committee of the issuer or registered investment company and approved prior to the completion of the audit by the audit committee or by one or more members of the audit committee who are members of the board of directors to whom authority to grant such approvals has been delegated by the audit committee.

(ii) A registered investment company's audit committee also must pre-approve its accountant's engagements for non-audit services with the registered investment company's investment adviser (not including a sub-adviser whose role is primarily portfolio management and is sub-contracted or overseen by another investment adviser) and any entity controlling, controlled by, or under common control with the investment adviser that provides ongoing services to the registered investment company in accordance with paragraph (c)(7)(i) of this section, if the engagement relates directly to the operations and financial reporting of the registered investment company, except that with respect to the waiver of the pre-approval requirement under paragraph (c)(7)(i)(C) of this section, the aggregate amount of all services provided constitutes no more than five percent of the total amount of revenues paid to the registered investment company's accountant by the registered investment company, its investment adviser and any entity controlling, controlled by, or under common control with the investment adviser that provides ongoing services to the registered investment company during the fiscal year in which the services are provided that would have to be pre-approved by the registered investment company's audit committee pursuant to this section.

(8) *Compensation.* An accountant is not independent of an audit client if, at any point during the audit and professional engagement period, any audit partner earns or receives compensation based on the audit partner procuring engagements with that audit client to provide any products or services other than audit, review or attest services. Any accounting firm with fewer than ten partners and fewer than five audit clients that are issuers (as defined in section 10A(f) of the Securities Exchange Act of 1934) shall be exempt from the requirement stated in the previous sentence.

(d) *Quality controls.* An accounting firm's independence will not be impaired solely because a covered person in the firm is not independent of an audit client provided:

(1) The covered person did not know of the circumstances giving rise to the lack of independence;

(2) The covered person's lack of independence was corrected as promptly as possible under the relevant circumstances after the covered person or accounting firm became aware of it; and

(3) The accounting firm has a quality control system in place that provides reasonable assurance, taking into account the size and nature of the accounting firm's practice, that the accounting firm and its employees do not lack independence, and that covers at least all employees and associated entities of the accounting firm participating in the engagement, including employees and associated entities located outside of the United States.

(4) For an accounting firm that annually provides audit, review, or attest services to more than 500 companies with a class of securities registered with the Commission under section 12 of the Securities Exchange Act of 1934, a quality control system will not provide such reasonable assurance unless it has at least the following features:

(i) Written independence policies and procedures;

(ii) With respect to partners and managerial employees, an automated system to identify their investments in securities that might impair the accountant's independence;

(iii) With respect to all professionals, a system that provides timely information about entities from which the accountant is required to maintain independence;

(iv) An annual or on-going firm-wide training program about auditor independence;

(v) An annual internal inspection and testing program to monitor adherence to independence requirements;

(vi) Notification to all accounting firm members, officers, directors, and employees of the name and title of the member of senior management responsible for compliance with auditor independence requirements;

(vii) Written policies and procedures requiring all partners and covered persons to report promptly to the accounting firm when they are engaged in employment negotiations with an audit client, and requiring the firm to remove immediately any such professional from that audit client's engagement and to review promptly all work the professional performed related to that audit client's engagement; and

(viii) A disciplinary mechanism to ensure compliance with this section. . . .

(f) *Definition of terms.* For purposes of this section:

(1) *Accountant,* as used in paragraphs (b) through (e) of this section, means a registered public accounting firm, certified public accountant or public accountant performing services in connection with an engagement for which independence is required. References to the accountant include any accounting firm with which the certified public accountant or public accountant is affiliated.

(2) *Accounting firm* means an organization (whether it is a sole proprietorship, incorporated association, partnership, corporation, limited liability company, limited liability partnership, or other legal entity) that is engaged in the practice of public accounting and furnishes reports or other documents filed with the Commission or otherwise prepared under the securities laws, and all of the organization's departments, divisions, parents, subsidiaries, and associated entities, including those located outside of the United States. Accounting firm also includes the organization's pension, retirement, investment, or similar plans.

(3)(i) *Accounting role* means a role in which a person is in a position to or does exercise more than minimal influence over the contents of the accounting records or anyone who prepares them.

(ii) *Financial reporting oversight role* means a role in which a person is in a position to or does exercise influence over the contents of the financial statements or anyone who prepares them, such as when the person is a member of the board of directors or similar management or governing body, chief executive officer, president, chief financial officer, chief operating officer, general counsel, chief accounting officer, controller, director of internal audit, director of financial reporting, treasurer, or any equivalent position.

(4) *Affiliate of the audit client* means:

(i) An entity that has control over the audit client, or over which the audit client has control, or which is under common control with the audit client, including the audit client's parents and subsidiaries;

(ii) An entity over which the audit client has significant influence, unless the entity is not material to the audit client;

(iii) An entity that has significant influence over the audit client, unless the audit client is not material to the entity; and

(iv) Each entity in the investment company complex when the audit client is an entity that is part of an investment company complex.

(5) *Audit and professional engagement period* includes both:

(i) The period covered by any financial statements being audited or reviewed (the "audit period"); and

(ii) The period of the engagement to audit or review the audit client's financial statements or to prepare a report filed with the Commission (the "professional engagement period"):

(A) The professional engagement period begins when the accountant either signs an initial engagement letter (or other agreement to review or audit a client's financial statements) or begins audit, review, or attest procedures, whichever is earlier; and

(B) The professional engagement period ends when the audit client or the accountant notifies the Commission that the client is no longer that accountant's audit client.

(iii) For audits of the financial statements of foreign private issuers, the "audit and professional engagement period" does not include periods ended prior to the first day of the last fiscal year before the foreign private issuer first filed, or was required to file, a registration statement or report with the Commission, provided there has been full compliance with home country independence standards in all prior periods covered by any registration statement or report filed with the Commission.

(6) *Audit client* means the entity whose financial statements or other information is being audited, reviewed, or attested and any affiliates of the audit client, other than, for purposes of paragraph (c)(1)(i) of this section, entities that are affiliates of the audit client only by virtue of paragraph (f)(4)(ii) or (f)(4)(iii) of this section.

(7)(i) *Audit engagement team* means all partners, principals, shareholders and professional employees participating in an audit, review, or attestation engagement of an audit client, including audit partners and all persons who consult with others on the audit engagement team during the audit, review, or attestation engagement regarding technical or industry-specific issues, transactions, or events.

(ii) *Audit partner* means a partner or persons in an equivalent position, other than a partner who consults with others on the audit engagement team during the audit, review, or attestation engagement regarding technical or industry-specific issues, transactions, or events, who is a member of the audit engagement team who has responsibility for decision-making on significant auditing, accounting, and reporting matters that affect the financial statements, or who maintains regular contact with management and the audit committee and includes the following:

(A) The lead or coordinating audit partner having primary responsibility for the audit or review (the "lead partner");

(B) The partner performing a second level of review to provide additional assurance that the financial statements subject to the audit or review are in conformity with generally accepted accounting principles and the audit or review and any associated report are in accordance with generally accepted auditing standards and rules promulgated by the Commission or the Public Company Accounting Oversight Board (the "concurring or reviewing partner");

(C) Other audit engagement team partners who provide more than ten hours of audit, review, or attest services in connection with the annual or interim consolidated financial statements of the issuer or an investment company registered under section 8 of the Investment Company Act of 1940; and

(D) Other audit engagement team partners who serve as the "lead partner" in connection with any audit or review related to the annual or interim financial statements of a subsidiary of the issuer whose assets or revenues constitute 20% or more of the assets or revenues of the issuer's respective consolidated assets or revenues.

(8) *Chain of command* means all persons who:

(i) Supervise or have direct management responsibility for the audit, including at all successively senior levels through the accounting firm's chief executive;

(ii) Evaluate the performance or recommend the compensation of the audit engagement partner; or

(iii) Provide quality control or other oversight of the audit.

(9) *Close family members* means a person's spouse, spousal equivalent, parent, dependent, nondependent child, and sibling.

(10) *Contingent fee* means, except as stated in the next sentence, any fee established for the sale of a product or the performance of any service pursuant to an arrangement in which no fee will be

charged unless a specified finding or result is attained, or in which the amount of the fee is otherwise dependent upon the finding or result of such product or service. Solely for the purposes of this section, a fee is not a "contingent fee" if it is fixed by courts or other public authorities, or, in tax matters, if determined based on the results of judicial proceedings or the findings of governmental agencies. Fees may vary depending, for example, on the complexity of services rendered.

(11) *Covered persons in the firm* means the following partners, principals, shareholders, and employees of an accounting firm:

(i) The "audit engagement team";

(ii) The "chain of command";

(iii) Any other partner, principal, shareholder, or managerial employee of the accounting firm who has provided ten or more hours of non-audit services to the audit client for the period beginning on the date such services are provided and ending on the date the accounting firm signs the report on the financial statements for the fiscal year during which those services are provided, or who expects to provide ten or more hours of non-audit services to the audit client on a recurring basis; and

(iv) Any other partner, principal, or shareholder from an "office" of the accounting firm in which the lead audit engagement partner primarily practices in connection with the audit.

(12) *Group* means two or more persons who act together for the purposes of acquiring, holding, voting, or disposing of securities of a registrant.

(13) *Immediate family members* means a person's spouse, spousal equivalent, and dependents. . . .

(15) *Office* means a distinct sub-group within an accounting firm, whether distinguished along geographic or practice lines.

(16) *Rabbi trust* means an irrevocable trust whose assets are not accessible to the accounting firm until all benefit obligations have been met, but are subject to the claims of creditors in bankruptcy or insolvency.

(17) *Audit committee* means a committee (or equivalent body) as defined in section 3(a)(58) of the Securities Exchange Act of 1934. . . .

Rule 2–02.   Accountants' reports and attestation reports.

(a) *Technical requirements for accountants' reports.* The accountant's report:

(1) Shall be dated;

(2) Shall be signed manually;

(3) Shall indicate the city and State where issued; and

(4) Shall identify without detailed enumeration the financial statements covered by the report.

(b) *Representations as to the audit included in accountants' reports.* The accountant's report:

(1) Shall state whether the audit was made in accordance with generally accepted auditing standards; and

(2) Shall designate any auditing procedures deemed necessary by the accountant under the circumstances of the particular case, which have been omitted, and the reasons for their omission. Nothing in this rule shall be construed to imply authority for the omission of any procedure which independent accountants would ordinarily employ in the course of an audit made for the purpose of expressing the opinions required by paragraph (c) of this section.

(c) *Opinions to be expressed in accountants' reports.* The accountant's report shall state clearly:

(1) The opinion of the accountant in respect of the financial statements covered by the report and the accounting principles and practices reflected therein; and

(2) the opinion of the accountant as to the consistency of the application of the accounting principles, or as to any changes in such principles which have a material effect on the financial statements.

(d) *Exceptions identified in accountants' reports.* Any matters to which the accountant takes exception shall be clearly identified, the exception thereto specifically and clearly stated, and, to the extent practicable, the effect of each such exception on the related financial statements given. . . .

(f) *Attestation report on internal control over financial reporting.* Every registered public accounting firm that issues or prepares an accountant's report for a registrant . . . that is included in an annual report required by section 13(a) or 15(d) of the Securities Exchange Act of 1934 containing an assessment by management of the effectiveness of the registrant's internal control over financial reporting must clearly state the opinion of the accountant, either unqualified or adverse, as to whether the registrant maintained, in all material respects, effective internal control over financial reporting, except in the rare circumstance of a scope limitation that cannot be overcome by the registrant or the registered public accounting firm which would result in the accounting firm disclaiming an opinion. The attestation report on internal control over financial reporting shall be dated, signed manually, identify the period covered by the report and indicate that the accountant has audited the effectiveness of internal control over financial reporting. The attestation report on internal control over financial reporting may be separate from the accountant's report.

Rule 2–02T. Accountants' reports and attestation reports on internal control over financial reporting. . . .

(a) The requirements of Rule 2–02(f) shall not apply to a registered public accounting firm that issues or prepares an accountant's report that is included in an annual report filed by a registrant that is neither a "large accelerated filer" nor an "accelerated filer," as those terms are defined in Rule 12b–2 [under the Securities Exchange Act], for a fiscal year ending on or after December 15, 2008 but before December 15, 2009.

(b) This rule expires on June 10, 2010.

Rule 2–07.   Communication with audit committees.

(a) Each registered public accounting firm that performs for an audit client that is an issuer (as defined in section 10A(f) of the Securities Exchange Act of 1934) . . . any audit required under the securities laws shall report, prior to the filing of such audit report with the Commission (or in the case of a registered investment company, annually, and if the annual communication is not within 90 days prior to the filing, provide an update, in the 90 day period prior to the filing, of any changes to the previously reported information), to the audit committee of the issuer or registered investment company:

(1) All critical accounting policies and practices to be used;

(2) All alternative treatments within Generally Accepted Accounting Principles for policies and practices related to material items that have been discussed with management of the issuer or registered investment company, including:

(i) Ramifications of the use of such alternative disclosures and treatments; and

(ii) The treatment preferred by the registered public accounting firm;

(3) Other material written communications between the registered public accounting firm and the management of the issuer or registered investment company, such as any management letter or schedule of unadjusted differences. . . .

REGULATION S–T—GENERAL RULES AND REGULATIONS FOR ELECTRONIC FILINGS

17 C.F.R. Part 232

§ 232.101. Mandated Electronic Submissions and Exceptions.

(a) *Mandated electronic submissions.*

(1) The following filings, including any related correspondence and supplemental information, except as otherwise provided, shall be submitted in electronic format:

(i) Registration statements and prospectuses filed pursuant to the Securities Act or registration statements filed pursuant to Sections 12(b) or 12(g) of the Exchange Act. . . .

(iii) Statements, reports and schedules filed with the Commission pursuant to sections 13, 14, 15(d) or 16(a) of the Exchange Act, and proxy materials required to be furnished for the information of the Commission in connection with annual reports on Form 10-K. . . .

REGULATION S–K—STANDARD INSTRUCTIONS FOR FILING FORMS UNDER SECURITIES ACT OF 1933 [AND] SECURITIES EXCHANGE ACT OF 1934 (SELECTED PROVISIONS)

17 C.F.R. §§ 229.10 et seq.

TABLE OF CONTENTS

SUBPART 100—GENERAL

Item		Page
10.	General	1320

SUBPART 200—SECURITIES OF THE REGISTRANT

201.	Market Price of and Dividends on Registrant's Common Equity and Related Stockholder Matters	1320

SUBPART 300—FINANCIAL INFORMATION

301.	Selected Financial Data	1322
303.	Management's Discussion and Analysis of Financial Condition and Results of Operations	1323
304.	Changes in and Disagreements with Accountants on Accounting and Financial Disclosure	1326
307.	Disclosure Controls and Procedures	1329
308.	Internal Control Over Financial Reporting	1329

SUBPART 400—MANAGEMENT AND CERTAIN SECURITY HOLDERS

401.	Directors, Executive Officers, Promoters and Control Persons	1330
402.	Executive Compensation	1332
403.	Security Ownership of Certain Beneficial Owners and Management	1346
404.	Transactions with Related Persons, Promoters and Certain Control Persons	1347
405.	Compliance with Section 16(a) of the Exchange Act	1350
406.	Code of Ethics	1351
407.	Corporate Governance	1352

SUBPART 500—REGISTRATION STATEMENT AND PROSPECTUS PROVISIONS

512.	Undertakings	1360

SUBPART 600—EXHIBITS

601.	Exhibits	1362

SUBPART 900—ROLL-UP TRANSACTIONS

901.	[Definitions]	1364
908.	Reasons for and Alternatives to the Roll-Up Transaction	1365
909.	Conflicts of Interest	1365
910.	Fairness of the Transaction	1366
911.	Reports, Opinions and Appraisals	1367

Subpart 100—General

Item 10.   General. . . .

(f) *Smaller reporting companies. . . .*

(1) *Definition of smaller reporting company.* As used in this part, the term *smaller reporting company* means an issuer that is not an investment company, an asset-backed issuer (as defined in Item 1101), or a majority-owned subsidiary of a parent that is not a smaller reporting company and that:

(i) Had a public float of less than $75 million as of the last business day of its most recently completed second fiscal quarter, computed by multiplying the aggregate worldwide number of shares of its voting and non-voting common equity held by non-affiliates by the price at which the common equity was last sold, or the average of the bid and asked prices of common equity, in the principal market for the common equity; or

(ii) In the case of an initial registration statement under the Securities Act or Exchange Act for shares of its common equity, had a public float of less than $75 million as of a date within 30 days of the date of the filing of the registration statement, computed by multiplying the aggregate worldwide number of such shares held by non-affiliates before the registration plus, in the case of a Securities Act registration statement, the number of such shares included in the registration statement by the estimated public offering price of the shares; or

(iii) In the case of an issuer whose public float as calculated under paragraph (i) or (ii) of this definition was zero, had annual revenues of less than $50 million during the most recently completed fiscal year for which audited financial statements are available. . . .

Subpart 200—Securities of the Registrant

Item 201.   Market Price of and Dividends on the Registrant's Common Equity and Related Stockholder Matters. . . .

(d) *Securities authorized for issuance under equity compensation plans.*

(1) In the following tabular format, provide the information specified in paragraph (d)(2) of this Item as of the end of the most recently completed fiscal year with respect to compensation plans (including individual compensation arrangements) under which equity securities of the registrant are authorized for issuance, aggregated as follows:

(i) All compensation plans previously approved by security holders; and

(ii) All compensation plans not previously approved by security holders.

Plan Category	Number of securities to be issued upon exercise of outstanding options, warrants and rights	Weighted-average exercise price of outstanding options, warrants and rights	Number of securities remaining available for future issuance under equity compensation plans (excluding securities reflected in column (a))
	(a)	(b)	(c)
Equity compensation plans approved by security holders			
Equity compensation plans not approved by security holders			
Total			

(2) The table shall include the following information as of the end of the most recently completed fiscal year for each category of equity compensation plan described in paragraph (d)(1) of this Item:

(i) The number of securities to be issued upon the exercise of outstanding options, warrants and rights (column (a));

(ii) The weighted-average exercise price of the outstanding options, warrants and rights disclosed pursuant to paragraph (d)(2)(i) of this Item (column (b)); and

(iii) Other than securities to be issued upon the exercise of the outstanding options, warrants and rights disclosed in paragraph (d)(2)(i) of this Item, the number of securities remaining available for future issuance under the plan (column (c)).

(3) For each compensation plan under which equity securities of the registrant are authorized for issuance that was adopted without the approval of security holders, describe briefly, in narrative form, the material features of the plan.

Instructions to Paragraph (d).

1.   Disclosure shall be provided with respect to any compensation plan and individual compensation arrangement of the registrant (or parent, subsidiary or affiliate of the registrant) under which equity securities of the registrant are authorized for issuance to employees or non-employees (such as directors, consultants, advisors, vendors, customers, suppliers or lenders) in exchange for consideration in the form of goods or services. . . .

(e) *Performance graph.* (1) Provide a line graph comparing the yearly percentage change in the registrant's cumulative total shareholder return on a class of common stock registered under section 12 of the Exchange Act (as measured by dividing the sum of the cumulative amount of dividends for the measurement period, assuming dividend reinvestment, and the difference between the registrant's share price at the end and the beginning of the measurement period, by the share price at the beginning of the measurement period) with:

(i) The cumulative total return of a broad equity market index assuming reinvestment of dividends, that includes companies whose equity securities are traded on the same exchange or are of comparable market capitalization; *provided, however*, that if the registrant is a company within the Standard & Poor's 500 Stock Index, the registrant must use that index; and

(ii) The cumulative total return, assuming reinvestment of dividends, of:

(A) A published industry or line-of-business index;

(B) Peer issuer(s) selected in good faith. If the registrant does not select its peer issuer(s) on an industry or line-of-business basis, the registrant shall disclose the basis for its selection; or

(C) Issuer(s) with similar market capitalization(s), but only if the registrant does not use a published industry or line-of-business index and does not believe it can reasonably identify a peer group. If the registrant uses this alternative, the graph shall be accompanied by a statement of the reasons for this selection.

(2) For purposes of paragraph (e)(1) of this Item, the term "measurement period" shall be the period beginning at the "measurement point" established by the market close on the last trading day before the beginning of the registrant's fifth preceding fiscal year, through and including the end of the registrant's last completed fiscal year. If the class of securities has been registered under section 12 of the Exchange Act (15 U.S.C. 78*l*) for a shorter period of time, the period covered by the comparison may correspond to that time period.

(3) For purposes of paragraph (e)(1)(ii)(A) of this Item, the term "published industry or line-of-business index" means any index that is prepared by a party other than the registrant or an affiliate and is accessible to the registrant's security holders; *provided, however*, that registrants may use an index prepared by the registrant or affiliate if such index is widely recognized and used.

(4) If the registrant selects a different index from an index used for the immediately preceding fiscal year, explain the reason(s) for this change and also compare the registrant's total return with that of both the newly selected index and the index used in the immediately preceding fiscal year.

Instructions to Item 201(e): . . . .

(6) *Smaller reporting companies*. A registrant that qualifies as a smaller reporting company, as defined by Item 10(f)(1), is not required to provide the information required by paragraph (e) of this Item.

Subpart 300—Financial Information

Item 301.   Selected Financial Data

Furnish in comparative columnar form the selected financial data for the registrant referred to below, for

(a) Each of the last five fiscal years of the registrant (or for the life of the registrant and its predecessors, if less), and

(b) Any additional fiscal years necessary to keep the information from being misleading.

Instructions to Item 301.

1.   The purpose of the selected financial data shall be to supply in a convenient and readable format selected financial data which highlight certain significant trends in the registrant's financial condition and results of operations.

2.   Subject to appropriate variation to conform to the nature of the registrant's business, the following items shall be included in the table of financial data: net sales or operating revenues; income (loss) from continuing operations; income (loss) from continuing operations per common share; total assets; long-term obligations and redeemable preferred stock. . . .

Briefly describe, or cross-reference to a discussion thereof, factors such as accounting changes, business combinations or dispositions of business operations, that materially affect the comparability of the information reflected in selected financial data. Discussion of, or reference to, any material uncertainties should also be included where such matters might cause the data reflected herein not to be indicative of the registrant's future financial condition or results of operations. . . .

(c) *Smaller reporting companies*. A registrant that qualifies as a smaller reporting company, as defined by Item 10(f)(1), is not required to provide the information required by this Item.

Item 303. **Management's Discussion and Analysis of Financial Condition and Results of Operations**

(a) *Full fiscal years.* Discuss registrant's financial condition, changes in financial condition and results of operations. The discussion shall provide information as specified in paragraphs (a)(1) through (a)(5) of this Item and also shall provide such other information that the registrant believes to be necessary to an understanding of its financial condition, changes in financial condition and results of operations. Discussions of liquidity and capital resources may be combined whenever the two topics are interrelated. Where in the registrant's judgment a discussion of segment information or of other subdivisions of the registrant's business would be appropriate to an understanding of such business, the discussion shall focus on each relevant, reportable segment or other subdivision of the business and on the registrant as a whole.

(1) *Liquidity.* Identify any known trends or any known demands, commitments, events or uncertainties that will result in or that are reasonably likely to result in the registrant's liquidity increasing or decreasing in any material way. If a material deficiency is identified, indicate the course of action that the registrant has taken or proposes to take to remedy the deficiency. Also identify and separately describe internal and external sources of liquidity, and briefly discuss any material unused sources of liquid assets.

(2) *Capital resources.* (i) Describe the registrant's material commitments for capital expenditures as of the end of the latest fiscal period, and indicate the general purpose of such commitments and the anticipated source of funds needed to fulfill such commitments.

(ii) Describe any known material trends, favorable or unfavorable, in the registrant's capital resources. Indicate any expected material changes in the mix and relative cost of such resources. The discussion shall consider changes between equity, debt and any off-balance sheet financing arrangements.

(3) *Results of operations.* (i) Describe any unusual or infrequent events or transactions or any significant economic changes that materially affected the amount of reported income from continuing operations and, in each case, indicate the extent to which income was so affected. In addition, describe any other significant components of revenues or expenses that, in the registrant's judgment, should be described in order to understand the registrant's results of operations.

(ii) Describe any known trends or uncertainties that have had or that the registrant reasonably expects will have a material favorable or unfavorable impact on net sales or revenues or income from continuing operations. If the registrant knows of events that will cause a material change in the relationship between costs and revenues (such as known future increases in costs of labor or materials or price increases or inventory adjustments), the change in the relationship shall be disclosed.

(iii) To the extent that the financial statements disclose material increases in net sales or revenues, provide a narrative discussion of the extent to which such increases are attributable to increases in prices or to increases in the volume or amount of goods or services being sold or to the introduction of new products or services.

(iv) For the three most recent fiscal years of the registrant . . . or for those fiscal years in which the registrant has been engaged in business, whichever period is shortest, discuss the impact of inflation and changing prices on the registrant's net sales and revenues and on income from continuing operations.

(4) *Off-balance sheet arrangements.* (i) In a separately-captioned section, discuss the registrant's off-balance sheet arrangements that have or are reasonably likely to have a current or future effect on the registrant's financial condition, changes in financial condition, revenues or expenses, results of operations, liquidity, capital expenditures or capital resources that is material to investors. The disclosure shall include the items specified in paragraphs (a)(4)(i)(A), (B), (C) and (D) of this Item to the extent necessary to an understanding of such arrangements and effect and shall also include such other information that the registrant believes is necessary for such an understanding.

(A) The nature and business purpose to the registrant of such off-balance sheet arrangements;

(B) The importance to the registrant of such off-balance sheet arrangements in respect of its liquidity, capital resources, market risk support, credit risk support or other benefits;

(C) The amounts of revenues, expenses and cash flows of the registrant arising from such arrangements; the nature and amounts of any interests retained, securities issued and other indebtedness incurred by the registrant in connection with such arrangements; and the nature and amounts of any other obligations or liabilities (including contingent obligations or liabilities) of the registrant arising from such arrangements that are or are reasonably likely to become material and the triggering events or circumstances that could cause them to arise; and

(D) Any known event, demand, commitment, trend or uncertainty that will result in or is reasonably likely to result in the termination, or material reduction in availability to the registrant, of its off-balance sheet arrangements that provide material benefits to it, and the course of action that the registrant has taken or proposes to take in response to any such circumstances.

(ii) As used in this paragraph (a)(4), the term off-balance sheet arrangement means any transaction, agreement or other contractual arrangement to which an entity unconsolidated with the registrant is a party, under which the registrant has:

(A) Any obligation under a guarantee contract that has any of the characteristics identified in FASB ASC paragraph 460–10–5–4. . . .

(B) A retained or contingent interest in assets transferred to an unconsolidated entity or similar arrangement that serves as credit, liquidity or market risk support to such entity for such assets;

(C) Any obligation, including a contingent obligation, under a contract that would be accounted for as a derivative instrument, except that it is both indexed to the registrant's own stock and classified in stockholders' equity in the registrant's statement of financial position, and therefore excluded from the scope of FASB ASC Topic 815 . . . ; or

(D) Any obligation, including a contingent obligation, arising out of a variable interest . . . in an unconsolidated entity that is held by, and material to, the registrant, where such entity provides financing, liquidity, market risk or credit risk support to, or engages in leasing, hedging or research and development services with, the registrant.

(5) *Tabular disclosure of contractual obligations.* (i) In a tabular format, provide the information specified in this paragraph (a)(5) as of the latest fiscal year end balance sheet date with respect to the registrant's known contractual obligations specified in the table that follows this paragraph (a)(5)(i). The registrant shall provide amounts, aggregated by type of contractual obligation. The registrant may disaggregate the specified categories of contractual obligations using other categories suitable to its business, but the presentation must include all of the obligations of the registrant that fall within the specified categories. A presentation covering at least the periods specified shall be included. The tabular presentation may be accompanied by footnotes to describe provisions that create, increase or accelerate obligations, or other pertinent data to the extent necessary for an understanding of the timing and amount of the registrant's specified contractual obligations.

Contractual Obligations	Payments due by period				
	Total	Less than 1 year	1–3 years	3–5 years	More than 5 years
[Long-term Obligations]	. . . .	. . . .	. . . .	. . . .	. . . .
[Capital (finance) Lease Obligations]	. . . .	. . . .	. . . .	. . . .	. . . .
[Operating Lease Obligations]	. . . .	. . . .	. . . .	. . . .	. . . .
[Purchase Obligations]	. . . .	. . . .	. . . .	. . . .	. . . .
[Other Long-Term Liabilities] Reflected on the Company's Balance Sheet under the GAAP of the primary financial statements	. . . .	. . . .	. . . .		. . . .
Total	. . . .	. . . .	. . . .	. . . .	. . . .

(ii) Definitions: The following definitions apply to this paragraph (a)(5):

(A) Long-Term Debt Obligation means a payment obligation under long-term borrowings referenced in FASB ASC Paragraph 470–10–50–1. . . .

(B) Capital Lease Obligation means a payment obligation under a lease classified as a capital lease pursuant to FASB ASC Topic 840. . . .

(C) Operating Lease Obligation means a payment obligation under a lease classified as an operating lease and disclosed pursuant to FASB ASC Topic 840.

(D) Purchase Obligation means an agreement to purchase goods or services that is enforceable and legally binding on the registrant that specifies all significant terms, including: fixed or minimum quantities to be purchased; fixed, minimum or variable price provisions; and the approximate timing of the transaction.

Instructions to Paragraph 303(a). . . .

3. The discussion and analysis shall focus specifically on material events and uncertainties known to management that would cause reported financial information not to be necessarily indicative of future operating results or of future financial condition. This would include descriptions and amounts of (A) matters that would have an impact on future operations and have not had an impact in the past, and (B) matters that have had an impact on reported operations and are not expected to have an impact upon future operations.

4. Where the consolidated financial statements reveal material changes from year to year in one or more line items, the causes for the changes shall be described to the extent necessary to an understanding of the registrant's businesses as a whole. . . .

7. Any forward-looking information supplied is expressly covered by the safe harbor rule for projections. See Rule 175 under the Securities Act. . . .

(b) *Interim periods.* If interim period financial statements are included or are required to be included [under] Regulation S–X . . . , a management's discussion and analysis of the financial condition and results of operations shall be provided so as to enable the reader to assess material changes in financial condition and results of operations. . . .

(c) *Safe harbor.* (1) The safe harbor provided in section 27A of the Securities Act of 1933 and section 21E of the Securities Exchange Act of 1934 ("statutory safe harbors") shall apply to forward-looking information provided pursuant to paragraphs (a)(4) and (5) of this Item, provided that the disclosure is made by: an issuer; a person acting on behalf of the issuer; an outside reviewer retained by the issuer making a statement on behalf of the issuer; or an underwriter, with respect to information provided by the issuer or information derived from information provided by the issuer.

(d) *Smaller reporting companies.* A smaller reporting company, as defined by Item 10(f)(1), may provide the information required in paragraph (a)(3)(iv) of this Item for the last two most recent fiscal years of the registrant if it provides financial information on net sales and revenues and on income from continuing operations for only two years. A smaller reporting company is not required to provide the information required by paragraph (a)(5) of this Item.

Item 304.   Changes in and Disagreements with Accountants on Accounting and Financial Disclosure

(a)(1) If during the registrant's two most recent fiscal years or any subsequent interim period, an independent accountant who was previously engaged as the principal accountant to audit the registrant's financial statements, or an independent accountant who was previously engaged to audit a significant subsidiary and on whom the principal accountant expressed reliance in its reports, has resigned (or indicated it has declined to stand for re-election after the completion of the current audit) or was dismissed, then the registrant shall:

(i) State whether the former accountant resigned, declined to stand for re-election or was dismissed and the date thereof.

(ii) State whether the principal accountant's report on the financial statements for either of the past two years contained an adverse opinion or a disclaimer of opinion, or was qualified or modified as to uncertainty, audit scope, or accounting principles; and also describe the nature of each such adverse opinion, disclaimer of opinion, modification, or qualification.

(iii) State whether the decision to change accountants was recommended or approved by:

(A) any audit or similar committee of the board of directors, if the issuer has such a committee; or

(B) the board of directors, if the issuer has no such committee.

(iv) State whether during the registrant's two most recent fiscal years and any subsequent interim period preceding such resignation, declination or dismissal there were any disagreements with the former accountant on any matter of accounting principles or practices, financial statement disclosure, or auditing scope or procedure, which disagreement(s), if not resolved to the satisfaction of the former accountant, would have caused it to make reference to the subject matter of the disagreement(s) in connection with its report. Also, (A) describe each such disagreement; (B) state whether any audit or similar committee of the board of directors, or the board of directors, discussed the subject matter of each of such disagreements with the former accountant; and (C) state whether the registrant has authorized the former accountant to respond fully to the inquiries of the successor accountant concerning the subject matter of each of such disagreements and, if not, describe the nature of any limitation thereon and the reason therefore. The disagreements required to be reported in response to this Item include both those resolved to the former accountant's satisfaction and those not resolved to the former accountant's satisfaction. Disagreements contemplated by this Item are those that occur at the decision-making level, i.e., between personnel of the registrant responsible for presentation of its financial statements and personnel of the accounting firm responsible for rendering its report.

(v) Provide the information required by paragraph (a)(1)(iv) of this Item for each of the kinds of events (even though the registrant and the former accountant did not express a difference of opinion regarding the event) listed in paragraphs (A) through (D) below, that occurred within the registrant's two most recent fiscal years and any subsequent interim period preceding the former accountant's resignation, declination to stand for re-election, or dismissal ("reportable events"). If the event led to a disagreement or difference of opinion, then the event should be reported as a disagreement under paragraph (a)(1)(iv) and need not be repeated under this paragraph.

(A) [t]he accountant's having advised the registrant that the internal controls necessary for the registrant to develop reliable financial statements do not exist;

(B) the accountant's having advised the registrant that information has come to the accountant's attention that has led it to no longer be able to rely on management's representations, or that has made it unwilling to be associated with the financial statements prepared by management;

(C)*(1)* the accountant's having advised the registrant of the need to expand significantly the scope of its audit, or that information has come to the accountant's attention during the time period covered by Item 304(a)(1)(iv), that if further investigated may *(i)* materially impact the fairness or reliability of either: a previously issued audit report or the underlying financial statements; or the financial statements issued or to be issued covering the fiscal period(s) subsequent to the date of the most recent financial statements covered by an audit report (including information that may prevent it from rendering an unqualified audit report on those financial statements), or *(ii)* cause it to be unwilling to rely on management's representations or be associated with the registrant's financial statements, and *(2)* due to the accountant's resignation (due to audit scope limitations or otherwise) or dismissal, or for any other reason, the accountant did not so expand the scope of its audit or conduct such further investigation; or

(D)*(1)* the accountant's having advised the registrant that information has come to the accountant's attention that it has concluded materially impacts the fairness or reliability of either *(i)* a previously issued audit report or the underlying financial statements, or *(ii)* the financial statements issued or to be issued covering the fiscal period(s) subsequent to the date of the most recent financial statements covered by an audit report (including information that, unless resolved to the accountant's satisfaction, would prevent it from rendering an unqualified audit report on those financial statements), and *(2)* due to the accountant's resignation, dismissal or declination to stand for re-election, or for any other reason, the issue has not been resolved to the accountant's satisfaction prior to its resignation, dismissal or declination to stand for re-election.

(2) If during the registrant's two most recent fiscal years or any subsequent interim period, a new independent accountant has been engaged as either the principal accountant to audit the registrant's financial statements, or as an independent accountant to audit a significant subsidiary and on whom the principal accountant is expected to express reliance in its report, then the registrant shall identify the newly engaged accountant and indicate the date of such accountant's engagement. In addition, if during the registrant's two most recent fiscal years, and any subsequent interim period prior to engaging that accountant, the registrant (or someone on its behalf) consulted the newly engaged accountant regarding (i) either: the application of accounting principles to a specified transaction, either completed or proposed; or the type of audit opinion that might be rendered on the registrant's financial statements, and either a written report was provided to the registrant or oral advice was provided that the new accountant concluded was an important factor considered by the registrant in reaching a decision as to the accounting, auditing or financial reporting issue; or (ii) any matter that was either the subject of a disagreement (as defined in paragraph 304(a)(1)(iv) and the related instructions to this item) or a reportable event (as described in paragraph 304(a)(1)(v)), then the registrant shall:

(A) so state and identify the issues that were the subjects of those consultations;

(B) briefly describe the views of the newly engaged accountant as expressed orally or in writing to the registrant on each such issue and, if written views were received by the registrant, file them as an exhibit to the report or registration statement requiring compliance with this Item 304(a);

(C) state whether the former accountant was consulted by the registrant regarding any such issues, and if so, provide a summary of the former accountant's views; and

(D) request the newly engaged accountant to review the disclosure required by this Item 304(a) before it is filed with the Commission and provide the new accountant the opportunity to furnish the registrant with a letter addressed to the Commission containing any new information, clarification of the registrant's expression of its views, or the respects in which it does not agree with the statements made by the registrant in response to Item 304(a). The registrant shall file any such letter as an exhibit to the report or registration statement containing the disclosure required by this Item.

(3) The registrant shall provide the former accountant with a copy of the disclosures it is making in response to this Item 304(a) that the former accountant shall receive no later than the day that the disclosures are filed with the Commission. The registrant shall request the former accountant to furnish the registrant with a letter addressed to the Commission stating whether it agrees with the statements made by the registrant in response to this Item 304(a) and, if not, stating the respects in which it does not agree. The registrant shall file the former accountant's letter as an exhibit to the report or registration statement containing this disclosure. If the former accountant's letter is unavailable at the time of filing such report or registration statement, then the registrant shall request the former accountant to provide the letter as promptly as possible so that the registrant can file the letter with the Commission within ten business days after the filing of the report or registration statement. Notwithstanding the ten business day period, the registrant shall file the letter by amendment within two business days of receipt; if the letter is received on a Saturday, Sunday or holiday on which the Commission is not open for business, then the two business day period shall begin to run on and shall include the first business day thereafter. The former accountant may provide the registrant with an interim letter highlighting specific areas of concern and indicating that a more detailed letter will be forthcoming within the ten business day period noted above. If not filed with the report or registration statement containing the registrant's disclosure under this Item 304(a), then the interim letter, if any, shall be filed by the registrant by amendment within two business days of receipt.

(b) If, (1) in connection with a change in accountants subject to paragraph (a) of this Item 304, there was any disagreement of the type described in paragraph (a)(1)(iv) or any reportable event as described in paragraph (a)(1)(v) of this Item; (2) during the fiscal year in which the change in accountants took place or during the subsequent fiscal year, there have been any transactions or events similar to those which involved such disagreement or reportable event and (3) such transactions or events were material and were accounted for or disclosed in a manner different from that which the former accountants apparently would have concluded was required, the registrant shall state the existence and nature of the disagreement or reportable event and also state the effect on the financial statements if the method had been followed which the former accountants apparently would have concluded was required. These disclosures need not be made if the method asserted by the former accountants ceases to be generally accepted because of authoritative standards or interpretations subsequently issued.

Instructions to Item 304. . . .

4. The term "disagreements" as used in this Item shall be interpreted broadly, to include any difference of opinion concerning any matter of accounting principles or practices, financial statement disclosure, or auditing scope or procedure which (if not resolved to the satisfaction of the former accountant) would have caused it to make reference to the subject matter of the disagreement in connection with its report. It is not necessary for there to have been an argument to have had a disagreement, merely a difference of opinion. For purposes of this Item, however, the term disagreements does not include initial differences of opinion based on incomplete facts or preliminary information that were later resolved to the former accountant's satisfaction by, and providing the registrant and the accountant do not continue to have a difference of opinion upon, obtaining additional relevant facts or information.

5. In determining whether any disagreement or reportable event has occurred, an oral communication from the engagement partner or another person responsible for rendering the accounting firm's opinion (or their designee) will generally suffice as the accountant advising the registrant of a reportable event or as a statement of a disagreement at the "decision-making level" within the accounting firm and require disclosure under this Item.

Item 307.   Disclosure Controls and Procedures

Disclose the conclusions of the registrant's principal executive and principal financial officers, or persons performing similar functions, regarding the effectiveness of the registrant's disclosure controls and procedures (as defined in Rule 13a–15(e) or Rule 15d–15(e)) as of the end of the period covered by the report, based on the evaluation of these controls and procedures required by paragraph (b) of Rule 13a–15 or Rule 15d–15.

Item 308.   Internal Control Over Financial Reporting

(a) *Management's annual report on internal control over financial reporting.* Provide a report of management on the registrant's internal control over financial reporting (as defined in Rule 13a–15(f) or Rule 15d–15(f)) that contains:

(1) A statement of management's responsibility for establishing and maintaining adequate internal control over financial reporting for the registrant;

(2) A statement identifying the framework used by management to evaluate the effectiveness of the registrant's internal control over financial reporting as required by paragraph (c) Rule 13a–15 or Rule 15d–15;

(3) Management's assessment of the effectiveness of the registrant's internal control over financial reporting as of the end of the registrant's most recent fiscal year, including a statement as to whether or not internal control over financial reporting is effective. This discussion must include disclosure of any material weakness in the registrant's internal control over financial reporting identified by management. Management is not permitted to conclude that the registrant's internal control over financial reporting is effective if there are one or more material weaknesses in the registrant's internal control over financial reporting; and

(4) If the registrant is an accelerated filer or a large accelerated filer (as defined in Rule 12b–2), or otherwise includes in its annual report a registered public accounting firm's attestation report on internal control over financial reporting, a statement that the registered public accounting firm that audited the financial statements included in the annual report containing the disclosure required by this Item has issued an attestation report on the registrant's internal control over financial reporting.

(b) *Attestation report of the registered public accounting firm.* If the registrant is an accelerated filer or a large accelerated filer (as defined in Rule 12b–2), provide the registered public accounting firm's attestation report on the registrant's internal control over financial reporting in the registrant's annual report containing the disclosure required by this Item.

(c) *Changes in internal control over financial reporting.* Disclose any change in the registrant's internal control over financial reporting identified in connection with the evaluation required by paragraph (d) of Rule 13a–15 or Rule 15d–15 that occurred during the registrant's last fiscal quarter (the registrant's fourth fiscal quarter in the case of an annual report) that has materially affected, or is reasonably likely to materially affect, the registrant's internal control over financial reporting.

Instructions to Item 308

1.   A registrant need not comply with paragraphs (a) and (b) of this Item until it either had been required to file an annual report pursuant to section 13(a) or 15(d) of the Exchange Act for the prior fiscal year or had filed an annual report with the Commission for the prior fiscal year. A registrant that does not comply shall include a statement in the first annual report that it files in substantially the following form: "This annual report does not include a report of management's assessment regarding internal control over financial reporting or an attestation report of the company's registered public accounting firm due to a transition period established by rules of the Securities and Exchange Commission for newly public companies."

2.   The registrant must maintain evidential matter, including documentation, to provide reasonable support for management's assessment of the effectiveness of the registrant's internal control over financial reporting. . . .

Subpart 400—Management and Certain Security Holders

Item 401.   Directors, Executive Officers, Promoters and Control Persons

(a) *Identification of directors.* List the names and ages of all directors of the registrant and all persons nominated or chosen to become directors; indicate all positions and offices with the registrant held by each such person; state his term of office as director and any period(s) during which he has served as such; describe briefly any arrangement or understanding between him and any other person(s) (naming such person(s)) pursuant to which he was or is to be selected as a director or nominee. . . .

(b) *Identification of executive officers.* List the names and ages of all executive officers of the registrant and all persons chosen to become executive officers; indicate all positions and offices with the registrant held by each such person; state his term of office as officer and the period during which he has served as such and describe briefly any arrangement or understanding between him and any other person(s) (naming such person) pursuant to which he was or is to be selected as an officer.

(c) *Identification of certain significant employees.* Where the registrant employs persons such as production managers, sales managers, or research scientists who are not executive officers but who make or are expected to make significant contributions to the business of the registrant, such persons shall be identified and their background disclosed to the same extent as in the case of executive officers. Such disclosure need not be made if the registrant was subject to section 13(a) or 15(d) of the Exchange Act or was exempt from section 13(a) by section 12(g)(2)(G) of such Act immediately prior to the filing of the registration statement, report, or statement to which this Item is applicable.

(d) *Family relationships.* State the nature of any family relationship between any director, executive officer, or person nominated or chosen by the registrant to become a director or executive officer.

Instruction to Paragraph 401(d).

The term "family relationship" means any relationship by blood, marriage, or adoption, not more remote than first cousin.

(e) *Business experience.* (1) *Background.* Briefly describe the business experience during the past five years of each director, executive officer, person nominated or chosen to become a director or executive officer, and each person named in answer to paragraph (c) of Item 401, including: each person's principal occupations and employment during the past five years; the name and principal business of any corporation or other organization in which such occupations and employment were carried on; and whether such corporation or organization is a parent, subsidiary or other affiliate of the registrant. In addition, for each director or person nominated or chosen to become a director, briefly discuss the specific experience, qualifications, attributes or skills that led to the conclusion that the person should serve as a director for the registrant at the time that the disclosure is made, in light of the registrant's business and structure. If material, this disclosure should cover more than the past five years, including information about the person's particular areas of expertise or other relevant qualifications. When an executive officer or person named in response to paragraph (c) of Item 401 has been employed by the registrant or a subsidiary of the registrant for less than five years, a brief explanation shall be included as to the nature of the responsibility undertaken by the individual in prior positions to provide adequate disclosure of his or her prior business experience. What is required is information relating to the level of his or her professional competence, which may include, depending upon the circumstances, such specific information as the size of the operation supervised.

(2) *Directorships.* Indicate any other directorships held, including any other directorships held during the past five years, by each director or person nominated or chosen to become a director in any company with a class of securities registered pursuant to section 12 of the Exchange Act or subject to the requirements of section 15(d) of such Act. . . .

(f) *Involvement in certain legal proceedings.* Describe any of the following events that occurred during the past ten years and that are material to an evaluation of the ability or integrity of any director, person nominated to become a director or executive officer of the registrant:

(1) A petition under the Federal bankruptcy laws or any state insolvency law was filed by or against, or a receiver, fiscal agent or similar officer was appointed by a court for the business or

property of such person, or any partnership in which he was a general partner at or within two years before the time of such filing, or any corporation or business association of which he was an executive officer at or within two years before the time of such filing;

(2) Such person was convicted in a criminal proceeding or is a named subject of a pending criminal proceeding (excluding traffic violations and other minor offenses);

(3) Such person was the subject of any order, judgment, or decree, not subsequently reversed, suspended or vacated, of any court of competent jurisdiction, permanently or temporarily enjoining him from, or otherwise limiting, the following activities:

(i) Acting as a futures commission merchant, introducing broker, commodity trading advisor, commodity pool operator, floor broker, leverage transaction merchant, any other person regulated by the Commodity Futures Trading Commission, or an associated person of any of the foregoing, or as an investment adviser, underwriter, broker or dealer in securities, or as an affiliated person, director or employee of any investment company, bank, savings and loan association or insurance company, or engaging in or continuing any conduct or practice in connection with such activity;

(ii) Engaging in any type of business practice; or

(iii) Engaging in any activity in connection with the purchase or sale of any security or commodity or in connection with any violation of Federal or State securities laws or Federal commodities laws. . . .

(7) Such person was the subject of, or a party to, any Federal or State judicial or administrative order, judgment, decree, or finding, not subsequently reversed, suspended or vacated, relating to an alleged violation of:

(i) Any Federal or State securities or commodities law or regulation; or

(ii) Any law or regulation respecting financial institutions or insurance companies including, but not limited to, a temporary or permanent injunction, order of disgorgement or restitution, civil money penalty or temporary or permanent cease-and-desist order, or removal or prohibition order; or

(iii) Any law or regulation prohibiting mail or wire fraud or fraud in connection with any business entity; or

(8) Such person was the subject of, or a party to, any sanction or order, not subsequently reversed, suspended or vacated, of any self-regulatory organization (as defined in Section 3(a)(26) of the Exchange Act (15 U.S.C. 78c(a)(26))), any registered entity (as defined in Section 1(a)(29) of the Commodity Exchange Act (7 U.S.C. 1(a)(29))), or any equivalent exchange, association, entity or organization that has disciplinary authority over its members or persons associated with a member.

(g) *Promoters and control persons.*

(1) Registrants, which have not been subject to the reporting requirements of section 13(a) or 15(d) of the Exchange Act for the twelve months immediately prior to the filing of the registration statement, report, or statement to which this Item is applicable, and which had a promoter at any time during the past five fiscal years, shall describe with respect to any promoter, any of the events enumerated in [paragraph (f)] of this Item that occurred during the past five years and that are material to a voting or investment decision.

(2) Registrants, which have not been subject to the reporting requirements of section 13(a) or 15(d) of the Exchange Act for the twelve months immediately prior to the filing of the registration statement, report, or statement to which this Item is applicable, shall describe with respect to any control person, any of the events enumerated in [paragraph (f)] that occurred during the past five years and that are material to a voting or investment decision. . . .

Item 402. Executive Compensation

(a) *General. . . .*

(2) *All compensation covered.* This Item requires clear, concise and understandable disclosure of all plan and non-plan compensation awarded to, earned by, or paid to the named executive officers designated under paragraph (a)(3) of this Item, and directors covered by paragraph (k) of this Item, by any person for all services rendered in all capacities to the registrant and its subsidiaries, unless otherwise specifically excluded from disclosure in this Item. All such compensation shall be reported pursuant to this Item, even if also called for by another requirement, including transactions between the registrant and a third party where a purpose of the transaction is to furnish compensation to any such named executive officer or director. No amount reported as compensation for one fiscal year need be reported in the same manner as compensation for a subsequent fiscal year; amounts reported as compensation for one fiscal year may be required to be reported in a different manner pursuant to this Item.

(3) *Persons covered.* Disclosure shall be provided pursuant to this Item for each of the following (the "named executive officers"):

(i) All individuals serving as the registrant's principal executive officer or acting in a similar capacity during the last completed fiscal year ("PEO"), regardless of compensation level;

(ii) All individuals serving as the registrant's principal financial officer or acting in a similar capacity during the last completed fiscal year ("PFO"), regardless of compensation level;

(iii) The registrant's three most highly compensated executive officers other than the PEO and PFO who were serving as executive officers at the end of the last completed fiscal year; and

(iv) Up to two additional individuals for whom disclosure would have been provided pursuant to paragraph (a)(3)(iii) of this Item but for the fact that the individual was not serving as an executive officer of the registrant at the end of the last completed fiscal year.

(4) *Information for full fiscal year.* If the PEO or PFO served in that capacity during any part of a fiscal year with respect to which information is required, information should be provided as to all of his or her compensation for the full fiscal year. If a named executive officer (other than the PEO or PFO) served as an executive officer of the registrant (whether or not in the same position) during any part of the fiscal year with respect to which information is required, information shall be provided as to all compensation of that individual for the full fiscal year.

(5) *Omission of table or column.* A table or column may be omitted if there has been no compensation awarded to, earned by, or paid to any of the named executive officers or directors required to be reported in that table or column in any fiscal year covered by that table.

(6) *Definitions.* For purposes of this Item:

(i) The term *stock* means instruments such as common stock, restricted stock, restricted stock units, phantom stock, phantom stock units, common stock equivalent units or any similar instruments that do not have option-like features, and the term *option* means instruments such as stock options, stock appreciation rights and similar instruments with option-like features. The term *stock appreciation rights* ("<u>SARs</u>") refers to SARs payable in cash or stock, including SARs payable in cash or stock at the election of the registrant or a named executive officer. The term *equity* is used to refer generally to stock and/or options.

(ii) The term *plan* includes, but is not limited to, the following: Any plan, contract, authorization or arrangement, whether or not set forth in any formal document, pursuant to which cash, securities, similar instruments, or any other property may be received. A plan may be applicable to one person. Except with respect to the disclosure required by paragraph (t) of this Item, registrants may omit information regarding group life, health, hospitalization, or medical reimbursement plans that do not discriminate in scope, terms or operation, in favor of executive officers or directors of the registrant and that are available generally to all salaried employees.

(iii) The term *incentive plan* means any plan providing compensation intended to serve as incentive for performance to occur over a specified period, whether such performance is measured by reference to financial performance of the registrant or an affiliate, the registrant's stock price, or any other performance measure. An *equity incentive plan* is an incentive plan or portion of an incentive plan under which awards are granted that fall within the scope of FASB ASC Topic 718. . . . A *non-equity incentive plan* is an incentive plan or portion of an incentive plan that is not an equity incentive plan. The term *incentive plan award* means an award provided under an incentive plan.

(iv) The terms *date of grant* or *grant date* refer to the grant date determined for financial statement reporting purposes pursuant to FASB ASC Topic 718.

(v) *Closing market price* is defined as the price at which the registrant's security was last sold in the principal United States market for such security as of the date for which the closing market price is determined.

(b) *Compensation discussion and analysis.*

(1) Discuss the compensation awarded to, earned by, or paid to the named executive officers. The discussion shall explain all material elements of the registrant's compensation of the named executive officers. The discussion shall describe the following:

(i) The objectives of the registrant's compensation programs;

(ii) What the compensation program is designed to reward;

(iii) Each element of compensation;

(iv) Why the registrant chooses to pay each element;

(v) How the registrant determines the amount (and, where applicable, the formula) for each element to pay;

(vi) How each compensation element and the registrant's decisions regarding that element fit into the registrant's overall compensation objectives and affect decisions regarding other elements; and

(vii) Whether and, if so, how the registrant has considered the results of the most recent shareholder advisory vote on executive compensation required by section 14A of the Exchange Act, or Rule 14a–20 in determining compensation policies and decisions and, if so, how that consideration has affected the registrant's executive compensation decisions and policies.

(2) While the material information to be disclosed under Compensation Discussion and Analysis will vary depending upon the facts and circumstances, examples of such information may include, in a given case, among other things, the following:

(i) The policies for allocating between long-term and currently paid out compensation;

(ii) The policies for allocating between cash and non-cash compensation, and among different forms of non-cash compensation;

(iii) For long-term compensation, the basis for allocating compensation to each different form of award (such as relationship of the award to the achievement of the registrant's long-term goals, management's exposure to downside equity performance risk, correlation between cost to registrant and expected benefits to the registrant);

(iv) How the determination is made as to when awards are granted, including awards of equity-based compensation such as options;

(v) What specific items of corporate performance are taken into account in setting compensation policies and making compensation decisions;

(vi) How specific forms of compensation are structured and implemented to reflect these items of the registrant's performance, including whether discretion can be or has been exercised (either to award compensation absent attainment of the relevant performance goal(s) or to reduce or increase the size of any award or payout), identifying any particular exercise of discretion, and stating whether it applied to one or more specified named executive officers or to all compensation subject to the relevant performance goal(s);

(vii) How specific forms of compensation are structured and implemented to reflect the named executive officer's individual performance and/or individual contribution to these items of the registrant's performance, describing the elements of individual performance and/or contribution that are taken into account;

(viii) Registrant policies and decisions regarding the adjustment or recovery of awards or payments if the relevant registrant performance measures upon which they are based are restated or otherwise adjusted in a manner that would reduce the size of an award or payment;

(ix) The factors considered in decisions to increase or decrease compensation materially;

(x) How compensation or amounts realizable from prior compensation are considered in setting other elements of compensation (*e.g.*, how gains from prior option or stock awards are considered in setting retirement benefits);

(xi) With respect to any contract, agreement, plan or arrangement, whether written or unwritten, that provides for payment(s) at, following, or in connection with any termination or change-in-control, the basis for selecting particular events as triggering payment (*e.g.*, the rationale for providing a single trigger for payment in the event of a change-in-control);

(xii) The impact of the accounting and tax treatments of the particular form of compensation;

(xiii) The registrant's equity or other security ownership requirements or guidelines (specifying applicable amounts and forms of ownership), and any registrant policies regarding hedging the economic risk of such ownership;

(xiv) Whether the registrant engaged in any benchmarking of total compensation, or any material element of compensation, identifying the benchmark and, if applicable, its components (including component companies); and

(xv) The role of executive officers in determining executive compensation.

(c) *Summary compensation table.*

(1) *General.* Provide the information specified in paragraph (c)(2) of this Item, concerning the compensation of the named executive officers for each of the registrant's last three completed fiscal years, in a Summary Compensation Table in the tabular format specified below.

SUMMARY COMPENSATION TABLE

Name and Principal Position	Year	Salary ($)	Bonus ($)	Stock Awards ($)	Option Awards ($)	Non-Equity Incentive Plan Compensation ($)	Change in Pension Value and Non-Qualified Deferred Compensation Earnings ($)	All Other Compensation ($)	Total ($)
(a)	(b)	(c)	(d)	(e)	(f)	(g)	(h)	(i)	(j)
PEO	— — —								
PFO	— — —								
A	— — —								
B	— — —								
C	— — —								

(2) The Table shall include:

(i) The name and principal position of the named executive officer (column (a));

(ii) The fiscal year covered (column (b));

(iii) The dollar value of base salary (cash and non-cash) earned by the named executive officer during the fiscal year covered (column (c));

(iv) The dollar value of bonus (cash and non-cash) earned by the named executive officer during the fiscal year covered (column (d));

(v) For awards of stock, the aggregate grant date fair value computed in accordance with FASB ASC Topic 718 (column (e));

(vi) For awards of options, with or without tandem SARs (including awards that subsequently have been transferred), the aggregate grant date fair value computed in accordance with FASB ASC Topic 718 (column (f)).

(vii) The dollar value of all earnings for services performed during the fiscal year pursuant to awards under non-equity incentive plans as defined in paragraph (a)(6)(iii) of this Item, and all earnings on any outstanding awards (column (g));

(viii) The sum of the amounts specified in paragraphs (c)(2)(viii)(A) and (B) of this Item (column (h)) as follows:

(A) The aggregate change in the actuarial present value of the named executive officer's accumulated benefit under all defined benefit and actuarial pension plans (including supplemental plans) from the pension plan measurement date used for financial statement reporting purposes with respect to the registrant's audited financial statements for the prior completed fiscal year to the pension plan measurement date used for financial statement reporting purposes with respect to the registrant's audited financial statements for the covered fiscal year; and

(B) Above-market or preferential earnings on compensation that is deferred on a basis that is not tax-qualified, including such earnings on nonqualified defined contribution plans;

(ix) All other compensation for the covered fiscal year that the registrant could not properly report in any other column of the Summary Compensation Table (column (i)). Each compensation item that is not properly reportable in columns (c)–(h), regardless of the amount of the compensation item, must be included in column (i). Such compensation must include, but is not limited to:

(A) Perquisites and other personal benefits, or property, unless the aggregate amount of such compensation is less than $10,000;

(B) All "gross-ups" or other amounts reimbursed during the fiscal year for the payment of taxes;

(C) For any security of the registrant or its subsidiaries purchased from the registrant or its subsidiaries (through deferral of salary or bonus, or otherwise) at a discount from the market price of such security at the date of purchase, unless that discount is available generally, either to all security holders or to all salaried employees of the registrant, the compensation cost, if any, computed in accordance with FASB ASC Topic 718;

(D) The amount paid or accrued to any named executive officer pursuant to a plan or arrangement in connection with:

(1) Any termination, including without limitation through retirement, resignation, severance or constructive termination (including a change in responsibilities) of such executive officer's employment with the registrant and its subsidiaries; or

(2) A change in control of the registrant;

(E) Registrant contributions or other allocations to vested and unvested defined contribution plans;

(F) The dollar value of any insurance premiums paid by, or on behalf of, the registrant during the covered fiscal year with respect to life insurance for the benefit of a named executive officer; and

(G) The dollar value of any dividends or other earnings paid on stock or option awards, when those amounts were not factored into the grant date fair value required to be reported for the stock or option award in column (e) or (f); and

(x) The dollar value of total compensation for the covered fiscal year (column (j)). With respect to each named executive officer, disclose the sum of all amounts reported in columns (c) through (i).

(d) *Grants of plan-based awards table.* (1) Provide the information specified in paragraph (d)(2) of this Item, concerning each grant of an award made to a named executive officer in the last completed fiscal year under any plan, including awards that subsequently have been transferred, in the following tabular format:

GRANTS OF PLAN-BASED AWARDS

Name	Grant Date	Estimated Future Payouts Under Non-Equity Incentive Plan Awards			Estimated Future Payouts Under Equity Incentive Plan Awards			All Other Stock Awards: Number of Shares of Stock or Units (#)	All Other Option Awards: Number of Securities Underlying Options (#)	Exercise or Base Price of Option Awards ($/Sh)	Grant Date Fair Value of Stock and Option Awards
		Thresh-old ($)	Target ($)	Maxi-mum ($)	Thresh-old (#)	Target (#)	Maxi-mum (#)				
(a)	(b)	(c)	(d)	(e)	(f)	(g)	(h)	(i)	(j)	(k)	(l)
PEO											
PFO											
A											
B											
C											

(2) The Table shall include:

(i) The name of the named executive officer (column (a));

(ii) The grant date for equity-based awards reported in the table (column (b)). If such grant date is different than the date on which the compensation committee (or a committee of the board of directors performing a similar function or the full board of directors) takes action or is deemed to take action to grant such awards, a separate, adjoining column shall be added between columns (b) and (c) showing such date;

(iii) The dollar value of the estimated future payout upon satisfaction of the conditions in question under non-equity incentive plan awards granted in the fiscal year, or the applicable range of estimated payouts denominated in dollars (threshold, target and maximum amount) (columns (c) through (e));

(iv) The number of shares of stock, or the number of shares underlying options to be paid out or vested upon satisfaction of the conditions in question under equity incentive plan awards granted in the fiscal year, or the applicable range of estimated payouts denominated in the number of shares of stock, or the number of shares underlying options under the award (threshold, target and maximum amount) (columns (f) through (h));

(v) The number of shares of stock granted in the fiscal year that are not required to be disclosed in columns (f) through (h) (column (i));

(vi) The number of securities underlying options granted in the fiscal year that are not required to be disclosed in columns (f) through (h) (column (j));

(vii) The per-share exercise or base price of the options granted in the fiscal year (column (k)). If such exercise or base price is less than the closing market price of the underlying security on the date of the grant, a separate, adjoining column showing the closing market price on the date of the grant shall be added after column (k); and

(viii) The grant date fair value of each equity award computed in accordance with FASB ASC Topic 18. If at any time during the last completed fiscal year, the registrant has adjusted or amended the exercise or base price of options, SARs or similar option-like instruments previously awarded to a named executive officer, whether through amendment, cancellation or replacement grants, or any other means ("repriced"), or otherwise has materially modified such awards, the incremental fair value, computed as of the repricing or modification date . . . shall be reported. . . .

(e) *Narrative disclosure to summary compensation table and grants of plan-based awards table.*

(1) Provide a narrative description of any material factors necessary to an understanding of the information disclosed in the tables required by paragraphs (c) and (d) of this Item. Examples of such factors may include, in given cases, among other things:

(i) The material terms of each named executive officer's employment agreement or arrangement, whether written or unwritten;

(ii) If at any time during the last fiscal year, any outstanding option or other equity-based award was repriced or otherwise materially modified (such as by extension of exercise periods, the change of vesting or forfeiture conditions, the change or elimination of applicable performance criteria, or the change of the bases upon which returns are determined), a description of each such repricing or other material modification;

(iii) The material terms of any award reported in response to paragraph (d) of this Item, including a general description of the formula or criteria to be applied in determining the amounts payable, and the vesting schedule. For example, state where applicable that dividends will be paid on stock, and if so, the applicable dividend rate and whether that rate is preferential. Describe any performance-based conditions, and any other material conditions, that are applicable to the award. For purposes of the Table required by paragraph (d) of this Item and the narrative disclosure required by paragraph (e) of this Item, performance-based conditions include both performance conditions and market conditions, as those terms are defined in FASB ASC Topic 18; and

(iv) An explanation of the amount of salary and bonus in proportion to total compensation.

(f) *Outstanding equity awards at fiscal year-end table.* (1) Provide the information specified in paragraph (f)(2) of this Item, concerning unexercised options; stock that has not vested; and equity incentive plan awards for each named executive officer outstanding as of the end of the registrant's last completed fiscal year in the following tabular format:

OUTSTANDING EQUITY AWARDS AT FISCAL YEAR END

Name	Option Awards					Stock Awards			
	Number of Securities Underlying Unexercised Options (#) Excercisable	Number of Securities Underlying Unexercised Options (#) Unexercisable	Equity Incentive Plan Awards: Number of Securities Underlying Unexercised Unearned Options (#)	Option Exercise Price ($)	Option Expiration Date	Number of Shares or Units of Stock That Have Not Vested (#)	Market Value of Shares or Units of Stock That Have Not Vested (#)	Equity Incentive Plan Awards: Number of Unearned Shares, Units or Other Rights That Have Not Vested (#)	Equity Incentive Plan Awards: Market or Payout Value of Unearned Shares, Units or Other Rights That Have Not Vested ($)
(a)	(b)	(c)	(d)	(e)	(f)	(g)	(h)	(i)	(j)
PEO									
PFO									
A									
B									
C									

(2) The Table shall include:

    (i) The name of the named executive officer (column (a));

    (ii) On an award-by-award basis, the number of securities underlying unexercised options, including awards that have been transferred other than for value, that are exercisable and that are not reported in column (d) (column (b));

    (iii) On an award-by-award basis, the number of securities underlying unexercised options, including awards that have been transferred other than for value, that are unexercisable and that are not reported in column (d) (column (c));

    (iv) On an award-by-award basis, the total number of shares underlying unexercised options awarded under any equity incentive plan that have not been earned (column (d));

    (v) For each instrument reported in columns (b), (c) and (d), as applicable, the exercise or base price (column (e));

    (vi) For each instrument reported in columns (b), (c) and (d), as applicable, the expiration date (column (f));

    (vii) The total number of shares of stock that have not vested and that are not reported in column (i) (column (g));

    (viii) The aggregate market value of shares of stock that have not vested and that are not reported in column (j) (column (h));

(ix) The total number of shares of stock, units or other rights awarded under any equity incentive plan that have not vested and that have not been earned, and, if applicable the number of shares underlying any such unit or right (column (i)); and

(x) The aggregate market or payout value of shares of stock, units or other rights awarded under any equity incentive plan that have not vested and that have not been earned (column (j)).

(g) *Option exercises and stock vested table.* (1) Provide the information specified in paragraph (g)(2) of this Item, concerning each exercise of stock options, SARs and similar instruments, and each vesting of stock, including restricted stock, restricted stock units and similar instruments, during the last completed fiscal year for each of the named executive officers on an aggregated basis in the following tabular format:

OPTION EXERCISES AND STOCK VESTED

	Option Awards		Stock Awards	
Name	Number of Shares Acquired on Exercise (#)	Value Realized on Exercise ($)	Number of Shares Acquired on Vesting (#)	Value Realized on Vesting ($)
(a)	(b)	(c)	(d)	(e)
PEO				
PFO				
A				
B				
C				

(2) The Table shall include:

(i) The name of the executive officer (column (a));

(ii) The number of securities for which the options were exercised (column (b));

(iii) For awards of stock, the dollar amount recognized for financial statement reporting purposes with respect to the fiscal year in accordance with FAS 123R (column (c));

(iv) For awards of stock options, with or without tandem SARs, the dollar amount recognized for financial statement reporting purposes with respect to the fiscal year in accordance with FAS 123R (column (d));

(v) The aggregate dollar value realized upon vesting of stock, or upon the transfer of an award for value (column (e)).

(h) *Pension benefits.*

(1) Provide the information specified in paragraph (h)(2) of this Item with respect to each plan that provides for payments or other benefits at, following, or in connection with retirement, in the following tabular format:

PENSION BENEFITS

Name	Plan Name	Number of Years Credited Service (#)	Present Value of Accumulated Benefit ($)	Payments During Last Fiscal Year ($)
(a)	(b)	(c)	(d)	(e)
PEO				
PFO				
A				
B				
C				

(2) The Table shall include:

(i) The name of the executive officer (column (a));

(ii) The name of the plan (column (b));

(iii) The number of years of service credited to the named executive officer under the plan, computed as of the same pension plan measurement date used for financial statement reporting purposes with respect to the registrant's audited financial statements for the last completed fiscal year (column (c));

(iv) The actuarial present value of the named executive officer's accumulated benefit under the plan, computed as of the same pension plan measurement date used for financial statement reporting purposes with respect to the registrant's audited financial statements for the last completed fiscal year (column (d)); and

(v) The dollar amount of any payments and benefits paid to the named executive officer during the registrant's last completed fiscal year (column (e)).

(i) *Nonqualified defined contribution and other nonqualified deferred compensation plans.*

(1) Provide the information specified in paragraph (i)(2) of this Item with respect to each defined contribution or other plan that provides for the deferral of compensation on a basis that is not tax-qualified in the following tabular format:

NONQUALIFIED DEFERRED COMPENSATION

Name	Executive Contributions in Last FY ($)	Registrant Contributions in Last FY ($)	Aggregate Earnings in Last FY ($)	Aggregate Withdrawals/ Distributions ($)	Aggregate Balance at Last FYE ($)
(a)	(b)	(c)	(d)	(e)	(f)
PEO					
PFO					
A					
B					
C					

(2) The Table shall include:

(i) The name of the executive officer (column (a));

(ii) The dollar amount of aggregate executive contributions during the registrant's last fiscal year (column (b));

(iii) The dollar amount of aggregate registrant contributions during the registrant's last fiscal year (column (c));

(iv) The dollar amount of aggregate interest or other earnings accrued during the registrant's last fiscal year (column (d));

(v) The aggregate dollar amount of all withdrawals by and distributions to the executive during the registrant's last fiscal year (column (e)); and

(vi) The dollar amount of total balance of the executive's account as of the end of the registrant's last fiscal year (column (f)).

(j) *Potential payments upon termination or change-in-control.* Regarding each contract, agreement, plan or arrangement, whether written or unwritten, that provides for payment(s) to a named executive officer at, following, or in connection with any termination, including without limitation resignation, severance, retirement or a constructive termination of a named executive officer, or a change in control of the registrant or a change in the named executive officer's responsibilities, with respect to each named executive officer:

(1) Describe and explain the specific circumstances that would trigger payment(s) or the provision of other benefits, including perquisites and health care benefits;

(2) Describe and quantify the estimated payments and benefits that would be provided in each covered circumstance, whether they would or could be lump sum, or annual, disclosing the duration, and by whom they would be provided;

(3) Describe and explain how the appropriate payment and benefit levels are determined under the various circumstances that trigger payments or provision of benefits;

(4) Describe and explain any material conditions or obligations applicable to the receipt of payments or benefits, including but not limited to non-compete, non-solicitation, non-disparagement or confidentiality agreements, including the duration of such agreements and provisions regarding waiver of breach of such agreements; and

(5) Describe any other material factors regarding each such contract, agreement, plan or arrangement.

(k) *Compensation of directors.*

(1) Provide the information specified in paragraph (k)(2) of this Item, concerning the compensation of the directors for the registrant's last completed fiscal year, in the following tabular format:

DIRECTOR COMPENSATION

Name	Fees Earned or Paid in Case ($)	Stock Awards ($)	Option Awards ($)	Non-Equity Incentive Plan Compensation ($)	Change in Pension Value and Nonqualified Deferred Compensation Earnings	All Other Compensation ($)	Total ($)
(a)	(b)	(c)	(d)	(e)	(f)	(g)	(h)
PEO							
PFO							
A							
B							
C							

(2) The Table shall include:

(i) The name of each director unless such director is also a named executive officer under paragraph (a) of this Item and his or her compensation for service as a director is fully reflected in the Summary Compensation Table pursuant to paragraph (c) of this Item and otherwise as required pursuant to paragraphs (d) through (j) of this Item (column (a));

(ii) The aggregate dollar amount of all fees earned or paid in cash for services as a director, including annual retainer fees, committee and/or chairmanship fees, and meeting fees (column (b));

(iii) For awards of stock, the aggregate grant date fair value computed in accordance with FASB ASC Topic 718 (column (c));

(iv) For awards of options, with or without tandem SARs (including awards that subsequently have been transferred), the aggregate grant date fair value computed in accordance with FASB ASC Topic 718 (column (d));

(v) The dollar value of all earnings for services performed during the fiscal year pursuant to non-equity incentive plans as defined in paragraph (a)(6)(iii) of this Item, and all earnings on any outstanding awards (column (e));

(vi) The sum of the amounts specified in paragraphs (k)(2)(vi)(A) and (B) of this Item (column (f)) as follows:

(A) The aggregate change in the actuarial present value of the director's accumulated benefit under all defined benefit and actuarial pension plans (including supplemental plans) from the pension plan measurement date used for financial statement reporting purposes with respect to the registrant's audited financial statements for the prior completed fiscal year to the pension plan measurement date used for financial statement reporting purposes with respect to the registrant's audited financial statements for the covered fiscal year; and

(B) Above-market or preferential earnings on compensation that is deferred on a basis that is not tax-qualified, including such earnings on nonqualified defined contribution plans;

(vii) All other compensation for the covered fiscal year that the registrant could not properly report in any other column of the Director Compensation Table (column (g)). Each compensation item that is not properly reportable in columns (b)–(f), regardless of the amount of the compensation item, must be included in column (g). Such compensation must include, but is not limited to:

(A) Perquisites and other personal benefits, or property, unless the aggregate amount of such compensation is less than $10,000;

(B) All "gross-ups" or other amounts reimbursed during the fiscal year for the payment of taxes;

(C) For any security of the registrant or its subsidiaries purchased from the registrant or its subsidiaries (through deferral of salary or bonus, or otherwise) at a discount from the market price of such security at the date of purchase, unless that discount is available generally, either to all security holders or to all salaried employees of the registrant, the compensation cost, if any, computed in accordance with FASB ASC Topic 718;

(D) The amount paid or accrued to any director pursuant to a plan or arrangement in connection with:

(*1*) The resignation, retirement or any other termination of such director; or

(*2*) A change in control of the registrant;

(E) Registrant contributions or other allocations to vested and unvested defined contribution plans;

(F) Consulting fees earned from, or paid or payable by the registrant and/or its subsidiaries (including joint ventures);

(G) The annual costs of payments and promises of payments pursuant to director legacy programs and similar charitable award programs;

(H) The dollar value of any insurance premiums paid by, or on behalf of, the registrant during the covered fiscal year with respect to life insurance for the benefit of a director; and

(I) The dollar value of any dividends or other earnings paid on stock or option awards, when those amounts were not factored into the grant date fair value required to be reported for the stock or option award in column (c) or (d); and

(viii) The dollar value of total compensation for the covered fiscal year (column (h)). With respect to each director, disclose the sum of all amounts reported in columns (b) through (g).

(3) *Narrative to director compensation table.*

Provide a narrative description of any material factors necessary to an understanding of the director compensation disclosed in this Table. While material factors will vary depending upon the facts, examples of such factors may include, in given cases, among other things:

(i) A description of standard compensation arrangements (such as fees for retainer, committee service, service as chairman of the board or a committee, and meeting attendance); and

(ii) Whether any director has a different compensation arrangement, identifying that director and describing the terms of that arrangement.

(*l*) *Smaller Reporting Companies.* [Subsections (*l*)–(r) provide for scaled-down disclosure of executive compensation in the case of smaller reporting companies, as defined in Item 10(f).]

(s) *Narrative disclosure of the registrant's compensation policies and practices as they relate to the registrant's risk management.* To the extent that risks arising from the registrant's compensation policies and practices for its employees are reasonably likely to have a material adverse effect on the registrant, discuss the registrant's policies and practices of compensating its employees, including non-executive officers, as they relate to risk management practices and risk-taking incentives. While the situations requiring disclosure will vary depending on the particular registrant and compensation policies and practices, situations that may trigger disclosure include, among others, compensation policies and practices: at a business unit of the company that carries a significant portion of the registrant's risk profile; at a business unit with compensation structured significantly differently than other units within the registrant; at a business unit that is significantly more profitable than others within the registrant; at a business unit where compensation expense is a significant percentage of the unit's revenues; and that vary significantly from the overall risk and reward structure of the registrant, such as when bonuses are awarded upon accomplishment of a task, while the income and risk to the registrant from the task extend over a significantly longer period of time. The purpose of this paragraph (s) is to provide investors material information concerning how the registrant compensates and incentivizes its employees that may create risks that are reasonably likely to have a material adverse effect on the registrant. While the information to be disclosed pursuant to this paragraph (s) will vary depending upon the nature of the registrant's business and the compensation approach, the following are examples of the issues that the registrant may need to address for the business units or employees discussed:

(1) The general design philosophy of the registrant's compensation policies and practices for employees whose behavior would be most affected by the incentives established by the policies and practices, as such policies and practices relate to or affect risk taking by employees on behalf of the registrant, and the manner of their implementation;

(2) The registrant's risk assessment or incentive considerations, if any, in structuring its compensation policies and practices or in awarding and paying compensation;

(3) How the registrant's compensation policies and practices relate to the realization of risks resulting from the actions of employees in both the short term and the long term, such as through policies requiring claw backs or imposing holding periods;

(4) The registrant's policies regarding adjustments to its compensation policies and practices to address changes in its risk profile;

(5) Material adjustments the registrant has made to its compensation policies and practices as a result of changes in its risk profile; and

(6) The extent to which the registrant monitors its compensation policies and practices to determine whether its risk management objectives are being met with respect to incentivizing its employees.

(t) *Golden Parachute Compensation.* (1) In connection with any proxy or consent solicitation material providing the disclosure required by section 14A(b)(1) of the Exchange Act or any proxy or consent solicitation that includes disclosure under Item 14 of Schedule 14A ..., with respect to each named executive officer of the acquiring company and the target company, provide the information specified in paragraphs (t)(2) and (3) of this section regarding any agreement or understanding, whether written or unwritten, between such named executive officer and the acquiring company or target company, concerning any type of compensation, whether present, deferred or contingent, that is based on or otherwise relates to an acquisition, merger, consolidation, sale or other disposition of all or substantially all assets of the issuer, as follows:

Golden Parachute Compensation							
Name	Cash ($)	Equity ($)	Pension/ NQDC ($)	Perquisites/ Benefits ($)	Tax Reimbursement ($)	Other ($)	Total ($)
(a)	(b)	(c)	(d)	(e)	(f)	(g)	(h)
PEO							
PFO							
A							
B							
C							

(2) The table shall include, for each named executive officer:

(i) The name of the named executive officer (column (a));

(ii) The aggregate dollar value of any cash severance payments, including but not limited to payments of base salary, bonus, and pro-rated non-equity incentive compensation plan payments (column (b));

(iii) The aggregate dollar value of:

(A) Stock awards for which vesting would be accelerated;

(B) In-the-money option awards for which vesting would be accelerated; and

(C) Payments in cancellation of stock and option awards (column (c));

(iv) The aggregate dollar value of pension and nonqualified deferred compensation benefit enhancements (column (d));

(v) The aggregate dollar value of perquisites and other personal benefits or property, and health care and welfare benefits (column (e));

(vi) The aggregate dollar value of any tax reimbursements (column (f));

(vii) The aggregate dollar value of any other compensation that is based on or otherwise relates to the transaction not properly reported in columns (b) through (f) (column (g)); and

(viii) The aggregate dollar value of the sum of all amounts reported in columns (b) through (g) (column (h)).

Item 403. **Security Ownership of Certain Beneficial Owners and Management**

(a) *Security ownership of certain beneficial owners.* Furnish the following information, as of the most recent practicable date, substantially in the tabular form indicated, with respect to any person (including any "group" as that term is used in section 13(d)(3) of the Exchange Act) who is known to the registrant to be the beneficial owner of more than five percent of any class of the registrant's voting securities. The address given in column (2) may be a business, mailing or residence address. Show in column (3) the total number of shares beneficially owned and in column (4) the percentage of class so owned. Of the number of shares shown in column (3), indicate by footnote or otherwise the amount known to be shares with respect to which such listed beneficial owner has the right to acquire beneficial ownership, as specified in Rule 13d–3(d)(1) under the Exchange Act. . . .

(1) Title of class	(2) Name and address of beneficial owner	(3) Amount and nature of beneficial ownership	(4) Percent of class

(b) *Security ownership of management.* Furnish the following information, as of the most recent practicable date, in substantially the tabular form indicated, as to each class of equity securities of the registrant or any of its parents or subsidiaries, including directors' qualifying shares, beneficially owned by all directors and nominees, naming them, each of the named executive officers as defined in Item 402(a)(3), and directors and executive officers of the registrant as a group, without naming them. Show in column (3) the total number of shares beneficially owned and in column (4) the percent of the class so owned. Of the number of shares shown in column (3), indicate, by footnote or otherwise, the amount of shares that are pledged as security and the amount of shares with respect to which such persons have the right to acquire beneficial ownership as specified in Rule 13d–3(d)(1).

(1) Title of Class	(2) Name of Beneficial Owner	(3) Amount and Nature of Beneficial Ownership	(4) Percent of Class

(c) *Changes in control.* Describe any arrangements, known to the registrant, including any pledge by any person of securities of the registrant or any of its parents, the operation of which may at a subsequent date result in a change in control of the registrant.

Item 404. Transactions with Related Persons, Promoters and Certain Control Persons

(a) *Transactions with related persons.* Describe any transaction, since the beginning of the registrant's last fiscal year, or any currently proposed transaction, in which the registrant was or is to be a participant and the amount involved exceeds $120,000, and in which any related person had or will have a direct or indirect material interest. Disclose the following information regarding the transaction:

(1) The name of the related person and the basis on which the person is a related person.

(2) The related person's interest in the transaction with the registrant, including the related person's position(s) or relationship(s) with, or ownership in, a firm, corporation, or other entity that is a party to, or has an interest in, the transaction.

(3) The approximate dollar value of the amount involved in the transaction.

(4) The approximate dollar value of the amount of the related person's interest in the transaction, which shall be computed without regard to the amount of profit or loss.

(5) In the case of indebtedness, disclosure of the amount involved in the transaction shall include the largest aggregate amount of principal outstanding during the period for which disclosure is provided, the amount thereof outstanding as of the latest practicable date, the amount of principal paid during the periods for which disclosure is provided, the amount of interest paid during the period for which disclosure is provided, and the rate or amount of interest payable on the indebtedness.

(6) Any other information regarding the transaction or the related person in the context of the transaction that is material to investors in light of the circumstances of the particular transaction.

Instructions to Item 404(a)

1.   For the purposes of paragraph (a) of this Item, the term *related person* means:

a.   Any person who was in any of the following categories at any time during the specified period for which disclosure under paragraph (a) of this Item is required:

i.   Any director or executive officer of the registrant;

ii.   Any nominee for director, when the information called for by paragraph (a) of this Item is being presented in a proxy or information statement relating to the election of that nominee for director; or

iii. Any immediate family member of a director or executive officer of the registrant, or of any nominee for director when the information called for by paragraph (a) of this Item is being presented in a proxy or information statement relating to the election of that nominee for director, which means any child, stepchild, parent, stepparent, spouse, sibling, mother-in-law, father-in-law, son-in-law, daughter-in-law, brother-in-law, or sister-in-law of such director, executive officer or nominee for director, and any person (other than a tenant or employee) sharing the household of such director, executive officer or nominee for director; and

b. Any person who was in any of the following categories when a transaction in which such person had a direct or indirect material interest occurred or existed:

i. A security holder covered by Item 403(a); or

ii. Any immediate family member of any such security holder, which means any child, stepchild, parent, stepparent, spouse, sibling, mother-in-law, father-in-law, son-in-law, daughter-in-law, brother-in-law, or sister-in-law of such security holder, and any person (other than a tenant or employee) sharing the household of such security holder.

2. For purposes of paragraph (a) of this Item, a *transaction* includes, but is not limited to, any financial transaction, arrangement or relationship (including any indebtedness or guarantee of indebtedness) or any series of similar transactions, arrangements or relationships.

3. The amount involved in the transaction shall be computed by determining the dollar value of the amount involved in the transaction in question, which shall include:

a. In the case of any lease or other transaction providing for periodic payments or installments, the aggregate amount of all periodic payments or installments due on or after the beginning of the registrant's last fiscal year, including any required or optional payments due during or at the conclusion of the lease or other transaction providing for periodic payments or installments; and

b. In the case of indebtedness, the largest aggregate amount of all indebtedness outstanding at any time since the beginning of the registrant's last fiscal year and all amounts of interest payable on it during the last fiscal year.

4. In the case of a transaction involving indebtedness:

a. The following items of indebtedness may be excluded from the calculation of the amount of indebtedness and need not be disclosed: amounts due from the related person for purchases of goods and services subject to usual trade terms, for ordinary business travel and expense payments and for other transactions in the ordinary course of business;

b. Disclosure need not be provided of any indebtedness transaction for the related persons specified in Instruction 1.b. to paragraph (a) of this Item; and

c. If the lender is a bank, savings and loan association, or broker-dealer extending credit under Federal Reserve Regulation T and the loans are not disclosed as nonaccrual, past due, restructured or potential problems . . . , disclosure under paragraph (a) of this Item may consist of a statement, if such is the case, that the loans to such persons:

i. Were made in the ordinary course of business;

ii. Were made on substantially the same terms, including interest rates and collateral, as those prevailing at the time for comparable loans with persons not related to the lender; and

iii. Did not involve more than the normal risk of collectibility or present other unfavorable features.

5. a. Disclosure of an employment relationship or transaction involving an executive officer and any related compensation solely resulting from that employment relationship or transaction need not be provided pursuant to paragraph (a) of this Item if:

i.   The compensation arising from the relationship or transaction is reported pursuant to Item 402; or

ii.   The executive officer is not an immediate family member (as specified in Instruction 1 to paragraph (a) of this Item) and such compensation would have been reported under Item 402 as compensation earned for services to the registrant if the executive officer was a named executive officer as that term is defined in Item 402(a)(3), and such compensation had been approved, or recommended to the board of directors of the registrant for approval, by the compensation committee of the board of directors (or group of independent directors performing a similar function) of the registrant.

b.   Disclosure of compensation to a director need not be provided pursuant to paragraph (a) of this Item if the compensation is reported pursuant to Item 402(k).

6.   A person who has a position or relationship with a firm, corporation, or other entity that engages in a transaction with the registrant shall not be deemed to have an indirect material interest within the meaning of paragraph (a) of this Item where:

a.   The interest arises only:

i.   From such person's position as a director of another corporation or organization that is a party to the transaction; or

ii.   From the direct or indirect ownership by such person and all other persons specified in Instruction 1 to paragraph (a) of this Item, in the aggregate, of less than a ten percent equity interest in another person (other than a partnership) which is a party to the transaction; or

iii. From both such position and ownership; or

b.   The interest arises only from such person's position as a limited partner in a partnership in which the person and all other persons specified in Instruction 1 to paragraph (a) of this Item, have an interest of less than ten percent, and the person is not a general partner of and does not hold another position in the partnership.

7.   Disclosure need not be provided pursuant to paragraph (a) of this Item if:

a.   The transaction is one where the rates or charges involved in the transaction are determined by competitive bids, or the transaction involves the rendering of services as a common or contract carrier, or public utility, at rates or charges fixed in conformity with law or governmental authority;

b.   The transaction involves services as a bank depositary of funds, transfer agent, registrar, trustee under a trust indenture, or similar services; or

c.   The interest of the related person arises solely from the ownership of a class of equity securities of the registrant and all holders of that class of equity securities of the registrant received the same benefit on a pro rata basis.

(b) *Review, approval or ratification of transactions with related persons.*

(1) Describe the registrant's policies and procedures for the review, approval, or ratification of any transaction required to be reported under paragraph (a) of this Item. While the material features of such policies and procedures will vary depending on the particular circumstances, examples of such features may include, in given cases, among other things:

(i) The types of transactions that are covered by such policies and procedures;

(ii) The standards to be applied pursuant to such policies and procedures;

(iii) The persons or groups of persons on the board of directors or otherwise who are responsible for applying such policies and procedures; and

(iv) A statement of whether such policies and procedures are in writing and, if not, how such policies and procedures are evidenced.

(2) Identify any transaction required to be reported under paragraph (a) of this Item since the beginning of the registrant's last fiscal year where such policies and procedures did not require review, approval or ratification or where such policies and procedures were not followed.

(c) *Promoters and certain control persons.*

(1) Registrants that are filing a registration statement on Form S-1 under the Securities Act or on Form 10 under the Exchange Act and that had a promoter at any time during the past five fiscal years shall:

(i) State the names of the promoter(s), the nature and amount of anything of value (including money, property, contracts, options or rights of any kind) received or to be received by each promoter, directly or indirectly, from the registrant and the nature and amount of any assets, services or other consideration [theretofore] received or to be received by the registrant; and

(ii) As to any assets acquired or to be acquired by the registrant from a promoter, state the amount at which the assets were acquired or are to be acquired and the principle followed or to be followed in determining such amount, and identify the persons making the determination and their relationship, if any, with the registrant or any promoter. If the assets were acquired by the promoter within two years prior to their transfer to the registrant, also state the cost thereof to the promoter.

(2) Registrants shall provide the disclosure required by paragraphs (c)(1)(i) and (c)(1)(ii) of this Item as to any person who acquired control of a registrant that is a shell company, or any person that is part of a group, consisting of two or more persons that agree to act together for the purpose of acquiring, holding, voting or disposing of equity securities of a registrant, that acquired control of a registrant that is a shell company. For purposes of this Item, *shell company* has the same meaning as in Rule 405 under the Securities Act and Rule 12b–2 under the Exchange Act.

(d) *Smaller reporting companies.* A registrant that qualifies as a "smaller reporting company," as defined by Item 10(f)(1), must provide the following information in order to comply with this Item:

(1) The information required by paragraph (a) of this Item for the period specified there for a transaction in which the amount involved exceeds the lesser of $120,000 or one percent of the average of the smaller reporting company's total assets at year end for the last two completed fiscal years;

(2) The information required by paragraph (c) of this Item; and

(3) A list of all parents of the smaller reporting company showing the basis of control and as to each parent, the percentage of voting securities owned or other basis of control by its immediate parent, if any.

Item 405.   Compliance with Section 16(a) of the Exchange Act

Every registrant having a class of equity securities registered pursuant to Section 12 of the Exchange Act . . . shall:

(a) Based solely upon a review of Forms 3 and 4 and amendments thereto furnished to the registrant under Rule 16a–3(e) during its most recent fiscal year and Forms 5 and amendments thereto furnished to the registrant with respect to its most recent fiscal year, and any written representation referred to in paragraph (b)(1) of this section:

(1) Under the caption "Section 16(a) Beneficial Ownership Reporting Compliance," identify each person who, at any time during the fiscal year, was a director, officer, [or] beneficial owner of more than ten percent of any class of equity securities of the registrant registered pursuant to Section 12 of the Exchange Act . . . ("reporting person") that failed to file on a timely basis, as disclosed in the above Forms, reports required by Section 16(a) of the Exchange Act during the most recent fiscal year or prior fiscal years.

(2) For each such person, set forth the number of late reports, the number of transactions that were not reported on a timely basis, and any known failure to file a required Form. A known failure to file would include, but not be limited to, a failure to file a Form 3, which is required of all reporting

persons, and a failure to file a Form 5 in the absence of the written representation referred to in paragraph (b)(1) of this section, unless the registrant otherwise knows that no Form 5 is required.

(b) With respect to the disclosure required by paragraph (a) of this section, if the registrant:

(1) Receives a written representation from the reporting person that no Form 5 is required; and

(2) Maintains the representation for two years, making a copy available to the Commission or its staff upon request, the registrant need not identify such reporting person pursuant to paragraph (a) of this section as having failed to file a Form 5 with respect to that fiscal year.

Item 406.   Code of Ethics

(a) Disclose whether the registrant has adopted a code of ethics that applies to the registrant's principal executive officer, principal financial officer, principal accounting officer or controller, or persons performing similar functions. If the registrant has not adopted such a code of ethics, explain why it has not done so.

(b) For purposes of this Item 406, the term code of ethics means written standards that are reasonably designed to deter wrongdoing and to promote:

(1) Honest and ethical conduct, including the ethical handling of actual or apparent conflicts of interest between personal and professional relationships;

(2) Full, fair, accurate, timely, and understandable disclosure in reports and documents that a registrant files with, or submits to, the Commission and in other public communications made by the registrant;

(3) Compliance with applicable governmental laws, rules and regulations;

(4) The prompt internal reporting of violations of the code to an appropriate person or persons identified in the code; and

(5) Accountability for adherence to the code.

(c) The registrant must:

(1) File with the Commission a copy of its code of ethics that applies to the registrant's principal executive officer, principal financial officer, principal accounting officer or controller, or persons performing similar functions, as an exhibit to its annual report;

(2) Post the text of such code of ethics on its Internet website and disclose, in its annual report, its Internet address and the fact that it has posted such code of ethics on its Internet Web site; or

(3) Undertake in its annual report filed with the Commission to provide to any person without charge, upon request, a copy of such code of ethics and explain the manner in which such request may be made.

(d) If the registrant intends to satisfy the disclosure requirement under Item 10 of Form 8-K regarding an amendment to, or a waiver from, a provision of its code of ethics that applies to the registrant's principal executive officer, principal financial officer, principal accounting officer or controller, or persons performing similar functions and that relates to any element of the code of ethics definition enumerated in paragraph (b) of this Item by posting such information on its Internet website, disclose the registrant's Internet address and such intention.

Instructions to Item 406.

1.   A registrant may have separate codes of ethics for different types of officers. Furthermore, a code of ethics within the meaning of paragraph (b) of this Item may be a portion of a broader document that addresses additional topics or that applies to more persons than those specified in paragraph (a). In satisfying the requirements of paragraph (c), a registrant need only file, post or provide the portions of a broader document that constitutes a code of ethics as defined in paragraph (b) and that apply to the persons specified in paragraph (a).

2.   If a registrant elects to satisfy paragraph (c) of this Item by posting its code of ethics on its website pursuant to paragraph (c)(2), the code of ethics must remain accessible on its Web site for as

long as the registrant remains subject to the requirements of this Item and chooses to comply with this Item by posting its code on its Web site pursuant to paragraph (c)(2). . . .

Item 407.   Corporate Governance

(a) *Director independence.* Identify each director and, when the disclosure called for by this paragraph is being presented in a proxy or information statement relating to the election of directors, each nominee for director, that is independent under the independence standards applicable to the registrant under paragraph (a)(1) of this Item. In addition, if such independence standards contain independence requirements for committees of the board of directors, identify each director that is a member of the compensation, nominating or audit committee that is not independent under such committee independence standards. If the registrant does not have a separately designated audit, nominating or compensation committee or committee performing similar functions, the registrant must provide the disclosure of directors that are not independent with respect to all members of the board of directors applying such committee independence standards.

(1) In determining whether or not the director or nominee for director is independent for the purposes of paragraph (a) of this Item, the registrant shall use the applicable definition of independence, as follows:

(i) If the registrant is a listed issuer whose securities are listed on a national securities exchange or in an inter-dealer quotation system which has requirements that a majority of the board of directors be independent, the registrant's definition of independence that it uses for determining if a majority of the board of directors is independent in compliance with the listing standards applicable to the registrant. When determining whether the members of a committee of the board of directors are independent, the registrant's definition of independence that it uses for determining if the members of that specific committee are independent in compliance with the independence standards applicable for the members of the specific committee in the listing standards of the national securities exchange or inter-dealer quotation system that the registrant uses for determining if a majority of the board of directors are independent. If the registrant does not have independence standards for a committee, the independence standards for that specific committee in the listing standards of the national securities exchange or inter-dealer quotation system that the registrant uses for determining if a majority of the board of directors are independent.

(ii) If the registrant is not a listed issuer, a definition of independence of a national securities exchange or of an inter-dealer quotation system which has requirements that a majority of the board of directors be independent, and state which definition is used. Whatever such definition the registrant chooses, it must use the same definition with respect to all directors and nominees for director. When determining whether the members of a specific committee of the board of directors are independent, if the national securities exchange or national securities association whose standards are used has independence standards for the members of a specific committee, use those committee specific standards.

(iii) If the information called for by paragraph (a) of this Item is being presented in a registration statement on Form S-1 under the Securities Act or on a Form 10 under the Exchange Act where the registrant has applied for listing with a national securities exchange or in an inter-dealer quotation system which has requirements that a majority of the board of directors be independent, the definition of independence that the registrant uses for determining if a majority of the board of directors is independent, and the definition of independence that the registrant uses for determining if members of the specific committee of the board of directors are independent, that is in compliance with the independence listing standards of the national securities exchange or inter-dealer quotation system on which it has applied for listing, or if the registrant has not adopted such definitions, the independence standards for determining if the majority of the board of directors is independent and if members of the committee of the board of directors are independent of that national securities exchange or inter-dealer quotation system.

(2) If the registrant uses its own definitions for determining whether its directors and nominees for director, and members of specific committees of the board of directors, are independent, disclose

whether these definitions are available to security holders on the registrant's Web site. If so, provide the registrant's Web site address. If not, include a copy of these policies in an appendix to the registrant's proxy statement or information statement that is provided to security holders at least once every three fiscal years or if the policies have been materially amended since the beginning of the registrant's last fiscal year. If a current copy of the policies is not available to security holders on the registrant's Web site, and is not included as an appendix to the registrant's proxy statement or information statement, identify the most recent fiscal year in which the policies were so included in satisfaction of this requirement.

(3) For each director and nominee for director that is identified as independent, describe, by specific category or type, any transactions, relationships or arrangements not disclosed pursuant to Item 404(a) . . . that were considered by the board of directors under the applicable independence definitions in determining that the director is independent.

Instructions to Item 407(a).

1.   If the registrant is a listed issuer whose securities are listed on a national securities exchange or in an inter-dealer quotation system which has requirements that a majority of the board of directors be independent, and also has exemptions to those requirements (for independence of a majority of the board of directors or committee member independence) upon which the registrant relied, disclose the exemption relied upon and explain the basis for the registrant's conclusion that such exemption is applicable. The same disclosure should be provided if the registrant is not a listed issuer and the national securities exchange or inter-dealer quotation system selected by the registrant has exemptions that are applicable to the registrant. Any national securities exchange or inter-dealer quotation system which has requirements that at least 50 percent of the members of a small business issuer's board of directors must be independent shall be considered a national securities exchange or inter-dealer quotation system which has requirements that a majority of the board of directors be independent for the purposes of the disclosure required by paragraph (a) of this Item. . . .

(b) *Board meetings and committees; annual meeting attendance.*

(1) State the total number of meetings of the board of directors (including regularly scheduled and special meetings) which were held during the last full fiscal year. Name each incumbent director who during the last full fiscal year attended fewer than 75 percent of the aggregate of:

(i) The total number of meetings of the board of directors (held during the period for which he has been a director); and

(ii) The total number of meetings held by all committees of the board on which he served (during the periods that he served).

(2) Describe the registrant's policy, if any, with regard to board members' attendance at annual meetings of security holders and state the number of board members who attended the prior year's annual meeting.

Instruction to Item 407(b)(2).

In lieu of providing the information required by paragraph (b)(2) of this Item in the proxy statement, the registrant may instead provide the registrant's Web site address where such information appears.

(3) State whether or not the registrant has standing audit, nominating and compensation committees of the board of directors, or committees performing similar functions. If the registrant has such committees, however designated, identify each committee member, state the number of committee meetings held by each such committee during the last fiscal year and describe briefly the functions performed by each such committee. Such disclosure need not be provided to the extent it is duplicative of disclosure provided in accordance with paragraph (c), (d) or (e) of this Item.

(c) *Nominating committee.* (1) If the registrant does not have a standing nominating committee or committee performing similar functions, state the basis for the view of the board of directors that it is appropriate for the registrant not to have such a committee and identify each director who participates in the consideration of director nominees.

(2) Provide the following information regarding the registrant's director nomination process:

(i) State whether or not the nominating committee has a charter. If the nominating committee has a charter, provide the disclosure required by Instruction 2 to this Item regarding the nominating committee charter;

(ii) If the nominating committee has a policy with regard to the consideration of any director candidates recommended by security holders, provide a description of the material elements of that policy, which shall include, but need not be limited to, a statement as to whether the committee will consider director candidates recommended by security holders;

(iii) If the nominating committee does not have a policy with regard to the consideration of any director candidates recommended by security holders, state that fact and state the basis for the view of the board of directors that it is appropriate for the registrant not to have such a policy;

(iv) If the nominating committee will consider candidates recommended by security holders, describe the procedures to be followed by security holders in submitting such recommendations;

(v) Describe any specific minimum qualifications that the nominating committee believes must be met by a nominating committee-recommended nominee for a position on the registrant's board of directors, and describe any specific qualities or skills that the nominating committee believes are necessary for one or more of the registrant's directors to possess;

(vi) Describe the nominating committee's process for identifying and evaluating nominees for director, including nominees recommended by security holders, and any differences in the manner in which the nominating committee evaluates nominees for director based on whether the nominee is recommended by a security holder, and whether, and if so how, the nominating committee (or the board) considers diversity in identifying nominees for director. If the nominating committee (or the board) has a policy with regard to the consideration of diversity in identifying director nominees, describe how this policy is implemented, as well as how the nominating committee (or the board) assesses the effectiveness of its policy;

(vii) With regard to each nominee approved by the nominating committee for inclusion on the registrant's proxy card (other than nominees who are executive officers or who are directors standing for re-election), state which one or more of the following categories of persons or entities recommended that nominee: security holder, non-management director, chief executive officer, other executive officer, third-party search firm, or other specified source. With regard to each such nominee approved by a nominating committee of an investment company, state which one or more of the following additional categories of persons or entities recommended that nominee: security holder, director, chief executive officer, other executive officer, or employee of the investment company's investment adviser, principal underwriter, or any affiliated person of the investment adviser or principal underwriter;

(viii) If the registrant pays a fee to any third party or parties to identify or evaluate or assist in identifying or evaluating potential nominees, disclose the function performed by each such third party; and

(ix) If the registrant's nominating committee received, by a date not later than the 120th calendar day before the date of the registrant's proxy statement released to security holders in connection with the previous year's annual meeting, a recommended nominee from a security holder that beneficially owned more than 5% of the registrant's voting common stock for at least one year as of the date the recommendation was made, or from a group of security holders that beneficially owned, in the aggregate, more than 5% of the registrant's voting common stock, with each of the securities used to calculate that ownership held for at least one year as of the date the recommendation was made, identify the candidate and the security holder or security holder group that recommended the candidate and disclose whether the nominating committee chose to nominate the candidate, *provided, however,* that no such identification or disclosure is required without the written consent of both the security holder or security holder group and the candidate to be so identified.

b.   If the security holder has filed a Schedule 13D, Schedule 13G, Form 3, Form 4, and/or Form 5, or amendments to those documents or updated forms, reflecting ownership of the securities as of or before the date of the recommendation, a copy of the schedule and/or form, and any subsequent amendments reporting a change in ownership level, as well as a written statement that the security holder continuously held the securities for the one-year period as of the date of the recommendation.

4.   For purposes of the registrant's obligation to provide the disclosure specified in paragraph (c)(2)(ix) of this Item, the security holder or group must have provided to the registrant, at the time of the recommendation, the written consent of all parties to be identified and, where the security holder or group members are not registered holders, proof that the security holder or group satisfied the required ownership percentage and holding period as of the date of the recommendation.

Instruction to Item 407(c)(2).

For purposes of paragraph (c)(2) of this Item, the term *nominating committee* refers not only to nominating committees and committees performing similar functions, but also to groups of directors fulfilling the role of a nominating committee, including the entire board of directors.

(3) Describe any material changes to the procedures by which security holders may recommend nominees to the registrant's board of directors, where those changes were implemented after the registrant last provided disclosure in response to the requirements of paragraph (c)(2)(iv) of this Item, or paragraph (c)(3) of this Item.

(d) *Audit committee.*

(1) State whether or not the audit committee has a charter. If the audit committee has a charter, provide the disclosure required by Instruction 2 to this Item regarding the audit committee charter.

(2) If a listed issuer's board of directors determines, in accordance with the listing standards applicable to the issuer, to appoint a director to the audit committee who is not independent . . . including as a result of exceptional or limited or similar circumstances, disclose the nature of the relationship that makes that individual not independent and the reasons for the board of directors' determination.

(3)(i) The audit committee must state whether:

(A) The audit committee has reviewed and discussed the audited financial statements with management;

(B) The audit committee has discussed with the independent auditors the matters required to be discussed by the statement on Auditing Standards No. 61, as amended (AICPA, *Professional Standards*, Vol. 1. AU section 380), as adopted by the Public Company Accounting Oversight Board in Rule 3200T;

(C) The audit committee has received the written disclosures and the letter from the independent accountants required by applicable requirements of the Public Company Accounting Oversight Board regarding the independent accountant's communications with the audit committee concerning independence . . . and has discussed with the independent accountant the independent accountant's independence; and

(D) Based on the review and discussions referred to in paragraphs (d)(3)(i)(A) through (d)(3)(i)(C) of this Item, the audit committee recommended to the board of directors that the audited financial statements be included in the company's annual report on Form 10-K. . . .

(ii) The name of each member of the company's audit committee (or, in the absence of an audit committee, the board committee performing equivalent functions or the entire board of directors) must appear below the disclosure required by paragraph (d)(3)(i) of this Item.

(4)(i) If the registrant meets the following requirements, provide the disclosure in paragraph (d)(4)(ii) of this Item:

(A) The registrant is a listed issuer, as defined in Rule 10A–3;

(B) The registrant is filing an annual report on Form 10-K or a proxy statement or information statement pursuant to the Exchange Act if action is to be taken with respect to the election of directors; and

(C) The registrant is neither:

(*1*) A subsidiary of another listed issuer that is relying on the exemption in Rule 10A–3(c)(2); nor

(*2*) Relying on any of the exemptions in Rule A–3(c)(4) through (c)(7) of this chapter.

(ii)(A) State whether or not the registrant has a separately-designated standing audit committee established in accordance with section 3(a)(58)(A) of the Exchange Act, or a committee performing similar functions. If the registrant has such a committee, however designated, identify each committee member. If the entire board of directors is acting as the registrant's audit committee as specified in section 3(a)(58)(B) of the Exchange Act, so state.

(B) If applicable, provide the disclosure required by Rule 10A–3(d) of this chapter regarding an exemption from the listing standards for audit committees.

(5) *Audit committee financial expert.*

(i)(A) Disclose that the registrant's board of directors has determined that the registrant either:

(*1*) Has at least one audit committee financial expert serving on its audit committee; or

(*2*) Does not have an audit committee financial expert serving on its audit committee.

(B) If the registrant provides the disclosure required by paragraph (d)(5)(i)(A)(*1*) of this Item, it must disclose the name of the audit committee financial expert and whether that person is *independent*, as independence for audit committee members is defined in the listing standards applicable to the listed issuer.

(C) If the registrant provides the disclosure required by paragraph (d)(5)(i)(A)(*2*) of this Item, it must explain why it does not have an audit committee financial expert.

(ii) For purposes of this Item, an *audit committee financial expert* means a person who has the following attributes:

(A) An understanding of generally accepted accounting principles and financial statements;

(B) The ability to assess the general application of such principles in connection with the accounting for estimates, accruals and reserves;

(C) Experience preparing, auditing, analyzing or evaluating financial statements that present a breadth and level of complexity of accounting issues that are generally comparable to the breadth and complexity of issues that can reasonably be expected to be raised by the registrant's financial statements, or experience actively supervising one or more persons engaged in such activities;

(D) An understanding of internal control over financial reporting; and

(E) An understanding of audit committee functions.

(iii) A person shall have acquired such attributes through:

(A) Education and experience as a principal financial officer, principal accounting officer, controller, public accountant or auditor or experience in one or more positions that involve the performance of similar functions;

(B) Experience actively supervising a principal financial officer, principal accounting officer, controller, public accountant, auditor or person performing similar functions;

(C) Experience overseeing or assessing the performance of companies or public accountants with respect to the preparation, auditing or evaluation of financial statements; or

(D) Other relevant experience.

(iv) *Safe harbor.*

(A) A person who is determined to be an audit committee financial expert will not be deemed an *expert* for any purpose, including without limitation for purposes of section 11 of the Securities Act, as a result of being designated or identified as an audit committee financial expert pursuant to this Item 407.

(B) The designation or identification of a person as an audit committee financial expert pursuant to this Item 407 does not impose on such person any duties, obligations or liability that are greater than the duties, obligations and liability imposed on such person as a member of the audit committee and board of directors in the absence of such designation or identification.

(C) The designation or identification of a person as an audit committee financial expert pursuant to this Item does not affect the duties, obligations or liability of any other member of the audit committee or board of directors.

Instructions to Item 407(d).

1. The information required by paragraphs (d)(1)–(3) of this Item shall not be deemed to be "soliciting material," or to be "filed" with the Commission or subject to Regulation 14A or 14C, other than as provided in this Item, or to the liabilities of section 18 of the Exchange Act. . . . Such information will not be deemed to be incorporated by reference into any filing under the Securities Act or the Exchange Act, except to the extent that the registrant specifically incorporates it by reference. . . .

(e) *Compensation committee.*

(1) If the registrant does not have a standing compensation committee or committee performing similar functions, state the basis for the view of the board of directors that it is appropriate for the registrant not to have such a committee and identify each director who participates in the consideration of executive officer and director compensation.

(2) State whether or not the compensation committee has a charter. If the compensation committee has a charter, provide the disclosure required by Instruction 2 to this Item regarding the compensation committee charter.

(3) Provide a narrative description of the registrant's processes and procedures for the consideration and determination of executive and director compensation, including:

(i)(A) The scope of authority of the compensation committee (or persons performing the equivalent functions); and

(B) The extent to which the compensation committee (or persons performing the equivalent functions) may delegate any authority described in paragraph (e)(3)(i)(A) of this Item to other persons, specifying what authority may be so delegated and to whom;

(ii) Any role of executive officers in determining or recommending the amount or form of executive and director compensation; and

(iii) Any role of compensation consultants in determining or recommending the amount or form of executive and director compensation (other than any role *limited* to consulting on any broad-based plan that does not discriminate in scope, terms, or operation, in favor of executive officers or directors of the registrant, and that is available generally to all salaried employees; or providing information that either is not customized for a particular registrant or that is customized based on parameters that are not developed by the compensation consultant, and about which the compensation consultant does not provide advice) during the registrant's last completed fiscal year, identifying such consultants, stating whether such consultants were engaged directly by the compensation committee (or persons performing the equivalent functions) or any other person, describing the nature and scope of their assignment, and the material elements of the instructions or directions given to the consultants with respect to the performance of their duties under the engagement:

(A) If such compensation consultant was engaged by the compensation committee (or persons performing the equivalent functions) to provide advice or recommendations on the amount or form of executive and director compensation (other than any role *limited* to consulting on any broad-based plan that does not discriminate in scope, terms, or operation, in favor of executive officers or directors of the registrant, and that is available generally to all salaried employees; or providing information that either is not customized for a particular registrant or that is customized based on parameters that are not developed by the compensation consultant, and about which the compensation consultant does not provide advice) and the compensation consultant or its affiliates also provided additional services to the registrant or its affiliates in an amount in excess of $120,000 during the registrant's last completed fiscal year, then disclose the aggregate fees for determining or recommending the amount or form of executive and director compensation and the aggregate fees for such additional services. Disclose whether the decision to engage the compensation consultant or its affiliates for these other services was made, or recommended, by management, and whether the compensation committee or the board approved such other services of the compensation consultant or its affiliates.

(B) If the compensation committee (or persons performing the equivalent functions) has not engaged a compensation consultant, but management has engaged a compensation consultant to provide advice or recommendations on the amount or form of executive and director compensation (other than any role *limited* to consulting on any broad-based plan that does not discriminate in scope, terms, or operation, in favor of executive officers or directors of the registrant, and that is available generally to all salaried employees; or providing information that either is not customized for a particular registrant or that is customized based on parameters that are not developed by the compensation consultant, and about which the compensation consultant does not provide advice) and such compensation consultant or its affiliates has provided additional services to the registrant in an amount in excess of $120,000 during the registrant's last completed fiscal year, then disclose the aggregate fees for determining or recommending the amount or form of executive and director compensation and the aggregate fees for any additional services provided by the compensation consultant or its affiliates.

(iv) With regard to any compensation committee consultant identified in response to item 407(e)(iii) whose work has raised a conflict of interest, disclose the nature of the conflict and how the conflict is being addressed.

(4) Under the caption "Compensation Committee Interlocks and Insider Participation":

(i) Identify each person who served as a member of the compensation committee of the registrant's board of directors (or board committee performing equivalent functions) during the last completed fiscal year, indicating each committee member who:

(A) Was, during the fiscal year, an officer or employee of the registrant;

(B) Was formerly an officer of the registrant; or

(C) Had any relationship requiring disclosure by the registrant under any paragraph of Item 404. In this event, the disclosure required by Item 404 shall accompany such identification.

(ii) If the registrant has no compensation committee (or other board committee performing equivalent functions), the registrant shall identify each officer and employee of the registrant, and any former officer of the registrant, who, during the last completed fiscal year, participated in deliberations of the registrant's board of directors concerning executive officer compensation.

(iii) Describe any of the following relationships that existed during the last completed fiscal year:

(A) An executive officer of the registrant served as a member of the compensation committee (or other board committee performing equivalent functions or, in the absence of any such committee, the entire board of directors) of another entity, one of whose executive officers served on the compensation committee (or other board committee performing equivalent functions or, in the absence of any such committee, the entire board of directors) of the registrant;

(B) An executive officer of the registrant served as a director of another entity, one of whose executive officers served on the compensation committee (or other board committee performing equivalent functions or, in the absence of any such committee, the entire board of directors) of the registrant; and

(C) An executive officer of the registrant served as a member of the compensation committee (or other board committee performing equivalent functions or, in the absence of any such committee, the entire board of directors) of another entity, one of whose executive officers served as a director of the registrant.

(iv) Disclosure required under paragraph (e)(4)(iii) of this Item regarding a compensation committee member or other director of the registrant who also served as an executive officer of another entity shall be accompanied by the disclosure called for by Item 404 with respect to that person.

(5) Under the caption "Compensation Committee Report:"

(i) The compensation committee (or other board committee performing equivalent functions or, in the absence of any such committee, the entire board of directors) must state whether:

(A) The compensation committee has reviewed and discussed the Compensation Discussion and Analysis required by Item 402(b) with management; and

(B) Based on the review and discussions referred to in paragraph (e)(5)(i)(A) of this Item, the compensation committee recommended to the board of directors that the Compensation Discussion and Analysis be included in the registrant's annual report on Form 10-K, proxy statement on Schedule 14A, or information statement on Schedule 14C.

(ii) The name of each member of the registrant's compensation committee (or other board committee performing equivalent functions or, in the absence of any such committee, the entire board of directors) must appear below the disclosure required by paragraph (e)(5)(i) of this Item.

Instructions to Item 407(e)(5).

1. The information required by paragraph (e)(5) of this Item shall not be deemed to be "soliciting material," or to be "filed" with the Commission or subject to Regulation 14A or 14C, other than as provided in this Item, or to the liabilities of section 18 of the Exchange Act, except to the extent that the registrant specifically requests that the information be treated as soliciting material or specifically incorporates it by reference into a document filed under the Securities Act or the Exchange Act. . . .

(f) *Shareholder communications.*

(1) State whether or not the registrant's board of directors provides a process for security holders to send communications to the board of directors and, if the registrant does not have such a process for security holders to send communications to the board of directors, state the basis for the view of the board of directors that it is appropriate for the registrant not to have such a process.

(2) If the registrant has a process for security holders to send communications to the board of directors:

(i) Describe the manner in which security holders can send communications to the board and, if applicable, to specified individual directors; and

(ii) If all security holder communications are not sent directly to board members, describe the registrant's process for determining which communications will be relayed to board members.

1.   In lieu of providing the information required by paragraph (f)(2) of this Item in the proxy statement, the registrant may instead provide the registrant's Web site address where such information appears.

2.   For purposes of the disclosure required by paragraph (f)(2)(ii) of this Item, a registrant's process for collecting and organizing security holder communications, as well as similar or related activities, need not be disclosed provided that the registrant's process is approved by a majority of the independent directors. . . .

4.   For purposes of this paragraph, security holder proposals submitted pursuant to Rule 14a–8, and communications made in connection with such proposals, will not be viewed as "security holder communications" . . . .

Instructions to Item 407 . . .

2.   With respect to paragraphs (c)(2)(i), (d)(1) and (e)(2) of this Item, disclose whether a current copy of the applicable committee charter is available to security holders on the registrant's Web site, and if so, provide the registrant's Web site address. If a current copy of the charter is not available to security holders on the registrant's Web site, include a copy of the charter in an appendix to the registrant's proxy or information statement that is provided to security holders at least once every three fiscal years, or if the charter has been materially amended since the beginning of the registrant's last fiscal year. If a current copy of the charter is not available to security holders on the registrant's Web site, and is not included as an appendix to the registrant's proxy or information statement, identify in which of the prior fiscal years the charter was so included in satisfaction of this requirement.

(g) *Smaller reporting companies.* A registrant that qualifies as a "smaller reporting company," as defined by Item 10(f)(1), is not required to provide:

(1) The disclosure required in paragraph (d)(5) of this Item in its first annual report filed pursuant to section 13(a) or 15(d) of the Exchange Act following the effective date of its first registration statement filed under the Securities Act or Exchange Act; and

(2) Need not provide the disclosures required by paragraphs (e)(4) and (e)(5) of this Item.

(h) *Board leadership structure and role in risk oversight.* Briefly describe the leadership structure of the registrant's board, such as whether the same person serves as both principal executive officer and chairman of the board, or whether two individuals serve in those positions, and, in the case of a registrant that is an investment company, whether the chairman of the board is an "interested person" of the registrant as defined in section 2(a)(19) of the Investment Company Act. If one person serves as both principal executive officer and chairman of the board, or if the chairman of the board of a registrant that is an investment company is an "interested person" of the registrant, disclose whether the registrant has a lead independent director and what specific role the lead independent director plays in the leadership of the board. This disclosure should indicate why the registrant has determined that its leadership structure is appropriate given the specific characteristics or circumstances of the registrant. In addition, disclose the extent of the board's role in the risk oversight of the registrant, such as how the board administers its oversight function, and the effect that this has on the board's leadership structure.

Subpart 500—Registration Statement and Prospectus Provisions. . . .

Item 512.   Undertakings

Include each of the following undertakings that is applicable to the offering being registered.

(a) *Rule 415 Offering.* Include the following if the securities are registered pursuant to Rule 415 under the Securities Act . . . :

The undersigned registrant hereby undertakes:

(1) To file, during any period in which offers or sales are being made, a post-effective amendment to this registration statement:

(i) To include any prospectus required by section 10(a)(3) of the Securities Act of 1933;

(ii) To reflect in the prospectus any facts or events arising after the effective date of the registration statement (or the most recent post-effective amendment thereof) which, individually or in the aggregate, represent a fundamental change in the information set forth in the registration statement. Notwithstanding the foregoing, any increase or decrease in volume of securities offered (if the total dollar value of securities offered would not exceed that which was registered) and any deviation from the low or high end of the estimated maximum offering range may be reflected in the form of prospectus filed with the Commission pursuant to Rule 424(b) . . . if, in the aggregate, the changes in volume and price represent no more than a 20% change in the maximum aggregate offering price set forth in the "Calculation of Registration Fee" table in the effective registration statement.

(iii) To include any material information with respect to the plan of distribution not previously disclosed in the registration statement or any material change to such information in the registration statement;

Provided, however, That . . .

(B) Paragraphs (a)(1)(i), (a)(1)(ii) and (a)(1)(iii) of this section do not apply if the registration statement is on Form S-3 . . . and the information required to be included in a post-effective amendment by those paragraphs is contained in reports filed with or furnished to the Commission by the registrant pursuant to section 13 or section 15(d) of the Securities Exchange Act of 1934 that are incorporated by reference in the registration statement, or is contained in a form of prospectus filed pursuant to Rule 424(b) [Filing of Prospectuses; Number of Copies] that is part of the registration statement.

(C) Paragraphs (a)(1)(i) and (a)(1)(ii) of this section do not apply if the registration statement is on Form S-3, Form S-8 or Form F-3, and the information required to be included in a post-effective amendment by those paragraphs is contained in periodic reports filed with or furnished to the Commission by the registrant pursuant to section 13 or section 15(d) of the Securities Exchange Act of 1934 that are incorporated by reference in the registration statement. . . .

(2) That, for the purpose of determining any liability under the Securities Act of 1933, each such post-effective amendment shall be deemed to be a new registration statement relating to the securities offered therein, and the offering of such securities at that time shall be deemed to be the initial bona fide offering thereof.

(3) To remove from registration by means of a post-effective amendment any of the securities being registered which remain unsold at the termination of the offering. . . .

(6) That, for the purpose of determining liability of the registrant under the Securities Act of 1933 to any purchaser in the initial distribution of the securities:

The undersigned registrant undertakes that in a primary offering of securities of the undersigned registrant pursuant to this registrant statement, regardless of the underwriting method used to sell the securities to the purchaser, if the securities are offered or sold to such purchaser by means of any of the following communications, the undersigned registrant will be a seller to the purchaser and will be considered to offer or sell such securities to such purchaser:

(i) Any preliminary prospectus or prospectus of the undersigned registrant relating to the offering required to be filed pursuant to Rule 424;

(ii) Any free writing prospectus relating to the offering prepared by or on behalf of the undersigned registrant or used or referred to by the undersigned registrant;

(iii) The portion of any other free writing prospectus relating to the offering containing material information about the undersigned registrant or its securities provided by or on behalf of the undersigned registrant; and

(iv) Any other communication that is an offer in the offering made by the undersigned registrant to the purchaser.

(b) *Filings incorporating subsequent Exchange Act documents by reference.* Include the following if the registration statement incorporates by reference any Exchange Act document filed subsequent to the effective date of the registration statement:

The undersigned registrant hereby undertakes that, for purposes of determining any liability under the Securities Act of 1933, each filing of the registrant's annual report pursuant to section 13(a) or section 15(d) of the Securities Exchange Act of 1934 (and, where applicable, each filing of an employee benefit plan's annual report pursuant to section 15(d) of the Securities Exchange Act of 1934) that is incorporated by reference in the registration statement shall be deemed to be a new registration statement relating to the securities offered therein, and the offering of such securities at that time shall be deemed to be the initial bona fide offering thereof. . . .

(h) *Request for acceleration of effective date or filing of registration statement becoming effective upon filing.* Include the following if acceleration is requested of the effective date of the registration statement pursuant to Rule 461 under the Securities Act, [or] if a Form S-3 . . . will become effective upon filing with the Commission pursuant to Rule 462 (e) or (f) [Immediate Effectiveness of Certain Registration Statements and Post-Effective Amendments] under the Securities Act, and: (1) any provision or arrangement exists whereby the registrant may indemnify a director, officer or controlling person of the registrant against liabilities arising under the Securities Act, or (2) the underwriting agreement contains a provision whereby the registrant indemnifies the underwriter or controlling persons of the underwriter against such liabilities and a director, officer or controlling person of the registrant is such an underwriter or controlling person thereof or a member of any firm which is such an underwriter, and (3) the benefits of such indemnification are not waived by such persons:

Insofar as indemnification for liabilities arising under the Securities Act of 1933 may be permitted to directors, officers and controlling persons of the registrant pursuant to the foregoing provisions, or otherwise, the registrant has been advised that in the opinion of the Securities and Exchange Commission such indemnification is against public policy as expressed in the Act and is, therefore, unenforceable. In the event that a claim for indemnification against such liabilities (other than the payment by the registrant of expenses incurred or paid by a director, officer or controlling person of the registrant in the successful defense of any action, suit or proceeding) is asserted by such director, officer or controlling person in connection with the securities being registered, the registrant will, unless in the opinion of its counsel the matter has been settled by controlling precedent, submit to a court of appropriate jurisdiction the question whether such indemnification by it is against public policy as expressed in the Act and will be governed by the final adjudication of such issue. . . .

Subpart 600—Exhibits

Item 601.   Exhibits. . . .

(b) Description of Exhibits . . .

    (10) Material Contracts . . .

        (ii) . . .

            (B) Any compensatory plan, contract or arrangement adopted without the approval of security holders pursuant to which equity may be awarded, including, but not limited to, options, warrants or rights (or if not set forth in any formal document, a written description thereof), in which any employee (whether or not an executive officer of the registrant) participates shall be filed unless immaterial in amount or significance. . . .

    (14) *Code of ethics.* Any code of ethics, or amendment thereto, that is the subject of the disclosure required by Item 406 of Regulation S–K or Item 10 of Form 8-K, to the extent that the registrant intends to satisfy the Item 406 or Item 10 requirements through filing of an exhibit. . . .

    (17) *Correspondence on departure of director.* Any written correspondence from a former director concerning the circumstances surrounding the former director's retirement, resignation, refusal to

stand for re-election or removal, including any letter from the former director to the registrant stating whether the former director agrees with statements made by the registrant describing the former director's departure. . . .

(31)(i) The certifications required by Rule 13a–14(a) or Rule 15d–14(a) exactly as set forth below. . . .

CERTIFICATIONS*

I, [identify the certifying individual], certify that:

1.   I have reviewed this [specify report] of [identify registrant];

2.   Based on my knowledge, this report does not contain any untrue statement of a material fact or omit to state a material fact necessary to make the statements made, in light of the circumstances under which such statements were made, not misleading with respect to the period covered by this report;

3.   Based on my knowledge, the financial statements, and other financial information included in this report, fairly present in all material respects the financial condition, results of operations and cash flows of the registrant as of, and for, the periods presented in this report;

4.   The registrant's other certifying officer(s) and I are responsible for establishing and maintaining disclosure controls and procedures (as defined in Exchange Act Rules 13a–15(e) and 15d–15(e)) and internal control over financial reporting (as defined in Exchange Act Rules 13a–15(f) and 15d–15(f)) for the registrant and have:

(a) Designed such disclosure controls and procedures, or caused such disclosure controls and procedures to be designed under our supervision, to ensure that material information relating to the registrant, including its consolidated subsidiaries, is made known to us by others within those entities, particularly during the period in which this report is being prepared;

(b) Designed such internal control over financial reporting, or caused such internal control over financial reporting to be designed under our supervision, to provide reasonable assurance regarding the reliability of financial reporting and the preparation of financial statements for external purposes in accordance with generally accepted accounting principles;

(c) Evaluated the effectiveness of the registrant's disclosure controls and procedures and presented in this report our conclusions about the effectiveness of the disclosure controls and procedures, as of the end of the period covered by this report based on such evaluation; and

(d) Disclosed in this report any change in the registrant's internal control over financial reporting that occurred during the registrant's most recent fiscal quarter (the registrant's fourth fiscal quarter in the case of an annual report) that has materially affected, or is reasonably likely to materially affect, the registrant's internal control over financial reporting; and

5.   The registrant's other certifying officer(s) and I have disclosed, based on our most recent evaluation of internal control over financial reporting, to the registrant's auditors and the audit committee of the registrant's board of directors (or persons performing the equivalent functions):

(a) All significant deficiencies and material weaknesses in the design or operation of internal control over financial reporting which are reasonably likely to adversely affect the registrant's ability to record, process, summarize and report financial information; and

---

*   Provide a separate certification for each principal executive officer and principal financial officer of the registrant. See Rules 13a–14(a) and 15d–14(a).

(b) Any fraud, whether or not material, that involves management or other employees who have a significant role in the registrant's internal control over financial reporting.

Date: . . . .

[Signature] . . . .

[Title] . . . .

(32) *Section 1350 Certifications.*

(i) The certifications required by Rule 13a–14(b) or Rule 15d–14(b) and Section 1350 of Chapter 63 of Title 18 of the United States.

(ii) A certification furnished pursuant to this item will not be deemed "filed" for purposes of Section 18 of the Exchange Act, or otherwise subject to the liability of that section. Such certification will not be deemed to be incorporated by reference into any filing under the Securities Act or the Exchange Act, except to the extent that the registrant specifically incorporates it by reference. . . .

Subpart 900—Roll-Up Transactions

Item 901. [Definitions] . . .

(b)(1) *Partnership* means any:

(i) Finite-life limited partnership; or

(ii) Other finite-life entity.

(2)(i) Except as provided in paragraph (b)(2)(ii) of this Item . . . , a limited partnership or other entity is "finite-life" if:

(A) It operates as a conduit vehicle for investors to participate in the ownership of assets for a limited period of time; and

(B) It has as a policy or purpose distributing to investors proceeds from the sale, financing or refinancing of assets or cash from operations, rather than reinvesting such proceeds or cash in the business (whether for the term of the entity or after an initial period of time following commencement of operations).

(ii) A real estate investment trust as defined in I.R.C. section 856 is not *finite-life* solely because of the distribution to investors of net income as provided by the I.R.C. if its policies or purposes do not include the distribution to investors of proceeds from the sale, financing or refinancing of assets, rather than the reinvestment of such proceeds in the business. . . .

(c)(1) Except as provided in paragraph (c)(2) or (c)(3) of this Item, *roll-up transaction* means a transaction involving the combination or reorganization of one or more partnerships, directly or indirectly, in which some or all of the investors in any of such partnerships will receive new securities, or securities in another entity.

(2) Notwithstanding paragraph (c)(1) of this Item, *roll-up transaction* shall not include:

(i) A transaction wherein the interests of all of the investors in each of the partnerships are repurchased, recalled, or exchanged in accordance with the terms of the preexisting partnership agreement for securities in an operating company specifically identified at the time of the formation of the original partnership;

(ii) A transaction in which the securities to be issued or exchanged are not required to be and are not registered under the Securities Act of 1933 . . . ;

(iii) A transaction that involves only issuers that are not required to register or report under Section 12 of the Securities Exchange Act of 1934, . . . both before and after the transaction;

(iv) A transaction that involves the combination or reorganization of one or more partnerships in which a non-affiliated party succeeds to the interests of a general partner or sponsor, if:

(A) Such action is approved by not less than 66⅔% of the outstanding units of each of the participating partnerships; and

(B) As a result of the transaction, the existing general partners will receive only compensation to which they are entitled as expressly provided for in the preexisting partnership agreements; . . . .

(C) For purposes of paragraph (c)(2)(v) of this item . . . , a *regularly traded* security means any security with a minimum closing price of $2.00 or more for a majority of the business days during the preceding three-month period and a six-month minimum average daily trading volume of 1,000 shares . . . ;

(vii) A transaction in which the investors in any of the partnerships involved in the transaction are not subject to a significant adverse change with respect to voting rights, the terms of existence of the entity, management compensation or investment objectives; or

(viii) A transaction in which all investors are provided an option to receive or retain a security under substantially the same terms and conditions as the original issue. . . .

Item 908. Reasons for and Alternatives to the Roll-Up Transaction

(a) Describe the reason(s) for the roll-up transaction.

(b)(1) If the general partner or sponsor considered alternatives to the roll-up transaction being proposed, describe such alternative(s) and state the reason(s) for their rejection.

(2) Whether or not described in response to paragraph (b)(1) of this Item, describe in reasonable detail the potential alternative of continuation of the partnerships in accordance with their existing business plans, including the effects of such continuation and the material risks and benefits that likely would arise in connection therewith, and, if applicable, the general partner's reasons for not considering such alternative.

(3) Whether or not described in response to paragraph (b)(1) of this Item, describe in reasonable detail the potential alternative of liquidation of the partnerships, the procedures required to accomplish liquidation, the effects of liquidation, the material risks and benefits that likely would arise in connection with liquidation, and, if applicable, the general partner's reasons for not considering such alternative.

(c) State the reasons for the structure of the roll-up transaction and for undertaking such transaction at this time.

(d) State whether the general partner initiated the roll-up transaction and, if not, whether the general partner participated in the structuring of the transaction.

(e) State whether the general partner recommends the roll-up transaction and briefly describe the reasons for such recommendation.

Item 909. Conflicts of Interest

(a) Briefly describe the general partner's fiduciary duties to each partnership subject to the roll-up transaction and each actual or potential material conflict of interest between the general partner and the investors relating to the roll-up transaction.

(b)(1) State whether or not the general partner has retained an unaffiliated representative to act on behalf of investors for purposes of negotiating the terms of the roll-up transaction. If no such representative has been retained, describe the reasons therefor and the risks arising from the absence of separate representation. . . .

Item 910.   **Fairness of the Transaction**

(a) State whether the general partner reasonably believes that the roll-up transaction is fair or unfair to investors and the reasons for such belief. Such discussion must address the fairness of the roll-up transaction to investors in each of the partnerships and as a whole. If the roll-up transaction may be completed with a combination of partnerships consisting of less than all partnerships, or with portions of partnerships, the belief stated must address each possible combination.

(b) Discuss in reasonable detail the material factors upon which the belief stated in paragraph (a) of this Item is based and, to the extent practicable, the weight assigned to each such factor. Such discussion should include an analysis of the extent, if any, to which such belief is based on the factors set forth in Instructions (2) and (3) to this Item, paragraph (b)(1) of Item 909 . . . and Item 911. . . . This discussion also must:

(1) Compare the value of the consideration to be received in the roll-up transaction to the value of the consideration that would be received pursuant to each of the alternatives discussed in response to Item 908(b) . . . ; and

(2) Describe any material differences among the partnerships (e.g., different types of assets or different investment objectives) relating to the fairness of the transaction.

(c) If any offer of the type described in Instruction (2)(viii) to this Item has been received, describe such offer and state the reason(s) for its rejection.

(d) Describe any factors known to the general partner that may affect materially the value of the consideration to be received by investors in the roll-up transaction, the values assigned to the partnerships for purposes of the comparisons to alternatives required by paragraph (b) of this Item and the fairness of the transaction to investors.

(e) State whether the general partner's statements in response to paragraphs (a) and (b) of this Item are based, in whole or in part, on any report, opinion or appraisal described in response to Item 911 of this subpart. If so, describe any material uncertainties known to the general partner that relate to the conclusions in any such report, opinion or appraisal including, but not limited to, developments or trends that have affected or are reasonably likely to affect materially such conclusions.

Instructions to Item 910.

(1) A statement that the general partner has no reasonable belief as to the fairness of the roll-up transaction to investors will not be considered sufficient disclosure in response to paragraph (a) of this Item.

(2) The factors which are important in determining the fairness of a roll-up transaction to investors and the weight, if any, which should be given to them in a particular context will vary. Normally such factors will include, among others, those referred to in paragraph (b)(1) of Item 909 and whether the consideration offered to investors constitutes fair value in relation to:

(i) Current market prices, if any;

(ii) Historic market prices, if any;

(iii) Net book value;

(iv) Going concern value;

(v) Liquidation value;

(vi) Purchases of limited partnership interests by the general partner or sponsor or their affiliates since the commencement of the partnership's second full fiscal year preceding the date of filing of the disclosure document for the roll-up transaction;

(vii) Any report, opinion, or appraisal described in Item 911; and

(viii) Offers of which the general partner or sponsor is aware made during the preceding eighteen months for a merger, consolidation, or combination of any of the partnerships; an acquisition of any of the partnerships or a material amount of their assets; a tender offer for or other acquisition of securities of any class issued by any of the partnerships; or a change in control of any of the partnerships.

(3) The discussion concerning fairness should specifically address material terms of the transaction including whether the consideration offered to investors constitutes fair value in relation to:

    (i) The form and amount of consideration to be received by investors and the sponsor in the roll-up transaction;

    (ii) The methods used to determine such consideration; and

    (iii) The compensation to be paid to the sponsor in the future.

(4) Conclusory statements, such as "The roll-up transaction is fair to investors in relation to net book value, going concern value, liquidation value and future prospects of the partnership," will not be considered sufficient disclosure in response to paragraph (b) of this Item. . . .

Item 911. Reports, Opinions and Appraisals

(a)(1) *All material reports, opinions or appraisals.* State whether or not the general partner or sponsor has received any report, opinion (other than an opinion of counsel) or appraisal from an outside party which is materially related to the roll-up transaction including, but not limited to, any such report, opinion or appraisal relating to the consideration or the fairness of the consideration to be offered to investors in connection with the roll-up transaction or the fairness of such transaction to the general partner or investors. . . .

(b) *Fairness Opinions:* (1) If any report, opinion or appraisal relates to the fairness of the roll-up transaction to investors in the partnerships, state whether or not the report, opinion or appraisal addresses the fairness of:

    (i) The roll-up transaction as a whole and to investors in each partnership; and

    (ii) All possible combinations of partnerships in the roll-up transaction (including portions of partnerships if the transaction is structured to permit portions of partnerships to participate). If all possible combinations are not addressed:

        (A) Identify the combinations that are addressed;

        (B) Identify the person(s) that determined which combinations would be addressed and state the reasons for the selection of the combinations; and

        (C) State that if the roll-up transaction is completed with a combination of partnerships not addressed, no report, opinion or appraisal concerning the fairness of the roll-up transaction will have been obtained.

(2) If the sponsor or the general partner has not obtained any opinion on the fairness of the proposed roll-up transaction to investors in each of the affected partnerships, state the sponsor's or general partner's reasons for concluding that such an opinion is not necessary in order to permit the limited partners or shareholders to make an informed decision on the proposed transaction. . . .

REGULATION M–A

TABLE OF CONTENTS

Item		Page
1000.	Definitions	1369
1001.	Summary Term Sheet	1369
1002.	Subject Company Information	1370
1003.	Identity and Background of Filing Person	1370
1004.	Terms of the Transaction	1371
1005.	Past Contacts, Transactions, Negotiations and Agreements	1372
1006.	Purposes of the Transaction and Plans or Proposals	1373
1007.	Source and Amount of Funds or Other Consideration	1373
1008.	Interest in Securities of the Subject Company	1374
1009.	Persons/Assets, Retained, Employed, Compensated or Used	1374
1010.	Financial Statements	1374
1011.	Additional Information	1375
1012.	The Solicitation or Recommendation	1376
1013.	Purposes, Alternatives, Reasons and Effects in a Going-Private Transaction	1376
1014.	Fairness of the Going-Private Transaction	1377
1015.	Reports, Opinions, Appraisals and Negotiations	1378
1016.	Exhibits	1378

Item 1000.   Definitions

The following definitions apply to the terms used in Regulation M–A, unless specified otherwise:

(a) *Associate* has the same meaning as in Rule 12b–2;

(b) *Instruction C* means General Instruction C to Schedule 13E-3 and General Instruction C to Schedule TO.

(c) *Issuer tender offer* has the same meaning as in Rule 13e–4(a)(2);

(d) *Offeror* means any person who makes a tender offer or on whose behalf a tender offer is made;

(e) *Rule 13e–3 transaction* has the same meaning as in Rule 13e–3(a)(3);

(f) *Subject company* means the company or entity whose securities are sought to be acquired in the transaction (e.g., the target), or that is otherwise the subject of the transaction;

(g) *Subject securities* means the securities or class of securities that are sought to be acquired in the transaction or that are otherwise the subject of the transaction; and

(h) *Third-party tender offer* means a tender offer that is not an issuer tender offer.

Item 1001.   Summary Term Sheet

Summary term sheet. Provide security holders with a summary term sheet that is written in plain English. The summary term sheet must briefly describe in bullet point format the most material terms of the proposed transaction. The summary term sheet must provide security holders with sufficient information to understand the essential features and significance of the proposed transaction. The bullet points must cross-reference a more detailed discussion contained in the disclosure document that is disseminated to security holders.

Item 1002.   Subject Company Information

(a) *Name and address.* State the name of the subject company (or the issuer in the case of an issuer tender offer), and the address and telephone number of its principal executive offices.

(b) *Securities.* State the exact title and number of shares outstanding of the subject class of equity securities as of the most recent practicable date. This may be based upon information in the most recently available filing with the Commission by the subject company unless the filing person has more current information.

(c) *Trading market and price.* Identify the principal market in which the subject securities are traded and state the high and low sales prices for the subject securities in the principal market (or, if there is no principal market, the range of high and low bid quotations and the source of the quotations) for each quarter during the past two years. If there is no established trading market for the securities (except for limited or sporadic quotations), so state.

(d) *Dividends.* State the frequency and amount of any dividends paid during the past two years with respect to the subject securities. Briefly describe any restriction on the subject company's current or future ability to pay dividends. If the filing person is not the subject company, furnish this information to the extent known after making reasonable inquiry.

(e) *Prior public offerings.* If the filing person has made an underwritten public offering of the subject securities for cash during the past three years that was registered under the Securities Act of 1933 or exempt from registration under Regulation A [under that Act], state the date of the offering, the amount of securities offered, the offering price per share (adjusted for stock splits, stock dividends, etc. as appropriate) and the aggregate proceeds received by the filing person.

(f) *Prior stock purchases.* If the filing person purchased any subject securities during the past two years, state the amount of the securities purchased, the range of prices paid and the average purchase price for each quarter during that period. Affiliates need not give information for purchases made before becoming an affiliate.

Item 1003.   Identity and Background of Filing Person

(a) *Name and address.* State the name, business address and business telephone number of each filing person. Also state the name and address of each person specified in Instruction C to the schedule (except for Schedule 14D-9). If the filing person is an affiliate of the subject company, state the nature of the affiliation. If the filing person is the subject company, so state.

(b) *Business and background of entities.* If any filing person (other than the subject company) or any person specified in Instruction C to the schedule is not a natural person, state the person's principal business, state or other place of organization, and the information required by paragraphs (c)(3) and (c)(4) of this section for each person.

(c) Business and background of natural persons. If any filing person or any person specified in Instruction C to the schedule is a natural person, provide the following information for each person:

(1) Current principal occupation or employment and the name, principal business and address of any corporation or other organization in which the employment or occupation is conducted;

(2) Material occupations, positions, offices or employment during the past five years, giving the starting and ending dates of each and the name, principal business and address of any corporation or other organization in which the occupation, position, office or employment was carried on;

(3) A statement whether or not the person was convicted in a criminal proceeding during the past five years (excluding traffic violations or similar misdemeanors). If the person was convicted, describe the criminal proceeding, including the dates, nature of conviction, name and location of court, and penalty imposed or other disposition of the case;

(4) A statement whether or not the person was a party to any judicial or administrative proceeding during the past five years (except for matters that were dismissed without sanction or settlement) that resulted in a judgment, decree or final order enjoining the person from future violations of, or prohibiting

activities subject to, federal or state securities laws, or a finding of any violation of federal or state securities laws. Describe the proceeding, including a summary of the terms of the judgment, decree or final order; and

(5) Country of citizenship.

(d) *Tender offer*. Identify the tender offer and the class of securities to which the offer relates, the name of the offeror and its address (which may be based on the offeror's Schedule TO filed with the Commission).

Item 1004.   Terms of the Transaction

(a) *Material terms*. State the material terms of the transaction.

(1) *Tender offers*. In the case of a tender offer, the information must include:

(i) The total number and class of securities sought in the offer;

(ii) The type and amount of consideration offered to security holders;

(iii) The scheduled expiration date;

(iv) Whether a subsequent offering period will be available, if the transaction is a third-party tender offer;

(v) Whether the offer may be extended, and if so, how it could be extended;

(vi) The dates before and after which security holders may withdraw securities tendered in the offer;

(vii) The procedures for tendering and withdrawing securities;

(viii) The manner in which securities will be accepted for payment;

(ix) If the offer is for less than all securities of a class, the periods for accepting securities on a pro rata basis and the offeror's present intentions in the event that the offer is oversubscribed;

(x) An explanation of any material differences in the rights of security holders as a result of the transaction, if material;

(xi) A brief statement as to the accounting treatment of the transaction, if material; and

(xii) The federal income tax consequences of the transaction, if material.

(2) *Mergers or similar transactions*. In the case of a merger or similar transaction, the information must include:

(i) A brief description of the transaction;

(ii) The consideration offered to security holders;

(iii) The reasons for engaging in the transaction;

(iv) The vote required for approval of the transaction;

(v) An explanation of any material differences in the rights of security holders as a result of the transaction, if material;

(vi) A brief statement as to the accounting treatment of the transaction, if material; and

(vii) The federal income tax consequences of the transaction, if material.

(b) *Purchases*. State whether any securities are to be purchased from any officer, director or affiliate of the subject company and provide the details of each transaction.

(c) *Different terms*. Describe any term or arrangement in the Rule 13e–3 transaction that treats any subject security holders differently from other subject security holders.

(d) *Appraisal rights*. State whether or not dissenting security holders are entitled to any appraisal rights. If so, summarize the appraisal rights. If there are no appraisal rights available under state law for security holders who object to the transaction, briefly outline any other rights that may be available to security holders under the law.

(e) *Provisions for unaffiliated security holders.* Describe any provision made by the filing person in connection with the transaction to grant unaffiliated security holders access to the corporate files of the filing person or to obtain counsel or appraisal services at the expense of the filing person. If none, so state.

(f) *Eligibility for listing or trading.* If the transaction involves the offer of securities of the filing person in exchange for equity securities held by unaffiliated security holders of the subject company, describe whether or not the filing person will take steps to assure that the securities offered are or will be eligible for trading on an automated quotations system operated by a national securities association.

Item 1005.   Past Contacts, Transactions, Negotiations and Agreements

(a) *Transactions.* Briefly state the nature and approximate dollar amount of any transaction, other than those described in paragraphs (b) or (c) of this section, that occurred during the past two years, between the filing person (including any person specified in Instruction C of the schedule) and;

(1) The subject company or any of its affiliates that are not natural persons if the aggregate value of the transactions is more than one percent of the subject company's consolidated revenues for:

(i) The fiscal year when the transaction occurred; or

(ii) The past portion of the current fiscal year, if the transaction occurred in the current year; and

(2) Any executive officer, director or affiliate of the subject company that is a natural person if the aggregate value of the transaction or series of similar transactions with that person exceeds $60,000.

(b) *Significant corporate events.* Describe any negotiations, transactions or material contacts during the past two years between the filing person (including subsidiaries of the filing person and any person specified in Instruction C of the schedule) and the subject company or its affiliates concerning any:

(1) Merger;

(2) Consolidation;

(3) Acquisition;

(4) Tender offer for or other acquisition of any class of the subject company's securities;

(5) Election of the subject company's directors; or

(6) Sale or other transfer of a material amount of assets of the subject company.

(c) *Negotiations or contacts.* Describe any negotiations or material contacts concerning the matters referred to in paragraph (b) of this section during the past two years between:

(1) Any affiliates of the subject company; or

(2) The subject company or any of its affiliates and any person not affiliated with the subject company who would have a direct interest in such matters.

(d) *Conflicts of interest.* If material, describe any agreement, arrangement or understanding and any actual or potential conflict of interest between the filing person or its affiliates and:

(1) The subject company, its executive officers, directors or affiliates; or

(2) The offeror, its executive officers, directors or affiliates.

(e) *Agreements involving the subject company's securities.* Describe any agreement, arrangement, or understanding, whether or not legally enforceable, between the filing person (including any person specified in Instruction C of the schedule) and any other person with respect to any securities of the subject company. Name all persons that are a party to the agreements, arrangements, or understandings and describe all material provisions.

Item 1006.   Purposes of the Transaction and Plans or Proposals

(a) *Purposes.* State the purposes of the transaction.

(b) *Use of securities acquired.* Indicate whether the securities acquired in the transaction will be retained, retired, held in treasury, or otherwise disposed of.

(c) *Plans.* Describe any plans, proposals or negotiations that relate to or would result in:

(1) Any extraordinary transaction, such as a merger, reorganization or liquidation, involving the subject company or any of its subsidiaries;

(2) Any purchase, sale or transfer of a material amount of assets of the subject company or any of its subsidiaries;

(3) Any material change in the present dividend rate or policy, or indebtedness or capitalization of the subject company;

(4) Any change in the present board of directors or management of the subject company, including, but not limited to, any plans or proposals to change the number or the term of directors or to fill any existing vacancies on the board or to change any material term of the employment contract of any executive officer;

(5) Any other material change in the subject company's corporate structure or business;

(6) Any class of equity securities of the subject company to be delisted from a national securities exchange or cease to be authorized to be quoted in an automated quotations system operated by a national securities association;

(7) Any class of equity securities of the subject company becoming eligible for termination of registration under section 12(g)(4) of the Securities Exchange Act;

(8) The suspension of the subject company's obligation to file reports under Section 15(d) of the Securities Exchange Act;

(9) The acquisition by any person of additional securities of the subject company, or the disposition of securities of the subject company; or

(10) Any changes in the subject company's charter, bylaws or other governing instruments or other actions that could impede the acquisition of control of the subject company.

(d) *Subject company negotiations.* If the filing person is the subject company:

(1) State whether or not that person is undertaking or engaged in any negotiations in response to the tender offer that relate to:

(i) A tender offer or other acquisition of the subject company's securities by the filing person, any of its subsidiaries, or any other person; or

(ii) Any of the matters referred to in paragraphs (c)(1) through (c)(3) of this section; and

(2) Describe any transaction, board resolution, agreement in principle, or signed contract that is entered into in response to the tender offer that relates to one or more of the matters referred to in paragraph (d)(1) of this section.

Item 1007.   Source and Amount of Funds or Other Consideration

(a) *Source of funds.* State the specific sources and total amount of funds or other consideration to be used in the transaction. If the transaction involves a tender offer, disclose the amount of funds or other consideration required to purchase the maximum amount of securities sought in the offer.

(b) *Conditions.* State any material conditions to the financing discussed in response to paragraph (a) of this section. Disclose any alternative financing arrangements or alternative financing plans in the event the primary financing plans fall through. If none, so state.

(c) *Expenses.* Furnish a reasonably itemized statement of all expenses incurred or estimated to be incurred in connection with the transaction including, but not limited to, filing, legal, accounting and appraisal fees, solicitation expenses and printing costs and state whether or not the subject company has paid or will be responsible for paying any or all expenses.

(d) *Borrowed funds.* If all or any part of the funds or other consideration required is, or is expected, to be borrowed, directly or indirectly, for the purpose of the transaction:

(1) Provide a summary of each loan agreement or arrangement containing the identity of the parties, the term, the collateral, the stated and effective interest rates, and any other material terms or conditions of the loan; and

(2) Briefly describe any plans or arrangements to finance or repay the loan, or, if no plans or arrangements have been made, so state.

Item 1008.   Interest in Securities of the Subject Company

(a) *Securities ownership.* State the aggregate number and percentage of subject securities that are beneficially owned by each person named in response to Item 1003 of Regulation M–A and by each associate and majority-owned subsidiary of those persons. Give the name and address of any associate or subsidiary.

(b) *Securities transactions.* Describe any transaction in the subject securities during the past 60 days. The description of transactions required must include, but not necessarily be limited to:

(1) The identity of the persons specified in the Instruction to this section who effected the transaction;

(2) The date of the transaction;

(3) The amount of securities involved;

(4) The price per share; and

(5) Where and how the transaction was effected.

Instructions to Item 1008(b):

1.   Provide the required transaction information for the following persons:

(a) The filing person (for all schedules);

(b) Any person named in Instruction C of the schedule and any associate or majority-owned subsidiary of the issuer of filing person (for all schedules except Schedule 14D-9). . . .

Item 1009.   Persons/Assets, Retained, Employed, Compensated or Used

(a) *Solicitations or recommendations.* Identify all persons and classes of persons that are directly or indirectly employed, retained, or to be compensated to make solicitations or recommendations in connection with the transaction. Provide a summary of all material terms of employment, retainer or other arrangement for compensation.

(b) Employees and corporate assets. Identify any officer, class of employees or corporate assets of the subject company that has been or will be employed or used by the filing person in connection with the transaction. Describe the purpose for their employment or use. Instruction to Item 1009(b): Provide all information required by this Item except for the information required by paragraph (a) of this section and Item 1007 of Regulation M–A.

Item 1010.   Financial Statements

(a) *Financial information.* Furnish the following financial information:

(1) Audited financial statements for the two fiscal years required to be filed with the company's most recent annual report under sections 13 and 15(d) of the Exchange Act;

(2) Unaudited balance sheets, comparative year-to-date income statements and related earnings per share data, statements of cash flows, and comprehensive income required to be included in the company's most recent quarterly report filed under the Exchange Act;

(3) Ratio of earnings to fixed charges . . . for the two most recent fiscal years and the interim periods provided under paragraph (a)(2) of this section; and

(4) Book value per share as of the date of the most recent balance sheet presented.

(b) *Pro forma information.* If material, furnish pro forma information disclosing the effect of the transaction on:

(1) The company's balance sheet as of the date of the most recent balance sheet presented under paragraph (a) of this section;

(2) The company's statement of income, earnings per share, and ratio of earnings to fixed charges for the most recent fiscal year and the latest interim period provided under paragraph (a)(2) of this section; and

(3) The company's book value per share as of the date of the most recent balance sheet presented under paragraph (a) of this section.

(c) *Summary information.* Furnish a fair and adequate summary of the information specified in paragraphs (a) and (b) of this section for the same periods specified. A fair and adequate summary includes:

(1) The summarized financial information specified in § 210.1–02(bb)(1) of this chapter;

(2) Income per common share from continuing operations (basic and diluted, if applicable);

(3) Net income per common share (basic and diluted, if applicable);

(4) Ratio of earnings to fixed charges . . . ;

(5) Book value per share as of the date of the most recent balance sheet; and

(6) If material, pro forma data for the summarized financial information specified in paragraphs (c)(1) through (c)(5) of this section disclosing the effect of the transaction.

Item 1011. Additional Information

(a) *Agreements, regulatory requirements and legal proceedings.* If material to a security holder's decision whether to sell, tender or hold the securities sought in the tender offer, furnish the following information:

(1) Any present or proposed material agreement, arrangement, understanding or relationship between the offeror or any of its executive officers, directors, controlling persons or subsidiaries and the subject company or any of its executive officers, directors, controlling persons or subsidiaries (other than any agreement, arrangement or understanding disclosed under any other sections of Regulation M–A);

(2) To the extent known by the offeror after reasonable investigation, the applicable regulatory requirements which must be complied with or approvals which must be obtained in connection with the tender offer;

(3) The applicability of any anti-trust laws;

(4) The applicability of margin requirements under section 7 of the [Securities Exchange] Act and the applicable regulations; and

(5) Any material pending legal proceedings relating to the tender offer, including the name and location of the court or agency in which the proceedings are pending, the date instituted, the principal parties, and a brief summary of the proceedings and the relief sought.

(b) Furnish the information required by Item 402(t)(2) and (3) and in the tabular format set forth in Item 402(t)(1) of this part with respect to each named executive officer

(1) Of the subject company in a Rule 13e–3 transaction; or

(2) Of the issuer whose securities are the subject of a third-party tender offer,

regarding any agreement or understanding, whether written or unwritten, between such named executive officer and the subject company, issuer, bidder, or the acquiring company, as applicable, concerning any type of compensation, whether present, deferred or contingent, that is based upon or otherwise relates to the Rule 13e–3 transaction or third-party tender offer.

(c) *Other material information.* Furnish such additional material information, if any, as may be necessary to make the required statements, in light of the circumstances under which they are made, not materially misleading.

Item 1012.   The Solicitation or Recommendation

(a) *Solicitation or recommendation.* State the nature of the solicitation or the recommendation. If this statement relates to a recommendation, state whether the filing person is advising holders of the subject securities to accept or reject the tender offer or to take other action with respect to the tender offer and, if so, describe the other action recommended. If the filing person is the subject company and is not making a recommendation, state whether the subject company is expressing no opinion and is remaining neutral toward the tender offer or is unable to take a position with respect to the tender offer.

(b) *Reasons.* State the reasons for the position (including the inability to take a position) stated in paragraph (a) of this section. Conclusory statements such as "The tender offer is in the best interests of shareholders" are not considered sufficient disclosure.

(c) *Intent to tender.* To the extent known by the filing person after making reasonable inquiry, state whether the filing person or any executive officer, director, affiliate or subsidiary of the filing person currently intends to tender, sell or hold the subject securities that are held of record or beneficially owned by that person.

(d) *Intent to tender or vote in a going-private transaction.* To the extent known by the filing person after making reasonable inquiry, state whether or not any executive officer, director or affiliate of the issuer (or any person specified in Instruction C to the schedule) currently intends to tender or sell subject securities owned or held by that person and/or how each person currently intends to vote subject securities, including any securities the person has proxy authority for. State the reasons for the intended action.

(e) *Recommendations of others.* To the extent known by the filing person after making reasonable inquiry, state whether or not any person specified in paragraph (d) of this section has made a recommendation either in support of or opposed to the transaction and the reasons for the recommendation.

Item 1013.   Purposes, Alternatives, Reasons and Effects in a Going-Private Transaction

(a) *Purposes.* State the purposes for the Rule 13e–3 transaction.

(b) *Alternatives.* If the subject company or affiliate considered alternative means to accomplish the stated purposes, briefly describe the alternatives and state the reasons for their rejection.

(c) *Reasons.* State the reasons for the structure of the Rule 13e–3 transaction and for undertaking the transaction at this time.

(d) *Effects.* Describe the effects of the Rule 13e–3 transaction on the subject company, its affiliates and unaffiliated security holders, including the federal tax consequences of the transaction.

Instructions to Item 1013:

1.   Conclusory statements will not be considered sufficient disclosure in response to this section.

2.   The description required by paragraph (d) of this section must include a reasonably detailed discussion of both the benefits and detriments of the Rule 13e–3 transaction to the subject company, its affiliates and unaffiliated security holders. The benefits and detriments of the Rule 13e–3 transaction must be quantified to the extent practicable.

3.   If this statement is filed by an affiliate of the subject company, the description required by paragraph (d) of this section must include, but not be limited to, the effect of the Rule 13e–3 transaction on the affiliate's interest in the net book value and net earnings of the subject company in terms of both dollar amounts and percentages.

Item 1014. Fairness of the Going-Private Transaction

(a) *Fairness*. State whether the subject company or affiliate filing the statement reasonably believes that the Rule 13e–3 transaction is fair or unfair to unaffiliated security holders. If any director dissented to or abstained from voting on the Rule 13e–3 transaction, identify the director, and indicate, if known, after making reasonable inquiry, the reasons for the dissent or abstention.

(b) *Factors considered in determining fairness*. Discuss in reasonable detail the material factors upon which the belief stated in paragraph (a) of this section is based and, to the extent practicable, the weight assigned to each factor. The discussion must include an analysis of the extent, if any, to which the filing person's beliefs are based on the factors described in Instruction 2 of this section, paragraphs (c), (d) and (e) of this section and Item 1015 of Regulation M–A.

(c) *Approval of security holders*. State whether or not the transaction is structured so that approval of at least a majority of unaffiliated security holders is required.

(d) *Unaffiliated representative*. State whether or not a majority of directors who are not employees of the subject company has retained an unaffiliated representative to act solely on behalf of unaffiliated security holders for purposes of negotiating the terms of the Rule 13e–3 transaction and/or preparing a report concerning the fairness of the transaction.

(e) *Approval of directors*. State whether or not the Rule 13e–3 transaction was approved by a majority of the directors of the subject company who are not employees of the subject company.

(f) *Other offers*. If any offer of the type described in paragraph (viii) of Instruction 2 to this section has been received, describe the offer and state the reasons for its rejection.

Instructions to Item 1014:

1.   A statement that the issuer or affiliate has no reasonable belief as to the fairness of the Rule 13e–3 transaction to unaffiliated security holders will not be considered sufficient disclosure in response to paragraph (a) of this section.

2.   The factors that are important in determining the fairness of a transaction to unaffiliated security holders and the weight, if any, that should be given to them in a particular context will vary. Normally such factors will include, among others, those referred to in paragraphs (c), (d) and (e) of this section and whether the consideration offered to unaffiliated security holders constitutes fair value in relation to:

(i) Current market prices;

(ii) Historical market prices;

(iii) Net book value;

(iv) Going concern value;

(v) Liquidation value;

(vi) Purchase prices paid in previous purchases disclosed in response to Item 1002(f) of Regulation M–A;

(vii) Any report, opinion, or appraisal described in Item 1015 of Regulation M–A; and

(viii) Firm offers of which the subject company or affiliate is aware made by any unaffiliated person, other than the filing persons, during the past two years for:

(A) The merger or consolidation of the subject company with or into another company, or vice versa;

(B) The sale or other transfer of all or any substantial part of the assets of the subject company; or

(C) A purchase of the subject company's securities that would enable the holder to exercise control of the subject company.

3.   Conclusory statements, such as "The Rule 13e–3 transaction is fair to unaffiliated security holders in relation to net book value, going concern value and future prospects of the issuer" will not be considered sufficient disclosure in response to paragraph (b) of this section.

Item 1015.   Reports, Opinions, Appraisals and Negotiations

(a) *Report, opinion or appraisal.* State whether or not the subject company or affiliate has received any report, opinion (other than an opinion of counsel) or appraisal from an outside party that is materially related to the Rule 13e–3 transaction, including, but not limited to: Any report, opinion or appraisal relating to the consideration or the fairness of the consideration to be offered to security holders or the fairness of the transaction to the issuer or affiliate or to security holders who are not affiliates.

(b) *Preparer and summary of the report, opinion or appraisal.* For each report, opinion or appraisal described in response to paragraph (a) of this section or any negotiation or report described in response to Item 1014(d) of Regulation M–A or Item 14(b)(6) of Schedule 14A concerning the terms of the transaction:

(1) Identify the outside party and/or unaffiliated representative;

(2) Briefly describe the qualifications of the outside party and/or unaffiliated representative;

(3) Describe the method of selection of the outside party and/or unaffiliated representative;

(4) Describe any material relationship that existed during the past two years or is mutually understood to be contemplated and any compensation received or to be received as a result of the relationship between:

(i) The outside party, its affiliates, and/or unaffiliated representative; and

(ii) The subject company or its affiliates;

(5) If the report, opinion or appraisal relates to the fairness of the consideration, state whether the subject company or affiliate determined the amount of consideration to be paid or whether the outside party recommended the amount of consideration to be paid; and

(6) Furnish a summary concerning the negotiation, report, opinion or appraisal. The summary must include, but need not be limited to, the procedures followed; the findings and recommendations; the bases for and methods of arriving at such findings and recommendations; instructions received from the subject company or affiliate; and any limitation imposed by the subject company or affiliate on the scope of the investigation.

(c) *Availability of documents.* Furnish a statement to the effect that the report, opinion or appraisal will be made available for inspection and copying at the principal executive offices of the subject company or affiliate during its regular business hours by any interested equity security holder of the subject company or representative who has been so designated in writing. This statement also may provide that a copy of the report, opinion or appraisal will be transmitted by the subject company or affiliate to any interested equity security holder of the subject company or representative who has been so designated in writing upon written request and at the expense of the requesting security holder.

Item 1016.   Exhibits

File as an exhibit to the schedule:

(a) Any disclosure materials furnished to security holders by or on behalf of the filing person, including:

(1) Tender offer materials (including transmittal letter);

(2) Solicitation or recommendation (including those referred to in Item 1012 of Regulation M–A);

(3) Going-private disclosure document;

(4) Prospectus used in connection with an exchange offer where securities are registered under the Securities Act of 1933; and

(5) Any other disclosure materials;

(b) Any loan agreement referred to in response to Item 1007(d) of Regulation M–A;

(c) Any report, opinion or appraisal referred to in response to Item 1014(d) or Item 1015 of Regulation M–A;

(d) Any document setting forth the terms of any agreement, arrangement, understanding or relationship referred to in response to Item 1005(e) or Item 1011(a)(1) of Regulation M–A;

(e) Any agreement, arrangement or understanding referred to in response to Item 1005(d), or the pertinent portions of any proxy statement, report or other communication containing the disclosure required by Item 1005(d) of Regulation M–A;

(f) A detailed statement describing security holders' appraisal rights and the procedures for exercising those appraisal rights referred to in response to Item 1004(d) of Regulation M–A;

(g) Any written instruction, form or other material that is furnished to persons making an oral solicitation or recommendation by or on behalf of the filing person for their use directly or indirectly in connection with the transaction; and

(h) Any written opinion prepared by legal counsel at the filing person's request and communicated to the filing person pertaining to the tax consequences of the transaction. . . .

SECURITIES EXCHANGE ACT OF 1934

15 U.S.C. §§ 78a et seq.

TABLE OF CONTENTS

Sec.		Page
1.	Short Title	1382
2.	Necessity for Regulation*	
3.	Definitions and Application	1382
3A.	Swap Agreements*	
4.	Securities and Exchange Commission	1385
4A.	Delegation of Functions by Commission*	
4B.	Transfer of Functions With Respect to Assignment of Personnel to Chairman*	
4C.	Appearance and Practice Before the Commission	1386
4E.	Deadline for Completing Enforcement Investigations and Compliance Examinations and Inspections*	
5.	Transactions on Unregistered Exchanges	1386
6.	National Securities Exchanges	1386
7.	Margin Requirements*	
8.	Restrictions on Borrowing and Lending by Members, Brokers, and Dealers*	
9.	Manipulation of Security Prices	1387
10.	Manipulative and Deceptive Devices	1389
10A.	Audit Requirements	1390
10B.	Position Limits and Position Accountability for Security-Based Swaps and Large Trader Reporting*	
10C.	Compensation Committees	1394
10D.	Recovery of Erroneously Awarded Compensation	1396
11.	Trading by Members of Exchanges, Brokers, and Dealers*	
11A.	National Market System for Securities; Securities Information Processors*	
12.	Registration Requirements for Securities	1396
13.	Periodical and Other Reports	1400
14.	Proxies	1405
14A.	Shareholder Approval of Executive Compensation	1412
14B.	Corporate Governance	1414
15.	Registration and Regulation of Brokers and Dealers	1414
15A.	Registered Securities Associations*	
15B.	Municipal Securities*	
15C.	Government Securities Brokers and Dealers*	
15D.	Security Analysts and Research Reports	1416
15E.	Registration of Nationally Recognized Statistical Rating Agencies*	
15F.	Registration and Regulation of Security-Based Swap Dealers and Major Security-Based Swap Participants*	
15G.	Credit Risk Retention*	
16.	Directors, Officers, and Principal Stockholders	1418
17.	Records and Reports*	
17A.	National System for Clearance and Settlement of Securities Transactions*	
17B.	Automated Quotation System for Penny Stocks*	
18.	Liability for Misleading Statements	1419
19.	Registration, Responsibilities, and Oversight of Self-Regulatory Organizations	1419
20.	Liability of Controlling Persons and Persons Who Aid and Abet Violations	1420
20A.	Liability to Contemporaneous Traders for Insider Trading	1421
21.	Investigations and Actions	1421

---

* Omitted.

21A.   Civil Penalties for Insider Trading 1423
21B.   Civil Remedies in Administrative Proceedings 1424
21C.   Cease-and-Desist Proceedings 1426
21D.   Private Securities Litigation 1426
21E.   Application of Safe Harbor for Forward-Looking Statements.................... 1434
21F.   Securities Whistleblower Incentives and Protection*
22.   Hearings by Commission*
23.   Rules, Regulations, and Orders; Annual Reports*
24.   Public Availability of Information*
25.   Court Review of Orders and Rules*
26.   Unlawful Representations*
27.   Jurisdiction of Offenses and Suits 1437
27A.   Special Provision Relating to Statute of Limitations on Private Causes of Action 1437
28.   Effect on Existing Law 1437
29.   Validity of Contracts 1440
30.   Foreign Securities Exchanges*
30A.   Prohibited Foreign Trade Practices by Issuers 1440
30B.   Prohibited Foreign Trade Practices by Domestic Concerns*
31.   Transaction Fees*
32.   Penalties 1442
33.   Separability of Provisions*
34.   Effective Date*
35.   Authorization of Appropriations*
35A.   Requirements for the EDGAR System*
36.   General Exemptive Authority 1443

_____

§ 1.   Short Title

This chapter may be cited as the "Securities Exchange Act of 1934." . . .

§ 3.   Definitions and Application

(a) Definitions

When used in this chapter, unless the context otherwise requires. . . .

(4) The term "broker" means any person engaged in the business of effecting transactions in securities for the account of others, but does not include a bank. . . .

(5) The term "dealer" means any person engaged in the business of buying and selling securities for his own account, through a broker or otherwise, but does not include a bank, or any person insofar as he buys or sells securities for his own account, either individually or in some fiduciary capacity, but not as a part of a regular business. . . .

(8) The term "issuer" means any person who issues or proposes to issue any security. . . .

(10) The term "security" means any note, stock, treasury stock, security future, bond, debenture, certificate of interest or participation in any profit-sharing agreement or in any oil, gas, or other mineral royalty or lease, any collateral-trust certificate, preorganization certificate or subscription, transferable share, investment contract, voting-trust certificate, certificate of deposit for a security, any put, call, straddle, option, or privilege on any security, certificate of deposit, or group or index of securities (including any interest therein or based on the value thereof), or any put, call, straddle, option, or privilege entered into on a national securities exchange relating to foreign currency, or in general, any instrument commonly known as a "security"; or any certificate of interest or participation in, temporary or interim certificate for, receipt for, or warrant or right to subscribe to or purchase, any of the foregoing; but shall not include currency or any note, draft, bill of exchange, or banker's acceptance which has a maturity at the time of

_____

*   Omitted.

issuance of not exceeding nine months, exclusive of days of grace, or any renewal thereof the maturity of which is likewise limited.

(11) The term "equity security" means any stock or similar security; or any security future on any such security; or any security convertible, with or without consideration, into such a security, or carrying any warrant or right to subscribe to or purchase such a security; or any such warrant or right; or any other security which the Commission shall deem to be of similar nature and consider necessary or appropriate, by such rules and regulations as it may prescribe in the public interest or for the protection of investors, to treat as an equity security.

(12)(A) The term "exempted security" or "exempted securities" includes—

(i) government securities, as defined in paragraph (42) of this subsection;

(ii) municipal securities, as defined in paragraph (29) of this subsection;

(iii) any interest or participation in any common trust fund or similar fund maintained by a bank exclusively for the collective investment and reinvestment of assets contributed thereto by such bank in its capacity as trustee, executor, administrator, or guardian;

(iv) any interest or participation in a single trust fund, or a collective trust fund maintained by a bank, or any security arising out of a contract issued by an insurance company, which interest, participation, or security is issued in connection with a qualified plan as defined in subparagraph (C) of this paragraph;

(v) any security issued by or any interest or participation in any pooled income fund, collective trust fund, collective investment fund, or similar fund that is excluded from the definition of an investment company under section 3(c)(10)(B) of the Investment Company Act of 1940; . . .

(vii) such other securities (which may include, among others, unregistered securities, the market in which is predominantly intrastate) as the Commission may, by such rules and regulations as it deems consistent with the public interest and the protection of investors, either unconditionally or upon specified terms and conditions or for stated periods, exempt from the operation of any one or more provisions of this chapter which by their terms do not apply to an "exempted security" or to "exempted securities". . . .

(13) The terms "buy" and "purchase" each include any contract to buy, purchase, or otherwise acquire. . . .

(14) The terms "sale" and "sell" each include any contract to sell or otherwise dispose of. . . .

(26) The term "self-regulatory organization" means any national securities exchange, registered securities association, or registered clearing agency. . . .

(27) The term "rules of an exchange", "rules of an association", or "rules of a clearing agency" means the constitution, articles of incorporation, bylaws, and rules, or instruments corresponding to the foregoing, of an exchange, association of brokers and dealers, or clearing agency, respectively, and such of the stated policies, practices, and interpretations of such exchange, association, or clearing agency as the Commission, by rule, may determine to be necessary or appropriate in the public interest or for the protection of investors to be deemed to be rules of such exchange, association, or clearing agency.

(28) The term "rules of a self-regulatory organization" means the rules of an exchange which is a national securities exchange, the rules of an association of brokers and dealers which is a registered securities association, the rules of a clearing agency which is a registered clearing agency or the rules of the Municipal Securities Rulemaking Board. . . .

(29) The term "municipal securities" means securities which are direct obligations of, or obligations guaranteed as to principal or interest by, a State or any political subdivision thereof, or any agency or instrumentality of a State or any political subdivision thereof, or any municipal corporate instrumentality of one or more States. . . .

(42) The term "government securities" means—

(A) securities which are direct obligations of, or obligations guaranteed as to principal or interest by, the United States;

(B) securities which are issued or guaranteed by corporations in which the United States has a direct or indirect interest and which are designated by the Secretary of the Treasury for exemption as necessary or appropriate in the public interest or for the protection of investors;

(C) securities issued or guaranteed as to principal or interest by any corporation the securities of which are designated, by statute specifically naming such corporation, to constitute exempt securities within the meaning of the laws administered by the Commission. . . .

(51)(A) The term "penny stock" means any equity security other than a security that is—

(i) registered or approved for registration and traded on a national securities exchange that meets such criteria as the Commission shall prescribe by rule or regulation for purposes of this paragraph;

(ii) authorized for quotation on an automated quotation system sponsored by a registered securities association, if such system (I) was established and in operation before January 1, 1990, and (II) meets such criteria as the Commission shall prescribe by rule or regulation for purposes of this paragraph;

(iii) issued by an investment company registered under the Investment Company Act of 1940;

(iv) excluded, on the basis of exceeding a minimum price, net tangible assets of the issuer, or other relevant criteria, from the definition of such term by rule or regulation which the Commission shall prescribe for purposes of this paragraph; or

(v) exempted, in whole or in part, conditionally or unconditionally, from the definition of such term by rule, regulation, or order prescribed by the Commission.

(B) The Commission may, by rule, regulation, or order, designate any equity security or class of equity securities described in clause (i) or (ii) of subparagraph (A) as within the meaning of the term "penny stock" if such security or class of securities is traded other than on a national securities exchange or through an automated quotation system described in clause (ii) of subparagraph (A).

(C) In exercising its authority under this paragraph to prescribe rules, regulations, and orders, the Commission shall determine that such rule, regulation, or order is consistent with the public interest and the protection of investors. . . .

(55)(A) The term "security future" means a contract of sale for future delivery of a single security. . . .

(56) The term "security futures product" means a security future or any put, call, straddle, option, or privilege on any security future. . . .

(58) Audit Committee.—The term "audit committee" means—

(A) a committee (or equivalent body) established by and amongst the board of directors of an issuer for the purpose of overseeing the accounting and financial reporting processes of the issuer and audits of the financial statements of the issuer; and

(B) if no such committee exists with respect to an issuer, the entire board of directors of the issuer.

(59) Registered Public Accounting Firm.—The term "registered public accounting firm" has the same meaning as in section 2 of the Sarbanes-Oxley Act of 2002. . . .

(79) Asset-backed security.—The term "asset-backed security"—

(A) means a fixed-income or other security collateralized by any type of self-liquidating financial asset (including a loan, a lease, a mortgage, or a secured or unsecured receivable) that allows the holder of the security to receive payments that depend primarily on cash flow from the asset, including—

(i) a collateralized mortgage obligation;

(ii) a collateralized debt obligation;

(iii) a collateralized bond obligation;

(iv) a collateralized debt obligation of asset-backed securities;

(v) a collateralized debt obligation of collateralized debt obligations; and

(vi) a security that the Commission, by rule, determines to be an asset-backed security for purposes of this section; and

(B) does not include a security issued by a finance subsidiary held by the parent company or a company controlled by the parent company, if none of the securities issued by the finance subsidiary are held by an entity that is not controlled by the parent company.

(80) Emerging growth company.—The term 'emerging growth company' means an issuer that had total annual gross revenues of less than $1,000,000,000 (as such amount is indexed for inflation every 5 years by the Commission to reflect the change in the Consumer Price Index for All Urban Consumers published by the Bureau of Labor Statistics, setting the threshold to the nearest 1,000,000) during its most recently completed fiscal year. An issuer that is an emerging growth company as of the first day of that fiscal year shall continue to be deemed an emerging growth company until the earliest of—

(A) the last day of the fiscal year of the issuer during which it had total annual gross revenues of $1,000,000,000 (as such amount is indexed for inflation every 5 years by the Commission to reflect the change in the Consumer Price Index for All Urban Consumers published by the Bureau of Labor Statistics, setting the threshold to the nearest 1,000,000) or more;

(B) the last day of the fiscal year of the issuer following the fifth anniversary of the date of the first sale of common equity securities of the issuer pursuant to an effective registration statement under the Securities Act of 1933;

(C) the date on which such issuer has during the previous 3-year period, issued more than $1,000,000,000 in non-convertible debt; or

(D) the date on which such issuer is deemed to be a 'large accelerated filer', as defined in Rule 12b–2.

(c) Other Definitions.—As used in this title, the following definitions shall apply:

(1) Commission.—The term Commission means the Securities and Exchange Commission.

(2) Initial public offering date.—The term initial public offering date means the date of the first sale of common equity securities of an issuer pursuant to an effective registration statement under the Securities Act of 1933.

(d) Effective date.—Notwithstanding section 2(a)(19) of the Securities Act of 1933 and section 3(a)(80) of the Securities Exchange Act of 1934, an issuer shall not be an emerging growth company for purposes of such Acts if the first sale of common equity securities of such issuer pursuant to an effective registration statement under the Securities Act of 1933 occurred on or before December 8, 2011.

(f) Consideration of promotion of efficiency, competition, and capital formation

Whenever pursuant to this chapter the Commission is engaged in rulemaking, or in the review of a rule of a self-regulatory organization, and is required to consider or determine whether an action is necessary or appropriate in the public interest, the Commission shall also consider, in addition to the protection of investors, whether the action will promote efficiency, competition, and capital formation. . . .

§ 4.   Securities and Exchange Commission

(a) Establishment; composition; limitations on commissioners; terms of office

There is hereby established a Securities and Exchange Commission (hereinafter referred to as the "Commission") to be composed of five commissioners to be appointed by the President by and with the advice and consent of the Senate. Not more than three of such commissioners shall be members of the same political party, and in making appointments members of different political parties shall be appointed alternately as nearly as may be practicable. . . .

§ 4C.   Appearance and Practice Before the Commission

(a)   Authority to censure

The Commission may censure any person, or deny, temporarily or permanently, to any person the privilege of appearing or practicing before the Commission in any way, if that person is found by the Commission, after notice and opportunity for hearing in the matter—

(1) not to possess the requisite qualifications to represent others;

(2) to be lacking in character or integrity, or to have engaged in unethical or improper professional conduct; or

(3) to have willfully violated, or willfully aided and abetted the violation of, any provision of the securities laws or the rules and regulations issued thereunder.

(b)   Definition

With respect to any registered public accounting firm or associated person, for purposes of this section, the term "improper professional conduct" means—

(1) intentional or knowing conduct, including reckless conduct, that results in a violation of applicable professional standards; and

(2) negligent conduct in the form of—

(A) a single instance of highly unreasonable conduct that results in a violation of applicable professional standards in circumstances in which the registered public accounting firm or associated person knows, or should know, that heightened scrutiny is warranted; or

(B) repeated instances of unreasonable conduct, each resulting in a violation of applicable professional standards, that indicate a lack of competence to practice before the Commission.

§ 5.   Transactions on Unregistered Exchanges

It shall be unlawful for any broker, dealer, or exchange, directly or indirectly, to make use of the mails or any means or instrumentality of interstate commerce for the purpose of using any facility of an exchange within or subject to the jurisdiction of the United States to effect any transaction in a security, or to report any such transaction, unless such exchange (1) is registered as a national securities exchange under section 6 of this title, or (2) is exempted from such registration upon application by the exchange because, in the opinion of the Commission, by reason of the limited volume of transactions effected on such exchange, it is not practicable and not necessary or appropriate in the public interest or for the protection of investors to require such registration.

§ 6.   National Securities Exchanges

(a)   Registration; Application

An exchange may be registered as a national securities exchange under the terms and conditions hereinafter provided in this section and in accordance with the provisions of section 19(a) of this title, by filing with the Commission an application for registration in such form as the Commission, by rule, may prescribe containing the rules of the exchange and such other information and documents as the Commission, by rule, may prescribe as necessary or appropriate in the public interest or for the protection of investors. . . .

(b)   Determination by Commission requisite to registration of applicant as national securities exchange. . . .*

An exchange shall not be registered as a national securities exchange unless the Commission determines that . . .

---

*   Section 6(b)(9) is effective December 17, 1994. (Footnote by ed.)

(9)(A) The rules of the exchange prohibit the listing of any security issued in a limited partnership rollup transaction (as such term is defined in paragraphs (4) and (5) of section 14(h)), unless such transaction was conducted in accordance with procedures designed to protect the rights of limited partners, including—

(i) the right of dissenting limited partners to one of the following:

(I) an appraisal and compensation;

(II) retention of a security under substantially the same terms and conditions as the original issue;

(III) approval of the limited partnership rollup transaction by not less than 75 percent of the outstanding securities of each of the participating limited partnerships;

(IV) the use of a committee of limited partners that is independent, as determined in accordance with rules prescribed by the exchange, of the general partner or sponsor, that has been approved by a majority of the outstanding units of each of the participating limited partnerships, and that has such authority as is necessary to protect the interest of limited partners, including the authority to hire independent advisors, to negotiate with the general partner or sponsor on behalf of the limited partners, and to make a recommendation to the limited partners with respect to the proposed transaction; or

(V) other comparable rights that are prescribed by rule by the exchange and that are designed to protect dissenting limited partners;

(ii) the right not to have their voting power unfairly reduced or abridged;

(iii) the right not to bear an unfair portion of the costs of a proposed limited partnership rollup transaction that is rejected; and

(iv) restrictions on the conversion of contingent interests or fees into non-contingent interests or fees and restrictions on the receipt of a non-contingent equity interest in exchange for fees for services which have not yet been provided.

(B) As used in this paragraph, the term "dissenting limited partner" means a person who, on the date on which soliciting material is mailed to investors, is a holder of a beneficial interest in a limited partnership that is the subject of a limited partnership rollup transaction, and who casts a vote against the transaction and complies with procedures established by the exchange, except that for purposes of an exchange or tender offer, such person shall file an objection in writing under the rules of the exchange during the period during which the offer is outstanding. . . .

(10)(A) The rules of the exchange prohibit any member that is not the beneficial owner of a security registered under section 12 from granting a proxy to vote the security in connection with a shareholder vote described in subparagraph (B), unless the beneficial owner of the security has instructed the member to vote the proxy in accordance with the voting instructions of the beneficial owner.

(B) A shareholder vote described in this subparagraph is a shareholder vote with respect to the election of a member of the board of directors of an issuer, executive compensation, or any other significant matter, as determined by the Commission, by rule, and does not include a vote with respect to the uncontested election of a member of the board of directors of any investment company registered under the Investment Company Act.

(C) Nothing in this paragraph shall be construed to prohibit a national securities exchange from prohibiting a member that is not the beneficial owner of a security registered under section 12 from granting a proxy to vote the security in connection with a shareholder vote not described in subparagraph (A).

§ 9. Manipulation of Security Prices

(a) Transactions relating to purchase or sale of security

It shall be unlawful for any person, directly or indirectly, by the use of the mails or any means or instrumentality of interstate commerce, or of any facility of any national securities exchange, or for any member of a national securities exchange—

(1) For the purpose of creating a false or misleading appearance of active trading in any security other than a government security, or a false or misleading appearance with respect to the market for any such security, (A) to effect any transaction in such security which involves no change in the beneficial ownership thereof, or (B) to enter an order or orders for the purchase of such security with the knowledge that an order or orders of substantially the same size, at substantially the same time, and at substantially the same price, for the sale of any such security, has been or will be entered by or for the same or different parties, or (C) to enter any order or orders for the sale of any such security with the knowledge that an order or orders of substantially the same size, at substantially the same time, and at substantially the same price, for the purchase of such security, has been or will be entered by or for the same or different parties.

(2) To effect, alone or with one or more other persons, a series of transactions in any security registered on a national securities exchange . . . creating actual or apparent active trading in such security or raising or depressing the price of such security, for the purpose of inducing the purchase or sale of such security by others.

(3) If a dealer or broker, or other person selling or offering for sale or purchasing or offering to purchase the security . . ., to induce the purchase or sale of any security other than a government security . . . by the circulation or dissemination in the ordinary course of business of information to the effect that the price of any such security will or is likely to rise or fall because of market operations of any one or more persons conducted for the purpose of raising or depressing the prices of such security.

(4) If a dealer or broker, or the person selling or offering for sale or purchasing or offering to purchase the security . . . with respect to such security, to make, regarding any security other than a government security . . ., for the purpose of inducing the purchase or sale of such security, any statement which was at the time and in the light of the circumstances under which it was made, false or misleading with respect to any material fact, and which he knew or had reasonable ground to believe was so false or misleading.

(5) For a consideration, received directly or indirectly from a dealer or broker, or other person selling or offering for sale or purchasing or offering to purchase the security . . . with respect to such security, to induce the purchase of any security registered on a national securities exchange or any security-based swap agreement . . . with respect to such security by the circulation or dissemination of information to the effect that the price of any such security will or is likely to rise or fall because of the market operations of any one or more persons conducted for the purpose of raising or depressing the price of such security.

(6) To effect either alone or with one or more other persons any series of transactions for the purchase and/or sale of any security other than a government security for the purpose of pegging, fixing, or stabilizing the price of such security in contravention of such rules and regulations as the Commission may prescribe as necessary or appropriate in the public interest or for the protection of investors.

(b)   Transactions relating to puts, calls, straddles, or options

It shall be unlawful for any person to effect, by use of any facility of a national securities exchange, in contravention of such rules and regulations as the Commission may prescribe as necessary or appropriate in the public interest or for the protection of investors—

(1) any transaction in connection with any security whereby any party to such transaction acquires (A) any put, call, straddle, or other option or privilege of buying the security from or selling the security to another without being bound to do so; or (B) any security futures product on the security; or

(2) any transaction in connection with any security with relation to which he has, directly or indirectly, any interest in any (A) such put, call, straddle, option, or privilege; or (B) such security futures product; or

(3) any transaction in any security for the account of any person who he has reason to believe has, and who actually has, directly or indirectly, any interest in any (A) such put, call, straddle, option, or privilege or (B) such security futures product with relation to such security. . . .

(d) Transactions relating to short sales of securities.—It shall be unlawful for any person, directly or indirectly, by the use of the mails or any means or instrumentality of interstate commerce, or of any facility of any national securities exchange, or for any member of a national securities exchange to effect, alone or with one or more other persons, a manipulative short sale of any security. The Commission shall issue such other rules as are necessary or appropriate to ensure that the appropriate enforcement options and remedies are available for violations of this subsection in the public interest or for the protection of investors.

(f) Persons liable; suits at law or in equity

Any person who willfully participates in any act or transaction in violation of subsections (a), (b), or (c) of this section, shall be liable to any person who shall purchase or sell any security at a price which was affected by such act or transaction, and the person so injured may sue in law or in equity in any court of competent jurisdiction to recover the damages sustained as a result of any such act or transaction. In any such suit the court may, in its discretion, require an undertaking for the payment of the costs of such suit, and assess reasonable costs, including reasonable attorneys' fees, against either party litigant. Every person who becomes liable to make any payment under this subsection may recover contribution as in cases of contract from any person who, if joined in the original suit, would have been liable to make the same payment. No action shall be maintained to enforce any liability created under this section, unless brought within one year after the discovery of the facts constituting the violation and within three years after such violation.

(g) Subsection (a) not applicable to exempted securities

The provisions of subsection (a) of this section shall not apply to an exempted security. . . .

(i) Limitations on practices that affect market volatility

It shall be unlawful for any person, by the use of the mails or any means or instrumentality of interstate commerce or of any facility of any national securities exchange, to use or employ any act or practice in connection with the purchase or sale of any equity security in contravention of such rules or regulations as the Commission may adopt, consistent with the public interest, the protection of investors, and the maintenance of fair and orderly markets—

(1) to prescribe means reasonably designed to prevent manipulation of price levels of the equity securities market or a substantial segment thereof; and

(2) to prohibit or constrain, during periods of extraordinary market volatility, any trading practice in connection with the purchase or sale of equity securities that the Commission determines (A) has previously contributed significantly to extraordinary levels of volatility that have threatened the maintenance of fair and orderly markets; and (B) is reasonably certain to engender such levels of volatility if not prohibited or constrained.

In adopting rules under paragraph (2), the Commission shall, consistent with the purposes of this subsection, minimize the impact on the normal operations of the market and a natural person's freedom to buy or sell any equity security. . . .

§ 10. Manipulative and Deceptive Devices

It shall be unlawful for any person, directly or indirectly, by the use of any means or instrumentality of interstate commerce or of the mails, or of any facility of any national securities exchange—

(a)(1) To effect a short sale, or to use or employ any stop-loss order in connection with the purchase or sale, of any security other than a government security, in contravention of such rules and regulations as the Commission may prescribe as necessary or appropriate in the public interest or for the protection of investors. . . .

(b) To use or employ, in connection with the purchase or sale of any security registered on a national securities exchange or any security not so registered, . . . any manipulative or deceptive device or contrivance in contravention of such rules and regulations as the Commission may prescribe as necessary or appropriate in the public interest or for the protection of investors. . . .

(c)(1) To effect, accept, or facilitate a transaction involving the loan or borrowing of securities in contravention of such rules and regulations as the Commission may prescribe as necessary or appropriate in the public interest or for the protection of investors. . . .

Rules promulgated under subsection (b) that prohibit fraud, manipulation, or insider trading (but not rules imposing or specifying reporting or recordkeeping requirements, procedures, or standards as prophylactic measures against fraud, manipulation, or insider trading), and judicial precedents decided under subsection (b) and rules promulgated thereunder that prohibit fraud, manipulation, or insider trading, shall apply to security-based swap agreements to the same extent as they apply to securities. Judicial precedents decided under section 17(a) of the Securities Act of 1933 and sections 9, 15, 16, 20, and 21A of this title, and judicial precedents decided under applicable rules promulgated under such sections, shall apply to security-based swap agreements to the same extent as they apply to securities.

§ 10A. Audit Requirements

(a) In general

Each audit required pursuant to this title of the financial statements of an issuer by a registered public accounting firm shall include, in accordance with generally accepted auditing standards, as may be modified or supplemented from time to time by the Commission—

(1) procedures designed to provide reasonable assurance of detecting illegal acts that would have a direct and material effect on the determination of financial statement amounts;

(2) procedures designed to identify related party transactions that are material to the financial statements or otherwise require disclosure therein; and

(3) an evaluation of whether there is substantial doubt about the ability of the issuer to continue as a going concern during the ensuing fiscal year.

(b) Required response to audit discoveries

(1) *Investigation and report to management.*—If, in the course of conducting an audit pursuant to this title to which subsection (a) applies, the registered public accounting firm detects or otherwise becomes aware of information indicating that an illegal act (whether or not perceived to have a material effect on the financial statements of the issuer) has or may have occurred, the firm shall, in accordance with generally accepted auditing standards, as may be modified or supplemented from time to time by the Commission—

(A)

(i) determine whether it is likely that an illegal act has occurred; and

(ii) if so, determine and consider the possible effect of the illegal act on the financial statements of the issuer, including any contingent monetary effects, such as fines, penalties, and damages; and

(B) as soon as practicable, inform the appropriate level of the management of the issuer and assure that the audit committee of the issuer, or the board of directors of the issuer in the absence of such a committee, is adequately informed with respect to illegal acts that have been detected or have otherwise come to the attention of such accountant in the course of the audit, unless the illegal act is clearly inconsequential.

(2) *Response to failure to take remedial action.*—If, after determining that the audit committee of the board of directors of the issuer, or the board of directors of the issuer in the absence of an audit committee, is adequately informed with respect to illegal acts that have been detected or have otherwise come to the attention of the firm in the course of the audit of such firm, the registered public accounting firm concludes that—

(A) the illegal act has a material effect on the financial statements of the issuer;

(B) the senior management has not taken, and the board of directors has not caused senior management to take, timely and appropriate remedial actions with respect to the illegal act; and

(C) the failure to take remedial action is reasonably expected to warrant departure from a standard report of the auditor, when made, or warrant resignation from the audit engagement;

the registered public accounting firm shall, as soon as practicable, directly report its conclusions to the board of directors.

(3) *Notice to commission; response to failure to notify.*—An issuer whose board of directors receives a report under paragraph (2) shall inform the Commission by notice not later than 1 business day after the receipt of such report and shall furnish the registered public accounting firm making such report with a copy of the notice furnished to the Commission. If the registered public accounting firm fails to receive a copy of the notice before the expiration of the required 1-business-day period, the registered public accounting firm shall—

(A) resign from the engagement; or

(B) furnish to the Commission a copy of its report (or the documentation of any oral report given) not later than 1 business day following such failure to receive notice.

(4) *Report after resignation.*—If a registered public accounting firm resigns from an engagement under paragraph (3)(A), the firm shall, not later than 1 business day following the failure by the issuer to notify the Commission under paragraph (3), furnish to the Commission a copy of the report of the firm (or the documentation of any oral report given).

(c) Auditor liability limitation

No registered public accounting firm shall be liable in a private action for any finding, conclusion, or statement expressed in a report made pursuant to paragraph (3) or (4) of subsection (b), including any rule promulgated pursuant thereto.

(d) Civil penalties in cease-and-desist proceedings

If the Commission finds, after notice and opportunity for hearing in a proceeding instituted pursuant to section 21C, that an independent public accountant has willfully violated paragraph (3) or (4) of subsection (b), the Commission may, in addition to entering an order under section 21C, impose a civil penalty against the registered public accounting firm and any other person that the Commission finds was a cause of such violation. The determination to impose a civil penalty and the amount of the penalty shall be governed by the standards set forth in section 21B.

(e) Preservation of existing authority

Except as provided in subsection (d), nothing in this section shall be held to limit or otherwise affect the authority of the Commission under this title.

(f) Definitions

As used in this section, the term "illegal act" means an act or omission that violates any law, or any rule or regulation having the force of law.

As used in this section, the term "issuer" means an issuer (as defined in section 3), the securities of which are registered under section 12, or that is required to file reports pursuant to section 15(d), or that files or has filed a registration statement that has not yet become effective under the Securities Act of 1933 (15 U.S.C. 77a et seq.), and that it has not withdrawn.

(g) Prohibited activities

Except as provided in subsection (h), it shall be unlawful for a registered public accounting firm (and any associated person of that firm, to the extent determined appropriate by the Commission) that performs for any issuer any audit required by this title or the rules of the Commission under this title or, beginning 180 days after the date of commencement of the operations of the Public Company Accounting Oversight Board established under section 101 of the Sarbanes-Oxley Act of 2002 (in this section referred to as the "Board"), the rules of the Board, to provide to that issuer, contemporaneously with the audit, any non-audit service, including—

(1) bookkeeping or other services related to the accounting records or financial statements of the audit client;

(2) financial information systems design and implementation;

(3) appraisal or valuation services, fairness opinions, or contribution-in-kind reports;

(4) actuarial services;

(5) internal audit outsourcing services;

(6) management functions or human resources;

(7) broker or dealer, investment adviser, or investment banking services;

(8) legal services and expert services unrelated to the audit; and

(9) any other service that the Board determines, by regulation, is impermissible.

(h) Preapproval required for non-audit services

A registered public accounting firm may engage in any non-audit service, including tax services, that is not described in any of paragraphs (1) through (9) of subsection (g) for an audit client, only if the activity is approved in advance by the audit committee of the issuer, in accordance with subsection (i).

(i) Preapproval requirements

(1) *In General.*—

(A) *Audit Committee Action.*—All auditing services (which may entail providing comfort letters in connection with securities underwritings or statutory audits required for insurance companies for purposes of State law) and non-audit services, other than as provided in subparagraph (B), provided to an issuer by the auditor of the issuer shall be preapproved by the audit committee of the issuer.

(B) *De Minimis Exception.*—The preapproval requirement under subparagraph (A) is waived with respect to the provision of non-audit services for an issuer, if—

(i) the aggregate amount of all such non-audit services provided to the issuer constitutes not more than 5 percent of the total amount of revenues paid by the issuer to its auditor during the fiscal year in which the non-audit services are provided;

(ii) such services were not recognized by the issuer at the time of the engagement to be non-audit services; and

(iii) such services are promptly brought to the attention of the audit committee of the issuer and approved prior to the completion of the audit by the audit committee or by 1 or more members of the audit committee who are members of the board of directors to whom authority to grant such approvals has been delegated by the audit committee.

(2) *Disclosure to Investors.*—Approval by an audit committee of an issuer under this subsection of a non-audit service to be performed by the auditor of the issuer shall be disclosed to investors in periodic reports required by section 13(a).

(3) *Delegation Authority.*—The audit committee of an issuer may delegate to 1 or more designated members of the audit committee who are independent directors of the board of directors, the authority to grant preapprovals required by this subsection. The decisions of any member to whom authority is delegated under this paragraph to preapprove an activity under this subsection shall be presented to the full audit committee at each of its scheduled meetings.

(4) *Approval of Audit Services for Other Purposes.*—In carrying out its duties under subsection (m)(2), if the audit committee of an issuer approves an audit service within the scope of the engagement of the auditor, such audit service shall be deemed to have been preapproved for purposes of this subsection.

(j) Audit partner rotation

It shall be unlawful for a registered public accounting firm to provide audit services to an issuer if the lead (or coordinating) audit partner (having primary responsibility for the audit), or the audit partner responsible for reviewing the audit, has performed audit services for that issuer in each of the 5 previous fiscal years of that issuer.

(k) Reports to audit committees

Each registered public accounting firm that performs for any issuer any audit required by this title shall timely report to the audit committee of the issuer—

(1) all critical accounting policies and practices to be used;

(2) all alternative treatments of financial information within generally accepted accounting principles that have been discussed with management officials of the issuer, ramifications of the use of such alternative disclosures and treatments, and the treatment preferred by the registered public accounting firm; and

(3) other material written communications between the registered public accounting firm and the management of the issuer, such as any management letter or schedule of unadjusted differences.

(*l*) Conflicts of interest

It shall be unlawful for a registered public accounting firm to perform for an issuer any audit service required by this title, if a chief executive officer, controller, chief financial officer, chief accounting officer, or any person serving in an equivalent position for the issuer, was employed by that registered independent public accounting firm and participated in any capacity in the audit of that issuer during the 1-year period preceding the date of the initiation of the audit.

(m) Standards relating to audit committees

(1) *Commission Rules.*—

(A) *In General.*—Effective not later than 270 days after the date of enactment of this subsection, the Commission shall, by rule, direct the national securities exchanges and national securities associations to prohibit the listing of any security of an issuer that is not in compliance with the requirements of any portion of paragraphs (2) through (6).

(B) *Opportunity to Cure Defects.*—The rules of the Commission under subparagraph (A) shall provide for appropriate procedures for an issuer to have an opportunity to cure any defects that would be the basis for a prohibition under subparagraph (A), before the imposition of such prohibition.

(2) *Responsibilities Relating to Registered Public Accounting Firms.*—The audit committee of each issuer, in its capacity as a committee of the board of directors, shall be directly responsible for the appointment, compensation, and oversight of the work of any registered public accounting firm employed by that issuer (including resolution of disagreements between management and the auditor regarding financial reporting) for the purpose of preparing or issuing an audit report or related work, and each such registered public accounting firm shall report directly to the audit committee.

(3) *Independence*

(A) *In General.*—Each member of the audit committee of the issuer shall be a member of the board of directors of the issuer, and shall otherwise be independent.

(B) *Criteria.*—In order to be considered to be independent for purposes of this paragraph, a member of an audit committee of an issuer may not, other than in his or her capacity as a member of the audit committee, the board of directors, or any other board committee—

(i) accept any consulting, advisory, or other compensatory fee from the issuer; or

(ii) be an affiliated person of the issuer or any subsidiary thereof.

(C) *Exemption Authority.*—The Commission may exempt from the requirements of subparagraph (B) a particular relationship with respect to audit committee members, as the Commission determines appropriate in light of the circumstances.

(4) *Complaints.*—Each audit committee shall establish procedures for—

(A) the receipt, retention, and treatment of complaints received by the issuer regarding accounting, internal accounting controls, or auditing matters; and

(B) the confidential, anonymous submission by employees of the issuer of concerns regarding questionable accounting or auditing matters.

(5) *Authority to Engage Advisers.*—Each audit committee shall have the authority to engage independent counsel and other advisers, as it determines necessary to carry out its duties.

(6) *Funding.*—Each issuer shall provide for appropriate funding, as determined by the audit committee, in its capacity as a committee of the board of directors, for payment of compensation—

(A) to the registered public accounting firm employed by the issuer for the purpose of rendering or issuing an audit report; and

(B) to any advisers employed by the audit committee under paragraph (5).

§ 10C. Compensation Committees

(a) Independence of compensation committees.—

(1) Listing standards.—The Commission shall, by rule, direct the national securities exchanges and national securities associations to prohibit the listing of any equity security of an issuer, other than an issuer that is a controlled company, limited partnership, company in bankruptcy proceedings, open-ended management investment company that is registered under the Investment Company Act of 1940, or a foreign private issuer that provides annual disclosures to shareholders of the reasons that the foreign private issuer does not have an independent compensation committee, that does not comply with the requirements of this subsection.

(2) Independence of compensation committees.—The rules of the Commission under paragraph (1) shall require that each member of the compensation committee of the board of directors of an issuer be—

(A) a member of the board of directors of the issuer; and

(B) independent.

(3) Independence.—The rules of the Commission under paragraph (1) shall require that, in determining the definition of the term 'independence' for purposes of paragraph (2), the national securities exchanges and the national securities associations shall consider relevant factors, including—

(A) the source of compensation of a member of the board of directors of an issuer, including any consulting, advisory, or other compensatory fee paid by the issuer to such member of the board of directors; and

(B) whether a member of the board of directors of an issuer is affiliated with the issuer, a subsidiary of the issuer, or an affiliate of a subsidiary of the issuer.

(4) Exemption authority.—The rules of the Commission under paragraph (1) shall permit a national securities exchange or a national securities association to exempt a particular relationship from the requirements of paragraph (2), with respect to the members of a compensation committee, as the national securities exchange or national securities association determines is appropriate, taking into consideration the size of an issuer and any other relevant factors.

(b) Independence of compensation consultants and other compensation committee advisers.—

(1) In general.—The compensation committee of an issuer may only select a compensation consultant, legal counsel, or other adviser to the compensation committee after taking into consideration the factors identified by the Commission under paragraph (2).

(2) Rules.—The Commission shall identify factors that affect the independence of a compensation consultant, legal counsel, or other adviser to a compensation committee of an issuer. Such factors shall be competitively neutral among categories of consultants, legal counsel, or other advisers and preserve the ability of compensation committees to retain the services of members of any such category, and shall include—

(A) the provision of other services to the issuer by the person that employs the compensation consultant, legal counsel, or other adviser;

(B) the amount of fees received from the issuer by the person that employs the compensation consultant, legal counsel, or other adviser, as a percentage of the total revenue of the person that employs the compensation consultant, legal counsel, or other adviser;

(C) the policies and procedures of the person that employs the compensation consultant, legal counsel, or other adviser that are designed to prevent conflicts of interest;

(D) any business or personal relationship of the compensation consultant, legal counsel, or other adviser with a member of the compensation committee; and

(E) any stock of the issuer owned by the compensation consultant, legal counsel, or other adviser.

(c)   Compensation committee authority relating to compensation consultants.—

(1) Authority to retain compensation consultant.—

(A) In general.—The compensation committee of an issuer, in its capacity as a committee of the board of directors, may, in its sole discretion, retain or obtain the advice of a compensation consultant.

(B) Direct responsibility of compensation committee.—The compensation committee of an issuer shall be directly responsible for the appointment, compensation, and oversight of the work of a compensation consultant.

(C) Rule of construction.—This paragraph may not be construed—

(i) to require the compensation committee to implement or act consistently with the advice or recommendations of the compensation consultant; or

(ii) to affect the ability or obligation of a compensation committee to exercise its own judgment in fulfillment of the duties of the compensation committee.

(2) Disclosure.—In any proxy or consent solicitation material for an annual meeting of the shareholders (or a special meeting in lieu of the annual meeting) occurring on or after the date that is 1 year after the date of enactment of this section, each issuer shall disclose in the proxy or consent material, in accordance with regulations of the Commission, whether—

(A) the compensation committee of the issuer retained or obtained the advice of a compensation consultant; and

(B) the work of the compensation consultant has raised any conflict of interest and, if so, the nature of the conflict and how the conflict is being addressed.

(d)   Authority to engage independent legal counsel and other advisers.—

(1) In general.—The compensation committee of an issuer, in its capacity as a committee of the board of directors, may, in its sole discretion, retain and obtain the advice of independent legal counsel and other advisers.

(2) Direct responsibility of compensation committee.—The compensation committee of an issuer shall be directly responsible for the appointment, compensation, and oversight of the work of independent legal counsel and other advisers.

(3) Rule of construction.—This subsection may not be construed—

(A) to require a compensation committee to implement or act consistently with the advice or recommendations of independent legal counsel or other advisers under this subsection; or

(B) to affect the ability or obligation of a compensation committee to exercise its own judgment in fulfillment of the duties of the compensation committee.

(e)   Compensation of compensation consultants, independent legal counsel, and other advisers.—

Each issuer shall provide for appropriate funding, as determined by the compensation committee in its capacity as a committee of the board of directors, for payment of reasonable compensation—

(1) to a compensation consultant; and

(2) to independent legal counsel or any other adviser to the compensation committee.

(f) Commission rules.—

(1) In general.—Not later than 360 days after the date of enactment of this section, the Commission shall, by rule, direct the national securities exchanges and national securities associations to prohibit the listing of any security of an issuer that is not in compliance with the requirements of this section.

(2) Opportunity to cure defects.—The rules of the Commission under paragraph (1) shall provide for appropriate procedures for an issuer to have a reasonable opportunity to cure any defects that would be the basis for the prohibition under paragraph (1), before the imposition of such prohibition.

(3) Exemption authority.—

(A) In general.—The rules of the Commission under paragraph (1) shall permit a national securities exchange or a national securities association to exempt a category of issuers from the requirements under this section, as the national securities exchange or the national securities association determines is appropriate.

(B) Considerations.—In determining appropriate exemptions under subparagraph (A), the national securities exchange or the national securities association shall take into account the potential impact of the requirements of this section on smaller reporting issuers.

(g) Controlled company exemption.—

(1) In general.—This section shall not apply to any controlled company.

(2) Definition.—For purposes of this section, the term "controlled company" means an issuer—

(A) that is listed on a national securities exchange or by a national securities association; and

(B) that holds an election for the board of directors of the issuer in which more than 50 percent of the voting power is held by an individual, a group, or another issuer. . . .

§ 10D. Recovery of Erroneously Awarded Compensation Policy

(a) Listing standards.—The Commission shall, by rule, direct the national securities exchanges and national securities associations to prohibit the listing of any security of an issuer that does not comply with the requirements of this section.

(b) Recovery of funds.—The rules of the Commission under subsection (a) shall require each issuer to develop and implement a policy providing—

(1) for disclosure of the policy of the issuer on incentive-based compensation that is based on financial information required to be reported under the securities laws; and

(2) that, in the event that the issuer is required to prepare an accounting restatement due to the material noncompliance of the issuer with any financial reporting requirement under the securities laws, the issuer will recover from any current or former executive officer of the issuer who received incentive-based compensation (including stock options awarded as compensation) during the 3-year period preceding the date on which the issuer is required to prepare an accounting restatement, based on the erroneous data, in excess of what would have been paid to the executive officer under the accounting restatement.

§ 12. Registration Requirements for Securities

(a) General requirement of registration

It shall be unlawful for any member, broker, or dealer to effect any transaction in any security (other than an exempted security) on a national securities exchange unless a registration is effective as to such security for such exchange in accordance with the provisions of this chapter and the rules and regulations thereunder. The provisions of this subsection shall not apply in respect of a security futures product traded on a national securities exchange.

(b) Procedure for registration; information

A security may be registered on a national securities exchange by the issuer filing an application with the exchange (and filing with the Commission such duplicate originals thereof as the Commission may require), which application shall contain—

(1) Such information, in such detail, as to the issuer and any person directly or indirectly controlling or controlled by, or under direct or indirect common control with, the issuer, and any guarantor of the security as to principal or interest or both, as the Commission may by rules and regulations require, as necessary or appropriate in the public interest or for the protection of investors, in respect of the following:

(A) the organization, financial structure, and nature of the business;

(B) the terms, position, rights, and privileges of the different classes of securities outstanding;

(C) the terms on which their securities are to be, and during the preceding three years have been, offered to the public or otherwise;

(D) the directors, officers, and underwriters, and each security holder of record holding more than 10 per centum of any class of any equity security of the issuer (other than an exempted security), their remuneration and their interests in the securities of, and their material contracts with, the issuer and any person directly or indirectly controlling or controlled by, or under direct or indirect common control with, the issuer;

(E) remuneration to others than directors and officers exceeding $20,000 per annum;

(F) bonus and profit-sharing arrangements;

(G) management and service contracts;

(H) options existing or to be created in respect of their securities;

(I) material contracts, not made in the ordinary course of business, which are to be executed in whole or in part at or after the filing of the application or which were made not more than two years before such filing, and every material patent or contract for a material patent right shall be deemed a material contract;

(J) balance sheets for not more than the three preceding fiscal years, certified if required by the rules and regulations of the Commission by a registered public accounting firm;

(K) profit and loss statements for not more than the three preceding fiscal years, certified if required by the rules and regulations of the Commission by a registered public accounting firm; and

(L) any further financial statements which the Commission may deem necessary or appropriate for the protection of investors.

(2) Such copies of articles of incorporation, bylaws, trust indentures, or corresponding documents by whatever name known, underwriting arrangements, and other similar documents of, and voting trust agreements with respect to, the issuer and any person directly or indirectly controlling or controlled by, or under direct or indirect common control with, the issuer as the Commission may require as necessary or appropriate for the proper protection of investors and to insure fair dealing in the security.

(3) Such copies of material contracts, referred to in paragraph (1)(I) above, as the Commission may require as necessary or appropriate for the proper protection of investors and to insure fair dealing in the security. . . .

(g) Registration of securities by issuer; exemptions

(1) Every issuer which is engaged in interstate commerce, or in a business affecting interstate commerce, or whose securities are traded by use of the mails or any means or instrumentality of interstate commerce shall— . . .

(A) within 120 days after the last day of its first fiscal year ended on which the issuer has total assets exceeding $10,000,000 and a class of equity security (other than an exempted security) held of record by either—

(i) 2,000 persons, or

(ii) 500 persons who are not accredited investors (as such term is defined by the Commission), and

(B) in the case of an issuer that is a bank or a bank holding company, as such term is defined in section 2 of the Bank Holding Company Act of 1956 (12 U.S.C. 1841), not later than 120 days after the last day of its first fiscal year ended after the effective date of this subsection, on which the issuer has total assets exceeding $10,000,000 and a class of equity security (other than an exempted security) held of record by 2,000 or more persons,

(C) within one hundred and twenty days after the last day of its first fiscal year . . . on which the issuer has total assets exceeding $1,000,000 and a class of equity security (other than an exempted security) held of record by five hundred or more . . . persons,

register such security by filing with the Commission a registration statement (and such copies thereof as the Commission may require) with respect to such security containing such information and documents as the Commission may specify comparable to that which is required in an application to register a security pursuant to subsection (b) of this section. Each such registration statement shall become effective sixty days after filing with the Commission or within such shorter period as the Commission may direct. Until such registration statement becomes effective it shall not be deemed filed for the purposes of section 18 of this title. Any issuer may register any class of equity security not required to be registered by filing a registration statement pursuant to the provisions of this paragraph. The Commission is authorized to extend the date upon which any issuer or class of issuers is required to register a security pursuant to the provisions of this paragraph.

(2) The provisions of this subsection shall not apply in respect of—

(A) any security listed and registered on a national securities exchange.

(B) any security issued by an investment company registered pursuant to section 80a–8 of this title. . . .

(G) any security issued by an insurance company if all of the following conditions are met:

(i) Such insurance company is required to and does file an annual statement with the Commissioner of Insurance (or other officer or agency performing a similar function) of its domiciliary State, and such annual statement conforms to that prescribed by the National Association of Insurance Commissioners or in the determination of such State commissioner, officer or agency substantially conforms to that so prescribed.

(ii) Such insurance company is subject to regulation by its domiciliary State of proxies, consents, or authorizations in respect of securities issued by such company and such regulation conforms to that prescribed by the National Association of Insurance Commissioners.

(iii) . . . [T]he purchase and sales of securities issued by such insurance company by beneficial owners, directors, or officers of such company are subject to regulation (including reporting) by its domiciliary State substantially in the manner provided in section 16 of this title. . . .

(3) The Commission may by rules or regulations or, on its own motion, after notice and opportunity for hearing, by order, exempt from this subsection any security of a foreign issuer, including any certificate of deposit for such a security, if the Commission finds that such exemption is in the public interest and is consistent with the protection of investors.

(4) Registration of any class of security pursuant to this subsection shall be terminated ninety days, or such shorter period as the Commission may determine, after the issuer files a certification with the Commission that the number of holders of record of such class of security is reduced to less than 300 persons, or, in the case of a bank or a bank holding company, . . . 1,200 persons. The Commission shall after notice

and opportunity for hearing deny termination of registration if it finds that the certification is untrue. Termination of registration shall be deferred pending final determination on the question of denial.

(5) For the purposes of this subsection the term "class" shall include all securities of an issuer which are of substantially similar character and the holders of which enjoy substantially similar rights and privileges. The Commission may for the purpose of this subsection define by rules and regulations the terms "total assets" and "held of record" as it deems necessary or appropriate in the public interest or for the protection of investors in order to prevent circumvention of the provisions of this subsection. For purposes of this subsection, a security futures product shall not be considered a class of equity security of the issuer of the securities underlying the security futures product. For purposes of determining whether an issuer is required to register a security with the Commission pursuant to paragraph (1), the definition of 'held of record' shall not include securities held by persons who received the securities pursuant to an employee compensation plan in transactions exempted from the registration requirements of section 5 of the Securities Act of 1933.

(6) *Exclusion for persons holding certain securities.*—The Commission shall, by rule, exempt, conditionally or unconditionally, securities acquired pursuant to an offering made under section 4(6) of the Securities Act of 1933 from the provisions of this subsection.

(h) Exemption by rules and regulations from certain provisions of section

The Commission may by rules and regulations, or upon application of an interested person, by order, after notice and opportunity for hearing, exempt in whole or in part any issuer or class of issuers from the provisions of subsection (g) of this section or from section 13, 14, or 15(d) of this title or may exempt from section 16 of this title any officer, director, or beneficial owner of securities of any issuer, any security of which is required to be registered pursuant to subsection (g) hereof, upon such terms and conditions and for such period as it deems necessary or appropriate, if the Commission finds, by reason of the number of public investors, amount of trading interest in the securities, the nature and extent of the activities of the issuer, income or assets of the issuer, or otherwise, that such action is not inconsistent with the public interest or the protection of investors. The Commission may, for the purposes of any of the above-mentioned sections or subsections of this chapter, classify issuers and prescribe requirements appropriate for each such class. . . .

(j) Denial, suspension, or revocation of registration; notice and hearing

The Commission is authorized, by order, as it deems necessary or appropriate for the protection of investors to deny, to suspend the effective date of, to suspend for a period not exceeding twelve months, or to revoke the registration of a security, if the Commission finds, on the record after notice and opportunity for hearing, that the issuer of such security has failed to comply with any provision of this chapter or the rules and regulations thereunder. No member of a national securities exchange, broker, or dealer shall make use of the mails or any means or instrumentality of interstate commerce to effect any transaction in, or to induce the purchase or sale of, any security the registration of which has been and is suspended or revoked pursuant to the preceding sentence.

(k) Trading suspensions; emergency authority

(1) *Trading Suspensions.* If in its opinion the public interest and the protection of investors so require, the Commission is authorized by order—

(A) summarily to suspend trading in any security (other than an exempted security) for a period not exceeding 10 business days, and

(B) summarily to suspend all trading on any national securities exchange or otherwise, in securities other than exempted securities, for a period not exceeding 90 calendar days.

The action described in subparagraph (B) shall not take effect unless the Commission notifies the President of its decision and the President notifies the Commission that the President does not disapprove of such decision. . . .

(2) *Emergency orders.* (A) The Commission, in an emergency, may by order summarily take such action to alter, supplement, suspend, or impose requirements or restrictions with respect to any matter or action

subject to regulation by the Commission or a self-regulatory organization under this title, as the Commission determines is necessary in the public interest and for the protection of investors—

    (i) to maintain or restore fair and orderly securities markets (other than markets in exempted securities); or

    (ii) to ensure prompt, accurate, and safe clearance and settlement of transactions in securities (other than exempted securities).

(B) An order of the Commission under this paragraph (2) shall continue in effect for the period specified by the Commission, and may be extended, except that in no event shall the Commission's action continue in effect for more than 10 business days, including extensions. . . .

(3) *Termination of Emergency Actions by president.* The President may direct that action taken by the Commission under paragraph (1)(B) or paragraph (2) of this subsection shall not continue in effect. . . .

    . . .

(6) *Definition of emergency.* For purposes of this subsection, the term "emergency" means a major market disturbance characterized by or constituting—

    (A) sudden and excessive fluctuations of securities prices generally, or a substantial threat thereof, that threaten fair and orderly markets, or

    (B) a substantial disruption of the safe or efficient operation of the national system for clearance and settlement of securities, or a substantial threat thereof.

(*l*) Issuance of any security in contravention of rules and regulations; application to annuity contracts and variable life policies

It shall be unlawful for an issuer, any class of whose securities is registered pursuant to this section or would be required to be so registered except for the exemption from registration provided by subsection (g)(2)(B) or (g)(2)(G) of this section, by the use of any means or instrumentality of interstate commerce, or of the mails, to issue, either originally or upon transfer, any of such securities in a form or with a format which contravenes such rules and regulations as the Commission may prescribe as necessary or appropriate for the prompt and accurate clearance and settlement of transactions in securities. The provisions of this subsection shall not apply to variable annuity contracts or variable life policies issued by an insurance company or its separate accounts. . . .

§ 13.   Periodical and Other Reports

(a)   Reports by issuer of security; contents

Every issuer of a security registered pursuant to section 12 of this title shall file with the Commission, in accordance with such rules and regulations as the Commission may prescribe as necessary or appropriate for the proper protection of investors and to insure fair dealing in the security—

    (1) such information and documents (and such copies thereof) as the Commission shall require to keep reasonably current the information and documents required to be included in or filed with an application or registration statement filed pursuant to section 12 of this title. . . .

    (2) such annual reports (and such copies thereof), certified if required by the rules and regulations of the Commission by independent public accountants, and such quarterly reports (and such copies thereof), as the Commission may prescribe.

Every issuer of a security registered on a national securities exchange shall also file a duplicate original of such information, documents, and reports with the exchange. In any registration statement, periodic report, or other reports to be filed with the Commission, an emerging growth company need not present selected financial data in accordance with Item 301 of Regulation S–K, for any period prior to the earliest audited period presented in connection with its first registration statement that became effective under this Act or the Securities Act of 1933 and, with respect to any such statement or reports, an emerging growth company may not be required to comply with any new or revised financial accounting standard until such date that a company that is not an issuer (as defined under section 2(a) of the Sarbanes-Oxley Act of 2002) is required to comply with such new or revised accounting standard, if such standard applies to companies that are not issuers.

(b) Form of report; books, records, and internal accounting; directives

(1) The Commission may prescribe, in regard to reports made pursuant to this chapter, the form or forms in which the required information shall be set forth, the items or details to be shown in the balance sheet and the earnings statement, and the methods to be followed in the preparation of reports, in the appraisal or valuation of assets and liabilities, in the determination of depreciation and depletion, in the differentiation of recurring and nonrecurring income, in the differentiation of investment and operating income, and in the preparation, where the Commission deems it necessary or desirable, of separate and/or consolidated balance sheets or income accounts of any person directly or indirectly controlling or controlled by the issuer, or any person under direct or indirect common control with the issuer. . . .

(2) Every issuer which has a class of securities registered pursuant to section 12 of this title and every issuer which is required to file reports pursuant to section 15(d) of this title shall—

(A) make and keep books, records, and accounts, which, in reasonable detail, accurately and fairly reflect the transactions and dispositions of the assets of the issuer;

(B) devise and maintain a system of internal accounting controls sufficient to provide reasonable assurances that—

(i) transactions are executed in accordance with management's general or specific authorization;

(ii) transactions are recorded as necessary (I) to permit preparation of financial statements in conformity with generally accepted accounting principles or any other criteria applicable to such statements, and (II) to maintain accountability for assets;

(iii) access to assets is permitted only in accordance with management's general or specific authorization; and

(iv) the recorded accountability for assets is compared with the existing assets at reasonable intervals and appropriate action is taken with respect to any differences. . . .

(d) Reports by persons acquiring more than five per centum of certain classes of securities

(1) Any person who, after acquiring directly or indirectly the beneficial ownership of any equity security of a class which is registered pursuant to section 12 of this title, or any equity security of an insurance company which would have been required to be so registered except for the exemption contained in section 12(g)(2)(G) of this title, or any equity security issued by a closed-end investment company registered under the Investment Company Act of 1940, is directly or indirectly the beneficial owner of more than 5 per centum of such class shall, within ten days after such acquisition or within such shorter time as the Commission may establish by rule, file with the Commission, a statement containing such of the following information, and such additional information, as the Commission may by rules and regulations, prescribe as necessary or appropriate in the public interest or for the protection of investors—

(A) the background, and identity, residence, and citizenship of, and the nature of such beneficial ownership by, such person and all other persons by whom or on whose behalf the purchases have been or are to be effected;

(B) the source and amount of the funds or other consideration used or to be used in making the purchases, and if any part of the purchase price is represented or is to be represented by funds or other consideration borrowed or otherwise obtained for the purpose of acquiring, holding, or trading such security, a description of the transaction and the names of the parties thereto, except that where a source of funds is a loan made in the ordinary course of business by a bank, . . . if the person filing such statement so requests, the name of the bank shall not be made available to the public;

(C) if the purpose of the purchases or prospective purchases is to acquire control of the business of the issuer of the securities, any plans or proposals which such persons may have to liquidate such issuer, to sell its assets to or merge it with any other persons, or to make any other major change in its business or corporate structure;

(D) the number of shares of such security which are beneficially owned, and the number of shares concerning which there is a right to acquire, directly or indirectly, by (i) such person, and (ii) by each associate of such person, giving the background, identity, residence, and citizenship of each such associate; and

(E) information as to any contracts, arrangements, or understandings with any person with respect to any securities of the issuer, including but not limited to transfer of any of the securities, joint ventures, loan or option arrangements, puts or calls, guaranties of loans, guaranties against loss or guaranties of profits, division of losses or profits, or the giving or withholding of proxies, naming the persons with whom such contracts, arrangements, or understandings have been entered into, and giving the details thereof.

(2) If any material change occurs in the facts set forth in the statement filed with the Commission, an amendment shall be filed with the Commission, in accordance with such rules and regulations as the Commission may prescribe as necessary or appropriate in the public interest or for the protection of investors.

(3) When two or more persons act as a partnership, limited partnership, syndicate, or other group for the purpose of acquiring, holding, or disposing of securities of an issuer, such syndicate or group shall be deemed a "person" for the purposes of this subsection.

(4) In determining, for purposes of this subsection, any percentage of a class of any security, such class shall be deemed to consist of the amount of the outstanding securities of such class, exclusive of any securities of such class held by or for the account of the issuer or a subsidiary of the issuer.

(5) The Commission, by rule or regulation or by order, may permit any person to file in lieu of the statement required by paragraph (1) of this subsection or the rules and regulations thereunder, a notice stating the name of such person, the number of shares of any equity securities subject to paragraph (1) which are owned by him, the date of their acquisition and such other information as the Commission may specify, if it appears to the Commission that such securities were acquired by such person in the ordinary course of his business and were not acquired for the purpose of and do not have the effect of changing or influencing the control of the issuer nor in connection with or as a participant in any transaction having such purpose or effect.

(6) The provisions of this subsection shall not apply to—

(A) any acquisition or offer to acquire securities made or proposed to be made by means of a registration statement under the Securities Act of 1933;

(B) any acquisition of the beneficial ownership of a security which, together with all other acquisitions by the same person of securities of the same class during the preceding twelve months, does not exceed 2 per centum of that class;

(C) any acquisition of an equity security by the issuer of such security;

(D) any acquisition or proposed acquisition of a security which the Commission, by rules or regulations or by order, shall exempt from the provisions of this subsection as not entered into for the purpose of, and not having the effect of, changing or influencing the control of the issuer or otherwise as not comprehended within the purposes of this subsection.

(e) Purchase of securities by issuer

(1) It shall be unlawful for an issuer which has a class of equity securities registered pursuant to section 12 of this title, or which is a closed-end investment company registered under the Investment Company Act of 1940, to purchase any equity security issued by it if such purchase is in contravention of such rules and regulations as the Commission, in the public interest or for the protection of investors, may adopt (A) to define acts and practices which are fraudulent, deceptive, or manipulative, and (B) to prescribe means reasonably designed to prevent such acts and practices. Such rules and regulations may require such issuer to provide holders of equity securities of such class with such information relating to the reasons for such purchase, the source of funds, the number of shares to be purchased, the price to be paid for such securities, the method of purchase, and such additional information, as the Commission deems necessary or

appropriate in the public interest or for the protection of investors, or which the Commission deems to be material to a determination whether such security should be sold.

(2) For the purpose of this subsection, a purchase by or for the issuer or any person controlling, controlled by, or under common control with the issuer, or a purchase subject to control of the issuer or any such person, shall be deemed to be a purchase by the issuer. The Commission shall have power to make rules and regulations implementing this paragraph in the public interest and for the protection of investors, including exemptive rules and regulations covering situations in which the Commission deems it unnecessary or inappropriate that a purchase of the type described in this paragraph shall be deemed to be a purchase by the issuer for purposes of some or all of the provisions of paragraph (1) of this subsection. . . .

(g) Statement of equity security ownership

(1) Any person who is directly or indirectly the beneficial owner of more than 5 per centum of any security of a class described in subsection (d)(1) of this section shall file with the Commission a statement setting forth, in such form and at such time as the Commission may, by rule, prescribe—

(A) such person's identity, residence, and citizenship; and

(B) the number and description of the shares in which such person has an interest and the nature of such interest.

(2) If any material change occurs in the facts set forth in the statement and filed with the Commission, an amendment shall be filed with the Commission, in accordance with such rules and regulations as the Commission may prescribe as necessary or appropriate in the public interest or for the protection of investors.

(3) When two or more persons act as a partnership, limited partnership, syndicate, or other group for the purpose of acquiring, holding, or disposing of securities of an issuer, such syndicate or group shall be deemed a "person" for the purposes of this subsection.

(4) In determining, for purposes of this subsection, any percentage of a class of any security, such class shall be deemed to consist of the amount of the outstanding securities of such class, exclusive of any securities of such class held by or for the account of the issuer or a subsidiary of the issuer.

(5) In exercising its authority under this subsection, the Commission shall take such steps as it deems necessary or appropriate in the public interest or for the protection of investors (A) to achieve centralized reporting of information regarding ownership, (B) to avoid unnecessarily duplicative reporting by and minimize the compliance burden on persons required to report, and (C) to tabulate and promptly make available the information contained in any report filed pursuant to this subsection in a manner which will, in the view of the Commission, maximize the usefulness of the information to other Federal and State agencies and the public.

(6) The Commission may, by rule or order, exempt, in whole or in part, any person or class of persons from any or all of the reporting requirements of this subsection as it deems necessary or appropriate in the public interest or for the protection of investors. . . .

(h) Large trader reporting

(1) *Identification requirements for large traders.*

For the purpose of monitoring the impact on the securities markets of securities transactions involving a substantial volume or a large fair market value or exercise value and for the purpose of otherwise assisting the Commission in the enforcement of this title, each large trader shall—

(A) provide such information to the Commission as the Commission may by rule or regulation prescribe as necessary or appropriate, identifying such large trader and all accounts in or through which such large trader effects such transactions; and

(B) identify, in accordance with such rules or regulations as the Commission may prescribe as necessary or appropriate, to any registered broker or dealer by or through whom such large trader directly or indirectly effects securities transactions, such large trader and all accounts directly or indirectly maintained with such broker or dealer by such large trader in or through which such transactions are effected.

(2) *Recordkeeping and reporting requirements for brokers and dealers.* Every registered broker or dealer shall make and keep for prescribed periods such records as the Commission by rule or regulation prescribes as necessary or appropriate in the public interest, for the protection of investors, or otherwise in furtherance of the purposes of this title, with respect to securities transactions that equal or exceed the reporting activity level effected directly or indirectly by or through such registered broker or dealer of or for any person that such broker or dealer knows is a large trader, or any person that such broker or dealer has reason to know is a large trader on the basis of transactions in securities effected by or through such broker or dealer. Such records shall be available for reporting to the Commission, or any self-regulatory organization that the Commission shall designate to receive such reports, on the morning of the day following the day the transactions were effected, and shall be reported to the Commission or a self-regulatory organization designated by the Commission immediately upon request by the Commission or such a self-regulatory organization. Such records and reports shall be in a format and transmitted in a manner prescribed by the Commission (including, but not limited to, machine readable form). . . .

(8) *Definitions.* For purposes of this subsection—

(A) the term "large trader" means every person who, for his own account or an account for which he exercises investment discretion, effects transactions for the purchase or sale of any publicly traded security or securities by use of any means or instrumentality of interstate commerce or of the mails, or of any facility of a national securities exchange, directly or indirectly by or through a registered broker or dealer in an aggregate amount equal to or in excess of the identifying activity level;

(B) the term "publicly traded security" means any equity security (including an option on individual equity securities, and an option on a group or index of such securities) listed, or admitted to unlisted trading privileges, on a national securities exchange, or quoted in an automated interdealer quotation system;

(C) the term "identifying activity level" means transactions in publicly traded securities at or above a level of volume, fair market value, or exercise value as shall be fixed from time to time by the Commission by rule or regulation, specifying the time interval during which such transactions shall be aggregated;

(D) the term "reporting activity level" means transactions in publicly traded securities at or above a level of volume, fair market value, or exercise value as shall be fixed from time to time by the Commission by rule, regulation, or order, specifying the time interval during which such transactions shall be aggregated; and

(E) the term "person" has the meaning given in section 3(a)(9) of this title and also includes two or more persons acting as a partnership, limited partnership, syndicate, or other group, but does not include a foreign central bank.

(i) Accuracy of financial reports

Each financial report that contains financial statements, and that is required to be prepared in accordance with (or reconciled to) generally accepted accounting principles under this title and filed with the Commission shall reflect all material correcting adjustments that have been identified by a registered public accounting firm in accordance with generally accepted accounting principles and the rules and regulations of the Commission.

(j) Off-balance sheet transactions

Not later than 180 days after the date of enactment of the Sarbanes-Oxley Act of 2002, the Commission shall issue final rules providing that each annual and quarterly financial report required to be filed with the Commission shall disclose all material off-balance sheet transactions, arrangements, obligations (including contingent obligations), and other relationships of the issuer with unconsolidated entities or other persons, that may have a material current or future effect on financial condition, changes in financial condition, results of operations, liquidity, capital expenditures, capital resources, or significant components of revenues or expenses.

(k)   Prohibition on personal loans to executives

(1) *In general.*—It shall be unlawful for any issuer (as defined in section 2 of the Sarbanes-Oxley Act of 2002), directly or indirectly, including through any subsidiary, to extend or maintain credit, to arrange for the extension of credit, or to renew an extension of credit, in the form of a personal loan to or for any director or executive officer (or equivalent thereof) of that issuer. An extension of credit maintained by the issuer on the date of enactment of this subsection shall not be subject to the provisions of this subsection, provided that there is no material modification to any term of any such extension of credit or any renewal of any such extension of credit on or after that date of enactment.

(2) *Limitation.*—Paragraph (1) does not preclude any home improvement and manufactured home loans (as that term is defined in section 5 of the Home Owners' Loan Act (12 U.S.C. 1464), consumer credit (as defined in section 103 of the Truth in Lending Act (15 U.S.C. 1602), or any extension of credit under an open end credit plan (as defined in section 103 of the Truth in Lending Act (15 U.S.C. 1602), or a charge card (as defined in section 127(c)(4)(e) of the Truth in Lending Act (15 U.S.C. 1637(c)(4)(e)), or any extension of credit by a broker or dealer registered under section 15 of this title to an employee of that broker or dealer to buy, trade, or carry securities, that is permitted under rules or regulations of the Board of Governors of the Federal Reserve System pursuant to section 7 of this title (other than an extension of credit that would be used to purchase the stock of that issuer), that is—

(A) made or provided in the ordinary course of the consumer credit business of such issuer;

(B) of a type that is generally made available by such issuer to the public; and

(C) made by such issuer on market terms, or terms that are no more favorable than those offered by the issuer to the general public for such extensions of credit. . . .

(*l*)   Real time issuer disclosures

Each issuer reporting under section 13(a) or 15(d) shall disclose to the public on a rapid and current basis such additional information concerning material changes in the financial condition or operations of the issuer, in plain English, which may include trend and qualitative information and graphic presentations, as the Commission determines, by rule, is necessary or useful for the protection of investors and in the public interest.

§ 14.   Proxies

(a)(1)   Solicitation of proxies in violation of rules and regulations

It shall be unlawful for any person, by the use of the mails or by any means or instrumentality of interstate commerce or of any facility of a national securities exchange or otherwise, in contravention of such rules and regulations as the Commission may prescribe as necessary or appropriate in the public interest or for the protection of investors, to solicit or to permit the use of his name to solicit any proxy or consent or authorization in respect of any security (other than an exempted security) registered pursuant to section 12 of this title. . . .

(2) The rules and regulations prescribed by the Commission under paragraph (1) may include—

(A) a requirement that a solicitation of proxy, consent, or authorization by (or on behalf of) an issuer include a nominee submitted by a shareholder to serve on the board of directors of the issuer; and

(B) a requirement that an issuer follow a certain procedure in relation to a solicitation described in subparagraph (A).

(b)(1)   Giving or refraining from giving proxy in respect of any security carried for account of customer; disclosure of beneficial owners

It shall be unlawful for any member of a national securities exchange, or any broker or dealer registered under this chapter, or any bank, association, or other entity that exercises fiduciary powers, in contravention of such rules and regulations as the Commission may prescribe as necessary or appropriate in the public interest or for the protection of investors, to give, or to refrain from giving a proxy, consent, authorization, or information statement in respect of any security registered pursuant to section 12 of this title, or any security issued by an investment company registered under the Investment Company Act of 1940, and carried for the account of a customer.

(2) With respect to banks, the rules and regulations prescribed by the Commission under paragraph (1) shall not require the disclosure of the names of beneficial owners of securities in an account held by the bank on December 28, 1985, unless the beneficial owner consents to the disclosure. The provisions of this paragraph shall not apply in the case of a bank which the Commission finds has not made a good faith effort to obtain such consent from such beneficial owners.

(c) Information to holders of record prior to annual or other meeting

Unless proxies, consents, or authorizations in respect of a security registered pursuant to section 12 of this title, or a security issued by an investment company registered under the Investment Company Act of 1940, are solicited by or on behalf of the management of the issuer from the holders of record of such security in accordance with the rules and regulations prescribed under subsection (a) of this section, prior to any annual or other meeting of the holders of such security, such issuer shall, in accordance with rules and regulations prescribed by the Commission, file with the Commission and transmit to all holders of record of such security information substantially equivalent to the information which would be required to be transmitted if a solicitation were made. . . .

(d) Tender offer by owner of more than five per centum of class of securities; exceptions

(1) It shall be unlawful for any person, directly or indirectly, by use of the mails or by any means or instrumentality of interstate commerce or of any facility of a national securities exchange or otherwise, to make a tender offer for, or a request or invitation for tenders of, any class of any equity security which is registered pursuant to section 12 of this title, or any equity security of an insurance company which would have been required to be so registered except for the exemption contained in section 12(g)(2)(G) of this title, or any equity security issued by a closed-end investment company registered under the Investment Company Act of 1940, if, after consummation thereof, such person would, directly or indirectly, be the beneficial owner of more than 5 per centum of such class, unless at the time copies of the offer or request or invitation are first published or sent or given to security holders such person has filed with the Commission a statement containing such of the information specified in section 13(d) of this title, and such additional information as the Commission may by rules and regulations prescribe as necessary or appropriate in the public interest or for the protection of investors. All requests or invitations for tenders or advertisements making a tender offer or requesting or inviting tenders of such a security shall be filed as a part of such statement and shall contain such of the information contained in such statement as the Commission may by rules and regulations prescribe. Copies of any additional material soliciting or requesting such tender offers subsequent to the initial solicitation or request shall contain such information as the Commission may by rules and regulations prescribe as necessary or appropriate in the public interest or for the protection of investors, and shall be filed with the Commission not later than the time copies of such material are first published or sent or given to security holders. Copies of all statements, in the form in which such material is furnished to security holders and the Commission, shall be sent to the issuer not later than the date such material is first published or sent or given to any security holders.

(2) When two or more persons act as a partnership, limited partnership, syndicate, or other group for the purpose of acquiring, holding, or disposing of securities of an issuer, such syndicate or group shall be deemed a "person" for purposes of this subsection.

(3) In determining, for purposes of this subsection, any percentage of a class of any security, such class shall be deemed to consist of the amount of the outstanding securities of such class, exclusive of any securities of such class held by or for the account of the issuer or a subsidiary of the issuer.

(4) Any solicitation or recommendation to the holders of such a security to accept or reject a tender offer or request or invitation for tenders shall be made in accordance with such rules and regulations as the Commission may prescribe as necessary or appropriate in the public interest or for the protection of investors.

(5) Securities deposited pursuant to a tender offer or request or invitation for tenders may be withdrawn by or on behalf of the depositor at any time until the expiration of seven days after the time definitive copies of the offer or request or invitation are first published or sent or given to security holders,

and at any time after sixty days from the date of the original tender offer or request or invitation, except as the Commission may otherwise prescribe by rules, regulations, or order as necessary or appropriate in the public interest or for the protection of investors.

(6) Where any person makes a tender offer, or request or invitation for tenders, for less than all the outstanding equity securities of a class, and where a greater number of securities is deposited pursuant thereto within ten days after copies of the offer or request or invitation are first published or sent or given to security holders than such person is bound or willing to take up and pay for, the securities taken up shall be taken up as nearly as may be pro rata, disregarding fractions, according to the number of securities deposited by each depositor. The provisions of this subsection shall also apply to securities deposited within ten days after notice of an increase in the consideration offered to security holders, as described in paragraph (7), is first published or sent or given to security holders.

(7) Where any person varies the terms of a tender offer or request or invitation for tenders before the expiration thereof by increasing the consideration offered to holders of such securities, such person shall pay the increased consideration to each security holder whose securities are taken up and paid for pursuant to the tender offer or request or invitation for tenders whether or not such securities have been taken up by such person before the variation of the tender offer or request or invitation.

(8) The provisions of this subsection shall not apply to any offer for, or request or invitation for tenders of, any security—

(A) if the acquisition of such security, together with all other acquisitions by the same person of securities of the same class during the preceding twelve months, would not exceed 2 per centum of that class;

(B) by the issuer of such security; or

(C) which the Commission, by rules or regulations or by order, shall exempt from the provisions of this subsection as not entered into for the purpose of, and not having the effect of, changing or influencing the control of the issuer or otherwise as not comprehended within the purposes of this subsection.

(e) Untrue statement of material fact or omission of fact with respect to tender offer

It shall be unlawful for any person to make any untrue statement of a material fact or omit to state any material fact necessary in order to make the statements made, in the light of the circumstances under which they are made, not misleading, or to engage in any fraudulent, deceptive, or manipulative acts or practices, in connection with any tender offer or request or invitation for tenders, or any solicitation of security holders in opposition to or in favor of any such offer, request, or invitation. The Commission shall, for the purposes of this subsection, by rules and regulations define, and prescribe means reasonably designed to prevent, such acts and practices as are fraudulent, deceptive, or manipulative.

(f) Election or designation of majority of directors of issuer by owner of more than five per centum of class of securities at other than meeting of security holders

If, pursuant to any arrangement or understanding with the person or persons acquiring securities in a transaction subject to subsection (d) of this section or subsection (d) of section 13 of this title, any persons are to be elected or designated as directors of the issuer, otherwise than at a meeting of security holders, and the persons so elected or designated will constitute a majority of the directors of the issuer, then, prior to the time any such person takes office as a director, and in accordance with rules and regulations prescribed by the Commission, the issuer shall file with the Commission, and transmit to all holders of record of securities of the issuer who would be entitled to vote at a meeting for election of directors, information substantially equivalent to the information which would be required by subsection (a) or (c) of this section to be transmitted if such person or persons were nominees for election as directors at a meeting of such security holders.

(g) Filing fees

(1)(A) At the time of filing such preliminary proxy solicitation material as the Commission may require by rule pursuant to subsection (a) of this section that concerns an acquisition, merger, consolidation, or proposed sale or other disposition of substantially all the assets of a company, the person making such filing, other than a company registered under the Investment Company Act of 1940 [15 U.S.C.A. § 80a–1 et seq.], shall pay to the Commission the following fees:

    (i) for preliminary proxy solicitation material involving an acquisition, merger, or consolidation, if there is a proposed payment of cash or transfer of securities or property to shareholders, a fee at a rate that, subject to paragraphs (5) and (6), is equal to $92 per $1,000,000 of such proposed payment, or of the value of such securities or other property proposed to be transferred; and

    (ii) for preliminary proxy solicitation material involving a proposed sale or other disposition of substantially all of the assets of a company, a fee at a rate that, subject to paragraphs (5) and (6), is equal to $92 per $1,000,000 of the cash or of the value of any securities or other property proposed to be received upon such sale or disposition.

    (B) The fee imposed under subparagraph (A) shall be reduced with respect to securities in an amount equal to any fee paid to the Commission with respect to such securities in connection with the proposed transaction under section 77f(b) of this title, or the fee paid under that section shall be reduced in an amount equal to the fee paid to the Commission in connection with such transaction under this subsection. Where two or more companies involved in an acquisition, merger, consolidation, sale, or other disposition of substantially all the assets of a company must file such proxy material with the Commission, each shall pay a proportionate share of such fee.

    (2) At the time of filing such preliminary information statement as the Commission may require by rule pursuant to subsection (c) of this section, the issuer shall pay to the Commission the same fee as required for preliminary proxy solicitation material under paragraph (1) of this subsection.

    (3) At the time of filing such statement as the Commission may require by rule pursuant to subsection (d)(1) of this section, the person making the filing shall pay to the Commission a fee at a rate that, subject to paragraphs (5) and (6), is equal to $92 per $1,000,000 of the aggregate amount of cash or of the value of securities or other property proposed to be offered. The fee shall be reduced with respect to securities in an amount equal to any fee paid with respect to such securities in connection with the proposed transaction under section 77f(b) of this title, or the fee paid under that section shall be reduced in an amount equal to the fee paid to the Commission in connection with such transaction under this subsection.

(4) Offsetting collections

Fees collected pursuant to this subsection for any fiscal year shall be deposited and credited as offsetting collections to the account providing appropriations to the Commission, and, except as provided in paragraph (9), shall not be collected for any fiscal year except to the extent provided in advance in appropriation Acts. No fees collected pursuant to this subsection for fiscal year 2002 or any succeeding fiscal year shall be deposited and credited as general revenue of the Treasury.

(5) Annual adjustment

For each of the fiscal years 2003 through 2011, the Commission shall by order adjust each of the rates required by paragraphs (1) and (3) for such fiscal year to a rate that is equal to the rate (expressed in dollars per million) that is applicable under section 77f(b) of this title for such fiscal year.

(6) Final rate adjustment

For fiscal year 2012 and all of the succeeding fiscal years, the Commission shall by order adjust each of the rates required by paragraphs (1) and (3) for all of such fiscal years to a rate that is equal to the rate (expressed in dollars per million) that is applicable under section 77f(b) of this title for all of such fiscal years.

(7) Pro rata application

The rates per $1,000,000 required by this subsection shall be applied pro rata to amounts and balances of less than $1,000,000.

(8) Review and effective date

In exercising its authority under this subsection, the Commission shall not be required to comply with the provisions of section 553 of Title 5. An adjusted rate prescribed under paragraph (5) or (6) and published under paragraph (10) shall not be subject to judicial review. Subject to paragraphs (4) and (9)—

(A) an adjusted rate prescribed under paragraph (5) shall take effect on the later of—

(i) the first day of the fiscal year to which such rate applies; or

(ii) five days after the date on which a regular appropriation to the Commission for such fiscal year is enacted; and

(B) an adjusted rate prescribed under paragraph (6) shall take effect on the later of—

(i) the first day of fiscal year 2012; or

(ii) five days after the date on which a regular appropriation to the Commission for fiscal year 2012 is enacted.

(9) Lapse of appropriation

If on the first day of a fiscal year a regular appropriation to the Commission has not been enacted, the Commission shall continue to collect fees (as offsetting collections) under this subsection at the rate in effect during the preceding fiscal year, until 5 days after the date such a regular appropriation is enacted.

(10) Publication

The rate applicable under this subsection for each fiscal year is published pursuant to section 77f(b)(10) of this title.

(11) Notwithstanding any other provision of law, the Commission may impose fees, charges, or prices for matters not involving any acquisition, merger, consolidation, sale, or other disposition of assets described in this subsection, as authorized by section 9701 of Title 31, or otherwise.

(h) Proxy solicitations and tender offers in connection with limited partnership rollup transactions

(1) Proxy rules to contain special provisions

It shall be unlawful for any person to solicit any proxy, consent, or authorization concerning a limited partnership rollup transaction, or to make any tender offer in furtherance of a limited partnership rollup transaction, unless such transaction is conducted in accordance with rules prescribed by the Commission under subsections (a) and (d) of this section as required by this subsection. Such rules shall—

(A) permit any holder of a security that is the subject of the proposed limited partnership rollup transaction to engage in preliminary communications for the purpose of determining whether to solicit proxies, consents, or authorizations in opposition to the proposed limited partnership rollup transaction, without regard to whether any such communication would otherwise be considered a solicitation of proxies, and without being required to file soliciting material with the Commission prior to making that determination, except that—

(i) nothing in this subparagraph shall be construed to limit the application of any provision of this chapter prohibiting, or reasonably designed to prevent, fraudulent, deceptive, or manipulative acts or practices under this chapter; and

(ii) any holder of not less than 5 percent of the outstanding securities that are the subject of the proposed limited partnership rollup transaction who engages in the business of buying and selling limited partnership interests in the secondary market shall be required to disclose such ownership interests and any potential conflicts of interests in such preliminary communications;

(B) require the issuer to provide to holders of the securities that are the subject of the limited partnership rollup transaction such list of the holders of the issuer's securities as the Commission may determine in such form and subject to such terms and conditions as the Commission may specify;

(C) prohibit compensating any person soliciting proxies, consents, or authorizations directly from security holders concerning such a limited partnership rollup transaction—

    (i) on the basis of whether the solicited proxy, consent, or authorization either approves or disapproves the proposed limited partnership rollup transaction; or

    (ii) contingent on the approval, disapproval, or completion of the limited partnership rollup transaction;

    (D) set forth disclosure requirements for soliciting material distributed in connection with a limited partnership rollup transaction, including requirements for clear, concise, and comprehensible disclosure with respect to—

    (i) any changes in the business plan, voting rights, form of ownership interest, or the compensation of the general partner in the proposed limited partnership rollup transaction from each of the original limited partnerships;

    (ii) the conflicts of interest, if any, of the general partner;

    (iii) whether it is expected that there will be a significant difference between the exchange values of the limited partnerships and the trading price of the securities to be issued in the limited partnership rollup transaction;

    (iv) the valuation of the limited partnerships and the method used to determine the value of the interests of the limited partners to be exchanged for the securities in the limited partnership rollup transaction;

    (v) the differing risks and effects of the limited partnership rollup transaction for investors in different limited partnerships proposed to be included, and the risks and effects of completing the limited partnership rollup transaction with less than all limited partnerships;

    (vi) the statement by the general partner required under subparagraph (E);

    (vii) such other matters deemed necessary or appropriate by the Commission;

    (E) require a statement by the general partner as to whether the proposed limited partnership rollup transaction is fair or unfair to investors in each limited partnership, a discussion of the basis for that conclusion, and an evaluation and a description by the general partner of alternatives to the limited partnership rollup transaction, such as liquidation;

    (F) provide that, if the general partner or sponsor has obtained any opinion (other than an opinion of counsel), appraisal, or report that is prepared by an outside party and that is materially related to the limited partnership rollup transaction, such soliciting materials shall contain or be accompanied by clear, concise, and comprehensible disclosure with respect to—

    (i) the analysis of the transaction, scope of review, preparation of the opinion, and basis for and methods of arriving at conclusions, and any representations and undertakings with respect thereto;

    (ii) the identity and qualifications of the person who prepared the opinion, the method of selection of such person, and any material past, existing, or contemplated relationships between the person or any of its affiliates and the general partner, sponsor, successor, or any other affiliate;

    (iii) any compensation of the preparer of such opinion, appraisal, or report that is contingent on the transaction's approval or completion; and

    (iv) any limitations imposed by the issuer on the access afforded to such preparer to the issuer's personnel, premises, and relevant books and records;

    (G) provide that, if the general partner or sponsor has obtained any opinion, appraisal, or report as described in subparagraph (F) from any person whose compensation is contingent on the transaction's approval or completion or who has not been given access by the issuer to its personnel and premises and relevant books and records, the general partner or sponsor shall state the reasons therefor;

    (H) provide that, if the general partner or sponsor has not obtained any opinion on the fairness of the proposed limited partnership rollup transaction to investors in each of the affected partnerships, such soliciting materials shall contain or be accompanied by a statement of such partner's or sponsor's reasons for concluding that such an opinion is not necessary in order to permit the limited partners to make an informed decision on the proposed transaction;

    (I) require that the soliciting material include a clear, concise, and comprehensible summary of the limited partnership rollup transaction (including a summary of the matters referred to in clauses (i) through (vii) of subparagraph (D) and a summary of the matter referred to in subparagraphs (F), (G), and (H)), with the risks of the limited partnership rollup transaction set forth prominently in the fore part thereof;

    (J) provide that any solicitation or offering period with respect to any proxy solicitation, tender offer, or information statement in a limited partnership rollup transaction shall be for not less than the lesser of 60 calendar days or the maximum number of days permitted under applicable State law; and

    (K) contain such other provisions as the Commission determines to be necessary or appropriate for the protection of investors in limited partnership rollup transactions.

(2) Exemptions

The Commission may, consistent with the public interest, the protection of investors, and the purposes of this chapter, exempt by rule or order any security or class of securities, any transaction or class of transactions, or any person or class of persons, in whole or in part, conditionally or unconditionally, from the requirements imposed pursuant to paragraph (1) or from the definition contained in paragraph (4).

(3) Effect on Commission authority

Nothing in this subsection limits the authority of the Commission under subsection (a) or (d) of this section or any other provision of this chapter or precludes the Commission from imposing, under subsection (a) or (d) of this section or any other provision of this chapter, a remedy or procedure required to be imposed under this subsection.

(4) Definition of limited partnership rollup transaction

Except as provided in paragraph (5), as used in this subsection, the term "limited partnership rollup transaction" means a transaction involving the combination or reorganization of one or more limited partnerships, directly or indirectly, in which—

    (A) some or all of the investors in any of such limited partnerships will receive new securities, or securities in another entity, that will be reported under a transaction reporting plan declared effective before December 17, 1993, by the Commission under section 11A of this title;

    (B) any of the investors' limited partnership securities are not, as of the date of filing, reported under a transaction reporting plan declared effective before December 17, 1993, by the Commission under section 11A of this title;

    (C) investors in any of the limited partnerships involved in the transaction are subject to a significant adverse change with respect to voting rights, the term of existence of the entity, management compensation, or investment objectives; and

    (D) any of such investors are not provided an option to receive or retain a security under substantially the same terms and conditions as the original issue.

(5) Exclusions from definition

Notwithstanding paragraph (4), the term "limited partnership rollup transaction" does not include—

    (A) a transaction that involves only a limited partnership or partnerships having an operating policy or practice of retaining cash available for distribution and reinvesting proceeds from the sale, financing, or refinancing of assets in accordance with such criteria as the Commission determines appropriate;

    (B) a transaction involving only limited partnerships wherein the interests of the limited partners are repurchased, recalled, or exchanged in accordance with the terms of the preexisting limited partnership agreements for securities in an operating company specifically identified at the time of the formation of the original limited partnership;

(C) a transaction in which the securities to be issued or exchanged are not required to be and are not registered under the Securities Act of 1933;

(D) a transaction that involves only issuers that are not required to register or report under section 12 of this title, both before and after the transaction;

(E) a transaction, except as the Commission may otherwise provide by rule for the protection of investors, involving the combination or reorganization of one or more limited partnerships in which a non-affiliated party succeeds to the interests of a general partner or sponsor, if—

(i) such action is approved by not less than 66⅔ percent of the outstanding units of each of the participating limited partnerships; and

(ii) as a result of the transaction, the existing general partners will receive only compensation to which they are entitled as expressly provided for in the preexisting limited partnership agreements; or

(F) a transaction, except as the Commission may otherwise provide by rule for the protection of investors, in which the securities offered to investors are securities of another entity that are reported under a transaction reporting plan declared effective before December 17, 1993, by the Commission under section 11A of this title, if—

(i) such other entity was formed, and such class of securities was reported and regularly traded, not less than 12 months before the date on which soliciting material is mailed to investors; and

(ii) the securities of that entity issued to investors in the transaction do not exceed 20 percent of the total outstanding securities of the entity, exclusive of any securities of such class held by or for the account of the entity or a subsidiary of the entity.

(i) **Disclosure of pay versus performance.**—The Commission shall, by rule, require each issuer to disclose in any proxy or consent solicitation material for an annual meeting of the shareholders of the issuer a clear description of any compensation required to be disclosed by the issuer under Item 402 of Regulation S–K (or any successor thereto), including, for any issuer other than an emerging growth company, information that shows the relationship between executive compensation actually paid and the financial performance of the issuer, taking into account any change in the value of the shares of stock and dividends of the issuer and any distributions. The disclosure under this subsection may include a graphic representation of the information required to be disclosed.

(j) **Disclosure of hedging by employees and directors.**—The Commission shall, by rule, require each issuer to disclose in any proxy or consent solicitation material for an annual meeting of the shareholders of the issuer whether any employee or member of the board of directors of the issuer, or any designee of such employee or member, is permitted to purchase financial instruments (including prepaid variable forward contracts, equity swaps, collars, and exchange funds) that are designed to hedge or offset any decrease in the market value of equity securities—

(1) granted to the employee or member of the board of directors by the issuer as part of the compensation of the employee or member of the board of directors; or

(2) held, directly or indirectly, by the employee or member of the board of directors.

§ 14A. Shareholder Approval of Executive Compensation

(a) **Separate resolution required.**—

(1) **In general**.—Not less frequently than once every 3 years, a proxy or consent or authorization for an annual or other meeting of the shareholders for which the proxy solicitation rules of the Commission require compensation disclosure shall include a separate resolution subject to shareholder vote to approve the compensation of executives, as disclosed pursuant to Item 402 of regulation S–K, or any successor thereto.

(2) Frequency of vote.—Not less frequently than once every 6 years, a proxy or consent or authorization for an annual or other meeting of the shareholders for which the proxy solicitation rules of the Commission require compensation disclosure shall include a separate resolution subject to shareholder vote to determine whether votes on the resolutions required under paragraph (1) will occur every 1, 2, or 3 years.

(3) Effective date.—The proxy or consent or authorization for the first annual or other meeting of the shareholders occurring after the end of the 6-month period beginning on the date of enactment of this section shall include—

(A) the resolution described in paragraph (1); and

(B) a separate resolution subject to shareholder vote to determine whether votes on the resolutions required under paragraph (1) will occur every 1, 2, or 3 years.

(b) Shareholder approval of golden parachute compensation.—

(1) Disclosure.—In any proxy or consent solicitation material (the solicitation of which is subject to the rules of the Commission pursuant to subsection (a)) for a meeting of the shareholders occurring after the end of the 6-month period beginning on the date of enactment of this section, at which shareholders are asked to approve an acquisition, merger, consolidation, or proposed sale or other disposition of all or substantially all the assets of an issuer, the person making such solicitation shall disclose in the proxy or consent solicitation material, in a clear and simple form in accordance with regulations to be promulgated by the Commission, any agreements or understandings that such person has with any named executive officers of such issuer (or of the acquiring issuer, if such issuer is not the acquiring issuer) concerning any type of compensation (whether present, deferred, or contingent) that is based on or otherwise relates to the acquisition, merger, consolidation, sale, or other disposition of all or substantially all of the assets of the issuer and the aggregate total of all such compensation that may (and the conditions upon which it may) be paid or become payable to or on behalf of such executive officer.

(2) Shareholder approval.—Any proxy or consent or authorization relating to the proxy or consent solicitation material containing the disclosure required by paragraph (1) shall include a separate resolution subject to shareholder vote to approve such agreements or understandings and compensation as disclosed, unless such agreements or understandings have been subject to a shareholder vote under subsection (a).

(c) Rule of construction.—The shareholder vote referred to in subsections (a) and (b) shall not be binding on the issuer or the board of directors of an issuer, and may not be construed—

(1) as overruling a decision by such issuer or board of directors;

(2) to create or imply any change to the fiduciary duties of such issuer or board of directors;

(3) to create or imply any additional fiduciary duties for such issuer or board of directors; or

(4) to restrict or limit the ability of shareholders to make proposals for inclusion in proxy materials related to executive compensation.

(d) Disclosure of votes.—Every institutional investment manager subject to section 13(f) shall report at least annually how it voted on any shareholder vote pursuant to subsections (a) and (b), unless such vote is otherwise required to be reported publicly by rule or regulation of the Commission.

(e) Exemption.—(1) In general. The commission may, by rule or order, exempt any other issuer or class of issuers from the requirement under subsection (a) or (b). In determining whether to make an exemption under this subsection, the Commission shall take into account, among other considerations, whether the requirements under subsections (a) and (b) disproportionately burdens small issuers.

(2) Treatment of emerging growth companies.—

(A) In general.—An emerging growth company shall be exempt from the requirements of subsections (a) and (b).

(B) Compliance after termination of emerging growth company treatment.—An issuer that was an emerging growth company but is no longer an emerging growth company shall include the first separate resolution described under subsection (a)(1) not later than the end of—

(i) in the case of an issuer that was an emerging growth company for less than 2 years after the date of first sale of common equity securities of the issuer pursuant to an effective registration statement under the Securities Act of 1933, the 3-year period beginning on such date; and

(ii) in the case of any other issuer, the 1-year period beginning on the date the issuer is no longer an emerging growth company.

§ 14B. Corporate Governance

. . . [T]he Commission shall issue rules that require an issuer to disclose in the annual proxy sent to investors the reasons why the issuer has chosen—

(1) the same person to serve as chairman of the board of directors and chief executive officer (or in equivalent positions); or

(2) different individuals to serve as chairman of the board of directors and chief executive officer (or in equivalent positions of the issuer).

§ 15.   Registration and Regulation of Brokers and Dealers

(a)   Registration of all persons utilizing exchange facilities to effect transactions; exemptions

(1) It shall be unlawful for any broker or dealer which is either a person other than a natural person or a natural person not associated with a broker or dealer which is a person other than a natural person (other than such a broker or dealer whose business is exclusively intrastate and who does not make use of any facility of a national securities exchange) to make use of the mails or any means or instrumentality of interstate commerce to effect any transactions in, or to induce or attempt to induce the purchase or sale of, any security (other than an exempted security or commercial paper, bankers' acceptances, or commercial bills) unless such broker or dealer is registered in accordance with subsection (b) of this section. . . .

(d)   Supplementary and periodic information

(1) In general. Each issuer which has filed a registration statement containing an undertaking which is or becomes operative under this subsection as in effect prior to August 20, 1964, and each issuer which shall after such date file a registration statement which has become effective pursuant to the Securities Act of 1933 . . . shall file with the Commission, in accordance with such rules and regulations as the Commission may prescribe as necessary or appropriate in the public interest or for the protection of investors, such supplementary and periodic information, documents, and reports as may be required pursuant to section 13 of this title in respect of a security registered pursuant to section 12 of this title. The duty to file under this subsection shall be automatically suspended if and so long as any issue of securities of such issuer is registered pursuant to section 12 of this title. The duty to file under this subsection shall also be automatically suspended as to any fiscal year, other than the fiscal year within which such registration statement became effective, if, at the beginning of such fiscal year, the securities of each class, other than any class of asset-backed securities to which the registration statement relates are held of record by less than 300 persons, or, in the case of bank or a bank holding company, ... For the purposes of this subsection, the term "class" shall be construed to include all securities of an issuer which are of substantially similar character and the holders of which enjoy substantially similar rights and privileges. The Commission may, for the purpose of this subsection, define by rules and regulations the term "held of record" as it deems necessary or appropriate in the public interest or for the protection of investors in order to prevent circumvention of the provisions of this subsection. . . .

(2) Asset-backed securities.—

(A) Suspension of duty to file.—The Commission may, by rule or regulation, provide for the suspension or termination of the duty to file under this subsection for any class of asset-backed security, on such terms and conditions and for such period or periods as the Commission deems necessary or appropriate in the public interest or for the protection of investors.

(B) Classification of issuers.—The Commission may, for purposes of this subsection, classify issuers and prescribe requirements appropriate for each class of issuers of asset-backed securities.

(e) Notices to customers regarding securities lending

Every registered broker or dealer shall provide notice to its customers that they may elect not to allow their fully paid securities to be used in connection with short sales. If a broker or dealer uses a customer's securities in connection with short sales, the broker or dealer shall provide notice to its customer that the broker or dealer may receive compensation in connection with lending the customer's securities. The Commission, by rule, as it deems necessary or appropriate in the public interest and for the protection of investors, may prescribe the form, content, time, and manner of delivery of any notice required under this paragraph. . . .

(g) Prevention of misuse of nonpublic information

Every registered broker or dealer shall establish, maintain, and enforce written policies and procedures reasonably designed, taking into consideration the nature of such broker's or dealer's business, to prevent the misuse in violation of this title, or the rules or regulations thereunder, of material, nonpublic information by such broker or dealer or any person associated with such broker or dealer. The Commission, as it deems necessary or appropriate in the public interest or for the protection of investors, shall adopt rules or regulations to require specific policies or procedures reasonably designed to prevent misuse in violation of this title (or the rules or regulations thereunder) of material, nonpublic information.

(h) Requirements for transactions in penny stocks

(1) *In general.* No broker or dealer shall make use of the mails or any means or instrumentality of interstate commerce to effect any transaction in, or to induce or attempt to induce the purchase or sale of, any penny stock by any customer except in accordance with the requirements of this subsection and the rules and regulations prescribed under this subsection.

(2) *Risk disclosure with respect to penny stocks.* Prior to effecting any transaction in any penny stock, a broker or dealer shall give the customer a risk disclosure document that—

(A) contains a description of the nature and level of risk in the market for penny stocks in both public offerings and secondary trading;

(B) contains a description of the broker's or dealer's duties to the customer and of the rights and remedies available to the customer with respect to violations of such duties or other requirements of Federal securities laws;

(C) contains a brief, clear, narrative description of a dealer market, including "bid" and "ask" prices for penny stocks and the significance of the spread between the bid and ask prices. . . .

(3) *Commission rules relating to disclosure.* The Commission shall adopt rules setting forth additional standards for the disclosure by brokers and dealers to customers of information concerning transactions in penny stocks. Such rules—

(A) shall require brokers and dealers to disclose to each customer, prior to effecting any transaction in, and at the time of confirming any transaction with respect to any penny stock, in accordance with such procedures and methods as the Commission may require consistent with the public interest and the protection of investors—

(i) the bid and ask prices for penny stock, or such other information as the Commission may, by rule, require to provide customers with more useful and reliable information relating to the price of such stock;

(ii) the number of shares to which such bid and ask prices apply, or other comparable information relating to the depth and liquidity of the market for such stock; and

(iii) the amount and a description of any compensation that the broker or dealer and the associated person thereof will receive or has received in connection with such transaction. . . .

(5) *Regulations.* It shall be unlawful for any person to violate such rules and regulations as the Commission shall prescribe in the public interest or for the protection of investors or to maintain fair and orderly markets—

(A) as necessary or appropriate to carry out this subsection; or

(B) as reasonably designed to prevent fraudulent, deceptive, or manipulative acts and practices with respect to penny stocks. . . .

(n)   Disclosures to retail investors.—

(1) In general.—Notwithstanding any other provision of the securities laws, the Commission may issue rules designating documents or information that shall be provided by a broker or dealer to a retail investor before the purchase of an investment product or service by the retail investor.

(2) Considerations.—In developing any rules under paragraph (1), the Commission shall consider whether the rules will promote investor protection, efficiency, competition, and capital formation.

(3) Form and contents of documents and information.—Any documents or information designated under a rule promulgated under paragraph (1) shall—

(A) be in a summary format; and

(B) contain clear and concise information about—

(i) investment objectives, strategies, costs, and risks; and

(ii) any compensation or other financial incentive received by a broker, dealer, or other intermediary in connection with the purchase of retail investment products.

(*o*)   Authority to restrict mandatory pre-dispute arbitration

The Commission, by rule, may prohibit, or impose conditions or limitations on the use of, agreements that require customers or clients of any broker, dealer, or municipal securities dealer to arbitrate any future dispute between them arising under the Federal securities laws, the rules and regulations thereunder, or the rules of a self-regulatory organization if it finds that such prohibition, imposition of conditions, or limitations are in the public interest and for the protection of investors.

§ 15D. Securities Analysts and Research Reports

(a)   Analyst protections

The Commission, or upon the authorization and direction of the Commission, a registered securities association or national securities exchange, shall have adopted, not later than 1 year after the date of enactment of this section, rules reasonably designed to address conflicts of interest that can arise when securities analysts recommend equity securities in research reports and public appearances, in order to improve the objectivity of research and provide investors with more useful and reliable information, including rules designed—

(1) to foster greater public confidence in securities research, and to protect the objectivity and independence of securities analysts, by—

(A) restricting the prepublication clearance or approval of research reports by persons employed by the broker or dealer who are engaged in investment banking activities, or persons not directly responsible for investment research, other than legal or compliance staff;

(B) limiting the supervision and compensatory evaluation of securities analysts to officials employed by the broker or dealer who are not engaged in investment banking activities; and

(C) requiring that a broker or dealer and persons employed by a broker or dealer who are involved with investment banking activities may not, directly or indirectly, retaliate against or threaten to retaliate against any securities analyst employed by that broker or dealer or its affiliates as a result of an adverse, negative, or otherwise unfavorable research report that may adversely affect the present or prospective investment banking relationship of the broker or dealer with the issuer that is the subject of the research report, except that such rules may not limit the authority of a broker or dealer to discipline a securities analyst for causes other than such research report in accordance with the policies and procedures of the firm;

(2) to define periods during which brokers or dealers who have participated, or are to participate, in a public offering of securities as underwriters or dealers should not publish or otherwise distribute research reports relating to such securities or to the issuer of such securities;

(3) to establish structural and institutional safeguards within registered brokers or dealers to assure that securities analysts are separated by appropriate informational partitions within the firm from the review, pressure, or oversight of those whose involvement in investment banking activities might potentially bias their judgment or supervision; and

(4) to address such other issues as the Commission, or such association or exchange, determines appropriate.

(b) Disclosure

The Commission, or upon the authorization and direction of the Commission, a registered securities association or national securities exchange, shall have adopted, not later than 1 year after the date of enactment of this section, rules reasonably designed to require each securities analyst to disclose in public appearances, and each registered broker or dealer to disclose in each research report, as applicable, conflicts of interest that are known or should have been known by the securities analyst or the broker or dealer, to exist at the time of the appearance or the date of distribution of the report, including—

(1) the extent to which the securities analyst has debt or equity investments in the issuer that is the subject of the appearance or research report;

(2) whether any compensation has been received by the registered broker or dealer, or any affiliate thereof, including the securities analyst, from the issuer that is the subject of the appearance or research report, subject to such exemptions as the Commission may determine appropriate and necessary to prevent disclosure by virtue of this paragraph of material non-public information regarding specific potential future investment banking transactions of such issuer, as is appropriate in the public interest and consistent with the protection of investors;

(3) whether an issuer, the securities of which are recommended in the appearance or research report, currently is, or during the 1-year period preceding the date of the appearance or date of distribution of the report has been, a client of the registered broker or dealer, and if so, stating the types of services provided to the issuer;

(4) whether the securities analyst received compensation with respect to a research report, based upon (among any other factors) the investment banking revenues (either generally or specifically earned from the issuer being analyzed) of the registered broker or dealer; and

(5) such other disclosures of conflicts of interest that are material to investors, research analysts, or the broker or dealer as the Commission, or such association or exchange, determines appropriate.

(c) Limitation.—Notwithstanding subsection (a) or any other provision of law, neither the Commission nor any national securities association registered under section 15A may adopt or maintain any rule or regulation in connection with an initial public offering of the common equity of an emerging growth company—

(1) restricting, based on functional role, which associated persons of a broker, dealer, or member of a national securities association, may arrange for communications between a securities analyst and a potential investor; or

(2) restricting a securities analyst from participating in any communications with the management of an emerging growth company that is also attended by any other associated person of a broker, dealer, or member of a national securities association whose functional role is other than as a securities analyst.

(d) Definitions.—In this section—

(1) the term "securities analyst" means any associated person of a registered broker or dealer that is principally responsible for, and any associated person who reports directly or indirectly to a securities analyst in connection with, the preparation of the substance of a research report, whether or not any such person has the job title of "securities analyst"; and

(2) the term "research report" means a written or electronic communication that includes an analysis of equity securities of individual companies or industries, and that provides information reasonably sufficient upon which to base an investment decision. . . .

§ 16.   Directors, Officers, and Principal Stockholders

(a)   Disclosures required

(1) *Directors, officers, and principal stockholders required to file.*—Every person who is directly or indirectly the beneficial owner of more than 10 percent of any class of any equity security (other than an exempted security) which is registered pursuant to section 12, or who is a director or an officer of the issuer of such security, shall file the statements required by this subsection with the Commission.

(2) *Time of filing.*—The statements required by this subsection shall be filed—

(A) at the time of the registration of such security on a national securities exchange or by the effective date of a registration statement filed pursuant to section 12(g);

(B) within 10 days after he or she becomes such beneficial owner, director, or officer, or within such shorter time as the Commission may establish by rule;

(C) if there has been a change in such ownership, or if such person shall have purchased or sold a security-based swap agreement (as defined in section 20 6(b) of the Gramm-Leach-Bliley Act (15 U.S.C. 78c note)) involving such equity security, before the end of the second business day following the day on which the subject transaction has been executed, or at such other time as the Commission shall establish, by rule, in any case in which the Commission determines that such 2-day period is not feasible.

(3) *Contents of statements.*—A statement filed—

(A) under subparagraph (A) or (B) of paragraph (2) shall contain a statement of the amount of all equity securities of such issuer of which the filing person is the beneficial owner; and

(B) under subparagraph (C) of such paragraph shall indicate ownership by the filing person at the date of filing, any such changes in such ownership, and such purchases and sales of the security-based swap agreements as have occurred since the most recent such filing under such subparagraph.

(4) *Electronic filing and availability.*—Beginning not later than 1 year after July 30, 2002—

(A) a statement filed under subparagraph (C) of paragraph (2) shall be filed electronically;

(B) the Commission shall provide each such statement on a publicly accessible Internet site not later than the end of the business day following that filing; and

(C) the issuer (if the issuer maintains a corporate website) shall provide that statement on that corporate website, not later than the end of the business day following that filing.

(b)   Profits from purchase and sale of security within six months

For the purpose of preventing the unfair use of information which may have been obtained by such beneficial owner, director, or officer by reason of his relationship to the issuer, any profit realized by him from any purchase and sale, or any sale and purchase, of any equity security of such issuer (other than an exempted security) . . . involving any such equity security within any period of less than six months, unless such security . . . was acquired in good faith in connection with a debt previously contracted, shall inure to and be recoverable by the issuer, irrespective of any intention on the part of such beneficial owner, director, or officer in entering into such transaction of holding the security . . . purchased or of not repurchasing the security . . . sold for a period exceeding six months. Suit to recover such profit may be instituted at law or in equity in any court of competent jurisdiction by the issuer, or by the owner of any security of the issuer in the name and in behalf of the issuer if the issuer shall fail or refuse to bring such suit within sixty days after request or shall fail diligently to prosecute the same thereafter; but no such suit shall be brought more than two years after the date such profit was realized. This subsection shall not be construed to cover any transaction where such beneficial owner was not such both at the time of the purchase and sale, or the sale and purchase, of the security . . . involved, or any transaction or transactions which the Commission by rules and regulations may exempt as not comprehended within the purpose of this subsection.

(c) Conditions for sale of security by beneficial owner, director, or officer

It shall be unlawful for any such beneficial owner, director, or officer, directly or indirectly, to sell any equity security of such issuer (other than an exempted security), if the person selling the security or his principal (1) does not own the security sold, or (2) if owning the security, does not deliver it against such sale within twenty days thereafter, or does not within five days after such sale deposit it in the mails or other usual channels of transportation; but no person shall be deemed to have violated this subsection if he proves that notwithstanding the exercise of good faith he was unable to make such delivery or deposit within such time, or that to do so would cause undue inconvenience or expense. . . .

§ 18. Liability for Misleading Statements

(a) Persons liable; persons entitled to recover; defense of good faith; suit at law or in equity; costs, etc.

Any person who shall make or cause to be made any statement in any application, report, or document filed pursuant to this chapter or any rule or regulation thereunder or any undertaking contained in a registration statement as provided in subsection (d) of section 15 of this title, which statement was at the time and in the light of the circumstances under which it was made false or misleading with respect to any material fact, shall be liable to any person (not knowing that such statement was false or misleading) who, in reliance upon such statement, shall have purchased or sold a security at a price which was affected by such statement, for damages caused by such reliance, unless the person sued shall prove that he acted in good faith and had no knowledge that such statement was false or misleading. A person seeking to enforce such liability may sue at law or in equity in any court of competent jurisdiction. In any such suit the court may, in its discretion, require an undertaking for the payment of the costs of such suit, and assess reasonable costs, including reasonable attorneys' fees, against either party litigant.

(b) Contribution

Every person who becomes liable to make payment under this section may recover contribution as in cases of contract from any person who, if joined in the original suit, would have been liable to make the same payment.

(c) Period of limitations

No action shall be maintained to enforce any liability created under this section unless brought within one year after the discovery of the facts constituting the cause of action and within three years after such cause of action accrued.

§ 19. Registration, Responsibilities, and Oversight of Self-Regulatory Organizations. . . .

(b) Proposed rule changes; notice; proceedings

(1) Each self-regulatory organization shall file with the Commission, in accordance with such rules as the Commission may prescribe, copies of any proposed rule or any proposed change in, addition to, or deletion from the rules of such self-regulatory organization (hereinafter in this subsection collectively referred to as a "proposed rule change") accompanied by a concise general statement of the basis and purpose of such proposed rule change. The Commission shall, upon the filing of any proposed rule change, publish notice thereof together with the terms of substance of the proposed rule change or a description of the subjects and issues involved. The Commission shall give interested persons an opportunity to submit written data, views, and arguments concerning such proposed rule change. No proposed rule change shall take effect unless approved by the Commission or otherwise permitted in accordance with the provisions of this subsection. . . .

(c) Amendment by Commission of rules of self-regulatory organizations

The Commission, by rule, may abrogate, add to, and delete from (hereinafter in this subsection collectively referred to as "amend") the rules of a self-regulatory organization (other than a registered clearing agency) as the Commission deems necessary or appropriate to insure the fair administration of the self-regulatory organization, to conform its rules to requirements of this chapter and the rules and regulations thereunder applicable to such organization, or otherwise in furtherance of the purposes of this chapter, in the following manner:

(1) The Commission shall notify the self-regulatory organization and publish notice of the proposed rulemaking in the Federal Register. The notice shall include the text of the proposed amendment to the rules of the self-regulatory organization and a statement of the Commission's reasons, including any pertinent facts, for commencing such proposed rulemaking.

(2) The Commission shall give interested persons an opportunity for the oral presentation of data, views, and arguments, in addition to an opportunity to make written submissions. A transcript shall be kept of any oral presentation.

(3) A rule adopted pursuant to this subsection shall incorporate the text of the amendment to the rules of the self-regulatory organization and a statement of the Commission's basis for and purpose in so amending such rules. This statement shall include an identification of any facts on which the Commission considers its determination so to amend the rules of the self-regulatory agency to be based, including the reasons for the Commission's conclusions as to any of such facts which were disputed in the rulemaking.

(4)(A) Except as provided in paragraphs (1) through (3) of this subsection, rulemaking under this subsection shall be in accordance with the procedures specified in section 553 of title 5 for rulemaking not on the record.

(B) Nothing in this subsection shall be construed to impair or limit the Commission's power to make, or to modify or alter the procedures the Commission may follow in making, rules and regulations pursuant to any other authority under this chapter.

(C) Any amendment to the rules of a self-regulatory organization made by the Commission pursuant to this subsection shall be considered for all purposes of this chapter to be part of the rules of such self-regulatory organization and shall not be considered to be a rule of the Commission. . . .

§ 20. Liability of Controlling Persons and Persons Who Aid and Abet Violations

(a) Joint and several liability; good faith defense

Every person who, directly or indirectly, controls any person liable under any provision of this chapter or of any rule or regulation thereunder shall also be liable jointly and severally with and to the same extent as such controlled person to any person to whom such controlled person is liable, unless the controlling person acted in good faith and did not directly or indirectly induce the act or acts constituting the violation or cause of action.

(b) Unlawful activity through or by means of any other person

It shall be unlawful for any person, directly or indirectly, to do any act or thing which it would be unlawful for such person to do under the provisions of this chapter or any rule or regulation thereunder through or by means of any other person.

(c) Hindering, delaying, or obstructing the making or filing of any document, report, or information

It shall be unlawful for any director or officer of, or any owner of any securities issued by, any issuer required to file any document, report, or information under this chapter or any rule or regulation thereunder without just cause to hinder, delay, or obstruct the making or filing of any such document, report, or information. . . .

(d) Liability for trading in securities while in possession of material nonpublic information

Wherever communicating, or purchasing or selling a security while in possession of, material nonpublic information would violate, or results in liability to any purchaser or seller of the security under any provision of this title, or any rule or regulation thereunder, such conduct in connection with a purchase or sale of a put, call, straddle, option, privilege, or security-based swap agreement . . . with respect to such security or with respect to a group or index of securities including such security, shall also violate and result in comparable liability to any purchaser or seller of that security under such provision, rule, or regulation.

(e) Prosecution of persons who aid and abet violations

For purposes of any action brought by the Commission under paragraph (1) or (3) of section 21(d), any person that knowingly or recklessly provides substantial assistance to another person in violation of a provision of this title, or of any rule or regulation issued under this title, shall be deemed to be in violation of such provision to the same extent as the person to whom such assistance is provided. . . .

§ 20A. Liability to Contemporaneous Traders for Insider Trading

(a) Private rights of action based on contemporaneous trading

Any person who violates any provision of this title or the rules or regulations thereunder by purchasing or selling a security while in possession of material, nonpublic information shall be liable in an action in any court of competent jurisdiction to any person who, contemporaneously with the purchase or sale of securities that is the subject of such violation, has purchased (where such violation is based on a sale of securities) or sold (where such violation is based on a purchase of securities) securities of the same class.

(b) Limitations on liability

(1) *Contemporaneous trading actions limited to profit gained or loss avoided.* The total amount of damages imposed under subsection (a) shall not exceed the profit gained or loss avoided in the transaction or transactions that are the subject of the violation.

(2) *Offsetting disgorgements against liability.* The total amount of damages imposed against any person under subsection (a) shall be diminished by the amounts, if any, that such person may be required to disgorge, pursuant to a court order obtained at the instance of the Commission, in a proceeding brought under section 21(d) of this title [Investigations; Injunctions and Prosecution of Offenses] relating to the same transaction or transactions.

(3) *Controlling person liability.* No person shall be liable under this section solely by reason of employing another person who is liable under this section, but the liability of a controlling person under this section shall be subject to section 20(a) of this title.

(4) *Statute of limitations.* No action may be brought under this section more than 5 years after the date of the last transaction that is the subject of the violation.

(c) Joint and several liability for communicating

Any person who violates any provision of this title or the rules or regulations thereunder by communicating material, nonpublic information shall be jointly and severally liable under subsection (a) with, and to the same extent as, any person or persons liable under subsection (a) to whom the communication was directed.

(d) Authority not to restrict other express or implied rights of action

Nothing in this section shall be construed to limit or condition the right of any person to bring an action to enforce a requirement of this title or the availability of any cause of action implied from a provision of this title.

(e) Provisions not to affect public prosecutions

This section shall not be construed to bar or limit in any manner any action by the Commission or the Attorney General under any other provision of this title, nor shall it bar or limit in any manner any action to recover penalties, or to seek any other order regarding penalties.

§ 21. Investigations and Actions . . .

(d)(1) Wherever it shall appear to the Commission that any person is engaged or is about to engage in acts or practices constituting a violation of any provision of this chapter, the rules or regulations thereunder, the rules of a national securities exchange or registered securities association of which such person is a member or a person associated with a member, the rules of a registered clearing agency in which such person is a participant, the rules of the Public Company Accounting Oversight Board, of which such person is a registered public accounting firm or a person associated with such a firm, or the rules of the Municipal Securities Rulemaking Board, it may in its discretion bring an action in the proper district court of the United States, the United States District Court for the District of Columbia, or the United States courts of any territory or other place subject to the jurisdiction of the United States, to enjoin such acts or practices, and upon a proper showing a permanent or temporary injunction or restraining order shall be granted without bond. The Commission may transmit such evidence as may be available concerning such acts or practices as may constitute a violation of any provision of this chapter or the rules or regulations thereunder to the Attorney General, who may, in his discretion, institute the necessary criminal proceedings under this chapter.

(2) *Authority of a court to prohibit persons from serving as officers and directors.* In any proceeding under paragraph (1) of this subsection, the court may prohibit, conditionally or unconditionally, and permanently or for such period of time as it shall determine, any person who violated section 10(b) of this title or the rules or regulations thereunder from acting as an officer or director of any issuer that has a class of securities registered pursuant to section 12 of this title or that is required to file reports pursuant to section 15(d) of this title if the person's conduct demonstrates unfitness to serve as an officer or director of any such issuer.

(3) *Money penalties in civil actions.*

(A) *Authority of commission.* Whenever it shall appear to the Commission that any person has violated any provision of this title, the rules or regulations thereunder, or a cease-and-desist order entered by the Commission pursuant to section 21C of this title, other than by committing a violation subject to a penalty pursuant to section 21A, the Commission may bring an action in a United States district court to seek, and the court shall have jurisdiction to impose, upon a proper showing, a civil penalty to be paid by the person who committed such violation.

(B) *Amount of penalty.*

(i) *First tier.* The amount of the penalty shall be determined by the court in light of the facts and circumstances. For each violation, the amount of the penalty shall not exceed the greater of (I) $7,500 for a natural person or $80,000 for any other person, or (II) the gross amount of pecuniary gain to such defendant as a result of the violation.

(ii) *Second tier.* Notwithstanding clause (i), the amount of penalty for each such violation shall not exceed the greater of (I) $80,000 for a natural person or $400,000 for any other person, or (II) the gross amount of pecuniary gain to such defendant as a result of the violation, if the violation described in subparagraph (A) involved fraud, deceit, manipulation, or deliberate or reckless disregard of a regulatory requirement.

(iii) *Third tier.* Notwithstanding clauses (i) and (ii), the amount of penalty for each such violation shall not exceed the greater of (I) $160,000 for a natural person or $750,000 for any other person, or (II) the gross amount of pecuniary gain to such defendant as a result of the violation, if—

(aa) the violation described in subparagraph (A) involved fraud, deceit, manipulation, or deliberate or reckless disregard of a regulatory requirement; and

(bb) such violation directly or indirectly resulted in substantial losses or created a significant risk of substantial losses to other persons. . . .

(4) *Prohibition of attorneys' fees paid from commission disgorgement funds*—Except as otherwise ordered by the court upon motion by the Commission, or, in the case of an administrative action, as otherwise ordered by the Commission, funds disgorged as the result of an action brought by the Commission in Federal court, or as a result of any Commission administrative action, shall not be distributed as payment for attorneys' fees or expenses incurred by private parties seeking distribution of the disgorged funds. . . .

(5) *Equitable relief.*—In any action or proceeding brought or instituted by the Commission under any provision of the securities laws, the Commission may seek, and any Federal court may grant, any equitable relief that may be appropriate or necessary for the benefit of investors.

(6) *Authority of a court to prohibit persons from participating in an offering of penny stock—*

(A) *In general.*—In any proceeding under paragraph (1) against any person participating in, or, at the time of the alleged misconduct who was participating in, an offering of penny stock, the court may prohibit that person from participating in an offering of penny stock, conditionally or unconditionally, and permanently or for such period of time as the court shall determine.

(B) *Definition.*—For purposes of this paragraph, the term "person participating in an offering of penny stock" includes any person engaging in activities with a broker, dealer, or issuer for purposes of issuing, trading, or inducing or attempting to induce the purchase or sale of, any penny stock. The Commission may, by rule or regulation, define such term to include other activities, and may, by rule, regulation, or order, exempt any person or class of persons, in whole or in part, conditionally or unconditionally, from inclusion in such term.

§ 21A. Civil Penalties for Insider Trading

(a) Authority to impose civil penalties

(1) *Judicial actions by commission authorized.* Whenever it shall appear to the Commission that any person has violated any provision of this title or the rules or regulations thereunder by purchasing or selling a security . . . while in possession of material, nonpublic information, or has violated any such provision by communicating such information in connection with, a transaction on or through the facilities of a national securities exchange or from or through a broker or dealer, and which is not part of a public offering by an issuer of securities other than standardized options or security futures products, the Commission—

(A) may bring an action in a United States district court to seek, and the court shall have jurisdiction to impose, a civil penalty to be paid by the person who committed such violation; and

(B) may, subject to subsection (b)(1), bring an action in a United States district court to seek, and the court shall have jurisdiction to impose, a civil penalty to be paid by a person who, at the time of the violation, directly or indirectly controlled the person who committed such violation.

(2) *Amount of penalty for person who committed violation.* The amount of the penalty which may be imposed on the person who committed such violation shall be determined by the court in light of the facts and circumstances, but shall not exceed three times the profit gained or loss avoided as a result of such unlawful purchase, sale, or communication.

(3) *Amount of penalty for controlling person.* The amount of the penalty which may be imposed on any person who, at the time of the violation, directly or indirectly controlled the person who committed such violation, shall be determined by the court in light of the facts and circumstances, but shall not exceed the greater of $1,525,000, or three times the amount of the profit gained or loss avoided as a result of such controlled person's violation. If such controlled person's violation was a violation by communication, the profit gained or loss avoided as a result of the violation shall, for purposes of this paragraph only, be deemed to be limited to the profit gained or loss avoided by the person or persons to whom the controlled person directed such communication.

(b) Limitations on liability

(1) *Liability of controlling persons.* No controlling person shall be subject to a penalty under subsection (a)(1)(B) unless the Commission establishes that—

(A) such controlling person knew or recklessly disregarded the fact that such controlled person was likely to engage in the act or acts constituting the violation and failed to take appropriate steps to prevent such act or acts before they occurred; or

(B) such controlling person knowingly or recklessly failed to establish, maintain, or enforce any policy or procedure required under section 15(f) of this title or section 204A of the Investment

Advisers Act of 1940 and such failure substantially contributed to or permitted the occurrence of the act or acts constituting the violation.

(2) *Additional restrictions on liability.* No person shall be subject to a penalty under subsection (a) solely by reason of employing another person who is subject to a penalty under such subsection, unless such employing person is liable as a controlling person under paragraph (1) of this subsection. Section 20(a) of this title shall not apply to actions under subsection (a) of this section. . . .

(e)   Authority to award bounties to informants

Notwithstanding the provisions of subsection (d)(1), there shall be paid from amounts imposed as a penalty under this section and recovered by the Commission or the Attorney General, such sums, not to exceed 10 percent of such amounts, as the Commission deems appropriate, to the person or persons who provide information leading to the imposition of such penalty. Any determinations under this subsection, including whether, to whom, or in what amount to make payments, shall be in the sole discretion of the Commission, except that no such payment shall be made to any member, officer, or employee of any appropriate regulatory agency, the Department of Justice, or a self-regulatory organization. Any such determination shall be final and not subject to judicial review.

(f)   Definition

For purposes of this section, "profit gained" or "loss avoided" is the difference between the purchase or sale price of the security and the value of that security as measured by the trading price of the security a reasonable period after public dissemination of the nonpublic information. . . .

§ 21B. Civil Remedies in Administrative Proceedings

(a)   Commission authority to assess money penalties

(1) **In general.** In any proceeding instituted pursuant to sections 15(b)(4), 15(b)(6), 15B, 15C, 15D, 15E or 17A of this title against any person, the Commission or the appropriate regulatory agency may impose a civil penalty if it finds, on the record after notice and opportunity for hearing that such penalty is in the public interest, that such person—

(A) has willfully violated any provision of the Securities Act of 1933, the Investment Company Act of 1940, the Investment Advisers Act of 1940, or this title, or the rules or regulations thereunder, or the rules of the Municipal Securities Rulemaking Board;

(B) has willfully aided, abetted, counseled, commanded, induced, or procured such a violation by any other person;

(C) has willfully made or caused to be made in any application for registration or report required to be filed with the Commission or with any other appropriate regulatory agency under this title, or in any proceeding before the Commission with respect to registration, any statement which was, at the time and in the light of the circumstances under which it was made, false or misleading with respect to any material fact, or has omitted to state in any such application or report any material fact which is required to be stated therein; or

(D) has failed reasonably to supervise, within the meaning of section 15(b)(4)(E) of this title, with a view to preventing violations of the provisions of such statutes, rules and regulations, another person who commits such a violation, if such other person is subject to his supervision.

(2) **Cease-and-desist proceedings.**—In any proceeding instituted under section 21C against any person, the Commission may impose a civil penalty, if the Commission finds, on the record after notice and opportunity for hearing, that such person—

(A) is violating or has violated any provision of this title, or any rule or regulation issued under this title; or

(B) is or was a cause of the violation of any provision of this title, or any rule or regulation issued under this title.

(b) Maximum amount of penalty

(1) *First tier.*—The maximum amount of penalty for each act or omission described in subsection (a) shall be $7,500 for a natural person or $80,000 for any other person.

(2) *Second tier.*—Notwithstanding paragraph (1), the maximum amount of penalty for each such act or omission shall be $80,000 for a natural person or $400,000 for any other person if the act or omission described in subsection (a) involved fraud, deceit, manipulation, or deliberate or reckless disregard of a regulatory requirement.

(3) *Third tier.*—Notwithstanding paragraphs (1) and (2), the maximum amount of penalty for each such act or omission shall be $160,000 for a natural person or $775,000 for any other person if—

(A) The act or omission described in subsection (a) involved fraud, deceit, manipulation, or deliberate or reckless disregard of a regulatory requirement; and

(B) such act or omission directly or indirectly resulted in substantial losses or created a significant risk of substantial losses to other persons or resulted in substantial pecuniary gain to the person who committed the act or omission.

(c) Determination of public interest

In considering under this section whether a penalty is in the public interest, the Commission or the appropriate regulatory agency may consider—

(1) whether the act or omission for which such penalty is assessed involved fraud, deceit, manipulation, or deliberate or reckless disregard of a regulatory requirement;

(2) the harm to other persons resulting either directly or indirectly from such act or omission;

(3) the extent to which any person was unjustly enriched, taking into account any restitution made to persons injured by such behavior;

(4) whether such person previously has been found by the Commission, another appropriate regulatory agency, or a self-regulatory organization to have violated the Federal securities laws, State securities laws, or the rules of a self-regulatory organization, has been enjoined by a court of competent jurisdiction from violations of such laws or rules, or has been convicted by a court of competent jurisdiction of violations of such laws or of any felony or misdemeanor described in section 15(b)(4)(B) of this title;

(5) the need to deter such person and other persons from committing such acts or omissions; and

(6) such other matters as justice may require.

(d) Evidence concerning ability to pay

In any proceeding in which the Commission or the appropriate regulatory agency may impose a penalty under this section, a respondent may present evidence of the respondent's ability to pay such penalty. The Commission or the appropriate regulatory agency may, in its discretion, consider such evidence in determining whether such penalty is in the public interest. Such evidence may relate to the extent of such person's ability to continue in business and the collectability of a penalty, taking into account any other claims of the United States or third parties upon such person's assets and the amount of such person's assets.

(e) Authority to enter an order requiring an accounting and disgorgement

In any proceeding in which the Commission or the appropriate regulatory agency may impose a penalty under this section, the Commission or the appropriate regulatory agency may enter an order requiring accounting and disgorgement, including reasonable interest. The Commission is authorized to adopt rules, regulations, and orders concerning payments to investors, rates of interest, periods of accrual, and such other matters as it deems appropriate to implement this subsection.

§ 21C. Cease-and-Desist Proceedings

(a) Authority of the Commission

If the Commission finds, after notice and opportunity for hearing, that any person is violating, has violated, or is about to violate any provision of this title, or any rule or regulation thereunder, the Commission may publish its findings and enter an order requiring such person, and any other person that is, was, or would be a cause of the violation, due to an act or omission the person knew or should have known would contribute to such violation, to cease and desist from committing or causing such violation and any future violation of the same provision, rule, or regulation. Such order may, in addition to requiring a person to cease and desist from committing or causing a violation, require such person to comply, or to take steps to effect compliance, with such provision, rule, or regulation, upon such terms and conditions and within such time as the Commission may specify in such order. Any such order may, as the Commission deems appropriate, require future compliance or steps to effect future compliance, either permanently or for such period of time as the Commission may specify, with such provision, rule, or regulation with respect to any security, any issuer, or any other person. . . .

(e) Authority to enter an order requiring an accounting and disgorgement

In any cease-and-desist proceeding under subsection (a), the Commission may enter an order requiring accounting and disgorgement, including reasonable interest. The Commission is authorized to adopt rules, regulations, and orders concerning payments to investors, rates of interest, periods of accrual, and such other matters as it deems appropriate to implement this subsection.

(f) Authority of the Commission to prohibit persons from serving as officers or directors

In any cease-and-desist proceeding under subsection (a), the Commission may issue an order to prohibit, conditionally or unconditionally, and permanently or for such period of time as it shall determine, any person who has violated section 10(b) or the rules or regulations thereunder, from acting as an officer or director of any issuer that has a class of securities registered pursuant to section 12, or that is required to file reports pursuant to section 15(d), if the conduct of that person demonstrates unfitness to serve as an officer or director of any such issuer.

§ 21D. Private Securities Litigation

(a) Private class actions

(1) *In general.*—The provisions of this subsection shall apply in each private action arising under this title that is brought as a plaintiff class action pursuant to the Federal Rules of Civil Procedure.

(2) *Certification filed with complaint.*—

(A) In General.—Each plaintiff seeking to serve as a representative party on behalf of a class shall provide a sworn certification, which shall be personally signed by such plaintiff and filed with the complaint, that—

(i) states that the plaintiff has reviewed the complaint and authorized its filing;

(ii) states that the plaintiff did not purchase the security that is the subject of the complaint at the direction of plaintiff's counsel or in order to participate in any private action arising under this title;

(iii) states that the plaintiff is willing to serve as a representative party on behalf of a class, including providing testimony at deposition and trial, if necessary;

(iv) sets forth all of the transactions of the plaintiff in the security that is the subject of the complaint during the class period specified in the complaint;

(v) identifies any other action under this title, filed during the 3-year period preceding the date on which the certification is signed by the plaintiff, in which the plaintiff has sought to serve as a representative party on behalf of a class; and

(vi) states that the plaintiff will not accept any payment for serving as a representative party on behalf of a class beyond the plaintiff's pro rata share of any recovery, except as ordered or approved by the court in accordance with paragraph (4).

(B) *Nonwaiver of attorney-client privilege.*—The certification filed pursuant to subparagraph (A) shall not be construed to be a waiver of the attorney-client privilege.

(3) *Appointment of lead plaintiff.*

(A) *Early notice to class members.*—

(i) *In General.*—Not later than 20 days after the date on which the complaint is filed, the plaintiff or plaintiffs shall cause to be published, in a widely circulated national business-oriented publication or wire service, a notice advising members of the purported plaintiff class—

(I) of the pendency of the action, the claims asserted therein, and the purported class period; and

(II) that, not later than 60 days after the date on which the notice is published, any member of the purported class may move the court to serve as lead plaintiff of the purported class.

(ii) *Multiple actions.*—If more than one action on behalf of a class asserting substantially the same claim or claims arising under this title is filed, only the plaintiff or plaintiffs in the first filed action shall be required to cause notice to be published in accordance with clause (i).

(iii) *Additional notices may be required under federal rules.*—Notice required under clause (i) shall be in addition to any notice required pursuant to the Federal Rules of Civil Procedure.

(B) *Appointment of lead plaintiff.*—

(i) *In general.*—Not later than 90 days after the date on which a notice is published under subparagraph (A)(i), the court shall consider any motion made by a purported class member in response to the notice, including any motion by a class member who is not individually named as a plaintiff in the complaint or complaints, and shall appoint as lead plaintiff the member or members of the purported plaintiff class that the court determines to be most capable of adequately representing the interests of class members (hereafter in this paragraph referred to as the "most adequate plaintiff") in accordance with this subparagraph.

(ii) *Consolidated actions.*—If more than one action on behalf of a class asserting substantially the same claim or claims arising under this title has been filed, and any party has sought to consolidate those actions for pretrial purposes or for trial, the court shall not make the determination required by clause (i) until after the decision on the motion to consolidate is rendered. As soon as practicable after such decision is rendered, the court shall appoint the most adequate plaintiff as lead plaintiff for the consolidated actions in accordance with this paragraph.

(iii) *Rebuttable presumption.*—

(I) *In general.*—Subject to subclause (II), for purposes of clause (i), the court shall adopt a presumption that the most adequate plaintiff in any private action arising under this title is the person or group of persons that—

(aa) has either filed the complaint or made a motion in response to a notice under subparagraph (A)(i);

(bb) in the determination of the court, has the largest financial interest in the relief sought by the class; and (cc) otherwise satisfies the requirements of Rule 23 of the Federal Rules of Civil Procedure.

(II) *Rebuttal evidence.*—The presumption described in subclause (I) may be rebutted only upon proof by a member of the purported plaintiff class that the presumptively most adequate plaintiff—

(aa) will not fairly and adequately protect the interests of the class; or

(bb) is subject to unique defenses that render such plaintiff incapable of adequately representing the class.

(iv) *Discovery.*—For purposes of this subparagraph, discovery relating to whether a member or members of the purported plaintiff class is the most adequate plaintiff may be conducted by a plaintiff only if the plaintiff first demonstrates a reasonable basis for a finding that the presumptively most adequate plaintiff is incapable of adequately representing the class.

(v) *Selection of lead counsel.*—The most adequate plaintiff shall, subject to the approval of the court, select and retain counsel to represent the class.

(vi) *Restrictions on professional plaintiffs.*—Except as the court may otherwise permit, consistent with the purposes of this section, a person may be a lead plaintiff, or an officer, director, or fiduciary of a lead plaintiff, in no more than 5 securities class actions brought as plaintiff class actions pursuant to the Federal Rules of Civil Procedure during any 3-year period.

(4) *Recovery by plaintiffs.*—The share of any final judgment or of any settlement that is awarded to a representative party serving on behalf of a class shall be equal, on a per share basis, to the portion of the final judgment or settlement awarded to all other members of the class. Nothing in this paragraph shall be construed to limit the award of reasonable costs and expenses (including lost wages) directly relating to the representation of the class to any representative party serving on behalf of a class.

(5) *Restrictions on settlements under seal.*—The terms and provisions of any settlement agreement of a class action shall not be filed under seal, except that on motion of any party to the settlement, the court may order filing under seal for those portions of a settlement agreement as to which good cause is shown for such filing under seal. For purposes of this paragraph, good cause shall exist only if publication of a term or provision of a settlement agreement would cause direct and substantial harm to any party.

(6) *Restrictions on payment of attorneys' fees and expenses.*—Total attorneys' fees and expenses awarded by the court to counsel for the plaintiff class shall not exceed a reasonable percentage of the amount of any damages and prejudgment interest actually paid to the class.

(7) *Disclosure of settlement terms to class members.*—Any proposed or final settlement agreement that is published or otherwise disseminated to the class shall include each of the following statements, along with a cover page summarizing the information contained in such statements:

(A) *Statement of plaintiff recovery.*—The amount of the settlement proposed to be distributed to the parties to the action, determined in the aggregate and on an average per share basis.

(B) *Statement of potential outcome of case.*—

(i) *Agreement on amount of damages.*—If the settling parties agree on the average amount of damages per share that would be recoverable if the plaintiff prevailed on each claim alleged under this title, a statement concerning the average amount of such potential damages per share.

(ii) *Disagreement on amount of damages.*—If the parties do not agree on the average amount of damages per share that would be recoverable if the plaintiff prevailed on each claim alleged under this title, a statement from each settling party concerning the issue or issues on which the parties disagree.

(iii) *Inadmissibility for certain purposes.*—A statement made in accordance with clause (i) or (ii) concerning the amount of damages shall not be admissible in any Federal or State judicial action or administrative proceeding, other than an action or proceeding arising out of such statement.

(C) *Statement of attorneys' fees or costs sought.*—If any of the settling parties or their counsel intend to apply to the court for an award of attorneys' fees or costs from any fund established as part of the settlement, a statement indicating which parties or counsel intend to make such an application, the amount of fees and costs that will be sought (including the amount of such fees and costs determined on an average per share basis), and a brief explanation supporting the fees and costs sought. Such information shall be clearly summarized on the cover page of any notice to a party of any proposed or final settlement agreement.

(D) *Identification of lawyers' representatives.*—The name, telephone number, and address of one or more representatives of counsel for the plaintiff class who will be reasonably available to answer questions from class members concerning any matter contained in any notice of settlement published or otherwise disseminated to the class.

(E) *Reasons for settlement.*—A brief statement explaining the reasons why the parties are proposing the settlement.

(F) *Other information.*—Such other information as may be required by the court.

(8) *Security for payment of costs in class actions.*—In any private action arising under this title that is certified as a class action pursuant to the Federal Rules of Civil Procedure, the court may require an undertaking from the attorneys for the plaintiff class, the plaintiff class, or both, or from the attorneys for the defendant, the defendant, or both, in such proportions and at such times as the court determines are just and equitable, for the payment of fees and expenses that may be awarded under this subsection.

(9) *Attorney conflict of interest.*—If a plaintiff class is represented by an attorney who directly owns or otherwise has a beneficial interest in the securities that are the subject of the litigation, the court shall make a determination of whether such ownership or other interest constitutes a conflict of interest sufficient to disqualify the attorney from representing the plaintiff class.

(b) Requirements for securities fraud actions

(1) *Misleading statements and omissions.*—In any private action arising under this title in which the plaintiff alleges that the defendant—

(A) made an untrue statement of a material fact; or

(B) omitted to state a material fact necessary in order to make the statements made, in the light of the circumstances in which they were made, not misleading;

the complaint shall specify each statement alleged to have been misleading, the reason or reasons why the statement is misleading, and, if an allegation regarding the statement or omission is made on information and belief, the complaint shall state with particularity all facts on which that belief is formed.

(2) *Required state of mind.*—(A) In general. Except as provided in Subparagraph (B) in any private action arising under this title in which the plaintiff may recover money damages only on proof that the defendant acted with a particular state of mind, the complaint shall, with respect to each act or omission alleged to violate this title, state with particularity facts giving rise to a strong inference that the defendant acted with the required state of mind.

(B) Exception.—In the case of an action for money damages brought against a credit rating agency or a controlling person under this title, it shall be sufficient, for purposes of pleading any required state of mind in relation to such action, that the complaint state with particularity facts giving rise to a strong inference that the credit rating agency knowingly or recklessly failed—

(i) to conduct a reasonable investigation of the rated security with respect to the factual elements relied upon by its own methodology for evaluating credit risk; or

(ii) to obtain reasonable verification of such factual elements (which verification may be based on a sampling technique that does not amount to an audit) from other sources that the credit rating agency considered to be competent and that were independent of the issuer and underwriter.

(3) *Motion to dismiss; stay of discovery.*—

(A) *Dismissal for failure to meet pleading requirements.*—In any private action arising under this title, the court shall, on the motion of any defendant, dismiss the complaint if the requirements of paragraphs (1) and (2) are not met.

(B) *Stay of discovery.*—In any private action arising under this title, all discovery and other proceedings shall be stayed during the pendency of any motion to dismiss, unless the court finds upon the motion of any party that particularized discovery is necessary to preserve evidence or to prevent undue prejudice to that party.

(C) *Preservation of evidence.*—

(i) In general.—During the pendency of any stay of discovery pursuant to this paragraph, unless otherwise ordered by the court, any party to the action with actual notice of the allegations contained in the complaint shall treat all documents, data compilations (including electronically recorded or stored data), and tangible objects that are in the custody or control of such person and that are relevant to the allegations, as if they were the subject of a continuing request for production of documents from an opposing party under the Federal Rules of Civil Procedure.

(ii) Sanction for willful violation.—A party aggrieved by the willful failure of an opposing party to comply with clause (i) may apply to the court for an order awarding appropriate sanctions.

(D) *Circumvention of stay of discovery.*—Upon a proper showing, a court may stay discovery proceedings in any private action in a State court, as necessary in aid of its jurisdiction, or to protect or effectuate its judgments, in an action subject to a stay of discovery pursuant to this paragraph.

(4) *Loss causation.*—In any private action arising under this title, the plaintiff shall have the burden of proving that the act or omission of the defendant alleged to violate this title caused the loss for which the plaintiff seeks to recover damages.

(c) Sanctions for abusive litigation

(1) *Mandatory review by court.*—In any private action arising under this title, upon final adjudication of the action, the court shall include in the record specific findings regarding compliance by each party and each attorney representing any party with each requirement of Rule 11(b) of the Federal Rules of Civil Procedure as to any complaint, responsive pleading, or dispositive motion.

(2) *Mandatory sanctions.*—If the court makes a finding under paragraph (1) that a party or attorney violated any requirement of Rule 11(b) of the Federal Rules of Civil Procedure as to any complaint, responsive pleading, or dispositive motion, the court shall impose sanctions on such party or attorney in accordance with Rule 11 of the Federal Rules of Civil Procedure. Prior to making a finding that any party or attorney has violated Rule 11 of the Federal Rules of Civil Procedure, the court shall give such party or attorney notice and an opportunity to respond.

(3) *Presumption in favor of attorneys' fees and costs.*—

(A) *In general.*—Subject to subparagraphs (B) and (C), for purposes of paragraph (2), the court shall adopt a presumption that the appropriate sanction—

(i) for failure of any responsive pleading or dispositive motion to comply with any requirement of Rule 11(b) of the Federal Rules of Civil Procedure is an award to the opposing party of the reasonable attorneys' fees and other expenses incurred as a direct result of the violation; and

(ii) for substantial failure of any complaint to comply with any requirement of Rule 11(b) of the Federal Rules of Civil Procedure is an award to the opposing party of the reasonable attorneys' fees and other expenses incurred in the action.

(B) *Rebuttal evidence.*—The presumption described in subparagraph (A) may be rebutted only upon proof by the party or attorney against whom sanctions are to be imposed that—

(i) the award of attorneys' fees and other expenses will impose an unreasonable burden on that party or attorney and would be unjust, and the failure to make such an award would not impose a greater burden on the party in whose favor sanctions are to be imposed; or

(ii) the violation of Rule 11(b) of the Federal Rules of Civil Procedure was de minimis.

(C) *Sanctions.*—If the party or attorney against whom sanctions are to be imposed meets its burden under subparagraph (B), the court shall award the sanctions that the court deems appropriate pursuant to Rule 11 of the Federal Rules of Civil Procedure.

(d) Defendant's right to written interrogatories

In any private action arising under this title in which the plaintiff may recover money damages, the court shall, when requested by a defendant, submit to the jury a written interrogatory on the issue of each such defendant's state of mind at the time the alleged violation occurred.

(e) Limitation on damages

(1) *In general.*—Except as provided in paragraph (2), in any private action arising under this title in which the plaintiff seeks to establish damages by reference to the market price of a security, the award of damages to the plaintiff shall not exceed the difference between the purchase or sale price paid or received, as appropriate, by the plaintiff for the subject security and the mean trading price of that security during the 90-day period beginning on the date on which the information correcting the misstatement or omission that is the basis for the action is disseminated to the market.

(2) *Exception.*—In any private action arising under this title in which the plaintiff seeks to establish damages by reference to the market price of a security, if the plaintiff sells or repurchases the subject security prior to the expiration of the 90-day period described in paragraph (1), the plaintiff's damages shall not exceed the difference between the purchase or sale price paid or received, as appropriate, by the plaintiff for the security and the mean trading price of the security during the period beginning immediately after dissemination of information correcting the misstatement or omission and ending on the date on which the plaintiff sells or repurchases the security.

(3) *Definition.*—For purposes of this subsection, the "mean trading price" of a security shall be an average of the daily trading price of that security, determined as of the close of the market each day during the 90-day period referred to in paragraph (1).

(f) Proportionate liability

(1) *Applicability.*—Nothing in this subsection shall be construed to create, affect, or in any manner modify, the standard for liability associated with any action arising under the securities laws.

(2) *Liability for damages.*—

(A) Joint and several liability.—Any covered person against whom a final judgment is entered in a private action shall be liable for damages jointly and severally only if the trier of fact specifically determines that such covered person knowingly committed a violation of the securities laws.

(B) Proportionate liability.—

(i) In general.—Except as provided in subparagraph (A), a covered person against whom a final judgment is entered in a private action shall be liable solely for the portion of the judgment that corresponds to the percentage of responsibility of that covered person, as determined under paragraph (3).

(ii) Recovery by and costs of covered person.—In any case in which a contractual relationship permits, a covered person that prevails in any private action may recover the attorney's fees and costs of that covered person in connection with the action.

(3) *Determination of responsibility.*—

(A) *In general.*—In any private action, the court shall instruct the jury to answer special interrogatories, or if there is no jury, shall make findings, with respect to each covered person and each of the other persons claimed by any of the parties to have caused or contributed to the loss incurred by the plaintiff, including persons who have entered into settlements with the plaintiff or plaintiffs, concerning—

(i) whether such person violated the securities laws;

(ii) the percentage of responsibility of such person, measured as a percentage of the total fault of all persons who caused or contributed to the loss incurred by the plaintiff; and

(iii) whether such person knowingly committed a violation of the securities laws.

(B) *Contents of special interrogatories or findings.*—The responses to interrogatories, or findings, as appropriate, under subparagraph (A) shall specify the total amount of damages that the plaintiff is entitled to recover and the percentage of responsibility of each covered person found to have caused or contributed to the loss incurred by the plaintiff or plaintiffs.

(C) *Factors for consideration.*—In determining the percentage of responsibility under this paragraph, the trier of fact shall consider—

(i) the nature of the conduct of each covered person found to have caused or contributed to the loss incurred by the plaintiff or plaintiffs; and

(ii) the nature and extent of the causal relationship between the conduct of each such person and the damages incurred by the plaintiff or plaintiffs.

(4) *Uncollectible share.*—

(A) *In general.*—Notwithstanding paragraph (2)(B), [if] upon motion made not later than 6 months after a final judgment is entered in any private action, the court determines that all or part of the share of the judgment of the covered person is not collectible against that covered person, and is also not collectible against a covered person described in paragraph (2)(A), each covered person described in paragraph (2)(B) shall be liable for the uncollectible share as follows:

(i) Percentage of net worth.—Each covered person shall be jointly and severally liable for the uncollectible share if the plaintiff establishes that—

(I) the plaintiff is an individual whose recoverable damages under the final judgment are equal to more than 10 percent of the net worth of the plaintiff; and

(II) the net worth of the plaintiff is equal to less than $200,000.

(ii) Other plaintiffs.—With respect to any plaintiff not described in subclauses (I) and (II) of clause (i), each covered person shall be liable for the uncollectible share in proportion to the percentage of responsibility of that covered person, except that the total liability of a covered person under this clause may not exceed 50 percent of the proportionate share of that covered person, as determined under paragraph (3)(B).

(iii) Net worth.—For purposes of this subparagraph, net worth shall be determined as of the date immediately preceding the date of the purchase or sale (as applicable) by the plaintiff of the security that is the subject of the action, and shall be equal to the fair market value of assets, minus liabilities, including the net value of the investments of the plaintiff in real and personal property (including personal residences).

(B) *Overall limit.*—In no case shall the total payments required pursuant to subparagraph (A) exceed the amount of the uncollectible share.

(C) *Covered persons subject to contribution.*—A covered person against whom judgment is not collectible shall be subject to contribution and to any continuing liability to the plaintiff on the judgment.

(5) *Right of contribution.*—To the extent that a covered person is required to make an additional payment pursuant to paragraph (4), that covered person may recover contribution—

(A) from the covered person originally liable to make the payment;

(B) from any covered person liable jointly and severally pursuant to paragraph (2)(A);

(C) from any covered person held proportionately liable pursuant to this paragraph who is liable to make the same payment and has paid less than his or her proportionate share of that payment; or

(D) from any other person responsible for the conduct giving rise to the payment that would have been liable to make the same payment.

(6) *Nondisclosure to jury.*—The standard for allocation of damages under paragraphs (2) and (3) and the procedure for reallocation of uncollectible shares under paragraph (4) shall not be disclosed to members of the jury.

(7) *Settlement discharge.*—

(A) *In general.*—A covered person who settles any private action at any time before final verdict or judgment shall be discharged from all claims for contribution brought by other persons. Upon entry of the settlement by the court, the court shall enter a bar order constituting the final discharge of all obligations to the plaintiff of the settling covered person arising out of the action. The order shall bar all future claims for contribution arising out of the action—

(i) by any person against the settling covered person; and

(ii) by the settling covered person against any person, other than a person whose liability has been extinguished by the settlement of the settling covered person.

(B) *Reduction.*—If a covered person enters into a settlement with the plaintiff prior to final verdict or judgment, the verdict or judgment shall be reduced by the greater of—

(i) an amount that corresponds to the percentage of responsibility of that covered person; or

(ii) the amount paid to the plaintiff by that covered person.

(8) *Contribution.*—A covered person who becomes jointly and severally liable for damages in any private action may recover contribution from any other person who, if joined in the original action, would have been liable for the same damages. A claim for contribution shall be determined based on the percentage of responsibility of the claimant and of each person against whom a claim for contribution is made.

(9) *Statute of limitations for contribution.*—In any private action determining liability, an action for contribution shall be brought not later than 6 months after the entry of a final, nonappealable judgment in the action, except that an action for contribution brought by a covered person who was required to make an additional payment pursuant to paragraph (4) may be brought not later than 6 months after the date on which such payment was made.

(10) *Definitions.*—For purposes of this subsection—

(A) a covered person "knowingly commits a violation of the securities laws"—

(i) with respect to an action that is based on an untrue statement of material fact or omission of a material fact necessary to make the statement not misleading, if—

(I) that covered person makes an untrue statement of a material fact, with actual knowledge that the representation is false, or omits to state a fact necessary in order to make the statement made not misleading, with actual knowledge that, as a result of the omission, one of the material representations of the covered person is false; and

(II) persons are likely to reasonably rely on that misrepresentation or omission; and

(ii) with respect to an action that is based on any conduct that is not described in clause (i), if that covered person engages in that conduct with actual knowledge of the facts and circumstances that make the conduct of that covered person a violation of the securities laws;

(B) reckless conduct by a covered person shall not be construed to constitute a knowing commission of a violation of the securities laws by that covered person;

(C) the term "covered person" means—

(i) a defendant in any private action arising under this title; or

(ii) a defendant in any private action arising under section 11 of the Securities Act of 1933, who is an outside director of the issuer of the securities that are the subject of the action; and

(D) the term "outside director" shall have the meaning given such term by rule or regulation of the Commission.

§ 21E. Application of Safe Harbor for Forward-Looking Statements

(a) Applicability

This section shall apply only to a forward-looking statement made by—

(1) an issuer that, at the time that the statement is made, is subject to the reporting requirements of section 13(a) or section 15(d);

(2) a person acting on behalf of such issuer;

(3) an outside reviewer retained by such issuer making a statement on behalf of such issuer; or

(4) an underwriter, with respect to information provided by such issuer or information derived from information provided by such issuer.

(b) Exclusions

Except to the extent otherwise specifically provided by rule, regulation, or order of the Commission, this section shall not apply to a forward-looking statement—

(1) that is made with respect to the business or operations of the issuer, if the issuer—

(A) during the 3-year period preceding the date on which the statement was first made—

(i) was convicted of any felony or misdemeanor described in clauses (i) through (iv) of section 15(b)(4)(B); or

(ii) has been made the subject of a judicial or administrative decree or order arising out of a governmental action that—

(I) prohibits future violations of the antifraud provisions of the securities laws;

(II) requires that the issuer cease and desist from violating the antifraud provisions of the securities laws; or

(III) determines that the issuer violated the antifraud provisions of the securities laws;

(B) makes the forward-looking statement in connection with an offering of securities by a blank check company;

(C) issues penny stock;

(D) makes the forward-looking statement in connection with a rollup transaction; or

(E) makes the forward-looking statement in connection with a going private transaction; or

(2) that is—

(A) included in a financial statement prepared in accordance with generally accepted accounting principles;

(B) contained in a registration statement of, or otherwise issued by, an investment company;

(C) made in connection with a tender offer;

(D) made in connection with an initial public offering;

(E) made in connection with an offering by, or relating to the operations of, a partnership, limited liability company, or a direct participation investment program; or

(F) made in a disclosure of beneficial ownership in a report required to be filed with the Commission pursuant to section 13(d).

(c) Safe harbor

(1) *In general.*—Except as provided in subsection (b), in any private action arising under this title that is based on an untrue statement of a material fact or omission of a material fact necessary to make the statement not misleading, a person referred to in subsection (a) shall not be liable with respect to any forward-looking statement, whether written or oral, if and to the extent that—

(A) the forward-looking statement is—

(i) identified as a forward-looking statement, and is accompanied by meaningful cautionary statements identifying important factors that could cause actual results to differ materially from those in the forward-looking statement; or

(ii) immaterial; or

(B) the plaintiff fails to prove that the forward-looking statement—

(i) if made by a natural person, was made with actual knowledge by that person that the statement was false or misleading; or

(ii) if made by a business entity; was—

(I) made by or with the approval of an executive officer of that entity; and

(II) made or approved by such officer with actual knowledge by that officer that the statement was false or misleading.

(2) *Oral forward-looking statements.*—In the case of an oral forward-looking statement made by an issuer that is subject to the reporting requirements of section 13(a) or section 15(d), or by a person acting on behalf of such issuer, the requirement set forth in paragraph (1)(A) shall be deemed to be satisfied—

(A) if the oral forward-looking statement is accompanied by a cautionary statement—

(i) that the particular oral statement is a forward-looking statement; and

(ii) that the actual results might differ materially from those projected in the forward-looking statement; and

(B) if—

(i) the oral forward-looking statement is accompanied by an oral statement that additional information concerning factors that could cause actual results to materially differ from those in the forward-looking statement is contained in a readily available written document, or portion thereof;

(ii) the accompanying oral statement referred to in clause (i) identifies the document, or portion thereof, that contains the additional information about those factors relating to the forward-looking statement; and

(iii) the information contained in that written document is a cautionary statement that satisfies the standard established in paragraph (1)(A).

(3) *Availability.*—Any document filed with the Commission or generally disseminated shall be deemed to be readily available for purposes of paragraph (2).

(4) *Effect on other safe harbors.*—The exemption provided for in paragraph (1) shall be in addition to any exemption that the Commission may establish by rule or regulation under subsection (g).

(d) Duty to update

Nothing in this section shall impose upon any person a duty to update a forward-looking statement.

(e) Dispositive motion

On any motion to dismiss based upon subsection (c)(1), the court shall consider any statement cited in the complaint and any cautionary statement accompanying the forward-looking statement, which are not subject to material dispute, cited by the defendant.

(f) Stay pending decision on motion

In any private action arising under this title, the court shall stay discovery (other than discovery that is specifically directed to the applicability of the exemption provided for in this section) during the pendency of any motion by a defendant for summary judgment that is based on the grounds that—

(1) the statement or omission upon which the complaint is based is a forward-looking statement within the meaning of this section; and

(2) the exemption provided for in this section precludes a claim for relief.

(g) Exemption authority

In addition to the exemptions provided for in this section, the Commission may, by rule or regulation, provide exemptions from or under any provision of this title, including with respect to liability that is based on a statement or that is based on projections or other forward-looking information, if and to the extent that any such exemption is consistent with the public interest and the protection of investors, as determined by the Commission.

(h) Effect on other authority of commission

Nothing in this section limits, either expressly or by implication, the authority of the Commission to exercise similar authority or to adopt similar rules and regulations with respect to forward-looking statements under any other statute under which the Commission exercises rulemaking authority.

(i) Definitions

For purposes of this section, the following definitions shall apply:

(1) *Forward-looking statement.*—The term "forward-looking statement" means—

(A) a statement containing a projection of revenues, income (including income loss), earnings (including earnings loss) per share, capital expenditures, dividends, capital structure, or other financial items;

(B) a statement of the plans and objectives of management for future operations, including plans or objectives relating to the products or services of the issuer;

(C) a statement of future economic performance, including any such statement contained in a discussion and analysis of financial condition by the management or in the results of operations included pursuant to the rules and regulations of the Commission;

(D) any statement of the assumptions underlying or relating to any statement described in subparagraph (A), (B), or (C);

(E) any report issued by an outside reviewer retained by an issuer, to the extent that the report assesses a forward-looking statement made by the issuer; or

(F) a statement containing a projection or estimate of such other items as may be specified by rule or regulation of the Commission.

(2) *Investment Company.*—The term "investment company" has the same meaning as in section 3(a) of the Investment Company Act of 1940.

(3) *Going Private Transaction.*—The term "going private transaction" has the meaning given that term under the rules or regulations of the Commission issued pursuant to section 13(e).

(4) *Person acting on behalf of an issuer.*—The term "person acting on behalf of an issuer" means any officer, director, or employee of such issuer.

(5) *Other terms.*—The terms "blank check company", "rollup transaction", "partnership", "limited liability company", "executive officer of an entity" and "direct participation investment program", have the meanings given those terms by rule or regulation of the Commission.

§ 27.   Jurisdiction of Offenses and Suits

(a)   In general.—The district courts of the United States, and the United States courts of any Territory or other place subject to the jurisdiction of the United States shall have exclusive jurisdiction of violations of this chapter or the rules and regulations thereunder, and of all suits in equity and actions at law brought to enforce any liability or duty created by this chapter or the rules and regulations thereunder. Any criminal proceeding may be brought in the district wherein any act or transaction constituting the violation occurred. Any suit or action to enforce any liability or duty created by this chapter or rules and regulations thereunder, or to enjoin any violation of such chapter or rules and regulations, may be brought in any such district or in the district wherein the defendant is found or is an inhabitant or transacts business, and process in such cases may be served in any other district of which the defendant is an inhabitant or wherever the defendant may be found. . . .

(b)   Extraterritorial jurisdiction.—The district courts of the United States and the United States courts of any Territory shall have jurisdiction of an action or proceeding brought or instituted by the Commission or the United States alleging a violation of the antifraud provisions of this title involving—

(1) conduct within the United States that constitutes significant steps in furtherance of the violation, even if the securities transaction occurs outside the United States and involves only foreign investors; or

(2) conduct occurring outside the United States that has a foreseeable substantial effect within the United States.

§ 27A.   Special Provision Relating to Statute of Limitations on Private Causes of Action

(a)   Effect on pending causes of action

The limitation period for any private civil action implied under section 10(b) of this Act that was commenced on or before June 19, 1991, shall be the limitation period provided by the laws applicable in the jurisdiction, including principles of retroactivity, as such laws existed on June 19, 1991.

(b)   Effect on dismissed causes of action

Any private civil action implied under section 10(b) of this Act that was commenced on or before June 19, 1991—

(1) which was dismissed as time barred subsequent to June 19, 1991, and

(2) which would have been timely filed under the limitation period provided by the laws applicable in the jurisdiction, including principles of retroactivity, as such laws existed on June 19, 1991,

shall be reinstated on motion by the plaintiff not later than 60 days after the date of enactment of this section.

§ 28.   Effect on Existing Law

(a)   Addition of rights and remedies; recovery of actual damages; State Securities Commissions

Except as provided in subsection (f), the rights and remedies provided by this chapter shall be in addition to any and all other rights and remedies that may exist at law or in equity; but no person permitted to maintain a suit for damages under the provisions of this chapter shall recover, through satisfaction of judgment in one or more actions, a total amount in excess of his actual damages on account of the act complained of. Except as otherwise specifically provided in this chapter, nothing in this chapter shall affect the jurisdiction of the securities commission (or any agency or officer performing like functions) of any State over any security or any person insofar as it does not conflict with the provisions of this chapter or the rules and regulations thereunder. No State law which prohibits or regulates the making or promoting of wagering or gaming contracts, or the operation of "bucket shops" or other similar or related activities, shall invalidate any put, call, straddle, option, privilege, or other security subject to this chapter, or apply to any activity which is incidental or related to the offer, purchase, sale, exercise, settlement, or closeout of any such security. . . .

(f)   Limitations on remedies—

(1) *Class action limitations.*—No covered class action based upon the statutory or common law of any State or subdivision thereof may be maintained in any State or Federal court by any private party alleging—

(A) a misrepresentation or omission of a material fact in connection with the purchase or sale of a covered security; or

(B) that the defendant used or employed any manipulative or deceptive device or contrivance in connection with the purchase or sale of a covered security.

(2) *Removal of covered class actions.*—Any covered class action brought in any State court involving a covered security, as set forth in paragraph (1), shall be removable to the Federal district court for the district in which the action is pending, and shall be subject to paragraph (1).

(3) *Preservation of certain actions.*—

(A) *Actions under the state law of state of incorporation.*—

(i) *Actions preserved.*—Notwithstanding paragraph (1) or (2), a covered class action described in clause (ii) of this subparagraph that is based upon the statutory or common law of the State in which the issuer is incorporated (in the case of a corporation) or organized (in the case of any other entity) may be maintained in a State or Federal court by a private party.

(ii) *Permissible actions.*—A covered class action is described in this clause if it involves—

(I) the purchase or sale of securities by the issuer or an affiliate of the issuer exclusively from or to holders of equity securities of the issuer; or

(II) any recommendation, position, or other communication with respect to the sale of securities of an issuer that—

(aa) is made by or on behalf of the issuer or an affiliate of the issuer to holders of equity securities of the issuer; and

(bb) concerns decisions of such equity holders with respect to voting their securities, acting in response to a tender or exchange offer, or exercising dissenters' or appraisal rights.

(B) *State actions.*—

(i) *In general.*—Notwithstanding any other provision of this subsection, nothing in this subsection may be construed to preclude a State or political subdivision thereof or a State pension plan from bringing an action involving a covered security on its own behalf, or as a member of a class comprised solely of other States, political subdivisions, or State pension plans that are named plaintiffs, and that have authorized participation, in such action.

(ii) *State pension plan defined.*—For purposes of this subparagraph, the term "State pension plan" means a pension plan established and maintained for its employees by the government of a State or political subdivision thereof, or by any agency or instrumentality thereof.

(C) *Actions under contractual agreements between issuers and indenture trustees.*— Notwithstanding paragraph (1) or (2), a covered class action that seeks to enforce a contractual agreement between an issuer and an indenture trustee may be maintained in a State or Federal court by a party to the agreement or a successor to such party.

(D) *Remand of removed actions.*—In an action that has been removed from a State court pursuant to paragraph (2), if the Federal court determines that the action may be maintained in State court pursuant to this subsection, the Federal court shall remand such action to such State court.

(4) *Preservation of state jurisdiction.*—The securities commission (or any agency or office performing like functions) of any State shall retain jurisdiction under the laws of such State to investigate and bring enforcement actions.

(5) *Definitions.*—For purposes of this subsection, the following definitions shall apply:

(A) *Affiliate of the issuer.*—The term "affiliate of the issuer" means a person that directly or indirectly, through one or more intermediaries, controls or is controlled by or is under common control with, the issuer.

(B) *Covered class action.*—The term "covered class action" means—

(i) any single lawsuit in which—

(I) damages are sought on behalf of more than 50 persons or prospective class members, and questions of law or fact common to those persons or members of the prospective class, without reference to issues of individualized reliance on an alleged misstatement or omission, predominate over any questions affecting only individual persons or members; or

(II) one or more named parties seek to recover damages on a representative basis on behalf of themselves and other unnamed parties similarly situated, and questions of law or fact common to those persons or members of the prospective class predominate over any questions affecting only individual persons or members; or

(ii) any group of lawsuits filed in or pending in the same court and involving common questions of law or fact, in which—

(I) damages are sought on behalf of more than 50 persons; and

(II) the lawsuits are joined, consolidated, or otherwise proceed as a single action for any purpose.

(C) *Exception for derivative actions.*—Notwithstanding subparagraph (B), the term "covered class action" does not include an exclusively derivative action brought by one or more shareholders on behalf of a corporation.

(D) *Counting of certain class members.*—For purposes of this paragraph, a corporation, investment company, pension plan, partnership, or other entity, shall be treated as one person or prospective class member, but only if the entity is not established for the purpose of participating in the action.

(E) *Covered security.*—The term "covered security" means a security that satisfies the standards for a covered security specified in paragraph (1) or (2) of section 18(b) of the Securities Act of 1933, at the time during which it is alleged that the misrepresentation omission, or manipulative or deceptive conduct occurred, except that such term shall not include any debt security that is exempt from registration under the Securities Act of 1933 pursuant to rules issued by the Commission under section 4(2) of that Act.

(F) *Rule of construction.*—Nothing in this paragraph shall be construed to affect the discretion of a State court in determining whether actions filed in such court should be joined, consolidated, or otherwise allowed to proceed as a single action.

§ 29.   Validity of Contracts

(a)   Waiver provisions

Any condition, stipulation, or provision binding any person to waive compliance with any provision of this chapter or of any rule or regulation thereunder, or of any rule of a self-regulatory organization, shall be void.

(b)   Contract provisions in violation of chapter

Every contract made in violation of any provision of this chapter or of any rule or regulation thereunder, and every contract (including any contract for listing a security on an exchange) heretofore or hereafter made, the performance of which involves the violation of, or the continuance of any relationship or practice in violation of, any provision of this chapter or any rule or regulation thereunder, shall be void (1) as regards the rights of any person who, in violation of any such provision, rule, or regulation, shall have made or engaged in the performance of any such contract, and (2) as regards the rights of any person who, not being a party to such contract, shall have acquired any right thereunder with actual knowledge of the facts by reason of which the making or performance of such contract was in violation of any such provision, rule, or regulation. . . .

§ 30A.   Prohibited Foreign Trade Practices by Issuers

(a)   Prohibition

It shall be unlawful for any issuer which has a class of securities registered pursuant to section 12 of this title or which is required to file reports under section 15(d) of this title, or for any officer, director, employee, or agent of such issuer or any stockholder thereof acting on behalf of such issuer, to make use of the mails or any means or instrumentality of interstate commerce corruptly in furtherance of an offer, payment, promise to pay, or authorization of the payment of any money, or offer, gift, promise to give, or authorization of the giving of anything of value to—

(1) any foreign official for purposes of—

(A)(i) influencing any act or decision of such foreign official in his official capacity, (ii) inducing such foreign official to do or omit to do any act in violation of the lawful duty of such official, or (iii) securing any improper advantage; or

(B) inducing such foreign official to use his influence with a foreign government or instrumentality thereof to affect or influence any act or decision of such government or instrumentality,

in order to assist such issuer in obtaining or retaining business for or with, or directing business to, any person;

(2) any foreign political party or official thereof or any candidate for foreign political office for purposes of—

(A)(i) influencing any act or decision of such party, official, or candidate in its or his official capacity, (ii) inducing such party, official, or candidate to do or omit to do an act in violation of the lawful duty of such party, official, or candidate, or (iii) securing any improper advantage; or

(B) inducing such party, official, or candidate to use its or his influence with a foreign government or instrumentality thereof to affect or influence any act or decision of such government or instrumentality

in order to assist such issuer in obtaining or retaining business for or with, or directing business to, any person; or

(3) any person, while knowing that all or a portion of such money or thing of value will be offered, given, or promised, directly or indirectly, to any foreign official, to any foreign political party or official thereof, or to any candidate for foreign political office, for purposes of—

(A)(i) influencing any act or decision of such foreign official, political party, party official, or candidate in his or its official capacity, (ii) inducing such foreign official, political party, party official, or candidate to do or omit to do any act in violation of the lawful duty of such foreign official, political party, party official, or candidate, or (iii) securing any improper advantage; or

(B) inducing such foreign official, political party, party official, or candidate to use his or its influence with a foreign government or instrumentality thereof to affect or influence any act or decision of such government or instrumentality

in order to assist such issuer in obtaining or retaining business for or with, or directing business to, any person.

(b)   Exception for routine governmental action

Subsections (a) and (g) of this section shall not apply to any facilitating or expediting payment to a foreign official, political party, or party official the purpose of which is to expedite or to secure the performance of a routine governmental action by a foreign official, political party, or party official.

(c)   Affirmative defenses

It shall be an affirmative defense to actions under subsections (a) and (g) of this section that—

(1) the payment, gift, offer, or promise of anything of value that was made, was lawful under the written laws and regulations of the foreign official's, political party's, party official's, or candidate's country; or

(2) the payment, gift, offer, or promise of anything of value that was made, was a reasonable and bona fide expenditure, such as travel and lodging expenses, incurred by or on behalf of a foreign official, party, party official, or candidate and was directly related to—

(A) the promotion, demonstration, or explanation of products or services; or

(B) the execution or performance of a contract with a foreign government or agency thereof. . . .

(f)   Definitions

For purposes of this section:

(1)(A) The term "foreign official" means any officer or employee of a foreign government or any department, agency, or instrumentality thereof, or of a public international organization, or any person acting in an official capacity for or on behalf of any such government or department, agency, or instrumentality, or for or on behalf of any such public international organization.

(B) For purposes of subparagraph (A), the term "public international organization" means—

(i) an organization that is designated by Executive order pursuant to section 1 of the International Organizations Immunities Act; or

(ii) any other international organization that is designated by the President by Executive order for the purposes of this section, effective as of the date of publication of such order in the Federal Register.

(2)(A) A person's state of mind is "knowing" with respect to conduct, a circumstance, or a result if—

(i) such person is aware that such person is engaging in such conduct, that such circumstance exists, or that such result is substantially certain to occur; or

(ii) such person has a firm belief that such circumstance exists or that such result is substantially certain to occur.

(B) When knowledge of the existence of a particular circumstance is required for an offense, such knowledge is established if a person is aware of a high probability of the existence of such circumstance, unless the person actually believes that such circumstance does not exist.

(3)(A) The term "routine governmental action" means only an action which is ordinarily and commonly performed by a foreign official in—

(i) obtaining permits, licenses, or other official documents to qualify a person to do business in a foreign country;

(ii) processing governmental papers, such as visas and work orders;

(iii) providing police protection, mail pick-up and delivery, or scheduling inspections associated with contract performance or inspections related to transit of goods across country;

(iv) providing phone service, power and water supply, loading and unloading cargo, or protecting perishable products or commodities from deterioration; or

(v) actions of a similar nature.

(B) The term "routine governmental action" does not include any decision by a foreign official whether, or on what terms, to award new business to or to continue business with a particular party, or any action taken by a foreign official involved in the decision-making process to encourage a decision to award new business to or continue business with a particular party.

(g) Alternative jurisdiction—

(1) It shall also be unlawful for any issuer organized under the laws of the United States, or a State, territory, possession, or commonwealth of the United States or a political subdivision thereof and which has a class of securities registered pursuant to section 12 of this title or which is required to file reports under section 15(d) of this title, or for any United States person that is an officer, director, employee, or agent of such issuer or a stockholder thereof acting on behalf of such issuer, to corruptly do any act outside the United States in furtherance of an offer, payment, promise to pay, or authorization of the payment of any money, or offer, gift, promise to give, or authorization of the giving of anything of value to any of the persons or entities set forth in paragraphs (1), (2), and (3) of subsection (a) of this section for the purposes set forth therein, irrespective of whether such issuer or such officer, director, employee, agent, or stockholder makes use of the mails or any means or instrumentality of interstate commerce in furtherance of such offer, gift, payment, promise, or authorization.

(2) As used in this subsection, the term "United States person" means a national of the United States (as defined in section 101 of the Immigration and Nationality Act), or any corporation, partnership, association, joint-stock company, business trust, unincorporated organization, or sole proprietorship organized under the laws of the United States or any State, territory, possession, or commonwealth of the United States, or any political subdivision thereof.

§ 32. Penalties

(a) Willful violations; false and misleading statements

Any person who willfully violates any provision of this chapter (other than section 30A of this title), or any rule or regulation thereunder the violation of which is made unlawful or the observance of which is required under the terms of this chapter, or any person who willfully and knowingly makes, or causes to be made, any statement in any application, report, or document required to be filed under this chapter or any rule or regulation thereunder or any undertaking contained in a registration statement as provided in subsection (d) of section 15 of this title, or by any self-regulatory organization in connection with an application for membership or participation therein or to become associated with a member thereof, which statement was false or misleading with respect to any material fact, shall upon conviction be fined not more than $5,000,000, or imprisoned not more than 20 years, or both, except that when such person is a person other than a natural person, a fine not exceeding $25,000,000 may be imposed; but no person shall be subject to imprisonment under this section for the violation of any rule or regulation if he proves that he had no knowledge of such rule or regulation.

(b) Failure to file information, documents, or reports

Any issuer which fails to file information, documents, or reports required to be filed under subsection (d) of section 15 of this title or any rule or regulation thereunder shall forfeit to the United States the sum of $210 for each and every day such failure to file shall continue. Such forfeiture, which shall be in lieu of any criminal penalty for such failure to file which might be deemed to arise under subsection (a) of this section, shall be payable into the Treasury of the United States and shall be recoverable in a civil suit in the name of the United States.

(c) Violations by issuers, officers, directors, stockholders, employees, or agents of issuers

(1)(A) Any issuer that violates subsection (a) or (g) of section 30A of this title shall be fined no more than $2,000,000.

(B) Any issuer that violates subsection (a) or (g) of section 30A of this title shall be subject to a civil penalty of not more than $16,000 imposed in an action brought by the Commission.

(2)(A) Any officer, director, employee, or agent of an issuer, or stockholder acting on behalf of such issuer, who willfully violates subsection (a) or (g) of section 30A of this title shall be fined not more than $100,000, or imprisoned not more than 5 years, or both.

(B) Any officer, director, employee, or agent of an issuer, or stockholder acting on behalf of such issuer, who violates subsection (a) or (g) of section 30A of this title shall be subject to a civil penalty of not more than $10,000 imposed in an action brought by the Commission.

(3) Whenever a fine is imposed under paragraph (2) upon any officer, director, employee, agent, or stockholder of an issuer, such fine may not be paid, directly or indirectly, by such issuer.

§ 36.   General Exemptive Authority

(a) Authority

(1) *In general.*—Except as provided in subsection (b) of this section, but notwithstanding any other provision of this chapter, the Commission, by rule, regulation, or order, may conditionally or unconditionally exempt any person, security, or transaction, or any class or classes of persons, securities, or transactions, from any provision or provisions of this chapter or of any rule or regulation thereunder, to the extent that such exemption is necessary or appropriate in the public interest, and is consistent with the protection of investors.

(2) *Procedures.*—The Commission shall, by rule or regulation, determine the procedures under which an exemptive order under this section shall be granted and may, in its sole discretion, decline to entertain any application for an order of exemption under this section.

(b) Limitation

The Commission may not, under this section, exempt any person, security, or transaction, or any class or classes of persons, securities, or transactions from section 15C [Government Securities Brokers and Dealers] or the rules or regulations issued thereunder. . . .

RULES AND FORMS UNDER THE SECURITIES EXCHANGE ACT OF 1934 (SELECTED PROVISIONS)

17 C.F.R. §§ 240.0–1 et seq.

TABLE OF CONTENTS

DEFINITIONS

Rule		Page
3a11–1.	Definition of the Term "Equity Security"	1448
3b–2.	Definition of "Officer"	1448
3b–6.	Liability for Certain Statements by Issuers	1448
3b–7.	Definition of "Executive Officer"	1449
3b–11.	Definitions Relating to Limited Partnership Roll-Up Transactions for Purposes of Sections 6(b)(9), 14(h) and 15A(b)(12)–(13)	1449

MANIPULATIVE AND DECEPTIVE DEVICES AND CONTRIVANCES

10b–5.	Employment of Manipulative and Deceptive Devices	1449
10b5–1.	Trading on the Basis of Material Nonpublic Information in Insider Trading Cases	1450
10b5–2.	Duties of Trust or Confidence in Misappropriation Insider Trading Cases	1451
10b–18.	Purchase of Certain Equity Securities by the Issuer and Others	1451

REPORTS UNDER SECTION 10A

10A–1.	Notice to the Commission Pursuant to Section 10A of the Act	1455
10A–2.	Auditor Independence	1456
10A–3.	Listing Standards Relating to Audit Committees	1456
10C–1.	Listing Standards Relating to Compensation Committees	1458

REGULATION 12B: REGISTRATION AND REPORTING

12b–2.	Definitions	1461

EXTENSIONS AND TEMPORARY EXEMPTIONS: DEFINITIONS

12g–1.	Exemption From Section 12(g)	1463
12g3–2.	Exemption for . . . Certain Foreign Securities	1463
12g–4.	Certification of Termination of Registration Under Section 12(g)	1464

REGULATION 13A: REPORTS OF ISSUERS OF SECURITIES REGISTERED PURSUANT TO SECTION 12

13a–1.	Requirements of Annual Reports	1465
13a–11.	Current Reports on Form 8-K	1465
13a–13.	Quarterly Reports on Form 10-Q	1465
13a–14.	Certification of Disclosure in Annual and Quarterly Reports	1465
13a–15.	Controls and Procedures	1465
13a–20.	Plain English Presentation of Specified Information	1466
Form 8-K.	Current Report Pursuant to Section 13 or 15(d) of the Securities Exchange Act of 1934	1468
Form 10-Q.		1482
Form 10-K.	Annual Report Pursuant to Section 13 or 15(d) of The Securities Exchange Act of 1934	1485
13b2–2.	Representations and Conduct in Connection With the Preparation of Required Reports and Documents	1488

SECURITIES EXCHANGE ACT OF 1934

REGULATION 13D–G

13d–1. Filing of Schedules 13D and 13G 1489
13d–2. Filing of Amendments to Schedules 13D or 13G 1491
13d–3. Determination of Beneficial Owner 1492
13d–4. Disclaimer of Beneficial Ownership 1493
13d–5. Acquisition of Securities 1493
13d–7. Dissemination 1493
Schedule 13D. Information to be Included in Statements Filed Pursuant to Rule 13d–1(a) and . . . Rule 13d–2(a) 1494
Schedule 13G. Information to be Included in Statements Filed Pursuant to Rule 13d–1(b), (c), and (d) 1496
13e–1. Purchase of Securities by the Issuer During a Third-Party Tender Offer 1496
13e–3. Going Private Transactions by Certain Issuers or Their Affiliates 1497
13e–4. Tender Offers by Issuers 1499
Schedule 13E–3. Transaction Statement Under Section 13(e) 1503
13h–1. Large Trader Reporting 1504

REGULATION 14A: SOLICITATION OF PROXIES

14a–1. Definitions 1508
14a–2. Solicitations to Which Rule 14a–3 to Rule 14a–15 Apply 1509
14a–3. Information to Be Furnished to Security Holders 1512
14a–4. Requirements as to Proxy 1513
14a–5. Presentation of Information in Proxy Statement 1516
14a–6. Filing Requirements 1516
14a–7. Obligations of Registrants to Provide a List of, or Mail Soliciting Material to, Security Holders 1518
14a–8. Shareholder Proposals 1520
14a–9. False or Misleading Statements 1525
14a–10. Prohibition of Certain Solicitations 1525
14a–12. Solicitation Before Furnishing a Proxy Statement 1525
14a–15. Differential and Contingent Compensation in Connection With Roll-Up Transactions 1526
14a–16. Internet Availability of Proxy Materials 1526
14a–17. Electronic Shareholder Forums 1530
14a–18. Disclosure Regarding Nominating Shareholders and Nominees Submitted for Inclusion in a Registrant's Proxy Materials Pursuant to Applicable State or Foreign Law, or a Registrant's Governing Documents 1530
14a–20. Shareholder Approval of Executive Compensation of TARP Recipients 1531
14a–21. Shareholder Approval of Executive Compensation, Frequency of Votes for Approval of Executive Compensation and Shareholder Approval of Golden Parachute Compensation 1531
Schedule 14A. Information Required in Proxy Statement 1531
—— [Form of] Notice of Exempt Solicitation—Information to Be Included in Statements Submitted by or on Behalf of a Person Pursuant to Rule 6(g) 1539
14b–1. Obligation of Registered Brokers and Dealers in Connection with the Prompt Forwarding of Certain Communications to Beneficial Owners 1539
14b–2. Obligation of Banks, Associations and Other Entities That Exercise Fiduciary Powers in Connection with the Prompt Forwarding of Certain Communications to Beneficial Owners 1540

REGULATION 14C: DISTRIBUTION OF INFORMATION PURSUANT TO SECTION 14(c)

14c–2. Distribution of Information Statement 1542
14c–3. Annual Report to Be Furnished Security Holders 1542
Schedule 14C. Information Required in Information Statement 1542

SELECTED RULES AND FORMS

REGULATION 14D

14d–1. Scope of and Definitions Applicable to Regulations 14D and 14E 1543
14d–2. Commencement of a Tender Offer 1544
14d–3. Filing and Transmission of Tender Offer Statement 1544
14d–4. Dissemination of Tender Offers to Security Holders 1544
14d–6. Disclosure of Tender Offer Information to Security Holders 1545
14d–7. Additional Withdrawal Rights 1546
14d–8. Exemption From Statutory Pro Rata Requirements 1547
14d–9. Recommendation or Solicitation by the Subject Company and Others 1547
14d–10. Equal Treatment of Security Holders 1548
14d–11. Subsequent Offering Period 1549
Schedule TO. Tender Offer Statement Under Section 14(d)(1) or 13(e)(1) 1550
Schedule 14D-9. Solicitation/Recommendation Statement Pursuant to Section 14(d)(4) of the
　　　Securities Exchange Act of 1934 1552

REGULATION 14E

14e–1. Unlawful Tender Offer Practices 1553
14e–2. Position of Subject Company With Respect to a Tender Offer 1553
14e–3. Transactions in Securities on the Basis of Material, Nonpublic Information in the
　　　Context of Tender Offers 1553
14e–4. Prohibited Transactions in Connection With Partial Tender Offers 1554
14e–5. Prohibiting Purchases Outside of a Tender Offer 1556
14e–7. Unlawful Tender Offer Practices in Connection With Roll-Ups 1558
14e–8. Prohibited Conduct in Connection with Pre-Commencement Communications 1558
14f–1. Change in Majority of Directors 1558

REGULATION 14N: FILINGS REQUIRED BY CERTAIN NOMINATING SHAREHOLDERS

14n–1. Filing of Schedule 14N 1559
14n–2. Filing of Amendments to Schedule 14N 1559
14n–3. Dissemination 1559

REGULATION 15D: REPORTS OF REGISTRANTS UNDER THE SECURITIES ACT OF 1933

15d–1. Requirement of Annual Reports 1561
15d–11. Current Reports on Form 8-K 1561
15d–13. Quarterly Reports on Form 10-Q 1561
15d–14. Certification of Disclosure in Annual and Quarterly Reports 1561
15d–15. Controls and Procedures 1562
15d–20. Plain English Presentation of Specified Information 1562

REPORTS OF DIRECTORS, OFFICERS, AND PRINCIPAL SHAREHOLDERS

16a–1. Definition of Terms 1563
16a–2. Persons and Transactions Subject to Section 16 1565
16a–3. Reporting Transactions and Holdings 1565
16a–4. Derivative Securities 1566
16a–6. Small Acquisitions 1566
16a–8. Trusts 1567
16a–9. Stock Splits, Stock Dividends, and Pro Rata Rights 1567
16a–10. Exemptions Under Section 16(a) 1567
16a–12. Domestic Relations Orders 1567
16a–13. Change in Form of Beneficial Ownership 1567

EXEMPTION OF CERTAIN TRANSACTIONS FROM SECTION 16(b)

16b–3.   Transactions Between Issuer and Its Officers or Directors... 1568
16b–5.   Bona Fide Gifts and Inheritance.. 1569
16b–6.   Derivative Securities 1570
16b–7.   Mergers, Reclassifications, and Consolidations 1570
Form 3.   Initial Statement of Beneficial Ownership of Securities 1572
Form 4.   Statement of Changes of Beneficial Ownership of Securities... 1576
Form 5.   Annual Statement of Beneficial Ownership of Securities... 1580

DEFINITIONS . . .

Rule 3a11–1. Definition of the Term "Equity Security"

The term "equity security" is hereby defined to include any stock or similar security, certificate of interest or participation in any profit sharing agreement, preorganization certificate or subscription, transferable share, voting trust certificate or certificate of deposit for an equity security, limited partnership interest, interest in a joint venture, or certificate of interest in a business trust; any security future on any such security; or any security convertible, with or without consideration into such a security, or carrying any warrant or right to subscribe to or purchase such a security; or any such warrant or right; or any put, call, straddle, or other option or privilege of buying such a security from or selling such a security to another without being bound to do so.

Rule 3b–2. Definition of "Officer"

The term "officer" means a president, vice president, secretary, treasurer or principal financial officer, comptroller or principal accounting officer, and any person routinely performing corresponding functions with respect to any organization whether incorporated or unincorporated.

Rule 3b–6. Liability for Certain Statements by Issuers

(a) A statement within the coverage of paragraph (b) of this section which is made by or on behalf of an issuer or by an outside reviewer retained by the issuer shall be deemed not to be a fraudulent statement (as defined in paragraph (d) of this section), unless it is shown that such statement was made or reaffirmed without a reasonable basis or was disclosed other than in good faith.

(b) This rule applies to the following statements:

(1) A forward-looking statement (as defined in paragraph (c) of this section) made in a document filed with the Commission, in Part I of a quarterly report on Form 10-Q, or in an annual report to security holders meeting the requirements of Rules 14a–3(b) and (c) or 14c–3(a) and (b), a statement reaffirming such forward-looking statement after the date the document was filed or the annual report was made publicly available, or a forward-looking statement made before the date the document was filed or the date the annual report was made publicly available if such statement is reaffirmed in a filed document, in Part I of a quarterly report on Form 10-Q, or in an annual report made publicly available within a reasonable time after the making of such forward-looking statement; *Provided*, that:

(i) At the time such statements are made or reaffirmed, either the issuer is subject to the reporting requirements of Section 13(a) or 15(d) of the Act and has complied with the requirements of Rule 13a-l or 15d-l thereunder, if applicable, to file its most recent annual report on Form 10-K . . . or if the issuer is not subject to the reporting requirements of Section 13(a) or 15(d) of the Act, the statements are made in a registration statement filed under the Securities Act of 1933, offering statement or solicitation of interest, written document or broadcast script under Regulation A or pursuant to Section 12 (b) or (g) of the Securities Exchange Act of 1934; and . . .

(2) Information that is disclosed in a document filed with the Commission in Part I of a quarterly report on Form 10-Q or in an annual report to security holders meeting the requirements of Rules 14a–3(b) and (c) or 14c–3(a) and (b) under the Act and that relates to:

(i) The effects of changing prices on the business enterprise . . . ; or

(ii) The value of proved oil and gas reserves. . . .

(c) For the purpose of this rule, the term *forward-looking statement* shall mean and shall be limited to:

(1) A statement containing a projection of revenues, income (loss), earnings (loss) per share, capital expenditures, dividends, capital structure or other financial items;

(2) A statement of management's plans and objectives for future operations;

(3) A statement of future economic performance contained in management's discussion and analysis of financial condition and results of operations included pursuant to Item 303 of Regulation S–K . . .

(4) Disclosed statements of the assumptions underlying or relating to any of the statements described in paragraphs (c)(1), (2), or (3) of this section.

(d) For the purpose of this rule the term *fraudulent statement* shall mean a statement which is an untrue statement of a material fact, a statement false or misleading with respect to any material fact, an omission to state a material fact necessary to make a statement not misleading, or which constitutes the employment of a manipulative, deceptive, or fraudulent device, contrivance, scheme, transaction, act, practice, course of business, or an artifice to defraud, as those terms are used in the Securities Exchange Act of 1934 or the rules or regulations promulgated thereunder.

Rule 3b–7. Definition of "Executive Officer"

The term "executive officer," when used with reference to a registrant, means its president, any vice president of the registrant in charge of a principal business unit, division or function (such as sales, administration, or finance), any other officer who performs a policy making function or any other person who performs similar policy making functions for the registrant. Executive officers of subsidiaries may be deemed executive officers of the registrant if they perform such policy making functions for the registrant.

Rule 3b–11. Definitions Relating to Limited Partnership Roll-Up Transactions for Purposes of Sections 6(b)(9), 14(h) and 15A(b)(12)–(13)

For purposes of Sections 6(b)(9), 14(h) and 15A(b)(12)–(13) of the Act . . . ;

(a) The term *limited partnership roll-up transaction* does not include a transaction involving only entities that are not "finite-life" as defined in Item 901(b)(2) of Regulation S–K. . . .

(c) The term "regularly traded" shall be defined as in Item 901(c)(2)(v)(C) of Regulation S–K.

MANIPULATIVE AND DECEPTIVE DEVICES AND CONTRIVANCES. . . .

Rule 10b–5. Employment of Manipulative and Deceptive Devices

It shall be unlawful for any person, directly or indirectly, by the use of any means or instrumentality of interstate commerce, or of the mails or of any facility of any national securities exchange,

(a) To employ any device, scheme, or artifice to defraud,

(b) To make any untrue statement of a material fact or to omit to state a material fact necessary in order to make the statements made, in the light of the circumstances under which they were made, not misleading, or

(c) To engage in any act, practice, or course of business which operates or would operate as a fraud or deceit upon any person, in connection with the purchase or sale of any security.

Rule 10b5–1. Trading on the Basis of Material Nonpublic Information in Insider Trading Cases

Preliminary Note to Rule 10b5–1: This provision defines when a purchase or sale constitutes trading "on the basis of" material nonpublic information in insider trading cases brought under Section 10(b) of the Act and Rule 10b–5 thereunder. The law of insider trading is otherwise defined by judicial opinions construing Rule 10b–5, and Rule 10b5–1 does not modify the scope of insider trading law in any other respect.

(a) *General.* The "manipulative and deceptive devices" prohibited by Section 10(b) of the Act and Rule 10b–5 thereunder include, among other things, the purchase or sale of a security of any issuer, on the basis of material nonpublic information about that security or issuer, in breach of a duty of trust or confidence that is owed directly, indirectly, or derivatively, to the issuer of that security or the shareholders of that issuer, or to any other person who is the source of the material nonpublic information.

(b) *Definition of "on the basis of."* Subject to the affirmative defenses in paragraph (c) of this section, a purchase or sale of a security of an issuer is "on the basis of" material nonpublic information about that security or issuer if the person making the purchase or sale was aware of the material nonpublic information when the person made the purchase or sale.

(c) *Affirmative defenses.*

(1)(i) Subject to paragraph (c)(1)(ii) of this section, a person's purchase or sale is not "on the basis of" material nonpublic information if the person making the purchase or sale demonstrates that:

(A) Before becoming aware of the information, the person had:

(1) Entered into a binding contract to purchase or sell the security,

(2) Instructed another person to purchase or sell the security for the instructing person's account, or

(3) Adopted a written plan for trading securities;

(B) The contract, instruction, or plan described in paragraph (c)(1)(i)(A) of this Section:

(1) Specified the amount of securities to be purchased or sold and the price at which and the date on which the securities were to be purchased or sold;

(2) Included a written formula or algorithm, or computer program, for determining the amount of securities to be purchased or sold and the price at which and the date on which the securities were to be purchased or sold; or

(3) Did not permit the person to exercise any subsequent influence over how, when, or whether to effect purchases or sales; provided, in addition, that any other person who, pursuant to the contract, instruction, or plan, did exercise such influence must not have been aware of the material nonpublic information when doing so; and

(C) The purchase or sale that occurred was pursuant to the contract, instruction, or plan. A purchase or sale is not "pursuant to a contract, instruction, or plan" if, among other things, the person who entered into the contract, instruction, or plan altered or deviated from the contract, instruction, or plan to purchase or sell securities (whether by changing the amount, price, or timing of the purchase or sale), or entered into or altered a corresponding or hedging transaction or position with respect to those securities.

(ii) Paragraph (c)(1)(i) of this section is applicable only when the contract, instruction, or plan to purchase or sell securities was given or entered into in good faith and not as part of a plan or scheme to evade the prohibitions of this section.

(iii) This paragraph (c)(1)(iii) defines certain terms as used in paragraph (c) of this Section.

(A) *Amount.* "Amount" means either a specified number of shares or other securities or a specified dollar value of securities.

(B) *Price.* "Price" means the market price on a particular date or a limit price, or a particular dollar price.

(C) *Date.* "Date" means, in the case of a market order, the specific day of the year on which the order is to be executed (or as soon thereafter as is practicable under ordinary principles of best execution). "Date" means, in the case of a limit order, a day of the year on which the limit order is in force.

(2) A person other than a natural person also may demonstrate that a purchase or sale of securities is not "on the basis of" material nonpublic information if the person demonstrates that:

(i) The individual making the investment decision on behalf of the person to purchase or sell the securities was not aware of the information; and

(ii) The person had implemented reasonable policies and procedures, taking into consideration the nature of the person's business, to ensure that individuals making investment decisions would not violate the laws prohibiting trading on the basis of material nonpublic information. These policies and procedures may include those that restrict any purchase, sale, and causing any purchase or sale of any security as to which the person has material nonpublic information, or those that prevent such individuals from becoming aware of such information.

Rule 10b5–2. Duties of Trust or Confidence in Misappropriation Insider Trading Cases

Preliminary Note to Rule 10b5–2: This section provides a non-exclusive definition of circumstances in which a person has a duty of trust or confidence for purposes of the "misappropriation" theory of insider trading under Section 10(b) of the Act and Rule 10b–5. The law of insider trading is otherwise defined by judicial opinions construing Rule 10b–5, and Rule 10b5–2 does not modify the scope of insider trading law in any other respect.

(a) *Scope of Rule.* This section shall apply to any violation of Section 10(b) of the Act and Rule 10b–5 thereunder that is based on the purchase or sale of securities on the basis of, or the communication of, material nonpublic information misappropriated in breach of a duty of trust or confidence.

(b) *Enumerated "duties of trust or confidence."* For purposes of this section, a "duty of trust or confidence" exists in the following circumstances, among others:

(1) Whenever a person agrees to maintain information in confidence;

(2) Whenever the person communicating the material nonpublic information and the person to whom it is communicated have a history, pattern, or practice of sharing confidences, such that the recipient of the information knows or reasonably should know that the person communicating the material nonpublic information expects that the recipient will maintain its confidentiality; or

(3) Whenever a person receives or obtains material nonpublic information from his or her spouse, parent, child, or sibling; provided, however, that the person receiving or obtaining the information may demonstrate that no duty of trust or confidence existed with respect to the information, by establishing that he or she neither knew nor reasonably should have known that the person who was the source of the information expected that the person would keep the information confidential, because of the parties' history, pattern, or practice of sharing and maintaining confidences, and because there was no agreement or understanding to maintain the confidentiality of the information.

Rule 10b–18. Purchase of Certain Equity Securities by the Issuer and Others

Preliminary Notes to Rule 10b–18

1.   Rule 10b–18 provides an issuer (and its affiliated purchasers) with a "safe harbor" from liability for manipulation under sections 9(a)(2) of the Act and Rule 10b–5 under the Act *solely* by reason of the manner, timing, price, and volume of their repurchases when they repurchase the issuer's common stock in the market in accordance with the section's manner, timing, price, and volume conditions. As a safe harbor, compliance with Rule 10b–18 is voluntary. To come within the safe harbor, however, an issuer's repurchases must satisfy (on a daily basis) each of the section's four conditions. Failure to meet any one of the four

conditions will remove all of the issuer's repurchases from the safe harbor for that day. The safe harbor, moreover, is not available for repurchases that, although made in technical compliance with the section, are part of a plan or scheme to evade the federal securities laws. . . .

(a) *Definitions.* Unless otherwise provided, all terms used in this section shall have the same meaning as in the Act. In addition, the following definitions shall apply:

(1) *ADTV* means the average daily trading volume reported for the security during the four calendar weeks preceding the week in which the Rule 10b–18 purchase is to be effected.

(2) *Affiliate* means any person that directly or indirectly controls, is controlled by, or is under common control with, the issuer.

(3) *Affiliated purchaser* means:

(i) A person acting, directly or indirectly, in concert with the issuer for the purpose of acquiring the issuer's securities; or

(ii) An affiliate who, directly or indirectly, controls the issuer's purchases of such securities, whose purchases are controlled by the issuer, or whose purchases are under common control with those of the issuer; *Provided, however,* that "affiliated purchaser" shall not include a broker, dealer, or other person solely by reason of such broker, dealer, or other person effecting Rule 10b–18 purchases on behalf of the issuer or for its account, and shall not include an officer or director of the issuer solely by reason of that officer or director's participation in the decision to authorize Rule 10b–18 purchases by or on behalf of the issuer. . . .

(5) *Block* means a quantity of stock that either:

(i) Has a purchase price of $200,000 or more; or

(ii) Is at least 5,000 shares and has a purchase price of at least $50,000; or

(iii) Is at least 20 round lots of the security and totals 150 percent or more of the trading volume for that security or, in the event that trading volume data are unavailable, is at least 20 round lots of the security and totals at least one-tenth of one percent (.001) of the outstanding shares of the security, exclusive of any shares owned by any affiliate;

Provided, however, That a block under paragraph (a)(5)(i), (ii), and (iii) shall not include any amount a broker or dealer, acting as principal, has accumulated for the purpose of sale or resale to the issuer or to any affiliated purchaser of the issuer if the issuer or such affiliated purchaser knows or has reason to know that such amount was accumulated for such purpose, nor shall it include any amount that a broker or dealer has sold short to the issuer or to any affiliated purchaser of the issuer if the issuer or such affiliated purchaser knows or has reason to know that the sale was a short sale.

(6) *Consolidated system* means a consolidated transaction or quotation reporting system that collects and publicly disseminates on a current and continuous basis transaction or quotation information in common equity securities pursuant to an effective transaction reporting plan. . . .

(7) *Market-wide trading suspension* means a market-wide trading halt of 30 minutes or more that is:

(i) Imposed pursuant to the rules of a national securities exchange or a national securities association in response to a market-wide decline during a single trading session; or

(ii) Declared by the Commission pursuant to its authority under section 12(k) of the Act. . . .

(9) *Principal market* for a security means the single securities market with the largest reported trading volume for the security during the six full calendar months preceding the week in which the Rule 10b–18 purchase is to be effected. . . .

(11) *Purchase price* means the price paid per share as reported, exclusive of any commission paid to a broker acting as agent, or commission equivalent, mark-up, or differential paid to a dealer.

(12) *Riskless principal transaction* means a transaction in which a broker or dealer after having received an order from an issuer to buy its security, buys the security as principal in the market at the same price to satisfy the issuer's buy order. The issuer's buy order must be effected at the same price per-share

at which the broker or dealer bought the shares to satisfy the issuer's buy order, exclusive of any explicitly disclosed markup or markdown, commission equivalent, or other fee. In addition, only the first leg of the transaction, when the broker or dealer buys the security in the market as principal, is reported under the rules of a self-regulatory organization or under the Act. For purposes of this section, the broker or dealer must have written policies and procedures in place to assure that, at a minimum, the issuer's buy order was received prior to the offsetting transaction; the offsetting transaction is allocated to a riskless principal account or the issuer's account within 60 seconds of the execution; and the broker or dealer has supervisory systems in place to produce records that enable the broker or dealer to accurately and readily reconstruct, in a time-sequenced manner, all orders effected on a riskless principal basis.

(13) *Rule 10b–18 purchase* means a purchase (or any bid or limit order that would effect such purchase) of an issuer's common stock (or an equivalent interest, including a unit of beneficial interest in a trust or limited partnership or a depository share) by or for the issuer or any affiliated purchaser (including riskless principal transactions). However, it does *not* include any purchase of such security:

(i) Effected during the applicable restricted period of a distribution that is subject to § 242.102 of this chapter;

(ii) Effected by or for an issuer plan by an agent independent of the issuer;

(iii) Effected as a fractional share purchase (a fractional interest in a security) evidenced by a script certificate, order form, or similar document;

(iv) Effected during the period from the time of public announcement (as defined in Rule 165(f)) of a merger, acquisition, or similar transaction involving a recapitalization, until the earlier of the completion of such transaction or the completion of the vote by target shareholders. This exclusion does *not* apply to Rule 10b–18 purchases:

(A) Effected during such transaction in which the consideration is solely cash and there is no valuation period; or

(B) Where:

(1) The total volume of Rule 10b–18 purchases effected on any single day does not exceed the lesser of 25% of the security's four-week ADTV or the issuer's average daily Rule 10b–18 purchases during the three full calendar months preceding the date of the announcement of such transaction;

(2) The issuer's block purchases effected pursuant to paragraph (b)(4) of this section do not exceed the average size and frequency of the issuer's block purchases effected pursuant to paragraph (b)(4) of this section during the three full calendar months preceding the date of the announcement of such transaction; and

(3) Such purchases are not otherwise restricted or prohibited;

(v) Effected pursuant to Rule 13e–1;

(vi) Effected pursuant to a tender offer that is subject to Rule 13e–4 or specifically excepted from Rule 13e–4; or

(vii) Effected pursuant to a tender offer that is subject to section 14(d) of the Act and the rules and regulations thereunder.

(b) *Conditions to be met.* Rule 10b–18 purchases shall not be deemed to have violated the anti-manipulation provisions of sections 9(a)(2) or 10(b) of the Act or Rule 10b–5 under the Act, solely by reason of the time, price, or amount of the Rule 10b–18 purchases, or the number of brokers or dealers used in connection with such purchases, if the issuer or affiliated purchaser of the issuer effects the Rule 10b–18 purchases according to each of the following conditions:

(1) *One broker or dealer.* Rule 10b–18 purchases must be effected from or through only one broker or dealer on any single day; *Provided, however,* that:

(i) The "one broker or dealer" condition shall not apply to Rule 10b–18 purchases that are not solicited by or on behalf of the issuer or its affiliated purchaser(s);

(ii) Where Rule 10b–18 purchases are effected by or on behalf of more than one affiliated purchaser of the issuer (or the issuer and one or more of its affiliated purchasers) on a single day, the issuer and all affiliated purchasers must use the same broker or dealer; and

(iii) Where Rule 10b–18 purchases are effected on behalf of the issuer by a broker-dealer that is not an electronic communication network (ECN) or other alternative trading system (ATS), that broker-dealer can access ECN or other ATS liquidity in order to execute repurchases on behalf of the issuer (or any affiliated purchaser of the issuer) on that day.

(2) *Time of purchases.* Rule 10b–18 purchases must not be:

(i) The opening (regular way) purchase reported in the consolidated system;

(ii) Effected during the 10 minutes before the scheduled close of the primary trading session in the principal market for the security, and the 10 minutes before the scheduled close of the primary trading session in the market where the purchase is effected, for a security that has an ADTV value of $1 million or more and a public float value of $150 million or more; and

(iii) Effected during the 30 minutes before the scheduled close of the primary trading session in the principal market for the security, and the 30 minutes before the scheduled close of the primary trading session in the market where the purchase is effected, for all other securities;

(iv) However, for purposes of this section, Rule 10b–18 purchases may be effected following the close of the primary trading session until the termination of the period in which last sale prices are reported in the consolidated system so long as such purchases are effected at prices that do not exceed the lower of the closing price of the primary trading session in the principal market for the security and any lower bids or sale prices subsequently reported in the consolidated system, and all of this section's conditions are met. However, for purposes of this section, the issuer may use one broker or dealer to effect Rule 10b–18 purchases during this period that may be different from the broker or dealer that it used during the primary trading session. However, the issuer's Rule 10b–18 purchase may not be the opening transaction of the session following the close of the primary trading session.

(3) *Price of purchases.* Rule 10b–18 purchases must be effected at a purchase price that:

(i) Does not exceed the highest independent bid or the last independent transaction price, whichever is higher, quoted or reported in the consolidated system at the time the Rule 10b–18 purchase is effected;

(ii) For securities for which bids and transaction prices are not quoted or reported in the consolidated system, Rule 10b–18 purchases must be effected at a purchase price that does not exceed the highest independent bid or the last independent transaction price, whichever is higher, displayed and disseminated on any national securities exchange or on any inter-dealer quotation system . . . that displays at least two priced quotations for the security, at the time the Rule 10b–18 purchase is effected; and

(iii) For all other securities, Rule 10b–18 purchases must be effected at a price no higher than the highest independent bid obtained from three independent dealers.

(4) *Volume of purchases.* The total volume of Rule 10b–18 purchases effected by or for the issuer and any affiliated purchasers effected on any single day must not exceed 25 percent of the ADTV for that security; *However*, once each week, in lieu of purchasing under the 25 percent of ADTV limit for that day, the issuer or an affiliated purchaser of the issuer may effect one block purchase if:

(i) No other Rule 10b–18 purchases are effected that day, and

(ii) The block purchase is *not* included when calculating a security's four week ADTV under this section.

(c) *Alternative conditions.* The conditions of paragraph (b) of this section shall apply in connection with Rule 10b–18 purchases effected during a trading session following the imposition of a market-wide trading suspension, except:

(1) That the time of purchases condition in paragraph (b)(2) of this section shall not apply, either:

(i) From the reopening of trading until the scheduled close of trading on the day that the market-wide trading suspension is imposed; or

(ii) At the opening of trading on the next trading day until the scheduled close of trading that day, if a market-wide trading suspension was in effect at the close of trading on the preceding day; and

(2) The volume of purchases condition in paragraph (b)(4) of this section is modified so that the amount of Rule 10b–18 purchases must not exceed 100 percent of the ADTV for that security.

(d) *Other purchases.* No presumption shall arise that an issuer or an affiliated purchaser has violated the anti-manipulation provisions of sections 9(a)(2) or 10(b) of the Act, or Rule 10b–5 under the Act, if the Rule 10b–18 purchases of such issuer or affiliated purchaser do not meet the conditions specified in paragraph (b) or (c) of this section.

REPORTS UNDER SECTION 10A

Rule 10A–1. Notice to the Commission Pursuant to Section 10A of the Act

(a)(1) If any issuer with a reporting obligation under the Act receives a report requiring a notice to the Commission in accordance with section 10A(b)(3) of the Act, the issuer shall submit such notice to the Commission's Office of the Chief Accountant within the time period prescribed in that section. The notice may be provided by facsimile, telegraph, personal delivery, or any other means, *provided* it is received by the Office of the Chief Accountant within the required time period.

(2) The notice specified in paragraph (a)(1) of this section shall be in writing and:

(i) Shall identify the issuer (including the issuer's name, address, phone number, and file number assigned to the issuer's filings by the Commission) and the independent accountant (including the independent accountant's name and phone number, and the address of the independent accountant's principal office);

(ii) Shall state the date that the issuer received from the independent accountant the report specified in section 10A(b)(2) of the Act;

(iii) Shall provide, at the election of the issuer, either:

(A) A summary of the independent accountant's report, including a description of the act that the independent accountant has identified as a likely illegal act and the possible effect of that act on all affected financial statements of the issuer or those related to the most current three-year period, whichever is shorter; or

(B) A copy of the independent accountant's report; and

(iv) May provide additional information regarding the issuer's views of and response to the independent accountant's report.

(3) Reports of the independent accountant submitted by the issuer to the Commission's Office of the Chief Accountant in accordance with paragraph (a)(2)(iii)(B) of this section shall be deemed to have been made pursuant to section 10A(b)(3) or section 10A(b)(4) of the Act, for purposes of the safe harbor provided by section 10A(c) of the Act.

(4) Submission of the notice in paragraphs (a)(1) and (a)(2) of this section shall not relieve the issuer from its obligations to comply fully with all other reporting requirements, including, without limitation:

(i) The filing requirements of Form 8-K . . . regarding a change in the issuer's certifying accountant and

(ii) The disclosure requirements of Item 304 of Regulation S–K.

(b)(1) Any independent accountant furnishing to the Commission a copy of a report (or the documentation of any oral report) in accordance with section 10A(b)(3) or section 10A(b)(4) of the Act, shall submit that report (or documentation) to the Commission's Office of the Chief Accountant within the time period prescribed by the appropriate section of the Act. The report (or documentation) may be submitted to the Commission's Office of the Chief Accountant by facsimile, telegraph, personal delivery, or any other means, provided it is received by the Office of the Chief Accountant within the time period set forth in section 10A(b)(3) or 10A(b)(4) of the Act, whichever is applicable in the circumstances.

(2) If the report (or documentation) submitted to the Office of the Chief Accountant in accordance with paragraph (b)(1) of this section does not clearly identify both the issuer (including the issuer's name, address, phone number, and file number assigned to the issuer's filings with the Commission) and the independent accountant (including the independent accountant's name and phone number, and the address of the independent accountant's principal office), then the independent accountant shall place that information in a prominent attachment to the report (or documentation) and shall submit that attachment to the Office of the Chief Accountant at the same time and in the same manner as the report (or documentation) is submitted to that Office.

(3) Submission of the report (or documentation) by the independent accountant as described in paragraphs (b)(1) and (b)(2) of this section shall not replace, or otherwise satisfy the need for, the newly engaged and former accountants' letters under Items 304(a)(2)(D) and 304(a)(3) of Regulation S–K, and shall not limit, reduce, or affect in any way the independent accountant's obligations to comply fully with all other legal and professional responsibilities, including, without limitation, those under generally accepted auditing standards and the rules or interpretations of the Commission that modify or supplement those auditing standards.

(c) A notice or report submitted to the Office of the Chief Accountant in accordance with paragraphs (a) and (b) of this section shall be deemed to be an investigative record and shall be non-public and exempt from disclosure pursuant to the Freedom of Information Act to the same extent and for the same periods of time that the Commission's investigative records are non-public and exempt from disclosure. . . . Nothing in this paragraph, however, shall relieve, limit, delay, or affect in any way, the obligation of any issuer or any independent accountant to make all public disclosures required by law, by any Commission disclosure item, rule, report, or form, or by any applicable accounting, auditing, or professional standard. . . .

Rule 10A–2. Auditor Independence

It shall be unlawful for an auditor not to be independent under Rule 2–01(c)(2)(iii)(B), (c)(4), (c)(6), (c)(7), and Rule 2–07.

Rule 10A–3. Listing Standards Relating to Audit Committees. . . .

(a) Pursuant to section 10A(m) of the [Securities Exchange] Act and section 3 of the Sarbanes-Oxley Act of 2002:

(1) *National securities exchanges.* The rules of each national securities exchange registered pursuant to section 6 of the Act must, in accordance with the provisions of this section, prohibit the initial or continued listing of any security of an issuer that is not in compliance with the requirements of any portion of paragraph (b) or (c) of this section.

(2) *National securities associations.* The rules of each national securities association registered pursuant to section 15A of the Act must, in accordance with the provisions of this section, prohibit the initial or continued listing in an automated inter-dealer quotation system of any security of an issuer that is not in compliance with the requirements of any portion of paragraph (b) or (c) of this section. . . .

(4) *Notification of noncompliance.* The rules required by paragraphs (a)(1) and (a)(2) of this section must include a requirement that a listed issuer must notify the applicable national securities exchange or national securities association promptly after an executive officer of the listed issuer becomes aware of any material noncompliance by the listed issuer with the requirements of this section. . . .

(b) *Required standards.*

(1) *Independence.*

(i) Each member of the audit committee must be a member of the board of directors of the listed issuer, and must otherwise be independent; . . . .

(ii) *Independence requirements for non-investment company issuers.* In order to be considered to be independent for purposes of this paragraph (b)(1), a member of an audit committee of a listed issuer that is not an investment company may not, other than in his or her capacity as a member of the audit committee, the board of directors, or any other board committee:

(A) Accept directly or indirectly any consulting, advisory, or other compensatory fee from the issuer or any subsidiary thereof, provided that, unless the rules of the national securities exchange or national securities association provide otherwise, compensatory fees do not include the receipt of fixed amounts of compensation under a retirement plan (including deferred compensation) for prior service with the listed issuer (provided that such compensation is not contingent in any way on continued service); or

(B) Be an affiliated person of the issuer or any subsidiary thereof. . . .

(2) *Responsibilities relating to registered public accounting firms.* The audit committee of each listed issuer, in its capacity as a committee of the board of directors, must be directly responsible for the appointment, compensation, retention and oversight of the work of any registered public accounting firm engaged (including resolution of disagreements between management and the auditor regarding financial reporting) for the purpose of preparing or issuing an audit report or performing other audit, review or attest services for the listed issuer, and each such registered public accounting firm must report directly to the audit committee.

(3) *Complaints.* Each audit committee must establish procedures for:

(i) The receipt, retention, and treatment of complaints received by the listed issuer regarding accounting, internal accounting controls, or auditing matters; and

(ii) The confidential, anonymous submission by employees of the listed issuer of concerns regarding questionable accounting or auditing matters.

(4) *Authority to engage advisers.* Each audit committee must have the authority to engage independent counsel and other advisers, as it determines necessary to carry out its duties.

(5) *Funding.* Each listed issuer must provide for appropriate funding, as determined by the audit committee, in its capacity as a committee of the board of directors, for payment of:

(i) Compensation to any registered public accounting firm engaged for the purpose of preparing or issuing an audit report or performing other audit, review or attest services for the listed issuer;

(ii) Compensation to any advisers employed by the audit committee under paragraph (b)(4) of this section; and

(iii) Ordinary administrative expenses of the audit committee that are necessary or appropriate in carrying out its duties. . . .

(e) *Definitions.* Unless the context otherwise requires, all terms used in this section have the same meaning as in the Act. In addition, unless the context otherwise requires, the following definitions apply for purposes of this section:

(1)(i) The term *affiliate* of, or a person *affiliated* with, a specified person, means a person that directly, or indirectly through one or more intermediaries, controls, or is controlled by, or is under common control with, the person specified.

(ii)(A) A person will be deemed not to be in control of a specified person for purposes of this section if the person:

(1) Is not the beneficial owner, directly or indirectly, of more than 10% of any class of voting equity securities of the specified person; and

(2) Is not an executive officer of the specified person.

(B) Paragraph (e)(1)(ii)(A) of this section only creates a safe harbor position that a person does not control a specified person. The existence of the safe harbor does not create a presumption in any way that a person exceeding the ownership requirement in paragraph (e)(1)(ii)(A)(1) of this section controls or is otherwise an affiliate of a specified person.

(iii) The following will be deemed to be affiliates:

(A) An executive officer of an affiliate;

(B) A director who also is an employee of an affiliate;

(C) A general partner of an affiliate; and

(D) A managing member of an affiliate. . . .

(3) In the case of a listed issuer that is a limited partnership or limited liability company where such entity does not have a board of directors or equivalent body, the term *board of directors* means the board of directors of the managing general partner, managing member or equivalent body.

(4) The term *control* (including the terms *controlling*, *controlled by* and under *common control with*) means the possession, direct or indirect, of the power to direct or cause the direction of the management and policies of a person, whether through the ownership of voting securities, by contract, or otherwise.

(6) The term *executive officer* has the meaning set forth in Rule 3b–7. . . .

(8) The term *indirect* acceptance by a member of an audit committee of any consulting, advisory or other compensatory fee includes acceptance of such a fee by a spouse, a minor child or stepchild or a child or stepchild sharing a home with the member or by an entity in which such member is a partner, member, an officer such as a managing director occupying a comparable position or executive officer, or occupies a similar position (except limited partners, non-managing members and those occupying similar positions who, in each case, have no active role in providing services to the entity) and which provides accounting, consulting, legal, investment banking or financial advisory services to the issuer or any subsidiary of the issuer.

(9) The terms *listed* and *listing* refer to securities listed on a national securities exchange or listed in an automated inter-dealer quotation system of a national securities association or to issuers of such securities.

Rule 10C–1. Listing Standards Relating to Compensation Committees

(a) Pursuant to section 10C(a) of the Act and section 952 of the Dodd-Frank Wall Street Reform and Consumer Protection Act of 2010:

(1) *National securities exchanges.* The rules of each national securities exchange registered pursuant to section 6 of the Act, to the extent such national securities exchange lists equity securities, must, in accordance with the provisions of this section, prohibit the initial or continued listing of any equity security of an issuer that is not in compliance with the requirements of any portion of paragraph (b) or (c) of this section.

(2) *National securities associations.* The rules of each national securities association registered pursuant to section 15A of the Act, to the extent such national securities association lists equity securities in an automated inter-dealer quotation system, must, in accordance with the provisions of this section, prohibit the initial or continued listing in an automated inter-dealer quotation system of any equity security of an issuer that is not in compliance with the requirements of any portion of paragraph (b) or (c) of this section.

(3) *Opportunity to cure defects.* The rules required by paragraphs (a)(1) and (a)(2) of this section must provide for appropriate procedures for a listed issuer to have a reasonable opportunity to cure any defects that would be the basis for a prohibition under paragraph (a) of this section, before the imposition of such prohibition. Such rules may provide that if a member of a compensation committee ceases to be independent in accordance with the requirements of this section for reasons outside the member's reasonable control, that person, with notice by the issuer to the applicable national securities exchange or national securities association, may remain a compensation committee member of the listed issuer until the earlier of the next annual shareholders meeting of the listed issuer or one year from the occurrence of the event that caused the member to be no longer independent.

(4) *Implementation.* (i) Each national securities exchange and national securities association that lists equity securities must provide to the Commission, no later than 90 days after publication of this section in the Federal Register, proposed rules or rule amendments that comply with this section. Each submission must include, in addition to any other information required under section 19(b) of the Act and the rules thereunder, a review of whether and how existing or proposed listing standards satisfy the requirements of this rule, a discussion of the consideration of factors relevant to compensation committee independence conducted by the national securities exchange or national securities association, and the definition of

independence applicable to compensation committee members that the national securities exchange or national securities association proposes to adopt or retain in light of such review.

(ii) Each national securities exchange and national securities association that lists equity securities must have rules or rule amendments that comply with this section approved by the Commission no later than one year after publication of this section in the Federal Register.

(b) *Required standards.* The requirements of this section apply to the compensation committees of listed issuers.

(1) *Independence.* (i) Each member of the compensation committee must be a member of the board of directors of the listed issuer, and must otherwise be independent.

(ii) *Independence requirements.* In determining independence requirements for members of compensation committees, the national securities exchanges and national securities associations shall consider relevant factors, including, but not limited to:

(A) The source of compensation of a member of the board of directors of an issuer, including any consulting, advisory or other compensatory fee paid by the issuer to such member of the board of directors; and

(B) Whether a member of the board of directors of an issuer is affiliated with the issuer, a subsidiary of the issuer or an affiliate of a subsidiary of the issuer.

(iii) *Exemptions from the independence requirements.* (A) The listing of equity securities of the following categories of listed issuers is not subject to the requirements of paragraph (b)(1) of this section:

(*1*) Limited partnerships;

(*2*) Companies in bankruptcy proceedings;

(*3*) Open-end management investment companies registered under the Investment Company Act of 1940; and

(*4*) Any foreign private issuer that discloses in its annual report the reasons that the foreign private issuer does not have an independent compensation committee.

(B) In addition to the issuer exemptions set forth in paragraph (b)(1)(iii)(A) of this section, a national securities exchange or a national securities association, pursuant to section 19(b) of the Act and the rules thereunder, may exempt from the requirements of paragraph (b)(1) of this section a particular relationship with respect to members of the compensation committee, as each national securities exchange or national securities association determines is appropriate, taking into consideration the size of an issuer and any other relevant factors.

(2) *Authority to retain compensation consultants, independent legal counsel and other compensation advisers.* (i) The compensation committee of a listed issuer, in its capacity as a committee of the board of directors, may, in its sole discretion, retain or obtain the advice of a compensation consultant, independent legal counsel or other adviser.

(ii) The compensation committee shall be directly responsible for the appointment, compensation and oversight of the work of any compensation consultant, independent legal counsel and other adviser retained by the compensation committee.

(iii) Nothing in this paragraph (b)(2) shall be construed:

(A) To require the compensation committee to implement or act consistently with the advice or recommendations of the compensation consultant, independent legal counsel or other adviser to the compensation committee; or

(B) To affect the ability or obligation of a compensation committee to exercise its own judgment in fulfillment of the duties of the compensation committee.

(3) *Funding.* Each listed issuer must provide for appropriate funding, as determined by the compensation committee, in its capacity as a committee of the board of directors, for payment of reasonable

compensation to a compensation consultant, independent legal counsel or any other adviser retained by the compensation committee.

(4) *Independence of compensation consultants and other advisers.* The compensation committee of a listed issuer may select a compensation consultant, legal counsel or other adviser to the compensation committee only after taking into consideration the following factors, as well as any other factors identified by the relevant national securities exchange or national securities association in its listing standards:

(i) The provision of other services to the issuer by the person that employs the compensation consultant, legal counsel or other adviser;

(ii) The amount of fees received from the issuer by the person that employs the compensation consultant, legal counsel or other adviser, as a percentage of the total revenue of the person that employs the compensation consultant, legal counsel or other adviser;

(iii) The policies and procedures of the person that employs the compensation consultant, legal counsel or other adviser that are designed to prevent conflicts of interest;

(iv) Any business or personal relationship of the compensation consultant, legal counsel or other adviser with a member of the compensation committee;

(v) Any stock of the issuer owned by the compensation consultant, legal counsel or other adviser; and

(vi) Any business or personal relationship of the compensation consultant, legal counsel, other adviser or the person employing the adviser with an executive officer of the issuer.

Instruction to paragraph (b)(4) of this section: A listed issuer's compensation committee is required to conduct the independence assessment outlined in paragraph (b)(4) of this section with respect to any compensation consultant, legal counsel or other adviser that provides advice to the compensation committee, other than in-house legal counsel.

(5) *General exemptions.* (i) The national securities exchanges and national securities associations, pursuant to section 19(b) of the Act and the rules thereunder, may exempt from the requirements of this section certain categories of issuers, as the national securities exchange or national securities association determines is appropriate, taking into consideration, among other relevant factors, the potential impact of such requirements on smaller reporting issuers.

(ii) The requirements of this section shall not apply to any controlled company or to any smaller reporting company.

(iii) The listing of a security futures product cleared by a clearing agency that is registered pursuant to section 17A of the Act or that is exempt from the registration requirements of section 17A(b)(7). . . .

(c) *Definitions.* Unless the context otherwise requires, all terms used in this section have the same meaning as in the Act and the rules and regulations thereunder. In addition, unless the context otherwise requires, the following definitions apply for purposes of this section:

(1) In the case of foreign private issuers with a two-tier board system, the term *board of directors* means the supervisory or non-management board.

(2) The term *compensation committee* means:

(i) A committee of the board of directors that is designated as the compensation committee; or

(ii) In the absence of a committee of the board of directors that is designated as the compensation committee, a committee of the board of directors performing functions typically performed by a compensation committee, including oversight of executive compensation, even if it is not designated as the compensation committee or also performs other functions; or

(iii) For purposes of this section other than paragraphs (b)(2)(i) and (b)(3), in the absence of a committee as described in paragraphs (c)(2)(i) or (ii) of this section, the members of the board of directors who oversee executive compensation matters on behalf of the board of directors.

(3) The term *controlled company* means an issuer:

(i) That is listed on a national securities exchange or by a national securities association; and

(ii) Of which more than 50 percent of the voting power for the election of directors is held by an individual, a group or another company.

(4) The terms *listed* and *listing* refer to equity securities listed on a national securities exchange or listed in an automated inter-dealer quotation system of a national securities association or to issuers of such securities.

(5) The term *open-end management investment company* means an open-end company, as defined by Section 5(a)(1) of the Investment Company Act of 1940, that is registered under that Act.

REGULATION 12B: REGISTRATION AND REPORTING
GENERAL

Rule 12b-2. Definitions

Unless the context otherwise requires, the following terms, when used in the rules contained in this regulation or in Regulation 13A or 15D or in the forms for statements and reports filed pursuant to sections 12, 13 or 15(d) of the act, shall have the respective meanings indicated in this rule:

Accelerated filer and large accelerated filer.

(1) *Accelerated filer.* The term *accelerated filer* means an issuer after it first meets the following conditions as of the end of its fiscal year:

(i) The issuer had an aggregate worldwide market value of the voting and non-voting common equity held by its non-affiliates of $75 million or more, but less than $700 million, as of the last business day of the issuer's most recently completed second fiscal quarter;

(ii) The issuer has been subject to the requirements of section 13(a) or 15(d) of the Act for a period of at least twelve calendar months;

(iii) The issuer has filed at least one annual report pursuant to section 13(a) or 15(d) of the Act;

(iv) The issuer is not eligible to use the requirements for smaller reporting companies in Regulation S–K of this chapter for its annual and quarterly reports.

(2) *Large accelerated filer.* The term *large accelerated filer* means an issuer after it first meets the following conditions as of the end of its fiscal year:

(i) The issuer had an aggregate worldwide market value of the voting and non-voting common equity held by its non-affiliates of $700 million or more, as of the last business day of the issuer's most recently completed second fiscal quarter;

(ii) The issuer has been subject to the requirements of section 13(a) or 15(d) of the Act for a period of at least twelve calendar months;

(iii) The issuer has filed at least one annual report pursuant to section 13(a) or 15(d) of the Act;

(iv) The issuer is not eligible to use the requirements for smaller reporting companies in Regulation S–K of this chapter for its annual and quarterly reports.

(3) *Entering and exiting accelerated filer and large accelerated filer status.*

(i) The determination at the end of the issuer's fiscal year for whether a non-accelerated filer becomes an accelerated filer, or whether a non-accelerated filer or accelerated filer becomes a large accelerated filer, governs the deadlines for the annual report to be filed for that fiscal year, the quarterly and annual reports to be filed for the subsequent fiscal year and all annual and quarterly reports to be filed thereafter while the issuer remains an accelerated filer or large accelerated filer.

(ii) Once an issuer becomes an accelerated filer, it will remain an accelerated filer unless the issuer determines at the end of a fiscal year that the aggregate worldwide market value of the voting and non-voting common equity held by non-affiliates of the issuer was less than $50 million, as of the last business day of the issuer's most recently completed second fiscal quarter. An issuer making this determination becomes a non-accelerated filer. The issuer will not become an accelerated filer again unless it subsequently meets the conditions in paragraph (1) of this definition.

(iii) Once an issuer becomes a large accelerated filer, it will remain a large accelerated filer unless the issuer determines at the end of a fiscal year that the aggregate worldwide market value of the voting and non-voting common equity held by non-affiliates of the issuer was less than $500 million, as of the last business day of the issuer's most recently completed second fiscal quarter. If the issuer's aggregate worldwide market value was $50 million or more, but less than $500 million, as of the last business day of the issuer's most recently completed second fiscal quarter, the issuer becomes an accelerated filer. If the issuer's aggregate worldwide market value was less than $50 million, as of the last business day of the issuer's most recently completed second fiscal quarter, the issuer becomes a non-accelerated filer. An issuer will not become a large accelerated filer again unless it subsequently meets the conditions in paragraph (2) of this definition.

(iv) The determination at the end of the issuer's fiscal year for whether an accelerated filer becomes a non-accelerated filer, or a large accelerated filer becomes an accelerated filer or a non-accelerated filer, governs the deadlines for the annual report to be filed for that fiscal year, the quarterly and annual reports to be filed for the subsequent fiscal year and all annual and quarterly reports to be filed thereafter while the issuer remains an accelerated filer or non-accelerated filer.

Affiliate. An "affiliate" of, or a person "affiliated" with, a specified person, is a person that directly, or indirectly through one or more intermediaries, controls, or is controlled by, or is under common control with, the person specified. . . .

Associate. The term "associate" used to indicate a relationship with any person, means (1) any corporation or organization (other than the registrant or a majority-owned subsidiary of the registrant) of which such person is an officer or partner or is, directly or indirectly, the beneficial owner of 10 percent or more of any class of equity securities, (2) any trust or other estate in which such person has a substantial beneficial interest or as to which such person serves as trustee or in a similar fiduciary capacity, and (3) any relative or spouse of such person, or any relative of such spouse, who has the same home as such person or who is a director or officer of the registrant or any of its parents or subsidiaries. . . .

Control. The term "control" (including the terms "controlling," "controlled by" and "under common control with") means the possession, direct or indirect, of the power to direct or cause the direction of the management and policies of a person, whether through the ownership of voting securities, by contract, or otherwise. . . .

Material. The term "material," when used to qualify a requirement for the furnishing of information as to any subject, limits the information required to those matters to which there is a substantial likelihood that a reasonable investor would attach importance in determining whether to buy or sell the securities registered.

Material weakness. The term *material weakness* is a deficiency, or a combination of deficiencies, in internal control over financial reporting such that there is a reasonable possibility that a material misstatement of the registrant's annual or interim financial statements will not be prevented or detected on a timely basis.

Significant deficiency. The term *significant deficiency* is a deficiency, or a combination of deficiencies, in internal control over financial reporting that is less severe than a material weakness, yet important enough to merit attention by those responsible for oversight of the registrant's financial reporting. . . .

Significant subsidiary. The term *significant subsidiary* means a subsidiary, including its subsidiaries, which meets any of the following conditions:

(1) The registrant's and its other subsidiaries' investments in and advances to the subsidiary exceed 10 percent of the total assets of the registrant and its subsidiaries consolidated as of the end of the most recently completed fiscal year (for a proposed combination between entities under common control, this condition is also met when the number of common shares exchanged or to be exchanged by the registrant exceeds 10 percent of its total common shares outstanding at the date the combination is initiated); or

(2) The registrant's and its other subsidiaries' proportionate share of the total assets (after intercompany eliminations) of the subsidiary exceeds 10 percent of the total assets of the registrant and its subsidiaries consolidated as of the end of the most recently completed fiscal year; or

(3) The registrant's and its other subsidiaries' equity in the income from continuing operations before income taxes, extraordinary items and cumulative effect of a change in accounting principle of the subsidiary exclusive of amounts attributable to any noncontrolling interests exceeds 10 percent of such income of the registrant and its subsidiaries consolidated for the most recently completed fiscal year.

Smaller reporting company: As used in this part, the term *smaller reporting company* means an issuer that is not an investment company, an asset-backed issuer (as defined in Item 1101 of Regulation S–K), or a majority-owned subsidiary of a parent that is not a smaller reporting company and that:

(1) Had a public float of less than $75 million as of the last business day of its most recently completed second fiscal quarter, computed by multiplying the aggregate worldwide number of shares of its voting and non-voting common equity held by non-affiliates by the price at which the common equity was last sold, or the average of the bid and asked prices of common equity, in the principal market for the common equity; or

(2) In the case of an initial registration statement under the Securities Act or Exchange Act for shares of its common equity, had a public float of less than $75 million as of a date within 30 days of the date of the filing of the registration statement, computed by multiplying the aggregate worldwide number of such shares held by non-affiliates before the registration plus, in the case of a Securities Act registration statement, the number of such shares included in the registration statement by the estimated public offering price of the shares; or

(3) In the case of an issuer whose public float as calculated under paragraph (1) or (2) of this definition was zero, had annual revenues of less than $50 million during the most recently completed fiscal year for which audited financial statements are available. . . .

Provided however, that an entity is not a small business issuer if it has a public float (the aggregate market value of the issuer's outstanding voting and non-voting common equity held by non-affiliates) of $25,000,000 or more.

NOTE: The public float of a reporting company shall be computed by use of the price at which the stock was last sold, or the average of the bid and asked prices of such stock, on a date within 60 days prior to the end of its most recent fiscal year. The public float of a company filing an initial registration statement under the Exchange Act shall be determined as of a date within 60 days of the date the registration statement is filed. In the case of an initial public offering of securities, public float shall be computed on the basis of the number of shares outstanding prior to the offering and the estimated public offering price of the securities.

Subsidiary. A "subsidiary" of a specified person is an affiliate controlled by such person directly, or indirectly through one or more intermediaries. . . .

EXTENSIONS AND TEMPORARY EXEMPTIONS: DEFINITIONS

Rule 12g–1. Exemption From Section 12(g)

An issuer shall be exempt from the requirement to register any class of equity securities pursuant to section 12(g)(1) if on the last day of its most recent fiscal year the issuer had total assets not exceeding $10 million and, with respect to a foreign private issuer, such securities were not quoted in an automated inter-dealer quotation system.

Rule 12g3–2. Exemptions for . . . Certain Foreign Securities. . . .

(b)(1) A foreign private issuer shall be exempt from the requirement to register a class of equity securities under section 12(g) of the Act if:

(i) The issuer is not required to file or furnish reports under section 13(a) of the Act or section 15(d) of the Act;

(ii) The issuer currently maintains a listing of the subject class of securities on one or more exchanges in a foreign jurisdiction that, either singly or together with the trading of the same class of the issuer's securities in another foreign jurisdiction, constitutes the primary trading market for those securities; and

(iii) The issuer has published in English, on its Internet Web site or through an electronic information delivery system generally available to the public in its primary trading market, information that, since the first day of its most recently completed fiscal year, it:

(A) Has made public or been required to make public pursuant to the laws of the country of its incorporation, organization or domicile;

(B) Has filed or been required to file with the principal stock exchange in its primary trading market on which its securities are traded and which has been made public by that exchange; and

(C) Has distributed or been required to distribute to its security holders. . . .

(3)(i) The information required to be published electronically under paragraph (b) of this section is information that is material to an investment decision regarding the subject securities, such as information concerning:

(A) Results of operations or financial condition;

(B) Changes in business;

(C) Acquisitions or dispositions of assets;

(D) The issuance, redemption or acquisition of securities;

(E) Changes in management or control;

(F) The granting of options or the payment of other remuneration to directors or officers; and

(G) Transactions with directors, officers or principal security holders.

(ii) At a minimum, a foreign private issuer shall electronically publish English translations of the following documents required to be published under paragraph (b) of this section if in a foreign language:

(A) Its annual report, including or accompanied by annual financial statements;

(B) Interim reports that include financial statements;

(C) Press releases; and

(D) All other communications and documents distributed directly to security holders of each class of securities to which the exemption relates. . . .

Rule 12g–4. Certification of Termination of Registration Under Section 12(g)

(a) Termination of registration of a class of securities under section 12(a) of the Act shall take effect in 90 days, or such shorter period as the Commission may determine, after the issuer certifies to the Commission on Form 15 that the class of securities is held of record by:

(1) Less than 300 persons; or

(2) Less than 500 persons, where the total assets of the issuer have not exceeded $10 million on the last day of each of the issuer's most recent three fiscal years. . . .

REGULATION 13A: REPORTS OF ISSUERS OF SECURITIES REGISTERED PURSUANT TO SECTION 12

Rule 13a–1. Requirements of Annual Reports

Every issuer having securities registered pursuant to section 12 of the Act shall file an annual report on the appropriate form authorized or prescribed therefor for each fiscal year after the last full fiscal year for which financial statements were filed in its registration statement. . . .

Rule 13a–11. Current Reports on Form 8-K

(a) Except as provided in paragraph (b) of this section, every registrant subject to Rule 13a–1 shall file a current report on Form 8-K within the period specified in that form. . . .

(c) No failure to file a report on Form 8-K that is required solely pursuant to Item 1.01, 1.02, 2.03, 2.04, 2.05, 2.06, 4.02(a), 5.02(e) or 6.03 of Form 8-K shall be deemed to be a violation of Securities Exchange Act § 10(b) or Rule 10b–5.

Rule 13a–13. Quarterly Reports on Form 10-Q . . .

(a) Except as provided in paragraphs (b) and (c) of this section, every issuer that has securities registered pursuant to section 12 of the Act and is required to file annual reports pursuant to section 13 of the Act. . . , shall file a quarterly report on Form 10-Q . . . for each of the first three fiscal quarters of each fiscal year of the issuer. . . .

Rule 13a–14. Certification of Disclosure in Annual and Quarterly Reports

(a) Each report . . . filed on Form 10-Q . . . [or] Form 10-K . . . must include certifications in the form specified in the applicable exhibit filing requirements of such report and such certifications must be filed as an exhibit to such report. Each principal executive and principal financial officer of the issuer, or persons performing similar functions, at the time of filing of the report must sign a certification. The principal executive and principal financial officers of an issuer may omit the portion of the introductory language in paragraph 4 as well as language in paragraph 4(b) of the certification that refers to the certifying officers' responsibility for designing, establishing and maintaining internal control over financial reporting for the issuer until the issuer becomes subject to the internal control over financial reporting requirements in Rule 13a–15 or Rule 15d–15.

(b) Each periodic report containing financial statements filed by an issuer pursuant to section 13(a) of the [Securities Exchange] Act must be accompanied by the certifications required by Section 1350 of Chapter 63 of Title 18 of the United States Code (18 U.S.C. 1350) and such certifications must be furnished as an exhibit to such report as specified in the applicable exhibit requirements for such report. Each principal executive and principal financial officer of the issuer (or equivalent thereof) must sign a certification. This requirement may be satisfied by a single certification signed by an issuer's principal executive and principal financial officers.

(c) A person required to provide a certification specified in paragraph (a) or (b) of this section may not have the certification signed on his or her behalf pursuant to a power of attorney or other form of confirming authority. . . .

Rule 13a–15. Controls and Procedures

(a) Every issuer that has a class of securities registered pursuant to section 12 of the Act . . . must maintain disclosure controls and procedures (as defined in paragraph (e) of this section) and, if the issuer either had been required to file an annual report pursuant to section 13(a) or 15(d) of the Act for the prior fiscal year or had filed an annual report with the Commission for the prior fiscal year, internal control over financial reporting (as defined in paragraph (f) of this section).

(b) Each such issuer's management must evaluate, with the participation of the issuer's principal executive and principal financial officers, or persons performing similar functions, the effectiveness of the issuer's disclosure controls and procedures, as of the end of each fiscal quarter. . . .

(c) The management of each such issuer that either had been required to file an annual report pursuant to section 13(a) or 15(d) of the Act for the prior fiscal year or previously had filed an annual report with the Commission for the prior fiscal year . . . must evaluate, with the participation of the issuer's principal executive and principal financial officers, or persons performing similar functions, the effectiveness, as of the end of each fiscal year, of the issuer's internal control over financial reporting. The framework on which management's evaluation of the issuer's internal control over financial reporting is based must be a suitable, recognized control framework that is established by a body or group that has followed due-process procedures, including the broad distribution of the framework for public comment.

(d) The management of each such issuer that either had been required to file an annual report pursuant to section 13(a) or 15(d) of the Act for the prior fiscal year or had filed an annual report with the Commission for the prior fiscal year . . . must evaluate, with the participation of the issuer's principal executive and principal financial officers, or persons performing similar functions, any change in the issuer's internal control over financial reporting, that occurred during each of the issuer's fiscal quarters, or fiscal year in the case of a foreign private issuer, that has materially affected, or is reasonably likely to materially affect, the issuer's internal control over financial reporting. . . .

(e) For purposes of this section, the term *disclosure controls and procedures* means controls and other procedures of an issuer that are designed to ensure that information required to be disclosed by the issuer in the reports that it files or submits under the [Securities Exchange] Act is recorded, processed, summarized and reported, within the time periods specified in the Commission's rules and forms. Disclosure controls and procedures include, without limitation, controls and procedures designed to ensure that information required to be disclosed by an issuer in the reports that it files or submits under the Act is accumulated and communicated to the issuer's management, including its principal executive and principal financial officers, or persons performing similar functions, as appropriate to allow timely decisions regarding required disclosure.

(f) The term *internal control over financial reporting* is defined as a process designed by, or under the supervision of, the issuer's principal executive and principal financial officers, or persons performing similar functions, and effected by the issuer's board of directors, management and other personnel, to provide reasonable assurance regarding the reliability of financial reporting and the preparation of financial statements for external purposes in accordance with generally accepted accounting principles and includes those policies and procedures that:

(1) Pertain to the maintenance of records that in reasonable detail accurately and fairly reflect the transactions and dispositions of the assets of the issuer;

(2) Provide reasonable assurance that transactions are recorded as necessary to permit preparation of financial statements in accordance with generally accepted accounting principles, and that receipts and expenditures of the issuer are being made only in accordance with authorizations of management and directors of the issuer; and

(3) Provide reasonable assurance regarding prevention or timely detection of unauthorized acquisition, use or disposition of the issuer's assets that could have a material effect on the financial statements.

Rule 13a–20.   Plain English Presentation of Specified Information

(a) Any information included or incorporated by reference in a report filed under section 13(a) of the Act that is required to be disclosed pursuant to Item 402, 403, 404 or 407 of Regulation S–K must be presented in a clear, concise and understandable manner. You must prepare the disclosure using the following standards:

(1) Present information in clear, concise sections, paragraphs and sentences;

(2) Use short sentences;

(3) Use definite, concrete, everyday words;

(4) Use the active voice;

(5) Avoid multiple negatives;

(6) Use descriptive headings and subheadings;

(7) Use a tabular presentation or bullet lists for complex material, wherever possible;

(8) Avoid legal jargon and highly technical business and other terminology;

(9) Avoid frequent reliance on glossaries or defined terms as the primary means of explaining information. Define terms in a glossary or other section of the document only if the meaning is unclear from the context. Use a glossary only if it facilitates understanding of the disclosure; and

(10) In designing the presentation of the information you may include pictures, logos, charts, graphs and other design elements so long as the design is not misleading and the required information is clear. You are encouraged to use tables, schedules, charts and graphic illustrations that present relevant data in an understandable manner, so long as such presentations are consistent with applicable disclosure requirements and consistent with other information in the document. You must draw graphs and charts to scale. Any information you provide must not be misleading. . . .

Note to Rule 13a–20

In drafting the disclosure to comply with this section, you should avoid the following:

1.   Legalistic or overly complex presentations that make the substance of the disclosure difficult to understand;

2.   Vague "boilerplate" explanations that are imprecise and readily subject to different interpretations;

3.   Complex information copied directly from legal documents without any clear and concise explanation of the provision(s); and

4.   Disclosure repeated in different sections of the document that increases the size of the document but does not enhance the quality of the information.

———————

SECURITIES EXCHANGE ACT OF 1934

FORM 8-K

Current Report

Pursuant to Section 13 or 15(d) of the Securities Exchange Act of 1934

* * * * *

GENERAL INSTRUCTIONS . . .

B.   Events to be Reported and Time for Filing of Reports.

1.   A report on this form is required to be filed or furnished, as applicable, upon the occurrence of any one or more of the events specified in the items in Sections 1–6 and 9 of this form. Unless otherwise specified, a report is to be filed or furnished within four business days after occurrence of the event. If the event occurs on a Saturday, Sunday or holiday on which the Commission is not open for business, then the four business day period shall begin to run on, and include, the first business day thereafter. A registrant either furnishing a report on this form under Item 7.01 (Regulation FD Disclosure) or electing to file a report on this form under Item 8.01 (Other Events) solely to satisfy its obligations under Regulation FD must furnish such report or make such filing, as applicable, in accordance with the requirements of Rule 100(a) of Regulation FD, including the deadline for furnishing or filing such report. A report pursuant to Item 5.08 is to be filed within four business days after the registrant determines the anticipated meeting date.

2.   The information in a report furnished pursuant to Item 2.02 (Results of Operations and Financial Condition) or Item 7.01 (Regulation FD Disclosure) shall not be deemed to be "filed" for purposes of Section 18 of the Exchange Act or otherwise subject to the liabilities of that section, unless the registrant specifically states that the information is to be considered "filed" under the Exchange Act or incorporates it by reference into a filing under the Securities Act or the Exchange Act. If a report on Form 8-K contains disclosures under Item 2.02 or Item 7.01, whether or not the report contains disclosures regarding other items, all exhibits to such report relating to Item 2.02 or Item 7.01 will be deemed furnished, and not filed, unless the registrant specifies, under Item 9.01 (Financial Statements and Exhibits), which exhibits, or portions of exhibits, are intended to be deemed filed rather than furnished pursuant to this instruction. . . .

6.   A registrant's report under Item 7.01 (Regulation FD Disclosure) or Item 8.01 (Other Events) will not be deemed an admission as to the materiality of any information in the report that is required to be disclosed solely by Regulation FD.

* * * * *

Information to Be Included in the Report

Section 1—Registrant's Business and Operations

Item 1.01.   Entry into a Material Definitive Agreement

(a) If the registrant has entered into a material definitive agreement not made in the ordinary course of business of the registrant, or into any amendment of such agreement that is material to the registrant, disclose the following information:

(1) the date on which the agreement was entered into or amended, the identity of the parties to the agreement or amendment and a brief description of any material relationship between the registrant or its affiliates and any of the parties, other than in respect of the material definitive agreement or amendment; and

(2) a brief description of the terms and conditions of the agreement or amendment that are material to the registrant.

(b) For purposes of this Item 1.01, a *material definitive agreement* means an agreement that provides for obligations that are material to and enforceable against the registrant, or rights that are material to the registrant and enforceable by the registrant against one or more other parties to the agreement, in each case whether or not subject to conditions.

Instructions

     1.   Any material definitive agreement of the registrant not made in the ordinary course of the registrant's business must be disclosed under this Item 1.01. An agreement is deemed to be not made in the ordinary course of a registrant's business even if the agreement is such as ordinarily accompanies the kind of business conducted by the registrant if it involves the subject matter identified in Item 601(b)(10)(ii)(A)–(D) of Regulation S–K. . . .

     2.   A registrant must provide disclosure under this Item 1.01 if the registrant succeeds as a party to the agreement or amendment to the agreement by assumption or assignment (other than in connection with a merger or acquisition or similar transaction). . . .

Item 1.02.   Termination of a Material Definitive Agreement

(a) If a material definitive agreement which was not made in the ordinary course of business of the registrant and to which the registrant is a party is terminated otherwise than by expiration of the agreement on its stated termination date, or as a result of all parties completing their obligations under such agreement, and such termination of the agreement is material to the registrant, disclose the following information:

(1) the date of the termination of the material definitive agreement, the identity of the parties to the agreement and a brief description of any material relationship between the registrant or its affiliates and any of the parties other than in respect of the material definitive agreement;

(2) a brief description of the terms and conditions of the agreement that are material to the registrant;

(3) a brief description of the material circumstances surrounding the termination; and

(4) any material early termination penalties incurred by the registrant.

(b) For purposes of this Item 1.02, the term *material definitive agreement* shall have the same meaning as set forth in Item 1.01(b).

Instructions

     1.   No disclosure is required solely by reason of this Item 1.02 during negotiations or discussions regarding termination of a material definitive agreement unless and until the agreement has been terminated.

     2.   No disclosure is required solely by reason of this Item 1.02 if the registrant believes in good faith that the material definitive agreement has not been terminated, unless the registrant has received a notice of termination pursuant to the terms of agreement. . . .

Item 1.03.   Bankruptcy or Receivership

(a) If a receiver, fiscal agent or similar officer has been appointed for a registrant or its parent, in a proceeding under the U.S. Bankruptcy Code or in any other proceeding under state or federal law in which a court or governmental authority has assumed jurisdiction over substantially all of the assets or business of the registrant or its parent, or if such jurisdiction has been assumed by leaving the existing directors and officers in possession but subject to the supervision and orders of a court or governmental authority, disclose the following information:

(1) the name or other identification of the proceeding;

(2) the identity of the court or governmental authority;

(3) the date that jurisdiction was assumed; and

(4) the identity of the receiver, fiscal agent or similar officer and the date of his or her appointment.

(b) If an order confirming a plan of reorganization, arrangement or liquidation has been entered by a court or governmental authority having supervision or jurisdiction over substantially all of the assets or business of the registrant or its parent, disclose the following;

(1) the identity of the court or governmental authority;

(2) the date that the order confirming the plan was entered by the court or governmental authority;

(3) a summary of the material features of the plan and, pursuant to Item 9.01 (Financial Statements and Exhibits), a copy of the plan as confirmed;

(4) the number of shares or other units of the registrant or its parent issued and outstanding, the number reserved for future issuance in respect of claims and interests filed and allowed under the plan, and the aggregate total of such numbers; and

(5) information as to the assets and liabilities of the registrant or its parent as of the date that the order confirming the plan was entered, or a date as close thereto as practicable.

Instructions

    1.   The information called for in paragraph (b)(5) of this Item 1.03 may be presented in the form in which it was furnished to the court or governmental authority. . . .

Section 2—Financial Information

Item 2.01.   **Completion of Acquisition or Disposition of Assets**

If the registrant or any of its majority-owned subsidiaries has completed the acquisition or disposition of a significant amount of assets, otherwise than in the ordinary course of business, disclose the following information:

(a) the date of completion of the transaction;

(b) a brief description of the assets involved;

(c) the identity of the person(s) from whom the assets were acquired or to whom they were sold and the nature of any material relationship, other than in respect of the transaction, between such person(s) and the registrant or any of its affiliates, or any director or officer of the registrant, or any associate of any such director or officer;

(d) the nature and amount of consideration given or received for the assets and, if any material relationship is disclosed pursuant to paragraph (c) of this Item 2.01, the formula or principle followed in determining the amount of such consideration;

(e) if the transaction being reported is an acquisition and if a material relationship exists between the registrant or any of its affiliates and the source(s) of the funds used in the acquisition, the identity of the source(s) of the funds unless all or any part of the consideration used is a loan made in the ordinary course of business by a bank as defined by Section 3(a)(6) of the Act, in which case the identity of such bank may be omitted provided the registrant:

(1) has made a request for confidentiality pursuant to Section 13(d)(1)(B) of the Act; and

(2) states in the report that the identity of the bank has been so omitted and filed separately with the Commission. . . .

Instructions

    1.   No information need be given as to:

    (i) any transaction between any person and any wholly-owned subsidiary of such person;

    (ii) any transaction between two or more wholly-owned subsidiaries of any person; or

    (iii) the redemption or other acquisition of securities from the public, or the sale or other disposition of securities to the public, by the issuer of such securities or by a wholly-owned subsidiary of that issuer.

    2.   The term *acquisition* includes every purchase, acquisition by lease, exchange, merger, consolidation, succession or other acquisition, except that the term does not include the construction or development of property by or for the registrant or its subsidiaries or the acquisition of materials for such purpose. The term *disposition* includes every sale, disposition by lease, exchange, merger, consolidation, mortgage, assignment or hypothecation of assets, whether for the benefit of creditors or otherwise, abandonment, destruction, or other disposition.

3.   The information called for by this Item 2.01 is to be given as to each transaction or series of related transactions of the size indicated. The acquisition or disposition of securities is deemed the indirect acquisition or disposition of the assets represented by such securities if it results in the acquisition or disposition of control of such assets.

4.   An acquisition or disposition shall be deemed to involve a significant amount of assets:

(i) if the registrant's and its other subsidiaries' equity in the net book value of such assets or the amount paid or received for the assets upon such acquisition or disposition exceeded 10% of the total assets of the registrant and its consolidated subsidiaries; or

(ii) if it involved a business . . . that is significant (see 17 CFR 210.11–01(b)).[*]

Acquisitions of individually insignificant businesses are not required to be reported pursuant to this Item 2.01 unless they are related businesses . . . and are significant in the aggregate.

5.   Attention is directed to the requirements in Item 9.01 (Financial Statements and Exhibits) with respect to the filing of:

(i) financial statements of businesses acquired;

(ii) *pro forma* financial information; and

(iii) copies of the plans of acquisition or disposition as exhibits to the report. . . .

Item 2.02.   Results of Operations and Financial Condition

(a) If a registrant, or any person acting on its behalf, makes any public announcement or release (including any update of an earlier announcement or release) disclosing material non-public information regarding the registrant's results of operations or financial condition for a completed quarterly or annual fiscal period, the registrant shall disclose the date of the announcement or release, briefly identify the announcement or release and include the text of that announcement or release as an exhibit.

(b) A Form 8-K is not required to be furnished to the Commission under this Item 2.02 in the case of disclosure of material non-public information that is disclosed orally, telephonically, by webcast, by broadcast, or by similar means if:

(1) the information is provided as part of a presentation that is complementary to, and initially occurs within 48 hours after, a related, written announcement or release that has been furnished on Form 8-K pursuant to this Item 2.02 prior to the presentation;

---

[*]   17 C.F.R./210.11–01(b) provides that:

A business combination or disposition of a business shall be considered significant if:

(1) A comparison of the most recent annual financial statements of the business acquired or to be acquired and the registrant's most recent annual consolidated financial statements filed at or prior to the date of acquisition indicates that the business would be a significant subsidiary pursuant to the conditions specified in § 210.1–02(w), substituting 20 percent for 10 percent for each place it appears therein; or

(2) The business to be disposed of meets the conditions of a significant subsidiary in § 210.1–02(w). . . .

17 C.F.R. § 210.1–02(w) provides that:

The term "significant subsidiary" means a subsidiary, including its subsidiaries, which meets any of the following conditions:

(1) The registrant's and its other subsidiaries' investments in and advances to the subsidiary exceed 10 percent of the total assets of the registrant and its subsidiaries consolidated as of the end of the most recently completed fiscal year (for a proposed business combination to be accounted for as a pooling of interests, this condition is also met when the number of common shares exchanged or to be exchanged by the registrant exceeds 10 percent of its total common shares outstanding at the date the combination is initiated); or

(2) The registrant's and its other subsidiaries' proportionate share of the total assets (after intercompany eliminations) of the subsidiary exceeds 10 percent of the total assets of the registrants and its subsidiaries consolidated as of the end of the most recently completed fiscal year; or

(3) The registrant's and its other subsidiaries' equity in the income from continuing operations before income taxes, extraordinary items and cumulative effect of a change in accounting principle of the subsidiary exceeds 10 percent of such income of the registrant and its subsidiaries consolidated for the most recently completed fiscal year. . . . (Footnote by ed.)

(2) the presentation is broadly accessible to the public by dial-in conference call, by webcast, by broadcast or by similar means;

(3) the financial and other statistical information contained in the presentation is provided on the registrant's website. . . ; and

(4) the presentation was announced by a widely disseminated press release, that included instructions as to when and how to access the presentation and the location on the registrant's website where the information would be available.

Instructions

1.   The requirements of this Item 2.02 are triggered by the disclosure of material non-public information regarding a completed fiscal year or quarter. Release of additional or updated material non-public information regarding a completed fiscal year or quarter would trigger an additional Item 2.02 requirement. . . .

3.   Issuers that make earnings announcements or other disclosures of material non-public information regarding a completed fiscal year or quarter in an interim or annual report to shareholders are permitted to specify which portion of the report contains the information required to be furnished under this Item 2.02.

4.   This Item 2.02 does not apply in the case of a disclosure that is made in a quarterly report filed with the Commission on Form 10-Q . . . or an annual report filed with the Commission on Form 10-K. . . .

Item 2.03.   **Creation of a Direct Financial Obligation or an Obligation under an Off-Balance Sheet Arrangement of a Registrant**

(a) If the registrant becomes obligated on a direct financial obligation that is material to the registrant, disclose the following information:

(1) the date on which the registrant becomes obligated on the direct financial obligation and a brief description of the transaction or agreement creating the obligation;

(2) the amount of the obligation, including the terms of its payment and, if applicable, a brief description of the material terms under which it may be accelerated or increased and the nature of any recourse provisions that would enable the registrant to recover from third parties; and

(3) a brief description of the other terms and conditions of the transaction or agreement that are material to the registrant.

(b) If the registrant becomes directly or contingently liable for an obligation that is material to the registrant arising out of an off-balance sheet arrangement, disclose the following information:

(1) the date on which the registrant becomes directly or contingently liable on the obligation and a brief description of the transaction or agreement creating the arrangement and obligation;

(2) a brief description of the nature and amount of the obligation of the registrant under the arrangement, including the material terms whereby it may become a direct obligation, if applicable, or may be accelerated or increased and the nature of any recourse provisions that would enable the registrant to recover from third parties;

(3) the maximum potential amount of future payments (undiscounted) that the registrant may be required to make, if different; and

(4) a brief description of the other terms and conditions of the obligation or arrangement that are material to the registrant.

(c) For purposes of this Item 2.03, *direct financial obligation* means any of the following:

(1) a long-term debt obligation, as defined in Item 303(a)(5)(ii)(A) of Regulation S–K;

(2) a capital lease obligation, as defined in Item 303(a)(5)(ii)(B) of Regulation S–K . . . ;

(3) an operating lease obligation, as defined in Item 303(a)(5)(ii)(C) of Regulation S–K . . . ; or

(4) a short-term debt obligation that arises other than in the ordinary course of business.

(d) For purposes of this Item 2.03, *off-balance sheet arrangement* has the meaning set forth in Item 303(a)(4)(ii) of Regulation S–K.

(e) For purposes of this Item 2.03, *short-term debt obligation* means a payment obligation under a borrowing arrangement that is scheduled to mature within one year, or, for those registrants that use the operating cycle concept of working capital, within a registrant's operating cycle that is longer than one year, as discussed in FASB ASC paragraph 210–10–43–3. . . .

Instructions

1.   A registrant has no obligation to disclose information under this Item 2.03 until the registrant enters into an agreement enforceable against the registrant, whether or not subject to conditions, under which the direct financial obligation will arise or be created or issued. If there is no such agreement, the registrant must provide the disclosure within four business days after the occurrence of the closing or settlement of the transaction or arrangement under which the direct financial obligation arises or is created.

2.   A registrant must provide the disclosure required by paragraph (b) of this Item 2.03 whether or not the registrant is also a party to the transaction or agreement creating the contingent obligation arising under the off-balance sheet arrangement. In the event that neither the registrant nor any affiliate of the registrant is also a party to the transaction or agreement creating the contingent obligation arising under the off-balance sheet arrangement in question, the four business day period for reporting the event under this Item 2.03 shall begin on the earlier of (i) the fourth business day after the contingent obligation is created or arises, and (ii) the day on which an executive officer, as defined in Rule 3b–7, of the registrant becomes aware of the contingent obligation.

3.   In the event that an agreement, transaction or arrangement requiring disclosure under this Item 2.03 comprises a facility, program or similar arrangement that creates or may give rise to direct financial obligations of the registrant in connection with multiple transactions, the registrant shall:

   (i) disclose the entering into of the facility, program or similar arrangement if the entering into of the facility is material to the registrant; and

   (ii) as direct financial obligations arise or are created under the facility or program, disclose the required information under this Item 2.03 to the extent that the obligations are material to the registrant (including when a series of previously undisclosed individually immaterial obligations become material in the aggregate).

4.   For purposes of Item 2.03(b)(3), the maximum amount of future payments shall not be reduced by the effect of any amounts that may possibly be recovered by the registrant under recourse or collateralization provisions in any guarantee agreement, transaction or arrangement.

5.   If the obligation required to be disclosed under this Item 2.03 is a security, or a term of a security, that has been or will be sold pursuant to an effective registration statement of the registrant, the registrant is not required to file a Form 8-K pursuant to this Item 2.03, *provided* that the prospectus relating to that sale contains the information required by this Item 2.03. . . .

Item 2.04.   Triggering Events That Accelerate or Increase a Direct Financial Obligation or an Obligation under an Off-Balance Sheet Arrangement

(a) If a triggering event causing the increase or acceleration of a direct financial obligation of the registrant occurs and the consequences of the event, taking into account those described in paragraph (a)(4) of this Item 2.04, are material to the registrant, disclose the following information:

(1) the date of the triggering event and a brief description of the agreement or transaction under which the direct financial obligation was created and is increased or accelerated;

(2) a brief description of the triggering event;

(3) the amount of the direct financial obligation, as increased if applicable, and the terms of payment or acceleration that apply; and

(4) any other material obligations of the registrant that may arise, increase, be accelerated or become direct financial obligations as a result of the triggering event or the increase or acceleration of the direct financial obligation.

(b) If a triggering event occurs causing an obligation of the registrant under an off-balance sheet arrangement to increase or be accelerated, or causing a contingent obligation of the registrant under an off-balance sheet arrangement to become a direct financial obligation of the registrant, and the consequences of the event, taking into account those described in paragraph (b)(4) of this Item 2.04, are material to the registrant, disclose the following information:

(1) the date of the triggering event and a brief description of the off-balance sheet arrangement;

(2) a brief description of the triggering event;

(3) the nature and amount of the obligation, as increased if applicable, and the terms of payment or acceleration that apply; and

(4) any other material obligations of the registrant that may arise, increase, be accelerated or become direct financial obligations as a result of the triggering event or the increase or acceleration of the obligation under the off-balance sheet arrangement or its becoming a direct financial obligation of the registrant.

(c) For purposes of this Item 2.04, the term *direct financial obligation* has the meaning provided in Item 2.03 of this form, but shall also include an obligation arising out of an off-balance sheet arrangement that is accrued under FASB ASC Section 450–20–25 . . . as a probable loss contingency.

(d) For purposes of this Item 2.04, the term *off-balance sheet arrangement* has the meaning provided in Item 2.03 of this form.

(e) For purposes of this Item 2.04, a *triggering event* is an event, including an event of default, event of acceleration or similar event, as a result of which a direct financial obligation of the registrant or an obligation of the registrant arising under an off-balance sheet arrangement is increased or becomes accelerated or as a result of which a contingent obligation of the registrant arising out of an off-balance sheet arrangement becomes a direct financial obligation of the registrant.

Instructions

1.   Disclosure is required if a triggering event occurs in respect of an obligation of the registrant under an off-balance sheet arrangement and the consequences are material to the registrant, whether or not the registrant is also a party to the transaction or agreement under which the triggering event occurs.

2.   No disclosure is required under this Item 2.04 unless and until a triggering event has occurred in accordance with the terms of the relevant agreement, transaction or arrangement, including, if required, the sending to the registrant of notice of the occurrence of a triggering event pursuant to the terms of the agreement, transaction or arrangement and the satisfaction of all conditions to such occurrence, except the passage of time.

3.   No disclosure is required solely by reason of this Item 2.04 if the registrant believes in good faith that no triggering event has occurred, unless the registrant has received a notice described in Instruction 2 to this Item 2.04.

4.   Where a registrant is subject to an obligation arising out of an off-balance sheet arrangement, whether or not disclosed pursuant to Item 2.03 of this form, if a triggering event occurs as a result of which under that obligation an accrual for a probable loss is required under SFAS No. 5, the obligation arising out of the off-balance sheet arrangement becomes a direct financial obligation as defined in this Item 2.04. In that situation, if the consequences as determined under Item 2.04(b) are material to the registrant, disclosure is required under this Item 2.04. . . .

Item 2.05.   Costs Associated with Exit or Disposal Activities

If the registrant's board of directors, a committee of the board of directors or the officer or officers of the registrant authorized to take such action if board action is not required, commits the registrant to an exit or disposal plan, or otherwise disposes of a long-lived asset or terminates employees under a plan of termination described in FASB ASC paragraph 420–10–25–4 . . . under which material charges will be incurred under generally accepted accounting principles applicable to the registrant, disclose the following information:

(a) the date of the commitment to the course of action and a description of the course of action, including the facts and circumstances leading to the expected action and the expected completion date;

(b) for each major type of cost associated with the course of action (for example, one-time termination benefits, contract termination costs and other associated costs), an estimate of the total amount or range of amounts expected to be incurred in connection with the action;

(c) an estimate of the total amount or range of amounts expected to be incurred in connection with the action; and

(d) the registrant's estimate of the amount or range of amounts of the charge that will result in future cash expenditures, *provided, however*, that if the registrant determines that at the time of filing it is unable in good faith to make a determination of an estimate required by paragraphs (b), (c) or (d) of this Item 2.05, no disclosure of such estimate shall be required; *provided further, however*, that in any such event, the registrant shall file an amended report on Form 8-K under this Item 2.05 within four business days after it makes a determination of such an estimate or range of estimates.

Item 2.06. Material Impairments

If the registrant's board of directors, a committee of the board of directors or the officer or officers of the registrant authorized to take such action if board action is not required, concludes that a material charge for impairment to one or more of its assets, including, without limitation, impairments of securities or goodwill, is required under generally accepted accounting principles applicable to the registrant, disclose the following information:

(a) the date of the conclusion that a material charge is required and a description of the impaired asset or assets and the facts and circumstances leading to the conclusion that the charge for impairment is required;

(b) the registrant's estimate of the amount or range of amounts of the impairment charge; and

(c) the registrant's estimate of the amount or range of amounts of the impairment charge that will result in future cash expenditures,

provided, however, that if the registrant determines that at the time of filing it is unable in good faith to make a determination of an estimate required by paragraphs (b) or (c) of this Item 2.06, no disclosure of such estimate shall be required; *provided further, however*, that in any such event, the registrant shall file an amended report on Form 8-K under this Item 2.06 within four business days after it makes a determination of such an estimate or range of estimates.

Instruction

No filing is required under this Item 2.06 if the conclusion is made in connection with the preparation, review or audit of financial statements required to be included in the next periodic report due to be filed under the Exchange Act, the periodic report is filed on a timely basis and such conclusion is disclosed in the report.

Section 3—Securities and Trading Markets

Item 3.01. Notice of Delisting or Failure to Satisfy a Continued Listing Rule or Standard; Transfer of Listing

(a) If the registrant has received notice from the national securities exchange or national securities association (or a facility thereof) that maintains the principal listing for any class of the registrant's common equity (as defined in Exchange Act Rule 12b–2) that:

- the registrant or such class of the registrant's securities does not satisfy a rule or standard for continued listing on the exchange or association;

- the exchange has submitted an application under Exchange Act Rule 12d2–2 to the Commission to delist such class of the registrant's securities; or

- the association has taken all necessary steps under its rules to delist the security from its automated inter-dealer quotation system,

the registrant must disclose:

(i) the date that the registrant received the notice;

(ii) the rule or standard for continued listing on the national securities exchange or national securities association that the registrant fails, or has failed to, satisfy; and

(iii) any action or response that, at the time of filing, the registrant has determined to take in response to the notice.

(b) If the registrant has notified the national securities exchange or national securities association (or a facility thereof) that maintains the principal listing for any class of the registrant's common equity (as defined in Exchange Act Rule 12b–2) that the registrant is aware of any material noncompliance with a rule or standard for continued listing on the exchange or association, the registrant must disclose:

(i) the date that the registrant provided such notice to the exchange or association;

(ii) the rule or standard for continued listing on the exchange or association that the registrant fails, or has failed, to satisfy; and

(iii) any action or response that, at the time of filing, the registrant has determined to take regarding its noncompliance.

(c) If the national securities exchange or national securities association (or a facility thereof) that maintains the principal listing for any class of the registrant's common equity (as defined in Exchange Act Rule 12b–2), in lieu of suspending trading in or delisting such class of the registrant's securities, issues a public reprimand letter or similar communication indicating that the registrant has violated a rule or standard for continued listing on the exchange or association, the registrant must state the date, and summarize the contents of the letter or communication.

(d) If the registrant's board of directors, a committee of the board of directors or the officer or officers of the registrant authorized to take such action if board action is not required, has taken definitive action to cause the listing of a class of its common equity to be withdrawn from the national securities exchange, or terminated from the automated inter-dealer quotation system of a registered national securities association, where such exchange or association maintains the principal listing for such class of securities, including by reason of a transfer of the listing or quotation to another securities exchange or quotation system, describe the action taken and state the date of the action.

Item 3.02.   Unregistered Sales of Equity Securities

(a) If the registrant sells equity securities in a transaction that is not registered under the Securities Act, furnish the information set forth in paragraphs (a) and (c) through (e) of Item 701 of Regulation S–K. For purposes of determining the required filing date for the Form 8-K under this Item 3.02(a), the registrant has no obligation to disclose information under this Item 3.02 until the registrant enters into an agreement enforceable against the registrant, whether or not subject to conditions, under which the equity securities are to be sold. If there is no such agreement, the registrant must provide the disclosure within four business days after the occurrence of the closing or settlement of the transaction or arrangement under which the equity securities are to be sold.

(b) No report need be filed under this Item 3.02 if the equity securities sold, in the aggregate since its last report filed under this Item 3.02 or its last periodic report, whichever is more recent, constitute less than 1% of the number of shares outstanding of the class of equity securities sold. In the case of a smaller reporting company, no report need be filed if the equity securities sold, in the aggregate since its last report filed under this Item 3.02 or its last periodic report, whichever is more recent, constitute less than 5% of the number of shares outstanding of the class of equity securities sold.

Instructions

1.   For purposes of this Item 3.02, "the number of shares outstanding" refers to the actual number of shares of equity securities of the class outstanding and does not include outstanding securities convertible into or exchangeable for such equity securities. . . .

Item 3.03.   Material Modification to Rights of Security Holders

(a) If the constituent instruments defining the rights of the holders of any class of registered securities of the registrant have been materially modified, disclose the date of the modification, the title of the class of securities involved and briefly describe the general effect of such modification upon the rights of holders of such securities.

(b) If the rights evidenced by any class of registered securities have been materially limited or qualified by the issuance or modification of any other class of securities by the registrant, briefly disclose the date of the issuance or modification, [and] the general effect of the issuance or modification of such other class of securities upon the rights of the holders of the registered securities.

Instruction

Working capital restrictions and other limitations upon the payment of dividends must be reported pursuant to this Item 3.03.

Section 4—Matters Related to Accountants and Financial Statements

Item 4.01.   Changes in Registrant's Certifying Accountant

(a) If an independent accountant who was previously engaged as the principal accountant to audit the registrant's financial statements, or an independent accountant upon whom the principal accountant expressed reliance in its report regarding a significant subsidiary, resigns (or indicates that it declines to stand for re-appointment after completion of the current audit) or is dismissed, disclose the information required by Item 304(a)(1) of Regulation S–K, including compliance with Item 304(a)(3) of Regulation S–K.

(b) If a new independent accountant has been engaged as either the principal accountant to audit the registrant's financial statements or as an independent accountant on whom the principal accountant is expected to express reliance in its report regarding a significant subsidiary, the registrant must disclose the information required by Item 304(a)(2) of Regulation S–K.

Instruction

The resignation or dismissal of an independent accountant, or its refusal to stand for re-appointment, is a reportable event separate from the engagement of a new independent accountant. On some occasions, two reports on Form 8-K are required for a single change in accountants, the first on the resignation (or refusal to stand for re-appointment) or dismissal of the former accountant and the second when the new accountant is engaged. Information required in the second Form 8-K in such situations need not be provided to the extent that it has been reported previously in the first Form 8-K.

Item 4.02.   Non-Reliance on Previously Issued Financial Statements or a Related Audit Report or Completed Interim Review

(a) If the registrant's board of directors, a committee of the board of directors or the officer or officers of the registrant authorized to take such action if board action is not required, concludes that any previously issued financial statements, covering one or more years or interim periods for which the registrant is required to provide financial statements under Regulation S–X, should no longer be relied upon because of an error in such financial statements as addressed in FASB ASC Topic 20 . . . , disclose the following information:

(1) the date of the conclusion regarding the non-reliance and an identification of the financial statements and years or periods covered that should no longer be relied upon;

(2) a brief description of the facts underlying the conclusion to the extent known to the registrant at the time of filing; and

(3) a statement of whether the audit committee, or the board of directors in the absence of an audit committee, or authorized officer or officers, discussed with the registrant's independent accountant the matters disclosed in the filing pursuant to this Item 4.02(a).

(b) If the registrant is advised by, or receives notice from, its independent accountant that disclosure should be made or action should be taken to prevent future reliance on a previously issued audit report or completed interim review related to previously issued financial statements, disclose the following information:

(1) the date on which the registrant was so advised or notified;

(2) identification of the financial statements that should no longer be relied upon;

(3) a brief description of the information provided by the accountant; and

(4) a statement of whether the audit committee, or the board of directors in the absence of an audit committee, or authorized officer or officers, discussed with the independent accountant the matters disclosed in the filing pursuant to this Item 4.02(b).

(c) If the registrant receives advisement or notice from its independent accountant requiring disclosure under paragraph (b) of this Item 4.02, the registrant must:

(1) provide the independent accountant with a copy of the disclosures it is making in response to this Item 4.02 that the independent accountant shall receive no later than the day that the disclosures are filed with the Commission;

(2) request the independent accountant to furnish to the registrant as promptly as possible a letter addressed to the Commission stating whether the independent accountant agrees with the statements made by the registrant in response to this Item 4.02 and, if not, stating the respects in which it does not agree; and

(3) amend the registrant's previously filed Form 8-K by filing the independent accountant's letter as an exhibit to the filed Form 8-K no later than two business days after the registrant's receipt of the letter.

Section 5—Corporate Governance and Management

Item 5.01.   Changes in Control of Registrant

(a) If, to the knowledge of the registrant's board of directors, a committee of the board of directors or authorized officer or officers of the registrant, a change in control of the registrant has occurred, furnish the following information:

(1) the identity of the person(s) who acquired such control;

(2) the date and a description of the transaction(s) which resulted in the change in control;

(3) the basis of the control, including the percentage of voting securities of the registrant now beneficially owned directly or indirectly by the person(s) who acquired control;

(4) the amount of the consideration used by such person(s);

(5) the source(s) of funds used by the person(s), *unless* all or any part of the consideration used is a loan made in the ordinary course of business by a bank as defined by Section 3(a)(6) of the Act, in which case the identity of such bank may be omitted provided the person who acquired control:

(i) has made a request for confidentiality pursuant to Section 13(d)(1)(B) of the Act; and

(ii) states in the report that the identity of the bank has been so omitted and filed separately with the Commission.

(6) the identity of the person(s) from whom control was assumed;

(7) any arrangements or understandings among members of both the former and new control groups and their associates with respect to election of directors or other matters. . . .

(b) Furnish the information required by Item 403(c) of Regulation S–K.

Item 5.02.   Departure of Directors or Certain Officers; Election of Directors; Appointment of Certain Officers; Compensation Arrangements of Certain Officers

(a)(1) If a director has resigned or refuses to stand for re-election to the board of directors since the date of the last annual meeting of shareholders because of a disagreement with the registrant, known to an executive officer of the registrant, as defined in Rule 3b–7, on any matter relating to the registrant's operations, policies or practices, or if a director has been removed for cause from the board of directors, disclose the following information:

(i) the date of such resignation, refusal to stand for re-election or removal;

(ii) any positions held by the director on any committee of the board of directors at the time of the director's resignation, refusal to stand for re-election or removal; and

(iii) a brief description of the circumstances representing the disagreement that the registrant believes caused, in whole or in part, the director's resignation, refusal to stand for re-election or removal.

(2) If the director has furnished the registrant with any written correspondence concerning the circumstances surrounding his or her resignation, refusal or removal, the registrant shall file a copy of the document as an exhibit to the report on Form 8-K.

(3) The registrant also must:

(i) provide the director with a copy of the disclosures it is making in response to this Item 5.02 no later than the day the registrant file the disclosures with the Commission;

(ii) provide the director with the opportunity to furnish the registrant as promptly as possible with a letter addressed to the registrant stating whether he or she agrees with the statements made by the registrant in response to this Item 5.02 and, if not, stating the respects in which he or she does not agree; and

(iii) file any letter received by the registrant from the director with the Commission as an exhibit by an amendment to the previously filed Form 8-K within two business days after receipt by the registrant.

(b) If the registrant's principal executive officer, president, principal financial officer, principal accounting officer, principal operating officer, or any person performing similar functions, or any named executive officer, retires, resigns or is terminated from that position, or if a director retires, resigns, is removed, or refuses to stand for re-election (except in circumstances described in paragraph (a) of this Item 5.02), disclose the fact that the event has occurred and the date of the event.

(c) If the registrant appoints a new principal executive officer, president, principal financial officer, principal accounting officer, principal operating officer, or person performing similar functions, disclose the following information with respect to the newly appointed officer:

(1) the name and position of the newly appointed officer and the date of the appointment;

(2) the information required by Items 401(b), (d), (e) and Item 404(a) of Regulation S–K; and

(3) a brief description of any material plan, contract or arrangement (whether or not written) to which a covered officer is a party or in which he or she participates that is entered into or material amendment in connection with the triggering event or any grant or award to any such covered person or modification thereto, under any such plan, contract or arrangement in connection with any such event.

(d) . . .

(5) a brief description of any material plan, contract or arrangement (whether or not written) to which the director is a party or in which he or she participates that is entered into or material amendment in connection with the triggering event or any grant or award to any such covered person or modification thereto, under any such plan, contract or arrangement in connection with any such event.

(e) If the registrant enters into, adopts, or otherwise commences a material compensatory plan, contract or arrangement (whether or not written), as to which the registrant's principal executive officer, principal financial officer, or a named executive officer participates or is a party, or such compensatory plan, contract or arrangement is materially amended or modified, or a material grant or award under any such plan, contract or arrangement to any such person is made or materially modified, then the registrant shall provide a brief description of the terms and conditions of the plan, contract or arrangement and the amounts payable to the officer thereunder. . . .

(f) If the salary or bonus of a named executive officer cannot be calculated as of the most recent practicable date and is omitted from the Summary Compensation Table as specified in Instruction 1 to Item 402(c)(2)(iii) and (iv) of Regulation S–K, disclose the appropriate information under this Item 5.02(f) when there is a payment, grant, award, decision or other occurrence as a result of which such amounts become calculable in whole or in part. Disclosure under this Item 5.02(f) shall include a new total compensation figure for the named executive officer, using the new salary or bonus information to recalculate the information that was previously provided with respect to the named executive officer in the registrant's Summary Compensation Table for which the salary and bonus information was omitted in reliance on Instruction 1 to Item 402(c)(2)(iii) and (iv) of Regulation S–K.

Instructions to Item 5.02 . . .

4. For purposes of this Item, the term "named executive officer" shall refer to those executive officers for whom disclosure was required in the registrant's most recent filing with the Commission under the Securities Act or Exchange Act that required disclosure pursuant to Item 402(c) of Regulation S–K.

Item 5.03.   Amendments to Articles of Incorporation or Bylaws; Change in Fiscal Year

(a) If a registrant with a class of equity securities registered under Section 12 of the Exchange Act amends its articles of incorporation or bylaws and a proposal for the amendment was not disclosed in a proxy statement or information statement filed by the registrant, disclose the following information:

(1) the effective date of the amendment; and

(2) a description of the provision adopted or changed by amendment and, if applicable, the previous provision.

(b) If the registrant determines to change the fiscal year from that used in its most recent filing with the Commission other than by means of:

(1) a submission to a vote of security holders through the solicitation of proxies or otherwise; or

(2) an amendment to its articles of incorporation or bylaws,

disclose the date of such determination, the date of the new fiscal year end and the form (for example, Form 10-K . . .) on which the report covering the transition period will be filed. . . .

Item 5.05.   Amendments to the Registrant's Code of Ethics, or Waiver of a Provision of the Code of Ethics

(a) Briefly describe the date and nature of any amendment to a provision of the registrant's code of ethics that applies to the registrant's principal executive officer, principal financial officer, principal accounting officer or controller or persons performing similar functions and that relates to any element of the code of ethics definition enumerated in Item 406(b) of Regulation S–K.

(b) If the registrant has granted a waiver, including an implicit waiver, from a provision of the code of ethics to an officer or person described in paragraph (a) of this Item 5.05, and the waiver relates to one or more of the elements of the code of ethics definition referred to in paragraph (a) of this Item 5.05, briefly describe the nature of the waiver, the name of the person to whom the waiver was granted, and the date of the waiver.

(c) The registrant does not need to provide any information pursuant to this Item 5.05 if it discloses the required information on its Internet website within four business days following the date of the amendment or waiver and the registrant has disclosed in its most recently filed annual report its Internet address and intention to provide disclosure in this manner. If the registrant elects to disclose the information required by this Item 5.05 through its website, such information must remain available on the website for at least a 12-month period. Following the 12-month period, the registrant must retain the information for a period of not less than five years. Upon request, the registrant must furnish to the Commission or its staff a copy of any or all information retained pursuant to this requirement. . . .

Item 5.07.   Submission of Matters to a Vote of Security Holders

If any matter was submitted to a vote of security holders, through the solicitation of proxies or otherwise, provide the following information:

(a) The date of the meeting and whether it was an annual or special meeting. This information must be provided only if a meeting of security holders was held.

(b) If the meeting involved the election of directors, the name of each director elected at the meeting, as well as a brief description of each other matter voted upon at the meeting; and state the number of votes cast for, against or withheld, as well as the number of abstentions and broker non-votes as to each such matter, including a separate tabulation with respect to each nominee for office. For the vote on the frequency of shareholder advisory votes on executive compensation required by section 14A(a)(2) of the Securities Exchange Act of 1934 and Rule 14a–21(b), state the number of votes cast for each of 1 year, 2 years, and 3 years, as well as the number of abstentions.

(c) A description of the terms of any settlement between the registrant and any other participant . . . terminating any solicitation subject to Rule 14a–12(c), including the cost or anticipated cost to the registrant.

(d) No later than one hundred fifty calendar days after the end of the annual or other meeting of shareholders at which shareholders voted on the frequency of shareholder votes on the compensation of executives as required by section 14A(a)(2) of the Securities Exchange Act of 1934, but in no event later than sixty calendar days prior to the deadline for submission of shareholder proposals under Rule 14a–8, as disclosed in the registrant's most recent proxy statement for an annual or other meeting of shareholders relating to the election of directors at which shareholders voted on the frequency of shareholder votes on the compensation of executives as required by section 14A(a)(2) of the Securities Exchange Act of 1934, by amendment to the most recent Form 8-K filed pursuant to (b) of this Item, disclose the company's decision in light of such vote as to how frequently the company will include a shareholder vote on the compensation of executives in its proxy materials until the next required vote on the frequency of shareholder votes on the compensation of executives.

Item 5.08.　　　Shareholder Director Nominations

(a) If the registrant did not hold an annual meeting the previous year, or if the date of this year's annual meeting has been changed by more than 30 calendar days from the date of the previous year's meeting, then the registrant is required to disclose the date by which a nominating shareholder or nominating shareholder group must submit the notice on Schedule 14N required pursuant to Rule 14a–11(b)(10), which date shall be a reasonable time before the registrant mails its proxy materials for the meeting. Where a registrant is required to include shareholder director nominees in the registrant's proxy materials pursuant to either an applicable state or foreign law provision, or a provision in the registrant's governing documents, then the registrant is required to disclose the date by which a nominating shareholder or nominating shareholder group must submit the notice on Schedule 14N required pursuant to Rule 14a–18.

(b) If the registrant is a series company as defined in Rule 18f–2(a) under the Investment Company Act, then the registrant is required to disclose in connection with the election of directors at an annual meeting of shareholders (or, in lieu of such an annual meeting, a special meeting of shareholders) the total number of shares of the registrant outstanding and entitled to be voted (or if the votes are to be cast on a basis other than one vote per share, then the total number of votes entitled to be voted and the basis for allocating such votes) on the election of directors at such meeting of shareholders as of the end of the most recent calendar quarter.

Section 7—Regulation FD

Item 7.01.　　　Regulation FD Disclosure

Unless filed under Item 8.01, disclose under this item only information that the registrant elects to disclose through Form 8-K pursuant to Regulation FD.

Section 8—Other Events

Item 8.01.　　　Other Events

The registrant may, at its option, disclose under this Item 8.01 any events, with respect to which information is not otherwise called for by this form, that the registrant deems of importance to security holders. The registrant may, at its option, file a report under this Item 8.01 disclosing the nonpublic information required to be disclosed by Regulation FD. . . .

FORM 10-Q
GENERAL INSTRUCTIONS

A. Rule as to Use of Form 10-Q.

1.   Form 10-Q shall be used for quarterly reports under Section 13 or 15(d) of the Securities Exchange Act of 1934, filed pursuant to Rule 13a–13 or Rule 15d–13. A quarterly report on this form pursuant to Rule 13a–13 or Rule 15d–13 shall be filed within the following period after the end of each of the first three fiscal quarters of each fiscal year, but no report need be filed for the fourth quarter of any fiscal year:

a.   40 days after the end of the fiscal quarter for large accelerated filers and accelerated filers (as defined in Rule 12b–2); and

b.   45 days after the end of the fiscal quarter for all other registrants.

Quarterly Report Under Section 13 or 15(d) of the Securities Exchange Act of 1934

For the Quarterly Period Ended   _____

* * *

Commission file number   _____

_____

(Exact name of registrant as specified in its charter)

_____

(State or other jurisdiction of incorporation or organization)   (I.R.S. Employer Identification No.)

_____

(Address of principal executive offices)   (Zip Code)

_____

(Registrant's telephone number, including area code)

_____

(Former name, former address and former fiscal year, if changed since last report.). . . .

PART 1—FINANCIAL INFORMATION

Item 1.   Financial Statements.

Provide the information required by Rule 10–01 of Regulation S–X [Interim Financial Statements]. . . .

Item 2.   Management's Discussion and Analysis of Financial Condition and Results of Operations.

Furnish the information required by Item 303 of Regulation S–K. . . .

Item 4.   Controls and Procedures.

Furnish the information required by Item 307 of Regulation S–K and 308(c) of Regulation S–K.

PART II—OTHER INFORMATION. . . .

Item 1.   Legal Proceedings.

Furnish the information required by Item 103 of Regulation S–K [Legal Proceedings]. As to such proceedings which have been terminated during the period covered by the report, provide similar information, including the date of termination and a description of the disposition thereof with respect to the registrant and its subsidiaries.

Item 1A.   Risk Factors.

Set forth any material changes from risk factors as previously disclosed in the registrant's Form 10-K in response to Item 1A. to Part I of Form 10-K. Smaller reporting companies are not required to provide the information required by this item.

Item 2.   Changes in Securities.

(a) If the constituent instruments defining the rights of the holders of any class of registered securities have been materially modified, give the title of the class of securities involved and state briefly the general effect of such modification upon the rights of holders of such securities.

(b) If the rights evidenced by any class of registered securities have been materially limited or qualified by the issuance or modification of any other class of securities, state briefly the general effect of the issuance or modification of such other class of securities upon the rights of the holders of the registered securities. . . .

Item 3.   Defaults Upon Senior Securities.

(a) If there has been any material default in the payment of principal, interest, a sinking or purchase fund installment, or any other material default not cured within 30 days, with respect to any indebtedness of the registrant or any of its significant subsidiaries exceeding 5 percent of the total assets of the registrant and its consolidated subsidiaries, identify the indebtedness and state the nature of the default. In the case of such a default in the payment of principal, interest, or a sinking or purchase fund installment, state the amount of the default and the total arrearage on the date of filing this report.

(b) If any material arrearage in the payment of dividends has occurred or if there has been any other material delinquency not cured within 30 days, with respect to any class of preferred stock of the registrant which is registered or which ranks prior to any class of registered securities, or with respect to any class of preferred stock of any significant subsidiary of the registrant, give the title of the class and state the nature of the arrearage or delinquency. In the case of an arrearage in the payment of dividends, state the amount and the total arrearage on the date of filing this report. . . .

Item 4.   Other Information. . . .

(a) The registrant must disclose under this item any information required to be disclosed in a report on Form 8-K during the period covered by this Form 10-Q, but not reported, whether or not otherwise required by this Form 10-Q. If disclosure of such information is made under this item, it need not be repeated in a report on Form 8-K which would otherwise be required to be filed with respect to such information or in a subsequent report on Form 10-Q; and

(b) Furnish the information required by Item 407(c)(3) of Regulation S–K.

Item 5.   Exhibits.

Furnish the exhibits required by Item 601 of Regulation S–K.

Form 10-Q   *SECURITIES EXCHANGE ACT OF 1934*

SIGNATURES

    Pursuant to the requirements of the Securities Exchange Act of 1934, the registrant has duly caused this report to be signed on its behalf by the undersigned thereunto duly authorized.

_____

(Registrant)

_____   _____

(Date)   (Signature)

_____   _____

(Date)   (Signature)

_____

FORM 10-K

Annual Report Pursuant to Section 13 or 15(d) of The Securities Exchange Act of 1934

GENERAL INSTRUCTIONS. . . .

A. Rule as to Use of Form 10-K.

(1) This Form shall be used for annual reports pursuant to Section 13 or 15(d) of the Securities Exchange Act of 1934 for which no other form is prescribed. This Form also shall be used for transition reports filed pursuant to Section 13 or 15(d) of the Act.

(2) Annual reports on this Form shall be filed within the following period:

(a) 60 days after the end of the fiscal year covered by the report . . . for large accelerated filers (as defined in Rule 12b–2):

(b) 75 days after the end of the fiscal year covered by the report for accelerated filers (as defined in Rule 12b–2); and

(c) 90 days after the end of the fiscal year covered by the report for all other registrants. . . .

For the fiscal year ended _____   Commission file number _____

_____
(Exact name of registrant as specified in its charter)

_____   _____
(State or other jurisdiction of incorporation   (I.R.S. Employer Identification No.)
            or organization)

_____   _____
(Address of principal executive offices)   (Zip Code)

(Registrant's telephone number, including area code) _____

Securities registered pursuant to Section 12(b) of the Act:

Title of each class	Name of each exchange on which registered
_____	_____
_____	_____

Securities registered pursuant to section 12(g) of the Act:

_____
(Title of class)

. . .

PART I . . .

Item 1. Business. . . .

Item 1A. Risk Factors.

Set forth, under the caption "Risk Factors," where appropriate, the risk factors described in Item 503(c) of Regulation S–K applicable to the registrant. Provide any discussion of risk factors in plain English in accordance with Rule 421(d) of the Securities Act of 1933. Smaller reporting companies are not required to provide the information required by this item.

Item 1B.   Unresolved Staff Comments.

If the registrant is an accelerated filer as defined in Rule 12b–2 of the Exchange Act or is a well-known seasoned issuer as defined in Rule 405 of the Securities Act and has received written comments from the Commission staff regarding its periodic or current reports under the Act not less than 180 days before the end of its fiscal year to which the annual report relates, and such comments remain unresolved, disclose the substance of any such unresolved comments that the registrant believes are material. Such disclosure may provide other information including the position of the registrant with respect to any such comment.

Item 2.   Properties. . . .

Item 3.   Legal Proceedings. . . .

Item 4.   Submission of Matters to a Vote of Security Holders.

If any matter was submitted during the fourth quarter of the fiscal year covered by this report to a vote of security holders, through the solicitation of proxies or otherwise, furnish the following information:

(a) The date of the meeting and whether it was an annual or special meeting.

(b) If the meeting involved the election of directors, the name of each director elected at the meeting and the name of each other director whose term of office as a director continued after the meeting.

(c) A brief description of each matter voted upon at the meeting and state the number of votes cast for, against or withheld, as well as the number of abstentions and broker non-votes as to each such matter, including a separate tabulation with respect to each nominee for office.

(d) A description of the terms of any settlement between the registrant and any other participant (as defined in Rule 14a–11 of Regulation 14A under the Act) terminating any solicitation subject to Rule 14a–11, including the cost or anticipated cost to the registrant.

PART II . . .

Item 5.   Market for Registrant's Common Equity and Related Stockholder Matters. . . .

Item 6.   Selected Financial Data.

Furnish the information required by Item 301 of Regulation S–K. . . .

Item 7.   Management's Discussion and Analysis of Financial Condition and Results of Operation.

Furnish the information required by Item 303 of Regulation S–K. . . .

Item 8.   Financial Statements and Supplementary Data. . . .

Furnish financial statements meeting the requirements of Regulation S–X. . . .

Item 9.   Changes in and Disagreements With Accountants on Accounting and Financial Disclosure.

Furnish the information required by Item 304 of Regulation S–K. . . .

Item 9A. Controls and Procedures.

Furnish the information required by Items 307 and 308 of Regulation S–K. . . .

PART III . . .

Item 10. Directors and Executive Officers of the Registrant.

Furnish the information required by Items 401, 405, 406, and 407(c)(3), (d)(4) and (d)(5) of Regulation S–K. . . .

Item 11. Executive Compensation.

Furnish the information required by Item 402 Regulation S–K and paragraphs (e)(4) and (e)(5) of Regulation S–K.

Item 12. Security Ownership of Certain Beneficial Owners and Management.

Furnish the information required by Item 201(d) of Regulation S–K and by Item 403 of Regulation S–K. . . .

Item 13. Certain Relationships and Related Transactions.

Furnish the information required by Item 404 of Regulation S–K and Item 407(a) of Regulation S–K.

Item 14. Principal Accountant Fees and Services.

Furnish the information required by Item 9(e) of Schedule 14A.

(1) Disclose, under the caption *Audit Fees*, the aggregate fees billed for each of the last two fiscal years for professional services rendered by the principal accountant for the audit of the registrant's annual financial statements and review of financial statements included in the registrant's Form 10-Q or services that are normally provided by the accountant in connection with statutory and regulatory filings or engagements for those fiscal years.

(2) Disclose, under the caption Audit-Related Fees, the aggregate fees billed in each of the last two fiscal years for assurance and related services by the principal accountant that are reasonably related to the performance of the audit or review of the registrant's financial statements and are not reported under Item 9(e)(1) of Schedule 14A. Registrants shall describe the nature of the services comprising the fees disclosed under this category.

(3) Disclose, under the caption Tax Fees, the aggregate fees billed in each of the last two fiscal years for professional services rendered by the principal accountant for tax compliance, tax advice, and tax planning. Registrants shall describe the nature of the services comprising the fees disclosed under this category.

(4) Disclose, under the caption All Other Fees, the aggregate fees billed in each of the last two fiscal years for products and services provided by the principal accountant, other than the services reported in Items 9(e)(1) through 9(e)(3) of Schedule 14A. Registrants shall describe the nature of the services comprising the fees disclosed under this category.

(5)(i) Disclose the audit committee's pre-approval policies and procedures. . . .

(ii) Disclose the percentage of services described in each of Items 9(e)(2) through 9(e)(4) of Schedule 14A that were approved by the audit committee. . . .

(6) If greater than 50 percent, disclose the percentage of hours expended on the principal accountant's engagement to audit the registrant's financial statements for the most recent fiscal year that were attributed to work performed by persons other than the principal accountant's full-time, permanent employees.

* * * * *

SIGNATURES . . .

Pursuant to the requirements of Section 13 or 15(d) of the Securities Exchange Act of 1934, the registrant has duly caused this report to be signed on its behalf by the undersigned, thereunto duly authorized.

(Registrant) _____

By (Signature and Title) _____

Date _____

Pursuant to the requirements of the Securities Exchange Act of 1934, this report has been signed below by the following persons on behalf of the registrant and in the capacities and on the dates indicated.

By (Signature and Title) _____

Date _____

By (Signature and Title) _____

Date _____

Rule 13b2–2. Representations and Conduct in Connection With the Preparation of Required Reports and Documents

(a) No director or officer of an issuer shall, directly or indirectly:

(1) Make or cause to be made a materially false or misleading statement to an accountant in connection with; or

(2) Omit to state, or cause another person to omit to state, any material fact necessary in order to make statements made, in light of the circumstances under which such statements were made, not misleading, to an accountant in connection with:

(i) Any audit, review or examination of the financial statements of the issuer required to be made pursuant to this subpart; or

(ii) The preparation or filing of any document or report required to be filed with the Commission pursuant to this subpart or otherwise.

(b)(1) No officer or director of an issuer, or any other person acting under the direction thereof, shall directly or indirectly take any action to coerce, manipulate, mislead, or fraudulently influence any independent public or certified public accountant engaged in the performance of an audit or review of the financial statements of that issuer that are required to be filed with the Commission pursuant to this subpart or otherwise if that person knew or should have known that such action, if successful, could result in rendering the issuer's financial statements materially misleading.

(2) For purposes of paragraphs (b)(1) and (c)(2) of this section, actions that, "if successful, could result in rendering the issuer's financial statements materially misleading" include, but are not limited to, actions taken at any time with respect to the professional engagement period to coerce, manipulate, mislead, or fraudulently influence an auditor:

(i) To issue or reissue a report on an issuer's financial statements that is not warranted in the circumstances (due to material violations of generally accepted accounting principles, generally accepted auditing standards, or other professional or regulatory standards);

(ii) Not to perform audit, review or other procedures required by generally accepted auditing standards or other professional standards;

(iii) Not to withdraw an issued report; or

(iv) Not to communicate matters to an issuer's audit committee. . . .

REGULATION 13D–G

Rule 13d–1. Filing of Schedules 13D and 13G

(a) Any person who, after acquiring directly or indirectly the beneficial ownership of any equity security of a class which is specified in paragraph (i) of this section, is directly or indirectly the beneficial owner of more than five percent of the class shall, within 10 days after such acquisition, file with the Commission, a statement containing the information required by Schedule 13D. . . .

(b)(1) A person who would otherwise be obligated under paragraph (a) of this section to file a statement on Schedule 13D may, in lieu thereof, file with the Commission, a short-form statement on Schedule 13G, provided, that:

(i) Such person has acquired such securities in the ordinary course of his business and not with the purpose nor with the effect of changing or influencing the control of the issuer, nor in connection with or as a participant in any transaction having such purpose or effect, including any transaction subject to Rule 13d–3(b), other than activities solely in connection with a nomination under Rule 14a–11; and

(ii) Such person is:

(A) A broker or dealer registered under section 15 of the Act;

(B) A bank as defined in section 3(a)(6) of the Act;

(C) An insurance company as defined in section 3(a)(19) of the Act;

(D) An investment company registered under section 8 of the Investment Company Act of 1940;

(E) Any person registered as an investment adviser under Section 203 of the Investment Advisers Act of 1940 or under the laws of any state;

(F) An employee benefit plan as defined in Section 3(3) of the Employee Retirement Income Security Act of 1974, as amended, 29 U.S.C. 1001 et seq. ("ERISA") that is subject to the provisions of ERISA, or any such plan that is not subject to ERISA that is maintained primarily for the benefit of the employees of a state or local government or instrumentality, or an endowment fund;

(G) A parent holding company or control person, provided the aggregate amount held directly by the parent or control person, and directly and indirectly by their subsidiaries or affiliates that are not persons specified in Rule 13d–1(b)(1)(ii)(A) through (J), does not exceed one percent of the securities of the subject class;

(H) A savings association as defined in Section 3(b) of the Federal Deposit Insurance Act (12 U.S.C. 1813);

(I) A church plan that is excluded from the definition of an investment company under section 3(c)(14) of the Investment Company Act of 1940;

(J) A non-U.S. institution that is the functional equivalent of any of the institutions listed in paragraphs (b)(1)(ii)(A) through (D) of this section, so long as the non-U.S. institution is subject to a regulatory scheme that is substantially comparable to the regulatory scheme applicable to the equivalent U.S. institution; and

(K) A group, provided that all the members are persons specified in Rule 13d–1(b)(1)(ii)(A) through (J).

(iii) Such person has promptly notified any other person (or group within the meaning of section 13(d)(3) of the Act) on whose behalf it holds, on a discretionary basis, securities exceeding five percent of the class, of any acquisition or transaction on behalf of such other person which might be reportable by that person under section 13(d) of the Act. This paragraph only requires notice to the account owner of information which the filing person reasonably should be expected to know and which would advise the account owner of an obligation he may have to file a statement pursuant to section 13(d) of the Act or an amendment thereto.

(2) The Schedule 13G filed pursuant to paragraph (b)(1) of this section shall be filed within 45 days after the end of the calendar year in which the person became obligated under paragraph (b)(1) of this section to report the person's beneficial ownership as of the last day of the calendar year, Provided, That it shall not be necessary to file a Schedule 13G unless the percentage of the class of equity security specified in paragraph (i) of this section beneficially owned as of the end of the calendar year is more than five percent; However, if the person's direct or indirect beneficial ownership exceeds 10 percent of the class of equity securities prior to the end of the calendar year, the initial Schedule 13G shall be filed within 10 days after the end of the first month in which the person's direct or indirect beneficial ownership exceeds 10 percent of the class of equity securities, computed as of the last day of the month. . . .

(c) A person who would otherwise be obligated under paragraph (a) of this section to file a statement on Schedule 13D may, in lieu thereof, file with the Commission, within 10 days after an acquisition described in paragraph (a) of this section, a short-form statement on Schedule 13G. *Provided,* That the person:

(1) Has not acquired the securities with any purpose, or with the effect of, changing or influencing the control of the issuer, or in connection with or as a participant in any transaction having such purpose or effect, including any transaction subject to Rule 13d–3(b), other than activities solely in connection with a nomination under Rule 14a–11; . . .

(3) Is not directly or indirectly the beneficial owner of 20 percent or more of the class. . . .

(d) Any person who, as of the end of any calendar year, is or becomes directly or indirectly the beneficial owner of more than five percent of any equity security of a class specified in paragraph (i) of this section and who is not required to file a statement under paragraph (a) of this section by virtue of the exemption provided by Section 13(d)(6)(A) or (B) of the Act, or because the beneficial ownership was acquired prior to December 22, 1970, or because the person otherwise (except for the exemption provided by Section 13(d)(6)(C) of the Act) is not required to file a statement, shall file with the Commission, within 45 days after the end of the calendar year in which the person became obligated to report under this paragraph (d), a statement containing the information required by Schedule 13G. . . .

(e)(1) Notwithstanding [paragraph (c)] of this section and Rule 13d–2(b), a person that has reported that it is the beneficial owner of more than five percent of a class of equity securities in a statement on Schedule 13G pursuant to paragraph . . . (c) of this section, or is required to report the acquisition but has not yet filed the schedule, shall immediately become subject to Rules 13d–1(a) and 13d–2(a) and shall file a statement on Schedule 13D within 10 days if, and shall remain subject to those requirements for so long as, the person:

(i) Has acquired or holds the securities with a purpose or effect of changing or influencing control of the issuer, or in connection with or as a participant in any transaction having that purpose or effect, including any transaction subject to Rule 13d–3(b); and

(ii) Is at that time the beneficial owner of more than five percent of a class of equity securities described in Rule 13d–1(i).

(2) From the time the person has acquired or holds the securities with a purpose or effect of changing or influencing control of the issuer, or in connection with or as a participant in any transaction having that purpose or effect until the expiration of the tenth day from the date of the filing of the Schedule 13D pursuant to this section, that person shall not:

(i) Vote or direct the voting of the securities described therein; or

(ii) Acquire an additional beneficial ownership interest in any equity securities of the issuer of the securities, nor of any person controlling the issuer.

(f)(1) Notwithstanding paragraph (c) of this section and Rule 13d–2(b), persons reporting on Schedule 13G pursuant to paragraph (c) of this section shall immediately become subject to Rule 13d–1(a) and Rule 13d–2(a) and shall remain subject to those requirements for so long as, and shall file a statement on Schedule 13D within 10 days of the date on which, the person's beneficial ownership equals or exceeds 20 percent of the class of equity securities.

(2) From the time of the acquisition of 20 percent or more of the class of equity securities until the expiration of the tenth day from the date of the filing of the Schedule 13D pursuant to this section, the person shall not:

(i) Vote or direct the voting of the securities described therein, or

(ii) Acquire an additional beneficial ownership interest in any equity securities of the issuer of the securities, nor of any person controlling the issuer. . . .

(g) Any person who has reported an acquisition of securities in a statement on Schedule 13G pursuant to paragraph (b) of this section, or has become obligated to report on the Schedule 13G (Rule 13d–102) but has not yet filed the Schedule, and thereafter ceases to be a person specified in paragraph (b)(1)(ii) of this section or determines that it no longer has acquired or holds the securities in the ordinary course of business shall immediately become subject to Rule 13d–1(a) or Rule 13d–1(c) (if the person satisfies the requirements specified in Rule 13d–1(c)), and Rule 13d–2 (a), (b) or (d), and shall file, within 10 days thereafter, a statement on Schedule 13D or amendment to Schedule 13G, as applicable, if the person is a beneficial owner at that time of more than five percent of the class of equity securities. . . .

(h) Any person who has filed a Schedule 13D pursuant to paragraph [(e) or (f)] of this section may again report its beneficial ownership on Schedule 13G pursuant to [paragraph] (c) of this section provided the person qualifies thereunder, as applicable, by filing a Schedule 13G once the person determines that the provisions of paragraph [(e) or (f)] of this section no longer apply.

(i) For the purpose of this regulation, the term "equity security" means any equity security of a class which is registered pursuant to section 12 of that Act, or any equity security of any insurance company which would have been required to be so registered except for the exemption contained in section 12(g)(2)(G) of the Act, or any equity security issued by a closed-end investment company registered under the Investment Company Act of 1940; *Provided,* Such term shall not include securities of a class of non-voting securities. . . .

(k)(1) Whenever two or more persons are required to file a statement containing the information required by Schedule 13D or Schedule 13G with respect to the same securities, only one statement need be filed: provided, that:

(i) Each person on whose behalf the statement is filed is individually eligible to use the Schedule on which the information is filed;

(ii) Each person on whose behalf the statement is filed is responsible for the timely filing of such statement and any amendments thereto, and for the completeness and accuracy of the information concerning such person contained therein; such person is not responsible for the completeness or accuracy of the information concerning the other persons making the filing, unless such person knows or has reason to believe that such information is inaccurate; and

(iii) Such statement identifies all such persons, contains the required information with regard to each such person, indicates that such statement is filed on behalf of all such persons, and includes, as an exhibit, their agreement in writing that such a statement is filed on behalf of each of them.

(2) A group's filing obligation may be satisfied either by a single joint filing or by each of the group's members making an individual filing. If the group's members elect to make their own filings, each such filing should identify all members of the group but the information provided concerning the other persons making the filing need only reflect information which the filing person knows or has reason to know.

Rule 13d–2. Filing of Amendments to Schedules 13D or 13G

(a) If any material change occurs in the facts set forth in the Schedule 13D required by Rule 13d–1(a), including, but not limited to, any material increase or decrease in the percentage of the class beneficially owned, the person or persons who were required to file the statement shall promptly file or cause to be filed with the Commission an amendment disclosing that change. An acquisition or disposition of beneficial ownership of securities in an amount equal to one percent or more of the class of securities shall be deemed "material" for purposes of this section; acquisitions or dispositions of less than those amounts may be material, depending upon the facts and circumstances. . . .

Rule 13d–3. Determination of Beneficial Owner

(a) For the purposes of sections 13(d) and 13(g) of the Act a beneficial owner of a security includes any person who, directly or indirectly, through any contract, arrangement, understanding, relationship, or otherwise has or shares:

(1) Voting power which includes the power to vote, or to direct the voting of, such security; and/or,

(2) Investment power which includes the power to dispose, or to direct the disposition of, such security.

(b) Any person who, directly or indirectly, creates or uses a trust, proxy, power of attorney, pooling arrangement or any other contract, arrangement, or device with the purpose or effect of divesting such person of beneficial ownership of a security or preventing the vesting of such beneficial ownership as part of a plan or scheme to evade the reporting requirements of section 13(d) or (g) of the Act shall be deemed for purposes of such sections to be the beneficial owner of such security.

(c) All securities of the same class beneficially owned by a person, regardless of the form which such beneficial ownership takes, shall be aggregated in calculating the number of shares beneficially owned by such person.

(d) Notwithstanding the provisions of paragraphs (a) and (c) of this rule:

(1)(i) A person shall be deemed to be the beneficial owner of a security, subject to the provisions of paragraph (b) of this rule, if that person has the right to acquire beneficial ownership of such security, as defined in Rule 13d–3(a) . . . within sixty days, including but not limited to any right to acquire: (A) Through the exercise of any option, warrant or right; (B) through the conversion of a security; (C) pursuant to the power to revoke a trust, discretionary account, or similar arrangement; or (D) pursuant to the automatic termination of a trust, discretionary account or similar arrangement; provided, however, any person who acquires a security or power specified in paragraphs (d)(1)(i)(A), (B) or (C), of this section, with the purpose or effect of changing or influencing the control of the issuer, or in connection with or as a participant in any transaction having such purpose or effect, immediately upon such acquisition shall be deemed to be the beneficial owner of the securities which may be acquired through the exercise or conversion of such security or power. Any securities not outstanding which are subject to such options, warrants, rights or conversion privileges shall be deemed to be outstanding for the purpose of computing the percentage of outstanding securities of the class owned by such person but shall not be deemed to be outstanding for the purpose of computing the percentage of the class [owned] by any other person.

(ii) Paragraph (d)(1)(i) of this section remains applicable for the purpose of determining the obligation to file with respect to the underlying security even though the option, warrant, right or convertible security is of a class of equity security, as defined in Rule 13d–1(i), and may therefore give rise to a separate obligation to file. . . .

(2) A member of a national securities exchange shall not be deemed to be a beneficial owner of securities held directly or indirectly by it on behalf of another person solely because such member is the record holder of such securities and, pursuant to the rules of such exchange, may direct the vote of such securities, without instruction, on other than contested matters or matters that may affect substantially the rights or privileges of the holders of the securities to be voted, but is otherwise precluded by the rules of such exchange from voting without instruction.

(3) A person who in the ordinary course of his business is a pledgee of securities under a written pledge agreement shall not be deemed to be the beneficial owner of such pledged securities until the pledgee has taken all formal steps necessary which are required to declare a default and determines that the power to vote or to direct the vote or to dispose or to direct the disposition of such pledged securities will be exercised, provided, that:

(i) The [pledge] agreement is bona fide and was not entered into with the purpose nor with the effect of changing or influencing the control of the issuer, nor in connection with any transaction having such purpose or effect, including any transaction subject to Rule 13d–3(b);

(ii) The pledgee is a person specified in Rule 13d–1(b)(ii), including persons meeting the conditions set forth in paragraph (G) thereof; and

(iii) The [pledge] agreement, prior to default, does not grant to the pledgee;

(A) The power to vote or to direct the vote of the pledged securities; or

(B) The power to dispose or direct the disposition of the pledged securities, other than the grant of such power(s) pursuant to a pledge agreement under which credit is extended subject to regulation T (12 CFR 220.1 to 220.8) and in which the pledgee is a broker or dealer registered under section 15 of the act.

(4) A person engaged in business as an underwriter of securities who acquires securities through his participation in good faith in a firm commitment underwriting registered under the Securities Act of 1933 shall not be deemed to be the beneficial owner of such securities until the expiration of forty days after the date of such acquisition.

Rule 13d–4. Disclaimer of Beneficial Ownership

Any person may expressly declare in any statement filed that the filing of such statement shall not be construed as an admission that such person is, for the purposes of sections 13(d) or 13(g) of the Act, the beneficial owner of any securities covered by the statement.

Rule 13d–5. Acquisition of Securities

(a) A person who becomes a beneficial owner of securities shall be deemed to have acquired such securities for purposes of section 13(d)(1) of the Act, whether such acquisition was through purchase or otherwise. . . .

(b)(1) When two or more persons agree to act together for the purpose of acquiring, holding, voting or disposing of equity securities of an issuer, the group formed thereby shall be deemed to have acquired beneficial ownership, for purposes of sections 13(d) and (g) of the Act, as of the date of such agreement, of all equity securities of that issuer beneficially owned by any such persons. . . .

Rule 13d–7. Dissemination

One copy of the Schedule filed pursuant to Rules 13d–1 and 13d–2 shall be sent to the issuer of the security at its principal executive office, by registered or certified mail. A copy of Schedules filed pursuant to Rules 13d–1(a) and 13d–2(a) shall also be sent to each national securities exchange where the security is traded.

SCHEDULE 13D. INFORMATION TO BE INCLUDED IN STATEMENTS FILED PURSUANT TO RULE 13d–1(a) AND . . . RULE 13d–2(a)

(Name of Issuer)

(Title of Class of Securities)

(CUSIP Number)

(Name, Address and Telephone Number of Person Authorized
to Receive Notices and Communications)

(Date of Event Which Requires Filing of This Statement). . . .

GENERAL INSTRUCTIONS . . .

Item 1.   Security and Issuer. State the title of the class of equity securities to which this statement relates and the name and address of the principal executive offices of the issuer of such securities.

Item 2.   Identity and Background. If the person filing this statement . . . is a corporation, general partnership, limited partnership, syndicate or other group of persons, state its name, the state or other place of its organization, its principal business, the address of its principal office and the information required by (d) and (e) of this Item. If the person filing this statement or any person enumerated in Instruction C is a natural person, provide the information specified in (a) through (f) of this Item with respect to such person(s).

(a) Name;

(b) Residence or business address;

(c) Present principal occupation or employment and the name, principal business and address of any corporation or other organization in which such employment is conducted;

(d) Whether or not, during the last five years, such person has been convicted in a criminal proceeding (excluding traffic violations or similar misdemeanors) and, if so, give the dates, nature of conviction, name and location of court, any penalty imposed, or other disposition of the case;

(e) Whether or not, during the last five years, such person was a party to a civil proceeding of a judicial or administrative body of competent jurisdiction and as a result of such proceeding was or is subject to a judgment, decree or final order enjoining future violations of, or prohibiting or mandating activities subject to, federal or state securities laws or finding any violation with respect to such laws; and, if so, identify and describe such proceedings and summarize the terms of such judgment, decree or final order; and

(f) Citizenship.

Item 3.   Source and Amount of Funds or Other Consideration. State the source and the amount of funds or other consideration used or to be used in making the purchases, and if any part of the purchase price is or will be represented by funds or other consideration borrowed or otherwise obtained for the purpose of acquiring, holding, trading or voting the securities, a description of the transaction and the names of the parties thereto. Where material, such information should also be provided with respect to prior acquisitions not previously reported pursuant to this regulation. If the source of all or any part of the funds is a loan made in the ordinary course of business by a bank . . . , the name of the bank shall not be made available to the public if the person at the time of filing the statement so requests in writing and files such request, naming such bank, with the Secretary of the Commission. If the securities were acquired other than by purchase, describe the method of acquisition.

Item 4.   Purpose of Transaction. State the purpose or purposes of the acquisition of securities of the issuer. Describe any plans or proposals which the reporting persons may have which relate to or would result in:

(a) The acquisition by any person of additional securities of the issuer, or the disposition of securities of the issuer;

(b) An extraordinary corporate transaction, such as a merger, reorganization or liquidation, involving the issuer or any of its subsidiaries;

(c) A sale or transfer of a material amount of assets of the issuer or any of its subsidiaries;

(d) Any change in the present board of directors or management of the issuer, including any plans or proposals to change the number or term of directors or to fill any existing vacancies on the board;

(e) Any material change in the present capitalization or dividend policy of the issuer;

(f) Any other material change in the issuer's business or corporate structure . . . ;

(g) Changes in the issuer's charter, bylaws or instruments corresponding thereto or other actions which may impede the acquisition of control of the issuer by any person;

(h) Causing a class of securities of the issuer to be delisted from a national securities exchange or to cease to be authorized to be quoted in an inter-dealer quotation system of a registered national securities association;

(i) A class of equity securities of the issuer becoming eligible for termination of registration pursuant to section 12(g)(4) of the Act; or

(j) Any action similar to any of those enumerated above.

Item 5.   Interest in Securities of the Issuer. (a) State the aggregate number and percentage of the class of securities identified pursuant to Item 1 . . . beneficially owned (identifying those shares which there is a right to acquire) by each person named in Item 2. The above mentioned information should also be furnished with respect to persons who, together with any of the persons named in Item 2, comprise a group within the meaning of section 13(d)(3) of the Act;

(b) For each person named in response to paragraph (a), indicate the number of shares as to which there is sole power to vote or to direct the vote, sole power to dispose or to direct the disposition, or shared power to dispose or to direct the disposition. Provide the applicable information required by Item 2 with respect to each person with whom the power to vote or to direct the vote or to dispose or direct the disposition is shared;

(c) Describe any transactions in the class of securities reported on that were effected during the past sixty days or since the most recent filing of Schedule 13D . . . whichever is less, by the persons named in response to paragraph (a). . . .

Item 6.   Contracts, Arrangements, Understandings or Relationships With Respect to Securities of the Issuer. Describe any contracts, arrangements, understandings or relationships (legal or otherwise) among the persons named in Item 2 and between such persons and any person with respect to any securities of the issuer, including but not limited to transfer or voting of any of the securities, finder's fees, joint ventures, loan or option arrangements, puts or calls, guarantees of profits, division of profits or loss, or the giving or withholding of proxies, naming the persons with whom such contracts, arrangements, understandings or relationships have been entered into. Include such information for any of the securities that are pledged or otherwise subject to a contingency the occurrence of which would give another person voting power or investment power over such securities except that disclosure of standard default and similar provisions contained in loan agreements need not be included. . . .

SCHEDULE 13G. INFORMATION TO BE INCLUDED IN STATEMENTS FILED PURSUANT TO RULE 13d–(1)(b), (c), AND . . . (d)

SECURITIES AND EXCHANGE COMMISSION
Washington, D. C. 20549
SCHEDULE 13G
Under the Securities Exchange Act of 1934

(Amendment No. _____)

_____
(Name of Issuer)

_____
(Title of Class of Securities)

_____
(CUSIP Number)

_____
(Date of Event Which Requires Filing of This Statement). . . .

Instructions . . .

Item 4

Ownership

Provide the following information regarding the aggregate number and percentage of the class of securities of the issuer. . . .

(a) Amount beneficially owned: _____

(b) Percent of class: _____

(c) Number of shares as to which the person has: _____

    (i) Sole power to vote or to direct the vote _____

    (ii) Shared power to vote or to direct the vote _____

    (iii) Sole power to dispose or to direct the disposition of _____

    (iv) Shared power to dispose or to direct the disposition of _____

Item 10

Certifications. . . .

(c) The following certification shall be included if the statement is filed pursuant to Rule 13d–1(c):

By signing below I certify that, to the best of my knowledge and belief, the securities referred to above were not acquired and are not held for the purpose of or with the effect of changing or influencing the control of the issuer of the securities and were not acquired and are not held in connection with or as a participant in any transaction having that purpose or effect other than activities solely in connection with a nomination under Rule 14a–11.

Rule 13e–1. Purchase of Securities by the Issuer During a Third-Party Tender Offer

An issuer that has received notice that it is the subject of a tender offer made under Section 14(d)(1) of the Act, that has commenced under Rule 14d–2 must not purchase any of its equity securities during the tender offer unless the issuer first:

(a) Files a statement with the Commission containing the following information:

(1) The title and number of securities to be purchased;

(2) The names of the persons or classes of persons from whom the issuer will purchase the securities;

(3) The name of any exchange, inter-dealer quotation system or any other market on or through which the securities will be purchased;

(4) The purpose of the purchase;

(5) Whether the issuer will retire the securities, hold the securities in its treasury, or dispose of the securities. If the issuer intends to dispose of the securities, describe how it intends to do so; and

(6) The source and amount of funds or other consideration to be used to make the purchase. If the issuer borrows any funds or other consideration to make the purchase or enters any agreement for the purpose of acquiring, holding, or trading the securities, describe the transaction and agreement and identify the parties; and

(b) Pays the fee required . . . when it files the initial statement.

(c) This section does not apply to periodic repurchases in connection with an employee benefit plan or other similar plan of the issuer so long as the purchases are made in the ordinary course and not in response to the tender offer.

Rule 13e–3. Going Private Transactions by Certain Issuers or Their Affiliates

(a) *Definitions.* Unless indicated otherwise or the context otherwise requires, all terms used in this section and in Schedule 13E-3 . . . shall have the same meaning as in the Act or elsewhere in the General Rules and Regulations thereunder. In addition, the following definitions apply:

(1) An "affiliate" of an issuer is a person that directly or indirectly through one or more intermediaries controls, is controlled by, or is under common control with such issuer. For the purposes of this section only, a person who is not an affiliate of an issuer at the commencement of such person's tender offer for a class of equity securities of such issuer will not be deemed an affiliate of such issuer prior to the stated termination of such tender offer and any extensions thereof;

(2) The term "purchase" means any acquisition for value including, but not limited to, (i) any acquisition pursuant to the dissolution of an issuer subsequent to the sale or other disposition of substantially all the assets of such issuer to its affiliate, (ii) any acquisition pursuant to a merger, (iii) any acquisition of fractional interests in connection with a reverse stock split, and (iv) any acquisition subject to the control of an issuer or an affiliate of such issuer;

(3) A "Rule 13e-3 transaction" is any transaction or series of transactions involving one or more of the transactions described in paragraph (a)(3)(i) of this section which has either a reasonable likelihood or a purpose of producing, either directly or indirectly, any of the effects described in paragraph (a)(3)(ii) of this section;

(i) The transactions referred to in paragraph (a)(3) of this section are:

(A) A purchase of any equity security by the issuer of such security or by an affiliate of such issuer;

(B) A tender offer for or request or invitation for tenders of any equity security made by the issuer of such class of securities or by an affiliate of such issuer; or

(C) A solicitation subject to Regulation 14A . . . of any proxy, consent or authorization of, or a distribution subject to Regulation 14C . . . of information statements to, any equity security holder by the issuer of the class of securities or by an affiliate of such issuer, in connection with: a merger, consolidation, reclassification, recapitalization, reorganization or similar corporate transaction of an issuer or between an issuer (or its subsidiaries) and its affiliate; a sale of substantially all the assets of an issuer to its affiliate or group of affiliates; or a reverse stock split of any class of equity securities of the issuer involving the purchase of fractional interests.

(ii) The effects referred to in paragraph (a)(3) of this section are:

(A) Causing any class of equity securities of the issuer which is subject to section 12(g) or section 15(d) of the Act to become eligible for termination of registration under Rule 12g–4 . . . or causing the reporting obligations with respect to such class to become eligible for . . . suspension under section 15(d); or

(B) Causing any class of equity securities of the issuer which is either listed on a national securities exchange or authorized to be quoted in an inter-dealer quotation system of a registered national securities association to be neither listed on any national securities exchange nor authorized to be quoted on an inter-dealer quotation system of any registered national securities association. . . .

(b) *Application of section to an issuer (or an affiliate of such issuer) subject to section 12 of the Act.* (1) It shall be a fraudulent, deceptive or manipulative act or practice, in connection with a Rule 13e–3 transaction, for an issuer which has a class of equity securities registered pursuant to section 12 of the Act or which is a closed-end investment company registered under the Investment Company Act of 1940, or an affiliate of such issuer, directly or indirectly

(i) To employ any device, scheme or artifice to defraud any person;

(ii) To make any untrue statement of a material fact or to omit to state a material fact necessary in order to make the statements made, in light of the circumstances under which they were made, not misleading; or

(iii) To engage in any act, practice or course of business which operates or would operate as a fraud or deceit upon any person.

(2) As a means reasonably designed to prevent fraudulent, deceptive or manipulative acts or practices in connection with any Rule 13e–3 transaction, it shall be unlawful for an issuer which has a class of equity securities registered pursuant to section 12 of the Act, or an affiliate of such issuer, to engage, directly or indirectly, in a Rule 13e–3 transaction unless:

(i) Such issuer or affiliate complies with the requirements of paragraphs (d), (e) and (f) of this section; and

(ii) The Rule 13e–3 transaction is not in violation of paragraph (b)(1) of this section. . . .

(d) *Material required to be filed.* The issuer or affiliate engaging in a Rule 13e–3 transaction must file with the Commission:

(1) A Schedule 13E-3, including all exhibits;

(2) An amendment to Schedule 13E-3 reporting promptly any material changes in the information set forth in the schedule previously filed; and

(3) A final amendment to Schedule 13E-3 reporting promptly the results of the Rule 13e–3 transaction.

(e) *Disclosure of information to security holders.*

(1) In addition to disclosing the information required by any other applicable rule or regulation under the federal securities laws, the issuer or affiliate engaging in a Rule 13e–3 transaction must disclose to security holders of the class that is the subject of the transaction, as specified in paragraph (f) of this section, the following:

(i) The information required by Item 1 of Schedule 13E-3 (Summary Term Sheet);

(ii) The information required by Items 7, 8 and 9 of Schedule 13E-3, which must be prominently disclosed in a "Special Factors" section in the front of the disclosure document;

(iii) A prominent legend on the outside front cover page that indicates that neither the Securities and Exchange Commission nor any state securities commission has: approved or disapproved of the transaction; passed upon the merits or fairness of the transaction; or passed upon the adequacy or accuracy of the disclosure in the document. The legend also must make it clear that any representation to the contrary is a criminal offense;

(iv) The information concerning appraisal rights required by Item 1016(f) of [Regulation S–K]; and

(v) The information required by the remaining items of Schedule 13E-3, except for Item 1016 of [Regulation S–K] (exhibits), or a fair and adequate summary of the information. . . .

Rule 13e–4. Tender Offers by Issuers

(a) *Definitions.* Unless the context otherwise requires, all terms used in this section and in Schedule TO . . . shall have the same meaning as in the Act or elsewhere in the General Rules and Regulations thereunder. In addition, the following definitions shall apply:

(1) The term "issuer" means any issuer which has a class of equity security registered pursuant to section 12 of the Act, or which is required to file periodic reports pursuant to section 15(d) of the Act, or which is a closed-end investment company registered under the Investment Company Act of 1940.

(2) The term "issuer tender offer" refers to a tender offer for, or a request or invitation for tenders of, any class of equity security, made by the issuer of such class of equity security or by an affiliate of such issuer. . . .

(b) *Filing, disclosure and dissemination.* As soon as practicable on the date of commencement of the issuer tender offer, the issuer or affiliate making the issuer tender offer must comply with:

(1) The filing requirements of paragraph (c)(2) of this section;

(2) The disclosure requirements of paragraph (d)(1) of this section; and

(3) The dissemination requirements of paragraph (e) of this section.

(c) *Material required to be filed.* The issuer or affiliate making the issuer tender offer must file with the Commission:

(1) All written communications made by the issuer or affiliate relating to the issuer tender offer, from and including the first public announcement, as soon as practicable on the date of the communication;

(2) A Schedule TO, including all exhibits;

(3) An amendment to Schedule TO reporting promptly any material changes in the information set forth in the schedule previously filed; and

(4) A final amendment to Schedule TO reporting promptly the results of the issuer tender offer.

Instructions to Rule 13e–4(c): . . .

5. "Public announcement" is any oral or written communication by the issuer, affiliate or any person authorized to act on their behalf that is reasonably designed to, or has the effect of, informing the public or security holders in general about the issuer tender offer.

(d) *Disclosure of tender offer information to security holders.*

(1) The issuer or affiliate making the issuer tender offer must disclose, in a manner prescribed by paragraph (e)(1) of this section, the following:

(i) The information required by Item 1 of Schedule TO (summary term sheet); and

(ii) The information required by the remaining items of Schedule TO for issuer tender offers, except for Item 12 (exhibits), or a fair and adequate summary of the information.

(2) If there are any material changes in the information previously disclosed to security holders, the issuer or affiliate must disclose the changes promptly to security holders in a manner specified in paragraph (e)(3) of this section.

(3) If the issuer or affiliate disseminates the issuer tender offer by means of summary publication as described in paragraph (e)(1)(iii) of this section, the summary advertisement must not include a transmittal letter that would permit security holders to tender securities sought in the offer and must disclose at least the following information:

(i) The identity of the issuer or affiliate making the issuer tender offer;

(ii) The information required by 1004(a)(1) and 1006(a) of [Regulation S–K];

(iii) Instructions on how security holders can obtain promptly a copy of the statement required by paragraph (d)(1) of this section, at the issuer or affiliate's expense; and

(iv) A statement that the information contained in the statement required by paragraph (d)(1) of this section is incorporated by reference.

(e) *Dissemination of tender offers to security holders.* An issuer tender offer will be deemed to be published, sent or given to security holders if the issuer or affiliate making the issuer tender offer complies fully with one or more of the methods described in this section.

(1) For issuer tender offers in which the consideration offered consists solely of cash and/or securities exempt from registration under section 3 of the Securities Act of 1933:

(i) *Dissemination of cash issuer tender offers by long-form publication*: By making adequate publication of the information required by paragraph (d)(1) of this section in a newspaper or newspapers, on the date of commencement of the issuer tender offer.

(ii) *Dissemination of any issuer tender offer by use of stockholder and other lists*:

(A) By mailing or otherwise furnishing promptly a statement containing the information required by paragraph (d)(1) of this section to each security holder whose name appears on the most recent stockholder list of the issuer;

(B) By contacting each participant on the most recent security position listing of any clearing agency within the possession or access of the issuer or affiliate making the issuer tender offer, and making inquiry of each participant as to the approximate number of beneficial owners of the securities sought in the offer that are held by the participant;

(C) By furnishing to each participant a sufficient number of copies of the statement required by paragraph (d)(1) of this section for transmittal to the beneficial owners; and

(D) By agreeing to reimburse each participant promptly for its reasonable expenses incurred in forwarding the statement to beneficial owners.

(iii) *Dissemination of certain cash issuer tender offers by summary publication*:

(A) If the issuer tender offer is not subject to Rule 13e–3, by making adequate publication of a summary advertisement containing the information required by paragraph (d)(3) of this section in a newspaper or newspapers, on the date of commencement of the issuer tender offer; and

(B) By mailing or otherwise furnishing promptly the statement required by paragraph (d)(1) of this section and a transmittal letter to any security holder who requests a copy of the statement or transmittal letter.

Instruction to paragraph (e)(1) . . .

(2) For tender offers in which the consideration consists solely or partially of securities registered under the Securities Act of 1933, a registration statement containing all of the required information, including pricing information, has been filed and a preliminary prospectus or a prospectus that meets the requirements of Section 10(a) of the Securities Act, including a letter of transmittal, is delivered to security holders. However, for going-private transactions (as defined by Rule 13e–3) and roll-up transactions (as described by Item 901 of Regulation S–K), a registration statement registering the securities to be offered must have become effective and only a prospectus that meets the requirements of Section 10(a) of the Securities Act may be delivered to security holders on the date of commencement. . . .

(f) *Manner of making tender offer.* (1) The issuer tender offer, unless withdrawn, shall remain open until the expiration of:

(i) At least twenty business days from its commencement; and

(ii) At least ten business days from the date that notice of an increase or decrease in the percentage of the class of securities being sought or the consideration offered or the dealer's soliciting fee to be given is first published, sent or given to security holders.

Provided, however, That, for purposes of this paragraph, the acceptance for payment by the issuer or affiliate of an additional amount of securities not to exceed two percent of the class of securities that is the subject of the tender offer shall not be deemed to be an increase. For purposes of this paragraph, the percentage of a class of securities shall be calculated in accordance with section 14(d)(3) of the Act.

(2) The issuer or affiliate making the issuer tender offer shall permit securities tendered pursuant to the issuer tender offer to be withdrawn:

(i) At any time during the period such issuer tender offer remains open; and

(ii) If not yet accepted for payment, after the expiration of forty business days from the commencement of the issuer tender offer.

(3) If the issuer or affiliate makes a tender offer for less than all of the outstanding equity securities of a class, and if a greater number of securities is tendered pursuant thereto than the issuer or affiliate is bound or willing to take up and pay for, the securities taken up and paid for shall be taken up and paid for as nearly as may be pro rata, disregarding fractions, according to the number of securities tendered by each security holder during the period such offer remains open; *Provided, however,* That this provision shall not prohibit the issuer or affiliate making the issuer tender offer from:

(i) Accepting all securities tendered by persons who own, beneficially or of record, an aggregate of not more than a specified number which is less than one hundred shares of such security and who tender all their securities, before prorating securities tendered by others; or

(ii) Accepting by lot securities tendered by security holders who tender all securities held by them and who, when tendering their securities, elect to have either all or none or at least a minimum amount or none accepted, if the issuer or affiliate first accepts all securities tendered by security holders who do not so elect;

(4) In the event the issuer or affiliate making the issuer tender increases the consideration offered after the issuer tender offer has commenced, such issuer or affiliate shall pay such increased consideration to all security holders whose tendered securities are accepted for payment by such issuer or affiliate.

(5) The issuer or affiliate making the tender offer shall either pay the consideration offered, or return the tendered securities, promptly after the termination or withdrawal of the tender offer.

(6) Until the expiration of at least ten business days after the date of termination of the issuer tender offer, neither the issuer nor any affiliate shall make any purchases, otherwise than pursuant to the tender offer, of:

(i) Any security which is the subject of the issuer tender offer, or any security of the same class and series, or any right to purchase any such securities; and

(ii) In the case of an issuer tender offer which is an exchange offer, any security being offered pursuant to such exchange offer, or any security of the same class and series, or any right to purchase any such security.

(7) The time periods for the minimum offering periods pursuant to this section shall be computed on a concurrent as opposed to a consecutive basis.

(8) No issuer or affiliate shall make a tender offer unless:

(i) The tender offer is open to all security holders of the class of securities subject to the tender offer; and

(ii) The consideration paid to any security holder for securities tendered in the tender offer is the highest consideration paid to any other security holder for securities tendered in the tender offer. . . .

(12)(i) Paragraph (f)(8)(ii) of this section shall not prohibit the negotiation, execution or amendment of an employment compensation, severance or other employee benefit arrangement, or payments made or to be made or benefits granted or to be granted according to such an arrangement, with respect to any security holder of the issuer, where the amount payable under the arrangement:

(A) Is being paid or granted as compensation for past services performed, future services to be performed, or future services to be refrained from performing, by the security holder (and matters incidental thereto); and

(B) Is not calculated based on the number of securities tendered or to be tendered in the tender offer by the security holder.

(ii) The provisions of paragraph (f)(12)(i) of this section shall be satisfied and, therefore, pursuant to this non-exclusive safe harbor, the negotiation, execution or amendment of an arrangement and any payments made or to be made or benefits granted or to be granted according to that arrangement shall not be prohibited by paragraph (f)(8)(ii) of this section, if the arrangement is approved as an employment compensation, severance or other employee benefit arrangement solely by independent directors as follows:

(A) The compensation committee or a committee of the board of directors that performs functions similar to a compensation committee of the issuer approves the arrangement, regardless of whether the issuer is a party to the arrangement, or, if an affiliate is a party to the arrangement, the compensation committee or a committee of the board of directors that performs functions similar to a compensation committee of the affiliate approves the arrangement; or

(B) If the issuer's or affiliate's board of directors, as applicable, does not have a compensation committee or a committee of the board of directors that performs functions similar to a compensation committee or if none of the members of the issuer's or affiliate's compensation committee or committee that performs functions similar to a compensation committee is independent, a special committee of the board of directors formed to consider and approve the arrangement approves the arrangement. . . .

Instruction to paragraph (f)(12)

The fact that the provisions of paragraph (f)(12) of this section extend only to employment compensation, severance and other employee benefit arrangements and not to other arrangements, such as commercial arrangements, does not raise any inference that a payment under any such other arrangement constitutes consideration paid for securities in a tender offer. . . .

(j)(1) It shall be a fraudulent, deceptive or manipulative act or practice, in connection with an issuer tender offer, for an issuer or an affiliate of such issuer, in connection with an issuer tender offer:

(i) To employ any device, scheme or artifice to defraud any person;

(ii) To make any untrue statement of a material fact or to omit to state a material fact necessary in order to make the statements made, in the light of the circumstances under which they were made, not misleading; or

(iii) To engage in any act, practice or course of business which operates or would operate as a fraud or deceit upon any person.

(2) As a means reasonably designed to prevent fraudulent, deceptive or manipulative acts or practices in connection with any issuer tender offer, it shall be unlawful for an issuer or an affiliate of such issuer to make an issuer tender offer unless:

(i) Such issuer or affiliate complies with the requirements of paragraphs (b), (c), (d), (e) and (f) of this section; and

(ii) The issuer tender offer is not in violation of paragraph (j)(1) of this section. . . .

SCHEDULE 13E-3.   TRANSACTION STATEMENT
UNDER SECTION 13(e). . . .

(Name of the Issuer)

(Name of Person(s) Filing Statement)

(Title of Class of Securities)

(CUSIP Number of Class of Securities)

(Name, address and telephone number of person authorized to receive
notices and communications on behalf of persons filing statement). . . .

General Instructions. . . .

C.   If the statement is filed by a general or limited partnership, syndicate or other group, the information called for by Items 3, 5, 6, 10 and 11 must be given with respect to: (i) each partner of the general partnership; (ii) each partner who is, or functions as, a general partner of the limited partnership; (iii) each member of the syndicate or group; and (iv) each person controlling the partner or member. If the statement is filed by a corporation . . . the information called for by the items specified above must be given with respect to: (a) each executive officer and director of the corporation; (b) each person controlling the corporation; and (c) each executive officer and director of any corporation or other person ultimately in control of the corporation. . . .

Item 1. Summary Term Sheet

Furnish the information required by Item 1001 of Regulation M–A unless information is disclosed to security holders in a prospectus that meets the requirements of Rule 421(d) [under the Securities Act].

Item 2. Subject Company Information

Furnish the information required by Item 1002(a) through (c) of Regulation M–A.

Item 3. Identity and Background of Filing Person

Furnish the information required by Item 1003(a) through (c) of Regulation M–A.

Item 4. Terms of the Transaction

Furnish the information required by Item 1004(a) of Regulation M–A.

Item 5. Past Contacts, Transactions, Negotiations and Agreements

Furnish the information required by Item 1005(a) and (b) of Regulation M–A.

Item 6. Purposes of the Transaction and Plans or Proposals

Furnish the information required by Item 1006(a) and (c)(1) through (7) of Regulation M–A.

Item 7. Purposes, Alternatives, Reasons and Effects

Furnish the information required by Item 1013 of Regulation M–A.

Item 8. Fairness of the Transaction

Furnish the information required by Item 1014 of Regulation M–A.

Item 9. Reports, Opinions, Appraisals and Negotiations

Furnish the information required by Item 1015 of Regulation M–A.

Item 10. Source and Amounts of Funds or Other Consideration

Furnish the information required by Item 1007 of Regulation M–A.

Item 11. Interest in Securities of the Subject Company

Furnish the information required by Item 1008 of Regulation M–A.

Item 12. The Solicitation or Recommendation

Furnish the information required by Item 1012(d) and (e) of Regulation M–A.

Item 13. Financial Statements

Furnish the information required by Item 1010(a) through (b) of Regulation M–A for the issuer of the subject class of securities.

Item 14. Persons/Assets, Retained, Employed, Compensated or Used

Furnish the information required by Item 1009 of Regulation M–A.

Item 15. Additional Information

Furnish the information required by Item 1011(b) and (c) of Regulation M–A.

Item 16. Exhibits

File as an exhibit to the Schedule all documents specified in Item 1016(a) through (d), (f) and (g) of Regulation M–A. . . .

Rule 13h–1. Large Trader Reporting

(a) *Definitions.* For purposes of this section:

(1) The term *large trader* means any person that:

(i) Directly or indirectly, including through other persons controlled by such person, exercises investment discretion over one or more accounts and effects transactions for the purchase or sale of any NMS security for or on behalf of such accounts, by or through one or more registered broker-dealers, in an aggregate amount equal to or greater than the identifying activity level; or

(ii) Voluntarily registers as a large trader by filing electronically with the Commission Form 13H of this chapter.

(2) The term *person* has the same meaning as in Section 13(h)(8)(E) of the Securities Exchange Act of 1934.

(3) The term *control* (including the terms *controlling, controlled by* and *under common control with*) means the possession, direct or indirect, of the power to direct or cause the direction of the management and policies of a person, whether through the ownership of securities, by contract, or otherwise. For purposes of this section only, any person that directly or indirectly has the right to vote or direct the vote of 25% or more of a class of voting securities of an entity or has the power to sell or direct the sale of 25% or more of a class of voting securities of such entity, or in the case of a partnership, has the right to receive, upon dissolution, or has contributed, 25% or more of the capital, is presumed to control that entity.

(4) The term *investment discretion* has the same meaning as in Section 3(a)(35) of the Securities Exchange Act of 1934. . . . A person's employees who exercise investment discretion within the scope of their employment are deemed to do so on behalf of such person.

(5) The term *NMS security* has the meaning provided for in Section 242.600(b)(46) of this chapter.

(6) The term *transaction* or *transactions* means all transactions in NMS securities, excluding the purchase or sale of such securities pursuant to exercises or assignments of option contracts. For the sole purpose of determining whether a person is a large trader, the following transactions are excluded from this definition:

(i) Any journal or bookkeeping entry made to an account in order to record or memorialize the receipt or delivery of funds or securities pursuant to the settlement of a transaction;

(ii) Any transaction that is part of an offering of securities by or on behalf of an issuer, or by an underwriter on behalf of an issuer, or an agent for an issuer, whether or not such offering is subject to registration under the Securities Act of 1933, provided, however, that this exemption shall not include an offering of securities effected through the facilities of a national securities exchange;

(iii) Any transaction that constitutes a gift;

(iv) Any transaction effected by a court appointed executor, administrator, or fiduciary pursuant to the distribution of a decedent's estate;

(v) Any transaction effected pursuant to a court order or judgment;

(vi) Any transaction effected pursuant to a rollover of qualified plan or trust assets subject to Section 402(a)(5) of the Internal Revenue Code;

(vii) Any transaction between an employer and its employees effected pursuant to the award, allocation, sale, grant, or exercise of a NMS security, option or other right to acquire securities at a pre-established price pursuant to a plan which is primarily for the purpose of an issuer benefit plan or compensatory arrangement; or 159

(viii) Any transaction to effect a business combination, including a reclassification, merger, consolidation, or tender offer subject to Section 14(d) of the Securities Exchange Act of 1934 (15 U.S.C. 78n(d)); an issuer tender offer or other stock buyback by an issuer; or a stock loan or equity repurchase agreement.

(7) The term *identifying activity level* means: aggregate transactions in NMS securities that are equal to or greater than:

(i) During a calendar day, either two million shares or shares with a fair market value of $20 million; or

(ii) During a calendar month, either twenty million shares or shares with a fair market value of $200 million.

(8) The term *reporting activity level* means:

(i) Each transaction in NMS securities, effected in a single account during a calendar day, that is equal to or greater than 100 shares;

(ii) Any transaction in NMS securities for fewer than 100 shares, effected in a single account during a calendar day, that a registered broker-dealer may deem appropriate; or

(iii) Such other amount that may be established by order of the Commission from time to time.

(9) The term *Unidentified Large Trader* means each person who has not complied with the identification requirements of paragraphs (b)(1) and (b)(2) of this section that a registered broker-dealer knows or has reason to know is a large trader. For purposes of determining under this section whether a registered broker-dealer has reason to know that a person is large trader, a registered broker-dealer need take into account only transactions in NMS securities effected by or through such broker-dealer.

(b) *Identification requirements for large traders.*

(1) *Form 13H.* Except as provided in paragraph (b)(3) of this section, each large trader shall file electronically Form 13H with the Commission, in accordance with the instructions contained therein:

(i) Promptly after first effecting aggregate transactions, or after effecting aggregate transactions subsequent to becoming inactive pursuant to paragraph (b)(3) of this section, equal to or greater than the identifying activity level;

(ii) Within 45 days after the end of each full calendar year; and

(iii) Promptly following the end of a calendar quarter in the event that any of the information contained in a Form 13H filing becomes inaccurate for any reason.

(2) *Disclosure of large trader status.* Each large trader shall disclose to the registered broker-dealers effecting transactions on its behalf its large trader identification number and each account to which it applies. A large trader on Inactive Status pursuant to paragraph (b)(3) of this section must notify broker-dealers promptly after filing for reactivated status with the Commission.

(3) *Filing requirement.*

(i) *Compliance by controlling person.* A large trader shall not be required to separately comply with the requirements of this paragraph (b) if a person who controls the large trader complies with all of the requirements under paragraphs (b)(1), (b)(2), and (b)(4) of this section applicable to such large trader with respect to all of its accounts.

(ii) Compliance by controlled person. A large trader shall not be required to separately comply with the requirements of this paragraph (b) if one or more persons controlled by such large trader collectively comply with all of the requirements under paragraphs (b)(1), (b)(2), and (b)(4) of this section applicable to such large trader with respect to all of its accounts.

(iii) Inactive status. A large trader that has not effected aggregate transactions at any time during the previous full calendar year in an amount equal to or greater than the identifying activity level shall become inactive upon filing a Form 13H and thereafter shall not be required to file Form 13H or disclose its large trader status unless and until its transactions again are equal to or greater than the identifying activity level. A large trader that has ceased operations may elect to become inactive by filing an amended Form 13H to indicate its terminated status.

(4) *Other information.* Upon request, a large trader must promptly provide additional descriptive or clarifying information that would allow the Commission to further identify the large trader and all accounts through which the large trader effects transactions.

(c) *Aggregation.*

(1) *Transactions.* For the purpose of determining whether a person is a large trader, the following shall apply:

(i) The volume or fair market value of transactions in equity securities and the volume or fair market value of the equity securities underlying transactions in options on equity securities, purchased and sold, shall be aggregated;

(ii) The fair market value of transactions in options on a group or index of equity securities (or based on the value thereof), purchased and sold, shall be aggregated; and 162

(iii) Under no circumstances shall a person subtract, offset, or net purchase and sale transactions, in equity securities or option contracts, and among or within accounts, when aggregating the volume or fair market value of transactions for purposes of this section.

(2) *Accounts.* Under no circumstances shall a person disaggregate accounts to avoid the identification requirements of this section.

(d) *Recordkeeping requirements for broker and dealers.*

(1) *Generally.* Every registered broker-dealer shall maintain records of all information required under paragraphs (d)(2) and (d)(3) of this section for all transactions effected directly or indirectly by or through:

(i) An account such broker-dealer carries for a large trader or an Unidentified Large Trader, or

(ii) If the broker-dealer is a large trader, any proprietary or other account over which such broker-dealer exercises investment discretion.

(iii) Additionally, where a non-broker-dealer carries an account for a large trader or an Unidentified Large Trader, the broker-dealer effecting transactions directly or indirectly for such large trader or Unidentified Large Trader shall maintain records of all of the information required under paragraphs (d)(2) and (d)(3) of this section for those transactions.

(2) *Information.* The information required to be maintained for all transactions shall include:

(i) The clearing house number or alpha symbol of the broker or dealer submitting the information and the clearing house numbers or alpha symbols of the entities on the opposite side of the transaction; 163

(ii) Identifying symbol assigned to the security;

(iii) Date transaction was executed;

(iv) The number of shares or option contracts traded in each specific transaction; whether each transaction was a purchase, sale, or short sale; and, if an option contract, whether the transaction was a call or put option, an opening purchase or sale, a closing purchase or sale, or an exercise or assignment;

(v) Transaction price;

(vi) Account number;

(vii) Identity of the exchange or other market center where the transaction was executed.

(viii) A designation of whether the transaction was effected or caused to be effected for the account of a customer of such registered broker-dealer, or was a proprietary transaction effected or caused to be effected for the account of such broker-dealer;

(ix) If part or all of an account's transactions at the registered broker-dealer have been transferred or otherwise forwarded to one or more accounts at another registered broker-dealer, an identifier for this type of transaction; and if part or all of an account's transactions at the reporting broker-dealer have been transferred or otherwise received from one or more other registered broker-dealers, an identifier for this type of transaction;

(x) If part or all of an account's transactions at the reporting broker-dealer have been transferred or otherwise received from another account at the reporting broker-dealer, an identifier for this type of transaction; and if part or all of an account's transactions at the reporting broker-dealer have been transferred or otherwise forwarded to one or more other accounts at the reporting broker-dealer, an identifier for this type of transaction; 164

(xi) If a transaction was processed by a depository institution, the identifier assigned to the account by the depository institution;

(xii) The time that the transaction was executed; and

(xiii) The large trader identification number(s) associated with the account, unless the account is for an Unidentified Large Trader.

(3) *Information relating to Unidentified Large Traders.* With respect to transactions effected directly or indirectly by or through the account of an Unidentified Large Trader, the information required to be maintained for all transactions also shall include such Unidentified Large Trader's name, address, date the account was opened, and tax identification number(s).

(4) *Retention.* The records and information required to be made and kept pursuant to the provisions of this section shall be kept for such periods of time as provided in Rule 17a–4(b) under the Securities Exchange Act.

(5) *Availability of information.* The records and information required to be made and kept pursuant to the provisions of this rule shall be available on the morning after the day the transactions were effected (including Saturdays and holidays).

(e) *Reporting requirements for brokers and dealers.* Upon the request of the Commission, every registered broker-dealer who is itself a large trader or carries an account for a large trader or an Unidentified Large Trader shall electronically report to the Commission, using the infrastructure supporting Rule 17a–25 under the Securities Exchange Act, in machine-readable form and in accordance with instructions issued by the Commission, all information required under paragraphs (d)(2) and (d)(3) of this section for all transactions effected directly or indirectly by or through accounts carried by such broker-dealer for large traders and Unidentified Large Traders, equal to or greater than the reporting activity level. Additionally, where a non-broker-dealer carries an account for a large trader or an Unidentified Large Trader, the broker-dealer effecting such transactions directly or indirectly for a large trader shall electronically report using the infrastructure supporting § 240.17a–25, in machine-readable form and in accordance with instructions issued by the Commission, all information required under paragraphs (d)(2) and (d)(3) of this section for such transactions equal to or greater than the reporting activity level. Such reports shall be submitted to the Commission no later than the day and time specified in the request for transaction information, which shall be no earlier than the opening of business of the day following such request, unless in unusual circumstances the same-day submission of information is requested.

(f) *Monitoring safe harbor.* For the purposes of this rule, a registered broker-dealer shall be deemed not to know or have reason to know that a person is a large trader if it does not have actual knowledge that a person is a large trader and it establishes policies and procedures reasonably designed to:

(1) Identify persons who have not complied with the identification requirements of paragraphs (b)(1) and (b)(2) of this section but whose transactions effected through an account or a group of accounts carried by such broker-dealer or through which such broker-dealer executes transactions, as applicable (and considering account name, tax identification number, or other identifying information available on the books and records of such broker-dealer) equal or exceed the identifying activity level;

(2) Treat any persons identified in paragraph (f)(1) of this section as an Unidentified Large Trader for purposes of this section; and

(3) Inform any person identified in paragraph (f)(1) of this section of its potential obligations under this section.

(g) *Exemptions.* Upon written application or upon its own motion, the Commission may by order exempt, upon specified terms and conditions or for stated periods, any person or class of persons or any transaction or class of transactions from the provisions of this section to the extent that such exemption is consistent with the purposes of the Securities Exchange Act of 1934.

REGULATION 14A: SOLICITATION OF PROXIES

Rule 14a–1. Definitions

Unless the context otherwise requires, all terms used in this regulation have the same meanings as in the Act or elsewhere in the general rules and regulations thereunder. In addition, the following definitions apply unless the context otherwise requires:

(a) *Associate.* The term "associate," used to indicate a relationship with any person, means:

(1) Any corporation or organization (other than the registrant or a majority owned subsidiary of the registrant) of which such person is an officer or partner or is, directly or indirectly, the beneficial owner of 10 percent or more of any class of equity securities;

(2) Any trust or other estate in which such person has a substantial beneficial interest or as to which such person serves as trustee or in a similar fiduciary capacity; and

(3) Any relative or spouse of such person, or any relative of such spouse, who has the same home as such person or who is a director or officer of the registrant or any of its parents or subsidiaries. . . .

(f) *Proxy.* The term "proxy" includes every proxy, consent or authorization within the meaning of section 14(a) of the Act. The consent or authorization may take the form of failure to object or to dissent.

(g) *Proxy statement.* The term "proxy statement" means the statement required by Rule 14a–3(a) whether or not contained in a single document. . . .

(j) *Registrant.* The term "registrant" means the issuer of the securities in respect of which proxies are to be solicited. . . .

(k) *Respondent bank.* For purposes of Rules 14a–13, 14b–1 and 14b–2, the term "respondent bank" means any bank, association or other entity that exercises fiduciary powers which holds securities on behalf of beneficial owners and deposits such securities for safekeeping with another bank, association or other entity that exercises fiduciary powers.

(*l*) *Solicitation.* (1) The terms "solicit" and "solicitation" include:

(i) Any request for a proxy whether or not accompanied by or included in a form of proxy;

(ii) Any request to execute or not to execute, or to revoke, a proxy; or

(iii) The furnishing of a form of proxy or other communication to security holders under circumstances reasonably calculated to result in the procurement, withholding or revocation of a proxy.

(2) The terms do not apply, however, to:

(i) The furnishing of a form of proxy to a security holder upon the unsolicited request of such security holder;

(ii) The performance by the registrant of acts required by Rule 14a–7;

(iii) The performance by any person of ministerial acts on behalf of a person soliciting a proxy; or

(iv) A communication by a security holder who does not otherwise engage in a proxy solicitation (other than a solicitation exempt under Rule 14a–2) stating how the security holder intends to vote and the reasons therefor, provided that the communication:

(A) is made by means of speeches in public forums, press releases, published or broadcast opinions, statements, or advertisements appearing in a broadcast media, or newspaper, magazine or other bona fide publication disseminated on a regular basis,

(B) is directed to persons to whom the security holder owes a fiduciary duty in connection with the voting of securities of a registrant held by the security holder, or

(C) is made in response to unsolicited requests for additional information with respect to a prior communication by the security holder made pursuant to this paragraph (*l*)(2)(iv).

Rule 14a–2. Solicitations to Which Rule 14a–3 to Rule 14a–15 Apply

Rules 14a–3 to 14a–15, except as specified below, apply to every solicitation of a proxy with respect to securities registered pursuant to Section 12 of the Act whether or not trading in such securities has been suspended. To the extent specified below, certain of these sections also apply to roll-up transactions that do not involve an entity with securities registered pursuant to Section 12 of the Act.

(a) Rules 14a–3 to 14a–15 do not apply to the following:

(1) Any solicitation by a person in respect to securities carried in his name or in the name of his nominee (otherwise than as voting trustee) or held in his custody, if such person—

(i) Receives no commission or remuneration for such solicitation, directly or indirectly, other than reimbursement of reasonable expenses,

(ii) Furnishes promptly to the person solicited (or such person's household in accordance with Rule 14a–3(e)(i)) a copy of all soliciting material with respect to the same subject matter or meeting received from all persons who shall furnish copies thereof for such purpose and who shall, if requested, defray the reasonable expenses to be incurred in forwarding such material, and

(iii) In addition, does no more than impartially instruct the person solicited to forward a proxy to the person, if any, to whom the person solicited desires to give a proxy, or impartially request from the person solicited instructions as to the authority to be conferred by the proxy and state that a proxy will be given if no instructions are received by a certain date.

(2) Any solicitation by a person in respect of securities of which he is the beneficial owner. . . .

(6) Any solicitation through the medium of a newspaper advertisement which informs security holders of a source from which they may obtain copies of a proxy statement, form of proxy and any other soliciting material and does no more than:

(i) Name the registrant,

(ii) State the reason for the advertisement, and

(iii) Identify the proposal or proposals to be acted upon by security holders.

(b) Rules 14a–3 to 14a–6 (other than paragraphs 14a–6(g)) and 14a–6(8), Rule 14a–8, 14a–10, and Rules 14a–12 to 14a–15 do not apply to the following:

(1) Any solicitation by or on behalf of any person who does not, at any time during such solicitation, seek directly or indirectly, either on its own or another's behalf, the power to act as proxy for a security holder and does not furnish or otherwise request, or act on behalf of a person who furnishes or requests, a form of revocation, abstention, consent or authorization. *Provided, however,* that the exemption set forth in this paragraph shall not apply to:

(i) the registrant or an affiliate or associate of the registrant (other than an officer or director or any person serving in a similar capacity);

(ii) an officer or director of the registrant or any person serving in a similar capacity engaging in a solicitation financed directly or indirectly by the registrant;

(iii) an officer, director, affiliate or associate of a person that is ineligible to rely on the exemption set forth in this paragraph (other than persons specified in paragraph (b)(1)(i) of this section), or any person serving in a similar capacity;

(iv) any nominee for whose election as a director proxies are solicited;

(v) any person soliciting in opposition to a merger, recapitalization, reorganization, sale of assets or other extraordinary transaction recommended or approved by the board of directors of the registrant who is proposing or intends to propose an alternative transaction to which such person or one of its affiliates is a party;

(vi) any person who is required to report beneficial ownership of the registrant's equity securities on a Schedule 13D, unless such person has filed a Schedule 13D and has not disclosed pursuant to Item 4 thereto an intent, or reserved the right, to engage in a control transaction, or any contested solicitation for the election of directors;

(vii) Any person who received compensation from an ineligible person directly related to the solicitation of proxies, other than pursuant to Rule 14a–13; . . .

(ix) any person who, because of a substantial interest in the subject matter of the solicitation, is likely to receive a benefit from a successful solicitation that would not be shared pro rata by all other holders of the same class of securities, other than a benefit arising from the person's employment with the registrant; and

(x) any person acting on behalf of any of the foregoing.

(2) Any solicitation made otherwise than on behalf of the registrant where the total number of persons solicited is not more than ten; and

(3) The furnishing of proxy voting advice by any person (the "advisor") to any other person with whom the advisor has a business relationship, if:

(i) The advisor renders financial advice in the ordinary course of his business;

(ii) The advisor discloses to the recipient of the advice any significant relationship with the registrant or any of its affiliates, or a security holder proponent of the matter on which advice is given, as well as any material interests of the advisor in such matter;

(iii) The advisor receives no special commission or remuneration for furnishing the proxy voting advice from any person other than a recipient of the advice and other persons who receive similar advice under this subsection; and

(iv) The proxy voting advice is not furnished on behalf of any person soliciting proxies or on behalf of a participant in an election subject to the provisions of Rule 14a–12(c).

(4) Any solicitation in connection with a roll-up transaction as defined in Item 901(c) of Regulation S–K . . . in which the holder of a security that is the subject of a proposed roll-up transaction engages in preliminary communications with other holders of securities that are the subject of the same limited partnership roll-up transaction for the purpose of determining whether to solicit proxies, consents, or authorizations in opposition to the proposed limited partnership roll-up transaction; *provided, however,* that:

(i) This exemption shall not apply to a security holder who is an affiliate of the registrant or general partner or sponsor; and

(ii) This exemption shall not apply to a holder of five percent (5%) or more of the outstanding securities of a class that is the subject of the proposed roll-up transaction who engages in the business of buying and selling limited partnership interests in the secondary market unless that holder discloses to the persons to whom the communications are made such ownership interest and any relations of the holder to the parties [to] the transaction or to the transaction itself, as required by Rule 14a–6(n)(1) and specified in the Notice of Exempt Preliminary Roll-up Communication (Rule 14a–104). If the communication is oral, this disclosure may be provided to the security holder orally. Whether the communication is written or oral, the notice required by Rule 14a–6(n) and Rule 14a–104 shall be furnished to the Commission.

(5) Publication or distribution by a broker or a dealer of a research report in accordance with Rule 138 or Rule 139 during a transaction in which the broker or dealer or its affiliate participates or acts in an advisory role.

(6) Any solicitation by or on behalf of any person who does not seek directly or indirectly, either on its own or another's behalf, the power to act as proxy for a shareholder and does not furnish or otherwise request, or act on behalf of a person who furnishes or requests, a form of revocation, abstention, consent, or authorization in an electronic shareholder forum that is established, maintained or operated pursuant to the provisions of Rule 14a–17, provided that the solicitation is made more than 60 days prior to the date announced by a registrant for its next annual or special meeting of shareholders. If the registrant announces the date of its next annual or special meeting of shareholders less than 60 days before the meeting date, then the solicitation may not be made more than two days following the date of the registrant's announcement of the meeting date. Participation in an electronic shareholder forum does not eliminate a person's eligibility to solicit proxies after the date that this exemption is no longer available, or is no longer being relied upon, provided that any such solicitation is conducted in accordance with this regulation.

(7) Any solicitation by or on behalf of any shareholder in connection with the formation of a nominating shareholder group pursuant to Rule 14a–11, provided that:

(i) The soliciting shareholder is not holding the registrant's securities with the purpose, or with the effect, of changing control of the registrant or to gain a number of seats on the board of directors that exceeds the maximum number of nominees that the registrant could be required to include under Rule 14a–11(d);

(ii) Each written communication includes no more than:

(A) A statement of each soliciting shareholder's intent to form a nominating shareholder group in order to nominate one or more directors under Rule 14a–11;

(B) Identification of, and a brief statement regarding, the potential nominee or nominees or, where no nominee or nominees have been identified, the characteristics of the nominee or nominees that the shareholder intends to nominate, if any;

(C) The percentage of voting power of the registrant's securities that are entitled to be voted on the election of directors that each soliciting shareholder holds or the aggregate percentage held by any group to which the shareholder belongs; and

(D) The means by which shareholders may contact the soliciting party.

(iii) Any written soliciting material published, sent or given to shareholders in accordance with this paragraph must be filed by the shareholder with the Commission, under the registrant's Exchange Act file number, . . . Three copies of the material must at the same time be filed with, or mailed for filing to, each national securities exchange upon which any class of securities of the registrant is listed and registered. The soliciting material must include a cover page in the form set forth in Schedule 14N and the appropriate box on the cover page must be marked.

(iv) In the case of an oral solicitation made in accordance with the terms of this section, the nominating shareholder must file a cover page in the form set forth in Schedule 14N, with the appropriate box on the cover page marked, under the registrant's Exchange Act file number . . . , no later than the date of the first such communication.

Rule 14a-3. Information to Be Furnished to Security Holders

(a) No solicitation subject to this regulation shall be made unless each person solicited is concurrently furnished or has previously been furnished with:

(1) A publicly-filed preliminary or definitive proxy statement, in the form and manner described in Rule 14a-16, containing the information specified in Schedule 14A; . . .

(3) A publicly-filed preliminary or definitive proxy statement, not in the form and manner described in Rule 14a-16, containing the information specified in Schedule 14A, if:

(i) The solicitation relates to a business combination transaction as defined in Rule 165 [under the Securities Act], as well as transactions for cash consideration requiring disclosure under Item 14 of Schedule 14A; or

(ii) The solicitation may not follow the form and manner described in Rule 14a-16 pursuant to the laws of the state of incorporation of the registrant;

(b) If the solicitation is made on behalf of the registrant and relates to an annual (or special meeting in lieu of the annual) meeting of security holders, or written consent in lieu of such meeting, at which directors are to be elected, each proxy statement furnished pursuant to paragraph (a) of this section shall be accompanied or preceded by an annual report to security holders as follows:

Note to Small Business Issuers. A "small business issuer," defined under Rule 12b-2 of the Exchange Act, shall refer to the disclosure items in Regulation S-B rather than Regulation S-K. If there is no comparable disclosure item in Regulation S-B, a small business issuer need not provide the information requested. A small business issuers shall provide the information in Item 310(a) of Regulation S-B in lieu of the financial information required by Rule 14a-3(b)(1). . . .

(1) The report shall include, for the registrant and its subsidiaries, consolidated and audited balance sheets as of the end of each of the two most recent fiscal years and audited statements of income and cash flows for each of the three most recent fiscal years prepared in accordance with Regulation S-X. . . .

(3) The report shall contain the supplementary financial information required by Item 302 of Regulation S-K. . . .

(4) The report shall contain information concerning changes in and disagreements with accountants on accounting and financial disclosure required by Item 304 of Regulation S-K. . . .

(5)(i) The report shall contain the selected financial data required by Item 301 of Regulation S-K. . . .

(ii) The report shall contain management's discussion and analysis of financial condition and results of operations required by Item 303 of Regulation S-K. . . .

(6) The report shall contain a brief description of the business done by the registrant and its subsidiaries during the most recent fiscal year which will, in the opinion of management, indicate the general nature and scope of the business of the registrant and its subsidiaries.

(7) The report shall contain information relating to the registrant's industry segments, classes of similar products or services, foreign and domestic operations and exports sales required by paragraphs (b), (c)(1)(i) and (d) of Item 101 of Regulation S-K [Description of Business]. . . .

(8) The report shall identify each of the registrant's directors and executive officers, and shall indicate the principal occupation or employment of each such person and the name and principal business of any organization by which such person is employed.

(9) The report shall contain the market price of and dividends on the registrant's common equity and related security holder matters required by Items 201(a), (b) and (c) of Regulation S-K. If the report precedes or accompanies a proxy statement or information statement relating to an annual meeting of security holders at which directors are to be elected (or special meeting or written consents in lieu of such meeting), furnish the performance graph required by Item 201(e).

(10) The registrant's proxy statement, or the report, shall contain an undertaking in bold face or otherwise reasonably prominent type to provide without charge to each person solicited upon the written request of any such person, a copy of the registrant's annual report on Form 10-K, including the financial

statements and the financial statement schedules, required to be filed with the Commission pursuant to Rule 13a-l under the Act for the registrant's most recent fiscal year, and shall indicate the name and address (including title or department) of the person to whom such a written request is to be directed. In the discretion of management, a registrant need not undertake to furnish without charge copies of all exhibits to its Form 10-K, provided that the copy of the annual report on Form 10-K furnished without charge to requesting security holders is accompanied by a list briefly describing all the exhibits not contained therein and indicating that the registrant will furnish any exhibit upon the payment of a specified reasonable fee, which fee shall be limited to the registrant's reasonable expenses in furnishing such exhibit. If the registrant's annual report to security holders complies with all of the disclosure requirements of Form 10-K and is filed with the Commission in satisfaction of its Form 10-K filing requirements, such registrant need not furnish a separate Form 10-K to security holders who receive a copy of such annual report.

(c) Seven copies of the report sent to security holders pursuant to this rule shall be mailed to the Commission, solely for its information, not later than the date on which such report is first sent or given to security holders or the date on which preliminary copies, or definitive copies, if preliminary filing was not required, of solicitation material are filed with the Commission pursuant to Rule 14a–6, whichever date is later. The report is not deemed to be "soliciting material" or to be "filed" with the Commission or subject to this regulation otherwise than as provided in this Rule, or to the liabilities of section 18 of the Act, except to the extent that the registrant specifically requests that it be treated as a part of the proxy soliciting material or incorporates it in the proxy statement or other filed report by reference. . . .

(e)(1)(i) A registrant will be considered to have delivered an annual report to security holders, proxy statement or Notice of Internet Availability of Proxy Materials, as described in Rule 14a–16, to all security holders of record who share an address if:

(A) The registrant delivers one annual report to security holders, proxy statement or Notice of Internet Availability of Proxy Materials, as applicable, to the shared address;

(B) The registrant addresses the annual report to security holders, proxy statement or Notice of Internet Availability of Proxy Materials, as applicable, to the security holders as a group (for example, "ABC Fund [or Corporation] Security Holders," "Jane Doe and Household," "The Smith Family"), to each of the security holders individually (for example, "John Doe and Richard Jones") or to the security holders in a form to which each of the security holders has consented in writing;

(C) The security holders consent, in accordance with paragraph (e)(1)(ii) of this section, to delivery of one annual report to security holders or proxy statement, as applicable;

(D) With respect to delivery of the proxy statement or Notice of Internet Availability of Proxy Materials, the registrant delivers, together with or subsequent to delivery of the proxy statement, a separate proxy card for each security holder at the shared address; and

(E) The registrant includes an undertaking in the proxy statement to deliver promptly upon written or oral request a separate copy of the annual report to security holders, proxy statement or Notice of Internet Availability of Proxy Materials, as applicable, to a security holder at a shared address to which a single copy of the document was delivered.

(f) The provisions of paragraph (a) of this section shall not apply to a communication made by means of speeches in public forums, press releases, published or broadcast opinions, statements, or advertisements appearing in a broadcast media, newspaper, magazine or other bona fide publication disseminated on a regular basis, provided that:

(1) no form of proxy, consent or authorization or means to execute the same is provided to a security holder in connection with the communication; and

(2) at the time the communication is made, a definitive proxy statement is on file with the Commission pursuant to Rule 14a–6(b).

Rule 14a–4. Requirements as to Proxy

(a) The form of proxy (1) shall indicate in bold-face type whether or not the proxy is solicited on behalf of the registrant's board of directors or, if provided other than by a majority of the board of directors, shall indicate in bold-face type on whose behalf the solicitation is made;

(2) Shall provide a specifically designated blank space for dating the proxy card; and

(3) Shall identify clearly and impartially each separate matter intended to be acted upon, whether or not related to or conditioned on the approval of other matters, and whether proposed by the registrant or by security holders. No reference need be made, however, to proposals as to which discretionary authority is conferred pursuant to paragraph (c) of this section.

(b)(1) Means shall be provided in the form of proxy whereby the person solicited is afforded an opportunity to specify by boxes a choice between approval or disapproval of, or abstention with respect to each separate matter referred to therein as intended to be acted upon, other than elections to office and votes to determine the frequency of shareholder votes on executive compensation pursuant to Rule 14a–21(b). A proxy may confer discretionary authority with respect to matters as to which a choice is not specified by the security holder provided that the form of proxy states in bold-face type how it is intended to vote the shares represented by the proxy in each such case.

(2) A form of proxy that provides for the election of directors shall set forth the names of persons nominated for election as directors, including any person whose nomination by a shareholder or shareholder group satisfies the requirements of Rule 14a–11, an applicable state or foreign law provision, or a registrant's governing documents as they relate to the inclusion of shareholder director nominees in the registrant's proxy materials. Such form of proxy shall clearly provide any of the following means for security holders to withhold authority to vote for each nominee:

(i) A box opposite the name of each nominee which may be marked to indicate that authority to vote for such nominee is withheld; or

(ii) An instruction in bold-face type which indicates that the security holder may withhold authority to vote for any nominee by lining through or otherwise striking out the name of any nominee; or

(iii) Designated blank spaces in which the security holder may enter the names of nominees with respect to whom the security holder chooses to withhold authority to vote; or

(iv) Any other similar means, provided that clear instructions are furnished indicating how the security holder may withhold authority to vote for any nominee.

(3) A form of proxy which provides for a shareholder vote on the frequency of shareholder votes to approve the compensation of executives required by section 14A(a)(2) of the Securities Exchange Act of 1934 shall provide means whereby the person solicited is afforded an opportunity to specify by boxes a choice among 1, 2 or 3 years, or abstain.

Such form of proxy also may provide a means for the security holder to grant authority to vote for the nominees set forth, as a group, provided that there is a similar means for the security holder to withhold authority to vote for such group of nominees. Any such form of proxy which is executed by the security holder in such manner as not to withhold authority to vote for the election of any nominee shall be deemed to grant such authority, provided that the form of proxy so states in bold-face type. Means to grant authority to vote for any nominees as a group or to withhold authority for any nominees as a group may not be provided if the form of proxy includes one or more shareholder nominees in accordance with Rule 14a–11, an applicable state or foreign law provision, or a registrant's governing documents as they relate to the inclusion of shareholder director nominees in the registrant's proxy materials.

Instructions.

1.   Paragraph (2) does not apply in the case of a merger, consolidation or other plan if the election of directors is an integral part of the plan.

2.   If applicable state law gives legal effect to votes cast against a nominee, then in lieu of, or in addition to, providing a means for security holders to withhold authority to vote, the registrant should provide a similar means for security holders to vote against each nominee.

(c) A proxy may confer discretionary authority to vote on any of the following matters:

(1) For an annual meeting of shareholders, if the registrant did not have notice of the matter at least 45 days before the date on which the registrant first sent its proxy materials for the prior year's annual meeting of shareholders (or date specified by an advance notice provision), and a specific statement to that

effect is made in the proxy statement or form of proxy. If during the prior year the registrant did not hold an annual meeting, or if the date of the meeting has changed more than 30 days from the prior year, then notice must not have been received a reasonable time before the registrant sends its proxy materials for the current years.

(2) In the case in which the registrant has received timely notice in connection with an annual meeting of shareholders (as determined under paragraph (c)(1) of this section), if the registrant includes, in the proxy statement, advice on the nature of the matter and how the registrant intends to exercise its discretion to vote on each matter. However, even if the registrant includes this information in its proxy statement, it may not exercise discretionary voting authority on a particular proposal if the proponent:

(i) Provides the registrant with a written statement, within the time-frame determined under paragraph (c)(1) of this section, that the proponent intends to deliver a proxy statement and form of proxy to holders of at least the percentage of the company's voting shares required under applicable law to carry the proposal;

(ii) Includes the same statement in its proxy materials filed under Rule 14a–6; and

(iii) Immediately after soliciting the percentage of shareholders required to carry the proposal, provides the registrant with a statement from any solicitor or other person with knowledge that the necessary steps have been taken to deliver a proxy statement and form of proxy to holders of at least the percentage of the company's voting shares required under applicable law to carry the proposal.

(3) For solicitations other than for annual meetings or for solicitations by persons other than the registrant, matters which the persons making the solicitation do not know, a reasonable time before the solicitation, are to be presented at the meeting, if a specific statement to that effect is made in the proxy statement or form of proxy.

(4) Approval of the minutes of the prior meeting if such approval does not amount to ratification of the action taken at that meeting;

(5) The election of any person to any office for which a bona fide nominee is named in the proxy statement and such nominee is unable to serve or for good cause will not serve.

(6) Any proposal omitted from the proxy statement and form of proxy pursuant to Rule 14a–8 or 14a–9 of this chapter.

(7) Matters incident to the conduct of the meeting.

(d) No proxy shall confer authority:

(1) To vote for the election of any person to any office for which a bona fide nominee is not named in the proxy statement,

(2) To vote at any annual meeting other than the next annual meeting (or any adjournment thereof) to be held after the date on which the proxy statement and form of proxy are first sent or given to security holders,

(3) To vote with respect to more than one meeting (and any adjournment thereof) or more than one consent solicitation or

(4) To consent to or authorize any action other than the action proposed to be taken in the proxy statement, or matters referred to in paragraph (c) of this rule. A person shall not be deemed to be a bona fide nominee and he shall not be named as such unless he has consented to being named in the proxy statement and to serve if elected.

Provided, however, that nothing in this Rule 4a–4 shall prevent any person soliciting in support of nominees who, if elected, would constitute a minority of the board of directors, from seeking authority to vote for nominees named in the registrant's proxy statement, so long as the soliciting party:

(i) seeks authority to vote in the aggregate for the number of director positions then subject to election;

(ii) represents that it will vote for all the registrant nominees, other than those registrant nominees specified by the soliciting party;

(iii) provides the security holder an opportunity to withhold authority with respect to any other registrant nominee by writing the name of that nominee on the form of proxy; and

(iv) states on the form of proxy and in the proxy statement that there is no assurance that the registrant's nominees will serve if elected with any of the soliciting party's nominees.

(e) The proxy statement or form of proxy shall provide, subject to reasonable specified conditions, that the shares represented by the proxy will be voted and that where the person solicited specifies by means of a ballot provided pursuant to paragraph (b) of this section a choice with respect to any matter to be acted upon, the shares will be voted in accordance with the specifications so made.

(f) No person conducting a solicitation subject to this regulation shall deliver a form of proxy, consent or authorization to any security holder unless the security holder concurrently receives, or has previously received, a definitive proxy statement that has been filed with the Commission pursuant to Rule 14a–6(b).

Rule 14a–5. Presentation of Information in Proxy Statement

(a) The information included in the proxy statement shall be clearly presented and the statements made shall be divided into groups according to subject matter and the various groups of statements shall be preceded by appropriate headings. The order of items and sub-items in the schedule need not be followed. Where practicable and appropriate, the information shall be presented in tabular form. All amounts shall be stated in figures. Information required by more than one applicable item need not be repeated. No statement need be made in response to any item or sub-item which is inapplicable.

(b) Any information required to be included in the proxy statement as to terms of securities or other subject matter which from a standpoint of practical necessity must be determined in the future may be stated in terms of present knowledge and intention. To the extent practicable, the authority to be conferred concerning each such matter shall be confined within limits reasonably related to the need for discretionary authority. Subject to the foregoing, information which is not known to the persons on whose behalf the solicitation is to be made and which it is not reasonably within the power of such persons to ascertain or procure may be omitted, if a brief statement of the circumstances rendering such information unavailable is made.

(c) Any information contained in any other proxy soliciting material which has been furnished to each person solicited in connection with the same meeting or subject matter may be omitted from the proxy statement, if a clear reference is made to the particular document containing such information.

(d) All printed proxy statements shall be in roman type at least as large and as legible as 10-point modern type, except that to the extent necessary for convenient presentation financial statements and other tabular data, but not the notes thereto, may be in roman type at least as large and as legible as 8-point modern type. All such type shall be leaded at least 2 points.

(e) All proxy statements shall disclose, under an appropriate caption, the following dates:

(1) The deadline for submitting shareholder proposals for inclusion in the registrant's proxy statement and form of proxy for the registrant's next annual meeting, calculated in the manner provided in Rule 14a–8(d) (Question 4); and

(2) The date after which notice of a shareholder proposal submitted outside the processes of Rule 14a–8 is considered untimely, either calculated in the manner provided by Rule 14a–4(c)(1) or as established by the registrant's advance notice provision, if any, authorized by applicable state law.

(f) If the date of the next annual meeting is subsequently advanced or delayed by more than 30 calendar days from the date of the annual meeting to which the proxy statement relates, the registrant shall, in a timely manner, inform shareholders of such change, and the new dates referred to in paragraphs (e)(1) and (e)(2) of this section, by including a notice, under Item 5, in its earliest possible quarterly report on Form 10-Q . . . , or, if impracticable, any means reasonably calculated to inform shareholders.

Rule 14a–6. Filing Requirements

(a) *Preliminary proxy statement.* Five preliminary copies of the proxy statement and form of proxy shall be filed with the Commission at least 10 calendar days prior to the date definitive copies of such material are first sent or given to security holders, or such shorter period prior to that date as the Commission may authorize upon a showing of good cause thereunder. A registrant, however, shall not file with the Commission a preliminary proxy statement, form of proxy or other soliciting material to be furnished to security holders concurrently therewith if the solicitation relates to an annual (or special meeting in lieu of the annual) meeting, . . . if the solicitation relates to any meeting of security holders at which the only matters to be acted upon are:

(1) the election of directors;

(2) the election, approval or ratification of accountant(s);

(3) a security holder proposal included pursuant to Rule 14a–8;

(4) A shareholder nominee for director included pursuant to Rule 14a–11, an applicable state or foreign law provision, or a registrant's governing documents as they relate to the inclusion of shareholder director nominees in the registrant's proxy materials.

(5) the approval or ratification of a plan as defined in paragraph (a)(6)(ii) of Item 402 of Regulation S–K or amendments to such a plan[; and/or]. . . .

(7) A vote to approve the compensation of executives as required pursuant to section 14A(a)(1) of the Securities Exchange Act of 1934 and Rule 14a–21(a), or pursuant to section 111(e)(1) of the Emergency Economic Stabilization Act of 2008 and Rule 14a–20, a vote to determine the frequency of shareholder votes to approve the compensation of executives as required pursuant to Section 14A(a)(2) of the Securities Exchange Act of 1934 and Rule 14a–21(b), or any other shareholder advisory vote on executive compensation.

This exclusion from filing preliminary proxy material does not apply if the registrant comments upon or refers to a solicitation in opposition in connection with the meeting in its proxy material.

(b) *Definitive proxy statement and other soliciting material.* Eight definitive copies of the proxy statement, form of proxy and all other soliciting materials, in the same form as the materials sent to security holders, must be filed with the Commission no later than the date they are first sent or given to security holders. Three copies of these materials also must be filed with, or mailed for filing to, each national securities exchange on which the registrant has a class of securities listed and registered.

(c) *Personal solicitation materials.* If part or all of the solicitation involves personal solicitation, then eight copies of all written instructions or other materials that discuss, review or comment on the merits of any matter to be acted on, that are furnished to persons making the actual solicitation for their use directly or indirectly in connection with the solicitation, must be filed with the Commission no later than the date the materials are first sent or given to these persons.

(d) *Release dates.* All preliminary proxy statements and forms of proxy filed pursuant to paragraph (a) of this section shall be accompanied by a statement of the date on which definitive copies thereof filed pursuant to paragraph (b) of this section are intended to be released to security holders. All definitive material filed pursuant to paragraph (b) of this section shall be accompanied by a statement of the date on which copies of such material were released to security holders, or, if not released, the date on which copies thereof are intended to be released. All material filed pursuant to paragraph (c) of this section shall be accompanied by a statement of the date on which copies thereof were released to the individual who will make the actual solicitation or if not released, the date on which copies thereof are intended to be released.

(e)(1) *Public availability of information.* All copies of preliminary proxy statements and forms of proxy filed pursuant to paragraph (a) of this section shall be clearly marked "Preliminary Copies," and shall be deemed immediately available for public inspection unless confidential treatment is obtained pursuant to paragraph (e)(2) of this section.

(2) *Confidential treatment.* If action will be taken on any matter specified in Item 14 of Schedule 14A, all copies of the preliminary proxy statement and form of proxy filed under paragraph (a) of this section will be for the information of the Commission only and will not be deemed available for public inspection until filed with the Commission in definitive form so long as:

(i) The proxy statement does not relate to a matter or proposal subject to Rule 13e–3 or a roll-up transaction as defined in Item 901(c) of Regulation S–K;

(ii) Neither the parties to the transaction nor any persons authorized to act on their behalf have made any public communications relating to the transaction except for statements where the content is limited to the information specified in Rule 135 [under the Securities Act]; and

(iii) The materials are filed in paper and marked "Confidential, For Use of the Commission Only." In all cases, the materials may be disclosed to any department or agency of the United States Government and to the Congress, and the Commission may make any inquiries or investigation into the materials as may be necessary to conduct an adequate review by the Commission.

(g) *Solicitations subject to Rule 14a–2(b)(1).*

(1) Any person who:

(i) engages in a solicitation pursuant to Rule 14a–2(b)(1), and

(ii) at the commencement of that solicitation owns beneficially securities of the class which is the subject of the solicitation with a market value of over $5 million, shall furnish or mail to the Commission, not later than three days after the date the written solicitation is first sent or given to any security holder, five copies of a statement containing the information specified in the [Form of] Notice of Exempt Solicitation which statement shall attach as an exhibit all written soliciting materials. Five copies of an amendment to such statement shall be furnished or mailed to the Commission, in connection with dissemination of any additional communications, not later than three days after the date the additional material is first sent or given to any security holder. Three copies of the Notice of Exempt Solicitation and amendments thereto shall, at the same time the materials are furnished or mailed to the Commission, be furnished or mailed to each national securities exchange upon which any class of securities of the registrant is listed and registered.

(2) Notwithstanding paragraph (g)(1) of this section, no such submission need be made with respect to oral solicitations (other than with respect to scripts used in connection with such oral solicitations), speeches delivered in a public forum, press releases, published or broadcast opinions, statements, and advertisements appearing in a broadcast media, or a newspaper, magazine or other bona fide publication disseminated on a regular basis. . . .

(n) *Solicitations subject to Rule 14a–2(b)(4).* Any person who:

(1) Engages in a solicitation pursuant to Rule 14a–2(b)(4), and

(2) At the commencement of that solicitation both owns five percent (5%) or more of the outstanding securities of a class that is the subject of the proposed roll-up transaction, and engages in the business of buying and selling limited partnership interests in the secondary market, shall furnish or mail to the Commission, not later than three days after the date an oral or written solicitation by that person is first made, sent or provided to any security holder, five copies of a statement containing the information specified in the Notice of Exempt Preliminary Roll-up Communication (Rule 14a–104). Five copies of any amendment to such statement shall be furnished or mailed to the Commission not later than three days after a communication containing revised material is first made, sent or provided to any security holder.

(o) *Solicitations before furnishing a definitive proxy statement.* Solicitations that are published, sent or given to security holders before they have been furnished a definitive proxy statement must be made in accordance with Rule 14a–12 unless there is an exemption available under Rule 14a–2.

(p) *Solicitations subject to Rule 14a–11.* Any soliciting material that is published, sent or given to shareholders in connection with Rule 14a–2(b)(7) or (b)(8) must be filed with the Commission as specified in that section.

Rule 14a–7. Obligations of Registrants to Provide a List of, or Mail Soliciting Material to, Security Holders

(a) If the registrant has made or intends to make a proxy solicitation in connection with a security holder meeting or action by consent or authorization, upon the written request by any record or beneficial holder of securities of the class entitled to vote at the meeting, or to execute a consent or authorization to provide a list of security holders or to mail the requesting security holder's materials, regardless of whether the request references this section, the registrant shall:

(1) deliver to the requesting security holder within five business days after receipt of the request:

(i) notification as to whether the registrant has elected to mail the security holder's soliciting materials or provide a security holder list if the election under paragraph (b) of this section is to be made by the registrant;

(ii) a statement of the approximate number of record holders and beneficial holders, separated by type of holder and class, owning securities in the same class or classes as holders which have been or are to be solicited on management's behalf, or any more limited group of such holders designated by the security holder if available or retrievable under the registrant's or its transfer agent's security holder data systems; and

(iii) the estimated cost of mailing a proxy statement, form of proxy or other communication to such holders, including to the extent known or reasonably available, the estimated costs of any bank, broker, and similar person through whom the registrant has solicited or intends to solicit beneficial owners in connection with the security holder meeting or action;

(2) perform the acts set forth in either paragraphs (a)(2)(i) or (a)(2)(ii) of this section, at the registrant's or requesting security holder's option, as specified in paragraph (b) of this section:

(i) Send copies of any proxy statement, form of proxy, or other soliciting material, including a Notice of Internet Availability of Proxy Materials (as described in Rule 14a–16), furnished by the security holder to the record holders, including banks, brokers, and similar entities, designated by the security holder. A sufficient number of copies must be sent to the banks, brokers, and similar entities for distribution to all beneficial owners designated by the security holder. The security holder may designate only record holders and/or beneficial owners who have not requested paper and/or e-mail copies of the proxy statement. If the registrant has received affirmative written or implied consent to deliver a single proxy statement to security holders at a shared address in accordance with the procedures in Rule 14a–3(e)(1), a single copy of the proxy statement or Notice of Internet Availability of Proxy Materials furnished by the security holder shall be sent to that address, provided that if multiple copies of the Notice of Internet Availability of Proxy Materials are furnished by the security holder for that address, the registrant shall deliver those copies in a single envelope to that address. The registrant shall send the security holder material with reasonable promptness after tender of the material to be sent, envelopes or other containers therefore, postage or payment for postage and other reasonable expenses of effecting such distribution. The registrant shall not be responsible for the content of the material; or

(ii) Deliver the following information to the requesting security holder within five business days of receipt of the request:

(A) A reasonably current list of the names, addresses and security positions of the record holders, including banks, brokers and similar entities holding securities in the same class or classes as holders which have been or are to be solicited on management's behalf, or any more limited group of such holders designated by the security holder if available or retrievable under the registrant's or its transfer agent's security holder data systems;

(B) The most recent list of names, addresses and security positions of beneficial owners as specified in Rule 14a–13(b), in the possession, or which subsequently comes into the possession, of the registrant;

(C) The names of security holders at a shared address that have consented to delivery of a single copy of proxy materials to a shared address, if the registrant has received written or implied consent in accordance with Rule 14a–3(e)(1); and

(D) If the registrant has relied on Rule 14a–16, the names of security holders who have requested paper copies of the proxy materials for all meetings and the names of security holders who, as of the date that the registrant receives the request, have requested paper copies of the proxy materials only for the meeting to which the solicitation relates.

(iii) All security holder list information shall be in the form requested by the security holder to the extent that such form is available to the registrant without undue burden or expense. The registrant shall furnish the security holder with updated record holder information on a daily basis or, if not available on a daily basis, at the shortest reasonable intervals; provided, however, the registrant need not provide beneficial or record holder information more current than the record date for the meeting or action.

(b)(1) The requesting security holder shall have the options set forth in paragraph (a)(2) of this section, and the registrant shall have corresponding obligations, if the registrant or general partner or sponsor is soliciting or intends to solicit with respect to:

(i) A proposal that is subject to Rule 13e–3;

(ii) A roll-up transaction as defined in Item 901(c) of Regulation S–K that involves an entity with securities registered pursuant to Section 12 of the Act;

(iii) A roll-up transaction as defined in Item 901(c) of Regulation S–K that involves a limited partnership. . . .

(2) With respect to all other requests pursuant to this section, the registrant shall have the option to either [send] the security holder's material or furnish the security holder list as set forth in this section.

(c) At the time of a list request, the security holder making the request shall:

(1) if holding the registrant's securities through a nominee, provide the registrant with a statement by the nominee or other independent third party, or a copy of a current filing made with the Commission and furnished to the registrant, confirming such holder's beneficial ownership; and

(2) provide the registrant with an affidavit, declaration, affirmation or other similar document provided for under applicable state law identifying the proposal or other corporate action that will be the subject of the security holder's solicitation or communication and attesting that:

(i) the security holder will not use the list information for any purpose other than to solicit security holders with respect to the same meeting or action by consent or authorization for which the registrant is soliciting or intends to solicit or to communicate with security holders with respect to a solicitation commenced by the registrant; and

(ii) the security holder will not disclose such information to any person other than a beneficial owner for whom the request was made and an employee or agent to the extent necessary to effectuate the communication or solicitation.

(d) The security holder shall not use the information furnished by the registrant pursuant to paragraph (a)(2)(ii) of this section for any purpose other than to solicit security holders with respect to the same meeting or action by consent or authorization for which the registrant is soliciting or intends to solicit or to communicate with security holders with respect to a solicitation commenced by the registrant; or disclose such information to any person other than an employee, agent, or beneficial owner for whom a request was made to the extent necessary to effectuate the communication or solicitation. The security holder shall return the information provided pursuant to paragraph (a)(2)(ii) of this section and shall not retain any copies thereof or of any information derived from such information after the termination of the solicitation.

(e) The security holder shall reimburse the reasonable expenses incurred by the registrant in performing the acts requested pursuant to paragraph (a) of this section.

Rule 14a–8. Shareholder Proposals

This section addresses when a company must include a shareholder's proposal in its proxy statement and identify the proposal in its form of proxy when the company holds an annual or special meeting of shareholders. In summary, in order to have your shareholder proposal included on a company's proxy card, and included along with any supporting statement in its proxy statement, you must be eligible and follow certain procedures. Under a few specific circumstances, the company is permitted to exclude your proposal, but only after submitting its reasons to the Commission. We structured this section in a question-and-answer format so that it is easier to understand. The references to "you" are to a shareholder seeking to submit the proposal.

(a) **Question 1: What is a proposal?**

A shareholder proposal is your recommendation or requirement that the company and/or its board of directors take action, which you intend to present at a meeting of the company's shareholders. Your proposal should state as clearly as possible the course of action that you believe the company should follow. If your proposal is placed on the company's proxy card, the company must also provide in the form of proxy means for shareholders to specify by boxes a choice between approval or disapproval, or abstention. Unless otherwise indicated, the word "proposal" as used in this section refers both to your proposal, and to your corresponding statement in support of your proposal (if any).

(b) **Question 2: Who is eligible to submit a proposal, and how do I demonstrate to the company that I am eligible?**

(1) In order to be eligible to submit a proposal, you must have continuously held at least $2,000 in market value, or 1%, of the company's securities entitled to be voted on the proposal at the meeting for at least one year by the date you submit the proposal. You must continue to hold those securities through the date of the meeting.

(2) If you are the registered holder of your securities, which means that your name appears in the company's records as a shareholder, the company can verify your eligibility on its own, although you will still have to provide the company with a written statement that you intend to continue to hold the securities through the date of the meeting of shareholders. However, if like many shareholders you are not a registered holder, the company likely does not know that you are a shareholder, or how many shares you own. In this case, at the time you submit your proposal, you must prove your eligibility to the company in one of two ways:

(i) The first way is to submit to the company a written statement from the "record" holder of your securities (usually a broker or bank) verifying that, at the time you submitted your proposal, you continuously held the securities for at least one year. You must also include your own written statement that you intend to continue to hold the securities through the date of the meeting of shareholders; or

(ii) The second way to prove ownership applies only if you have filed a Schedule 13D, Schedule 13G, Form 3, Form 4 and/or Form 5, or amendments to those documents or updated forms, reflecting your ownership of the shares as of or before the date on which the one-year eligibility period begins. If you have filed one of these documents with the SEC, you may demonstrate your eligibility by submitting to the company:

(A) A copy of the schedule and/or form, and any subsequent amendments reporting a change in your ownership level;

(B) Your written statement that you continuously held the required number of shares for the one-year period as of the date of the statement;

(C) Your written statement that you intend to continue ownership of the shares through the date of the company's annual or special meeting.

(c) **Question 3: How many proposals may I submit?**

Each shareholder may submit no more than one proposal to a company for a particular shareholders' meeting.

(d) **Question 4: How long can my proposal be?**

The proposal, including any accompanying supporting statement, may not exceed 500 words.

(e) **Question 5: What is the deadline for submitting a proposal?**

(1) If you are submitting your proposal for the company's annual meeting, you can in most cases find the deadline in last year's proxy statement. However, if the company did not hold an annual meeting last year, or has changed the date of its meeting for this year more than 30 days from the last year's meeting, you can usually find the deadline in one of the company's quarterly reports on Form 10-Q. . . . In order to avoid controversy, shareholders should submit their proposals by means, including electronic means, that permit them to prove the date of delivery.

(2) The deadline is calculated in the following manner if the proposal is submitted for a regularly scheduled annual meeting. The proposal must be received at the company's principal executive offices not less than 120 calendar days before the date of the company's proxy statement released to shareholders in connection with the previous year's annual meeting. However, if the company did not hold an annual meeting the previous year, or if the date of this year's annual meeting has been changed by more than 30

days from the date of the previous year's meeting, then the deadline is a reasonable time before the company begins to print or send its proxy materials.

(3) If you are submitting your proposal for a meeting of shareholders other than a regularly scheduled annual meeting, the deadline is a reasonable time before the company begins to print and send its proxy materials.

(f) **Question 6: What if I fail to follow one of the eligibility or procedural requirements explained in answers to Questions 1 through 4 of this section?**

(1) The company may exclude your proposal, but only after it has notified you of the problem, and you have failed adequately to correct it. Within 14 calendar days of receiving your proposal, the company must notify you in writing of any procedural or eligibility deficiencies, as well as of the time frame for your response. Your response must be postmarked, or transmitted electronically, no later than 14 days from the date you received the company's notification. A company need not provide you such notice of a deficiency if the deficiency cannot be remedied, such as if you fail to submit a proposal by the company's properly determined deadline. If the company intends to exclude the proposal, it will later have to make a submission under Rule 14a–8 and provide you with a copy under Question 10 below, Rule 14a–8(j).

(2) If you fail in your promise to hold the required number of securities through the date of the meeting of shareholders, then the company will be permitted to exclude all of your proposals from its proxy materials for any meeting held in the following two calendar years.

(g) **Question 7: Who has the burden of persuading the Commission or its staff that my proposal can be excluded?**

Except as otherwise noted, the burden is on the company to demonstrate that it is entitled to exclude a proposal.

(h) **Question 8: Must I appear personally at the shareholders' meeting to present the proposal?**

(1) Either you, or your representative who is qualified under state law to present the proposal on your behalf, must attend the meeting to present the proposal. Whether you attend the meeting yourself or send a qualified representative to the meeting in your place, you should make sure that you, or your representative, follow the proper state law procedures for attending the meeting and/or presenting your proposal.

(2) If the company holds its shareholder meeting in whole or in part via electronic media, and the company permits you or your representative to present your proposal via such media, then you may appear through electronic media rather than traveling to the meeting to appear in person.

(3) If you or your qualified representative fail to appear and present the proposed, without good cause, the company will be permitted to exclude all of your proposals from its proxy materials for any meetings held in the following two calendar years.

(i) **Question 9: If I have complied with the procedural requirements, on what other bases may a company rely to exclude my proposal?**

(1) **Improper under state law:** If the proposal is not a proper subject for action by shareholders under the laws of the jurisdiction of the company's organization;

Note to paragraph (i)(1): Depending on the subject matter, some proposals are not considered proper under state law if they would be binding on the company if approved by shareholders. In our experience, most proposals that are cast as recommendations or requests that the board of directors take specified action are proper under state law. Accordingly, we will assume that a proposal drafted as a recommendation or suggestion is proper unless the company demonstrates otherwise.

(2) **Violation of law:** If the proposal would, if implemented, cause the company to violate any state, federal, or foreign law to which it is subject;

Note to paragraph (i)(2): We will not apply this basis for exclusion to permit exclusion of a proposal on grounds that it would violate foreign law if compliance with the foreign law would result in a violation of any state or federal law.

(3) **Violation of proxy rules:** If the proposal or supporting statement is contrary to any of the Commission's proxy rules, including Rule 14a–9, which prohibits materially false or misleading statements in proxy soliciting materials;

(4) **Personal grievance; special interest:** If the proposal relates to the redress of a personal claim or grievance against the company or any other person, or if it is designed to result in a benefit to you, or to further a personal interest, which is not shared by the other shareholders at large;

(5) **Relevance:** If the proposal relates to operations which account for less than 5 percent of the company's total assets at the end of its most recent fiscal year, and for less than 5 percent of its net earnings and gross sales for its most recent fiscal year, and is not otherwise significantly related to the company's business;

(6) **Absence of power/authority:** If the company would lack the power or authority to implement the proposal;

(7) **Management functions:** If the proposal deals with a matter relating to the company's ordinary business operations;

(8) **Director elections:** If the proposal:

(i) Would disqualify a nominee who is standing for election;

(ii) Would remove a director from office before his or her term expired;

(iii) Questions the competence, business judgment, or character of one or more nominees or directors;

(iv) Seeks to include a specific individual in the company's proxy materials for election to the board of directors; or

(v) Otherwise could affect the outcome of the upcoming election of directors.

(9) **Conflicts with company's proposal:** If the proposal conflicts in substance with one of the company's own proposals to be submitted to shareholders at the same meeting;

Note to paragraph (i)(9): A company's submission to the Commission under this section shall specify the points of conflict with the company's proposal.

(10) **Substantially implemented:** If the company has already substantially implemented the proposal;

(11) **Duplication:** If the proposal substantially duplicates another proposal previously submitted to the company by another proponent that will be included in the company's proxy materials for the same meeting;

(12) **Resubmissions:** If the proposal deals with substantially the same subject matter as another proposal or proposals that has or have been previously included in the company's proxy materials within the preceding 5 calendar years, a company may exclude it from its proxy materials for any meeting held within 3 calendar years of the last time it was included if the proposal received:

(i) Less than 3% of the vote if proposed once within the preceding 5 calendar years;

(ii) Less than 6% of the vote on its last submission to shareholders if proposed twice previously within the preceding 5 calendar years; or

(iii) Less than 10% of the vote on its last submission to shareholders if proposed three times or more previously within the preceding 5 calendar years; and

(13) **Specific amount of dividends:** If the proposal relates to specific amounts of cash or stock dividends.

(j) **Question 10: What procedures must the company follow if it intends to exclude my proposal?**

(1) If the company intends to exclude a proposal from its proxy materials, it must file its reasons with the Commission no later than 80 calendar days before it files its definitive proxy statement and form of

proxy with the Commission. The company must simultaneously provide you with a copy of its submission. The Commission staff may permit the company to make its submission later than 80 days before the company files its definitive proxy statement and form of proxy, if the company demonstrates good cause for missing the deadline.

(2) The company must file six paper copies of the following:

(i) The proposal;

(ii) An explanation of why the company believes that it may exclude the proposal, which should, if possible, refer to the most recent applicable authority, such as prior Division letters issued under the rule; and

(iii) A supporting opinion of counsel when such reasons are based on matters of state or foreign law.

(k) **Question 11: May I submit my own statement to the Commission responding to the company's arguments?**

Yes, you may submit a response, but it is not required. You should try to submit any response to us, with a copy to the company, as soon as possible after the company makes its submission. This way, the Commission staff will have time to consider fully your submission before it issues its response. You should submit six paper copies of your response.

(*l*) **Question 12: If the company includes my shareholder proposal in its proxy materials, what information about me must it include along with the proposal itself?**

(1) The company's proxy statement must include your name and address, as well as the number of the company's voting securities that you hold. However, instead of providing that information, the company may instead include a statement that it will provide the information to shareholders promptly upon receiving an oral or written request.

(2) The company is not responsible for the contents of your proposal or supporting statement.

(m) **Question 13: What can I do if the company includes in its proxy statement reasons why it believes shareholders should not vote in favor of my proposal, and I disagree with some of its statements?**

(1) The company may elect to include in its proxy statement reasons why it believes shareholders should vote against your proposal. The company is allowed to make arguments reflecting its own point of view, just as you may express your own point of view in your proposal's supporting statement.

(2) However, if you believe that the company's opposition to your proposal contains materially false or misleading statements that may violate our anti-fraud rule, Rule 14a–9, you should promptly send to the Commission staff and the company a letter explaining the reasons for your view, along with a copy of the company's statements opposing your proposal. To the extent possible, your letter should include specific factual information demonstrating the inaccuracy of the company's claims. Time permitting, you may wish to try to work out your differences with the company by yourself before contacting the Commission staff.

(3) We require the company to send a copy of its statements opposing your proposal before it sends its proxy materials, so that you may bring to our attention any materially false or misleading statements, under the following timeframes.

(i) If our no-action response requires that you make revisions to your proposal or supporting statement as a condition to requiring the company to include it in its proxy materials, then the company must provide you with a copy of its opposition statements no later than 5 calendar days after the company receives a copy of your proposal; or

(ii) In all other cases, the company must provide you with a copy of its opposition statements no later than 30 calendar days before its files definitive copies of its proxy statement and form of proxy under Rule 14a–6.

Rule 14a–9. False or Misleading Statements

(a) No solicitation subject to this regulation shall be made by means of any proxy statement, form of proxy, notice of meeting or other communication, written or oral, containing any statement which, at the time and in the light of the circumstances under which it is made, is false or misleading with respect to any material fact, or which omits to state any material fact necessary in order to make the statements therein not false or misleading or necessary to correct any statement in any earlier communication with respect to the solicitation of a proxy for the same meeting or subject matter which has become false or misleading.

(b) The fact that a proxy statement, form of proxy or other soliciting material has been filed with or examined by the Commission shall not be deemed a finding by the Commission that such material is accurate or complete or not false or misleading, or that the Commission has passed upon the merits of or approved any statement contained therein or any matter to be acted upon by security holders. No representation contrary to the foregoing shall be made. . . .

(c) No nominee, nominating shareholder or nominating shareholder group, or any member thereof, shall cause to be included in a registrant's proxy materials, either pursuant to the federal proxy rules, an applicable state or foreign law provision, or a registrant's governing documents as they relate to including shareholder nominees for director in a registrant's proxy materials, include in a notice on Schedule 14N, or include in any other related communication, any statement which, at the time and in the light of the circumstances under which it is made, is false or misleading with respect to any material fact, or which omits to state any material fact necessary in order to make the statements therein not false or misleading or necessary to correct any statement in any earlier communication with respect to a solicitation for the same meeting or subject matter which has become false or misleading.

Rule 14a–10. Prohibition of Certain Solicitations

No person making a solicitation which is subject to Rules 14a–1 to 14a–10 shall solicit:

(a) Any undated or postdated proxy; or

(b) Any proxy which provides that it shall be deemed to be dated as of any date subsequent to the date on which it is signed by the security holder.

Rule 14a–12. Solicitation Before Furnishing a Proxy Statement

(a) Notwithstanding the provisions of Rule 14a–3(a), a solicitation may be made before furnishing security holders with a proxy statement meeting the requirements of Rule 14a–3(a) if:

(1) Each written communication includes:

(i) The identity of the participants in the solicitation (as defined in Instruction 3 to Item 4 of Schedule 14A) and a description of their direct or indirect interests, by security holdings or otherwise, or a prominent legend in clear, plain language advising security holders where they can obtain that information; and

(ii) A prominent legend in clear, plain language advising security holders to read the proxy statement when it is available because it contains important information. The legend also must explain to investors that they can get the proxy statement, and any other relevant documents, for free at the Commission's web site and describe which documents are available free from the participants; and

(2) A definitive proxy statement meeting the requirements of Rule 14a–3(a) is sent or given to security holders solicited in reliance on this section before or at the same time as the forms of proxy, consent or authorization are furnished to or requested from security holders.

(b) Any soliciting material published, sent or given to security holders in accordance with paragraph (a) of this section must be filed with the Commission no later than the date the material is first published, sent or given to security holders. Three copies of the material must at the same time be filed with, or mailed for filing to, each national securities exchange upon which any class of securities of the registrant is listed and registered. The soliciting material must include a cover page in the form set forth in Schedule 14A and the appropriate box on the cover page must be marked. Soliciting material in connection with a registered offering is required to be filed only under Rule 424 or Rule 425 [under the Securities Exchange Act], and will be deemed filed under this section.

(c) Solicitations by any person or group of persons for the purpose of opposing a solicitation subject to this regulation by any other person or group of persons with respect to the election or removal of directors at any annual or special meeting of security holders also are subject to the following provisions:

(1) *Application of this rule to annual report to security holders.* Notwithstanding the provisions of Rule 14a–3 (b) and (c), any portion of the annual report to security holders referred to in Rule 14a–3(b) that comments upon or refers to any solicitation subject to this rule, or to any participant in the solicitation, other than the solicitation by the management, must be filed with the Commission as proxy material subject to this regulation. This must be filed in electronic format. . . .

(2) *Use of reprints or reproductions.* In any solicitation subject to this Rule 14a–12(c), soliciting material that includes, in whole or part, any reprints or reproductions of any previously published material must:

(i) State the name of the author and publication, the date of prior publication, and identify any person who is quoted without being named in the previously published material.

(ii) Except in the case of a public or official document or statement, state whether or not the consent of the author and publication has been obtained to the use of the previously published material as proxy soliciting material.

(iii) If any participant using the previously published material, or anyone on his or her behalf, paid, directly or indirectly, for the preparation or prior publication of the previously published material, or has made or proposes to make any payments or give any other consideration in connection with the publication or republication of the material, state the circumstances.

Rule 14a–15. Differential and Contingent Compensation in Connection With Roll-Up Transactions

(a) It shall be unlawful for any person to receive compensation for soliciting proxies, consents, or authorizations directly from security holders in connection with a roll-up transaction as provided in paragraph (b) of this section, if the compensation is:

(1) Based on whether the solicited proxy, consent, or authorization either approves or disapproves the proposed roll-up transaction; or

(2) Contingent on the approval, disapproval, or completion of the roll-up transaction.

(b) This section is applicable to a roll-up transaction as defined in Item 901(c) of Regulation S–K, except for a transaction involving only:

(1) Finite-life entities that are not limited partnerships. . . .

Rule 14a–16. Internet Availability of Proxy Materials

(a)(1) A registrant shall furnish a proxy statement pursuant to Rule 14a–3(a), or an annual report to security holders pursuant to Rule 14a–3(b), to a security holder by sending the security holder a Notice of Internet Availability of Proxy Materials, as described in this section, 40 calendar days or more prior to the security holder meeting date, or if no meeting is to be held, 40 calendar days or more prior to the date the votes, consents or authorizations may be used to effect the corporate action, and complying with all other requirements of this section.

(2) Unless the registrant chooses to follow the full set delivery option set forth in paragraph (n) of this section, it must provide the record holder or respondent bank with all information listed in paragraph (d) of this section in sufficient time for the record holder or respondent bank to prepare, print and send a Notice of Internet Availability of Proxy Materials to beneficial owners at least 40 calendar days before the meeting date.

(b)(1) All materials identified in the Notice of Internet Availability of Proxy Materials must be publicly accessible, free of charge, at the Web site address specified in the notice on or before the time that the notice is sent to the security holder and such materials must remain available on that Web site through the conclusion of the meeting of security holders.

(2) All additional soliciting materials sent to security holders or made public after the Notice of Internet Availability of Proxy Materials has been sent must be made publicly accessible at the specified Web site address no later than the day on which such materials are first sent to security holders or made public.

(3) A clear and impartial identification of each separate matter intended to be acted on and the soliciting person's recommendations, if any, regarding those matters, but no supporting statements;

(4) The registrant must provide security holders with a means to execute a proxy as of the time the Notice of Internet Availability of Proxy Materials is first sent to security holders.

(c) The materials must be presented on the Web site in a format, or formats, convenient for both reading online and printing on paper.

(d) The Notice of Internet Availability of Proxy Materials must contain the following:

(1) A prominent legend in bold-face type that states "Important Notice Regarding the Availability of Proxy Materials for the Shareholder Meeting To Be Held on [insert meeting date]";

(2) An indication that the communication is not a form for voting and presents only an overview of the more complete proxy materials, which contain important information and are available on the Internet or by mail, and encouraging a security holder to access and review the proxy materials before voting;

(3) The Internet Web site address where the proxy materials are available;

(4) Instructions regarding how a security holder may request a paper or email copy of the proxy materials at no charge, including the date by which they should make the request to facilitate timely delivery, and an indication that they will not otherwise receive a paper or email copy;

(5) The date, time, and location of the meeting, or if corporate action is to be taken by written consent, the earliest date on which the corporate action may be effected;

(6) A clear and impartial identification of each separate matter intended to be acted on and the soliciting person's recommendations regarding those matters, but no supporting statements;

(7) A list of the materials being made available at the specified Web site;

(8) A toll-free telephone number, an e-mail address, and an Internet Web site where the security holder can request a copy of the proxy statement, annual report to security holders, and form of proxy, relating to all of the registrant's future security holder meetings and for the particular meeting to which the proxy materials being furnished relate;

(9) Any control/identification numbers that the security holder needs to access his or her form of proxy;

(10) Instructions on how to access the form of proxy, provided that such instructions do not enable a security holder to execute a proxy without having access to the proxy statement and, if required by Rule 14a–3(b), the annual report to security holders; and

(11) Information on how to obtain directions to be able to attend the meeting and vote in person.

(e)(1) The Notice of Internet Availability of Proxy Materials may not be incorporated into, or combined with, another document, except that it may be incorporated into, or combined with, a notice of security holder meeting required under state law, unless state law prohibits such incorporation or combination.

(2) The Notice of Internet Availability of Proxy Materials may contain only the information required by paragraph (d) of this section and any additional information required to be included in a notice of security holders meeting under state law; provided that:

(i) The registrant must revise the information on the Notice of Internet Availability of Proxy Materials, including any title to the document, to reflect the fact that:

(A) The registrant is conducting a consent solicitation rather than a proxy solicitation; or

(B) The registrant is not soliciting proxy or consent authority, but is furnishing an information statement pursuant to Rule 14c–2; and

(ii) The registrant may include a statement on the Notice to educate security holders that no personal information other than the identification or control number is necessary to execute a proxy.

(f)(1) Except as provided in paragraph (h) of this section, the Notice of Internet Availability of Proxy Materials must be sent separately from other types of security holder communications and may not accompany any other document or materials, including the form of proxy.

(2) Notwithstanding paragraph (f)(1) of this section, the registrant may accompany the Notice of Internet Availability of Proxy Materials with:

(i) A pre-addressed, postage-paid reply card for requesting a copy of the proxy materials; . . .

(ii) A copy of any notice of security holder meeting required under state law if that notice is not combined with the Notice of Internet Availability of Proxy Materials. . . .

(iv) An explanation of the reasons for a registrant's use of the rules detailed in this section and the process of receiving and reviewing the proxy materials and voting as detailed in this section.

(g) *Plain English.*

(1) To enhance the readability of the Notice of Internet Availability of Proxy Materials, the registrant must use plain English principles in the organization, language, and design of the notice.

(2) The registrant must draft the language in the Notice of Internet Availability of Proxy Materials so that, at a minimum, it substantially complies with each of the following plain English writing principles:

(i) Short sentences;

(ii) Definite, concrete, everyday words;

(iii) Active voice;

(iv) Tabular presentation or bullet lists for complex material, whenever possible;

(v) No legal jargon or highly technical business terms; and

(vi) No multiple negatives.

(3) In designing the Notice of Internet Availability of Proxy Materials, the registrant may include pictures, logos, or similar design elements so long as the design is not misleading and the required information is clear.

(h) The registrant may send a form of proxy to security holders if:

(1) At least 10 calendar days or more have passed since the date it first sent the Notice of Internet Availability of Proxy Materials to security holders and the form of proxy is accompanied by a copy of the Notice of Internet Availability of Proxy Materials; or

(2) The form of proxy is accompanied or preceded by a copy, via the same medium, of the proxy statement and any annual report to security holders that is required by Rule 14a–3(b).

(i) The registrant must file a form of the Notice of Internet Availability of Proxy Materials with the Commission pursuant to Rule 14a–6(b) no later than the date that the registrant first sends the notice to security holders.

(j) *Obligation to provide copies.*

(1) The registrant must send, at no cost to the record holder or respondent bank and by U.S. first class mail or other reasonably prompt means, a paper copy of the proxy statement, information statement, annual report to security holders, and form of proxy (to the extent each of those documents is applicable) to any record holder or respondent bank requesting such a copy within three business days after receiving a request for a paper copy.

(2) The registrant must send, at no cost to the record holder or respondent bank and via e-mail, an electronic copy of the proxy statement, information statement, annual report to security holders, and form of proxy (to the extent each of those documents is applicable) to any record holder or respondent bank requesting such a copy within three business days after receiving a request for an electronic copy via e-mail.

(3) The registrant must provide copies of the proxy materials for one year after the conclusion of the meeting or corporate action to which the proxy materials relate, provided that, if the registrant receives the request after the conclusion of the meeting or corporate action to which the proxy materials relate, the

registrant need not send copies via First Class mail and need not respond to such request within three business days.

(4) The registrant must maintain records of security holder requests to receive materials in paper or via e-mail for future solicitations and must continue to provide copies of the materials to a security holder who has made such a request until the security holder revokes such request.

(k) *Security holder information.*

(1) A registrant or its agent shall maintain the Internet Web site on which it posts its proxy materials in a manner that does not infringe on the anonymity of a person accessing such Web site.

(2) The registrant and its agents shall not use any e-mail address obtained from a security holder solely for the purpose of requesting a copy of proxy materials pursuant to paragraph (j) for any purpose other than to send a copy of those materials to that security holder. The registrant shall not disclose such information to any person other than an employee or agent to the extent necessary to send a copy of the proxy materials pursuant to paragraph (j).

(*l*) A person other than the registrant may solicit proxies pursuant to the conditions imposed on registrants by this section, provided that:

(1) A soliciting person other than the registrant is required to provide copies of its proxy materials only to security holders to whom it has sent a Notice of Internet Availability of Proxy Materials; and

(2) A soliciting person other than the registrant must send its Notice of Internet Availability of Proxy Materials by the later of:

(i) 40 calendar days prior to the security holder meeting date or, if no meeting is to be held, 40 calendar days prior to the date the votes, consents, or authorizations may be used to effect the corporate action; or

(ii) The date on which it files its definitive proxy statement with the Commission, provided its preliminary proxy statement is filed no later than 10 calendar days after the date that the registrant files its definitive proxy statement.

(3) *Content of the soliciting person's Notice of Internet Availability of Proxy Materials.*

(i) If, at the time a soliciting person other than the registrant sends its Notice of Internet Availability of Proxy Materials, the soliciting person is not aware of all matters on the registrant's agenda for the meeting of security holders, the soliciting person's Notice on Internet Availability of Proxy Materials must provide a clear and impartial identification of each separate matter on the agenda to the extent known by the soliciting person at that time. The soliciting person's notice also must include a clear statement indicating that there may be additional agenda items of which the soliciting person is not aware and that the security holder cannot direct a vote for those items on the soliciting person's proxy card provided at that time.

(ii) If a soliciting person other than the registrant sends a form of proxy not containing all matters intended to be acted upon, the Notice of Internet Availability of Proxy Materials must clearly state whether execution of the form of proxy will invalidate a security holder's prior vote on matters not presented on the form of proxy.

(m) This section shall not apply to a proxy solicitation in connection with a business combination transaction, as defined in [Rule 165 under the Securities Act], as well as transactions for cash consideration requiring disclosure under Item 14 of Schedule 14A.

(n) *Full Set Delivery Option.*

(1) For purposes of this paragraph (n), the term *full set of proxy materials* shall include all of the following documents:

(i) A copy of the proxy statement;

(ii) A copy of the annual report to security holders if required by Rule 14a–3(b); and

(iii) A form of proxy.

(2) Notwithstanding paragraphs (e) and (f)(2) of this section, a registrant or other soliciting person may:

(i) Accompany the Notice of Internet Availability of Proxy Materials with a full set of proxy materials; or

(ii) Send a full set of proxy materials without a Notice of Internet Availability of Proxy Materials if all of the information required in a Notice of Internet Availability of Proxy Materials pursuant to paragraphs (d) and (n)(4) is incorporated in the proxy statement and the form of proxy.

(3) A registrant or other soliciting person that sends a full set of proxy materials to a security holder pursuant to this paragraph (n) need not comply with

(i) The timing provisions of paragraphs (a) and (*l*)(2); and

(ii) The obligation to provide copies pursuant to paragraph (j).

(4) A registrant or other soliciting person that sends a full set of proxy materials to a security holder pursuant to this paragraph (n) need not include in its Notice of Internet Availability of Proxy Materials, proxy statement, or form of proxy the following disclosures:

(i) Instructions regarding the nature of the communication pursuant to paragraph (d)(2) of this section;

(ii) Instructions on how to request a copy of the proxy materials; and

(iii) Instructions on how to access the form of proxy pursuant to paragraph (d)(10).

Rule 14a–17. Electronic Shareholder Forums

(a) A shareholder, registrant, or third party acting on behalf of a shareholder or registrant may establish, maintain, or operate an electronic shareholder forum to facilitate interaction among the registrant's shareholders and between the registrant and its shareholders as the shareholder or registrant deems appropriate. Subject to paragraphs (b) and (c) of this section, the forum must comply with the federal securities laws, including Section 14(a) of the Act and its associated regulations, other applicable federal laws, applicable state laws, and the registrant's governing documents.

(b) No shareholder, registrant, or third party acting on behalf of a shareholder or registrant, by reason of establishing, maintaining, or operating an electronic shareholder forum, will be liable under the federal securities laws for any statement or information provided by another person to the electronic shareholder forum. Nothing in this section prevents or alters the application of the federal securities laws, including the provisions for liability for fraud, deception, or manipulation, or other applicable federal and state laws to the person or persons that provide a statement or information to an electronic shareholder forum.

(c) Reliance on the exemption in Rule 14a–2(b)(6) to participate in an electronic shareholder forum does not eliminate a person's eligibility to solicit proxies after the date that the exemption in Rule 14a–2(b)(6) is no longer available, or is no longer being relied upon, provided that any such solicitation is conducted in accordance with this regulation. . . .

Rule 14a–18. Disclosure Regarding Nominating Shareholders and Nominees Submitted for Inclusion in a Registrant's Proxy Materials Pursuant to Applicable State or Foreign Law, or a Registrant's Governing Documents

To have a nominee included in a registrant's proxy materials pursuant to a procedure set forth under applicable state or foreign law, or the registrant's governing documents addressing the inclusion of shareholder director nominees in the registrant's proxy materials, the nominating shareholder or nominating shareholder group must provide notice to the registrant of its intent to do so on a Schedule 14N and file that notice, including the required disclosure, with the Commission on the date first transmitted to the registrant. This notice shall be postmarked or transmitted electronically to the registrant by the date specified by the registrant's advance notice provision or, where no such provision is in place, no later than 120 calendar days before the anniversary of the date that the registrant mailed its proxy materials for the prior year's annual meeting, except that, if the registrant did not hold an annual meeting during the prior year, or if the date of the meeting has changed by more than 30 calendar days from the prior year, then the nominating shareholder or nominating shareholder group must provide notice a reasonable time before the registrant mails its proxy materials, as specified by the registrant in a Form 8-K filed pursuant to Item 5.08 of Form 8-K.

Rule 14a–20. Shareholder Approval of Executive Compensation of TARP Recipients

If a solicitation is made by a registrant that is a *TARP recipient*, as defined in section 111(a)(3) of the Emergency Economic Stabilization Act of 2008 (12 U.S.C. § 5221(a)(3)), during the period in which any obligation arising from financial assistance provided under the *TARP*, as defined in section 3(8) of the Emergency Economic Stabilization Act of 2008 (12 U.S.C. § 5202(8)), remains outstanding and the solicitation relates to an annual (or special meeting in lieu of the annual) meeting of security holders for which proxies will be solicited for the election of directors, as required pursuant to section 111(e)(1) of the Emergency Economic Stabilization Act of 2008, the registrant shall provide a separate shareholder vote to approve the compensation of executives, as disclosed pursuant to Item 402 of Regulation S–K, including the compensation discussion and analysis, the compensation tables, and any related material.

Rule 14a–21. Shareholder Approval of Executive Compensation, Frequency of Votes for Approval of Executive Compensation and Shareholder Approval of Golden Parachute Compensation

(a) If a solicitation is made by a registrant and the solicitation relates to an annual or other meeting of shareholders at which directors will be elected and for which the rules of the Commission require executive compensation disclosure pursuant to Item 402 of Regulation S–K, . . . include a separate resolution subject to shareholder advisory vote to approve the compensation of its named executive officers, as disclosed pursuant to Item 402 of Regulation S–K.

(b) If a solicitation is made by a registrant and the solicitation relates to an annual or other meeting of shareholders at which directors will be elected and for which the rules of the Commission require executive compensation disclosure pursuant to Item 402 of Regulation S–K, the registrant shall . . . include a separate resolution subject to shareholder advisory vote as to whether the shareholder vote required by paragraph (a) of this section should occur every 1, 2 or 3 years. Registrants required to provide a separate shareholder vote pursuant to Rule 14a–20 shall include the separate resolution required by this section for the first annual or other meeting of shareholders after the registrant has repaid all obligations arising from financial assistance provided under the TARP, as defined in section 3(8) of the Emergency Economic Stabilization Act of 2008, and thereafter no later than the annual or other meeting of shareholders held in the sixth calendar year after the immediately preceding vote under this subsection.

(c) If a solicitation is made by a registrant for a meeting of shareholders at which shareholders are asked to approve an acquisition, merger, consolidation or proposed sale or other disposition of all or substantially all the assets of the registrant, the registrant shall include a separate resolution subject to shareholder advisory vote to approve any agreements or understandings and compensation disclosed pursuant to Rule 402(t) of Regulation S–K, unless such agreements or understandings have been subject to a shareholder advisory vote under paragraph (a) of this section. Consistent with section 14A(b) of the Exchange Act, any agreements or understandings between an acquiring company and the named executive officers of the registrant, where the registrant is not the acquiring company, are not required to be subject to the separate shareholder advisory vote under this paragraph.

SCHEDULE 14A. INFORMATION REQUIRED IN PROXY STATEMENT. . . .

Item 1.   *Date, time and place information.* (a) State the date, time and place of the meeting of security holders, and the complete mailing address, including ZIP Code, of the principal executive offices of the registrant, unless such information is otherwise disclosed in material furnished to security holders with or preceding the proxy statement. If action is to be taken by written consent, state the date by which consents are to be submitted if state law requires that such a date be specified or if the person soliciting intends to set a date.

(b) On the first page of the proxy statement, as delivered to security holders, state the approximate date on which the proxy statement and form of proxy are first sent or given to security holders.

(c) Furnish the information required to be in the proxy statement by Rule 14a–5(e). . . .

Item 2.   Revocability of proxy. State whether or not the person giving the proxy has the power to revoke it. If the right of revocation before the proxy is exercised is limited or is subject to compliance with any formal procedure, briefly describe such limitation or procedure.

Item 3.   Dissenters' right of appraisal. Outline briefly the rights of appraisal or similar rights of dissenters with respect to any matter to be acted upon and indicate any statutory procedure required to be followed by dissenting security holders in order to perfect such rights. Where such rights may be exercised only within a limited time after the date of adoption of a proposal, the filing of a charter amendment or other similar act, state whether the persons solicited will be notified of such date.

> *Instruction.* Indicate whether a security holder's failure to vote against a proposal will constitute a waiver of his appraisal or similar rights and whether a vote against a proposal will be deemed to satisfy any notice requirements under State law with respect to appraisal rights. If the State law is unclear, state what position will be taken in regard to these matters.

Item 4.   Persons Making the Solicitation—(a) Solicitations not subject to Rule 14a–12(c). . . . (1) If the solicitation is made by the registrant, so state. Give the name of any director of the registrant who has informed the registrant in writing that he intends to oppose any action intended to be taken by the registrant and indicate the action which he intends to oppose.

(2) If the solicitation is made otherwise than by the registrant, so state and give the names of the participants in the solicitation, as defined in paragraphs (a)(iii), (iv), (v) and (vi) of Instruction 3 to this Item.

(3) If the solicitation is to be made otherwise than by the use of the mails or pursuant to Rule 14a–16, describe the methods to be employed. If the solicitation is to be made by specially engaged employees or paid solicitors, state (i) the material features of any contract or arrangement for such solicitation and identify the parties, and (ii) the cost or anticipated cost thereof.

(4) State the names of the persons by whom the cost of solicitation has been or will be borne, directly or indirectly.

(b) *Solicitations subject to Rule 14a–12(c).* . . . (1) State by whom the solicitation is made and describe the methods employed and to be employed to solicit security holders.

(2) If regular employees of the registrant or any other participant in a solicitation have been or are to be employed to solicit security holders, describe the class or classes of employees to be so employed, and the manner and nature of their employment for such purpose.

(3) If specially engaged employees, representatives or other persons have been or are to be employed to solicit security holders, state (i) the material features of any contract or arrangement for such solicitation and the identity of the parties, (ii) the cost or anticipated cost thereof and (iii) the approximate number of such employees or employees of any other person (naming such other person) who will solicit security holders.

(4) State the total amount estimated to be spent and the total expenditures to date for, in furtherance of, or in connection with the solicitation of security holders.

(5) State by whom the cost of the solicitation will be borne. If such cost is to be borne initially by any person other than the registrant, state whether reimbursement will be sought from the registrant, and, if so, whether the question of such reimbursement will be submitted to a vote of security holders.

(6) If any such solicitation is terminated pursuant to a settlement between the registrant and any other participant in such solicitation, describe the terms of such settlement, including the cost or anticipated cost thereof to the registrant. . . .

> *Instructions.* . . .
>
> 3.   For purposes of this Item 4 and Item 5 of this Schedule 14A:
>
> (a) The terms "participant" and "participant in a solicitation" include the following:

(i) the registrant;

(ii) any director of the registrant, and any nominee for whose election as a director proxies are solicited;

(iii) any committee or group which solicits proxies, any member of such committee or group, and any person whether or not named as a member who, acting alone or with one or more other persons, directly or indirectly takes the initiative, or engages, in organizing, directing, or arranging for the financing of any such committee or group;

(iv) any person who finances or joins with another to finance the solicitation of proxies, except persons who contribute not more than $500 and who are not otherwise participants;

(v) any person who lends money or furnishes credit or enters into any other arrangements, pursuant to any contract or understanding with a participant, for the purpose of financing or otherwise inducing the purchase, sale, holding or voting of securities of the registrant by any participant or other persons, in support of or in opposition to a participant; except that such terms do not include a bank, broker or dealer who, in the ordinary course of business, lends money or executes orders for the purchase or sale of securities and who is not otherwise a participant; and

(vi) any person who solicits proxies.

(b) The terms "participant" and "participant in a solicitation" do not include:

(i) any person or organization retained or employed by a participant to solicit security holders and whose activities are limited to the duties required to be performed in the course of such employment;

(ii) any person who merely transmits proxy soliciting material or performs other ministerial or clerical duties;

(iii) any person employed by a participant in the capacity of attorney, accountant, or advertising, public relations or financial adviser, and whose activities are limited to the duties required to be performed in the course of such employment;

(iv) any person regularly employed as an officer or employee of the registrant or any of its subsidiaries who is not otherwise a participant; or

(v) any officer or director of, or any person regularly employed by, any other participant, if such officer, director or employee is not otherwise a participant.

Item 5.   Interest of certain persons in matters to be acted upon—

(a) *Solicitations not subject to Rule 14a–12(c).* . . . Describe briefly any substantial interest, direct or indirect, by security holdings or otherwise, of each of the following persons in any matter to be acted upon, other than elections to office:

(1) If the solicitation is made on behalf of the registrant, each person who has been a director or executive officer of the registrant at any time since the beginning of the last fiscal year.

(2) If the solicitation is made otherwise than on behalf of the registrant, each participant in the solicitation, as defined in paragraphs (a)(iii), (iv), (v), and (vi) of Instruction 3 to Item 4 of this Schedule 14A.

(3) Each nominee for election as a director of the registrant.

(4) Each associate of any of the foregoing persons. . . .

(5) If the solicitation is made on behalf of the registrant, furnish the information required by Item 402(t) of Regulation S–K.

(b) *Solicitation subject to Rule 14a–12(c).* With respect to any solicitation subject to Rule 14a–12(c):

(1) Describe briefly any substantial interest, direct or indirect, by security holdings or otherwise, of each participant as defined in paragraphs (a)(ii), (iii), (iv), (v) and (vi) of Instruction 3 to Item 4 of this Schedule 14A, in any matter to be acted upon at the meeting, and include with respect to each participant the following information, or a fair and accurate summary thereof:

(i) Name and business address of the participant.

(ii) The participant's present principal occupation or employment and the name, principal business and address of any corporation or other organization in which such employment is carried on.

(iii) State whether or not, during the past ten years, the participant has been convicted in a criminal proceeding (excluding traffic violations or similar misdemeanors) and, if so, give dates, nature of conviction, name and location of court, and penalty imposed or other disposition of the case. A negative answer need not be included in the proxy statement or other soliciting material.

(iv) State the amount of each class of securities of the registrant which the participant owns beneficially, directly or indirectly.

(v) State the amount of each class of securities of the registrant which the participant owns of record but not beneficially.

(vi) State with respect to all securities of the registrant purchased or sold within the past two years, the dates on which they were purchased or sold and the amount purchased or sold on each such date.

(vii) If any part of the purchase price or market value of any of the shares specified in paragraph (b)(1)(vi) of this Item is represented by funds borrowed or otherwise obtained for the purpose of acquiring or holding such securities, so state and indicate the amount of the indebtedness as of the latest practicable date. If such funds were borrowed or obtained otherwise than pursuant to a margin account or bank loan in the regular course of business of a bank, broker or dealer, briefly describe the transaction, and state the names of the parties.

(viii) State whether or not the participant is, or was within the past year, a party to any contract, arrangements or understandings with any person with respect to any securities of the registrant, including, but not limited to joint ventures, loan or option arrangements, puts or calls, guarantees against loss or guarantees of profit, division of losses or profits, or the giving or withholding of proxies. If so, name the parties to such contracts, arrangements or understandings and give the details thereof.

(ix) State the amount of securities of the registrant owned beneficially, directly or indirectly, by each of the participant's associates and the name and address of each such associate.

(x) State the amount of each class of securities of any parent or subsidiary of the registrant which the participant owns beneficially, directly or indirectly.

(xi) Furnish for the participant and associates of the participant the information required by Item 404(a) of Regulation S–K.

(xii) State whether or not the participant or any associates of the participant have any arrangement or understanding with any person—

(A) with respect to any future employment by the registrant or its affiliates; or

(B) with respect to any future transactions to which the registrant or any of its affiliates will or may be a party.

If so, describe such arrangement or understanding and state the names of the parties thereto.

(2) With respect to any person, other than a director or executive officer of the registrant acting solely in that capacity, who is a party to an arrangement or understanding pursuant to which a nominee for election as director is proposed to be elected, describe any substantial interest, direct or indirect, by security holdings or otherwise, that such person has in any matter to be acted upon at the meeting, and furnish the information called for by paragraphs (b)(1)(xi) and (xii) of this Item. . . .

(3) If the solicitation is made on behalf of the registrant, furnish the information required by Item 402(1) of Regulation S–K.

Item 6.   Voting securities and principal holders thereof. (a) As to each class of voting securities of the registrant entitled to be voted at the meeting (or by written consents or authorizations if no meeting is held), state the number of shares outstanding and the number of votes to which each class is entitled.

(b) State the record date, if any, with respect to this solicitation. If the right to vote or give consent is not to be determined, in whole or in part, by reference to a record date, indicate the criteria for the determination of security holders entitled to vote or give consent.

(c) If action is to be taken with respect to the election of directors and if the persons solicited have cumulative voting rights: (1) Make a statement that they have such rights, (2) briefly describe such rights, (3) state briefly the conditions precedent to the exercise thereof, and (4) if discretionary authority to cumulate votes is solicited, so indicate.

(d) Furnish the information required by Item 403 of Regulation S–K . . . to the extent known by the persons on whose behalf the solicitation is made.

(e) If, to the knowledge of the persons on whose behalf the solicitation is made, a change in control of the registrant has occurred since the beginning of its last fiscal year, state the name of the person(s) who acquired such control, the amount and the source of the consideration used by such person or persons; the basis of the control, the date and a description of the transaction(s) which resulted in the change of control and the percentage of voting securities of the registrant now beneficially owned directly or indirectly by the person(s) who acquired control; and the identity of the person(s) from whom control was assumed. If the source of all or any part of the consideration used is a loan made in the ordinary course of business by a bank . . . , the identity of such bank shall be omitted provided a request for confidentiality has been made . . . by the person(s) who acquired control. In lieu thereof, the material shall indicate that the identity of the bank has been so omitted and filed separately with the Commission.

Instruction. 1. State the terms of any loans or pledges obtained by the new control group for the purpose of acquiring control, and the names of the lenders or pledgees.

2. Any arrangements or understandings among members of both the former and new control groups and their associates with respect to election of directors or other matters should be described.

Item 7. Directors and executive officers. If action is to be taken with respect to the election of directors, furnish the following information in tabular form to the extent practicable. If, however, the solicitation is made on behalf of persons other than the registrant, the information required need be furnished only as to nominees of the persons making the solicitation.

(a) The information required by instruction 4 to Item 103 of Regulation S–K [Legal Proceedings] . . . with respect to directors and executive officers.

(b) The information required by Items 401, 404(a) and (b), 405 and 407(d)(4), (d)(5) and (h) of Regulation S–K.

(c) The information required by Item 407(a) of Regulation S–K.

(d) The information required by Item 407(b), (c)(1), (c)(2), (d)(1), (d)(2), (d)(3), (e)(1), (e)(2), (e)(3) and (f) of Regulation S–K. . . .

(e) If a shareholder nominee or nominees are submitted to the registrant for inclusion in the registrant's proxy materials pursuant to Rule 14a–11 and the registrant is not permitted to exclude the nominee or nominees pursuant to the provisions of Rule 14a–11, the registrant must include in its proxy statement the disclosure required from the nominating shareholder or nominating shareholder group under Item 5 of the Schedule 14N with regard to the nominee or nominees and the nominating shareholder or nominating shareholder group.

(f) If a registrant is required to include a shareholder nominee or nominees submitted to the registrant for inclusion in the registrant's proxy materials pursuant to a procedure set forth under applicable state or foreign law, or the registrant's governing documents providing for the inclusion of shareholder director nominees in the registrant's proxy materials, the registrant must include in its proxy statement the disclosure required from the nominating shareholder or nominating shareholder group under Item 6 of Schedule 14N with regard to the nominee or nominees and the nominating shareholder group. . . .

Item 8. Compensation of directors and executive officers. Furnish the information required by Item 402 of Regulation S–K and paragraphs (e)(4) and (e)(5) of Item 407 of Regulation S–K if action is to be taken with regard to:

(a) the election of directors;

(b) any bonus, profit sharing or other compensation plan, contract or arrangement in which any director, nominee for election as a director, or executive officer of the registrant will participate;

(c) any pension or retirement plan in which any such person will participate; or

(d) the granting or extension to any such person of any options, warrants or rights to purchase any securities, other than warrants or rights issued to security holders as such, on a pro rata basis. However, if the solicitation is made on behalf of persons other than the registrant, the information required need be furnished only as to nominees of the persons making the solicitation and associates of such nominees. . . .

However, if the solicitation is made on behalf of persons other than the registrant, the information required need be furnished only as to nominees of the persons making the solicitation and associates of such nominees. . . .

Item 9.   *Independent public accountants.* If the solicitation is made on behalf of the registrant and relates to: (1) The annual (or special meeting in lieu of annual) meeting of security holders at which directors are to be elected, or a solicitation of consents or authorizations in lieu of such meeting or (2) the election, approval or ratification of the registrant's accountant, furnish the following information describing the registrant's relationship with its independent public accountant:

(a) The name of the principal accountant selected or being recommended to security holders for election, approval or ratification for the current year. If no accountant has been selected or recommended, so state and briefly describe the reasons therefor.

(b) The name of the principal accountant for the fiscal year most recently completed if different from the accountant selected or recommended for the current year or if no accountant has yet been selected or recommended for the current year.

(c) The proxy statement shall indicate: (1) Whether or not representatives of the principal accountant for the current year and for the most recently completed fiscal year are expected to be present at the security holders' meeting, (2) whether or not they will have the opportunity to make a statement if they desire to do so, and (3) whether or not such representatives are expected to be available to respond to appropriate questions.

(d) If during the registrant's two most recent fiscal years or any subsequent interim period, (1) an independent accountant who was previously engaged as the principal accountant to audit the registrant's financial statements, or an independent accountant on whom the principal accountant expressed reliance in its report regarding a significant subsidiary, has resigned (or indicated it has declined to stand for re-election after the completion of the current audit) or was dismissed, or (2) a new independent accountant has been engaged as either the principal accountant to audit the registrant's financial statements or as an independent accountant on whom the principal accountant has expressed or is expected to express reliance in its report regarding a significant subsidiary, then, notwithstanding any previous disclosure, provide the information required by Item 304(a) of Regulation S–K.

(e)(1) Disclose, under the caption *Audit Fees*, the aggregate fees billed for each of the last two fiscal years for professional services rendered by the principal accountant for the audit of the registrant's annual financial statements and review of financial statements included in the registrant's Form 10-Q or services that are normally provided by the accountant in connection with statutory and regulatory filings or engagements for those fiscal years.

(2) Disclose, under the caption Audit-Related Fees, the aggregate fees billed in each of the last two fiscal years for assurance and related services by the principal accountant that are reasonably related to the performance of the audit or review of the registrant's financial statements and are not reported under paragraph (e)(1) of this section. Registrants shall describe the nature of the services comprising the fees disclosed under this category.

(3) Disclose, under the caption Tax Fees, the aggregate fees billed in each of the last two fiscal years for professional services rendered by the principal accountant for tax compliance, tax advice, and tax planning. Registrants shall describe the nature of the services comprising the fees disclosed under this category.

(4) Disclose, under the caption All Other Fees, the aggregate fees billed in each of the last two fiscal years for products and services provided by the principal accountant, other than the services reported in paragraphs (e)(1) through (e)(3) of this section. Registrants shall describe the nature of the services comprising the fees disclosed under this category.

(5)(i) Disclose the audit committee's pre-approval policies and procedures described in 17 CFR 210.2–01(c)(7)(i).

(ii) Disclose the percentage of services described in each of paragraphs (e)(2) through (e)(4) of this section that were approved by the audit committee pursuant to 17 CFR 210.2–01(c)(7)(i)(C).

(6) If greater than 50 percent, disclose the percentage of hours expended on the principal accountant's engagement to audit the registrant's financial statements for the most recent fiscal year that were attributed to work performed by persons other than the principal accountant's full-time, permanent employees. . . .

Item 10.   Compensation Plans. If action is to be taken with respect to any plan pursuant to which cash or noncash compensation may be paid or distributed, furnish the following information:

(a) *Plans Subject to Security Holder Action.*

(1) Describe briefly the material features of the plan being acted upon, identify each class of persons who will be eligible to participate therein, indicate the approximate number of persons in each such class, and state the basis of such participation.

(2)(i) In the tabular format specified below, disclose the benefits or amounts that will be received by or allocated to each of the following under the plan being acted upon, if such benefits or amounts are determinable:

NEW PLAN BENEFITS

| | Plan Name | |
Name and Position	Dollar Value ($)	Number of Units
CEO		
A		
B		
C		
D		
Executive Group		
Non-Executive Director Group		
Non-Executive Officer Employee Group		

(ii) The table required by paragraph (a)(2)(i) of this Item shall provide information as to the following persons:

(A) Each person (stating name and position) specified in paragraph (a)(3) of Item 402 of Regulation S–K;

(B) All current executive officers as a group;

(C) All current directors who are not executive officers as a group; and

(D) All employees, including all current officers who are not executive officers, as a group. . . .

(b)(1) *Additional Information Regarding Specified Plans Subject to Security Holder Action.* With respect to any pension or retirement plan submitted for security holder action, state:

(i) The approximate total amount necessary to fund the plan with respect to past services, the period over which such amount is to be paid and the estimated annual payments necessary to pay the total amount over such period; and

(ii) The estimated annual payment to be made with respect to current services. In the case of a pension or retirement plan, information called for by paragraph (a)(2) of this Item may be furnished in the format specified by paragraph (h)(2) of Item 402 of Regulation S–K.

(2)(i) With respect to any specific grant of or any plan containing options, warrants or rights submitted for security holder action, state:

(A) The title and amount of securities underlying such options, warrants or rights;

(B) The prices, expiration dates and other material conditions upon which the options, warrants or rights may be exercised;

(C) The consideration received or to be received by the registrant or subsidiary for the granting or extension of the options, warrants or rights;

(D) The market value of the securities underlying the option, warrants, or rights as of the latest practicable date; and

(E) In the case of options, the federal income tax consequences of the issuance and exercise of such options to the recipient and the registrant; and

(ii) State separately the amount of such options received or to be received by the following persons if such benefits or amounts are determinable:

(A) Each person (stating name and position) specified in paragraph (a)(3) of Item 402 of Regulation S–K;

(B) All current executive officers as a group;

(C) All current directors who are not executive officers as a group;

(D) Each nominee for election as a director;

(E) Each associate of any of such directors, executive officers or nominees;

(F) Each other person who received or is to receive 5 percent of such options, warrants or rights; and

(G) All employees, including all current officers who are not executive officers, as a group. . . .

(c) *Information regarding plans and other arrangements not subject to security holder action.* Furnish the information required by Item 201(d) of Regulation S–K. . . .

Item 18.   Matters not required to be submitted. If action is to be taken with respect to any matter which is not required to be submitted to a vote of security holders, state the nature of such matter, the reasons for submitting it to a vote of security holders and what action is intended to be taken by the registrant in the event of a negative vote on the matter by the security holders. . . .

Item 20.   Other proposed action. . . . Registrants required to provide a separate shareholder vote pursuant to section 111(e)(1) of the Emergency Economic Stabilization Act of 2008 and Rule 14a–20 shall disclose that they are providing such a vote as required pursuant to the Emergency Economic Stabilization Act of 2008, and briefly explain the general effect of the vote, such as whether the vote is non-binding.

Item 21.   Voting Procedures. As to each matter which is to be submitted to a vote of security holders, furnish the following information:

(a) State the vote required for approval or election, other than for the approval of auditors.

(b) Disclose the method by which votes will be counted, including the treatment and effect of abstentions and broker non-votes under applicable state law as well as registrant charter and by-law provisions. . . .

Item 24.   Shareholder Approval of Executive Compensation. Registrants required to provide any of the separate shareholder votes pursuant to Rule 14a–21 of this chapter shall disclose that they are providing each such vote as required pursuant to section 14A of the Securities Exchange Act, briefly explain the general effect of each vote, such as whether each such vote is non-binding, and, when applicable, disclose the current frequency of shareholder advisory votes on executive compensation required by Rule 14a–21(a) and when the next such shareholder advisory vote will occur.

[FORM OF] NOTICE OF EXEMPT SOLICITATION— INFORMATION TO BE INCLUDED IN STATEMENTS SUBMITTED BY OR ON BEHALF OF A PERSON PURSUANT TO RULE 6(g)

Notice of Exempt Solicitation

1.   Name of the Registrant:

2.   Name of person relying on exemption:

3.   Address of person relying on exemption:

4.   Written materials. Attach written material required to be submitted pursuant to Rule 14a–6(g)(1).

Rule 14b–1. Obligation of Registered Brokers and Dealers in Connection with the Prompt Forwarding of Certain Communications to Beneficial Owners

(a) *Definitions.* Unless the context otherwise requires, all terms used in this section shall have the same meanings as in the Act and, with respect to proxy soliciting material, as in Rule 14a–1 thereunder and, with respect to information statements, as in Rule 14c–1 thereunder. In addition, as used in this section, the term "registrant" means:

(1) The issuer of a class of securities registered pursuant to Section 12 of the Act. . . .

(2) An investment company registered under the Investment Company Act of 1940.

(b) *Dissemination and beneficial owner information requirements.* A broker or dealer registered under Section 15 of the Act shall comply with the following requirements for disseminating certain communications to beneficial owners and providing beneficial owner information to registrants.

(1) The broker or dealer shall respond, by first class mail or other equally prompt means, directly to the registrant no later than seven business days after the date it receives an inquiry . . . by indicating, by means of a search card or otherwise:

(i) The approximate number of customers of the broker or dealer who are beneficial owners of the registrant's securities that are held of record by the broker, dealer, or its nominee;

(ii) The number of customers of the broker or dealer who are beneficial owners of the registrant's securities who have objected to disclosure of their names, addresses, and securities positions if the registrant has indicated . . . that it will distribute the annual report to security holders to beneficial owners of its securities whose names, addresses and securities positions are disclosed pursuant to paragraph (b)(3) of this section; . . .

(2) The broker or dealer shall, upon receipt of the proxy, other proxy soliciting material, information statement, and/or annual report to security holders from the registrant or other soliciting person, forward such materials to its customers who are beneficial owners of the registrant's securities no later than five business days after receipt of the proxy material, information statement or annual report to security holders.

(3) The broker or dealer shall, through its agent or directly:

(i) Provide the registrant, upon the registrant's request, with the names, addresses, and securities positions, compiled as of a date specified in the registrant's request which is no earlier than five business days after the date the registrant's request is received, of its customers who are beneficial owners of the registrant's securities and who have not objected to disclosure of such information . . . ; and

(ii) Transmit the data specified in paragraph (b)(3)(i) of this section to the registrant no later than five business days after the record date or other date specified by the registrant. . . .

(c) *Exceptions to dissemination and beneficial owner information requirements.* . . .

(2) A broker or dealer need not satisfy:

(i) Its obligations under paragraphs (b)(2), (b)(3) . . . of this section if the registrant or other soliciting person, as applicable, does not provide assurance of reimbursement of the broker's or dealer's reasonable expenses, both direct and indirect, incurred in connection with performing the obligations imposed by paragraphs (b)(2), (b)(3) and (d) of this section. . . .

Rule 14b–2. Obligation of Banks, Associations and Other Entities That Exercise Fiduciary Powers in Connection with the Prompt Forwarding of Certain Communications to Beneficial Owners

(a) *Definitions.* Unless the context otherwise requires, all terms used in this section shall have the same meanings as in the Act and, with respect to proxy soliciting material, as in Rule 14a–1 thereunder and, with respect to information statements, as in Rule 14c–1 thereunder. In addition, as used in this section, the following terms shall apply:

(1) The term "bank" means a bank, association, or other entity that exercises fiduciary powers.

(2) The term "beneficial owner" includes any person who has or shares, pursuant to an instrument, agreement, or otherwise, the power to vote, or to direct the voting of a security. . . .

(3) The term "registrant" means:

(i) The issuer of a class of securities registered pursuant to Section 12 of the Act.

(ii) . . . .

(b) *Dissemination and beneficial owner information requirements.* A bank shall comply with the following requirements for disseminating certain communications to beneficial owners and providing beneficial owner information to registrants.

(1) The bank shall:

(i) Respond, by first class mail or other equally prompt means, directly to the registrant, no later than one business day after the date it receives an inquiry . . . by indicating the name and address of each of its respondent banks that holds the registrant's securities on behalf of beneficial owners, if any; and

(ii) Respond, by first class mail or other equally prompt means, directly to the registrant no later than seven business days after the date it receives an inquiry . . . by indicating, by means of a search card or otherwise:

(A) The approximate number of customers of the bank who are beneficial owners of the registrant's securities that are held of record by the bank or its nominee;

(B) If the registrant has indicated . . . that it will distribute the annual report to security holders to beneficial owners of its securities, whose names, addresses, and securities positions are disclosed pursuant to paragraphs (b)(4)(ii) and (iii) of this section:

(1) With respect to customer accounts opened on or before December 28, 1986, the number of beneficial owners of the registrant's securities who have affirmatively consented to disclosure of their names, addresses, and securities positions; and

(2) With respect to customer accounts opened after December 28, 1986, the number of beneficial owners of the registrant's securities who have not objected to disclosure of their names, addresses, and securities positions; and

(C) The identity of its designated agent, if any, acting on its behalf in fulfilling its obligations under paragraphs (b)(4)(ii) and (iii) of this section; . . .

(2) Where proxies are solicited, the bank shall, within five business days after the record date:

(i) Execute an omnibus proxy, including a power of substitution, in favor of its respondent banks and forward such proxy to the registrant; and

(ii) Furnish a notice to each respondent bank in whose favor an omnibus proxy has been executed that it has executed such a proxy, including a power of substitution, in its favor pursuant to paragraph (b)(2)(i) of this section.

(3) Upon receipt of the proxy, other proxy soliciting material, information statement, and/or annual report to security holders from the registrant or other soliciting person, the bank shall forward such materials to each beneficial owner on whose behalf it holds securities, no later than five business days after the date it receives such material and, where a proxy is solicited, the bank shall forward, with the other proxy soliciting material and/or the annual report to security holders, either:

(i) A properly executed proxy:

(A) indicating the number of securities held for such beneficial owner;

(B) bearing the beneficial owner's account number or other form of identification, together with instructions as to the procedures to vote the securities;

(C) briefly stating which other proxies, if any, are required to permit securities to be voted under the terms of the instrument creating that voting power or applicable state law; and

(D) being accompanied by an envelope addressed to the registrant or its agent, if not provided by the registrant; or

(ii) A request for voting instructions (for which registrant's form of proxy may be used and which shall be voted by the record holder bank or respondent bank in accordance with the instructions received), together with an envelope addressed to the record holder bank or respondent bank.

(4) The bank shall:

(i) Respond, by first class mail or other equally prompt means, directly to the registrant no later than one business day after the date it receives an inquiry made in accordance with Rule 14a–13(b)(1) or Rule 14c–7(b)(1) by indicating the name and address of each of its respondent banks that holds the registrant's securities on behalf of beneficial owners, if any;

(ii) Through its agent or directly, provide the registrant, upon the registrant's request, and within the time specified in paragraph (b)(4)(iii) of this section, with the names, addresses, and securities position, compiled as of a date specified in the registrant's request which is no earlier than five business days after the date the registrant's request is received, of:

(A) With respect to customer accounts opened on or before December 28, 1986, beneficial owners of the registrant's securities on whose behalf it holds securities who have consented affirmatively to disclosure of such information, subject to paragraph (b)(5) of this section; and

(B) With respect to customer accounts opened after December 28, 1986, beneficial owners of the registrant's securities on whose behalf it holds securities who have not objected to disclosure of such information; . . .

(iii) Through its agent or directly, transmit the data specified in paragraph (b)(4)(ii) of this section to the registrant no later than five business days after the date specified by the registrant. . . .

(5) For customer accounts opened on or before December 28, 1986, unless the bank has made a good faith effort to obtain affirmative consent to disclosure of beneficial owner information pursuant to paragraph (b)(4)(ii) of this section, the bank shall provide such information as to beneficial owners who do not object to disclosure of such information. A good faith effort to obtain affirmative consent to disclosure of beneficial owner information shall include, but shall not be limited to, making an inquiry:

(i) Phrased in neutral language, explaining the purpose of the disclosure and the limitations on the registrant's use thereof:

(ii) Either in at least one mailing separate from other account mailings or in repeated mailings; and

(iii) In a mailing that includes a return card, postage paid enclosure.

(c) *Exceptions to dissemination and beneficial owner information requirements....*

(2) The bank need not satisfy:

(i) Its obligations under paragraphs (b)(2), (b)(3), (b)(4) ... of this section if the registrant or other soliciting person, as applicable, does not provide assurance of reimbursement of its reasonable expenses, both direct and indirect, incurred in connection with performing the obligations imposed by paragraphs (b)(2), (b)(3), (b)(4) of this section....

REGULATION 14C: DISTRIBUTION OF INFORMATION PURSUANT TO SECTION 14(c) ...

Rule 14c-2. Distribution of Information Statement

(a)(1) In connection with every annual or other meeting of the holders of the class of securities registered pursuant to section 12 of the Act ... including the taking of corporate action by the written authorization or consent of security holders, the registrant shall transmit to every security holder of the class that is entitled to vote or give an authorization or consent in regard to any matter to be acted upon and from whom proxy authorization or consent is not solicited on behalf of the registrant pursuant to section 14(a) of the Act:

(i) A written information statement containing the information specified in Schedule 14C;

(ii) A publicly-filed information statement, in the form and manner described in Rule 14c-3(d), containing the information specified in Schedule 14C....

(d) A registrant shall transmit an information statement to security holders pursuant to paragraph (a) of this section by satisfying the requirements set forth in Rule 14a-16; provided, however, that the registrant shall revise the information required in the Notice of Internet Availability of Proxy Materials, including changing the title of that notice, to reflect the fact that the registrant is not soliciting proxies for the meeting.

Rule 14c-3. Annual Report to Be Furnished Security Holders

(a) If the information statement relates to an annual (or special meeting in lieu of the annual) meeting, or written consent in lieu of such meeting, of security holders at which directors are to be elected, it shall be accompanied or preceded by an annual report to such security holders....

(1) The annual report to security holders shall contain the information specified in paragraphs (b)(1) through (b)(11) of Rule 14a-3....

(d) A registrant shall furnish an annual report to security holders pursuant to paragraph (a) of this section by satisfying the requirements set forth in Rule 14a-16.

SCHEDULE 14C. INFORMATION REQUIRED IN INFORMATION STATEMENT ...

Note: Where any item, other than Item 4, calls for information with respect to any matter to be acted upon at the meeting or, if no meeting is being held, by written authorization or consent, such item need be answered only with respect to proposals to be made by the registrant....

Item 1.   Information required by Items of Schedule 14A..... Furnish the information called for by all of the items of Schedule 14A of Regulation 14A (other than Items 1(c), 2, 4 and 5 thereof) which would be applicable to any matter to be acted upon at the meeting if proxies were to be solicited in connection with the meeting....

Item 2.   Statement that proxies are not solicited. The following statement shall be set forth on the first page of the information statement in bold-face type:

WE ARE NOT ASKING YOU FOR A PROXY AND YOU ARE REQUESTED NOT TO SEND US A PROXY

Item 3.   Interest of certain persons in or opposition to matters to be acted upon. (a) Describe briefly any substantial interest, direct or indirect, by security holdings or otherwise, of each of the following persons in any matter to be acted upon, other than elections to office:

(1) Each person who has been a director or officer of the registrant at any time since the beginning of the last fiscal year;

(2) Each nominee for election as a director of the registrant;

(3) Each associate of any of the foregoing persons.

(b) Give the name of any director of the registrant who has informed the registrant in writing that he intends to oppose any action to be taken by the registrant at the meeting and indicate the action which he intends to oppose.

(c) Furnish the information required by Item 402(t) of Regulation S–K.

Item 4.   Proposals by security holders. If any security holder entitled to vote at the meeting or by written authorization or consent has submitted to the registrant a reasonable time before the information statement is to be transmitted to security holders a proposal, other than elections to office, which is accompanied by notice of his intention to present the proposal for action at the meeting the registrant shall, if a meeting is held, make a statement to that effect, identify the proposal and indicate the disposition proposed to be made of the proposal by the registrant at the meeting. . . .

REGULATION 14D

Rule 14d–1. Scope of and Definitions Applicable to Regulations 14D and 14E

(a) *Scope.* Regulation 14D shall apply to any tender offer that is subject to section 14(d)(1) of the Act, including, but not limited to, any tender offer for securities of a class described in that section which is made by an affiliate of the issuer of such class. Regulation 14E (Rules 14e–1 and 14e–2) shall apply to any tender offer for securities (other than exempted securities) unless otherwise noted therein. . . .

(2) *Definitions.* Unless the context otherwise requires, all terms used in Regulation 14D and Regulation 14E have the same meaning as in the Act and in Rule 12b–2 . . . promulgated thereunder. In addition, for purposes of sections 14(d) and 14(e) of the Act and Regulations 14D and 14E, the following definitions apply:

(1) The term *bidder* means any person who makes a tender offer or on whose behalf a tender offer is made: *Provided, however,* That the term does not include an issuer which makes a tender offer for securities of any class of which it is the issuer;

(2) The term *subject company* means any issuer of securities which are sought by a bidder pursuant to a tender offer;

(3) The term *security holders* means holders of record and beneficial owners of securities which are the subject of a tender offer; . . .

(5) The term *tender offer material* means:

(i) The bidder's formal offer, including all the material terms and conditions of the tender offer and all amendments thereto;

(ii) The related transmittal letter (whereby securities of the subject company which are sought in the tender offer may be transmitted to the bidder or its depositary) and all amendments thereto; and

(iii) Press releases, advertisements, letters and other documents published by the bidder or sent or given by the bidder to security holders which, directly or indirectly, solicit, invite or request tenders of the securities being sought in the tender offer;

(6) The term *business day* means any day, other than Saturday, Sunday or a federal holiday. . . .

Rule 14d-2. Commencement of a Tender Offer

(a) *Date of commencement.* A bidder will have commenced its tender offer for purposes of section 14(d) of the Act and the rules under that section at 12:01 a.m. on the date when the bidder has first published, sent or given the means to tender to security holders. For purposes of this section, the means to tender includes the transmittal form or a statement regarding how the transmittal form may be obtained.

(b) *Pre-commencement communications.* A communication by the bidder will not be deemed to constitute commencement of a tender offer if:

(1) It does not include the means for security holders to tender their shares into the offer; and

(2) All written communications relating to the tender offer, from and including the first public announcement, are filed under cover of Schedule TO with the Commission no later than the date of the communication. The bidder also must deliver to the subject company and any other bidder for the same class of securities the first communication relating to the transaction that is filed, or required to be filed, with the Commission.

Instructions to paragraph (b)(2) . . .

5.   "Public announcement" is any oral or written communication by the bidder, or any person authorized to act on the bidder's behalf, that is reasonably designed to, or has the effect of, informing the public or security holders in general about the tender offer.

(c) *Filing and other obligations triggered by commencement.* As soon as practicable on the date of commencement, a bidder must comply with the filing requirements of Rule 14d-3(a), the dissemination requirements of Rule 14d-4(a) or (b), and the disclosure requirements of Rule 14d-6(a).

Rule 14d-3. Filing and Transmission of Tender Offer Statement

(a) *Filing and transmittal.* No bidder shall make a tender offer if, after consummation thereof, such bidder would be the beneficial owner of more than 5 percent of the class of the subject company's securities for which the tender offer is made, unless as soon as practicable on the date of the commencement of the tender offer such bidder:

(1) Files with the Commission a Tender Offer Statement on Schedule TO . . . , including all exhibits thereto;

(2) Delivers a copy of such Schedule TO, including all exhibits thereto:

(i) To the subject company at its principal executive office; and

(ii) To any other bidder, which has filed a Schedule TO with the Commission relating to a tender offer which has not yet terminated for the same class of securities of the subject company, at such bidder's principal executive office or at the address of the person authorized to receive notices and communications (which is disclosed on the cover sheet of such other bidder's Schedule TO);

(3) Gives telephonic notice of the information required by Rule 14d-6(d)(2)(i) and (ii) and mails by means of first class mail a copy of such Schedule TO, including all exhibits thereto:

(i) To each national securities exchange where such class of the subject company's securities is registered and listed for trading . . . which telephonic notice shall be made when practicable prior to the opening of each such exchange; and

(ii) To the National Association of Securities Dealers, Inc. ("NASD") if such class of the subject company's securities is authorized for quotation in the NASDAQ interdealer quotation system. . . .

Rule 14d-4. Dissemination of Tender Offers to Security Holders

As soon as practicable on the date of commencement of a tender offer, the bidder must publish, send or give the disclosure required by Rule 14d-6 to security holders of the class of securities that is the subject of the offer, by complying with all of the requirements of any of the following:

(a) *Cash tender offers and exempt securities offers.* For tender offers in which the consideration consists solely of cash and/or securities exempt from registration under section 3 of the Securities Act of 1933:

(1) *Long-form publication.* The bidder makes adequate publication in a newspaper or newspapers of long-form publication of the tender offer.

(2) *Summary publication.* (i) If the tender offer is not subject to Rule 13e–3 . . . , the bidder makes adequate publication in a newspaper or newspapers of a summary advertisement of the tender offer; and

(ii) Mails by first class mail or otherwise furnishes with reasonable promptness the bidder's tender offer materials to any security holder who requests such tender offer materials pursuant to the summary advertisement or otherwise. . . .

(b) *Registered securities offers.* For tender offers in which the consideration consists solely or partially of securities registered under the Securities Act of 1933, a registration statement containing all of the required information, including pricing information, has been filed and a preliminary prospectus or a prospectus that meets the requirements of section 10(a) of the Securities Act, including a letter of transmittal, is delivered to security holders. However, for going-private transactions (as defined by Rule 13e–3) and roll-up transactions (as described by Item 901 of Regulation S–K), a registration statement registering the securities to be offered must have become effective and only a prospectus that meets the requirements of section 10(a) of the Securities Act may be delivered to security holders on the date of commencement.

(c) *Adequate publication.* Depending on the facts and circumstances involved, adequate publication of a tender offer pursuant to this section may require publication in a newspaper with a national circulation or may only require publication in a newspaper with metropolitan or regional circulation or may require publication in a combination thereof: *Provided, however,* That publication in all editions of a daily newspaper with a national circulation shall be deemed to constitute adequate publication. . . .

Rule 14d–6. Disclosure of Tender Offer Information to Security Holders

(a) *Information required on date of commencement.*—(1) Long-form publication. If a tender offer is published, sent or given to security holders on the date of commencement by means of long-form publication under Rule 14d–4(a)(1), the long-form publication must include the information required by paragraph (d)(1) of this section.

(2) *Summary publication.* If a tender offer is published, sent or given to security holders on the date of commencement by means of summary publication under Rule 14d–4(a)(2):

(i) The summary advertisement must contain at least the information required by paragraph (d)(2) of this section; and

(ii) The tender offer materials furnished by the bidder upon request of any security holder must include the information required by paragraph (d)(1) of this section.

(3) *Use of stockholder lists and security position listings.* If a tender offer is published, sent or given to security holders on the date of commencement by the use of stockholder lists and security position listings under Rule 14d–4(a)(3):

(i) The summary advertisement must contain at least the information required by paragraph (d)(2) of this section; and

(ii) The tender offer materials transmitted to security holders pursuant to such lists and security position listings and furnished by the bidder upon the request of any security holder must include the information required by paragraph (d)(1) of this section.

(4) *Other tender offers.* If a tender offer is published or sent or given to security holders other than pursuant to Rule 14d–4(a), the tender offer materials that are published or sent or given to security holders on the date of commencement of such offer must include the information required by paragraph (d)(1) of this section.

(b) *Information required in other tender offer materials published after commencement.* Except for tender offer materials described in paragraphs (a)(2)(ii) and (a)(3)(ii) of this section, additional tender offer materials published, sent or given to security holders after commencement must include:

(1) The identities of the bidder and subject company;

(2) The amount and class of securities being sought;

(3) The type and amount of consideration being offered; and

(4) The scheduled expiration date of the tender offer, whether the tender offer may be extended and, if so, the procedures for extension of the tender offer.

(c) *Material changes.* A material change in the information published or sent or given to security holders must be promptly disclosed to security holders in additional tender offer materials.

(d) *Information to be included.*—(1) *Tender offer materials other than summary publication.* The following information is required by paragraphs (a)(1), (a)(2)(ii), (a)(3)(ii) and (a)(4) of this section:

(i) The information required by Item 1 of Schedule TO (Summary Term Sheet); and

(ii) The information required by the remaining items of Schedule TO for third-party tender offers, except for Item 12 (exhibits) of Schedule TO, or a fair and adequate summary of the information.

(2) *Summary Publication.* The following information is required in a summary advertisement under paragraphs (a)(2)(i) and (a)(3)(i) of this section:

(i) The identity of the bidder and the subject company;

(ii) The information required by Item 1004(a)(1) of Regulation M–A;

(iii) If the tender offer is for less than all of the outstanding securities of a class of equity securities, a statement as to whether the purpose or one of the purposes of the tender offer is to acquire or influence control of the business of the subject company;

(iv) A statement that the information required by paragraph (d)(1) of this section is incorporated by reference into the summary advertisement;

(v) Appropriate instructions as to how security holders may obtain promptly, at the bidder's expense, the bidder's tender offer materials; and

(vi) In a tender offer published or sent or given to security holders by use of stockholder lists and security position listings under Rule 14d–4(a)(3), a statement that a request is being made for such lists and listings. The summary publication also must state that tender offer materials will be mailed to record holders and will be furnished to brokers, banks and similar persons whose name appears or whose nominee appears on the list of security holders or, if applicable, who are listed as participants in a clearing agency's security position listing for subsequent transmittal to beneficial owners of such securities. If the list furnished to the bidder also included beneficial owners pursuant to Rule 14d–5(c)(1) and tender offer materials will be mailed directly to beneficial holders, include a statement to that effect.

(3) *No transmittal letter.* Neither the initial summary advertisement nor any subsequent summary advertisement may include a transmittal letter (the letter furnished to security holders for transmission of securities sought in the tender offer) or any amendment to the transmittal letter.

Rule 14d–7. Additional Withdrawal Rights

(a)(1) *Rights.* In addition to the provisions of section 14(d)(5) of the Act, any person who has deposited securities pursuant to a tender offer has the right to withdraw any such securities during the period such offer, request or invitation remains open.

(2) *Exemption during subsequent offering period.* Notwithstanding the provisions of section 14(d)(5) of the Act and paragraph (a) of this section, the bidder need not offer withdrawal rights during a subsequent offering period.

(b) *Notice of withdrawal.* Notice of withdrawal pursuant to this section shall be deemed to be timely upon the receipt by the bidder's depositary of a written notice of withdrawal specifying the name(s) of the tendering stockholder(s), the number or amount of the securities to be withdrawn and the name(s) in which the certificate(s) is (are) registered, if different from that of the tendering security holder(s). A bidder may impose other reasonable requirements, including certificate numbers and a signed request for withdrawal accompanied by a signature guarantee, as conditions precedent to the physical release of withdrawn securities.

Rule 14d–8. Exemption From Statutory Pro Rata Requirements

Notwithstanding the pro rata provisions of section 14(d)(6) of the Act, if any person makes a tender offer or request or invitation for tenders, for less than all of the outstanding equity securities of a class, and if a greater number of securities are deposited pursuant thereto than such person is bound or willing to take up and pay for, the securities taken up and paid for shall be taken up and paid for as nearly as may be pro rata, disregarding fractions, according to the number of securities deposited by each depositor during the period such offer, request or invitation remains open.

Rule 14d–9. Recommendation or Solicitation by the Subject Company and Others

(a) *Pre-commencement communications.* A communication by a person described in paragraph (e) of this section with respect to a tender offer will not be deemed to constitute a recommendation or solicitation under this section if:

(1) The tender offer has not commenced under Rule 14d–2; and

(2) The communication is filed under cover of Schedule 14D-9 with the Commission no later than the date of the communication.

(b) *Post-commencement communications.* After commencement by a bidder under Rule 14d–2, no solicitation or recommendation to security holders may be made by any person described in paragraph (e) of this section with respect to a tender offer for such securities unless as soon as practicable on the date such solicitation or recommendation is first published or sent or given to security holders such person complies with the following:

(1) Such person shall file with the Commission a Tender Offer Solicitation/Recommendation Statement on Schedule 14D-9 . . . and

(2) If such person is either the subject company or an affiliate of the subject company,

(i) Such person shall hand deliver a copy of the Schedule 14D-9 to the bidder at its principal office . . . ; and

(ii) Such person shall give telephonic notice (which notice to the extent possible shall be given prior to the opening of the market) of the information required by Items 1003(d) and 1012(a) of Regulation M–A and shall mail a copy of the Schedule to each national securities exchange where the class of securities is registered and listed for trading and, if the class is authorized for quotation in the NASDAQ interdealer quotation system, to the National Association of Securities Dealers, Inc. ("NASD").

(3) If such person is neither the subject company nor an affiliate of the subject company,

(i) Such person shall mail a copy of the schedule to the bidder at its principal office . . . ; and

(ii) Such person shall mail a copy of the Schedule to the subject company at its principal office. . . .

(d) *Information required in solicitation or recommendation.* Any solicitation or recommendation to holders of a class of securities referred to in section 14(d)(1) of the Act with respect to a tender offer for such securities shall include the name of the person making such solicitation or recommendation and the information required by Items 1 through 8 of Schedule 14D-9 . . . or a fair and adequate summary thereof: *Provided, however,* That such solicitation or recommendation may omit any of such information previously furnished to security holders of such class of securities by such person with respect to such tender offer.

(e) *Applicability.* (1) Except as is provided in paragraphs (e)(2) and (f) of this section, this section shall only apply to the following persons:

(i) The subject company, any director, officer, employee, affiliate or subsidiary of the subject company;

(ii) Any record holder or beneficial owner of any security issued by the subject company, by the bidder, or by any affiliate of either the subject company or the bidder; and

(iii) Any person who makes a solicitation or recommendation to security holders on behalf of any of the foregoing or on behalf of the bidder other than by means of a solicitation or recommendation to security holders which has been filed with the Commission pursuant to this section or Rule 14d–3. . . .

(2) Notwithstanding paragraph (e)(1) of this section, this section shall not apply to the following persons:

(i) A bidder who has filed a Schedule TO . . . pursuant to Rule 14d–3 . . . ;

(ii) Attorneys, banks, brokers, fiduciaries or investment advisers who are not participating in a tender offer in more than a ministerial capacity and who furnish information and/or advice regarding such tender offer to their customers or clients on the unsolicited request of such customers or clients or solely pursuant to a contract or a relationship providing for advice to the customer or client to whom the information and/or advice is given. . . .

(f) *Stop-look-and-listen communication.* This section shall not apply to the subject company with respect to a communication by the subject company to its security holders which only:

(1) Identifies the tender offer by the bidder;

(2) States that such tender offer is under consideration by the subject company's board of directors and/or management;

(3) States that on or before a specified date (which shall be no later than 10 business days from the date of commencement of such tender offer) the subject company will advise such security holders of (i) whether the subject company recommends acceptance or rejection of such tender offer; expresses no opinion and remains neutral toward such tender offer; or is unable to take a position with respect to such tender offer and (ii) the reason(s) for the position taken by the subject company with respect to the tender offer (including the inability to take a position); and

(4) Requests such security holders to defer making a determination whether to accept or reject such tender offer until they have been advised of the subject company's position with respect thereto pursuant to paragraph (f)(3) of this section.

(g) *Statement of management's position.* A statement by the subject company of its position with respect to a tender offer which is required to be published or sent or given to security holders pursuant to Rule 14e–2 shall be deemed to constitute a solicitation or recommendation within the meaning of this section and section 14(d)(4) of the Act.

Rule 14d–10.   **Equal Treatment of Security Holders**

(a) No bidder shall make a tender offer unless:

(1) The tender offer is open to all security holders of the class of securities subject to the tender offer; and

(2) The consideration paid to any security holder for securities tendered in the tender offer is the highest consideration paid to any other security holder for securities tendered in the tender offer. . . .

(d)(1) Paragraph (a)(2) of this section shall not prohibit the negotiation, execution or amendment of an employment compensation, severance or other employee benefit arrangement, or payments made or to be made or benefits granted or to be granted according to such an arrangement, with respect to any security holder of the subject company, where the amount payable under the arrangement:

(i) Is being paid or granted as compensation for past services performed, future services to be performed, or future services to be refrained from performing, by the security holder (and matters incidental thereto); and

(ii) Is not calculated based on the number of securities tendered or to be tendered in the tender offer by the security holder.

(2) The provisions of paragraph (d)(1) of this section shall be satisfied and, therefore, pursuant to this non-exclusive safe harbor, the negotiation, execution or amendment of an arrangement and any payments made or to be made or benefits granted or to be granted according to that arrangement shall not be prohibited by paragraph (a)(2) of this section, if the arrangement is approved as an employment compensation, severance or other employee benefit arrangement solely by independent directors as follows:

(i) The compensation committee or a committee of the board of directors that performs functions similar to a compensation committee of the subject company approves the arrangement, regardless of whether the subject company is a party to the arrangement, or, if the bidder is a party to the arrangement, the compensation committee or a committee of the board of directors that performs functions similar to a compensation committee of the bidder approves the arrangement; or

(ii) If the subject company's or bidder's board of directors, as applicable, does not have a compensation committee or a committee of the board of directors that performs functions similar to a compensation committee or if none of the members of the subject company's or bidder's compensation committee or committee that performs functions similar to a compensation committee is independent, a special committee of the board of directors formed to consider and approve the arrangement approves the arrangement; or

(iii) If the subject company or bidder, as applicable, is a foreign private issuer, any or all members of the board of directors or any committee of the board of directors authorized to approve employment compensation, severance or other employee benefit arrangements under the laws or regulations of the home country approves the arrangement.

Instruction to paragraph (d)

The fact that the provisions of paragraph (d) of this section extend only to employment compensation, severance and other employee benefit arrangements and not to other arrangements, such as commercial arrangements, does not raise any inference that a payment under any such other arrangement constitutes consideration paid for securities in a tender offer.

Rule 14d–11. Subsequent Offering Period

A bidder may elect to provide a subsequent offering period of at least three business days during which tenders will be accepted if:

(a) The initial offering period of at least 20 business days has expired;

(b) The offer is for all outstanding securities of the class that is the subject of the tender offer, and if the bidder is offering security holders a choice of different forms of consideration, there is no ceiling on any form of consideration offered;

(c) The bidder immediately accepts and promptly pays for all securities tendered during the initial offering period;

(d) The bidder announces the results of the tender offer, including the approximate number and percentage of securities deposited to date, no later than 9:00 a.m. Eastern time on the next business day after the expiration date of the initial offering period and immediately begins the subsequent offering period;

(e) The bidder immediately accepts and promptly pays for all securities as they are tendered during the subsequent offering period; and

(f) The bidder offers the same form and amount of consideration to security holders in both the initial and the subsequent offering period.

SCHEDULE TO. TENDER OFFER STATEMENT UNDER SECTION 14(d)(1) OR 13(e)(1) . . .

Schedule TO

Tender Offer Statement under Section 14(d)(1) or 13(e)(1) of the Securities Exchange Act of 1934 . . .

_____

(Name of Subject Company (user))

_____

(Names of Filing Persons (identifying status as offeror, issuer or other person))

_____

(Title of Class of Securities)

_____

(CUSIP Number of Class of Securities)

_____

(Name, address, and telephone numbers of person authorized to receive notices and communications on behalf of filing persons) . . .

General Instructions. . . .

    C. If the statement is filed by a general or limited partnership, syndicate or other group, the information called for by Items 3, 5, 6, 10 and 11 must be given with respect to: (i) each partner of the general partnership; (ii) each partner who is, or functions as, a general partner of the limited partnership; (iii) each member of the syndicate or group; and (iv) each person controlling the partner or member. If the statement is filed by a corporation . . . the information called for by the items specified above must be given with respect to: (a) each executive officer and director of the corporation; (b) each person controlling the corporation; and (c) each executive officer and director of any corporation or other person ultimately in control of the corporation. . . .

    Item 1. *Summary Term Sheet*

Furnish the information required by Item 1001 of Regulation M–A unless information is disclosed to security holders in a prospectus that meets the requirements of Rule 421(d) [under the Securities Act].

    Item 2. *Subject Company Information*

Furnish the information required by Item 1002 of Regulation M–A.

    Item 3. *Identity and Background of Filing Person*

Furnish the information required by Item 1003(a) through (c) of Regulation M–A for a third-party tender offer and the information required by Item 1003(a) of Regulation M–A.

    Item 4. *Terms of the Transaction*

Furnish the information required by Item 1004(a) of Regulation M–A for a third-party tender offer and the information required by Item 1004(a) through (b) of Regulation M–A for an issuer tender offer.

    Item 5. *Past Contacts, Transactions, Negotiations and Agreements*

Furnish the information required by Item 1005(a) and (b) of Regulation M–A for a third-party tender offer and the information required by Item 1005(e) of Regulation M–A for an issuer tender offer.

Item 6. *Purposes of the Transaction and Plans or Proposals*

Furnish the information required by Item 1006(a) and (c)(1) through (7) of Regulation M–A for a third-party tender offer and the information required by Item 1006(a) through (c) of Regulation M–A for an issuer tender offer.

Item 7. *Source and Amount of Funds or Other Consideration*

Furnish the information required by Item 1007(a), (b) and (d) of Regulation M–A.

Item 8. *Interest in Securities of the Subject Company*

Furnish the information required by Item 1008 of Regulation M–A.

Item 9. *Persons/Assets, Retained, Employed, Compensated or Used*

Furnish the information required by Item 1009(a) of Regulation M–A.

Item 10. *Financial Statements*

If material, furnish the information required by Item 1010(a) and (b) of Regulation M–A for the issuer in an issuer tender offer and for the offeror in a third-party tender offer.

Instructions to Item 10:

1. Financial statements must be provided when the offeror's financial condition is material to security holder's decision whether to sell, tender or hold the securities sought. The facts and circumstances of a tender offer, particularly the terms of the tender offer, may influence a determination as to whether financial statements are material, and thus required to be disclosed.

2. Financial statements are not considered material when: (a) The consideration offered consists solely of cash; (b) the offer is not subject to any financing condition; and either: (c) the offeror is a public reporting company under Section 13(a) or 15(d) of the Act that files reports electronically. . . . , or (d) the offer is for all outstanding securities of the subject class. Financial information may be required, however, in a two-tier transaction. . . .

Item 11. *Additional Information*

Furnish the information required by Item 1011(a) and (c) of Regulation M–A.

Item 12. *Exhibits*

File as an exhibit to the Schedule all documents specified by Item 1016 (a), (b), (d), (g) and (h) of Regulation M–A.

Item 13. *Information Required by Schedule 13E-3*

If the Schedule TO is combined with Schedule 13E-3, set forth the information required by Schedule 13E-3 that is not included or covered by the items in Schedule TO. . . .

SCHEDULE 14D-9. SOLICITATION/RECOMMENDATION STATEMENT UNDER SECTION 14(d)(4) OF THE SECURITIES EXCHANGE ACT OF 1934

_____

(Name of Subject Company)

_____

(Names of Persons Filing Statement)

_____

(Title of Class of Securities)

_____

(CUSIP Number of Class of Securities)

_____

(Name, address and telephone number of person authorized to receive notices and communications on behalf of persons filing statement). . . .

Item 1. Subject Company Information

Furnish the information required by Item 1002(a) and (b) of Regulation M–A.

Item 2. Identity and Background of Filing Person

Furnish the information required by Item 1003(a) and (d) of Regulation M–A.

Item 3. Past Contacts, Transactions, Negotiations and Agreements

Furnish the information required by Item 1005(d) of Regulation M–A.

Item 4. The Solicitation or Recommendation

Furnish the information required by Item 1012(a) through (c) of Regulation M–A.

Item 5. Person/Assets, Retained, Employed, Compensated or Used

Furnish the information required by Item 1009(a) of Regulation M–A.

Item 6. Interest in Securities of the Subject Company

Furnish the information required by Item 1008(b) of Regulation M–A.

Item 7. Purposes of the Transaction and Plans or Proposals

Furnish the information required by Item 1006(d) of Regulation M–A.

Item 8. Additional Information

Furnish the information required by Item 1011(b) and (c) of Regulation M–A.

Item 9. Exhibits

File as an exhibit to the Schedule all documents specified by Item 1016(a), (e) and (g) of Regulation M–A. . . .

_____

REGULATION 14E

Note: For the scope of and definitions applicable to Regulation 14E, refer to Rule 14d–1.

Rule 14e–1. Unlawful Tender Offer Practices

As a means reasonably designed to prevent fraudulent, deceptive or manipulative acts or practices within the meaning of section 14(e) of the Act, no person who makes a tender offer shall:

(a) Hold such tender offer open for less than twenty business days from the date such tender offer is first published or sent or given to security holders . . . ;

(b) Increase or decrease the percentage of the class of securities being sought or the consideration offered or the dealer's soliciting fee to be given in a tender offer unless such tender offer remains open for at least ten business days from the date that notice of such increase or decrease is first published or sent or given to security holders. . . .

(c) Fail to pay the consideration offered or return the securities deposited by or on behalf of security holders promptly after the termination or withdrawal of a tender offer. . . .

Rule 14e–2. Position of Subject Company With Respect to a Tender Offer

(a) *Position of subject company.* As a means reasonably designed to prevent fraudulent, deceptive or manipulative acts or practices within the meaning of section 14(e) of the Act, the subject company, no later than 10 business days from the date the tender offer is first published or sent or given, shall publish, send or give to security holders a statement disclosing that the subject company:

(1) Recommends acceptance or rejection of the bidder's tender offer;

(2) Expresses no opinion and is remaining neutral toward the bidder's tender offer; or

(3) Is unable to take a position with respect to the bidder's tender offer. Such statement shall also include the reason(s) for the position (including the inability to take a position) disclosed therein.

(b) *Material change.* If any material change occurs in the disclosure required by paragraph (a) of this section, the subject company shall promptly publish or send or give a statement disclosing such material change to security holders. . . .

Rule 14e–3. Transactions in Securities on the Basis of Material, Nonpublic Information in the Context of Tender Offers

(a) If any person has taken a substantial step or steps to commence, or has commenced, a tender offer (the "offering person"), it shall constitute a fraudulent, deceptive or manipulative act or practice within the meaning of section 14(e) of the Act for any other person who is in possession of material information relating to such tender offer which information he knows or has reason to know is nonpublic and which he knows or has reason to know has been acquired directly or indirectly from:

(1) The offering person,

(2) The issuer of the securities sought or to be sought by such tender offer, or

(3) Any officer, director, partner or employee or any other person acting on behalf of the offering person or such issuer,

to purchase or sell or cause to be purchased or sold any of such securities or any securities convertible into or exchangeable for any such securities or any option or right to obtain or to dispose of any of the foregoing securities, unless within a reasonable time prior to any purchase or sale such information and its source are publicly disclosed by press release or otherwise.

(b) A person other than a natural person shall not violate paragraph (a) of this section if such person shows that:

(1) The individual(s) making the investment decision on behalf of such person to purchase or sell any security described in paragraph (a) of this section or to cause any such security to be purchased or sold by or on behalf of others did not know the material, nonpublic information; and

(2) Such person had implemented one or a combination of policies and procedures, reasonable under the circumstances, taking into consideration the nature of the person's business, to ensure that individual(s) making investment decision(s) would not violate paragraph (a) of this section, which policies and procedures may include, but are not limited to, (i) those which restrict any purchase, sale and causing any purchase and sale of any such security or (ii) those which prevent such individual(s) from knowing such information.

(c) Notwithstanding anything in paragraph (a) of this section to the contrary, the following transactions shall not be violations of paragraph (a) of this section:

(1) Purchase(s) of any security described in paragraph (a) of this section by a broker or by another agent on behalf of an offering person; or

(2) Sale(s) by any person of any security described in paragraph (a) of this section to the offering person.

(d)(1) As a means reasonably designed to prevent fraudulent, deceptive or manipulative acts or practices within the meaning of section 14(e) of the Act, it shall be unlawful for any person described in paragraph (d)(2) of this section to communicate material, nonpublic information relating to a tender offer to any other person under circumstances in which it is reasonably foreseeable that such communication is likely to result in a violation of this section *except* that this paragraph shall not apply to a communication made in good faith.

(i) To the officers, directors, partners or employees of the offering person, to its advisors or to other persons, involved in the planning, financing, preparation or execution of such tender offer;

(ii) To the issuer whose securities are sought or to be sought by such tender offer, to its officers, directors, partners, employees or advisors or to other persons, involved in the planning, financing, preparation or execution of the activities of the issuer with respect to such tender offer; or

(iii) To any person pursuant to a requirement of any statute or rule or regulation promulgated thereunder.

(2) The persons referred to in paragraph (d)(1) of this section are:

(i) The offering person or its officers, directors, partners, employees or advisors;

(ii) The issuer of the securities sought or to be sought by such tender offer or its officers, directors, partners, employees or advisors;

(iii) Anyone acting on behalf of the persons in paragraph (d)(2)(i) of this section or the issuer or persons in paragraph (d)(2)(ii) of this section; and

(iv) Any person in possession of material information relating to a tender offer which information he knows or has reason to know is nonpublic and which he knows or has reason to know has been acquired directly or indirectly from any of the above.

Rule 14e–4. Prohibited Transactions in Connection With Partial Tender Offers

(a) *Definitions.* For purposes of this section:

(1) The amount of a person's "net long position" in a subject security shall equal the excess, if any, of such person's "long position" over such person's "short position." For the purposes of determining the net long position as of the end of the proration period and for tendering concurrently to two or more partial tender offers, securities that have been tendered in accordance with the Rule and not withdrawn are deemed to be part of the person's long position.

(i) Such person's "long position," is the amount of subject securities that such person:

(A) or his agent has title to or would have title to but for having lent such securities; or

(B) has purchased, or has entered into an unconditional contract, binding on both parties thereto, to purchase but has not yet received; or

(C) has exercised a standardized call option for; or

(D) has converted, exchanged, or exercised an equivalent security for; or

(E) is entitled to receive upon conversion, exchange, or exercise of an equivalent security.

(ii) Such person's "short position," is the amount of subject securities or subject securities underlying equivalent securities that such person:

(A) has sold, or has entered into an unconditional contract, binding on both parties thereto, to sell; or

(B) has borrowed; or

(C) has written a non-standardized call option, or granted any other right pursuant to which his shares may be tendered by another person; or

(D) is obligated to deliver upon exercise of a standardized call option sold on or after the date that a tender offer is first publicly announced or otherwise made known by the bidder to holders of the security to be acquired, if the exercise price of such option is lower than the highest tender offer price or stated amount of the consideration offered for the subject security. For the purpose of this paragraph, if one or more tender offers for the same security are ongoing on such date, the announcement date shall be that of the first announced offer.

(2) The term "equivalent security" means:

(i) Any security (including any option, warrant, or other right to purchase the subject security), issued by the person whose securities are the subject of the offer, that is immediately convertible into, or exchangeable or exercisable for, a subject security, or

(ii) Any other right or option (other than a standardized call option) that entitles the holder thereof to acquire a subject security, but only if the holder thereof reasonably believes that the maker or writer of the right or option has title to and possession of the subject security and upon exercise will promptly deliver the subject security.

(3) The term "subject security" means a security that is the subject of any tender offer or request or invitation for tenders.

(4) For purposes of this rule, a person shall be deemed to "tender" a security if he:

(i) Delivers a subject security pursuant to an offer,

(ii) Causes such delivery to be made,

(iii) Guarantees delivery of a subject security pursuant to a tender offer,

(iv) Causes a guarantee of such delivery to be given by another person, or

(v) Uses any other method by which acceptance of a tender offer may be made.

(5) The term "partial tender offer" means a tender offer or request or invitation for tenders for less than all of the outstanding securities subject to the offer in which tenders are accepted either by lot or on a *pro rata* basis for a specified period, or a tender offer for all of the outstanding shares that offers a choice of consideration in which tenders for different forms of consideration may be accepted either by lot or on a *pro rata* basis for a specified period.

(6) The term "standardized call option" means any call option that is traded on an exchange, or for which quotation information is disseminated in an electronic interdealer quotation system of a registered national securities association.

(b) It shall be unlawful for any person acting alone or in concert with others, directly or indirectly, to tender any subject security in a partial tender offer:

(1) For his own account unless at the time of tender, and at the end of the proration period or period during which securities are accepted by lot (including any extensions thereof), he has a net long position equal to or greater than the amount tendered in:

(i) the subject security and will deliver or cause to be delivered such security for the purpose of tender to the person making the offer within the period specified in the offer; or

(ii) an equivalent security and, upon the acceptance of his tender will acquire the subject security by conversion, exchange, or exercise of such equivalent security to the extent required by the terms of the offer, and will deliver or cause to be delivered the subject security so acquired for the purpose of tender to the person making the offer within the period specified in the offer; or

(2) For the account of another person unless the person making the tender:

(i) Possesses the subject security or an equivalent security, or

(ii) Has a reasonable belief that, upon information furnished by the person on whose behalf the tender is made, such person owns the subject security or an equivalent security and will promptly deliver the subject security or such equivalent security for the purpose of tender to the person making the tender.

(c) This rule shall not prohibit any transaction or transactions which the Commission, upon written request or upon its own motion, exempts, either unconditionally or on specified terms and conditions.

Rule 14e–5. Prohibiting Purchases Outside of a Tender Offer

(a) *Unlawful activity.* As a means reasonably designed to prevent fraudulent, deceptive or manipulative acts or practices in connection with a tender offer for equity securities, no covered person may directly or indirectly purchase or arrange to purchase any subject securities or any related securities except as part of the tender offer. This prohibition applies from the time of public announcement of the tender offer until the tender offer expires. . . .

(b) *Excepted activity.* The following transactions in subject securities or related securities are not prohibited by paragraph (a) of this section:

(1) *Exercises of securities.* Transactions by covered persons to convert, exchange, or exercise related securities into subject securities, if the covered person owned the related securities before public announcement;

(2) *Purchases for plans.* Purchases or arrangements to purchase by or for a plan that are made by an agent independent of the issuer;

(3) *Purchases during odd-lot offers.* . . .

(4) *Purchases as intermediary.* Purchases by or through a dealer-manager or its affiliates that are made in the ordinary course of business and made either:

(i) On an agency basis not for a covered person; or

(ii) As principal for its own account if the dealer-manager or its affiliate is not a market maker, and the purchase is made to offset a contemporaneous sale after having received an unsolicited order to buy from a customer who is not a covered person;

(5) *Basket transactions.* Purchases or arrangements to purchase a basket of securities containing a subject security or a related security if the following conditions are satisfied:

(i) The purchase or arrangement to purchase is made in the ordinary course of business and not to facilitate the tender offer;

(ii) The basket contains 20 or more securities; and

(iii) Covered securities and related securities do not comprise more than 5% the value of the basket;

(6) *Covering transactions.* Purchases or arrangements to purchase that are made to satisfy an obligation to deliver a subject security or a related security arising from a short sale or from the exercise of an option by a non-covered person if:

(i) The short sale or option transaction was made in the ordinary course of business and not to facilitate the offer;

(ii) In the case of a short sale, the short sale was entered into before public announcement of the tender offer; and

(iii) In the case of an exercise of an option, the covered person wrote the option before public announcement of the tender offer;

(7) *Purchases pursuant to contractual obligations.* Purchases or arrangements to purchase pursuant to a contract if the following conditions are satisfied:

(i) The contract was entered into before public announcement of the tender offer;

(ii) The contract is unconditional and binding on both parties; and

(iii) The existence of the contract and all material terms including quantity, price and parties are disclosed in the offering materials;

(8) *Purchases or arrangements to purchase by an affiliate of the dealer-manager.* Purchases or arrangements to purchase by an affiliate of a dealer-manager if the following conditions are satisfied:

(i) The dealer-manager maintains and enforces written policies and procedures reasonably designed to prevent the flow of information to or from the affiliate that might result in a violation of the federal securities laws and regulations;

(ii) The dealer-manager is registered as a broker or dealer under Section 15(a) of the Act;

(iii) The affiliate has no officers (or persons performing similar functions) or employees (other than clerical, ministerial, or support personnel) in common with the dealer-manager that direct, effect, or recommend transactions in securities; and

(iv) The purchases or arrangements to purchase are not made to facilitate the tender offer. . . .

(c) *Definitions.* For purposes of this section, the term:

(1) *Affiliate* has the same meaning as in Rule 12b–2; . . .

(3) *Covered person* means:

(i) The offeror and its affiliates;

(ii) The offeror's dealer-manager and its affiliates;

(iii) Any advisor to any of the persons specified in paragraph (c)(3)(i) and (ii) of this section, whose compensation is dependent on the completion of the offer; and

(iv) Any person acting, directly or indirectly, in concert with any of the persons specified in this paragraph (c)(3) in connection with any purchase or arrangement to purchase any subject securities or any related securities; . . .

(5) *Public announcement* is any oral or written communication by the offeror or any person authorized to act on the offeror's behalf that is reasonably designed to, or has the effect of, informing the public or security holders in general about the tender offer;

(6) *Related securities* means securities that are immediately convertible into, exchangeable for, or exercisable for subject securities;

(7) *Subject securities* has the same meaning as in [Regulation M–A, Item 1000]. . . .

(d) *Exemptive authority.* Upon written application or upon its own motion, the Commission may grant an exemption from the provisions of this section, either unconditionally or on specified terms or conditions, to any transaction or class of transactions or any security or class of security, or any person or class of persons.

Rule 14e–7. Unlawful Tender Offer Practices in Connection With Roll-Ups

In order to implement Section 14(h) of the Act:

(a)(1) It shall be unlawful for any person to receive compensation for soliciting tenders directly from security holders in connection with a roll-up transaction as provided in paragraph (a)(2) of this section, if the compensation is:

(i) Based on whether the solicited person participates in the tender offer; or

(ii) Contingent on the success of the tender offer.

(2) Paragraph (a)(1) of this section is applicable to a roll-up transaction as defined in Item 901(c) of Regulation S–K, structured as a tender offer, except for a transaction involving only:

(i) Finite-life entities that are not limited partnerships. . . .

(b)(1) It shall be unlawful for any finite-life entity that is the subject of a roll-up transaction as provided in paragraph (b)(2) of this section to fail to provide a security holder list or mail communications related to a tender offer that is in furtherance of the roll-up transaction, at the option of a requesting security holder, pursuant to the procedures set forth in Rule 14a–7.

(2) Paragraph (b)(1) of this section is applicable to a roll-up transaction as defined in Item 901(c) of Regulation S–K, structured as a tender offer, that involves:

(i) An entity with securities registered pursuant to Section 12 of the Act; or

(ii) A limited partnership. . . .

Rule 14e–8. Prohibited   Conduct   in   Connection   with   Pre-Commencement Communications

It is a fraudulent, deceptive or manipulative act or practice within the meaning of section 14(e) of the Act for any person to publicly announce that the person (or a party on whose behalf the person is acting) plans to make a tender offer that has not yet been commenced, if the person:

(a) Is making the announcement of a potential tender offer without the intention to commence the offer within a reasonable time and complete the offer;

(b) Intends, directly or indirectly, for the announcement to manipulate the market price of the stock of the bidder or subject company; or

(c) Does not have the reasonable belief that the person will have the means to purchase securities to complete the offer.

Rule 14f–1. Change in Majority of Directors

If, pursuant to any arrangement or understanding with the person or persons acquiring securities in a transaction subject to section 13(d) or 14(d) of the Act, any persons are to be elected or designated as directors of the issuer, otherwise than at a meeting of security holders, and the persons so elected or designated will constitute a majority of the directors of the issuer, then, not less than 10 days prior to the date any such person take office as a director, or such shorter period prior to that date as the Commission may authorize upon a showing of good cause therefor, the issuer shall file with the Commission and transmit to all holders of record of securities of the issuer who would be entitled to vote at a meeting for election of directors, information substantially equivalent to the information which would be required by Items 6(a), (d) and (e), 7 and 8 of Schedule 14A of Regulation 14A . . . to be transmitted if such person or persons were nominees for election as directors at a meeting of such security holders. Eight copies of such information shall be filed with the Commission.

REGULATION 14N: FILINGS REQUIRED BY CERTAIN NOMINATING SHAREHOLDERS

Rule 14n–1. Filing of Schedule 14N

(a) A shareholder or group of shareholders that submits a nominee or nominees in accordance with Rule 14a–11 or a procedure set forth under applicable state or foreign law, or a registrant's governing documents providing for the inclusion of shareholder director nominees in the registrant's proxy materials shall file with the Commission a statement containing the information required by Schedule 14N and simultaneously provide the notice on Schedule 14N to the registrant. . . .

Rule 14n–2. Filing of Amendments to Schedule 14N. . . .

Rule 14n–3. Dissemination. . . .

Schedule 14N—Information to be included in Statements. . . .

(1) Names of reporting persons: _____ . . .

(2) Mailing address and phone number of each reporting person (or, where applicable, the authorized representative): _____

(3) Amount of securities held that are entitled to be voted on the election of directors held by each reporting person (and, where applicable, amount of securities held in the aggregate by the nominating shareholder group), but including loaned securities and net of securities sold short or borrowed for purposes other than a short sale: _____

(4) Number of votes attributable to the securities entitled to be voted on the election of directors represented by amount in Row (3) (and, where applicable, aggregate number of votes attributable to the securities entitled to be voted on the election of directors held by group):

_____ . . .

Item 3. Ownership

Provide the following information. . . .

(a) Amount of securities held and entitled to be voted on the election of directors (and, where applicable, amount of securities held in the aggregate by the nominating shareholder group):

_____.

(b) The number of votes attributable to the securities referred to in paragraph (a) of this Item:

_____.

(c) The number of votes attributable to securities that have been loaned but which the reporting person:

(i) has the right to recall; and

(ii) will recall upon being notified that any of the nominees will be included in the registrant's proxy statement and proxy card: _____.

(d) The number of votes attributable to securities that have been sold in a short sale that is not closed out, or that have been borrowed for purposes other than a short sale: _____.

(e) The sum of paragraphs (b) and (c), minus paragraph (d) of this Item, divided by the aggregate number of votes derived from all classes of securities of the registrant that are entitled to vote on the election of directors, and expressed as a percentage: _____.

Item 4. Statement of Ownership from a Nominating Shareholder or Each Member of a Nominating Shareholder Group Submitting this Notice Pursuant to Rule 14a–11

(a) If the nominating shareholder, or each member of the nominating shareholder group, is the registered holder of the shares, please so state. Otherwise, attach to the Schedule 14N one or more written statements from the persons (usually brokers or banks) through which the nominating shareholder's securities are held, verifying that, within seven calendar days prior to filing the shareholder notice on Schedule 14N with the Commission and transmitting the notice to the registrant, the nominating shareholder continuously held the amount of securities being used to satisfy the ownership threshold for a period of at least three years. In the alternative, if the nominating shareholder has filed a Schedule 13D, Schedule 13G, Form 3, Form 4, and/or Form 5, or amendments to those documents, reflecting ownership of the securities as of or before the date on which the three-year eligibility period begins, so state and incorporate that filing or amendment by reference.

(b) Provide a written statement that the nominating shareholder, or each member of the nominating shareholder group, intends to continue to hold the amount of securities that are used for purposes of satisfying the minimum ownership requirement of Rule 14a–11(b)(1) through the date of the meeting of shareholders, as required by Rule 14a–11(b)(4). Additionally, provide a written statement from the nominating shareholder or each member of the nominating shareholder group regarding the nominating shareholder's or nominating shareholder group member's intent with respect to continued ownership after the election of directors, as required by Rule 14a–11(b)(5).

Item 5. Disclosure Required for Shareholder Nominations Submitted Pursuant to § 240.14a–11

If a nominating shareholder or nominating shareholder group is submitting this notice in connection with the inclusion of a shareholder nominee or nominees for director in the registrant's proxy materials pursuant to Rule 14a–11, provide the following information:

(a) A statement that the nominee consents to be named in the registrant's proxy statement and form of proxy and, if elected, to serve on the registrant's board of directors;

(b) Disclosure about the nominee as would be provided in response to the disclosure requirements of Items 4(b), 5(b), 7(a), (b) and (c) . . . ;

(c) Disclosure about the nominating shareholder or each member of a nominating shareholder group as would be required of a participant in response to the disclosure requirements of Items 4(b) and 5(b) of Schedule 14A, as applicable;

(d) Disclosure about whether the nominating shareholder or any member of a nominating shareholder group has been involved in any legal proceeding during the past ten years, as specified in Item 401(f) of Regulation S–K. Disclosure pursuant to this paragraph need not be provided if provided in response to Item 5(c) of this section;

(e) Disclosure about whether, to the best of the nominating shareholder's or group's knowledge, the nominee meets the director qualifications, if any, set forth in the registrant's governing documents;

(f) A statement that, to the best of the nominating shareholder's or group's knowledge, in the case of a registrant other than an investment company, the nominee meets the objective criteria for "independence" of the national securities exchange or national securities association rules applicable to the registrant, if any. . . .

(g) The following information regarding the nature and extent of the relationships between the nominating shareholder or nominating shareholder group, the nominee, and/or the registrant or any affiliate of the registrant:

(1) Any direct or indirect material interest in any contract or agreement between the nominating shareholder or any member of the nominating shareholder group, the nominee, and/or the registrant or any affiliate of the registrant (including any employment agreement, collective bargaining agreement, or consulting agreement);

(2) Any material pending or threatened legal proceeding in which the nominating shareholder or any member of the nominating shareholder group and/or the nominee is a party or a material participant, and that involves the registrant, any of its executive officers or directors, or any affiliate of the registrant; and

(3) Any other material relationship between the nominating shareholder or any member of the nominating shareholder group, the nominee, and/or the registrant or any affiliate of the registrant not otherwise disclosed;

(h) The Web site address on which the nominating shareholder or nominating shareholder group may publish soliciting materials, if any; and

(i) Any statement in support of the shareholder nominee or nominees, which may not exceed 500 words for each nominee, if the nominating shareholder or nominating shareholder group elects to have such statement included in the registrant's proxy materials. . . .

———

REGULATION 15D. REPORTS OF REGISTRANTS UNDER THE SECURITIES ACT OF 1933

Rule 15d–1. Requirement of Annual Reports

Every registrant under the Securities Act of 1933 shall file an annual report, on the appropriate form authorized or prescribed therefor, for the fiscal year in which the registration statement under the Securities Act of 1933 became effective and for each fiscal year thereafter, unless the registrant is exempt from such filing by section 15(d) of the Act or rules thereunder. . . .

Rule 15d–11.   Current Reports on Form 8-K . . .

(a) Except as provided in paragraph (b) of this section, every registrant subject to Rule 15d–1 shall file a current report on Form 8-K within the period specified in that form unless substantially the same information as that required by Form 8-K has been previously reported by the registrant. . . .

(c) No failure to file a report on Form 8-K that is required solely pursuant to Item 1.01, 1.02, 2.03, 2.04, 2.05, 2.06, 4.02(a), 5.02(e) or 6.03 of Form 8-K shall be deemed to be a violation of 15 U.S.C. § 10(b) and Rule 10b–5.

Rule 15d–13.   Quarterly Reports on Form 10-Q

(a) Except as [otherwise] provided . . . every issuer that has securities registered pursuant to the Securities Act and is required to file annual reports pursuant to section 15(d) of the Act on Form 10-K shall file a quarterly report on Form 10-Q . . . for each of the first three fiscal quarters of each fiscal year of the issuer. . . .

Rule 15d–14.   Certification of Disclosure in Annual and Quarterly Reports

(a) Each report, including transition reports, filed on Form 10-Q [or] . . . Form 10-K under section 15(d) of the Act . . . must include certifications in the form specified in the applicable exhibit filing requirements of such report and such certifications must be filed as an exhibit to such report. Each principal executive and principal financial officer of the issuer, or persons performing similar functions, at the time of filing of the report must sign a certification. The principal executive and principal financial officers of an issuer may omit the portion of the introductory language in paragraph 4 as well as language in paragraph 4(b) of the certification that refers to the certifying officers' responsibility for designing, establishing and maintaining internal control over financial reporting for the issuer until the issuer becomes subject to the internal control over financial reporting requirements in Rule 13a–15 or Rule 15d–15.

(b) Each periodic report containing financial statements filed by an issuer pursuant to section 15(d) of the Act must be accompanied by the certifications required by Section 1350 of Chapter 63 of Title 18 of the United States Code and such certifications must be furnished as an exhibit to such report as specified in the applicable exhibit requirements for such report. Each principal executive and principal financial officer of the issuer (or equivalent thereof) must sign a certification. This requirement may be satisfied by a single certification signed by an issuer's principal executive and principal financial officers.

(c) A person required to provide a certification specified in paragraph [(a) or (b)] of this section may not have the certification signed on his or her behalf pursuant to a power of attorney or other form of confirming authority. . . .

Rule 15d–15.   Controls and Procedures

(a) Every issuer that files reports under section 15(d) of the Act . . . must maintain disclosure controls and procedures (as defined in paragraph (e) of this section) and, if the issuer either had been required to file an annual report pursuant to section 13(a) or 15(d) of the Act for the prior fiscal year or had filed an annual report with the Commission for the prior fiscal year, internal control over financial reporting (as defined in paragraph (f) of this section).

(b) Each such issuer's management must evaluate, with the participation of the issuer's principal executive and principal financial officers, or persons performing similar functions, the effectiveness of the issuer's disclosure controls and procedures, as of the end of each fiscal quarter. . . .

(c) The management of each such issuer that either had been required to file an annual report pursuant to section 13(a) or 15(d) of the Act for the prior fiscal year or had filed an annual report with the Commission for the prior fiscal year . . . must evaluate, with the participation of the issuer's principal executive and principal financial officers, or persons performing similar functions, the effectiveness, as of the end of each fiscal year, of the issuer's internal control over financial reporting. The framework on which management's evaluation of the issuer's internal control over financial reporting is based must be a suitable, recognized control framework that is established by a body or group that has followed due-process procedures, including the broad distribution of the framework for public comment.

(d) The management of each such issuer that previously either had been required to file an annual report pursuant to section 13(a) or 15(d) of the Act for the prior fiscal year or previously had filed an annual report with the Commission for the prior fiscal year . . . must evaluate, with the participation of the issuer's principal executive and principal financial officers, or persons performing similar functions, any change in the issuer's internal control over financial reporting, that occurred during each of the issuer's fiscal quarters, or fiscal year in the case of a foreign private issuer, that has materially affected, or is reasonably likely to materially affect, the issuer's internal control over financial reporting. . . .

(e) For purposes of this section, the term *disclosure controls and procedures* means controls and other procedures of an issuer that are designed to ensure that information required to be disclosed by the issuer in the reports that it files or submits under the Act (15 U.S.C. 78a *et seq.*) is recorded, processed, summarized and reported, within the time periods specified in the Commission's rules and forms. Disclosure controls and procedures include, without limitation, controls and procedures designed to ensure that information required to be disclosed by an issuer in the reports that it files or submits under the Act is accumulated and communicated to the issuer's management, including its principal executive and principal financial officers, or persons performing similar functions, as appropriate to allow timely decisions regarding required disclosure.

(f) The term *internal control over financial reporting* is defined as a process designed by, or under the supervision of, the issuer's principal executive and principal financial officers, or persons performing similar functions, and effected by the issuer's board of directors, management and other personnel, to provide reasonable assurance regarding the reliability of financial reporting and the preparation of financial statements for external purposes in accordance with generally accepted accounting principles and includes those policies and procedures that:

(1) Pertain to the maintenance of records that in reasonable detail accurately and fairly reflect the transactions and dispositions of the assets of the issuer;

(2) Provide reasonable assurance that transactions are recorded as necessary to permit preparation of financial statements in accordance with generally accepted accounting principles, and that receipts and expenditures of the issuer are being made only in accordance with authorizations of management and directors of the issuer; and

(3) Provide reasonable assurance regarding prevention or timely detection of unauthorized acquisition, use or disposition of the issuer's assets that could have a material effect on the financial statements.

Rule 15d–20.   Plain English Presentation of Specified Information

(a) Any information included or incorporated by reference in a report filed under section 15(d) of the Act that is required to be disclosed pursuant to Item 402, 403, 404 or 407 of Regulation S–K must be presented in a clear, concise and understandable manner. You must prepare the disclosure using the following standards:

(1) Present information in clear, concise sections, paragraphs and sentences;

(2) Use short sentences;

(3) Use definite, concrete, everyday words;

(4) Use the active voice;

(5) Avoid multiple negatives;

(6) Use descriptive headings and subheadings;

(7) Use a tabular presentation or bullet lists for complex material, wherever possible;

(8) Avoid legal jargon and highly technical business and other terminology;

(9) Avoid frequent reliance on glossaries or defined terms as the primary means of explaining information. Define terms in a glossary or other section of the document only if the meaning is unclear from the context. Use a glossary only if it facilitates understanding of the disclosure; and

(10) In designing the presentation of the information you may include pictures, logos, charts, graphs and other design elements so long as the design is not misleading and the required information is clear. You are encouraged to use tables, schedules, charts and graphic illustrations that present relevant data in an understandable manner, so long as such presentations are consistent with applicable disclosure requirements and consistent with other information in the document. You must draw graphs and charts to scale. Any information you provide must not be misleading. . . .

REPORTS OF DIRECTORS, OFFICERS, AND PRINCIPAL SHAREHOLDERS

Rule 16a–1. Definition of Terms

Terms defined in this Rule shall apply solely to Section 16 of the Act and the rules thereunder. These terms shall not be limited to Section 16(a) of the Act but also shall apply to all other subsections under Section 16 of the Act.

(a) The term "beneficial owner" shall have the following applications:

(1) Solely for purposes of determining whether a person is a beneficial owner of more than ten percent of any class of equity securities registered pursuant to Section 12 of the Act, the term "beneficial owner" shall mean any person who is deemed a beneficial owner pursuant to Section 13(d) of the Act and the rules thereunder; *provided, however,* that the following institutions or persons shall not be deemed the beneficial owner of securities of such class held for the benefit of third parties or in customer or fiduciary accounts in the ordinary course of business . . . as long as such shares are acquired by such institutions or persons without the purpose or effect of changing or influencing control of the issuer or engaging in any arrangement subject to Rule 13d–3(b):

(i) A broker or dealer . . . ;

(ii) A bank . . . ;

(iii) An insurance company . . . ;

(iv) An investment company . . . ;

(v) . . . an investment adviser . . . ;

(vi) An employee benefit plan. . . .

(vii) A parent holding company or control person, provided the aggregate amount held directly by the parent or control person, and directly and indirectly by their subsidiaries or affiliates that are not persons specified in paragraphs (a)(1)(i) through (x), does not exceed one percent of the securities of the subject class. . . .

Note to paragraph (a). Pursuant to this section, a person deemed a beneficial owner of more than ten percent of any class of equity securities registered under Section 12 of the Act would file a Form 3, but the securities holdings disclosed on Form 3, and changes in beneficial ownership reported on subsequent Forms 4 or 5, would be determined by the definition of "beneficial owner" in paragraph (a)(2) of this section.

(2) Other than for purposes of determining whether a person is a beneficial owner of more than ten percent of any class of equity securities registered under Section 12 of the Act, the term "beneficial owner" shall mean any person who, directly or indirectly, through any contract, arrangement, understanding, relationship or otherwise, has or shares a direct or indirect pecuniary interest in the equity securities, subject to the following:

(i) The term "pecuniary interest" in any class of equity securities shall mean the opportunity, directly or indirectly, to profit or share in any profit derived from a transaction in the subject securities.

(ii) The term "indirect pecuniary interest" in any class of equity securities shall include, but not be limited to:

(A) securities held by members of a person's immediate family sharing the same household; *provided, however,* that the presumption of such beneficial ownership may be rebutted . . . ,

(B) a general partner's proportionate interest in the portfolio securities held by a general or limited partnership. . . .

(E) A person's interest in securities held by a trust . . . ; and

(F) A person's right to acquire equity securities through the exercise or conversion of any derivative security, whether or not presently exercisable.

(iii) A shareholder shall not be deemed to have a pecuniary interest in the portfolio securities held by a corporation or similar entity in which the person owns securities if the shareholder is not a controlling shareholder of the entity and does not have or share investment control over the entity's portfolio. . . .

(b) The term "call equivalent position" shall mean a derivative security position that increases in value as the value of the underlying equity increases, including, but not limited to, a long convertible security, a long call option, and a short put option position.

(c) The term "derivative securities" shall mean any option, warrant, convertible security, stock appreciation right, or similar right with an exercise or conversion privilege at a price related to an equity security, or similar securities with a value derived from the value of an equity security. . . .

(d) The term "equity security of such issuer" shall mean any equity security or derivative security relating to an issuer, whether or not issued by that issuer.

(e) The term "immediate family" shall mean any child, stepchild, grandchild, parent, stepparent, grandparent, spouse, sibling, mother-in-law, father-in-law, son-in-law, daughter-in-law, brother-in-law, or sister-in-law, and shall include adoptive relationships.

(f) The term "officer" shall mean an issuer's president, principal financial officer, principal accounting officer (or, if there is no such accounting officer, the controller), any vice-president of the issuer in charge of a principal business unit, division or function (such as sales, administration or finance), any other officer who performs a policy-making function, or any other person who performs similar policy-making functions for the issuer. Officers of the issuer's parent(s) or subsidiaries shall be deemed officers of the issuer if they perform such policy-making functions for the issuer. . . .

(g) The term "portfolio securities" shall mean all securities owned by an entity, other than securities issued by the entity.

(h) The term "put equivalent position" shall mean a derivative security position that increases in value as the value of the underlying equity decreases, including, but not limited to, a long put option and a short call option position.

Rule 16a–2. Persons and Transactions Subject to Section 16

Any person who is the beneficial owner, directly or indirectly, of more than ten percent of any class of equity securities ("ten percent beneficial owner") registered pursuant to Section 12 of the Act, any director or officer of the issuer of such securities, and any person specified in Section 17(a) of the Public Utility Holding Company Act of 1935 or Section 30(h) of the Investment Company Act of 1940, . . . shall be subject to the provisions of Section 16 of the Act. The rules under Section 16 of the Act apply to any class of equity securities of an issuer whether or not registered under Section 12 of the Act. . . . With respect to transactions by persons subject to Section 16 of the Act:

(a) A transaction(s) carried out by a director or officer in the six months prior to the director or officer becoming subject to Section 16 of the Act shall be subject to Section 16 of the Act and reported on the first required Form 4 only if the transaction(s) occurred within six months of the transaction giving rise to the Form 4 filing obligation and the director or officer became subject to Section 16 of the Act solely as a result of the issuer registering a class of equity securities pursuant to Section 12 of the Act.

(b) A transaction(s) following the cessation of director or officer status shall be subject to section 16 of the Act only if:

(1) Executed within a period of less than six months of an opposite transaction subject to section 16(b) of the Act that occurred while that person was a director or officer; and

(2) Not otherwise exempted from section 16(b) of the Act pursuant to the provisions of this chapter.

Note to paragraph (b): For purposes of this paragraph, an acquisition and a disposition each shall be an opposite transaction with respect to the other.

(c) The transaction that results in a person becoming a ten percent beneficial owner is not subject to Section 16 of the Act unless the person otherwise is subject to Section 16 of the Act. A ten percent beneficial owner not otherwise subject to Section 16 of the Act must report only those transactions conducted while the beneficial owner of more than ten percent of a class of equity securities of the issuer registered pursuant to Section 12 of the Act. . . .

Rule 16a–3. Reporting Transactions and Holdings

(a) Initial statements of beneficial ownership of equity securities required by Section 16(a) of the Act shall be filed on Form 3. Statements of changes in beneficial ownership required by that Section shall be filed on Form 4. Annual statements shall be filed on Form 5. At the election of the reporting person, any transaction required to be reported on Form 5 may be reported on an earlier filed Form 4. All such statements shall be prepared and filed in accordance with the requirements of the applicable form. . . .

(e) Any person required to file a statement under Section 16(a) of the Act shall, not later than the time the statement is transmitted for filing with the Commission, send or deliver a duplicate to the person designated by the issuer to receive such statements, or, in the absence of such a designation, to the issuer's corporate secretary or person performing equivalent functions.

(f)(1) A Form 5 shall be filed by every person who at any time during the issuer's fiscal year was subject to Section 16 of the Act with respect to such issuer, except as provided in paragraph (2) below. The Form shall be filed within 45 days after the issuer's fiscal year end, and shall disclose the following holdings and transactions not reported previously on Forms 3, 4 or 5:

(i) All transactions during the most recent fiscal year that were exempt from section 16(b) of the Act, except:

(A) Exercises and conversions of derivative securities exempt under either Rule 16b–3 or Rule 16b–6(b), and any transaction exempt under Rule 16b–3(d), Rule 16b–3(e), or Rule 16b–3(f) (these are required to be reported on Form 4);

(B) Transactions exempt from section 16(b) of the Act pursuant to Rule 16b–3(c), which shall be exempt from section 16(a) of the Act; and

(C) Transactions exempt from section 16(a) of the Act pursuant to another rule;

(ii) Transactions that constituted small acquisitions pursuant to Rule 16a–6(a);

(iii) all holdings and transactions that should have been reported during the most recent fiscal year, but were not; and

(iv) with respect to the first Form 5 requirement for a reporting person, all holdings and transactions that should have been reported in each of the issuer's last two fiscal years but were not, based on the reporting person's reasonable belief in good faith in the completeness and accuracy of the information.

(2) Notwithstanding the above, no Form 5 shall be required where all transactions otherwise required to be reported on the Form 5 have been reported before the due date of the Form 5.

Note: Persons no longer subject to Section 16 of the Act, but who were subject to the Section at any time during the issuer's fiscal year, must file a Form 5 unless paragraph (f)(2) is satisfied. See also Rule 16a–2(b) regarding the reporting obligations of persons ceasing to be officers or directors.

(g)(1) A Form 4 must be filed to report: all transactions not exempt from section 16(b) of the Act; all transactions exempt from section 16(b) of the Act pursuant to 16b–3(d), 16b–3(e), or 16b–3(f); and all exercises and conversions of derivative securities, regardless of whether exempt from section 16(b) of the Act. Form 4 must be filed before the end of the second business day following the day on which the subject transaction has been executed.

(2) Solely for purposes of section 16(a)(2)(C) of the Act and paragraph (g)(1) of this section, the date on which the executing broker, dealer or plan administrator notifies the reporting person of the execution of the transaction is deemed the date of execution for a transaction where the following conditions are satisfied:

(i) the transaction is pursuant to a contract, instruction or written plan for the purchase or sale of equity securities of the issuer (as defined in Rule 16a–1(d)) that satisfies the affirmative defense conditions of Rule 10b5–1(c) of this chapter; and

(ii) the reporting person does not select the date of execution.

(3) Transactions that are exempted by operation of any rule pursuant to Section 16(b) of the Act, other than exercises and conversions of derivative securities exempted pursuant to Rule 16b–6(b), shall be reported on either Form 5, or, at the option of the reporting person, Form 4, but in no event later than the due date of the Form 5 with respect to the fiscal year in which the transaction occurred. . . .

(k) Any issuer that maintains a corporate website shall post on that website by the end of the business day after filing any Form 3, 4 or 5 filed under section 16(a) of the Act as to the equity securities of that issuer. Each such form shall remain accessible on such issuer's website for at least a 12-month period. In the case of an issuer that is an investment company and that does not maintain its own website, if any of the issuer's investment adviser, sponsor, depositor, trustee, administrator, principal underwriter, or any affiliated person of the investment company maintains a website that includes the name of the issuer, the issuer shall comply with the posting requirements by posting the forms on one such website.

Rule 16a–4. Derivative Securities

(a) For purposes of Section 16 of the Act, both derivative securities and the underlying securities to which they relate shall be deemed to be the same class of equity securities, *except that* the acquisition or disposition of any derivative security shall be separately reported. . . .

Rule 16a–6. Small Acquisitions

(a) Any acquisition of an equity security or the right to acquire such securities, other than an acquisition from the issuer (including an employee benefit plan sponsored by the issuer), not exceeding $10,000 in market value shall be reported on Form 5, subject to the following conditions:

(1) Such acquisition, when aggregated with other acquisitions of securities of the same class (including securities underlying derivative securities, but excluding acquisitions exempted by rule

from section 16(b) or previously reported on Form 4 or Form 5) within the prior six months, does not exceed a total of $10,000 in market value; and

(2) The person making the acquisition does not within six months thereafter make any disposition, other than by a transaction exempt from section 16(b) of the Act.

(b) If an acquisition no longer qualifies for the reporting deferral in paragraph (a) of this section, all such acquisitions that have not yet been reported must be reported on Form 4 before the end of the second business day following the day on which the conditions of paragraph (a) of this section are no longer met.

Rule 16a–8.   Trusts

(a) *Persons Subject to Section 16.*

(1) *Trusts.* A trust shall be subject to section 16 of the Act with respect to securities of the issuer if the trust is a beneficial owner, pursuant to Rule 16a–1(a)(1), of more than ten percent of any class of equity securities of the issuer registered pursuant to section 12 of the Act ("ten percent beneficial owner").

(2) *Trustees, Beneficiaries, and Settlors.* In determining whether a trustee, beneficiary, or settlor is a ten percent beneficial owner with respect to the issuer:

(i) such persons shall be deemed the beneficial owner of the issuer's securities held by the trust, to the extent specified by Rule 16a–1(a)(1); and

(ii) settlors shall be deemed the beneficial owner of the issuer's securities held by the trust where they have the power to revoke the trust without the consent of another person. . . .

Rule 16a–9.   Stock Splits, Stock Dividends, and Pro Rata Rights

The following shall be exempt from Section 16 of the Act:

(a) The increase or decrease in the number of securities held as a result of a stock split or stock dividend applying equally to all securities of a class, including a stock dividend in which equity securities of a different issuer are distributed; and

(b) the acquisition of rights, such as shareholder or preemptive rights, pursuant to a pro rata grant to all holders of the same class of equity securities registered under Section 12 of the Act. . . .

Rule 16a–10.   Exemptions Under Section 16(a)

Except as provided in Rule 16a–6, any transaction exempted from the requirements of Section 16(a) of the Act, insofar as it is otherwise subject to the provisions of Section 16(b), shall be likewise exempt from Section 16(b) of the Act.

Rule 16a–12.   Domestic Relations Orders

The acquisition or disposition of equity securities pursuant to a domestic relations order, as defined in the Internal Revenue Code or Title I of the Employee Retirement Income Security Act, or the rules thereunder, shall be exempt from section 16 of the Act.

Rule 16a–13.   Change in Form of Beneficial Ownership

A transaction, other than the exercise or conversion of a derivative security or deposit into or withdrawal from a voting trust, that effects only a change in the form of beneficial ownership without changing a person's pecuniary interest in the subject equity securities shall be exempt from section 16 of the Act.

EXEMPTION OF CERTAIN TRANSACTIONS
FROM SECTION 16(b) . . .

Rule 16b–3.   Transactions Between an Issuer and Its Officers or Directors

(a) *General.* A transaction between the issuer (including an employee benefit plan sponsored by the issuer) and an officer or director of the issuer that involves issuer equity securities shall be exempt from section 16(b) of the Act if the transaction satisfies the applicable conditions set forth in this section.

(b) *Definitions.*

(1) A *Discretionary Transaction* shall mean a transaction pursuant to an employee benefit plan that:

(i) Is at the volition of a plan participant;

(ii) Is not made in connection with the participant's death, disability, retirement or termination of employment;

(iii) Is not required to be made available to a plan participant pursuant to a provision of the Internal Revenue Code; and

(iv) Results in either an intra-plan transfer involving an issuer equity securities fund, or a cash distribution funded by a volitional disposition of an issuer equity security.

(2) An *Excess Benefit Plan* shall mean an employee benefit plan that is operated in conjunction with a Qualified Plan, and provides only the benefits or contributions that would be provided under a Qualified Plan but for any benefit or contribution limitations set forth in the Internal Revenue Code of 1986, or any successor provisions thereof.

(3)(i) A *Non-Employee Director* shall mean a director who:

(A) Is not currently an officer (as defined in Rule 16a–1(f)) of the issuer or a parent or subsidiary of the issuer, or otherwise currently employed by the issuer or a parent or subsidiary of the issuer;

(B) Does not receive compensation, either directly or indirectly, from the issuer or a parent or subsidiary of the issuer, for services rendered as a consultant or in any capacity other than as a director, except for an amount that does not exceed the dollar amount for which disclosure would be required pursuant to Item 404(a) [under Regulation S–K]; and

(C) Does not possess an interest in any other transaction for which disclosure would be required pursuant to Item 404(a) [under Regulation S–K].

(4) A *Qualified Plan* shall mean an employee benefit plan that satisfies the coverage and participation requirements of sections 410 and 401(a)(26) of the Internal Revenue Code of 1986, or any successor provisions thereof.

(5) A *Stock Purchase Plan* shall mean an employee benefit plan that satisfies the coverage and participation requirements of sections 423(b)(3) and 423(b)(5), or section 410, of the Internal Revenue Code of 1986, or any successor provisions thereof.

(c) *Tax-conditioned plans.* Any transaction (other than a Discretionary Transaction) pursuant to a Qualified Plan, an Excess Benefit Plan, or a Stock Purchase Plan shall be exempt without condition.

(d) *Acquisitions from the issuer.* Any transaction, other than a Discretionary Transaction, involving an acquisition from the issuer (including without limitation a grant or award), whether or not intended for a compensatory or other particular purpose, shall be exempt if:

(1) The transaction is approved by the board of directors of the issuer, or a committee of the board of directors that is composed solely of two or more Non-Employee Directors;

(2) The transaction is approved or ratified, in compliance with section 14 of the Act, by either: the affirmative votes of the holders of a majority of the securities of the issuer present, or represented, and entitled to vote at a meeting duly held in accordance with the applicable laws of the state or other

jurisdiction in which the issuer is incorporated; or the written consent of the holders of a majority of the securities of the issuer entitled to vote; *provided that* such ratification occurs no later than the date of the next annual meeting of shareholders; or

(3) The issuer equity securities so acquired are held by the officer or director for a period of six months following the date of such acquisition, *provided that* this condition shall be satisfied with respect to a derivative security if at least six months elapse from the date of acquisition of the derivative security to the date of disposition of the derivative security (other than upon exercise or conversion) or its underlying equity security.

(e) *Dispositions to the issuer.* Any transaction, other than a Discretionary Transaction, involving the disposition to the issuer of issuer equity securities, whether or not intended for a compensatory or other particular purpose, shall be exempt, provided that the terms of such disposition are approved in advance in the manner prescribed by either paragraph (d)(1) or paragraph (d)(2) of this section.

(f) *Discretionary Transactions.* A Discretionary Transaction shall be exempt only if effected pursuant to an election made at least six months following the date of the most recent election, with respect to any plan of the issuer, that effected a Discretionary Transaction that was:

(1) An acquisition, if the transaction to be exempted would be a disposition; or

(2) A disposition, if the transaction to be exempted would be an acquisition.

Notes to Rule 16b–3:

Note (1): The exercise or conversion of a derivative security that does not satisfy the conditions of this section is eligible for exemption from section 16(b) of the Act to the extent that the conditions of Rule 16b–6(b) are satisfied.

Note (2): Section 16(a) reporting requirements applicable to transactions exempt pursuant to this section are set forth in Rule 16a–3(f) and (g) and Rule 16a–4.

Note (3): The approval conditions of paragraphs (d)(1), (d)(2) and (e) of this section require the approval of each specific transaction, and are not satisfied by approval of a plan in its entirety except for the approval of a plan pursuant to which the terms and conditions of each transaction are fixed in advance, such as a formula plan. Where the terms of a subsequent transaction (such as the exercise price of an option, or the provision of an exercise or tax withholding right) are provided for in a transaction as initially approved pursuant to paragraphs (d)(1), (d)(2) or (e), such subsequent transaction shall not require further specific approval.

Note (4): For purposes of determining a director's status under those portions of paragraph (b)(3)(i) that reference Item 404(a) of Regulation S–K of this chapter, an issuer may rely on the disclosure provided under Item 404(a) of this chapter for the issuer's most recent fiscal year contained in the most recent filing in which disclosure required under Item 404(a) is presented. Where a transaction disclosed in that filing was terminated before the director's proposed service as a Non-Employee Director, that transaction will not bar such service. The issuer must believe in good faith that any current or contemplated transaction in which the director participates will not be required to be disclosed under Item 404(a) of this chapter, based on information readily available to the issuer and the director at the time such director proposes to act as a Non-Employee Director. At such time as the issuer believes in good faith, based on readily available information, that a current or contemplated transaction with a director will be required to be disclosed under Item 404(a) in a future filing, the director no longer is eligible to serve as a Non-Employee Director; provided, however, that this determination does not result in retroactive loss of a Rule 16b–3 exemption for a transaction previously approved by the director while serving as a Non-Employee Director consistent with this Note. In making the determinations specified in this Note, the issuer may rely on information it obtains from the director, for example, pursuant to a response to an inquiry.

Rule 16b–5. Bona Fide Gifts and Inheritance

Both the acquisition and the disposition of equity securities shall be exempt from the operation of Section 16(b) of the Act if they are: (a) bona fide gifts; or (b) transfers of securities by will or the laws of descent and distribution.

Rule 16b–6. Derivative Securities

(a) The establishment of or increase in a call equivalent position or liquidation of or decrease in a put equivalent position shall be deemed a purchase of the underlying security for purposes of Section 16(b) of the Act, and the establishment of or increase in a put equivalent position or liquidation of or decrease in a call equivalent position shall be deemed a sale of the underlying securities for purposes of Section 16(b) of the Act. . . .

(b) The closing of a derivative security position as a result of its exercise or conversion shall be exempt from the operation of Section 16(b) of the Act, and the acquisition of underlying securities at a fixed exercise price due to the exercise or conversion of a call equivalent position or the disposition of underlying securities at a fixed exercise price due to the exercise of a put equivalent position shall be exempt from the operation of Section 16(b) of the Act. . . .

(c) In determining the short-swing profit recoverable pursuant to Section 16(b) of the Act from transactions involving the purchase and sale or sale and purchase of derivative and other securities, the following rules apply:

(1) Short-swing profits in transactions involving the purchase and sale or sale and purchase of derivative securities that have identical characteristics (*e.g.*, purchases and sales of call options of the same strike price and expiration date, or purchases and sales of the same series of convertible debentures) shall be measured by the actual prices paid or received in the short-swing transactions.

(2) Short-swing profits in transactions involving the purchase and sale or sale and purchase of derivative securities having different characteristics but related to the same underlying security (*e.g.*, the purchase of a call option and the sale of a convertible debenture) or derivative securities and underlying securities shall not exceed the difference in price of the underlying security on the date of purchase or sale and the date of sale or purchase. . . .

Rule 16b–7. Mergers, Reclassifications, and Consolidations

(a) The following transactions shall be exempt from the provisions of section 16(b) of the Act:

(1) The acquisition of a security of a company, pursuant to a merger, reclassification or consolidation, in exchange for a security of a company that before the merger, reclassification or consolidation, owned 85 percent or more of either:

(i) The equity securities of all other companies involved in the merger, reclassification or consolidation, or in the case of a consolidation, the resulting company; or

(ii) The combined assets of all the companies involved in the merger, reclassification or consolidation, computed according to their book values before the merger, reclassification or consolidation as determined by reference to their most recent available financial statements for a 12 month period before the merger, reclassification or consolidation, or such shorter time as the company has been in existence.

(2) The disposition of a security, pursuant to a merger, reclassification or consolidation, of a company that before the merger, reclassification or consolidation, owned 85 percent or more of either:

(i) The equity securities of all other companies involved in the merger, reclassification or consolidation or, in the case of a consolidation, the resulting company; or

(ii) The combined assets of all the companies undergoing merger, reclassification or consolidation, computed according to their book values before the merger, reclassification or consolidation as determined by reference to their most recent available financial statements for a 12 month period before the merger, reclassification or consolidation.

(b) A merger within the meaning of this section shall include the sale or purchase of substantially all the assets of one company by another in exchange for equity securities which are then distributed to the security holders of the company that sold its assets.

(c) The exemption provided by this section applies to any securities transaction that satisfies the conditions specified in this section and is not conditioned on the transaction satisfying any other conditions.

(d) Notwithstanding the foregoing, if a person subject to section 16 of the Act makes any non-exempt purchase of a security in any company involved in the merger, reclassification or consolidation and any non-exempt sale of a security in any company involved in the merger, reclassification or consolidation within any period of less than six months during which the merger, reclassification or consolidation took place, the exemption provided by this section shall be unavailable to the extent of such purchase and sale.

Form 3

UNITED STATES SECURITIES AND EXCHANGE COMMISSION

Washington, D.C. 20549

FORM 3

INITIAL STATEMENT OF BENEFICIAL OWNERSHIP OF SECURITIES ...

GENERAL INSTRUCTIONS

1. Who Must File

(a) This Form must be filed by the following persons ("reporting person"):

(i) any director or officer of an issuer with a class of equity securities registered pursuant to Section 12 of the Securities Exchange Act of 1934 ("Exchange Act"); (*Note:* Title is not determinative for purposes of determining "officer" status. See Rule 16a–1(f) for the definition of "officer");

(ii) any beneficial owner of greater than 10% of a class of equity securities registered under Section 12 of the Exchange Act, as determined by voting or investment control over the securities pursuant to Rule 16a–1(a)(1) ("ten percent holder"); . . .

(v) any trust, trustee, beneficiary or settlor required to report pursuant to Rule 16a–8. . . .

(c) If a person described above does not beneficially own any securities required to be reported (*see* Rule 16a–1 and Instruction 5), the person is required to file this Form and state that no securities are beneficially owned.

2. When Form Must Be Filed

. . . This Form must be filed within 10 days after the event by which the person becomes a reporting person (*i.e.,* officer, director, ten percent holder or other person). . . .

3. Where Form Must Be Filed

(a) A reporting person must file this Form in electronic format via the Commission's Electronic Data Gathering Analysis and Retrieval System (EDGAR). . . .

(b) At the time this Form or any amendment is filed with the Commission, file one copy with each Exchange on which any class of securities of the issuer is registered. . . .

4. Class of Securities Reported

. . . Persons reporting pursuant to Section 16(a) of the Exchange Act shall include information as to their beneficial ownership of any class of equity securities of the issuer, even though one or more of such classes may not be registered pursuant to Section 12 of the Exchange Act. . . .

5. Holdings Required to Be Reported

(a) *General Requirements*

Report holdings of each class of securities of the issuer beneficially owned as of the date of the event requiring the filing of this Form. See Instruction 4 as to securities required to be reported.

(b) *Beneficial Ownership Reported (Pecuniary Interest)*

(i) Although, for purposes of determining status as a ten percent holder, a person is deemed to beneficially own securities over which that person has voting or investment control (*see* Rule 16a–1(a)(1)), for reporting purposes, a person is deemed to be the beneficial owner of securities if that person has or shares the opportunity, directly or indirectly, to profit or share in any profit derived from a transaction in the securities ("pecuniary interest"). *See* Rule 16a–1(a)(2). . . .

(ii) Both direct and indirect beneficial ownership of securities shall be reported. Securities beneficially owned directly are those held in the reporting person's name or in the name of a bank, broker or nominee for the account of the reporting person. In addition, securities held as joint tenants, tenants in common, tenants by the entirety, or as community property are to be reported as held directly. If a person has a pecuniary interest, by reason of any contract, understanding or relationship (including a family relationship or arrangement), in securities held in the name of another person, that person is an indirect beneficial owner of those securities. *See* Rule 16a–1(a)(2)(ii) for certain indirect beneficial ownerships.

(iii) Report securities beneficially owned directly on a separate line from those beneficially owned indirectly. Report different forms of indirect ownership on separate lines. The nature of indirect ownership shall be stated as specifically as possible; for example, "By Self as Trustee for X," "By Spouse," "By X Trust," "By Y Corporation," etc.

(iv) In stating the amount of securities owned indirectly through a partnership, corporation, trust, or other entity, report the number of securities representing the reporting person's proportionate interest in securities beneficially owned by that entity. . . .

FORM 3

UNITED STATES SECURITIES AND EXCHANGE COMMISSION
Washington, D.C. 20549
Form 3

INITIAL STATEMENT OF BENEFICIAL OWNERSHIP OF SECURITIES

Filed pursuant to Section 16(a) of the Securities Exchange Act of 1934, Section 17(a) of the Public Utility
Holding Company Act of 1935 or Section 30(h) of the Investment Company Act of 1940

(Print or Type Responses)

1. Name and Address of Reporting Person*	2. Date of Event Requiring Statement (Month/Day/Year)	3. Issuer Name and Ticker or Trading Symbol

(Last) (First) (Middle)		4. Relationship of Reporting Person(s) to Issuer (Check all applicable)	5. If Amendment, Date Original Filed (Month/Day/Year)
(Street)		___ Director ___ 10% Owner ___ Officer (give title below) ___ Other (specify below)	6. Individual or Joint/Group Filing (Check Applicable Line) Form filed by One Reporting Person Form filed by More than One Reporting Person
(City) (State) (Zip)			

Table I — Non-Derivative Securities Beneficially Owned

1. Title of Security (Instr. 4)	2. Amount of Securities Beneficially Owned (Instr. 4)	3. Ownership Form: Direct (D) or Indirect (I) (Instr. 5)	4. Nature of Indirect Beneficial Ownership (Instr. 5)

Reminder. Report on a separate line for each class of securities beneficially owned directly or indirectly
* If the form is filed by more than one reporting person, see Instruction 5(b)(v).

Potential persons who are to respond to the collection of information contained in this form are not
required to respond unless the form displays a currently valid OMB control number.

OMB APPROVAL
OMB Number: 3235-0104
Expires: January 31, 2005
Estimated average burden
hours per response......0.5

(Over)

SEC 1473 (6-03)

FORM 3 (continued)

Table II — Derivative Securities Beneficially Owned (*e.g.*, puts, calls, warrants, options, convertible securities)

1. Title of Derivative Security (Instr. 4)	2. Date Exercisable and Expiration Date (Month/Day/Year)		3. Title and Amount of Securities Underlying Derivative Security (Instr. 4)		4. Conversion or Exercise Price of Derivative Security	5. Ownership Form of Derivative Security Direct (D) or Indirect (I) (Instr. 5)	6. Nature of Indirect Beneficial Ownership (Instr. 5)
	Date Exercisable	Expiration Date	Title	Amount or Number of Shares			

Explanation of Responses:

** Intentional misstatements or omissions of facts constitute Federal Criminal Violations. *See* 18 U.S.C. 1001 and 15 U.S.C. 78ff(a).

Note: File three copies of this Form, one of which must be manually signed. If space is insufficient. *See* Instruction 6 for procedure.

****Signature of Reporting Person**   Date

Page 2

Form 4

UNITED STATES SECURITIES AND EXCHANGE COMMISSION

Washington, D.C. 20549

FORM 4

STATEMENT OF CHANGES OF BENEFICIAL OWNERSHIP OF SECURITIES . . .

GENERAL INSTRUCTIONS

1.   When Form Must Be Filed

(a) This Form must be filed before the end of the second business day following the day on which a transaction resulting in a change in beneficial ownership has been executed (see Rule 16a–1(a)(2) and Instruction 4 regarding the meaning of "beneficial owner," and Rule 16a–3(g) regarding determination of the date of execution for specified transactions). This Form and any amendment is deemed filed with the Commissions or the Exchange on the date it is received by the Commission or the Exchange, respectively. *See,* however, Rule 16a–3(h) regarding delivery to a third party business that guarantees delivery of the filing no later than the specified due date.

(b) A reporting person no longer subject to Section 16 of the Securities Exchange Act of 1934 ("Exchange Act") must check the exit box appearing on this Form. However, Form 4 and 5 obligations may continue to be applicable. *See* Rule 16a–3(f); *see also* Rule 16a–2(b) (transactions after termination of insider status). Form 5 transactions to date may be included on this Form and subsequent Form 5 transactions may be reported on a later Form 4 or Form 5, provided all transactions are reported by the required date.

(c) A separate Form shall be filed to reflect beneficial ownership of securities of each issuer, except that a single statement shall be filed with respect to the securities of a registered public utility holding company and all of its subsidiary companies.

(d) If a reporting person is not an officer, director, or ten percent holder, the person should check "other" in Item 6 (Relationship of Reporting Person to Issuer) and describe the reason for reporting status in the space provided.

2.   Where Form Must Be Filed . . .*

3.   Class of Securities Reported . . .

4.   Transactions and Holdings Required to be Reported

(a) *General Requirements*

(i) Report, in accordance with Rules 16a–3(g):

(1) all transactions not exempt from § 16(b);

(2) all transactions exempt from Section 16(b) pursuant to Rule 16b–3(d), Rule 16b–3(e), or Rule 16b–3(f); and

(3) all exercises and conversions of derivative securities, regardless of whether exempt from Section 16(b) of the Act.

Every transaction must be reported even though acquisitions and dispositions are equal. Report total beneficial ownership following the reported transaction(s) for each class of securities in which a transaction was reported. . . .

(b) *Beneficial Ownership Reported (Pecuniary Interest)*

(i) Although for purposes of determining status as a ten percent holder, a person is deemed to beneficially own securities over which that person exercises voting or investment control (*see* Rule 16a–1(a)(1)), for reporting transactions and holdings, a person is deemed to be the beneficial owner of

---

* Instructions 2, 3, and 4(b) parallel instructions 3, 4, and 5(b) for Form 3, supra. (Footnote by ed.)

securities if that person has the opportunity, directly or indirectly, to profit or share in any profit derived from a transaction in the securities ("pecuniary interest"). *See* Rule 16a–1(a)(2). *See also* Rule 16a–8 for the application of the beneficial ownership definition to trust holdings and transactions.

(ii) Both direct and indirect beneficial ownership of securities shall be reported. Securities beneficially owned directly are those held in the reporting person's name or in the name of a bank, broker or nominee for the account of the reporting person. In addition, securities held as joint tenants, tenants in common, tenants by the entirety, or as community property are to be reported as held directly. If a person has a pecuniary interest, by reason of any contract, understanding or relationship (including a family relationship or arrangement), in securities held in the name of another person, that person is an indirect beneficial owner of the securities. *See* Rule 16a–1(a)(2)(ii) for certain indirect beneficial ownerships. . . .

FORM 4

☐ Check this box if no longer subject to Section 16. Form 4 or Form 5 obligations may continue. See Instruction 1(b).

OMB APPROVAL

OMB Number: 3235-0287
Expires: January 31, 2005
Estimated average burden
hours per response ... 0.5

UNITED STATES SECURITIES AND EXCHANGE COMMISSION
Washington, D.C. 20549

STATEMENT OF CHANGES IN BENEFICIAL OWNERSHIP

Filed pursuant to Section 16(a) of the Securities Exchange Act of 1934, Section 17(a) of the Public Utility Holding Company Act of 1935 or Section 30(th) of the Investment Company Act of 1940

1. Name and Address of Reporting Person* (Print or Type Responses)	2. Issuer Name and Ticker or Trading Symbol	5. Relationship of Reporting Person(s) to Issuer (Check all applicable)
(Last) (First) (Middle)		___ Director ___ 10% Owner ___ Officer (give title below) ___ Other (specify below)
(Street)	3. Date of Earliest Transaction Required to be Reported (Month/Day/Year)	4. If Amendment, Date Original Filed(Month/Day/Year)
(City) (State) (Zip)		6. Individual or Joint/Group Filing (Check Applicable Line) ___ Form filed by One Reporting Person ___ Form filed by More than One Reporting Person

Table 1 — Non-Derivative Securities Acquired, Disposed of, or Beneficially Owned

1. Title of Security (Instr. 3)	2. Transaction Date (Month/Day/Year)	2A. Deemed Execution Date, if any (Month/Day/Year)	3. Transaction Code (Instr. 8)		4. Securities Acquired (A) or Disposed of (D) (Instr. 3, 4 and 5)			5. Amount of Securities Beneficially Owned Following Reported Transaction(s) (Instr. 3 and 4)	6. Ownership Form: Direct (D) or Indirect (I) (Instr. 4)	7. Nature of Indirect Beneficial Ownership (Instr. 4)
			Code	V	Amount	(A) or (D)	Price			

Reminder: Report on a separate line for each class of securities beneficially owned directly or indirectly.

* If the form is filed by more than one reporting person, see Instruction 4(b)(v).

(Over)   SEC 1474 (06-03)

FORM 4 (continued)

Table II — Derivative Securities Acquired, Disposed of, or Beneficially Owned
(*e.g.*, puts, calls, warrants, options, convertible securities)

1. Title of Derivative Security (Instr. 3)	2. Conversion or Exercise Price of Derivative Security	3. Transaction Date (Month/Day/Year)	3A. Deemed Execution Date, If any (Month/Day/Year)	4. Transaction Code (Instr. 8)		5. Number of Derivative Securities Acquired (A) or Disposed of (D) (Instr. 3, 4, and 5)			6. Date Exercisable and Expiration Date (Month/Day/Year)		7. Title and Amount of Underlying Securities (Instr. 3 and 4)		8. Price of Derivative Security (Instr. 5)	9. Number of Derivative Securities Beneficially Owned following Reported Transaction(s)(Instr. 4)	10. Ownership Form of Derivative Security: Direct (D) or Indirect (I) (Instr. 4)	11. Nature of Indirect Beneficial Ownership (Instr. 4)
				Code	V	(A)	(D)		Date Exercisable	Expiration Date	Title	Amount or Number of Shares				

Explanation of Responses:

_____
**Signature of Reporting Person

_____
Date

** Intentional misstatements or omissions of facts constitute **Federal Criminal Violations.** See 18 U.S.C. 1001 and 15 U.S.C. 78ff(a).

Note: File three copies of this Form, one of which must be manually signed. If space is insufficient, *see* Instruction 6 for procedure.

Potential persons who are to respond to the collection of information contained in this form are not required to respond unless the form displays a currently valid OMB Number.

Form 5

UNITED STATES SECURITIES AND EXCHANGE COMMISSION

Washington, D.C. 20549

FORM 5

ANNUAL STATEMENT OF BENEFICIAL OWNERSHIP OF SECURITIES . . .

GENERAL INSTRUCTIONS

1.   When Form Must Be Filed

(a) This Form must be filed on or before the 45th day after the end of the issuer's fiscal year in accordance with Rule 16a–3(f). . . .

(b) A reporting person no longer subject to Section 16 of the Securities Exchange Act of 1934 ("Exchange Act") must check the exit box appearing on this Form. Transactions and holdings previously reported are not required to be included on this Form. Form 4 or Form 5 obligations may continue to be applicable. *See* Rules 16a–3(f) and 16a–2(b). . . .

2.   Where Form Must Be Filed . . .*

3.   Class of Securities Reported . . .

4.   Transactions and Holdings Required to Be Reported

(a) *General Requirements*

(i) Pursuant to Rule 16a–3(f), if not previously reported, the following transactions, and total beneficial ownership as of the end of the issuer's fiscal year (or the earlier date applicable to a person ceasing to be an insider during the fiscal year) for any class of securities for which a transaction is reported, shall be reported:

(A) any transaction during the issuer's most recent fiscal year that was exempt from Section 16(b) of the Act, except: (1) any transaction exempt from Section 16(b) pursuant to Rule 16b–3(d), Rule 16b–3(e) or Rule 16b–3(f) (these are required to be reported on Form 4); (2) any exercise or conversion of derivative securities exempt under either Rule 16b–3 or Rule 16b–6(b) (these are required to be reported on Form 4); (3) any transaction exempt from Section 16(b) of the Act pursuant to Rule 16b–3(c), which is exempt from Section 16(a) of the Act; and (4) any transaction exempt from Section 16 of the Act pursuant to another Section 16(a) rule;

(B) any small acquisition or series of acquisitions in a six month period during the issuer's fiscal year not exceeding $10,000 in market value (*see* Rule 16a–6);

(C) any transactions or holdings that should have been reported during the issuer's fiscal year on a Form 3 or Form 4, but were not reported. The first Form 5 filing obligation shall include all holdings and transactions that should have been reported in each of the issuer's last two fiscal years but were not. . . .

---

* Instructions 2, 3, and 4(b) generally parallel the corresponding instructions 3, 4, and 5(b) for Form 3, supra. (Footnote by ed.)

FORM 5

☐ Check box if no longer subject to
Section 16. Form 4 or Form 5 obligations may continue. *See Instruction 1(b).*
☐ Form 3 Holdings Reported
☐ Form 4 Transactions Reported

UNITED STATES SECURITIES AND EXCHANGE COMMISSION
Washington, D.C. 20549

ANNUAL STATEMENT OF CHANGES IN BENEFICIAL OWNERSHIP OF
SECURITIES

Filed pursuant to Section 16(a) of the Securities Exchange Act of 1934, Section 17(a) of the Public Utility
Holding Company Act of 1935 or Section 30(h) of the Investment Company Act of 1940

OMB APPROVAL
OMB Number: 3235-0362
Expires: January 31, 2005
Estimated average burden
hours per response...... 1.0

1. Name and Address of Reporting Person*

(Last)   (First)   (Middle)

(Street)

(City)   (State)   (Zip)

2. Issuer Name and Ticker or Trading Symbol

3. Statement for Issuer's Fiscal Year Ended (Month/Day/Year)

4. If Amendment, Date Original Filed (Month/Day/Year)

5. Relationship of Reporting Person(s) to Issuer (Check all applicable)

___ Director   ___ 10% Owner
___ Officer (give title below)   ___ Other (specify below)

6. Individual or Joint/Group Reporting (check applicable line)

___ Form Filed by One Reporting Person
___ Form Filed by More than One Reporting Person

Table I — Non-Derivative Securities Acquired, Disposed of, or Beneficially Owned

1. Title of Security (Instr. 3)	2. Transaction Date (Month/Day/Year)	2A. Deemed Execution Date, if any (Month/Day/Year)	3. Transaction Code (Instr. 8)	4. Securities Acquired (A) or Disposed of (D) (Instr. 3, 4 and 5)			5. Amount of Securities Beneficially Owned at end of Issuer's Fiscal Year (Instr. 3 and 4)	6. Ownership Form: Direct (D) or Indirect (I) (Instr. 4)	7. Nature of Indirect Beneficial Ownership (Instr. 4)
				Amount	(A) or (D)	Price			

Reminder: Report on a separate line for each class of securities beneficially owned directly or indirectly.
* If the form is filed by more than one reporting person, see instruction 4(b)(v).

Potential persons who are to respond to the collection of information contained in this form are not required to respond unless the form displays a currently valid OMB control number.

SEC 2270 (7-03)   (Over)

FORM 5 (continued)

Table II — Derivative Securities Acquired, Disposed of, or Beneficially Owned
(e.g., puts, calls, warrants, options, convertible securities)

1. Title of Derivative Security (Instr. 3)	2. Conversion or Exercise Price of Derivative Security	3. Transaction Date (Month/Day/Year)	3A. Deemed Execution Date, if any (Month/Day/Year)	4. Transaction Code (Instr. 8)	5. Number of Derivative Securities Acquired (A) or Disposed of (D) (Instr. 3, 4, and 5)		6. Date Exercisable and Expiration Date (Month/Day/Year)		7. Title and Amount of Underlying Securities (Instr. 3 and 4)		8. Price of Derivative Security (Instr. 5)	9. Number of Derivative Securities Beneficially Owned at End of Issuer's Fiscal Year (Instr. 4)	10. Ownership Form of Derivative Securities: Direct (D) or Indirect (I) (Instr. 4)	11. Nature of Indirect Beneficial Ownership (Instr. 4)
					(A)	(D)	Date Exercisable	Expiration Date	Title	Amount or Number of Shares				

Explanation of Responses:

** Intentional misstatements or omissions of facts constitute Federal Criminal Violations.
See 18 U.S.C. 1001 and 15 U.S.C. 78ff(a).

Note: File three copies of this Form, one of which must be manually signed.
If space provided is insufficient, see Instruction 6 for procedure.

_____   _____
** Signature of Reporting Person   Date

Page 2

JOBS ACT PROVISIONS NOT AMENDING
OTHER FEDERAL STATUTES

§ 101. DEFINITIONS . . .

(c) OTHER DEFINITIONS.—As used in this title, the following definitions shall apply:

(1) COMMISSION.—The term "Commission" means the Securities and Exchange Commission.

(2) INITIAL PUBLIC OFFERING DATE.—The term "initial public offering date" means the date of the first sale of common equity securities of an issuer pursuant to an effective registration statement under the Securities Act of 1933. . . .

(d) EFFECTIVE DATE.—Notwithstanding section 2(a)(19) of the Securities Act of 1933 and section 3(a)(80) of the Securities Exchange Act of 1934, an issuer shall not be an emerging growth company for purposes of such Acts if the first sale of common equity securities of such issuer pursuant to an effective registration statement under the Securities Act of 1933 occurred on or before December 8, 2011.

§ 102. DISCLOSURE OBLIGATIONS . . .

(c) OTHER DISCLOSURES.—An emerging growth company may comply with section 303(a) of Regulation S–K, by providing information required by such section with respect to the financial statements of the emerging growth company for each period presented pursuant to section 7(a) of the Securities Act of 1933. An emerging growth company may comply with Item 402 of Regulation S–K, by disclosing the same information as any issuer with a market value of outstanding voting and nonvoting common equity held by non-affiliates of less than $75,000,000.

§ 105. AVAILABILITY OF INFORMATION ABOUT EMERGING GROWTH COMPANIES . . .

(d) POST OFFERING COMMUNICATIONS.—Neither the Commission nor any national securities association registered under section 15A of the Securities Exchange Act of 1934 may adopt or maintain any rule or regulation prohibiting any broker, dealer, or member of a national securities association from publishing or distributing any research report or making a public appearance, with respect to the securities of an emerging growth company, either—

(1) within any prescribed period of time following the initial public offering date of the emerging growth company; or

(2) within any prescribed period of time prior to the expiration date of any agreement between the broker, dealer, or member of a national securities association and the emerging growth company or its shareholders that restricts or prohibits the sale of securities held by the emerging growth company or its shareholders after the initial public offering date.

§ 107. OPT-IN RIGHT FOR EMERGING GROWTH COMPANIES . . .

(a) IN GENERAL.—With respect to an exemption provided to emerging growth companies under this title, or an amendment made by this title, an emerging growth company may choose to forgo such exemption and instead comply with the requirements that apply to an issuer that is not an emerging growth company.

(b) SPECIAL RULE.—Notwithstanding subsection (a), with respect to the extension of time to comply with new or revised financial accounting standards provided under section 7(a)(2)(B) of the Securities Act of 1933 and section 13(a) of the Securities Exchange Act of 1934, as added by section 102(b), if an emerging growth company chooses to comply with such standards to the same extent that a non-emerging growth company is required to comply with such standards, the emerging growth company—

(1) must make such choice at the time the company is first required to file a registration statement, periodic report, or other report with the Commission under section 13 of the Securities Exchange Act of 1934 and notify the Securities and Exchange Commission of such choice;

(2) may not select some standards to comply with in such manner and not others, but must comply with all such standards to the same extent that a non-emerging growth company is required to comply with such standards; and

(3) must continue to comply with such standards to the same extent that a non-emerging growth company is required to comply with such standards for as long as the company remains an emerging growth company.

REGULATION FD

Rule 100.   General Rule Regarding Selective Disclosure.

(a) Whenever an issuer, or any person acting on its behalf, discloses any material nonpublic information regarding that issuer or its securities to any person described in paragraph (b)(1) of this section, the issuer shall make public disclosure of that information as provided in Rule 101(e):

(1) Simultaneously, in the case of an intentional disclosure; and

(2) Promptly, in the case of a non-intentional disclosure.

(b)(1) Except as provided in paragraph (b)(2) of this section, paragraph (a) of this section shall apply to a disclosure made to any person outside the issuer:

(i) Who is a broker or dealer, or a person associated with a broker or dealer, as those terms are defined in Section 3(a) of the Securities Exchange Act of 1934;

(ii) Who is an investment adviser, as that term is defined in Section 202(a)(11) of the Investment Advisers Act of 1940; an institutional investment manager, as that term is defined in Section 13(f)(5) of the Securities Exchange Act of 1934 . . . or a person associated with either of the foregoing. . . .

(iii) Who is an investment company, as defined in Section 3 of the Investment Company Act of 1940 (15 U.S.C. 80a–3), or who would be an investment company but for Section 3(c)(1) (15 U.S.C. 80a–3(c)(1)) or Section 3(c)(7) (15 U.S.C. 80a–3(c)(7)) thereof, or an affiliated person of either of the foregoing. For purposes of this paragraph, "affiliated person" means only those persons described in Section 2(a)(3)(C), (D), (E), and (F) of the Investment Company Act of 1940 (15 U.S.C. 80a–2(a)(3)(C), (D), (E), and (F)), assuming for these purposes that a person who would be an investment company but for Section 3(c)(1) (15 U.S.C. 80a–3(c)(1)) or Section 3(c)(7) (15 U.S.C. 80a–3(c)(7)) of the Investment Company Act of 1940 is an investment company; or

(iv) Who is a holder of the issuer's securities, under circumstances in which it is reasonably foreseeable that the person will purchase or sell the issuer's securities on the basis of the information.

(2) Paragraph (a) of this section shall not apply to a disclosure made:

(i) To a person who owes a duty of trust or confidence to the issuer (such as an attorney, investment banker, or accountant);

(ii) To a person who expressly agrees to maintain the disclosed information in confidence;

(iii) In connection with a securities offering registered under the Securities Act, other than an offering of the type described in any of Rule 415(a)(1)(i) through (vi) under the Securities Act (except an offering of the type described in Rule 415(a)(1)(i) under the Securities Act also involving a registered offering, whether or not underwritten, for capital formation purposes for the account of the issuer (unless the issuer's offering is being registered for the purpose of evading the requirements of this section)), if the disclosure is by any of the following means:

(A) A registration statement filed under the Securities Act, including a prospectus contained therein;

(B) A free writing prospectus used after filing of the registration statement for the offering or a communication falling within the exception to the definition of prospectus contained in clause (a) of section 2(a)(10) of the Securities Act;

(C) Any other Section 10(b) prospectus;

(D) A notice permitted by Rule 135 under the Securities Act;

(E) A communication permitted by Rule 134 under the Securities Act; or

(F) An oral communication made in connection with the registered securities offering after filing of the registration statement for the offering under the Securities Act.

Rule 101.   Definitions.

This section defines certain terms as used in Regulation FD (Rules 100–103).

(a) *Intentional.* A selective disclosure of material nonpublic information is "intentional" when the person making the disclosure either knows, or is reckless in not knowing, that the information he or she is communicating is both material and nonpublic.

(b) *Issuer.* An "issuer" subject to this regulation is one that has a class of securities registered under Section 12 of the Securities Exchange Act of 1934, or is required to file reports under Section 15(d) of the Securities Exchange Act of 1934. . . .

(c) *Person acting on behalf of an issuer.* "Person acting on behalf of an issuer" means any senior official of the issuer (or, in the case of a closed-end investment company, a senior official of the issuer's investment adviser), or any other officer, employee, or agent of an issuer who regularly communicates with any person described in Rule 100(b)(1)(i), (ii), or (iii), or with holders of the issuer's securities. An officer, director, employee, or agent of an issuer who discloses material nonpublic information in breach of a duty of trust or confidence to the issuer shall not be considered to be acting on behalf of the issuer.

(d) *Promptly.* "Promptly" means as soon as reasonably practicable (but in no event after the later of 24 hours or the commencement of the next day's trading on the New York Stock Exchange) after a senior official of the issuer (or, in the case of a closed-end investment company, a senior official of the issuer's investment adviser) learns that there has been a non-intentional disclosure by the issuer or person acting on behalf of the issuer of information that the senior official knows, or is reckless in not knowing, is both material and nonpublic.

(e) *Public disclosure.* (1) Except as provided in paragraph (e)(2) of this section, an issuer shall make the "public disclosure" of information required by Rule 100(a) by furnishing to or filing with the Commission a Form 8-K disclosing that information.

(2) An issuer shall be exempt from the requirement to furnish or file a Form 8-K if it instead disseminates the information through another method (or combination of methods) of disclosure that is reasonably designed to provide broad, non-exclusionary distribution of the information to the public.

(f) *Senior official.* "Senior official" means any director, executive officer [as defined in Rule 3b–7 under the Securities Act], investor relations or public relations officer, or other person with similar functions.

(g) *Securities offering.* For purposes of Rule 100(b)(2)(iv):

(1) *Underwritten offerings.* A securities offering that is underwritten commences when the issuer reaches an understanding with the broker-dealer that is to act as managing underwriter and continues until the later of the end of the period during which a dealer must deliver a prospectus or the sale of the securities (unless the offering is sooner terminated);

(2) *Non-underwritten offerings.* A securities offering that is not underwritten:

(i) If covered by Rule 415(a)(1)(x) [under the Securities Act], commences when the issuer makes its first bona fide offer in a takedown of securities and continues until the later of the end of the period during which each dealer must deliver a prospectus or the sale of the securities in that takedown (unless the takedown is sooner terminated);

(ii) If a business combination as defined in Rule 165(f)(1) [under the Securities Act], commences when the first public announcement of the transaction is made and continues until the completion of the vote or the expiration of the tender offer, as applicable (unless the transaction is sooner terminated);

(iii) If an offering other than those specified in paragraphs (a) and (b) of this section, commences when the issuer files a registration statement and continues until the later of the end of the period during which each dealer must deliver a prospectus or the sale of the securities (unless the offering is sooner terminated).

Rule 102.   No Effect on Antifraud Liability.

No failure to make a public disclosure required solely by Rule 100 shall be deemed to be a violation of Rule 10b–5 under the Securities Exchange Act.

Rule 103.   No Effect on Exchange Act Reporting Status.

A failure to make a public disclosure required solely by Rule 100 shall not affect whether:

(a) For purposes of Forms S-2, S-3 and S-8 under the Securities Act, an issuer is deemed to have filed all the material required to be filed pursuant to Section 13 or 15(d) of the Securities Exchange Act of 1934 or, where applicable, has made those filings in a timely manner; or

(b) There is adequate current public information about the issuer for purposes of Rule 144(c) [under the Securities Act].

SECURITIES AND EXCHANGE COMMISSION
RELEASE NO. 33–7881 (2000)

SELECTIVE DISCLOSURE AND INSIDER TRADING . . .
II.   Selective Disclosure: Regulation FD

A.   Background

. . . [W]e we have become increasingly concerned about the selective disclosure of material information by issuers. As reflected in recent publicized reports, many issuers are disclosing important nonpublic information, such as advance warnings of earnings results, to securities analysts or selected institutional investors or both, before making full disclosure of the same information to the general public. Where this has happened, those who were privy to the information beforehand were able to make a profit or avoid a loss at the expense of those kept in the dark.

We believe that the practice of selective disclosure leads to a loss of investor confidence in the integrity of our capital markets. Investors who see a security's price change dramatically and only later are given access to the information responsible for that move rightly question whether they are on a level playing field with market insiders.

Issuer selective disclosure bears a close resemblance in this regard to ordinary "tipping" and insider trading. In both cases, a privileged few gain an informational edge—and the ability to use that edge to profit—from their superior access to corporate insiders, rather than from their skill, acumen, or diligence. Likewise, selective disclosure has an adverse impact on market integrity that is similar to the adverse impact from illegal insider trading: Investors lose confidence in the fairness of the markets when they know that other participants may exploit "unerodable informational advantages" derived not from hard work or insights, but from their access to corporate insiders. The economic effects of the two practices are essentially the same. Yet, as a result of judicial interpretations, tipping and insider trading can be severely punished under the antifraud provisions of the federal securities laws, whereas the status of issuer selective disclosure has been considerably less clear.

Regulation FD is also designed to address another threat to the integrity of our markets: the potential for corporate management to treat material information as a commodity to be used to gain or maintain favor with particular analysts or investors. . . . [I]n the absence of a prohibition on selective disclosure, analysts may feel pressured to report favorably about a company or otherwise slant their analysis in order to have continued access to selectively disclosed information. We are concerned, in this regard, with reports that analysts who publish negative views of an issuer are sometimes excluded by that issuer from calls and meetings to which other analysts are invited.

Finally, . . . technological developments have made it much easier for issuers to disseminate information broadly. Whereas issuers once may have had to rely on analysts to serve as information intermediaries, issuers now can use a variety of methods to communicate directly with the market. In addition to press releases, these methods include, among others, Internet webcasting and teleconferencing. Accordingly, technological limitations no longer provide an excuse for abiding the threats to market integrity that selective disclosure represents.

To address the problem of selective disclosure, we proposed Regulation FD. It targets the practice by establishing new requirements for full and fair disclosure by public companies. . . .

B.   Discussion of Regulation FD

Rule 100 of Regulation FD sets forth the basic rule regarding selective disclosure. Under this rule, whenever:

(1) an issuer, or person acting on its behalf,

(2) discloses material nonpublic information,

(3) to certain enumerated persons (in general, securities market professionals or holders of the issuer's securities who may well trade on the basis of the information),

(4) the issuer must make public disclosure of that same information:

> (a) simultaneously (for intentional disclosures), or
>
> (b) promptly (for non-intentional disclosures).

As a whole, the regulation requires that when an issuer makes an intentional disclosure of material nonpublic information to a person covered by the regulation, it must do so in a manner that provides general public disclosure, rather than through a selective disclosure. For a selective disclosure that is non-intentional, the issuer must publicly disclose the information promptly after it knows (or is reckless in not knowing) that the information selectively disclosed was both material and nonpublic. . . .

1.   Scope of Communications and Issuer Personnel Covered by the Regulation . . .

[Regulation FD] is designed to address the core problem of selective disclosure made to those who would reasonably be expected to trade securities on the basis of the information or provide others with advice about securities trading. Accordingly, Rule 100(a) of Regulation FD . . . makes clear that the general rule against selective disclosure applies only to disclosures made to the categories of persons enumerated in Rule 100(b)(1).

Rule 100(b)(1) enumerates four categories of persons to whom selective disclosure may not be made absent a specified exclusion. The first three are securities market professionals—(1) broker-dealers and their associated persons, (2) investment advisers, certain institutional investment managers and their associated persons, and (3) investment companies, hedge funds, and affiliated persons. These categories will include sell-side analysts, many buy-side analysts, large institutional investment managers, and other market professionals who may be likely to trade on the basis of selectively disclosed information. The fourth category of person included in Rule 100(b)(1) is any holder of the issuer's securities, under circumstances in which it is reasonably foreseeable that such person would purchase or sell securities on the basis of the information. Thus, as a whole, Rule 100(b)(1) will cover the types of persons most likely to be the recipients of improper selective disclosure, but should not cover persons who are engaged in ordinary-course business communications with the issuer, or interfere with disclosures to the media or communications to government agencies.

Rule 100(b)(2) sets out four exclusions from coverage. The first, as proposed, is for communications made to a person who owes the issuer a duty of trust or confidence—*i.e.*, a "temporary insider"—such as an attorney, investment banker, or accountant. The second exclusion is for communications made to any person who expressly agrees to maintain the information in confidence. Any misuse of the information for trading by the persons in these two exclusions would thus be covered under either the "temporary insider" or the misappropriation theory of insider trading. This approach recognizes that issuers and their officials may properly share material nonpublic information with outsiders, for legitimate business purposes, when the outsiders are subject to duties of confidentiality.

The third exclusion from coverage in Rule 100(b)(2) is for disclosures to an entity whose primary business is the issuance of credit ratings, provided the information is disclosed solely for the purpose of developing a credit rating and the entity's ratings are publicly available. . . . [R]atings organizations often obtain nonpublic information in the course of their ratings work. We are not aware, however, of any incidents of selective disclosure involving ratings organizations. Ratings organizations, like the media, have a mission of public disclosure; the objective and result of the ratings process is a widely available publication of the rating when it is completed. And under this provision, for the exclusion to apply, the ratings organization must make its credit ratings publicly available. For these reasons, we believe it is appropriate to provide this exclusion from the coverage of Regulation FD.

The fourth exclusion from coverage is for communications made in connection with most offerings of securities registered under the Securities Act. . . .

b.   Disclosures by a Person Acting on an Issuer's Behalf . . .

. . . We define the term ["person acting on behalf of an issuer"] to mean: (1) Any senior official of the issuer[1] or (2) any other officer, employee, or agent of an issuer who regularly communicates with any of the

---

[1]   "Senior official" is defined in Rule 101(f) as any director, executive officer, investor relations or public relations officer, or other person with similar functions. . . .

persons described in Rule 100(b)(1)(i), (ii), or (iii), or with the issuer's security holders. [Under this definition, Regulation FD covers senior management, investor relations professionals, and others who regularly interact with securities market professionals or security holders]. Of course, neither an issuer nor such a covered person could avoid the reach of the regulation merely by having a non-covered person make a selective disclosure. Thus, to the extent that another employee had been *directed* to make a selective disclosure by a member of senior management, that member of senior management would be responsible for having made the selective disclosure. *See* Section 20(b) of the Exchange Act. In addition . . . the definition expressly states that a person who communicates material nonpublic information in breach of a duty to the issuer would not be considered to be acting on behalf of the issuer. Thus, an issuer is not responsible under Regulation FD when one of its employees improperly trades or tips.

2. *Disclosures of Material Nonpublic Information*

[Regulation FD] applies to disclosures of "material nonpublic" information about the issuer or its securities. The regulation does not define the terms "material" and "nonpublic," but relies on existing definitions of these terms established in the case law. Information is material if "there is a substantial likelihood that a reasonable shareholder would consider it important" in making an investment decision. To fulfill the materiality requirement, there must be a substantial likelihood that a fact "would have been viewed by the reasonable investor as having significantly altered the total mix of information made available." Information is nonpublic if it has not been disseminated in a manner making it available to investors generally. . . .

. . . While it is not possible to create an exhaustive list, the following items are some types of information or events that should be reviewed carefully to determine whether they are material: (1) Earnings information; (2) mergers, acquisitions, tender offers, joint ventures, or changes in assets; (3) new products or discoveries, or developments regarding customers or suppliers (*e.g.,* the acquisition or loss of a contract); (4) changes in control or in management; (5) change in auditors or auditor notification that the issuer may no longer rely on an auditor's audit report; (6) events regarding the issuer's securities—*e.g.,* defaults on senior securities, calls of securities for redemption, repurchase plans, stock splits or changes in dividends, changes to the rights of security holders, public or private sales of additional securities; and (7) bankruptcies or receiverships.

By including this list, we do not mean to imply that each of these items is *per se* material. The information and events on this list still require determinations as to their materiality (although some determinations will be reached more easily than others). For example, some new products or contracts may clearly be material to an issuer; yet that does not mean that *all* product developments or contracts will be material. This demonstrates, in our view, why no "bright-line" standard or list of items can adequately address the range of situations that may arise. Furthermore, we do not and cannot create an exclusive list of events and information that have a higher probability of being considered material.

One common situation that raises special concerns about selective disclosure has been the practice of securities analysts seeking "guidance" from issuers regarding earnings forecasts. When an issuer official engages in a private discussion with an analyst who is seeking guidance about earnings estimates, he or she takes on a high degree of risk under Regulation FD. If the issuer official communicates selectively to the analyst nonpublic information that the company's anticipated earnings will be higher than, lower than, or even the same as what analysts have been forecasting, the issuer likely will have violated Regulation FD. This is true whether the information about earnings is communicated expressly or through indirect "guidance," the meaning of which is apparent though implied. Similarly, an issuer cannot render material information immaterial simply by breaking it into ostensibly non-material pieces.

At the same time, an issuer is not prohibited from disclosing a non-material piece of information to an analyst, even if, unbeknownst to the issuer, that piece helps the analyst complete a "mosaic" of information that, taken together, is material. Similarly, since materiality is an objective test keyed to the reasonable investor, Regulation FD will not be implicated where an issuer discloses immaterial information whose significance is discerned by the analyst. Analysts can provide a valuable service in sifting through and extracting information that would not be significant to the ordinary investor to reach material conclusions. We do not intend, by Regulation FD, to discourage this sort of activity. The focus of Regulation FD is on whether the issuer discloses material nonpublic information, not on whether an analyst, through some combination of persistence, knowledge, and insight, regards as material information whose significance is not apparent to the reasonable investor.

. . . Rule 101(a) states that a person acts "intentionally" only if the person knows, or is reckless in not knowing, that the information he or she is communicating is both material and nonpublic. . . . [T]his aspect of the regulation provides additional protection that issuers need not fear being second-guessed by the Commission in enforcement actions for mistaken judgments about materiality in close cases.

3. *Intentional and Non-intentional Selective Disclosures: Timing of Required Public Disclosures*

A key provision of Regulation FD is that the timing of required public disclosure differs depending on whether the issuer has made an "intentional" selective disclosure or a selective disclosure that was not intentional. For an "intentional" selective disclosure, the issuer is required to publicly disclose the same information simultaneously.

a. *Standard of "Intentional" Selective Disclosure.* Under the regulation, a selective disclosure is "intentional" when the issuer or person acting on behalf of the issuer making the disclosure either knows, or is reckless in not knowing, prior to making the disclosure, that the information he or she is communicating is both material and nonpublic. . . .

b. *"Prompt" Public Disclosure After Non-intentional Selective Disclosures.*

Under Rule 100(a)(2), when an issuer makes a covered non-intentional disclosure of material nonpublic information, it is required to make public disclosure promptly. . . .

Commenters expressed varying views on the definition of "promptly" provided in the rule. Some said that the time period provided for disclosure was appropriate; others said it was too short; and still others said that it was too specific, and should require disclosure only as soon as reasonably possible or practicable. We believe that it is preferable for issuers and the investing public that there be a clear delineation of when "prompt" disclosure is required. We also believe that the 24-hour requirement strikes the appropriate balance between achieving broad, non-exclusionary disclosure and permitting issuers time to determine how to respond after learning of the non-intentional selective disclosure. However, recognizing that sometimes non-intentional selective disclosures will arise close to or over a weekend or holiday, we have slightly modified the final rule to state that the outer boundary for prompt disclosure is the later of 24 hours or the commencement of the next day's trading on the New York Stock Exchange, after a senior official learns of the disclosure and knows (or is reckless in not knowing) that the information disclosed was material and nonpublic. . . .

4. *"Public Disclosure" Required by Regulation FD*

Rule 101(e) defines the type of "public disclosure" that will satisfy the requirements of Regulation FD. As proposed, Rule 101(e) gave issuers considerable flexibility in determining how to make required public disclosure. The proposal stated that issuers could meet Regulation FD's "public disclosure" requirement by filing a Form 8-K, by distributing a press release through a widely disseminated news or wire service, or by any other non-exclusionary method of disclosure that is reasonably designed to provide broad public access—such as announcement at a conference of which the public had notice and to which the public was granted access, either by personal attendance, or telephonic or electronic access. This definition was designed to permit issuers to make use of current technologies, such as webcasting of conference calls, that provide broad public access to issuer disclosure events. . . .

We believe that issuers could use the following model, which employs a combination of methods of disclosure, for making a planned disclosure of material information, such as a scheduled earnings release:

- First, issue a press release, distributed through regular channels, containing the information;

- Second, provide adequate notice, by a press release and/or website posting, of a scheduled conference call to discuss the announced results, giving investors both the time and date of the conference call, and instructions on how to access the call; and

- Third, hold the conference call in an open manner, permitting investors to listen in either by telephonic means or through Internet webcasting.[2]

By following these steps, an issuer can use the press release to provide the initial broad distribution of the information, and then discuss its release with analysts in the subsequent conference call, without fear that if it should disclose additional material details related to the original disclosure it will be engaging in a selective disclosure of material information. . . .

5. Issuers Subject to Regulation FD

Regulation FD will apply to all issuers with securities registered under Section 12 of the Exchange Act, and all issuers required to file reports under Section 15(d) of the Exchange Act, including closed-end investment companies, but not including other investment companies, foreign governments, or foreign private issuers. . . .

7. Liability Issues

We recognize that the prospect of private liability for violations of Regulation FD could contribute to a "chilling effect" on issuer communications. Issuers might refrain from some informal communications with outsiders if they feared that engaging in such communications, even when appropriate, would lead to their being charged in private lawsuits with violations of Regulation FD. . . .

. . . Rule 102 . . . expressly provides that no failure to make a public disclosure required solely by Regulation FD shall be deemed to be a violation of Rule 10b–5. This provision makes clear that Regulation FD does not create a new duty for purposes of Rule 10b–5 liability. Accordingly, private plaintiffs cannot rely on an issuer's violation of Regulation FD as a basis for a private action alleging Rule 10b–5 violations.

Rule 102 is designed to exclude Rule 10b–5 liability for cases that would be based "solely" on a failure to make a public disclosure required by Regulation FD. As such, it does not affect any existing grounds for liability under Rule 10b–5. Thus, for example, liability for "tipping" and insider trading under Rule 10b–5 may still exist if a selective disclosure is made in circumstances that meet the *Dirks* "personal benefit" test. In addition, an issuer's failure to make a public disclosure still may give rise to liability under a "duty to correct" or "duty to update" theory in certain circumstances. And an issuer's contacts with analysts may lead to liability under the "entanglement" or "adoption" theories. In addition, if an issuer's report or public disclosure made under Regulation FD contained false or misleading information, or omitted material information, Rule 102 would not provide protection from Rule 10b–5 liability.

Finally, if an issuer failed to comply with Regulation FD, it would be subject to an SEC enforcement action alleging violations of Section 13(a) or 15(d) of the Exchange Act . . . and Regulation FD. We could bring an administrative action seeking a cease-and-desist order, or a civil action seeking an injunction and/or civil money penalties.[3] In appropriate cases, we could also bring an enforcement action against an individual at the issuer responsible for the violation, either as "a cause of" the violation in a cease-and-desist proceeding,[4] or as an aider and abettor of the violation in an injunctive action.[5]

---

[2]   Giving the public the opportunity to listen to the call does not also require that the issuer give all members of the public the opportunity to ask questions.

[3]   Regulation FD does not expressly require issuers to adopt policies and procedures to avoid violations, but we expect that most issuers will use appropriate disclosure policies as a safeguard against selective disclosure. We are aware that many, if not most, issuers already have policies and regarding disclosure practices, the dissemination of material information, and the question of which issuer personnel are authorized to speak to analysts, the media, or investors. The existence of an appropriate policy, and the issuer's general adherence to it, may often be relevant to determining the issuer's intent with regard to a selective disclosure.

[4]   Section 21C of the Exchange Act, *15 U.S.C. 78u–3*. A failure to file or otherwise make required public disclosure under Regulation FD will be considered a violation for as long as the failure continues; in our enforcement actions, we likely will seek more severe sanctions for violations that continue for a longer period of time.

[5]   Section 20(e) of the Exchange Act, *15 U.S.C. 78t*(e).

III. Insider Trading Rules . . .

A.   Rule 10b5–1: Trading "On the Basis of" Material Nonpublic Information

1.   *Background*

. . . [O]ne unsettled issue in insider trading law has been what, if any, causal connection must be shown between the trader's possession of inside information and his or her trading. In enforcement cases, we have argued that a trader may be liable for trading while in "knowing possession" of the information. The contrary view is that a trader is not liable unless it is shown that he or she "used" the information for trading. Until recent years, there has been little case law discussing this issue. Although the Supreme Court has variously described an insider's violations as trading "on"[6] or "on the basis of"[7] material nonpublic information, it has not addressed the use/possession issue. Three recent courts of appeals cases addressed the issue but reached different results.[8]

. . . [I]n our view, the goals of insider trading prohibitions—protecting investors and the integrity of securities markets—are best accomplished by a standard closer to the "knowing possession" standard than to the "use" standard. At the same time, we recognize that an absolute standard based on knowing possession, or awareness, could be overbroad in some respects. The new rule attempts to balance these considerations by means of a general rule based on "awareness" of the material nonpublic information, with several carefully enumerated affirmative defenses. This approach will better enable insiders and issuers to conduct themselves in accordance with the law. . . .

. . . Scienter remains a necessary element for liability under Section 10(b) of the Exchange Act and Rule 10b–5 thereunder, and Rule 10b5–1 does not change this.

2.   *Provisions of Rule 10b5–1*

We are adopting . . . the general rule set forth in Rule 10b5–1(a), and the definition of "on the basis of" material nonpublic information in Rule 10b5–1(b). A trade is on the basis of material nonpublic information if the trader was aware of the material, nonpublic information when the person made the purchase or sale.

. . . The awareness standard reflects the common sense notion that a trader who is aware of inside information when making a trading decision inevitably makes use of the information. Additionally, a clear awareness standard will provide greater clarity and certainty than a presumption or "strong inference" approach.[9] Accordingly, we have determined to adopt the awareness standard. . . .

. . . [T]he affirmative defense [in Rule 10b5–1] allows purchases and sales pursuant to contracts, instructions, and plans. [The defense provides] appropriate flexibility to persons who wish to structure securities trading plans and strategies when they are not aware of material nonpublic information, and do not exercise any influence over the transaction once they do become aware of such information.

As adopted, paragraph (c)(1)(i) sets forth an affirmative defense from the general rule, which applies both to individuals and entities that trade. To satisfy this provision, a person must establish several factors.

- First, the person must demonstrate that before becoming aware of the information, he or she had entered into a binding contract to purchase or sell the security, provided instructions to another person to execute the trade for the instructing person's account, or adopted a written plan for trading securities.

- Second, the person must demonstrate that, with respect to the purchase or sale, the contract, instructions, or plan either: (1) expressly specified the amount, price, and date; (2) provided a

---

[6]   *See Dirks v. SEC*, 463 U.S. 646, 654 (1983).

[7]   *See O'Hagan*, 521 U.S. at 651–52.

[8]   *Compare United States v. Teicher*, 987 F.2d 112, 120–21 (2d Cir.), cert. denied, 510 U.S. 976 (1993) (suggesting that "knowing possession" is sufficient) with *SEC v. Adler*, 137 F.3d 1325, 1337 (11th Cir.1998) ("use" required, but proof of possession provides strong inference of use) and *United States v. Smith*, 155 F.3d 1051, 1069 & n. 27 (9th Cir.1998), cert. denied, 525 U.S. 1071 (1999) (requiring that "use" be proven in a criminal case).

[9]   Some commenters stated that "aware" was an unclear term that may be interpreted to mean something less than "knowing possession." We disagree. "Aware" is a commonly used and well-defined English word, meaning "having knowledge; conscious; cognizant." We believe that "awareness" has a much clearer meaning that "knowing possession," which has not been defined by case law.

written formula or algorithm, or computer program, for determining amounts, prices, and dates; or (3) did not permit the person to exercise any subsequent influence over how, when, or whether to effect purchases or sales; provided, in addition, that any other person who did exercise such influence was not aware of the material nonpublic information when doing so.

- • Third, the person must demonstrate that the purchase or sale that occurred was pursuant to the prior contract, instruction, or plan. A purchase or sale is not pursuant to a contract, instruction, or plan if, among other things, the person who entered into the contract, instruction, or plan altered or deviated from the contract, instruction, or plan or entered into or altered a corresponding or hedging transaction or position with respect to those securities.[10]

Under paragraph (c)(1)(ii), . . . the exclusion provided in paragraph (c)(1)(i) will be available only if the contract, instruction, or plan was entered into in good faith and not as part of a scheme to evade the prohibitions of this section.

Paragraph (c)(1)(iii) defines several key terms in the exclusion. . . . ["Amount"] means either a specified number of shares or a specified dollar value of securities. . . . [Price] means market price on a particular date or a limit price or a particular dollar price. "Date" means either the specific day of the year on which a market order is to be executed, or a day or days of the year on which a limit order is in force.

Taken as a whole, the . . . defense is designed to cover situations in which a person can demonstrate that the material nonpublic information was not a factor in the trading decision. We believe this provision will provide appropriate flexibility to those who would like to plan securities transactions in advance at a time when they are not aware of material nonpublic information, and then carry out those pre-planned transactions at a later time, even if they later become aware of material nonpublic information.

For example, an issuer operating a repurchase program will not need to specify with precision the amounts, prices, and dates on which it will repurchase its securities. Rather, an issuer could adopt a written plan, when it is not aware of material nonpublic information, that uses a written formula to derive amounts, prices, and dates. Or the plan could simply delegate all the discretion to determine amounts, prices, and dates to another person who is not aware of the information—provided that the plan did not permit the issuer to (and in fact the issuer did not) exercise any subsequent influence over the purchases or sales.

Similarly, an employee wishing to adopt a plan for exercising stock options and selling the underlying shares could, while not aware of material nonpublic information, adopt a written plan that contained a formula for determining the specified percentage of the employee's vested options to be exercised and/or sold at or above a specific price. The formula could provide, for example, that the employee will exercise options and sell the shares one month before each date on which her son's college tuition is due, and link the amount of the trade to the cost of the tuition.

An employee also could acquire company stock through payroll deductions under an employee stock purchase plan or a Section 401(k) plan. The employee could provide oral instructions as to his or her plan participation, or proceed by means of a written plan. The transaction price could be computed as a percentage of market price, and the transaction amount could be based on a percentage of salary to be deducted under the plan. The date of a plan transaction could be determined pursuant to a formula set forth in the plan. Alternatively, the date of a plan transaction could be controlled by the plan's administrator or investment manager, assuming that he or she is not aware of the material, nonpublic information at the time of executing the transaction, and the employee does not exercise influence over the timing of the transaction. . . .

The [rule includes] an additional affirmative defense available only to trading parties that are entities. . . . [T]his defense is available to entities as an alternative to the other enumerated defenses described above.

Under this provision, an entity will not be liable if it demonstrates that the individual making the investment decision on behalf of the entity was not aware of the information, and that the entity had implemented reasonable policies and procedures to prevent insider trading. . . .

---

[10] Rule 10b5–1(c)(1)(i)(C). However, a person acting in good faith may modify a prior contract, instruction, or plan before becoming aware of material nonpublic information. In that case, a purchase or sale that complies with the modified contract, instruction, or plan will be considered pursuant to a new contract, instruction, or plan.

B.   *Rule 10b5–2: Duties of Trust or Confidence in
        Misappropriation Insider Trading Cases*

1.   Background

... [A]n unsettled issue in insider trading law has been under what circumstances certain non-business relationships, such as family and personal relationships, may provide the duty of trust or confidence required under the misappropriation theory. Case law has produced the following anomalous result. A family member who receives a "tip" (within the meaning of *Dirks*) and then trades violates Rule 10b–5. A family member who trades in breach of an express promise of confidentiality also violates Rule 10b–5. A family member who trades in breach of a reasonable expectation of confidentiality, however, does not necessarily violate Rule 10b–5.

... [W]e think that this anomalous result harms investor confidence in the integrity and fairness of the nation's securities markets. The family member's trading has the same impact on the market and investor confidence in the third example as it does in the first two examples. In all three examples, the trader's informational advantage stems from "contrivance, not luck," and the informational disadvantage to other investors "cannot be overcome with research or skill." Additionally, the need to distinguish among the three types of cases may require an unduly intrusive examination of the details of particular family relationships. Accordingly, we believe there is good reason for the broader approach we adopt today for determining when family or personal relationships create "duties of trust or confidence" under the misappropriation theory.

... [Rule 10b5–2] is not designed to interfere with particular family or personal relationships; rather, its goal is to protect investors and the fairness and integrity of the nation's securities markets against improper trading on the basis of inside information. Moreover, we do not believe that the rule will require a more intrusive examination of family relationships than would be required under existing case law without the rule. Current case law ... already establishes a regime under which questions of liability turn on the nature of the details of the relationships between family members, such as their prior history and patterns of sharing confidences. By providing more of a bright-line test for certain enumerated close family relationships, we believe the rule will mitigate, to some degree, the need to examine the details of particular relationships in the course of investigating suspected insider trading.

2.   Provisions of Rule 10b5–2

[Rule 10b5–2] sets forth a non-exclusive list of three situations in which a person has a duty of trust or confidence for purposes of the "misappropriation" theory of the Exchange Act and Rule 10b–5 thereunder.

First ... we provide that a duty of trust or confidence exists whenever a person agrees to maintain information in confidence.

Second, we provide that a duty of trust or confidence exists when two people have a history, pattern, or practice of sharing confidences such that the recipient of the information knows or reasonably should know that the person communicating the material nonpublic information expects that the recipient will maintain its confidentiality. This is a "facts and circumstances" test based on the expectation of the parties in light of the overall relationship. Some commenters were concerned that, as proposed, this provision examined the reasonable expectation of confidentiality of the person communicating the material nonpublic information rather than examining the expectations of the recipient of the information and/or both parties to the communication. We believe that mutuality was implicit in the proposed rule because an inquiry into the reasonableness of the recipient's expectation necessarily involves considering the relationship as a whole, including the other party's expectations. Nevertheless, we have revised the provision to make this mutuality explicit. ...

Third, we are adopting as proposed a bright-line rule that states that a duty of trust or confidence exists when a person receives or obtains material nonpublic information from certain enumerated close family members: spouses, parents, children, and siblings. An affirmative defense permits the person receiving or obtaining the information to demonstrate that under the facts and circumstances of that family relationship, no duty of trust or confidence existed. Some commenters noted that the enumerated relationships do not include domestic partners, step-parents, or step-children. We have determined not to include these relationships in this paragraph, although paragraphs (b)(1) and (b)(2) could reach them. Our experience in this area indicates that most instances of insider trading between or among family members involve spouses, parents and children, or siblings; therefore, we have enumerated these relationships and not others. . . .

EXAMPLE OF SEC NO-ACTION LETTER: SELECTED ITEMS FROM JOHNSON & JOHNSON ARBITRATION BYLAW PROPOSAL

SKADDEN, ARPS, SLATE, MEAGHER & FLOM LLP
1440 NEW YORK AVENUE, N.W. WASHINGTON, D.C.   20005-2111

TEL: (202) 371-7000
FAX: (202) 393-5760
www.skadden.com

FIRM/AFFILIATE OFFICES

BOSTON
CHICAGO HOUSTON LOS ANGELES NEW YORK PALO ALTO WILMINGTON
BEIJING BRUSSELS
FRANKFURT
HONG KONG
LONDON
MOSCOW
MUNICH
PARIS
SÃO PAULO
SEOUL
SHANGHAI SINGAPORE TOKYO TORONTO

marc.gerber@skadden.com

BY EMAIL (shareholderproposals@sec.gov)

December 11, 2018

U.S. Securities and Exchange Commission Division of Corporation Finance
Office of Chief Counsel 100 F Street, N.E. Washington, D.C. 20549

RE: Johnson & Johnson – 2019 Annual Meeting Omission of Shareholder Proposal of The <u>Doris Behr 2012</u>
<u>Irrevocable Trust</u>

Ladies and Gentlemen:

Pursuant to Rule 14a-8(j) promulgated under the Securities Exchange Act of 1934, as amended (the "Exchange Act"), we are writing on behalf of our client, Johnson & Johnson, a New Jersey corporation, to request that the Staff of the Division of Corporation Finance (the "Staff") of the U.S. Securities and Exchange Commission (the "Commission") concur with Johnson & Johnson's view that, for the reasons stated below, it may exclude the shareholder proposal and supporting statement (the "Proposal") submitted by The Doris Behr 2012 Irrevocable Trust (the "Proponent") from the proxy materials to be distributed by Johnson & Johnson in connection with its 2019 annual meeting of shareholders (the "2019 proxy materials").

In accordance with Section C of Staff Legal Bulletin No. 14D (Nov. 7, 2008) ("SLB 14D"), we are emailing this letter and its attachments to the Staff at shareholderproposals@sec.gov. In accordance with Rule 14a-8(j), we are simultaneously sending a copy of this letter and its attachments to the Proponent as notice of Johnson & Johnson's intent to omit the Proposal from the 2019 proxy materials.

Rule 14a-8(k) and Section E of SLB 14D provide that shareholder proponents are required to send companies a copy of any correspondence that the shareholder proponents elect to submit to the Commission or the Staff. Accordingly, we are taking this opportunity to remind the Proponent that if the Proponent submits correspondence to the Commission or the Staff with respect to the Proposal, a copy of that correspondence should concurrently be furnished to Johnson & Johnson.

I.   The Proposal

The text of the resolution in the Proposal is set forth below:

Resolved: The shareholders of Johnson & Johnson request the Board of Directors take all practicable steps to adopt a mandatory arbitration bylaw that provides:

- for disputes between a stockholder and the Corporation and/or its directors, officers or controlling persons relating to claims under federal securities laws in connection with the purchase or sale of any securities issued by the Corporation to be exclusively and finally settled by arbitration under the Commercial Rules of the American Arbitration Association (AAA), as supplemented by the Securities Arbitration Supplementary Procedures;

- that any disputes subject to arbitration may not be brought as a class and may not be consolidated or joined;

- an express submission to arbitration (which shall be treated as a written arbitration agreement) by each stockholder, the Corporation and its directors, officers, controlling persons and third parties consenting to be bound;

- unless the claim is determined by the arbitrator(s) to be frivolous, the Corporation shall pay the fees of the AAA and the arbitrator(s), and if the stockholder party is successful, the fees of its counsel;

- a waiver of any right under the laws of any jurisdiction to apply to any court of law or other judicial authority to determine any matter or to appeal or otherwise challenge the award, ruling or decision of the arbitrator(s);

- that governing law is federal law; and

- for a five-year sunset provision, unless holders of a majority of Corporation shares vote for an extension and the duration of any extension.

II.   Basis for Exclusion

We hereby respectfully request that the Staff concur in Johnson & Johnson's view that it may exclude the Proposal from the 2019 proxy materials pursuant to Rule 14a-8(i)(2) because implementation of the Proposal would cause Johnson & Johnson to violate federal law.

III.   Background

On November 12, 2018, Johnson & Johnson received the Proposal, accompanied by a cover letter from the Proponent dated November 9, 2018, and a letter from Fifth Third Bank dated November 9, 2018, verifying the Proponent's stock ownership as of such date (the "Broker Letter"). Copies of the Proposal, the cover letter and the Broker Letter are attached hereto as Exhibit A.

IV.   The Proposal May be Excluded Pursuant to Rule 14a-8(i)(2) Because Implementation of the Proposal Would Cause Johnson & Johnson to Violate Federal Law.

Rule 14a-8(i)(2) permits a company to exclude a shareholder proposal if implementation of the proposal would cause the company to violate any state, federal or foreign law to which it is subject. For the reasons discussed below, Johnson & Johnson believes that adoption of a bylaw amendment as described in the Proposal would be contrary to the public policy interests underlying the federal securities laws and would cause Johnson & Johnson to violate federal law. Accordingly, the Proposal is excludable under Rule 14a-8(i)(2) as a violation of law.

Johnson & Johnson believes that adoption of a bylaw amendment as described in the Proposal would be in violation of Section 29(a) of the Exchange Act. Section 29(a) of the Exchange Act broadly states that "[a]ny condition, stipulation, or provision binding any person to waive compliance with any provision of this title or of any rule or regulation thereunder, or of any rule of a self-regulatory organization, shall be void." In the context of arbitration, the U.S. Supreme Court has limited the broad scope of Section 29(a) of the Exchange Act to prohibit only waivers of the substantive obligations imposed by the Exchange Act and has concluded that in the narrow circumstance where the prescribed procedures are subject to the oversight authority of the Commission, an agreement to arbitrate does not constitute a waiver of the protections of the Exchange Act. *Shearson/Am. Exp. Inc. v. McMahon*, 482 U.S. 220, 228–29, 234 (1987). The Staff has previously concurred with the exclusion, pursuant to Rule 14a-8(i)(2), of a shareholder proposal relating to a bylaw amendment where the company argued that the bylaw amendment would, if implemented, cause the company to violate Section 29(a) of the Exchange Act. *See, e.g., Gannett Co., Inc.* (Feb. 22, 2012) (shareholder proposal requesting that the company adopt a bylaw amendment to provide that certain controversies or claims, including those arising under the federal securities laws, shall be settled by arbitration); *Pfizer Inc.* (Feb. 22, 2012) (same); *see also Alaska Air Group, Inc.* (Mar. 11, 2011) (shareholder proposal requesting that the company initiate the appropriate process to amend its charter to provide for a partial waiver of the "fraud-on-the-market" presumption of reliance excludable pursuant to Rule 14a-8(i)(2) because the proposed charter amendment would violate Section 29(a) of the Exchange Act).

As in the precedent described above, adoption of a bylaw amendment as requested by the Proposal would weaken the ability of investors in Johnson & Johnson's securities to pursue a private right of action under Exchange Act Section 10(b) and Rule 10b-5. In particular, Section (e) of the bylaw amendment contained in the proposal in *Gannett* and *Pfizer* would have prevented any shareholder who had a claim subject to arbitration from bringing a claim in a representative capacity on behalf of a class of Gannett or Pfizer shareholders, effectively waiving shareholders' abilities to bring claims under Exchange Act Section 10(b) and Rule 10b-5.

Similarly, in this instance, the second bullet point of the Proposal seeks to prevent any shareholder who has a claim subject to arbitration from bringing the claim on behalf of a class of Johnson & Johnson shareholders or by consolidation or joinder in order to resolve the dispute. In addition, the fifth bullet point of the Proposal provides a waiver of any right under the laws of any jurisdiction to apply to any court of law or other judicial authority to determine any matter or to appeal or otherwise challenge the award, ruling or decision of the arbitrator(s), thus effectively waiving shareholders' abilities to bring claims under Exchange Act Section 10(b) and Rule 10b-5. The expression in the supporting statement that "[the Proponent] believe[s] arbitration is an effective alternative to class actions" further emphasizes the Proposal's request for mandatory arbitration of certain claims and the prevention of shareholders from maintaining an arbitration in a representative capacity on behalf of similarly situated shareholders. Moreover, claims arbitrated under the bylaw amendment as described in the Proposal will be governed by the Commercial Rules of the American Arbitration Association, as supplemented by the Securities Arbitration Supplementary Procedures, none of which are subject to the Commission's oversight. Given the substantial similarities between the Proposal and the proposal in *Gannett* and *Pfizer*, including, the lack of any meaningful distinction between the two proposals with respect to the ability of investors to recover damages in a dispute alleging a violation of Exchange Act Rule 10b-5, it is clear that the Proposal should be excludable under Rule 14a-8(i)(2) because implementation of the Proposal would cause Johnson & Johnson to violate the federal securities laws.

The Staff has long taken the view that including arbitration clauses in the governing documents of U.S. public companies is contrary to public policy. *See* Thomas L. Riesenberg, *Arbitration and Corporate Governance: A Reply to Carl Schneider*, 4 Insights 8 (1990). Mr. Riesenberg, then Assistant General Counsel of the Commission, outlined his views that mandatory pre-dispute arbitration of shareholder claims would "be contrary to the public interest to require investors who want to participate in the nation's equity markets to waive access to a judicial forum for vindication of federal or state law rights, where such a waiver is made through a corporate charter rather than through an individual investor's decision." In addition, the U.S. Supreme Court "has long recognized that meritorious private actions to enforce federal antifraud securities laws are an essential supplement to criminal prosecutions and civil enforcement actions brought, respectively, by the Department of Justice and the Securities and Exchange Commission." *Tellabs, Inc. v. Makor Issues & Rights, Ltd.*, 551 U.S. 308, 308 (2007).

Furthermore, no indication has been given that this policy position has changed since 1990. In fact, in an April 24, 2018 response letter to Congresswomen Carolyn B. Maloney, Commission Chairman Jay Clayton provided a detailed account of his views on the idea of mandatory arbitration of shareholder claims, stating that the matter is "complex" and involves important issues under federal securities laws and state corporate laws, as well as "many public policy considerations."[1] Although Chairman Clayton noted that the U.S. Supreme Court has "affirmed the strong federal interest in promoting the arbitration of claims under federal laws," he expressed recognition that "[t]he federal securities laws provide a basis for private rights of action by investors" and that "[t]here is a long history of claims of this type" in federal and state courts, "including as class actions." Ultimately, Chairman Clayton explained that in his view a number of pressing and significant matters other than the inclusion of mandatory arbitration clauses in the governing documents of U.S. public companies more urgently require the Commission's limited rulemaking and other related resources. Accordingly, in light of the Staff's historical view and the various legal and policy considerations, Chairman Clayton stated that any review of a mandatory arbitration clause in the context of a U.S. company's initial public offering registration statement under the Securities Act of 1933, as amended, for example, "should be conducted in a measured and deliberative manner" and "the decision about whether to declare the filing effective should be made by the Commission, not the Division of Corporation Finance by delegated authority." Similar to Chairman Clayton's views with respect to an initial public offering of a U.S. company, Johnson & Johnson believes that its 2019 annual meeting proxy statement and the Staff's Rule 14a-8 no-action letter process is not the right forum to address the issue and instead believes the appropriate course of action is for the issue to be analyzed, debated and decided by Congress, through an amendment to the Exchange Act, or by the Commission, through the appropriate notice and comment rulemaking process.

Accordingly, consistent with the precedent described above, the Proposal should be excluded from Johnson & Johnson's 2019 proxy materials pursuant to Rule 14a-8(i)(2) because implementation of the Proposal would cause Johnson & Johnson to violate federal law.

---

[1] Letter from Chairman Jay Clayton to The Honorable Carolyn B. Maloney (Apr. 24, 2018) is available at https://maloney.house.gov/sites/maloney.house.gov/files/MALONEY%20ET%20AL%20-%20FORCED%20ARBITRATION%20-%20ES156546%20Response.pdf.

V. Conclusion

Based upon the foregoing analysis, Johnson & Johnson respectfully requests that the Staff concur that it will take no action if Johnson & Johnson excludes the Proposal from its 2019 proxy materials.

Should the Staff disagree with the conclusions set forth in this letter, or should any additional information be desired in support of Johnson & Johnson's position, we would appreciate the opportunity to confer with the Staff concerning these matters prior to the issuance of the Staffs response. Please do not hesitate to contact the undersigned at (202) 371-7233.

Very truly yours,

Marc S. Gerber

EXHIBIT A

Resolved: The shareholders of Johnson & Johnson request the Board of Directors take all practicable steps to adopt a mandatory arbitration bylaw that provides:

- for disputes between a stockholder and the Corporation and/or its directors, officers or controlling persons relating to claims under federal securities laws in connection with the purchase or sale of any securities issued by the Corporation to be exclusively and finally settled by arbitration under the Commercial Rules of the American Arbitration Association (AAA), as supplemented by the Securities Arbitration Supplementary Procedures;

- that any disputes subject to arbitration may not be brought as a class and may not be consolidated or joined;

- an express submission to arbitration (which shall be treated as a written arbitration agreement) by each stockholder, the Corporation and its directors, officers, controlling persons and third parties consenting to be bound;

- unless the claim is determined by the arbitrator(s) to be frivolous, the Corporation shall pay the fees of the AAA and the arbitrator(s), and if the stockholder party is successful, the fees of its counsel;

- a waiver of any right under the laws of any jurisdiction to apply to any court of law or other judicial authority to determine any matter or to appeal or otherwise challenge the award, ruling or decision of the arbitrator(s);

- that governing law is federal law; and

- for a five-year sunset provision, unless holders of a majority of Corporation shares vote for an extension and the duration of any extension.

Supporting Statement

The United States is the only developed country in which stockholders of public companies can form a class and sue their own company for violations of securities laws. As a result, U.S. public companies are exposed to litigation risk that, in aggregate, can cost billions of dollars annually. The costs (in dollars and management time) of defending and settling these lawsuits are borne by stockholders. Across the corporate landscape, this effectively recirculates money within the same investor base, minus substantial attorneys' fees. Lawsuits are commonly filed soon after merger or acquisition announcements, or stock price changes, based on little more than their happening.

We believe arbitration is an effective alternative to class actions. It can balance the interests and rights of plaintiffs to bring federal securities law claims, with cost-effective protections for the corporation and its stockholders.

The Supreme Court has held that mandatory individual arbitration provisions are not in conflict with any provision of the federal securities laws, and the SEC has no basis to prohibit mandatory arbitration provisions that apply to federal securities law claims. Furthermore, New Jersey law establishes that the bylaws of a corporation are to be interpreted as a contract between the corporation and its stockholders.

A bylaw providing for mandatory individual arbitration of federal securities law claims would permit stockholders and corporations to opt-out of a flawed system that often seems more about the lawyers than the claimants and invariably wastes stockholder funds on expensive litigation costs.

The Doris Behr 2012 Irrevocable Trust
Hal Scott, Trustee
Harvard Law School, Lewis 339, 1557 Massachusetts Ave, Cambridge, MA 02138

November 9, 2018

Mr. Thomas J. Spellman III
Assistant General Counsel and Corporate Secretary Johnson & Johnson
One Johnson & Johnson Plaza New Brunswick, NJ 08933
Dear Mr. Spellman:

The undersigned, as trustee of The Doris Behr 2012 Irrevocable Trust (the "Stockholder"), is providing this notice in accordance with Rule 14a-8 of the Securities Exchange Act of 1934, as amended ("Rule 14a-8"). The Stockholder offers the attached proposal (the "Proposal") for the consideration and vote of shareholders at the 2019 annual meeting of shareholders (the "Annual Meeting") of Johnson & Johnson (the "Company"). The Stockholder requests that the Company include the Proposal in the Company's proxy statement for the Annual Meeting.
Letters from the Stockholder's custodian and sub-custodian documenting the Stockholder's continuous ownership of the requisite amount of the Company's stock for at least one year prior to the date of this letter are attached. The Stockholder intends to continue its ownership of at least the minimum number of shares required by Rule 14a-8 through the date of the Annual Meeting.

I represent that the Stockholder or its agent intends to appear in person or by proxy at the Annual Meeting to present the attached Proposal.

Very truly yours,

Hal Scott Trustee

Enclosures: Shareholder Proposal
Custodian and Sub-Custodian Letters

November 9, 2018

To whom it may concern:

    Goulstorrs & Co., Inc., which is wholly owned by Goulston & Storrs LLP, is the custodian for the Doris Behr 2012 Irrevocable Trust and holds shares on behalf of the Doris Behr 2012 Irrevocable Trust in our account at Fifth Third Bank. This letter is in response to a request by the Doris Behr 2012 Irrevocable Trust and verifies that the Doris Behr 2012 Irrevocable Trust has been a beneficial owner of 1,050 shares of Johnson and Johnson (CUSIP 478160104) continuously for at least one year as of and including November 9, 2018. Verification of this ownership from a DTC participating bank (Number 2116), Fifth Third Bank, is enclosed.

Sincerely,

Michelle M. Porter Assistant Secretary Goulstorrs & Co., Inc.

FIFTH THIRD
INSTITUTIONAL SERVICES

November 9, 2018

To whom it may concern:

Fifth Third Bank is the sub-custodian for Goulstorrs & Co., Inc., which in turn is the custodian for the Doris Behr 2012 Irrevocable Trust. This letter is in response to a request by the Doris Behr 2012 Irrevocable Trust regarding confirmation from Fifth Third Bank as sub-custodian. Per statement provided by Goulstorrs & Co, Inc., Doris Behr 2012 Irrevocable Trust has been a beneficial owner of 1,050 shares of Johnson and Johnson (CUSIP 478160104) stock continuously for at least one year as of and including November 9, 2018.

We verify, as custodian for Goulstorrs & Co, Inc., that as of November 9, 2018, the Doris Behr 2012 Irrevocable Trust held, and has continuously held for at least one year, 1,050 shares of Johnson and Johnson. Fifth Third Bank is a DTC participant 2116.

SiRcerely,

*c/ tl.,oc /l/cf2Z_*

Anoopa4<'1cKim
Senior Relationship Manager Fifth Third Institutional Services

SKADDEN, ARPS, SLATE, MEAGHER & FLOM LLP
1440 NEW YORK AVENUE, N.W. WASHINGTON, D.C. 20005-2111

TEL: (202) 371-7000
FAX: (202) 393-5760
www.skadden.com

FIRM/AFFILIATE OFFICES

BOSTON
CHICAGO HOUSTON LOS ANGELES NEW YORK PALO ALTO WILMINGTON

BEIJING BRUSSELS

FRANKFURT
HONG KONG
LONDON
MOSCOW
MUNICH
PARIS

SÃO PAULO
SEOUL
SHANGHAI SINGAPORE TOKYO TORONTO

marc.gerber@skadden.com

January 16, 2019

BY EMAIL (shareholderproposals@sec.gov)

U.S. Securities and Exchange Commission Division of Corporation Finance
Office of Chief Counsel 100 F Street, N.E. Washington, D.C. 20549

RE: Johnson & Johnson – 2019 Annual Meeting Supplement to Letter dated December 11, 2018 Relating to
        Shareholder Proposal of The Doris Behr 2012 Irrevocable Trust

Ladies and Gentlemen:

We refer to our letter dated December 11, 2018 (the "No-Action Request"), submitted on behalf of our client, Johnson & Johnson, a New Jersey corporation, pursuant to which we requested that the Staff of the Division of Corporation Finance (the "Staff") of the U.S. Securities and Exchange Commission (the "Commission") concur with Johnson & Johnson's view that the shareholder proposal and supporting statement (the "Proposal") submitted by The Doris Behr 2012 Irrevocable Trust (the "Proponent") may be excluded from the proxy materials to be distributed by Johnson & Johnson in connection with its 2019 annual meeting of shareholders (the "2019 proxy materials").

This letter supplements the No-Action Request. In accordance with Rule 14a-8(j), we are simultaneously sending a copy of this letter and its attachment to the Proponent.

I.   The Proposal May be Excluded Pursuant to Rule 14a-8(i)(2) Because Implementation of the Proposal Would Cause Johnson & Johnson to Violate State Law.

As described in the No-Action Request, Rule 14a-8(i)(2) permits a company to exclude a shareholder proposal if implementation of the proposal would cause the company to violate any state, federal or foreign law to which it is subject. For the reasons described below and based upon the legal opinion of Lowenstein Sandler LLP, attached hereto as Exhibit A (the "New Jersey Opinion"), Johnson & Johnson believes that implementation of the Proposal would cause Johnson & Johnson to violate New Jersey law. Accordingly, the Proposal is excludable under Rule 14a-8(i)(2) as a violation of law.

Johnson & Johnson is incorporated in the State of New Jersey and, as explained in both the No-Action Request and the New Jersey Opinion, adoption of a bylaw amendment requested by the Proposal would prohibit any shareholder from bringing claims arising under the federal securities laws in connection with the purchase or sale of any securities issued by Johnson & Johnson in court (including New Jersey courts) and instead require such persons to arbitrate such claims. For the reasons provided in the New Jersey Opinion, Johnson & Johnson believes that adoption of a bylaw amendment as described in the Proposal violates New Jersey law and that adoption of such a bylaw amendment would be subject to legal challenges. Johnson & Johnson believes that it should not be required to include a proposal to adopt such a bylaw amendment in the 2019 proxy materials where the bylaw amendment requested would, if adopted, likely be the subject of costly litigation. Furthermore, even if the Staff believes that the legality of the bylaw amendment requested by the Proposal is an open question, the Staff has previously concurred with the exclusion of shareholder proposals to amend a company's bylaws under Rule 14a-8(c)(1), the predecessor to Rule 14a-8(i)(1), a sister rule to Rule 14a-8(i)(2), where the Staff found that the proposed bylaw amendments were of "questionable validity." *See Radiation Care, Inc.* (Dec. 22, 1994) (permitting exclusion under Rule 14a-8(c)(1) of a proposal to amend the bylaws to, among other things, authorize the expenditure of corporate funds effected by shareholders without any concurring action by the board of directors, noting that even if the proposal were recast in precatory terms, it would nevertheless constitute an improper subject for shareholder action because the proposal contained a provision of questionable validity under Delaware law) and *Pennzoil Corp.* (Feb. 24, 1993, recon. denied, Mar. 22, 1993) (same).

As more fully described in the New Jersey Opinion, a New Jersey corporation's bylaws may not contain a provision that is inconsistent with law, and the New Jersey Opinion expresses the view that a New Jersey court, if presented the question, would likely conclude that New Jersey corporations may not lawfully mandate arbitration in their constitutive documents as the forum to resolve claims of shareholders for alleged violations of the federal securities laws. In addition, a New Jersey court presented with the question would likely conclude that shareholders who did not approve an arbitration provision in a New Jersey corporation's bylaws would not have provided the mutual assent required to enforce an arbitration agreement, as determined under customary principles of contract law, such that a mandatory arbitration bylaw would likely be held inconsistent with New Jersey law and, therefore, invalid. Accordingly, Johnson & Johnson believes that implementation of the Proposal would violate New Jersey law.

On numerous occasions, the Staff, pursuant to Rule 14a-8(i)(2), has permitted exclusion of shareholder proposals regarding bylaw amendments (either mandatory amendments or precatory proposals) that, if implemented, would cause the company to violate state law. *See, e.g., Vail Resorts, Inc.* (Sept. 16, 2011) (permitting exclusion under Rule 14a-8(i)(2) of a proposal to amend the bylaws to "make distributions to shareholders a higher priority than debt repayment or asset acquisition" because the proposal would cause the company to violate state law); *Citigroup, Inc.* (Feb. 18, 2009) (permitting exclusion under Rule 14a-8(i)(2) of a proposal to amend the bylaws to establish a board committee on U.S. economic security because the proposal would cause the company to violate state law); *Monsanto Co.* (Nov. 7, 2008, recon. denied, Dec. 18, 2008) (permitting exclusion under Rule 14a-8(i)(2) of a proposal to amend the bylaws to require directors to take an oath of allegiance to the U.S. Constitution because the proposal would cause the company to violate state law); *Hewlett-Packard Co.* (Jan. 6, 2005) (permitting exclusion under Rule 14a-8(i)(2) of a proposal recommending that the company amend its bylaws so that no officer may receive annual compensation in excess of certain limits without approval by a vote of "the majority of the stockholders" because the proposal would cause the company to violate state law).

Finally, as noted in the New Jersey Opinion, Johnson & Johnson acknowledges that no New Jersey court has considered the issue of whether a mandatory arbitration bylaw requiring shareholders to arbitrate claims under the federal securities laws would be legal as a matter of New Jersey law. However, as is typically the case, the New Jersey Opinion uses legal reasoning from existing New Jersey statutes and case law, and analogizes to case law from Delaware and the U.S. Court of Appeals for the Third Circuit, to come to an opinion as to how a New Jersey court would likely view a novel question presented by adoption of a bylaw amendment as described in the Proposal. The Staff has previously allowed for the exclusion of shareholder proposals pursuant to Rule 14a-8(i)(2) where there was no case law directly on point. *See General Motors Corp.* (Apr. 19, 2007) (permitting exclusion under Rule 14a-8(i)(2) of a proposal requiring directors to oversee certain functional groups excludable even though the company's Delaware counsel expressly noted that there was "no Delaware case that specifically addresses the validity of the Proposed Bylaw or a similar bylaw"); *Citigroup Inc.* (Feb. 18, 2009) (permitting exclusion under Rule 14a-8(i)(2) of a proposal to amend the bylaws to establish a board committee on U.S. economic security excludable where the proponent argued that, because there had not been a court decision regarding the matters addressed in the Delaware law opinion related to the no-action request, the Staff should not grant no-action relief to the company).

Accordingly, consistent with the precedent described above, Johnson & Johnson believes the Proposal should be excluded from the 2019 proxy materials pursuant to Rule 14a-8(i)(2) because implementation of the Proposal would cause Johnson & Johnson to violate state law.

II.   Conclusion

For the reasons stated above and in the No-Action Request, Johnson & Johnson respectfully requests that the Staff concur that it will take no action if Johnson & Johnson excludes the Proposal from the 2019 proxy materials.

Should the Staff disagree with the conclusions set forth in this letter, or should any additional information be desired in support of Johnson & Johnson's position, we would appreciate the opportunity to confer with the Staff concerning these matters prior to the issuance of the Staffs response. Please do not hesitate to contact the undersigned at (202) 371-7233.

Very truly yours,

Marc S. Gerber

State of New Jersey
OFFICE OF THE ATTORNEY GENERAL DEPARTMENT OF LAW AND
PUBLIC SAFETY PO Box 080
TRENTON, NJ 08625-0080

PHILIP D. MURPHY
Governor

SHEILA Y. OLIVER
Lt. Governor

GURBIR S. GREWAL
Attorney General

January 29, 2019

Via Email to: shareholderproposals@sec.gov
U.S. Securities and Exchange Commission Division of Corporation Finance
Office of Chief Counsel 100 F Street
Washington, DC 20549

Re: Johnson & Johnson – 2019 Annual Meeting – Omission of Shareholder Proposal of
      The Doris Behr 2012 Irrevocable Trust

Ladies and Gentlemen:

I write, as the Attorney General of the State of New Jersey, in support of the request by Johnson & Johnson that the staff of the U.S. Securities and Exchange Commission concur that the company may exclude from its 2019 proxy materials a shareholder proposal and supporting statement ("Proposal") submitted by the Doris Behr 2012 Irrevocable Trust. Johnson & Johnson, a New Jersey corporation, made its request for such a "no-action" letter in correspondence dated December 11, 2018, and submitted pursuant to Rule 14a-8(j).

The Proposal includes a resolution requesting that the company's "Board of Directors take all practicable steps to adopt a mandatory arbitration bylaw" governing "disputes between a stockholder and the Corporation and/or its directors, officers or controlling persons relating to claims under federal securities laws in connection with the purchase or sale of any securities issued by the Corporation." In addition to stating that such disputes shall be "exclusively and finally settled by arbitration," the proposed bylaw would provide, among other things, that "any disputes subject to arbitration may not be brought as a class and may not be consolidated or joined."

Johnson & Johnson's correspondence explains that the Proposal may be excluded from the company's proxy materials under Rule 14a-8(i)(2) because "the adoption of a bylaw as described in the Proposal would be contrary to the public policy interests underlying the federal securities laws and would cause Johnson & Johnson to violate federal law." I agree that the Proposal would be contrary to the public policy interests underlying the federal securities laws, and that it would seriously undermine the goals of investor protection and transparency on the part of those who issue and sell securities. I write separately, however, to advise the Commission that the Proposal is also excludable under Rule 14a-8(i)(2) for the additional reason that adoption of the proposed bylaw would cause Johnson & Johnson to violate applicable *state* law.

Longstanding principles of New Jersey law limit the subject matter of corporate bylaws to matters of internal concern to the corporation. Under New Jersey law, as under Delaware law, forum-selection provisions relating to claims under the federal securities laws do not address matters of internal concern, and bylaw provisions purporting to dictate the forum for such claims—including but not limited to mandatory arbitration provisions—are void. This conclusion is reinforced by recent amendments to the New Jersey Business Corporation Act ("NJBCA"), N.J.S.A. §§ 14A:1-1 *et seq.*, which specifically address forum-selection bylaws and do not authorize forum-selection bylaws relating to federal securities law claims. Thus, New Jersey law provides a sufficient and independent basis for Commission staff to concur with Johnson & Johnson's no-action request.[1]

A. State Law May Make a Shareholder Proposal Excludable from Proxy Materials

Analysis of whether a proposal is excludable from proxy materials requires an assessment of applicable state law. In particular, Rule 14a-8(i)(2) makes a proposal excludable "[i]f the proposal would, if implemented, cause the company to violate any state, federal, or foreign law to which it is subject." 17 C.F.R. § 240.14a-8(i)(2). Rule 14a-8(i)(2) reflects the Commission's determination that it would not be "appropriate to allow the inclusion in proxy materials of any proposal which, if implemented, would violate an applicable law." *Adoption of Amendments Relating to Proposals by Security Holders*, 41 Fed. Reg. 52,994, 52,996 (Dec. 3, 1976).

Accordingly, Commission staff must consider applicable state law before advising a company whether a proposal is excludable under Rule 14a-8(i)(2). And, where state law provides an independent and adequate ground for excluding a proposal, it becomes unnecessary for the agency even to consider whether the proposal would be excludable as conflicting with federal law. *See, e.g.*, Johnson & Johnson, SEC No-Action Letter (Feb. 16, 2012), https://www.sec.gov/divisions/ corpfin/cf-noaction/14a-8/2012/kennethsteiner021612-14a8.pdf (finding it unnecessary to address an alternative basis for omission after concurring that a proposal was excludable because it would cause the company to violate state law).

B. The Proposal Is Excludable Under Rule 14a-8(i)(2) Because It Would Cause Johnson & Johnson to Violate New Jersey State Law

The Proposal, if adopted, would cause Johnson & Johnson to violate the NJBCA and should be excluded from the company's 2019 proxy materials on that basis. *See id.* (concurring that Johnson & Johnson may omit a proposal from its proxy materials under Rule 14a-8(i)(2) because the proposal would cause the company to violate the NJBCA).

1. The New Jersey Business Corporation Act (Pre-2018 Amendment)

The NJBCA grants each business corporation the power "to make and alter by-laws for the administration and regulation of the affairs of the corporation," subject to any limitations imposed by the NJBCA or any other New Jersey statute or by the corporation's certificate of incorporation. N.J.S.A. § 14A:3-1. Section 14A:2-9 of the NJBCA addresses the making and altering of bylaws, and provides generally that "by-laws made by the board may be altered or repealed, and new by-laws made, by the shareholders." *Id.* § 14A:2-9(1). However, "[a] by-law or an amendment to a by-law which is repugnant to any part of our Corporation Act is illegal and void." *Penn-Tex. Corp. v. Niles-Bement-Pond Co.*, 34 N.J. Super. 373, 378 (Ch. Div. 1955).

Under longstanding New Jersey case law, the right to amend bylaws is "a limited rather than an absolute right." *Lambert v. Fisherman's Dock Co-op., Inc.*, 61 N.J. 597, 600 (1972). Among other limitations, "in general the exercise of such a right should be confined to matters touching the administrative policies and affairs of the corporation, the relations of members and officers with the corporation and among themselves, and like matters of internal concern." *Id.* (citing 8 Fletcher, Cyclopedia Corporations (Perm. Ed.) § 4177; 1 Hornstein, Corporation Law & Practice (1959) § 269).

---

[1] The State of New Jersey and its Attorney General have a substantial interest in New Jersey business corporations' compliance with the NJBCA, and the Attorney General in particular plays an important role in the administration of the NJBCA. *See, e.g.*, N.J.S.A. § 14A:12-6.

Here, as discussed in greater detail below, the Proposal's provisions on mandatory arbitration of federal securities law claims are not ones which New Jersey law permits to be set forth in the bylaws of a business corporation. These provisions would not address the internal concerns of Johnson & Johnson, but rather would seek to regulate external relationships of the company that are governed by federal law. Accordingly, the proposed bylaw amendment would violate New Jersey corporate law.

2. Delaware Case Law

The conclusion that New Jersey law does not authorize a business corporation's bylaws to provide for mandatory arbitration of federal securities law claims finds support in case law from Delaware, to which New Jersey courts frequently look for guidance on matters of corporate law in the absence of controlling New Jersey authority. *See, e.g., Pogostin v. Leighton*, 216 N.J. Super. 363, 373 (App. Div. 1987).

Just as New Jersey corporate law generally confines bylaw amendments to "matters of internal concern," Delaware corporate law generally limits bylaw amendments to provisions addressing the corporation's "internal affairs." *See, e.g., Sciabacucchi v. Salzberg*, C.A. No. 2017-0931-JTL, 2018 Del. Ch. LEXIS 578 (Del. Ch. Dec. 18, 2018); *Boilermakers Local 154 Ret. Fund v. Chevron Corp.*, 73 A.3d 934, 952 (Del. Ch. 2013). This limitation is reflected in § 109(b) of the Delaware General Corporation Law ("DGCL"), which provides in pertinent part: "The bylaws may contain any provision, not inconsistent with law or with the certificate of incorporation, relating to the business of the corporation, the conduct of its affairs, and its rights or powers or the rights or powers of its stockholders, directors, officers or employees." 8 Del. C. § 109(b). Section 102(b)(1) of the DGCL contains a substantially similar provision applicable to certificates of incorporation.

The Delaware Court of Chancery recently addressed, in the *Sciabacucchi* case, the validity of corporate charter and bylaw provisions—like the Proposal's mandatory arbitration bylaw—that would dictate the forum for litigation of claims arising under the federal securities laws. *See Sciabacucchi*, at *2. At issue in *Sciabacucchi* were provisions in three companies' certificates of incorporation, each of which required any claims under the Securities Act of 1933 to be filed in federal court. *Id.* Applying principles common to Sections 102(b)(1) and 109(b) of the DGCL – which, again, respectively govern certificates of incorporation and bylaws – the Court held the federal forum-selection provisions to be "ineffective and invalid." *Id.* at *8.

The basis for the holding in *Sciabacucchi* was the court's conclusion that "[t]he constitutive documents of a Delaware corporation cannot bind a plaintiff to a particular forum when the claim does not involve rights or relationships that were established by or under Delaware's corporate law." *Id.* Corporate charter and bylaw provisions may not bind a plaintiff to a particular forum with respect to a federal securities law claim, the court determined, because such a claim "does not arise out of the corporate contract and does not implicate the internal affairs of the corporation." *Id.* at *7. Indeed, with respect to purchases of a corporation's shares, "[a]t the time the predicate act occurs, the purchaser is not yet a stockholder and lacks any relationship with the corporation that is grounded in corporate law." *Id.* at *8. "Because the claim exists outside of the corporate contract," the court concluded that "it is beyond the power of state corporate law to regulate." *Id.* at *6. Put differently, "the corporate contract can only regulate claims involving the corporate contract. It cannot regulate external activities, nor the behavior of parties in other capacities." *Id.* at *46. "In light of these principles," the court concluded "there is no reason to believe that corporate governance documents, regulated by the law of the state of incorporation, can dictate mechanisms for bringing claims that do not concern corporate internal affairs, such as claims alleging fraud in connection with a securities sale." *Id.* (quoting Ann M. Lipton, *Manufactured Consent: The Problem of Arbitration Clauses in Corporate Charters and Bylaws*, 104 Geo. L.J. 583, 598 (2016)). Under *Sciabacucchi*, therefore, federal securities fraud claims are distinguishable from the kinds of state corporate law claims that may properly be addressed in forum-selection bylaw provisions.

The Court of Chancery's earlier decision in *Boilermakers* further illustrates the distinction between "internal affairs" claims, which may properly be addressed in forum-selection bylaw provisions, from "external" claims, which may not. The court in *Boilermakers* upheld a corporate bylaw provision which identified the Delaware Court of Chancery as the sole and exclusive forum for: (i) any derivative action or proceeding brought on behalf of the corporation; (ii) any action asserting a claim of breach of a fiduciary duty; (iii) any action asserting a claim arising pursuant to any provision of the DGCL; or (iv) any action asserting a claim governed by the internal affairs doctrine. *Id.* at 939. In reaching that result, the court distinguished this provision from bylaw provisions purporting to regulate "external matters," such as a forum-selection provision for tort or contract claims against the company, which would be beyond the permissible subject matter for bylaws under Section 109. *Id.* at 952. Indeed, the court emphasized that the bylaws at issue in *Boilermakers* did not purport "in any way to foreclose a plaintiff from exercising any statutory right of action created by the federal government." *Id.* at 962.[2]

Thus, Delaware law does not authorize bylaw amendments that dictate the forum for litigation arising under the federal securities laws.

3. 2018 Amendments to the NJBCA

Recent legislation amending the NJBCA should eliminate any doubt that New Jersey law, like Delaware law, does not permit forum-selection bylaw amendments relating to federal securities law claims. This legislation, which took effect on January 16, 2018, added two new subsections to N.J.S.A. § 14A:2-9, the section of the NJBCA on making and altering bylaws. *See* P.L.2017, c.356 (attached hereto as Exhibit A). Both new subsections support the conclusion that the Proposal should be excluded from Johnson & Johnson's proxy materials under Rule 14a-8(i)(2) because the proposed bylaw would be invalid under New Jersey law.

First, new subsection (4) incorporates – nearly verbatim – the first sentence of Section 109(b) of the DGCL. *See* N.J.S.A. § 14A:2-9(4) ("The by-laws may contain any provision, not inconsistent with law or the certificate of incorporation, relating to the business of the corporation, the conduct of its affairs, and its rights or power or the rights or power of its shareholders, directors, officers or employees."). Thus, the New Jersey State Legislature borrowed, and adopted for the State of New Jersey, the very same statutory language that the Delaware Court of Chancery has interpreted to prohibit forum-selection provisions addressing federal securities law claims. *See* Exhibit A at 2 ("This language is based upon a provision of Delaware law.").

Second, new subsection (5) identifies categories of forum-selection provisions that may permissibly be included in a New Jersey business corporation's bylaws. That new subsection states in relevant part:

Without limiting [N.J.S.A. § 14A:2-9(4)], the by-laws may provide that the federal and State courts in New Jersey shall be the sole and exclusive forum for:

(i)   any derivative action or proceeding brought on behalf of the corporation;

(ii)   any action by one or more shareholders asserting a claim of a breach of fiduciary duty owed by a director or officer, or former director or officer, to the corporation or its shareholders, or a breach of the certificate of incorporation or by-laws;

(iii)   any action brought by one or more shareholders asserting a claim against the corporation or its directors or officers, or former directors or officers, arising under the certificate of incorporation or the "New Jersey Business Corporation Act," N.J.S.A. 14A:1-1 et seq.;

(iv)   any other State law claim, including a class action asserting a breach of a duty to disclose, or a similar

---

[2]   Delaware later codified the holding of *Boilermakers*, providing that certificates of incorporation and bylaws may require "that any or all *internal corporate claims* shall be brought solely and exclusively in any or all of the courts in this State, and no provision of the certificate of incorporation or the bylaws may prohibit bringing such claims in the courts of this State." 8 Del. C. § 115 (emphasis added); *see Sciabacucchi*, at *30.

claim, brought by one or more shareholders against the corporation, its directors or officers, or its former directors or officers; or

(v)   any other claim brought by one or more shareholders which is governed by the internal affairs or an analogous doctrine.

Id. § 14A:2-9(5)(a). All of the actions and claims that may be subject to forum-selection bylaw provisions under new § 14A:2-9(5)(a) may be characterized as types of "internal affairs" claims—reinforcing § 14A:2-9(4)'s limitations on the subject matter appropriate for bylaws. *See* Exhibit A at 2 ("The bill specifically allows the by-laws of a New Jersey corporation to contain exclusive forum clauses to provide that the federal and State courts in New Jersey are the sole and exclusive forum for disputes related to the 'internal affairs' of the corproation").

In contrast, forum-selection provisions relating to actions or claims arising under the federal securities laws are notably absent from the list of permissible forum-selection provisions. This omission is significant for purposes of statutory construction because New Jersey courts traditionally recognize the "canon of statutory construction, *expression unius est exclusion alterius*—expression of one thing suggests the exclusion of another left unmentioned." *Brodsky v. Grinnell Haulers, Inc.*, 181 N.J. 102, 112 (2004); *see, e.g.*, *Feuer v. Merck & Co.*, 455 N.J. Super. 69, 85 (App. Div. 2018). Had the Legislature intended to authorize bylaws that would dictate the forum for federal securities law actions and claims, it would have said so when it amended the NJBCA just a year ago.

Thus, if there were any doubt as to whether New Jersey law permits a business corporation's bylaws to include a forum-selection provision governing federal securities law actions or claims, the 2018 amendments to the NJBCA provide a clear answer: "No."

* * *

Because the Proposal, if adopted, would cause Johnson & Johnson to violate New Jersey state law, in the opinion of my Office, the Proposal should be excluded under Rule 14a-8(i)(2). Accordingly, I respectfully request that the Commission take no action against Johnson & Johnson if the company excludes the Proposal from its forthcoming proxy materials.

Sincerely,

GURBIR S. GREWAL ATTORNEY GENERAL

EXAMPLE OF SEC NO-ACTION LETTER

UNITED STATES
SECURITIES AND EXCHANGE COMMISSION
WASHINGTON, D.C. 20549

DIVISION OF
CORPORATION FINANCE

February 11, 2019

Marc S. Gerber
Skadden, Arps, Slate, Meagher & Flom LLP marc.gerber@skadden.com

Re: Johnson & Johnson
Incoming letter dated December 11, 2018

Dear Mr. Gerber:

This letter is in response to your correspondence dated December 11, 2018 and January 16, 2019 concerning the shareholder proposal (the "Proposal") submitted to Johnson & Johnson (the "Company") by The Doris Behr 2012 Irrevocable Trust (the "Proponent") for inclusion in the Company's proxy materials for its upcoming annual meeting of security holders. We have received correspondence on the Proponent's behalf dated December 24, 2018, January 23, 2019 and February 1, 2019. We also have received correspondence from the Attorney General of the State of New Jersey dated January 29, 2019. Copies of all of the correspondence on which this response is based will be made available on our website at http://www.sec.gov/divisions/corpfin/cf-noaction/14a-8.shtml. For your reference, a brief discussion of the Division's informal procedures regarding shareholder proposals is also available at the same website address.

Sincerely,

M. Hughes Bates Special Counsel

Enclosure

cc: Hal Scott
The Doris Behr 2012 Irrevocable Trust hscott@law.harvard.edu

February 11, 2019

Response of the Office of Chief Counsel <u>Division of Corporation Finance</u>

Re: Johnson & Johnson
Incoming letter dated December 11, 2018

      The Proposal requests that the board take all practicable steps to adopt a bylaw provision to require disputes between a shareholder and the Company, its directors, officers or controlling persons relating to certain claims under the federal securities laws to be exclusively and finally settled by arbitration.

      The Company requested that the staff concur in the Company's view that it may exclude the Proposal from its 2019 proxy materials pursuant to rule 14a-8(i)(2), which permits a company to exclude a shareholder proposal "[i]f the proposal would, if implemented, cause the company to violate any state, federal, or foreign law to which it is subject." The Company argued that the Proposal would cause the Company to violate federal and state law.

      As to state law, the Company argued that implementation of the Proposal would cause the Company to violate the state law of New Jersey, where it is incorporated, and provided a New Jersey legality opinion from counsel supporting its view. The Proponent raised arguments in rebuttal. We carefully considered the parties' submissions.

      When parties in a rule 14a-8(i)(2) matter have differing views about the application of state law, we consider authoritative views expressed by state officials. Here, the Attorney General of the State of New Jersey, the state's chief legal officer, wrote a letter to the Division stating that "the Proposal, if adopted, would cause Johnson & Johnson to violate New Jersey state law." We view this submission as a legally authoritative statement that we are not in a position to question.

      In light of the submissions before us, including in particular the opinion of the Attorney General of the State of New Jersey that implementation of the Proposal would cause the Company to violate state law, we will not recommend enforcement action to the Commission if the Company omits the Proposal from its proxy materials in reliance on rule 14a-8(i)(2). To conclude otherwise would put the Company in a position of taking actions that the chief legal officer of its state of incorporation has determined to be illegal. In granting the no-action request, the staff is recognizing the legal authority of the Attorney General of the State of New Jersey; it is not expressing its own view on the correct interpretation of New Jersey law. The staff is not "approving" or "disapproving" the substance of the Proposal or opining on the legality of it. Parties could seek a more definitive determination from a court of competent jurisdiction.

      We are also not expressing a view as to whether the Proposal, if implemented, would cause the Company to violate federal law. Chairman Clayton has stated that questions regarding the federal legality or regulatory implications of mandatory arbitration provisions relating to claims arising under the federal securities laws should be addressed by the Commission in a measured and deliberative manner.[1]

Sincerely,

Jacqueline Kaufman Attorney-Adviser

---

[1]   See letter from Chairman Jay Clayton to the Honorable Carolyn B. Maloney dated April 28, 2018, *available at* https://maloney.house.gov/sites/maloney.house.gov/files/MALONEY%20ET%20AL%20-%20FORCED%20ARBITRATION%20-%20ES156546%20Response.pdf; S. Hrg. 115-176, Hearing Before the S. Comm. on Banking, Housing, and Urban Affairs, Feb. 6, 2018, *available at* https://www.govinfo.gov/content/pkg/CHRG-115shrg28854/pdf/CHRG-115shrg28854.pdf at 146-151; Remarks before the SEC Investor Advisory Committee (March 8, 2018), *available at* https://www.sec.gov/news/public-statement/statement-clayton-2018-3-8.

DIVISION OF CORPORATION FINANCE, SECURITIES AND EXCHANGE COMMISSION

Shareholder Proposals

Staff Legal Bulletin No. 14I (CF)

Action: Publication of CF Staff Legal Bulletin

Date: November 1, 2017

Summary: This staff legal bulletin provides information for companies and shareholders regarding Rule 14a–8 under the Securities Exchange Act of 1934.

Supplementary Information: The statements in this bulletin represent the views of the Division of Corporation Finance (the "Division"). This bulletin is not a rule, regulation or statement of the Securities and Exchange Commission (the "Commission"). Further, the Commission has neither approved nor disapproved its content.

Contacts: For further information, please contact the Division's Office of Chief Counsel by submitting a web-based request form at https://www.sec.gov/forms/corp_fin_interpretive.

A. The purpose of this bulletin

This bulletin is part of a continuing effort by the Division to provide guidance on important issues arising under Exchange Act Rule 14a–8. Specifically, this bulletin contains information about the Division's views on:

- the scope and application of Rule 14a–8(i)(7);
- the scope and application of Rule 14a–8(i)(5);
- proposals submitted on behalf of shareholders; and
- the use of graphs and images consistent with Rule 14a–8(d).

You can find additional guidance about Rule 14a–8 in the following bulletins that are available on the Commission's website: SLB No. 14, SLB No. 14A, SLB No. 14B, SLB No. 14C, SLB No. 14D, SLB No. 14E, SLB No. 14F, SLB No. 14G and SLB No. 14H.

B. Rule 14A–8(i)(7)

1. Background

Rule 14a–8(i)(7), the "ordinary business" exception, is one of the substantive bases for exclusion of a shareholder proposal in Rule 14a–8. It permits a company to exclude a proposal that "deals with a matter relating to the company's ordinary business operations." The purpose of the exception is "to confine the resolution of ordinary business problems to management and the board of directors, since it is impracticable for shareholders to decide how to solve such problems at an annual shareholders meeting."[2]

2. The Division's application of Rule 14A–8(i)(7)

The Commission has stated that the policy underlying the "ordinary business" exception rests on two central considerations.[3] The first relates to the proposal's subject matter; the second, the degree to which the proposal "micromanages" the company. Under the first consideration, proposals that raise matters that are "so fundamental to management's ability to run a company on a day-to-day basis that they could not, as a practical matter, be subject to direct shareholder oversight" may be excluded, unless such a proposal focuses on policy issues that are sufficiently significant because they transcend ordinary business and would be

---

[2] Release No. 34–40018 (May 21, 1998).

[3] *Id.*

appropriate for a shareholder vote.[4] Whether the significant policy exception applies depends, in part, on the connection between the significant policy issue and the company's business operations.[5]

At issue in many Rule 14a–8(i)(7) no-action requests is whether a proposal that addresses ordinary business matters nonetheless focuses on a policy issue that is sufficiently significant. These determinations often raise difficult judgment calls that the Division believes are in the first instance matters that the board of directors is generally in a better position to determine. A board of directors, acting as steward with fiduciary duties to a company's shareholders, generally has significant duties of loyalty and care in overseeing management and the strategic direction of the company. A board acting in this capacity and with the knowledge of the company's business and the implications for a particular proposal on that company's business is well situated to analyze, determine and explain whether a particular issue is sufficiently significant because the matter transcends ordinary business and would be appropriate for a shareholder vote.

Accordingly, going forward, we would expect a company's no-action request to include a discussion that reflects the board's analysis of the particular policy issue raised and its significance. That explanation would be most helpful if it detailed the specific processes employed by the board to ensure that its conclusions are well-informed and well-reasoned. We believe that a well-developed discussion of the board's analysis of these matters will greatly assist the staff with its review of no-action requests under Rule 14a–8(i)(7).

C. Rule 14A–8(i)(5)

1. Background

Rule 14a–8(i)(5), the "economic relevance" exception, is one of the substantive bases for exclusion of a shareholder proposal in Rule 14a–8. It permits a company to exclude a proposal that "relates to operations which account for less than 5 percent of the company's total assets at the end of its most recent fiscal year, and for less than 5 percent of its net earnings and gross sales for its most recent fiscal year, and is not otherwise significantly related to the company's business."

2. History of Rule 14A–8(i)(5)

Prior to adoption of the current version of the exclusion in Rule 14a–8(i)(5), the rule permitted companies to omit any proposal that "deals with a matter that is not significantly related to the issuer's business." In proposing changes to that version of the rule in 1982, the Commission noted that the staff's practice had been to agree with exclusion of proposals that bore no economic relationship to a company's business, but that "where the proposal has reflected social or ethical issues, rather than economic concerns, raised by the issuer's business, and the issuer conducts any such business, no matter how small, the staff has not issued a no-action letter with respect to the omission of the proposal."[6] The Commission stated that this interpretation of the rule may have "unduly limit[ed] the exclusion," and proposed adopting the economic tests that appear in the rule today.[7] In adopting the rule, the Commission characterized it as relating "to proposals concerning the functioning of the economic business of an issuer and not to such matters as shareholders' rights, e.g., cumulative voting."[8]

Shortly after the 1983 amendments, however, the District Court for the District of Columbia in *Lovenheim v. Iroquois Brands, Ltd.*, 618 F. Supp. 554 (D.D.C. 1985) preliminarily enjoined a company from excluding a proposal regarding sales of a product line that represented only 0.05% of assets, $79,000 in sales and a net loss of ($3,121), compared to the company's total assets of $78 million, annual revenues of $141 million and net earnings of $6 million. The court based its decision to grant the injunction "in light of the ethical and social significance" of the proposal and on "the fact that it implicates significant levels of sales." Since that time, the Division has interpreted *Lovenheim* in a manner that has significantly narrowed the scope of Rule 14a–8(i)(5).

---

[4] *Id.*

[5] *See* Staff Legal Bulletin No. 14H (Oct. 22, 2015), *citing* Staff Legal Bulletin No. 14E (Oct. 27, 2009) (stating that a proposal generally will not be excludable "as long as a sufficient nexus exists between the nature of the proposal and the company").

[6] Release No. 34–19135 (Oct. 14, 1982).

[7] *Id.*

[8] Release No. 34–20091 (Aug. 16, 1983).

3. The Division's application of Rule 14A–8(I)(5)

Over the years, the Division has only infrequently agreed with exclusion under the "economic relevance" exception. Under its historical application, the Division has not agreed with exclusion under Rule 14a–8(i)(5), even where a proposal has related to operations that accounted for less than 5% of total assets, net earnings and gross sales, where the company conducted business, no matter how small, related to the issue raised in the proposal. The Division's analysis has not focused on a proposal's significance to the company's business. As a result, the Division's analysis has been similar to its analysis prior to 1983, with which the Commission expressed concern.

That analysis simply considered whether a company conducted any amount of business related to the issue in the proposal and whether that issue was of broad social or ethical concern. We believe the Division's application of Rule 14a–8(i)(5) has unduly limited the exclusion's availability because it has not fully considered the second prong of the rule as amended in 1982—the question of whether the proposal "deals with a matter that is not significantly related to the issuer's business" and is therefore excludable. Accordingly, going forward, the Division's analysis will focus, as the rule directs, on a proposal's significance to the company's business when it otherwise relates to operations that account for less than 5% of total assets, net earnings and gross sales. Under this framework, proposals that raise issues of social or ethical significance may be included or excluded, notwithstanding their importance in the abstract, based on the application and analysis of each of the factors of Rule 14a–8(i)(5) in determining the proposal's relevance to the company's business.

Because the test only allows exclusion when the matter is not "otherwise significantly related to the company," we view the analysis as dependent upon the particular circumstances of the company to which the proposal is submitted. That is, a matter significant to one company may not be significant to another. On the other hand, we would generally view substantive governance matters to be significantly related to almost all companies.

Where a proposal's significance to a company's business is not apparent on its face, a proposal may be excludable unless the proponent demonstrates that it is "otherwise significantly related to the company's business."[9] For example, the proponent can provide information demonstrating that the proposal "may have a significant impact on other segments of the issuer's business or subject the issuer to significant contingent liabilities."[10] The proponent could continue to raise social or ethical issues in its arguments, but it would need to tie those to a significant effect on the company's business. The mere possibility of reputational or economic harm will not preclude no-action relief. In evaluating significance, the staff will consider the proposal in light of the "total mix" of information about the issuer.

As with the "ordinary business" exception in Rule 14a–8(i)(7), determining whether a proposal is "otherwise significantly related to the company's business" can raise difficult judgment calls. Similarly, we believe that the board of directors is generally in a better position to determine these matters in the first instance. A board acting with the knowledge of the company's business and the implications for a particular proposal on that company's business is better situated than the staff to determine whether a particular proposal is "otherwise significantly related to the company's business." Accordingly, we would expect a company's Rule 14a–8(i)(5) no-action request to include a discussion that reflects the board's analysis of the proposal's significance to the company. That explanation would be most helpful if it detailed the specific processes employed by the board to ensure that its conclusions are well-informed and well-reasoned.

In addition, the Division's analysis of whether a proposal is "otherwise significantly related" under Rule 14a–8(i)(5) has historically been informed by its analysis under the "ordinary business" exception, Rule 14a–8(i)(7). As a result, the availability or unavailability of Rule 14a–8(i)(7) has been largely determinative of the availability or unavailability of Rule 14a–8(i)(5). Going forward, the Division will no longer look to its analysis under Rule 14a–8(i)(7) when evaluating arguments under Rule 14a–8(i)(5). In our view, applying separate analytical frameworks will ensure that each basis for exclusion serves its intended purpose.

---

[9] Proponents bear the burden of demonstrating that a proposal is "otherwise significantly related to the company's business." *See* Release No. 34–39093 (Sep. 18, 1997), *citing* Release No. 34–19135.

[10] Release No. 34–19135.

We believe the approach going forward is more appropriately rooted in the intended purpose and language of Rule 14a–8(i)(5), and better helps companies, proponents and the staff determine whether a proposal is "otherwise significantly related to the company's business."

D. Proposals submitted on behalf of shareholders

While Rule 14a–8 does not address shareholders' ability to submit proposals through a representative, shareholders frequently elect to do so, a practice commonly referred to as "proposal by proxy." The Division has been, and continues to be, of the view that a shareholder's submission by proxy is consistent with Rule 14a–8.[11]

The Division is nevertheless mindful of challenges and concerns that proposals by proxy may present. For example, there may be questions about whether the eligibility requirements of Rule 14a–8(b) have been satisfied. There have also been concerns raised that shareholders may not know that proposals are being submitted on their behalf. In light of these challenges and concerns, and to help the staff and companies better evaluate whether the eligibility requirements of Rule 14a–8(b) have been satisfied, going forward, the staff will look to whether the shareholders who submit a proposal by proxy provide documentation describing the shareholder's delegation of authority to the proxy.[12] In general, we would expect this documentation to:

- identify the shareholder-proponent and the person or entity selected as proxy;
- identify the company to which the proposal is directed;
- identify the annual or special meeting for which the proposal is submitted;
- identify the specific proposal to be submitted (e.g., proposal to lower the threshold for calling a special meeting from 25% to 10%); and
- be signed and dated by the shareholder.

We believe this documentation will help alleviate concerns about proposals by proxy, and will also help companies and the staff better evaluate whether the eligibility requirements of Rule 14a–8(b) have been satisfied in connection with a proposal's submission by proxy. Where this information is not provided, there may be a basis to exclude the proposal under Rule 14a–8(b).[13]

E. Rule 14A–8(d)

1. Background

Rule 14a–8(d) is one of the procedural bases for exclusion of a shareholder proposal in Rule 14a–8. It provides that a "proposal, including any accompanying supporting statement, may not exceed 500 words."

2. The use of images in shareholder proposals

Questions have recently arisen concerning the application of Rule 14a–8(d) to proposals that include graphs and/or images.[14] In two recent no-action decisions,[15] the Division expressed the view that the use of "500 words" and absence of express reference to graphics or images in Rule 14a–8(d) do not prohibit the inclusion of graphs and/or images in proposals. Just as companies include graphics that are not expressly permitted under the disclosure rules, the Division is of the view that Rule 14a–8(d) does not preclude shareholders from using graphics to convey information about their proposals.[16]

---

[11] We view a shareholder's ability to submit a proposal by proxy as largely a function of state agency law provided it is consistent with Rule 14a–8.

[12] This guidance applies only to proposals submitted by proxy after the date on which this staff legal bulletin is published.

[13] Companies that intend to seek exclusion under Rule 14a–8(b) based on a shareholder's failure to provide some or all of this information must notify the proponent of the specific defect(s) within 14 calendar days of receiving the proposal so that the proponent has an opportunity to cure the defect. *See* Rule 14a–8(f)(1).

[14] Rule 14a–8(d) is intended to limit the amount of space a shareholder proposal may occupy in a company's proxy statement. *See* Release No. 34–12999 (Nov. 22, 1976).

[15] *General Electric Co.* (Feb. 3, 2017, *recon. granted* Feb. 23, 2017); *General Electric Co.* (Feb. 23, 2016).

[16] Companies should not minimize or otherwise diminish the appearance of a shareholder's graphic. For example, if the company includes its own graphics in its proxy statement, it should give similar prominence to a shareholder's

The Division recognizes the potential for abuse in this area. The Division believes, however, that these potential abuses can be addressed through other provisions of Rule 14a–8. For example, exclusion of graphs and/or images would be appropriate under Rule 14a–8(i)(3) where they:

- make the proposal materially false or misleading;

- render the proposal so inherently vague or indefinite that neither the stockholders voting on the proposal, nor the company in implementing it, would be able to determine with any reasonable certainty exactly what actions or measures the proposal requires;

- directly or indirectly impugn character, integrity or personal reputation, or directly or indirectly make charges concerning improper, illegal, or immoral conduct or association, without factual foundation; or

- are irrelevant to a consideration of the subject matter of the proposal, such that there is a strong likelihood that a reasonable shareholder would be uncertain as to the matter on which he or she is being asked to vote.[17]

Exclusion would also be appropriate under Rule 14a–8(d) if the total number of words in a proposal, including words in the graphics, exceeds 500.

---

graphics. If a company's proxy statement appears in black and white, however, the shareholder proposal and accompanying graphics may also appear in black and white.

[17] *See General Electric Co.* (Feb. 23, 2017).

DIVISION OF CORPORATION FINANCE, SECURITIES AND EXCHANGE COMMISSION: STAFF LEGAL BULLETIN NO. 14C

Date: June 28, 2005

. . . C.   Under rule 14a–8(i)(6), when do we concur with a company's view that there is a basis for excluding a proposal calling for director independence?

1.   Rule 14a–8(i)(6)

Rule 14a–8(i)(6) is one of the substantive bases for exclusion in rule 14a–8. It permits a company to exclude a proposal that the company would lack the power or authority to implement.

2.   Our analysis of no-action requests from companies that intend to rely on rule 14a–8(i)(6) to exclude proposals calling for director independence

Our analysis of whether a proposal that seeks to impose independence qualifications on directors is beyond the power or authority of the company to implement focuses primarily on whether the proposal requires continued independence at all times. In this regard, although we would not agree with a company's argument that it is unable to ensure the election of independent directors, we would agree with the argument that a board of directors lacks the power to ensure that its chairman or any other director will retain his or her independence at all times. As such, when a proposal is drafted in a manner that would require a director to maintain his or her independence at all times, we permit the company to exclude the proposal under rule 14a–8(i)(6) on the basis that the proposal does not provide the board with an opportunity or mechanism to cure a violation of the standard requested in the proposal. In contrast, if the proposal does not require a director to maintain independence at all times or contains language permitting the company to cure a director's loss of independence, any such loss of independence would not result in an automatic violation of the standard in the proposal and we, therefore, do not permit the company to exclude the proposal under rule 14a–8(i)(6).

We believe that our approach is consistent with Commission rules relating to director independence. Specifically, Exchange Act rule 10A–3, adopted pursuant to Exchange Act Section 10A(m), mandates various audit committee requirements for most exchange-listed issuers, including a requirement that audit committees consist entirely of independent directors. Although rule 10A–3 requires entirely independent audit committees for most listed issuers, the rule also contemplates that a director may cease to be independent. In addition, both Section 10A(m) and rule 10A–3 require that an issuer have an opportunity to cure any non-compliance with the applicable audit committee independence requirements before such non-compliance may serve as a basis for prohibiting the listing of the issuer's securities. Therefore, we believe that our view that a board lacks the power to ensure that a director maintains his or her independence at all times is consistent with Section 10A(m) and rule 10A–3, which not only contemplate that a board member may lose independence, but require that mechanisms exist to allow an issuer to cure such a loss.

The following chart illustrates our analysis of the application of rule 14a–8(i)(6) to proposals calling for director independence, and demonstrates that . . . differing language in proposals may result in different no-action responses.

Company	Proposal	Date of our response	Our response
Allied Waste Industries, Inc.	"The shareholders . . . urge the Board of Directors . . . to amend the by-laws to require that an independent director who has not served as the chief executive of the Company serve as Board Chair."	Mar. 21, 2005	We concurred in Allied Waste's view that it could exclude the proposal under rule 14a–8(i)(6). In doing so, our response noted that the proposal did not provide the board with an opportunity or mechanism to cure a violation of the independence standard requested in the proposal.
Merck & Co., Inc.	"The shareholders . . . request that the Board of Directors establish a policy of separating the roles of Board Chair and Chief Executive Officer (CEO) whenever possible, so that an independent director who has not served as an executive officer of the Company serves as Chair of the Board of Directors."	Dec. 29, 2004	We did not concur in Merck's view that it could exclude the proposal under rule 14a–8(i)(6). The proposal provided the board with an opportunity or mechanism to cure a violation of the independence standard requested in the proposal.
The Walt Disney Co.	"[T]he shareholders . . . urge the Board of Directors to amend the Corporate Governance Guidelines, and take whatever other actions are necessary to set as a company policy that the Chairman of the Board of Directors will always be an independent member of the Board of Directors, except in rare and explicitly spelled out, extraordinary circumstances."	Nov. 24, 2004	We did not concur in Disney's view that it could exclude the proposal under rule 14a–8(i)(6). The proposal provided the board with an opportunity or mechanism to cure a violation of the independence standard requested in the proposal.

D. Under rule 14a–8(i)(7), when do we concur with a company's view that there is a basis for excluding a proposal referencing environmental or public health issues as relating to the ordinary business matter of evaluating risk?

1. Rule 14a–8(i)(7)

Rule 14a–8(i)(7) is another of the substantive bases for exclusion in rule 14a–8. It permits a company to exclude a proposal that deals with a matter relating to the company's ordinary business operations. The fact that a proposal relates to ordinary business matters does not conclusively establish that a company may exclude the proposal from its proxy materials. As the Commission stated in Exchange Act Release No. 40018, proposals that relate to ordinary business matters but that focus on "sufficiently significant social policy issues . . . would not be considered to be excludable, because the proposals would transcend the day-to-day business matters. . . ."

2. Our analysis of no-action requests from companies that intend to rely on rule 14a–8(i)(7) to exclude proposals as relating to an evaluation of risk

Each year, we are asked to analyze numerous proposals that make reference to environmental or public health issues. In determining whether the focus of these proposals is a significant social policy issue, we consider both the proposal and the supporting statement as a whole. To the extent that a proposal and supporting statement focus on the company engaging in an internal assessment of the risks or liabilities that the company faces as a result of its operations that may adversely affect the environment or the public's health, we concur with the company's view that there is a basis for it to exclude the proposal under rule 14a–8(i)(7) as relating to an evaluation of risk. To the extent that a proposal and supporting statement focus on the company minimizing or eliminating operations that may adversely affect the environment or the public's health, we do not concur with the company's view that there is a basis for it to exclude the proposal under rule 14a–8(i)(7). The following chart illustrates this distinction.

Company	Proposal	Date of our response	Our response
Xcel Energy Inc.	"That the Board of Directors report . . . on (a) the economic risks associated with the Company's past, present, and future emissions of carbon dioxide, sulphur dioxide, nitrogen oxide and mercury emissions, and the public stance of the company regarding efforts to reduce these emissions and (b) the economic benefits of committing to a substantial reduction of those emissions related to its current business activities (i.e. potential improvement in competitiveness and profitability)."	Apr. 1, 2003	We concurred in Xcel's view that it could exclude the proposal under rule 14a–8(i)(7), as relating to an evaluation of risks and benefits.
Exxon Mobil Corp.	"[S]hareholders request . . . a report . . . on the potential environmental damage that would result from the company drilling for oil and gas in protected areas. . . ."	Mar. 18, 2005	We did not concur in ExxonMobil's view that it could exclude the proposal under rule 14a–8(i)(7).

DIVISION OF CORPORATION FINANCE, SECURITIES AND EXCHANGE COMMISSION: STAFF LEGAL BULLETIN NO. 14H

Date: October 22, 2015

A. The purpose of this bulletin

This bulletin is part of a continuing effort by the Division to provide guidance on important issues arising under Exchange Act Rule 14a–8. Specifically, this bulletin contains information about the Division's views on:

- the scope and application of Rule 14a–8(i)(9); and

- the scope and application of Rule 14a–8(i)(7) in light of *Trinity Wall Street v. Wal-Mart Stores, Inc.*[1]

B. Rule 14a–8(i)(9)

1. Background

Rule 14a–8(i)(9) is one of the substantive bases for exclusion of a shareholder proposal in Rule 14a–8. It permits a company to exclude a proposal "[i]f the proposal directly conflicts with one of the company's own proposals to be submitted to shareholders at the same meeting."

During the most recent proxy season, questions arose about the Division's interpretation of Rule 14a–8(i)(9). . . .

2. History of Rule 14a–8(i)(9)

This exclusion was first adopted in 1967. . . .

In 1998, the Commission revised Rule 14a–8 into its current Q&A, plain English format. In connection with these amendments, the Commission replaced the language in Rule 14a–8(c)(9) with Rule 14a–8(i)(9)'s current language, which allows the exclusion of a proposal that "directly conflicts with one of the company's own proposals to be submitted to shareholders at the same meeting."[7] The Commission also added a note to the rule stating that a "company's submission to the Commission under this section should specify the points of conflict with the company's proposal." In proposing this revision, the Commission stated that the amended rule would "reflect the Division's long-standing interpretation permitting omission of a shareholder proposal if the company demonstrates that its subject matter directly conflicts with all or part of one of management's proposals." At adoption, the Commission clarified that "by revising the rule we do not intend to imply that proposals must be identical in scope or focus for the exclusion to be available."

3. The Division's application of Rule 14a–8(i)(9)

Based on our review of the history of the exclusion, we believe that it was intended to prevent shareholders from using Rule 14a–8 to circumvent the proxy rules governing solicitations. When a shareholder solicits in opposition to a management proposal, the Commission's proxy rules contain additional procedural and disclosure requirements that are not required by Rule 14a–8. We do not believe the shareholder proposal process should be used as a means to conduct a solicitation in opposition without complying with these requirements. Several commenters agreed with this view.

Many of the Division's response letters granting no-action relief under the exclusion have expressed the view that a shareholder proposal was excludable if including it, along with a management proposal, could present "alternative and conflicting decisions for the shareholders" and create the potential for "inconsistent and ambiguous results." . . .

After reviewing the history of Rule 14a–8(i)(9) and based on our understanding of the rule's intended purpose, we believe that any assessment of whether a proposal is excludable under this basis should focus

---

[1] 792 F.3d 323 (3d Cir. 2015).

[7] Release No. 34–40018 (May 21, 1998).

on whether there is a direct conflict between the management and shareholder proposals. For this purpose, we believe that a direct conflict would exist if a reasonable shareholder could not logically vote in favor of both proposals, *i.e.*, a vote for one proposal is tantamount to a vote against the other proposal. While this articulation may be a higher burden for some companies seeking to exclude a proposal to meet than had been the case under our previous formulation, we believe it is most consistent with the history of the rule and more appropriately focuses on whether a reasonable shareholder could vote favorably on both proposals or whether they are, in essence, mutually exclusive proposals.

In considering no-action requests under Rule 14a–8(i)(9) going forward, we will focus on whether a reasonable shareholder could logically vote for both proposals. For example, where a company seeks shareholder approval of a merger, and a shareholder proposal asks shareholders to vote against the merger, we would agree that the proposals directly conflict. Similarly, a shareholder proposal that asks for the separation of the company's chairman and CEO would directly conflict with a management proposal seeking approval of a bylaw provision requiring the CEO to be the chair at all times.

We will not, however, view a shareholder proposal as directly conflicting with a management proposal if a reasonable shareholder, although possibly preferring one proposal over the other, could logically vote for both. For example, if a company does not allow shareholder nominees to be included in the company's proxy statement, a shareholder proposal that would permit a shareholder or group of shareholders holding at least 3% of the company's outstanding stock for at least 3 years to nominate up to 20% of the directors would not be excludable if a management proposal would allow shareholders holding at least 5% of the company's stock for at least 5 years to nominate for inclusion in the company's proxy statement 10% of the directors. This is because both proposals generally seek a similar objective, to give shareholders the ability to include their nominees for director alongside management's nominees in the proxy statement, and the proposals do not present shareholders with conflicting decisions such that a reasonable shareholder could not logically vote in favor of both proposals.

Similarly, a shareholder proposal asking the compensation committee to implement a policy that equity awards would have no less than four-year annual vesting would not directly conflict with a management proposal to approve an incentive plan that gives the compensation committee discretion to set the vesting provisions for equity awards. This is because a reasonable shareholder could logically vote for a compensation plan that gives the compensation committee the discretion to determine the vesting of awards, as well as a proposal seeking implementation of a specific vesting policy that would apply to future awards granted under the plan.

In the preceding examples, the board of directors may have to consider the effects of both proposals if both the company and shareholder proposals are approved by shareholders. We do not believe, however, that such a decision represents the kind of "direct conflict" the rule was designed to address.[16]

Commenters generally agreed that Rule 14a–8(i)(9) is designed to ensure that Rule 14a–8 is not used as a means to circumvent the Commission's proxy rules governing solicitations, and suggested several alternatives for administering the exclusion going forward. We agree that proponents should not be able to use Rule 14a–8 to circumvent the proxy rules governing solicitations and believe that focusing on whether a reasonable shareholder could logically vote for both proposals effectively addresses such concerns.

Some commenters suggested that the Division should take the view that precatory proposals do not directly conflict with management proposals because they are not binding. We believe that a precatory shareholder proposal, while not binding, may nevertheless directly conflict with a management proposal on the same subject if a vote in favor is tantamount to a vote against management's proposal. Other commenters suggested that the exclusion should not apply when a shareholder submits his or her proposal before the company approves its proposal. This approach would not necessarily prevent a shareholder from submitting

---

[16] We recognize, however, that there may be instances in which a binding shareholder and management proposal would directly conflict. We do not believe that a reasonable shareholder would logically vote for two proposals, each of which has binding effect, that contain two mutually exclusive mandates. However, consistent with the Division's practice under Rule 14a–8(i)(1), our no-action response may allow proponents to revise a proposal's form from binding to nonbinding. If revised within a specified time, and a reasonable shareholder could otherwise logically vote for both proposals, the shareholder proposal would not be excludable under Rule 14a–8(i)(9). In addition, a binding shareholder proposal on the same subject as a binding management proposal may be excludable under Rules 14a–8(i)(1) or 14a–8(i)(2) to the extent a company demonstrates that it is excludable under one of those bases.

a proposal opposing a management proposal, in contravention of the proxy rules governing solicitations. Finally, other commenters suggested that the Division either continue its historic application of the exclusion or adopt a broader, subject matter exclusion. We believe that these approaches do not take full account of the language of the exclusion because they may allow the exclusion of proposals that propose different means of accomplishing an objective, but do not directly conflict. In our view, granting no-action relief only if a reasonable shareholder could not logically vote in favor of both proposals is more appropriately rooted in the exclusion's intended purpose and language, and better helps companies, proponents and the staff determine when two proposals "directly conflict."[22]

C. Rule 14a–8(i)(7)

In *Trinity Wall Street v. Wal-Mart Stores, Inc.*, the U.S. Court of Appeals for the Third Circuit addressed the application of Rules 14a–8(i)(3) and 14a–8(i)(7).[23] Reversing a decision by the U.S. District Court for the District of Delaware which ruled that a shareholder proposal could not be excluded, a three-judge panel held that a shareholder proposal submitted to Wal-Mart Stores, Inc. ("Wal-Mart") was excludable under Rules 14a–8(i)(3)[24] and 14a–8(i)(7). The staff had previously agreed that Wal-Mart could exclude the proposal under Rule 14a–8(i)(7).[25]

In analyzing whether the proposal was excludable under Rule 14a–8(i)(7), the Third Circuit concluded that the proposal's subject matter related to Wal-Mart's ordinary business operations—specifically, "a potential change in the way Wal-Mart decides which products to sell." This conclusion was the same as our conclusion when responding to Wal-Mart's no-action request. We believe our analysis in this matter is consistent with the views the Commission has expressed on how to analyze proposals under the ordinary business exclusion, *i.e.*, the analysis should focus on the underlying subject matter of a proposal's request for board or committee review regardless of how the proposal is framed.[26]

The panel also considered whether the significant policy exception to the ordinary business exclusion applied. The majority opinion employed a new two-part test, concluding that "a shareholder must do more than focus its proposal on a significant policy issue; the subject matter of its proposal must 'transcend' the company's ordinary business."[27] The majority opinion found that to transcend a company's ordinary business, the significant policy issue must be "divorced from how a company approaches the nitty-gritty of its core business."[28] This two-part approach differs from the Commission's statements on the ordinary business exclusion and Division practice.

In contrast, the concurring judge analyzed Rule 14a–8(i)(7) in a manner consistent with the approach articulated by the Commission and applied by the Division, including in Wal-Mart's no-action request. Summarizing the Commission's history on this exclusion, the judge noted that "whether a proposal focuses on an issue of social policy that is sufficiently significant is not separate and distinct from whether the proposal transcends a company's ordinary business. Rather, a proposal is sufficiently significant 'because'

---

[22] Where a shareholder proposal is not excluded and companies are concerned that including proposals on the same topic could potentially be confusing, we note that companies can, consistent with Rule 14a–9, explain in the proxy materials the differences between the two proposals and how they would expect to consider the voting results. As always, we expect companies and proponents to respect the Rule 14a–8 process and encourage them to find ways to constructively resolve their differences.

[23] Rule 14a–8(i)(3) permits a company to exclude a shareholder proposal "[i]f the proposal or supporting statement is contrary to . . . [Rule] 14a–9, which prohibits materially false or misleading statements in proxy soliciting materials" and Rule 14a–8(i)(7) permits a company to exclude a shareholder proposal "[i]f the proposal deals with a matter relating to the company's ordinary business operations."

[24] Two judges concluded that the proposal could be excluded under Rule 14a–8(i)(3). The Division was not asked to express a view on the application of Rule 14a–8(i)(3) to this proposal in the no-action process and therefore we do not express a view in this bulletin.

[25] *Wal-Mart Stores, Inc.* (Mar. 20, 2014). In our view, the proposal was excludable because it related to the company's ordinary business operations and did not focus on a significant policy issue.

[26] Release No. 34–20091 (Aug. 16, 1983).

[27] Trinity, 792 F.3d at 346–347.

[28] Id. at 347.

it transcends day-to-day business matters."[29] The judge also explained that the Commission "treats the significance and transcendence concepts as interrelated, rather than independent."[30]

Although we had previously concluded that the significant policy exception does not apply to the proposal that was submitted to Wal-Mart, we are concerned that the new analytical approach introduced by the Third Circuit goes beyond the Commission's prior statements and may lead to the unwarranted exclusion of shareholder proposals. Whereas the majority opinion viewed a proposal's focus as separate and distinct from whether a proposal transcends a company's ordinary business, the Commission has not made a similar distinction. Instead, as the concurring judge explained, the Commission has stated that proposals focusing on a significant policy issue are not excludable under the ordinary business exception "*because* the proposals would transcend the day-to-day business matters and raise policy issues so significant that it would be appropriate for a shareholder vote."[31] Thus, a proposal may transcend a company's ordinary business operations even if the significant policy issue relates to the "nitty-gritty of its core business." Therefore, proposals that focus on a significant policy issue transcend a company's ordinary business operations and are not excludable under Rule 14a–8(i)(7).[32] The Division intends to continue to apply Rule 14a–8(i)(7) as articulated by the Commission and consistent with the Division's prior application of the exclusion, as endorsed by the concurring judge, when considering no-action requests that raise Rule 14a–8(i)(7) as a basis for exclusion.

---

[29] Id. at 353 (Schwartz, J., concurring).

[30] *Id.*

[31] Release No. 34–40018 (emphasis added).

[32] Whether the significant policy exception applies depends, in part, on the connection between the significant policy issue and the company's business operations. *See* Staff Legal Bulletin No. 14E (Oct. 27, 2009) (stating that a proposal generally will not be excludable as long as a sufficient nexus exists between the nature of the proposal and the company).

DIVISION OF CORPORATION FINANCE, SECURITIES AND EXCHANGE COMMISSION: STAFF LEGAL BULLETIN NO. 14J (CF)

Action: Publication of CF Staff Legal Bulletin

Date: October 23, 2018

Summary: This staff legal bulletin provides information for companies and shareholders regarding Rule 14a–8 under the Securities Exchange Act of 1934.

Supplementary Information: The statements in this bulletin represent the views of the Division of Corporation Finance (the "Division"). This bulletin is not a rule, regulation or statement of the Securities and Exchange Commission (the "Commission"). Further, the Commission has neither approved nor disapproved its content.

Contacts: For further information, please contact the Division's Office of Chief Counsel by submitting a web-based request form at https://www.sec.gov/forms/corp_fin_interpretive.

A. The purpose of this bulletin

This bulletin is part of a continuing effort by the Division to provide guidance on important issues arising under Exchange Act Rule14a–8. Specifically, this bulletin contains information about the Division's views on:

- board analyses provided in no-action requests that seek to rely on Rules 14a–8(i)(5) or 14a–8(i)(7) as a basis to exclude shareholder proposals;

- the scope and application of micromanagement as a basis to exclude a proposal under Rule14a–8(i)(7); and

- the scope and application of Rule 14a–8(i)(7) for proposals that touch upon senior executive and/or director compensation matters. . . .

B. Board Analysis

1. Background

In SLB No. 14I, the Division addressed the scope and application of Rule14a–8(i)(5), the "economic relevance" exception, and Rule 14a–8(i)(7), the "ordinary business" exception. Specifically, the bulletin noted that evaluating whether a proposal raises an issue that is "otherwise significantly related" to a company's business, in the case of Rule 14a–8(i)(5), or transcends ordinary business matters, in the case of Rule 14a–8(i)(7), often raises difficult judgment calls that the Division believes are matters that the board of directors generally is well-situated to analyze. To assist the staff with its review of these types of no-action requests, the bulletin invited companies to include in their no-action requests a discussion reflecting the board's analysis of the particular policy issue raised by the proposal and its significance in relation to the company.

2. Discussion of a board's analysis

During the most recent proxy season, a number of no-action requests included a discussion of the board's analysis. Overall, we found these discussions helpful in evaluating the requests, even where we did not ultimately agree with the company's position. The discussions we found most helpful focused on the board's analysis and the specific substantive factors the board considered in arriving at its conclusion. Less helpful were those that described the board's conclusions or process without discussing the specific factors considered.

We continue to believe that a well-developed discussion of the board's analysis of whether the particular policy issue raised by the proposal is otherwise significantly related to the company's business, in the case of Rule 14a–8(i)(5), or is sufficiently significant in relation to the company, in the case of Rule 14a–8(i)(7), can assist the staff in evaluating a company's no-action request. The absence of a board analysis will not create a presumption against exclusion; however, without having the benefit of the board's views on the matters raised, the staff may find it difficult in some instances to agree that a proposal may be excluded. This is especially the case where the significance of a particular issue to a particular company and its shareholders may depend on factors that are not self-evident and that the board may be well-positioned to consider and evaluate. Likewise, the presence of a board analysis will not create a presumption of exclusion.

In our view, a well-developed discussion will describe in sufficient detail the specific substantive factors the board considered in arriving at its conclusion that an issue is not otherwise significantly related to its business, in the case of Rule 14a–8(i)(5), or is not sufficiently significant in relation to the company, in the case of Rule 14a–8(i)(7). These may include:

- The extent to which the proposal relates to the company's core business activities.

- Quantitative data, including financial statement impact, related to the matter that illustrate whether or not a matter is significant to the company.

- Whether the company has already addressed the issue in some manner, including the differences—or the delta—between the proposal's specific request and the actions the company has already taken, and an analysis of whether the delta presents a significant policy issue for the company.

- The extent of shareholder engagement on the issue and the level of shareholder interest expressed through that engagement.

- Whether anyone other than the proponent has requested the type of action or information sought by the proposal.

- Whether the company's shareholders have previously voted on the matter and the board's views as to the related voting results.

These factors are not exclusive or exhaustive, nor is it necessary for a board analysis to address each one of the above factors.

As noted above, to the extent a company's shareholders have previously voted on a matter, we would expect any board discussion accompanying the request to adequately address the related voting results. We will consider these results as part of the total mix of information, and the weight given to them will depend on the specific facts and circumstances. For example, if a previously voted-on matter received significant shareholder support, we will consider whether the company has taken any subsequent actions and/or whether other intervening events have occurred since the vote that may have mitigated the issue's significance to the company. Similarly, if a previously voted-on matter received insignificant shareholder support, we will consider whether any subsequent company actions or intervening events may have increased the issue's significance to the company. In addition, we will consider the length of time that has passed since a matter was last voted on by shareholders. In our view, the more recent a vote is, the more likely that such vote is indicative of the topic's significance to a company and its shareholders.

The submission of a board analysis is voluntary and the inclusion or absence of an analysis will not be dispositive in the staff's evaluation of a company's request. The staff will also consider the proponent's analysis of the issue. Determinations as to whether we agree that a proposal may be excluded "will be made on a case-by-case basis, taking into account factors such as the nature of the proposal and the circumstances of the company to which it is directed." Thus, a proposal that the staff agrees is excludable for one company may not be excludable for another; conversely, a proposal that is not excludable by one company would not be dispositive as to whether it is excludable by another.

As we indicated in SLB No. 14I, we generally view substantive governance matters to be significantly related to almost all companies. Thus, we would not expect to agree with exclusion of proposals that focus on substantive governance matters.

C. Rule 14a–8(i)(7)

1. Background

Rule 14a–8(i)(7), the "ordinary business" exception, permits a company to exclude a proposal that "deals with a matter relating to the company's ordinary business operations." The purpose of the exception is "to confine the resolution of ordinary business problems to management and the board of directors, since it is impracticable for shareholders to decide how to solve such problems at an annual shareholders meeting."

2. Micromanagement

The Commission has stated that the policy underlying the "ordinary business" exception rests on two central considerations. The first relates to the proposal's subject matter; the second, the degree to which the proposal "micromanages" the company "by probing too deeply into matters of a complex nature upon which shareholders, as a group, would not be in a position to make an informed judgment." The Commission has explained that the second consideration "may come into play in a number of circumstances, such as where the proposal involves intricate detail, or seeks to impose specific time-frames or methods for implementing complex policies."

Unlike the first consideration, which looks to a proposal's subject matter, the second consideration looks only to the degree to which a proposal seeks to micromanage. Thus, a proposal that may not be excludable under the first consideration may be excludable under the second if it micromanages the company. Determinations as to excludability of proposals "will be made on a case-by-case basis, taking into account factors such as the nature of the proposal and the circumstances of the company to which it is directed."

As the Commission has explained, a proposal may probe too deeply into matters of a complex nature if it "involves intricate detail, or seeks to impose specific time-frames or methods for implementing complex policies." The Division applies this framework when evaluating whether a proposal micromanages a company and is therefore excludable. For example, the Division agreed that a proposal to generate a plan to reach net-zero greenhouse gas emissions by the year 2030, which sought to impose specific timeframes or methods for implementing complex policies, was excludable on the basis of micromanagement.

This framework also applies to proposals that call for a study or report. For example, a proposal that seeks an intricately detailed study or report may be excluded on micromanagement grounds. In addition, the staff would, consistent with Commission guidance, consider the underlying substance of the matters addressed by the study or report. Thus, for example, a proposal calling for a report may be excludable if the substance of the report relates to the imposition or assumption of specific timeframes or methods for implementing complex policies.

We believe that the above framework is consistent with the Commission's guidance in this area and, accordingly, we will continue to apply it when evaluating whether a proposal micromanages. It is important to note, however, that the staff's concurrence with a company's micromanagement argument does not necessarily mean that the subject matter raised by the proposal is improper for shareholder consideration. Rather, in that case, it is the manner in which a proposal seeks to address an issue that results in exclusion on micromanagement grounds.

3. The Division's application of Rule 14a–8(i)(7) to proposals that address senior executive and/or director compensation

Under Rule 14a–8(i)(7), proposals that raise matters that are "so fundamental to management's ability to run a company on a day-to-day basis that they could not, as a practical matter, be subject to direct shareholder oversight" may be excluded, unless such a proposal focuses on policy issues that are sufficiently significant because they transcend ordinary business and would be appropriate for a shareholder vote. Whether this exception applies depends, in part, on the connection between the issue raised and the company's business operations.

The Commission has said that proposals involving "the management of the workforce, such as the hiring, promotion, and termination of employees," generally relate to ordinary business matters. Consistent with this guidance, proposals that relate to general employee compensation and benefits are excludable under Rule 14a–8(i)(7). On the other hand, proposals that focus on significant aspects of senior executive and/or director compensation generally are not excludable under Rule 14a–8(i)(7). In determining whether the focus of a proposal is senior executive and/or director compensation or, instead, an ordinary business matter, we consider both the resolved clause and supporting statement as a whole.

We are providing the additional guidance below to clarify the Division's views with respect to proposals that implicate senior executive and/or director compensation.

a. Proposals that address senior executive and/or director compensation and ordinary business matters

At issue in some Rule 14a–8(i)(7) requests is whether the focus of a proposal is senior executive and/or director compensation, or whether its underlying concern relates primarily to ordinary business matters that are not sufficiently related to senior executive and/or director compensation. We have concurred in the exclusion of proposals that, while styled as senior executive and/or director compensation proposals, have had as their underlying concern ordinary business matters. For example, the staff agreed with the exclusion of a proposal requesting that the board prohibit payment of incentive compensation to executive officers unless the company first adopted a process to fund the retirement accounts of certain retired employees. In that instance, the staff agreed that the company could exclude the proposal under Rule14a–8(i)(7) on the grounds that the focus of the proposal was on the ordinary business matter of employee benefits, rather than senior executive compensation matters.

In evaluating proposals that raise both ordinary business and senior executive and/or director compensation matters, the staff examines whether the focus of the proposal is an ordinary business matter or aspects of senior executive and/or director compensation. Where the focus appears to be on the ordinary business matter, the proposal may be excludable under Rule 14a–8(i)(7). This framework ensures that form is not elevated over substance and that a proposal is not included simply because it addresses an excludable matter in a manner that is connected to or touches upon senior executive or director compensation matters. Including an aspect of senior executive or director compensation in a proposal that otherwise focuses on an ordinary business matter will not insulate a proposal from exclusion under Rule 14a–8(i)(7).

b. Proposals that address aspects of senior executive and/or director compensation that are also available or applicable to the general workforce

The Division believes that a proposal that addresses senior executive and/or director compensation may be excludable under Rule 14a–8(i)(7) if a primary aspect of the targeted compensation is broadly available or applicable to a company's general workforce and the company demonstrates that the executives' or directors' eligibility to receive the compensation does not implicate significant compensation matters. For example, a proposal that seeks to limit when senior executive officers will receive golden parachutes may be excludable under Rule14a–8(i)(7) if the company's golden parachute provision broadly applies to a significant portion of its general workforce. This is because the availability of certain forms of compensation to senior executives and/or directors that are also broadly available or applicable to the general workforce does not generally raise significant compensation issues that transcend ordinary business matters. In this regard, it is difficult to conclude that a proposal does not relate to a company's ordinary business when it addresses aspects of compensation that are broadly available or applicable to a company's general workforce, even when the proposal is framed in terms of the senior executives and/or directors.

In SLB No. 14A, we took the position that where the focus of a proposal is on aspects of compensation that are available or apply only to the general workforce, companies may generally rely on Rule14a–8(i)(7) to omit the proposal from their proxy materials. Similar to the approach in SLB No. 14A with respect to Rule14a–8(i)(7) submissions concerning proposals that relate to shareholder approval of equity compensation plans, we will take the following approach with respect to proposals that address aspects of senior executive and/or director compensation that are also available or applicable to a company's general workforce:

- *Proposals where the focus is on aspects of compensation that are available or apply only to senior executive officers and/or directors.* Companies may generally not rely on Rule 14a–8(i)(7) to omit these proposals from their proxy materials.

- *Proposals where the focus is on aspects of compensation that are available or apply to senior executive officers, directors, and the general workforce.* Companies may generally rely on Rule 14a–8(i)(7) to omit the proposal from their proxy materials.

c. Proposals that micromanage senior executive and/or director compensation practices

As discussed above, one of the central considerations underlying the "ordinary business" exception "relates to the degree to which the proposal seeks to 'micro-manage' the company." Historically, the Division has not agreed with the exclusion of proposals addressing senior executive and/or director compensation on the basis of micromanagement. We have further considered the Commission's statements on micromanagement discussed above, however, and we do not believe there is a basis for treating executive compensation proposals differently than other types of proposals. Consistent with the Division's treatment of shareholder proposals on other topics, therefore, the Division may agree that proposals addressing senior executive and/or director compensation that seek intricate detail, or seek to impose specific timeframes or methods for implementing complex policies can be excluded under Rule 14a–8(i)(7) on the basis of micromanagement. For example, a proposal detailing the eligible expenses covered under a company's relocation expense policy such as the type and duration of temporary living assistance, as well as the scope of eligible participants and amounts covered, could well be excludable on the basis of micromanagement.

As discussed above, micromanagement addresses the manner in which a proposal raises an issue, and not whether a proposal's subject matter itself is proper for a shareholder proposal under Rule 14a–8. Proposals that focus on significant executive and/or director compensation matters and do not micromanage will continue not to be excludable under Rule 14a–8(i)(7).

PROXY VOTING: DISCLOSURE OF PROXY VOTING POLICIES AND PROXY VOTING RECORDS BY MUTUAL FUNDS AND OTHER REGISTERED MANAGEMENT INVESTMENT COMPANIES

(Forms N1-A and N-PX)

Form N-1A (Registration Statement of Open-End Management Investment Companies)

Item 13. Management of the Fund ...

(f) *Proxy Voting Policies.* Unless the Fund invests exclusively in non-voting securities, describe the policies and procedures that the Fund uses to determine how to vote proxies relating to portfolio securities, including the procedures that the Fund uses when a vote presents a conflict between the interests of Fund shareholders, on the one hand, and those of the Fund's investment adviser; principal underwriter; or any affiliated person of the Fund, its investment adviser, or its principal underwriter, on the other. Include any policies and procedures of the Fund's investment adviser, or any other third party, that the Fund uses, or that are used on the Fund's behalf, to determine how to vote proxies relating to portfolio securities. Also, state that information regarding how the Fund voted proxies relating to portfolio securities during the most recent 12-month period ended June 30 is available (1) without charge, upon request, by calling a specified toll-free (or collect) telephone number; or on or through the Fund's Web site at a specified Internet address; or both; and (2) on the Commission's Web site at http://www.sec.gov.

Instructions.

1. A Fund may satisfy the requirement to provide a description of the policies and procedures that it uses to determine how to vote proxies relating to portfolio securities by including a copy of the policies and procedures themselves.

2. If a Fund discloses that the Fund's proxy voting record is available by calling a toll-free (or collect) telephone number, and the Fund (or financial intermediary through which shares of the Fund may be purchased or sold) receives a request for this information, the Fund (or financial intermediary) must send the information disclosed in the Fund's most recently filed report on Form N-PX, within three business days of receipt of the request, by first-class mail or other means designed to ensure equally prompt delivery.

3. If a Fund discloses that the Fund's proxy voting record is available on or through its Web site, the Fund must make available free of charge the information disclosed in the Fund's most recently filed report on Form N-PX on or through its Web site as soon as reasonably practicable after filing the report with the Commission. ...

Item 22. Financial Statements ...

(b) *Annual Report ...*

(7) A statement that a description of the policies and procedures that the Fund uses to determine how to vote proxies relating to portfolio securities is available (i) without charge, upon request, by calling a specified toll-free (or collect) telephone number; (ii) on the Fund's Web site, if applicable; and (iii) on the Commission's Web site at http://www.sec.gov.

(8) A statement that information regarding how the Fund voted proxies relating to portfolio securities during the most recent 12-month period ended June 30 is available (i) without charge, upon request, by calling a specified toll-free (or collect) telephone number; or on or through the Fund's Web site at a specified Internet address; or both; and (ii) on the Commission's Web site at http://www.sec.gov.

PROXY VOTING

Form N-PX (Annual Report of Proxy Voting Record of Registered Management Investment Company) . . .

Form N-PX is to be used by a registered management investment company . . . to file reports with the Commission, not later than August 31 of each year, containing the registrant's proxy voting record for the most recent twelve-month period ended June 30. . . .

Item 1.   Proxy Voting Record

Disclose the following information for each matter relating to a portfolio security considered at any shareholder meeting held during the period covered by the report and with respect to which the registrant was entitled to vote:

(a) The name of the issuer of the portfolio security;

(b) The exchange ticker symbol of the portfolio security;

(c) The Council on Uniform Securities Identification Procedures ("CUSIP") number for the portfolio security;

(d) The shareholder meeting date;

(e) A brief identification of the matter voted on;

(f) Whether the matter was proposed by the issuer or by a security holder;

(g) Whether the registrant cast its vote on the matter;

(h) How the registrant cast its vote (e.g., for or against proposal, or abstain; for or withhold regarding election of directors); and

(i) Whether the registrant cast its vote for or against management.

VOTING ACTIVITIES BY
INVESTMENT ADVISERS

**[17 C.F.R. Part 275—Rules 204–2, 275–6
Under the Investment Advisers Act]**

Rule 204–2. Books and Records to be Maintained by Investment Advisers. . . .

(c) . . .

(2) Every investment adviser [registered or required to be registered under section 203 of the Investment Advisers Act] that exercises voting authority with respect to client securities shall, with respect to those clients, make and retain the following:

(i) Copies of all policies and procedures required by Rule 275.

(ii) A copy of each proxy statement that the investment adviser receives regarding client securities. An investment adviser may satisfy this requirement by relying on a third party to make and retain, on the investment adviser's behalf, a copy of a proxy statement (provided that the adviser has obtained an undertaking from the third party to provide a copy of the proxy statement promptly upon request) or may rely on obtaining a copy of a proxy statement from the Commission's Electronic Data Gathering, Analysis, and Retrieval (EDGAR) system.

(iii) A record of each vote cast by the investment adviser on behalf of a client. An investment adviser may satisfy this requirement by relying on a third party to make and retain, on the investment adviser's behalf, a record of the vote cast (provided that the adviser has obtained an undertaking from the third party to provide a copy of the record promptly upon request).

(iv) A copy of any document created by the adviser that was material to making a decision how to vote proxies on behalf of a client or that memorializes the basis for that decision.

(v) A copy of each written client request for information on how the adviser voted proxies on behalf of the client, and a copy of any written response by the investment adviser to any (written or oral) client request for information on how the adviser voted proxies on behalf of the requesting client. . . .

(e)(1) All books and records required to be made under the provisions of [paragraph (c)(2)] shall be maintained and preserved in an easily accessible place for a period of not less than five years from the end of the fiscal year during which the last entry was made on such record, the first two years in an appropriate office of the investment adviser.

Rule 275–6. Proxy Voting.

If you are an investment adviser registered or required to be registered under section 203 of the [Investment Advisors] Act, it is a fraudulent, deceptive, or manipulative act, practice or course of business within the meaning of section 206(4) of the Act, for you to exercise voting authority with respect to client securities, unless you:

(a) Adopt and implement written policies and procedures that are reasonably designed to ensure that you vote client securities in the best interest of clients, which procedures must include how you address material conflicts that may arise between your interests and those of your clients;

(b) Disclose to clients how they may obtain information from you about how you voted with respect to their securities; and

(c) Describe to clients your proxy voting policies and procedures and, upon request, furnish a copy of the policies and procedures to the requesting client.

REGULATION AC
(ANALYST CERTIFICATION)

17 C.F.R. §§ 242.500–505

TABLE OF CONTENTS

Rule		Page
500.	Definitions	1643
501.	Certifications in Connection with Research Reports	1644
502.	Certifications in Connection with Public Appearances	1644
503.	Certain Foreign Research Reports	1645
504.	Notification to Associated Persons	1645
505.	Exclusion for News Media	1645

Rule 500.   Definitions.

For purposes of Regulation AC the term:

Covered person of a broker or dealer means an associated person of that broker or dealer but does not include:

(1) An associated person:*

(i) If the associated person has no officers (or persons performing similar functions) or employees in common with the broker or dealer who can influence the activities of research analysts or the content of research reports; and

(ii) If the broker or dealer maintains and enforces written policies and procedures reasonably designed to prevent the broker or dealer, any controlling persons, officers (or persons performing similar functions), and employees of the broker or dealer from influencing the activities of research analysts and the content of research reports prepared by the associated person. . . .

Foreign person means any person who is not a U.S. person.

Foreign security means a security issued by a foreign issuer for which a U.S. market is not the principal trading market.

Public appearance means any participation by a research analyst in a seminar, forum (including an interactive electronic forum), or radio or television or other interview, in which the research analyst makes a specific recommendation or provides information reasonably sufficient upon which to base an investment decision about a security or an issuer.

Registered broker or dealer means a broker or dealer registered or required to register pursuant to section 15 or section 15B of the Securities Exchange Act of 1934 or a government securities broker or government securities dealer registered or required to register pursuant to section 15C(a)(1)(A) of the Securities Exchange Act of 1934.

Research analyst means any natural person who is primarily responsible for the preparation of the content of a research report.

Research report means a written communication (including an electronic communication) that includes an analysis of a security or an issuer and provides information reasonably sufficient upon which to base an investment decision.

---

* The term "person associated with a broker or dealer" is defined in section 3(a)(18) of the Securities Exchange Act to mean ". . . any partner, officer, director, or branch manager of such broker or dealer (or any person occupying a similar status or performing similar functions), any person directly or indirectly controlling, controlled by, or under common control with such broker or dealer, or any employee of such broker or dealer. . . ." (Footnote by ed.)

Third party research analyst means:

(1) With respect to a broker or dealer, any research analyst not employed by that broker or dealer or any associated person of that broker or dealer; and

(2) With respect to a covered person of a broker or dealer, any research analyst not employed by that covered person, by the broker or dealer with whom that covered person is associated, or by any other associated person of the broker or dealer with whom that covered person is associated. . . .

Rule 501.   Certifications in Connection with Research Reports.

(a) A broker or dealer or covered person that publishes, circulates, or provides a research report prepared by a research analyst to a U.S. person in the United States shall include in that research report a clear and prominent certification by the research analyst containing the following:

(1) A statement attesting that all of the views expressed in the research report accurately reflect the research analyst's personal views about any and all of the subject securities or issuers; and

(2)(i) A statement attesting that no part of the research analyst's compensation was, is, or will be, directly or indirectly, related to the specific recommendations or views expressed by the research analyst in the research report; or

(ii) A statement:

(A) Attesting that part or all of the research analyst's compensation was, is, or will be, directly or indirectly, related to the specific recommendations or views expressed by the research analyst in the research report;

(B) Identifying the source, amount, and purpose of such compensation; and

(C) Further disclosing that the compensation could influence the recommendations or views expressed in the research report.

(b) A broker or dealer or covered person that publishes, circulates, or provides a research report prepared by a third party research analyst to a U.S. person in the United States shall be exempt from the requirements of this section with respect to such research report if the following conditions are satisfied:

(1) The employer of the third party research analyst has no officers (or persons performing similar functions) or employees in common with the broker or dealer or covered person; and

(2) The broker or dealer (or, with respect to a covered person, the broker or dealer with whom the covered person is associated) maintains and enforces written policies and procedures reasonably designed to prevent the broker or dealer, any controlling persons, officers (or persons performing similar functions), and employees of the broker or dealer from influencing the activities of the third party research analyst and the content of research reports prepared by the third party research analyst.

Rule 502.   Certifications in Connection with Public Appearances.

(a) If a broker or dealer publishes, circulates, or provides a research report prepared by a research analyst employed by the broker or dealer or covered person to a U.S. person in the United States, the broker or dealer must make a record within 30 days after any calendar quarter in which the research analyst made a public appearance that contains the following:

(1) A statement by the research analyst attesting that the views expressed by the research analyst in all public appearances during the calendar quarter accurately reflected the research analyst's personal views at that time about any and all of the subject securities or issuers; and

(2) A statement by the research analyst attesting that no part of the research analyst's compensation was, is, or will be, directly or indirectly, related to the specific recommendations or views expressed by the research analyst in such public appearances.

(b) If the broker or dealer does not obtain a statement by the research analyst in accordance with paragraph (a) of this section:

(1) The broker or dealer shall promptly notify in writing its examining authority, designated pursuant to section 17(d) of the Securities Exchange Act of 1934 and Rule 17d–2 of this chapter, that the research analyst did not provide the certifications specified in paragraph (a) of this section; and

(2) For 120 days following notification pursuant to paragraph (b)(1) of this section, the broker or dealer shall disclose in any research report prepared by the research analyst and published, circulated, or provided to a U.S. person in the United States that the research analyst did not provide the certifications specified in paragraph (a) of this section.

(c) In the case of a research analyst who is employed outside the United States by a foreign person located outside the United States, this section shall only apply to a public appearance while the research analyst is physically present in the United States.

(d) A broker or dealer shall preserve the records specified in paragraphs (a) and (b) of this section in accordance with Rule 17a–4 of this chapter and for a period of not less than 3 years, the first 2 years in an accessible place.

Rule 503.   Certain Foreign Research Reports.

A foreign person, located outside the United States and not associated with a registered broker or dealer, who prepares a research report concerning a foreign security and provides it to a U.S. person in the United States in accordance with the provisions of § 240.15a–6(a)(2) of this chapter shall be exempt from the requirements of this regulation.

Rule 504.   Notification to Associated Persons.

A broker or dealer shall notify any person with whom that broker or dealer is associated who publishes, circulates, or provides research reports:

(a) Whether the broker or dealer maintains and enforces written policies and procedures reasonably designed to prevent the broker or dealer, any controlling persons, officers (or persons performing similar functions), or employees of the broker or dealer from influencing the activities of research analysts and the content of research reports prepared by the associated person; and

(b) Whether the associated person has any officers (or persons performing similar functions) or employees in common with the broker or dealer who can influence the activities of research analysts or the content of research reports and, if so, the identity of those persons.

Rule 505.   Exclusion for News Media.

No provision of this Regulation AC shall apply to any person who:

(a) Is the publisher of any bona fide newspaper, news magazine or business or financial publication of general and regular circulation; and

(b) Is not registered or required to be registered with the Commission as a broker or dealer or investment adviser.

SARBANES-OXLEY ACT

15 U.S.C.A. §§ 7201 et seq.

TABLE OF CONTENTS

Sec.		Page
1.	Short title	1649
2.	Definitions	1649
3.	Commission rules and enforcement	1651

TITLE I—PUBLIC COMPANY ACCOUNTING OVERSIGHT BOARD

101.	Establishment; administrative provisions	1651
102.	Registration with the Board	1654
103.	Auditing, quality control, and independence standards and rules	1655
104.	Inspections of registered public accounting firms	1657
105.	Investigations and disciplinary proceedings	1659
106.	Foreign public accounting firms*	
107.	Commission oversight of the Board	1663
108.	Accounting standards	1665
109.	Funding*	
110.	Definitions	1665

TITLE II—AUDITOR INDEPENDENCE

201.	Services outside the scope of practice of auditors	1666
202.	Preapproval requirements	1666
203.	Audit partner rotation	1666
204.	Auditor reports to audit committees	1666
205.	Conforming amendments*	
206.	Conflicts of interest	1666
207.	Study of mandatory rotation of registered public accounting firms	1666
208.	Commission authority	1666
209.	Considerations by appropriate State regulatory authorities	1667

TITLE III—CORPORATE RESPONSIBILITY

301.	Public company audit committees	1667
302.	Corporate responsibility for financial reports	1667
303.	Improper influence on conduct of audits	1668
304.	Forfeiture of certain bonuses and profits	1668
305.	Officer and director bars and penalties	1668
306.	Insider trades during pension fund blackout periods	1668
307.	Rules of professional responsibility for attorneys	1670
308.	Fair funds for investors	1670

TITLE IV—ENHANCED FINANCIAL DISCLOSURES

401.	Disclosures in periodic reports	1670
402.	Enhanced conflict of interest provisions	1670
403.	Disclosures of transactions involving management and principal stockholders	1671
404.	Management assessment of internal controls	1671
405.	Exemption*	
406.	Code of ethics for senior financial officers	1671

---

* Omitted.

407. Disclosure of audit committee financial expert 1671
408. Enhanced review of periodic disclosures by issuers 1672
409. Real time issuer disclosures 1672

TITLE V—ANALYST CONFLICTS OF INTEREST

501. Treatment of securities analysts by registered securities associations and national securities exchanges 1672

TITLE VI—COMMISSION RESOURCES AND AUTHORITY

601. Authorization of appropriations*
602. Appearance and practice before the Commission 1672
603. Federal court authority to impose penny stock bars 1672
604. Qualifications of associated persons of brokers and dealers*

TITLE VII—STUDIES AND REPORTS*

701. GAO study and report regarding consolidation of public accounting firms*
702. Commission study and report regarding credit rating agencies*
703. Study and report on violators and violations*
704. Study of enforcement actions*
705. Study of investment banks*

TITLE VIII—CORPORATE AND CRIMINAL FRAUD ACCOUNTABILITY

801. Short title*
802. Criminal penalties for altering documents*
803. Debts nondischargeable if incurred in violation of securities fraud laws*
804. Statute of limitations for securities fraud*
805. Review of Federal Sentencing Guidelines for obstruction of justice and extensive criminal fraud*
806. Protection for employees of publicly traded companies who provide evidence of fraud 1673
807. Criminal penalties for defrauding shareholders of publicly traded companies 1674

TITLE IX—WHITE-COLLAR CRIME PENALTY ENHANCEMENTS

901. Short title*
902. Attempts and conspiracies to commit criminal fraud offenses*
903. Criminal penalties for mail and wire fraud*
904. Criminal penalties for violations of the Employee Retirement Income Security Act of 1974*
905. Amendment to sentencing guidelines relating to certain white-collar offenses*
906. Corporate responsibility for financial reports 1674

TITLE X—CORPORATE TAX RETURNS*

1001. Sense of the Senate regarding the signing of corporate tax returns by chief executive officers*

TITLE XI—CORPORATE FRAUD AND ACCOUNTABILITY

1101. Short title 1674
1102. Tampering with a record or otherwise impeding an official proceeding 1675
1103. Temporary freeze authority for the Securities and Exchange Commission*
1104. Amendment to the Federal Sentencing Guidelines*
1105. Authority of the Commission to prohibit persons from serving as officers or directors 1675

---

* Omitted.

1106.   Increased criminal penalties under Securities Exchange Act of 1934 1675
1107.   Retaliation against informants 1675

§ 1.   SHORT TITLE

(a) SHORT TITLE.—This Act may be cited as the "Sarbanes-Oxley Act of 2002" . . .

§ 2.   DEFINITIONS

(a) IN GENERAL.—Except as otherwise specifically provided in this Act, in this Act, the following definitions shall apply:

(1) APPROPRIATE STATE REGULATORY AUTHORITY.—The term "appropriate State regulatory authority" means the State agency or other authority responsible for the licensure or other regulation of the practice of accounting in the State or States having jurisdiction over a registered public accounting firm or associated person thereof, with respect to the matter in question.

(2) AUDIT.—The term "audit" means an examination of the financial statements of any issuer by an independent public accounting firm in accordance with the rules of the Board or the Commission (or, for the period preceding the adoption of applicable rules of the Board under section 103, in accordance with then-applicable generally accepted auditing and related standards for such purposes), for the purpose of expressing an opinion on such statements.

(3) AUDIT COMMITTEE.—The term "audit committee" means—

(A) a committee (or equivalent body) established by and amongst the board of directors of an issuer for the purpose of overseeing the accounting and financial reporting processes of the issuer and audits of the financial statements of the issuer; and

(B) if no such committee exists with respect to an issuer, the entire board of directors of the issuer.

(4) AUDIT REPORT.—The term "audit report" means a document or other record—

(A) prepared following an audit performed for purposes of compliance by an issuer with the requirements of the securities laws; and

(B) in which a public accounting firm either—

(i) sets forth the opinion of that firm regarding a financial statement, report, or other document; or

(ii) asserts that no such opinion can be expressed.

(5) BOARD.—The term "Board" means the Public Company Accounting Oversight Board established under section 101.

(6) COMMISSION.—The term "Commission" means the Securities and Exchange Commission.

(7) ISSUER.—The term "issuer" means an issuer (as defined in section 3 of the Securities Exchange Act of 1934 (15 U.S.C. 78c)), the securities of which are registered under section 12 of that Act (15 U.S.C. 78l), or that is required to file reports under section 15(d) (15 U.S.C. 78o(d)), or that files or has filed a registration statement that has not yet become effective under the Securities Act of 1933 (15 U.S.C. 77a et seq.), and that it has not withdrawn.

(8) NON-AUDIT SERVICES.—The term "non-audit services" means any professional services provided to an issuer by a registered public accounting firm, other than those provided to an issuer in connection with an audit or a review of the financial statements of an issuer.

(9) PERSON ASSOCIATED WITH A PUBLIC ACCOUNTING FIRM.—

(A) IN GENERAL.—The terms "person associated with a public accounting firm" (or with a "registered public accounting firm") and "associated person of a public accounting firm" (or of a "registered public accounting firm") mean any individual proprietor, partner, shareholder, principal, accountant, or other professional employee of a public accounting firm, or any other independent contractor or entity that, in connection with the preparation or issuance of any audit report—

(i) shares in the profits of, or receives compensation in any other form from, that firm; or

(ii) participates as agent or otherwise on behalf of such accounting firm in any activity of that firm.

(B) EXEMPTION AUTHORITY.—The Board may, by rule, exempt persons engaged only in ministerial tasks from the definition in subparagraph (A), to the extent that the Board determines that any such exemption is consistent with the purposes of this Act, the public interest, or the protection of investors.

(10) PROFESSIONAL STANDARDS.—The term "professional standards" means—

(A) accounting principles that are—

(i) established by the standard setting body described in section 19(b) of the Securities Act of 1933, as amended by this Act, or prescribed by the Commission under section 19(a) of that Act (15 U.S.C. 17a(s)) or section 13(b) of the Securities Exchange Act of 1934 (15 U.S.C. 78a(m)); and

(ii) relevant to audit reports for particular issuers, or dealt with in the quality control system of a particular registered public accounting firm; and

(B) auditing standards, standards for attestation engagements, quality control policies and procedures, ethical and competency standards, and independence standards (including rules implementing title II) that the Board or the Commission determines—

(i) relate to the preparation or issuance of audit reports for issuers; and

(ii) are established or adopted by the Board under section 103(a), or are promulgated as rules of the Commission.

(11) PUBLIC ACCOUNTING FIRM.—The term "public accounting firm" means—

(A) a proprietorship, partnership, incorporated association, corporation, limited liability company, limited liability partnership, or other legal entity that is engaged in the practice of public accounting or preparing or issuing audit reports; and

(B) to the extent so designated by the rules of the Board, any associated person of any entity described in subparagraph (A).

(12) REGISTERED PUBLIC ACCOUNTING FIRM.—The term "registered public accounting firm" means a public accounting firm registered with the Board in accordance with this Act.

(13) RULES OF THE BOARD.—The term "rules of the Board" means the bylaws and rules of the Board (as submitted to, and approved, modified, or amended by the Commission, in accordance with section 107), and those stated policies, practices, and interpretations of the Board that the Commission, by rule, may deem to be rules of the Board, as necessary or appropriate in the public interest or for the protection of investors.

(14) SECURITY.—The term "security" has the same meaning as in section 3(a) of the Securities Exchange Act of 1934 (15 U.S.C.A. § 78c(a)).

(15) SECURITIES LAWS.—The term "securities laws" means the provisions of law referred to in section 3(a)(47) of the Securities Exchange Act of 1934 (15 U.S.C.A. § 78c(a)(47)), as amended by this Act, and includes the rules, regulations, and orders issued by the Commission thereunder.

(16) STATE.—The term "State" means any State of the United States, the District of Columbia, Puerto Rico, the Virgin Islands, or any other territory or possession of the United States. . . .

§ 3.   COMMISSION RULES AND ENFORCEMENT

(a) REGULATORY ACTION.—The Commission shall promulgate such rules and regulations, as may be necessary or appropriate in the public interest or for the protection of investors, and in furtherance of this Act.

(b) ENFORCEMENT.—

(1) IN GENERAL.—A violation by any person of this Act, any rule or regulation of the Commission issued under this Act, or any rule of the Board shall be treated for all purposes in the same manner as a violation of the Securities Exchange Act of 1934 (15 U.S.C.A. §§ 78a et seq.) or the rules and regulations issued thereunder, consistent with the provisions of this Act, and any such person shall be subject to the same penalties, and to the same extent, as for a violation of that Act or such rules or regulations. . . .

(c) EFFECT ON COMMISSION AUTHORITY.—Nothing in this Act or the rules of the Board shall be construed to impair or limit—

(1) the authority of the Commission to regulate the accounting profession, accounting firms, or persons associated with such firms for purposes of enforcement of the securities laws;

(2) the authority of the Commission to set standards for accounting or auditing practices or auditor independence, derived from other provisions of the securities laws or the rules or regulations thereunder, for purposes of the preparation and issuance of any audit report, or otherwise under applicable law; or

(3) the ability of the Commission to take, on the initiative of the Commission, legal, administrative, or disciplinary action against any registered public accounting firm or any associated person thereof.

TITLE I—PUBLIC COMPANY ACCOUNTING OVERSIGHT BOARD

§ 101.   ESTABLISHMENT; ADMINISTRATIVE PROVISIONS

(a) ESTABLISHMENT OF BOARD.—There is established the Public Company Accounting Oversight Board, to oversee the audit of companies that are subject to the securities laws, and related matters, in order to protect the interests of investors and further the public interest in the preparation of informative, accurate, and independent audit reports. The Board shall be a body corporate, operate as a nonprofit corporation, and have succession until dissolved by an Act of Congress.

(b) STATUS.—The Board shall not be an agency or establishment of the United States Government, and, except as otherwise provided in this Act, shall be subject to, and have all the powers conferred upon a nonprofit corporation by, the District of Columbia Nonprofit Corporation Act. No member or person employed by, or agent for, the Board shall be deemed to be an officer or employee of or agent for the Federal Government by reason of such service.

(c) DUTIES OF THE BOARD.—The Board shall, subject to action by the Commission under section 107, and once a determination is made by the Commission under subsection (d) of this section—

(1) register public accounting firms that prepare audit reports for issuers, in accordance with section 102;

(2) establish or adopt, or both, by rule, auditing, quality control, ethics, independence, and other standards relating to the preparation of audit reports for issuers, brokers and dealers in accordance with section 103;

(3) conduct inspections of registered public accounting firms, in accordance with section 104 and the rules of the Board;

(4) conduct investigations and disciplinary proceedings concerning, and impose appropriate sanctions where justified upon, registered public accounting firms and associated persons of such firms, in accordance with section 105;

(5) perform such other duties or functions as the Board (or the Commission, by rule or order) determines are necessary or appropriate to promote high professional standards among, and improve the quality of audit services offered by, registered public accounting firms and associated persons thereof, or otherwise to carry out this Act, in order to protect investors, or to further the public interest;

(6) enforce compliance with this Act, the rules of the Board, professional standards, and the securities laws relating to the preparation and issuance of audit reports and the obligations and liabilities of accountants with respect thereto, by registered public accounting firms and associated persons thereof; and

(7) set the budget and manage the operations of the Board and the staff of the Board.

(d) COMMISSION DETERMINATION.—The members of the Board shall take such action (including hiring of staff, proposal of rules, and adoption of initial and transitional auditing and other professional standards) as may be necessary or appropriate to enable the Commission to determine, not later than 270 days after the date of enactment of this Act, that the Board is so organized and has the capacity to carry out the requirements of this title, and to enforce compliance with this title by registered public accounting firms and associated persons thereof. The Commission shall be responsible, prior to the appointment of the Board, for the planning for the establishment and administrative transition to the Board's operation.

(e) BOARD MEMBERSHIP.—

(1) COMPOSITION.—The Board shall have 5 members, appointed from among prominent individuals of integrity and reputation who have a demonstrated commitment to the interests of investors and the public, and an understanding of the responsibilities for and nature of the financial disclosures required of issuers, brokers and dealers under the securities laws and the obligations of accountants with respect to the preparation and issuance of audit reports with respect to such disclosures.

(2) LIMITATION.—Two members, and only 2 members, of the Board shall be or have been certified public accountants pursuant to the laws of 1 or more States, provided that, if 1 of those 2 members is the chairperson, he or she may not have been a practicing certified public accountant for at least 5 years prior to his or her appointment to the Board.

(3) FULL-TIME INDEPENDENT SERVICE.—Each member of the Board shall serve on a full-time basis, and may not, concurrent with service on the Board, be employed by any other person or engage in any other professional or business activity. No member of the Board may share in any of the profits of, or receive payments from, a public accounting firm (or any other person, as determined by rule of the Commission), other than fixed continuing payments, subject to such conditions as the Commission may impose, under standard arrangements for the retirement of members of public accounting firms.

(4) APPOINTMENT OF BOARD MEMBERS.—

(A) INITIAL BOARD.—Not later than 90 days after the date of enactment of this Act, the Commission, after consultation with the Chairman of the Board of Governors of the Federal Reserve System and the Secretary of the Treasury, shall appoint the chairperson and other initial members of the Board, and shall designate a term of service for each.

(B) VACANCIES.—A vacancy on the Board shall not affect the powers of the Board, but shall be filled in the same manner as provided for appointments under this section.

(5) TERM OF SERVICE.—

(A) IN GENERAL.—The term of service of each Board member shall be 5 years, and until a successor is appointed, except that—

(i) the terms of office of the initial Board members (other than the chairperson) shall expire in annual increments, 1 on each of the first 4 anniversaries of the initial date of appointment; and

(ii) any Board member appointed to fill a vacancy occurring before the expiration of the term for which the predecessor was appointed shall be appointed only for the remainder of that term.

(B) TERM LIMITATION.—No person may serve as a member of the Board, or as chairperson of the Board, for more than 2 terms, whether or not such terms of service are consecutive.

(6) REMOVAL FROM OFFICE.—A member of the Board may be removed by the Commission from office, in accordance with section 107(d)(3), for good cause shown before the expiration of the term of that member.

(f) POWERS OF THE BOARD.—In addition to any authority granted to the Board otherwise in this Act, the Board shall have the power, subject to section 107—

(1) to sue and be sued, complain and defend, in its corporate name and through its own counsel, with the approval of the Commission, in any Federal, State, or other court;

(2) to conduct its operations and maintain offices, and to exercise all other rights and powers authorized by this Act, in any State, without regard to any qualification, licensing, or other provision of law in effect in such State (or a political subdivision thereof);

(3) to lease, purchase, accept gifts or donations of or otherwise acquire, improve, use, sell, exchange, or convey, all of or an interest in any property, wherever situated;

(4) to appoint such employees, accountants, attorneys, and other agents as may be necessary or appropriate, and to determine their qualifications, define their duties, and fix their salaries or other compensation (at a level that is comparable to private sector self-regulatory, accounting, technical, supervisory, or other staff or management positions);

(5) to allocate, assess, and collect accounting support fees established pursuant to section 109, for the Board, and other fees and charges imposed under this title; and

(6) to enter into contracts, execute instruments, incur liabilities, and do any and all other acts and things necessary, appropriate, or incidental to the conduct of its operations and the exercise of its obligations, rights, and powers imposed or granted by this title.

(g) RULES OF THE BOARD.—The rules of the Board shall, subject to the approval of the Commission—

(1) provide for the operation and administration of the Board, the exercise of its authority, and the performance of its responsibilities under this Act;

(2) permit, as the Board determines necessary or appropriate, delegation by the Board of any of its functions to an individual member or employee of the Board, or to a division of the Board, including functions with respect to hearing, determining, ordering, certifying, reporting, or otherwise acting as to any matter, except that—

(A) the Board shall retain a discretionary right to review any action pursuant to any such delegated function, upon its own motion;

(B) a person shall be entitled to a review by the Board with respect to any matter so delegated, and the decision of the Board upon such review shall be deemed to be the action of the Board for all purposes (including appeal or review thereof); and

(C) if the right to exercise a review described in subparagraph (A) is declined, or if no such review is sought within the time stated in the rules of the Board, then the action taken by the holder of such delegation shall for all purposes, including appeal or review thereof, be deemed to be the action of the Board;

(3) establish ethics rules and standards of conduct for Board members and staff, including a bar on practice before the Board (and the Commission, with respect to Board-related matters) of 1 year for former members of the Board, and appropriate periods (not to exceed 1 year) for former staff of the Board; and

(4) provide as otherwise required by this Act.

(h) ANNUAL REPORT TO THE COMMISSION.—The Board shall submit an annual report (including its audited financial statements) to the Commission, and the Commission shall transmit a copy of that report to the Committee on Banking, Housing, and Urban Affairs of the Senate, and the Committee on Financial Services of the House of Representatives, not later than 30 days after the date of receipt of that report by the Commission.

§ 102.   REGISTRATION WITH THE BOARD

(a) MANDATORY REGISTRATION.—It shall be unlawful for any person that is not a registered public accounting firm to prepare or issue, or to participate in the preparation or issuance of, any audit report with respect to any issuer, broker, or dealer.

(b) APPLICATIONS FOR REGISTRATION.—

(1) FORM OF APPLICATION.—A public accounting firm shall use such form as the Board may prescribe, by rule, to apply for registration under this section.

(2) CONTENTS OF APPLICATIONS.—Each public accounting firm shall submit, as part of its application for registration, in such detail as the Board shall specify—

(A) the names of all issuers, brokers, or dealers for which the firm prepared or issued audit reports during the immediately preceding calendar year, and for which the firm expects to prepare or issue audit reports during the current calendar year;

(B) the annual fees received by the firm from each such issuer, broker, or dealer for audit services, other accounting services, and non-audit services, respectively;

(C) such other current financial information for the most recently completed fiscal year of the firm as the Board may reasonably request;

(D) a statement of the quality control policies of the firm for its accounting and auditing practices;

(E) a list of all accountants associated with the firm who participate in or contribute to the preparation of audit reports, stating the license or certification number of each such person, as well as the State license numbers of the firm itself;

(F) information relating to criminal, civil, or administrative actions or disciplinary proceedings pending against the firm or any associated person of the firm in connection with any audit report;

(G) copies of any periodic or annual disclosure filed by an issuer with the Commission during the immediately preceding calendar year which discloses accounting disagreements between such issuer, broker, or dealer and the firm in connection with an audit report furnished or prepared by the firm for such issuer, broker, or dealer, and

(H) such other information as the rules of the Board or the Commission shall specify as necessary or appropriate in the public interest or for the protection of investors.

(3) CONSENTS.—Each application for registration under this subsection shall include—

(A) a consent executed by the public accounting firm to cooperation in and compliance with any request for testimony or the production of documents made by the Board in the furtherance of its authority and responsibilities under this title (and an agreement to secure and enforce similar consents from each of the associated persons of the public accounting firm as a condition of their continued employment by or other association with such firm); and

(B) a statement that such firm understands and agrees that cooperation and compliance, as described in the consent required by subparagraph (A), and the securing and enforcement of such consents from its associated persons, in accordance with the rules of the Board, shall be a condition to the continuing effectiveness of the registration of the firm with the Board.

(c) ACTION ON APPLICATIONS.—

(1) TIMING.—The Board shall approve a completed application for registration not later than 45 days after the date of receipt of the application, in accordance with the rules of the Board, unless the Board, prior to such date, issues a written notice of disapproval to, or requests more information from, the prospective registrant.

(2) TREATMENT.—A written notice of disapproval of a completed application under paragraph (1) for registration shall be treated as a disciplinary sanction for purposes of sections 105(d) and 107(c).

(d) PERIODIC REPORTS.—Each registered public accounting firm shall submit an annual report to the Board, and may be required to report more frequently, as necessary to update the information contained in its application for registration under this section, and to provide to the Board such additional information as the Board or the Commission may specify, in accordance with subsection (b)(2).

(e) PUBLIC AVAILABILITY.—Registration applications and annual reports required by this subsection, or such portions of such applications or reports as may be designated under rules of the Board, shall be made available for public inspection, subject to rules of the Board or the Commission, and to applicable laws relating to the confidentiality of proprietary, personal, or other information contained in such applications or reports, provided that, in all events, the Board shall protect from public disclosure information reasonably identified by the subject accounting firm as proprietary information.

(f) REGISTRATION AND ANNUAL FEES.—The Board shall assess and collect a registration fee and an annual fee from each registered public accounting firm, in amounts that are sufficient to recover the costs of processing and reviewing applications and annual reports.

§ 103. AUDITING, QUALITY CONTROL, AND INDEPENDENCE STANDARDS AND RULES

(a) AUDITING, QUALITY CONTROL, AND ETHICS STANDARDS.—

(1) IN GENERAL.—The Board shall, by rule, establish, including, to the extent it determines appropriate, through adoption of standards proposed by 1 or more professional groups of accountants designated pursuant to paragraph (3)(A) or advisory groups convened pursuant to paragraph (4), and amend or otherwise modify or alter, such auditing and related attestation standards, such quality control standards, such ethics standards, and such independence standards to be used by registered public accounting firms in the preparation and issuance of audit reports, as required by this Act or the rules of the Commission, or as may be necessary or appropriate in the public interest or for the protection of investors.

(2) RULE REQUIREMENTS.—In carrying out paragraph (1), the Board—

(A) shall include in the auditing standards that it adopts, requirements that each registered public accounting firm shall—

(i) prepare, and maintain for a period of not less than 7 years, audit work papers, and other information related to any audit report, in sufficient detail to support the conclusions reached in such report;

(ii) provide a concurring or second partner review and approval of such audit report (and other related information), and concurring approval in its issuance, by a qualified person (as prescribed by the Board) associated with the public accounting firm, other than the person in charge of the audit, or by an independent reviewer (as prescribed by the Board); and

(iii) in each audit report for an issuer, describe the scope of the auditor's testing of the internal control structure and procedures of the issuer, required by section 404(b), and present (in such report or in a separate report)—

(I) the findings of the auditor from such testing;

(II) an evaluation of whether such internal control structure and procedures—

(aa) include maintenance of records that in reasonable detail accurately and fairly reflect the transactions and dispositions of the assets of the issuer;

(bb) provide reasonable assurance that transactions are recorded as necessary to permit preparation of financial statements in accordance with generally accepted accounting principles, and that receipts and expenditures of the issuer are being made only in accordance with authorizations of management and directors of the issuer; and

(III) a description, at a minimum, of material weaknesses in such internal controls, and of any material noncompliance found on the basis of such testing.

(B) shall include, in the quality control standards that it adopts with respect to the issuance of audit reports, requirements for every registered public accounting firm relating to—

(i) monitoring of professional ethics and independence from issuers, brokers, or dealers on behalf of which the firm issues audit reports;

(ii) consultation within such firm on accounting and auditing questions;

(iii) supervision of audit work;

(iv) hiring, professional development, and advancement of personnel;

(v) the acceptance and continuation of engagements;

(vi) internal inspection; and

(vii) such other requirements as the Board may prescribe, subject to subsection (a)(1).

(3) AUTHORITY TO ADOPT OTHER STANDARDS.—

(A) IN GENERAL.—In carrying out this subsection, the Board—

(i) may adopt as its rules, subject to the terms of section 107, any portion of any statement of auditing standards or other professional standards that the Board determines satisfy the requirements of paragraph (1), and that were proposed by 1 or more professional groups of accountants that shall be designated or recognized by the Board, by rule, for such purpose, pursuant to this paragraph or 1 or more advisory groups convened pursuant to paragraph (4); and

(ii) notwithstanding clause (i), shall retain full authority to modify, supplement, revise, or subsequently amend, modify, or repeal, in whole or in part, any portion of any statement described in clause (i).

(B) INITIAL AND TRANSITIONAL STANDARDS.—The Board shall adopt standards described in subparagraph (A)(i) as initial or transitional standards, to the extent the Board determines necessary, prior to a determination of the Commission under section 101(d), and such standards shall be separately approved by the Commission at the time of that determination, without regard to the procedures required by section 107 that otherwise would apply to the approval of rules of the Board.

(4) ADVISORY GROUPS.—The Board shall convene, or authorize its staff to convene, such expert advisory groups as may be appropriate, which may include practicing accountants and other experts, as well as representatives of other interested groups, subject to such rules as the Board may prescribe to prevent conflicts of interest, to make recommendations concerning the content (including proposed drafts) of auditing, quality control, ethics, independence, or other standards required to be established under this section.

(b) INDEPENDENCE STANDARDS AND RULES.—The Board shall establish such rules as may be necessary or appropriate in the public interest or for the protection of investors, to implement, or as authorized under, title II of this Act.

(c) COOPERATION WITH DESIGNATED PROFESSIONAL GROUPS OF ACCOUNTANTS AND ADVISORY GROUPS.—

(1) IN GENERAL.—The Board shall cooperate on an ongoing basis with professional groups of accountants designated under subsection (a)(3)(A) and advisory groups convened under subsection

(a)(4) in the examination of the need for changes in any standards subject to its authority under subsection (a), recommend issues for inclusion on the agendas of such designated professional groups of accountants or advisory groups, and take such other steps as it deems appropriate to increase the effectiveness of the standard setting process.

(2) BOARD RESPONSES.—The Board shall respond in a timely fashion to requests from designated professional groups of accountants and advisory groups referred to in paragraph (1) for any changes in standards over which the Board has authority.

(d) EVALUATION OF STANDARD SETTING PROCESS.—The Board shall include in the annual report required by section 101(h) the results of its standard setting responsibilities during the period to which the report relates, including a discussion of the work of the Board with any designated professional groups of accountants and advisory groups described in paragraphs (3)(A) and (4) of subsection (a), and its pending issues agenda for future standard setting projects.

§ 104. INSPECTIONS OF REGISTERED PUBLIC ACCOUNTING FIRMS

(a) IN GENERAL.—The Board shall conduct a continuing program of inspections to assess the degree of compliance of each registered public accounting firm and associated persons of that firm with this Act, the rules of the Board, the rules of the Commission, or professional standards, in connection with its performance of audits, issuance of audit reports, and related matters involving issuers. . .

(2) Inspections of audit reports for brokers and dealers.—

(A) The Board may, by rule, conduct and require a program of inspection in accordance with paragraph (1), on a basis to be determined by the Board, of registered public accounting firms that provide one or more audit reports for a broker or dealer. The Board, in establishing such a program, may allow for differentiation among classes of brokers and dealers, as appropriate.

(B) If the Board determines to establish a program of inspection pursuant to subparagraph (A), the Board shall consider in establishing any inspection schedules whether differing schedules would be appropriate with respect to registered public accounting firms that issue audit reports only for one or more brokers or dealers that do not receive, handle, or hold customer securities or cash or are not a member of the Securities Investor Protection Corporation.

(C) Any rules of the Board pursuant to this paragraph shall be subject to prior approval by the Commission pursuant to section 107(b) before the rules become effective, including an opportunity for public notice and comment.

(D) Notwithstanding anything to the contrary in section 102 of this Act, a public accounting firm shall not be required to register with the Board if the public accounting firm is exempt from the inspection program which may be established by the Board under subparagraph (A).

(b) INSPECTION FREQUENCY.—

(1) IN GENERAL.—Subject to paragraph (2), inspections required by this section shall be conducted—

(A) annually with respect to each registered public accounting firm that regularly provides audit reports for more than 100 issuers; and

(B) not less frequently than once every 3 years with respect to each registered public accounting firm that regularly provides audit reports for 100 or fewer issuers.

(2) ADJUSTMENTS TO SCHEDULES.—The Board may, by rule, adjust the inspection schedules set under paragraph (1) if the Board finds that different inspection schedules are consistent with the purposes of this Act, the public interest, and the protection of investors. The Board may conduct special inspections at the request of the Commission or upon its own motion.

(c) PROCEDURES.—The Board shall, in each inspection under this section, and in accordance with its rules for such inspections—

(1) identify any act or practice or omission to act by the registered public accounting firm, or by any associated person thereof, revealed by such inspection that may be in violation of this Act, the

rules of the Board, the rules of the Commission, the firm's own quality control policies, or professional standards;

(2) report any such act, practice, or omission, if appropriate, to the Commission and each appropriate State regulatory authority; and

(3) begin a formal investigation or take disciplinary action, if appropriate, with respect to any such violation, in accordance with this Act and the rules of the Board.

(d) CONDUCT OF INSPECTIONS.—In conducting an inspection of a registered public accounting firm under this section, the Board shall—

(1) inspect and review selected audit and review engagements of the firm (which may include audit engagements that are the subject of ongoing litigation or other controversy between the firm and 1 or more third parties), performed at various offices and by various associated persons of the firm, as selected by the Board;

(2) evaluate the sufficiency of the quality control system of the firm, and the manner of the documentation and communication of that system by the firm; and

(3) perform such other testing of the audit, supervisory, and quality control procedures of the firm as are necessary or appropriate in light of the purpose of the inspection and the responsibilities of the Board.

(e) RECORD RETENTION.—The rules of the Board may require the retention by registered public accounting firms for inspection purposes of records whose retention is not otherwise required by section 103 or the rules issued thereunder.

(f) PROCEDURES FOR REVIEW.—The rules of the Board shall provide a procedure for the review of and response to a draft inspection report by the registered public accounting firm under inspection. The Board shall take such action with respect to such response as it considers appropriate (including revising the draft report or continuing or supplementing its inspection activities before issuing a final report), but the text of any such response, appropriately redacted to protect information reasonably identified by the accounting firm as confidential, shall be attached to and made part of the inspection report.

(g) REPORT.—A written report of the findings of the Board for each inspection under this section, subject to subsection (h), shall be—

(1) transmitted, in appropriate detail, to the Commission and each appropriate State regulatory authority, accompanied by any letter or comments by the Board or the inspector, and any letter of response from the registered public accounting firm; and

(2) made available in appropriate detail to the public (subject to section 105(b)(5)(A), and to the protection of such confidential and proprietary information as the Board may determine to be appropriate, or as may be required by law), except that no portions of the inspection report that deal with criticisms of or potential defects in the quality control systems of the firm under inspection shall be made public if those criticisms or defects are addressed by the firm, to the satisfaction of the Board, not later than 12 months after the date of the inspection report.

(h) INTERIM COMMISSION REVIEW.—

(1) REVIEWABLE MATTERS.—A registered public accounting firm may seek review by the Commission, pursuant to such rules as the Commission shall promulgate, if the firm—

(A) has provided the Board with a response, pursuant to rules issued by the Board under subsection (f), to the substance of particular items in a draft inspection report, and disagrees with the assessments contained in any final report prepared by the Board following such response; or

(B) disagrees with the determination of the Board that criticisms or defects identified in an inspection report have not been addressed to the satisfaction of the Board within 12 months of the date of the inspection report, for purposes of subsection (g)(2).

(2) TREATMENT OF REVIEW.—Any decision of the Commission with respect to a review under paragraph (1) shall not be reviewable under section 25 of the Securities Exchange Act of 1934 (15

U.S.C. 78y), or deemed to be "final agency action" for purposes of section 704 of title 5, United States Code.

(3) TIMING.—Review under paragraph (1) may be sought during the 30-day period following the date of the event giving rise to the review under subparagraph (A) or (B) of paragraph (1).

§ 105. INVESTIGATIONS AND DISCIPLINARY PROCEEDINGS

(a) IN GENERAL.—The Board shall establish, by rule, subject to the requirements of this section, fair procedures for the investigation and disciplining of registered public accounting firms and associated persons of such firms.

(b) INVESTIGATIONS.—

(1) AUTHORITY.—In accordance with the rules of the Board, the Board may conduct an investigation of any act or practice, or omission to act, by a registered public accounting firm, any associated person of such firm, or both, that may violate any provision of this Act, the rules of the Board, the provisions of the securities laws relating to the preparation and issuance of audit reports and the obligations and liabilities of accountants with respect thereto, including the rules of the Commission issued under this Act, or professional standards, regardless of how the act, practice, or omission is brought to the attention of the Board.

(2) TESTIMONY AND DOCUMENT PRODUCTION.—In addition to such other actions as the Board determines to be necessary or appropriate, the rules of the Board may—

(A) require the testimony of the firm or of any person associated with a registered public accounting firm, with respect to any matter that the Board considers relevant or material to an investigation;

(B) require the production of audit work papers and any other document or information in the possession of a registered public accounting firm or any associated person thereof, wherever domiciled, that the Board considers relevant or material to the investigation, and may inspect the books and records of such firm or associated person to verify the accuracy of any documents or information supplied;

(C) request the testimony of, and production of any document in the possession of, any other person, including any client of a registered public accounting firm that the Board considers relevant or material to an investigation under this section, with appropriate notice, subject to the needs of the investigation, as permitted under the rules of the Board; and

(D) provide for procedures to seek issuance by the Commission, in a manner established by the Commission, of a subpoena to require the testimony of, and production of any document in the possession of, any person, including any client of a registered public accounting firm, that the Board considers relevant or material to an investigation under this section.

(3) NONCOOPERATION WITH INVESTIGATIONS.—

(A) IN GENERAL.—If a registered public accounting firm or any associated person thereof refuses to testify, produce documents, or otherwise cooperate with the Board in connection with an investigation under this section, the Board may—

(i) suspend or bar such person from being associated with a registered public accounting firm, or require the registered public accounting firm to end such association;

(ii) suspend or revoke the registration of the public accounting firm; and

(iii) invoke such other lesser sanctions as the Board considers appropriate, and as specified by rule of the Board.

(B) PROCEDURE.—Any action taken by the Board under this paragraph shall be subject to the terms of section 107(c).

(4) COORDINATION AND REFERRAL OF INVESTIGATIONS.—

(A) COORDINATION.—The Board shall notify the Commission of any pending Board investigation involving a potential violation of the securities laws, and thereafter coordinate its work with the work of the Commission's Division of Enforcement, as necessary to protect an ongoing Commission investigation.

(B) REFERRAL.—The Board may refer an investigation under this section—

(i) to the Commission;

(ii) to a self-regulatory organization, in the case of an investigation that concerns an audit report for a broker or dealer that is under the jurisdiction of such self-regulatory organization; and

(iii) to any other Federal functional regulator (as defined in section 509 of the Gramm-Leach-Bliley Act (15 U.S.C. 6809)), in the case of an investigation that concerns an audit report for an institution that is subject to the jurisdiction of such regulator; and

(iv) at the direction of the Commission, to—

(I) the Attorney General of the United States;

(II) the attorney general of 1 or more States; and

(III) the appropriate State regulatory authority.

(5) USE OF DOCUMENTS.—

(A) CONFIDENTIALITY.—Except as provided in subparagraphs (B) and (C), all documents and information prepared or received by or specifically for the Board, and deliberations of the Board and its employees and agents, in connection with an inspection under section 104 or with an investigation under this section, shall be confidential and privileged as an evidentiary matter (and shall not be subject to civil discovery or other legal process) in any proceeding in any Federal or State court or administrative agency, and shall be exempt from disclosure, in the hands of an agency or establishment of the Federal Government, under the Freedom of Information Act (5 U.S.C. 552a), or otherwise, unless and until presented in connection with a public proceeding or released in accordance with subsection (c).

(B) AVAILABILITY TO GOVERNMENT AGENCIES.—Without the loss of its status as confidential and privileged in the hands of the Board, all information referred to in subparagraph (A) may—

(i) be made available to the Commission; and

(ii) in the discretion of the Board, when determined by the Board to be necessary to accomplish the purposes of this Act or to protect investors, be made available to—

(I) the Attorney General of the United States;

(II) the appropriate Federal functional regulator (as defined in section 509 of the Gramm-Leach-Bliley Act (15 U.S.C. 6809)), other than the Commission, with respect to an audit report for an institution subject to the jurisdiction of such regulator;

(III) State attorneys general in connection with any criminal investigation;

(IV) any appropriate State regulatory authority, each of which shall maintain such information as confidential and privileged; and

(V) a self-regulatory organization, with respect to an audit report for a broker or dealer that is under the jurisdiction of such self-regulatory organization. . . .

(6) IMMUNITY.—Any employee of the Board engaged in carrying out an investigation under this Act shall be immune from any civil liability arising out of such investigation in the same manner and to the same extent as an employee of the Federal Government in similar circumstances.

(c) DISCIPLINARY PROCEDURES.—

(1) NOTIFICATION; RECORDKEEPING.—The rules of the Board shall provide that in any proceeding by the Board to determine whether a registered public accounting firm, or an associated person thereof, should be disciplined, the Board shall—

(A) bring specific charges with respect to the firm or associated person;

(B) notify such firm or associated person of, and provide to the firm or associated person an opportunity to defend against, such charges; and

(C) keep a record of the proceedings.

(2) PUBLIC HEARINGS.—Hearings under this section shall not be public, unless otherwise ordered by the Board for good cause shown, with the consent of the parties to such hearing.

(3) SUPPORTING STATEMENT.—A determination by the Board to impose a sanction under this subsection shall be supported by a statement setting forth—

(A) each act or practice in which the registered public accounting firm, or associated person, has engaged (or omitted to engage), or that forms a basis for all or a part of such sanction;

(B) the specific provision of this Act, the securities laws, the rules of the Board, or professional standards which the Board determines has been violated; and

(C) the sanction imposed, including a justification for that sanction.

(4) SANCTIONS.—If the Board finds, based on all of the facts and circumstances, that a registered public accounting firm or associated person thereof has engaged in any act or practice, or omitted to act, in violation of this Act, the rules of the Board, the provisions of the securities laws relating to the preparation and issuance of audit reports and the obligations and liabilities of accountants with respect thereto, including the rules of the Commission issued under this Act, or professional standards, the Board may impose such disciplinary or remedial sanctions as it determines appropriate, subject to applicable limitations under paragraph (5), including—

(A) temporary suspension or permanent revocation of registration under this title;

(B) temporary or permanent suspension or bar of a person from further association with any registered public accounting firm;

(C) temporary or permanent limitation on the activities, functions, or operations of such firm or person (other than in connection with required additional professional education or training);

(D) a civil money penalty for each such violation, in an amount equal to—

(i) not more than [$120,000]* for a natural person or [$2,375,000] for any other person; and

(ii) in any case to which paragraph (5) applies, not more than [$900,000] for a natural person or [$17,800,000] for any other person;

(E) censure;

(F) required additional professional education or training; or

(G) any other appropriate sanction provided for in the rules of the Board.

(5) INTENTIONAL OR OTHER KNOWING CONDUCT.—The sanctions and penalties described in subparagraphs (A) through (C) and (D)(ii) of paragraph (4) shall only apply to—

(A) intentional or knowing conduct, including reckless conduct, that results in violation of the applicable statutory, regulatory, or professional standard; or

(B) repeated instances of negligent conduct, each resulting in a violation of the applicable statutory, regulatory, or professional standard.

---

* The bracketed figures in this section have been adjusted for inflation by the SEC under the Debt Collection Act of 1996, which requires the Commission to make inflationary adjustments to civil penalties in the Securities Act, the Exchange Act, and other Acts that the Commission administers. (Footnote by ed.)

(6) FAILURE TO SUPERVISE.—

(A) IN GENERAL.—The Board may impose sanctions under this section on a registered accounting firm or upon any person who is, or at the time of the alleged failure reasonably to supervise was, a supervisory person at such firm, if the Board finds that—

(i) the firm has failed reasonably to supervise an associated person, either as required by the rules of the Board relating to auditing or quality control standards, or otherwise, with a view to preventing violations of this Act, the rules of the Board, the provisions of the securities laws relating to the preparation and issuance of audit reports and the obligations and liabilities of accountants with respect thereto, including the rules of the Commission under this Act, or professional standards; and

(ii) such associated person commits a violation of this Act, or any of such rules, laws, or standards.

(B) RULE OF CONSTRUCTION.—No current or former supervisory person of a registered public accounting firm shall be deemed to have failed reasonably to supervise any associated person for purposes of subparagraph (A), if—

(i) there have been established in and for that firm procedures, and a system for applying such procedures, that comply with applicable rules of the Board and that would reasonably be expected to prevent and detect any such violation by such associated person; and

(ii) such person has reasonably discharged the duties and obligations incumbent upon that person by reason of such procedures and system, and had no reasonable cause to believe that such procedures and system were not being complied with.

(7) EFFECT OF SUSPENSION.—

(A) ASSOCIATION WITH A PUBLIC ACCOUNTING FIRM.—It shall be unlawful for any person that is suspended or barred from being associated with a registered public accounting firm under this subsection willfully to become or remain associated with any registered public accounting firm, or for any registered public accounting firm that knew, or, in the exercise of reasonable care should have known, of the suspension or bar, to permit such an association, without the consent of the Board or the Commission.

(B) ASSOCIATION WITH AN ISSUER, BROKER, OR DEALER.—It shall be unlawful for any person that is suspended or barred from being associated with a registered public accounting firm under this subsection willfully to become or remain associated with any issuer, broker, or dealer in an accountancy or a financial management capacity, and for any issuer that knew, or in the exercise of reasonable care should have known, of such suspension or bar, to permit such an association, without the consent of the Board or the Commission.

(d) REPORTING OF SANCTIONS.—

(1) RECIPIENTS.—If the Board imposes a disciplinary sanction, in accordance with this section, the Board shall report the sanction to—

(A) the Commission;

(B) any appropriate State regulatory authority or any foreign accountancy licensing board with which such firm or person is licensed or certified; and

(C) the public (once any stay on the imposition of such sanction has been lifted).

(2) CONTENTS.—The information reported under paragraph (1) shall include—

(A) the name of the sanctioned person;

(B) a description of the sanction and the basis for its imposition; and

(C) such other information as the Board deems appropriate.

(e) STAY OF SANCTIONS.—

(1) IN GENERAL.—Application to the Commission for review, or the institution by the Commission of review, of any disciplinary action of the Board shall operate as a stay of any such disciplinary action, unless and until the Commission orders (summarily or after notice and opportunity for hearing on the question of a stay, which hearing may consist solely of the submission of affidavits or presentation of oral arguments) that no such stay shall continue to operate.

(2) EXPEDITED PROCEDURES.—The Commission shall establish for appropriate cases an expedited procedure for consideration and determination of the question of the duration of a stay pending review of any disciplinary action of the Board under this subsection.

§ 107. COMMISSION OVERSIGHT OF THE BOARD

(a) GENERAL OVERSIGHT RESPONSIBILITY.—The Commission shall have oversight and enforcement authority over the Board, as provided in this Act. The provisions of section 17(a)(1) of the Securities Exchange Act of 1934 (15 U.S.C. 78q(a)(1)), and of section 17(b)(1) of the Securities Exchange Act of 1934 (15 U.S.C. 78q(b)(1)) shall apply to the Board as fully as if the Board were a "registered securities association" for purposes of those sections 17(a)(1) and 17(b)(1).

(b) RULES OF THE BOARD.—

(1) DEFINITION.—In this section, the term "proposed rule" means any proposed rule of the Board, and any modification of any such rule.

(2) PRIOR APPROVAL REQUIRED.—No rule of the Board shall become effective without prior approval of the Commission in accordance with this section, other than as provided in section 103(a)(3)(B) with respect to initial or transitional standards.

(3) APPROVAL CRITERIA.—The Commission shall approve a proposed rule, if it finds that the rule is consistent with the requirements of this Act and the securities laws, or is necessary or appropriate in the public interest or for the protection of investors.

(4) PROPOSED RULE PROCEDURES.—The provisions of paragraphs (1) through (3) of section 19(b) of the Securities Exchange Act of 1934 (15 U.S.C.A. § 78s(b)) shall govern the proposed rules of the Board, as fully as if the Board were a "registered securities association" for purposes of that section 19(b), except that, for purposes of this paragraph—

(A) the phrase "consistent with the requirements of this title and the rules and regulations thereunder applicable to such organization" in section 19(b)(2) of that Act shall be deemed to read "consistent with the requirements of title I of the Sarbanes-Oxley Act of 2002, and the rules and regulations issued thereunder applicable to such organization, or as necessary or appropriate in the public interest or for the protection of investors"; and

(B) the phrase "otherwise in furtherance of the purposes of this title" in section 19(b)(3)(C) of that Act shall be deemed to read "otherwise in furtherance of the purposes of title I of the Sarbanes-Oxley Act of 2002".

(5) COMMISSION AUTHORITY TO AMEND RULES OF THE BOARD.—The provisions of section 19(c) of the Securities Exchange Act of 1934 (15 U.S.C. 78s(c)) shall govern the abrogation, deletion, or addition to portions of the rules of the Board by the Commission as fully as if the Board were a "registered securities association" for purposes of that section 19(c), except that the phrase "to conform its rules to the requirements of this title and the rules and regulations thereunder applicable to such organization, or otherwise in furtherance of the purposes of this title" in section 19(c) of that Act shall, for purposes of this paragraph, be deemed to read "to assure the fair administration of the Public Company Accounting Oversight Board, conform the rules promulgated by that Board to the requirements of title I of the Sarbanes-Oxley Act of 2002, or otherwise further the purposes of that Act, the securities laws, and the rules and regulations thereunder applicable to that Board".

(c) COMMISSION REVIEW OF DISCIPLINARY ACTION TAKEN BY THE BOARD.—

(1) NOTICE OF SANCTION.—The Board shall promptly file notice with the Commission of any final sanction on any registered public accounting firm or on any associated person thereof, in such form and containing such information as the Commission, by rule, may prescribe.

(2) REVIEW OF SANCTIONS.—The provisions of sections 19(d)(2) and 19(e)(1) of the Securities Exchange Act of 1934 (15 U.S.C. 78s (d)(2) and (e)(1)) shall govern the review by the Commission of final disciplinary sanctions imposed by the Board (including sanctions imposed under section 105(b)(3) of this Act for noncooperation in an investigation of the Board), as fully as if the Board were a self-regulatory organization and the Commission were the appropriate regulatory agency for such organization for purposes of those sections 19(d)(2) and 19(e)(1), except that, for purposes of this paragraph—

(A) section 105(e) of this Act (rather than that section 19(d)(2)) shall govern the extent to which application for, or institution by the Commission on its own motion of, review of any disciplinary action of the Board operates as a stay of such action;

(B) references in that section 19(e)(1) to "members" of such an organization shall be deemed to be references to registered public accounting firms;

(C) the phrase "consistent with the purposes of this title" in that section 19(e)(1) shall be deemed to read "consistent with the purposes of this title and title I of the Sarbanes-Oxley Act of 2002";

(D) references to rules of the Municipal Securities Rulemaking Board in that section 19(e)(1) shall not apply; and

(E) the reference to section 19(e)(2) of the Securities Exchange Act of 1934 shall refer instead to section 107(c)(3) of this Act.

(3) COMMISSION MODIFICATION AUTHORITY.—The Commission may enhance, modify, cancel, reduce, or require the remission of a sanction imposed by the Board upon a registered public accounting firm or associated person thereof, if the Commission, having due regard for the public interest and the protection of investors, finds, after a proceeding in accordance with this subsection, that the sanction—

(A) is not necessary or appropriate in furtherance of this Act or the securities laws; or

(B) is excessive, oppressive, inadequate, or otherwise not appropriate to the finding or the basis on which the sanction was imposed.

(d) CENSURE OF THE BOARD; OTHER SANCTIONS.—

(1) RESCISSION OF BOARD AUTHORITY.—The Commission, by rule, consistent with the public interest, the protection of investors, and the other purposes of this Act and the securities laws, may relieve the Board of any responsibility to enforce compliance with any provision of this Act, the securities laws, the rules of the Board, or professional standards.

(2) CENSURE OF THE BOARD; LIMITATIONS.—The Commission may, by order, as it determines necessary or appropriate in the public interest, for the protection of investors, or otherwise in furtherance of the purposes of this Act or the securities laws, censure or impose limitations upon the activities, functions, and operations of the Board, if the Commission finds, on the record, after notice and opportunity for a hearing, that the Board—

(A) has violated or is unable to comply with any provision of this Act, the rules of the Board, or the securities laws; or

(B) without reasonable justification or excuse, has failed to enforce compliance with any such provision or rule, or any professional standard by a registered public accounting firm or an associated person thereof.

(3) CENSURE OF BOARD MEMBERS; REMOVAL FROM OFFICE.—The Commission may, as necessary or appropriate in the public interest, for the protection of investors, or otherwise in furtherance of the purposes of this Act or the securities laws, remove from office or censure any person who is, or at the time of the alleged misconduct was, a member of the Board, if the Commission finds, on the record, after notice and opportunity for a hearing, that such member—

(A) has willfully violated any provision of this Act, the rules of the Board, or the securities laws;

(B) has willfully abused the authority of that member; or

(C) without reasonable justification or excuse, has failed to enforce compliance with any such provision or rule, or any professional standard by any registered public accounting firm or any associated person thereof.

§ 108. ACCOUNTING STANDARDS

(a) AMENDMENT TO SECURITIES ACT OF 1933. [This section amends Securities Act § 19. See this Supplement, supra.]

(b) COMMISSION AUTHORITY.—The Commission shall promulgate such rules and regulations to carry out section 19(b) of the Securities Act of 1933, as added by this section, as it deems necessary or appropriate in the public interest or for the protection of investors.

(c) NO EFFECT ON COMMISSION POWERS.—Nothing in this Act, including this section and the amendment made by this section, shall be construed to impair or limit the authority of the Commission to establish accounting principles or standards for purposes of enforcement of the securities laws. . . .

§ 110. DEFINITIONS

For the purposes of this title, the following definitions shall apply:

(1) Audit.—The term "audit" means an examination of the financial statements, reports, documents, procedures, controls, or notices of any issuer, broker, or dealer by an independent public accounting firm in accordance with the rules of the Board or the Commission, for the purpose of expressing an opinion on the financial statements or providing an audit report.

(2) Audit report.—The term "audit report" means a document, report, notice, or other record—

(A) prepared following an audit performed for purposes of compliance by an issuer, broker, or dealer with the requirements of the securities laws; and

(B) in which a public accounting firm either—

(i) sets forth the opinion of that firm regarding a financial statement, report, notice, or other document, procedures, or controls; or

(ii) asserts that no such opinion can be expressed.

(3) Broker.—The term "broker" means a broker (as such term is defined in section 3(a)(4) of the Securities Exchange Act of 1934) that is required to file a balance sheet, income statement, or other financial statement under section 17(e)(1)(A) of such Act, where such balance sheet, income statement, or financial statement is required to be certified by a registered public accounting firm.

(4) Dealer.—The term "dealer" means a dealer (as such term is defined in section 3(a)(5) of the Securities Exchange Act of 1934) that is required to file a balance sheet, income statement, or other financial statement under section 17(e)(1)(A) of such Act, where such balance sheet, income statement, or financial statement is required to be certified by a registered public accounting firm.

(5) Professional standards.—The term "professional standards" means—

(A) accounting principles that are—

(i) established by the standard setting body described in section 19(b) of the Securities Act of 1933, as amended by this Act, or prescribed by the Commission under section 19(a) of that Act or section 13(b) of the Securities Exchange Act of 1934; and

(ii) relevant to audit reports for particular issuers, brokers, or dealers, or dealt with in the quality control system of a particular registered public accounting firm; and

(B) auditing standards, standards for attestation engagements, quality control policies and procedures, ethical and competency standards, and independence standards (including rules implementing title II) that the Board or the Commission determines—

(i) relate to the preparation or issuance of audit reports for issuers, brokers, or dealers; and

(ii) are established or adopted by the Board under section 103(a), or are promulgated as rules of the Commission.

(6) Self-regulatory organization.—The term 'self-regulatory organization' has the same meaning as in section 3(a) of the Securities Exchange Act of 1934.

TITLE II—AUDITOR INDEPENDENCE

§ 201. SERVICES OUTSIDE THE SCOPE OF PRACTICE OF AUDITORS

[This section adds Securities Exchange Act § 10A(g). See this Supplement, supra.]

(b) EXEMPTION AUTHORITY.—The Board may, on a case by case basis, exempt any person, issuer, public accounting firm, or transaction from the prohibition on the provision of services under section 10A(g) of the Securities Exchange Act of 1934 (as added by this section), to the extent that such exemption is necessary or appropriate in the public interest and is consistent with the protection of investors, and subject to review by the Commission in the same manner as for rules of the Board under section 107.

§ 202. PREAPPROVAL REQUIREMENTS

[This section adds Securities Exchange Act § 10A(i). See this Supplement, supra.]

§ 203. AUDIT PARTNER ROTATION

[This section adds Securities Exchange Act § 10A(j). See this Supplement, supra.]

§ 204. AUDITOR REPORTS TO AUDIT COMMITTEES

[This section adds Securities Exchange Act § 10A(k). See this Supplement, supra.]

§ 206. CONFLICTS OF INTEREST

[This section adds Securities Exchange Act § 10A(*l*). See this Supplement, supra.]

§ 207. STUDY OF MANDATORY ROTATION OF REGISTERED PUBLIC ACCOUNTING FIRMS

(a) STUDY AND REVIEW REQUIRED.—The Comptroller General of the United States shall conduct a study and review of the potential effects of requiring the mandatory rotation of registered public accounting firms.

(b) REPORT REQUIRED.—Not later than 1 year after the date of enactment of this Act, the Comptroller General shall submit a report to the Committee on Banking, Housing, and Urban Affairs of the Senate and the Committee on Financial Services of the House of Representatives on the results of the study and review required by this section.

(c) DEFINITION.—For purposes of this section, the term "mandatory rotation" refers to the imposition of a limit on the period of years in which a particular registered public accounting firm may be the auditor of record for a particular issuer.

§ 208. COMMISSION AUTHORITY

(a) COMMISSION REGULATIONS.—Not later than 180 days after the date of enactment of this Act, the Commission shall issue final regulations to carry out each of subsections (g) through (*l*) of section 10A of the Securities Exchange Act of 1934, as added by this title.

(b) AUDITOR INDEPENDENCE.—It shall be unlawful for any registered public accounting firm (or an associated person thereof, as applicable) to prepare or issue any audit report with respect to any issuer, if the firm or associated person engages in any activity with respect to that issuer prohibited by any of subsections (g) through (*l*) of section 10A of the Securities Exchange Act of 1934, as added by this title, or any rule or regulation of the Commission or of the Board issued thereunder.

§ 209. CONSIDERATIONS BY APPROPRIATE STATE REGULATORY AUTHORITIES

In supervising nonregistered public accounting firms and their associated persons, appropriate State regulatory authorities should make an independent determination of the proper standards applicable, particularly taking into consideration the size and nature of the business of the accounting firms they supervise and the size and nature of the business of the clients of those firms. The standards applied by the Board under this Act should not be presumed to be applicable for purposes of this section for small and medium sized nonregistered public accounting firms.

TITLE III—CORPORATE RESPONSIBILITY

§ 301. PUBLIC COMPANY AUDIT COMMITTEES

[This section adds Securities Exchange Act § 10A(m). See this Supplement, supra.]

§ 302. CORPORATE RESPONSIBILITY FOR FINANCIAL REPORTS

(a) REGULATIONS REQUIRED.—The Commission shall, by rule, require, for each company filing periodic reports under section 13(a) or 15(d) of the Securities Exchange Act of 1934 (15 U.S.C. 78m, 78o(d)), that the principal executive officer or officers and the principal financial officer or officers, or persons performing similar functions, certify in each annual or quarterly report filed or submitted under either such section of such Act that—

(1) the signing officer has reviewed the report;

(2) based on the officer's knowledge, the report does not contain any untrue statement of a material fact or omit to state a material fact necessary in order to make the statements made, in light of the circumstances under which such statements were made, not misleading;

(3) based on such officer's knowledge, the financial statements, and other financial information included in the report, fairly present in all material respects the financial condition and results of operations of the issuer as of, and for, the periods presented in the report;

(4) the signing officers—

(A) are responsible for establishing and maintaining internal controls;

(B) have designed such internal controls to ensure that material information relating to the issuer and its consolidated subsidiaries is made known to such officers by others within those entities, particularly during the period in which the periodic reports are being prepared;

(C) have evaluated the effectiveness of the issuer's internal controls as of a date within 90 days prior to the report; and

(D) have presented in the report their conclusions about the effectiveness of their internal controls based on their evaluation as of that date;

(5) the signing officers have disclosed to the issuer's auditors and the audit committee of the board of directors (or persons fulfilling the equivalent function)—

(A) all significant deficiencies in the design or operation of internal controls which could adversely affect the issuer's ability to record, process, summarize, and report financial data and have identified for the issuer's auditors any material weaknesses in internal controls; and

(B) any fraud, whether or not material, that involves management or other employees who have a significant role in the issuer's internal controls; and

(6) the signing officers have indicated in the report whether or not there were significant changes in internal controls or in other factors that could significantly affect internal controls subsequent to

the date of their evaluation, including any corrective actions with regard to significant deficiencies and material weaknesses.

(b) FOREIGN REINCORPORATIONS HAVE NO EFFECT.—Nothing in this section 302 shall be interpreted or applied in any way to allow any issuer to lessen the legal force of the statement required under this section 302, by an issuer having reincorporated or having engaged in any other transaction that resulted in the transfer of the corporate domicile or offices of the issuer from inside the United States to outside of the United States.

(c) DEADLINE.—The rules required by subsection (a) shall be effective not later than 30 days after the date of enactment of this Act.

§ 303. IMPROPER INFLUENCE ON CONDUCT OF AUDITS

(a) RULES TO PROHIBIT.—It shall be unlawful, in contravention of such rules or regulations as the Commission shall prescribe as necessary and appropriate in the public interest or for the protection of investors, for any officer or director of an issuer, or any other person acting under the direction thereof, to take any action to fraudulently influence, coerce, manipulate, or mislead any independent public or certified accountant engaged in the performance of an audit of the financial statements of that issuer for the purpose of rendering such financial statements materially misleading.

(b) ENFORCEMENT.—In any civil proceeding, the Commission shall have exclusive authority to enforce this section and any rule or regulation issued under this section.

(c) NO PREEMPTION OF OTHER LAW.—The provisions of subsection (a) shall be in addition to, and shall not supersede or preempt, any other provision of law or any rule or regulation issued thereunder.

(d) DEADLINE FOR RULEMAKING.—The Commission shall—

(1) propose the rules or regulations required by this section, not later than 90 days after the date of enactment of this Act; and

(2) issue final rules or regulations required by this section, not later than 270 days after that date of enactment.

§ 304. FORFEITURE OF CERTAIN BONUSES AND PROFITS

(a) ADDITIONAL COMPENSATION PRIOR TO NONCOMPLIANCE WITH COMMISSION FINANCIAL REPORTING REQUIREMENTS.—If an issuer is required to prepare an accounting restatement due to the material noncompliance of the issuer, as a result of misconduct, with any financial reporting requirement under the securities laws, the chief executive officer and chief financial officer of the issuer shall reimburse the issuer for—

(1) any bonus or other incentive-based or equity-based compensation received by that person from the issuer during the 12-month period following the first public issuance or filing with the Commission (whichever first occurs) of the financial document embodying such financial reporting requirement; and

(2) any profits realized from the sale of securities of the issuer during that 12-month period.

(b) COMMISSION EXEMPTION AUTHORITY.—The Commission may exempt any person from the application of subsection (a), as it deems necessary and appropriate.

§ 305. OFFICER AND DIRECTOR BARS AND PENALTIES

[This section amends Securities Exchange Act §§ 20(3), 21(d). See this Supplement, supra.]

§ 306. INSIDER TRADES DURING PENSION FUND BLACKOUT PERIODS

(a) PROHIBITION OF INSIDER TRADING DURING PENSION FUND BLACKOUT PERIODS—

(1) IN GENERAL.—Except to the extent otherwise provided by rule of the Commission pursuant to paragraph (3), it shall be unlawful for any director or executive officer of an issuer of any equity

security (other than an exempted security), directly or indirectly, to purchase, sell, or otherwise acquire or transfer any equity security of the issuer (other than an exempted security) during any blackout period with respect to such equity security if such director or officer acquires such equity security in connection with his or her service or employment as a director or executive officer.

(2) REMEDY.—

(A) IN GENERAL.—Any profit realized by a director or executive officer referred to in paragraph (1) from any purchase, sale, or other acquisition or transfer in violation of this subsection shall inure to and be recoverable by the issuer, irrespective of any intention on the part of such director or executive officer in entering into the transaction.

(B) ACTIONS TO RECOVER PROFITS.—An action to recover profits in accordance with this subsection may be instituted at law or in equity in any court of competent jurisdiction by the issuer, or by the owner of any security of the issuer in the name and in behalf of the issuer if the issuer fails or refuses to bring such action within 60 days after the date of request, or fails diligently to prosecute the action thereafter, except that no such suit shall be brought more than 2 years after the date on which such profit was realized.

(3) RULEMAKING AUTHORIZED.—The Commission shall, in consultation with the Secretary of Labor, issue rules to clarify the application of this subsection and to prevent evasion thereof. Such rules shall provide for the application of the requirements of paragraph (1) with respect to entities treated as a single employer with respect to an issuer under section 414(b), (c), (m), or (o) of the Internal Revenue Code of 1986 to the extent necessary to clarify the application of such requirements and to prevent evasion thereof. Such rules may also provide for appropriate exceptions from the requirements of this subsection, including exceptions for purchases pursuant to an automatic dividend reinvestment program or purchases or sales made pursuant to an advance election.

(4) BLACKOUT PERIOD.—For purposes of this subsection, the term "blackout period", with respect to the equity securities of any issuer—

(A) means any period of more than 3 consecutive business days during which the ability of not fewer than 50 percent of the participants or beneficiaries under all individual account plans maintained by the issuer to purchase, sell, or otherwise acquire or transfer an interest in any equity of such issuer held in such an individual account plan is temporarily suspended by the issuer or by a fiduciary of the plan; and

(B) does not include, under regulations which shall be prescribed by the Commission—

(i) a regularly scheduled period in which the participants and beneficiaries may not purchase, sell, or otherwise acquire or transfer an interest in any equity of such issuer, if such period is—

(I) incorporated into the individual account plan; and

(II) timely disclosed to employees before becoming participants under the individual account plan or as a subsequent amendment to the plan; or

(ii) any suspension described in subparagraph (A) that is imposed solely in connection with persons becoming participants or beneficiaries, or ceasing to be participants or beneficiaries, in an individual account plan by reason of a corporate merger, acquisition, divestiture, or similar transaction involving the plan or plan sponsor.

(5) INDIVIDUAL ACCOUNT PLAN.—For purposes of this subsection, the term "individual account plan" has the meaning provided in section 3(34) of the Employee Retirement Income Security Act of 1974 (29 U.S.C. 1002(34)), except that such term shall not include a one-participant retirement plan (within the meaning of section 101(i)(8)(B) of such Act).

(6) NOTICE TO DIRECTORS, EXECUTIVE OFFICERS, AND THE COMMISSION.—In any case in which a director or executive officer is subject to the requirements of this subsection in connection with a blackout period (as defined in paragraph (4)) with respect to any equity securities, the issuer of such equity securities shall timely notify such director or officer and the Securities and Exchange Commission of such blackout period. . . .

§ 307.   RULES OF PROFESSIONAL RESPONSIBILITY FOR ATTORNEYS

Not later than 180 days after the date of enactment of this Act, the Commission shall issue rules, in the public interest and for the protection of investors, setting forth minimum standards of professional conduct for attorneys appearing and practicing before the Commission in any way in the representation of issuers, including a rule—

(1) requiring an attorney to report evidence of a material violation of securities law or breach of fiduciary duty or similar violation by the company or any agent thereof, to the chief legal counsel or the chief executive officer of the company (or the equivalent thereof); and

(2) if the counsel or officer does not appropriately respond to the evidence (adopting, as necessary, appropriate remedial measures or sanctions with respect to the violation), requiring the attorney to report the evidence to the audit committee of the board of directors of the issuer or to another committee of the board of directors comprised solely of directors not employed directly or indirectly by the issuer, or to the board of directors.

§ 308.   FAIR FUNDS FOR INVESTORS

(a) CIVIL PENALTIES ADDED TO DISGORGEMENT FUNDS FOR THE RELIEF OF VICTIMS.—If in any judicial or administrative action brought by the Commission under the securities laws (as such term is defined in section 3(a)(47) of the Securities Exchange Act of 1934) the Commission obtains an order requiring disgorgement against any person for a violation of such laws or the rules or regulations thereunder, or such person agrees in settlement of any such action to such disgorgement, and the Commission also obtains pursuant to such laws a civil penalty against such person, the amount of such civil penalty shall, on the motion or at the direction of the Commission, be added to and become part of the disgorgement fund for the benefit of the victims of such violation.

(b) ACCEPTANCE OF ADDITIONAL DONATIONS.—The Commission is authorized to accept, hold, administer, and utilize gifts, bequests and devises of property, both real and personal, to the United States for a disgorgement fund described in subsection (a). Such gifts, bequests, and devises of money and proceeds from sales of other property received as gifts, bequests, or devises shall be deposited in the disgorgement fund and shall be available for allocation in accordance with subsection (a). . . .

TITLE IV—ENHANCED FINANCIAL DISCLOSURES

§ 401.   DISCLOSURES IN PERIODIC REPORTS

(a) DISCLOSURES REQUIRED.—[This section adds Securities Exchange Act § 13(i), (j). See this Supplement, supra.]

(b) COMMISSION RULES ON PRO FORMA FIGURES.—Not later than 180 days after the date of enactment of the Sarbanes-Oxley Act of 2002, the Commission shall issue final rules providing that pro forma financial information included in any periodic or other report filed with the Commission pursuant to the securities laws, or in any public disclosure or press or other release, shall be presented in a manner that—

(1) does not contain an untrue statement of a material fact or omit to state a material fact necessary in order to make the pro forma financial information, in light of the circumstances under which it is presented, not misleading; and

(2) reconciles it with the financial condition and results of operations of the issuer under generally accepted accounting principles. . . .

§ 402.   ENHANCED CONFLICT OF INTEREST PROVISIONS

[This section adds Securities Exchange Act § 13(k). See this Supplement, supra.]

§ 403. DISCLOSURES OF TRANSACTIONS INVOLVING MANAGEMENT AND PRINCIPAL STOCKHOLDERS

[This section adds Securities Exchange Act § 16(a). See this Supplement, supra.]

§ 404. MANAGEMENT ASSESSMENT OF INTERNAL CONTROLS

(a) RULES REQUIRED.—The Commission shall prescribe rules requiring each annual report required by section 13(a) or 15(d) of the Securities Exchange Act of 1934 to contain an internal control report, which shall—

(1) state the responsibility of management for establishing and maintaining an adequate internal control structure and procedures for financial reporting; and

(2) contain an assessment, as of the end of the most recent fiscal year of the issuer, of the effectiveness of the internal control structure and procedures of the issuer for financial reporting.

(b) INTERNAL CONTROL EVALUATION AND REPORTING.—With respect to the internal control assessment required by subsection (a), each registered public accounting firm that prepares or issues the audit report for the issuer shall attest to, and report on, the assessment made by the management of the issuer. An attestation made under this subsection shall be made in accordance with standards for attestation engagements issued or adopted by the Board. Any such attestation shall not be the subject of a separate engagement.

§ 406. CODE OF ETHICS FOR SENIOR FINANCIAL OFFICERS

(a) CODE OF ETHICS DISCLOSURE.—The Commission shall issue rules to require each issuer, together with periodic reports required pursuant to section 13(a) or 15(d) of the Securities Exchange Act of 1934, to disclose whether or not, and if not, the reason therefor, such issuer has adopted a code of ethics for senior financial officers, applicable to its principal financial officer and comptroller or principal accounting officer, or persons performing similar functions.

(b) CHANGES IN CODES OF ETHICS.—The Commission shall revise its regulations concerning matters requiring prompt disclosure on Form 8-K (or any successor thereto) to require the immediate disclosure, by means of the filing of such form, dissemination by the Internet or by other electronic means, by any issuer of any change in or waiver of the code of ethics for senior financial officers.

(c) DEFINITION.—In this section, the term "code of ethics" means such standards as are reasonably necessary to promote—

(1) honest and ethical conduct, including the ethical handling of actual or apparent conflicts of interest between personal and professional relationships;

(2) full, fair, accurate, timely, and understandable disclosure in the periodic reports required to be filed by the issuer; and

(3) compliance with applicable governmental rules and regulations. . . .

§ 407. DISCLOSURE OF AUDIT COMMITTEE FINANCIAL EXPERT

(a) RULES DEFINING "FINANCIAL EXPERT".—The Commission shall issue rules, as necessary or appropriate in the public interest and consistent with the protection of investors, to require each issuer, together with periodic reports required pursuant to sections 13(a) and 15(d) of the Securities Exchange Act of 1934, to disclose whether or not, and if not, the reasons therefor, the audit committee of that issuer is comprised of at least 1 member who is a financial expert, as such term is defined by the Commission.

(b) CONSIDERATIONS.—In defining the term "financial expert" for purposes of subsection (a), the Commission shall consider whether a person has, through education and experience as a public accountant or auditor or a principal financial officer, comptroller, or principal accounting officer of an issuer, or from a position involving the performance of similar functions—

(1) an understanding of generally accepted accounting principles and financial statements;

(2) experience in—

    (A) the preparation or auditing of financial statements of generally comparable issuers; and

    (B) the application of such principles in connection with the accounting for estimates, accruals, and reserves;

(3) experience with internal accounting controls; and

(4) an understanding of audit committee functions. . . .

§ 408. ENHANCED REVIEW OF PERIODIC DISCLOSURES BY ISSUERS

(a) REGULAR AND SYSTEMATIC REVIEW.—The Commission shall review disclosures made by issuers reporting under section 13(a) of the Securities Exchange Act of 1934 (including reports filed on Form 10-K), and which have a class of securities listed on a national securities exchange or traded on an automated quotation facility of a national securities association, on a regular and systematic basis for the protection of investors. Such review shall include a review of an issuer's financial statement.

(b) REVIEW CRITERIA.—For purposes of scheduling the reviews required by subsection (a), the Commission shall consider, among other factors—

(1) issuers that have issued material restatements of financial results;

(2) issuers that experience significant volatility in their stock price as compared to other issuers;

(3) issuers with the largest market capitalization;

(4) emerging companies with disparities in price to earning ratios;

(5) issuers whose operations significantly affect any material sector of the economy; and

(6) any other factors that the Commission may consider relevant.

(c) MINIMUM REVIEW PERIOD.—In no event shall an issuer required to file reports under section 13(a) or 15(d) of the Securities Exchange Act of 1934 be reviewed under this section less frequently than once every 3 years.

§ 409. REAL TIME ISSUER DISCLOSURES

[This section adds Securities Exchange Act § 13(*l*). See this Supplement, supra.]

TITLE V—ANALYST CONFLICTS OF INTEREST

§ 501. TREATMENT OF SECURITIES ANALYSTS BY REGISTERED SECURITIES ASSOCIATIONS AND NATIONAL SECURITIES EXCHANGES

[This section adds Securities Exchange Act § 15D. See this Supplement, supra.]

TITLE VI—COMMISSION RESOURCES AND AUTHORITY

§ 602. APPEARANCE AND PRACTICE BEFORE THE COMMISSION

[This section adds Securities Exchange Act § 4C. See this Supplement, supra.]

§ 603. FEDERAL COURT AUTHORITY TO IMPOSE PENNY STOCK BARS

[This section adds Securities Exchange Act §§ 20, 21(d). See this Supplement, supra.]

TITLE VIII—CORPORATE AND CRIMINAL FRAUD ACCOUNTABILITY

§ 806. PROTECTION FOR EMPLOYEES OF PUBLICLY TRADED COMPANIES WHO PROVIDE EVIDENCE OF FRAUD

(a) IN GENERAL.—Chapter 73 of title 18, United States Code, is amended by inserting after section 1514 the following:

"§ 1514A. Civil action to protect against retaliation in fraud cases

"(a) WHISTLEBLOWER PROTECTION FOR EMPLOYEES OF PUBLICLY TRADED COMPANIES.—No company with a class of securities registered under section 12 of the Securities Exchange Act of 1934 or that is required to file reports under section 15(d) of the Securities Exchange Act of 1934, or any officer, employee, contractor, subcontractor, or agent of such company, may discharge, demote, suspend, threaten, harass, or in any other manner discriminate against an employee in the terms and conditions of employment because of any lawful act done by the employee—

"(1) to provide information, cause information to be provided, or otherwise assist in an investigation regarding any conduct which the employee reasonably believes constitutes a violation of section 1341, 1343, 1344, or 1348, any rule or regulation of the Securities and Exchange Commission, or any provision of Federal law relating to fraud against shareholders, when the information or assistance is provided to or the investigation is conducted by—

"(A) a Federal regulatory or law enforcement agency;

"(B) any Member of Congress or any committee of Congress; or

"(C) a person with supervisory authority over the employee (or such other person working for the employer who has the authority to investigate, discover, or terminate misconduct); or

"(2) to file, cause to be filed, testify, participate in, or otherwise assist in a proceeding filed or about to be filed (with any knowledge of the employer) relating to an alleged violation of section 1341, 1343, 1344, or 1348, any rule or regulation of the Securities and Exchange Commission, or any provision of Federal law relating to fraud against shareholders.

"(b) ENFORCEMENT ACTION.—

"(1) IN GENERAL.—A person who alleges discharge or other discrimination by any person in violation of subsection (a) may seek relief under subsection (c), by—

"(A) filing a complaint with the Secretary of Labor; or

"(B) if the Secretary has not issued a final decision within 180 days of the filing of the complaint and there is no showing that such delay is due to the bad faith of the claimant, bringing an action at law or equity for de novo review in the appropriate district court of the United States, which shall have jurisdiction over such an action without regard to the amount in controversy.

"(2) PROCEDURE.—

"(A) IN GENERAL.—An action under paragraph (1)(A) shall be governed under the rules and procedures set forth in section 42121(b) of title 49, United States Code.

"(B) EXCEPTION.—Notification made under section 42121(b)(1) of title 49, United States Code, shall be made to the person named in the complaint and to the employer.

"(C) BURDENS OF PROOF.—An action brought under paragraph (1)(B) shall be governed by the legal burdens of proof set forth in section 42121(b) of title 49, United States Code.

"(D) STATUTE OF LIMITATIONS.—An action under paragraph (1) shall be commenced not later than 90 days after the date on which the violation occurs.

"(c) REMEDIES.—

"(1) IN GENERAL.—An employee prevailing in any action under subsection (b)(1) shall be entitled to all relief necessary to make the employee whole.

"(2) COMPENSATORY DAMAGES.—Relief for any action under paragraph (1) shall include—

"(A) reinstatement with the same seniority status that the employee would have had, but for the discrimination;

"(B) the amount of back pay, with interest; and

"(C) compensation for any special damages sustained as a result of the discrimination, including litigation costs, expert witness fees, and reasonable attorney fees.

"(d) RIGHTS RETAINED BY EMPLOYEE.—Nothing in this section shall be deemed to diminish the rights, privileges, or remedies of any employee under any Federal or State law, or under any collective bargaining agreement. . . ."

§ 807. CRIMINAL PENALTIES FOR DEFRAUDING SHAREHOLDERS OF PUBLICLY TRADED COMPANIES

[This section adds 18 U.S.C. § 1348. See this Supplement, infra.]

TITLE IX—WHITE-COLLAR CRIME PENALTY ENHANCEMENTS

§ 906. CORPORATE RESPONSIBILITY FOR FINANCIAL REPORTS

(a) IN GENERAL.—Chapter 63 of title 18, United States Code, is amended by inserting after section 1349, as created by this Act, the following:

"§ 1350. Failure of corporate officers to certify financial reports

"(a) CERTIFICATION OF PERIODIC FINANCIAL REPORTS.—Each periodic report containing financial statements filed by an issuer with the Securities Exchange Commission pursuant to section 13(a) or 15(d) of the Securities Exchange Act of 1934 shall be accompanied by a written statement by the chief executive officer and chief financial officer (or equivalent thereof) of the issuer.

"(b) CONTENT.—The statement required under subsection (a) shall certify that the periodic report containing the financial statements fully complies with the requirements of section 13(a) or 15(d) of the Securities Exchange Act of 1934 and that information contained in the periodic report fairly presents, in all material respects, the financial condition and results of operations of the issuer.

"(c) CRIMINAL PENALTIES.—Whoever—

"(1) certifies any statement as set forth in subsections (a) and (b) of this section knowing that the periodic report accompanying the statement does not comport with all the requirements set forth in this section shall be fined not more than $1,000,000 or imprisoned not more than 10 years, or both; or

"(2) willfully certifies any statement as set forth in subsections (a) and (b) of this section knowing that the periodic report accompanying the statement does not comport with all the requirements set forth in this section shall be fined not more than $5,000,000, or imprisoned not more than 20 years, or both.".

TITLE XI—CORPORATE FRAUD ACCOUNTABILITY

§ 1101. SHORT TITLE

This title may be cited as the "Corporate Fraud Accountability Act of 2002".

§ 1102. TAMPERING WITH A RECORD OR OTHERWISE IMPEDING AN OFFICIAL PROCEEDING

Section 1512 of title 18, United States Code, is amended . . .

(2) by inserting after subsection (b) the following new subsection:

"(c) Whoever corruptly—

"(1) alters, destroys, mutilates, or conceals a record, document, or other object, or attempts to do so, with the intent to impair the object's integrity or availability for use in an official proceeding; or

"(2) otherwise obstructs, influences, or impedes any official proceeding, or attempts to do so, shall be fined under this title or imprisoned not more than 20 years, or both.

§ 1105. AUTHORITY OF THE COMMISSION TO PROHIBIT PERSONS FROM SERVING AS OFFICERS OR DIRECTORS

[This section adds Securities Exchange Act §§ 21C(f), 8A(f). See this Supplement, supra.]

§ 1106. INCREASED CRIMINAL PENALTIES UNDER SECURITIES EXCHANGE ACT OF 1934

[This section amends Securities Exchange Act § 32(a). See this Supplement, supra.]

§ 1107. RETALIATION AGAINST INFORMANTS

(a) IN GENERAL.—Section 1513 of title 18, United States Code, is amended by adding at the end the following:

"(e) Whoever knowingly, with the intent to retaliate, takes any action harmful to any person, including interference with the lawful employment or livelihood of any person, for providing to a law enforcement officer any truthful information relating to the commission or possible commission of any Federal offense, shall be fined under this title or imprisoned not more than 10 years, or both."

FEDERAL MAIL FRAUD ACT

18 U.S.C. §§ 1341 et seq.

TABLE OF CONTENTS

Sec.		Page
1341.	Frauds and Swindles	1677
1343.	Fraud by Wire, Radio, or Television	1677
1348.	Securities Fraud	1677

---

§ 1341. Frauds and Swindles

Whoever, having devised or intending to devise any scheme or artifice to defraud, or for obtaining money or property by means of false or fraudulent pretenses, representations, or promises, or to sell, dispose of, loan, exchange, alter, give away, distribute, supply, or furnish or procure for unlawful use any counterfeit or spurious coin, obligation, security, or other article, or anything represented to be or intimated or held out to be such counterfeit or spurious article, for the purpose of executing such scheme or artifice or attempting so to do, places in any post office or authorized depository for mail matter, any matter or thing whatever to be sent or delivered by the Postal Service, or deposits or causes to be deposited any matter or thing whatever to be sent or delivered by any private or commercial interstate carrier, or takes or receives therefrom, any such matter or thing, or knowingly causes to be delivered by mail according to the direction thereon, or at the place at which it is directed to be delivered by the person to whom it is addressed, any such matter or thing, shall be fined under this title or imprisoned not more than 20 years, or both. If the violation affects a financial institution, such person shall be fined not more than $1,000,000 or imprisoned not more than 30 years, or both.

§ 1343. Fraud by Wire, Radio, or Television

Whoever, having devised or intending to devise any scheme or artifice to defraud, or for obtaining money or property by means of false or fraudulent pretenses, representations, or promises, transmits or causes to be transmitted by means of wire, radio, or television communication in interstate or foreign commerce, any writings, signs, signals, pictures, or sounds for the purpose of executing such scheme or artifice, shall be fined under this title or imprisoned not more than 20 years, or both. If the violation affects a financial institution, such person shall be fined not more than $1,000,000 or imprisoned not more than 30 years, or both.

§ 1348. Securities Fraud

Whoever knowingly executes, or attempts to execute, a scheme or artifice—

(1) to defraud any person in connection with any security of an issuer with a class of securities registered under section 12 of the Securities Exchange Act of 1934 or that is required to file reports under section 15(d) of the Securities Exchange Act of 1934; or

(2) to obtain, by means of false or fraudulent pretenses, representations, or promises, any money or property in connection with the purchase or sale of any security of an issuer with a class of securities registered under section 12 of the Securities Exchange Act of 1934;

shall be fined under this title, or imprisoned not more than 25 years, or both.

U.S.C. § 1658

[Statute of Limitations]

(a) Except as otherwise provided by law, a civil action arising under an Act of Congress enacted after the date of the enactment of this section may not be commenced later than 4 years after the cause of action accrues.

(b) Notwithstanding subsection (a), a private right of action that involves a claim of fraud, deceit, manipulation, or contrivance in contravention of a regulatory requirement concerning the securities laws, as defined in section 3(a)(47) of the Securities Exchange Act of 1934, may be brought not later than the earlier of—

(1) 2 years after the discovery of the facts constituting the violation; or

(2) 5 years after such violation.

RACKETEER INFLUENCE AND CORRUPT ORGANIZATIONS (RICO)

18 U.S.C. § 1961 et seq.

TABLE OF CONTENTS

Sec.		Page
1961.	Definitions	1681
1962.	Prohibited Activities	1681
1963.	Criminal Penalties	1682
1964.	Civil Remedies	1682
1965.	Venue and Process*	
1966.	Expedition of Actions*	
1967.	Evidence*	
1968.	Civil Investigative Demand*	

§ 1961. Definitions

As used in this chapter—

(1) "racketeering activity" means (A) any act or threat involving murder, kidnaping, gambling, arson, robbery, bribery, [or] extortion, . . . which is chargeable under State law and punishable by imprisonment for more than one year; . . . (D) any offense involving fraud connected with a case under title 11 . . . [or] fraud in the sale of securities, . . . [or] (E) any act which is indictable under the Currency and Foreign Transactions Reporting Act. . . .

(4) "enterprise" includes any individual, partnership, corporation, association, or other legal entity, and any union or group of individuals associated in fact although not a legal entity;

(5) "pattern of racketeering activity" requires at least two acts of racketeering activity, one of which occurred after the effective date of this chapter and the last of which occurred within ten years (excluding any period of imprisonment) after the commission of a prior act of racketeering activity. . . .

§ 1962. Prohibited Activities

(a) It shall be unlawful for any person who has received any income derived, directly or indirectly, from a pattern of racketeering activity . . . to use or invest, directly or indirectly, any part of such income, or the proceeds of such income, in [the] acquisition of any interest in, or the establishment or operation of, any enterprise which is engaged in, or the activities of which affect, interstate or foreign commerce. A purchase of securities on the open market for purposes of investment, and without the intention of controlling or participating in the control of the issuer, or of assisting another to do so, shall not be unlawful under this subsection if the securities of the issuer held by the purchaser, the members of his immediate family, and his or their accomplices in any pattern or racketeering activity . . . do not amount in the aggregate to one percent of the outstanding securities of any one class, and do not confer, either in law or in fact, the power to elect one or more directors of the issuer.

(b) It shall be unlawful for any person through a pattern of racketeering activity . . . to acquire or maintain, directly or indirectly, any interest in or control of any enterprise which is engaged in, or the activities of which affect, interstate or foreign commerce.

---

* Omitted.

(c) It shall be unlawful for any person employed by or associated with any enterprise engaged in, or the activities of which affect, interstate or foreign commerce, to conduct or participate, directly or indirectly, in the conduct of such enterprise's affairs through a pattern of racketeering activity. . . .

(d) It shall be unlawful for any person to conspire to violate any of the provisions of subsection (a), (b), or (c) of this section.

§ 1963. Criminal Penalties

(a) Whoever violates any provision of section 1962 of this chapter shall be fined under this title or imprisoned not more than 20 years (or for life if the violation is based on a racketeering activity for which the maximum penalty includes life imprisonment), or both, and shall forfeit to the United States, irrespective of any provision of State law—

(1) any interest the person has acquired or maintained in violation of section 1962;

(2) any—

(A) interest in;

(B) security of;

(C) claim against; or

(D) property or contractual right of any kind affording a source of influence over;

any enterprise which the person has established, operated, controlled, conducted, or participated in the conduct of in violation of section 1962; and

(3) any property constituting, or derived from, any proceeds which the person obtained, directly or indirectly, from racketeering activity . . . in violation of section 1962. . . .

§ 1964. Civil Remedies

(a) The district courts of the United States shall have jurisdiction to prevent and restrain violations of section 1962 of this chapter by issuing appropriate orders, including, but not limited to: ordering any person to divest himself of any interest, direct or indirect, in any enterprise; imposing reasonable restrictions on the future activities or investments of any person, including, but not limited to, prohibiting any person from engaging in the same type of endeavor as the enterprise engaged in, the activities of which affect interstate or foreign commerce; or ordering dissolution or reorganization of any enterprise, making due provision for the rights of innocent persons.

(b) The Attorney General may institute proceedings under this section. Pending final determination thereof, the court may at any time enter such restraining orders or prohibitions, or take such other actions, including the acceptance of satisfactory performance bonds, as it shall deem proper.

(c) Any person injured in his business or property by reason of a violation of section 1962 of this chapter may sue therefor in any appropriate United States district court and shall recover threefold the damages he sustains and the cost of the suit, including a reasonable attorney's fee, except that no person may rely upon any conduct that would have been actionable as fraud in the purchase or sale of securities to establish a violation of section 1962. The exception contained in the preceding sentence does not apply to an action against any person that is criminally convicted in connection with the fraud, in which case the statute of limitations shall start to run on the date on which the conviction becomes final.

(d) A final judgment or decree rendered in favor of the United States in any criminal proceeding brought by the United States under this chapter shall estop the defendant from denying the essential allegations of the criminal offense in any subsequent civil proceeding brought by the United States. . . .

HART-SCOTT-RODINO ANTITRUST
IMPROVEMENTS ACT

15 U.S.C. § 18a, Clayton Act § 7A

§ 18a.   Premerger Notification and Waiting Period

(a)   Filing

Except as exempted pursuant to subsection (c), no person shall acquire, directly or indirectly, any voting securities or assets of any other person, unless both persons (or in the case of a tender offer, the acquiring person) file notification pursuant to rules under subsection (d)(1) and the waiting period described in subsection (b)(1) has expired, if—

(1) the acquiring person, or the person whose voting securities or assets are being acquired, is engaged in commerce or in any activity affecting commerce;

(2) as a result of such acquisition, the acquiring person would hold an aggregate total amount of the voting securities and assets of the acquired person—

(A) in excess of $359,900,000 [adjusted periodically based on percentage changes in the gross national product];

(B)(i) in excess of $90,000,000 (as so adjusted . . .) but not in excess of $359,900,000 (as so adjusted . . .); and

(ii)(I) any voting securities or assets of a person engaged in manufacturing which has annual net sales or total assets of $18,000,000 (as so adjusted . . .) or more are being acquired by any person which has total assets or annual net sales of $180,000,000 (as so adjusted . . .) or more;

(II) any voting securities or assets of a person not engaged in manufacturing which has total assets of $18,000,000 (as so adjusted . . .) or more are being acquired by any person which has total assets or annual net sales of $180,000,000 (as so adjusted . . .) or more; or

(III) any voting securities or assets of a person with annual net sales or total assets of $180,000,000 (as so adjusted . . .) or more are being acquired by any person with total assets or annual net sales of $18,000,000 (as so adjusted . . .) or more.

In the case of a tender offer, the person whose voting securities are sought to be acquired by a person required to file notification under this subsection shall file notification pursuant to rules under subsection (d).

(b)   Waiting period; publication; voting securities

(1) The waiting period required under subsection (a) of this section shall—

(A) begin on the date of the receipt by the Federal Trade Commission and the Assistant Attorney General in charge of the Antitrust Division of the Department of Justice (hereinafter referred to in this section as the "Assistant Attorney General") of—

(i) the completed notification required under subsection (a), or

(ii) if such notification is not completed, the notification to the extent completed and a statement of the reasons for such noncompliance,

from both persons, or, in the case of a tender offer, the acquiring person; and

(B) end on the thirtieth day after the date of such receipt (or in the case of a cash tender offer, the fifteenth day), or on such later date as may be set under subsection (e)(2) or (g)(2).

(2) The Federal Trade Commission and the Assistant Attorney General may, in individual cases, terminate the waiting period specified in paragraph (1) and allow any person to proceed with any acquisition

subject to this section, and promptly shall cause to be published in the Federal Register a notice that neither intends to take any action within such period with respect to such acquisition.

(3) As used in this section—

(A) The term "voting securities" means any securities which at present or upon conversion entitle the owner or holder thereof to vote for the election of directors of the issuer or, with respect to unincorporated issuers, persons exercising similar functions.

(B) The amount or percentage of voting securities or assets of a person which are acquired or held by another person shall be determined by aggregating the amount or percentage of such voting securities or assets held or acquired by such other person and each affiliate thereof.

(c)   Exempt transactions

The following classes of transactions are exempt from the requirements of this section—

(1) acquisitions of goods or realty transferred in the ordinary course of business;

(2) acquisitions of bonds, mortgages, deeds of trust, or other obligations which are not voting securities;

(3) acquisitions of voting securities of an issuer at least 50 per centum of the voting securities of which are owned by the acquiring person prior to such acquisition;

(4) transfers to or from a Federal agency or a State or political subdivision thereof;

(5) transactions specifically exempted from the antitrust laws by Federal statute;

(6) transactions specifically exempted from the antitrust laws by Federal statute if approved by a Federal agency, if copies of all information and documentary material filed with such agency are contemporaneously filed with the Federal Trade Commission and the Assistant Attorney General; . . .

(9) acquisitions, solely for the purpose of investment, of voting securities, if, as a result of such acquisition, the securities acquired or held do not exceed 10 per centum of the outstanding voting securities of the issuer;

(10) acquisitions of voting securities, if, as a result of such acquisition, the voting securities acquired do not increase, directly or indirectly, the acquiring person's per centum share of outstanding voting securities of the issuer; . . .

(12) such other acquisitions, transfers, or transactions, as may be exempted under subsection (d)(2)(B).

(d)   Commission rules

The Federal Trade Commission, with the concurrence of the Assistant Attorney General . . . consistent with the purposes of this section—

(1) shall require that the notification required under subsection (a) be in such form and contain such documentary material and information relevant to a proposed acquisition as is necessary and appropriate to enable the Federal Trade Commission and the Assistant Attorney General to determine whether such acquisition may, if consummated, violate the antitrust laws; and

(2) may—

(A) define the terms used in this section;

(B) exempt, from the requirements of this section, classes of persons, acquisitions, transfers, or transactions which are not likely to violate the antitrust laws; and

(C) prescribe such other rules as may be necessary and appropriate to carry out the purposes of this section.

(e)   Additional information; waiting period extensions

(1)(A) The Federal Trade Commission or the Assistant Attorney General may, prior to the expiration of the 30-day waiting period (or in the case of a cash tender offer, the 15-day waiting period) specified in subsection (b)(1) of this section, require the submission of additional information or documentary material relevant to the proposed acquisition, from a person required to file notification with respect to such acquisition under subsection (a) of this section prior to the expiration of the waiting period specified in subsection (b)(1) of this section, or from any officer, director, partner, agent, or employee of such person. . . .

(2) The Federal Trade Commission or the Assistant Attorney General, in its or his discretion, may extend the 30-day waiting period (or in the case of a cash tender offer, the 15-day waiting period) specified in subsection (b)(1) of this section for an additional period of not more than 30 days (or in the case of a cash tender offer, 10 days) after the date on which the Federal Trade Commission or the Assistant Attorney General, as the case may be, receives from any person to whom a request is made under paragraph (1), or in the case of tender offers, the acquiring person, (A) all the information and documentary material required to be submitted pursuant to such a request, or (B) if such request is not fully complied with, the information and documentary material submitted and a statement of the reasons for such noncompliance. . . .

(g) Civil penalty; compliance; power of court

(1) Any person, or any officer, director, or partner thereof, who fails to comply with any provision of this section shall be liable to the United States for a civil penalty of not more than $10,000 for each day during which such person is in violation of this section. Such penalty may be recovered in a civil action brought by the United States.

(2) If any person, or any officer, director, partner, agent, or employee thereof, fails substantially to comply with the notification requirement under subsection (a) or any request for the submission of additional information or documentary material under subsection (e)(1) of this section within the waiting period specified in subsection (b)(1) and as may be extended under subsection (e)(2), the United States district court—

(A) may order compliance;

(B) shall extend the waiting period specified in subsection (b)(1) and as may have been extended under subsection (e)(2) until there has been substantial compliance, except that, in the case of a tender offer, the court may not extend such waiting period on the basis of a failure, by the person whose stock is sought to be acquired, to comply substantially with such notification requirement or any such request; and

(C) may grant such other equitable relief as the court in its discretion determines necessary or appropriate,

upon application of the Federal Trade Commission or the Assistant Attorney General. . . .

REGULATIONS UNDER THE HART-SCOTT-RODINO ANTITRUST IMPROVEMENTS ACT

16 C.F.R. § 800.1 et seq.

TABLE OF CONTENTS

Sec.		Page
801.1	Definitions	1687
801.13	Voting Securities or Assets to Be Held as a Result of Acquisition	1687
802.21	Acquisitions of Voting Securities Not Meeting or Exceeding Greater Notification Threshold	1688

---

§ 801.1 Definitions

When used in the act and these rules . . .

(h) *Notification threshold.* The term "notification threshold" means:

(1) An aggregate total amount of voting securities of the acquired person valued at greater than $90 million (as adjusted) but less than $180.0 million (as adjusted);

(2) An aggregate total amount of voting securities of the acquired person valued at $180 million (as adjusted) or greater but less than $899.8 million (as adjusted);

(3) An aggregate total amount of voting securities of the acquired person valued at $899.8 million (as adjusted) or greater;

(4) Twenty-five percent of the outstanding voting securities of an issuer if valued at greater than $1.799.5 billion (as adjusted); or

(5) Fifty percent of the outstanding voting securities of an issuer if valued at greater than $90 million (as adjusted).

(i)(1) *Solely for the purpose of investment.* Voting securities are held or acquired "solely for the purpose of investment" if the person holding or acquiring such voting securities has no intention of participating in the formulation, determination, or direction of the basic business decisions of the issuer. . . .

(n) (*as adjusted*). The parenthetical "(as adjusted)" refers to the adjusted values published in the Federal Register notice titled "Revised Jurisdictional Threshold for Section 7A of the Clayton Act." This Federal Register notice will be published in January of each year and the values contained therein will be effective as of the effective date published in the Federal Register notice and will remain effective until superseded in the next calendar year. The notice will also be available at http://www.ftc.gov. Such adjusted values will be calculated in accordance with Section 7A(a)(2)(A) and will be rounded up to the next highest $100,000.

§ 801.13 Voting Securities or Assets to Be Held as a Result of Acquisition

(a) *Voting securities.* (1) Subject to the provisions of § 801.15, and paragraph (a)(3) of this section, all voting securities of the issuer which will be held by the acquiring person after the consummation of an acquisition shall be deemed voting securities held as a result of the acquisition. The value of such voting securities shall be the sum of the value of the voting securities to be acquired . . . and the value of the voting securities held by the acquiring person prior to the acquisition, determined in accordance with paragraph (a)(2) of this section. . . .

(3) Voting securities held by the acquiring person prior to an acquisition shall not be deemed voting securities held as a result of that subsequent acquisition if:

(i) The acquiring person is, in the subsequent acquisition, acquiring only assets; and

(ii) The acquisition of the previously acquired voting securities was subject to the filing and waiting requirements of the act (and such requirements were observed) or was exempt pursuant to § 802.21. . . .

§ 802.21   Acquisitions of Voting Securities Not Meeting or Exceeding Greater Notification Threshold

(a) An acquisition of voting securities shall be exempt from the requirements of the act if:

(1) The acquiring person and all other persons required by the act and these rules to file notification filed notification with respect to an earlier acquisition of voting securities of the same issuer;

(2) The waiting period with respect to the earlier acquisition has expired . . . and the acquisition will be consummated within 5 years of such expiration or termination; and

(3) The acquisition will not increase the holdings of the acquiring person to meet or exceed a notification threshold (as adjusted) greater than the greatest notification threshold met or exceeded in the earlier acquisition.

Agency Outline:

- **agency**: the relationship that arises when P manifests assent that another (A) shall act on their behalf and under their control (A consents)

- **capacity**: ① P must have contractual capacity (<u>not</u> minor or diminished capacity)
  - ↳ capacity to contract
  ② A only needs minimal capacity (any person may be an A, includes minor, incompetent

- **formalities**: ① Consent of both A + P, ② <u>no</u> consideration required, ③ writing generally <u>not</u> required (unless by statute)

- **modes of creation**: ① by act of parties (agreement of two, P holds another out as A, ratification by P), ② operation of law
  - ↳ <u>estoppel</u>: P may be estopped from denying existence of the agency, depends on 3P reliance, a remedy to protect 3P from loss

- **Rights and Duties:**
  (A to P)
  ① Duty of loyalty (can't have interests adverse to P's, breach by failing to disclose
  ② Duty of obedience (<u>must</u> obey all lawful rules of P)
  ③ Duty of care (notify P - imputed, compensated /) gratuitous A

- **Remedies of P**: ① Action for damages (breach of contract or tort)
  ② Action for secret profits (breaches duty and secretly profit)
    - ↳ P gets actual profits)
  §8.01 ③ Accounting (ct determines exact amount of P's funds A has that <u>must</u> be returned)
  ④ Withholding compensation (intentional tort / breach, P may refuse to pay A unapportioned compensation
  ⑤ termination of agency (A's breach allows P to terminate prior to date in contract)

- **Duties of subagent to P and A**: same duties as agent would owe

- **subagent**: a person appointed by A to perform functions assigned to A by P

- **co-agency**: another A of P (A doesn't delegate their powers like subagent)

- **liability of A for subagent**: A will also be held liable to P for breaches of sub

- **liability of sub to A**: ① general rule: sub owes A same duties owed to P
  ② unauthorized subs: if appointed w/out authority, A liable to P, A's only recourse against sub

- **Duties of P to A**: ① operation of law (compensate & reimburse (indemnify))
  ② by contract (comply w/ contract terms)
  ③ duty to cooperate (help A carry out agency function →) provide w/ opportunities, don't interfere

Agency Power

- **actual authority**: P bound even if 3P didn't know of authority,

(A belief)   A not liable to P for breach → A reasonably thinks they possess the authority based on P's dealings with them

   ① **Express** – communication from P to A either written or oral

   ② **Implied** – from express, custom or usage (must have knowledge of it) or through acquiescence (P accepts or fails to object)

- **apparent authority**: P can still be held liable if 3P can show that A had apparent authority, P holds out another as

(3P belief)   having authority thereby, inducing others to believe authority existed

   ↳ **lingering apparent** – if actual authority terminated, then P must notify 3P of termination, if fails to & so are 3P would not have reasonably known, then A still has apparent

- **general A**: authorized to engage in a series of transactions (continuity of service)
  special A: authorized to engage in one or two transactions (no continuity)
  universal A: authority to do anything for P

- **Inherent authority**: derived solely from agency relationship (results in P being bound by A's acts in certain situations even though A has no actual or apparent) → protect 3P

Ratification

- **effect** – ① P bound when P ratifies an unauthorized transaction by A
  ② A relief of warranty liability – A relieved of this liability if P ratifies

- **prerequisites** – ① P must know material facts ② P must accept entire transaction
  ③ P must have capacity, ④ no consideration needed

- **methods**: ① express affirmance, ② Implied (acceptance of benefits, silence, lawsuit)

- **liabilities of parties**: ① 3P to P – if A had authority, P liable to 3P, ② 3P to A – depends on whether P was disclosed, unidentified or undisclosed
  a) disclosed – always liable on contract with A, but A generally not liable, only P can hold 3P liable
  b) unidentified/undisclosed – both P & A liable, both can hold 3P liable
  $\S 602$ $\S 603$

Tort Liability

- **general rule** – P is vicariously liable to 3P for torts committed by A

- **theories of vicarious**: ① respondeat superior (employee, within scope)
  ② apparent – P can still be vicariously liable if A had apparent
  $\S 7.08$

- **Respondeat Superior** ① Indep K or employee?
  ↳ indep K – calling of own, particular job, paid given amount
  ↳ employee – full time, paid by time, supervised work
  $\S 7.07(f)$ ↙ ② determination of right to control: characterization by parties, extent of supervision, skill, tools, period of employment, compensation, business purpose

- **Scope** ① frolic & detour (frolic – major deviation, fall outside of scope)
  (detour – small deviations from directions ...

Dissociation / Dissolution Chart

Basis of Differences	Dissociation of Partner	Dissolution of Partner	
		At will	Definite term/task
Definition or Meaning	Person has power to dissociate as partner anytime rightfully or wrongfully by withdrawing as partner by express will § 602(a)	Partnership is dissolved and business must be wound up upon triggering event § 801	
Triggering Events			
Acts of Partners			
Assignment of Partner's interest	§ 601(4)(B)		
Member Min. 2		§ 801(6)	§ 801(6)
Withdrawal	§ 601(1)	§ 801(1)	
Bankruptcy	§ 601(6)		
Incapacity	§ 601(7)(B)(C)		*
Death	§ 601(7)(8)(9)		*
Expulsion of Partner	§ 601(3)(4)		*
Expiration of term			
Event specified in Agreement	§ 601(2)		§ 801(2)(C)
Unanimous to Dissolve	(& wind up done) § 601(15)	§ 801(3)	§ 801(3)
Operation of Law			§ 801(2)(B)
Illegality	§ 601(4)(A)		
Court Order		§ 801(4)(A)	§ 801(4)(A)
Judicial Expulsion of Partner	§ 601(5)		
Judicial Determination of Partner's incapacity to perform duties	§ 601(7)(B)(C)		* *
Judicial Determination of economic frustration or impracticability		§ 801(4)(B),(C),(D)	§ 801(4)(B)(C),(D)
Application by transferee of partner's interest if equitable		§ 801(5)(B)	§ 801(5)(A)

	Dissociation	Dissolution
Formalities	May file statement of dissociation §704(a)	May file statement of dissolution §802(b)(2)(A) May file statement of termination §802(b)(2)(F) May give notice to creditors §807, §808
Recission	N/A if dissociated person must buy back (asset or skill) into partnership	May rescind unless termination statement has been filed or court has ordered dissolution of partnership §803
Power to bind	Dissociation immediately the persons actual authority to act for partnership, unless results in dissolution and winding up §702 comments	Both a partner and a dissociated partner can bind a partnership if the act is appropriate for winding up, the 3P didn't know of dissolution, partnership would have been liable prior to dissolution and if dissociated must have been dissociated less than two years §804
Disposition of assets	N/A Partnership not ending *distribution to partner determined as if dissolution is occurring §701(b)	In winding up assets to be applied to debt obligations and surplus to be distributed §806(a)(b)
Liabilities	A person who withdraws and wrongfully dissociates is liable to partnership and partners for damages caused §602(c) - Generally a person dissociated as partner not liable for obligations incurred after §703(a) - Exceptions: §703(b), 305	If partner knows of dissolution or it dissociates, and incurs debt not appropriate for winding up, they are liable to partnership §805
Effects	Person dissociated as partner right to participate in management duties and obligation end (except winding up) BUT doesn't discharge debts, obligations or liability to partnership §603(b)(1)(2),(c) - Switching provision if result in dissolution use Art 8, otherwise use Art 7 §603(a)	Dissolution of the Partnership does not end existence of partnership purpose of partnership changes to terminating (winding up) partnership §801 comments

⁕ = Dissolution will occur if within 90 days of dissociation, at least half of the remaining partners desire to wind up business §801(2)(A)

→ When grounds exist for both dissociation and dissolution, the act has discretion to choose between them §601 pg 101 comments

Dissociation occurs when any partner ceases to be involved in the business of the firm, and "dissolution" happens when RUPA requires the partnership to wind up and terminate; dissociation does not necessarily cause dissolution

⁕ if sole proprietor, you are personally liable for all debts
↳ there is no distinction between this and individual owner

* piercing veil only applies to a limited partnership and a
closely held corp

* partnership piercing → perpetrate fraud, circumvent statute,
or for other wrongful purpose / inequitable

* if ct doesn't find corp is de facto, then it is automatically general
partnership or agency

* de facto :

* de jure :

* state where incorporated governs internal affairs of corp

* state where bad act occurred governs external affairs of corp

* governing law of corp hierarchy: state laws, articles of incorp, bylaws

Piercing Factors:

① Substantial stock ownership → is the corp entity responsible for
the debt or obligation seeking to be satisfied
(important factor but not conclusive)

② undercapitalization → lack of sufficient capital (money and resources)
(not sufficient alone) → strong factor favoring piercing
↳ doesn't have enough to satisfy its obligations
↳ key indicators — inability to pay dividends, lack of insurance
customary for industry doing business in, lack capital assets

③ failure to observe corporate formalities (hold meetings)

④ Absence of corporate records (minutes, records of stock ownership)

⑤ Commingling → corp assets and corp identities (when attempt to
separate identity of corp from identity of shareholders, cts reluctant
to pierce) → when intertwined likely to pierce

⑥ Siphoning → of corp assets, a shareholder is using the assets of
corp for own personal benefit or for purpose not intended

⑦ proof of fraud unnecessary → no need to prove fraud to prove
piercing appropriate (evidence of injustice or deception
increase likelihood of sh)

⑧ uphill battle → should only be used (pierce doctrine) in
extreme cases to advance fairness and equity

⑨ K v. tort victims —

Essay Outline

Agency: ① <u>Contract</u> or <u>Tort</u>

- Agency created?
- capacity?
- formalities?
- how created

- Indp. K v Employee,
- Scope

Rights + Duties of ____ ⟨relationship⟩ A or P or 3P

Fiduciary Duties
Remedies

<u>Enforceable</u>

Authority
Scope
Termination
Ratification
Liability

<u>Liability</u>

Relationship
Authority
Scope
Intentional
Ratification

Liability → A = A→P; A→3P, P→3P

C = Cv. Cr, Cv. 3, C v. BOD

BOD v. Cr, BOD v. 3

Reverse (SH cr v. C) → Pierce = Cr v. SH, Cr v PC, Cr v Sibs ⟨parent corp'n⟩ ⟨sibling⟩ (horizontal)

P = Psh v. 3, Psh v P, P v. 3

partnership

Pierce (to prevent (fraud or injustice).

↳ LP v 3

Agency → Agent/Principle (Limited Ø Agents) (BOD Ø Agents)

Corp = Dejure or Defacto/Estoppel

Gen partnership

P = f. Ud or Gen ⟨act of P or Law⟩

imp Exp

Partnership

① partnership created?
   ↳ formalities
   ↳ agency law / relationship

② Rights and Duties
   ↳ fiduciary Duties
   ↳ Partnership Agreement

Liability

Notice/Knowledge
Authority
Scope
K/Tort/Crime

Distribution

Dissol/Disso
transfer sub
interes
contribut
cred. tors

* §407 RUPA, 504 ULPA, 640 MBCA

Equity + Balance Sheet tests!

Piercing Cases:

Contract:

① **Bartle** — π is Bartle (trustee in Westerlea bankruptcy),
Δ is Home Owner Co-op - claim Δ liable for the
K debts of Westerlea, their wholly-owned subsidiary.

Westerlea created after Δ couldn't get contractors
for housing construction (costs higher than
expected so creditors took over responsibilities)
years later Westerlea went bankrupt

Holding: agree w/
lower ct., law permits
incorporation for the
purpose of escaping
personal liability)

π claims lower ct. erred by refusing to pierce
Westerlea's corp existence → doctrine is invoked to
prevent fraud or to achieve equity - none in case)

Dissent: Westerlea is an A of A's. Δ is
rendered liable for A's indebtedness

② **Dewitt** — two-prong test (fraud and other eg.)
- if fraud then you can pierce
- if other eg. (gross undercapitalized insolvency,

Flemming personally
distributing money /
as primary shareholder
to many things
by this made corp have
no assets

lack of dividends, payment if corp funds to
primary stockholders, lack of corp formalities,
non-functioning corp officers, lack of corp records,
evidence that corp is a facade for a stockholders
activities) then pierce allowed

③ **Bagel Bros** — bros operated chain of stores, same trade name
but diff. entity or struct, name attached, kept
separate books and records, adhered to corp frame
- OH farmers provided product to OH stores
- NY stores merged into Maple for admin purposes
so corp headquarters moved there

holding: no piercing
- OH stores closed, left unpaid debt to OH farmers
so filed claim in Maple bankruptcy case, which
Maple rejected (separate corp entities)
- judge allowed OH claim, appealed decision (no
evidence that farmers would have known only
OH stores could be liable)
↳ farmers should've been confused by the
trade name same b/c separate books and records

Tort:

① **Minton** — Seminole opened a swimming pool (leased)
- π's daughter drowned → want to hold Leavy
personally liable for judgment against Seminole
- Seminole used his office to keep records
(kept records there which indicates Leavy
actively participated in business)

holding: reversed,
Leavy wasn't party
to original suit for opportunity
to contest claims
- undercapitalization
factor

② **Baatz** — corp purchased the bar, executed a promissory note
personally guaranteeing remaining amount after down payment
also obtained financing for park and made another guarantee
- π's were injured in car accident struck by McBride (drank at
corp's bar) → claim that they negligently served McBride
- ct entered summary judgment dismissing Novotny as indiv. D's
so Baatz appealed
- ct may not pierce if no evidence that recognition of
corp entity would produce injustice and inequitable consequence
to hold individual shareholders liable

Enterprise Liability: hold one company liable for debts of another as both
are part of common entity (parent)

① **Walkowszky** = Carlton D owned a taxicab business
(shareholder of 10 corps)
π claims he was injured by one of Carlton's owned cabs
(sued Carlton, the corp and Carlton's other corps, claiming
all were a single enterprise)
- π must show that a shareholder used the corp as
his agent to conduct business in own indiv. capacity
- did not pierce (can't sue it because someone
put insufficient $ in the corps)

Piercing Notes: (aka disregard of corp entity)
- arises when a corp entity has liability for an obligation
but doesn't have the assets to satisfy that liability → π seeks
to hold some other entity/individual personally liable (typically
shareholder)
- sibling or enterprise: π may seek to impose liability on a party
that is related to original corp entity
- piercing is an exception to general rule that shareholders
of corps have limited liability and thus cannot be
held personally liable for corp obligations
- common piercing forms:
① from corp to indiv. shareholder
② from corp to corp parent
③ from corp to subsidiary of corp
④ from corp to another corp w/ same corp parent

Questions to ask:
④ under what
circumstances
would it be
willing to pierce?
① why is π seeking to pierce?
② what indiv or entity would be liable if ct pierced?
③ what is relationship between indiv or entity that π
seeking to hold responsible and entity liable?

Meinhard – Co-adventurers w/ Salmon, lease was offered
to be extended, Salmon did so not tg Meinhard it
opportunity and extended lease on his own

↳ is notification required w/ joint ventures?

↳ owe duty of loyalty to one another while enterprise
continues

↳ Salmon in management provided, so duty to disclose
but did not (defrauded Meinhard)

↳ dissent: Salmon did everything required to in
agreement so meinhard not entitled to
equity in new extension

Kovacik – Co-adventurers, Kovacik financed while Reed provided
services, resulted in losses, Reed never agreed
to pay losses

– if only contributes services are required to pay losses

↳ no, not liable to each other for losses if
one gives money and other services

↳ only lose what you gave

↳ lower ct's decision forcing half losses to
kovacik reversed

Equal Dignities Rule – requires A to have in writing their
authority to enter into contracts

Business Judgment Rule – act is good faith, is interested
(pg 640)   corp (whoever is is doing this to
overcome this)

Schlensky v. Wrigley – cubs lost lots of money
§301 (business   – more fans at night games w/
issue)   white sox because they had lights
                      – filed derivative suit
                      – claimed that by failing to provide
                        lights, the directors of corp breached
                        following duty
                      – schlensky claimed Wrigley believed
                        games better in day time, directors gut
                        (short profits)
                      – holding: schlensky had no claim b/c can
                        only bring claim against directors if fraud

✱ ct won't second-
guess directors
choices unless
illegality, fraud,
or conflict of
interest
not
here

Theory Characteristics (helps separate partnership from corp)

A) Associates (need more than one person) - partnership

B) Purpose (partnership statute) graph

→ based on what the rational economic person would do (always based on price)

C) Centralized Management (management is separate from ownership)

D) Continuity of Life (outlives me, corp continues after death - aka Perpetual existence)

E) Limited Liability (lose only what you invest)

F) Transferable interests (separate management and financial interests can be) - cannot be sold

G) Regulatory Concerns / Include Tax SEC

* rule 10b-5 → anyone who breaches a duty not to use inside information for personal benefit can be held liable